The Concise Corsini Encyclopedia *of* Psychology *and* Behavioral Science

The Concise Corsini Encyclopedia *of* Psychology *and* Behavioral Science

Third Edition

W. Edward Craighead and
Charles B. Nemeroff
Editors

John Wiley & Sons, Inc.

WB

This book is printed on acid-free paper. ♾

Published by John Wiley & Sons, Inc., Hoboken, New Jersey.
Published simultaneously in Canada.

For general information on our other products and services please contact our Customer Care Department within the U.S. at (800) 762-2974, outside the United States at (317) 572-3993 or fax (317) 572-4002.

Wiley also publishes its books in a variety of electronic formats. Some content that appears in print may not be available in electronic books. For more information about Wiley products, visit our website at www.wiley.com.

Library of Congress Cataloging-in-Publication Data:

The concise Corsini encyclopedia of psychology and behavioral science / W. Edward Craighead and Charles B. Nemeroff, editors.— 3rd ed.
p. cm.
Rev. ed. of: Concise encyclopedia of psychology. c1996.
Includes bibliographical references and index.
ISBN 0-471-22036-1 (cloth)
1. Psychology—Encyclopedias. I. Craighead, W. Edward. II. Nemeroff, Charles B. III. Concise encyclopedia of psychology.

BF31.E52 2004
150'.3—dc22

2003059558

Printed in the United States of America

10 9 8 7 6 5 4 3 2 1

4/24/08

FOR:

Linda Wilcoxon Craighead

Gayle Applegate Nemeroff

PREFACE

It seems like only a few short months since we co-edited *The Corsini Encyclopedia of Psychology and Behavioral Science.* We have now compiled the materials for the "Concise" edition of these volumes. In this edition, we have asked previous authors to update their material to reflect the most recent ideas and research findings on their topics. This edition also contains new entries because the fields of psychology and neuroscience continue to flourish. Although each entry is shorter than those of the four volume Encyclopedia, we trust they are thorough enough to be informative to the reader. Numerous authors have referred to other publications relevant to their entries in this book, and we trust these will be useful to the reader in gathering additional details about the topics of interest. The purpose of the Encyclopedia is to provide succinct summaries of information regarding the most important topics in Psychology and Neuroscience for the reader. We hope this concise edition will make that material available to an even wider audience.

We would like to thank our numerous contributors (about 800) who have provided materials for this book. Although deciding on topics to be included and collating and editing the entries is an extensive undertaking, it is the authors who have provided the actual information in the book, and to them we are extremely grateful. We are also grateful to Alinne Barrera, our Managing Editor, for her excellent attention to detail in monitoring the entries as they came and went and for corresponding with the numerous contributors to the volume. We are also grateful to Wade and Margaret Craighead for their assistance in managing various details of keeping us on track in the production of this book. Finally, we are grateful to the staff at John Wiley & Sons, particularly former Wiley editor Jennifer Simon, and current Vice President and Publisher Peggy Alexander for their support of this project and bringing the book into existence, and to Kelly Franklin who brought us to Wiley in the first place.

ABNORMALITY

From time immemorial, individuals have recognized a small minority of members of their societies as psychologically "abnormal." The research of Jane Murphy (1976) further demonstrates that people in non-Western cultures, such as the Yorubas of Nigeria and the Yupic-speaking Eskimos of Alaska, readily recognize certain behaviors as abnormal. Moreover, many of these behaviors, such as talking to oneself, are similar to those regarded as abnormal in Western society. Murphy's findings suggest that the concept of abnormality is not entirely culturally relative.

Nevertheless, these observations leave unanswered a crucial question: What is abnormality? Surprisingly, a definitive answer to this question remains elusive. In this entry, we examine several conceptualizations of abnormality and their strengths and weaknesses. All of these conceptualizations strive to provide a definition of abnormality that encompasses both physical and mental disorders, although most place primary emphasis on the latter.

The first and most radical conception examined here is that abnormality is entirely a function of societal values. According to this *subjective values* model, which has been championed by Thomas Szasz (1960), abnormal conditions are those deemed by society to be undesirable in some way. Although this model touches on an important truth—namely, that many or most abnormal conditions are perceived as undesirable—it does not explain why many socially undesirable behaviors, such as rudeness, laziness, and even racism, are not perceived as pathological. A comprehensive definition of abnormality involves more than subjective values. This fact helps to explain in part why Harvard psychiatrist Alvin Poussaint's (2002) recent efforts to include extreme racism in the current diagnostic manual have met with little success.

Proponents of a *statistical* approach, such as Henry Cohen (1981), posit that abnormality can be defined as statistical deviation from a norm. Thus, any behavior that is rare is abnormal. Although this conceptualization is appealing in its simplicity, it suffers from several shortcomings. First, the cutoff points for abnormality are scientifically arbitrary. Should abnormality be defined as the uppermost 1% of the population, the uppermost 3%, or some other figure? Second, a statistical approach provides no guidance regarding which dimensions are relevant to psychopathology. As a consequence, it erroneously classifies high levels of certain socially desirable dimensions, such as creativity and altruism, as abnormal. Third, a statistical approach mistakenly classifies all common conditions as normal. For example, it implies that the bubonic plague ("Black Death"), which killed approximately one third of Europe's population in the fourteenth century, was not abnormal because it was widespread.

Some writers, such as F. Kraupl Taylor (1971), have embraced the pragmatic position that abnormality is nothing more than the set of conditions that professionals treat. According to this view of disorder as whatever professionals treat, psychologically abnormal conditions are those that elicit intervention from mental health professionals. Although this view avoids many of the conceptual pitfalls of other definitions, it does not explain why many conditions treated by professionals, such as pregnancy, a misshapen nose corrected by plastic surgery, and marital conflict, are not per se regarded as pathological.

Advocates of a *subjective discomfort* model maintain that abnormal conditions are those that produce suffering in affected individuals. Although many psychopathological conditions, such as Major Depressive Disorder, clearly produce considerable subjective distress, several others, such as psychopathy (a condition characterized by guiltlessness, callousness, and dishonesty) and the manic phase of bipolar disorder (a condition characterized by extreme levels of elation, energy, and grandiosity), are often associated with minimal subjective distress. Moreover, like the statistical model, the subjective discomfort model provides no guidance concerning what cutoffs should be used to define abnormality. How much discomfort is required for a condition to be pathological?

Most of the aforementioned definitions focus on subjective judgments concerning the presence of abnormality. In contrast, proponents of a *biological model,* such as R. E. Kendell (1975), contend that abnormality should be defined by strictly biological criteria, particularly those derived from evolutionary theory. For example, Kendell argued that abnormal conditions are characterized by a reduced life span, reduced biological fitness (the capacity of an organism to transmit its genes to future generations), or both. Despite its potentially greater scientific rigor relative to other models, a biological model is subject to numerous counterexamples. For example, being a soldier in a war tends to reduce one's longevity but is not a disorder; priesthood (which results in having no children) tends to reduce one's fitness but is similarly not a disorder. Moreover, a biological model falls victim to the same problem of arbitrary cutoffs that bedevils the statistical model: How much below average must life span or fitness be for a condition to be abnormal?

Whereas some of the preceding conceptualizations of abnormality invoke primarily social criteria, such as value judgments, others invoke primarily biological criteria. Jerome Wakefield (1992) suggests that the proper definition of abnormality requires both social and biological criteria. Specifically, he posits that all abnormal conditions are "harmful dysfunctions." The harm component of Wakefield's conceptualization refers to social values regarding a condition's undesirability, whereas the *dysfunction* component refers to the failure of a system to function as "designed" by natural selection. For example, Panic Disorder is abnormal, according to Wakefield, because (1) it is viewed by society as harmful and (2) the fear system was not evolutionarily designed to respond with intense anxiety in the absence of objective danger. Wakefield's analysis is a significant advance in the conceptualization of abnormality, because it distinguishes those features of abnormality that are socially constructed from those that are scientifically based. Nevertheless, his analysis assumes that all disorders involve failures of psychological or physiological systems. Yet some disorders, such as Post-Traumatic Stress Disorder and perhaps other anxiety disorders, probably represent evolved defensive reactions to subjectively perceived threats. Moreover, Wakefield's analysis presumes the existence of a clear-cut demarcation between adaptive function and dysfunction. But the functioning of many systems, such as the anxiety system, may be distributed continuously, with no unambiguous dividing line between normality and abnormality.

In response to the problems with earlier efforts to provide an adequate definition of abnormality, some authors, such as David Rosenhan and Martin Seligman (1995) and Scott Lilienfeld and Lori Marino (1995), have proposed a *family resemblance* model of abnormality. According to this model, the concept of abnormality cannot be explicitly defined, because abnormality is an inherently fuzzy concept with indefinite boundaries. Instead, conditions perceived as abnormal share a loosely related set of characteristics, including statistical rarity, maladaptiveness, impairment, and the need for treatment. The family resemblance view implies that all efforts to construct a clear-cut conceptualization of abnormality are doomed to failure. Nevertheless, this view implies that there will often be substantial consensus regarding which conditions are perceived as abnormal, because individuals rely on similar features when identifying abnormality.

REFERENCES

Cohen, H. (1981). The evolution of the concept of disease. In A. Caplan, H. Engelhardt, & J. McCarthy (Eds.), *Concepts of health and disease: Interdisciplinary perspectives* (pp. 209–220). Reading, MA: Addison-Wesley.

Kendell, R. E. (1975). The concept of disease and its implications for psychiatry. *British Journal of Psychiatry, 127,* 305–315.

Kraupl Taylor, F. (1971). A logical analysis of the medico-psychological concept of disease. *Psychological Medicine, 1,* 356–364.

Lilienfeld, S. O., & Marino, L. (1995). Mental disorder as a Roschian concept: A critique of Wakefield's "harmful dysfunction" analysis. *Journal of Abnormal Psychology, 104,* 411–420.

Murphy, J. M. (1976). Psychiatric labeling in cross-cultural perspective. *Science, 191,* 1019–1028.

Poussaint, A. F. (2002). Yes: It can be a delusional symptom of psychotic disorders. *Western Journal of Medicine, 176,* 4.

Rosenhan, D., & Seligman, M. (1995). *Abnormal psychology* (3rd ed.). New York: Norton.

Szasz, T. S. (1960). The myth of mental illness. *American Psychologist, 15,* 113–118.

Wakefield, J. C. (1992). The concept of mental disorder: On the boundary between biological facts and social values. *American Psychologist, 47,* 373–388.

Scott O. Lilienfeld
Emory University

ACCOMMODATION

The term *accommodation* is used in various areas of study relevant to psychology and neuroscience. Several applications are considered here.

Visual Accommodation

Visual accommodation is the automatic adjustment process by which the lens of the eye adjusts to *focus* on objects at different distances. The lens is a pliant transparent elliptical structure that refracts, or bends, rays of light inward, thus focusing them on the retina. When the eye is at rest, the *suspensory ligaments* hold the lens firmly in a relatively flattened position. The normal resting eye is then in a far-point vision position and can focus on objects that are at least 20 feet (6 meters) distant, without any accommodative adjustment of the lens. Light rays passing through the cornea and aqueous humor then enter the pupil of the eye and pass through the lens, after which they pass through the vitreous humor and reach the retina in focus.

For near vision, closer than 20 feet, accommodation for focusing takes place: The *ciliary muscles,* located around and attached to the suspensory ligaments, contract. This causes relaxation of the suspensory ligaments, which then allow the flattened lens to thicken and bulge, becoming more convex, or rounded. The light rays are thus bent and fall, sharply focused, on the retina.

The ability to focus changes with age. In early childhood, children can focus on objects as close as 2.5 inches (6.3 centimeters). As age increases, accommodation becomes less possible due to progressive hardening of the lens. By 30 years of age, near vision is usually not clear at less than 6 inches (15 centimeters) from the eye. During the 40s, visual articles usually have to be moved farther and farther away in order to be clearly seen. *Presbyopia* is the term given to decreasing ability to focus with advancing age. This leads to the need for near-vision-lensed eyeglasses for most senior citizens for activities requiring close vision. *Hyperopia,* or farsightedness, and *myopia,* or nearsightedness, may also be related to problems of accommodation.

Illumination level has been found to have an effect upon accommodation. There have been various theories of the *physiological mechanism* for accommodation. Some researchers consider the sympathetic nervous system to be responsible for a basic tonal background, through vascular innervation. The oculomotor nerve, through increased or decreased innervation, leads to positive and negative accommodation, or specific adjustment for focusing.

Nerve Accommodation

When a constant stimulus, such as an electric current, is applied to a nerve, the excitability of the nerve under the cathode, or negative electrode, increases quickly. With continued stimulation by current flow, there is a slow decrease in nerve excitability, known as *accommodation,* followed by a sudden drop when the current is stopped. Following cessation of the stimulating current, the nerve briefly becomes less sensitive to stimulation than it was before the current was turned on. Following a resting period, the original level of excitability tends to be restored. During the adaptation period, or time of decrease in excitability, it may be possible to stimulate the nerve by changing either the length or strength of the stimulus.

Accommodation in Auditory Theory

The ear consists of three main divisions: the outer ear, middle ear, and inner ear. The *outer ear* is the portion that allows sound waves to be transmitted, via the *tympanic membrane,* or *eardrum,* to the *middle ear.* In the middle ear are three tiny bones, the *ossicles,* comprising the *ossicular chain.* Here, the sound waves are transduced into mechanical energy, the ossicular chain rocking back and forth. The two tiny muscles of the middle ear, the *tensor tympani* and the *stapedius,* have attachments to the ossicles. The ossicles interface with the *inner ear,* which includes the *cochlea,* a snail-shaped structure that ultimately contains the electrochemical mechanisms for changing the mechanical waves into nerve impulses traveling along the eighth cranial, or *auditory* (*acoustic*), *nerve* to the brain.

The function of the middle-ear muscles has been debated over the years. One of at least five theories has been termed the frequency-selection or accommodation theory. This theory presumes that contraction of the muscles increases the sharpness of hearing by acting as a damping mechanism that selectively absorbs acoustic energy at particular frequencies. The other theories are the intensity-control or protective theory, the fixation theory, the labyrinthine-pressure theory, and a less-accepted theory that the middle-ear muscles are involved in the formation of overtones.

The middle-ear muscles are usually not under voluntary control but contract in response to sound energy in what has been called the *acoustic reflex. Electromyography* has been an important laboratory technique for its study. The acoustic reflex alters the mechanical properties of the middle ear transmission system; *acoustic impedence* is the term given to the consequent mechanical resistance. It may be measured indirectly by audiologists and auditory researchers and has become a notable means of studying hearing in humans for both research and clinical purposes.

Accommodation in Infant Development

The term *accommodation* was also used by Jean Piaget as part of his theoretical view of how infants develop cognitively. Accommodation refers to the infant's modification of concepts or of notions of the world as a response to new experiences or to experiences inconsistent with a previously held notion. *Assimilation* refers to the incorporation into the child's cognitive structure of notions from elements of environmental experience. When an organized cognitive pattern develops through the processes of assimilation and accommodation, a *schema* or *scheme* is said to have developed. Schemata develop, according to Piaget, during the first 2 years, or *sensorimotor period,* during which the infant develops mainly through sensorimotor activities. Piaget differentiated six stages of sensorimotor development.

Piaget's theories have been applied, among other ways, as a partial model of infant and childhood development of language and prelanguage behaviors. With this model, speech-language pathologists and others working with speech and language development can assess very early development for signs of problems. Early intervention aims to aid the prevention of later, larger-magnitude difficulty and thus to promote more adequate functioning later on in areas such as listening, speaking, reading, and writing.

Barbara B. Mates
City College of New York, CUNY

See also: **Adaptation; Depth Perception; Eye; Perception; Piaget's Theory**

ACHIEVEMENT NEED

The most thoroughly studied of the 20 psychological needs identified by H. A. Murray in his seminal study, *Explo-*

rations in Personality, is what Murray termed "need achievement." In early research studies, the need to achieve (*n Ach*) was assumed to be present in any situation marked by competition with a standard of excellence. (The standard of excellence could of course be set by others' performance or by one's own aspirations.) In most of these studies, especially the ones conducted by D. C. McClelland and his associates, *n Ach* was measured by analyses of stories told by subjects in response to pictures included in or resembling those of the Thematic Apperception Test (TAT). The concurrent validity of the TAT measure was shown by a study in which McClelland and Atkinson found that naval cadets who had been made to "fail" (because of false information given them about their performance on seemingly important tests) introduced more achievement themes in their TAT stories than did members of a control group. The predictive validity of the TAT method was demonstrated by McClelland, who found that college students who made high *n Ach* scores were more likely to enter entrepreneurial occupations in later years than were students who scored low.

McClelland maintained that the level of economic achievement attained by a society is determined by the way it raises its children. This is the theme of his best-known work, *The Achieving Society,* in which he maintained that achievement themes identified in such diverse modes of expression as pottery designs, literature, and children's textbooks predicted levels of economic achievement decades later in various countries and cultures, ancient, medieval, and modern. The effect of child-rearing practices can, however, be reversed. McClelland and Winter report field studies conducted in India of businessmen with initially low levels of *n Ach* who were coached in order to raise their levels of aspiration, and who consequently expanded their business activities and made significant economic contributions to their community.

The work of McClelland and his associates has been criticized on a number of grounds. M. S. Weinstein observed that he, as well as other researchers, found TAT measures to be of low reliability and questionable validity. Maehr and Nicholls objected to the McClelland group's emphasis on personality as a critical variable in determining behavior, to the narrowness of their achievement criteria, and to their failure to obtain significant results regarding achievement motivation in women.

Many researchers have also been unable to find significant relationships between women's *n Ach* scores and achievement-related variables. Horner suggested that women are likely to believe that ambition is inappropriate for them, especially in fields dominated by men, and that, as a consequence, they are inhibited by a "fear of success." Subsequent research by Sid and Lindgren, however, indicated that fear of success has inhibiting effects on men as well as women.

One reason for researchers' inability to relate *n Ach* scores to women's achievement may lie in the way *n Ach* is usually assessed. These measures, both of the TAT and questionnaire type, have typically attempted to cover all components of what has come to be recognized as achievement motivation: task orientation, positive attitudes toward problems and challenges, responsiveness to the Zeigarnik effect, preference for medium-risk ventures (as contrasted with high- or low-risk ventures), competitiveness, and the desire to work independently for self-determined goals rather than for group goals. The unsatisfactory reliability and validity of *n Ach* measures may be the result of attempting to measure too broad a spectrum of traits. Lindgren proposed that problems inherent in such measures could be bypassed by employing a forced-choice questionnaire which would require subjects to choose between achievement-related personal styles and those that were affiliation-related. The rationale for this juxtaposition of factors was found in a number of studies that showed needs for achievement and affiliation to be negatively correlated. Research by Lindgren and by Sadd and colleagues with the resulting questionnaire reported (1) no significant differences between mean scores of men and women undergraduates, and (2) positive correlations between *n Ach* scores and academic performance.

The strong emphasis on cognitive psychology that appeared in the 1970s had a marked effect on achievement motivation research. During this period, Maehr and Nicholls pointed out, researchers became interested in subjects' cognitions about the nature of achievement, their purposes in performing achievement-related acts, and their attributions as to causes of outcomes. Cross-cultural studies, for example, turned up both differences and similarities between national cultures and the way in which their members interpreted "success" and "failure" and attributed the antecedents and consequences of success.

By the early 1980s, the question of whether achievement motivation may be appropriately studied as a personality trait or whether it should be studied cognitively had not been resolved; thus, personality and cognitive psychologists continued to pursue their separate ways. The earlier questions that had been raised by Weinstein as to whether achievement motivation could be measured, or indeed whether it existed at all, seemed to have been resolved, for research activity in this area actually increased during the 1970s and 1980s. Weinstein's criticism of the reliability of TAT measures may, however, have stimulated the development of questionnaire measures, for the majority of studies of achievement motivation in the 1980s employed this potentially more reliable type of assessment.

Henry C. Lindgren

See also: **Affiliation Need; Optimal Functioning**

ACQUIRED DRIVES

One of the raging controversies in the history of psychology once centered on the aspect of the nature-nurture issue, which asks whether motives are inborn or learned. Some psychologists, of whom William McDougall was the most important, took the instinctivist position that motives are inborn, unlearned, universal within species, and—at least to a degree—continuous between species. Other psychologists, for whom John B. Watson was the most important spokesman, argued that motives are acquired through learning and therefore differ from individual to individual, culture to culture, and species to species. As occurred generally with the nature-nurture issue, the intensity of this controversy has lessened with time. It is now clear that all motives are a joint product of biological and environmental forces. If the question is asked at all, it is in terms of the relative importance of these two contributions.

Certain motives, sometimes called *primary drives,* are chiefly biological. Hunger, thirst, pain avoidance, and sex are examples. Even in these cases, however, experience plays a part. Rhythms of feeding and drinking, sensitivity to pain, and preferences in sexual partners are all influenced in this way. Other motives, sometimes called *secondary* or *acquired drives,* are determined primarily by experience, as for instance fears, affection for parents, drug addictions, and functionally autonomous habits such as miserliness. These examples show something of the variety of acquired drives. They also suggest that different acquired drives may depend on forms of learning that differ at least superficially.

Acquisition of Fear

One of the forms of learning just referred to is *classical conditioning.* Experimental evidence that some motives are acquired as the result of this process dates at least to the famous study of Watson and Rayner, who conditioned the boy "little Albert" to fear a white rat. The rat (CS) was shown to the child, simultaneously with a loud and unpleasant sound (US) produced by the striking of a steel bar behind his head. The sound caused the child to cry (UR). After a few repetitions, Albert cried at the sight of the rat (CR), and this fear generalized to other furry objects, such as a fur neckpiece or a Santa Claus mask. Attempts to repeat the Watson and Rayner study were not always successful, and Valentine made the cogent point that fears might be much more easily conditioned to furry objects such as a caterpillar or a rat than to others such as a pair of opera glasses. In spite of these criticisms, the impact of the Watson and Rayner study on the history of psychology was considerable. It indicated that reactions once thought to be instinctive were more properly seen as the result of learning.

Affectional Responses

The young of many species come to treat the first large, moving, noisy object they see as if it were a parent. In most cases this object is in fact a parent, but the process of *imprinting,* as it is called, may produce such attachments to other species and even inanimate objects.

Various lines of evidence indicate that an essential component of imprinted reactions is motivational. The hatchlings of precocial birds, if imprinted on any object, stay near that object and will climb over obstacles to get near it; further, they make distress calls in its absence. The process of learning involved in imprinting bears a strong resemblance to classical conditioning and may be the same thing.

Social Techniques

Literature in the area of acquired motivation suggests that some motives may be acquired by a process that is more like instrumental learning. E. C. Tolman has given us an account that is fairly representative. Figure 1 summarizes his view, which holds that, in infancy, the individual has only a set of biological drives. Inevitably these drives are subjected to frustration, and new techniques are developed to satisfy them. Whatever techniques lead to relief from frustration are learned, and they become characteristic of the individual's repertory of responses to the world. As Tolman's drive-conversion diagram (Figure 1) also suggests, these first primitive adjustments achieved by the individual are not adequate to deal with all situations. They too are frustrated, with the result that new learning occurs and the individual's reactions to the world are modified further.

It should be noted that, so far in this account, nothing has been said about motives. Yet a glance at Figure 1 will reveal that several of the social techniques are ones that we often describe in motivational terms. Aggression, hostility, social approval, loyalty, identification, and self-punishment are all terms that probably occur more often in psychological literature in the context of motive than in that of habit. This suggests that there must be some sense in which habits are, or can become, motives. Gordon Allport once suggested in an article that such is the case, and he offered the concept of functional autonomy, whereby well-established habits become ends in themselves—that is, motives. It should be noted, however, that functional autonomy does not explain such effects; it only describes them.

Addictions

Addictions to tobacco, alcohol, and other substances are of special interest because they dramatize certain features of the psychology of acquired motivation. The motivational power of the addictions is obvious: Lives have been devoted to, and even lost to, activities performed to support an addiction. Established addictions no doubt represent a change in the physiology of the addicted person, probably a change in how certain neurotransmitters function. But at the same time, addictions are clearly acquired. This testifies to the power that experience may sometimes have over biological processes.

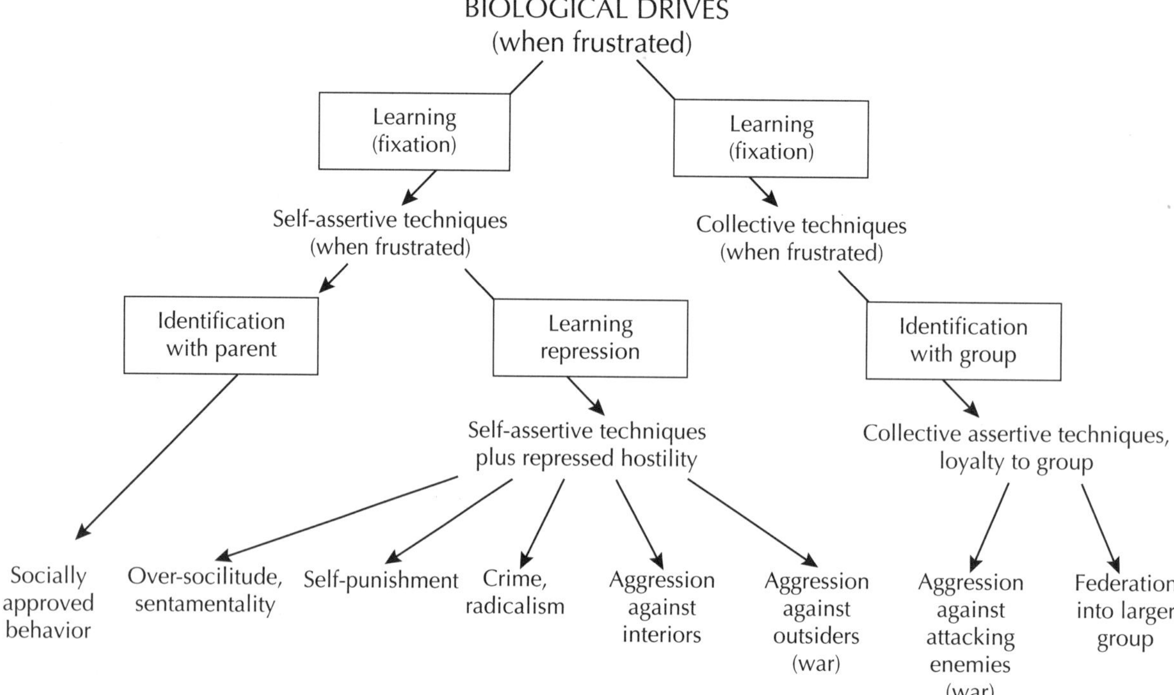

Figure 1. Tolman's drive-conversion diagram.
Source: Figure adapted from G. A. Kimble (1961). Based on E. C. Tomlin (1942).

The mechanism of learning an addiction appears to be a two-stage process. In the first stage, the future addict experiments with the addictive substance out of curiosity or a yielding to peer pressure, or for some other reason that soon becomes irrelevant. In the case of some drugs, like the opiates, only a few such encounters are required to leave the individual with a powerful craving after the initial euphoria produced by the drug wears off. The only ways to relieve this craving are either painful waiting for the craving to subside or taking more of the substance in question. People who become addicted choose the latter alternative, thus beginning the vicious circle: drug—euphoria—agonized craving—drug again. In abstract terms, the learning process appears to be of the operant or instrumental variety, with the relief from craving and the agony of abstinence playing a greater role than the positively reinforcing euphoric experience initiated by the drug.

Motivation and Emotion

The literature on the various acquired drives and drugs provides a particularly straightforward way of making a methodological point. Although common speech and some psychological theories make a distinction between motives and emotions, it is clear that these terms refer to different aspects of the same process. *Motivation* refers to the power of an acquired drive to promote certain kinds of behavior, chiefly those of reaching certain goals—relief from fear, being near a parent, achieving certain social goals, or avoiding withdrawal symptoms. *Emotion* refers to the subjective experiences associated with the arousal of these states.

These points are all very nicely integrated in R. L. Solomon's *opponent-process theory* of emotion. The essential ideas in this theory are the following: (1) the conditions that arouse a motivational/emotional state (State A) also call out a more sluggishly acting opposed state (State B); (2) State B is a "slave" state, which occurs as an inevitable accompaniment of State A; (3) termination of the original emotional circumstances leaves State B as the individual's dominating emotional state; and (4) State B, but not State A, increases with use and decreases with disuse.

Solomon and others have applied this opponent-process theory to many different motivational/emotional reactions. The application provides a rich account of the details of such behavior and a means of understanding the changes in such reactions after many arousals of the emotion. In opiate addiction, for instance, at first the effect of the drug (State A) is a feeling of euphoria, a "rush"; when the drug wears off, its aftereffect (State B) is craving. With continued usage and the strengthening of State B, the effect of the drug is less intense and is often described as a feeling of contentment. Its aftereffect is now much more intense—an excruciatingly painful set of withdrawal symptoms. Similar accounts are put forward for other emotional experiences.

Greg A. Kimble

See also: **Functional Autonomy; Specific Hungers**

ACTION POTENTIAL

The action potential is a self-propagating change in membrane voltage conducted sequentially along the axon of a neuron that transmits information from the neuron cell body or sensory ending to the axon terminal. The action potential is initiated either as the consequence of summation of local electronic potentials in the region where the axon arises from the neuron cell body (axon hillock), or as a result of a sufficiently large generator potential in the sensory ending. Once initiated, the action potential is conducted without change in magnitude along the axon until it invades the axon terminal and causes release of quanta of neurotransmitter molecules.

To understand the action potential it is necessary to understand the resting membrane potential. To record the resting membrane potential and the action potential one electrode is inserted into the cell while a second electrode remains outside the cell. The voltage potential between the two electrodes is amplified and measured. For most neurons the measured resting membrane potential is from –60 to –70 millivolts (mV); the inside of the cell is negative relative to the outside of the cell.

The resting membrane potential is determined by the relative distribution of positively or negatively charged ions near the extracellular and intracellular surfaces of the cell membrane. Positive sodium (Na^+) and potassium (K^+) ions and negative chloride (Cl^-) and organic (A^-) ions are important for both the resting membrane potential and the action potential. The positively charged ions are called *cations,* and the negatively charged ions are called *anions.* The organic anions are mostly proteins and organic acids.

During the resting state Na^+ and Cl^- have higher extracellular than intracellular concentrations, and K^+ and A^- are more highly concentrated within the cell. The organic ions never leave the intracellular compartment, and in most neurons Cl^- is relatively free to pass through the membrane. Three factors contribute to determining the ionic distribution across the membrane. The first factor is the relative permeability of the membrane to each ion species. The second factor is the concentration gradient of each ion species. The third factor is the electromotive force created by the separation of charges across the semipermeable membrane.

Because the inside of the cell is negative relative to the outside, and there is a lower intracellular concentration of Na^+, the sodium cations would flood into the cell if the membrane were freely permeable to Na^+. At rest, however, the cell membrane is not freely permeable to Na^+. Permeability of a membrane to any given ion species is controlled by the number of membrane channels available for that particular species. Membrane channels are made of proteins that extend from the extracellular to the intracellular surface of the membrane (i.e., they are membrane-spanning). The membrane channels may be always open, or nongated, or open only under certain conditions. Channels that open or close depending on conditions are called *gated channels.* Whether gated channels are open or closed depends on the conformation of the proteins that form the walls of the channel. When the neuron membrane is at rest the gated channels for Na^+ are closed. The Na^+ that does enter flows through the nongated, nonspecific channels in the membrane, but it is actively extruded from the cell by the sodium-potassium pump. This pump is made of carrier proteins and uses metabolic energy supplied by adenosine triphosphate (ATP). Na^+ and K^+ are linked in transmembrane transportation such that three Na^+ ions are transported out of the cell for every two K^+ ions that are transported into the cell. The Na^+–K^+ pump maintains the intracellular and extracellular concentrations of these ions, which is necessary for homeostatic osmotic equilibrium across the cell membrane as well as creation of the resting membrane potential.

During the resting state the membrane channels do not allow movement of Na^+ into the cell. However, some Na^+ does enter the cell through nonspecific membrane channels. Na^+ does this because it has a higher concentration outside than inside and, therefore, flows down its concentration gradient. Additionally, the electromotive force created by the relative intracellular negativity propels Na^+ inward. The sodium-potassium ATP-coupled pump counteracts the influx of Na^+ ions in the resting state.

The membrane is also not fully permeable to K^+ in the resting state, but K^+ ions are, compared to Na^+ ions, freer to move through the cell membrane. That is, the neuron membrane is more permeable to K^+ than to Na^+. For this reason K^+ moves more readily down its concentration gradient than Na^+, and the resting membrane potential is, therefore, closer to the K^+ equilibrium potential than the Na^+ equilibrium potential.

To summarize, in the resting state the paucity of open membrane channels for Na^+ and K^+ and the Na^+–K^+ pump serve to maintain an excess of extracellular Na^+ and intracellular K^+. The magnitude of the resting membrane potential is the result of the degree of separation of these cations and the presence of the organic anions within the cell. Because the membrane is more permeable to K^+ than Na^+, the resting membrane potential more closely approximates the equilibrium potential for K^+ than for Na^+.

The Na^+ and K^+ channels are voltage-gated. This means that a change in voltage across the membrane changes the conformation of the channel protein to either open or close the channel. If the membrane depolarizes and the membrane potential becomes more positive, the Na^+ channels begin to open. On dendrites and cell bodies, channels are opened by neurotransmitters released at the synapse from other cells. The neurotransmitters bind to receptors on the target neuron and open chemically gated ion channels. If the neurotransmitter is excitatory, the postsynaptic membrane is slightly depolarized in the area of the synapse. This depolarization is less than required for generation of an action potential. However, depolarizing excitatory postsynaptic potentials (EPSPs) sum at the axon hillock with hyperpolarizing inhibitory postsynaptic potentials (IPSPs). If the resulting change in membrane polarity at the hillock is a depolarization that exceeds about 10 mV an action potential is initiated.

Depolarization at the axon hillock causes voltage-gated Na^+ channels to open. The number of Na^+ channels opened by the depolarization is proportional to the amount of positive change in membrane potential until threshold for action potential initiation is exceeded, at which time essentially all of the Na^+ channels in the area of threshold depolarization open and Na^+ rushes into the axon. The membrane potential then moves rapidly (about 0.5 ms) toward Na^+ equilibrium potential until it becomes about +55 mV. This is the rising phase of the action potential; when it reaches its peak, Na^+ channels close and voltage-gated K^+ channels open. K^+ leaves the cell and, in combination with decreased Na^+ conductance, reverses the depolarization. The K^+ channels stay open long enough not only to return the membrane potential to its resting level, but to cause a brief (about 2 ms) overshoot hyperpolarization. During the early part of the hyperpolarizing phase of the action potential, Na^+ channels can not reopen and another action potential can not be generated. This is known as the *absolute refractory period.* This prevents action potentials from summating. As the membrane continues to repolarize, an action potential can be generated if a stronger than normal stimulus is applied to the axon. This is known as the *relative refractory period.* Within 2.5 ms after peak depolarization of the action potential, the resting Na^+–K^+ concentrations are restored and the system is ready for reactivation.

The action potential propagates because the ionic current flow at one point of the membrane causes changes in current flow in the adjacent membrane toward the axon terminal. The current flow changes the transmembrane voltage potential and opens Na^+ channels. The entire sequence just described is then repeated. In myelinated axons, the current flow occurs only at the nodes of Ranvier. In addition to lacking the electrical insulation provided by myelin, the nodes of Ranvier also have a far greater concentration of Na^+ channels than do the parts of the axon covered by myelin. The result of the presence of myelin is that the action potential jumps from one node to the next (saltatory conduction). This produces more rapid conduction of the action potential than is possible in nonmyelinated axons.

SUGGESTED READING

Koester, J. (1991a). Membrane potential. In E. R. Kandel, J. H. Schwartz, & T. M. Jessell (Eds.), *Principles of neural science* (3rd ed., pp. 81–94). New York: Elsevier.

Koester, J. (1991b). Voltage-gated ion channels and the generation of the action potential. In E. R. Kandel, J. H. Schwartz, & T. M. Jessell (Eds.), *Principles of neural science* (3rd ed., pp. 104–118). New York: Elsevier.

Siegelbaum, S. S., & Koester, J. (1991). Ion channels. In E. R. Kandel, J. H. Schwartz, & T. M. Jessell (Eds.), *Principles of neural science* (3rd ed., pp. 66–79). New York: Elsevier.

Shepherd, G. M. (1994). The membrane potential: The action potential. In *Neurobiology* (3rd ed., pp. 87–121). New York: Oxford University Press.

Smock, T. K. (1999). Communication among neurons: The membrane potential. In *Physiological psychology: A neuroscience approach* (pp. 47–87). Upper Saddle River, NJ: Prentice Hall.

Michael L. Woodruff
East Tennessee State University

ADAPTATION

Like many other words in psychology, *adaptation* has multiple meanings. At the basis of all the meanings, however, is the concept carried by its Latin root, *adaptare:* to fit.

Among ethologists, who think that characteristic species-typical behaviors are distillations of evolutionary processes, each physical and behavioral characteristic of a species is the product of and contributes to its adaptive radiation, the multiplication of individuals that can survive in the changing environment, and the diversification of the species in a diverse environment. Such adaptation is genetically based and requires numerous generations to be accomplished.

In contrast to this genetic adaptation are phenotypic adaptations, often only seconds in duration, which occur within the life span of an individual. The results of these adaptations are not transmitted to the offspring, although the capacity for such adaptation is. Implicit in the concept is the alteration of an individual by the presence of a persistent, nontoxic or nontraumatic, nonfatiguing stimulus, or by the prolonged cessation and absence of a customary, persistent stimulus, such as weightlessness. Examples of such adaptation include the gradual diminution in the coldness of water after we immerse our hand in it; the reduction in loudness of a tone after a few seconds; and the return of sight (though colorless) after a period in a darkened room following exposure to bright lights, and the return of comfortable color vision after reexposure to a brightly lighted environment. The mechanisms involved in these examples are all different: stimulus (receptor) failure in the cold; activation of an acoustic reflex (plus receptor change); and bleaching and regeneration of photopigments plus neural change in the retina. In general, scientists tend to think of this kind of adaptation as occurring in or affecting the receptor, whereas the term for a similar phenomenon—*habituation*—is reserved for those situations in which more central events are at least involved if not prominent.

A so-called "General Adaptation Syndrome" was proposed by Selye (1950) as part of our typical response to dangerous environmental challenge. This syndrome is an extension of Cannon's Emergency Syndrome (1932/1960) the "flee, fright, or fight" syndrome, consisting of a rapid total body response to the challenge. Many manifestations of the adaptation syndrome have been observed in lower animals, but they often are difficult to detect in humans. Other concepts (e.g., acclimatization) have been proposed to account for many of the data.

REFERENCES

Cannon, W. B. (1960). *The wisdom of the body.* New York: Norton. (Original work published 1932)

Selye, H. (1950). *Stress.* Montreal, Canada: Acta.

Arthur J. Riopelle

See also: **Accommodation; General Adaptation Syndrome**

ADDICTION

Addiction is a term widely used to indicate any type of excessive repetitive involvement with an activity or substance, and it is applied as readily to exercise, reading, and television viewing as to alcohol, cocaine, or heroin use. Such broad use of the term detracts from its technical value, and in this entry the term will be used to refer only to substance use. When considering problematic patterns of use, two distinct patterns, abuse and dependence, are described (American Psychiatric Association, 1994). Substance Abuse refers to life problems from substance use—use in situations in which it is physically dangerous, use interfering with occupational roles or with family and other social relationships, or use resulting in legal difficulties. In contrast, Substance Dependence is more syndromal. Physiological components of dependence may include tolerance—the need for increasing amounts of the substance to attain the same behavioral and subjective effects—or withdrawal, a physical syndrome activated by cessation of use of the substance. Behavioral components include using larger amounts of the substance over longer periods of times than intended; spending excessive amounts of time obtaining, using, and recovering from use of the substance; or using instead of engaging in other recreational and social pursuits. Psychological components include continued use despite knowledge of medical or psychological conditions caused or worsened by substance use, and desire or actual attempts to cut down or stop using the substance. Use of a range of substances, including alcohol, other sedative/hypnotic/anxiolytic drugs, cocaine, other stimulants, heroin, cannabis, hallucinogens, inhalants, and nicotine, can lead to Substance Abuse or Dependence. A withdrawal syndrome is associated only with alcohol, sedative/hypnotic/anxiolytic drugs, heroin, and nicotine.

Epidemiology

Use of alcohol is common; regular use or abuse of other drugs is less common (Grant & Dawson, 1999). At some time in their adult lives two thirds of Americans have been regular drinkers (consumed at least 12 drinks in a year). In contrast, just under 16% of Americans are regular drug users (illicit use of a drug at least 12 times in a year) at some point in their lives. The lifetime prevalence of Substance Abuse and Dependence varies by substance, with different prevalence rates for men and women. Alcohol Abuse or Dependence is most common, with a lifetime prevalence for men of 25.5% and for women of 11.4%. In contrast, 8.1% of men and 4.2% of women have had any form of drug abuse or dependence at some time in their lives. The most common drug of abuse or dependence is cannabis, followed by prescription drugs, cocaine, amphetamines, hallucinogens, opiates, and sedatives.

Etiology

The causes of addiction are complex and involve an interplay among three dimensions—the biological, the psychological, and the social. The relative importance of each dimension varies with the specific substance of abuse and with the individual user. Considerable research has attempted to identify the causes of dependence at the cellular or molecular level. A number of different neuronal changes have been suggested as causing Alcohol Dependence, including changes in neuronal membranes, changes in the excitability and function of nerve cells mediated through the calcium and GABA receptor/chloride channels, changes in the activity of excitatory neurotransmitter systems, and changes in second messenger systems (Moak & Anton, 1999). Research on opiate dependence has failed to find changes in opiate receptors associated with addiction. However, at the subcellular level, chronic exposure to opiates has been demonstrated to lead to long-term changes in specific G protein subunits (Stine & Kosten, 1999).

Substance use disorders run in families, and research has attempted to distinguish genetic from familial aspects of etiology. Both twin and adoption studies suggest a heritable component to Alcohol Dependence. With other drugs, some studies are suggestive of genetic elements, such as evidence of common drug preferences in monozygotic twins, and increased risk for drug dependence in families (Hesselbrock, Hesselbrock, & Epstein, 1999). The relationship between family history and the development of alcohol or other substance dependence, however, is not absolute—the majority of offspring from families with Alcohol Abuse or Dependence do not develop problems, and the majority of those with Alcohol Abuse or Dependence do not have a clear family history (Fingarette, 1988).

Among those with familial alcohol or drug problems, the mechanisms by which inherited risk is expressed are not clear. The most common mechanism appears to be through specific temperament or personality—persons high in sensation seeking, low in harm avoidance, and low in reward dependence. Consequently, those with inherited risk for alcohol or drug dependence are at greater risk for Conduct Disorder or Antisocial Personality Disorder.

Psychological research has demonstrated the importance of interactions between the individual and environment. Repeated exposure to drug use situations can lead to conditioned physiological responses to the situations that are similar to physiological responses to the actual drug (Rohsenow et al., 1994). The development of strong positive expectancies about the effects of certain drugs can also contribute to continued use (Brown, Christiansen, & Goldman, 1987). Individuals may use substances to enhance positive moods as well as to cope with negative emotions, and those with other psychological problems are at particularly high risk for the development of substance use disorders as well.

Alcohol and drug use occurs in a social context. Introduction to alcohol and drug use most commonly occurs with either peers or family members. Individuals who are at high risk for using drugs and for other problem behaviors often join with peers of a similarly high risk level, and these peer groups then may influence those within the group to continue to use or experiment with other substances and other high-risk behaviors.

Prevention

Prevention of addiction has taken many forms, including broad-brush prevention programs in schools; prevention targeted at specific populations, such as pregnant women; and environmentally focused interventions that change laws and policies, decrease access to the substance, and increase penalties. Individually and environmentally focused interventions have been successful in preventing or delaying the onset of use, decreasing use among those already using, and decreasing harmful consequences to the individual or to others.

Treatment

Treatment efforts include both psychological and pharmacological approaches. A number of psychological therapies are effective in the treatment of Substance Abuse or Dependence. Brief, motivationally focused interventions are effective for individuals with milder problems, and they also may enhance treatment outcomes when combined with ongoing treatments (Bien, Miller, & Tonigan, 1993). Cognitive-behavioral therapies, including community reinforcement treatment, relapse prevention, social skills training, and behavioral couples therapy, have good support for their effectiveness in treating Alcohol Dependence (McCrady & Langenbucher, 1996). Community reinforcement combined with the use of vouchers (Higgins et al., 1994), and family therapy (Liddle & Dakof, 1995) are effective in treating drug dependence. Outcomes for those who complete long-term treatment in therapeutic communities are good, but dropout rates are high (Simpson & Curry, 1997). Treatments to facilitate involvement with self-help groups such as Alcoholics Anonymous or Narcotics Anonymous also are effective (Project MATCH Research Group, 1997), and continued active participation in self-help groups is correlated with better outcomes.

Separate from medications for withdrawal, effective pharmacotherapies to treat substance use disorders are somewhat limited in number. Naltrexone, acamprosate, and disulfiram have evidence supporting their use in the treatment of alcohol dependence. Methadone, LAAM (1-a-acetylmethadol), and buprenorphine have strong evidence of effectiveness in the treatment of opioid dependence. Nicotine replacement products are effective in the initial phases of treatment for nicotine dependence, and bupropion appears to be effective for longer-term pharmacotherapy (Barber & O'Brien, 1999).

Conclusions

The term *addiction* is overused, but it is useful in referring to a range of substance use problems. Etiology of these problems is complex, with multiple biological, psychological, and social factors contributing. Prevention is possible, and a number of effective treatments are available.

REFERENCES

American Psychiatric Association. (1994). *Diagnostic and statistical manual of mental disorders* (4th ed.). Washington, DC: Author.

Barber, W. S., & O'Brien, C. P. (1999). Pharmacotherapies. In B. S. McCrady & E. E. Epstein (Eds.), *Addictions: A comprehensive guidebook* (pp. 347–369). New York: Oxford University Press.

Bien, T. H., Miller, W. R., & Tonigan, J. S. (1993). Brief interventions for alcohol problems: A review. *Addiction, 88,* 315–336.

Brown, S. A., Christiansen, B. A., & Goldman, M. S. (1987). The Alcohol Expectancy Questionnaire: An instrument for the assessment of adolescent and adult expectancies. *Journal of Studies on Alcohol, 48,* 483–491.

Fingarette, H. (1988). *The myth of heavy drinking as a disease.* Berkeley: University of California Press.

Grant, B. F., & Dawson, D. A. (1999). Alcohol and drug use, abuse, and dependence: Classification, prevalence, and comorbidity. In B. S. McCrady & E. E. Epstein (Eds.), *Addictions: A comprehensive guidebook* (pp. 9–29). New York: Oxford University Press.

Hesselbrock, M., Hesselbrock, V., & Epstein, E. (1999). Theories of etiology of alcohol and other drug use disorders. In B. S. McCrady & E. E. Epstein (Eds.), *Addictions: A comprehensive guidebook* (pp. 50–74). New York: Oxford University Press.

Higgins, S. T., Budney, A. J., Bickel, W. K., Foerg, F. E., Donham, R., & Badger, G. J. (1994). Incentives improve outcome in outpatient behavioral treatment of cocaine dependence. *Archives of General Psychiatry, 51,* 568–576.

Liddle, H., & Dakof, G. A. (1995). Family-based treatment for adolescent drug use: State of the science [Monograph]. In E. Rahdert & D. Czechowicz (Eds.), *Adolescent drug abuse: Clinical assessment and therapeutic interventions* (pp. 218–254). Rockville, MD: National Institute on Drug Abuse Research.

McCrady, B. S., & Langenbucher, J. W. (1996). Alcoholism treatment and health care reform. *Archives of General Psychiatry, 53,* 737–746.

Moak, D., & Anton, R. (1999). Alcohol. In B. S. McCrady & E. E. Epstein (Eds.), *Addictions: A comprehensive guidebook* (pp. 75–94). New York: Oxford University Press.

Project MATCH Research Group. (1997). Matching alcoholism treatments to client heterogeneity: Project MATCH posttreatment drinking outcomes. *Journal of Studies on Alcohol, 58,* 7–29.

Rohsenow, D. J., Monti, P. M., Rubonis, A. V., Sirota, A. D., Niaura, R. S., Colby, S. M., et al. (1994). Cue reactivity as a predictor of drinking among male alcoholics. *Journal of Consulting and Clinical Psychology, 62,* 620–626.

Simpson, D. D., & Curry, S. J. (Eds.). (1997). Drug abuse treatment outcome study [Special issue]. *Psychology of Addictive Behaviors, 11*(4), 211–337.

Stine, S. M., & Kosten, T. R. (1999). Opioids. In B. S. McCrady & E. E. Epstein (Eds.), *Addictions: A comprehensive guidebook* (pp. 141–161). New York: Oxford University Press.

Barbara S. McCrady

ADHD (ATTENTION-DEFICIT/ HYPERACTIVITY DISORDER)

Description

Attention-Deficit/Hyperactivity Disorder (ADHD) is most commonly characterized by persistent and chronic inattention and/or excessive motor restlessness and impulsive behavior. Earlier names for ADHD included Minimal Brain Dysfunction, Hyperkinetic Impulse Disorder, and Attention Deficit Disorder with or without Hyperactivity. Since the 1994 publication of the fourth edition of the *Diagnostic and Statistical Manual of Mental Disorders* (*DSM-IV*), ADHD has been reorganized into three subtypes: predominantly inattentive (ADHD-I), predominantly hyperactive-impulsive (ADHD-HI), and combined (ADHD-C). The inattentive subtype requires six or more symptoms of inattention and five or fewer hyperactive-impulsive symptoms. The hyperactive-impulsive subtype consists of six or more symptoms of hyperactivity-impulsivity and five or fewer inattentive symptoms. The combined subtype requires six or more out of nine symptoms from both the inattentive and hyperactive-impulsive categories. Symptoms on the inattentive list are related to poor attention and organizational skills, forgetfulness, and distractibility. Symptoms on the hyperactive-impulsive list refer to restlessness, excessive talking, and interrupting. According to *DSM-IV,* the symptoms must be present for at least 6 months and observable by 7 years of age. For the purpose of diagnosis, symptom manifestation should be developmentally inappropriate and exhibited in two or more settings (e.g., home and school).

Prevalence

Prevalence rates of ADHD in the childhood population vary, with expert opinion most often citing an incidence of approximately 3–5% (American Psychiatric Association, 1994). Prevalence rates in adults are more speculative, but are estimated to be about 4.7% (Barkley, 1998). The disorder is more common in males, with Barkley (1998) citing three males to one female for nonreferred samples.

Diagnosis

The diagnosis of ADHD remains difficult, with no single test to assess it and a heavy reliance on subjective measures. A comprehensive evaluation of ADHD in adults or children should assess the presence or absence of symptomatology, differential diagnosis from other disorders that mimic ADHD, and the possibility of comorbid psychiatric disorders. At a minimum, the evaluation should include a clinical interview, a medical evaluation conducted within the past year, standardized behavior rating scales from parents and teachers, and direct observation of the patient. The evaluation for both children and adults includes a family history as well as documentation regarding developmental, social, and academic functioning. An evaluation for adults should also include information regarding their childhood via academic records and transcripts and retrospective-childhood ratings by the adult patient and a parent or another individual who knew the patient as a child. Common conditions that may coexist with ADHD and warrant screening include Oppositional Defiant Disorder, Conduct Disorder, Bipolar Disorder, Antisocial Personality Disorder (for adults), and learning disorders. An assessment of intellectual, academic, neuropsychological, and attentional functioning is desirable for purposes of differential diagnosis, as well as for pointing out individual strengths and weaknesses. Psychoeducational testing can also be useful when a low level of intellectual functioning or a learning disability mimics or coexists with ADHD.

Treatment

Treatment of ADHD should be individualized depending upon the presenting concerns. Treatment approaches may include behavioral interventions combined with medication. Interventions begin with education about ADHD, its etiology, and its treatment. Behavioral interventions for children include social skills training, school interventions, and parent training in contingency management. Behavioral treatments for adults often focus on developmentally appropriate self-monitoring techniques (e.g., a self-prescribed reward for completing a goal), time management skills, organizational skills, social skills, and vocational counseling. Adults may also choose to have an individual therapist or coach to monitor daily progress.

The use of pharmacological interventions is warranted if the symptoms are interfering significantly with functioning at home, school, or work. Psychostimulant medications (e.g., methylphenidate and dextroamphetamine) are considered safe and effective treatments for ADHD and are used to treat children as well as adults whose diagnoses have been confirmed. Stimulants, typically considered the first line of defense, can produce improvements in impulse control, attention, on-task behavior, and social behavior. A number of new delivery systems for psychostimulant medications have become available that have the potential to reduce dosing from the older regimen of two to three times a day to once a day.

Other medications, including bupropion and tricyclic antidepressants, are considered when there are concerns regarding substance abuse or coexisting depression, or when the stimulants produce significant side effects. There are several new nonstimulant compounds under development for the disorder. These compounds target the norepinephrinergic, histaminergic, and dopaminergic systems.

Neurobiologic Bases of ADHD

The etiology of ADHD is unknown, although the disorder is now considered a disorder of the brain and development. There has been a wave of recent genetic studies that suggest that a substantial genetic component contributes to the disorder. Most of the genetic research has focused on candidate genes involved in dopaminergic transmission.

Dysfunction in both dopaminergic and norepinephrinergic neurotransmitter systems are implicated in ADHD. Both clinical and preclinical pharmacological studies support the role of these neurotransmitters in ADHD, with additional confirmation for the role of catecholamine's involvement arising from the observation that compounds known to improve ADHD symptoms affect catecholamine transmission. Neuroimaging research into brain structure and the function of ADHD in children and adults has shown significant differences between subjects with ADHD and controls in frontal, basal ganglia, and cerebellar anatomy and function. A number of functional imaging studies demonstrate decreased neuronal activity in the anterior cingulate and associated projection areas in subjects with ADHD. A combination of methods using behavioral, imaging, and genetic techniques should increase our understanding of the etiology of the disorder in the future.

REFERENCES

American Academy of Child and Adolescent Psychiatry. (1997). Practice parameters for the assessment and treatment of children, adolescents, and adults with Attention-Deficit/Hyperactivity Disorder. *Journal of the American Academy of Child and Adolescent Psychiatry, 36*(Supp.), 85S–121S.

American Psychiatric Association. (1994). *Diagnostic and statistical manual of mental disorders* (4th ed.). Washington, DC: Author.

Barkley, R. A. (1998). *Attention Deficit Hyperactivity Disorder* (2nd ed.). New York: Guilford Press.

Julie B. Schweitzer
Maryland Psychiatric Research Center

See also: **Behavior Therapy; Genetics; Neurotransmitters; Self-control**

ADOLESCENT DEVELOPMENT

Adolescence can be defined as the period in life when most of a person's biological, cognitive, psychological, and social characteristics are changing in an interrelated manner from what is considered childlike to what is considered adultlike (Lerner & Spanier, 1980). When most of one's characteristics are in this state of change one is an adolescent.

Adolescence requires adjustments to changes in the self, family, peer group, and institutions. There are individual differences in the timing, speed, and outcomes of these transitions, changes caused by variation in the timing of connections among biological, psychological, and societal factors, and not merely *one* of these factors acting alone (Brooks-Gunn & Petersen, 1983; Lerner, 2002). A major source of diversity in development is the systemic relations adolescents have with people and institutions in their context (Bandura, 1964; Block, 1971; Douvan & Adelson, 1966; Lerner, 2002; Offer, 1969).

Multiple Levels of Context are Influential During Adolescence

Adolescence is a period of rapid transitions in physical characteristics. The quality and timing of hormonal or other biological changes influence, and are influenced by, psychological, social, cultural, and historical factors (Elder, 1998; Gottlieb, 1997; Magnusson & Stattin, 1998; Tanner, 1991).

Biological effects interact with contextual and experiential factors to influence psychological and social functioning—for example, academic achievement (Lerner, 2002; Lerner & Galambos, 1998; Simmons & Blyth, 1987). Evidence does not support the claim that behavioral disturbances are a universal part of adolescence (e.g., Hall, 1904;

Freud, 1969) or that general psychological or social disruptions mark adolescence. For example, the biological changes of early pubertal maturation have been linked to delinquency in adolescent girls, but only among those who attended mixed-sex schools (Caspi, Lynam, Moffitt & Silva, 1993) or among girls who socialized with older peers (Magnusson & Stattin, 1998).

Changing Relations among Adolescents and Their Contexts Produce Development in Adolescence

The varying relations between adolescents and their contexts constitute the basic process of development in this period and underlie both positive and negative outcomes that occur (Lerner, 2002). Most developmental trajectories across adolescence involve positive adjustment on the part of the adolescent. For most youth there is a continuation of warm and accepting relations with parents (Grotevant, 1998). The most optimal development occurs among youth who are afforded the individual and ecological assets needed not only for positive development but also for thriving (Benson, 1997; Damon, 1997).

Conclusions

To advance basic knowledge and the applications aimed at enhancing youth development, scholarship should be directed toward elucidating the developmental course of diverse adolescents and how their individual and ecological strengths—and those of families and communities—result in healthy, positive development. Policies and programs must be aimed not only at the amelioration or prevention of problems; rather, actions must be directed toward promoting positive youth development (Lerner, Fisher, & Weinberg, 2000).

The stereotype that there is only one type of pathway across adolescence is not viable in the face of current knowledge about adolescent diversity. In future research and applications, scholars and practitioners must extend their conception of adolescence to focus on changing relations between individual youth characteristics and their distinct ecologies. Understanding these relations may enable the strengths of all young people to be translated into actions, resulting in successful contributions to self, family, community, and civil society.

REFERENCES

Bandura, A. (1964). The stormy decade: Fact or fiction? *Psychology in the School, 1,* 224–231.

Benson, P. (1997). *All kids are our kids: What communities must do to raise caring and responsible children and adolescents.* San Francisco: Jossey Bass.

Block, J. (1971). *Living through time.* Berkeley, CA: Bancroft Books.

Brooks-Gunn, J., & Petersen, A. C. (1983). *Girls at puberty: Biological and psychosocial perspectives.* New York: Plenum Press.

Caspi, A., Lynam, D., Moffitt, T. E., & Silva, P. A. (1993). Unraveling girls' delinquency: Biological, dispositional, and contextual contributions to adolescent misbehavior. *Developmental Psychology, 29,* 19–30.

Damon, W. (1997). *The youth charter: How communities can work together to raise standards for all our children.* New York: Free Press.

Douvan, J. D., & Adelson, J. (1966). *The adolescent experience.* New York: Wiley.

Elder, G. H., Jr. (1998). The life course and human development. In W. Damon (Series Ed.) & R. M. Lerner (Vol. Ed.), *Handbook of child psychology: Vol 1. Theoretical models of human development* (5th ed., pp. 939–991). New York: Wiley.

Freud, A. (1969). Adolescence as a developmental disturbance. In G. Caplan & S. Lebovier (Eds.), *Adolescence* (pp. 5–10). New York: Basic Books.

Gottlieb, G. (1997). *Synthesizing nature-nurture: Prenatal roots of instinctive behavior.* Mahwah, NJ: Erlbaum.

Grotevant, H. D. (1998). Adolescent development in family contexts. In W. Damon (Series Ed.), *Handbook of child psychology: Vol. 3* (pp. 1097–1149). New York: Wiley.

Hall, G. S. (1904). *Adolescence: Its psychology and its relations to psychology, anthropology, sociology, sex, crime, religion, and education.* New York: Appleton.

Lerner, R. M. (2002). *Adolescence: Development, diversity, context, and application.* Upper Saddle River, NJ: Pearson.

Lerner, R. M., Fisher, C., & Weinberg, R. A. (2000). Toward a science for and of the people: Promoting civil society through the application of developmental science. *Child Development, 71,* 11–20.

Lerner, R. M., & Galambos, N. L. (1998). Adolescent development: Challenges and opportunities for research, programs, and policies. In J. T. Spence (Ed.), *Annual review of psychology* (Vol. 49, pp. 413–446). Palo Alto, CA: Annual Reviews.

Lerner, R. M., & Spanier, G. B. (1980). A dynamic interactional view of child and family development. In R. M. Lerner & G. B. Spanier (Eds.), *Child influences on marital and family interaction: A life-span perspective* (pp. 1–20). New York: Academic Press.

Magnusson, D., & Stattin, H. (1998). Person-context interaction theories. In W. Damon (Series Ed.) & R. M. Lerner (Vol. Ed.), *Handbook of child psychology: Vol. 1. Theoretical models of human development* (5th ed., pp. 685–759). New York: Wiley.

Offer, D. (1969). *The psychological world of the teen-ager.* New York: Basic Books.

Simmons, R. G., & Blyth, D. A. (1987). *Moving into adolescence: The impact of pubertal change and school context.* Hawthorne, NJ: Aldine.

Tanner, J. (1991). Menarche, secular trend in age of. In R. M. Lerner, A. C. Petersen, & J. Brooks-Gunn (Eds.), *Encyclopedia of adolescence* (Vol. 1, pp. 637–641). New York: Garland.

Richard M. Lerner
Aida B. Balsano
Deborah L. Bobek
Tufts University

See also: **Contextualism; Individual Differences; Peer Influences**

ADOLESCENT SEX OFFENDERS

Historically, sexual offenses by adolescents have been minimized and viewed as innocent sex play, experimentation, curiosity, or a normal aspect of sexual development. In the early 1980s, however, clinicians and the judicial system determined that aberrant juvenile sexual behaviors were unacceptable and would be considered criminal actions in need of appropriate psychological treatment. Although incidence rates vary, Uniform Crime Report (UCR) statistics indicate that 20% of rapes and about 50% of reported cases of child molestation are committed by adolescents. Confirmatory data from treatment settings show that child victims of sexual abuse report an adolescent perpetrator in 40 to 60% of cases. Most adolescent sex offenders are male. The incidence rate is about 5% for females; such offenses predominantly occur with siblings or in baby-sitting situations.

The most common offenses among male offenders are fondling, rape, and exhibitionism, with 50% of the offenses involving some form of penetration. Nearly 66% of the victims are children under 10 years of age. Most of the victims of adolescent sexual offenses are known by the offender; the majority are either family members, extended family members, or acquaintances. It is noteworthy that the majority of adolescent sex offenders had themselves been sexually abused as children or came from families in which spousal violence, child abuse, or sexual molestation had occurred. The high incidence of childhood victimization suggests a reactive, conditioned behavior pattern that demonstrates the cyclical nature of sexual abuse. There is no evidence that adolescent sex offenders are more prevalent in the lower socioeconomic strata, although several studies implicate the problems of the father-absent household.

Earlier studies on the etiologies of juvenile sexual abuse revealed that the adolescent child molester is a loner, has few friends or social peers, prefers interaction with younger children, has a limited occupational history, is an underachiever, is immature, and identifies with a dominating mother. More recent research has suggested other clinical dimensions of the adolescent offender (i.e., feelings of male inadequacy; low self-esteem; fear of rejection; anger toward women; aberrant erotic fantasies; and identification with adult models of aggression, violence, and intimidation). A central characteristic of the offender is poor psychological adjustment and adaptation, which is evident in poor social skills, social isolation, lack of appropriate assertiveness, and deficits in communication skills.

Differential diagnosis is a major concern in the evaluation of sex offenders. It is difficult to distinguish between the diagnosis of "sex offender" and related disorders of delinquency, impulsivity, conduct disturbances, hyperactivity, and Substance Abuse. Frequently, a dual diagnosis seems in order. A related problem arises when clinicians or researchers must differentiate between the psychological and criminal nature of the offense. A review of the literature by G. E. Davis and H. Leitenberg emphasizes that empirical research on the characteristics and profile of the adolescent sex offender is still at the rudimentary stage.

In recent years, several studies have reported on the psychological assessment of juvenile sex offenders versus nonsex adolescent offenders. Studies using the Minnesota Multiphasic Personality Inventory and the Rorschach Inkblot Test found few differences between sex offenders and juvenile offenders. This has led researchers to conclude that adolescent sex offenders are actually a subgroup of juvenile delinquents or sociopaths. On the Rorschach, however, the former group gave more anatomy responses, which reflected repressed hostility and destructive impulses.

An increasing number of rehabilitation programs are now available for the specific treatment of the adolescent sex offender. A National Adolescent Perpetrator Network has been established with guidelines for treatment components and goals. These include confronting denial, accepting responsibility, understanding the pattern or cycle of sexually offensive behaviors, developing empathy for victims, controlling deviant sexual arousal, combating cognitive distortions that trigger offending, expressing emotions and the self, developing trust, remediating social skills deficits, and preventing relapse. In addition, these intensive treatment programs focus on didactic instruction on normal human sexuality, training in interpersonal and dating skills, and the teaching of anger control techniques. Psychodynamic-oriented therapy has shown disappointing results, whereas various behavioral, cognitive-behavioral, and prescriptive approaches have proved to be most efficacious. Many programs use a multicomponent treatment approach, which usually includes family therapy. However, biological treatment modalities such as antiandrogenic medications are not indicated in the treatment of adolescent offenders. Residential treatment and community-based programs are showing much promise. J. Bingham and C. Piotrowski discuss the usefulness and rehabilitative aspects of a house arrest program in Florida as an option to incarceration for young sex offenders. Unfortunately, few controlled outcome studies have been reported on the long-term effectiveness of these types of treatment programs.

C. Piotrowski

See also: **Adolescent Development; Antisocial Personality Disorder; Sexual Deviations**

ADOPTED CHILDREN

Intra- and Extrafamilial Adoption

A distinction is made between intrafamilially and extrafamilially adopted children. In intrafamilial or kinship adoption, children are adopted either by blood relatives or by family members by marriage, frequently a stepparent of the adopted child. A genuine desire to adopt is, normally, not the primary motivating force in kinship adoptions, except when childless family members adopt. The classical intrafamilial adoption occurs (a) to protect children whose parents are not available to care for them, (b) to prevent children from ever being returned to an unfit parent (addiction, violence, etc.), or (c) to change the legal status of stepchildren. The majority of adoptions are extrafamilial ones, whose goals include building a family (e.g., in the case of infertile couples), balancing a single-gender sibling constellation, or making a foster child or a child in need into a family member. Selfish goals include securing cheap labor, acquiring a permanent baby-sitting service for younger siblings, or, in the worst-case scenario, acquiring a sex object.

Known or presumed reasons for the adoption can play a major role in the parent-adoptee relationship. Complications in stepchild adoptions can be predicted when a child resents the family merger and insists on keeping the biological father's name or when a reluctant stepparent fears adverse financial consequences. Children deal well with unequal status among siblings, if it is a result of the children's own choices. Equal treatment of children in daily life is more important than equality of legal status.

Special Needs Children

Twenty-five percent of domestic adopted children in the United States are reported to be special needs (SN) children. Many parents cannot foresee the impact such children can have on the family. SN children include children with physical or emotional (including behavioral and delinquency) problems. Parental estimates of physically ill or handicapped children's effect on their lives are often more realistic than the outcome projection of adopting children with mental or emotional deficits or handicaps. Families are rarely prepared for the enormous consequences mental illness, acting-out behavior, addiction, and delinquency can have on them. The fact that many of the older adoptees already have multiple rejections behind them further impedes successful bonding and family integration. Family breakups can result from unrelenting stress. Successful outcomes are related to parent/family qualities including flexible expectations, coping and listening skills, resourcefulness, rejection tolerance, sense of humor, willingness to forgive, applause readiness, patience, and love.

Telling Children About Adoption: How and When

Informing children about their adoption status is of major importance. It eliminates the risk that the child might find out from nonfamily sources, which could jeopardize the adoptee's trust in the parents. Where adoption is a familiar, positively valued household subject even before the child grasps the meaning of the word, concept comprehension grows naturally with the child's cognitive development and evokes positive emotions. Even inadvertently portraying adoption as an inferior, last-resort way of building a family devalues the wanted child to a means to an end. Late disclosure, even in adulthood, can seriously affect the adoptee's sense of self and create identity problems.

Acceptance, Rejection, Identification

Depending on their preadoption history, adoptees may experience acceptance, rejection, identification, and separation issues in a magnified way, as these issues can activate concerns about the loss of the biological parents and the reasons for and permanence of their being wanted by their new parents. Identifying with the adopting parents may be a complex task, if truth and fantasy about the lost parents interfere or if strong differences, such as skin color or IQ, set them apart. Parental counteridentification problems can be felt. Not convinced that family bonds are forever, adoptees appear especially vulnerable to even a semblance of rejection. Even normal parental limit setting can be interpreted as a rejection. Being sensitive to weak, unstable, or conditional parent-child bonding, adopted children can act out and seriously test parental love. While actually seeking confirmation of the unconditional acceptance they had hoped for, they sometimes precipitate the very rejection they feared. Children traumatized by the instability of ever-changing caretakers in early childhood may have difficulty bonding successfully and face exceptionally turbulent times when seeking to separate from their parents in adolescence. Reassuring adoptees of having been chosen, not merely wanted, can increase their self-esteem and experience of being secure. A comparison of normal children—both adopted and nonadopted—revealed no difference in self-concept between the two groups. Adoption becomes a negligible factor in individuals who are able to make a positive adjustment.

Search For Biological Parents

Despite the presumed rejection by their birth parents, many adopted children start to search for their biological parents, typically during adolescence. Motivating goals include the wish to meet the parent(s) and additional family members; to learn about their lives; to replace the birth parents' presumed rejection with an acceptable scenario; and to gain genetic information and clarify identity issues. Outcomes can be positive, but adoptees can also uncover parents who are in negative life circumstances or unwilling to enter a personal relationship for fear of destabilizing their present social balance.

Understanding parents assist their adopted children in finding their birth parents. Search interests vary: out of a group of transracially adopted children, all of the Black children, but only some of the Asian and Caucasian ones, initiated a search.

Searches can be hampered by laws governing the disclosure of information on birth parents, some of which are intended to protect not only adoptees but also the privacy of the biological parents.

Open, Closed, and Mediated Adoption

Closed or confidential adoption was standard practice in the past. In response to the psychological problems and genetic information gap caused by this practice, open adoption is becoming the mode of choice, and mediated adoption offers an intermediate solution.

Open adoption refers to information sharing and/or actual contacts between biological and adoptive parents. Communication may be limited to the time before the child is placed with the new parents, or it may continue as long as the parties involved remain interested in maintaining contact. Open adoption offers the opportunity to meet biological relatives or to maintain established ties if the child had lived with biological family members prior to adoption. Children in open adoption situations typically feel less rejected, have higher self-esteem, and adjust better. Changes to reduce or discontinue contact were initiated more often by birth parents than by adoptive families.

It appears wise to allow children who never knew or do not remember their birth parents to meet them early. Very young children take facts as they are and need no explanation. Having one mother who gave birth to the adoptee and another mother to live with is perfectly acceptable, particularly if in the child's mind it has always been that way.

In *mediated adoption* a third party shares information between biological and adoptive families without disclosing identities. Families who are unwilling to reveal their name or whereabouts can share information so as not to deprive the adoptee. Later, the child will be able to initiate contact with the birth mother, if desired. Concerns include possible misunderstandings or misinterpretations regarding birth parent–related information.

Nationally, states that permit open adoption seem to have a significantly higher adoption rate. This suggests that both biological and adopting parents may be more comfortable with having firsthand information about the child's family background or future prospects.

Matchmaking: Facilitating Adoption Informally

In line with open adoption and a less secretive approach to the adoption process, as well as governmental promotion of adoption, two innovative approaches have brought some success. First, children available for adoption are featured on the Internet, which provides broad, even interstate, access to them. The second approach features organized events, such as outings, that give potential parents or families a chance to meet children who are available for adoption in a casual setting. The benefit here is not merely that children receive targeted exposure, but that a setting is created where spontaneous emotional connections can occur and where both sides have a chance to assess compatibility. The drawback is that many children who participate in these get-to-know-each-other parties and repeatedly are not chosen tend to feel like rejects.

Interracial Adoption

In the United States, Caucasian couples willing to adopt outnumber adoptable Caucasian children. This situation is a factor in the increase in interethnic, interracial, and international adoptions. The Multiethnic Placement Act of 1994 outlaws racial or ethnic bias in selections of adoption and foster care placements. Foster parents who have bonded with a child of a different race can no longer be prevented from adopting on racial grounds. Contrary to the objections raised against interracial adoptions, research has shown that no psychological harm came to African American children adopted into White families: They developed a positive racial identity, and their adjustment was excellent. Black adoptees found to have more problems than Whites had been older when adopted and had come from more unstable and abusive backgrounds. While the color of loving parents seems to matter less, interracial adoptees are more comfortable in ethnically and racially integrated schools and communities. These children prefer interracial adoption over being farmed out to foster homes and child care facilities.

International Adoption

Legalized abortion, a decrease in the number of adoptable Caucasian children, social acceptance of single parenthood, and financial support from the government have caused the number of adoptable children in the United States to drop significantly, reportedly by 30,000 in 20 years. Consequently, many couples, especially Caucasian ones, looked for children abroad, including in Asian countries. Most prevalent among foreign adoptees were Korean, Romanian, and Russian children.

Since the Korean War, Korean children have been favorite adoptees, the most sought after for about 30 years. Initially adoptees were war orphans or unwanted Amerasians, and later they were mostly abandoned girls and children born into poverty. As a group they made excellent adjustments, had good self-esteem, and were quiet, high-achieving, responsible, socially mature, and without emotional problems. Although the majority of these children were past the noncritical stages of adoption on arrival in the States, they did better than U.S.-born Caucasian adoptees.

Later, Romanian and, more recently, Russian children became popular U.S. adoptees. In the 1990s, after news reports on neglected and abused children in Romania were broadcast, many U.S. families adopted Romanian children. Most Romanian adoptees had endured serious hardships, including institutionalization, neglect, serious malnutrition at developmentally critical times, and, in some cases, abuse. As a result of social deprivation, many of the adoptees suffered from disinhibited attachment disorder, displaying indiscriminate friendliness with strangers. Many children older than 6 months showed cognitive impairments, but not the younger adoptees. However, some children, though equally deprived during critical phases, overcame their problems. Similar reports came from families with children adopted from Russian orphanages.

Specific parental stress can be created by foreign country officials and government-sanctioned red tape, which can delay the adoption (e.g., through extortion or in an effort to solicit bribes), and can also occur when transplanted children, surrounded by strangers and unable to communicate in English, manifest (at least initially) regressive, anxious, or rejecting behavior instead of the joy and gratefulness the parents naively expected.

Mental Health and Related Issues

Adoptees have been reported to be overrepresented in clinical populations, but there is no evidence that being adopted is a major factor affecting mental health, as attested to by the history of Korean adoptees. Overrepresentation may relate to the fact that parents may more readily refer adoptees to mental health clinics because many have unrealistic expectations about child behavior or because the lack of genetic ties presumably exempts them from a connection to the problem. Although some reports indicate that there is no significant difference between biological and adopted children in prevalence of psychological problems or serious psychopathology, others found that natural children may more often develop internalizing problems, whereas in adopted children problems like lying, stealing, and aggressive and/or sexual acting out predominate. These findings may relate to an adoptee's age at the time of permanent placement. Research suggested that, based on the age at placement, the probability of an adoptee's acting out was found to be as follows: up to 3 months: none; 3 to 12 months: possible; 12 months on: expected. The core issue, though, is not time, but how the time was spent. Exposure to depersonalizing institutions, multiple rejections, or abusive foster care placements, or the experience of being given up for adoption only after becoming unmanageable, tends to intensify any propensity for maladjustment or delinquency and may trigger a mental illness for which biological prerequisites are met. Another etiology of potential problems has been connected to the possibility that at least some adopted children come from an undesirable genetic background, given that many adoptees are conceived and born outside of socially responsible circumstances.

In adoptees who became schizophrenic, genetic lineage, not adoption, was key. Research from Finland showed that a healthy adoptive home safeguards children with a genetic vulnerability to schizophrenia. Even depression could not be tied to adoption. Instead, depression in adoptees was related to individual life events, like friendship problems or personal losses. The problems observed among Romanian and Russian adoptees were related not to adoption but to preceding events.

Overall, mental health problems are not readily tied to adoption. Heredity and environmental circumstances are factors with adoptees as with other children. Even an established factor, like age at adoption, is not the correct indicator for the link to maladjustment. Factors likely to play an etiological role in maladjustment and mental illness, although equally applicable to all children, may be somewhat more prevalent in the adoptable population, with the exception of Korean children.

Identity confusion may be the one condition that can be related directly to adoption. It is difficult to construct a cohesive sense of identity when the initial building blocks consist of negative messages (absent birth family, abandonment, neglectful institutions, rejecting or abusive foster settings), which contradict positive messages from adoptive family, teachers, and social environment, and it is likewise difficult to build on speculations to fill the information gap in cases of closed adoption. Interracial adoptees seeking to identify with their parents gain from concentrating on shared interests and values and on deemphasizing differences in appearance. Fusing confusing and contrasting experiences and knowledge into one coherent entity is the goal of the adoptees' search for an identity congruent with the inner self.

Adoptive Parent Status

Traditionally children were adopted by married couples. Some states eventually allowed single individuals to become adoptive parents. Although the subject remains controversial, there are increasingly more gay and lesbian couples who adopt. However, in some states this is not a legal option. Research to date has not shown any negative effects on the adoptees, either in identification with parents or in influence on the children's sexual orientation.

Government Interest in Adoption

Since the Adoption Assistance and Child Welfare Act (1980) brought about an increase in kinship adoptions, government efforts to promote adoptions overall have increased. In 1998, 100,000 children were reported to be waiting for adoption. The government goal for adoption was set at 56,000 in 2002.

On behalf of adoptable and adopted children, it needs to be noted, *de lege ferenda,* that it must become illegal for governmental authorities and particularly the legal system to disrupt strong psychological bonds between young children and their caregivers. If a parent has not been concerned enough to be cognizant of the existence of a child he fathered, or if biological parents are reconsidering their decision to give a child up for adoption and demand the return of this child who is now emotionally rooted elsewhere, their claim has to be denied in the interest of the child. The right to maintain strong psychological bonds has to supersede the presumed rights of blood relatives that were never executed to establish firm mutual psychological attachments.

Erika Wick
St. John's University, New York

ADRENAL CORTEX

The adrenal glands are located superior to the kidneys and consist of two anatomically and chemically distinct structures: an outer cortical region in which steroid hormones are synthesized, and an inner medullary area in which catecholamines are produced. The cortex is divided into three zones: the zona fasciculata, which secretes glucocorticoids; the zona reticularis, which is responsible for adrenal androgen production; and the zona glomerulosa, which releases mineralocorticoids.

The glucocorticoids represent the end product of the hypothalamic-pituitary-adrenal (HPA) axis and are involved in a myriad of functional responses in the organism. These hormones serve as major regulators of carbohydrate and lipid metabolism, in adaptation to stress; in linking sleep and waking states; in food-seeking and cognitive behaviors; in controlling emotional states; in mediating anaphylactic and immune responses; in modulating the responses to neurochemicals, hormones, and growth factors; and in the differentiation and development of cells (Munck, Guyre, & Holbrook, 1984; Tsigos and Chrousos, 1994). Cortisol is the principal natural glucocorticoid in humans, whereas in many animals corticosterone is the primary glucocorticoid.

Regulation of Glucocorticoid Secretion

The main driving force behind glucocorticoid secretion is corticotropin-releasing hormone (CRH) acting in synergy with arginine-vasopressin (AVP), both of which are primarily released from the paraventricular nucleus (PVN) of the hypothalamus. The CRH stimulates the corticotroph cells in the anterior pituitary to secrete corticotropin (ACTH), which, in turn, influences the adrenal cortex. Three separate regulatory forces are involved in the secretion of glucocorticoids under physiological conditions and during times of stress. A circadian rhythm of basal activity is under the influence of the suprachiasmatic nucleus. Stress-induced responses are more complex and involve afferent inputs from numerous brain regions, including the locus ceruleus and autonomic systems in the brain stem, the amygdala-hippocampus complex, and the cerebral cortex. Finally, a feedback inhibitory input is provided by glucocorticoids.

Circadian Rhythm of Cortisol

In general, changes in plasma cortisol occur in parallel with those of ACTH. The rhythm of ACTH secretion results, in turn, from periodic changes in CRF. Cortisol levels peak in the early morning just prior to awakening, marking the onset of circadian activation. There is a gradual decline throughout the day until it reaches a nadir during early hours of nocturnal sleep, to abruptly rise during the later part of sleep (Van Cauter & Turek, 1995).

Glucocorticoid Secretion Under Stressful Conditions

Living organisms survive by maintaining a complex dynamic equilibrium that is constantly challenged by intrinsic or extrinsic disturbing forces. In response to a stressor that exceeds a threshold magnitude, the organism changes its behavior and physiology to maintain homeostasis. Behavioral adaptation includes increased arousal and alertness, heightened attention, and suppression of feeding and sexual behavior. Concomitantly, physical adaptation occurs and includes functions that redirect energy sources to the stressed body site, where they are needed most. In this adaptive process, glucocorticoids, along with catecholamines, form the frontline of defense.

Glucocorticoid secretion during stress also is dependent upon the release of CRH and AVP, although the magnitude of PVN activity is influenced by the nature and intensity of the stressor. Simultaneously, the locus ceruleus/norepinephrine-sympathetic system (autonomic-arousal system) becomes activated during stress, thus facilitating the release of epinephrine and norepinephrine from the adrenal medulla and the peripheral sympathetic nervous system. The PVN and the autonomic-arousal system are anatomically and functionally connected to each other and to the mesocortical/mesolimbic systems and the hippocampus.

Glucocorticoids and the Pathophysiology of Stress Response. Generally, the stress response, with the resultant elevation of glucocorticoid levels, is meant to last only for a limited duration. The time-limited nature of this process renders its accompanying catabolic and immunosuppressive effects beneficial, with no adverse consequences. Chronic activation of the stress system, however, is detrimental. For example, prolonged exposure to elevated glucocorticoid levels results in suppression of anabolic processes, muscle atrophy, reduced sensitivity to insulin and a risk for diabetes, hypertension, hyperlipidemia, arterial disease, peptic ulcers, amenorrhea, impotence, immunosuppression, and the impairment of growth and tissue repair (Munck et al., 1984). In addition, elevated glucocorticoid levels are associated with psychopathology, neuronal damage, and impaired cognitive function (McEwen, 1994; Tsigos & Chrousos, 1994). An efficient endocrine response to stress is one that is rapidly mobilized in the presence of a threat and effectively terminated once the threatening condition is no longer present.

Regulation of Glucocorticoid Secretion Through Negative Feedback

Inhibition of glucocorticoid secretion is achieved primarily through the action of glucocorticoids themselves. This negative feedback inhibition is achieved partly by glucocorticoid binding to specific corticoid receptors in the brain. Based on biochemical and functional characteristics, two types of corticoid receptors have been described (Reul & De Kloet, 1985). The glucocorticoid receptor (GR) is widely distributed in the brain but is most abundant in hypothalamic CRH neurons and pituitary corticotrophs. The mineralocorticoid receptor (MR) is densely localized in hippocampal and septal neurons. The MR binds glucocorticoids with a tenfold higher affinity than the GR. The receptor characteristics and distribution complement each other, thus providing the organism with the ability to modulate HPA responses. The MR operates at low glucocorticoid concentrations and exerts a tonic inhibition. When glucocorticoid levels are high, the MR receptors become saturated and the corticosteroids then bind to GR receptors, thereby ensuring a return to homeostasis.

Association Between Glucocorticoid Regulation and Psychopathology

Several lines of research support the association between glucocorticoid regulation and psychiatric disorders (Holsboer, 1989; Tsigos & Chrousos, 1994). Both physical and psychological stressors have been shown to be temporally related to psychiatric illness. Because glucocorticoids are intricately linked to the neurobiology of stress, alterations in glucocorticoid levels and/or activity are expected in association with psychiatric conditions. Indeed, altered HPA function has been shown in a variety of psychiatric disorders, including depression, Anxiety Disorders, Substance Abuse, Anorexia Nervosa, and Schizophrenia. Pharmacological studies indicate that glucocorticoids directly modulate neurotransmitter function and behavioral systems, as well as the activity of psychotropic agents. Moreover, there is evidence that glucocorticoids exert genomic effects in the brain and regulate transcription of many genes, including those that code for behaviorally active neuropeptides. Therefore, a greater understanding of the effects of glucocorticoids at the molecular level, and their interactions with different neurotransmitter systems, should provide important clues into the pathophysiology and treatment of these disorders.

Summary

Because glucocorticoids target almost all organ systems to regulate a myriad of functional responses, alterations in their level and/or activity can lead to diverse functional consequences.

REFERENCES

Holsboer, F. (1989). Psychiatric implications of altered limbic-hypothalamic-pituitary-adrenocortical activity. *Psychiatry and Neurological Sciences, 238,* 302–322.

McEwen, B. S. (1994). Corticosteroids and hippocampal plasticity. *Annals of the New York Academy of Sciences, 746,* 134–142.

Munck, A., Guyre, P. M., & Holbrook N. J. (1984). Physiological functions of glucocorticoids in stress and their relation to pharmacological actions. *Endocrine Reviews, 5,* 25–44.

Reul, J. M. H. M., & De Kloet, E. R. (1985). Two receptor systems for corticosterone in the rat brain: Microdistribution and differential occupation. *Endocrinology, 117,* 2505–2512.

Tsigos, C., & Chrousos, G. P. (1994). Physiology of the hypothalamic-pituitary-adrenal axis in health and dysregulation in psychiatric and autoimmune disorders. *Endocrinology and Metabolism Clinics of North America, 23,* 451–466.

Van Cauter, E., & Turek, F. W. (1995). Endocrine and other biological rhythms. In L. J. DeGroot (Ed.), *Endocrinology: Vol. 3* (pp. 2487–2548). Philadelphia: W. B. Saunders.

Uma Rao
Russell E. Poland
UCLA Neuropsychiatric Institute

ADULT INTELLECTUAL DEVELOPMENT

Why do some individuals retain their behavioral competence well into advanced old age, whereas others show early decline? This question has long been a central topic in the psychology of adult development and aging. Five central questions and relevant research findings address this issue:

1. Does intelligence change uniformly through adulthood, or are there different life course ability patterns?
2. At what age is there a reliably detectable age decrement in ability, and what is the magnitude of that decrement?
3. What are the patterns of generational differences, and what are their magnitudes?
4. What accounts for individual differences in age-related change in adulthood?
5. Can cognitive decline in old age be reversed?

The Measurement of Adult Intelligence

Most large-scale studies of adult intelligence conducted during the past few decades have used either the Wechsler Adult Intelligence Scale (WAIS), one of its derivatives, or a derivative of Thurstone's work on the primary mental abilities. Findings of these studies differ markedly, however, depending on whether age comparisons have been made cross-sectionally or whether the same individuals have been followed longitudinally over time.

Differential Patterns of Change

There is no uniform pattern of age-related changes across all intellectual abilities. Studies of overall intellectual ability (IQ) are therefore insufficient to monitor age changes and age differences in intellectual functioning for either individuals or groups. Age difference work with the WAIS suggests that verbal abilities are maintained well, whereas performance tests show early age differences favoring younger adults. Longitudinal data on the WAIS also show high levels of stability of verbal behaviors into advanced old age, whereas performance scores begin to decline in midlife. Studies of the primary mental abilities indicate that active or fluid abilities tend to decline earlier than passive or crystallized abilities. These findings are complicated by ability-by-age and ability-by-cohort interactions. For example, women tend to decline earlier in the active abilities, whereas men do so on the passive abilities. Although fluid abilities begin to decline earlier, crystallized abilities appear to show steeper decrement once the late 70s are reached.

Age Level And Magnitude of Age-Related Intellectual Decline

Cross-sectional studies with the WAIS suggest that significant age differences favoring young adults can be found by the 30s for performance tests and by the 60s for verbal tests. These differences, however, confound cohort effects in education and health status. By contrast, in longitudinal studies, reliably replicable average age decrements in intellectual abilities are rarely found before age 60, but they are observed for all intellectual functions at least by age 74. Analyses of individual differences in intellectual change, however, demonstrate that even at age 81 less than half of all observed individuals showed reliable decremental change over the preceding 7 years.

Generational Differences

The existence of generational (cohort) differences in intellectual abilities has been conclusively demonstrated. Almost linear positive cohort shifts have been observed for inductive reasoning, with more spasmodic positive shifts for verbal ability and spatial orientation. A curvilinear cohort pattern has been found for number skills, which reach a peak for birth cohorts born in the 1920s and then follow a largely negative slope. A similar curvilinear cohort pattern has been observed for word fluency. As a consequence, cross-sectional studies of intellectual aging underestimate age changes before age 60 for abilities with negative cohort gradients and overestimate age changes for abilities with positive cohort gradients.

Individual Differences in Age-Related Change in Adulthood

Individual differences are large at all ages, such that substantial overlap among samples can be found from young adulthood into the mid-70s (cf. Schaie, 1988b). Very few individuals decline on all or most abilities. Indeed, maintenance of functioning on one or more abilities is characteristic for most individuals well into advanced old age. A number of factors account for individual differences in decline, some of which have been shown to be amenable to experimental intervention. Predictors of favorable cognitive aging include (1) absence of cardiovascular and other chronic disease; (2) favorable environment, as indicated by high socioeconomic status; (3) involvement in a complex and intellectually stimulating environment; (4) flexible personality style at midlife; (5) high cognitive status of spouse; and (6) maintenance of level of perceptual processing speed.

Reversibility of Cognitive Decline

Present understanding of individual differences in cognitive decline suggests that unless neurological pathology is present, cognitive interventions may serve to remediate known intellectual decline and reduce cohort differences in those individuals who have remained stable in their own performance over time but who have become disadvantaged compared with younger peers. The effectiveness of cognitive interventions has been demonstrated in various laboratory studies as well as in a recent major clinical trial. Cognitive decline in many older people may well be the result of disuse of specific skills that can be reserved by appropriate training regimens. In two studies, approximately 66% of the experimental subjects showed significant improvement, and about 40% of those who had declined significantly over 14 years were returned to their predecline level.

K. Warner Schaie
Pennsylvania State University

See also: **Age Differences; Primary Mental Abilities**

ADULTHOOD AND AGING: SOCIAL PROCESSES AND DEVELOPMENT

One of the most reliable findings in social gerontology is that with age, people report fewer social partners. Assuming that cultural ageism is responsible, researchers had construed this phenomenon as society's rejection of older adults. Laura Carstensen's (1999) socioemotional selectivity theory, however, posits that decrease in social network size is a developmental process of social selection that begins in early adulthood. According to the theory, this decrease is the direct result of people's actively reducing the number of peripheral social partners with whom they interact; in contrast, the number of emotionally close social partners stays relatively constant with age. The age-related preference for close social partners, as opposed to acquaintances, is documented in many studies of men and women using ethnicity diverse groups of Americans and samples from Germany, Hong Kong, and mainland China.

Close social partners provide emotionally meaningful interactions, and satisfaction with family members, including siblings, spouse, and children, increases with age. The sibling relationship represents one of the longest, more enduring relationships in life, and Victor Cicirelli's (1989) research reveals that people who report positive relationships with siblings, particularly their sisters, also report lower levels of depression. In addition, the marital tie is also important to overall well-being. Across the life span, marital satisfaction follows a curvilinear pattern: high in the early years of marriage, decreasing slightly into middle adulthood, and then rising again toward the end of middle age. People whose marriages survived into old age report high levels of marital happiness and contentment. Although they reported that difficult times did occur, they attribute their marriage's longevity to strong levels of mutual commitment and friendship.

Children are sources of high satisfaction for parents of all ages. Karen Fingerman's (2003) research reveals that middle-aged mothers enjoy watching their daughters enter adulthood, and older mothers benefit from the intergenerational kinship that their children and grandchildren provide. The relationships between parents and children are marked by reciprocity, with both generations reporting high levels of shared emotional and instrumental support. The type of instrumental support, however, varies by age, such that older parents are more likely to provide financial support, and their middle-aged children are more likely to provide practical assistance.

Although the most emotionally meaningful relationships often include family members, the strain of caregiving can create tension. With the exception of a minority of adults who experience increases in their sense of purpose and life satisfaction, most caregivers experience decreases in well-being. For both men and women, rates of depression are higher among caregivers than the general population, and physical complaints often increase with the added physical and emotional strain of caregiving, especially for those caring for a family member with a dementing illness. These family caregivers are most often women—wives, daughters, or daughters-in-law. When men are caregivers, they often receive more instrumental help but less emotional support from friends and family members than their female counterparts.

The majority of research has focused predominantly on the insular traditional family group of children and parents, but the definition of family is changing, and Vern Bengtson (2001) has written about several influences that are altering the picture of family relationships and age. With greater longevity, intergenerational connections will become more important to family members to fulfill emotional and practical needs. In addition, higher rates of divorce and remarriage introduce understudied unions that will also influence social networks of older adults. Finally, non-European-American family systems often include extended kin networks, and the importance of these family members has been relatively ignored in the literature.

In addition to family members, friends play a significant role in social processes and well-being across adulthood for both men and women. Although findings are conflicting, men generally report larger social networks than women, and women's friendships are marked by greater intimacy, mutual self-disclosure, and greater emotional support. Men often report less satisfaction with their friendships than women, but the greater emotional bonds women experience may also be detrimental: Women are more likely to report more burden from their friendships than men.

Friendships comprise many different types of associations, from casual relationships to more intimate, collaborative, and enduring bonds. Friends serve as confidants, model coping strategies, enhance self-esteem, and buffer stressful life events. Although friendships are important for all age groups, research by the laboratories of Antonnuci, Levitt, and Carstensen indicates that types of relationships vary in importance over the adult life span. Young adults tend to have many friends and a wide circle of affiliations, and happiness is related to larger networks comprised of many acquaintances. By middle adulthood, people selectively reduce their number of friends and form close, long-term relationships with those remaining in their network. In late adulthood, as spouses and old friends die, maintaining relationships with close friends becomes especially central to well-being. Karen Rook's (1995) work, however, emphasizes that older adults also rely on companions for recreational activities, even if these casual friends do not provide emotional support per se.

Whether with family or friends, social connection is necessary and essential to overall well-being. Having meaningful relations is associated with decreased reactivity to stressors, greater immune functioning, decreased risk of some diseases such as hypertension, faster recovery from illness, lower chances of relapse, and even lower risk of mortality. In fact, measures of social support, such as the absence or loss of social ties, are as important in predicting mortality as other known medical indicators, such as cholesterol level and smoking history. Social connection is also important to emotional well-being, including lower rates of depression, anxiety, and sleep disturbance. Of course, not all social interactions are beneficial. Karen Rook's research indicates that negative social exchanges have stronger associations with well-being than do positive social exchanges. Such findings clarify the importance of positive social relations on well-being, and the potential risks incurred by negative exchanges.

Current knowledge suggests that social processes do not diminish in importance across the adult life span. For every age group, social connections are necessary for physical and mental well-being. Developmental processes, however, alter the structure and meaning of social relationships; over time, the number of social partners decreases, but the meaning of close friends and family members becomes even more central to the daily lives of older men and women.

REFERENCES

Bengston, V. L. (2001). Beyond the nuclear family: The increasing importance of multigenerational bonds (The Burgess Award Lecture). *Journal of Marriage & the Family, 63,* 1–16.

Carstensen, L. L., Isaacowitz, D. M., & Charles, S. T. (1999). Taking time seriously: A theory of socioemotional selectivity theory. *American Psychologist, 54,* 165–181.

Cicirelli, V. G. (1989). Feelings of attachment to siblings and well-being in later life. *Psychology & Aging, 4*(2), 211–216.

Fingerman, K. (2003). *Mothers and their adult daughter: Mixed emotions, enduring bonds.* Amherst, NY: Prometheus Books.

Rook, K. S. (1995). Support, companionship, and control in older adults' social networks: Implications for well-being. In J. F. Nussbaum & J. Coupland (Eds.), *Handbook of communication and aging research.* LEA's communication series (pp. 437–463). Hillsdale, NJ: Erlbaum.

Susan T. Charles
Melanie Horn
University of California, Irvine

AFFECT

Affect is typically considered to reflect the feelings associated with emotional processes, which are related in presently unknown ways to the other major components of emotions—expressive, autonomic, and cognitive. Affective experience has been among the most difficult aspects of mind to understand scientifically because it is so thoroughly subjective. Its importance in human economic, political, and social affairs has long been subsumed under the concept of *utility*—the recognition that societies must aspire to the greatest good (and the least suffering) for the greatest number. As Jeremy Bentham (1789, *Introduction to the Principles of Morals and Legislation*) famously said: "Utility is . . . that property in any object, whereby it tends to produce benefit, advantage, pleasure, good, or happiness . . . or . . . to prevent the happening of mischief, pain, evil, or unhappiness." Experienced affect is the neural currency for such cost-benefit "calculations" in the economy of the brain. When linked to specific perceptions, affective feelings typically signal the survival utility of objects.

There are, of course, an enormous number of affects, and it is by no means certain how any are instantiated within the brain. Although emotional feelings often appear related to objects of the world (since brains project feelings onto sensory/perceptual processes), affects are actually elaborated by specific brain systems. To the best of our knowledge, the critical systems are concentrated in ancient brain areas also found in many other animals.

Conceptually, affects may be divided into those that reflect bodily needs and disturbances—the hungers, thirst, and various other pains and pleasures of the world—while others are more closely related to instinctual actions—the expressive emotional urges of the mind. To understand the former, a guiding principle is that objects of the world that support survival are generally experienced as delightful and pleasant, while those incompatible with survival are experienced as aversive and unpleasant. The "sensory-linked affects" are typically studied as perceptual experiences of the brain; for instance, the taste of chocolate or the disgust engendered by the smell of feces. Such valenced experiences—the varieties of goodness and badness—are mediated by specific brain circuits that course upward through brain stem, thalamus, and hypothalamus to ancient limbic cortical areas of the brain. For instance, people with *insular* cortical damage are deficient in experiencing negative feelings such as pain, disgust, and coldness. Yet other cortical areas (e.g., orbitofrontal cortex) help distinguish many sensory pleasures.

The other major category of affective experience is more closely linked to emotional systems that allow organisms to generate adaptive instinctual behaviors during various life-challenging situations. Thus, all mammals have brain systems for: (1) seeking resources, (2) becoming angry if access to resources is thwarted, (3) becoming scared when one's bodily well-being is threatened, (4) various sexual desires that are somewhat different in males and females, (5) urges to exhibit loving and attentive care toward one's offspring, (6) feelings of panic and distress when one has lost contact with loved ones, and (7) the boisterous joyousness of rough-and-tumble playfulness. Each is manifested through characteristic action patterns that reflect the dynamics of the associated feelings. All other mammals may experience such basic feelings because of brain systems they share with humans. For instance, other mammals are attracted to the drugs that humans commonly overuse and abuse, and they dislike similar drug-induced experiences. Of course, there are many socially-derived feelings as various basic emotions are thwarted and blended in real life situations (yielding frustrations and feelings such as shame, jealousy, guilt, or embarrassment, many of which may be uniquely human).

The vast human capacity to think and to symbolize experience in language and culture has added subtle layers of complexity to our feelings, especially our aesthetic experiences. As scientists categorize the diverse affective dimensions of life, many are tempted to simplify emotional complexities into holistic schemes (e.g., positive and negative affects) that may partly reflect our linguistic capacity to oversimplify. But there may also be superordinate brain systems for such global feelings.

Although humans have many special feelings ranging from awe to zoophobia, scientific understanding of the evolved nature of feelings is best obtained through the study of ancient brain systems we share with other animals. Recent evidence indicates these systems do have chemical codes, such as the neuropeptides, which help conduct specific neuroaffective tunes. Most of these substances, which barely cross blood–brain barriers, must be placed directly into animals' brains. However, as related medicinal agents are developed, we can anticipate the emergence of new and selective psychiatric drugs to control troublesome or excessive human feelings. For millennia, humankind had only one such drug, opium, which could alleviate physical pain as well as the painful grief arising from social loss.

So what, in a deep neural sense, are emotional feelings? They reflect the various types of neurodynamics that establish characteristic, mentally experienced "forces" that regulate and reflect action readiness within the nervous system—the pounding force of anger, the shivery feelings of fear, the caress of love, the urgent thrusting of sexuality, the painful pangs of grief, the exuberance of joy, and the persistent "nosy" poking about of organisms seeking resources. Moods and many psychiatric disorders may reflect the long-term balance or imbalance of the various positive and negative affective systems.

And how do the material events of the brain get converted into the mystery of subjective experience? No one is certain, but some have suggested that the core of our being is organized around neurosymbolic motor–action coordinates of the brain. The various basic neurodynamics of such a core "self," evident in the instinctual action dynamics of each animal, may be critical for the transformation of brain activities into emotional experiences. If this is the case, then certain affective values were built in at the very core of mammalian brain evolution, thereby providing a solid grounding for mental life. This view of brain–mind organization, not widely accepted by certain schools of materialist (e.g., behaviorist) thought, has the potential to contribute to a more accurate and admirable scientific image of life than was evident during the twentieth century.

Jaak Panksepp
Bowling Green State University

AFFECTIVE DEVELOPMENT

Affect, as a feature or type of behavior, and hence a focus of psychology, is one of the least understood and most difficult problems in the field. *Affect* relates to or encompasses a wide range of concepts and phenomena, including feelings, emotions, moods, motivation, and certain drives and instincts. Anger, joy, fear, laughter, sadness, anxiety, pride, love, hate, and so on—all are so central to human experience, yet so little understood by psychology. Theorists and researchers have approached affect in numerous ways, often using idiosyncratic, contradictory, or mutually exclusive conceptualizations and operational definitions that have resulted in confusion and limited progress in our understanding of affect or any of these other related or synonymous constructs.

The psychology of *affective development* seeks to describe, map out, and explain the processes, continuities, and changes in the experience, differentiation, and expression of affect. Most often, affective development is placed in dichotomy, or even counterpoint, with cognitive development, reflecting an age-old concern with mind-body dualism (thinking vs. feeling). Much of the discussion centers around the primacy of one over the other or the nature of their interaction or mutual influence. Referents and resolutions are often sought in the social domain, whether in terms of social cognition or object relations, because of the complexity and salience of interpersonal and intrapersonal relations for ideas, attitudes, feelings, and behavior. Whatever categorizations may be hypothesized for the sake of theory building or empirical inquiry, it is important to bear in mind the complexity of affective development and the limited state of our current knowledge.

From its early days, psychoanalysis, as a clinical and developmental psychology, has centered on affective development. Psychologists influenced by the organismic developmental psychology proposed by Heinz Werner in 1940 have also had a long-standing interest in affective development. In the 1970s and 1980s a number of conceptual and methodological advances converged, bringing about a resurgence of interest, priority, and legitimacy for the study of affective development, and it remains a productive domain of inquiry as the twenty-first century unfolds.

Models of affective development vary in the degree to which they emphasize biological elements or socialization elements. Darwinian and ethological models are especially interested in unlearned complex behavior and often posit central nervous system specificity and correspondence between stimulus or elicitors and an individual's affective response. Socialization models emphasize learning processes, especially in the infant-caregiver interaction, and situational or environmental influences on affective experience or expression. Reliance on one or the other model type, of course, influences the manner in which affective development is understood or studied. For instance, biological researchers might be more likely to measure electrophysiological responsiveness or neurophysiological correlates of specific emotions, whereas socialization researchers might be more interested in observing the quality of parent-child attachment and separation reactions over time. It is likely that multiple models and perspectives will be essential to furthering our understanding of affective development, and indeed such comprehensive and integrative approaches are evident in current theories of affective development such as Sroufe's organizational perspective and Tomkins's and Izard's differential emotions theory.

In his review of current knowledge on affective development, Yarrow states:

> Emotional expression can best be understood in a developmental context, in the framework of psychological changes accompanying the infant's increased autonomy, increasing awareness of a capacity to control people, objects, and self, and in the context of cognitive changes associated with a developing memory and the acquisition of object permanence. Similarly motor expression of emotion and the ability to inhibit and modulate responses to emotional stimuli are dependent on the maturation of the central nervous system. In examining the developmental course of emotional expression, it becomes evident that some aspects of emotional and cognitive development are on parallel lines; in other instances the cognitive skill is a prerequisite for emotional expression. Chronological age is not a simple variable; it is only a rough index of the psychological changes associated with the changing capacities of the child.

Donald L. Wertlieb
Tufts University

See also: **Cognitive Theories of Emotions**

AFFERENT

Axons that are presynaptic to a neuron are commonly called *afferents*. In their terminal knobs is stored the neurotransmitter, which will be released into the synaptic cleft and which will bind to receptors on the postsynaptic dendrites and soma. Thus, the topic of afferents is extremely broad. Much information about afferent function has been obtained from the study of primary afferents.

Primary Afferents

The term *primary afferents* refers to the cells whose axons serve somatosensory receptors and that proceed to the central nervous system (CNS) through the dorsal roots of sensory nerve input to the spinal cord. The cell bodies of primary afferents are dorsal root ganglion cells located in the peripheral nervous system. The central axon synapses to postsynaptic cells at the segment level, at close segments, or at some distance from the entry point, even to the first synapse being in the brain stem at the dorsal column nuclei.

Primary afferents serve receptors for touch, thermal sensations, proprioceptive sensations from displacement of muscles and joints, and pain. Their sensory nerve classification is into groups I, II, III, and IV, on the basis of decreasing axonal diameter and decreasing conduction velocity. Most human physiology texts have a table showing these parameters, and most are currently incorrect (Peters & Brooke, 1998). This is because the data were obtained using feline nerves, which conduct much faster than human ones. A very rough rule of thumb is to halve the velocity and diameter to translate from cat to human. Human Ia fibers conduct in the approximate range of 40 to 60 meters per second.

Complexity of Primary Afferent Effects

Human physiology texts describe some of the common connections between primary afferents and motoneurons, serving the stretch reflex, the flexor withdrawal reflex, the inverse myotatic reflex, and so forth. What is not usually addressed is that these are simple paths surrounded by extremely complex additional projections of those afferents to other motoneurons and interneurons of the spinal cord (Baldissera, Hultborn, & Illert, 1981), and powerful modulating inputs onto those paths from spinal interneuronal pools (Jankowska, 1992; Pierrot-Deseilligny, Morin, Bergego, & Tankov, 1981; Brooke et al., 1997). It is clear that specific somatosensory receptor discharge can have widespread effects over neuronal pools of the spinal cord and brain and that the strength of the effect can be modulated from profound to minimal (Brooke et al., 1997).

Regulatory Effects of Primary Afferents in Motor Control

Primary afferents play a significant role in motor control (Pearson, 1993). In locomotion, primary afferents transmit sensory information on load bearing, muscle stretch, joint position, and cutaneous sensations and are involved in such matters as the transition from stance to swing or from static to dynamic balance in the initiation of stepping. Their reflex effects, ipsi- and contralaterally through Ia and cutaneous afferent activation, in the human are substantially modulated over cycles of activities such as walking (Brooke et al., 1997). In addition to spinal paths from sensory receptors to motoneurons and motor interneurons, it is clear that primary afferent activity regulates the activity of other primary afferents in complex and organized ways (Rudomin, Romo, & Mendell, 1998). Often, this involves presynaptic inhibition (Stein, 1995). Such sensorisensory conditioning is seen across much of the animal kingdom (Watson, 1992).

Gain Control in Human Primary Afferent Transmission Over Spinal Paths

In humans, Ia transmission monosynaptically to leg motoneurons—for example, the Hoffmann (H) reflex—is attenuated by muscle spindle activation of Ia afferents serving uniarticular extensor muscles of the hip or knee or, probably, ankle. The inhibitory pathway is, at least in part, spinal through presynaptic inhibitory interneurons (Brooke et al., 1997). Such centripetal sensorisensory conditioning is complemented by centrifugal conditioning arising from the brain and from central pattern-generating networks of the spinal cord and brain stem (Rudomin et al., 1998). For example, immediately before voluntary plantar flexion movement, H-reflex magnitudes in the plantar flexor muscle soleus increase considerably.

There seems to be clear separation of the control of Ia afferents and cutaneous afferents during locomotion. Locomotor-induced modulation of cutaneous afferent affects on motoneurons appears to arise from centrifugal conditioning but, unlike the Ia pathways previously described, not as attenuation from centripetal conditioning from somatosensory afferents activated as a consequence of the movement per se (Brooke, McIlroy, Staines, Angerilli, & Peritore, 1999).

Primary afferent activation can also reveal novel membrane characteristics of motoneurons. A brief burst of Ia afferent firing can reset membrane currents so that plateau potentials occur in mammalian motoneurons (e.g., in stance), being a rapid series of action potentials from a depolarized plateau (Kiehn, 1991). Such repetitive motoneuronal firing, continuing well beyond the duration of the Ia afferent burst, can then be terminated by a brief burst of firing of high threshold primary afferents.

Gain Control in Human Primary Afferent Transmission Over Ascending Paths

Excitation of primary afferents in peripheral nerves at low stimulus intensities rapidly results (from arms, in 15+ ms; from legs, in 25+ ms) in somatosensory evoked potentials (SEPs) measured from scalp electrodes recording from the somatosensory reception areas of the cerebral cortex. As previously described for spinal Ia reflexes, the ascending path from fast-conducting afferents to the brain can be attenuated at spinal levels by activation of other Ia afferents (Staines, Brooke, Misiaszek, & McIlroy, 1997). The effect is observed as reduced magnitudes of SEPs, despite nonvarying stimulation. Further, just as the brain can centrifugally control primary afferent transmission in Ia spinal reflexes, so it can also control the transmission through the ascending path (Rudomin et al., 1998). For example, SEPs are attenuated following learning that involves those pathways online (Nelson, Brooke, McIlroy, Bishop, & Norrie, 2001).

The attenuation reduces SEP magnitudes by as much as 50% of initial control values. Accompanying behavioral evidence of failure to use the pathways in predictable conditions suggests that the brain control of transmission from the primary afferents is linked to a switch from reactive to predictive control using an internal model (Nelson, 1996). Such a switch probably reflects a difference in brain sites involved in the motor control for the tasks. Thus, stimulation of primary afferents and observation of subsequent neural response shed light on the neural organization for skilled behavior.

REFERENCES

Baldissera, F., Hultborn, H., & Illert, M. (1981). Integration in spinal neuronal systems. In V. B. Brooks (Ed.), *Handbook of physiology: Section 1. The nervous system: Vol. II. Motor control* (pp. 509–595). Bethesda, MD: American Physiological Society.

Brooke, J. D., Cheng, J., Collins, D. F., McIlroy, W. E., Misiaszek, J. E., & Staines, W. R. (1997). Sensori-sensory afferent conditioning with leg movement: Gain control in spinal reflex and ascending paths. *Progress in Neurobiology, 51,* 393–421.

Brooke, J. D., McIlroy, W. E., Staines, W. R., Angerilli, P. A., & Peritore, G. F. (1999). Cutaneous reflexes of the human leg during passive movement. *Journal of Physiology, 15,* 619–628.

Jankowska, E. (1992). Interneuronal relay in spinal pathways from proprioceptors. *Progress in Neurobiology, 38,* 335–378.

Kiehn, O. (1991). Plateau potentials and active integration in the "final common pathway" for motor behaviour. *Trends in Neuroscience, 14,* 68–73.

Nelson, A. J., Brooke, J. D., McIlroy, W. E., Bishop, D. C., & Norrie, R. G. (2001). The gain of initial somatosensory evoked potentials alters with practice of an accurate motor task. *Brain Research, 890,* 272–279.

Nelson, R. (1996). Interactions between motor commands and somatic perception in sensorimotor cortex. *Current Opinion in Neurobiology, 6,* 801–810.

Pearson, K. G. (1993). Common principles of motor control in vertebrates and invertebrates. *Annual Reviews of Neuroscience, 16,* 265–297.

Peters, M. H., & Brooke, J. D. (1998). Comment on conduction velocity in muscle and cutaneous nerve afferents in humans. *Journal of Motor Behavior, 30,* 285–287.

Pierrot-Deseilligny, E., Morin, C., Bergego, C., & Tankov, N. (1981). Pattern of group I fibre projections from ankle flexor and extensor muscles in man. *Experimental Brain Research, 42,* 337–350.

Rudomin, P., Romo, R., & Mendell, L. M. (Eds.). (1998). *Presynaptic inhibition and neural control.* Oxford, UK: Oxford University Press.

Staines, W. P., Brooke, J. D., Misiaszek, J. E., & McIlroy, W. E. (1997). Movement-induced gain modulation of somatosensory potentials and soleus H reflexes evoked from the leg: II. Correlation with rate of stretch of knee extensor muscles. *Experimental Brain Research, 115,* 156–164.

Stein, R. B. (1995). Presynaptic inhibition in humans. *Progress in Neurobiology, 47,* 533–544.

Watson, D. H. D. (1992). Presynaptic modulation of sensory afferents in the invertebrate and vertebrate nervous system. *Comparative Biochemistry and Physiology, 103A,* 227–239.

John D. Brooke
Feinberg School of Medicine, Northwestern University

AFFILIATION NEED

Need for affiliation (*n Aff*) was 1 of 20 psychological needs identified by H. A. Murray and measured through his Thematic Apperception Test (TAT). The *n Aff* is scored when one or more of the characters in a subject's TAT story shows concern "over *establishing, maintaining, or restoring a positive affective relationship with another person*" (italics in the original). Individuals scoring high on *n Aff* on Gough's Adjective Check List tend to describe themselves in such terms as friendly, warm, trusting, talkative, cheerful, kind, loyal, helpful, praising, accepting, and generous. These characteristics are more likely to be associated with feminine than with masculine personality stereotypes. S. Miller and K. M. Nardini found, for example, that women scored higher than men on a measure of affiliation tendency, while Bose, Das Gupta, and Lindgren observed that female undergraduates in Calcutta who took a Bengali test measuring *n Aff* and need for achievement (*n Ach*) scored higher on *n Aff* and lower on *n Ach* than male undergraduates did.

There is considerable evidence to show that *n Ach* and *n Aff* are negatively correlated, probably because the two motives are generally expressed in mutually incompatible forms of behavior.

Studies generally confirm hypotheses based on *n Aff* theory. Lansing and Heyns, for instance, found that *n Aff* was significantly related to frequency of local telephone calls made by subjects, although it was only weakly related to numbers of letters written or frequency of visits to relatives and close friends living at a distance. Sid and Lindgren found that women students majoring in nursing and education rated higher on a measure of *n Aff* than did students in other major fields, and that the *n Aff* of expectant mothers was higher than that of any other group tested.

The possibility that affiliation tendency is characterized by sensitivity to rejection was explored by Mehrabian, who found the two traits to be essentially unrelated. Both variables were negatively correlated with a measure of achieving tendency, but affiliation tendency was positively correlated with measures of empathy and arousal-seeking tendency, whereas sensitivity to rejection was negatively correlated with arousal-seeking tendency and social desirability. Mehrabian found, however, that scores on measures of affiliative tendency and sensitivity to rejection could be combined to produce a single measure of dependency.

Henry C. Lindgren

See also: **Prosocial Behavior**

AGE DIFFERENCES

Behavioral changes with age are as striking as changes in physical appearance. Both training and altered structures contribute to these psychological differences. Differences that occur throughout the life span are mainly studied by *cross-sectional* and *longitudinal* methods.

Age differences in intelligence have been extensively studied. Mental age (MA) as measured by standard intelligence tests increases with chronological age (CA), and because of the way age scales are constructed, the relation is linear. An average child shows an increase of 1 year in MA for each year of CA until about 15 to 18 years of age, when MA is assumed to level off. There is evidence, however, that the intellectual ability of some individuals may continue to increase at least until they are in their early 20s.

The question of the growth of MA with age is complicated by two factors: (1) the difficulty level of items for young adults, and (2) the different composition of abilities tested at different age levels. If there are few difficult items at the upper end of the scale, older subjects cannot show improvement: The ceiling of the test is too low. If the same functions are not being tested at different age levels, what does it mean to say that MA *increases* with age?

The constancy of IQ across time has long been an age-related issue. In general, IQs of schoolchildren and adults have been found to be constant enough to allow satisfactory prediction over several years. And within limits, the older the subjects, the longer the test scores remain relatively constant (within 4 to 5 IQ points). At the opposite extreme, preschool IQs are very poor predictors of scores obtained later in life. It should be emphasized, however, that, even when test-retest correlations are high for a group, sizable systematic shifts in IQ can occur in particular individuals. A change of 30 or more points in a mean of 12 years has been found in 9% of the cases studied by Honzik, Macfarlane, and Allen.

Interestingly, there is often a large drop in IQ a few years before death, regardless of when death occurs. Such a drop in IQ can even be used to predict death.

The fact that recognition memory and recall show decided improvement in children, say, between ages 6 and 9 is probably related to an increase in mental age. The older children use implicit verbalization more—labeling, rehearsing, and comparing stimuli. Age seems to affect recall performance more than recognition, improving performance in children and hindering it in old age.

A fair number of generalizations can be made about behavior changes in later life.

1. Since behavior is in part a product of the central nervous system, the loss of brain cells with age is probably a relevant consideration. By the age of 80 or 90, 40% of cortical cells may be lost. Also, water content declines and fats increase in the brain over the life span.
2. Older people definitely have more health problems than the young, which inevitably modifies their behavior.
3. Visual acuity and accommodation decline because of the increase in opacity and loss of elasticity of the lens of the eye in middle age. Changes in the retina later in life also impair color vision and increase sensitivity to glare.
4. Similarly, in audition, perception of higher frequencies disappears in the middle years, and after age 65 many adults require (although they do not necessarily use) hearing aids. Stress due to hearing loss can produce depression and other emotional disorders.
5. There is also declining sensitivity in taste, smell, and pain in the later years.
6. Older people seem to take longer to learn verbal material than do the young. However, when the learning of older people is self-paced and meaningful, they perform well. They also improve in learning and long-term memory when instructed to use mediating or mnemonic devices.
7. Older people's deficit in long-term memory seems to be mainly one of retrieval; short-term memory is impaired only when the task requires divided attention (e.g., dichotic listening). Span remains essentially intact until very advanced years.
8. Individual variability in all intellectual tasks increases over the life span, but this does not pose an educational problem until around 70 years of age or later.
9. With increasing age the central nervous system slows down. This change appears to account for the gradual decrease in speed of responding across the life span for a wide range of tasks, including reaction time, sorting objects, copying, canceling, and other similar processing functions.
10. Although there are few studies on problem solving and creativity as functions of aging, some hypotheses have emerged:
    - Older subjects tend to ask uninformative questions, to be disrupted by irrelevant and redundant information, and to treat both positive and negative instances of a concept as positive. Failure to profit from negative information can make a person seem rigid.
    - If memory load is kept low and older people are given strategy hints and the like, age-related deficits in problem solving can be substantially reduced (Sanders et al., 1975).
    - Although Lehman (1953) concluded that most creative achievements occur early in a scientist's or artist's career, considerable evidence indicates that some of the most valuable contributions come late in life. For example, Claude Monet began his famed "Water Lily" series at age 73; Benjamin Franklin invented the bifocal lens at 78; Sophocles wrote *Oedipus Rex* at 75; and George Bernard Shaw wrote his first play at 48. When the quality of works by Bach and Beethoven is assessed by the number of times a piece has been recorded, the latest works excel.
11. As one grows older, interests change; for example, the participant in sports becomes a spectator, and the incidence of crime declines steadily.
12. Finally, well-conducted sequential studies suggest that a person's personality is characterized more by continuity than by change. Cohort differences appear to be more prevalent than age changes.

M. R. Denny

See also: **Alzheimer's Disease; Human Development; Lifespan Development; Longitudinal Studies**

AGING AND INTELLIGENCE

Phenomena of aging effects on intellectual and cognitive functioning are investigated by research approaches at the psychometric, information-processing, and biological levels. These approaches complement each other and should be considered conjointly for a comprehensive overview of aging and intelligence. Recent neurocomputational approaches help to integrate theory and data across these levels.

The Behavioral Psychometric Approach

Extant psychometric data on aging and intelligence indicate three major phenomena. First, intellectual aging is multifaceted. Multifactorial models of intelligence (e.g., the *Gf-Gc* theory; Cattell, 1971; Horn, 1982; the dual-process model of life span intellectual development, Baltes, Staudinger, & Lindenberger, 1999) suggest that abilities in the *fluid-mechanics* (*Gf*) domain, which reflect an individual's capacity for problem solving, information organization, and concentration, are more biology based. In contrast, abilities in the *crystallized-pragmatic* (*Gc*) domain reflect the acquisition and use of culture-based information.

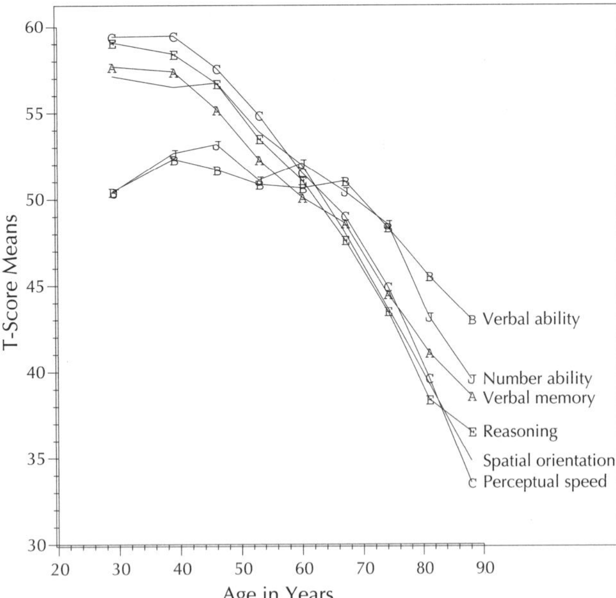

Figure 1. Cross-sectional age gradients in six primary mental abilities (N = 1,628). Abilities were assessed with three to four different tests and are scaled in a T-score metric.

Source: Data based on Schaie & Willis (1993); figure adapted from Lindenberger & Baltes (1994).

Figure 1 shows that cross-sectional age gradients of primary mental abilities (Thurstone & Thurstone, 1949) in the fluid-mechanics domain (i.e., verbal memory, reasoning, spatial orientation, and perceptual speed) decline linearly beginning in the 40s. However, abilities in the crystallized-pragmatic domain (i.e., verbal and numeric abilities) remain stable up to the 60s or 70s (Schaie & Willis, 1993).

Second, cross-sectional age differences are generally more pronounced than longitudinal age changes. Whereas modest *cross-sectional negative age differences* are found by the 40s for some abilities and by the 60s for most abilities, moderate *longitudinal negative age changes* in most abilities are usually not evident until the mid-70s or early 80s (Hayslip, 1994; Schaie, 1983, 1996). Discrepancies between cross-sectional and longitudinal age gradients are due to cohort effects (Schaie, 1965), practice effects, and selective attrition in longitudinal studies (Lindenberger & Baltes, 1994). After controlling for cohort and historical time effects, discrepancies between cross-sectional age differences and longitudinal age changes are reduced (Schaie, 1996). In addition, studies extending to very old age have provided opportunities for observing age differences and age changes in the 90s and beyond (e.g., the Berlin Aging Study, Baltes & Mayer, 1998; the Georgia Centenarian Study, Poon, Sweaney, Clayton, & Merriam, 1992; and the Kungsholmen Project, Small & Bäckman, 1997).

Third, aging contracts the factor space of intellectual abilities. Ample cross-sectional data show that correlations among subscales are generally larger in older samples, indicating an increasing degree of ability dedifferentiation (e.g., Babcock, Laguna, & Roesch, 1997; Balinsky, 1941; Baltes, Cornelius, Spiro, Nesselroade, & Willis, 1980; Lindenberger & Baltes, 1997; Lienert & Crott, 1964). Similar patterns have also been found in longitudinal studies, although the trends of dedifferentiation are not as strong as in the cross-sectional findings (McHugh & Owens, 1954; Schaie et al., 1998). Furthermore, ability dedifferentiation generalizes beyond the intellectual domain. A series of recent studies using simple measures of sensory acuity (Baltes & Lindenberger, 1997; Lindenberger & Baltes, 1994; Salthouse, Hancock, Meinz, & Hambrick, 1996), contrast sensitivity, and muscle strength (Anstey, Lord, & Williams, 1997) report an increase in the sensory-cognitive correlation with advancing age in age-heterogeneous samples. The strengthening of the sensory-cognitive link in old age has been interpreted as an indication of general neurological decline affecting both domains of functioning (e.g., Baltes & Lindenberger, 1997). The nature of the sensory-cognitive link is, however, still under debate. A few recent studies took the experimental, instead of the correlational, methodology to study the sensory-cognitive link. Findings from these studies suggest that as people grow older they seem to allocate an increasing amount of resources to tasks that require maintaining balance in an upright posture or walking (e.g., Lindenberger, Marsiske, & Baltes, 2000; K. Z. H. Li, Lindenberger, Freund, & Baltes, 2001).

The Behavioral Information-Processing Approach

In formulating theories of intelligence, researchers have examined several information-processing mechanisms or resources that may mediate age-related differences in intelligence. A common hypothesis of cognitive aging is that aging constrains general cognitive resources (GCRs). Three related types of GCRs—working memory, processing speed, and inhibitory mechanisms—have been investigated most extensively in relation to the fluid-mechanics domain of intelligence.

Working Memory

Working memory (WM) refers to the ability to simultaneously hold information in immediate memory while transforming the same or other information (Baddeley, 1986). Associated with higher-level cognition, WM is involved in language processing, problem solving, and concurrent task performance. Age-related declines in WM performance have been well documented (Craik & Jennings, 1992; Zacks, Hasher, & Li, 2000). Furthermore, large-scale studies show that a substantial portion of age-related variance in *Gf* abilities is shared with age-related differences in WM (e.g., Salthouse, 1991).

Processing Speed

In this view, age-related intellectual declines have biological underpinnings, such as neuronal slowing, which lead to the slowing of basic cognitive operations and exacerbated effects in complex tasks (Birren, 1964; Cerella, 1990; Jensen, 1993). Correlational analyses show that the observed age-associated variance in *Gf* abilities is greatly reduced or eliminated after individual differences in processing speed are controlled for (e.g., Park et al., 1996; Salthouse, 1996).

Attention and Inhibitory Mechanisms

It has also been proposed that aging impairs attention and inhibitory processes, leading to greater interference and difficulty in suppressing previously relevant information and habitual responses, as measured using tasks such as Stroop color naming, negative priming, and response stopping (e.g., Hasher & Zacks, 1988; Hasher, Zacks, & May, 2000). Measures of interference proneness have accounted for significant proportions of age-related variance in cognitive performance (e.g., Salthouse & Meinz, 1995), although fewer efforts have been made to link intelligence tests to measures of inhibition in comparison to the processing speed literature. Nonetheless, strong theoretical and empirical links appear to exist among all three GCRs, which may be best conceptualized as basic mechanisms (speed, inhibition) nested within more complex cognitive functions (WM).

The Cognitive and Computational Neuroscience Approaches

Recent developments in cognitive neuroscience have motivated researchers to investigate functional relationships between aging deficits in basic cognitive mechanisms and their biological underpinnings (Figure 2). The biological correlates of aging effects on intelligence examined so far involve molecular and neuronal mechanisms.

Molecular Correlates

ApoE is a plasma protein involved in cholesterol transportation. There is recent consensus that the ε_4 variant of ApoE is a risk factor for developing Alzheimer's disease. It may also relate to milder forms of nonclinical cognitive impairment (see Small, Basun, & Bäckman, 1998, for reviews).

Neuronal Correlates

Besides anatomical changes (Raz, 2000), there is consensus that during the course of normal aging the concentration of neurotransmitters—for instance, dopamine—in the frontal cortex, striatum, and basal ganglia decreases by 5–10% in each decade of life (e.g., Kaasinen et al., 2000). Functional relationships between aging-related deficits in the dopaminergic system and age-related decrements in various aspects of information processing have also been documented. For instance, the density of dopamine receptors in the nigrostriatum associates negatively with reaction time (RT)

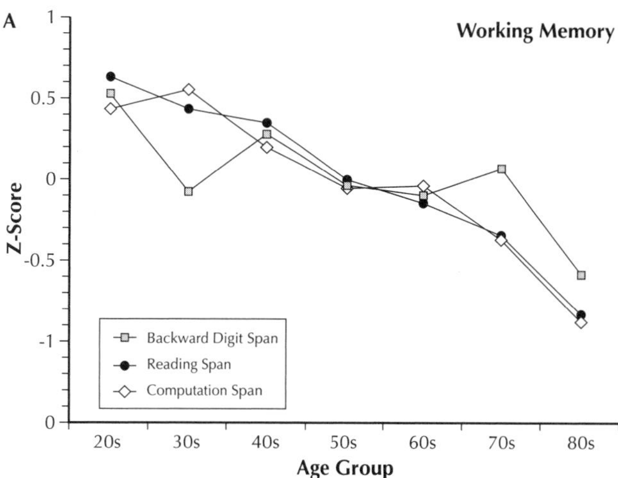

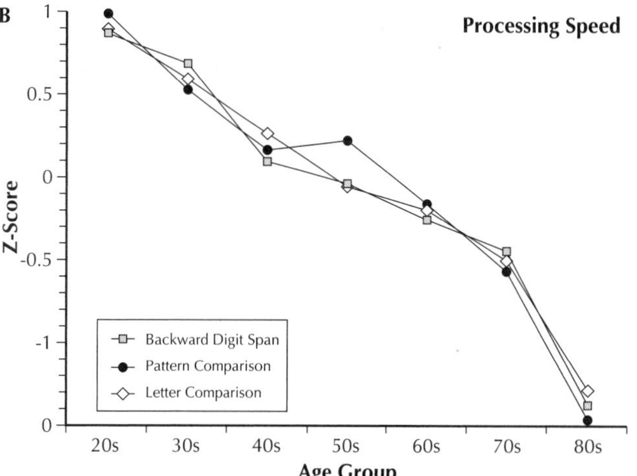

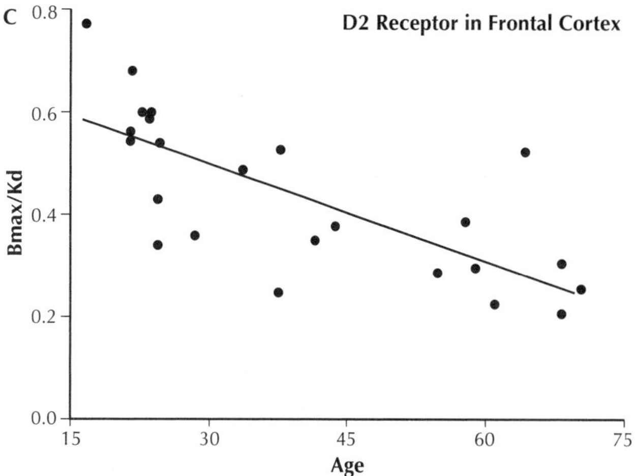

Figure 2. Aging-related declines in information processing and neurotransmitter density.
Negative adult age differences in working memory (A), processing speed (B), and dopamine D2-like receptor availability in the frontal cortex (C).
Source: Data based on Park et al. (1996) and Kaasinen et al. (2000); figure adapted from Li, Lindenberger, & Sikström (2001).

and positively with RT variance (Spirduso, Mayfield, Grant, & Schallert, 1989). Other studies have demonstrated that WM function is reduced in aged monkeys due to attenuated dopaminergic function (for review see Arnsten, 1998).

Recent *neurocomputational approaches* provide computational explications for linking aging-related decline in neuromodulation and cognitive deficits. For instance, simulations show that declines in dopaminergic modulation could be related to reduced neural information-processing fidelity, cortical representation distinctiveness, and various aspects of cognitive aging deficits (S.-C. Li, Lindenberger, & Sikström, 2001). Other models relate deficits in dopamine modulation more specifically to aging effects on memory context representation and maintenance (Braver et al., 2001) and on error processing (Nieuwenhuis et al., 2002).

Conclusions

Psychometric studies conducted since the 1920s indicate that intellectual aging is not a unitary process. Culture-based intelligence is maintained into the 70s, whereas biology-based intellectual abilities begin declining in the 40s. There is growing interest in understanding cognitive and neurobiological mechanisms that may underlie age-related declines in *Gf* abilities. At the information-processing level, factors such as WM, processing speed, and inhibition mechanisms are correlated with age differences in intelligence. Furthermore, there is emerging consensus that the prefrontal cortex and its supporting neuromodulation mechanisms underlie such cognitive functions. At present, the cross-level link from brain aging to intellectual aging continues to be refined.

REFERENCES

Baltes, P. B., & Mayer, U. (1998). *The Berlin Aging Study.* Cambridge, UK: Cambridge University Press.

Craik, F. I. M., & Salthouse, T. A. (2000). *The handbook of aging and cognition.* Mahwah, NJ: Erlbaum.

Kaasinen, V., et al. (2000). Age-related dopamine D2/D3 receptor loss in extrastriatal regions of human brain. *Neurobiology of Aging, 21,* 683–688.

Li, K. Z. H., Lindenberger, U., Freund, A. M., & Baltes, P. B. (2001). Walking while memorizing: Age-related differences in compensatory behavior. *Psychological Science, 12,* 230–237.

Li, S.-C., Lindenberger, U., & Sikström. S. (2001). Aging cognition: From neuromodulation to representation. *Trends in Cognitive Sciences, 5,* 479–486.

Lindenberger, U., & Baltes, P. B. (1994). Aging and intelligence. In R. J. Sternberg (Ed.), *Encyclopedia of human intelligence* (Vol. 1, pp. 52–66). New York: MacMillan.

Lindenberger, U., Marsiske, M., & Baltes, P. B. (2000). Memorizing while walking: Increase in dual-task costs from young adulthood to old age. *Psychology & Aging.*

Park, D. C., et al. (1996). Mediators of long-term memory performance across the lifespan. *Psychology & Aging, 4,* 621–637.

Schaie, K. W. (1996). *Intellectual development in adulthood: The Seattle Longitudinal Study.* Cambridge, UK: Cambridge University Press.

Schneider, E. L., Rowe, J. W., Johnson, T. E., Holbrook, N. J., & Morrison, J. H. (Eds.). (1996). *Handbook of the biology of aging* (4th ed.). Academic Press.

Shu-Chen Li
Max Planck Institute for Human Development

Karen Z. H. Li
Concordia University, Montreal, Canada

See also: **Aging and Intelligence; Geriatric Psychology**

AGRAPHIA

Definition

Agraphia (dysgraphia) is a systematic disorder of written language due to cerebral disease (Benson & Cummings, 1985; Bub & Chertkow, 1988; Hinkin & Cummings, 1996). It denotes a disturbance of writing in various physical forms; spatial or apraxic disorders may also contribute. It is not contingent on motor or sensory impairment, although combinations occur. Callosal lesions may cause unilateral agraphia (Roeltgen, 1993, 1997). Accompanying aphasia, agraphia usually reflects its pattern and severity; it is considered part of the supramodal language deficit (Kaplan, Gallagher, & Glosser, 1998; Ulatowska, Baker, & Stern, 1979).

Occurrence

Agraphia rarely coexists with alexia or occurs in isolation. Its hallmarks are paragraphias, on either a letter (literal) or word (verbal or semantic) level. Additionally, automatisms, perseverations, and syntactic or word-finding difficulties may occur as with spoken language.

Model of Writing

The model of a central language system comprises three components: phonology (speech sound production), lexicon (vocabulary), and syntax (sentence construction). Within the secondary language system of writing, an additional phoneme-to-grapheme conversion system is necessary, triggering the motor patterns for letters and an orthographic system.

While strings of letters are generated via the phonological route, entire words are produced via the semantic route. Various readers may rely more or less on one or the other, but usually they work in parallel fashion (the dual-

Figure 1. Handwriting of a 66-year-old right-handed man who had suffered a left temporal cerebral hematoma one month previously, developing transcortical-sensory aphasia. On dictation ("Wohin wird sie es mir bringen?" [Where is she going to take it for me?]) he wrote: "wi nin gricht es sich," producing literal (first three words) and verbal (last word) paragraphias.

route hypothesis). They may, however, be impaired selectively, yielding to different agraphia types.

Clinical Examination

Examination for agraphia includes spontaneous writing, writing to dictation (Figure 1), and written naming. If the dominant arm is paralyzed, writing may be attempted with the nondominant arm. A distinction between linguistic and spatial components of agraphia is best made by copying. To compensate for impaired motor abilities, letter or word synthesis using printed material may be used. Testing for kinesthetic reading, letter synthesis using sticks (matches), oral spelling, and reading may also be helpful.

Clinical Varieties

Pure Agraphia

This consists of severe inability to write without gross aphasia or alexia, leading to scribbling or misspelling. Production of single words in a barely legible fashion may be possible. Lesions are found in the left parieto-occipital region or second frontal gyrus (Exner's center). The distinction between pure and apraxic agraphia is questioned by some authors (Kaplan et al., 1998).

Aphasic Agraphia

This is part of aphasia, whose type and severity it reflects. Therefore, screening for agraphia may be used in testing for aphasia. Lesions are located in the classical language zones (i.e., in the distribution of the middle cerebral artery; Figure 2).

Neurolinguistically, three types may be defined. *Lexical agraphia* consists of a disability to convert phonemes to graphemes, especially with irregular spelling, resulting in phonetic writing without lexical control. Lesion sites are the posterior superior parietal lobule and the angular gyrus. *Phonologic agraphia* consists of holistic writing of words with occasional failure to produce entire words that cannot be written in a letter-by-letter fashion. The patient fails in dictated pronounceable nonsense words while succeeding in well-known imageable words. Lesions are in the

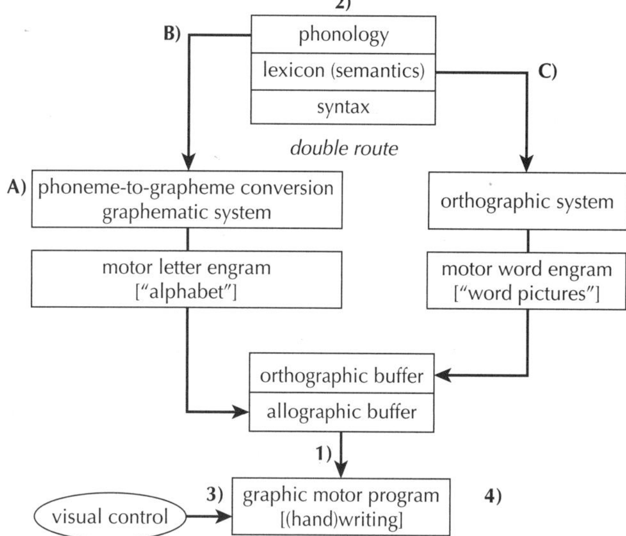

Figure 2. Proposed neurolinguistic model of writing. The letters and numbers indicate the presumed sites of disruption.

anterior inferior supramarginal gyrus or the adjoining insula. Patients with *semantic agraphia* may successfully write real and nonsense words to dictation but have difficulties in written confrontation naming or description.

In analogy to deep and surface alexia, deep and surface agraphia have been distinguished. *Deep agraphia* is characterized by semantic paragraphias (e.g., *airplane* for *propeller;* Roeltgen, 1997), whereas in *surface agraphia* mostly literal paragraphias are produced (e.g., *propettle* for *propeller*). In languages with irregular orthography such as English, surface agraphia seems to be more frequent than in languages with regular orthography.

Spatial Agraphia

Letters or words are incorrectly placed, closed in, omitted, of quite unequal shape and size, or augmented by superfluous strokes. In *neglect agraphia* words or letters at the margin of a page are omitted, or the lines show a marked slope toward one side. Patients often suffer from right parietal brain injury presenting with spatial deficits in nonlanguage tasks.

Apraxic Agraphia

Single letters are malformed or confused according to their graphic (e.g., M and W) rather than their phonetic similarity. This variety is consequent to the loss of graphic motor programs necessary for writing. Apraxic agraphia resembling pure agraphia has been described in terms of a modality-specific apraxia, but (ideomotor) apraxia is usually present in nonlanguage tasks. In Gerstmann's syndrome, elements of aphasic, spatial, and apraxic agraphia mingle. Lesions are found in the left parietal lobe, especially near the angular and supramarginal gyri.

REFERENCES

Benson, D. F., & Cummings, J. L. (1985). Agraphia. In J. A. M. Frederiks (Ed.), *Handbook of clinical neurology: Vol. 1. Clinical neuropsychology* (pp. 457–472). Amsterdam: Elsevier.

Bub, D., & Chertkow, D. (1988). Agraphia. In F. Boller & J. Grafman (Eds.), *Handbook of neuropsychology: Vol. 1* (pp. 393–414). Amsterdam: Elsevier.

Hinkin, C. H., & Cummings, J. L. (1996). Agraphia. In J. G. Beaumont, P. M. Kenealy, & M. J. C. Rogers (Eds.), *The Blackwell dictionary of neuropsychology* (pp. 21–31). Cambridge: Blackwell.

Kaplan, E., Gallagher, R. E., & Glosser, G. (1998). Aphasia-related disorders. In M. T. Sarno (Ed.), *Acquired aphasia* (3rd ed., pp. 309–339). San Diego, CA: Academic Press.

Roeltgen, D. (1993). Agraphia. In K. M. Heilman & E. Valenstein (Eds.), *Clinical neuropsychology* (3rd ed., pp. 63–89). New York: Oxford University Press.

Roeltgen, D. (1997). Agraphia. In T. E. Feinberg & M. J. Farah (Eds.), *Behavioral neurology and neuropsychology* (pp. 209–217). New York: McGraw-Hill.

Ulatowska, H. K., Baker, T., & Stern, R. F. (1979). Disruption of written language in aphasia. In H. Whitaker & H. A. Whitaker (Eds.), *Studies in neurolinguistics: Vol. 4* (pp. 241–268). New York: Academic Press.

Christoph J. G. Lang
University of Erlangen-Nuremberg, Erlangen, Germany

AGRICULTURAL PSYCHOLOGY

In contrast to other social sciences that have developed specialized applications to agriculture, psychology is not known for its concern with rural issues. For instance, there are no psychological counterparts to specialties such as agricultural economics, rural sociology, agricultural marketing, or rural geography. Nonetheless, psychological perspectives have interacted with agriculture in several domains: (1) assessment of therapeutic needs of rural populations, (2) investigation of farming tasks and skills, (3) analysis of expert agricultural judges, (4) evaluation of farming decisions, and (5) statistics and experimental design.

Therapeutic Needs

Rural life is often portrayed as idyllic and down-to-earth. Rural communities are assumed to be less stressful and more humane. However, epidemiological studies reveal serious mental health problems in rural settings. In fact, many psychopathologies have higher rates of incidence in agricultural areas. Despite their need, rural communities often lack mental health services taken for granted in cities.

One major reason for the lack of mental health services is that most therapists are trained in urban universities. Faculty (and students) are unfamiliar with the values, concerns, and language of rural living. Consequently, specialized programs and methods (e.g., traveling clinics and in-school programs) are necessary to prepare mental health care providers with the strategies they need to cope with problems encountered in rural communities.

One issue receiving attention in rural communities is child abuse. Rural environments are different in many respects from urban environments, which are more widely understood. It should not be surprising, therefore, to find that rural child abuse is perceived differently and frequently goes unreported. Nonetheless, home-based early intervention programs are successful in helping at-risk children.

Farming Tasks and Skills

Traditionally, farmers and ranchers were expected to be skilled in many manual and physical tasks. Work psychologists found that dairy workers are proficient in nine separate tasks, ranging from operating milking machines to evaluating the health of cows. Thus, a traditional farmer needed to be a jack of all trades, with general skills in many areas.

However, with increased mechanization and computerization in agriculture, there is a shift. Instead of many general abilities, fewer specialized skills are necessary now. Instead of emphasizing manual skills, modern agribusiness places greater demand on cognitive abilities: For example, a combine harvester involves simultaneous control of at least seven tasks. Given this complexity, the high rate of farm accidents may be due, in part, to overstressed human factors components.

With the trend away from small family farms to large corporate farming, there is also a greater need for farmers with sophisticated problem-solving and management skills. This has produced changes in both the education and the practice of farmers. As a result, behavioral investigators turned their interests toward analysis of higher thought processes.

Agricultural Expertise

Initial insights into the psychology of expertise arose from studies of agricultural workers. For instance, H. D. Hughes conducted one of the earliest studies of experts in 1917. He found that corn rated highest by expert corn judges did not produce the highest yield. Henry Wallace (later vice president under Franklin D. Roosevelt) reanalyzed Hughes's data using path analysis. He showed that (1) corn judges largely agreed with each other, but (2) their ratings correlated only slightly with crop yields.

In similar research, licensed grain inspectors were found to misgrade nearly one third of wheat samples and, when grading a second time, gave over one third a different grade. Also, increased experience made judges more confident but did not necessarily increase accuracy. Finally, more experienced judges tended to overgrade wheat samples (perhaps the original "grade inflation").

One source of errors in agricultural judgment is the presence of irrelevant factors. Gary Gaeth and James Shanteau found that nondiagnostic material (e.g., excessive moisture) had a significant impact on decisions by soil judges. However, cognitive training successfully compensated for these irrelevant materials. Another approach to improving expert judgment was used in weather forecasting: Precipitation forecasts were improved using Brier scores (a quadratic scoring system). Recently, accuracy of short-term weather forecasts has increased dramatically.

Farm Management Decisions

There have been analyses of the choices needed to manage a farm. Most of this work is concerned with how economic decisions should be made. Various methods have been proposed to help farmers choose more effectively. For instance, farmers often make suboptimal allocations when buying crop insurance. However, farmers can be persuaded to make more effective decisions by taking a longer time perspective.

Insights into marketing and consumer behavior have arisen from studies in agriculture. For instance, the pioneering analysis of new-product diffusion by Everett Rogers in 1962 was based on farmers' willingness to adopt new agricultural equipment. His classification of consumers into "innovators, early adopters, early majority, late majority, and laggards" is now widely accepted.

Statistics and Experimental Design

One area with a long-standing interface between psychology and agriculture is statistical analysis and design. A century ago, psychologists such as Francis Galton were instrumental in developing modern statistical thinking. Later psychologists (e.g., James McKeen Cattell and L. L. Thurstone) extended the application of statistics in behavioral research.

Statisticians working in agriculture (such as R. A. Fisher) developed much of what is now standard experimental design and analysis. For instance, random assignment and factorial designs were initially originally devised for agricultural science. Many terms used in statistics—for example, *split-plot designs*—reflect this agricultural origin.

In summary, although agricultural psychology is not normally recognized as a subfield of psychology, there have been many applications of psychology in agriculture. Moreover, agricultural issues have affected psychology in many often unappreciated ways.

REFERENCE

Rogers, E. M. (1962). *Diffusion of innovations.* New York: Free Press.

SUGGESTED READING

Childs, A. W., & Melton, G. B. (1983). *Rural psychology.* New York: Plenum Press.

Husaini, B. A., Neff, J. A., & Stone, R. H. (1979). Psychiatric impairment in rural communities. *Journal of Community Psychology, 7,* 137–146.

Phelps, R. H., & Shanteau, J. (1978). Livestock judges: How much information can an expert use? *Organizational Behavior and Human Performance, 21,* 209–219.

James Shanteau
Kansas State University

AKATHISIA

The term *akathisia* (literally, "not to sit") was introduced by the Bohemian neuropsychiatrist Lad Haskovec in 1901 (Haskovec, 1901). Akathisia represents a complex psychomotor syndrome that consists of a subjective (emotional) and an objective (motor) component (Brüne & Bräunig,

Table 1. Subjective Symptoms of Akathisia

- Inner restlessness
- Urge to move (tasikinesia)
- Inability to remain still
- General unease
- Discomfort
- Inability to relax
- Poor concentration
- Dysphoria
- Anxiety
- Fear
- Terror, rage
- Suicidal ideation
- Aggressive thoughts

Table 2. Objective Symptoms of Akathisia

Sitting Position	Standing Position
Fidgetiness of arms and hands	Marching on the spot
Rubbing face	Changing stance
Rubbing, caressing, or shaking arms or hands	Flexing and extending knees
	Rocking from foot to foot
Rubbing or massaging legs	Pacing, walking repetitively
Tapping, picking on clothes	
Crossing and uncrossing arms	
Crossing and uncrossing legs	
Swinging or kicking crossed legs	
Tapping toes	
Frequently squirming in chair, making straightening motions	
Rocking and twisting the body	

Table 3. Differential Diagnosis of Akathisia

Subjective Component Prominent	Objective Component Prominent
Psychotic agitation	Restless-legs syndrome
Anxiety	Tardive dyskinesia
Agitation due to affective disorder	Stereotypies
	Tremor
Drug withdrawal syndromes	Myoclonus
Neuroleptic dysphoria	Restless, repetitive movements due to organic disorder (e.g., pacing in dementia, hyperactivity in Tourette's syndrome)
Agitation due to organic disorder (e.g., dementia, hypoglycemia)	

1997; Sachdev, 1995; see Tables 1 and 2). Subjectively distressing inner restlessness and repetitive movements of the legs are the most frequent symptoms, predominantly emerging when the patient is in a standing or sitting position, with some relief taking place when the patient is lying. However, none of the symptoms is pathognomonic, making it difficult to distinguish akathisia from other forms of restlessness as well as from other movement disorders (Sachdev, 1994, 1995; see Table 3).

Although probably first mentioned in postencephalitic parkinsonism and in idiopathic Parkinson's disease long before neuroleptics became available, akathisia is nowadays mostly associated with the administration of antipsychotic drugs. "Classical" antipsychotics with a high affinity to dopamine D2 receptors are much more likely to produce akathisia than are atypical antipsychotics. However, agents targeting serotonin receptors are also suspected of causing an akathisialike syndrome. Akathisia is of specific clinical relevance because it may complicate the treatment by inducing noncompliant and impulsive behaviors, which may include assaultive and suicidal actions (Van Putten, 1975). Moreover, akathisia is sometimes mistaken as psychotic agitation or even overlooked (Van Putten, 1975; Weiden, Mann, Haas, Mattson, & Frances, 1987). Since the 1980s, several clinically useful rating scales for akathisia have been published to improve systematic evaluation (details in Brüne & Bräunig, 1997; Sachdev, 1995).

Akathisia generally has an acute beginning within hours or days after initiation of antipsychotic treatment. High initial dosages and rapid dose increment are predisposing factors to produce acute akathisia (Sachdev & Kruk, 1994). Other subtypes of akathisia have been described according to the time of onset during antipsychotic treatment with more ambiguous risk factors (see Table 4). When a patient is taking a chronic course, subjective distress may decrease and the movement patterns look more like stereotypies, suggesting an overlap with tardive dyskinesia (Barnes & Braude, 1985).

The reported prevalence and incidence rates vary considerably, depending on the applied diagnostic criteria (Brüne & Bräunig, 1997; Sachdev, 1995; Van Putten, May, & Marder, 1984).

Table 4. Subtypes of Drug-Induced Akathisia

Subtype	Description
Acute akathisia	Onset within 6 weeks of initiation of treatment, dose increment, or change of drug type; concurrent medication not decreased or discontinued
Chronic akathisia	Symptoms persist for over 3 months; specify acute, tardive, or withdrawal onset
Tardive akathisia	Onset at least 3 months after initiation of treatment, dose increment, or change of drug type; no dose increment or change of drug within 6 weeks prior to onset; concurrent medication not decreased or discontinued
Withdrawal akathisia	Onset within 6 weeks of discontinuation or marked reduction of dose; prior to onset, duration of treatment at least 3 months; concurrent medication not decreased or discontinued
Pseudoakathisia	Typical objective symptoms without subjective distress

Source: Modified from Sachdev (1994).

The pathophysiology of akathisia is far from being fully understood. Akathisia may best be viewed as resulting from the interaction of dopaminergic neurones with noradrenergic, serotonergic, cholinergic, GABAergic, glutamatergic, and opioid systems in mesolimbic and mesocortical pathways (Sachdev, 1995).

Early diagnosis is critical due not only to the possible complications associated with akathisia but also to the impending dilemma of insufficient or delayed treatment response. Thus, preventive measures, such as choosing the lowest effective dose and employing the stepwise increment of dose, are indispensable (Sachdev, 1995). Moreover, routine clinical checks for extrapyramidal side effects and behavioral observation (e.g., during occupational therapy or other group therapies) are recommended (Brüne & Bräunig, 1997).

If akathisia is present, stopping the offending drug or at least reducing the dose is considered to be the best option (Sachdev, 1995). However, in highly agitated patients, waiting for a spontaneous wearing-off may be impracticable. Anticholinergic drugs, receptor antagonists, and benzodiazepines are effective for acute treatment, yet response rates are variable. If onset of akathisia is less acute, a change of antipsychotic class or administration of modern agents is proposed. Treating chronic or tardive akathisia is probably less effective (Brüne & Bräunig, 1997; Sachdev, 1995).

REFERENCES

Barnes, T. R. E., & Braude, W. M. (1985). Akathisia variants and tardive dyskinesia. *Archives of General Psychiatry, 42,* 874–878.

Brüne, M., & Bräunig, P. (1997). Akathisie [Akathisia]. *Fortschritte der Neurologie und Psychiatrie, 65,* 396–406.

Haskovec, L. (1901). L'Akathisie [Akathisia]. *Revue Neurologique, 9,* 1107–1109.

Sachdev, P. (1994). Research diagnostic criteria for drug-induced akathisia: Conceptualization, rationale and proposal. *Psychopharmacology, 114,* 181–186.

Sachdev, P. (1995). *Akathisia and restless legs.* New York: Cambridge University Press.

Sachdev, P., & Kruk, J. (1994). Clinical characteristics and predisposing factors in acute drug-induced akathisia. *Archives of General Psychiatry, 51,* 963–974.

Van Putten, T. (1975). The many faces of akathisia. *Comprehensive Psychiatry, 16,* 43–47.

Van Putten, T., May, P. R. A., & Marder, S. R. (1984). Akathisia with haloperidol and thiothixene. *Archives of General Psychiatry, 41,* 1036–1039.

Weiden, P. J., Mann, J., Haas, G., Mattson, M., & Frances, A. (1987). Clinical nonrecognition of neuroleptic-induced movement disorders: A cautionary study. *American Journal of Psychiatry, 144,* 1148–1153.

Martin Brüne
Centre for Psychiatry and Psychotherapy, University of Bochum, Germany

ALEXIA/DYSLEXIA

In an increasingly literate world, the inability to read becomes a significant disability that may affect academic success, employment, and self-concept. Because widespread literacy is a recent historical development, it should not be surprising that it was only about 100 years ago that the first case of alexia or "word blindness" was described. By definition, the term *alexia* describes a condition where reading ability is lost as the result of some neurological insult, such as head injury or stroke. With alexia, it is assumed that the individual had adequate reading achievement prior to the neurological insult.

The clinical and experimental literature on alexia has greatly increased understanding of dyslexia. The term *dyslexia* refers to an inborn or congenital inability to learn to read. The term rose out of the medical literature and is not completely accepted by many educators who work with children with reading difficulties. Many educators and psychologists prefer the terms *developmental reading disorder* or *reading disability,* because they avoid the implication that the etiology of the reading disorder is due to neurological deficits. Consequently, the term *dyslexia* is most appropriate when it describes a severe reading disability presumed to be neurologic in origin. Although prevalence estimates vary, the incidence of dyslexia has been estimated at 3% to 8% of the school-aged population. Although definitions of dyslexia vary across contexts, most definitions center on a significant discrepancy between reading achievement, particularly word recognition ability, and a measure of general cognitive ability or intellectual functioning.

The biological bases of dyslexia have gained significant research attention since the early 1990s. Many researchers have targeted the left hemisphere's perisylvian region, or the area surrounding the Sylvian fissure on the lateral surface of the cortex, in research examining morphology and planum temporale symmetry. *Morphology* refers to the pattern of gyri and sulci on the surface of the brain. Subtle deviations in perisylvian morphology, although not at a level of gross neurological significance, have been associated with dyslexia. Research on the biological basis of dyslexia has also focused on the planum temporale. Symmetry or rightward asymmetry in the length or size of the planum temporale have been associated with dyslexia. Polymicrogyri, additional small folds in the cortical surface, and heterotopias, neuronal migration errors, in this region have also been associated with dyslexia.

Although the perisylvian region has received significant research attention, it is not entirely clear why brains with symmetry or atypical morphology are more likely to be found in individuals with dyslexia. The symmetry noted in these brains may result from neuronal migration errors or poor pruning of redundant pathways. Because the individual has fewer functionally connected cells, those that are functional may be less able to compensate for other cortical atypicalities. Additionally, the individual may have fewer pathways available to compensate for the atypicalities.

Reading is a complex cognitive task that combines numerous skills, including attention, memory, phonological processing, rapid naming, and so forth. Consequently, any findings related to individual chromosomal involvement in the development of dyslexia might actually pertain to language tasks in general. Despite this caveat, research has implicated chromosomes 6 and 15 in dyslexia, resulting from the action of an autosomal dominant gene with variable expression and incomplete penetrance. Although there is significant evidence to support genetic involvement in dyslexia, environmental factors also play a role. Behavioral genetics research has suggested that slightly more than 50% of the variance in reading performance is the result of differences in genetic heritability.

Although research supports the involvement of genetics and the differences in the brain as being risk factors for dyslexia, these areas do not answer questions about the underlying cognitive processes that are involved in reading and that are aberrant in dyslexia. Research on dyslexia suggests that phonological processing and orthographic coding are two cognitive processes that play significant roles in reading ability and dyslexia.

Phonological processing allows an individual to hear and manipulate individual sounds in spoken language. Although there are only 26 letters in the English language, there are 44 phonemes. Phonological processing is part of the larger skill of auditory perception and discrimination, but it is involved only with sounds used in speech. Rather than being one unitary skill demonstrable in a single behavior, phonological processing skills are actually a group of skills, including letter-sound association, rhyming, blending, segmenting, and sound replacement. Phonological processing skills are developing in children before they enter school, and these early skills appear to predict future reading achievement. Furthermore, these skills continue to develop as the child learns to read, such that the relationship between phonological processing and reading is symbiotic. Research with dyslexic children suggests that phonological deficits may be the core deficits impeding their reading acquisition. Furthermore, there is evidence to suggest that these skills are influenced by genetics and the underlying brain structures in the perisylvian region.

Orthographic processing is a second area of research investigation. It involves the interpretation of abstract representations, specifically, series of letters that form words during the reading process. Orthographic processing is most closely related to sight word reading, in which the individual does not use decoding strategies to read words but, rather, recognizes the entire word on sight. It appears to be influenced mostly by environmental factors, such as home reading environment, rather than genetic heritability. Functional magnetic resonance imaging (fMRI) has been employed to chart possible deficiencies in phonological and orthographic processes in the brain.

Intervention for dyslexia typically consists of remediation and compensation strategies. When children are diagnosed with dyslexia during the early school years, the emphasis is on teaching them phonetic skills to improve their decoding ability and teaching them to recognize sight words to increase reading speed. For many children, their reading improves and they are able to experience normal developmental outcomes, such as employment and, in some cases, higher-level education. For those individuals who do not develop adequate reading ability by adolescence and adulthood, the emphasis changes to include compensatory strategies. As adults, dyslexic individuals typically have access to books on tape and other compensatory approaches.

Carlin J. Miller
City University of New York, Queens College

George W. Hynd
Purdue University

ALIENATION (POLITICAL)

Political alienation, or disaffection, is basically a feeling of dissatisfaction, disillusionment, and detachment regarding political leaders, governmental policies, and the political system.

Feelings of political disaffection comprise at least five components: *powerlessness* ("People like me don't have any say in what the government does"); *discontentment* ("For the most part, the government serves the interests of a few organized groups such as business or labor, and isn't very concerned about the needs of people like me"); *distrust* ("A large number of city and county politicians are political hacks"); *estrangement* ("When I think about the government in Washington, I don't feel as if it's my government"); and *hopelessness* ("The future of this country seems dark to me").

Three research findings seem germane to this conceptualization of political disaffection. First, these five components of disaffection are highly interrelated, with high levels of disaffection in one component correlating with high levels of disaffection in the other four. Second, two attitudinal dimensions appear to underlie these five components, with political powerlessness and estrangement forming a personal dimension of disaffection, while political discontentment, distrust, and hopelessness constitute a systemic dimension of disaffection. Third, in exploring the attribution of responsibility for political disaffection, one finds that individuals attribute the condition of the political system to the unintentional behavior of private citizens ("Citizens are uninformed about politics and public affairs because the government lies to them") rather than to the intentional behavior of public officials ("Politicians are unqualified for the positions they hold").

Two demographic factors have been fairly consistently found to relate to feelings of political disaffection: socioeconomic status and race. Thus, political alienation is more prevalent among the lower and working classes than among the middle and upper classes, and Blacks are more politically alienated than Whites.

Theories

At least seven explanations have been advanced to account for people's feelings of political alienation. *Complex organization theory* states that political disaffection will occur when people are unable or unwilling to participate politically in society, large formal organizations, or their communities. Two key causes of political alienation in society are a lack of primary relationships and an inability to belong to and participate in voluntary associations. When these two phenomena occur, feelings of political alienation result. *Mass society theory,* the principal variant of this explanation, suggests that modern society cannot be understood, does not offer achievable goals, is composed of people with dissimilar values, permits few personal satisfactions, and offers no sense of personal control. These societal characteristics lead in turn to political disaffection.

Social disadvantages theory, by comparison, holds that

people's social positions do not produce political disaffection; rather, disaffection results from the perceptions that people occupying social positions have of their relations with other people and other social entities. This theory would be supported by the evidence that socioeconomic status—that is, education, income, and occupation—is related to political disaffection, with such feelings occurring more frequently among individuals with less formal education, lower income levels, and blue-collar, manual occupations.

Personal failure theory postulates three preconditions for political alienation: (1) the individual must occupy a social position that limits his or her actions, (2) these limited opportunities must preclude the achievement of major life goals, and (3) the individual must perceive him- or herself as a failure in these attempts at goal attainment. In this case, failure to attain personal life goals does not engender political alienation; such a failure must be both socially caused and recognized by the individual for political alienation to occur.

Social isolation theory of alienation suggests that feelings of political disaffection are related to isolation from, or a lack of assimilation to, the political system. This lack of assimilation pertains to any social ties to any social object, not necessarily to society itself, and can be either cognitive or behavioral in nature. In addition, the social isolation can be either involuntary or voluntary, unconscious or conscious. In this instance, disaffection would be predicted from disinterest in politics, political apathy, weak partisanship, political ignorance, and a failure to vote.

In contrast to these sociological theories of political alienation, the *social deprivation model of disaffection* postulates that personal feelings of social deprivation lead to low self-esteem, which in turn results in high levels of political alienation. The two key elements in this theory—the linkage between perceived social deprivation and feelings of low self-esteem, and between low self-esteem and felt political alienation—have not been supported in surveys of White and Black adolescents.

Conversely, the *sociopolitical reality explanation* of political disaffection has been repeatedly supported in empirical research. This theory posits a direct link between perceptions of the sociopolitical system's functioning and feelings of political disaffection, with critical views of the system's operation being directly linked to felt disaffection. Although the sociopolitical reality model of political disaffection receives strong support, it manifests a major shortcoming, in that no account is provided for the nexus between a person's critical perceptions of systemic functioning and that person's feelings of political disaffection.

This connection is provided by the *systemic disaffection theory,* which suggests that three causal factors contribute to political alienation. First, critical perceptions of sociopolitical reality—that is, of economic and racial discrimination—must occur. Second, a politically irrational, perfectionistic response to the operations of the sociopolitical system must next occur, typically of a moralistic, rigid, grandiose nature. Third, psychological reactance, or perceived threat from the sociopolitical system, must also be elicited. This perceived threat to and/or loss of freedom will be particularly salient if the individual feels particularly susceptible to such a threat or loss, or views himself or herself as being comparable to others who have experienced a threat to or loss of freedom.

These three preconditions follow a specific causal sequence. Thus, critical perceptions of sociopolitical reality not only directly contribute to feelings of alienation from the sociopolitical system, but also lead to irrational political ideation and to psychological reactance. Next, irrational political ideation fosters high levels of psychological reactance and generates political alienation. Then feelings of psychological reactance also contribute to political alienation.

Consequences

A major concern among theories on the political disaffection process is the consequences of disaffection for the political system. Of the four attitudinal and behavioral consequences of political disaffection that are most frequently cited in the literature—attitudinal rightism and negativism, and behavioral apathy and extremism—only behavioral apathy has been firmly established in the research literature on conventional political activity. Thus it can be concluded that the politically disaffected, in their political attitudes and behavior, differ little from the politically allegiant. It also follows that the stability and viability of democratic political systems are not jeopardized by politically alienated segments of the population who may remain more politically apathetic than their peers.

S. Long

ALL-OR-NONE LAW

Applied to the axon (single, relatively lengthy process) of a nerve cell or neuron, the all-or-none law states that transmission of a nerve impulse occurs either all the way or not at all. If the changes that produce the nerve impulse—that is, the movement of charged particles or ions—reach a certain threshold level, then the impulse (also called the *action potential* or *spike potential*) is conducted at a constant level from its origin to the end of the axon.

Another way the law is sometimes expressed is that axonal transmission is independent of the intensity of the stimulus that produces it. As long as the stimulus causes enough ionic movement to exceed a threshold, the nerve impulse occurs all the way, without decreasing as it travels the length of the axon. A mild stimulus that surpasses the threshold produces the same nerve impulse as an intense stimulus. The nervous system codes the intensity of a stimulus by the rate of generation of action potentials, not by whether they occur, and also by the number of neurons activated in a given area. The greater the intensity, the larger the number of neurons activated and the more rapidly they generate action potentials. A neuron's action potentials are analogous to signals from a telegraph key: A neuron cannot send bigger or faster action potentials any more than a telegraph operator can send bigger or faster signals with the telegraph key.

The all-or-none concept applies to other excitable tissue as well, and the principle was first demonstrated in 1871 in heart muscle by American physiologist Henry P. Bowditch. In 1902, English physiologist F. Gotch discovered evidence for an all-or-none effect in nerves, but the effect was not convincingly proven until Edgar Douglas Adrian's work, for which he received a Nobel prize in physiology in 1932. Adrian's research was preceded by studies performed by K. Lucas, who actually named the law in a 1909 article.

Like most of the nervous system's so-called laws, the all-or-none law has exceptions. For example, some neurons can produce a series of action potentials that grow successively smaller, thus disobeying the law.

B. Michael Thorne
Mississippi State University

ALPHA RHYTHMS

Ensembles of synchronously active cortical neurons generate electromagnetic field potentials that can be measured by electroencephalography (EEG) or magnetoencephalography (MEG). The alpha frequency band is defined to be between 8 and 13 Hz (Berger, 1929; Adrian & Mathews, 1934). The classical alpha rhythm is prominent at electrodes overlying the occipital (visual) cortex and to a lesser extent over the posterior temporal and parietal areas. Alpha rhythm occurs in a condition of relaxed wakefulness with eyes closed, and it is depressed upon eye opening. The alpha rhythm disappears gradually during drowsiness, and different types of alpha activity appear in rapid eye movement (REM) sleep (Cantero, Atienza, & Salas, 2002).

Blind children do not develop the alpha rhythm. The alpha frequency matures and reaches the approximate average values of 8 Hz at age 3, 9 Hz at age 9, and 10 Hz at age 15. The interindividual variability is quite large. About 6–10% of healthy subjects have "low-voltage alpha activity," below 20 μV. In general, alpha amplitude is higher in children than in adults. Consistent amplitude asymmetries exceeding 2:1 are usually considered to be abnormal. Alpha variant rhythms with frequency of half or double the normal frequency may occur in some healthy subjects (Markand, 1990).

Alpha rhythm peak frequency correlates with cerebral blood flow and metabolism (Sulg, 1984), and low frequency is found in metabolic, infectious, and degenerative disorders, such as dementia of the Alzheimer type. Unilateral slowing or loss of alpha rhythm occurs in the presence of traumatic, neoplastic, infectious, or vascular lesions of one occipital lobe. Abnormal "alpha coma pattern" occurs in some comatose patients. The outcome is variable, depending on the underlying condition, but it is most often poor.

Other physiological rhythms within the alpha frequency band are the mu rhythm (9–11 Hz) recorded over the sensorimotor cortex (Niedermeyer, 1999) and the tau rhythm (Hari, 1999). Mu may be the only routinely recorded alpha-band rhythm in EEG of infants and small children. In order to see the proper alpha rhythm, passive eye closure or recording in darkness should by attempted.

Subdural and intracortical recordings, as well as source localization studies, have shown that the alpha rhythm has multiple generators within the cerebral cortex (Williamson, Kaufmann, Lu, Wang, & Karron, 1997). Although early studies suggested that the alpha rhythm was driven by feedback inhibition of thalamic relé cells (Andersen & Andersson, 1968), more recent studies suggest that both cortico-cortical and thalamo-cortical connections are of importance. It has been suggested that both intrinsic membrane ion channel properties and local neuron network properties determine rhythmic behavior (Lopes da Silva, 1991).

The coherence-function has become a popular tool because it reveals information about functional connectivity between different parts of the brain during various tasks and states (Gevins, Leong, Smith, Le, & Du, 1995). Volume conduction and the EEG-reference montage must be considered during interpretation. Event-related desynchronization (ERD) of central and occipital alpha rhythms represent activation of those cortical areas that are active in vision, motor preparation or selective attention (Pfurtscheller, Stancák, & Neuper, 1996). Event-related alpha-oscillations in visual and auditory cortex following visual and auditory stimuli respectively have been described (Basar, Basar-Eroglu, Karakas, & Schürmann, 1999).

Conflicting results have been published regarding the possible relationship between alpha frequency and cognitive performance (Markand, 1990; Klimesch, 1999). A recent study found no correlation between alpha peak frequency and intelligence dimensions (Posthuma, Neale, Boomsma, & de Geus, 2001). Some evidence suggest that slow (8–10 Hz) and fast (11–12 Hz) alphas reflect functionally different processes (Verstraeten & Cluydts, 2002). Biofeedback treatment aimed at alpha enhancement may relieve anxiety (Moore, 2000). The existence of a relationship between depression and frontal alpha asymmetry has been challenged recently (Debener et al., 2000).

Considerable progress has been made toward a better understanding of the basic mechanisms behind alpha rhythms and brain function during recent years. Some data regarding alpha coherence seem to challenge the concept that cognitive events only are associated with gamma (30–100 Hz) activity (Nunez, Wingeier, & Silberstein, 2001). High-resolution EEG and MEG recording combined with mathematical methods and individual magnetic resonance brain imaging are exciting tools for future brain function research.

REFERENCES

Andersen, P., & Andersson, S. (1968). *Physiological basis of the alpha rhythm.* New York: Appleton-Century-Croft.

Adrian, E. D., & Mathews, B. H. C. The Berger rhythm: Potential changes from the occipital lobes in man. *Brain, 57,* 354–385.

Basar, E., Basar-Eroglu, C., Karakas, S., & Schürmann, M. (1999). Are cognitive processes manifested in event-related gamma, alpha, theta and delta oscillations in the EEG? *Neuroscience Letters, 259,* 165–168.

Berger, H. (1929). Über das elektroenkephalogramm des Menschen. *Archives of Psychiatry Nervenkr, 87,* 527–570.

Cantero, J. L., Atienza, M., & Salas, R. M. (2002). Spectral features of EEG alpha activity in human REM sleep: Two variants with different functional roles? *Sleep, 23,* 746–750.

Debener, S., Beauducel, A., Nessler, D., Brocke, B., Heilemann, H., & Kayser, J. (2000). Is resting anterior EEG alpha asymmetry a trait marker for depression? Findings for healthy adults and clinically depressed patients. *Neuropsychobiology, 41,* 31–37.

Gevins, A., Leong, H., Smith, M. E., Le, J., & Du, R. (1995). Mapping cognitive brain function with modern high-resolution electroencephalography. *Trends in Neurosciences, 18,* 429–436.

Hari, R. (1999). Magnetoencephalography as a tool of clinical neurophysiology. In E. Niedermeyer & F. H. da Silva (Eds.), *Electroencephalography: Basic principles, clinical applications and related fields* (4th ed., pp. 1107–1134). Baltimore: Williams & Wilkins.

Klimesch, W. (1999). EEG alpha and theta oscillations reflect cognitive and memory performance: A review and analysis. *Brain Research Reviews,* 169–195.

Lopes da Silva, F. (1991). Neural mechanisms underlying brain waves: From neural membranes to networks. *Electroencephalography and Clinical Neurophysiology, 7,* 81–93.

Markand, O. N. (1990). Alpha rhythms. *Journal of Clinical Neurophysiology, 7,* 163–189.

Moore, N. C. (2000). A review of EEG biofeedback treatment of anxiety disorders. *Clinical Electroencephalography, 31,* 1–6.

Niedermeyer, E. (1999). The normal EEG in the waking adult. In E. Niedermeyer & F. H. da Silva (Eds.), *Electroencephalography: Basic principles, clinical applications and related fields* (4th ed., pp. 149–173). Baltimore: Williams & Wilkins.

Nunez, P. L., Wingeier, B. M., & Silberstein, R. B. (2001). Spatial-temporal structures of human alpha rhythms: Theory, microcurrent sources, multiscale measurements, and lobal binding of local networks. *Human Brain Mapping, 13,* 125–164.

Pfurtscheller, G., Stancák, Jr., A., & Neuper, C. H. (1996). Event-related synchronization (ERS) in the alpha band—An electrophysiological correlate of cortical idling: A review. *International Journal of Psychophysiology, 24,* 39–46.

Posthuma, D., Neale, M. C., Boomsma, D. I., & de Geus, E. J. C. (2001). Are smarter brains running faster? Heritability of alpha peak frequency, IQ, and their interrelation. *Behaviour Genetics, 31,* 567–579.

Sulg, I. (1984). Quantitative EEG as a measure of brain dysfunction. In G. Pfurtscheller, E. H. Jonkman, & F. H. Lopes da Silva (Eds.), *Progress in neurobiology: Vol. 62. Brain ischemia: Quantitative EEG and imaging techniques* (pp. 65–84). Amsterdam: Elsevier.

Verstraeten, E., & Cluydts, R. (2002). Attentional switching-related human EEG alpha oscillations. *Neuroreport, 13,* 681–684.

Williamson, S. J., Kaufmann, L., Lu, Z. L., Wang, J. Z., & Karron, D. (1997). Study of human occipital alpha rhythm: The alphon hypothesis and alpha suppression. *International Journal of Psychophysiology, 26,* 63–76.

TROND SAND
Trondheim University Hospital, Norway

ALZHEIMER'S DISEASE

Alzheimer's disease (AD) is a progressive neurodegenerative disease, affecting memory, intellectual functions, and behavior. The prevalence of Alzheimer's disease is increasing with the growing percentage of the population over age 65. Remarkably, 15% of persons over age 65, and up to 50% of persons over age 80, may meet diagnostic criteria for AD (Evans et al., 1996; Pfeffer, Afifi, & Chance, 1987). Approximately 14 million persons are expected to have AD by the middle of the twenty-first century.

The pathology of AD involves the degeneration of select cortical regions and ascending brain-stem systems, including the cholinergic basal forebrain. These structures exhibit pathological hallmarks of neurofibrillary tangles within neurons and extracellular senile plaques containing Aβ40 and Aβ42. There are other pathological changes, however, including synaptic and neuronal loss, vascular changes, granulovacuolar degeneration and alterations to endosomal/lysosomal systems, and signs of inflammation and oxidative stress (Terry, 1994).

Genetic research has provided key insights into the biology of AD. Early-onset familial AD is linked to mutations in the β amyloid precursor protein (APP), presenilin 1, and presenilin 2 (Hardy & Selkoe, 2002). Late-onset familial and sporadic AD is associated with Apo E. Increased amounts of Aβ42, derived from APP, resulting from mutations in APP and presenilins alike (Hardy & Selkor, 2002), may enhance Aβ aggregation (Jarrett & Lansbury, 1993). Apo E genotype influences AD susceptibility, perhaps via increased Aβ deposition (Schmechel et al., 1993). Numerous studies confirm that the ε4 allele increases AD risk and decreases age of onset (Corder et al., 1993; Farrer et al., 1997).

The clinical presentation of AD usually begins with

Table 1. NINDS-ARDA Criteria for Probable Alzheimer's Disease and *DSM-IV* Criteria for Dementia of the Alzheimer's Type

A. Include the following:
   1. Dementia established by clinical examination and documented by the Mini-Mental Test, Blessed Dementia Scale, or some similar examination, and confirmed by neuropsychological tests
   2. Deficits in two or more areas of cognition
   3. Progressive worsening of memory and other cognitive functions
   4. No disturbance of consciousness
   5. Onset between ages 40–90, most often after age 65
   6. Absence of systemic disorders or other brain diseases that in and of themselves could account for the progressive deficits in memory and cognition

B. The diagnosis is supported by the following:
   1. Progressive deterioration of specific cognitive functions, such as language (aphasia), motor skills (apraxia), and perception (agnosia)
   2. Impaired activities of daily living and altered patterns of behavior
   3. Family history of similar disorders, especially if confirmed neurohistopathologically

A. The development of multiple cognitive deficits manifested by both:
   1. Memory impairment (impaired ability to learn new information or to recall previously learned information) and
   2. One (or more) of the following cognitive disturbances:
      a. Aphasia (language disturbance)
      b. Apraxia (impaired ability to carry out motor activities despite intact motor function)
      c. Agnosia (failure to recognize or identify objects despite intact sensory function)
      d. Disturbance in executive functioning (i.e., planning organizing, sequencing)

B. Each of the cognitive deficits in Criteria A1 and A2 causes significant impairment in social or occupational functioning and represents a decline from a previous level of functioning.

C. The course is characterized by gradual onset and continuing cognitive decline.

D. The cognitive deficits in Criteria A1 and A2 are not due to any of the following:
   1. Other central nervous system conditions that cause progressive deficits in memory and cognition (e.g., cerebrovascular disease, Parkinson's disease, Huntington's disease, subdural hematoma, normal pressure hydrocephalus, brain tumor)
   2. Systemic conditions that are known to cause dementia (e.g., hypothyroidism, vitamin B12 or folic acid deficiency, hypercalcemia, neurosyphilis, HIV infection)
   3. Substance-induced conditions

E. The deficits do not occur exclusively during the course of a delirium.

F. The disturbance is not better accounted for by another Axis I disorder (e.g., Major Depressive Disorder, Schizophrenia)

memory loss and mild cognitive impairment, which slowly worsen over years (Cummings & Cole, 2002). In early stages there is frequent repetition of stories and questions, misplacing of belongings, geographic disorientation, dysnomia, and difficulty managing finances or handling complex tasks. Sleep disturbances, depression, psychosis, and other neuropsychiatric problems commonly evolve. Assistance is eventually needed for dressing, bathing, meals, and other activities. Individuals often become lost in familiar surroundings and have reduced comprehension. Late stages often bring agitation and aggression, profound cognitive impairment, and loss of control of bodily functions. These disabilities often lead to institutionalization, increased risk of decubitus ulcers, aspiration pneumonia, and urosepsis from indwelling catheters.

Diagnosis of AD is based on the clinical features and the exclusion of other etiologies (Knopman et al., 2001). Two commonly used diagnostic criteria are listed in Table 1. Confirmation of cognitive impairment is important. Common screening tools for dementia include the Mini-Mental State Exam, the Mattis Dementia Rating Scale, and the clock drawing test (Folstein, Folstein, & McHugh, 1975; Kirby et al., 2001; Mattis, 1976).

Laboratory testing is important in evaluation of cognitively impaired individuals to rule out other causes of dementia (Table 2). Blood tests evaluate metabolic, hormonal, and nutritional derangements. New tests can aid in diagnosis of atypical cases. Cerebrospinal fluid analysis of tau and Aβ42 provides reasonable sensitivity and specificity for AD (Andreasen et al., 2001; Hulstaert et al., 1999) but is limited by its invasiveness. Genetic testing for Apo E and presenilin is commercially available, but its role in AD diagnosis is often misunderstood. Apo E genotyping is not indicated for AD diagnostic testing (Liddell, Lovestone, & Owen, 2001; Post et al., 1997) and adds little to the sensitivity and specificity of clinical judgement. Many patients with sporadic late-onset AD do not have an ε4 allele, and many patients with an ε4 allele do not have AD. In families with autosomal dominant early-onset AD, genetic testing can often determine the mutation (Lidell et al., 2001), but these cases collectively account for less than 2% of all AD (Saunders, 2001). Presenilin testing should only be performed with appropriate genetic counseling.

Neuroimaging is essential to rule out conditions such as subdural hematomas, hydrocephalus, and space-occupying lesions (Small & Leiter, 1998). Noncontrast computed tomography or magnetic resonance imaging are suitable for most cases. Positron emission tomography and single photon emission computerized tomography scanning of patients with AD characteristically reveals hypometabolism in the parietotemporal region, even in preclinical individuals at high genetic risk for disease (Small et al., 1995). However, these studies are expensive and not widely available. They are most useful when attempting to discriminate AD from other neurodegenerative conditions that show distinct regional patterns of hypometabolism. Imaging research is

Table 2. Disease Processes That Should Be Considered in the Differential Diagnosis of Dementia and Their Principle Method of Evaluation

Treatable causes of dementia that must be excluded primarily by serologic studies:

- Neurosyphilis
- Hypothyroidism
- Vitamin B12 deficiency
- Folate deficiency
- Hypercalcemia
- Hypo- or hypernatremia
- Renal dysfunction
- Liver dysfunction
- Chronic drug intoxication
- HIV infection

Treatable causes of dementia that must be excluded primarily by neuroimaging studies:

- Normal pressure hydrocephalus
- Subdural hematoma
- Multi-infarct dementia
- Subcortical arteriosclerotic encephalopathy (Binswanger's disease)
- Space-occupying lesions (tumor, abscess, etc.)
- Demyelinating diseases (multiple sclerosis, PML)

Other causes of dementia that may be excluded by EEG:

- Subclinical seizures
- Creutzfeld-Jakob disease (CSF 14-3-3 protein also diagnostic)

Other causes of dementia that must be excluded primarily by clinical features:

- Pseudodementia (depression)
- Pick's disease and Frontotemporal dementias
- Parkinson's disease
- Progressive Supranuclear Palsy
- Diffuse Lewy Body disease
- Cortical-basal-ganglionic degeneration
- Huntington's disease

evolving rapidly, promising more sensitive and specific tools for future clinical use.

Current therapies for AD are primarily based on augmenting the central cholinergic system (Doody et al., 2001). Available acetylcholinesterase inhibitor drugs have similar efficacy. Donepezil, rivastigmine, and galantamine have been shown to be effective in several large double-blind placebo-controlled clinical trials (Dooley & Lamb, 2000; Lamb & Goa, 2001; Olin & Schneider, 2002). Many patients may not show immediate clinical benefit, but over time (e.g., 6–12 months) they tend to show less decline than untreated subjects. These drugs have efficacy for cognitive symptoms as well as for behavioral problems; they delay the need for institutionalization and also reduce the overall economic burden.

Other therapies employed in the treatment of AD include the use of vitamin E, an antioxidant that appears to delay progression of the disease (Sano et al., 1997). Epidemiological studies have provided indirect evidence that other medications are associated with reduced AD risk, including estrogen, nonsteroidal anti-inflammatory drugs (NSAIDs), statins, folic acid, and vitamin supplementation (Cummings & Cole, 2002; DeKosky, 2001; Kukull & Bowen, 2002). However, prospective clinical studies are essential to determine if these treatments are effective and safe. Unfortunately, prospective double-blind studies have failed to show efficacy of estrogen replacement or NSAIDs (Aisen, 2002; Mulnard et al., 2000); further study is necessary. Until safety and efficacy issues are addressed with prospective studies, precautions against use of any unproven agents for AD should be heeded because of the risk of serious adverse events.

Finally, psychotherapy and education are often needed to help families as they come to terms with a patient's changing abilities and experience the grief associated with perceived loss, and to provide more effective care (Cooke et al., 2001; Gitlin et al., 2001; Hepburn et al., 2001). Although the diagnosis may be perceived by some as catastrophic news, education and contact with community support such as the Alzheimer's Association and other such groups may help lessen the anxiety and fear of the unknown, and enable individuals to function better and longer within their families and in their own homes.

REFERENCES

Aisen, P. S. (2002). Evaluation of selective COX-2 inhibitors for the treatment of Alzheimer's disease. *Journal of Pain and Symptom Management, 23*(4 Suppl.), S35–S40.

Andreasen, N., et al. (2001). Evaluation of CSF-tau and CSF-Abeta42 as diagnostic markers for Alzheimer disease in clinical practice. *Archives of Neurology, 58*(3), 373–379.

Cooke, D. D., et al. (2001). Psychosocial interventions for caregivers of people with dementia: A systematic review. *Aging & Mental Health, 5*(2), 120–135.

Corder, E. H., Saunders, A., Strittmatter, W., Schmedel, D., Gaskell, P., Small, G., Roses, A., Haines, J., & Pericak-Vance, M., et al. (1993). Gene dose of apolipoprotein E type 4 allele and the risk of Alzheimer's disease in late onset families. *Science, 261,* 921–923.

Cummings, J. L., & Cole, G. (2002). Alzheimer disease. *Journal of the American Medical Association, 287*(18), 2335–2338.

DeKosky, S. T. (2001). Epidemiology and pathophysiology of Alzheimer's disease. *Clinical Cornerstone, 3*(4), 15–26.

Doody, R. S., et al. (2001). Practice parameter: Management of dementia (an evidence-based review). Report of the Quality Standards Subcommittee of the American Academy of Neurology. *Neurology, 56*(9), 1154–1166.

Dooley, M., & Lamb, H. M. (2000). Donepezil: A review of its use in Alzheimer's disease. *Drugs & Aging, 16*(3), 199–226.

Evans, D. A., Funkenstein, H. H., Albert, M. S., Scherr, P. A., Cook, N. R., et al. (1989). Prevalence of Alzheimer's disease in a community population of older persons. *Journal of the American Medical Association, 262,* 2551–2556.

Farrer, L. A., Ouppics, L. A., Haines, J. L., Hyman, B., Kukull, W., Mayeux, R., et al. (1997). Effects of age, sex, and ethnicity on the association between apolipoprotein E genotype and Alzheimer disease: A meta-analysis. APOE and Alzheimer Disease Meta Analysis Consortium. *Journal of the American Medical Association, 278*(16), 1349–1356.

Folstein, M. F., Folstein, S. E., & McHugh, P. R. (1975). "Mini-Mental State": A practical method for grading the cognitive state of patients for the clinician. *Journal of Psychiatric Research, 12,* 189–198.

Gitlin, L. N., et al. (2001). A randomized, controlled trial of a home environmental intervention: Effect on efficacy and upset in caregivers and on daily function of persons with dementia. *Gerontologist, 41*(1), 4–14.

Hardy, J., & Selkoe, D. J. (2002). The amyloid hypothesis of Alzheimer's disease: Progress and problems on the road to therapeutics. *Science, 297*(5580), 353–356.

Hepburn, K. W., et al. (2001). Dementia family caregiver training: Affecting beliefs about caregiving and caregiver outcomes. *Journal of the American Geriatrics Society, 49*(4), 450–457.

Hulstaert, F., et al. (1999). Improved discrimination of AD patients using beta-amyloid(1–42) and tau levels in CSF. *Neurology, 52*(8), 1555–1562.

Jarrett, J. T., & Lansbury, Jr., P. T. (1993). Seeding "one-dimensional crystallization" of amyloid: A pathogenic mechanism in Alzheimer's disease and scrapie? *Cell, 73*(6), 1055–1058.

Kirby, M., et al. (2001). The clock drawing test in primary care: Sensitivity in dementia detection and specificity against normal and depressed elderly. *International Journal of Geriatric Psychiatry, 16*(10), 935–940.

Knopman, D. S., et al. (2001). Practice parameter: Diagnosis of dementia (an evidence-based review). Report of the Quality Standards Subcommittee of the American Academy of Neurology. *Neurology, 56*(9), 1143–1153.

Kukull, W. A., & Bowen, J. D. (2002). Dementia epidemiology. *Medical Clinics of North America, 86*(3), 573–590.

Lamb, H. M., & Goa, K. L. (2001). Rivastigmine: A pharmacoeconomic review of its use in Alzheimer's disease. *Pharmacoeconomics, 19*(3), 303–318.

Liddell, M. B., Lovestone, S., & Owen, M. J. (2001). Genetic risk of Alzheimer's disease: Advising relatives. *British Journal of Psychiatry, 178*(1), 7–11.

Mattis, S. (1976). Mental status examination for organic mental syndrome in the elderly patient. In L. Bellak & T. Karasu (Eds.), *Geriatric psychiatry: A handbook for psychiatrists and primary care physicians* (pp. 77–121). New York: Grune & Stratton.

Mulnard, R. A., et al. (2000). Estrogen replacement therapy for treatment of mild to moderate Alzheimer disease: A randomized controlled trial. Alzheimer's Disease Cooperative Study. *Journal of the American Medical Association, 283*(8), 1007–1015.

Olin, J., & Schneider, L. (2002). Galantamine for Alzheimer's disease (Cochrane Review). *Cochrane Database of Systematic Reviews, 3.*

Pfeffer, R. I., Afifi, A. A., & Chance, J. M. (1987). Prevalence of Alzheimer's disease in a retirement community. *American Journal of Epidemiology, 125*(3), 420–436.

Post, S. G., et al. (1997). The clinical introduction of genetic testing for Alzheimer disease: An ethical perspective. *Journal of the American Medical Association, 277*(10), 832–836.

Sano, M., Ernesto, C., Thomas, R., Klauber, M., Schafer, K., Grundman, M., et al. (1997). A controlled trial of selegiline, alpha-tocopherol, or both as treatment for Alzheimer's disease. The Alzheimer's Disease Cooperative Study. *New England Journal of Medicine, 336*(17), 1216–1222.

Saunders, A. M. (2001). Gene identification in Alzheimer's disease. *Pharmacogenomics, 2*(3), 239–249.

Schmechel, D., et al. (1993). Increased amyloid b-peptide deposition in cerebral cortex as a consequence of apolipoprotein E genotype in late-onset Alzheimer disease. *Proceedings of the National Academy of Science, 90,* 9649–9653.

Small, G. W., et al. (1995). Apolipoprotein E type 4 allele and cerebral glucose metabolism in relatives at risk for familial Alzheimer disease. *Journal of the American Medical Association, 273,* 942–947.

Small, G. W., & Leiter, F. (1998). Neuroimaging for diagnosis of dementia. *Journal of Clinical Psychiatry, 59*(Suppl. 11), 4–7.

Terry, R. D. (1994). Neuropathological changes in Alzheimer disease. *Progress in Brain Research, 101,* 383–390.

ALLAN LEVEY

AMERICAN PSYCHOLOGICAL ASSOCIATION

The American Psychological Association (APA) is a scientific and professional membership association incorporated in the District of Columbia. Founded in 1892, the APA was the world's first national psychological association, and it remains the largest. In 1945, it reorganized to encompass several smaller psychological groups, broadening its mission but retaining the APA name.

The APA's expanded mission included professional as well as scientific issues and a concern for psychology's contributions to the public interest. A multifaceted structure was developed to reflect the diversity of the APA's membership and its expanded mission. These changes, and the growth of membership, also prompted the establishment in 1946 of a central office with an executive officer and staff to provide membership services.

Membership

In 2002, the APA had 155,000 members and affiliates. The members exercise their authority over Association affairs by voting directly for bylaw changes and for the APA president, and through the election of members to serve on the Council of Representatives. The membership consists of several classes: member, fellow, associate member, and affiliate. Affiliates, who are not members, include international members, students, and high school teachers.

Council of Representatives

The Council of Representatives (hereafter referred to as the Council) has full authority over Association affairs and funds. Its members are elected by the APA's two primary constituencies: divisions, which are an integral part of the APA's structure, and state and provincial psychological associations (SPPAs), which are affiliates of the APA. The Council elects the recording secretary, the treasurer, and members of all standing boards and committees. It also confirms the appointment of the chief executive officer (CEO).

Board of Directors

The Council elects six of its members to serve with elected officers (president, past president, president elect, treasurer, recording secretary, and CEO ex officio), as members at large of the 12-person board of directors (hereafter, the Board), which manages affairs of the Association. Subject to the final authority of the Council, the Board oversees the Association's business, monitoring the annual budget and any budget deviations during the year, and acting for the Council between the Council's biennial meetings.

Boards and Committees

Much of the Association's work is done by volunteer members serving on boards, committees, and other groups, such as ethics, membership, accreditation, and so on. Committees generate proposals for new policies or new activities, which are submitted for review by the Board and then sent to the Council for final determination.

Divisions

When the APA reorganized in 1945, 19 divisions were established to reflect special interests of its members. By 2002, the APA had 53 divisions, ranging in size from 300 to 7,500 members, representing areas of specialization (e.g., clinical, counseling, developmental), special interest (e.g., international affairs, women's issues, psychology, law), and employment (public service, independent practice, the military). Each division has officers, bylaws, a newsletter, and an annual business meeting. Some have staff, administrative offices, and divisional journals and other publications.

State and Provincial Associations

Each state, two U.S. territories, and six Canadian provinces have psychological associations affiliated with the APA and are entitled to seek representation on the Council. These SPPAs range in size from 25 to 6,000 members. Most SPPAs have offices, a paid executive director, newsletters, annual meetings, and officers.

Central Office

The APA's central office is located a few blocks from the U.S. capitol. With nearly 500 employees, it provides staff for all boards and committees, operates a large publishing house, invests in stocks, manages real estate, and interacts with private, state, and federal agencies and organizations. In addition to annual revenues of $12 million in member dues and fees and $11 million from publications, it generates additional income of almost $15 million. General dues represent only 18% of the revenues needed to run the APA.

The executive vice president and CEO is responsible for the management and staffing of the central office and for running the business aspects of the APA. The Board oversees the work of the CEO and annually evaluates his or her performance.

Directorates

Central office activities are organized into eight units titled directorates and offices. The professional concerns of the membership are reflected in the four directorates: science, practice, education, and public interest. Each directorate has an executive director who is responsible for staff, programs, and a budget of several million dollars, and who reports to the CEO. Each directorate has a standing board or committee to provide general oversight for its activities.

Activities not fitting into one of the directorates are managed by one of four major offices: Public Communications, Central Programs, Financial Affairs, Publications and Communications, and the executive office.

The executive office provides coordination among the APA's offices and directorates, oversees all central office operations, maintains contact with national and international organizations, conducts all elections, and provides support to the officers, the Board, the Council, and APA governance.

APA Graduate Students

The APA graduate student organization (APAGS) is a student affiliate category, providing psychology students with the *Monitor* and the *American Psychologist,* and access to APA publications and services. APAGS permits psychology graduate students to participate actively in APA, to elect their own officers, and to carry out projects of interest. In 2002, there were approximately 59,700 student affiliates.

Annual Convention

The annual convention is held every August in different parts of the country, attracting 12,000 to 20,000 participants. The divisions primarily organize the program, each having an allotment of hours based on its size and previous member convention participation.

Federal Advocacy

Because of the importance of congressional actions and the activities of many federal agencies to psychology, the APA employs staff who specialize in advocacy and are trained to provide information and assistance in policy development. They review proposed legislation, identify areas relevant to psychology's agenda, advocate on behalf of psychologists, and work with federal agencies to ensure that psychology participates in appropriate programs.

Interorganizational Activities

The APA maintains communication with a large number of psychology and related organizations worldwide. Each directorate maintains contact with U.S. psychological organizations relating to its domain, and the APA participates in many interdisciplinary coalitions for advocacy and information exchange. The Office of International Affairs publishes a newsletter for several thousand APA international affiliates, maintains contact with virtually all national psychological societies, and participates actively in international congresses, including sponsoring and organizing the 1998 International Congress of Applied Psychology.

Raymond D. Fowler

AMERICAN PSYCHOLOGICAL ASSOCIATION *CODE OF ETHICS*

The American Psychological Association (APA) promulgated the first *Code of Ethics* for psychologists in 1953. Based on the work of a committee organized in 1947 (Canter, Bennett, Jones, & Nagy, 1994), this publication had further basis in the work of another committee, this one formed in 1938 and devoted to ethical concerns. The formalization and codification of ethical standards was ultimately a response to the increasing professionalization of psychology, a development that began during World War II.

The first *Code of Ethics* (APA, 1953) was developed using an empirical, critical-incident methodology (Hobbs, 1948), which had been unprecedented among associations. Rather than using an a priori method to determine ethical principles, the authors surveyed the membership of the association for descriptions of past incidents in which decisions with ethical implications had been made, and requested a discussion of the ethical issues involved. This material then formed the basis for many drafts of the first *Code of Ethics,* each of which was distributed to the membership for commentary before the final version was adopted.

Since the introduction of the original *Code of Ethics,* numerous revisions, either minor or major, have been adopted. These changes, regardless of scope, serve to keep the *Code* current and responsive to new issues, to changing views on traditional issues, and to legal imperatives that influence ethical behavior. It would be accurate to describe the *Code of Ethics* as a living document whose approach to ethics is influenced by current events rather than being based on universal ethical principles. Each revision of the *Code of Ethics* contains a set of ethical principles (or standards) without the inclusion of illustrative incidents.

The *Code of Ethics* presently in force was published in 1992 (APA, 1992), although a committee currently is working on a new revision. Although the critical-incident methodology was not employed for the 1992 edition, the revision was informed by the history of ethical complaints that had been filed, so that an empirical basis was built into the revision process. The alterations to the *Code* took 6 years and involved many iterations of the APA membership, the Ethics Committee, the Revision Comments Subcommittee, and the Council of Representatives of APA. The resulting document was intended to be accessible both to psychologists and to consumers of psychological services, and to provide guidelines that would increase the quality of psychological services and also reduce the risk of harm to the consumers.

The code of ethics of any professional association is enforceable only with regard to members of the association, yet such a code also informs the basis of many state boards' conceptions of ethics. Board members, in turn, are asked to make judgments on the professional conduct of licensed professionals. In psychology, the *Code* is the foundation of the ethical instruction mandated by accreditation for its students. Thus, the influence of the *Code* is far broader than its scope of enforceability. Similarly, although the maximum penalty that can be exacted for a serious violation of the *Code* is simply expulsion from the organization, this expulsion is publicly noted, other groups with relevant jurisdiction are informed (and may take independent action), and matters such as insurability are affected, so that the penalty is much more severe than expulsion by itself.

The 1992 *Code of Ethics* has two major sections, as well as introductory material. The first section of the *Code* consists of six General Principles, which, although aspirational rather than enforceable, can be used to interpret the enforceable standards that follow. These principles are concerned with the areas of competence, integrity, professional and scientific responsibility, respect for people's rights and dignity, concern for others' welfare, and social responsibility. Their approach informs the rest of the document, particularly the more specific principles that make up the largest portion of the document.

The General Principles' specific, directly enforceable translation is the Ethical Standards. The 102 standards are contained in eight sections; the first, General Standards, is potentially applicable to the professional and scientific activities of all psychologists, and is amplified in many of the subsequent standards. This section indicates, among other things, that the *Code* applies only to the professional, and not the personal, activities of psychologists, and that, when the *Code* conflicts with the law, the psychologist may choose to conform with the law, but *must* attempt to resolve the conflict in a manner consistent with the *Code.*

The second standard concerns evaluation, assessment,

or intervention. It is predominantly, but not exclusively, applicable to clinical activities. The standard concerning advertising and other public standards is much more permissive than previous Codes had been and was heavily influenced by rulings of the Federal Trade Commission. The fourth standard concerns therapy and may be the area of major concern to most practitioners. It is complemented by the next standard, which concerns privacy and confidentiality, although the latter standard goes beyond the clinical activities of psychologists. The sixth standard concerns teaching, training supervision, research, and publishing. Its presence makes clear that the *Code of Ethics* is not restricted in its scope to professional practice but is intended to be applicable to the activities of all psychologists. The seventh standard, forensic activities, is new, and reflects the increasing involvement of psychologists in forensic activities. It applies to all forensic activities, and not just the activities of forensic psychologists. This section has been an area of disproportionate action, perhaps because of the adversarial nature of the arena in which this activity takes place. The last standard addresses resolving ethical issues and indicates the responsibility of psychologists to be familiar with and to help uphold the ethical standards of the discipline.

Although the *Code* itself consists only of bare statements, an excellent commentary has been developed (Canter et al., 1994) for those who wish for further information about the meaning of the principles. It is only through the commitment of the individual psychologist to the *Code of Ethics* that psychology can progress toward a firm foundation in ethical and responsible conduct.

REFERENCES

American Psychological Association. (1953). *Ethical standards of psychologists.* Washington, DC: Author.

American Psychological Association. (1992). Ethical principles of psychologists and code of conduct. *American Psychologist, 47,* 1597–1611.

Canter, M. B., Bennett, B. E., Jones, S. E., & Nagy, T. F. (1994). *Ethics for psychologists: A commentary on the APA Ethics Code.* Washington, DC: American Psychological Association.

Hobbs, N. (1948). The development of a code of ethical standards for psychology. *American Psychologist, 3,* 80–84.

George Stricker
Adelphi University

AMPA RECEPTORS

Introduction

AMPA ([RS]-alpha-amino-3-hydroxy-5-methyl-4-isoxazole propionic acid) receptors belong to the subclass of glutamate receptors known as ionotropic or ion channel receptors (iGluRs), in addition to the kainic acid (KA), and *N*-methyl-D-aspartate (NMDA) families. AMPA receptors were originally called *quisqualate receptors* because of their affinity for quisqualic acid, derived from the Cambodian quisquala tree. However, the seaweed toxin kainic acid (KA) was also found to activate these receptors to a lesser degree. Further studies then found that [^{3}H]AMPA distinguished this group of receptors more clearly from [^{3}H]KA binding sites in brain tissue. Glutamic acid is the major endogenous ligand for the iGluRs, although additional so-called EAAs (excitatory amino acids), named for their generation of excitatory postsynaptic potentials (EPSPs), are also present in the brain, including L-aspartate, quinolinate, and homocysteate. The other current major subclass of receptors activated by glutamate, the metabotropic type (mGluRs), are guanine nucleotide binding protein (G-protein)–coupled and are voltage-gated as opposed to ion-gated. The AMPA receptor/channel complex and the KA and NMDA iGluR channel types are the main mediators of excitatory neurotransmission in the brain. They also have many roles outside the central nervous system.

Molecular Diversity of Structure

AMPA-type glutamate ion channels are synthesized in vivo from four subunits (GluR1-4 or GluRA-D). The GluR1-4 subunits are assembled in various combinations to form the protein structure of a channel, which is either homomeric (all the same subunit) or heteromeric (more than one type of subunit). The types of subunits assembled determine the functional characteristics of the channel, as will be noted further. The AMPA-type channels function in the neuronal or glial cell membrane to conduct the influx of ions (particularly Na^+, K^+, Ca^{++}) and rapidly desensitize in the ongoing presence of ligands.

The GluR1-4 subunit proteins belong to a single family of genes (based on sequence homology), yet each subunit is coded by a different gene, namely *GRIA1* (GluR1) at chromosome 5q32-33, *GRIA2* (GluR2) at 4q32-33, *GRIA3* (GluR3) at Xq25-26, and *GRIA4* (GluR4) at 11q22-33 (Dingledine, Borges, Bowie, & Traynelis, 1999).

The AMPA receptor subunits are structurally similar and have a similar transmembrane topology, possessing three transmembrane (M1, M3, and M4) domains and one reentrant membrane domain facing the cytoplasm (M2). The N-terminus is extracellular and the C-terminus is intracellular (Figure 1). The binding domain for ligand such as glutamate is in the pocket formed by S1 and S2. S1 is before M1, and S2 is after M3 in the transmembrane topology (Figure 1). Each of these four GluR1-4 subunits is diverse in its molecular variation via posttranscriptional and posttranslational mechanisms, which result in significant functional variations depending on brain region, developmental stage, and states of health or disease.

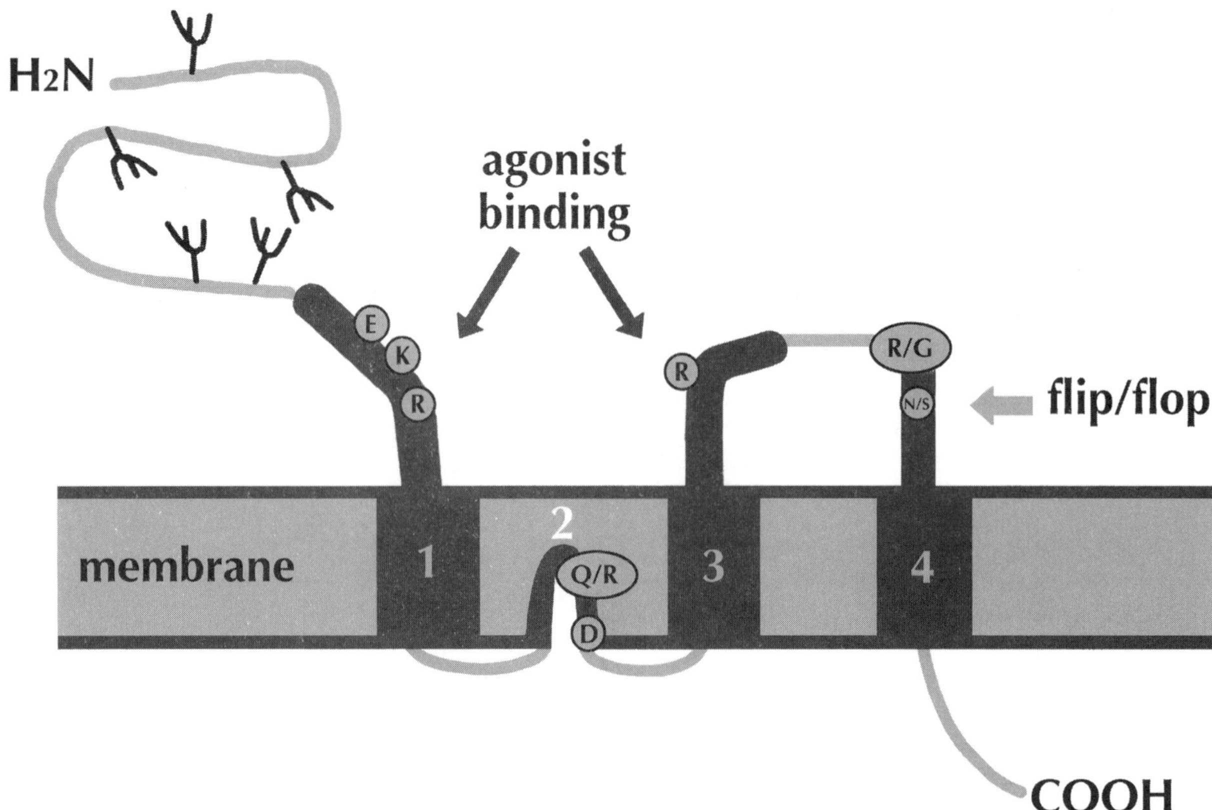

Figure 1. AMPA receptor topology. Q/R (glutamine/arginine) and R/G (arginine/glycine) are editing sites; N/S are asparagine (N) and serine (S) residues that confer specific desensitization properties (via cyclothiazide sensitivity) to the flip and flop modules; E (glutamate), K (lysine), and R (arginine) are amino acid residues that determine the binding site for glutamate and other EAAs.
Source: Borges (1998). Reproduced by Permission.

Posttranscriptional (RNA) Modifications

Each subunit undergoes posttranscriptional modifications involving at least two mechanisms. One of these is the *alternative splicing* of mRNA. The resulting splice variants called *flip* (i) and *flop* (o) result from the splicing out of one of two possible modules within the mRNA. Flip and flop splice variants are responsible for significant structural and functional channel variation on the extracellular side of the membrane preceding TM4 (Figure 1). They are of vital importance in determining the desensitization properties of the receptor/channel complex. Another source of structural and functional variation is *RNA editing* at the *Q/R* and *R/G* sites in the mRNA. In domain TM2 of GluR1-4, a particular glutamine (Q607; codon CAG) may be edited enzymatically to an arginine (R607; codon CIG). This Q/R editing process is regulated by an adenosine deaminase enzyme (ADARA) by yet-unknown mechanisms and is more than 99% efficient in editing GluR2 in almost all brain regions (a physiologically important exception being Bergmann glial cells in the cerebellum), conferring the property of near impermeability to calcium ions, low single-channel conductance, and a nearly linear current-voltage relation. Calcium ion impermeability in most brain regions is essential for survival to prevent excitotoxic injury to neurons. A single edited GluR2 subunit in a heteromeric AMPA channel is sufficient to confer this protection. Recent evidence also shows that GluR2 release from the endoplasmic reticulum seems to be regulated by this editing process, lending dual importance to its role. GluR2-4 are also edited at an additional site called the R/G site, located near the flip/flop coding region, resulting in diminished and more rapid desensitization.

Posttranslational (Protein) Modifications

AMPA ion channels undergo *phosphorylation,* which may affect synaptic plasticity and is tightly regulated by phosphokinases such as PKA, PKC, CaMKII, and others. Phosphorylation generally potentiates AMPA receptor activation, with evidence that it occurs by keeping the channel open longer or more often. AMPA receptors also contain 4 to 6 *N-glycosylation* sites that influence binding of ligands to the receptor pocket, with effects that depend on the type of ligand and the subunit's flip/flop specification.

Protein-Protein Interactions Involving AMPA Receptor Proteins

Recent experimental findings have begun to outline a rich complex of protein interactions involved in the trafficking, assembly, clustering, and membrane anchoring of AMPA subunits, presumably crucial to maintenance of the appropriate number and functional types of AMPA channels. Important interacting proteins include the PDZ-domain bearing proteins GRIP1 (glutamate receptor interacting protein), GRIP2, PICK1 (protein interacting with C kinase), ABP (AMPA binding protein), EphrinB1, liprin/SYD2 family proteins; the secreted lectin and immediate early gene Narp (neuronal activity-regulated pentraxin); and NSF (N-ethylmaleamide-sensitive factor). The protein-protein interactions carried out by these entities in the AMPA family appear to be analogous to those in other glutamate receptor subclasses (e.g., PSD-95 and NMDA channels) and in other receptor families (e.g., agrin and acetylcholine receptors).

Developmental Aspects of Diversity

The GluR1-4 subunits and their molecular variants (Figure 2) appear to follow specific ontogenetic, regional, and disease-specific patterns presumably to meet the current needs of the organism. For example, the edited (i.e., calcium ion impermeable) form of GluR2 becomes increasingly prevalent with maturity, as required to restrict calcium ion flux through the AMPA-type channels. Vulnerability to the development of seizure disorders is hypothesized to be related to the lower concentrations of edited GluR2 early in development. The flip and flop isoforms are also observed to follow developmental lines. Flip forms are more prevalent before birth and continue their expression into adulthood in rodents, whereas flop forms begin at low levels of expression until postnatal day 8 and then upregulate to a level similar to the flip variants. The flip forms tend to desensitize more slowly and to a lesser degree than flop forms.

AMPA Receptors in Health

Glutamate receptors contribute to processes of normal development, synaptic plasticity, learning, and excitatory neurotransmission of humans, nonhuman primates, rodents, Drosophila species (fruit fly), and C. elegans (roundworm). AMPA receptors participate with NMDA receptors in the coordination of long-term potentiation (LTP) and long-term depression (LTD), which are strongly suspected to subserve memory functions, including working memory, and govern experience-dependent synaptic plasticity by the rapid cycling of AMPA receptors into and out of the cell membrane via complex protein-protein interaction mechanisms (Luscher, Nicoll, Malenka, & Muller, 2000) Glutamate neurons project from most cerebral cortical regions to other areas of cortex, the basal ganglia, the brain stem ventral tegmental area, and other sites. This strongly suggests powerful local and global organizational and regulatory functions for the AMPA and other glutamate receptor subtypes in the brain.

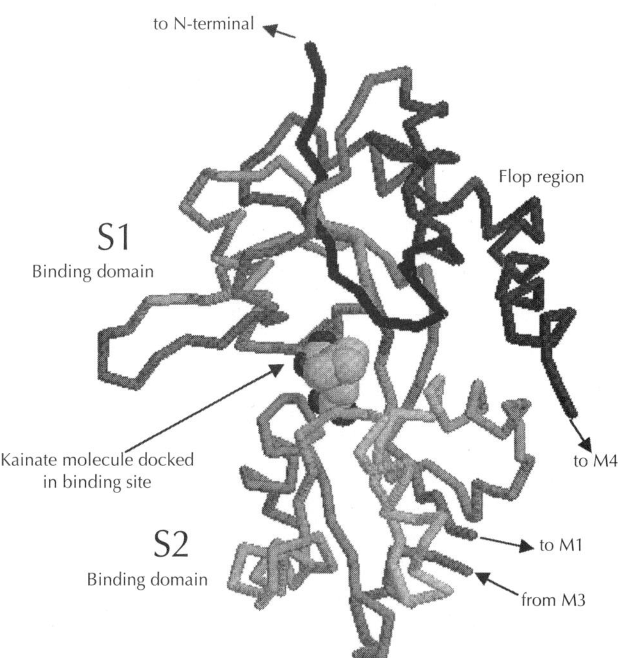

Figure 2. Crystal structure of the GluR2 subunit.
Source: Labels adapted with permission from Dingledine et al. (1999); protein structure 1GR2 from Protein Data Bank, Brookhaven, CT using Chime 2.2.

AMPA Receptors in Disease

A recently proposed model of glutamate excitotoxicity highlights the importance of molecular diversity of AMPA subunit expression. It hypothesizes that cells are vulnerable to injury from excessive Ca^{++} influx after any of a number primary insults affecting the expression of edited GluR2 subunits (such as ischemia, hypoxia, hypoglycemia, or epilepsy). AMPA receptor expression is also altered under conditions of stress in the hippocampus. Perhaps a peak in the expression of AMPA receptors at 20 to 22 weeks of gestation in the human may increase vulnerability to excitoxicity at that time, because AMPA receptors have been shown to increase during the prenatal period in rats, when there is also observed a greater vulnerability to excitotoxic injury.

In Rassmussen's encephalitis, a severe childhood form of epilepsy often requiring cerebral hemispherectomy because of its poor response to available anticonvulsive regimens, recent evidence supports an autoimmune mechanism involving the GluR3 subunit as an autoantigen.

Thus, current evidence supports roles for AMPA receptor involvement in excitotoxic injury through various pathophysiologic mechanisms such as epilepsy, stroke, ischemia, hypoxia, trauma, extreme stress, hypoglycemia, or hypercortisolemia, as well as in neurodegenerative diseases (e.g., Huntington's disease, Alzheimer's disease, Parkinson's disease). Pathophysiological roles for AMPA receptors have been suggested, and are under continuing study, in other neuropsychiatric disorders such as mood disorders, Schizophrenia, and anxiety disorders.

AMPA Receptors as Pharmacotherapeutic Sites

AMPA receptors are widespread in the brain, including most regions of the cerebral cortex, hippocampus, amygdala, thalamus, hypothalamus, brain stem, and spinal cord. The regional variations in expression of the subunits, splice variants, and editing efficiency are apparent and are probably involved in local and global network function. AMPA receptors are being studied as potential therapeutic targets in diseases such as Alzheimer's disease, cerebrovascular disease (preventive and poststroke), epilepsy, schizophrenia, neural trauma, and other conditions involving cognitive impairments. Such promise has been raised by the successes reported for AMPA agonists (*AMPAmimetics* or *AMPAkines*) to enhance maze learning in age-associated memory impairment in mice and for antagonists (*blockers*) to prevent the spread of necrosis in ischemic events. Agonists (such as CX516 and aniracetam) and antagonists of varying specificity for AMPA receptor variants are being studied, with goals of safer and more effective treatments for direct injury prevention due to toxins, ischemia, hypoxia, physical and emotional trauma, hypoglycemia, hypercortisolemia, neurodegenerative mechanisms, neurodevelopmental disorders, cognitive disorders, and epilepsy. A whole new array of selective clinical pharmacotherapeutics are based on allosteric modulators that are noncompetitive AMPA receptor antagonists, such as the 2,3-benzodiazepines GYKI 52466, GYKI 53773, and LY404187 may be clinically useful for treatment of movement disorders (like spasticity and Parkinson's disease), epilepsy, ischemia, and a wide variety of neurodegenerative diseases. Cognition enhancers such as aniracetam and CX516 may be useful for improvement of the cognitive deficits of disorders ranging from Alzheimer's disease to Schizophrenia. Pharmaceutical chemistry is advancing to the level of GluR1-4 subunit and splice form specificity, which is bringing a large number of drugs closer to clinical trials for some of the most common and devastating brain pathologies. Future work will hopefully also begin to elucidate the regulatory mechanisms behind GluR1-4 subunit and splice form assembly, homeostasis, regional specificity, and region-to-region signaling, of which very little is currently known.

REFERENCES

Dingledine, R., Borges, K., Bowie, D., & Traynelis, S. F. (1999). The glutamate receptor ion channels. *Pharmacological Reviews, 51*(1), 7–61.

Luscher, C., Nicoll, R. A., Malenka, R. C., & Muller, D. (2000). Synaptic plasticity and dynamic modulation of the postsynaptic membrane. *Nature Neuroscience, 3,* 545–550.

J. Thomas Noga
Emory University

AMPUTEES AND PHANTOM LIMB PAIN

Amputation of a body part can result in several forms of disordered sensation. These can be characterized as phantom sensation (nonpainful sensation referred to the amputated limb or body part), stump pain (pain at the amputation site), and phantom pain (pain referred to the amputated limb or body part). Phantom pain is defined as "pain referred to a surgically removed limb or portion thereof" by the International Association for the Study of Pain Task Force on Taxonomy (Merskey & Bogduk, 1994). It is characterized by continuous cramping, aching, burning sensations and painful loss of sensation often described as "pins and needles." It is often associated with stump pain. Prevalence varies, with reports of pain experience in up to 80% of amputees (Warton, Hamann, Wedley, & McColl, 1997). Episodes may last seconds to days and recur from a few times per year to hourly. Further information on the topic can be obtained from a recent review (Nikolajsen & Jensen, 2001).

The mechanism for development of phantom pain is debated, but there is agreement that it is related to pain in the limb prior to amputation, often referred to as "pain memory" (Nikolajsen, Ilkajaer, Kroner, Christensen, & Jensen, 1997). It has been stated in several case reports that the pain may be similar to that experienced several years before the amputation. Indications from the Nikolajsen study are an increased incidence of phantom pain in the first six months following amputation in patients who experienced preoperative pain, compared to those who did not. This correlation no longer existed 2 years following amputation. The authors concluded that there may be a relationship between intensity of preamputation pain and presence of phantom pain, but presence of preamputation pain may not be related to duration or nature of phantom pain.

Painful conditions of a neurogenic nature often present with similar symptoms, but the diversity of etiology of the conditions is too great to permit them to be described in global terms. In an attempt to describe the development of phantom phenomena, Melzack described the concept of a "neuromatrix" (Melzack, 1990). This involves a network of neurons that link different areas of the brain, including the somatosensory cortex, the thalamocortical area, and the limbic system. Input from the periphery and the cortex itself is coprocessed by these areas and shared with other regions of the brain to develop an overall picture of the intact body. Melzack suggested that the neuromatrix may maintain a long-term representation of the amputated limb.

Cortical reorganization has been implicated in the etiology of phantom pain and may help to explain why some patients experience phantom pain while others do not (Birbaumer et al., 1997). For many years it has been demonstrated in case reports that sensations in the phantom limb can be elicited by stimulating anatomically unrelated areas. For example, touching an area on the face may cause the patient to experience sensation in the phantom finger. This suggests that the cortex is receiving stimuli that, via neuronal reorganization, it perceives to originate in the phantom limb. Advanced neuromagnetic imaging techniques have permitted the demonstration of cortical reorganization in patients experiencing phantom pain. No corresponding cortical reorganization has been demonstrated in amputees not experiencing phantom pain. Cortical reorganization in patients with phantom pain was reversed following the administration of a regional anaesthetic block in those patients whose pain was resolved by the block (Birbaumer et al., 1997). This capacity to reverse cortical reorganization, even after prolonged periods of time, provides hope that effective treatments for phantom pain could be developed. *Telescoping,* described as the gradual shrinking and eventual disappearance of the phantom limb, has also been described. It is thought that this phenomenon may also be attributed to ongoing cortical reorganization over time.

Phantom limb pain is difficult to manage, with no individual treatment gaining universal acceptance. Treatment approaches for phantom pain include surgery, pharmacological management, physical therapies, and psychological interventions. Surgical procedures that attempt to cut or ablate the pain pathways have little if any benefit. However, surgical implantation of electrodes to stimulate the spinal cord and various parts of the brain may be of value in treating patients with phantom limb pain that is unresponsive to other treatments (Saitoh et al., 2000). Pharmacological management of phantom limb pain can involve drugs from many different classes, such as tricyclic antidepressants, opioids, benzodiazepines, antiarrythmics, anticonvulsants, antipsychotics, peptides (e.g., calcitonin), and NMDA-receptor antagonists (e.g., ketamine). In all cases, successful management in small-scale studies has been reported. Drug combination therapies are also used. In addition, regional anaesthetic nerve blocks (Birbaumer et al., 1997) and epidural and intrathecal blocks (Omote, Ohmori, Kawamata, Matsumoto, & Namiki, 1995) have been used to manage phantom limb pain. In many cases the effect of regional, epidural, or intrathecal block significantly outlasts the duration of the block, suggesting a long-term modulatory influence on the pain mechanism. One of the most common physical therapy approaches has been use of transcutaneous electrical nerve stimulation (TENS) for symptomatic relief. Acupuncture has also been used. Recent studies have demonstrated that active use of a functional limb prosthesis is effective in reducing phantom limb pain, possibly due to reversal of cortical reorganization resulting from activity of the limb (Weiss, Miltner, Adler, Bruckner, & Taub, 1999). Psychological issues related to loss the of limb, such as grief, may increase pain. Development of effective coping strategies has been shown to reduce pain in small studies (Pucher, Kickinger, & Frischenschlager, 1999).

It is likely that a multifaceted approach to pain management will be most effective, but further research is required to better understand the pain-causing mechanisms and determine effective treatment protocols for this common and difficult clinical problem.

REFERENCES

Birbaumer, N., Lutzenberger, W., Montoya, P., Larbig, W., Unertl, K., Topfner, S., et al. (1997). Effects of regional anaesthesia on phantom limb pain are mirrored in changes in cortical reorganisation. *Journal of Neuroscience, 17,* 5503–5508.

Melzack, R. (1990). Phantom limbs and the concept of a neuromatrix. *Trends in Neuroscience, 13,* 88–92.

Merskey, H., & Bogduk, N. (1994). *Classification of chronic pain: Descriptions of chronic pain syndromes and definitions of pain terms* (2nd ed.). Seattle: International Association for the Study of Pain.

Nikolajsen, L., Ilkajaer, S., Kroner, K., Christensen, J. H., & Jensen, T. S. (1997). The influence of preamputation pain on postamputation stump and phantom pain. *Pain, 72,* 393–405.

Nikolajsen, L., & Jensen, T. S. (2001). Phantom limb pain. *British Journal of Anaesthesiology, 87,* 107–116.

Omote, K., Ohmori, H., Kawamata, M., Matsumoto, M., & Namiki, A. (1995). Intrathecal buprenorphine in the treatment of phantom limb pain. *Anesthesia and Analgesia, 80,* 1030–1032.

Pucher, I., Kickinger, W., & Frischenschlager, O. (1999). Coping with amputation and phantom limb pain. *Journal of Psychosomatic Research, 46,* 379–383.

Saitoh, Y., Shibata, M., Hirano, S., Hirata, M., Mashimo, T., & Yoshimine, T. (2000). Motor cortex stimulation for central and peripheral deafferentation pain: Report of eight cases. *Journal of Neurosurgery, 92,* 150–155.

Warton, S. W., Hamann, W., Wedley, J. R., & McColl, I. (1997). Phantom pain and sensations among British veteran amputees. *British Journal of Anaesthesiology, 78,* 652–659.

Weiss, T., Miltner, W. H., Adler, T., Bruckner, L., & Taub, E. (1999). Decrease in phantom limb pain associated with prosthesis-induced increased use of an amputation stump in humans. *Neuroscience Letters, 272,* 131–134.

Heather A. E. Benson
Anthony Wright
Curtin University of Technology

AMYGDALA

The amygdala is a collection of nuclei located along the medial wall of the temporal lobe. Amygdaloid nuclei are classified as either cortexlike or noncortexlike based on neuronal morphology. The cortexlike nuclei, which include the lateral, basal, accessory basal, periamygdaloid, amygdalo-hippocampal area, and cortical nuclei, possess pyramidal-like neurons similar to the pyramidal neurons of the cortex. The noncortexlike nuclei, which include the central and medial nuclei, possess neurons similar to the medium spiny neurons of the striatum and do not possess pyramidal-like neurons. Each of the amygdaloid nuclei has distinct inputs and outputs, suggesting that they serve distinct functional roles. However, the amygdaloid nuclei are also interconnected, suggesting that circuitry within the amygdaloid nuclei allows the amygdala to function as a unit in processing information. In regard to information processing within the amygdala, sensory input is received primarily through the cortexlike nuclei, and output is relayed primarily through the noncortexlike nuclei.

The amygdala is a component of the limbic system, which is thought to be involved in learning, memory, emotion, and motivation. The amygdala receives highly integrated unimodal and polymodal sensory information and sends information to cortical, limbic, endocrine, autonomic, and motor areas. These anatomical connections suggest that the amygdala is ideally located for monitoring the environment and modifying physiological and behavioral responses accordingly. Indeed, the amygdala has been implicated in processing emotional stimuli, associative learning, memory, attention, arousal, and social behavior.

One of the first clues regarding the function of the amygdala was that symptoms of the Klüver-Bucy syndrome, including a loss of reactivity to emotional stimuli, were produced by amygdala lesions in monkeys. These monkeys willingly approached fear-inducing stimuli. This finding suggested that the amygdala is involved in processing the emotional significance of environmental stimuli. Several additional lines of evidence support this idea. Unilateral lesions of the amygdala along with cuts through the optic chiasm and forebrain commissures produce a disconnection of visual input from one eye to the amygdala. Monkeys restricted to viewing threatening stimuli through the eye disconnected from the amygdala remain calm and fail to show defensive reactions to the stimuli. When the same monkeys are allowed to view the fearful stimuli through the other eye, however, they exhibit appropriate defensive reactions, which suggests that the intact amygdala processes the emotional significance of the stimuli. The amygdala also plays a role in processing reward, because animals will perform an operant response to obtain mild stimulation of the amygdala, and lesions of the amygdala disrupt appropriate responding to changes in reward magnitude. Electrophysiological studies indicate that amygdala neurons are more responsive to complex emotional stimuli than simple neutral stimuli. In humans, imaging studies have demonstrated that the amygdala is activated by photographs of facial expressions and is more strongly activated by fearful faces than angry or happy faces. Furthermore, patients with amygdala damage have difficulty comprehending the emotional category and intensity of facial expressions. Moreover, stimulation of the amygdala in humans and animals evokes emotional responses and species-specific defense reactions, respectively.

The amygdala is also involved in associative learning through which initially neutral stimuli gain biological significance (i.e., survival value). The best-documented example of this associative learning is fear conditioning, in which a fearful event or stimulus (unconditioned stimulus) is paired with an initially neutral stimulus (conditioned stimulus). Subsequently, the conditioned stimulus comes to elicit conditioned fear responses in the absence of the unconditioned stimulus. These responses include conditioned freezing behavior, startle reactivity, and autonomic responses. There are strong and converging lines of evidence that the amygdala is involved in fear conditioning.

Although the amygdala may play a prepotent role in information processing and associative learning involving aversive fearful stimuli, its function is not limited to aversively motivated learning, because it also plays a role in stimulus-reward associations. For instance, monkeys exhibit emotional reactions when presented with familiar palatable foods; however, they exhibit relatively little interest when presented with novel palatable foods. Upon tasting the novel foods, the monkeys learn to associate other sensory aspects of the foods with the taste of the foods. Subsequently, exposure to the foods elicits learned emotional responses and preferences for certain foods over other foods. Amygdala lesions disrupt acquisition of emotional responses and preferences for the novel palatable foods, suggesting that the animals are unable to associate the appearance of a new food with its palatability. Through stimulus-reward associations, initially neutral environmental stimuli gain incentive salience via their ability to predict reward. Consequently, these stimuli come to produce incentive motivation, reflected by approach behaviors, as well as secondary reinforcing effects. These behavioral effects are also disrupted in animals with amygdala lesions, particularly lesions of the basolateral amygdaloid nuclei. For instance, animals with basolateral amygdala lesions fail to acquire operant responding reinforced by presentation of a stimulus light (secondary reinforcer) that had been paired previously with delivery of a water reinforcer (primary reinforcer).

Memory for emotional events is superior to memory of nonemotional events. This phenomenon may be due, at least in part, to hormones that are released in response to stress that modulate effects on memory by binding to receptors in the amygdala. Stress hormones, such as epinephrine and corticosterone, produce a dose-dependent enhancement of memory when given after training. Posttraining administration corresponds to the time at which these hormones are naturally released in response to a stressful event and at which consolidation of the memory for the event occurs. Amygdala lesions abolish the memory-enhancing effects of these hormones, and direct injection of the hormones into the amygdala produces memory-enhancing effects. Psychomotor stimulants, such as amphetamine, may also modulate learning and memory evident as enhancement of responding for secondary reinforcers. Lesions of the central amygdala disrupt psychomotor stimulant-induced enhancement of responding for secondary reinforcers.

The amygdala, particularly the central nucleus, is involved in modulating attention and arousal. The central nucleus of the amygdala projects to several brain regions that are thought to be involved in attention and arousal, including cholinergic basal forebrain neurons, autonomic regulatory nuclei in the medulla, and the lateral tegmental area of the brainstem. In rabbits, a conditioned stimulus predictive of an aversive shock produces an increase in spontaneous firing of amygdala neurons that correlates with excitability of cortical neurons as measured by cortical electroencephalogram (EEG) activity. The cortical EEG activity is thought to reflect an increase in attention. Evidence from functional magnetic resonance imaging studies in humans suggests that the amygdala responds to stimuli processed at a subconscious level. Specifically, subjects given very brief presentations of happy or fearful faces followed immediately by longer presentations of neutral faces report seeing only the neutral faces, yet the amygdala is more strongly activated when the neutral faces are preceded by fearful faces rather than happy faces. These findings suggest that the amygdala constantly monitors the environment for biologically relevant stimuli and may modulate moment-to-moment levels of attention. Many conditioned responses mediated by the amygdala, including conditioned autonomic responses and an arrest of ongoing activity, may serve to enhance attention to environmental stimuli. Furthermore, lesion and brain stimulation studies across species suggest that the amygdala is involved in orienting responses to environmental stimuli.

The amygdala plays an important role in social behavior. In general, stimulation of the amygdala elicits rage and attack behaviors, whereas lesions of the amygdala decrease aggressive behaviors across species. Stimulation and lesion studies also suggest that the amygdala is involved in social rank and affiliation, as well as sexual and maternal behaviors. Radiotelemetry data from a social group suggest that electrical activity of the amygdala is strongest when animals are being chased or aggressed upon or given ambiguous social information.

Amygdala dysfunction has been implicated in a number of neurological and psychiatric disorders. The amygdala is among several structures in the temporal lobe that are involved in epileptic seizure disorders. Repeated electrical or pharmacological stimulation of the amygdala induces the development of seizures. This experimentally induced seizure activity is referred to as *kindling* and is used as an animal model of epilepsy. The amygdala has also been implicated in other disorders known to involve temporal lobe pathology, including Schizophrenia and Alzheimer's disease. Imaging studies have indicated that amygdala volume is reduced in patients presenting these disorders. The amygdala likely plays a role in depression, anxiety, and Post-Traumatic Stress Disorder. Most antidepressant and anxiolytic medications produce effects via either benzodiazepine, norepinephrine, or serotonin receptors; the amygdala has a large population of these receptors. Furthermore, direct amygdaloid injection of benzodiazepine anxiolytic drugs reduces behavioral reactions that are thought to reflect fear and anxiety. Moreover, imaging studies have found that depressed patients exhibit an increase in metabolic activity in the amygdala that correlates with measures of depressive symptoms and is reduced by antidepressant treatments. The amygdala has also been implicated in the reinforcing effects of drugs of abuse. Furthermore, imaging studies suggest that the amygdala probably plays a role in the ability of drug-associated stimuli (e.g., drug paraphernalia) to elicit drug craving.

SUGGESTED READING

Aggleton, J. P. (Ed.). (2000). *The amygdala: A functional analysis.* New York: Oxford University Press.

McGinty, J. F. (Ed.). (1999). Advancing from the ventral striatum to the extended amygdala. *Annals of the New York Academy of Sciences, 877.*

JANET NEISEWANDER
Arizona State University

ANALYSIS OF COVARIANCE

The analysis of covariance (ANCOVA) has goals similar to those of analysis of variance; that is, it uses estimates of variability to test hypotheses about group means. However, ANCOVA differs from standard analysis of variance (ANOVA) because it uses not only information about the dependent variable, Y, but also information about an additional variable, X, called the *covariate,* which is correlated with the dependent variable. The ANCOVA procedure attempts to control statistically for differences in the covariate that would result in error variability and hence would reduce the efficiency of an ANOVA. The potentially greater efficiency of ANCOVA is obtained at the cost of additional complexity and stronger assumptions that must be made about the data. ANCOVA results are also frequently misunderstood.

Consider an example. Suppose we wish to test the effectiveness of four different software packages designed to develop problem-solving skills in fourth graders. Children are randomly assigned to work with each of the packages, and the dependent variable, Y, is the score on a problem-solving test given after the students have worked with the packages for 3 months. We also have available scores, X, on a pretest of problem-solving skills given before the children started working with the packages. Suppose we use ANOVA to test the null hypothesis that the software packages are equally effective. The means of the instructional groups will reflect not only the effects of the software packages, but also other sources of variability, including individual differences in problem-solving ability. The ANOVA can be thought of as a test of whether a model in which there is a treatment effect—that is, a component corresponding to the effect of working with one of the packages,

$$Y_{ij} = \mu + \alpha_j + \varepsilon_{ij}$$

—accounts for the data better than a restricted model in which there are no treatment effects,

$$Y_{ij} = \mu + \varepsilon_{ij}$$

where Y_{ij} is the test score of the ith participant in the jth treatment (here, software package) group, m is a common component, α_j is the effect of the jth treatment, and ε_{ij} is the error variability associated with the score. The larger the error variability, the more the treatment effects will be obscured. Because the children were *randomly* assigned to treatment groups, preexisting individual differences in problem-solving ability will not differ systematically across groups; however, they will contribute to the error variability and, thus, to the between-group variability. If all children had equal problem-solving ability (indicated by equal scores on the covariate) before working with the software packages, we would have a much better chance of assessing how effective the packages were. ANCOVA attempts to remove the component of the dependent variable predictable on the basis of the pretest by adding a regression component to each of the above models. It tests the model

$$Y_{ij} = \mu + \alpha_j + \beta(X_{ij} - \overline{X}) + \varepsilon_{ij}$$

against the restricted model

$$Y_{ij} = \mu + \beta(X_{ij} - \overline{X}) + \varepsilon_{ij}$$

where β is the regression coefficient or slope. An increase of power may be achieved because, if the treatment and error components are adjusted by removing the variability accounted for by the regression on X, the test statistic may be much larger. In effect, the ANOVA tries to assess whether there would be a treatment effect if all of the children had equal scores on the covariate.

Assumptions and Interpretation

Assumptions of normality and homogeneity of variance similar to those in ANOVA are made. However, additional assumptions that follow from the attempt to statistically control for differences in the covariate are required.

Linearity and Homogeneity of Regression Slopes

ANCOVA adjusts for differences in the covariate by removing variability accounted for by a linear regression on the covariate. If there is a nonlinear component to the relationship between X and Y, the ANCOVA tests will be biased. Moreover, it is assumed that the same regression adjustment is appropriate for each treatment group. Unless the slopes of the regression equations of Y on X are the same for each treatment group, ANCOVA should not be used. If there are different slopes, the interesting question is not what would happen if all the participants had the same score on the covariate, but rather, what would happen at different values of the covariate. A test for homogeneity of regression slopes should be conducted before an ANCOVA is performed.

Assumption of the Independence of Treatment and Covariate

It is not possible to interpret the results of an ANCOVA if the covariate varies systematically with the treatment effect. Using X as a covariate removes any part of Y predictable by a linear regression on X. However, if the value of X depends on the treatment condition, performing an ANCOVA will remove not only "error" variability, but also part of the effect of the treatment itself.

Suppose that in the example of the software packages students could choose to spend extra time working with the packages, and we desired to control for the amount of time they spent. However, time spent working with each package might reflect how understandable, interesting, and helpful the package was. Therefore, any adjustment based on the covariate would tend to remove part of the treatment effect. There is no substitute for conducting a true experiment in which both software package and time spent are independent variables.

Random Assignment to Treatment Conditions as Opposed to Using Intact Nonequivalent Groups

In ANCOVA, the distinction between randomized and nonequivalent group designs is important. When participants are randomly assigned to groups, groups should not vary systematically on the covariate, and interpretation is straightforward. However, when intact groups that differ on the covariate are assigned to different treatments, the treatment is confounded with characteristics of the group, and the results of an adjustment may be not be interpretable. Any adjustment based on the covariate will result in adjustments of any correlated characteristics as well, and will result in the kinds of difficulties of interpretation that occur in correlational research.

SUGGESTED READING

Huitema, B. E. (1980). *The analysis of covariance and alternatives.* New York: Wiley.

Myers, J. L., & Well, A. D. (2002). *Research design and statistical analysis* (2nd ed.). Mahwah, NJ: Erlbaum.

Arnold D. Well
University of Massachusetts

See also: **Analysis of Variance**

ANALYSIS OF VARIANCE

Analysis of variance (ANOVA) is one of the most commonly used statistical techniques in psychological research. The basic approach (and the reason for the name of the procedure) is to use estimates of variability to test hypotheses about group means.

To be more specific, consider an experimental design with a single factor (independent variable) that has, say, four levels. Suppose that the scores at each level are the numbers of items correctly recalled by participants in a memory experiment and the factor is learning strategy; that is, the levels of the factor correspond to different learning strategies. Each learning strategy can be thought of as being associated with a hypothetical population of scores: all the scores that have been, or could be, obtained using the strategy if the experiment were conducted over and over again. If the participants in the current experiment are appropriately chosen and assigned to the learning groups, the scores actually obtained in the four groups can be thought of as random samples from the populations associated with the different strategies. ANOVA can be used to test the null hypothesis that the means of the populations corresponding to the different strategies are all the same. That is, ANOVA provides a procedure for deciding whether the data collected in the experiment provide sufficient evidence to reject the null hypothesis, so that the strategy factor can be considered to be *statistically significant.*

Even if the null hypothesis was true, we would not expect all the sample means in our experiment to be equal. Any true differences among the different strategies will be obscured by random error variability in the obtained scores. That is, scores may differ from one another not only because they are associated with different learning strategies, but also because of a possible host of additional variables. For example, some participants might be better learners than others or be more motivated to perform well in the experiment. Perhaps for some participants there was background noise or other factors that interfered with learning present during the experiment. Because of this uncontrolled "error" variability, even if participants were assigned randomly to groups so that the groups would not differ systematically, the more talented or motivated participants would not be distributed exactly evenly across the groups, so the group means would be expected to differ from one another. The ANOVA procedure attempts to determine whether the group means associated with the different levels of an independent variable or factor differ from one another by more than would be expected on the basis of the error variability.

The mean of the variances of the scores *within* each group provides one estimate of the error variability. If the null hypothesis is true, the variability *among* the group means can be used to generate another estimate of the error variability. Under certain assumptions, the ratio of these two estimates is distributed as the F distribution if the null hypothesis is true. If the null hypothesis is *not* true, the estimate based on the group means should be larger than that based on the within-group variability because it includes not only random variability but all systematic variability due to the difference in the population means, and the ratio of the estimates should be larger than would be expected from the F distribution. In standard usage, if the value obtained for the ratio of the two estimates would place it in the extreme upper tail (the usual criterion is the upper 5%) of the F distribution, the null hypothesis is rejected.

ANOVA can deal with the effects of several factors in the same analysis. If we apply ANOVA to a design with two factors, we can test whether each is significant. Moreover, we can test whether there is a significant *interaction* between the factors—that is, whether there is a joint effect of the two factors that cannot be determined by considering each factor separately (see the entry dealing with factorial designs).

The null hypotheses tested by an ANOVA are very general. For tests of a *main effect,* the null hypothesis is that the population means of a factor are all equal. For tests of the interactions of two or more factors, the null hypothesis is that the joint effects—that is, the effects that cannot be obtained by adding up the main effects of the factors in question—are all 0.

There are many different kinds of ANOVA designs. When each subject provides a single score at only one combination of levels of the factors in the design, we have what is called a pure *between-subjects design.* When each subject provides a score at every combination of levels of the factors in the design, we have a pure *within-subjects* or *repeated-measures design.* It is common to encounter *mixed designs,* in which a given subject provides scores at all levels of one or more within-subjects factors, but at only one level of one or more between-subjects factors.

ANOVA is commonly employed to analyze the data from experiments. It is less appropriate for data obtained from observational research, because ANOVA treats all factors as categorical and uncorrelated.

SUGGESTED READING

Keppel, G. (1991). *Design and analysis: A researcher's handbook.* Englewood Cliffs, NJ: Prentice Hall.

Moore, D. S. (2000). *The basic practice of statistics* (2nd ed.). New York: Freeman.

Myers, J. L., & Well, A. D. (2002). *Research design and statistical analysis* (2nd ed.). Mahwah, NJ: Erlbaum.

Arnold D. Well
University of Massachusetts

ANALYTICAL PSYCHOLOGY

Analytical Psychology is the name Swiss psychologist Carl Gustav Jung (1875–1961) gave to his theoretical and methodological approach to the psychology of the unconscious following his break with Freud and psychoanalysis in 1913. Unlike psychoanalysis, analytical psychology does not understand the structure of the unconscious to be limited to contents that were initially a part of consciousness. Although it does not deny the psychoanalytic view that the unconscious includes contents that were once conscious, it holds that in addition to these the unconscious includes contents not yet capable of becoming conscious (i.e., symptoms) and contents incapable of ever becoming fully conscious (i.e., the symbolic manifestation of the archetypes of the collective unconscious). Moreover, analytical psychology maintains that the dynamics at issue in the formation of the unconscious are not exhausted by repression. Analytical psychology contests neither the psychoanalytic account of the *felt* incompatibility between conscious and preconscious (as well as unconscious) contents, nor the consequent mechanism of repression resulting in the dissociation of the latter contents from consciousness. However, it maintains that an additional dynamic, rooted in the inability of consciousness to *apperceive* psychic contents, also results in psychic contents having a subliminal and therefore an unconscious status. Apperception is defined by analytical psychology as the psychic process whereby new contents are assimilated into consciousness on the basis of their similarity to the contents already existing in consciousness.

Attitude Types and the Four Functions of Consciousness

Analytical psychology diverges from psychoanalysis in its theory of the qualitative factors at issue in the blocking of psychic contents—whose energy is sufficient for conscious entrance—from entering consciousness. According to analytical psychology, in addition to psychoanalysis's theoretical formulation of this qualitative factor in terms of conflicts between the so-called ego instincts and sexually charged libido, there are also qualitative factors that involve the apperceptive conflict between the two basic attitudes that govern the flow of psychic energy (introversion and extroversion) and the apperceptive conflict between the four basic functions of consciousness (thinking, feeling, sensation, and intuition).

Theory of Complexes

Analytical psychology's theory of complexes is rooted in its understanding of apperception as the psychic process by which a new content is articulated with similar, already existing contents in such a way that it becomes understood, apprehended, and clear. As such, apperception is the bridge that connects the already existing constellated contents with the new one. According to analytical psychology, apperception is either "active" or "passive." When apperception is active, the bridge between the already existing and new contents is fashioned by the association of similar contents. When the apperception is passive, the conditions are lacking for an associative bridge based upon the similarity of the already existing contents and new contents. This has as its result the dissociation between the former and latter contents, which, paradoxically, functions apperceptively to link the two. The paradoxically apperceptive apprehension of new contents that occurs in dissociation manifests these contents as symptoms.

The absence of an associative link between ego-consciousness and unconscious contents (i.e., the symptoms) in passive apperception does not preclude for analytical psychology the existence of associations with respect to the latter contents. Rather, the theory of complexes maintains that the existence of associations that refer psychic contents to other such dissociated contents and therefore *not* to the ego can be both observed and investigated. By the term *complex,* analytical psychology understands the loose association of passively apperceived contents, which lack an associative link to ego-consciousness.

Personal and Collective Unconscious

Analytical psychology understands the personal character of the associations yielded by the symptomatic (i.e., dissociated) images of the complex to provide evidence for a *personal unconscious.* Moreover, it understands the transpersonal character of those associations yielded by the symptomatic images that refer not to ego consciousness but to other images to provide evidence for a *collective unconscious.* The methodical unfolding of the transpersonal context of the associations at issue in the collective unconscious involves what analytical psychology calls the *amplification* of the associations of images that refer not to ego consciousness but to other images. Speaking of this method, Jung writes that "I adopt the method of the philologist, which is far from being free association, and apply a logical principle which is called *amplification.* It is simply the seeking of parallels" (Jung, 1935/1970). Proceeding in this manner, the initial appearance of associated images is guided by *parallel material* drawn from dreams, literature, myth, religion, and art. The point of departure for the amplification of associations is always the question "How does the thing appear?" The guidance provided by the parallel material with respect to the initially appearing associated images functions to facilitate a conscious propensity to assimilate, and therefore to apperceive actively, hints or fragments of lightly toned unconscious complexes and, by associating them with parallel elements, to elaborate them in a clearly visual form.

Archetypes and Individuation

Analytical psychology unfolds a topology of the collective associative designs—termed *archetypes*—that surround the nucleus of the complex. The most basic archetypes identified by analytical psychology include the persona (the socially accepted mask assumed by the ego); the shadow (the undeveloped and therefore infantile aspects of the ego); the anima and animus (countersexual images in men and women, respectively, which apperceptively link their personal unconsciouses to the collective unconscious); and the Self (the transpersonal basis of the ego and therefore of the conscious personality). The therapeutic goal of analytical psychology is the self-conscious differentiation of ego-consciousness from the various archetypes that become constellated in the course of the life of an individual. The process of striving to realize this goal is termed *individuation*. The crucial role of the "analytical" distinction between ego-consciousness and the archetypal contents of the collective unconscious in the process of individuation is signaled in the name Jung gave to his psychology in order to distinguish it from psychoanalysis: analytical psychology.

REFERENCE

Jung, C. G. (1970). *Analytic psychology: Its theory and practice.* New York: Vintage Books. (Original work published 1935)

SUGGESTED READING

Jung, C. G. (1918). *Studies in word association.* London: Routledge & Kegan Paul.

Jung, C. G. (1969a). On psychic energy. In *The structures and dynamics of the psyche.* Princeton: Princeton University Press. (Original work published 1928)

Jung, C. G. (1969b). On the nature of the psyche. In *The structures and dynamics of the psyche.* Princeton: Princeton University Press. (Original work published 1947)

Jung, C. G. (1970). *Two essays on analytical psychology.* Princeton: Princeton University Press. (Original work published 1917)

Jung, C. G. (1973). *Aion: Researches into the phenomenology of the self.* Princeton: Princeton University Press. (Original work published 1951)

Jung, C. G. (1976). *Psychological types.* Princeton: Princeton University Press. (Original work published 1920)

Burt Hopkins
Seattle University

See also: **Archetypes; Individuation; Introversion/Extraversion**

ANDROGENS, ESTROGENS, AND BEHAVIOR

Androgens and estrogens are the primary sex hormones. Males and females produce and respond to both hormones but in different amounts, especially during prenatal life, at puberty, and in adulthood. Males have higher androgen levels and lower estrogen levels than do females. Androgens and estrogens produce physical sex differences and contribute to sex differences in psychological characteristics.

Studies In Nonhuman Mammals

Experimental studies in mammals convincingly demonstrate that androgens and estrogens affect behaviors that show sex differences. Hormones affect behavior in two ways, depending on when they are present.

In early life, when the brain is developing, hormones produce permanent changes in brain structure that affect behavior (*organizational* effects). High levels of androgen during critical developmental periods are associated with high levels of male-typical behavior (higher in level or frequency in males than in females) and low levels of female-typical behavior (higher in level or frequency in females than in males). Female rodents and primates who are treated with high doses of androgen during prenatal and neonatal periods when the brain develops show sexual behavior more typical of males than of other females. Compared to typical females, they also engage in more rough play, are more aggressive, and perform better in mazes in which males excel. Conversely, males deprived of androgen during these sensitive periods behave in ways more typical of females than of other males. Excess or reduced androgen also produce changes in the hypothalamus, which is involved in sexual behavior, and hippocampus, involved in spatial learning.

Behavior is also affected by hormones circulating in the body throughout adolescence and adulthood (*activational* effects). Studies in animals show that both sexual and nonsexual behaviors are affected by circulating hormones acting on neural activity. For example, changes in estrogen across the estrous cycle in female rats are associated with variations in motor function, perception, and learning and memory. These effects are mediated by estrogen action on underlying brain regions, including striatum, cerebellum, and hippocampus.

Human Studies of Behavioral Effects of Androgens and Estrogens

In people, as in other species, behavior is affected by hormones in two ways: organizational changes to the brain during early development and activation of brain systems later in life.

Organizational effects of sex hormones occur during prenatal development. Sex differences in hormone concentrations are greatest during prenatal weeks 8 to 24, following the development of the genitalia. Because prenatal hormones cannot be manipulated, knowledge about human behavioral effects of hormones comes from "experiments of nature," in which hormones are altered by disease in the fetus or the mother's exposure to drugs. Studies of hormone effects on human behavior are consistent with studies in other species in suggesting that behavior is affected by androgen present early in development.

The best-studied experiment of nature is congenital adrenal hyperplasia (CAH), a genetic disease in which the fetus is exposed to high levels of androgen beginning early in gestation. If sexual differentiation of human behavior is affected by androgen present during critical periods of development (as occurs for human physical sexual differentiation and for both physical and behavioral sexual differentiation in other mammals), then females with CAH should be behaviorally more masculine and less feminine than a comparison group of females without CAH. And they are in many, but not all, ways. Compared to female controls, females with CAH are more interested in boys' toys and activities and less interested in girls' toys and activities in childhood and in adolescence, are more likely to report using physical aggression in conflict situations, have higher spatial ability, are less interested in infants and feminine appearance, and are less likely to engage in heterosexual activity and more likely to be sexually aroused by other women. However, most females with CAH have female-typical gender identity.

Findings from females with CAH have been confirmed in other ways. For example, girls exposed to masculinizing hormones because their mothers took medication during pregnancy are more likely than their unexposed sisters to report using aggression in conflict situations. Converging evidence for these special cases comes from normal individuals with typical variations in prenatal hormones: 7-year-old girls who had high testosterone in utero (determined from amniotic fluid at prenatal weeks 14 to 16) had better spatial ability than girls who had low testosterone.

The neural mechanisms mediating behavioral effects of prenatal androgen are currently not known. There are sex differences in brain structure and function, but these have not yet been well studied in relation to sex differences in behavior or to prenatal hormone exposure.

Sex hormones continue to affect behavior later in life, probably by activating neural circuits organized early in development. Androgen affects aggression, but the effect is small and bidirectional: That is, aggression itself can increase androgen. Androgen also facilitates spatial ability in a curvilinear fashion. High spatial ability is associated with relatively high androgen in females but relatively low androgen in males, but keep in mind that males on the low end of normal still have higher androgen than females on the high end of normal.

Estrogen also affects behavior later in life. Cognition changes with variations in estrogen levels resulting from the menstrual cycle, oral contraceptives, menopause, and estrogen treatment. Estrogen facilitates aspects of motor function, perhaps by modulating left-hemisphere regions involved in praxis. Estrogen also facilitates memory, so that postmenopausal women receiving estrogen supplementation have better memory than women not taking estrogen. There are associated changes in brain activity, especially in regions involved in memory, including frontal lobes and hippocampus.

Conclusions

Androgens and estrogens have powerful effects on human behavior, as they do on human physical characteristics and on behavioral and physical characteristics in nonhuman mammals. Androgens and estrogens exert some effects directly on the brain, by changing structure early in life and activity throughout life. Sex hormones may also affect behavior indirectly. For example, hormones might alter sensory thresholds, facilitating performance through improved sensation or perception, or increasing sensitivity to environmental input. Exposure to high levels of prenatal androgen may affect not only the behavior of the individual but social responses to the individual. For example, a predisposition to play with cars produced by exposure to high prenatal androgen may be increased over time by gifts received from adults. Hormones affect behavior in complex ways, as one of a set of influences, not as determinants.

SUGGESTED READING

Becker, J. B., Breedlove, S. M., Crews, D., & McCarthy, M. M. (Eds.). (2002). *Behavioral endocrinology* (2nd ed.). Cambridge, MA: MIT Press.

Berenbaum, S. A. (Ed.). (1998). Gonadal hormones and sex differences in behavior [Special issue]. *Developmental Neuropsychology, 14.*

Collaer, M. L., & Hines, M. (1995). Human behavioral sex differences: A role for gonadal hormones during early development? *Psychological Bulletin, 118,* 55–107.

Goy, R. W. (Ed.). (1996). Sexual differences in behavior [Special issue]. *Hormones and Behavior, 30.*

Kimura, D. (1999). *Sex and cognition.* Cambridge, MA: MIT Press.

Wallen, K. (1996). Nature needs nurture: The interaction of hormonal and social influences on the development of behavioral sex differences in rhesus monkeys. *Hormones and Behavior, 30,* 364–378.

Williams, C. L. (Ed.). (1998). Estrogen effects on cognition across the lifespan [Special issue]. *Hormones and Behavior, 14.*

Sheri A. Berenbaum
Pennsylvania State University

ANESTHESIA

The use of anesthesia to prevent pain during surgery began in the United States in the 1800s. Surgeons turned to the nurses with whom they worked to administer the anesthetic. Anesthesia is now a recognized specialty of nursing and medicine.

Three different types of anesthesia are provided for surgical and diagnostic procedures: sedation, regional anesthesia, and general anesthesia.

Sedative drugs depress the central nervous system, causing a decrease in awareness and reducing anxiety. Some sedative drugs also cause amnesia. Sedation is most often administered prior to surgery to relieve anxiety, during unpleasant diagnostic procedures, or during regional anesthesia and surgery. Most people do not easily accept the idea of being awake during surgery. Sedation allows patients to feel as if they are asleep during a regional or local anesthetic and often prevents memory of the surgical experience.

The type and amount of sedation administered are based on the procedure being performed and the patient's physical condition, weight, and level of anxiety. Sedation necessitates close observation of the patient. Sedation and general anesthesia exist on a continuum. At some point, as more medication is administered, sedation becomes general anesthesia. Oversedation results in respiratory depression. All but the lightest sedation should be administered by an anesthetist or other health care provider skilled and experienced in airway management and the assessment of oxygenation and breathing.

Local anesthetic drugs temporarily disable the function of nerves. Regional anesthesia can be used to numb a small area of skin, a single nerve, or a large region of the body. Regional anesthesia can be used for minor procedures as well as some types of major surgery. Local anesthesia is commonly used around a wound edge before stitches are sewn in. A common nerve block is used by dentists to numb a large area of the mouth with a single injection. Epidural blocks are commonly used to anesthetize a large area of the body during labor pains or cesarean section.

Regional blocks wear off gradually; sensations such as touch, pressure, and pain, and the ability to use muscles in the anesthetized area, return to normal at different speeds. The individual will usually experience a pins-and-needles feeling before normal sensation completely returns.

General anesthetics temporarily depress brain function and result in a loss of consciousness. This produces insensibility to pain, prevents awareness, and relaxes or paralyzes voluntary muscles. A general anesthetic diminishes the brain's ability to regulate essential functions like breathing and body temperature. In addition to administering an anesthetic, the anesthetist monitors, supports, and, when necessary, controls these vital functions.

Although the initiation of general anesthesia is quick, it is a time when many critical tasks are performed. For adults, anesthetic drugs are usually injected into an intravenous line to put the patient to sleep, and then anesthetic vapor is inhaled through a breathing circuit. For infants and young children, the anesthetic vapor is often inhaled first and an intravenous line started after the child is asleep.

Many surgeries benefit from relaxation of skeletal muscles. In these cases drugs are administered that paralyze voluntary muscles. Such drugs make it impossible for patients to breathe on their own, but anesthetists are very skilled at ventilating patients. Paralysis is eliminated prior to the end of anesthesia either by allowing paralyzing drugs to wear off or by administering other drugs to counter their effects.

Awaking from general anesthesia occurs when anesthetic drugs are allowed to wear off. Anesthetists carefully control the drugs given in order that the patient emerges from general anesthesia at but not before the desired time. This takes experience and a detailed understanding of the drugs used and the patient's response to those drugs. If the patient must be left on a ventilator with a breathing tube in place, the anesthetist may take the patient to an intensive care unit asleep rather than awaking him or her from the anesthetic.

Recovery from general anesthesia continues after the patient awakens. Inhaled anesthetics are eliminated through the lungs. Small amounts are exhaled for amounts of time ranging from hours to days. Patients commonly remain amnestic for minutes or hours after awaking. Some difficulty with complex mental tasks may last several days.

In addition to administering anesthesia, anesthetists provide emergency airway management and establish circulatory access with arterial and intravenous lines. Anesthetists are skilled at placing and using artificial airway devices and ventilating patients. When patients outside the operating suite experience life-threatening breathing problems, anesthetists are often summoned to establish an airway.

Pain management is provided by physicians, surgeons, and anesthetists. Patient-controlled analgesia (PCA) allows patients to push a button that injects pain medicine into their intravenous line. The PCA pump is programmed to deliver a set dose when the patient pushes the button. A preset time interval must pass between each dose. Once the total dose given for an hour reaches the programmed limit, the PCA pump will not give any more until the next hour.

PCA allows the patient control over when pain medicine is received, which helps reduce anxiety. PCA also results in better pain relief than intermittent injections.

When a regional block is produced, whether it completely eliminates sensation and muscle tone from an area (anesthetic) or simply reduces pain sensation in that area (analgesia) depends upon the drug(s) used, as well as dose and strength. Regional anesthesia can be used for pain relief after surgery in many cases. Local anesthetics, either alone or combined with opioids, are commonly used for pain relief. When regional pain blocks affect the legs, patients are usually confined to bed. Even dilute concentrations of local anesthetic affect muscle strength enough to increase the risk of falling.

When opioids are added to a spinal or epidural anesthetic they provide pain relief that persists after the anesthetic block has stopped working. Some opioids provide hours of postoperative pain relief when used in this way. Regional analgesia often provides better pain relief than injections or PCA.

Michael A. Fiedler
Samford University

ANIMAL MODELS

When medical or psychological phenomena in animals are studied as analogues to those phenomena in humans, one is said to be using an *animal model.* Models are basic and powerful tools in biological and behavioral sciences, and this explains in part why so much research aimed at understanding human physiology, brain, and behavior is actually done with animals. The key word for understanding models is *analogy.* Use of a model is *not* a claim of identity with that being modeled. Rather, a model is a convergent set of analogies between the human phenomenon and the system that is being studied as a model for that phenomenon. Animal models are widely used in neuroscience and psychology to explore and understand new relationships and interactions among the environment, central nervous system, and behavior and to study these interrelations under simpler and more controlled conditions than can be achieved in research with humans. Animals models often allow for the discovery of causal relations not possible in research on humans.

Animal models have a long and distinguished history in studies of both normal and abnormal behavior. Life scientists (e.g., anatomists, physiologists, pharmacologists, and psychologists) broadly accept the homological and analogical bases for the use of animal models that are rooted in the evolutionary theory of Charles Darwin. Evolutionary theory projects a continuity of morphology, physiology, and the emergent emotions and "mind" from animals to humans.

At the more biological end of the continuum of behavioral neuroscience and psychological research and application, the use of animal models finds general acceptance and is largely noncontroversial. These uses include research on neural mechanisms of reflexes, motivation, emotion, learning, perception, and memory. Animal models are an established integral component of the progress of understanding in these areas. Contemporary animal models make clear that neuroscience, emotion, and behavior do not exist in a linear chain from one to the other but in a continuously interdependent interacting circle. More controversially, animal models have been and continue to be extended with success into the behavioral neuroscience of memory dysfunction in aging, problem solving and thinking, social interactions and cultural structures, drug dependency and addiction, psychopharmacology, and psychiatry.

Animal modeling is more difficult and controversial when it addresses dysfunctional behavior and psychopathology. Animal models promise an understanding of human psychopathology, not as bizarre distortions of behavior but, rather, as the consequence of lawful psychological processes whose principles and mechanisms *can* be elucidated scientifically. Ivan Pavlov was perhaps the first to argue that experimentally induced abnormal behavior in animals might teach us about human dysfunction. Behavioral scientists continued with principled analysis and research with animals in an attempt to define the potential for the emotional hazards in animals and humans that might arise "accidentally" in the course of normal learning experiences and result in the development of psychopathology. One illustrative example showed that punishment of cats' consummatory behavior resulted in persistent fears analogous to phobic neuroses but that these fears were treatable by a forced extinction procedure and concurrent feedings. This result proved particularly seminal for contemporary clinical psychologists, because it was from this that the principles for *reciprocal inhibition* were derived; reciprocal inhibition is the basis for the systematic desensitization therapy for phobias so widely used today with human patients. This example clearly demonstrates the applied value of animal models in contemporary psychopathology research.

Numerous models of human psychopathologies have been developed, some more complete and useful than others. Well-accepted and productive models include those on maternal separation, Post-Traumatic Stress Disorder, depression, alcoholism, stress and consequent psychosomatic disorders, psychosocial dwarfism, Korsokoff syndrome, and dementias of aging, among many.

Although the development of animal models is not without difficulty even at the level of systems physiology, human psychopathology can be especially difficult to model in animals. For example, schizophrenia has proved to be a challenge; part of the problem here is the plethora of human symptoms, each imperfectly associated with schizophrenia, and a lack of agreement about what should be focused upon in the analogy. Moreover, in schizophrenia, some of the most important diagnostic criteria relate to verbal behaviors—something for which there is no easy analogue in animal behavior.

Biobehavioral dysfunctions, psychiatric disorders, and neurological diseases must continue to be studied to bring relief to literally hundreds of millions of sufferers. And, until the processes involved are better understood, scientists are deterred from classes of research with human subjects and patient populations, such as experimentation with etiologies or with therapies that involve physiological changes that are not yet understood, because they involve unwarranted risk. Animal research can help, because understanding is to be gained only through the use of living organisms.

It is particularly surprising that animal models should today be the focus of philosophical hostility in a society in which psychological problems and mental disease pose such a large threat to human well-being and for which history provides so much evidence of the scientific power and therapeutic success through the use of animal models. There are, of course, ethical considerations in the use of animals for research. The species employed must be chosen with care and knowledge of its basic physiology, the design of the research and numbers of animals necessary for a successful experimental test should be carefully determined, and the research should be performed strictly within the guidelines laid down by legal authorities and prior peer review. Scientists are obligated to demonstrate that the modeling processes are understood and that the analogies in the model developed are sound. Such models may sometimes necessarily involve the induction of distress; after all, physical and emotional distress are fundamental to the etiology of many common forms of human pathology.

Despite the conceptual, scientific, and societal challenges associated with the use of animals, the need for animal models for the advancement of physiology, neuroscience, and psychology is increasing and perhaps greater in the twenty-first century than ever before.

J. Bruce Overmier
University of Minnesota

R. Murison
University of Bergen, Bergen, Norway

ANIMAL PARENTAL BEHAVIOR

Evolution requires reproduction, but for reproduction to be successful in an evolutionary sense, offspring must survive to reproduce themselves. Parental behavior is any behavior that contributes to the survival of the offspring. Among birds and mammals, species can generally be classified into *uniparental* or *biparental* depending on who is taking care of the young. Approximately 90% of bird species are biparental, meaning that both males and females participate in the care of the offspring. There is great variation in how species divide these tasks between males and females, but a general rule is that the demands of protecting and feeding the young have made biparental care highly adaptive for birds. In contrast to birds, over 90% of mammals are uniparental. Indeed, the uniquely female specialization of nursing partly defines mammals. But even among mammals, there are several monogamous species that provide biparental care. Paternal care can include all aspects of care of the young except for nursing and may involve specialized forms of grooming or defense. In many species (especially primates), *alloparenting*—that is, parental behavior from kin or even unrelated conspecifics—is an important adjunct to either uniparental or biparental care.

Much of what we know about the neurobiology of maternal care comes from studies of laboratory rats. Rats are particularly useful for such studies because nulliparous (literally "never parturient"—a female that has never given birth) adult rats do not display maternal behavior and will either avoid or attack pups. Late in the gestation period, which for a rat is 22 days, the pregnant female becomes interested in pups and begins to display full maternal behavior, including nest building, retrieving, grouping, grooming, and nursing the young. Although maternal behavior is often described as a composite, the various components may be dissociated under experimental conditions. Most research has focused on retrieval, because this behavior appears superficially to reflect maternal motivation. However, there are important aspects of maternal behavior that are not directed at pups. Not only are maternal rats more aggressive toward intruders, but they are also less fearful and markedly less responsive to stress than virgin females.

We now understand that the onset of maternal behavior in the rat depends on specific experiential, sensory, and hormonal factors, although we still do not know how these specific factors regulate each of the components of maternal care. The following conclusions can be taken from four decades of research in this area: (1) experience appears important for both the onset and the maintenance of maternal behavior, (2) sensory inputs regulate different aspects of maternal care, and (3) hormones appear more important for the onset than the maintenance of maternal behavior.

Experience

The process of giving birth to and raising young appears to result in permanent changes in behavior. Recent research has looked in great detail at individual differences in the style of mothering in rats. High licking-grooming dams spend more time grooming their pups than do low licking-grooming dams. It now appears, from cross-fostering studies, that this style of mothering is transmitted to subsequent generations, as offspring of a low licking-grooming dam that are raised by a high licking-grooming dam will show high levels of licking and grooming toward their own pups. Thus, experiential factors that influence maternal care include not only the dam's previous experience as a mother but her own experience of being mothered as an infant.

Sensory Factors

What determines whether a female will approach or avoid a pup? Given that rats are predominantly olfactory animals, it's a reasonable bet that she responds to the odor of pups. Surprisingly, lesions of the olfactory system actually facilitate the onset of maternal behavior in virgin female rats. Presumably this is because females find pup odors aversive, so that reducing olfactory processing facilitates maternal approach, permitting ventral and oral-buccal stimulation to stimulate maternal responsiveness. In primates, visual and auditory cues (i.e., cries) may be more important than olfactory cues for stimulating maternal care.

Hormonal Factors

The onset of maternal behavior in the pregnant female rat is coincident with a sharp decrease in progesterone and an increase in estrogen and prolactin. These changes in hormones appear to be both necessary and sufficient for the onset of maternal behavior because, after pregnancy termination, estrogen facilitates and progesterone delays the onset of maternal behavior. How does estrogen prime the brain to influence behavior? It is now clear that the effects of estradiol on behavior may be due to its actions on the estrogen receptors, which are hormone-dependent transcription factors. Thus, estrogen is best considered as an early step in a cascade of cellular events that can ultimately lead to neuronal activation, recruitment of a neural system, and ultimately behavioral change.

The most important genes that are targets of estrogen action are likely to be oxytocin and prolactin and their respective receptors. Not only are these hormones important for parturition and lactation, but receptors for these hormones within the brain appear to support the onset of maternal behavior. Oxytocin given to estrogen-primed females can induce maternal care within 30 minutes. Prolactin had similar effects, although the onset takes place over days rather than minutes.

Although there is not a single brain area that represents the neuroanatomical locus of maternal behavior, lesions of the medial preoptic area (MPOA) in the most anterior aspect of the hypothalamus impair nest building and retrieval of pups, although females show no retrieval deficits for nonpup stimuli. The MPOA is not the only region involved in maternal behavior, but it is of particular interest because of its potential role in the hormonal regulation of the onset of maternal care. The MPOA is rich in estrogen and progesterone receptors as well as oxytocin and prolactin receptors. All of these receptors increase in number during gestation, and estrogen implanted directly in the MPOA facilitates the onset of pup retrieval.

In primates, including humans, it is generally assumed that hormonal factors are less important than experiential factors. In marked contrast to rats, maternal behavior in primates is generally not restricted to the postpartum period but can be observed in females of any endocrine status. Other factors such as social rank or environmental stress may be more important for primate maternal behavior.

Parental care provides an extraordinary opportunity to explore how genes and hormones influence the brain to modify behavior. In particular, the diversity of parental care, while discouraging simple generalizations across species, offers several remarkable experiments of nature, which, properly analyzed, should yield important insights into the mechanisms by which parental care evolved.

Thomas R. Insel
National Institute of Mental Health

ANOMIC APHASIA

Anomia refers to the inability to name things: that is, an impairment in retrieving words for things such as concrete entities (named by nouns), actions (named by verbs), or spatial relationships (named by prepositions). Anomia is a frequent part of the symptom complex that characterizes patients with *aphasia* (Goodglass & Wingfield, 1997; Tranel & Anderson, 1999), which refers to disturbances of the comprehension and formulation of verbal messages caused by acquired damage to language-related brain structures (typically in the left hemisphere). In some patients, however, anomia occurs as an isolated manifestation of acquired brain dysfunction, and in this situation the designation of *anomic aphasia* applies.

The ability to name—that is, to retrieve a particular word to designate an entity or event—is different from the ability to retrieve conceptual knowledge regarding that entity or event (Caramazza & Shelton, 1998; Gainotti, Silveri, Daniele, & Giustolisi, 1995; Pulvermüller, 1999; Tranel, 2001; Tranel, Damasio, & Damasio, 1997). Knowing what something is (its meaning, sometimes termed *semantics*) is referred to as *recognition,* and this is distinct from knowing what something is called (referred to as *naming*). In anomic aphasia, patients have lost the ability to retrieve names of things, but they have not lost the ability to recognize what things are. Hence, even when they cannot name things, anomic aphasics can usually produce accurate descriptions of those things or indicate by gestures that they have normal knowledge of things. For example, when shown a picture of a camel, the patient may say, "That is an animal that has humps on its back, lives in the desert, and can go for a long time without water." Or when shown a picture of Bill

Clinton, the patient may say, "That guy was a president, had an affair, had a southern accent." A related phenomenon occurs fairly frequently in the realm of normal experience, particularly under conditions of fatigue, distraction, or in connection with normal aging—that is, normal individuals may experience the inability to retrieve a particular name (especially proper names) even though they know perfectly well what it is that they are attempting to name (Burke, MacKay, Worthley, & Wade, 1991). This is sometimes referred to as a "tip-of-the-tongue" state (Schwartz, 1999).

Anomia can occur in connection with any sensory modality—for example, when attempting to name a picture of something, a sound, a smell, or something that is felt by the hand. Also, anomia can occur in the course of verbal discourse, as when one is speaking and suddenly cannot retrieve the name for a particular concept that is part of the intended utterance. The majority of scientific inquiries into the phenomenon of anomia, however, have focused on the visual modality and have used paradigms in which subjects are presented pictures (or actual objects) and asked to name them (Goodglass & Wingfield, 1997). This format, known as *visual confrontation naming,* is also the standard paradigm for assessing naming in patients with brain injuries. As a consequence, most of our current knowledge regarding the brain underpinnings of word retrieval (H. Damasio, Tranel, Grabowski, Adolphs, & Damasio, in press), and most theoretical accounts of this process (Dell, Schwartz, Martin, Saffran, & Gagnon, 1997; Levelt, Roelofs, & Meyer, 1999), are heavily tied to the visual modality.

The classic aphasia syndromes, including Broca's ("nonfluent") and Wernicke's ("fluent") aphasia, which include anomia as part of the symptom complex but which also involve other defects in speech and language, are associated with brain damage in the vicinity of the sylvian fissure in the left hemisphere (the left hemisphere being dominant for language in the vast majority [about 98%] of right-handed individuals and in the majority [about 70%] of left-handed individuals). Isolated defects in naming, though, which define anomic aphasia, are associated primarily with damage to structures in the left hemisphere outside the classic language regions. Specifically, anomic aphasia is most often caused by damage to the left anterior temporal lobe, to the inferior and lateral aspect of the left temporal lobe, or to the left occipitotemporal junction. Scientific investigations of patients with anomic aphasia, using modern neuroanatomical and neuropsychological techniques, have revealed a number of intriguing associations between specific brain structures and specific types of naming abilities (Caramazza & Hillis, 1991; Damasio & Tranel, 1993; H. Damasio, Grabowski, Tranel, Hichwa, & Damasio, 1996; H. Damasio et al., in press; Hart & Gordon, 1992; Hillis & Caramazza, 1995; Tranel, Adolphs, Damasio, & Damasio, 2001). Studies in normal subjects, using functional neuroimaging procedures (positron emission tomography, functional magnetic resonance imaging), have corroborated several of these findings (Chao & Martin, 2000; H. Damasio et al., 1996, in press; Grabowski et al., 2001; Grafton, Fadiga, Arbib, & Rizzolatti, 1997; Martin, Haxby, Lalonde, Wiggs, & Ungerleider, 1995; Martin, Wiggs, Ungerleider, & Haxby, 1996; Warburton et al., 1996).

The evidence from this research indicates that the retrieval of proper nouns—that is, names denoting unique entities such as persons and places—is associated with the temporal polar region in the anterior left temporal lobe. Immediately behind the temporal pole, in the inferior and lateral aspect of the temporal lobe, is a region that has been associated with the retrieval of names for animals. And further back, in the vicinity of the temporal-occipital junction, is a region that has been associated with the retrieval of names for tools. These associations may appear arbitrary or even bizarre, but there are principled accounts of why the human brain may be organized in such a fashion (H. Damasio et al., 1996, in press; Forde & Humphreys, 1999; Gainotti et al., 1995; Gordon, 1997; Humphreys & Forde, 2001; Saffran & Sholl, 1999; Tranel, Logan, Frank, & Damasio, 1997). For example, factors such as whether an entity is unique (e.g., Tom Hanks) or nonunique (e.g., a screwdriver), whether it is living (e.g., a pig) or nonliving (e.g., a hammer), whether it is manipulable (e.g., a wrench) or nonmanipulable (e.g., a giraffe), or whether it makes a distinctive sound (e.g., a rooster) or not (e.g., a thimble), are important in determining which neural structures will be used in the mapping and retrieval of knowledge for entities, including their names (H. Damasio et al., in press; Tranel, Logan, et al., 1997). Interestingly, the modality in which a stimulus is perceived may *not* make much difference: For example, retrieving the name *rooster* when confronted with a picture of a rooster, or when confronted with the characteristic sound of a rooster, appears to depend on the same left temporal lobe region (Tranel, Damasio, Eichhorn, Grabowski, Ponto, & Hichwa, 2003).

There are also intriguing distinctions between words that come from different grammatical categories, for example, nouns versus verbs. The brain regions that are important for retrieving nouns are partially separate from those that are important for retrieving verbs. As noted earlier, the retrieval of nouns is related to structures in the left temporal lobe. The retrieval of verbs, by contrast, is related to structures in the left frontal lobe, in the frontal operculum (in front of the Rolandic sulcus). And some studies have suggested that noun-verb homophones—for example, words like *hammer* or *duck,* which are used frequently as either nouns or verbs—are retrieved by the brain system that fits the context in which the word is being used: If *hammer* is being used as a noun, the temporal lobe system will be used, but if *hammer* is being used as a verb, the frontal lobe system will be used (Tranel, 2001). Again, such dissociations may appear rather curious on the surface, but there are compelling explanations of why the brain has organized knowledge in different regions to subserve words from different grammatical categories (Caramazza &

Hillis, 1991; Damasio & Tranel, 1993; Kemmerer, Tranel, & Barrash, 2001; Tranel et al., 2001).

Pure forms of anomic aphasia—that is, severe naming impairments unaccompanied by other speech or linguistic deficits—are relatively rare, occurring far less frequently than most of the so-called classic aphasia syndromes. Nonetheless, patients with anomic aphasia have provided a unique opportunity to learn how the brain operates the processes associated with word retrieval, and how different brain structures are specialized for different types of words and different categories of entities. Thus, while anomic aphasia is important as a clinical disorder, its particular interest lies in the realm of scientific study of how the human brain operates language processes. This, in turn, can help inform rehabilitation efforts aimed at patients with acquired disturbances of naming.

REFERENCES

Burke, D. M., MacKay, D. G., Worthley, J. S., & Wade, E. (1991). On the tip of the tongue: What causes word finding failures in young and older adults? *Journal of Memory and Language, 30,* 542–579.

Carammaza, A., & Hillis, A. (1991). Lexical organization of nouns and verbs in the brain. *Nature, 349,* 788–790.

Caramazza, A., & Shelton, J. R. (1998). Domain-specific knowledge systems in the brain: The animate-inanimate distinction. *Journal of Cognitive Neuroscience, 10,* 1–34.

Chao, L. L., & Martin, A. (2000). Representation of manipulable man-made objects in the dorsal stream. *NeuroImage, 12,* 478–484.

Damasio, A. R., & Tranel, D. (1993). Nouns and verbs are retrieved with differently distributed neural systems. *Proceedings of the National Academy of Sciences, 90,* 4957–4960.

Damasio, H., Grabowski, T. J., Tranel, D., Hichwa, R., & Damasio, A. (1996). A neural basis for lexical retrieval. *Nature, 380,* 499–505.

Damasio, H., Tranel, D., Grabowski, T. J., Adolphs, R., & Damasio, A. R. (in press). Uncovering neural systems behind word and concept retrieval. *Cognition.*

Dell, G. S., Schwartz, M. F., Martin, N., Saffran, E. M., & Gagnon, D. A. (1997). Lexical access in aphasic and nonaphasic speakers. *Psychological Review, 104,* 801–838.

Forde, E. M. E., & Humphreys, G. W. (1999). Category-specific recognition impairments: A review of important case studies and influential theories. *Aphasiology, 13,* 169–193.

Gainotti, G., Silveri, M. C., Daniele, A., & Giustolisi, L. (1995). Neuroanatomical correlates of category-specific semantic disorders: A critical survey. *Memory, 3,* 247–264.

Goodglass, H., & Wingfield, A. (Eds.). (1997). *Anomia: Neuroanatomical and cognitive correlates.* New York: Academic Press.

Gordon, B. (1997). Models of naming. In H. Goodglass & A. Wingfield (Eds.), *Anomia: Neuroanatomical and cognitive correlates* (pp. 31–64). New York: Academic Press.

Grabowski, T. J., Damasio, H., Tranel, D., Ponto, L. L. B., Hichwa, R. D., & Damasio, A. R. (2001). A role for left temporal pole in the retrieval of words for unique entities. *Human Brain Mapping, 13,* 199–212.

Grafton, S. T., Fadiga, L., Arbib, M. A., & Rizzolatti, G. (1997). Premotor cortex activation during observation and naming of familiar tools. *NeuroImage, 6,* 231–236.

Hart, J., & Gordon, B. (1992). Neural subsystems for object knowledge. *Nature, 359,* 60–64.

Hillis, A. E., & Caramazza, A. (1995). Representations of grammatical categories of words in the brain. *Journal of Cognitive Neuroscience, 7,* 396–407.

Humphreys, G. W., & Forde, E. M. E. (2001). Hierarchies, similarity, and interactivity in object recognition: "Category-specific" neuropsychological deficits. *Behavioral and Brain Sciences, 24,* 453–509.

Kemmerer, D., Tranel, D., & Barrash, J. (2001). Patterns of dissociation in the processing of verb meanings in brain-damaged subjects. *Language and Cognitive Processes, 16,* 1–34.

Levelt, W. J. M., Roelofs, A., & Meyer, A. S. (1999). A theory of lexical access in speech production. *Behavioral and Brain Sciences, 22,* 1–75.

Martin, A., Haxby, J. V., Lalonde, F. M., Wiggs, C. L., & Ungerleider, L. G. (1995). Discrete cortical regions associated with knowledge of color and knowledge of action. *Science, 270,* 102–105.

Martin, A., Wiggs, C. L., Ungerleider, L. G., & Haxby, J. V. (1996). Neural correlates of category-specific knowledge. *Nature, 379,* 649–652.

Pulvermüller, F. (1999). Words in the brain's language. *Behavioral and Brain Sciences, 22,* 253–336.

Saffran, E. M., & Sholl, A. (1999). Clues to the functional and neural architecture of word meaning. In C. M. Brown & P. Hagoort (Eds.), *The neurocognition of language* (pp. 241–272). New York: Oxford University Press.

Schwartz, B. L. (1999). Sparkling at the end of the tongue: The etiology of tip-of-the-tongue phenomenology. *Psychological Bulletin Review, 6,* 379–393.

Tranel, D. (2001). Combs, ducks, and the brain. *The Lancet, 357,* 1818–1819.

Tranel, D., Adolphs, R., Damasio, H., & Damasio, A. R. (2001). A neural basis for the retrieval of words for actions. *Cognitive Neuropsychology, 18,* 655–670.

Tranel, D., & Anderson, S. (1999). Syndromes of aphasia. In F. Fabbro (Ed.), *Concise encyclopedia of language pathology* (pp. 305–319). Oxford, UK: Elsevier Science.

Tranel, D., Damasio, H., & Damasio, A. R. (1997). A neural basis for the retrieval of conceptual knowledge. *Neuropsychologia, 35,* 1319–1327.

Tranel, D., Damasio, H., Eichhorn, G. R., Grabowski, T. J., Ponto, L. L. B., & Hichwa, R. D. (2003). Neural correlates of naming animals from their characteristic sound. *Neuropsychologia, 41,* 847–854.

Tranel, D., Logan, C. G., Frank, R. J., & Damasio, A. R. (1997). Explaining category-related effects in the retrieval of conceptual and lexical knowledge for concrete entities: Operationalization and analysis of factors. *Neuropsychologia, 35,* 1329–1339.

Warburton, E., Wise, R. J. S., Price, C. J., Weiller, C., Hadar, U., Ramsay, S., et al. (1996). Noun and verb retrieval by normal subjects: Studies with PET. *Brain, 119,* 159–179.

Daniel Tranel
University of Iowa College of Medicine

ANOREXIA NERVOSA

Definition and Clinical Descriptions

The disorder of anorexia nervosa (AN) is defined by four major criteria.

1. Refusal to maintain body weight at a minimally normal weight for age and height.
2. An intense fear of gaining weight. This fear, present even in an emaciated condition, may be denied, but it is demonstrated by an intense preoccupation with thoughts of food, irrational worries about gaining weight, and rigorous exercising programs, with severe restriction of total food intake in order to prevent weight gain.
3. A disturbance of body conceptualization. Parts of the body such as the thighs and abdomen are experienced as being excessively large; evaluation of the self is mainly in terms of body weight and shape; and the denial of illness or the underweight condition is a hallmark symptom of this disorder.
4. Amenorrhea or cessation of menstrual cycles.

There are two subtypes of AN: the restrictor type (AN-R) and the binge-purge type (AN-BP). The restrictors lose weight by restricting food intake and exercising; the binge-purge type engages in binge eating, purging behavior (such as self-induced vomiting), laxative abuse, and diuretic abuse.

Impulsive behaviors including stealing, drug abuse, suicide attempts, self-mutilations, and mood lability are more prevalent in AN-BP than in AN-R. The AN-BP types also have a higher prevalence of premorbid obesity, familial obesity, and debilitating personality traits (Halmi, 1999).

Most of the physiological and metabolic changes in AN are secondary to the starvation state or purging behavior. These changes revert to normal with nutritional rehabilitation and the cessation of purging behavior. Hypokalemic alkalosis occurs with purging. These patients may have hypokalemia and physical symptoms of weakness, lethargy, and cardiac arrhythmias, which may result in sudden cardiac arrest. Persistent vomiting causes severe erosion of the enamel of teeth, with consequent loss of teeth, and produces parotid gland enlargement (Halmi, 1999). Chronic food restriction produces osteoporosis and fractures.

Epidemiology

There was a consistent increase in the incidence of AN over the period from 1931 to 1986 in industrialized countries (Hoek, 1993). A study conducted in northeastern Scotland (Eagles et al., 1995) showed that between 1965 and 1991 there was almost a sixfold increase in the incidence of anorexia (from 3 in 100,000 to 17 in 100,000 cases). The male-female ratio for eating disorders lies consistently between 1/10 and 1/20 (Hoek, 1993).

AN is rare in non-Western, poorly industrialized countries (Lee, Leung, & Lee, 1996). Individuals and groups who are exposed to the ideal of a slender body type seem to be a risk for developing an eating disorder (Crago, Schisslak, & Estes, 1996). A review of eight studies in the 1980s (Gard & Freeman, 1996) failed to support a higher social economic class prevalence in AN.

Etiology and Risk Factors

AN is best conceptualized by a multidimensional model that emphasizes the interaction of biological, psychological, and cultural factors. Within each of these areas, research has identified factors that predispose, precipitate, or maintain the eating disorder.

Genetic Factors

In a series of 67 twin probands, the concordance for restricting AN was markedly higher for monozygotic twins, 66%, than for dizygotic, 0%. A familial aggregation of AN and Bulimia Nervosa is present in AN probands (Treasure & Holland, 1989).

A genomewide linkage analysis of 192 families with one AN member and another with any related eating disorder identified in the *Diagnostic and Statistic Manual of Mental Disorders* (fourth edition) showed a modest linkage on chromosome 4. When a subset of 37 families containing 2 with restricting AN was analyzed, a more robust linkage was found on chromosome 1p (Devlin et al., 2002; Grice et al., 2002).

A vulnerability for destabilization of the endocrine and metabolic mechanisms affecting eating behavior may cause the full-blown eating disorder under stresses such as severe dieting. Neurotransmitter serotonin pathways modulate feeding and inhibitory behaviors. There is evidence of aberrations in this neurotransmitter system in anorectic patients.

Because AN predominately starts during puberty (there is a bimodal peak for age onset at ages 14–15 and age 18), Crisp (1970) developed the hypothesis that AN reflects an attempt to cope with maturational problems through the mechanism of avoidance of biological maturity.

A genetic predisposition to develop AN could be a particular personality type. There is evidence that a rigid, inhibited, and perfectionistic personality may be at risk for developing AN-R (Halmi, 1999).

Two behavior variables, obsessionality and drive for thinness, showed high and concordant values in a cluster of AN pairs. These variables in the AN pairs showed suggestive linkages on chromosome 1, 2, and 13 (Devlin et al., 2002).

Family Functioning

Studies of anorectic families show they have more rigidity in their family organization, less clear interpersonal boundaries, and a tendency to avoid open discussions of disagreements among themselves compared with control families (Humphrey, 1988).

Stressful Events

Stressful life events may be a risk factor for developing AN. Studies investigating the relationship between sexual abuse and eating disorders have produced highly discrepant results (Connors & Morse, 1993). A low rate of sexual abuse has been reported among anorectic restrictors relative to either bulimic anorectics or to normal-weight bulimics (Waller, Halek, & Crisp, 1993).

Normative developmental events, such as the onset of puberty, departure from home, or a change of school, can precipitate an eating disorder. Adverse life events, such as the death of a close relative, the breakup of a relationship, or illness, may also precipitate an eating disorder (Tobin et al., 1995).

Course of Illness

Long-term follow-up research indicates that about one fourth of those with AN recover from the disorder, one fourth stay chronically ill with no improvement, and about half have partial improvement. Most of the latter have bulimic behaviors. Mortality rates at 10 years are 6.6% and at 30 years are 18% to 20% after presentation for treatment (Eckert et al., 1995).

Patients with an earlier onset, between ages 13 and 18, recover from the disorder more quickly. Most studies have found purging behavior to be a poor outcome predictor.

Treatment

There are few outpatient controlled treatment studies of AN. Open studies have indicated that a multifaceted treatment approach is the most effective. This includes medical management, psycho-education, and individual therapy utilizing both cognitive and behavioral therapy principles. Controlled studies have shown that children under the age of 18 do better if they have family therapy (Russell et al., 1987). Nutritional counseling and pharmacological intervention can also be useful components of the treatment plan.

Treatment levels range from a specialized eating disorder inpatient unit to a partial hospitalization or day program to outpatient care, depending on the weight, medical status, and other psychiatric comorbidity of the patient. Medical management usually requires weight restoration, nutritional rehabilitation, rehydration, and correction of serum electrolytes for hospitalized patients. Cyproheptadine in high doses can facilitate weight gain in AN-R, and serotonin reuptake inhibitors may be effective in preventing relapse (Halmi, 1999).

Cognitive and behavioral therapy principles can be applied with both inpatients and outpatients. Behavioral therapy is effective for inducing weight gain. Cognitive therapy techniques for AN have been extensively described (Kleifield, Wagner, & Halmi, 1996). These include the monitoring of food intake, feelings and emotions, binge/purge behaviors, and problems in interpersonal relationships. Cognitive therapy also uses the techniques of cognitive restructuring and problem solving.

Family Therapy

A family analysis should be done on all AN patients who are living with their families and a decision made as to what type of family therapy or counseling is advisable. Most clinicians find it necessary to combine individual therapy with some sort of family counseling.

At the present time no treatment modality can predict recovery in a specific AN patient.

REFERENCES

Connors, M. E., & Morse, W. (1993). Sexual abuse in eating disorders: A review. *International Journal of Eating Disorders, 13,* 1–11.

Crago, M., Schisslak, C. M., & Estes, L. S. (1996). Eating disturbances among American minority groups: A review. *International Journal of Eating Disorders, 19,* 239–248.

Crisp, A. H. (1970). Premorbid factors in adult disorders of weight, with particular reference to primary AN (weight phobia). *Journal of Psychosomatic Research, 14,* 1–22.

Devlin, B., Bacanu, S. A., Klump, K., Bulik, C., Fichter, M., Halmi, K. A., et al. (2002). Linkage analysis of anorexia nervosa incorporating behavioral covariates. *Human Molecular Genetics, 11,* 689–696.

Diagnostic and Statistical Manual of Mental Disorders (DSM-IV). (1994). Washington, DC: American Psychiatric Association.

Eagles R., Johnston M., Hunter D., et al. (1995). Increasing incidences of AN in the female population of northeast Scotland. *American Journal Psychiatry, 152,* 1266–1271.

Eckert, E. D., Halmi, K. A., Marchi, E. P., & Cohen, J. (1995). Ten-year follow-up of AN: Clinical course and outcome. *Psychological Medicine, 25,* 143–156.

Gard, M. C., & Freeman, C. P. (1996). The dismantling of a myth: A review of eating disorders and social economic status. *International Journal of Eating Disorders, 20,* 1–12.

Grice, D. E., Halmi, K. A., Fichter, M. M., Strober, M., Woodside, B. B., Treasure, J. T., et al. (2002). Evidence for a susceptibility gene for anorexia nervosa on chromosome 1. *American Journal of Human Genetics, 70,* 787–792.

Halmi, K. A. (1999). Eating disorders: AN, bulimia nervosa and obesity. In K. E. Hales, S. C. Yudofsky, & J. Talbot (Eds.), *American psychiatric textbook of psychiatry* (3rd ed., pp. 983–1002). Washington, DC: American Psychiatry Association.

Hoek, H. (1993). Review of the epidemiological studies of eating disorders. *International Reviews of Psychiatry, 5,* 61–64.

Humphrey, L. L. (1988). Relationship within subtypes of anorectic, bulimic, and normal families. *J. Am Acad Child Adol Psychiatry, 27,* 544–551.

Kleifield, E. I., Wagner, S., & Halmi, K. A. (1996). Cognitive-behavioral treatment of AN. *Psychiatric Clinics of North America, 19,* 715–737.

Lee, S., Leung, T., & Lee, A. M. (1996). Body dissatisfaction among Chinese undergraduates and its implication for eating disorders in Hong Kong. *International Eating Disorders Journal, 20,* 77–84.

Russell, G. F. M., Szmukler, G. I., & Dore, C. (1987). An evaluation of family therapy in anorexia and bulimia nervosa. *Arch. Gen Psych, 44,* 1047–1056.

Tobin, D. L., Moltemi, A. L., & Elin, M. D. (1995). Early trauma, dissociation, and late onset in the eating disorders. *International Eating Disorders Journal, 17,* 305–315.

Treasure, J., & Holland, A. J. (1989). Genetic vulnerability to eating disorders: Evidence from twin and family studies. In M. H. Remschmidt & M. Schmidt (Eds.), *Child and youth psychiatry: European prospectives* (pp. 59–68). New York: Hogrefe and Hubert.

Waller, G., Halek, C., & Crisp, A. H. (1993). Sexual abuse as a factor in AN: Evidence from two separate case series. *Journal of Psychosomatic Research, 37,* 873–879.

Katherine Halmi
Cornell University Medical College

See also: **Bulimia; Family Therapy**

ANTABUSE (Disulfiram) AND OTHER ANTI-ALCOHOLISM DRUGS

Antabuse (disulfiram), a drug used as a supplementary therapy for alcoholism, was originally used in the manufacture of rubber. When the chemical got into the air in one factory and settled on the workers' skin, many developed dermatitis (Schwartz & Tulipan, 1933). If they inhaled the disulfiram, they discovered that they could no longer tolerate alcohol. Beginning in the 1940s, therapists tried using the drug as a therapy for alcoholism, on the theory that alcoholics would learn to avoid alcohol because of its now unpleasant aftereffects.

Antabuse alters the metabolism of alcohol. Ethanol (ethyl alcohol) is metabolized in the liver by the enzyme alcohol dehydrogenase into acetaldehyde, a toxic chemical. Acetaldehyde is then metabolized by the enzyme aldehyde dehydrogenase (also known as aldehyde NAD-oxidoreductase) into acetate (acetic acid), which is a source of energy. Antabuse and a similar drug, Temposil (calcium carbimide), bind to the copper ion of acetaldehyde dehydrogenase and thereby inactivate it. Consequently, after someone drinks ethanol, it is converted as usual to aldehyde, but the aldehyde then accumulates instead of being converted to acetate. Symptoms of acetaldehyde accumulation include flushing of the face, increased heart rate, nausea and vomiting, headache, abdominal pain, and labored breathing. People using Antabuse are advised to take a 200 to 500 mg pill daily and warned that drinking alcohol within a day or two after taking a pill can cause severe illness. They need to avoid even using shampoos containing alcohol, because of the danger of skin rashes. Giving someone Antabuse without his or her knowledge would be unethical and hazardous because of the likelihood that the person would unknowingly drink enough alcohol to become severely ill.

For genetic reasons, some people produce lower than average amounts of the enzyme aldehyde dehydrogenase. Drinking alcohol produces for them symptoms similar to, although generally milder than, those associated with Antabuse. About half of Chinese and Japanese people have low amounts of this enzyme, and partly because of this lack alcohol abuse has historically been less common in China and Japan than in most other countries (Tu & Israel, 1995).

Many sources state that Antabuse is not significantly more effective than a placebo, citing a study by Fuller and Roth (1979). That criticism is misleading, however. The study included one group who were correctly told that they were taking a placebo and one who were given placebos but intentionally misinformed that they were taking Antabuse. The group taking Antabuse and the placebo group who believed they were taking Antabuse fared similarly: In both cases about one fourth of the individuals abstained completely throughout the year, whereas the others quit taking the drug and resumed drinking. Both of these groups did far better than the group who knew they were taking a placebo, who unsurprisingly continued drinking heavily. In other words, taking Antabuse, or believing one is taking Antabuse, is an effective deterrent to drinking and a useful adjunct to a decision not to drink. The pharmacological properties of Antabuse were irrelevant in this study, simply because those alcoholics who wished to resume drinking stopped taking the pill.

One review of 24 studies concluded that Antabuse on the average decreases the number of drinking days and the total consumption of alcohol but does not significantly increase the probability of remaining abstinent over the long term (Hughes & Cook, 1997). The problem in evaluating the effectiveness of Antabuse is the high frequency of noncompliance among participants in most of the research. Many alcoholics, even if they begin with good intentions, quit taking the pills or take them only sporadically. When therapists have taken measures to increase compliance, such as having someone's friend or relative supervise the daily pill-taking, the results have been more encouraging (Azrin, Sisson, Meyers, & Godley, 1982). A review of just those studies that maintained enough supervision to assure compliance concluded that supervised Antabuse is statistically and clinically effective in preventing relapse of alcoholism (Brewer, Meyers, & Johnsen, 2000). One possible way to improve compliance is to develop an implant that would provide sustained release in controlled quantities. However, effective and reliable implants have not yet been developed (Hughes & Cook, 1997).

The other drug approved in the United States for use against alcoholism is naltrexone, which blocks opioid receptors in the brain. Naltrexone is an antidote for excessive heroin use and helps decrease heroin cravings. Alcohol indirectly activates opioid pathways, and naltrexone decreases cravings for alcohol (Swift, 1999). The drug acamprosate (Campral) is sometimes used against alcohol in Europe, but as of 2002 it was not available in the United States. Acamprosate increases activity at glutamate type NMDA receptors in the nucleus accumbens, in contrast to alcohol, which decreases glutamate transmission (Berton, Francesconi, Madamba, Zieglgansberger, & Siggins, 1998). Acamprosate has shown promise in helping abstaining alcoholics to avoid relapse, with an effectiveness approximately equal to that of naltrexone (Kranzier & Van Kirk, 2001). Another drug used in Europe is tiapride, which blocks dopamine receptors (Swift, 1999). Dopamine activity is critical for nearly all types of reinforcement, so although blocking it may have potential for decreasing alcoholism, it runs the risk of decreasing other motivations as well.

For all of these drugs used against alcoholism, the problem is compliance. Many alcoholics have mixed feelings about quitting alcohol and decreasing their own cravings and at various times many of them quit taking the drugs. In short, any of these drugs can be a useful supplement to other forms of treatment, but only under conditions of adequate supervision to assure compliance.

REFERENCES

Azrin, N. H., Sisson, R. W., Meyers, R., & Godley, M. (1982). Alcohol treatment by disulfiram and community reinforcement therapy. *Journal of Behavior Therapy and Experimental Psychiatry, 13,* 105–112.

Berton, F., Francesconi, W. G., Madamba, S. G., Zieglgansberger, W., & Siggins, G. R. (1998). Acamprosate enhances N-methyl-D-aspartate receptor-mediated neurotransmission but inhibits presynaptic GABA(B) receptors in nucleus accumbens neurons. *Alcoholism: Clinical and Experimental Research, 22,* 183–191.

Brewer, C., Meyers, R. J., & Johnsen, J. (2000). Does disulfiram help to prevent relapse in alcohol abuse? *CNS Drugs, 14,* 329–341.

Fuller, R. K., & Roth, H. P. (1979). Disulfiram for the treatment of alcoholism: An evaluation in 128 men. *Annals of Internal Medicine, 90,* 901–904.

Hughes, J. C., & Cook, C. C. H. (1997). The efficacy of disulfiram: A review of outcome studies. *Addiction, 92,* 381–395.

Kranzier, H. R., & Van Kirk, J. (2001). Efficacy of naltrexone and acamprosate for alcoholism treatment: A meta-analysis. *Alcoholism: Clinical and Experimental Research, 25,* 1335–1341.

Schwartz, L., & Tulipan, L. (1933). An outbreak of dermatitis among workers in a rubber manufacturing plant. *Public Health Reports, 48,* 808–814.

Swift, R. M. (1999). Medications and alcohol craving. *Alcohol Research & Health, 23,* 207–213.

Tu, G. C., & Israel, Y. (1995). Alcohol consumption by Orientals in North America is predicted largely by a single gene. *Behavior Genetics, 25,* 59–65.

James W. Kalat
North Carolina State University

ANTHROPOLOGY

The Nature of Anthropology as a Discipline

Anthropology is an outgrowth of the sixteenth-, seventeenth-, and eighteenth-century European discoveries of the remains of ancient civilizations and fossil ancestors as well as Europeans' encounters with contemporary cultures that differed greatly from those of Europe. The need to explain, understand, and deal with these discoveries as a means of better understanding their own cultures gave rise to anthropology as an academic and museum discipline.

It was not until the late nineteenth and early twentieth centuries, however, that a coherent intellectual structure emerged for the discipline. In the United States Franz Boas, of Columbia University, helped combine four subfields into what we now see in most major U.S. university departments of anthropology: cultural anthropology, archaeology, anthropological linguistics, and physical (biological) anthropology. Combined research in these four subfields has achieved a broad coverage of human biological and cultural evolution in its study of the world's cultures, past and present—the most distinguishing feature of anthropology. The concept of culture has become the unifying theoretical framework that allows the subdisciplines of the field to interact in research and teaching.

Cultural anthropology deals with the description and analysis of the forms and styles of human social life. One subdiscipline of anthropology, ethnography, systematically describes societies and cultures. Another subdiscipline, ethnology, is the closely related theoretical comparison of these descriptions that provides the basis for broad-based cultural generalizations.

Archaeology and its systematic excavation of the interred remains of the past reveal sequences of social and cultural adaptations and evolution under diverse natural and cultural conditions. Archaeology makes substantial contributions to the study of man in its quest to understand prehistory and in its investigation of the full cultural record of mankind.

Anthropological linguistics provides yet another essential perspective with its investigation of world languages. A major objective of this field is reconstructing historical changes that have led to the formation of contemporary languages and families of languages. In a more fundamental sense, anthropological linguistics is concerned with the nature of language and its functions in human and prehuman cultures. Anthropological linguistics is also concerned with the relationships between the evolution of language and the evolution of cultures. Finally, anthropological linguistics is essential for the cultural anthropologist seeking to understand and to write heretofore unwritten languages.

The subfield of physical (biological) anthropology concentrates on man's prehuman origins and takes into account both genetically and culturally determined aspects of human beings. Physical anthropology seeks to identify the processes of human evolution by studying the fossil remains of ancient human and prehuman species and by describing and analyzing the distribution of hereditary variations among contemporary populations increasingly by means of genetic research.

The Relevance of Anthropology as a Discipline

Anthropology does not achieve its general and fundamental significance by organizing the data of other disciplines or by synthesizing higher-level theories from the other disciplines' concepts and principles. Anthropologists are interested in the facts and theories of other disciplines that apply to the study of man. Certainly there are many collaborative efforts and fruitful exchanges between anthropologists and biologists, psychologists, sociologists, social psychologists, geologists, historians, and economists, as well as scholars in the humanities. It should also be noted that as research and publications accumulate in each of the four subfields of anthropology, fewer and fewer anthropologists are masters of the entire discipline. In fact, anthropologists increasingly find themselves working not only with fellow anthropologists but also with members of entirely different scientific and humanistic disciplines. For example, cultural anthropologists interested in the relationships between cultural practices and the natural environment must study the principles of ecology. Physical anthropologists studying the relationships between human and protohuman fossils may, because of the importance of teeth in the fossil record, become more familiar with dentistry journals than with journals devoted to ethnography or linguistics. Cultural anthropologists who focus on the relationships between culture and an individual's personality are sometimes more at home professionally with psychologists than with archaeologists in their own university departments. Likewise, anthropology makes great contributions to museums, and many anthropologists spend their careers as museologists. In general it may be said that the working links between anthropological specialties and other disciplines are quite pragmatic. Ongoing specialization requires branching out in many directions in response to research opportunities, scholarly interests, and new discoveries and research techniques.

An important feature of anthropology as a discipline is that its scope is panhuman in its theoretical foundation. It is systematically and uncompromisingly diachronic and comparative in its insistence that the proper study of man can only be undertaken successfully through a general study of mankind. The anthropological impulse is, first and foremost, to insist that conclusions based upon the study of one particular human group or civilization be checked against the evidence gleaned from other groups under both similar and different conditions. In this way the relevance of anthropology transcends the interests of American, Western, or any other culture. In anthropological perspective, all civilizations are particular, local, and evanescent; thus, anthropology opposes the ethnocentrism of those who would have themselves and none other represent humanity, stand at the pinnacle of progress, or be chosen by God or history to fashion the world in their own image.

Because of its diachronic and comparative perspectives anthropology holds the key to answering the recurring fundamental questions of contemporary relevance to humanity. It lies peculiarly within the province of anthropology to contextualize the place of man's animal heritage in modern society, to define what is distinctively human about humans, and to differentiate between cultural and noncultural reasons for conditions such as competition, conflict, and war.

Anthropological facts and concepts are essential to an understanding of the origins of social inequality, racism, exploitation, poverty, underdevelopment, and other human problems. Of decisive importance to the entire anthropological enterprise is the question of the nature and significance of human racial variation. Because of its combination of biological, archaeological, linguistic, and cultural perspectives, general anthropology is uniquely suited to address this problem.

In addition to its basic research mission, anthropology has become an applied science with applications in most areas of contemporary life. Techniques of applied anthropology may now be seen in problem-solving activities across the spectrum of virtually all cultural and biological domains. Applied anthropologists in the United States alone number in the thousands and are employed as professionals and scientists in government, business, the military, health, education, and various other fields. It is now predicted that half of all graduating doctorates in anthropology will pursue nonacademic careers.

Underlying all of anthropology's other contributions to the sciences and humanities is its abiding search for the causes of social and cultural differences and similarities in the family of man. This enduring quest to understand both the biological and cultural nature of mankind in a diachronic and comparative framework continues to distinguish anthropology as an essential and vital component of a sound education for the modern world.

Deward E. Walker, Jr.
University of Colorado, Boulder

ANTIDEPRESSANT MEDICATIONS

Medications effective in reducing the symptoms of major depression are called *antidepressants.* The Food and Drug Administration requires controlled, double-blind studies showing safety and efficacy before approving an antidepressant medication to be available in the United States.

Major Depressive Disorder is characterized by sadness and an inability to experience pleasure. Associated symptoms include decreased self-esteem, feelings of hopelessness and worthlessness, excessive guilt, and difficulty with concentration, memory, and decision making. Anxiety manifested as fear, nervousness, or excessive worry is also common in depression. A greater focus on bodily sensations can result in somatic symptoms. Sleep difficulties marked by reduced or excessive sleep, and a change in appetite with consequent weight loss or gain, are also present. Suicidal ideas can lead to suicidal attempts with the potential to succeed. The diagnosis of major depression requires these symptoms to be present fairly continuously for a minimum of 2 weeks and to be associated with significant distress or impairment in role function.

There are different forms of major depression, including one seen in bipolar disorder in which individuals have episodes of not only depression but also forms of mania; melancholia, characterized by symptoms like a distinct quality of sadness, inability to experience pleasure, and early morning awakening; and atypical depression, which is more responsive to environmental events and associated with an increase in appetite and need for sleep. The presence of depressive symptoms that fall below the threshold of criteria for major depression is called by various names: *dysthymia* (which is a chronic lower-grade depression and still impairing), depressive symptoms in response to negative life events, and minor depression.

Depression is believed to arise from a combination of genetic vulnerabilities and environmental factors. Traumatic experiences, particularly if they occur in childhood, are a potential environmental risk factor for the development of depression.

Medications to treat depression are classified based on their chemical structure and pharmacological effect. Three major classes of antidepressants are available in the United States. These are the tricyclic antidepressants (TCAs), monoamine oxidase inhibitors (MAOIs), and selective serotonin reuptake inhibitors (SSRIs). The initial effects of these medications in the brain are primarily on two chemical messengers called neurotransmitters—norepinephrine and serotonin. The TCAs have a prominent effect in blocking the recycling of norepinephrine. Commonly used TCAs included imipramine (trade name Tofranil), amitryptaline (Elavil), doxepin (Sinequan), desipramine (Norpramin), and nortriptyline (Pamelor and Aventyl). One TCA, clomipramine (Anafranil), also powerfully blocks the recycling of serotonin. The MAOIs inhibit an enzyme, monoamine oxidase, that is important in the physiological breakdown of norepinephrine and serotonin. Commonly used MAOIs include phenelzine (Nardil) and tranylcypramine (Parnate). The SSRIs selectively block the recycling of serotonin. These include fluoxetine (Prozac), sertraline (Zoloft), paroxetine (Paxil), fluvoxamine (Luvox), and citalopram (Celexa).

Some antidepressant medications do not fall easily into the above groups. Buproprion (Wellbutrin) is believed to block the recycling of norepinephrine as well as another neurotransmitter, dopamine. Venlafaxine (Effexor) blocks the recycling of both serotonin and norepinephrine. Nefazodone (Serzone) blocks the recycling of serotonin and additionally a specific serotonin receptor. Mirtazapine (Remeron) impacts a specific norepinephrine receptor on the serotonin cell, increasing its firing rate while simultaneously blocking some serotonin receptors.

The benefits of antidepressant medications are rarely immediate but accrue gradually over several weeks. They appear to modulate primary negative emotional responses like anxiety in structures like the amygdala, such that cognitive and executive choices are more available to drive behavioral responses. The maximum benefit may not plateau until several months. The initial effect of antidepressants begins a cascade of events in critical neurons that are ultimately believed to alter the expression of specific genes. Recent studies suggest that antidepressants enhance the activity of neurotropic agents that impact neurogenesis. This process is gradual, thus the delay in obtaining the full benefits of antidepressant medications.

In addition to their therapeutic benefits, antidepressant medications also have unwanted effects. These side effects can be explained by their pharmacological effects in areas other than the sites involved in their beneficial effects, or by their effects on other receptors. The TCAs appear to have the largest number of such unwanted effects, including potential effects on the electrical conduction system in the heart. This effect makes them particularly dangerous if taken in overdose. The TCAs' effects on the cholinergic, histaminergic, and alpha-1 adrenergic receptors mediate the majority of their adverse effects. MAOIs indiscriminately inhibit the monoamine oxidase enzyme, and as a result they have the potential to interact with other specific medications or with food substances like cheese. Such an interaction may increase blood pressure, which, if high enough, can cause strokes and even death. The newer antidepressants like the SSRIs, because of their greater selectivity in their pharmacological actions, are less likely to cause serious side effects. However, with the exception of buproprion, nefazodone, and mirtazapine, their potential for causing sexual side effects seems to be greater.

Antidepressants have been increasingly recognized as being effective in a variety of other conditions other than major depression. These include dysthymia and the anxiety disorders like Generalized Anxiety Disorder, Panic Disorder, Obsessive-Compulsive Disorder, Post-Traumatic Stress Disorder, and Social Anxiety Disorder.

In a general group of patients with major depression,

roughly 10–20% are intolerant to the first antidepressant tried. Of the remaining, roughly half are able to tolerate the medications without any significant side effects. Side effects, when they occur, may fade as the individual gets used to the medication. Occasionally, side effects develop gradually over time.

An adequate trial of an antidepressant requires a minimum of a month or two on an adequate dose. Roughly two thirds of the individuals will obtain at least a 50% reduction in the severity of their depressive symptoms. One quarter to one third may achieve remission, which is considered a full or close to a full level of response. Those who fail to respond might respond to either switching the medication to another class of antidepressants or augmenting the first antidepressant with one of several choices. Individuals who fail to respond to antidepressant medications may respond to electroconvulsive therapy, believed to be the most powerful treatment available for major depression.

Philip T. Ninan
Emory University School of Medicine

See also: **Anxiety Disorders; MAO Inhibitors; Tricyclic Antidepressants**

ANTISOCIAL PERSONALITY DISORDER

Antisocial Personality Disorder (ASP) is characterized by a pattern of socially irresponsible, exploitative, and guiltless behavior that begins in early childhood or early adolescence. Typical behaviors include criminality and failure to conform to the law, failure to sustain consistent employment, manipulation of others for personal gain, frequent deception of others, and a lack of empathy for others.

Antisocial behavior has been described throughout recorded history, yet formal descriptions date only to the early nineteenth century. Philippe Pinel, founding father of modern psychiatry, used the term *manie sans delire* to describe persons who were not insane but had irrational outbursts of rage and violence. In the late nineteenth century, German psychiatrists coined the term *psychopathy* to describe a broad range of deviant behaviors and eccentricities. The term was later popularized by the American psychiatrist Hervey Cleckley in the now-classic *Mask of Sanity,* originally published in 1941 (1941/1976). The term *sociopathic personality disturbance* was introduced in the first edition of the *Diagnostic and Statistical Manual of Mental Disorders (DSM-I)*, published in 1952, and was replaced by *Antisocial Personality Disorder* in 1968 in the second edition of the *DSM,* a term whose use has continued to the present in the fourth edition of the *DSM.* The term *antisocial* implies that the disturbance is directed against society.

Clinical Findings

Antisocials typically report a history of childhood behavior problems, such as fights with peers, conflicts with adults, lying, cheating, stealing, vandalism, fire setting, running away from home, and cruelty to animals or other children. As the antisocial youth achieves adult status, other problems develop that reflect a lack of age-appropriate responsibilities, such as uneven job performance, being undependable, changing jobs frequently, and being fired. Criminal behavior, pathological lying, and the use of aliases are also characteristic.

Survey data show that from 2% to 4% of men and 0.5% to 1% women in the United States are antisocial. The percentages are much higher in prisons and psychiatric hospitals and clinics, and among homeless and alcohol- and drug-addicted persons.

Natural History

The disorder is chronic, although it tends to be worse early in its course, and patients tend to improve with advancing age. In a 30-year follow-up study, Robins (1966) found that of 82 antisocial subjects, 12% were in remission, and another 20% were deemed improved; the remaining subjects were considered as disturbed, or more disturbed than at the study onset. The median age for improvement was 35 years.

Psychiatric comorbidity is common, and many antisocial persons suffer from an alcohol or drug use disorder, a mood disorder, an anxiety disorder, or an attention-deficit disorder (ADD). Sexual dysfunction, paraphilias, other personality disorders (e.g., borderline personality), and impulse control disorders (e.g., pathological gambling) are also frequent. Risk for death from suicide or homicide is elevated.

Etiology

ASP may be genetically transmitted to some extent. Family studies show that nearly one fifth of first-degree relatives of antisocials are themselves antisocials. ASP is more commonly found in both identical twins than among nonidentical twins, and offspring of an antisocial parent who are adopted in childhood are more likely to develop ASP than adoptees without an antisocial parent.

Chronic nervous system underarousal is thought by some researchers to underlie ASP. This theory is supported by evidence that antisocials have low resting pulse rates, low skin conductance, and an increased amplitude on event-related potentials.

The central nervous system (CNS) neurotransmitter serotonin has been linked with impulsive and aggressive behavior. Low levels of cerebrospinal fluid 5-hydroxyindolacetic acid (5-HIAA)—a metabolite of serotonin—have been found in men who killed with unusual cruelty or committed arson and in newborns with a family history of ASP.

Other evidence points toward abnormal CNS functioning in ASP. Positron emission tomography scans in a group of criminals who had either committed or attempted murder showed abnormal function in the prefrontal cortex. In another study, which used structural magnetic resonance imaging, antisocial men had a reduction in prefrontal gray matter volume.

The social and home environment also contributes to the development of antisocial behavior. Parents of troubled children show a high level of antisocial behavior themselves, and their homes are frequently broken by domestic abuse, divorce, separation, or the absence of a parent. Antisocial persons often have a history of childhood abuse.

Managing ASP

Antisocial patients who seek help can be evaluated on an outpatient basis. A careful psychiatric interview supplemented by information from informants is the best way to assess ASP, because there are no diagnostic tests. Cognitive therapy has recently been used to treat ASP and involves helping patients to recognize and correct situations in which their distorted beliefs and attitudes interfere with their functioning. Antisocial patients can be very difficult to treat because they typically blame others for their problems, have a low tolerance for frustration, are impulsive, and rarely form trusting relationships.

Several drugs have been shown to reduce aggression, the chief problem of many antisocials, but no medications are routinely used or specifically approved for the treatment of ASP. Lithium carbonate and phenytoin have both been found to reduce anger, threatening behavior, and assaultiveness among prisoners. Other drugs used have been used to treat aggression primarily in brain-injured or mentally retarded patients, including carbamazepine, valproate, propranolol, buspirone, trazodone, and the antipsychotics. Medication targeted at comorbid major depression, anxiety disorders, or ADD may help to reduce antisocial behavior. Antisocial substance abusers who stop abusing are less likely to engage in antisocial or criminal behaviors, and they have fewer family conflicts and emotional problems.

Antisocials with spouses and families may benefit from marriage and family counseling. Bringing family members into the counseling process may help antisocial patients recognize the impact of their disorder on others. Therapists who specialize in family counseling may be helpful in addressing antisocials trouble in maintaining enduring attachments to their spouse or partner, their inability to be effective parents, their problems with honesty and responsibility, and the anger and hostility that can lead to domestic violence.

Prevention of ASP

Preventive measures should focus on teaching children how to recognize and reject bad behavior, how to make acceptable judgments between right and wrong, and how to connect actions with consequences. Parents of troubled children may need special training to show them how to identify and correct misbehavior as it occurs and how to steer their children away from negative influences like delinquent peers. Antiviolence programs such as those offered in some public schools may help children find alternatives to lashing out.

REFERENCES

Cleckley, H. (1976). *The mask of sanity: An attempt to clarify some issues about the so-called psychopathic personality* (5th ed.). St. Louis: Mosby. (Original work published 1941)

Robins, L. (1966). *Deviant children grown up.* Baltimore: Williams & Wilkins.

SUGGESTED READING

Black, D. W. (1999). *Bad boys, bad men: Confronting Antisocial Personality Disorder.* New York: Oxford University Press.

Hare, R. D. (1993). *Without conscience: The disturbing world of the psychopaths among us.* New York: Pocket Books.

Raine, A., Lencz, T., Bihrle, S., La Casse, L., Colletti, P., et al. (2000). Reduced prefrontal gray matter volume and reduced antonomic activity in Antisocial Personality Disorder. *Archives of General Psychiatry, 57,* 119–127.

Donald W. Black
University of Iowa College of Medicine

See also: **Conduct Disorder**

ANXIETY

Introduction

One of the best definitions of anxiety, put forth over fifteen years ago by Kandel (1983), remains highly apt and appropriate today: "Anxiety is a normal inborn response either to threat—to one's person, attitudes, or self-esteem—or to the absence of people or objects that assure and signify safety" (p. 1277).

Anxiety is an emotion and state of mind characterized by aversive cognitive (apprehensive expectation of negative experience or consequences), physiologic (autonomic hyperarousal with multiple somatic symptoms), and behavioral (hypervigilance, avoidance, paralysis of action) components. Its relationship to fear states in animals is ambiguous. Fear is an adaptive response to a clear-cut, external threat; anxiety is excessive or inappropriate in relation to the stimulus and often extends well beyond the provoking situation (i.e., the cognitive aspect of anxious anticipation and uncertainty about the future). This distinction may simply reflect the highly complex and more developed human brain, whose frontal lobes allow for a degree of planning and rehearsal of future events not possible in animals, along with a capacity for symbolism that facilitates multiple higher-order contextual associations with negative affect. Although a certain amount of anxiety, analogous to fear, is adaptive in helping the organism prepare a response to a demanding situation, excess anxiety is maladaptive, characterizes a number of the clinical anxiety disorders, and also occurs as a significant symptom complex in other psychiatric disorders, most notably depression.

Psychological Approaches

Until recently, theories of anxiety were largely psychological (Craig, Brown, & Baum 1995). Psychoanalysis emphasized the importance of early childhood experience as it was stored in the brain or mind. Internal conflicts and/or damaged self-esteem based on these memories and recollections served as a cognitive stimulus for anxiety.

Learning and behavior theorists conceptualized anxiety as a response to a specific environmental stimulus that could be maintained by reinforcing consequences, and they used this understanding of the immediate triggers and consequences of anxiety to design specific treatment interventions. This strictly behavioral approach was most applicable to the treatment of phobias (i.e., excessively fearful responses to concrete environmental situations and cues). Later theorists added a cognitive element to these concepts, focusing on the role of internal cognitive stimuli as potential triggers or reinforcing factors. This development moved discussion more into the realm of psychoanalysts, and at the same time this cognitive focus allowed learning theorists to bridge the gap between the more behaviorally concrete animal fear and the more human (i.e., cognitive) element in anxiety.

Neuroscience Perspectives

Recent developments in understanding the basic neurobiology of anxiety have allowed theorists to combine a neuroscience and behavioral/learning perspective to understand the role of both nature and nurture in determining the anxiety response. In this conceptualization, both external and internal (i.e., cognitive) environments play important roles in modulating activity in key brain areas that control the processing of environmental signals and the propensity for an anxiety response. This dual contribution is consistent with the equal and important role of both medication and psychotherapeutic approaches to the treatment of the various anxiety disorders.

The amygdala is an almond-shaped brain structure below the cerebral cortex and deep inside the temporal lobes. It serves as a central integrative brain center that coordinates both stimulus processing and anxiety response generation (LeDoux, 1996). This coordination is made possible by a rich set of reciprocal connections to higher cortical centers that process and compare multiple sensory and cognitive signals and to lower brain-stem centers that regulate blood pressure, pulse, respiration, digestion, and other arousal-related functions. In animals, lesioning the amygdala prevents acquisition of a conditioned emotional response (so that animals cannot learn the association between, for example, an electric shock and a light signal). Thus, the amygdala is a key brain structure modulating the ability to learn an association between various environmental contexts and danger, anxiety, or apprehension.

Many studies of the anxiety and stress response have implicated key hormones and neurotransmitters. Prominent among these are corticotropin-releasing hormone (CRH), which modulates adrenal cortisol response; norepinephrine, which controls the ratio of signal to noise, thereby alerting the organism to the relevance of certain stimuli; and serotonin, which plays a key "braking" role in controlling sensory input to the amygdala as well as modulating anxiety responsivity. Brain norepinephrine synergizes with CRH in activating arousal of the peripheral sympathetic nervous system and central nervous system, the amygdala plays a key role in orchestrating this response, and these hormones may provide feedback to the amygdala that potentiates the anxiety response.

It is of some interest that the responsivity of a number of these stress hormones has been linked to developmental experience by an elegant series of studies. These studies show that early adverse life experiences appear to set thresholds for activity of these various stress response systems. Separation and loss, hardship, and abuse serve to increase the individual's tendency for hormone/neurotransimitter-related hyperarousal (Coplan et al., 1998). These findings are consistent with studies showing an increased rate of early adverse life experiences, especially separation and loss, in patients with various pathologic anxiety disorders.

There are significant genetic contributions to anxiety (Plomin, DeFries, McClearn, & Rutter, 1997). Twin studies have shown heritability in children for a dimension of fearfulness called *behavioral inhibition,* as well as shyness, and in adults for the personality characteristics of neuroticism. Behavioral inhibition before 1 year of age is associated with an increased cortisol and heart rate response (Kagan, 1997) consistent with the setting of lower thresholds for stress response system activation previously noted. However, twin studies also show a significant role for the environment (e.g., a proportion of behaviorally inhibited infants improve by age seven, whereas some noninhibited infants acquire this response at age seven).

In the context of this neurobiologic system that modulates anxiety response, the dual roles of medication and psychotherapy can be readily appreciated. Antidepressant medications (which also have potent anti-anxiety effects) work on neurotransmitter systems in lower brain-stem centers that control input and outflow from the amygdala. More purely anti-anxiety medications (e.g., benzodiazepine tranquilizers) work in the amygdala itself, directly dampening certain inputs and perhaps affecting output. In contrast, psychotherapy probably works at higher cortical centers, which will affect sensory input to the amygdala as well as modifying amygdala processing itself via the reciprocal connections, thereby affecting the proclivity to generate an anxiety response and the likelihood that this response can be extinguished with new experience and learning. The greater effectiveness of combined treatment with both modalities, often observed in studies of anxious patients, can be readily appreciated from this point of view.

REFERENCES

Craig, K. J., Brown, K. J., & Baum A. (1995). Environmental factors in the etiology of anxiety. In F. E. Bloom & D. J. Kupfer (Eds.), *Psychopharmacology: The fourth generation of progress* (pp. 1325–1337). New York: Raven.

Coplan, J. D., Trost, R., Owens, M. J., Cooper, T., Gorman, J. M., Nemeroff, C. B., et al. (1998). Cerebrospinal fluid concentrations of somatostatin and biogenic amines in grown primates reared by mothers exposed to manipulated foraging conditions. *Archives of General Psychiatry, 55,* 473–477.

Kagan, J. (1997). Temperament and the reactions to unfamiliarity. *Child Development, 68,* 139–143.

Kandel, E. R. (1983). From metapsychology to molecular biology: Explorations into the nature of anxiety. *American Journal of Psychiatry, 140*(10), 1277–1293.

LeDoux, J. E. (1996). *The emotional brain.* New York: Simon and Schuster.

Plomin, R, DeFries, J. C., McClearn, G. E., & Rutter, M. (1997). *Behavioral genetics.* New York: Freeman.

Peter Roy-Byrne
University of Washington, Harborview Medical Center, Seattle, WA

See also: **Antidepressant Medications; Cognitive Therapy; Neurotransmitters**

ANXIETY DISORDERS

Anxiety disorders are among the most prevalent of psychological disorders, affecting up to 20% of the population. The key features shared by the anxiety disorders include excessive or unrealistic fear and anxiety, avoidance of feared objects and situations, and excessive attempts to reduce discomfort or to protect oneself from potential threat. In addition, for an anxiety disorder to be diagnosed, the person has to report considerable distress over having the anxiety symptoms, or the symptoms have to cause significant interference in the individual's life. In fact, in severe cases, people with anxiety disorders may be unable to work, develop relationships, or even leave their homes. Anxiety disorders often pose an enormous financial burden on society. For example, they often lead to lower work productivity and considerable increases in health care utilization.

Types of Anxiety Disorders

The fourth edition of the American Psychiatric Association's *Diagnostic and Statistical Manual of Mental Disorders* (*DSM-IV*) describes 11 different anxiety disorders. Each of these is listed in Table 1, along with their most important defining features. Although other psychological problems may be associated with extreme fear or anxiety (e.g., eating disorders are associated with a fear of gaining weight), only the conditions listed in Table 1 are officially classified as anxiety disorders in the *DSM-IV.*

Demographic Features of the Anxiety Disorders

Anxiety disorders can occur across a wide range of cultures, ages, sexes, and income levels. In most cases, anxiety disorders are more common in women than in men. The more frequent occurrence in women is most pronounced for Panic Disorder with Agoraphobia and certain specific phobias (particularly animals and storms). For other anxiety disorders, such as Social Anxiety Disorder, blood and needle phobias, and Obsessive-Compulsive Disorder (OCD), the differences between men and women are smaller. The typical onset of anxiety disorders varies, with some tending to begin in early childhood (e.g., animal phobias), others beginning, on average, during the teen years (e.g., Social Anxiety Disorder, OCD), and others tending to begin in early adulthood (e.g., Panic Disorder).

Causes of Anxiety Disorders

Although there are still many unanswered questions about how anxiety disorders begin, a number of contributing factors have been identified. From a biological perspective, there is mounting evidence supporting the role of genetics. In addition, certain neurotransmitters in the brain appear to play a role. For example, OCD appears to be associated with abnormal levels of serotonin, whereas Panic Disorder appears to be associated with abnormalities in the norepinephrine system, as well as others. Differences have also been shown in patterns of blood flow in the brains of individuals with and without anxiety disorders. Interestingly, these patterns may normalize following treatment, either with medication or with psychological treatment.

From a psychological perspective, life experiences appear to play a role in the onset and exacerbation of anxiety disorders. For example, life stress can contribute to the development of Panic Disorder and other anxiety disorders. In addition, traumatic events in particular situations may trigger the onset of Post-Traumatic Stress Disorder (PTSD), a specific phobia, or another anxiety-related problem.

In addition to the role of life events, there is significant

Table 1. Key Features of the Anxiety Disorders

Anxiety Disorder	Key Features
Panic Disorder With or Without Agoraphobia	• The presence of unexpected or uncued *panic attacks* (a panic attack is a rush of fear or discomfort that peaks quickly and is accompanied by four or more associated symptoms, such as racing heart, dizziness, breathlessness, and others). • The presence of anxiety over the panic attacks, worry about the possible consequences of attacks (e.g., dying, losing control, "going crazy"), or a change in behavior related to the attacks. • *Agoraphobia* often occurs with Panic Disorder. This refers to anxiety about, or avoidance of, situations in which escape might be difficult or help unavailable in the event of a panic attack or paniclike symptoms. Feared situations may include crowded places, travel, driving, enclosed places, and others.
Agoraphobia Without History of Panic Disorder	• The presence of Agoraphobia, without ever having met the full diagnostic criteria for Panic Disorder.
Specific Phobia	• An excessive or unrealistic fear of a specific object or situation, such as an animal, heights, blood, needles, elevators, or flying.
Social Anxiety Disorder (Social Phobia)	• An excessive or unrealistic fear of one or more social or performance situations, such as public speaking, conversations, or meeting new people, The fear is of being embarrassed, humiliated, or judged by others.
Obsessive-Compulsive Disorder (OCD)	• The presence of *obsessions* (i.e., thoughts, images, or impulses that are perceived as intrusive and distressing), such as fears of being contaminated, doubts about one's actions, or irrational fears of hurting others). • The presence of *compulsions* (i.e., repetitive behaviors, such as checking, washing, or counting, that are used to reduce anxiety or to prevent something bad from happening).
Post-Traumatic Stress Disorder (PTSD)	• The experience of a trauma in which an individual has been confronted with a threat to his or her physical well-being or to the physical well-being of another individual (e.g., experiencing a rape, assault, or accident; witnessing an act of violence). • 1 month or more in which the individual experiences recurrent recollections of the trauma, avoidance of situations that remind him or her of the trauma, emotional numbing, symptoms of arousal, and hypervigilance.
Acute Stress Disorder	• Similar to PTSD, except with a duration of between 2 days and 4 weeks.
Generalized Anxiety Disorder (GAD)	• Frequent worry about a number of different areas (e.g., work, family, health) with difficulty controlling the worry and a number of associated symptoms (e.g., muscle tension, sleep problems, poor concentration).
Anxiety Disorder Due to a General Medical Condition	• Significant problems with anxiety that are directly caused by a medical condition (e.g., panic attack symptoms triggered by hyperthyroidism).
Substance-Induced Anxiety Disorder	• Significant problems with anxiety that are directly caused by a substance (e.g., panic attack symptoms triggered by cocaine use, caffeine, or alcohol withdrawal).
Anxiety Disorder Not Otherwise Specified	• Significant problems with anxiety that do not meet the official criteria for another anxiety disorder or for some other psychological disorder.

evidence that anxious biases in a person's beliefs, assumptions, and predictions can contribute to anxiety symptoms. For example, individuals with Social Anxiety Disorder tend to be overly concerned that others will judge them in a negative way. Likewise, individuals with Panic Disorder tend to misinterpret normal physical sensations, such as dizziness or breathlessness, as being dangerous.

Treatment of Anxiety Disorders

Anxiety disorders are among the most treatable of psychological problems. Most individuals who receive appropriate treatment experience a significant reduction in symptoms. For Substance-Induced Anxiety Disorders and Anxiety Disorders Due to a General Medical Condition, the focus is generally on reducing the substance use or on treating the medical condition that is causing the problem. However, for the other anxiety disorders, evidence-based treatments include medications, cognitive-behavioral therapy (CBT), or a combination of these approaches.

The selective serotonin reuptake inhibitors (SSRIs), such as paroxetine, fluoxetine, and sertraline, have been shown to be useful for treating most of the anxiety disorders. Other antidepressants (e.g., venlavaxine, imipramine) are also useful for particular anxiety disorders. Anxiolytic medications (especially the benzodiazepines, such as alprazolam and diazepam) are also effective for reducing anxiety, although they are usually prescribed with caution due to the potential for abuse and the difficulty that some people have discontinuing these drugs. All of the anxiety disorders, except perhaps specific phobias, have been shown to improve following treatment with medications.

CBT includes a number of components. First, patients are encouraged to expose themselves to the situations they fear until their fear subsides. For example, individuals with Social Anxiety Disorder may practice meeting new people, engaging in conversations, or purposely making minor mistakes in social situations. Individuals with Panic Disorder are encouraged to expose themselves to the physical feelings they fear (e.g., running in place until their fear of a racing heart decreases), in addition to the feared agoraphobic situations. In the case of OCD, the exposure is combined with prevention of the compulsive rituals (e.g., touching "contaminated" objects without washing one's hands).

Second, cognitive therapy is often used to help individuals to replace their anxious thoughts with more balanced, realistic perspectives. For example, an individual with Generalized Anxiety Disorder (GAD) who worries whenever his or her spouse is late would be encouraged to consider all of the possible factors that may contribute to the lateness, rather than assuming the worst.

Third, treatment may include teaching the individual other relevant skills. For example, people with GAD often benefit from relaxation or meditation-based treatments. Individuals with Social Anxiety Disorder may benefit from learning to communicate more effectively.

Finally, treatment often includes a combination of medication and CBT. Generally, CBT, medications, and combined treatments are equally effective on average, although some individuals respond better to one approach than another. In the long term, after treatment has been discontinued, symptoms are more likely to return following treatment with medications than they are following treatment with CBT.

Martin M. Antony
Anxiety Treatment and Research Centre, St. Joseph's Hospital

APPIC (ASSOCIATION OF PSYCHOLOGY POSTDOCTORAL AND INTERNSHIP CENTERS)

Founded and incorporated in 1968, the Association of Psychology Internship Centers (APIC) was originally constituted as an informal group of psychologists involved in internship training. These trainers banded together for the purpose of sharing information about mutual problems. Over time, the organization expanded to include postdoctoral residency training directors as well as internship training directors, and in 1992 it was renamed the Association of Psychology Postdoctoral and Internship Centers (APPIC).

According to the current mission statement, the APPIC (1) facilitates the achievement and maintenance of high-quality training in professional psychology; (2) fosters the exchange of information among institutions and agencies offering doctoral internships or postdoctoral training in professional psychology; (3) develops standards for such training programs; (4) provides a forum for exchanging views; establishing policies, procedures, and contingencies on training matters and selection of interns; and resolving other problems and issues for which common agreement is either essential or desirable; (5) offers assistance in matching students with training programs; and (6) represents the views of training agencies to groups and organizations whose functions and objectives relate to those of APPIC and develops and maintains relationships with colleagues in those groups and organizations.

The APPIC has a central office in Washington, D.C., which is headed by a full-time executive director. The APPIC board of directors includes seven psychologist members elected by APPIC-member internship and postdoctoral programs and one public member chosen by the other board members. The APPIC also has a number of standing committees whose members are APPIC-member training directors.

The APPIC is a membership and not an accrediting organization. To be accepted for APPIC membership, internship and postdoctoral residency programs must meet specific membership criteria. Membership is automatic for programs accredited by the American Psychological Association (APA) or the Canadian Psychological Association (CPA). The APPIC sponsors a mentoring program to assist new and developing programs in meeting the criteria for APPIC membership. In addition, doctoral-level professional psychology academic programs may choose to become APPIC subscribers, a status that provides specific services to the program and its students.

The APPIC offers a multitude of services. The first APPIC directory was developed for the 1972–1973 training year. At that time, there were 90 internship programs listed and no postdoctoral programs. In the 2002–2003 APPIC directory, a total of 666 APPIC-member programs (588 internships and 78 postdoctoral residency programs) were listed. In addition to the printed APPIC directory, an online and more comprehensive version of the directory was launched in the summer of 2000. The online directory may be updated at any time by training directors, and users may search for programs using a variety of criteria.

Another major service is the facilitation of the internship matching process. For the 1972–1973 through 1998–1999 training years, the APPIC conducted a standardized internship selection process, which utilized a uniform notification date, to structure a previously unregulated process (Stedman, 1989). In 1999, the APPIC instituted a computer-based internship matching program (called the APPIC Match) to place applicants into available positions (Keilin, 1998). Furthermore, beginning in 1986, the APPIC has operated a postselection clearinghouse to assist both unplaced students and programs with unfilled positions. The matching process further improved in 1996, when the APPIC developed a uniform application for internship, the APPIC Application for Psychology Internships (AAPI).

The provision of information is another key service offered by APPIC, and this occurs in multiple ways. The first APPIC newsletter was published in 1980, and it has served as a major communication forum regarding internship and postdoctoral training issues for member and subscriber programs. The APPIC web site (www.appic.org), along with a variety of e-mail news and discussion lists for trainers and students, also aids in the dissemination of information to member and subscriber programs, intern applicants, interns, and postdoctoral residents. The web site currently has sections covering upcoming APPIC events, the directory, APPIC Match, the clearinghouse, training resources for students and trainers, e-mail lists, and problem resolution. Some of the e-mail lists offer the opportunity for discussion of questions related to the internship and postdoctoral residency application process, jobs, and handling of complex training issues, whereas other lists provide information regarding such diverse topics as the APPIC Match, new funding opportunities, and legislative advocacy efforts. More in-depth sharing of information also occurs at biannual membership conferences and biannual continuing education programs.

One service that the APPIC has provided for many years is the handling of formal complaints from APPIC members, subscribers, or students regarding violations of APPIC policies and procedures. The APPIC Standards and Review Committee (ASARC) investigates these complaints and makes recommendations to the APPIC board regarding the appropriate course of action. More recently, an informal problem resolution mechanism has been implemented. This mechanism is available to all relevant constituency groups and offers members, subscribers, and students an opportunity to seek consultation, guidance, and assistance in resolving conflicts and problems related to APPIC policies and procedures and other internship and postdoctoral residency training issues.

The publication of research data relevant to internship and postdoctoral training has been another service offered by the APPIC research committee. Research findings have been made available on such topics as the supply and demand imbalance or balance (Keilin, Thorn, Rodolfa, Constantine, & Kaslow, 2000), the internship matching process (Keilin, 1998, 2000), and the value of formalized postdoctoral training (Logsdon-Conradsen et al., 2001).

There are myriad ways in which the APPIC has been actively involved in the larger national and multinational psychology education, training, and credentialing communities. The APPIC has ongoing liaison relationships with doctoral, internship, and postdoctoral training councils, as well as credentialing organizations. The APPIC participates actively in various interorganizational groups, including the Council of Chairs of Training Councils, Psychology Executive Roundtable, Council of Credentialing Organizations in Professional Psychology, Trilateral Forum on Professional Issues in Psychology, and Commission on Education and Training Leading to Licensure. The APPIC also has two seats on the Committee on Accreditation of the American Psychological Association (APA).

The APPIC has taken a leadership role in national and multinational psychology conferences. In 1992, the APPIC hosted the National Conference on Postdoctoral Training in Professional Psychology in Ann Arbor (Belar et al., 1993). This conference led to the formation of the Interorganizational Council (IOC), of which the APPIC was a member. The IOC utilized the Ann Arbor document as the basis for formulating recommendations for the accreditation of postdoctoral training programs. As a result of the work of the IOC, since 1996 the Committee on Accreditation of the APA has been accrediting postdoctoral residencies. In response to the supply and demand crisis in psychology, which was related in part to the imbalance in the number of intern applicants and internship positions (Dixon & Thorn, 2000; Keilin, 2000; Keilin et al., 2000; Oehlert & Lopez, 1998; Thorn & Dixon, 1999), in 1996 the APPIC and APA cosponsored the National Working Conference on Supply and Demand: Training and Employment Opportunities in Professional Psychology (Pederson et al., 1997). This conference drew attention to the crisis and led to the development and implementation of multiple strategies designed to reduce this imbalance. Current data suggest that, at least with regard to internship positions, this crisis has improved significantly. In November 2002, APPIC took the lead, hosting, with multiple other sponsoring groups, Competencies 2002: Future Directions in Education and Credentialing in Professional Psychology in Scottsdale.

REFERENCES

Belar, C. D., Bieliauskas, L. A., Klepac, R. K., Larsen, K. G., Stigall, T. T., & Zimet, C. N. (1993). National Conference on Postdoctoral Training in Professional Psychology. *American Psychologist, 48,* 1284–1289.

Dixon, K. E., & Thorn, B. E. (2000). Does the internship shortage portend market saturation? 1998 placement data across the four major national training councils. *Professional Psychology: Research and Practice, 31,* 276–280.

Keilin, W. G. (1998). Internship selection 30 years later: An overview of the APPIC matching program. *Professional Psychology: Research and Practice, 29,* 599–603.

Keilin, W. G. (2000). Internship selection in 1999: Was the Association of Psychology Postdoctoral and Internship Centers' match a success? *Professional Psychology: Research and Practice, 31,* 281–287.

Keilin, W. G., Thorn, B. E., Rodolfa, E. R., Constantine, M. G., & Kaslow, N. (2000). Examining the balance of internship supply and demand: 1999 Association of Psychology Postdoctoral and Internship Centers' match implications. *Professional Psychology: Research and Practice, 31,* 288–294.

Logsdon-Conradsen, S., Sirl, K. S., Battle, J., Stapel, J., Anderson, P. L., Ventura-Cook, E., et al. (2001). Formalized postdoctoral fellowships: A national survey of postdoctoral fellows. *Professional Psychology: Research and Practice, 32,* 312–318.

Oehlert, M. E., & Lopez, S. J. (1998). APA-accredited internships: An examination of the supply and demand issue. *Professional Psychology: Research and Practice, 29,* 189–194.

Pederson, S. L., DePiano, F., Kaslow, N. J., Klepac, R. K., Hargrove, D. S., & Vasquez, M. (1997). *Proceedings from the National Working Conference on Supply and Demand: Training and Employment Opportunities in Professional Psychology.* Paper presented at the National Working Conference on Supply and Demand: Training and Employment Opportunities in Professional Psychology, Orlando, FL.

Stedman, J. M. (1989). The history of the APIC selection process. *APIC Newsletter, 14,* 35–43.

Thorn, B. E., & Dixon, K. E. (1999). Issues of supply and demand: A survey of academic, counseling, and clinical programs. *Professional Psychology: Research and Practice, 30,* 198–202.

NADINE J. KASLOW
Emory University School of Medicine

W. GREGORY KEILIN
The University of Texas at Austin

APPLIED RESEARCH

Definition and Background

Applied research uses the scientific method to solve problems and resolve issues of direct relevance to a given societal need or question. Because it is focused on problem solving within society, it is distinct from basic research, which focuses on pursuit of scientific knowledge for the sole purpose of extending scientific understanding and the knowledge base.

Applied psychologists are Ph.D. graduates of universities where they received extensive training in the scientific method. Within this experimental method, the scientist develops an hypothesis based on existing knowledge and observations. The researcher then formulates an experiment to test the hypothesis, conducting systematic empirical observation and data gathering under carefully controlled conditions. Data are analyzed using appropriate, established statistical methods, and the outcome of the analysis determines whether the hypothesis is supported or rejected.

The distinction between applied and basic research forms a continuum rather than a dichotomy. A neuroscientist, for example, may seek to determine whether neuronal lesions in the hippocampus accelerate neuronal sprouting—a basic psychology question to further knowledge about the way the brain functions. As the scientist applies drug treatments to these lesions, she or he may discover a drug that effectively accelerates the sprouting process. This discovery, in turn, may prove to have long-range applicability for patients who have suffered some form of spinal injury and resulting paralysis. Although the beginning point was not to address a societal problem, the findings may prove to have direct societal applicability. On this basic/applied continuum, many outcomes of basic research have proved relevant in addressing given societal problems. The distinction lies in the starting point—whether the societal problem was directly addressed within the research or whether the research sought solely to extend the existing scientific knowledge base.

History

As early as 1908, Hugo Munsterberg stated, "The time for . . . Applied Psychology is surely near, and work has been started from most various sides. Those fields of practical life which come first in question may be said to be education, medicine, art, economics, and law" (Marciano, 1999). Hailed as "the first all-around applied psychologist in America," Munsterberg shaped the field, brought definition to it, and outlined its potential uses in business and industry (Spillman & Spillman, 1993). Equally significant was the pioneering influence of Walter Dill Scott. In the same year that Munsterberg predicted applied psychology's era, Scott was bringing that era still closer to fruition with his book *The Psychology of Advertising.* Seven years later he again pioneered as the first psychologist to receive an appointment as professor of applied psychology at an American university (Carnegie Institute of Technology).

The early branches of applied research reflected closely the industrial orientation of their pioneers. Three of the basic research disciplines gave early birth to applied research offspring. Psychological testing produced personnel selection and classification; experimental psychology parented human factors engineering; and personality/social psychology provided the background setting for work in employee relations. The early history of applied research is, in effect, the history of industrial psychology as well.

World War II Landmark

Prior to the 1940s, the vast majority of psychologists were associated with universities and were conducting basic research. World War II brought with it an unprecedented range of problems that required rapid scientific attention. Not all aviator recruits were created equal in their ability to fly planes, and selection methods were needed to determine those best suited for piloting. Elsewhere in the war scenario, a highly sophisticated Nazi propaganda network challenged our effective counterresponse. American citizens' attitudes toward given food and product consumption needed to be changed in support of the war effort. And returning war veterans brought with them psychological and emotional problems in massive numbers unprecedented within the U.S. mental health community. The pressure of such severe mental and emotional distress in such mammoth proportions confronted a formerly basic research discipline with a real-world clinical problem of incredible magnitude. In these areas and others, applied research came to the front line and needed to respond scientifically, effectively, and rapidly.

Range of Applied Research Settings

The range of applied research settings spans the broad range of society itself. Problems are scientifically addressed in settings ranging from hospitals, clinics, and other human service facilities to the areas of business and industry, courts and correctional institutions, law enforcement and community policing, government and military services, consulting and research organizations, clinical and counseling practice, and community planning.

The problems and questions are as wide-ranging as the settings themselves. Hospitals and clinics may need help in addressing problems that relate to preparing patients and their families for major surgery or working with those who have experienced a specific type of trauma. Business and industry may need assistance in personnel selection for given positions "on the line" or in upper-level management. A given industry may need to determine how to most effectively design a work space within a factory or the controls within an airplane cockpit to minimize fatigue and maximize performance efficiency. Community planners may need to know what elements and architectural designs to build into their communities in order to create living spaces and communities conducive to positive social interaction and emotional health. Schools may need to effectively test student strengths and counsel these students on compatible career matches. All of these and related questions require the knowledge, expertise, and training of applied psychology and applied research.

Basic/Applied Tension

The formally stated goal of the American Psychological Association (APA) gives testimony to the tension and growth that applied research has brought to the discipline. The APA's goal is "to advance psychology as a science, a profession, and as a means of promoting human welfare."

No members of the profession felt this implication more prominently than did clinical psychologists. Unable to meet their applied-research and psychotherapy-orientation needs within the APA, they formed state and national splinter groups (e.g., the American Association of Applied Psychology, Psychologists Interested in the Advancement of Psychotherapy) where their applied research interests and activities could be effectively and meaningfully shared. The fact that splinter groups and their members now live under the APA roof is prominent evidence of the professional growth that has occurred within the APA. It is also a tribute to the efforts of pioneers such as Carl Rogers who devoted extensive time and personal energy to the task of unifying. The threefold goal—science, profession, human welfare—has now attained a visible balance within the professional activity and commitments of the APA.

Concurrently, basic researchers within colleges, universities, and research centers created a mirror image of the earlier splintering. Convinced that the APA had now become a predominantly applied professional organization, they founded the American Psychological Society (APS). The organization's stated purpose, resonant of the APA's, sets the goal "To promote, protect, and advance the interests of scientifically oriented psychology in research, application, and the improvement of human welfare." Many psychologists hold membership in both organizations, and only the future can determine whether the APA and APS will continue as separate identities.

Rapid Growth and Societal Need

The growth and complexity of societal questions and needs have spawned a corresponding growth in applied research. Whereas only a few applied research divisions existed in the American Psychological Association 50 years ago, several applied research divisions exist today. Among them one finds such divisions as The Society for the Psychological Study of Social Issues, Consulting Psychology, The Society for Industrial and Organizational Psychology, and Education/School/Counseling Psychology. Other divisions relate to such areas as public service, military psychology, adult development and aging, rehabilitation, consumer psychology, psychopharmacology and substance abuse, mental retardation and developmental disabilities, and population and environment. The divisions are as vast and wide-ranging as societal needs themselves.

As one views the vast range of areas and divisions it becomes readily apparent that applied research will continue its rapid growth. Within this growth there is the ever-present danger that psychologists may fragment into their respective avenues of applied issues and problems. At the same time, it is well to remember that all are united in their scientific background training and their commitment to the scientific method, empirical observation, and systematic data gathering and analysis.

SUGGESTED READING

Anastasi, A. (1979). *Fields of applied psychology.* New York: McGraw-Hill.

Davidson, M. A. (1977). The scientific/applied debate in psychology: A contribution. *Bulletin of the British Psychological Society, 30,* 273–278.

Hartley, J., & Braithwaite, A. (1989). *Applied psychologist.* New York: Open University Press/Taylor & Francis.

Kazdin, A. (2001). *Behavior modification in applied settings* (6th ed.). Belmont, CA: Wadsworth/Thomson Learning.

Marciano, P. (1999, Nov. 12). The Early History of Industrial/Organizational Psychology. Presented at the Psychology Colloquium at Davidson College, Davidson, North Carolina.

Schultz, D. P., & Schultz, S. E. (1997). *Psychology and work today.* New York: Prentice Hall.

Spillman, J., & Spillman, L. (1993). The rise and fall of Hugo Munsterberg. *Journal of the History and Systems of Psychology, 29,* 322–338.

Edward L. Palmer
Davidson College, Davidson, North Carolina

See also: **Consumer Research**

APPROACH-AVOIDANCE CONFLICT

Approach-avoidance conflict occurs when approach and avoidance tendencies of similar strength are opposed to each other. More generally, "conflict occurs when two or more incompatible reaction tendencies are instigated simultaneously" (Kimble, 1961). Conflict can involve approach-approach, avoidance-avoidance, approach-avoidance or multiple combinations of these. "Approach-avoidance conflict is by far the most important and the most common form of conflict in animal behavior" (McFarland, 1987). Both approach and avoidance can be produced by stimuli that generally do so in a particular species without previous experience. The kind of behavior produced by these "innate" stimuli helps us understand function. Other stimuli produce approach and avoidance only after learning. Their effects can help us understand control mechanisms. Approach-avoidance conflict is currently important for identifying antianxiety drugs (File, 1992) and for analyzing the brain areas involved in human anxiety disorders.

By looking at natural conflict in the wild (ethology), observers have discovered some complex patterns of behavior. Suppose food is close to danger. Animals will approach while they are far from the food (and danger) but will move away again when too close to the danger (and food). They will usually finish up in an ambivalent posture at some intermediate distance (see, e.g., McFarland, 1987). The problem is how to get your lunch without becoming lunch for someone else. The high survival value of solving this problem has led to ritualization of behavior in many conflicts. "Conflict behaviour is [also] often replaced by other seemingly irrelevant, behaviour . . . termed displacement activity" (McFarland, 1987). So conflict can produce a mixture of approach and avoidance behavior. In a simple robot this mixture would result in unending oscillation at an intermediate distance, but it often produces a variety of complicated and sometimes apparently bizarre behaviors. These behaviors can resolve the conflict by providing new information or by allowing the animal to ignore an insoluble problem and get on with other business.

Analysis of approach-avoidance conflict in the laboratory provides some explanation of the ethological observations. In 1944, Miller (Miller, 1944; Kimble, 1961; Gray, 1987) proposed a model, the details of which have since been essentially confirmed. Both the tendency to approach a desired object and the tendency to avoid a feared object increase as the object gets closer to the animal. This has been measured in terms of the strength with which the animal will pull toward or away from the object (Gray, 1987). The avoidance gradient is steeper than the approach gradient. Thus, at large distances the animal approaches, whereas at short distances it avoids, and at equilibrium conflict behavior is observed (see Gray, 1987, for cases in which the avoidance gradient may be reduced).

Recently, ethoexperimental analysis (Blanchard & Blanchard, 1989) has extended this picture to include temporal as well as spatial distance. (Ethoexperimental analysis involves the use of ethological measures and experimental manipulations within an ecologically consistent laboratory setting.) When a cat is present, rats avoid an arena containing food. When there is no sign of a cat, rats enter the arena and eat the food. When a cat has recently been present or when the smell of a cat is present, the rats engage in an approach-avoidance oscillation accompanied by risk analysis behavior. Here, extensive assessment of the environment and the use of a stretch-attend posture may be seen not as ritualization or displacement activity but as behavior that will actively resolve the conflict (in favor of approach or avoidance) by gathering new information.

Blanchard and Blanchard (1989) ascribe pure avoidance to fear and distinguish this from risk analysis in the presence of threat, which they ascribe to anxiety. The implied relation between these behaviors and equivalent human clinical dysfunction is supported by the fact that the former are sensitive to antipanic agents and the latter to antianxiety agents (Blanchard, Griebel, Henrie, & Blanchard, 1997). Much conventional experimental analysis suggests that avoidance within an approach-avoidance conflict (resulting from either fear or frustration) is sensitive to antianxiety drug action, whereas pure avoidance (resulting from fear or frustration) is not (Gray, 1977). As with the ethological analysis, this suggests that approach-avoidance conflict involves more than a simple balance between approach and avoidance. It involves special mechanisms to produce ritualized behavior and displacement activity. The drug data show that conflict increases avoidance tendencies. In the wild, this would produce a more "safety-first" attitude than if approach and avoidance were simply allowed to sum arithmetically.

A shift toward risk taking in approach-avoidance conflict with little change in pure approach or pure avoidance is characteristic not only of antianxiety drug action but also of septal and hippocampal lesions. Thus, antianxiety drugs appear to change approach-avoidance conflict by impairing hippocampal function (Gray, 1982). The septo-hippocampal system appears to receive information about approach and avoidance tendencies, to detect conflicts, and (particularly with approach-avoidance conflict) to increase avoidance tendencies (Gray & McNaughton, 2000). Given the previous distinction made by Blanchard and Blanchard (1989) between fear and anxiety, this theory holds that Generalized Anxiety Disorder (but not simple phobia or panic) involves hyperactivity of the septo-hippocampal system (McNaughton, 1997). This hyperactivity can be viewed as increasing the level of fear (or of anticipation of loss of reward). It thus moves the point of intersection of the approach and avoidance gradients further from sources of threat.

Approach-avoidance conflict, then, has been under detailed investigation for many decades; a clear picture is now emerging of its structure, function, and psychological properties. Dysfunction of the mechanisms controlling approach-avoidance conflict appears fundamental to Anxiety Disorders. Detailed neural mechanisms, and sites of action of therapeutic drugs on those neural mechanisms, are now being discovered as substrates of the psychological processes involved (Crestani et al., 1999). Of particular cause for optimism, ethology, behavior analysis, cognitive psychology, psychopharmacology, and behavioral neuroscience appear to be combining to produce a single, coherent, integrated, story in this area.

REFERENCES

Blanchard, R. J., & Blanchard, D. C. (1989). Antipredator defensive behaviors in a visible burrow system. *Journal of Comparative Psychology, 103*(1), 70–82.

Blanchard, R. J., Griebel, G., Henrie, J. A., & Blanchard, D.C. (1997). Differentiation of anxiolytic and panicolytic drugs by effects on rat and mouse defense test batteries. *Neuroscience and Biobehavioral Reviews, 21*(6), 783–789.

Crestani, F., Lorez, M., Baer, K., Essrich, C., Benke, D., Laurent, J. P., et al. (1999). Decreased $GABA_A$-receptor clustering results in enhanced anxiety and a bias for threat cues. *Nature Neuroscience, 2*(9), 833–839.

File, S. E. (1992). Behavioural detection of anxiolytic action. In J. M. Elliott, D. J. Heal, & C. A. Marsden (Eds.), *Experimental approaches to anxiety and depression* (pp. 25–44). London: Wiley.

Gray, J. A. (1977). Drug effects on fear and frustration: Possible limbic site of action of minor tranquilizers. In L. L. Iversen, S. D. Iversen, & S. H. Snyder (Eds.), *Handbook of psychopharmacology: Vol. 8. Drugs, neurotransmitters and behavior* (pp. 433–529). New York: Plenum Press.

Gray, J. A. (1982). *The neuropsychology of anxiety: An enquiry into the functions of the septo-hippocampal system* (1st ed.). Oxford, UK: Oxford University Press.

Gray, J. A. (1987). *The psychology of fear and stress.* London: Cambridge University Press.

Gray, J. A., & McNaughton, N. (2000). *The neuropsychology of anxiety: An enquiry into the functions of the septo-hippocampal system* (2nd ed.). Oxford, UK: Oxford University Press.

Kimble, G. A. (1961). *Hilgard and Marquis' conditioning and learning* (2nd ed.). New York: Appleton-Century-Crofts.

McFarland, D. (1987). *The Oxford companion to animal behaviour.* Oxford, UK: Oxford University Press.

McNaughton, N. (1997). Cognitive dysfunction resulting from hippocampal hyperactivity: A possible cause of anxiety disorder. *Pharmacology, Biochemistry and Behavior, 56,* 603–611.

Miller, N. E. (1944). Experimental studies of conflict. In J. M. Hunt (Ed.), *Personality and the behavioural disorders.* New York: Ronald.

Neil McNaughton
University of Otago, Dunedin, New Zealand

APTITUDE TESTING, IMPORTANCE OF

Aptitude testing involves estimating an individual's potential to perform a criterion of interest on the basis of measures of that individual's knowledge, skills, abilities, and other attributes. Such testing is important for selection efforts, such as determining who has the greatest likelihood of excelling in a school, career, or training program. Aptitude testing also is central to personnel classification—that is, matching individuals to jobs or job tasks on the basis of aptitudes. Since many aptitudes exhibit developmental change, aptitude testing also is important for validating theories of the nature and course of such change (English, 1998).

Assessment can be *concurrent,* in which case the aptitude test, or *predictor,* and the outside criterion against which the predictor is being validated occur at the same point in time. The assessment can be *predictive.* In these efforts, the predictor occurs in the present, and the criterion will occur in the future. Alternatively, the assessment can be *postdictive,* as when the predictor occurs in the present, and the criterion has occurred in the past.

The results of aptitude assessment can fruitfully be linked to interventions in educational, occupational, and clinical settings (Sternberg, Torff, & Grigorenko, 1998). In addition to measuring learning, tests can be *agents* of learning. Such *learning tests* are designed to foster learning during assessment (Dempster, 1997).

Issues In Aptitude Test Design and Development

Researchers are interested in elucidating (1) relationships between aptitudes and the criterion measures that the aptitudes predict, (2) types of aptitudes being measured and interrelationships between the aptitudes, (3) the manner in which the aptitudes are measured, and (4) the psychometric properties of tests in given testing sessions. Psychometric issues include standardizability, reliability, validity, and adverse impact.

Test administration issues include the time available for testing, resources and technology needed for administration and scoring of aptitude tests, and adaptability of tests and testing equipment for different test sites. *Test utility* issues include ease of administration, costs associated with training test administrators, maintaining test sites and equipment, and preparing test materials. *Implementation* of testing programs that have broad applicability in a timely manner remains an important challenge. Furthermore, tests should be designed so that the resulting information, when used in selection and classification efforts, minimizes attrition.

Conceptions of Aptitude

Theoretical notions regarding the origins of aptitude guide approaches to aptitude testing and directly address the above issues (Dillon, 1997; Flanagan, McGrew, & Ortiz, 2000). Performance on aptitude tests may result from a range of biological, cognitive, and social factors including (1) activation of competence, (2) trainability, (3) changes in learning and development resulting from mediated learning experiences, (4) guided experience, and (5) direct experience (Gottfredson, 1997).

Aptitude Testing Framework

Testing paradigms can be considered along four dimensions: aptitudes, methods, measures, and timing.

Aptitude Dimensions

The level of specificity of predictors, domains tapped, and the prior-knowledge demands of aptitude tests are all important factors in aptitude testing. Aptitude dimensions range from neurophysiological, electrophysiological, and perceptual processes to information-processing components (Dillon, 1997) and metacomponents (Sternberg, 1998; Sternberg, Torff, & Grigorenko, 1998); knowledge and reasoning aptitudes (Dillon & Vineyard, 1999); school subject aptitudes (Jacobs, 1998; Skehan, 1998; Sparks & Ganschow, 1996); sociocultural attributes (Lopez, 1997); personality, temperament, attitude, and motivational attributes; and interpersonal attributes such as social problem-solving aptitudes, including environmental adaptation aptitudes.

Information-processing theory and methodologies have enabled researchers to decompose reasoning and other IQ test-type tasks into their distinct information-processing components, such as encoding, rule inference, rule application, and confirmation. Researchers have studied the functioning of these component processes during complex thinking and problem solving (e.g., Dillon, 1997; Sternberg, 2000), and they have developed methods and measures to test attributes that occur in everyday life, such as tacitly acquired knowledge (e.g., John & Mashna, 1997). Considerable attention has been paid to issues in special education testing (Carver & Clark, 1998; Forness, Keogh, & MacMillan, 1998; Greenspan & McGrew, 1996) and aptitude testing in gifted education programs (Sternberg, 1998). In addition to enhancing understanding of one's possession of various abilities, research in cognitive flexibility has helped scientists to understand the manner in which individuals select and deploy tactics as the demands of a task or situation warrant (Dillon & Vineyard, 1999; Fox, 1997).

Methods of Test Administration and Measures Taken From Tests

Methods of test administration and data collection include computerized adaptive testing, dynamic testing (Dillon, 1997; Sternberg & Grigorenko, 2002), paper-and-pencil testing, observational data collection, document analysis, portfolio assessment, and job sample measures. Conceptions of aptitude differ in the nature of the databases on which the different models rest. Some researchers use complex and extensive statistical methods to uncover mental structures and processes. Other researchers base their conceptions of aptitude on interpretations of psychological observations and experimental findings. Still other researchers employ psychophysiological, neurophysiological, electrophysiological, or information-processing paradigms, sometimes coupled with experimental manipulations. Finally, some researchers use *curriculum-based assessment* (CBA) or *performance assessment* (PA) paradigms, which boast connections between assessment, curriculum development, and instruction (Cantor, 1997; Elliot, Braden, & White, 2001; Elliott, Kratochwill, & McKevitt, 2001).

Timing

Aptitude tests can be given to determine who has the highest probability of succeeding in a particular education or training program. Aptitude tests also can be given prior to initial job selection. Subsequent to job selection, testing is used for the purpose of classification to particular jobs. Testing also is undertaken for job enhancement, such as for retention, promotion, or selection to advanced training programs.

Aptitude models are validated against a variety of school and occupational arenas. Common criterion measures include performance in (1) high school and college, (2) military training, (3) medical school preparation courses and medical school, and (4) complex workplace activities.

Testing in the Twenty-First Century

According to Kyllonen (1996), researchers should develop testing systems that are broad-based, precise, quick, and implemented in a short time frame. In addition, important technology, including computer delivery; item-generation technology; multidimensional adaptive technology; comprehensive cognitive aptitudes and abilities measurement; time-parameterized testing; and latent factor-centered design should be utilized.

REFERENCES

Cantor, A. S. (1997). The future of intelligence testing in the schools. *The School Psychology Review, 26,* 255–261.

Carver, R. P., & Clark, S. W. (1998). Investigating reading disabilities using the rauding diagnostic system. *Journal of Learning Disabilities, 31,* 453–471, 481.

Dempster, F. N. (1997). Using tests to promote classroom learning. In R. F. Dillon (Ed.), *Handbook on testing* (pp. 332–346). Westport, CN: Greenwood.

Dillon, R. F. (Ed.). (1997). *Handbook on testing.* Westport, CN: Greenwood.

Dillon, R. F., & Vineyard, G. M. (1999). *Cognitive flexibility: Further validation of flexible combination.* U.S. Illinois. Accession No: ED435727.

Dillon, R. F., & Vineyard, G. M. (1999). Convergent and discriminant validation of flexible combination ability. *Resources in Education.*

Elliott, S. N., Braden, J. P., & White, J. L. (2001). *Assessing one and all.* College Station: Texas A&M University Press.

Elliott, S. N., Kratochwill, T. R., & McKevitt, B. C. (2001). Experimental analysis of the effects of testing accommodations on the scores of students with and without disabilities. *Journal of School Psychology, 39*(1), 3–24.

English, Y. N. (1998). Uncovering students' analytic, practical, and creative intelligences: One school's application of Sternberg's triarchic theory. *School Administrator, 55,* 28–29.

Flanagan, D. P., McGrew, K. S., & Ortiz, S. O. (2000). *The Wechsler Intelligence Scales and Gf-Gc theory: A contemporary interpretive approach.* Boston: Allyn & Bacon.

Forness, S. R., Keogh, B. K., & MacMillan, D. L. (1998). What is so special about IQ? The limited explanatory power of abilities in the real world of special education. *Remedial and Special Education, 19,* 315–322.

Fox, C. M. (1997). A confirmatory factor analysis of the structure of tacit knowledge in nursing. *Journal of Nursing Education, 36,* 459–466.

Gottfredson, L. S. (1997). Why g matters: The complexity of everyday life. *Intelligence, 24,* 79–132.

Greenspan, S., & McGrew, K. S. (1996). Response to Mathias and Nettelbeck on the structure of competence: Need for theory-based methods to test theory-based questions. *Research in Developmental Disabilities, 17,* 145–160.

Jacobs, E. L. (1998). KIDTALK: A computerized language screening test. *Journal of Computing in Childhood Education, 9,* 113–131.

John, B. E., & Mashna, M. M. (1997). Evaluating a multimedia authoring tool. *Journal of the American Society for Information Science, 48,* 1005–1022.

Kyllonen, P. (1996). Smart testing. In R. F. Dillon (Ed.), *Handbook on testing* (pp. 347–368). Westport, CT: Greenwood.

Lopez, R. (1997). The practical impact of current research and issues in intelligence test interpretation and use for multicultural populations. *The School Psychology Review, 26,* 249–254.

Skehan, P. (1998). *A cognitive approach to language learning.* Oxford, UK: Oxford University Press.

Sparks, R. L., & Ganschow, L. (1996). Teachers' perceptions of students' foreign language academic skills and affective characteristics. *The Journal of Educational Research, 89,* 172–185.

Sternberg, R. J. (1998). Teaching and assessing for successful intelligence. *School Administrator, 55,* 26–27, 30–31.

Sternberg, R. J. (2000). *Handbook of intelligence.* New York: Cambridge University Press.

Sternberg, R. J., & Grigorenko, E. L. (2002). *Dynamic testing.* New York: Cambridge University Press.

Sternberg, R. J., Torff, B., & Grigorenko, E. L. (1998). Teaching triarchically improves school achievement. *Journal of Experimental Psychology, 90*(3), 1–11.

Ronna F. Dillon
Southern Illinois University

ARCHETYPES

Carl Jung introduced the term *archetype* into psychological theory, and he is primarily responsible for the development of the concept to which it refers. Jung recognized two basic layers in the unconscious—the personal unconscious, whose contents are derived from present lifetime experience, and the collective unconscious, whose contents are inherited and essentially universal within the species. The collective unconscious consists of archetypes. Jung described these as primordial images that have existed from the remotest times, but images that lack clear content. Their specific content as realized images is supplied by the material of conscious experience. Thus, the archetype as such is an empty form that must be inferred, or derived by abstraction, from a class of experienced images or symbols.

Jung (1969) noted that the term was first used by Philo Judaeus and later appeared in the writings of Irenaeus and Dionysius the Areopagite. In such ancient uses, it had a meaning close to that of Plato's *ideas.* A similar concept recurs over the centuries in idealistic philosophy and was emphasized by Romantic philosophers of the nineteenth century.

Jung acknowledged an intellectual lineage that can be traced to Plato, but he contended that his use of the term *archetype* is more empirical and less metaphysical than the use of the same or corresponding terms by idealistic philosophers. He arrived at the concept initially through a study of psychotic patients and augmented his understanding through a more comprehensive study of symbol systems. To the extent that he used experience as a springboard for theory, Jung can be regarded as more Aristotelian than Platonic. Yet, to the extent that Jung's theory of archetypes is valid, it leads to the paradoxical conclusion that only a limited empiricism is possible. For Jung, the archetypes are the most fundamental ingredients of the whole psyche. They are the forms that underlie everything we perceive, imagine, and think. Through progressive accumulation and elaboration of specific contents, the archetype becomes manifest in the image and then in the conscious idea, and even the basic concepts of philosophy and science can be regarded as ultimately rooted in archetypal forms. Thus, while Jung's concept of the archetype may be partly empirical, it necessarily rests on its own archetypal base.

Jung noted that this concept is akin to that of the instinct. Each term refers to an inborn predisposition, and in each case it is a predisposition that must be inferred from a certain class of effects. The term *instinct* refers to a predisposition to act in a certain way, whereas *archetype* refers to a predisposition toward a certain kind of "psychic apprehension." One might surmise that in both cases we are dealing with a tendency that has evolved and become universal within a species because it has survival value. Jung, however, did not provide a biological rationale for the archetype, and he considered it rather futile to speculate on its origin. He merely suggested that if the archetype ever "originated," its origin must have coincided with that of the species.

Jung began to develop the archetype concept during his early work at the Burghölzli Hospital, where he observed that some of his relatively uneducated psychotic patients experienced universal religious and mythological symbols. In many instances it was clear that the patient could not have learned of the symbol through formal study, and the appearance of the symbol in the patient's ideation or imagery had to represent a spontaneous eruption of unconscious material not derived from experience during the present lifetime. Jung subsequently explored the archetypal realm through an intensive examination of his own dreams and waking fantasies. He developed a method of "active imagination," by which he was able to secure a spontaneous flow of dreamlike material in a waking state. He studied religious symbolism, mythology, tribal lore, and such occult disciplines as alchemy in quest of evidence of universal motifs. Thus, his conclusions can be said to rest on an extremely broad base of observational data.

The archetypes to which Jung devoted the greatest amount of attention in his writings include the shadow, the anima and animus, the wise old man, the magna mater (or great earth mother), the child, and the self (Jung, 1968). Each of these archetypes collects a great deal of associated content, which varies according to the experience of the individual and colors a large portion of our total experience. The behavioral, intellectual, and perceptual qualities over which we fail to develop much conscious control remain with us as a kind of unexamined dark side and become associated with the shadow. The feminine qualities that a man fails to realize consciously in himself become associated with his anima, while the unrealized masculine qualities of the woman become associated with her animus. Thus, each archetype becomes the core of a system of content that varies a bit from one individual to another.

The archetypes noted above tend to be experienced in personified form. They may appear as figures in our dreams, and they provide the source of such cultural symbols as gods and goddesses. They also enter extensively into our interpersonal experience, for we frequently project them onto other people. Each of these archetypes can be expressed in a great variety of personifications. A given anima image, for example, may be positive or negative and may emphasize any of a number of possible qualities—sexuality, beauty, wisdom, spirituality, moral virtue, destructiveness, and so forth. There are other archetypes, which Jung (1969) called archetypes of transformation, that do not appear in a personal form. They are expressed in many of the situations, places, implements, and events of our dreams, and they govern corresponding motifs in folklore. Jung believed he had identified the most important archetypes. Yet, if his basic assumptions are valid, it may be assumed that the total number of archetypes is indefinitely large and that an exhaustive inventory is not feasible.

REFERENCES

Jung, C. G. (1968). *The collected works of C. G. Jung: Vol. 9, Pt. II. Aion: Researches into the phenomenology of the self.* Princeton, NJ: Princeton University Press.

Jung, C. G. (1969). *The collected works of C. G. Jung: Vol. 9, Pt. I. The archetypes and the collective unconscious.* Princeton, NJ: Princeton University Press.

Richard Welton Coan
University of Arizona

ASIAN PSYCHOLOGIES

Within the new global context of our lives, Western psychology will need to be repositioned as one of many psychologies worldwide, rather than as the only or dominant psychology.

—Marsella (1998, p. 1286)

Overview

Until recently, Western psychologists assumed that their own psychologies were the only ones worthy of serious consideration, but this unfortunate attitude is changing rapidly.

We will limit discussion here to four Asian psychologies—the Yogic and Buddhist psychologies of India and the Taoist and neo-Confucian systems of China. These also display significant commonalities and have therefore been referred to as aspects of the "perennial wisdom," "perennial psychology," or "consciousness disciplines."

Researchers increasingly describe development as proceeding through three major stages: preconventional, conventional, and postconventional (or prepersonal, personal, and transpersonal). Psychotherapies address three correlative levels of health: pathology reduction, existential issues, and transpersonal concerns. Western psychologies have developed sophisticated prepersonal and personal maps and therapies. By contrast, Asian psychologies focus almost exclusively on existential and transpersonal concerns and offer little on early development or severe psychopathology.

Personality

Asian psychologies both derive from and lead to ideas about human nature, health, pathology, and potential that in certain ways differ significantly from traditional Western views. We can summarize the Asian claims under the headings of consciousness, identity, motivation, psychopathology, and psychological health.

Consciousness

In *The Varieties of Religious Experience* William James (1958, p. 298) concluded:

> Our normal waking consciousness . . . is but one special type of consciousness, whilst all about it, parted from it by the filmiest of screens, there lie potential forms of consciousness entirely different. . . . No account of the universe in its totality can be final which leaves these other forms of consciousness quite disregarded.

Asian psychologies agree completely. They recognize multiple states and that some states of consciousness may be associated with specific functions and abilities not available in our usual state. Perceptual sensitivity, attention, and the sense of identity, as well as affective, cognitive, and perceptual processes may all vary with the state of consciousness in precise and predictable ways.

"Higher" states possess the effective functions of the usual states, plus heightened perceptions, insights, or affects outside the realm of day-to-day experience. If higher states exist, then our usual state must be suboptimal. This is exactly the claim of Asian psychologies. They argue that our usual state of consciousness is underdeveloped, constricted, and dreamlike, to a remarkable but usually unrecognized degree. Thus the normal person is seen as "asleep" or "dreaming." When the dream is especially painful or disruptive, it becomes a nightmare and is recognized as psychopathology. However, since the vast majority of the population "dreams," the true state of affairs goes unrecognized. When individuals permanently disidentify or "awaken" from "dreams," they are able to recognize the true nature of both their former state and that of the population. This awakening, known variously as *wu, moksha* liberation, or enlightenment, is a central aim of Asian psychologies.

In part, this is an extension of traditional Western psychology, which has long recognized a broad range of perceptual distortions, unrecognized by naive subjects. But Asian psychologies assert that these distortions are more pervasive and harmful than usually recognized but that these distortions can be recognized and reduced by specific mental training and that doing so fosters psychological development to transconventional, transpersonal levels.

Identity

Western psychologists usually assume that our natural and optimal identity is "egoic," implying a sense of self inextricably linked to the body and separate from other people and things. Asian psychologies suggest that our egoic identity is unnecessarily constricted, resulting in egocentricity, selfishness, and suffering. They also suggest that a more mature, expansive identity is possible and that this claim is directly testable by anyone willing to cultivate perceptual sensitivity via meditative-Yogic practices.

Asian psychologies also suggest that existential and psychoanalytic claims about the impossibility of resolving psychodynamic conflicts and existential givens such as finitude, meaning, and suffering are indeed correct at the egoic level. Existentialists might be said to have rediscovered part of the Buddha's first Noble Truth: that unsatisfactoriness is part of life and (for the untrained mind) is accompanied by angst. However, the Buddha went further, and in the remaining three Noble Truths pointed to a crucial cause of suffering (addiction or craving) and the means for escaping it.

Motivation

Asian psychologies, especially Yogic psychology, tend to see motives as hierarchically organized in a manner analogous to that suggested by Abraham Maslow (1971) and Ken Wilber (2002). However, Asian psychologies emphasize the importance of "higher motives," such as self-transcendence and selfless service, which are rarely recognized in Western psychology.

One motivational factor that is given great emphasis and viewed as a major determinant of pathology and suffering is attachment (or addiction). From this perspective, psychological suffering is a feedback signal, indicating the existence of attachments and the need to let them go.

Attachment invariably gives rise to its mirror image: aversion. Whereas attachment says "I must have something in order to be happy," aversion says "I must avoid something in order to be happy." Aversion is said to underlie anger and aggression.

Psychopathology

The Asian view of psychopathology centers on three ideas: immaturity, unhealthy mental qualities, and the "three poisons" of greed, hatred, and delusion.

Asian psychologies regard our usual adult state as a form of arrested development and would agree with Abraham Maslow (1968, p. 16) that "it seems more and more clear that what we call 'normal' in psychology is really a psychopathology of the average, so undramatic and so widely spread that we don't even notice it ordinarily." From this perspective, development has proceeded from preconventional to conventional but has then faltered and ground to a premature halt. At this stage the mind operates suboptimally, many potentials and capacities remain unrealized, and various unhealthy mental qualities flourish.

These unhealthy qualities include, for example, attentional difficulties such as distractibility and agitation, cognitive deficits such as mindlessness, disruptive emotions such as anger and jealousy, and problematic motives such as sloth and selfishness. The most fundamental pathological factors are sometimes said to be the three poisons of delusion, attachment and aversion.

Psychological Health

The Asian ideal of health extends beyond pathology reduction to encompass existential and transpersonal concerns. Health is defined primarily in terms of three changes: (1) the reduction of unhealthy qualities, especially the three poisons, (2) cultivation of healthy qualities, and (3) maturation to transpersonal stages of development.

Asian psychologies emphasize that specific healthy mental qualities must be deliberately cultivated to ensure psychological health and maturity, for example, concentration, compassion, and mindfulness. The quality of mindfulness—precise awareness of the nature of the stimuli being observed—might be regarded as a highly developed form of the Freudian "observing ego."

Psychological health also includes maturation to transpersonal stages and capacities. These include, for example, postformal operational cognition and wisdom, postconventional morality, transpersonal emotions such as encompassing love and compassion, and metamotives such as self-transcendence and selfless service.

Asian Disciplines and Therapies

The applied side of Asian psychologies focuses on disciplines and therapies designed to foster psychological and spiritual development and well-being. The best-known disciplines are meditation and yoga. Meditation refers to a family of techniques that train awareness and attention in order to bring mental processes under greater voluntary control. This control is used to reduce destructive mental qualities; to cultivate beneficial qualities such as concentration, compassion, and insight; and to enhance psychological and spiritual growth and well-being. Yogas are more inclusive disciplines that encompass meditation, ethics, lifestyle modification, body postures, breath control, and intellectual study.

In addition to specific meditative and Yogic techniques, Asian systems, like contemplative traditions around the world, emphasize seven central practices and goals.

1. Redirecting motivation and moving up the hierarchy of needs, especially by reducing attachment and aversion
2. Transforming emotions, especially reducing problematic ones such as anger and fear, and cultivating beneficial emotions such as love and compassion
3. Living ethically so as to reduce destructive mental qualities such as greed and attack, and to foster helpful qualities such as empathy and generosity
4. Developing concentration
5. Enhancing awareness
6. Fostering wisdom
7. Increasing generosity and altruism

To give just two examples of Asian techniques and resultant skills—which until recently Western psychologists considered impossible—consider the cultivation of love and lucid dreaming. Several meditations are specifically designed to cultivate the encompassing, unconditional love known as *bhakti* in the East and *agape* in the West. Dream yoga is a 2,000-year-old discipline for developing lucid dreaming: the ability to know one is dreaming while still asleep. Advanced practitioners claim to maintain awareness and continue meditation and mind training throughout the night, a claim now supported by electroencephalographic studies. These capacities hint at the remarkable abilities, developmental possibilities, and powers of mind—some as yet unrecognized by Western psychologists—that Asian psychologies have discovered in their 3,000-year-long exploration of our inner universe. The Swiss psychiatrist Medard Boss (1963, p. 188), one of the first Westerners to examine Asian practices, suggested that compared with the extent of Yogic self-exploration "even the best Western training analysis is not much more than an introductory course." However, even modest amounts of practice can produce significant psychological, physiological, and therapeutic changes, as several hundred experiments and clinical studies have shown.

Because they focus on different aspects of health and development, Asian and Western psychologies may be partly complementary. One of the major challenges for the twenty-first century will be to synthesize Asian and Western systems into an overarching integral psychology that honors and includes both. The writings of Ken Wilber provide the best example to date of this possibility.

REFERENCES

Boss, M. (1963) *A psychiatrist discovers India* (p. 188). New York: Basic Books.

James, W. (1958). *The varieties of religious experience.* New York: New American Library.

Marsella, A. (1998). Toward a "Global Community Psychology: Meeting the needs of a changing world." *American Psychologist, 43,* 1282–1291.

Maslow, A. (1971). *The farther reaches of human nature.* New York: Viking.

Wilber, K. (2002). *Integral psychology: Consciousness, spirit, psychology, therapy.* Boston: Shambala.

Roger Walsh
University of California College of Medicine

ASSERTIVENESS TRAINING

Assertiveness training (AT) was introduced by Andrew Salted, developed by Joseph Wolpe, and popularized by Wolpe and Lazarus. Rarely used alone, AT is used most frequently as one aspect of a broader therapeutic program. The goals of AT include (1) increased awareness of personal rights; (2) differentiating between nonassertiveness, assertiveness, aggressiveness, and passive-aggressiveness; and (3) learning both verbal and nonverbal assertiveness skills. Assertiveness skills involve saying "no"; asking for favors or making requests; expressing positive and negative feelings; and initiating, continuing, and terminating conversations.

Assertiveness training, as generally practiced, requires determining the specific situations where the client characteristically behaves maladaptively, that is, either unassertively, aggressively, or passive-aggressively. While self-report inventories are available for assessing the client's general responses to situations that require assertiveness, most contemporary assertiveness inventories are constructed to be situation specific. Behaviorally, though it is desirable to observe the client in the actual problematic situation, it is routine to role-play the unassertive or passive interaction with the therapist.

If assessment demonstrates that the client is always unassertive, aggressive, or passive-aggressive, then more traditional therapies are recommended. However, if there are specific troublesome situations where the client could perform with increased assertiveness, AT is indicated. Clients are often resistant to AT because of cultural, familial, or religious proscriptions against being assertive. These reservations require careful consideration and discussion, if AT is to proceed efficiently.

There is no universally formulated program called Assertiveness Training. The personal predilections of the therapist determine the course of therapy. However, the following five methods are commonly utilized to generate increased assertiveness in specific situations. First, *response acquisition learning* involves increasing assertiveness through modeling and behavioral instruction. The focus is on the verbal, nonverbal, cognitive, and affective components of assertiveness. Second, *response reproduction* includes performing the new responses using role-playing, behavior rehearsal, or response practice. Third, *response refining* uses shaping and strengthening the new behavior with appropriate feedback and coaching. Fourth, *cognitive restructuring* challenges irrational beliefs that interfere with assertiveness and generates cognitions that promote assertive behavior. Finally, *generalization instruction* involves attempting new behavior in vivo and encourages transfer to new situations. The above procedures are continued until the client demonstrates appropriate assertiveness. Typically, there are five steps in AT: (1) recognize your own feelings (e.g., disappointment), (2) recognize the other person's feelings, (3) reflect the other person's feelings, (4) express your own feelings, and (5) request a behavior or behavioral change from the other person.

Early formulations about the theoretical basis for AT assumed either an anxiety-produced response inhibition or an unassertive response skills deficit. Current research has established the importance of cognitive and information-processing factors in generating assertive behavior. Cognitions that limit assertion include unassertive irrational beliefs, inappropriately stringent self-evaluative standards, and faulty expectations concerning the consequences of behaving assertively.

Recent AT research has focused on reducing anxiety in psychiatric patients, providing stress management training, using AT in school settings to reduce aggressive behavior, enhancing social skills training, developing sex education programs, and increasing self-confidence in college students. Assertiveness training is also being used in Behavioral Health and Behavioral Medicine programs for lowering blood pressure, smoking cessation, and anger control.

Chet H. Fischer
Radford University

ASSISTIVE TECHNOLOGY

Definition

Assistive technology (AT) is anything scientifically or technically manufactured that serves to assist or improve normal function. It can include manufactured items that serve humans, ranging from clothing that enhances functioning in cold weather to airplanes that speed movement from one place to another. The term is not restricted to its use by people with disabilities (PWDs) for technological devices or programs that are useful to them. However, the field of rehabilitation of people with physical or sensory disabilities has co-opted the term to some extent to refer to utilization by PWDs without actually defining the nature or the extent of the disability. Thus the term, as used in rehabilitation, includes all types of devices and programs, regardless of complexity or technical level, from eyeglasses to mechanical ventilators and from computer-assisted communications to programmed heart monitors, that may improve the physical and psychosocial conditions of a PWD. According to the U.S. Technology Act, reauthorized in 1998, AT is defined as "[a]ny item, piece of equipment or product system, whether acquired commercially off the shelf, modified, or customized, that is used to increase, maintain, or improve functional capabilities of individuals with disabilities." While the act refers only to the functional capabilities of AT, the thrust of research by psychologists into AT in rehabilitation has been AT's psychosocial impact.

The interest of psychology in AT is twofold. The first is to study the effects of AT on the life of its consumer, especially the effects on psychosocial aspects such as quality of life (QOL). The second is in outcome research, especially to explore reasons for the adoption of assistive devices and for the high level of their abandonment.

Quality of Life

Enhancement of QOL is an accepted goal of rehabilitation, and its study is becoming very important in the field of rehabilitation psychology. Originally, QOL was an area that had been dominated by economists, sociologists, and some other social scientists. The first public mention of QOL was in a speech by an early spokesperson for President Johnson in which it was stated:

> The task of the Great Society is to ensure our people the environment, the capacities, and the social structures that will give them a meaningful chance to pursue their individual happiness. Thus the Great Society is concerned not with how much, but with how good—not with the quantity of the goods, but with the quality of our lives.

But a close reading of the speech suggests that what was really discussed was *standard of life* rather than its quality, as noted in the emphasis on the interaction between the person and the environment. In fact, the people assigned to assess whether people were getting what was being promised were economists and sociologists, and they defined QOL in terms of the nature of the environment and the assets that people possessed. Thus they would include "domains," such as "number and quality of parks in the district," "the number of robberies in the community," and "the number of television sets in the home." Different people chose to include different domains in their final indices of QOL, and so the index varied with the researcher. Although this seemed to them to be an acceptable way of conceptualizing and measuring QOL, it was rejected by others in different countries who argued that one could have an equally high QOL without the greater abundance of goods and conditions found in the United States. In fact, comparisons of QOL of people in different communities generally failed to indicate significant differences.

Psychologists also argued that one should avoid concentration on being "well-off" and focus on a concern of "well-being." Furthermore, they argued that personal satisfaction with one's standard of life was the key to understanding the meaning of QOL and that one might possess very little but be satisfied or dissatisfied with whatever one had.

If we are to understand the impact of AT on a consumer, we must be aware that there are different impacts, each of which depends on the nature of the consumer and that of the device or program. The best analogy is probably that of the pyramid postulated by Maslow to illustrate the hierarchy of needs. In the bottom levels, he argued, are found the biological needs, and these must be gratified before the next levels become potent. The middle levels are the person-environment interactions in which the individual strives to gain reward from the surrounding world, including both external and internal environments. Finally, at the peak, which Maslow termed *self-actualization,* is the need for inner satisfaction from life as a whole and the search for fulfillment of the needs for satisfaction in life experience.

Similarly, AT impacts on comparable levels. At the lowest level we find that the impact is biological and serves to extend life biologically. This can be termed *quantity of life.* Mechanical ventilation for people with ALS disease is an example of where AT has its strongest impact. At the intermediate level one finds that the impact is mainly on the standard of life. Wheelchairs, for example, impact on consumers so that they can interact more easily with the environment. At the peak of the pyramid, the impact is on the QOL, a term that should be reserved to denote the inner satisfaction derived from the assessment of the whole life process. Consumers find that by utilizing AT they are more satisfied with their lives and have greater self-confidence in their actions. Although AT can impact on all three levels, most AT devices impact on both the standard of life and the QOL levels.

Measurement of Impact on QOL

Change in QOL is an outcome variable that has import on the acceptance or abandonment of an AT device or program. The measurement of impact on QOL therefore becomes an important line of research. Commonly, the person interested in demonstrating effectiveness of an intervention will fashion an index of QOL that includes those domains that are expected to be impacted the most. The researcher will give the identical questionnaire both pre- and postintervention and will demonstrate that the intervention was successful. But the changes may be due to concurrent events and not to the intervention itself. Moreover, the new index is rarely transferable across time and conditions.

In 1996, the Psychosocial Impact of Assistive Devices Scale (PIADS) was produced. This is a 26-item generic questionnaire designed to measure the impact of AT devices in terms of three generally accepted QOL factors, *competence, adaptability,* and *self-esteem.* A number of studies have demonstrated that the PIADS is a reliable, valid, and responsive measure of a variety of AT devices (e.g., eyeglasses, electronic aids for daily living, and mechanical ventilators). One finding is that the impact on QOL remains stable over time, and, in a number of studies, significant differences on the QOL factors were found between retainers and abandoners of AT devices, leading to the prediction of abandonment of various AT.

Abandonment

There is a great deal of dissatisfaction among AT adopters with currently prescribed ATs. Simple ones, such as contact lenses, are abandoned at a high rate (up to 50%), hearing aids and wheel chairs are frequently traded in for other models, and even mechanical ventilators are sometimes abandoned by a PWD with no alternative but death. The reasons for abandonment are many and have been studied recently by a growing number of psychologists.

The most common reason for abandonment is that the device or program is not flexible for a PWD who is undergoing change. For example, a person using a walker may lose more control over his or her gait and is forced to adopt a wheelchair instead of the walker, or someone wearing eyeglasses may resort to laser surgery that results in abandonment of the AT because the person's vision has now improved. But many other reasons for abandonment can be identified that are specific to the AT and the individual's interaction. Although early research focused mainly on the physical properties of the AT device, more recently the direction has shifted to looking also at person variables and the fit between the two, termed the Matching Person and Technology Model, designed to measure satisfaction, including the motivational, personality, gender, and psychosocial factors that affect this fit. A number of questionnaires are now available to measure satisfaction of consumers with ATs as an outcome variable. While concerned with satisfaction derived from adopting an AT, they focus directly on positive and negative aspects of the psychosocial life of the consumer and attempt to account for the high rate of dissatisfaction.

H. I. Day
York University, Toronto, Ontario

***See also:* Aging and Intelligence; Quality of Life**

ASSOCIATION FOR BEHAVIOR ANALYSIS

The Association for Behavior Analysis (ABA) is an organization that includes psychologists, educators, behavioral health practitioners, and practitioners working in other settings (e.g., the private sector) whose scholarly activities and practice derive from the seminal work of psychologist B. F. Skinner (e.g. 1938, 1953, 1974). Its mission is to "develop, enhance, and support the growth and vitality of behavior analysis through research, education, and practice." There are 3,922 members, of whom 1,212 are full members, 1,412 are student members, and 1,006 are associate members. Those remaining are chapter-adjunct or emeritus members. The association has 39 affiliated chapters, including 15 international chapters. Members of ABA are located in 41 countries around the world.

History

ABA was incorporated in 1974, the year in which it held its first annual meeting, which was in Chicago, Illinois. In 1978, ABA added the subtitle "An International Organization" to its name in response to a growing membership from countries outside the United States. In 1980, the Society for the Advancement of Behavior Analysis was created to provide foundational support to ABA. The immediate past president of ABA serves as president of the Society. ABA's central office was housed on the campus of Western Michigan University from its inception until 2002, when it moved to ABA's own building in Kalamazoo, Michigan.

The members of the original 1974 organization committee (which later became the executive council) were Sidney Bijou, James Dinsmoor, Israel Goldiamond, Bill Hopkins, Neil Kent, Kenneth Lloyd, Richard Malott, Gerald Mertens, Jack Michael, Roger Ulrich, and Scott Wood (Peterson, 1978).

Since its founding, ABA has held an annual convention in cities across the United States and in Canada. In November 2001, it sponsored its first international meeting, in Venice, Italy.

Membership

There are several classes of membership, including full membership in ABA, which requires (1) a master's degree in experimental or applied behavior analysis or a related field, and (2) contributions to the field of behavior analysis; affiliate membership, which is designed for persons who have an interest in behavior analysis or who have completed undergraduate credit but do not meet full member requirements; student membership, which is for full-time undergraduate or graduate students, residents, or interns; chapter-adjunct membership, which allows members of affiliated chapters to join ABA; supporting or sustaining membership, which is for full members of ABA who support the organization financially through higher dues; and emeritus membership, which is for voting members who have retired.

Governance and Organization

The organization is governed by an executive council comprised of seven members elected by the full (voting) membership at large; an international representative, elected by international voting members; and a student representative, elected by the student members. The council members reflect the diverse interests of the membership in that one council member is elected to represent each of the following interests: the international community, applied behavior analysis, and the experimental analysis of behavior. There also are two elected members-at-large. The other elected members of the council are the immediate past president, the president, and the president-elect. Presidents thus serve a 3-year term on the council and serve as president of the organization for 1 year.

The executive council oversees the work of a number of boards, each with committees and special-purpose task forces that represent the diverse interests and concerns of the organization. The boards are the Science Policy and Research Board; the Education Board; the Standards, Accreditation, and Professional Affairs Board; the Affiliated Chapters Board; the Membership Board; the Program Board; and the Publication Board.

The ABA is administered by an executive director and a staff at its central office in Kalamazoo.

Association Activities and Their Impact

The activity with the most visible impact is ABA's annual convention, which attracts more than 2,800 behavior analysts, who attend workshops, invited addresses, symposia, round-table discussions, addresses, and poster sessions on a range of topics relevant to the advancement of the basic science of behavior, and to the application of behavioral principles, in a variety of settings with a number of different populations. Continuing education credit for both psychologists and behavior analysts is available during the convention. ABA sponsors an annual award series, with the recipients recognized at the annual convention, to acknowledge distinguished contributions both to the discipline of behavior analysis and to the dissemination of behavior analysis among both professional and lay audiences.

In addition to the annual convention, ABA is the leading advocate in the United States for the efficacy of behavior analysis and behavioral psychology in applied settings. This advocacy takes several forms, including legislative-influence efforts, programs of public education, and support of the Behavior Analyst Certification Board (BACB), the national certification organization for behavior analysts, designed to ensure the quality of individuals offering their services in both the public and private sector as behavior analysts. Certification of individual members as Certified Behavior Analysts requires an advanced degree relevant to behavior analysis and the passing of a written and oral certification examination administered by the BACB.

To complement the BACB certification program for individual behavior analysts, ABA helps assure the quality of educational programs offering training in behavior analysis. Through its accreditation program, both doctoral and master's-level training programs can be accredited by ABA by meeting a set of requirements. Such accreditation involves a self-study by the applicant program, followed by a formal visit to the program by representatives of the accreditation committee. Approval of the program's accreditation is decided by the executive council.

Leadership and support are provided to the academic community in other ways as well. For example, ABA is a member of the Federation of Behavioral, Psychological, and Cognitive Sciences, an organization of scientific societies that supports research in the disciplines represented by the member societies. This support takes the form of efforts to educate and impact the legislative branch of the federal government and such federal agencies as the National Institutes of Health and the National Science Foundation.

Two professional journals are published by ABA: *The Behavior Analyst* and *The Analysis of Verbal Behavior.* The former publishes both scholarly articles and articles on professional issues relevant to the general discipline of behavior analysis, and the latter publishes articles relevant to the understanding of language, in the tradition of B. F. Skinner's (1957) book *Verbal Behavior,* from a behavior-analytic perspective.

REFERENCES

Peterson, M. E. (1978). The midwestern association on behavior analysis: Past, present, future. *The Behavior Analyst, 1,* 3–15.

Skinner, B. F. (1938). *The behavior of organisms: An experimental analysis.* New York: Appleton Century-Crofts.

Skinner, B. F. (1953). *Science and human behavior.* New York: Macmillan.

Skinner, B. F. (1957). *Verbal behavior.* New York: Appleton-Century-Crofts.

Skinner, B. F. (1974). *About behaviorism.* New York: Knopf.

Kennon A. Lattal
West Virginia University

***See also:* Behaviorism**

ASSOCIATIONISM

Association of ideas is the intuitive notion that ideas are grouped together, or associated, in explicable ways. For example, if someone says "horse," one is likely to think "animal," "rider," or "race," but not "shelf," "battery," or "floor." The first set of ideas are all associated with horses, the latter are not. Associationism embraces association of ideas and turns it into a general systematic account of mind or behavior.

John Locke coined the phrase "association of ideas" in the fourth edition of his *Essay Concerning Human Understanding.* He regarded associations as a kind of "madness," as they get in the way of rational, directed thinking. Notwithstanding Locke's condemnation, several eighteenth-century philosophers turned association of ideas into associationism, a view of mind and behavior that places association at the heart of thinking and tends to reduce all psychological principles to the principle of association.

Foremost among these philosophers were David Hume and David Hartley. Hume proudly reduced the mind to the association of ideas, maintaining that the mind contains either perceptions or their copies and ideas, and that ideas are glued together by two laws of association, similarity and contiguity (whereby two ideas that occur together become linked).

The tendency signaled by Hume and Hartley to elevate the principle of associative learning was continued by the nineteenth-century British associationists James Mill, his son John Stuart Mill, and his son's friend, Alexander Bain. James Mill proposed a mechanical theory of association in which ideas are stuck together like tinkertoys. J. S. Mill recognized the unwieldiness of this arrangement and proposed mental chemistry, in which several ideas can merge into one and reveal emergent properties, as when hydrogen and oxygen merge to make water. Bain placed Hartley's project on a better foundation, uniting association philosophy with up-to-date physiology to produce a real association psychology.

It was then only a short step to psychological experiments on association formation, or learning and memory. Thomas Brown had already put forward an empirically researchable form of associationism in his secondary laws of association, which further specified the operation of the primary laws (contiguity, similarity). For example, Brown argued that the more frequently two ideas were contiguously experienced, the stronger would be the associative bond between them, but this law of frequency is open to empirical test.

In the twentieth century, association of ideas transmuted into association of stimulus and response under the influence of behaviorism. The laws of association became the laws of learning; the law of frequency became the gradually rising learning curve; the law of similarity became the generalization gradient; and contiguity of ideas became the contiguity of unconditioned and conditioned stimuli. More recently, eighteenth-century concepts have revived with cognitive psychology, which views memory as an associative network of ideas (e.g., in J. R. Anderson and G. H. Bower's *Human Associative Memory*) embedded in a complex information-processing system, rather like the old mental faculties.

The doctrine of association has not gone unchallenged. The Gestalt psychologists completely renounced it, and various psychologists have periodically attacked it. Nevertheless, association of ideas has proven the most durable of psychological concepts, having maintained an unbroken record of influence from Plato to cognitive science.

Thomas H. Leahey
Virginia Commonwealth University

ATHLETIC COACHING

At all levels of sport, coaches function as educators, leaders, and strategists. In these roles, they can strongly influence the performance and personal development of the athletes with whom they come in contact. The teaching techniques coaches employ, the goal priorities they establish, the values they exhibit and reinforce, and the relationships they form with athletes have all been topics of psychological research.

One important area of research is coach instructional techniques. Behavioral researchers have observed and analyzed the techniques employed by outstanding coaches at all levels of competition. They have found that such coaches tend to use approaches that have proven successful in enhancing performance in other performance domains, such as education and business. Systematic goal setting has proven to be a powerful technique for positive skill development. Coaches who employ this technique analyze the task requirements and current skills of the athlete, set specific behavioral (not outcome) goals, develop individualized action plans for developing the needed skills, set timelines for attainment, and closely monitor the targeted behaviors to assess change. This approach has proven effective from youth sports to the professional level. Other research has shown that behavioral feedback and the use of positive reinforcement enhance the development of sport skills. In general, a positive approach to strengthening desired behaviors through encouragement, sound technical instruction, and positive reinforcement of desired behaviors is preferred by athletes to a negative one featuring criticism, punishment, and an emphasis on avoiding mistakes. Athletes expect coaches to exert control and maintain discipline, but they prefer that it occur within the context of a basically positive coach-athlete relationship.

Much research has focused on youth-sport coaches in recent years. Behavioral coding techniques have been developed, enabling researchers to observe coaches during practices and games, assess their responses to particular classes of situations (e.g., positive and negative athlete behaviors and game developments), and generate behavioral profiles of the coaches based on thousands of their behaviors. They can also obtain athletes' and coaches' ratings of how often the coach engaged in the various behaviors that were coded. Such research has shown that even child athletes are more accurate perceivers of coaching behaviors than are the coaches themselves. Studies have also shown that coaching behaviors are more strongly related to athletes' attitudes toward the coach than are won-lost records. Although winning becomes more important in adolescence than at earlier ages, behaviors continue to be more powerful predictors of athletes' evaluations of coaches and desire to play for them again. In line with the positive approach described above, coaches who create a supportive environment through their use of encouragement, technical instruction, positive reinforcement of desired athlete behaviors (including compliance with team rules), and avoidance of punitive behaviors are best liked by athletes. On teams coached by positive coaches, athletes also like their teammates more, possibly because of the socially supportive atmosphere encouraged and modeled by the coach.

Such findings have inspired a number of coach-training programs designed to help coaches create an athletic environment that is enjoyable and that fosters positive psychosocial outcomes. Such programs give coaches specific behavioral guidelines, show them how to engage in the positive behaviors and find alternatives for punitive ones, and often teach coaches how to monitor their own behavior to make them more self-aware. Although most of these programs have not been formally evaluated, one program, Coach Effectiveness Training (CET), has yielded encouraging results. Behavioral observations and athletes' ratings of their coaches' behaviors indicated that, compared with untrained coaches, those trained in CET behaved in a more supportive and encouraging manner. Although their teams did not win more games, the trained coaches were evaluated more positively by their athletes, and their athletes showed significant increases in self-esteem and decreases in performance anxiety by the end of the season. They also showed a lower rate of dropping out of sports the following season (6% attrition rate compared with a 27% dropout rate among athletes who played for untrained coaches). The latter finding is important because research also shows that children and adolescents who remain involved in sports are less likely to engage in delinquent and other self-defeating behaviors.

An important focus of current research is the motivational climate created by coaches. Analyses of achievement-related goals in children and adults have identified two important goal orientations, known as task- and ego-orientation. Task-oriented people feel successful and competent when they have learned something new, witnessed skill improvement in themselves, mastered the task at hand, or given their best effort. In contrast, ego-oriented people feel successful when they demonstrate superiority over others or avoid feeling inferior to others. Although both orientations can lead to successful performance, research in educational and sport settings indicate that task-oriented people place relatively more emphasis on effort than outcome, are more likely to persist in the face of adversity or failure, and select more challenging goals. They can feel successful even when the desired outcome has not been attained, if they believe that they gave maximum effort and learned important things from the experience. Ego-oriented individuals show less persistence in the face of adversity and are more likely to experience distress and eventually avoid settings in which they do not win out over others.

Most people have both task- and ego-orientations to varying degrees. The situational context or motivational climate that exists in achievement settings can differ in the extent to which task- or ego-involving goals are emphasized. A mastery-oriented motivational climate supports and strengthens task orientation; an ego-oriented climate fosters competitiveness and comparisons with others. Much educational research has shown that mastery-oriented climates promote higher academic performance and intrinsic learning motivation, as well as lower levels of fear of failure. This research is now being applied within the athletic domain by encouraging coaches and parents to establish a mastery-based motivational climate. The principle is that if athletes are oriented toward becoming as proficient as possible ("their" best rather than "the" best), are not shackled by fear of failure, and are prepared and technically well-coached, winning will take care of itself within the limits of their ability. Research shows that mastery-oriented sport environments provide more enjoyable and fulfilling settings for the majority of athletes. More importantly, the lessons learned in mastery environments may have salutary carryover to other achievement domains as well.

Ronald E. Smith
Frank L. Smoll
University of Washington

ATTACHMENT STYLES

Observational studies of parent-child bonding revealed the existence of four distinctive styles of relational behavior exhibited by infants in distress. Further research conducted with older children, adolescents, and adults has supported the ongoing development of similar response styles across the lifespan. These *attachment styles* classify the majority of individuals as *secure* and specify three varieties of *insecure* or *anxious* attachment patterns. Individuals classified as *securely attached* consistently demonstrate superior levels of psychosocial adjustment across a variety of domains when compared to people classified into one of the three insecure categories.

Attachment Theory

British psychoanalyst John Bowlby (1958, 1969), strongly influenced by ethological theories of primate evolution, formulated *attachment theory* to explain how selection pressures supported the survival of offspring whose behavior elicited and maintained maternal protection. He further theorized that early attachment experiences generate *internal working models* that encode aspects of relational behavior and expectations.

Empirical support for attachment theory later emerged in Ainsworth's observational studies of *separation anxiety.* She and her collaborators (Ainsworth, Blehar, Waters, & Wall, 1978) were the first to classify children's attachment styles based upon each child's behavior during a series of separations and reunions with that child's mother. These original attachment styles were labeled *secure, avoidant,* and *resistant/ambivalent.* A more recently accepted attachment classification, termed *disorganized/disoriented* (Main & Solomon, 1986), was created to capture the behavior patterns of children who fit poorly into the other attachment categories.

More recently, attachment theory has been extended as a broad explanatory framework for understanding close personal relationships in adulthood (Hazan & Shaver, 1987). However, as the applications of attachment theory are increasingly extended, there is a danger that its principles will be distorted to fit so many aims that a corresponding loss of coherency will result.

Typology of Child and Adult Attachment Styles

Infants whose signals of distress consistently receive nurturing care tend to develop a style of responding well to soothing behavior from others. Such children appear to expect nurturance and demonstrate a balance of exploratory interest in their environment and reliance upon the caregiver as a secure base in times of insecurity or distress. The attachment style of children fitting this description is designated as *secure.* Adults who are comfortable with depending on others and having relational partners depend on them are considered to exhibit a secure *adult attachment pattern.* Patterns of attachment behavior at any age that deviate substantially from this model are characterized as *anxious* or *insecure.*

Anxious attachment styles have been defined by various terms including ambivalent, avoidant, and disorganized/disoriented among children and preoccupied, dismissive, and fearful among adults. Children who seldom seek parental care and who may even show somewhat more interest in the attention of adult strangers are classified as *avoidant.* The corresponding style of adults who adopt an extremely self-reliant attitude and who express little interest in close relationships with others is termed *dismissive.* If the person's attitude toward relationships contains evidence of both devaluing relationships and showing distrust toward partners, the *fearful* attachment classification is indicated.

Some children heartily protest the absence of their caregivers but are difficult to soothe when their signals of distress are responded to. This style of anxious attachment is classified as *ambivalent* because the child appears to relate to the parent as alternately desirable and aversive. When adults perceive relationships as highly desirable, but seem prone to anxious concerns about rejection or require excessive reassurance from their partners, they are likely to be classified as exhibiting a *preoccupied* attachment style.

Children who display idiosyncratic and contradictory sequences of attachment responses have been termed *disorganized/disoriented.* These children may appear confused and lacking a coherent strategy for obtaining and maintaining comfort and protection. Measures of adult attachment are likely to classify such individuals under the *fearful* attachment style.

Methods of Assessing Attachment Styles

While the classification of attachment in infants is still conducted almost exclusively by means of the *strange situation test,* a variety of interviews and self-report measures are now employed to assess attachment styles in adults. The Adult Attachment Interview (George, Kaplan, & Main, 1985) is the most prominent example of the interview approach. Researchers needing measures that lend themselves to use with larger samples have developed self-report measures yielding various indices of attitudes and reactions in close, personal relationships.

Early examples of this method included the three-category approach of Hazan and Shaver (1987) and the four-category approach of Bartholomew and Horowitz (1991). Later developments of similar measures have departed from categorical assignment and allowed individuals to rate the degree of correspondence between themselves and each of the attachment style prototypes. These scores could then be combined to develop a more complex picture of individual differences in adult attachment styles.

An alternative innovation has been to construct multi-item self-report measures consisting of statements about oneself in relational contexts. This method improves the reliability of the measures, and the items are sorted according to various theoretical dimensions that have received support in factor-analytic studies. Extensive analyses performed on both categorical and dimensional measures of attachment (Fraley & Waller, 1998) supported the conceptual and empirical superiority of the dimensional approach.

Implications of Attachment Styles for Social Adjustment

Insecure attachment in early childhood predicts a variety of undesirable outcomes, including poor peer relationships, difficulties in regulating negative affect, and impulsive, aggressive, and disruptive behavioral patterns. Moreover, maltreatment in childhood has been consistently shown to be a risk factor for the development of insecure attachment styles.

Adolescents and adults with insecure patterns of attachment exhibit higher rates of affective disorders, anxiety disorders, and personality disorders than securely attached peers. Insecure attachment has also been implicated as a risk factor for poor relational quality in marriage and other intimate relationships (Kobak & Hazan, 1991).

REFERENCES

Ainsworth, M. D. S., Blehar, M. C., Waters, E., & Wall, S. (1978). *Patterns of attachment: Assessed in the strange situation and at home.* Hillsdale, NJ: Erlbaum.

Bartholomew, K., & Horowitz, L. M. (1991). Attachment styles among young adults: A test of a four-category model. *Journal of Personality and Social Psychology, 61,* 226–244.

Bowlby, J. (1958). The nature of a child's tie to his mother. *International Journal of Psychoanalysis, 39,* 350–373.

Bowlby, J. (1969). *Attachment and loss: Vol. 1. Attachment.* Middlesex, UK: Penguin Books.

Fraley, R. C., & Waller, N. G. (1998). Adult attachment patterns: A test of the typological model. In J. A. Simpson & W. S. Rholes (Eds.), *Attachment theory and close relationships* (pp. 77–114). New York: Guilford Press.

George, C., Kaplan, N., & Main, M. (1985). *The adult attachment interview.* Unpublished manuscript, University of California, Berkeley.

Hazan, C., & Shaver, P. R. (1987). Romantic love conceptualized as an attachment process. *Journal of Personality and Social Psychology, 52,* 511–524.

Kobak, R. R., & Hazan, C. (1991). Attachment in marriage: Effects of security and accuracy of working models. *Journal of Personality and Social Psychology, 60,* 861–869.

Main, M., & Solomon, J. (1986). Discovery of a new, insecure-disorganized/disoriented attachment pattern. In M. Yogman & T. B. Brazelton (Eds.), *Affective development in infancy* (pp. 95–124). Norwood, NJ: Ablex.

Gilbert Reyes
University of South Dakota

ATTITUDES

Throughout the history of social psychology, the attitude construct has played a central role in the explanation of social behavior. Attitude is defined as a disposition to respond favorably or unfavorably to an object, person, institution, or event. An unobservable, hypothetical construct, attitude must be inferred from measurable responses that reflect positive or negative evaluations of the attitude object. People can be asked to express their attitudes directly, by judging the object of the attitude as *good* or *bad* or by rating their degree of liking for it. Alternatively, attitudes can be inferred more indirectly from *cognitive responses* or beliefs (reflecting the individual's perception of and information about the attitude object); *affective responses* (feelings toward the object); and *conative responses* (behavioral intentions, tendencies, and actions with respect to the object). For example, attitudes toward an ethnic group can be inferred from beliefs (whether valid or biased) that attribute certain traits, abilities, opinions, and lifestyles to members of the group in question; from such affective or emotional responses as expressions of admiration or contempt for the ethnic group; and from intentions or overt actions that reflect tendencies to approach or avoid members of the group under consideration.

Although people are generally aware of their attitudes, research has shown that conscious or *explicit* attitudes can be accompanied by evaluatively discrepant *implicit* attitudes. Thus, when well-established attitudes change, the old implicit attitude is not necessarily replaced but may coexist with the new explicit attitude, and for such socially sensitive topics as racial prejudice, an explicit liberal or egalitarian attitude toward a minority group can coexist with a more negative implicit stereotype. Subtle response latency measures are used to uncover such implicit attitudes.

Attitude Formation

Functional Approach

Early attempts to identify the origins of attitudes focused on the needs or functions they may serve. Thus, attitudes were assumed to have instrumental or utilitarian functions (helping people attain rewards and avoid punishments); knowledge functions (organizing and simplifying people's experiences); expressive functions (enabling emotional release); and ego-defensive functions (protecting and enhancing the self). Although it generated considerable interest, the functional approach to attitudes has produced only a modest amount of research and has been of limited practical value.

Behavioral Approach

Behaviorally oriented social psychologists have used principles of classical conditioning to describe and explain attitude formation. Repeated and systematic association between the attitude object (conditioned stimulus) and a positively or negatively valued event (unconditioned stimulus) is assumed to produce a favorable or unfavorable implicit reaction (attitude) to the object. Controversy revolves around the question of awareness—the extent to which awareness of the object-event contingencies is a necessary requirement for conditioning of attitude. Although the issue has not been completely resolved, few studies have clearly demonstrated automatic conditioning of attitude without contingency awareness.

Cognitive Approach

A general trend toward cognitive or information-processing explanations of social behavior has brought a concomitant decline in the importance accorded to needs and automatic conditioning processes. Instead, stress is now placed on the role of information as a basis of attitude formation. According to this view, beliefs—representing people's subjective knowledge about themselves and their world—are the primary determinants of attitudes. Each belief links the attitude object to a positively or negatively valued attribute; thus smoking (the object) causes lung cancer (the attribute). Generally speaking, the greater the number of beliefs that associate the object with positive attributes, and the smaller the number of beliefs that associate it with negative attributes, the more favorable is the resultant attitude toward the object.

Attitudes and Behavior

Because attitudes are considered to be behavioral dispositions, it is natural to assume that they direct, and in some sense determine, social action. However, by the late 1960s there was growing evidence that a strong relation between verbal expressions of attitude and overt behavior could not be taken for granted. Controlled studies failed to find relations between racial attitudes and such actions as accepting members of the racial group in a hotel or restaurant, conforming with their views or behaviors, or extending an invitation to members of that group; attitudes toward cheating failed to predict actual cheating behavior; attitudes toward another person were unrelated to cooperation or competition with that person; work-related attitudes had little to do with absenteeism, tardiness, or turnover; and so forth.

Under the weight of this negative evidence, social psychologists were forced to reexamine the nature of attitude and its relation to social behavior. It was concluded that a strong relation between verbal and overt actions can be expected only if the two types of responses are compatible with each other in terms of their generality or specificity. Thus, although unrelated to any single action, verbal expressions of general liking or disliking for an ethnic group are found to be strongly related to aggregate measures of discriminatory behavior that involve different actions toward various members of that group, observed in different contexts and on different occasions. By the same token, degree of religiosity often fails to predict single church-related activities, but it is strongly related to religious behavior that aggregates across different types of religious activities, contexts, and occasions.

Single behaviors, on the other hand, can be predicted from attitudes toward the behaviors themselves—for example, attitudes toward smoking marijuana (rather than global attitudes toward the counterculture), attitudes toward attending church services (as opposed to attitudes toward the church), or attitudes toward donating blood (instead of global attitudes concerning altruism). However, response tendencies reflected in attitudes toward specified actions can change as a result of situational demands or unanticipated events. Moreover, individuals vary in their susceptibility to the influence of such external factors. Thus, while attitudes toward behaviors tend to produce corresponding behavioral intentions, the extent to which these intentions are actually carried out is moderated by situational factors and individual difference variables. Nevertheless, barring unforeseen events, behavioral attitudes and intentions are usually found to be quite accurate predictors of subsequent actions.

SUGGESTED READING

Ajzen, I. (1988). *Attitudes, personality, and behavior.* Chicago: Dorsey Press.

Eagly, A. H., & Chaiken, S. (1993). *The psychology of attitudes.* Fort Worth, TX: Harcourt Brace.

Greenwald, A. G., & Banaji, M. R. (1995). Implicit social cognition: Attitudes, self-esteem, and stereotypes. *Psychological Review, 102,* 4–27.

Icek Ajzen
University of Massachusetts

See also: **Interpersonal Perception**

ATTRIBUTION THEORY

Consider questions such as "Why did I fail my exam?" "Why won't Mary go out with Jim?" "Did he hit me on purpose?" Attribution theory refers to a set of propositions and hypotheses regarding how laypersons arrive at answers to these questions and what the consequences are of their causal beliefs. Philosophers including Hume, Kant, and Mill, who have guided some attributional thinking, have written extensively about questions of causality. However, they address these issues logically and prescriptively rather than describing how the layperson arrives at a causal understanding. In addition, philosophers have not been interested in the psychological importance and functions of perceptions of causality, whereas these concerns are central to attribution theorists.

The originator of attribution theory, Fritz Heider, primarily introduced his ideas in the 1950s. Attributional thinking then reached its zenith in the 1970s, when it was the dominant topic in social psychology and influenced clinical, educational, motivational, and personality psychology as well. In that era, the ideas of Edward Jones, Harold Kelley, Bernard Weiner, and others supplemented the thinking of Heider and, to some extent, moved away from the focus on naive psychology.

Reaching Causal Inferences

One goal of attribution theorists has been to identify the personal and situational determinants of causal understanding. It has been assumed that humans want to attain a cognitive mastery of their world. Further, people are regarded as naive scientists, logical and rational—albeit not infallible—and subject to systematic biases and errors. The following discussion introduces a few specific research directions and some empirical findings regarding causal inferences.

In the desire for understanding, it has been documented

that causal search is not undertaken in all instances but is most likely given an important, unexpected, and negative event or outcome. This might be failure at a crucial exam, rejection of a marriage proposal, and the like. Principles found in covariation analyses regarding the presence and absence of causes and effects are important sources of causal information to help determine the answers to "why" questions. For example, failure at an exam is more likely to be self-attributed if there have been many prior personal failures and knowledge of the successes of others. In addition, causal rules are used such that, for example, if beliefs of multiple causality are elicited, then even in the presence of insufficient effort there will be additional attributions to lack of ability or to some environmental factors as causes of the failure. Further, the presence of some causes may result in other causes being discounted. One controversy associated with the latter process concerns the hypothesis that rewarding pupils for successful achievement performance reduces their motivation because the extrinsic reward results in a discounting of their intrinsic interest.

It also has been reasoned (again, with controversy) that the behavior of others tends to be ascribed to a stable disposition or trait inasmuch as explanations that capture enduring aspects of the world often are preferred, and the other is dominant in social perception. The underestimation of the situation as a perceived cause of the behavior of others and overattribution to the person has been labeled "the fundamental attribution error." This principle has been challenged in cross-cultural research, for it has been argued that situational attributions are more salient among Asians.

Another bias that has been documented in attribution research concerns beliefs about the causes of positive and negative events. Self-attributions tend to be given for positive outcomes ("I succeeded because I studied hard"), whereas negative outcomes elicit external attributions ("I failed because the exam was unfair"). This pattern of attributions has been labeled the "hedonic bias" inasmuch as positive self-directed emotions and the maintenance of self-esteem are fostered.

Consequences of Causal Beliefs

The research concerning the consequences of perceived causality is less voluminous than that associated with the reaching of causal inferences, but it nonetheless is very substantial, particularly in disciplines other than social psychology. Here, again, only a small sample of the research directions is presented.

In the field of clinical psychology, it has been suggested that ascribing negative events to something about the self that also is not subject to personal control produces a state of "learned helplessness," which promotes and/or accompanies depression. Hence, failure perceived as due to lack of aptitude may be an antecedent (or correlate) of depression. Attribution-guided research within clinical psychology also has revealed that when the behavior of a mentally ill family member is ascribed to a cause under personal control ("He is just being lazy")—in other words, when the cause implicates personal blame—then the likelihood increases that the ill person will return to institutionalization because of the negative emotions this elicits among family members.

Assignment of responsibility and blame is central in many other contexts as well, suggesting that in addition to being naive scientists, humans also act as naive judges. Other-blame, which is one indicator of marital distress, also is elicited by a variety of stigmas, including alcoholism and obesity, and decreases help giving. The anticipation of the negative consequences of being perceived as responsible gives rise to a variety of impression-management techniques that deflect this inference. For example, students publicly claim lack of ability rather than low effort as the cause when explaining their failure to authority figures (but not when ascribing the cause of failure to peers).

Adaptive and maladaptive attributions also have been identified in studies of coping with stress. Following a negative life stressor, such as rape, individuals ascribing this event to their character ("I am a risk taker") do not cope as well as those attributing the event to a particular behavior ("I accidentally was in the wrong place at the wrong time").

Individual differences in coping with aversive circumstances are linked with disparate beliefs about the perceived causes of negative events. For these reasons, attributional therapies have been devised that attempt to change causal beliefs so they are more adaptive.

In sum, causal beliefs play an important role in self- and other-understanding and significantly influence emotions and subsequent actions. The study of causal attributions therefore provides one of the foundations for social psychology and also has great relevance for other subareas within psychology.

Bernard Weiner
University of California, Los Angeles

AUTOMATIC THOUGHTS

Automatic thoughts are spontaneous ideas—ideations or thoughts typically indicated by internal self-statements or self-talk. Cognitive theories emphasize the roles of belief systems, cognitive schematas, intellectual processes, and automatic thoughts in behavioral operations. Each individual has a frame of reference, variously called personality, lifestyle, worldview, and so on, within which one copes with life. One's inner belief structure depends on past experiences, learnings, goals, purposes, and core belief structures. Automatic thoughts differ from belief structures. Merluzzi and Boltwood (1989) state, "an important distinction between automatic thoughts or self statements and underlying schemata or belief systems [is] automatic thoughts are spontaneous self statements or ruminations. . . . In contrast cognitive schematas are seen as relatively stable, enduring traits like cognitive patterns" (p. 256). Similarly, Beck and Weishaar (1989b) distinguish between automatic and voluntary thoughts. Voluntary thoughts are fully conscious self-determined decisions. Automatic thoughts "are more stable and less accessible than voluntary thoughts [and] are generally quite powerful" (Beck & Weishaar, 1989a, p. 28). Both voluntary thoughts and automatic thoughts are consistent with one's core beliefs or schematas.

Beck and Weishaar (1989b) point out that a variety of situations, events, or circumstances may trigger underlying core beliefs and generate automatic thoughts. More specifically, automatic thoughts "intercede between a stimulus event and one's emotional and behavioral reactions to it" (Beck & Weishaar, 1989a, p. 28).

Unconscious Processes

Automatic thoughts are considered to be unconscious or lying below the surface of immediate conscious awareness. They are spontaneous self-statements, stemming from core beliefs out of conscious awareness.

Applications

Use of automatic thoughts in psychology center on changing belief systems through psychotherapy. In cognitive and cognitive-behavioral therapies, the primary focus is on changing the client's "distorted" or dysfunctional belief systems. Client's belief systems are explored and accessed. Albert Ellis outlines 12 irrational beliefs (Criddle, 1975), and Beck outlines primarily six cognitive distortions or distorted thoughts—belief processes (Beck & Weishaar, 1989a, 1989b). Others have added to and modified irrational beliefs and cognitive distortions (McMullin, 1986).

Core beliefs can be accessed by having people monitor their own spontaneous self-statements or automatic thoughts. These are then challenged and changed. Therapy problems can be resolved by changing one's views of the problems via automatic thoughts, a kind of paradigmatic shift in thinking, known in psychotherapy jargon as *reframing*.

REFERENCES

Beck, A., & Weishaar, M. (1989a). Cognitive therapy. In A. Freeman, K. J. Simon, L. E. Beutler, & H. Arkowitz (Eds.), *Comprehensive handbook of cognitive therapy.* New York: Plenum.

Beck, A., & Weishaar, M. (1989b). Cognitive therapy. In R. Corsini & D. Wedding (Eds.), *Current psychotherapies.* Itasca, NY: Peacock.

Criddle, W. (1975). Guidelines for challenging irrational beliefs. *Rational Living, 9*(1), 8–13.

McMullin, R. E. (1986). *Handbook of cognitive therapy techniques.* New York: Norton.

Merluzzi, T. V., & Boltwood, M. D. (1989). Cognitive assessment. In A. Freeman, K. M. Simon, L. E. Beutler, & H. Arkowitz (Eds.), *Comprehensive handbook of cognitive therapy.* New York: Plenum.

M. S. Carich
Adler School of Professional Psychology

AUTORECEPTORS

Autoreceptors are defined as receptors located on neurons that release a transmitter that activates such presynaptic receptors. They may be located on the neuronal cell body and/or the nerve terminals. In general, they exert a negative feedback influence on the function of their neuron. That is, when overactivated by their neurotransmitters, an inhibitory influence is triggered. Autoreceptors are determinant in controlling the function of neurons. Under most physiological conditions, they are tonically activated. This can be put into evidence by the administration of an antagonist, which will increase neuronal output. Using exogenous agonists, it is sometimes possible to obtain, upon their maximal activation, a complete shutdown of the neuronal process to which they are coupled. They have, therefore, been targets for drug development. The scope of this brief synopsis is to review some neuronal systems for which autoreceptors have been clearly identified and for which selective ligands have been developed for actual or potential therapeutic use.

Noradrenaline Autoreceptors

Noradrenaline (NE) neurons are endowed with autoreceptors on their cell bodies, where they exert a negative feedback role on firing rate. They are of the α_{2A} subtype as confirmed by genetic cloning experiments. Such autoreceptors are also located on NE terminals throughout the brain, where they inhibit the release of NE. The prototypical agonist of such receptors is clonidine, which is commercialized mainly for the treatment of high blood pressure. Its hypotensive effect would not, however, be exclusively mediated by its action on autoreceptors as α_2-adrenoceptors are also located postsynaptically. Yohimbine, among several agents capable of blocking α_2-adrenoceptors, is a relatively selective agent used mainly to treat erectile dysfunction. The antidepressant drugs mirtazapine and mianserin antagonize α_2-adrenoceptors, leading to enhanced NE release that contributes to their therapeutic actions in major depression. While mirtazapine acts in part by enhancing indirectly the activation of excitatory α_1-adrenoceptors located on serotonin (5HT) neurons, mianserin antagonizes α_1-adrenoceptors.

Serotonin Autoreceptors

As for NE neurons, 5HT neurons are endowed with cell body and terminal autoreceptors that exert a negative feedback influence on neuronal firing and release, respectively. The somatodendritic ones that inhibit firing rate are of the $5HT_{1A}$ subtype, and the ones located on terminals are mainly of the $5HT_{1B}$ subtype. The former subtypes of autoreceptors play a crucial role in the antidepressant effect of 5HT reuptake blockers and monoamine oxidase inhibitors because they desensitize after 2 to 3 weeks of treatment. This permits a recovery of the firing rate of 5HT neurons to normal in the presence of inhibited reuptake or monoamine oxidase inhibition, then producing a net increase in neurotransmission. The time course for this recovery in firing activity is consistent with the onset of the therapeutic action of such drugs in major depression. This observation has recently been put to clinical use by accelerating the antidepressant response of such drugs with the $5HT_{1A}$ autoreceptor antagonist pindolol. Eight of the first ten placebo-controlled studies documented a 7- to 14-day acceleration with this strategy.

There are $5HT_{1D}$ autoreceptors at the level of the cell body of 5HT neurons that exert an inhibitory role on 5HT release in the midbrain and thus, indirectly, on terminal 5HT release through a $5HT_{1A}$ autoreceptor interaction. Finally, $5HT_3$ receptor activation, under certain experimental conditions, enhances 5HT release and was prematurely attributed to an autoreceptor function. Subsequent experiments have, however, revealed that these receptors are not located on 5HT neurons and, until proven otherwise, should not be considered autoreceptors.

Dopamine Autoreceptors

Dopamine neurons have autoreceptors of the D_2 subtype located on their soma and dendrites. When activated by dopamine itself or by exogenous D_2 agonists, such as apomorphine, neuronal firing is attenuated. On the contrary, their antagonism with the prototypical antipsychotic drug haloperidol leads not only to an increased firing rate but also to a discharge pattern characterized by bursts that produce a greater release of dopamine than would the same number of action potentials occurring at regular intervals. Prolonged D_2 antagonism leads to a depolarization of these neurons and thus a shutting off of their firing activity. Such a silencing of the mesolimbic-dopamine neurons likely plays an important role in mediating the antipsychotic response because it leads to a decrease of dopamine in postsynaptic structures, contributing to decreased dopamine neurotransmission. Because long-term administration of the atypical antipsychotic agent clozapine depolarizes mesolimbic-dopamine neurons without affecting substantia-nigra-dopamine neurons, which give rise to projections to the striatum, this differential activity may account for the lack of movement disorders of clozapine. In support of this possibility, typical antipsychotic agents such as haloperidol, which produce such extrapyramidal side effects, depolarize both populations of dopamine neurons.

Other Chemospecific Neurons with Autoreceptors

Cholinergic terminals have inhibitory receptors of the muscarinic 2 subtype, which exert a negative feedback influence on release. Considerable evidence also exists for nicotinic receptors exerting a positive influence on acetylcholine release. As acetylcholine is a key neurotransmitter in Alzheimer's disease, these two types of receptors represent targets for the development of drugs to enhance acetylcholine release from the remaining fibers, that is, muscarinic type 2 antagonists and nicotinic agonists.

Glutamatergic terminals have autoreceptors of the metabotropic subtype 2 that, when overactivated, attenuate glutamate release. Recently, agonists have been developed in the hope of helping treat conditions such as opiate withdrawal symptoms, given that this condition increases glutamatergic activity that stimulates NE activity. Indeed, this condition cannot be controlled using only the α_2-adrenergic agonist clonidine to attenuate physical and psychological agitation.

GABA neurons inhibit the release of their own neurotransmitter via $GABA_B$ autoreceptors. However, the exact role that the GABA agonist baclofen exerts on these autoreceptors to mediate the antispasmodic effect of this drug in patients with spinal cord lesions remains to be clarified.

Finally, histamine neurons bear autoreceptors of the H_3 subtype that inhibit histamine release. Although selective H_3 antagonists have been developed and demonstrated to increase arousal and decrease food intake in animals, they have not yet reached the therapeutic armamentarium. They are interestingly devoid of peripheral side effects because H_3 receptors are virtually absent outside the central nervous system.

In summary, autoreceptors are crucial neuronal elements because they are intimately involved in modulating the overall function of their neurons. As for most types of neurons, their presence probably represents more the rule than the exception. They have been exploited in human therapeutics using either agonists, mainly to decrease neurotransmitter release, or antagonists, to promote neuronal output. Their discovery and characterization have already led to advances of certain disorders and should yield further therapeutic indications in the future.

SUGGESTED READING

Blier, P., & Bergeron, R. (1998). The use of pindolol to potentiate antidepressant medication. *Journal of Clinical Psychiatry, 59,* 16–23.

Langer, S. Z. (1997). 25 years since the discovery of presynaptic receptors: Present knowledge and future perspectives. *Trends in Pharmacological Sciences, 18,* 95–99.

Piñeyro, G., & Blier, P. (1999). Autoregulation of serotonin neurons: Role in antidepressant drug action. *Pharmacological Reviews, 51,* 533–591.

Starke, K., Göthert, M., & Kilbinger, H. (1989). Modulation of neurotransmitter release by presynaptic autoreceptors. *Physiological Reviews, 69,* 864–988.

Pierre Blier
University of Florida

See also: **Neurotransmitters**

AUTOSHAPING

Autoshaping refers to the process whereby biologically primed stimulus-response relations interact with and occasionally override operantly learned, potentially incompatible response-reinforcer relations. It may also be referred to as *misbehavior of organisms.* The name is derived from quick operant shaping (i.e., automatic shaping) that occurred without apparent reinforcement of successive approximations. Typically, the behavior observed depends upon the object or goal received. For example, food appears to release eating behavior and water appears to release drinking behavior. Although initially thought to manifest only among simpler mammals, autoshaping may occur in humans (Siegel, 1978). Consensus regarding etiology is lacking, though this is not a result of irregularities in data; the phenomenon of autoshaping is valid and reliable.

Example

Pigeons quickly learn key pecking responses when a key is illuminated and provides a reliable and salient cue for the delivery of food (Brown & Jenkins, 1968). However, attempts to operantly extinguish or negatively punish pecking generally fail, leading one to question whether the behavior was acquired through operant training or some other modality.

Theories of Autoshaping

Autoshaping resides in the gap between nature and nurture. It has been posited that autoshaping represents interactions between organism and environment, phylogeny and ontogeny, and respondent and instrumental processes. Each of these represents a different level of analysis to the puzzle of autoshaping.

Though the formal study of autoshaping largely began in the late 1960s, the existence of the phenomenon may have been foreshadowed by Darwin's theory of evolution (1859). Darwin posited natural selection as the mechanism whereby species-specific morphogenesis and behavior would need to show environmental adaptation (i.e., functionality) with regard to subsistence and reproduction. In simple terms, as long the new structure or behavior did not impair the animal's relative ability to compete for basic resources, it would continue to exist. Influenced by Darwin's work, William James (1890) similarly implied the existence of autoshaping in discussions of instinct. According to James, an instinct was defined as "the faculty of acting in a such a way as to produce certain ends, without foresight of the ends, and without previous education in the performance" (p. 383). But instincts were not to be considered immutable stimulus-response relations; they were to be considered "blind" to the resultant consequences of the action on the first occurrence of the behavior, after which they could be "disguised" or "modified." Hence, fixed action patterns, an interchangeable term for instinct used by ethologists, may be more or less fixed depending upon the effect of the behavior as well as the species under consideration. James implicated the existence of a process whereby innate, hard-wired behavior might interact with and be modified by resultant environmental stimuli.

Lorenz (1957), an early ethologist, posited the more widely held view that due to the simplicity of the nervous system of lower animals, constraints on stimulus perception and response are more likely than in humans and that those responses would be adaptive to the survival of the animal. This view on instinct proposed a mechanism whereby the animal perceived a stimulus that *released* a species-specific response (e.g., pecking) designed to provide a specific consequence (e.g., food). This paradigm also adhered to the assumption that instinctive responses were unlearned, yet were modifiable, although the modification would only be found in the offspring. Lorenz postulated that the fixed action pattern released by a specific stimulus should be referred to as an instinct; all supporting, orienting, or learned behaviors maintaining or modifying an instinct are to be considered appetitive responses. But, in practice, the line between instinctive and appetitive behaviors remained blurred, perhaps because the etiology of instincts or phylogenically predisposed fixed action patterns was not well understood.

Better understood are ontogenic models for acquiring behavior within the life of the animal. Two specific forms of learning, classical and operant conditioning, appear relevant to autoshaping. In the aforementioned example with autoshaped pecking in pigeons, it was originally thought that innate aspects of the bird provided for, or predisposed the bird for, rapid shaping via reinforcement of successive approximations of pecking. However, introducing terms like *innate aspect* or *predisposition* weakened the scientific explanation, as those terms were not operationally defined, did little to advance the understanding of the data, and were usually tautological (i.e., based on circular reasoning). Brown and Jenkins (1968) were the first to report that noncontingent food presentation temporally contiguous with key illumination resulted in pigeon pecking. Furthermore,

Williams and Williams (1969) conducted the first example of omission training with pigeons, whereby the presentation of food was contingent upon the nonoccurrence of pecking. Under an omission training model, behavior under operant control would cease or become greatly reduced. However, the pigeons continued to exhibit pecking over many trials without food. This study underscored the implausibility that autoshaping was maintained by contingent reinforcement with food, even if intermittently or superstitiously. This prompted researchers to investigate the possibility that key pecking was classically conditioned.

The rationale for considering classical conditioning as the mechanism of action for autoshaping stems from the fact that within each operant there resides the potential for simultaneous classical conditioning (for in-depth discussion, refer to texts by Davis & Hurwitz, 1977; Honig & Staddon, 1977; Rachlin, 1976; Schwartz, 1989). Due to the stimulus properties of consequences, particularly primary consequences, neutral stimuli that reliably precede and predict delivery may become conditioned. In other words, reinforcers and punishers may also serve as unconditioned stimuli–unconditioned response (US-UR) pairs, inadvertently creating conditioned stimuli (CS) and conditioned responses (CR). In the example with pigeons, the food pellet was contingently delivered upon pecking at the key when illuminated. This food pellet, both a potential reinforcer and paired US-UR, might allow the light inside the key to become a CS that elicits a key-pecking response (CR) that closely approximates a normal unconditioned eating response (UR). This model fits the data well, as autoshaped behaviors closely approximate the normal phylogenic response released by the goal stimulus. In a further testing of this model, noncontingent delivery of the food maintained key pecking as long as the illumination preceded and was temporally contiguous to the food delivery, that is, CS continued to evoke the CR when it reliably predicted the US-UR delivery (Brown & Jenkins, 1968). Later, Jenkins (1977) altered the predictability of the CS so that it no longer preceded the food delivery. Classical conditioning extinction curves were noted, as were spontaneous remission curves when contiguity was reestablished. Jenkins also noted that maintenance of the pecking response was best when both contiguity and contingency were in place (i.e., classical and operant conditioning may be additive processes).

In summary, autoshaping appears to be primarily a function of classical conditioning in that underlying US-UR relations are a requisite condition. However, operant consequences may also serve as US-UR pairs, allowing the occurrence of classical conditioning. Autoshaping per se only manifests when operant training appears to be overriding US-UR patterns, or in the terms of James and Lorenz, attempting to modify instinctive fixed action patterns for obtaining goals. Hence, behaviors exhibited during autoshaping continue to defy simple categorization and precise etiologic explanation.

REFERENCES

Brown, P., & Jenkins, H. (1968). Auto-shaping of the pigeon's key peck. *Journal of the Experimental Analysis of Behavior, 11,* 1–8.

Darwin, C. A. (1859). *The origin of species by means of natural selection.* London: John Murray.

Davis, H., & Hurwitz, H. M. B. (1977). *Operant-Pavlovian interactions.* New York: Wiley.

Hergenhahn, B. R., & Olson, M. H. (1997). *An introduction to theories of learning* (5th ed.). Upper Saddle River, NJ: Prentice Hall.

Honig, W. K., & Staddon, J. E. R. (1977). *Handbook of operant behavior.* Englewood Cliffs, NJ: Prentice Hall.

James, W. (1890). *Principles of psychology* (reprint 1990). Birmingham: Smith Peter.

Jenkins, H. (1977). Sensitivity to different response systems to stimulus-reinforcer and response-reinforcer relations. In H. Davis & H. M. B. Hurwitz (Eds.), *Operant-Pavlovian interactions* (pp. 47–66). New York: Wiley.

Lorenz, K. (1957). Companions in the life of birds. In C. Schiller (Ed.), *Instinctive behavior.* New York: International Universities Press.

Rachlin, H. (1976). *Behavior and learning* (pp. 83–128). San Francisco: W. H. Freeman.

Schwartz, B. (1989). *Psychology of learning and behavior* (3rd ed.). New York: W. W. Norton.

Siegel, R. K. (1978). Stimulus selection and tracking during urination: Autoshaping directed behavior with toilet targets. *Journal of Applied Behavior Analysis, 10*(2), 255–265.

Williams, D., & Williams, H. (1969). Auto-maintenance in the pigeon: Sustained pecking despite contingent non-reinforcement. *Journal of the Experimental Analysis of Behavior, 12,* 511–520.

David B. Hatfield
Devereux Cleo Wallace,
Colorado Springs, CO

***See also:* Operant Conditioning**

AVOIDANCE LEARNING

Avoidance learning occurs when an individual's behavior prevents exposure to an unpleasant consequence. This arrangement, or contingency, is pervasive in everyday life. For example, in writing a mortgage check each month, the homeowner does so not because this behavior is immediately pleasurable but, rather, it avoids conflict with, and possible foreclosure by, a financial lender. Or, consider the motorist who is traveling above the speed limit posted on a highway. Upon seeing the blinking light of a police vehicle ahead, the driver slows down to avoid a negative encounter with law enforcement. It might be said, in fact, that learning by avoidance is what motivates most people most of the time.

Avoidance learning has its roots in experimental psychology and conditioning theory. This chapter describes its theoretical basis, reviews conceptual issues, and discusses the role of avoidance learning in clinical psychology.

Theory

B. F. Skinner was a psychologist who, among other things, studied the effects of behavior consequences on animal and human learning. Although he wrote extensively about many topics, he is most commonly associated with the principles of positive and negative reinforcement. Positive reinforcement is the presentation of a pleasurable consequence following a behavior, with the result being an increase in the future probability of that behavior. By contrast, negative reinforcement is the behavior-contingent *removal* or *postponement* of a nonpleasurable experience, which also produces an increase in responding.

As noted, negative reinforcement can operate in two ways. When one's behavior stops or reduces ongoing contact with an unpleasant experience, it functions as "escape." To illustrate, turning up the thermostat at home during winter months will terminate the cold temperature in a room. With the second operation, the individual is not confronted with a contemporaneous unpleasant situation but behaves to prevent or avoid its occurrence. Escape responding, therefore, requires that the behavior be demonstrated in the presence of the nonpreferred (negative) situation, whereas avoidance responding occurs in the absence of the nonpreferred (negative) situation.

Avoidance learning can be traced to the study of *discriminated avoidance* that emerged from animal research. A neutral stimulus, such as a light or tone, was presented to a rat in an experimental chamber preceding the delivery of electric shock through a grid floor. If the rat pressed a lever during a preset interval between onset of the stimulus and the noxious stimulation, the electric shock would be prevented. The behavior of lever pressing is "discriminated" because it does not occur in the absence of the light or tone, which have become a warning signal.

Other Considerations in Avoidance Learning

As revealed in the preceding example with lower organisms, avoidance learning is predicated on exposure to aversive stimulation that subsequently can be predicted by an exteroceptive cue or signal. Among humans, however, similar learning can be promoted without direct contact with an unpleasant situation. On one hand, an individual's behavior may adhere to the avoidance paradigm by *observing* the performance of other people. Avoiding interpersonal difficulties with a supervisor on the job, for instance, might be the outcome for a worker who sees colleagues chastised or rebuked, or receive similar harsh consequences, when they interact with that individual.

Learning through avoidance without actually experiencing negative situations also can be the result of giving an individual verbal instructions, directions, or explanations. Such is the case when a parent informs a young child, "Don't touch the stove," in order to prevent injury. Similarly, the visibility of "Do" and "Don't" signs abundant in our environment provides explicit warnings for the purpose of avoiding untoward (and possibly fatal) consequences. Verbal and written language is said to mediate or control behavior through rule governance.

Avoidance Learning in Clinical Psychology

Within clinical psychology, avoidance learning is pertinent in both understanding the causes of maladaptive behaviors and formulating methods to intervene therapeutically. Relative to etiology, psychologists have long posited that experiential avoidance is at the heart of many clinical disorders. Thus, a person who struggles to cope effectively may abuse alcohol or use illicit drugs to avoid confronting sources of stress and discomfort.

When implemented for therapeutic purposes, avoidance learning is promoted according to a five-step process: (1) identifying a problem behavior to be reduced or eliminated, (2) selecting a response to serve as replacement for the problem behavior, (3) choosing a negative consequence, (4) pairing the negative consequence with the problem behavior, and (5) allowing the person receiving treatment to avoid the negative consequence. Although this step-wise progression looks like a straightforward process, it is not without complications. First, there are ethical concerns when proposing or using negative and distressing events with individuals who already have adjustment difficulties. Second, even if an avoidance learning approach to treatment seems appropriate, it can be an arduous task arranging contiguous behavior and unpleasant conditions. And third, negative reinforcement generally would not be considered the sole basis of treatment, but instead it would be combined with other therapeutic procedures to prompt and maintain compensatory skills.

Avoidance learning for therapeutic purposes is employed typically by professionals from the disciplines of behavior therapy and behavior modification. Beginning in the early 1960s, several research reports by behavioral psychologists described examples of avoidance conditioning that incorporated extremely aversive stimulation. In one demonstration, children who had autism and were unresponsive to social interaction learned to avoid electric shock by approaching a therapist who called to them, "Come here." Faradic and other noxious stimuli such as foul odors and tastes also were programmed with individuals to condition avoidance of cues and situations associated with alcohol ingestion, drug use, and "deviant" sexual orientation. By contemporary standards these approaches would be unacceptable and viewed by some as dehumanizing. In fact, the majority of behavioral practitioners have essentially abandoned aversive treatment procedures in favor of positively oriented and skill-building strategies.

Although avoidance learning is still included in many current therapies, the types of negative experiences are more benign than those found in the historical record. As a whole, and when contrasted to other behavior-change procedures, avoidance learning and training is used less frequently in clinical practice. Again, because avoidance must be produced by exposure (real or threatened) to unpleasant conditions, it should be considered cautiously and applied with great care on those occasions when it can be justified clinically.

Summary

Avoidance learning is a powerful influence on human behavior. It is generated by encountering a negative situation, observing other people in similar circumstances, or being informed about the consequences of behavior. Verbal and written language serve frequently as warning stimuli that occasion avoidance-maintained responding. In a clinical context, avoidance learning has been incorporated to overcome problems and teach compensatory skills.

James K. Luiselli
The May Institute, Inc., Norwood, MA

AVOIDANT PERSONALITY

Avoidant personality, or Avoidant Personality Disorder (APD), is a label included in the *Diagnostic and Statistical Manual of Mental Disorders* of the American Psychiatric Association to describe a condition in which a person

1. Avoids occupational activities that involve significant interpersonal contact because of fears of criticism, disapproval, or rejection
2. Is unwilling to get involved with people unless certain of being liked
3. Shows restraint within intimate relationships because of the fear of being shamed or ridiculed
4. Is preoccupied with being criticized or rejected in social situations
5. Is inhibited in new interpersonal situations because of feelings of inadequacy
6. Views self as socially inept, personally unappealing, or inferior to others
7. Is unusually reluctant to take personal risks or to engage in any new activities because of potential embarrassment (*DSM-IV,* 1994, pp. 664–665)

Avoidant Personality Disorder is found in approximately 1% of the general population and in 10% of individuals seeking outpatient treatment from mental health clinics. This personality pattern occurs equally in men and women. Although APD can begin when people are in their teens, many avoidant individuals report that they have been socially anxious for as long as they can remember. Individuals with APD commonly display a variety of other clinical disorders, in particular, the anxiety disorders, mood disorders, and schizophrenic-spectrum disorders. Empirical studies also indicate that between 15% and 30% of people who abuse alcohol meet the criteria for APD, which suggests that long-standing social avoidance may increase vulnerability to substance dependence.

Personality types characterized by social sensitivity and withdrawal appear in earlier clinical descriptions of personality disorders; however, contemporary views of avoidant personality disorder have their origins in Theodore Millon's biosocial learning theory. In his book *Disorders of Personality* (1981), Millon proposed that the avoidant pattern develops when a child with a fearful or anxious temperament is exposed to early social experiences characterized by persistent deprecation, rejection, and humiliation. Avoidant individuals learn what Millon labeled an *active-detached* coping pattern. This consists of behavioral strategies designed to protect the person from the painful emotions he or she expects to result from interpersonal encounters.

Cognitive and interpersonal models of APD have also been developed. In their book *Cognitive Therapy of Personality Disorders* (1990), Aaron Beck and Arthur Freeman emphasized the role of cognitive schemas that develop in response to traumatic early social experiences and/or biological sensitivities. According to these writers, schemas—the cognitive structures that organize experience—include beliefs and rules of conduct, which for the avoidant person take such forms as "If people get close to me they will reject me" and "Don't stick your neck out." Although accurate in an historical sense, these schemas are hypothesized to lead to distortions in processing current social information and to the adoption of maladaptive interpersonal strategies.

Interpersonal writers emphasize the contribution of self-perpetuating transactional cycles to the onset and maintenance of APD. According to these writers, early social experiences lead avoidant individuals to develop beliefs about people that color their interpretations of current interactions. As a result, they adopt behaviors that provoke negative reactions from others, thereby confirming their original beliefs. In short, people with APD are caught in a cycle of unwittingly reenacting the early significant relationships that led to the development of their underlying fears. Consistent with all of these theories, research indicates that childhood maltreatment, particularly neglect, increases the likelihood that a person will develop APD.

There are similarities between APD and personality traits such as shyness and behavioral inhibition. The primary distinction is that APD is characterized by greater distress and impairment. Shyness and behavioral inhibition have been shown to arise in part from innate differences in physiological reactivity to environmental change. This suggests that individuals with APD either have stronger biological dispositions toward anxiety than do shy people or have experienced more negative social developmental events that exacerbate innate biological vulnerabilities.

Avoidant Personality Disorder also shares features with several other clinical conditions, most notably generalized Social Phobia (GSP) and Dependent Personality Disorder (DPD). A substantial number of individuals with APD also meet diagnostic criteria for GSP, and as many as 60% of patients with GSP meet criteria for APD. Comparative studies indicate that patients with APD report greater social anxiety and depression and lower self-esteem, and they display more comorbid diagnoses than do patients with GSP alone, but few other differences emerge. Avoidant Personality Disorder also overlaps with DPD. Research suggests that only the symptom of social withdrawal reliably discriminates the two conditions, and in practice, diagnoses of APD and DPD often co-occur. Distinctions between APD, GSP, and DPD require further study.

A variety of treatment strategies for APD have been evaluated, including cognitive-behavioral, interpersonal, and pharmacological regimens. Empirical studies show that behavioral and cognitive-behavioral treatment programs produce significant improvement in social comfort and activity in avoidant individuals and may be more effective than psychodynamic therapies. Overall, psychological treatments produce significant gains in avoidant patients, and these gains are maintained, at least over the year following treatment termination. On a less positive note, many APD individuals remain at the low end or below normative levels of social functioning even after treatment. This suggests that avoidant individuals may require a longer course of treatment or that biological factors or early trauma limit change. Pharmacological regimens have also been examined, primarily in the context of treating patients with Social Phobia. The monoamine oxidase inhibitors (MAOIs), particularly phenelzine, and the serotonin-reuptake inhibitors (SRIs) are considered the most effective pharmacological interventions presently available. Even patients who respond to medication, however, can continue to have some problems with social avoidance, and further work on the treatment of this long-standing condition is required.

SUGGESTED READING

Alden, L. E., Laposa, J. M., Taylor, C. T., & Ryder, A. G. (2002). Avoidant personality disorder: Current status and future directions. *Journal of Personality Disorders, 16,* 1–29.

Beck, A. T., & Freeman, A. (1990). *Cognitive therapy of Personality Disorders.* New York: Guilford Press.

Millon, T. (1981). *Disorders of Personality, DSM-III: Axis II.* New York: Wiley Interscience.

Lynn Alden
University of British Columbia, Vancouver, Canada

See also: Shyness

B

BABINSKI SIGN

In 1896, Joseph François Félix Babinski (1857–1932) reported the clinical sign that now bears his name. Babinski noted that stimulation of the soles of the feet of some patients with unilateral paralysis induced, not the expected flexion, but rather the extension of the great toe on the paralyzed side (Babinski, 1896). Others had seen this reflex response, but Babinski was the first to recognize and call attention to its diagnostic importance, for example, in differentiating structural from hysterical paralysis (Babinski, 1898). He later pointed out that fanning of the lateral toes may accompany extension of the great toe (Babinski, 1903).

The sign is best elicited by having the patient lie supine with the leg uncovered and supported by the examiner. After informing the patient about what is to happen, a stimulus (ranging from light touch to moderately firm and slightly noxious pressure from a blunt object like a wooden applicator stick or key) is applied to the lateral plantar surface of the foot in a gentle, sweeping motion from heel to ball (van Gijn, 1995). The hallmark positive (extensor) response is mediated by contraction of the long extensor of the great toe (*extensor hallucis longus*). Careful observation for tightening of the *extensor hallucis longus* tendon may resolve doubts about whether the sign is present. Extensor responses can be evoked by stimuli applied to a number of other loci on the foot or leg, but the interpretation of the response is the same. Extension of the toe (away from the noxious stimulus on the sole) is part of a generalized flexion response of the stimulated limb, so visible flexion of thigh on hip, leg on knee, and foot on ankle may occur, brought about by contraction of the tibialis anterior, hamstrings, tensor fasciae latae, and iliopsoas muscles, respectively (Bassetti, 1995).

The clinical significance of the Babinski sign is found by reviewing its developmental course. A positive response has been reported in 10–90% of normal newborns (Hogan & Milligan, 1971; Jaynes, Gingold, Hupp, Mullett, & Bodensteiner, 1997). The pyramidal tracts of the central nervous system, carrying neurons from the motor cortex into the spinal cord, subserve voluntary muscle function throughout the body. As these tracts mature during the first 6 months of life, the toe response changes from extensor to flexor by the age of 9–12 months (Katiyar, Sen, & Agarwal, 1976); the entire flexion response of the lower extremity is extinguished along with the Babinski response (van Gijn, 1995).

Since maturation of the pyramidal tracts underlies the developmental disappearance of the Babinski response, it is not surprising that persistence of the response after the first year of life—or its later reappearance, especially if laterally asymmetrical—indicates disease affecting the pyramidal tract. As Babinski knew, the sign often accompanies destructive lesions of the motor fibers innervating the foot; in these patients careful testing may reveal weakness of the affected limb or at least disturbances of fine motor function (Bassetti, 1995).

Now, more than 100 years after its initial description, the extensor response of the great toe remains one of the best known and clinically useful of the eponymic signs in clinical medicine. Its unilateral presence almost always indicates serious structural abnormalities of the upper motor neurons serving the affected limb. The finding of a positive Babinski response after the first year of life should be considered abnormal and appropriate neurological investigation should be undertaken to identify the nature and location of the abnormal process.

REFERENCES

Babinski, J. (1896). Sur le réflexe cutané plantaire dans certains affections organiques du système nerveux central. *Comptes Rendus de la Société de Biologie, 48,* 207–208.

Babinski, J. (1898). Du phénomène des orteils et de sa valeur sémiologique. *Semaine Médicale, 18,* 321–322.

Babinski, J. (1903). De l'abduction des ortreils. *Revue Neurologique (Paris), 11,* 728–729.

Bassetti, C. (1995). Babinski and Babinski's sign. *SPINE, 20,* 2591–2594.

Hogan, G. R., & Milligan, J. E. (1971). The plantar reflex of the newborn. *New England Journal of Medicine, 285,* 502–593.

Jaynes, M. E., Gingold, M. K., Hupp, A., Mullett, M. D., & Bodensteiner, J. B. (1997). The plantar response in normal newborn infants. *Clinical Pediatrics, 36,* 649–651.

Katiyar, G. P., Sen, S., & Agarwal, K. N. (1976). Plantar response during infancy. *Acta Neurologica Scandinavica, 53,* 390–394.

van Gijn, J. (1995). The Babinski reflex. *Postgraduate Medical Journal, 71,* 645–648.

Francis A. Neelon
Duke University Medical Center

THE BECK DEPRESSION INVENTORY-II

The Beck Depression Inventory-II (BDI-II; Beck, Steer, & Brown, 1996) is a 21-item self-report instrument for measuring the severity of depression in adolescents and adults according to symptoms corresponding to the criteria for diagnosing major depressive disorders listed in the fourth edition of the American Psychiatric Association's (1994) *Diagnostic and Statistical Manual of Mental Disorders* (*DSM-IV*). It is the upgraded version of the amended Beck Depression Inventory (BDI-IA; Beck & Steer, 1993), which, in turn, replaced the original instrument developed by Beck, Ward, Mendelson, Mock, and Erbaugh (1961).

The BDI-II is scored by summing the highest rating for each of the 21 symptoms, and a 4-point scale ranging from 0 to 3 is employed for each item. Respondents are asked to rate each symptom for the past 2 weeks, through that day. This instrument generally requires between 5 and 10 minutes to complete. Beck, Steer, and Brown (1996) suggested the following cutoff score guidelines for evaluating the severity of self-reported depression in patients diagnosed with major depressive disorders: Total scores from 0 to 13 are "minimal," and those from 14 to 19 are "mild." Scores from 20 to 28 are "moderate," and scores from 29 to 63 are "severe."

Reliability

The internal consistency of the BDI-II has repeatedly been described as high with a coefficient alpha of approximately .90 in adolescent (Steer, Kumar, Ranieri, & Beck, 1998) and adult psychiatric patients (Steer, Ball, Ranieri, & Beck, 1997) and college students (Dozois, Dobson, & Ahnberg, 1998; Osman, Downs, Barrios, Kopper, Gutierrez, & Chiros, 1997; Steer & Clark, 1997). Beck, Steer, and Brown (1996) reported that the 1-week test-retest reliability was also high ($r = .93$) for 26 outpatients who completed the BDI-II before their first and second cognitive therapy sessions.

Validity

For their normative samples of 500 outpatients who were diagnosed with various psychiatric disorders and 120 college students, Beck, Steer, and Brown (1996) described a number of analyses that supported the convergent and discriminant validities of the BDI-II. For example, the BDI-II was more positively correlated with the revised Hamilton Psychiatric Rating Scale for Depression (Riskind, Beck, Brown, & Steer, 1987; $r = .71$) than it was with the revised Hamilton Rating Scale for Anxiety (Riskind et al., 1987; $r = .47$) in 87 outpatients.

Factor Structure

Beck, Steer, and Brown (1996) found that the BDI-II was composed of two positively correlated *cognitive* and *noncognitive* (*somatic-affective*) dimensions for both psychiatric outpatients and students. The noncognitive factor is represented by somatic symptoms, such as loss of energy, and affective symptoms, such as irritability, whereas the cognitive factor is composed of psychological symptoms, such as self-dislike and worthlessness. Steer, Ball, Ranieri, and Beck (1999) also identified these two factors in 210 adult outpatients (age 18 or older) who were diagnosed with *DSM-IV* depressive disorders, as did Steer, Kumar, Ranieri, and Beck (1998) in 210 adolescent psychiatric outpatients and Steer, Rissmiller, and Beck (2000) in 130 depressed geriatric inpatients (age 55 or older). These two dimensions were also reported by Steer and Clark (1997) and Dozois, Dobson, and Ahnberg (1998) for college students and by Arnau, Meagher, Norris, and Bramson (2001) for primary-care medical patients. However, Osman and colleagues (1997) found three factors representing *negative attitudes, performance difficulty,* and *somatic elements* in 230 college students, and Buckley, Parker, and Heggie (2001) also found three factors representing *cognitive, affective,* and *somatic* dimensions in 416 male substance abusers.

REFERENCES

American Psychiatric Association. (1994). *Diagnostic and statistical manual of mental disorders* (4th ed.). Washington, DC: Author.

Arnau, R. C., Meagher, M. W., Norris, M. P., & Bramson, R. (2001). Psychometric evaluation of the Beck Depression Inventory-II with primary care medical patients. *Health Psychology, 20,* 112–119.

Beck, A. T., Steer, R. A., & Brown, G. K. (1996). *Manual for the Beck Depression Inventory-II.* San Antonio, TX: The Psychological Corporation.

Beck, A. T., & Steer, R. A. (1993). *Manual for the Beck Depression Inventory.* San Antonio, TX: The Psychological Corporation.

Beck, A. T., Ward, C. H., Mendelson, M., Mock, J., & Erbaugh, J. (1961). An inventory for measuring depression. *Archives of General Psychiatry, 4,* 561–571.

Buckley, T. C., Parker, J. D., & Heggie, J. (2001). A psychometric evaluation of the BDI-II in treatment-seeking substance abusers. *Journal of Substance Abuse Treatment, 20,* 197–204.

Dozois, D. J. A., Dobson, K. S., & Ahnberg, J. L. (1998). A psychometric evaluation of the Beck Depression Inventory-II. *Psychological Assessment, 10,* 83–89.

Osman, A., Downs, W. R., Barrios, F. X., Kopper, B. A., Gutierrez, P. M., & Chiros, C. E. (1997). Factor structure and psychometric characteristics of the Beck Depression Inventory-II. *Journal of Psychopathology and Behavioral Assessment, 19,* 359–375.

Riskind, J. H., Beck, A. T., Brown, G., & Steer, R. A. (1987). Taking the measure of anxiety and depression: Validity of the reconstructed Hamilton scales. *Journal of Nervous and Mental Disease, 175,* 474–479.

Steer, R. A., Ball, R., Ranieri, W. F., & Beck, A. T. (1997). Further evidence for the construct validity of the Beck Depression Inventory-II with psychiatric outpatients. *Psychological Reports, 80,* 443–446.

Steer, R. A., Ball, R., Ranieri, W. F., & Beck, A. T. (1999). Dimensions of the Beck Depression Inventory-II in clinically depressed outpatients. *Journal of Clinical Psychology, 55,* 117–128.

Steer, R. A., & Clark, D. A. (1997). Psychometric characteristics of the Beck Depression Inventory-II with college students. *Measurement and Evaluation in Counseling and Development, 30,* 128–136.

Steer, R. A., Kumar, G., Ranieri, W. F., & Beck, A. T. (1998). Use of the Beck Depression Inventory-II with adolescent psychiatric outpatients. *Journal of Psychopathology and Behavioral Assessment, 20,* 127–137.

Steer, R. A., Rissmiller, D. F., & Beck, A. T. (2000). Use of the Beck Depression Inventory-II with depressed geriatric inpatients. *Behaviour Research and Therapy, 38,* 311–318.

Robert A. Steer
University of Medicine and Dentistry of New Jersey School of Osteopathic Medicine

Aaron T. Beck
Beck Institute for Cognitive Therapy and Research

See also: **Depression; Reliability; Self-report**

BEHAVIOR GENETICS

The past two decades have produced an exponential increase in research examining the genetic and environmental factors that influence both normal and atypical patterns of behavior. This rapid accumulation of new knowledge illustrates the broad impact of behavioral and molecular genetic methods. However, the results of these studies have also underscored the complexity of the etiological pathways for all psychological traits and demonstrate clearly how much is yet to be learned.

The first section of this entry provides a brief overview of behavioral genetic methods that can be used to determine the extent to which a psychological trait or disorder is due to genetic or environmental influences. The second section describes molecular genetic techniques that can then be applied to localize genes that increase risk for the disorder. Finally, the concluding section summarizes several key implications and future directions of behavioral genetic studies.

Behavioral Genetic Methods

Behavioral genetic methods are designed to estimate the relative influence of genetic and environmental factors on individual differences in a trait or in symptoms of a disorder. The influence of genes is quantified by estimating *heritability,* the proportion of the population variance in a trait that is attributable to genetic influences. The proportion of variance due to environmental factors can be subdivided into *shared* and *nonshared environmental influences.* Shared environmental influences are those that similarly influence members of a family, thereby increasing the similarity of individuals within a family in comparison to unrelated individuals in the population. In contrast, nonshared environmental influences either affect just one individual in a family or have a different effect on different family members. In either case, nonshared environmental influences are those that lead to differences among individuals in a family.

Family Studies

Because individuals cannot be randomly assigned to different environmental or genetic backgrounds, family, adoption, and twin studies take advantage of different naturally occurring events to estimate the extent to which a trait or disorder is due to genetic or environmental influences. In the family study design the rate of a disorder is compared among the biological relatives of individuals with and without the disorder. If the disorder occurs more often in the family members of individuals with the disorder, this suggests that familial factors increase risk for the disorder.

Previous family studies have found that most psychological traits and disorders are significantly familial. However, because a disorder could run in families because of either genetic influences or shared environmental factors, adoption and twin studies are necessary to disentangle their relative contributions.

Adoption Studies

The adoption study design compares the prevalence of a disorder among adoptive and biological relatives of individuals with the disorder. The biological relatives of an individual who has been adopted are related genetically to the individual but have not shared any environmental influences. In contrast, adoptive relatives live in the same family environment but are biologically unrelated to the individual. Therefore, if a disorder is due to genetic factors, the biological relatives of individuals with the disorder should exhibit a higher rate of the disorder than the population base rate, whereas an elevated rate of the disorder among adoptive relatives would suggest that family environmental influences play a role in the etiology of the disorder.

The adoption design is quite elegant and has been helpful for some disorders, but two specific constraints have limited the utility of adoption studies. Most importantly, in societies in which adoption records are closed, it is often quite difficult to obtain information from the biological relatives of individuals who are adopted. Moreover, adoptive parents may not be representative of the overall population of parents due to the laudable desire of adoption agencies to place adopted children in an optimal environment with high-functioning parents with many available resources.

Twin Studies

By comparing the similarity of monozygotic (identical) twins, who share all of their genes, to dizygotic (fraternal) twins, who share half of their segregating genes on average, the twin-study methodology facilitates the estimation of the proportion of the total variance in a trait that is attributable to the influence of genes, shared environment, and nonshared environment. Results of large population-based twin studies have shown that genetic influences are significant for virtually all psychological traits and disorders. Similarly, environmental factors also play an important role in the etiology of nearly every trait or disorder that has been studied, although nonshared environmental influences are often slightly stronger. Therefore, the question is no longer whether a trait is due to nature *or* nurture, but instead the extent to which each of these factors and the interactions between them influence the development of the trait. In the next section we turn to methods that can be used to identify the specific genes that influence these behaviors.

Molecular Genetic Approaches

Although an estimated 99.8% of the deoxyribonucleic acid (DNA) sequence that comprises the human genetic code is identical among all people, the genetic sequence varies at thousands of locations across the remaining 0.2% of the human genome. Many of these sequence differences cause individual differences in protein production, which may then lead to individual differences in neural development or adult brain functioning if the sequence differences occur in a gene that are expressed in the central nervous system. Two primary methods can be used to identify the approximate location of genes that contain sequence differences that influence a trait.

Candidate Genes

The candidate gene approach is useful if previous research has identified specific biological substrates that are associated with the disorder. For example, if a disorder is known to be associated with elevated or depleted levels of a specific neurotransmitter, plausible candidate genes can be identified that influence some aspect of this neurotransmitter system. Candidate gene studies have identified several intriguing associations between genes in the dopamine and serotonin systems and psychological traits and disorders such as novelty seeking, neuroticism, Attention-Deficit/Hyperactivity Disorder, Schizophrenia, and Bipolar Disorder. However, subsequent studies often fail to replicate the initial results, suggesting that these genes may have relatively small effects.

Linkage and Association

Although the candidate gene approach is useful when viable candidates can be identified based on previous research, the etiology of many disorders is not understood sufficiently well to identify likely candidate genes. In the absence of an a priori reason to examine specific candidate genes, family-based linkage analysis can be used to screen broad sections of the genome to identify regions that may contain a gene that increases susceptibility to a disorder, and association analyses can be used to narrow further the region that contains a gene that influences the trait or disorder. Linkage and association analysis take advantage of the fact that genes that are close together on a chromosome tend to be transmitted together across many generations. Although these methods typically do not identify a gene with functional significance for the disorder of interest, they facilitate the identification of smaller regions of the genome that may be fruitful targets for further focused studies.

Determining Gene Function

After a gene that influences behavior has been identified, the function of the gene must be determined. This can be accomplished by first mapping the entire sequence of the gene to identify specific sequences that vary among people. These sequence differences are then used to determine the specific proteins that are produced by the gene, and a variety of techniques can be applied in studies of humans or animals to determine the function of the gene.

The Future of Behavior Genetic Research

Implications for Psychiatric Diagnoses and Diagnostic Systems

In contrast to conditions such as Parkinson's Disease that are caused by a single gene, increasingly, data suggest that virtually all psychological traits and disorders are caused by a combination of many genetic and environmental risk factors. Moreover, it is likely that many of these genes increase risk for more than one disorder, suggesting that the boundaries between putatively distinct diagnoses may prove to be blurry. Behavioral and molecular genetic methods will provide an essential tool to improve the nosology of psychiatric diagnoses by revealing the common and unique risk factors that contribute to the development of complex disorders.

Prevention and Treatment

Results of future behavioral and molecular genetic studies are likely to facilitate the development and application of effective primary prevention and early intervention techniques that would be impossible without understanding of the etiology of the disorder. For example, if a screening revealed that an infant had significant genetic susceptibility to reading difficulties, tutoring could be implemented to improve important reading-related language processes before the child even began to learn to read. Similarly, knowledge about the specific genetic or environmental etiology of a disorder will enable tertiary treatments that target directly these causal factors.

Accessibility

In closing, it is worth noting that procedures for DNA collection and genetic analysis continue to become more automated and efficient. It is rapidly becoming possible for researchers with even relatively modest budgets to include a behavior genetic component within their study. The ability to apply these methods to a broad new set of psychological questions will facilitate an extraordinary kind of collaborative synergy between behavior genetic researchers and investigators in other areas of psychology and psychiatry that can only serve to strengthen the studies in both domains.

Erik Willcutt
University of Colorado at Boulder

See also: **Nature/Nurture Controversy**

BEHAVIOR MODIFICATION

Behavior modification is the field of study that focuses on using principles of learning and cognition to understand and change people's behavior (Sarafino, 1996). Although not all experts in this field would include cognitive processes in the definition (see Lee, 1992; Sweet & Loizeaux, 1991; Wolpe, 1993), these processes have been widely adopted and applied by behavior modification professionals since the early 1970s (Dobson, 1988; Kazdin, 1978; Mahoney, 1993; Williams, Watts, MacLeod, & Mathews, 1988).

Defining Characteristics of Behavior Modification

The field of behavior modification has several characteristics that make its approach unique (Kazdin, 1978; Wixted, Bellack, & Hersen, 1990). First, professionals in this field focus on people's *behavior,* which can be *overt,* such as motor or verbal acts, or *covert,* such as feelings, thoughts, or physiological changes. As a result, their approach typically involves (1) defining people's current status and progress in terms of behavior rather than traits or other broad features, (2) measuring the behavior in some way, and (3) whenever possible, assessing covert behaviors, such as fear, in terms of overt actions. Efforts to improve behavior can be directed at a *behavioral deficit*—that is, the behavior occurs with insufficient frequency, strength, or quality—or a *behavioral excess*—that is, it occurs too frequently or strongly. The behavior to be changed is called the *target behavior.*

Second, although behavior modification professionals recognize that injury and heredity can limit the abilities of an individual, they assume that human behavior is, for the most part, *learned* and influenced by the environment. The most basic types of learning are *respondent (classical) conditioning*—in which a stimulus gains the ability to elicit a particular response by being paired with an unconditioned stimulus that already elicits that response—and *operant conditioning*—in which behavior is changed by its consequences. The methods applied in behavior modification generally involve altering the *antecedents* and *consequences* of the target behavior.

Third, behavior modification has a strong scientific orientation. As a result, there is a major focus on carefully gathering empirical data, analyzing and interpreting the data, and specifying the precise methods used to gather and analyze the data. The field is also quite pragmatic, emphasizing the need to find and use techniques that work, as indicated by carefully conducted research. Fourth, behavior modification techniques for changing behavior often have clients or subjects become active participants, such as by performing "homework" and "self-management" activities, in the process of modifying their behavior.

History of Behavior Modification

Behavior modification developed from the perspective called *behaviorism,* which emerged with the work of John B. Watson (1913, 1930) and B. F. Skinner (1938, 1953). This perspective emphasizes the study of observable and measurable behavior and proposes that nearly all behavior is the product of learning, particularly operant and respondent conditioning. Three lines of research laid the foundation for behaviorism. Ivan Pavlov (1927) demonstrated the process of respondent conditioning. John Watson and Rosalie Rayner (1920) showed that an infant, "Little Albert," learned to fear a white rat through respondent conditioning. And Edward Thorndike (1898, 1931) studied how "satisfying" and "annoying" consequences—which we now call *reinforcement* and *punishment*—affect learning. Other studies formed the basis for applying the ideas of behaviorism by showing that conditioning techniques could effectively reduce fears (Jones, 1924) and improve problem behaviors of psychiatric patients (Ayllon & Michael, 1959; Lindsley, 1956). The field of behavior modification now includes the areas of the *experimental analysis of behavior,* which examines basic theoretical processes in learning, *applied behavior analysis,* which emphasizes application to socially important problems in various settings, and *behavior therapy,* which focuses on application in psychotherapy settings.

Application and Techniques of Behavior Modification

Behavior modification techniques have been applied successfully in a wide variety of settings and with many types of behaviors and populations (Sarafino, 1996). They have been used to improve general parenting skills, help parents correct children's problem behaviors, enhance instructional methods in schools, improve classroom conduct, train developmentally disabled children in self-help skills, reduce substance abuse, reduce depression and anxiety, promote people's health and prevent illness, and improve worker productivity and safety.

The techniques used in modifying behavior are quite varied. Operant techniques include some that deal with the consequences of behavior. In *reinforcement,* consequences strengthen the target behavior. *Positive reinforcement* involves introducing a pleasant event after the target behavior, and *negative reinforcement* involves removing or reducing an aversive circumstance if the target behavior occurs. *Extinction* is a procedure whereby eliminating the reinforcers of a target behavior weakens that behavior. When *punishment* is used as a consequence, it suppresses the target behavior. Operant techniques also address the antecedents of the target behavior. For instance, *prompting* involves using a stimulus to remind individuals to perform a behavior they know how to do or help them perform a behavior they do not do well. Other operant methods concentrate on the behavior itself. *Shaping* improves a target behavior by requiring better and better performance to receive reinforcement, and *chaining* is used to develop complex motor behaviors by organizing simple responses into a sequence.

Respondent techniques are usually applied to reduce conditioned emotional responses, such as fear or anger. One technique is *extinction,* in which a conditioned response is weakened by repeatedly presenting the conditioned stimulus without the unconditioned stimulus. Another method is *systematic desensitization,* whereby a conditioned emotional response is reduced by having the person experience increasingly strong conditioned stimuli while maintaining a relaxation response. The conditioned stimuli are arranged in a hierarchy from a very weak stimulus to a very intense one.

Other behavior modification techniques include *modeling,* a vicarious process in which individuals learn a behavior by watching someone else perform it; biofeedback; and various cognitive methods, such as relaxation training, thought stopping, and covert sensitization. *Biofeedback* is a technique that teaches people to regulate physiological functioning by presenting moment-by-moment information about the status of the body system. The form of relaxation that is most commonly applied in behavior modification is *progressive muscle relaxation,* which has the person alternately tense and relax separate muscle groups. Once the relaxation response is mastered, the procedure can be used by itself or as part of systematic desensitization. *Thought stopping* is a technique in which individuals interrupt distressing thoughts by saying "Stop" emphatically, either aloud or covertly. *Covert sensitization* is a method that is used to teach a person to dislike a liked event, such as drinking alcohol, by pairing it repeatedly with an aversive event in an imagined situation.

Applying behavior modification is a creative enterprise that organizes techniques into programs that are tailored to meet the needs of specific clients in particular circumstances.

REFERENCES

Ayllon, T., & Michael, J. (1959). The psychiatric nurse as a behavioral engineer. *Journal of the Experimental Analysis of Behavior, 2,* 323–334.

Dobson, K. S. (Ed.). (1988). *Handbook of cognitive-behavioral therapies.* New York: Guilford Press.

Jones, M. C. (1924). The elimination of children's fears. *Journal of Experimental Psychology, 7,* 382–390.

Kazdin, A. E. (1978). *History of behavior modification: Experimental foundations of contemporary research.* Baltimore: University Park Press.

Lee, C. (1992). On cognitive theories and causation in human behavior. *Journal of Behavior Therapy and Experimental Psychiatry, 23,* 257–268.

Lindsley, O. R. (1956). Operant conditioning methods applied to research in chronic schizophrenia. *Psychiatric Research Reports, 5,* 118–139.

Mahoney, M. J. (1993). Introduction to special section: Theoretical developments in the cognitive psychotherapies. *Journal of Consulting and Clinical Psychology, 61,* 187–193.

Pavlov, I. P. (1927). *Conditioned reflexes* (G. V. Anrep, Trans.). New York: Oxford University Press.

Sarafino, E. P. (1996). *Principles of behavior change: Understanding behavior modification techniques.* New York: Wiley.

Skinner, B. F. (1938). *The behavior of organisms.* New York: Appleton-Century-Crofts.

Skinner, B. F. (1953). *Science and human behavior.* New York: Macmillan.

Sweet, A. A., & Loizeaux, A. L. (1991). Behavioral and cognitive treatment methods: A critical comparative review. *Journal of Behavior Therapy and Experimental Psychiatry, 22,* 159–185.

Thorndike, E. L. (1898). Animal intelligence: An experimental study of the associative processes in animals. *Psychological Review Monograph Supplements, 2*(8).

Thorndike, E. L. (1931). *Human learning.* New York: Century.

Watson, J. B. (1913). Psychology as the behaviorist views it. *Psychological Review, 20,* 158–177.

Watson, J. B. (1930). *Behaviorism.* New York: Norton.

Watson, J. B., & Rayner, R. (1920). Conditioned emotional reactions. *Journal of Experimental Psychology, 3,* 1–14.

Williams, J. M. G., Watts, F. N., MacLeod, C., & Mathews, A. (1988). *Cognitive psychology and emotional disorders.* New York: Wiley.

Wixted, J. T., Bellack, A. S., & Hersen, M. (1990). Behavior therapy. In A. S. Bellack & M. Hersen (Eds.), *Handbook of compar-*

ative treatments for adult disorders (pp. 17–33). New York: Wiley.

Wolpe, J. (1993). Commentary: The cognitivist oversell and comments on symposium contributions. *Journal of Behavior Therapy and Experimental Psychiatry, 24,* 141–147.

Edward P. Sarafino
The College of New Jersey

See also: **Reinforcement**

BEHAVIOR THERAPY: PROBLEMS AND ISSUES

Behavior therapy is an increasingly accepted part of the mental health establishment, bringing with it an influx of professional issues pertaining to clinical strategies, training, licensing, guidelines, accountability, legal constraints, and a host of problems encountered in the hurly-burly of daily practice.

Behavioral procedures go back to antiquity. What is new is the systematic application and formulation of the principles in terms of scientific methodology. This methodology contains within it the following features: objectivity, quantification, replicability, validation, hypothesis testing, reliance on data and reason rather than appeal to authority, and an obligation to submit feasible alternative explanations to scientific scrutiny.

For some behavior therapists, the conceptual framework is Pavlovian classical conditioning translated into practice by such techniques as aversion therapy and systematic desensitization. For other behavior therapists, the primary influence is Skinnerian operant conditioning and an empirical analysis of behavior, leading to behavioral shaping, token economies, and so forth. For yet others, the uniqueness of behavior therapy lies in its emphasis on the application of experimental methodology to individual cases. For social learning theorists, modeling and conditioning principles have been incorporated into a performance-based schema with the individual and the environment exerting reciprocal and interactive influences.

Some behavior therapists accept trait theories; others do not. For some, the environment is all-encompassing; for others, physiological and constitutional factors are paramount. Some view behavior therapy as in large part an exercise in self-actualization, but for others, self-control is a delusion. For this latter group, there is no such thing as a self; the guiding principle is radical or metaphysical behaviorism, with a complete denial of any intervening variable between stimulus and response. For some behavior therapists, data are sufficient and theory is of little or no consequence; for others, theory is essential if behavior therapy is to advance.

Most behavior therapists share certain characteristics in addition to or arising out of methodology. These include a focus on current rather than historical determinants of behavior, an emphasis on overt behavior change as a main criterion by which treatment is to be evaluated, the delineation of treatment in objective terms to make replication possible, a reliance on basic research as a source of hypotheses about treatment and specific techniques of intervention, and a specificity in defining, treating, and measuring target populations.

The definition of behavior therapy tentatively adopted by the Association for Advancement of Behavior Therapy in the early 1970s was as follows:

> Behavior therapy involves primarily the application of principles derived from research in experimental and social psychology for the alleviation of human suffering and the enhancement of human functioning. Behavior therapy involves a systematic evaluation of the effectiveness of these applications. Behavior therapy involves environmental change and social interaction rather than the direct alteration of bodily processes by biological procedures. The aim is primarily educational. The techniques facilitate improved self-control. In the conduct of behavior therapy, a contractual agreement is negotiated, in which mutually agreeable goals and procedures are specified. Responsible practitioners using behavior therapy are guided by generally accepted principles.

Behavior therapy started in the 1950s. Its first decade was characterized by ideology and polemics, the second by consolidation, and the third by the development of sophisticated methodology, innovative conceptual models, and a search for new horizons. These developments involve an increasing acceptance of inner processes (the so-called cognitive revolution), a growing interdisciplinary basis, and a broadening interface with the community. Because of this expanded domain, and because behavior therapy is not a unitary system with circumscribed therapeutic procedures, conceptual problems and issues arise.

Stimulus-Response Learning Theory and Conditioning in Behavior Therapy

There is increasing evidence that behavior therapy is firmly based on neither theories nor principles of conditioning. Conditioning is devoid of precise meaning. The differentiation between classical and operant conditioning remains equivocal. The relationships between conditioning in the laboratory, conditioning in the clinic, and conditioning in daily life are complex and open to diverse interpretations. No general factor of conditionability has as yet been demonstrated, even though it is an implicit assumption underlying much of behavior therapy. Neither classical conditioning, operant conditioning, nor applied behavioral analysis accounts adequately for the many complexities of neuroses. Attempts to update conditioning theory in terms of cognition, subjective experience, or interaction response patterns could complicate rather than clarify the issue.

Thus the evidence for conditioning as an explanatory concept in behavior therapy is, at best, equivocal.

Were it to be granted that behavior therapy is based on theories of learning, there is still little agreement about which learning theories or principles are applicable. Whether the prevailing concepts of conditioning are adequate to account for covert, inner-directed processes is yet unresolved. It is occasionally proposed that the foundation of behavior therapy be broadened to include knowledge drawn from social psychology, physiology, and sociology rather than relying exclusively on conditioning-based learning theory. To do so would be to change radically some of the premises on which behavior therapy is based.

A unifying factor in behavior therapy is generally considered to be its derivation from experimentally established procedures and principles that conform to the characteristic methodology of the behavioral scientist. Unfortunately, much of behavior therapy rests on limited scientific evidence. At best, behavior therapy is based on empirical validation rather than derivation from theory, and occasionally on little more than prevailing notions arising out of the clinical experience of the practitioner. Swan and MacDonald found that behavior therapy as actually conducted is not always consistent with the theories and principles espoused by the practitioners concerned.

Role of Cognition in Behavior Therapy

Perhaps because of a desire to discard anything that smacked of mentalism or inner processes, early behavior therapists resolutely rejected all forms of cognitive influence. Within two decades this situation changed drastically so that behavior therapy in the 1980s was in the throes of what was termed the "cognitive revolution." The emphasis on the role of cognition aroused considerable dispute and dialogue within the ranks of behavior therapy. For some behavior therapists, cognitions are not behaviors, but are hypothetical constructs used to account for relationships between the environment and behavior. For others, cognition is an integral part of behavior therapy, to be accounted for either in terms of some form of conditioning or by the introduction of an as yet undetermined additional explanatory concept.

The precise relationship between cognition and behavior remains equivocal. All therapies are probably simultaneously cognitive and behavioral to a greater or lesser extent. Further clarification must await the development of an appropriate technology of brain-behavior-cognitive function.

Virtually all current procedures in behavior therapy involve some cognitive influence. Most behavior therapists reject the radical or metaphysical approach in favor of some form of methodological behaviorism. It is more appropriate to regard contemporary behavior therapists as behavioral rather than behavioristic. Nevertheless, the debate about the behaviorism in behavior therapy is far from resolved, and the issue of what is and what is not philosophically legitimate remains a matter of lively controversy.

Certain individuals recognize the impossibility of philosophical or conceptual integration between psychoanalysis and behavior therapy but insist that some form of interaction is both feasible and desirable at the level of practice.

Cyril M. Franks
Rutgers University

See also: **Behaviorism; Cognitive Therapies; Operant Conditioning**

BEHAVIORAL INHIBITION

Behavioral inhibition is a consequence of an animal's capacity to learn both positive and negative relationships, whether these relationships involve stimuli or responses. The term arises from the seminal work of Pavlov (1927) in his studies of conditioned reflexes in hungry dogs. Pavlov found that an initially neutral conditioned stimulus (CS), such as the sound of a metronome, could acquire significance if it predicted the delivery of an unconditioned stimulus (US), such as meat powder. After a number of CS-US pairings, the CS would come to evoke a conditioned response (CR), such as salivation. This form of behavioral adaptation, known as excitatory conditioning, allowed the animal to prepare for the arrival of the US. Inhibitory conditioning is the counterpart of excitatory conditioning. Pavlov found that an initially neutral CS would acquire the ability to suppress the salivary CR (behavioral inhibition) if the CS signaled the absence of an expected US.

In *Conditioned Reflexes* (1927), Pavlov listed four experimental conditions under which responding is inhibited: (1) suppression of the CR evoked by an excitatory CS in the presence of a second "inhibitory" CS, (2) the gradual loss of the CR in extinction, (3) decreased generalized responding to an unreinforced CS when trained concurrently with a reinforced CS (called *differential conditioning*), and (4) diminution of the CR in the early portion of a long-duration CS. The first procedure is now the paradigmatic instance of what is called inhibitory conditioning.

Although Pavlov emphasized the importance of inhibitory conditioning, the idea was not initially well received. Interest in inhibitory conditioning was reawakened with the incorporation of inhibitory conditioning into correlative accounts of conditioning (e.g., Rescorla, 1967). During this time, the concept of inhibition also proved to be a powerful vehicle for understanding a wide range of clinically relevant behavioral phenomena. Of special interest was the persistence of phobic avoidance in the absence of further traumatic events. But the key development was Rescorla's (1969) introduction of the summation and retardation tests. These special tests could be applied to detect the presence of inhibition independently of the conditions under which it was observed.

Since its first introduction, the idea that a CS may possess inhibitory properties has stirred a great deal of controversy. How can a CS be declared inhibitory merely on the basis of a reduction in the probability of the CR? To resolve such a controversy, it is necessary to exclude alternative accounts. Historically, three general types of alternatives have been offered. One invokes competition between incompatible reactions. The second possibility is that an inhibitory CS draws attention away from other excitatory stimuli and is merely an attentional distractor. The third is that reduced responding is not a matter of inhibition but rather of less excitation.

Rescorla (1969) argued that an inhibitory CS should acquire properties opposite to those of an excitatory CS, if inhibition involved learning that a CS and US were negatively correlated. One test designed to show the oppositional properties of an inhibitory CS was called *summation.* If a CS were truly inhibitory, it should reduce the probability that an excitatory CS would evoke its usual CR when the two stimuli were presented in compound for the first time. To rule out attentional distraction, the reductions obtained should be greater than those produced by a control CS that was uncorrelated with the US. Further evidence of inhibition would be shown by retardation of acquisition in which the inhibitory CS is transformed into an excitatory CS. The required finding is that conditioning should proceed more slowly than transformation of a neutral CS into an excitor. These two tests, taken together, are still accepted by most in the field as firm evidence of inhibition.

Equipped with tests for verifying the status of an inhibitory CS, researchers turned to the question of the psychological basis for behavioral inhibition. On the basis of Pavlov's work, one might speculate that an inhibitory CS signals a period during which the US is absent. This can be shown to be false. If two distinctive CSs are paired on separate trials with the same US, and both CSs together are then combined with a third CS and the triplet is reinforced, it turns out that the third CS acquires the properties of a conditioned inhibitor, even though it does not signal the absence of the US (Kremer, 1978). However, this procedure also suggests an answer. When two excitatory CSs are combined, unusually high levels of excitation are elicited—much higher than can be sustained by a single US. Hence, although the third CS does not predict the nonoccurrence of the US, it does predict that the single US received will be less than is predicted by the two excitatory CSs. Thus, conditioned inhibition seems to develop when the US received is less than that anticipated. This is currently the most accepted psychological account (Wagner & Rescorla, 1972).

Experimentation has also revealed that an extinguished CS does not actually lose its excitatory power as the term *extinction* suggests. Instead, the excitatory CS acquires a new inhibitory association that joins the already present excitatory association. That extinction does not erase the original excitatory association is abundantly clear if one reminds the animal of the earlier association. For example, if acquisition takes place in a different experimental context than extinction, a return to the context of acquisition causes *renewal* of the original CR (Bouton, 1993). Renewal is of obvious importance for our understanding and treatment of anxiety disorders. Conditioned fears are never truly lost (extinguished) but are only inhibited. It should be apparent from this last example that behavioral inhibition is a rich area for the application of basic research to psychological dysfunctions.

REFERENCES

Bouton, M. E. (1993). Context, time, and memory retrieval in interference paradigms in Pavlovian learning. *Psychological Bulletin, 114,* 80–99.

Kremer, E. F. (1978). The Rescorla-Wagner model: Losses in associative strength in compound conditioned stimuli. *Journal of Experimental Psychology: Animal Behavior Processes, 4,* 22–36.

Pavlov, I. P. (1927). *Conditioned reflexes.* Oxford, UK: Oxford University Press.

Rescorla, R. A. (1967). Pavlovian conditioning and its proper control procedures. *Psychological Review, 74,* 71–80.

Rescorla, R. A. (1969). Pavlovian conditioned inhibition. *Psychological Bulletin, 72,* 77–94.

Wagner, A. R., & Rescorla, R. A. (1972). Inhibition in Pavlovian conditioning: Application of a theory. In R. A. Boakes & M. S. Halliday (Eds.), *Inhibition and learning.* London: Academic Press.

Douglas A. Williams
University of Winnipeg, Winnipeg, Canada

BEHAVIORAL MODELING

Much human learning occurs from sitting and watching, or from just happening to notice what someone else is doing. Indeed, more *social learning* occurs from observing others than from physically or verbally interacting and experiencing positive or negative outcomes. Observation provides information about what may be learned (alternative behaviors, potential consequences, etc.). When observation occurs under the right circumstances, it can result in immediate changes to learning or performance.

Modeling is defined as the process by which an individual (the model) serves to illustrate behavior that can be imitated or adapted in the behavior of another individual (the observer). It may also influence thoughts and attitudes. The model may be live; filmed; described in any other medium, such as print; or even imagined. The term *behavioral modeling* is distinguished from mathematical modeling and so on. Otherwise, the simpler term *modeling* is used.

When the observers are used as their own models, the process is called *self-modeling*. This process is procedurally very different, although there is a connecting theoretical thread (Dowrick, 1999; see encyclopedia entry "Video: Major Applications in Behavioral Science").

Applications

Modeling has been widely applied and evaluated in a variety of areas. Representative examples are described below under headings in six broad categories.

Professional Training

Modeling is often used in the training of human service personnel. For example, videotaped modeling has been used as a key component in training health care personnel to handle psychiatric emergencies and in training job coaches. Other popular training areas range from counselors to military special services, where it accounts for larger gains in skill acquisition than role-playing or feedback.

Social Skills and Daily Living

Modeling by in vivo demonstration is widely used as part of social skills training. Video modeling is the staple of many standard programs. It has been the primary component in a diverse range of training programs, from teaching young, isolated children to overcome their shyness, to providing alternatives to social behavior related to drug abuse, aggression, and other illicit or unhealthy activity. For example, films of age-appropriate students coping with social pressure to smoke cigarettes have been effective in programs at junior high schools. It may be noted that the programs with greatest effectiveness are those that illustrate adaptive coping (resisting coercion without destroying friendships), not negative consequences (early, gruesome death by cancer).

Parent and Child Issues

Different forms of modeling have been widely used in programs for parent training. While there is no substitute for realistic practice in acquiring skills for child care, it is equally clear that observing effective models is essentially valuable to begin such practice. Most parent training is requested because of the child's so-called problems. Therefore, children are taught communication and self-control skills as well. Modeling also proves effective for this purpose, using either peers or adults.

Preparing for Medically Related Treatments

The need to prepare people, especially children, for potentially invasive or scary treatment procedures has been extensively served by modeling strategies. Information (e.g., what steps are involved in the procedure) is important to emotional and long-term attitudes, but modeling is more essential to the immediate situation.

Physical Performance

Sport and other body coordination skills are widely taught using some form of demonstration by peers, coaches, and experts. Physical therapists also use modeling as the major component in rehabilitation through therapeutic exercises. The commercial video market is replete with examples, usually by experts, for the development of individual skills (golf, tennis, aerobics, skiing, etc.). Participants in team sports watch videotapes of opponents, not just to find weaknesses, but to seek out and imitate superior team playing strategies. Special effects (e.g., slow motion, still frames) in video modeling are most useful in motor performance applications.

Diverse Populations

Appropriately designed modeling has obvious application to individuals with disabilities and other diversity who may lack suitable models in their natural environment. Well-documented examples exist in the teaching of daily living skills, such as shopping by young adults with autism. Other types of skills for which modeling-based training has been developed include social skills, recreation, communication (e.g., sign language), vocational skills, and academics. Although it would seem best to use peers as models, often the models are expert adults from the dominant culture. Such demonstrations must be carefully constructed to match the individuality of the intended trainees.

General Principles

A modeling procedure focuses on the skill to be learned, its context, and its consequences. The modeled event is effective if the observer (1) absorbs the skill information, and later (2) has the opportunity, motive, and self-belief to use it (Bandura, 1997). Much research in the last 40 years has contributed to an understanding of these components.

The characteristics of the model contribute to the effectiveness of the procedure. The use of similar models, multiple models, and coping (as opposed to *mastery*) performances have been shown to assist effectiveness. These factors contribute to the ability of the viewer to absorb the skill information. They help to ensure that some of the skills demonstrated are attainable at an appropriate level of use by the observer.

When the model is similar, the observer will pay more attention and is more likely to be motivated to replicate the demonstrated behavior. Because the *activity* is important, behavioral similarity counts more than looks, social background, and so on, and unusual models, such as clowns, can gain attention without effective absorption of the skill information. The use of multiple models can boost the magnitude of effect and its generalization to other settings.

Coping (better called *struggling*) models are sometimes more effective than mastery models, who demonstrate only expert performance. High-status models can also be effective. These potentially contrary results are understood by considering how the modeled skills are relevant to the observer's ability level and how the specific model may contribute to motivation and sense of self-efficacy.

The characteristics of the observer and the setting also affect the efficacy of modeling. Sometimes observational learning must first be taught as a skill in itself—for example, young children with autism may not have learned to imitate others. Emphasizing a positive outcome or reward for the target behavior can enhance the effectiveness of a model. But it is important to note the frequent failure of negative modeling to act as a deterrent. The reverse is often the case, sometimes tragically. More than once, for example, televised dramatizations of teenage suicides, intended to be a deterrent, have been followed by increases in suicides of young people.

Modeling is well documented as a powerful intervention in its own right, but it is mostly used along with other procedures, such as opportunity to practice. It will normally take its place early in the learning sequence: basic information, *modeling,* practice, feedback, and feedforward. It can also be used as a sophisticated component in advanced learning applications.

REFERENCES

Bandura, A. (1997). *Self-efficacy: The exercise of control.* New York: Freeman.

Dowrick, P. W. (1999). A review of self modeling and related interventions. *Applied and Preventive Psychology, 8,* 23–39.

Peter W. Dowrick
University of Hawaii, Manoa

See also: **Self-efficacy; Video: Major Applications in Behavioral Science**

BEHAVIORISM

Behaviorism was the most significant movement in experimental psychology for the first three quarters of the twentieth century. It was launched by Watson in 1913, but had already begun in the work of psychologists such as Thorndike and Pavlov, and it remains influential today despite an increasing chorus of criticism after about 1960.

The history of behaviorism is told elsewhere in this encyclopedia; this article is a rational reconstruction of the movement, focusing on psychological rather than philosophical behaviorism. The name *behaviorism* implies that there is only one kind of behaviorism, but this is far from the case. There have been many behaviorisms, and they can be classified and defined in several ways. Several rational reconstructions of behaviorism are therefore possible, and some are listed at the end of this article.

Mentalism: What Behaviorism Rejects

Prior to behaviorism, experimental psychologists studied the mind, which they defined as conscious experience, and their research tool was one or another form of introspection. Among themselves they disagreed over what counted as scientific introspection: Wundt insisted on a highly controlled form of self-report, whereas Titchener and the Würzburg group allowed retrospective analyses of mental processes, and William James advocated ordinary armchair introspection. They also disagreed about how to explain conscious experience. Some advocated a reductionist approach, in which experience was to be explained by reference to underlying physiological processes. Others preferred to cite unconscious mental processes as the cause of experience. Still others advocated pure phenomenology, in which experience was described but not causally explained. In any case, all were mentalists in taking mind as the subject matter of psychology to be investigated by introspection. Behaviorism rejects the mentalistic definition of psychology and, therefore, mentalism's research method of introspection. Behaviorists define psychology as the science of behavior, and they study behavior, eschewing attempts to enter their subjects' minds.

Varieties of Behaviorism

Classical Behaviorism

Historically, the most important distinction among versions of behaviorisms is that between Watson's original classical behaviorism—boldly stated but imprecisely worked out—and a variety of more sophisticated systems inspired by him, known collectively as *neobehaviorism.* In his paper "Psychology as the Behaviorist Views It," Watson (1913, p. 158) spelled out the fundamental faith of all behaviorists:

> Psychology as the behaviorist views it is a purely objective experimental branch of natural science. Its theoretical goal is the prediction and control of behavior. Introspection forms no essential part of its methods, nor is the scientific value of its data dependent upon the readiness with which they lend themselves to interpretation in terms of consciousness. The behaviorist, in his efforts to get a unitary scheme of animal response, recognizes no dividing line between man and brute. The behavior of man, with all of its refinement and complexity, forms only a part of the behaviorist's total scheme of investigation.

Watson sets out the essential contrasts with mentalism: The subject matter of psychology is to be behavior, not mind or consciousness; its methods are objective, and introspection is to be rejected; and behavior is not to be interpreted or explained by reference to mental processes. Watson laid down the behaviorist's creed, but although he continued to expound his own version of behaviorism (see his *Behaviorism*), the movement was taken in different directions by his successors, the neobehaviorists.

Methodological Versus Metaphysical Behaviorism

Philosophically, one must distinguish two main justifications for rejecting mentalism and choosing behaviorism. A methodological behaviorist concedes that mental events and processes are real, but maintains that they cannot be studied scientifically. The data of science, says the methodological behaviorist, must be public events, such as the motions of the planets or chemical reactions that all researchers can observe. Conscious experience, however, is necessarily private; introspection may describe it (often inaccurately), but does not make it public for all to see. Therefore, to be scientific, psychology must study only overt behavior and reject introspection. However real and however fascinating, consciousness, methodologically speaking, cannot be scientific psychology's subject matter. The exploration of subjective experience is left to the arts.

The metaphysical behaviorist makes a more sweeping assertion: Just as the physical sciences have rejected demons, spirits, and gods, showing them to be myths, so the psychologist must reject mental events and mental processes as mythical. This is not to say that mental concepts such as "idea" are necessarily meaningless (although they may be), any more than the concept "Zeus" is meaningless. We can describe Zeus and account for why people believed in him, while nevertheless asserting that the word *Zeus* never referred to anything that ever existed. Similarly, says the radical behaviorist, we can describe the conditions under which people use "idea" or any other mental concept, and account for why they believe they have minds, and still assert that "idea" or "mind" and so on do not refer to anything that really exists, except perhaps certain behaviors and certain stimuli. Therefore, psychology must be behavioristic because there is no mind to investigate: Behavior is all there is.

Watson's own position is unclear. He typically defended behaviorism on methodological grounds but, especially in his later writings, asserted the metaphysical claim, too. The various neobehaviorists came down on different sides.

Varieties of Neobehaviorism

Once begun by Watson, the movement of behaviorism—like all movements—was changed by its later adherents. The major varieties of neobehaviorism are formal behaviorism, including logical behaviorism and purposive (or cognitive) behaviorism; informal behaviorism; and radical behaviorism. All but the last are forms of methodological behaviorism; radical behaviorists uphold metaphysical behaviorism.

Formal Behaviorism. While the behaviorist takes the subject matter of psychology to be behavior, he does not necessarily rule out talking about unobserved processes that may be used to explain observed behavior. Indeed, under the influence of logical positivism and operationalism the formal behaviorist made it his job to explain observed behavior in terms of a theory consisting of just such unobserved entities. However, these entities were not conceived as mental processes actually taking place in a person (or animal) and perhaps accessible to introspection, but were defined *behavior-theoretically;* that is, a given unobserved theoretical construct was operationally defined in terms of either manipulations performed on the animal or some aspect of its stimulus environment, or a measurable aspect of its behavior. In this way formal behaviorists hoped to gain scientific status by accepting methodological behaviorism, while aspiring to the same kind of explanatory theory found in physics or chemistry, where unobserved theoretical terms are commonplace.

The logical behaviorism of Hull and his associates was the most completely developed program of formal behaviorism. Following the lead of Newton and physics generally, Hull set out a hypothetico-deductive learning theory proposed to be valid for all mammals. The theory was stated as a set of axioms from which, via operational definition, predictions about behavior were derived that could then be put to the test.

To exemplify the method, consider the following (simplified) axiom from Hull's *Principles of Behavior* (1943):

$$_SE_R = {_SH_R} \times D$$

or in words, *reaction potential* ($_SE_R$) is equal to *habit strength* ($_SH_R$) times *drive* (D).

Reaction potential refers to the momentary tendency of an organism (e.g., a rat) to make a particular response (e.g., run down an alley). It may be measured, or operationally defined, in several ways, including latency (how long after we let him go does he get started), speed, strength (how much weight will he pull to get to the other end), or resistance to extinction of the response. The concept of habit strength claims that, when an organism learns something, it is learning something we cannot see except for when it happens to occur—namely, as a habit—and that the strength of the habit may be great or small. Operationally, habit strength was defined in terms of the number of times the organism has been reinforced for making a response such as running down an alley and finding food at the other end. Finally, drive refers to the motivational state of the organism and may be operationally defined in terms of number of hours without food or water. In doing an experiment, we can manipulate the values of $_SH_R$ and D, predict the value of $_{S}E_{R}$, measure its actual value, and check the prediction with the result.

The expressions $_{S}E_{R}$, $_{S}H_{R}$, and D are theoretical constructs or intervening variables. We do not observe reaction potential, habit strength, or drive directly; rather, we define them on the basis of what we do to the organism or on the basis of our measurement of its behavior. The theoretical strategy of formal behaviorism, then, is to permit theorizing about unobservable entities as long as one does not conceive of them mentalistically as something the organism has inside. Instead, theoretical constructs should be conceived of as intervening variables defined over stimuli and responses.

Tolman's purposive or cognitive behaviorism, when contrasted with Hull's logical behaviorism, shows how different two behaviorisms can be in detail while retaining allegiance to Watson's broad creed. Tolman rejected the mechanistic "muscle-twitchism" of Watson and Hull. For them, learning consisted in associating certain stimuli with specific motor responses, thus eliminating reference to purpose or cognition, which they regarded as mysterious and mentalistic. Tolman, on the other hand, conceived of behavior as ineluctably purposive (in that animals are always acting to move toward or away from some goal) and of learning as ineluctably cognitive (its purpose being not to respond to stimuli, but to learn about one's environment).

Nevertheless Tolman, like all behaviorists, shunned introspection and the study of consciousness. He constructed a theory that was much less fully elaborated than Hull's, despite the fact that it was he who introduced intervening variables to psychology. Tolman claimed that purpose, cognition, and expectancies could be defined theoretically through behavior. Tolman maintained that purposiveness was a property of behavior itself, or it could be treated as an operationally defined intervening variable.

Therefore, although Hull's and Tolman's learning theories were ever at odds, both are different theoretical and research strategies carried out within methodological, formal behaviorism. Following Watson, they abandoned mentalism for the objective study of behavior and, following the logical positivists, constructed theories of learning containing unobserved but nonmental, operationally defined theoretical constructs.

It needs to be said, however, that while Hull and Tolman theoretically followed operationalist and logical positivist guidelines, each one deviated sharply from them. Hull had a secret agenda to create a learning machine, and his theory was a description of that machine dressed in postulate form. Although Tolman, too, talked like a logical positivist, he thought of cognitive maps and expectancies as real things inside organisms' heads, not just as operationally defined constructs having no reality beyond theoretical convenience. In a narrow sense, then, neither Hull nor Tolman was a practicing formal behaviorist, because their theories were about something other than behavior: for Hull, the processes inside his learning machine, and for Tolman, cognitive processes inside living organisms. Their followers were truer to the behaviorist creed.

Informal Behaviorism. In any case, after the golden age of theory in the 1930s and 1940s, behaviorism went through further evolution. This was more true of Hull's logical behaviorism than of Tolman's purposive behaviorism, because Hull had more followers and left behind a more fully developed theory. The neo-Hullian behaviorism of the post–World War II era is sometimes called neobehaviorism, but a more descriptive phrase would be informal behaviorism or "liberalized Stimulus-Response theory." The major hallmark of the movement was lessened concern with axiomatic grand theory and increased willingness to talk about the higher mental processes in human beings, if done in S-R mediational terms. Formal behaviorism thus became less rigidly formal and more flexible in handling important human phenomena such as language and problem solving.

The informal behaviorists developed one of Hull's notions into a central cognitive process. Hull had explained some learning phenomena by postulating that organisms sometimes make fractional, unobservable responses (r) which have stimulus consequences (S), so that part of a learned S-R behavior chain is covert: S → r → s → R. Hull conceived mediating r-s pairs as covert peripheral responses (e.g., a rat might slightly salivate at even the beginning of a well-learned maze). The informal behaviorists, including Miller, Berlyne, Kendler, and Kendler, conceived r-s pairs as central brain processes that nevertheless followed the usual laws of S-R learning, and so could be incorporated into operational S-R theories of learning with no abandonment of behaviorism.

The informal behaviorists were thus able to talk about thinking, memory, problem solving, and language in S-R behavior theory terms, treating them as covert parts of learned S-R connections. In this way the range of behavior explicable in S-R terms was increased. A notable result was social learning theory, a marriage of neo-Hullian behaviorism and psychoanalysis, with some of Freud's postulated mental mechanisms being treated as covert mediating behaviors.

Historically, informal behaviorism has proven less a substantive position than a bridge from formal behaviorism to more cognitive, information-processing viewpoints. Once permitted to step inside the organism, as the central mediating response allowed behaviorists to do, there is little reason to think of the brain as an S-R device beyond mere prejudice in favor of S-R language. Once the prejudice is overcome, the attraction of the increased flexibility of information-processing language, accompanied by no loss of theoretical vigor, becomes irresistible. Whether one ceases to be a behaviorist upon giving in is an open question.

Radical Behaviorism. The purest form of behaviorism is Skinner's radical behaviorism—essentially the same as the less-well-known interbehaviorism of Kantor. Skinner rejected methodological behaviorism for the more radical assertion of metaphysical behaviorism: Mind and mental talk are cultural myths to be exploded and discarded.

Methodological behaviorists identified the mental with the private and made the latter off-limits for science. Skinner rejected the identification, recognizing that private events must figure in scientific psychology. A toothache is a private event, or stimulus, that powerfully controls one's behavior, leading one to take aspirin and visit the dentist. Radical behaviorism does not therefore reject an organism's private world, but studies it scientifically. However, it is a behaviorism because it rejects the mind and aims at the prediction and control of behavior.

Ordinary, everyday mentalistic talk is explained in three ways. First, some alleged mental events like toothaches are really just physical processes in the body that we have learned to label. There is no difference in principle between a public stimulus like a pinprick and a private one like toothache except that one person alone has access to the latter event. Second, some mental events, especially feelings, are just collateral by-products of environmental influence and resulting behavior but play no role in determining behavior. So one may "feel satisfied" if praised by one's boss, but what controls the behavior is the praise itself—the reinforcer—and not the collateral feeling. Unlike private stimuli, which may exert control over behavior, collateral feelings do not, and they may be ignored by scientific psychology, however much they fascinate the phenomenologist. Finally, many mentalistic terms are simply rejected outright as myths, being regarded as verbal operants taught by our culture and entirely devoid of reference. So, for example, free will is regarded as a myth (since all behavior is determined), invented largely in the Enlightenment as a reaction to the pain control used by oppressive, authoritarian governments. Such myths Skinner and his followers regard as dangerous because they stand in the way of effective application of behavioral technology and a scientific pursuit of happiness.

In its essence, though not at all in its details, radical behaviorism is the closest of all the neobehaviorisms to Watson's classical behaviorism. For the radical behaviorists, as for Watson, talk of mind is something to be exorcised by all, not just by scientists, as a relic of our superstitious, prescientific past. With positivism, radical behaviorists assert that whatever cannot be observed does not exist and that the world and its people would be better off abandoning comforting illusions to face bravely the material facts of life. Mind, they hold, should go the way of Zeus, Odin, and the imaginary friends of our childhood.

Behaviorism Today

Radical behaviorism is the only behaviorism exerting serious influence today. It has its own division within the American Psychological Association and its own journals, *The Experimental Analysis of Behavior* and *Applied Behavior Analysis*. The other behaviorisms have passed into history, their founders' intellectual descendents having altered them beyond recognition.

But behaviorism as a philosophy and an historical movement remains an object of interest to psychologists, philosophers, and historians. An important unresolved question is the current status of behaviorism. Although formal and informal behaviorism are clearly gone and radical behaviorism's importance is waning, it is clear that there has been no return to prebehavioristic mentalism. Cognitive psychologists still aim for the prediction and control of behavior, reject introspection for objective methods, have relatively little to say about consciousness, and study both humans and animals (as well as computers). In other words, they still could subscribe to Watson's basic creed, while rejecting his "muscle-twitchism" as did Tolman and the informal behaviorists. It is possible, then, that cognitive psychology is a new form of behaviorism with historical roots in Tolman's purposive behaviorism and Hull's fascination with learning machines. Or, if one insists that cognitive science's willingness to postulate real inner processes sets it off sharply from behaviorism, perhaps a new term is needed that encompasses both behaviorism and cognitive science, distinguishing both from traditional mentalism. Edmund Ions has coined a possible name: *behavioralism.*

REFERENCES

Hull, C. L. (1943). *Principles of behavior.* New York: Appleton-Century-Crofts.

Skinner, B. F. (1974). *About behaviorism.* New York: Knopf.

Watson, J. B. (1913). Psychology as the behaviorist views it. *Psychological Review, 20,* 158–177.

SUGGESTED READING

Leahey, T. H. (2000). *A history of psychology.* Upper Saddle River, NJ: Prentice Hall.

O'Donohue, W., & Kitchener, R. (Eds.). (1998). *Handbook of behaviorism.* Orlando, FL: Academic Press.

Thomas H. Leahey
Virginia Commonwealth University

See also: **Logical Positivism; Mind/Body Problem; Operationalism; Religion and Mental Health; Structuralism**

BELIEF IN A JUST WORLD

The Concept

The belief in a just world (BJW) refers to beliefs and processes that convey and maintain faith in the idea that the world is a fair and just place, a place where people get what they deserve and deserve what they get—a concept first described by Melvin J. Lerner in the 1960s. Lerner's interest in the concept came from his efforts to understand why highly educated university students consistently condemned victims of poverty as "lazy and no good," while denying evidence showing them to be victims of socioeconomic powers beyond their control. According to Lerner, in order to maintain psychological equanimity, engage in goal-directed behavior, and plan for the future, people need to believe that they live in a just world, a place where they will get what they deserve, at least in the long run.

The BJW serves several functions. First, it helps reduce existential terror (i.e., concerns resulting from our ability to comprehend a meaninglessness world and our own mortality). Specifically, without assurance that victims deserve their fates or that they will ultimately be compensated, people would be overcome by the suffering that surrounds them and be terrified that a similar fate could befall them. Second, the BJW encourages people to commit to long-range goals and facilitates the socially regulated behavior of day-to-day life. The belief encourages goal-directed, instrumental behavior by providing the rationalization necessary to engage in such behaviors. Specifically, without the knowledge that hard work will be rewarded, there is little rationale for exerting such effort. Finally, the belief that violators of societal regulations will be punished helps people to feel safe and keeps society orderly.

Maintenance Process and Reactions to Injustice

According to Lerner, instances of injustice arouse strong emotional reactions and defensive coping reactions. Typical emotional reactions range from empathic pain, concern, or pity, to revulsion, fear, or even panic (Lerner, 1980). People have developed sophisticated ways of warding off such negative emotions and maintaining their belief in a just world. Lerner outlines *rational* and *nonrational* strategies that function to eliminate or neutralize threats to the belief in a just world. Rational strategies include prevention and restitution. Here, social devices (e.g., social agencies) or one's own efforts may prevent injustice, restore justice, or at least compensate the victims of injustice. Acceptance of one's limitations is a cognitive strategy where the individual convinces him- or herself that if given infinite time and resources, justice could have been achieved; however, there is only so much that one person can do.

Nonrational strategies include denial of and withdrawal from the unjust situation and several varieties of cognitive reinterpretation, including reinterpretation of the outcome, reinterpretation of the cause, and reinterpretation of the character of the victim. Denial involves selective perception of the environment so as to avoid evidence of injustice, whereas withdrawal involves physically removing oneself from areas of potential injustice or, as a preventative measure, structuring one's life so as to avoid situations likely to reveal injustice. Overall, reinterpretation strategies involve reevaluating an unjust situation in a way that removes the injustice. Reinterpretation of the outcome may involve maintaining that unjust suffering promotes long-term benefits, that suffering makes one a better person, or that some people are happy in their suffering. Reinterpretation of the cause, or behavioral blame, refers to attributing the victim's fate to something he or she did or failed to do. Thus, justice would have prevailed, if only the victim had done the right thing. Finally, reinterpretation of the character of the victim, or characterological blame, refers to denigrating the personality of the victim so as to make him or her the type of person who deserves his or her unjust fate.

Lerner contends that people also develop long-term strategies to maintain BJW. Such strategies include developing a sense of ultimate justice, where despite short-term setbacks, justice wins out in the long run or where victims are compensated (or punished) in the afterlife. People may also compartmentalize cultures or subcultures into just and unjust ones. Therefore, not all cultures need be just, and injustices are acceptable and not personally threatening as long as they occur outside one's own culture.

Research on Belief in a Just World

Research on the BJW remains strong. Furthermore, and as a testimony to his original insight, Lerner's theory remains largely unchanged from his original statements. Theoretical advancements have been at the margins: What are the boundary conditions for belief in a just world? Are there multiple just and unjust worlds? What is the nature of the person who believes in a just world?

Overall, research on BJW falls into one of several categories. For example, a large number of studies have examined how people cope with injustice, including how they react emotionally, behaviorally, and cognitively to victims of injustice. Included are investigations of behavioral and characterological blame, with victimized groups including victims of rape or incest, the homeless, victims of spouse abuse, members of stereotyped groups, and people with diseases such as cancer or AIDS. A second category of research examines the role of BJW in other social processes. Included are studies examining how BJW relates to perceived risk assessment, facilitates coping with acute stress, is associated with life and marital satisfaction, contributes to practice of health behaviors, is associated with investment in long-term goals and motivation, relates to religiosity, and predicts recovery from illness. In contrast to the victim derogation work, these studies usually assess the adaptive side of BJW. A final category of research includes studies of the nature of the belief (e.g., is there a just world for self versus for others?), development and revision of individual difference measures, studies of the relation of BJW to political beliefs and ideologies, and cross-cultural studies of BJW.

REFERENCE

Lerner, M. J. (1980). *The belief in a just world: A fundamental delusion.* New York: Plenum Press.

JOE TOMAKA
University of Texas, El Paso

BELL-MAGENDIE LAW

The Bell-Magendie Law refers to the discovery, in the early 1800s, that sensory nerves enter the spinal cord by way of the dorsal roots of the spinal nerves, and motor nerves exit the spinal cord by way of the ventral roots. Recognition for making the discovery was attributed jointly to Charles Bell and François Magendie. Prior to this observation, it was held that nerves were tubular conduits that served both sense and motor functions. The discovery of functionally distinct sensory and motor nerves revealed, for the first time, clear evidence of the basic structure of the nervous system. Articulation of the physiology of the spinal reflex arc and the architecture of the nervous system in terms of the specific function of sensory and motor nerves developed directly and swiftly from this first fact of neural localization.

Charles Bell (1774–1842) was an accomplished Scottish anatomist and surgeon. In 1811, he wrote a pamphlet titled *Idea of a New Anatomy of the Brain: Submitted for the Observation of His Friends.* The pamphlet was privately printed and distributed to 100 friends and colleagues. In this letter, he outlined a rationale for the study of brain function, and he speculated about the location of higher mental functions in the brain. He considered that the functions of specific nerves were determined from their origin in different parts of the brain. During this discourse, he noted that spinal roots emerging from the vertebra fused together to form larger nerves. His opinion that these spinal nerve roots were functionally distinct was put to the test in a simple experiment. When he severed the posterior (dorsal) root, the muscles of the back did not convulse, but he observed a convulsion of the muscle when he touched the anterior (ventral) root.

In 1822 François Magendie (1783–1855), a French physician and physiologist, published his findings from experiments in which he cut unilaterally some of the posterior spinal roots, anterior spinal roots, or both posterior and anterior roots. Magendie had devised a clever procedure that enabled him to cut anterior roots without damaging the posterior roots. He noted that sensation (pain) was not elicited when the severed posterior root was touched, whereas the limb moved spontaneously when the anterior root was intact. Severing the anterior roots, however, caused the limb to go flaccid, whereas sensibility remained when the posterior root was intact. Magendie concluded that the anterior and posterior roots of the nerves emanating from the spinal cord have different functions, with the posterior root pertaining to sensibility, whereas the anterior root was linked to movement.

Following the publication of Magendie's article in 1822, a challenge to the priority of the discovery was issued by Charles Bell, and subsequently by his brothers-in-law John Shaw and Alexander Shaw in various texts and journals. Bell's unpublished 1811 pamphlet was cited as the basis for his claim to be the first to establish that sensory and motor nerves were distinct entities. This campaign to assign priority for the discovery to Bell was quite successful. Bell was lauded for the discovery by many eminent physiologists and scholars throughout the nineteenth century, such as Sherrington, who made seminal contributions to the physiology of spinal reflex arcs; Neuberger, a respected medical historian; and even by some of Magendie's contemporary French physicians, such as Flourens. Scholars who have more recently examined documents relevant to the discovery, however, dispute Bell's claim for priority.

An analysis of the controversy was thoroughly documented by Cranefield (1974), in a text that includes a facsimile of Bell's annotated letter to his friends, as well as facsimiles of all of the material by Bell, John Shaw, and Magendie on which the claim for priority can be based. Clearly, there is no challenge to Magendie's experiment that is precise, elegant, and unambiguous in demonstrating, and correctly interpreting, the sensory function of the posterior spinal root and the motor function of the anterior spinal root. Several issues were raised that cast aspersions on Bell's claim. That Bell's pamphlet was privately printed and circulated, rather than published in a scientific journal that was open to public scrutiny, certainly detracts from the authority of discovery. Second, during the period from 1816 to 1823, Bell and John Shaw published numerous articles on the anatomy of the brain and nerves, but in none of these was there a specific statement about the functions of the spinal nerve roots. This indifference is in marked contrast to the importance of the discovery claimed by Bell after Magendie's publication in 1822. Finally, following the procedure described in *Idea of a New Anatomy of the Brain* (Bell, 1811/1974), there was no basis for suggesting the sensory function for the anterior spinal roots.

REFERENCES

Bell, Charles. (1974). Idea of a new anatomy of the brain: Submitted for the observations of his friends. In P. F. Cranefield, *The way in and the way out: François Magendie, Charles Bell and the roots of the spinal nerves.* New York: Futura Publishing. (Original work published 1811)

Brazier, M. A. B. (1988). *A history of neurophysiology in the 19th century.* New York: Raven Press.

Cranefield, P. F. (1974). *The way in and the way out: François Magendie, Charles Bell and the roots of the spinal nerves.* New York: Futura Publishing.

Magendie, François. (1822a). Expériences sur les fonctions des racines des nerfs rachidiens. *Journal de Physiologie Expérimentale et Pathologique, 2,* 276–279.

Magendie, François. (1822b). Expériences sur les fonctions des racines des nerfs qui naissent de la moelle épinière. *Journal de Physiologie Expérimentale et Pathologique, 2,* 366–371.

Robert M. Stelmack
University of Ottawa, Ottawa, Canada

BENDER GESTALT

The Visual Motor Gestalt Test was developed by Lauretta Bender in 1938. Both conceptually and methodologically, the test was heavily built on concepts and materials derived from the founders of Gestalt psychology: Max Wertheimer, Kurt Koffka, and Wolfgang Köhler. "The gestalt function may be defined as that function of the integrated organism whereby it responds to a given constellation of stimuli as a whole; the response itself being a constellation, or pattern, or gestalt" (Bender, 1938, p. 3).

Stimuli

Bender (1938) carefully chose nine of Wertheimer's (1923) original designs for the Visual Motor Gestalt Test on the basis of principles (laws) put forward by the founders of Gestalt psychology.

Administration

The ease of administration of the Bender Test certainly contributes to its popularity among psychologists. Variations in administration procedures, however, are not uncommon even for the standard administration (Lezak, 1995). Other modalities of test administration include the stress modality, which involves the repetition of the test under the stress of time pressure, as described by Lezak (1995) and standardized by Brito and Santos (1996), and the immediate and delayed recall of all designs collectively, as reported by Brito, Alfradique, Pereira, Porto, and Santos (1998) in an extensive normative study.

Scoring Procedures

Bender (1938) used her test mainly as a clinical tool to observe the performance of her patients. Nevertheless, several scoring procedures were developed over the years to tap into the potential of the test to assess visuoperceptive cortical functions or as a projective technique for the study of personality.

The best known scoring procedure seems to be the one devised by Pascal and Suttell (1951) who identified over 100 scorable characteristics of the Bender Test in adolescents and adults. Keogh and Smith (1961) and Koppitz (1975), among others, devised scoring systems for kindergarten and elementary school children. Furthermore, Koppitz (1975) included emotional indicators in the analysis of test protocols. Other researchers have developed scoring procedures centered on whole performance rather than on the analysis of individual reproductions. A prototypical example of such a scoring system would be the Psychopathology Scale devised by Hutt (1985). Hutt, in addition, developed another scale that taps into the projective potential of the Bender Test: the Adience-Abience Scale.

Test Properties

Developmental studies on the Bender Test have shown that age, social class, cultural factors, ethnic group, and academic standing impact significantly on test performance (Koppitz, 1975; Brito et al., 1998). Additionally, developmental Bender and IQ test scores are significantly correlated, but only within the average and below-average IQ range (Koppitz, 1975). The finding of Brito and Santos (1996) that the number of emotional indicators significantly correlates with factor scores derived from the Composite Teacher Rating Scale (Brito & Pinto, 1991) suggests that the number of emotional indicators is a valid measure.

Bender Test and Child Neuropsychopathology

Bender (1938) reported on the abnormal test productions of Francine, a schizophrenic child. Additionally, the Bender Test has been used in the identification of children with learning difficulties (Koppitz, 1975), determination of the neuropsychological correlates of hyperactivity and inattention in school children (Brito, Pereira, & Santos-Morales, 1999), and neuropsychological assessment of the effects of stimulant medication (Brown & Borden, 1989) and biofeedback training of children with Attention Deficit/Hyperactivity Disorder (Hodes, 1989).

Bender Test and Adult and Geriatric Neuropsychopathology

Bender and the Gestalt psychologists considered that pathological integrative dysfunctions would be revealed by ruptures or modifications in the final products of the visual motor reproductions of the original stimuli. Bender (1938) presented a significant amount of information on the abnormal test results of patients with Schizophrenia and manic depressive psychoses. Furthermore, Bender (1938) showed that patients with organic brain disease (e.g., aphasia and Korsakoff syndrome) also produced abnormal reproductions of the test stimuli. Lezak (1995) considers that poor performance on the test is most likely in patients with right parietal lesions, although a normal performance cannot be construed to rule out organic brain pathology.

Flexible and creative adaptations for the administration of the Bender Test will guarantee its continued use as a valuable tool in the clinical behavioral neurosciences.

REFERENCES

Bender, L. (1938). *A visual motor Gestalt test and its clinical use* (Research Monographs No. 3). New York: The American Orthopsychiatric Association.

Brito, G. N. O., Alfradique, G. M. N., Pereira, C. C. S., Porto, C. M. B., & Santos, T. R. (1998). Developmental norms for eight instruments used in the neuropsychological assessment of children: Studies in Brazil. *Brazilian Journal of Medical and Biological Research, 31,* 399–412.

Brito, G. N. O., Pereira, C. C. S., & Santos-Morales, T. R. (1999). Behavioral and neuropsychological correlates of hyperactivity and inattention in Brazilian school children. *Developmental Medicine and Child Neurology, 41,* 732–739.

Brito, G. N. O., & Pinto, R. C. A. (1991). A composite teacher rating scale: Analysis in a sample of Brazilian children. *Journal of Clinical and Experimental Neuropsychology, 13,* 417–418.

Brito, G. N. O., & Santos, T. R. (1996). The Bender Gestalt Test for 5- to 15-year old Brazilian children: Norms and validity. *Brazilian Journal of Medical and Biological Research, 29,* 1513–1518.

Brown, R. T., & Borden, K. A. (1989). Neuropsychological effects of stimulant medication on children's learning and behavior. In C. R. Reynolds & E. Fletcher-Janzen (Eds.), *Handbook of clinical child neuropsychology.* New York: Plenum Press.

Hodes, R. L. (1989). The biofeedback treatment of neuropsychological disorders of childhood and adolescence. In C. R. Reynolds & E. Fletcher-Janzen (Eds.), *Handbook of clinical child neuropsychology.* New York: Plenum Press.

Hutt, M. L. (1985). *The Hutt adaptation of the Bender Gestalt Test: Rapid screening and intensive diagnosis* (4th ed.). Orlando, FL: Grune & Stratton.

Keogh, B., & Smith, C. E. (1961). Group techniques and proposed scoring system for the Bender Gestalt Test with children. *Journal of Clinical Psychology, 17,* 172–175.

Koppitz, E. M. (1975). *The Bender Gestalt Test for young children: Vol. 2. Research and application.* New York: Grune & Stratton.

Lezak, M. D. (1995). *Neuropsychological assessment* (3rd ed.). New York: Oxford University Press.

Pascal, G., & Suttell, B. (1951). *The Bender Gestalt Test.* New York: Grune & Stratton.

Gilberto N. O. Brito
Instituto Fernandes Figueira, Niteroi, Brazil

See also: **Gestalt Psychology; Neuropsychology**

BETA AND GAMMA RHYTHMS

Beta and gamma rhythms were first studied in the human electroencephalogram (EEG) recorded from the scalp. Beta rhythm is defined in general as any EEG rhythm over 13 Hz (The International Federation of Societies for Electroencephalography and Clinical Neurophysiology [IFSECN] 1974). Typically, it is a rhythm from 13 to 35 Hz. Gamma rhythm is commonly used by neuroscientists to designate neural activity of frequency of about 30–100 Hz, including the 40-Hz oscillations. Beta and gamma EEGs are of relatively low amplitude (less than 30 μV) in the EEG, and their quantification normally requires computer analysis with careful separation of muscle artifacts (Niedermeyer, 1999).

Three main types of beta rhythms are commonly observed in the scalp EEG of human adult subjects: (1) a fronto-central beta rhythm that can be blocked by contralateral movement or tactile stimulation, (2) a diffused beta rhythm without specific reactivity, and (3) a posterior beta rhythm that can be blocked by visual activity, similar to the occipital alpha rhythm (Kuhlo, 1976). An increase in beta rhythm has been reported in neuropsychiatric patients, but Kuhlo (1976) concluded that "no adequate evidence exists at present of any relationship between normal or excessive beta activity and psychiatric disorders." A pronounced increase in beta-frequency EEG was found with drugs that enhance gamma-aminobutyric acid-A (GABA-A) receptor functions, including sedative doses of barbiturates and benzodiazepines (Kozelka & Pedley, 1990) and the anesthetic propofol. Neural circuitry that involves GABAergic interneurons in the cortex is probably responsible for the generation of the drug-induced beta and gamma rhythms (Leung, 1998; Traub, Jefferys, & Whittington, 1999). The regional loss of the spontaneous or the barbiturate-induced beta rhythm is a sign of local cortical dysfunction.

After Jasper and Andrews (1938), the term *gamma rhythm* has not been adopted for use in clinical EEG (IFSECN, 1974). The recent interest in gamma rhythm stems from animal experiments that have shown the importance of gamma rhythm in sensory information processing in the brain (Freeman, 1991; Singer & Gray, 1995). In the visual cortex, single neurons may code for various features of a visual object, like size, form, and orientation. It is proposed that the spatially dispersed neurons that code for different features may synchronize through gamma oscillations, thus forming a dynamic assembly of neurons that represents an object uniquely (Singer & Gray, 1995). Similar processes may exist in the olfactory, auditory, somatosensory, and motor cortices. Gamma rhythms have also been found in subcortical structures, including the thalamus (Ribary et al., 1991; Steriade, Contreras, Amzica, & Timofeev, 1996) and basal forebrain nuclei. In the hippocampus, gamma waves may mediate neural processing and enhance interactions among the entorhinal cortex and various subfields of the hippocampus (Leung, 1998; Bragin et al., 1995). An increase in hippocampal gamma waves after seizure or phencyclidine is thought to drive behavioral hyperactivity, a feature of psychosis in animals (Ma & Leung, 2000; Ma &

Leung, 2002). Gamma waves are implicated in the maintenance of consciousness (Engel & Singer, 2001), and gamma waves are suppressed during general anesthesia (Traub et al., 1999; Ma, Shen, Stewart, Herrick, & Leung, 2002).

Multiple mechanisms underlie the high-frequency oscillations in the brain. Synaptic interactions among excitatory and inhibitory neurons (Freeman, 1991) or among inhibitory interneurons only (Traub et al., 1999) have been purported to generate gamma oscillations. Llinas, Grace, and Yarom (1991) discovered that single neurons may oscillate at various frequencies including beta and gamma frequencies. In the brain, local neural circuits generate beta or gamma activity that may synchronize with other local and distant circuits. Many parts of the brain respond preferentially to gamma rather than other frequencies, and thus temporal synchronization across spatially distributed domains may be achieved dynamically.

REFERENCES

Bragin, A., Jando, G., Nadasdy, Z., Hetke, J., Wise, K., & Buzsaki, G. (1995). Gamma (40–100 Hz) oscillation in the hippocampus of the behaving rat. *Journal of Neuroscience, 15,* 47–60.

Engel, A. K., & Singer, W. (2001). Temporal binding and the neural correlates of sensory awareness. *Trends in Cognitive Sciences, 5,* 16–25.

Freeman, W. J. (1991). The physiology of perception. *Scientific American, 264,* 78–85.

The International Federation of Societies for Electroencephalography and Clinical Neurophysiology (IFSECN). (1974). A glossary of terms commonly used by clinical electroencephalographers. *Electroencephalography and Clinical Neurophysiology, 37,* 538–548.

Jasper, H. H., & Andrews, H. L. (1938). Electroencephalography: III. Normal differentiation of occipital and precentral regions in man. *Archives of Neurology & Psychiatry, 39,* 96–115.

Kozelka, J. W., & Pedley, T. A. (1990). Beta and mu rhythms. *Journal of Clinical Neurophysiology, 7,* 191–207.

Kuhlo, W. (1976). Typical normal rhythms and significant variants: C. The beta rhythms. In G. E. Chatrian & G. C. Lairy (Eds.), *Handbook of electroencephalography and clinical neurophysiology* (Vol. 6a, pp. 29–46). Amsterdam: Elsevier.

Leung, L. S. (1998). Generation of theta and gamma rhythms in the hippocampus. *Neuroscience Biobehavior Review, 22,* 275–290.

Llinas, R. R., Grace, A. A., & Yarom, Y. (1991). In vitro neurons in mammalian cortical layer 4 exhibit intrinsic oscillatory activity in the 10- to 50-Hz frequency range. *Proceedings of the National Academy of Sciences, USA, 88,* 897–901.

Ma, J., & Leung, L. S. (2000). Relation between hippocampal gamma waves and behavioral disturbances induced by phencyclidine and methamphetamine. *Behavioral Brain Research, 111,* 1–11.

Ma, J., Shen, B., Stewart, L. S., Herrick, I. A., & Leung, L. S. (2002). The septohippocampal system participates in general anesthesia. *Journal of Neuroscience, 22,* 1–6.

Niedermeyer, E. (1999). The normal EEG of the waking adult. In E. Niedermeyer & F. H. Lopes da Silva (Eds.), *Electroencephalography* (4th ed.). Baltimore: Williams & Wilkins.

Ribary, U., Ioannides, A. A., Singh, K. D., Hasson, R., Bolton, J. P., Lado, F., Mogilner, A., & Llinas, R. (1991). Magnetic field tomography of coherent thalamocortical 40-Hz oscillations in humans. *Proceedings of the National Academy of Sciences, USA, 88,* 11037–11041.

Singer, W., & Gray, C. (1995). Visual feature integration and the temporal correlation hypothesis. *Annual Review of Neuroscience, 18,* 555–586.

Steriade, M., Contreras, D., Amzica, F., & Timofeev, I. (1996). Synchronization of fast (30–40 Hz) spontaneous oscillations in intrathalamic and thalamocortical networks. *Journal of Neuroscience, 16,* 2788–2808.

Traub, R. D., Jefferys, J. G. R., & Whittington, M. A. (1999). *Fast oscillations in cortical circuits.* Cambridge, MA: MIT Press.

L. Stan Leung
University of Western Ontario, London, Canada

BIOFEEDBACK

Biofeedback is best understood as a closed feedback loop consisting of a person or other animal, a response, a means to detect the response, and a mechanism for displaying the response to the person or animal—the response is thus fed back. For example, a person can be instructed to increase his or her heart rate; the heart rate is displayed by a monitor and fed back to the person; a feedback loop is thereby established. Biological systems have numerous, reflexive feedback loops to maintain homeostatic integrity—for example, body temperature, blood sugar, blood pressure, and endocrine levels. Fluctuations are kept within narrow limits by such feedback loops. However, biofeedback learning is not reflexive; it is more closely associated with higher-order learning processes.

One motive for the development of biofeedback was to devise therapies for volitional control over processes considered automatic and reflexive. Processes such as heart rate, blood pressure, and gastric secretion change along their respective dimensions, depending upon metabolic needs and emotional states. But when such processes move beyond certain limits, then health and proper functioning of the organism become compromised. Biofeedback self-regulation, as a therapy, can be viewed as a learning technique to help keep systems within proper limits with little of the side effects of more traditional medical therapies. A second stimulus for biofeedback development came from theorists concerned with disproving the hypothesis that responses innervated by the autonomic nervous system were not modifiable by reward learning. This position held that such responses were capable of being modified only through the conditional response techniques crafted by I. P. Pavlov.

A third reason for exploration came from interest in the self-control of conscious states. The fact that electroencephalographic (EEG) rhythms might be modifiable by providing information to an observer regarding EEG activity led to increased biofeedback research. Finally, the idea that self-regulation of neuromuscular function might help alleviate certain types of pain, such as headache, or lead to recovery of muscular function following trauma or disease, further helped the development of biofeedback.

Early experimental reports indicated that human subjects could control vasomotor responses, electrodermal activity, and heart rate. In the first of these studies a Russian investigator, Lisina (in Razran), claimed that when individuals were allowed to view a polygraph displaying their vasomotor responses to electric shock, they learned to produce vasodilation to escape the shock—the usual response to cutaneous electrical stimulation is vasoconstriction. Following these early studies, a number of laboratories began publishing data claiming to have effected reward learning in a variety of autonomically mediated responses with both humans and animals. Besides the usual methodological objections, criticism centered on the mechanisms responsible for the learning. A mediation issue was proposed that held that true reward learning was not occurring. Instead, it was argued, the subjects were somehow mediating the autonomic response through either cognition (i.e., thinking either calming or emotional thoughts) or covert striate muscular activity (either intended, with no movement, or actual, with movement). Although this issue remains unresolved, studies on subjects paralyzed by spinal lesions and plagued by hypotension indicated that neither cognitions, small muscular twitches, nor actual movement could account entirely for the biofeedback-produced changes. Autonomic reward learning is also influenced by such variables as type of feedback, awareness, instructions, homeostatic restraints, and links between somatic and autonomic response systems.

Biofeedback has been applied to athletic performance, Raynaud's disease, cardiac abnormalities, migraine headache, functional diarrhea, tension headache, temporomandibular disorder, essential hypertension, diabetes mellitus, Attention-Deficit/Hyperactivity Disorder, gait disorders, urinary incontinence, nocturnal enuresis, irritable bowel syndrome, tinnitus, fibromyalgia, and asthma, as well as to other problems with autonomic involvement such as anxiety, eczema, and sexual arousal. The applications continue to expand, and biofeedback is, in fact, the method of choice in treating Raynaud's disease.

The application of biofeedback techniques to problems resulting from neuromuscular dysfunction has shown considerable promise. Many reports are available on a wide array of disorders, ranging from headache to foot drop. Neuromuscular feedback has shown impressive specificity of control by successfully training subjects to either activate or inhibit activity of single motor muscle units as well as to control fecal incontinence.

Attempts have been made to modulate EEG activity through either biofeedback or manipulation of cognitive states thought to underlie a specific range of EEG frequencies. Results of these studies showed that biofeedback for alpha (8–12 Hz) did change and was accompanied by changes in psychological state. Increased alpha was related to feelings of relaxed attention and absence of anxiety. Whether increases in alpha produced psychological changes or the psychological states produced the EEG changes became part of the mediation issue. Evidence available strongly implicates the role of eye movement in the production or suppression of alpha, and this oculomotor hypothesis is the most salient explanation regarding alpha control. Convergence, divergence, and focusing of the eyes are related to the amount of alpha produced. In addition, correlated psychological states with such changes are at least partly due to expectations. Attempts have also been made to relate theta EEG (4–7 Hz) to the psychological states of dreamlike imagery and creative insight. Finally, some research has focused on modification of the sensorimotor rhythm (12–14 Hz) to reduce epileptic seizures. Results showed that when modification occurred in the 6–8-Hz band there was a concomitant reduction of seizures.

SUGGESTED READING

Gatchel, R. J., & Blanchard, E. B. (Eds.). (1993). *Psychophysiological disorders: Research and clinical applications.* Washington, DC: American Psychological Association.

Hatch, J. P., Fisher, J. G., & Ruch, J. D. (Eds.). (1987). *Biofeedback: Studies in clinical efficacy.* New York: Plenum Press.

Razran, G. (1961). The observable unconscious and the inferable conscious in current Soviet psychophysiology: Interoceptive conditioning, and the orienting reflex. *Psychological Review, 68,* 81–147.

Schwartz, M. S. (Ed.). (1998). *Biofeedback: A practitioner's guide* (2nd ed.). New York: Guilford Press.

William A. Greene
Eastern Washington University, Spokane

BIOGRAPHICAL DATA

Biography—the writing of a life (from Greek *graphein* and bio)—is an ancient concern of humankind. *The Odyssey,* the Bible, and Plutarch's *Lives* provide examples. In everyday life even a short conversation on meeting a person is probably going to include questions about background. Professionals working with people obtain histories of health events, employment, and education. In psychological lore, it is often said that the best predictor of future behavior is past behavior—especially under similar circumstances. Despite this widespread and age-old interest, there are no widely accepted tests or inventories and little psychological research using systematic scoring of personal histories over the life span.

Five major sources for constructing possible scores or indexes from life-history data are the following: (1) interviews with the target person and his or her acquaintances; (2) written biographies and autobiographies; (3) personal documents and products such as diaries or works of artists and others; (4) institutional records such as hospital charts, application forms, and school records; and (5) specially constructed biographical inventories and checklists. The first four are mainly used impressionistically and informally, but they may be quantified by judges counting frequencies of specified events or by rating or coding the nature of the material. As an interesting example, Gordon Allport in his 1965 *Letters from Jenny* coded for emotions and thoughts the 301 letters written when Jenny was aged 58–70.

Organizational and industrial psychologists have taken the lead in biodata research, often using standardized application blanks quantified by attaching weights to items. As early as 1894, an insurance company used standard forms for selecting salespeople. Later, military and industrial psychologists developed forms. In World War II, psychologists demonstrated good validity, with coefficients ranging from 0.25 to 0.45, in predicting success in training U.S. pilots, navigators, and army officers. Weights of items on a biodata form, sometimes called a *biographical information blank* (BIB), can be validated against outcome criteria such as supervisors' ratings or productivity. Such a biodata score may contain a variety of items, such as marital status, previous job tenure, health conditions, or hobbies. Care must be taken to specify the relevance of items to the position and to avoid misleading or illegal bias from background factors, such as minority status, sex, age, or disability.

A biographical inventory or checklist is a set of items representative of life-history events or experiences that are pertinent to the purpose of assessment. Psychometric techniques using such indicators as health status, social adjustment, and job success will select and weight items. Items on inventories emphasize factual events or conditions, but some items may verge on the attitudes and subjective impressions found in personality inventories. All of these self-report procedures are subject to the usual criticisms of the reporting of life histories, such as poor recall, intentional or unintentional distortion, and various test-taking attitudes. Especially if biographical items are transparently related to the situation of assessment, subjects may slant responses, for instance, to get a job or to avoid incarceration. These problems are similar to those found on all self-report inventories. Intensive interviewing compared with checklists and inventories would improve accuracy of reports, but interviews take costly professional time.

Personality inventories often include life-history items, but there are few published inventories specific to biography. Child development tests and inventories cover only part of the life span. For adults, the Minnesota-Briggs History Record provides seven scales having titles such as "Social Misfit" and "Introversion." There is also a verbal projective technique, Bruhn's Early Memories Procedure, which, however, produces no scores. Another more limited approach is that of checklists and inventories of life changes on which subjects indicate whether they have had various stressful events, but these refer only to the last few weeks or months and are not life histories. Clinicians may use the informal technique of having clients draw a lifeline marked by major shifts or decisions for better or worse. As life span theory develops and recognizes the changing conditions surrounding the person, it seems likely that inventories and other procedures will be produced to measure important variables over a long period of time. Until then we will depend mainly on reported life stories, often very interesting, but judged impressionistically. Some psychologists, instead of pursuing factual life histories, frankly acknowledge that much of what passes as life history is really narrative and should be analyzed as stories are.

REFERENCES

Allport, G. W. (1965). *Letters from Jenny.* New York: Harcourt Brace.

Briggs, P. F. (1959). Eight item clusters for use with the M-B History Record. *Journal of Clinical Psychology, 1,* 22–28.

Bruhn, A. R. (1992). The Early Memories Procedure: A projective test of autobiographical memory: I. *Journal of Personality Assessment, 58,* 1–15.

Norman D. Sundberg
University of Oregon, Eugene

BIOLOGICAL CLOCKS AND SEASONAL BEHAVIOR

The biological rhythms, detectable at all levels of organization, constitute a temporal structure in all animal species. These rhythms concern many biological parameters and have clinical implications, mainly in psychiatry.

Human rhythms are determined by endogenous pacemakers, which are located in the hypothalamus. The hypothalamus is in interrelation with other elements of complex human biology such as the endocrine system, which is affected, via the cortex cerebri, by environmental factors such as light, darkness, seasons, noise, food, and stress. Thus, endogenous pacemakers adapt their impulses to other environmental rhythms. These complex interferences regulate our biological clocks. A dysfunction of one factor may induce a rhythm modification, which alters another rhythm, and so on, and may result in a clinical disorder, often a psychiatric illness. In this manner, our living patterns are controlled by the interrelation between endogenous pacemakers and exogenous rhythms.

The biological rhythms of different functions become apparent at different times after birth. In the infant, the development of rhythmicity must represent a combination of the genetic potential of the maturation process in the brain and of the varying influences of environment. The alternation of light and darkness is perhaps the most obvious of external rhythms, but similar alternations of noise and silence and the attention that the infant receives from adults may also be of importance. In the adult, the biological rhythms are represented by the periodic regular cyclic variations of the biological processes, describing a sinusoidal function with individual characteristics of periodicity and amplitude.

The human rhythms are represented mainly by circadian and circannual rhythms, characterized, respectively, by a period of 21 to 27 hours and a longer period of more than 27 hours, such as a month or season. The human circadian system is composed of at least two oscillators, which are self-sustained and coupled to each other. One of these oscillators is strong and controls body temperature, REM-sleep propensity, and cortisol secretion; the other is weak and controls the sleep-wake cycle and sleep related neuroendocrine activity. These oscillator systems may be affected by many factors such as organic diseases, drugs, and environmental factors, which may lead to psychological disorders.

Studies of seasonal patterns of incidence of psychiatric disorders have highlighted the role of seasonally regulated environmental factors on internal biological processes. Since ancient times the relationship between seasons and mood has been noted, and numerous investigations have indicated a seasonal variation in the incidence of affective illness.

Depression has been described as most common in spring and autumn, and the influence of climatological factors (mainly photoperiod) on seasonal affective disorders (SADs) have been shown. One study reported cases of SAD with summer depression and winter hypomania, and Lemoine described summer SAD (or SAD reverse) in which the temperature factor was more implicated than the daylight factor. One biological explanation has been a seasonal variation in human brain serotonin concentrations, which has been implicated in the biochemistry of affective disorders.

But if seasonal rhythms influence depressive illness, a dysregulation of circadian rhythms was found as well. There is evidence that the sleep and neuroendocrine dysfunctions observed in depressive patients are correlated with a phase advance of the circadian strong oscillator with respect to the weak oscillator. Clinical studies suggest that antidepressants can slow or delay circadian rhythms. Other therapies modifying biological rhythms may improve depressive mood. Sleep deprivation, for example, has been found to lead to rapid improvement of depressive symptomatology, and reports have shown that artificial lengthening of the photoperiod (phototherapy) may have therapeutic effects in depressive illness. The biological parameter implicated in the mechanism of action of this therapy is melatonin, for which rhythm appears to be an endocrine code of the environmental light-dark cycle conveying photic information that is used by an organism for both circadian and seasonal temporal organization.

Some authors have suggested a relationship between the season of one's birth and the occurrence of affective disorders. Season of birth/conception has also been examined as a possible factor in the depression of women who have given birth. However, although a significant seasonal variation in the occurrence of postnatal depression has been found with the largest peak occurring in autumn, there are discrepancies in the data concerning the influence of the season of conception on the frequency of postpartum mental illness.

The seasonal variation in suicides has been studied in several countries. Suicides were found to be most frequent in spring and summer in Finland and in May and September in France. Seasonal variations of other psychiatric illnesses have been less studied, although a possible link between season of birth and schizophrenia (winter and spring peaks) has been described. Biological reasons may exist, as dopamine has been implicated in the biochemistry of schizophrenia, and there is a seasonal variation in human brain dopamine concentrations.

The number of hospitalizations for alcoholism seems to peak in the spring, and there seem to be peaks in spring and summer births among alcoholics.

Human performance efficiency also has circadian rhythms in healthy individuals. One study determined that a simple manual dexterity task is almost entirely under the control of the temperature rhythm oscillator, whereas a more complex cognitive task demonstrates a periodicity that appears to be influenced by those oscillators controlling temperature and the sleep/wake cycle.

Even for human sexuality seasonal variations exist, as they do in other mammals, with a peak in autumn, probably linked to the seasonal variation of testosterone activity.

A better knowledge of all these rhythm interferences and their clinical implications brings to mind the possibility that by modifying these influences we may be able to alleviate the patient's symptoms. New approaches to the treatment of all these disorders involve direct manipulation of the biological rhythms.

SUGGESTED READING

Ballard, C. G., & Mohan, R. N. C. (1993). Seasonal variation in the prevalence of postnatal depression. *European Journal of Psychiatry, 7,* 73–76s.

Castrogiovanni, P., Iapichino, S., Pacchierotti, C., & Pieraccini, F. (1998). Season of birth in psychiatry: A review. *Neuropsychobiology, 37*(4), 175–181.

Fossey, E., & Shapiro, C. M. (1992). Seasonality in psychiatry: A review. *Canadian Journal of Psychiatry, 37*(5), 299–308.

Lemoine, P. (1995). Chronobiology and chronotherapy. In J. L. Senon, D. Sechter, & D. Richard (Eds.), *Thérapeutique psychiatrique* (pp. 471–492). Paris: Hermann.

Mills, J. N. (1975). Development of circadian rhythms in infancy. *Chronobiologia, 2,* 363–371.

Modestin, J., Ammann, R., & Wurmle, O. (1995). Season of birth: Comparison of patients with schizophrenia, affective disorders and alcoholism. *Acta Psychiatrica Scandinavia, 91*(2), 140–143.

Pevet, P. (1998). Mélatonine et rhythmes biologiques. *Thérapie, 53,* 411–420.

Rosenthal, N. E., Sack, D. A., Gillin, J. C., Lewy, A. J., Goodwin, F. K., Davenport, Y., et al. (1984). Seasonal affective disorder: A description of the syndrome and preliminary findings with light therapy. *Archives of General Psychiatry, 41,* 72–80.

Sechter, D., Bonin, B., & Bizouard, P. (1996). Phototherapy: A treatment for mood disorders? In H. Greppin, R. Degli Agosti, & M. Bozon (Eds.), *Vistas on biorhythmicity* (pp. 295–301). Geneva, Switzerland: University of Geneva.

Souêtre, E., Salvati, E., Belugou, J. L., Douillet, P., Braccini, T., & Darcourt, G. (1987). Seasonality of suicides: Environmental, sociological and biological covariations. *Journal of Affective Disorders, 13,* 215–225.

Wehr, T. A., & Goodwin, F. K. (1981). Biological rhythms and psychiatry. In S. Arieti & H. K. H. Brodie, *American handbook of psychiatry* (Vol. 7, pp. 46–74). New York: Basic Books.

Wirz-Justice, A., Graw, P., Krauchi, K., Sarrafzadeh, A., English, J., & Sand, L. (1996). "Natural" light treatment of seasonal affective disorder. *Journal of Affective Disorders, 37,* 109–120.

Wirz-Justice, A., & Wehr, T. A. (1983). Neuropsychopharmacology and biological rhythms. *Advances in Biological Psychiatry, 11,* 20–34.

Pierre Vandel
Hospital Saint-Jacques, Bensançon, France

BIPOLAR AFFECTIVE DISORDER (MANIC-DEPRESSIVE ILLNESS)

Clinical Description and Course

Bipolar affective disorder, formerly known as manic-depressive illness, is a psychiatric disorder involving wide-ranging fluctuations in mood, activity, and cognition. It affects between 0.8% and 1.4% of the population. When depressed, bipolar persons experience a sad mood, loss of interests, fatigue, psychomotor retardation or agitation, loss of concentration, insomnia, feelings of worthlessness, and suicidality. During manias, patients experience euphoric, elevated or irritable mood states, racing of thoughts (or the verbal concomitant, "flight of ideas"), pressure of speech, increased activity and energy, impulsive and high-risk behaviors, an inflated sense of self-worth or grandiose delusions, distractibility, and a decreased need for sleep (American Psychiatric Association, 2000). Manic episodes are generally more damaging to bipolar persons and those around them than are depressive episodes.

Bipolar I patients alternate between the two extremes of mania and depression, or they experience mania and depression simultaneously in *mixed* affective episodes. Bipolar II patients experience debilitating depressions that alternate with *hypomanic* episodes. Hypomania is an attenuated form of mania. It is not associated with significant functional impairment, psychosis, or the need for hospitalization.

Bipolar I Disorder affects men and women with equal frequency, but bipolar II patients are more frequently women. Women appear to have a preponderance of depressive episodes over manic or hypomanic episodes, whereas the reverse appears true of men. Similarly, the first onset of bipolar disorder is usually a depressive episode in a woman and a manic episode in a man.

The course of the disorder varies considerably from person to person. Some bipolar persons return to a *euthymic,* normal mood state between episodes. However, by some estimates (e.g., Harrow, Goldberg, Grossman, & Meltzer, 1990), more than half of patients have significant symptoms during the intervals between major episodes. The average duration of episodes varies from 4 to 13 months, with longer durations reported in studies from the pre-pharmacological era (Goodwin & Jamison, 1990). Episode duration has decreased significantly since the advent of mood-stabilizing agents such as lithium carbonate or the anticonvulsants (see following). But even with active medication, about 40% of bipolar patients have a recurrence of their illness in a 1-year period, and 73% over 5 years (Gitlin, Swendsen, Heller, & Hammen, 1995).

Between 13% and 20% of patients are *rapid cyclers* (Calabrese, Fatemi, Kujawa, & Woyshville, 1996), who experience four or more episodes of depression, mania, hypomania, or mixed affective disorder in a single year; these patients are disproportionately women. There are several known predictors of increased cycling of the disorder, including medication nonadherence, presence of psychosis, alcohol and drug abuse, sleep deprivation, and, in some patients, the use of antidepressant medications.

Bipolar disorder is associated with high personal, social, and economic costs. About 33% of bipolar I patients cannot maintain employment in the 6 months after a manic episode; over 50% show declines in occupational functioning over the 5 years after an episode. The suicide rate is believed to be about 30 times greater than the normal population. Bipolar disorder is also associated with marital dysfunction and high rates of divorce, general health complications, legal problems, and problems in the adjustment of children (Coryell, Andreasen, Endicott, & Keller, 1987; Coryell et al., 1993; Goldberg, Harrow, & Grossman,

1995; Dion, Tohen, Anthony, & Waternaux, 1988; Hammen, Burge, Burney, & Adrian, 1990; Silverstone & Romans-Clarkson, 1989). In 1991, the economic costs of bipolar disorder were $45 billion in the United States alone (Wyatt & Henter, 1995).

Most bipolar patients develop the illness between the ages of 19 and 23. However, prepubertal and adolescent onsets of the disorder are being increasingly recognized. In fact, the age at onset of the disorder is becoming younger in successive generations. Between 20% and 40% of bipolar patients have their first onset in childhood or adolescence, and about 20% of depressed adolescents eventually switch into mania. The early-onset form of the disease appears to have a stronger genetic liability (greater familial aggregation) than the later-onset forms. It is also frequently characterized by mixed symptoms, rapid cycling, psychosis, and other poor prognostic attributes. If bipolar teenagers are not treated early, they can fall behind, sometimes irreparably, in social, school, and work functioning (Geller & Luby, 1997; McClellan & Werry, 1997).

Etiology

Genetic and Biological Predispositions

Bipolar disorder unquestionably runs in families. Concordance rates between identical twins average 57% and between fraternal twins, 14% (Alda, 1997). The family pedigrees of bipolar probands are characterized by increased rates of bipolar disorder, unipolar disorder, and alcoholism. At least 20% of the first-degree relatives of bipolar patients have major affective disorders (Gershon, 1990). Although several gene loci have been identified, there is a particularly promising set of findings linking bipolar disorder to loci on the long arm of chromosome 18. This linkage is strongest among families of bipolar patients who are comorbid for Panic Disorder (MacKinnon et al., 1998). There is also growing evidence that a variant in the serotonin transporter gene, which might lead to instabilities in the regulation of serotonin within the CNS, may be related to the onset of bipolar disorder (Collier et al., 1996).

Bipolar disorder is presumed to involve imbalances in the activity of neurotransmitter (e.g., dopamine, serotonin) and neurohormonal (e.g., glucorticoid) systems. A recent theory of dysfunction in the activity of signal-transducing guanine nucleotide-binding proteins (G-proteins) is gaining credibility. Bipolar patients have higher platelet levels of stimulatory G-protein subunits than do normal comparison subjects, even when patients are examined in the remitted state (Mitchell et al., 1997). Lithium carbonate—the primary medication used in treating bipolar disorder—has been found to reduce G-protein function in animals (Avissar, Schreiber, Danon, & Belmaker, 1988) and in normal humans (Risby et al., 1991). Other research has focused on the protein kinase C signaling cascade, a mediator of signals within cells when receptors are stimulated by neurotransmitters. Drugs used to treat bipolar disorder, including lithium carbonate and divalproex sodium, reduce activity of the protein kinase C signaling cascade (Manji, 2001).

Psychosocial Factors

Bipolar disorder is affected by psychosocial stress. Two domains have been studied: negative affective relationships within the patient's family, and stressful life events. Regarding the former, prospective studies indicate that bipolar patients who, following an acute illness episode, return to family or marital environments that are high in "expressed emotion" (containing relatives who are highly critical, hostile, or emotionally overinvolved) are more likely to relapse at 9-month or 1-year follow-up than patients who return to low-key family environments (for a review, see Miklowitz, Wendel, & Simoneau, 1998). It is not clear whether stress within the family is a primary eliciting factor for symptoms, whether bipolar symptoms in patients evoke family conflicts, or whether patients' symptoms and family conflicts are both traceable to third variables such as a shared genetic vulnerability to mood disorder.

Episodes of bipolar disorder often follow major life events (Johnson & Roberts, 1995). Various theories have been advanced for explaining this association. One model views the core dysfunction in bipolar disorder as one of instability and postulates that mood disorders are strongly affected by changes in the circadian clock (Ehlers, Frank, & Kupfer, 1988; Ehlers, Kupfer, Frank, & Monk, 1993). Life events that affect sleep/wake rhythms and other daily routines (e.g., the birth of a baby) do appear potent in eliciting manic, but not depressive, episodes (Malkoff-Schwartz et al., 1998). Another model postulates that life events interact with a faulty "behavioral activation system" that is sensitive to reward cues. Life events that involve goal striving (e.g., a job promotion) may stimulate this system, which then produces an aroused state associated with greater motivation for rewards, heightened affect, and increased sociability or risk taking (Johnson & Roberts, 1995; Johnson et al., 2000).

A third model, the "kindling hypothesis" (Post, 1992), postulates that bipolar episodes are often precipitated by an external agent (i.e., life stress) at the beginning phases of the illness, but patients become increasingly sensitized to stress over time. In later stages of the disorder, episodes occur spontaneously, without external stressors. Eventually the illness takes on an autonomous, self-perpetuating course. Evidence for the kindling hypothesis is inconsistent. Hammen and Gitlin (1997) found that among bipolar patients who had had recurrences, those with a greater number of prior episodes were more likely to have experienced a major stressor in the 6 months prior to their recurrence, and relapsed more quickly after the stressor, than patients with fewer prior episodes.

Treatment

Biological Approaches

The primary treatments for bipolar disorder are pharmacological. Lithium carbonate was the first mood stabilizer to come into wide use. It appears to be effective for about 50–60% of patients in controlling the acute symptoms of the disorder and preventing future episodes. Anticonvulsant medications such as divalproex sodium (Depakote), carbamazepine (Tegretol), oxcarbazepine (Trileptal), and lamotrigine (Lamictal) are now used as substitutes for or in conjunction with lithium, usually for lithium-refractory patients, patients who complain of lithium's side effects, or patients with atypical presentations (e.g., mixed episodes or rapid cycling). Atypical antipsychotic agents such as olanzapine (Zyprexa) are also in use as primary, first-line agents.

Most mood stabilizers appear more effective in controlling and preventing manic symptoms than depressive symptoms. For this reason, they are often combined with antidepressants. Although often effective in controlling depressive symptoms, antidepressants pose risk to bipolar patients because they can elicit hypomanic or manic episodes or lead to an acceleration of mood cycling.

Antipsychotic agents and anxiolytic compounds are often added to patients' lithium or anticonvulsant regimes, depending upon the patients' clinical presentation. Electroconvulsive therapy (shock treatment) is recommended for treatment-refractory patients, particularly when they are in severe depressive states. Other treatment approaches that require more investigation include bright light treatment and omega-3 fatty acids (fish oil).

Medications for bipolar disorder have negative side effects. For example, lithium and divalproex sodium are associated with weight gain, nausea, and trembling. One study found that almost 60% of patients were inconsistent with their medicines in the year after their first hospitalized episode (Strakowski et al., 1998). Nonadherence is not only the result of side effects, however. Some patients miss their high, euphoric periods and dislike having their moods controlled by medication (Jamison, Gerner, & Goodwin, 1979). Some complain of a loss of creativity due to medications. Indeed, there is evidence of a linkage between bipolar disorder and artistic creativity, as evidenced by the number of writers, artists, and musicians who have had the disorder or a mild form of it (Jamison, 1993).

Psychosocial Approaches

Psychosocial therapy is used as an adjunct to drug treatment. Its purposes are to mollify the symptomatic course of the disorder, enhance patients' compliance with medications, enhance social and occupational functioning, and increase patients' ability to manage stressors that evoke symptoms. There are three treatments that have received some, albeit limited, empirical support. One is family or marital therapy, particularly psychoeducational approaches that focus on teaching patients and their family members about bipolar disorder and how to manage it and effective ways to communicate and solve family problems (Miklowitz & Goldstein, 1997; Miklowitz et al., 2000). A second is interpersonal and social rhythm therapy, an individual therapy that focuses on helping the patient understand and renegotiate the interpersonal context associated with mood disorder symptoms (Frank, Swartz, & Kupfer, 2000). Patients learn to stabilize sleep/wake rhythms and other daily routines, particularly in the face of environmental triggers for disruption. A third treatment is individual cognitive-behavioral therapy, in which patients learn to identify, evaluate, and restructure cognitive distortions, and develop illness management strategies such as behavioral activation, drug compliance monitoring, and the appropriate use of support systems (Cochran, 1984; Lam et al., in press; Otto, Reilly-Harrington, & Sachs, in press).

Conclusion

Bipolar disorder is a genetically- and biologically-based illness of mood states. It takes a tremendous economic, social, and personal toll on sufferers and their family members. Recent advances in biological psychiatry and psychosocial research have clarified some of the predisposing factors for the disorder and have identified triggers for the disorder's cycling. Advances in its pharmacological and psychological management are being translated into treatment algorithms that have the potential to improve community-based care for this often debilitating disorder.

REFERENCES

Alda, M. (1997). Bipolar disorder: From families to genes. *Canadian Journal of Psychiatry, 42,* 378–387.

American Psychiatric Association. (2000). *Diagnostic and statistical manual of mental disorders* (4th ed., text revision; DSM-IV-TR). Washington, DC: Author.

Avissar, S., Schreiber, G., Danon, A., & Belmaker, R. H. (1988). Lithium inhibits adrenergic and cholinergic increases in GTP binding in rat cortex. *Nature, 331,* 440–442.

Calabrese, J. R., Fatemi, S. H., Kujawa, M., & Woyshville, M. J. (1996). Predictors of response to mood stabilizers. *Journal of Clinical Psychopharmacology, 16*(Suppl. 1), 24–31.

Cochran, S. D. (1984). Preventing medical noncompliance in the outpatient treatment of bipolar affective disorders. *Journal Consult Clinical Psychology, 52,* 873–878.

Collier, D. A., Arranz, M. J., Sham, P., Battersby, S., Vallada, H., Gill, P., et al. (1996). The serotonin transporter is a potential susceptibility factor for bipolar affective disorder. *Neuroreport, 7,* 1675–1679.

Coryell, W., Andreasen, N. C., Endicott, J., & Keller, M. (1987). The significance of past mania or hypomania in the course and outcome of major depression. *American Journal of Psychiatry, 144,* 309–315.

Coryell, W., Scheftner, W., Keller, M., Endicott, J., Maser, J., & Klerman, G. L. (1993). The enduring psychosocial consequences of mania and depression. *American Journal of Psychiatry, 150,* 720–727.

Dion, G., Tohen, M., Anthony, W., & Waternaux, C. (1988). Symptoms and functioning of patients with bipolar disorder six months after hospitalization. *Hospital and Community Psychiatry, 39,* 652–656.

Ehlers, C. L., Frank, E., & Kupfer, D. J. (1988). Social zeitgebers and biological rhythms: A unified approach to understanding the etiology of depression. *Archives of General Psychiatry, 45,* 948–952.

Ehlers, C. L., Kupfer, D. J., Frank, E., & Monk, T. H. (1993). Biological rhythms and depression: The role of zeitgebers and zeitstorers. *Depression, 1,* 285–293.

Frank, E., Swartz, H. A., & Kupfer, D. J. (2000). Interpersonal and social rhythm therapy: Managing the chaos of bipolar disorder. *Biological Psychiatry, 48,* 593–604.

Geller, B., & Luby, J. (1997). Child and adolescent bipolar disorder: A review of the past 10 years. *Journal of the American Academy of Child and Adolescent Psychiatry, 36,* 1168–1176.

Gershon, E. S. (1990). Genetics. In F. K. Goodwin & K. R. Jamison (Eds.), *Manic-depressive illness* (pp. 373–401). New York: Oxford University Press.

Gitlin, M. J., Swendsen, J., Heller, T. L., & Hammen, C. (1995). Relapse and impairment in bipolar disorder. *American Journal of Psychiatry, 152*(11), 1635–1640.

Goldberg, J. F., Harrow, M., & Grossman, L. S. (1995). Course and outcome in bipolar affective disorder: A longitudinal follow-up study. *American Journal of Psychiatry, 152,* 379–385.

Goodwin, F. K., & Jamison, K. R. (1990). *Manic-depressive illness.* New York: Oxford University Press.

Hammen, C., Burge, D., Burney, E., & Adrian, C. (1990). Longitudinal study of diagnoses in children of women with unipolar and bipolar affective disorder. *Archives of General Psychiatry, 47,* 1112–1117.

Hammen, C., & Gitlin, M. J. (1997). Stress reactivity in bipolar patients and its relation to prior history of the disorder. *American Journal of Psychiatry, 154,* 856–857.

Harrow, M., Goldberg, J. F., Grossman, L. S., & Meltzer, H. Y. (1990). Outcome in manic disorders: A naturalistic follow-up study. *Archives of General Psychiatry, 47,* 665–671.

Jamison, K. R. (1993). *Touched with fire: Manic-depressive illness and the artistic temperament.* New York: Maxwell Macmillan International.

Jamison, K. R., Gerner, R. H., & Goodwin, F. K. (1979). Patient and physician attitudes toward lithium: Relationship to compliance. *Archives of General Psychiatry, 36,* 866–869.

Johnson, S. L., & Roberts, J. E. (1995). Life events and bipolar disorder: Implications from biological theories. *Psychological Bulletin, 117,* 434–449.

Johnson, S. L., Sandrow, D., Meyer, B., Winters, R., Miller, I., Solomon, D., et al. (2000). Increases in manic symptoms following life events involving goal-attainment. *Journal of Abnormal Psychology, 109,* 721–727.

Lam, D. H., Watkins, E. R., Hayward, P., Bright, J., Wright, K., Kerr, N., et al. (in press). A randomised controlled study of cognitive therapy of relapse prevention for bipolar affective disorder: Outcome of the first year. *Archives of General Psychiatry.*

MacKinnon, D. F., Xu, J., McMahon, F. J., Simpson, S. G., Stine, O. C., McInnis, M. G., et al. (1998). Bipolar disorder and Panic Disorder in families: An analysis of chromosome 18 data. *American Journal of Psychiatry, 155*(6), 829–831.

Malkoff-Schwartz, S., Frank, E., Anderson, B., Sherrill, J. T., Siegel, L., Patterson, D., et al. (1998). Stressful life events and social rhythm disruption in the onset of manic and depressive bipolar episodes: A preliminary investigation. *Archives of General Psychiatry, 55,* 702–707.

Manji, H. K. (2001). The neurobiology of bipolar disorder. *The Economics of Neuroscience, 3,* 37–44.

McClellan, J., & Werry, J. S. (1997). Practice parameters for the assessment and treatment of children and adolescents with bipolar disorder. *Journal of the American Academy of Child and Adolescent Psychiatry, 36*(Suppl. 10), 157–176.

Miklowitz, D. J., & Goldstein, M. J. (1997). *Bipolar disorder: A family-focused treatment approach.* New York: Guilford Press.

Miklowitz, D. J., Simoneau, T. L., George, E. L., Richards, J. A., Kalbag, A., Sachs-Ericsson, N., et al. (2000). Family-focused treatment of bipolar disorder: 1-year effects of a psychoeducational program in conjunction with pharmacotherapy. *Biological Psychiatry, 48,* 582–592.

Miklowitz, D. J., Wendel, J. S., & Simoneau, T. L. (1998). Targeting dysfunctional family interactions and high expressed emotion in the psychosocial treatment of bipolar disorder. *In Session: Psychotherapy in Practice, 4,* 25–38.

Mitchell, P. B., Manji, H. K., Chen, G., Jolkovsky, L., Smith-Jackson, E., Denicoff, K., et al. (1997). High levels of Gs alpha in platelets of euthymic patients with bipolar affective disorder. *American Journal of Psychiatry, 154*(2), 218–223.

Otto, M. W., Reilly-Harrington, N., & Sachs, G. (in press). Psychoeducational and cognitive-behavioral strategies in the management of bipolar disorder. *Journal of Affective Disorders.*

Post, R. M. (1992). Transduction of psychosocial stress into the neurobiology of recurrent affective disorder. *American Journal of Psychiatry, 149,* 999–1010.

Risby, E. D., Hsiao, J. K., Manji, H. K., Bitran, J., Moses, F., Zhou, D. F., et al. (1991). The mechanisms of action of lithium: II. Effects on adenylate cyclase activity and beta-adrenergic receptor binding in normal subjects. *Archives of General Psychiatry, 48,* 513–524.

Silverstone, T., & Romans-Clarkson, S. (1989). Bipolar affective disorder: Causes and prevention of relapse. *British Journal of Psychiatry, 154,* 321–335.

Strakowski, S. M., Keck, P. E., McElroy, S. L., West, S. A., Sax, K. W., Hawkins, J. M., et al. (1998). Twelve-month outcome after a first hospitalization for affective psychosis. *Archives of General Psychiatry, 55,* 49–55.

Wyatt, R. J., & Henter, I. (1995). An economic evaluation of manic-depressive illness. *Social Psychiatry and Psychiatric Epidemiology, 30,* 213–219.

David J. Miklowitz
University of North Carolina

See also: **Family Therapy; Interpersonal Psychotherapy**

BIRTH ORDER

Birth order refers to the ordinal sequence of birth for each child in the family. Some researchers identify five positions: (only, first, second, middle, and last), while others use four positions (only, first, middle, and last). Alfred Adler was the first theorist in modern psychology to note the significance of psychological birth order position in the dynamics of personality development. Adler recognized that the addition of each child to the family would have a profound effect on the family system, noting that the birth of each child would alter the interactions, roles, and responsibilities of each family member.

Although birth order is important, Adler suggested, the "psychological order" of the child might be more important than the ordinal position. The psychological birth order position is a vantage point from which a child perceives and evaluates itself and forms convictions about what is required to belong to society. The term *family constellation* is used to describe the family environment—the parents, siblings, and others living in the family of origin.

Variables

A number of family variables influence the child's perception of the birth order and create a different psychological order from the ordinal position. These variables influence how the child will evaluate the birth order position and decide whether that birth order is the best or the worst position in the family; for example, a first born may evaluate the heavy responsibilities expected of the oldest child and decide that it is easier to be lazy than assume leadership. A middle child may see that the leadership demonstrated by the oldest child is inferior and decide to leapfrog into a role as the leader of the group. Each child will evaluate his or her birth-order position in relation to the other siblings and decide on a pattern of behavior to enable that child to become unique in the family structure.

Corsini and Manaster (1982) maintain that the important factor relative to birth order and personality development is the child's perception of the role to be played and its demands and expectations. Age spacing and the other variables subsequently listed may influence such perceptions, but in the final analysis, the child is responsible for these perceptions.

In the study of birth order, the sex of the child is an important variable because each child searches to establish his or her sex-role identity by finding a role model in the family. Parents have different sex-role expectations for each child and reinforce or reward the child's behaviors in accordance with their expectations.

The structure of the family is important to consider when examining the various influences on the child. The family structure includes a description of the sex of each child and the sequence of birth of each child. A family of four children could have a birth order and sequence combination to form sixteen different family structures. A family of four boys (boy, boy, boy, boy) is very different from a family of four girls (girl, girl, girl, girl). Another family of four children (girl, boy, girl, boy) is quite different from another family of four children (girl, girl, boy, boy). The sequence of birth and the gender of each child will influence how siblings are likely to group and interact.

The age separation between siblings is another important consideration in the development of personality. Closely spaced children have a strong influence on each other because they are likely to play together extensively. Children who are born several years apart have less influence on each other than those who are closely spaced. Two or more families can exist within the family unit; when children are born (at least) five years apart, the family can be considered to have a second generation of children within the same family unit.

Parents hold different expectations for each child based on the sex, age, and size of the child. A first-born daughter is often required to assume responsibilities and act as the "Junior Mom" by supervising the younger siblings. Similarly, a first-born son is often expected to be the "Junior Dad" to the younger siblings. A last-born child is recognized as the "baby" and may utilize learned helplessness to keep other people busy with his or her problems. Parents may pamper their youngest child and give it many privileges that the older siblings did not receive.

Parents may choose a favorite child based on their own birth order. A last-born parent may identify with the last-born child and say, "I know what that child is going through; I know what it feels like to be picked on by those older kids." When one parent and a child establish a strong bond, the remaining children will seek other role models.

How parents interact with the child is often influenced by the age of the parents. Teenage parents are very energetic and are likely to play with the child, whereas parents in their late 30s are more likely to be academic and will read to the child. Mature parents provide their first-born child a different socioeconomic environment than teenage parents.

A family with multiple births (twins, triplets, quadruplets, and quintuplets) will have special circumstances because of their shared environment. Multiple-birth siblings often bond closely and develop private language or symbols for communication. Identical twins experience similar family environments and develop common traits, yet they find subtle ways to differentiate themselves.

A child who requires special care, for example, a child with a disability, will alter the expectations for each member of the family. Each family member will have some role in the care of this child.

Any conditions that may lead the parents to give special consideration or protection to a child may have an influence on the family environment. A parent who has several miscarriages before the successful birth of a child may become an overprotective parent. The death of a sibling during childhood will have a profound effect on each of the surviving family members.

REFERENCE

Manaster, G., & Corsini, R. (1982). *Individual psychology: Theory and practice.* Itasca, IL: Peacock.

C. Reginald Brasington
University of South Carolina, Columbia

BISEXUALITY

Bisexuality is a word applied to an adult whose desire for, and/or choice of, sexual partners includes persons of both the opposite and the same sex. In conception, the bisexual person should have no preference, being equally attracted to both males and females, but the term is often misapplied to individuals who have partners of both sexes and also have a clear preference for one or the other sex.

The prototype bisexual is the "3" on the 7-point scale of sexual preference proposed by Alfred Kinsey and his associates in their classic book, *Sexual Behavior in the Human Male.*

While individuals who have sexual contact with persons of both sexes are not uncommon, true bisexuals are relatively rare. Kinsey and his colleagues found that just more than 3% of adult White males fit his definition of *bisexual.* Among females, a little more than 1% of the single females were 3s.

Eugene E. Levitt
Seton Hall University

See also: **Homosexuality; Sexual Deviation**

BLOOD-BRAIN BARRIER

The blood-brain barrier (BBB) is the interface between blood and brain and, therefore, plays an important role in many disciplines, including psychology, psychiatry, nutrition, general metabolism, as well as pharmacology, neurology, and neurosurgery (Pardridge, 2001). The BBB evolved in parallel with myelination of the brain, is present in the brain of all vertebrates, and is formed within the first trimester of human fetal life. The anatomical localization of the BBB is the capillary endothelium of brain. Unlike capillary endothelial cells in peripheral tissues, the endothelial cells of capillaries perfusing the brain and spinal cord are joined together by epithelial-like, high-resistance tight junctions that eliminate the normal paracellular pathway of solute flux from blood to the organ interstitium (Brightman, Reese, & Feder, 1970). There is also a 99% reduction in the pinocytosis in endothelia of the central nervous system (CNS), and this eliminates the normal transcellular pathway of free solute exchange between blood and the organ interstitial space.

The paracellular and transcellular pathways for free solute exchange across the capillary wall that are present in the microcirculation of peripheral organs are absent in the capillaries perfusing the brain and spinal cord. Therefore, circulating molecules gain access to brain or spinal cord by only one of two processes: (1) free diffusion based on the lipid solubility and molecular weight of the molecule, and (2) catalyzed transport (Oldendorf, 1974). The latter involves either carrier-mediated transport (CMT) for small molecular weight nutrients such as glucose or amino acids, or receptor-mediated transcytosis (RMT) for certain circulating peptides such as insulin, leptin, or transferrin (Pardridge, 2001). The CMT and RMT systems are individual proteins expressed by specific genes within the capillary endothelium. The CMT and RMT systems mediate the transport of nutrients or some endogenous peptides across both the luminal plasma membrane of the capillary endothelium, at the blood surface, and the abluminal membrane of the capillary endothelium, at the side of the brain interstitial fluid. The luminal and abluminal membranes are separated by approximately 300 nm of endothelial cytoplasm. Therefore, transport across the BBB is a process of molecular transfer through two membranes in series: the capillary endothelial luminal and abluminal plasma membranes. If a molecule does not have access to one of the specialized CMT or RMT systems within the BBB membranes, then there is no significant uptake of the molecule by brain.

The capillaries within the brain are approximately 40 microns apart, and it takes a small molecule such as glucose to diffuse 40 microns around 1 second. The capillary transit time in brain is approximately 1 second. Therefore, the angioarchitecture of brain has evolved to allow for instantaneous solute equilibration throughout the brain interstitium once the molecule crosses the limiting membrane, which is the BBB. The endothelial cell shares a capillary basement membrane with the pericyte, which sits on the abluminal side of the endothelium. The pericyte has an antigen presentation role in the CNS (Pardridge, 2001). More than 99% of the brain surface of the capillary basement membrane is invested by astrocyte foot processes, and the distance between the astrocyte foot process and the capillary endothelium is only 20 nm or 200 angstroms, and this distance is equal to the thickness of the capillary basement membrane. There are no tight junctions between astrocyte foot processes, and the astrocyte foot process constitutes no permeability barrier in brain. While the permeability of the

BBB is strictly regulated by the endothelial cell, the total function of the brain microvasculature is determined by the paracrine interactions between the endothelial cell, the pericyte, the astrocyte foot process, and the occasional nerve ending that terminates directly on the brain side of the capillary.

CNS Drug Development

Molecules that are lipid soluble and have a molecular weight under a 500 Dalton threshold are able to cross the BBB in pharmacologically significant amounts (Pardridge, 2001). All present-day CNS drugs in clinical practice fulfill these dual criteria of (1) lipid solubility and (2) molecular weight under a 500 Dalton threshold. If a molecule lacks both of these criteria, it is unlikely that the molecule will cross the BBB in pharmacologically significant amounts, unless the molecule has affinity for one of the CMT or RMT systems in the BBB. In the absence of this, the molecule will need a brain drug delivery system if the drug is to be used as a neuropharmaceutical. Since more than 98% of the drugs that emanate from high throughput receptor-based CNS drug discovery programs will not cross the BBB, the presence of the BBB poses a significant problem for future CNS drug development. On this basis, it is important that there be parallel progress in both CNS drug discovery *and* CNS drug delivery so that these two pathways can be merged in the overall CNS drug development process. Unfortunately, less than 1% of present-day CNS drug development is devoted to CNS drug delivery, and more than 99% is applied to CNS drug discovery.

Blood-Brain Barrier Function in Psychologic Stress

Blood-brain barrier disruption occurs in pathologic states such as the recovery from stroke, infection of the brain, or brain tumors. In addition, there is evidence that the BBB is disrupted in states of severe stress or emotionality. This phenomenon may occur in patients who are acutely admitted to a hospital under severe stress. In this setting of transitory BBB disruption, drugs that are normally excluded from the brain may cross the disrupted BBB. This process may underlie the high incidence of CNS neurotoxicity in acutely hospitalized patients. The biochemical basis of BBB disruption is poorly understood and is an area in need of additional research. Once the biochemical basis of this process is elucidated, new drugs may be developed to prevent BBB disruption in states of severe emotionality.

REFERENCES

Brightman, M. W., Reese, T. S., & Feder, N. (1970). Assessment with the electron-microscope of the permeability to peroxidase of cerebral endothelium and epithelium in mice and sharks. In C. Crone & N. A. Lassen (Eds.), *Capillary permeability* (p. 463). Copenhagen: Munksgaard.

Oldendorf, W. H. (1974). Blood-brain barrier permeability to drugs. *Annual Review of Pharmacology and Toxicology, 14,* 239–248.

Pardridge, W. M. (2001). *Brain drug targeting: The future of brain drug development.* Cambridge, UK: Cambridge University Press.

William M. Pardridge
University of California, Los Angeles

BOGARDUS SOCIAL DISTANCE SCALE

The Bogardus Social Distance Scale was one of the first techniques for measuring attitudes toward racial and ethnic groups. The basic concept behind the Bogardus scale is that the more prejudiced an individual is against a particular group, the less that person will wish to interact with members of that group (R. M. Dawes, 1972). Thus, the items that compose a Bogardus scale describe relationships into which a respondent might be willing to enter with a member of the specified cultural group (e.g., spouse, friend, neighbor, coworker, citizen, visitor to our country, etc.). Items are worded in terms of either inclusion or exclusion. “Would you accept an *X* as a spouse?” is an example of an inclusion-type question. “Would you keep all *Y*s out of America?” is an example of an exclusion-type question. The attitude or esteem with which the respondent holds the specified group is defined as the closeness of relationship that the respondent reports as being willing to accept with a member of that group.

In E. S. Bogardus's (1928) early work, he found that White Americans maintained relatively small social distances from groups such as the British, Canadians, and northern Europeans, but greater social distances from southern Europeans. Groups that differed racially (e.g., Blacks and Orientals) were subject to even larger social distances. Extending the typical use of Bogardus scales, H. C. Triandis and L. M. Triandis (1960) used multifactor experimental designs to separate the independent effects of varying aspects of group membership (e.g., race, religion, and occupation). Triandis and Triandis (1962) later showed that various aspects of group membership of the respondents interact with the social distances they assign various other groups. Thus, Americans were found to consider race an important variable, whereas Greeks considered religion to be more critical. Personality factors such as dogmatism have also been shown to be related to one's proclivity to desire relatively large social distances from groups other than one's own.

The Bogardus scale is a type of Guttman scale. Thus, someone willing to accept members of a certain group as friends would also be willing to accept them as neighbors, coworkers, fellow citizens, and all other more distant relationships. While the responses of some individuals do occasionally reverse the rank-ordered nature of the items, average responses of groups (e.g., cultural or racial groups) tend to maintain the order in a well-constructed Bogardus scale (H. C. Triandis & L. M. Triandis, 1965). Hence, the Bogardus approach to attitude measurement is an effective means of estimating the esteem with which a group of individuals is held by other distinct groups of people.

Although the Bogardus approach to measuring attitudes between and among groups is primarily of historical importance, it continues to be used in recent years. It has generally been employed to assess attitudes in the sense of social distances among both ethnic and racial groups (e.g., Adler, 1985; Kleg & Yamamoto, 1998; Kunz & Yaw, 1989; Law & Lane, 1987), as has been the case historically, and among various psychologically defined groups (Maddux, Scheiber, & Bass, 1982) and groups representing those with various disabilities (Eisenman, 1986; Tolor & Geller, 1987).

REFERENCES

Adler, L. L. (1985). Projected social distances as an indicator of attitudes. In P. Pedersen (Ed.), *Handbook of cross-cultural counseling and therapy* (pp. 247–255). Westport, CT: Greenwood.

Bogardus, E. S. (1928). *Immigration and race attitudes.* Boston: Heath.

Dawes, R. M. (1972). *Fundamentals of attitude measurement.* New York: Wiley.

Eisenman, R. (1986). Social distances toward Blacks and the physically disabled. *College Student Journal, 20,* 189–190.

Kleg, M., & Yamamoto, K. (1998). As the world turns: Ethno-racial distances after 70 years. *Social Science Journal, 35,* 183–190.

Kunz, P. R., & Yaw, O. S. (1989). Social distance: A study of changing views of young Mormons toward Black individuals. *Psychological Reports, 65,* 195–200.

Law, S. G., & Lane, D. S. (1987). Multicultural acceptance by teacher education students: A survey of attitudes toward 12 ethnic and national groups and a comparison with 60 years of data. *Journal of Instructional Psychology, 14,* 3–9.

Maddux, C. D., Scheiber, L. M., & Bass, J. E. (1982). Self-concept and social distance in gifted children. *Gifted Child Quarterly, 26,* 77–81.

Tolor, A., & Geller, D. (1987). Psychologists' attitudes toward children having various disabilities. *Psychological Reports, 60,* 1177–1178.

Triandis, H. C., & Triandis, L. M. (1960). Race, social class, religion and nationality as determinants of social distance. *Journal of Abnormal and Social Psychology, 61,* 110–118.

Triandis, H. C., & Triandis, L. M. (1962). A cross-cultural study of social distance. *Psychological Monographs, 76*(540).

Triandis, H. C., & Triandis, L. M. (1965). Some studies of social distance. In I. D. Steiner & M. Fishbein (Eds.), *Current studies in social psychology.* New York: Holt, Rinehart and Winston.

Kurt F. Geisinger
University of St. Thomas

BONDING AND ATTACHMENT

John Bowlby introduced the term *attachment,* which was established as the essential concept for a new theoretical approach that combines ethology and psychoanalysis for understanding the origins of a child's bond to the mother.

Ethological Theory and Attachment

Animal studies suggest that lasting attachments are formed by a process of *imprinting* that occurs in a short time span at an early critical period of life. Ethology assumes that genetically preprogrammed behaviors important for species survival interact with the environment to produce bonding.

Konrad Lorenz, a pioneer in the study of imprinting, demonstrated that newly hatched fowl such as goslings would become fixed upon and follow the first moving proximal object or person they encountered shortly after birth. Niko Tinbergen demonstrated that the fight-flight response in animals evolves into socialized ritualistic behaviors. Robert Zaslow concluded from studies of the pathology of attachment found in infantile autism that the formation of attachment depends on two bonding networks of behavior: (1) the body–contact bond, necessary for intimacy and basic trust; and (2) the eye–face–contact bond, necessary for integration, focus, and direction of behavior.

Learning Theory and Attachment

Learning theorists have stressed the importance of feeding as a primary drive-reducing reinforcement mechanism for the development of attachment to the mother as a learned process. The satisfaction of the primary drive of hunger results in a positive attachment to the mother through a secondary reinforcement in the feeding situation. A new development in learning theory appeared when Harry Harlow stated that oral gratification through feeding was not sufficient to develop attachment and affection when mannequin monkey mothers were used.

Development of Attachment

In general, attachment emerges in a series of developmental steps that are species-specific. In the beginning, the infant is attached to all humans who exhibit species behaviors that are effectively compatible. Bowlby describes the development of attachment behavior as having four phases: (1) orientation and signals as a general reaction with no discrimination of a specific person, (2) orientation and signals directed to one or more discriminated people, (3) maintenance of proximity to a person by means of locomotion and signals, and (4) formation of a reciprocal relationship with people. Strong attachments to specific persons appear at approximately 7 months of age and are exhibited as a fear of strangers. Infants display protest behavior in the form of anger and resistance when separated from a person to whom they are attached. The protest behavior is increased in an unfamiliar environment, indicating attachment to place as well as to people. As cognition and memory develop in the child, the intensity of protest and the need for physical proximity are reduced because the separation is seen as temporary.

Quality of Attachment

The stability and strength of attachment depends on the quality of parental–infant interaction patterns. A positive attachment is developed by a combination of nurturant-affectionate behaviors and the expression of resistant-angry behaviors in the infant and child. Chronic unresolved anger in parent and child disturbs attachment formation. Rhythm and timing have been found to affect the quality of attachment. Infants are more attached to the parent who responds quickly and spontaneously initiates interactions. Later studies by Ainsworth reveal that the quality of attachment depends on stimulation and control of the environment and child. Ainsworth stated that infants may be securely or anxiously attached, thus affecting the quality and stability of attachment.

Attachment and Psychopathology

Bowlby showed that after the initial positive bond is formed between mother and infant at about 6 months, the infant reacts to loss of the mother in three characteristic stages. First, there is *protest*—crying and anger that serve to bring mother back. If this is unsuccessful, a period of *despair* follows, characterized by withdrawal, depression, and decrease in activity. Finally, a stage of *detachment* appears in which the infant is relatively unresponsive to people. The child's anger toward the mother figure is a central feature of this pattern. The anger is expressed openly in the protest phase and indirectly in the detachment phase. Bowlby stated that the separation experience elicits intense and violent hatred of the mother figure.

Bowlby's observations on separation and loss are supported by the infant studies of Ainsworth and a number of infrahuman primate studies. René Spitz described anaclitic depression as a condition in which the infant, when separated from the mother, dies because of hospitalization. Zaslow and Breger made an attachment analysis of early infantile autism that is followed by separation and loss. They derived several theoretical conclusions applicable to normal human attachment and the psychopathology of attachment. The first was that holding a child in a state of protest behavior, characteristic of infant-child crying, forms a stress-to-relaxation cycle that is a fundamental unit of positive attachment. The greater the intensity of protest, the greater the relaxation and the stronger the bond between child and parent. The second conclusion was that social-affective human attachment is to the face and not to the breast. The human species-specific behaviors important for the maintenance of face-to-face interactions, such as smiling, crying with tears, talking, and listening, are not found in the autistic child, who strongly resists eye-face contact. These provide an alternative behavioral network to the fight-flight response that results from the stress of prolonged eye-face contact found in lower species.

Bowlby reached a general conclusion about attachment theory and its relationship to psychopathology with the view that attachment theory is a scientifically valid system that incorporates concepts derived from psychoanalysis, ethology, cognitive theory, and control theory.

R. W. Zaslow

See also: **Affiliation Need; Avoidant Personality; Deindividuation; Z Process**

BOREDOM AND BOREDOM PRONENESS

Boredom is an emotional state ranging from mild to severe discontent that people describe as a feeling of tedium, monotony, ennui, apathy, meaninglessness, emptiness, lack of interest, and disconnection with the current environment. Boredom is the state—the current condition. Boredom proneness is the trait—a tendency to experience tedium and little personal involvement and enthusiasm, a general or frequent lack of sufficient interest in one's life surroundings and future. The most commonly used measure of boredom and boredom proneness, as with many internal emotional conditions, such as depression and anxiety, is some form of self-report. Behavioral indicators could include yawning, "glazed" eyes, slumped posture, restlessness, and such signs of inattention as looking around the room. Emotions or states opposite to boredom include interest, enthusiasm, involvement, engagement, and optimal stimulation.

Paradoxically, boredom is interesting for both practical and theoretical reasons. Boredom is of practical importance because of its relation to many social problems, such as delinquency, dropping out of school, drug abuse, low morale, poor industrial production, job turnover, and problems of living in institutions such as prisons, mental hospitals, military settings, and nursing homes. Being boring is a condition that all lecturers, entertainers, and advertisers try to avoid. Although boredom is an emotion that probably everyone has experienced, it has received much less research attention than emotions such as depression and anger. One review, covering 1926 to 1980, found less than one article per year on boredom. However, between 1992 and 2002, the pace of research and theoretical activity had increased, and PsycINFO citations occurred at the rate of ten per year.

In addition to practical reasons, there are important theoretical reasons to understand boredom as a motivational concept connecting inner feelings and motives with environmental conditions. Theories relate boredom to attention, arousal, information processing, and stimulus underload. In 1960 Berlyne (1960, p. 187) stated that boredom is "a drive that is reduced through divertive exploration and aroused when external stimuli are excessively scarce or excessively monotonous." The most common theoretical approach construes boredom as occurring in situations with less than the optimal level of stimulation. Theorists tend to emphasize either external conditions or internal predispositions or characteristics. Industrial research is mainly concerned with external conditions as they affect productivity. Among others, Zuckerman emphasized internal elements and saw boredom susceptibility as a part of a stimulus-seeking model. For existentialists, a distinction may be made between existential boredom (the sense of lack of intrinsic meaning in life) and neurotic boredom (an anxious lack of interest or purpose). Some psychoanalytic thought brings another possible research-generating element—sense of control. In 1951 Fenichel stated that boredom occurs "when we must not do what we want to do, or must do what we do not want to do." (Fenichel 1959, p. 359).

Boredom involves ongoing person-environment relationships—the fit of the individual's characteristics to the situation's characteristics. Csikszentmihalyi explored the balance of boredom with anxiety, both being mismatches between environmental challenge and personal competence. Boredom occurs in situations in which a person's capabilities are greater than situational opportunities for expression, whereas anxiety comes when the environment demands more of the person that he or she is able to perform at the time. The achievement of balance occurs in "flow," a condition of pleasurable absorption in an activity. Cross-cultural issues, such as collectivism versus individualism, offer additional theoretical challenges for exploring boredom as an important relation between persons and social environments.

Research on boredom mainly falls into two general categories: (1) experiments in which conditions are manipulated using a stimulus situation assumed to be boring, such as vigilance tasks (e.g., watching radar screens for long periods) or other monotonous tasks (e.g., crossing out a given letter on pages of random letters); and (2) correlation of ratings or questionnaires about boredom with other measures or conditions. A few tests have been developed. Zuckerman's Stimulus Seeking Scale included a Boredom Susceptibility subscale. Another is the Boredom Proneness Scale, or BPS, by Farmer and Sundberg, a 28-item self-report scale that shows good reliability and some evidence of validity but does not correlate significantly with the Zuckerman subscale. Vodanovich and Kass identified five factors in the BPS conceptually very similar to those discussed in the literature: external stimulation, internal stimulation, affective responses to boredom, perception of time (slowness), and constraints (on self-initiated actions). In several studies males are more boredom prone than females. Boredom may be highest in adolescence and may decrease with age. The BPS relates to disinclination to vote, narcissism, forms of self-absorption, and pathological gambling. Several studies have shown a moderate overlap between boredom and negative emotions, such as depression and loneliness.

Physiological factors in relation to boredom have been explored. Zuckerman advocated a physiological basis for boredom and sensation seeking in line with Eysenck's theory. Eysenck postulated that the arousal systems of extroverted people require more stimulation than those of introverts; therefore, in seeking optimal levels of stimulation, extroverts are more outgoing, carefree, and impulsive. In a 1981 review, Smith noted that the most consistent finding was that extroverts were especially vulnerable to boredom. Others reviewing the biological evidence related to monotony avoidance and impulsiveness (which are aspects of extroversion) concluded that there is an association between certain neurochemical activities (especially that of monoamine oxidase, or MAO) and impulsiveness and sensation seeking. Hamilton found increases in capacity for sustained attention in relation to biological indicators during development in later childhood and adolescence.

Coping with boredom is another area of study. Hamilton developed a brief self-report measure of intrinsic enjoyment and boredom coping. She and her colleagues have found these measures to be related to ability to attend to a performance task for long periods—an important element in many industrial and military situations. Fantasy is one way of coping with monotonous situations, and a paucity of fantasy may be related to boredom proneness. Addictive behaviors may be used in coping with boredom, including overeating. Reported boredom is related to school performance. Boredom also appears to be a signal of problems with creativity. Clinicians have been concerned about coping with boredom during psychotherapy either on the part of the patient or the therapist, seeing it as an indicator of problems in transference or countertransference. The positive function of boredom may be to alert a person to do something different.

In conclusion, boredom seems to be generating more and more research attention. At this point, the findings suggest hypotheses for many kinds of studies. There is a strong need for further theoretical development integrating the empirical results with a larger theory of emotions.

REFERENCES

Berlyne, D. E. (1960). *Conflict, arousal and curiosity.* New York: McGraw-Hill.

Farmer, R., & Sundberg, N. D. (1986). Boredom proneness—The development and correlates of a new scale. *Journal of Personality Assessment, 50,* 4–17.

Fenichel, O. (1951). On the psychology of boredom. In D. Rappaport (Ed.), *Organization and pathology of thought* (pp. 349–361). New York: Columbia University Press.

Smith, R. P. (1981). Boredom: A review. *Human Factors, 23,* 329–340.

Vodanovich, S. J., & Kass, S. J. (1990a). A factor analytic study of the Boredom Proneness Scale. *Journal of Personality Assessment, 55,* 115–123.

Zuckerman, M. (1979). *Sensation seeking: Beyond the optimal level of arousal.* Hillsdale, NJ: Erlbaum.

Norman D. Sundberg
University of Oregon, Eugene

See also: **Depression**

BRAIN

The human brain is a complex aggregate of billions of cells working together to process stimuli, to monitor needs, and to direct behavior. Developmentally, the brain begins at the most rostral extension of the neural tube; it bends over and convolutes as it expands within the confines of the skull (cranium). The brain's expansion is disproportionate relative to the growth of the spinal cord, the most caudal extension of the central nervous system. Figure 1 illustrates the development of the human brain, showing its major subdivisions.

There are three major sections of the brain: the *prosencephalon* or forebrain, the *mesencephalon* or midbrain, and the *rhombencephalon* or hindbrain. The forebrain is the largest and most expansive and is made up of two subdivisions: the telencephalon (endbrain) and the diencephalon (interbrain). Telencephalic structures account for about 75% of the weight of the entire human central nervous system. These structures include the two cerebral hemispheres that are connected by a mass of crossing fiber tracts (the corpus callosum). The surface of the hemispheres is a multicellular layer of brain tissue about 4.5 centimeters thick, called the *cerebral cortex.* The cortex is divided into subregions according to gross anatomical landmarks called *sulci* and *gyri.* The largest subregions are called *lobes,* of which there are four in each hemisphere: frontal, parietal, temporal, and occipital. The location of the four lobes and other major brain structures can be seen in Figures 1 and 2. The occipital lobes have visual functions. The temporal lobes are important for audition, learning and memory, and, on the left side of the brain, for understanding language. The parietal lobes control visuospatial and somatosensory functions, and at the junction with the temporal lobe, the left parietal cortex is important for language comprehension. Frontal cortex is polysensory; it is known to be important in movement, impulse control, emotional behavior, problem solving, and, on the left side, language expression.

In the cerebral hemispheres the cortex has a laminar architecture with the different neuronal cell types organized in layers. From an evolutionary standpoint, the layered cor-

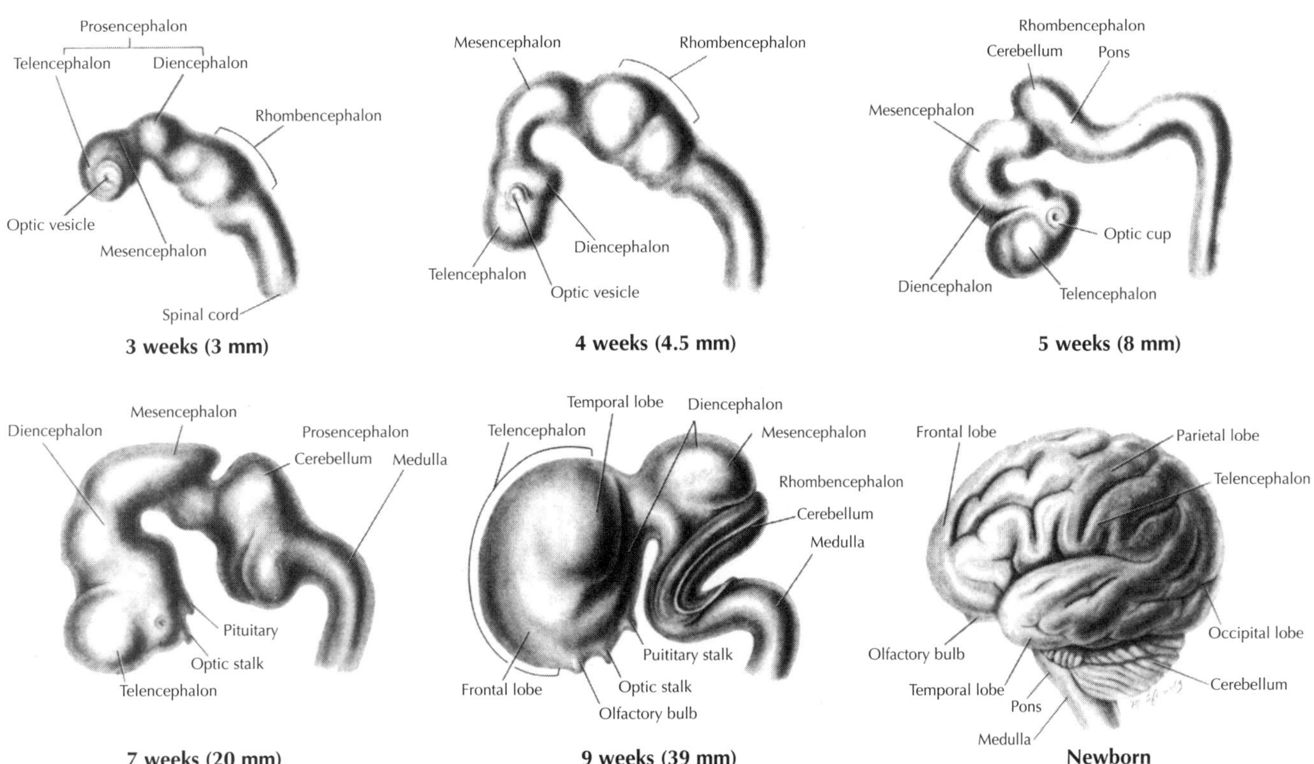

Figure 1. The development of the human brain, showing its major subdivisions.

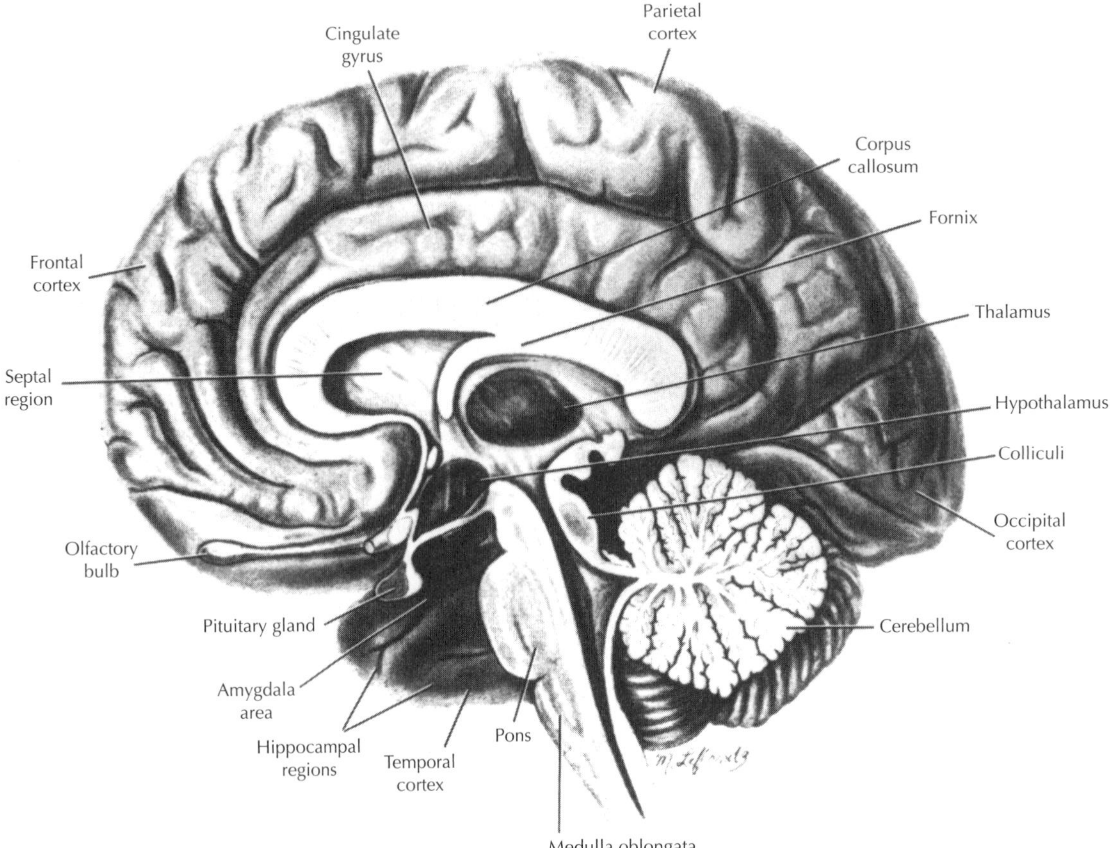

Figure 2. The location of the four lobes and other major brain structures of the adult brain.

tical areas have changed in complexity across the phylogenetic scale. Cortical nerve cell bodies collectively appear gray, thus accounting for the fact that cerebral cortex is commonly called *gray matter.* Likewise, nerve fibers emanating from the cell bodies, because of their collective white appearance subcortically, have been referred to as *white matter.* These fibers connect with other nerve cells that are aggregated in clusters called *subcortical nuclei.* In the telencephalon, the subcortical nuclei include the septum, the amygdaloid complex, and nuclei of the basal ganglia (caudate, putamen, and globus pallidus). Septal and amygdala regions are intimately connected to each other and are important in emotional and motivational functions. The basal ganglia are concerned largely with various aspects of motor control.

The cerebral hemispheres are attached to the diencephalon by massive fiber bundles, the corona radiata. Major structural components present in the diencephalon include the thalamus (a way station for incoming neurons); the subthalamus (a way station between the thalamus and the cortex); the hypothalamus (literally, "under the thalamus"); and the epithalamus (containing the pineal body and the habenular complex).

The middle section of the developing brain is called the *mesencephalon* or midbrain. At maturity the mesencephalon resembles its early embryonic form more closely than do either the prosencephalon or the rhombencephalon. The mesencephalon is made up of three main parts, the tectum (containing auditory and visual relay stations called the *inferior and superior colliculi*), the tegmentum (containing the midbrain reticular formation that activates attention, the substantia nigra that subserves motor functions, and numerous other nuclear groups), and the crus cerebri (a descending bundle of fibers).

The third major section of the brain, part of which eventually exits into the spinal cord at the base of the skull, is the rhombencephalon or hindbrain. It is composed of two subparts, the metencephalon (consisting of the pons and cerebellum) and the myelencephalon (the medulla oblongata). The cerebellum is a prominent eminence; it is the center for motor skills and also subserves certain types of learned activities. The pons and medulla oblongata contain clusters of cranial nerve nuclei that connect the nerves going to and from the face and head. Because of the shape and position of the pons and medulla at the base of the brain, they often are referred to as the *brain stem,* although this term usually includes structures in the midbrain and lower diencephalon as well.

The various components of the brain are interconnected through a very complicated network of neuronal pathways, and neurons are in continuous communication (through specialized chemicals called neurotransmitters). Nuclei within the brain seldom act autonomously. Instead, several nuclei and their fiber tracts may act together to organize and modulate complex behaviors. The functions subserved by these many diverse structures and systems are generally similar in all normal, healthy adults. Sensory systems regulate information coming from outside and inside the body; attentional systems not only keep us alert, but also allow us to ignore stimulus information that may be irrelevant and to rest when we need to; motor systems regulate how we respond and move about; and emotional and motivational systems monitor drives and needs and homeostasis. Other systems help us to learn and to remember or forget. Together, the functioning brain is essential to every aspect of life and consciousness.

Marlene Oscar-Berman
Boston University School of Medicine and Department of Veterans Affairs Health Care System

BRAIN-DERIVED NEUROTROPHIC FACTOR

Brain-derived neurotrophic factor (BDNF) is one of a series of peptide growth factors secreted from neurons and having its own specific receptor. Nerve growth factor (NGF) has TRKA as its receptor, BDNF has TRKB, and neurotrophic factor 3 (NT-3) acts at the TRKC receptor. These neurotrophic factors appear to have different functions at different stages of neurogenesis and development.

It appears that they are crucial for the initial neuronal and synaptic connectivity of the central nervous system (CNS), during which cells that "fire together, wire together." At this stage of development, many of the neurotrophic factors are secreted by the cell bodies of the stimulated (postsynaptic) neurons, picked up by axon terminals, and retrogradely transported back to the nucleus of the innervating neuron; in this manner they alter the patterns of gene expression for maintenance of synaptic efficacy and even neuronal survival. In addition to a role in the basic wiring diagram of the CNS, it would appear that they are also involved in a more subtle sculpting and resculpting of the CNS based on experience-dependent neural plasticity.

In the adult animal, BDNF appears to be integrally involved in long-term potentiation and other models of learning and memory. For example, in genetically modified mice in which BDNF is knocked out, long-term potentiation fails. This failure appears to be physiologically and functionally relevant to the animal because it is unable to navigate based on spatial cues to find a previously discovered submerged platform in the Morris water maze test.

Although it has not been definitively demonstrated, considerable new evidence suggests that BDNF and related neurotrophic factors may be released in a feed-forward fashion with neuronal firing, rather than simply having uptake and retrograde transfer back to the innervating neuron. This is potentially of considerable interest in the dentate granule cells of the hippocampus, which not only are involved in the trisynaptic glutamate-based excitatory circuitry important for learning and memory, but also are capable of producing (and likely releasing) BDNF from their presynaptic terminals.

In the amygdala kindling paradigm wherein repeated subthreshold stimulations of the amygdala eventually come to evoke full-blown tonic-clonic seizures, the dentate granule cells show dendritic sprouting as well as axonal sprouting onto the CA3 pyramidal cells. While kindling induces increases in BDNF mRNA expression, stresses decrease in the same area of the dentate granule cells of the hippocampus.

There is some specificity of the effects on BDNF as a function of both anatomical area involved and specific type of neurotrophic factor. Thus, although stress decreases BDNF in the hippocampus, it increases NT-3, and the effects on BDNF are in the opposite direction in the hypothalamic-pituitary-adrenal axis, which hypothetically could contribute to the increased size of the pituitary and adrenal glands in patients with major depression.

In neonatal rat pups, 24 hours of maternal deprivation results in substantial decrements in BDNF in the hippocampus and a doubling in the rate of the diffuse neuronal apoptosis that occurs in the 12-day-old animal. Repeated experiences of maternal deprivation for 3 hours in the first 10 days of life result in an animal that is permanently hyperactive and hypercortisolemic, as well as prone to alcohol and cocaine self-administration as compared with its non-deprived litter mates. These biochemical and behavioral defects are reversed by chronic treatment with serotonin-selective antidepressants but return when these treatments are discontinued. While alterations in BDNF or other neurotrophic factors have not been definitively linked to these long-term biochemical and behavioral changes in this psychosocial stressor paradigm, they provide a plausible mechanism.

The potential bidirectionality of such experiential effects is further emphasized by the work of Meaney and colleagues, who observed that 15 minutes of maternal deprivation resulted in increased maternal attention and licking upon reunion and subsequently thereafter, and thus engendered protective effects against stress-related hypercortisolemia and even age-related decline in hippocampal structure and memory loss. Parallel effects were observed in the offspring of mothers who were high natural lickers of their infants compared with those who naturally engaged in lesser degrees of this grooming and contact behavior.

Many of the currently utilized psychotropic agents have effects on neurotrophic factor gene expression, including that of BDNF. Smith and colleagues were the first to demonstrate the opposite effects of stress and antidepressants on BDNF mRNA in the hippocampus; these data were replicated and extended by Duman and colleagues at Yale.

They found that antidepressants as a class, including electroconvulsive therapy, increase BDNF gene expression following chronic administration. Moreover, there is partial amelioration of some of the stress-induced decrements in BDNF gene expression if antidepressants are used prior to or concurrently with the stress induction.

From the clinical perspective, this raises the potential of different types of benefit from long-term antidepressant prophylaxis in individuals with recurrent unipolar depression. They prevent recurrent depression, and to the extent that the preclinical data in animals are relevant to the human condition—and some preliminary autopsy data from the Stanley Foundation brain collection are at least consistent with this perspective—it is possible that antidepressants could be partially protective to the effects of stressors on BDNF gene expression. This might be useful and neuroprotective in its own right, but to the extent that some types of stressors are involved in the triggering of affective episodes, this could be involved in depression prophylaxis.

Preliminary evidence also suggests that BDNF is positive in some animal paradigms predictive of the efficacy of antidepressants, further raising the speculation that more direct targeting of BDNF specifically for therapeutic purposes, either by increasing BDNF itself or increasing activity at its TRKB receptor, may ultimately provide a new approach to the therapeutics of depression, possibly at a level of primary as well as secondary prevention.

SUGGESTED READING

Alter, C. A., Cai, N., Bliven, T., Juhasz, M., Conner, J. M., Acheson, A. L., et al. (1997). Anterograde transport of brain-derived neurotrophic factor and its role in the brain. *Nature, 389,* 856–860.

Duman, R. S., Heninger, G. R., & Nestler, E. J. (1997). A molecular and cellular theory of depression. *Archives of General Psychiatry, 54,* 597–606.

Gaiddon, C., Loeffler, J. P., & Larmet, Y. (1996). Brain-derived neurotrophic factor stimulates AP-1 and cyclic AMP-responsive element dependent transcriptional activity in central nervous system neurons. *Journal of Neurochemistry, 66,* 2279–2286.

Korte, M., Staiger, V., Griesbeck, O., Thoenen, H., & Bonhoeffer, T. (1996). The involvement of brain-derived neurotrophic factor in hippocampal long-term potentiation revealed by gene targeting experiments. *Journal of Physiology, 90,* 157–164.

Korte, M., Kang, H., Bonhoeffer, T., & Schuman, E. (1998). A role for BDNF in the late-phase of hippocampal long-term potentiation. *Neuropharmacology, 37,* 553–559.

Nibuya, M., Morinobu, S., & Duman, R. S. (1995). Regulation of BDNF and TRKB mRNA in rat brain by chronic electroconvulsive seizure and antidepressant drug treatments. *Journal of Neuroscience, 15,* 7539–7547.

Nowak, R. (1992). Cells that fire together, wire together. *Journal of the National Institutes of Health Research, 4,* 60–64.

Siuciak, J. A., Lewis, D. R., Wiegand, S. J., & Lindsay, R. M. (1997). Antidepressant-like effect of brain-derived neurotrophic factor (BDNF). *Pharmacology, Biochemistry and Behavior, 56,* 131–137.

Smith, M. A., Makino, S., Kvetnansky, R., & Post, R. M. (1995a). Effects of stress on neurotrophic factor expression in the rat brain. *Annals of the New York Academy of Sciences, 771,* 234–239.

Smith, M. A., Makino, S., Kvetnansky, R., & Post, R. M. (1995b). Stress and glucocorticoids affect the expression of brain-derived neurotrophic factor and neurotrophin-3 mRNAs in the hippocampus. *Journal of Neuroscience, 15,* 1768–1777.

Robert M. Post
National Institute of Mental Health

***See also:* Central Nervous System**

BRAIN EVOLUTION

Most neurons have long processes that allow rapid cell-to-cell communication over long distances within an organism. The evolutionary gain of neurons allowed an explosive new radiation of multicellular animals, most of which have bilateral symmetry and a centralized nervous system. The rostral part of centralized nervous systems is composed either of a localized collection of ganglia or a unitary brain; the term *brain* will be used here loosely to refer to both conditions.

Brain Elaboration: A Repeating Theme

Brain evolution is a story of brain diversity. Brains have independently evolved multiple times in the many separate lines of invertebrate and vertebrate groups. In some groups, brains are simply organized, and many species with relatively simple brain organization have been evolutionarily successful. In many other instances, brains have become enlarged and elaborated with more distinct neuronal cell groups (nuclei), more extensive interconnections of these cell groups, lamination of the neurons and fiber (axonal) systems in some regions, and a greater variety of neuronal cell types.

Among invertebrates, brain enlargement and elaboration have occurred independently multiple times (Breidbach & Kutsch, 1995)—within molluscs such as *Nautilus,* squid, and octopus and within arthropods such as insects. Among jawed vertebrates, brain enlargement and elaboration have occurred independently for some members within each major group—cartilaginous fishes, ray-finned (including bony) fishes, and tetrapods. Often, anatomical complexity appears to be correlated with behavioral complexity.

Seminal Events in Vertebrate History

In the line leading to vertebrates, several major evolutionary events occurred that established the basis for most parts of our nervous systems, including major gains in sensory system structure and the motor neuron–musculature system (Butler & Hodos, 1996; Nieuwenhuys, ten Donkelaar, & Nicholson, 1998). The brain and spinal cord were greatly enlarged, and the vertebrate sensory systems—including olfactory, visual, somatosensory, auditory, vestibular, gustatory, and lateral line (mechanosensory and electrosensory)—were gained (Northcutt, 1996). Motor neuronal pools for the muscles of the face and throat (pharynx) regions and, subsequently, for eye muscles and then jaw and neck muscles were gained. In the ancestral line leading to tetrapods, sets of paired appendages and a muscular tongue were gained along with their respective motor nuclei, while the lateral line system was lost.

Brain Evolution in Vertebrates

In those groups with enlarged and elaborated brains, the more dorsal (alar plate–derived) parts of the brain tend to show more variation than the more ventral (basal plate–derived) parts. Structural elaboration is often correlated with a major exploitation of a particular sensory aspect of the world or with the gain of complex behaviors (see Butler & Hodos, 1996, and references therein). For example, mormyrid fishes utilize an expanded cerebellum and lateral line lobe, which are alar plate–derived, in their complex electrosensory communication system for individual recognition, nest building, and care of their young. Many tropical reef fish have greatly enlarged forebrains and complex territorial, courtship, and parental behaviors. Some cartilaginous fishes also have substantially enlarged forebrains used in complex sensory processing.

Within the brain stem across amniotes (reptiles, birds, and mammals), similarities exist for many of the nuclei, but the alar plate–derived, sensory part of the trigeminal nerve is very versatile. It generally supplies touch, position sense, pain, and temperature for the face but also innervates mechanosensory and electrosensory receptors in platypuses, infrared receptors in some snakes, and magnetic-sensitive receptors in birds. The cerebellum likewise varies markedly. In primates the neocerebellar hemispheres are greatly expanded for control of limb movements as well as some aspects of sensory processing. The midbrain roof, or tectum, is also highly variable. Its rostral part, the superior colliculus, is involved in visual localization functions. Of modest size in mammals, it reaches its apogee in birds. The caudal tectum, the inferior colliculus, processes auditory stimuli and is elaborately developed in bats as part of their echolocation sonar system and in birds, such as owls, that hunt in darkness and localize their prey by sound.

Among amniotes, major differences occur in forebrain structure. In mammals, the elaborately layered neocortex (Bock & Cardew, 1999) receives sensory input relayed from dorsal thalamic nuclei, whereas in reptiles and birds, some of the telencephalic cell populations that receive thalamic input are organized as nuclei rather than in layers. Whether these nuclei are equivalent (homologous) to neocortex is an unresolved question (Karten, 1991; Northcutt & Kaas, 1995; Butler & Hodos, 1996; Puelles et al., 2000). All modern mammals are derived from an ancestral stock with somatomotor, auditory, and visual cortical regions occupying similar relative positions on the cerebral hemispheres. Within various orders of mammals, the number of cortical sensory areas has independently increased, and each area has become dedicated to the analysis of specific aspects of the sensory input (Bock & Cardew, 1999). Many primates, for example, have over 20 visual cortical areas that each analyze different aspects and combinations of the visual input. Bats have specialized auditory cortical areas for analyzing the Doppler shift in constant frequency to determine prey velocity and for analyzing frequency modulated sounds with time delay to determine range. Some mammals with prominent whiskers, such as rodents, have specialized, cylindrically shaped regions in the somatosensory cortex called *barrels* that each receive the input from a single whisker.

Neocortex in humans has few truly unique features vis à vis other primate brains. The volume of neocortex relative to the total volume of the brain is only what one would expect for a generalized primate (Passingham, 1979). Language was arguably the most important evolutionary gain for our species (Deacon, 1997), but even here, the parts of the brain used for language comprehension and motor speech have precedent areas in other primates. It is possible that small differences in the volume of cortex in a given region allow for dramatic differences in function. Current research includes new insights gleaned from comparative embryological studies, indicating that small changes in the genome and in the complex developmental program can have profound effects on the phenotype. Some of the most difficult persistent questions concern the complex relationships between cytoarchitecture and function.

REFERENCES

Bock, G., & G. Cardew (Eds.). (1999). Evolutionary developmental biology of the cerebral cortex. *Novartis Foundation Symposium, 228.* New York: Wiley.

Breidbach, O., & Kutsch, W. (Eds.). (1995). *The nervous system of invertebrates: An evolutionary and comparative approach.* Basel, Switzerland: Birkhäuser Verlag.

Butler, A. B., & Hodos, W. (1996). *Comparative vertebrate neuroanatomy: Evolution and adaptation.* New York: Wiley-Liss.

Deacon, T. W. (1997). *The symbolic species: The co-evolution of language and the brain.* New York: W. W. Norton.

Karten, H. J. (1991). Homology and evolutionary origins of the "neocortex." *Brain Behavior and Evolution, 38,* 264–272.

Nieuwenhuys, R., ten Donkelaar, H., & Nicholson, C. (1998). *The central nervous system of vertebrates.* Berlin, Germany: Springer-Verlag.

Northcutt, R. G. (1996). The origin of craniates: Neural crest, neurogenic placodes, and homeobox genes. *Israel Journal of Zoology, 42,* S273–S313.

Northcutt, R. G., & Kaas, J. (1995). The emergence and evolution of mammalian neocortex. *Trends in Neurosciences, 18,* 373–379.

Passingham, R. E. (1979). Brain size and intelligence in man. *Brain Behavior and Evolution, 16,* 253–270.

Puelles, L., Kuwana, E., Puelles, E., Bulfone, A., Shimamura, K., Keleher, J., et al. (2000). Pallial and subpallial derivatives in the embryonic chick and mouse telencephalon, traced by the expression of the genes *Dlx-2, Emx-1, Nkx-2.1, Pax-6,* and *Tbr-1. Journal of Comparative Neurology, 424,* 409–438.

Ann B. Butler
George Mason University

See also: Neocortex

BRAIN IMAGING IN AFFECTIVE NEUROSCIENCE

Emotions are action-related feelings of positive or negative valence that are associated with approach or avoidance behaviors and neurophysiological changes. They are learned, innate, or a combination between the two; and they may be transient states such as fear, anger, or happiness; or they may be enduring moods such as depression. Basic knowledge about the neural underpinnings of emotion stems from several decades of animal research utilizing lesion, electrical stimulation, single cell recording, and pharmacological manipulation techniques. During recent years, functional neuroimaging has been applied to study normal and pathological emotions in humans. Together, these streams of research have contributed to the emergence of *affective neuroscience* (Davidson & Sutton, 1995).

Neuroimaging

Brain imaging includes techniques such as electroencephalography (EEG), magnetoencephalography (MEG), positron emission tomography (PET), single photon emission tomography (SPECT), computerized axial tomography (CT), functional magnetic spectroscopy (MRS), and structural (MRI) and functional magnetic resonance imaging (fMRI). Imaging tools may reveal both structure and function and permit measures of electrical, magnetic, metabolic, and neuroreceptor and neurotransmitter characteristics. The first wave of neuroimaging studies concerned basic research on cognitive processes as well as psychopathology, for example, by imaging dopamine receptors in schizophrenic patients or regional cerebral blood flow (rCBF) in individuals with anxiety disorders. A main lesson from the early imaging literature is that the notion of centers, whether cognitive or emotional, is too simplified because even simple tasks may require widespread activation in neural networks.

Affective Style

Imaging studies typically report data that are averaged over groups of individuals. However, individuals vary in quality and intensity of their reactions to similar emotional stimuli. This is often referred to as *affective style* (Davidson & Irwin, 1999), presumably reflecting differences in temperament, personality, and psychopathological vulnerability. Electrocortical studies of affective style have suggested that left frontal brain activity is associated with positive emotions and approach behavior, whereas right frontal activation predicts negative emotions and avoidance. Affective style has also been related to emotionally determined differences in amygdala activation. Activity in the amygdala has been shown to correlate with aversive emotional reactions in general and fear in particular (Davidson & Irwin, 1999).

Emotional Perception and Experience

Emotions may be induced internally though imagination or self-generation, or externally in perceptually driven emotions. Kosslyn and colleagues (1996) reported that the negative emotional content of stimuli increased activity in the occipital cortex both during perception and imagery. Thus, the neural circuits underlying self-generated and perceptually driven emotion may overlap. While self-generated emotions unequivocally involve feelings, perceiving emotion in others may tax cognitive processes rather than generating an emotional experience. Hence, it is important not to equate perception with experience of emotion. Imaging studies of emotional perception have explored the neural networks involved in perceiving facial expressions of primary emotions like fear and disgust presented both consciously and unconsciously, that is, subliminally (Adolphs, 2002). Neuronal activity in the amygdala seems to undergo rapid habituation both in emotional perception and induction studies (for reviews see Whalen, 1998; Davis & Whalen, 2001). It has been argued that the amygdala respond to biologically significant stimuli but predominantly in ambiguous situations (Wahlen, 1998).

Studies of emotional induction have focused mainly on unpleasant emotions, often involving pharmacological probes (e.g., yohimbine, procaine, cholecystokinin tetrapetide [CCK-4] administration) or sensory stimulation using visual (e.g., films or pictures) or auditory (e.g., scripts or tapes) stimuli. Only a small number of studies have extended into other domains such as the olfactory, gustatory, and somatosensory modalities. In an examination of 25 neuroimaging publications on brain and emotion in healthy individuals, Maddock (1999) noted that the inferior frontal and posterior cingulate cortex, in particular the right retrosplenial cortex, were the regions most frequently activated by emotional conditions.

Emotional Learning and Memory

In classical fear conditioning the emotional impact of a stimulus is altered, that is, it is transformed into a conditioned stimulus capable of eliciting fear reactions after pairings with aversive unconditioned stimuli such as electric shocks. Numerous animal studies support a crucial role for the amygdala in the expression and acquisition of such associative fear memories (Davis & Whalen, 2001). Lesion and neuroimaging studies have indicated that the amygdala is involved in fear conditioning processes in humans as well (Davis & Whalen 2001). The amygdala may also participate in the formation of declarative memory for emotional events (e.g., Cahill et al., 1996). However, the exact role of the amygdala and its subnuclei in the formation and storage of emotional memory is debated and a matter of active research.

Neuropsychiatric Applications

Emotional dysregulation is especially prominent in Anxiety and Mood Disorders. Patients with various Anxiety Disorders have been scanned during symptom provocation to elucidate the pathophysiology of anxiety. Metabolic abnormalities in the orbitofrontal cortex, the cingulate, and the caudate nucleus have been noted in Obsessive-Compulsive Disorder (Rauch & Shin, 1997). For other Anxiety Disorders, findings are mixed although the anterior paralimbic cortex and the amygdala region have been implicated, particularly in Posttraumatic Stress Disorder (Rauch & Shin, 1997), and Social Phobia (Tillfors et al., 2001). The amygdala region may be a common site of action for behavioral and pharmacological treatments of Social Phobia (Furmark et al., 2002).

In major depression, metabolic abnormalities have been reported mainly in the prefrontal, cingulate, amygdala, and thalamic regions. Functional imaging data suggest that depression is associated both with mood-dependent and traitlike neurophysiological abnormalities in brain regions that are at least partly related to anatomical abnormalities revealed by structural imaging techniques (Drevets, 2000).

Studies of pain are also relevant for affective neuroscience because pain regulates mood and motivational behavior. Human pain imaging has shown involvement of the anterior cingulate, anterior insula, and prefrontal and posterior parietal cortices, as well as subcortical regions like the thalamus (Ingvar, 1999). Recent imaging findings suggest that placebo effects mimic brain alterations resulting from opioid analgesia (Petrovic, Kalso, Peterson, & Ingvar, 2002).

Future Directions

While measures of oxygen consumption, glucose metabolism, and regional cerebral blood may reveal the neural correlates of thoughts and feelings, dynamic receptor imaging could enhance our understanding of the associated neurochemistry. By comparing the effect of psychological and pharmacological treatments on receptor or transmitter characteristics, future investigations may reveal whether separate or common neurochemical mechanisms operate. By studying receptor characteristics we could better understand the dynamics of neural transmission during emotional activation and regulation.

REFERENCES

Adolphs, R. (2002). Neural systems for recognizing emotion. *Current Opinion in Neurobiology, 12,* 169–177.

Cahill, L., Haier, R. J., Fallon, J., Alkire, M. T., Tang, C., Keator, D., et al. (1996). Amygdala activity at encoding correlated with long-term free recall of emotional information. *Proceedings of the National Academy of Sciences, USA, 93,* 8016–8021.

Davidson, R. J., & Sutton, S. K. (1995). Affective neuroscience: The emergence of a discipline. *Current Opinion in Neurobiology, 5,* 217–224.

Davidson, R. J., & Irwin, W. (1999). The functional neuroanatomy of emotion and affective style. *Trends in Cognitive Sciences, 3,* 11–21.

Davis, M., & Whalen, P. J. (2001). The amygdala: Vigilance and emotion. *Molecular Psychiatry, 6,* 13–34.

Drevets, W. C. (2000). Neuroimaging studies of Mood Disorders. *Biological Psychiatry, 48,* 813–829.

Furmark, T., Tillfors, M., Marteinsdottir, I., Fischer, H., Pissiota, A., Långström, B., et al. (2002). Common changes in cerebral blood flow in patients with Social Phobia treated with citalopram or cognitive-behavioral therapy. *Archives of General Psychiatry, 59,* 425–433.

Ingvar, M. (1999). Pain and functional imaging. *Philosophical Transactions of the Royal Society of London: Series B. Biological Sciences, 354,* 1347–1358.

Kosslyn, S. M., Shin, L. M., Thompson, W. L., McNally, R. J., Rauch, S. L., Pitman, R. K., et al. (1996). Neural effects of visualizing and perceiving aversive stimuli: A PET investigation. *Neuroreport, 7,* 1569–1576.

Maddock, R. J. (1999). The retrosplenial cortex and emotion: New insights from functional neuroimaging of the human brain. *Trends in Neuroscience, 22,* 310–316.

Petrovic, P., Kalso, E., Peterson, K. M., & Ingvar, M. (2002). Placebo and opioid analgesia: Imaging a shared neuronal network. *Science, 295,* 1737–1740.

Rauch, S. L., & Shin, L. M. (1997). Functional neuroimaging studies in Posttraumatic Stress Disorder. *Annals of the New York Academy of Sciences, 821,* 83–98.

Tillfors, M., Furmark, T., Marteinsdottir, I., Fischer, H., Pissiota, A., Långström, B., et al. (2001). Cerebral blood flow in subjects with Social Phobia during stressful speaking tasks: A PET study. *American Journal of Psychiatry, 158,* 1220–1226.

Whalen, P. J. (1998). Fear, vigilance, and ambiguity: Initial neuroimaging studies of the human amygdala. *Current Directions in Psychological Science, 7,* 177–188.

Mats Fredrikson
Tomas Furmark
Uppsala University, Uppsala, Sweden

BRAIN INJURIES

The brain can suffer injury in diverse ways: metabolic or structural abnormalities that are genetically inherited or perinatally induced; trauma from civilian accidents or military combat; toxicity from drugs, heavy metals, or poisonous gases; malnutrition; infections or diseases; tumors; cerebrovascular accidents (stroke); surgical removal of brain tissue for relief of epilepsy, intractable pain, or serious psychiatric symptomatology; and aging-related disorders (e.g., Alzheimer's disease).

Early perinatal brain lesions tend to be more extensive and diffuse than those incurred later in life. Early lesions often are detected by abnormalities in behavior observed during later development, and the time of onset of the damage can only be approximated in relation to presumed prenatal events. By contrast, lesions incurred beyond infancy often can be linked to a specific event or to an approximate onset in the symptomatology, and premorbid behavior can be compared with postinjury behavior. Some injuries in adulthood can produce clearer abnormalities than others. For example, destruction of an area of the cerebral cortex in the anterior region of the left frontal lobe may cause a noticeable disruption in normal speech, whereas a lesion in the analogous area in the right frontal lobe may produce only subtle changes in emotional functions and personality. Similarly, a lesion in the left frontal lobe near the junction with the parietal lobe can result in loss of language comprehension, but no such problem occurs after an analogous lesion on the right side of the brain.

Brain damage can have divergent effects, depending upon the locus and extent of the damage. For example, clinically it has been noted that lesions in distinctly different areas of the brain will disrupt visual perception at different levels of processing. Damage in the optic nerve, superior colliculi, certain thalamic way stations, and cortex of the occipital lobes will interfere with visual functioning at the level of stimulus input, or processing of stimulus features. Damage in the temporal lobes adjacent to the occipital lobes will disrupt visual perception at a higher level of analysis, such as evaluating the importance or meaningfulness of stimuli, or remembering what the stimuli are. If the damage is on the left side, verbal comprehension of written material (e.g., reading) is impaired. Finally, damage in the frontal lobes may interfere with the expression of responses to stimuli. Not surprisingly, left frontal damage can interfere with language expression (e.g., speaking or writing words).

Because brain damage does not always result in immediately apparent symptoms, localization of the site and extent of damage may be difficult. For example, while an analysis of a specific sensory function, such as the integrity of the visual fields, can reveal basic sensory defects, more subtle cognitive and intellectual defects may require careful scrutiny. Functions involved in attention, motivation, emotion, and language often must be measured through the skillful administration and interpretation of tests specifically designed to show the impairments. Descriptions of many of these tests can be found in books by Lezak (1995), Mesulam (2000), and Spreen and Strauss (1998), as well as in a chapter by Oscar-Berman and Bardenhagen (1998).

Accidental head trauma, generally called *traumatic brain injury* or *TBI,* is a common yet severely disabling disorder. Because of the shape of the skull and the way the brain rests inside this bony case, violent blows to the head often seriously impact the prefrontal cortex and its connections with other brain regions. Severe frontal dysfunction leads to relaxed inhibitory control over appetitive or sexual drives and thus to inappropriate social behaviors that can prevent the TBI patient from returning to full functional independence.

Neurologists rely on a variety of imaging and recording techniques for visualizing brain abnormalities in their patients. The techniques are used to measure parameters such as cerebral blood-flow patterns and obstructions, ventricular size, regional glucose utilization, the presence of abnormal tissue masses, and seizure activity. Such techniques include angiography, X-ray computerized tomography (CT scans), structural and functional magnetic resonance imaging (MRI and fMRI scans), positron emission tomography (PET scans), single photon emission computed tomography (SPECT scans), electroencephalography (EEG), evoked potentials (EP), and magnetoencephalography (MEG). Each technique provides the neurologist and neuroscientist with a particular type of information about the structure or function of the brain. The various techniques also are used to monitor changes in the brain with the progression of a disease, or during recovery from an illness.

Some techniques use X rays to reveal images of abnormal blood flow through cerebral arteries (carotid angiography) or lesions produced by stroke or brain tumors (CT scans). MRI scans provide images of the brain without X rays, and because of the nature of the magnetic signals that produce MRI images, the scans can easily visualize small tumors, multiple sclerosis plaques, and infarctions. Another group of imaging techniques such as PET, SPECT, and fMRI provide images of regional cerebral blood flow, blood volume, or glucose metabolism, all of which are closely coupled and correlated with neuronal activity and are thus indirect measures of brain functioning. Normal electrical changes in the brain, as well as abnormal electrical activity such as in epilepsy, can be measured with another set of techniques, which include EEG, EP, and MEG. These procedures generally entail the attachment of electrodes to the scalp at standard locations in order to pick up electrical signals reflecting brain functioning. The signals are amplified and interpreted for the presence of abnormalities. For a comparison of various neuroimaging techniques, see a recent paper by Dale and Halgren (2001).

REFERENCES

Dale, A. M., & Halgren, E. (2001). Spatiotemporal mapping of brain activity by integration of multiple imaging modalities. *Current Opinion in Neurobiology, 11,* 202–208.

Lezak, M. D. (1995). *Neuropsychological assessment* (3rd ed.). New York: Oxford University Press.

Mesulam, M.-M. (Ed.). (2000). *Principles of behavioral and cognitive neurology* (2nd ed.). New York: Oxford University Press.

Oscar-Berman, M., & Bardenhagen, F. (1998). Nonhuman primate models of memory dysfunction in neurodegenerative disease: Contributions from comparative neuropsychology. In A. Tröster (Ed.), *Memory in neurodegenerative disease* (pp. 3–20). New York: Cambridge University Press.

Spreen, O., & Strauss, E. (1998). *A compendium of neuropsychological tests* (2nd ed.). New York: Oxford University Press.

Marlene Oscar-Berman
Boston University School of Medicine

BRAIN SPECIALIZATION

Specialization and Integration

The brain adheres to two fundamental principles of organization, *functional integration* and *functional specialization.* The integration among specialized cortical areas depends upon cortico–(sub)cortical connections and the neuronal interactions they mediate. The characterization of functional specialization is important in many areas of neuroscience and provides an infrastructure within which normal brain function can be understood (e.g., cognitive neuroscience) and how things might go wrong (e.g., neuropsychology and clinical neuroscience). The distinction between specialization and integration relates to the distinction between localizationism and (dis)connectionism that dominated thinking about brain function in the nineteenth century. Since the early anatomic theories of Gall, the identification of a particular brain region with a specific function has become a central theme in neuroscience. However, functional localization per se was not easy to demonstrate: for example, a meeting entitled "Localization of Function in the Cortex Cerebri" in 1881 addressed the difficulties of attributing function to a cortical area, given the dependence of cerebral activity on underlying connections (Phillips, Zeki, & Barlow, 1984). Goltz (1881), although accepting the results of electrical stimulation in dog and monkey cortex, considered the excitation method inconclusive in that the movements elicited might have originated in related pathways or current could have spread to distant areas. In short, the excitation method could not be used to infer functional localization because localizationism discounted interactions among areas. It was concluded that lesion studies should supplement excitation experiments. Ironically, it was observations on patients with brain lesions (Absher & Benson, 1993) some years later that led to the concept of disconnection syndromes and the refutation of localizationism as a sufficient account of cortical organization.

Functional localization implies that a function is localized in an area, whereas specialization suggests that a cortical area is specialized for some aspects of cognitive, perceptual, or sensorimotor processing. The cortical infrastructure supporting a single function may involve many specialized areas whose union is mediated by functional integration. In this view functional specialization is only meaningful in the context of functional integration and vice versa.

The Nature of Functional Specialization

The functional role played by any component (e.g., cortical area, subarea, or neuronal population) of the brain is defined by its connections. Certain patterns of cortical projections are so common that they could amount to rules of connectivity. "These rules revolve around one, apparently, overriding strategy that the cerebral cortex uses—that of functional specialization" (Zeki, 1990). Functional specialization demands that cells with common functional properties be grouped together. This architectural constraint necessitates both convergence and divergence of cortical connections. Extrinsic connections between cortical regions are not continuous but occur in patches or clusters. This patchiness has a clear relationship to functional specialization. For example, a visual area at the back of the brain (V2) has a distinctive cytochrome oxidase staining pattern, consisting of thick stripes, thin stripes, and interstripes. When recordings are made in V2, directionally selective (but not wavelength- or color-selective) neurons are found exclusively in the thick stripes. Retrograde (i.e., backwards) labeling of cells in a functionally homogeneous area that is specialized for visual motion (V5) is limited to these thick stripes. Evidence of this nature supports the notion that patchy connectivity is the anatomical substrate of functional specialization. If neurons in a given area share a common responsiveness (by virtue of their connections) to some sensorimotor or cognitive attribute, then this functional specialization is also an anatomical one.

The search for specialized cortical areas still rests upon the axis established in the nineteenth century, namely the lesion-deficit model and brain excitation methods. Current

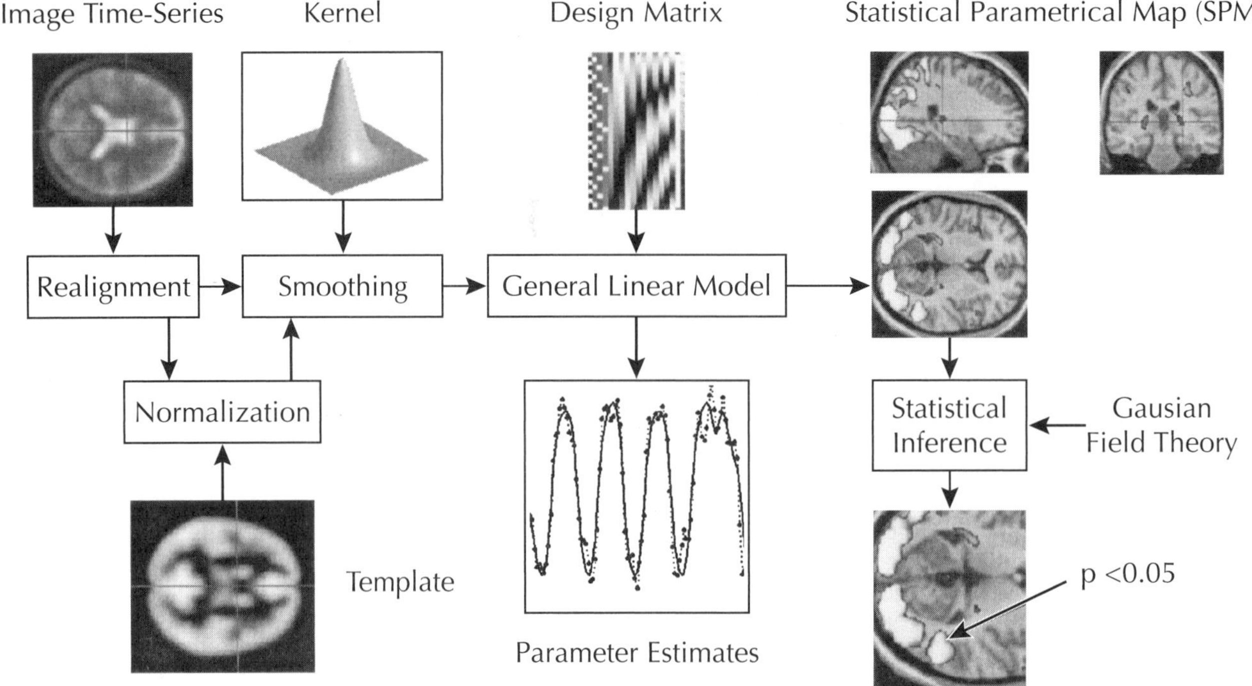

Figure 1. Mapping specialization in the brain.
The transformations that constitute an analysis of functional images create a statistical parametric map (SPM). SPMs can be thought of as X rays of the significance of an effect (e.g., activation in a specialized area revealed by subtracting scans obtained in one condition from those obtained in another). After realignment the images are subject to nonlinear warping to match a template that conforms to some standard anatomical space. After smoothing, the general linear model is employed to perform the appropriate statistical test at every voxel (i.e., volume element). The test statistics that ensue (usually *t*- or *F* statistics) constitute the SPM. SPMs are used to make inferences about brain responses that are then characterized using the fitted responses or parameter estimates. Adjustments to *p*-values, for the enormous number of tests implicit in an SPM, are usually made using distributional approximations from the theory of Gaussian fields.

approaches rely on (1) the functional deficits following circumscribed brain injury (neuropsychology), and (2) functional neuroimaging. Although important, the inferences about neuronal architectures, based solely on the lesion-deficit model, are fundamentally limited. The integration of neuropsychology, psychophysics, and neuroimaging has revolutionized our view of the brain, literally and conceptually. Challenging subjects with the appropriate sensorimotor attribute or cognitive process leads to activity changes in, and only in, the relevant specialized areas. This is the model upon which functional imaging is based.

Specialization and Functional Imaging

The tenet of functional neuroimaging is that the difference between two tasks can be formulated as a separable cognitive or sensorimotor component and that the regionally specific differences in brain activity identify the corresponding specialized area. The first applications addressed the functional anatomy of word processing (Peterson, Fox, Posner, Mintun, & Raichle, 1989) and functional specialization in extrastriate cortex (Lueck et al., 1989). The latter studies involved presenting visual stimuli with and without some sensory attribute (e.g., color, motion, etc.). The areas highlighted, by comparing the ensuing scans, were identified with homologous areas in monkeys that showed selective electrophysiological responses to equivalent stimuli. Most studies of functional specialization employ statistical parametric mapping (Friston, 1997) to provide what can be thought of as X rays of significant brain responses (see Figure 1). These statistical parametric maps (SPMs) are constructed using a series of brain scans acquired from subjects under experimentally induced changes in brain state, designed to isolate the function of interest. The cortical area in the lower right of Figure 1 is visual area V5 and shows significant motion-sensitive responses elicited by alternate presentations of stationary and moving dots.

REFERENCES

Absher, J. R., & Benson, D. F. (1993). Disconnection syndrome: An overview of Geschwind's contributions. *Neurology, 43,* 862–867.

Friston, K. J. (1997). Imaging cognitive anatomy. *Trends in Cognitive Sciences, 1,* 21–27.

Goltz, F. (1881). In W. MacCormack (Ed.), *Transactions of the 7th International Medical Congress: Vol. 1* (pp. 218–228). London: J. W. Kolkmann.

Lueck, C. J., Zeki, S., Friston, K. J., Deiber, N. O., Cope, P., Cunningham, V. J., et al. (1989). The colour centre in the cerebral cortex of man. *Nature, 340,* 386–389.

Peterson, S. E., Fox, P. T., Posner, M. I., Mintun, M., & Raichle, M. E. (1989). Positron emission tomographic studies of the processing of single words. *Journal of Cognitive Neuroscience, 1,* 153–170.

Phillips, C. G., Zeki, S., & Barlow, H. B. (1984). Localization of function in the cerebral cortex: Past, present, and future. *Brain, 107,* 327–361.

Zeki, S. (1990). The motion pathways of the visual cortex. In C. Blakemore (Ed.), *Vision: Coding and efficiency* (pp. 321–345). Cambridge, UK: Cambridge University Press.

Karl J. Friston
Wellcome Department of Cognitive Neurology, London, England

BRAIN STEM

The brain stem, which consists of the midbrain, pons, and medulla oblongata, connects the cerebrum above to the spinal cord below. It is a highly organized structure that, in addition to conveying ascending and descending tracts, contains the nuclei of the cranial nerves III to XII and is responsible for a number of complex functions, including control of respiratory and cardiovascular activity and regulation of the level of consciousness.

The *midbrain* is the shortest segment of the brain stem. It consists of a ventral and a dorsal portion separated by the ventricular space. The dorsal or posterior portion is called the *tectum* and consists of four rounded swellings, the paired superior and inferior colliculi. The ventral or anterior portion is called the *tegmentum* and contains the reticular formation, the nuclei of cranial nerves III and IV, and ascending and descending pathways.

The *pons* is readily identified from the midbrain and from the medulla oblongata (whose description follows) as a large bulge on the ventral surface of the brain stem lying on the dorsum sellae of the sphenoid bone. The dorsal or posterior surface of the pons is taken up superiorly by the superior cerebellar peduncles, while inferiorly it forms the upper part of the floor of the fourth ventricle. The pons contains ascending and descending tracts and connections with the cerebellum, as well as the nuclei of cranial nerves V to VIII.

The *medulla oblongata* extends from the lower limit of the pons to a level just above the first pair of cervical nerves, where it is continuous with the spinal cord. It is somewhat pyriform in shape, larger superiorly than inferiorly. The dorsal surface of the medulla oblongata forms the lower part of the floor of the fourth ventricle in the cephalad half. The ventral surface is made up of the pyramids containing the corticospinal tracts. The medulla oblongata contains the nuclei of cranial nerves IX through XII, which exit along its lateral aspects. The caudal half of the medulla oblongata represents a transition to the spinal cord, with cross-sectional organization and a central canal similar to the cord.

Given the complexity of the structure of the brain stem and the proximity of the motor and sensory tracts and cranial nerve nuclei, it is not surprising that disturbances in brain-stem function can be seen with very small lesions. Until the advent of computerized tomography (CT) in the late 1970s, the brain stem could be imaged only by indirect means. Even CT is not ideal, primarily because of distortions of the image caused by the surrounding bone. Magnetic resonance imaging (MRI) is now the imaging modality of choice for patients in whom a lesion in the brain stem is suspected.

Lesions that may affect the brain stem include vascular malformations such as angiomas, which may be a cause of spontaneous hemorrhage; infectious diseases such as tuberculosis, although this is rare in developed countries; demyelinating diseases such as multiple sclerosis; and tumors.

Classically occurring in children at a median age of between 5 and 10 years, brain-stem tumors account for as many as 15% of all brain tumors in this age group. Evidence suggests that the incidence of brain-stem tumors has been increasing, although this is probably due in large part to better detection using MRI of lesions that in the past may have gone undiagnosed.

There are several types of brain-stem tumors, each characterized by a distinct clinical presentation and MRI appearance. These include focal tumors, most often seen in the midbrain; dorsal exophytic tumors that grow from the dorsal aspect of the medulla into the fourth ventricle; and cervicomedullary tumors that originate in the upper cervical cord or medulla and grow posteriorly to project into the fourth ventricle. These types account for approximately 20% of all brain-stem tumors. Some, notably focal tumors arising in the tectum, may do well without any therapeutic intervention. Others may do well after surgery alone or, if this is not possible, after treatment with radiotherapy. In contrast, approximately 80% of all brain-stem tumors are of the so-called "diffuse intrinsic kind." These are high-grade astrocytomas that grow very rapidly and cause multiple neurological deficits. Surgery is not indicated, and these patients are treated with radiotherapy alone. In spite of a satisfactory early response to treatment, outcome is very poor. The median time to progression after treatment with radiotherapy is only of the order of 6 months, and the median survival time is less than 1 year. Less than 10% of patients will be alive 2 years or more after treatment. Several groups are actively undertaking research studies using various types and combinations of chemotherapy and biological agents given along with radiotherapy in the hope of achieving an improved outcome for children with these tumors, as yet without success.

Carolyn R. Freeman
McGill University Health Center / Montreal General Hospital, Montreal, Quebec, Canada

BUFFERING HYPOTHESIS

The buffering hypothesis asserts that social support provides protection against the stress that produces psychological or physiological disorder or disease or reduces job performance. The stress-buffering function of social support has been of considerable interest to behavioral and medical scientists, especially since a 1979 Alameda County study showed that social conditions, such as marriage and group membership, were related to mortality.

Several issues emerge in research on the buffering hypotheses. Of particular importance is the definition and measurement of three variables: stress, social support, and outcome. Psychological *stress* is often measured on a checklist or inventory by self-report of major life events of the last few months, such as death in the family, divorce, and changes in work. Using weights from experts' ratings of stress, the experimenter obtains a total score. A less used kind of measure is called *daily hassles,* such as burdensome household chores and waiting in traffic. *Social support* is measured in three ways: (1) social network membership (sometimes called social integration), such as living with a family, belonging to a club, or attending a church; (2) perceived social support, such as self-report of availability of people to discuss problems or provide material aid; and (3) support behaviors, such as reported or observed actions of helping the specified person. The first two methods have received the most research attention. The *outcome* or dependent variables are usually physical or psychological disorders (or health), such as depression, recovery from surgery, smoking cessation, and development of cancer or AIDS symptoms in infected people. Productivity may be used as an outcome in industrial settings.

In general the findings across many studies with the first two social support measures have been positive. In a 1991 review, Sheldon Cohen (pp. 1–2) concluded, "The epidemiological data on the role of social integration in morbidity and mortality have clearly established that the social environment plays an important role in health and well being . . . [and] when a perceived availability of a social support measure is used, these effects reliably occur in the prediction of psychological and physical symptoms." It appears that the body's immune system is affected by social support, and people who get colds readily are likely to have poor social supports. An overview of abstracts of articles since Cohen's conclusions show a majority of studies with positive results, but not all. A few studies of animals also support the buffering hypothesis.

Beyond these generally positive findings, many theoretical and research questions remain. One is the issue of whether the results are due to main effects or buffering effects. Is social support a true buffering effect having no influence of its own but being entirely conditional upon the presence of stress? Another related issue is the place of social support in the chain of multiple cause and effect as represented in the diathesis-stress theories of psychopathology. *Diathesis* refers to predispositions to disorder from biological or early experiential causes. Throughout the life cycle, social support and nonsupport interact with other variables to protect or not protect against stress.

An important theoretical task in clarifying the buffering hypothesis is the integration of the many possible variables into a model explaining why social support works. Cohen has presented a transactional model that includes core concepts about social networks, stressful events, and personality factors, including perceived social support, stress appraisal, and support behaviors ultimately affecting the development of a disorder. Basing his conclusion on several studies, Cohen indicates that one personality feature that seems particularly important to include in addition to social support is the sense of internalized control or self-efficacy (a person's sense of capability and effectiveness). Coping styles and genetic predispositions are other psychological variables that need to be included in an integrated theory of the relation between stress and disorder surrounding the buffering hypothesis.

On a larger than individual scale, community settings and institutions, such as churches, schools, and senior centers, can provide buffers for stress. Group interventions, such as workshops on stress inoculation for people in dangerous occupations or students facing examinations, may provide social support as well as increasing self-efficacy.

REFERENCE

Cohen, S. (1991). Social supports and physical health: Symptoms, health behaviors, and infectious disease. In E. M. Cummings, A. L. Greene, & K. H. Harraker (Eds.), *Life-span developmental psychology: Perspectives on stress and coping* (pp. 213–234). Hillsdale, NJ: Erlbaum.

Norman D. Sundberg
University of Oregon, Eugene

BULIMIA

Bulimia, more accurately known as Bulimia Nervosa, is an eating disorder characterized by three primary symptoms: recurrent episodes of binge eating, inappropriate compensatory behaviors, and extreme concern about body weight and shape. Binge eating involves the consumption of a large amount of food in a relatively short period of time along with a perception of loss of control over eating. Binge eating may be triggered by a number of factors, including hunger, negative mood, interpersonal stressors, and thoughts about weight and shape. Inappropriate compensatory behaviors are strategies aimed at controlling body weight and shape, including self-induced vomiting, misuse of laxatives and/or diuretics, excessive exercising, and fasting. The *Diagnostic and Statistical Manual of Mental Disorders* (*DSM-IV;* American Psychiatric Association, 1994) divides Bulimia Nervosa into two subtypes. The *purging* subtype is distinguished by the presence of purging compensatory behaviors such as self-induced vomiting or laxative misuse. The *nonpurging* subtype is diagnosed in the presence of only nonpurging compensatory behaviors (e.g., excessive exercise). Individuals with Bulimia Nervosa also exhibit overconcern about their body weight and shape and usually engage in extreme dietary restriction outside of binge-eating episodes in order to control weight and shape. The dysfunctional concerns about weight and shape are typically conceptualized as the central feature or core psychopathology of Bulimia Nervosa.

Bulimia Nervosa typically begins with rigid and unhealthy dieting that is motivated by the desire to be thin and lose weight. Individuals with Bulimia Nervosa attempt to limit the amount and type of food that they consume, particularly during the early stages of the disorder. Over time, they become increasingly preoccupied with thoughts of food, and episodes of binge eating alternate with periods of restriction. Vomiting, laxative misuse, and other inappropriate compensatory behaviors usually follow the onset of binge eating.

Bulimia Nervosa most commonly occurs in women and usually begins in adolescence or early adulthood. Approximately 1–2% of young women meet criteria for the disorder. In contrast to Anorexia Nervosa, individuals with Bulimia Nervosa maintain normal weight. As a result, Bulimia Nervosa is more difficult to detect than Anorexia Nervosa as physical signs are not readily apparent to the casual observer. Bulimia is often a secretive disorder, and individuals with Bulimia Nervosa typically experience guilt and shame about their behavior. Individuals with Bulimia Nervosa display rigid patterns of thinking and tend to view the world and their experiences from an "all or nothing" perspective. For example, bulimics often describe eating as being either "in control" or "out of control" and weight or appearance as either "thin" or "fat."

The medical complications associated with Bulimia Nervosa are generally regarded as less severe than those associated with the low body weight of Anorexia Nervosa. Electrolyte disturbances represent the most serious medical complication and may lead to cardiac irregularities and, in some cases, heart failure. Inflammation and rupture of the esophagus is another serious potential complication resulting from repeated vomiting. Additional medical complications include laxative dependence, fatigue, enlargement of salivary glands leading to puffy cheeks, headaches, dry skin, abrasions to fingers from inducing vomiting, and dental erosion.

Numerous causal factors have been proposed as being related to the development of Bulimia Nervosa. Disturbances in such neurotransmitter systems as those of serotonin and norepinephrine have been observed, but it remains unclear whether these biological irregularities cause Bulimia Nervosa or result from the disturbed eating behaviors that characterize the disorder. Findings from several studies suggest that Bulimia Nervosa may result, in part, from dieting-based changes in serotonin functioning in vulnerable individuals. Neurochemical abnormalities appear to persist after recovery. A genetic basis for bulimia is supported by family studies, which examine the clustering of disorders within families. Family studies find increased rates of eating disorders in the families of individuals with Bulimia Nervosa as compared to the families of individuals without Bulimia Nervosa. The exact role genetic factors play in the development of Bulimia Nervosa, however, remains unclear, and environmental factors clearly influence the development of the disorder.

Although it is widely believed that childhood sexual abuse causes Bulimia Nervosa, there is little evidence for a specific relationship between a history of sexual abuse and the development of the disorder. Childhood sexual abuse appears to increase one's risk for psychological disorders in general, not Bulimia Nervosa specifically. Cultural factors do appear to play a role in the development of Bulimia Nervosa. The ideal female weight in Western society, often referred to as the *thin ideal,* has continued to decrease even as the average female weight increases. As a result, more and more women experience normative body dissatisfaction secondary to a discrepancy between their ideal and actual weight. Body dissatisfaction is widespread among adolescent girls, and research links body dissatisfaction, along with acceptance of the thin ideal, to the development of Bulimia Nervosa. Prospective research has also found a strong relationship between dieting and the later development of an eating disorder. Other potential risk factors include early onset of menstruation, a personal or parental history of obesity, parental dieting, and personality traits such as perfectionism. Bulimia Nervosa often co-occurs with other psychological disorders including depression, Anxiety Disorders, substance abuse disorders, or some Personality Disorders such as Borderline Personality Disorder.

According to the *DSM-IV,* Bulimia Nervosa is typically either intermittent, with binge eating and/or purging alternating with periods of remission, or chronic. Treatment, however, can significantly affect outcome. Cognitive-behavioral therapy (CBT), a psychological treatment, is widely viewed as the treatment of choice for Bulimia Nervosa. CBT for Bulimia Nervosa includes education about Bulimia Nervosa, self-monitoring of eating behaviors, establishing a regular pattern of eating, strategies to reduce binge eating and compensatory behaviors (e.g., vomiting), problem solving, and cognitive restructuring. Cognitive restructuring is a strategy designed to help patients identify and challenge their patterns of thinking. Numerous studies have demonstrated that the majority of patients treated with CBT benefit from treatment and that improvement is maintained over time. Interpersonal psychotherapy is another psychological treatment that is supported by research, although fewer studies have examined this form of psychotherapy. Antidepressant medications also appear to reduce bulimic symptoms.

REFERENCE

American Psychiatric Association. (1994). *Diagnostic and statistical manual of mental disorders* (4th ed.). Washington, DC: Author.

Carolyn Black Becker
Trinity University

BUROS MENTAL MEASUREMENTS YEARBOOK

As a young professor at Rutgers University in the mid-1930s, Oscar Krisen Buros developed the idea for a book series that would insure test users an indispensable reference for in-depth descriptions and critiques of all commercially produced tests developed in the English language. Soon to become *The Mental Measurements Yearbook* (*MMY*) series, his publication of "candidly critical" reviews of tests, Buros believed, would serve a variety of public interests. For test users, the series would afford valuable access to the expertise of scholars and professionals. Buros also held that test users would gradually become informed consumers of testing products and would increasingly select tests that met or exceeded minimal standards of psychometric adequacy. For test designers and publishers, Buros maintained that the publication of critical reviews would "cause authors and publishers to publish fewer but better tests" (Buros, 1938, p. xiii).

Buros was undaunted by substantial pressures to curtail publication of the *MMY* series. The logistics of recruiting qualified professionals and securing their reviews for large numbers of testing instruments promised to be (and has remained) an enormous undertaking. In addition, test authors and publishers sometimes provided limited cooperation for securing information about tests and related testing materials. Occasionally, Buros was threatened with lawsuits over critical reviews. To sustain him in this endeavor, Buros enlisted the considerable talents of his wife, Luella, and small group of devoted staff. Funding to create a consumer's research bureau whereby specially trained teams of psychometricians would independently evaluate tests did not materialize. Instead, Buros continued to rely upon large numbers of academics and specialized professionals to serve in the role of test reviewers.

Despite the name *The Mental Measurements Yearbook* and the desire of its editor to publish new volumes annually, the exacting standards of Buros and the size of the undertaking mandated a production schedule for the *MMY* averaging once every 5 years. Besides the publication of the *MMY,* Buros also edited special monographs on testing in distinct subject areas (e.g., vocations, personality) and initiated production of the *Tests in Print (TIP)* series. *TIP* was designed to serve the testing community as a compendium of all currently available tests and to provide a quick reference to test reviews published in the *MMY* series. Whereas new editions of the *MMY* both describe and review new tests, each edition of the *TIP* series contains descriptive entries of all known tests currently available in the English language.

The publication process for the books edited by Buros began with *Educational, Psychological, and Personality Tests of 1936* and *The 1938 Mental Measurements Yearbook* and had continued through *The Eighth Mental Measurements Yearbook* (1978) when Buros passed away. After a nationwide search to determine a successor location, Luella Buros selected the University of Nebraska-Lincoln to continue the work begun by her late husband over 40 years earlier. The world's largest collection of tests and testing material was subsequently crated and shipped to a new location halfway across the United States. Publication commenced in 1983 with *Tests in Print III,* followed soon afterward by *The Ninth Mental Measurements Yearbook.*

The dream of Oscar Buros for fewer, better quality tests has been partially realized in several ways. A current count of in-print tests has suggested a small reduction in the number of commercially available instruments being offered for sale since 1983. In addition, many of the sophisticated methodological strategies designed to insure test reliability, validity, and appropriate standardization had not been developed in the days when Buros made his initial proclamation on tests. With the advent of testing standards first articulated in 1954 (and most recently in 1999) by the American Educational Research Association, the American Psychological Association, and the National Council on Measurement in Education, test authors and publishers alike have greater guidance by which to judge the adequacy of their products.

Shortly before her death in 1995, Luella Buros funded the Buros Center for Testing. Mrs. Buros believed that, in order to speed advances in the field of testing and measurement, it was essential to create a consultation service that would share test development expertise with both the public and private sectors. Working as the umbrella organization, the center has acted to combine the historic objectives of the Buros Institute of Mental Measurements for improved testing with consultation services from the newly created Buros Institute for Assessment Consultation and Outreach.

In response to continual requests to make test reviews more accessible to the public, *Test Reviews Online* was launched in September, 2001. This Internet service (available at *www.unl.edu/buros*) was designed to provide, for a modest fee, immediate access to over 2,000 testing instruments in a wide variety of subject areas. Additional test reviews are being added each month. The Buros Center for Testing continues the work of improving tests and assessments that was first articulated by Oscar Buros over 65 years ago.

Brief History of the Buros Institute of Mental Measurements

1938—*The 1938 Mental Measurements Yearbook;* Oscar K. Buros (Editor)

1940—*The 1940 Mental Measurements Yearbook;* Oscar K. Buros (Editor)

1949 to 1978—The third through eighth *Mental Measurements Yearbooks,* and *Tests in Print* and *Tests in Print II;* Oscar K. Buros (Editor)

1978—Oscar K. Buros passes away. Luella Gubrud Buros relocates the Buros Institute of Mental Measurements to the University of Nebraska-Lincoln.

1983 to 1985—*Tests in Print III* and *The Ninth Mental Measurements Yearbook;* James V. Mitchell, Jr. (Editor)

1989—*The Tenth Mental Measurements Yearbook;* Jane Close Conoley & Jack J. Kramer (Editors)

1992—*The Eleventh Mental Measurements Yearbook;* Jack J. Kramer & Jane Close Conoley (Editors)

1994—The Oscar and Luella Buros Center for Testing is created as a parent organization, adding the Buros Institute for Assessment Consultation and Outreach to the Buros Institute of Mental Measurements. *Tests in Print IV;* Linda L. Murphy, Jane Close Conoley, & James C. Impara (Editors)

1995—*The Twelfth Mental Measurements Yearbook;* Jane Close Conoley & James C. Impara (Editors)

1998—*The Thirteenth Mental Measurements Yearbook;* James C. Impara & Barbara S. Plake (Editors)

1999—*Tests in Print V;* Linda L. Murphy, James C. Impara, & Barbara S. Plake (Editors)

2001—*The Fourteenth Mental Measurements Yearbook;* Barbara S. Plake & James C. Impara (Editors). *Test Reviews Online* (a collection of over 2,000 recent test descriptions and reviews from *The Mental Measurements Yearbook* and *Tests in Print* series) becomes available via the Internet.

2002—*Tests in Print VI;* Linda L. Murphy, Barbara S. Plake, James C. Impara, & Robert A. Spies (Editors)

2003—*The Fifteenth Mental Measurements Yearbook;* Barbara S. Plake, James C. Impara, & Robert A. Spies (Editors) with subsequent editions to be completed at 18-month intervals

REFERENCES

American Educational Research Association, American Psychological Association, & National Council on Measurement in Education. (1999). *Standards for educational and psychological testing.* Washington, DC: American Educational Research Association.

Buros, Oscar K. (Ed). (1938). *The 1938 mental measurements yearbook.* New Brunswick, NJ: Rutgers University Press.

Robert A. Spies
University of Nebraska, Lincoln

Linda L. Murphy
Buros Institute of Mental Measurements

BYSTANDER INVOLVEMENT

In March 1964 Kitty Genovese was brutally murdered in New York while 38 of her neighbors watched from their apartment windows. Even though the attack lasted over 30 minutes, no one called the police until it was over. As a direct result of this incident, a great deal of empirical and theoretical knowledge has been generated on the topic of bystander involvement.

According to a model developed by Latane and Darley (1970), the decision to intervene consists of a series of decisions. First, the bystander must notice that something is happening. Second, the bystander must interpret or label what has been noticed as an emergency. Third, the bystander must decide that he or she has a responsibility to become involved. Fourth, the bystander must decide what form of assistance to render. And fifth, the bystander must decide how to implement the previous decision. Research findings supporting the model attest to the important role played by social influence factors at two stages of the model—labeling the event as an emergency and feeling responsible for becoming involved. Bystanders may use the actions of others in the situation to help them interpret the event. If the others are unsure themselves about what is happening and hesitate to take action, each may use this seeming passivity of others to label the event as a nonemergency. Even when a bystander is certain that the event is an emergency, the presence of others may diffuse responsibility for taking action. As a result, bystanders are less likely to aid the victim. This diffusion of responsibility explanation of bystander involvement is supported by a wide range of empirical findings showing that the greater the number of bystanders present, the less likely a victim is to receive aid (Latane & Nida, 1981).

Another model of bystander involvement for which there

is considerable empirical support is the Arousal: Cost-Reward Model first proposed by I. M. Piliavin, Rodin, and J. A. Piliavin (1969), and more recently expanded to cover nonemergency helping (J. A. Piliavin, Dovidio, Gaertner, & Clark, 1981). The model consists of two components—an arousal component and a cost-reward component. The components are conceptually distinct but functionally related. The model proposes that bystanders are aversively aroused by the victim's distress, that they are motivated to reduce their arousal, and that helping the victim is one way to accomplish this. According to the model, "arousal is a function of the clarity and severity of the crisis and of the psychological and physical closeness of the bystander to the victim" (Dovidio, J. A. Piliavin, Gaertner, Schroeder, & Clark, 1991, p. 89). In their search for ways to reduce their arousal, bystanders are guided by their assessment of the rewards and costs of each option. The model proposes that they will prefer responses that most rapidly and completely reduce arousal and that yield the most favorable costs-rewards ratio. For example, the costs of intervening could include effort and physical harm, whereas rewards could include feelings of efficacy and expressions of gratitude from the victim.

The model is sufficiently broad to account for the influence of a wide array of personality and situational variables. A recent review of relevant research indicates strong empirical support for many aspects of the model (Dovidio et al., 1991). While successive versions of the model have added to its breadth, the model has become increasingly complex (the current version has eight boxes and 17 arrows), making causal analysis more difficult.

Batson and his colleagues have challenged the Arousal: Cost-Reward Model, claiming that it assumes bystanders are egoistically motivated (Batson, 1987). That is, it assumes that bystanders' primary concern is to reduce their own distress and helping the victim is a means for achieving this goal. In contrast, Batson proposes a model of helping based on empathic concern. According to his Empathy-Altruism Hypothesis, witnessing another individual in distress can lead to empathic concern, involving feelings of sympathy, compassion, and tenderness. Such emotions can "evoke motivation with an ultimate goal of benefitting the person for whom the empathy is felt—that is, altruistic motivation" (Batson, 1998, p. 300). In a series of experiments that controlled for alternative egoistic motivation, Batson (1987) demonstrated strong support for altruistically motivated helping. The research thus suggests that there can be multiple motives for bystanders' reactions and that their helping behavior can best be viewed as a weighted function of egoistic and altruistic motives.

Two important moderators of bystander reactions are attributions and type of relationship. The types of attributions bystanders make about the victim and about themselves (e.g., their arousal) can influence their helping behavior. For example, bystanders have been found to be less likely to aid a victim if they view the victim as being responsible for his or her fate (Lerner, 1980). The type of relationship that the bystander has with the victim can also moderate helping. Bystanders who feel a sense of "we-ness" with the victim, or who are in a communal relationship with the victim (Clark & Mills, 1979), may feel more empathy for the victim and thus experience greater arousal and distress than bystanders who perceive the victim as being different or as being a member of an out-group.

Personality factors have been found to provide a poorer accounting of bystander involvement than have features of the situation. Although there has been some recent success in identifying dispositional predictors of helping, correlations rarely exceed 0.30–0.40, leaving about 85–90% of the variance unaccounted for (Batson, 1998).

REFERENCES

Batson, C. D. (1987). Prosocial motivation: Is it ever truly altruistic? In L. Berkowitz (Ed.), *Advances in experimental social psychology* (Vol. 20, pp. 65–122). New York: Academic Press.

Batson, C. D. (1998). Altruism and prosocial behavior. In D. T. Gilbert, S. T. Fiske, & G. Lindzey (Eds.), *The handbook of social psychology* (Vol. 2, pp. 282–316). New York: McGraw-Hill.

Clark, M. S., & Mills, J. (1979). Interpersonal attraction in exchange and communal relationships. *Journal of Personality and Social Psychology, 37,* 12–24.

Dovidio, J. F., Piliavin, J. A., Gaertner, S. L., Schroeder, D. A., & Clark, R. D., III. (1991). The Arousal: Cost-Reward Model and the process of intervention: A review of the evidence. In M. S. Clark (Ed.), *Prosocial behavior* (pp. 86–118). Newbury Park, CA: Sage.

Latane, B., & Darley, J. M. (1970). *The unresponsive bystander: Why doesn't he help?* New York: Appleton-Century-Croft.

Latane, B., & Nida, S. A. (1981). Ten years of group size and helping. *Psychological Bulletin, 89,* 308–324.

Lerner, M. J. (1980). *The belief in a just world: A fundamental delusion.* New York: Plenum.

Piliavin, I. M., Rodin, J., & Piliavin, J. A. (1969). Good Samaritanism: An underground phenomenon. *Journal of Personality and Social Psychology, 13,* 289–299.

Piliavin, J. A., Dovidio, J. F., Gaertner, S. L., & Clark, R. D., III. (1981). *Emergency intervention.* New York: Academic Press.

Martin S. Greenberg
University of Pittsburgh

C

CANADIAN PSYCHOLOGICAL ASSOCIATION

A motion creating the Canadian Psychological Association (CPA) was moved and passed at a dinner meeting in Ottawa in June 1938, which was held in conjunction with a meeting of the American Association for the Advancement of Science. Subsequently, a constitution was adopted in December 1940; however, the usual date reported for the inception of the organization is 1939. There were 38 founding members. Although there is some debate about the impetus for the establishment of the CPA, one school of thought holds that the organization was created so that psychologists might contribute more effectively to the war effort.

In general the CPA's mandate is to represent the interests of and provide leadership in all aspects of psychology in Canada. More particularly, CPA aims to promote the unity, coherence, and sense of identity among the diverse scientific and professional interests and geographical disparities of all psychologists in the country. Current members number over 5,100. Full members must possess a master's degree in psychology, while student members may be graduate or undergraduate students studying psychology on a full- or part-time basis. Affiliates are those who have shown an active interest in psychology and have all the perks of membership but may not hold office.

The governance of the CPA consists of an appointed honorary president plus an 11-person board of directors (including the president, president elect, and past president) assisted by an executive director and head office staff. (Administrative offices are located in Ottawa.) Two directors, one representing the Canadian Society for Brain, Behaviour, and Cognitive Science and the other the Council of Canadian Departments of Psychology, have designated seats, while other directors and the president are elected. The Council of Provincial Associations of Psychologists (CPAP), the Canadian Council of Professional Psychology Programs, and the Association of State and Provincial Psychology Boards enjoy observer status at board meetings. Various functions are assigned to committees of the board, with a director serving as chair. Included among the 15 extant committees are By-Laws, Rules and Procedures; Convention; Education and Training; Ethics; Fellows and Awards; International Relations; Membership; Professional Affairs; Publications; Scientific Affairs; and Sections. There are 24 sections affiliated with the CPA that span the myriad subspecialties in the discipline, from Adult Development and Aging to Women and Psychology. These sections have official status under the bylaws and are the primary agents through which the particular and special needs of members are met and interests served. The CPA also maintains close ties with provincial associations of psychologists and regulatory bodies through membership on CPAP.

The CPA publishes three scholarly journals (*Canadian Psychology, Canadian Journal of Behavioural Science,* and *Canadian Journal of Experimental Psychology*), each of which produces four issues annually. A newsletter, *Psynopsis,* sent to all members, also appears four times a year. Access to these publications is available online for members. More episodic publications include the Strengthening Psychology series. This series consists of relatively brief articles, commissioned by CPA, that address specific issues in the health care field (e.g., home and community care, medicare, pharmacare, and primary care). The organization has also been active in the development of national standards and ethical principles, and a number of documents pertain to these efforts (e.g., *A Canadian Code of Ethics for Psychologists,* 1991; *A Companion Manual of the Canadian Code of Ethics for Psychologists,* 1992; *Guidelines for Non-Discriminatory Practice,* 1996; *Guidelines for Therapy and Counselling with Women,* 1980; *Guidelines for Professional Practice for School Psychologists,* 2002). A number of position statements have also been approved by CPA members over the years recognizing the legitimacy of psychology of women courses and research, the need for more affordable quality child care, opposition to the reintroduction of the death penalty, and various other matters. The Association also maintains a web site at http://cpa.ca.

The CPA annually hosts a 3-day convention with a varied program of invited speakers, symposia, and paper and poster sessions. A number of continuing education workshops typically precede the convention proper. Sections and committees hold their annual business meetings at the convention, and sections have significant responsibilities for convention content. Another publication of the CPA is the annual convention issue of *Canadian Psychology,* which contains abstracts of convention submissions.

In addition to recognizing the contributions of members through election to fellowship, the CPA offers a number of other awards for distinguished contributions to the application of psychology; to public or community service; to psychology as a profession; to psychology as a science; and to education and training in psychology. There are also a number of New Researcher awards and a Gold Medal award for lifetime contributions to Canadian psychology. Students producing outstanding honors, master's, and doctoral theses at each university across the country are recognized with a Certificate of Excellence award. Many sections also provide awards; several of these are designed to applaud the best student presentation at the convention.

One of the many important functions performed by the CPA is the accreditation of university-based professional doctoral programs in clinical, clinical neuropsychology and counselling (22 accredited), and predoctoral internship programs (26 accredited). A recent initiative of the CPA is the inauguration of the CPA Foundation. Donations to the Foundation are intended to provide support for students in psychology, for psychological research, and for public policy development. A mentoring program for junior faculty is another member service offered by the CPA. The purpose of this initiative is to offer new academic faculty an opportunity to contact and communicate with more experienced, tenured colleagues (from another university) who are willing to provide advice and direction relevant to the role of a university professor.

Representing psychology to the government is a priority of the CPA. The CPA has maintained a high profile in both consulting and lobbying with the Canadian federal government on issues affecting the ability of psychology to contribute to the welfare of Canadian society (for example, in the areas of health, the criminal justice system, research funding, and education). This work frequently represents collaborative efforts with other groups such as the Canadian Consortium for Research and the Health Action Lobby. *Psychology and Public Policy: An Advocacy Guide for Psychologists* (1999) and *Working With the Media: A Guide for Psychologists* (2000) are excellent how-to documents designed to encourage greater political participation on the part of Canadian psychologists.

In the interests of fulfilling its mandate of fostering cohesion among the disparate national and provincial organizations of psychology, the CPA has been an active participant, along with 17 other organizations, in seeking to integrate these diverse groups so that Canadian psychology might speak with one voice.

Sandra W. Pyke
York University, Canada

See also: **American Psychological Association**

CAREER COUNSELING

Career counseling is one of several interventions used to assist clients with career issues and problems. Other interventions include career appraisal and testing and the use of computer-assisted career guidance systems, the Internet, job simulations, gaming, and a variety of self-directed initiatives designed to help clients clarify their personal strengths and weaknesses, as well as their aptitudes, interests, values, personality types, and aspirations. Both self-directed and counselor-directed processes focus on helping the client explore available jobs, occupations, and other career options, evaluate them, and examine their congruence with client preferences and abilities.

Historically, career counseling was treated as separate from psychotherapy or personal counseling. Within the past two decades, however, the use and content of career counseling have broadened in their application throughout the life span to populations experiencing an increasingly comprehensive array of career concerns. Thus, whereas traditional models of career counseling tend to focus on career exploration, job selection, clarification of life and career goals, and improvement in decision-making skills, more recent applications of career counseling tend to address problems that require a fusion of career and personal counseling. In the latter approaches, career counseling may address providing support to persons experiencing job stress, job loss, and major (often involuntary) career transitions; helping clients deal with work adjustment issues, such as coping with negative relations with a supervisor or coworkers; teaching clients to deal with anger management; restructuring work dysfunctions; modifying irrational career beliefs; or resolving conflicts between work and family roles.

Definitions of Career Counseling

As the problems clients bring to career counselors have expanded and become more complex, the definitions of career counseling have changed. These definitions have increasingly shifted from viewing career problems as rational, objective, and unaffected by emotional crises outside the workplace to examining the interaction of work-related problems with those of personal identity, family concerns, mental health, and related issues. Krumboltz (1993), for example, has stated emphatically that "career and personal counseling are inextricably intertwined. Career problems have a strong emotional component" (p. 143).

Brown and Brooks (1991, p. 5) have defined career counseling as follows:

> Career counseling is an interpersonal process designed to assist individuals with career development problems. Career development is that process of choosing, entering, adjusting to and advancing in an occupation. It is a life-long psychological process that interacts dynamically with other life roles. Career problems include but are not limited to career indecisions and undecidedness, work performance, stress and adjustment, incongruence of the person and work environment, and inadequate or unsatisfactory integration of life roles (e.g., parent, friend, citizen).

In essence, career counseling is used with individuals and with groups, represents a continuum of approaches tailored to the career concerns and needs of individual clients, and is likely to be part of a program of interventions that include career assessments, self-directed activities, assistance with skill development, and related functions.

Approaches to Career Counseling

Whatever the precise theoretical framework used, career counseling emphasizes maximum collaborative efforts between the counselor and the client to clarify the current situation of concern (e.g., needs for career planning, choice among possible options, an untenable work environment, work-family issues); clarify the client's personal role within the situation; identify action goals to be pursued in the career counseling process; identify information of relevance to the situation; develop insight about behavioral options available; and engage in problem solving to develop a plan of action. Within this general outline of a career counseling process, there are variations in what goals are emphasized, depending on individual differences and on theoretical orientations. For example, Brown and Brooks (1991) emphasize that many persons lack *cognitive clarity,* the ability to assess objectively one's own strengths and weaknesses and relate the assessment to environmental situations. In this view, persons who lack cognitive clarity also possess faulty logic systems that may result in what theorists describe as irrational beliefs, negative self-talk, or faulty private rules for decision making.

Beyond helping the client to achieve cognitive clarity or to confront faulty logic and negative cognitions about their career development, career counseling may include other approaches. Perhaps the most venerable is what has historically been called *trait and factor,* and more recently *person-environment fit* (Chartrand, 1991). Such an approach helps clients match individual traits to the performance requirements and work culture of particular jobs, occupations, or training. The intent is to increase the congruence between the client's abilities, interests, and values and the technical and psychosocial aspects of the job, occupation, or training option chosen (Holland, 1997). Embedded in such an approach is the goal of helping the client evaluate the probabilities or odds of gaining access to and being successful in different jobs, occupations, or educational opportunities. Such an approach is typically information and assessment driven. It often involves considerable analysis of the client's self-understanding, abilities, and preferences as an evaluative base to which to relate possible career options. Trait and factor (person-environment fit) approaches also are likely to help clients gain insight into the elasticity of their previous work experience with other jobs or occupations for which there is compatibility and fit.

Although there are also client-centered, psychodynamic, behavioral, cognitive, and constructivist approaches to career counseling, the final major approach to be discussed is the developmental approach. This approach emphasizes the client's coping with developmental tasks in the past and in the current choice situation. Such an analysis may focus on the client's readiness to cope with emerging roles and skill requirements, relinquishing roles that are no longer appropriate, and acquiring the attitudinal and behavioral elements of career adaptability required in the current life stage: planfulness, exploration, time perspective, assertiveness, flexibility, reality orientation, and so forth.

Evaluation of Career Counseling

A large number of studies have reported positive effects for career interventions on diverse career outcomes (Sexton, Whiston, Bleuer, & Walz, 1995). Within the positive effects found for career interventions in general, individual counseling has constantly been found to be the most effective intervention per unit of time involved (Oliver & Spokane, 1988; Sexton, Whiston, Bleuer, & Walz, 1997). Other researchers have concluded that although individual and group counseling and other techniques yield positive outcomes, they may be differentially effective for different types of clients (Herr & Cramer, 1996; Swanson, 1995).

REFERENCES

Brown, D., & Brooks, L. (1991). *Career counseling techniques.* Boston: Allyn & Bacon.

Chartrand, J. M. (1991). The evolution of trait and factor career counseling: A person x environment fit approach. *Journal of Counseling and Development, 69,* 518–524.

Herr, E. L., & Cramer, S. H. (1996). *Career guidance and counseling through the lifespan: Systematic approaches* (5th ed.). New York: Harper Collins.

Holland, J. L. (1997). *Making vocational choices: A theory of vocational personalities and work environments* (3rd ed.). Odessa, FL: Psychological Assessment Resources.

Krumboltz, J. D. (1993). Integrating career and personal counseling. *The Career Development Quarterly, 42*(2), 143–148.

Oliver, L. W., & Spokane, A. R. (1988). Career intervention outcome: What contributes to client gain? *Journal of Counseling Psychology, 35*(4), 447–462.

Sexton, T. L, Whiston, S. C., Bleuer, J. C., & Walz, G. R. (1995). *A critical review of the counseling outcomes research.* Technical report for the Human Development Foundation, American Counseling Association, Alexandria, VA.

Sexton, T. L., Whiston, S. C., Bleuer, J. C., & Walz, G. R. (1997). *Integrating outcome research into counseling practice and training.* Alexandria, VA: American Counseling Association.

Swanson, J. L. (1995). The process and outcome of career counseling. In W. B. Walsh & S. H. Osipow (Eds.), *Handbook of vocational psychology: Theory, research and practice* (pp. 217–259). Mahway, NJ: Erlbaum.

EDWIN L. HERR
Pennsylvania State University

CAREER DEVELOPMENT

Virtually all persons engage in multiple forms of career behavior throughout their life. Examples include preparing for a work role, choosing and entering a job or occupation, dealing with the dynamics of work adjustment, moving from one job to another, becoming unemployed, and making plans for retirement. Although there are similarities in how persons approach such work-related tasks, there are also significant variations between males and females, persons of different educational or socioeconomic levels, persons of different racial and ethnic backgrounds, and persons with physical and mental disabilities. The term *career development* describes the processes and factors that influence how individuals develop a personal identity in regard to work, and how their beliefs, values, interests, and aptitudes are reflected in the transition, induction, and adjustment to work.

Career Defined

In order to understand the term *career development,* it is useful to consider the term *career.* Jobs and occupations are part of one's career but are not synonymous with this concept. Jobs and occupations describe groups of tasks or work performances that occur within a workplace and that constitute paid positions that can be identified, applied for, and achieved. But the term *career* means more than work performance. Among the classic definitions of career is that of Super (1976):

> The course of events which constitutes a life; the sequence of occupations and other life roles which combine to express one's commitment to work in his or her total pattern of self-development. . . . Careers exist only as people pursue them. (p. 4)

In a more abstract sense, the term *career* "can refer to the individual's movement through time and space . . . [and] the intersection of individual biography and social structures" (Collin & Young, 2000, p. 3).

These definitions affirm that careers are unique to each person and created by what one chooses or does not choose. They are dynamic and unfold throughout life. They include not only jobs and occupations but prevocational concerns (school courses, job training) and postvocational concerns (retirement) as well as integration of other roles: family, community, and leisure.

Perspectives On Career Development

Career development can be understood as one of the many aspects of socialization that combine to create human development; in this case the focus is on occupational or work socialization. In psychological terms, the individual acquires motivation to act in certain ways related to his or her beliefs about personal self-efficacy to achieve in particular work domains, to the likelihood that certain valued outcomes will occur from some choices and not others, and to the salience of work to his or her personal identity. In sociological terms, however, individual career development is also a product of the constraints on and barriers to choices that individuals might prefer to make. Such constraints can occur because of limitations on individual choice that arise from political conditions or from economic circumstances. Sociological effects on choice also can be seen in family and cultural influences. Families with differing educational and socioeconomic backgrounds tend to reinforce different educational and occupational goals and belief systems related to career choice. Nations and cultural groups also differ in how particular types of education, work, or family roles are valued, and these perceptions tend to be internalized by group members and reflected in their choices.

Career development can be thought of in both structural and developmental terms (Herr & Cramer, 1996). The structure of career development refers to the elements that comprise concepts like career maturity, career adaptability, career planfulness, and person-job congruence (Holland, 1997). Career maturity, for example, in adolescence and career adaptability in adulthood tend to include five factors: planfulness or time perspective, exploration, information, decision making, and reality orientation. These five factors are structural components of career maturity, and each factor has its own structural sub-elements.

In addition to a structural approach to career development, there is also a developmental approach. In such an approach, the questions are different: Does career maturity change over time? Is behavior described as career mature at age 18 the same as career adaptability at age 25 or 45? What are the factors that influence career behavior at different life stages: childhood, adolescence, young adult, mid-career adult, older adult?

Further perspectives view career development as a lifestyle concept. In essence, the work roles that one implements throughout the life span are not independent of other life roles; indeed, they may be in conflict with them. For example, being a workaholic, a spouse, and a parent may be problematic if the amount of energy or time given to the work role is significantly out of balance with that given to these other life roles.

Theories of Career Development

The theories that offer explanations of career behavior are multidisciplinary. This is true in part because career identity and the socialization to work are such important aspects of human development in the developed nations of the world, and in part because the factors that influence career development take many forms. In capturing such a perspective, Super (1990) contended that

> The pioneers of career are people from four disciplines: differential psychologists interested in work and occupations, developmental psychologists interested in the "life course," sociologists focusing on occupational mobility as a function of social class, and personality theorists who view individuals as organizers of experience. (p. 197)

To these theorists of different aspects of career development, one can add the growing attention of political scientists, economists, and organizational theorists as persons concerned about career development. As a result of this disciplinary diversity focused on career behavior, some theory and research are primarily applied to job or occupational choice at a specific period in time (Holland, 1997), to the role or interests or other personal characteristics, to adjustment within a work setting, or to the decision-making process used by different persons. Some research is concerned with the structure of choice, work behavior, or career maturity within a particular life stage; other theories are concerned with how such structures change over time, the role of chance in career choice, and the continuities and discontinuities in career patterns throughout the life span (Super (1990). Some theories are more focused on the roots of career behavior in childhood and adolescence; other theories give greater attention to career behavior in middle and late adulthood. Growing attention is being given to the unique dimensions of career development in women and in different cultural groups and as it relates to mental health.

The changing nature of work (e.g., organizational downsizing, the pervasive use of advanced technology to increase productivity, the increasing use of part-time workers, international economic competition) and of career paths is providing new challenges to theories of career theory in the twenty-first century. Some theories in the twentieth century focused on career behavior that was linear and predictable within stable organizations. Such conditions are rapidly changing as workplaces use new means to remain competitive. The result is a widening diversity of career patterns and experiences, more frequent career transitions, and increased expectations that workers must become their own career managers. Such dynamics are not yet fully captured in career development theories.

REFERENCES

Collin, A., & Young, R. A. (Eds.). (2000). *The future of career.* Cambridge, UK: Cambridge University Press.

Herr, E. L., & Cramer, S. H. (1996). *Career guidance and counseling through the lifespan: Systematic approaches.* New York: HarperCollins.

Holland, J. L. (1997). *Making vocational choices: A theory of vocational personalities and work environments* (3rd ed.). Odessa, FL: Psychological Assessment Resources.

Super, D. E. (1976). *Career education and the meaning of work* (Monographs on Career Education). Washington, DC: The Office of Career Education, the U.S. Office of Education.

Super, D. E. (1990). A life-span, life-space approach to career development. In D. Brown & L. Brooks (Eds.), *Career choice and development: Applying contemporary theories to practice* (pp. 197–261). San Francisco: Jossey-Bass.

Edwin L. Herr
Pennsylvania State University

See also: **Career Counseling; Communication Skills Training**

CATHARSIS

Catharsis is a term used in aesthetics and the psychology of art with reference to spectator response, and in psychotherapy with reference to the release of repressed affect or psychic energy.

In ancient Greek, *katharsis* most commonly meant physical or spiritual purgation, ridding one of uncleanliness or guilt. Empedocles used it to speak of religious purification; Plato, to speak of purification of the soul by means of philosophy; and Hippocrates and his followers, to speak of the evacuation of morbid humors. But its most notable use in ancient times occurs in Aristotle's cryptic definition of tragedy as drama which "accomplishes through pity and fear the catharsis of such feelings" (*Poetics* 1449b). For literally centuries, philosophers, art theorists and critics, and psychologists have argued about what Aristotle meant, notably over whether the emotions are aroused in spectators or simply depicted in the drama and, if the former, whether they are purged, sublimated, or in some other way resolved. The term has been applied to a wide range of art forms and emotional responses or representations. According to philosopher Richard Kuhns (1998), "The spirit of catharis as an aesthetic principle"—though often not mentioned explicitly—"informs the work of [critics] I. A. Richards, F. R. Leavis, and Wolfgang Iser, and energizes the artistic achievements of many of our modern poets" such as Lawrence, Hardy, Eliot, Auden, and Stevens.

In psychoanalytic literature the term first appeared in *Studies on Hysteria* by Breuer and Freud, although both the naming and the therapeutic method initially associated with it are credited to Breuer (perhaps unjustly; Jacob Bernays, uncle to Freud's wife, believed that "catharsis" referred to a medical healing process, and his articulated view may well have influenced both Breuer and Freud). Breuer had apparently cured patients of hysterical symptoms by inducing them, under hypnosis, to relive or remember forgotten childhood events—often but not always traumatic—and the affects associated with them. Freud hypothesized that in such cases the mental or nervous energy that would have led to the original affect was diverted into hysterical symptoms, and that memories of the experiences were repressed into the unconscious. When, under hypnosis, both the memory and the associated affect were brought into consciousness, the affect was thereby discharged and the symptom eliminated. The process of affective discharge was also called *abreaction.*

Although Freud soon replaced hypnosis with free association and enlarged his theory, he stated in "A Short Account of Psycho-Analysis" (1961) that the cathartic method was both the precursor and the ongoing nucleus of psychoanalysis. Catharsis thus remains a basic concept, even though the term itself has lost favor among psychoanalysts. In its psychoanalytic context—referring to the release of repressed ideas and affects—it has also been an important and fruitful concept in theorizing about spectator responses to works of art by thinkers within the psychoanalytic tradition (such as Kris), outside it (such as Vygotsky), and partly in and partly out (such as Wollheim).

In contemporary psychotherapy outside the psychoanalytic tradition, *catharsis* is often defined much more loosely as referring in a general way to the therapeutic release of emotions or tensions, including some that might be conscious or related to conscious experiences. A central concept in psychodrama, catharsis is also a major aspect of Gestalt and primal therapies and of most brief and crisis-oriented therapies. Sometimes it is called "talking out," "acting out," or "ventilation." In implosive therapy there is a deliberate attempt to elicit strong emotions in order to bring about cathartic release of tension.

Controversy persists concerning the effectiveness of catharsis as merely emotional release rather than its more fundamental role in a psychotherapeutic process of reintegration.

REFERENCES

Breuer, J., & Freud, S. (1957). *Studies on hysteria.* New York: Basic Books. (Original work published 1895)

Freud, S. (1961). A short account of psycho-analysis. In *The standard edition of the complete psychological works of Sigmund Freud* (Vol. 19). London: Hogarth Press. (Original work published 1924)

Kuhns, R. (1998). Katharsis. *Encyclopedia of aesthetics* (Vol. 3, pp. 62–63). New York: Oxford University Press.

Forest W. Hansen

CENTRAL LIMIT THEOREM

The central limit theorem concerns the distribution of a linear composite. Y is a linear composite of a set of variables ($X1$, $X2$, $X3$, etc.) if $Y = a1\,X1 + a2\,X2 + a3\,X3 + \ldots$, where the a's are weights. For example, if Y equals $3X1 + 4X2$, then $a1$ equals 3 and $a2$ equals 4. The central limit theorem states that the shape of the distribution of Y becomes more and more like the normal distribution as the number of variables included in the composite increases. Specifically, the central limit theorem states that Y is asymptotically normal as the number of composited variables approaches infinity. The central limit theorem is one of the principal reasons that psychologists and statisticians make regular use of the normal distribution.

Table 1. Distribution of X

Value of X	Probability of X
0	.50
1	.50

Table 2. Distribution of Y

Value of Y	Probability of Y
0	.001
1	.010
2	.044
3	.117
4	.205
5	.246
6	.205
7	.117
8	.044
9	.010
10	.001

Notice that the theorem does not require that the variables in the composite be normally distributed. Y is asymptotically normal even when the composited variables have very nonnormal distributions. Perhaps this is most easily illustrated by compositing a set of coin tosses. Imagine tossing a fair (unbiased) coin one time, recording 0 for a tail and 1 for a head. This experiment has two possible outcomes, each equally likely. If we call the experiment's outcome X, it can be concluded that $P(X = 0) = 0.5$ and $P(X = 1) = 0.5$. The distribution of X is given in Table 1.

Repeat this simple experiment 10 times, generating values for $X1, X2, X3 \ldots X10$. Each of the X's has the same distribution. It is possible to create a new variable that is a linear composite of the X's. Let $Y = X1 + X2 + X3 + \ldots + X10$. Y is the number of heads in 10 tosses of a fair coin, and the distribution of Y is given in Table 2. Notice that with only 10 variables in our composite, Y resembles the normal distribution; probabilities are highest in the middle of the distribution and gradually decrease for more extreme scores. If the coin were tossed 1,000 times and the outcomes were summed, the distribution of this sum would be almost indistinguishable from the normal distribution.

The central limit theorem frequently is introduced as a special case, to describe the distribution of the sample mean. The sample mean is a linear composite of the scores in the sample, with each score weighted by $1/N$, where N is the sample size. If N is large enough, the distribution of the sample mean will be normal, so the normal distribution can be used to build confidence interval estimates of the population mean and to test hypotheses concerning the sample mean. Researchers generally assume the sample mean has a normal distribution if N is at least 30, but how quickly the distribution assumes the normal shape depends on how normal the X's are. If the X scores are normally distributed, their mean always will be normally distributed. If the X scores are very nonnormal, N may have to be larger than 30 for the distribution to be normal.

The central limit theorem also can explain why many physical measurements are normally distributed. Human heights and weights are determined by many factors, probably including hundreds of genes and thousands of variables related to nutritional and psychological history. Heights or weights can be thought of as composite of thousands of variables, so they should be normally distributed. Many psychological traits, such as intelligence, also are normally distributed, probably because they are influenced by thousands of genes and prenatal and postnatal events. Deviations from normality suggest the heavy influence of one event that overrides the linear composite. For example, people who are so extremely short that their presence is not consistent with the normal distribution may have heights determined by a pituitary problem. Their heights are not influenced by the genes and events that under other circumstances would have made them taller. Similarly, people with extremely low intelligence may have a rare genetic defect or may have been subject to some trauma that damaged the central nervous system.

Mary J. Allen
California State University

See also: **Probability**

CENTRAL NERVOUS SYSTEM

The central nervous system (CNS) refers to the portion of the nervous system that lies within the skull and spinal column and receives nervous impulses from sense receptors throughout the organism, regulates bodily processes, and organizes and directs behavior. Anatomically, the CNS comprises the brain and spinal cord, which float within the cranial cavity of the skull and the vertebral canal of the spinal column in a liquid matrix called *cerebrospinal fluid,* which also fills their hollows and serves as a protective cushion against damage. CNS tissue is further protected by three enfolding membranes called the *meninges.* The outer and toughest, the dura mater, attaches to skull and spine, encasing the spongy arachnoid membrane within which the cerebrospinal fluid circulates. The soft pia mater is contiguous with the outer layer of brain and cord.

The basic structural unit of nervous tissue is the nerve cell or neuron, a specialized body cell of elongated shape (from a few microns to several feet in length), whose enhanced reactivity and conductivity permit it to propagate or conduct an electrical impulse along its length and to chemically stimulate adjacent neurons to do likewise at specialized junctions called *synapses.* The nervous system is made up of billions of neurons, which interconnect every part of the organism to monitor and regulate it. Receptor neurons lead like the twigs of a tree inward to branches and thence to great trunks, called *nerves,* which enter the CNS and ascend into the brain. There, effector neurons originate and descend to exit the CNS as nerves branching repeatedly out to regulate all muscle tissue and therefore all bodily activity. Twelve bilateral pairs of cranial nerves enter the brain directly. The cord is the origin of 31 bilateral pairs of spinal nerves, which exit the CNS through openings between adjacent vertebrae. Each spinal nerve contains both entering receptor fibers and departing effector fibers. The nerve divides on reaching the cord, with sensory fibers entering on the back and motor fibers exiting on the front.

The spinal cord is thus a great pathway for ascending and descending nerve tracts, but connectedness is a property of the CNS, within which a third type of neuron, the interneuron, is found. Interneurons connect effector and receptor neurons, and by repeated branchings of their tips may synapse at either end with many hundreds of other neurons. The functional unit of the nervous system is the reflex arc, which so links receptor and effector neurons that a stimulus at a sense receptor capable of causing its nerve to conduct will automatically trigger an effector neuron to produce a response in a muscle or gland. Some reflexes are extremely simple, but most are not. The CNS is hierarchically organized, with higher centers being stimulated by and acting upon lower centers, so that progressively more complex reflexes are organized progressively higher in the CNS. Certain muscle stretch reflexes operate spinally for the most part. Respiratory reflexes are largely centered in the brain stem, the part of the brain that is contiguous to the spinal cord. Homeostatic reactions depend upon reflexes organized higher yet, in the hypothalamus, which may give rise to motivational states such as hunger and thirst. It is thought that by means of progressively more complex reflexes (some inborn, but most acquired through learning) all functions of the CNS are conducted, including the higher mental functions, the seat of which is the brain. The CNS is also symmetrically organized. Midline structures like the cord have two symmetrical halves. Other structures are duplicated, such as the two cerebral hemispheres. Most fibers cross the midline (e.g., the left brain controls the right hand).

The brain is an organ of unparalleled complexity of parts and function, a reality that may be obscured by summary description. A great deal has nevertheless been learned about the pathways that are followed by ascending and descending nerve tracts. Much of the CNS is white matter, the encased processes or extensions of nerve cells, bundles of which indicate pathways called tracts. The nerve bodies are not encased and are present as gray matter, clusters of which indicate centers of activity called *nuclei*. Evolutionary influences have given characteristic shapes to the complex arrangements of neurons in the CNS, permitting to be named and located on charts or in living tissue.

The gross anatomy of the brain, in greatly oversimplified summary, may be divided into three regions: (1) the brain stem, the parts of which (medulla, pons, mesencephalon) contain the nuclei of the brain stem reticular formation, which is vital in consciousness and the level of arousal of the brain above; (2) the cerebellum, a center for the smooth regulation of motor behavior; and (3) the cerebrum, which is of greatest interest to psychology for its organizing role in the higher mental functions and emotion. Between brain stem and cerebrum are the thalamus and hypothalamus, which some authorities class with the brain stem, some with the cerebrum. Thalamic nuclei largely integrate and relay sensory impulses upward to the cerebrum. Hypothalamic nuclei, however, are vital in the regulation of homeostatic reactions and in integrating the reflexes of the nuclei of the limbic system, structures embedded deep within the cerebrum that give rise to emotional experience and expression.

The cerebrum's deeply fissured gray outer surface, the hemispheres of its cerebral cortex, is the terminus of sensory processes and the origin of motor processes. Much of this area is given over to association areas of interneurons, whose complex interconnections give rise to memory, speech, purposive behavior, and, generally, the higher mental functions.

The pathways, relays, and sensory and motor areas of the brain have been mapped by largely physical and physiological methods. But the nature of the higher mental processes of humans remains elusive because they cannot be charted thus. As J. Minckler observed, the structure and function of nervous tissue are so intertwined that they must be studied together. At some levels of the CNS, the appropriate units of function are physiological. Other levels are best studied through discrete behaviors. Still more complex functions of brain, however, require the scrutiny of complex patterns or styles of behavior, and the highest levels of brain function shade into issues of intelligence, logic, purpose, and consciousness, themselves as little understood as the brain.

The study of the CNS in humans is thus the study of brain-behavior and brain-mind relationships, a field in which psychology is heavily involved. That there is a relationship between brain and mind is well established and has been observed for a very long time. C. J. Golden noted that Pythagoras, in 500 B.C., linked brain and human reasoning. In the second century A.D., Galen of Pergamum observed the effects on consciousness of brain injury in gladiators and described animals rendered senseless by pressure on their brains.

Galen was incorrect in attributing mental processes to the fluid-filled hollows of the brain, a view which nevertheless endured until the Renaissance. Modern concepts regarding brain functions did not begin to develop until the 1800s. This delay resulted from vitalistic and imprecise views of both brain and mind, and it endured until a more scientific and reductionistic view of both brain and behavior emerged. Rarnón y Cajal forwarded neuron theory in the late 1800s and received a Nobel Prize in physiology in 1906, the same year that C. S. Sherrington, who developed the concept of the reflex arc, published on integrative mechanisms of the nervous system. Galton's work with the behavioral measurement of individual differences contributed greatly to the emerging science of psychometrics or mental measurement. In the early 1900s, J. B. Watson moved psychology toward the study of behavior rather than mental states. He and B. F. Skinner both contributed to a science and technology of behavior that has meshed well with biology in permitting brain behavior studies. But the complexities of mind or behavior and brain are such that the more we learn, the more there remains to be learned. In 1974, G. Sommerhoff put it thus: "The peculiar fascination of the brain lies in the fact that there is probably no other object of scientific enquiry about which we know so much and yet understand so little."

At the heart of the problem lies the fact that the nervous system, so simple in basic elements, is so complex in arrangements. As Hubbard observed in 1975, it is easy to imagine neuronal arrangements capable of causing muscles to contract or glands to empty, but it is difficult to imagine such arrangements permitting the aging Beethoven to compose works he could no longer hear. The sheer complexity of interconnections, which could well permit such complex behaviors, virtually defies understanding. Some five million neurons, for example, may lie beneath a single square centimeter of brain surface, each of which synapses with perhaps 600 other neurons. Virtually the entire depth and surface of the brain may be involved in any given behavior.

To be understood, the brain (and possibly all the CNS) must be understood as a whole. Yet owing to limits in theory, knowledge, and perhaps capacity, we must approach the whole through study of the parts, viewed at many levels and from many perspectives. Full understanding of the CNS thus lies beyond any one discipline. Psychology, however, contributes in many ways to the expanding interdisciplinary study of the CNS, called *neuroscience*. Psychologists have put forward or contributed to models of mind compatible with known facts of brain function and have helped develop new models of neural function drawing on and contributing to computer modeling. They have also used neuroscientific findings to develop broad models of human behavior. Psychologists also commonly contribute directly to knowledge of brain-behavior relationships through experimental and clinical neuropsychology.

Experimental neuropsychologists have long studied such things as the behavioral derangements caused by known lesions and other disturbances of CNS tissue in animals. Clinical neuropsychologists have increasingly used qualitative and quantitative aspects of behavior on special tasks to deduce or infer the probable locus and nature of brain tissue impairment in individuals. The accuracy of such assessments reached very substantial levels by the 1970s, and behavioral mappings of the strengths and deficits of brain-injured individuals contribute significantly to current treatment and rehabilitation efforts.

Ongoing developments in knowledge and methodology continue to require new connections among the disciplines comprising the evolving field of neuroscience.

REFERENCES

Golden, C. J. (1980). Organic brain syndromes. In R. H. Wood, (Ed.), *Encyclopedia of clinical assessment* (Vol. 1). San Francisco: Jossey-Bass

Hubbard, J. I. (1975). *The biological basis of mental activity.* Reading, MA: Addison-Wesley.

Minkler, J. (Ed.). (1972). *Introduction to neuroscience.* St. Louis, MO: Mosby.

Summerhoff, G. (1974). *Logic of the living brain.* New York: Putnam's.

Roger E. Enfield
*West Central GA Regional Hospital
Columbus, GA*

See also: **Homeostasis; Limbic System; Reticular Activating System**

CENTRAL NERVOUS SYSTEM DISORDERS

The central nervous system (CNS) is composed of the brain and the spinal cord. The spinal cord controls movement and feeling of body regions located below the brain. The brain also plays a role in movement and feeling. However, the brain's role is more complex than that of the spinal cord, and the brain controls complex psychological processes as well (e.g., attention, perception, motivation, emotion, language, cognition, and purposeful behaviors). When certain parts of the brain are damaged, specific functions may be lost. The type and extent of functional loss depend upon the age of the individual, the location of the brain damage, its etiology, and the amount of brain tissue that is compromised. For example, damage to a strip of cortex in the posterior part of the frontal lobes controlling movement of parts of the body will result in paralysis of those body parts. Lesions within relay stations along the visual sensory system—from the optic nerves to the occipital lobes—will result in visual field defects such as scotomas (blind spots). Lesions deep in the hypothalamus may produce hunger, uncontrolled eating, and obesity. Destruction of areas involved in arousal may result in a permanent comatose state. Finally, damage early in life can be less devastating than analogous damage in late adulthood.

Disorders of the CNS usually are classified according to lesion location (e.g., abnormalities occurring after frontal lobe damage) or according to etiology, symptomatology, and functional loss (e.g., amnesia). The following discussion focuses on two exemplars of CNS disorders. The first, frontal system disorders, exemplifies possible consequences of damage to the anterior regions of the frontal lobes (Stuss & Knight, 2002). The second, amnesia after long-term alcoholism (Oscar-Berman, 2000), exemplifies a disorder recognized by abnormalities of memory, especially memory for recent events (anterograde amnesia). Keep in mind that the distinction between structure and function is not a mutually exclusive one. The brain has many highly interconnected parts, and when one part is damaged, other parts will be affected as well. Similarly, behavioral abnormalities are complex; they involve a broad spectrum of perceptual and cognitive deficits that may be integral to the presenting symptoms of many disorders of the CNS (Armengol & Jamieson, 2001; Lezak, 1995; Mesulam, 2000; Spreen & Strauss, 1998).

Frontal System Dysfunction

The frontal lobes are connected with all of the other lobes of the brain, and they receive and send fibers to numerous subcortical structures as well (Fuster, 1997). Control of motor function takes place in the posterior region of the frontal lobes. The anterior region of the frontal lobes (prefrontal cortex) plays a kind of executive regulatory role within the CNS, inhibiting the occurrence of unnecessary or unwanted behaviors. Disruptions of normal inhibitory functions of frontal lobe neuronal networks often will have the interesting effect of releasing previously inhibited behaviors from frontal control. The resultant aberrant conduct of a frontal patient may be due to the freely unregulated functioning of the released brain regions (disinhibition).

Early evidence for a role of the frontal lobes in supporting the ability to inhibit impulsivity came from the 1868 report of a physician on his patient Phineas Gage. Gage, a railway workman, survived an explosion that blasted an iron bar (about four feet long and an inch wide) through his frontal lobes. After he recovered from the accident, Gage's personality changed. He became irascible, impatient, impulsive, unruly, and inappropriate. The damage had mostly been in the orbital frontal region of Gage's frontal lobes (Mesulam, 2000; Stuss & Knight, 2002).

Damage to frontal brain systems occurs in a number of CNS disorders, including stroke, brain tumors, dementing diseases (e.g., Alzheimer's), and head trauma (Lichter & Cummings, 2001). Patients with bilateral frontal disorders often display a pull to nearby objects (e.g., grabbing at doorknobs) as well as a remarkable tendency to imitate the actions of people nearby (echopraxia). The behaviors of a frontal patient appear not to be based on rational decisions; rather, some responses are under the control of salient objects around them (i.e., objects that capture the attention). In other words, the patient's behaviors are environmentally driven rather than personally chosen. Such behaviors may extend to otherwise embarrassing gestures such as urinating in public or chewing paper.

Alcohol-Induced Persisting Amnesiic Disorder (Korsakoff's Syndrome)

Amnesia, especially *anterograde amnesia,* or memory loss for recent events, is an intriguing but serious disorder. When amnesia occurs as a consequence of long-term alcoholism, it is referred to as *alcoholic Korsakoff's syndrome.* Patients with Korsakoff's syndrome are permanently unable to remember new information for more than a few seconds. However, memories that were formed prior to the onset of alcohol-related brain damage are relatively well preserved. Because new events are forgotten a few seconds after they occur, virtually nothing new is learned, and the patient with Korsakoff's syndrome lives in the past.

The critical brain lesions of alcoholic Korsakoff's syndrome are thought to include the mammillary bodies of the hypothalamus and/or medial thalamic nuclei (Oscar-Berman & Evert, 1997). Damage to these or to other regions of the brain (hippocampus, fornix, anterior thalamus) has long been associated with memory impairments (Mesulam, 2000). The impairments include severe anterograde amnesia for recent events, and some retrograde amnesia (i.e., loss of memory for events that happened prior to the appearance of obvious symptomatology). Damage to basal forebrain structures (important in the production of neurotransmitters, which are needed for normal memory functions) may also be involved.

Although anterograde amnesia is the most obvious presenting symptom in Korsakoff patients, these individuals have other cognitive impairments as well. Like patients with bilateral prefrontal cortical lesions, Korsakoff patients are abnormally sensitive to distractions (proactive interference). This sensitivity may be due to alcoholism-related prefrontal dysfunction, which impairs the ability to counteract the effects of cognitive interruptions. In addition to their memory problems and their sensitivity to interference, Korsakoff patients also tend to repeat unnecessary behaviors (perseverative responding) and have restricted attention, retarded perceptual processing abilities, and decreased sensitivity to reward contingencies (Oscar-Berman & Evert, 1997). These additional abnormalities reflect widespread cerebral atrophy accompanying sustained alcohol abuse. Thus, consideration should be given to sensory and cognitive deficits that may be integral to the disease process caused by chronic alcoholism.

REFERENCES

Armengol, C. G., & Jamieson, W. (2001). The screening versus the comprehensive neuropsychological examination. In C. G. Armengol, E. Kaplan, & E. J. Moes (Eds.), *The consumer-oriented neuropsychological report* (pp. 61–81). Lutz, FL: Psychological Assessment Resources.

Fuster, J. M. (1997). *The prefrontal cortex* (3rd ed.). New York: Lippincott-Raven.

Lezak, M. D. (1995). *Neuropsychological assessment* (3rd ed.). New York: Oxford University Press.

Lichter, D. G., & Cummings, J. L. (Eds.). (2001). *Frontal-subcortical circuits in psychiatric and neurological disorders.* New York: Guilford Press.

Mesulam, M.-M. (2000). Behavioral neuroantomy: Large-scale networks, association cortex, frontal syndromes, the limbic system, and hemispheric specializations. In M.-M. Mesulam (Ed.), *Principles of behavioral and cognitive neurology* (2nd ed., pp. 1–120). New York: Oxford University Press.

Oscar-Berman, M. (2000). Neuropsychological vulnerabilities in chronic alcoholism. In A. Noronha, M. Eckardt, & K. Warren (Eds.), *Review of NIAAA's neuroscience and behavioral research portfolio* (National Institute on Alcohol Abuse and Alcoholism [NIAAA] Research Monograph no. 34, pp. 149–158). Bethesda, MD: NIAAA.

Oscar-Berman, M., & Evert, D. L. (1997). Alcoholic Korsakoff's syndrome. In P. D. Nussbaum (Ed.), *Handbook of neuropsychology and aging* (pp. 201–215). New York: Plenum.

Spreen, O., & Strauss, E. (1998). *A compendium of neuropsychological tests* (2nd ed.). New York: Oxford University Press.

Stuss, D. T., & Knight, R. T. (Eds.). (2002). *Principles of frontal lobe function.* New York: Oxford University Press.

Marlene Oscar-Berman
Boston University School of Medicine and Department of Veterans Affairs Healthcare System

CENTRAL TENDENCY MEASURES

We often wish to provide summary numbers that best describe a set or distribution of scores. These include measures of *location,* which indicate a typical or average value for the scores; measures of *dispersion,* which indicate how spread out the scores are; and measures that describe the *shape* of the distribution.

A measure of central tendency is a measure of location; the goal is to provide a single number that best describes the values of a set of scores. The terms *measure of central tendency* and *average* are often used interchangeably, although some authors use *average* only to refer the arithmetic mean. Although there are many measures of central tendency, those most commonly encountered are the mode, median, and mean.

Given a set of scores, the *mode* is simply the score that

occurs most often. If scores are grouped into classes, the mode is considered to be the midpoint of the class that contains the largest number of scores. The mode is not a very useful summary measure because it does not take into account scores that do not have the modal value; also, there may be two or more values that occur with high frequency.

The *median* is the middle score of a distribution. If the scores are ordered from smallest to largest, the median is the middle score. If there are an even number of scores, the median is considered to be halfway between the two middle scores. For example, given sets of scores A (6, 8, 4, 9, 11) and B (6, 8, 4, 9, 11, 14), the median of A is 8 and of B is 8.5. For grouped data, the median is taken be the 50th percentile point—the value below which 50 percent of the scores fall. Because the median is insensitive to the values of scores at the extremes of the distribution, it is useful for characterizing distributions that include outliers, extreme scores that are quite different from the scores in the center of the distribution. The median for (6, 8, 4, 9, 11) is the same as for (6, 8, 4, 9, 11944).

The *arithmetic mean* is the most commonly encountered measure of central tendency. It is obtained by adding up all of the scores in the set and dividing by the number of scores. The mean depends on all the scores in the set; as a result, the mean is sensitive to extreme values. Although the medians for the sets (6, 8, 4, 9, 11) and (6, 8, 4, 9, 11944) are the same, 8, the means are 7.6 and 2394.2, respectively. Here the median does a better job of characterizing the typical value of the scores.

It is useful to think of the mean of a distribution of scores as the balance point of the distribution. Imagine that scores are represented by weights placed on a balance beam at locations corresponding to their values. Then the location of the balance point of the set of scores corresponds to the value of the mean. For example, suppose that equal weights are placed at locations 4, 6, 8, 9, and 11 units from the left edge of a weightless, rigid beam; then, if the beam is placed on a fulcrum located 7.6 units from the left edge the beam, it will balance. Another way of thinking about this is that if we find the deviation of each score from the mean, then add up all these deviations, they will sum to zero.

Another useful characteristic of the mean is that it is the value that minimizes the *sum of squared deviations.* That is, if we find the deviation of each score from a value M, square each deviation, then add all these squared deviations together, the sum is smaller if M is the mean than if it is for other value. The median is the value that minimizes the sum of the *absolute values* of the deviations.

For a symmetrical distribution of scores, the mean and median will have similar values. If the distribution of scores is skewed to the right (that is, if the distribution is asymmetrical, with a short tail on the left side of center and a longer tail on the right), the mean will be larger than the median. If the distribution is skewed to the left, so that it has a longer tail on the left side, the mean will be smaller than the median.

We are very often interested in estimating the mean of a population of scores on the basis of samples of scores selected from the population. We can use a measure of central tendency of the sample, such as the sample mean or median, as an estimator of the population mean. If we take a number of samples of the same size, these sample means and medians will vary from sample to sample because of the variability in the scores selected to be in each sample. If the population is bell-shaped (i.e., if the scores are distributed like the normal distribution), it can be shown that the sample mean is a more efficient estimator than the sample median. The mean is more efficient in the sense that the means of samples can be shown to cluster more closely around the population mean than the sample medians, and so they tend to be better estimates of the population mean. If, on the other hand, the population is asymmetric or heavy-tailed (i.e., it tends to contain extreme scores), the sample mean may not be as good an estimator as the sample median or certain kinds of trimmed means (that is, sample means obtained after discarding some of the smaller and larger scores in the sample).

SUGGESTED READING

Moore, D. S. (2000). *The basic practice of statistics* (2nd ed.). New York: Freeman.

Myers, J. L., & Well, A. D. (2002). *Research design and statistical analysis* (2nd ed.). Hillsdale, NJ: Erlbaum.

Arnold D. Well
University of Massachusetts

CEREBELLUM

The cerebellum is one of the two largest structures in the mammalian brain, and, like the cerebum, it has two hemispheres. The cerebellum receives a full range of sensory information directly from the peripheral sensors (including auditory and visual). It also receives motor and sensory information from the cerebral cortex. It is involved with the learning-based control and elaboration of reflex homeostatic responses at the brain stem and spinal cord level and may operate in parallel with the cerebral cortex in controlling motor performance. However, the cerebellar system is thought to be particularly important for the control of frequently executed or rehearsed movements that become automatized and are performed without conscious effort.

The cerebellum is considered to be able to represent and process both sensory and motor information and to do so in a unified manner, that is, as a *sensorimotor system.* It is capable of rapid information processing and real-time regulation of coordinated sensorimotor activity. On the basis of its microstructural and functional characteristics it is considered that the cerebellum is essentially a *parallel distributed* or *connectionist* type of system that represents and processes information in a probabilistic manner. As a consequence of its parallel distributed amodal representation and processing, the cerebellum is considered to be an analog or holistic type of system and to facilitate associative storage. However, another consequence is that it lacks potential for highly specialized analysis of sensory-specific information: That is, it is a relatively low-discrimination system.

Based on parallel distributed representation and processing models of cerebellar function, a number of other processing or computational features have been inferred. The cerebellum may detect and respond to patterns or features, which may be determined partly on the basis of the relative frequency with which they occur. Parallel processing facilitates the automatic statistical revelation and statistical evaluation of features that are to varying extents common to a number of information inputs or experiences. In this respect the cerebellum may be considered to separate "figure" from "ground" and function like a *Gestalt system*. When a significant part of a frequently occurring feature or pattern is received as an input, the cerebellar system will recognize that part as though it is the whole, thus in effect completing or generating the expected pattern. This phenomenon may be involved in nonverbal analogical reasoning.

In a similar manner, when part of a familiar sequence is received as an input, the cerebellar system will respond so as to complete the expected temporal pattern. This is a kind of predictive mechanism and facilitates anticipatory responses based on the learned response sequences (sensorimotor schemata). These processing characteristics could facilitate associative learning in the form of classical conditioning or operant conditioning and would allow for sensory stimuli to act as retrieval cues for stored information concerning the response that past experience suggests is the most probably beneficial. The cued or released sensorimotor information would automatically, through its motor component, involve a behavioral response. Such responses generated by the cerebellum would appear to be released in an all-or-none fashion—that is, as wholes. It is thought that the cerebellum does not allow for the erasure of recorded information. The only way that information can in effect be forgotten is by functionally overlaying the information to be forgotten with the information to be remembered in preference (similar to the behaviorist notion of extinction).

Over the years there has been a steady accumulation of evidence that the cerebellum is critically involved in the classical conditioning of simple motor responses. Thompson et al. (1997) have shown that the essential memory traces for a range of classical conditioning responses are formed in, and reside in, the cerebellum. It is now generally assumed that the cerebellum plays a major role in sensorimotor learning. This form of learning is evident at the earliest stage in human cognitive development and is typified by the developmental concepts of enactive representation (Bruner) and sensorimotor intelligence (Piaget). Given this, one might expect that the cerebellum would be involved in cognitive processing at a fundamental level.

A range of research (including Tomographic regional cerebral blood flow [rCBF], regional cerebral metabolic rate [rCMR], and position emission tomography [PET] studies) indicates that in humans the cerebellum contributes to various cognitive process. It appears to be involved with verbal processing, including speech, writing, and reading, not only in the direct motor expression of these skills, but also in the mental simulation and rehearsal of these skills, and in related nonmotor aspects such as word association. It also appears to be involved with visual processing, including imagined motor expression (tennis movements, writing, speech), visual discrimination, mental rotation of simple drawings, and visuospatial organization tasks. Studies have indicated that cerebellum contributes to IQ, mainly visual IQ (performance scale IQ test ability on the Wechsler Adult Intelligence Scale, in particular, picture completion, picture arrangement, and object assembly). Other higher-order cognitive processes in which the cerebellum has been implicated include the skilled manipulation of symbols, conceptual reasoning, and complex planning activities. In summary, several publications have suggested that the cerebellum is involved in a range of cognitive processes, including what has been described as "pure mental activity" and "pure cognitive activity." Data suggest that for verbal processing, including writing and spoken language (verbal working memory and non-motor processing of words such as semantic association tasks), it is the right cerebellar hemisphere that is most involved. The lateralization to the right cerebellar hemisphere is consistent with observations that each cerebellar hemisphere is anatomically and functionally related to the contralateral (in this case the left, language-dominant) cerebral hemisphere. In contrast, complex cognitive spatial operations and visual reasoning are associated with processing in the left cerebellar hemisphere. The cerebellum and cerebrum may be considered complementary and facilitate optimal cognitive performance by the brain as a whole.

In the execution of motor processes, it is considered that the cerebellum does not operate at the level of normal consciousness but, relative to the cerebrum, operates at an unconscious level. Similarly, it is considered that its sensory processing operates not at a conscious level but rather as an unconscious mind's eye. Cerebellar contributions to cognitive processing skills could therefore constitute part of what has been called the "cognitive unconscious."

The cerebellum is one of two cortical subsystems capable of cognitive processing of information from the environment and of controlling the behavior of the organism; in evolutionary terms it is, in part, the earliest to develop and therefore, in part, relates to later stages of cognitive development; it is particularly associated with unconscious control and cognition. In information representation and processing terms it may be described as a parallel processing sensorimotor subsystem of relatively low level of discrimination, and from this perspective it is complementary to the cerebrum.

REFERENCE

Thompson, R. F., et al. (1997). Associative learning. *International Review of Neurobiology, 41,* 151–89.

Eric J. Parkins
University of Nottingham

See also: **Brain; Cerebrum**

CEREBRAL LOCALIZATION

The theory that different parts of the brain subserve different functions is known as *localization theory.* It is consistent with the basic biological principle that structures that do not look alike should have different functions. Localization of function is the theoretical backbone of modern neuropsychology, neurology, and related disciplines, all of which attempt to correlate specific behaviors with specific brain parts.

In the history of the brain sciences, it is possible to conceive of the theory of localization as being applied to the whole and then to increasingly smaller parts (Finger, 1994). At first the question seemed to be "Why is the brain special and how is it different from other organs, such as the heart?" This was an important question in classical and Hellenistic Greece, where opinions were divided. Aristotle (384–322 B.C.), the greatest of the Greek naturalist philosophers, believed that the heart was the seat of sensory and cognitive functions and that the brain simply tempered "the heat and seething" of the heart. In this regard, he was consistent with the archaic Greeks and the Egyptians. In contrast, Plato (c. 429–348 B.C.), in agreement with the thoughts of the Hippocratic physicians, believed that intellect belonged not in the heart but in the head.

During the Roman period, Galen (130–200 A.D.) reasoned that the seat of the highest soul, and hence the seat of intellect, had to be the brain itself. He listed imagination, cognition, and memory as basic components of intellect, but in his surviving writings he did not localize these functions in different parts of the brain (Finger, 2000). What he did write was that the soft front of the brain is likely to be sensory (better able to receive impressions), whereas the harder back (cerebellar) region is likely to be motor.

The church fathers of the fourth and fifth centuries A.D. went one step further when they localized imagination, intellect, and memory in the different hollow ventricles of the brain. One of the earliest advocates of ventricular localization was Nemesius (fl. 390 A.D.), a bishop in Syria. He localized perception in the two lateral ventricles, cognition in the middle ventricle, and memory in the posterior ventricle. This early localization theory was also embraced by St. Augustine (354–430), and it was broadly accepted in its general form for more than 1,000 years (i.e., some writers varied the ventricles that were associated with these particular functions).

During the Renaissance, as scientists returned to dissection and experimentation, observation began to replace conjecture. Leonardo Da Vinci (1472–1519) made molds of the ventricles to reveal their shape, and Andreas Vesalius (1514–1564) showed that the ventricles vary little across mammals. Consequently, the idea of ventricular localization slowly gave way, and increased attention began to be given to differences in the size and makeup of the brain itself.

The freer thinking and questioning of the Renaissance set the stage for Thomas Willis (1621–1675), an Oxford physician, who published his *Cerebri Anatome* in 1664 (Finger, 2000). Willis proposed that the corpus striatum, which he defined as all white matter between the basal ganglia and the cortex, plays a role in sensation and muscle movement, and that the cerebral cortex controls memory and the will. The cerebellum (which was broadly defined to include some pons and midbrain) was thought to regulate involuntary, smooth motor functions, such as breathing. This division of the brain into working parts, based partly on comparative anatomy, partly on clinical material, and partly on speculative theories, helped to change thinking about the functional organization of the brain.

The opening decades of the 1800s proved to be an especially important time in the history of localization theory. First, Julien Jean César Legallois (1770–1840) provided the first accepted localization within a region of the brain. In 1812, he pinpointed the area responsible for respiration within the medulla. In addition, the seeds were planted for modern cortical localization theory when Franz Gall (1757–1828) presented his theory of organology (his assistant Spurzheim preferred the word *phrenology*) at about the same time (Finger, 1994, 2000; Young, 1970). Gall maintained that different areas of the cerebral cortex govern different mental faculties and that cranial features reflect the development of these different organs of mind. Among other things, Gall was convinced that humanity's highest functions (e.g., speech) belong in the front of the cerebrum.

The theories of Gall and his followers stimulated great debate. Some scientists thought they had merit, others found them absurd, and still others believed that cortical localization made sense but that cranioscopy was a dead end that must be replaced by careful neurological examinations. The latter position was advocated by Jean-Baptiste Bouillaud (1794–1881). This Frenchman began to localize speech in the anterior lobes in 1825, and he then spent decades collecting clinical and autopsy material supportive of speech localization.

The debates over cortical localization continued to heat

up until 1861, when Paul Broca (1824–1880) presented his celebrated case of M. Leborgne ("Tan") in Paris (Finger, 2000). His sickly, hospitalized patient had lost his capacity for articulate language (among other things), and an autopsy revealed a lesion involving the third frontal convolution of the left hemisphere. Broca's localization of a center for articulate language toward the back of the frontal lobes went further than Bouillaud's broader anterior lobe idea, and it became the first cortical localization to receive broad acceptance.

In 1865, Broca published another landmark paper. As his collection of cases continued to grow, he had recognized that the left hemisphere must be special for speech. Left hemispheric dominance for speech was something that Marc Dax (1770–1837) had written about in 1836. Unfortunately, Dax failed to make his findings public in his lifetime. Thanks to his son Gustave, however, his report on more than 40 cases also appeared in print in 1865, the same year as Broca's own paper on the subject (Finger & Roe, 1996; Joynt & Benton, 1964).

In 1870, Gustav Fritsch (1838–1927) and Eduard Hitzig (1838–1907) discovered the motor cortex of the dog, first by stimulation and then by ablation (Finger, 2000). This was a significant accomplishment, because it showed that cortical localization could be studied under controlled conditions in laboratory animals. In the wake of this paper, lesion studies were conducted to localize sensory functions, such as vision and hearing, as well as higher intellectual functions, such as attention and memory. The leader of the new localization movement was David Ferrier (1843–1928), a Scottish physiologist-physician who moved to London. His most influential book, *The Functions of the Brain,* was first published in 1876 (Finger, 2000). Three other early contributors to the cortical localization movement were Hermann Munk (1839–1912), a German, and Victor Horsley (1857–1916) and Edward Schäfer (1850–1935), two Englishmen.

The success of localization theory was not, however, based solely on pathological (brain lesion) material—it also received good support from other sources. In 1875, Richard Caton (1842–1926) of Liverpool reported that cortical electrical activity varied in accord with Ferrier's maps when animals chewed, looked at flashing lights, and so forth. In addition, Paul Flechsig (1847–1929) showed that different cortical areas become myelinated at different times, a finding he correlated with the gradual attainment of different functions. Cytoarchitectonic studies of the cerebral cortex, such as those of Korbinian Brodmann (1868–1918), represented another significant source of support for localization theory.

Today, efforts continue to divide the brain into smaller functional units, albeit with positron emission tomography (PET) and functional magnetic resonance imaging (fMRI) scans and other sophisticated tools that could not even have been imagined when Broca was living. In this regard, localization theory is alive and well. However, so is the moderate holistic notion, which holds that the brain is not a collection of independent functional parts but a remarkably unified organ made up of interacting specialized parts that are laid down by the genes and shaped by experience.

REFERENCES

Finger, S. (1994). *Origins of neuroscience.* New York: Oxford University Press.

Finger, S. (2000). *Minds behind the brain.* New York: Oxford University Press.

Finger, S., & Roe, D. (1996). Gustave Dax and the early history of cerebral dominance. *Archives of Neurology, 53,* 806–813.

Joynt, R. A., & Benton, A. L. (1964). The memoir of Marc Dax on aphasia. *Neurology, 14,* 851–854.

Young, R. M. (1970). *Mind, brain and adaptation in the 19th century.* Oxford, UK: Clarendon Press.

Stanley Finger
Washington University

CEREBRUM

The cerebrum is the larger of the two cortical subsystems in the mammalian brain, the other, smaller subsystem being the cerebellum. Most of the cerebrum is the cortex, which has two hemispheres, each containing four lobes (frontal, parietal, temporal, and occipital). As a whole, the cerebral cortex is the most recent brain structure to evolve. It normally operates as the highest-level subsystem within the brain and is associated with conscious and volitional control of behavior.

Most basically, the cerebrum is involved with the control and elaboration of reflex homeostatic responses at the brain stem and spinal cord level. This control may be directly from the cerebrum to the brain stem and spinal system, or it may be indirectly through control of cerebellar output. The cerebrum is particularly involved with motor control that is under conscious volition and with discrete and precisely refined movement. These voluntary movements will be controlled by the cerebrum and will rely on feedback to the cerebrum from sensory organs. However, after repeated execution through habit, or through deliberate practice, control of the motor output sequence may be carried out by the cerebellum and may then be performed more quickly and more automatically with less conscious effort. Conscious practice may be seen as subprogramming of the cerebellum by the cerebrum. Such practiced action sequences may thereafter be switched on by the cerebrum and then released automatically from the cerebellum without further involving the cerebrum.

Sensory input direct from the peripheral sensors first reaches the cerebral cortex in the various unimodal primary areas. The most basic cerebrocortical processing is therefore concerned with sensory processing limited to a single modality. Within the cerebral cortex there is directionality of information flow from primary sensory areas, through secondary association areas and tertiary amodal regions that integrate information, and eventually to output areas that control motor function. Anatomic, physiological, and behavioral studies have all emphasized that there is a clear *sequential processing* built into cerebrocortical organization. The unimodal primary reception areas of the cerebral cortex result in a process of information abstraction by sensory modality. In addition, the cerebral cortex can selectively control its own input via the thalamus, and most of this control is inhibitory (i.e., of a filtering kind). Through its ability to abstract information (facilitated partly by unimodal primary representation and partly by input filtering) the cerebral cortex is thought to provide the brain with a system for high-level discrimination and for the analytical and abstract processing that is characteristic of logical thought or formal operational reasoning.

Evolution of the cerebral cortex, with its cerebrocortical primary sensory and motor areas, may be viewed as providing the brain with a second cortical subsystem with a higher level of discrimination than the cerebellum, capable of abstracting detail and of analytical sequential processing, and with the ability for more refined and elaborated control. Until recently the prevailing view in contemporary brain research is that cognitive functions are mediated almost exclusively by the cerebral cortex. The cerebrum is thought to be involved in the whole range of cognitive processes, including nonverbal communication, recognition and expression of emotion, visuospatial skills, imagination, mathematical processing, language skills (speaking, reading, writing), problem solving, planning, analytical and logical reasoning, and aspects of memory and recall.

There is evidence that the two cerebral hemispheres represent and process information in different ways and have different roles. The dominant (most often left) cerebral hemisphere is associated with information representation and processing, which is sequential or in series, digital, and abstract. It is characterized by analytical and logical processing that deals with detail. It plays a major role in the processing of verbal information, and in particular digital or abstract linguistic representation. Of the two cerebral hemispheres the dominant one is considered to be involved with consciousness, especially self-consciousness.

The minor (most often right) cerebral hemisphere is associated with information representation and processing, which is simultaneous or in parallel, analog, and holistic. It is characterised by Gestalt, analogical, and integrative processing, which deals with more spatial and global information and with novel or unfamiliar information. It plays a major role in the processing of naturomorphic or imagistic representations and in particular the processing of nonverbal and emotional information, spatial and pictorial information, and music and other non-language sounds.

One reason given for hemispheric specialization within the cerebral cortex is that it allows for the coexistence of two incompatible but complementary modes of information processing. To some extent this may be true; however, the two cerebral hemispheres have the same fundamental cytoarchitecture, have unimodal primary reception areas, and receive filtered input. In fact, much of the currently available information points to differences between the cerebral hemispheres that are merely relative or quantitative rather than qualitative. Furthermore, there is evidence from various sources that indicates that the cognitive processes attributed to one or the other of the cerebral hemispheres are not exclusive to that hemisphere. Most basically, the two cerebral hemispheres are both abstract in-series processors, but they appear to have different patterns of development. As a result of this differential development the dominant hemisphere appears to represent and process information at a much higher and relatively incompatible level of abstraction than that of the minor hemisphere.

Association areas within the minor hemisphere temporal lobe, particularly the inferotemporal region, are thought to be involved in emotional processes, experiential memory, and imagination. There is some evidence that the temporal lobe may not be the location of the experiential memory record, but that this information may be transmitted to the temporal lobe from subcerebral areas. Transmission from subcortical regions appears to involve the hippocampus and the brain stem monoamine systems. As noted earlier, the cerebrum projects to the cerebellar cortex and can contribute to cerebellar processing. However, it is also evident that the cerebellum projects to the cerebral cortex, including association areas, and can contribute to cerebral processing in the cognitive domain. Reciprocal interaction between the cerebral neocortex and the cerebellar cortex involves the hippocampus and the brain stem monoamine systems. A range of evidence supports the suggestion that Norepinephrine or its precursor Dopamine faciilitates excitatory output from the cerebellum to the cerebrum whereas 5-Hydroxytryptamine appear inhibit output from the cerebellar to the cerebrum. There is evidence of lateralization of neurotransmitter activity and lateralization of interaction between the cerebellum and cerebrum. It is therefore possible that some of the subcerebral input to association cortex processing is of cerebellar origin and that some of the cognitive processes attributed to the minor hemisphere cerebral hemispheres are of cerebellar origin.

In summary, the cerebrum is one of two cortical subsystems capable of cognitive processing of information from the environment and of controlling the behavior of the organism; in evolutionary terms, as a whole, it is the most recent to develop and therefore relates to later stages of cognitive development. It is particularly associated with conscious control and cognition. In information representation and processing terms the cerebrum may be described as a sequential processing abstract subsystem of relatively high discrimination, and from this perspective it is complementary to the cerebellum.

SUGGESTED READING

Parkins, E. J. (1997). Cerebellum and cerebrum in adaptive control and cognition: A review. *Biological Cybernetics, 77,* 79–87.

Parkins, E. J. (1990). *Equilibration, mind and brain: Toward an integrated psychology.* New York: Praeger.

Thompson, R. (1993). Centrencephalic theory, the general learning system, and subcortical dementia. *Annals of New York Academy of Sciences, 702,* 197–223.

Zaidel, E., et al. (1990). Hemispheric independence: A paradigm case for cognitive neuroscience. In A. B. Scheibel & A. F. Wechsler (Eds.), *Neurobiology of higher cognitive function* (pp. 297–355). New York: Guilford Press.

Eric J. Parkins
University of Nottingham

See also: **Brain; Cerebellum**

CHARACTER DISORDER

The conception of character reflects mankind's understanding of human nature. Plato (427–347 B.C.) and Aristotle (284–322 B.C.) recognized individual differences; Hippocrates (460–377 B.C.) and Galen (130–200 A.D.) offered humoral theories of temperament, whereas Theophrastus (372–287 B.C.) described 30 character types, some of which resemble modern personality typologies. By the early nineteenth century psychopathology became linked to character. For example, Pinel (1801/1962) described insanity without delirium, Rush (1812) wrote about moral depravity, and Prichard (1835) advanced the concept of moral insanity.

According to Pierce's (1924) *The Philosophy of Character,* personality and character are equivalent; both reflect the sum of attributes of the person and the agglomeration of all knowledge, innate and acquired, teleological and nonteleological, which forces action, and thus, taken with the environment, determines the conduct of individuals. Similarly, Roback's *The Psychology of Character* (1927) defined character as the disposition to inhibit impulse and narrow self-seeking in light of some value principle.

From this traditional definition, the concept of character disorders evolved to include four rather diverse patterns of abnormal behavior: alcoholism, drug addiction, sexual deviancy, and psychopathy. Despite their diversity, several characteristics common to individuals so categorized were cited as justification for viewing them within a single conceptual framework. The behavior patterns typically constitute a violation of the codes and conventions of society. The problem behaviors most often result in immediate positive reinforcing consequences, although the delayed effects are usually negative. Finally, these individuals do not seem to experience guilt over repeated violation of societal conventions and are rarely motivated to change their behavior.

A slightly different meaning to the term *character* can be found within psychoanalytic theory. Early analysts began by investigating neurotic symptoms, phenomena that do not fit within a customary mode of behavior. Realizing the importance of these customary modes of "character" in the analysis of symptoms of therapeutic resistances, analysts began describing the nature of character and the role it played within the ego (see Fenichel, 1945). The publication of Reich's *Character Analysis* in 1933 was an impetus for the serious study of character types. It represented a shift in psychoanalytic theory away from unconscious material and toward the characteristic behavior that is used as a defense against analytic insight and unconscious material (Reich, 1972).

The most common example of character disorder is the condition classically designated as the psychopathic or sociopathic personality, the history of which has been comprehensively recounted elsewhere (Millon, Simonsen, & Birket-Smith, 1998). The psychopath seems to regard others not as persons, with feelings and rights comparable to his or her own, but as things to be used, exploited, and manipulated. H. Cleckley in *The Mask of Sanity* (1941) describes the psychopath as having superficial charm, untruthfulness, insincerity, poor judgment, failure to learn from experience, unresponsiveness in interpersonal relationships, and a failure to follow any life plan. Frequent involvement with criminal justice systems is common, along with participation in fraud and swindling activities. Modern assessment, such as Hare's (1991) checklist, preserves a set of core attributes: glib and superficial charm; grandiose sense of self-worth; need for stimulation or proneness to boredom; tendency toward pathological lying, conning, and manipulativeness; lack of remorse or guilt; shallow affect; callousness and lack of empathy; parasitic lifestyle; poor behavior controls; promiscuous sexual behavior; early behavior problems; lack of realistic, long-term goals; impulsivity; irresponsibility; failure to accept responsibility for own actions; many short-term marital relationships; juvenile delinquency; revocation of conditional release; and criminal versatility. Confusingly, the term *psychopath* is almost absent from widely accepted modern nomenclature, replaced by the more ubiquitous *Antisocial Personality Disorder,* which substituted more reliable behavioral criteria of lawlessness and deviance for richer, albeit less reliable, etiologic and theoretic formulations.

Alcoholism and drug abuse have traditionally been included under the heading of character disorders. Individuals with these symptoms generally show many dependency-autonomy conflicts and problems in the area of impulse control, conformity to social expectations, and personal value commitments that are common to a disorder of character. Similarly, sexual behaviors including exhibitionism, transvestitism, voyeurism, sadomasochism, fetishism, rape, homosexuality, pedophilia, and incest have historically been included in this category. Modern classification systems have discarded the notion of character as defining in these disorders and have separated substance abuse and sexual paraphilias into discrete diagnostic categories. Likewise, in psychology's more recent history, *character disorder* is used as a generic term to refer to disorders of personality. Such disorders represent any deeply ingrained inflexible, maladaptive patterns of relating to, perceiving, and thinking about the environment and oneself. They may cause either significant impairment in adaptive functioning or subjective distress. Thus they are pervasive personality traits and are exhibited in a wide range of social and personal contexts. *The Diagnostic and Statistical Manual of Mental Disorders* (American Psychiatric Association, 1994) is one system of describing these conditions.

Finally, it is important to recognize that character disorders need not be exclusively defined by their clinical, symptomatic, or maladaptive components. Indeed, there are examples of constellations of traits that might be considered maladaptive in one setting but adaptive, perhaps even richly rewarding, in another setting. Widom (1977), for instance, has studied the personality profiles of noninstitutionalized psychopaths, ones who have never been caught. Works such as Lasch's (1978) *The Culture of Narcissism* and Smith's (1978) *The Psychopath in Society* have taken an even broader view by implicating certain character "disorders" as ascendant over aspects of modern culture and commerce.

In summary, character disorders, a slightly archaic term by standards of contemporary nomenclature, have their origin in conceptions of human nature and individual difference. As a class, character disorders subsumed a number of conditions for which a moral defect was believed responsible: alcoholism, drug addiction, sexual deviancy and psychopathy. Modern conceptions of character disorders are relegated to descriptions of Antisocial Personality Disorder, personality disorders in general, or Substance Abuse and Sexual Disorders.

REFERENCES

American Psychiatric Association. (1994). *Diagnostic and statistical manual of mental disorders* (4th ed.). Washington, DC: Author.

Cleckley, H. (1941). *The mask of sanity.* St. Louis, MO: Mosby.

Fenichel, O. (1945). *The psychoanalytic theory of neurosis.* New York: W. W. Norton.

Hare, R. D. (1991). *The Hare psychopathy checklist—revised.* Toronto, Canada: Multi-Health Systems.

Lasch, C. (1978). *The culture of narcissism: American life in an age of diminishing expectations.* New York: W. W. Norton.

Millon, T., Simonsen, E., & Birket-Smith, M. (1998). Historical conceptions of psychopathy in the United States and Europe. In T. Millon, E. Simonsen, M. Birket-Smith, & R. D. Davis (Eds.), *Psychopathy: Antisocial, criminal and violent behavior* (pp. 3–31). New York: Guilford Press.

Pierce, E. (1924). *The philosophy of character.* Cambridge, MA: Harvard University Press.

Pinel, P. (1962). *A treatise on insanity* (D. Davis, Trans.). New York: Hafner. (Original work published 1801)

Prichard, J. C. (1835). *A treatise on insanity and other disorders affecting the mind.* London: Sherwood, Gilbert & Piper.

Reich, W. (1972). *Character analysis* (3rd ed.). New York: Orgone Institute Press.

Roback, A. A. (1927). *The psychology of character.* New York: Harcourt Brace.

Rush, B. (1812). *Medical inquires and observations upon the diseases of the mind.* Philadelphia: Kimber & Richardson.

Smith, R. J. (1978). *The psychopath in society.* New York: Academic Press.

Widom, C. S. (1977). A methodology for studying noninstitutionalized psychopaths. *Journal of Consulting and Clinical Psychology, 45,* 674–83.

Richard M. Ashbrook
Capital University

See also: **Antisocial Personality Disorders; Individual Differences**

CHI-SQUARE TEST

The chi-square (χ^2) test was developed by Karl Pearson in 1900, an event often regarded as one of the most important breakthroughs in the history of statistics. The test and the statistical distribution on which it is based have a wide variety of applications in psychological research. Its two principal uses are to test the independence of two variables and to assess how well a theoretical model or set of a priori probabilities fits a set of data. In both cases the chi-square test is typically thought of as a nonparametric procedure involving observed (O) and expected (E) frequencies. The expected frequencies may be determined either theoretically or empirically. The basic formula for calculating the chi-square statistic is

$$\chi^2 = \sum_{1}^{k} \left[\frac{(O-E)^2}{E} \right].$$

The χ^2 test is commonly applied to a wide variety of designs, including $k \times 1$ groups, $2 \times k$ groups, 2×2 contingency tables, and $R \times C$ contingency tables. It is most appropriately used with nominal-level (categorical) data but is frequently used with ordinal-level data as well. The χ^2 statistic is related to several measures of association, including the phi coefficient (ϕ), contingency coefficient (C), and Cramer's phi (ϕ' or ϕ_C). $\phi^2 = \chi^2/N$ is frequently used as a measure of practical significance or effect size for 2×2 tables.

Historically, there has been concern over the use of the chi-square test when any E was small (e.g., < 5–10) because the underlying χ^2 distribution is continuous whereas the distribution of observations is discrete. For 2×2 tables this led to the development of the widely used and recommended Yates' correction for continuity. However, most recent evidence seems to suggest that the use of Yates' correction is unnecessary even with very small E.

The χ^2 distribution is related to the normal distribution, such that the square of a standard normal deviate (z^2) is distributed as a χ^2 with one degree of freedom. The chi-square distribution also describes the sampling distribution of the variance, s^2, such that $\chi^2 = (N - 1)\, s^2/\sigma^2$ with $N - 1$ degrees of freedom. These relationships form the basis for many tests of statistical significance. For example, the analysis of variance F statistic may be thought of as the ratio of two χ^2 statistics. The χ^2 statistic is also used in many multivariate statistical tests and in calculating multinomial probabilities, especially for log-linear models. Multivariate statistics that use both generalized least squares and maximum likelihood procedures also rely on the χ^2 statistic. For example, in structural equation modeling, the χ^2 statistic forms the basis for many goodness-of-fit tests. In the 1930s, Fisher developed a procedure using the χ^2 test to combine the results of several independent tests of the same hypothesis, an early version of meta-analysis.

Joseph S. Rossi
University of Rhode Island

CHILD AND ADOLESCENT DEPRESSION

Clinical depression as seen in children and adolescents is characterized by depressed mood and/or loss of interest in activities as well as related symptoms such as difficulties with sleep, appetite changes, a sense of hopelessness, decreased energy, increased aches and pains, loss of self-esteem, difficulties with concentration, and thoughts of death and dying, sometimes with active suicidal plans. In some cases, young people do not complain of depressed mood or loss of interest in activities but instead have extreme irritability along with other symptoms. Most children, just like adults, have brief periods of depressed or irritable mood. Clinical depression (Major Depression) requires that several symptoms occur at the same time; persist for most of the day, nearly every day for a period of at least 2 weeks; and be associated with significant impairment in the child's ability to function. When clinical depression is causing impairment, parents and teachers may notice loss of interest in activities, increased arguments with others, decreased school attendance or performance, and loss of friends. Thus, many children may have brief periods of time (a few days) when they feel down in the dumps, typically after a disappointment. Parents and caretakers need to worry about clinical depression when many symptoms occur at the same time, persist over a period of a week or more, and are associated with a decline in school or family functioning and social participation.

Significant depression has been observed in young children, but depression appears to become more of a problem for children as they move into the adolescent years. At any point in time about 1 to 2% of children meet the criteria previously outlined for clinical depression; this rate increases to 4 to 8% of adolescents, and some research studies indicate that 25% of adolescents will have experienced a significant depression by the time they turn 18. Although rates of depression increase during adolescence for both boys and girls, gender differences begin to emerge between ages 13 and 15, with more girls than boys reporting depressive symptoms.

Periods of clinical depression can last for many months in some young people and can interfere significantly with a child's ability to keep up in school and remain active with friends. They can also be recurrent: As many as 40% of children and adolescents experience a second episode of depression within 2 years. Finally, depression is associated with substantial negative changes and risks both during and after the episode; these include difficulties in school and interpersonal relationships, increased risk of tobacco and substance abuse, suicide attempts, and completed suicide.

Although the cause of depression is not yet determined, it is thought that depression is most likely to occur when a number of risk factors come together. Biological vulnerability is one of these factors: Children whose parents have had significant depression are at a markedly increased risk for depression as well as other behavioral and emotional problems. Children may inherit a genetic risk for depression or temperamental qualities such as sensitivity to negative emotions, or they may learn depressive coping styles from their parents. Both adults and young people who are depressed share a depressive or negative way of thinking that leads them to view themselves, the world, and their future in a negative way. This is frequently described as seeing the cup as half empty, while others can look at the same situation and see the cup as half full. Many times depressed individuals come to see all failures as due to their own inherent faults but any success as pure chance or a fluke. This is called *negative attributional or explanatory style.* It is widely believed that depression affects a vulnerable person (based on biological, cognitive, or a combination of factors) when he or she is faced with stressful life events. For young people these events frequently include parental separation or divorce, geographic moves, loss of a friendship or romance, or exposure to abuse or neglect. Antidotes for depression include increased social support and social activity and learning skills needed to manage stress.

Efforts to both prevent the onset of depression in at-risk young people and treat depression in children and adolescents have been promising. A series of studies have described the use of school-based, small group programs geared to increase problem-solving skills, decrease negative or depressive thinking patterns, and increase social supports in youths at risk for depression. Risk is typically determined based on the presence of a parent who is struggling with depression or a child's report of initial signs of depressive symptoms.

Two structured psychotherapeutic approaches have also shown promise in the treatment of youths who are clinically depressed. Cognitive-behavioral therapy (CBT) is a 12- to 16-week individual treatment approach that focuses on teaching how to identify and then challenge (change) negative thought patterns as well as how to increase participation in pleasant events and improve stress management and social support. CBT has been effective in reducing the negative thinking patterns of depressed youths. Interpersonal psychotherapy (IPT), another brief treatment (12–16 weeks), also has initial outcome data suggesting positive treatment effects. IPT stresses the importance of the youth's social relationships and sees depression as occurring when a young person is in the midst of a change in social role (i.e., the adolescent transition) or does not have the social skills or social support to maintain a sense of well-being. Initial studies of this approach indicate success in improving overall social function, which may in turn lead to a decrease in depressed mood. Finally, initial studies suggest that medication also plays an important role in the treatment of depression. Although carefully controlled studies are few, there is some evidence to suggest that the selective serontonin reuptake inhibitors, such as Prozac, are effective in reducing symptoms of depression, especially symptoms of sleep and appetite disturbance and the tendency to be caught up in recurrent worries and negative thoughts. At this time the recommended treatment approach for clinical depression in children and adolescents is psychotherapy with pharmacotherapy as an additional component when indicated, such as when sleep or appetite disturbance or recurrent worry is present or when the depressed mood is so severe that it interferes with psychotherapeutic efforts.

Elizabeth McCauley
Cindy Smith
University of Washington

See also: **Antidepressant Medication; Gender Roles**

CHILD CUSTODY

Throughout history, different trends have occurred in custody determination. Prior to the 1920s, children were considered to be the property of the father, who almost always received custody. Starting in the 1920s, the Tender Years Doctrine was advanced, which assumed that young children were better in their mother's care. Consequently, a strong preference was given to the mother in regard to custody. This continued until 1970, when the focus shifted to the best interests of the child. At the present time, all states use this standard. However, specific criteria vary from state to state. Some common criteria include parenting capacity; mental and physical status of the parents; wishes of the parents and children regarding custody; home, school, and community adjustment of the children; and the willingness of each parent to facilitate the children's relationship with the other parent.

There are two major types of custody: legal and physical. Legal custody refers to decision-making power. Sole legal custody means that one parent holds all legal rights to decision making regarding the children, along with physical placement. Joint legal custody means the parents have equal legal rights and responsibilities for the children. Most states strongly support joint legal custody unless there is clear and convincing evidence that it would be detrimental. This position is advocated because it keeps both parents actively involved in major decision making regarding their children.

Physical custody refers to the physical placement of the children. Shared placement or joint physical custody means an equal or nearly equal distribution of time with the children. This is a workable plan when the parents live close to each other, conflict between the parents is minimal, children are able to deal with transition, and the children's age and developmental needs support such a plan. However, in the majority of cases, the children reside predominately with one parent, with designated parenting time (e.g., visitation) with the other parent. Parenting time plans vary widely and need to be developed to meet the individual needs of the parties. Some factors often considered are work schedule(s) and availability of the parents, geographic distance between the parents, age and developmental needs of the children, special needs of the parents and children, degree of cooperation between the parents, and desires of the parents and children. A couple of common plans are (1) the noncustodial parent having the children every Wednesday evening and every other weekend, and (2) the noncustodial parent having the children every weekend or three of the four weekends per month and one evening before and after the nonvisitation weekend. During the summer, the parenting plan may continue, or the time may be equally divided between the parents. Holidays and vacation breaks are usually divided or alternated between the parents.

In the overwhelming majority of child custody cases, the parents are able to come to an agreement regarding legal and physical custody. However, in about 10% of the cases, custody becomes contentious. In these cases, the court sometimes orders a child custody evaluation. This type of forensic evaluation is performed by a clinic affiliated with the court or by a private practice mental health professional with specialized training and experience in the child custody field. Evaluations performed by a court clinic are usually brief, taking 4 to 8 hours to complete, with a two- to five-page report to the court. Cost is usually minimal or determined by a sliding scale. Evaluations performed by private mental health professionals are usually very comprehensive and costly. Private practice doctoral-level psychologists usually take 25–30 hours to complete the evaluation. Reports to the court are typically about 20 pages but may vary depending on the complexity of the case.

The court should appoint the child custody evaluator, thereby allowing the evaluator to function in an independent, objective, and impartial role. The evaluator should not have a prior relationship with the family (i.e., as therapist). The focus of the evaluation is the best interests of the children. The evaluator needs to address the specific best-interest criteria established by state law. All parties need to be involved in the evaluation process, because the evaluator needs to critically evaluate both sides of the dispute. Also, an evaluator cannot provide an opinion about a person not seen. In contrast to therapy, court-ordered evaluations have limited confidentiality, meaning that all information gathered during the evaluation may be reported to the court. Guidelines for performing child custody evaluations are provided by professional organizations. For example, the American Psychological Association has published the *Guidelines for Child Custody Evaluations in Divorce Proceedings,* which outlines parameters for professional practice in this area.

Multiple methods of data collection are used in child custody evaluations. The following components are critical in the evaluation process: (1) interviews with each parent to gather a comprehensive psychosocial history and explore the marital history and dispute; (2) interviews with each child; (3) parent-child observations; (4) psychological testing of the parents, and children if needed; (5) collateral contacts with important individuals, such as new partners, therapists, teachers, or babysitters; and (6) review of pertinent documents and court records. In terms of psychological testing, parents are frequently given personality measures to assess personality traits and characteristics, along with signs of mental illness. Also, parenting inventories are increasingly being used to assess parenting attitudes and beliefs.

Many times in these contentious cases an allegation of sexual abuse, domestic violence, substance abuse, or parent alienation is made. Many different motives are involved in these allegations. Sometimes it is a genuine concern for the children's welfare; however, at other times the allegation is used in a vengeful, vindictive way to gain leverage in the dispute. These types of allegations require much investigation and a high level of expertise on the evaluator's part.

The average amount of time to complete a child custody evaluation is usually 2 months. A report is provided to the court regarding the findings and recommendations. Judges consider the report, along with other data, in making the ultimate decisions regarding custody and parenting time.

REFERENCE

American Psychological Association. (1994). Guidelines for child custody evaluations in divorce proceedings. *American Psychologist, 49,* 677–680.

James N. Bow

See also: **Expert Testimony; Forensic Psychology; Psychology and the Law**

CHILD GUIDANCE CLINICS

The National Committee for Mental Hygiene marshaled the child guidance clinic movement, which spanned the decades of the 1920s to 1940s. Child guidance clinics were established for the psychiatric study, treatment, and prevention of juvenile delinquency, other social ills, and conduct and personality disorders in 3- to 17-year-old non–mentally retarded children. The child guidance clinic approach to children's mental health represented a shift from traditional treatment models of the era, which were largely individual psychoanalytically oriented play therapy sessions conducted by a psychiatrist or psychologist, toward more innovative modes of intervention. Child guidance clinics' comprehensive, community-based approach to children's mental health service was carried out by multidisciplinary teams of psychologists, psychiatrists, psychiatric social workers, speech therapists, and psychiatric occupational therapists. In the 1940s the mental health focus shifted from the child guidance clinic movement to World War II–related mental health issues.

The next large impact on children's mental health services was the Community Mental Health Centers (CMHCs) Act of 1963. Like child guidance clinics, CMHCs sought to address both the treatment and prevention of mental illness within communities. However, unlike child guidance clinics, CMHCs were not solely child focused, rather, they addressed mental health issues across development, from prenatal health to coordination of services for the elderly at individual, family, and community levels. CMHCs were responsible for a comprehensive menu of services including outpatient treatment, primary and secondary prevention efforts, 24-hour crisis response, and community mental health education. CMHCs fulfilled their community education responsibility through consultation with schools in the area of early child risk evaluation.

Partly in response to changes in insurance reimbursement systems such as health maintenance organizations, mental health services for children have continued to evolve. Currently they include varied theoretical orientations and treatment approaches. Current work with children emphasizes child-centered, family-focused, community-based efforts in the planning and implementation of treatment. Mental health services strive to be both culturally competent and responsive to the cultural, racial, and ethnic differences within varied service populations. Services available to children within the mental health system include inpatient and outpatient psychiatric and psychological treatment facilities, partial programs, mobile therapy, crisis teams, foster care, juvenile justice, education, social welfare, primary health care, emergency shelter, and home-based interventions. In addition, wraparound services that meet a child's mental and physical health needs across his or her varied environments have been added to the children's mental health service menu. Case managers, whose job it is to coordinate children's mental health services within this complex system, have emerged to ensure that services are not fragmented and work in an interactive therapeutic manner to meet children's mental health needs. Undoubtedly, the mental health service system will continue to evolve in an effort to meet children's ever-changing physical, emotional, social, and educational needs.

SUGGESTED READING

Horn, M. (1989). *Before it's too late: The child guidance movement in the United States, 1922–1945.* Philadelphia: Temple University Press.

Stephen A. Erath
Kelly S. Flanagan
Pennsylvania State University

CHILD NEGLECT

Child abuse and child neglect are the two forms of child maltreatment. Abuse requires deliberate action; neglect is a failure to act in ways necessary to nurture or protect a child. The forms are similar in that they can be emotional, educational, medical, sexual, or physical, and both are extremely harmful. Abuse might seem worse and more common. However, neglect is actually more common, more destructive, and more deadly.

More than half a million children in the United States are severely neglected each year (these are reported and substantiated cases; millions more are not reported). Worldwide, 1 billion children are neglected annually, a number that becomes believable if you remember that, of the world's 2 to 3 billion children, many suffer chronic malnutrition, exposure to violence, or lack of medicine.

Within the United States, for every child who is abusively murdered, at least four die of neglect: They starve, die of illness, or perish in preventable accidents. Fortunately, if neglect is recognized early on as pervasive and destructive, it is preventable before permanent damage to a child occurs.

Emotional Neglect

From a psychological perspective, *emotional neglect* is the most serious form of neglect, in that the consequences of ongoing emotional neglect are lifelong: An emotionally deprived child becomes an adult who rarely experiences the joy, love, and intimacy that make life worth living. Emotional neglect begins in infancy. If babies cannot establish normal attachments, perhaps because their caregivers are depressed, drug-addicted, emotionally immature, or overwhelmed by their own survival needs, then infants and toddlers become detached from social relationships. The damage occurs within the brain, during formation of synapses and dendrites, and thus is difficult to reverse later on.

Typically, neglectful caregivers continue their emotional distancing throughout early childhood, never teaching the child about love, fear, anger, or sadness. By the time they reach school age, emotionally neglected children cannot regulate their emotions: They are too fearful, too depressed, or too aggressive. They become bullies, or victims, or friendless. They have never learned to distinguish hostile anger from innocent mistakes, genuine warmth from superficial friendliness. As adolescents and adults they befriend people who exploit them or provoke people who will hurt them, often becoming antisocial, bitter, and lonely.

Educational, Medical, and Sexual Neglect

Another type of neglect is *educational neglect.* All children are eager to learn, from the moment they are born. Early on, they need to learn language, which means that someone must talk to them and listen to them many hours every day. A 1-year-old who is not speaking, or a 2-year-old who is not using simple sentences, may be the victim of educational neglect. Preschoolers learn through active play and safe exploration; they are neglected if they sit alone or watch television for many hours each day instead of playing. Parents who do not send their school-age children to school, and schools that do not teach every child all the basic skills, are educationally neglectful.

Medical neglect is failure to meet a child's medical needs for protection against disease and for treatment. Basic immunizations against polio, tetanus, whooping cough, mumps, measles, and even chicken pox, as well as treatment for high fevers, painful earaches, broken bones, deep cuts, concussions, diarrhea, and so on are part of good care for every child. When they are not provided, parents, doctors, and communities are neglectful. One sign of child abuse is missed immunizations and untreated traumas, because medical neglect is often the first warning sign for later abuse.

Sexual neglect occurs when a child is not protected from sexual exploitation. Children not only need privacy, but they also need to develop respect for their own bodies. Before puberty, children need to know not only how to avoid sexual diseases and unwanted pregnancy, but also how to love themselves and another person. Loving mothers and fathers teach them this by example.

Physical Neglect

Failure to meet basic food, rest, and shelter needs is *physical neglect,* the most commonly reported form of neglect. If an infant grows very slowly, that can be *failure to thrive.* Slightly older children (aged 2–10) may suffer *deprivation dwarfism:* They are unusually short because too much stress (especially when it occurs at night, when most growth occurs) slows down their growth.

Children also need ample sleep, not only for growth but also for brain maturation and intellectual alertness. Cultures vary in sleeping arrangements: Some families believe children need their own rooms, and other families believe children should never sleep alone. From a psychological perspective, neither practice is necessarily neglect. However, failure to shield a child from witnessing domestic strife and violence may cause posttraumatic stress, with one symptom being vivid nightmares. Routinely waking the child from a sound sleep is also neglectful. Schools that begin early in the morning may ignore normal body rhythms (many teenagers are at least half asleep until noon).

Exposure to hazards—motor vehicles, swimming pools (drowning is the leading cause of accidental death for 1- to 4-year-olds in 10 states, including California, Florida, Arizona, and Texas), fires, poisons and so on—is neglect as well. Most accidents to children are preventable. For example, laws requiring car seats and safety belts have reduced the child motor vehicle death rate by half. Fatal fires could be much less common—they are seven times more likely if a caregiver is drunk, five times more likely when dwellings are run-down and crowded, and three times more likely if there is no working smoke detector. This is just one example that reveals that social neglect underlies many child deaths.

Note that we have not stressed psychological disorders as a cause of child neglect. Some parents have severe emotional disturbances; some children are hyperactive, or rebellious, or learning disabled. Such inadequacies are real, and they increase the risk of child neglect. However, psychologists consider neglect more of a social and community problem than an individual one; everyone needs to recognize it and take whatever action he or she can. When caregivers are inadequate, the entire community can prevent the harm that occurs from child neglect.

Kathleen Stassen Berger
City University of New York

CHILD PSYCHOLOGY

Child psychology deals with the personality and behavior of children, typically from conception to puberty. In the past *child psychology* has referred to both normal and abnormal behavior, to both theory and research, and also to the psychotherapy or counseling of disturbed children. Current usage, however, limits the term to a branch of the *science* of developmental psychology, specifying "child clinical" when referring to the professional practice of child psychology.

Childhood can be divided into substages: prenatal, infancy, toddlerhood, preschool, middle childhood, and later childhood. Some researchers, however, argue that development is best understood in the context of the total span of life and propose a "life span developmental psychology." Additionally, current research has focused on the contexts that influence development, including the family, school, and peers (see Bronfenbrenner, 1989, 1993).

History

Four sorts of history can be considered. Ontogenetic history, the history of the organism from conception to death, is the basic material of human development. Phylogenetic history refers to the evolutionary development of the species. According to one theory—proposed by G. Stanley Hall in his treatise *Adolescence* (1904), but now largely discounted—the ontogenetic history of individuals represented a "recapitulation" or repeating of the species's phylogenetic history.

A third sort of history refers to changes over time in the concept of childhood, corresponding to the sociocultural history of the family. Philippe Müller (1969) identified four periods in the cultural history of the family that corresponded to changing conceptions of the child.

A fourth kind of history in child psychology is the history of the field itself. Early Greek writers were concerned with stages of development, the socialization process, and the proper education of children. The origins of child psychology as a science, however, can be traced to the careful observations recorded in early "baby biographies," such as those written by Tiedemann (1787), Darwin (1877), and Preyer (1888/1882). Despite their shortcomings as scientific data, these biographies paved the way for more careful observation, for attention to psychological processes, and finally for experiments dealing with child behavior.

More recent influences on child psychology have been the testing movement and the development of child guidance clinics and major university centers for research on child behavior. Current literature emphasizes developmentally appropriate guidance, that is, optimal ways to work with and parent children.

Theories

Early theories of child psychology were largely implicit, children being thought of as miniature adults. Not until the late nineteenth century and the emergence of a formal discipline of psychology did theories about child behavior become prominent. An early psychologist, G. Stanley Hall, proposed a biogenetic theory emphasizing biological growth and genetic predispositions.

Freud, the father of psychoanalysis, emphasized environmental and especially social factors in the development of child behavior and personality. One of the first to stress the influence of early experience on later behavior, Freud assigned a major role to the unconscious. He postulated a series of psychosexual stages defined by the characteristic way in which libido, or mental sexual energy, gets expressed (see "Psychosexual Stages").

Jean Piaget developed a major theory of cognitive development. For Piaget, the stages of development concern the increasingly complex way in which the individual can incorporate and process information and assimilate it into his or her own previously developed mental structures.

Learning theorists have tended to view children's behavior as based on environmental rather than organismic factors and, like Freud, see the organism as passive rather than active in its own development. The emergence of social learning theory was in some respects a combination of psychoanalytic and learning theory concepts.

Research Methods

Since the days of the baby biographies, child psychology has progressed in methodology as well as theory. Using a *longitudinal* approach, investigators follow the same subjects over the years of interest and observe age changes. With the *cross-sectional* approach, the researcher tests subjects of different ages. A combination of the two procedures has been suggested (Schaie, 1970) as a more powerful approach.

Research methods have included questionnaires; ratings and rankings by teachers, peers, parents, and oneself; interviews; observation; projective tests; personality and intelligence tests; and direct experimentation. A good source for understanding the basic information on research methods in child psychology is *Research Methods in Human Development* (Brown, Cozby, Kee, & Worden, 1999).

Issues In Developmental Psychology

The contrasting views of the child as an active agent or a recipient remain a salient issue in child psychology. The relative influence of environmental factors, contrasted with genetic predispositions, is also an important dimension to child psychologists. Finally, child psychologists differ in the importance they place on stages in development: While some theorists perceive development as proceeding by discrete stages, other assume a more continuous unfolding of personality and behavior.

REFERENCES

Bronfenbrenner, U. (1989). Ecological systems theory. In R. Vasta (Ed.), *Six theories of child development: Annals of child development* (Vol. 6, pp. 187–249). Greenwich, CT: JAI Press.

Bronfenbrenner, U. (1993). The ecology of cognitive development: Research models and fugitive findings. In R. H. Wozniak & K. W. Fischer (Eds.), *Development in context: Acting and thinking in specific environments* (pp. 3–44). Hillsdale, NJ: Erlbaum.

Brown, K. W., Cozby, P. C., Kee, D. W., & Worden, P. E. (1999). *Research methods in human development* (2nd ed.). Mountain View, CA: Mayfield Publishing.

Darwin, C. A. (1877). A biographical sketch of an infant. *Merid, 2,* 285–294.

Hall, G. S. (1904). *Adolescence: Its psychology and its relations to physiology, anthropology, sociology, sex, crime, religion, and education* (Vol. I). Englewood Cliffs, NJ: Prentice Hall.

Müller, P. (1969). *The tasks of childhood.* New York: McGraw-Hill.

Preyer, W. (1888). *The mind of the child.* New York: Appleton-Century. (Original work published 1882)

Schaie, K. W. (1970). A reinterpretation of age-related changes in cognitive structure and functioning. In L. R. Goulet & P. B. Baltes (Eds.), *Life-span developmental psychology: Research and theory.* (pp. 485–507). New York: Academic Press.

Tiedemann, D. (1787). *Beobachtungen über die Entwicklung der Seelenfähigkeiten bei Kindern.* Altenburg: Bonde.

John Paul McKinney
Michigan State University, Professor Emeritus

See also: **Life-span Development; Psychosexual Stages; Theories of Family Development**

CHILDHOOD DEPRESSION

Diagnosis, Prevalence, and Prognosis

A depressive disorder is defined by a disturbance in mood and a cluster of emotional, cognitive, vegetative, and behavioral symptoms that result in functional impairment. Typically, depressive disorders are episodic. There are two diagnoses of unipolar depressive disorders: Major Depressive Disorder and Dysthymic Disorder. Major depression is a more severe disorder in terms of the number and quality of symptoms and the extent of functional impairment. Dysthymic Disorder is less severe but longer lasting. A child may experience both of these disorders at once.

Prevalence rates are increasing with each successive generation. Prevalence increases with age and differs across subgroups and diagnostic categories. Depressive disorders are rare among preschool children. Among children, rates of 2% are reported for major depression and 2–3% for Dysthymic Disorder. Twenty percent of adolescents report symptoms of major depression, with the rate increasing dramatically at puberty. Females, African American children, and children with a medical condition or learning disability are at greater risk for developing depression.

Children's depressive disorders tend to be longer and more severe than those of adults. Although most children will recover, depression can leave them socially, cognitively, and educationally impaired. Several variables including severity, family dysfunction, and gender predict the duration of a depressive episode. The average duration of a major depressive episode is reported to be 32 to 36 weeks, with longer durations in females. The rate of recovery is slow, with the greatest improvement starting between the 24th and 36th week. Within 6 months of onset, the depressive episode has remitted for 40% of the children. At one year, 80% of the children are no longer experiencing a depressive episode. The average duration of dysthymia is 3 years. A chronic course is reported for a significant percentage of depressed children. Depressive disorders are recurrent, with about 75% experiencing another episode within 5 years. Most depressed youths simultaneously experience additional psychological disorders. Occurrence of a psychotic depression or comorbid Attention-Deficit/Hyperactivity Disorder (ADHD) may be risk factors for later development of bipolar disorder.

Etiology

There are a number of possible biological and psychosocial causes of depression. The most widely accepted theories of depressive disorders are stress diathesis models, in which stress interacts with a genetic or psychosocial vulnerability to produce a depressive episode.

Most biological theories of depression assume that the diathesis is a dysfunction of one or more neurochemical systems in the brain. The biogenic amine theory suggests that depression is caused by depletion of monoamines (norepinephrine, serotonin, and dopamine) at critical synapses in the brain (Schildkraut, 1965). There is an increasing appreciation of the synergistic action of multiple neurotransmitter systems. Hormonal, neuroendocrine, and hypothalamic-thyroid systems may also be involved in depression.

A number of psychosocial models of childhood depression are empirically supported. The cognitive model suggests that a depressive disorder originates with a disturbance in the child's thinking. Beck's (1967) cognitive theory of depression describes a disturbance in the memory structures that guide an individual's attention, construction of experiences, and other thought processes. According to the learned hopelessness model of depression (Abramson, Metalsky, & Alloy, 1989), the individual questions the occurrence of a negative or stressful event; the answer to the question is referred to as an *attribution* and affects the youngster's emotional adjustment. Depressed individuals have an attributional style that leads to feeling helpless. Additional theories focus on deficits in areas such as (1) interpersonal relationships, (2) emotion regulation, (3) social skills and problem solving, and (4) personal competence. No single theory seems to account for all cases of depression.

Assessment

Clinicians use a multitrait, multi-informant, and multimethod approach to assess childhood depression. These assessments usually consist of paper-and-pencil measures and a diagnostic interview completed by the child and parents. The questionnaires and interview are designed to assess the presence and severity of depressive symptoms. The experience of depression is subjective, so the child is the primary informant, with parents providing information about the onset and duration.

Treatment

Both medication and psychological treatments have been successfully employed with children. Currently, there are four main classes of antidepressants that may be prescribed to youths: tricyclics, monoamine oxidase inhibitors, selective serotonin reuptake inhibitors (SSRIs), and second-generation antidepressants. The antidepressants act on the monoamine neurotransmitter system, more specifically the neurotransmitters acetylcholine, norepinephrine, serotonin, and to a lesser extent dopamine. Antidepressant medications influence the metabolization and/or reuptake of the neurotransmitters producing increased levels of functionally available neurotransmitters. Most antidepressants have a broad spectrum effect, influencing the metabolization and/or reuptake of acetylcholine, norepinephrine, serotonin, and dopamine. A few are more focused, targeting specific brain monoamine systems. Current research indicates that SSRI treatments are beneficial for many depressed youngsters due to their efficacy, safety profile, and fewer reported side effects (Ambrosini, Emslie, Greenhill, Kutcher, & Weller, 1995). The presence and types of comorbid conditions are important determinants in choosing an appropriate medication. The recommended length of a medication trial is 6 to 10 weeks. If the medication does not show results during this period, then another antidepressant or an augmentation strategy with a different class of medications may be initiated. In a successful medication regimen, the recommended duration of treatment ranges from 2 months to 2 years.

Research has also supported the efficacy of cognitive-behavioral treatments for depressed youths. Cognitive-behavioral interventions are time-limited, structured interventions designed to change the depressed youngster's maladaptive thinking, behavior, and coping patterns. The child and therapist form a collaborative team in which the child is taught emotion regulation skills, coping skills, social skills, problem solving, and strategies for identifying and altering negative thoughts. The overall treatment goal is changing the individual's basic rules for interpreting daily interactions. Caregivers or the entire family may be included in the treatment program.

REFERENCES

Abramson, L.Y, Metalsky, G. I., & Alloy, L. B. (1989). Hopelessness depression: A theory-based subtype of depression. *Psychological Review, 96,* 358–372.

Ambrosini, P. J., Emslie, G. J., Greenhill, L. L., Kutcher, S., & Weller, E. B. (1995). Selecting a sequence of antidepressants for treating depression in youth. *Journal of Child and Adolescent Psychopharmacology, 5,* 233–240.

Beck, A. T. (1967). *Depression: Clinical, experimental, and theoretical aspects.* New York: Harper & Row.

Schildkraut, J. (1965). The catecholamine hypothesis of affective disorders: A review of supporting evidence. *American Journal of Psychiatry, 122,* 508–522.

Kevin D. Stark
Dawn Sommer
Mary G. Yancy
Jennifer Hargrave
University of Texas

See also: **Antidepressant Medications; Neurotransmitters**

CHILDREN'S BEHAVIORAL STAGES

Studies of human development indicate basic principles underlying all developmental processes that lead to a series of stages that all individuals can be expected to go through. These principles are related to heredity as it interacts with environment and time during critical or sensitive periods and maturation. Indications of a stage development approach can be found in the work of Arnold Gesell, Jean Piaget, Lawrence Kolberg, Sigmund Freud, Erik Erickson, and others. These theorists generally think of development as a genetically determined sequence interacting in a continuous and, so to speak, creative fashion with the environment.

From birth onward there are new stages in motor, cognitive (thinking), and personality development to be considered. The organism is now in a position to be observed, and much more rigorous research is possible. At birth every infant has a repertoire of reflex behaviors to carry on everyday activities. In addition, sensory awareness begins to develop at a faster pace. Touch appears to be the only completely active sense at birth, but vision and hearing are even more advanced in their development than specialists considered possible only a short time ago.

Development in the womb and after birth follows three basic sequences. The first goes from the head downward in the body and is known in the literature as *cephalocaudal development.* The second is from the center of the body outward, known in the literature as *proximodistal development.* The third is the change from the massive generalized responses seen initially to the more specific later responses, indicated in the literature as a movement from gross to refined movements.

Arnold Gesell, who was interested in the genetically determined or maturational aspects of development, founded the Yale Clinic of Child Development at Yale University. He was concerned with the unfolding of inner tendencies rather than the changes resulting from learning or experience. Gesell concluded that behavior occurred in an unvarying sequence and that maturational changes made new kinds of behavior possible. He believed that knowledge about the maturational readiness of a child was essential for developing the best educational and training programs.

Behavioral norms for many aspects of child development were obtained and published in *Developmental Diagnoses: Normal and Abnormal Child Development,* by A. Gesell and C. Amatruda. The behaviors described in this publication are set up on a normative basis in such a way that 50% of the children examined at a particular age level will demonstrate the behavior under consideration, 25% will not have achieved that level of behavior as yet, and 25% will be beyond it. The norms are developed and presented in this form to help parents make decisions in regard to their own children. The norms enable parents to know what normal behavior can be expected and to be aware of developmental problems that may exist. Although Gesell stressed these norms in his work, he was also sensitive to differences among children and did not want the norms to obscure individuality of development.

Some psychologists think that Gesell overgeneralized in reporting his developmental growth stages. However, some conclude that his work on sequential levels of development, and his indication that growing stages are major periods of reorganization followed by periods of integration of the changes that have taken place, added a great deal to our understanding of how a child changes while maturing.

Jean Piaget considered development to be a continuous and creative interaction between the organism and the environment. He noted that both body and sensory activities contribute to a child's development of intelligence, and he stressed the need for adequate stimulation in the early years. Piaget concluded that the child's developmental stages dealt with specific cognitive behaviors that gradually and predictably changed in some specific order.

Piaget found four major stages, each of which contained consistent ways of dealing with the world different from the other three. The stages are sequential, and an individual must pass through all four of them. At the same time the stages are not rigidly fixed in a time sequence: They can overlap to some extent, and the ages at which a stage is to appear are only approximate.

The four stages that Piaget identified were (1) the sensorimotor stage, from birth to approximately 2 years of age; (2) the preoperational stage, from approximately 2 to 7 years of age; (3) the concrete operations stage, from approximately 7 to 11 years of age; and (4) the formal operations stage, from approximately 11 to 15 years of age.

In the *sensorimotor stage* the infant is learning to use the body and is gaining immediate experiences through the senses. All activity is practical and based on immediate experiences.

The *preoperational stage* finds the child beginning to use words and solve more complex problems. Children can move from one- or two-word sentences, at age 2 years, to eight- or ten-word sentences at around 5 years of age.

The *concrete operations stage* brings a literal, concrete way of thinking and a tendency to give up the magical thinking of the previous stage. Reasoning during this period is based on concrete examples, and each experience is considered as unique and not related to another experience.

The *formal operations stage* is when rational patterns of thinking are able to develop. Symbolic meanings are understood, and abstract strategies are possible. Hidden meanings can be understood, and generalizations from stories and games become a possibility.

Piaget sees these changes as part of an individual's movement toward a state of equilibrium. A well-balanced set of ideas organized into a workable mental system can be used to solve new problems.

Children assimilate particular kinds of experience at each stage of development, as they perform activities they already know how to do by using their new level of awareness. Accommodation occurs when children internalize these experiences and make them a part of their new capability.

Freud is considered a major developmental theorist with a stage-dependent approach. His theory of psychosexual development stresses the fact that certain early experiences during sensitive periods have lasting effects on the individual. He hypothesized five basic stages of development, with each stage characterized by a new socialization problem facing the individual. Stage 1 is the *oral stage,* which goes from birth to 1½ years of age; stage 2 is the *anal stage,* which lasts from 1½ to 3 years of age: stage 3 is the *phallic stage,* which lasts from 3 to 7 years of age, during which the child becomes aware of genital differences and the pleasures related to the genital area, such as masturbation. The Oedipus complex and the castration complex appear at this time. Stage 4, the *latency stage,* lasts from 7 to 12 years of age, a period when primary love interests are diverted to individuals outside the home. The basic personality has been formed by this time and becomes more or less stabilized during this stage. This period is often considered a calm before the storm of pubertal change. Stage 5 is the *genital stage,* which lasts from 12 years of age into the adult period of life. This is a period when the instinctual sexual drives increase, parental attachments are dissolved, and adolescent conflicts develop.

Freud believed that if the first three stages are completed without psychic trauma, the individual will tend to be psychologically healthy. If, however, some of the basic needs are frustrated, personality development will be arrested or fixation will occur and the personality will be affected at all later stages.

Similar to Piaget and Freud, the neo-Freudian Erik Erikson believed in a stage-dependent approach. He disagreed with Freud's psychosexual concepts because he believed that they were too narrowly conceived and that personality is not totally defined in early childhood but continues to develop throughout life. He evolved an eight-stage psychosocial development sequence, with his early childhood stages almost a duplicate of Freud's.

Lawrence Kolberg sees moral development as a universal cognitive process that proceeds from one stage to the next in a definite and fixed fashion at a pace determined by the individual's opportunities and experiences.

Frederick D. Breslin
WFB Enterprises

See also: **Adolescent Development; Development of Human Social Behavior; Eriksonian Developmental Stages; Moral Development**

CHILDREN'S FEARS

Because fear is an emotional response to a perceived threat, it provides a protective survival mechanism by alerting the individual to danger. Mild or moderate fear reactions are viewed as normal and adaptive, promoting caution when real danger is present. However, fears become maladaptive when they are intense and persistent, alerting the child in the absence of potential danger, and interfering with normal physical, social, and intellectual functioning.

Psychologists generally distinguish between two types of fear: (1) *phobia,* an intense and to some extent irrational fear directly associated with specific objects, events, or situations; and (2) *anxiety,* a vague feeling of apprehension, uneasiness, or impending doom that has a relatively uncertain or unspecific source. Although the particular fears a child will develop—and their severity—cannot be predicted accurately, some generalizations about gender and age factors in the development of fears can be made.

Gender and Age Differences

Researchers have found consistently that girls report a greater number of fears than do boys. However, one cannot tell from these studies whether this gender difference is due to a higher inborn fear reactivity in females or whether other factors, such as sex-role influences, are responsible.

Several studies have found age-related changes in the *type* of fear children report. An overview of this developmental trend reveals that, as children grow older, their fears tend to become (1) more abstract and (2) more anticipatory, rather than being tied to immediate occurrences. For instance, compared to young children, older children tend to be less afraid of animals but more fearful of school and social relations.

Infancy and the Toddler Stage

Normal babies are born with startle or fright reactions to pain, to loss of physical support, and to sudden loud noises and flashes of light. Two common fears of infancy and the toddler stage are fear of strangers and fear of separations.

Preschool and Early School Years

Among the more common fears that develop in early childhood are (listed alphabetically) animals and insects; dark, especially at bedtime; death, often related to separation distress; doctors and dentists; heights; monsters and imaginary creatures such as ghosts and witches; school, often related to separation distress; storms and other natural events; and deep water.

Middle Childhood to Adolescence

In later childhood, a frequent theme underlying children's fears is the threat of physical injury from criminals and from machinery such as cars and airplanes. However, the most distinctive trend during this age period is toward increasing worry about school, individual competence, and social relationships—worries that continue into adolescence.

Sources of Fear

The process by which fears are acquired seems to involve three factors:

1. *Inborn sources.* Each baby enters the world with certain dispositions or basic personality traits, called *temperaments.* The temperamental styles of individuals seem to be enduring and appear to make some children vulnerable to the development of fear. These children may be more affected by and less able to cope with stressful experiences.
2. *Experiences.* Direct encounters with negative events can lead to fear by way of classical conditioning: The ability of a previously unfeared stimulus to elicit fear is increased when it becomes associated with an event that already elicits a fear reaction.
3. *Thinking and imagination.* Fears can also arise out of children's imagination, particularly when incorrect ideas and faulty reasoning are involved.

Treatment

Children can be helped to cope with fears before they become serious problems. When therapy is needed, two of the most effective treatments for fear reduction are counterconditioning and modeling. In *counterconditioning* a calm, relaxation, or coping response is substituted for the fear response by way of classical conditioning procedures, in which the feared object is gradually paired with pleasant or neutral events. Therapeutic *modeling* is a procedure in which the child observes other people in progressively more active or direct encounters with the feared object.

Edward P. Sarafino
College of New Jersey

CHRONIC FATIGUE SYNDROME: CLINICAL DISORDER

Chronic fatigue syndrome (CFS) is a disabling condition characterized by severe, relentless fatigue that does not improve with sleep or rest and often worsens with physical or mental activity. Individuals with CFS are unable to perform activities that they were once able to perform without difficulty, such as working a full-time job or maintaining the tasks of daily living, such as household chores or grocery shopping. Specifically, CFS involves 6 or more months of unexplained fatigue that interferes with previous levels of occupational, educational, or social performance. According to the most recent U.S. diagnostic criteria issued by an international panel of experts headed by Dr. Keji Fukuda in 1994, at least four of eight additional physical and cognitive symptoms persist with the fatigue for at least 6 months. These include sore throat, swollen or tender lymph nodes, difficulties with short-term memory and concentration, muscle pain, multijoint pain, increased fatigue and symptoms following exertion, headaches, and unrefreshing sleep. In addition to these eight primary symptoms, a number of other symptoms have been reported by 20–50% of CFS patients, and may include nausea, abdominal pain, diarrhea, alcohol intolerance, dizziness, lightheadedness, weakness, dry eyes or mouth, bloating, chest pain, irregular heartbeat, chronic cough, and psychological distress involving feelings of depression and anxiety.

CFS can exhibit drastic fluctuations in symptom severity and level of impairment between and within individuals. A person who had been unable to leave his or her home may occasionally feel well enough to leave the house, take short walks, and converse with others. On the other hand, a usually high-functioning individual may experience a "crash" and be unable to perform his or her usual responsibilities for weeks or even months. A significant portion of these patients report some level of improvement over time but only a minority (less than 10%) appear to achieve substantial recovery. Although prevalence estimates vary between studies, the average estimate is 200–422 individuals per 100,000 persons. The syndrome affects a wide range of individuals from varying racial, ethnic, and socioeconomic backgrounds. It affects both sexes, but it tends to be more common in women than men. Although less prevalent, CFS has been found to exist in adolescents and school-aged children. The level of co-occurrence of CFS with conditions such as fibromyalgia and multiple chemical sensitivities appears to be high. Because these conditions show moderate symptomatic overlap with each other, some have suggested that they are variations of the same underlying disorder. However, factor analytic studies suggest that, despite commonalities in symptomatology, these illnesses can be considered distinct entities.

The cause of CFS has not yet been determined, and as yet there is no specific diagnostic procedure or laboratory test that can definitively diagnose CFS. Debate regarding the medical legitimacy of CFS has entered into a number of important domains involving assessment and treatment. Some emphasize the role of psychological agents in the etiology and course of CFS and consider individuals with CFS as having a form of somatic depression or a variant of hypochondriasis. Others underscore the role of social-environmental factors in CFS, employing models of a dialectical relationship between body and society, in which somatic symptoms are interpreted as the sequelae of painful or otherwise exploitative social interactions. Still others emphasize the biomedical correlates of CFS, highlighting distinctions between CFS and psychiatric disorders such as depression. Although CFS is generally associated with higher than expected rates of psychiatric comorbidity as compared to the general population, research suggests that rates of psychiatric disorder observed in individuals with these conditions are no higher than those observed in other medically ill populations. Moreover, the failure to identify symptomatic overlap between these illnesses and psychiatric disorders may result in misleading overestimations of psychiatric comorbidity in psychodiagnostic studies. It is likely that some of the psychiatric disorders that are observed in some individuals with these illnesses are triggered by the personal devastation resulting from symptoms, functional impairments, and resource losses. Despite this controversy, a majority of researchers and practitioners acknowledge some distinction between CFS and psychiatric illness or support a biopsychosocial model for understanding the etiology and course of CFS in which biological, psychological, and social variables interact in the onset and maintenance of the syndrome.

Pathophysiological findings in microbiology, immunology, endocrinology, and neuroscience suggest that CFS cannot be explained solely by psychiatric factors, and laboratory studies have detected differences between individuals with CFS and those with primary depression on a number of indices. Almost every investigation of psychiatric comorbidity conducted to date has found an absence of diagnosable psychiatric illness in at least one quarter to one third of individuals with CFS (Wessely, 1998). Currently, research supports the idea that multiple precipitants may converge to form a single causal pathway to CFS. Some of these causal agents include viral and bacterial infectious agents, immune dysfunction, abnormalities of blood pressure and heart rate regulation, nutritional deficits, and other acute physical or emotional stressors: Alterations in the hypothalamic-pituitary-adrenal (HPA) axis that perhaps lead to abnormalities in immune functioning have also been postulated.

No curative medical interventions are available for any of these conditions. In part, this problem explains why many individuals with these conditions report negative experiences with treatment providers and with physicians in particular. Many physicians rely solely on palliative pharmacological agents, refer individuals with CFS for psychotherapy, or recommend no treatment whatsoever. Pharmacological management has been found to be helpful for certain individuals. Activity pacing, energy conservation training, and cognitive-behavioral therapy with graded activity have been used effectively to improve coping and in some cases improve functioning. Multidisciplinary approaches that include medical supervision, nutritional counseling, physical therapy, social support, psychotherapy, and medication management may produce the most favorable outcomes. In addition to these approaches, many patients dissatisfied with Western medicine have utilized alternative medical treatments, such as acupuncture and massage therapy for pain reduction.

REFERENCE

Wessely, S. (1998). The epidemiology of chronic fatigue syndrome. *Epidemiologia e Psichiatria Sociale, 7*(1), 19–24.

Renee R. Taylor
University of Illinois, Chicago

CHRONIC FATIGUE SYNDROME: RESEARCH

Clinical Presentation

Although diseases similar to chronic fatigue syndrome (CFS) have been recognized for centuries under various rubrics, strict diagnostic criteria for conditions dominated by medically unexplained chronic fatigue were first proposed in 1988. Current diagnostic criteria were crafted in 1994 by an International Chronic Fatigue Syndrome Study Group as an attempt to standardize patient populations included in research studies. The International CFS Research Case Definition requires the presence of at least 6 months of persistent, unexplained fatigue that interferes with multiple domains of daily life, is not relieved by rest, and is accompanied by at least four of the following symptoms: cognitive impairment, sore throat, tender neck or lymph nodes, muscle pain, joint pain, headaches, unrefreshing sleep, and more than 24 hours of post-exertional malaise. Importantly, the research case definition precludes classification as CFS if a patient has an identifiable medical cause to be fatigued. Similarly, subjects with certain psychiatric conditions cannot be classified as CFS in research studies. Exclusionary psychiatric conditions include Schizophrenia, bipolar disorder, or melancholic major depression. It is important to realize that the CFS case definition was devised for research purposes, and the concept of exclusionary conditions is critical to avoid confounding CFS with other medical disorders. In clinical settings the list of exclusionary conditions is most useful as a list of differential diagnoses. In clinical practice, patients with various exclusionary conditions may also be diagnosed and managed as having CFS based on the physician's medical opinion.

Prevalence and Prognosis

Fatigue is a common complaint. Community-based epidemiological studies suggest that at any given time approximately 10% of women and 5% of men suffer from fatigue of greater than 6 months' duration. However, because CFS requires severe, medically unexplained fatigue that is not resolved by rest, cannot be explained by medical or psychiatric illness, and is accompanied by specific symptoms, CFS itself is far less common. Prevalence rates vary significantly across studies, probably as a result of differences in diagnostic criteria and experimental design. Nevertheless, it appears that 0.3 to 1.6% of the population meet criteria for CFS. In the largest community-based epidemiological study conducted to date, researchers at the Centers for Disease Control and Prevention (CDC) found that 2% of women and 0.9% of men met CFS criteria based on phone interviews. However, when carefully evaluated by a trained clinician, most of these individuals failed to qualify for CFS because symptoms had changed or a potential medical or psychiatric exclusion was identified. Based upon these careful assessments, the CDC now estimates the prevalence of CFS to be 235 per 100,000 adults 18 to 69 years of age, or 0.24%.

Traditionally the prevalence rates for CFS have been thought to be highest in middle- and upper middle-class White females. It is now clear that this reflects a bias in early studies that recruited patients from medical practices. Large community-based epidemiological studies in the United States indicate that CFS is equally or more common in African Americans, Hispanics, and Native Americans and among individuals who earn less than $40,000 per year. However, in all these groups, women are two to four times more likely than men to have CFS.

CFS is a chronic illness that waxes and wanes over time, and although patients report significant improvement, it is unclear if the illness completely resolves. Patients with CFS are strikingly disabled: Between 40 and 70% are unable to work or attend school, and 93% report severe impairment in their ability to perform daily life activities. Some evidence suggests that patients who develop CFS suddenly may have a better outcome than those who develop the illness insidiously over time.

Etiology

Despite several decades of research, the etiology of CFS remains unclear. In any potential etiological domain, studies reporting positive findings are nearly always counterbalanced by studies that are negative. Nonetheless, tentative conclusions can be drawn concerning physiological systems that may be abnormal in at least some patients with CFS. It is important to remember, however, that it remains unknown whether any given abnormality represents a cause or a consequence of CFS.

Early etiological theories of the disorder focused on the immune system and infection with Epstein Barr and other latent viruses. Although cases of CFS may follow such infections, it is clear that specific viral infections are not a primary cause of the disorder. A variety of immune system abnormalities have also been reported, including decreases in natural killer cell activity and increases in proinflammatory cytokines, especially in patients with sudden-onset CFS. A recent study indicated that CFS patients have increased delayed type hypersensitivity reactions, suggesting an abnormality in T-cell-mediated immunity.

Patients with CFS also may exhibit decreased activity of the hypothalamic-pituitary-adrenal (HPA) axis, the body's primary stress response system. Several studies report decreased levels of circulating cortisol and decreased adrenocortical reserve. Concordant with this observation, one study reported that CFS patients demonstrate adrenocortical atrophy on CT scan. In addition to decreased functioning, the HPA axis has also been reported to lose its normal circadian rhythm in CFS patients. Clinical improvement has been associated with normalization of this rhythm.

Other physiological abnormalities have been reported in patients with CFS. Many patients with CFS complain of unrefreshing sleep. In keeping with this, fibromyalgia, which has symptoms that overlap with those of CFS, has been characterized by an increase in awake-state (alpha) brain rhythms during deep (stage 4) sleep. It has also been reported that abnormal autonomic nervous system functioning may be common in patients with CFS, based on the fact that at least some CFS patients demonstrate orthostatic intolerance when subjected to tilt table testing. Conversely, patients with postural orthostatic intolerance syndrome often manifest symptoms similar to those seen in CFS. Alterations in central nervous system serotonin, arginine vasopressin, and growth hormone have also been described.

Finally, psychological and stress-related factors have been associated with CFS. Many patients report an increase in life stress in the year prior to disease development, especially when the illness develops slowly. Recent work with identical twins suggests that patients with CFS are more affected by similar levels of somatic distress than are genetically identical but unaffected persons.

Treatment

Numerous treatments have been applied to CFS patients, with various results. Those with the best experimental data to support efficacy include graded exercise training and cognitive-behavioral therapy. Low-dose corticosteroids have been reported to improve symptoms in two studies. Trials of antidepressants have yielded a confusing welter of positive and negative results, but in general these agents appear to be significantly less effective for CFS than for mood or anxiety disorders. Other CFS treatments with at least one positive study to their credit include growth hormone, selegiline, immunoglobulin, ampligen, nicotinamide adenine dinucleotide (NADH), and omega-3 fatty acids. Although treatments may ameliorate symptoms, to date, none will resolve the disorder.

Charles L. Raison
Andrew H. Miller
Dimitris Papanicolaou
Emory University School of Medicine

William C. Reeves
Centers for Disease Control and Prevention

CLINICAL GEROPSYCHOLOGY

Overview

Clinical geropsychology is a subfield of psychology concerned with the psychosocial issues that affect the mental health and quality of life of people aged 65 and older and their caregivers. Clinical geropsychologists provide assessment and treatment of a complex set of problems among older adults in a wide variety of service settings such as medical clinics, community mental health clinics, assisted living facilities, and nursing homes.

Clinical geropsychology has grown substantially in the past 20 years, a timely increase given that recent population demographic estimates suggest that in the year 2030, 20% of the U.S. population is expected to be 65 years and older. In recent years, economic forces such as new opportunities for Medicare reimbursement for psychological services have also served to increase practice in geropsychology. Unfortunately, the burgeoning numbers of older adults in American society suggest that without a substantial increase in both the availability of, and interest in the pursuit of, geropsychological training, increased funding for psychological treatment research, and insurance parity for mental health services, the future mental health needs of many older adults may not be adequately met.

Mental Health In Late Life

Epidemiological studies have found that mental health problems such as depression are not a natural consequence of growing older. However, there are a number of challenges that occur primarily in later life and that may increase the disability and burden of mental health problems among the elderly. For example, serious medical illnesses and related functional decline are much more common in later life. Bereavement related to the loss of a spouse, although not uncommon among younger adults, is very common among married or partnered older cohorts. Likewise, the functional and emotional challenges to individuals and family members posed by dementing illnesses such as Alzheimer's disease largely occur during later life.

Stressful life events and hassles, medical illness, physical and functional decline, and decreasing social activity are all associated with causing or worsening a wide variety of mental disorders among older adults. When mental disorders, medical illness, and functional decline co-occur, older adults face a greatly increased risk of hospitalization and placement in long-term care facilities. It is important to note, however, that older adults vary substantially in terms of their mental and physical health, physical abilities, level of cognition (e.g., memory skills), independent living skills, community functioning, family and social relationships, and overall well-being. Some older adults are relatively healthy and active well into their 80s and 90s.

Assessment

Diagnostic and functional assessments provide a comprehensive understanding of older adults' needs and typically include critical information about psychiatric diagnosis and social and environmental factors that influence older adults' emotions and behavior. Quality assessments are needed to ensure that an appropriate intervention is chosen for treatment. Geropsychologists use standardized interview and self-report instruments that have been specifically designed for use with older adults to diagnose psychiatric disorders such as depression, anxiety, and Substance Abuse. In the case of dementing illnesses such as Alzheimer's disease, which affect approximately 50% of older adults over the age of 85, psychological assessment evaluations determine the extent of problems with functions such as attention and memory skills and the extent to which the disease has adversely impacted important day-to-day activities such as self-care, household care, financial management, driving skills, and social activities. Evaluations of the possibility of elder abuse by caregivers and assessment of the medically ill older adult's competence to make legal, financial, and medical decisions are also elements of practice that may fall under the scope of the geropsychologist.

Treatment of Late-Life Psychopathology

Many older adults with recognized mental health problems are prescribed medications by their treating physicians in primary care settings. However, a substantial body of geropsychotherapy research over the past two decades has resulted in the development of a variety of psychological treatments for some of the most common mental health problems faced by older adults. Clinical geropsychologists provide psychotherapy or so-called talking treatments for these problems. For example, a number of theoretically and practically distinct treatments (e.g., psychodynamic or insight-oriented, cognitive-behavioral or learning-based, interpersonal therapy) have been found to be effective in the treatment of depression among healthy older adults. Psychological treatments are also available for anxiety disorders and sleep disorders such as Insomnia. There is a nascent but growing body of clinical research for older adults with Schizophrenia and older adults who engage in health-damaging substance abuse behavior (e.g., alcohol abuse). The few medical and psychosocial treatments currently available for dementia are focused on managing problem behaviors such as wandering and agitation. New treatments currently under development focus on managing the emotional problems such as depression that often co-occur with dementia. Given the literature documenting the substantial negative emotional and health impacts associated with caregiving for an older adult suffering from a dementia, geropsychologists may also administer psychological interventions to improve the functioning and emotional well-being of family caregivers. Effective caregiver interventions may serve the beneficial purpose of delaying the older adult's entry into a long-term care setting.

Future of Clinical Geropsychology

The future of clinical geropsychology depends on the achievement of a number of tasks, such as increasing the number of qualified clinicians, expanding the number of available treatments for late-life psychiatric disorders, increasing funding and expanding access for mental health services for older adults, and figuring out how to make mental health interventions acceptable and easily available for as many older adults as possible. Prevention and treatment programs must be incorporated into the health care and community settings where older adults are already receiving services, as this may partly bypass the stigma that many older people currently associate with mental health treatment. Geropsychologist involvement in key public policy initiatives such as creating parity for mental health coverage in insurance plans may also lead to improved access to mental health services for older adults.

Future geropsychological research should focus on identifying factors associated with healthy and adaptive aging, characterizing late-life psychiatric disorders, and clarifying the differences between early- and later-onset disorders. Future psychotherapy treatment research should improve upon and expand the number of useful psychotherapy treatments for late-life mental health problems. Finally, in order to generate treatments for older adults whose well-being is most at risk, psychotherapy research should extend its focus beyond diagnostic categories, to older adults whose mental disorders and symptoms place them most at risk for disabling functional impairment.

Beth L. Cook
Patricia Aveán
University of California

See also: **Aging and Intelligence; Geriatric Psychology; Human Development**

CLINICAL GRADUATE TRAINING IN PSYCHOLOGY

Clinical graduate training has undergone many changes during the past 50 years. The American Psychological Association (APA) responded to an increased need for psychological services after World War II by developing a model curriculum for the training of psychologists. In 1948, the APA granted accreditation to 35 doctoral programs. In 1949, the Boulder Conference promulgated a scientist-practitioner model for instruction. Although many institutions continue to adhere to this model, the 1973 Vail Conference proffered a scholar-practitioner approach that ultimately led to the granting of the Doctor of Psychology (Psy.D.) degree. This model emphasized practice-related skills with less focus on the production of research. U.S.-trained doctoral-level applied psychologists may have the Ph.D., Psy.D., or Ed.D., and all complete a 12-month applied internship as an integral component of their education. Many new graduates elect to complete postdoctoral training to specialize or enhance skills.

New Mexico became the first state to pass legislation that grants psychologists the authority to prescribe psychotropic medication. As psychopharmacology becomes an aspect of psychological expertise, the type of graduate training psychologists undergo may significantly change. It is possible that an increased emphasis on the biological aspects of behavior and psychopharmacology may occur.

This may lead some departments to require natural science prerequisites for admission. However, if training to prescribe is limited to postdoctoral education, there may be little change in the graduate curriculum. The course work heavily emphasizing psychopharmacology would, in that model, take place only within specialty training after completion of the graduate degree.

The APA guidelines for professional psychology programs (APA, 1996) focus on student competencies. This requires doctoral programs and internship centers to determine the skills they want their trainees to demonstrate and to develop evaluative methodologies.

Competencies

Competencies are practical, flexible, observable, and measurable (Stratford, 1994). To be practical, a competency must consist of a manageable number of subskills. To be flexible, it must allow for a variety of approaches. This allows students to follow through with the task in a manner that best suits their development and the circumstances or that most effectively addresses the research topic.

After relevant skills are determined, a method of measuring designated target behaviors is developed. For example, competency in the administration of the Wechsler Scale may be verified by use of the Administrative Checklist for the WAIS-III (Sattler & Ryan, 2001). The competency approach understands that a minimal standard must be set and that, if that standard is not met, one is not considered competent (Fantuzzo, 1984).

Developmental Issues in Competency Assessment

Many (e.g., Hogan, 1964; Stoltenberg, 1981) consider the acquisition of psychotherapeutic skills and their evaluation from a developmental perspective. Novices need information and are learning to comprehend fundamental principles. Thus, entry-level skills are best evaluated by the use of tests (Chambers & Glassman, 1997).

Students who are more advanced can be assessed through simulation. This may entail an evaluation of the individual's breadth of knowledge as well as hands-on performance in scenarios that closely emulate actual practice. Training methods might include problem-based learning, close supervision in practica, and the writing of research proposals.

When students' competency levels will soon allow them to function autonomously, direct evaluation is required. This may involve research studies, record reviews, a portfolio approach, case presentations, or some combination of these (Chambers & Glassman, 1997).

Core Body of Knowledge

The APA (1996) criteria concerning the elements of psychological knowledge that should be acquired by students include the biological, cognitive, affective, and social aspects of behavior. Additional domains of study include the history of the field, psychological assessment, research methods, individual differences, ethics, human development, psychopathology, psychodiagnosis, intervention, cultural differences, and the attitudes that facilitate problem solving, scholarly investigation, and lifelong learning.

Building on a strong psychological knowledge base, the National Council of Schools and Programs in Professional Psychology (Peterson et al., 1991) proposed competency areas presented here in a modified form (Sumerall, Lopez, & Oehlert, 2000):

Relationship refers to the capacity to develop and maintain a constructive working alliance with clients.

Assessment is an ongoing, interactive, and inclusive process that serves to describe, conceptualize, characterize, and predict relevant aspects of a client.

Intervention consists of activities that promote, restore, sustain, or enhance positive functioning in clients through preventive, developmental, or remedial services. The concept of empirically validated treatments has gained acceptance, and a task force within Division 12 (Clinical) of the APA has published a listing of such interventions (Task Force, 1993).

Intervention competencies may be divided into those for individuals, couples, families, and groups as well as infants, children, adolescents, adults, and the elderly. They may be classified according to complexity or acuteness of the presenting problem. Areas to consider include dual diagnoses, cognitive impairment, social or familial impairment, chronic psychosis, and severe personality disorders.

Research involves a systematic inquiry that focuses on problem identification and the acquisition, organization, and interpretation of information pertaining to psychological phenomena. Students become involved in research early in the educational process and assist with ongoing studies prior to initiating the thesis or dissertation.

Education is the enhancement of knowledge, skills, and attitudes in the learner, whether a student, client, allied professional, or family caregiver.

Management includes activities that direct, organize, or control the services that psychologists and other professionals offer or render to the public.

Advanced clinical skills are areas of expertise represented by specialties such as neuropsychology, forensic practice, and, possibly in the future, psychopharmacology.

Ethics involves the acquisition of strategies for addressing conflicts in principle ethics (e.g., how one should act in specific situations; Meara, Schmidt, & Day,

1996) and virtue ethics (educating professionals to be a certain type of person (e.g., competent, honest, etc.).

Attitudes can refer to professionalism and professional development.

Summary

Graduate education in professional psychology involves training in a broad array of psychological skills, knowledge areas, and applied experiences. As the field matures, new clinical interventions, possibly including psychopharmacology, will be incorporated into the training students receive. The creation of new knowledge and the ability to evaluate and utilize research literature will continue to be an important component of graduate education.

REFERENCES

American Psychological Association (APA), Office of Program Consultation and Accreditation. (1996). *Book 1: Guidelines and principles for accreditation of programs in professional psychology.* Washington, DC: Author.

American Psychological Association (APA), Task Force on Promotion and Dissemination of Psychological Procedures. (1993). *A report adopted by Division 12 Board.* Washington, DC: Author.

Chambers, D. W., & Glassman, P. (1997). A primer on competency-based evaluation. *Journal of Dental Education, 61,* 651–666.

Fantuzzo, J. W. (1984). Mastery: A competency-based training model for clinical psychologists. *The Clinical Psychologist, 37*(1), 29–30.

Hogan, R. A. (1964). Issues and approaches in supervision. *Psychotherapy: Theory, Research, and Practice, 1,* 139–141.

Meara, N. M., Schmidt, L. D., & Day, J. D. (1996). Principles and virtues: A foundation for ethical decisions, policies, and character. *The Counseling Psychologist, 24,* 4–77.

Peterson, R. L., McHolland, J. D., Bent, R. J., Davis-Russell, E., Edwall, G. E., Polite, K., et al. (Eds.). (1991). *The core curriculum in professional psychology.* Washington, DC: American Psychological Association.

Sattler, J. M., & Ryan, J. J. (2001). Wechsler Adult Intelligence Scale-III: WAIS-III description. In J. M. Sattler (Ed.), *Assessment of children: Cognitive applications* (4th ed., pp. 375–414). San Diego, CA: Jerome M. Sattler.

Stoltenberg, C. (1981). Approaching supervision from a developmental perspective: The counselor complexity model. *Journal of Counseling Psychology, 28,* 59–65.

Stratford, R. (1994). A competency approach to educational psychology practice: The implications for quality. *Educational and Child Psychology, 11,* 21–28.

Sumerall, S. W., Lopez, S. J., & Oehlert, M. E. (2000). *Competency-based education and training in psychology: A primer.* Springfield, IL: Charles C. Thomas.

Scott W. Sumerall
William Jewell College

Joseph J. Ryan
Central Missouri State University

CLINICAL JUDGMENT

Clinical judgment is the cognitive process by which a clinician estimates a clinically relevant parameter for an individual patient or client; it also refers to the product of that process (the parameter itself). Accuracy in clinical judgment is presumed to be acquired through experience and to be associated with expertise.

Although there are many parameters that a clinician might estimate, the two most important classes of parameters are, broadly speaking, probabilities of a clinical event and values for clinical states. Clinical probability judgment comprises judgments of probabilities in the absence of individuating information and judgments of probabilities conditional on individuating information. In several clinical fields, the clinical judgment of the probability of an outcome is referred to as the *index of suspicion* associated with the outcome.

In the first case, the clinician must estimate the likelihood of some outcome on the basis of his or her knowledge of and previous experience with the outcome (e.g., that a new patient will be schizophrenic or allergic to penicillin). In principle, the novice clinician ought to do this by retrieving information about the frequency of the outcome that he or she has learned during his or her clinical education, while the more experienced clinician is likely to treat the judgment as a pattern-matching task and assess the likelihood of outcomes on the basis of their similarity to prototypical outcomes with which the clinician has familiarity and whose relative frequency the clinician knows. In medicine, Geoff Norman, Georges Bordage, and Larry Gruppen have been influential in the description of the semantic and cognitive structures underlying these pattern-matching judgments.

The psychological literature, particularly the work of Daniel Kahneman and Amos Tversky in the 1970s and 1980s, suggests that probability judgments are often subject to systematic biases, particularly those produced by the availability heuristic (the probability of recent and memorable outcomes is overestimated). In medicine, students are often given maxims like "when you hear hoofbeats, think of a horse, not a zebra" to encourage them to consider common diseases before rare ones.

In the second case, the clinician is attempting to revise his or her belief about the patient's status on the basis of individuating information, such as patient history, physical examination, or diagnostic testing. For example, a clinical psychologist may wish to estimate the probability that the client is schizophrenic, conditional on the score of the client's Minnesota Multiphasic Personality Inventory (MMPI). Bayes' theorem is the normative model for revision of probability judgments on the basis of new evidence, but formal Bayesian calculations require the clinician to specify not only his or her prior belief about the patient's status but also the likelihood ratio associated with the individuating information, and Bayes' theorem makes independence assumptions that can be difficult to meet in clinical practice. Hal Arkes and several other psychological researchers have characterized clinical judgment as insufficiently Bayesian and reported both inappropriate conservatism in judgments (failure to revise beliefs sufficiently) and inappropriate disregard for prior probabilities (resulting in too much revision). The use of pattern-matching strategies based on a representative heuristic (how representative the case is of the prototype) can also lead to systematic biases. However, it is unclear how frequently these biases impact clinical judgments in the real world and how important their impact is.

Probability judgments alone are rarely sufficient to make a clinical decision, because the values of a correct diagnosis, a correctly rejected misdiagnosis, a missed diagnosis (a false negative), and a false positive diagnosis are often different. Accordingly, the other major class of clinical judgments is estimations of the value that patients or clients will place on an outcome. Although clinicians can often directly ask their patients to evaluate the impact of outcomes on their quality of life, in many circumstances clinicians find themselves acting as surrogate judges of value as well as probability.

As with probability judgments, clinical value judgments have been shown to be susceptible to several systematic biases. Arthur Elstein and his colleagues have documented several of these biases since their research program began in the late 1960s. Most of these biases, however, are also at work in patients or clients making their own value judgments, and they are not specific to clinical judgment. Although some studies have demonstrated that surrogate clinical judgments are poor predictors of direct judgment by patients, other studies have found good correspondence between surrogate and personal values in some aspects of value judgment, such as the rate at which future events are discounted in evaluations.

Several approaches to the measurement of the quality of clinical judgment have been suggested. The most common is to measure calibration of probability judgments. In a well-calibrated clinician, events judged to have a given probability actually occur with that relative frequency. For example, events that the clinician considers 70% likely should actually occur 70% of the times that the clinician makes the judgment. Neal Dawson has reviewed three more sophisticated approaches: receiver operating characteristic curves, mean probability scores, and Brunswickian lens model analyses. The quality of clinical value judgments must usually be assessed by their association with direct judgments of outcome values by the patients or clients involved. Multiattribute utility approaches can also be applied to attempt to determine if the clinician places the same relative weights on the dimensions of the outcome that the patient or client does.

Because unaided clinical judgment may be subject to several systematic biases, many clinical areas rely on guidelines, scoring rules, or other algorithms as judgmental aids. These aids may call attention to important cues or dimensions to consider in the judgment, warn against the use of irrelevant cues, or even prescribe a formula for combining observed cues and prior beliefs to provide an estimate of the object of judgment. Research by Paul Meehl, Robyn Dawes, and other psychologists has repeatedly demonstrated that even simplified statistical prediction rules can outperform clinical prediction in a variety of situations. Although some guidelines have been successfully introduced in clinical fields, many are applied inconsistently or run afoul of practitioners' beliefs that their clinical judgment is likely to be superior to a guideline.

Alan Schwartz
University of Illinois, Chicago

COGNITIVE MAPS

A cognitive map represents the relative locations of points in space, making it possible for an animal to orient itself toward a point that has no distinctive cues. Tolman appears to have coined the term and to have applied it to maze learning in rats. His cognitive map hypothesis was tentatively supported by data from his laboratory, namely the sudden drop in errors with the initial introduction of a food reward in a previously explored complex maze and appropriate responding in so-called insight and alternative path studies. Similarly, Maier's three-table-reasoning problem assumed that a successful rat knew the position of each table with respect to the other two tables.

Later, Olton provided somewhat more convincing evidence for the hypothesis of cognitive maps. Using an eight-arm radial maze, Olton and associates studied spatial memory in the rat by removing the food pellet at the end of each alley once it had been visited on the trial. The rats soon learned, to almost an errorless level, to enter only an arm that had not been previously visited. Rats perform well with controlled odor cues or odor trails, go to the appropriate spatial location even when the maze is rotated, and do not learn fixed sequences that could function independently of spatial memories.

Morris tested the cognitive map hypothesis directly by requiring rats to locate a slightly submerged platform in a tank of water made opaque by adding milk. Once the maze is learned from the one starting point, the rat can be dropped into any point in the tank and it sets a course more or less directly toward the platform, as consistent with a cognitive map.

One animal that clearly has a cognitive map, one that may be superior to that of humans, is the chimpanzee. This was first observed by Tinklepaugh in his study of multiple delayed response using 16 different containers situated as equally spaced pairs in a large circle. One member of each pair, on the left or the right, was baited while the subject (chimpanzee, human adult, or human child) watched. After a short delay, the subject was free to find the hidden object for each pair. Children did very poorly on this task, and chimpanzees were slightly superior to human adults, having a success rate of more than 70%, even when the baiting was done in a random fashion, which would seem to rule out unintentional cuing by the experimenters because they did not remember where things were either.

Birds also seem to have cognitive maps. For example, marsh tits exhibit good spatial memory for seeds that they have hoarded in a variety of cache locations. They also avoid earlier used but now empty holes. These memories probably reflect species-specific adaptations. The birds are very poor in finding seeds stored in holes by an experimenter, which rules out smell as a basis for detecting seed locations.

Bees clearly use landmarks around sources of nectar to locate the substance, but recent evidence suggests that this local map consists of route-based memories rather than a cognitive map of a familiar landscape, as with humans and other vertebrates. A study by Whishaw on latent learning in a swimming pool task raises questions about the rats' use of cognitive mapping, because of strong evidence for the use of associative processing.

Denny provides information on how cognitive maps are established. Visual recognition and ability to move about in a spatial layout were tested following single-route or multiple-route training of the space solely through kinesthesis (by means of blind hand movements among points on a plane). Single-route training, in spite of much more practice on the target route, failed to yield better learning of the route than multiple-route training and produced a much poorer cognitive map, as judged from kinesthetic and visual transfer tasks. Certain conclusions seem justified: (1) the more varied the initial experience, the more abstract and less egocentric (individual-referenced) the representation of space becomes, and (2) active experiencing of space produces a representation of the space as a coordinated whole—one that transcends the individual links (paths) between locations. The whole is known better than its parts.

M. R. Denny

See also: **Reinforcement**

COGNITIVE NEUROSCIENCE

The study of the neural basis of cognition, or cognitive neuroscience, has evolved rapidly in the last 10 years. In large part this has resulted from the parallel advances in imaging technology and raw computing power. Indeed, the exponential growth and concomitant movement of extraordinarily powerful computers to the desktop has made routine the analysis of large, complex data sets. Cognitive neuroscience is an enterprise that depends heavily on the use of modern imaging technologies such as positron emission tomography and functional magnetic resonance imaging (fMRI), and because of this reliance on technology, the ability to look noninvasively at the functionings of the human brain has only become possible very recently.

The fundamental goal of the cognitive neuroscientist is to understand the neural basis of the human mind. Historically, the mind had been thought to be separate from the body. Rene Descartes, the eighteenth-century French philosopher-mathematician, was perhaps the most vociferous advocate of mind-body dualism. The question of where the human mind, perhaps even the soul, resides has plagued humanity for at least as long as written records exist. Until recently, there was no reason to suspect that the mind might have components that were tied to the body. After all, this notion might be discordant with the belief of the immortality of the soul—if the body dies, then so does the mind. Descartes circumvented the problem by separating the mind from the body, and therefore the brain.

Mind-body dualism did not last long. Neurologists of the nineteenth century began to notice that patients with specific brain injuries, either from stroke or trauma, displayed consistent behavioral deficits. Pierre Paul Broca, a French neurologist, systematically described the effect of lesions in the left frontal cortex on language. Insightfully, he was the first to state that language was localized to the left cerebral hemisphere. This opened the door for an explosion of cognitive localization in the brain. In its extreme form, phrenology, every function of the human mind could be localized to some bump or valley in the brain (and skull). The use of brain lesions to deduce brain function subsequently became the predominant method for exploring the mind/brain for the next 100 years.

The lesion method truly was the first cognitive neuroscience technique. Its growth paralleled the recognition of other types of deficiency syndromes in medicine. The lesion method relied solely on the power of observation and a ready supply of patients with various types of brain injury. The history of the field is full of references to famous patients whose unfortunate circumstances led to some insight about the functioning of some particular brain region. Phineas Gage, perhaps the first famous patient, was a nineteenth-century railroad worker who had an iron rod accidentally driven upwards from just below his left eye out through the top of his skull. Remarkably, he lived for another decade, and his subsequent change in personality from a reliable and steady worker to a profane, erratic, and irascible man was aptly characterized by his physician at the time: "Gage was no longer Gage."

The father of modern psychology, William James, was

attuned to these advancements in understanding the brain in the late nineteenth century. Further evidence linking brain function to cognitive processing continued to amass. The observation that regional changes in cerebral blood flow were tied to mental function can be traced to the fortuitous discovery in a patient with an arteriovenous malformation in his frontal lobe. This patient (and his physician) noticed an increase in audible blood pulsation when performing mental calculation. This observation, that local changes in cerebral blood flow are linked to neural activity, underlies all of modern functional imaging techniques.

The parallel development of new imaging technologies with increased computational power in the late twentieth century resulted in the development of two new methods to study human brain function. Positron emission tomography (PET) developed as an outgrowth of autoradiography. Unlike its predecessor, PET could be performed without the requirement of sacrificing the animal. PET takes advantage of the fact that when a positron (a positively charged electron) encounters an electron, the two particles annihilate each other, and two high-energy gamma rays are emitted in exactly opposite directions. When a series of gamma-ray detectors are arranged in a ring, the origin of the particle can be computed. Positron emitters can be synthesized into common molecules, like water or 2-deoxyglucose, and when injected into a subject they can be used to map cerebral blood flow or metabolism respectively. Similarly, fMRI relies on the coupling of neural activity to local cerebral blood flow. Current thinking suggests that transient increases in neural activity result in a hyperremic blood flow response. Oxygenated hemoglobin and deoxygenated hemoglobin have different magnetic properties, and because the increase in blood flow results in a transient increase in the oxy-deoxy ratio, this can be detected with MRI. By rapidly acquiring MRIs while a subject is performing a cognitive task in the scanner, one can correlate the changes in blood flow to what the subject is doing.

Although PET and fMRI typically measure only relative changes in brain activity, through careful experimental design it is possible to isolate the neural circuits associated with specific cognitive processes. The basis for this is called *subtractive design*. When an experiment is designed with at least two cognitive conditions, one of which is a control state, the brain activity maps obtained during the control state can be subtracted from the brain activity during the condition of interest. In actual practice, a statistical test is usually performed instead of a simple subtraction, but the assumption is that whatever brain regions show different activity between the conditions represent the circuit associated with processing the extra information. It is critical that the control state be chosen appropriately. Otherwise, one might be subtracting cognitive states that are so different from one another that the assumptions of this method are violated. In particular, subtraction assumes that cognitive process behave linearly: that is, that processes can be added and subtracted without interacting with each other. This may be true under some circumstances, but not all.

In general, the subtractive approach to imaging has confirmed what was known from the lesion method, but recent advances in fMRI have allowed the description of more subtle processes. By presenting subjects with very brief stimuli, we can measure the cerebral blood flow response and correlate it with individual events. This goes beyond the subtractive approach, which often requires the subject to maintain a cognitive state for tens of seconds to minutes. Event-related fMRI measures the brain response on a scale less than a second, which is much closer to the time scale at which the brain operates. New computational algorithms are also revealing the complex correlations that occur between different brain regions, which begins to reveal the choreography of brain activity that must be the hallmark of cognition. With the combination of rapid imaging and new algorithms, perhaps the elusive goal of identifying the neural basis of the mind will be achieved.

Gregory S. Berns
Emory University School of Medicine

COGNITIVE NEUROSCIENCE OF LEARNING AND MEMORY

Cognitive neuroscience approaches, with their focus on relating neural substrates to cognitive functions, have advanced our understanding of the neural basis of learning and memory. In turn, our understanding of the neural basis has informed the way we think about the functional organization of memory systems. One of the most prominent themes in cognitive neuroscience has been trying to understand which kinds of learning and memory are spared, and which are impaired, with damage to the *hippocampus* (a specialized brain structure in the medial temporal lobe).

We have known for many decades that the hippocampus plays a disproportionately important role in learning and memory, since Scoville and Milner (1957) presented the famous patient HM. HM had severe memory impairments following bilateral medial temporal lobe lesions that included the hippocampus. Despite these severe impairments, including the inability to learn all kinds of factual information (names, places, facts, etc.), HM was nevertheless able to learn to perform new tasks (e.g., tracing while looking into a mirror). Many different attempts have been made to precisely characterize what distinguishes these preserved learning abilities from those that are impaired (e.g., Squire, 1992; Schacter, 1987; Sutherland & Rudy, 1989; Cohen & Eichenbaum, 1993; Rolls, 1990). Many of these ideas emphasize a *procedural* (e.g., sensorimotor task learning) or *implicit* (i.e., not explicitly verbalizable) aspect of preserved learning abilities, which is consistent with the data from HM.

Computational neural network models, which simulate cognitive functions using networks of neuron like processing units constrained according to known properties of different brain areas, have provided a more precise language for understanding the unique contribution of the hippocampus in learning in memory (O'Reilly & Rudy, 2001). These models show that there is a basic computational conflict between two essential kinds of learning: the ability to rapidly learn specific novel information without interfering with previous knowledge, and the ability to learn about the generalities or regularities of the environment. Therefore, it makes sense that two different brain areas should each separately achieve these learning objectives. Biological and behavioral evidence coincide with this computational argument in suggesting that the hippocampus is specialized for the rapid learning of specific information, while the cortex is better suited for learning generalities.

The computationally motivated division of labor between the cortex and hippocampus is consistent with recent data from individuals who suffered selective hippocampal damage early in life. These people were able to learn all kinds of general information (e.g., language skills, semantic knowledge about the world) and had IQ scores in the normal range, yet they suffered from the inability to rapidly encode novel information as measured by *episodic* memory tests (Vargha-Khadem et al., 1997). Note that these data violate earlier notions that hippocampal damage spares only procedural or implicit learning, whereas the computational notions based on underlying neural mechanisms provide a more general framework that encompasses these data.

The cognitive neuroscience–based theories can inform our understanding of performance on the kinds of basic memory tasks that psychologists have been studying for many years. For example, many are now arguing that recognition memory (the ability to recognize an item as having been recently studied or not) can be subserved by two different neural systems having different functional properties (e.g., Aggleton & Brown, 1999; Norman & O'Reilly, in press; Yonelinas, 2002). One of these systems is the hippocampus, which can provide an explicit *recollection* signal (i.e., recalling specific aspects of the study episode), while the other is subserved by cortical areas surrounding the hippocampus, which can provide an indistinct sense of *familiarity.* As recent brain imaging techniques (functional magnetic resonance imaging [fMRI], positron emission tomography [PET], and event-related potentials [ERP]) improve their ability to resolve active representations in various memory tasks (e.g., Buckner & Koutstaal, 1998; Henson, Rugg, & Dolan, 1999), we should be able to test even more sophisticated and nuanced theories of the cognitive neuroscience of learning and memory.

REFERENCES

Aggleton, J. P., & Brown, M. W. (1999). Episodic memory, amnesia, and the hippocampal-anterior thalamic axis. *Behavioral and Brain Sciences, 22,* 425–490.

Buckner, R. L., & Koutstaal, W. (1998). Functional neuroimaging studies of encoding, priming, and explicit memory retrieval. *Proceedings of the National Academy of Sciences, 95,* 891.

Cohen, N. J., & Eichenbaum, H. (1993). *Memory, amnesia, and the hippocampal system.* Cambridge, MA: MIT Press.

Henson, R. N. A., Rugg, M. D., & Dolan, R. J. (1999). Recollection and familiarity in recognition memory: An event-related functional magnetic resonance imaging study. *Journal of Neuroscience, 19,* 3962–3972.

Norman, K. A., & O'Reilly, R. C. (2003). Modeling hippocampal and neocortical contributions to recognition memory: A complementary learning systems approach. *Psychological Review, 110,* 601–643

O'Reilly, R. C., & Rudy, J. W. (2001). Conjunctive representations in learning and memory: Principles of cortical and hippocampal function. *Psychological Review, 108,* 311–345.

Rolls, E. T. (1990). Principles underlying the representation and storage of information in neuronal networks in the primate hippocampus and cerebral cortex. In S. F. Zornetzer, J. L. Davis, & C. Lau (Eds.), *An introduction to neural and electronic networks* (pp. 73–90). San Diego, CA: Academic Press.

Schacter, D. L. (1987). Implicit memory: History and current status. *Journal of Experimental Psychology: Learning, Memory, and Cognition, 13*(3), 501–518.

Scoville, W. B., & Milner, B. (1957). Loss of recent memory after bilateral hippocampal lesions. *Journal of Neurology, Neurosurgery, and Psychiatry, 20,* 11–21.

Squire, L. R. (1992). Memory and the hippocampus: A synthesis from findings with rats, monkeys, and humans. *Psychological Review, 99,* 195–231.

Sutherland, R. J., & Rudy, J. W. (1989). Configural association theory: The role of the hippocampal formation in learning, memory, and amnesia. *Psychobiology, 17*(2), 129–144.

Vargha-Khadem, F., Gadian, D. G., Watkins, K. E., Connelly, A., Van Paesschen, W., & Mishkin, M. (1997). Differential effects of early hippocampal pathology on episodic and semantic memory. *Science, 277,* 376–380.

Yonelinas, A. P. (2002). The nature of recollection and familiarity: A review of 30 years of research. *Journal of Memory and Language, 46,* 441–517.

Randall C. O'Reilly
University of Colorado, Boulder

COGNITIVE PSYCHOPHYSIOLOGY

Cognitive psychophysiology is an interdisciplinary field overlapping psychology and physiology in which efforts are made to solve the classical problem of "mind" through modern electronic technology. The primary thesis is that mental processes are generated when selective bodily systems interact and that they can be directly studied with sufficiently sensitive equipment. The bodily systems include the receptors (eyes, ears, etc.), central nervous system (principally the brain), skeletal musculature, autonomic system (the gastrointestinal tract, the cardiovascular system, etc.), and their neural interconnections. The field's interdisciplinary nature is exemplified by the presence of researchers from psychology, physiology, medicine, and biomedical engineering.

Approaches to the problem of mind, dating from the time of ancient philosophers, may be summarily classified as either *dualistic* or *monistic.* Traditionally, dualistic positions have been the most popular, even as they are today in everyday thinking. The basic assumption of dualism is that there are two kinds of entities in the world, those of a physical (material) and those of a mental (nonmaterial) nature; furthermore, in dualism only physical events are knowable by science. Monism, however, holds that the universe consists of only one kind of entity. The principal monistic position is that of strict materialism, which holds that there are only physical phenomena in the universe. According to materialistic monism, therefore, mental processes are physical phenomena generated within the body and can therefore be directly observed through scientific technology.

Contemporary Assessment of the Problem of Mind

In considering where in the body thoughts occur, objectivity demands that we avoid predisposing biases and consider that any bodily system might serve some cognitive function until empirically established otherwise. However, the reactions of these systems are often so subtle that they are referred to as *covert* (versus *overt*). Covert reactions are such small-scale bodily processes that they cannot be observed with the naked eye; hence they must be amplified in the laboratory to be studied, as in the case of brain waves or heart activity.

Cognitive psychophysiologists, specializing in different bodily systems and using extremely sensitive procedures, have now been successful in measuring covert reactions *throughout* the body during cognitive activities. Furthermore, it has been established that these events occur in close temporal proximity to one another and are systematically (often causally) related. The conclusion is inescapable that widespread covert reactions in the receptors, brain, muscles, and autonomic system are intricately linked through complex neuromuscular circuits that have cybernetic (feedback or servoloop) characteristics.

The Transition From Mechanical to Electronic Methods

Around the turn of the twentieth century, researchers eagerly attempted to construct "thought-reading machines" with what tools were then available. With the advent of the vacuum tube, these crude mechanical methods gave way to the sensitive electronic techniques that were critical for the advancement of cognitive psychophysiology. Thus, about 1921, primitive electromyographs for recording electrical components of muscle activity became available. The first recording of electroencephalograms was by Hans Berger in 1929, empirically establishing that the brain generates electrical signals (although Berger's findings were greeted with skepticism for many years). The galvanic skin response and other measures of autonomic activity during emotion had been initiated in the late nineteenth century (especially with Feré in 1888); such autonomic measures were important in the early development of cognitive psychophysiology, as they continue to be today.

There are four essential features of a cognitive psychophysiological laboratory for electrically studying covert bodily events: (1) *sensors,* usually electrodes placed over the brain and on the surface of the skin to detect electrical components of neural, muscular, and glandular phenomena; (2) *amplifiers,* which increase the amplitude of the body signal sensed; (3) *readout devices,* such as cathode ray oscilloscopes or recorders, which can display the covert body signals; and (4) *quantification systems,* which render numerical values for those signals.

A number of the more commonly measured psychophysiological events are classified in Table 1. The primary division is between *responses* of the muscular and glandular systems and *neurophysiological* processes of the central nervous system.

The first two response classes in Table 1, those of the skeletal musculature in the speech and somatic regions, are best measured electrically through electromyography. *Myo,* standing for muscle, and *graph,* for writing, form the term for recording electrical components of muscle activity.

Covert eye behavior, the third response category in Table

Table 1. Covert Psychophysiological Events in Humans

I. Covert Responses (muscular and glandular events)
   A. Covert speech responses: electromyographic measures from the tongue, lip, chin, cheek, laryngeal, and jaw regions
   B. Covert somatic responses: electromyographic measures of the skeletal musculature from the fingers, arms, legs, etc.
   C. Covert eye responses, principally through electrooculography
   D. Covert autonomic responses
      1. Cardiovascular measures such as heart rate, electrocardiogram, finger pulse volume, and blood pressure
      2. Visceral muscle activity principally from the intestines, as the electrogastrogram
      3. Electrodermal measures from the surface of the skin (galvanic skin response, skin conductance, etc.)

II. Neurophysiological Processes
   Electrical activity from the brain, recorded with electroencephalography, through signal averaging, yields average evoked potentials, and the contingent negative variation.

1, is typically recorded through electrooculography, where *oculo* refers to the eyes.

The last response class, that for autonomic behavior, consists of a variety of subcategories. Common autonomic components include: (1) measures of heart (cardiac) activity through electrocardiography; (2) activity of the intestinal portion of the gastrointestinal tract, which, when electrically recorded, yields the electrogastrogram; and (3) electrodermal measures of skin (dermal) activity, most prominently the galvanic skin response measured with the psychogalvanometer.

The second major category in Table 1 is for electrical signals from the brain. These include such well-known events as alpha waves (large amplitude, cyclical waves) and beta waves (lower in amplitude than alpha waves but greater in frequency).

With the entrance of the small electronic computer into the laboratory, however, it became possible to *average* brain waves to expose intrinsic signals not discernible in the raw traces.

Direct Electrical Measurement of Mental Processes

Individual experiments have established that each of the events specified in Table 1 occurs during cognitive experiences (although the grand experiment of simultaneously recording all those measures has not been attempted). The various mental events are *similar,* then, in that they all involve covert activities throughout the body, including the brain.

The *unique* mentalistic terms for mental events exist because the experiences occur under different environmental and organismic conditions. Night dreams, daydreams, and directed rational thought all differ, for instance, because of the degree to which they are influenced by environmental input. During "sleep thoughts" or images of night dreams, most environmental stimulation is physiologically shut off, apparently at the reticular activating system. Consequently, the mental activity of dreaming is chaotic, since it is not directed by external reality, or, as one psychiatrist put it, a night dream allows us all to go safely insane for a brief period of time. Similar mental processes occur in the daydream, but they are partially influenced by the external environment. During directed problem solving, rational thought processes are largely controlled by repeated reference to the environment.

Hallucinations—false perceptions that the patient confuses with real ones—are akin to night dreams in that they are controlled by internal stimuli, although they are mistakenly ascribed to external forces. Neuromuscular circuits that generate visual hallucinations presumably include the occipital lobe at the back of the brain and the eyes. Auditory hallucinations are similarly thought to be generated when auditory and linguistic regions of the brain interact with muscles of the ears and speech. Auditory hallucinations, for instance, seem to be produced when the patient subvocalizes, as indicated by auditory and electromyographical recording of covert speech (Figure 1).

Figure 1. A sample tracing of the report of a hallucination. The 2-sec intervals before and after the report are marked on the event line at the top. Next in order are the pneumogram, arm electromyogram, chin electromyogram, tongue electromyogram, and the sound record. The increase in chin electromyographic activity and in subvocalization (bottom trace) coincide with the hallucinatory experience.

Auditory components of night dreams are apparently generated by neuromuscular circuits like those for auditory hallucinations. Figure 2 illustrates small-scale, rapid covert muscle activity in the lips and chin when one experiences conversations in dreams. These covert speech responses are not present during visual dreams or nondreaming periods.

Deaf individuals who are not proficient in oral speech use dactylic ("sign" or "manual") language for communication. The muscles for the fingers therefore are the locus of

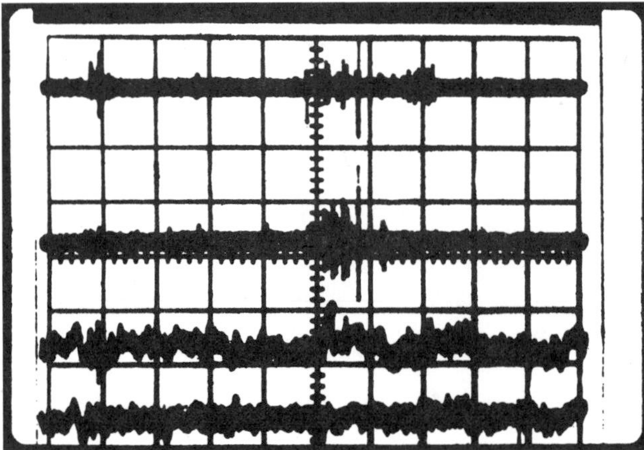

Figure 2. Illustration of signals during a conversational dream. From the top down, the signals are lip electromyogram, chin electromyogram, horizontal eye placement, and frontal electroencephalogram. Amplitude for the top three traces is 50 μV/division, and 100 μV/division for the electroencephalogram. Time is 1 sec/division.

their linguistic response mechanisms. For them, consequently, the speech musculature is not engaged during thought. Instead, they make covert finger responses when thinking. In addition, individuals who are proficient in both oral and manual language processes engage both the speech musculature and the fingers covertly during thought.

Technological Consequences

As from all scientific fields, a number of practical applications flow from cognitive psychophysiology, perhaps the most important being principles for self-regulation. As one continuously meets the stresses of life, there often eventuates some bodily malfunction. The primitive reaction of the body to stress is characterized as the startle reflex, a major component of which is the tensing of the skeletal musculature for fight or flight. Chronic states of excess tension throughout the skeletal musculature can result in two classes of bodily malfunctions: (1) psychiatric difficulties such as anxiety states, phobias, and depression; and (2) psychosomatic maladies such as ulcers, headaches, spastic colon, and elevated blood pressure. The original and apparently most effective method for alleviating these tension maladies is progressive relaxation, developed by Edmund Jacobson from 1908 on. In progressive relaxation one relaxes the skeletal muscle system, which in turn produces a state of tranquility throughout the central and autonomic nervous systems. Jacobson has shown that habitual relaxation can thereby alleviate many psychiatric and psychosomatic maladies such as those mentioned previously. However, perhaps the prophylactic application of progressive relaxation has even greater beneficial consequences. For this purpose Jacobson has advocated that tension control be universally taught to children while in the primary grades.

Another prominent method aimed at the development of self-regulation is biofeedback, in which internal processes are transduced to make them publicly observable. The strategy is to monitor and thus control such internal events as brain waves, muscle signals, and electrodermal responses by visually observing them as on a cathode ray oscilloscope or by hearing them through an external speaker. Biofeedback holds considerable promise for helping us to better understand our internal world; much research is currently in progress in this important area. There are, however, difficulties in its clinical application, such as the dependency of the learner on a biofeedback signal. Consequently, if the desired changes in behavior occur in the clinic, they may not be lasting and generalized to the patient's everyday world. Nevertheless, a revolutionary consequence of biofeedback and progressive relaxation is that they provide the opportunity to study a person's internal world, just as classical psychology has concentrated on our relationship with the external environment.

Another application has been in the understanding of reading and of the teaching of silent reading. It is a common myth that subvocalization—or, more technically, covert speech behavior—retards reading proficiency. Popular speed-reading courses, for instance, seek to increase reading rate by short-circuiting the speech musculature. Some teachers have attempted to prevent subvocalization by taping lips or filling the mouths of pupils with marbles, by wrapping the tongue around a pencil, and so forth. However, such efforts to inhibit subvocalization are futile, for the speech musculature still responds during silent reading even when so inhibited. The empirical generalization is that covert speech behavior occurs in all silent readers and is necessary for comprehending what is being read. Actually, as the reading rate becomes faster, the amount of covert speech behavior does not *decrease,* but *increases.* However, if speech muscles are well relaxed during reading through progressive relaxation, the reader fails to understand the meaning of the text. The implication for teachers, therefore, is that they should not tamper with the child's subvocalization, for the child needs to subvocalize while reading. Actually, subvocalization becomes naturally reduced over time, although it still persists in the adult at a very reduced level.

Lie detection, or more precisely the detection of deception, is a widespread application for espionage purposes, for the identification of criminals, and even as a criterion for employment. The polygraph, which relies heavily on cardiovascular measures, is the most widely used instrument for these purposes. Unfortunately the traditional polygraph, like newer variations of lie detectors such as the psychological stress evaluator and the voice stress analyzer, does not have sufficient validity to justify its standard use. However, techniques and principles are available within the field of cognitive psychophysiology to develop successful deception detection systems, and these systems will undoubtedly be made.

F. J. McGuigan

See also: **Lie Detection; Neurolinguistics; Neuropsychology**

COGNITIVE THEORIES OF EMOTION

Theories of emotion try to explain how emotion is aroused, how it produces physiological changes, and how one emotion differs from another. The answer to the first question distinguishes cognitive theories from other theories of emotion.

Theorists of all persuasions usually agree that anger, fear, or both are aroused when a situation is interpreted as annoying and/or dangerous. Many insist that such arousal is programmed into the nervous system during evolutionary prehistory and serves biological survival. For cognitive psychologists, every emotion is aroused by knowing something and appraising it. No doubt, some appraisals are preprogrammed: Infants like anything sweet the first time they taste it. However, older children and adults appraise what they encounter not only as it affects their bodily well-being but also as it affects them as persons. The child is angry when teased by buddies; the young man, when his pals show him up before his girlfriend. If emotions depend on appraisals, there will be as many different emotions as there are different appraisals. Emotions may be classified, but they need not be derived from one another.

Not surprisingly, cognitive theories have a long history. In the third century B.C., Aristotle suggested in his *De Anima (About the Soul)* that human beings and animals can make sensory judgments (through what he called the *vis estimativa*) of things as being good or bad for them; this estimate arouses an emotion, liking, or dislike. Thomas Aquinas, in his *Commentary,* followed Aristotle in this explanation of emotional arousal.

Descartes insisted that all emotions are aroused directly by exciting the "animal spirits," or by arousing inherent reflex actions together with the physiological changes necessary for survival—a notion shared by Darwin. William James and Carl Lange later reversed the commonsense view that emotion produces bodily changes, by insisting that bodily changes follow directly on the perception of the exciting object: Our sensation of these changes *is* the emotion.

The James-Lange theory of emotion was accepted unquestioningly and soon fatally reduced the interest of academic psychologists in the analysis of emotion.

To say that some situations arouse hereditary patterns is no solution. Fear or anger may arouse flight or attack, but both still depend on a realization that something is threatening or annoying, which is an appraisal, however rudimentary.

M. B. Arnold introduced the notion of appraisal into academic psychology. She defined emotion as "a felt action tendency toward anything intuitively appraised as good, or away from anything intuitively appraised as bad for me here and now," which is "accompanied by a pattern of physiological changes organized toward a specific kind of approach or withdrawal." Arnold distinguished a few basic emotions, simple reactions to the appraisal of basic situations: liking (love), dislike, desire, aversion, joy, sorrow, daring, fear, anger, hope, and despair.

In her book *Emotion and Personality,* Arnold pointed out that emotions depend not only on the intuitive appraisal of something as "good or bad for me," but also on the spontaneous appraisal of possible responses as suitable or unsuitable. Something threatening may be seen as difficult to escape and so arouses fear, or it may be appraised as something that can be anticipated by bold action and so is overcome by a daring attack. Arnold emphasized that the intuitive spontaneous appraisal is supplemented by a deliberate value judgment, at least in the older child and adult, just as sensory knowledge is complemented by conceptual knowledge. Because we use intuitive and reflective appraisals concurrently, even our intuitive judgments generating emotion can be educated. Because the person is a unit, every reflective value judgment will be accompanied by an intuitive appraisal. Value judgments are seldom if ever coldly objective: What is valued, attracts. Hence emotions can be socialized, influenced by social attitudes and customs.

Like other cognitive theorists, Arnold recognizes the importance of the physiological changes that accompany emotion. When these changes are felt, they are again appraised and may either reinforce or change the original emotion. When a person appraises an increased pulse rate during fear as indicating heart disease, the original fear is now overlaid by a fear of illness. By definition, heart disease weakens the body. The fear aroused by the increased pulse rate then dictates the appraisal that, being ill, one will not be able to cope with the situation, which increases the original fear.

Important research in emotion is reported by Richard Lazarus and his coworkers. These scientists make appraisal the cornerstone of their theory of emotion. Lazarus suggests that each emotion is based on a particular kind of cognitive appraisal accompanied by motor-behavioral and physiological changes. He distinguishes primary appraisal, secondary appraisal, and reappraisal. The secondary appraisal is an evaluation of a person's relation to the environment and so leads to an altered emotional response. Reappraisal can occur as a simple evaluation of the significance of this altered relation to the environment, or it may be a psychological attempt at coping with stress. Such a reappraisal is not necessarily based on factual information; it can be an attempt to look at the situation from a more congenial point of view. In Lazarus's terms, it may be a "defensive reappraisal." A reappraisal may also be an attempt at coping when direct action is impossible.

Lazarus and his associates found that the appraisal of a situation and therefore a person's emotional reaction could be manipulated experimentally. Before they showed a harrowing subincision film to the experimental subjects, they read a passage to one group that described the painful procedure at length, and they told another group that the boys in the picture were willing to undergo this initiation ritual and were proud of their stoic endurance. To a third group, finally, they gave intellectualizing information that emphasized the anthropological significance of the ritual. The first group was strongly affected by the film, while the other two groups remained comparatively unaffected.

Although the influence of cognition on appraisal is well documented, the distinction between intuitive and reflective appraisal is more difficult to substantiate. In his article "Feeling and Thinking: Preferences Need no Inferences," R. B. Zajonc pointed out that the notion of the primacy of feeling has languished since Wundt's time. In cognitive psychology it has been replaced by an information-processing scheme in which an affective reaction occurs only after considerable processing. Hence major works on cognition disregard affect or feeling and concentrate exclusively on cognitive processing. Yet, says Zajonc, "affect . . . is the major currency in which social intercourse is transacted." Hence, "to arouse affect, objects need to be cognized very little, in fact, minimally." In recall as in perception, the affective reaction is the first element to emerge. As Zajonc points out, although affect may mark the end of considerable cognitive activity (in listening to a joke, for instance), this need not imply that cognitive activity is a necessary component of affect.

According to Zajonc, there is a separation between affect and cognition. Judgments of similarity and judgments of preference have different dimensions. Early in the twentieth century, T. Nakashima reported in his "Contribution to the Study of Affective Processes" that judgments of pleasantness and unpleasantness are independent of sensory qualities and so cannot be mediated by them. Aesthetic judgments and preferences of all kinds do not depend on cognitive analysis. Experimental investigations have shown that judgments of like and dislike are made and recalled with great certainty, while judgments that a given stimulus word is new or a repeat are made with noticeable uncertainty. Hence Zajonc concludes that the perceptual process, starting from sensory experience, arouses first an unconscious affective reaction, and next produces the recognition of familiar features (also unconscious) before the reflective cognitive processing begins.

We may conclude that Zajonc has exposed a chink in the armor of cognitive psychology. Thinking and reflective judgment seem to depend as much on affect as on sensory experience. Because affect is a conscious experience of attraction/repulsion that is not generated by a reflective value judgment, it must be aroused by the spontaneous (unconscious) appraisal of good/bad objects and suitable/unsuitable responses. Emotions are usually accompanied by reflective judgments, can themselves be appraised as suitable/unsuitable, and can be changed by corrective experiences but rarely by reflection or persuasion.

M. B. Arnold

See also: **Learned Helplessness; Thought Disturbances; Unconscious**

COGNITIVE THERAPY

Definition

Cognitive therapy is a psychotherapeutic approach that teaches individuals that their interpretations of situations influence their emotions, physiological reactions, behaviors, and motivations. Cognitive therapy is a time-effective, structured, collaborative form of treatment that utilizes psychoeducation and psychological skills acquisition. Treatment focuses on helping patients to recognize thematic biases in their thinking; to generate alternative, adaptive viewpoints; and to use new cognitive, behavioral, and experiential strategies to improve mood and enhance problem-solving skills.

History

Aaron T. Beck developed cognitive therapy starting in the early 1960s. While empirically testing Freud's "anger turned inward" theory of depression, Beck instead found that depression involved a negative bias in thinking that often led patients to feel despondent and hopeless. Through clinical observations and research, Dr. Beck refined his cognitive theory of depression and developed techniques (e.g., Socratic questioning, hypothesis testing, cognitive reevaluation, behavioral experiments) to treat patients by modifying their biased thought processes. Beck's developing theory was influenced by ego-oriented psychodynamic psychotherapy (Adler, 1936), developmental cognitive psychology (Piaget, 1954), personal construct therapy (Kelly, 1955), social-learning theory (Bandura, 1977), behavior therapy (Mahoney, 1974), and the phenomenological school of psychology (Frankl, 1985). Beck integrated these diverse approaches into a powerful, new clinical methodology.

Although initially developed as a treatment for unipolar depression (A. T. Beck, Rush, Shaw, & Emery, 1979), cognitive therapy subsequently has been applied to a wider range of psychological disorders (e.g., personality disorders), daily living difficulties, medical problems, and other clinical populations. Cognitive therapy can be used in individual, couples, family, and group formats, with adults, adolescents, and children.

Theory

According to the cognitive model, negatively biased perceptions adversely affect mood and behavior. For example, an individual suffering from depression may experience automatic thoughts centering on self-criticisms or hopelessness about the self, the world, and the future (the *cognitive triad;* see A. T. Beck et al., 1979). These automatic thoughts may demoralize the patient, leading to inertia and a worsening condition, rather than to improvement through active coping. In addition to being identifiable by their *contents,* cognitive biases can be addressed and studied in terms of their *process.* An example is *fortune telling,* in which the individuals assume they know that the outcome of an event necessarily will be negative. This may lead them not only to be pessimistic, but also to prematurely give up trying to attain the goal. This unfavorable outcome reinforces the negative belief, thus causing a vicious cycle that solidifies the emotional distress.

Automatic thoughts are theorized to be produced by more basic, fundamental, all-encompassing beliefs called "negative schemas" (Young, 1999). For example, an individual with an *incompetency* schema, upon being presented with a difficult task, may feel defeated, hopeless, and dysphoric even before trying to accomplish the task. In order to cope with the activation of this core negative schema, the individual develops compensatory behaviors, such as procrastination or other forms of avoidance. Sometimes these compensatory strategies can shield an individual from immediate distress, but more commonly they grow to cause their own set of difficulties. It is at this point that people typically decide that they need to seek therapy. A specific treatment plan is then developed from a conceptualization of the patient's automatic thoughts, underlying schemas, and compensatory strategies (J. S. Beck, 1995). Following this, realistic goals are set and are pursued via the use of individually tailored interventions.

Clinical Applications

Patients are taught to systematically examine and modify distorted thinking to gain a more objective and manageable view of their problems. Therapists conduct a comprehensive diagnostic evaluation and formulate a cognitive conceptualization (Persons, 1989) that is continually reshaped by new data throughout treatment. From this, the treatment plan and goals are set, pursued, and evaluated periodically.

An agenda is set each session and includes assessing the patient's mood, reviewing the main points from the previous session as well as the homework assignment, applying new cognitive and behavioral skills to ongoing issues and goals, summarizing the main ideas from the present session, getting and giving feedback about the session, and collaboratively generating ideas for new homework assignments. The therapist and patient collaborate to understand the patient's worldview and empirically evaluate specific target areas (e.g., social avoidance, procrastination, impulsivity). Cognitive therapists use a variety of cognitive, behavioral, and experiential interventions to monitor, test, and modify problematic beliefs and their concomitant emotions; to strengthen problem-solving skills; to replace compensatory behaviors with more adaptive strategies; and to develop an adaptive coping repertoire. Homework is assigned to reinforce work done in session, apply therapy lessons to the outside world, and design behavioral experiments for examination in the next session. Cognitive therapy patients learn important skills that maximize long-term maintenance of therapeutic gains.

REFERENCES

Adler, A. (1936). The neurotic's picture of the world. *International Journal of Individual Psychology, 2,* 3–10.

Bandura, A. (1977). *Social learning theory.* Englewood Cliffs, NJ: Prentice Hall.

Beck, A. T., Rush, A. J., Shaw, B. F., & Emery, G. (1979). *Cognitive therapy of depression.* New York: Guilford Press.

Beck, J. S. (1995). *Cognitive therapy: Basics and beyond.* New York: Guilford Press.

Frankl, V. E. (1985). Logos, paradox, and the search for meaning. In M. J. Mahoney & A. Freeman (Eds.), *Cognition and psychotherapy* (pp. 3–49). New York: Plenum Press.

Kelly, G. (1955). *The psychology of personal constructs.* New York: W. W. Norton.

Mahoney, M. (1974). *Cognition and behavior modification.* Cambridge, MA: Ballinger.

Persons, J. B. (1989). *Cognitive therapy in practice: A case formulation approach.* New York: W. W. Norton.

Piaget, J. (1954). *The construction of reality in the child.* New York: Basic Books.

Young J. E. (1999). *Cognitive therapy for personality disorders: A schema-focused approach* (3rd ed.). Sarasota, FL: Professional Resource Press/Professional Resource Exchange.

Marci Gittes Fox
Beck Institute for Cognitive Therapy & Research

Cory F. Newman
University of Pennsylvania

See also: **Behavior Therapy; Cognitive Theory; Personal Construct Theory; Psychotherapy**

COGNITIVE TRIAD

According to cognitive theory, many of the disturbances associated with depression result from the activation of a set of cognitive patterns that forces the individual to view his or her situation in an idiosyncratic, negative, and pessimistic way (Beck, 1967, 1976; Clark, Beck, & Alford, 1999). This set of negative cognitions is referred to as the *cognitive triad,* as it consists of thought patterns about the world, the self, and the future. The cognitive triad remains active in depressed individuals because such individuals selectively and inappropriately interpret experiences as being negative in some substantive way. Typical cognitions of depressed individuals show a variety of deviations from logical thinking, including making arbitrary inferences of negative meaning, selectively focusing on negative events, overgeneralizing from one negative experience, employing dichotomous thinking, and catastrophizing. As a consequence of these errors in information processing, the patient automatically makes negative interpretations of situ-

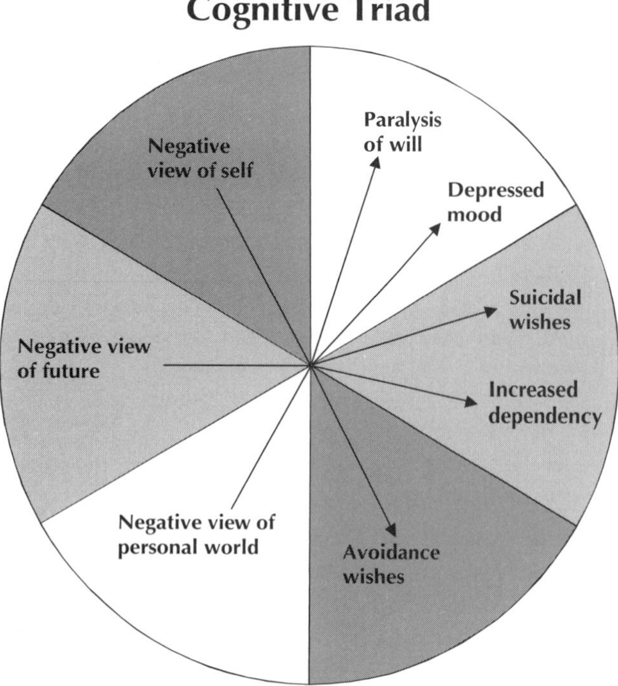

Figure 1. Cognitive triad.

ations even though more plausible explanations are readily apparent. The continued activation and dominance of the negative cognitive triad leads to other phenomena associated with the depressive state, such as sad affect and the lack of motivation.

Negative View of the Personal World

The first component of the cognitive triad (Figure 1) is the tendency of the depressed individual to interpret ongoing experiences in a negative way. Interactions with the environment are often misinterpreted as representing some form of defeat or deprivation. Automatic reactions to problems or difficulties are likely to be thoughts such as "I'm beaten," "I'll never be able to do this," or "I'm blocked no matter what I do." Any problem seems insoluble, and any delay in reaching a goal seems indefinite. For example, a depressed woman who had some difficulty finding a pencil in her purse immediately had the thought, "I'll never be able to find it." She experienced a strong sense of frustration even though she was able to find it in a few seconds.

Many patients with depression are particularly prone to react to achievement-oriented situations with a sense of failure or to make negative attributions whenever they are in a competitive situation. One patient had the highest standing in class, but whenever the teacher called on another student to answer a question, the patient thought, "He doesn't really think I'm smart or he would have called on me." If the professor complimented other students, the patient would have the thought that the professor had a low opinion of him.

Making comparisons with other people is especially likely to activate feelings of dissatisfaction and deprivation. Many depressed patients have thoughts such as "I don't have anything" when a friend acquires something new. In addition to feeling deprived, the depressed patient is prone to interpret comments from others as devaluing and is likely to read insults, ridicule, or disparagement into what other people say. In summary, the world of the depressed individual is filled with themes of defeat, deprivation, and devaluation.

Negative View of the Self

Depressed patients not only interpret their experiences as negative, but they devalue themselves as well. If a depressed individual does not do as well as expected on a test or a business venture, a likely immediate reaction is to think of himself or herself as ineffective and undesirable. A striking feature of the depressed patient is the tendency to overgeneralize from a particular incident. A student who had difficulty getting a date on a single occasion thought, "I must be repulsive to girls." A highly successful businessman who made one transaction that lost money became obsessed by the idea that he was stupid. A mother whose child was untidy on one occasion thought, "I'm a terrible parent."

Depressed patients often see themselves solely in terms of their deficiencies. Further, these negative self-evaluations are usually associated with self-rejection. Patients often will not only see themselves as inferior, but will criticize, reproach, and castigate themselves for being so inferior. Thoughts of ineffectiveness, inferiority, and inadequacy abound in individuals with depression.

Negative View of the Future

Depressed patients often show considerable preoccupation with thoughts about the future, and these ideations may occur in the form of pictorial fantasies or obsessive ruminations. Such thoughts have a negative cast and are usually an extension of the patient's view of the present state, often to the point that the patient sees no possibility for improvement. If patients regard themselves as currently deprived, immobilized, or rejected, then they are likely to visualize a future of continual deprivation, immobilization, or rejection. Not only are long-range forecasts pessimistic, but short-term predictions are similarly negative. When contemplating whether or not to perform a task, they predict that they will make a mess of it. When a suggestion is made that they engage in an ordinarily enjoyable activity, they assume they will not have a good time. One patient, for example, frequently had elaborate fantasies of failure before engaging in any activity. When driving to the psychiatrist's office for an appointment, she pictured herself making a wrong turn and getting lost. If she decided to go shopping, she imagined herself losing her purse or making the wrong purchases. Like the present, the future is seen as containing one failure and defeat after another.

Implications

Identifying the automatic negative evaluations that depressed individuals make about their world, self, and future has significant implications for the diagnosis, assessment, and treatment of the condition. Cognitive therapists help patients identify such thoughts and then work to develop ways of challenging these faulty, overly negative evaluations. Such therapy has been demonstrated to be quite effective at alleviating symptoms of depression (Clark et al., 1999).

REFERENCES

Beck, A. T. (1967). *Depression: Clinical, experimental, and theoretical aspects.* New York: Harper & Row.

Beck, A. T. (1976). *Cognitive therapy and the emotional disorders.* New York: International Universities Press.

Clark, D. A., Beck, A. T., & Alford, B. A. (1999). *Scientific foundations of cognitive theory and therapy of depression.* New York: Wiley.

Gregg Henriques
University of Pennsylvania

See also: **Attribution Theory; Psychotherapy**

COMMUNICATION SKILLS TRAINING

Therapists of diverse theoretical positions have long realized that numerous clients with a variety of psychopathological complaints are deficient in interpersonal or communication skills. Persons diagnosed as schizophrenic, neurotic, or mildly mentally retarded, as well as alcoholics, those having marital difficulties, and parents with child management problems, have all been seen as having difficulties in interpersonal communication. In the period from 1970 to 1980, three major trends led to the increased emphasis upon communication skills training as an important therapeutic and preventive tool. The first and perhaps most important trend was the disenchantment of many psychologists and other therapists with the medical model of therapeutic intervention. As Goldstein has noted in *Psychological Skills Training* (1981), an increasing number of therapists turned to a different set of assumptions. Basic to this new approach is the assumption that the client is suffering from a skill performance deficit and that the role of the therapist is to teach or train the client to perform the requisite set of skills.

The second trend was the increasing application of behavioral strategies to the treatment of a diversity of behavioral problems. It was quickly recognized that before psychiatric clients could be deinstitutionalized or normalized they would have to learn an extensive array of communication skills, such as conversational skills and job acquisition and maintenance skills. Those behaviorists working with neurotic clients quickly learned that many of their clients required assertiveness training.

The third trend involved the use of microcounseling procedures to train counselors and psychotherapists in interviewing skills. To those using this method of training and to those trained by it, it quickly became obvious that similar methods could be used to train clients in interpersonal communication skills. Thus, the microcounseling technology has been used to train institutionalized psychiatric clients, parents, marital partners, and families in communication skills.

Communication skills training usually is focused upon two broad sets of interpersonal skills: skills for interacting with one or more persons, and skills involving interpersonal or shared problem solving. Conversational skill training is directed toward the enhancement of an individual's ability to initiate and maintain conversations with other people. This form of training has been employed with institutionalized and formerly institutionalized persons and with individuals experiencing social anxiety. Communication skills training is a central component of most assertiveness-training procedures, since effective communication is seen as an important precursor to assertive behavior.

Another specific form of communication skills training is job interview training directed toward chronically unemployed persons and students about to enter, and others reentering, the job market. Most premarital, marital, and parenting programs, whether developed for therapeutic or preventive/educative purposes, include communication skills training in both interactional and shared problem-solving skills. Many organizational development programs, directed toward increasing the quality of working life, include communication skills training as a critical component. Programs concerned with facilitating interpersonal communication or shared problem solving have been developed for managers, supervisors, and coworkers. With the increasing realization that primary prevention programs are best directed at the younger members of our society, social skills training programs have been developed for use from prekindergarten to high school. Kelly, in *Social-Skills Training,* has presented an excellent review of many of these varied communication skills training programs.

As the various communication skills training programs developed, it became increasingly obvious that there is perhaps a common set of communication skills that pervade the many and varied interpersonal activities in which people engage. Thus, the same communication skills are important in interactions with a person's spouse, children, family, friends, and coworkers. There is a need to identify these skills more precisely and then to develop a modular program, elements of which can be used to train individuals who are deficient in one or more skills. This approach assumes that assessment methods exist to assess an individual's skill level in each area of expertise.

With the shift from the assumptions of the medical model of intervention to the assumptions of an education or training model has come greater reliance on the principles of instructional psychology. Most communication skills training programs are based on a very similar model of training that involves an instructional sequence, a practice sequence, and a generalization sequence. Gagne and Briggs, in *Principles of Instructional Design,* summarize many of the important characteristics of instruction included in various communication skills training programs.

Initial research in this area involved the demonstration that communication skills training methods produced significant increments in performance during training. A current focus of research involves the demonstration that increments in communication skills performance lead to changes in other behaviors, such as decreased delinquency, reduced drug and alcohol abuse, improved marital and parent-child relations, and improved academic performance. A subsequent concern of researchers is the demonstration that educationally based methods of communication skills training are superior to methods based upon other assumptions, such as sensitivity training. Yet another focus of research has been the specification of the skills that should be included in communication skills training programs and the best methods of training the constituent skills. It can be concluded that communication skills training programs are effective; however, research is still required to develop programs that enhance the generalization of the skills to different situations and over time.

REFERENCES

Gagne, R. M., & Briggs, L. (1979). *Principles of instructional design.* New York: Holt Rinehart & Winston. (Original work published 1974)

Goldstein, A. P. (1981). *Psychological skills training.* New York: Pergamon.

David R. Evans
University of Western Ontario, Canada

See also: **Behavior Therapy; Social Support**

COMMUNITY PSYCHOLOGY: PREVENTION AND INTERVENTION

Community psychology is the study of the interaction between the individual and the environment (Dalton, Elias, & Wandersman, 2001). Community psychologists are interested in examining and improving the quality of life of individuals, communities, and society through collaborative research and action (Jason & Glenwick, 2002). Duffy and Wong (2000) characterized this field as emphasizing prevention over treatment; underscoring strengths and competencies over weaknesses; adopting an ecological perspective that examines the relationships among people and their environment; valuing and respecting diversity and differences; stressing empowerment, which involves enhancing the processes by which people gain control over their lives; emphasizing action research and social change, which provide more alternatives; stressing collaboration with other disciplines; examining how social support can act as a buffer against stress; and focusing on interventions that build a sense of community.

The field grew out of concern for the social and community problems confronting the United States during the 1960s and 1970s (Duffy & Wong, 2000; Tolan, Keys, Chertok, & Jason, 1990). It was formally founded in 1965 at a conference in Swampscott, Massachusetts (Levine & Perkins, 1997), where psychologists stressed the need to emphasize prevention and the importance of targeting the social environment. A core belief of this approach was that the flow of human casualties could be reduced by modifying social systems to make them more responsive and health-inducing or by teaching persons how to live behaviorally healthy lifestyles (Cowen, 1973). Thus, through community-based prevention and promotion, it was hoped that cost-effective services could be implemented, with fewer resources ultimately devoted to remediating hard-to-cure, entrenched problems.

From a more theoretical perspective, several models of prevention have been advanced, the principal ones being social competence, empowerment, and an ecological approach. Some theorists focus on a social competence model, where the goal is to prevent disorders by enhancing individuals' competencies (Duffy & Wong, 2000). Favored by many behaviorally oriented psychologists because of its emphasis on explicit skills, the social competence approach can assist persons in gaining more resources and increasing their competence and independence (Bogat & Jason, 2000; Glenwick & Jason, 1980).

Another approach is the empowerment model, which attempts to enhance people's sense of control over their own destinies (Rappaport, 1981). Empowerment is action-oriented and goes beyond the individual level as emphasized in the social competence model. Individuals, organizations, and communities can be empowered, and in the process they gain greater access to, and power and influence over, decisions and resources (Zimmerman, 2000). One difficulty for practitioners of the empowerment model involves deciding which groups to empower. In many communities, there are opposing groups, with each regarding its perspective as correct.

Another paradigm that has captured the attention of many prevention practitioners and community psychologists is the ecological model (Kelly, 1985, 1990), which was adapted from the biological field of ecology. Kelly's theory includes four ecological principles that describe characteristics of settings and systems. For example, various components of a system are interdependent, in that change in one part influences change in another. One aspect of the ecological approach for increasing the validity of our understanding of social phenomena is its emphasis on the collaborative relationship between researchers and participants. In such a relationship, concepts and hypotheses are developed and tested jointly by investigators and participants. Individuals should be involved in research projects as participants, not as subjects, with the process of being understood and represented considered to be empowering. Also, including community members in the research and intervention process enables them to receive support, learn to identify resources, and become better problem solvers.

There are many significant problems that our planet is facing, including the need to feed an escalating population, increasing poverty in many countries and excessive waste of resources in others, and environmental degradation. The field of community psychology is committed to finding ways to focus on improving the quality of life through research and action (Jason, 1997). As Albee (1986) argued, in the absence of social change, psychopathology will continue to exist as long as there is excessive concentration of economic power, nationalism, and institutions that perpetuate powerlessness, poverty, sexism, racism, ageism, and other forms of oppression.

REFERENCES

Albee, G. W. (1986). Toward a just society. *American Psychologist, 41,* 891–898.

Bogat, G. A., & Jason, L. A. (2000). Towards an integration of behaviorism and community psychology: Dogs bark at those they do not recognize. In J. Rappaport & E. Seidman (Eds.), *Handbook of community psychology* (pp. 101–114). New York: Plenum.

Cowen, E. L. (1973). Social and community interventions. In P. Mussen & M. Rosenzweig (Eds.), *Annual review of psychology* (Vol. 24, pp. 423–472). Palo Alto, CA: Annual Reviews.

Dalton, J. H., Elias, M. J., & Wandersman, A. (2001). *Community psychology: Linking individuals and communities.* Belmont, CA: Wadsworth.

Duffy, K. G., & Wong, F. Y. (2000). *Community psychology* (2nd ed.). Boston: Allyn & Bacon.

Glenwick, D. S., & Jason, L. A. (Eds.). (1980). *Behavioral community psychology: Progress and prospects.* New York: Praeger.

Jason, L. A. (1997). *Community building: Values for a sustainable future.* Westport, CT: Praeger.

Jason, L. A., & Glenwick, D. S. (Eds.). (2002). *Innovative strategies for promoting health and mental health across the lifespan.* New York: Springer.

Kelly, J. G. (1985). The concept of primary prevention: Creating new paradigms. *Journal of Primary Prevention, 5,* 269–272.

Kelly, J. G. (1990). Changing contexts and the field of community psychology. *American Journal of Community Psychology, 18,* 769–792.

Levine, M., & Perkins, D. V. (1997). *Principles of community psychology: Perspectives and applications* (2nd ed.). New York: Oxford University Press.

Rappaport, J. (1981). In praise of paradox: A social policy of empowerment over prevention. *American Journal of Community Psychology, 9,* 1–25.

Tolan, P., Keys, C., Chertok, F., & Jason, L. (Eds.). (1990). *Researching community psychology: Issues of theories and methods.* Washington, DC: American Psychological Association.

Zimmerman, M. (2000). Empowerment theory: Psychological, organizational and community levels of analysis. In J. Rappaport & E. Seidman (Eds.), *Handbook of community psychology* (pp. 43–63). New York: Plenum.

Leonard A. Jason
Bernadette Sanchez
DePaul University

COMPARATIVE NEUROPSYCHOLOGY

Results of nonhuman animal research can provide new information that human experimentation does not permit, usually for ethical considerations or because of limited control over complex environmental and genetic influences. The new knowledge can then be used to help understand human disorders. One approach to understanding interspecies brain functions, comparative neuropsychology, involves the direct evaluation of human clinical populations by employing experimental paradigms originally developed for nonhuman animals (Oscar-Berman & Bardenhagen, 1998). Over many decades of animal research, the paradigms were perfected to study the effects of well-defined brain lesions on specific behaviors, and later the tasks were modified for human use. Generally the modifications involve changing the reward from food to money, but standard administration of the tasks in humans still involves minimal instructions, thus necessitating a degree of procedural learning in human and nonhuman animals alike. Currently, comparative neuropsychological paradigms are often used with neurological patients to link specific deficits with localized areas of neuropathology (Fuster, 1997; Oscar-Berman & Bardenhagen, 1998).

The comparative neuropsychological approach employs simple tasks that can be mastered without relying upon language skills. Precisely because these simple paradigms do not require linguistic strategies for solution, they are especially useful for working with patients whose language skills are compromised or whose cognitive skills may be minimal. Comparative neuropsychology contrasts with the traditional approach of using tasks that rely upon linguistic skills and that were designed to study human cognition

(Lezak, 1995). Because important ambiguities about its heuristic value had not been addressed empirically, only recently has comparative neuropsychology become popular for implementation with brain-damaged patients (e.g., see reviews by Oscar-Berman & Bardenhagen, 1998; Squire, 1992). Within the past decade, it has had prevalent use as a framework for comparing and contrasting the performances of disparate neurobehavioral populations on similar tasks.

Although many paradigms have been employed, two popular tasks are classical delayed-reaction tests such as delayed response (DR) and delayed alternation (DA). Both tasks measure a subject's ability to bridge a time gap (see Fuster, 1997). This ability has been termed *working memory,* which is a transient form of memory. Working memory is multimodal in nature, and it serves to keep newly incoming information available online; it acts much like a mental clipboard for use in problem solving, planning, and the like. In the classical DR task, the experimenter places a small reward into a reinforcement well under one of two identical stimuli. The subject is able to see the experimenter put a reward there but cannot reach it. After the experimenter covers the reinforcement wells with the stimuli, he or she lowers a screen, obscuring the stimulus tray. After a delay period, usually between 0 and 60 seconds, the experimenter raises the screen to allow the subject to make a choice. The subject then pushes one of the stimuli away and, with a correct choice, takes the reward; attentional and spatial memory skills are needed to do this. Some investigators have used automated versions of the tasks in which the cues presented to the subjects are lights or sounds, and the subjects are required to respond, after a delay period, by pressing a key or a lever (Oscar-Berman & Bardenhagen, 1998).

DA shares important features with DR. Both are spatial tasks, and both have a delay between stimulus presentation and the opportunity to make a response. In DA, however, subjects must learn to alternate responding from left to right. On each trial, the side not previously chosen is rewarded, and a brief delay (usually 5 seconds) is interposed between trials. Instead of having to notice and remember the location of a reward placed there by the experimenter (in DR), in DA, subjects must remember the side last chosen and whether or not a reward had been available. Subjects must also learn to inhibit, on each trial, the previously rewarded response (i.e., they must not perseverate with consecutive responses to one side only). Rankings of the performance levels of a wide range of mammals, including children, on delayed-reaction tasks have been reported to parallel the phylogenetic scale.

Comparative neuropsychological tasks such as DR and DA are simple to administer and do not rely on intact language abilities. Both tasks also are sensitive to abnormalities after damage to frontal brain systems. Furthermore, successful performance on DR and DA tasks is known to rely upon different underlying neuroanatomical and neuropsychological mechanisms. Thus, the prefrontal cortex is host to at least two subsystems: dorsolateral and orbitofrontal (on the ventral surface). While the dorsolateral system contains intimate connections with other neocortical sites, its connections with limbic sites are less striking than the orbitofrontal system's. The dorsolateral system, although important for successful performance on both DR and DA, is especially important for DR performance, in which visuospatial, mnemonic, and attentional functions are considered critical. By contrast, functions involved in response inhibition have been linked more to the orbitofrontal system. With an inability to inhibit unintended responses comes abnormal perseverative responding, a salient characteristic of orbitofrontal damage. The orbitofrontal system is intimately connected with basal forebrain and limbic structures; its connections with other neocortical regions are not as extensive as the dorsolateral system's. The orbitofrontal system, like the dorsolateral system, supports successful performance on both DA and DR, but it is especially important for DA performance.

Comparative neuropsychological research has provided a framework that is helpful for understanding memory dysfunction in neurodegenerative disorders. In some neurodegenerative diseases (e.g., Parkinson's disease and progressive supranuclear palsy), patients may have working-memory and attentional impairments resulting from prefrontal system damage. In other disorders (e.g., Korsakoff's syndrome and herpes encephalopathy), there are new-learning impairments suggestive of limbic system damage (Oscar-Berman & Bardenhagen, 1998).

Implicit in nonhuman research models of human brain functioning is the assumption of homologous structural-functional relationships among the species (e.g., Milner, 1998; Wasserman, 1993). Research on brain mechanisms that underlie behaviors across species contributes to the discovery of common and divergent principles of brain-behavior relationships.

REFERENCES

Fuster, J. M. (1997). *The prefrontal cortex* (3rd ed.). New York: Lippincott-Raven.

Lezak, M. D. (1995). *Neuropsychological assessment* (3rd ed.). New York: Oxford University Press.

Milner, A. D. (Ed.). (1998). *Comparative neuropsychology.* New York: Oxford University Press.

Oscar-Berman, M., & Bardenhagen, F. (1998). Nonhuman primate models of memory dysfunction in neurodegenerative disease: Contributions from comparative neuropsychology. In A. Tröster (Ed.), *Memory in neurodegenerative disease* (pp. 3–20). New York: Cambridge University Press.

Squire, L. R. (1992). Memory and the hippocampus: A synthesis from findings with rats, monkeys, and humans. *Psychological Review, 99*(2), 195–231.

Wasserman, E. A. (1993). Comparative cognition: Beginning the second century of the study of animal intelligence. *Psychological Bulletin, 113,* 211–228.

Marlene Oscar-Berman
Boston University School of Medicine and Department of Veterans Affairs Healthcare System

COMPARATIVE PSYCHOLOGY

Animal behavior is the subject matter of comparative psychology. The first goal of comparative psychology is to identify principles and theories that govern animal behavior. The second goal is to understand how an animal's behavior contributes to its total evolutionary fitness. Historically, comparative psychology has focused on generalizations across species, and ethology has focused on detailed descriptions of particular species.

History

Behaviors and antics of animals have evoked curiosity and amusement in people since antiquity. Pre-nineteenth-century literature and natural history are punctuated with stories, anecdotes, and nonscientific speculations about animal behavior.

The strict separation of animal and human behavior ended with Charles Darwin's theory of evolution, which was the starting point for present-day comparative psychology. Evolutionary development had two important implications: first, that elements of human mentality would occur in animals; and second, that elements of animal mentality would occur in humans. Darwin, well aware of these implications, addressed the first in *The Descent of Man* (1871) and the second in *The Expression of Emotions in Man and Animals* (1872).

Phylogenetic Trees and Phylogenetic Scales

Darwin recognized that the evolutionary process was one of constant diversification. Therefore, evolution can be likened to an enormously elaborated branching tree, with living species represented by the tips of the branches, while the remainder of the tree represents extinct species. In no sense has evolution been an orderly process that produces organisms of increasing subtlety and complexity, culminating in humans. Comparative psychology, therefore, has the virtue of illuminating human behavior as only a small part of a wider context involving enormous interspecies variation.

Similarities in behavioral characteristics of two species with a common ancestor may arise in two different ways. The characteristics may have been present in the common ancestor and survived down to the current descendents, in which case the similarities are homogenous. Alternatively, the characteristics may have been absent in the common ancestor but evolved independently in lines leading to the current species, in which case the behaviors are analogous. Indirect techniques are usually required to infer phylogenetic development of a behavioral trait. For example, if several species sharing a common ancestor all display a behavioral trait, then the shared trait was probably present in the common ancestor (Alcock, 2001). Evolutionary considerations can also lead to questions about how a behavior affected a species's adaptation to its environment and about the role of the behavior in the evolutionary history of the species. Alcock (2001) describes techniques for empirically testing hypotheses about the evolutionary adaptiveness of particular behaviors.

The How and Why of Animal Behavior

There are two fundamental types of explanations for animal behavior. Ultimate explanations are based on evidence suggesting reasons why the behaviors contributed to the fitness of individuals over the evolutionary history of the species. Therefore, ultimate explanations are closely related to the effects of the behaviors in solving a species's problems in its natural habitat.

Proximate explanations address the questions of how a behavior occurs. These explanations answer questions about a behavior's ontogenetic development and how it was affected by learning, physiological and neurological variables, genes, and environmental stimulation. Proximate explanations incorporate variables that exert effects within an animal's lifetime. In contrast, ultimate explanations incorporate mechanisms that have been affecting natural selection long into the phylogenetic past of the species (Alcock, 2001).

Both ultimate and proximate explanations are legitimate scientific approaches to understanding animal behavior. There has been considerable recent interest in finding ultimate or evolutionary explanations for basic learning phenomena that had previously been explained only in terms of proximate causes (Shettleworth, 1998).

Minds and Language

The possibilities and manifestations of mind and consciousness in animals were topics of active speculation in the early post-Darwinian period of comparative psychology. *The Animal Mind* by Margaret Flow Washburn, published in four editions from 1908 to 1936, was a popular and widely used textbook in comparative psychology. But the increasing influence of behaviorism and the warnings of Morgan's canon relegated mind, consciousness, and similar attributes to the dustbin of comparative psychology.

In 1966 Gardner and Gardner (1971) began tutoring a young chimpanzee, Washoe, in American Sign Language. The project was far more successful than earlier attempts to teach chimpanzees a spoken language.

In the more than 35 years since the original Washoe study, several other ape language projects have been reported, some with manual signing, others in which the ape directed manual responses toward abstract symbols (Rumbaugh & Savage-Rumbaugh, 1994).

In 1993, Savage-Rumbaugh described a remarkable experiment with the bonobo Kanzi showing that he could respond appropriately to a large number of spoken English sentences that he had not previously heard. Kanzi's ability to understand novel spoken sentences is the most impressive evidence to date that apes' language capabilities can closely approximate those of humans who are first acquiring language.

A second important issue in recent comparative psychology is whether apes and possibly monkeys have a theory of mind. Having a theory of mind implies an ability to understand the intentions, mental states, personalities, and perceptions of other animals (Whiten & Byrne, 1997). Tactical deception based on deliberately or knowingly presenting incorrect, deceptive information to another animal is one example of using a theory of mind. Whiten and Byrne (1997) presented evidence of tactical deception in nonhuman primates.

REFERENCES

Alcock, J. (2001). *Animal behavior* (7th ed.). Sunderland, MA: Sinauer Associates.

Gardner, B. T., & Gardner, R. A. (1971). Two-way communications with an infant chimpanzee. In A. M. Schrier & F. Stollnitz (Eds.), *Behavior of nonhuman primates* (Vol. 4, pp. 117–184). New York: Academic Press.

Rumbaugh, D. M., & Savage-Rumbaugh, E. S. (1994). Language in comparative perspective. In N. J. MacKintosh (Ed.), *Animal learning and cognition* (pp. 307–334). San Diego, CA: Academic Press.

Shettleworth, S. J. (1998). *Cognition, evolution and behavior.* New York: Oxford University Press.

Whiten, A., & Byrne, R. W. (1997). *Machiavellian intelligence II: Extensions and evaluations.* Cambridge, UK: Cambridge University Press.

SUGGESTED READING

Greenberg, G., & Haraway, M. M. (1998). *Comparative psychology: A handbook.* New York: Garland.

Dewsbury, D. A. (1984). *Comparative psychology in the twentieth century.* Stroudsburg, PA: Hutchinson Ross.

James E. King
University of Arizona

COMPETENCY TO STAND TRIAL

A defendant can be found incompetent to stand trial, under provisions in criminal law, if he or she is unable to understand or participate adequately in his or her defense. If the defendant is found incompetent, further judicial proceedings are suspended until his or her competency is restored. The purpose behind this procedure is to ensure that a defendant receives a fair trial and, in addition, to preserve the dignity of the adversarial process (Melton, Petrila, Poythress, & Slogobin, 1997). The competency standard that is currently recognized by the courts was established in *Dusky v. United States* (362 U.S. 402, 1960), which holds that defendants must be able to consult with an attorney and have a rational and factual understanding of the proceedings.

Competency and criminal responsibility are often confused. However, while competency is concerned with a defendant's present ability to participate in the defense, criminal responsibility refers to a defendant's mental state at the time of the alleged crime. It is quite possible that a defendant could be found to be competent to stand trial and then later successfully raise the insanity defense. Indeed, if the competency issue were to be raised, a defendant would have to be considered competent before being allowed to proceed with an insanity defense.

Based on a thorough review of case law, Bonnie (1992) outlines two types of competence, *competency to assist counsel* and *decisional competency.* Competency to assist counsel refers to the minimum capacities a defendant would need to assist in his or her defense, such as the capacity to understand the criminal charges and the role of defense counsel. These capacities are different from those capacities that may be needed to make decisions that arise in a particular case. Decisional competency refers to the ability to understand and choose among alternative courses of action. In Bonnie's view, it is possible that some defendants could be considered competent to assist their attorney but incompetent to make certain decisions that arise during the course of the defense, such as whether to enter a guilty plea, to waive constitutional rights, or to employ an insanity defense.

Both defense and prosecution can raise the issue of competence. The courts have historically used mental health professionals, including psychologists and psychiatrists, to evaluate competency. Since competency is a legal issue, a judge makes the final determination, but evaluators have considerable influence (Roesch & Golding, 1980). Only a small proportion of defendants referred for fitness evaluations is found incompetent, usually about 10–25%.

Competency evaluations may be intentionally misused by attorneys to delay the trial, investigate the feasibility of an insanity plea, or discover new information about the defendant (Roesch & Golding, 1980). Competency evaluations may also be used as a "back door" to the hospital when a mentally ill individual does not meet the dangerousness criteria for civil commitment.

Robey's (1965) competency checklist is considered to be the first formalized measure of competency. Following this, the National Institute of Mental Health funded a research project that enabled the development of both the Competency Screening Test (Laboratory of Community Psychiatry, 1973), a 22-item screening test, and the Competency Assessment Instrument (Laboratory of Community Psychiatry, 1973), a more thorough semistructured interview. Other structured and semistructured interviews include the Georgia Court Competency Test-R (Johnson & Mullett, 1987), the Interdisciplinary Fitness Interview (Golding, Roesch, & Schreiber, 1984), the Fitness Interview Test (Roesch, Zapf, Eaves, & Webster, 1998), and the MacArthur Competency Assessment Tool—Criminal Adjudication (Poythress, Bonnie, Monahan, Otto, & Hoge, 2002). Psychosis and, to a lesser extent, mental retardation are the basis for an incompetency determination.

Treatment of competency is, in general, successful. Nicholson and McNulty (1992) found that competency could not be restored for only 10% of defendants. In such cases alternative dispositions, including dismissal of charges or civil commitment, are considered. The most common form of treatment is psychotropic medication (Roesch, Hart, & Zapf, 1996). However, while psychotropic medication may affect a defendant's mental disorder, it does not address his or her psycholegal impairments (Siegel & Elwork, 1992). In contrast, psycholegal education programs do address psycholegal impairments, focusing on topics such as the roles of key players and courtroom procedures (e.g., Pendleton, 1980).

REFERENCES

Bonnie, R. (1992). The competence of criminal defendants: A theoretical reformulation. *Behavioral Sciences and the Law, 10,* 291–316.

Golding, S. L., Roesch, R., & Schreiber, J. (1984). Assessment and conceptualization of competency to stand trial: Preliminary data on the Interdisciplinary Fitness Interview. *Law and Human Behavior, 8,* 321–334.

Johnson, W. G., & Mullett, N. (1988). Georgia Court Competency Test–R. In M. Hersen & A. S. Bellack (Eds.), *Dictionary of behavioral assessment techniques* (pp. 217–227). New York: Pergamon.

Laboratory of Community Psychiatry, Harvard Medical School. (1973). *Competency to stand trial and mental illness.* Rockville, MD: Department of Health, Education, and Welfare.

Melton, G. B., Petrila, J., Poythress, N. G., & Slogobin, C. (1997). *Psychological evaluations for the courts: A handbook for mental health professionals and lawyers* (2nd ed.). New York: Guilford Press.

Nicholson, R. A., & McNulty, J. L. (1992). Outcome of hospitalization for defendants found incompetent to stand trial. *Behavioral Sciences and the Law, 10,* 371–383.

Pendleton, L. (1980). Treatment of persons found incompetent to stand trial. *American Journal of Psychiatry, 137,* 1098–1100.

Poythress, N. G., Bonnie, R. J., Monahan, J., Otto, R. K., & Hoge, S. K. (2002). *Adjudicative competence: The MacArthur studies.* New York: Kluwer/Plenum.

Robey, A. (1965). Criteria for competency to stand trial: A checklist for psychiatrists. *American Journal of Psychiatry, 122,* 616–623.

Roesch, R., & Golding, S. L. (1980). *Competency to stand trial.* Urbana: University of Illinois Press.

Roesch, R., Hart, S. D., & Zapf, P. A. (1996). Conceptualizing and assessing competency to stand trial: Implications and applications of the MacArthur Treatment Competence Model. *Psychology, Public Policy, and Law, 2,* 96–113.

Roesch, R., Zapf, P. A., Eaves, D., & Webster, C. D. (1998). *Fitness Interview Test* (Rev. ed.). Burnaby, BC: Mental Health, Law, and Policy Institute.

Siegel, A., & Elwork, A. (1990). Treating incompetence to stand trial. *Law and Human Behavior, 14,* 57–65.

Ronald Roesch
Jodi Viljoen
Simon Fraser University

See also: **Expert Testimony; Forensic Psychology; Psychological Assessments; Psychology and the Law**

COMPLEXES

The concept of the complex has been used by a number of theorists associated with the psychoanalytic movement. It was introduced by Carl Jung, who is largely responsible for the development of the concept. Jung borrowed the term and the original formulation of the concept from Theodor Ziehen. In studying word association, Ziehen had observed that an individual's reaction time was often long when a stimulus word relating to something unpleasant was presented. He reasoned that such a stimulus was associated with a feeling-toned complex of representations.

In 1900 Jung went to work at the Burghölzli Hospital, where his chief, Eugen Bleuler, introduced the word association test and asked Jung to do research with it. Jung soon came to see his task as the detection and study of complexes. He believed that complexes could be inferred not only from long reaction times but also from physiological reactions, such as the galvanic skin response and changes in respiratory pattern, to certain stimulus words. Jung regarded the complex as a constellation of associated ideas, affects, and images. The constellation can often be viewed as centering on an image corresponding to the idea or situation at the core of the complex—in some cases, an image of a traumatic event that created the complex. The central idea or image tends in some way to be incompatible with the habitual attitude of consciousness. Since we are inclined to repress such contents or avoid awareness of them, these contents remain largely unconscious. At the same time, they possess a certain wholeness and inner coherence. Because the complex is relatively unconscious, and because some of the energy that would otherwise be available to consciousness is bound up in it, it acts as a somewhat autonomous part of the psyche. In a sense, it can act as a separate subpersonality or splinter personality within the psyche, at odds with the conscious personality.

In the word association test, Jung observed the interference of the complex with the performance of a task undertaken in consciousness. He conjectured that the complex could have similar effects on action and physiological processes in other situations. Thus, he viewed the complex as responsible for slips of the tongue, for gaps in our memory, for the forgetting of names, for accidents—in short, for the various phenomena that Sigmund Freud described as evidence for the operation of unconscious motives.

Traumatic events are evidently one source of complexes. The formative experience might consist of either a single painful incident or repeated episodes of criticism, rejection, or embarrassment in childhood. Jung believed complexes might also arise as a result of moral conflict, a clash between instinctual impulses and acquired values. As he developed the concept of the archetype in his later writings, he came to regard the complex as having an archetypal core as well as ingredients stemming from present-lifetime experience.

Jung regarded neurosis as a dissociation of the personality due to complexes and contended that the symptoms of the neurotic can be understood as the expression of complexes. He recognized, however, that complexes are not necessarily pathological and that they may have both harmful and beneficial effects. He believed that every personality, or psyche, contains a number of semi-independent systems that can be considered complexes.

Jung developed the concept of the complex before his involvement in the psychoanalytic movement. After he became familiar with Freud's work, he sought to relate his own ideas about the complexes to Freud's views of the unconscious. In the subsequent work of Freud, the concept was assimilated into a theoretical system that emphasizes sexuality. Alfred Adler also adopted the concept, but his writings emphasize the striving for power and the sense of inferiority that results from a lack of power. The one complex of importance to Adler was the inferiority complex, which he regarded as a characteristic feature of neurosis.

Richard Welton Coan

See also: **Analytical Psychology; Archetypes**

COMPULSIONS

Definition

Compulsions, along with obsessions, are a hallmark feature of Obsessive-Compulsive Disorder (OCD). According to the fourth edition of the *Diagnostic and Statistic Manual of Mental Disorders* (*DSM-IV;* American Psychiatric Association, 1994), compulsions are "repetitive behaviors . . . or mental acts . . . the goal of which is to prevent or reduce anxiety or distress" (p. 418). Although behaviors resembling compulsions occur at a range of frequencies in the normal population, in order to be considered pathological the compulsions must be associated with either intense distress or functional impairment. Impairment from compulsions can be quite severe, with some individuals spending several hours per day performing rituals, feeling unable to stop and attend to their daily responsibilities. Although the label *compulsion* has been applied to a broad range of repetitive behaviors, including excessive drinking, gambling, shopping, and so on, these behaviors are differentiated from true compulsions by the function they serve. This function will be described in detail later.

Types of Compulsions

While many different classifications of compulsive behavior have been proposed, two of the most common compulsions are cleaning and checking. Hodgson and Rachman (1977) reported that 52% of OCD patients reported checking compulsions and 48% reported cleaning compulsions. Although cleaning and checking appear to be the most common forms of compulsion, other forms of compulsive behavior are also reported frequently. These include collecting or hoarding useless objects, ordering and arranging objects, repeating actions, and seeking reassurance from others (Foa et al., 1995).

Early definitions of OCD maintained that obsessions were mental events and compulsions were overt behaviors. Under this definition, some OCD patients without overt rituals were labeled "pure obsessives." However, current theories recognize that compulsions can be either actions or thoughts; nearly 80% of OCD patients describe mental compulsions (Foa & Kozak, 1995). Mental compulsions are differentiated from obsessions according to their function: that is, whether they elicit distress or reduce it (Foa et al., 1995). Whereas obsessions elicit anxiety or distress, compulsions are defined as overt (behavioral) or covert (mental) actions that reduce or prevent distress elicited by obsessions. Examples of mental compulsions include attempting to think "good thoughts"; counting objects or counting up to a certain number; saying certain prayers in a rigid, repetitive manner; and mentally reviewing past actions or conversations to hunt for mistakes or other infractions. Thus, it appears that nearly all OCD patients have some form of compulsion, either overt or covert.

Association Between Obsessions and Compulsions

For most patients with OCD, obsessions are followed by compulsions. Usually, the compulsions are thematically related to the obsessions; however, there is a broad range of logical coherence of this connection. Washing rituals, for example, are usually motivated by fears of contamination or illness. Checking rituals are usually prompted by worries that an action (e.g., turning off the stove) was performed incorrectly and that some catastrophic event (e.g., fire) will occur as a result. Other connections are less logical: for example, turning a light switch off and on several times in order to prevent one's family from dying in a car accident.

Functional Significance of Compulsions

Given their often bizarre appearance, compulsions are often difficult to understand. Why would an individual choose to engage in such behavior, and why does the behavior persist despite marked functional impairment and distress? Compulsions are best understood within the context of the function they serve. Learning theory models of OCD (e.g., Kozak & Foa, 1997) have traditionally been based to some extent on Mowrer's (1960) two-factor theory of fear. Briefly, two-factor theory posits that classically conditioned fear motivates avoidance behavior. When the organism avoids the feared stimulus successfully, anxiety is reduced and the avoidance is therefore negatively reinforced. The avoidance also prevents extinction of fear by limiting exposure to the feared stimulus; therefore, the fear is maintained. OCD theorists have suggested that compulsions are a form of active avoidance, which are cued by obsessive fears. When the individual performs a compulsion, fear is reduced. Thus, compulsions are negatively reinforced, and obsessive fear is increased. Although there is little evidence for the role of classical conditioning in OCD, studies have supported the anxiety-reduction hypothesis of compulsions: Exposure to feared stimuli increased participants' anxiety, whereas performing compulsions led to decreased anxiety (Hodgson & Rachman, 1972). One problem with a two-factor model of compulsions is the fact that some individuals with OCD report that compulsions are associated with increased, rather than decreased, fear. For example, Röper, Rachman, and Hodgson (1973) found that a subsample of compulsive checkers reported higher levels of fear after checking. Cases such as these might be better explained by Herrnstein's (1969) learning theory, which suggests that mildly anxiety-evoking behaviors might be considered avoidant if they serve to prevent the occurrence of strong anxiety. Thus, although checking may elicit anxiety in some patients, refraining from checking is perceived as even more aversive. In summary, the specific function of compulsions may vary, but the general function appears to be one of anxiety reduction and/or prevention. In this manner, compulsive behavior is negatively reinforced, and extinction of fear is blocked.

Attention to the function of compulsion may help with the differential diagnosis of OCD. Many *DSM-IV* impulse control disorders have been classified as part of an "OCD spectrum." These disorders include "compulsive" overeating, gambling, and sex. However, these problems tend to be functionally distinct from compulsions: They are not triggered by obsessions or fears and are not negatively reinforced by fear reduction. On the contrary, disinhibited behaviors are more likely to be triggered by feelings of tension or boredom, and because the behaviors are satisfying, they are positively, rather than negatively, reinforced (e.g., Steketee, 1993). Although Goldsmith, Shapira, Phillips, and McElroy (1998) point out that this distinction does not apply to every patient, until more convincing data are produced, the term *compulsion* is best reserved to indicate a specific functional relationship between behavior and fear.

REFERENCES

American Psychiatric Association. (1994). *Diagnostic and statistical manual of mental disorders* (4th ed.). Washington, DC: Author.

Foa, E. B., Franklin, M. E., & Kozak, M. J. (1998). Psychosocial treatments for Obsessive-Compulsive Disorder. In R. P. Swinson, M. M. Antony, S. Rachman, & M. A. Richter (Eds.), *Obsessive-Compulsive Disorder: Theory, research, and treatment* (pp. 258–276). New York: Guilford Press.

Foa, E. B., & Kozak, M. J. (1996). Psychological treatment for Obsessive-Compulsive Disorder. In M. R. Mavissakalian & R. F. Prien (Eds.), *Long-term treatments of anxiety disorders* (pp. 285–309). Washington, DC: American Psychiatric Association Press.

Foa, E. B., Kozak, M. J., Goodman, W. K., Hollander, E., Jenike, M. A., & Rasmussen, S. A. (1995). *DSM-IV* field trial: Obsessive-Compulsive Disorder. *American Journal of Psychiatry, 152,* 90–96.

Goldsmith, T., Shapira, N. A., Phillips, K. A., & McElroy, S. L. (1998). Conceptual foundations of obsessive-compulsive spectrum disorders. In R. P. Swinson, M. M. Antony, S. Rachman, & M. A. Richter (Eds.), *Obsessive-Compulsive Disorder: Theory, research, and treatment* (pp. 397–425). New York: Guilford Press.

Herrnstein, R. J. (1969). Method and theory in the study of avoidance. *Psy chological Review, 76,* 49–69.

Hodgson, R. J., & Rachman, S. (1972). The effects of contamination and washing in obsessional patients. *Behaviour Research and Therapy, 10,* 111–117.

Hodgson, R. J., & Rachman, S. (1977). Obsessional-compulsive complaints. *Behaviour Research and Therapy, 15,* 389–395.

Kozak, M. J., & Foa, E. B. (1997). *Mastery of Obsessive-Compulsive Disorder: A cognitive-behavioral approach.* Albany, NY: Graywind.

Mavissakalian, M., Turner, S. M., & Michelson, L. (1985). Future directions in the assessment and treatment of Obsessive-Compulsive Disorder. In M. Mavissakalian, S. M. Turner, & L. Michelson (Eds.), *Psychological and pharmacological treatment of Obsessive-Compulsive Disorder.* New York: Plenum Press.

Mowrer, O. H. (1960). *Learning theory and behavior.* New York: Wiley.

Röper, G., Rachman, S., & Hodgson, R. (1973). An experiment on obsessional checking. *Behaviour Research and Therapy, 11,* 271–277.

Steketee, G. S. (1993). *Treatment of Obsessive-Compulsive Disorder.* New York: Guilford Press.

David F. Tolin
The Institute of Living

COMPUTED AXIAL TOMOGRAPHY (CAT SCAN)

Imaging technology has been very useful in the development of the fields of psychiatry and neuroscience. The past two decades have seen an explosion of this technology, so that we now have a window into the brain and other bodily organs. Much of the early work in this area began with computed tomography (CT), which provided important information about the structure of the brain in various neuropsychiatric disorders, including schizophrenia and affective disorders. Although magnetic resonance imaging (MRI) has largely replaced CT for imaging brain structure in psychiatric disorders, many of the fundamental findings in psychiatry (e.g., enlarged ventricular-brain ratios in schizophrenia) are based on CT research.

The past century's advances in the field of imaging sciences that led directly to CT and other modalities have their basis in the discovery and development of X rays for the imaging of the human body. At the turn of the twentieth century, a physician named Roentgen discovered that passing X rays through the human hand with a photographic plate on the other side created a ghostly image on the photographic plate that represented the bones of the hand, which are hidden from the naked eye. Soon, physicians discovered that X rays could provide a wealth of information about the structure of the human body, both in sickness and in health. The principle of X rays is based on the creation of an X-ray beam. The X-ray beam is created when electrons travel from an anode to a cathode. X rays travel through space like light or sound and have their own specific energy.

X rays travel through different parts of the body at different speeds, depending on the type of tissue that is present. Tissue that is denser or has physical properties will slow down, or attenuate, the X-ray beam to a greater extent than will tissue that is less dense. For example, bone is denser than water (which is basically what the cerebrospinal fluid—the fluid that bathes the brain—is made of, and in fact most of the brain has a density that is fairly close to water). X rays will have a harder time traveling through bone than through water. Fewer of the X-ray photons that travel through bone will be able to make it to the other side of the skull and hit the photographic film in the area corresponding to where bone is present, making the part of the film corresponding to the location of bone look different from the area where there is brain and cerebrospinal fluid. This basic principle, of what are essentially variant forms of light waves (or photons), passing through the body, and the degree to which the photons are slowed down or deflected in their path, providing information about the physical properties of the body that can be used to provide a picture or image of our insides that we cannot see with our naked eye, underlies most of the radiological sciences.

An advance over the use of simple X rays came with the development of the computer after World War II. Hounsfield, an engineer working in London, found in 1967 that images of the interior of the body could be produced by passing X rays through the body at multiple angles and measuring the degree to which the tissues of the body attenuated the X rays. With computers, X rays could be passed through the body at multiple angles, and the information could be reconstructed in an image that provided a map of the interior of the body in exquisite detail. This new technique was used to turn the X-ray images into displays of fine slices, or *tomographs,* throughout the human body, hence the term *computed tomography* (CT). This technology provided images of not only normal human anatomy but also of disease, often giving clues of very small tumors in the body that were less than half an inch in size. Another advance that boosted the resolution of CT over earlier X-ray imaging techniques was the use of photomultiplier tubes over regular radiographic film. With photomultiplier tubes, the radiation reaching the other side of the body interacts with other electrons, resulting in a shower of electrons for each radiation that penetrates the body, effectively amplifying the signal as much as 100 times over the old technique. The improvement is in a parameter known as *sensitivity,* or the ability to detect small amounts of radiation. Another factor that is important in imaging is called *resolution,* or the ability to image very small objects or to determine that two objects that are very close together actually represent two distinct objects. Sensitivity and resolution have been steadily improving in all of the imaging modalities over the past 40 years, which has led to increasingly precise maps of the body's structure and the function of the body.

In the 1970s and 1980s, the development of CT added to our understanding of psychiatric disorders. Scientists used CT to study patients with the diagnosis of affective disorders. CT studies showed that patients with affective disorders, including major depression and manic depression, had atrophy of the brain and enlargement of the large fluid-filled cavities of the brain, called *ventricles,* that also indicated atrophy of the brain. Some patients with depression have an increase in the stress hormone cortisol, and stress has been linked to the development of depression. CT showed that treatment with steroids related to cortisol led to atrophy of the brain. CT studies in patients with depression showed atrophy and enlargement of the ventricles similar to that seen in patients treated with steroids. In some cases, patients with the highest levels of cortisol had the greatest amount of brain atrophy.

An even larger number of studies have been conducted in Schizophrenia. At least 75% of the 50 or more CT studies in patients with Schizophrenia have found widening of the lateral ventricles compared to control groups. Various methods have been used to measure ventricular size, including computer-based and manual tracing methods. Some studies measured the linear width of the ventricles at their widest point, others measured the volume on several slices, and still others measured volume throughout the brain. The most sensitive method for measuring ventricular size has been the assessment of ventricular volume to brain volume ratios (VBR). Although not all patients with Schizophrenia develop enlarged ventricles, and although these differences are not always large enough to visualize with the naked eye, clearly the majority of studies that use quantitative measures have shown that the mean values of precisely measured lateral ventricular volumes differ from those of normal controls. Other findings that have been consistently found on CT in Schizophrenia include enlargement of the third ventricle, widening of the cortical sulci, and cerebellar atrophy. Positive associations have been found between enlarged ventricles and clinical status (poor social adjustment, poor outcomes, negative or defect symptoms) and cognitive status (neuropsychological deficits). No relationship has been found with treatment history or duration of illness. The significance of these findings is unclear, but many authors have posited a neurodevelopmental hypothesis for neuroanatomical abnormalities in schizophrenia. However, enlarged ventricles have been found in new-onset patients, suggesting that this finding has developed before the onset of clinical recognizable symptoms.

The meaning of enlarged ventricular volumes is unclear. Ventricular enlargement could be related to atrophy of a number of structures that surround the ventricles, including the hippocampus, amygdala, thalamus, striatum, and corpus callosum. Atrophy of structures more removed could also cause ventricular enlargement. The correlation of clinical symptoms with ventricular enlargement, however, is consistent with the idea that these are clinically relevant changes in the brains of psychiatric patients.

In summary, ventricular enlargement in affective disorders and Schizophrenia has been an important and well-replicated finding in psychiatry that was based on the use of CT technology. Although other techniques, such as MRI, have received more widespread use for measurement of brain structure, CT remains an important technique for psychiatry and psychology. The recent development of combined positron emission tomography–computed technology (PET-CT) devices may bring CT back into the realm of research and clinical applications in the future.

J. Douglas Bremner
Emory University School of Medicine

COMPUTER-ASSISTED PSYCHOTHERAPY

Computer-assisted psychotherapy can be defined as (1) the application of computer tools as an adjunct to clinician-administered psychotherapy, or (2) the use of a computer to enhance the efficiency, cost-effectiveness, or delivery of psychotherapy. Attempts were made to adapt computers for use in psychotherapy applications as early as the 1960s (O'Dell & Dickson, 1984; Weizenbaum, 1966; Wright & Wright, 1997). The first program ("Eliza") was intended as an exercise in computer programming, not as a serious effort to conduct psychotherapy on a computer. Although "Eliza" was a fascinating demonstration project, it was not able to communicate reliably with humans using natural language (O'Dell & Dickson, 1984). Most subsequent developers have not attempted to program computers to conduct interviews that simulate communication with a human therapist. Instead, the unique attributes of computer technology have been tapped to design programs that use a variety of media (e.g., text, video and audio, interactive voice response, virtual reality) to educate, give feedback to, and involve users in highly interactive learning exercises (Wright & Wright, 1997).

It has been suggested that therapeutic software could lower the cost of treatment by reducing the number or length of sessions with a clinician required for effective treatment (Wright & Wright, 1997). Several controlled investigations have documented this advantage of computer-assisted therapy (Kenwright, Liness, & Marks, 2001; Newman et al., 1997; Wright et al., 2001). Other possible benefits include improved access to psychotherapy; effective provision of psychoeducation; ability to store, analyze, and display data; systematic feedback to the user; and promotion of the self-monitoring, homework, and self-help components of treatment (Locke & Rezza, 1996; Wright & Wright, 1997).

One of the concerns raised about computer-assisted psychotherapy is that patients could experience being referred to a computer as a dehumanizing experience. However, research with therapeutic software has demonstrated that patients usually report high levels of satisfaction with their experiences in using a computer as part of treatment (Colby, 1995; O'Dell & Dickson, 1984; Wright, Wright, Salmon, et al., 2002). Another concern is that a computer program could never be programmed to have the empathy, wisdom, or creativity of the human therapist. Contemporary developers of computer-assisted therapy programs agree with this observation, and thus do not attempt to simulate the traditional therapeutic interview (Wright & Wright, 1997).

Computers, unlike human therapists, do not have inherent values or ethical standards. However, developers convey their theoretical orientation, values, and ethics in writing software for computer programs. Sampson and Pyle (1983) have offered ethical guidelines for computerized psychotherapy programs that include the following: (1) adequate protection of confidentiality; (2) up-to-date and accurate information; (3) well-functioning hardware and software; and (4) supervision of the treatment process by a clinician. Some developers of therapeutic software have produced professional and self-help editions (Colby & Colby, 1990; Wright, Wright, & Beck, 2002). The professional edition is intended for use in clinician-directed computer-assisted therapy, whereas the self-help edition is designed to be utilized in a manner similar to a self-help book.

Computer programs for psychotherapy have been based most commonly on cognitive and behavioral methods because these forms of treatment use specific interventions, emphasize psychoeducation, and employ self-help as a primary ingredient of therapy (O'Dell & Dickson, 1984). An example of a computer program oriented toward cognitive-behavioral therapy (CBT) is the software developed in the 1980s by Selmi and coworkers (Selmi, Klein, & Greist, 1982). This program relied completely on written text to communicate with users and is no longer produced. However, Selmi and coworkers demonstrated that computerized CBT could be as effective as standard CBT (Selmi, Klein, & Greist, 1990). Other early software not available for clinical use includes two behavior therapy interventions for anxiety disorders based on the book *Living With Fear* (Ghosh, Marks, & Carr, 1984; Carr, Ghosh, & Marks, 1988; Marks, 1978).

Colby and coworkers (Colby, Gould, & Aronson, 1989; Colby, Gould, Aronson, & Colby, 1991) developed software that integrates computerized instruction with group discussions. The Therapeutic Learning Program identifies problematic interpersonal situations and offers coaching for proactive behavior. It has been used extensively for employee assistance programs. Colby also developed "Overcoming Depression," which utilizes written text and a natural language-based dialogue format (Colby, 1995; Colby & Colby, 1990). A study of this software with depressed inpatients found that the dialogue component of the program did not always communicate effectively with patients and that use of the software did not enhance treatment efficacy (Bowers, Stuart, MacFarlane, & Gorman, 1993; Stuart & LaRue, 1996).

The most recent computer programs for psychotherapy have incorporated new technologies geared toward heightening the power of the learning experience and improving ease of use. For example, Wright and coworkers have designed and tested the first multimedia program for computer-assisted CBT (Kenwright et al., 2001; Colby, 1995; Colby & Colby, 1990). Research with this software demonstrated high acceptance ratings by patients, significant increases in learning of cognitive therapy, and equivalent efficacy to standard CBT (Kenwright et al., 2001; Colby, 1995). Video, audio, and other multimedia elements are used to engage the user and stimulate affect. Users participate in a variety of interactive self-help exercises and are assigned homework to encourage use of CBT in real-life situations. A revised, DVD-ROM version of this software ("Good Days Ahead: The Multimedia Program for Cognitive Therapy") is now available (Colby & Colby, 1990).

Rothbaum (Rothbaum, Anderson, Hodges, Price, & Smith, 2002; Rothbaum, Hodges, & Kooper, 1995; Rothbaum et al., 2001) has pioneered virtual reality technology applications for fear of heights, fear of flying, and Post-Traumatic Stress Disorder (PSTD) in Vietnam War veterans. Controlled trials have found evidence for the efficacy of virtual reality based exposure therapy (Rothbaum et al., 1995, 2001, 2002), but the need for specialized equipment has limited the use of these methods. A more conventional computer program, "Fear Fighter," was developed in Great Britain by Marks and coworkers (Kenwright et al., 2001; Shaw, Marks, & Toole, 1999). This software utilizes text, graphics, and audio to help users plan self-exposure to feared situations and to endure anxiety until it diminishes. Preliminary research suggests that it can substantially reduce the amount of clinician time required for effective treatment of anxiety.

Hand-held computers also have been found to be useful for computer-assisted psychotherapy. Newman and coworkers (1997) found that long-term outcome of computer-assisted CBT for Panic Disorder was equal to standard CBT, even though clinician contact time was reduced to four sessions in those that received the computer adjunct. Gruber and associates (2001) demonstrated the efficacy and cost saving potential of a hand-held computer program added to cognitive-behavioral group treatment for social phobia. Computer-controlled, interactive voice response systems are another possible application of computer technology to perform psychotherapy functions (Greist et al., 2002; Marks et al., 1998). These systems use a conventional telephone instead of a computer terminal or a hand-held device to communicate with the user. Interactive voice response programs for Obsessive-Compulsive Disorder ("BT Steps") and depression ("Cope with Life") have been developed and tested by a team of British and American investigators (Greist et al., 2002; Marks et al., 1998; Osgood-Hines et al., 1998).

Currently, computer programs are not used widely in psychotherapy applications. However, technological advances, increased use of computers in society, and changes in the economics of health care delivery may lead to growth in the use of computer-assisted therapy. If preliminary studies demonstrating patient acceptance, efficacy, and cost-efficiency are confirmed in future research, computer-assisted treatment could become a standard therapeutic tool.

REFERENCES

Bowers, W., Stuart, S., MacFarlane, R., & Gorman, L. (1993). Use of computer-administered cognitive-behavior therapy with depressed inpatients. *Depression, 1,* 294–299.

Carr, A., Ghosh, A., & Marks, I. (1988). Computer supervised exposure treatment for phobias. *Canadian Journal of Psychiatry, 33,* 112–117.

Colby, K. M. (1995). A computer program using cognitive therapy to treat depressed patients. *Psychiatric Services, 46,* 1223–1225.

Colby, K. M., & Colby, P. M. (1990). *Overcoming depression.* Malibu, CA: Malibu Artificial Intelligence Works.

Colby, K. M., Gould, R. I., & Aronson, G. (1989). Some pros and cons of computer-assisted psychotherapy. *Journal of Nervous and Mental Disease, 177,* 105–108.

Colby, K. M., Gould, R. I., Aronson, G., & Colby, P. M. (1991). A model of common-sense reasoning underlying intentional nonaction in stressful interpersonal situations and its application in the technology of computer based psychotherapy. *Journal of Intelligent Systems, 3,* 259–272.

Ghosh, A., Marks, I. M., & Carr, A. C. (1984). Controlled study of self-exposure treatment for phobics: Preliminary communications. *Journal of the Royal Society of Medicine, 77,* 483–487.

Greist, J. H., Marks, I. M., Baer, L., Kobak, K. A., Wenzel, K. W., Hirsch, M. J., Mantle, J. M., & Clary, C. M. (2002). Behavior therapy for OCD guided by a computer or by a clinician compared with relaxation as a control. *Journal of Clinical Psychiatry, 63*(2), 138–145.

Gruber, K., Moran, P., Roth, W., et al. (2001). Computer-assisted CBT for Social Phobia. *Behavior Therapy, 32,* 155–165.

Kenwright, M., Liness, S., & Marks, I. (2001). Reducing demands on clinicians by offering computer-aided self-help for phobia-panic: Feasibility study. *British Journal of Psychiatry, 11,* 456–459.

Locke, S. E., & Rezza, M. E. H. (1996). Computer-based education in mental health. *MD Computing, 13,* 10–45.

Marks, I. M. (1978). *Living with fear.* New York: McGraw Hill.

Marks, I., Baer, L, Greist, J. H., Park, J., Bachifen, M., Nakagawa, A., et al. (1998). Home self-assessment of Obsessive-Compulsive Disorder. Use of a manual and computer-conducted telephone interviews: Two UK-US studies. *British Journal of Psychiatry, 172*(5), 406–412.

Newman, M. G., Kenardy, J., Herman, S., et al. (1997). Comparison of palm top-computer assisted brief cognitive-behavioral treatment for Panic Disorder. *Journal of Consulting and Clinical Psychology, 65,* 178–183.

O'Dell, J. W., & Dickson, J. (1984). "Eliza" as a therapeutic tool. *Computerized Psychotherapy, 40,* 942–945.

Osgood-Hynes, D. J., Greist, J. H., Marks, I. M., Baer, L, Heneman, S. W., Wenzel, K. W., Manzo, P. A., Parkin, J. R., Spierings, C. J., Dottl, S. L., & Vitse, H. M. (1998). Self-administered psychotherapy for depression using a telephone-accessed computer system plus booklets: An open U.S.-U.K. study. *Journal of Clinical Psychiatry, 59*(7), 358–365.

Rothbaum, B., Anderson, P., Hodges, L., Price, L., & Smith, S. (2002). Twelve-month follow-up of virtual reality and standard exposure therapies for the fear of flying. *Journal of Counseling and Clinical Psychology, 70*(2), 428–432.

Rothbaum, B., Hodges, L., & Kooper, R. (1995). Effectiveness of computer-generated virtual reality exposure in the treatment of acrophobia. *American Journal of Psychiatry, 152,* 626–628.

Rothbaum, B., Hodges, L., Ready, D., Graap, K., et al. (2001). Virtual reality exposure therapy for Vietnam veterans with PTSD. *Journal of Clinical Psychiatry, 62*(8), 617–622.

Sampson, J. P., & Pyle, K. R. (1983). Ethical issues involved in with the use of computer assisted counseling, testing and guidance systems. *Personnel and Guidance Journal, 61,* 283–287.

Selmi, P. M, Klein, M. H., & Greist, J. H. (1982). An investigation of computer assisted cognitive-behavioral therapy in the treatment of depression. *Behavior Research Methods and Instruments, 14,* 181–185.

Selmi, P. M, Klein, M. H., & Greist, J. H. (1990). Computer-administered cognitive-behavioral therapy for depression. *American Journal of Psychiatry, 147,* 51–56.

Shaw, S. C., Marks, I. M., & Toole, S. (1999). Lessons from pilot tests of computer self-help for Agoraphobia/claustrophobia and panic. *MD Computing, 7/8,* 44–48.

Stuart, S., & LaRue, S. (1996). Computerized cognitive therapy: The interface between man and machine. *Journal of Cognitive Psychotherapy, 10,* 181–191.

Weizenbaum, J. (1966). Computational linguistics. *Communications of the ACM, 9,* 36–45.

Wright, J. H., & Wright, A. (1997). Computer-assisted psychotherapy. *Journal of Psychotherapy Practice and Research, 6,* 315–329.

Wright, J. H., Wright, A. S., Basco, M. R., Albano, A. M., Raffield, T., Goldsmith, J., et al. (2001, July). *Controlled trial of computer-assisted cognitive therapy for depression.* Poster presented at the World Congress of Cognitive Therapy, Vancouver, Canada.

Wright, J. H., Wright, A. S., & Beck, A. T. (2002). *Good days ahead: The multimedia program for cognitive therapy.* Louisville, KY: Mindstreet.

Wright, J. H., Wright, A. S., Salmon, P., Beck, A. T., Kuykendall, J., Goldsmith, J., et al. (2002). Development and initial testing of a multimedia program for computer-assisted cognitive therapy. *American Journal of Psychotherapy, 56*(1), 76–86.

Jesse H. Wright
Marina Katz
University of Louisville School of Medicine

The author may receive a portion of profits from sale of computer software (The DVD-ROM, "Good Days Ahead") reviewed in this article. A portion of profits from the sale of this software is donated to the Norton Foundation and the Foundation for Cognitive Therapy and Research.

See also: **Anxiety Disorders; Compulsions; Obsessions**

COMPUTERIZED PSYCHOLOGICAL AND BEHAVIORAL ASSESSMENT

The technology boom of the late twentieth century and early twenty-first century was not lost on psychologists and behavior therapists. Researchers have been quick to recognize the potential computers offer in the assessment and treatment of individuals with mental health problems. Efforts to computerize the assessment process, or some component of it, have been made by researchers in all the major theoretical orientations. Computer applications take many forms and are not easily categorized. However, in psychological and behavioral assessment, the following types of applications have emerged.

Computer-assistant programs include software that assists clinicians in collecting client data and/or making diagnostic decisions. For example, researchers have designed *computerized behavior observation systems* to facilitate naturalistic and analog observation of individuals. *Expert systems* are computer-assistant programs that include algorithm structures that are designed to simulate diagnostic-decision making. For example, one group of researchers created a smoking cessation expert system that analyzed assessment data, integrated the information, and made individualized recommendations for treatment strategies in a short report. *Case formulation software* helps clinicians organize important variables operating in a client's life and assists the clinician in developing hypotheses about client functioning. Stephen Haynes and his colleagues have developed a computer program that helps clinicians identify target behavior problems, the effects of those problems, and the causal variables that precede the behavior problems.

Researchers have also developed programs that interactively administer interviews. *Direct computer interviews* are software programs that administer traditional paper-and-pencil questionnaires or structured interviews without the clinician present. These programs typically aggregate data and print reports that assist clinicians in making diagnostic and treatment decisions. Clients may complete the interviews at the beginning of treatment or throughout treatment. For example, Albert Farrell and his colleagues have developed a software program that clients complete at each treatment session to help clinicians monitor client behavior problems.

Virtual reality programs are often used to simulate challenging or feared environments for individuals and can be used in both assessment and treatment contexts. For example, researchers have developed virtual reality programs for phobic individuals that simulate experiences with a feared stimulus. Recently, one research team concluded that phobic individuals are readily immersed in virtual environments and report levels of fear and anxiety similar to what one would expect to see in an exposure therapy session. From a treatment perspective, initial results suggest that exposure therapy conducted via virtual reality is at least as effective as in vivo exposure. Virtual reality systems have also been used with disabled children to assess acquisition of motor behaviors.

Self-monitoring computer programs have taken a variety of formats prior to the computer revolution. *Ecological momentary assessment,* or EMA, refers to the collection of self-monitoring or psychophysiological data in the client's natural environment. Researchers often use handheld computers to administer one or more questionnaires to an individual several times per day at scheduled intervals. The questionnaires are typically brief and usually take no more than a few minutes. Researchers then examine the data for relationships between variables of interest (e.g., mood level and activity). One of the most interesting results from EMA studies thus far is the lack of congruence between client ratings of their own behavior in the natural environment and clinician ratings of client behavior in a structured interview. For example, one group of researchers found in individuals diagnosed with Obsessive-Compulsive Disorder that mean clinician ratings of client symptom severity were almost one standard deviation higher than levels reported by clients in their natural environment.

Computer-based test interpretations (CBTIs) are software programs that generate interpretive reports after assimilating data that are collected by a clinician or a computer. For example, a client might complete a paper-and-pencil administration of a psychological test (e.g., the Minnesota Multiphasic Personality Inventory). The clinician then enters the client's responses into the computer program, and the software generates an interpretive report based on a predetermined algorithm. Alternatively, report generation may be included as an additional feature of a direct computer interview. CBTIs can greatly expedite the process of report writing, but critics argue that they are not sensitive to an individual's unique circumstances, use report-writing rules that are of questionable validity, and tend to produce reports that vague and not clinically meaningful. Most researchers have concluded that CBTIs can be valuable adjuncts to, rather than substitutes for, more individualized clinical assessment and judgment.

Issues In Computerized Assessment

Equivalence

For computer programs that are designed to replicate more cumbersome and time-consuming paper-and-pencil measures or structured interviews, an important consideration is the equivalence of results between the computer version and its parent instrument. How one concludes that data are equivalent is a matter still open to debate. For example, failure to find statistically significant differences between groups using traditional hypothesis testing strategies (e.g., *t*-tests) does not mean that data between groups are equivalent. Currently, there is no commonly held standard for assessing degree of equivalence. The equivalency issue is of more than passing interest because some researchers have found that research participants respond differently when interviewed by a computer. For example, some researchers have found that individuals are more likely to report occurrences of embarrassing, sensitive, or illegal behaviors to a computer than to a human interviewer.

Reactions To Computerized Assessment

Critics of computerized psychological and behavioral assessment have sometimes contended that clients will respond negatively to computer interviews and will be alienated from treatment as a result. Generally, researchers have not found this to be the case. For example, one group of researchers found that neither college students nor Vietnam veterans showed a preference for a computerized or human-administered format for Post-Traumatic Stress Disorder interviews. Other researchers have reported a trend toward clients' *preferring* the computer interview.

Summary and Conclusion

Computerized psychological and behavioral assessment is a field experiencing exponential growth, which is catalyzed by technological advances and promises to deliver tremendous gains in the coming years. The field will prosper as long as the software applications are developed that help clinicians rapidly and accurately assess client functioning.

David C. S. Richard
Eastern Michigan University

CONCEPTUAL LEARNING AND DEVELOPMENT

Bruner, Goodnow, and Austin (1956) presented a theory of thinking that stimulated widespread interest in concept learning. The high interest continued into the 1980s but then lessened except as it related to science concepts. Piagetian theory on children's development of the concept of *number* (Piaget 1952) and of *space* (Piaget & Inhelder 1956), reported in books in English, generated worldwide interest in children's conceptual development. His theory remains a predominant theory of child development.

Klausmeier and his associates began programmatic research in 1960 directed toward testing the theories of both Bruner and Piaget. They found concept learning and concept development to be inseparably related. In turn, Klausmeier reported a rudimentary theory of conceptual learning and development in a 1971 journal article and a refined theory in 1992. The main propositions of the refined theory follow.

Concepts are the fundamental agents of intellectual activity, the basic component of a maturing individual's continuously enlarging cognitive structure. A concept consists of a person's organized information about an item or a class of items. Item as used here refers to an object (e.g. cutting tool), event (e.g., birthday), action (e.g., run), quality (e.g., thick), relationship (e.g., taxonomic), or abstract construct (e.g., eternity).

Concepts that have two or more instances are attained at four successively higher levels of understanding. Specific mental operations that emerge with neural maturation and learning and then become more powerful with further maturation and learning make possible the attainment of each successively higher level.

The four consecutive levels are *concrete, identity, classificatory,* and *formal.* Attainment of the prior level is prerequisite for attaining the next level.

A concept has been attained at the concrete level when the learner recognizes an item (e.g., a clock on the wall) as the same one previously encountered in the identical spatial context or other context in which it was initially encountered. The mental operations involved in attaining a concept at the concrete level are selectively attending to an item, discriminating the item as an entity different from its surroundings, representing the item in long-term memory, attending to the item when it is again encountered in the identical context, retrieving the representation, and using it in recognizing the item as the same one encountered earlier.

Attaining a concept at the identity level involves recognizing an item as the same one previously encountered when it is observed from a different spatiotemporal perspective or when it is sensed in a different modality. The new mental operation that enables attaining the identity level is generalizing that the item, although experienced differently, is the same one cognized earlier.

Attaining the classificatory level requires recognizing at least two items (e.g., the clock on the wall and one on the desk) as being equivalent. Generalizing that at least two items are equivalent is the new operation that enables attaining the classificatory level. Concept attainment of the classificatory level continues until the learner can recognize any instance or noninstance of the concept.

Concept attainment of the formal level is inferred when the individual can identify any instance of the concept and any noninstance, give the name of the concept and the names of its defining attributes, state how any instance of the concept differs from any noninstance in terms of defining attributes, and give the experts' definition of the concept. Abstract thinking with words and other symbols facilitates learning the formal level.

Not all concepts can be learned at all four levels. Concepts for which there is only one instance (e.g., the Earth's moon) are learned only at the concrete and identity levels. Abstract concepts that have no observable instances (e.g., soul) are learned only at the formal level.

Focused instruction accelerates the learning of concepts. The learning aspect of conceptual learning and development theory is based on classroom experiments (Klausmeier, Ghatala, & Frayer, 1974; Klausmeier & Sipple, 1980). Major findings follow.

Repeated presentation of an item is necessary for attaining the concrete and identity levels of a concept. Experience with concept examples and nonexamples is essential for learning to classify correctly. The examples and nonexamples are most effective when the examples differ from one another in their nondefining, or variable, attributes; range from easy to difficult; and are presented concurrently. Providing the learner (1) examples and nonexamples that have nearly the same defining attributes, (2) the name of the concept, (3) the names of its defining attributes, and (4) a definition of the concept facilitates attainment of the formal level.

Giving the learner the name of the concept facilitates attainment of all four levels. Providing a definition reduces the number of examples and nonexamples required. Teaching students a strategy accelerates learning markedly, especially at the classificatory and formal levels.

The time required for attaining the four levels of concepts varies greatly. The time is longer for abstract concepts (e.g., noun) than for concrete concepts (e.g., cutting tool) and for slower cognitive developers than rapid developers.

Students vary greatly in the attainment of concepts. To illustrate, 20% of third-grade students had attained the formal level of *noun* while 21% of 12th-grade students had not.

As a concept is attained from the identity to the formal level it can be used more effectively to (1) recognize instances and noninstances of the concept, (2) understand principles of which the concept is a part, (3) understand relationships of the taxonomy of which the concept is a part, and (4) solve problems requiring understanding of the concept.

There are numerous theories of category learning, one being prototype theory, which was formulated by Rosch (1975, 1978). According to this theory, newly encountered objects are identified as members of a category by comparing them with a prototype that is the best or most typical instance of the concept that was learned earlier.

REFERENCES

Bruner, J. S., Goodnow, J. J., & Austin, G. A. (1956). *A study of thinking.* New York: Wiley

Klausmeier, H. J. (1971). Cognitive operations in concept learning. *Educational Psychologist, 9,* 1–8.

Klausmeier, H. J. (1992). Concept learning and concept teaching. *Educational Psychologist, 27,* 267–286

Klausmeier, H. J., & Allen, P. S. (1978). *Cognitive development of children and youth: A longitudinal study.* New York: Academic Press.

Klausmeier, H. J., et al. (1979). *Cognitive learning and development: Information-processing and Piagetian perspectives.* Cambridge, MA: Ballinger.

Klausmeier, H. J., Ghatala, E. S., & Frayer, D. A. (1974). *Conceptual learning and development: A cognitive view.* New York: Academic Press.

Klausmeier, H. J., & Sipple, T. S. (1980). *Learning and teaching process concepts: A strategy for testing applications of theory.* New York: Academic Press.

Piaget, J. (1952). *The child's conception of number.* New York: Humanities Press.

Piaget, J., & Inhelder, B. (1956). *The child's conception of space.* London: Routledge.

Rosch, E. (1975). Cognitive representation of semantic categories. *Journal of Experimental Psychology, General, 104,* 192–233.

Rosch, E. (1978). Principles of categorization. In E. Rosch & B. Lloyd (Eds.), *Cognition and categorization* (pp. 9–31). Hillsdale, NJ: Erlbaum.

Herbert J. Klausmeier

***See also:* Piaget's Theory; School Learning**

CONDITIONED FOOD AVERSION

A conditioned food aversion is a learned dislike for and rejection of particular flavors that have been associated with illness. The strength of such learning depends on the procedure used to pair the food with the illness in time, the characteristics of the food, and the nature of the illness.

Conditioning Procedure

The procedure used to produce conditioned food aversions resembles classical conditioning. The conditioned stimulus (CS) is usually a novel flavor, and the unconditioned stimulus (US) is often an emetic agent. The unconditioned response (UR) is not well defined and is assumed to be related to the nausea, malaise, or other internal disruptions induced by the US. After one or more pairings with the US, the CS then comes to elicit a conditioned response (CR) that presumably resembles the illness of the UR, and the animal acts as if the CS is aversive and avoids further contact with it. An important control procedure is an unpaired group that receives equivalent experience with both the CS and US but at sufficiently different times that conditioning to the CS does not occur.

Two types of tests commonly used to evaluate the effects of conditioning are the preference test and the taste reactivity test. In the preference test, animals are given access to a choice between the CS and another neutral substance, such as their normal diet or water. After conditioning, intake of the CS is selectively reduced. In the taste reactivity test (Grill & Norgren 1978), the CS is infused directly into the mouth of the subject, and species-typical ingestive or rejection reactions are quantified. After aversion conditioning with emetic agents, subjects increase their rejection reactions and decrease their ingestive reactions.

In sharp contrast to the traditional classical conditioning procedure, the interval from the CS to US in food aversion conditioning can be as long as a few hours and still produce robust conditioning in a single trial (Garcia, Hankins, & Rusiniak, 1974). These features of aversion conditioning help an animal to learn to avoid poisonous foods without multiple experiences with the poison even if the poison does not immediately make the animal sick.

Characteristics of the Food

The phenomenon of conditioned food aversion is also known as *conditioned taste* or *flavor aversion, poison-based avoidance conditioning, bait shyness,* or *aversion therapy* depending on the interests of the investigator. A taste aversion implies that the aversion is limited to a gustatory CS: that is, one that is sensed by the tongue. A flavor aversion implies that both taste and odor cues compose the CS and that both contribute to the conditioning.

Substances having a bitter, sour, or putrid flavor may evoke an unconditioned aversion, but investigators in food aversion studies typically use flavors that produce positive ingestive responses, such as a dilute solution of saccharin. After administration of an emetic agent such as lithium chloride (LiCl), a decrease in ingestion rapidly emerges in animals that received the CS and US paired closely in time. Any distinctive taste or flavor can be the target of a conditioned aversion, but some types of flavors seem to be particularly prone to the development of aversions. For example, proteins such as eggs, cheese, and meat are more likely to become targets of conditioned food aversions than carbohydrates, and novel foods are more likely to become targets than familiar foods (Bernstein, 1999).

Nature of the Illness

Unconditioned stimuli that are known to induce food aversions usually produce some type of gastric distress, including nausea, vomiting, or malaise. LiCl is commonly used for experimental treatments in rats. Emetic agents used for conditioned aversion therapy in humans with alcohol dependency include apomorphine, emetidine, syrup of ipecac, disulfiram, ethanol, and others (Howard & Jenson, 1990). Nondrug experimental procedures that produce conditioned aversions include rotational dizziness and some abdominal surgical procedures such as a subdiaphragmatic vagotomy or a bile duct ligation (Lane, Starbuck, & Fitts, 1997). Accidental pairings of harmless novel foods with subsequent gastrointestinal illness probably account for many food aversions in humans, as when persons experience nausea as a result of cancer or cancer chemotherapy.

Other types of treatments that may induce avoidance when they are paired with certain foods or tastes include drugs such as amphetamine, cocaine, morphine, and phencyclidine. Curiously, and in great contrast to the emetic drugs, rats will self-administer these drugs under certain experimental circumstances. The avoidance of a food after its pairing with a rewarding drug may be fundamentally different from the avoidance induced by emetic drugs: After conditioning with a rewarding drug, rats still drink less of a CS in preference tests, but they fail to show large increases in rejection reactions in the taste reactivity test (Parker, 1995).

Neurobiology of Conditioned Food Aversions

Certain parts of the brain related to autonomic activity and emesis become active following administration of an emetic US, and an analysis of such brain activity is improving our understanding of what constitutes the US, UR, and CR in food aversion studies (Bernstein, 1999). The nucleus of the solitary tract (NTS) in the hindbrain receives much afferent input from both the abdominal viscera and the gustatory system, and an injection of LiCl, the US, in rats produces a characteristic pattern of neural activation in NTS as measured by expression of the immediate early gene c-Fos. Intraoral infusions of a preferred solution such as saccharin or of a noxious tastant such as quinine do not by themselves induce c-Fos expression in the NTS, but once saccharin has been paired with LiCl, an intraoral infusion of saccharin alone, the CS, thereafter evokes activity in the NTS as if LiCl had been given instead (Swank & Bernstein, 1994). Thus, the CR as measured by c-Fos expression in the brain resembles the UR. This activation of the NTS results from descending information from the forebrain, suggesting a learning interpretation, and does not result simply from conditioned fear or autonomic arousal (Bernstein 1999; Schafe, Fitts, Thiele, LeDoux & Bernstein, in press).

The neural substrates of conditioned food aversions differ considerably depending on the procedures used to elicit them. Lesions in the amygdala abolish aversions conditioned by intraoral infusion of a CS but do not disrupt those conditioned by drinking the CS from a bottle (Schafe, Thiele, & Bernstein, 1998); lesions of the inferior olive disrupt aversions conditioned by a concurrent acquisition procedure but not by a sequential procedure (Mediavilla, Molina, & Puerto, 1999); and lesions of the area postrema eliminate aversions conditioned by emetic agents such as LiCl (Ritter, McGlone & Kelley, 1980) but not those conditioned by amphetamine or apomorphine (Berger, Wise & Stein, 1973; Van der Kooy, Swerdlow, & Koob, 1983). Clearly, conditioned food aversions are not a unitary phenomenon but represent several different neural processes that may reflect different kinds of learning (i.e., classical and instrumental conditioning).

REFERENCES

Berger, B. D., Wise, C. D., & Stein, L. (1973). Area postrema damage and bait shyness. *Journal of Comparative Physiology and Psychology, 82,* 475–479.

Bernstein, I. L. (1999). Taste aversion learning: A contemporary perspective. *Nutrition, 15,* 229–234.

Garcia, J., Hankins, W. G., & Rusiniak, K. W. (1974). Regulation of the milieu interne in man and rat. *Science, 185,* 823–831.

Grill, H. J., & Norgren, R. (1978). The taste reactivity test: I. Mimetic responses to gustatory stimuli in neurologically normal rats. *Brain Research, 143,* 263–279.

Howard, M. O., & Jenson, J. M. (1990). Chemical aversion treatment of alcohol dependence: II. Future research directions for the '90s. *International Journal of the Addictions, 25,* 1403–1414.

Lane, J. R., Starbuck, E. M., & Fitts, D. A. (1997). Ethanol preference, metabolism, blood pressure, and conditioned taste aversion in experimental cholestasis. *Pharmacology, Biochemistry, and Behavior, 57,* 755–766.

Mediavilla, C., Molina, F., & Puerto, A. (1999). Inferior olive lesions impair concurrent taste aversion learning in rats. *Neurobiology of Learning and Memory, 72,* 13–27.

Parker, L. A. (1995). Rewarding drugs produce taste avoidance, but not taste aversion. *Neuroscience and Biobehavioral Reviews, 19,* 143–151.

Ritter, R. C., McGlone, J. J., & Kelley, K. W. (1980). Absence of lithium-induced taste aversion after area postrema lesion. *Brain Research, 201,* 501–506.

Schafe, G. E., Fitts, D. A., Thiele, T. E., LeDoux, J. E., & Bernstein, I. L. (2000). The induction of c-Fos in NTS following taste aversion learning is not correlated with measures of conditioned fear. *Behavioral Neuroscience, 114,* 99–106.

Schafe, G. E., Thiele, T. E., & Bernstein, I. L. (1998). Conditioning method dramatically alters the role of amygdala in taste aversion learning. *Journal of Experimental Psychology: Learning, Memory, and Cognition, 5,* 481–492.

Swank, M. W., & Bernstein, I. L. (1994). C-Fos induction in response to a conditioned stimulus after single trial taste aversion learning. *Brain Research, 636,* 202–208.

Van der Kooy, D., Swerdlow, N. R., & Koob, G. F. (1983). Paradoxical reinforcing properties of apomorphine: Effects of nucleus accumbens and area postrema lesions. *Brain Research, 259,* 111–118.

Douglas A. Fitts
University of Washington

See also: **Operant Conditioning**

CONDUCT DISORDER

Conduct Disorder is a repetitive and persistent pattern of behavior that violates societal norms or the basic rights of others (American Psychiatric Association [ApA], 1994), covering four symptom areas: (1) aggressive behavior that threatens or causes physical harm to other people or animals (e.g., bullies, threatens, or intimidates others;), (2) nonaggressive conduct that causes property loss or damage (e.g., fire setting), (3) deceitfulness or theft (e.g., breaking into someone's house or car), and (4) serious violation of rules (e.g., truancy). To be diagnosed, at least 3 of 15 possible symptoms must have been displayed during the past 12 months. Childhood-onset Conduct Disorder is differentiated from adolescent-onset when at least one of the behavioral characteristics is evident before age 10.

Although some forms of aggressive behaviors are relatively common in mild forms during early childhood years, such behaviors become clinically significant if the instances are highly intense, high in frequency, or characterized by notably violent elements in later years. Estimated rates of Conduct Disorder are 6 to 16% for boys and 2 to 9% for girls (ApA, 1994), with boys outnumbering girls about three to one (Kazdin, 1998; Lochman & Szczepanski, 1999). Loeber (1990) hypothesized that aggressive behavior in elementary school years is part of a developmental trajectory that can lead to adolescent delinquency and Conduct Disorder. Similarly, the fourth edition of the *Diagnostic and Statistical Manual of Mental Disorders* (*DSM-IV;* ApA, 1994) indicates that Oppositional Defiant Disorder can evolve into childhood-onset Conduct Disorder and then into Antisocial Personality Disorder in adults. Longitudinal research has documented that aggressive behavior and rejection by children's peers can be additive risk markers for subsequent maladjusted behavior in the middle school years (Coie, Lochman, Terry, & Hyman, 1992) and for substance use, overt delinquency, and police arrests in later adolescent years (Coie, Terry, Zakriski, & Lochman, 1995; Lochman & Wayland, 1994). Children are more at risk for continued aggressive and antisocial behavior if they display aggressive behavior in multiple settings and if they develop so-called versatile forms of antisocial behavior, including both overt and covert behaviors by early to mid-adolescence (Lochman & Szszepanski, 1999).

The developmental trajectory leading to childhood-onset Conduct Disorder may start very early among inflexible infants with irritable temperaments (Loeber, 1990). These children are at risk for failing to develop positive attachments with caregivers, displaying high rates of hyperactivity and inattention in the preschool years, and becoming involved in increasingly coercive interchanges with parents and significant adults, such as teachers. Moffitt (1993) has suggested that life-course-persistent delinquents ("early starters") are at risk because of combined biological and family factors. In some children, family dysfunction may be sufficient to initiate this sequence of escalating aggressive behavior. Parents of aggressive, conduct problem children often display high rates of harsh, inconsistent discipline, have unclear rules and expectations, and have low rates of positive involvement, adaptive discipline strategies, and problem-solving skills (Lochman & Wells, 1996; Patterson, 1986).

Loeber (1990) hypothesized that children begin to generalize their use of coercive behaviors to other social interactions, leading to increasingly aggressive behavior with peers and adults and to dysfunctional social-cognitive processes, which in turn serve to maintain problem behavior sequences. For example, aggressive children tend to have hostile attributional biases and problem-solving strategies that rely on forceful, direct action rather than verbal, negotiation strategies, and they expect that aggressive solutions will work (Crick & Dodge, 1994). These information-processing difficulties are made worse for aggressive children because of their dominance-oriented social goals, pervasive schema-based expectations for others' behavior, and strong physiological reactivity in response to provocation (Dodge, Lochman, Harnish, Bates, & Pettit, 1997; Lochman & Dodge, 1998; Lochman & Szczepanski, 1999), as well as their poor verbal fluency and abstract reasoning abilities (Kazdin, 1998). Furthermore, children displaying aggressive behavior are often socially rejected by their peer group and can become more withdrawn and isolated. By early to middle adolescence, they are prone to meeting their affiliation needs by gravitating toward deviant peer groups, which can become an additional proximal cause for delinquent behavior (Coie et al., 1995; Patterson, Reid, & Dishion, 1992).

Historically, psychosocial treatment of antisocial, conduct-disordered youths has been perceived to be difficult and not very productive. However, in recent years randomized clinical research trials have identified empirically supported treatments for Oppositional Defiant Disorder and Conduct Disorder. Brestan and Eyberg (1998) have identified two parent-training intervention programs with well-established positive effects (Patterson et al., 1992; Webster-Stratton, 1994) and ten other programs as probably efficacious for treating Conduct Disorder. Kazdin (1998; Kazdin & Weisz, 1998) has similarly identified several positive treatment approaches for Conduct Disorder, including Parent Management Training, Functional Family Therapy, Cognitive Problem-Solving Skills Training, and Multisystemic Therapy. Parent Management Training and Functional Family Therapy are directed at dysfunctional parenting processes and have produced significant improvements in parenting practices and reductions in children's aggressive conduct problem behavior (Alexander & Parsons, 1973; Eyberg, Boggs, & Algina, 1995; Peed, Roberts, & Forehand, 1977; Webster-Stratton, 1994; Wiltz & Patterson, 1974). Cognitive-behavioral treatments designed to assist children's anger management, perspective-taking, and problem-solving skills have produced improvements in children's abilities to accurately perceive others' intentions and to generate more competent problem solutions and have led to reductions in problem behaviors (Feindler, Marriott, & Iwata, 1984; Kazdin, Siegel, & Bass, 1992; Lochman, Burch, Curry, & Lampron, 1984). Multisystemic treatment relies on individualized assessments of antisocial youths and the impaired systems around them (e.g., parents, peer groups, school bonding) and uses intense, individualized treatment plans to affect these systems, producing significant reductions in antisocial behavior among seriously delinquent youth (Henggeler, Melton, & Smith, 1992). In recent years, there has been a focus on developing and evaluating effective multicomponent interventions that target both the social-cognitive and parenting skill deficits evident in Conduct-Disordered youths and their families (Kazdin et al., 1992; Webster-Stratton & Hammond, 1997). Intensive, comprehensive prevention programs have also been developed and evaluated with high-risk children starting as early as first grade, and the results indicate that aggressive behavior and Conduct Disorder can be reduced through early intervention (Conduct Problems Prevention Research Group, 1999; Vitaro, Brendgen, Pagani, Tremblay, & McDuff, 1999).

REFERENCES

Alexander, J. F., & Parsons, B. V. (1973). Short-term behavioral intervention with delinquent families: Impact on family process and recidivism. *Journal of Abnormal Psychology, 81,* 219–225.

American Psychiatric Association. (1994). *Diagnostic and statistical manual of mental disorders* (4th ed.). Washington, DC: Author.

Brestan, E. V., & Eyberg, S. M. (1998). Effective psychosocial treatments of Conduct-Disordered children and adolescents: 29 years, 82 studies, and 5,272 kids. *Journal of Clinical Child Psychology, 27,* 180–189.

Coie, J. D., Lochman, J. E., Terry, R., & Hyman, C. (1992). Predicting early adolescent disorder from childhood aggression and peer rejection. *Journal of Consulting and Clinical Psychology, 60,* 783–792.

Coie, J. D., Terry, R., Zakriski, A., & Lochman, J. E. (1995). Early adolescent social influences on delinquent behavior. In J. McCord (Ed.), *Coercion and punishment in long-term perspectives* (pp. 229–244). Cambridge, UK: Cambridge University Press.

Conduct Problems Prevention Research Group. (1999). Initial impact of the Fast Track prevention trial for conduct problems: I. The high-risk sample. *Journal of Consulting and Clinical Psychology, 67,* 631–647.

Crick, N. R., & Dodge, K. A. (1994). A review and reformulation of social information-processing mechanisms in children's social adjustment. *Psychological Bulletin, 115,* 74–101.

Dodge, K. A., Lochman, J. E., Harnish, J. D., Bates, J. E., & Pettit, G. S. (1997). Reactive and proactive aggression in school children and psychiatrically impaired chronically assaultive youth. *Journal of Abnormal Psychology, 106,* 37–51.

Eyberg, S. M., Boggs, S., & Algina, J. (1995). Parent-child interaction therapy: A psychosocial model for the treatment of young children with conduct problem behavior and their families. *Psychopharmacology Bulletin, 31,* 83–91.

Feindler, D. L., Marriott, S. A., & Iwata, M. (1984). Group anger control training for junior high school delinquents. *Cognitive Therapy and Research, 8,* 299–311.

Henggeler, S. W., Melton, G. B., & Smith, L. A. (1992). Family preservation using Multisystemic Therapy: An effective alternative to incarcerating serious juvenile offenders. *Journal of Consulting and Clinical Psychology, 60,* 953–961.

Kazdin, A. E. (1998). Conduct disorder. In R. J. Morris & T. R. Kratochwill (Eds.), *The practice of child therapy* (3rd ed., pp. 199–230). Boston: Allyn & Bacon.

Kazdin, A. E., Siegel, T. C., & Bass, D. (1992). Cognitive problem-solving skills training and parent management training in the treatment of antisocial behavior in children. *Journal of Consulting and Clinical Psychology, 60,* 733–747.

Kazdin, A. E., & Weisz, J. R. (1998). Identifying and developing empirically supported child and adolescent treatments. *Journal of Consulting and Clinical Psychology, 66,* 19–36.

Lochman, J. E., Burch, P. R., Curry, J. F., & Lampron, L. B. (1984). Treatment and generalization effects of cognitive-behavioral and goal-setting interventions with aggressive boys. *Journal of Consulting and Clinical Psychology, 52,* 915–916.

Lochman, J. E., & Dodge, K. A. (1998). Distorted perceptions in dyadic interactions of aggressive and nonaggressive boys: Effects of prior expectations, context, and boys' age. *Development and Psychopathology, 10,* 495–512.

Lochman, J. E., & Szczepanski, R. G. (1999). Externalizing conditions. In V. L. Schwean & D. H. Saklofske (Eds.), *Psychosocial correlates of exceptionality* (pp. 219–246). New York: Plenum.

Lochman, J. E., & Wayland, K. K. (1994). Aggression, social acceptance and race as predictors of negative adolescent outcomes. *Journal of the American Academy of Child and Adolescent Psychiatry, 33,* 1026–1035.

Lochman, J. E., & Wells, K. C. (1996). A social-cognitive intervention with aggressive children: Prevention effects and contextual implementation issues. In R. D. Peters & R. J. McMahon

(Eds.), *Prevention of childhood disorders, substance abuse, and delinquency* (pp. 111–143). Thousand Oaks, CA: Sage.

Loeber, R. (1990). Development and risk factors of juvenile antisocial behavior and delinquency. *Clinical Psychology Review, 10,* 1–42.

Moffitt, T. E. (1993). Adolescence-limited and life-course persistent antisocial behavior: A developmental taxonomy. *Psychology Review, 100,* 674–701.

Patterson, G. R. (1986). Performance models for antisocial boys. *American Psychologist, 41,* 145–166.

Patterson, G. R., Reid, J. B., & Dishion, T. J. (1992). *Antisocial boys.* Eugene, OR: Castalia.

Peed, S., Roberts, M., & Forehand, R. (1977). Evaluation of the effectiveness of a standardized parent training program in altering the interaction of mothers and their noncompliant children. *Behavior Modification, 1,* 323–350.

Vitaro, F., Brendgen, M., Pagani, L., Tremblay, R. E., & McDuff, P. (1999). Disruptive behavior, peer association, and Conduct Disorder: Testing the developmental links through early intervention. *Development and Psychopathology, 11,* 287–304.

Webster-Stratton, C. (1994). Advancing videotape parent training: A comparison study. *Journal of Consulting and Clinical Psychology, 62,* 583–593.

Webster-Stratton, C., & Hammond, M. (1997). Treating children with early-onset conduct problems: A comparison of child and parent training interventions. *Journal of Consulting and Clinical Psychology, 65,* 93–109.

Wiltz, N. A., & Patterson, G. R. (1974). An evaluation of parent training procedures designed to alter inappropriate aggressive behavior of boys. *Behavior Therapy, 5,* 215–221.

John E. Lochman
University of Alabama

Tammy D. Barry
Texas A&M University

See also: **Antisocial Personality Disorder; Parent Management Training**

CONDUCTION APHASIA

Definition and Clinical Findings

Conduction aphasia is a specific language deficit that consists of impaired repetition that is disproportionate to any defects in fluency or comprehension. Literal paraphasias—errors in which incorrect syllables are substituted within words for correct ones—are frequent and are exacerbated by attempts at repetition. In contrast to patients with Wernicke's aphasia, these patients are aware of their deficit and have no difficulty in comprehension. Ideomotor apraxias—inability to perform a manual task despite comprehending its goal—can also be present. To neurologists conduction aphasia is an important clinical finding because it reliably indicates a brain lesion involving the dominant posterior perisylvian region. To cognitive neuroscientists, conduction aphasia stands at the center of a long-standing debate on whether complex behaviors are created from joining of simple cortical regions or are mediated by more specialized cortex.

Localization

Classically, conduction aphasia results from lesions of the arcuate fasciculus that disconnect receptive from expressive language regions. The arcuate fasiculus is a white matter tract that runs from Wernicke's area in the posterior superior temporal gyrus, arches around the sylvian fissure, and runs anteriorly to the inferior frontal lobe of Broca's region.

Many lesions that cause conduction aphasia not only involve the arcuate fasciculus but also include the supramarginal gyrus and, sometimes, the posterior superior temporal gyrus, the left auditory complex, and portions of the insula. Most cases of conduction aphasia follow cerebral infarcts of the dominant hemisphere involving thromboembolic occlusion of a posterior branch of the middle cerebral artery. It is relatively rare in comparison to other major aphasias (global, expressive, and receptive) because thromboemboli usually lodge more proximally, causing more anterior or widespread infarcts.

Carl Wernicke postulated that a lesion of the arcuate fasciculus that disconnected receptive from expressive centers would produce a deficit in repetition, or *conduction aphasia.* Others proposed that a single cortical center was responsible for integration of receptive and expressive regions yet was independent of them (Goldstein, 1948). This hypothesis lead to adoption of the alternative term *central aphasia* because the specific cortical region mediated central or inner speech.

Evidence Supporting Disconnection

Evidence from subjects with conduction aphasia usually supports the concept of disconnection. In these studies (usually patients with strokes examined at autopsy or by neuroimaging), disruption of the arcuate fasiculus is obligate with variable involvement of adjacent regions of supra- or subsylvian cortex (Benson et al., 1973; Damasio & Damasio, 1980). Studies of cortical strokes in determinations of cortical versus subcortical mechanisms can be misleading, however, because regions of destruction involve both cortex and the arcuate fasciculus.

Circumscribed lesions of the arcuate fasiculus that spare overlying cortex also support disconnection (Aihara et al., 1995; Arnett, Rao, Hussian, Swanson, & Hammeke, 1996; Tanabe et al., 1987), but with white matter lesions (caused by multiple sclerosis, for example) it is not possible to differentiate between the relative importance of disruption of the arcuate fasiculus and disconnections of overlying neurons along its course.

Physiological findings have also supported disconnection

as the mechanism of conduction aphasia. Regional blood flow determined by xenon CT-scan was absent in Broca's region in stroke patients with conduction aphasia, suggesting functional disconnection (Demeurisse & Capon, 1991).

Electrical stimulation, unlike clinical-pathological correlations in stroke, can more selectively separate cortical from white matter dysfunction. Electrical stimulation of eloquent cortex produced both Broca's and Wernicke's aphasias but not conduction aphasia (Schäffler, Lüders, & Beck, 1996), suggesting that conduction aphasia is not cortically mediated. Notably, in this series of patients with implanted subdural electrodes, the testing paradigm involved mainly reading aloud, and repetition may not have been tested (Schäffler et al., 1996).

Evidence Supporting Cortical Specialization

Other studies suggest that disconnection may not be the only mechanism of conduction aphasia. Some cases of conduction aphasia were caused by lesions that clearly spared the arcuate fasciculus (Marshall, Lazar, Mohr, Van Heertum, & Mast, 1996; Mendez & Benson, 1985). Similarly, lesions confined to the arcuate fasciculus have not always resulted in conduction aphasia (Shuren et al., 1995).

Physiologic data provided by positron emission tomography (PET) imaging does not clearly support the disconnection theory. In one study of stroke and conduction aphasia, cerebral metabolic patterns had no clear correlation to clinical findings (Kempler et al., 1988), suggesting that functional disconnection is not necessary to produce conduction aphasia.

PET studies are correlated by two independent reports of cortical mapping using electrical stimulation of implanted electrodes. In these cases, impaired repetition, with other features of conduction aphasia, was transiently elicited by stimulations of the posterior superior temporal gyrus (Anderson et al., 1999; Quigg & Fountain, 1999). The selective and reversible impairment of a specific region of cortex suggests that conduction aphasia is mediated by regions of specialized cortex.

Although the classic Wernicke model is insufficient to account for all cases of conduction aphasia, it remains a clinically useful means by which to organize deficits in language.

REFERENCES

Aihara, M., Oba, H., Ohtomo, K., Uchiyama, G., Hayashibe, H., & Nakazawa, S. (1995). MRI of white matter changes in the Sjogren-Larsson syndrome. *Neuroradiology, 37,* 576–577.

Anderson, J. M., Gilmore, R., Roper, S., Crosson, B., Bauer, R. M., Nadeau, S., Beuersdorf, D. Q., & Heilman, K. M. (1999), Conduction aphasia and the arcuate fasiculus: A reexamination of the Wernicke-Geschwind model. *Brain and Language, 70,* 1–12.

Arnett, P., Rao, S., Hussian, M., Swanson, S., & Hammeke, T. (1996). Conduction aphasia in multiple sclerosis: A case report with MRI findings. *Neurology, 47,* 576–578.

Benson, D., Sheremata, W., Bouchard, R., Segarra, J., Price, D., & Geschwind, N. (1973). Conduction Aphasia. *Archives Neurology, 28,* 339–346.

Damasio, H., & Damasio, A. (1980). The anatomic basis of conduction aphasia. *Brain, 103,* 337–350.

Demeurisse, G., & Capon, A. (1991). Brain activation during a linguistic task in conduction aphasia. *Cortex, 27,* 285–294.

Goldstein, K. (1948). *Language and language disturbances.* New York: Grune and Stratton.

Kempler, D., Metter, E., Jackson, C., Hanson, W., Riege, W., Mazziotta, J., & Phelps, M. (1988). Disconnection and cerebral metabolism: The case of conduction aphasia. *Archives Neurology, 45,* 275–279.

Marshall, R., Lazar, R., Mohr, J., Van Heertum, R., & Mast, H. (1996). "Semantic" conduction aphasia from a posterior insular cortex infarction. *Journal of Neuroimaging, 6,* 189–191.

Mendez, M., & Benson, D. (1985). Atypical conduction aphasia: A disconnection syndrome. *Archives of Neurology, 42,* 886–891.

Quigg, M., & Fountain, N. B. (1999). Conduction aphasia elicited by cortical stimulation of the posterior superior temporal gyrus. *Journal of Neurology, Neurosurgery and Psychiatry, 66,* 393–396.

Schäffler, L., Lüders, H., & Beck, G. (1996). Quantitative comparison of language deficits produced by extraoperative electrical stimulation of Broca's, Wernicke's, and basal temporal language areas. *Epilepsia, 37,* 463–475.

Shuren, J., Schefft, B., Yeh, H., Privitera, M., Cahill, W., & Houston, W. (1995). Repetition and the arcuate fasciculus. *Journal of Neurology, 242,* 596–598.

Tanabe, H., Sawada, T., Inoue, N., Ogawa, M., Kuriyama, Y., & Shiraishi, J. (1987). Conduction aphasia and arcuate fasciculus. *ACTA Neurologica Scandinavica, 76,* 422–427.

Mark Quigg
University of Virginia

CONFIDENCE INTERVAL

The concept of the confidence interval was introduced and developed theoretically by Neyman in the 1930s. The confidence interval represents the range of values around a parameter estimate that indicates the degree of certainty that the range contains the true value of the population parameter. The upper and lower boundaries of the range are the confidence limits. The width of the confidence interval indicates the degree of precision associated with the parameter estimate. Wider intervals indicate less precision, and narrower intervals indicate greater precision. The width of the interval can never be zero, because there will always be some sampling error associated with estimating a population parameter from sample data. Sampling error may be due to measurement unreliability or other chance factors that cause fluctuations from sample to sample. The result is that no matter how carefully a sample is drawn or how large it is, there can be no certainty that the sample estimate is exactly equal to the parameter (population) value.

The calculation of the confidence interval for any parameter is based on the standard error of the relevant sampling distribution. For a simple observation, X, assuming an underlying normal distribution with mean μ and standard deviation σ, the confidence limits on the observation can be stated simply as $X = \mu \pm z\sigma$, where z represents the standard normal deviate associated with any particular level of confidence. Any confidence level may be specified, but in practice the most commonly used intervals are the 95%, 99%, and 99.9% levels:

$$\text{95\% confidence limits: } -1.96\sigma \le X - \mu \le 1.96\sigma$$

$$\text{99\% confidence limits: } -2.58\sigma \le X - \mu \le +2.58\sigma$$

$$\text{99.9\% confidence limits: } -3.29\sigma \le X - \mu \le +3.29\sigma$$

During the early decades of research in experimental psychology, confidence intervals of 50% were commonly reported, based on the concept of the probable error ($\mu \pm 0.6745\sigma$). It is now seldom used and is generally considered obsolete.

Confidence limits can be computed for any sample statistic for which the sampling distribution is known. For example, for the mean (M), the standard error of the mean (σ_m) is used, so that $M = \mu \pm z\sigma_m$. If the population mean and standard error are not known, which is often the case, estimates of the mean and standard error based on observed samples may be substituted. However, in this situation, the confidence limits must be set using the t-distribution rather than the normal (z) distribution. When sampling distributions are unknown or seriously depart from the normal distribution, various advanced techniques can be employed to estimate the standard error from observed data, such as bootstrapping, jackknifing, and computer simulation. Confidence intervals are most commonly reported for well-known statistics such as sample means, correlation and regression coefficients, proportions, and predicted scores, but they should also be determined for less commonly used statistics, such as measures of effect size and goodness-of-fit indexes.

As an example of the use of confidence intervals, consider an incoming class of 750 college freshman with an average recorded Scholastic Aptitude Test (SAT) score of 550. Assuming an underlying normal distribution with $\mu = 500$ and $\sigma = 100$, then $\sigma_m = 3.65$. The resulting 95% confidence interval is 543–557. This interval is typically interpreted as meaning that there is a 95% chance that the interval 543–557 contains the "true" value of the freshman class SAT score. However, since any specifically computed interval either does or does not contain the true score, it is probably fairer to say that if a very large number—in principle, an infinite number—of such group means were sampled, 95% of the resulting confidence intervals would contain the true score.

The use of confidence intervals is increasingly being recommended as a substitute for statistical significance testing. This position received its first major explication by Rozeboom in 1960 and has been elaborated by others since, especially Cohen. This position holds that null hypothesis significance testing is a barrier to progress in behavioral science, especially with respect to the accumulation of knowledge across studies. The use of confidence intervals, in conjunction with other techniques such as meta-analysis, is proposed to replace traditional significance testing. The idea here is that confidence intervals can provide all of the information present in a significance test while yielding important additional information as well.

JOSEPH S. ROSSI
University of Rhode Island

***See also:* Probability**

CONFIDENTIALITY

Confidentiality is fundamental to effective diagnosis and treatment of mental illness. Although privacy and confidentiality are important to many aspects of health care, mental illness is among those disorders that evoke special concerns for privacy on the part of people who suffer from them, because of stigma, shame, feelings of failure, and possible detrimental effects if their mental and emotional conditions were to be known. Loss of employment, public embarrassment, disrupted relationships, and loss of insurability are among the potential consequences that people fear. Even more sensitive are the revelations that patients make in the course of psychotherapy, where complete openness and honesty are vital to the treatment process.

Some definitions are in order. *Confidentiality* characterizes a mutually understood, societally defined relationship between two parties, in which full disclosure and trust that the disclosed information will not be revealed are essential to the recognized function of the relationship. Such relationships may be professional, as in the case of doctor-patient, attorney-client, or clergy-penitent relationships, or they may be personal, as with husband and wife. Because of its characterization as part of a special relationship, confidentiality is distinct from *privacy,* which is a broader right not to have one's personal life, person, property, financial status, and so on invaded by or exposed to others. It is also distinct from *privilege,* which refers to legal protection of specified information from disclosure in certain judicial proceedings or governmental hearings. To relate these three concepts, one may view confidentiality as a particular, relationship-specific form of privacy, which may be protected by the laws of privilege in legal proceedings.

Confidentiality in medical settings has long been recognized as a key element of medical ethics. The Hippocratic Oath of ancient Greece is the foundation of modern ethical codes for not only medicine but also other healing professions. One translation of this code is that "Whatsoever I see and hear concerning the life of men, in my attendance of the sick or even apart therefrom, which ought not to be noised abroad, I will keep silence thereon, counting such things as holy secrets." A related principle of the medical profession is *primum non nocere:* First and foremost, do no harm. A breach of confidentiality can do great harm and expose the offending professional to significant liability. The highly trained professionals who treat mental illness—psychiatric physicians, psychologists, social workers, mental health counselors, nurses—are bound by the ethical standard of guarding confidentiality. Even the fact that a patient or client is receiving treatment for mental illness is subject to this constraint.

The disclosures of a patient in psychotherapy are especially sensitive. Although various methods of psychotherapy require differing degrees of personal disclosure, patients generally expect to speak freely about the private details of their mental and emotional life. This is especially true of psychotherapy based on psychoanalytic principles and methods. The laws of all states protect the confidentiality of disclosures in psychotherapy. The U.S. Supreme Court strongly affirmed the special protection of the contents of psychotherapy in its historic 1996 decision in *Jaffee v. Redmond,* in which the court declined to permit access to information from the psychotherapy of a policewoman who was sued for killing a suspect in the line of duty. The court's rationale recognized psychotherapy as a personal and social good that could not take place without confidentiality. The decision declared that "Effective psychotherapy . . . depends upon an atmosphere of confidence and trust in which the patient is willing to make a frank and complete disclosure of facts, emotions, memories, and fears. Because of the sensitive nature of the problems for which individuals consult psychotherapists, disclosure of confidential communications made during counseling sessions may cause embarrassment or disgrace. For this reason, the mere possibility of disclosure may impede development of the confidential relationship necessary for successful treatment." The court established an absolute privilege protecting confidentiality in court proceedings—absolute in the sense that a judge is not free in an individual trial to balance the adverse effects of disclosing confidential material from psychotherapy against other considerations such as the possible value of such a disclosure in seeking the truth in the trial.

The Privacy Rule promulgated in 2000 by the U.S. Department of Health and Human Services as mandated by the Health Insurance Portability and Accountability Act (HIPAA) of 1996, which took effect in April 2003, established additional governmental protection of personal disclosures in psychotherapy. Mental health professionals may document the contents of psychotherapy sessions in "psychotherapy notes," a part of the medical record kept separate from the rest of the record. Only with the patient's specific authorization may a therapist disclose the contents of those notes. Authorized disclosure may not be coerced as a condition of rendering or paying for the treatment, as by an insurance company or a managed care organization. Limited exceptions include disclosure to "avert a serious and imminent threat to health and safety," for a medical examiner determining the cause of a patient's death, for defense of the therapist if sued by the patient, or for oversight of the professional by governmental bodies. The privacy rule outlines basic elements to be documented in the general medical record in contrast to what would usually appear in the protected psychotherapy notes at the therapist's discretion.

Much controversy took place in the development of the HIPAA privacy rule, particularly about a provision that the patient's written consent would be prerequisite for all disclosures for purposes of "treatment, payment, and health care operations." This applied to all medical situations, including mental health care. Over the strong objections of privacy advocates, who contended that having no choice regarding consent for disclosures would deter patients from seeking care, the government removed that requirement in 2002. In so doing, the government yielded to those who contended that strict application of the rule would severely interfere with communications essential for emergency care or the efficient delivery and management of services. Patients must instead be informed of their privacy rights and protections. Individual practitioners remain free to request the patient's consent, although under the regulation they are not necessarily bound by the patient's decision. The change did not alter the protection of psychotherapy notes. More stringent protections imposed by individual states would take precedence. The privacy rule also mandates that disclosure must be limited to the minimum amount of information necessary to the purpose of the disclosure. The privacy rule applies only to entities that communicate medical information by electronic means. Many details of the implementation of HIPAA regulations for security and electronic communications remain to be worked out.

Norman A. Clemens

See also: **Psychotherapy**

CONSTANCY

We perceive objects and events by their effects on our sense organs—the light they provide the eye, the pressure waves that enter the ear, and so on. An object's physical attributes, such as its size, shape, and reflectance, are *distal* stimuli: properties that are relatively invariant for a given object, and important to our dealings with the world. To perceive these properties, we must extract information about them from the patterns of stimulus energies at our sense organs—the *proximal* stimulation, which changes constantly. Thus, varying the viewing distance, viewing angle, and illumination changes the size, shape, and brightness of the object's proximal stimulus. Nevertheless, things do not generally seem to expand when approached or become less reflective when moved from light to shade. These phenomena are given appropriate names: *size constancy, lightness constancy, position constancy,* and so forth.

This general rule, as formulated by Hermann von Helmholtz, can be paraphrased as follows: One perceives that state of affairs in the world that would, under normal conditions, have given rise to the pattern of proximal stimulation that one's sense organs receive.

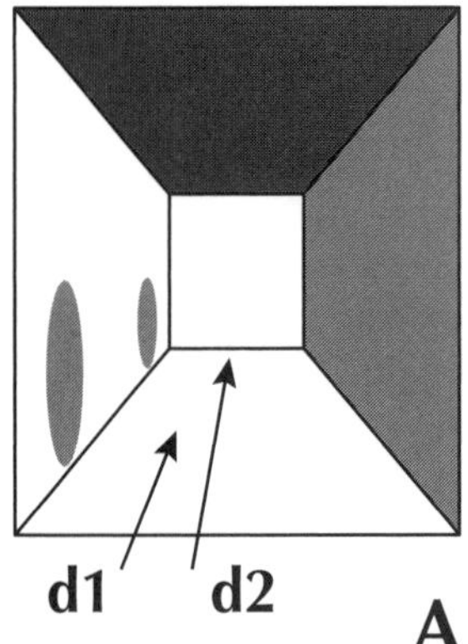

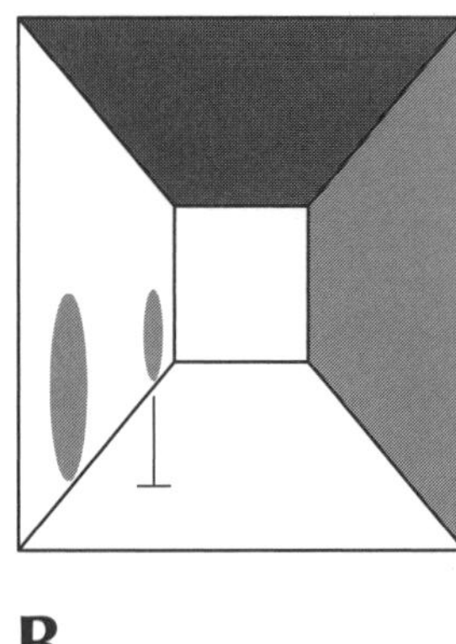

Figure 1. Size constancy and attention: (a) If seen in perspective against the left wall, at the different distances d1 and d2, the two ovals look like disks of equal sizes against the left wall. (b) If you can see them as at the same distance, by attending to the stand under the right-hand one, they appear of very different size.

Theories and Implications of Constancy

There have been several general approaches, differing in purpose and scope, to explaining how the perception of unchanging distal attributes is achieved, given the changing proximal stimulation.

Classical Theory of Constancy

The first explanation, central to the Helmholtzian classical theory of perception, is that we apply (usually unconsciously) what we have learned from our experiences with physical regularities of the world, and we thereby infer (also unconsciously) what the distal situation around us must be. Thus, we use the information about the distances (**d1, d2**) implied by the *perspective* in Figure 1A to estimate the gray disks' distal sizes, given their proximal sizes as picked up by the receptors in the retina. Similarly, we take the differences in illumination and our knowledge about how light bounces off surfaces to estimate the reflectance in each case of color or lightness constancy.

Note that this theory of the constancies assumes the viewer has considerable mental structure available beyond the information in the proximal stimulation and has learned the ecological likelihoods involved. It does explain many other perceptual phenomena as well, including contrast and other illusions, and many of the Gestalt phenomena of organization.

Direct Theories of Constancy

We now know that the classical explanation of the constancies is not the whole story, because animals with no prior visual experience nevertheless display adequate perceptual competence. The perceptual approaches known as Gestalt theory and direct theory, both strongly opposed to the classical view, hold that so long as the distal stimulus is invariant, some aspects of proximal stimulation will be invariant, in spite of changing size and luminance in the retinal image. This argument had been offered earlier by Ewald Hering and Ernst Mach, and it has since formed the core of two quite different direct theories of constancy.

The first of these are what can be termed *physiological theories of constancy.* Hering and Mach had proposed that innate networks of lateral connections exist between the receptors, as well as in the higher levels of the nervous system, and these might contribute to some of the perceptual constancies (particularly color constancy).

Such interconnections have now been demonstrated and measured, and they must surely affect how we perceive. Put simply, a more strongly illuminated region in the retinal image reduces the response of adjacent regions of the retina through a process of *lateral inhibition.* When the illumination falling both on an object and on its surroundings increases, there is an increase in both the light reflected to the eye from the object and the light from its surround, so the inhibition from the latter reduces the neural response to the former. The response to the light from the object therefore normally remains relatively unchanged, despite changes in the illumination, so long as the objects' and surroundings' reflectances remain constant. (Several common illusions are covered by the same explanation, notably examples of *contrast,* as when a bright surround makes a gray object look darker.) L. Hurvich and D. Jameson developed and tested a quantitative model of chromatic color constancy for simple patterns, thereby testing as well their model of red/green, yellow/blue, white/black opponent pairs, which itself was based originally on Hering's theory of color receptors.

Of course, there are reasons aside from testing underlying theories to study the constancies, like the needs of imaging technologies. For example, mathematical algorithms in the fields of color science and computer vision, notably by B. Wandell and colleagues, have recently been aimed at separately estimating surface colors and their illumination, using pictures of natural scenes. More generally, the attempt to explain *constancies as direct responses to stimulus invariances* avoids both questions of physiological mechanisms and questions of Helmholtzian inference. Thus, when the illumination changes, both the light reaching the eye from an object and the light from its surround change, but the *ratio* of their intensities remains invariant. It has

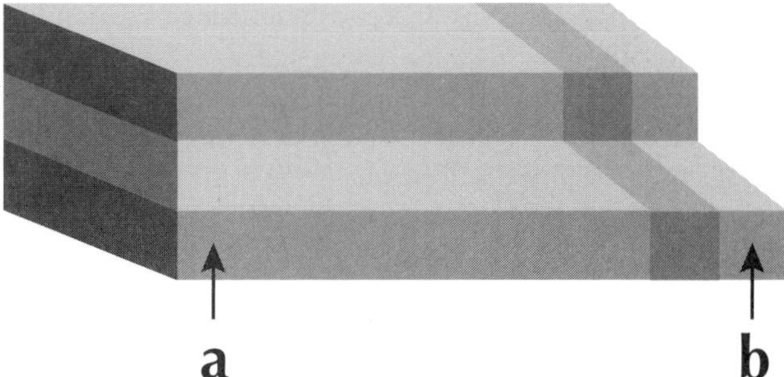

Figure 2. Adelson's impossible staircase.

been recognized since Hering that if sensed lightness were a response only to such a ratio, lightness constancy (and lightness contrast) would then be a direct response to that variable of stimulation.

Most generally, J. J. Gibson argued that for most properties the changing proximal stimulus pattern received by a perceiver moving around in an evolutionarily normal environment offers invariants that reflect the structure of the physical world and therefore make any inferencelike processes wholly unnecessary.

Inference and Attention in Constancy

Although the direct approach is potentially highly useful, there is no evidence that most constancies are direct responses to such invariances. Moreover, many examples of attention-dependent taking-into-account processes remain, needing explanation. In Figure 2, devised by E. Adelson, although **a** and **b** are identical as printed, **a** looks like a dark (paint-striped) surface and **b** looks like a light surface in shadow, depending on where one attends; similar attention-dependent examples can be shown in judging size, shape, and the like. Thus, in Figure 1B, the right disk looks smaller than in 1A, if you attend its dim stand. Attention (and perceptual inference) remain involved.

REFERENCES

Adelson, E. H. (2000). Lightness perception and lightness illusions. In M. Gazzaniga (Ed.), *The new cognitive neurosciences* (2nd ed., pp. 339–351). Cambridge, MA: MIT Press.

Hochberg, J. (in press). Acts of perceptual inquiry: Parsing objects by diagnostic coupling and consequences. *ACTA Psychologica.*

Julian Hochberg
Columbia University

CONSTRUCTIVISM

In traditional philosophy, the commodity that goes by the name of *knowledge,* whether based on information conveyed by the senses or on insights of intuitive reason, is always expected to represent an external reality in some way analogous to the way pictures represent what they are supposed to depict. The constructivist theory of knowing breaks with this tradition and posits a different relationship between knowledge and the real world. The activity of knowing is seen rather like that of a river that finds its way through the constraints presented by a landscape. The river does not discover what the landscape is like, but by trial and error it finds a way to flow. The path the river takes is determined on the one hand by the constraints of the landscape and on the other by the constraints implicit in the "logic" of water, which prevents the river from flowing uphill. In the constructivist view, then, knowledge does not regard what may or may not exist, but focuses (like the pragmatists' view) on what has proven successful.

Instead of speaking of truth, indicating that a piece of knowledge matches reality, constructivists speak of *functional fit,* by which they mean that their knowledge is expected to fit into the world of their experience. A concept, a way of thinking, or a theory is therefore said to be *viable* if experience shows that it does what is expected of it.

This change of perspective entails two basic principles: (1) Knowledge is not passively received but actively built up by the cognizing subject; and (2) the function of cognition is adaptive and serves the organization of the experiential world, not the discovery of ontological reality.

The Swiss psychologist Jean Piaget, the father of the constructivist school in the 20th century, characterized the situation by saying: "The mind organizes the world by organizing itself." This is often erroneously interpreted as an expression of philosophical idealism. It is a misinterpretation because it disregards the fact that Piaget considered knowledge a form of adaptation, and the world the mind organizes is not what idealist philosophers call reality, but the world of the individual's practical experience. Such a pragmatic position is perfectly compatible with views expressed by the great physicists of the 20th century, who held that physical theories are *models* of the experiential world, not descriptions of an observer-independent reality.

The constructivist theory of cognition, although formulated a decade earlier, has two obvious parallels to conceptions in the discipline of cybernetics. On the one hand, the process of cognition is a prime example of *self-organization* and can be seen as a continuous chain of *feedback loops* in search of viable ways of acting and thinking. On the other hand, the constructivist theory of language and its meanings is in agreement with Shannon's theory of communication, according to which signals (or words) do not carry meaning in themselves but are given it by the sender and the receiver on the basis of their individual experience in social and linguistic interaction.

Relinquishing the view of communication as a form of transportation (meanings being conveyed from sender to receiver) makes it necessary to consider that students' interpretation of texts and teachers' discourse is inevitably subjective and driven by the natural desire to organize their own experiential world in a reasonable, manageable fashion. This has several important consequences for the practice of education. First, a radical distinction has to be made between educational procedures that aim at generating understanding (teaching) and those that disregard conceptual development and aim at generating the repetition of specific phrases and behaviors (training). Second, the researcher's as well as the educator's interest will be focused on what can be inferred to be going on inside the student's head, rather than on overt responses. Third, the teacher will realize that knowledge cannot be transferred ready-made to students because conceptual structures can be built up only by them. Language, therefore, cannot serve as a means of transmission but only as a tool in the process of orienting each student's construction. Finally, students' "errors" and instances in which their answers deviate from the teacher's expectations will be of particular interest, because these deviations tend to throw light on how the students, at the particular point in their conceptual development, are organizing their experiential world.

During the last 20 years, constructivism has had an acknowledged influence on the teaching of mathematics and science. Instances in which it was put it in practice have been generally successful, and the relevant literature is full of such evidence. But there has also been the inevitable backlash and attempts to mitigate the school's adamant agnosticism with regard to ontological reality. One of these attempts is called *constructionism* and holds that the conceptions of language and society reflect things that have an independent existence beyond the constructions of individual minds. However, the assumption of any such correspondence remains a metaphysical fiction as long as no indication is given as to how its viability could be experientially achieved or confirmed. Constructivism, the school of thought discussed in this entry, is a theory of cognition and concerns, not what might exist, but only what can rationally be known.

Ernst von Glasersfeld
University of Massachusetts

CONSUMER RESEARCH

Each one of us is a consumer. We eat, sleep, bathe, dress, exercise, gather, read, travel, and perform a host of other daily and weekly activities. In an earlier era it was a major challenge to find any product or service to meet a given need. If a product or service was available and affordable, it was readily accessed and used. This reality continues to be true in underdeveloped, third world countries; but industrialized nations—those that commonly comprise the world's Group of Eight (G8)—provide a very different picture and challenge. In these countries, every item and service comes in a vast array of brands representing an equally vast array of companies. The challenge is no longer simply to get a specific product or service to market and consumers. Now the challenge becomes one of assuring that the consumer will prefer and will purchase a specific brand of product or service . . . the chosen one among the available many. To meet this challenge, companies invest heavily in research to learn about their prospective consumers, their habits, their personalities, and their preferences. To misread the consumer can spell millions of dollars in company losses and, in some instances, bankruptcy. Because the stakes are high, methodical information-gathering becomes essential and critical.

Definition and Evolution

Consumer research systematically studies the many aspects of human behavior related to the purchase and use of economic goods and services. The product-related focus includes research in advertising effectiveness, product features, and marketing techniques. Focus upon the consumer has included the study of attitudes, feelings, preferences, and the many group influences upon the decision-making process of the individual consumer. The field also studies the consumer as a citizen and a central figure in social/environmental problem solving. This scope and range make consumer research highly interdisciplinary. It integrates theoretical concepts and research approaches from social psychology, sociology, and economics.

Although in one sense consumer research is as old as the dawn of recorded human history, in still another sense it is as young as the last few decades. Not until the 1920s did consumer research begin to focus on two-way communication: gathering information from consumers to prepare more effective advertisements. Still later, attention was given to consumer attitudes and opinions prior to product design. As this consumer focus steadily grew, it marked the appearance of a newly independent member of the advertising family: consumer psychology. Official recognition came in 1960 when the Division of Consumer Psychology was formed within the American Psychological Association.

The early-era, primitive question was one of "What do people need?" Economic growth and increased personal income spawned the more probing questions of "What do people want?" and "What can people be enticed to want?" It is these questions that form the basis of consumer research today.

Consumer research takes many forms and spans many different settings. Prevalent forms include a variety of survey and polling methods, in-depth projective techniques, and behavioral studies.

Research Methods

Survey and Polling Techniques

Most research utilizes some form or variation of survey or polling. It has the advantage of gathering input from large groups of consumers quickly and relatively inexpensively. This research approach assumes that consumers know their likes, dislikes, and preferences and will be forthright in expressing them.

The method is premised on random selection of consumers within a target market. Where this market is the U.S. population at large, the survey or polling typically focuses on carefully selected communities that, taken collectively, proportionally represent the various constituencies comprising the broader community. Where the market is more product-line-specific, a select group of consumers in a given demographic or socioeconomic group becomes the focus. For example, parents of young children might be surveyed to check cereal or other food preferences.

The survey and polling methods themselves are wide-ranging. Selected consumers may receive a survey by mail, may be visited at home by an interviewer, may be telephoned, or may be computer-accessed by the Internet. Other consumers may be surveyed within a grocery store or a shopping mall. They may be asked about a specific product, sizes, colors, textures, and shapes. They may be asked to come into a mall-based test room where they express actual preferences of products or features. Or, in the case of food items or personal hygiene products, they may be asked to try different samples and register preferences. Logical consumers of a given product (e.g., mothers with infants, where the product is baby-care-related) may be gathered in focus groups to determine product features and preferences.

Rapid technological advances have brought prominent growth in surveying by Internet and the prospect of virtually instant response via integrated systems combining cable, computer, and television. Although the technologies will rapidly change, the basic principles underlying surveying and polling will remain constant—principles of random sampling within representative general or target-market populations.

In notable instances, polling or surveying will target those consumers who have purchased a given product or brand. What attracted them to the product, why they selected it, how satisfied they are with its features and performance, and related questions hold central interest for the company whose product was selected or, in some instances, a competing company who seeks to win the consumer in the future. The questionnaire may come in the just-purchased box of shoes, radio alarm clock, or computer. Purchaser surveying is the only consumer research method used by Japan. It is their belief that random surveying within the broader consumer population is too capricious and subject to change.

Depth/Projective Techniques

Projective techniques probe below the surface of a consumer's cognizant behaviors, preferences, and motivations. These techniques are premised on the belief that consumers in the marketplace are motivated by desires they do not know and cannot express consciously. To access these motivations, the technique, in effect, removes the question from the person through interpretation of abstract stimuli or pictures, sentence or story completion, questions about what their neighbor would consider most important in selecting a given product, descriptions of the personality of a consumer who would select a given product or grouping of products, and so on. Through techniques such as these the consumer unwittingly expresses her or his own underlying motivations while responding on the basis of stimuli, sentences, or other individuals.

Historically, projective techniques have been very meaningful in designing advertising campaigns to effectively move beyond a marketing problem or roadblock. When Duncan Hines introduced a cake mix that required only adding water, it sat quietly on supermarket shelves. Projective techniques revealed the guilt homemakers felt at baking a cake so easily, and the product was reformulated to require adding an egg. Similar projective techniques have been useful in revealing and overcoming resistances in a wide variety of product areas including microwave dinners and instant coffee, to name but a few.

Behavioral Techniques

Behavioral techniques examine the actions of the prospective consumer in several facets of the purchasing arena. Children and their parents may be invited to shop in a mock grocery or toy store. Consumers and their actions in store aisles may be observed firsthand or through one-way-mirrors. Selected consumers may be given scanner cards that register all their purchases at designated scanner-cable-equipped supermarkets. These scanner-cable panels of consumers provide important data to major food manufacturers.

Conclusion

Although this discussion has focused upon the commercial marketplace, the techniques of consumer research are used extensively in broader nonprofit and societal orientations as well. Questions of consumer welfare, product safety, and truth-in-packaging legislation have been central among these broader concerns. Equally central have been issues relating to quality of life and the reciprocal nature of consumer behavior: (1) the responsibility of society toward the individual consumer, and (2) the responsibility of the individual consumer toward society. Society's responsibility encompasses areas such as health care delivery systems, education, and cultural and recreational facilities. The individual consumer's responsibility encompasses respect for the environment, for communities, and for natural resources.

Edward L. Palmer
Davidson College, Davidson, North Carolina

CONTEXTUALISM

Contextualism is a philosophy of science based on modern variants of American pragmatism. The core analytic unit of contextualism or pragmatism is the ongoing act in context: the common sense–situated action. It is doing as it is being done, such as in hunting, shopping, or making love. This has sometimes been termed the *historical act,* but not in the sense of a thing done in the past. Rather, the term *historical act* recognizes that acts occur not just in a current situational context, but also as part of a stream of purposive acts in an individual life. In practical terms, contextualists (1) focus on the whole behavioral event, (2) are continuously sensitive to the role of context in understanding the nature and function of this event, and (3) maintain a firm grasp on a pragmatic truth criterion. Contextualism is commonly distinguished from mechanism, formism, and organicism as other broad philosophical approaches.

To contextualistic psychologists, a psychological act-in-context cannot be explained by an appeal to actions of various parts of the organism such as its brain or muscles. Legs do not go shopping, brains do not go hunting, and penises do not make love. People do these things, and people are integrated organisms. This does not mean that information about the operation of the brain or other parts of the organism are not relevant, but that the whole event is always primary and reductionism and expansionism are rejected. Contextualism is applicable at all levels of analysis. If one were to become interested in the action of a part of the organism (say, the brain) then this would become the new whole and all else would be context at this new level of analysis. What is learned at one level of organization will not, however, fully explain events at other levels of organization.

Each participant in a whole event defines the qualities of the other participants, much as the front of a coin implies a back and vice versa. For example, going shopping implies a place to go from and to, a reason to go, a method of going, and future events that shopping will enable. All of these facets working together are the whole event, and none can be examined out of context and be fully understood. The legs may move in a particular fashion as one goes to the store, but moving legs are not "shopping," and the same leg movements may participate in completely different acts in other contexts (e.g., dancing, exercising). To a contextualist, the whole behavioral event cannot be built up from its components, because qualities of the whole event exist only in the totality.

What creates the whole event is the purpose of the behaving organism and, at another level, the purpose of the person doing the analysis. In other words, units of action are entirely functional. It is not assumed that there are "true" units, only useful ones. The universe is the ultimate context, but the universe is not something that can be described, so all units are taken to be convenient analytic fictions. The specific contextual or behavioral features to be abstracted are those that contribute to the achievement of the goals of the therapist or scientist in doing an analysis.

The truth criterion of contextualism emerges from the core analytic unit itself: *successful working.* Going shopping implies a place to shop, and when that place has been reached and shopping has occurred, the act is complete. Similarly, a pragmatic truth criterion implies a goal to be reached, and when that goal is reached the analysis is complete. Since successful working is the means by which contextualists evaluate events, and goals allow this criterion to be applied, analytic goals themselves cannot ultimately be evaluated or justified. They can only be stated. To evaluate a goal via successful working would require yet another goal, but then that second goal could not be evaluated, and so on *ad infinitum.*

Logically this means there are as many forms of contextualism as there are sets of scientific goals. Nevertheless, in psychology we can organize contextualists into two rough groups. *Descriptive contextualists* seek a full and personal appreciation of the participating factors in a whole event. They are like historians, wanting to appreciate a unique historical event by examining closely all the strands that make up the whole story. Dramaturgy, hermeneutics, narrative psychology, interbehaviorism, feminist psychology, and social constructionism are all examples of this type of contextualism. *Functional contextualists* seek the prediction and influence of events as an integrated goal. Contextualistic behavior analysis, some forms of Marxist psychology, and some forms of psychobiological thinking are examples.

The choice of a goal in contextualism is pre-analytic. It is a means of analysis, not the result of analysis. Thus, neither descriptive nor functional contextualists can claim that their goal is the "right" goal. But we can examine what happens when these different goals are adopted.

Consider, for example, the environmentalism that is so characteristic of behavior analysis. Initially this focus seems dogmatic, since obviously behavior influences the environment as much as environment influences behavior. The dogmatism is removed when one realizes that the contextual features to be abstracted in any contextualistic analysis are those that contribute to the achievement of the goals of the analysis. Functional contextualists want analyses that achieve prediction and influence as an *integrated* goal. Only contextual features that are (1) external to the behavior of the individual being studied and (2) manipulable, at least in principle, could possibly lead *directly* to behavioral influence as an outcome. Verbal analyses generate rules for people, not rules for the world. To accomplish prediction *and* influence, rules must start with the environment, in the sense of the "world outside of the behavior," because that is where the consumers of these rules are. The environmentalism in behavior analysis is thus made more coherent (and nondogmatic) when it is seen as part of a particular contextualistic system.

In the hands of a contextualist, mundane clinical statements can lead to unusual outcomes. For example, suppose a client says "I can't leave my home or I will have an anxiety attack." A more mechanistic therapist might wonder why the person is anxious or how the panic can be alleviated. Among several other steps, contextualistic clinician might (1) look for the larger contexts that are implied by this formulation (e.g., that anxiety is bad); (2) examine the context in which the client would say such a thing (e.g., what the person is accomplishing in therapy by this speech act—is the person asking for support, explaining dependence, etc.?); (3) look for contexts that exist or could be created in which panic and staying home are unrelated events (for example, if anxiety was no longer avoided, would anxiety still lead to staying inside?); or (4) see if there are parts of this statement that could be supported therapeutically, and so on. Several new forms of intervention in the behavioral and cognitive therapies (e.g., Acceptance and Commitment Therapy, Functional Analytic Psychotherapy) are contextualistic, taking advantage of the new light contextualism casts on old issues.

Steven C. Hayes
University of Nevada

See also: **Functional Analysis**

CONTROL THERAPY

Control therapy is an integrated approach to psychotherapy and health care that combines theory, research, and practice. It is based on the premise that issues of control (e.g., fear of loss of control, desire for control, power struggles) underlie most concerns brought to therapy. A reliable and valid standardized psychological assessment inventory (the Shapiro Control Inventory, or SCI) was developed to both measure the theory and provide an individual client "control profile." Control-based therapeutic techniques, including an assertive change mode of control and an accepting/yielding mode of control, are matched to the client's control profile and taught as interventions. The theory, test construction, and interventions have been developed and empirically tested over a period of 25 years involving research and clinical work with thousands of individuals in over a dozen countries.

A Unifying Theory of Control

The theoretical basis of control therapy builds upon and integrates several literatures, including self-efficacy; learned helplessness; optimism; competence; dyscontrol; reactance; will to meaning; will to superiority; cybernetic feedback models and disregulation; internal and external locus of control; self-determination; and self-control/delay of gratification.

Thus, control theory is based on an unifying bio-psychosocial theory of human control and self-control and has three postulates: (1) All individuals want a sense of control in their lives; (2) there are healthy and unhealthy ways by which they attempt to gain or regain that sense of control; and (3) there are individual differences in control profiles of individuals and in how they face this central issue of maintaining a healthy sense of control in their lives.

Developing a Client Control Profile: Assessing the Theory

A client control profile is based on clinical assessment with the SCI, which has undergone extensive reliability and validity testing (including an investigation of neurobiological correlates of control using positron emission tomography). The 187-item, nine-scale SCI inventory is a clinically reliable and valid multidimensional instrument that measures four primary and interrelated components of clients' control profiles: (1) desire for control (i.e., where they want control and why they want it); (2) current sense of control in both general and specific domains; (3) the modes by which they seek control (assertive/change and yielding/accepting); and (4) use of both self and other agencies in gaining control. Research shows that this method of assessing client control profiles is the most sensitive inventory yet devised to differentiate among clinical disorders and between clinical and normative populations.

Assessment also includes methods for listening to clients' speech—including the clients' narratives (their "control stories"), control-related beliefs and assumptions, and assaults to their sense of control—and identifying and monitoring domains where they feel a lack of control.

Control-Based Interventions

Control therapy consists of an 8- to 12-week step-by-step treatment program that involves defining the area of concern, performing assessment, monitoring, goal setting, determining the appropriate strategies, teaching the strategies, and performing evaluation.

Therapeutic interventions involve detailed and well-defined clinical instructions for matching treatment strategy to the client's control profile, thus offering both standardized, replicable techniques and providing flexibility and sensitivity to each client's individual needs and style.

Based on the goal selected, individually tailored cognitive and behavioral strategies are utilized to help clients regain a sense of control through one or both of the positive modes of control. The assertive/change mode of control, which has historically been emphasized by Western scientific psychology, involves having individuals learn to identify, monitor, and gain active control of those aspects of their lives that are or should be amenable to change.

The yielding, accepting mode, which has historically been emphasized by non-Western philosophical and psychological traditions, helps clients learn the value of surrendering, accepting, and letting go with serenity (i.e., without feelings of helplessness or resignation) of those aspects of their lives that are not under personal control, or of inappropriate active control efforts. Practical instructions in each mode are explained, as well as ways to integrate and achieve balance between the two positive modes.

A Control-Based View of Psychological Health: Suboptimal, Normal, and Optimal

Traditional Western psychology argues that loss of control and learned helplessness are unhealthy and suboptimal. Normal control is defined as gaining control (which even includes an illusion of control) and is equated with mental health. This traditional view argues that instrumental control is good, and that the more control, the better.

The theory, research, and practice of control therapy agree that "normal" control is better than suboptimal. However, normal control strategies (e.g., external attributions for failure) can also be problematic. They can keep individuals from being aware of the unconscious, reflexive, and reactive nature of many of their control desires and efforts; they are often insular and self-serving; and they can keep people from learning about their mistakes.

Therefore, a concept of optimal control is needed. Optimal control, according to Control Therapy, involves the following:

- Increased conscious awareness of one's control dynamics, including affective, cognitive, and somatic experiences, in order to learn when and how desire and efforts for control are expressed; when control beliefs, goals, desires, and strategies are reflexive, limiting, and potentially destructive; and when they should be increased, decreased, or channeled
- A balanced and integrated use of assertive/change and yielding/accepting modes of control matched to situation and goals, desires, and temperament
- The ability to gain a sense of control from both self (self-regulation of cognitions, affect, and behavior) and others (including religious and spiritual beliefs)

Benefits of Control Therapy

Control therapy has been shown to be effective in both assessment (sensitivity and specificity) and treatment (clinical outcome) with a wide range of mental disorder diagnoses and health-related concerns. Clinical areas investigated include Generalized Anxiety Disorder, panic attack, depression, borderline personality, eating disorders, and adult children of alcoholics. Control issues have also been investigated in type-A individuals with myocardial infarction, women with breast cancer, and individuals at high cardiovascular risk.

There are several advantages to control therapy and the unifying theory upon which it is based. First, a unifying theory helps clinicians understand control as a central component underlying all schools of therapy; the analytic view that humans are governed by unknown and uncontrolled forces; the cognitive-behavioral schools' emphasis on self-control; and the humanistic or existential focus on personal choice, individual freedom, and self-determination.

Second, in addition to the theory's universality and parsimony, it also can be operationalized, thereby providing an empirical foundation for assessing a client's control profile. Based on individual variations in control profiles, specific techniques can be matched to client needs and clinical problem.

Third, drawing from both Eastern and Western psychological traditions, control therapy involves specific assertive/change and yielding/accepting modes of control intervention techniques, and the matching of these techniques to a client's control profile, goals, and clinical problem.

Finally, control therapy articulates a control-based vision of mental, physical, and interpersonal health involving suboptimal, normal, and optimal control profiles. Thus, although control therapy was designed to specifically address individual mental and physical health problems, it can also be used as a means to help promote growth, including intrapersonal, interpersonal, and even societal health, healing, and well-being.

Deane H. Shapiro
University of California College of Medicine

John A. Astin
California Pacific Medical Center

Shauna L. Shapiro
University of Santa Clara

See also: **Psychological Health; Psychotherapy**

CONSTRUCTIVIST PSYCHOTHERAPY

Constructivism refers to a group of theories (originally stemming from George Kelly's personal construct theory) holding the philosophical position that so-called reality is, in some ways, created by persons. Rather than imposing some objective truth on persons seeking help, constructivist therapists attempt experientially to grasp the lived reality of each client. Constructivist therapy is a cocreated experience between therapist and client, mutual experts on different aspects of the reality being created between them. This relationship is more egalitarian and client-empowering than approaches in which the more powerful therapist imposes diagnostic and treatment "realities" on the less powerful client. Consistent with Kelly's theory, constructivist psychotherapy can be seen as a part of the broader group of humanistic, existential, and postmodern therapies.

While all constructivists agree that reality cannot be known directly, different theoretical groups disagree on the exact nature of the relationship between the person and the world. *Radical constructivists* argue that one cannot even speak of a reality outside of the meanings the person has created. *Social constructionists* might argue that we are saturated with meanings created by cultures and imposed upon us. Occupying a middle ground, *critical constructivists* believe that meanings are cocreated in the dynamic interaction between the person and the world.

Although there are numerous specific approaches (a few of which are described later), constructivist therapies generally share certain attitudes about therapy. Most constructivists will listen to clients with the assumption that everything the client says is true in the sense of revealing important aspects of the client's experiential meaning system (Kelly's *credulous approach*). There is a respect for contrast, oppositionality, or the dialectic in meaning making. Most constructivists also are attuned to making therapy a safe place for clients to experience life, explore, and grow, and they emphasize seeing the client as a *process of meaning creation* rather than a static entity composed of specific meanings. The client's process of construction is seen as active as opposed to reactive and underscores the agency of the person, again emphasizing the humanistic and existential roots of the approach.

Different constructivist therapists employ these attitudes in different therapeutic approaches. In Kelly's *fixed-role therapy,* for example, the client first writes a character sketch that is open, revealing, yet sympathetic. This sketch is written in the third person, from the perspective of a friend who might know the client most intimately. The therapist and client then cocreate an alternate sketch for the client to enact, typically for a 2-week period. Fixed-role therapy is viewed as a failure if the client sees it as a behavioral prescription; it is designed to free the client to experiment with alternative ways of experiencing life.

Experiential personal construct psychotherapy (EPCP) is based upon the relational, experiential, and existential foundations of personal construct psychology. EPCP construes persons as simultaneously needing and being terrified of depths of emotional closeness. On the one hand, such intimate relationships can affirm the meanings that have formed the foundation of our existence. On the other hand, we can experience devastating disconfirmation in intimate relationships. Clients then struggle with needing to connect with others, risking terror to gain profound richness, versus retreating from intimacy, buying safety at the cost of the empty objectification of self and others. Therapeutic growth can occur if the therapist experiences *optimal therapeutic distance,* a blending of profound connection and separateness, when the therapist is close enough to feel the client's experience yet distant enough to recognize those feelings as the client's and not the therapist's own.

Other constructivist therapists employ narrative approaches to therapy. These therapists believe that narratives give meaning and continuity to the lived experience of clients. Gaps, incompleteness, and incoherence in the client's life story may indicate struggles in creating an integrated experience of self-in-the-world. Goncalves illustrates constructivist narrative therapy with his "moviola" technique, in which the therapist's attention scans the settings of a client's life, much like a camera in a movie. The therapist can zoom in on a detail or back off and get a more panoramic view. For example, a therapist might start by having the client describe the entire room in which he or she was abused. Eventually, the therapist might help the client see in detail his or her face, filled with fear and horror, while the abuse occurred. Because people innately create meanings to understand their experiences, the experience of re-viewing the abuse with an empathic therapist allows for new constructions to be created. These newer meanings, in turn, allow for newer experiences as clients' lives move into the future.

Depth-oriented brief therapy (DOBT) applies constructivist principles to help clients understand and engage in radical change in a very short-term treatment. DOBT understands the symptom as painful because of the ways it invalidates important aspects of our experience. At the same time, there are other constructions, often at a lower level of consciousness, making the symptom absolutely necessary for the client. DOBT uses specific experiential techniques to help the client gain access to these deeper meanings. The client then can more consciously decide whether to keep or abandon these more unconscious meanings.

Constructivist therapy has been used with a wide range of problems, from mild adjustment issues to the most severely disturbed clients. It has been used with specific symptoms (e.g., stuttering, obesity, bulimia, posttraumatic flashbacks) as well as more general life distress. It also has been useful with young children as well as elderly clients. Specific constructivist techniques have been developed for family therapy (e.g., systemic bow-ties to help each client understand how their actions, based upon their deepest fears, confirm the deepest fears of other family members).

There have been numerous methodologically sound studies exploring the effectiveness of constructivist therapies across different countries, ages, and types of problems. Effect sizes for client change in these studies were at least as large as those reported in the cognitive-behavioral and psychoanalytic literature. In other words, good constructivist therapy respects the lived experiences of persons and has been empirically supported by studies that meet the most rigorous of experimental criteria.

L. M. Leitner
D. J. Domenici
Miami University

See also: **Existential Psychology; Personal Construct Psychology; Postmodernism**

CONVULSANTS

Convulsants are substances that induce seizurelike paroxysmal behaviors by producing patterns of electrical activity in the brain that resemble those seen in human epilepsy.

Epilepsy is characterized by recurring episodes in which the electrical activity of many thousands of neurons becomes abnormally elevated and pathologically synchronized. This discharge interrupts normal brain function and leads, in some forms of epilepsy, to alterations in behavior (seizures). Seizures come in many varieties, ranging from brief, barely detectable losses of consciousness in what are called absence or petit mal epilepsies, to uncontrollable tonic-clonic contractions of large muscle groups in the so-called grand mal epilepsies. The behavioral manifestations and severity of the seizure reflect primarily the size and localization of the abnormal electrical discharge.

One remarkable aspect of the human epilepsies is the diversity of underlying etiological factors, including perinatal trauma, brain infection, drug and alcohol withdrawal, tumors, and stroke. Our current understanding of epilepsy is that epileptiform brain activity and the behavioral seizures produced by that activity arise as the symptom of some underlying brain pathology. Perhaps it not surprising, therefore, that an incredibly diverse group of chemical substances can produce convulsions when given centrally or applied directly to brain tissue.

The study of the mechanism of action of convulsants has led to the formulation of one of the more enduring hypotheses of the generation of epilepsy (Traub & Miles, 1991). There seems to be a delicate balance between the strength of inhibitory and excitatory synaptic transmission in the brain. Any disturbance in this balance that favors excitation will lead to the uncontrolled spread of excitation between cells so that their discharge becomes rapidly synchronous. In this sense, epilepsy is a disease of populations of cells, rather than individual cells. In fact, not all brain regions are equally likely to be identified as sites of epileptiform discharge in patients, and not all brain regions are equally sensitive to convulsants. It is thought that the ability of a convulsant to trigger seizures in a given brain region depends on a number of factors. First, the convulsant's appropriate target must be present. The convulsant strychnine, for example, will be inactive in nuclei lacking glycinergic inhibition. Second, the necessary neuronal circuitry must be present. In particular, there must be local excitatory axon collaterals so that excitation can spread between cells. These connections are particularly prominent between pyramidal cells in the hippocampal formation and neocortex—two regions that are highly sensitive to most convulsants and in which epileptic discharge is typically initiated in human epilepsy patients. Finally, some output connections capable of influencing behavior and/or consciousness must be present.

Several of the most widely used and better understood convulsants are listed in Table 1 (for reviews see Fisher, 1989; Löscher & Schmidt, 1988), and they have been classified by their actions on the balance of excitatory and inhibitory synaptic transmission, when known. It should be noted that the patterns of seizures and electrical abnormalities are not the same for all convulsants and may vary for any one convulsant depending on where and how the substance is applied.

Convulsants That Decrease Inhibition

Much of our understanding of the cellular basis of epilepsy comes from the application of convulsants to the brain, in whole animal experiments and, more recently, to isolated slices of brain tissue maintained ex vivo. Penicillin, the first widely used convulsant, is a weak antagonist of the recep-

Table 1. Widely Used Convulsants and Their Mechanism of Action

Class of Action	Target System	Mechanism of Action	Examples
Decrease inhibition:	1. g-aminobutyric acid	a. Receptor antagonists	penicillin, bicuculline, picrotoxin,
		b. Synthesis inhibitors	methoxypyridoxine, isoniazid, 3-mecaptoproprionic acid
		c. Benzodiazepine receptor	inverse agonists
		d. Release inhibitors	opioid peptides
	2. Glycine	a. Receptor antagonists	strychnine
Enhance excitation:	1. Excitatory amino acids (e.g. glutamate)	a. NMDA receptors	magnesium-free saline
		b. non-NMDA receptors	kainic acid
		c. Potassium channel blockers	tetraethylammonium, 4-aminopyridine, various peptide toxins
	2. Acetylcholine	a. Receptor agonists	pilocarpine
		b. Cholinesterase inhibitors	soman
Unknown		a. Neurotoxins	cholera toxin, tetanus toxin
		b. Injury/Trauma	alumina hydroxide, cobalt
		b. CNS Stimulant	p entylenetetrazol

tors for the predominant brain inhibitory neurotransmitter, γ-aminobutyric acid (GABA). More potent antagonists, such as bicuculline and the ion channel-blocker picrotoxin, are now more typically used. Seizures and epileptiform discharge can also be elicited by blocking the synthesis or release of GABA. In addition, substances active at modulatory sites on GABA receptors can also exert convulsant activity, such as inverse agonists of the benzodiazepine receptor.

Convulsants That Increase Excitation

Substances that directly or indirectly increase excitation are powerful convulsants. For example, application of saline containing a lower than physiological concentration of Mg^{2+} relieves the normal block of the ion channels gated by N-methyl-D-aspartate (NMDA)–preferring excitatory amino acid receptors, and thus considerably enhances the synaptic excitation of cells. Application of kainic acid, an agonist of non-NMDA excitatory amino acid receptors, is also widely used to trigger seizures in whole animals, by injection either into the cerebral vesicles or directly into the tissue. The release of endogenous excitatory amino acids can also be triggered by increasing the excitability of neurons with substances that block repolarizing K^+ conductances. Neurons have perhaps hundreds of such K^+ conductances, and numerous antagonists of these channels are effective convulsants, including tetraethylammonium, 4-amminopyridine, and various naturally occurring peptide toxins. Finally, modulators of central cholinergic synaptic function are also employed as convulsants, including direct agonists such as pilocarpine as well as acetylcholinesterase inhibitors, and are believed to act by increasing neuronal excitability.

Other Convulsants

Although the mechanism of action of these convulsants fits well with the hypothesized balance of synaptic excitation and inhibition in epilepsy-prone brain regions, it is less well understood how other important convulsants exert their effects. Cholera toxin is an activator of adenylate cyclase and may therefore trigger seizures by mimicking any of the many cellular actions of cAMP and cAMP-dependent protein kinase, including reduction of K^+ conductance and facilitation of transmitter release. Tetanus toxin inhibits the release of both excitatory and inhibitory neurotransmitters. Epileptiform activity elicited by focal application of alumina hydroxide or cobalt has been used as a model for posttraumatic epilepsy, although the mechanisms underlying seizure generation remain unclear. Pentylenetetrazol is a powerful and widely used convulsant whose mechanism of action is also unknown.

REFERENCES

Fischer, R. S. (1989). Animal models of the epilepsies. *Brain Research Reviews, 14,* 245–278.

Löscher, W., & Schmidt, D. (1988). Which animal models should be used in the search for new antiepileptic drugs? A proposal based on experimental and clinical observations. *Epilepsy Research, 2,* 145–181.

Traub, R. D., & Miles, R. (1991). *Neuronal networks of the hippocampus.* New York: Cambridge University Press.

Scott M. Thompson
University of Maryland

CORRELATION METHODS

Correlation and regression deal with (1) how closely variables are related, and (2) the prediction of one variable from another. If we are dealing with *bivariate* (i.e., two variables) correlation and regression, the correlation coefficient assesses the degree to which the variables X and Y have a linear relationship, when standardized; and regression refers to the prediction of one variable—say, Y—from another—say, X—using a linear equation of the form

$$\hat{Y} = b_0 + b_1X$$

The Correlation Coefficient

The Pearson product-moment correlation coefficient for X and Y is most easily thought of as the mean of the summed cross-products of the z-scores of X and Y; that is,

$$r_{XY} = \frac{1}{N}\sum_i z_{X_i} z_{Y_i} \quad \text{where } z_{X_i} = \frac{X_i - \text{mean of } X}{\text{standard deviation of } X},$$

although it can be written in many other forms. This coefficient takes on a value of +1 if all of the data points (X, Y) fall exactly on a straight line with a positive slope, so that Y increases as X increases, and –1 if they all fall on a straight line with a negative slope. If there is no linear component to the relationship between Y and X, the correlation coefficient will have a value of close to 0.

The size of the correlation coefficient stays the same if either or both of X and Y undergo linear transformations in which each value is multiplied by a constant and another constant is then added to or subtracted from the product. Therefore, the correlation coefficient stays the same if units are changed, so that the correlation between height and weight would be the same if height was measured in inches or meters.

The correlation coefficient is often misinterpreted. Among issues to consider are the following: First, the correlation coefficient is an index of *linear* relationship, not relationship in general; therefore, a correlation of 0 does not rule out the existence of a systematic nonlinear relationship between the variables. Second, if X and Y are correlated, it does not necessarily follow that there is a direct causal relationship between them; the correlation could occur because of the influence of other variables. For example, among elementary school students, vocabulary size is strongly correlated with height because both are related to chronological age. Finally, although the correlation coefficient is an index of linear relationship, unless the variances of X and Y are equal, r doesn't by itself provide information about the nature of the best-fitting linear function. In particular, the slope, or rate of change, of Y with X is given by

$$b_{YX} = \frac{r_{XY}s_Y}{s_X},$$

that is, the correlation coefficient multiplied by the ratio of the standard deviations. So if in two groups the rates of change of Y with changes in X are the same, the correlations may well be different if there is more variability in the values of X and Y in one group than in the other. For this reason, r is often referred to as a *sample-specific* measure.

Correlational Versus Experimental Research

A distinction is often made between experimental and correlational (or observational) research. In true experiments, independent variables are manipulated; that is, the assignment of subjects to the level of the independent variable is under control of the experimenter. If the experiment is conducted properly, it is possible to make causal statements about the effect of the independent variable on the dependent variable. In correlational studies, values are simply observed, no attempt is made to manipulate the independent variables, and it is not possible to make causal statements. Suppose we wanted to compare the effectiveness of two methods of teaching reading. If we simply measured the reading ability of students taught by the two methods, we could not be sure whether any differences were due to the teaching methods themselves or to other factors "correlated" with the use of the methods. Perhaps one of the methods tended to be used more in neighborhoods that had schools with smaller class sizes and families who provided more support to students.

Some Other Correlation Coefficients

A number of other correlation coefficients are also encountered. Some of these are simply the Pearson coefficient applied to specific classes of data. Examples are the *Spearman rank-order correlation coefficient,* which is just the Pearson coefficient applied to ranked data, and the *point-biserial correlation coefficient,* which can be thought of as the regular Pearson coefficient applied to data in which Y is continuous and X is dichotomous (i.e., X takes on only two possible values). The so-called *phi coefficient* is just the Pearson coefficient applied to data in which both X and Y are dichotomous.

Several other measures make assumptions of underlying normality to estimate what the correlation would have been if one or both variables had not been artificially dichotomized. Suppose we wish to correlate math and verbal ability. Assume we have normally distributed scores on a verbal ability test but all we know about math ability is whether or not each student passed the test. If we assume that math ability is normally distributed, we can generate the biserial correlation coefficient, which is an estimate of what the correlation coefficient would be if we had continuous scores on both dimensions. The tetrachoric correlation coefficient results if we apply the same logic to two dichotomous variables.

Multiple Correlation

Suppose we wish to predict a criterion variable Y from a number of predictor variables $X_1, X_2, \ldots X_p$. For example, we may wish to predict a measure of success in graduate school on the basis of undergraduate grades and verbal and quantitative Graduate Record Exam scores. Using the procedures of multiple regression, we can find the equation of the form

$$\hat{Y} = b_0 + b_1X_1 + b_2X_2 + \ldots + b_pX_p$$

that optimally predicts Y. The multiple correlation coefficient, $R_{Y12..p}$, is simply the Pearson product-moment correlation coefficient between the predicted and actual Y scores.

SUGGESTED READING

Cohen, J., & Cohen, P. (1983). *Applied multiple regression/correlation analysis for the behavioral sciences.* Hillsdale, NJ: Erlbaum.

Myers, J. L., & Well, A. D. (2002). *Research design and statistical analysis* (2nd ed.). Mahwah, NJ: Erlbaum.

Arnold D. Well
University of Massachusetts

COUNSELING

The term *counseling* has both a generic and a more specific meaning. Generally speaking, counseling represents a set of problem-solving actions—developing a working relationship, assessing the problem, initiating behavior change, maintaining change, and evaluating the outcomes. These generic actions are used by "counselors" working in a variety of professions, including business, law, education, health, and so on. Thus, we have financial counselors, legal counsel, academic advisors, and nutritional consultants—all of whom are identified as doing counseling. From a more specific stance, counseling also represents a professional identity and tradition with ethical codes, licensure procedures, scholarly journals, professional organizations, and academic requirements. Counseling in the professional sense and as the topic of this narrative has been associated with education and medicine, which provide the historical traditions through which counseling has evolved. Counseling as an educational intervention has been associated with schools and guidance programs, whereas counseling as a more medically oriented intervention has become interchangeable with psychotherapy practiced in clinical settings. While such diversity is viewed as a strength by some, others note the lack of consensus reflected in professional identity problems.

Counseling as Education

Counseling as education—or guidance, as it is often called—is related to the historical use of the term *counseling*. Dictionary definitions of counseling emphasize giving advice and exchanging information. Since the earliest times, people have sought advice and counsel—from Old Testament prophets, Greek philosophers, and ancient healers. Although such earlier antecedents can be identified, guidance developed in the industrialized Middle West and East. The merger of vocational guidance and psychological testing established an important foundation of counseling. Before the development of testing, vocational guidance relied on vocational education that stressed occupational information and advice. With the development of testing in the areas of ability, interests, occupations, and personality, vocational guidance obtained a scientific means to realize its common-sense notion of improving the worker-occupation relationship. As articulated by the leaders of vocational guidance, perhaps most persuasively by Frank Parsons in *Choosing a Vocation,* worker-occupation relationships depended on a suitable match between the worker and the job. This match was predicated on the ability to gather accurate information about the individual, his or her abilities and interests, and the job. Scientific methods helped transform guidance workers into professionals, established the respectability of vocational counseling, and facilitated its acceptance by public institutions such as the schools and, later, the Veterans Administration. Such a transformation was largely carried out at the University of Minnesota through the pioneering work of Donald Patterson and his colleagues and students, especially E. G. Williamson.

In the 1950s and 1960s, counseling as guidance—while less popular than psychotherapy—was stimulated by the development of professional organizations (e.g., American Personnel and Guidance Association and now the American Counseling Association) and the reemergence of the importance of schooling (with Russian Sputnik I) and work (with the Vocational Rehabilitation Act of 1954). As a result, there was a great demand for school counselors (spurred by the National Defense Act of 1958) and rehabilitation counselors. In response, professional organizations lobbied for funds and later established accreditation programs (e.g., the Council for the Accreditation of Counseling and Related Programs) for the preparation of counselors. Through their respective journals, the concerns of counselors were given a voice.

On the other hand, another organization with members representing the guidance tradition—originally the Division of Counseling and Guidance, in 1952 renamed the Division of Counseling Psychology (American Psychological Association) and now, the Society of Counseling Psychology, a division of the American Psychological Association—competed for psychological services (e.g., the Veterans Administration). These activities contributed to the further decline of the guidance tradition and to a separation of counseling psychologists with doctoral-level training from school and rehabilitation counselors with subdoctoral-level training.

During this time period, advances in social sciences brought significant conceptual developments (self-concept theory, stage theory) that transformed vocational guidance into career development (with the work of Donald Super, John Holland, Anne Roe, and others). Today the emphasis is on addressing the theoretical and empirical inadequacies of this tradition that neglected the roles of gender, race, class, sexual orientation, and disability. New programs are being developed to address these deficiencies, such as the school-to-work transition movement.

Counseling as Therapy

Around 1940, the dominance of the guidance model began to erode; by the end of the decade it was replaced by psychotherapy, an intervention often associated with a more medically oriented setting. A number of factors contributed to the decline. Part of the downfall coincided with social changes brought on by the end of the Depression and the beginning of World War II. People were confronted with rapid social change that seemed to broadly affect their lives.

Effects went beyond educational or occupational problems as people sought help with all types of personal adjustment issues. In this Age of Psychotherapy, the publication of Carl Rogers's *Counseling and Psychotherapy* was important. Rogers, trained as a clinical psychologist, brought psychotherapy from the medical clinic to non-medical practitioners. He transformed therapy as a medical intervention by framing therapy in terms of a humanistic philosophy, an approach more congenial to counselors.

This psychotherapy tradition represented by Rogers had multiple sources. Perhaps the central experience for Rogers was his work with clients. From these experiences, Rogers formulated and reformulated his approach to counseling and psychotherapy. Although there have been changes and shifts of emphasis, the basic outlook has been a person-centered approach in which the self-determination capacities of the client are the focus of attention, concern, activity, and acceptance conveyed through a therapeutic relationship. Like Parsons's conceptual contribution to the guidance tradition, Rogers focused on individual assets. Both of these traditions, guidance and therapy, highlight the worldview of counseling, a focus on strengths rather than pathology.

Since Rogers, there have been numerous counseling and psychotherapy approaches advanced. As the twenty-first century begins, there is renewed emphasis on counseling that works, with most attention focusing on competing models of treatment—cognitive-behavioral treatment versus a common-factors position. For psychotherapy, the challenge in a rapidly changing health care market is to document the effectiveness of counseling practices, especially the validity of our treatments for racial and ethnic minorities.

Challenges

Up to this point, counseling has been seen as evolving as a field through vocational guidance and psychotherapy. Although *counseling* often has multiple meanings, it continues to represent a disciplined mode of action of working with people. Counseling faces numerous future challenges, but diversity and managed health care appear to have the largest potential for influencing the nature of counseling in the new millennium. The growing diversity of our population and the inadequacy of our traditional counseling world view have stimulated a multicultural revolution. Beginning with the unmet need for counseling women, counselors have struggled to develop approaches that are effective with various oppressed groups in our society (racial and ethnic minorities; gay, lesbian, bisexual, and transgender-identified individuals; persons with disabilities). The traditional counseling competencies—relationship, assessment, interviewing, intervention, and research skills—need a cultural transformation from a set of competencies reflecting a universal cultural myth to a set of cultural practices appropriate to a worldview of multiple perspectives. The other challenge, managed care, has focused attention on examining the effectiveness of counseling practices. In putting these challenges together, the big question is not if counseling works, but if counseling works for neglected groups of our society.

Gerald L. Stone

See also: **Behavior Therapy; Psychotherapy**

COUNSELING PSYCHOLOGY

Counseling psychology has undergone significant developments since its formal inception as a distinct helping profession in 1946. Originally devoted to assisting individuals in the search for appropriate occupations, it broadened into a profession that assists relatively intact persons in maximizing their developmental potential in all areas of their lives. In doing so, it makes use of a wide variety of sophisticated psychological interventions designed not only to assist people in adjusting to their environment, but also to modify environments to make them more suited to human needs.

Definitional Models of Counseling Psychology

The definition of counseling psychology has consisted of several emphases that distinguish it from related helping professions. First, counseling psychology has consistently followed an educational rather than a clinical, remedial, or medical model. Clients (not patients) are viewed as normal individuals who need assistance in coping with stresses and tasks of everyday life. The task of the counseling psychologist is to teach clients coping strategies and new behaviors that they can use in making maximum use of their already existing resources or in developing more adequate resources.

Other methods may be used for reeducating clients besides the dyadic interview. Thus, counseling psychologists may lead groups designed to enhance the lives of each of the members, or they may design and conduct workshops on various aspects of life planning, such as assertion skills or communications skills. The counseling psychologist may intervene in the client's immediate environment to facilitate client change and growth, and he or she may relate to the client in real-life situations in addition to an office setting.

Counseling psychology's educational base is seen most clearly in public schools and in college and university counseling centers. There, however, the counselor's role has broadened from an almost exclusive concern with the vocational and educational guidance of youths to an increasing focus on the creation of a total educational environment conducive to learning. In the process, counselors find themselves doing not only vocational counseling but also personal and emotional counseling in an attempt to maximize students' receptivity to education. Counselors may also act as consultants with faculty and administration to help create a total school environment that facilitates learning. School counselors generally are trained at the master's degree level, while college and university counseling psychologists typically possess a doctorate degree.

Counseling psychology stresses a developmental model. It attempts to assist clients in achieving their optimal development and in removing blocks to normal growth.

Counseling psychology has advocated preventive approaches to developmental problems in addition to, but not to the exclusion of, remedial approaches. The strategy in prevention is to identify individuals, groups, or settings that, according to theory and research, are seen as being particularly at risk, and to intervene with appropriate individuals or in appropriate settings *before* a crisis occurs. This is analogous to public health measures designed to prevent the outbreak of disease rather than to cure it.

Counseling psychology, alone among the helping professions, pays particular attention to the role of occupation in the lives of people. Indeed, the profession derives much of its identity from the vocational guidance movement. With the post–World War II rise of affluence and the decline of the work ethic as a source of personal and societal values, counseling psychology broadened its aim to include personal development in areas other than work. The profession's methodology has likewise become more sophisticated, moving from a relatively straightforward one-time matching of persons and jobs to a consideration of psychological needs fulfilled by work, the selection of different occupations throughout the life span as a function of developmental stages, the differing career patterns of men and women, and an exploration of the meaning and value of work in relation to other activities such as leisure.

Professional Identity of Counseling Psychology

As counseling psychology evolved from its original base of vocational guidance, it overlapped with other helping professions. Thus, as psychotherapy increasingly was practiced by counseling psychologists without reference to occupational selection, the overlap with clinical psychology grew. As counseling psychologists intervened in the client's network of social relations, their function overlapped with that of social workers. Meanwhile, clinical psychologists moved increasingly out of the mental hospitals, away from assessment of mental functioning as a primary activity, and toward a greater involvement with relatively intact individuals. Similarly, social workers moved away from case management and toward therapeutic counseling. There has thus been simultaneous movement of the three largest helping professions toward one another, resulting in a blurring of previously distinct role definitions and functions.

Exacerbating the identity problem is the historical linkage of counseling psychology with colleges of education, due in large part to the original mission of counseling departments to train school counselors. As, on the one hand, counselor education broadened in scope into counseling psychology and, on the other hand, vocational guidance became increasingly psychologically sophisticated, counseling psychology programs were often caught between education and psychology. The result is that the majority of counseling psychology programs approved by the American Psychological Association currently are located in colleges of education rather than in departments of psychology. Although this makes sense in terms of the educational model of the profession, among counseling psychologists it has resulted in a split loyalty between the field of counselor education, which may not be psychologically oriented, and the field of applied psychology, which may follow a remedial, quasi-medical model. As the issues of licensing and credentialing, specialty guidelines, and third-party payments become important, counseling psychologists are being forced to choose between education and psychology as their main knowledge base and source of professional identity. As a result, counseling psychology programs have taken on a greater emphasis on training in basic psychology, and the gulf between counseling psychology and counselor education appears to be growing.

Theoretical Models of Counseling Psychology

The original Minnesota model of vocational counseling began during the 1930s with Edmund G. Williamson in the Student Counseling Bureau at the University of Minnesota and served as a model for most later university counseling centers. This model was basically a rational decision-making process in which test interpretation figured prominently and that resulted in an educational or occupational selection. With the rise of the psychotherapy movement, counseling psychology models focused more on the *process* of the counseling relationship than on the *outcome.*

Two theoretical models in particular—the decision-making and the counselor social influence models—warrant further discussion, as they represent a unique contribution of counseling psychology to applied psychology. Decision-making counseling involves the translation into the counseling process of the concepts and practices underlying decision theory, and in general it attempts to teach clients, either individually or in groups, overt procedures and strategies for effective decision making. The decision-making model is especially suitable for vocational and career counseling, as illustrated by Mitchell, Jones, and Krumboltz in *Social Learning and Career Decision Making.* Counseling psychology's stress on prevention is nicely illustrated by the decision-making model; formal classes as well as other methods of teaching decision-making skills have been used to teach these skills to potentially high-risk populations *before* major decisions must be made.

Problem solving is closely related to decision making. In *Problem-Solving Counseling,* David Dixon and John Glover have integrated the pragmatic problem-solving methodology that characterizes a number of counseling psychology approaches with the research and conceptual literature on problem solving. Both decision-making and problem-solving integrations represent a movement to include cognitive dimensions along with behavioral counseling.

The social influence model of the counseling process was originally proposed by Stanley R. Strong in the late 1960s. Strong drew on the interpersonal influence literature in social psychology to conceptualize the counselor's influence over the client as a result of the former's perceived expertness and credibility. Much research has since been done regarding the behaviors that contribute to counselor social influence; the conditions under which counselor social influence can be maximized; the relationship of social influence measures to other measures of counseling process and outcome; and social influence as a function of specific counselor and client attributes such as race, sex, and social class. Currently, social influence is one of the most influential models of the counseling process.

Research In Counseling Psychology

Research in counseling psychology has changed over time. The largest change has been the ratio of empirical studies to conceptual or theoretical articles; in 1954, the ratio was 1:1, although in the 1980s there were more than nine empirical studies to one nonempirical study. Another change has been in the relative proportion of outcome research to process research, the former declining to a small proportion while the latter has risen to about 25% of the total. Process-outcome research has likewise shown a substantial increase, making the journal a major publication outlet for process-oriented research in applied psychology. Reflecting counseling psychology's deemphasis on vocational counseling, the percentage of research on vocational behavior has declined somewhat over the years, although this has been offset by the increase in research relating to counseling with special populations. Finally, social influence research has accounted for a significant portion of recent issues of the journal, thus emphasizing its prominent place as a process model in counseling psychology.

The quality and specificity of research in counseling psychology have likewise increased. Studies are much more likely now to use multifactorial designs, to make use of multivariate statistics, to provide tight experimental controls in order to eliminate extraneous sources of variance, and to investigate the effects of specific interventions on specific measures of change. There has been an increasing focus on what technique used by what counselor with what client results in what outcome under what conditions.

E. Thomas Dowd
Kent State University

See also: **Career Development; Counseling**

COUNTERCONDITIONING

In 1924, Mary Cover Jones, a student of John Watson, published a paper describing the successful treatment of a fear of rabbits in a 3-year-old boy named Peter. Under Watson's supervision, she exposed the child to a caged rabbit while the boy was eating one of his favorite foods. The rabbit was at first kept at a distance but gradually was moved closer to Peter over a period of several sessions. Eventually Peter was able to pet the rabbit and allow it to nibble his fingers without any sign of fear.

Counterconditioning is a procedure in which a response to a stimulus is replaced or countered by pairing that stimulus with a new stimulus of differing valence. In the case of Peter, Jones presented the feared stimulus (the rabbit) in conjunction with a pleasant stimulus (food), with the result that the fear response was eliminated. It is important to note that the feared stimulus was introduced in a gradual fashion, to ensure that at no time was a fear response elicited that was more powerful than the response of eating. Had this occurred, the fear of rabbits would not have been removed, and a conditioned fear response to the food (or other associated cues) might have been established.

Counterconditioning is somewhat similar to extinction in the classical (Pavlovian) conditioning paradigm. Both procedures result in diminution or elimination of a response to a stimulus. However, in extinction the conditioned stimulus is presented alone without the unconditioned stimulus, whereas in counterconditioning the conditioned stimulus is presented with a *different* unconditioned stimulus.

The term *counterconditioning* has been used in two different ways, which are often confused. Letting S stand for stimulus and R for response, consider two reflexes, $S_1 \rightarrow R_1$ and $S_2 \rightarrow R_2$, where it is impossible for R_1 and R_2 to occur simultaneously. In one usage, counterconditioning is a *procedure* involving the pairing of S_1 with S_2. The result of such a procedure is usually the elimination of the weaker of the two reflexes. In the second usage, counterconditioning is an inferred *process* proposed to explain this result. This process is stimulus substitution: The stronger response is substituted for the weaker one. When the counterconditioning procedure is successful in eliminating a reflex, it is not necessarily the case that the process responsible is simple stimulus substitution. Other possible explanations that have been proposed are conditioned inhibition, habituation, and extinction.

Two types of counterconditioning have been widely used for therapeutic purposes with humans. These procedures are distinguished chiefly by whether the goal is to increase or decrease the attractiveness of a stimulus. In appetitive counterconditioning, the desired outcome is an increase in attractiveness, as in the case of Peter and the feared rabbit. Systematic desensitization is the most widely used technique based on this type of counterconditioning. Instead of using food as the positive countering stimulus, desensitization employs muscle relaxation. The goal is to reduce a fear response to a specific stimulus.

In aversive counterconditioning, a stimulus becomes less attractive as a result of being paired with an aversive stimulus. An example is the use of electric shock paired with sexually deviant pictures to reduce sexual attraction.

Jones was not the first to appreciate the therapeutic potential of counterconditioning. In a paper describing the conditioning of a fear response in an 11-month-old child, J. B. Watson and R. Rayner (1920) suggested a procedure similar to the one used with Peter. And in a study reported after Jones's paper was published but almost certainly conducted prior to it, Ivan Pavlov (1927) treated a dog who became agitated when placed in an experimental stand by feeding him while the dog was in the apparatus. None of this early work had an impact on clinical practice, and widespread use of treatments based on counterconditioning did not occur until Joseph Wolpe developed systematic desensitization some 30 years later.

Stuart G. Fisher

See also: **Behavior Therapy; Psychotherapy**

COUNTERTRANSFERENCE

Countertransference refers to feelings that arise in the therapist in response to the patient during the course of the patient's treatment. In its narrowest sense, the term *countertransference* is defined as the therapist's transferential reactions to the patient. Like all transferential reactions, countertransference involves a displacement onto the patient of feelings, beliefs, or impulses that were experienced previously by the therapist toward another person or persons.

The term *counter-transference* was first articulated by Freud to describe the therapist's affective reactions to the patient: "We have begun to consider the 'counter-transference,' which arises in the physician as a result of the patient's influence on his unconscious feelings, and have nearly come to the point of requiring the physician to recognize and overcome this counter-transference in himself" (1910/1961, pp. 144–145). Although Freud never explicitly defined the scope and nature of countertransference feelings, his work has largely been interpreted to mean that countertransference interferes with the progress of therapy. Accordingly, the neutrality required of the therapist in the therapeutic setting cannot be achieved unless countertransference feelings are contained or eliminated. This interpretation of Freudian theory conforms with the classical definition of countertransference feelings as deriving solely from the therapist's unresolved conflicts, without regard for the patient's contribution to the therapist's affective response.

The classical definition of countertransference went largely unchallenged until the middle of the twentieth century, when relational models of psychoanalytic thought began to reconceptualize the meaning of emotional experience as a reflection of self in relation to other. This shift from intrapsychic drive to interpersonal interaction was accompanied by a shift in the theory of therapy that recast the therapist in the role of "participant-observer" in the therapeutic process (Sullivan, 1953). The relational model of psychotherapy viewed the therapist's countertransference feelings as both relevant and inevitable. In contrast to classical theory, the feelings aroused in the therapist provided a critical source of information about both the patient and the therapeutic process. Furthermore, the distinction between real and distorted countertransference responses was rejected as a false one. A new definition, variously termed "totalist" or "objective" countertransference, broadened countertransference to include the therapist's total response to the patient, conscious and unconscious, real and distorted.

The role of countertransference in therapy varies depending on whether countertransference is defined from a classical or totalist perspective. According to the classical approach, countertransference derives solely from the therapist's own, unresolved conflicts and must be avoided or controlled if the therapist is to work effectively with the patient. The task of the classical therapist is to become a tabula rasa, free of subjective distortions. This means that the therapist strives to banish emotional reactions to the patient in order more effectively to attend to the patient's unconscious communications. Only by maintaining neutrality can the therapist accurately interpret the patient's transference distortions. For example, a therapist who finds the patient to be flirtatious will strive to banish from the therapist's own affective responses and actions any reciprocal response. In this way, the material remains untarnished by the therapist's countertransference reactions.

By contrast, the totalist approach includes in its definition of countertransference both "real" and distorted reactions to the patient and considers these reactions to be unavoidable. Far from impeding the interpretation of the patient's unconscious communications, the totalist view regards countertransference as a mechanism by which the patient's unconscious communications may be understood. The relational therapist, therefore, attends carefully to countertransference feelings to expand his or her awareness of the relational patterns that manifest themselves in the therapeutic setting. The therapist who becomes aware of a patient's flirtation, for example, might then use his or her awareness of the flirtation as a source of data with regard to the patient's relational experience.

The neutrality of the classical therapist removes countertransference feelings from the realm of therapeutic inquiry. Because the therapist disregards emotional reactions to the patient, the patient's experience of the therapist is necessarily transferential. In other words, the patient's primary experience of the therapist has nothing to do with the therapist's actual behavior, thoughts, or feelings, but instead reflects some aspect of the patient's past that has been transferred into the therapeutic relationship. The manifestation of countertransference feelings, if it does occur, is a mistake that must be rectified. The classical approach avoids discussion of countertransference feelings by interpreting the patient's experience of the therapist as a manifestation of transference. For example, the therapist might interpret the patient's experience of irritation on the part of the therapist to be a transferential reaction stemming from the patient's aggressive wishes.

Because the totalist view considers countertransference reactions to be an inevitable component of the therapeutic process, the patient's observations of the therapist always reflect some mixing of objective reality and transferential distortions. Rather than assuming the patient's reactions to be transferential, the therapist examines the nature of the transference-countertransference interactions to see how they reflect the patient's relational history and experience. Whereas the classical approach is to keep countertransference feelings out of the room, the totalist sees the inevitable unfolding of the transference-countertransference enactment as a potential road map to the patient's intrapsychic experience. In the example of the patient who experiences the therapist as irritated, the therapist might consider whether the therapeutic interaction comprises an unconscious enactment of aggressive behavior. Rather than viewing the patient's experience as a reflection of transferential material, the therapist might interpret the intrapsychic function of the enactment to the patient. In this way the totalist approach steers clear of the "reality" versus "distortion" dichotomy and focuses instead on the meaning of inevitable affective exchanges in the therapeutic relationship.

How do the differences between classical and totalist approaches to countertransference manifest themselves in the current practice of psychodynamic psychotherapy? This question was addressed in a survey of attitudes toward countertransference among experienced analysts whose theoretical orientations, classical and interpersonal, were believed to correspond, respectively, with the classical and totalist approaches to countertransference (Mendelsohn, Bucci, & Chouhy, 1992). Classical analysts continued to understand countertransference as a distorted and inappropriate response to the patient, and they therefore viewed countertransference as an obstacle to the therapeutic work. Interpersonalist analysts defined countertransference as the total emotional reaction to the patient and viewed it as an important treatment tool. However, with respect to therapeutic technique, classical and interpersonalist analysts were in agreement that the analyst's emotional responses, including dreams, unconscious associations, and fantasies, should be used as sources of information about the patient's dynamics and transferences. Classical analysts differed from interpersonalist analysts in reporting both significantly less frequent use of their emotional reactions to the patient and significantly less frequent communication to the patient of their emotions and associations. Although this survey suggests that the debate between classical and totalist camps regarding the role of countertransference reflects in part a semantic difference regarding the term *countertransference,* it also demonstrates that the different understandings of countertransference conform to different uses of countertransference in current analytic practice (Mendelsohn et al., 1992).

REFERENCES

Freud, S. (1961). The future prospects of psycho-analytic therapy. In J. Strachey (Ed. and Trans.), *The standard edition of the complete psychological works of Sigmund Freud* (Vol. 11, pp. 144–151). London: Hogarth Press. (Original work published 1910)

Mendelsohn, R., Bucci, W., & Chouhy, R. (1992). Transference and countertransference: A survey of attitudes. *Contemporary Psychoanalysis, 28,* 364–390.

Sullivan, H. S. (1953). *The interpersonal theory of psychiatry.* New York: W. W. Norton.

Sally Keller
George Stricker
Adelphi University

CREATIVITY

Most Asian, African, and Native American traditions used creative imagination to enrich and enhance everyday life; original contributions were typically seen as gifts from deities or spirits, who used humans as "channels." These insights would often come in nighttime dreams or daytime visions, and they were thought to recreate divine truth rather than to innovate. In some of these societies, an individual who produced something unprecedented (such as a mask or weapon) would be hailed as a hero, but in others he or she would be censured for breaking with tradition. Even in Western societies, women's creativity often was undervalued, and women were given few opportunities to develop the skills, the education, or the life circumstances on which creative productivity depends.

The English word *creativity* is linked with the concept of origin itself (from the Latin *creare,* to make, and the ecclesiastical Latin, *creator* or Creator). Some psychologists focus on creative *products,* requiring that they be of social value or have attained some other type of consensual agreement if they are to be called creative. Others emphasize the *process* by which the products (artwork, technology, ideas, etc.) come into being. Others conceptualize creativity as the unique *achievement, ability,* and/or *attitude* of a person or a consortium. In each of these perspectives, there can be levels of accomplishment, utility, or originality, implying that some persons or groups can be more or less creative than others. The concept of *everyday creativity* directs attention to creative outcomes in office management, child rearing, home repairs, food preparation, or community service, as well as the dark side of creativity, innovative but destructive acts. Thus, from a Western standpoint, *creativity* is a term that can be used to describe the process of bringing something new into being by becoming sensitive to gaps in human knowledge, identifying these deficiencies, searching for their solutions, making guesses as to a potential solution, testing one's hypotheses, and communicating the final results. However, the creative process is imperfectly understood; these steps may be linear or overlap, may occur in a planned sequence or spontaneously, and may be intentional or largely unconscious. Finally, the term *creativity* is a social construct used to describe various outcomes in a number of domains, such as linguistic, musical, logical, spatial, kinesthetic, interpersonal, and intrapersonal (Gardner, 1993).

Attempts to measure the creative *process* have led to the development of various tests and measures of "divergent thinking" and other cognitive skills. Biographical inventories and personality measures have been devised in an attempt to identify the creative *person.* The creative *environment* has been assessed by various scales and questionnaires focusing on the classroom or the workplace, while creative *products* have been rated by a variety of scales (Runco, 1999). Some of these attempts at assessment have been used to identify highly creative individuals in order to offer them special instruction; in the United States, entire programs—some of them statewide—have been based on pupils' test results. However, creativity measures have been criticized on the basis of content validity, construct validity, reliability, relevance to different populations, comprehensiveness, and the proclivity for their results to be influenced by situational or contextual factors. Some positive outcomes have resulted from assessing level or type of creativity through the use of such naturalistic assignments as writing a short story, assembling collages, or engaging in spontaneous problem solving. Despite their shortcomings, creativity tests have been utilized in many important research projects (Barron & Harrington, 1981).

Creative training programs assume that creative behavior can be enhanced, an assumption that has not gained acceptance among those psychologists for whom biological determinants and early learning are important variables. Some approaches admit that key creativity skills cannot be affected within a short span of time, since these components include such elements as knowledge of the topic, technical skills, and working and cognitive styles. As a result, these programs emphasize task motivation through modeling, fantasy, and a deemphasis on evaluation. Other programs take a more optimistic view, focusing on cognitive rather than social psychological methods; for example, brainstorming and creative problem solving teach people how to generate unusual ideas. Some programs for school children have been found effective in improving scores on standard creativity tests (Amabile, 1983). Several elements converge to form creativity (e.g., intelligence, accumulated knowledge, cognitive styles, personality traits, motivation, and environmental variables; Sternberg & Lubart, 1995), and training programs need to address these elements in a systematic manner.

When personality characteristics of people identified as creative are observed, a common set of characteristics usually emerges, such as broad interests, high energy levels, attraction to complexity, independence of judgment, autonomy, use of intuition, ability to resolve paradoxes or to accommodate apparently opposite or conflicting aspects of one's self-concept, and a firm sense of one's self as creative (Barron & Harrington, 1981). However, there appear to be important differences among groups of creative people: Artists have been described as more emotionally sensitive, tense, and impractical than scientists; many scientists grew up as "intellectual rebels"; musicians have suffered more problems with substance abuse, poets more mania and psychosis, and writers more bipolar disorders (Ludwig, 1995).

Future research studies need to identify the genetic markers for creative activity, reconcile personality and cognitive research data in creativity, evaluate the role played by altered states of consciousness in creative ideation, determine the part played by mental illness in blocking or facilitating creative expression, and specify what home and school variables are critical factors in creative development. The need for creative solutions to the world's many social, economic, and environmental problems reflects the importance of this field and of the psychologists who dedicate themselves to studying it.

REFERENCES

Amabile, T. M. (1983). *The social psychology of creativity.* New York: Springer-Verlag.

Barron, F., & Harrington, D. M. (1981). Creativity, intelligence, and personality. *Annual Review of Psychology, 32,* 439–476.

Gardner, H. (1993). *Creating minds.* New York: Basic Books.

Ludwig, A. (1995). *The price of greatness.* New York: Guilford Press.

Runco, M. A. (1999). Tests of creativity. In M. A. Runco & S. R. Pritzker (Eds.), *Encyclopedia of creativity* (Vol. 2, pp. 189–202). San Diego, CA: Academic Press.

Sternberg, R. J., & Lubart, T. I. (1995). *Defying the crowd: Cultivating creativity in a culture of conformity.* New York: Free Press.

Stanley Krippner
Saybrook Graduate School

CRITICAL INCIDENT TECHNIQUE

The critical incident technique is a job analysis method first described by John Flanagan in 1954. The method involves the collection of hundreds of anecdotal descriptions of effective and ineffective job behaviors that job incumbents, supervisors, and others have actually observed in the work setting. These anecdotes, called *critical incidents,* must be specific behaviors that exemplify success or failure in some aspect of the job being analyzed. For example, a critical ineffective incident for a truck driver would be "The driver failed to look in his rear-view mirror when backing up the truck and consequently hit a parked car." The observer reporting the critical incident is typically asked to describe (1) what led up to the incident and the context in which it occurred; (2) exactly what the individual did that was effective or ineffective; (3) the apparent consequences of this behavior; and (4) whether or not the consequences were under the individual's control.

After several hundred critical incidents are collected, they are content-analyzed and sorted by one or more judges into categories or dimensions of critical job behavior. These dimensions then serve as the basis for the identification or construction of job-related tests and other selection devices. They can also be used as a basis for the development of training programs.

In *Applied Psychology in Personnel Management,* Cascio

(1982) noted that a major advantage of the critical incident technique as a job analysis method is that it focuses on observable, measurable job behaviors. Disadvantages of the method include the considerable amount of time and effort required to implement it and its neglect of average job performance.

The critical incident technique has been employed for several purposes other than job analysis. In 1959 Herzberg and his coworkers (Herzberg, Mausner, & Snyderman, 1959) used the method to research work motivation and satisfaction. Flanagan and Burns (1955) showed how the critical incident technique could be adapted for use as a work performance appraisal and development tool. The application of Thurstone scaling to critical incidents, suggested most notably by Smith and Kendall (1963), has led to the development of several work performance appraisal techniques, including behaviorally anchored rating scales, mixed standard rating scales, and weighted checklists. In "Spin-Offs From Behavior Expectation Scale Procedures," Blood (1974) showed how critical incidents could be used to investigate organizational policy. The critical incident technique has also been used to improve workplace and product safety and efficiency.

REFERENCES

Blood, M. R. (1974). Spin-offs from behavior expectation scale procedures. *Journal of Applied Psychology, 59,* 513–515.

Cascio, W. F. (1982). *Applied psychology in personnel management* (2nd ed.). Reston, VA: Reston.

Flanagan, J. C., & Burns, R. K. (1955). The employee performance record: A new appraisal and development tool. *Harvard Business Review, 33*(5), 95–102.

Herzberg, F., Mausner, B., & Snyderman, B. (1959). *The motivation to work.* New York: Wiley.

Smith, P. C., & Kendall, L. M. (1963). Retranslation of expectations: An approach to the construction of unambiguous anchors for rating scales. *Journal of Applied Psychology, 47,* 149–155.

WILLIAM. I. SAUSER, JR.
Auburn University

See also: **Applied Research; Industrial-Organizational Psychology**

CROSS-CULTURAL COUNSELING

Cross-cultural counseling describes any psychological helping relationships in formal or informal settings where a trained provider provides a helping human service to a culturally different client-consumer. Historically, cross-cultural counseling has adapted Western, dominant-culture methods to meet the needs of non-Western, minority clients.

Whereas the fields of psychoanalysis and anthropology were initially the focus of interest in studying cultures and mental health, the focus has since shifted from the anthropological study of remote and exotic cultures to cultural variations in modern pluralistic and complex societies. Psychology has conventionally assumed that there is a fixed or absolutist perspective of mental functioning and that culture distorts that universal definition of normal behavior. The contrasting perspective of anthropology assumed that cultural differences illuminate attitudes, values, and perspectives that differ across cultures in a relativist perspective. Cross-cultural counseling attempts to reconcile these two extreme positions.

The cultural context can be narrowly defined to include only ethnic or national aspects, but *culture* may also be broadly defined to include ethnographic and demographic status and formal or informal affiliations. Cross-cultural counseling has generally been used to describe the national and international applications of counseling across all cultural boundaries (Pedersen, Draguns, Lonner, & Trimble, 2001; Ponterotto, Casas, Suzuki & Alexander, 2002; Sue & Sue, 1999). A weakness of the *cross-cultural counseling* term is that it implies the comparison of cultures, with an implicit judgment that some cultures are better than others. In recent years the term *multicultural counseling* has been preferred over *cross-cultural counseling* to emphasize the multiplicity of equally valued cultural groups and contexts in which counseling occurs.

As non-Western countries and cultures have modernized and urbanized on a global scale, sources of traditional village, religious, and family authority and social support have been weakened, and Westernized models of counseling services have become more popular. As an alternative to the transfer of Western models, indigenous therapies are also becoming more popular. The transfer of counseling outside the Euro-American cultural context has revealed cultural biases in the conventional descriptions of counseling and therapy.

The presence of cultural bias in counseling has been well documented. Wrenn (1962) defined the "culturally encapsulated counselor" as one who had substituted symbiotic modal stereotypes for the real world, disregarded cultural variations among clients, and dogmatized technique-oriented definitions of counseling and therapy. Western-trained counselors are likely to promote the individualistic assumptions of a dominant culture intentionally or unintentionally as they transfer the dominant culture perspective of counseling to their clients.

The Basic Behavioral Science Task Force of the National Advisory Mental Health Council (1996) has identified specific examples of how social and cultural beliefs influence diagnosis and treatment, how diagnostic categories reflect majority culture values, how diagnosis differs across cultures, how symptoms are expressed differently across cultures, and the effect of most providers' being from a majority culture background while most clients come from minority cultural groups.

In the 1970s research demonstrated that mental health services were being underutilized by minority groups and that behavior described as pathological in a minority culture, such as individualistic assertiveness, may be viewed as adaptive in a majority culture client. Asian Americans, Blacks, Chicanos, American Indians, and other minority groups terminate counseling significantly earlier than Anglo clients (Sue & Sue, 1999). In most of the research literature these examples of underutilization are explained by cultural barriers that hinder the formation of good counseling relationships, language barriers, class-bound values, and culture-bound attitudes.

Cross-cultural counselors have failed to develop grounded theory based on empirical data for several reasons. First, the emphasis has been on abnormal rather than normal behavior across cultures. Second, only in the 1970s did a pancultural core emerge for the more serious categories of disturbance such as Schizophrenia and affective psychoses, so that they are recognizable according to uniform symptoms across cultures, even though tremendous cultural variations continue to exist. Third, the complexity of research on therapy across cultural lines is difficult to measure. Fourth, the research has lacked an applied emphasis related to practical concerns of program development, service delivery, and techniques of treatment. Fifth, there has been insufficient interdisciplinary collaboration across psychology, psychiatry, and anthropology, and each approaches culture and mental health from a different perspective. Sixth, the emphasis of research has been on the symptom as a basic variable, to the neglect of the interaction with the community's needs (Pedersen et al., 2002).

Culturally sensitive competencies were developed from the mid-1980s describing a three-stage developmental sequence beginning with multicultural awareness, then moving to multicultural knowledge and finally to multicultural skill competencies (Sue et al., 1982). This framework has been elaborated by Sue and colleagues (1998). These multicultural competencies have been adopted by Division 17 (Counseling) of the American Psychological Association as well as the American Counseling Association as standards for professional conduct.

The future of cross-cultural counseling will depend on advances in four areas: (1) Conceptual and theoretical approaches need to be developed (Sue, Ivey, & Pedersen, 1996); (2) a more focused research effort is needed to identify those primary variables that will explain what has happened, interpret what is happening, and perhaps predict what is going to happen in the migration of persons and ideas across cultures; (3) criteria of expertise for the education and training of professionals to work across cultures need to be defined to adequately prepare providers to deal with the problems of a pluralistic society; and (4) revolutionary modes of providing services need to be developed based on new theory, research, and training so that counseling is equitably and appropriately provided to all members of our pluralistic society.

REFERENCES

Basic Behavioral Science Task Force of the National Advisory Mental Health Council. (1996). Basic behavioral science research for mental health: Sociocultural and environmental processes. *American Psychologist, 51,* 722–731.

Pedersen, P., Draguns, J., Lonner, W., & Trimble, J. (2002). *Counseling across cultures* (5th ed.). Thousand Oaks, CA: Sage.

Ponterotto, J. G., Casas, J. M., Suzuki, L. A., & Alexander, C. M. (2001). *Handbook of multicultural counseling* (2nd ed.). Thousand Oaks, CA: Sage.

Sue, D. W., & Sue D. (1999). *Counseling the culturally different: Theory and practice* (3rd ed.). New York: Wiley Interscience.

Sue, D. W., Bernier, J. E., Durran, A., Fineberg, L., Pedersen, P., Smith, C. J., et al. (1982). Cross-cultural counseling competencies. *The Counseling Psychologist, 19*(2), 45–52.

Sue, D. W., Carter, R. T., Casas, J. M., Fouad, N. A., Ivey, A. E., Jensen, M., et al. (1998). *Multicultural counseling competencies.* Thousand, Oaks, CA: Sage.

Sue, D. W., Ivey, A. E., & Pedersen, P. B. (1996). *Multicultural counseling theory.* Pacific Grove, CA: Brooks/Cole.

Wrenn, G. (1962). The culturally encapsulated counselor. *Harvard Educational Review, 32,* 444–449.

Paul B. Pedersen
Professor Emeritus, Syracuse University and Visiting Professor at the Department of Psychology, University of Hawaii

See also: **Multicultural Counseling**

CROSS-CULTURAL PSYCHOLOGY

Introduction and Overview

The study of human behavior must include observations made all around the world, not just in the few highly industrialized nations where most research has historically been done. The concept of culture summarizes many of the major influences on human behavior and the bases for concepts of self and group identity that people hold. Further, aspects of culture have major effects on the formulation, dissemination, and acceptance of programs designed to deliver psychological services or to use psychological principles. Cross-cultural research is also central to theory development and to programs aimed at applying the lessons learned from research (Brislin, 2000; Berry, Poortinga, & Pandey, 1997; Triandis & Suh, 2002).

Definitions of Culture

As with many complex concepts long studied by psychologists, such as personality, intelligence, and abnormal behavior, no one definition of *culture* is widely accepted. Psychologists have not spent much effort developing definitions of culture but have benefited from the efforts of their colleagues in anthropology. Alfred Kroeber and Clyde Kluckhohn, in "Culture: A Critical Review of Concepts and Definitions," concluded by suggesting that many definitions contained "patterns, explicit and implicit, of or for behavior transmitted by symbols, constituting the distinctive achievements of human groups . . . [and] ideas and their attached values" (Kroeber & Kluckhohn, 1952, p. 181). Melville Herskovits, in *Man and His Works* (1948, p. 17), proposed the equally influential generalization that culture is "the man-made part of the human environment."

In *The Analysis of Subjective Culture,* Harry Triandis (1972) benefited from Herskovits's contribution and made a distinction between physical and subjective culture. The former would include man-made objects such as houses and tools, while the latter comprises people's responses to those objects in the form of values, roles, and attitudes. It is important to delimit the concept of culture, lest it be so all-encompassing as to explain little or nothing in particular. Violent storms are not best conceptualized as part of a culture, even though a certain society may inhabit an area in a hurricane belt. However, people's reactions to storms, in the form of preparations or collective action following a disaster, are indeed part of their culture.

Since much cross-cultural research has the goal of understanding concepts as seen by people in the culture under study, the influence of cognitive psychology has been strong. Much research has focused on people's knowledge about their world, their communication with one another given this shared knowledge, and the transmittal of this knowledge to the next generation. Given this emphasis, a third definition of culture suggested by Clifford Geertz (1973, p. 89) captures the flavor of much cross-cultural research: "Culture denotes an historically transmitted pattern of meanings embodied in symbols, a system of inherited conceptions expressed in symbolic forms by means of which men communicate, perpetuate, and develop their knowledge about and attitudes toward life."

In research programs, many psychologists use aspects of all three definitions. In studies of ethnocentrism, for instance, the fact that ideas have "attached value"—suggested by Kroeber and Kluckhohn—should be added to the concept of "symbolic forms," which Geertz formulated. The fact that people's symbols are valued leads to ethnocentric thinking, especially concerning subjective elements such as ideology, religion, morality, or law. *Ethnocentrism* refers to the deeply held belief that one's own culture is the best (defined by that culture's own standards) and that others are inferior in many ways. People almost uniformly believe that what they do is good or right and that members of other cultures are somewhat backward and/or illogical concerning their customs, rituals, food, interpersonal relationships, and other aspects of everyday behavior.

Goals of Cross-Cultural Psychology

Cross-cultural psychology is the study of culture's effects on human behavior. More formally, cross-cultural psychology is the empirical study of members of various culture groups with identifiable experiences that lead to predictable and significant similarities and differences in behavior. People's experiences take place in various social contexts, and so the study of culture often includes analysis of the social contexts in which people find themselves.

Social context has been notoriously difficult to operationalize (Markus & Kitayama, 1998). The study of social context has been an active research focus for cross-cultural psychologists (Cole & Means, 1981; Kagitcibasi, 1997). In their own culture, investigators are so close to the same social contexts as the participants in their research projects that separation of person from context is difficult. In other cultures, since visiting investigators have not had much experience with various everyday social contexts, they can more easily separate themselves from social situations and formulate hypotheses about the relative contributions of individual and contextual factors (Hall, 1977; Brislin, 2000).

At times, psychologists interested in the applications of research knowledge can take advantage of knowledge about social context. Jordan and Tharp (1979) developed programs to teach Hawaiian and part-Hawaiian children to read. They had little success after importing methods found to be effective in the United States or Western Europe. They did research, however, on children's everyday behavior in their homes and in their communities, and found that the children spent large amounts of time sitting around telling stories to one another and listening to adults tell such stories. The researchers then used knowledge of this practice, called *talk story* in Hawaii, in the classroom. They found that if children read their books as members of small groups and then discussed what they had just read, reading skills improved dramatically.

Conclusion

Any definition of psychology must take into account observations made in various parts of the world, not just those few countries in which most psychological research has historically been done. Cross-cultural studies, then, are central to the development of psychology. Cross-cultural contributions should increase in the future, as more and more psychologists in various countries free themselves from the shackles of imposed theories from Euro-American sources (Draguns, 2001). Psychologists in various countries can develop their own theories to explain research findings that differ from predictions based on Euro-American theories.

REFERENCES

Berry, J., Poortinga, Y., & Pandey, J. (Eds.). (1997). *Handbook of cross-cultural psychology: Vol. 1. Theory and method* (2nd ed.). Boston: Allyn & Bacon.

Brislin, R. (2000). *Understanding culture's influence on behavior* (2nd ed.). Fort Worth, TX: Harcourt Brace.

Cole, M., & Means, B. (1981). *Comparative studies of how people think.* Cambridge, MA: Harvard University Press.

Draguns, J. (2001). Towards a truly international psychology: Beyond English only. *American Psychologist, 56,* 1019–1031.

Geertz, C. (1973). *The interpretation of cultures.* New York: Basic Books.

Hall, E. (1977). *Beyond culture.* Garden City, NY: Anchor Books.

Herskovits, M. (1948). *Man and his works.* New York: Knopf.

Jordan, C., & Tharp, R. (1979). Culture and education. In A. Marsella, R. Tharp, & T. Ciborowski (Eds.), *Perspectives on cross-cultural psychology* (pp. 265–285). New York: Academic Press.

Kagitcibasi, C. (1997). Individualism and collectivism. In J. Berry, M. Segall, & C. Kagitcibasi (Eds.), *Handbook of cross-cultural psychology: Vol. 3. Behavior and applications* (2nd ed., pp. 1–49). Boston: Allyn & Bacon.

Kroeber, A., & Kluckhohn, C. (1952). Culture. *Papers of the Peabody Museum, 47*(1).

Markus, H., & Kitayama, S. (1998). The cultural psychology of personality. *Journal of Cross-Cultural Psychology, 29,* 63–87.

Triandis, H. (1972). *The analysis of subjective culture.* New York: Wiley.

Triandis, H., & Suh, E. (2002). Cultural influences on personality. *Annual Review of Psychology, 53,* 133–160.

Richard W. Brislin
University of Hawaii

See also: **Attribution Theory; Cross-Culture Psychology: Culture-Universal and Culture-Specific Frameworks; Culture and Psychotherapy; Multicultural Counseling**

CROSS-CULTURAL RESEARCH: COMMUNICATING WITH PARTICIPANTS

Cross-cultural research methods have become a specialized study area and have been the focus of entire texts (Brislin, Lonner, & Thorndike, 1973; Triandis & Berry, 1980; Berry, Poortinga, & Pandey, 1997). A basic aspect of good methodology is communicating with subjects. Without clear understanding of instructions directed from the researcher to the participants, and without clear understanding of what responses mean, a research study not only may be misleading but may also possibly be damaging (Bhawuk, 2001).

Various techniques have been devised to ensure good communication between researchers and participants. Irvine and Carroll (1980) suggest a number of steps in testing, such as separation of individual subtests to avoid confusion; oral instructions with visual aids; translation of instructions carried out by typical members of the respondent group; supervised practice on sample items; commencement of each test session with items already familiar to respondents; and creation of an enjoyable atmosphere for testing. If the subject matter under study is a complex concept, such as the stage reached according to Piagetian theories of mental development, training studies can be introduced (Dasen, Lavallee, & Retschitzki, 1979). The acquisition of Piagetian stages is influenced by people's previous experiences; people in various cultures do not have the same everyday experiences that might lead (at least at the same rate) to the various stages. Realizing this, Dasen and his colleagues (working among the Baoule in West Africa) created training studies in which the same sorts of experiences, theoretically posited as triggering a given stage, were emulated. Compared to a control group that did not have the training experience, experimental subjects scored higher on independently assessed Piagetian tasks. Without the training study—one example of researchers' attempts to empathize with respondents, so that competencies and not just atypical performances are assessed—conclusions about "slower development" might have been made.

A little creativity may ensure researcher-participant communication. De Lacey (1970) made sure that Australian aboriginal children understood such terms as *red, circle,* and *round* by showing them wooden replicas and inviting them to handle the different shapes that were painted different colors. They were also asked to indicate examples of the terms before the actual experiment on classification ability began. In another study, Price-Williams (1961) tested the acquisition of various Piagetian concepts among the Tiv of Central Africa. In his experiment on the conservation of discontinuous qualities, the normal Piagetian method is to use beads in containers. Price-Williams tried his method but found communication difficulties were prevalent, so he changed the materials to nuts, which are far more familiar in the Tiv culture. Results showed a degree of conservation similar to acculturated European groups of children. In many cross-cultural studies of theoretical ideas where Euro-American children might be compared with children from other cultures, there is a factor that can be called *explicit attention to communication with subjects.* When this factor is clearly present in a study, there is a much greater probability of similar Euro-American and other-culture results (e.g., Dasen & Heron, 1981).

If researchers are attentive to communication issues, they will be alert to an important fact: If a person cannot perform a task or do well on a test, this does not mean there is a deficiency in ability. This implication contrasts with the normal inference that if a person does not perform well, then there is no competence or ability. The preferred interpretation, supported vigorously by Cole and Scribner (1974), is that the task itself or the situational nature of the testing situation may well be causing the poor performance. These situational elements include uncommon materials involved in the task; unfamiliar time pressures to complete the task; the presence of a nervousness-producing, high-status outsider doing the testing; and so forth. Cole has used the research technique of redesigning the testing situation until the person performs well on the task, taking the original poorer performance only as a starting point. Sometimes this is a very difficult research procedure to implement, but when successful it gives infinitely more information about the exact reasons and exact cues for good performance than if one stops immediately after the first testing. The cues that brought out good performance, such as those that encourage effective organization of information rather than rote memorization, can then be used in other learning situations.

In cross-cultural studies, research instruments have to be prepared in languages other than the researchers' own. One of the most important recommendations in such studies is to "decenter" instruments (Brislin, 2000). Instruments should not be prepared in one language with the expectation that they be translated without modifications into other languages. Such a procedure often forces the use of stilted, unfamiliar phrases in other languages that leads to poor communication. In decentering, materials are prepared at the earliest stages so that the wordings chosen will lead to clear and familiar wordings in all the languages that are part of the research study. There is no "center" to the research (e.g., instruments from the United States that must be translated verbatim) in this recommended procedure. Researchers should work closely with translators and should ask them to identify phrases that are difficult to translate or that will lead to wordings unfamiliar to the eventual respondents in the research study.

Cross-cultural data can edit findings found in only a few countries and thus point to the specific limitations of theories. Further, cross-cultural data can provide a stimulus to new thinking, which in turn leads to new and more powerful theories. As more and more psychologists accept the necessity of taking a worldwide view of human behavior, the necessity for a special section on cross-cultural studies will vanish.

REFERENCES

Berry, J., Poortinga, Y., & Pandey, J. (Eds.). (1997). *Handbook of cross-cultural psychology: Vol. 1. Theory and method* (2nd ed.). Boston: Allyn & Bacon.

Bhawuk, D. (2001). Evolution of culture assimilators: Toward theory-based assimilators. *International Journal of Intercultural Relations, 25,* 141–163.

Brislin, R. (2000). *Understanding culture's influence on behavior* (2nd ed.). Fort Worth, TX: Harcourt Brace.

Brislin, R., Lonner, W., & Thorndike, R. (1973). *Cross-cultural research methods.* New York: Wiley.

Cole, M., & Scribner, S. (1974). *Culture and thought: A psychological introduction.* New York: Wiley.

Dasen, P., Lavallee, M., & Retschitzki, J. (1979). Training conservation of quantity (liquids) in West African (Baoule) children. *International Journal of Psychology, 14,* 57–68.

Dasen, P., & Heron, A. (1981). Cross-cultural tests of Piaget's theory. In H. Triandis & A. Heron (Eds.), *Handbook of cross-cultural psychology: Vol. 4.* (pp. 295–342). Boston: Allyn & Bacon.

De Lacey, P. (1970). A cross-cultural study of classificatory ability in Australia. *Journal of Cross-Cultural Psychology, 1,* 293–304.

Irvine, S., & Carroll, W. (1980). Testing and assessment across cultures: Issues in methodology and theory. In H. Triandis & J. Berry (Eds.), *Handbook of cross-cultural psychology: Vol. 2. Methodology* (pp. 181–244). Boston: Allyn & Bacon.

Price-Williams, D. (1961). A study concerning concepts of conservation of quantities among primitive children. *ACTA Psychologica, 18,* 297–305.

Triandis, H., & Berry, J. (Eds.). (1980). *Handbook of cross-cultural psychology: Vol. 2. Methodology.* Boston: Allyn & Bacon.

Richard W. Brislin
University of Hawaii

See also: **Cross-Cultural Training Programs; Multicultural Counseling; Research Methodologies**

CROSS-CULTURAL TRAINING PROGRAMS

Cross-cultural training programs refer to formal efforts designed to prepare people to live and work in cultures other than their own (Bhawuk, 2001; Brislin & Yoshida, 1994; Cushner & Brislin, 1996; Landis & Bhagat, 1996; Paige, 1992). Ideally, such programs are structured, staffed by professionals with relevant training and experience, designed with an adequate budget, and conducted in a setting designed to create an atmosphere conducive to learning. The nature of cross-cultural training is made clearer when its opposite is considered. Before going overseas on a business assignment, good training can prepare people for the stresses of adjusting to another culture and differing ways of carrying out business negotiations in other cultures, and can provide advice on accomplishing one's goals. The opposite is to simply send people abroad with no preparation and to let them sink or swim on their own.

The vast majority of research and careful thinking about cross-cultural training has taken place since World War II. Reasons include the greater movement of students who take advantage of educational opportunities in countries other than their own, increases in technical assistance programs, the increased availability of jet travel, the development of global marketplaces, increases in the number of programs aimed at person-to-person contact across cultural boundaries (e.g., the Peace Corps and youth exchange programs), and increases in the number of independent countries, which necessitates greater amounts of diplomatic contact. In addition to preparing people to live in countries other than their own, cross-cultural training programs also are designed to help people work effectively with culturally different individuals within their own country. For example, programs have been designed for Anglo social workers who are about to work with refugees from Southeast Asia and for Japanese-American teachers in Hawaii who have large numbers of students of Hawaiian ancestry. People skillful in designing and implementing cross-cultural training programs can be found in colleges and universities, the personnel departments of large businesses, government service, public school systems, churches, social welfare agencies, counseling centers, and private consulting firms.

Goals of Training

Training programs are commonly designed with four goals in mind (Brislin, 2000; Hammer, 1989, 1992). For the sake of convenience, programs to prepare people for overseas assignments will be treated here, although very similar arguments can be made about programs to increase effective intercultural contact *within* any one large country. The first goal of training programs is to prepare people to enjoy and to benefit from their overseas assignment, not simply to tolerate an unpleasant interruption in their lives. Because few people can enjoy their assignments without cordial and effective interactions with others, programs should give guidance on developing good interpersonal relations with host country nationals, both in the workplace and during voluntary leisure time. One way of measuring progress toward this goal is that people on overseas assignments should be able to list people with whom they work well, with whom they interact during their leisure time, and whom they can call on in times of need. Second, and at the same time, the host country's point of view needs to be given attention. Good training increases the probability that people in the host country will have positive attitudes about the sojourners in their country. By examining these two goals, trainers can avoid the mistake of making conclusions based on people's *reports* of positive relations with hosts. In some cases, people can make a list of friends, but those purported friends might report that the people are insensitive, ethnocentric, and condescending.

The third goal is to provide guidance on how participants in training programs can accomplish their goals. Virtually all sojourners have concrete goals in addition to enjoying and personally benefiting from their assignments. Overseas students want to obtain university degrees within a reasonable amount of time; overseas businesspeople want to enter into trade agreements; diplomats want to develop treaties acceptable to all sides in a conflict; technical assistance advisers want to construct sanitation facilities, irrigation systems, or medical centers; cross-cultural researchers want to establish collegial relations so that information can be gathered and shared; and so forth. Training can give people guidance on such topics as working through bureaucracies, negotiating with counterparts, keeping legal requirements in mind, identifying the resources needed for project completion, and so forth. Many times, training must be culturally specific, depending on the types of participants in programs. Foreign students working in the United States need to be prepared for the independence in scholarly inquiry that professors expect. American businesspeople working in Asia need to be more sensitive to the effects of their actions on the collective identity of their hosts (Hofstede, 2001; Triandis, Brislin, & Hui, 1988). Diplomats need to be aware of the long history of animosities that various ethnic groups within a country may bring to the bargaining table.

The fourth and final goal is to assist program participants to deal with the stress that overseas assignments can bring. The most commonly used term associated with such stress is *culture shock,* or the set of strong emotions that result from having the familiar structures of one's own culture taken away (Bochner, 1994). *People do not interact with each other in familiar ways! How they make decisions is a mystery! They never are clear when they try to communicate! They seem to talk about me all the time!* All of these feelings are very common, and cross-cultural trainers have adopted such stress-reduction methods as relaxation, cognitive restructuring, development and maintenance of valued leisure time activities, exercise, and the avoidance of health-threatening behaviors (e.g., increased alcohol use). Trainers frequently introduce the concept that program participants should not feel singled out for negative self-judgments. The feeling that "I am the only one" who is having difficulties adjusting to the other culture is common. If participants learn that most sojourners experience adjustment difficulties and feel the temptation to engage in negative self-thoughts, then the resulting stress is decreased.

Given increases in the same factors that lead to the need for effective intercultural communication, such as immigration, global business, the needs of international students, and the demands of various ethnic groups to be heard in the political arena, the future will undoubtedly see even more attention to cross-cultural training programs.

REFERENCES

Bhawuk, D. P. S. (2001). Evolution of culture assimilators: Toward theory-based assimilators. *International Journal of Intercultural Relations, 25,* 141–163.

Bochner, S. (1994). Culture shock. In W. Lonner & R. Malpass (Eds.), *Psychology and culture* (pp. 245–251). Needham Heights, MA: Allyn & Bacon.

Brislin, R. (2000). *Understanding culture's influence on behavior* (2nd ed.). Fort Worth, TX: Harcourt.

Brislin, R., & Yoshida, T. (1994). *Intercultural communication training: An introduction.* Thousand Oaks, CA: Sage.

Cushner, K., & Brislin, R. (1996). *Intercultural interactions: A practical guide* (2nd ed.). Thousand Oaks, CA: Sage.

Hammer, M. (1989). Intercultural communication competence. In M. Asante & W. Gudykunst (Eds.), *Handbook of international and intercultural communication* (pp. 247–260). Newbury Park, CA: Sage.

Hammer, M. (1992). Intercultural communication skills. *Communique, 21*(1), 6–15.

Hofstede, G. (2001). *Culture's consequences: Comparing values, behaviors, institutions, and organizations across cultures* (2nd ed.). Thousand Oaks, CA: Sage.

Landis, D., & Bhagat, R. (Eds.). (1996). *Handbook of intercultural training* (2nd ed.). Thousand Oaks, CA: Sage.

Paige, M. (Ed.). (1992). *Education for the intercultural experience.* Yarmouth, ME: Intercultural Press.

Triandis, H., Brislin, R., & Hui, C. H. (1988). Cross-cultural training across the individualism-collectivism divide. *International Journal of Intercultural Relations, 12,* 269–289.

Richard W. Brislin
University of Hawaii

See also: **Career Counseling; Cross-Cultural Psychology; Group Counseling**

CROSS-CULTURE PSYCHOLOGY: CULTURE-UNIVERSAL AND CULTURE-SPECIFIC FRAMEWORKS

Emics and Etics

The jargon of cross-cultural specialists includes the terms *emics* and *etics,* which summarize an important central concept and analytical tool (Berry, 1969; Poortinga, 1997; Brislin, 2000). To best explain this concept, a problem that can be analyzed with the help of it will first be posed. Emics and etics will then be introduced in their abstract form and subsequently applied to the problem.

The problem involves drought and starvation in East Africa (Talbot, 1972). A group of European consultants recommended that development projects be established to increase water availability and grasslands for the Masai, an East African culture long involved in raising cattle. Instead of leading to healthier herds and better grazing areas, however, the development projects led to starvation for the cattle and eventually for some of the Masai. How can this be explained? The cross-cultural concepts of emics and etics are useful.

Emics and *etics* refer to the two goals of cross-cultural research. One is to document valid principles in all cultures and to establish theoretical frameworks useful in comparing human behavior in various cultures (Triandis & Suh, 2002). These frameworks have the goal of being culture general, useful in examining human behavior anywhere in the world. This is the *etic* goal—a term that comes from phonetic analysis. In linguistics, a phon*etic* system is one that documents and analyzes all meaningful sounds present in all languages and integrates them into a general framework. The other goal of cross-cultural research is to document valid principles of behavior within any one culture, with attention to what the people themselves value as important as well as what is familiar to them. These principles will be part of culture-specific frameworks, useful in examining behavior in one culture but with no claims about generality to other cultures. Such an analysis has to reject the importation and imposition of frameworks from outside a culture since, by definition, a researcher cannot gain insight into emics by using foreign tools; the tools must be indigenous (Kim & Berry, 1993). This latter type is an *emic* analysis—a term from phonemics. In linguistics, a phon*emic* analysis document sounds meaningful in a specific language.

An example from linguistics may be helpful. A phonetic system will have an initial *ng* sound, an initial *l* sound, and an initial *r* sound, since these are important in at least one of the world's languages. In addition, these sounds can be integrated into a general framework based on such concepts as activation of vocal cords and parts of the mouth used in making the sounds. An English phonemic system will have the *l* and *r* sounds, but not the initial *ng* sound, since the latter is not part of the English language. Japanese does not have the initial *l* and the initial *r* sound, since the language does not make a distinction between them (a fact that leads to ethnic jokes). English speakers thus have to put special effort into learning the initial *ng* sound—a task faced by many Peace Corps volunteers assigned to Pacific island cultures. Japanese speakers have to work hard on the *l-r* distinction, as most teachers of English as a second language will testify. The metaphor of emics and etics for cross-cultural research contains the elements referred to previously: what is present and absent, what is meaningful, what has to be given special attention since it is common in one system but not another, and what can be systematized into integrative frameworks.

Cross-cultural researchers have attempted to deal with both etics and emics in their research. A system proposed by Brislin (1976, 2000), drawing upon earlier work by Przeworski and Teune (1966, 1970), represents such an attempt. The researcher starts by examining concepts that may have cross-cultural validity but keeps in mind that not all aspects of those concepts will be the same in all cultures under study. Aspects may be different both for cultures across nations as well as for various cultures or subcultures within a country.

In discussing the effects of range development on the Masai culture of East Africa, Talbot (1972) analyzed the concept of "uses and care of cattle" from the perspective of the Masai and from the perspective of people from Europe and North America in charge of the development (Table 1). Members of both cultures have similar conceptualizations about several core connotations, and these are the proposed etics: provision of milk, fertilizer, and demands placed on humans for caring of cattle. But in addition to this etic core, there are differences that can be called the emics within each group.

The emphasis on quantity was a major problem in the range development projects. Prior to European contact, natural conditions such as droughts and fires effectively limited the size of herds, so the intelligent practice was to always have as many cattle as possible. But when water and grasslands became more common after development,

Table 1. Uses and Care of Cattle

North America, Europe Emics	Masai Emics
Cattle used for meat	Cattle not primarily used for meat
Cattle raised for sale	Cattle not generally raised for sale
Grazing over a large area	Grazing over small areas (to protect from predators)
Emphasis on quantity as much as quality	Emphasis on quality
Other signs of wealth and prestige available besides cattle	Cattle are a major sign of wealth and prestige
Experience with conservation	Always a struggle to maintain limited herds, hence no opportunity to think about conservation when large numbers of cattle are present

the Masai norm of "desirability of quantity," without a self-imposed norm of "desirability of limitations for the purpose of conservation," led to herds of unreasonable size. The cattle then overgrazed and destroyed the available range. In turn, cattle then died for lack of food, and the Masai themselves faced starvation. This case is frequently cited as an example of failure of technology (range development) due to ignorance of a human variable (norm of quantity). If people know these terms, advice for them as they move across cultures is to know culture general frameworks (the etics) but to constantly keep in mind that there will be culture-specific issues (emics) that must be understood (Cheung & Leung, 1998).

REFERENCES

Berry, J. (1969). On cross-cultural comparability. *International Journal of Psychology, 4,* 119–128.

Brislin, R. (1976). Comparative research methodology: Cross-cultural studies. *International Journal of Psychology, 1,* 215–229.

Brislin, R. (2000). *Understanding culture's influence on behavior* (2nd ed.). Fort Worth, TX: Harcourt.

Cheung, F., & Leung, K. (1998). Indigenous personality measures: Chinese examples. *Journal of Cross-Cultural Psychology, 29,* 233–248.

Kim, U., & Berry, J. (Eds.). (1993). *Indigenous psychologies.* Newbury Park, CA: Sage.

Poortinga, Y. (1997). Towards convergence? In J. Berry, Y. Poortinga, & J. Pandey (Eds.), *Handbook of Cross-Cultural Psychology: Vol. 1. Theory and method* (2nd ed., pp. 347–387). Boston: Allyn & Bacon.

Przeworski, A., & Teune, H. (1966). Equivalence in cross-national research. *Public Opinion Quarterly, 30,* 33–43.

Przeworski, A., & Teune, H. (1970). *The logic of comparative social inquiry.* New York: Wiley.

Talbot, L. (1972). Ecological consequences of rangeland development in Masailand, East Africa. In M. Farvar & J. Milton (Eds.), *The careless technology: Ecology and international development* (pp. 694–711) Garden City, NY: Natural History Press.

Triandis, H., & Suh, E. (2002). Cultural influences on personality. *Annual Review of Psychology, 53,* 133–160.

Richard W. Brislin
University of Hawaii

CULTURE AND DEPRESSION

Research interest in cross-cultural variations of major depression has increased over the past 25 years. Major depression is a worldwide problem and a leading cause of disability and mortality, particularly in developing regions where the pervasiveness is high (Murray & Lopez, 1997). Despite its worldwide existence, the prevalence and clinical presentation of depressive symptomatology remain heterogeneous.

Prevalence Rates

Epidemiological surveys indicate that the rate of lifetime major depression varies across countries and across ethnocultural groups within the same country. In the general population of the United States, the lifetime prevalence rate is approximately 17%; the lifetime risk for women ranges from 10 to 25% and from 5 to 12% for men. In five European countries (Finland, Ireland, Norway, Spain, and the United Kingdom) the prevalence rate is approximately 9% (Ayuso-Mateos et al., 2001). A cross-national comparison of affective disorders in community samples of nine countries (Canada, France, Italy, Korea, Lebanon, New Zealand, Puerto Rico, Taiwan, the United States, and West Germany) indicated annual prevalence rates ranging from 0.8% in Taiwan to 5.8% in Christchurch, New Zealand (Weissman et al., 1996). Lifetime rates of depression were lowest in Taiwan (1.5%) and highest in Beirut, Lebanon (19%). The low prevalence rate of depression in Taiwan remains less clear but is consistent with other reports that have found lifetime prevalence rates as low as 1.14% in Taiwan and 0.19% in China (Hwu et al., 1996). In addition, college students in Taiwan reported lower mean scores of depressive symptoms when they were compared to similar samples in Korea, the Philippines, and the United States (Crittenden, Fugita, Bae, Lamug, & Lin, 1992).

As noted, prevalence rates of depression also vary between ethnocultural groups within the same country. The United States is a good example of this phenomenon, given its multiethnic composition and high rate of immigration each year. Large epidemiological studies have revealed that prevalence rates differ between ethnocultural groups residing in the United States. For instance, African Americans tend to report lower lifetime prevalence rates of depression than their Caucasian counterparts (Kessler et al., 1994; Zhang & Snowden, 1999); a similar trend has been demonstrated among Asian-American individuals. The prevalence rate among Latino individuals, however, is less consistent. Reports have stated that Latino (e.g. Burnam et al., 1987) individuals tend to report lower 1-year (Oquendo et al., 2001) and lifetime prevalence rates of depression when compared to Caucasian individuals; others have demonstrated that Latinos have significantly higher rates of lifetime depression than non-Latino whites (Kessler et al., 1994).

Symptom Presentation

Cultural factors can influence the expression of depressive symptomatology and often function as the lens through which we interpret and define reality. Although misdiagnosis, underdiagnosis, and overestimation of psychiatric disorders continue to be problems when patient and clinician are from different cultural backgrounds (Paniagua, 2000), they can be greatly diminished if we increase our awareness of cultural factors, particularly as they relate to the presentation of major depression.

The importance of considering the effect of cultural factors in the expression of depression is manifold. In the United States, for example, it is estimated that by the year 2050, half of the population will be composed of Latino, African American, Asian American, and Native American peoples (U.S. Bureau of the Census). The number of ethnic minorities seeking mental health services is likely to increase as well. It is important for clinicians to educate themselves about the difficulties of applying diagnostic criteria to individuals with varying cultural backgrounds.

Proper diagnosis requires a clinician's highest level of cultural understanding. Somatic complaints, such as nerves (*nervios;* Latino) and heart pain (Hopi Indians), are common manifestations of depressive experiences among these ethnocultural groups; furthermore, major depression fails to correspond to any category of illness within certain Native American cultures. The presentation of Western-derived symptomatology used to define diagnostic criteria for depression (i.e., in the *Diagnostic and Statistic Manual of Mental Disorders,* fourth edition [*DSM-IV*] and the *International Statistical Classification of Diseases and Related Health Problems,* 10th revision [*ICD-10*]) varies across different countries as well. For instance, insomnia, loss of energy, concentration difficulties, and thoughts of death or suicide were the most common symptoms of depression reported in the previously mentioned cross-national study. Appetite problems were most common in Beirut, Taiwan, and Korea; meanwhile, feelings of worthlessness and excessive guilt were less likely to be reported in Beirut, Taiwan, and Puerto Rico. Finally, among Asian countries, Korean individuals appear to be more likely to manifest their depressive experiences in somatic and psychological terms rather than with affective complaints (Crittenden et al., 1992).

Conclusion

The differences in prevalence rates and expression of major depression suggest that a person's culture functions as a factor that influences the expression and meaning of major depression. Understanding the meanings attached to concepts such as emotional distress, mind-body dualism, and intragroup categories of illness is likely to further our knowledge and understanding of major depression. Furthermore, demographic variables such as socioeconomic status, acculturation, and language use, for instance, need to be considered when we attempt to understand cultural influences attached to the meaning of major depression. Finally, the global popularity of the *DSM-IV* and *ICD-10* demands the inclusion of more cultural principles and considerations in light of their application to both U.S. ethnic minority and majority populations as well as populations around the world (Alarcón, 1995).

REFERENCES

Alarcón, R. D. (1995). Culture and psychiatric diagnosis: Impact on DSM-IV and ICD-10. *Psychiatric Clinics of North America, 18*(3), 449–465.

Ayuso-Mateos, J. L., Vazquez-Barquero, J. L., Dowrick, C., Lehtinen, V., Dalgard, O. S., Casey, P., Wilkinson, C., Lasa, L., Page, H., Dunn, G., & Wilkinson, G. (2001) Depressive disorders in Europe: Prevalence figures from the ODIN study. *British Journal of Psychiatry, 179*(4), 308–316.

Burnam, M. A., Houch, R. L., Karno, M., Escobar, J. I., & Telles, C. A. (1987). Acculturation and lifetime prevalence of psychiatric disorders among Mexican Americans in Los Angeles. *Journal of Health and Social Behavior, 28,* 89–102.

Crittenden, K. S., Fugita, S. S., Bae, H., Lamug, C. B., et al. (1992). A cross-cultural study of self-report depressive symptoms among college students. *Journal of Cross-Cultural Psychology, 23*(2), 163–178.

Hwu, H.-G., Chang, I.-H., Yeh, E.-K., Chang, C.-J., & Yeh, L.-L. (1996). Major depressive disorder in Taiwan defined by the Chinese Diagnostic Interview Schedule. *Journal of Nervous & Mental Disease, 184*(8), 497–502.

Murray, C., & López, A. (1997). Alternative projections of mortality and disability by cause 1990–2020: Global Burden of Disease Study. *Lancet, 349,* 1498-15-4.

Oquendo, M. A., Ellis, S. P., Greenwald, S., Malone, K. M., Weissman, M. M., & Mann, J. J. (2001). Ethnic and sex differences in suicide rates relative to major depression in the United States. *American Journal of Psychiatry, 158*(10), 1652–1658.

Paniagua, F. A. (2000). Culture-bound syndromes, cultural variations, and psychopathology. In I. Cuéllar, F. A. Paniagua, et al. (Eds.), *Handbook of multicultural mental health* (pp. 139–169). San Diego, CA: Academic Press.

U.S. Bureau of Census. (1999). *The Hispanic population in the United States: Population characteristics.* Washington, DC: Government Printing Office.

Weissman, M. M., Bland, R. C., Canino, G. J., Faravelli, C., Greenwald, S., Hwu, H., Joyce, P. R., Karam, E. G., Lee, C., Lellouch, J., Lepine, J., Newman, S. C., Rubio-Stipec, M., Wells, J. E., Wickramaratne, P. J., Wittchen, H., & Yeh, E. (1996). Cross-national epidemiology of major depression and bipolar disorder. *JAMA, 276,* 293–299.

Zhang, A. Y., & Snowden, L. R. (1999). Ethnic characteristics of mental disorders in five U.S. communities. *Cultural Diversity and Ethnic Minority Psychology, 5*(2), 132–146.

Alinne Z. Barrera
University of Colorado, Boulder

See also: **Cross-cultural Therapy; Depression**

CULTURE AND HEALTH

Culture is both a product of human behavior and a regulator of behavior. It refers to the particular beliefs, customs, norms, and values of a set of people, usually defined by a special history, geography, and dialect or language. Almost all countries have different cultural groups, often called *ethnic groups,* within their borders. The United States and Indonesia are multicultural or multiethnic, whereas Japan is relatively monocultural.

Health is not just the absence of disease or infirmity but a state of physical, psychological, and social well-being. Health psychology is an applied discipline closely related to public health. It aims to improve human functioning, especially through better health care and prevention programs. Each culture has its own definition of health and health service. The Western industrialized countries tend to use a biomedical model for their services, emphasizing individual physical health. Developing countries, especially Asian ones, have a more collectivist, family-oriented, and holistic view of health and health service. Separation between mind and body is less distinct. Although Western ideas have penetrated deeply into many areas of the rest of the world, there remain strong influences from widespread folk beliefs about health. For instance, most Chinese believe that healthy nutrition requires a balance between hot and cold foods, and they accept and expect traditional Chinese medical practices such as herbal remedies, massage, and acupuncture. Within the United States the many ethnic subcultures vary in their willingness to accept Western medicine and in their faith in traditional healers such as Latino curanderos.

How many people around the world do share information regarding health? Obviously, in physical matters (as epidemics and organ transplants demonstrate) there is much in common, but what about psychological and sociocultural characteristics? One major debate in cross-cultural theorizing is between universalists and relativists (the etic-emic distinction). Psychologists tend to try to find categories and principles that apply to all cultures in varying amounts and intensity; anthropologists point out the unique patterns of each particular culture. Attempting to create a universal system, the World Health Organization (WHO) lately has put forth an international classification system for diseases and indicators of health. The measurable indicators cover health status, policies, social and economic factors, and primary care services. Reports from over 150 WHO member states are useful, but questions remain about the consistency of diagnoses and practices across countries and cultures. Particularly problematic are misdiagnoses because of poor cross-cultural understanding.

Some health-related practices are dramatically culture-bound, such as infanticide and malnutrition in girl children because of boy preference in several Asian countries. Mothers in West Papua do not take ferum tablets due to the fear of having large babies, since they have to deliver their babies by themselves in the hut in the back yard outside their homes. Certain mental illnesses, such as *amok* (sudden frenzy), *koro* (fear of penis constriction), and *taijin-kyofusho* (fear of being looked at) are thought to be culture-specific rather than universal. Anorexia Nervosa (self-starvation and distorted body image) is mainly confined to Western countries, but more recently it has been showing up in Asian locations.

Beliefs about causation of mental illness differ among cultures. For instance, Bedouin Arabs in Israel believe that symptoms occur because of supernatural powers, such as God's will or sorcery. The degree of acculturation is another aspect of understanding meanings in cross-cultural work. One American study showed a difference between normative beliefs of adolescents with Middle Eastern backgrounds who were born in the United States versus those who immigrated. The American-born adolescents were more accepting of aggression. On the positive end of health, that is, life satisfaction, there are strong differences between poorer and wealthier nations, with poor people valuing financial success and people from wealthier countries valuing home life and self-esteem. The research questions about health and ethnicity are numerous and intriguingly complex, especially when they overlap with economic and educational factors. Kazarian and Evans edited a cultural clinical psychology book in 1998. They propose a combination of clinical psychology and cultural psychology in theory, research, and practice to accommodate multicultural societies needs in mental health services.

One example of health and cultural issues from Indonesia is the overuse of injections not related to diagnosis. Such injections, especially with reuse of needles, increase the risk of communicable diseases such as hepatitis B and HIV. It is important to understand that Indonesians like ceremonies. From birth to death, Indonesians are accustomed to rituals. The practice of injection by a medical worker is like a ritual. The provider has to go through a certain sequence in the injection preparation and process. The patients feel the pain as the soluble preparation is inserted in their bodies. This ritual seems to give both parties satisfaction. The providers have done something, and the patients have received something directly into their bodies.

Such a ritual might seem strange to people from developed countries. They are accustomed to being informed and giving consent before medical intervention takes place, yet for people in Indonesia who are not well educated, the health service provider is the authority for the treatment. The patients do not have to know anything.

Since health is multidimensional worldwide, using only the biomedical model for explaining health issues is limiting and inadequate. Many different disciplines need to take part. Specifically, social sciences, such as anthropology, demography, economics, education, ethics, political science, psychology, and sociology, have been involved in health-related studies and policy making for decades. To accomplish communication and cooperation among so many disciplines covering many cultures and countries is not an easy task. Questions arise as to what names to use and how these different disciplines and traditions should be together. The involvement of social sciences in health is reflected in names, with specialties such as medical anthropology, medical ethics, medical geography, and medical psychology. The approach is still mostly within the given discipline. Medical psychology, for example, has applied different psychological theories, research, assessment instruments, and therapies to physical diseases. The needed approach for many projects, nonetheless, is more interdisciplinary so that social scientists and health scientists are contributing together to research teams.

Johana E. P. Hadiyono
Gadjah Mada University, Indonesia

See also: **Cross-Cultural Therapy**

CULTURE AND INTELLIGENCE

Introduction

Today, the recognition among many within the academy of the interdependence of genetic and environmental influences on human intelligence has to some degree quieted the nature-nurture controversy about the genesis of intelligence. This essay focuses on two issues: (1) the attributes of culture that have psychological relevance for understanding the meaning of intelligence and (2) the delineation of certain types of learning experiences within cultural niches as the mechanism by which intellectual potentials develop and find expression in behavior as developed intelligence.

Definition of Intelligence

There is no universal agreement concerning the definition of intelligence. One of the major reasons for this is the fact that the construct has differential meaning in different cultural groups. As Homo sapiens, we are born into the world with certain biologically constrained potentials to learn from and adapt to the environment in which we live. Although there continues to be endless debate about the nature, number, type, and level of these genetically programmed potentials, the search for consensus about these potentials is pointless, for two reasons. First, it is the culture in which we are born that invents a definition of intelligence to make sense of observed differences among its members and to define what its members believe and value as a culture. Secondly, it is the culture that gives structure, direction, and regulation to these embryonic potentials and to a large extent determines which ones will develop and become crystallized, which ones will atrophy, and which ones will remain unrealized. There are at least three attributes of psychologically salient attributes of culture that serve these socializing functions: values and beliefs, communicative conventions and courtesies, and symbolic modes of representation. A brief elaboration of each follows.

Values and Beliefs

Values and beliefs are overarching norms or principles that govern the daily lives of members of a social group and are reflected in the standards and expectations of what is considered right, desirable, or worthwhile. They are often tacitly embodied in tasks and social interactions in which children engage and therefore serve a socializing role in determining what potentials are worth developing, how, and what conditions are most conducive to their fullest possible expression.

Communicative Conventions and Courtesies

Communicative conventions and courtesies are the idiosyncratic modes of discourse that members of a social group use to communicate ideas, skills, emotions, and attitudes to each other in different situations. Capacities to learn and adapt to one's environment are developed and find expression as developed intelligence through social interactions. Consequently, individuals who engage in tasks requiring the deployment of intellectual processes must be familiar with and understand their implicit or explicit conventions and courtesies of communication.

Symbolic Modes of Representation

Symbolic modes of representation are to the media (e.g., linguistic, spatial, gestural) that members of a social group use for dealing with the tasks in various situations they encounter in their daily lives. Some tasks embody more than one symbolic modality (e.g., visual-spatialization, auditory-spatialization, or kinesthetic-auditory). How well individuals are able to develop their intellectual potentials depends, in part, on their familiarity with these culturally grounded modes of representation.

In sum, because tasks requiring intellectual engagement and behavior are so culturally grounded in the values, beliefs, communicative conventions, and symbolic modes of representation, intelligence is considered a culturally dependent construct. We turn now to a discussion of the role of learning experiences and cultural niches in the development of biologically constrained intellectual potentials.

Learning Experiences

Learning experiences are salient characteristics of intellectual tasks in which the child engages as well as the nature and quality of the social interactions in which he or she participates while doing such tasks. It is through the frequency and consistency of learning experiences over time that biologically constrained intellectual potentials are transformed into culturally dependent developed intelligence.

Apart from the values and beliefs embedded in tasks and the symbolic modes in which they are represented, there are two other features of tasks that must be considered: motivational appeal and level of cognitive complexity. Also, besides the mode of discourse used in communicating about intellectual tasks, the caliber of mediation to which the child is exposed must be noted as well.

Motivation Appeal

Motivational appeal describes the tacit power within tasks to arouse individuals' interest and attention, sustain the intensity of their effort, and ultimately direct their energies to use intellectual processes in successful completion of the intellectual task at hand.

Level of Cognitive Complexity

Level of complexity refers to the degree of difficulty of the intellectual task as reflected in the amount and type of intellectual processing as well as the knowledge demands required for successful completion.

Mediation

Mediation is an interactive clinical involvement in which an adult or capable peer teaches the child how to find and use the rules underlying an intellectual task. Using techniques such as cognitive modeling, scaffolding, and prompting with feedback and reinforcement, the adult or capable peer helps the child to transform the biologically constrained intellectual potentials into developed intelligence.

Cultural Niches

Biologically constrained intellectual potentials develop and find expression as developed intelligence within particular contexts in the environment that may be described as *cultural niches.* The term *niche* is borrowed from biology to describe the growth-fostering interactions or relationships that occur between organisms and their environments. The niche is described as cultural because the learning experiences that unfold with it are themselves culturally grounded. The home, the peer group, and the classroom may be described as cultural niches to the extent that the nature and quality of the learning experiences with them allow for the development and eventual transformation of biologically constrained potentials into fully developed intelligence.

Conclusion

This essay has made the case that intelligence is a biocultural construct. Humans are born with a set of biologically constrained intellectual potentials, but they develop and find expression as developed intelligence through particular types of learning experiences that unfold over time in various cultural niches in the environment.

Eleanor Armour-Thomas
Queens College, New York

CULTURE AND PSYCHOTHERAPY

Despite their widely different trappings, psychotherapeutic interventions are practiced in all regions of the world. Moreover, these efforts share certain general objectives, above all the relief of human suffering and distress (Prince, 1980). According to Draguns (1975), psychotherapy is crucially concerned with the establishment or restoration of a workable and stable balance between the person and his or her social milieu. Cultural considerations are thus relevant to all psychotherapy encounters. On the basis of this recognition, Pedersen (2002) has construed the cultural perspective as the fourth force in therapeutic psychology, on a par with psychodynamic, behavioral, and humanistic orientations.

These formulations are germane both to ethnic differences in multicultural environments and to variations among cultures that are geographically removed and culturally distinct. Observations of procedures of healers in other cultures, such as shamans in the Arctic, witch doctors in Africa, and modern therapists in Japan and elsewhere adapting indigenous techniques have been important sources of information. In North America, the documented underutilization of mental health services by major sociocultural minority groups has provided a stimulus for developing effective and culturally meaningful modes of therapy (Sue, 1977). Another practical challenge has been the influx of refugees, immigrants, and sojourners, some of them traumatized and in urgent need of workable and culturally sensitive therapy. Even across interrelated Euro-American cultures, subtle yet consequential differences in responsiveness to psychotherapy have been noted. Moreover, psychotherapy has been increasingly recognized as a valuable source of data on the intertwining of personal dynamics and cultural precepts (Seeley, 1999).

Divergent expectations often obtrude from the very start. Across cultural barriers, clients often seek quick relief, in the form of direction, advice, and/or medication. Their complaints tend to focus on physical pain and distress. Western therapists, however, are trained to facilitate search for and discovery of the person's own solutions to problems of living, whereas their clients' cultural experience predisposes them to rely on their family's consensus and on the judgment of elders and other authority figures (Pfeiffer, 1995). More generally, North American helping services have been described as placing emphasis upon the individual, promoting action orientation, and focusing on the exploration of the client's unique and intrapsychic self (Katz, 1985).

Culturally sophisticated therapists favor flexibility, adaptability, and improvisation. Going beyond that, on the basis of experience with African clients in Paris Nathan (1994) has exhorted cross-cultural therapists to shed their ingrained preconceptions and embark upon psychotherapy with an open mind. Specifically, he recommends taking clients' beliefs seriously even when they appear to be in conflict with Western science and to respect traditional modes of problem solving and decision making. In British Columbia, Jilek (1982) has successfully incorporated Salish Indian healing rituals into therapy programs and has collaborated with traditional healers.

Experiencing and communicating empathy across a cultural gulf poses a major challenge. Stereotypes may interfere with the therapist's ability to feel a culturally different client's emotional state and to share his or her perspective. Enhancing the perceptiveness of therapists in training of the subjective experience of their culturally diverse clientele remains an urgent and ambitious objective in supervision, to be pursued both academically and experientially.

Most of the information on the role of culture in psychotherapy is based on clinical observation. On the basis of personal experience, Fish (1996) has offered five practical recommendations applicable in a variety of cultural contexts: (1) Focus upon goals rather than problems; (2) encourage talk about solutions rather than problems; (3) help the client see the problem as controllable and soluble; (4) find exceptions to the problem and use them as a wedge; and (5) promote expectations of change. Proceeding from several recent accounts of therapy across cultures, Draguns (2002) has cautioned against equating cultural differences with deficits and symptoms.

Still, there is no substitute for systematic research on psychotherapy in relation to culture, an enterprise that has barely begun. Hall (2002) has pointed out that empirically supported therapies have rarely been investigated in ethnocultural minority samples in the United States. Internationally, potentially relevant constructs have been proposed but as yet not empirically tested. Readiness for self-disclosure may vary across cultures (Toukmanian & Browers, 1998), and cultural variations in self-experience may be relevant to psychotherapy (Draguns, 2002). Attention has been focused upon the five cultural dimensions intensively investigated by Hofstede (2001): individualism-collectivism, power distance, uncertainty avoidance, masculinity-femininity, and long-term versus short-term time orientation. Specific hypotheses have been formulated, but not yet validated, concerning therapist preferences and client expectations in relation to these five constructs (Draguns, 2002). A promising multinational research project (Orlinsky, 1999) is focused on changes in the experience of psychotherapists during their careers. Qualitative, ethnographic methods have also been systematically applied in elucidating the role of culture in all aspects and phases of psychotherapy (Seeley, 2000). As these efforts are completed and extended, a more differentiated and specific body of knowledge will emerge on the interplay of culture and psychotherapy.

REFERENCES

Draguns, J. G. (1975). Resocialization into culture: The complexities of taking a worldwide view of psychotherapy. In R. W. Brislin, S. Bochner, & W. J. Lonner (Eds.), *Cross-cultural perspectives in learning* (pp. 273–289). Beverly Hills, CA: Sage.

Draguns, J. G. (2002). Universal and cultural aspects of counseling and psychotherapy. In P. B. Pedersen, J. Draguns, W. Lonner, & J. Trimble (Eds.), *Counseling across cultures* (5th ed., pp. 29–50). Thousand Oaks, CA: Sage.

Fish, J. M. (1996). *Culture and therapy: An integrative approach.* Northvale, NJ: Jason Aronson.

Hall, G. N. (2002). Psychotherapy research with ethnic minorities: Empirical, ethical, and conceptual issues. *Journal of Consulting and Clinical Psychology, 69,* 502–510.

Hofstede, G. (2001). *Culture's consequences* (2nd ed.). Thousand Oaks, CA: Sage.

Jilek, W. (1982). *Indian healing: Shamanistic ceremonialism in the Pacific Northwest.* Vancouver, BC: Hancock House.

Katz, J. H. (1985). The sociopolitical nature of counseling. *Counseling Psychologist, 13*(4), 615–624.

Nathan, T. (1994). *L'influence qui guérit* [The healing influence]. Paris: Odile Jacob.

Orlinsky, D. (1999). Development of psychotherapists: Concepts, questions, and methods of a collaborative international study. *Psychotherapy Research, 9*(2), 127–153.

Pedersen, P. B. (2002). Ethics, competence, and other professional issues in culture-centered counseling. In P. B. Pedersen, J. Draguns, W. Lonner, & J. Trimble (Eds.), *Counseling across cultures* (5th ed., pp. 3–28). Thousand Oaks, CA: Sage.

Pfeiffer, W. M. (1995). Kulturpsychiatrische Aspekte der Migration [Culturally psychiatric aspects of migration]. In E. Koch, M. Özek, & W. M. Pfeifer (Eds.), *Psychologie und Pathologie der Migration* (pp. 17–30). Freiburg, Germany: Lambertus.

Prince, R. H. (1980). Variations in psychotherapeutic procedures. In H. C. Triandis & J. G. Draguns (Eds.), *Handbook of cross-cultural psychology: Vol. 6. Psychopathology* (pp. 291–349). Boston: Allyn & Bacon.

Seeley, K. M. (1999). *Cultural psychotherapy.* Northvale, NJ: Jason Aronson.

Sue, S. (1977). Community mental health services to minority groups: Some optimism, some pessimism. *American Psychologist, 32,* 616–624.

Toukmanian, S. G., & Brouwers, M. C. (1998). Cultural aspects of self-disclosure and psychotherapy. In S. S. Kazarian & D. R. Evans (Eds.), *Cultural clinical psychology: Theory, research, and practice* (pp. 106–127). New York: Oxford University Press.

Juris G. Draguns
Pennsylvania State University

See also: Psychotherapy

CULTURE-BOUND DISORDERS

The term *culture-bound disorders* refers to psychological disorders limited to members of distinct ethnocultural settings and traditions. Both the term and the concept are controversial and have been the topic of considerable debate, because they raise fundamental questions about the universality of psychological disorders. For some researchers, culture-bound disorders are simply variants of disorders found among Western people. For others, however, they represent disorders specific to non-Western people that cannot be classified among Western disorders.

A major part of the debate surrounds the question of cultural influences on psychopathology. Most psychiatric researchers have considered cultural variables unimportant. Thus, if culture-bound disorders exist, culture must be assigned an important role. This poses problems for biological conceptions of mental disorders.

A number of terms have been used to describe culture-bound disorders: (1) exotic psychoses, (2) atypical psychoses, (3) esoteric disorders, (4) hysterical psychoses, (5) ethnic psychoses, (6) culture-bound reactive syndromes, and (7) culture-specific disorders. All these terms reflect the confusion regarding the nature of these disorders. Should they be considered psychotic or neurotic disorders? Do they have biogenic or psychogenic origins? Are they simply variants of mental disorders found in Western cultures, or are they culturally unique patterns of disorder? The answers are complex. For culture-bound disorders, case observations have been limited in number and quality. Often the research material is strong on opinion and weak on fact. Because many investigators have not even had access to cases, there has been a frequent reliance on secondary information from poorly trained informants.

Types of Culture-Bound Disorders

More than 30 culture-bound disorders have been reported in the clinical and research literature. However, among these disorders only a handful have received substantive attention, of which this article limits the discussion to *latah, amok, susto,* and *koro.*

Latah

Latah is found primarily among populations residing in Malaysia and Indonesia. It is present in both males and females, but it is more frequent among the latter. Its two major components are a startle reaction and subsequent imitative behavior including echolalia (repeating what someone says), echopraxia (repeating what someone does), automatic obedience coprolalia (involuntary utterance of obscene words), altered consciousness, and fear. These behaviors can occur repeatedly. In most instances, the disorder is precipitated by a sudden stress.

H. B. M. Murphy, an anthropologist and transcultural psychiatrist, proposed a number of theories about the origins of *latah* and its relationship to cultural factors. He posits that certain Malaysian and Indonesian child-rearing practices predispose individuals toward hypersuggestibility, which then becomes linked to sexual functioning.

Researchers have speculated that *latah* is similar to hysterical disorders found in Southeast Asia, Siberia, and various parts of Japan. Pow Meng Yap, a transcultural psychiatrist who wrote extensively on culturebound disorders, noted that *latah* is similar to the following disorders: *myriachit, amurakh, olonism, imu, imubacco, young-dah-hte, bahtschi, yuan, mali-mali,* jumping, and Arctic hysteria. Of all culture-bound syndromes, *latah* has been the most popular subject among researchers.

Amok

According to Murphy, the term *amok* first appeared in the European literature in 1552 among accounts of Portuguese travelers to Southeast Asia who were describing religious zealots who had taken vows to sacrifice their lives in battle against the enemy. Over time, the term came to refer to individuals who emerge from periods of withdrawal and apathy with a sudden outburst of mania, agitation, and violent physical attacks on nearby people. Frequently, the attack ends when the *amok* individual is shot or killed by others in self-defense.

A number of theories of *amok* were advanced, variously attributing it to febrile diseases (e.g., malaria), nonfebrile diseases (e.g., syphilis), opium addiction, chronic disorders (e.g., brain damage), and sociopsychological distress. No theory has achieved lasting acceptance, and some researchers have come to conclude that *amok* does not represent a distinct disease syndrome but rather an explosive dissociative state that can occur from a number of causes.

Pfeiffer noted that *amok* can be caused by a variety of factors, including chronic illness, infections, sleep deprivation, sexual arousal, environmental stress, or heat. He claims it proceeds through three phases. In the first phase, the individual is withdrawn, passive, and neurasthenic. In the second phase, he (virtually all victims are male) experiences depersonalization, derealization, paranoia, rage, and somatic symptoms. In the third or *amok* phase, there is sudden violent behavior, amnesia, screaming, rage, and assault with a weapon (e.g., a machete). If the *amok*-runner is not killed, this phase is followed by exhaustion and a return to normal consciousness. Kiev observed that *amok* is similar to disorders encountered in other parts of the world, including malignant anxiety in Africa, *cathard* in Polynesia, *psuedonite* in the Sahara desert, and *negi-negi* in the New Guinea highlands.

Susto

Susto—also known as *espanto*—is found among Hispanic populations in Central and South America and also among Hispanic migrants in North America. It has been discussed by Rubel and by Gobeil. Although *susto* occurs across both sexes and all age groups, it is most common among children and young women. The term *susto* is applied to a wide array of phenomena.

In general, *susto* refers to "soul loss." It begins with a strong sense of fear and is followed by weight loss, appetite loss, skin pallor, fatigue, lethargy, untidiness, and excessive thirst.

Several theories of *susto* have been proposed. Kiev suggested that *susto* is an anxiety disorder caused by unacceptable impulses that produce a reliance on projection, isolation, and displacement. In addition, he claims it provides a "sick" role that affords much secondary gain in the way of attention and affection. He states: "Susto is . . . a culturally meaningful anxiety hysteria syndrome that affords the sick the opportunity of being recognized." Gobeil contends that its occurrence in children may be due to insecurities and fears related to parental abandonment, especially under conditions of frequent mobility and migration.

Koro

Koro (sometimes known as *shook yong*) is found among Chinese populations in Southeast Asia and Hong Kong. In men, it is characterized by an intense fear that one's penis is withdrawing into the body. In women, it can be experienced as a fear that breasts are shrinking or labia are withdrawing into the body. However, it is primarily a male disorder. It has been described by Yap and by Rin, who attribute it to beliefs about the balance of yin (female) and yang (male) forces related to sexual excesses. The intense fear takes the form of panic attacks or even a fear of death. In addition, there is sometimes shame over one's action, especially if there is frequent resort to prostitutes or masturbation.

Classification of Culture-Bound Disorders

Although some researchers believe culture-bound disorders represent dysfunctions specific to the ethnocultural settings and traditions in which they occur, others believe they are variants of disorders found in the Western world. The latter group have suggested several classification systems for the culture-bound disorders.

Kiev offered the following classification system for the culture-bound disorders: (1) anxiety states: *koro, susto;* (2) phobic states: *malojo,* voodoo death; (3) depressive disorders: *hiwa-itchk, windigo* psychosis, malignant anxiety; (4) hysterical disorders: *latah;* (5) obsessional-compulsive neuroses: *shinkeishitsu,* frigophobia; (6) dissociative states: *amok, pibloktoq, hsieh ping,* spirit possession. For Kiev, the culture-bound disorders can be included among the subcategories of Western neurotic disorders.

Yap considered many culture-bound disorders to be variants of reactive psychoses. He suggested that they constitute four basic patterns of psychopathology: (1) primary fear reactions: *susto,* magical death, *latah, mali-mali, imu, miryachit, young-dah-hte,* and magical fright; (2) hypereridic rage reactions: *amok; negi-negi;* (3) culturally imposed nosophobias: *koro;* and (4) trance dissociation states: *windigo* psychosis, *hsieh ping.* These patterns then can be placed among the three major categories of psychogenic or reactive psychoses suggested by K. Schneider (1959): emotional syndromes (*koro, susto*), paranoid syndromes, and disordered consciousness syndromes (*latah, amok, negi-negi, hsieh ping, windigo*).

The role of cultural factors in the etiology, onset, manifestation, course, and outcome of psychological disorders is well established (Marsella & White, 1982; Triandis & Draguns, 1981). Thus it should not be surprising that distinct cultural settings and traditions should be associated with specific disorders. A major problem for Western psychiatry has been its inability to accommodate its assumptions and knowledge to the finding that every culture fosters and maintains distinct disorders. There are disorders that are universal, but even they cannot escape cultural influences. Thus in this respect all psychological disorders are culture-bound. This is the case for Schizophrenia and depression as much as it is for *koro, latah, amok,* and the other "culture-bound" disorders. Culture-bound disorders call our attention to the ethnocentric biases of Western psychiatry and thereby provide us with the opportunity to clarify the puzzle of all psychological disorders.

A. J. Marsella
University of Hawaii

***See also:* Cross-Cultural Psychology**

CULTURE SHOCK

The psychological and physiological impact on an individual of the process of initial adjustment to an unfamiliar culture is frequently labeled *culture shock.* In a multicultural situation, culture shock has been defined as the nonspecific state of tension causing a person to be in a state of readiness for any demand made by the new cultural environment. Kalvero Oberg (1960) invented the term *culture shock* to describe the anxiety resulting from losing one's sense of when to do what and how in a new culture. A visitor to a foreign culture experiencing culture shock discovers that familiar cues have been replaced by strange or unfamiliar cues.

Oberg (1960) mentioned six aspects of culture shock: (1) strain, resulting from the effort of psychological adaptation; (2) a sense of loss and deprivation, referring to former friends, status, profession, and possessions; (3) rejection by or of the culture; (4) confusion, referring to role, role expectations, feelings, and self-identity; (5) surprise, anxiety, disgust, or indignation regarding the cultural differences between old and new ways; and (6) feelings of impotence, as a result of the inability to cope in the new environment. Others have applied Oberg's term more widely to include culture fatigue, language shock, and role shock. More recently (Berry & Sam, 1997) *acculturative stress* has become the preferred term for culture shock "because it is closely linked to psychological models of stress as a response to environmental stressors" (p. 298).

Acculturation research describes three levels of difficulty for the individual in culture shock (Berry & Sam, 1997). The first level considers psychological changes that can be accomplished by simple behavioral shifts, culture learning, or the acquisition of social skills. The second level involves more difficult changes of behavior, which may result in psychosomatic problems that accompany acculturative stress. The third level involves psychopathology where changes in behavior exceed the individual's ability to cope.

Any new situation, such as a new job, new relationship, new lifestyle, or new residence, may involve some adjustment of role and change of identity resembling culture shock. *Culture shock* has come to mean the general condition in which any individual is forced to adjust to a new environment in which previously and culturally learned behaviors are no longer appropriate (Ward, 2001).

The problems of culture shock can be identified by at least six characteristics (Pedersen, 1995). First, familiar cues about how the person is supposed to behave are missing, or they now have different meanings. Second, values the person considered desirable may no longer be honored. Third, the disorientation of culture shock creates an emotional state of anxiety, depression, or even hostility, ranging from a mild uneasiness to the "white furies" of unreasonable and uncontrollable rage. Fourth, there is a dissatisfaction with the new ways and an idealization of the way things were back home. Fifth, recovery skills that used to work before do not seem to work any more. Sixth, there is a sense that this is a permanent condition that will never go away.

Peter Adler (1975) was among the early authors to hypothesize a sequence of stages in the culture shock experience in a five-stage process. The initial contact, or the honeymoon stage, is when the newly arrived individual experiences the curiosity and excitement of a tourist without any corresponding sense of responsibility for his or her own behavior. The second stage involves disintegration of familiar cues and overwhelms the individual with the requirements of the new culture. The individual typically experiences self-blame and a sense of personal inadequacy for difficulties encountered. The third stage reintegrates new cues with an increased ability to function in the new culture. However, the emotions associated with this third stage are typically anger, blame, and resentment toward the new culture for having caused difficulties unnecessarily. The fourth stage continues the process of reintegration toward gradual autonomy and increased ability to see both bad and good elements of the old and new cultures. The fifth stage is when the individual has achieved a bicultural identity and is able to function in both the old and the new cultures.

This sequence of stages has been referred to as a *U-curve,* an expression that describes the adjustment process as it moves from higher to lower and back to higher levels of competency. Although the research support for a U-curve adjustment process is controversial, the model continues to have heuristic value. Furnham and Bochner (1986) are critical of the U-curve for being simplistic. First, there are many dependent variables to consider in the adjustment process, such as depression, loneliness, and homesickness. Second, each individual begins culture shock at a different point in his or her adjustment and changes at a different rate.

Pedersen (1995) suggests several coping strategies for managing culture shock. First, the visitor needs to recognize that any important life transition is likely to result in stress and discomfort as a normal consequence. Second, the maintenance of personal integrity and self-esteem is an important resource for someone experiencing culture shock. Third, time must be allowed for the adjustment to take place without pressure or urgency. Fourth, recognizing the patterns of adjustment will help the visitor develop new skills and insights. Fifth, labeling the symptoms of culture shock will help the visitor interpret emotional responses to stress in adjustment. Sixth, being well-adjusted back home does not ensure an easy adjustment in a foreign culture. Seventh, although culture shock cannot be prevented, it is possible to prepare persons for transition and ease the adjustment process. In all instances the development of a support system is essential to helping the visitor cope with the adjustment process. The visitor learns important lessons from culture shock that cannot be learned in any other way, and to that extent culture shock contributes toward the long-term bicultural or multicultural adjustment of the visitor (Berry & Sam, 1997).

REFERENCES

Adler, P. S. (1975). The transitional experience: An alternative view of culture shock. *Journal of Humanistic Psychology, 15*(4), 13–23.

Berry, J. W., & Sam, D. (1997). Acculturation and adaptation. In J. W. Berry, M. H. Segall, & C. Kagitcibasi (Eds.), *Handbook of cross-cultural psychology: Vol 3* (pp. 291–326). Boston: Allyn & Bacon.

Furnham, A., & Bochner, S. (1986). *Culture shock: Psychological reactions to unfamiliar environments.* London: Methuen.

Oberg, K. (1960). Cultural shock: Adjustment to new cultural environments. *Practical Anthropology, 7,* 177–182.

Pedersen, P. (1995). *The five stages of culture shock: Critical incidents around the world.* Westport, CT: Greenwood.

Ward, C. (2001). Acculturation. In D. Matsumoto (Ed.), *Handbook of culture and psychology.* New York: Oxford University Press.

Paul B. Pedersen
University of Hawaii

CURRENT PSYCHOTHERAPIES

Several popular and classical different systems of psychotherapy are outlined in this article, although for the sake of brevity some important systems and techniques are omitted.

Psychoanalytic Psychotherapy

Classical psychoanalysis was originated by Sigmund Freud in the mid-1890s and has since been modified—and often turned into analytically oriented psychotherapy by many neo-Freudians.

According to psychoanalysis, emotional disturbances and behavioral dysfunction mainly arise from (1) early childhood experiences; (2) unconscious attitudes and experiences, often deeply repressed; (3) biologically based erotic and aggressive drives that create conflicts; (4) fixations on early sexual stages of development such as oral, anal, and genital stages; and (5) defensive maneuvers and avoidances that block people from changing.

To get at the main sources of the analysands' unconscious conflicts and to undo their serious fixations, psychoanalysts use various therapeutic techniques: (1) free association; (2) dream analysis and interpretation; (3) the development of and working through of an intense transference relationship between the analyst and analysand; (4) interpretation of the analysands' unconscious feelings and conflicts; and (5) helping clients to surrender their defenses.

Adlerian Psychotherapy or Individual Psychology

Individual psychology, originated by Alfred Adler, has been followed fairly closely but has also been significantly augmented by many psychotherapists.

According to Adlerian theory, emotional disturbances are largely related to (1) feelings of inferiority; (2) individuals' striving for their own greater glory rather than for social interest; (3) hesitancy to take risks and make full commitments to life; (4) refusal to give constructive meaning to one's existence; and (5) distorted perceptions and beliefs, leading to failure of learning.

Adlerian techniques include (1) showing clients what their life goals are and how they can change their dysfunctional lifestyles; (2) confronting them with their self-defeating ideas; (3) urging clients to take constructive actions that will change their self-sabotaging life goals; (4) encouraging clients to assume responsibility for directing their lives into more positive channels; (5) helping clients achieve the courage to be imperfect; and (6) showing clients how to develop their social interests.

Analytical (Jungian) Psychotherapy

Carl G. Jung broke with Freud around 1913. He viewed libido as general psychic energy instead of sexual energy and emphasized mythological and other symbols of causation and treatment of emotional disturbance.

According to Jungian theory, emotional disturbances largely stem from (1) interference with the individual's strong instinct of individuation; (2) complexes springing from strong unconscious compulsions; (3) guiding symbolic messages from the unconscious that lead people astray; and (4) inheritable predispositions that arise from the malfunctioning of the collective unconscious.

Jungian techniques include (1) showing clients that all suffering is a loss of meaning and that archetypes can provide healing powers; (2) helping clients symbolically understand the symptoms of their neurosis; (3) emphasizing the purposive, prospective functioning of the psyche; (4) revealing to clients the creative and healing powers of the unconscious; (5) making dream interpretations, with emphasis on the symbolic meanings of the clients' dreams; and (6) encouraging experiencing rather than mere intellectual understanding and persistently encouraging clients to pay heed to and value their own inner world.

Person-Centered Therapy

Person-centered therapy was originated by Carl Rogers in the early 1940s. Although not practiced fully by many therapists today, it is incorporated in the theory and practice of a number of theorists and therapists.

According to the Rogerian view, emotional disturbance largely arises from (1) people's acquiring a negative self-concept because others do not sufficiently accept them and provide them with suitable conditions of growth; (2) people's refusing to directly and freely admit to awareness-aspects of themselves that are not consistent with their self-concepts; and (3) self-devaluation or feelings of worthlessness.

Person-centered therapeutic techniques include (1) engaging in a deep, intense caring relationship with the clients; (2) consistently displaying genuineness, congruence, and empathic understanding of the clients and their problems in the course of this relationship; (3) maintaining nondirective and nonintrusive dialogue between therapist and client; and (4) helping clients to achieve unconditional positive regard for themselves, largely through their experiencing the therapist's unconditional positive regard for them.

Cognitive-Behavioral Therapy and Rational-Emotive Behavior Therapy

Modern cognitive-behavioral therapy (CBT) originated in 1955 with Albert Ellis's Rational-Emotive Behavior Therapy (REBT). Following the lead of many philosophers, ancient and modern, CBT and REBT take a constructivist view that people largely make themselves disturbed and integrate this with the behaviorist views of John D. Watson and B. F. Skinner.

According to the theories of REBT and CBT, human disturbances stem from (1) a strong tendency, both innate and acquired, for people to act both for and against their own and their social group's interest; (2) misperceptions and unrealistic observations and conclusions; (3) absolutist and irrational beliefs that unpleasant conditions must not exist, that people absolutely cannot stand them, and that people who bring about such conditions are worthless individuals; (4) people's unreasonable escalation of their strong desires into godlike demands; and (5) pronounced interactions among people's unrealistic and absolutistic thinking, their emoting, and their self-defeating behaviors.

Therapeutic techniques include (1) showing clients that unfavorable conditions by themselves do not upset them but that they consciously or unconsciously choose to upset themselves; (2) teaching clients a number of cognitive, emotive, and behavioral methods to change their dysfunctional thinking, feelings, and behaviors; (3) agreeing with clients that they do cognitive, affective, and behavioral homework; (4) applying forceful methods such as strong self-statements and shame-attacking exercises; (5) using problem solving to change adversities in people's lives; (6) applying a variety of psychoeducational techniques such as self-monitoring and gradual change of thoughts and beliefs; (7) using skill training to improve clients' abilities, interests, and achievements; and (8) employing cognitive restructuring and relaxation methods.

Behavioral Psychotherapy

Behavioral methods in psychotherapy started with applications of the learning theories of John B. Watson and B. F. Skinner and their followers. During the 1950s and 1960s clinical applications of these principles were developed.

Behavior therapy theories hold that emotional problems largely arise from (1) ineffective or maladaptive learning; (2) conditioning by others; (3) self-conditioning and self-practice of dysfunctional actions; (4) avoidance of situations that help to create anxiety; and (5) lack of skills that lead to poor performances.

Main techniques used in Behavior therapy include (1) focusing on changing clients' present behavior; (2) actively and directively teaching clients how to change their dysfunctional behaviors and how to practice more functional ones; (3) applying imaginal and in vivo systematic desensitization of anxieties and fears; (4) showing clients how to use stimulus control in the situations that cause them problems; (5) performing skill training; (6) using contingencies of reinforcements for adaptive behavior and aversive conditioning for maladaptive behaviors; and (7) teaching relaxation techniques.

Gestalt Therapy

Gestalt therapy originated with the clinical work of Fritz Perls in the 1940s.

Gestalt therapy sees emotional disturbance as largely caused by (1) a "should" attitude toward life; (2) obsession with thinking rather than feeling and doing; (3) refusing to live in the present and centering oneself in the past or future; (4) trying to reform others instead of being oneself and accepting oneself as one is; and (5) refusing to accept responsibility for one's own decisions.

Some of the main Gestalt therapy techniques include (1) helping clients to be fully aware of their feelings in the here and now; (2) showing them how to reject cognitive interpretations and explanations of their difficulties; (3) teaching breathing and body work; and (4) helping clients achieve integration.

Experiential and Humanistic Psychotherapy

Experiential, humanistic, and existential psychotherapy began with the philosophic writings of Martin Heidegger and Martin Buber and includes a variety of theories and techniques.

Experiential, humanistic, and existential therapists generally hold that emotional disturbance has these main roots: (1) refusal to take the risk of living fully and of accepting the inevitability of death; (2) inability to own one's own life and conduct and to be fairly autonomous even though living in a community or social group; (3) overconformity, leading to continual pressure to ignore one's own experience; and (4) refusing to experiment with one's desires and wishes and instead forcing oneself into a narrow mode of experiences.

Experiential, humanistic, and existential therapists use the following techniques: (1) emphasizing clients' felt senses and their inner processes of change and development; (2) helping clients to have a profound inner sense of experience; (3) using body work and physical methods of emotional release; (4) teaching risk taking, so that clients learn to change by forcing themselves to exist differently;

(5) relating caringly and fully to clients, which encourages clients to relate caringly and fully to others; and (6) helping clients achieve unconditional positive regard or full acceptance, authenticity, self-honesty, and openness.

Transactional Analysis

Transactional analysis (TA), originated by Eric Berne in the mid-1950s, originally was designed to supplement psychoanalysis.

According to TA theory, the main causes of emotional disturbance include (1) children's receiving early messages or "tapes" from their "parent" ego states that encourage them to act in their "child" ego state instead of their more sensible and productive "adult" state; (2) the innate tendency of people to make the transactions among their ego states all-important and rigid; (3) resulting stereotyped habit patterns and lack of personal autonomy; (4) lack of early stroking or loving recognition by others; and (5) the tendency to use defensive maneuvers or games to retain and reinforce early script decisions.

Transactional therapists use a variety of techniques, especially the following: (1) tracing clients' disturbed feelings back to their early decisive moments, then reeducating the clients to feel differently; (2) helping clients to achieve a balance of ego states; (3) showing clients how to reexperience decision moments and redecide important issues through self-orientation; and (4) revealing and interrupting clients' defensive maneuvers or games.

As can be seen, all these kinds of psychotherapies seem different in many respects but also overlap with each other in several other important respects. They also include several important variations, such as interpersonal relationship therapy, which was pioneered by Harry Sullivan in the 1950s, and solution-focused therapy, which was pioneered by Steven DeShazer in 1985.

In the 1970s Arnold Lazarus attempted to integrate many leading techniques of psychotherapy into his multimodal therapy, which includes several main modalities. This was followed in the 1980s by several other leading psychotherapists, like Marvin Goldfried and Paul Wachtel, who started a popular movement to integrate and interrelate many of the major theories and practices of psychotherapy.

Albert Ellis

See also: **Behavior Therapy; Gestalt Therapy; Rational Emotive Behavior Therapy**

CUTANEOUS SENSES

Cutaneous or skin senses are aspects of what is often referred to as the "sense of touch." Studies indicate that there are four different cutaneous senses: pressure (including light touch), pain, warmth, and cold. Although they are not completely understood, it is thought that other cutaneous sensations, such as tickle and itch, are varieties of the four primary cutaneous senses.

In order for an organism to receive information, specific types of nerve endings, called *sensory receptors,* respond to particular external or internal environmental stimuli. In animal organisms, the process of sensory reception transduces, or converts, the stimuli into nerve signals that are transmitted via neurons for further processing and interpretation in the central nervous system (CNS). This provides the mechanism for a living organism to perceive and/or react to stimuli. The brain interprets these signals as feelings of light touch, pressure, heat, and cold. Other responses, such as the involuntary knee-jerk reflex, may take place at lower levels in the CNS (e.g., at the spinal cord). Still other involuntary responses may be endocrine in nature.

For the cutaneous senses, certain types of sensory receptors respond to specific stimuli. These receptors are found in the tissue that underlies the skin. Some are also found with other receptors in muscles, tendons, ligaments, and joints for kinesthetic proprioception, or awareness of body position, as we move. Body balance or equilibrium, the vestibular sense, has mechanisms in the semicircular canals of the inner ear.

There are several ways to classify sensory receptors. One way is to view them in terms of the *source* of the information to which they respond. Cutaneous receptors which respond to stimuli from the external environment are *exteroceptors,* which are affected by pain, temperature, touch, and pressure. *Interoceptors* respond to changes in the internal bodily environment, while *proprioceptors* are stimulated by changes in movement, position, and tension.

Another receptor classification plan is in terms of the *information,* or stimuli, to which specific receptor types react. Using this classification, cutaneous sense *thermoreceptors* serve for heat, *nociceptors* for painful stimuli, and *mechanoreceptors* for touch and pressure. Mechanical stimuli serve to bring about reflexes such as knee jerks. Other categories include *photoreceptors,* which respond to light, and *chemoreceptors* for smell and taste.

Dermatomes

Cutaneous receptors are not evenly distributed throughout the body in the dermis, or inner layer of the skin. The nerve pathway to the brain from the cutaneous receptors is arranged in terms of areas of the skin known as *dermatomes,* which are connected with the nerves to the spinal cord.

Two-Point Threshold

Two stimulated points on the skin cannot be distinguished from a single stimulated skin point when only one receptor or the same nerve serves the two stimulated points. The *two-point threshold* varies with the part of the body and is related to dermatome size, the largest being for the center of the back and the smallest for the tongue tip.

Local Sign

Local sign is a term that refers to the ability of an individual to localize, without looking, the portion of the body surface at which the skin has been stimulated. Scientists have not agreed as to whether or not local sign is unlearned (innate) or learned (acquired). Both innate and acquired factors may be involved.

Light Touch and Heavy Pressure

The receptors for *light touch* are believed to comprise Meissner's corpuscles, hair follicle bulbs, and some free nerve endings. *Heavy pressure* is believed to have as its receptors the Pacinian corpuscles, which appear as onionlike bulbs, each with a central nerve fiber. Changes of pressure, rather than constant application of pressure, appear to lead to receptor function that senses vibratory pressure and touch. Adaptation to pressure takes place, as may be indicated by individuals' rapid loss of awareness of the pressure of their wearing apparel. Merkel's discs, which also respond to touch, do not quickly adapt.

Pain

More remains to be learned about both reception of *pain* from the body and the site of reception of pain in the brain. Free nerve endings appear to be receptors for skin pain. Pain functions as a warning of injury to the body. Some of these receptors send impulses into the CNS to form a two-neuron spinal-level reflex arc by way of impinging upon outgoing nerve cells to muscles. This can be seen for acute pain, for example, when the hand is withdrawn from scalding water (or following a pinprick) before the brain, which takes more neural connections to reach, receives the sensation of heat. Such intense, acute stimulation is carried by quick-transmitting nerve fibers called type A delta fibers. Slow conducting fibers called type C fibers are believed to be responsible for a sense of persistent pain. Methods of study of pain include the use of radiant heat, in order to separate the stimulation of pain from stimulation of pressure receptors. A small amount of adaptation to slight skin pain has been observed.

Warm and Cold

Receptors remain to be definitively identified for *warm and cold* stimuli, despite the fact that there are distinctly separate reception spots for such stimuli. Ruffini's corpuscles and free nerve endings are believed to be receptors for heat, although they are thought also to be involved in deep, continuous pressure. The end-bulbs of Krause, also called Krause's terminal bulbs, are believed to be thermoreceptors for cold. The sensation of *hot* does not have a separate receptor but is felt when both warm and cold receptors are stimulated simultaneously. The sensation of cold that often occurs just prior to the feeling of hot to a hot stimulus is termed *paradoxical cold.* One explanation is that it represents the reception of faster transmission to the brain from the cold receptors than from the warm receptors, although both have been stimulated together. Usually, adaptation occurs to or toward the currently prevailing temperature. A change from this adapted neutral point is then felt relatively as warm or cold. Together with sensors that respond to internal bodily environmental changes, cutaneous thermoreceptors contribute to maintenance of a consistent body temperature. In response to sensed thermal changes, to help regulate body temperature, the pores of the skin may be made larger or smaller. Observable bodily responses to thermal changes include perspiring, shivering, and panting.

Barbara B. Mates
City College of New York, CUNY, and New School University, New York

See also: **Central Nervous System; Neuromuscular Disorders; Pain; Psychophysiology**

CYBERNETICS

The concept of cybernetics was originally adapted from biology, computers, communication theory, and mathematics and applied to human social systems. In psychology, it first was adopted by family therapists. Cybernetics and cybernetic systems have not been fully applied to personality theories. "Cybernetics is primarily concerned with understanding and managing the organization of systems" (Keeney & Thomas, 1986, p. 263). Emphasis is placed on discerning and managing specific patterns of the organization of a social system. Cybernetics is concerned with recursive feedback loops or ongoing patterns that connect within a system. The focus is on the relationships between elements within the system. "Cybernetic systems are therefore patterns of organization that maintain stability through processes of change" (Keeney & Ross, 1983, p. 51).

Cybernetic and cybernetic systems have similarities to and differences from general systems theory, viewing organisms as systems within systems (called *suprasystems;* Keeney & Thomas, 1986; Laszlo, 1980). According to a general systems theoretical view, a system is a Gestalt with the whole being more than the sum of its parts, meanwhile maintaining a balanced, homeostatic steady state (Speer, 1970). Keeney (1983) refers to general systems theory as simple cybernetics or a lower-level cybernetics.

When using a cybernetic systems perspective, it is necessary to make an epistemological shift, changing the way causality is viewed.

An Epistemological Shift

An age-old question among philosophers refers to the causes of human behavior. When using concepts of systems theory, cybernetics, and cybernetic systems, one must shift to an unusual view of causality. A linear view states that A causes B (Keeney, 1983), or one event causes another, for example, as in the stimulus-response concept. Cybernetics and systems theory, on the other hand, are based on circular views of causality, reflected by mutually feeding patterns of behavior (Keeney, 1983): A causes B and B causes A. Keeney (1983) and Keeney and Ross (1983) refer to circular causality as simple cybernetics.

Key Concepts

Cybernetic systems theory consists of several key dynamics: self-reference, feedback patterns, homeostasis, and self-autonomy.

Self-Reference

Perception can be viewed in terms of relationships, that is, self-reference, or placing the perceiver in the observation. The relationship between the observer-perceiver and perceived reality can be analyzed in terms of patterns of relationships, because the observer is always part of the context by definition.

Feedback Patterns

Any living or mechanical system is organized by patterns connecting each element within the system. These patterns are referred to as *feedback loops* (Gerson & Barsky, 1976) or recursive (ongoing circularly fed) communicative patterns of behavior. There are positive and negative feedback loops (Gerson & Barsky, 1976; Speer, 1970). Positive feedback loops initiate change by dumping new information into the system. Negative feedback loops are patterns that help maintain the system's status quo or sameness. Balance or equilibrium can be restored through the calibration of feedback loops. At the highest level of a cybernetic system, equilibrium or homeostasis is continuously maintained through the complementary relationship between patterns of positive and negative feedback loops.

Homeostasis: A Dynamic Balance

Systems maintain a continuous ongoing dynamic balance referred to as *homeostasis* (Keeney, 1983; Speer, 1970). Keeney (1983) emphasized that all living systems maintain a dynamic balance at their highest level, or else they would self-destruct and perish. According to the views postulated by early general systems theorists, change facilitates a state of disequilibrium, and then the organism returns to equilibrium. Change is encompassed by a recursive loop of stability (Keeney, 1983). Change and stability fit together like two sides of a coin; they cannot be separated. Negative and positive feedback loops also are complementary.

Self-Autonomy

The cybernetic system is self-autonomous and self-maintained at the highest level of observation (Keeney, 1983). It also is a closed system at the highest level. Self-autonomy is maintained through the processes of *morphostasis* (patterned processes of change and stability; Speer, 1970). Paradoxically, a system's structure is maintained through calibrated patterns of change and stability.

REFERENCES

Gerson, M., & Barsky, M. (1976). The new family therapist: A glossary of terms. *American Journal of Family Therapy, 4*(1), 15–30.

Keeney, B. P. (1983). *Aesthetic of change.* New York: Guilford Press.

Keeney, B. O., & Ross, J. M. (1983). Cybernetics of brief family therapy. *Journal of Marital and Family Therapy, 9*(4), 375–382.

Keeney, B. P., & Thomas, F. (1986). Cybernetic foundations of family therapy. In F. P. Piercy & D. H. Sprenkle (Eds.), *Family therapy sourcebook* (pp. 262–287). New York: Guilford Press.

Laszlo, E. (1980). *The systems of the world.* New York: Braziller.

Speer, D. (1970). Family systems morphostasis and morphogenesis, or is "homeostasis" enough? *Family Process, 9*(1), 259–278.

M. S. Carich
Adler School of Professional Psychology

CYCLOTHYMIC DISORDER

Cyclothymic personality, or Cyclothymic Disorder, as it is called in the *Diagnostic and Statistical Manual of Mental Disorders,* fourth edition (*DSM-IV;* American Psychiatric Association, 1994), is characterized by recurrent and intermittent mood episodes in which the individual oscillates or cycles between periods of depression and hypomania, with or without normal periods in between. Cyclothymic depressions include symptoms such as sadness, anhedonia, low energy, pessimism, poor concentration, and sleep and appetite changes resembling those observed in episodes of major depression, whereas cyclothymic hypomanic periods involve symptoms such as euphoria; high energy or activity; talkativeness; high self-confidence or grandiosity; decreased sleep; and impulsive, reckless behaviors typically observed in mania. However, unlike major depression and mania, both types of cyclothymic mood episodes are of subsyndromal intensity and duration (2–3 days on average). Cyclothymic personality can present as predominantly depressed, predominantly hypomanic, or balanced with approximately equal proportions of high and low periods (Goodwin & Jamison, 1990).

Historically, controversy surrounded the issue of whether cyclothymia is best conceptualized as a personality temperament/disorder or a subsyndromal mood disorder (Goodwin & Jamison, 1990). Indeed, cyclothymic patients are often perceived as exhibiting features of personality disorder rather than mood disorder at first clinical presentation. Family members often describe them as "moody," "high-strung," "hyperactive," and "explosive" (Akiskal, Djenderedjian, Rosenthal, & Khani, 1977). Moreover, cyclothymics exhibit social role impairment and considerable problems in interpersonal relations (Klein, Depue, & Krauss, 1986).

Kraepelin (1921) emphasized that cyclothymia is on a continuum with full-blown bipolar (manic-depressive) disorder and, indeed, may be a precursor to it. Four lines of evidence strongly support this continuum model and suggest that cyclothymia is an integral part of the bipolar disorder spectrum. First, the behavior of cyclothymics is qualitatively similar to that of patients with full-blown bipolar disorder; cyclothymia merges imperceptibly with Bipolar II (individuals who exhibit major depressive and hypomanic episodes, but not manic episodes), and sometimes Bipolar I (individuals who exhibit both major depressive and manic episodes), Disorder at the behavioral level (Akiskal et al., 1977; Akiskal, Khani, & Scott-Strauss, 1979; Depue et al., 1981). Second, equivalent rates of bipolar disorder have been reported in the first- and second-degree relatives of cyclothymic and Bipolar I patients (Akiskal et al., 1977; Depue et al., 1981; Dunner, Russek, Russek, & Fieve, 1982), and increased rates of cyclothymia are found in the offspring of Bipolar I patients (Klein, Depue, & Slater, 1985). In addition, among monozygotic twins, when one twin had manic-depression, the other, if not also manic-depressive, was frequently cyclothymic (Bertelsen, Harvald, & Hauge, 1977). These findings suggest that cyclothymia shares a common genetic diathesis with bipolar disorder. Third, cyclothymics, like Bipolar I patients, often experience an induction of hypomanic episodes when treated with tricyclic antidepressants (Akiskal et al., 1977). In turn, lithium prophylaxis leads to clinical improvement in a significant proportion of cyclothymics, as it does in bipolar patients (Akiskal et al., 1979). Finally, up to 80% of bipolar patients exhibit cyclothymic premorbid personalities (Goodwin & Jamison, 1990; Waters, 1979). Moreover, cyclothymics are at increased risk for developing full-blown bipolar disorder. Among cyclothymics followed from 1 to 3 years, 35–40% have developed Bipolar II or I Disorder (Abramson, Alloy, Donovan, Hogan, & Whitehouse, 2003; Akiskal et al., 1977).

The onset of cyclothymia usually occurs in mid-adolescence (mean age 14 years; Akiskal et al., 1977, 1979), whereas the onset of full-blown Bipolar I or II Disorder occurs around 24 years on average (Goodwin & Jamison, 1990). Thus, there is approximately a 10-year risk period in which cyclothymics could be identified prior to the onset of full-blown bipolar disorder. Depue and colleagues (1981; Depue, Krauss, Spoont, & Arbisi, 1989) have developed the General Behavior Inventory (GBI) as a first-stage screening instrument for this purpose. The GBI has been found to identify cyclothymics in the general population reliably and validly, with high sensitivity and specificity.

Cyclothymia often presents a problem in differential diagnosis (Goodwin & Jamison, 1990). Symptoms such as hyperactivity and distractability that are part of cyclothymic hypomanic periods are easily confused with Attention-Deficit/Hyperactivity Disorder (ADHD). The key difference is that when these symptoms are part of cyclothymia, they are more episodic and more characterized by rapid swings in attention and activity level than when they are part of ADHD. The impulsive, reckless behaviors (e.g., shoplifting, substance abuse, hostility) seen in cyclothymic hypomanic periods can also be mistaken for Antisocial Personality Disorder. Here, the association of these behaviors with elevated or irritable mood states is central to the differential diagnosis.

Several personality characteristics and cognitive styles have been associated with cyclothymia. Among the offspring of bipolar patients, obsessional personality traits correlated with the presence of cyclothymia (Klein & Depue, 1985). An association between genetic liability for bipolar disorder and creativity has also been reported (Jamison, 1993), with an increased propensity for creativity being most strongly expressed in individuals with subsyndromal manifestations of the bipolar spectrum (i.e., cyclothymia; Andreason, 1987; Richards, Kinney, Lunde, Benet, & Merzel, 1988; Shapiro & Weissberg, 1999). Recent evidence indicates that cyclothymic individuals exhibit stable negative cognitive styles similar to those observed among unipolar depressed people (Alloy, Abramson, Donovan, Whitehouse, & Hogan, 2001; Alloy, Reilly-Harrington, Fresco, Whitehouse, & Zechmeister, 1999). Alloy and colleagues (1999) reported that cyclothymic individuals exhibited dysfunctional attitudes and attributional styles (styles for explaining the causes of positive and negative life events) as negative as those of dysthymic individuals and that cyclothymics' dysfunctional attitudes and attributional styles remained stable across large changes in mood and symptomatology over time.

Recent evidence suggests that the extreme mood swings observed among cyclothymic and other bipolar individuals may be attributable to both a behavioral and a biological hypersensitivity to stress. Alloy and colleagues (1999) and Reilly-Harrington, Alloy, Fresco, and Whitehouse (1999) found that cyclothymic and bipolar individuals' dysfunctional attitudes and negative attributional styles interacted with stressful life events to predict longitudinally depressive and hypomanic mood swings. Specifically, cyclothymic and bipolar participants with negative cognitive styles were the most likely to experience depressive and hypomanic mood swings in response to stressful events. Similarly, Depue and colleagues (Depue, Kleiman, Davis, Hutchinson, & Krauss, 1985; Goplerud & Depue, 1985) found that cyclothymics showed slower behavioral recovery following a stressful life event and slower recovery of cortisol secretion following a laboratory stressor than did normal controls.

REFERENCES

Abramson, L. Y., Alloy, L. B., Donovan, P., Hogan, M. E., & Whitehouse, W. G. (2003). *The Wisconsin-Temple Longitudinal Investigation of Bipolar Spectrum Disorders (LIBS) Project: The prospective prediction of conversion to Bipolar II and I Disorder among individuals with subsyndromal bipolar disorder.* Manuscript in preparation, University of Wisconsin, Madison.

Akiskal, H. S., Djenderedjian, A. H., Rosenthal, R. H., & Khani, M. K. (1977). Cyclothymic disorder: Validating criteria for inclusion in the bipolar affective group. *American Journal of Psychiatry, 134,* 1227–1233.

Akiskal, H. S., Khani, M. K., & Scott-Strauss, A. (1979). Cyclothymic temperamental disorders. *Psychiatric Clinics of North America, 2,* 527–554.

Alloy, L. B., Abramson, L. Y., Donovan, P., Whitehouse, W. G., & Hogan, M. E. (2001). *Cognitive styles and self-referent information processing in individuals with bipolar spectrum disorders.* Paper presented at the Association for the Advancement of Behavior Therapy Meeting, Philadelphia, PA.

Alloy, L. B., Reilly-Harrington, N., Fresco, D. M., Whitehouse, W. G., & Zechmeister, J. S. (1999). Cognitive styles and life events in subsyndromal unipolar and bipolar disorders: Stability and prospective prediction of depressive and hypomanic mood swings. *Journal of Cognitive Psychotherapy: An International Quarterly, 13,* 21–40.

American Psychiatric Association. (1994). *Diagnostic and statistical manual of mental disorders* (4th ed.). Washington, DC: Author.

Andreason, N. C. (1987). Creativity and mental illness: Prevalence rates in writers and their first degree relatives. *American Journal of Psychiatry, 144,* 1288–1292.

Bertelsen, A., Harvald, B., & Hauge, M. (1977). A Danish twin study of manic-depressive disorders. *British Journal of Psychiatry, 130,* 330–351.

Depue, R. A., Kleiman, R. M., Davis, P., Hutchinson, M., & Krauss, S. P. (1985). The behavioral high-risk paradigm and bipolar affective disorder: VIII. Serum free cortisol in nonpatient cyclothymic subjects selected by the General Behavior Inventory. *American Journal of Psychiatry, 142,* 175–181.

Depue, R. A., Krauss, S., Spoont, M. R., & Arbisi, P. (1989). General Behavior Inventory identification of unipolar and bipolar affective conditions in a nonclinical university population. *Journal of Abnormal Psychology, 98,* 117–126.

Depue, R. A., Slater, J., Wolfstetter-Kausch, H., Klein, D., Goplerud, E., & Farr, D. (1981). A behavioral paradigm for identifying persons at risk for bipolar depressive disorder: A conceptual framework and five validation studies (Monograph). *Journal of Abnormal Psychology, 90,* 381–437.

Dunner, D. L., Russek, F. D., Russek, B., & Fieve, R. R. (1982). Classification of bipolar affective disorder subtypes. *Comprehensive Psychiatry, 23,* 186–189.

Goodwin, F. K., & Jamison, K. R. (1990). *Manic-depressive illness.* New York: Oxford University Press.

Goplerud, E., & Depue, R. A. (1985). Behavioral response to naturally occurring stress in cyclothymia and dysthymia. *Journal of Abnormal Psychology, 94,* 128–139.

Jamison, K. R. (1993). *Touched with fire: Manic-depressive illness and the artistic temperament.* New York: Free Press.

Klein, D. N., & Depue, R. A. (1985). Obsessional personality traits and risk for bipolar affective disorder: An offspring study. *Journal of Abnormal Psychology, 94,* 291–297.

Klein, D. N., Depue, R. A., & Krauss, S. P. (1986). Social adjustment in the offspring of parents with bipolar affective disorder. *Journal of Psychopathology and Behavior Assessment, 8,* 355–366.

Klein, D. N., Depue, R. A., & Slater, J. F. (1985). Cyclothymia in the adolescent offspring of parents with bipolar affective disorder. *Journal of Abnormal Psychology, 94,* 115–127.

Kraepelin, E. (1921). *Manic-depressive insanity and paranoia* (R. M. Barclay, Trans., G. M. Robertson, Ed.). Edinburgh: E & S Livingstone.

Reilly-Harrington, N. A., Alloy, L. B., Fresco, D. M., & Whitehouse, W. G. (1999). Cognitive styles and life events interact to predict bipolar and unipolar symptomatology. *Journal of Abnormal Psychology, 108,* 567–578.

Richards, R. L., Kinney, D. K., Lunde, I., Benet, M., & Merzel, A. (1988). Creativity in manic-depressives, cyclothymes, their normal relatives, and control subjects. *Journal of Abnormal Psychology, 97,* 281–288.

Shapiro, P. J., & Weissberg, R. W. (1999). Creativity and bipolar diathesis: Common behavioral and cognitive components. *Cognition and Emotion, 13,* 741–762.

Waters, B. G. H. (1979). Early symptoms of bipolar affective psychosis: Research and clinical implications. *Canadian Psychiatric Association Journal, 2,* 55–60.

Lauren B. Alloy
Temple University

Lyn Y. Abramson
University of Wisconsin, Madison

***See also:* Bipolar Disorder**

D

DAYDREAMING

Daydreaming has been defined as "a dream indulged in while awake, esp. one of happiness or gratified hope or ambition; a reverie, castle in the air" (*Oxford English Dictionary*) or "a visionary fancy indulged in while awake" (*Webster's Dictionary*). Obviously, daydreaming is not a very precisely defined or discrete entity. Daydreaming can be thought of as including a number of other terms in daily parlance, such as reverie, fantasy, imagination, playful thinking, wandering thoughts, and free association.

Taken in its broadest sense, including all the aforementioned terms, daydreaming clearly occupies a great deal of our time. A long-term study of daydreaming, using a variety of questionnaire techniques, suggests that we probably spend at least half of our waking lives in daydreaming activity, and even when we are engaged in an intense waking mental task, we still spend at least 10% of the time daydreaming.

Daydreaming may be especially important in terms of our scientific study of the brain and mind because it can be thought of as the background activity of the waking mind. Daydreaming is what the mind (and the underlying brain) does naturally when it is not paying attention—when it is not constrained into performing one of the specific tasks our brains have been trained to do.

Daydreaming has been studied by a number of different techniques, most often using a variety of questionnaires asking what people daydream about and when. There have also been a series of studies designed to "catch" daydream content by having subjects wear a device which buzzes or signals them at random intervals as a signal to write down or dictate whatever was going through their minds.

More recently, there have also been studies of brain activity dealing with types of mental activity (see Brain Imaging, elsewhere in this volume). These studies are most advanced relating to rapid eye movement (REM) sleep, which is when most dreaming occurs. Daydreaming per se has not yet been clearly demonstrated to involve particular brain regions or systems, but work is in progress in that direction. Over many years, there have been studies of peripheral physiology—such measures as pulse, blood pressure, skin resistance. All of these show that emotionally arousing material produces clear-cut changes in physiological measures. These can differentiate highly emotional or charged daydreams from bland daydreams, but do not identify daydreams as such.

Overall these studies have produced many suggestive findings on daydreams. First, as previously mentioned, a large amount of total time is spent daydreaming. On the other hand, studies attempting to examine an individual daydream, insofar as it can be delineated, find that it is surprisingly short—usually 5–14 seconds in length. Studies on the content of daydreams invariably show that they are influenced by emotional concerns. We daydream especially of current concerns and, to a lesser degree, of past concerns. The more emotionally important a concern is, the more likely we are to daydream about it at the time.

A number of distinct daydreaming styles have been identified in daydreaming research. One classification divides people into (1) basically happy daydreamers, (2) unpleasant or anxious daydreamers, whose daydreams include a lot of guilt, depression and fear of failure, and (3) erratic or distractible daydreamers, whose daydreams are unfettered, ranging rapidly over many areas. Not surprisingly, the studies tend to show that daydreaming styles are related closely to results on personality tests of many kinds so that persons who are "happy daydreamers" tend to be people who score "happy" on various tests.

Can daydreams be distinguished from dreams? The very word, daydream, suggests that we all see some sort of connection. A daydream is a dream we have while awake. In fact, this is a very important question, because although we started off above thinking of daydreams as something occurring in the waking mind or as the most unconstrained state possible during waking, it may be that what happens during waking is not so different from what happens during sleep.

I was personally struck by this in one of my previous studies of nightmares. In a series of long interviews with people who had a great many nightmares at night, I realized that a number of them also talked about "daymares"—daydreams that developed in a frightening direction, went out of the subject's control, and became increasingly frightening until the subject "woke up" or snapped out of it. This made me realize that conscious control, which we often use to distinguish our waking life from our dreaming life, is not an absolute, and at least for some people daydreams take on lives of their own and are, at least temporarily, out of the dreamer's control.

Along these lines, it can be useful to think of all mental activity along a continuum, from focused waking activity at one end to dreaming at the other. The continuum would run from focused waking activity, such as doing an arithmetic problem or figuring out where to run to catch a frisbee, to the somewhat looser thinking that characterizes much of our lives, then to clear-cut daydreaming or reverie, and finally to dreaming at the other end. This continuum has a number of strands. In terms of material dealt with, focused waking activity deals with perceptional material and with imposed tasks. As we go further toward dreaming, these drop out and the material dealt with is chiefly memory. In terms of style or content, the focused waking end, at least for many people, involves simple perception or thought without definite evoked imagery (though some people are never without imagery). Then moving along the continuum imagery (especially visual imagery) becomes more and more prominent. In terms of how material is handled, we can think of the left hand end as a serial processing, moving from A to B to C to D in a straight line, whereas the right hand end involves more parallel processing. For those who think in terms of connectionist nets, on the left end of the continuum the mind acts as a "feed-forward net," and toward the right end, more of an "auto-associative net." The role of emotion, too, is important. Our emotions always influence our lives, but they have least influence on our focused waking thoughts, and an increasing influence as we move toward daydreams and dreams.

Among the studies that support the continuum point of view is a study showing that the longer subjects spend in a state of quiet relaxed sensory isolation (usually a dimly lit room or something that imposes a grey field over their vision), the more dreamlike their mental activity becomes, so that when people are in such situations for 15–30 minutes or more, what they report experiencing is very like a dream.

We recently performed a study in which students simply wrote down the most recent dream and the most recent daydream they could remember. The dreams and daydreams were then scored on a number of well-known scales by scorers blind as to condition. It was found that there was considerable overlap in the sense that the daydreams of some students were just as "dreamlike" and "bizarre" as the night dreams of other students, or more so, and this was in fact related to the personality of the student. When the students were divided into those with "thick boundaries" (solid, definite, keeping everything separate, thinking in black and white) and those with "thin boundaries" (allowing more merging, looseness, thinking in shades of grey), it turned out that both the dreams and daydreams of those with thin boundaries were considerably more dreamlike and bizarre than those with thick boundaries, and overall the daydreams of students with thin boundaries were scored on the average just as dreamlike and bizarre as the night dreams of students with thick boundaries.

Thus, in terms of our continuum from focused waking at one end to daydreaming and finally dreaming at the other end, we note that some people naturally function more at one end, and some more at the other. This may be important in overall studies of mental functioning, since it recently has become clear that night dreams do not always occur during REM sleep. REM sleep is the ideal place to find typical night dreams. Such dreams are sometimes reported from non-REM sleep, quite often from sleep onset, and from special conditions such as always preceding epileptic seizures. Neuropsychological studies suggest that there are certain areas in the cortex and other portions of the forebrain that are necessary for dreaming to occur and that REM sleep is just one way—certainly the most common way—to activate these forebrain regions. This may be relevant to daydreaming since, among the large numbers of patients studied who have brain lesions producing cessation of dreaming, most also note a cessation or paucity of daydreaming. These studies strongly suggest that daydreaming will probably turn out to involve activation of the same regions in the forebrain or very similar regions as those activated in dreaming.

I hope the above discussion makes it clear that daydreaming is part of our normal mental activities. There is nothing pathological about daydreaming per se. Nevertheless, excessive daydreaming—very hard to define—is sometimes considered a symptom of disorders such as Attention-Deficit/Hyperactivity Disorder (ADHD) and other conditions. I suggest that the problem is not daydreaming itself, but rather the deficit in attention mechanisms.

Finally, we can ask briefly whether daydreaming has a function. We cannot provide a definite answer, of course, since at this point we do not know with any certainty the functions of dreaming or even of sleep. However, it seems clear that something we spend as much time doing as daydreaming probably has some adaptive use. Thinking phylogenetically, the function may have been simply the increased success in food gathering, hunting, and so on in someone who is able to imagine possible results and to foresee possible futures. More generally, daydreaming or imagination, in the sense of developing new ideas or new possibilities, is obviously useful for the preservation of the species. In this sense, daydreaming clearly plays a part in creativity, and creativity has adaptive uses.

Ernest Hartmann
Director, Sleep Disorders Center, Newton-Wellesley Hospital, Newton, MA

DEAFNESS AND HEARING LOSS

Estimates of the prevalence of hearing loss vary widely within and across countries. As one indicator, 23 million Americans (almost 10% of the population) have significant, chronic hearing losses, and 1.5 million are deaf in both ears.

Variation in the degree of hearing loss, age of hearing loss onset, and the etiologies of the losses influence the way and extent to which deafness affects psychological functioning.

Hearing losses are categorized as *conductive,* involving the middle ear; *sensorineural,* involving the inner ear and auditory nerve; or *central,* involving auditory centers of the brain. Speech perception (which directly relates to ability to interact with others, learn a spoken language, and succeed in school) is most affected by losses at frequencies 500 hertz (Hz), 1,000 Hz, and 2,000 Hz. Etiologies of hearing loss range from hereditary losses to adventitious losses that are associated with birth complications, illness, and accidents. Adventitious losses may be accompanied by damage to other sensory systems or related neurological effects. Statistics concerning the academic success of deaf children, literacy rates, intelligence, and so on thus are based on heterogeneous samples and do not purely reflect consequences of deafness. Similarly, lack of early language exposure, social interaction, and experiential diversity can affect development, but studies involving deaf children of deaf parents reveal them to be indirect effects and not a function of hearing loss per se.

The terms *deaf* and *hard of hearing* refer not only to quantitative descriptions of hearing loss but also to cultural identity. Audiologically, hearing losses from 26 to 40 decibels (dB) in the better ear are categorized as *mild,* those from 41 to 55 dB as *moderate,* from 56 to 70 dB as *moderately severe,* from 71 to 90 dB as *severe,* and losses greater than 90 dB in the better ear are categorized as *profound.* Whatever the quantitative loss, individuals may consider themselves members of the Deaf community, depending on the degree to which they identify with members and institutions in that community and whether they prefer to use signed or spoken language. Most countries have such communities, although their visibility varies.

Over 95% of deaf children have hearing parents, a situation that significantly influences language, social, and cognitive development. Deaf children of deaf parents reach developmental milestones at rates similar to hearing peers. They also exhibit the same patterns of language acquisition (e.g., errors such as overgeneralizations and pronoun reversals) as hearing children of hearing-parents peers and even have some advantages (e.g., in vocabulary size, through the one-word stage). Many deaf children of hearing parents, in contrast, show delays in various domains, particularly language and literacy. Developing a sense of identity and self-esteem may be especially challenging as many deaf children do not have exposure to deaf peers or deaf adults.

Hearing mothers tend toward overcontrol of their deaf children, but patterns of mother-child attachment generally are similar in deaf and hearing dyads. The quality of hearing parent–deaf child interactions is strongly related to effective communication, often accomplished through sign language. Natural sign languages such as American Sign Language (ASL), British Sign Language (BSL), or Italian Sign Language (LIS) are as difficult for parents to learn as any foreign language, but for children with greater hearing losses, they generally are more successful than either spoken language or the various forms of signing based on the vernacular (e.g., Signed English, Signed Mandarin).

Through the early twentieth century, psychologists believed that severe hearing loss predisposed individuals to psychopathology and intellectual inferiority. In fact, distributions in both mental health and intellectual domains are largely comparable for deaf and hearing populations. While some reports suggest that the prevalence and severity of mental illness among deaf people are greater than in the general population, that situation appears largely due to the lack of mental health services for deaf individuals and poor communication between health personnel and deaf clients. Recent studies suggest that less than 2% of deaf individuals who need mental health treatment receive it, a problem particularly acute for deaf individuals from ethnic minorities. Deaf children are still often misdiagnosed as mentally retarded due to communication barriers.

Contrary to assumptions about *sensory compensation,* hearing loss generally does not result in superior visual processing abilities. Among deaf children and adults who use natural sign languages, however, significant visual processing advantages are seen in domains such as mental rotation, face recognition, visual attention, and image generation. These differences appear to be direct results of various aspects of sign language use (i.e., deaf people who use spoken language do not exhibit them). There is also a more general enhanced sensitivity to visual signals in the periphery—evidenced in both behavioral and neurological assessments—a result of reliance on visual rather than auditory stimuli in the environment.

Early research indicated that deaf people had shorter memory spans than hearing people, a result that reinforced assumptions about intellectual deficiency. Recent research has revealed those results to result not from underlying capacity differences, but to the fact that signs consume more space in the limited-capacity working memory system (the phonological loop) relative to spoken words, a finding with parallels across spoken languages that vary in their pronunciation times for digits and words. Still, deaf individuals tend to remember less than hearing individuals in a variety of memory paradigms. In part, such results reflect more heterogeneous and less well-interconnected conceptual information in semantic memory on the part of deaf individuals, despite considerable overlap in the organizational structure of their knowledge. Deaf adults and children are also less likely to apply conceptual knowledge in various tasks, due to either their educational histories (and lower expectations of parents and teachers) or to differences in their strategic approaches to problem solving. Tasks that require relational processing or the simultaneous consideration of multiple dimensions of a stimulus appear particularly problematic, a result that has general implications for learning and psychological functioning.

Deaf children's educational success depends on early language exposure and effective communication with parents. Early exposure to sign language appears to lead to linguistic and cognitive advantages, but acquisition of literacy skills remains a significant challenge to deaf individuals. Many deaf people acquire mental representations functionally equivalent to the phonological codes that underlie reading in hearing individuals, and literacy subskills such as spelling often approach hearing norms. Nevertheless, vocabulary, grammar, and other components of reading and writing in the vernacular remain difficult for deaf children to acquire, even when they are skilled in sign language. Thus far, neither the provision of vernacular-based sign systems nor bilingual programs that involve both spoken and sign language have proven effective in significantly enhancing literacy rates among deaf individuals, and the median reading level for deaf 18-year-olds in the United States remains comparable to that of hearing 9-year-olds.

Marc Marschark
National Technical Institute for the Deaf, Rochester, New York
University of Aberdeen

John A. Albertini
National Technical Institute for the Deaf, Rochester, New York

DEATH, LOSS, AND TRAUMA

Major Loss as a Unifying Construct

This article will provide a brief survey of the fields of work on death, loss, and trauma. The field of death and dying focuses almost exclusively on the dying process and various aspects of death. The field of loss and trauma is broader, encompassing both death and various types of major loss events, including dissolution of close relationships, loss of health, loss of possessions, violation of self as in rape, and losses occurring in traumatic events. Traumatic events are those that inflict major loss, frequently involving violence and multiple deaths.

The idea of experiencing a major loss is common to these literatures and integrates a variety of death and loss and trauma concepts and findings. A major loss may be defined as a reduction in resources in which the person is emotionally invested. As an example of this synthesis, bereavement and adaptation often are conceived as involving steps common to death and other forms of major loss. Such steps include emotional and cognitive processing of the event and its implications and development of an understanding of the event. This understanding may involve an account of the nature of the losses, why the event happened, and perceived consequences. Adaptation usually occurs when people are able to express their feelings about the loss, as by talking or writing about it. An important part of the adaptive process may be finding a confidant who will listen and be there as the individual tells her or his story of loss.

Death and Grief

Death and major loss in general usually result in the process of bereavement or grieving. *Grief* is defined as a person's emotional reaction to the event of loss, and as a process of realization, of making real inside the self an event that has already occurred in reality outside. The *Diagnostic and Statistical Manual of Mental Disorders* (4th ed.) of the American Psychiatric Association defines bereavement as a psychiatric disorder if it includes symptoms characteristic of "a major depressive episode . . . such as insomnia, poor appetite, and weight loss . . ." that last at least 2 months after the loss. As C. S. Lewis suggested in his 1961 book *A Grief Observed,* grief is a type of experience that most people anticipate with dread. Lewis himself died within two years of the death of his wife Joy, and it is believed that Lewis's profound grief hastened his death. In principle, however, grief is an adaptive reaction and essential to recovery. Scholars have argued that grief instinctively occurs and is focused on resolution and adaptation. When the degree of intense grieving is quite prolonged and interferes with normal functioning, the grieving person is conceived to be experiencing chronic grief.

As many scholars have noted, different types of loss and resulting grief directly affect the length and depth of the grieving experience. A distinction between *high-grief* deaths versus *low-grief* deaths often is made. A high-grief death is characterized by intense emotional and physical reactions to loss. A low-grief death is less affecting emotionally, and the bereaved is able to cope more readily. The death of a child would be the classic high-grief death. The death of a person who had reached a quite advanced age and who had lived a long and fulfilling life would be a low-grief death.

One view of grief is that it can be the prelude to positive developments in a survivor's life. In C. S. Lewis's book on grief, he wrote, "Still, there are enormous gains" (p. 49). It has been recognized that a key activity of grieving is a search for meaning that leads to insights, glimmers of understanding, and the learning of principles that help us clarify our philosophy of living and provide a more mature view of oneself and other people.

Adaptation may differ according to type of major loss. Death of a loved one is irrevocable. Nonetheless, the grieving person may continue to feel guilt, anger, and a sense of unfinished business in adapting to the loss. Loss of close relationships, as in divorce, may also elicit these responses. However, there is the possibility that the grieving person may continue to interact with the lost other, thus providing an opportunity to work on emotions such as guilt and anger. Some types of loss, including those associated with aging and prejudice, may be subtle, leading to a feeling of disenfranchised grief. The loss connected with this type of grief is not appreciated very well by others, and there may be little support available to the individual experiencing such grief.

Trauma

Trauma is a specific term referring to unusual psychological and physiological reactions to major losses, such as the death of close others. Traumatic reactions may be so severe as to constitute Posttraumatic Stress Disorder (PTSD), which is a particular diagnostic category in psychology and psychiatry. The field that now is called traumatology began with an ancient Egyptian physician's reports of hysterical reactions that were published in 1900 B.C. in *Kunyus Papyrus* (quoted in Figley, 1993, p. 3) and that became one of the first medical texts. Traumatology may be defined as the investigation and application of knowledge about the immediate and long-term psychosocial consequences of highly stressful events and the factors that affect those consequences. This field evolved mainly within the last 2 decades, with foci both on research and therapy and application. The onslaught of studies of PTSD after the Vietnam War was a major factor in contributing to development and refinements of this field.

Conclusion

Major loss is a broad construct that helps connect the findings and ideas of literatures on different types of loss (including divorce), death, and trauma. Death and dying and traumatology are large, growing fields. With events such as the terrorism of September 11, 2001, dominating public attention in the early twenty-first century, these fields are likely to grow and become even more prominent in years to come.

REFERENCE

Figley, C. R. (1978). Introduction. In C. R. Figley (Ed.), *Disorders among Vietnam veterans: Theory, research, and treatment* (pp. 3–10). New York: Bruner/Mazel.

John H. Harvey
University of Iowa, Iowa City

DECEPTION

Deception refers to inducing a false belief in another. Although it is often successful and rewarded when undetected, targets are often subject to the influences of deception even when they know the message may be faked. False praise and adoration, as well as concealment of dislike and loathing, allow smooth interaction with others—a social lubricant. Many who distort do not consider themselves to be faking. The remainder of this paper concerns deliberate deception and its attempted measurement by psychologists in clinical and forensic contexts.

Deception can occur anywhere within the context of the psychological evaluation. The two temporal foci of distortion are the times of the evaluation and of a previous relevant event. This means that deception for the present (i.e., the time of the evaluation) may be quite different from that presented for the past (e.g., clinical, criminal, or civil event). Patients sometimes deceive to get into treatment and deny psychopathology in order to leave it. Criminal defendants may fake insanity to avoid prison and minimize deficiencies to obtain release into the community.

Simple response styles are used occasionally by the faker, for example, denying or fabricating everything possible. Usually, however, mixed response styles are used, whereby people lie selectively in different ways about different things. An individual will sometimes change styles within one evaluation session, for example, from denying problems to honest responding as fatigue increases. This makes the assessment of deception more difficult, but not impossible, for the rigorous evaluator.

Evaluation for Deception

The purposes of a deception analysis within a psychological evaluation are as follows:

1. To examine the reliability and validity of database information
2. To detect the possible existence of misrepresentation
3. To determine the response style(s) utilized by the evaluatee
4. To determine the magnitude of deception
5. To place symptoms, behaviors, or mental conditions associated with deception into clear perspective
6. To generate hypotheses for further evaluation/investigation
7. To communicate the decision path and the findings to the referral source
8. To eventually standardize the deception analysis process

In the clinical area, applications include assessment of (1) who to select for treatment, (2) readiness for discharge, (3) treatment motivation, (4) transference and countertransference, and (5) honesty of collaterals. In forensic applications, there is a wide relevance. Within the criminal area, these include (1) identification of perpetrators, (2) competency to proceed, (3) criminal responsibility, (4) violence prediction, and (5) community monitoring of treatment after release. In the civil area, applications include evaluation for: (1) competency, (2) witness credibility, (3) child custody and divorce actions, (4) personal injury and wrongful death, and (5) employment screening and dishonesty.

Professional Misconceptions Regarding Deception

Throughout the history of the mental health-law disciplines, misbeliefs about deception include the following:

Most spoken words and behavior can be taken literally. Many mental-health professionals believe that deception does not occur in their evaluations. The frequency of deception in clinical settings and situations is unknown, but assumed to be high. In forensic settings, Malingering has been confirmed or suspected in more than 20% of criminal defendants, with another 5% showing substantial unintentional distortion. The deception rates for litigants in civil actions may be even higher.

The evaluator cannot be fooled (other people can). In general, mental-health professionals are not good at detecting faking. Worse yet, an inverse relationship is suggested: The greater the confidence, the lower the accuracy in detecting faking.

Deception, when it does occur, means that the faker is mentally sick. Desperate people often resort to desperate measures to survive or adapt. A person who fakes insanity is not necessarily mentally ill, but may want to avoid prison, an aversive stimulus environment under the best of conditions.

The current DSM *allows for deception analysis.* The last three *DSMs* state that Malingering should be suspected if (1) there is a forensic context to the evaluation, (2) a discrepancy between reported disability and objective findings exists, (3) there is lack of cooperation, or (4) the patient has an Antisocial Personality Disorder.

These criteria for detecting malingering are too limited, failing to take into account different styles of deception (of which Malingering is only one), extant methods of detection, and other population groups who fake. An explicit disclaimer to the use of the mental diagnoses in forensic contexts is presented in the *DSM.*

Some conditions, such as Amnesia, hallucinations, and posttrauma reactions, are easily faked and nearly impossible to prove. Faked Amnesia has been detected with promising degrees of accuracy, hovering at about 75%–85% accuracy. Other conditions can be scrutinized for deception. Claimed hallucinations are hard to disprove, yet base rates for comparison and decision criteria are available to assist the evaluator. Posttraumatic Stress Disorder (PTSD) can be assessed by psychometrics or arousal methods with built-in features to assess deception.

Detecting faking is an art and cannot be taught. The reverse appears to be true. Following a few simple rules increases the accuracy rate substantially above chance. Deception analysis is a trainable skill. The average mental health professional of any culture can be taught to adequately detect faking in a relatively short period of time.

Near absolute accuracy of detecting faking can never be achieved. It is a dangerous untruth to believe that near absolute accuracy of detecting faking can never be achieved. Recent technologies, such as DNA fingerprinting and P300 wave analysis, are nearly 100% accurate. The latter method is based on brain waves associated with stimulus familiarity rather than arousal, in contrast to methods with lower accuracy such as polygraphy, voice stress analysis, and penile plethysmography.

Psychologists face a moral dilemma much like those in the physical sciences in their development of harmful technologies. There appears to be an increased acceptance of deception as a means of exploiting others on the parts of both institutions and individuals. This issue of "too little" versus "too much" accuracy in detecting deception suggests a balancing of ethics versus efficacy. Whether the resolution of moral issues outweighs the benefits of continued technological improvements in deception analysis is a value judgment regarding the rights of the target individuals versus the needs and security issues of the larger community.

Harold V. Hall
Pacific Institute for the Study of Conflict and Aggression, Kamuela, Hawaii

DECLARATIVE MEMORY

Declarative memory involves representations of facts and events that are subject to conscious recollection, verbal reflection, and explicit expression. Sometimes also called explicit memory, declarative memory is contrasted with procedural, implicit, or (simply) nondeclarative memory. The distinguishing features of declarative memory involve a combination of two major features. One of these features is its mode of expression, which is characterized by the ability to bring facts and experiences to mind, that is, the ability to consciously recall items in memory. The second feature involves the ability to express a recalled memory in a variety of ways, most prominently by verbal reflection on a learned fact or past experience, but also by using the memory to answer a variety of questions or solve any of a variety of problems. By contrast, nondeclarative memory is characterized by its inaccessibility to conscious recall and by expression only through implicit measures of performance, typically increases in the speed or shift in choice bias during repetition of a mental procedure (Eichenbaum & Cohen, 2001). Although several dichotomies of human memory have been proposed, most are consensual in these properties that distinguish a conscious, declarative memory from forms of unconscious memory. Finally, declarative memory is sometimes divided into two subtypes—episodic memory for specific autobiographical experiences and semantic memory for general world knowledge.

Conscious and explicit memory can be dissociated from other types of memory expression in normal human subjects (Richardson-Klavehn & Bjork, 1988; Metcalfe, Mencl, & Cottrell, 1994; Schacter, 1987) and in amnesia (e.g., Corkin, 1984; Butters & Delis, 1995; Squire, Knowlton, & Musen, 1993), leading several investigators to propose that declarative memory is a distinct form of memory. Studies on normal subjects have shown that manipulation of memory testing demands can differentially affect performance on declarative and nondeclarative memory. For example, study instructions that emphasize semantic processing over superficial phonemic processing of verbal material differentially improve success in declarative but not in nondeclarative memory, even for the same materials. In addition, manipulation of the retention interval and exposure to interfering information can differentially affect declarative memory as compared to nondeclarative memory performance. Conversely, changes in the modality of learning materials from initial exposure to memory testing, for example, by a change in the typeface of printed words or by a shift from auditory to visual presentation, can affect nondeclarative memory performance, whereas these manipulations have little affect on declarative memory. Yet other studies have dissociated declarative memory from nondeclarative memory by demonstrating stochastic independence, that is, lack of statistical correlation, between performance success in typical declarative and implicit expression of memory for the same items.

Studies on human Amnesia have also revealed numerous dissociations between performance in declarative and nondeclarative memory. In particular a profound impairment in declarative memory, but not nondeclarative memory, results from damage to the medial temporal lobe region. For example, following removal of most of the hippocampal formation and its associated medial temporal lobe structures, the famous patient H. M. suffered a profound impairment in recall and recognition that was remarkable in its severity, pervasiveness, and selectivity. H. M.'s memory was severely impaired regardless of the form of the learning materials or modality of their presentation. Yet, even the early observations on H. M. indicated that the hippocampal region was important to only some aspects of memory and spared other aspects of memory performance. With regard to the distinction between declarative and nondeclarative memory, the range of spared learning capacities in Amnesia includes motor, perceptual, and cognitive skills; sensory adaptations; and priming of perceptual and lexical stimuli. Even learning involving the identical materials may be either severely impaired or fully spared in H. M. and other amnesic subjects, depending on whether they were asked to use conscious recollection to recall or recognize the study phase, as is typical in most memory tasks, or whether memory was assessed by more subtle measures such as changes in response bias or speed after exposure to the test materials (for review, see Eichenbaum & Cohen, 2001).

We are only beginning to understand the structure of declarative memory and its neurobiological mechanisms. Some success in this understanding has come from the development of animal models of declarative memory, where behavioral, anatomical, and neurophysiological manipulations and measures can be pursued at a level of selectivity and resolution not possible in human subjects. In particular, recent studies in rodents have shown that damage to the hippocampus or its connections results in memory impairments that are severe in degree, pervasive in scope, and selective in the nature of the memory deficit, similar to observations on human Amnesia (Eichenbaum, 2000). Furthermore, these studies have offered insights into the nature of the cognitive mechanisms that underlie declarative memory. Thus, animals with hippocampal region damage are impaired at a variety of spatial, olfactory, and other learning tasks, but the memory impairment depends on the testing demands and on the type of memory expression, as it does in humans. Impairments are observed when subjects are required to combine and relate multiple independent experiences obtained across distinct events and then to express their memory flexibly by inferential use of information acquired in a situation different from that original learning.

For example, rats with hippocampal damage can learn to localize an important place in an environment when they are allowed to navigate directly to a particular complex of spatial cues. However, unlike normal rats, rats with hippocampal damage are impaired when they must learn to combine and relate spatial information obtained across different experiences, viewing the environment from different perspectives, or when they must express their knowledge of the relevant location from a new perspective. Similarly, rats with hippocampal damage can acquire responses to each of a set of particular odors. However, unlike normal rats, rats with hippocampal damage cannot acquire and inferentially express indirect relations among odor memories learned in separate episodes. These qualities of hippocampal dependent memory in animals bear similarity with William James's (1890/1918) characterization of conscious memory as involving numerous diverse connections among individual memories, allowing memories to be retrieved via many routes. Such a characterization suggests that the fundamental basis of declarative memory involves the networking of memories acquired across distinct episodes and the consequent capacity to surf such a memory network to retrieve and express memories in a flexible way.

REFERENCES

Butters, N., & Delis, D.C. (1995). Clinical assessment of memory disorders in amnesia and dementia. *Annual Review of Psychology, 46,* 493–523.

Corkin, S. (1984). Lasting consequences of bilateral medial temporal lobectomy: Clinical course and experimental findings in H. M. *Seminars in Neurology, 4,* 249–259.

Eichenbaum, H. (2000). A cortical-hippocampal system for declarative memory. *Nature Reviews Neuroscience, 1,* 41–50.

Eichenbaum, H., & Cohen, N. J. (2001). *From conditioning to conscious recollection: Memory systems of the brain.* New York: Oxford University Press.

James, W. (1918). *The principles of psychology.* New York: Holt. (Original work published 1890)

Metcalfe, J., Mencl, W. E., & Cottrell, G. W. (1994). Cognitive binding. In D. L. Schacter & E. Tulving (Eds.), *Memory Systems 1994* (pp. 369–394). Cambridge, MA: MIT Press.

Richardson-Klavehn, A., & Bjork, R. A. (1988). Measures of memory. *Annual Review of Psychology, 39,* 475–543.

Schacter, D. L. (1987). Implicit memory: History and current status. *Journal of Experimental Psychology: Learning, Memory, and Cognition, 13,* 501–518.

Squire, L. R., Knowlton, B., & Musen, G. (1993). The structure and organization of memory. *Annual Review of Psychology, 44,* 453–495.

Howard Eichenbaum
Boston University

DEFENSIVE PESSIMISM

Defensive pessimists strategically adopt and benefit from a negative outlook toward upcoming events or performances. Although they acknowledge a history of success in situations such as academic or social settings, they nevertheless enter those situations expecting the worst. Their pessimism is strategic because it serves two major goals: (1) a self-protective goal of helping the person brace for or be buffered from possible negative outcomes, and (2) a motivational goal of inducing increased effort and preparation in order to enhance the prospect of actually doing well. Defensive pessimism is measured using a scale called the Defensive Pessimism Questionnaire (DPQ; Norem & Cantor, 1986b), which has been extended for use in a variety of settings (Spencer & Norem, 1996).

Anticipatory Versus Retrospective Strategies

Defensive pessimists are characterized by anticipatory coping strategies, that is, those used *before* entering a performance setting. A hallmark of defensive pessimism is setting low performance expectations, which serves the self-protective goal. By thinking about how the worst might happen, they may cushion themselves preemptively against potential bad outcomes. If something bad does happen, defensive pessimists are able to think, "I expected it all along," making the outcome seem less deleterious. Convincing themselves that they will do poorly also serves a motivational goal by impelling them to redouble their efforts and preparation to ensure that they actually will do well. This helps to harness the anxiety or negative affect over possible failure (Norem & Cantor, 1986b; Sanna, 1996, 1998, 2000; Showers & Rubin, 1990).

Defensive pessimists' use of anticipatory strategies may appear ironic. First, they are very high performers, and in fact they have usually performed well in the past (Norem & Cantor, 1986b). Setting low performance expectations seems to be at odds with their actual performance histories. Second, convincing themselves that poor performances will happen does not actually make it happen. Low performance expectations are not self-fulfilling because of the buffering and motivational strategies (Norem & Cantor, 1986a).

Defensive pessimism is often contrasted with the strategy of optimism (Sanna, 1996, 2000; Spencer & Norem, 1996). Rather than using defensive pessimists' anticipatory strategies, optimists rely more on retrospective coping strategies, that is, strategies that are used *after* performance outcomes are known. Optimists do not set low expectations before performing as do defensive pessimists, but are more likely instead to engage in cognitive restructuring of performances after the fact (e.g., by using "self-serving attributional biases"; Cantor & Norem, 1989; Showers, 1992), particularly when those outcomes are poor.

Defensive pessimism also differs from true pessimism and depression; true pessimists and depressives do not use their negative outlooks strategically, and their ability to cope does not benefit from negative worldviews (Cantor & Norem, 1989; Showers & Ruben, 1990).

Mental Simulations as Strategies

Particular types of mental simulations appear to be a key part of defensive pessimists' strategies. Mental simulations can differ on the basis of timing (before versus after performance) and direction (better or worse than expected versus actuality; Sanna, 2000).

Defensive pessimists are most likely to use *upward-prefactual* thoughts as part of their preferred strategy (Sanna, 1996, 1998). Prefactuals are mental simulations of what may be. Upward prefactuals, which occur prior to performance, are alternative preoutcome mental simulations that are better than what one expects to actually happen (e.g., "If only I had more study time, I could do better on tomorrow's exam").

By comparison, optimists are likely to use *downward-counterfactual* thoughts as part of their strategies. Counterfactuals are mental simulations of what might have been (Sanna, Stocker, & Clarke, 2003). Downward counterfactual thoughts, which occur after performance, are alternative postoutcome simulations that are worse than actuality (e.g., "At least I bought the study guide, or my grade might have been worse").

In the case of defensive pessimists, low performance expectations function as an anchor from which mental simulations are generated. That is, if one expects the worst (to perform poorly), one's *alternative* simulated possible performance outcome is most likely to be upward, or better than expected. Concomitant with upward simulations is higher anxiety and bad moods (Sanna, 1996, 1998). By comparison, optimists use downward counterfactuals after performing to maintain or restore good moods. In short, defensive pessimists use strategies that lower expectations and increase bad moods before performing, including upward prefactuals, but they do not use many retrospective strategies. Optimists do not use many anticipatory strategies, but employ downward counterfactuals retrospectively to maintain or restore good moods.

Strategy Usage and Effective Coping

Defensive pessimists effectively use their preferred strategies when coping with life events. However, when the use of strategy is unavailable or not possible, performance suffers. There are several examples of this. First, defensive pessimists prefer to think through (Norem & Illingworth, 1993) possible outcomes using such tactics as upward prefactuals. When thinking through alternate outcomes is interfered with by other demands, performance suffers for defensive pessimists, but not for optimists (Norem & Illingworth, 1993; Sanna, 1998; Spencer & Norem, 1996). Second, defensive pessimists' performance and coping are less effective when they are forced to focus on positive possibilities before performing (Sanna, 1996; Showers, 1992), because thinking about bad things is their usual tactic. By comparison, thinking about positive alternatives does not adversely affect optimists (Showers, 1992).

One reason defensive pessimists' strategies can be interfered with is that mental simulations and affect are linked (Sanna, 1996, 1999, 2000). When defensive pessimists are given encouragement and support (Norem & Illingworth, 1993), they ironically perform poorly. Encouragement puts them in good moods and takes them out of their normal strategy of having high anxiety and bad moods. Forcing defensive pessimists to think about good things (Sanna, 1996; Showers, 1992) may analogously put them in good moods and interfere with their usual strategies. However, being forced to think about negative possibilities puts defensive pessimists in bad moods, and they perform well. Directly putting them into bad moods (Sanna, 1998) also seems to improve performances. In short, defensive pessimists cope effectively using moods and mental simulations that facilitate their use of preferred anticipatory strategies.

REFERENCES

Cantor, N., & Norem, J. K. (1989). Defensive pessimism and stress and coping. *Social Cognition, 7,* 92–112.

Norem, J. K., & Cantor, N. (1986a). Anticipatory and post hoc cushioning strategies: Optimism and defensive pessimism in "risky" situations. *Cognitive Therapy and Research, 10,* 347–362.

Norem, J. K., & Cantor, N. (1986b). Defensive pessimism: "Harnessing" anxiety as motivation. *Journal of Personality and Social Psychology, 51,* 1208–1217.

Norem, J. K., & Illingworth, K. S. S. (1993). Strategy-dependent effects of reflecting on self and tasks: Some implications of optimism and defensive pessimism. *Journal of Personality and Social Psychology, 65,* 822–835.

Sanna, L. J. (1996). Defensive pessimism, optimism, and simulating alternatives: Some ups and downs of prefactual and counterfactual thinking. *Journal of Personality and Social Psychology, 71,* 1020–1036.

Sanna, L. J. (1998). Defensive pessimism and optimism: The bittersweet influence of mood on performance and prefactual and counterfactual thinking. *Cognition and Emotion, 12,* 635–665.

Sanna, L. J. (1999). Mental simulations, affect, and subjective confidence: Timing is everything. *Psychological Science, 10,* 339–345.

Sanna, L. J. (2000). Mental simulation, affect, and personality: A conceptual framework. *Current Directions in Psychological Science, 9,* 168–173.

Sanna, L. J., Stocker, S. L., & Clarke, J. A. (2003). Rumination, imagination, and personality: Specters of the past and future in the present. In E. C. Chang & L. J. Sanna (Eds.), *Virtue, vice, and personality: The complexity of behavior* (pp. 105–124). Washington, DC: American Psychological Association.

Showers, C. (1992). The motivational and emotional consequences of considering positive or negative possibilities for an upcoming event. *Journal of Personality and Social Psychology, 63,* 474–484.

Showers, C., & Ruben, C. (1990). Distinguishing defensive pessimism from depression: Negative expectations and positive coping mechanisms. *Cognitive Therapy and Research, 14,* 385–399.

Spencer, S. M., & Norem, J. K. (1996). Reflection and distraction: Defensive pessimism, strategic optimism, and performance. *Personality and Social Psychology Bulletin, 22,* 354–365.

Lawrence J. Sanna
Eulena M. Small
University of North Carolina, Chapel Hill

DEINDIVIDUATION

In his classic book *The Crowd* (1895/1960), French sociologist Gustave Le Bon postulated the concept of a group mind. He suggested that in some circumstances persons lose their individuality and merge into the crowd. Such deindividuation was associated with a loss of inhibitions and a tendency to uncharacteristic and antinormative behavior. From a historical perspective, human beings have only slowly escaped from a deindividuated existence immersed in extended kinship relations, bonds, and tribes. In *Escape From Freedom* (1965) Eric Fromm examined the emergence of individuality in human history and the sense of uniqueness and freedom that accompanied this development. However, according to Fromm, individuation is accompanied by a feeling of isolation that often motivates people to join various groups.

Festinger, Pepitone, and Newcomb (1952) proposed that the person's focus on the group, which is associated with his or her attraction to the group, lessens the attention given to individuals. The focus on the group deindividuates its members, who are submerged and, in a sense, hidden within the group. Deindividuation, therefore, lowers the person's inhibitions toward engaging in counternormative actions. Thus, according to this formulation, attraction to a group increases deindividuation, which in turn encourages behavior that is normally inhibited.

In 1964, Ziller suggested that persons learn to associate individuation with rewarding situations and deindividuation with potentially punishing ones. A person learns to expect rewards for performing certain tasks well and wants to appear uniquely responsible for such actions. On the other hand, whenever the person expects punishment, there will be a tendency to hide or diffuse responsibility by submerging the self into a group. Ziller's emphasis was on the rewards and satisfaction that are gained through self-definition and uniqueness.

In still another version of deindividuation theory, Zimbardo (1969) argued that the expression of normally inhibited behavior may include loving and creative behavior as well as counternormative or negative actions. Furthermore, Zimbardo proposed that a large number of factors may lead to deindividuation, in addition to focus on the group or desire to avoid negative evaluation of moral responsibility. Among the deindividuating factors are anonymity (however created), the size of the group, level of emotional arousal, the novelty or ambiguity of the situation, altered time perspectives (such as during drug or alcohol use), degree of involvement in group activities, and so on.

All these factors lead to a loss of identity or self-consciousness which in turn causes the individual to become unresponsive to inhibiting stimuli and to lose cognitive control over emotions and motivations. As a consequence, the deindividuated person is less compliant to positive or negative sanctions from agents outside the group. Hence, behavior is less apt to conform to external rules and standards.

In 1980 Diener offered a further theoretical modification by associating deindividuation with self-awareness. Deindividuated individuals do not attend to their own behaviors and lack awareness of themselves as distinct entities. The result is a failure to monitor or reflect upon their own behaviors and a failure to retrieve appropriate norms of conduct from storage in long-term memory. Deindividuated persons also lack foresight, and their behavior lacks premeditation or planning. When there is little self-regulation, individuals are more apt to respond to immediate stimuli, emotions, and motives. Thus, their behaviors tend to be impulsive. In Diener's view the term *deindividuation* is a construct describing a set of relationships among situations, cognitive mechanisms, emotional states, and behavioral reactions.

A rather wide scope of antinormative behaviors has been associated with individuation and deindividuation. For example, drug abuse has been associated with social isolation from friends and family. Riots, lynchings, and other forms of mob violence have been attributed to deindividuation. A loss of inhibitions by members of encounter, marathon, and other noncognitive therapy groups has frequently been observed, and this may also be attributed to a loss of self-awareness.

REFERENCES

Diener, E. (1980). Deindividuation: The absence of self-awareness and self-regulation in group members. In P. B. Paulus (Ed.), *Psychology of group influence.* Hillsdale, NJ: Erlbaum.

Festinger, L., Pepitone, A., & Newcomb, T. (1952). Some consequences of deindividuation in a group. *Journal of Abnormal and Social Psychology, 47,* 382–289.

Fromm, E. (1965). *Escape from freedom.* New York: Avon Books.

Le Bon, G. (1960). *The crowd.* New York: Viking. (Original work published 1895)

Ziller, R. C. (1964). Individuation and socialization. *Human Relations, 17,* 341–360.

Zimbardo, P. G. (1969). The human choice: Individuation, reason, and order versus deindividuation, impulse, and chaos. In W. J. Arnold & D. Levine (Eds.), *Nebraska Symposium on Motivation.* Lincoln: University of Nebraska Press.

James T. Tedeschi
University of Illinois, Urbana-Champaign

DELTA RHYTHMS AND ACTIVITY

Electrical activity in the brain varies along qualitative and quantitative dimensions. Differences in the frequency of cortical rhythms have long attracted attention because of their relationships with normal and pathological conditions. This article focuses on delta rhythms and will be divided into three main sections. The biological basis of delta rhythms will be described first, followed by a brief discussion of its role in normal function, and then its involvement in selected neurological and psychiatric conditions.

Biological Bases of Delta Waves

Cortical rhythms, as measured by an electroencephalogram (EEG), largely reflect the algebraic summation of postsynaptic potentials of apical dendrites in cortical neurons. During periods of higher neural activity (e.g., alert

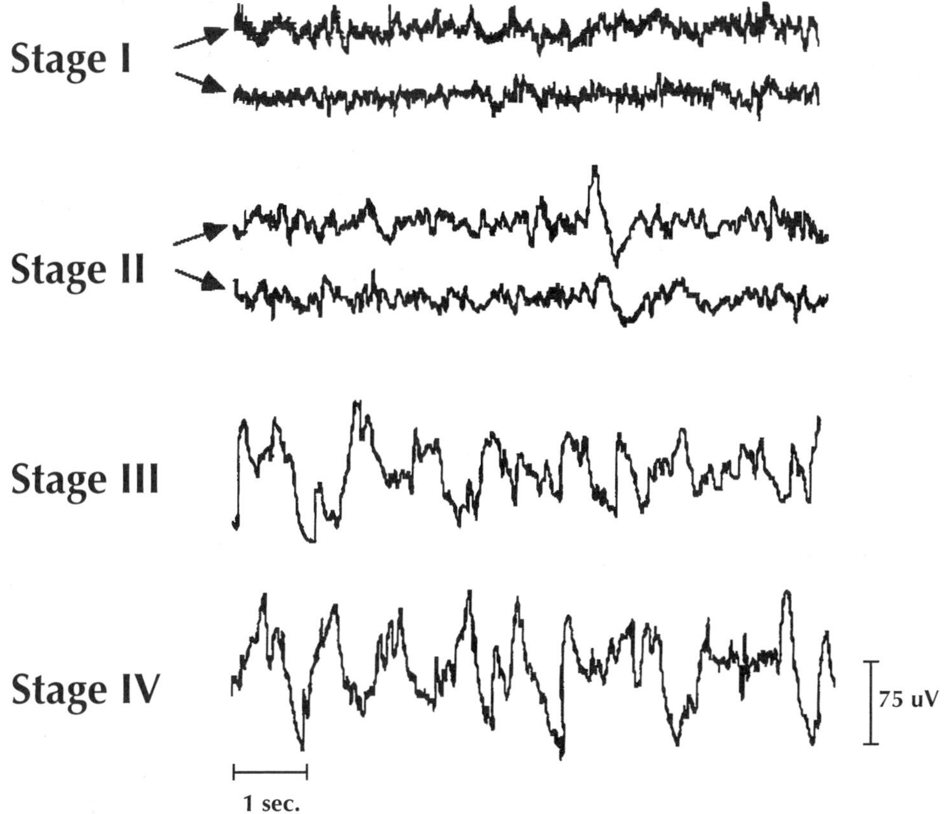

Figure 1. The stages of human sleep.
Note that the amplitudes of the waves increase while their frequencies decrease in the deeper stages (III and IV; noted as 3 and 4 in the text). This reflects reductions in cortical activity. Delta waves are most common in stages III and IV (see text).
Source: Figure courtesy of Dr. Robert Stickgold, Harvard Medical School.

wakefulness), waveforms are relatively heterogeneous and desynchronized from each other. Consequently, waveforms cancel each other out and appear on the EEG with low amplitudes and high frequencies. In periods of lower neural activity (e.g., deep sleep) waveforms are *relatively* more homogeneous and synchronized with each other. This synchrony appears on the EEG with higher amplitudes and lower frequencies. At least three distinct types of delta rhythms have been identified (Amzica & Steriade, 1998), including a slow one (less than 1 Hz) that is generated cortically in large neuronal networks, a second one that is generated in a clocklike fashion by thalamocortical neurons across a broader frequency (1–4 Hz), and a third one that is generated by cortical neurons with intrinsic bursting properties across a broader frequency. These separate rhythms integrate to produce polymorphic delta waves on EEGs in the range of 0.5–4 Hz.

Delta rhythms occur with the greatest intensity during deep sleep in humans (stages 3 and 4, that together is also termed *delta sleep;* see Figure 1) and are relatively localized to the prefrontal cortex (Buchsbaum et al., 1982). For this reason, the functions of delta waves are often linked to those of this region of the brain (Horne, 1993), although it should be stressed that delta waves are not limited to either one part of the brain or to one state of arousal. Recent data in mice show that delta power (i.e., a measure of delta EEG activity) is influenced both by duration of prior wakefulness and by genotype (Franken, Chollet, & Tafti, 2001).

Delta Waves in Normal Functions

Because delta waves occur with the greatest intensity and regularity during deep sleep (an EEG period, or epoch, is typically classified as stage 3 sleep if delta waves comprise at least 20% of the epoch, and it is classified as stage 4 sleep if delta waves comprise at least 50% of the epoch), their function has most often been linked to the function of sleep. The latter is a very complex issue that remains largely unsolved (Rechtschaffen, 1998), although it is likely that the primary benefits of sleep are to the brain (Horne, 1988).

In particular, the value of deep sleep has been related to the restoration of cerebral function, especially in the prefrontal lobes. Studies of sleep deprivation, for example, support this view because associated neuropsychological deficits are similar to those seen in frontal lobe dysfunction (e.g., diminished verbal fluency and intonation, poor planning, poor organization and encoding of new material—especially in regard to solving novel problems, diminished affect, vulnerability to interference and distraction, perceptual distortions, perseverations, and concrete thinking; e.g.,

Harrison & Horne, 1997; Horne, 1988; Kimberg, D'Esposito, & Farah, 1997). Moreover, when subjects are allowed to sleep freely following periods of deprivation (i.e., recovery sleep), most of the lost sleep is not made up, with the exception of deep sleep (and to a lesser extent, rapid eye movement sleep), which is then followed by the return of predeprivation levels of cognitive abilities (e.g., Horne, 1988).

Relationships between delta waves—usually measured in the context of deep sleep—and other biological processes are even less clear than they are in the restorative aspects of sleep. For example (Rechtschaffen, 1998), a variety of substances that stimulate immune responses, such as interferon alpha-2, interleukin-1, and tumor necrosis factor, also stimulate delta sleep (e.g., Krueger, Shoham, & Davenne, 1986), which underlies the hypothesis that immune responses are impaired by the loss of delta sleep and facilitated by its presence. The effects are far from general, however, with little direct evidence to link delta sleep to immune function (e.g., Benca & Quintans, 1997; Rechtschaffen, 1998). Similarly, hypotheses of causal relationships between pain thresholds (notably in fibromyalgia syndrome) and delta sleep remain unconfirmed (Older et al., 1998).

Delta Waves in Pathological Functions

Delta waves are related to pathological functions in at least two ways. The first of these involves the presence of abnormal delta activity. For example, impairments in cortical areas (e.g., due to deafferentation, abnormal development, or necrosis) promote delta waves in regions contiguous to cortical tumors (Amzica & Steriade, 1998), in Down syndrome (which reflects slow and deficient brain development; Kaneko, Phillips, Riley, & Ehlers, 1996), and in cerebrovascular disease (Inui, Motomura, Kaige, & Nomura, 2001). Because these rhythms (during wakefulness) are often related to dysfunction in specific areas, they may facilitate intervention strategies, such as the presurgical localization of temporal lobe (Jan, Sadler, & Rahey, 2001) and extratemporal lobe (primarily frontal; Geyer, Bilir, Faught, Kuzniecky, & Gilliam, 1999) epilepsies.

A second way in which delta activity is related to pathological processes is by its absence or unexpectedly low levels during sleep. This occurs in psychiatric disorders that include, for instance, Schizophrenia and depression. Several studies that augmented visual EEG scoring with automated counts of delta activity showed reduced delta waves in Schizophrenia, especially in the greater than or equal to 1–2 Hz range (Ganguli, Reynolds, & Kupfer, 1987; Keshavan et al., 1998), although not all patients demonstrate the abnormality (e.g., Hoffmann, Hendrickse, Rush, & Armitage, 2000). These findings are interesting in that Schizophrenia provides another example of a disorder that often involves prominent frontal lobe pathology, related neuropsychological deficits (Seidman et al., 1996), and impaired delta activity reductions. Moreover, deficits in delta activity occur in major depression (Benca, Obermeyer, Thisted, & Gillin, 1992; Hoffmann et al., 2000), which may also include frontal lobe dysfunction. Although other, non-delta sleep deficits occur in these disorders as well, these findings raise the possibility that deficits in delta activity during sleep might serve as markers for psychiatric as well as neurological disorders.

REFERENCES

Amzica, F., & Steriade, M. (1998). Electrophysiological correlates of delta waves. *Electroencephalography and Clinical Neurophysiology, 107,* 69–83.

Benca, R. M., Obermeyer, W. H., Thisted, R. A., & Gillin, J. C. (1992). Sleep and psychiatric disorders. *Archives of General Psychiatry, 49,* 661–668.

Benca, R. M., & Quintans, J. (1997). Sleep and host defenses: A review. *Sleep, 20,* 1027–1037.

Buchsbaum, M. S., Mendelson, W. B., Duncan, W. C., Coppola, R., Kelsoe, J., & Gillin, J. C. (1982). Topographical cortical mapping of EEG sleep states during daytime naps in normal subjects. *Sleep, 5,* 248–255.

Franken, P., Chollet, D., & Tafti, M. (2001). The homeostatic regulation of sleep need is under genetic control. *Journal of Neuroscience, 21,* 2610–2621.

Ganguli, R., Reynolds, C. F., & Kupfer, D. J. (1987). Electroencephalographic sleep in young, never-medicated schizophrenics. *Archives of General Psychiatry, 44,* 36–44.

Geyer, J. D., Bilir, E., Faught, R. E., Kuzniecky, R., & Gilliam, F. (1999). Significance of interictal temporal lobe delta activity for localization of the primary epileptogenic region. *Neurology, 52,* 202–205.

Harrison, Y., & Horne, J. A. (1997). Sleep deprivation affects speech. *Sleep, 10,* 871–877.

Hoffmann, R., Hendrickse, W., Rush, A. J., & Armitage, R. (2000). Slow-wave activity during non-REM sleep in men with Schizophrenia and Major Depressive Disorders. *Psychiatry Research, 95,* 215–225.

Horne, J. A. (1988). *Why we sleep: The functions of sleep in humans and other mammals.* Oxford, UK: Oxford University Press.

Horne, J. A. (1993). Human sleep, sleep loss and behavior: Implications for the prefrontal cortex and psychiatric behavior. *British Journal of Psychiatry, 162,* 413–419.

Inui, K., Motomora, E., Kaige, H., & Nomura, S. (2001). Temporal slow waves and cerebrovascular diseases. *Psychiatry and Clinical Neurosciences, 55,* 525–531.

Jan, M. M., Sadler, M., & Rahey, S. R. (2001). Lateralized post-ictal EEG delta predicts the side of seizure surgery in temporal lobe epilepsy. *Epilepsia, 42,* 402–405.

Kaneko, W. M., Phillips, E. L., Riley, E. P., & Ehlers, C. L. (1996). EEG findings in fetal alcohol syndrome and Down's syndrome children. *Electroencephalography and Clinical Neurophysiology, 98,* 20–28.

Keshavan, M. S., Reynolds, C. F., III, Miewald, J. M., Montrose, D. M., Sweeney, J. A., Vasko, R. C., et al. (1998). Delta sleep deficits in Schizophrenia. *Archives of General Psychiatry, 55,* 443–448.

Kimberg, D. Y., D'Esposito, M., & Farah, M. J. (1997). Frontal lobes: Cognitive neuropsychological aspects. In T. E. Feinberg

& M. J. Farah (Eds.), *Behavioral neurology and neuropsychology* (pp. 409–418). New York: McGraw-Hill.

Krueger, J. M., Shoham, S., & Davenne, D. (1986). Immune modulators as promoters of slow wave sleep. *Clinical Neuropharmacology, 9*(Suppl. 4), 462–464.

Older, S. A., Battafarano, D. F., Danning, C. L., Ward, J. A., Grady, E. P., Derman, S., et al. (1998). The effects of delta wave sleep interruption on pain thresholds and fibromyalgia-like symptoms in healthy subjects: Correlations with insulin-like growth factor I. *The Journal of Rheumatology, 25,* 1180–1186.

Rechtschaffen, A. (1998). Current perspectives on the function of sleep. *Perspectives in Biology and Medicine, 41,* 359–390.

Seidman, L. J., Oscar-Berman, M., Kalinowski, A. G., Ajilore, O., Kremen, W. S., Faraone, S. V., et al. (1996). Neuropsychological measures of prefrontal dysfunction in Schizophrenia. *Biological Psychiatry, 39,* 578.

William S. Stone
Harvard Medical School

DEPENDENCY

Dependency is the seeking of identity, support, security, or permission from outside the self. The dependency object may be another person; a social unit such as an extended family or a religious or fraternal order; an entity beyond the five senses such as a spirit guardian; or even a belief system in itself, for example, nonviolence, to which the dependent is devoted and from which the dependent receives nurture in return.

By definition, dependency is reciprocal. The dependent seeks, expecting and receiving a dependency response: To give is to receive and to receive is to give. It is also obligatory: Dependents are *expected* to seek and receive return support. Failure to participate in this circle of obligation may result in a range of responses from verbal disapproval to ostracism.

Dependency differs from the related process of interdependence in which separate entities reciprocally seek identity, support, security, or permission from one another.

In "dependency societies," such as Japan, the fledgling ego is taught to defer inside a vertical authority system. The ideal of conformity is intended to strengthen the individual's sense of self-respect. In "independence societies," such as modern mainstream America, the fledgling ego is expected to move out of obligatory relationships in a horizontal authority system, rather than to defer. The ideal of self-focus is intended to strengthen the individual's sense of self-respect.

Key characteristics of dependency are bonding, obligation, reciprocity, trust, continuity, and involvement. Every culture or subculture defines "normal" dependency on the basis of its own value system.

Whereas Western thought minimizes continuity between the living and ancestors, dependency cultures tend to consider discontinuity as threatening.

Even though there are cultural variations, there seem also to be certain universals in dependency. Key characteristics fall into three clusters.

The first cluster may be viewed as negative dependency, which hinders psychosexual development, crippling the ability to handle a variety of life situations. The second cluster can be considered positive, enhancing the maturing process by aiding individuals and groups to function in ways that support their sense of well being. The third cluster relates to an absence or termination of dependency relationships, which may also cripple development.

It is useful to divide dependency theory into three culture-time phases: (1) preliterate, tribal, and folk (beginning to present), (2) modern colonial (1500–1945), and (3) post-colonial (1945 to present).

Preliterate, Tribal, and Folk Studies

Early ethnological studies tended to view dependency as structural networking based on tribal, village, folk, and extended family patterns that were seen, on the whole, as positive. They were thought to reflect security and other needs in a life setting severely limited by a prescientific world-view and technical development.

In such a society individuals define themselves or are defined as they relate to others, rather than by how they fulfill or express themselves. Success in these interactions is considered the most important measure of mature self-expression.

Modern Colonial

The interruption of traditional dependency patterns has been a major and often underestimated effect of colonial contact since the fifteenth century. As Mannoni has shown, a major factor in the conquest of native peoples was their own tendency to transfer dependency expectations from familiar authority figures to European authority substitutes.

Aggressive European cultures exploited native dependency while at the same time exporting values of independence, individualism, and progress, which did as much to weaken native resistance as the horses of Cortez or the firearms of the British. With its emphasis on competition, the Protestant work ethic dealt a heavy psychological blow to traditional notions of reciprocity, obligation, and trust. Under long-term colonization, the native personality is thought to have been severely stressed by the need to reconcile warring dependency-belief systems.

During this same period in the Western world, dependency appears to have been systematically downgraded to neurotic behavior. Sigmund Freud theorized that the helplessness of the infant was the source of lifelong dependency bonds against which the maturing ego must implacably struggle.

Furthermore, Freud held that the psychological structures and functions of societies paralleled those of individuals. In modern thought—strongly influenced by Freudian theory—individuals must struggle to break free from dependence on groups as well as from a variety of others, beginning with Mother. What had earlier been seen as reciprocity came to be regarded as helplessness.

Postcolonial

In the Western world since about 1945, the belief has begun to emerge that undue stress on independence, change, and competition has contributed to massive alienation, anomie, and even morbidity rates. One response has been a trend toward the reinterpretation of dependency, as seen in a variety of recent developments. Carl Rogers, through his work on group dynamics, has encouraged a variety of lay and professional approaches that stress dependency interaction. More recently, "networking" has become a major drive among persons who recognize their need to relate to other individuals, especially in urban settings.

Another dependency development is affiliated families, in which nonblood kin members of two or three generations pool their needs and resources in a common dwelling or at least in the same community.

J. Gurian

See also: **Affiliation Need; Alienation (Political); Bonding and Attachment; Cross-cultural Psychology; Prosocial Behavior**

DEPENDENT VARIABLES

Dependent variable is a term used in research methods and refers to the attribute being measured. In experimental research the dependent variable is what is being assessed to determine the effect of manipulating an independent variable. The dependent variable may involve behavioral, physiological, or social characteristics depending on the nature of the study. It may involve assessment of performance, such as the amount of information a subject might learn as measured by the number of correct responses on a test. A dependent variable is what is being measured to ascertain the effects of some treatment in an investigation or to use as a description of the status of subjects in the study. For example, suppose two methods of math instruction were being compared: the dependent variable might be the number of correct responses on a math test administered after instruction is completed.

The choice of a dependent measure is often given inadequate attention when researchers are designing studies. However, selection of an appropriate dependent variable is very important to the overall strength, outcome, and interpretation of an investigation. A number of matters should be considered in determining the appropriateness of the dependent variable selected.

One obvious concern is that a dependent measure should reflect the construct being studied. If a researcher is investigating anxiety, the dependent variable should relate to the construct of anxiety. A dependent variable should also be both sensitive and reliable in the context of the phenomenon under study. The measure should be sufficiently sensitive to detect accurately behavioral or performance changes when they occur. The dependent measure should be able to reflect such changes in a reliable fashion. Generally, a researcher will select the most sensitive and reliable dependent variable possible. The only circumstance when this rule of thumb is not appropriate is when such a measure is obtrusive, that is, when the act of obtaining the measure alters a subject's behavior. If using a particular measure appears to be obtrusive, another dependent variable may be preferred so that the data obtained are not contaminated. Thus, the measure of choice is one that is maximally sensitive, reliable, and unobtrusive.

Another consideration related to selection of a dependent variable involves avoiding ceiling or floor effects in the data. A ceiling effect occurs when the performance range of the task is limited so that subjects "top out." A floor effect reflects a task so difficult that many subjects cannot perform the task at all. Ceiling and floor effects generate inaccurate results or artifactual data. In circumstances where either ceiling or floor effects exist, the data reflect the limits of the task rather than subjects' ability to perform.

SUGGESTED READING

Drew, C. J., Hardman, M. L., & Hart, A. W. (1996). *Designing and conducting research: Inquiry in education and social science.* Boston: Allyn & Bacon.

Martella, R. C., Nelson, J. R., & Marchand-Martella, N. E. (1999). *Research methods: Learning to become a critical research consumer.* Boston: Allyn & Bacon.

Schloss, P. J., & Smith, M. A. (1999). *Conducting research.* Columbus, OH: Prentice Hall.

Clifford J. Drew
University of Utah

See also: **Reliability; Validity**

DEPRESSION

Description

In the United States, the word *depression* refers to everything from a transient mood state (feeling down) to a clinical disorder, Major Depressive Disorder (MDD). In order to receive a diagnosis of MDD, a person must experience marked distress and a decrease in level of functioning. In addition, the 2 weeks preceding the examination must be characterized by the almost daily occurrence of a dysphoric mood (e.g., sadness) or a loss of interest or pleasure (anhedonia) in almost all activities. The individual must also experience at least four (only three if both dysphoric mood and anhedonia are both present) of the following seven symptoms nearly every day for the 2-week period: significant weight change or change in appetite; Insomnia or Hypersomnia; psychomotor agitation or retardation; fatigue or loss of energy; feelings of worthlessness or excessive or inappropriate guilt; decreased concentration or indecisiveness; and suicidal ideation, plan, or attempt (*Diagnostic and Statistical Manual of the American Psychiatric Association*). Related disorders (i.e., other Mood Disorders) include Bipolar I and II Disorder (manic-depressive disorder), dysthymia, and cyclothymia.

Prevalence and Costs

MDD is the most commonly diagnosed psychiatric disorder among adults, with lifetime prevalence rates of 20–25% for women and 9–12% for men. At any given point in time, the prevalence rates are about 6% for women and 3% for men. MDD is fairly rare among children, but it begins to manifest itself at puberty. Depression has been diagnosed with increased frequency among young people, so that in the current 16-to-25 age group, about 20% have already suffered from a MDD. After late adolescence, the prevalence rates and gender differences are fairly constant over the human life span.

Depression tends to be a cyclical disorder. Among those who have one episode, the probability of a second episode is 50%, and among those with two episodes, the probability of a third episode is 75–80%. After the third episode, the disorder is likely to plague the person on a chronic basis, although episodes of the disorder may come and go even without treatment. The episodes are painful for the individuals with the disorder and those around them. As noted, the disorder interferes with functioning in both social situations and jobs. The costs are enormous to both the individual and society; for example, MDD is regularly rated among the top five most expensive health problems.

Treatments

There are two major approaches to treatment of MDD—biological interventions and psychotherapies. The major biological intervention is antidepressant medications. The first major classification of antidepressants was called *tricyclics* because of the chemical structure of the medicines. Included in this group were such familiar medicines as amitriptyline (Elavil), imipramine (Tofranil), desipramine (Norpramin), and nortriptyline (Pamelor). These medications worked with about 55–65% of patients with MDD, but they have fairly severe side effects, including blurred vision, constipation, and orthostatic hypotension; furthermore, an overdose of these medications is likely to be lethal. Thus, they are currently used less frequently as a first line of treatment. Another class of antidepressant medications is the monoamine oxidase inhibitors (MAO inhibitors); examples include phenelzine (Nardil) and tranylcypromine (Parnate). These medications are as effective as the tricyclics for MDD and probably slightly more effective for a form of the disorder called *atypical depression* (e.g., symptoms of mood reactivity, extreme sensitivity to rejection, extreme fatigue, increased sleep, and weight gain or appetite increase). However, MAO inhibitors necessitate abstinence from several popular foods, so they are not very well tolerated. By far the most popular class of antidepressant medications currently is the selective serotonin reuptake inhibitors (SSRIs), which includes fluoxetine (Prozac), paroxetine (Paxil), sertraline (Zoloft), and citalopram (Celexa). These medications work with 60–70% of individuals with the disorder, and the side effects are *relatively* minor. However, one major drawback to the SSRIs is their fairly frequent side effect of inhibiting orgasm. There are several other less frequently utilized antidepressants, which do not fall into one of the preceding classes. One of those is buproprion (Wellbutrin), which may not be quite as effective as some of the other antidepressants, but it does have the advantage of facilitating sexual performance in some patients. For extremely difficult to treat depressions, electric convulsant therapy (ECT) and transcranial magnetic stimulation (TMS) may be employed. The latter therapies work very well, but there are fairly severe side effects, and the rates of relapse following the treatments are fairly high.

There are innumerable psychotherapies, but there are two that have been fairly extensively evaluated as treatments for MDD. Both of these therapies are short-term (16–20 sessions), conducted over a period of 12–16 weeks. Both therapies focus on current life problems and are fairly directive (i.e., the therapist takes an active role in identifying and suggesting possible solutions to problems). The first of these is interpersonal psychotherapy (IPT). This therapy was designed to address interpersonal difficulties associated with MDD and focuses on one or more interpersonal problems. The topics of therapy include life transitions, losses, lack of social skills, and role conflicts.

The second effective psychotherapy for MDD is cognitive-behavioral therapy (CBT). This therapy focuses on the behavioral deficiencies (e.g., a lack of social skills) and cognitive styles (e.g., the belief that the depressed person causes bad things to happen, has always caused bad things to happen, and causes bad things to happen in many areas of his or her life) associated with MDD. With outpatients suffering from MDD, IPT and CBT are about equally effective.

Each is about as effective as antidepressant medications for mild to moderate depressions. Current studies are under way to determine if these psychotherapies are as effective as the antidepressant medications for more severe depressions. The limited available data suggest that a combination of antidepressant medications and one of these psychotherapies is both the most effective and the most enduring treatment for MDD.

Pharmacological interventions with children with MDD have been very disappointing; however, recent work has shown that fluoxetine (Prozac) is effective with adolescents who are age 15 or older. CBT has been used in small-sample studies with children, and it seems to be reasonably effective. CBT has been implemented in both the school and family settings.

At least two large research projects have suggested that behavioral marital therapy is an effective treatment for MDD when the depressed person is a partner in an unhappy marriage. It has been found that 50% of married depressed individuals are in unhappy marriages and that 50% of individuals in unhappy marriages are depressed. Thus, behavioral marital therapy may be useful to many married patients suffering from MDD.

One of the problems that has plagued the treatment of MDD is that a fairly large percentage of successfully treated individuals suffer from a relapse or recurrence of the disorder. Because the relapse rate is so great when antidepressants are taken for a fairly brief period of time (e.g., 3 months), it is strongly recommended that once an antidepressant medication is taken, it should be continued for at least 9–12 months. Combining antidepressant medication and psychotherapy (IPT or CBT) appears to decrease the relapse rate following treatment. It does appear that the most effective treatment for recurrent (three or more episodes) MDD is likely to be continued antidepressant medications.

Because of the increasing rates of MDD among young people, it is becoming increasingly important to prevent first episodes and recurrences of the disorder. Prevention programs, focused on individuals with some but not all the symptoms of MDD and individuals with pessimistic cognitive styles, have shown some promise. Small studies also suggest that combined CBT and IPT for individuals who have had an episode of MDD but are not currently depressed may decrease the recurrence rates of MDD.

W. Edward Craighead
University of Colorado, Boulder

Benjamin H. Craighead
*Medical College of Virginia
Richmond, VA*

See also: **Antidepressant Medications; Cognitive Behavior Therapy; Interpersonal Psychotherapy; Major Depressive Disorder**

DEPRESSION AND BIPOLAR SUPPORT ALLIANCE

The Depression and Bipolar Support Alliance (DBSA) is the largest patient-directed, illness-specific organization in the United States. Incorporated in 1985 and headquartered in Chicago, DBSA has a nationwide grassroots network of chapters and support groups. It is governed by a 15-member board of directors and guided by a 65-member scientific advisory board comprised of the leading researchers and clinicians in the field of mood disorders. The organization does not endorse or recommend the use of any specific treatment or medication, but rather encourages patients to make informed choices with their health care providers.

DBSA's mission is to improve the lives of people living with mood disorders. Efforts to accomplish that mission include:

- *Encouraging people to seek diagnosis and treatment.* By communicating information about depression and bipolar disorder, especially about symptom recognition, DBSA encourages people to take the first step to seek help and assists them in adhering to their treatment plan once a diagnosis has been made. DBSA's programs and services also reduce the fear and isolation associated with mental illness by delivering a strong message of hope and community, and reinforcing the critical message that mood disorders are real, treatable illnesses, not personality flaws or character weaknesses. Visitors to the organization's web site, www.DBSAlliance.org, can also take the Mood Disorder Questionnaire (MDQ), the first bipolar disorder self-assessment tool ever available, as a way to take their first steps in seeking diagnosis.
- *Raising awareness to eliminate stigma.* The stigma surrounding mental illnesses is so strong it can prevent people from seeking help, weaken their already fragile self-image, or put their employment in jeopardy. It has also hampered efforts to achieve insurance parity for mental illness. DBSA effectively battles stigma through public education. Its public service announcements have been broadcast on the radio and have appeared on television and in dozens of national magazines. The organization's educational video, *Dark Glasses and Kaleidoscopes,* can be rented free of charge at Blockbuster Video stores across the country. Its web site features stories of real people and how they have worked to overcome stigma and the challenges of their illness. In addition, DBSA keeps a close eye on the media and responds to stigmatizing material. The organization keeps its constituents informed and encourages them to respond to stigma in their communities.
- *Enhancing health care professional and patient communication to maximize treatment success.* The cre-

ation of effective dialogue between patients and professionals can lead to a higher quality of care and more positive outcomes. Health care providers will be better able to care for and communicate with patients if they can understand mood disorders from the patients' perspective. In addition, patients can become empowered to play an important role in the management of their own illnesses by receiving information about treatment options, possible side effects, and expected outcomes. DBSA provides this information in a variety of free brochures, and offers books and audio and video tapes for purchase, all of which are carefully reviewed for accuracy and relevance.

- *Answering questions about the illness, treatment, and side effects.* It is sometimes difficult for patients to understand what health care professionals are saying. The information DBSA provides is presented in a clear, easy-to-understand way. Patients who receive clear, jargon-free information about treatment and side effects are much more likely to continue treatment as prescribed. DBSA's web site and local DBSA support groups are often the first places people go for answers to their questions, and can be lifelines for patients living outside major metropolitan areas.
- *Providing groups for peer-to-peer and family member support.* The more than 1,000 DBSA peer-run support groups motivate people to follow treatment plans; help patients understand that their illnesses do not define who they are; provide a forum for mutual acceptance, understanding, and self-discovery; and offer the opportunity for patients and their families to reach out to others and benefit from the experience of those who have "been there." Many support group participants say that their groups have brought meaning back to their lives and have been the first place where they were able to connect with caring friends who truly understood them.
- *Serving as a champion for mental health care reform.* DBSA is constantly working to change laws, increase funding for research, and advance the fight for such critical issues as patient confidentiality and insurance parity. DBSA keeps constituents informed about pending legislation through its newsletter and web site, and it offers ideas and assistance for writing letters to members of Congress to make constituents' collective voice heard.
- *Encouraging patient-centered research that results in better treatment and eventually facilitates a cure or prevention.* DBSA keeps lawmakers and government decision-makers aware of the great need for increased research, and therefore increased funding. In addition, the organization represents and protects patients by serving on the advisory boards of many clinical trials. DBSA also convenes annual conferences of preeminent mood disorder researchers to share knowledge in the field and come to consensus on best practices. The organization also gives awards to outstanding researchers.

As a patient-run and patient-focused organization, DBSA plays a critical role in advocating for the individuals and families touched by these devastating illnesses. In addition to raising awareness, encouraging timely and accurate diagnosis and treatment, providing patient-focused information to enhance doctor/patient communication, advocating for health care reform, and helping people to share experiences with our network of support groups, DBSA provides hope. The hope that recovery is possible and that others can understand their pain makes a lifesaving difference to the millions of patients and their families struggling with mood disorders.

Lydia Lewis
Laura Hoofnagle
Depression and Bipolar Support Alliance

DEPROGRAMMING

J. Clark defined extremist religious cults as being characterized by the following: (1) wealthy living leaders who consider themselves to be messiahs or claim to possess special powers, (2) philosophies based on a system of dogmatic and absolutist beliefs, (3) a totalitarian system of governance, (4) requirements to obey group regulations without question, (5) a strong emphasis on acquiring wealth for the cult, and (6) little concern for the welfare of the individual cult member.

Potential converts are rarely made aware of these characteristics but are usually given information quite different or even in direct opposition to what actually takes place. M. Singer and R. J. Lifton claim that once recruits are drawn far enough into a cult to be affected by group pressure, they are subjected to brainwashing strategies.

The end product of the indoctrination process is simplistic and stereotyped thought. As in hypnotic states, thought content is controlled largely from without rather than from within, resulting in blind obedience to the cult leader.

Comprehensive personality change can be effected by extremist religious cults within a few days to a few weeks, while J. Clark reported that after 4 to 7 years of cult life such changes may be irreversible.

Deprogramming consists of the facilitation of critical, flexible, creative, and independent thinking, and the correction of misconceptions about cult life. This is accomplished by encouraging the cult member to examine the cult ideology in the light of logic and empirical data. This examination can be catalyzed through a series of leading questions whereby the recruit is guided toward a systematic examination of issues on the basis of data available through his or her own life experience.

Straightforward filling of information gaps is also useful. For example, recruits may not know the true identity of the group they have joined, the fact that creative community projects give nothing to the community, that they will be expected to devote their life to the group, or that their marriage partner and the date of the marriage will be chosen for them. Of particular usefulness is a description and explanation of the indoctrination process.

Throughout the process the recruit's curiosity, questioning, and reasoning builds momentum until a point is reached that marks a change in the process. During this time the recruit may suddenly pause and become quiet and reflective, or express signs of shock. The recruit then usually "snaps." This moment is characterized by such sensations as tingling and shaking. Affectively, it may involve agonized crying and fear; cognitively, it is associated with a sudden change in worldview and a decision to leave the cult.

Treatment does not end with the snapping moment because for a period following it termed the *floating phase,* a chance meeting, phone call, or even a word may result in the recruit snapping just as quickly back to the cult worldview. To prevent this, individuals usually require continued support and guidance until critical thought capacities are strengthened enough to be self-supportive.

George K. Lockwood

DEPTH PERCEPTION

We perceive the world around us as containing different objects that are separated from each other and from us by varying distances. This three-dimensional awareness of the space around us is termed *depth perception* and is made possible by the use of several sensory input channels that provide the cues indicating the respective distances between us and these other objects in space. Human perceivers attend primarily (in most cases) to visual depth cues that are typically classified as either monocular (requiring at least one eye for cue interpretation) or binocular (requiring at least two eyes).

Monocular Cues

Through visual experiences we have learned to associate familiar objects of known size as being near or far depending upon the consequent retinal image size. Thus, *size* is one cue. Similarly, near objects tend to be more clearly seen than distant objects because of atmospheric degradation; thus *clarity* is another cue. *Aerial perspective* is a special case of the loss of clarity found with increasing distance above viewed objects. *Linear perspective* is a cue based on multiple familiar objects subtending smaller angles as they represent greater viewer-to-object distances. Linear perspective is illustrated frequently by the apparent decrease in road width seen as the road diminishes into the distance. An object partially positioned behind another (opaque) object gives rise to the cue of *interposition,* resulting in a partially seen view of the more distant object. As a consequence of *accommodation* (changing thickness of the lens as one focuses the eye for varying distances), kinesthetic feedback may indicate different (short-range) distances. *Motion parallax* is a cue based on the greater amount of retinal image movement for close objects than for far objects when the eye moves laterally. *Chromostereopsis* (illusion of depth that results from changing the focus of the eye for coplanar objects of different hues because of chromatic aberration) is a nonveridical form of apparent depth that may be noticed on computer color monitors. A sudden increase in size—called *looming*—results in a retinal image that may be veridical or illusory in indicating object approach.

Binocular Cues

Two eyes separated in space receive different views of the visual field. These different views form slightly different images on the separate retinas of the eyes and serve as the basis for the cue of *retinal disparity.* In human visual development this cue becomes effective (on average) at an age of 4 months (although in cases where there is a failure of the eyes to work together, as in uncorrected strabismus, the child may, if not functionally blind in one eye, nevertheless become stereoblind). When the two eyes are directed toward and become focused upon objects at varying distances, several changes occur. Specifically, as the distance to an object is reduced, each eye rotates inward through the activation (mainly) of the medial rectus and inhibition of the lateral rectus extraocular muscles of the eye. This is the binocular cue of *convergence.* A second physiologically linked response is that of *accommodation* (mentioned previously as a *monocular cue*). Both of these provide kinesthetic feedback indicating depth. Pupillary constriction occurs as an associated third response with the increased depth of field possibly serving as an additional depth cue. Several of these cues may be simultaneously operating, each one corroborating the others. It is difficult experimentally to identify which cues are operating at a given time.

Visual depth perception is studied in several ways. One approach is to have the subject (under binocular or monocular conditions) adjust a rod or needle such that it is equally distant relative to a standard. The visual cliff (a platform device with a glass floor extending out over an apparently deep side and shallow side) can be used to test depth perception in human and nonhuman subjects by ascertaining the amount of preference for the shallow side. Three-dimensional perception can be provided by the stereoscope, which presents two nearly identical views separately to the two eyes. A later development has been Bela Julesz's invention (1971) of random-dot stereograms: computer-generated patterns of random dots with pattern pairs that are identical except for a laterally displaced region. This region, when viewed with a stereoscope, appears to stand above or below the rest of the pattern.

Auditory depth cues are used by blind people who can approach and stop before colliding with a wall by (unconsciously) attending to reflected sounds. Echolocation in bats and cetaceans represents an elaboration of this capability. Additional auditory cues for depth are amount of reverberation, spectral characteristics (atmospheric absorption is greater for higher frequencies), motion parallax, and relative loudness of known sounds.

Depth cues provided by other senses include proximity detection because of the strength of a familiar odor, thermal detection in pit vipers, and the electric field sensitivity found in some fish.

REFERENCE

Julesz, B. (1971). *Foundations of cyclopean perception.* Chicago: University of Chicago Press.

SUGGESTED READING

Boring, E. G. (1942). *Sensation and perception in the history of experimental psychology.* New York: Appleton-Century-Crofts.

Graham, C. H. (Ed.). (1965). *Vision and visual perception.* New York: Wiley.

Griffin, D. R. (1986). *Listening in the dark: The acoustic orientation of bats and men.* Ithaca, NY: Cornell University Press.

Howard, I. P. (2002). Depth perception. In H. Pashler (Series Ed.) & S. Yantis (Vol. Ed.), *Stevens' handbook of experimental psychology: Vol. 1. Sensation and perception* (3rd ed., pp. 77–120). New York: Wiley.

Marr, D. (1982). *Vision.* New York: W. H. Freeman.

Schöne, H. (1984). *Spatial orientation: The spatial control of behavior in animals and man* (C. Strausfeld, Trans.). Princeton, NJ: Princeton University Press. (Original work published 1980)

George H. Robinson
University of North Alabama

DETERMINISM AND INDETERMINISM

The concept of determinism in philosophy has in it the element of necessity: Things must be just as they are because of antecedent causes. This notion is central to science, which maintains that, were one to know all factors involved in some forthcoming event, one could predict it exactly; or conversely, if an event occurs, that it is inevitable. Every thing and event in creation is the result, and will always be the result, of natural laws that can be determined by means of the scientific method.

When it comes to human behavior, an interesting set of alternative positions has been established that has real relevance outside psychology as a science or profession and that relates to general human behavior and institutions, including the laws of society and the dogmas of religion. What has occurred is an interesting set of contradictions. As noted, scientists view life as determined and generally believe in the inevitability of behavior: Were one to know everything about an individual, one could predict his or her every movement. However, throughout the history of society the common-sense view has been one of individual responsibility.

Indeterminism generally is taken to mean that the individual has freedom of choice, that people can predict the consequences of their actions and can decide how to operate, for example, in terms of their own selfish gain versus the good of the community. The purest example of indeterminism is the belief in free will, which holds that all conscious behavior is decided by responsible people. The laws of most societies and the dogma of many religions, especially the Judaeo-Christian ones, are based on the notion of individual responsibility: The consequences of punishment—whether in this world or in the next—are justified in terms of a person's moral judgments and behavior.

Psychologists take a variety of positions in this age-old controversy. Strict behaviorists tend to be strict determinists, whereas those with an existential bent tend to be indeterminists. However, perhaps in an illogical manner, most psychologists sit on both sides of this fence, asserting as part of the scientific method the necessity of determinism, but nevertheless operating in terms of indeterminism.

Fairly recent events in the world of physics cast doubt on the scientific legitimacy of determinism. Essentially, the issue has to do with the impossibility of determining at the same time the momentum of an electron particle as well as its position. Apparently, there will always be an area of uncertainty. Werner Heisenberg, who received the Nobel prize in 1932, developed from this observation what is generally known as the Heisenberg indeterminacy principle, demonstrating that Newtonian physics simply does not apply at the level of atoms. If we view the single human as the equivalent of an atom, we may now say that, while determinancy is true for the human species, leading to a deterministic nomothetic position, indeterminancy is also true for the human individual, whose behavior would be only partially explainable in terms of preceding events. In other words, the individual is impossible to predict with complete success.

W. S. Sutton

See also: **Empiricism; Logical Positivism**

DEVELOPMENT OF HUMAN SOCIAL BEHAVIOR

Social behavior occupies a place of paramount importance in the lives of human beings and its development therefore commands attention. Social behavior encompasses a human being's interaction not only with other persons but also with the world of things, which have acquired their meaning and status from the customs and practices of the culture.

The development of social behavior depends on and keeps pace with the development of such biological and psychological processes as maturation, perception, attention, memory, and learning, as these processes are modified by experience. Further, its development depends on the same processes of learning (taken in its broadest meaning) as the development of any other class of behavior, including trial-and-error learning, conditioning and the law of effect, social learning theory with its emphasis on imitation and modeling, and the comprehension of language. Thus, no child, no more than any human being, can behave socially in the absence of motor, cognitive, or linguistic skills.

Social behavior is by definition an interactive process; the behavior of any partner to the interaction modifies the behavior of the other person, even as it is being modified by the response of the other person. The interaction begins at birth, hence it may fairly be claimed that the human infant qualifies from birth as a social being.

Not only do human infants, requiring constant provision and care, depend for their survival on the ministrations of others, but they are in fact treated as social beings at birth. Mothers and fathers, for example, smile and vocalize to their newborn infants, and an analysis of the speech of hospital personnel to newborns provided ample evidence that even these unrelated persons viewed and treated newborns as fellow human beings.

From birth on, the uneven development of the human infants' sensory and motor systems, compared with the young of many other mammalian species, plays a special role in the development of their social behavior. In their ability to respond to visual, auditory, and tactile stimuli, they resemble precocial animals; in their inability to locomote and so secure nourishment or mingle with other members of their species by their own efforts, they resemble altricial animals. During the long period until effortless locomotion is achieved, what they see and hear, the objects and persons with whom they have contact, as well as the routines of care, are provided by their parents. The gaze, speech, smiles, and other acts of caretakers not only evoke responses from the infants but just as often follow (are contingent on) the infants' looking at them, smiling, vocalizing, crying, and so on.

Development During the First 6 Months

Scales of infant development document many early social behaviors. Infants pay attention to people who approach them, show facial brightening and smiles in response to a person who smiles and talks to them, and are quiet when held. Even in the first month or so of life they vocalize in response to another's vocalizations. By 16 weeks of age they are already initiating social play. They have also learned that their crying brings people to their side, even as people learn what they should do to alleviate the cause.

During this early period, infants achieve the major accomplishment of learning to distinguish between the animate and the inanimate, between people and things. Although many objects in the world provide as varied visual and auditory stimulation as do people, people respond more often to the infant's behavior and, being human, their responses are more variable and less predictable. Especially the faces of people, on which infants fasten very early in life, not only present an ever-changing set of stimuli, but are almost always accompanied by speech appropriate to their own feelings and actions, as well as to those of the infants. It is people, finally, who minister to the infants' basic biological needs.

The infants' ability to distinguish between familiar and unfamiliar persons constitutes another major accomplishment of these early months. Although infants this young respond positively to all persons, the social responses to familiar persons are more expansive and come more readily.

These social accomplishments reveal the infants' growing perceptual abilities and the presence of a considerable memory.

The Second 6 Months

The social accomplishments of the infants' earliest days become richer and more varied as their perceptions deepen, their motor skills improve, and their knowledge increases. They repeat behaviors others laugh at, imitate sounds, and respond to their names. They learn the rules of the game of give-and-take and, whereas at 6 months of age they enjoy playing peek-a-boo, by 12 months of age they are already initiating a number of simple games.

About midway in this period infants begin to show distress when separated from their mothers and often from their fathers—a behavior that reaches prominence especially when they are ill or otherwise upset. The phenomenon was labeled *separation anxiety* by Spitz and described in hospitalized children by James Robertson and John Bowlby. These observations gave rise to the concept of attachment first sketched by Bowlby. Subsequently, attachment was studied empirically by Mary Ainsworth. Although Robert Cairns supplied a straightforward learning theory explanation of the disruption of behavior caused by the removal of familiar stimuli, the reliance of the concept of attachment on psychoanalytic and ethological theory remains strong.

As the concept evolved, component behaviors were delineated. The infant's seeking to maintain proximity to the mother, by staying close or by following her, was proposed as the primary indexing behavior. Then, as everyday observation showed that infants often wandered away at the beck and call of an enticing environment, such behavior was incorporated and labeled *exploration from a secure base.* The other component behaviors included the aforementioned distress at separation from the mother and the display of fear in the presence of strangers. In a later development, three types of attachment—secure, avoidant, and resistant—were proposed, based on differences in the infants' responses to the mothers' return after a series of experimentally manipulated events that ended in the infants' being left alone in an unfamiliar environment. The nature of the infants' responses was attributed to differences in the mothers' sensitivity to the needs of their infants.

Attractive as the concept of attachment is, some qualifications are in order. The concept scants the differential contribution to the interaction made by different infants; infants vary as much as caretakers, and both contribute to the interaction. Also, infants are not always cared for exclusively by their mothers, and room must be allowed for attachment to other persons, as first proposed by Rudolph Schaffer and Peggy Emerson. Furthermore, infants not only crawl away from their parents, but do so in most unusual and hence unfamiliar settings (e.g., airports). Even when free to follow a parent, they often stop first to play with toys and on occasion will follow an unknown person. Thus, even for infants, a world of difference lies between a voluntary and a forced separation from loved ones. Finally, although infants may scrutinize unknown persons more intently and do not always smile at unsmiling persons, they do not show fear. Approached playfully or even normally, most infants respond positively. When fearful responses are reported, they have been experimentally produced by socially invasive procedures.

As children approach their first birthday, they show unmistakable signs that they are becoming aware of themselves as actors among other actors, signs that suggest the beginnings of a self-concept. Even when infants repeat an act the parents laughed at, a dawning sense of themselves as individuals can be surmised. A similar claim can be made for the behavior, common at about 10 months of age, of the infants' holding objects out to other persons with the apparent intent of drawing their attention to the object—a behavior followed sometimes now, but always in the second year, by actually giving them objects. Such behavior had long been practiced in the give-and-take game and is so well consolidated in the next few months as to qualify as a gesture of sharing one's possessions with another. Drawing other persons' attention to distant objects by pointing with the index finger is a related accomplishment. Now, when they themselves point to interesting spectacles, they also vocalize and look back at the person's face as though to check that the message is received. Infants, then, recognize other persons not only as separate from themselves, but also as persons with whom they can share an experience.

The Child's Wider Social Environment

Even though fathers generally have spent less time with their infants than mothers and have been less responsible for meeting their moment-by-moment needs, what actually does occur during these intermittent interactions is especially highlighted. As actual studies of the nature of the interaction between fathers and infants now reveal, fathers are just as responsive to their newborn infants as mothers. Although fathers are as capable as mothers in ministering to the physical needs of their offspring, and often do so, their style undoubtedly differs from that of mothers. Certainly differences in how mothers and fathers play with their young children have been remarked: Fathers' play is more physical, including more rough-and-tumble, while mothers' is more vocal. Yet here as elsewhere, when engaging in comparisons, one fastens on differences and forgets the similarities that greatly outnumber them. Thus, the responses of children to their fathers resemble those to their mothers.

As soon as investigators turned their attention to fathers, the larger picture came into view: Members of the family—mother, father, and siblings if present—not only interact with the youngest member of the family in their own individual fashion, but each separate interaction is affected by all the others. The social behavior of the infant and young child develops and is refined in a complex and multifaceted web of social relations.

Interestingly, attendance in day-care or nursery school settings does not seem to result in the loss of the emotional bond between children and their parents, which supports the contention that what is important is not the amount of time spent in interactions, but the nature of the interactions.

Interactions with Other Children

Even very young infants respond as socially to children as to their caretakers. It cannot be supposed that these very young children recognize other children as fellow creatures of their own small size and status. Rather, children being more lively than adults, they present more interesting stimuli, are more often playful, and may be more easily imitated.

Siblings, both older and younger, constitute a special class of children, distinguished by their familiarity and even more important by their contribution to the social web of the family. Although rivalry between siblings was vividly portrayed by David Levy in 1937, this does not tell the whole story. Naturalistic and laboratory studies, building on anecdotes, reveal many positive interactions. Older siblings entertain, talk to, and play with their infant siblings. As the infants become toddlers, their siblings help and comfort them, and in turn the younger siblings find their older brothers and sisters attractive models, following where they go and imitating what they do.

Unrelated children also engage in congenial social interactions. Even infants smile and reach out to other infants, and older, but still young, children play together, with and without toys, and engage each other in true conversations. Early experience with other children of their own age, as well as with those older and younger, is often considered as important for young children's social development as association with adults. They learn the rules of a more egalitarian interaction, and by comparing themselves with others of their own age acquire knowledge of their own capabilities—knowledge that contributes to their developing concept of self.

Aggressive Behavior

Although the play groups of little children conjure up images of a melee of squalling, fighting children, the truth is quite otherwise. Conflicts do occur, usually over the possession of toys, but these are few relative to more positive interactions and are more often resolved by sociable acts than by force.

Development of Speech

Of the many activities composing the category of social behavior, speech occupies a preeminent position. Not only are newborns spoken to, but throughout the children's lives almost every subsequent contact with the parents, as well as with all other persons, is accompanied by speech. Even within the first months of life they vocalize in turn, setting the stage for a dialogue, a term that can well stand as a metaphor for all social interactions. While children are very young, adults carry the main burden of the conversation, marking their speech by a lively intonation, many repetitions, and much asking of questions. In turn, the vocalizations of the infant come to resemble the sounds and especially the intonations they hear.

By the end of the first year infants have acquired a word or two, and soon thereafter many words, as attentive bystanders label not only the objects and events in the environment but also the infants' own behavior. The adults' labeling of the infants' gestures—in particular, the infants' pointing to objects—plays an important part in establishing the meaning of their first words.

In studies of the semantic and syntactic properties of the child's speech, its social origins and pragmatic properties tend to be overlooked. The sine qua non of social behavior is communicating with others, and the modes of communicating are many, nonverbal and vocal as well as verbal. The child's use of the verbal mode, as of the other modes, originates in social interaction and, once acquired, plays a role of increasing importance in all social encounters.

Early Acquisition of Prosocial Behavior

During the second year of the child's life a number of behaviors such as comforting, sharing, and helping make their appearance and, with appreciation and reinforcement, develop into socially valued behaviors. These positive behaviors, being common, low-key, and undemanding, tend to go unremarked, posing as they do no problems for parents and teachers.

From an early age little children become emotionally upset at the distress of others and offer them sympathy by word and deed. They often spontaneously share their toys and possessions, and the objects they find, with other people and children, both familiar and unfamiliar. In extending such nurturant acts to both animate and inanimate objects, they creatively reenact the care they themselves had experienced at the hands of their parents.

Among the prosocial behaviors, obedience to the words of the parents deserves separate attention. Although here, too, more attention has been paid by parents and investigators to incidents when children do not obey, complying with verbal requests is the more common response. In fact, complying begins early and appears to develop without coercion. By the middle of the second year little children carry out many simple commands not only readily but often with pleasure, stemming apparently from their newfound ability to fit their behavior to the words of others.

Differences Between Boys and Girls

The sex of the child from birth is of paramount consequence to the beholder, if not yet to the child. No question is asked more consistently at the birth of a child than its sex.

Although many major attributes studies show no major differences in how parents rear their sons and daughters, nevertheless some do exist. For example, large differences fitting the culture's stereotypes were found in the type of toys parents provided for their young children. Parents of very young children profess to an intention to treat their children alike regardless of sex; they have been conditioned by a whole lifetime in a culture that has fairly definite ideas about sex-appropriate behavior. Furthermore, by 2 or 3 years of age children come to know, or at least to label, themselves as *boys* or *girls,* the first in a series of cognitive stages leading to gender identity sometime between 5 and 7 years of age.

Yet in the area of social behavior, no clear evidence has been presented of major differences in the interactions of boys and girls with parents, other adults, or children. Beyond infancy, as children come together in play groups and nursery schools, physical aggression, although on the whole infrequent relative to peaceable interchanges, is seen more often in boys than in girls.

Harriet L. Rheingold

See also: **Affective Development; Bonding and Attachment; Early Childhood Development; Prosocial Behavior**

DEVIANCE

The study of deviance is based on two different points of view. The first has viewed deviance as an exceptional, but consistent, variation from statistical norms. In other words consistent performance, behavior, or cognition, which is an unusual occurrence in relation to the overall population, is considered deviant. This definition has been prominently used in the psychological study of deviance.

The second prominent position has seen deviance as defined by the occurrence of single critical events. The occurrence of unusual and high-intensity behaviors characterized by mental illness and violence exemplify this point of view. The critical event view of deviance is the basis of legal definitions of deviance.

Deviance has been the thrust of major aspects of personality theory, clinical psychology, and social psychology. The study of deviance can be classified into four major positions. The first posits that deviance is a function of internal factors. Deviance is seen as *differences among individuals.* The individual differences point of view suggests that individuals or groups of individuals possessing certain levels of characteristics are more likely to become deviant. Individual differences are further posited to be causally related to deviance.

A second major explanation of deviance posits *social structural differences* as major precursors. Officially codified forms of deviance tend to be disproportionately represented among the lower socioeconomic strata in our society. From a social structural point of view, it is suggested that differential access to legitimate opportunity, differential access to illegitimate opportunity, and alienation or enmity tend to be the critical ingredients causing deviance. From this point of view, deviance has both individual components that are a result of differential social structures, and environmental aspects.

A third major explanation of deviance takes an *interactionist point of view.* Formally entitled *labeling theory,* deviance is created by the reaction of critical individuals to a given act. Psychological disturbance, criminality, and underachievement are both formally and informally labeled as deviant. From the labeling perspective deviance is clearly an interaction between individual performances and society's reactions to those performances.

A fourth major point of view is that expressed by *learning theory.* Learning theory suggests that all actions, deviant and normal, are learned according to the laws of modeling, reinforcement, and punishment. Those individuals who display deviant behavioral patterns have received differential reward for such actions. From the learning theory point of view there is no inherent difference between deviant and normal behavior. Criminal behavior, abnormal behavior, and learning disabilities are learned.

William S. Davidson II
Michigan State University

See also: **Alienation (Political)**

DIAGNOSIS

Diagnosis is the act of identifying and naming a disorder or disease by using an agreed-upon system of categorization. In North America, mental and emotional syndromes are currently diagnosed according to the *Diagnostic and Statistical Manual of Mental Disorders,* fourth edition (*DSM-IV;* American Psychiatric Association [ApA], 1994).

Roots of the *DSM-IV*

The roots of the *DSM-IV* extend back to nineteenth-century German psychiatrist Emil Kraepelin, who believed strongly in the detailed medical and psychiatric histories of patients, emphasized thorough observation of signs and symptoms, and considered some disorders, including prominently the psychoses, to be diseases of the brain. Despite a few earlier unsuccessful efforts, it was not until the end of World War II that representatives of the War Department, the Veterans Administration, and the civilian psychiatric community in the United States began discussing the creation of a national nomenclature that could simultaneously serve their diverse needs. The result was a syndromally based nomenclature, the *DSM-I* (ApA, 1952).

The DSM-I *and the* DSM-II

The *DSM-I* was designed to permit mental health professionals across the United States to use a common diagnostic language for the first time. Notwithstanding the *DSM-I* and its similar successor, the *DSM-II* (ApA, 1968), had serious deficiencies. Because they provided only brief descriptions of each disorder, the reliability of resultant diagnoses was low. Moreover, syndrome descriptions were not empirically based and often failed to correspond to the clinical experience of those working in clinical settings.

The DSM-III

The roots of the *DSM-III* lie in (1) late 1960s research by psychiatrist R. L. Spitzer at the New York State Psychiatric Institute that led to the development of a series of structured diagnostic interviews (e.g., Spitzer, Fleiss, Endicott, & Cohen, 1967) designed to gather the data on signs and symptoms on which an empirically based nomenclature could be built, (2) an influential article by Feighner and colleagues (1972) that proposed explicit, empirically derived diagnostic criteria for 16 major diagnostic categories, and (3) publication of the *Research Diagnostic Criteria (RDC;* Spitzer, Endicott, & Robins, 1975), which allowed empirical testing of the reliability of the Feighner criteria.

The *DSM-III* (ApA, 1980) represented a breakthrough in efforts to heighten the reliability and, to a lesser extent, the validity and utility of syndromal diagnosis. The instrument's diagnostic criteria, and those of its successors, the *DSM-III-R* (ApA, 1987) and the *DSM-IV* (ApA, 1994), represent its major departure from its predecessors. Modeled after the *RDC,* the diagnostic criteria organized each syndrome's signs and symptoms in a consistent format. As a result, the reliability of *DSM-III* diagnoses selectively improved.

The clinical utility of the *DSM-III* also improved. The *DSM-III* text, and those of its successors, contained several times as many pages and words as its predecessors, permitting far greater explication of each of the more than 300 sets of operational criteria (more than 3 times as many as its predecessors), as well as information on associated features, age of onset, course, nature and extent of impairment, complications, predisposing features, prevalence, sex ratio, familiar pattern, and differential diagnostic issues.

The *DSM-III* also introduced the multiaxial system, which assesses each patient along five axes, rather than only one, as in the *DSM-I* and the *DSM-II.* Not only are patients assessed on psychopathology on Axes I and II, but also on the physical conditions which might have contributed to their psychopathology (Axis III), the severity of the psychological stressors to which the patient was exposed (Axis IV), and the patient's highest level of adaptive functioning during the preceding year (Axis V).

The DSM-IV

A principal goal of the *DSM-IV* process was to create a nomenclature based even more than the *DSM-III* on empirical research. Thirteen work groups, one for each major diagnostic grouping, first undertook systematic literature reviews designed to address unresolved diagnostic questions. When literature reviews failed to resolve questions, the work groups sought to locate clinical data sets that would do so; 40 analyses of existing patient data sets were ultimately carried out. The work groups also designed and carried out extensive field trials to generate new clinical data; 12 large-scale field trials at more than 70 sites worldwide, involving more than 7,000 participants, were completed.

Reliability and Validity of *DSM-IV* Diagnoses

Most data reported to date on the reliability and validity of *DSM-IV* categories have come from the field trials. They suggest modest increments in the reliability of a few diagnostic categories (e.g., Oppositional Defiant Disorder and Conduct Disorder in children and adolescents, Substance Abuse and Dependence) and in validity (e.g., Autistic Disorder; Oppositional Defiant Disorder in childhood and adolescence). However, little progress was made in addressing the substantial reliability problems of the Personality Disorders, the Sleep Disorders, the disorders of childhood and adolescence, and some of the disorders within the schizophrenic spectrum.

Criticisms of the *DSM-IV*

In a response to criticisms that professional issues overshadowed scientific ones in the creation of the *DSM-IV* (e.g., Caplan, 1991), Widiger and Trull (1993) admitted that the *DSM-IV* Task Force was sensitive to a variety of professional issues. Nonetheless, they see it as primarily an empirically driven instrument. As well, Guze expressed concern in 1995 that many *DSM-IV* diagnostic conditions continue to fail to meet Robins and Guze's (1970) criteria for diagnostic validity; this is a theme others (e.g., Kirk & Kutchins, 1992) have also sounded.

Comorbidity of Diagnoses

There is substantial overlap among disorders in the *DSM-IV.* With others, Klein and Riso (1993) have asked whether these disorders represent discrete, "natural" classes or artificial categories created by the establishment of arbitrary cutoffs on a continuum. In a report from the National Comorbidity Survey (NCS), Blazer and his colleagues (Blazer, Kessler, McGonagle, & Swartz, 1994) confirmed the high rates of co-occurrence between major depression and a range of other psychiatric disorders. Kessler and colleagues (Kessler, Sonnega, Bromet, Hughes, & Nelson, 1995), in a second NCS article, reported that Posttraumatic Stress Disorder is strongly comorbid with other lifetime *DSM-III-R* disorders in both men and women, especially the affective disorders, the Anxiety Disorders, and the Substance Use Disorders. Magee and his colleagues (Magee, Eaton, Wittchen, McGonagle, & Kessler, 1996) report that lifetime phobias are highly comorbid with each other, with other Anxiety Disorders, and with affective disorders.

The Categorical Versus Dimensional Debate

Categorical versus dimensional classification first became a matter of concern when the *DSM-III* tripled the number of diagnoses described by its predecessors, thereby raising the question of boundaries between old and new diagnostic entities. As diagnoses proliferated, the frequency of comorbidity increased, causing clinicians to ask whether comorbidity represents the co-occurrence of two or more mental disorders or a single disorder that has simply been labeled in different ways. As a consequence, the advantages and disadvantages of dimensional and categorical approaches to personality and diagnosis are now being explored extensively (e.g., Widiger, 1997). The focus of these efforts is on the Personality Disorders, where symptom overlap is greatest.

REFERENCES

American Psychiatric Association. (1952). *Diagnostic and statistical manual of mental disorders* (1st ed.). Washington, DC: Author.

American Psychiatric Association. (1968). *Diagnostic and statistical manual of mental disorders* (2nd ed.). Washington, DC: Author.

American Psychiatric Association. (1980). *Diagnostic and statistical manual of mental disorders* (3rd ed.). Washington, DC: Author.

American Psychiatric Association. (1987). *Diagnostic and statistical manual of mental disorders* (3rd ed., rev. ed.). Washington, DC: Author.

American Psychiatric Association. (1994). *Diagnostic and statistical manual of mental disorders* (4th ed.). Washington, DC: Author.

Blazer, D. G., Kessler, R. C., McGonagle, K. A., & Swartz, M. S. (1994). The prevalence and distribution of major depression in a national community sample: The National Comorbidity Survey. *American Journal of Psychiatry, 151,* 979–986.

Caplan, P. J. (1991). How do they decide who is normal? The bizarre, but true, tale of the *DSM* process. *Canadian Psychology, 32,* 162–170.

Feighner, J. R., Robins, E., Guze, S. B., Woodruff, R. A., Winokur, G., & Munoz, R. (1972). Diagnostic criteria for use in psychiatric research. *Archives of General Psychiatry, 26,* 57–63.

Guze, S. B. (1995). Review of American Psychiatric Association *Diagnostic and Statistical Manual of Mental Disorders,* 4th ed. *American Journal of Psychiatry, 152,* 1228.

Kessler, R. C., Sonnega, A., Bromet, E., Hughes, M., & Nelson, C. B. (1995). Posttraumatic Stress Disorder in the National Comorbidity Survey. *Archives of General Psychiatry, 52,* 1048–1060.

Kirk, S. A., & Kutchins, H. (1992). *The selling of* DSM. *The rhetoric of science in psychiatry.* Hawthorne, NY: Aldine de Gruyter.

Klein, D. N., & Riso, L. P. (1993). Psychiatric disorders: Problems of boundaries and comorbidity. In C. G. Costello (Ed.), *Basic issues in psychopathology* (pp. 19–66). New York: Guilford Press.

Magee, W. J., Eaton, W. W., Wittchen, H.-U., McGonagle, K. A., & Kessler, R. C. (1996). Agoraphobia, simple phobia, and Social Phobia in the National Comorbidity Survey. *Archives of General Psychiatry, 53,* 159–168.

Robins, E., & Guze, S. (1970). Establishment of diagnostic validity in psychiatric illnesses: Its application to Schizophrenia. *American Journal of Psychiatry, 126,* 983–987.

Spitzer, R. L., Endicott, J., & Robins, E. (1975). *Research diagnostic criteria (RDC) for a selected group of functional disorders.* New York: New York State Psychiatric Institute.

Spitzer, R. L., Fleiss, J. L., Endicott, J., & Cohen, J. (1967). Mental Status Schedule: Properties of a factor-analytically derived scale. *Archives of General Psychiatry, 16,* 479–493.

Widiger, T. A. (1997). Mental disorders as discrete clinical conditions: Dimensional versus categorical classification. In S. M. Turner & M. Hersen (Eds.), *Adult psychopathology and diagnosis* (pp. 3–23). New York: Wiley.

Widiger, T. A., & Trull, T. J. (1993). The scholarly development of *DSM-IV.* In J. A. C. de Silva & C. C. Nadelson (Eds.), *International review of psychiatry* (pp. 59–78). Washington, DC: American Psychiatric Press.

Peter E. Nathan
University of Iowa, Iowa City

See also: **Diagnosis; Reliability**

DIAGNOSTIC INTERVIEW SCHEDULE FOR *DSM-IV (DIS-IV)*

The ability to diagnose psychiatric disorders accurately has improved dramatically over the last 20 years. Structured interviews have played a major role in this advancement, and the *Diagnostic Interview Schedule for DSM-IV (DIS-IV;* Robins, Cottler, Bucholz, Compton, North, & Rourke, 1999) is among the most prominent and popular of these instruments.

Overview and History

The *DIS-IV* is a fully structured interview designed to assess the presence or absence of major psychiatric disorders. It was crafted to be administered in a reliable and valid fashion by nonclinician interviewers. Computerized administration of the *DIS-IV (C-DIS)* is standard. Computerized administration may be interviewer-administered or self-administered. In both formats, the exact wording of all questions and probes are presented to the respondent in a standardized order on a computer screen, and rephrasing of questions is discouraged, although *DIS* interviewers can repeat questions as necessary to ensure that they are understood by the respondent. All questions are written to be closed-ended, and replies are coded with a forced choice yes or no format, which eliminates the need for clinical judgment to rate responses. The *DIS* gathers all necessary information about the subject from the subject; collateral sources of information are not used. The *DIS* is self-contained and covers all necessary symptoms to make many *Diagnostic and Statistical Manual of Mental Disorders,* fourth edition *(DSM-IV)* diagnoses (American Psychiatric Association, 1994). Responses are directly entered into a database during the interview, and the diagnosis is made according to the explicit rules of the *DSM-IV* diagnostic system.

In 1978, development of the original *DIS* was begun by researchers at the Washington University Department of Psychiatry in St. Louis at the request of the National Institute of Mental Health (NIMH). At that time, the NIMH Division of Biometry and Epidemiology was planning a set of large-scale, multicenter epidemiological investigations of mental illness in the general adult population in the United States as part of its Epidemiological Catchment Area Program. Variables under study included incidence and prevalence of many psychiatric disorders and utilization profiles of health and mental health services. With this grand purpose in mind, development of a structured interview that could be administered by nonclinicians was imperative due to the prohibitive cost of using professional clinicians as interviewers. As a result, the *DIS* was designed as a fully structured diagnostic interview that minimizes the amount of clinical experience required to administer it.

Since its initial development, the *DIS* has undergone several major revisions. For example, the original *DIS* (Robins, Helzer, Croughan, & Ratcliff, 1981) covered criteria for only 31 *DSM-III* diagnoses, with later versions adding more disorders. Another refinement was the addition of a comprehensive set of training materials including training videotapes and extensive training courses. Perhaps most importantly, *DIS* questions and diagnostic algorithms were revamped to match new criteria in *DSM-III-R* (called Version DIS-III-R; Robins, Helzer, Cottler, & Goldring, 1989), and most recently in *DSM-IV* (ApA, 1994).

Features of the *DIS*

Since the *DIS* was designed for epidemiological research with normative samples, interviewers do not elicit a presenting problem from the respondent, as would be typical in unstructured clinical interviews. Rather, *DIS* interviews begin by asking questions about symptoms in a standardized order. Like other structured interviews, the *DIS* has sections that cover different disorders. Each diagnostic section is independent, except where one diagnosis preempts another. Once a symptom is reported to be present, further closed-ended questions are pursued to assess additional diagnostically relevant information such as severity, frequency, time frame, and possibility of organic etiology of the symptom. The *DIS* includes a set of core questions that are asked of each respondent. Core questions are followed by contingent questions that are administered only if the preceding core question is endorsed. *DIS* interviewers utilize a probe flow chart that indicates which probes to use in which circumstances.

For each symptom, the respondent is asked to state whether it has ever been present and how recently. All data about presence or absence of symptoms and time frames of occurrence are coded and entered into the computer. Consistent with its use of nonclinician interviewers, the diagnostic output of the *DIS* is generated by a computer program which analyzes data from the completed interview. The output provides estimates of prevalence for two time periods: current and lifetime.

Due to its highly specified format, full administration of the *DIS-IV* interview typically takes 75–150 minutes. To shorten administration time, the modular format makes it possible to drop evaluation of disorders that are not of interest in a particular study. Another option is to drop further questioning for a particular disorder once it is clear that the threshold number of symptoms needed for diagnosis will not be met. Modules can be dropped, shortened, or asked in full depending on the specific research needs.

Although designed for use by nonclinician administrators, training for competent administration of the *DIS* is intensive. Trainees typically attend a 1-week training program at Washington University during which they review the *DIS* manual, listen to didactic presentations about the structure and conventions of the *DIS,* view videotaped vignettes, complete workbook exercises, and conduct several practice interviews followed by feedback and review. Additional supervised practice is also recommended.

The psychometric properties of the original *DIS* and its revisions have been evaluated in numerous investigations, with encouraging results. The interested reader is referred to Segal and Coolidge (2003) for a full discussion of reliability and validity data for the *DIS*. Overall, the *DIS* has proven to be a popular and useful diagnostic assessment tool, especially for large-scale epidemiological research. The *DIS* has been translated into over a dozen languages. It is used in many countries for epidemiological research and served as the basis for the Composite International Diagnostic Interview used by the World Health Organization. Presently, the *DIS-IV* is the only well-validated case finding strategy that can make *DSM-IV* diagnoses in large-scale epidemiological research. Like earlier versions, the *DIS-IV* can be expected to enjoy widespread application in psychiatric research, service, and training for many years to come. Given the history of the *DIS,* its continued evolution will likely make it a popular and effective instrument for psychiatric diagnosis in the twenty-first century. For further information, see the *DIS* web site at http://epi.wustl.edu.

REFERENCES

American Psychiatric Association. (1994). *Diagnostic and statistical manual of mental disorders* (4th ed.). Washington, DC: Author.

Robins, L. N., Cottler, L. B., Bucholz, K. K., Compton, W. M., North, C., & Rourke, K. (1999). *The Diagnostic Interview Schedule for DSM-IV (DIS-IV).* St. Louis, MO: Washington University School of Medicine. Last revision, 1-2000.

Robins, L. N., Helzer, J. E., Cottler, L. B., & Goldring, E. (1989). *The Diagnostic Interview Schedule, Version III-R.* St. Louis, MO: Washington University School of Medicine.

Robins, L. N., Helzer, J. E., Croughan, J., & Ratcliff, K. S. (1981). National Institute of Mental Health Diagnostic Interview Schedule: Its history, characteristics, and validity. *Archives of General Psychiatry, 38,* 381–389.

Segal, D. L., & Coolidge, F. L. (2003). Structured interviewing and DSM classification. In M. Hersen & S. Turner (Eds.), *Adult psychopathology and diagnosis* (4th ed., pp. 72–103).

Daniel L. Segal
University of Colorado, Colorado Springs

DICTIONARY OF OCCUPATIONAL TITLES

First produced by the U.S. Department of Labor in 1939, the *Dictionary of Occupational Titles* (*DOT*) provides standardized occupational information useful to individuals and professionals in the job-seeking process. The *DOT* represents an extremely wide variety of occupational activities related to the full range of service provided by the U.S. employment services.

Among the items included are descriptions of more than 20,000 occupations, covering almost all jobs in the U.S. economy. Because it groups occupations into a systematic classification structure based on how jobs are related with respect to their tasks and requirements, it is extremely useful as a job placement tool. It enhances the ability of the personnel worker to match worker skills with job requirements.

Occupational titles are arranged by groups, by industries, and alphabetically. Definitions are organized into six basic components: occupational code number, occupational title, industry designation, any alternate titles, the definition itself, and any undefined related title.

The occupational code is a nine-digit number. The first three digits identify an occupational group. The first digit identifies a broad occupational category; the second, some subdivision within the category; and the third, the occupation within the broader subdivision.

The second three digits of the code describe worker function. These are defined in terms of data, which are the fourth digit; people, the fifth digit; and things, the sixth digit. Together, they describe the degree of involvement that the job has with data, people, and things.

The last set of three digits differentiates a particular occupation from any other occupations that might have the same first six digits. No two occupations, therefore, can have the same nine digits.

The total system has many very useful features. The *DOT* can identify, for example, tasks that workers might have to perform in a particular occupation, the kinds of machines or tools that might be used, the amount of independent judgment that a worker might have to exercise in the performance of a job, and the setting in which the work might be done. In addition, each occupation is described in terms of its exertional requirements and skill level, as well as the level of proficiency in general level of intelligence, verbal, and computations skills it requires.

This system is subject to replacement at some future date by a system called *O-Net.*

REFERENCE

U.S. Department of Labor. (1991). *Dictionary of Occupational Titles* (4th ed.). Washington, DC: U.S. Government Printing Office.

Samuel H. Osipow
Ohio State University, Columbus

See also: **Career Counseling**

DIFFERENTIAL PSYCHOLOGY

This branch of psychology is concerned with the nature and origins of individual and group differences in behavior. Measurement of such differences has produced an extensive body of descriptive data of considerable scientific and practical interest in its own right. More basically, however, differential psychology represents one avenue to an understanding of behavior; its characteristic approach is through the comparative analysis of behavior under varying biological and environmental conditions. By relating observed behavioral differences to known concomitant circumstances, it is possible to investigate the relative contributions of different variables to behavior development.

As an organized field of scientific endeavor, differential psychology began to take shape during the last quarter of the nineteenth century. Francis Galton contributed significantly to the investigation of individual differences, devising tests for the measurement of sensorimotor and other simple functions, gathering data in a variety of settings, and developing appropriate statistical techniques for data analysis. James McKeen Cattell, an American student of Wilhelm Wundt, extended Galton's work in test development and incorporated this approach in the emerging field of experimental psychology.

The first systematic description of the aims, scope, and methods of a psychology of individual differences appeared in an 1895 article by Alfred Binet and Victor Henri, "La psychologie individuelle" (Individual psychology). A fuller development of relevant topics, together with summaries of available findings, was provided in 1900 by William Stern. The term *differential psychology,* first introduced in the subtitle of his book, was incorporated formally in the revised and enlarged later editions, whose title reads, *Die Differentielle Psychologie in Ihren Methodischen Grundlagen*

(Methodological Foundations of Differential Psychology). Subsequent progress in the study of individual and group differences parallels closely the growth of psychological testing, as well as advances in related fields, notably genetics, developmental psychology, and cross-cultural psychology, all of which have made significant contributions to the methodology, data, and concepts of differential psychology.

Scope and Distribution of Individual Differences

Individual differences in behavioral characteristics are not limited to the human species, but occur throughout the animal scale. Investigations of animal behavior, from unicellular organisms to anthropoid apes, reveal wide individual differences in learning, motivation, emotionality, and other measurable traits. So large are these differences that the distributions of individual performance overlap even when widely separated species are compared.

Although in popular descriptions persons are often placed into distinct categories, such as bright or dull and excitable or calm, actual measurement of any psychological trait shows individuals to vary in degree along a continuous scale. In most traits, the distributions approximate the bell-shaped normal probability curve, with the greatest clustering of cases near the center of the range and a gradual decrease in numbers as the extremes are approached. First derived by mathematicians in their study of probability, the normal curve is obtained whenever the measured variable depends on a very large number of independent and equally weighted factors. Because of the extremely large number of hereditary and environmental factors that contribute to the development of most psychological traits, the normal curve is generally accepted as the most appropriate model for trait distribution, and psychological tests are generally constructed so as to conform to this model.

Heredity and Environment

Concepts

The origins of individual differences in behavioral characteristics are to be found in the innumerable interactions between heredity and environment that occur throughout one's life span. An individual's heredity consists of the genes received from each parent at conception. Genes are units of complex chemical substances transmitted on the chromosomes of the ovum and spermatozoon that unite to form the new organism. If there is a chemical deficiency or imbalance in one of these genes, a seriously defective organism may result, with physical pathology and severe mental retardation, as in phenylketonuria (PKU). Except for such pathological deviates, however, heredity sets broad limits to behavior development, and the limits are broader in the human than in lower species. Within these limits, what individuals actually become depends on their environment.

The environment comprises the sum total of stimuli to which the individual responds from conception to death. It covers a vast multiplicity of agents, ranging from air and food to the intellectual and emotional climate of home and community and the beliefs and attitudes of one's associates. Environmental influences begin to operate before birth. Nutritional deficiencies, toxins, and other chemical or physical conditions of the prenatal environment may have profound and lasting effects on both physical and mental development. Such terms as *inborn, innate,* and *congenital* are often misused with the false implication that all characteristics present at birth are hereditary. Another common confusion is the difference between organic and hereditary conditions. Mental retardation resulting from early brain injury, for instance, may be properly said to have an organic but not a hereditary origin.

Methodology

The many methods used to investigate the operation of hereditary and environmental influences in behavior development may be subsumed under three major approaches: *selective breeding, experiential control,* and *statistical studies of family resemblances.* Selective breeding for behavioral characteristics has been successfully applied to several species. From a single initial group of rats, for example, it proved possible to breed two strains comprising good and poor maze learners, respectively. That the two strains did not differ in general learning capacity, however, was demonstrated by the finding that both strains performed equally well in other learning problems. Still another study of these selectively bred strains provided a clear example of the interaction of heredity and environment. When reared in restrictive environments, both strains performed almost as poorly as did the genetically "dull" rats reared in a natural environment. In contrast, an enriched environment, providing a variety of stimulation and opportunities for motor activity, improved the performance of the "dull" strain, both groups now performing at about the level of the "bright" rats in a natural environment.

Later selective breeding experiments extended these procedures to other species and other types of behavior. Of particular significance was the development of techniques for measuring individual differences in behavior among such organisms as the fruit fly *Drosophila.* It thus became possible to capitalize on the mass of available genetic knowledge regarding the morphology of *Drosophila,* as well as on such other advantages as the short time span between generations and the abundance of progeny. Through these procedures, a strain of fruit flies was bred that would fly *toward* a source of light and another that would fly *away* from it.

A second approach to the study of heredity and environment is concerned with the behavioral effects of systematic, controlled variations in experience. Experimental investigations of this question either provide special training or prevent the normal exercise of a particular function. This method has frequently been followed with animals to study a wide variety of activities, ranging from the swimming of tadpoles and the singing of birds to sexual behavior and care of the young. Significant effects of such experiential manipulations have been reported for nearly all types of behavior, including perceptual, motor, learning, emotional, and social reactions. Through such experiments, activities formerly regarded as completely unlearned or "instinctive," such as nest building and grooming of the young by rats, have been shown to depend on the animal's prior experiences. Even when the animal has no opportunity to learn the specific activity in question, its behavior may be influenced by the exercise of other related functions.

In studies of infants and young children, one group of experiments utilized the method of cotwin control, in which one identical twin is given intensive training in, for example, stair climbing, while the other serves as the control. The results generally show that, if training is introduced when the child is physically ready for it, progress will be faster than if training is given earlier. Other studies have compared the development of children reared in experientially restricted environments, such as orphanages, with that of children reared in more stimulating environments. Marked differences have been found as a function of the amount of adult contact as well as the extent of physical stimulation and opportunities for motor activity. There is evidence, however, that appropriate educational programs, particularly when initiated in early childhood, may counteract the detrimental effects of such deprived environments on intellectual development.

The third major approach is based on statistical analyses of familial resemblance. Similarity of performance on both aptitude and personality tests have been investigated for parents and children, siblings, and both fraternal and identical twin pairs. In general, the closer the hereditary relation, the more similar the test scores. On most intelligence tests, for instance, identical twin correlations are close to .90, being nearly as high as the correlations between test and retest scores of the same persons. Fraternal twin correlations cluster around 0.70; those between siblings cluster around 0.50, as do those between parents and children. It should be noted, however, that a family is a cultural as well as a biological unit. In general, the more closely two persons are related by heredity, the greater will be the similarity of their environments and the extent of their influence on each other. Special studies of foster children and identical twins reared apart permit some separation of hereditary and environmental contributions, but several uncontrolled conditions in these studies preclude definitive conclusions.

Nature of Intelligence

Composition

Intelligence has been commonly identified with the intelligence quotient (IQ) obtained on a standardized intelligence test. Such tests reflect at least partly the concept of intelligence prevalent in the culture in which they were developed. Modern intelligence testing originated with Alfred Binet's development of a test to assess intellectual retardation among schoolchildren. Intelligence tests have frequently been validated against such academic criteria as school grades, teachers' ratings of intelligence, promotion and graduation data, and amount of schooling completed. In content, most intelligence tests are predominantly verbal, with some coverage of arithmetic skills and quantitative reasoning. Different intelligent tests, however, may sample somewhat different combinations of abilities. Nonlanguage and performance tests, for instance, often make much heavier demands on spatial visualization, perceptual speed and accuracy, and nonverbal reasoning than do the usual verbal-type tests.

With the increasing participation of psychologists in vocational counseling and personnel selection came the realization that supplementary tests were needed to measure aptitudes not covered by traditional intelligence tests. As a result, so-called special aptitude tests were developed for mechanical, clerical, and other occupationally useful abilities. At the same time, basic research on the nature of intelligence was being conducted by the techniques of factor analysis. Essentially, these techniques involve statistical analyses of the intercorrelations among test scores in the effort to identify the smallest number of independent factors that can account for the intercorrelations. Among the aptitudes, or factors, thus identified are verbal comprehension, word fluency, arithmetic skills, quantitative reasoning, perceptual speed, spatial visualization, and mechanical comprehension. Through factor analysis, the functions measured by intelligence tests were themselves sorted into relatively independent verbal and numerical aptitudes. These aptitudes, in combination with those underlying special aptitude tests, now provide a more comprehensive picture of human abilities. Several of these abilities are incorporated in what are generally designated multiple-aptitude batteries.

From another angle, the increasing accumulation of data from cross-cultural research indicated that intelligence can have different meanings in different cultures. Both traits constitute intelligence, and the relative level of development of these traits reflects the demands and the contingent reinforcements provided by the cultures in which people function. Investigations in preliterate cultures show that those members who have been exposed to a substantial amount of Western-type schooling are more likely to respond in terms of abstract concepts and are less context-bound than are their more traditionally reared age peers. Within a cross-cultural frame of reference, available intelligence tests can be most appropriately described as measures of academic intelligence or scholastic aptitude. These skills represent a limited segment of intelligence, but a segment that is broadly applicable and widely demanded in modern, technologically advanced societies. Within such societies, academic intelligence correlates substantially, not only with school achievement, but also with achievement in most occupations and in other major societal activities.

The intellectual functions tapped by traditional intelligence tests have also been investigated by cognitive psychologists within the framework of information processing and computer simulation of human thinking. Although this area of research is still in its early stages, it is contributing to an understanding of what intelligence tests measure by focusing attention on processes rather than end-products in problem solving. *What* does the examinee do when responding to test items? Analyzing intelligence test performance in terms of elementary component processes may eventually help to identify each person's sources of strength and weakness. Such analysis should enhance the diagnostic use of tests and facilitate the tailoring of training programs to fit each individual's needs.

Life-Span Development

Longitudinal studies of age changes with respect to performance on traditional intelligence tests reveal a slow rise in infancy, followed by more rapid progress and eventual slowing down as maturity is approached. It should be noted, however, that the trait cluster measured by intelligence tests varies with age. In infancy, the IQ is based largely on sensorimotor development, whereas in childhood, it depends increasingly on verbal and other abstract functions. During the period of uniform formal schooling, the content of intelligence tests closely reflects what is learned in school. Later, changing patterns of intellectual development associated with progressive educational and occupational specialization may not be fully identified through available intelligence tests; they may require a broader spectrum of tests and other assessment procedures.

Average performance on traditional intelligence tests shows continuing improvement with age through the 20s. Among high-scoring groups, especially college graduates and those engaged in intellectually demanding occupations, such improvements may continue throughout life. In more nearly average samples, tested abilities tend to decline beyond the 30s, the drop being largest in tasks involving speed, visual perception, and abstract spatial relations. In cross-sectional studies, which use different samples at different age levels, age differences are likely to be confounded with cultural changes in the population because of lack of comparability of the different age groups in amount of education and other changing life conditions. Well-designed longitudinal studies of adults indicate that the decline attributable to age is much smaller than are the differences attributable to educational and cultural changes over time.

Intellectual Deviates

The mentally retarded and the gifted represent the lower and upper extremes of the distribution of intelligence. Because the distribution is continuous, there is no sharp separation between these groups and the norm. In terms of intelligence test performance, mental retardation is customarily identified with IQs below 70, representing about 2–3% of the general population. Decisions regarding the disposition and treatment of individual cases are based not only on the IQ but also on a comprehensive study of the individual's intellectual development, educational history, social competence, physical condition, and familial situation. Although a few rare forms of mental retardation result from defective genes, the large majority of cases can be traced to environmental conditions operating before or after birth and including both physical and psychological influences.

At the other end of the scale, the intellectually gifted have been investigated by various procedures and from several points of view. In a major, long-term project conducted by Lewis M. Terman and his associates at Stanford University, approximately 1,000 children with Stanford-Binet IQs of 140 or higher were intensively examined and subsequently followed up at several life stages. IQs as high as these are found in slightly more than 1% of the general population. The results of the Stanford study, which have been corroborated in several investigations conducted elsewhere, revealed the gifted child as typically successful in school, healthy, emotionally stable, and having a wide range of interests. As they grew into maturity, these gifted children on the whole maintained their superiority in adult achievements.

The concept of intelligence was thereby broadened to include several creative abilities, such as ideational fluency and originality. Motivation, interests, and other personality variables were also found to play important parts in creative achievement, as did the psychological climate of the environment in which the individual was reared and in which he or she functioned as an adult.

Group Differences

Sex Differences

The investigation of any group differences in behavioral characteristics presents several methodological and interpretive problems. In group comparisons, individual differences *within* each group have proved far greater than average differences *between* groups. The distributions of different groups overlap to a marked extent. Even when there are large, statistically significant differences between the mean scores of two groups, individuals can be found in the lower-scoring group who outperform individuals in the higher-scoring group. It follows that one's group membership is not a dependable indicator of one's standing in psychological traits.

Another problem arises from the use of unrepresentative samples in which selective factors may have operated differentially for the populations under investigation. Insofar as more boys than girls may drop out of school, for example, a comparison of the intelligence test scores of high school boys and girls will show a mean difference in favor of boys. This difference would disappear if we were to include dropouts, who tend to score toward the low end of the distribution. A similar interpretive error in the opposite direction is illustrated by surveys of institutionalized mental retardates, which have generally shown an excess of males. Although once regarded as evidence for the higher incidence of mental retardation among males, these findings were later traced to selective admission policies. For various social and economic reasons, mentally retarded females were more likely to remain in the community than were males of the same intellectual levels.

The use of total scores on intelligence tests may also be misleading in group comparisons. In the construction of several intelligence tests, such as the Stanford-Binet, sex differences were ruled out by omitting or balancing out items that favored either sex. Even when this practice is not followed in selecting items, a composite score on a heterogeneous test may obscure existing group differences in specific abilities.

Psychological test surveys have demonstrated significant mean differences between the sexes in a number of aptitudes and personality traits. Females as a group excel in finger dexterity, perceptual speed and accuracy, verbal fluency and other tasks involving the mechanics of language, and rote memory for most types of content. Males excel in speed and coordination of gross bodily movements, spatial orientation, mechanical comprehension, and mathematical reasoning. Among personality differences, one of the best established is the greater aggression of the male. This difference is manifested early in life and is found consistently across cultural groups. It has also been observed in animals, notably subhuman primates and most other mammalian species. Several investigations indicated a stronger achievement drive in the male, but this difference was subsequently found to vary with the conditions under which it was assessed; the results may reflect in part the extent to which the context is task-oriented or person-oriented. There is considerable evidence that females exhibit a stronger social orientation and desire for social approval than do males, as well as less self-confidence and a higher level of anxiety in various situations.

Most investigations of sex differences yield only descriptive data about existing differences within a given culture. The origins of such differences must be sought in the complex interactions of biological and cultural factors. From a biological viewpoint, the different roles men and women play in the reproductive function undoubtedly contribute to sex differentiation in psychological development. The long period of childbearing and child rearing, which falls biologically on the female, has had far-reaching effects on sex differences in interests, attitudes, emotional traits, occupational goals, and achievement. Sex differences in aggression are associated with the greater body size, muscular strength, and physical endurance of the male. There is also considerable experimental evidence that aggressive behavior is related to the level of sex hormones. Another significant sex difference is to be found in the developmental acceleration of girls. Not only do girls reach puberty earlier than boys, but throughout childhood they are also further advanced toward their own adult status in all physical traits. In infancy, the developmental acceleration of girls may be an important factor in their more rapid acquisition of language and may give them a head start in verbal development as a whole.

The contributions of culture can be readily illustrated. Although living in the same homes, girls and boys in most societies are reared in different subcultures. In countless ways they receive differential treatment from parents, other adults, and age peers. The personalities of mother and father are themselves important factors in the child's developing concept of sex roles, providing models of what is expected of each sex in the particular culture. Sex-role stereotypes are likely to influence sex differentiation in motivation, interests, and attitudes. There is also some evidence that performance on cognitive tasks, such as problem solving and achievement tests in reading and arithmetic, is significantly related to the degree of individuals' sex-role identification and their own evaluation of the sex-appropriateness of various activities. Most of the descriptive data regarding sex differences in psychological traits were gathered in the United States and other contemporary Western nations prior to the advent of the current feminist movement. The educational, occupational, and social changes promoted by that movement may be reflected in changes in the relative development of males and females in both cognitive and noncognitive areas.

Racial and Cultural Differences

Race is a biological concept referring to subdivisions of a species. It corresponds to such classifications as breed, stock, or strain in animals. Human races are formed when a group becomes relatively isolated, through either geographic or social barriers, so that mating among its members is more frequent than mating with outsiders. Over many generations, this process produces populations that differ in the relative frequency of certain genes. Because these differences are relative and not absolute, however, any racial group exhibits some variation in hereditary racial characteristics and overlaps with other populations in such characteristics. For this reason, the concept of race can be properly applied to populations, but not to individuals.

When persons are classified according to such categories as socioeconomic level, nationality, or ethnic identity, significant group differences are often found in child-rearing practices, sexual behavior, emotional responses, interests, and attitudes, as well as in performance on many aptitude tests. In all such comparisons, the direction and amount of group difference depend on the particular trait that is investigated. Because each culture or subculture fosters the development of its own characteristic pattern of aptitudes and personality traits, comparisons in terms of such global measures as IQ or general emotional adjustment can have little meaning.

Isolation of groups leads to cultural as well as racial differentiation. Hence, it is difficult to disentangle the contributions of biological and cultural factors to race differences in psychological traits. Test performance of hybrid, or racially mixed, groups has been investigated for this purpose. It has been argued that, if one race is intellectually superior to another because of genetic factors, the hybrid offspring of both races should be intermediate in intelligence. As commonly tested, this hypothesis is questionable because it assumes complete linkage between the genes determining skin color or other racial indexes and the genes determining intelligence. With incomplete linkage, the correlation between racial characteristics and intelligence would disappear within a few generations of cross-breeding. The results are further complicated by the fact that race mixture is usually selective within either or both races, as well as by the tendency toward greater cultural assimilation of hybrids into the majority population. In groups that were fairly homogeneous in their assimilation of the majority culture, and in which individuals were classified according to ancestry records rather than appearance, the correlation between test scores and extent of race mixture was negligible.

Another approach is concerned with changes in the comparative test performance of racial groups with age. Studies of Black infants and preschool children in the United States, for example, revealed little or no retardation in terms of White norms. Tests administered to schoolchildren in the same regions and time periods, however, showed significant mean retardation that increased with age. These findings are similar to those obtained with various other groups reared in educational and culturally restricted environments. The age decrement has been attributed to the cumulative effects of experiential limitations and to the increasing inadequacy of such environments to meet the expanding intellectual needs of the growing child. From a broader viewpoint, such an age decrement in relation to test norms may be said to occur when a test assesses cognitive functions not fostered in a particular culture or subculture.

A third approach compares samples of the same race reared in different environments. In general, such studies have yielded larger differences in test performance among subgroups of a single race living in different milieus than among different racial groups living under more nearly similar conditions. That the regional differences found within a racial population are associated with cultural differences rather than with selective migration has been demonstrated in several studies.

Studies of so-called equated groups of different races generally show substantial reduction in mean IQ differences, although some difference remains. Such studies are subject to several methodological difficulties. One is statistical regression toward the mean, which occurs whenever a matched-sample experimental design is employed with populations that differ in the equating variable, such as socioeconomic level. The effect of this procedure is to produce mean differences in, for example, IQ in the samples chosen, simply as a statistical artifact of the selection procedure. Another difficulty arises from the use of very broad categories for classifying such variables as socioeconomic and educational levels. With broad categories, it is likely that the individuals from one population cluster at the low end *within* each category, whereas those in the other population cluster at the high end, even though they were selected so that the total number within each category was the same.

A related difficulty pertains to the use of such traditional equating variables as parental occupation and education, whose relation to the child's psychological development may be too indirect and remote. There is an increasing tendency to construct home environment scales that are more detailed and more immediately relevant to the development of specified traits, such as scholastic aptitude. Use of such scales in comparative studies of Black and White preschool children and high school students yielded promising evidence of the dependence of group differences in intellectual development on the relevant characteristics of home environments.

In light of available knowledge, only a few conclusions can be drawn with confidence. First, no biological basis has as yet been clearly identified for any existing psychological race difference. Second, there is considerable evidence, from both racial studies and other types of investigations in differential psychology, showing the part played by cultural factors in producing the sort of behavioral differences commonly found among racial groups. Finally, in all psychological traits, the range of individual differences within each race is far larger than the mean difference between races.

With regard to group differences in general, we can say that empirically established *group differences* become *group stereotypes* when (1) mean differences are ascribed indiscriminately to all individuals within the group, and (2) the observed differences are assumed to be rigidly fixed, unchangeable, and hereditary.

Anne Anastasi
Fordham University

See also: **Adopted Children; Behavioral Genetics; Human Intelligence; Individual Differences; Psychological Assessment; Sex Differences**

DIGESTIVE SYSTEM

The *digestive system* refers to those organs involved in the process of breaking down ingested food into molecules that are used to nourish the body. The digestive system includes all portions of the gastrointestinal tract—mouth, esophagus, stomach, small intestine, large intestine, rectum, and anus—and the organs that secrete chemical juices necessary for the digestive process: salivary glands, liver, gall bladder, and pancreas.

In the mouth, the food is chewed into relatively small particles and mixed with saliva, which contains ptyalin, an enzyme which converts some starches to sugar. After the food passes through the esophagus and into the stomach, it is vigorously mixed with hydrochloric acid and the enzyme pepsin. This initiates the digestion of proteins. The food, which is now a thick liquid, is called *chyme.* When the particle size and chemical nature of the chyme is at the appropriate level, a sphincter opens, allowing the chyme to pass into the small intestine. In the small intestine, pancreatic juice containing the enzymes trypsin, amylase, and lipase continue the breakdown of the partially digested food. The complete digestive process is aided by additional secretions in the small intestine including bile, which is produced in the liver and stored in the gall bladder.

When the food is completely digested, it is absorbed in the walls of the small intestine and carried by the circulatory system to all parts of the body. The role of the large intestine is to store nondigestible waste products and to absorb small amounts of water and minerals.

The psychophysiology of the gastrointestinal (GI) system is a relatively unexplored area. We note the 1943 landmark work of Wolf and Wolff in which they described the secretory and motility changes of their fistulated subject to various stress situations, and the very recent work of GI psychophysiologists who have demonstrated that behavioral stressors, which influence autonomic and cardiovascular reactivity, also influence gastric activity, but there were few studies reported in between. However, the paucity of psychophysiology research on the GI system is not so surprising when we consider the instrumentation and measurement problems of obtaining data from far inside this constantly changing many-meter-long system.

As a consequence of these problems, no psychophysiological studies of absorption are known to the author, and few studies of gastric acid secretion have been conducted by psychophysiologists. However, several studies of motor activity have been conducted, particularly in the more easily accessible two ends of the GI tract, the esophagus and rectum, and also in the stomach. An increasing number of studies have recently been published by psychophysiologists in which the motor activity of the stomach was measured with the noninvasive method of electrogastrography.

Electrogastrography refers to the recording of electrogastrograms (EGGs). Electrogastrograms reflect gastric myoelectrical activity as it is recorded from the abdominal surface with cutaneous electrodes. EGGs are sinusoidal waves recurring at a rate of 3 cycles per minute (cpm) in healthy humans. This predominant frequency is usually discernable by visual inspection of the signal, but computer analysis is essential for quantitative study of EGG recordings. The stomach is also the source of abnormally fast or slow usually dysrhythmic myoelectrical signals, the tachygastrias (4–10 cpm) and bradygastrias (1–2.5 cpm). Acute or chronic shifts from normal 3 cpm EGG signals to the gastric dysrhythmias are associated with a variety of clinical syndromes and symptoms, particularly nausea. In contrast to the abnormalities in frequency such as the gastric dysrhythmias, the amplitude, duration, wave form, and wave propagation characteristics of the EGG have been infrequently studied.

EGG, because of its noninvasive nature, will continue to aid basic researchers in their quest for additional information about gastric myoelectric activity, gastric motility, and their relationship in normal and pathophysiological conditions. Applied research using the EGG by gastroenterologists is increasing rapidly, largely due to the ease and reliability of its use in detecting gastric dysrhythmias and the recently established relationship between gastric dysrhythmias and upper GI disorders, including delayed gastric emptying and nausea. A related exciting new area that requires EGG recording in order to assess results is electrical pacing of the stomach. Research is currently being carried out on dogs and on a small number of humans in cases of gastric paresis where the stomach has ceased contracting and no drugs are helpful. A less dramatic but related area of research that is currently underway is biofeedback of EGG for individuals with gastric dysrhythmias in an effort to restore normal 3 cpm activity and thereby relieve nausea. The recent increase in the use of the EGG by gastroenterologists has brought with it refinements in both hardware and software, including ambulatory units that have flown on Space Shuttle flights. It is predicted that with the availability of this new equipment, additional psychophysiologists will soon be using the EGG to study the effects of stress and emotions on gastric activity.

REFERENCE

Wolf, S. & Wolff, H. G. (1943). *Human gastric function.* New York: Oxford University Press.

Robert M. Stern
Pennsylvania State University

DISCRIMINATION

Discrimination is negative behavior directed at individuals or at groups of individuals because of their social group membership. Discrimination is based on social categories that individuals do not generally choose to belong to, including gender, race, religion, disability, sexual orientation, stigma, age, and physical appearance. Although it is normal to favor people who are similar to us (young children frequently play within gender groups and people date and marry primarily within their own race), discrimination involves unfair, unwarranted, and unjustifiable treatment of others.

Discrimination occurs in both *explicit* and *subtle* forms. Explicit discrimination ranges from actions such as making negative comments to or about people or excluding them from activities, to verbal and sexual abuse or physical harm. Subtle discrimination includes actions that are normally more difficult to detect, such as failing to make eye contact with someone, staring at or avoiding someone, or ignoring them entirely. Explicit discrimination is usually assessed through survey methodology in organizations or through examination of historical records. Subtle discrimination is frequently assessed in laboratory contexts using unobtrusive measures of verbal and nonverbal behavior, such as how much help research participants give to another person, how long they converse with them, or how far away from them they sit.

Discrimination is multiply determined at psychological and sociological levels. At the level of the individual, some people are more likely to discriminate than others. Discrimination is closely related to holding negative stereotypes about members of other groups and to being prejudiced toward them, and it occurs when people choose to act on their negative stereotypes and prejudices. Discrimination also occurs in part because it helps maintain individuals' personal esteem and social identity. People may feel better about themselves and their own groups when they put down, insult, or degrade members of another group. People may also assume that individuals from other groups hold different beliefs and values and therefore dislike them.

At a social level, discrimination is in large part the result of social conformity. If people perceive that the relevant social norms favor discrimination, then they will discriminate themselves; if they perceive that the norms do not allow discrimination, they will not discriminate. Interventions designed to alleviate discrimination frequently attempt to change social norms, with the expectation that this will reduce discrimination. At a societal level, discrimination occurs more frequently when economic conditions are poor. As one example, lynching of Blacks in the South during the early twentieth century was inversely correlated with the price of cotton (an indicator of economic prosperity). This relationship is in part due to the frustration caused by hardship and in part due to realistic conflict caused by employment scarcity. Discrimination may be socially sanctioned because high-status, powerful, individuals are motivated to retain their status by discriminating against lower-status groups.

It is frequently difficult to identify discrimination (even if it is explicit) because most instances leave room for interpretation. In a case where a more qualified female is passed over for a position and a male is hired instead, one can only be certain that discrimination has occurred when gender is the sole difference between the two candidates or if there is a continuing pattern of unequal treatment by the employer over time. In many cases, there is not enough information to allow an unambiguous attribution. Thus, even though discrimination may have occurred, it may not be easily interpreted as such, and therefore may not be perceived or reported.

Although members of targeted groups (for instance, women and African Americans) report that there is discrimination directed at their group as a whole, they do not generally report experiencing it personally. People may deny personal discrimination because admitting that they are victims is psychologically costly. There are also many social costs to reporting discrimination (such as embarrassment, ostracism, and employment harassment) that make people unlikely to do so.

Discrimination can be both psychologically and physically harmful to those who endure it. Individuals who report frequent exposure to discrimination or unfair treatment also report experiencing more psychological distress, depression, and lower levels of life satisfaction. Discrimination may contribute to the high percentage of minority group members who live in poverty and lack access to high-paying jobs. Discrimination also is responsible in part for higher mortality rates, access to less and poorer quality healthcare, delayed diagnoses, or failure to manage chronic diseases for members of minority groups.

If the targets are aware of the discrimination they are experiencing, they may place the blame internally, and this may result in lowered self-esteem, self-blame, and disidentification with the ingroup. On the other hand, they may also place the blame externally, which can lead to either individual action (such as leaving the negative situation or reporting or confronting perpetrators) or collective action (such as mobilizing political or other organizations).

Political policies in the United States, including the Civil Rights Act of 1964, which established the Equal Employment Opportunities Commission and prohibited discrimination in employment, have reduced the frequency of explicit discrimination in recent years. The courts have ruled that even unintentional discrimination violates equal status laws. If targets are harmed, degraded, or treated differently than others as a function of their group membership, then discrimination has occurred. These laws have also required reparations for violations of the laws, including awarding employment, promotions and back salary, and have in some cases requested employers to establish practices that require a certain number or percentage of members of victimized social groups to be hired or promoted. Despite a reduction in explicit discrimination, implicit forms of discrimination continue to be common. Current research shows that women and minorities generally report experiencing discrimination on a weekly basis.

Charles Stangor
University of Maryland

Gretchen B. Sechrist
State University of New York, Buffalo

DISPLACEMENT

Displacement of aggression refers to a redirection of harm-doing behavior from a primary to a secondary target or victim. An early theory of displacement was proposed by Sigmund Freud in *Beyond the Pleasure Principle* (1950). Freud suggested that persons tend to attack the sources of frustration, but if an individual cannot attack such a source because the target is unavailable or too powerful, a substitute target may become the victim of the pent-up anger. This mechanism explained apparently irrational behavior, such as a person's killing a total stranger for no apparent reason. Frustration causes a buildup of inner tension, which is expended when the individual expresses aggression toward a target. The amount of aggression is postulated to be directly related to the amount of cumulated inner energy. A sudden release of energy through aggressive action is referred to as catharsis.

In *Frustration and Aggression* (1939), Dollard, Doob, Miller, Mowrer, and Sears converted the literary and metaphoric language of Freud into the scientifically more acceptable, positivistic language of laboratory-oriented behavioristic psychologists. According to Dollard and his colleagues, aggressive behavior—like all other kinds of behavior—should be considered subject to the laws of learning. They defined *frustration* as any stimulus that blocked the goal attainment of an organism striving to attain a goal. Frustration causes a buildup of aggressive drive, which presses for behavioral expression in the form of harm-doing. When a person directs an aggressive response at a frustrating agent and the response is successful in removing the barrier to goal attainment, aggression is rewarded. A rewarded response is more likely to recur the next time the individual faces a similar situation. Thus, while harm-doing behavior reduces aggressive drive and additional immediate aggression, it is rewarding and increases the likelihood of harm-doing when the individual is frustrated again in the future.

Rewarding an individual for inhibiting an aggressive response or punishing harm-doing behavior may teach self-control. As a result of learned inhibition, the aggressive energy generated by frustration either continues to build up or is expressed in indirect ways. While fear of punishment inhibits aggressive behavior, the cumulated internal energy pushes for its expression. These two conflicting forces were conceptualized by Miller (1948) in terms of a model incorporating approach and avoidance forces, but this conflict model has had little subsequent impact on research. Displacement is essentially a principle of substitution of responses or of targets and may be viewed in terms of response or stimulus generalization.

The concept of displacement has been used to explain a wide variety of behaviors; for example, ethnic prejudice and discrimination may be considered a form of displacement. Thus, researchers have tried to show that historically a decline in cotton prices in the southern United States was associated with an increase in lynchings of African Americans. The reasoning is that bad economic results were frustrating to farmers, who took out their anger on Blacks—a type of scapegoating theory. Similarly, wars have been considered to be a result of the cumulated frustrations of many people manifested in an aggression toward a substitute target: the enemy nation. The importance of understanding displacement effects is certainly underlined by the frequent reference of the concept to ethnic, racial, and religious conflicts; child abuse, lynchings, riots, suicides, revolutions, and many other important social behaviors.

The establishment of the frustration-aggression interpretation is undermined by evidence failing to demonstrate catharsis effects (the reduction of subsequent aggression immediately following aggressive behavior). Furthermore, there is no evidence of a buildup of more intense aggressive behavior over a series of frustrating experiences. The fact of displacement-like effects is indisputable, and alternative theories are being developed that rely on concepts drawn from factors related to interpersonal interactions rather than intrapsychic dynamics. Among these alternative explanations are active downward comparisons, self-presentation, negative equity, and guilt by association. Active downward comparison refers to an individual's efforts to lower the performance or identity of another person or group so as to enhance his or her own identity (Wills, 1981). For example, acting to block the opportunities of others (such as providing them with inferior schools) serves to maintain the relative superiority of the discriminating person or group. The desire for positive self-esteem is considered the motivating factor.

Tedeschi and Norman (1985), however, argued that putting others down raises the self up, not so much for internal self-esteem reasons but for the purpose of presenting oneself to others as better or superior in some way. In this formulation, individuals are highly motivated to establish and maintain desirable identities in order to foster positive and rewarding interactions with other people. As a result, an individual is willing to harm someone else if doing so will help promote a positive identity for the individual in the eyes of others. The victims of such harm-doing may have done nothing to provoke or justify the action. For example, a group of teenage boys, each one of them motivated by the desire to impress the other boys with his willingness to use violence, may attack someone at random.

Motivation to restore equity may also produce displacement-like behavior. Members of most groups expect rewards to be fairly distributed. The rule of equity prescribes that each member should receive a share of the rewards proportional to his or her contribution to the group's success in attaining the rewards. It is assumed that people are motivated to maintain justice and that, when an injustice occurs, something should be done to restore justice. When rewards are unfairly distributed in a group, disadvantaged members may be motivated to restore equity. If for some reason no action can be taken against the source of the inequity, other means of restoring equity may be undertaken. For example, if a boss distributes Christmas bonuses to his or her workers, and a few of the workers believe they received unfairly low bonuses, they should be motivated to restore equity. They cannot punish the boss for fear of losing their jobs, but they might take out their anger by harming (probably in some nonviolent way) the relatively advantaged workers. Such action restores equity in the sense that the advantaged workers are made to suffer, detracting from the monetary gain and thus making outcomes more fair.

Anthropologists and historians have noted that retaliation is often visited upon coconspirators, blood relatives, or friends of instigators, rather than directly against the instigator. Victims sometimes hold all members of an outgroup equally responsible for harm done to them and may retaliate against one of the weaker members of the outgroup. Thus, retaliation may be directed against any member of a rival gang, or in blood feuds, against any member of the target family. Hate groups may randomly target any member of the hated group. The representative target chosen from the category of believed enemies may be completely innocent and unaware of any harm done to the aggressor. The attack represents a displacementlike effect, since revenge is not taken against a frustrating agent but against an innocent third party—although such an attack may serve to punish the frustrating agent by harming a loved one, or it may be motivated to deter future harm-doing by that agent.

REFERENCES

Dollard, J., Doob, N., Miller, N. E., Mowrer, O. H., & Sears, R. R. (1939). *Frustration and aggression.* New Haven, CT: Yale University Press.

Freud, S. (1950). *Beyond the pleasure principle* (J. Strachey, Trans.). New York: Liveright.

Miller, N. E. (1948). Theory and experiment relating psychoanalytic displacement to stimulus-response generalization. *Journal of Abnormal and Social Psychology, 43,* 155–178.

Tedeschi, J. T., & Norman, N. (1985). Social mechanisms of displaced aggression. In E. J. Lawler (Ed.), *Advances in group processes: Theory and research* (Vol. 2, pp. 29–56). Greenwich, CT: JAI Press.

Wills, T. A. (1981). Downward comparison principles in social psychology. *Psychological Bulletin, 90,* 245–271.

James T. Tedeschi
University of Illinois, Urbana-Champaign

DOCTOR OF PSYCHOLOGY DEGREE (PsyD)

The Doctor of Psychology degree (PsyD) is awarded to psychologists whose education and training are designed to prepare them for careers in professional practice. With considerable variation in content and emphasis, the training programs that lead to the degree all include education in basic facts and principles of psychology, extensive supervised experience in application of procedures for the assessment and modification of psychological functioning, and an internship. Early proposals for PsyD programs did not include a doctoral dissertation requirement, but nearly all the programs now in operation do so. Systematic inquiry is regarded as a form of practice rather than an end in itself, and the range of topics is broader than has traditionally characterized PhD dissertations in psychology. Community needs analyses, case studies, and theoretical inquiries, among other kinds of investigations, are all acceptable, so long as each project contributes to improved understanding or constructive change in the way psychologists do their work. A typical program requires 5 years of graduate study beyond the baccalaureate degree.

The first proposal for use of the PsyD was advanced by Leta Hollingworth in 1918. Similar proposals were put forward by Loyal Crane in 1925 and A. T. Poffenberger in 1938. All argued that education in the science of psychology was insufficient for the practice of psychology and that the PhD degree, traditionally used as a scholarly credential across all disciplines, was inappropriate as a certificate of knowledge and competence in professional psychology. They urged development of programs expressly designed to prepare people for practice, and awarding a professional doctorate analogous to the MD, DDS, and other professional degrees upon completion of graduate studies. The proposals were not cordially received in the academic community, however, and only two practitioner programs, both in Canada and both short-lived, were attempted before the 1960s.

A conference on training in clinical psychology at Boulder, Colorado in 1949 established the scientist-practitioner model as the dominant pattern for the education of professional psychologists and the PhD as the standard qualifying credential. In the Boulder model, as it came to be called, students were to be prepared as researchers as well as clinicians, in the belief that each form of activity would enhance the other. The Boulder model was widely adopted in American universities and remains the most common design for the education of professional psychologists.

By the middle of the 1960s, however, expressions of discontent with prevailing PhD programs were often heard. According to critics, most clinical programs in academic departments overemphasized research at the expense of training for practice, and psychologists entering professional careers, as more than half of them were doing by that time, were poorly prepared for the challenges they faced in their work. After lengthy deliberations, an American Psychological Association (APA) committee on the scientific and professional aims of psychology recommended the establishment of practitioner programs leading to the PsyD degree. The proposal was debated at a conference on training in clinical psychology in Chicago in 1965, where it was not generally endorsed, although the majority recognized that programs of this kind might be attempted in some universities and that the results of those efforts would provide a basis for evaluation at a later time. Shortly after the Chicago conference, the faculty of the Urbana-Champaign campus of the University of Illinois voted to inaugurate a PsyD program, and the first program in the United States was established there in 1968.

Five years later, still another conference on training in professional psychology was held in Vail, Colorado. There the concept of direct education for the practice of psychology was endorsed, as was the use of the PsyD degree to certify completion of graduate work in practitioner programs. In the years that followed, additional PsyD programs were developed in universities and professional schools throughout the United States, although the initial program at the University of Illinois was discontinued in 1980.

Beginning in the 1980s and continuing into the 1990s, long-standing educational policies that restricted use of the PhD to mark the highest level of achievement in preparation for careers of creative research and scholarship, and to mandate the use of professional doctoral degrees to recognize completion of academic preparation for professional practice, were actively enforced by agencies responsible for accrediting educational institutions in the United States. During this period, a considerable number of practitioner programs that had previously awarded the PhD were required to employ the PsyD degree to maintain approval. This change, along with continuing development of new programs, led to substantial expansion in the number of PsyD programs in the United States and Canada. Toward the end of the twentieth century, some 60 programs were in operation. Approximately half of these were in universities, half were in free-standing professional schools, and two-thirds had been fully or provisionally approved by the APA Committee on Accreditation.

SUGGESTED READING

Peterson, D. R. (1997). *Educating professional psychologists: History and guiding conception.* Washington, DC: APA Books.

Donald R. Peterson
Rutgers University

DOPAMINE SYSTEMS

Perhaps more than any other neurotransmitter, dopamine has received attention for its potential involvement in psychiatric disorders ranging from Substance Abuse to Schizophrenia. This focus relies primarily on the capacity of drugs that manipulate dopamine transmission to ameliorate or exacerbate psychiatric conditions. However, our emerging comprehension of brain circuitry and function permits an understanding of dopamine transmission in the brain that is both more integrated and accurate. This short description of dopamine systems will explicate the components of dopamine transmission, such as synthesis, release, and receptor signaling, and using brain circuitry to assemble the dopamine neurons and projections into overall brain functions.

Dopamine: The Neurotransmitter

Anatomical Organization

Akin to other monoaminergic transmitter systems, the dopamine neurons are located in discrete brain nuclei and are not widely distributed throughout the brain. The largest cluster of dopamine cells is located in the ventral midbrain. The medial portion of cells is located in the ventral tegmental area, while the lateral cluster is in the substantia nigra. In addition, another large group of cells is located in the hypothalamus. This latter group functions primarily to regulate prolactin secretion from the pituitary, while the midbrain neurons project to areas of the forebrain and cortex involved in motor, emotional, and cognitive processing. This includes projections to aspects of the extrapyramidal motor system, prefrontal cortex, and various limbic structures such as the amygdala and hippocampus. These projections are topographically organized, with the more medial neurons providing innervation to the cortex and limbic nuclei, and the more lateral cell group providing innervation primarily to the caudate. Moreover, within certain axon terminal fields there is a medial to lateral topography. For example, in the ventral pallidum or subthalamus, the ventral tegmental area innervates the medial aspect of the nucleus, whereas the substantia nigra innervates the lateral compartment.

Synthesis, Degradation, and Release

Dopamine synthesis is a multiple enzymatic process involving the hydroxylation and decarboxylation of tyrosine. The rate-limiting enzyme in the synthesis of dopamine is tyrosine hydroxylase, which catabolizes tyrosine into dopa. This is a highly regulated enzyme susceptible to end-product feedback by cytosolic dopamine as well as by released dopamine via stimulation of dopamine autoreceptors. Following synthesis, dopamine is transported from the cytosol into synaptic vesicles via a proton-dependent vesicular monoamine transporter and is then sequestered pending release into the synaptic cleft. The physiological release of dopamine is voltage- and calcium-dependent and is regulated by the frequency and pattern of action potentials as well as by dopamine autoreceptors. A burst pattern of action potentials is most efficient at releasing dopamine. Dopamine in the synaptic cleft is eliminated by one of three mechanisms: (1) The vast majority of dopamine undergoes reuptake into the presynaptic terminal via the dopamine transporter; (2) A minor metabolic inactivation in the synaptic cleft involves methylation via catecho-O-methyltransferase to form 3-methoxytyramine; or (3) Dopamine can diffuse into the perisynaptic extracellular space. Following transport into the presynaptic terminal, dopamine is either transported into synaptic vesicles or oxidized by monoamine oxidase. Monoamine oxidase is primarily located in the mitochondria and exists as two isozymes (MAO-A and MAO-B). The two isozymes are differentially distributed in the brain and have different affinities for monoamines. Monoamine oxidase-B is of greater importance in metabolizing dopamine in the nigrostriatal pathway, whereas MAO-A may be of greater importance elsewhere.

Dopamine Receptors

Receptor Subtypes

Dopamine receptors can be localized on neurons postsynaptic to dopamine terminals (postsynaptic receptors), on dopamine axon terminals (autoreceptors), on nondopaminergic axon terminals (heteroreceptors), or on dopamine cell bodies and dendrites (somatodendritic autoreceptors). Dopamine receptors are synthesized from five different genes and, based upon sequence homology and pharmacological specificity, have been divided into two receptor families. The D1 receptor family consists of the D1 and D5 receptors while the D2 family consists of D2, D3, and D4 receptors. Two splice variants of the D2 receptor subtype have been characterized: D2S and D2L.

Receptor Localization

The various dopamine receptor subtypes are heterogeneously distributed in the nervous system. The D2 receptors are found both postsynaptically and as presynaptic autoreceptors, while the D1 receptors are located postsynaptically and heterosynaptically on nondopaminergic axon terminals. Thus D2 receptors, notably the D2 and perhaps D3 subtypes, regulate the release and synthesis of dopamine in response to stimulation by extracellular dopamine. Remarkably, in certain areas where dopamine receptors are in highest density, such as the striatum and substantia nigra, the cells expressing each receptor subtype are distinct. Within each family there also exist distinct distributions of receptors. For example, in the D1 family the D1 subtype is highest in the striatum, olfactory tubercle, amygdala, and parts of the cortex, whereas the D5 subtype is most dense in the thalamus and hippocampus. Similarly, for the D2 family, D2 receptors are dense throughout the basal ganglia, whereas D3 receptors are localized to the more limbic, ventral portions to the striatum and olfactory tubercle, and D4 receptors are found primarily in the prefrontal cortex and hippocampus.

Receptor Signaling

All of the dopamine receptor subtypes are metabotropic, G-protein coupled receptors. The two families of receptors have distinct intracellular signaling mechanisms. The D1 family couples with Gs to activate adenylate cyclase and cAMP production. The ensuing activation of protein kinase A results in the phosphorylation of numerous proteins leading to changes in enzyme activity, signaling in other receptor systems and gene expression. Notably, there is a heterosynaptic inhibition or stimulation of the release of other neurotransmitters, as well as a stimulatory effect on voltage-dependent calcium channels. The transduction pathway for the D2 family of receptors is more complicated, but involves coupling to Gi and Go. The two most well-studied signaling pathways are the inhibition of adenylate cyclase and the opening of potassium channels. These actions result in numerous changes in cell functioning. Notably there is a hyperpolarization of membrane potential, due primarily to the opening of potassium channels, which accounts for the inhibition dopamine release by D2 autoreceptors and the inhibition of postsynaptic neurons.

Receptor Pharmacology

The pharmacological stimulation of dopamine receptors can be produced by two types of agonist. Direct agonists have affinity for the dopamine receptors themselves, whereas the indirect agonists stimulate dopamine receptors by increasing the concentrations of dopamine in the synaptic cleft. Both types of agonist have clinical utility. The indirect agonists produce increases in extracellular dopamine by binding to the dopamine transporter and either preventing dopamine transport or acting as a false substrate. Amphetamine typifies a false substrate that is transported in place of dopamine. Additionally, the false substrates promote the heteroexchange of dopamine, causing reverse transport through the transporter. Therefore, drugs like amphetamine not only prevent the elimination of dopamine from the synaptic cleft but also induce release of cytosolic dopamine via reversal of the transporter. Cocaine and methylphenidate are prototypic drugs that bind to the transporter to prevent the reuptake of dopamine but are not themselves transported. Therefore, the increased release of dopamine by these latter drugs relies solely on the accumulation of dopamine released from synaptic vesicles and does not result from heteroexchange. Direct agonists bind to dopamine receptors and may or may not be selective for the D1 or D2 family of receptors. Given the heterogeneity of receptor localization (discussed previously), the development of highly selective compounds would seem to provide for relatively subtle manipulations of dopamine transmission. While drugs exist to clearly distinguish the D1 and D2 families, no drugs are universally accepted to distinguish between the receptor subtypes within each family. However, progress has been made recently in developing drugs to distinguish the D2 from the D3 receptor. Similarly, dopamine receptor family selective antagonists are well characterized, but the development of antagonists selective for the receptor subtypes within each family is not well evolved. Nonetheless, as outlined in the next section, certain drugs are somewhat preferential for one receptor subtype versus another and the relative clinical utility of these drugs has led to considerable speculation regarding involvement of one versus the other subtype in psychiatric disease processes.

Physiology of Dopamine Systems

Dopamine neuronal activity is regulated by a variety of neurotransmitters in the ventral midbrain. The neurons themselves are what one might call *leaky* and will initiate spontaneous action potentials in addition to being driven by various inputs. In general, the activity of dopamine neurons responds to changes in an organism's environment. A novel stimulus activates dopamine cells regardless of whether the stimulus is of positive (e.g., reward) or negative (e.g., stress) valence to the organism. Thus, activation of dopaminergic pathways serves to cue the animal that an important environmental event has occurred in preparation for engaging in an adaptive behavior. Given this function it is rational that the most dense dopaminergic innervation is to the limbic and motor regions of the forebrain. For example, when an animal undergoes a stress or is exposed to a cue, such as the possibility of sex or food, that signals a positive reward, there is an increase in dopamine release in the nucleus accumbens (a portion of the ventral striatum thought to be a particularly critical interface for integrating emotions with adaptive motor responses).

Pathophysiology of Dopamine Systems

Parkinson's Disease

Parkinson's disease is characterized as a degenerative movement disorder that very clearly results from a loss of dopamine neurons in the substantia nigra and an ensuing loss of dopamine innervation to the basal ganglia. The motor disorder progresses from tremor and slurred speech to akinesia and rigidity. The treatment of Parkinson's disease is initially dopamine replacement in the form of the dopamine precursor l-dopa. However, to be effective, sufficient dopamine synthetic capacity must be available in axon terminals in the basal ganglia. Thus, as the degeneration progresses, l-dopa becomes a progressively less effective treatment. Based upon understanding of basal ganglia circuitry, manipulating other neurotransmitters such as acetylcholine is also useful in ameliorating the motor symptoms of Parkinson's disease. However, no treatment is available that reverses or inhibits the neurodegeneration.

Substance Abuse

The dopamine projection from the midbrain to the nucleus accumbens is thought to be critical in the development of addiction to most drugs of abuse. Indeed, many drugs such as cocaine, amphetamine, ecstasy, and nicotine have been shown to directly activate dopamine neurons or release dopamine. Even drugs such as alcohol or heroin that do not directly bind to dopamine neurons are thought to produce addiction, at least in part, via indirect stimulation of mesoaccumbens dopamine release. The release of dopamine by these drugs elevates dopamine substantially higher than the level that occurs following physiological response to a stress or a natural reward (mentioned earlier). Such aphysiological elevations precipitate changes in gene expression in dopamine cells and elsewhere in limbic and motor circuits and ultimately mediate the behavioral changes associated with addiction. Given the apparent role of dopamine in addiction it would be predicted that dopamine antagonists might be useful in treating addiction. However, this has not proven to be the case, presumably because the repeated use of drugs in addiction produces neuroplastic changes beyond dopamine transmission that can mediate the cravings and sensitivity to stress that cause relapse to drug taking.

Schizophrenia

The dopamine hypothesis of Schizophrenia remains a well considered postulate of both the etiology and symptomatology of Schizophrenia. The primary buttresses of this hypothesis are that certain symptoms of Schizophrenia are ameliorated by D2 family dopamine blockers, and that dopamine agonists exacerbate these symptoms. Moreover, there is some evidence to indicate that prophylactic administration of dopamine antagonists inhibits the progressive amplification of psychosis that sometimes occurs in Schizophrenia. Although dopamine is no doubt involved in Schizophrenia it appears that defects in different pathways mediate different symptoms and that the primary defect may be in transmitters that regulate the dopamine systems. For example, a deficit in dopamine transmission in the prefrontal cortex may mediate certain cognitive symptoms, whereas enhanced dopamine transmission in the nucleus accumbens likely plays an important role in mediating the positive symptoms of psychosis, such as paranoia. Indeed, a number of current hypotheses regarding the etiology of Schizophrenia rely on the primary defect residing in limbic excitatory input to the prefrontal cortex.

Conclusions

Dopamine is a monoamine transmitter that has been linked to a surprising number of neuropsychiatric disorders. It is among the most well-characterized transmitter systems, and drugs manipulating dopamine release and receptor occupation profoundly modify behavior in both a therapeutic and maladaptive manner. Physiologically, dopamine appears to function in linking emotional state with adaptive behavioral responses. Thus, dopamine is perfectly situated to be at least indirectly involved in many psychiatric disorders that are manifested as a maladaptive mismatch between environmental stimulus and behavioral response.

SUGGESTED READING

Cooper, J. R., Bloom, F. E., & Roth, R. H. (1997). *The biochemical basis of neuropharmacology.* New York: Oxford University Press.

Nemeroff, C. B., & Schatzberg, A. F. (1998). *Textbook of psychopharmacology.* Washington, DC: American Psychiatric Press.

Neve, K. A., & Neve, R. L. (1997). *The dopamine receptors.* New Jersey: Humana Press.

Weinberger, D. R. (1995). Neurodevelopment perspectives on Schizophrenia. In F. E. Bloom & D. J. Kupper (Eds.), *Psychopharmacology: The fourth generation of progress.* New York: Raven Press.

Peter W. Kalivas
Medical University of South Carolina

See also: **Neurotransmitter Release**

DOUBLE BIND

Double bind is a concept characterizing an ongoing pattern of communication that imposes painful no-win situations upon its victim through two processes: first, through contradictory demands made at different levels of communication, and second, by preventing the victim from either discriminating and commenting on the bind or withdrawing from it. Originally studied in the relationships between schizophrenic adults and their families, the double bind was viewed as having had causal relevance for their Schizophrenia through having impaired their capacities to derive clear meaning from communications and to participate in normal social relationships.

The original clinical studies leading to the double bind concept were conducted in Palo Alto, California, in the 1950s and 1960s by Gregory Bateson, Don D. Jackson, Jay Haley, and John H. Weakland (1956), a group of clinicians and scholars who collectively introduced a communication theory approach to the mental health field through pioneering contributions to the development of family therapy. Their work emphasized that there are, within families as within the individual's internal environment, homeostatic or stability-making processes that regulate their functioning and contribute to their survival. Within families, communication serves this function.

A single, complex human communication can contain many messages of different logical types, often involving separate modalities that can contradict or reinforce one another. An aggressive utterance might, for example, be qualified by movements, postures, or voice tones conveying that "this is all in fun." Even the relationship of the message to surrounding events or shared past experience may contribute to its meaning. Put entirely into words, this multilevel message might mean that "I pretend to show aggression in jest because our relationship is such that, under the circumstances, you will find it funny and feel warmly toward me."

In its regulatory role in human interaction, communication carries substantial responsibility for defining the nature and limits of the relationships between or among people and, therefore, the roles appropriately played by each person in a given interaction. The communicational approach holds that each transaction between the parties to a communication involves a relationship message proffering or affirming a relationship of a particular sort and a response that accepts, modifies, or negates the definition communicated. Thus by the act of scolding, a parent affirms the right to scold in the relationship with that child. The angry transactions between adolescents and their parents may well have less to do with the apparent content of the quarrel than with the relationship changes being forged and contested.

Considerable learning, often nonverbal, is involved in the capacity to decode communications, particularly those involving apparent contradictions between levels, as with angry words said laughingly. When meaning is not apparent, people learn to shift to a more abstract level and to communicate about communication, thereby clarifying the meaning of ambiguous messages. Children initially lack this capacity; if they are blocked from learning how to learn about meaning, serious adulthood disorders may result. The double bind involves a communication style which is pernicious in its reliance upon internal contradictions and blocked learning. As studied in the families of schizophrenics, it appeared often in mother-child relationships in which the mothers seemed not to want to be understood: They could accept neither their children nor their rejection of those children. The double bind describes their covert pursuit of distant relationships disguised by reciprocal shows of loving behavior. Such parents appeared to invite closeness at one level while negating it at another. A child who responded by approaching was covertly rebuffed, yet efforts to withdraw were also punished. In addition, efforts to shift levels and to question the meaning of the interactions were punished, impairing the child's capacity to form and trust impressions of reality.

While the double bind as an ongoing pattern cannot be fully represented in a single transaction, the following vignette illustrates many of its features. A young woman hospitalized for Schizophrenia improved enough to select and purchase clothing for her first hospital leave. When her parents came for her, however, her mother showed immediate distress over her juvenile taste in clothing and agitatedly undressed her and regarbed her in items of the mother's own choosing. "There," the mother said, "now you look all grown up!" The leave went badly and the daughter was soon back in an acutely psychotic condition.

The mother's emphatic behavioral rejection of her daughter's independence was belied by the verbal message that she urgently must look grown up, indicating to hospital staff a probable conflict regarding the relationship: The patient must be an adult and therefore independent, yet a child and therefore dependent. In responding to movement toward independence, the injunction never to be independent was more emphatic than that to be always independent. Enjoined to be a woman and a child, independent and dependent, close and far, the patient responded with disturbed, psychotic behavior. A woman made childlike by an illness, she was incapable of independence, yet too disturbed to be at home: She was neither too close nor too far. Her relationship to her mother was preserved.

In the decades since the concept of the double bind was introduced, it has found widespread use in and beyond our culture as a means to describe patterns of covertly contradictory communications and their pernicious effects on the targeted person. The difficulties of studying these sorts of complex family communications, the complexities of Schizophrenia research, and a pendulum swing toward biological explanations hindered double bind research. Interest has apparently faded regarding the original concept that a predisposition to Schizophrenia can be created by prolonged participation in double binds within the family. Even so, research on this topic continues here and abroad, with periodic demonstrations of its relevance to understanding Schizophrenia.

REFERENCE

Bateson, G., Jackson, D., Haley, J., & Weakland, J. (1956). Towards a theory of schizophrenia. *Behavioral Science, 1,* 251–264.

Roger E. Enfield
West Central Georgia Regional Hospital
Columbus, GA

See also: **Family Therapy; Schizophrenia**

DREAMS

The study of dreams has changed its focus from meaning to the underlying neuroscience mechanisms that are involved in their generation. Current research suggest that cortical areas involved in dreaming reflect those areas associated with emotional and sensory processing and lack involvement of higher-level logical thinking.

Historical Introduction

Since the beginning of recorded history dreams have played a role in humans' attempt to make meaning of the world and ourselves. Dreams have represented the other, the aspects of ourselves and our world that stood outside of human knowledge or could not be understood within the current paradigm. As illustrated in a variety of religious texts over the last few thousand years, dreams have foretold future events as well as allowed for communication with the gods. Still, during this period others, including the Roman poet Lucretius in 44 B.C., suggested that dreams are common in all animals. Darwin echoed a similar theme in his *The Descent of Man* (1871), in which he suggests that all higher animals, including birds, have dreams. Within the last 100 years the understanding of dreams has been brought into a more theoretical perspective within dynamic and analytic psychology and more recently within the context of the neurosciences. Although a topic of heated debate, an initial contribution was Freud's perspective that dreams could be understood within the context of instinctual functioning and the neurology outlined in the *Project for a Scientific Psychology.* As articulated in the *Project,* dreams offered an understanding of previously established networks of neurons and pointed to the manner in which ideas and events had come to be associated with one another in the brain. In this way dreams were reflective of an individual's psychology during the waking state. Jung had a more evolutionary perspective in which he viewed specific processes in our environment as triggers for bringing forth action patterns, or *archetypes* as he called them, much in the same manner as described by the ethologists. Dreams in this context reflect these evoked archetypical patterns.

Beginnings of Empirical Research

Many view the scientific study of dreams beginning in 1953 with the discovery by Aserinsky and Kleitman of an association between dreaming and rapid eye movement (REM) sleep. Sleep generally is characterized by four different stages as reflected in the electroencephalogram (EEG). In contrast to the higher-voltage more-patterned EEG activity found in sleep, REM sleep appears to have an EEG pattern more like that of the waking state, also is referred to as *paradoxical sleep,* and is characterized by low-voltage random-appearing EEG activity. Awaking an individual during REM sleep is more likely to result in a dream report than any other sleep stage. Following the discovery of the association between REM sleep and dreams, a variety of labs examined the dream state. The work included a variety of foci including the nature of the dream itself, factors involved in dream recall, the influence of external factors on dreaming, and other factors associated with dreaming. For example, following a natural disaster such as an earthquake, researchers have found an increase in nightmares, suggesting that trauma can be related to dreaming. Another type of research has shown increased REM sleep when learning a new task in both humans and animals, which suggests that activity during REM sleep may be associated with consolidating new information into long-term memory. Dream research has used a variety of theoretical perspectives including a more cognitive one. The main characteristics of dream process include emotionally laden sensory processes and images without a sense of individual control. Less well understood is the so-called *lucid dream,* in which an individual realizes while dreaming that he or she is part of a dream and may even experience control of the dream. Lucid dreams are rare and occur in only 1–2% of all reported dreams.

Neuroscience Studies

More recently, dream processes have been examined within the context of current neuroscience work with the goal of determining brain areas involved in dreaming and the manner in which dreaming and other cognitive processes (e.g., visual imagery) are related. Early speculation suggested that dreams were related to brain-stem functioning especially the pons with its generators for REM sleep. However, neuropsychological case studies have shown that damage to the pons does not stop dream reports, whereas damage to the forebrain areas does. Current brain-imaging studies suggest that a variety of brain areas are active during brain states associated with dreaming. These areas include the brain stem, which is responsible for basic arousal; the limbic system, which is highly involved in emotionality; and forebrain areas involved in sensory processing. Areas involved in higher-level cognitive processes such as planning and logical thinking showed decreased activation during these dream periods. Further explorations suggest that pathways between areas involved in emotional processing and those involved in visual processing are active, whereas those between visual processing and higher-level logical thinking are not. This may help to explain the nature of dreams in which emotional and nonlogical sequencing of imagery are accepted without reflective awareness. One implication that can be drawn from the brain-imaging work is that a variety of processes are involved in the creation of dreams and that such work helps to characterize the nature of the subjective experience of dreaming.

REFERENCES

Aserinsky, E., & Kleitman, N. (1955). Two types of ocular motility occurring in sleep. *Journal of Applied Physiology, 8,* 1–10.

Freud, S. (1966). Project for a scientific psychology. *Standard edition* (Vol. 1, pp. 281–397). (Original work published 1895)

William J. Ray
Pennsylvania State University

See also: **Rapid Eye Movement (REM) Sleep**

DRUG REHABILITATION

In 2000, the National Household Survey on Drug Abuse estimated that approximately 14 million Americans, or 6.3% of the population, used an illicit drug during the previous month (Office of Applied Studies, Substance Abuse and Mental Health Services Administration, 2001). Of those 14 million people, approximately 4.3 million met the American Psychiatric Association's *Diagnostic and Statistical Manual of Mental Disorders* (*DSM-IV;* American Psychiatric Association, 1994) diagnostic criteria for Substance Abuse or Dependence. Thus, the treatment and rehabilitation of drug abusers remains a pressing public-health need and a challenge for mental health professionals.

To some, drug rehabilitation refers primarily to the treatment of intravenous heroin users or daily users of cocaine. However, treatment and prevention efforts targeting lower levels of drug use have also become widely available. The *DSM-IV* recognizes 11 categories of Substance Use Disorders: alcohol; amphetamines; caffeine; cannabis; cocaine; hallucinogens; inhalants; nicotine; opioids; phencyclidine (PCP); and sedatives, hypnotics, or anxiolytics. Moreover, patients can be diagnosed with Substance Abuse (recurrent and significant adverse consequences related to use) or, in more serious cases, Substance Dependence (continues use despite negative consequences, tolerance, withdrawal, and compulsive use). Thus, a random selection of patients in drug rehabilitation might include a heroin addict, a chronic marijuana user, a person who abuses prescription pain medications, or an adolescent who uses ecstasy every weekend. The expanded range of individuals seeking or being referred to drug rehabilitation has necessitated the development and evaluation of an increasingly diverse group of treatment strategies.

In most cases, the ultimate goal of treatment is helping the patient achieve lasting abstinence. More immediate goals often include reducing drug use; improving interpersonal, occupational, and community functioning; and reducing the negative medical and social consequences of drug use.

Pharmacotherapy, or the use of medications, can be an important element of treatment for certain types of Substance Dependence. One of the best examples of pharmacotherapy is the use of methadone in the treatment of heroin dependence. Methadone is an opiate agonist, meaning that it is chemically similar to heroin and produces some of the same effects. The use of methadone in the treatment of opiate dependence has several advantages, including the prevention of opiate withdrawal, reduction or elimination of the euphoric effects of heroin, reduced use of illicit drugs, and stabilization of other life domains. However, it is generally recognized that pharmacotherapy work best when used within the context of a more comprehensive treatment plan.

Group and individual counseling, and other behaviorally based treatments, are also critical components of drug rehabilitation. Group therapy attempts to foster a supportive atmosphere in which patients can learn from one another as they try to make positive life changes. Groups can consist entirely of current or former drug abusers, such as those employed by Alcoholics Anonymous, Narcotics Anonymous, and other self-help organizations. Groups that are directed by a mental health professional and follow a more structured format are also widely available.

Individual counseling tends to combine strategies directly aimed at reducing drug use with the discussion of other life domains. Increasing motivation, understanding the antecedents and consequences of drug use, severing ties with other drug users, and the development of drug-refusal skills are some of the commonly used techniques that counselors use to help patients reduce their drug use. Other life areas that often need to be addressed over the course of counseling include physical and mental health, interpersonal and family relationships, education and occupational achievement, involvement in the community and other drug-free activities, spirituality, development of effective problem-solving skills, and help with legal and financial difficulties.

In 1999, the National Institute of Drug Abuse (NIDA) distilled the last 25 years of drug rehabilitation research into a set of guiding principles. These principles included the endorsement of a number of scientifically based, empirically validated forms of individual counseling. The following are examples of highly regarded, NIDA approved counseling approaches.

Motivational Enhancement Therapy (*MET*) is a client-centered counseling approach designed to resolve the ambivalence many patients have about entering treatment and stopping drug use. This approach employs a number of specific interviewing techniques to increase internal motivation to change. Motivational Enhancement Therapy can be used to reduce drug use, or, in cases with a history of treatment failure, to prepare patients for more intensive forms of treatment.

The *Community Reinforcement Approach* (*CRA*) is an intensive outpatient therapy for the treatment of cocaine addiction. Through weekly counseling, patients learn to reduce drug use and increase involvement in drug-free recreational activities and social relationships. The CRA approach also makes use of contingency management, a behaviorally based strategy that uses a system of rewards and punishments to reinforce abstinence and make drug use less attractive. Patients submit urine samples over the course of treatment, and they receive vouchers for drug-free samples. Vouchers can then be exchanged for goods and services that help promote a drug-free lifestyle.

Multidimensional Family Therapy (*MDFT*) for adolescents is an outpatient family-based treatment for teenagers. In this approach, adolescent drug use is believed to be influenced by factors related to the individual, the family, the peer group, and the larger community. Treatment includes both individual and family sessions and may occur in the clinic, the patient's home, or in the community (e.g., court, school). Both the adolescent drug user and his or her family members are encouraged to take an active role in achieving drug abstinence.

Relapse Prevention Therapy uses a variety of cognitive-behavioral strategies to facilitate abstinence and reduce the risk of a return to drug use. Relapse Prevention Therapy's approach recognizes that many patients will resume drug use after treatment and that most patients will require multiple treatment episodes before they are able to achieve sustained abstinence. Thus, a central element of this approach is helping patients anticipate and prepare for situations that may trigger a relapse.

Drug rehabilitation can occur in various settings, including hospitals and specialty clinics, or with individual mental health professionals in private practice. Treatment for a Substance Use Disorder can also be incorporated into the treatment of other coexisting psychiatric disorders. Short-term residential programs require patients to live at the treatment facility for anywhere from 3 to 6 weeks. Therapeutic Communities (TC) are a special case of the residential treatment program. In the TC, patients with long histories of drug dependence and criminal behavior reside in a highly structured environment for up to 12 months. Prison-based drug rehabilitation programs have also shown some promise and appear to work best when paired with community-based programs that continue treatment after the patient leaves prison.

REFERENCES

American Psychiatric Association. (1994). *Diagnostic and statistical manual of mental disorders* (4th ed.). Washington, DC: Author.

Office of Applied Studies, Substance Abuse and Mental Health Services Administration. (2001). *Summary of Findings from the 2000 National Household Survey on Drug Abuse* (DHHS Publication No. SMA 01-3549, NHSDA Series H-13). Rockville, MD: Substance Abuse and Mental Health Services Administration, Office of Applied Studies.

Christopher J. Correia
Auburn University

See also: **Psychotherapy**

DYNAMIC ASSESSMENT

Dynamic assessment refers to an approach to conducting psychoeducational or speech and language assessments that most characteristically involves interacting with the client during the course of the assessment and using the responsiveness of the client to this interaction as a primary source of information.

While there are a number of models and developing procedures that vary on dimensions of content and degree of standardization (Lidz & Elliott, 2000), dynamic assessments often follow a pretest-intervene-retest format. The assessor first determines what the client is able to do without assistance, then proceeds to offer assistance, and finally evaluates the degree and nature of the client's responsiveness to this assistance.

The roots of dynamic assessment extend back into the early twentieth century, where many writers expressed their dissatisfaction with the available approaches to the measurement of intelligence (Lidz, 1987). More specifically, the fatherhood of dynamic assessment is generally assigned to both Vygotsky (1978) and Feuerstein (Feuerstein, Rand, & Hoffman, 1979). Vygotsky's notions of the "zone of actual development" and the "zone of proximal development" are definitive of these procedures. Feuerstein's descriptions of "mediated learning experiences" have influenced the development of the interventions offered during the assistance phases of the procedures. It was also Feuerstein who operationalized the notion of dynamic assessment in his Learning Potential Assessment Device.

Research and development regarding these procedures had been essentially parallel in the United States, Europe, and Israel. However, more recently, with European publications increasingly available in English, these developments have cross-seminated and current publications tend to present articles and chapters from multiple and diverse sources.

There are essentially four primary models of dynamic assessment. The first, which is characteristic of Feuerstein and colleagues' approach, is the most loosely structured and diagnostically oriented. The intervention provided to the examinee is tailored to the responses and responsiveness of the examinee, with little preprescription. The second, which characterizes the approach designed by Budoff (1987), offers a standardized intervention to all examinees, based on predetermined strategies relevant to the task. The third, exemplified by the Campione and Brown (1987) approach, operationalizes the zone of proximal development as a series of graduated prompts, predetermined on the basis of increasing explicitness in the teaching of the task. The fourth, described by Lidz (1991) is curriculum-based dynamic assessment that utilizes referral-relevant curriculum content and bases the intervention and interpretation on the degree of match between the process analysis of the demands of the task on the learner and the intactness of the processes the learner applies to the task. Most available specific procedures can be characterized in terms of one of these four models. While varying with the model, the information provided by dynamic assessment procedures can include in-depth descriptions of the strengths and weaknesses of the learner's cognitive processing, responsiveness of the learner to intervention, intensity of the effort required to facilitate change, and the linkage of assessment with intervention.

There are several books that provide a broad sample of available models and procedures of dynamic assessment from both American, Israeli, and European sources, as well as discussions regarding their applications. These include Carlson (1995), Gupta and Coxhead (1986), Hamers, Sijtsma, and Ruijssenaars (1993), Haywood and Tzuriel (1992), Lidz (1987, 1991), and Lidz and Elliott (2000). Reviews of research studies involving this approach are available in Lidz (1991, 1997).

REFERENCES

Budoff, M. (1987). Measures for assessing learning potential. In C. S. Lidz (Ed.), *Dynamic assessment: An interactional approach to evaluating learning potential* (pp. 173–195). New York: Guilford Press.

Campione, J. C., & Brown, A. L. (1987). Linking dynamic assessment with school achievement. In C. S. Lidz (Ed.), *Dynamic assessment: An interactional approach to evaluating learning potential* (pp. 82–11). New York: Guilford Press.

Carlson, J. S. (Ed.). (1995). *European contributions to dynamic assessment.* London: JAI Press.

Feuerstein, R., Rand, Y., & Hoffman, M. (1979). *Dynamic assessment of retarded performers.* Baltimore: University Park Press.

Gupta, R. M., & Coxhead, P. (Eds.). (1986). *Cultural diversity and learning efficiency: Recent developments in assessment.* New York: St. Martin's Press.

Hamers, J. H. M., Sijtsma, K., & Ruijssenaars, A. J. J. M. (Eds.). (1993). *Learning potential assessment: Theoretical, methodological, and practical issues.* Amsterdam: Swets & Zeitlinger.

Haywood, H. C., & Tzuriel, D. (Eds.). (1992). *Interactional assessment.* New York: Springer-Verlag.

Lidz, C. S. (Ed.). (1987). *Dynamic assessment: An interactional approach to evaluating learning potential.* New York: Guilford Press.

Lidz, C. S. (1991). *Practitioner's guide to dynamic assessment.* New York: Guilford Press.

Lidz, C. S. (1997). Dynamic assessment approaches. In D. P. Flanagan, J. L. Genshaft, & P. L. Harrison (Eds.), *Contemporary approaches to assessment of intelligence* (pp. 281–296). New York: Guilford Press.

Lidz, C. S., & Elliott, J. (2000). *Dynamic assessment: Prevailing models and practices.* Amsterdam: JAI/Elsevier.

Vygotsky, L. S. (1978). *Mind in society: The development of higher psychological processes* (M. Cole, V. John-Steiner, S. Scribner, & E. Souberman, Eds.). Cambridge, MA: Harvard University Press.

Carol S. Lidz
Freidman Associates,
Bala Cynwyd, Pennsylvania

See also: **Reliability**

DYNAMIC PSYCHOLOGY

The term *dynamic* relates to forces acting on a system. These forces include ongoing processes within the system as well as those external to the system. In psychology, *dynamics* relates to the interplay among motivating or driving forces that acts as a determinant of an organism's behavior. Thus, the term reflects a concern with the specification of motives and principles of motivated functioning. The term is also frequently associated with particular theories that emphasize the interplay among conscious and unconscious forces—drives, motives, needs, instincts, and wishes—in the direction of behavior. Such theories are known as psychoanalytic or psychodynamic theories of personality.

Theories of motivation are concerned, then, with specifying the motives characteristic of organisms and the principles of motive functioning that determine the initiation, maintenance, and termination of behavior.

Over the years a great variety of theories of motivation have been developed. These may be viewed as falling into three broad categories: (1) hedonic or pleasure theories; (2) cognitive or need-to-know theories; and (3) growth or actualization theories. A fourth category might also be noted that concerns the role of brain structures and neural mechanisms in motivated behavior. Research in this category typically is found in areas defined as psychobiology, biopsychology, or neurobiology.

Hedonic or Pleasure Theories of Motivation

Hedonic or pleasure theories form the largest category of theories of motivation. In one form or another, theories in this group emphasize the guiding role of pleasure in the organization of activity. A number of subclassifications within this category are possible. Perhaps the largest subgroup of hedonic theories consists of those that emphasize the organism's efforts toward *tension reduction.* Such theories emphasize the disquieting state of affairs caused by internal tension and the pleasure derived from the reduction of tension through the discharge of energy, expression of an instinct, or reduction in the level of a drive.

Woodworth took the concept of drive from the field of mechanics and viewed it as the source of motive power or force in organismic functioning. Thereafter, until the 1960s, this concept was used extensively by psychologists interested in human or animal behavior. Often distinctions were made between innate and acquired drives, primary and secondary drives, and viscerogenic and psychogenic drives.

In the area of animal behavior, the concept of drive played a major role in the learning theory of Clark L. Hull. According to Hull's stimulus-response (SR) theory, learning involves motivational variables such as drives. The organism has primary or innate drives such as pain and hunger, as well as learned or secondary drives such as the desire for money and fears—both learned during the course of development. Although the concept of drive referred to an internal process, it could be used by behaviorist-oriented psychologists because it was tied to specific external conditions manipulated by the experimenter. Variations in drive level, manipulated by the experimenter, were then related to objectively defined and measured overt responses.

Hull's work was extended by Miller and Dollard, among others. They made a particular contribution in emphasizing the role of learned, secondary drives in human behavior. For example, anxiety was viewed as a secondary drive based on the primary drive of pain. The anxiety drive is important because it can be learned quickly, become a strong motivating force, and lead to a variety of behaviors relevant to normal and abnormal behavior. Considerable attention was directed by Miller and Dollard to the relation between frustration and aggression, as well as to the importance of drive conflicts in clinical phenomena. Thus, the approach-avoidance conflict between two drives was viewed as the basic ingredient for the development of neurotic behavior. Dollard and Miller attempted to integrate the achievements of learning theory as expressed in the works of Hull with the achievements of psychoanalysis as expressed in the works of Freud.

A concept of motivation related to that of drive and used by many personality theorists is that of *need.* An important representative of such a view was Kurt Lewin, who viewed all behavior as driven by states of need or tension in the organism. As with Hull, needs could be primary and biologically determined or secondary and acquired through experience. Lewin viewed the existence of a need as leading to tension; it was a force that pushed the organism into action. The organism was viewed as a dynamic system in that ordinarily multiple needs enter into action. The forces associated with these needs have the qualities of strength, direction, and point of application.

The operation of these forces, in Lewin's view, takes place in a dynamic field where the state of any part of the field depends on and influences other parts of the field. The valence of objects, in association with states of organismic need or tension, pulls the organism in various directions and sets the stage for gratification, frustration, or conflict. Where multiple needs and environmental objects exist, the organism may experience an approach–approach conflict, an avoidance–avoidance conflict, or an approach–avoidance conflict.

Another representative of the hedonic, tension-reduction view was Henry Murray. The basic motivational concept in Murray's system was that of need. Needs could be primary and viscerogenic, or secondary and psychogenic, and represented forces for action. Murray distinguished between needs and traits in that needs represented a potential for action, whereas traits were defined in terms of actual behavior. Murray also attended to the role of environmental objects, suggesting that the environment could be defined in terms of press or characteristics associated with the potential for need gratification.

The concept of *incentive* is important, yet independent of its relation to drive theory, and forms a second subcategory of hedonic theories of motivation. In the incentive theories there is an emphasis on the association of stimuli with pleasure or pain and the goal-directed striving of the organism to achieve various outcomes. Thus, these theories are hedonic, like drive theories, in their emphasis on pleasure, but, unlike most drive theories, they emphasize the orientation of the organism toward future goals or end points. McDougall rejected a mechanistic, reflex, stimulus-determined view of behavior in favor of an emphasis on active strivings toward anticipated goals associated with pleasure.

Theories of motivation emphasizing goals often are criticized as being teleological. However, goals operate in the present in terms of mental representations of desired outcomes or end points. Most recently, the concept of goals has returned to play an important role in cognitive, information-processing models of human behavior.

A third variant of the hedonic model of motivation is that based on *affect.* Here the emphasis is on the organism's efforts to maximize pleasurable affect and minimize unpleasant affect, although there is no necessary association of affect with physiological need or drive. One of the early significant theorists to emphasize the role of emotion in motivation was P. T. Young. According to Young, stimuli (internal and external) acquire incentive value through their association with affective arousal, which is experienced primarily as positive or negative in nature. Through the gradual accumulation of experience, involving the association of various stimuli with affective arousal, the person develops a value system. Affective processes play the central role in organizing, activating, regulating, and sustaining learned patterns of behavior.

It is important to recognize an overlap among groups. Thus, for example, many drive theorists have emphasized the importance of affect; McDougall emphasized the role of affect in goal development, and many affect theorists emphasize the importance of affects in the development and maintenance of goal system functioning.

Cognitive or Need-to-Know Theories of Motivation

Indeed, by the 1950s, the concept of drive had almost been dropped entirely from the literature because of several reasons: problems in developing reliable measures of drives, particularly in humans; findings that did not support a tension-reduction point of view; and the growth of interest in information-processing theories associated with the cognitive revolution. In some ways, cognition replaced motivation as an important issue in the field. Some cognitive theories remained basically tension-reduction models.

Other cognitive theories, however, emphasized the motivation inherent in the information-processing activity of the organism. For example, J. M. Hunt, influenced by Jean Piaget, suggested that the organism always seeks to integrate new information with what is already known. Incoming information may be congruent or incongruent with what is known. Hunt cited evidence that incongruous or novel information instigates approach behavior, but, when the disparity between incoming and already stored information becomes too great, withdrawal behavior may also occur. Hunt not only emphasized intrinsic motivation but also suggested that differing degrees of incongruity between new and old information lead to various degrees of arousal and positive or negative hedonic tone. Thus, too little incongruity would be boring and too much would similarly lead to negative hedonic tone, whereas a moderate or optimum amount of incongruity would lead to a moderate degree of arousal, positive hedonic tone, and approach behavior. A cognitive model of motivation, then, was tied to a hedonic one.

George A. Kelly represents a theorist emphasizing a more purely cognitive theory of motivation. Kelly specifically rejected what he believed were the dominant "carrot and stick" theories of motivation—those emphasizing incentives that pulled the organism toward them and those emphasizing drives that pushed the organism. Instead, Kelly suggested that every person is a scientist seeking to gain better predictability concerning events. According to him, people are always active, so a theory of motivation does not have to account for activity per se. In terms of direction of movement, people choose to act in ways that promise the greatest potential for elaboration of their construct system, thereby leading to enhanced prediction. People may experience negative affect in the sense of anxiety when they cannot predict events or experience threat when their entire construct (predictive) system is in danger. Furthermore, such negative affect will lead to corrective action.

The emphasis on cognition led many psychologists to be concerned with information processing in the absence of motivational considerations. To this day, work in the area of cognition, for the most part, remains disconnected from work in the areas of emotion and motivation.

Growth or Actualization Theories of Motivation

The third major theoretical approach emphasizes growth or actualization. Representative theorists include Andras Angyal, Kurt Goldstein, Abraham Maslow, and Carl Rogers. The common theme here is a rejection of the view that all human activity occurs in the service of tension reduction. Instead, there is an emphasis on activity stimulated by growth or self-fulfilling tendencies, and that may at times involve increases in tension. These theorists, often linked together as part of the human potential movement, generally do not reject the idea that some activity may occur in the service of reducing tension. However, the most important and basic striving of the organism is seen as directed toward actualizing and enhancing the experiencing organism. Maslow, for example, suggested a hierarchy of needs involving both biological needs (hunger, sleep, thirst) and psychological needs (self-esteem, affection, belongingness). When biological needs are satisfied, psychological needs predominate. In fact, however, psychological needs may even override biological needs in importance. Thus, Rogers suggests that the basic actualizing tendency is the only motive that needs to be postulated and that people are most human when functioning in relation to this motive. Although theories that are part of the human potential movement have been important in personality and were quite popular during the 1960s and 1970s, the concept of actualization has proven to be highly abstract and difficult to measure in any systematic way.

Psychoanalytic Theory

Finally, we can consider the specific theory most often linked with dynamic psychology—psychoanalytic theory. Psychoanalytic theory is dynamic in the sense that it emphasizes the importance of sexual and aggressive drives and the derivatives from these drives in human behavior. However, it also is a dynamic theory in its emphasis on the interplay among drives as expressed in concepts such as conflict, anxiety and the mechanisms of defense, cathexes and anticathexes, and compromise formations. According to such a view, the same phenomena may be the result of different combinations of forces, and a slight shift in energy may result in a dramatic alteration in the nature of the system.

Freud based his theory on the clinical phenomena presented to him by his patients and on the principles then current in biological science. Subsequent analytic theorists such as Alfred Adler and Carl Jung split with Freud over the nature of the fundamental motives in human behavior, although most held to a dynamic psychology in the sense of a system involving the interplay among motives or forces. Most recently there has been the beginning of an effort to focus on the clinical observations of Freud and to reformulate the theory in terms that are less metatheoretical and less tied to what is now considered an outmoded energy point of view. Concepts such as cognitions, purposes, meaning, and action, rather than those of instinct, drive, force, and energy, are emphasized.

General Systems Theory

Having considered various theories of motivation, we may turn to the broadest meaning of the term *dynamic* as found in general systems theory. Originally developed in biology and associated with Ludwig von Bertalanffy, general systems theory represents an effort to formulate principles of functioning that are characteristic of all biological systems. A system consists of interconnecting parts or units, the action of one having implications for the actions of others, whereas certain processes are characteristic of the whole. General systems theory distinguishes between open systems engaged in continuous exchanges with the environment and closed systems unaffected by external forces. Also, a distinction is made between living systems, which are open systems capable of regeneration and growth, and nonliving systems, which may be either open or closed, but which are not capable of regeneration or growth.

Certain concepts and principles are seen as being useful in the understanding of all living systems. Such concepts and principles in particular relate to the dynamic aspects of organismic functioning. For example, the concept of *feedback* emphasizes the ability of the organism to make use of information resulting from its own actions. Associated with this is an emphasis on the purposive or goal-directed aspects of organismic functioning, in particular the process of *adaptation*. Finally, in relation to the goal-directed quality of behavior, there is the concept of *equifinality*—the potential for the same goal or end point to be reached through multiple paths or means.

The dynamic aspects of general systems theory may be seen in its emphasis on ongoing processes within the organism and between the organism and its external environment. However, it does not tell us about the specific forces acting on the organism or the principles under which such forces operate. In terms of the more specific meaning of the term *dynamic,* general systems theory tells us little about the motives that instigate and direct action.

Conclusion

The emphasis here has been on dynamic psychology as it relates to human behavior and in particular to personality theory. However, it is important to recognize that concern with problems of motivation exists in the areas of brain research, physiological psychology, and animal psychology (ethology) as well. Particularly in the latter, concern has increasingly focused on the interplay among motives rather than on the operation of single motives, and on the organization of behavioral processes over time rather than on the specific factors that determine behavior at a specific moment in time. It is processes such as these that general systems theory has tried to capture and that lie at the heart of a dynamic psychology.

Lawrence A. Pervin

See also: **Teleological Psychology**

DYSPLASIA

The clinical term *dysplasia* has been used to describe a variety of anomalies in normal brain development that are associated commonly with mild to severe cognitive impairments and epilepsy. *Dysplasias* are best defined as microscopic abnormalities in brain cytoarchitecture. These abnormalities can be focal, for example, ectopias and heterotopias which appear as islands within an otherwise normal brain, or general, for example, lissencephaly or micro- or macrogyria, which affect large portions of the brain, if not the entire brain.

With few exceptions, dysplasias have been associated with anomalies in the cerebral or the cerebellar cortex. This association may reflect, in part, the fact that dysplasias are detected more easily in these two brain structures rather than a paucity of dysplasias in other brain regions. The cerebral cortex and cerebellum share a well-delineated stratified cytoarchitecture that results from a complex developmental history. Classically, neural development is divided into three major stages: neurogenesis (cell proliferation), neuronal migration, and neuronal maturation (including differentiation and synapse formation). In the development of both the cerebral and the cerebellar cortex, young neurons must migrate through layers of previously generated neurons before they begin differentiating and forming synaptic connections. During the migration phase, there are a number of developmental cues that occur between neuronal populations. After migration, neurons differentiate into cells with distinct shapes and synaptic connections. In both the cerebral and the cerebellar cortex, the stages of neuronal development are precisely timed and are delicately sensitive to disruption. The dysplasias discussed here result primarily from perturbations in normal neuronal migration and neuronal maturation that lead to malformations in the architecture of cerebral and cerebellar cortex. It is also possible, however, that particular neuronal groups migrate or mature at abnormal times because they were generated aberrantly.

In dysplasias that result from *abnormal neuronal migration,* small groups of neurons or entire populations may fail to migrate past previously generated neurons. Alternatively, the neurons may move defectively past their normal locations into regions of white matter, for example, into the cortical molecular layer. In the cerebellum, the failure of granule cells to migrate through Purkinje neurons will lead to malformations in cerebellar cytoarchitecture, as well as abnormal Purkinje cell development. Such dysplasias can affect motor coordination, as well as some aspects of learning and memory. In the cerebral cortex, focal migrational defects appear to disrupt local synaptic circuitry, in particular inhibitory circuitry, and are regarded as a predominant cause of early onset epilepsy. In humans, multiple focal ectopias in the cerebral cortex that result from altered neuronal migration are associated with developmental dyslexia. Migrational abnormalities are often compounded by alterations in neuronal generation and/or neuronal maturation, making it impossible to correlate specific behavioral abnormalities with a particular stage of development. In rodent and other primate studies, however, migrational abnormalities disrupt synaptic connectivity and produce cognitive abnormalities that correlate roughly with the magnitude of the cytoarchitectural abnormalities. Thus, cortical abnormalities that affect larger portions of cortex, such as micro- and macrogyria, ordinarily have more profound behavioral consequences than small focal anomalies.

Abnormal neuronal maturation, despite normal migration, is frequently the source of dysplasias that can lead to profound developmental disabilities, including mental retardation. Examples include genetic disorders, such as Down syndrome and Rett syndrome, as well as many unclassified amentias. In these dysplasias, entire brain regions fail to elaborate normally shaped dendritic trees and spines and display altered synaptic densities. Alterations in cortical dendritic length and number of spines have been reported in postmortem tissue from individuals with Down syndrome, a developmental disorder that almost invariably is associated with cognitive deficits. In recent years, with the advent of in vivo imaging techniques, dysplasias can be studied in living individuals and correlated more directly with behavioral changes. Increases in the width of the cerebral cortex in autism and fragile-X syndrome, as well as decreases in width of cortex in Down syndrome, have been observed. These findings strengthen the hypothesis that abnormal cortical morphology underlies some of the abnormal cognitive behaviors seen in these developmental disabilities. These changes in cortical widths likely reflect alterations in neuropil (dendrites and synapses) or glia cell populations and presumably lead to alterations in synaptic connections within cortex and between cortical and subcortical regions.

The causes for morphological changes leading to dysplasias are only partially understood. Migrational abnormalities may be the consequence of altered cell-cell interactions but can also result secondarily from radiation exposure. Altered cell-cell interactions can be caused either by mutations in the genes coding for cell surface proteins or by environmental factors that change the expression of cell surface proteins. Neuronal differentiation is controlled by a plethora of factors including cell surface interactions, neurotrophins, cytokines, neurotransmitters and neuromodulators, and, last but not least, synaptic activity. Disruptions of any one, or any combination, of these factors may induce altered neuronal maturation. In addition to genetic mutations, aberrant neuronal migration and maturation may be caused by environmental factors, such as heavy metals (for example, lead); ethanol and other psychoactive drugs of abuse; or gestational and perinatal insults, such as hypoxia and ischemia.

SUGGESTED READING

Bayer, S. A., Altman, J., Russon, R. J., & Zhang, X. (1993). Timetables of neurogenesis in the human brain based on experimentally determined patterns in rat. *Neurotoxicology, 14,* 83–144.

Berger-Sweeney, J., & Hohmann, C. F. (1997). Behavioral consequences of abnormal cortical development: Insights into developmental disabilities. *Behavioural Brain Research, 86,* 121–142.

Capone, G. T. (1996). Human brain development. In A. J. Capute & P. J. Accardo (Eds.), *Developmental disabilities in infancy and childhood: Vol. 1. Neurodevelopmental diagnosis and treatment* (2nd ed., pp. 25–75). Baltimore: Paul Brooks.

McKay, R. (1997). Stem cells in the central nervous system. *Science, 276,* 66–71.

Porter, B. E., Brooks-Kayal, A., & Golden, J. A. (2002). Disorders of cortical development and epilepsy. *Archives of Neurology, 59,* 361–365.

Prayson, R. A., Spreafico, R., & Vinters, H. V. (2002). Pathologic characteristics of the cortical dysplasias. *Neurosurgery Clinics of North America, 13,* 17–25.

Joanne Berger-Sweeney
Wellesley College

C. F. Hohmann
Morgan State University

DYSTHYMIC DISORDER

Dysthymic Disorder is a form of mood disorder that is characterized by mild, chronic depression. The current diagnostic criteria for dysthymia require chronic depressed mood (i.e., depressed most of the day, for more days than not, for at least 2 years). In addition, the individual must experience at least two of the following six depressive symptoms: low self-esteem, feelings of hopelessness, low energy or fatigue, difficulty concentrating or making decisions, sleep disturbance (insomnia or sleeping too much), and appetite disturbance (poor appetite or overeating). The symptoms must be persistent (i.e., the individual is never without depressive symptoms for more than 2 months at a time during this period), have a gradual (or insidious) onset, and cause significant distress or impairment in social or occupational functioning. Finally, the diagnosis cannot be made if the individual has a psychotic or bipolar (manic-depressive) disorder, or if the symptoms are due to medication, substances of abuse, or a general medical condition (*Diagnostic and Statistical Manual of Mental Disorders,* third edition, revised [*DSM-III-R*]; American Psychiatric Association, 1987).

Dysthymic disorder is closely related to the diagnosis of Major Depressive Disorder. However, episodes of major depression tend to be more severe, have a more rapid (or acute) onset, and are not generally chronic.

Dysthymic Disorder is relatively common, with approximately 3% of adults in the community meeting criteria during the past 12 months, and 6% meeting criteria at some point in their lives (Kessler et al., 1997). Like many forms of depression, dysthymia is approximately twice as common in women as in men. It is evident in all age groups (Kovacs, Akiskal, Gatsonis, & Parrone, 1994). Persons with an onset of dysthymia in childhood or adolescence are more likely to have other co-occurring psychiatric disorders and a greater family history of Mood Disorders than individuals with an adult onset.

Dysthymic Disorder frequently co-occurs (or is comorbid) with other psychiatric disorders. Approximately 75% of persons with dysthymia experience episodes of major depression that are superimposed on the preexisting Dysthymic Disorder. This pattern has been referred to as *double depression* (Keller, Lavori, Endicott, Coryell, & Klerman, 1983). Although this term implies that such individuals suffer from two different kinds of Depressive Disorders, it is likely that it is a single disorder that waxes and wanes, often in response to stress. Persons with dysthymia also frequently experience Anxiety Disorders, Substance Abuse Disorders, and Personality Disorders (particularly Borderline and Avoidant Personality Disorders).

As dysthymia is, by definition, a chronic condition, it is not surprising that recovery rates are low. In naturalistic follow-up studies (in which there is no attempt to control treatment), approximately 50% of outpatients with dysthymia recover (defined as having no or almost no symptoms for at least 2 consecutive months) during the course of the next 5 years. Approximately 50% of patients who recover experience a relapse, meeting full criteria for another episode of dysthymia within the next 5 years (Klein, Schwartz, Rose, & Leader, 2000).

Dysthymic Disorder runs in families, along with major depression. Persons with dysthymia have increased rates of both dysthymia and major depression in their first-degree relatives. There also appears to be a higher rate of some Personality Disorders in the families of persons with dysthymia (Klein et al., 1995).

Few studies have been conducted to distinguish the role of genetic from environmental factors in the familial transmission of Dysthymic Disorder. However, there is evidence that persons with dysthymia are more likely to have grown up in adverse early home environments, with increased rates of physical and sexual abuse and poor parenting (Lizardi et al., 1995). Although there is a large literature on the biological, psychological, and social variables that may be involved in the etiology and development of major depression, much less is known about the role that these variables play in dysthymia.

There are a number of studies indicating that dysthymic disorder is responsive to most types of antidepressant medication (Thase et al., 1996). In addition, several studies have indicated that maintenance treatment (i.e., continuing on medication after recovery) for dysthymia and double depression can reduce the risk of recurrences (Kocsis et al., 1996).

Various forms of psychotherapy are also used to treat Dysthymic Disorder. Although there are few controlled trials, there is preliminary evidence suggesting that several forms of psychotherapy, including cognitive therapy and interpersonal therapy, may also be effective in treating dysthymia and double depression (Markowitz, 1995). Moreover, a recent study indicates that in double depression the combination of medication and psychotherapy is more effective than either pharmacotherapy or psychotherapy alone (Keller et al., 2000).

REFERENCES

American Psychiatric Association. (1987). *Diagnostic and Statistical Manual of Mental Disorders* (3rd ed., rev. ed.). Washington, DC: Author.

Keller, M. B., Lavori, P. W., Endicott, J., Coryell, W., & Klerman, G. L. (1983). "Double depression": Two-year follow-up. *American Journal of Psychiatry, 140,* 689–694.

Keller, M. B., McCullough, J. P., Klein, D. N., Arnow, B., Dunner, D. L., & Gelenberg, A. J., et al. (2000). A comparison of Nefazodone, the Cognitive Behavioral Analysis System of Psychotherapy, and their combination for the treatment of chronic depression. *New England Journal of Medicine, 342,* 1462–1470.

Kessler, R. C., McGonagle, K. A., Zhao, S., Nelson, C. B., Hughes, M., & Eshleman, S., et al. (1994). Lifetime and 12-month prevalence of *DSM-III-R* psychiatric disorders in the United States. *Archives of General Psychiatry, 51,* 8–19.

Klein, D. N., Riso, L. P., Donaldson, S. K., Schwartz, J. E., Anderson, R. L., Ouimette, P. C., et al. (1995). Family study of early-onset dysthymia. *Archives of General Psychiatry, 52,* 487–496.

Klein, D. N., Schwartz, J. E., Rose, S., & Leader, J. B. (2000). Five-year course and outcome of early-onset Dysthymic Disorder: A prospective, naturalistic follow-up study. *American Journal of Psychiatry, 157,* 931–939.

Kocsis, J. H., Friedman, R. A., Markowitz, J. C., Leon, A. C., Miller, N. L., Gniwesch, L., et al. (1996). Maintenance therapy for chronic depression. *Archives of General Psychiatry, 53,* 769–774.

Kovacs, M., Akiskal, H. S., Gatsonis, C., & Parrone, P. L. (1994). Childhood-onset Dysthymic Disorder: Clinical features and prospective naturalistic outcome. *Archives of General Psychiatry, 51,* 365–374.

Lizardi, H., Klein, D. N., Ouimette, P. C., Riso, L. P., Anderson, R. L., & Donaldson, S. K. (1995). Reports of the childhood home environment in early-onset dysthymia and episodic major depression. *Journal of Abnormal Psychology, 104,* 132–139.

Markowitz, J. C. (1995). Psychotherapy of Dysthymic Disorder. In J. H. Kocsis & D. N. Klein (Eds.), *Diagnosis and treatment of chronic depression* (pp. 146–168). New York: Guilford Press.

Thase, M. E., Fava, M., Halbreich, U., Kocsis, J. H., Koran, L., Davidson, J., et al. (1996). A placebo-controlled, randomized clinical trial comparing sertraline and imipramine for the treatment of dysthymia. *Archives of General Psychiatry, 53,* 777–784.

Daniel N. Klein
State University of New York, Stony Brook

See also: **Depression**

E

EARLY CHILDHOOD DEVELOPMENT

Childhood is a culturally defined period in human development between infancy and adulthood, and, in historical perspective, it is a relatively recent social construction. Only in the past 400 years or so has the idea of childhood been a part of Western culture, with the recognition of this special class of people and special phase in the growth of each individual (French historian Philippe Aries analyzes the emergence of these ideas in *Centuries of Childhood*). Early childhood, as a special and important subperiod of childhood, most often refers to the months and years between infancy and school age or middle childhood: age 2 to 5 years.

These preschool years, sometimes extended to include infancy and toddlerhood or even lengthened into middle childhood to about age 8 years, are a time of significant and complex advances and reorganizations in behavior, and thus they figure centrally in most theories of human development. Learning, perception, reasoning, memory, and social relations undergo important changes and progressions in early childhood.

Many complex milestones and achievements have been described by numerous researchers. Gesell and his colleagues described the steps of development across domains, including physical growth, motor behavior, adaptive responsiveness, language, and personal/social behavior in their classic book *The First Five Years of Life*. Language is among the most impressive achievements in early childhood as the infant's babbling transforms itself into the very sophisticated language of the youngster at age 5. White describes the physical, emotional, and intellectual growth of preschool children in *The First Three Years of Life*. Similarly, other authors have described the equally remarkable complex of behavioral development and reorganization between ages 5 and 7.

Psychoanalytic developmental psychology posits early childhood as the critical period in development during which major personality orientations emerge that will continue into childhood, adolescence, and adulthood, forming boundaries and constraints on later modifications of intrapsychic organization, interpersonal relationships, and ego development. A person's sense of self and his or her gender identity are formed during this period of development. Freud's theory of psychosexual development describing the oral, anal, and phallic/Oedipal phases of early childhood development, and Erikson's theory of psychosocial development describing the tasks and crises of early childhood—trust versus mistrust, autonomy versus shame and doubt, initiative versus guilt, industry versus inferiority—are among the most influential psychoanalytic contributions toward understanding early childhood development. Bowlby's theory of attachment, further elaborated by Ainsworth, Harlow, and others, applies Erikson's theory to the special relationship between parent or primary caregiver and the developing child. These writers suggest that successful negotiation of the early parent-child relationship has lifelong implications for successful personality development, interpersonal relationships, and mental well-being.

In addition to learning to get along with others, a young child must learn to regulate his or her own behavior. Self-regulation refers to the capacity to monitor and direct one's activities in order to achieve goals or meet demands imposed by others. Self-control is the ability to regulate oneself even when the caregiver is absent, and may be considered a sign of emerging moral development. Learning to use a toilet and refraining from grabbing toys are examples of emerging self-regulation and self-control skills.

Cognitive developmental theories espoused by the Swiss psychologist Jean Piaget and his followers (Piaget & Inhelder, 1969) also emphasize early childhood development as a period of major steps in a child's construction of reality and knowledge. The infant in the sensorimotor stage of intelligence develops knowledge of self and the world through a complex series of interactions with the environment that emphasize sensory and motor experience. In early childhood the child achieves preoperational and then concrete operational thinking. With the increase in a child's capacity for imaginative and logical thought, important levels of symbolic and representational thinking develop as a basis for classification and categorization of information, essential to appreciation of important rules about the physical and interpersonal world. Recent controversies regarding the validity of children's memories of either traumatic or routine events are partly based on Piaget's descriptions of the limitations in reasoning skills during this stage of development and subsequent extensions of his theory.

Changes in family structure in the United States have dramatically altered the way many young children are raised. Mothers of young children are more likely to work outside the home for a variety of reasons, and both mothers and fathers are working longer hours. Although some laypeople worry about the long-term implications of extensive out-of-home care during early childhood, accumulating evidence suggests that good, high-quality day care with appropriate ratios of staff to children can actually enhance some aspects of cognitive and social development. Increasing awareness of the influence of diverse family structures and multicultural family contexts for the multivariate processes of early childhood development characterizes contemporary research and practice.

The theoretical centrality of early childhood as a critical period in human development is applied in early childhood education and intervention. Great teachers and theorists such as J. A. Comenius (1592–1670), Jean-Jacques Rousseau (1712–1778), J. H. Pestalozi (1746–1827), Friedrich Froebel (1782–1852), John Dewey (1859–1952), Maria Montessori (1870–1952), and Anna Freud (1895–1982) long ago recognized the importance of learning and development in early childhood. Nursery schools, kindergartens, and early intervention programs such as Headstart are manifestations of an appreciation of early childhood development, not only in education and psychology, but also in social reform and public policy. With increases in the number of children and the number of hours spent in structured day-care settings, opportunities to observe and apply the knowledge gleaned from the study of early child development have expanded in the past two decades.

REFERENCES

Aries, P. (1962). *Centuries of childhood.* New York: Knopf.

Damon, W., & Lerner, R. (1997). *Handbook of child psychology.* New York: Wiley.

Gessel, A. (1940). *The first five years of life.* New York: Harper

Piaget, J., & Inhelder, B. (1969). *The psychology of the child.* New York: Basic Books.

White, B. (1975). *The first three years of life.* Englewood Cliffs, NY: Prentice Hall.

Dante S. Spetter
Harvard University

Donald L. Wertlieb
Tufts University

See also: **Child Psychology**

EAST-WEST PSYCHOLOGY

East-West psychology is a term used to describe the integration of Eastern or Oriental religions, philosophical disciplines, and psychological practices with Western psychological theory and practice. Confucianism, Taoism, Hinduism, Buddhism, and Islam are among the approaches included in the Eastern tradition. The Western psychological tradition includes the major psychoanalytic, behavioral, and humanistic theories.

The inquiry includes some states that go beyond limits of the ego and personality levels as defined in traditional Western psychology, such as ordinary and altered states of consciousness, meta- or optimal health, self-actualization and human potential, and the full range of human existence and development.

Boundaries of Western Psychology

The West has basically derived its understanding of phenomena from an intellectual and objective approach. In the classical Greek concept, the universe was viewed as comprehensible by reductionism, divisible, static, nonrelativistic, and atomistic. As defined in the philosophy of Descartes, matter and spirit are seen as being fundamentally different.

Roger Walsh and others ("Paradigms in Collision") described the different levels and aims of psychotherapeutic intervention as (1) traditionally therapeutic—reducing pathology and enhancing adjustment; (2) existential—confronting the questions and problems of existence; and (3) soteriological—enlightenment, transcendence of the problems first confronted at the existential level. He said that Western psychologies and therapies focus on the first two levels, while the third is the chief goal of the consciousness disciplines that incorporate Eastern thought.

Western psychology recognized distortions of reality as pathological but equated "reality" with the world as perceived in the waking state of awareness and perceived the self as separate from what is perceived. Daniel Goleman stated that this viewpoint denied access or credibility to reality as perceived in other states of consciousness.

Carl Jung, whose investigation of psychology included Eastern religions, began to widen understanding of the unconscious to incorporate a collective dimension common to all cultures and races. In asserting the existence of "impersonal" levels of consciousness, he took a step beyond former reductionistic and mechanistic theories. Jung commented on the boundaries of Western psychology when he said, "Western consciousness is by no means the only kind of consciousness there is; it is an historically conditioned and geographically limited factor, and representative of only one part of mankind."

The Eastern Perspective

The Eastern worldview is dynamic and organic, seeing the cosmos as one inseparable reality, spirit and material at the same time.

According to the Eastern orientation, the usual state of consciousness is an illusory distortion of perception (maya) arising from a dualistic distinction between subject and object, between self and the other, and between the organism and the environment.

The aim of Eastern practices is to penetrate the veil of the accustomed reality and emerge into an awakened state or enlightenment. It is possible to transcend ego conflicts, view ego demands with detachment, and understand human experience in the light of an awakened state of mind.

Buddhist teachings indicate the necessity of freeing oneself from the analytic mind, from all conditioning and compulsive functioning of the mind and body, and from habitual emotional responses. These teachings discuss developing awareness in terms of fractions of a second, to awaken people to the fleeting glimpses of an open, precognitive spaciousness that occur before things are interpreted in a particular perspective. Gaps in the stream of thought permit a direct experience of pure awareness that, according to the Buddhist perspective, is the individual's true nature.

Eastern tradition has emphasized a personal, empirical approach to knowledge different from the Western path of scientific, impersonal, objective knowledge. As opposed to analytic and logical thinking, direct experiential knowledge is stressed.

In the Eastern tradition, the contemplative-meditative mode of knowing has been valued as accurate, whereas traditional Western science and philosophy have used only sensation-empirical and cognition-conceptual modes.

Meditation is one of the primary practices in the East for shifting away from the active, linear mode and toward the receptive and process-oriented mode. Meditation serves to dismantle the automatism and selectivity of ordinary awareness.

Emergence of East-West Psychology

As mental health professionals felt more and more limited by the theories of behaviorism and psychoanalysis, which were mainly derived from studies of psychopathology, and ignored certain areas—such as value, will, and consciousness—necessary for a full inquiry into human nature, humanistic psychology emerged in the 1960s as a model based on health and the whole person. Humanistic psychology recognized the individual's drive toward self-actualization and the ways in which this idea could be fostered in individuals, groups, and organizations.

Western science in the twentieth century found that the classical concept of reductionism and an atomistic divisible universe were inadequate as explanation. Modern theoretical physics has adopted a model of the universe that is holistic, indivisible, interconnected, and dynamic, unlike the former reductionistic and static view, and supports the findings of mystical insight. This view is consistent with and supportive of the emergence of East-West psychology.

Western psychology was compelled to encompass a broader scope by the development in the culture at large of the human potential movement, cross-cultural exposure, disillusionment with the materialistic dream, and the use of psychedelic drugs and technologies for the induction of higher states of consciousness. This scope incorporated these experiences and values, which were domains already explored and described in Eastern thought.

Technological advances have permitted researchers to describe the physiological and biochemical correlates of altered states of consciousness. As mental health professionals have individually and collectively been influenced and affected by their contact with Eastern philosophy, they have synthesized this awareness into their own theory and practice of psychology.

The evidence of this synthesis was seen in the development of transpersonal psychology, documented by the publication of its first journal in 1969. A. Maslow foresaw as a fourth force of psychology a psychology that would be "transpersonal, transhuman, centered in the cosmos rather than in human needs and interest, going beyond humanness, identity, self-actualization, and the like." Transpersonal psychology is conceived of as promoting and facilitating growth and as expanding awareness beyond limits prescribed by most traditional Western models of mental health.

The transpersonal psychology movement brought together insights from other traditions and from modern depth psychology, and validated and influenced an emerging paradigm that incorporated a health- rather than disease-oriented model, transcendence rather than adjustment focus, and a transpersonal rather than a personality-level approach.

In the field of health care and health psychology, disciplines from the East have been incorporated into traditional Western medicine and health care delivery. Research in biofeedback has expanded the scope of behavioral and physiological psychology.

As a specific method of training the mind, increasing awareness, and directing human attention, meditation has gained widespread recognition in the areas of personal growth, health, and stress management. It is estimated that by 1980 more than 6 million people in the United States alone had learned some form of meditation. Clinically, meditation is being taught as a tool for stress reduction, control of addiction, and increased coping ability.

Educational psychology has been influenced by the awareness that both hemispheres of the brain must be stimulated and that the development of creativity, imagery, and fantasy through the receptive mode is as important as the development of logic and reasoning in the active mode.

Susan F. Wallock

EDUCATIONAL MAINSTREAMING AND INCLUSION

Early advocacy for mainstreaming in education has become increasingly focused on inclusion, with frequent confusion and failure to distinguish between the two ideas. Although at times the terms are used synonymously, *mainstreaming* refers most frequently to the return of children from special education to regular education, and *inclusion* refers to meeting the needs of children within the regular classroom setting without assignment to a special education setting. In the case of the use of support services, inclusion implies the provision of services within the classroom or on a consultative basis to the teacher ("push in"), in contrast to "pull out" approaches, which typically involve removal of children from the classroom for involvement in specialized support services. Both mainstreaming and inclusion reflect the federal mandates concerning placement of children with special needs in the "least restrictive" environment (IDEA, PL101-476, Sec. 612 (5)(B)).

Inclusion has been most strongly advocated for children with mild handicapping, but it has been viewed by some as appropriate for children with moderate to severe disabilities as well. The meaning of inclusion may vary from full to part time, and from applying to some or all children with disabilities. The move toward mainstreaming was given impetus by the landmark article by Dunn in 1968, and the move toward inclusion was catalyzed by the Regular Education Initiative proposed by Madeleine Will (e.g., 1986).

The success of students with disabilities in regular education relies to a great extent upon introduction of a number of curriculum modifications and supports within the classroom. Classroom size and the degree of disruptiveness and depth of need of the included students are likely to affect the success of inclusion as well. Mere proximity of handicapped and nonhandicapped children does not result in a successful mainstreaming experience (Guralnick, Connor, Hammond, Gottman, & Kinnish, 1996; Zigmond & Baker, 1990). The evidence suggests that children need to interact in order to modify their attitudes toward peers with disabilities (Voeltz, 1980; Weinberg, 1978). Teachers need to intervene both personally and programmatically to promote inclusion, and to do so effectively requires supportive consultative services and training experiences.

Teachers need staff development opportunities, consultative support, and in-class help in order to address the needs of these students (Johnson & Cartwright, 1979; Naor & Milgram, 1980). The attitudes of teachers toward mainstreaming appear to reflect their feelings regarding their ability to succeed in teaching students with special needs, and their success in this requires adequate support services (Galis & Tanner, 1995; Larrivee & Cook, 1979).

Evidence regarding the effectiveness of inclusion depends upon the population and the nature of the variables studied. Baker, Wang, & Walberg (1995) conducted a meta-analysis documenting small to moderate positive effects for children with special needs in favor of inclusion, with no significant negative effects on students without disabilities. The effectiveness of inclusion as an educational intervention remains to be seen and may in fact vary, depending upon the student and the attitudes, experience, and practices of the teaching and support staff (Galis & Tanner, 1995). Parents and educators, as well as individuals with disabilities, seem to have very different points of view about their preferences for settings (Vaughn & Klingner, 1998). The most valid conclusion appears to be that assignments to educational treatments and settings needs to be carried out in a highly individualistic way that takes into consideration evidence of effectiveness, the needs of the learner, and the preferences of the family and student.

REFERENCES

Baker, E. T., Wang, M. C., & Walberg, H. J. (1995). The effects of inclusion on learning. *Educational Leadership, 42,* 33–35.

Dunn, L. M. (1968). Special education for the mildly retarded: Is much of it justifiable? *Exceptional Children, 35,* 5–22.

Galis, S. A., & Tanner, C. K. (1995). Inclusion in elementary schools: A survey and policy analysis. *Education Policy Analysis Archives, 3.* Available at http://olam.ed.asu.edu/epaa.v3n15.html.

Guralnick, M. J., Connor, R. T., Hammond, M., Gottman, J. M., & Kinnish, K. (1996). Immediate effects of mainstreamed settings on the social interactions and social integration of preschool children. *American Journal on Mental Retardation, 100,* 359–377.

Johnson, A. B., & Cartwright, C. A. (1979). The roles of information and experience in improving teachers' knowledge and attitudes about mainstreaming. *Journal of Special Education, 13,* 453–462.

Larrivee, B., & Cook, L. (1979). Mainstreaming: A study of the variables affecting teacher attitude. *Journal of Special Education, 13,* 315–324.

Naor, M., & Milgram, R. M. (1980). Two preservice strategies for preparing regular class teachers for mainstreaming. *Exceptional Children, 47,* 126–129.

Vaughn, S., & Klingner, J. K. (1998). Students' perceptions of inclusion and resource room settings. *Journal of Special Education, 32,* 79–88.

Voeltz, L. M. (1980). Children's attitudes toward handicapped peers. *American Journal of Mental Deficiency, 84,* 455–464.

Weinberg, N. (1978). Modifying social stereotypes of the physically disabled. *Rehabilitation Counseling Bulletin, 22,* 114–124.

Will, M. C. (1986). Educating children with learning problems: A shared responsibility. *Exceptional Children, 52,* 411–415.

Zigmond, N., & Baker, J. (1990). Mainstream experiences for learning disabled students (Project MELD): Preliminary report. *Exceptional Children, 57,* 176–185.

Carol S. Lidz

EFFECTIVE COMPONENTS OF PSYCHOTHERAPY

All forms of psychotherapy, by and large, are followed by more benefit in more people than is informal help or the simple passage of time. This strongly suggests that, despite the clamor of conflicting claims by different therapeutic schools and their doctrinal and procedural differences, all must share certain therapeutic features—features, moreover, that distinguish psychotherapies from other forms of help from friends, relatives, or others.

Three major distinguishing features can be noted: (1) the helper is a professional; (2) the proceedings are confidential; and (3) the therapy is grounded in a theory that "explains" the patient's distress and prescribes certain procedures for alleviating it. In addition, the therapeutic medium of all psychotherapies is symbolic communication, usually by words but sometimes by exercises and other bodily rituals that have a large symbolic component.

The forms of distress and disability assumed to be amenable to psychotherapy share significant psychological components. These range from emotional states exacerbating chronic illnesses to psychoses, but most patients in psychotherapy suffer primarily from so-called neurotic symptoms such as anxiety, depression, phobias, and obsessions. The specific aim of all forms of psychotherapy is to relieve symptoms, but this invariably includes implicitly strengthening patients' self-esteem, improving their coping strategies, and the like.

The Demoralization Hypothesis

Since all forms of psychotherapy are helpful, their shared features must counteract a type of distress and disability common to most seekers of psychotherapy. This condition may be termed *demoralization*—a sense of incompetence based on inability to solve some internal conflict or external problem, coupled with feelings of distress. Why some persons are more prone to demoralization than others is largely unknown. Inborn characteristics such as lack of stamina or hardihood probably have much to do with it, as does the extent of support from others.

An empirical definition of demoralization has been provided by the following list of complaints, scales of which a series of population surveys found to be as highly correlated as the probable error of each scale permitted: poor self-esteem, hopelessness/helplessness, dread (including fear of insanity), confused thinking, sadness, anxiety, psychophysiological symptoms, and perceived physical health. These include the most frequent complaints of patients in psychotherapy.

Except possibly for some phobias, some depressions, and obesity, no convincing evidence has emerged that one therapeutic approach is more successful overall than any other. A plausible hypothesis, then, is that patients seek therapy because of both demoralization and specific symptoms. Although both patients and therapists believe the aims of therapy to be relief of symptoms, successful therapy in fact counteracts the patient's demoralization, and this is the main source of benefit.

From the standpoint of the demoralization hypothesis, patients' complaints can be grouped into three classes. The first and most common are direct expressions of demoralization, notably anxiety and depression. They are also the most responsive to any therapeutic intervention. Second are symptoms related to pathologic organic processes such as cyclical depressions, hallucinations, delusions, and the like. Demoralization may often play an etiological role in these, because stressing the patient readily exacerbates them.

The final group includes so-called neurotic symptoms such as phobias, compulsions, obsessions, amnesias, and the like, currently believed to be symbolic self-perpetuating and self-defeating efforts to solve internal conflicts or persistent difficulties with others resulting from distorted perceptions of self and others. Their origin is customarily attributed to deficient or damaging learning experiences in early childhood.

Shared Features of All Psychotherapies That Counteract Demoralization

All therapies combat demoralization by seeking to counteract patients' feelings of discouragement, isolation, loss of self-confidence, and feelings of failure. Morale-enhancing features of all psychotherapies can be divided into those inherent in the therapist-patient relationship and the therapeutic setting, and those related to the processes of therapy.

Therapist-Patient Relationship

At the most general level, demoralization is combatted by the therapist's being a professional in the broadest sense of the term—the possessor of an expertise either recognized by society as a whole (as in the case of psychologists, psychiatrists, and social workers) or acknowledged by a group whose values are shared by the patient.

Furthermore, as a professional the therapist is expected to assume some responsibility for the patient's welfare, and the therapist's professional status reassures the patient that the therapist will not exploit the patient and that the patient need not fear that what he or she says or does will disrupt the therapeutic relationship through angering, seducing, or otherwise causing the therapist to abandon the professional role. The therapist counteracts demoralization by conveying continuing willingness to listen to and respect the patient.

By accepting the patient for treatment, the therapist implies that the therapist believes the patient can be helped. This in itself inspires the patient's hope—an emotion that powerfully counteracts demoralization and is often probably healing in itself. Arousal of hope at the first therapeutic contact may account in large part for the large proportion of outpatients (60 to 80%) who improve significantly after one interview. The therapist also provides a consistent outlook, value system, and standards of behavior that help the patient to reduce confusion.

In addition to these general therapeutic features of the patient-therapist relationship, the therapist may influence the patient in specific ways through the therapeutic procedure. However "nondirective" the procedure may seem to be, patients tend to follow therapists' leads, even when therapists are not aware of giving any. The influencing power of therapists rests on the patients' dependence on them for help, intensified by the patients' concern about the therapists' opinion of them. *Evaluation apprehension,* as it has been termed, has been shown to heighten a person's susceptibility to influence.

Therapeutic Setting

A private office or a clinic conveys the atmosphere of a place of healing. Because what occurs in therapy is confidential—that is, confined to the therapeutic setting—the patient is free to reveal thoughts, feelings, and attitudes, including shameful or repressed aspects of the self, without fear of consequences beyond the therapeutic situation. Thus, the setting in itself facilitates morale-enhancing experiences such as increased self-awareness and the relief following revelation of information or exploration of personal problems that the patient fears mentioning in settings of daily life.

Morale-Enhancing Aspects of the Therapeutic Process

Emotional Arousal

Although the reason is unclear, clinical experience indicates that beneficial change in the patient is facilitated by the emotional arousal accompanying therapy. This arousal may be caused by feelings toward the therapist; by reexperiencing repressed feelings toward self and family; in behavior therapies, by attempting to change habitual behaviors; by particular maneuvers to elicit strong emotions; or in other ways.

Cognitive and Experiential Learning

All therapies convey new information by helping patients to bring to awareness hitherto unavailable knowledge about themselves. To be most effective, these discoveries must provide a new emotional experience.

As models, guides, and advisors, all psychotherapists provide the patient with a variety of opportunities for learning better ways of coping with problems. By the type of questions asked, the therapist offers a model of rational decision making, including consideration of alternatives before acting.

Enhancement of the Sense of Self-Efficacy

Patients in psychotherapy typically believe themselves to be more or less at the mercy of inner feelings or external stresses. This state of mind is coupled with a sense of failure, as well as dysphoric emotions that further reduce the patient's coping capacity. Thus, strengthening the patient's sense of mastery or self-efficacy is probably the strongest morale-enhancing component of all psychotherapies. To this end, all therapies typically emphasize that therapeutic gains result primarily from the patient's own efforts.

Implications of the Demoralization Hypothesis for Training

The likelihood that all psychotherapeutic procedures are followed by essentially similar overall improvement rates should not be taken to imply that training of therapists is unnecessary. Therapeutic skill may be compared to musical talent: Not everyone can be a virtuoso, but—except for the few who are tone-deaf—anyone can learn to play an instrument and improve with practice. Similarly, mastery of one or more procedures maintains the therapist's own sense of competence and thereby the patient's faith in the therapist—states of mind crucial for the success of all therapies. The feeling of competence also sustains the therapist's self-confidence in the face of the inevitable failures experienced by practitioners of all therapeutic schools. Finally, only through persistent, expert application of specific therapies can any hitherto undiscovered beneficial effects be discovered for different clinical conditions or personality types.

Ideally, then, training programs should teach several forms of therapy, so the student can pick those that are most congenial. The more a therapist can master, the better; but in any case the therapist can rest assured that, for most if not all patients, the chosen method will not be less effective than alternative approaches.

Jerome D. Frank

See also: **Psychotherapy; Psychotherapy Research**

EFFECTIVENESS OF PSYCHOTHERAPY, EFFICACY OF PSYCHOTHERAPY

Scientific Evaluation of Psychotherapy

Two methods have been utilized to conduct scientific evaluations of psychotherapy. Efficacy and effectiveness research are both important and provide us with distinct information about how psychotherapy works. Although both methods are used, to date, efficacy studies have dominated the field. As a result, most of what we know about how well psychotherapy works comes from efficacy rather than effectiveness research.

Efficacy studies test psychotherapy in a controlled experimental design and typically utilize a structured, manualized session format delivered over a fixed number of sessions. Patients are selected carefully, with the bulk carrying single, uncomplicated diagnoses, falling into specific age ranges, and meeting other strict inclusion and exclusion criteria. Patients are randomly assigned to different treatments, and ideally the treatment being studied is also compared to a placebo control. The strict design in efficacy studies provides strong internal validity and thereby enables researchers to be confident that the treatment under investigation causes the observed effect. However, because of the tightly controlled format, efficacy studies are associated with weaker external validity, suggesting that obtained findings may not generalize to the clinical populations for whom they are ultimately intended.

Effectiveness studies, by contrast, evaluate the outcome of therapy directly on clinical populations, but in doing so sacrifice the rigors of efficacy research. Effectiveness research is conducted as it is actually delivered in a variety of settings, including hospitals, clinics, and private practice. Patients are heterogeneous, typically have multiple diagnoses, and may or may not be randomly assigned to treatment groups. The choice of treatments or therapists is often determined by patients themselves, manuals are typically not utilized, and the length of treatment is not fixed. Treatment is usually terminated once the therapist or patient determines that progress has occurred or as a function of insurance constraints. As a result, effectiveness research, although not as internally rigorous as efficacy research, provides us with information about how well treatment works when it is carried out in clinical practice.

Efficacy Research on Psychotherapy

Comprehensive reviews have been undertaken of psychotherapies with demonstrated efficacy in controlled studies (e.g., Chambless et al., 1998; Nathan & Gorman, 1998; Weissman, Markowitz, & Klerman, 2000). Chambless and Ollendick (2001) recently completed the most extensive review of the efforts of eight work groups (from the United States, United Kingdom, and Canada) focused on identifying psychotherapies with existing efficacy data or evidence-based treatments (EBT). Although the criteria used to define EBTs were not the same for each work group, overall the criteria used tended to be conservative. For a treatment to be defined as evidence-based, support from at least one rigorous randomized clinical trial was necessary. Based upon Chambless and Ollendick's (2001) "review of reviews" it is accurate to say that at least one EBT (and sometimes several) exists for the full spectrum of psychiatric disorders, including the following (see Chambless & Ollendick, 2001, for complete list):

Anxiety and Stress
Agoraphobia/Panic with Agoraphobia
Blood injury phobia
Generalized Anxiety Disorder
Geriatric anxiety and depression
Obsessive-Compulsive Disorder
Panic Disorder
Posttraumatic Stress Disorder
Public speaking anxiety
Social Anxiety Disorder (Social Phobia)
Specific Phobia
Chemical Abuse and Dependence
Alcohol Abuse and Dependence
Benzodiazepine withdrawal
Cocaine Abuse
Opiate Dependence
Bipolar disorder
Major Depressive Disorder
Anorexia Nervosa
Binge-Eating Disorder
Borderline Personality Disorder
Bulimia Nervosa
Chronic pain
Irritable-bowel syndrome
Marital discord
Migraine headache
Obesity
Schizophrenia
Smoking cessation
Sexual dysfunction

Psychotherapies are not efficacious for all conditions (for example, interpersonal psychotherapy (IPT) has been shown to be ineffective in two studies with opiate abusers). However, for several disorders, psychotherapies have been shown to be as effective as psychotropic interventions (e.g., cognitive-behavioral therapy [CBT] for Panic Disorder, CBT and IPT for Bulimia Nervosa). For other disorders, psychotherapy is an invaluable adjunct to medication (e.g., bipolar disorder, Schizophrenia).

In this section we highlight data on the efficacy of psychotherapies for three commonly occurring psychiatric disorders.

Depression. Both IPT (Weissman et al., 1979; Elkin et al., 1989) and CBT (cf. Glaoguen, Cottraux, & Cucherat, 1998; Elkin et al., 1989) have been shown to be as effective as psychotropic medication for the treatment of depression (Depression Guideline Panel, 1993) and have also demonstrated efficacy in decreasing relapse and recurrences in depression (Frank et al., 1990; Jarrett, Basco, & Ritter, 1998; see Sanderson & McGinn, 2001, for a comprehensive review). An amalgam of the two (cognitive-behavioral analysis system of psychotherapy) has demonstrated efficacy in treating chronic depression (Keller et al., 2000).

Anxiety Disorders. A considerable body of evidence has shown that CBT is as effective as, or more effective than, medications in the treatment of the full range of anxiety disorders (cf. Nathan & Gorman, 1998, for a comprehensive review), Agoraphobia (e.g., Chambless, Foa, Groves, & Goldstein, 1979), Generalized Anxiety Disorder (e.g., Barlow, Rapee, & Brown, 1992), Obsessive-Compulsive Disorder (e.g., Fals-Stewart, Marks, & Schafer, 1993), Panic Disorder (e.g., Barlow, Gorman, Shear, & Woods, 2000), Social Phobia (e.g., Heimberg et al., 1998), and Posttraumatic Stress Disorder (e.g., Foa, Rothbaum, Riggs, & Murdock, 1991).

Schizophrenia. Efficacy studies for Schizophrenia focus on relapse prevention and typically compare two or more psychotherapies in patients also receiving antipsychotic medication. Overall, when compared to treatment as usual, behavioral, supportive, and systems-based family therapies and social skills training have demonstrated efficacy in reducing relapse in Schizophrenia (e.g., Falloon et al., 1984; Hogarty, Anderson, & Reiss, 1986; Leff, Kuipers, Berkowitz, & Sturgeon, 1985; Schooler et al., 1997). The different family-based interventions appear to be equivalent to each other (Baucom, Shoham, Mueser, Daiuto, & Stickle, 1998; Brent et al., 1997) except that family therapy utilizing insight-oriented techniques and focusing on the past has not demonstrated efficacy in reducing relapse (Kottgen, Sonnichsen, Mollenhauer, & Jurth, 1984) and can be associated with negative outcomes (McFarlane, Link, Dushay, Marchal, & Crilly, 1995).

Effectiveness. The next challenge is determining how well these treatments generalize to clinical practice, where patients often do not have a single diagnosis, where practitioners in the community must be used, and where training programs must be simple and cost-efficient (effectiveness research). Although effectiveness research is in its infancy, the existing data generated thus far support the use of EBTs in clinical practice (Wade, Treat, & Stuart, 1998; Sanderson, Raue, & Wetzler, 1998; Franklin, Abramowitz, Kozac, Levitt, & Foa, 2000; Tuschen-Caffier, Pook, & Frank, 2001; Antonuccio, Thomas, & Danton, 1997; Otto, Pollack, & Maki, 2000).

REFERENCES

Antonuccio, D. A., Thomas, M., & Danton, W. G. (1997). A cost-effectiveness analysis of cognitive behavior therapy and fluoxetine in the treatment of depression. *Behavior Therapy, 28,* 187–210.

Barlow, D. H., Gorman, J. M., Shear, M. K., & Woods, S. W. (2000). Cognitive-behavioral therapy, imipramine, and their combination in Panic Disorder. *Journal of the American Medical Association, 283,* 2529–2536.

Barlow, D. H., Rapee, R., & Brown, T. (1992). Behavioral treatment of Generalized Anxiety Disorder. *Behavior Therapy, 23,* 551–570.

Baucom, D. H., Shoham, V., Mueser, K. T., Daiuto, A. D., & Stickle, T. R. (1998). Empirically supported couple and family interventions for marital distress and adult mental health problems. *Journal of Consulting and Clinical Psychology, 66,* 53–88.

Brent, D. A., Holder, D., Kolko, D., Birmaher, B., Baugher, M., Roth, C., et al. (1997). A clinical psychotherapy trial for adolescent depression comparing cognitive, family, and supportive treatments. *Archives of General Psychiatry, 54,* 877–885.

Chambless, D. L., Baker, M. J., Baucom, D., Beutler, L. E., Calhoun, K. S., Crits-Christoph, P., et al. (1998). Update on empirically validated therapies II. *The Clinical Psychologist, 51*(1), 3–16.

Chambless, D. L., Foa, E. B., Groves, G. A., & Goldstein, A. J. (1979). Flooding with brevital in the treatment of agoraphobia: Countereffective? *Behavior Research and Therapy, 17,* 243–25.

Chambless, D. L., & Ollendick, T. H. (2001). Empirically supported psychological interventions: Controversies and evidence. *Annual Review of Psychology, 52,* 685–716.

Depression Guideline Panel. (1993). *Depression in Primary Care: Volume 2. Treatment of Major Depression. Clinical Practice Guideline, Number 5* (AHCPR Publication No. 93-0551). Department of Health and Human Services, Public Health Service, Agency for Healthcare Policy and Research, Rockville, MD. Washington, DC: U.S. Government Printing Office.

Elkin, I., Shea, M. T., Watkins, J. T., Imber, S. D., Sotsky, S. M., Collins, J. F., et al. (1989). National Institute of Mental Health treatment of depression collaborative research program. *Archives of General Psychiatry, 46,* 971–982.

Falloon, I. R. H., Boyd, J. L., McGill, C. W., Williamson, M., Razani, J., Moss, J. B., et al. (1985). Family management in the prevention of morbidity in schizophrenia: Clinical outcome of a two-year longitudinal study. *Archives of General Psychiatry, 42,* 887–896.

Fals-Stewart, W., Marks, A. P., & Schafer, J. A. (1993). A comparison of behavioral group therapy and individual behavior therapy in treating Obsessive-Compulsive Disorder. *Journal of Nervous & Mental Disease, 181*(3), 189–193.

Foa, E. B., Rothbaum, B. O., Riggs, D. S., & Murdock, T. B. (1991). Treatment of Post-Traumatic Stress Disorder in rape victims. *Journal of Consulting and Clinical Psychology, 59,* 715–723.

Frank, E., Kupfer, D. J., Perel, J. M., Cornes, C., Jarret, D. B., Mallinger, A. G., et al. (1990). Three-year outcomes for maintenance therapies in recurrent depression. *Archives of General Psychiatry, 47,* 1093–1099.

Franklin, M. E., Abramowitz, J. S., Kozak, M. J., Levitt, J. T., & Foa, E. B. (2000). Effectiveness of exposure and response prevention for Obsessive-Compulsive Disorder: Randomized compared with nonrandomized samples. *Journal of Consulting and Clinical Psychology, 68,* 594–602.

Glaoguen, V., Cottraux, J., & Cucherat, M. (1998). A meta-analysis of the effects of cognitive therapy in depressed patients. *Journal of Affective Disorders, 49,* 59–72.

Heimberg, R. G., Liebowitz, M. R., Hope, D. A., Schneier, F. R., Holt, C. S., Welkowitz, L. A., et al. (1998). Cognitive behavioral group therapy vs. phenelzine therapy for Social Phobia. *Archives of General Psychiatry, 55,* 1133–1141.

Hogarty, G. E., Anderson, C. M., & Reiss, D. J. (1986). Family psychoeducation, social skills training and maintenance chemotherapy in the aftercare treatment of Schizophrenia. *Archives of General Psychiatry, 43,* 633–642.

Jarrett, R. B., Basco, M. R., & Risser, R. (1998). Is there a role for continuation phase cognitive therapy for depressed outpatients? *Journal of Consulting and Clinical Psychology, 66,* 1036–1040.

Keller, M. B., McCullough, J. P., Klein, D. N., Arnow, B., Dunner, D. L., Gelenberg, A. J., et al. (2000). A comparison of nefazodone, the cognitive behavioral-analysis system of psychotherapy, and their combination in the treatment of chronic depression. *New England Journal of Medicine, 342*(20), 1426–1470.

Kottgen, C., Sonnichsen, I., Mollenhauer, K., & Jurth, R. (1984). Group therapy with the families of schizophrenic patients: Results of the Hamburg Camberwell Family Interview Study III. *International Journal of Family Psychiatry, 5,* 84–94.

Leff, J., Kuipers, L., Berkowitz, R., & Sturgeon, D. (1985). A controlled trial of social intervention in the families of schizophrenic patients: Two-year follow-up. *British Journal of Psychiatry, 146,* 594–600.

McFarlane, W. R., Link, B., Dushay, R., Marchal, J., & Crilly, J. (1995). Psychoeducational multiple family groups: Four-year outcome in Schizophrenia. *Family Process, 34,* 127–144.

Nathan, P. E., & Gorman, J. M. (Eds.). (1998). *A guide to treatments that work.* New York: Oxford University Press.

Otto, M. W., Pollack, M. H., & Maki, K. M. (2000). Empirically supported treatments for Panic Disorder: Costs, benefits, and stepped care. *Journal of Consulting and Clinical Psychology, 68,* 556–563.

Schooler, N. R., Keith, S. J., Severe, J. B., Mathews, S. M., Bellack, A. S., Glick, I. D., et al. (1997). Relapse and rehospitalization during maintenance treatment of schizophrenia: The effects of dose reduction and family therapy. *Archives of General Psychiatry, 54,* 453–463.

Sanderson, W. C., & McGinn, L. K. (2001). Cognitive behavior therapy of depression. In M. W. Weissman (Ed.), *Treatment of depression: Bridging the 21st century* (pp. 249–280). American Psychological Association.

Sanderson, W. C., Raue, P. J., & Wetzler, S. (1998). The generalizability of cognitive behavior therapy for Panic Disorder. *Journal of Cognitive Psychotherapy, 12,* 323–330.

Tuschen-Caffier, B., Pook, M., & Frank, M. (2001). Evaluation of manual-based cognitive-behavioral therapy for Bulimia Nervosa in a service setting. *Behaviour Research and Therapy, 39,* 299–308.

Wade, W. A., Treat, T. A., & Stuart, G. L. (1998). Transporting an empirically supported treatment for Panic Disorder to a service clinic setting: A benchmarking strategy. *Journal of Consulting and Clinical Psychology, 66,* 231–239.

Weissman, M. M., Markowitz, J. C., & Klerman, G. L. (2000). *Comprehensive guide to interpersonal therapy.* New York: Basic Books.

Weissman, M. M., Prusoff, B. A., DiMascio, A., Neu, C., Goklaney, M., & Klerman, G. L. (1979). The efficacy of drugs and psychotherapy in the treatment of acute depressive episodes. *American Journal of Psychiatry, 136,* 555–558.

Lata K. McGinn
Yeshiva University

William C. Sanderson
Hofstra University

***See also:* Interpersonal Psychotherapy; Psychotherapy**

EFFERENT

Axons leaving the neuronal soma are often referred to as *efferents.* The observations made on the efferents of alpha spinal motoneurons have contributed to our understanding of motor control. In natural recruitment of motoneurons, Ohm's law applies, so neurons with the smallest-diameter somas are recruited first. In contrast, electrical stimulation of a mixed peripheral nerve results in the largest diameter axons being activated at the lowest threshold, that is, first if stimulation current is gradually increased. The diameters of the largest-diameter axons of alpha motoneurons are similar to those of Ia afferents, although the largest of the latter are usually slightly larger than the largest motoneuronal axons.

M Waves in EMG from Motoneuronal Axon Stimulation

When motoneuronal axons are stimulated, an M wave results in the electromyogram (EMG) after the brief interval required for nerve conduction from the stimulus site to the muscle electrodes. This wave appears before the H-reflex waveforms that result from stimulating Ia afferents, as the effects of the latter must be exerted over a longer path, through the synapse with motoneurons in the spinal cord (Brooke et al., 1997). The constancy of M wave magnitudes is used as a biocalibration of the stability of stimulating Ia axons in reflex studies. The technique works because of the similarity in diameter of these efferents and afferents. Using this technique Misiaszek, Cheng, and Brooke (1995) showed that passive movement-induced attenuation of H-reflexes occurred over all stimulus strengths, from that at the threshold for M waves to that eliciting Mmax. It was inferred that the same afferent group, probably Ia, was involved in the expression of the reflex over the range of stimulation.

The M wave is the orthodromic outcome of stimulating motoneuronal axons. However, there is also an antidromic action potential set up at that time. This potential may collide with antidromically proceeding motoneuronal action potentials resulting from H-reflex activation. Accordingly, as M wave magnitudes rise, H-reflex magnitudes diminish. A further nuance results when alpha motoneuronal action potentials for voluntary movement are occurring. Then, (1) M waves may be diminished due to refractory motoneuronal axons; (2) H-reflexes may be diminished due to antidromic activation of alpha efferents and/or to refractory motoneurons; and (3) H-reflexes or M waves may be maximized under a recently-cleared-line principle. Thus, a contraction and high stimulus intensity to elicit Mmax results in distributions of M wave and H-reflex magnitudes that range from zero to maximal (Brooke & McIlroy, 1985). It is noteworthy that with normal stimulus recruitment curves, the maximal H-reflexes obtained seem to actually be maximal, as the collision technique described in the previous sentence does not appear to produce any larger H-reflexes. This collision technique has the potential to describe the ongoing ebb and flow of temporal recruitment of motoneurons over time.

Clinical Evaluation Using Efferent Stimulation

M waves are used for assessment of the number of motor units in a muscle and thus for estimation of the number of alpha motoneurons serving a muscle (the motoneuronal pool for that muscle). When the intensity of transcutaneous electrical stimulation of a mixed nerve is gradually increased, a current is reached at which the first small M wave is seen at the appropriate latency in the EMG. This M wave represents the muscular result of activation of the axon of a motoneuron. If the current is then gradually increased, at a certain point the M wave will become larger and its shape will alter. The muscular response to the activation response of a second motoneuron has been added to the first. This process and identification in the M wave shape can be continued for a number of motoneurons. If the current is reduced, the M wave decreases in discreet steps. At a high current, the maximum M wave is obtained, and further increases in current elicit no further increase in M wave magnitude. These phenomena have been combined by McComas and colleagues (McComas, 1996) to estimate the number of motoneurons in a pool. The mean M wave magnitude (mV) from a small sample of early recruited motoneurons is divided into the magnitude of Mmax (mV), the result being the estimate of the number of motoneurons serving the muscle. The procedure is now computerized. The technique has revealed the very large losses of motoneurons with advanced aging and during diseases such as amyotrophic lateral sclerosis (McComas, 1996).

F waves in the EMG are used to establish motoneuronal integrity (Ma & Liveson, 1983). With high intensities of transcutaneous stimulation of motoneuronal efferents, antidromic activation can produce action potentials that, arising from the soma, course orthodromically back down the axon to lead eventually to excitation of the muscle fibers. These F waves have latencies very similar to H-reflexes. Separation from H-reflexes usually relies on the high variability in being able to produce F waves, compared to H-reflexes, and the high stimulation intensity required for the former compared to the latter. Morphological differences in wave forms of reflex and F wave may also help.

Completeness of maximum voluntary contraction can be established using the sequelae of Mmax stimulation. If a patient is not making a maximum voluntary contraction when requested, the Mmax stimulation will still produce a muscle twitch (McComas, 1996).

In some diseases, such as myasthenia gravis, the adequacy of release of acetylcholine (the neurotransmitter at the myoneuronal junction) is compromised. In diagnosing this deficiency, it is common to test with a series of four or five Mmax stimuli closely spaced in time (interstimulus rate can range from 3 to 50Hz; Walton, 1987). The later stimuli in the time series result in markedly reduced M waves in the EMG in the patient with transmitter deficiency, compared to the healthy person. This contrasts with the availability of glutamate at the Ia-motoneuronal synapse. In the latter case, even as few as two closely spaced stimuli will result in the second H-reflex being much reduced in magnitude or even nonexistent. This is the phenomenon of homosynaptic depression (Capek & Esplin, 1977).

REFERENCES

Brooke, J. D., & McIlroy, W. E. (1985). M wave distribution shift and concomitant H reflex increase with contraction efference. *The Physiologist, 28,* 282.

Brooke, J. D., Cheng, J., Collins, D. F., McIlroy, W. E., Misiaszek, J. E., & Staines, W. R. (1997). Sensori-sensory afferent conditioning with leg movement: Gain control in spinal reflex and ascending paths. *Progress in Neurobiology, 51,* 393–421.

Capek, R., & Esplin, B. (1977). Homosynaptic depression and transmitter turnover in spinal monosynaptic pathway. *Journal of Neurophysiology, 40,* 95–105.

Ma, D. M., & Liveson, J. A. (1983). *Nerve conduction handbook.* Philadelphia: Davis.

McComas, A. J. (1996). *Skeletal muscle: Form and function.* Champaign, IL: Human Kinetics.

Misiaszek, J. E., Cheng, J., & Brooke, J. D. (1995). Movement-induced depression of soleus H-reflexes is consistent in humans over the range of excitatory afferents involved. *Brain Research, 702,* 271–274.

Walton, J. (1987). *Introduction to clinical neuroscience* (2nd ed., p. 91). London: Balliere Tindall.

John D. Brooke
Feinberg School of Medicine, Northwestern University

EGO DEVELOPMENT

The term *ego development* is used in different ways by different authors. Most psychoanalysts use it in one of three ways: (1) to describe the period of formation of the self or ego in the first 2 or 3 years of life; (2) to describe the development of all ego functions, including what Heinz Hartmann called the "conflict-free ego sphere," that is, locomotion, speech, and so on; (3) to describe aspects of ego development such as those described by Erik Erikson as psychosocial tasks, entwined with psychosexual development (i.e., the development of drives and drive derivatives) and tied to age-specific life tasks. In clinical psychoanalytic use, disorders of ego development usually refer to problems arising in the period of ego formation; they are likely to lead to profound maladjustment or to "borderline" personality types.

Psychologists have delineated a different conception that has roots in Harry Stack Sullivan's *interpersonal theory of psychiatry.* This conception, in addition to being a developmental sequence, is a dimension of individual differences that applies in principle at any age, although higher stages are never found in early childhood and the lowest stages are rare in maturity. Terms such as *moral development, interpersonal reliability,* and *cognitive complexity* have been used for aspects of the sequence.

Stages

The earliest stage (or stages)—the *period of ego formation*—occurs in infancy. This stage is presocial, at first autistic, later symbiotic with the mother or mother figure. Acquisition of language is believed to be an important factor in bringing the period to an end.

The *impulsive stage* is next: The child confirms a separate existence from the mother by willfulness and is dependent on others for control of impulses. Persons at this stage are preoccupied with their own needs, often bodily ones, and see others as a source of supply. They live in a universe conceptually oversimplified, at least as to its interpersonal features. Rules are seen as specific prohibitions or as frustration of wishes rather than as a system of social regulation.

Growth at first is in terms of ensuring more certain gratification by tolerating some delay and detour, which leads to the *self-protective stage.* Children at this stage will often assert some degree of autonomy to free themselves from excessive dependence; however, their interpersonal relations remain exploitative. They are concerned with power and control, dominance and submission. In early childhood this period is normally negotiated with the help of rituals; when a person remains at this stage into adolescence and adult life, there may be a marked opportunism. Rules are understood but are manipulated to the person's advantage.

Normally in late childhood there is a sea-change. One identifies oneself and one's own welfare with that of the group. Rules are partly internalized and are adhered to precisely because they are group-accepted and endorsed. This is the *conformist stage,* which has been widely recognized and described as a personality type. Conformity is valued for its own sake, and people tend to perceive others and themselves as conforming.

Many people seem to advance beyond the conformist stage by perceiving that they themselves do not always live up to the high standards of conduct that society endorses and do not always have the approved emotions in some situations. This period is called the *conscientious-conformist level,* or the *self-aware level.* Whether it is a transition between the conformist stage and the conscientious stage or a true stage is an unsettled point. The person at this level sees multiple possibilities as appropriate.

At the *conscientious stage* rules are truly internalized. The person obeys rules not just because the group approves, but because they have been self-evaluated and accepted as personally valid. Interpersonal relations are understood in terms of feelings and motives rather than merely actions. The person has a richly differentiated inner life and—in place of stereotyped perceptions of others—a rich vocabulary of differentiated traits with which to describe people. Thus, their parents are described as real people with both virtues and failings, rather than as idealized portraits or as entirely hateful persons. Self-descriptions are also modulated; the person does not describe the self either as perfect or as worthless, but sees circumscribed faults that he or she aspires to improve. Achievement is valued, not purely as competitive or as social recognition, but as measured by the person's own standards. Persons at this stage may feel excessively responsible for shaping the lives of others.

In moving beyond the conscientious stage, the person begins to appreciate individuality for its own sake; thus this transitional level is called *individualistic.* It is characterized by increased conceptual complexity: Life is viewed in terms of many-faceted possibilities instead of diametrically opposed dichotomies. There is spontaneous interest in human development and an appreciation of psychological causation.

At the *autonomous stage* the characteristics of the individualistic level are developed further. The name *autonomous* is somewhat arbitrary, as are all the stage names. No aspect of behavior arises suddenly in one era and perishes immediately on passage to the next. What characterizes this stage particularly is respect for the autonomy of others. A crucial case is the subject's own children, especially acknowledging their right to make their own mistakes. The person at this stage is often aware of functioning differently in different roles. One copes with inner conflict such as that between one's own needs and duties. Conflict is viewed as an inevitable part of the human condition rather than as a failing of self, other family members, or society.

Beginning at the conscientious stage and especially

characteristic of higher stages is seeing oneself in a larger social context. This is particularly true of persons at the *integrated stage,* who are able to unite concern for society and for self in a single complex thought.

Related Domains

Many authors have sketched stages of development closely related to the foregoing sequence. Clyde Sullivan, Marguerite Q. Grant, and J. Douglas Grant refer to their stages as "interpersonal integration." Their conception has been used in studies of differential treatment of different subtypes of delinquents.

Kohlberg has developed a system of stages for the development of moral judgment; his ideas have been widely applied. In schools they have been the basis for curricula to encourage moral development, including the forming of alternative schools on the model of "just communities."

Selman labels his stages "interpersonal perspective taking." He has studied school-age children; thus his work applies chiefly to early stages. He has also studied a small clinical sample.

Perry's sequence corresponds to some of the higher stages. John M. Broughton covered a wide age range. He was concerned with development of "natural epistemologies"—conceptions of mind, self, reality, and knowledge.

Methods of Study

Although the idea of character development goes back at least to Socrates, modern study begins with Jean Piaget. Kohlberg, Selman, and others have adapted Piaget's method of clinical interviewing. Kohlberg presents his subjects with an unfinished story ending in a moral dilemma. When the subject finishes the story, there follows a probing interview during which reasons for choices are explored; the stage assigned depends on the reasoning. Rest has evolved an objectively scored test that is an adaptation of Kohlberg's instrument. Broughton and Perry have worked out interviews beginning with broad, unstructured questions.

Loevinger, Wessler, and Redmore's scoring manual for a sentence completion test is sufficiently detailed as to be semi-objective and includes self-teaching exercises. Marguerite Warren (formerly Grant) and others working with the interpersonal integration system of C. Sullivan and colleagues have used a variety of instruments including interviews, sentence completion tests, and objective tests.

Theories

There are two major theoretical issues: Why is the ego (or self) as stable as it is? How and why does it manage to change at all?

The theories of ego stability are all variations of H. S. Sullivan's "anxiety-gating" theory. What Sullivan calls the "self-system" acts as a kind of filter, template, or frame of reference for one's perception and conception of the interpersonal world. Any observations not consonant with one's current frame of reference cause anxiety. However, the main purpose of the self-system is to avoid or attenuate anxiety. Therefore, such perceptions are either distorted so as to fit the preexisting system or—in Sullivan's phrase—they are "selectively inattended to." Thus, the theory states that because the self-system or ego is a structure, it is self-perpetuating.

Kohlberg has a structural theory of change. When a person at one stage repeatedly encounters and grapples with reasoning and arguments just one stage higher, conditions are optimal for assimilating the reasoning and hence advancing toward that stage.

Identification is the key to the current psychoanalytic theory of ego development. One moves ahead in part because one identifies with some admired model who is (or is perceived as being) at a slightly higher level. Although Kohlberg's theory is primarily cognitive and the psychoanalytic theory is affective, both imply a Piagetian model of equilibrium, disequilibration, and re-equilibration. Both are, in effect, "social learning" theories, although they differ radically from what is usually called social learning theory.

There is another element in the psychoanalytic theory that originates as social learning but becomes wholly internal to the individual. The ideal or model toward which the person strives or aspires need not be embodied in the environment. The capacity for constructing one's own model is what is called the *ego ideal.*

Ausubel presents another theory of some aspects of ego development. Infants believe themselves to be omnipotent because their wishes are magically realized. (Here Ausubel is following Ferenczi's essay.) As children learn of their total dependence on their parents, they face a catastrophic loss of self-esteem. To escape that fate, they assign their former omnipotence to their parents and so become their satellites, shining in their reflected glory. In late childhood and early adolescence one should "desatellize," or learn to derive self-esteem from one's own achievements. Satellization and desatellization may miscarry at several points, resulting in various patterns of psychopathology.

Perry depicts many factors as contributing to both stability and change in the college years. His model of change has implications for a dynamic explanation. The student whose world view is, say, dualistic (right vs. wrong, us vs. them) at first learns to perceive some special field as more complicated and multiplistic (many possibilities, everyone has a right to his or her own opinion). As the fields of application for the multiplistic view increase, those where the dualistic view applies correspondingly shrink, until the multiplistic view becomes the predominant one, with only isolated areas of life still seen in dualistic terms. The same paradigm applies for the transition from multiplistic to relativistic thinking (some views are better because they are grounded in better data or sounder reasoning). One of the generally accepted aims of a liberal education is to encourage acceptance of the relativistic nature of all knowledge. In Perry's view, relativism should be followed by acceptance of some commitments.

J. Loevinger

See also: **Eriksonian Developmental Stages; Identity Formation**

ELDER ABUSE AND NEGLECT

Of all the facets of gerontology, elder abuse and neglect is one of the least well understood. Even the definitions of abuse and neglect are debated and vary from locality to locality across the United States. Often the term *abuse* or *abuse and neglect* is used generically to refer to a variety of behaviors that are not strictly abuse or neglect (e.g., financial exploitation) or that do not involve a second party (e.g., self-neglect). Here the discussion will be restricted largely to the infliction of physical or emotional harm or serious threat of such harm on a vulnerable individual (abuse) or the withholding of needed care or attention from such an individual (neglect) by a second person or persons in a trust relationship that occurs in a domestic setting. Abuse and neglect occurring in institutional settings are not covered. Even abuse and neglect in domestic settings, some experts have argued, deserve separate treatment because they are very different—the former being a criminal justice matter and the latter a civil justice issue or even a health, mental health, or social service issue often stemming from some type of caregiving crisis. Both will be treated here as forms of elder mistreatment.

Numbers reflecting prevalence suggest the magnitude of abuse and neglect, while recent research suggesting substantially increased death rates among those mistreated reflects its seriousness. Although neither the prevalence nor the incidence of elder mistreatment in the United States is known with any precision, the best research suggests that 2–4% of the population 65 years and older suffer abuse or neglect.

Prevalence of abuse and neglect, it must be emphasized, is extremely difficult to measure. Not only are victims often reluctant to reveal mistreatment, especially by a relative, but also the "victim" as judged by legal standards or professional practice may not view himself or herself as a victim. Furthermore, perception of what constitutes mistreatment may differ markedly according to the cultural background of an individual. Moreover, mistreatment can flow both ways, or even emanate from the elder "victim," especially where an elder care recipient suffers from dementia and exhibits aggressive behavior.

Of all of the types of mistreatment, neglect appears to be the most prevalent, and emotional abuse almost certainly exceeds, in number of episodes, physical abuse of all types. Self-neglect, not covered here, may well be more prevalent than any type of mistreatment by a second party.

The second-party perpetrator is most likely a family member and, most often, an adult child or a spouse. Conceptually, elder mistreatment by a spouse that takes the form of abuse, at least, also can be considered domestic or intimate partner violence. However, it is rarely treated as such by governmental authorities or service providers, largely because the sociocultural and statutory histories of the domestic violence arena are very different from those that give rise to concerns surrounding elder abuse. The domestic or intimate partner violence rubric is almost always reserved for violence against women of childbearing age.

There is no want to the list of suggested explanations for elder mistreatment. Neglect is almost always diagnosed within the context of caregiving, and in that context it seems somewhat easier to explain than physical abuse. Physical or mental incapacity of the caregiver, and in some cases simple ignorance of the underlying needs of a frail elder or, more often, of appropriate ways to address those needs, seem adequate explanations. In perhaps a very substantial proportion of cases, the abuse or neglect that transpires reflects a poor emotional relationship between victim and perpetrator that, in many instances, may have a relatively long history.

Until at least the 1980s, caregiver stress was offered as the leading explanation for elder abuse and neglect, a sort of blame-the-victim approach. More recent studies, however, have cast doubt on that as the major explanatory factor, and scholars have turned largely from attempting simple explanations to focusing on the nature of the interaction or relationship between the victim and the perpetrator and on identifying risk factors for or indicators of mistreatment.

Being a victim of abuse or neglect in the past appears to be the single best predictor of future victimization. Beyond that, principal risk factors seem to be poor mental (and perhaps physical) functioning of the victim (both of which tend to be associated with advanced age); financial dependence of the abuser on the victim; poor emotional health of the perpetrator, including substance abuse; social isolation of the family; and, for married victims, a history of marital violence. Even on these factors, however, agreement is less than perfect.

The absence of consensus and the presence of disparate findings from research studies regarding explanations or risk factors for elder abuse and neglect undoubtedly reflect not only the complexity of human behavior overall but also the potential reality that the explanation or even the risk factor varies by type of mistreatment involved. Further complexity is added by the fact that each type does not necessarily occur in isolation but may be perpetrated in various combinations of mistreatment and exploitative behaviors.

Following the principle of assumed power of *parens patriae,* public responsibility in the United States for addressing elder mistreatment has devolved under federal mandate to the states. States have set up mechanisms (typically an abuse hot line) for reporting instances of elder mistreatment of any type (often including financial exploitation and self-neglect) as well as Adult Protective Services offices to investigate these reports. This reporting function has been modeled on that established earlier for reporting child abuse, and in many states reporting is mandatory for anyone who strongly suspects mistreatment has occurred. The service response to confirmed mistreatment cases typically is the provision of long-term care services, such as a homemaker or personal care, that were designed for cases of self-neglect. Due to budget constraints reflecting the add-on nature of services and infrastructure to deal with elder abuse and neglect existing in most states, however, these purportedly long-term care services are actually provided for a brief period of time, usually for only a few days or weeks until the immediate crisis is past. Moreover, in stark contrast to governmental actions taken to address domestic abuse or violence, the only public responsibility commonly assumed in the case of elder abuse is for the victim. Typically, the state takes little if any action with respect to the perpetrator other than perhaps Adult Protective Service investigators reporting to the police cases in which they suspect a crime has been committed. Criminal prosecution of elder abusers is rarely pursued.

Elder abuse and neglect or mistreatment is a complex phenomenon that has received too little research or public policy attention. As a consequence, our knowledge base surrounding it is rudimentary. Unfortunately, and in part also as a consequence, the intervention to address it typically is too narrow and, at the same time, too imprecise. This social problem calls for a multidisciplinary approach in research and a multispecialty approach to applying the results of that research in prevention, treatment, and adjudication.

Burton D. Dunlop
Max B. Rothman
Florida International University

ELECTRODERMAL ACTIVITY

Many who record electrodermal activity (EDA) today share the basic belief expressed by Carl Jung in 1907 and by some present-day lie detector operators that verbal responses do not tell all, but that EDA does reveal the secrets of "mental life."

The skin has a special significance because it both receives outside information and responds to signals from within. As one EDA investigator stated, "We can listen in on such signals by taking advantage of the fact that their arrival at the skin is heralded by measurable electrified changes that we call electrodermal activity." If we think of our skin as a giant receptor separating us from the rest of the world, is it any wonder that responses obtained from it would be of interest to psychologists? Today we think of EDA as a measure of the state of the organism's interaction with its environment. EDA reflects not only emotional responding; it is also elicited by cognitive activity.

Terminology

The terms used to describe EDA have changed over the years. The term used at the turn of the nineteenth century was *psychogalvanic reflex* (PGR). Later the term *galvanic skin response* (GSR) was used. Today most psychophysiologists have dropped this term in favor of *electrodermal activity* (EDA).

The electrical activity of the skin can be measured in two ways. First, a small current can be passed through the skin from an external source, and the resistance to the passage of current is then measured. This technique was first used by Feré in 1888 and is referred to as the *exosomatic method.* The second method, the *endosomatic technique,* was first used by Tarchanoff in 1889; it measures the electrical activity at the surface of the skin, with no externally imposed current. The exosomatic method has been modified today into the measurement of *skin conductance* (SC), the reciprocal of skin resistance. The endosomatic method is still used to measure skin potential (SP), but skin conductance recording is used today by most researchers.

When describing EDA, one can discuss basal activity (tonic) versus the response to a stimulus (phasic). When referring to tonic electrodermal activity, the convention is to use the word *level* (L) and when discussing phasic activity to use the word *response* (R). Therefore, the four common descriptions of electrodermal activity are as follows: skin conductance level (SCL), skin conductance response (SCR), skin potential level (SPL), and skin potential response (SPR).

Psychophysiological recordings show a third type of activity in addition to tonic and phasic activity. Spontaneous electrodermal activity appears in records obtained using both the SC and SP techniques.

Physiological Basis

We still don't know a great deal about the complex relationship of the central nervous system to EDA. Peripherally, we know that eccrine sweat glands, a special type of sweat gland, are intimately involved in EDA. Eccrine sweat glands are concentrated in the palms of the hands and soles of the feet. What makes them of particular interest to psychologists is that they respond primarily to "psychic" stimulation, whereas other sweat glands respond more to increases in temperature. The eccrine sweat glands are innervated by the sympathetic branch of the autonomic nervous system, but the chemical transmitter at the postganglionic synapse is acetylcholine, not noradrenaline, as would be expected in the sympathetic nervous system.

The eccrine sweat glands, which can be thought of as tiny tubes with their openings at the surface of the skin, act as variable resistors wired in parallel. Depending upon the degree of sympathetic activation, sweat rises toward the surface of the skin in varying amounts and in varying numbers of sweat glands. The higher the sweat rises in a given gland, the lower the resistance in that variable resistor. In some cases, but certainly not all, sweat overflows onto the surface of the skin. This hydration of the skin with salty sweat increases SCL and SPL. Years ago, it was thought that EDA was determined solely by the amount of sweat on the surface of the skin. We now know this is not so. Even in those cases where stimulation does not result in sweat at the surface of the skin, changes in EDA are often found, because even a slight rise of the sweat in the glands will change the values of the variable resistors. If we wished to quantify the EDA at a given moment, we would sum the values of all the active resistors that are wired in parallel. The sum of resistors in parallel equals the sum of their reciprocals, or conductance. This is one reason for using skin conductance rather than skin resistance when describing exosomatic EDA. A second reason is that skin conductance, unlike skin resistance, does not have to be corrected for base level. In addition to the hydration of the skin and the number of active sweat glands, other factors that may be involved in EDA include a membrane in the sweat duct wall that affects the reabsorption of sweat, and changes in pressure in the duct that affect the opening of the pores in the skin. For skin potential, it has been demonstrated that SPL of extremely relaxed subjects is determined largely by the concentration of potassium at the surface.

Factors to Control When Recording or Interpreting EDA Data

The following subject variables have been found to affect EDA: age, sex, race, and stage of menstrual cycle. Environmental factors that effect EDA include temperature, humidity, time of day, day of week, and season.

Robert M. Stern

See also: **Psychophysiology; Sympathetic Nervous System**

EMOTIONAL CONTAGION

Emotional contagion has been defined as "The tendency to automatically mimic and synchronize expressions, vocalizations, postures, and movements with those of another person and, consequently, to converge emotionally" (Hatfield, Cacioppo, & Rapson, 1993). The Emotional Contagion Scale is designed to measure the extent to which men and women tend to catch expressions of joy, love, anger, fear, and sadness in others.

Theoretically, emotions can be caught in a variety of ways. Some researchers have argued that conscious reasoning, analysis, and imagination account for the phenomenon. Others contend that people must *learn* to share others' emotions. Most, however, assume that emotional contagion is an even more primitive process—that it happens automatically, outside of conscious awareness.

The process of emotional contagion is thought to operate like this:

> *Proposition 1:* In conversation, people automatically and continuously mimic and synchronize their facial expressions, voices, postures, movements, and instrumental behaviors with those of others.
> *Proposition 2:* Subjective emotional experience is affected moment to moment by the feedback from such mimicry/synchrony.

Theoretically, emotional experience could be influenced by (1) the central nervous system commands that direct such mimicry/synchrony in the first place; (2) the afferent feedback from such facial, verbal, or postural mimicry/synchrony; or (3) conscious self-perception processes, wherein individuals draw inferences about their own emotional states on the basis of the emotional expressions and behaviors evoked in them by the emotional states of others.

> *Proposition 3:* Consequently, people tend, from moment to moment, to "catch" others' emotions.

Researchers have collected considerable evidence in support of these propositions.

Proposition 1

Researchers have found evidence that people do tend to imitate the facial expressions, postures, voices, and instrumental behaviors of others.

Social psychophysiologists find that people are capable of mimicking others' emotional expressions (as measured by electromyographic [EMG] procedures) with surprising speed and accuracy. When people observe happy facial expressions, they show increased muscular activity over the zygomaticus major (cheek) muscle region. When they observe angry facial expressions, they show increased muscular activity over the corrugator supercilli (brow) muscle region.

Such mimicry begins almost at birth. Developmental psychologists find that 10-week-old infants imitate their mothers' facial expressions of happiness, sadness, and anger. Mothers mimic their infants' expressions of emotion as well.

There also is voluminous evidence that people mimic and synchronize their vocal utterances. Communication researchers find that there is interspeaker influence on utterance durations, speech rate, latencies of response, and a host of other speech characteristics. People also tend to mimic and synchronize their postures and movements with others.

Proposition 2

Researchers have found that emotions are tempered to some extent by somatic and skeletal feedback.

Researchers interested in testing the facial feedback hypothesis have employed a variety of strategies for inducing people to adopt various emotional expressions. Sometimes they simply ask them to fake an emotional expression. Sometimes they ask them to exaggerate or to hide any emotional reactions they may have. Sometimes they try to trick them into adopting various facial expressions. Sometimes they try to arrange things so they will unconsciously mimic others' emotional and facial expressions.

In all cases, however, scientists have found that people's subjective emotional experiences *are* affected by feedback from the facial expressions they adopt.

Scientists have assembled an impressive array of evidence supporting the proposition that people's subjective emotional experiences are affected, moment to moment, by feedback from facial, vocal, postural, and movement mimicry.

Proposition 3

Researchers from a variety of disciplines provide evidence that emotional contagion exists. The majority of work has come from animal researchers; child psychologists interested in primitive emotional contagion, empathy, and sympathy; clinicians exploring the process of transference and countertransference; social psychologists; and historians.

Individual Differences

Do people differ in the capacity to share the joy, love, sadness, fear, and anger of others? It seems that they do. Theorists have proposed a variety of characteristics that may increase individuals' susceptibility to emotional contagion. Scientists contend that people are more likely to catch others' emotions if they are attentive to others' feelings; if they feel closely linked to others; if they are skilled at reading facial expressions, voices, and gestures; if they tend to mimic others' facial, vocal, and postural expressions; if they are sensitive to their own emotions; and if they are emotionally expressive. Conversely, people who rarely attend to others, who construe themselves as distinct and unique from others, who are unable to read others' emotions, who fail to mimic, or whose subjective emotional experiences are unaltered by peripheral feedback should be fairly resistant to contagion.

Researchers also propose that people should be most vulnerable to contagion in certain kinds of *relationships*. Caretakers and infants should be especially prone to share one another's emotions. Men and women ought to be more likely to catch one another's emotions when they are passionately or companionately in love and when they possess similar attitudes and beliefs. People who have power over others should be resistant to contagion. Those they control should be more vulnerable to soaking up emotions.

As yet, however, there is only sparse evidence in favor of these reasonable-sounding hypotheses.

Implications

Cognitive psychologists have discovered that people are able to use multiple means to gain information about others' cognitive and emotional states. Conscious analytic skills can assist people in figuring out what makes other people "tick." But if people pay careful attention to the emotions they experience in the company of others, they may well gain an extra edge into "feeling themselves into" others' cognitive and emotional states, as well.

There is evidence that both what people think and what they feel may provide valuable, and different, information about others. In one study, for example, researchers found that people's conscious assessments of what others must be feeling were heavily influenced by what the others *claimed* to feel. People's own emotions, however, were more influenced by the others' nonverbal clues as to what the others were *really* feeling.

REFERENCE

Hatfield, E., Cacioppo, J. T., & Rapson, R. L. (1993). *Emotional contagion*. New York: Cambridge University Press.

Elaine Hatfield
Richard L. Rapson
University of Hawaii

EMOTIONAL DEVELOPMENT

Emotions play a significant role in the development of the child. Not only are they central to the process of attachment and other social interactions, but they also influence how well a child does in other developmental domains. This brief review discusses developmental theories of emotion and the developmental course of specific emotions. As the child matures, he or she gains new perspectives on how emotions are used. These processes are reviewed here.

Although there are several different perspectives on the development of emotion, the two that dominate the literature differ as to the mechanisms by which emotions emerge. The evolutionary/functionalist developmental theory (Darwin, 1872/1965; Izard & Malatesta, 1987; Barrett & Campos, 1987) proposes that emotions emerge when they are adaptive. The cognitive theory of emotional development (Lewis, 1993), on the other hand, suggests that emotions emerge or differentiate depending upon the development of certain cognitive skills. Interestingly, these mechanisms often converge.

At birth, the infant is capable of feeling distress, disgust, pain, and interest, although there is debate as to whether interest is an emotion. By 3 months of age, when the infant perceives and differentiates familiar from unfamiliar persons, he or she expresses happiness or joy. Smiling functions to maintain social contact. At approximately the same time, when the infant begins to self-initiate reaching and grasping, anger emerges. Anger is an emotion generated when an obstacle (barrier) prevents the child from obtaining a goal (interesting toy) and thus motivates the child to remove the obstacle. When the infant begins to move out into the environment on his or her own, usually at around 7 to 9 months of age, a new emotion emerges that serves to protect the infant from new and potentially dangerous persons and objects—fear. This emotion is often reflected in the infant's newfound avoidance of strangers; however, not all infants exhibit what is often called stranger anxiety.

Emotions such as embarrassment, shame, pride, guilt, and empathy are proposed to emerge after the development of self-awareness. Self-recognition, which emerges between the ages of 18 and 24 months, has been shown to be a necessary condition for embarrassment. Self-conscious emotions such as pride and guilt require the child to evaluate his or her own behavior against a standard. This ability occurs around the 2-year age mark.

Toddlers and preschoolers undergo significant progress in all areas of development, particularly with respect to the emotional domain. Component skills of emotional development include the expression, understanding, and regulation of emotion (Denham, 1998).

Emotional expression involves the communication of nonverbal emotional signals in appropriate contexts and in socially appropriate ways. Expression of an emotion may be characterized by its intensity, duration, and frequency. The complexity of the emotions expressed, the knowledge of the appropriate emotion for a given situation, and the cultural rules for displaying a given emotion in a social situation are a result of within-person differences, as well as interpersonal interactions that contribute to the child's abilities. By 3 years of age, children are able to interpret others' emotions correctly. Five- and 6-year-olds are also very capable of assessing the events likely to have caused another's emotional state. The complexity of children's understanding of *display rules,* the culture rules that suggest when it might be best to mask or substitute a felt emotion for prosocial reasons, is difficult to untangle. However, these skills appear to develop rapidly in preschoolers and school-age children, and girls appear to assimilate these rules into their repertoire sooner than boys.

Emotion regulation is the complex process of appropriately coping with positive and negative emotions and the situations that elicit these emotions. The regulatory or coping process may occur at the level of the emotion, the perceptions or cognitions about the emotion, or the behavior associated with the emotion. Even very young babies are capable of modulating their emotions to some extent, for example, by sucking on their fingers. In early childhood, competence in emotion regulation is marked by the gradual shift from external sources of regulation, such as parents, to internal sources of regulation. They learn strategies to reduce emotionally charged information, such as thinking of something pleasant, looking away, or reinterpreting the event.

The abilities to label emotions, including the more complex emotions, understand the causes and consequences of emotion and emotional situations, discern the independence of one's own emotions from others' emotional experience, and communicate with others about emotion are all aspects of *emotion understanding.* Children gather this important information as they increasingly interact with others and find themselves with the opportunity to label or relate to another person's emotion. Each of these interrelated emotional skills is intricately associated with social development, as emotional competence is vital in understanding one's own experiences and negotiating successful interactions with others.

These skills are not traits that young children simply develop at specified time points; rather, their development is the result of interactions that socialize the child over time. Conversations and interactions with parents, other caregivers, siblings, and peers assist children's development of an understanding of emotion. These interactions are embedded within the larger cultural context, which also exerts a socializing force (Saarni, 1999). Three mechanisms proposed in the process of emotion socialization are modeling, coaching, and contingency (Halberstadt, 1991). *Modeling* occurs whenever someone expresses an emotion and it is witnessed or observed by the child in context. When modeling occurs, it contributes to the overall emotional climate of any family or social group. *Coaching* of emotions includes any talk or teaching about emotions and their consequences. For example, talk about emotion in the family is an important vehicle for teaching young children about emotions in themselves and others, and dealing with emotionally charged events (Dunn & Brown, 1991; Dunn, Bretherton, & Munn, 1987). *Contingency* includes others' emotional and behavioral reactions to a child's emotions. These reactions may increase or decrease the likelihood of the child's patterns of expressiveness and the coping styles they use for handling emotions on their own (Halberstadt, 1991). The complexities of the process of emotion socialization are many. The individual characteristics of the parent and the child, and the child's age, sex, and siblings, are just some of the many factors that may influence this essential but complicated developmental process.

REFERENCES

Barrett, K., & Campos, J. (1987). Perspectives on emotional development II: A functionalist approach to emotions. In J. Osofsky (Ed.), *Handbook of infant development* (Vol. 2, pp. 555–578). New York: Wiley.

Darwin, C. (1965). *The expression of the emotions in man and animals.* Chicago: University of Chicago Press. (Original work published 1872)

Denham, S. A. (1998). *Emotional development in young children.* New York: Guilford Press.

Dunn, J., & Brown, J. R. (1991). Relationships, talk about feelings, and the development of affect regulation in early childhood. In J. Garber & K. Dodge (Eds.), *The development of emotion regulation and dysregulation* (pp. 89–108). Cambridge, UK: Cambridge University Press.

Dunn, J., Bretherton, I., & Munn, P. (1987). Conversations about feeling states between mothers and their young children. *Developmental Psychology, 23,* 132–139.

Halberstadt, A. (1991). Socialization of expressiveness: Family influences in particular and a model in general. In R. S. Feldman & S. Rimé (Eds.), *Fundamentals of emotional expressiveness* (pp. 106–162). Cambridge, UK: Cambridge University Press.

Izard, C., & Malatesta, C. (1987). Perspectives on emotional development: I. Differential emotions theory of early emotional development. In J. Osofsky (Ed.), *Handbook of infant development* (Vol. 2, pp. 494–554). New York: Wiley.

Lewis, M. (1993). The emergence of human emotions. In M. Lewis & J. Haviland (Eds.), *Handbook of emotions* (pp. 223–235). New York: Guilford Press.

Saarni, C. (1999). *The development of emotional competence.* New York: Guilford Press.

Cynthia A. Stifter
Heather K. Warren
Pennsylvania State University

EMPIRICISM

Empiricism is one of several rival doctrines in the philosophical field of epistemology, the study of knowledge. Epistemology's main concern is how to establish the truth of knowledge claims. If someone advances a proposition or group of propositions—for example, a scientific theory—how are we to determine that it is true? Empiricism holds that knowledge arises from and is to be justified by perceptual experience. Although empiricism seems straightforward enough, it faces challenges that have created its epistemological competitors.

Plato offered the first influential critique of experience as the basis for knowledge claims, pointing out that experience is frequently mistaken. If one person enters a room from a blizzard and another enters it having stoked a fire, they will disagree about whether the room is hot or cold. Perception is a source only of opinions, of beliefs that might be true or false. Knowledge, Plato said, must be absolutely and demonstrably true for all times and all places. Plato advanced two important alternatives to empiricism: rationalism and nativism. Rationalism locates the truth of knowledge claims in logic. Plato was influenced by Pythagoras and his followers, who created the notion of logical proof. When one works through the proof of the Pythagorean theorem, for example, one arrives at a truth that cannot be doubted because it has been formally proved. Mathematical proofs derive their authority from reason, not experience, and Plato hoped to extend a similar level of provable certainty to all knowledge claims.

Plato was also influenced by the Eastern religions infiltrating Greece from the fifth century B.C.E. onward. These religions taught that humans had immortal souls; some taught that a soul went through a cycle of reincarnations. Plato taught that, while out of the body, the soul sees eternal, transcendental Forms, heavenly prototypes of the objects of ordinary experience. Thus, a cat is a cat because it resembles the Form of the Cat, while a dog resembles the Form of the Dog. Knowledge of the Forms remains latent in the soul upon reincarnation and is merely awakened by perceptual experience. In Plato's philosophy, right use of reason makes knowledge demonstrably true, while existence of the Forms makes knowledge true eternally and transcendentally.

Plato's student Aristotle defended the validity of experience. He advanced a version of perceptual realism, asserting that we perceive things as they really are. Error arises from mistaken judgments we make about our experience, not from experience itself. Seeing a man on the street, one might mistake him for a friend, but the error impugns the viewer's judgment, not his or her perception. In a broad sense, Aristotle was an empiricist because he said that knowledge arises from experience; but in the modern sense, he was not an empiricist because he did not share its representational theory of perception.

Modern empiricism in philosophy and psychology began with Locke and Descartes. Because of Descartes' emphasis on reason and his belief in innate ideas he is typically lumped together with Plato as a rationalist and nativist, but his theory of perception is also the starting point for modern empiricism as developed by Locke. Descartes proposed that we do not experience the world directly, but through a veil of ideas that represent objects. In this representational theory of perception, one does not directly perceive the book he or she is now reading (as Aristotle taught), but only a representation of it, an idea held in consciousness. Locke's empiricism held that knowledge is the mind's acquaintance with its ideas.

Unfortunately, representational empiricism runs up against the problem that, because one does not perceive things directly, one cannot be certain—cannot *know*—that one's ideas are, in fact, accurate copies of things outside consciousness, raising the possibility that the world is very different than it seems to be, or even that the external world is a dream or hallucination. In the 17th and 18th centuries, different philosophers responded to the shortcomings of empiricism in different ways. Hume developed the skeptical possibilities in empiricism, concluding that knowledge is, in fact, never provably true, thus anticipating the American philosophy of pragmatism. Other Scottish philosophers attempted to revive realism and a new form of nativism. They taught that God endowed us with mental powers—faculties—enabling us to perceive and know His creation as it really is.

Perceptual realism, however, remained a minority viewpoint, surfacing in the philosophy of Brentano and American Neorealism and in Gestalt and Gibson's ecological theory of perception. Nativism was slain by evolution—that is, innate ideas and faculties, if they exist at all, are implanted not by God but by the vagaries of natural selection. In psychology, nativism has returned in Noam Chomsky's linguistics and in evolutionary psychology, but researchers in these fields seek in the genes, not truth, only certain mental dispositions we inherit from our hominine ancestors.

Empiricism became and remains the dominant epistemology in Great Britain and in the United States. The most important alternative to empiricism, idealism, arose with Kant, and it exerted great influence in nineteenth- and early twentieth-century Germany. Kant was shocked by Hume's conclusion that all knowledge claims are fallible, and he attempted to synthesize empiricism and rationalism into an epistemology more worldly than the former but more certain than the latter. Kant thought of science as the paradigm of human knowledge and acknowledged that it begins with and systematizes experience. However, Kant held that human experience is shaped by logically necessary (not God-given) characteristics of the human mind, which yield the orderly phenomena studied by science. Science therefore rests on a rationally provable foundation that is inherent in the mind and therefore exists prior to experience. Kantian idealism affected the psychology of Jean Piaget, who proposed that formal logical structures of the mind determine how children and adults perceive and think about the world.

Thomas H. Leahey
Virginia Commonwealth University

See also: **Logical Positism**

EMPLOYEE ASSISTANCE PROGRAMS

Employee assistance programs (EAPs) are workplace programs offered by employers to employees that assist troubled employees and their family members with a variety of issues, ranging from financial and legal concerns to mental health and substance abuse problems. EAPs traditionally focus on these problems as they affect workplace performance, but EAPs are broadening their focus with the rise in managed care. The EAP movement in the United States grew out of industrial alcohol programs in the 1950s and saw its biggest growth during the 1980s. It was during the 1980s that most EAPs moved from primarily alcohol-focused programs to the multi-issue or broad-brush programs that they are today.

EAPs offer a broad array of services to employees and their family members to assist with their problems. Comprehensive EAPs engage in identification, assessment, motivation, referral, short-term counseling, monitoring, and follow-up activities and help with a variety of personal problems, including family, emotional, financial, legal, and substance abuse concerns. EAPs do not provide long-term treatment or health care services. Several attempts have been made to determine a core set of services, or technologies, that define an EAP. The traditional core technologies of EAPs were defined by Paul Roman and Terry Blum in the late 1980s and early 1990s as the following seven activities:

1. Identify employee behavioral problems based on workplace performance concerns.
2. Provide consultation to supervisors, managers, and union representatives on how to use and refer employees to the EAP.
3. Use constructive confrontation strategies when appropriate.
4. Create micro-linkages with treatment, counseling, and community resources.
5. Create and maintain macro-linkages between the work site and treatment, counseling, and community resources.
6. Focus on employee alcohol and substance abuse problems as a strategy that offers the most promise for recovery and cost savings to the work site.
7. Serve as a consultant to the work site on personal problems affecting employee welfare.

Recently, changes to these traditional core technologies have been proposed by various authors to better match the current role of EAPs in the workplace. Attempts at defining a new set of core technologies have been hampered, however, by the ever-changing role of EAPs. Many EAPs now serve as behavioral health care gatekeepers for managed care plans, further complicating efforts to define a core set of EAP services.

Regardless of core services, EAPs fall into two primary types: internal and external. Internal EAPs are owned by the sponsoring employer, and EAP staff members are company employees. Internal EAPs can be housed at the work site but often have separate offices to increase the perception of confidentiality and independence from company management. External EAPs are separate companies that the employer contracts with to provide EAP services. External EAPs may have on-site representatives, but these representatives are not company employees. Both internal and external EAPs typically offer assessment and referral, but internal EAPs are more likely to offer counseling services. Early on, most EAPs were internal EAPs that evolved from other workplace programs, often through the efforts of a single dedicated employee. More recently, however, large external EAPs have begun to dominate the industry. These EAPs often have affiliate networks that include small providers that service specific employers.

Several studies have attempted to assess the prevalence of EAPs. In the late 1980s, the Bureau of Labor Statistics (BLS) conducted a survey of employer antidrug programs, including EAPs. The BLS estimated that approximately 31% of U.S. employees had EAP services available to them. These employees were concentrated within large work sites, however. Seventy-six percent of establishments with more than 1,000 employees had EAPs, while only 9% of establishments with fewer than 50 employees had EAPs. Two surveys conducted by the Research Triangle Institute (RTI) in the mid-1990s showed that the prevalence of EAPs had grown substantially since the BLS survey. By 1996, EAPs reached well over half of the U.S. workforce, but EAPs were still concentrated within large work sites. Much of the growth in EAPs occurred in external providers, with external EAPs providing approximately 81% of EAP services in 1993. More recently, a benefit survey by the Society for Human Resource Management showed that EAP growth has continued through today. Estimates suggest that EAPs are one of the most common employee benefits. Only dental plans, life insurance, and health-related insurance and managed care plans exceed the coverage of EAPs.

Estimates of the extent to which employees use EAP services when they are available are less common than estimates of the prevalence of EAPs. Anecdotal evidence and research conducted at individual work sites suggest that approximately 5–12% of employees use EAP services annually. Evidence suggests that EAP utilization is slightly lower among females and among minorities, possibly because of confidentiality concerns but also due in part to EAPs' traditional focus on workplace rather than family issues. To date, however, no nationally representative survey has attempted to estimate the rate at which employees use EAP services or examine differences in utilization rates by demographic groups.

Cost estimates of EAP service, which are most often presented as the cost per eligible employee, suggest that EAPs are an affordable workplace program in most cases. The RTI surveys found that in 1993 the cost of EAP services ranged from about $18 per eligible employee for external EAPs to approximately $22 per eligible employee for internal EAPs. A case study of seven EAPs, however, suggests that cost may vary widely depending on program characteristics and on the number of employees served. Intramarket competition among external EAPs, combined with the movement toward involving EAPs in managed care activities, has kept the costs of external EAPs relatively low over the past decade. Internal EAPs may have seen somewhat more of a rise in costs, but anecdotal evidence suggests that internal EAPs may be even more integrated in managed care and other workplace health promotion programs so that any rise in costs has been accompanied by an increase in services offered. Importantly, however, very little research has been done to estimate the cost *per service* of EAPs so that EAP services can be compared with other potential providers of comparable services.

Studies on the effectiveness and cost-effectiveness of EAPs suggest that they are effective in addressing employee problems and do so for relatively low cost, but this literature suffers from several shortcomings that preclude making definitive conclusions. Most notable are methodological problems, such as inadequate sample sizes and nonequivalent comparison samples. Perhaps as serious a limitation, however, is that many EAP effectiveness studies are conducted by EAPs themselves in an effort to demonstrate their value to company management.

Although more rigorous studies on EAP effectiveness are needed, the realities of workplace research often hamper efforts to design and conduct such studies. First and foremost is the changing role of EAPs. Because both the role of EAPs in the workplace and the services they offer have changed so dramatically over the past decade, EAPs represent a moving target that is very difficult to study. EAPs have moved from providing simple assessment and referral to providing short-term counseling, and then have moved back to assessment and referral but with a gatekeeper or case management role. Another factor limiting EAP research is the willingness of work sites to participate in an extended research study. Even if researchers obtain high-level cooperation, changes in workplace management can often result in workplaces' pulling out of studies before adequate data are collected.

In summary, EAPs represent an inexpensive gateway to mental health and substance abuse services. As the behavioral health care system in the United States has changed, so has the role of EAPs and the services they offer. These changes have often thwarted attempts to quantify the effectiveness of EAPs in helping with employee problems. Nonetheless, the continuing increase in the number of employers offering EAPs suggests that these employers view EAPs as a beneficial service for their employees.

Jeremy W. Bray
Research Triangle Institute

ENCOPRESIS

Encopresis is generally regarded as a disorder of childhood. The term refers to repeated fecal soiling. The fourth edition of the *Diagnostic and Statistical Manual of Mental Disorders* (*DSM-IV;* American Psychiatric Association [ApA], 1994) gives four criteria for diagnosis of Encopresis: repeated passage of feces into inappropriate places; the occurrence of this behavior at least once a month for at least three months; a chronological age of the child of at least 4 years, or if there has been a developmental delay, a mental age of at least 4 years; and an inability to attribute the fecal incontinence to a general medical condition (except constipation) or to the effects of substances (e.g., a laxative).

The *DSM-IV* recognizes that fecal soiling may be voluntary or involuntary, but many family physicians and pediatricians would not diagnose voluntary fecal soiling as Encopresis, and would most often diagnose Encopresis as a consequence of constipation. The *DSM-IV* defines two subtypes of Encopresis. The first is with constipation and the inappropriate passage of feces due to overflow of fecal matter. About 80% of cases of Encopresis fall into this category, which may be called *Retentive Encopresis.* It is often the case that a child suffering from Retentive Encopresis has experienced pain or discomfort associated with bowel movements, leading to voluntary retention of stool. As large amounts of fecal material are retained, the rectum stretches to accommodate the increased mass. The larger the mass, the more painful the elimination, and the greater the motivation to hold the stool. Ultimately, the mass becomes large enough that the rectum is stretched to the point that the sensation of needing to have a bowel movement disappears. Indeed, the abdominal mass that results from this series of events is large enough to externally palpate in about half of the children with Encopresis (Loening-Baucke, 1994). The inappropriate soiling in Retentive Encopresis occurs as fecal matter leaks around the mass and escapes from the anus without the child's knowing that this has occurred.

The second form of Encopresis occurs without constipation and overflow incontinence (ApA, 1994) and accounts for about 20% of all cases of Encopresis (Kuhn, Marcus, & Pitner, 1999). It may be called *Nonretentive Encopresis.* Nonretentive Encopresis is usually associated with other behavioral problems, such as Oppositional Defiant Disorder or Conduct Disorder (ApA, 1994).

In addition to the distinction between Retentive and Nonretentive Encopresis, this disorder is further defined as being either primary or secondary. If a child has not been continent of stool for at least 1 year the disorder is referred to as *Primary Encopresis.* If a 1-year period of continence can be documented, the disorder is classified as *Secondary Encopresis.* Fifty to 60% of all children with Encopresis have Secondary Encopresis (Howe & Walker, 1992). Secondary Encopresis may be traced to a significant change in the life of the child, such as the birth of a sibling, a move to a new house, or beginning school.

The prevalence of Encopresis varies by age and by sex. Boys are three to four times more likely than girls to develop Encopresis, and, not surprisingly, the frequency decreases with age. Between the ages of 4 and 5 years about 3.5 to 4% of boys and 1 to 1.5% of girls are encopretic, whereas by age 8, the frequency is about 2.3% in boys and 0.7% in girls. By age 12 the frequency is 1.3% in boys and 0.3% in girls (Kaplan & Sadock, 1991). In rare cases, Encopresis may continue into adulthood.

In making the differential diagnosis of Encopresis it is important to distinguish the disorder from others caused by organic pathology. Hirschprung's disease, or aganglionic megacolon, is chief among the organic disorders that may be confused with functional Encopresis. Aganglionic megacolon is a congenital disorder in which the colon becomes dilated due to lack of neural supply. The patient may have an uncontrollable overflow of feces, but the rectum will often be empty. One of the symptoms of other medical disorders, including hypothyroidism, diabetes insipidus, and early inflammatory bowel disease also may mimic some aspects of Encopresis, but the other signs and symptoms associated with these conditions make differential diagnosis relatively easy.

Because Encopresis is probably caused by the interaction of a number of variables, including physiological predisposition, pain upon defecation, and difficulties in toilet training, treatment will often be multifaceted (Levine & Bakow, 1976). The family as well as the child should be involved in the treatment. Family counseling and therapy directed toward reducing conflict between the parents and child is advised. Family therapy sessions may also be useful in identifying precipitating factors within the child's psychosocial milieu and changing attitudes toward toilet training, if the problem is Primary Encopresis and the child has not been continent for an extended period of time.

In addition to family counseling therapy and a full developmental and behavioral analysis of the child, the treatment strategy should take into account the type of Encopresis. For example, treatment of Nonretentive Encopresis will primarily utilize behavioral therapies, with the use of laxatives only if the stool is not soft enough to produce comfortable bowel movements. Daily, scheduled, positive toilet sits should then be conducted and reinforcement given for successful defecation during these sits (Kuhn et al., 1999).

In treating cases of Retentive Encopresis medical treatment is employed on a regular basis. This treatment involves using enemas for disimpaction and laxatives to promote bowel movements. However, relying on medical intervention alone diminishes the success rate of treatment of Encopresis. Cox and colleagues (Cox, Sutphen, Borowitz, Kovatchev, & Ling, 1998) compared the effectiveness of (1) 3 months of treatment for Retentive Encopresis by medical treatment alone (enemas and laxatives); (2) medical treatment and enhanced toilet training employing reinforcement, scheduled toilet sits, and instruction and modeling to promote appropriate straining; or (3) medical treatment, toilet training, and biofeedback directed at relaxing the external anal sphincter during attempted defecation. They found that medical care alone reduced soilings per child by

21%, whereas enhanced toilet training and medical treatment caused a 76% reduction, and biofeedback and medical treatment yielded a 65% reduction. Additionally, Cox and colleagues reported that enhanced toilet training significantly benefitted more children than either of the other two treatment regimens and that fewer laxatives and fewer training sessions were necessary. The results of this study of 87 children are in general agreement with many other studies that behavioral therapy is a necessary addition to medical therapy in treating Retentive Encopresis.

REFERENCES

American Psychiatric Association. (1994). *Diagnostic and Statistical Manual of Mental Disorders* (4th ed.). Washington, DC: Author.

Cox, D. J., Sutphen, J., Borowitz, S., Kovatchev, B., & Ling, W. (1998). Contribution of behavior therapy and biofeedback to laxative therapy in the treatment of pediatric encopresis. *Annals of Behavioral Medicine, 20,* 70–76.

Howe, A. C., & Walker, C. E. (1992). Behavioral management of toilet training, enuresis, and encopresis. *Pediatric Clinics of North America, 39,* 413–432.

Kaplan, H. I., & Sadock, B. J. (1991). *Synopsis of psychiatry* (6th ed.). Baltimore: Williams & Wilkins.

Kuhn, B. R., Marcus, B. A., & Pitner, S. L. (1999). Treatment guidelines for primary nonretentive encopresis and stool toileting refusal. *American Family Physician, 59,* 2171–2178.

Levine, M. D., & Bakow, H. (1976). Children with encopresis: A study of treatment outcome. *Pediatrics, 58,* 845–852.

Loening-Baucke, V. (1994). Assessment, diagnosis and treatment of constipation in childhood. *Journal of the WOCN, 21,* 49–58.

Michael L. Woodruff
East Tennessee State University

EPIDEMIOLOGY OF MENTAL DISORDERS

Definition of Epidemiology

Epidemiology is the health science that studies patterns of occurrence of disease and disorder, as well as causal factors that influence such patterns in human or animal populations.

Prevalence and Incidence

Two principal types of rates are employed by epidemiologists: prevalence and incidence.

Prevalence

Prevalence rate has been likened to a snapshot insofar as it describes the health of a group within a specified time interval. This interval can either be an instance in time, most typically a day (point prevalence), or an interval of months, years, or even decades (period prevalence). The time interval need not be a point or period in calendar time but can refer to an event or events that happen to different individuals at different periods in calendar time. Within the designated time period, prevalence is defined as the number of individuals who are determined to have the disorder divided by the total number of individuals comprising the population of interest:

Prevalence rate =
Number of persons with the disorder during a specified time period/Total number of persons in the population during a specified time period

One frequently reported rate, lifetime prevalence, refers to a measure of the proportion of persons who have had the disorder at any time during their lives. Lifetime prevalence rates are nearly always based on retrospective reports and are susceptible to the inaccuracies characteristic of such reports.

Incidence

Incidence describes the rate of development of a disorder within a group over a designated period of time. This time period is factored into the formula defining incidence as follows:

Incidence rate =
Total number of new cases/Total number in the population at risk per time interval

In contrast to prevalence, which describes a proportion of *all* cases of the disorder in a designated population, incidence describes the continuing occurrence of *new* cases. Incidence is typically more difficult to determine than prevalence because persons who already have the disorder at the beginning of the study's time period must be identified and excluded from the incidence numerator. Because these individuals also are not at risk for developing the disease, they must also be excluded from the incidence denominator.

Risk Factors

It is possible to calculate the risk of developing a mental disorder on the basis of prevalence and incidence rates and a systematic account of other factors operating in the situation. Risk metrics indicate an associative or causal relationship between the presence of specific biological, environmental, or psychosocial factors and the occurrence of a disorder. *Relative risk* refers to the ratio of the incidence of a disorder among individuals known to have been exposed to a risk factor divided by the incidence among individuals known not to have been exposed to that risk factor. *Attributable risk* is the absolute incidence of the disorder that can be attributed to exposure to the risk factor. Attributable risk is typically calculated by subtracting the incidence of the disorder among an exposed group from its total incidence among an unexposed group. It is a useful indication of what might result were the risk factor(s) to be removed.

Risks vary in the degree to which they are associated with disorders and in the degree to which they cause disorders. *Factor-related risks* are risks that are frequently, although not always, observed in conjunction with a disorder. *Factor-specific risks* are necessary, although not sufficient, prerequisites to developing a disorder. Patterns that suggest a causal connection between a risk factor and a mental disorder include consistent association, precedence, and specificity of effect. In consistent association, a clear relationship is reported between the risk factor and the mental disorder over repeated studies. Elimination of the risk factor eliminates or markedly ameliorates the disorder. Introduction of the risk factor precipitates or exacerbates the disorder. In precedence, the risk factor is observed to be present before the disorder is observed. In specificity of effect, the effect of the risk factor is specific to the disorder under investigation. A major goal of the epidemiology of mental disorders is the identification of risk factors that contribute to, precipitate, or maintain mental disorders.

Comparing rates of disorder between various groups is considerably important. Such comparisons are frequently expressed as differences between rates, as ratios of one rate to another, or of many rates to a standard rate.

Types of Studies

There are two fundamental types of epidemiological studies. *Descriptive studies* are undertaken to document the occurrence of disorders or disorder-related phenomena in a group. Descriptive studies generally measure the disorder and its related attributes in a somewhat diffuse or superficial manner. They provide observations concerning the relationship of disorders to such basic characteristics as age, gender, ethnic background, socioeconomic status, geographic location and distribution, time of occurrence, and so forth. *Analytic studies* are conducted to explain the observed pattern of the disorder within the group and thereby clarify the etiological factors involved in precipitating, maintaining, or alleviating the disorder. In contrast to descriptive studies, analytic studies tend to be more narrowly focused on a specific set of hypotheses and often require more rigorous study designs and more sophisticated quantitative analyses of findings. The three most basic types of analytic observational studies are prevalence studies, case-control studies, and cohort studies.

Prevalence studies investigate the relationship between disorders and other attributes of interest such as they exist in the population of interest during a particular time period. The presence, absence, or severity of the disorder is determined for each individual sampled, and the relationship between the attribute and the disease can be determined in either of two ways: (1) in terms of the presence, absence, or severity of the disorder in different population subgroups defined by the attribute, or (2) in terms of the presence, absence, or severity of symptoms for those determined to have the disorder versus those who were not.

Case-control studies are similar to prevalence studies in that they investigate the correlations between indicators of existing symptoms with other variables or attributes. The presence or absence of the disorder is determined for each member of the study and is systematically related to other factors or attributes. Typically, following an initial process of case determination, an appropriate control group of individuals without the disorder is identified. Correlations of other attributes to the disorder are determined by comparing the disordered group with controls for presence or severity of the attribute.

Cohort studies are undertaken to investigate more directly factors related to the development of the disorder. A group of individuals who are determined to be free of the disorder is identified at a particular time. Attributes of interest are measured in this cohort, then these individuals are followed up at various times to determine the development of the disorder(s) under study. The correlation of an attribute with the disorder is determined by splitting the population into subgroups according to the presence or level of the attribute initially and comparing the incidence of disorder among the various subgroups formed.

In actual practice, the neat distinction between descriptive and analytical studies is often blurred. A carefully designed and implemented descriptive study may provide a clear resolution of specific hypotheses. An analytic study focused on a specific hypothesis may coincidentally provide descriptive data of considerable interest.

Special Issues in the Epidemiology of Mental Disorders

The difficulties inherent in the diagnosis of mental disorders within modern American society are compounded when individuals from various minority groups or from non-Western cultural backgrounds are studied. Psychiatric epidemiologists have long appreciated that many mental disorders manifest as patterns of thought, affect, or behavior that deviate from dominant cultural beliefs and expectations and are found to be disturbing by those who think, feel, or act them out or to others around them. Because different cultures have established different standards and upheld different expectations for their members, it follows that what might be considered disturbing or disordered in one culture may fall comfortably within the normal range of experience for another culture. Some of the most influential studies in the history of mental health epidemiology have addressed these issues.

The Value of Epidemiology to the Mental Health Community

The value of properly conducted epidemiological studies for theory building and for the therapeutic practice of psychology is unquestionable. Valid epidemiological rates are of fundamental importance in alerting the mental health community to those types of individuals most likely to be afflicted with a particular disorder, where the disorder is most likely to occur geographically, and when it is most likely to manifest for the individual case or come to the attention of the professional mental health care community. Thus, valid epidemiological information helps guide the individual diagnostic process and also may aid in the selection of appropriate and effective intervention strategies. Reliable epidemiological information also is obviously valuable for efficient planning of community mental health services and facilities. By providing information regarding the etiology of mental disorders and by raising new hypotheses regarding the nature of their antecedents, course, and consequents, epidemiological data make fundamental contributions to theory building for both fundamental understanding and treatment of mental disorders.

E. H. Spain

See also: **Diagnosis**

ERIKSONIAN DEVELOPMENTAL STAGES

The developmental theory of Erik Erikson (1950, 1968) provides a life-span account of psychosocial development, which emphasizes the autonomous or conflict-free development of an adaptive ego that organizes experience. He postulates that human beings have a need to categorize and integrate their experiences, as well as a need to satisfy their basic biological needs. A consolidated sense of ego identity—a perceived sense of personal wholeness and "continuity of experience"—is considered to be necessary for optimal personal functioning.

The building and integrating of personality follows an eight-stage life-span sequence governed by what Erikson calls the *epigenetic principle,* which states that "anything that grows has a ground plan, and that out of this ground plan the parts arise, each part having its time of special ascendancy, until all parts have arisen to form a functioning whole" (Erikson 1968, p. 92). Each stage, from birth to old age, is marked by a normative crisis that must be confronted and negotiated. These bipolar crises are psychosocial in nature. Crisis resolutions have residual effects on the developing person, with each contributing to the totally formed personality. Ideally, resolutions should not be completely one-sided: A positively balanced ratio of the two poles indicates optimal progress.

The stages, which are assumed to be interdependent, build upon one another in a cumulative manner. Each stage contributes a unique personal quality of strength or virtue, such as hope or faith, to the evolving personality. The achievement of ego identity during adolescence is the central concept in this developmental scheme; it entails the synthesis and integration of prior experiences and developments and provides the foundation upon which future progress occurs.

Stage 1: Trust Versus Mistrust (Infancy)

At birth, infants are dominated by biological needs and drives. The reliability and quality of their relationship with caregivers will influence the extent to which they develop a sense of trust (or mistrust) in others, themselves, and the world in general. The virtue of *hope* is associated with this stage.

Stage 2: Autonomy Versus Doubt and Shame (Early Childhood)

Social demands for self-control and bodily regulation (toilet training) influence feelings of self-efficacy versus self-doubt. The quality of *will,* the willful self-discipline to do what is expected and expectable, emerges at stage two.

Stage 3: Initiative Versus Guilt (Preschool Age)

Here children begin actively exploring their environment. Will they sense guilt about these self-initiated activities, or will they feel justified in planning and asserting control over their activities? The virtue of *purpose*—the courage to pursue personally valued goals in spite of risks and possible failure—now ascends.

Stage 4: Industry Versus Inferiority (School Age)

The societal context in which the first three psychosocial conflicts are negotiated is predominantly the home and immediate family. In stage four, however, children begin formal instruction of some sort. Mastery of tasks and skills valued by one's teachers and the larger society becomes focal. The quality of *competence* is said to develop.

Stage 5: Identity and Diffusion (Adolescence)

This is the linchpin in Erikson's scheme, a time when adolescents actively attempt to synthesize their experiences in an effort to formulate a stable sense of identity. Although this process is psychosocial in nature—a social fit or "solidarity with group ideals" must occur—Erikson emphasizes reality testing and the acquisition of credible self-knowledge. Youths come to view themselves as products of their previous experiences, and a unified sense of temporal self-continuity is experienced. Positive resolutions of prior crises—being trusting, autonomous, willful, and industrious—facilitate identity formation; previous failures may lead to identity diffusion. *Fidelity,* the ability to maintain commitments in spite of contradictory value systems, is the virtue that emerges during adolescence.

In Erikson's theory, development continues throughout life. The three adult stages, however, are directly affected by the identity achieved during adolescence.

Stage 6: Intimacy Versus Isolation (Young Adulthood)

In this stage, one must be able and willing to unite his or her identity with that of another. Since authentic disclosure and mutuality leave people vulnerable, a firm sense of identity is prerequisite. The quality that ascends during this stage is *love.*

Stage 7: Generativity Versus Stagnation (Middle Adulthood)

This is the time in the life span when one strives to actualize the identity that has been formed and shared with selected others. The generation or production of offspring, artifacts, ideas, products, and so forth is involved. The virtue of *care* emerges: Generative adults care for others through parenting, teaching, supervising, and so forth, whereas stagnating adults become self-absorbed in immediate personal needs and interests.

Stage 8: Integrity Versus Despair (Maturity)

The final stage focuses on the perceived completion or fulfillment of one's life cycle. *Wisdom* is the last virtue to emerge. Wise people understand the relativistic nature of knowledge and accept that their life had to be the way it was.

As a heuristic scheme, Erikson's theory has had a profound impact on contemporary psychology, especially adolescent development. Despite its popularity and apparent face validity, the empirical foundation for the stage theory is relatively weak. The imprecise nature of the theoretical constructs—for instance, hope or wisdom—as defined by Erikson has made it difficult for researchers to independently test specific predictions derived from the theory. Another obstacle has been the need for long-term longitudinal studies to evaluate Erikson's claims about the sequential nature of psychosocial stages and the processes responsible for life-span personality development. Nonetheless, productive lines of research based on and generally consistent with Erikson's views relevant to particular stages have emerged (see, for example, Berzonsky & Adams, 1999; Marcia, 1993; McAdams, Ruetzel, & Foley, 1986; Orlofsky, 1993).

REFERENCES

Berzonsky, M. D., & Adams, G. R. (1999). The identity status paradigm: Still useful after thirty-five years. *Developmental Review, 19,* 557–590.

Erikson, E. H. (1950). *Childhood and society.* New York: Norton.

Erikson, E. H. (1968). *Identity: Youth and crisis.* New York: Norton.

Marcia, J. E. (1993). The status of the statuses: Research review. In J. E. Marcia, A. S. Waterman, D. R. Matteson, S. L. Archer, & J. L. Orlofsky (Eds.), *Ego identity: A handbook for psychosocial research* (pp. 22–41). New York: Springer-Verlag.

McAdams, D. P., Ruetzel, K., & Foley, J. M. (1986). Complexity and generativity at mid-life: Relations among social motives, ego development, and adults' plans for the future. *Journal of Personality and Social Psychology, 50,* 800–807.

Orlofsky, J. L. (1993). Intimacy statuses: Theory and research. In J. E. Marcia, A. S. Waterman, D. R. Matteson, S. L. Archer, & J. L. Orlofsky (Eds.), *Ego identity: A handbook for psychosocial research* (pp. 111–133). New York: Springer-Verlag.

Michael D. Berzonsky
State University of New York, Cortland

See also: **Human Development; Life-span Development**

ERRORS (TYPE I AND II)

Statistical tests, which attempt to infer whether or not variables are related in a population by evaluating data from smaller samples, are by no means foolproof. Occasionally sample information would seem to imply that, say, variable X is related to variable Y in the population, when in fact no such population relation exists. For example, a random sample of subjects receiving a treatment may get considerably higher scores on some outcome measure than a comparable random (control) group of subjects not receiving the treatment, although in fact the treatment is completely ineffective and these two samples only differ because higher-scoring subjects were randomly assigned to the treatment group. In this case, inferring that X (presence/absence of treatment) is related to Y (outcome measure) is an example of a *Type I error.* On the other hand, sample data may seem to imply that X and Y are unrelated when indeed they do have a relation in the population. For example, a treatment group may get very similar outcome scores to those from a control group, although in fact the treatment is effective and these two samples are similar only because fairly high-scoring subjects were randomly assigned to the control group. In this case, inferring that X (presence/absence of treatment) is unrelated to Y (score) is an example of a *Type II error.* These two types of errors are discussed briefly in this entry.

For the generic experimental example just described,

	Truth in population	
Inference	H_0 is true (X and Y unrelated)	H_0 is false (X and Y related)
X and Y sample relation not statistically significant; retain H_0 as tenable	accurate inference	inaccurate inference (Type II error)
X and Y sample relation statistically significant; reject H	inaccurate inference (Type I error)	accurate inference

Figure 1. Errors (type I and II).

two possible truths exist at the population level, and two possible conclusions may be derived from the sample information. For the populations, either the treatment has some average effect or it has none. This latter notion, that there is no average difference between scores from a population receiving a treatment and a control population, is termed the *null hypothesis* (symbolized H_0). Thus, a genuinely benign treatment means that H_0 is true, whereas a treatment that affects outcome Y means that H_0 is false. As for conclusions drawn from samples, if the two sample means (averages) are relatively similar (i.e., not differing statistically significantly) the guarded inference would be made that H_0 remains tenable. One need not actually believe that the treatment is completely ineffective in the population; one may merely feel that sufficient evidence has not been gathered to the contrary, thus retaining H_0 as a tenable explanation for the lack of statistical significance associated with the observed difference between the two sample means. Conversely, if the two sample means are statistically significantly different, then one would infer that H_0 is false and that the treatment has some effect (positive or negative, accordingly).

Crossing the two population and two sample conditions previously outlined defines four possible outcomes of a research endeavor, two representing accurate inference and two representing inaccurate inference (i.e., Type I and Type II errors). These are depicted in Figure 1. Consider first the cells on the left side of the figure, in which H_0 is true (i.e., treatment has no effect on outcome). The top left cell results when the observed sample relation between treatment (presence/absence) and outcome is not statistically significant; that is, the observed difference between sample means falls in the realm of what one would comfortably expect by chance if two population means truly do not differ. In this situation one would infer that H_0 remains tenable, and in fact the inference would be accurate because H_0 is true. In short, the study would have gathered no evidence that the treatment is effective, and in truth it has no effect in the population.

The bottom left cell, on the other hand, results when the observed sample relation between the variables of interest is statistically significant; that is, the observed difference between sample means falls outside the realm of what one would comfortably expect by chance when two population means truly do not differ. In this situation one would infer that H_0 should be rejected as false; however, the inference would be inaccurate because H_0 is true, and it is thus labeled a Type I error. Such an event would be an unfortunate random occurrence, in which two samples happened to be selected whose outcome measure scores were extremely disparate, but this disparity was merely a random occurrence and in no way reflective of any beneficial or detrimental treatment effect.

Now consider the right column of the figure, in which H_0 is false (i.e., treatment has some effect on outcome). The bottom right cell results when the observed sample relation between the variables of interest is statistically significant. In this situation one would infer that H_0 should be rejected as false, and in fact the inference would be accurate. Thus, the study would have gathered evidence that the treatment is related to test performance, and in truth such a relation does exist in the population.

The top right cell, on the other hand, results when the observed sample relation between treatment and outcome score is not statistically significant. In this situation one would infer that H_0 remains tenable; however, the inference would be inaccurate because H_0 is false, and it is thus labeled a Type II error. Such an event would be an unfortunate random occurrence, in which two samples happened to be selected whose outcome scores were not particularly disparate, but this lack of disparity was not reflective of the actual treatment effect.

In practice, researchers never know in which cell they fall because they never know if H_0 is true or false. Thus, the best strategy is to minimize the chance of making either error in inference. To reduce Type I errors, researchers often select an "alpha level" in which statistical significance will be proclaimed (and H_0 rejected) such that one seldom infers a population relation where none truly exists. A common choice is the .05 level, thus deeming statistically significant a sample relation that is so unlikely as to be observed less than 5% of the time when no such relation exists in the population. To reduce Type II errors, and thereby increase the chance of inferring the existence of population relations when they truly exist (i.e., increase "statistical power"), researchers can use highly reliable outcome measures, use statistical techniques to reduce variability in *Y* unrelated to *X*, and use samples of adequate size. The reader is referred to any introductory social science statistics text for further discussion of these and related issues.

Gregory R. Hancock
University of Maryland, College Park

See also: **Hypothesis Testing**

ESCAPE-AVOIDANCE LEARNING

Avoidance learning and extinction are typically studied in the rat with electric foot shock as the aversive stimulus. In active avoidance, the rat is often placed in a runway, the floor of which is electrified at one end and is, at least temporarily, safe at the other end. The rat must move to the opposite end to escape or avoid shock. Before shock is delivered, the subject has several seconds in which to respond. A naive subject, however, fails to avoid and is shocked on at least one trial before escaping the shock chamber. Thus traditional avoidance learning always includes escape behavior and is appropriately called *escape-avoidance learning.*

When the situation is arranged so that the subject cannot avoid but can only escape shock, the termination of shock is considered reinforcing (termed *negative reinforcement* by Skinnerians), and learning to escape is usually measured by a reduction in latency with successive shocks (trials). In a one-way situation (described later), a series of, say, 8 or 10 escape trials also can mediate perfect avoidance learning when the opportunity to avoid is provided.

With a two-way, or shuttlebox, situation avoidance learning is slow, escape responses prevail, and perfect performance is rarely, if ever, attained. In a shuttle situation, the subject must learn to shuttle from one end of the alley to the other every time a warning signal (buzzer or light) is presented. This is difficult to do because no section of the alley is uniquely associated with either shock or safety. Thus fear is conditioned to the whole apparatus, engendering freezing; the rat has no distinguishable place to go to relax or escape fear, and after each escape trial it must learn to avoid by running right back into the region where it just got shocked.

In a one-way box, however, the rat is placed in a start chamber specifically associated with shock to which fear is conditioned, and the rat avoids by approaching a particular chamber that is consistently safe (i.e., where fear is clearly reduced or relaxation can occur). Some subjects in a one-way box learn to avoid in one trial, and learning to a 100% level in a mean of three or four trials is not unusual. Here the use of distinctive chambers and increasing the shock level up to a point facilitates learning. Presumably fear and safety are thereby segregated better, and reinforcement is enhanced (greater fear reduction), whereas the opposite is true in a shuttlebox, where conditioned fear (competition from freezing and the like) is enhanced by these manipulations. The same manipulations that facilitate or hinder avoidance learning have been shown to have parallel effects in pure escape learning by Franchina and associates.

In passive avoidance, the subject avoids shock by not making a particular response. For example, the rat is placed on a small platform surrounded by an electrified grid. If it remains on the platform without stepping down, the rat avoids passively. Because it yields fast learning and is simple to use, many studies of amnesia and other behavioral effects of biological intervention use the passive technique for assessment purposes. Basically, the use of punishment, in which an aversive stimulus is contingent on a particular response, is the same as passive avoidance. Passive avoidance is impeded if an alternative safe place to approach actively is available after the rat has been shocked for stepping down, and the more so the longer the rat remains in this safe place.

Mowrer's two-factor theory, or fear hypothesis, provides the main explanation of avoidance learning. Fear is conditioned to the shock area or warning signal, and escape from fear or the reduction of fear when the shock area or warning signal is removed is the reinforcement for the avoidance response (this is called *secondary negative reinforcement* by Skinnerians, and the concept of fear is not invoked). Research by Denny and associates indicates that 2.5 min away from shock or fear-provoking stimuli on each trial provides a good opportunity to relax, confers optimal approach value to the nonshock or safe area, and yields optimal avoidance learning in one-way situations. Also, the concept of relaxation in this context is especially valuable for explaining the extinction of fear-related behaviors such as escape and avoidance. Relaxation is directly incompatible with fear and presumably constitutes the competing response that extinguishes fear. In one-way situations, extinction appears to originate in the safe area, where the longer the subject is confined, the more it relaxes, and the faster fear extinguishes, especially if the safe area is similar to the shock region.

Tortora, working with vicious dogs that had presumably learned to avoid punishment by being aggressive, trained them to avoid shock by promptly following 15 different commands (e.g., down, here, and heel). For many dogs a tone (safety signal) followed each correct response and was associated with a long shock-free, relaxation period. The safety tone clearly facilitated training, producing manageable, prosocial animals.

Results from a number of recent escape-avoidance studies indicate that without fear there is no tendency to avoid or to approach safety.

M. R. Denny

See also: **Behavior Modification; Conceptual Learning; Inhibitory Conditioning; Operant Behavior; Stress Consequences**

ETHICAL TREATMENT OF ANIMALS

In the quarter century since the publication of Peter Singer's *Animal Liberation* (1975) reopened discussion of our use of animals other than humans (hereafter, animals) in scientific research, three major developments have occurred.

First, within moral philosophy, several theories have been expounded regarding the ethics of this use. In addition to Singer's utilitarian ethic, Regan's (1983) eponymous rights theory ("animal rights movement") and, more recently, feminist, communitarian, and contractarian theories, together have assured a secure place for this topic in courses on moral philosophy.

The theories all attempt to answer the question of the moral considerability of animals and to infer the policy and practices that follow from the standing claimed for them. For example, beyond that moral consideration due a sentient being, Wise (2000) argues that some animals (e.g., chimpanzees) are persons and this status obligates us to give them legal as well as ethical standing.

Second, in the area of institutional self-regulation and governmental regulation, following the passage of federal legislation in 1966 and subsequent amendments, review committees now oversee almost all laboratories engaged in animal research. Although this mechanism is modeled after the successful institutional review boards for research involving human subjects, its adequacy is hotly debated. Do the preponderance of animal researchers on these review boards and the exclusion of rodents and birds (the most frequent objects of study in psychological animal research) from the committees' purview undermine effectiveness and credibility? Or, does the exercise of requirements such as the search for alternatives that replace animals, or at least reduce their numbers and extent of suffering, and the provision that both husbandry and procedures ensure the well-being of primates constitute adequate policing and reforming practices?

Animal Studies

Symbolized by Singer's acceptance of the position of Decamp Professor of Bioethics at Princeton University, the third development in the discussion of animals' use in research is the emergence of a field of Animal Studies, which provides academic foundation to a progressive social movement. Scholars in the social and natural sciences as well as the humanities apply the methods of their respective disciplines to the study of nonhuman animals and human-animal interfaces. Books published by major publishing houses, book series, journals (e.g., *Society and Animals* and *Anthrozoos*), and university programs, courses, and chairs devoted to animal studies constitute a robust intellectual infrastructure. The defining feature of Animal Studies is the shift from the study of nonhuman animals as representative objects, models, cultural artifacts, and symbols of human phenomena to subjects in the full sense of that term.

Psychology's Ambivalence

The role of psychology in these three developments has been mixed. Plous (1996) found a high level of support for research involving observation and even confinement. However, when asked about research involving pain or death to primates and rats, many psychologists (62.1% and 44.4%, respectively, for the two animal groups) indicate that such research is unjustified even when the research is described as "institutionally approved and deemed of scientific merit" (p. 1171).

On the negative side of psychology's role, several writers, including Singer, single out psychological research for criticism beyond its proportionate share of the research enterprise. Psychology also contributed a cause célèbre of abuse (the Silver Spring monkeys) as a psychology laboratory had its major federal support grant suspended. Regarding the field's general response to the issue of psychological animal research, two psychologists chided the field for adopting a "strategic defensive posture" (Gluck & Kubacki, 1991, p. 158).

More positively, two British psychologists contributed conceptual advances in the debate: Ryder coined the term *speciesism,* while Heim articulated the notion that there are ethical limits on our use of animals that are independent of any beneficial ends. A number of psychologists have conducted noninvasive animal research with primates and other animals that demonstrates the sophisticated capabilities of these animals, such as communication, self-reflection, and attribution of mind. The findings have raised the ethical bar to the use of animals in invasive research.

Psychologists also have contributed to the critique of animal research by adding science-based evidence and argument to the debate within ethics (e.g., Shapiro, 1998). They also have developed scales to measure degree of pain and harm, and provided empirical studies demonstrating the link between violence toward humans and other animals.

Increasingly, clinical psychologists are capitalizing on the empirically demonstrated social support, interpersonal facilitation, and other beneficial and therapeutic effects of involvement in a compassionate and respectful human-animal relation. Therapists use animals as adjuncts in individual therapy (animal-assisted therapy). Residential group settings also use caring for animals as a vehicle for developing mutual, responsible relationships. A number of psychologists have chosen careers working in organizations in which the mission is the abolition or reform of invasive animal research, and one group of psychologists (Psychologists for the Ethical Treatment of Animals) has organized as animal advocates. In response to legislation in 18 states allowing the judge to require counseling for convicted animal abusers, Jory and Randour (1999) have developed a treatment manual for this population. Through these and other avenues, psychology is moving from a defensive to a constructive and progressive position on the issue of the ethical treatment of animals.

REFERENCES

Gluck, J. P., & Kubacki, S. R. (1991). Animals in biomedical research: The undermining effect of the rhetoric of the besieged. *Ethics & Behavior, 1*(3), 157–173.

Jory, B., & Randour, M. (1999). *The Anicare model of treatment for animal abuse.* Washington Grove, MD: Psychologists for the Ethical Treatment of Animals.

Plous, S. (1996). Attitudes toward the use of animals in psychological research and education: Results from a national survey of psychologists. *American Psychologist, 51,* 1167–1180.

Regan, T. (1983). *The case for animal rights.* Berkeley: University of California.

Shapiro, K. (1998). *Animal models of human psychology: Critique of science, ethics, and policy.* Gottingen, Germany: Hogrefe and Huber.

Singer, P. (1975). *Animal liberation: A new ethic for our treatment of animals.* New York: Avon.

Wise, S. (2000). *Rattling the cage: Toward legal rights for animals.* Cambridge, MA: Perseus.

Kenneth J. Shapiro
Psychologists for the Ethical Treatment of Animals

ETHNOCENTRISM

The term *ethnic* has been in use in the written English language at least since the fifteenth century and was derived from *ethnos* in Greek, which was interpreted variously as people, race, culture, or nation. The term was also used by the Greeks to denote heathens, as the term *ethnos* itself was derived from *ethnikos.* The term *ethnocentric* was used in the literature as early as 1898, though the term *ethnicity* is supposed to have been introduced in the 1940s (Sollors, 1996). The concept of ethnocentrism was defined by Sumner in 1906 as "this view of things in which one's own group is the center of everything, and all others are scaled and rated with reference to it. . . . Each group nourishes its own pride and vanity, boasts itself superior, exalts its own divinities, and looks with contempt on outsiders" (Sumner, 1959). The Greeks and Romans, for example, considered all outsiders barbarians. Sumner's use of the term *ethnocentrism* has also been interpreted more broadly as an ethnocentric syndrome (Le Vine & Campbell, 1972). Ethnocentrism is not limited to racial or geographic factors alone; it is based on many other social, cultural, and linguistic factors. It can even be based on ideologies. The boundaries between different ethnic groups are not always clearly demarcated, as ethnicity is often subjective in nature. There are different levels of ethnocentricity, and the extent of ethnocentrism varies considerably (Brewer & Campbell, 1976). The concept of social distance introduced in the 1920s enabled researchers to measure the extent of perceived distance among different ethnic groups. Although the concept of ethnocentrism was originally used as a group-based concept, it is now used to measure individual views and perspectives as well. Concepts such as "the stranger" and "marginal man" introduced by Simmel convey the idea of an individual who generally provided a bridge between the in-group and out-groups. The authoritarian personality studies have addressed the problem of relationship between ethnocentrism and discernible personality traits and characteristics (Forbes, 1985). Attitude scales such as the F scale provide other examples of an authoritarian personality measurement (Brewer & Campbell, 1976). Ethnocentrism, however, needs to be clearly distinguished from xenophobia, jingoism, and chauvinism, although they are all based on ethnocentric views.

Causes, Consequences, and Reduction of Ethnocentrism

The causes and manifestation of ethnocentrism can take different forms. One type of explanation would be based on personality factors of individuals. Another form of ethnocentric behavior is contextual or situational, such as the loss of jobs due to competition from a neighboring state or groups. One group or nation can be transformed from a friend to an enemy and vice versa after the end of a war. The reasons for another type of ethnocentrism may vary from mistrust of the stranger to the aims of conquest and subjugation of another group for various reasons.

The more serious negative aspects of ethnocentrism have often been manifested throughout history as violent conflicts, wars, slavery, ethnic cleansing, and genocide. The protohistorical accounts of warfare were based on tribal affiliations. The crusades in the Middle Ages, conflict in Northern Ireland, and the Nazi holocaust were based on religion. In addition to tribal and religious basis of ethnocentrism, race, colonialism, and ethnonationalism have contributed toward distinctly negative and sometimes savage consequences. Prejudicial attitudes and discriminatory behavior of Whites and African Americans in the United States are examples of ethnocentrism based on racial lines.

The apartheid practices in South Africa constituted an example of colonial ethnocentrism and concomitant racism that was common in most colonial situations. Even in multiracial or multicultural colonies, the primary White and non-White grouping, along with the dichotomy of the master and the subjugated, persisted because of the convergence of power, color, race, language, and class differences. The colonial perspective was often Eurocentric, with hierarchical and discriminatory lines drawn between the European colonizer and the colonized. The perceived distinctions of superiority and inferiority of groups became a self-fulfilling prophecy. Race relations in the United States have often been described as internal colonialism by Marxists and non-Marxists alike. The minority ethnic groups are often disrespectful of their own ethnicity in contrast with the ethnic group that is in power, a phenomenon often noticed in the colonial context. Ethnonationalism has manifested in the creation of more new nations in the last century than any other century in history. Many of these nations were created as a result of violent conflicts, atrocities, and civil wars.

Ethnocentrism has also been utilized as a means to bolster the in-group feelings and group solidarity built along ethnic lines. Terms of reference such as "brother," "sister," or "white man's burden" and the development of ethnic literature, clubs, and distinct modes of dressing are examples of activities intended to maintain the separate identity and self-respect of minorities. Socialization through the family, schools, media, peer groups, and religious teachings is a major avenue of germination and indoctrination of ethnocentrism. However, it must be strongly emphasized that all ethnic relations are not necessarily violent. There are many long-standing examples of peaceful coexistence of different ethnic groups in spite of their ethnocentric beliefs.

Ethnocentrism is a learned behavior, rooted in differences covering a variety of characteristics, and thus can be unlearned. Cultural contact has been tried as one of the approaches to reduce ethnocentrism, with the Olympic games being one example. Another solution that has been suggested is the submerging of local ethnic groups into a larger collective such as a nationality. This was the assumption made in the case of countries with intertribal or intergroup conflicts or rivalries, such as Nigeria. It was often wrongly believed that these conflicts would be subordinated or submerged in the superordinate collective such as that of nationhood. Education and socialization of children in schools through the emphasis on multicultural perspectives is another technique used to reduce ethnocentric biases. Legal measures have sometimes been effective in reducing discriminatory behavior in a few cases, but they are not likely to make an impact in case of long-standing distrust or animosities among different groups. Social changes may reduce or enhance ethnocentrism between two groups. Cross-cutting loyalties, such as different religious affiliations but a common language, would oftentimes result in lowered levels of ethnocentrism. However, regardless of many efforts, different and new types of ethnocentric conflicts keep cropping up in many places all around the world, as it recently did in the form of terrorism. The inherent differences in the worldviews, cultural values, and belief systems are always vying for legitimization. In spite of the importance of the subject of ethnocentrism, the research on this topic is surprisingly sparse so far.

REFERENCES

Brewer, M. B., & Campbell, D. T. (1976). *Ethnocentrism and intergroup attitudes: East African studies.* New York: Halstead Press.

Forbes, H. D. (1985). *Nationalism, ethnocentrism and personality: Social science and critical theory.* Chicago: University of Chicago Press.

LeVine, R. A., & Campbell, D. T. (1972). *Ethnocentrism: Theories of conflict, ethnic attitudes, and group behavior.* New York: Wiley.

Sollors, W. (Ed). (1996). *Theories of ethnicity: A classical reader.* New York: New York University Press.

Sumner, W. G. (1959). *Folkways.* New York: Dover Publications.

Subhash R. Sonnad
Western Michigan University

ETHNOCULTURAL PSYCHOTHERAPY

Ethnocultural psychotherapy integrates ethnicity and culture into assessment and treatment. Complementing targeted mental health interventions with historical and current cultural practices, ethnocultural psychotherapy employs multigenerational genograms, transitional maps, fables, testimonies, and other indigenous psychological techniques to acknowledge the concept of self as an internal ethnocultural representation.

Ethnocultural psychotherapy pays particular attention to issues prevalent among culturally diverse individuals, including translocation and adaptation, inclusion and exclusion, power and powerlessness, and identity transformation. One of the tools of this therapy, the ethnocultural assessment, explores the developmental stages that contribute to the ethnocultural identity. Used in both diagnosis and treatment, the ethnocultural assessment examines heritage, myth, niche, adjustment, and relationships.

The genetic, biological, and sociocultural familial heritage provides a backdrop for exploration of the family myth: the circumstances that led to the client's (and multigenerational family's) cultural transitions. The niche—derived from a posttransition analysis—is based on the client's intellectual and emotional perception of his or her family's ethnocultural identity in the host society since the translocation. The adjustment stage refers to the client's own perceived adaptation in the host culture as an individual distinct from the rest of the family. This involves a therapeutic exploration of the contrasts between the client's ethnocultural identity and that of his or her work and social milieus. Finally, the relationships stage examines transference and countertransference, considering the therapist's own ethnocultural assessment to determine specific areas of similarity and difference. Besides obtaining a wealth of information crucial for therapeutic intervention, performance of the assessment often opens new channels of recognition of the self in the other.

Ethnocultural psychotherapy facilitates a cultural analysis, which aims at critical consciousness, or the process of transformation that oppressed individuals experience while educating themselves in a dialectic conversation with their world. Through this process clients learn to read their condition as well as authoring their own reality. The therapeutic relationship functions as the dialogue that helps clients to express their truth, assert their identity, heal, and achieve autonomy.

Lillian Comas-Díaz
George Washington University

Frederick M. Jacobsen
Transcultural Mental Health Institute, George Washington University

ETHOLOGY

Ethology is defined as the study of animal behavior in its natural environment, including its physical, biological, and social aspects. Ethology is also concerned with the role of Darwinian natural selection in shaping animal behavior. This implies that the behavior is related to genotypes that are in turn a product of the species's evolutionary history. Furthermore, gene selection is assumed to have been influenced by the consequences of naturally occurring behaviors. Jaynes (1969) has written a comprehensive review of ethology's origins.

Concepts in Classic Ethology

The starting point for ethological study has been *ethograms,* which are extensive, highly detailed descriptions of a species's behaviors in its natural environment. They originated in the work of European naturalists such as O. Heinroth, J. H. Fabre, and D. Spaulding during the late nineteenth and early twentieth centuries. These early ethologists were impressed by the constant, stereotyped nature of many adaptive behaviors that were often labeled as innate or instinctive.

Fixed-action patterns are specific, stereotyped behaviors characteristic of a species. Fixed-action patterns are so constant that they have been used as criteria for taxonomic classification of species (Hinde, 1970). Furthermore, fixed-action patterns are usually elicited by specific stimuli (called *releasers* or *sign stimuli*). Occasionally, an artificial stimulus termed a *supranormal stimulus* is more effective than the naturally occurring one in releasing a fixed-action pattern.

The ethological deprivation experiment is a type of restriction that differs from the typical deprivation experiment in American experimental psychology. In the ethological deprivation experiment only a small, carefully chosen set of stimuli are withheld from the subjects in order to prevent practice of a target behavior. The ethologist makes a point of imposing no more deprivation than necessary to prevent the occurrence of the target behavior. If, following the deprivation, the animal shows the full fixed-action pattern in response to the appropriate releasing stimulus, then the behavior did not depend on previous practice. Early ethologists further concluded that the behavior was innate and did not depend on any prior learning, an inference that is not necessarily justified.

Later Developments in Ethology

Following Lorenz and Tinbergen's establishment of a basic theoretical foundation for ethology in the 1930s, several major changes occurred in the theoretical and empirical approaches of ethologists to animal behavior. A major change in classic ethological theory has been an increasing awareness of the strong influence of learning in animal behavior, including many fixed-action patterns. The best-known example is imprinting, which was initially regarded by Lorenz as an innately released following behavior in recently born or hatched animals of some species. Later research showed that a simple and rapid conditioning probably underlies imprinting (Moltz, 1963).

The sophistication of ethological research has increased dramatically during the past 40 years. One facet of modern ethological research is a focus on quantification of the adaptive value of behavior. The study of territoriality in golden-winged sunbirds (Gill & Wolf, 1975) was an early example that showed how territorial defense could be predicted by analysis of calories expended in foraging or defending territories and caloric values of food sources in alternative territories. Optimality theory assumes that natural selection has adjusted animal behavior, such as foraging for food in the natural habitat, so as to achieve an optimum balance between costs and benefits (Krebs & Davis, 1993). Feeding, predator-prey relationships, and population regulation have been frequent issues addressed by behavioral ecologists.

The field of behavioral ecology has also emerged from classic ethology. Behavioral ecology is focused on the interactions of animals within their entire ecological communities, including the inorganic environment, plants, other animal species, and their own species (Krebs & Davis, 1993).

One of the most dramatic findings to emerge from recent ethological research is the increasingly abundant evidence of evolved behavioral dispositions that promote group cohesion and reduce aggression (de Waal, 1996). These processes include reconciliation, reciprocity of both positive and negative acts, and consolation, as well as processes having some resemblance to sympathy and altruism. The power of these prosocial processes was shown by the observation that when the population density of rhesus monkeys was increased by a factor of 646, there was no increase in aggression but marked increases in appeasement and submissive gestures (de Waal, 1996).

Ethological studies in recent years have also overlapped with the domain of sociobiology, wherein a large variety of behaviors are explained in terms of an expanded definition of evolutionary fitness that includes natural selection for benefits that accrue to all genetic relatives (kin selection: Trivers, 1985).

Elements of game theory have been introduced in ethology based on evidence that the old idea that a single set of species-specific behaviors characterizes all species is incorrect. In fact, behavioral polymorphism (distinctly different types of behaviors in different animals within the same species) has been identified in several species. These polymorphisms may be determined by an animal's social and environmental circumstances or may be genetically determined. Behaviors displaying polymorphic variation are often different reproductive strategies, with each having the same evolutionary fitness.

REFERENCES

de Waal, F. B. M. (1996). *Good natured: The origins of right and wrong in humans and other animals.* Cambridge, MA: Harvard University Press.

Gill, F. B., & Wolf, L. L. (1975). Economics of feeding territoriality in the golden-winged sunbird. *Ecology, 56,* 333–345.

Hinde, R. A. (1970). *Animal behavior: A synthesis of ethology and comparative psychology.* New York: McGraw-Hill.

Jaynes, J. (1969). The historical origins of "ethology" and "comparative psychology." *Animal Behavior, 17,* 601–606.

Krebs, J. R., & Davis, N. B. (1993). *An introduction to behavioral ecology.* Boston: Blackwell Scientific Publications.

Moltz, H. (1963). Inprinting: An epigenetic approach. *Psychological Review, 70,* 123–138.

Trivers, R. (1985). *Social evolution.* Menlo Park, CA: Benjamin/Cummings.

SUGGESTED READING

Dawkins, R. (1999). *The extended phenotype: The long reach of the gene.* New York: Oxford University Press.

Gould, J. L. (1982). *Ethology: The mechanisms and evolution of behavior.* New York: Norton.

Hinde, R. A. (1982). *Ethology, its nature and relations with other sciences.* New York: Oxford University Press.

McFarland, D. (1985). *Animal behavior: psychobiology, ethology, and evolution.* Menlo Park, CA: Benjamin/Cummings.

James E. King
University of Arizona

EVERYDAY COGNITION

Everyday cognition refers to the study of thinking—memory, reasoning, and judgment—in naturalistic settings and with real-world content. Examples of such thinking include the way in which we form impressions of people in our everyday lives, how we retrieve memories from our childhood, how we decide which brand is the best buy at the supermarket, and how we judge the likelihood of landing a job that we've applied for. The study of everyday cognition can be contrasted with traditional laboratory research on memory and thinking, where cognitive processes are studied outside of their everyday context and are assumed to be completely general (even universal) across contexts and materials. Thus, for example, rather than studying general problem-solving processes in the lab, researchers in everyday cognition have examined how grocery shoppers use nonstandard math in making their buying decisions and how dairy workers fill orders and determine the price of these orders. Similarly, rather than looking at the degree to which lab participants reason with abstract probability problems or simulations of lotteries or gambles, researchers in naturalistic decision making have looked at the real-world decision making of urban firefighters and military commanders in the field.

Everyday cognition research is also notable for the wide variety of methods used, in contrast to traditional laboratory research. Thus, for example, these methods include diary keeping, survey research, field studies, analyzing think-aloud protocols, and the use of archival data, to name just a few (in addition to traditional laboratory techniques). Everyday cognition research also often involves a focus on special populations (e.g., amnesia patients, experts in everyday skills such as typewriting or baseball) and applied problems (e.g., eyewitness testimony, adherence to schedules of medication).

Two prototypical topics in the area of everyday cognition that illustrate some of these differences from traditional laboratory research on memory and cognition, as well as the variety of different techniques used in the former area, are *autobiographical memory* and the study of *practical reasoning* in work settings. The topic of autobiographical memory (AM) is concerned with what we recall about our personal life history: how accurate or distorted these memories are, how they are distributed over the different periods of our lives (e.g., early childhood, adolescence, middle age), how events are represented and organized in memory, and how such memories are retrieved. In general, studies of AM differ from traditional laboratory studies of memory in that researchers on AM typically have little control over the conditions under which such memories are acquired and rehearsed and, in many cases, no way of judging their accuracy. In addition, AMs are typically months, years, or even decades old rather than being acquired in the same research session, and, unlike the memories studied in most lab research, AMs typically have significant personal meaning for the participant.

Studies on AM have used a variety of different research methods. For example, much traditional research has used a cue word method in which participants are asked to retrieve personal memories that match a given cue (e.g., an emotion or an object). In one particular version of this sort of study, participants were asked to recall AMs that met certain criteria, such as a memory of a time when they drove on the freeway and nearly had an accident. By presenting cues in different orders and measuring the time it took for participants to retrieve a memory, this research concluded that AMs are represented primarily in terms of activities (e.g., going to a restaurant) rather than in terms of general actions that are associated with a variety of contexts and activities (e.g., paying the bill), emotions, people, or the like.

In addition to studies using this sort of more familiar experimental manipulation, research on AM has also used long-term diary studies with single or small numbers of participants. For example, in two classic studies individual researchers recorded samples of events and experiences over 6-year periods of their lives, along with ratings of these events (e.g., in terms of salience and emotionality) and, in one case, details of the who, what, when, and where of the event. These researchers then tested their memory for randomly sampled examples of these events, either on a monthly basis or in the final year of the 6-year period. A common finding of both of these studies is that the diarists' memory for events proved to be much better than would be expected from traditional lab studies of memory. A subsequent study in which the recorded events were randomly sampled (i.e., by having participants write a description of whatever they were doing and thinking when a beeper they were carrying went off) found somewhat greater forgetting, though still better recall than that found in most lab studies of memory. Finally, some recent diary studies have focused on the involuntary, automatic recall of AMs, such as memories elicited by some odor or song or scene, as opposed to deliberate, strategic memory searches.

A second example of everyday cognition research can be found in a set of studies by Sylvia Scribner on the practical problem solving engaged in by workers at a dairy plant. This research looked at product assembly workers who had to fill orders by retrieving cases and partial cases of dairy products from a large ice box, drivers who had to calculate the price for specific quantities of milk and other dairy products, and inventory workers who took stock of existing supplies in the ice box. This research is of interest for a couple of different reasons. First, Scribner began with ethnographic observations of these workers performing their everyday tasks in a "natural" setting (i.e., the dairy) rather than trying to abstract some general processes out of that setting. From these observations Scribner formulated a conception of the workers' practical problem-solving strategies, which she then tested by means of task simulations with these same workers, as well as by comparing the experienced workers' performance with that of relative novices on the same tasks. Based on this evidence, Scribner concluded that the dairy workers typically reformulated the problem facing them in such a way that they could perform the task with optimal efficiency and flexibility and with minimal effort, for example, by completing an order by moving the minimal number of units. These workers also used properties of the environment (e.g., known dimensions of the ice box) in problem solving.

In general, Scribner, like so many other researchers in everyday cognition, has been at pains to point out how this sort of practical reasoning differs from the sorts of problem-solving tasks studied in traditional laboratory research. Thus, for example, practical, everyday problems typically relate to the overall goals and activities of the problem solver, rather than simply being isolated tasks to be solved for their own sake. Similarly, the workers' use of the environment in their problem solutions differs from the usual emphasis in laboratory studies (or school settings) on participants (or students) solving problems symbolically or "in the head."

Research on everyday cognition clearly takes a variety of different forms and, at this point in time, is still a work in progress. Nevertheless, the study of cognitive processes in real-world settings and with everyday materials presently offers a significant challenge to traditional research on memory and cognition.

Stanley Woll
California State University

EVOLUTIONARY PSYCHOLOGY

Human psychology is a product of the human nervous system. Neural mechanisms, often clustered in the brain, gather and process information from the environment, interact, and execute all actions. Every conscious and unconscious mental phenomenon—motivations, emotions, plans, and so on—derives from neural activity. Even the most mundane behaviors require precise unconscious calculations. Walking, for instance, requires extensive feedback and sensory integration in order to coordinate intricate muscle movement.

The only known process resulting in complex biological systems, such as the human nervous system, is evolution by natural selection. Natural selection is the process whereby genetically heritable traits within a population that directly or indirectly increase the bearer's reproduction pass more frequently into the next generation than less beneficial genetically heritable traits. Environmental features (food, conspecifics, substrate, etc.) that affect reproduction determine the direction of natural selection. Because human psychology is a product of the nervous system, and because evolution by natural selection is the only known mechanism that creates complex biological systems, all human psychology is a product of evolution by natural selection.

Natural selection produces adaptations: genetically heritable traits that serve context-specific purposes. Some adaptations perform functions that are helpful in modern contexts—reflexively pulling one's hand away from sudden intense heat before recognizing pain still minimizes tissue damage. Some adaptations, however, no longer function well in modern human environments. Our taste preference for fats now leads to obesity and increases our chance of suffering from cardiovascular disease and diabetes. It is difficult to understand adaptations, such as a preference for fats, without understanding their functions.

The fundamental function of every adaptation is to facilitate the reproduction of its host, ultimately to propagate the gene or genes that code for that adaptation. Adaptations exist over time because they propagated more numerously than other traits or forms of the same trait in a certain environment and withstood some measure of natural selection. Because natural selection eliminates traits that inferiorly propagate themselves compared to other traits (adaptations), the tautological function of an adaptation is to facilitate reproductive success in the environment in which it evolved. Adaptations such as the human nervous system, and thus all psychological mechanisms, are ultimately designed to propagate the genes for which they code.

Reproductive success can be subtle: An adaptation that grants a 1% reproductive advantage over other adaptations (or other forms of the same adaptation) can come to dominate a population after many generations. Reproductive success is context specific; that which is successful in one environment is often unsuccessful in different environments. Human reproductive success is often specifically difficult to understand due to the gap between the environment in which our psychology evolved and our modern environment.

Some aspects of modern human environments remain very similar to the environments in which human psychological mechanisms evolved, such as pair bonding in short- and long-term relationships, language use, and kinship networks. However, significant features of our current environment differ greatly from that of our ancestors. Among other environmental features, our ancestors did not benefit from the use of electricity, safe and easily acquired food, and indoor plumbing. Consequently, we possess no psychological adaptations designed to handle the problems associated with these new environmental features. Evolutionary psychology considers how human ancestral environments might be responsible for seemingly irrational modern human cognition and behavior. Many features of human psychology do not make adaptive sense because human behavior evolved in a sometimes drastically different environment.

Human taste preference for fatty foods illustrates the discrepancy between the environment in which human psychology evolved and modern environments. It is illogical in modern times to possess strong fat taste preferences because fat is easily accessible and high fat intake often leads to various diseases. Evolved fat preference makes adaptive sense only when we consider the famine conditions recurrent over human evolutionary history and the great difficulty ancestral humans would have faced in securing fatty foods. Ancestral humans that preferred fat (which is calorically dense) were more likely to survive and reproduce than those who did not prefer fats when food became intermittently available. The added caloric benefit of heritable fat preference outweighed fat's deleterious effects because fat was not widely available and thus not consumed in the manner and amounts that now induce health problems. The fat preference that was beneficial for our ancestors is now often harmful due to differences between modern environments and the environment in which this element of human psychology evolved.

Relatively rapid and inconsistent environmental change typifies the last 10,000 years of human existence, yet new adaptations regularly take 1,000 to 10,000 generations (15,000 to 150,000 human years) to spread throughout a population. Genes for adaptations specific to modern environments have not had sufficient time to propagate, even if such adaptations could exist. As William Allman suggests, our modern skulls house a "Stone Age mind" (Allman, 1994).

The indelible marks of evolution by natural selection pervade human psychology. However, the complexities of evolutionary theory and human behavior delayed a synthesis of the two fields until the latter part of the twentieth century. Because human behavioral scientists have not yet largely utilized evolutionary principles, many productive advances await evolutionarily informed researchers. Evolution provides insight into the design and purpose of behavior across realms of behavioral science, be it clinical psychology, neuroscience, linguistics, or otherwise. Perhaps we may one day achieve that which Darwin predicted in *The Origin of Species* (1859): "In the distant future I see open fields for far more important researches. Psychology will be based on a new foundation."

REFERENCE

Allman, W. F. (1994). *The stone age present: How evolution has shaped modern life—from sex, violence, and language to emotions, morals, and communities.* New York: Simon & Schuster.

RUSSELL JACKSON
University of Texas, Austin

See also: Adaptation; Anthropology

EXCITATORY AND INHIBITORY SYNAPSES

Chemical synapses—that is, synapses that use a chemical neurotransmitter to transfer information from one neuron to another—can be excitatory or inhibitory, depending on their effect on the postsynaptic neuron. Synapses releasing a neurotransmitter that brings the membrane potential of the postsynaptic neuron toward the threshold for generating action potentials are said to be excitatory. Alternatively, inhibitory synapses drive the membrane potential of the postsynaptic neuron away from the threshold for generating action potentials. The effect of a synapse is determined by its neurotransmitter content and the properties of the receptors present on the postsynaptic membrane. For example, in the adult mammalian brain, glutamate synapses are known to be excitatory, whereas gamma-aminobutyric acid (GABA) synapses are inhibitory. Meanwhile, synapses containing acetylcholine can be either excitatory or inhibitory, depending on the type of receptors present at a given synapse. Thus, at the neuromuscular junction, acetylcholine produces synaptic excitation by acting on a nicotinic receptor, while in the heart it acts on the inhibitory muscarinic receptor, resulting in slowing of the heart rate. Moreover, acetylcholine can have both excitatory and inhibitory effects in the same region, as described in the hippocampus (Ben-Ari, Krnjević, Reinhardt, & Ropert, 1981; Dodd, Dingledine, & Kelly, 1981). Even more complex is the case of neurons releasing two neurotransmitters with opposing action, for example, glutamate and GABA in hippocampal granule cells (Walker, Ruiz, & Kullmann, 2001), and dopamine and glutamate in ventral midbrain neurons (Sulzer et al., 1998). Postsynaptic factors may be involved in regulating the differential release of such cotransmitters, as demonstrated in sympathetic neurons, producing both norepinephrine (excitatory) and acetylcholine (inhibitory). In these neurons, brain-derived neurotrophic factor (BDNF) favors the secretion of acetylcholine, and its presence can thus transform an excitatory synapse into an inhibitory one within minutes (Yang, Slonimsky, & Birren, 2002).

In many instances, excitatory and inhibitory synapses appear to differ morphologically. In the cerebral cortex, Gray (1959) described two morphological types of synapses, type 1 and type 2, which were later correlated to excitatory and inhibitory synapses (Eccles, 1964). Type 1 synapses have a prominent postsynaptic density and a synaptic cleft about 20 nm wide. They are also called *asymmetric synapses,* because the postsynaptic membrane specialization is thicker than the presynaptic one (Colonnier, 1968). Most type 1 or asymmetric synapses contain round synaptic vesicles, so they are also termed S-type (S for spheroid vesicles). The great majority of type 1 synapses in the cerebral cortex use glutamate as a neurotransmitter, and they are excitatory. Type 2 synapses are characterized by a less pronounced postsynaptic density and a narrower synaptic cleft of about 12 nm. They are also known as *symmetric,* because the pre- and postsynaptic membrane specializations have a similar appearance. These synapses contain both round and flat synaptic vesicles after aldehyde fixation, hence the term F-type (F for flat vesicles). In the cerebral cortex, the vast majority of type 2 or symmetric synapses contain GABA as a neurotransmitter and are inhibitory. Glycine, another major inhibitory neurotransmitter of the brain, is also found in symmetric synapses in the spinal cord, cochlear nucleus, and other regions of the brain (reviewed in Legendre, 2001).

Although this correlation between morphology and function essentially holds true for the synapses in the adult cerebral cortex, this is not always the case during development or in other regions of the brain. For example, in the very young cerebral cortex, GABA cannot be detected by immunocytochemistry in as many as three quarters of the symmetric synapses (Micheva & Beaulieu, 1996). In some regions of the brain, such as the spinal cord, basal ganglia, and inferior olive, GABA terminals have been observed to also form asymmetric synapses. Thus, although the correlation between the two morphological types of synapses and their function holds true in a significant number of cases, it has to be used with caution, and always in conjunction with an immunocytochemical identification of the neurotransmitter type.

The excitatory and inhibitory synapses have been the object of many studies in different regions of the brain. For example, in the cerebral cortex, it was found that these two types of synapses differ in both their quantity and their distribution. The excitatory synapses represent the majority of synapses (more than 80%) and contact predominantly distal parts of the neuron, such as dendritic spines (i.e., the protoplasmic protrusions extending from the dendrites of some cells). Inhibitory synapses, meanwhile, are much less numerous and are most often found on proximal parts of the neuron such as dendritic shafts and cell bodies (e.g., Beaulieu, Kisvárday, Somogyi, Cynader, & Cowey, 1992). These morphological data appear to contradict physiological studies that indicate the existence of a balance between the excitatory and inhibitory neurotransmission in the cortex. However, even though the excitatory connections are much more abundant, the cortical inhibitory neurons fire at much higher rates than the excitatory pyramidal neurons (reviewed in Connors and Gutnick, 1990). The fact that inhibitory neurons make much more contacts on or near the cell bodies is also important since the spatial location of a synapse determines its relative contribution to the electrical state of the cell (i.e., the closer the synapse to the site of generation of action potentials, presumably the axon hillock, the greater its effect). Therefore, the inhibitory system, by way of its distribution and pattern of activity, can efficiently balance excitatory neurotransmission in the cerebral cortex. The inhibitory system is also in a position to exert a very focused effect on a single excitatory input, since some dendritic spines receive both an excitatory and inhibitory synapse (Jones and Powell, 1969; Qian and Sejnowski, 1990). In this case, the interaction between the two synaptic inputs would occur locally, at the level of the dendritic spine that is relatively isolated from the rest of the neuron.

It thus becomes clear that studying the distribution and physiology of the excitatory and inhibitory synapses, as well as their development and plasticity, is essential for understanding the overall organization and functioning of the brain.

REFERENCES

Beaulieu, C., Kisvárday, Z., Somogyi, P., Cynader, M., & Cowey, A. (1992). Quantitative distribution of GABA-immunopositive and -immunonegative neurons and synapses in the monkey striate cortex (area 17). *Cerebral Cortex, 2,* 295–309.

Ben-Ari, Y., Krnjević, K., Reinhardt, W., & Ropert, N. (1981). Intracellular observations on the disinhibitory action of acetylcholine in the hippocampus. *Neuroscience, 6,* 2475–2484.

Colonnier, M. (1968). Synaptic patterns of different cell types in the different laminae of the cat visual cortex: An electron microscope study. *Brain Research, 9,* 268–287.

Connors, B. W., & Gutnick, M. J. (1990). Intrinsic firing patterns of diverse neocortical neurons. *Trends in Neuroscience, 13,* 99–104.

Dodd, J., Dingledine, R., & Kelly, J. S. (1981). The excitatory action of acetylcholine on hippocampal neurons of the guinea pig and rat maintained in vitro. *Brain Research, 207,* 109–127.

Eccles, J. C. (1964). *The physiology of synapses.* Berlin: Springer-Verlag.

Gray, E. G. (1959). Axo-somatic and axo-dendritic synapses of the cerebral cortex: An electron microscope study. *Journal of Anatomy, 93,* 420–433.

Jones, E. G., & Powell, T. P. S. (1969). Morphological variations in the dendritic spines of the neocortex. *Journal of Cell Science, 5,* 509–529.

Legendre, P. (2001). The glycinergic inhibitory synapse. *Cellular and Molecular Life Sciences, 58,* 760–793.

Micheva, K. D., & Beaulieu, C. (1996). Quantitative aspects of synaptogenesis in the rat barrel field cortex with special reference to GABA circuitry. *Journal of Comparative Neurology, 373,* 340–354.

Qian, N., & Sejnowski, T. J. (1990). When is an inhibitory synapse effective? *Proceedings of the National Academy of Sciences, USA, 87,* 8145–8149.

Sulzer, D., Joyce, M. P., Lin, L., Geldwert, D., Haber, S. N., Hattori, T., et al. (1998). Dopamine neurons make glutamatergic synapses in vitro. *Journal of Neuroscience, 18,* 4588–602.

Walker, M. C., Ruiz, A., & Kullmann, D. M. (2001). Monosynaptic GABAergic signaling from dentate to CA3 with a pharmacological and physiological profile typical of mossy fiber synapses. *Neuron, 29,* 703–715.

Yang, B., Slonimsky, J. D., & Birren, S. J. (2002). A rapid switch in sympathetic neurotransmitter release properties mediated by the p75 receptor. *Nature Neuroscience, 5,* 539–545.

Kristina D. Micheva
Stanford University School of Medicine

EXISTENTIAL PSYCHOLOGY

Existential psychology assumes that the meaning of one's life derives from the accumulation of decisions one makes. Everything one does involves making a decision, whether one recognizes it or not. Decisions involve mental and action components. Mentally, when one mulls over and reaches conclusions about experiences through the processes of symbolization, imagination, and judgment, decisions are being made. And when one takes action based on these mental processes, decisions are also being made.

Although decisions vary enormously in magnitude and content, they all share an invariant form, namely, one can choose the future or the past. Choosing the future involves striking out in a new direction, whereas choosing the past involves shrinking back into what is familiar and already known. Choosing the future regularly is the way of personal growth and development through new experiences that provide a continual sense of vibrant, unfolding meaning. Ongoing new experiences also satisfy the constant stimulation needs of the huge human brain, needs that have evolved over the centuries.

Given all this, why would anyone characteristically avoid choosing the future? The reason is that choosing the future brings with it ontological anxiety, or fear of uncertainty and failure. One cannot be sure whether what transpires will be pleasurable, effective, successful, or what one hoped for. If what happens is positive, that will further your self-esteem, but if it is negative, you will have no one to blame but yourself.

Choosing the past, however, is not really a viable alternative, because it arouses ontological guilt, or the sense of missed opportunity. If one chooses the past regularly, one declines to mull over experience to see what it might involve, preferring instead to categorize it in old, established ways. Further, choosing the past involves taking only routine, habitual actions, regardless of the circumstances. If this process continues, the resulting sense of missed opportunities understandably accumulates into boredom, stagnation, bitterness, and meaninglessness. The eventual outcome is the conclusion that life is not worthwhile and that you are inconsequential. Further, choosing the past characteristically will be a constant source of frustration to that huge human brain, so needy of the new information that comes through symbolization, imagination, judgment, and novel action.

Needless to say, the most authentic way of life is regularly to choose the future, despite the ontological anxiety this brings. To do this well, one needs existential courage, or the recognition and acceptance that growth and development is not only a vibrant but also a painful experience. Existential courage has been operationalized as hardiness, which is a motivational set of attitudes comprising the three Cs of challenge, commitment, and control. Persons strong in challenge see change as normal and something to be learned from rather than a threat to be avoided. They do not expect easy comfort and security in life. Persons strong in commitment are inclined to stay involved with the people and events around them, seeing this as the most interesting and worthwhile way. They see withdrawal into isolation as a waste of time. Persons strong in control keep trying to influence the outcomes of which they are part, and they feel that sinking into powerlessness is too easy a way out.

As existential courage, hardiness (1) is not considered inborn, but rather is learned through encouragement to struggle with stresses, and (2) leads to resiliency, such that there is not only survival but also enhancement of performance and health under stress. Accumulating research findings provide support for these hypotheses. In this research, a wide range of stressful contexts have been used, from life-threatening events of military combat, through the culture shock of immigration or work missions abroad, to everyday work, school, or sports pressures and demands. Across such contexts, hardiness leads to enhanced performance, leadership, conduct, morale, stamina, and health. Further, the early lives of people strong in hardiness are characterized not only by many ongoing stresses, but also by being designated by their parents as the family's hope and having accepted that role.

In adulthood, the personality type resulting from regularly choosing the future is called *authenticity,* or individualism. Characteristics of this type include defining (1) oneself as someone who can, through decision making and interpretation, influence ongoing experiencing, and (2) society as formed out of the actions of individuals and, therefore, changeable by them. Authentic persons can learn by failures, and their lifestyle shows unity and innovativeness. Their biological and social experiencing shows subtlety, taste, intimacy, and love. Because of hardiness, doubt (ontological anxiety) is regarded as a natural concomitant of creating meaning and does not undermine the decision-making process. Although authentic people can fall into self-deception, they tend to correct this rapidly through their commitment to self-scrutiny and reflectiveness.

In contrast, the personality type resulting from regularly choosing the past is the conformist. This type is characterized by defining (1) oneself as nothing more than a player of social roles, and (2) society as an unchangeable, incontrovertible source of meaning and rules. Expression of symbolization, imagination, and judgment is inhibited, leading to stereotypic, fragmentary functioning. Biological and social experiencing is unsubtle and contractual, rather than discerning and intimate. Conformists feel worthless and insecure because of the buildup of ontological guilt through choosing the past rather than the future. Their worldview emphasizes materialism and pragmatism, and they deny and persist in failures rather than learning from them.

These two personality types refer to everyday functioning, rather than expressions of psychopathology. Existential psychology defines psychopathology in terms of massive breakdowns of one's everyday functioning, precipitated by major stresses. These major stresses are of three sorts, namely, experiencing significant social upheavals, life-threatening circumstances, and unavoidable and insistent indications of personal superficiality. Conformists are especially vulnerable to these major stresses, whereas individualists tend to use them as springboards to further growth and development. The most extreme form of psychopathology resulting from the breakdown of the conformist lifestyle in reaction to major stresses is *vegetativeness,* which is characterized by the inability to believe in the value of anything one can do or imagine doing, constant boredom, and actions that are listless and aimless. A less extreme form of existential psychopathology is *nihilism,* characterized by the sole cogency of paradoxical (or anti) meaning, feelings of anger and disgust, and the pursuit of hurtful actions against any positive meaning and those who believe in it. Least extreme is the psychopathology of *adventurousness,* wherein only extreme or dangerous activities retain any meaningfulness, and there are resulting wide swings in mood and action as the person tries to avoid everyday circumstances and pursue more dramatic experiences.

Salvatore R. Maddi
University of California, Irvine

See also: **Psychopathology**

EXIT INTERVIEWS

Exit interviews are used in employment settings, focusing specifically on those employees who are leaving the organization. Two distinct purposes can be identified for such interviews: information gathering and information giving. In addition, the exit interview can be a good way to show support for the departing employee's decision or to stay in touch with employees after they leave.

Information gathering is an attempt to curb financial

losses associated with excessive turnover and to collect diagnostic information regarding organizational functioning. Why are employees seeking other jobs? Are departing employees the best or worst workers? In contrast, information given to employees helps smooth their transition. An employee may wonder, for example, what the status of his or her benefits is. This is also an opportunity for the employer to make certain that the employee has checked in all keys and other company property.

Maintaining good relations with past employees is a more recent consideration in the literature on the exit interview, but in an era of declining employee loyalty to organizations, it is always possible to have an employee work in or around the organization again, either as a rehire or as an employee of an organization that does business with the former employer. The value of exit interviews is open to question. Research has shown that these interviews and a later follow-up questionnaire gave different reasons for leaving, with questionnaire results being more negative toward the company. The same general results have been found in a study comparing exit interviews to results obtained by an interview with an outside consultant.

Perhaps the best time to collect information (e.g., "What would it take to get you to consider employment elsewhere?" "Why do you stay here?") is before the decision is made to leave, or 6 months after the employee has left. At the actual time of departure, the employee may well not give accurate or honest information, because he or she is emotionally elsewhere—the new job. In short, employees may be reluctant to help the employer.

In spite of such problems, exit interviews should be used. In order for them to be effective, the organization should carefully consider the information to be gathered, who should be doing the interview, how that interviewer should be prepared for the task, and what kinds of organizational support are required (Finney, 1999). Interpretation of any information obtained should carefully consider biases, but ignoring the problem altogether is not a generally preferable alternative.

REFERENCE

Finney, M. (1999). Debriefing departing employees: Tips on conducting exit interviews. *Employment Managament Today, 4*(2), 22–27.

Philip G. Benson
New Mexico State University

EXORCISM

An exorcism is a ritual, formalized by the Catholic Church during the seventeenth century, performed on a person exhibiting signs of demonic possession. Possession is said to occur when the Devil enters and takes over the physical and mental faculties of the victim. The purpose of exorcism is to remove the Devil from the possessed person. This ritual, described in the *Ritual Romanum* in 1614 and still accepted as the official procedure, was directed at the Devil or "unclean spirit" assumed to inhabit the body of the possessed. One of the most popular and dramatic explanations of disordered behavior, demonic possession was mentioned only once in the Old Testament of the Bible. Possession, however, is referred to frequently in the New Testament of the Bible. The possessed person may be either an innocent victim or targeted by the Devil because of previous evil behavior. Four complete cases of exorcism were reported to have been performed by Jesus. Explanations relying on demonic possession have been reported in most countries at various times throughout history.

Accepted signs of demonic possession may include any of the following: an offensive stench, tight lips, inability to pray, the vomiting of strange objects, rolling of the eyes, the display of powers beyond one's physical capacity, the shouting of obscenities, personality changes, prophetic wisdom, convulsions, the capacity to speak or understand a strange language, repulsion by the sight of the cross, repulsion by holy water, and the refusal to enter a sanctified place of worship. Most of those persons found possessed were women.

During the early Christian era, exorcistic skills were considered to be a special talent. Later, during the middle of the third century, the Catholic Church created the position of exorcist. The exorcist was typically a minor cleric who exhibited the necessary piety, judgment, and character for the position. Exorcism consisted of two parts. First, the exorcist strengthened himself by praying. The Devil was subsequently attacked, insulted, and commanded to leave the body of the possessed. Recovery was assumed to have occurred when the person returned to a prepossessed state. Contemporary Roman Catholic belief distinguishes between major and minor exorcisms, depending upon the degree of possession. A brief exorcistic rite is often included in the baptismal ceremony of the Catholic Church. The Catholic Church updated the guidelines for exorcism in 1999. The new guidelines encourage making a thorough medical and psychological evaluation before recommending an exorcism. The psychological literature regarding exorcisms is limited primarily to case studies and anecdotal reports.

Chet H. Fischer
Radford University

EXPERIENTIAL PSYCHOTHERAPY

Experiential therapy refers to a way of conducting therapy rather than to a therapy specific to one theory of persons or personality. Experiential therapy comprises a method for applying theory, and in this way it is metatheoretical.

A central focus in conducting therapy experientially is the client's moment-to-moment experiencing. Experiencing is seen as the entry point to processes leading to personality change and psychological improvement. It is the primary navigational aid regarding a productive course of therapeutic interaction.

Therapeutic moves (empathic response, interpretation, suggestion, question, confrontation, chair work, psychoeducation, etc.) can be immediately evaluated by their effect on client experiencing: When subsequent experiencing becomes more closed, defensive, abstract, or out of control for the client, the move has had an experiential effect of dubious value. When experiencing becomes more open, emotional, complex, intricate, sensation based, and accurately expressible in words or other symbols, the move has had a desirable experiential effect.

Attending to this experiential feedback protects the therapist against the pitfall of selectively perceiving data anticipated by the therapist's particular theoretical or personal expectations. The experiential therapist can thereby quickly correct unhelpful moves, rather than persisting with faulty plans and generating problems in the therapeutic relationship.

References to the experiential way of doing therapy are found in the works of many major early psychotherapists. Carl Rogers developed a method of psychotherapy in which client experiencing is centrally relied upon to guide the course of therapy, as counterpoint to the widely held belief that the doctor should guide the therapy. Carl Whitaker and T. P. Malone may have been the first to use the term *experiential psychotherapy* to describe their approach. Eugene Gendlin, who worked closely with Rogers, developed the philosophical basis that makes systematic the experiential method. Gendlin cites the existential and phenomenological philosophers S. Kirkegaard, W. Dilthey, E. Husserl, M. Heidegger, M. Buber, J.-P. Sartre, and M. Merleau-Ponty as precursors of his experiential philosophy.

Rogers drew on biologist Kurt Goldstein's observation and conceptualization of an actualizing tendency. This is the tendency, found in any living organism, to behave in ways that fulfill and further perfect the capacities, according to its nature, of the organism as a whole.

The client's moment-to-moment experiencing is seen as the real-time expression of the actualizing tendency. Experiencing is wider and deeper than conscious experience. Subjectively, experiencing is found in the person's "inner space." It is generally vague and and often elusive, with physical sensations and emotional qualities attendant to relevant cognition. This inner sense of intricacy is called the *bodily felt sense.* Experiencing is considered inherently life-promoting for both the individual and the social group, and generally more so with more awareness.

The actualization of healthy potentials implicit in experiencing does not depend only on the individual, but is seen as highly dependent on the interpersonal (and other environmental) conditions with which the person interacts currently and with which the person has interacted historically.

Things go awry when factors in a person's environment interfere with healthy awareness and symbolization of experiencing that would carry it forward to meet the person's needs, especially if the interference is systematic over a long time. Certain patterns of relating to experiencing (or avoiding it) may result; these patterns shape the positive potential of experiencing into negative and ineffective forms of expression.

Therapy, then, is very much about changing problematic attitudes toward experiencing. The therapeutic relationship establishes a safe climate within which, aided by the expertise of the therapist, the client can better articulate, express, and live out experiencing. The process of doing this takes time and involves many little successes before major and lasting change is accomplished. When something in experiencing that has been poorly symbolized is finally approached with an empathic attitude that results in more accurate symbolization, there is a bodily sigh of relief known as a *felt shift.*

When a person regularly and reliably relates to experiencing so as to get these felt shifts, he or she is said to have a high level of experiencing. There is evidence that a high-experiencing way of working with one's feeling about a traumatic experience has a positive effect on physical health, in the form of improved immune function. Many studies have found psychological benefits associated with high levels of experiencing.

Regardless of his or her theoretical training, the experiential therapist remains alert for the words, images, behavioral strategies, or situational changes that have a positive resonating power with the client's bodily felt sense. Thus many different approaches to helping the client are usable, limited only by what the therapist knows and can work with skillfully. Therapist and client both rely on responses from their body senses to the steps of therapeutic interaction in order to guide the way toward improvement that is both uniquely right for the client and in the theoretically and interpersonally desirable direction.

James R. Iberg

See also: **Psychotherapy**

EXPERIMENTAL CONTROLS

Edwin G. Boring (1954) developed three meanings in psychology for the word *control:* (1) a check, in the sense of verification; (2) a restraint, in the sense of maintaining constancy; and (3) a guide or direction. Controlled observations, and controls on experimental variables or checks on observations, are as old as science. The use in psychology, however, of an experimental control group as such—a separate group of individuals against which comparisons of the experimental group's observations are made—began during the twentieth century.

Since people not in psychological experiments do learn, mature, and change from experiences in daily living, experimental control groups for comparison purposes are valuable, almost necessary, in most of psychology in order to have a context in which to interpret meaningful research findings. In addition, the almost inherent lack of ability to measure with precision in psychology has a decided influence on changes in observations over time. The research context in which the observations are made, the possible reaction of participants to the somewhat unusual conditions of the psychological research study, and motivational differences between the experimental and control groups can also reduce the quality of the comparisons needed for interpretation. These concerns are also the subject of experimental design and research methodology.

Early attempts to develop experimental controls in psychological research included attempting to hold all variables constant except those being deliberately manipulated. This is difficult to do with human participants; it can be done only within rather broad limits, and it often makes the experimental conditions so artificial that generalizations to the everyday psychological world are difficult.

Participants in psychological research are sometimes used as their own experimental controls; they are observed, an experimental condition is applied, and then they are observed again. This method is useful if a large number of observations are made prior to and after the experimental condition. Such observations can be used to establish the stability of the participants' behavior and its typical range. When the experimental treatment can be applied and withdrawn over time—again with many observations made in each interval between conditions—the experimental control is better. If a stable change can be observed after each of the conditions, then good comparisons and interpretations can be made.

In psychology, experimenters often match participants on one or more variables or group participants by characteristics or prior conditions. Then some of these groups have the experimental treatment and some do not. If the groups are matched on variables such as gender, residential area, or other accurately observed characteristics, the method is acceptable. If the matching or grouping can be followed by a chance allocation of participants (i.e., at random) to experimental and control groups, the resulting experimental controls and comparisons are quite good. If not, there can be major errors.

Sometimes statistical adjustments are attempted as a control method in psychological research. Unless accompanied by allocation of participants to experimental and control groups by chance, these methods often are less than adequate to obtain good research comparisons.

During this century psychology has developed a rather mature, rigorous, and sometimes elaborate set of experimental controls for its research methodology, taking into account the special characteristics and problems associated with human participants and psychological variables. Its research methodology is still growing, however, and undoubtedly more and better experimental controls will be developed.

J. William Asher
Purdue University

See also: **Analysis of Covariance**

EXPERIMENTAL METHODS

Experimental methods are among the scientific methods used in psychological research. True experiments involve the careful observation of the effects of one or more variables (independent variables) on one or more outcome variables (dependent variables) under carefully controlled conditions with subjects randomly assigned to treatments. For example, a study of the effect of adrenaline on activity level could be done by randomly assigning subjects to an experimental group (who receive adrenaline) or to a control group (who receive an inert substance, a placebo) and then recording their activity levels in an objective way. The independent variable (drug dosage) has two levels (drug vs. placebo), and the dependent variable (activity level) is measured using an operational definition (a description of how activity level scores are assigned). More levels of the independent variable could be used; for example, subjects might be given 0-mg, 3-mg, 10-mg, or 25-mg doses of adrenaline, so that the independent variable would have four levels.

The experiment could be made more complex by adding additional independent or dependent variables. For example, time of day might be used as a second independent variable with three levels (morning, afternoon, evening), so that subjects might be randomly assigned to any of 12 different conditions (0 mg in the morning, 10 mg in the evening, etc.). It is clear that the number of subjects required for more complex designs would be greater than for simpler designs because the number of subjects under each condition (e.g., 10 mg in the afternoon) must be sufficient to generalize about that condition.

Although other scientific methods exist, the true experiment is the only method that allows researchers to make conclusions about cause-and-effect relationships. In the simple experiment with one independent variable (drug dosage) with two levels, if subjects in both the experimental and the control group are treated in identical ways (except for the independent variable), and if subjects are randomly assigned to treatment conditions (drug vs. placebo), then any differences between the activity level scores can be attributed to the independent variable. To infer causation, it is essential that the subject groups not differ with respect to anything other than the independent variable. For example, if only men were in the experimental group and only women were in the control group, observed differences might reflect gender rather than dosage differences.

Sometimes independent variables cannot be manipulated by the researcher. For example, a researcher with gender, ethnicity, political party, frequency of marijuana use, or educational level as an independent variable cannot randomly assign subjects to levels of independent variables. Such variables sometimes are called *nonmanipulated variables.* The study of such variables cannot make use of a true experiment, but they are frequently studied in quasi-experiments. Interpretation of results for nonmanipulated variables is complicated, since various additional variables generally are confounded with them. For example, social class, intelligence, and a number of personality variables are confounded with educational level, so observed difference between high school and college graduates may reflect these confounded variables rather than the effect of education. One way to facilitate interpretation of nonmanipulated independent variables is to match subjects on relevant confounding variables. For example, each high school graduate could be paired with a college graduate who matches in age, gender, social class, intelligence, and personality measures. The more complete the matching, the more comfortable the researcher can be in interpreting the effects of the independent variable.

Sometimes research strategies involve repeatedly testing the same subjects. A longitudinal study of human development may test the same group of children at ages 2, 5, 10, and 20, or a learning study may test subjects after every stimulus presentation. This introduces another complication: an order effect. For example, if subjects are asked to rate the physical attractiveness of 10 people, with slides showing the stimuli presented to all subjects in the same order, the rating of the third slide may reflect an order effect as well as the stimulus. If the second slide, for example, is of a particularly attractive person, the third slide may be undervalued because of a contrast effect. If the third slide were in a different ordinal position, its ratings would be different. Clearly, the solution to such problems involves manipulation of the order, so that different subjects receive the stimuli in different sequences. This is the technique of *counterbalancing.*

Experimental designs vary across experiments and depend upon a number of factors: the number of independent and dependent variables; whether independent variables are manipulated or nonmanipulated; whether subjects are matched or tested once or repeatedly; and how subjects are assigned to experimental conditions.

All experimental methods must be used carefully and cautiously, with attention to ethical, practical, and statistical considerations. Scientific theory is built upon repeated, consistent research results; a single study represents only one piece of information for scientific evaluation.

SUGGESTED READING

Allen, M. J. (1995). *Introduction to psychological research.* Itasca, IL: Peacock.

MARY J. ALLEN
California State University

EXPERT TESTIMONY

It has been over a century since lively debate began in scientific journals and law reviews on the psychology of testimony and the value of psychology to the judicial process (Goldofski, 1904; Jaffe, 1903; Lobsien, 1904). Hugo Munsterberg brought together a number of essays on psychology and crime, first publishing these in the *New York Times* magazine and then as the book *On the Witness Stand* (1908). In his enthusiasm Munsterberg stated, "my only purpose is to turn the attention of serious men to an absurdly neglected field which demands the full attention of the social community." He then presented a series of essays on illusions, the memory of witnesses, the detection of crime, untrue confessions, hypnotism and crime, and the prevention of crime.

Munsterberg's effort was interesting, enthusiastic, and predictive of the increasing overlap of psychology and law. It was, unfortunately, somewhat premature, but it did not go unnoticed. John H. Wigmore, professor of the Law of Evidence at Northwestern University, wrote a scathing parody of *On the Witness Stand* that was published in the *Illinois Law Review* in 1909. The critique reported a mythical suit filed in the city of "Windyville, Illiania" against Munsterberg for having "caused to be printed, published, and circulated in Illiania and throughout the country . . . [a book that] contained . . . certain assertions, erroneous, incorrect and untrue concerning the said plaintiffs, in their capacity as members of the bar."

Wigmore confronted Munsterberg with the lack of published evidence to support the claim that the law was ready for psychology, as Munsterberg had cited no references in his pioneer text. The mock complaint cited 127 learned treatises to justify the proceedings. The mock trial ended with a finding against Munsterberg, the jury assessing damages of one dollar.

Wigmore's attack was telling: Few references to psychologists as expert witnesses appeared for a quarter of a century. Then in 1931 Lewis M. Terman, a professor of psychology at Stanford University, appeared before the Los Angeles Bar Association to present an address, "Psychology and the Law." Terman took pains to refer to Munsterberg's

On the Witness Stand and Wigmore's scathing response. He suggested that Munsterberg's error was in exaggerating the importance of psychology's contributions based on the then-existing research. Termin indicated, however, that the ultimate significance of psychology for the legal profession could hardly be overstated considering the scientific advances made during the first quarter of the century. Terman emphasized the value of experimental psychology in clarifying errors of testimony. He suggested psychology may be useful in developing, researching, evaluating, or clarifying lie detection, eyewitness testimony, the vagaries of the insanity plea, and jury selection. Terman ended his presentation with a critique similar to that presented by Hugo Munsterberg nearly a quarter of a century before: "Our law, like our proverbs and adages, are the product of folk-thinking and like those, they are a mixture of shred wisdom, childish error, superstition, and folly" (Terman, 1935).

By this time, Wigmore's *On Evidence* was considered the definitive work, as it was being used and cited by attorneys and judges throughout the United States. Yet psychology's most bitter critic in the law at that time modified his position in the last edition of his master work: "Both law and practice permit the calling of any expert scientist whose method is acknowledged in his science to be a sound and trustworthy one. Whenever the Psychologist is ready for the Courts, the Courts are ready for him" (Wigmore, 1937). Clearly, Wigmore was demonstrating the flexibility, awareness, and practicality psychologists are likely to find among lawyers and judges when presented with psychological data, techniques, and methods generally acceptable to colleagues and concordant with the standards of the profession.

One of the earliest reviews of the legal and psychological literature regarding the psychologist as expert witness was published by D. W. Louisell in 1955. An appendix to this article presented the testimony of Dr. Kenneth E. Clark in the trademark infringement case of *Robinsdale Amusement Co. v. Warner Brothers Pictures Distributing Corp. et al.;* Clark testified as an expert in public opinion techniques.

During the 1950s psychologists were sometimes qualified as experts and sometimes dismissed by the judge. In 1954, Dr. Michael H. P. Finn, then chief psychologist at the Springfield State Hospital, appeared in *Hidden v. Mutual Life Insurance of New York.* The judge refused to allow Finn to testify. On appeal, the U.S. Court of Appeals reversed this decision on the ground that Finn was qualified to give expert testimony.

In the earliest formal text on private practice in clinical psychology, T. G. Blau (1959) included a chapter entitled "The Clinical Psychologist and the Legal Profession." Blau suggested that psychologists would do well to prepare themselves to be competent expert witnesses within their field. Several court transcripts were included to illustrate direct examination and cross-examination of psychologists in personal injury and competency cases.

The role of the psychologist as expert witness in matters of mental disease or defect was addressed in considerable detail in the landmark case of *Jenkins v. United States* in 1962. After indictment for housebreaking with intent to commit an assault, assault with intent to rape, and assault with a dangerous weapon, Jenkins was committed to a hospital in Washington, D.C., for a mental examination on September 4, 1959. The purpose of the examination was to determine his competence to stand trial and his mental state at the time of the alleged offense. Jenkins was given a series of psychological tests by staff psychologists under the supervision of Bernard I. Levy. Jenkins was also examined by several psychiatrists, who informed the District Court that he was incompetent. He was then committed to St. Elizabeth's Hospital until mentally competent to stand trial. At St. Elizabeth's he was tested extensively by Lawrence Tirnauer, PhD, who concluded Jenkins was schizophrenic. Two other psychiatrists found "no evidence of mental disease or defect." Margaret Ives, PhD, administered additional tests and concluded that Tirnauer's diagnosis was correct. The trial court, *sua sponte* (on its own motion), instructed the jury to disregard the testimony of the three defense psychologists' opinions that the defendant had had a mental disease when allegedly committing the crimes.

On appeal, Judge Bazelon of the U.S. Court of Appeals held that the lower court had erred on several points, including rejection of qualified psychologists as experts on the presence or absence of mental disease. This decision was rendered in spite of an *amicus curiae* brief submitted by the American Psychiatric Association, urging the court not to allow psychologists to qualify as experts. Bazelon's scholarly opinion defined the fully trained psychologist. In a rare concurrence, Judge Warren Burger (who later became a Chief Justice of the U.S. Supreme Court) agreed with Bazelon. Since the *Jenkins* decision, the rejection of psychologists by the court as experts in their fields of specialization has been considered trial error.

Not all psychologists are likely to be accepted by the court as expert witnesses in all areas of psychological practice. The psychologist must be qualified before the court as an expert in the area about which he or she will testify. Furthermore, as legal scholars have pointed out, the issue must be such that the expert may answer by giving an opinion that is a reasonable probability, rather than conjecture or speculation (Ladd, 1952).

The credibility of any expert's testimony in some jurisdictions continues to follow the admonition delineated in *Frye v. United States* (1923), in which the court reasoned:

> Just when a scientific principle of discovery crosses the line between the experimental and demonstrable stages is difficult to define. Somewhere in this twilight zone the evidential force of the principle must be recognized, and while courts will go a long way in admitting expert testimony deduced from a well-recognized scientific principle or discovery, the thing from which the deduction is made must be sufficiently established to have gained general acceptance in the particular field which it belongs.

The admissibility of expert testimony was predicted to change drastically subsequent to the 1993 case *Daubert v. Merrell-Dow Pharmaceuticals.* A majority opinion by the U.S. Supreme Court indicated that the *Frye* test was too austere and that a new standard based on the Federal Rules of Evidence should be adopted. Admissibility of testimony based on the Federal Rules of Evidence tended to be more flexible than the *Frye* rule. It indicated that a qualified expert could provide scientific, technical, or specified knowledge that would assist the trier of fact or law in determining an issue that was based on material that was reliably accepted by the scientific community. The *Daubert* ruling basically made the trial judge the gatekeeper to the admissibility of expert testimony. Several criteria were enumerated by Justice Blackman for trial judges to use in determining the admissibility of testimony, and include (1) whether the hypothesis that formed the basis for the testimony was testable (falsifiability), (2) whether it had been published, (3) whether there was a known error rate for the procedure, (4) whether it had been peer-reviewed, and (5) whether it was generally accepted in the field. Interestingly, the *Frye* test of whether a particular scientific principle is "generally accepted in the relevant scientific community" bears considerable similarity to the last criterion enumerated in *Daubert* regarding whether such a principle is generally accepted in the field.

In 1999, the trial judge's gatekeeper status was reaffirmed by the U.S. Supreme Court in the case of *Kumho Tire Company v. Carmichael.* The Supreme Court upheld exclusion of testimony based on the unreliability of the methodology.

The Revised Ethical Principles of Psychologists and Code of Conduct (American Psychological Association, 1992) addresses forensic activities. Specialty guidelines for forensic psychologists published in 1991 by the Committee on Ethical Guidelines for Forensic Psychologists more specifically address the ethical obligations of psychologists providing expert testimony.

Since the *Jenkins* decision, psychologists have appeared more frequently in the courts as experts. Most published reports of psychologists as expert witnesses involve competency evaluations and the sanity plea. In this narrow area of expert testimony, psychologists have entered into a domain once belonging exclusively to psychiatrists. Data suggest that psychologists are successful and well regarded as expert witnesses in matters of competence and sanity (Perlin, 1980). Psychologists testify in civil matters, including personal injury, wrongful death, trademark infringement, product liability, and other issues. Psychologists have testified in criminal courts in matters of change of venue, death-qualified juries, prison conditions, and capacity to form criminal intent.

Judges are increasingly aware of the potential of psychologists to assist the courts. Patricia McGowan Wald (1982), circuit judge for the U.S. Court of Appeals, District of Columbia, has stated: "I find that after a decade or more of increasing awareness among psychologists and lawyers about what litigation can and cannot accomplish, the era of their most productive relationships built on mutual respect and realistic idealism may be only just beginning."

More graduate and postgraduate training is being offered to prepare psychologists to function as expert witnesses in the courts. Psychologists who currently expect to function in this role must acquire education, training, and experience ad lib or, more appropriately, from continuing education at the postdoctoral level. Interest in this area is burgeoning; it seems likely that doctoral students in professional training programs will, in the future, have a greater opportunity to prepare to function as experts for the courts. Joint PhD/JD programs are producing psychologist-lawyers who, one hopes, will bridge the gap of knowledge and issues of mutual distrust between the two professions (Wolinksy, 1982).

One way to assess the importance of appropriately given expert testimony is by the number of books and chapters dedicated thereto. The interested reader is referred to the Suggested Reading section that follows.

REFERENCES

American Psychological Association. (1992). Ethical principles of psychologists and code of conduct (Rev. ed.). *American Psychologist, 47*(1), 1597.

Daubert v. Merrell-Dow Pharmaceuticals, Inc. 509 U.S. 579 589 (1993).

Frye v. United States, 293 F. 1013 (DC 1923).

Goldofski, O. B. (1904). The psychology of testimony. *Vyestnik Prava,* No. 16–18, 185.

Hidden v. Mutual Life Insurance Co., 217F. 2d 818, 821 (4th Cir. 1954).

Jaffe, S. (1903). Ein psychologisches experiment in Kriminalistischen seminar der universitaet Berlin [A psychological experiment in criminality seminar at the University of Berlin]. *Beitraege zur Psychologie der Aussage, mit besonderer Bereuecksrchitigung der Rechtspflege, Paedogogik, Psychiatrie und Geschichts forschung, 1,* 79.

Jenkins v. United States, 307 F. 2d 637 (1962).

Kumho Tire Company v. Carmichael, 67 U.S. L.W. 4179 (1999).

Ladd, J. (1952). Expert testimony. *Vanderbilt Law Review, 5,* 414, 419.

Lobsien, M. (1904). Veber psychologie der aussage. *Zeit schrift feur Paedagogische Psychologie, VI,* 161.

Louisell, D. W. (1955). The psychologist in today's legal world. *Minnesota Law Review, 39*(3), 235–272.

Munsterberg, H. (1908). *On the witness stand.* New York: Doubleday.

Perline, M. L. (1980). The legal status of the psychologist in the courtroom. *Mental Disabilities Law Review, 3*(4), 194–200.

Robinsdale Amusement Co. v. Warner Brothers, Civil #4584 (4th Division, Minneapolis).

Terman, L. M. (1935). Psychology and the law. *Commercial Law Journal, 40,* 639–646.

Wald, P. M. (1982). Become a real "friend of the court." *APA Monitor, 13*(2), 5.

Wigmore, J. H. (1909). Professor Munsterberg and the psychology of testimony. *Illinois Law Review, 3*(7), 399–445.

Wigmore, J. H. (1940). On evidence (3rd ed.). Boston: Little, Brown.

Wolinksy, J. (1982). Programs join "distrustful" disciplines. *APA Monitor, 13*(2), 15.

SUGGESTED READING

Blau, T. H. (1998). *The psychologist as expert witness* (2nd ed.). New York: Wiley.

Brodsky, S. L. (1991). *Testifying in court: Guidelines and maxims for the expert witness.* Washington, DC: American Psychological Association.

Hess, A. K., & Weiner, I. B. (Eds.). (1999). *The handbook of forensic psychology* (2nd ed.). New York: Wiley.

Lubet, S. (1998). *Expert testimony: A guide for expert witnesses and the lawyers who examine them.* Chicago: National Institute for Trial Advocacy.

Melton, G. B., Petrila, J., Poythress, N. G., & Slobogin, C. (1997). *Psychological evaluations for the courts: A handbook for mental health professionals and lawyers* (2nd ed.). New York: Guilford Press.

THEODORE H. BLAU
J. T. SUPER

EXTRASENSORY PERCEPTION (ESP)

Awareness of information that occurs independently of known sensory channels such as sight, hearing, taste, smell, or touch, is referred to as *extrasensory perception* (ESP). Examples of ESP claims include the detection of hidden objects (clairvoyance), thought transference between people (telepathy), and knowledge of future events (precognition). Some experiences may give the appearance of extrasensory awareness, yet ESP phenomena require scientific support to verify their authenticity (Irwin, 1999). Historically, anecdotes of spontaneous cases of anomalous experiences constituted the basis of ESP claims. *Spontaneous cases* are subjective reports of everyday life experiences categorized in terms of clairvoyance, telepathy, or precognition (L. E. Rhine, 1953). When distinctions between clairvoyance, telepathy, and precognition became ambiguous, the concept known as *general extrasensory perception* (GESP) was proposed by Joseph B. Rhine (1948), an American pioneer in conducting research on ESP. Moreover, the term *psi* embraces both ESP and psychokinesis (PK), that is, mental influence on physical events ("mind over matter"; Schmidt, 1973). Concerns over the precision and proliferation of terminology in ESP have persisted for over a century (Zingrone & Alvarado, 1987).

Rhine's Research Efforts at Duke University

Joseph Banks Rhine was a botanist who joined the faculty at Duke University in 1927. In 1934, Rhine published a monograph based on his laboratory studies, entitled *Extra-Sensory Perception,* in which he claimed overwhelming statistical evidence for the existence of ESP. These lab studies conducted by Rhine were empirical in design, and his data were statistically analyzed, which provided greater objectivity compared to the spontaneous-case approach. Yet Rhine's observations were not experimental because his research did not employ control groups or conditions. ESP research continued at Duke until 1962 when Rhine reestablished his laboratory in Durham, North Carolina, close to the campus. Rhine called his new location the Foundation for Research on the Nature of Man (FRNM), and it is now referred to as the Rhine Research Center.

Learning to Use ESP with Automation?

Principles of conditioning and learning models in psychology have been applied to the possibility of teaching people to increase their ESP skills. Giving immediate feedback to subjects after each trial has led to a reduction in the *decline effect* (a gradual decrease in the number of hits over many series of tests), yet these scores are not consistently above chance (Tart, 1976). Attempts to automate ESP research designs and rid them of extraneous sources of physical cues called *sensory leakage* prompted the use of computers (Broughton, 1982). Moreover, useful control tests can be done with a computer (Gaither & Zusne as cited in Zusne & Jones, 1982).

Remote Viewing Experiments

The Stanford Research Institute (SRI) conducted a series of experiments to determine whether subjects could accurately describe a randomly selected outdoor location that was at a distance and not visible from the subject's laboratory room (Targ & Puthoff, 1978). The Central Intelligence Agency financed an independent study of possible uses of remote viewing, such as for governmental spying, only to abandon this program in the late 1970s in the absence of encouraging findings (Hyman, 1996). Suggestions of methodological and statistical flaws and concerns that the judges of subjects' reports were not totally ignorant of the identity of the target locations cast doubt on the validity of remote-viewing data (Irwin, 1999).

Beliefs in the Existence of ESP

The term *sheep* was chosen to refer to people who believe in the possibility of ESP and *goats* refers to those who doubt or deny its existence (Schmeidler & McConnell, 1958; Thalbourne & Delin, 1993). The persistence of belief in the existence of ESP despite only occasional hits compared with the many trials of failure reported in controlled lab research has been analyzed. Rationales for such tenacity of belief include the cognitive need for people to structure many puzzling events in life so that they appear comprehensible (Irwin, 1999) and the *partial reinforcement effect,* in which occasional hits of ESP hidden targets compared to numerous misses result in a strong "resistance to extinction" of ESP beliefs (Vitulli, 1997).

Future Status of Research and Theory in ESP

The *ganzfeld* procedure deprives the subject of normal sensory stimulation (Bem and Honorton, 2001). ESP-conducive data have been reported under *ganzfeld,* yet apparent methodological flaws result in controversial interpretations. Scientific theories are characterized as having aesthetic value or beauty in rough proportion to the degree of empirical data in support of that theory (McAllister, 1998). The absence of reliable demonstrations, upon demand, of the existence of ESP leaves this area of inquiry in a state of limbo. Nevertheless, the spirit of human curiosity serves as a beacon for scientific progress. Despite paranormal claims, research in anomalous experiences such as ESP continues to occur for the sake of knowledge, regardless of where it may lead.

Selected Journals Dedicated to ESP-Related Research

European Journal of Parapsychology
Journal of Parapsychology
Journal of the American Society of Psychical Research
Journal of the Society for Psychical Research
Skeptical Inquirer
Zetetic Scholar

REFERENCES

Bem, D. J., & Honorton, C. (2001). Does psi exist? Replicable evidence for an anomalous process of information transfer. In K. R. Rao (Ed.), *Basic research in parapsychology* (pp. 345–380). Jefferson, NC: McFarland.

Broughton, R. S. (1982). Computer methodology: Total control with a human face. *Parapsychology Review, 13,* 1–6.

Hyman, R. (1996). Evaluation of the military's twenty-year program on psychic spying. *Skeptical Inquirer, 20,* 21–23.

Irwin, H. J. (1999). *An introduction to parapsychology* (3rd ed.). Jefferson, NC: McFarland.

McAllister, J. W. (1998). Is beauty a sign of truth in scientific theories? *American Scientist, 86,* 174–183.

Rhine, J. B. (1934). *Extra-sensory perception.* Boston: Boston Society for Psychic Research.

Rhine, J. B. (1948). *The reach of the mind.* London: Faber & Faber.

Rhine, L. E. (1953). Subjective forms of spontaneous psi experiences. *Journal of Parapsychology, 17,* 77–114.

Schmeidler, G. R. (1952). Personal values and ESP scores. *Journal of Abnormal and Social Psychology, 47,* 757–761.

Schmeidler, G. R., & McConnell, R. A. (1958). *ESP and personality patterns.* New Haven, CT: Yale University Press.

Schmidt, H. (1973). PK tests with a high-speed random number generator. *Journal of Parapsychology, 37,* 105–118.

Targ, R., & Puthoff, H. (1978). *Mind reach.* London: Granada.

Tart, C. T. (1976). *Learning to use extrasensory perception.* Chicago: University of Chicago Press.

Thalbourne, M. A., & Delin, P. S. (1993). A new instrument for measuring the sheep-goat variable: Its psychometric properties and factor structure. *Journal of the Society for Psychical Research, 59,* 172–186.

Vitulli, W. F. (1997). Beliefs in parapsychological events or experiences among college students in a course in experimental parapsychology. *Perceptual and Motor Skills, 85,* 273–274.

Zingrone, N. L., & Alvarado, C. S. (1987). Historical aspects of parapsychological terminology. *Journal of Parapsychology, 51,* 49–74.

Zusne, L., & Jones, W. H. (1982). *Anomalistic psychology.* Hillsdale, NJ: Erlbaum.

William F. Vitulli
University of South Alabama

EXTRAVERSION AND INTROVERSION, CONCEPT OF

The words *extraversion* and *introversion* have been in use for several centuries. Considered etymologically, they may be construed respectively as an "outward turning" and an "inward turning." They have been used, in fact, with essentially those meanings, both in a physical sense and in a psychological sense. The psychological usage can be found in writings dating as far back as the seventeenth century, where extraversion referred to the turning of thoughts toward outer objects and introversion referred to the turning of thoughts inward to one's own mind or soul or to the spiritual realm.

The work of Jung (1921/1976) is largely responsible for directing the attention of psychologists to these concepts. Jung viewed extraversion versus introversion as the most basic dimension of human temperament and believed many major fluctuations and controversies in Western thought could be understood in terms of a clash between these opposing outlooks. He also believed that Western thought on the whole, in comparison with that of the Orient, stressed extraversion.

Jung defined extraversion as an outward turning of libido, or psychic energy. This is equivalent to saying that extraversion means a directing of interest toward objects (other people or things) in the environment and functioning in relation to those objects. In an extraverted state one perceives, thinks, feels, and acts in relation to the object. We might also say that action and experience are determined directly by the object. Introversion is defined as an inward turning of libido. This implies a directing of interest away from the object toward the subject—toward the individual's own conscious experience. In an introverted state, perception, thinking, feeling, and action are determined more directly by subjective factors than by the object. The extravert, the individual who is habitually in an extraverted state, tends to respond immediately and directly to stimuli from without. Habitually in an introverted state, the introvert tends to withhold immediate responses and act on the basis of subjective considerations that follow the external stimulus.

Jung (1921/1976) reviewed a variety of earlier dichotomous typologies and concluded that many of them represented equivalent expressions of the same basic dimension. He regarded hysteria and psychasthenia respectively as extraverted and introverted forms of psychoneurosis, and he suggested that manic-depressive psychosis and Schizophrenia represented a similar parallel in the realm of psychosis. He also concluded that the polarity of tough-minded versus tender-minded, which James (1907) applied to a basic division within the field of philosophy, was basically the same as his own dimension. It can be argued, however, that James's dimension is more concerned with ingredients of the psychic function dimensions described by Jung (thinking versus feeling and sensation versus intuition). There is evidence that the most basic division of perspectives evident in the histories of both philosophy and psychology is better characterized by the dimension postulated by James than by that of Jung (Coan, 1979). Many other theorists have proposed dichotomous typologies that involve some sort of inner-outer contrast, but it is a mistake to assume that these all involve the same underlying temperament dimension.

The dimension of extraversion versus introversion itself has been subject to a variety of interpretations. Upon learning of Jung's use of these terms, Freud concluded that extraversion was the healthy condition, while introversion constituted a predisposition to psychopathology. To Freud, an "inward turning of libido" implied narcissism, while an "outward turning of libido" implied the possibility of forming a true object-cathexis, hence the achievement of the genital level of development. Jung, however, did not construe extraversion and introversion in quite this way and considered neither to be preferable to the other. The Freudian perspective tends to prevail in any society, such as the United States, that favors extraversion over introversion.

There has been a tendency among American psychologists and educators to view extraversion as preferable and to reinterpret the dimension in terms of social behavior. Thus, extraversion has often been understood in terms of sociability, while introversion has been regarded as a tendency to withdraw from social contacts. Jung thought of the dimension primarily in terms of modes of experience or consciousness, and the behavioral definition itself reflects a more extraverted approach to psychology. Most efforts to construct questionnaire scales for the dimension reflect this shift in orientation, for the items have often contained extraversive scale content that pertains to sociability and introversive scale content that pertains to shyness, reserve, and anxiety. Even scales purported to measure the Jungian dimension usually focus on social behavior, because it is more difficult to formulate items that will evoke self-descriptions that directly express the variables conceptualized by Jung (Coan, 1978). A different method of assessment may be needed.

Murray (1938/1962) contended that Jung's concepts encompassed a number of component variables that might be distinguished and separately assessed. He suggested a component dimension of exocathection versus endocathection, which is concerned with the extent to which the individual attaches value to either the outer world or the inner world. He also posited a component dimension of extraception versus intraception. This is concerned with the extent to which perception, judgment, and action are governed either by observable, physical conditions or by subjective factors (feelings, fantasies, speculations, and aspirations).

Murray offered a rational analysis of Jung's concepts, but the work of some of the major factor-analytic researchers—including Cattell, Guilford, and Eysenck—indicates that semi-independent components of the extraversion-introversion dimension can be distinguished by statistical methods. These researchers concur in finding evidence for a broad general dimension of this sort, a dimension that enters into a large number of the specific individual differences we find in human personality. They differ in their identification and labeling of the components, but in the research findings of all three there is evidence of constituents of extraversion entailing such things as high activity level, sociability, impulsiveness, dominance, and dependence on the group. In contrast, such features as low activity level, deliberateness, and self-reliance are found to be associated with the introversive end of the dimension. Since the bulk of relevant factor-analytic research has focused on questionnaire responses, it is not surprising that the most obvious ingredients of the dimension lie in the realm of social behavior. In contrast, Murray's analysis remained closer to the polarity conceptualized by Jung.

Eysenck (1967) devoted particular attention to this dimension and, in interpreting it, borrowed a couple of physiological concepts from Pavlov. While studying temperamental variations among dogs, Pavlov concluded that some animals were characterized by a predominance of excitatory cortical processes, while others were characterized by a predominance of inhibitory cortical processes. Pavlov suggested a relationship between these processes and the four classical temperament types of Hippocrates and

Galen. Eysenck rejected Pavlov's rationale for this relationship, but he felt the process concepts could be used to explain the extraversion-introversion dimension. According to Eysenck, introverts are characterized by very sensitive cortical excitation processes. They tend, therefore, to feel intellectually and emotionally overwhelmed by moderate social and physical stimulation, and they are relatively prone to the experience of anxiety and despair. As a consequence, they often resort to a self-protective retreat from their surroundings and may limit interaction by means of self-control or behavioral inhibition. Extraverts are characterized by less sensitive cortical processes or by a predominance of inhibitory cortical processes. Consequently, they require more stimulation from the social environment and may actively seek it to overcome their own cortical inertia.

REFERENCES

Coan, R. W. (1978). Myers-Briggs Type Indicator. In O. K. Buros (Ed.), *The eighth mental measurements yearbook* (Vol. I). Highland Park, NJ: Gryphon.

Coan, R. W. (1979). *Psychologists: Personal and theoretical pathways.* New York: Irvington.

Eysenck, H. J. (1967). *The biological basis of personality.* Springfield, IL: Thomas.

James, W. (1907). *Pragmatism: A new name for some old ways of thinking.* New York: Longman Green.

Jung, C. G. (1976). *Psychological types.* Princeton, NJ: Princeton University Press. (Original work published 1921)

Murray, H. A. (1962). *Explorations in personality: A clinical and experimental study of fifty men of college age.* New York: Oxford University Press. (Original work published 1938)

Richard Welton Coan
University of Arizona

See also: **Introversion-Extraversion**

EYE

The eye performs three fundamental functions. Its optical components collect light energy. Its neural components transduce that light energy into electrochemical events and use these electrochemical events to produce meaningful neural signals that become the subjective sense of sight when further processed by the brain. All of the structures that make up the eye either contribute in some way to these functions or provide protection to the eye.

The protective tissue of the eye includes the lids and the transparent epithelial membrane known as the conjunctiva that lines the lids and continues to cover the white (sclera) of the eyeball. The tear or lacrimal glands and the fatty tissue of the orbit, which acts to absorb shock, also contribute protection to the eye.

The optical tissues of the eye include the cornea, the lens, the aqueous humor, and the vitreous humor or body. The cornea is the main structure responsible for refraction of light as it enters the eye. It normally does not have a blood supply. In addition to its refractive function, the cornea acts to protect the other optical structures of the eye and aids the sclera in giving the eye form and rigidity. The sclera is the tough white coat that forms the posterior four-fifths of the eye. The cornea is continuous with the sclera, and when the two structures are subjected to routine histological staining, the anatomical appearance of the cornea does not differ markedly from that of the sclera. The transparent quality of the cornea is due to a continual pumping of interstitial fluid across the cell surfaces, which prevents the cornea from becoming cloudy.

The lens of the eye lies behind the cornea and the pigmented iris. The lens is held in place by suspensory ligaments called the zonule fibers. The zonule fibers are connected to the ciliary body containing the ciliary muscle. When the ciliary muscle contracts, the lens bulges, thereby increasing the refraction of light. This happens, along with pupillary constriction and convergence of the eyes, as part of the accommodation reflex that occurs when an object close to the eyes is viewed. The image focused on the retina by the cornea and lens is upside down and reversed right to left.

The aqueous humor is secreted into the posterior chamber of the eye by epithelial cells that cover the ciliary body. Aqueous humor flows through the pupil to the anterior chamber of the eye, where it can exit the eye through the canals of Schlemm. Schlemm's canals are located in the angle of the anterior chamber where the iris contacts the cornea.

Both the posterior and anterior chambers of the eye lie in front of the lens and zonule fibers. The zonule fibers that encircle the lens consist of individual strands of connective tissue, and for this reason the fluid in the posterior chamber is in contact with the gelatinous substance called vitreous humor that fills the area of the eyeball between the lens and the retina. If the aqueous humor cannot drain through Schlemm's canals the resulting accumulation increases pressure within the eye, and this pressure is transmitted by the vitreous humor to the retina. This condition is called *glaucoma,* and the pressure on the retina can cause blindness.

The uvea, or vascular tunic, of the eye is composed of the iris, the ciliary body, and the choroid. The choroid is vascularized and pigmented. It lies between the retina and the sclera. Its pigmentation prevents the scattering of light in the eye. The iris lies posterior to the cornea and anterior to the lens. Light causes the iris to constrict. This reduces the amount of light that enters the eye but also enhances the depth of focus when the eye focuses on a near object. Thus, the iris constricts not only in response to increases in light but also as part of the accommodation reflex.

The retina is the photoreceptive and integrative portion of the eye. Embryologically, it is an outpouching of the surface of the brain. At the retina a light stimulus is converted into a neural code and transmitted over the optic nerve and tract to the brain. The neural organization of the retina is sufficiently complex to allow a fair amount of integration of visual information. The rods and cones are the photoreceptive cells of the retina and are located at the very back of the retina (i.e., in its most posterior aspect). The cones function during daylight and are responsible for color vision. The rods function best in dim light and present the world in shades of gray. Rods are most numerous in the periphery of the retina, while cones are concentrated toward the focal center. The fovea, or macula, is found in the focal center of the retina and contains only cones. The rods and cones make contact with the bipolar cells. In turn, the bipolar cells of the retina synapse with the ganglion cells. The ganglion cells give rise to axons which form the optic nerve. The point where all of the ganglion cell axons come together and leave the eye is called the papilla or optic nerve head. Because there are no receptors at this point, the papilla is a "blind spot" in the retina. Other neurons in the retina are associated with the bipolar layer and perform associative functions; they are known as horizontal and amacrine cells. The photoreceptive rods and cones are located behind the other retinal cells and the axons of the ganglion cells, such that light must pass through the axons, nonphotoreceptive neurons, and supporting glial cells before reaching the rods and cones.

The process of visual perception is initiated when light is absorbed by the photopigments contained within the outer segment of the rods and cones. Rhodopsin is contained within rods. The cones appear to utilize at least three separate photopigments, which have peak absorptions at wavelengths of light corresponding to the colors blue, green, and yellow. There is, however, considerable overlap in absorption among these pigments. Chemical changes initiated in the photopigments of the rods and cones when light is absorbed produce the rod and cone generator potentials.

SUGGESTED READING

Geneser, F. (1986). *Textbook of histology.* Copenhagen, Denmark: Munksgaard.

Hutchins, J. B., & Corbett, J. J. (1997). The visual system. In D. E. Haines (Ed.), *Fundamental neuroscience* (pp. 266–271). New York: Churchill Livingstone.

Koretz, J. F., & Handelman, G. H. (1988). How the human eye focuses. *Scientific American, 259,* 92–99.

May, P. J., & Corbett, J. J. (1997). Visual motor system. In D. E. Haines (Ed.), *Fundamental neuroscience* (pp. 399–416). New York: Churchill Livingstone.

Michael L. Woodruff
East Tennessee State University

EYE MOVEMENTS

The eyes are rarely stationary. To the viewer, the world seems quite stable and the eyes seem to be directed at will, but it is not so. Even when we intently view or fixate an object or scene, our eyes are free of large movements for only about 250 to 300 milliseconds, and fine movements are superimposed on even these seemingly stationary periods. Eye movements are generally functional in that they bring new information to central or foveal vision, and they change the scene so that receptors do not adapt and cease providing information to the visual cortex. Some eye movements such as fine tremors may be the result of muscle tension from the dense musculature servicing the visual system.

Each optical orbit is served by six muscles located in the medial aspect of the orbit. Anatomically they form three complement pairs. The medial rectus (nasal) and lateral rectus (temporal) allow for horizontal movement about the vertical axis. The superior rectus and inferior rectus provide practical complements for vertical movement, but they also have horizontal and torsional components allowing for oblique movement as well. The inferior and superior obliques, located slightly diagonal to one another, control torsional movements along with the superior and inferior rectus. Not only do these muscle groups provide for a great deal of latitude in movement, but their density also provides a greater amount of musculature for the weight of movable organs than does any other structure in the body. Consequently, there result great speed and great resiliency to fatigue.

Generally, the eyes move conjugately or in parallel; one exception is the vergence movement system, where the eyes move in opposite directions toward or away from the nose. Movements of the eyes are classified as catching, holding, and fine.

The next surge of interest in eye movements and reading came in the mid-1970s. Emphasis shifted to greater specificity on the parts of words on which the eye movements landed, and on the flexibility of eye movements to change dynamics between sentences within passages, based upon the reader's cognitive processing ability—that is, the perceived importance of text selections. Measuring devices have become much more comfortable, even though bite boards and head restraints are needed to achieve accuracy levels exceeding 1 min of arc and recording msec by msec. Other devices are aimed at more natural viewing with no encumbrances or awareness by the viewer, in order to get more naturalistic estimates of behavior with slight trade-offs in precision. Driving behavior, pilots' view of the ground and instruments, learning disabilities, psychopathologies, and many other areas of research interest involve recording of eye movements.

For nearly a century, principal empirical emphasis has been directed at verifying one of four proposed purposes for the eye movement sequence. First, eye movements may maintain vision: Without them, receptors adapt, and scenes and pictures fade from view. Second, eye movements and their fixations may be responsible for perception: They seem to exhibit a psychomotor program directly related to a particular picture or scene that is viewed. Third, eye movements and their fixations may be directed by perception: Because fixations seem to fall in locations judged to contain high information, such as contours, objects, and shadings, it is believed that some overall semantic content directs the eye movement pattern. Fourth, the eye movement sequence may provide a means for the encoding, storing, and subsequent reconstruction of the successive retinal images of the detail found in a scene or picture: Each individual provides an idiosyncratic eye movement pattern as a reflection of that individual's own viewing and interpretation of the scene. The possibility also exists that all these alternatives at one time or another are correct.

Dennis F. Fisher

EYSENCK PERSONALITY QUESTIONNAIRE

The Eysenck Personality Questionnaire–Revised Edition (EPQ-R) is the most recent version of the personality questionnaire designed to measure the three personality factors identified by Hans J. Eysenck (1916–1997) and others. These factors, known as psychoticism, extraversion, and neuroticism, comprise what is termed the P.E.N. Personality Model. The P.E.N. model holds that these three personality factors account for the bulk of human personality variation. That is, the model states that the personalities of humans differ primarily with respect to these three factors. Each personality factor is composed of a large number of specific traits. The EPQ-R is composed of 94 self-report items, such as "Do you like to arrive at appointments in plenty of time?" and "Do you worry a lot about your looks?" to which respondents either agree or disagree. The number of affirmative responses to items that compose each scale are summed to arrive at the scores on the three personality dimensions.

Individuals who have high scores on the Psychoticism subscale (27 items) have the potential to develop a psychotic disorder, as they may exhibit similar characteristics to those who have had a break with reality. These individuals may also have high levels of anger and are inclined to exhibit some types of conduct or behavioral disorders. They may be described as hostile or unempathic, and they may disregard societal conventions via nonconformity, recklessness, manipulation of others, and impulsivity. Other potential traits of people with high psychoticism scores include tough-mindedness, aggression, egocentrism, assertiveness, and dogmatism. Although there has been limited research on the biological basis of psychoticism, it has been suggested that these individuals have increased testosterone levels.

The Extraversion scale (22 items) measures one's level of sociability and affect. Individuals who have high scores on this subscale tend to be gregarious, carefree, and exciting. These individuals enjoy parties and feel the need to have other people with whom to talk. They are likely to be involved in social activities, and they may lose control quickly. Additional traits of people with high extroversion scores include irresponsibility, dominance, sensation seeking, and engagement in risk-taking behaviors. Individuals with low extraversion scores (a.k.a. introverts) are often characterized as reliable, somewhat pessimistic, and highly ethical. The biological correlates of extraversion include a high level of cortical arousal and general physiological arousal.

Individuals who score high on the Neuroticism scale (24 items) of the EPQ-R generally have a temperament reflective of negative affect. More specifically, they often possess high levels of anxiety and/or depression. These types of people may be frequently worried or nervous, often sleep poorly, and have high susceptibility to develop psychosomatic disorders. In addition, they may be overly emotional and react too strongly to events in their environment. Other traits that high scorers on the Neuroticism scale may have include feelings of guilt, moodiness, tenseness, obsessive thoughts, low self-esteem, and dependence. In terms of biological associations, it has been suggested that the basis for neuroticism is the sympathetic nervous system, which controls our "fight or flight" response to threatening environmental stimuli.

Self-report measures like the EPQ-R are, of course, subject to the honesty and accuracy of the respondent. Therefore, the EPQ-R also includes a "lie" scale (21 items) to detect inaccurate or socially desirable responding. If the respondent is not able to admit to a number of everyday human foibles or is trying to present him- or herself in an overly positive manner, the lie scale score will be high. When the lie scale score is high, the other scores are not interpreted.

The EPQ-R and its earlier versions have been used extensively in psychological research. That being the case, the psychometric properties of the EPQ-R have been the subject of much study. Studies of the psychometric properties of self-report questionnaires like the EPQ-R examine questions of reliability (i.e., are the scores repeatable or stable from one administration or time to the next?) and validity (i.e., do the scores really reflect levels individual differences in levels of the hypothesized construct—e.g., neuroticism—and not something else—e.g., anger?). Although the Neuroticism and Extraversion scales of the EPQ-R have received a substantial amount of empirical psychometric support, the Psychoticism scale has not. Specifically, scores on the Psychoticism scale have been shown to have low reliability. The construct of psychoticism has not been as extensively studied as neuroticism or extraversion, which may explain the psychometric weaknesses of the psychoticism scale.

In summary, the EPQ-R provides scores that allow for the clinical use of Hans J. Eysenck's P.E.N. model, which attempts to explain human personality variation. The EPQ-R has also been used extensively for psychological research. The extraversion and neuroticism scores have good reliability and validity for a variety of purposes. Scores on the psychoticism domain have been the focus of far less study, but even so it can be stated that they do not possess the same level of psychometric quality. The P.E.N. model is but one of many models used to explain and describe human personality, although it has enjoyed a prominent place among them. Perhaps the most important distinguishing characteristic of the P.E.N. model is the emphasis that P.E.N. supporters have placed on the biological basis of personality (see the earlier description of each personality factor). According to the leading P.E.N. researchers, personality is based in biology, and a personality factor can only be confirmed as such when biological markers or correlates are identified. This is in direct contrast to other personality models, like the Big Five Model or models based on "psychological type," where biological causes of personality are not required for the identification of a construct as a personality factor. Because P.E.N. theorists have placed this emphasis on biology, cross-species research has been more productive, even resulting in the thought-provoking notion that rats have the same three personality factors as humans!

John C. Caruso
J. D. Gottlieb
University of Montana

F

FACE RECOGNITION

Face recognition is an important and arguably unique human ability. Some researchers assert that face recognition is specific and neurally encapsulated (Fodor, 1983) or "special" (Ellis & Young, 1989), whereas others describe face recognition as a general, well-practiced perceptual skill (Bushnell, 1998). Although face recognition is rapid and seemingly effortless, it involves several levels of analysis. Numerous studies have detailed the workings of this process, its failure, and its development.

Accuracy

Bahrick, Bahrick, and Wittlinger (1975) documented that adults could distinguish the faces of high school classmates from others long after graduation. Fifty years later, participants recognized 75% of classmates' faces. Even brief exposures lead to extremely accurate recognition, although studies of eyewitness testimony indicate that recognition is not perfect (Goldstein, 1977). Specific modifications to face recognition tasks may affect performance. For example, recognition accuracy decreases when faces are inverted relative to pictures of objects such as houses or dogs (Scapinello & Yarmey, 1970; but see Diamond & Carey, 1986).

Prosopagnosia

Failure to recognize faces, prosopagnosia, is a rare but fascinating disorder that yields information about mechanisms. Prosopagnosics fail to recognize faces of persons they knew before onset of the disorder and the faces of those encountered frequently afterwards. The cause appears to be damage to the occipito-temporal regions of the central visual system, especially in the right hemisphere. Although *prosopagnosia* is meant to describe a face-processing deficit, individuals with this diagnosis may have difficulty with any stimulus that requires specific and context-related recognition (Damasio, Damasio, & Van Hoesen, 1982). More generalized deficits may reflect more widespread damage.

Nonhuman Primates

Nonhuman primates also show face recognition, for both human and nonhuman primate faces. Humans and squirrel monkeys recognize upright human and great ape faces better than inverted faces (Phelps & Roberts, 1994). Gross, Rocha-Miranda, and Bender (1972) discovered that some cells in monkeys' temporal cortex were selectively responsive to stimuli such as hands and faces. Similarly, Perrett and colleagues (1984) found cells that were especially responsive to a particular human face often seen by the monkey. Single neurons in the primate temporal lobe visual cortex respond primarily to faces and differentially to familiar faces (Rolls, Treves, Tovee, & Panzeri, 1998). Such evidence suggests that mechanisms have evolved that allow for early steps in a facial recognition process without extensive learning.

Development

Initially, human infants attend preferentially to faces. Goren, Sarty, and Wu (1975) discovered that newborns would visually track facelike images further than images that contained facial features but in noncanonical patterns. Newborns also recognize their mother's face. Infants at 12 to 36 hours produced more sucking responses upon viewing an image of their mother's face compared to an unfamiliar face matched for eye color, complexion, and hair color and style (Walton, Bower, & Bower, 1992).

A major developmental question is whether children treat faces as sets of independent features or as unified wholes. Cashon and Cohen (1999) found that after repeated exposure to two unfamiliar faces, 7-month-olds treated a composite face that combined the internal features of the two faces as novel. This configurational effect disappeared when it was inverted, suggesting that infants (like adults) process an *inverted* face as a set of features.

Summary

Human adults are highly skilled in the face detection, discrimination, and recognition. Infants show similar skills, recognizing their mothers' faces when newborns and using configurational information to discriminate faces by 7 months. Unequivocal evidence that face recognition is "special" or simply expert is not yet available, although neurophysiological data are becoming increasingly useful.

REFERENCES

Bahrick, H. P., Bahrick, P. O., & Wittlinger, R. P. (1975). Fifty years of memory for names and faces: A cross-cultural approach. *Journal of Experimental Psychology: General, 104,* 54–75.

Bushnell, I. W. R. (1998). The origins of face perception. In F. Simion & G. Butterworth (Eds.), *The development of sensory, motor and cognitive capacities in early infancy* (pp. 69–86). Hove, UK: Psychology Press.

Cashon, C. H., & Cohen, L. B. (1999, April). *Infant face perception: Do infants process independent features or the face as a whole?* Poster session presented at the meetings of the Society for Research in Child Development, Albuquerque, NM.

Diamond, R., & Carey, S. (1986). Why faces are and are not special: An effect of expertise. *Journal of Experimental Psychology: General, 115,* 107–117.

Damasio, A. R., Damasio, H., & Van Hoesen, G. W. (1982). Prosopagnosia: Anatomic basis and behavioural mechanisms. *Neurology, 32,* 331–341.

Ellis, H. D., & Young, A. W. (1989). Are faces special? In A. W. Young & H. D. Ellis (Eds.), *Handbook of research on face processing.* Amsterdam: North Holland.

Fodor, J. A. (1983). *The modularity of mind.* Cambridge, MA: MIT Press.

Goldstein, A. G. (1977). The fallibility of eyewitness: Psychological evidence. In B. D. Sales (Ed.), *Psychology in the legal process* (pp. 223–247). New York: Spectrum.

Goren, C. C., Sarty, M., & Wu, P. Y. K. (1975). Visual following and pattern discrimination of face-like stimuli by newborn infants. *Pediatrics, 56,* 544–549.

Gross, C. G., Rocha-Miranda, C. E., & Bender, D. B. (1972). Visual properties of neurons in inferotemporal cortex of the macaque. *Journal of Neurophysiology, 35,* 96–111.

Perrett, D., Smith, P. A. J., Potter, D. D., Mistlin, A. J., Head, A. S., Milner, A. D., et al. (1984). Neurones responsive to faces in the temporal cortex: Studies of functional organization, sensitivity to identity and relation to perception. *Human Neurobiology, 3,* 197–208.

Phelps, M. T., & Roberts, W. A. (1994). Memory for pictures of upright and inverted primate faces in humans (Homo sapiens), squirrel monkeys (Saimiri sciureus), and pigeons (Columba livia). *Journal of Comparative Psychology, 108,* 114–125.

Rolls, E. T., Treves, A., Tovee, M. J., & Panzeri. S. (1997). Information in the neuronal representation of individual stimuli in the primate temporal visual cortex. *Journal of Computational Neuroscience, 4,* 309–333.

Scapinello, K. I., & Yarmey, A. S. (1970). The role of familiarity and orientation in immediate and delayed recognition of pictorial stimuli. *Psychonomic Science, 21,* 329–330.

Walton, G., Bower, N. J. A., & Bower, T. G. R. (1992). Recognition of familiar faces by newborns. *Infant Behavior and Development, 15,* 265–269.

Arlene S. Walker-Andrews
Rutgers—The State University of New Jersey

FACE VALIDITY

Face validity refers to a characteristic associated with a psychological test and its individual items. Distinct from more technical types of validity, face validity is the appropriateness, sensibility, or relevance of the test and its items as they appear to the person answering the test. That is, do a test and its items look valid and meaningful to the individual taking the test? More formally, face validity has been defined as the degree to which a test respondent views the content of a test and its items as relevant to the situation being considered (Wiggins, 1973).

Three factors are important in the definition of face validity. First, face validity is based not on the judgments of psychologists or experts, but rather on the opinions of test takers who may be quite naive about the domain being assessed by the test. Second, face validity depends on the obviousness of the test item content (e.g., the test items may imply that a personality trait, such as neatness, is being measured). Third, the situation in which a test is given will influence face validity. Most important, however, in determining the face validity of a test or test item is the combination of these three factors. Consider the statement "Trying something new is scary," to which a test taker must answer either "true" or "false." If this item appeared on an employment test being given to job candidates who were applying to work for a manufacturing company, the applicants might feel that the test item is irrelevant or inappropriate for that testing situation (i.e., the item is not face valid). Further, if the entire employment test consisted of statements with similar content, then the test as a whole might be viewed as lacking face validity. Now, consider the same item being given on a test to patients newly admitted to a psychiatric hospital. For test takers in such a mental health setting, the test item might well seem to be quite appropriate and situationally relevant (i.e., the item is face valid).

Should test developers strive to construct tests that are face valid? The answer to this question depends on the test developer's theoretical orientation as well as on considerations of technical validity, public relations, and possible litigation.

The content of face-valid tests is readily identifiable by test takers and is susceptible to faking, either consciously or unconsciously. Test developers whose theoretical orientation emphasizes test respondent defensiveness (e.g., psychoanalytically oriented test developers), or test administrators who are employed in defensiveness-inducing situations (e.g., personnel or forensic settings) in which there is an assumption that individuals will not present themselves openly and honestly, believe that face-valid tests will result in inaccurate responses and, consequently, that such tests should be avoided. Alternatively, test constructors who possess a theoretical perspective that people will present themselves openly and honestly believe that direct, transparent (i.e., face-valid) tests are those of choice.

Research on technical validity has shown significant positive associations between face validity and test item accuracy (Holden & Jackson, 1979). Test items having face validity, on average, tend to be more technically valid or accurate (i.e., they are better items because they tend to be more strongly associated with a relevant criterion) than those items not possessing face validity. Further, research also indicates that, in circumstances under which test takers have been asked to fake responses, face-valid items (which are supposedly more susceptible to faking) are no less accurate than items that are not face valid (Holden & Jackson, 1985). Although the positive association between face validity and technical validity is significant and stable, it is not perfect, and consequently, cautions are warranted. Face validity may be related to better test items, but it does not guarantee other, more technical and desirable forms of validity. Thus, the mere appearance of relevance or face validity (e.g., as regularly found in tests published in popular magazines) fails to ensure a test's accuracy. Furthermore, the absence of face validity does not necessarily mean that a test or its items are inaccurate.

The face validity of a test is an important factor for issues of public relations and litigation (Nevo, 1985). Psychological testing should not be an antagonistic and seemingly irrelevant exercise for test respondents. Cooperation and good rapport between testers and test takers is sound practice in all assessment circumstances. The presence of face validity enhances test takers' motivation and effort (Bornstein, 1996) and the perceived relevance of a psychological test. Further, face validity reduces the likelihood of feelings of depersonalization and resentment in the individual being tested. The absence of face validity (regardless of technical validity or accuracy) may result in feelings of anger and frustration and of being cheated. Such feelings may well be acted on, resulting in negative media publicity, public demands for the cessation of testing programs (e.g., in schools), labor-management conflict, or even costly legal proceedings.

REFERENCES

Bornstein, R. F. (1996). Face validity in psychological assessment: Implications for a unified model of validity. *American Psychologist, 51,* 983–984.

Holden, R. R., & Jackson, D. N. (1979). Item subtlety and face validity in personality assessment. *Journal of Consulting and Clinical Psychology, 47,* 459–468.

Holden, R. R., & Jackson, D. N. (1985). Disguise and the structured self-report assessment of psychopathology: I. An analogue investigation. *Journal of Consulting and Clinical Psychology, 53,* 211–222.

Nevo, B. (1985). Face validity revisited. *Journal of Educational Measurement, 22,* 287–293.

Wiggins, J. S. (1973). *Personality and prediction: Principles of personality assessment.* Reading, MA: Addison-Wesley.

Ronald R. Holden
Queen's University, Ontario

See also: **Reliability; Validity**

FACTORIAL DESIGNS

A factorial design is one in which the effects of *two or more factors* are studied simultaneously. Because the factors are considered in the same design, both their individual effects (called *main effects*) and their joint effects (called *interactions*) on the dependent variable can be assessed.

Single-Factor Designs

First consider a design in which there is only one factor. Suppose an investigator wishes to assess the effects of fatigue on test performance by using three groups of subjects: low, moderate, and high fatigue. Because fatigue is the variable that is manipulated, it is referred to as the *independent variable* or *factor* in the design. The fatigue factor is said to have three *levels,* one for each fatigue group. More generally, the single factor in this experiment may be referred to as A and the levels as A_1, A_2, and A_3.

Test performance is measured for each participant and is referred to as the *dependent variable.* Even if the fatigue factor had no effect, we would not expect the mean test performance to be exactly the same at each level of fatigue, because of random variability. Analysis of variance (ANOVA) is a general statistical procedure for testing the null hypothesis that the population means at each level of a factor are equal.

Two-Factor Designs

We can change the one-factor design into a factorial design by adding a second factor, say, test difficulty, with levels low and high. More generally, we can say that a second factor B with levels B_1 and B_2 has been added to the design (see Table 1).

In this 3×2 factorial design (so called because factor A has thee levels and factor B has two), the effects of fatigue and test difficulty can be studied as well as their joint effects. There are six combinations of levels of fatigue and difficulty, each corresponding to a cell in the table. Now consider the idealized data presented in Table 1. We assume that there are equal numbers of participants in each condition and that there are no effects of random variability or measurement error, so that any differences obtained among groups will be due to *real* effects.

The number in each cell represents the mean test score for participants at the corresponding combination of levels of A and B. For example, the mean score for medium fatigue and low test difficulty is 70. The numbers outside the table are called *marginal* means, and they represent the means of rows and columns of the table.

Main Effects

If there is no error variability, we say that a factor has a main effect if the means of the levels of the factor are not all the same. In our example, there are main effects of both

Table 1. A 3 × 2 Factorial Design With no Interaction

Test Difficulty	Level of Fatigue			Averages
	Low	Medium	High	
Low	80	70	60	70
High	60	50	40	50
Averages	70	60	50	

Table 2. A 3 × 2 Factorial Design With an Interaction

Test Difficulty	Level of Fatigue			Averages
	Low	Medium	High	
Low	75	70	65	70
High	65	50	35	50
Averages	70	60	50	

fatigue and test difficulty. For test difficulty, the mean score for the low-difficulty test condition, 70, is 10 points higher than the average of the low and high difficulty levels, whereas the mean score in the high-difficulty test condition is 10 points lower. Therefore, the effects associated with the low- and high-difficulty conditions are +10 and –10. The corresponding effects for the low-, medium-, and high-fatigue conditions are +10, 0, and –10.

Interactions

In Table 1, the data are additive; that is, the effect of being in the A_1B_1 cell is the sum of the effects of being at level A_1 of A and level B_1 of B. However, in many cases particular combinations of levels of factors may have joint effects that cannot be obtained by adding the main effects of the factors. In Table 2 the marginal means, and hence the main effects for both factors are exactly the same as in Table 1. However, some of the cell means are different. The effect of the combination of high fatigue and high test difficulty (35 – 60 = –25) is not the same as the sum of the high fatigue and high test difficulty effects (–10 and –10). In this case there is a nonzero joint effect, and we say that there is a Difficulty × Fatigue interaction. There would be no Difficulty × Fatigue interaction if the differences between the low- and high-difficulty condition were the same for each level of fatigue.

Interactions and main effects are logically independent. Knowing whether or not there are A and B main effects does not tell us anything about whether or not there is an $A \times B$ interaction. It is possible to investigate interactions among factors only if they are considered in the same design.

Higher-Order Factorial Designs

In designs with more than two factors, there may be different kinds of interactions. If we have a design with three factors A, B, and C, we could have three *first-order interactions*, $A \times B$, $A \times C$, and $B \times C$. If we wished to consider, say, the $A \times B$ interaction, we could average over the levels of C. Similarly, if we wished to investigate the $B \times C$ interaction, we could average over levels of A, and so on. Higher-order interactions involve more than two factors. With factors A, B, and C it would be possible to have a second-order interaction, $A \times B \times C$. This would occur if, for example, the simple $A \times B$ interactions at each level of C were not all the same.

Arnold D. Well
University of Massachusetts

FAMILY THERAPY

The field of family therapy began to burgeon in the 1950s, partially because those who were to become the early pioneers were not satisfied with the slow progress they made when doing individual therapy or psychoanalysis, and because they recognized that the impact that changes in the patient had on family members could be great. If the significant others had no place to discuss what was occurring and their reactions to it, they might sabotage treatment; therefore, it would be better if they were part of the process. Moreover, there were huge waiting lists at agencies after World War II, so seeing couples or families together seemed a justifiable way to cut the patient backlog. Earlier roots of the family therapy movement existed in the child guidance movement, even though in child guidance clinics a psychiatrist usually saw the child while a social worker saw the parent, concurrently and not conjointly, and conjoint sessions would be the model in the emerging field of family therapy. Another tributary was the early approach to social work with troubled, multi-problem families (Richmond, 1917); however, this often entailed home visits rather than having whole families come to the therapist's office, which was to evolve as the most frequent practice in the ensuing 40-plus years. (For histories of the field see Guerin, 1976; Kaslow, 1982, 1987; Kaslow, Kaslow, & Farber, 1999). Interestingly, since the early 1990s there has been a resurgence of the practice of home-based treatment, both in the United States and other countries, with poor and multi-problem families who are unable or unwilling to get to therapists' offices (Sharlin & Shamai, 1999).

The fact that the field of family therapy had come into its own was marked by the birth of the journal *Family Process* in 1961, and the field's status was solidified by the subsequent inauguration of at least half a dozen other major family journals in the United States and several dozen additional ones in numerous other countries during the 1970s and 1980s. Books on this mammoth topic also have proliferated exponentially. The United States has spawned two major organizations that are dedicated to the field of family therapy. The American Association for Marriage and Family Therapy (AAMFT) began in 1942 as the American

Association of Marriage Counselors, which reflected its focus then. It was not changed to AAMFT until the late 1970s. The American Family Therapy Academy (AFTA) began in the mid-1970s as the American Family Therapy Association. The Division of Family Psychology (#41) of the American Psychological Association (APA) began in the mid-1980s and now has several thousand members, and is about double the size of AFTA. The American Psychiatric Association (ApA) also has a separate unit focused on the family. Other countries have established similar national and regional organizations.

There are also two major international organizations devoted to this discipline: the International Family Therapy Association (IFTA), started in 1987, and the International Academy of Family Psychology (IAFP), inaugurated in 1990. Using organization memberships, journal subscriptions, and the number of books published annually as a quantitative measure of the field's importance and stature, we can conclude that family therapy/psychology is indeed thriving in many countries of the world.

Some of the fundamental tenets of family therapy that have evolved and continue to be salient include the following: (1) The members of a family constitute a system, with all parts interdependent and interrelated; (2) change in any part (member) of the system causes corresponding changes in all other members of the system; (3) families range on a continuum from dysfunctional, through mid-range, to quite functional and healthy; (4) some members of families seek to retain the existing homeostatic balance or equilibrium, whereas other members, usually the younger ones, try to alter that balance; (5) many dysfunctional families are characterized by rigid alliances, schisms, and secrets; (6) healthy families exhibit good problem-solving skills, integrity, and open communication styles; (7) boundaries between generations should be clear and should not be crossed inappropriately; and (8) some patterns are transmitted intergenerationally, and these can be detrimental or healthy, depending on the pattern. There are additional basic principles; the ones presented here comprise just a representative sample of the core tenets.

Over the years a variety of schools of family therapy have emerged (Becvar & Becvar, 1996). Each theory or school has had its major progenitor(s) and its second-, third-, and fourth-generation leaders and staunch followers (Kaslow et al., 1999). Each theory promulgates a somewhat different viewpoint as to the definition of therapy and how treatment should be conducted—that is, the process and techniques that it advocates. Each school is predicated upon ideas about what makes change occur, and most articulate the interventions to use, which should be consonant with the theory's underlying assumptions and beliefs (Goldenberg & Goldenberg, 1996; Nichols & Schwartz, 1995).

We have divided and organized the theories into four categories and subsumed the most prominent of the contemporary approaches under the heading that seems most appropriate. The various theories have fluctuated in popularity; once having waned, they occasionally experience a resurgence of interest and again come to occupy a central position within the spectrum of available explanatory theories of family dynamics, structure, and functioning. Different theories have adherents in different countries, depending on where they were generated initially, which leaders have come to that region to present workshops on their own approaches, and which therapeutic styles and methodologies are most compatible with their cultural context. Our typology follows (Kaslow et al, 1999).

I. Transgenerational schools
   A. Psychodynamically informed (including object relations approaches)
   B. Bowenian
   C. Contextual/relational
   D. Symbolic/experiential
II. Systems models
   A. Communications
   B. Strategic
   C. Structural
   D. Systemic
   E. Brief and solution focused
III. Cognitive and behavioral models
   A. Behavioral
   B. Functional
   C. Cognitive-behavioral
IV. Miscellaneous
   A. Psychoeducational
   B. Narrative
   C. Social constructionist (including postmodern linguistic approaches)
   D. Integrative (including comprehensive and multimodal models)

The field to date has witnessed the ascendance of a bevy of charismatic leaders, some of whom attain guru status and garner disciples. However, in the last two decades at least part of the field, noticeably the more research-trained psychologists, has pushed for analysis and validation of what works through both qualitative and quantitative research on process and outcome variables, reaching beyond what people believe works based mainly on clinical evidence and personal testimonials.

Another controversial area in the field is the issue of whether graduate and professional students should first be trained broadly, learning many of the theories and only then going on to gain greater knowledge and competence in one or several theories and a set of techniques they believe have greatest efficacy, or whether they should learn one theory and its accompanying techniques in depth before being exposed to multiple approaches. Some see this latter training model as akin to indoctrination with a catechism, yet others deliberately select such curriculum and model.

Family theoreticians and practitioners, supervisors, and

researchers continue to be drawn from the fields of psychology, psychiatry, social work, marriage and family therapy, sociology, counseling and guidance, and nursing. Such diversity enriches the field, yet it also contributes to interdisciplinary tensions and conflicts around licensing—that is, the issue of who can use the title and practice marriage and family therapy. These turf conflagrations are apt to continue.

Since we are all born into a family and grow up in our family of origin or an adoptive or foster family, and most people later move on to create their own families, the fascination with the family as a system and as a unit that merits professional and societal attention no doubt will continue unabated for many decades to come. Therapists of all disciplines and theoretical persuasions share this fascination and find doing family therapy challenging, stimulating, frustrating, rewarding, and quite gratifying.

REFERENCES

Becvar, D. S., & Becvar, R. J. (1996). *Family therapy: A systemic integration* (3rd ed.). Needham Heights, MA: Allyn & Bacon.

Goldenberg, I., & Goldenberg, H. (1996). *Family therapy: An overview* (4th ed.). Pacific Grove, CA: Brooks/Cole.

Guerin, P. J. (1976). Family therapy: The first twenty-five years. In P. J. Guerin (Ed.), *Family therapy and practice* (pp. 2–22). New York: Gardner Press.

Kaslow, F. W. (1982). History of family therapy in the United States: A kaleidoscopic overview. In F. W. Kaslow (Ed.), *The international book of family therapy* (pp. 5–40). New York: Bruner/Mazel.

Kaslow, F. W. (1987). Marital and family therapy. In M. B. Sussman & S. K. Steinmetz (Eds.), *Handbook of marriage and the family* (pp. 835–860). New York: Plenum Press.

Kaslow, N. J., Kaslow, F. W., & Farber, E. W. (1999). Theories and techniques of marital and family therapy. In M. B. Sussman, S. K. Steinmetz, & G. W. Peterson (Eds.), *Handbook of marriage and the family* (2nd ed., pp. 767–793). New York: Plenum Press.

Nichols, M. P., & Schwartz, R. C. (1995). *Family therapy: Concepts and methods* (3rd ed.). Boston, MA: Allyn & Bacon.

Richmond, M. (1917). *Social diagnosis.* New York: Russell Sage Foundation.

Sharlin, S. A., & Shamai, M. (1999). *From distress to hope: Intervening with poor and disorganized families.* New York: Haworth.

Florence W. Kaslow
Florida Couples and Family Institute

FAST AXOPLASMIC TRANSPORT

Fast axoplasmic transport (also known as *fast axonal transport*) is defined as the movement of vesicles in the axon and dendrites of nerve cells at speeds that range between 200 and 400 mm/day. Vesicle transport occurs in both directions along the axon and dendrites. The fast speed of movement distinguishes vesicle transport from the transport of soluble proteins that move along the axon at speeds of 0.5–3 mm/day (slow axonal transport). Schematically, a nerve cell can be subdivided into a cell body (perikaryon), short-branched dendrites, and a long axon. The diameter of the axon is small compared to the diameter of the cell body and the axon can reach a length of many centimeters. Therefore the end of the axon or axon terminal is often located a long distance from the cell body. The membrane proteins of axoplasmic vesicles are synthesized in the cell body where the rough endoplasmic reticulum (ER) and Golgi apparatus reside. Therefore transport of vesicles into the axon is required to supply synaptic vesicles at the axon terminal and for axon survival and regeneration. Fast axonal transport is also the mechanism by which membrane components are returned to the cell body for degradation.

The diameter of vesicles that are transported in the axon ranges in size from very small (50 nm, e.g., synaptic vesicles) to very large (1,000 nm, e.g., multivesicular bodies). The transport of vesicles originating in the cell body and traveling toward the axon terminal is defined as *anterograde transport.* The transport of vesicles originating at the axon terminal and traveling toward the cell body is defined as *retrograde transport.* The vesicles in transit along the axon represent the cargo transported by molecular motors as they travel on filaments of the cytoskeleton. There are three types of cytoskeletal filaments in neurons, called neurofilaments (10 nm in diameter), microtubules (25 nm), and actin filaments (6 nm). Only the latter two types of filaments are known to function as tracks or rails on which molecular motors transport cargo. Molecular motors require chemical energy in the form of ATP (adenosine triphosphate) to transport vesicles, and therefore the proteins are called *ATPases.* Molecular motors are filament-type specific. Kinesin and cytoplasmic dynein are the molecular motors that transport vesicles along microtubules (Hirokawa, 1998), and myosin is the motor that transports vesicles on actin filaments (DePina & Langford, 1999; Mermall, Post, & Mooseker, 1998).

Microtubules are usually long filaments (> 25 μm) and have an intrinsic polarity due to the identical orientation of the tubulin subunits within the filaments. To distinguish the two ends of the microtubule, one is called the plus end (fast-growing end) and the other the minus end (slow-growing). All microtubules in the axon are aligned parallel to the long axis of the axon with their plus ends distal relative to the cell body. The molecular motor kinesin is a plus end-directed motor—that is, it transports vesicles toward the plus end of the microtubule or away from the cell body (anterograde transport). Cytoplasmic dynein is a minus end-directed motor and is responsible for vesicle transport from the axon terminal (retrograde transport). The specific type of motor attached to a vesicle determines the direction in which it will be transported in the axon. Kinesin has been shown to be associated with synaptic vesicles, synaptic precursor vesicles, mitochondria, multivesicular bodies, and presynaptic membrane precursor vesicles. Cytoplasmic dynein has been shown to be associated with retrogradely transported vesicles in axons including early and late endosomes and lysosomes.

Actin filaments in the axon are short (1 μm) compared to the length of microtubules (Fath & Lasek, 1988), and they too have an intrinsic polarity due to the identical orientation of the actin subunits that make up the filaments. The terms *plus end* and *minus end* are used to distinguish the two ends of the actin filaments. The two ends of actin filament are sometimes referred to as *barbed* (plus) and *pointed* (minus) ends like the two ends of an arrow. Actin filaments form a cross-linked network near the cell membrane (the cell cortex). The plus ends of some actin filaments are attached to the plasma membrane. The molecular motors that transport vesicles on actin filaments are part of a large superfamily of myosins. Most myosins are plus end-directed motors and therefore move vesicles toward the plus ends of actin filaments.

Vesicles move over long distances in the axon on microtubules and transition onto actin filaments provides short-range movement in the cell cortex (Langford & Molyneaux, 1998). Therefore short-range movement functions to localize vesicles to membrane sites for capture, docking and fusion with the plasma membrane (DePina & Langford, 1999). Examples of vesicles that move on actin filaments are synaptic vesicles at the presynaptic terminal of the axon (Prekeris & Terrian, 1997) and smooth ER vesicles within the spines of neuronal dendrites and along the axon membrane (Dekker-Ohno et al., 1997; Tabb, Molyneaux, Cohen, Kuznetsov, & Langford, 1998). The class of myosin shown to transport endoplasmic reticulum (ER) vesicles in the squid giant axon (Tabb et al., 1998), synaptic vesicles in the axon terminal (Prekeris & Terrian, 1997), and ER in the spines of Purkinje cell dendrites (Dekker-Ohno et al., 1996; Takagishi et al., 1996) is myosin-V. Recent studies have shown that myosin-V interacts with kinesin, a microtubule-based motor. The functional significance of the interactions between kinesin and myosin-V has not been established. However, one plausible hypothesis is that interactions between these motors provide feedback and thereby allow coordination of motor activity during the transition of vesicles from microtubules to actin filaments. Such feedback between motors could explain the seamless transition of vesicles from microtubules to actin filaments observed in squid neurons. Therefore the direct interaction of motors from both filament systems may represent the mechanism by which the transition of vesicles from microtubules to actin filaments is regulated during fast axonal/dendritic transport.

REFERENCES

Dekker-Ohno, K., Hayasaka, S., Takagishi, Y., Oda, S., Wakasugi, N., Mikoshiba, K., et al. (1996). Endoplasmic reticulum is missing in dendritic spines of Purkinje cells of the ataxic mutant rat. *Brain Research, 714,* 226–230.

DePina, A. S., & Langford, G. M. (1999). Vesicle transport: The role of actin filaments and myosin motors. *Microscopy Research Technique, 47,* 1–14.

Fath, K. R., & Lasek, R. J. (1988). Two classes of actin microfilaments are associated with the inner cytoskeleton of axons. *Journal of Cell Biology, 107,* 613–621.

Hirokawa, N. (1998). Kinesin and dynein superfamily proteins and the mechanism of organelle transport. *Science, 279,* 519–526.

Langford, G. M., & Molyneaux, B. (1998). Myosin V in the brain: Mutations lead to neurological defects. *Brain Research Review, 28,* 1–8.

Mermall, V., Post, P. L., & Mooseker, M. S. (1998). Unconventional myosins in cell movement, membrane traffic, and signal transduction. *Science, 279,* 527–533.

Prekeris, R., & Terrian, D. M. (1997). Brain myosin V is a synaptic vesicle-associated motor protein: Evidence for a Ca^{2+}-dependent interaction with the synaptobrevin-synaptophysin complex. *Journal of Cell Biology, 137,* 1589–1601.

Tabb, J. S., Molyneaux, B. J., Cohen, D. L., Kuznetsov, S. A., & Langford, G. M. (1998). Transport of ER vesicles on actin filaments in neurons by myosin V. *Journal of Cellular Science, 111,* 3221–3234.

Takagishi, Y., Oda, S., Hayasaka, S., Dekker-Ohno, K., Shikata, T., Inouye, M., et al. (1996). The dilute-lethal (dl) gene attacks a Ca^{2+} store in the dendritic spine of Purkinje cells in mice. *Neuroscience Letters, 215,* 169–172.

George M. Langford
Dartmouth College

FECHNER'S LAW

Gustav T. Fechner (1801–1887), professor of physics at the University of Leipzig, sought to measure the mind quantitatively. In approaching this task he studied stimuli and the sensations they aroused. His interest was in ascertaining how sensations changed with changing stimulation. While lying in bed on the morning of October 22, 1850, he conceived the essential idea of what was later to be called Fechner's law. In his subsequent derivation of the law (which appears at the beginning of the second volume of *Elemente der Psychophysik*), he began with Weber's law (that the just noticeable difference in stimulation is a constant proportion of the stimulus magnitude, or $JND = kI$) and the assumption that the sensation (R) of a stimulus is the cumulative sum of equal sensation increments. Translating this into differential form, he started with $dR = dI/I$ and integrated, under the assumption that $R = 0$ at absolute threshold (I_0), to get the equation $R = c \log(I/I_0)$. This equation is Fechner's law, where R is the sensation magnitude, c is a constant (which depends on the logarithmic base and the Weber ratio), I is the stimulus intensity, and I_0 is the absolute threshold intensity. The law states that sensations follow a negatively accelerated increasing (logarithmic) curve. For example, the increase in brightness experienced in going from 1 to 10 lamps would be the same as the increase in brightness in going from 10 to 100 lamps. This is a special case of the general relationship, algebraically derivable from his law, that the stimulus magnitude (I_b) required to generate a sensation midway in magnitude to those sensations generated by stimuli of magnitudes I_a and I_c is exactly equal to the square root of the product of I_a and I_c (i.e., the geometric mean). Sensation magnitudes increase arithmetically when stimulus magnitudes increase geometrically.

In order to work with his formulation Fechner needed to know the value of the absolute threshold, I_0. In the first volume of his *Elemente der Psychophysik* Fechner describes methods for measuring differential sensitivity to stimuli (and later suggests their application to absolute sensitivity). These are the classical psychophysical methods that have been used by psychologists and others to determine thresholds (absolute and difference) for the various senses. They have also been used (with modifications) for clinical assessment of hearing, vision, and (to a limited extent) other senses. Fechner's law influences everyday life through applications in acoustics. A standard measure of sound is the sound pressure level (SPL) scale defined by the (Fechnerian) equation $SPL = 20 \log (P/P_0)$, where P is the pressure of the sound being measured and P_0 is the absolute threshold pressure. The volume control used in radio and television receivers (among other audio devices) is a variable resistor that has a logarithmic (or approximately logarithmic) variation in resistance in order to provide a positively accelerating audio amplitude output to counteract the negatively accelerated sensation response specified by Fechner's law, thereby resulting in a fairly even increase in loudness as the amplitude is increased by adjusting the volume control.

SUGGESTED READING

Boring, E. G. (1942). *Sensation and perception in the history of experimental psychology.* New York: Appleton-Century-Crofts.

Fechner, G. T. (1964). *Elemente der Psychophysik.* Amsterdam: E. J. Bonnet. (Original work published 1860)

Fechner, G. T. (1966). *Elements of psychophysics* (D. H. Howes & E. G. Boring, Eds., H. E. Adler, Trans.). New York: Holt, Rinehart and Winston. (Original work published 1860)

Marks, L. E., & Gescheider, G. A. (2002). Psychophysical scaling. In H. Pashler (Ed. in Chief) & J. Wixted (Vol. Ed.), *Stevens' handbook of experimental psychology: Vol. 4. Methodology in experimental psychology* (pp. 91–138). New York: Wiley.

Uttal, W. R. (1973). *The psychobiology of sensory coding.* New York: Harper & Row.

G. H. Robinson

FEMALE SEX THERAPY

Sex therapy starts with the correct diagnosis of the sexual dysfunction presented by the patient. This is not an easy task considering the vague diagnoses provided by the fourth edition of the *Diagnostic and Statistical Manual of Mental Disorders* (*DSM-IV;* American Psychiatric Association, 2000), the high comorbidity of sexual dysfunctions, and the lack of age-related norms for the female sexual response. The common agreement is to look at medical etiology of the sexual complaints and then to follow with the investigation of personal and relational aspects. After this initial phase, the most liberal therapists discuss potential goals and patient's expectations, which are not limited to sexual intercourse but could include skills such as communication and assertiveness, or feelings of enjoyment and comfort during sexual behaviors. The techniques used in sex therapy vary according to treatment goals, dysfunction, and patient characteristics. Because sex therapy is a symptom-oriented approach, much of the rational is borrowed from the cognitive-behavioral school. In order to select the most appropriate form of sex therapy and therapy goals, patient characteristics such as age, sexual orientation, ethnic background, and cultural expectations need to be considered.

Sexual Desire Disorders

Hypoactive Sexual Desire Disorder

Women with hypoactive sexual desire disorder (HSDD) complain of a low interest in general sexual activities. There are currently no empirically validated treatments for HSDD. Sex therapy techniques generally consist of 15 to 45 sessions of cognitive therapy aimed at restructuring thoughts or beliefs that may adversely impact sexual desire (e.g., "women should not initiate sexual activities," "sex is dirty") and addressing negative underlying relationship issues. Behavioral approaches are utilized to teach patients to express intimacy and affection in both nonsexual (e.g., holding hands, hugging) and sexual ways, to incorporate new techniques into their sexual repertoire that may enhance their sexual pleasure, and to increase sexual communication. Testosterone is effective in restoring sexual desire in women with abnormally low testosterone levels (e.g., secondary to removal of the adrenal glands, bilateral removal of the ovaries, menopause).

Sexual Aversion Disorder

Defined as the avoidance of sexual genital contact with a partner, sexual aversion disorder (SAD) has a high comorbidity with history of sexual abuse, vaginismus, and dyspareunia. Treatment for this condition often combines couples and cognitive therapy and focuses on solving the couple's conflict areas, emotional differences, and issues of control. Anxiety reduction techniques such as systematic desensitization are used when the aversion is accompanied by strong feelings of anxiety. Systematic desensitization consists of identifying a hierarchy of sexual activities that provoke anxiety and then pairing relaxation techniques with imagining the sexual activity. The goal is for the patient to feel relaxed while imagining each sexual activity and eventually while actually engaging in each sexual activity. Some therapists feel that, when treating sexual abuse survivors, trauma-related issues need to be resolved before addressing SAD.

Arousal Disorders

Female Sexual Arousal Disorder

Female sexual arousal disorder (FSAD) is operationalized as the difficulty in reaching and maintaining vaginal lubrication or genital swelling until the completion of the sexual activity (ApA, 2000). Recently, theorists have argued that diagnosis of FSAD should consider not only the physiological dimension of sexual arousal (i.e., lubrication) but the psychological experience as well. Women of all ages may experience difficulty lubricating, although it tends to be more of a problem in later life, typically after menopause. Female sexual arousal disorder is generally assessed and treated in conjunction with female orgasmic disorder or HSDD. To date, there are no validated treatments that focus exclusively on treating female arousal problems, although a number of pharmacological agents for enhancing vaginal engorgement and lubrication are currently under investigation. Techniques are often employed to help the patient become aware of her anxiety or her sexual turn-off thoughts, emotions, or behaviors. To help facilitate arousal, the patient is sometimes trained in the development of sexual fantasies, communication skills, sexual assertiveness, sensate focus, and the use of erotica or vibrators. Lubricants such as KY Jelly or Astroglide are often recommended to help compensate for decreased lubrication. Recently, the Federal Drug Administration approved a hand-held battery-operated device called EROS-CTD for the treatment of FSAD. This suction device is placed over the clitoral tissue and draws blood into the genital tissue.

Orgasm Disorders

Female Orgasmic Disorder

Female orgasmic disorder (FOD) is defined in the *DSM-IV* (ApA, 2000) as the delay or absence of orgasm following a normal sexual excitement phase. The cognitive-behavioral treatment approach has received the greatest amount of empirical support for treating FOD. Reported success rates range between 88% and 90%. This therapy technique aims at reducing anxiety-producing thoughts associated with sexual activities and increasing positive behavioral experiences. The treatment is moderately short, averaging 10 to 20 sessions. The major treatment components include sensate focus, directed masturbation, and systematic desensitization. Sensate focus involves exchanging physical caresses, moving from nonsexual to increasingly sexual touching of one another's body over an assigned period of time. Directed masturbation involves a series of at-home exercises that begin with visual and tactile total body exploration and move toward increased genital stimulation with the eventual optional use of a vibrator. Directed masturbation is the technique with the best success rates; systematic desensitization is particularly useful when anxiety plays a primary role in the dysfunction. Couples therapy that focuses on enhancing intimacy and increasing communication has also been used for the treatment of FOD, but the success rates of this approach have not been well established.

Sexual Pain Disorders

Dyspareunia

Dyspareunia refers to genital pain associated with intercourse (APA, 2000). Vulvar vestibulitis is the most common type of premenopausal dyspareunia, whereas vulvar or vaginal atrophy is mostly reported by postmenopausal women. Women with these types of dyspareunia complain of pain in the vulvar area or anterior portion of the vagina upon penetration. The assessment of the type of dyspareunia should include information on the location, quality, intensity, time course, and meaning of the pain. The few studies that have examined treatment efficacy showed a moderate success rate of cognitive-behavioral techniques and biofeedback. The cognitive-behavioral approach includes education and information about dyspareunia, training in progressive muscle relaxation and abdominal breathing, Kegel exercises to train the patient to identify vaginal tenseness and relaxation, use of vaginal dilators, distraction techniques to direct the patient's focus away from pain cues, communication training, and cognitive restructuring of negative thoughts. During biofeedback, the patient is instructed to contract and relax her vaginal muscles while a surface electromyographic sensor inserted in her vagina provides her with feedback on muscular tenseness.

Vaginismus

Vaginismus is the involuntary contraction of the outer third of the vagina, which impedes penetration of fingers, tampons, or penis. Sex therapy for vaginismus often consists of a form of systematic desensitization that involves instructing the woman to insert graded vaginal dilators into her vagina. The woman's control over the insertion of the dilators is an important aspect of the therapy. The role of the partner in the exercise is passive if present at all. The emotional and psychological aspects of vaginismus are approached through patient education and control. Exercises that reduce anxiety and replace anxiety-provoking thoughts with positive sexual thoughts are sometimes used in conjunction with the behavioral techniques.

REFERENCE

American Psychiatric Association. (2000). *Diagnostic and statistical manual of mental disorders* (4th ed., text revision). Washington, DC: Author.

Cindy M. Meston
Alessandra Rellini
University of Texas, Austin

FEMALE SEXUAL DYSFUNCTION

Dysfunctions in female sexuality may occur in each phase of the sexual response cycle: desire, arousal, and orgasm or resolution. In addition, there may be pain or muscle spasm that prevents penile penetration or enjoyment of coitus. All can occur at random, during specific situations, or as a primary dysfunction in which the disorder has always been present.

Sexual dysfunctions in females, as in males, may stem from anxiety. Helen S. Kaplan described the causes as either current or remote. Current or ongoing causes occur during the sexual experience and create distraction, fear, anger, or other unpleasant emotional states; these interfere with the ability to relax and allow sexual arousal to build. Such immediate causes might include fear of failure, performance anxiety, lack of effective sexual technique, failure to communicate desires, or *spectatoring*—a term coined by William Masters and Virginia Johnson to describe conscious monitoring and judging of sexual behavior. Remote causes are derived from previous childhood experiences, intrapsychic conflict, and/or serious problems within the relationship between sexual partners. Guilt about past sexual experiences, extremely restrictive family and religious backgrounds, a history of traumatic sexual experiences such as incest or sexual assault, or unconscious conflicts that evoke anxiety at the time of sexual encounters may result in maladaptive sexual functioning. Because sexual activities are more discouraged for females in Western cultures, there may be more difficulties in sexual functioning for adult women than for men. When the sexual disorder is absolute and arousal or orgasm has never occurred, remote causes are highly suspect in etiology. Current factors creating anxiety are more typically responsible for random or situational dysfunctions.

Relationship variables are frequent etiological factors. Communication problems, anger, lack of attraction to or love for the partner, power struggles, and lack of trust and respect create rejection, hostility, and distance between sexual partners. This impairs the woman's ability to abandon herself to sexual pleasure.

Disorders of Desire

Disorders of desire were identified later than were other dysfunctions, when the scope of sexual performance was expanded to include the preliminary emotional and physical reactions of arousal and desire. Kaplan states that inhibited or hypoactive sexual desire may be the most common, sexual dysfunction.

Inhibited sexual desire (ISD) is referred to in the *Diagnostic and Statistical Manual of Mental Disorders,* fourth edition (*DMS-IV*) as a "persistent and pervasive inhibition of sexual desire" (i.e., the woman experiences low libido, lack of sexual response to genital stimulation, and lack of or very limited interest in and satisfaction with sexual activities). Women may react to this dysfunction with any of a wide range of emotions, from nonchalant acceptance to worry and acute distress. Sexual dysfunction is diagnosed when the individual experiences distress with the symptom. Absolute or primary inhibited desire is rare; situational ISD is more common.

Orgasmic Dysfunction

Orgasmic dysfunction is present when the female has great difficulty in experiencing orgasm or is unable to do so with effective sexual stimulation. Adequate desire and physiological and emotional arousal may be present, but anxiety interrupts the arousal buildup prior to the orgasmic relief.

Controversy reigned for many years about the types of female orgasm and the desirability of each. Vaginal and clitoral orgasms were alleged before the work of Masters and Johnson in 1966. With laboratory data, they concluded that all orgasms are essentially similar and consist of sensory input from the clitoris and muscle contractions by the vagina. Conclusive data do not exist concerning the incidence of women who have orgasms during coitus without concurrent clitoral stimulation, although estimates range from 30 to 50%.

Vaginismus

Vaginismus is an involuntary spasm of the vaginal muscles that prevents penile penetration. Arousal and orgasm may be present, but penetration is impossible. This spasm is a conditioned response to the anticipation of pain with intercourse; phobic avoidance of intercourse is often present. Etiology may include incidents of rape, painful attempts at coitus, vaginal and pelvic conditions that engender pain with sexual contact (vaginal infections, endometriosis, pelvic inflammatory disease), or misinformation or ignorance about sex. Vaginismus is a major factor in unconsummated marriages and is accompanied by fantasies of physical injury and pain. Gradual dilation of the vagina in a short time span (a few days) can often eliminate the muscle spasm and allow for penetration.

Dyspareunia

Dyspareunia is similar to vaginismus in that there is pain associated with sexual intercourse; however, the involuntary vaginal muscle spasm is absent. Dyspareunia may be caused by insufficient vaginal lubrication due to lack of sexual arousal, senile vaginitis, or reactions to medication. It may also result from gynecological disorders such as herpes, vaginal infection, endometriosis, rigid hymen, or hymeneal tags. When pain accompanies intercourse, anxiety results, arousal diminishes, and there is avoidance of sexual encounter. Complete physical and pelvic examinations are required in the assessment and treatment of dyspareunia because of the many physical factors that could contribute to the pain.

Sexual dysfunction typically is treated with some form of sex therapy. Often this is brief, behaviorally focused therapy that aims at symptom removal. Barriers to effective sexual functioning are identified, and a combination of communication and sensual touching assignments are given.

DIANNE GERARD

See also: **Anxiety; Nymphomania**

FETAL ALCOHOL SYNDROME: BACKGROUND, TREATMENT, AND PREVENTION

Historical Background

Suggested adverse effects of maternal drinking appeared in seventeenth-century England, and several observers reported that mothers who drank heavily during the early eighteenth-century "gin epidemic" had children who were small, sickly, and mentally slow. In the nineteenth-century, reports linked stillbirth, infant mortality, and mental retardation to maternal drinking during pregnancy. However, claims of ancient descriptions of damaging effects of maternal alcohol consumption appear to be erroneous (Abel, 1984).

Formal studies in the early 1900s failed to find adverse effects of maternal drinking. Montagu's conclusion seemed well founded in 1965: "[I]t now can be stated categorically . . . that no matter how great the amount of alcohol taken by the mother . . . neither the germ cells nor the development of the child will be affected" (p. 114). However, Lemoine, Harousseau, Borteryu, and Menuet (1968) reported abnormalities in the three areas now associated with fetal alcohol syndrome (growth retardation, low intelligence, and facial anomalies) in children of alcoholic parents, and in 1973 fetal alcohol syndrome (FAS) was named and thoroughly described (e.g., Jones, Smith, Ulleland, & Streissguth, 1973).

Incidence and Risk Factors

Incidence of FAS is approximately 1 in 1,000 live births worldwide and many times higher in the United States (Abel, 1998). Estimates vary widely across study and country, reflecting national or regional differences, sampling errors, and differing diagnostic criteria. Combined incidence of FAS and less severe fetal alcohol effects (FAE) or alcohol-related neurodevelopmental disorder (ARND) may be 9 in 1,000 births (Sampson et al., 1997).

Full FAS apparently occurs only with heavy maternal drinking, and incidence and degree of FAE/ARND increases with amount of prenatal maternal alcohol consumption (e.g., Abel, 1998). Animal experiments confirm that the damage is from prenatal alcohol and not secondary to another factor (e.g., Abel, 1998; Sampson et al., 1997). Although some (e.g., Abel, 1998) claim that prenatal alcohol exposure has a threshold effect, considerable research suggests that many effects show a continuous dose-response relationship (e.g., Sampson et al., 1997). Indeed, alcohol-exposed children without characteristic FAS features show significant deficits in IQ relative to normal children (Mattson & Riley, 1998).

FAS occurs much more commonly in offspring of mothers of lower socioeconomic status (SES) even after equating alcohol intake in different SES women (Abel & Hannigan, 1995). Binge drinking is a particularly high risk factor; other factors include minority ethnic status, smoking, maternal age, and undernutrition (e.g., Abel, 1998; Abel & Hannigan, 1995).

Genetic factors in both offspring and mothers also play a role. Fraternal twins of alcoholic mothers show differential development and performance (e.g., Streissguth, 1986). Pregnant mice from two different strains given comparable doses of alcohol had different blood-alcohol levels, and offspring of the higher-level strain had more anomalies, implicating maternal factors (Chernoff, 1980).

FAS Effects from Childhood to Adulthood

FAS effects persist into adulthood (e.g., Streissguth et al., 1991). FAS/FAE adolescents and adults average about 2 standard deviations below the mean in height and head circumference. Mean IQ is in the mildly retarded range, but variability is high. Those with the most severe physical symptoms in childhood have the lowest later IQ scores. The characteristic low weight of FAS/FAE children largely disappears. FAS facial dysmorphologies become less distinctive with age, although features such as short palpebral fissure length remain. Only a few affected children or adolescents can cope in regular classes without special help; many are in self-contained special education classes. Although academic deficits are broad, arithmetic deficits are particularly large. Many adults are not employed and are in sheltered workshops or institutions.

Children and adolescents with FAS/FAE, even those without mental retardation, show behavioral deficits and excesses that present serious management challenges (e.g., Carmichael Olson & Burgess, 1997; Mattson & Riley, 1998). Common features include hyperactivity, inattention, impaired learning of verbal material, receptive and expressive language problems, difficulty conforming to social norms, and fine motor deficits. Temper tantrums in younger children and serious conduct disorders in older ones are a particular concern. Streissguth and Kanter (1997) described "secondary characteristics" that intervention might reduce and "protective factors" that reduce the those characteristics. The secondary factors are serious mental health problems; disrupted school experience; trouble with the law; inpatient or prison confinement for mental health, substance abuse, or crime problems; inappropriate sexual behavior; and alcohol or drug problems. Protective factors are a stable and nurturant home, particularly from 8 to 12 years of age; diagnosis before age 6; not having been abused; staying in living situations for extensive periods; diagnosis of FAS rather than FAE (apparently paradoxically, lower IQ was associated with fewer secondary characteristics); and having basic needs met for at least 13% of life.

Treatment

Early intervention may reduce some behavioral problems. Pharmacological and behavioral interventions have had varied success (e.g., Carmichael Olson & Burgess, 1997; Streissguth & Kanter, 1997). A highly structured and relatively low-stimulating environment improves attention and reduces problem behavior in both adults and children (e.g., Carmichael Olson & Burgess, 1997). The high level of Attention-Deficit/Hyperactivity Disorder in FAS/FAE individuals suggests that stimulant medication would be effective, but one study found highly variable response to stimulants: Generally, medication reduced hyperactivity but did not increase attention (Snyder, Nason, Snyder, & Block, 1997). Given the variety and extent of problems manifested by FAS/FAE individuals and the effect of these problems on others, Clarren and Astley (1997) suggest that clinics specifically devoted to FAS/FAE individuals may be needed.

Prevention

Although FAS is completely preventable theoretically, alcohol abuse is resistant to treatment, and relapse rates are high. Education programs may lower consumption by moderately drinking women during pregnancy but are unlikely to affect alcohol-abusing women, whose infants are most at risk. Treatment and prevention programs targeted specifically at alcohol-abusing women (e.g., Kilbey & Asghar, 1992; National Institute on Alcohol Abuse and Alcoholism, 1987) may be necessary to decrease the incidence.

More information is available from the National Organization on Fetal Alcohol Syndrome's web site, http://www.nofas.org/.

REFERENCES

Abel, E. L. (1984). *Fetal alcohol syndrome and fetal alcohol effects.* New York: Plenum.

Abel, E. L. (1998). *Fetal alcohol abuse syndrome.* New York: Plenum.

Abel, E. L., & Hannigan, J. H. (1995). Maternal risk factors in fetal alcohol syndrome: Provocative and permissive influences. *Neurotoxicology and Teratology, 17,* 445–462.

Carmichael Olson, H., & Burgess, D. M. (1997). Early intervention for children prenatally exposed to alcohol and other drugs. In M. J. Guralnick (Ed.), *The effectiveness of early intervention* (pp. 109–145). Baltimore: Paul H. Brookes.

Chernoff, G. F. (1980). The fetal alcohol syndrome in mice: Maternal variables. *Teratology, 22,* 71–75.

Clarren, S., & Astley, S. (1997). Development of the FAS diagnostic and prevention network in Washington State. In A. Streissguth & J. Kanter (Eds.), *The challenge of fetal alcohol syndrome: Overcoming secondary disabilities* (pp. 40–51). Seattle, WA: University of Washington Press.

Jones, K. L., Smith, D. W., Ulleland, C. N., & Streissguth, A. P. (1973). Pattern of malformation in offspring of chronic alcoholic mothers. *Lancet, 1,* 1267–1271.

Kilbey, M. M., & Asghar, K. (Eds.). (1992). *Methodological issues in epidemiological, prevention, and treatment research on drug-exposed women and their children* (Research monograph 117). Rockville, MD: National Institute on Drug Abuse.

Lemoine, P., Harousseau, H., Borteryu, J. P., & Menuet, J. C. (1968). Les enfants de parents alcoholiques: Anomalies observées a propos de 127 cas [Children of alcoholic parents: Anomalies observed in 127 cases]. *Ouest Medical, 21,* 476–482.

Mattson, S. N., & Riley, E. P. (1998). A review of the neurobehavioral deficits in children with fetal alcohol syndrome or prenatal exposure to alcohol. *Alcoholism: Clinical and Experimental Research, 22,* 279–294.

Montagu, A. (1965). *Life before birth.* New York: Signet.

National Institute on Alcohol Abuse and Alcoholism. (1987). *Program strategies for preventing fetal alcohol syndrome and alcohol-related birth defects.* Rockville, MD: National Institute on Alcohol Abuse and Alcoholism.

Sampson, P. D., Streissguth, A. P., Bookstein, F. L., Little, R. E., Clarren, S. K., Dehaene, P., et al. (1997). Incidence of fetal alcohol syndrome and prevalence of alcohol-related neurodevelopmental disorder. *Teratology, 56,* 317–326.

Snyder, J., Nason, J., Snyder, R., & Block, G. (1997). A study of stimulant medication in children with FAS. In A. Streissguth & J. Kanter (Eds.), *The challenge of fetal alcohol syndrome: Overcoming secondary disabilities* (pp. 25–39). Seattle: University of Washington Press.

Streissguth, A. P. (1986). The behavioral teratology of alcohol: Performance, behavioral, and intellectual deficits in prenatally exposed children. In J. R. West (Ed.), *Alcohol and brain development* (pp. 3–44). New York: Oxford University Press.

Streissguth, A. P., Aase, J. M., Clarren, S. K., Randels, S. P., LaDue, R. A., & Smith, D. F. (1991). Fetal alcohol syndrome in adolescents and adults. *Journal of the American Medical Association, 265,* 1961–1967.

Streissguth, A., & Kanter, J. (Eds.). (1997). *The challenge of fetal alcohol syndrome: Overcoming secondary disabilities.* Seattle: University of Washington Press.

Robert T. Brown
University of North Carolina, Wilmington

FETAL ALCOHOL SYNDROME: DIAGNOSIS AND DESCRIPTION

Fetal alcohol syndrome (FAS) is a complex of physical anomalies and neurobehavioral deficits that may affect offspring of heavy-drinking mothers. First described in 1973 (e.g., Jones, Smith, Ulleland, & Streissguth), FAS is the most prevalent environmental and preventable type of mental retardation in the Western world. Prenatal exposure to alcohol has a continuum of effects: less serious ones, termed *fetal alcohol effects* (FAE), and alcohol-related neurodevelopmental disorder (ARND) among others (see Table 1).

Diagnosis, which is based on clinical signs and family history, may be difficult. Diagnostic criteria themselves are controversial. Even offspring of mothers who drank heavily during pregnancy show widely varying and nonunique effects, and numerous lifelong behavior problems may develop in those with minimal physical signs (e.g., Sampson, Streissguth, Bookstein, & Barr, 2000). Full FAS is associated with three major effects, "the triad of the FAS" (Rosett & Weiner, 1984, p. 43):

1. Prenatal and/or postnatal growth retardation below 10th percentile, corrected for gestational age. Although it is generally viewed as FAS's most common characteristic, some suggest that growth retardation may not be either a primary or a defining characteristic (Carmichael Olson & Burgess, 1997).

2. Central nervous system (CNS) dysfunction (neurological abnormality, developmental delay, or mental impairment < 10th percentile). Mental retardation or subnormality is the most common indicator. Variability of IQ is high, with average IQ estimated at about 65 (Mattson & Riley, 1998). Children with the most severe morphology and growth indicators have the most severe intellectual and other CNS deficits. Prenatal alcohol has many adverse effects on the developing CNS (e.g., Abel, 1998; Stratton, Howe, & Battaglia, 1996). Affected infants and children may show failure to thrive, poor sucking, retarded speech/motor development, repetitive self-stimulating behaviors,

Table 1. Summary of IOM's (1997) Diagnostic Criteria for Fetal Alcohol Syndrome (FAS) and Alcohol-Related Effects

I. Category 1: FAS with confirmed maternal alcohol exposure
   A. Confirmed maternal alcohol exposure
   B. Characteristic pattern of facial anomalies such as short palpebral fissures and abnormalities in the premaxillary zone (e.g., flat upper lip, flattened philtrum, and flat midface)
   C. Growth retardation as indicated by at least one of the following: low birth weight for gestational age; decelerating weight over time not due to nutrition; disproportional low weight to height
   D. CNS neurodevelopmental abnormalities, including at least one of the following: decreased cranial size at birth; structural brain abnormalities (e.g., microcephaly, partial or complete agenesis of the corpus callosum, cerebellar hypoplasia); neurological hard or soft signs (as age appropriate), such as impaired fine motor skills, neurosensory hearing loss, poor tandem gait, poor eye-hand coordination

II. Category 2: FAS without confirmed maternal alcohol exposure
   A. Characteristic pattern of facial anomalies
   B. Growth retardation
   C. CNS neurodevelopmental abnormalities as in Category 1.

III. Category 3: Partial FAS with confirmed maternal alcohol exposure
   A. Confirmed maternal alcohol exposure
   B. Some components of characteristic pattern of facial anomalies as in Category 1.
   C. Growth retardation and CNS neurodevelopmental abnormalities, as in Category 1, or complex pattern of behavior or cognitive abnormalities that is inconsistent with developmental level and cannot be explained by familial background or environment alone, such as learning difficulties; deficits in school performance; poor impulse control; problems in social perception; deficits in higher-level receptive and expressive language; poor capacity for abstraction or metacognition; specific deficits in mathematical skills; or problems in memory, attention, or judgment

IV. Category 4: Alcohol-related effects
   A. Alcohol-related birth defects (ARBD): Presence of a subset of an extensive list of congenital anomalies, including cardiac, skeletal, renal, ocular, auditory, and numerous other malformations and dysplasias
   B. Alcohol-related neurodevelopmental disorder (ARND): Presence of any one CNS neurodevelopmental abnormality as described in Category 1 and/or the complex pattern of behavior or cognitive abnormalities, as in Category 3

auditory deficits, Attention-Deficit/Hyperactivity Disorder, oppositional defiant and conduct disorders, and seizures. Many of the behavior deficits and excesses reflect deficits in rule-governed behavior suggestive of impaired frontal-lobe functioning (Sampson et al., 2000).

3. Characteristic facies (at least two of three facial dysmorphologies: microcephaly [head circumference < 3rd percentile]; microphthalmia and/or short palpebral fissures; or

poorly developed philtrum, thin upper lip, and flattening of the maxillary area). According to the Institute of Medicine (IOM), "At present, the facial features observed in FAS remain the most unique feature. . . . No one can receive an FAS diagnosis without an experienced clinician's assertion that the face, *taken as a whole,* appears to be the FAS face" (Stratton et al., 1996, p. 72, italics in original).

The IOM (Stratton et al., 1996) proposed the diagnostic categories shown in Table 1, which have been largely adopted by the American Academy of Pediatrics (2000). However, the categories have been criticized for several reasons (e.g., Abel, 1998; Sampson et al., 2000): (1) The distinction between FAS and alcohol-related effects is questionable, owing to high overlap between them in neurobehavioral effects—indeed, similar IQ deficits occur in alcohol-exposed children with or without FAS physical features (Mattson & Riley, 1998); (2) prenatal alcohol exposure during only a narrow period leads to facial deformities, whereas exposure over a much wider range leads to CNS and consequential behavioral defects; (3) requiring a history of maternal drinking during pregnancy is problematic because women may underreport their drinking and adopted infants may have no maternal histories; thus, underdiagnosis is a concern. Researchers are attempting to identify clear biological markers of prenatal alcohol exposure. At this time, except in cases with clear and distinct infant features and a known history of maternal drinking during pregnancy, practitioners should consult with expert diagnosticians before making a diagnosis. Because milder phenotypes characteristic of FAS/FAE may result from problems other than alcohol (Streissguth, Sampson, Barr, Clarren, & Martin, 1986), pregnant women who occasionally drank small amounts of alcohol and have slightly deformed infants should not be made to feel that alcohol necessarily caused the deformities.

More information is available from the National Organization on Fetal Alcohol Syndrome's web site, http://www.nofas.org/.

REFERENCES

Abel, E. L. (1998). *Fetal alcohol abuse syndrome.* New York: Plenum.

American Academy of Pediatrics, Committee on Substance Abuse and Committee on Children with Disabilities. (2000). Fetal alcohol syndrome and alcohol-related neurodevelopmental disorders. *Pediatrics, 106,* 358–361.

Carmichael Olson, H., & Burgess, D. M. (1997). Early intervention for children prenatally exposed to alcohol and other drugs. In M. J. Guralnick (Ed.), *The effectiveness of early intervention* (pp. 109–145). Baltimore: Brookes.

Jones, K. L., Smith, D. W., Ulleland, C. N., & Streissguth, A. P. (1973). Pattern of malformation in offspring of chronic alcoholic mothers. *Lancet, 1,* 1267–1271.

Mattson, S. N., & Riley, E. P. (1998). A review of the neurobehavioral deficits in children with fetal alcohol syndrome or prenatal exposure to alcohol. *Alcoholism: Clinical and Experimental Research, 22,* 279–294.

Rosett, H. L., & Weiner, L. (1984). *Alcohol and the fetus.* New York: Oxford University Press.

Sampson, P. D., Streissguth, A. P., Bookstein, F. L., & Barr, H. M. (2000). On categorizations in analyses of alcohol teratogenesis. *Environmental Health Perspectives Supplements, 108*(3), 421–428.

Stratton, K., Howe, C., & Battaglia, F. C. (Eds.). (1996). Fetal alcohol syndrome: Diagnosis, epidemiology, prevention, and treatment. Washington, DC: National Academy Press. Available online at http://www.nap.edu/books/0309052920/html/index.html.

Streissguth, A. P., Sampson, P. D., Barr, H. M., Clarren, S. K., & Martin, D.C. (1986). Studying alcohol teratogenesis from the perspective of the fetal alcohol syndrome: Methodological and statistical issues. In H. M. Wisniewski & D. A. Snider (Eds.), *Mental retardation: Research, education, and technology transfer* (pp. 63–86). *Annals of the New York Academy of Sciences, 477.* New York: New York Academy of Sciences.

Robert T. Brown
University of North Carolina, Wilmington

FIGHT/FLIGHT REACTION

Fighting and fleeing are the two basic responses available to most animals, including humans, when they are dealing with danger. A threat to the survival of an organism will be met with one or both of these behaviors. The threat may be real or perceived, and the response may be physical or, in the case of humans, abstract or intellectual. Further, the fight/flight response may be by an individual alone or by a group acting together.

A genetic basis for fight/flight behaviors shares an argument for the more general topic of aggression. That is, these behaviors have been prevalent throughout history; they are shown by almost all species of animals; they appear early in childhood; and they appear to be of some survival value. In contrast, learning is an important factor influencing aggressive acts.

W. R. Bion incorporated fight/flight behavior into an elaborate theory of human behavior. This theory has had great impact on the understanding of individuals' actions, especially as they occur in a social context. W. R. Bion and others such as Henry Ezriel brought greatly increased understanding of the relationship that exists between the basic biological drives in man, such as fear and anxiety, and other observed behaviors, both abnormal and normal.

Stanley Berent
University of Michigan

See also: **Learned Helplessness**

FIVE-FACTOR MODEL OF PERSONALITY

Introduction

Personality traits describe individual differences in human beings' typical ways of perceiving, thinking, feeling, and behaving that are generally consistent over time and across situations. Beginning with the work of Allport and Odbert (1936), trait psychologists have attempted to identify a set of basic traits that adequately describe variation in human personality. This effort has employed two strategies, the analysis of descriptive adjectives across human languages (the lexical approach) and the measurement of various traits derived from personality theories (the questionnaire approach). For nearly 50 years competing sets of fundamental traits (e.g., by Cattell, Eysenck, and Guilford), typically derived through factor analysis, created disagreement about which traits were basic. However, in the 1980s, a convergence of the lexical and questionnaire strategies generated a consensus among many trait psychologists that five basic broad traits provided an adequate description of individual differences (McCrae & John, 1992). This set of basic traits is referred to as the Five-Factor Model of Personality (FFM).

Contemporary factor analytic investigations have recovered the FFM traits in diverse languages spoken around the world (McCrae & Costa, 1997) and demonstrated that most traits assessed by personality questionnaires, regardless of their original theoretical roots and applied purposes, can be subsumed by the FFM (McCrae, 1989). The major advantages of this consensus include the provision of a common language for psychologists of different traditions to use in describing individual differences, and the ability to focus research on the roles traits play in diverse human phenomena rather than on endless debates over which traits are basic (Wiggins, 1992).

Description

Although differences of opinion regarding the names of the five basic traits exist, I use the labels associated with the most popular articulation of the FFM (Costa & McCrae, 1992).

Neuroticism versus Emotional Stability. High neuroticism suggests a proneness to psychological distress and emotional reactivity, reflected in chronic experiences of anxiety, depression, self-consciousness, low self-esteem, and ineffective coping. Low neuroticism does not guarantee psychological health but does suggest a calm, even-tempered emotional style.

Extraversion versus Introversion. High extraversion suggests an interpersonal style marked by preferences for social interaction, high activity levels, and the capacity to experience positive emotions. Low extraversion suggests a preference for solitude and a reserved, quiet, and independent interpersonal style, but not an inherently unhappy or unfriendly individual.

Openness to Experience versus Closed to Experience. High openness suggests an active pursuit and appreciation of experiences for their own sake, reflecting curiosity, imagination, tolerance of diverse values and beliefs, novelty-seeking, and attraction to aesthetic experiences. Low openness suggests a preference for conventional attitudes, conservative tastes, dogmatic views, and little interest in the unfamiliar or markedly different.

Agreeableness versus Antagonism. High agreeableness suggests a friendly, cooperative, trustworthy, and nurturant interpersonal style. Low agreeableness suggests a cynical, rude, abrasive, suspicious, uncooperative, and irritable interpersonal style.

Conscientiousness versus Unconscientiousness. This trait describes individual differences in the degree of organization, persistence, control, and motivation in goal-directed behavior. High conscientiousness reflects a tendency to be organized, reliable, hard-working, self-directed, deliberate, ambitious, and persevering. Low conscientiousness reflects a tendency to be disorganized, aimless, lazy, careless, lax, negligent, and hedonistic.

Theory

Although it is empirically derived through factor analytic investigations of language and personality questionnaires, it is erroneous to conceive of the FFM as atheoretical. The emerging consensus led to the question "Why are these five basic traits universal descriptors of human individual differences?" Several theoretical viewpoints have been applied to this question (Wiggins, 1996), including the lexical hypothesis, the dyadic-interactional perspective, socioanalytic personality theory, evolutionary theory, and personality metatheory.

Assessment

The FFM can be assessed through self-reports, observer ratings, and a structured interview. Individuals interested in assessing the FFM should consider important differences among instruments and methods (Widiger & Trull, 1997).

Applications

The FFM has been widely applied in diverse domains of psychological science and practice. Clinical psychologists have demonstrated the advantages of using the FFM for treatment planning and understanding the psychotherapy process. The FFM has also been linked to both symptom-based psychopathologies and the personality disorders. Beyond clinical psychology, the FFM has been widely used in industrial/organizational psychology, cross-cultural psychology, health psychology, social psychology, developmental psychology, counseling, and close relationships. Finally, the FFM dimensions are likely to be reliable and valid predictors of many everyday behaviors of potential interest to investigators.

Criticisms

Although the FFM has been successfully applied in diverse areas of psychology, criticisms of the model have been raised (Block, 1995, McAdams, 1992; Westen, 1995). These largely focus on the inherent vulnerabilities of factor analysis, the lack of validity scales for most FFM inventories, and the limitations of the descriptive scope of the FFM.

REFERENCES

Allport, G. W., & Odbert, H. S. (1936). Trait names: A psycho-lexical study. *Psychological Monographs, 47*(1, Whole no. 211).

Block, J. (1995). A contrarian view of the five-factor approach to personality description. *Psychological Bulletin, 117,* 187–215.

Costa, P. T., Jr., & McCrae, R. R. (1992). *NEO-PI-R / NEO-FFI professional manual.* Odessa, FL: Psychological Assessment Resources.

McAdams, D. P. (1992). The Five-Factor Model in personality: A critical appraisal. *Journal of Personality, 60,* 329–361.

McCrae, R. R. (1989). Why I advocate the Five-Factor Model: Joint analyses of the NEO-PI and other instruments. In D. M. Buss & N. Cantor (Eds.), *Personality psychology: Recent trends and emerging directions* (pp. 237–245). New York: Springer-Verlag.

McCrae, R. R., & Costa, P. T., Jr. (1997). Personality trait structure as a human universal. *American Psychologist, 52,* 509–516.

McCrae, R. R., & John, O. P. (1992). An introduction to the Five-Factor Model and its applications. *Journal of Personality, 60,* 175–215.

Westen, D. (1995). A clinical-empirical model of personality: Life after the Mischelian ice age and the NEO-Lithic era. *Journal of Personality, 64,* 495–524.

Widiger, T. A., & Trull, T. J. (1997). Assessment of the Five-Factor Model of Personality. *Journal of Personality Assessment, 68,* 228–250.

Wiggins, J. S. (1992). Have model, will travel. *Journal of Personality, 60,* 527–532.

Wiggins, J. S. (1996). *The Five-Factor Model of Personality: Theoretical perspectives.* New York: Guilford Press.

Aaron Lee Pincus
Pennsylvania State University

FORENSIC PSYCHOLOGISTS: ROLES AND ACTIVITIES

Forensic psychology deals with the interface of psychology and the law, and with the application of psychology to legal issues. This specialty includes a wide range of clients and settings, including individuals of all ages, couples, groups, organizations and industries, government agencies, schools, universities, inpatient and outpatient mental health settings, and correctional institutions. Forensic psychologists may become involved in such diverse areas as criminal competency and responsibility, tort liability and/or damages, the effects of workplace discrimination or harassment, products liability, mental hospital commitment and treatment, divorce and custody litigation, risk assessment for future aggressive behavior, treatment of offenders, rights of patients and offenders, special education, eyewitness identification, the effect of suggestibility on children's testimony in cases of alleged child sex abuse, jury selection, police selection and training, workers' compensation, and professional liability. Events of recent years have led to increased attention to prediction of violence in the workplace and in schools. Although few forensic psychologists are qualified in all these areas, all are expected to have a basic knowledge of certain core areas as well as a thorough knowledge of their specialization.

Although psychiatry has had a role within the legal system for many years, it was not until Judge Bazelon's decision in *Jenkins v. United States* in 1962 that psychology obtained firm legal status. In *Jenkins,* a criminal case, the trial judge had ordered the jury to disregard the psychologist's testimony regarding mental disease. He did so on the basis that a psychologist is not qualified to give a medical opinion. The Court of Appeals ruled that the judge was in error and stated that "some psychologists are qualified to render expert testimony in the field of mental disorder." The court went on to suggest criteria for qualifying a psychologist as an expert. In the years since that decision, other cases and the Federal Rules of Evidence have substantially broadened the issues included within psychologists' legally defined expertise. Today, though there are some differences among states, and between the states and federal government, psychologists are regularly accorded expert status in practically every appropriate area of criminal, civil, family, and administrative law.

The growth of forensic psychology has been manifested in a variety of other ways. Some interdisciplinary programming between law schools and psychology departments began in the 1960s. The early 1970s witnessed the development of joint PhD-JD degree programs and psychology PhD programs with a specialty in forensic or correctional psychology. Today there are a substantial number of such programs, and also a growing trend within psychology graduate schools to include law-related courses in the curriculum.

A number of professional organizations have also emerged. In 1980 the American Psychological Association membership approved the creation of a Division of Psychology and Law (Division 41). The American Board of Forensic Psychology was established in 1978. Its purpose is to identify qualified practitioners to the public and to promote forensic psychology as a recognized discipline. Applicants for diplomate status must, among other criteria, have at least 1,000 hours of experience in forensic psychology in a 5-year period in order to qualify. They then must submit a work sample, which, when approved, allows them to take a 3-hour oral peer-review examination.

Another manifestation of growth is the publication of journals and books specific to the field. Among the important journals are *Law and Human Behavior, Behavioral Science and the Law, The American Journal of Forensic Psychology,* and *Psychology, Public Policy and Law,* although many other journals also publish relevant articles. Among books that provide an overview of the field are Heilbrun, Marczyk, and DeMatteo's *Forensic Mental Health Assessment: A Casebook* (Oxford University Press, 2002) and Hess and Weiner's *The Handbook of Forensic Psychology* (Wiley, 1999). A further aspect of the growth of forensic psychology has been the development of specialized forensic instruments to assess issues such as criminal competency, criminal responsibility, and parenting capacity.

Specific Issues Addressed by Forensic Psychologists

In most forensic cases the questions that the psychologist is called upon to answer fall into three categories: (1) diagnostic questions: personality dynamics, presence of psychosis or organicity, evidence of malingering, and so on; (2) questions involving inference from the diagnostic level to opinions regarding specific legal questions, such as competency to stand trial, the relationship of a psychological disorder to an accident, the best interests of the child, and so forth; and (3) questions regarding disposition: need for treatment and prognosis with and without treatment, potential for future dangerous behavior, and the like. To address these questions, the forensic psychologist must not only possess the usual evaluation skills, but also be aware of special forensic instruments and relevant case law. Also, there will be important confidentiality/privilege issues, which will vary from situation to situation. The psychologist must be aware of these and take the necessary steps to protect clients. The psychologist must also work with attorneys prior to the evaluation to determine the question to be addressed and to help them understand what the evaluation can and cannot do. For example, an attorney may incorrectly request that the evaluation answer the question of whether the person is telling the truth regarding the commission of a crime. The attorney must also understand that the payment of a fee is for the evaluation only and that there is no commitment on the part of the psychologist to testify on behalf of the client. Whether testimony occurs depends on the findings of the evaluation.

It is also necessary for the psychologist to take a *forensic history,* which is more comprehensive than the usual history and is likely to include such information as hospital records, police reports, and statements of witness. These sources of information will then be referenced in the report based on the evaluation.

Testifying in Court

In some cases the report of the forensic psychologist will be accepted without an appearance in court. But at other times the psychologist may be called to testify. Giving testimony can be a traumatic experience: The key to minimizing difficulties is thorough preparation. This preparation takes place on several levels. The first level involves a thorough knowledge of the relevant law, the tests used, and the test findings. The psychologist must also be able to articulate findings without using excessive jargon and by utilizing behavioral examples that will illustrate the statements made. The second level of preparation involves meeting with the attorney. The forensic psychologist must abide by ethical principles and must retain personal integrity. However, the psychologist also has the responsibility to present the findings as effectively as possible. The attorney, on the other hand, is required to advance the client's interest. The attorney has been taught never to ask a witness a question to which the attorney does not already know the answer. Preparation, therefore, includes an agreement between the psychologist and the attorney on the order in which the findings will be presented, on what questions will be asked, and on what the psychologist's answers will be. It is also helpful to review likely cross-examination questions and for the psychologist to indicate what the answers would be.

The credibility of the psychologist in the courtroom will depend on several factors. The first of these is credentials: The psychologist should provide the attorney with a curriculum vitae, which the attorney can use when presenting the psychologist's qualifications. The credibility of the psychologist will also depend on courtroom demeanor. The psychologist on the witness stand must remember that the cross-examining attorney is only doing a job when questioning the credibility of the psychologist and of the findings. The cross-examination is not a personal attack, although if one loses perspective, it is easy to feel personally attacked. In giving testimony, the psychologist should not hesitate to say that he or she did not understand the question or does not know the answer, or that there is insufficient information to answer the question.

Forensic Treatment

Forensic treatment covers as wide a range of cases as forensic evaluation. In criminal cases, treatment may consist of therapy focused on returning an incompetent individual to competency. Or it may provide emotional support to the person who must face imprisonment. Treatment in criminal cases sometimes includes therapy focused on personality problems or on aggressive or sexual behavior while the individual is incarcerated, or outpatient therapy as a condition of probation or parole. Treatment of offenders requires special knowledge about the criminal justice system, the nature and effects of the prison environment, the probation-parole system, and the personality characteristics and/or behavior frequently observed in offenders. Group therapy or behavioral therapy techniques are often valuable in treating sexual offenders, offenders with alcohol problems, and others.

In a civil damage situation, treatment may consist of insight-oriented or supportive psychotherapy. In addition, special methods such as behavior therapy, cognitive therapy, or biofeedback may be used for pain management or to treat anxiety or depression. The therapist must be aware that testimony may be required in court, and this may at times influence both the mental status of the client and the course of therapy. Often in such cases the therapist may find the legal situation to be at odds with the therapeutic situation. For example, it is often therapeutic for a patient who has been unable to work to return to work as soon as possible. However, this is often inconsistent with the approach being taken by the attorney. In such cases, the therapist has a responsibility to make the patient and the attorney aware of the recommendations, but the final decision as to whether to proceed on those recommendations lies with the patient.

In the child custody situation, treatment is often ordered by the court either to avoid full custody litigation or as part of the resolution of the conflict. The focus of treatment is to help the child make a positive adjustment, and this of course requires treatment of the child. However, treatment of the parents is almost always required as well. The treatment of the parents focuses on such issues as communication in dealing with the child, unconscious or conscious derogation of the other parent to the child, and resolution of conflicts between the parents. Conflicts often arise over visitation issues, so that the child becomes the focal point of conflict between the parents. Resolving such issues often requires joint sessions with the parents, which, though often explosive, may be necessary and productive.

Research in Forensic Psychology

Many of the questions asked of the forensic psychologist require only description of the present status of an individual. But many other questions make an explicit or implicit request for a prediction of future behavior. For example, the answers to such questions as the probability of future dangerous behavior, the likely response to treatment, or the adjustment of a child under various possible alternative custodial situations require not only thorough clinical evaluations, but also a knowledge of relevant research. The research may often reveal that clinical lore is incorrect. On the other hand, the state of the art is such that it is often difficult to support a clinical opinion within the framework of available research findings. It is, therefore, incumbent on the forensic psychologist to be both the recipient and the provider of research on these questions. The psychologist may not be called upon to provide research support for clinically based opinions, but he or she should be prepared to do so if necessary. In other types of cases, such as those involving eyewitness identification, the primary basis on which opinions are offered is the research.

The forensic psychologist must keep abreast of new information which emerges from research. Such effort, along with up-to-date knowledge of the law and modifications of the law by new cases, provides a perspective that, when combined with a thorough clinical approach, allows the forensic psychologist to be of greatest services to the legal system.

SUGGESTED READING

Brodsky, S. L. (1991). *Testifying in court: Guidelines and maxims for the expert witness.* Washington, DC: American Psychological Association.

Ceci, S. J., & Hembrooke, H. (1998). *Expert witness in child abuse cases.* Washington, DC: American Psychological Association.

Gerald Cooke

See also: **Expert Testimony; Psychology and the Law**

FORENSIC PSYCHOLOGY

Forensic psychology refers to the burgeoning field in which psychology and law share interest. Called *psycho-legal studies, psychology and law,* or *criminal and legal psychology,* among other terms, forensic psychology encompasses three basic and overlapping areas of collaboration between psychology and law. They are psychology *in* the law, psychology *and* the law, and psychology *by* the law.

Psychology in the law refers to the way that psychology has been used by the law to solve problems. Traditionally, these problems include determining sanity; assessing competency in both civil court (e.g., assessing the ability to take of one's affairs, or providing child custody recommendations in divorce proceedings) and criminal matters (e.g., the ability to contribute to one's defense at trial); classifying prisoners' risks in determining level of custody; assessing whether educational and employment practices are discriminatory; determining disability; recommending probation and parole suitability; and providing criminal behavioral analysis. When people think about psychologists in forensic matters, they are typically considering how psychologists work in the law.

As forensic psychology has grown, novel application of psychological expertise have developed. For example, a cognitive psychologist's consultation and testimony would be most helpful in determining whether targeted consumers would be confused by a trademark or logo from a company that was similar to a well-recognized company. Would there be trademark infringement if a new company was named "Tidee Soap Flakes," possibly capitalizing on the trademark of a more established company with a similar name? Also, experimental psychologists would be helpful in determining the optimal amount and complexity of information on a highway sign that drivers whizzing by could process without distraction. When signs are poorly done or badly placed, suits might arise in which the testimony of psychologists specializing in forensic human factors might be essential. Psychologists also assess community attitudes to determine whether a fair trial can be conducted regarding highly publicized and notorious events. Psychologists assist attorneys in the selection of jurors during voir dire and can conduct focus groups to see how a jury might consider different legal arguments when confronting facts of a case. These innovative applications of psychology are helping further the growth in this area of forensic psychology.

Psychology of the law is centered on research about legal issues and how the law functions. For example, psychologists have determined that the usual way of conducting lineups (that is, the simultaneous display of six people for an eyewitness to view) is inferior to the sequential lineup, in which the eyewitness makes an individual judgment about one person at a time before viewing the second, third, fourth, and so on. The sequential lineup results in fewer misidentifications of innocent people with no loss of accuracy in detecting guilty parties. Psychologists have also studied how people view privacy. Most people think that only the owner or renter can grant entry into a home and allow seizure of items police may want. However, the law allows that anyone in a home, including a worker painting the house or repairing a refrigerator, may grant entry and allow seizure of property. Interestingly, police typically view privacy not as the law regards it but as citizens think of it.

Psychology of the law involves studying the decision-making processes of litigants (e.g., should I sue, and should I settle?); criminals (e.g., what makes a target vulnerable?); victims (e.g., have I been the victim of a crime, and is it worth pressing charges?); police (e.g., should I ticket or arrest this person?); prosecutors (e.g., is this crime worth prosecuting?); judges and juries (e.g., determining liability in civil cases and guilt in criminal cases, setting awards or sentences); and corrections (e.g., what degree of security is needed for this convict, and when should parole be granted?). Recent innovative research includes examinations of how jury instructions affect awards in tort cases. If the results of this research are applied, then we may not need legislatures to reform tort law. Psychology of the law concerns applying behavioral research strategies to legal phenomena in order to increase the fairness and effectiveness of the administration of justice in our society.

Psychology by the law refers to the laws, statutes, regulations, and ordinances that affect the practice of psychology. The psychologist who teaches must be aware of organizational procedure for handling such matters as admitting students into a program in a nonbiased fashion; apprehending student cheaters and according them appropriate due process as the institution has set forth; and recruiting and treating research participants in ethically and legally appropriate ways. Recently, the privacy of research data has come under attack, so that psychologists conducting research need to know what they can or cannot promise in terms of confidentiality of data gathered in research. The psychologist in practice needs to know about licensing and about confidentiality and privilege, as well as understanding the limits of each of these (e.g., most states have mandatory child abuse reporting statutes and require warnings of a patient's homicidal threats if such threats present an imminent danger to an identifiable third party). Psychologists who hire other professional staff need to know about employment and personnel law, and if services are rendered to the public, the psychologists need to provide reasonable accommodations to people with disabilities.

Each of these three areas of forensic psychology has grown explosively in recent years. The growth in the subscriptions to psychology journals, the popularity of forensic psychology workshops, the development of forensic psychology graduate programs, the Diplomate in forensic psychology, the publication of such works as the second edition of *The Handbook of Forensic Psychology* (Hess and Weiner, 1999), and even television shows portraying forensic psychologists are signs of interest in this area.

REFERENCES

Hess, A. K., & Wiener, I. B. (1999). *The handbook of forensic psychology* (2nd ed.). New York: Wiley.

Allen K. Hess
Auburn University, Montgomery, Alabama

FORM/SHAPE PERCEPTION

Form/shape perception refers to how figure (as distinct from its background) information is specified so that object recognition and shape matching are possible and object-oriented actions can be made accurately. It is difficult to distinguish form from shape as, generally speaking, the terms are used synonymously (henceforth we will use *shape* to refer to form and shape). Shape information is available from vision and touch, although most research has focused on shape perception in vision.

As shape can readily been seen in monochrome line drawings and silhouettes, shape can be established without reference to color, motion, or depth information. Consequently, most research on shape perception has concentrated on how shape can be computed from edge-based stimuli. However, it is important to know that shape can also be computed from patterns of motion (shape-from-motion) by using Gestalt principles such as common fate (Johansson, 1973). Given certain constraints, shape can also be perceived from shadow (e.g., Ramachandran, 1988). Therefore, how we perceive shape in the real world will be determined from at least three sources of visual information: edge, movement, and shadow.

Cognitive Processes

Processes of shape representation are usually thought to operate in a bottom-up or data-driven fashion (e.g., Marr, 1982; Biederman, 1987). Particular attention has been given to understanding whether shapes are processed as global entities or broken down into parts and shape constancy. Although some have claimed that it is the global aspects of a shape that are important for understanding its structure (e.g., Cave & Kosslyn, 1993), most authors believe that shapes are usually described in terms of parts and the relationships between parts. Specifying what the constitute parts of shapes are has been a theoretical challenge. Some authors have suggested a role for stored primitives or templates (Marr, 1982; Biederman, 1987) and others that parts are computed online using physical properties of the image (Hoffman & Singh, 1997). The weight of evidence is currently in favor of the latter approach with segmentation between parts being made at boundary cusps. The rule describing the places where shapes are divided into parts is called the *minima rule* (see Hoffman & Richards, 1984).

The representations of three-dimensional shapes must exhibit constancy such that their perceived shapes do not change with viewpoint, and various schemes have been proposed to achieve this. For example, objects might be described with reference to their principle axes (e.g., Marr, 1982) or from information directly available in the image (e.g., Biederman, 1987).

Not all shape processing can be bottom-up: Recent studies have shown that object recognition affects figure-ground segmentation (e.g., Peterson & Gibson, 1991; Peterson, de Gelder, Rapcsak, Gerhardstein, & Bachoud-Levi, 2000) and the perception of ambiguous and incomplete figures (Rock, 1983). Therefore, top-down processes are also likely to be critical for shape perception. However, exactly what top-down information is used in shape perception and the mechanisms through which it is exploited remain unknown.

Neuropsychology of Shape Perception

Patients exhibiting failures to properly specify shape information are said to suffer from *apperceptive agnosia.* In such cases, sensory loss is either absent or unable to account for their perceptual loss. It is also critical that patients are shown to have retained stored knowledge of object form and function. The classic test of shape perception is the Efron test (Efron, 1968). In the Efron test, patients have to judge whether two orthogonally oriented rectangles, matched for overall flux (luminance and area), have the same or different dimensions. Failure on this test can only be because of an inability to compute shape information. The locus of brain damage usually considered sufficient to produce apperceptive agnosia is diffuse damage of parieto-occipital cortex of the right hemisphere (Bradshaw & Mattingley, 1995).

The failure to consciously perceive shape does not necessarily imply that shape is not computed. There is good evidence that the conscious experience of shape doubly dissociates from the ability to reach and grasp appropriately for objects. Patients with optic ataxia cannot reach and grasp objects but can report accurately the shape of a stimulus along with the shape's location, size, and orientation (Perenin & Vighetto, 1988), whereas patients with visual form agnosia cannot report accurately the shape, size, or orientation of an object. Nevertheless, they can reach and grasp for objects automatically and without error (Goodale, Milner, Jakobsen, & Carey 1991). Therefore, a failure to consciously perceive shape does not mean that it has not been processed.

Neuroanatomy of Shape Perception

The cortical loci responsible for shape analysis have also been studied using functional imaging. The critical design for such a study must ensure that shape analysis is isolated from feature processing and activation of semantic memory using a subtractive methodology (see Peterson, Fox, Snyder, & Raichle, 1990). In studies where these conditions have been met, the cortical areas activated only during shape analysis are on the inferolateral surface of the brain near the junction of occipital and temporal lobes in both right and left hemispheres (e.g., Kanwisher, Woods, Iacoboni, & Mazziotta, 1997).

In conclusion, shape perception refers to a complex set of processes through which two- and three-dimensional figures come to be represented in order that recognition, matching, and actions can be supported. These processes are mostly driven by bottom-up considerations such that part decomposition and shape constancy can be achieved. However, shape processing is affected by top-down factors, as evidenced by its role in figure-ground segmentation and the perception of ambiguous figures. Shape processing can break down following brain damage to posterior regions of the right hemisphere, and the awareness of shape can be lost, although shape processing can still allow accurate grasping of objects. Functional imaging studies concur with the studies of brain-damaged patients in highlighting the role of posterior cortex in shape perception but suggest a role for both right and left hemispheres.

REFERENCES

Biederman, I. (1987). Recognition-by-components: A theory of human image understanding. *Psychological Review, 94,* 115–147.

Bradshaw, J. L., & Mattingley, J. B. (1995). *Clinical neuropsychology.* San Diego, CA: Elsevier Science/Academic Press.

Cave, C. B., & Kosslyn, S. M. (1993). The role of parts and spatial relations in identification. *Perception, 22,* 229–248.

Efron, R. (1968). What is perception? *Boston Studies in Philosophy of Science, 4,* 137–173.

Goodale, M. A., Milner, A. D., Jakobsen, L. S., & Carey, D. P. (1991). A neurological dissociation between perceiving objects and grasping them. *Nature, 349,* 154–156.

Hoffman, D. D., & Richards, W. A. (1984). Parts of recognition. *Cognition, 18,* 65–96.

Hoffman, D. D., & Singh, M. (1997). Salience of visual parts. *Cognition, 63,* 29–78.

Johansson, G. (1973). Visual perception of biological motion and a model for its analysis. *Perception and Psychophysics, 14,* 210–211.

Kanwisher, N., Woods, R. P., Iacoboni, M., & Mazziotta, J. C. (1997). A locus in human extrastriate cortex for visual shape analysis. *Journal of Cognitive Neuroscience, 9,* 133–142.

Marr, D. (1982). *Vision.* San Francisco: Freeman.

Perenin, M.-T., & Vighetto, A. (1988). Optic ataxia: A specific disruption in visuomotor mechanisms. *Brain, 111,* 643–674.

Petersen, S. E., Fox, P. T., Snyder, A. Z., & Raichle, M. E. (1990). Activation of extrastriate and frontal cortices by visual words and word-like stimuli. *Science, 249,* 1041–1044.

Peterson, M. A., de Gelder, B., Rapcsak, S. Z., Gerhardstein, P. C., & Bachoud-Levi, A.-C. (2000). Object memory effects on figure assignment: Conscious object recognition is not necessary or sufficient. *Vision Research, 40,* 1549–1567.

Peterson, M. A., & Gibson, B. S. (1991). The initial organization of figure-ground relationships: Contributions from shape recognition processes. *Bulletin of the Psychonomic Society, 29,* 199–202.

Ramachandran, V. S. (1988). The perception of shape from shading. *Nature, 331,* 163–166.

Rock, I. (1983). *The logic of perception.* Cambridge, MA: MIT Press.

Nick Donnelly
University of Southampton

FRAGILE X SYNDROME

Little known until a new technique facilitated identification in the 1980s, Fragile X, or fra(X), is the most common heritable cause of mental retardation (MR). Fra(X) owes to a weak site on the X chromosome, is sex-linked, and is largely responsible for higher prevalence of MR in males than females. Discovery of the responsible gene has led to replacement of cytogenetic tests with more effective and less expensive DNA ones, which identify affected individuals and carriers (Hagerman & Lampe, 1999). Prevalence estimates of full expression in males and females are about 1 in 4,000–6,250 and 1 in 8,000–12,500, respectively (Saul & Tarleton, 2000). Fra(X) may account for 5% of children receiving special education services for mental retardation. Individuals with MR of unknown cause are routinely screened for Fra(X).

History

Martin and Bell's (1943) description of a family with an X-linked inheritance MR pattern in males helped to explain the long-known higher incidence of males with MR. Lubs's (1969) description of the fragile-X site drew little interest until accurate diagnosis led to recognition of its frequency (e.g., Sutherland & Hecht, 1985). The family studied by Martin and Bell is now known to be affected by fra(X), and Martin-Bell and Fragile X syndromes are synonymous.

Genetics

Fra(X) is unusual genetically (see Meyer & Batshaw, 2002). In typical X-linked disorders, a carrier female expresses no characteristics of the disorder but passes the defective gene, on average, to half of her children. Males who inherit the defective gene express its effects, whereas females are unaffected carriers. In fra(X), carrier females may manifest some fra(X) characteristics, including impaired intelligence and learning disabilities, and about 20% of fra(X) males show no apparent effects but pass the defective chromosome on to their daughters, who may have affected sons.

The underlying mutated defective fragile-X MR (FMR1) gene interferes with a particular protein apparently important in brain development. Normally, the genetic code shows some repetition in three nucleotide base pairs (triplet repeats), which on many chromosomes may expand abnormally over generations into fragile sites. The fragile-X site (FRAXA) normally contains 6–50 repeats of the cytosine-guanine-guanine (CGG) triplet base pair sequence. Asymptomatic transmitting, or permutation, males and carrier females have 50–90 and 50–200 CGG repeats, respectively, and do not show a fragile X site. Premutations occur in about 1 in 500 males and 1 in 250 females. Premutations of more than 100 CGG repeats almost always expand into full (200–3,000 CGG repeats) mutations in the next generation. Males and females with full mutations have observable fragile-X sites and symptoms. All males and 50% of females show MR. However, fra(X) involves the phenomenon of genomic imprinting, in which the sex of the transmitting parent influences expression of a mutation. Daughters of pre- or full mutation males generally have only premutations and are asymptomatic, whereas sons and daughters of pre- or full mutation females have further expanded CGG repeats. Offspring of full mutation females will always have full mutations, and those of permutation females have increased likelihood full mutations.

Characteristics of Affected Individuals

Expressivity of fra(X) is highly variable and can only be summarized here. Detailed descriptions are in Hagerman & Lampe (1999), Meyer and Batshaw (2002), and Online Mendelian Inheritance in Man (OMIM, 2002). About two thirds of postpubertal males show a "clinical triad": (1) moderate-severe MR; (2) craniofacial features (large forehead, protruding chin, coarse facies, long face, macrocephaly, and elongated ears); and (3) large testes (e.g., Sutherland & Hecht, 1985). Females and prepubertal males are more variable. Most prepubertal males show overgrowth from birth, with head size, fontanel, and body measurements exceeding the 97th percentile, but less distinct macroorchidism and craniofacial features. Fra(X) children may also show hyperextensible joints, high arched palate, mitral valve prolapse (a form of heart murmur), flat feet, scoliosis, strabismus, and low muscle tonus. Female carriers, particularly those with subnormal intelligence, may also show facial features, including high broad forehead and long face, and hyperextensibility.

Approximately 95% of affected males have mild to profound MR and some form of communication disorder. Affected males have particular difficulty with processing and short-term memory of serial information. Auditory memory and reception are poor. General language development is delayed relative to intelligence, and specific problems such as perseverations, repetitions, echolalia, cluttered speech, and dysfluencies are often shown. Many fully affected males show an apparently unique complex of behaviors, including stereotypies, particularly hand flapping, gaze aversion, avoidance of touch, hyperactivity, inattentiveness, aggression, and anxiety (Meyer & Batshaw, 2002).

About 70% of carrier females show no clear physical, cognitive, or behavioral problems. The rest show a variety of symptoms, less severe than in males, including mild MR, learning disabilities, communication problems, and emotional disturbances. Frequent learning disabilities include problems in visual-spatial skills, executive function, and simultaneous processing. Language problems, similar to those of males, include cluttered and perseverative speech.

Relationship to Autism

Many of fra(X)'s characteristics are similar to those of autism and other pervasive developmental disorders. About 7% of children with autism have fra(X), and 15–28% of those with fra(X) meet criteria for autism (Meyer & Batshaw, 2002). Thus, boys diagnosed with autism are now routinely screened for fra(X). However, the disorders appear to be separate. For example, severe autism rarely occurs with fra(X) (Bailey et al., 1998), and a study (Klauck et al., 1997) of a large sample of autistic boys found no true association between fra(X) and autism.

Treatment

A team approach is recommended (e.g., Hagerman & Lampe, 1999). Stimulant medications, clonidine, and folic acid are commonly used to reduce Attention-Deficit/Hyperactivity Disorder symptoms and temper tantrums, but owing to differential response, no one drug regimen is effective. Antiseizure medications may help control not only seizures but also mood swings and aggression. Selective serotonin reuptake inhibitors are often effective for mood swings, anxiety, and aggression. Speech/language, physical, and occupational therapy are almost always helpful. Fra(X) children respond well to highly structured multimodal learning environments, including computer-assisted instruction that provides immediate feedback. Behavioral therapy is particularly effective in managing problem behaviors. Given the variable characteristics of fra(X) children, detailed psychological assessment is important for the design of appropriate individualized instruction.

REFERENCES

Bailey, D. B., Jr., Mesibov, G. B., Hatton, D. D., Clark, R. D., Roberts, J. E., & Mayhew, L. (1998). Autistic behavior in young boys with fragile X syndrome. *Journal of Autism and Developmental Disorders, 28,* 499–508.

Hagerman, R. J., & Lampe, M. E. (1999). Fragile X syndrome. In S. Goldstein & C. R. Reynolds (Eds.), *Handbook of neurodevelopmental and genetic disorders of children* (pp. 298–316). New York: Guilford Press.

Klauck, S. M., Munstermann, E., Bieber-Martig, B., Ruhl, D., Lisch, S., Schmotzer, G., et al. (1997). Molecular genetic analysis of the FRM-1 gene in a large collection of autistic patients. *Human Genetics, 100,* 224–229.

Lubs, H. A. (1969). A marker X chromosome. *American Journal of Human Genetics, 21,* 231–244.

Martin, J. P., & Bell, J. (1943). A pedigree of mental defect showing sex-linkage. *Journal of Neurology, Neurosurgery, and Psychiatry, 6,* 154–157.

Meyer, G. A., & Batshaw, M. L. (2002). Fragile X syndrome. In M. L. Batshaw (Ed.), *Children with disabilities* (5th ed., pp. 321–331). Baltimore: Paul H. Brookes.

Online Mendelian Inheritance in Man (OMIM). (2002). Fragile site mental retardation 1; FMR1. MIM No. 309550. Baltimore: Johns Hopkins University. Available at http://www3.ncbi.nlm.nih.gov/htbin-post/Omim/dispmim?309550.

Saul, R. A., & Tarleton, J. C. (2000). Fragile X syndrome. *GeneReviews.* Available at http://www.geneclinics.org/servlet/access?id=39439&key=UYtJgjTLopnv7&gry=INSERTGRY&fcn=y&fw=dDAB&filename=/profiles/fragilex/details.html.

Sutherland, G. R., & Hecht, F. (1985). *Fragile sites on human chromosomes.* New York: Oxford University Press.

Robert T. Brown
University of North Carolina, Wilmington

FREE WILL

In psychology and in psychologically oriented philosophy two extreme positions have been taken on the question of free will. One—widely associated at present with psychology and often presented as a basic assumption in introductory textbooks of general psychology—is that free will is entirely illusory and that in order to be scientific psychologists must believe that all human behavior or experience is absolutely determined by causal processes that are in principle knowable. The other extreme, especially associated in this century with the existentialist movement in philosophy, is that human free will is real and ubiquitous in the sense that all experience and action involve some element of free choice, that with no change in the antecedent conditions one could always have experienced or acted somewhat differently from the way one did.

Among psychologists, the extreme deterministic position often seems to be based on the belief that it is taken by, and is somehow essential to, the physical sciences, and that it must be a basic assumption of any genuinely scientific enterprise. Quantum physics has accepted some degree of indeterminacy as an inevitable principle. Conditions, the knowledge of which would be needed for perfect predictability in psychology, would often include internal processes that could not be accurately known without interventions that would change them and hence the outcome; this seems sufficiently analogous to the basis for indeterminacy in quantum physics to argue for extension of the principle to psychology. Once indeterminacy is granted to be inevitable, a distinction between free will and a determinism that cannot possibly be verified may become scientifically meaningless.

The argument for free will is most often empirical. Having acted, a person often feels certain that he or she could have acted differently, could have made a different choice; free will, it is argued, is thus a basic fact of experience. This argument cannot escape the objection that causal determinants may simply not yet be sufficiently identified and understood.

Another pragmatic basis for a choice of positions on the issue of free will is the effect of various positions on general human welfare. Advocates of rigid determinism sometimes consider acceptance of their position necessary for convincing people that human behavior can be predicted and controlled, so that the future of humanity can be influenced by "human engineering" just as physical events can be influenced by engineering based on the physical sciences. Opponents of rigid determinism argue that acceptance of that position eliminates hope of deliberate change and thus has a detrimental influence.

I. L. Child

See also: **Behaviorism**

FRIENDSHIP

Friendships are important relationships in all cultures and throughout the lifespan. Friendships are characterized by several defining features: (1) they are dyadic relationships; (2) there is an affective bond that is reciprocated; (3) they are voluntary; (4) they are typically egalitarian in nature; and (5) almost all entail some shared activities and companionship. Friendships often meet other functions as well, such as serving as a source of support and providing opportunities for self-disclosure and intimacy.

These features differentiate friendships from several related phenomena. The fact that they are dyadic relationships distinguishes them from cliques or groups of peers. (Of course, many members of cliques are also friends with other members.) Similarly, having friendships is different from being popular. Individuals who are not popular may have close friendships, and, less commonly, a popular person may not have a close friendship. The reciprocal nature of friendship differentiates actual friendships from relationships in which one person thinks or wishes it were a friendship. The strong affective bond distinguishes friendships from acquaintanceships. Friends provide individuals with more support than acquaintances, although friends do not necessarily engage in less conflict than acquaintances. Finally, romantic relationships are considered a special form of friendship, and in fact romantic partners are commonly seen as one's best friend.

Friendship Selection

Who becomes friends? Two key predictors of friendship formation are proximity and similarity. Friends usually live near each other, attend the same school, or work near each other. Proximity makes it more likely that individuals will have the opportunities to interact with each other and to develop a friendship. In addition, contrary to the adage "opposites attract," friends are usually similar to one another. They tend to be of the same age, gender, and socioeconomic and ethnic background. Moreover, friends commonly share interests and tend to develop more similar interests and values over the course of being friends. Individuals who are dissimilar are less likely to remain friends.

Friendships Across the Lifespan

Individuals of almost all ages develop friendships. Approximately 75% of preschoolers report having friends, and the percentage increases to over 90% by adulthood; the proportion remains high through adulthood, although about 15% of the elderly report not having friends. It is debatable whether very young children have true friendships, although even toddlers prefer some playmates to others. Preschoolers' friendships are typically based on shared activities and tend to be less long-lasting than friendships later in life. One of the most striking developmental changes in friendships occurs in preadolescence, when children begin to develop *chumships*. These relationships are usually with a same-sex peer and involve more intimacy, self-disclosure, support, and acceptance than earlier friendships. Chumships are thought to be a precursor for adult friendships and romantic relationships. In adolescence, other-sex friendships become more commonplace, and romantic relationships begin to emerge. In addition, adolescents and adults often develop specialized friendships wherein one turns to different friends for different purposes. Throughout adulthood, friendships remain important, although they may not be as central as a romantic relationship.

Friendship and Gender

Friendships develop more often between members of the same gender than between males and females. Other-sex friendships are particularly infrequent during the elementary school years, accounting for less than 20% of friendships during this time. These friendships occur less commonly because of structural barriers and cultural norms. Differences also exist in the typical nature of friendships of males and females. For instance, female friendships tend to be characterized by more intimacy and self-disclosure than male friendships, and this distinction becomes particularly notable in adolescence. Closeness in male friendships may occur through shared activities; sometimes experiencing a very stressful event together can also foster closeness. During childhood and adolescence, girls tend to be more exclusive in their friendships than boys are.

Significance of Friendships

Friendships play an important role in development and adjustment in several ways. One reason is that they are egalitarian in nature. Whereas parents ultimately have more power in parent-child relationships, friends are on equal footing. Accordingly, what friends do together or how they behave toward each other is more open to negotiation. As a result, children obtain valuable experience in learning how to express their own wishes and compromise with another person in a way that they can't learn by interacting with a parent or other authority figure. In addition, friendships provide a ready venue for communicating information about peer norms and values, as well as about taboo topics such as sex.

These contrasts between friendships and parent-child relationships do not mean that friends and parents are opposing social influences. Contrary to some depictions in the popular media, friends and parents more commonly have similar influences on children and adolescents. Typically children select friends whose values are congruent with their parents' values. Moreover, both parents and friends are likely to affect individuals' behavior. For example, whether both an adolescent's friends and parents smoke influences the likelihood of his or her choosing to smoke. The strongest clashes between the influences of friends versus parents occur when relationships with parents are strained.

Empirical research has repeatedly found links between healthy adjustment and having friendships. Well-adjusted individuals are more likely to develop friendships, and friendships seem to promote adjustment. It seems particularly important that one have at least one close friendship. Although friendships are generally thought to have a positive influence on adjustment, the specific effects vary as a function of who the friend is. Thus, having a friend who is deviant or antisocial is likely to foster deviant or antisocial behavior. Similarly, conflictual, problematic friendships can have deleterious effects.

Both having friendships and being accepted (versus rejected) by one's peers contribute to well-being. Similarly, the characteristics of relationships with both parents and friends contribute to adjustment and development. In effect, friendships share features with other close relationships but also have their own unique features and make their own contribution to individuals' lives.

Wyndol Furman
Lauren E. Berger
University of Denver

See also: **Human Development; Social Support; Socialization**

FROMM'S THEORY

Eric Fromm was concerned about a diversity of topics related to his search for the essence of human nature. He combined several humanist approaches to define human nature as essentially dynamic and dialectic. According to Fromm, the essential in man is his capacity to act with freedom and to understand love as an objective communion. He considered people essentially equal, without sexual or status differences.

Self-awareness, reason, and imagination disrupt the harmony that characterizes animal existence. The emergence of these traits made humankind into an anomaly, a freak of the universe. Part of nature, subject to physical laws and unable to change them, humans transcend the rest of nature. Being aware of ourselves, we realize our powerlessness and the limitations of our existence. We visualize our own end—death.

Fromm referred to needs rooted in the peculiarity of human existence. These include the need for relationship, because feeling isolated leads to disintegration just as inanition leads to death. Also, there is the need to transcend, to rise above the possivity and accidentality of our existence; this need makes us become original and look for freedom.

The need to transcend offers us the option to create or to destroy, to love or to hate. The satisfaction of the need to create induces us to happiness, destruction, or suffering. A third need is rootedness, which leads us to security and helps us to avoid anxiety and loneliness. A fourth need, identification, gives us a concept of self, since we need to feel and say, "I am myself." A fifth need, orientation, is a peculiar need based on our existential situation, humanity, imagination, and reason; it refers to the purpose of finding a sense for or a value to existence.

For Fromm, social character implied the adaptation of free individuals to social conditions that develop the character traits inducing them to behave in the same way that, within their culture, most people do. Social character internalizes the external needs, orienting individuals toward tasks required by the socioeconomic system.

Rafael Nuñez
Capital University

FUNCTIONAL ANALYSIS

Definition

Functional analysis is a strategy for the assessment and treatment of mental health problems with origins in behaviorism. It is generally viewed as a subfield within the larger realm of behavioral assessment and behavior therapy. More specifically, functional analysis is a set of procedures that attempts to identify important contextual variables such as history and environment that help to cause and/or maintain problematic behaviors or behavior-environment interactions. The goal of functional analysis is to effectively identify targets of intervention that are alterable such that appropriate treatments may be rapidly implemented and evaluated through concentrated intervention efforts.

History

When a client seeks psychological or psychiatric intervention for a mental health or behavioral problem, the obvious questions are "what created and maintains the problem?" and "how can the problem be solved?" Assessment procedures are the data-gathering tools that are used to investigate the former question and to inform the latter one. Assessment is sifting through the multitude of facts that comprise a person's life and determining which historical and current aspects are relevant to the development and/or maintenance of the problem. Traditionally this process resulted in classifying problems and, by extension, individuals with those problems into diagnostic categories based on commonalities in apparently relevant variables. These categories are designed to describe syndromes and to guide clinical interventions.

Behaviorists have questioned the usefulness of diagnosis and syndromal classification systems such as the *Diagnostic and Statistical Manual* of the American Psychiatric Association on many grounds. Of particular relevance to functional analysis are the significant varieties in symptom presentation that comprise a single category. It is argued that symptom overlap does not equate with a unique, full-fledged kind of mental disorder. As a result, newer approaches to assessment that consider the function of behaviors over the topographical form of the behaviors, and that attend more closely to individual differences in behavior, have been explored. The product of this desire to understand behavior functionally and idiographically is functional analysis.

Functional analysis is a term that has been used interchangeably with several others in the behavioral literature, including *behavioral analysis, behavioral assessment, functional behavioral analysis,* and *behavioral case formulation.* Compounding the confusion is that just as many terms are used to refer to the same procedures, *functional analysis,* is used to refer to a diversity of procedures in the literature. This phrase has been used to describe any part of the process that includes discovering the variables of which behavior is a function, designing an intervention for the environment or behaviors, implementing the intervention, reevaluating the case conceptualization based on response to treatment, and recycling the process until the problem subsides. Although some behavior analysts focus exclusively on the assessment portion of this intervention process, others consider the whole process to be a complete functional analysis.

Procedures

Functional analysis derived from basic behavioral principles. It attends to the antecedents, stimuli, responses, consequences, and contingencies that produce and/or maintain effective or ineffective behaviors. The identification of pertinent, controllable variables in this sequence and the effective treatment of those variables to produce different outcomes are its challenges. The basic form of a functional analysis is as follows.

1. Identify aspects of the client and his or her environment or history that may be relevant to the problem.
2. Organize information about potentially relevant variables according to behavioral principles in order to identify possible causal relationships among variables.
3. Collect additional detailed information about potential causal variables in order to complete the analysis.
4. Identify or create a treatment hypothesized to produce a desired increase or decrease in the frequency

or intensity of the causal variables based on the case conceptualization of how the variable functions for the individual.

5. Implement the intervention for one variable at a time and observe any change in the problem.
6. If there is no change in the target behavior, remove the original intervention, move to the next suspected causal variable, and implement and evaluate the treatment of that variable.
7. If the problem is not alleviated, return to the case conceptualization to identify alternative variables that may be pertinent or alternative causal relationships and continue with the steps of the functional analysis.
8. Continue to revise the conceptualizations and interventions until the problem is solved.

Strengths and Weaknesses

Strengths

The strengths of functional analysis are the precision with which cases may be conceptualized and the direct link to treatment implementation. Instead of relying on imprecise diagnostic categories as heuristics to guide conceptualizations of the problem, both case conceptualizations and treatment planning focus on the unique aspects of the particular problem. These unique aspects of the problem are the points of customized clinical interventions instead of a generic syndrome-level intervention.

Weaknesses

The weaknesses of functional analysis stem from its lack of specificity. Communication between mental health professionals and replication of assessment, treatment, and treatment evaluations are impeded by the imprecision of functional analysis language and procedures. When different terms are being used for functional analyses, relevant information may not be shared because it is not identified as belonging to the functional analysis category. Similarly, when *functional analysis* is used to refer to overlapping or altogether different procedures, miscommunications may occur because the discussants are working from different assumptions about the procedures that are involved. Moreover, as communication is increasingly removed from direct observations of client behaviors, there are greater opportunities for miscommunications to arise. If clinicians that are familiar with functional analysis have difficulties communicating effectively with one another, how much more difficult it is to create and maintain clear lines of communication with administrators and insurance representatives. Functional analysis is therefore difficult to administer and justify from a systemic perspective.

A related problem is replication. *Functional analysis* currently refers to a range of assessment and intervention procedures. Without a standard of practice for the subfield, clinicians may perform different sets of procedures and call each of them a functional analysis. As a result, there is no guarantee that one clinician's conclusions are going to match another professional's conclusions in the same case. This lack of replicability distills confidence from the assessment procedures, which dilutes their effectiveness. Furthermore, if a functional analysis cannot be replicated, doubt is cast on the ability to reliably study the phenomenon. This replicability problem ironically renders an assessment and intervention procedure that arose out of the behavioral empirical literature untestable.

Future Directions

The field of behavior analysis acknowledges the strengths and weaknesses of functional analysis and is beginning to propose improvements. Suggestions have been made that promote standardizing the definition of functional analysis and the procedures that comprise such an analysis in order to advance communication and replication. Additional proposals have been made to strengthen the communication aspect of the procedure. The development of a nomothetic classification system that is based on functional analysis has been offered. Proposed variations of this taxonomy include expert systems, logical functional analytic systems, or functional diagnostic systems, each based on functional analyses.

In addition to more advanced clinical applications, researchers have segued into an expanded use of functional analysis as a research strategy. Compiling and analyzing functional analytic data within and across clients may contribute to the basic understanding of many behaviors and behavior-environment interactions.

SUGGESTED READING

Cone, J. (1997). Issues in functional analysis in behavioral assessment. *Behaviour Research and Therapy, 35,* 259–275.

Haynes, S., & O'Brien, W. (1990). Functional analysis in behavior therapy. *Clinical Psychology Review, 10,* 649–668.

Iwata, B., Kahng, S., Wallace, M., & Lindberg, J. (2001). The functional analysis model of behavioral assessment. In J. Austin & J. Carr (Eds.), *Handbook of applied behavior analysis* (pp. 61–90). Reno, NV: Context Press.

Kanfer, F., & Saslow, G. (1969). Behavioral diagnosis. In C. M. Franks (Ed.), *Behavior therapy: Appraisal and status* (pp. 417–444). New York: McGraw-Hill.

Sturmey, P. (1996). *Functional analysis in clinical psychology.* Chichester, UK: Wiley.

William T. O'Donohue
University of Nevada, Reno

Tamara Penix Sbraga
Central Michigan University

***See also:* Operant Conditioning**

FUNCTIONAL AUTONOMY

Gordon W. Allport coined the term *functional autonomy* to refer to motives that have become independent of the needs on which they were originally based.

When first introduced, this concept of functional autonomy was both radical and controversial. The motivational theories prevailing in North American psychology focused almost exclusively on mechanisms directly linked to basic physiological needs. In contrast, Allport's functional autonomy raised the possibility that motives could function quite independently of any physiological need or drive. This liberalized conceptualization of motivation had important implications for several key issues in psychology. It provided an image of the individual as an active agent rather than a passive entity entirely under the control of biological needs and immediate stimuli. It allowed for explanations of behavior that emphasized the present and the future rather than the past. It also pointed to the role of complex and unique patterns of motives in shaping and defining individual personality.

In contemporary psychology, the idea of functionally autonomous motives has been accepted into the mainstream of psychology.

R. E. Goranson

See also: **Intrinsic Motivation; Motivation**

FUNDAMENTAL ATTRIBUTION ERROR

Attribution theory is concerned with the causes that people assign to behaviors in their attempts to explain them. The inferences about causation of a person's actions fall into two broad categories: internal (characteristics of the person) and external (characteristics of the social or physical environment). The fundamental attribution error (FAE), sometimes called *actor-observer asymmetry* or *overattribution,* is the general tendency of an observer to perceive another person's behavior to be caused by internal, personal characteristics or dispositions, rather than external, situational influences. Conversely, the behaving person (the actor) tends to see his or her own behavior as caused by the situation. The concept of FAE grew out of an extensive body of research on social perception and cognition, and in turn the idea has stimulated much research. There may even be attributional thinking in primates. In human beings, this well-established observer overemphasis on personal traits and underemphasis on context raises serious questions about bias in many situations in which people judge other people, such as jury decisions, voting for political candidates, and clinical assessment and treatment.

This prominent tendency to overattribute internal causes had been recognized by early social psychologists, such as Fritz Heider in 1958, as an actor-observer effect, and in further research Lee Ross in 1977 gave FAE its name. Typical experiments might involve judging statements allegedly made by persons under various conditions, or comparing subjects' explanations for their own choices and the choices made by others. Subjects might report causes of actions while viewing themselves or another person on videotapes. The FAE process is so strong that even when the observer is told something about the situational conditions of the actors, there is a tendency to attribute others' actions to personal traits. In daily life, this seems related to "blaming the victims" of rape, poverty, and other social problems. In organizations, people may overattribute responsibility to individuals, such as leaders, when there are structural or system faults. Since psychology in general focuses on individual variables, there is a strong likelihood that psychologists will overattribute observed results to individual dispositions. Some measures of individual differences are available, for instance, the Attributional Style Questionnaire and the Causal Dimension Scale.

There are several approaches to explaining FAE. A common explanation involves differences in the amount and type of information available to actors and observers. Persons looking at their own behavior have much previous behavior against which to compare it. When people make attributions to others, they seldom have the same amount or kind of information available. Also, actors and observers differ in information that is salient or striking to them—what is figure and what is ground.

The application of attribution theory to clinical work is of considerable importance. Some studies have shown that a dispositional or individualistic bias may exist among professional helpers, but this bias has not been clearly proven. Since, however, the tendency to overattribute problems to personal characteristics is common in the general population, it would seem important in clinical training to help students examine their explanations of clients' feelings and behaviors. Conversely, counselors and clinicians may use FAE as part of "attribution therapy," helping the client to reframe self-attributions. Depressed patients tend to use self-blame much more than others. Some studies have shown that cognitive therapeutic instruction to decrease overattribution of negative events helps to reduce depression or immunize people against a sense of helplessness.

Other interesting areas of application of the FAE principle are in legal and international situations. Questions such as the following arise: What was the intent of an individual alleged to have committed a crime? What does he or she see as reasons or causes for doing the deed? How about witnesses and attribution errors? In regard to the security problems of nations, FAE exacerbates attribution of hostile intentions to others and leads even peaceful states to arm excessively. Policy makers see arming themselves as a defensive action and assume that others' military buildups are aggressive. Social identity theory suggests that observers will tend to perceive in-group members as similar to themselves and therefore give situational explanations for discrepant behavior but will attribute out-group responsibilities differently.

There are several cautions and limitations about the FAE bias. It is important to note that FAE refers to a relative tendency of observers to attribute to the actor more responsibility for behavior than does the actor; it does not say anything about accuracy of causal claims. There are few research attempts to determine the reality or truth of attributions; questions may be raised about the accuracies of the observer, the actor, or both. Another caution is that oftentimes observers make personal attributions because of efficiency; if information about the actor's situation is not available, it may not be possible or practical to take the complexity of the actor's view into account. Attitudes in the attributional process are also important; the actor-observer differences may be diminished by an observer's empathic attitude or personal acquaintance with the actors and their situations. There seem to be cultural differences in the FAE tendency; North Americans and Westerners in general may have a bias toward blaming the individual in contrast with people in India and China or other collectivist or more holistic cultures. Easterners may tend to take situational information more into account when that is available. Sabini claims that FAE is pancultural in that it involves saving face and embarrassment.

Considerable work needs to be done to clear up the theoretical confusions about how FAE relates to similar concepts such as general social identity, theories of mind, self-efficacy, and internal and external locus of control. There is a difference between giving "mere causes" for behaviors as compared with reasons that involve intentions and show the logic that was used in the process.

Norman D. Sundberg
University of Oregon

***See also:* Forensic Psychology**

G

GABA RECEPTORS

It is now universally recognized that γ-aminobutyric acid (GABA) synthesized by the two molecular forms of glutamic acid decarboxylase (GAD65 or 67) expressed in neurons functions as a key neurotransmitter from crustaceans to mammals.

$GABA_A$ Receptors

In the brains of vertebrates, GABA mediates synaptic inhibitory events by binding to specific recognition sites located in various members of a pentameric protein family, including a transmembrane anion channel, which is termed $GABA_A$. When two molecules of GABA bind to a $GABA_A$ receptor molecule, the opening frequency of the anionic channels increases and, most of the time, Cl^- ions flow inwardly. In 1952, Hodgkin and Huxley suggested that in voltage-operated Na^+ and K^+ channels, the gating and its ion permeation are two independent processes. The idea that the gating opens and closes the channels but pays scant attention to the behavior of fully activated channels might also apply to the $GABA_A$-gated receptor channels. The binding of the two GABA molecules to a $GABA_A$ receptor molecule activates that Cl^- channel; in contrast, the binding to positive or negative allosteric modulatory sites of hormones (neurosteroids) or endogenous modulatory ligands (endozepines) affects the ohmic behavior of the channel by changing either the open time duration or the opening frequency of the Cl^- channels gated by GABA. Some of these modulatory sites also function as the high-affinity binding sites for important drugs used during surgery to induce anesthesia (barbiturates) or in psychiatry for the treatment of Anxiety or Mood Disorders (benzodiazepines [BZ]). Both drugs amplify the GABA-gated Cl^- current intensity and thereby decrease retention of recent memories, reduce learning speed, and induce sedation. Anesthesia is induced by barbiturates and not by BZs because only barbiturates can gate the $GABA_A$ receptor channels in the absence of GABA.

$GABA_B$ Receptors

The family of metabotropic GABA receptors was identified after the ionotropic $GABA_A$ receptor family. The activation of $GABA_B$ receptors by GABA decreases the rate of cAMP formation and this metabotropic function differentiates these receptors from ionotropic $GABA_A$ receptors. The $GABA_B$ receptors were further characterized by their insensitivity to bicuculline inhibition and muscimol stimulation (typical of $GABA_A$ receptors) by a specific inhibition by a number of selective antagonists inactive on $GABA_A$ receptors and by their selective stimulation by baclofen, which does not stimulate $GABA_A$ receptors. Confirmation of the metabotropic nature and of their functional association to G proteins has been accomplished by cloning two specific DNA sequences (each encoding for a slightly different 7-transmembrane domain protein) which, functioning as dimers, inhibit adenylate cyclase or gate K^+ channels using various G protein subtypes as second messengers.

The complete structural and functional distinction between $GABA_A$ (ionotropic) and $GABA_B$ (metabotropic) receptors has a clear parallel to that between nicotinic (ionotropic) and muscarinic (metabotropic) acetylcholine receptors and ionotropic and metabotropic receptors for the transmitter glutamate.

$GABA_C$ Receptors

This third family of ionotropic receptors ligated by GABA is insensitive to bicuculline inhibition, baclofen or muscimol stimulation, and positive allosteric modulation by BZs.

The ionotropic responses elicited by GABA acting on $GABA_C$ receptors are also of the fast type associated with an opening of an anion channel. The $GABA_C$ receptor structure results from homomeric assembly of ρ (ρ_1, ρ_2, ρ_3) subunits. The only organ that expresses ρ subunits in both rat and human is the retina. Since these ρ subunits have a 27% homology to $GABA_A$ receptor subunits, they have been considered a subgroup of these receptor subunits. However, unlike $GABA_A$ receptors, when ρ subunits combine to form $GABA_C$ receptors, they form only homomeric receptors. Thus, the function of homomeric ρ receptors sharply differs from that of $GABA_A$ receptors because ρ subunits lack the regulatory sites that are expressed in α, β, and γ subunits. The resistance of $GABA_C$ receptors to bicuculline inhibition or muscimol stimulation and the absence of allosteric modulation sites for barbiturates and BZs justify maintaining a functional distinction between $GABA_C$ and $GABA_A$ receptors.

Characterization of $GABA_A$ Receptor Functional Modifications by Various Anxiolytic Drugs Acting on the BZ Recognition Site

There is considerable interest in the availability of an effective $GABA_A$ receptor-acting anxiolytic drug that will not share the problems of presently available medications. These problems are tolerance, dependence liability, and several inconvenient side effects such as sedation, induction of recent memory deficit, barbiturate or ethanol potentiation, and ataxia. The high-affinity binding site for BZs located in $GABA_A$ receptors has specific structural features. One consists of a binding pocket formed by the contiguity of an α subunit (not present in α_6 and with low intrinsic activity in α_5) with a γ_2 or γ_3 subunit (which is not expressed by a γ_1 subunit). These requirements should predict which $GABA_A$ receptors are susceptible to positive allosteric modulation by ligands to the BZ recognition sites, that is subunit isomerism and sequence. Unfortunately, we do not have suitable methods to fulfill either task. It is presently believed that BZs amplify the actions of GABA by facilitating the opening of channels in monoligated $GABA_A$ receptors that, in order to open the channels in the absence of BZs, require two molecules of GABA bound to the receptor.

SUGGESTED READING

Costa, E., Auta, J., & Guidotti, A. (2001). Tolerance and dependence to ligands of the benzodiazepine recognition sites expressed by $GABA_A$ receptors. In H. Möhler (Ed.), *Pharmacology of GABA and glycine neurotransmission* (pp. 227–247). Berlin: Springer-Verlag.

Möhler, H. (2001). Functions of $GABA_A$ receptors: Pharmacology and pathophysiology. In H. Möhler (Ed.), *Pharmacology of GABA and glycine neurotransmission* (pp. 101–112). Berlin: Springer-Verlag.

Erminio Costa
University of Illinois, Chicago

GAMBLING, PROBLEM

Gambling in the United States

The past 2 decades have witnessed significant increases in legalized gambling opportunities in the United States. These opportunities have been accompanied by record levels of gambling expenditures. Over 10% of every dollar that Americans spend on leisure is spent on gambling.

Increase in gambling availability has also been accompanied by an increase in problem gambling behavior. Over 5% of adults have experienced significant problems related to gambling, and 1% of adults meet criteria for Pathological Gambling Disorder. Higher rates of problem gambling have been reported among males, youth, college students, African Americans, and individuals with easy access to gambling.

Problems Associated with Excessive Gambling

The most basic consequence of excessive gambling is financial. To deal with their debts, problem gamblers often must turn to other sources for money, including family; friends; or criminal activities, such as embezzlement. As a result of insufficient financial resources many gamblers file for bankruptcy. Arrest and incarceration due to illegal activities aimed at securing more money are also common.

Problem gamblers are more likely to suffer from depression or alcohol problems. They report greater rates of psychological distress and more use of psychiatric treatment. Problem gamblers often experience serious relationship difficulties. Spouses and family members must cope with the consequences of the gambler's behavior, including absence from the home, distrust of the gambler, and stress over family finances. Among problem gamblers, divorce rates are higher than the national average.

Pathological Gambling Disorder

Pathological Gambling Disorder was officially recognized as an impulse control disorder by the American Psychiatric Association in 1980 (*Diagnostic and Statistical Manual of Mental Disorders,* third edition [*DSM-III*]). *DSM-III* criteria include (1) preoccupation with gambling, (2) wagering larger amounts of money to experience excitement, (3) feelings of withdrawal when trying to control gambling, (4) gambling to escape problems, (5) chasing losses, (6) lying to others to conceal gambling involvement, (7) committing illegal acts to obtain money to gamble, (8) jeopardizing important relationships or opportunities because of gambling, (9) relying on financial assistance from others to pay gambling debts, and (10) unsuccessful efforts to limit gambling. These criteria were fashioned after the criteria for Substance Use Disorders and are based on the assumption that gambling may be similar to addictive behaviors.

Models of Problem Gambling: Medical

A variety of explanatory models for problem gambling have been developed. The disease model views problem gambling as a medical illness. Excessive gambling behavior is considered a chronic condition that manifests itself in clear signs and symptoms. Many explanations for the cause of the disease have been offered. Psychodynamic theorists have explained that gambling may fulfill an individual's instinctual drives; however, the nature of the psychodynamic position has not allowed researchers to support or refute it.

Genetic research has suggested that problem gamblers may inherit a genetic predisposition to gamble excessively. However, genetic factors appear to be only one important component in the development of gambling problems.

Models of Problem Gambling: Psychological

Psychologists have attempted to understand the role of psychological factors in the development of gambling problems. Theorists who have examined the relationship between gambling and personality traits, such as sensation-seeking, extroversion, and locus of control have generated only limited support for the role of personality in gambling.

Behavioral theorists have used learning models to explain how individuals develop gambling-related problems. According to operant conditioning theory, individuals gamble because they have been reinforced on a variable ratio schedule. Occasional wins serve to maintain the gambling behavior. Behavioral theories have difficulty with the seemingly irrational basis of gambling behavior.

In recent years, models of problem gambling have increasingly focused on the role of cognition. These cognitive models are based on empirical evidence that irrational beliefs are related to gambling behavior. According to cognitive theory, many gamblers hold beliefs that lead them to continue to gamble, despite the odds and their mounting losses. Belief in luck and the ability to control chance events are examples of irrational beliefs that may lead to problematic gambling behavior.

At the core of problem gambling behavior is a lack of self-regulation. Problem gamblers fail to control their gambling behavior and experience the resulting consequences. Although early treatment models were based on medical models of problem gambling, more recent treatment strategies have shifted to cognitive and behavioral perspectives.

Treatment of Problem Gambling

For the small number of problem gamblers who seek treatment, the most available option is Gamblers Anonymous (GA). GA is a self-help group based on the disease model of problem gambling and is focused on a 12-step program emphasizing group support, faith, and commitment. GA members share with the group their story about how excessive gambling led to problems. Complete abstinence from gambling is considered the only viable treatment goal. Members are encouraged to be actively involved in the program even after extensive periods of abstinence to avoid relapse. Research has suggested that GA is beneficial for a small percentage of those who attend.

A variety of behavior therapy strategies have been administered to problem gamblers including aversion therapy, in vivo desensitization, imaginal desensitization, and cue exposure and response prevention. Although most of these programs lack stringent evaluation, outcome data have generally supported their efficacy.

More recent therapy developments have focused on a cognitive model of problem gambling. These treatments use cognitive restructuring techniques designed to change gamblers' irrational beliefs about gambling. Cognitive strategies are often combined with problem-solving skills training and training to identify and cope with situations that present a high risk of relapse.

It is likely that future treatment strategies for problem gambling will build on contemporary models that have been developed in the alcohol treatment field or models that are specific to problem gambling. For example, brief, motivationally based treatment programs, which have received empirical support as effective alternatives to traditional abstinence-based interventions for alcohol problems, are now being adapted and tested to help problem gamblers.

The growing availability of gambling, the recognition of individual and societal problems associated with excessive gambling, and the increasing attention of scientists and clinicians suggest that the area of problem gambling will be a dynamic one.

Andrew W. Meyers
University of Memphis

Timothy A. Steenbergh
Indiana Wesleyan University

GATE CONTROL THEORY OF PAIN

The theory of pain that we inherited in the twentieth century was proposed by Descartes three centuries earlier. Descartes's specificity theory of pain proposed that injury activates specific pain fibers that, in turn, project pain signals through a spinal pain pathway to a pain center in the brain. The psychological experience of pain, therefore, was virtually equated with peripheral injury. In the 1950s, there was no room for psychological contributions to pain, such as attention, past experience, and the meaning of the situation. Instead, pain experience was held to be proportional to peripheral injury or pathology. Patients who suffered chronic pain syndromes without presenting signs of organic disease were labeled as crocks and sent to psychiatrists. The picture, in short, was simple. However, to thoughtful clinical observers, it was clearly wrong (Livingston, 1943; Noordenbos, 1959).

In 1965, Melzack and Wall proposed the gate control theory of pain, based on the following propositions:

1. The transmission of nerve impulses from afferent fibers to spinal cord transmission cells is modulated by a spinal gating mechanism in the dorsal horn.
2. The spinal gating mechanism is influenced by the relative amount of activity in large-diameter and small-diameter fibers: Activity in large fibers tends to inhibit transmission (close the gate), whereas small-fiber activity tends to facilitate transmission (open the gate).

3. A specialized system of large-diameter, rapidly conducting fibers (the central control trigger) activates selective cognitive processes that then influence, by way of descending fibers, the modulating properties of the spinal gating mechanism.
4. When the output of the spinal cord transmission cells exceeds a critical level, it activates the action system—those neural areas that underlie the complex, sequential patterns of behavior and experience characteristic of pain.

When the gate control theory was published, it generated vigorous (sometimes vicious) debate as well as a great deal of research to disprove or support the theory. It was not until the mid-1970s that the gate control theory was presented in almost every major textbook in the biological and medical sciences. At the same time there was an explosion in research on the physiology and pharmacology of the dorsal horns and the descending control systems.

The theory's emphasis on the modulation of inputs in the spinal dorsal horns and the dynamic role of the brain in pain processes had both a clinical and a scientific impact. Psychological factors, which were previously dismissed as reactions to pain, were now seen to be an integral part of pain processing, and new avenues for pain control were opened. Similarly, cutting nerves and spinal pathways was gradually replaced by a host of methods to modulate the input. Physical therapists and other health care professionals, who use a multitude of modulation techniques, were brought into the picture. The current status of pain research and therapy has recently been evaluated (Melzack & Wall, 1996) and indicates that, despite the addition of a massive amount of detail, the theory has remained basically intact up to the present time.

The gate control theory's most important contribution to pain research and therapy is its emphasis on the central, rather than peripheral, nervous system (Melzack & Wall, 1996; Melzack, 1998, 1999). The great challenge at present is to understand brain mechanisms. Melzack and Casey (1968) made a start by proposing that specialized systems are involved in the sensory-discriminative, motivational-affective, and evaluative dimensions of pain. The McGill Pain Questionnaire, which taps into subjective experience, is widely used to measure pain (Melzack & Torgerson, 1971; Melzack, 1975). We have also begun to understand the different pathways and neural mechanisms that underlie acute and chronic pain—again, by invoking complex spinal and brain mechanisms—and we have gained a far better understanding of analgesic drugs (Wall & Melzack, 1999).

In 1978, Melzack and Loeser described severe pains in the phantom body of paraplegics with verified total sections of the spinal cord, and proposed a central "pattern generating mechanism" above the level of the section. They focused more powerfully than ever before on central nervous system (CNS) mechanisms. Recent studies have explored new theoretical concepts to explain phantom body experiences—from pain to orgasm—in people with total spinal sections (Melzack, 1989). These experiences reveal important features of brain function because the brain is completely disconnected from the cord. Psychophysical specificity, in such a concept, makes no sense, and we must explore how patterns of nerve impulses generated in the brain can give rise to somesthetic experience.

REFERENCES

Livingston, W. K. (1943). *Pain mechanisms.* New York: Macmillan.

Melzack, R. (1975). The *McGill Pain Questionnaire* major properties and scoring methods. *Pain, 277,* 277–299.

Melzack, R. (1989). Phantom limbs, the self, and the brain (The D. O. Hebb Memorial Lecture). *Canadian Psychology, 30,* 1–14.

Melzack, R. (1998). Pain and stress: Clues toward understanding chronic pain. In M. Sabourin, F. Craik, & M. Robert (Eds.), *Advances in psychological science: Vol. 2. Biological and cognitive aspects.* Hove, UK: Psychology Press.

Melzack, R. (1999). Pain and stress: A new perspective. In R. J. Gatchel & D.C. Turk (Eds.), *Psychosocial factors in pain* (pp. 89–106). New York: Guilford Press.

Melzack, R., & Casey, K. L. (1968). Sensory, motivational, and central control determinants of pain: A new conceptual model. In D. Kenshalo (Ed.), *The skin senses* (pp. 423–443). Springfield, IL: Thomas.

Melzack, R., & Loeser, J. D. (1978). Phantom body pain in paraplegics: Evidence for a central "pattern generating mechanism" for pain. *Pain, 4,* 195–210.

Melzack, R., & Torgerson, W. S. (1971). On the language of pain. *Anesthesiology, 34,* 50–59.

Melzack, R., & Wall, P. D. (1965). Pain mechanisms: A new theory. *Science, 150,* 971–979.

Melzack, R., & Wall, P. D. (1996). *The challenge of pain* (2nd ed.). London: Penguin.

Noordenbos, W. (1959). *Pain.* Amsterdam: Elsevier Press.

Wall, P. D., & Melzack, R. (Eds.). (1999). *Textbook of pain* (4th ed.). Edinburgh, Scotland: Churchill Livingston.

Ronald Melzack
McGill University, Montreal, Quebec, Canada

See also: **Pain: Coping Strategies**

GENDER ROLES

Gender roles are the set of expectations a society has about males and females. These expectations are multifaceted and include specifications about appearance, personality traits, emotions, interests, abilities, and occupations. For example, in Western societies men are generally expected to be more agentic and less emotional than women, and women are expected to be more communal and less aggressive than men. Furthermore, men are often assumed to have paid occupations and to be financially responsible for their families, whereas women are assumed to be homemakers with primary responsibility for the children. Such beliefs serve to define what behaviors are considered appropriate or inappropriate for each gender. Thus, gender roles do more than merely describe the way things are; they describe how things should be.

Gender roles serve both social and intrapsychic functions. With respect to the former function, gender role expectations guide people's judgments and evaluations of others. When one assumes that another person possesses certain characteristics on the basis of his or her gender, one is engaging in *gender stereotyping.* Gender stereotyping is pervasive and can influence judgments in a subtle, nonconscious, and unintended manner. Gender roles also influence interpersonal evaluation directly: A person who conforms to the appropriate gender role is likely to be evaluated positively, whereas deviation from that role may result in avoidance, disapproval, or even outright hostility. Gender roles serve an intrapsychic function by helping people to define themselves as individuals and to guide their behavior. Importantly, however, people do vary in the extent to which they identify with a given gender role. That is, not all men view themselves in traditionally masculine terms, nor do all women identify with a traditionally feminine image. The extent to which one shares the constellation of characteristics associated with a particular gender role is known as *gender role identity.*

The measurement of gender role identity typically focuses upon personality traits (e.g., agentic versus communal), with individuals indicating on a paper-and-pencil survey the degree to which each trait provides a true description of themselves. Note, however, that measurement of gender role identity is not without some debate. Traditionally, masculinity and femininity are considered to be opposite ends of a single continuum (i.e., if you are high in femininity, you must be low in masculinity). More modern theorists, however, view masculinity and femininity as independent characteristics (i.e., you can be high or low on both dimensions, as well as high on one and low on the other). Persons describing themselves as being both strongly masculine and strongly feminine are labeled *androgynous.* Alternately, gender role identification may be conceptualized as a stagelike process wherein androgynous individuals are those who have transcended or rejected traditional gender roles. In this case, androgyny is viewed as the last stage of gender role identification.

There are a number of theories regarding how individuals become gender identified (also known as *gender typed*). One of the earliest formal theories, proposed by Freud, suggested that individuals must pass through a series of stages (oral, anal, phallic, genital, and latency) in order to become appropriately gender typed. According to this view, successful gender typing was argued to occur when children learn to identify with their same-sex parent and, in doing so, adopt the qualities and characteristics of that parent. Despite the popular attention paid to this theory, there is little empirical evidence to support it. More modern theories generally fall within the nature or nurture traditions. The theory that best represents the biological or nature tradition focuses upon the role of evolution in shaping each gender's interests, traits, and behaviors. In particular, this theory suggests that contemporary differences in male and female gender roles are, in effect, carryovers from those interests, traits, and behaviors that were adaptive for our ancestors. For example, the observed gender difference in the number of sexual partners desired is thought to have originated from gender differences in the sexual strategies found to be successful in the ancestral environment.

On the other hand, the socialization or nurture account argues that parents and other adults influence behavior by rewarding appropriate gender role behavior and punishing inappropriate role behavior. For example, parents may praise obedience and punish aggressiveness in their daughters and praise risk taking and punish crying in their sons. This theoretical account has more recently included *cognition* as an important intervening variable. Rather than suggesting that children are merely shaped by external forces, social cognitive learning theory argues that the process of receiving reinforcements and punishments for gender-appropriate and gender-inappropriate behavior results in the creation of cognitive expectancies that come to guide future behavior. Furthermore, this account suggests that receiving rewards and punishments is not the only means by which children learn gender-appropriate behavior. Significant adults may also impact gender typing by modeling behavior. Children learn to imitate those behaviors they see adults of their same sex performing. Although theories tend to follow one or the other tradition (nature versus nurture), these two general accounts need not be antagonistic or independent. Today, most psychologists who study gender typing recognize that biology and socialization likely work together to shape gendered behavior; it is no longer necessary to decide between nature *or* nurture, but to acknowledge the influence of nature *and* nurture.

Regardless of origin, it is important to convey that gender roles are neither static nor invariant. For example, male and female gender roles are far more discrepant from one another in some cultures than in others, with men and women sharing little in the way of daily activities. Furthermore, what may be considered masculine in one culture may be perceived as feminine in another. For example, while Western cultures expect women to be more emotionally expressive than men, Middle Eastern cultures expect the reverse. Gender roles also vary over time. Within the United States alone, gender roles have changed tremendously in the last 50 years, with far fewer people expecting, for example, married women to confine their activities to the home. Gender roles also change as we age. Research indicates that both women and men adhere less to gender roles as they mature beyond middle age, an occurrence that could be explained by either nature (hormones) or nurture (differential role demands).

Scientists have long debated the degree to which males and females differ in their traits, interests, and behavior. Consensus is emerging, however, that observed gender differences must be considered in the context of situational norms, gender stereotypes, and gender identity. Although each individual is unique, gender roles exert a powerful influence that should not be ignored in any attempt to understand human behavior.

Alison P. Lenton
Irene V. Blair
University of Colorado, Boulder

See also: **Socialization**

GENERAL ADAPTATION SYNDROME

The General Adaptation Syndrome (GAS) is a cluster of bodily responses to severe, prolonged stressors that was described by Hans Selye. Selye observed that rats exposed to a wide variety of noxious agents exhibited a nonspecific syndrome consisting of enlargement of the adrenal cortex; shrinkage of the thymus, spleen, and lymph glands; and the appearance of ulcers in the stomach and small intestine. This response was seen in animals exposed to extreme cold and heat, intense sound or light, forced exercise, injections of various organ extracts or formalin, or a variety of other intense biological challenges to normal homeostatic function. Selye suggested that the GAS consisted of three phases of response to a stressor. The initial stage consisted of an alarm reaction during which the adrenal cortex enlarged and released large amounts of the adrenoglucocorticoid hormone cortisol into the bloodstream, the lymphatic tissues shrunk, the number of white blood cells declined, the gastrointestinal tract developed ulcers, heart rate and blood pressure increased, and the animals lost weight. During the second stage, the stage of resistance, the adrenal cortex remained enlarged, but instead of releasing cortisol, the gland retained the hormone, other tissues and physiological functions appeared relatively normal, and the body weight returned to near normal levels. With continued application of the severe stressor, according to the GAS, the animals eventually entered a third stage, called the stage of exhaustion. Here again, similar to the body's responses during the alarm reaction, substantial amounts of cortisol were released into the blood, lymphatic tissues shrank, and body weight again fell. This stage ended with the animal's death.

Selye's GAS and the research that followed from this early notion of a nonspecific response to challenges from the environment was an important idea that launched the study of biological stress. Indeed, Selye himself used the term *stress,* which he had borrowed from physics to refer to this syndrome of responses to a noxious agent. However, more recent studies of the concept of stress have broadened the definition of *stressors* to include less potent challenges to an organism's normal function, including psychological stressors. Thus, it is now clear that the GAS does not occur following all events that one would reasonably consider stressors and does not occur in all individuals. As Selye himself noted, organisms may not experience all three stages of the GAS and stressors sometimes may produce only limited features of the alarm reaction (e.g., cortisol release without gastric ulceration). Thus, the GAS does not appear to apply to any but the most intense, prolonged, and painful physical stressors. Despite these criticisms, Selye's GAS was an important concept in the history of research on stress because it suggested that in addition to the specific, finely tuned bodily changes induced by aversive physical challenges to homeostasis, there was also a more generalized bodily response elicited by any one of a diverse array of intense stressors that threatened the organism's survival.

SUGGESTED READING

Selye, H. (1936). A syndrome produced by diverse nocuous agents. *Nature, 138,* 32.

Selye, H. (1956). *The stress of life.* New York: McGraw-Hill.

Weiner, H. (1992). *Perturbing the organism: The biology of stressful experience.* Chicago: Chicago University Press.

Karen S. Quigley
University of Medicine and Dentistry of New Jersey
New Jersey Medical School and
East Orange VA Medical Center

See also: **Homeostasis**

GENETIC APPROACHES TO MEMORY

Genetic approaches fall into two general categories: forward and reverse genetics. Forward genetics is concerned with the identification of genes and the starting point is usually the identification of mutant organisms with interesting phenotypes. In reverse genetic studies, the gene is already at hand, and the goal is to define its functions. This normally involves the study of organisms with defined genetic changes. Recently, animals with genetically engineered mutations have been used to develop and test theories of memory. Additionally, novel molecular techniques have accelerated the identification of new genes required for memory.

Forward Genetics

Long before we had the ability to directly manipulate genes in animals such as flies and mice, geneticists were busy using chemical mutagens to alter genetic information in living systems (forward genetics). The goal of classical or forward genetics, which continues to be used extensively to this day, is to identify the genes critical for biological processes of interest. The idea is that study of those genes is often a critical first hint in unraveling underlying biological processes. In forward genetic screens, animals are first exposed to a mutagen—for example, the DNA-altering compound ethyl-nitroso-urea—and then mated; the progeny are screened for phenotypic changes of interest. The phenotype of a mutant is the sum total of observed biological changes caused by a genetic manipulation. Recent application of this approach in the study of mammalian circadian rhythms resulted in the identification of *clock,* a crucial link in the cascade of transcriptional events that marks molecular time in organisms as diverse as drosophila and mice (Wilsbacher & Takahashi, 1998). Other molecular components of this pathway, such as *per,* were isolated in mutagenesis screens in drosophila. By identifying novel and unexpected molecular components of biological processes of interest, forward genetics has often reshaped entire fields of research. At times, science can go in circles, obsessively chasing its own tail of half-truths. Forward genetics, in the hands of masters such as Edward Lewis (developmental mutants) and Seymor Benzer (learning mutants), has the ability to turn paradigms upside down and initiate new lines of scientific inquiry.

The First Screens for Learning and Memory Mutants

Seymor Benzer and colleagues working with drosophila at the California Institute of Technology designed the first successful screen for learning and memory mutants in the 1970s. Benzer and colleagues developed a behavioral procedure with operant and Pavlovian components. During training the flies were allowed to enter two chambers, each with a different odorant, but they only got shocked in one of the chambers. During testing approximately two thirds of the trained flies avoided the chamber with the odorant that previously had been paired with shock. With this procedure, Benzer and colleagues tested a number of *Drosophila* lines derived from flies treated with ethylmethane sulfonate (EMS). The first mutant line isolated from this screen was *dunce* (Dudai, 1988).

Remarkably, three out of the four learning and memory mutations first discovered in genetic screens in drosophila code for members of the cAMP-signaling pathway. For example, *dunce,* lacks a phosphodiesterase that degrades cAMP. In the early 1970s, Eric Kandel and his colleagues at Colombia University, while studying learning in the sea snail *Aplysia,* also uncovered evidence that cAMP signaling is critical for learning and memory (Byrne & Kandel, 1996). Importantly, these findings have recently been extended into vertebrates, where electrophysiological and behavioral studies have confirmed the critical importance of cAMP signaling to learning and memory (Silva, Kogan, et al., 1998). This is a fascinating example of convergent evidence in science, but it also serves to illustrate that genetics, like any other tool in science, is most successful when used in parallel with other approaches. Besides identifying new genes, genetics can also be used to test hypotheses about the function of cloned genes (reverse genetics).

Reverse Genetics

In classical genetics an interesting phenotype is usually the driving force behind the molecular experiments required to identify the underlying mutant gene(s). In contrast, in reverse genetics, the interesting molecular properties of a gene usually drive the generation and study of the mutant animal (hence, the word *reverse*). It is now possible to delete and add genes to many species, ranging from bacteria to mice. For example, mice can be derived with the deletion (knockouts) or overexpression (transgenics) of almost any cloned gene (collectively referred to as *transgenetic approaches*). These manipulations can involve whole genes or they can target specific domains or even single base pairs.

With classical knockout and transgenic techniques it is not possible to regulate the time and the regions affected by the mutation or transgene. However, recent techniques have circumvented these limitations. For example, the expression of the gene of interest can be regulated by gene promoters that can be controlled by exogenously provided substances, such as tetracycline derivatives (Mayford, Mansuy, et al., 1997). Alternatively, it is also possible to regulate the function of a protein of interest by fusing it with another protein that can be regulated by synthetic ligands, such as tamoxifen (Picard, 1993). For example, our laboratory has recently showed that a mutant transcription factor called $CREB^r$ can be activated in the brain at will when fused with a ligand-binding domain (LBD^m) of a modified estrogen receptor; activation of this fusion protein represses memory without affecting short-term memory or learning (Kida, Josselyn, et al., 2002). It is important to note that irrespective of the exact method used, the general idea of reverse genetic studies is that the function of a gene can be deduced from the phenotype of the mutant animal.

Knockouts, Transgenics, and Memory

The first knockout transgenic study of learning and memory analyzed mice with a targeted mutation of the α isoform of CaMKII (Grant & Silva, 1994) and showed that this kinase mediates the strengthening synapses, a process critical for learning. Many studies since then have identified more than 100 other molecules required for synaptic function and learning. These molecules include members of all of the principal signaling pathways known, including cAMP, PKC, Ras/Raf/MAPK, and so on. These studies have provided compelling evidence that the molecular mechanisms responsible for the induction and stability of synaptic changes have a critical role in the acquisition and storage of information in brain structures such as the hippocampus. This finding is of critical significance because it is the cornerstone of our understanding of the molecular and cellular basis of learning and memory. The idea that synaptic plasticity is important for learning can be traced back to luminary neuroanatomical studies by Ramon Cajal; elegant experiments in a number of species such as *Aplysia* and *Hermissenda* helped to establish it as a dominant theory of learning and memory. However, the sheer number of convergent data from transgenetic experiments in mice helped to consolidate this theory and provided a means to explore its implications and significance.

The Future of Genetic Manipulations

In the near future it will be possible to delete or modify any gene, anywhere in most organisms of interest, and at any time of choice. Additionally, more powerful forward genetic strategies will allow the isolation of entire pathways of genes involved in any neurobiological phenomenon of interest, including learning, attention, emotion, addition, and so on. Microarray techniques and other molecular cloning approaches will allow the identification of gene profiles in mutant mice. These molecular profiles will be critical to delineating the molecular changes behind the expression of a mutant phenotype. In parallel with expected advances in genetics, there will also be advances in the methods used to analyze mutants, including the use of whole-brain imaging methods such as Positron Emission Tomography (PET) and Magnetic Resonance Imaging (MRI). It is important to note that genetics allows us to reprogram the biology of organisms. The finer and more sophisticated the phenotypic and genotypic tools that we have at our disposal, the deeper we may be able to probe the magical natural programs embedded in our genes.

REFERENCES

Byrne, J. H., & Kandel, E. R. (1996). Presynaptic facilitation revisited: State and time dependence. *Journal of Neuroscience, 16*(2), 425–435.

Dudai, Y. (1988). Neurogenetic dissection of learning and short-term memory in drosophila. *Annual Review of Neuroscience, 11,* 637–563.

Grant, S. G., & Silva, A. J. (1994). Targeting learning. *Trends in Neurosciences, 17*(2), 71–75.

Kida, S., Josselyn, S., Ortiz, S. P., Kogan, J. H., Chevere, I., Masushige, S., & Silva, A. (2002). CREB required for the stability of new and reactivated fear memories. *Nature Neuroscience, 5,* 348–355.

Mayford, M. I., Mansuy, M., et al. (1997). Memory and behavior: A second generation of genetically modified mice. *Current Biology, 7*(9), R580–R589.

Picard, D. (1993). Steroid-binding domains for regulating functions of heterologous proteins in cis. *Trends in Cell Biology, 3,* 278–280.

Silva, A. J., Kogan, J. H., Frankland, & P. W., Kida, S. (1998). CREB and memory. *Annual Review of Neuroscience, 21,* 127–148.

Wilsbacher, L. D., & Takahashi, J. S. (1998). Circadian rhythms: Molecular basis of the clock. *Current Opinion in Genetics and Development, 8*(5), 595–602.

Alcino J. Silva
Psychology and Brain Research Institute, Los Angeles, California

GENETICS AND GENERAL INTELLIGENCE

The discussions and the disputes about the contributions to general intelligence from heredity and environment have gone on for many years, but today we can reach an understanding. Progress has been made by behavioral geneticists and will be summarized. Also, a definition of *general intelligence* that is based on observable behavior will be used. It will, in genetic words, be a phenotypic definition.

The Construct of General Intelligence

The construct is derived by factor analysis, using objective methods from a wide variety of cognitive tests. By a method described by Schmid and Leiman in 1957, the factoring results in a matrix of factors that are orthogonal and hierarchical in structure. The general factor of intelligence is at the top of the hierarchy. This structure is replicable from one set of cognitive measures to another, from one sample of a population to another, and from one population to another that has had the minimum cultural exposure needed, for example, American Whites and Blacks. Note that all of the factors in the hierarchy, including the general factor, are necessarily phenotypic constructs. Factors defined by raw scores on tests do not suddenly become pure measures of hypothetical entities within the organism. The construct places the contributions of behavioral geneticists in a setting that leads to understanding. The correlates of this phenotypic score provide dependable evidence for widespread use of the score and the construct that it measures for individuals and groups.

Behavioral Genetics Data

Behavioral geneticists are using a program of correlations among different degrees of genetic resemblance of relatives to estimate three sources of individual differences in the phenotypic trait. One of these is genetic, two are environmental. The two are called *between families* and *within families*. The nature of the between families variance is indicated by the socioeconomic status (SES) of the parents, but it is broader than traditional measures of SES. Within families depends on the abilities and motivation of the child. Children seek environmental situations that they are comfortable with. These vary from child to parent and from child to child within a family. Opportunities for such exploration are essential.

These three categories of sources of individual differences in the phenotypic trait have different properties. Genetic endowment does not change with chronological age, but some effects may appear with age. Between families makes a substantial contribution in young children, but the effects diminish as children age. Children of parents who produce the original effect do get a head start at the time of school entrance, but it shrinks with age toward zero. Within family variance substantially increases in adulthood. Increases are expected to be somewhat specialized as a result of the child's interests, genetic endowment, and the variety of opportunities the child's society and family make available. Free public education and free public libraries make important opportunities available.

The changes of the three phenotypic traits with advancing age are highly congruent with available data on the stability of individual differences in intelligence from year to year. The correlation from one year to another shows a great deal of stability of the phenotype trait but does so imperfectly. Stability increases with advancing age. Children change their positions within their own population but do so unpredictably.

Correlates of the Phenotypic Measure

There are many correlates of general intelligence, so many as to justify the name. Before proceeding to characterize them, it is necessary to correct the most common and egregious error made by psychologists and others when interpreting correlations: the automatic squaring of r to obtain r^2. The appropriate measure of effect size r is parallel to the d used for differences in means by experimental psychologists.

Properties of the Correlation Between Means

When r is used to predict the performance of individuals, the estimate of the performance score is made with a good deal of error in most circumstances. The spread of individuals around their estimated mean is given by $(1 - r^2)$. It has also been shown, however, that the correlation between the distributions of the means of X estimated from Y, r, and the means of the scores on X can be very high. The reason is that most regressions of individual differences on good measure are linear. In large Ns the correlation between means approaches 1.00. Furthermore, the slope of the regression of the means is given by the size of the r in the individual differences data. A modest r of four tenths of the difference in those data estimates a performance mean in standard score units of the actual mean from the mean of the means.

Breadth of Correlates

The generality of the correlates of general intelligence has been supplied in a lengthy list by Brand. Traits of physique, temperament, attitudes, and interests are found to be related to general intelligence. Many of these correlations are of a size similar to those for simple and discriminatory reaction time and the speed of nerve conduction. Correlations with highly speeded performance are not as high as those with correct answers. General intelligence can be defined primarily by the cognitive skills, problem solving, and information processed by a child at a particular moment in time. As stated earlier, change does take place. Intelligence is not the speed and accuracy with which data can be processed; it is the learning, storing and retrieving of data.

The generality with which an intelligence test can be used on different groups is broad but not independent of twentieth-century American and closely related cultures. It does depend on more than a minimal acquaintance with the common language. Today's Hispanic children may not be measured validly by a test heavily dependent on the use of English. Most Black children meet the minimum requirement, as do Asian children. Children with a family handicap at 6 years old may gain more than those with a family bonus by age 18, but the test is still a valid measure of phenotype at age 6.

Accuracy of the Phenotypic Test

The items of intelligence tests have been investigated looking for differential item performance (DIS). For tests that measure well, any effects appear to be small and balanced. The conclusions of regressions total scores of two groups being compared.

Data on Blacks are most extensive. There is little differences in slopes. A test valid for Whites is valid for Blacks. Not infrequently there are small differences in intercepts of the lines. Cases in which this occurs typically overpredict performance for Blacks. The amount of this overprediction is about the size that is expected when two groups with different means have scores compared that are somewhat imperfectly reliable. There is little error in concluding that a given phenotypic score on a test of general intelligence can be used to interpret accurately without knowledge of the race, White or Black, of the person who obtained it.

Lloyd G. Humphreys
University of Illinois, Urbana-Champaign

GENIUS

As a concept, genius is closely related to *giftedness, creativity,* and *precocity.* From F. Galton's 1869 study of eminent men onward, definitions have been problematic. Although *genius* and *giftedness* are sometimes seen as synonyms, *genius* connotes exceptionally rare and prodigious achievement, whereas *giftedness,* especially in the context of identifying and encouraging academic or creative talent, has been defined in less restrictive ways. Albert's productivity-based definition of *genius* referred to the person who "produces, over a long period . . . a large body of work that has significant influence on many [others] for many years"—work creating a "major shift" in perceptions or ideas.

Biographical studies from 1869 to the 1940s focused on historically eminent persons, reporting that they tended to come from families of high occupational level and had histories of good health and character. Little support for a link between genius and either pathology or physical frailty was found, challenging long-held notions.

Intensive studies were undertaken of living scientists, artists, and professionals recognized as unusually productive or creative. Other than high intelligence, some common features of personality, work motivation, and perceptual style characterized these subjects. This work overlapped research on creativity, expanding the concept of giftedness beyond traditional IQ-based definitions to include originality and imaginativeness. Various measures of creative ability were designed and investigated.

Ann B. Pratt
State University of New York, Albany

See also: **Human Intelligence**

GERIATRIC PSYCHOLOGY

Interdisciplinary in nature and process, geriatric psychology is the science of the behavior of the aged. Geriatric psychology, with its medical, neurological, psychiatric, and physiological emphases, involves the behavioral, biological, and social sciences. The importance of cross-cultural and cross-national studies in geriatric psychology is increasingly patent in research.

Geriatric psychology is a rather new area of interest: Experimental studies of aging became a matter of concern only in the last 60 years. In 1947 George Lawton wrote comprehensively on a philosophy for maturity, proposing a bill of rights for old age. There are now delicate interpersonal situations in the multigeneration family in which the older group, conventionally defined as 65 years and over, increasingly calls for the attention, interest, and commitment of mental health workers. Geriatric psychology must be concerned with the terrors of loneliness in old age, worry about illness or shelter, anxiety over finances, or the unhappiness that results when one generation infringes on the life of another. Geriatric psychology must deal with the fact that aging is not synonymous with disease; that aging is not a state of ill health; and that a disabling, lengthy sickness is not an inevitable part of growing old. It must, however, promote understanding of the mental and emotional problems of the later years of life because accumulated physical handicaps, plus a general deterioration in bodily functions, superimpose a heavier burden on whatever emotional traumas may have developed earlier within the individual.

While the scientific body of knowledge pertaining to aging is called *gerontology,* Ignaz L. Rascher, in 1914, coined the term *geriatrics* for that branch of medicine dealing with the health problems of the aged. Rascher declared that medicine's challenge is to restore a diseased organ or tissue to a state that is normal in senility, *not* in a state that is normal in maturity; the ideal, in other words, is adding life to years rather than merely years to life.

In *Pain Management: A Practical Guide for Clinicians,* sixth edition (2002), Richard S. Weiner offers directly the most up-to-date information available on multidisciplinary pain diagnosis, treatment, and management—both traditional and alternative approaches for geriatric patients.

Geriatric psychology recognizes that the outstanding sign of aging is found in body tissues, where *stroma* (connective tissue, or nonfunctional elements) increases while *parenchyma* (functional tissue) decreases. The geriatric psychologist knows that every organ of the human body pursues its individual pattern of aging, and that, neuropsychologically, a decrease in hormones may be as important in aging as a flagging vascular system. A full understanding of the entire relationship between glands and aging still awaits full experimental findings.

The Task Panel on the Elderly of the President's Commission on Mental Health (1979) reported that the graying of America is one of the most significant demographic trends of this century. Every day 5,000 Americans join the ranks of those over 65, while only 3,600 die—a net gain of 1,400 elderly a day. The total number of older Americans is expected to increase from 23 million today to 55 million by 2030 (U.S. Census Bureau, 1977). The 75-plus age group is the fastest-growing segment of the population. Most recent census data confirm this trend.

Mental illness is more prevalent in the elderly than in younger adults. An estimated 15–25% of older persons have significant mental health problems. Psychosis increases after age 65, and even more so beyond age 75. Twenty-five percent of all reported suicides in this country are committed by elderly persons. The chronic health problems that afflict 86% of the aged, and the financial difficulties faced by many, clearly contribute to increasing stress (G. D. Cohen, 1977). The stresses affecting the mental health of the elderly are multiple and pervasive.

W. D. Poe and D. A. Holloway (1980, p. 147) quote Leonard Hayflick of Stanford University on population and longevity:

> . . . [I]f zero population growth can be achieved, it can be predicted that by 2025 A. D. those over 65 will number nearly 40 million and will constitute more than 20% of the total population.
>
> The inevitable consequence would be a further acceleration of current trends in which the government would be providing more health care, food, housing, recreation, and income to the elderly. Since it could safely be assumed that the proportion of those in government over 65 would also increase, the closest thing to a gerontocracy could prevail in 2025.

Frederick Sierles (1982, p. 206) wrote:

> Aging (senescence) is a gradual decline in physiological functioning as the years progress. It is debatable whether it begins with birth or in adulthood, and its causes are not known for sure. The decline in function varies in degree from individual to individual, and competence or excellence in behavior or other physiological functioning can be maintained by some at any age. For example, Vinci, Titian, Durer, Michelangelo, Voltaire, Goethe, Verdi, Renoir, and Picasso are examples of artistic genius that continued to flower in old age.

Thomas Crook and Gene D. Cohen (1981, p. 43) of the National Institute of Mental Health point out:

> Although many individuals remain physically and emotionally healthy into and beyond the seventh and eight decades of life, the prevalence of a broad range of physical and emotional disorders is increased in these years. Persons over age 65% account for a disproportionate number of visits to primary care physicians, for example, more than 30% of visits to specialists in internal medicine, and a substantial proportion of the prescriptions written for a number of drugs, including many psychotherapeutic compounds.

A basic geriatric problem of a psychological nature concerns elderly individuals who share households with kin. Charles H. Mindel's study (1979) indicated that while there has been a definite decline in the number and proportion of multigenerational households, the decline has been greater for the "young-old" (65–74) than the "old-old" (75-plus), with only slight differences in the proportion of "single" elderly males and "single" elderly females living in multigenerational families. In spite of the decline, the multigenerational household is still viable for approximately 2 million elderly persons.

K. E. Reever, J. M. Bach-Peterson, and S. H. Zarit (1979) reported on the impact of the elderly on relatives in a family constellation. The principal reason for institutionalizing cognitively impaired older persons is the caregivers' inability to continue providing help and not the severity of deficits. Feelings of burden were significantly correlated with the frequency of visits made by others but not with other variables such as the severity of cognitive impairment and frequency of memory and natural support systems as an essential part of providing services to the families of the impaired elderly. To be sure, the physical manifestations of aging are only a small part of the process of growing old. Changing attitudes, behavior, and overall personality—often the result of societal pressure—are now recognized as equally important considerations in the study of geriatric psychology.

David S. Baldwin and Jon Birtwistle in *An Atlas of Depression* (2002) present a graphical review of the diagnosis, management, and treatment of affective disorders in older populations, exploring the overlap of anxiety and the depressive syndromes in care settings.

In their *Handbook of Mental Health and Aging,* James E. Birren and R. Bruce Sloane (1980) write: "A national health problem which is most severe in terms of its prevalence and cost is a group of mental disorders and dysfunctions which are associated with aging. More important perhaps is a cost that cannot be measured or tabulated the loss of human potential and of the affected person's capacity for adaptation and ability to contribute to human welfare."

Geriatric psychology also concerns itself experimentally and theoretically with the signs and symptoms of disease processes. Widespread inflammation, muscular rigidity, cough, pain, and fever in the elderly are not minor but acute processes. Senile persons cannot bear extremes such as heat, cold, overeating, starvation, and dehydration. The older individual has accumulated many scars from the hazards of life: injurious habits, poor nutrition, intoxications, infections, and actual injuries, including the psychological traumas incident to a long life.

Steven Steury and Marie L. Blank (1981, p. 105), writing on retirement, state:

> In contrast to the popular view of the post-menopausal, empty-nest phase of a woman's life, it is typically experienced as a productive period with increased levels of satisfaction.
>
> Retirement in men is often considered an equivalent of menopause and may be viewed as marking the end of a productive life. Retirement is a new phenomenon in the history of man. In preindustrial societies men continued to work until poor health or death intervened. Some persons view work and satisfactions derived from work—apart from the income itself—as the ralson d'etre for men, much as they do childbearing for women.
>
> For many men, however, work is not the central life concern by middle age. Its meaning varies substantially by occupational level. For many men retirement is not feared but anticipated.

Another important aspect of geriatric psychology is the sexuality of the older person. Katie Ludeman (1981) reports that research refutes the pervasive cultural myth of asexual age. Men and women continue to be physiologically capable of sexual functioning, although in most older persons interest in sexual activity and actual performance decline with age. Older men are more interested in sex and more active sexually than older women.

In *Innovative Approaches to Health Psychology* (2002), edited by Margaret A. Chesney and Michael H. Antoni, it is pointed out that in our era of vaccinations, angioplasty, and gene therapy, there is the ongoing need for behavioral change in improving health on all age levels.

D. L. Parron, F. Solomon, and J. Rodin (1981) emphasize the need to direct the behavioral sciences toward a wider range of health problems than the mental health issues with which they have traditionally been concerned, to link the biomedical and behavioral sciences, and to stimulate interdisciplinary clinical and basic research. They point out that new research initiatives should be undertaken with respect to the changing vulnerabilities of the elderly to disease, the relationship of attitudes and beliefs regarding health and illness that influence the health care provider to the elderly, and the relationship of the health care provider to the elderly patient.

Appropriate attention should be given by mental health practitioners to the immunologic status of the elderly, for example, the impact of behavioral processes of adaptation on immune function, the impact of age-related changes in immunologic competence on behavior, and the role of the immune system in mediating relationships between behavioral processes of adaptation and the maintenance of health and the development of disease.

One of the major problems in the work of the geriatric psychologist is that of chronic, degenerative diseases, which include gout, arthritis, arteriosclerosis, and nutritional disorders (e.g., diabetes, anemia, and gonadal deficiency). Most of the disorders of old age are of doubtful etiology. They usually arise from factors within the patient, are highly variable, and are in operation years before they are overtly manifested. Unless and until the causative factors are unequivocally established, geriatric psychology must aim at *control* rather than cure and at *prevention* through better supervision and living. James A. Brussel (1967), writing on environmental stress in later years, quotes Claude Bernard, the father of modern physiology: "Health comes from harmony between the external environment and the internal milieu." This implies that geriatrical and gerontological knowledge, if it is to be truly scientific, must embrace all aspects of the process of aging.

Herbert Pardes wrote: "It is the challenge, and often the quandary, of behavioral scientists to assimilate a vast variety of influences and forces into a coherent portrayal of the whole person. A comprehensive model for studying and understanding the process of human development across the lifespan is essential for progress in all areas of understanding mental health and illness" (Greenspan & Pollock, 1981).

Christopher Foote and Christine Stanners in their *An Integrated System of Care for Older People* (2002) express the thesis for a multiagency approach to the support of older people, including coordinates of medical, social, and community services.

W. A. Knaus and others (1982) refer to the need for improved systematic data collection on acute and chronic health status to help make the intricate relationships among age, intensive care, and outcome easier to investigate and thereby improve.

The keynote in geriatric psychology is *individualization*. Each elderly person must be separately assessed and inventoried. The changes psychologically produced by old age are many: changes in emotional reactions, in intellectual functioning, response to stress, immunity, biochemical equilibrium, metabolism, structure, and so forth. In fact, recognition of "abnormal" mental and emotional features in persons of advanced years still remains one of the real perplexities of medical practice. Nowhere in the fields of psychiatry, neurology, and geriatric psychology are holistic principles of practice more meaningful than in treating geriatric individuals, for the aged person's mental condition will always be complicated by organic disorders of some kind.

Studies of health behavior in the elderly must take into account the social conditions as well as the underlying physical and psychological changes that occur with age. These changes function as a substrate for the influence of age and the presentation of disease, response to treatment, and complications that ensue. The same is true for the study of alcohol and drug use in the elderly. Of particular interest in both domains is the variability of physiological changes within and among individuals. Understanding the relationship among central nervous system, endocrine, and immune function may help in identifying one of the bases for this variability.

Research is needed to determine how adaptation to environmental situations may be interrelated with psychological defenses, coping, and social supports because these factors affect health and disease in older persons. Geriatric psychologists should look at specific components of the immune response and at substances such as thymic factors—especially important because they change with aging—that have powerful influences on immune function. Many of the important questions concerning the effect of aging on the interaction of health and behavior demand ongoing multidisciplinary research.

REFERENCES

Baldwin, D. S., & Birtwistle, J. (2002). *An atlas of depression.* CRC Press–Parthenon Publishers.

Birren, J. E. (Ed.). (1996a). *Encyclopedia of gerontology: Age, aging, and the aged.* New York: Academic. Volumes 1 and 2, particularly sections "Ageism and discrimination," by T. G. Gowan (71–81); "Autonomic nervous system," by S. Borst (141–149); "Cognitive-behavioral interventions," by H. M. DeVries (289–299); "Creativity," by D. K. Simonton (341–353); "Epidemiology," by K. G. Manton (493–505), of Volume 1; and "Memory," by A. D. Smith (107–119); "Personality," by J. E. Ruth (281–295); "Psychological well-being," by C. D. Ryff (365–371), of Volume II. See also: Academic American Encyclopedia (1995). Danbury, CT: Grolier. Section on Geriatrics, 122ff.

Birren, J. E., & Sloan, R. B. (Eds.). (1980). *Handbook of mental health and aging.* Englewood Cliffs, NJ: Prentice Hall.

Brussel, J. A. (1967). *The layman's guide to psychiatry* (2nd ed.). New York: Barnes and Noble.

Chesney, M. A., & Antoni, M. H. (Eds.). *Innovative approaches to health psychology.* Washington, DC: American Psychological Association.

Cohen, G. D. (1977). Mental health and the elderly. Unpublished paper, National Institute of Mental Health. Bethesda, MD.

Crook, T., & Cohen, G. D. (Eds.). (1981). *Physicians' handbook on psychotherapeutic drug use in the aged.* New Canaan, CT: Pawley.

Foote, C., & Stanners, C. (2002). *An integrated system of care for older people.* London: Jessica Kingsley Pub.

Knaus, W. A., Wagner, D. F., & Portnoi, V. A. (1982). Intensive treatment for the elderly. *Journal of the American Medical Association, 247*(23), 3185–3186.

Lawton, G. (1947). *Aging successfully.* New York: Columbia University Press.

Mindel, C. H. (1979). Multigenerational family households: Recent trends and implications for the future. *The Gerontologist, 19*(5), 456–463.

Pardes, H. (1981). Concepts of the Aging Process. In S. I. Greenspan & G. H. Pollock (Eds.), *The course of life: Volume III. Adulthood and the aging process.* Adelphi, MD: U.S. Department of Health and Human Services, National Institute of Mental Health.

Parron, D. L., Solomon, F., & Rodin, J. (Eds.). (1981). *Health, behavior and aging.* Interim Report, Number 5. Washington, DC: National Academy Press.

Poe, W. D., & Holloway, D. A. (1980). *Drugs and the aged.* New York: McGraw-Hill.

President's Commission on Mental Health (1979). *Task Panel on the Elderly.* Washington, DC.

Reever, K. E., Beck-Peterson, J. M., & Zarit, S. H. (1979). Relatives of the impaired elderly. In *32nd Annual Scientific Meeting Program,* Part II. Washington, DC: Gerontological Society.

Sierles, F. (Ed.). (1982). *Clinical behavioral sciences.* New York: Spectrum.

Silverman, H. L. (1996). On the meaning of psychotherapy: A survey and evaluation. *PAMA Journal, 1*(1), 32–39.

Steury, S., & Blank, M. L. (Eds.). (1981). *Readings in psychotherapy with older people.* Rockville, MD: U.S. Department of Health and Human Services, National Institute of Mental Health.

Weiner, R. S. (2001). *Pain management: A practical guide for clinicians* (6th ed.). Saint Lucie Press.

Hirsch Lazaar Silverman

See also: **Adaptation; Gerontology; Life-span Development; Quality of Life**

GERONTOLOGY

Increasing life expectancy has led to remarkable growth in the older adult population. According to the 2000 U.S. Census, 35 million older Americans, or 12.4% of the U.S. population, is over the age of 65. The over-85 age group includes 4.2 million Americans, the fastest growing age group in the United States. With the aging of the baby boom cohort, there will be 70.3 million Americans over age 65 in the year 2030. The rapidly growing older population and the significant impact of aging on physical, psychological, and social functioning suggest that knowledge about gerontology (normal aging) and geriatrics (clinical aging) will become vital for researchers, clinicians, and policy makers.

Successful Aging, Normal Aging, and Age Related Disease

Gerontologists distinguish between age-related disease, normal aging (typical changes without such disease), and successful aging (aging under optimal conditions). Each age cohort experiences a unique set of historical events, socialization, and education that shapes the experience of aging. Future cohorts of older adults are likely to have higher educational attainment, higher rates of Mood and Substance Abuse Disorders, and more favorable attitudes about mental health services than today's cohort of older persons. Societal changes also produce different contexts for aging, such as changing expectations about retirement and the roles of women. Therefore, descriptions of the characteristics and problems of older persons should be examined with some caution, as the older adults of the future may have some very different challenges and resources than are seen at present.

Aging increases risk for many disabling chronic diseases, including osteoarthritis, coronary heart disease, cancer, stroke, and Alzheimer's disease. Even in the absence of significant disease, normal aging is associated with loss of reserve capacity in systems including cardiovascular, pulmonary, and muskuloskeletal systems. This loss of reserve capacity leads to losses of strength, increases in body fat, and poorer aerobic capacity in the absence of sustained efforts to maintain fitness, which in turn increases risk for loss of functioning and independence, especially with illness or trauma. Recent studies of successful aging have shown that older adults who engage in aerobic and strength training can make considerable gains in capacity that are important in maintaining daily functioning. However, even world-class senior athletes, who may be genetically gifted and trained to optimal capacity, do not perform at the level of younger athletes.

In normal aging, many cognitive functions are well maintained including crystallized intelligence (vocabulary, overlearned information and behaviors, reasoning and judgment), immediate memory, and recognition memory.

Aging is associated with declines in fluid intelligence, or the ability to rapidly solve novel problems; slowing of cognitive functions; and declines in memory, especially difficult tasks requiring the use of free recall. However, normal age-related changes in cognition may be of minimal importance in the daily functioning of older persons unless they remain active in extremely demanding occupations. Most older persons find successful ways of compensating for these age changes or select activities that suit the changes in their intellectual skills, such as the scientist who transitions into mentoring and administration.

Aging, Stress, and Mental Disorders

Aging is associated with increased risk for a number of important stressful life events and chronic strains, including declines in health, death of spouse or significant others, and caregiving for impaired family members. However, common conceptions of late-life as generally stressful or unpleasant are incorrect. For example, recent studies of retirement show no negative effects on health or psychological functioning once preretirement physical and emotional functioning are considered. Older adults have lower rates of some stressful life events than younger persons because of their retirement status. Older persons are also often found to cope as successfully with problems as younger persons, and in some cases better, in part due to their prior experience with adversity and the fact that certain problems (such as spousal bereavement) are normative in late life.

The present cohort of older persons has lower rates of major depression, substance abuse, and some other mental disorders than younger cohorts. Older persons are at increased risk for a number of mental disorders, including the dementias (of which Alzheimer's disease is most common) and subsyndromal depressive and anxiety disorders. Future projections suggest we will see increased prevalence of late-life mental disorders when the baby boom cohort reaches advanced age. Mental disorder in older adults is distinct in that it is often comorbid with multiple physical disorders and complicating social factors. Older persons are often taking multiple medications and seeing multiple health care providers. These changes mean that mental health or behavioral health services should be carefully coordinated with medical and social services, ideally through multidisciplinary teams.

Clinical Assessment and Intervention

Psychological assessment of older adults should include attention to medical, social, and cultural issues, and clinicians should assure that assessment instruments are culturally sensitive and appropriately normed for older populations. Without attention to differences in educational attainment, older adults may be inappropriately diagnosed with cognitive and mental disorders. Comorbid medical problems may complicate the assessment process as well. Special measures designed to provide brief and valid assessments of common problems in older adults include the Geriatric Depression Scale, Mini-Mental State Exam, and Mattis Dementia Rating Scale.

Contrary to common conceptions, research has demonstrated the effectiveness of a variety of psychological interventions for older persons and their family caregivers for problems such as geriatric depression, family caregiver distress, managing incontinence, and reducing disruptive behaviors in patients with dementia. Interventions for older adults should be tailored to their values and perspectives. For example, the current cohort of older persons tends to fear psychiatric stigma and prefer treatment in medical settings. Innovative approaches that integrate psychological services into primary care and other medical settings hold considerable promise for reaching older adults that would resist referral to traditional psychiatric settings.

Future Issues

Given the projected growth of the older population, mental health professionals should attend to several important issues. First, all professionals providing mental health services to older adults need to receive basic education and training in geriatrics and gerontology with supervised practicum in order to meet the unique and various mental health services needs of future cohorts of older adults. Due to increased rates of disorders in younger cohorts and the aging of the baby boom population, we must also develop a larger cadre of geriatric specialists in all professions to work with patients with complex problems, conduct research, and train other professionals in the field of aging.

The 2000 U.S. Census data suggest that 25.4% of the elderly population in 2030 will be members of racial and ethnic minority groups. Increasing life expectancy among racial and ethnic minority groups means an increasingly diverse aging population and thus, interventions for older adults should be developed and provided in culturally sensitive and appropriate ways. Clinicians should consider factors such as cohort-specific discrimination and different values concerning caregiving and mental health issues held among different ethnic minority elderly groups.

Issues regarding reimbursement and public education need more attention as well. While Medicare is the primary insurer of older adults it requires higher copays for mental health than for other services. At the same time, many older adults are not aware that psychological services are covered under Medicare. Thus, it is important that the public is educated more about aging and mental health issues.

Our society is poorly prepared to provide for the growing numbers of older adults who will be increasingly diverse in their demographic and sociocultural characteristics and will also need medical, psychological, social, and long-term care services. Public policy must evolve to find ways to distribute resources to the special needs of older adults and their families while attending to issues of generational equity.

William E. Haley
Jung Kwak
University of South Florida

See also: **Human Development**

GESTALT PSYCHOLOGY

Early in the twentieth century, Gestalt psychology came about as an amendment to the traditional method of scientific analysis. The accepted way of analyzing a complex phenomenon scientifically had been that of describing the parts and arriving at the whole by adding up the descriptions thus obtained. Recent developments in biology, psychology, and sociology had begun to suggest, however, that such a procedure could not do justice to phenomena that are field processes—entities made up of interacting forces. The need for a revision was felt first in the life sciences, but inevitably extended to the physical sciences as well. Gestalt psychology thus became a component of a more broadly conceived Gestalt theory concerning scientific method in general.

This extension into the physical sciences became an integral aspect of the Gestalt approach for two reasons. First, many psychological phenomena, especially those in perception, could be described but not explained by what was observable at the level of conscious experience. It was possible to determine by laws or rules which conditions led to which consequences, but the only way to indicate the causes of such happenings was by reference to the physiological counterpart of the observed phenomena.

This procedure, then, implied a parallelism between psychological experience and correlated processes in the nervous system. The laws governing the functioning of the brain and, by extension, the physical universe in general, were assumed to be reflected in mental activity as well. Such a view—a second reason for Gestalt psychologists to stress the link with the physical sciences—made it possible to coordinate the functioning of the mind with the organic and inorganic world as a whole.

In textbooks of psychology the Gestalt approach is often exemplified by the "rules of grouping." Although easily reconciled with traditional analysis, these rules were presented by Wertheimer in preparation of what might be called a Copernican switch from a mere linking of elements "from below" to a primary concern "from above" with the total structure of the phenomenon.

In his paper "Laws of organization in perceptual forms," Wertheimer showed that the formation of Gestalt patterns is governed by a supreme principle which he referred to as the tendency toward the "good Gestalt" or the *Prägnanz* principle meant to describe a strictly objective tendency toward the greatest simplicity and regularity.

This tendency toward the simplest structure available under given circumstances or, to use a related criterion, toward the lowest available level of tension, has been of great explanatory value, especially in the exploration of sensory perception. Nevertheless, the simplicity principle alone was insufficient to account for perceptual Gestalten. If it ruled unopposed, it would reduce percepts to an amorphous homogeneity, to the limiting case of structure. What was needed was a counteragent, an anabolic tendency that offered constraints to the organizing forces in the field. In perception, the principal supplier of such constraints was the world of stimuli impinging on the receptor organs of the senses, especially those of vision, hearing, and touch.

At the retinal level, little if any of the Gestalt organization takes place. (The more recently discovered receptive fields in the retinae or the cerebral cortex of animals do not activate Gestalt processes.) At the higher levels of the visual apparatus, the stimulus configuration constrains the physiological field process, which is determined first of all by the tendency toward simplest structure (i.e., the physiological counterpart of the percept assumes the simplest structure compatible with the stimulus situation). A Gestalt has come about through the interaction between the stimulus configuration and the organizing powers of the visual field.

It is this interaction between tension-enhancing and tension-reducing forces that brings about the state of what Wertheimer called *Prägnanz.*

Gestalt structures vary all the way on a scale extending between two hypothetical poles. At the one extreme, there would be the state of total interaction. At the other extreme, the parts of a whole would be totally independent of one another, so that what happened at one place in the constellation would have no effect on the remainder.

Interaction in a Gestalt context is the very opposite of the functioning of machines, in which, in Köhler's formulation, the form of action in the system is entirely prescribed by the constraint. All action takes place along preordained channels. Machines can serve also as illustrative models for the networks of defined concepts that constitute intellectual reasoning, such as scientific theories. It must be made clear that although field processes in psychology and elsewhere must be understood as Gestalten, a scientific statement itself, by its very nature, can never be a Gestalt. Gestalten exist in perception, in mental imagery, in the dynamics of the human personality, in physiological and physical states of interaction, but they can be conceptualized only through networks of relations. The validity of the scientific description depends on how faithful an equivalent it offers, with its own means, of the Gestalt structures it undertakes to match.

The Gestalt approach requires that the subdivision of a whole into its components be effected in strict obedience to the cleavings inherent in the given structure itself. As a practical consequence, the range of a problem singled out for investigation cannot be arbitrarily staked out, but depends strictly on what is relevant for the processes under scrutiny. To discover the proper range of a problem is nearly tantamount to finding its solution.

Gestalt structure extends in the time dimension as readily as in the space dimensions, and the principles governing time and space are similar. The Gestalt analyses of spatial relations have had very little competition, but when it came to sequences in time, Gestalt psychology had to cope with a powerful tradition that explained all temporal connections by the laws of association. In its original form—in Aristotle—associative connections were based on something either similar or contrary to what we seek, or else on that which was contiguous with it. Such criteria were compatible with the Gestalt effort to derive connection from structural organization. When, however, it was asserted that associations come about by mere frequency of occurrence, Gestalt psychologists raised objections. A doctrine according to which anything could become associated with anything if it had been its neighbor often enough replaced meaningful belonging with a whimsical subjectivity.

Gestalt psychologists denounced conditioning by mere repetition as the lowest form of learning and opposed it with learning through understanding. Productive learning was now asserted to occur when a person or animal acted according to the demands of a given structure. Effective learning could come about only when the learner perceived the connections among the decisive elements of a given situation by what was called *insight.*

A decisive difference between the purely perceptual grasp of a given structure and a *problem situation* in the more particular sense of the term should be mentioned here. In simple perception, problem solving is limited to finding the structure inherent in the stimulus data. A harder task challenges the observer when a situation presents itself as organized in a way that conceals the connections needed for a solution. Restructuring may consist in merely looking at the situation differently or may require an actual rearrangement of the components.

The restructuring of a Gestalt is an eminently dynamic activity of field forces, but so is all structuring in the first place. In fact, a structure by definition never ceases to be a constellation of forces. Just as an apparently stable social pattern such as a family group never ceases to be a more or less balanced arrangement of various motivational tendencies, so a visual pattern presents to the sensitive eye a system of variously directed vectors that keep one another in balance. This reflection of the corresponding physiological field forces in experience is what Gestalt psychologists describe as perceptual expression. Expressive qualities are authentic and objective properties of all percepts. They can even be called the primary qualities conveyed by perceptual shape, size, movement, intensity, timbre, and so on.

Perhaps the most characteristic aspect of the Gestalt view is its profound respect for the "givenness" of the world as an objectively existing cosmos held together by law and order. It is a view that leads to a theory of value based on the criterion of objective requirement. Whether it be the irrational pressure of an instinct or the demands of the categorical imperative, value in Gestalt psychology is considered a field force—one that by no means issues always from the ego needs of the person who is doing the valuing. Gestalt psychology is therefore in strong philosophical opposition to a worldview that describes values as purely subjective and arbitrary, and therefore as idiosyncrasies to be excluded from the scientific image of the world.

Rudolf Arnheim

See also: **Perception**

GESTALT THERAPY

Origins

Gestalt therapy is an existential and phenomenological approach, emphasizing the principles of present-centered awareness and immediate experience. To discover how one blocks one's flow of awareness and aliveness, the individual in therapy is directed to fully experience current thoughts, feelings, and body sensations. Gestalt therapy was developed by Frederick S. (Fritz) Perls, M.D., who was trained in classical Freudian psychoanalysis. Perls's broad interests in existentialism, Eastern religions, and Gestalt psychology led him away from the Freudian viewpoint toward his own theory and method of therapy. Perls saw the human being as a unified organism, an integration of mental, physical, emotional, and sensory processes expressed in the present moment. Wulf (1998) notes that together with Perls, two other cofounders, Laura Perls and Paul Goodman, also were instrumental in creating the new synthesis.

Gestalt is a German word with no exact English equivalent. It means a configuration or whole, an entity which is more than the sum of its parts. In his first book, Perls presented the preliminary outlines of his approach (Perls, 1947). Later works elaborated and extended these early formulations (Perls, 1969; Perls, 1973; Perls, Hefferline, & Goodman, 1951).

Major Theoretical Concepts

Gestalt theory suggests that a continuing flow of needs and wishes comes into awareness, each of which can be thought of as a Gestalt, a figure or focus which emerges out of an undifferentiated background of experience. In healthy functioning, the organism mobilizes to meet each need, making contact with aspects of the environment appropriate to need satisfaction. For this self-regulating process to function, it is essential that the organism has sufficient *awareness*—that is, be in touch with thoughts, feelings, and sensations as they occur from moment to moment.

Perls emphasized the importance of accepting responsibility for one's own behavior. Instead of denying, blaming, projecting, and displacing responsibility for one's experience, the individual is encouraged to accept thoughts, feelings, and actions as parts of the self. Another key concept is *unfinished business,* incomplete situations from the past, accompanied by unexpressed feelings never fully experienced or discharged. Unfinished business can be resolved by reenacting (either directly or in fantasy) the original situation and allowing the associated effect to be experienced and expressed.

Therapeutic Goals and Role of the Therapist

The Gestalt therapist assists the patient to achieve greater self-acceptance, to assume more personal responsibility, to reintegrate disowned or split-off aspects of personality, and to be more authentic and less manipulative in relating to others.

The Gestalt therapist brings his or her own individuality into the encounter and takes responsibility for being present in a direct, spontaneous, and self-disclosing manner. Perls summed up the relationship between therapist and patient succinctly in his dictum, "I and Thou, Here and Now" (Yontef, 1993, p. 66).

Techniques of Gestalt Therapy

Gestalt therapists have described a variety of techniques to sharpen direct experience, heighten conflicts and polarities, foster freer expression, or to bring into awareness blocks and avoidance mechanisms. *Continuum of awareness* is a technique which encourages the patient to focus on the now, the ever-shifting midpoint of experience. The Gestalt therapist avoids "why" questions which encourage theorizing, rationalizing, and justifying. Instead, the therapist encourages the patient to "stay with" whatever is in the foreground and bring full awareness to the experience. The resolution of an unpleasant situation lies in experiencing it fully, not trying to avoid it.

In Gestalt therapy as practiced by Fritz Perls, *taking the hot seat* indicated a person's willingness to engage with the therapist. In this case the *hot seat* was a chair facing the therapist. An additional empty chair next to the patient might be used to imagine the presence of a significant other or disowned part of self for the purpose of initiating a dialogue. As the interplay between these conflicting parts is heightened and more fully experienced, integration through greater self-acceptance becomes possible. In the Gestalt method of *dream-work,* each dream is thought to contain an existential message—an expression of aspects of the dreamer's present state of being. By becoming every object and character in the dream (both animate and inanimate), the dreamer can identify with and thereby reown projections, conflicts, and unfinished situations reflected in the dream.

Applications of Gestalt Therapy

As originally practiced by Fritz Perls, Gestalt therapy was primarily an individual form of treatment. Other Gestaltists have applied the principles to group therapy (e.g., Glass, 1972; Feder & Ronall, 1980). Going beyond Perls's unique personal style of therapy, the work has been extended to a broad spectrum of client populations. Brown (1975) and Oaklander (1978) have described Gestalt work with children and adolescents. Gestalt family therapy is presented in the works of Kempler (1981) and Resnikoff (1995). Herman and Korenich's applications to management (1977) further increased the breadth and scope of Gestalt theory and practice.

Evaluation and Current Status

Gestalt therapy at its best can be energizing and enlivening through its emphasis on direct contact, expressiveness, focus on feelings, and minimal theorizing and interpreting. Critics, however, have pointed out that this approach can be technique-dependent, overly confrontive, and suitable only to well-motivated, verbal clients.

In the 50 years since its inception, Gestalt therapy has undergone considerable evolution. Yontef (1999) describes a growing movement toward a more relational trend in Gestalt therapy characterized by increased support and greater gender and culture sensitivity and away from the confrontation, catharsis, and dramatic emphases of the 1960s and 1970s. Gestalt therapy has become truly international with active practioners, institutes, training centers, and university-based programs throughout the United States and in many other countries.

Diversity in therapeutic styles, adaptations to varied client populations, and a burgeoning literature all point to Gestalt therapy's continuing vitality and development, as it finds its place in the mainstream of contemporary psychotherapy.

REFERENCES

Brown, G. I. (1975). *The live classroom: Innovation through confluent education and Gestalt.* New York: Viking Press.

Feder, B., & Ronall, R. (Eds.). (1980). *Beyond the hot seat: Gestalt approaches to group.* New York: Bruner/Mazel.

Glass, T. A. (1972). *The Gestalt approach to group therapy.* Paper presented at the 80th Annual convention of the American Psychological Association, Honolulu.

Herman, S. M., & Korenich, M. (1977). *Authentic management: A Gestalt orientation to organizations and their development.* Reading, MA: Addison-Wesley.

Kempler, W. (1981). *Experiential psychotherapy within families.* New York: Bruner/Mazel.

Oaklander, V. (1978). *Windows to our children.* Moab, UT: Real People Press.

Perls, F. S. (1947). *Ego, hunger, and aggression.* New York: Vintage Books.

Perls, F. S. (1969). *Gestalt therapy verbatim.* Lafayette, CA: Real People Press.

Perls, F. S. (1973). *The Gestalt approach and eye witness to therapy.* Ben Lomond, CA: Science and Behavior Books.

Perls, F. S., Hefferline, R. F., & Goodman, P. (1951). *Gestalt therapy: excitement and growth in the human personality.* New York: Julian Press.

Resnikoff, R. (1995). Gestalt family therapy. *The Gestalt Journal, 18*(2), 55–75.

Wulf, R. (1998). The historical roots of Gestalt therapy theory. *The Gestalt Journal, 21*(1), 81–92.

Yontef, G. (1993). *Awareness, dialogue and process: Essays on Gestalt therapy.* Highland, NY: The Gestalt Journal Press.

Yontef, G. (1999). Preface to the 1998 edition of *Awareness, dialogue and process. The Gestalt Journal, 22*(1), 9–20.

Thomas A. Glass, Ph.D.
Clinical Psychologist
Private Practice
Honolulu, Hawaii

See also: **Psychotherapy; Gestalt Psychology**

GLANDS AND BEHAVIOR

Glands may be classified as either exocrine or endocrine. Exocrine glands have ducts. Their products perform their functions in the immediate vicinity of the secreting gland, but outside the tissues of the body, although this may mean within the mouth or gastrointestinal tract. Sweat glands, salivary glands, and the exocrine pancreas, which secretes peptides involved in digestion, are examples. They have little direct influence on behavior. Endocrine, or ductless, glands secrete their products into the bloodstream and exert their effect on organs distant from the secreting gland. Several can produce profound direct effects on (1) maintenance of homeostasis; (2) modulation of emotional behaviors, especially those related to stress; and (3) sexual and gender-related behaviors.

There are six endocrine glands, and two of them have structurally and functionally distinct divisions. The pituitary, one of these latter two glands also known as the hypophysis, lies at the base of the brain and is connected to the hypothalamus by the infundibular or pituitary stalk. The anterior division of the pituitary is significantly larger than the posterior division and is called the adenohypophysis. The adenohypophysis is truly a gland and secretes growth hormone, adrenocorticotropic hormone, thyroid-stimulating hormone, prolactin, and the gonadotropins. Levels of hormones secreted by the adenohypophysis are controlled by the hypothalamus through its connections to the median eminence where axons from the cells of the parvicellular system of the hypothalamus release factors that either stimulate or inhibit release of anterior pituitary hormones.

The posterior division of the pituitary, the neurohypophysis, receives direct innervation from the hypothalamic magnocellular neurosecretory system. The cells of origin of the magnocellular neurosecretory system are located in the supraoptic and paraventricular nuclei of the hypothalamus, and they send axons to the neurohypophysis. The terminals of these axons release oxytocin and vasopressin that enter the bloodstream.

The adrenal gland also has two parts. Its outside is the cortex. Releasing hormones from the pituitary stimulate cells of the adrenal cortex to release either mineralocorticoids or glucocorticoids. Mineralocorticoids such as aldosterone work on the kidney to enable conservation of salt and water. Glucocorticoids are involved in the body's response to stress. The inside of the adrenal gland is the medulla. Its cells are the target of preganglionic sympathetic axons from the spinal cord and release adrenalin and noradrenalin into the bloodstream.

The testis of the male and the ovaries of the female comprise the gonads. Both the female and male gonads secrete estrogen, progesterone, and testosterone. The relative amounts of these hormones determine the sexual characteristics that distinguish the two genders.

The remaining endocrine glands are the pancreas, thyroid, and parathyroid. The endocrine pancreas secretes insulin necessary for glucose and fats to enter cells so that the cells can use them for energy or, in the case of fat cells, store them. The thyroid gland secretes thyroxin, which regulates metabolic rate and protein synthesis by cells throughout the body. The parathyroid secretes a hormone involved in the regulation of calcium concentration in blood. This gland has little direct influence on behavior.

The activity of virtually all endocrine glands, with the exception of the adrenal medulla, is directly modulated by hormones released from the pituitary, whereas the pituitary is regulated by the hypothalamus. Although the adrenal medulla receives direct input from the sympathetic division of the autonomic nervous system, even the release of adrenalin and noradrenalin by this gland is influenced by the hypothalamus because of its ability to control the autonomic nervous system. Any discussion of the role of glands in the regulation of behavior must include the hypothalamus.

Hormonal Influences on Homeostatic Mechanisms

The concept of homeostatic mechanism refers to any activity or group of activities designed to maintain a cell, an organ, or an entire organism in a steady state optimal for survival known as homeostasis. At the cellular level, an example of such an activity would be activation of the sodium-potassium pump to regain intracellular and extracellular concentrations of these two ions appropriate for the resting membrane. Eating and drinking behaviors are examples of homeostatic mechanisms at the level of the whole organism. Neural and hormonal systems are involved in maintaining organism homeostasis in mammals.

To maintain homeostasis, the body requires a variety of substances such as vitamins, minerals, trace elements, fats, carbohydrates, and proteins. If excess amounts of any of these substances are present in the circulation, they may be either excreted or stored. If too small an amount is present, it is necessary, in most cases, to ingest the missing substance. However, inadequate levels of vitamins, minerals, and trace elements (with the possible exception of salt) do not induce hunger. Hunger and consequent behaviors related to finding food and eating are induced by low levels of carbohydrates, fats, and possibly proteins.

The endocrine pancreas is the gland involved in the modulation of feeding. The islands of Langerhans scattered throughout the pancreas compose its endocrine division. Three different cell types within the islands of Langerhans secrete three hormones involved in regulating the availability of glucose to cells. These are glucagon, which raises blood glucose; insulin, which lowers the level of blood glucose by binding with cell membranes throughout the body and brain to permit entry of glucose into the cell; and somatostatin, which appears to regulate the release of glucagon and insulin. Insulin is the hormone of the endocrine pancreas most directly related to eating behavior.

Insulin is secreted in response to increased levels of blood glucose. This may occur after a meal or if glucagon is released and circulating glucose increases. Increased insulin levels cause glucose to enter cells more quickly where it is either used for fuel or, in the case of fat cells, is converted to triglycerides and stored. Blood glucose levels then drop. Data support the contention that hunger and eating are initiated when nutrient levels, especially glucose levels, decrease in the blood. Thus a high insulin level could lead to hunger because it decreases blood glucose. Furthermore, insulin levels can be influenced by the hypothalamus, and disruption of this control by hypothalamic lesions may explain some of the effects of such lesions on eating behavior and body weight.

The dorsal motor nucleus of the vagus nerve provides input from the brain to the pancreas. Neurons of the lateral hypothalamus send input to the dorsal motor nucleus, and stimulation of the lateral hypothalamus increases circulating insulin levels. Neurons in the lateral hypothalamus appear to be sensitive to changes in blood glucose use, either because they have glucoreceptors themselves or receive neural feedback from liver glucoreceptors. Bilateral destruction of the lateral hypothalamus produces an animal that will not eat and will starve unless it is carefully nursed back to health. It has been suggested that this effect is due to loss of lateral hypothalamic stimulation of the vagal nucleus, which leads to increased levels of insulin. Thus an animal without its lateral hypothalamus has continued levels of low insulin and low rates of glucose utilization. Therefore, its brain does not sense that it is hungry, and eating is not initiated. This is, of course, not a complete account of the neural control of hunger and eating, nor is it the only mechanism by which the lateral hypothalamus influences eating, but it does provide the first example of how the hypothalamus and a product of an endocrine gland interact to modify homeostatic behavior.

A second example is provided by drinking, which is part of a homeostatic mechanism designed to regulate body water content, salt concentration, and blood pressure. When blood volume decreases as a consequence of water loss, as might occur during heavy exercise that results in excessive sweating, blood volume drops, and blood flow slows down. This decrease in blood flow is sensed by the kidney, which responds by releasing renin, which in turn is converted to angiotensin in the bloodstream. Angiotensin does two things: It stimulates the adrenal cortex to release the hormone aldosterone, which stimulates the kidney to return sodium to the bloodstream. As the sodium is returned to the bloodstream, water is carried with it, and blood volume is partially restored by this mechanism. Angiotensin also stimulates the subfornical organ in the brain. Neurons in the subfornical organ in turn stimulate the circuitry in the medial preoptic area that mediates drinking behavior via connections to the midbrain. In addition, loss of extracellular water stimulates osmoreceptive neurons in the nucleus circularis of the hypothalamus that stimulate the supraoptic nucleus. This causes antidiuretic hormone (ADH) to be released from the posterior pituitary. ADH causes the kidney to concentrate urine and return water to the bloodstream. Therefore, thirst and drinking are also homeostatic mechanisms greatly influenced by glands.

Hormonal Responses to Emotional Stress

The two principal kinds of emotional behavior influenced by endocrine glands are those related to stress and those related to gender-specific sexual behavior. Gender-specific behaviors are not only those behavioral patterns involved in mating and care of the young, but also acts such as intermale aggression not directly involved in reproduction of the species. Certain of the gonadotropins are necessary to organize the development of the neuronal circuits that underlie these behaviors.

Terms used to classify emotions generally include happiness, love, grief, guilt, and joy. However, most of these are impossible to define with sufficient operational rigor to permit scientific study, especially when animal models are used to unravel the neural and endocrine contributions to the emotional state and accompanying behavior. This is because these categories of emotion have not been constructed and refined from empirical observation. Rather, they are words taken from everyday language that describe either the speaker's introspective state or the internal state of another individual inferred from that individual's behavior. Therefore, the contribution of the neuroendocrine systems to many emotional states commonly described in everyday terms is not known. However, the relationship between stress and the neuroendocrine system is well established, and this relationship may be extended to the states of fear and anxiety.

Fear may be usefully regarded as a response to a specific stimulus present in the environment, whereas anxiety is an anticipatory response to a possible threatening event. Fear, then, is generally a shorter-lived state, whereas anxiety may be chronic and generalize to the degree to which it is not bound to a specific stimulus. However, both of these states produce similar endocrine responses. The simplest of these responses involves discharge from the sympathetic neurons located in the spinal cord. The axons of the sympathetic neurons terminate on visceral organs, including arteries. Their activity during periods of stress increases blood pressure, heart and respiratory rates, and the release of liver glucose stores, while gastrointestinal motility is decreased. In addition, sympathetic activation of the adrenal medulla increases the release of adrenalin and noradrenalin into the bloodstream.

The adrenal cortex also is involved in response to either acute (fear) or chronic (anxiety) stress. However, the adrenal cortex is not directly activated by the sympathetic nervous system. As noted earlier, the adrenal cortex is activated by adrenocorticotropic hormone (ACTH). ACTH is released from the adenohypophysis (anterior pituitary) and stimulates the adrenal cortex to release glucocorticoids (cortisol, cortisone, and corticosterone). The glucocorticoids increase cardiac and vascular muscle tone, enhance the release of nutrients into the blood, decrease inflammation, and inhibit protein synthesis. The release of ACTH by the anterior pituitary is controlled by the hypothalamic hormone, corticotropin-releasing factor (CRF). CRF is manufactured by neurons in the paraventricular nucleus of the hypothalamus and is transported down the axons of these neurons and released into the portal circulation of the adenohypophysis where it stimulates release of ACTH. The paraventricular nucleus is strongly influenced by structures in the limbic system, such as the amygdala, that are involved in modulation of fear responses. The secretion of glucocorticoids by the adrenal cortex is closely linked to parts of the brain involved in elaboration of fear states and intensification of behaviors that accompany them.

Activation of both the sympathetic-adrenal medullary response and the hypothalamic-pituitary-adrenal cortical response are obviously adaptive in the face of immediate, comparatively short-term threat. These responses help the organism to fight or flee. However, as described by Selye, continual activation of these systems by chronic stress can lead to serious consequences for health. Selye referred to the changes produced by long-term stress as the general adaptation syndrome (GAS) and divided it into three stages. The first stage is the alarm reaction during which the body significantly increases the production and release of the stress hormones. This first stage lasts only a few hours, but the second stage, resistance, may continue for days or weeks. During this stage, blood levels of adrenalin, noradrenalin, and the glucocorticoids remain high. The final stage is exhaustion when the body can no longer respond to the stress.

GAS may be brought about by any stressful situation, including chronic physical stress (e.g., from exposure to extreme cold or in times of real physical danger), but it also may occur as a result of continual psychological stress. As originally described by Selye, the physical correlates of GAS include enlarged adrenal glands, with a marked increased in size of the adrenal cortex as its cells respond to the actions of ACTH and attempt to produce ever larger quantities of the glucocorticoids, as well as a shrunken thymus, weight loss, and gastric ulcers. Gastric ulcers are caused by chronic decrease in blood flow to the gut. Substantial rates of blood flow are necessary for maintenance of the mucosal lining that protects the stomach from the digestive acids. As a consequence of chronic activation of the body's stress response, the gut's blood flow is so decreased that its mucosal lining deteriorates, and the stomach's hydrochloric acid produces ulcers.

The cause of the shrinkage of the thymus noted in GAS is not known. The thymus is responsible for producing many of the lymphocytes (key cells in the immunologic defense of the body from infection), and chronic stress decreases the ability of the immune system to respond. The mechanism for stress-induced reduction in immune responsiveness is known and involves the increased amounts of circulating glucocorticoids present during stress.

Enhanced levels of glucocorticoids decrease protein synthesis. As a short-term part of a response to threat this is useful because it conserves metabolic energy. However, the decreased protein synthesis extends to those proteins that form the receptors on cells that recognize foreign elements in the blood. These receptors constitute antibodies, and the cells are the white blood cells (leukocytes), including the lymphocytes. During stress, production of both the antibody receptors and the cells that carry these receptors decreases. Prolonged periods of stress results in immunosuppression and increased susceptibility to infectious disease and the development of cancer.

Abnormally high levels of the glucocorticoid cortisol also have been found in 40–60% of depressed patients and is known to be caused by enhanced secretion of CRF by the hypothalamus. The hypersecretion of CRF by the hypothalamus is probably a specific effect of the general dysfunction of the ascending aminergic neurotransmitter systems (dopamine, norepinephrine, and serotonin) thought to be the biological cause of depression.

The overall effect of activation of the neuroendocrine systems involved in response to stress is to produce a state of enhanced readiness for physical action without necessarily activating specific neural circuits that produce directed behaviors. Although such activation may be beneficial for survival in the face of real threat, prolonged activation of these systems is detrimental to health.

Gender-Specific Behavior

Gonadal hormones exert effects on the nervous system and consequently on behavior that depend on the stage of development of the organism. During critical developmental periods, gonadal hormones produce permanent changes in the organization of neuronal circuitry that results in sexual differentiation of behavior. In the adult, gonadal hormones can activate gender-typical behaviors, but the behaviors do not persist in the absence of the hormone, and structural changes in the brain are not produced.

One gene determines whether the fetal animal or human will differentiate into a male or a female adult. Sexual dimorphism includes obvious body characteristics such as the form of the external genitalia as well as the organization of various neural systems and is determined by whether the sperm contributes an X or a Y sex chromosome when it fertilizes the egg. If the sperm contains an X chromosome, the resulting XX mix causes the fetus to develop as a phenotypic female. When the ovaries begin to secrete gonadotropins, the secondary sex characteristics and the brain will be feminine. If the sex chromosomes are XY, testis will develop, and the secondary sex characteristics and the brain will be masculine.

The critical gene that determines whether or not the gonads will become either ovaries or testes is located in the middle of the short arm of the Y chromosome. The gene is called the sex-determining region of Y and encodes for production of testes-determining factor (TDF). The presence of TDF causes the testes to develop. The testes in turn secrete two hormones that are responsible for the phenotypic development of the fetus as a male. If these hormones are lacking, no signals are sent to alter the intrinsic default developmental sequence, and the fetus develops as a female. Testosterone, secreted by the Leydig cells of the testes, changes the sex organs, mammary gland anlage, and nervous system into the male pattern. The second hormone is secreted by the Sertoli cells of the testes and is called Müllerian duct-inhibiting hormone (MIS). MIS causes the tissues that would become the oviducts, uterus, cervix, and vagina to be resorbed.

Although conducted before the discovery of MIS, an early experiment by Phoenix, Goy, Gerall, and Young serves to distinguish the roles of these two hormones and demonstrates the importance of testosterone for masculization of adult behavior. Fetuses of both sexes are exposed to high estrogen levels from the mother's circulation. Thus the primary secretion of the fetal ovaries is reinforced by estrogen from the mother. Phoenix and colleagues wondered what would happen if female fetuses were exposed to higher than normal levels of testosterone. To answer this question, they injected large amounts of testosterone into pregnant guinea pigs. The external genitalia were unequivocally male, but the internal genitalia were female. These animals were now pseudohermaphroditic. The explanation of this phenomenon is that the external genitalia were shaped as male by the influence of the testosterone; however, the oviducts, uterus, cervix, and vagina existed because these guinea pigs were not exposed to the second testicular hormone, MIS, so development of the internal genitalia proceeded according to the default female plan.

The second observation was more important. In normal adult female guinea pigs, administration of estrogen and progesterone produces strong lordosis when the female is mounted by the male. Lordosis is a gender-specific behavior activated in the adult female by the presence of estrogens in the circulation. Phoenix and colleagues found that the female guinea pigs exposed to testosterone in utero demonstrated little lordotic behavior when injected with estrogen and progesterone as adults. However, although they had functioning ovaries, they displayed as much mounting behavior as male litter mates when injected with testosterone. Mounting behavior is often used as an experimental index of the male behavior pattern and is seldom seen in normal adult females, even with testosterone injections. Prenatal exposure to testosterone may have not only produced masculine external genitalia but may also have changed parts of the circuitry of the brain to the masculine pattern.

There are relatively short critical periods in the development of the animal when manipulation of levels of sex steroids makes a difference in development of adult patterns of sexual behavior. Rats have a 21-day gestation period. The testes appear on the 13th day of embryonic life and secrete androgens until the 10th day after birth. Androgen secretion then virtually ceases until puberty. Castration at the day of birth causes male rats to display female sexual behavior as adults when injected with estrogen and progesterone and mounted by normal males. Male rat pups castrated after postnatal day 10 will not display lordosis as adults. This suggests that there is a short critical period when the brain is influenced by testosterone to develop circuitry for male sexual behavior.

Furthermore, the anterior pituitary of both males and females secretes luteinizing hormone (LH) and follicle-stimulating hormone (FSH). As noted previously, release of hormones from the anterior pituitary is under control of the hypothalamus. In males, LH and FSH are released at a steady rate, but in females, the release of these hormones is cyclical, and their levels are related to the cyclical activation of the reproductive organs. If male rats are castrated shortly after birth, cyclical release of LH and FSH will occur. If ovaries are implanted into adult genetic males that were castrated within 1 day of birth, these ovaries can cyclically ovulate, and the host male rats demonstrate behavior normally shown by females in estrus.

Exposure to higher-than-normal levels of androgens at

critical periods clearly can produce male behavior in genetic females, and lack of exposure to these hormones can feminize genetic males. Thus females exposed to high levels of testosterone during the critical developmental periods will exhibit mounting behavior at a rate similar to that of genetic males, and males lacking testosterone during the critical period will fail to exhibit mounting behavior, but will exhibit lordosis when exposed as adults to estrogen. A correlated observation to the results of these experimental manipulations is that in normal males and females, exposure to homotypic hormones (i.e., hormones appropriate to the sex of the animal) can trigger sex-specific behaviors (e.g., lordosis on exposure of a normal female to estrogen and progesterone). These observations suggest that the brain (1) must be responsive to sex steroids, and (2) there should be differences in organization of at least some parts of the brain between males and females.

For the central nervous system to respond to gonadal hormones, receptors for androgens, estrogen, and progesterone must exist in neural tissue. Such receptors are located in neurons found in several regions of the central nervous system of the rat and monkey. These areas include not only the hypothalamus, but also the frontal and cingulate cortex, amygdala, hippocampus, midbrain, and spinal cord. Unlike receptors for neurotransmitters, receptors for sex steroids are typically found in the cell nucleus, not in the cell-limiting membrane. Therefore, rather than changing plasma membrane properties, gonadal hormones influence DNA and the transcription of genes. This action permits these hormones potentially to exert influence over many functions of the cell.

The presence of receptors for the different gonadal hormones in the brain differs between the sexes. For example, it was noted previously that in females LH is released in relationship to the cyclical activation of the reproductive organs, whereas in males LH release is continuous at a steady level. Release of LH is regulated by neurosecretory cells of the anterior pituitary that secrete LH-releasing hormone (LHRH). The LHRH neurosecretory cells do not have sex-steroid receptors. These cells, however, receive neural input from neurons in the preoptic area of the hypothalamus. These preoptic neurons do have receptors for estrogen. Thus in normal females, as the ovarian follicles grow, the secreted estrogen stimulates neurons in the preoptic hypothalamus, which in turn stimulate LHRH neurosecretory cells to produce LH. In the brains of genetic females that have been exposed to high levels of androgens either prenatally or immediately postnatally, the preoptic cells do not express estrogen receptors and do not respond to estrogen activation. Therefore, the male pattern of LH secretion ensues.

The structure of the brain differs between males and females. The most obvious example is the sexually dimorphic nucleus located in the preoptic area of the hypothalamus. This nucleus is much larger in males. Unfortunately, its function is not known. Raisman and Field observed differences in organization of input to the preoptic area of the hypothalamus.

In addition to their influence on reproductive behaviors, the gonadal hormones also may have organizing and triggering effects on other types of behavior. For example, aggression between males is positively related to testosterone levels, whether the males are competing for a female. These effects may be related to neural events taking place in the medial and preoptic hypothalamus. Aggressive play is much more prevalent in male animals, and the incidence of this form of play is sharply reduced in male rats if they are castrated before postnatal day 6, but not if they are castrated later in life. Conversely, female rats given large doses of testosterone within the first 6 days of life exhibit as much aggressive play as males when this activity develops several weeks later. Similar findings have been reported for monkeys, but the manipulations must be made prenatally.

In summary, gonadal hormones have the capability of organizing behaviors if administered during certain critical periods of development of the organism. Presumably, this organization is due to the influence of these hormones on the developing brain circuitry, but the exact causal sequence between hormonal release and final brain circuit is not known. The exact timing of the critical periods when gonadal hormones can permanently influence behavior varies according to species, but critical periods occur either late during gestation or immediately after birth. The behaviors organized are those related to sexual activity but also include other behavioral patterns, particularly those reflecting aggression. Exposure to gonadal hormones also can activate behaviors such as mounting or lordosis in adults if appropriate sensory events, such as a receptive female in the case of male mounting behavior, are present. Gonadal hormones also influence the actual morphology of the sexual organs and secondary sex characteristics. Alterations in external sex characteristics might also influence behavioral expression, particularly in humans for whom sex roles are heavily influenced by gender assignment based on external appearance and consequent social learning.

Michael L. Woodruff
East Tennessee State University, Johnson City

See also: **Behavioral Genetics; General Adaptation Syndrome; Homeostasis; Neurochemistry; Pituitary; Stress Consequences; Transsexualism; Weight Control**

GOLDMAN EQUATION

In 1943, the chemist David Goldman studied salt flow through artificial membranes and described his results with an equation now known as the Goldman equation. His work remains important in psychology because the difference between sadness and happiness, good mood and bad mood, and even sanity and mental illness depends on the flow of charged salts (ions) through the protein channels puncturing neural membranes. For example, cocaine opens some Ca^{+2} channels; a mutation in some K^+ channels is thought to be associated with Schizophrenia; and general anesthetics keep GABA-sensitive Cl^- channels open longer.

Much of any cell's function is controlled by changes in the voltage across its ultrathin insulating wall. For a typical voltage of 100 mV across the 10 nm-thick membrane, the electric field strength is about 10 million V/m (about ten million volts across a doorway!). It should not be surprising, then, that small voltage changes can alter cell function by contorting the charged channel proteins. This is particularly true of voltage-controlled channels. Similarly, changes in the local electric field within stretch-sensitive channels due to slight membrane stretch alters ion flow through them, making them useful in cell volume regulation and detection of atomic movements throughout the body (in the ear, skin, muscle spindles, joints, etc.). For ligand-mediated channels, ion flow is altered by changes in the local electric field caused by bound hormones, drugs, or neurotransmitters. Because all of these channels are crucial in the electrical and chemical communication within and between cells, we clearly need to understand how channels open and close, how membrane voltages determine ion flow, and how ion flow determines membrane voltage.

Equilibrium

If an ion x (say, Na^+, K^+, or Cl^-) passes through a particular type of channel, the electrochemical potential energy difference (μ_x) driving the ion through the channel is given by $\mu_x = z_x V + E_{10} \log_{10} (x_o/x_i)$, where V is the voltage across the membrane, z_x is the ion's charge, and x_o and x_i are its concentrations, or activities, inside and outside the cell. $E_{10} =$ (2.303kT/q), where q is the proton charge in Coulomb, k is the Boltzmann constant, and T is absolute temperature in degrees Kelvin (Adamson, 1973; Hille, 1992). At 38°C, E_{10} = 60 mV. Diffusion of ion x is equal in both directions (equilibrium occurs) when $\mu_x = 0$ for $V = E_x = (E_{10}/z)\log_{10} (x_o/x_i)$, where E_i is the equilibrium voltage for x.

Nonequilibrium

While important, this last Nernst equation has limited practical application because ions are not often at equilibrium (except after death). Most often $V \neq E_x$, and there is a net ion flow or current through channels, approximated by the modified Goldman-Hodgkin-Katz (GHK) current equation

$$I_x = (n_x g_x p_o)[(z^2{}_x q/E_{10})V(x_i - x_o 10^{-z_x V/E_{10}})/(1 - 10^{-z_x V/E_{10}})]$$
$$= P_x \mathrm{GHK}_x$$

where n_x is the number of channels in the membrane, with a probability of opening of p_o and a single-channel conductance of g_x. The product $P_x = (n_x g_x p_o)$ is the membrane's permeability to ion x.

Graphical Interpretation

While the GHK equation appears daunting, it is most easily appreciated in its graphical form, in which it describes the current-versus-voltage (IV) curve for the ion/channel combination. As shown in Figure 1A, the shape of the IV curve is defined by the complex term within square brackets (GHK_x) and varies with the concentration ratio (x_o/x_i), and the magnitude of the current is scaled by the permeability P_x (Figure 1B). The IV curve passes through the ordinate ($I_x = 0$) at equilibrium, where $V = E_x$. As for P_x, the channel density n_x is determined genetically, is often up- and down-regulated during cell function, and may also be altered with drugs; and the channel conductance g_x may change with drugs or a genetic mutation (e.g., cystic fibrosis or Schizophrenia). For voltage-controlled channels, p_o often follows a simple Boltzmann function $p_o = 1/[1 + 10^{(V - V_{1/2})/V_{11}}]$, where $V_{1/2}$ is the voltage at which $p_o = 1/2$, and V_{11} is the voltage change from $V_{1/2}$ required to increase p_o from 1/2 to 10/11, or decrease it from 1/2 to 1/11 in the other direction. Because p_o is a strong function of V for voltage-controlled channels, their IV curve can take on complex shapes, often either N-shaped (Figure 1C) or L-shaped (Figure 1D). For stretch-sensitive channels, p_o is often described by a Boltzmann function, with $p_o = 1/[1 + 10^{(d - d_{1/2})/d_{11}}]$, where d is the membrane deformation, $d_{1/2}$ is the membrane deformation at which $p_o = 1/2$, and d_{11} is the displacement away from $d_{1/2}$ required to increase the opening probability from 1/2 to 10/11, or from 1/2 to 1/11 if the displacement is in the other direction. For ligand-mediated channels the opening probability is often a saturating function of the concentration (C) of the molecular ligand, and if n (the Hill coefficient) ligand molecules must bind to the channel receptor to open the channel, the opening probability is given by $p_o = [C/(C + K_{sat})]^n$, where K_{sat} is a binding parameter that determines the onset of saturation, and n is the Hill coefficient.

All Ions Combined

Of course, the parameters are different for different channel types, and different values of z_x, x_o, and x_i apply to each ion x. Nevertheless, if all ions flowing through a membrane share the same V (assuming no local charge screening), and we ignore ionic currents through membrane pumps and carrier molecules, then the total current is the sum of all channel currents, and the total IV curve is the vertical sum of each separate IV curve. Assuming only one type of fixed channel for each major ion (Na^+, K^+, and Cl^-), with permeabilities P_{Na}, P_K, and P_{Cl}, the total current would be $I_{tot} =$

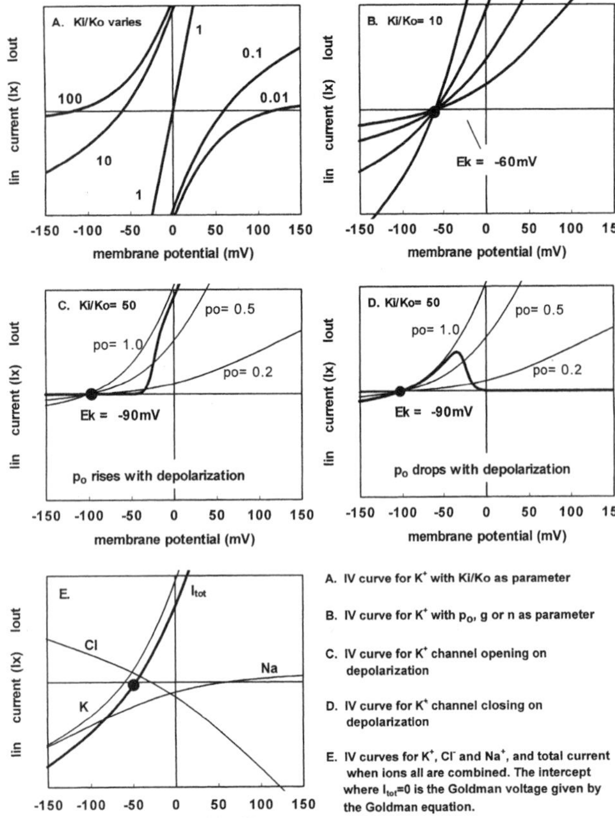

Figure 1. Membrane potentials.

$P_{Na}GHK_{Na} + P_{K}GHK_{Na} + P_{Cl}GHK_{Cl}$ (Figure 1E), and the net current is zero at a particular voltage, V_m, which is not necessarily equal to E_{Na}, E_K, or E_{Cl}. This resting membrane voltage is important because it is the only voltage that is stable: When $I_{tot} = 0$, the membrane is neither charging nor discharging, and the voltage remains constant as long as the concentrations remain fixed. It can be shown that $I_{tot} = 0$ for a value of V_m given by the Goldman equation $V_m = E_{10}\log_{10}[(P_{Na}Na_i^+ + P_K K_i^+ + P_{Cl}Cl_o^-)/(P_{Na}Na_o^+ + P_K K_o^+ + P_{Cl}Cl_i^-)]$ Clearly the resting membrane voltage changes with the concentration ratios (as in sensory cells, like Na^+ detection on the tongue), or permeabilities (as in sensory cells, in neurotransmission, and during drug action).

Problems with the Goldman Equation

While useful as a first approximation, the Goldman equation is not applicable when cells or their environments are asymmetrical, because different permeabilities and ion concentrations apply around the cell's perimeter. The equation is also inappropriate when significant current flows through membrane pumps or carriers, as in salt transport epithelia. Nevertheless, in symmetric cells dominated by channel currents, the Goldman equation estimates the membrane voltage. If ion x dominates because of its large concentration or high permeability, the Goldman equation simplifies to the Nernst equation, and V_m tends to E_x. Finally, if an ion is not being pumped through a membrane, it ultimately distributes passively across the membrane according to its charge and the membrane voltage, and cancels itself out of the Goldman equation. It is common, then, for such passive ions to be excluded from the equation at the outset. This is problematic because the passive redistribution of passive ions takes time, and passive ions can still modify rapid voltage changes such as action potentials or postsynaptic potentials.

Robert Patuzzi
University of Western Australia

GRIEF

Grief is usually defined as a person's constellation of responses to loss and bereavement. As a universal human phenomenon, it has biological, cultural, and unique individual components.

Grief's biological aspects can be seen as having roots in the behaviors of animals. Greylag geese were observed by ethologist Konrad Lorenz (1952) as having a pattern of restless searching for a lost mate. Bereaved primates such as rhesus monkeys exhibit patterns of depressed behavioral activity, lowered bodily temperature, and whimpering. Elephants have been reported to bury dead animals (including humans). Thus, it can be said that grief is not limited to the realm of the human but is deeply rooted in animal experience.

Cultural determinants of grief are seen in the great range of grief reactions throughout history. For example, today's Western cultural norms of grieving are very different from earlier practices largely because witnessing death is a relatively rare experience. In the Middle Ages, an individual might have known, every year, about 100 people who died of childhood illnesses, of plagues, or of a variety of other causes that are uncommon today. Rituals such as the *nuntius mortis* (asking a close friend to play the role of letting you know when you looked like you might be getting mortally ill so that you could prepare for a good death) were commonplace.

Individual aspects of grief are the result of many factors in addition to the cultural and biological. These include the personality and coping history of each griever, his or her relationship with the deceased, and the circumstances surrounding the loss.

John Bowlby (1980) had demonstrated the importance of affectional bonds or attachments. We form such bonds through simple close contact with another. Many of our needs, especially needs for safety and security, are met through our attachments to intimate others. As a result, the death of someone to whom we have been attached is a painful experience.

The experience of losing someone to whom we have been

attached occurs on at least four levels, according to thanatologist J. William Worden (2001). Thus, grief is normally seen in the many ways that reflect these levels of experiencing. Knowing that these are normal reactions can sometimes bring a measure of reassurance to the grieving person.

1. Normal *feelings* include sadness (the most common feeling), shock, numbness, yearning, loneliness, guilt, anxiety, helplessness, fatigue, and anger.
2. Normal *cognitions* include confusion, difficulty concentrating, disbelief, preoccupation, and hallucinations (thinking one has just seen or heard the deceased).
3. Normal *behaviors* include crying, sleep disturbance, eating disturbance, restlessness, and searching and calling out to or dreaming of the deceased.
4. Normal *physical sensations* include oversensitivity to noise, a lump in the throat, tightness in the chest, shortness of breath, dry mouth, lack of energy, and muscle weakness.

Others, notably Corr, Nabe, and Corr (2000), have included two additional levels.

5. *Social* disturbances include withdrawal, problems in relationships, and problems working in groups (e.g., at work).
6. *Spiritual* disturbances include anger with God, a search for meaning, and a sense that previous ways of making sense of life are now inadequate.

It is important, according to research by Thomas Attig (1996) and others, to recognize that grieving is a process of coping. It is a process that demands energy and presents the grieving person with tasks, choices, and opportunity for growth.

The grieving process has been characterized by several theorists as occurring in phases or stages. Perhaps the best-known phase model has been that of Colin Murray Parkes (1987). Drawing on the work of Bowlby, Parkes (1987) described four phases:

1. Shock and numbness (an initial reaction of feeling dazed)
2. Yearning and searching (protesting the reality of the loss)
3. Disorganization and despair (questioning one's sense of self and disorganized cognitive schemas)
4. Reorganization (making sense of one's life, including integrating the loss into one's scheme of things)

Phase models have considerable face validity because they seem to describe experiences common to many people. However, their emphasis on sequence may not best describe the process of grieving. It may be more accurate to describe the phases as overlapping and often repeating events following a loss.

A different approach to grieving has emphasized the tasks involved in the process. Worden (2001) has offered the best-known of the task models. In its stressing the importance of tasks in the grieving process, this approach can be therapeutic. The active accomplishment of tasks frames grieving as a process in which the individual exercises his or her self-determination of the outcome. The tasks of mourning are

- Accepting the reality of the loss—the facts of the loss as well as the meaning of the loss
- Experiencing the pain;
- Adjusting to an environment in which the deceased is missing—learning new skills, taking on the roles of the deceased, and otherwise adapting
- Emotionally relocating the deceased and moving on with life—reinvesting one's emotional energy without forgetting the deceased

Grieving can often be an active process with opportunities for growth and self-definition. Catherine Sanders (1998) has contributed the concept of a "decision point" that most people seem to reach after the early (perhaps more biologically influenced) aspects of grieving. She points out that a grieving person makes a decision, sometimes unconsciously, to survive and go on with a new life or to remain in a state of bereavement.

A widely accepted approach to grieving and grief therapy focuses on the individual's reconstruction of meaning. Robert Neimeyer (2000), the editor of *Death Studies,* has articulated this idiographic model that emphasizes each individual's unique experience of grieving. The revision of one's life story is the central process in grieving, and grief therapy is an opportunity for grieving persons to tell their life stories in ways that will help them make sense of loss and of life.

Human life can be seen as a process of telling one's story. Through telling and revising our stories, people develop a sense of meaning, purpose, and self. Losses and deaths disrupt our stories. They can threaten assumptions that have given meaning and order to our lives. Significant losses can initiate a search for meaning. Recent studies indicate that at least 70–85% of bereaved persons engage in a search for meaning in their lives. Research by Davis, Nolen-Hoeksema, and Larson (1998) has found that this search usually centers on two kinds of questions. Early questions try to make sense of the loss: "Why did this happen? What is the meaning of this loss (death)?" Later questions try to find benefits from the loss: "What can I learn from this experience?" or "What is the meaning of this experience in my life?" Neimeyer (2000) has said that such new meanings become part of the grieving person's broad scheme of things. Thus, for most people bereavement can be a time for looking at such existential questions as "What is the purpose of my life? Who am I?"

Grieving can ultimately be a time of learning about oneself. We learn about ourselves by observing our own behaviors following a loss, by listening to our own answers to existential questions, and by revising our life stories following the urgent experience of bereavement. A growth outcome of grieving can be increased self-perception and self-definition.

REFERENCES

Attig, T. (1996). *How we grieve: Relearning the world.* New York: Oxford University Press.

Bowlby, J. (1980). *Attachment and loss: Vol. 3. Loss, sadness, and depression.* New York: Basic Books.

Corr, C. A., Nabe, C. M., & Corr, D. M. (2000). *Death and dying, life and living* (3rd ed.). Belmont, CA: Wadsworth/Thomson Learning.

Davis, C. G., Nolen-Hoeksema, S., & Larson, J. (1998). Making sense of loss and benefiting from the experience: Two construals of meaning. *Journal of Personality and Social Psychology, 75*(2), 561–574.

Lorenz, K. (1952). *King Solomon's ring.* London: Methuen.

Neimeyer, R. A. (2000). Searching for the meaning of meaning: Grief therapy and the process of reconstruction. *Death Studies, 24*(6), 541–558.

Parkes, C. M. (1987). *Bereavement: Studies of grief in adult life* (2nd ed.). Madison, CT: International Universities Press.

Sanders, C. M. (1998). *Grief the mourning after: Dealing with adult bereavement* (2nd ed.). New York: Wiley.

Worden, J. W. (2001). *Grief counseling and grief therapy: A handbook for the mental health professional* (3rd ed.). New York: Springer.

SUGGESTED READING

Robak, R. W. (1999). *Loss and bereavement counseling.* South Orange, NJ: Hemlock Falls Press.

Rostyslaw Robak
Pace University

See also: **Depression**

GROSS MOTOR SKILL LEARNING

The acquisition of motor skill, sometimes referred to as *motor learning,* has been the object of a great deal of experimental work. By far the most popular apparatus for such study has been the pursuit rotor or rotary pursuit test.

The most important variable affecting performance during the acquisition of skill is *distribution of practice.* Typically, performance is very much better with spaced practice than with massed practice. Special procedures employed along with distribution of practice reveal certain other important phenomena. For example, a rest of 10 minutes or more following a series of massed-practice trials produces an increase in performance called *reminiscence.* This spontaneous improvement means that the reduced performance under massed practice is an effect on performance exclusively; massed-practice subjects have learned just as much as distributed-practice subjects.

Sometimes this last fact is partially obscured by the subjects' need to warm up after the rest following massed practice. The theory that the effects of distribution are on performance rather than on learning is further supported by the data obtained following a test for reminiscence. If the subjects are returned to a massed-practice schedule of trials, their performance decreases. Somewhat surprising, this decrease typically continues until the learning curve has returned approximately to the level where it would have been if no rest period had been introduced; then performance begins to increase. If subjects switch to distributed practice following the rest, their performance shows no trace of the previous experience on massed practice after the necessary warmup.

Greg A. Kimble

GROUP COHESIVENESS

Group cohesiveness has been defined in many ways. Leon Festinger defined the concept in terms of forces that lead an individual to remain in or leave a given group. One way to understand group cohesiveness rests on the idea of "task." Implicitly or explicitly, every group has a task or tasks it must accomplish. Many schemes have been presented for categorizing group tasks. Some approaches have emphasized the unconscious motives harbored by group members. Others have specified aspects of communication among group members. Still others have focused on the content of observed aspects of the work of the group. The extent to which members of a group identify with and work toward a common task is a measure of group cohesiveness.

What influences group cohesiveness? Although Rabbie and colleagues have suggested that competition between groups has no more effect on ingroup cohesion than does intergroup cooperation, the majority of writers over the years have agreed that hostility toward an outside person or persons serves to strengthen cohesiveness within a group.

Bion suggested that group tasks often derive from members' unconscious and primitive needs and expectations. He classified these activities as *dependence, fight–flight,* and *pairing.* These activities reflect assumptions shared by all in the group. The task or purpose of the *dependent group* is to be sustained by a leader. In the *fight–flight group* the purpose is simply to defend against some threat, either by fighting someone or something or by running away. In the *pairing group* the members act as if their purpose is union and some new entity will derive from that unity. Bion believed that it was necessary to attend to both work and basic aspects of group activity to fully comprehend a given group and such group considerations as cohesiveness.

To explain how individuals in a group come together to behave toward some common end, Thomas French developed the concept of "focal conflict." Similar ideas have been postulated by other writers as well. In general, such notions refer to a tendency for groups to attend to topics that have relevance, often by reducing anxiety for all members. Many specialties have concerned themselves with group phenomena. Personality and psychotherapy theorists, social and organizational psychologists, anthropologists, and educational specialists are but a number of professions interested in this topic. Diverse methods and emphases have influenced conclusions. An integration of findings about group cohesiveness has not yet been achieved.

Stanley Berent
University of Michigan

GROUP COUNSELING

Group counseling is typically conducted with a small number of people, usually seven to ten, depending upon the ages of the group members. The individuals in the group provide the subject matter for discussion by sharing their personal thoughts, feelings, and behavior. Group members are expected to be involved in the process by reacting to each other through feedback, support, and problem solving.

The leader usually has had special training in group counseling techniques and strives to create an atmosphere of trust, openness, responsibility, and interdependency. The leader typically models appropriate behavior and guides group members through the processes of understanding, caring, and conflict management.

Differences between group counseling and group psychotherapy center on the composition of group membership, the degree of personality change expected, and the nature of the group leader's training. Methods, procedures, and theories used in counseling and therapy groups are often quite similar.

Members of a counseling group can come from virtually any walk of life and typically fall within the normal ranges of adjustment and ability to cope with life situations. They join counseling groups to gain deeper personal insights or to develop their personal potentials. Psychotherapy group members bring more severe personality problems to the group and may be mildly to chronically neurotic, with limited ability to deal with life problems. They usually require more intensive personal work in restructuring basic personality patterns.

Both counseling and therapy group leaders require special training in the conduct of groups. Counselors typically focus their training on normal life-span development. Psychotherapists usually spend more training time with abnormal populations and in the study of psychopathology.

Group counseling owes its historical roots to the influence of group dynamics and the more established procedures used with group guidance and group psychotherapy. Groups are a natural phenomenon in human history. Forerunners of organized groups include various religious movements, drama, and morality plays. Some historians cite Mesmer's work as a precursor of group treatment.

Most, however, note the "class method" work of J. H. Pratt as the beginning of scientific group treatment in the United States. Pratt used a directive-teaching methodology with his tubercular patients as he instructed them in hygiene, nutrition, and rest. His original intention was to boost their morale through more effective cleanliness. It soon became clear that his patients were deriving more benefit from the supportive atmosphere of the group than from the information imparted in the lectures. The method more resembled what we think of as a psychoeducational group today (Berg, Landreth, & Fall, 1998).

Alfred Adler and J. L. Moreno began using group methods in Europe. Adler would counsel children in front of a group, with the primary purpose of instructing other professionals in individual psychology. The observation was made that the group or audience, as they asked questions and interacted, had a positive impact on the counseling.

Moreno used group techniques with the street people of Vienna. He worked with children, displaced persons, and prostitutes as he found them in their environments. Moreno introduced sociometry and psychodrama to the United States; he also coined the terms *group therapy* and *group psychotherapy.*

Others who have had great influence on group work in the United States include S. R. Slavson who introduced methods known as activity group therapy, initially developed with socially maladjusted children. Rudolph Dreikurs applied Adlerian principles in his work with family groups and children in Chicago. Carl Rogers and his person-centered or phenomenological approach helped further popularize group work.

Owing to influences of group psychotherapy and group dynamics, many early writers used the terms *guidance, counseling,* and *psychotherapy* interchangeably. Continuing clarification of terms and procedures along with the professionalization of school counselors and counselors in public agencies and private practice has added acceptability and credibility to group counseling.

Other influences in the acceptance of group counseling as a viable treatment include the Human Potential Movement and professional counselor organizations such as the American Counseling Association (ACA) and the American Psychological Association. Each of these major organizations has ethics codes that specifically address the area of group work.

In 1973, under the leadership of George Gazda, the Association for Specialists in Group Work was officially formed as a division of the American Personnel and Guidance Association (APGA) now the (ACA). The ACA was and is very active in the promotion of ethical guidelines for leaders and professional standards for the training of group leaders.

Yalom (1995) addressed what he termed therapeutic factors that operate in every type of counseling or therapy group. They include (1) the *imparting of information*—Included is didactic instruction, advice, suggestions, or direct guidance about life problems; (2) the *instillation of hope*—High expectations for success, hope, and faith in the treatment model have been related to positive outcomes in groups; (3) *universality*—Participation often teaches people that they are not alone or isolated with the "uniqueness" of their problems, frequently producing a sense of relief; (4) *altruism*—Group members help one another by offering support, suggestions, reassurance, and insights; (5) the *corrective recapitulation of the primary family group*—Groups resemble families in several significant ways. Many group members have had unsatisfactory experiences in their original families; the group offers an opportunity to work through and restructure important family relationships in a more encouraging environment; (6) the *development of socializing techniques*—Social learning takes place in all groups. The development of basic social or interpersonal skills is a product of the group counseling process that is encouraged by member-to-member feedback; (7) *imitative behavior*—A group member often observes the work of another member with similar problems. Through vicarious therapy the group member can incorporate or try out new behaviors; (8) *interpersonal learning*—The group is a social microcosm providing the necessary therapeutic factors to allow corrective emotional experiences. Group members, through validation and self-observation, become aware of their interpersonal behavior. The group, through feedback and encouragement, helps the member see maladaptive social and interpersonal behavior and provides the primary supportive environment for change; (9) *group cohesiveness*—It is defined as the attractiveness a group has for its members, a "we-ness," "groupness," or "togetherness." Cohesiveness in a group is analogous to connectedness or relationship between individuals. Acceptance and support demonstrated by the group can be a potent healing force; and (10) *catharsis*—The group provides members with a safe place to vent their feelings rather than holding them inside. The process encourages learning how to express feelings in general and to express both negative and positive feelings.

While these therapeutic factors are cited as advantages for the use of groups as a treatment method, there are also several risks and limitations. Corey and Corey (2002) caution that groups are not "cure-alls" and that not all people are suited for groups. Some potential members may be too suspicious, hostile, or fragile to gain benefits from a group experience. Additionally, there is often a subtle pressure to conform to group norms.

When a group member accepts the process of the group, there is the possibility of some psychological hazard. As members open up, they may become vulnerable, particularly with the significant people in their lives.

Also, absolute confidentiality is difficult to ensure: Some members may talk about what they have heard outside the group. Any treatment system as potent as a group can cause major life disruptions. Changes can occur in lifestyle and values, and in loss of security. Potential group members should be aware of these risks and limitations.

While it is doubtful that many group leaders practice from a pure theoretical position, preferring an eclectic approach, theoretical positions with the widest currency include the *person-centered model,* developed by Carl Rogers and his proponents. It is based on the assumption that human beings have an innate ability to reach their full potential. This includes the potential to solve their own problems, given a free and permissive atmosphere. Frederick S. Perls and his followers developed the *Gestalt therapy model.* Group experience focuses upon an intensive here-and-now orientation. The experiencing of the present moment provides insight into personal behavior and creates the basis upon which new decisions for behavior change can be made. Group members are taught to take personal responsibility for all of their feelings and behavior. The *Rational-Emotive Behavior Therapy model* developed by Albert Ellis uses an educational rather than a medical or psychodynamic system. Direct behavioral actions taken upon one's belief in irrational ideas that result from verbal self-indoctrination form the bases for behavior change. The goal of therapy is to assist group members in internalizing a more rational philosophy of life and thus to behave and live life more fully.

Other theoretical approaches that have gained some measure of acceptance, but that may be limited to certain distinct settings, include the psychoanalytic model, transactional analysis, cognitive therapy models, the development approach, and Adlerian lifestyle approaches.

REFERENCES

Berg, R. C., Landreth, G. L., & Fall, K. A. (1998). *Group counseling: Concepts and procedures* (3rd ed.). Philadelphia: Taylor and Francis.

Corey, M. S., & Corey, G. (2002). *Groups: Process and practice* (6th ed.). Pacific Grove, CA: Brooks/Cole.

Yalom, I. D. (1995). *The theory and practice of group psychotherapy* (4th ed.). New York: Basic Books.

Robert C. Berg
University of North Texas

See also: **Counseling; Psychotherapy**

GROWTH HORMONE ([GH] SOMATOTROPIN)

The human anterior pituitary gland contains 5–10mg growth hormone (GH), which is synthesized and stored in cells referred to as *somatotropes,* which are located in the lateral wings of the gland. The human GH gene is on chromosome 17 and its mRNA transcript possesses 5 exons separated by 4 introns. The peptide contains 191 amino acids and has a plasma half-life of 20 minutes (Dinan, 1998). GH plays an important role in the regulation of growth and trophic metabolic processes. The peripheral physiology of GH and its salutary effects in models of peripheral nerve injury (Scheepens et al., 2001) is not the focus of the current summary; the focus is how GH function may inform us about central nervous system (CNS) function in psychiatric disorders (Coplan et al., 1995).

The release of GH by the pituitary gland is regulated by many of the monoamine and neuropeptide systems, also involved in mood and anxiety regulation, acting through the hypothalamus. The release of GH, by either a provocative stimulus or a spontaneous release as part of a physiological process (e.g., sleep) has therefore been viewed as a potential window into CNS trophic function. The neuroscientific challenge remains to wholly integrate frontolimbic dysfunction, which current technology are increasingly well equipped to detect, with previously documented hypothalamic-pituitary dysfunction, which, to date, is most readily apparent with psychoneuroendocrine evaluation.

Regulation of GH Secretion

The regulation of the hypothalamic-pituitary-somatomedin (HPS) axis, responsible for GH release, occurs primarily through two main limbs—stimulation through the hypothalamic peptide growth hormone releasing-factor (GRF) and inhibition through the 14 amino-acid peptide, somatostatin (SOM). Numerous factors impact upon these two limbs, and in fact, the degree to which neurotransmitter systems impact upon either limb may vary according to interspecies differences (see Uhde, Tancer, & Rubinow, 1992). It appears that clonidine, a widely studied α_2 adrenoceptor agonist, may produce its GH secretory effect in healthy control humans either through α_2 mediated stimulation of GRF or α_2 mediated inhibition of somatostatin release. Growth hormone secretion is inhibited by high plasma GH levels, as well as somatomedin-C, which is released by the liver in response to circulating GH. Other neurotransmitter systems that impact on the regulation of GH response to clonidine include the cholinergic, dopaminergic, GABAergic, the Hypothalamic-hypopituitary-adrenal (HPA) axis (specifically corticotropin-releasing factor [CRF]) and serotonergic systems (for review, see Dinan, 1998). Age, obesity, alcoholism, phase of menstrual cycle, and postmenopausal status may also influence stimulated GH response. Less clear-cut factors influencing GH response to GH secretagogues include heavy smoking, which may increase GH secretion; lifetime exposure to tricyclic antidepressants and recent exposure to benzodiazepines.

Possible Mechanisms for Blunted GH Secretion to GH Secretagogues in Anxiety and Mood Disorders

Blunted GH responses to GH secretagogues, such as clonidine, desipramine, the insulin tolerance test, and others, were thought to detect down-regulation of postsynaptic alpha-2 receptors following excessive central noradrenaline (NA) activity in major depressive disorder (Coplan et al., 1995; Siever et al., 1982). That GH responses are blunted in response to both clonidine and growth hormone releasing factor (GRF) in Panic Disorder (PD) refuted the view that reduced GH response to clonidine simply reflects a specific alpha-2 abnormality. Uhde, Tancer, and Rubinow (1992) have reviewed the possible site(s) where blunting of GH may occur. These include (1) reduced availability of pituitary GH stores secondary to reduced synthesis or excessive secretion (this option seems unlikely as GH responses to the dopamine agonist, apomorphine, are exaggerated in PD); (2) overall hypersecretion of GH with secondary inhibition of GH secretion to secretory stimuli; (3) an abnormally enhanced negative feedback system, that is, increased pituitary sensitivity to the inhibitory effects of GH or somatomedin-C; (4) subsensitivity of the pituitary to the secretory effect of GRF or reduced GRF; (5) failure of clonidine to reduce the inhibitory effect of somatostatin neurons on the pituitary; and (6) abnormal function of a host of other factors previously enumerated. It should be noted that blunted GH secretion is not only observed in PD and depression but also in Generalized Anxiety Disorder (GAD) and possibly Social Phobia. GH responses to GRF and clonidine in childhood depression also tend to be blunted. However, the abnormality is not observed in Schizophrenia or Obsessive-Compulsive Disorder.

Investigators have argued that reduced GH responses to chemical or physiological stimuli in Anxiety and Mood Disorders may represent a trait marker of vulnerability to Mood and Anxiety Disorders. Coplan, Pine, Papp, and Gorman (1997) have presented evidence in both patients with PD as well as in unpredictably reared nonhuman primates that the GH response to the GH secretagogue, clonidine, varies inversely with the degree of HPA axis activation. More recent work with nonhuman primates has provided even stronger evidence of a negative correlation between CRF and GH secretion (Coplan et al., 2000a). Examining juvenile neurochemical levels of CSF, CRF, 5 hydroxy-indole-acetic acid (serotonon metabolite) (5-HIAA), HVA, SOM, 3-methoxy-4-hydroxy phenylglycol (noradrenaline metabolite) (MHPG), and CSF cortisol revealed that only levels of CSF and CRF were significantly correlated with GH response to clonidine. An inverse relationship involving the CRF and HPA axis and GH may be an enduring, trait-like feature observed in association with both stressful early rearing and Mood and Anxiety Disorders.

Nocturnal Growth Hormone Secretion

Sleep onset represents a highly evolved, dynamic biological process, involving the reduction and ultimate cessation of noradrenergic and serotonergic neuronal activity, the onset of cholinergic "bursts" of firing from pontine nuclei and the increased secretion of GH primarily through muscarinic inhibition of SOM, the GH secretagogue suppressant. During the early phases of sleep, increases of spontaneous GH secretion have been associated with slow wave (delta) sleep, the former subsiding several hours following sleep onset. The elevations of CRF and cortisol increases that are frequently evident in Mood Disorders are inhibitory towards GH secretion and imply a ratio increase of CRF to GRF in adult depression (Holsboer, 1994).

Thus, adults with acute Major Depressive Disorder (MDD) quite consistently *hyposecrete* GH around the time of sleep onset. Studies followed depressed subjects into a drug-free recovery phase and found persistence of sleep-related GH hyposecretion, suggesting that this may be a trait marker for MDD. Investigators have proposed that secretion of growth hormone at night may be phase advanced in depression such that secretion occurs just prior to sleep onset instead of during the first few hours of sleep. Of interest, one group of investigators has reported that the phase-advanced GH peak is phase-delayed into the normal range after recovery from the depressive state, in contrast to the persistent, trait-like nature of the blunted nocturnal GH secretion in adult depression.

Puig-Antich (1987) hypothesized that a serotonin deficit state with cholinergic dominance could lead to sleep-related GH hypersecretion in prepubertal depressives. Coplan and colleagues (2000) examined unperturbed serial GH measurements over a 24-hour period in depressed and normal control adolescents in light of 10 years of clinical follow-up data. A reanalysis of diagnoses demonstrated that lifetime-depressive subjects (subjects who were initially depressed and those who became depressed over the 10-year period) exhibited low levels of GH in the 100 minutes before sleep relative to lifetime depression-free subjects.

Growth Hormone and Neurogenesis

GH also appears to play an important role in the newly described phenomenon termed *neurogenesis,* or new neuronal division in the CNS. A major mediator of the trophic effects of GH throughout the body is a mediating hormone, insulin-like growth factor-I (IGF-I), with increased gene expression of IGF-I through GH exposure (Pankov, 1999). It has been recently demonstrated that IGF-I has a clear stimulatory effect on both cell proliferation and neurogenesis in the rodent hippocampus (Anderson, Aberg, Nilsson, & Eriksson, 2002), providing indirect confirmation of GH involvement in neurotrophic processes. Because it appears a range of antidepressant and mood stabilizing interventions increase neurogenesis, the blunted GH response to clonidine observed in PD, depression, and GAD should be considered within the context of GH-sensitive IGFs as promoters of neuroprotection and neurogenesis. Studies of GH secretion hyposecretion are therefore informative as a peripheral index of central neuroprotection and also a possible site for neuroprotective deficits in Mood and Anxiety Disorders.

REFERENCES

Anderson, M. F., Aberg, M. A., Nilsson, M., & Eriksson, P. S. (2002). Insulin-like growth factor-I and neurogenesis in the adult mammalian brain. *Brain Research. Developmental Brain Research, 134,* 115–122.

Coplan, J. D., Papp, L. A., Martinez, J., Pine, D., Rosenblum, L. A., Cooper, T., et al. (1995). Persistence of blunted human growth hormone response to clonidine in fluoxetine-treated patients with panic disorder. *American Journal of Psychiatry, 152*(4), 619–622.

Coplan, J. D., Pine, D., Papp, L., & Gorman, J. M. (1997). A window on noradrenergic, hypothalamic-pituitary-adrenal axis and corticotropin releasing-factor function in Anxiety and affective disorders: The growth hormone response to clonidine. *Psychopharmacology Bulletin, 33*(2), 193–204.

Coplan, J. D., Smith, E. L., Trost, R. C., Scharf, B. A., Altemus, M., Bjornson, L., et al. (2000a). Growth hormone response to clonidine in adversely reared young adult primates: Relationship to serial cerbrospinal fluid corticotropin-releasing factor concentrations. *Psychiatry Research, 95,* 93–102.

Coplan, J. D., Wolk, S. I., Goetz, R. R., Ryan, N. D., Dahl, R. E., Mann, J. J., et al. (2000ba). Nocturnal growth hormone secretion studies in adolescents with or without major depression reexamined: Integration of adult clinical follow-up data. *Biological Psychiatry, 47*(7), 594–604.

Dinan, T. G. (1998). Psychoneuroendocrinology of depression: Growth hormone. In C. B. Nemeroff (Ed.), *The psychiatric clinics of North America: Psychoneuroendocrinology* (pp. 325–340).

Holsboer, F. (1994). Neuroendocrinology of mood disorders. In F. E. Bloom & D. J. Kupfer (Eds.), *Neuropsychopharmacology: The fourth generation of progress* (pp. 957–970). New York: Raven Press.

Pankov, Y. A. (1999). Growth hormone and a partial mediator of its biological action, insulin-like growth factor I. *Biochemistry, 64*(1), 1–7.

Puig-Antich, J. (1987). Affective disorders in children and adolescents: Diagnostic validity and psychobiology. In H. Y. Meltzer (Ed.), *Psychopharmacology: The third generation of progress* (pp. 843–859). New York: Raven Press.

Scheepens, A., Sirimanne, E. S., Breier, B. H., Clark, R. G., Gluckman, P. D., & Williams, C. E. (2001). Growth hormone as a neuronal rescue factor during recovery from CNS injury. *Neuroscience, 104*(3), 677–687.

Siever, L. J., Uhde, T. W., Silberman, E. K., Jimerson, D.C., Aloi, J. A., Post, R. M., et al. (1982). Growth hormone response to clonidine as a probe of noradrenergic receptor responsiveness in affective disorder patients and controls. *Psychiatry Research, 6,* 171–183.

Uhde, T. W., Tancer, M. E., Rubinow, D. R., Roscow, D. B., Boulenger, J. P., Vittone, B., Gurguis, G., Geraci, M., Black, B., & Post, R. M. (1992). Evidence for hypothalamo-growth hormone dysfunction in Panic Disorder: Profile of growth hormone responses to clonidine, yohimbine, caffeine, glucose, GRF and TRH in Panic Disorder patients versus healthy volunteers. *Neuropsychopharmacology, 6*(2), 101–118.

Jeremy D. Coplan
Muhammad Arif
State University of New York, Brooklyn

Curtis Wittmann
Washington University in St. Louis School of Medicine

See also: **Depression, Neurotransmitter**

HALFWAY HOUSES

Halfway houses are locales where all activities and interactions may be viewed as having potentially healing, rehabilitative, and supportive properties and where all members may consciously or unconsciously contribute to therapy. Halfway houses typically work to prepare individuals to move from institutionalized settings to becoming able to function independently. Also, it is the goal of halfway houses to integrate or reintegrate their residents into independent living members of their communities. In some cases, the halfway house may be the first referral source or an intermediary step before a person is institutionalized. Halfway houses are commonly affiliated with churches, private organizations, hospitals, and the government and may differ greatly in the number, gender, and age of residents they serve, as well as the type of therapeutic approach they offer residents.

History

For many years, there have been organizations and individuals that have sought to help people dealing with any number of situations and conditions adjust to living and being functioning members of society. After World War II there were homes set up to help soldiers make the transitions from war to living in their respective communities. During the 1960s, with the impetus toward deinstitutionalization of the mentally ill, the advances made with psychotropic medications, and the new community mental health legislation, the number of halfway houses increased greatly. As the emphasis on transitional facilities for the mentally ill grew, there was an increased amount of attention paid to helping individuals in the criminal justice system and with substance abuse problems make the transition from institutional life to becoming acclimated to the community. Today, there are halfway houses serving a variety of populations with a variety of issues.

Types of Residents Served By Halfway Houses

The Mentally Ill

Residents are usually required to attend some type of treatment, whether it is on site or off. The staff ensures that residents take their required prescription medication regularly and properly. A great deal of treatment focus is placed on social and vocational skills. In some cases, aftercare for these clients is provided after they leave the house.

Substance Abusers

Individuals recovering from addiction are often sent to halfway houses after they have completed time in a residential treatment facility. Enrollment in a treatment program is mandatory, and no alcohol or drugs are allowed to be used by residents. The halfway house facilitates sobriety, provides support from people with similar problems, and helps residents to readjust to living in the community.

Criminal Offenders

Incarcerated individuals are often sent to halfway houses to serve out the remainder of their sentences if they have demonstrated good behavior, or they are sent to halfway houses after they are released from prison. These homes can be for either adult or youthful offenders. There is an emphasis on finding and maintaining employment. Sobriety is also usually required for these residents.

Troubled Adolescents

Children with severe behavioral problems, emotional problems, or volatile home situations are often sent to halfway houses. These children are normally residents until they can be provided with alternative stable housing or until their behavior changes. Training children in social skills is a large component of these programs. The halfway house is staffed by personnel around the clock who monitor the children's schoolwork, chores, and recreations.

The Developmentally Disabled

In halfway houses for the developmentally disabled, the staff works to help the residents function independently. Residents learn skills such as how to manage their money, cook, clean, and utilize different modes of public transportation. Some residents attain and maintain jobs while staying at the home. Many of the residents go on to live on their own or function well with minimal help from others.

Methods

There are four basic theoretical approaches taken by halfway houses: democratization, communalism, permissiveness, and reality confrontation. *Democratization* refers to involvement of the staff and patients in the important decisions made in the running of the house. House administrators who subscribe to this approach believe that democratization may decrease resident dependence on the staff and foster independence and inventiveness in the residents. Halfway houses that follow a *communalism* model encourage staff and residents to take part in the activities of the home together. The interaction of staff and residents provides more instances to model and teach desired behaviors. Houses that follow the *permissiveness* model allow a greater expression of emotional and behavioral displays than most traditional settings before physical or behavioral restraints are used. In houses that apply the *reality confrontation* model, patients receive the same response to and consequence from their actions and behaviors that they would in the community.

Halfway house staff members employ several techniques within these modalities to aid in the adjustment of their residents to community life. Group and individual therapy, 12-step programs, social skills training, development of financial management skills, social outings, job training, and moral support are used by many house staffs to foster the independence of their residents. Many houses use some type of reward system, whether it is a token economy, gaining of privileges as skills are mastered, or acquisition of rewards and privileges with seniority as one moves through the program of the house. These tools are used in many combinations, often depending on the population of residents and the philosophical orientation of the organization, to help the residents to be able to become integrated into the community.

The ideals on which the halfway house model is built may seem quite laudable. Nonetheless, the efficacy of such programs has not yet been adequately demonstrated. There has been a wide array of studies producing various results. Several methodological issues, such as the lack of control groups in research and the lack of random assignment, have been raised in relation to studies done on halfway houses. Also, due to the various modalities of treatment and different populations served, it has been difficult to conduct research and determine effectiveness. Greater emphasis should be placed on using empirically supported methods in working with residents instead of using antiquated methods that may not be appropriate for the population.

Joseph R. Ferrari
DePaul University, Chicago

HALLUCINATIONS

Hallucinations are involuntary sensory experiences that are perceived as emanating from the external environment, in the absence of stimulation of relevant sensory receptors. Hallucinations can occur in a variety of contexts but are perhaps most striking and debilitating in the setting of Schizophrenia, where they are generally experienced as real, emotionally significant, and related to concurrent delusions, and represent a form of psychosis. Hallucinations can occur in any sensory modality or can involve multiple modalities, with auditory hallucinations being most common in Schizophrenia and other illnesses that are traditionally termed psychiatric, and visual hallucinations being most common in illnesses termed neurologic. Hallucinations can be described at multiple levels of analysis, including cognitive, neurochemical, computational, and social/psychological. This article will present a functional neuroanatomic approach to hallucinations, describing and analyzing them in terms of disorders of sensory input, subcortical (midbrain/thalamus), and higher brain regions including cortical sensory, limbic, and frontal regions. It will touch also upon treatment considerations.

Disorders of Sensory Input Associated with Hallucinations

Hallucinations produced by disorders of the peripheral sensory system appear to result from ongoing cortical sensory processing in the setting of degraded or absent sensory input. In this setting, perception may be dominated by the cortically generated expectations (top-down processing) that interact with peripheral input (bottom-up processing) in the generation of normal perception. Hallucinations of this sort are most frequently seen in the visual system, where they are termed the *Charles Bonnet Syndrome.* These are usually vivid, colorful representations of people, animals, trees, and so on that appear smaller than normal (Lilliputian) and are often engaged in activities. Notably, the individuals experiencing these hallucinations are aware that they do not represent reality, and generally they have no strong emotional reaction to them. Similar hallucinations can occur in conditions, such as stroke, that involve destruction of primary visual cortex, as this region provides input to unimodal association areas involved in the generation of complex hallucinations. When lesions are limited to one hemisphere, hallucinations may occur only in the affected contralateral visual field.

In the somatosensory system, a striking example of hallucinations caused by disordered sensory input occurs in the phantom limb syndrome, in which an amputated limb continues to be experienced as present, able to move in space, and able to feel pain or tingling. In the auditory system, individuals with peripheral dysfunction (including deafness) can develop complex hallucinations such as music or voices, or simple hallucinations such as ringing, buzzing, or isolated tones.

Midbrain/Thalamic Disorders Associated with Hallucinations

Hallucinations similar to those produced by peripheral lesions can occur with lesions of the upper midbrain and adjacent thalamus. Originally attributed to a lesion in the midbrain peduncular region, they remain known as *peduncular* hallucinations. Like Charles Bonnet hallucinations, they are usually vivid visual hallucinations, frequently of people or animals, sometimes Lilliputian, often moving. Unlike those produced by peripheral lesions, peduncular hallucinations are generally associated with disturbances in sleep and arousal and may at times be interpreted as real.

These disturbances in sleep and arousal provide clues to the mechanism by which hallucinations are generated by midbrain and thalamic lesions. Frequency-specific oscillations in thalamocortical circuits have been associated with the temporal binding of perception, and with dreaming—a normal condition involving perception in the absence of external stimuli. During the awake state, thalamic relay nuclei faithfully transmit inputs to the cortex; during dreaming, they do not. Neurotransmitters, notably acetylcholine and serotonin, play an important role in initiating this switch in relay mode. Abnormalities of cholmergic and serotonergic transmission brought on by disease, medication, or drug use are frequently accompanied by hallucinations. Similarly, transitions between states of sleep and wakefulness are associated with hallucinations, usually in the setting of sleep disorders. These are generally multimodal, vivid, and emotionally charged. Common examples are the feeling of being about to fall into an abyss or be attacked, of being caught in a fire, or of sensing a presence in the room. Hallucinations in the settings of delirium and sedative drug withdrawal are also associated with disturbances in sleep and arousal. Such hallucinations should be distinguished from illusions, which are misinterpretations of actual sensory stimuli.

Disorders of Higher Brain Regions Associated with Hallucinations

Hallucinations, such as those that occur in migraine, epilepsy, and Schizophrenia, may also be associated with primary pathology at higher levels of the brain. In recent years, studies employing functional neuroimaging techniques have implicated a number of higher brain regions in the generation of hallucinations, corresponding to their form, content, and setting.

Cortical Sensory Activity Associated with Hallucinations

Regardless of the mechanism by which they are generated, hallucinations appear to be associated with activity in cortical sensory regions corresponding to their modality and complexity. The hallucinations previously described may be categorized as complex or formed. Noncomplex hallucinations are referred to interchangeably as simple, unformed, or crude. In the visual system, these are known as *photopsias.* Occurring most frequently with migraines, they may also be seen at the onset of partial seizures, for the first few days following an infarction of the central visual system, and with disorders of visual input. Photopsias may consist of colored or colorless glittering spots, or black and white zigzag patterns known as *fortification lines.* They often occur unilaterally, but they may fill the entire visual field. Simple hallucinations are believed to reflect activity in primary sensory or adjacent early unimodal association areas and to correspond, in form, to the area's functional specialization. For example, colored photopsias would be associated with activity in occipital subregions involved in color processing.

Complex hallucinations are associated with activity in sensory association areas, with or without involvement of primary sensory cortex. As with simple hallucinations, their form and content correspond to the location of activity. For example, in a functional neuroimaging study of an individual experiencing ongoing auditory-visual hallucinations in the setting of Schizophrenia, we detected activations in association cortices mediating higher-order visual perception, speech perception, and intermodal processing.

Limbic/Paralimbic Activity Associated with Hallucinations

The study just cited included other subjects with Schizophrenia, all of whom experienced frequent auditory hallucinations. Although each had a somewhat different pattern of sensory cortical activation, perhaps reflecting differences in the form and content of their hallucinations, group analysis revealed a significant pattern of common activations in thalamic (see earlier discussion), limbic, and paralimbic areas—regions involved in the processing of emotion, memory, and their integration with sensory information. Just as abnormal activity in sensory cortex is correlated with the form and content of hallucinations, it is likely that aberrant activity in limbic/paralimbic regions gives rise to the marked emotional significance of hallucinations in the setting of Schizophrenia.

Further evidence of a role for thalamic and limbic system dysfunction in the generation of schizophrenic symptoms is provided by postmortem, neuropsychological, electrophysiologic, and neuroimaging studies that reveal structural and functional abnormalities of thalamic and limbic regions in individuals with Schizophrenia, including hyperactivity of temporal regions, left greater than right, associated with psychosis. Additionally, activity of the limbic system is closely interconnected with that of dopamine, a neurotransmitter implicated in the generation of hallucinations and delusions in the settings of Schizophrenia, medication toxicity, and drug abuse. Recently, dysfunction in the glutamatergic excitatory transmitter system has also been implicated. Hallucinations that arise in the context of severe emotional stress may also involve abnormal limbic activity.

Temporolimbic structures also play a role in the generation of hallucinations associated with epilepsy. The onset of partial seizures can be accompanied by simple hallucinations in any modality, reflecting ictal discharges in primary sensory areas, or by complex hallucinations reflecting discharges in limbic and sensory association areas. Olfactory hallucinations can also be seen in this setting. These complex hallucinations most often involve temporolimbic regions, including hippocampus and amygdala, which have the lowest seizure thresholds of all brain structures, as well as sensory association areas. Like the hallucinations seen in Schizophrenia, these are often emotionally charged. Unlike those seen in Schizophrenia, they are more often visual than auditory and are not usually believed by the person experiencing them to represent reality. Individuals who suffer from epilepsy over prolonged periods may also develop hallucinations between seizure episodes. These may resemble more closely those seen in Schizophrenia, because they are frequently emotionally charged, accompanied by delusions, and believed to represent reality, and they are as often auditory as visual. As in Schizophrenia, they appear to be associated with temporal lobe abnormalities, left more often than right.

Frontal/Executive Activity Associated with Hallucinations

The lack of awareness that hallucinatory experience does not correspond to reality is a striking feature of Schizophrenia. In addition to temporal lobe abnormalities, numerous studies have revealed frontal dysfunction and abnormal frontotemporal connectivity associated with Schizophrenia. The frontal lobes, in concert with interconnected regions, mediate the higher, more complex aspects of cognition, termed *executive functions,* that include judgment, insight, and self-monitoring. Although relevant studies have produced mixed results, there is evidence to suggest that frontal dysfunction may contribute to the inability of individuals with Schizophrenia to identify the internal origin of their hallucinatory experience and its relation to their illness. Temporal lobe epilepsy may also be accompanied by executive as well as other forms of cognitive dysfunction, and by abnormalities of frontal activity.

Treatment of Hallucinations

For hallucinations accompanying Schizophrenia or other primary psychiatric disorders, medications that alter transmission of dopamine and related neurotransmitters (such as serotonin), termed *antipsychotics,* are the mainstay of treatment. In other settings, the first step in the treatment of hallucinations is to address the condition that underlies their existence. Where this is impossible or ineffective, antipsychotic medications may be tried. However, these tend to be less effective in conditions that do not involve limbic, striatal, or dopaminergic pathology. Fortunately, hallucinations in the setting of sensory input disorders, where antipsychotics are least effective, are often less disturbing to those experiencing them, as previously described. Such hallucinations sometimes respond to carbamazepine, a medication used to treat a variety of neuropsychiatric conditions. Where hallucinations are distressing and unresponsive to medication, psychological treatments, including cognitive-behavioral and supportive therapies, may be helpful. Future developments in the treatment of hallucinations are likely to be guided by the functional neuroanatomic approach, altering neurotransmission (via medications) or cortical activity (via techniques such as transcranial magnetic stimulation) in specific cerebral regions.

Jane Epstein
Emily Stern
David Silbersweig
Weill Medical College of Cornell University

HALLUCINOGENIC DRUGS

Many drugs can produce hallucinations (e.g., LSD, scopolamine, phencyclidine, methamphetamine, bromides, alcohol withdrawal, corticosteroids), but only a few can do so without producing delirium, and those few, with LSD being the prototype, are termed *hallucinogens.* Even LSD does not usually produce true hallucinations, because the user usually remains aware that the sensory distortions are drug-induced pseudohallucinations, but this label has persisted. Hallucinogens are also called *phantastica,* psychedelics, and psychotomimetics. (Sometimes, but not herein, phencyclidine [PCP] and ketamine are called hallucinogens, but, because of their unique pharmacological properties, they are best considered in a class of their own—the dissociative anesthetics.)

The hallucinogens fall into two broad chemical classes, indoleamines (e.g., lysergic acid diethylamide, abbreviated LSD from the original German name, Lyserg-Säure-Diäthylamid; psilocybin; ibogaine; and harmaline) and phenethylamines (e.g., mescaline, methylenedioxymethamphetamine [MDMA or ecstasy], 4-methyl-2,5-dimethoxyamphetamine [DOM or STP]). Some are plant constituents (mescaline from the peyote cactus, psilocybin from *Psilocybe* mushrooms), whereas others are synthetic (MDMA; LSD is semisynthetic, since the lysergic acid moiety is derived from the ergot fungus). The most potent is LSD, with a typical oral dose of 100 micrograms. Some other hallucinogens are as powerful but not as potent as LSD (mescaline is at least as powerful); that is, they are capable of exerting effects that are as profound as those of LSD, though at a much higher dose (e.g., 200–400 milligrams of mescaline). Hallucinogens are usually taken orally. Illicit LSD is often absorbed on small squares of paper printed with cartoons (in this form it is known as *blotter acid*).

Most hallucinogens, including LSD, are believed to induce their cognitive, perceptual, and mood distortions by directly activating certain subtypes of brain serotonin receptors (5-HT_{2A} and other 5-HT_2 receptors), resulting in (1) decreased tonic activity of noradrenergic neurons (via GABAergic afferents) and facilitation of the activation of noradrenergic neurons by sensory stimuli (via glutamatergic afferents) in the locus coeruleus, and (2) enhanced glutamate release throughout the neocortex (Aghajanian & Marek, 1999). There is a significant correlation between hallucinogenic potency in humans and drug agonist potency for these serotonin receptor subtypes in vitro (Glennon, 1996; Sanders-Bush, 1994). These same subtypes of serotonin receptors have been implicated in the pathogenesis of Schizophrenia. A few hallucinogens (e.g., MDMA) work primarily by releasing serotonin. Most recently, a number of genes implicated in synaptic plasticity, glutamatergic signaling, and cytoskeletal architecture have been reported to be activated upon acute LSD administration. Some of these changes are speculated to represent early sequelae in the pathways that may lead to long-term effects of LSD (Nichols & Sanders-Bush, 2002).

The psychological effects of LSD are unpredictable. They depend on the amount ingested and the user's personality, mood, expectations, and surroundings. Sensations and feelings are affected much more dramatically than somatic signs. The user may feel several different emotions (including euphoria) at once, or may switch rapidly from one emotion to another. Visual delusions, distortions, and pseudohallucinations usually occur. Colors, sounds, odors, and other sensations appear to be intensified, and pseudohallucinations of movements, forms, and events may follow. The user's perceptions of time and self are distorted, including feelings of time slowing, one's body changing shape (e.g., arms very long), and out-of-body experience. Sensations may seem to cross over (synesthesia), giving the user the feeling of hearing colors and seeing sounds. Old memories may be vividly recalled. Anxiety often occurs while using LSD and other hallucinogens, and some users experience terrifying thoughts, nightmarish feelings, despair, and fears of insanity, death, and losing control. Fatal accidents have occurred during LSD use. However, there are no documented toxic fatalities directly occurring from LSD. The somatic effects of LSD are mainly sympathetic and relatively slight. They include dilated pupils, hyperthermia, increased heart rate and blood pressure, sweating, loss of appetite, restlessness, dry mouth, dizziness, and tremors.

Users refer to LSD and other hallucinogen experiences as "trips" and to the acute adverse experiences as "bad trips," although most hallucinogen trips have both pleasant and unpleasant aspects. LSD trips are long—typically they begin to clear after 8–12 hours. Most users of hallucinogens feel that their experiences have a mystical, perception-expanding, epiphanous character. Lasting benefits, if any, of the trips have not been scientifically demonstrated. Works of authors closely associated with hallucinogens (e.g., Aldous Huxley, Timothy Leary, Alan Watts) are widely available and easy to find via the Internet.

LSD was synthesized at the Sandoz Company pharmaceutical-chemical research laboratories in Basel, Switzerland in 1938 by Albert Hofmann, who discovered its pharmacological properties in 1943, at first by accidentally ingesting a small amount and then by self-experimentation (Hofmann, 1980). Hallucinogens did not become popular until the 1960s. Their abuse declined in the 1970s but persists. LSD and MDMA are now considered to be *club drugs.* Club drugs are used by young adults at all-night dance parties such as raves or trances, dance clubs, and bars. Abuse and popularity of most club drugs are rising, whereas use of LSD has been dropping slightly since a brief increase in the mid-1990s. It may be that the dramatic increase in use of MDMA (the prototypical club drug) and ketamine displaced LSD. The 2001 Monitoring the Future Survey, funded by the National Institute on Drug Abuse, estimates that 16% of young adults (ages 19–28) have used LSD at least once, and 13% of young adults have used MDMA at least once. In 2001, among 40-year-old high school graduates, 20% reported some experience during their lifetime with LSD, but virtually no active use of LSD at this age (Johnston, O'Malley, & Bachman, 2002).

The hallucinogens are not known to produce brain damage, except MDMA, which damages brain serotonergic neurons in man and animals, and ibogaine and harmaline, both of which produce cerebellar Purkinje neuron degeneration, at least in rats. However, LSD and other hallucinogens may produce a subtle neurotoxicity not yet detected in experiments. There are two long-term disorders associated with LSD, which could possibly be caused by subtle damage to the brain-persistent psychosis and hallucinogen persisting perception disorder (HPPD; Abraham, Aldridge, & Gogia, 1996). A user of LSD may suffer a devastating psychological experience, resulting in a long-lasting psychosis. Post-LSD psychoses are unpredictable, sometimes following a single dose, but they are more common in people with prior psychopathology. Post-LSD psychoses resemble schizoaffective disorders and are frequently accompanied by visual disturbances. The extent of this problem with the other hallucinogens is not known. However, MDMA, which does not produce the profound sensory disruptions characteristic of LSD and mescaline but instead produces primarily alterations in emotions and a feeling of empathy with others, is believed to be less likely to produce long-lasting psychoses (or HPPD). The most effective treatments for post-LSD psychoses are electroconvulsive therapy and lithium.

In the 1950s, flashbacks (spontaneous, disturbing recurrences of aspects of LSD experiences, long after the use of LSD has stopped) began to be reported, sometimes months after LSD use. The work of Henry Abraham (Abraham et al., 1996) demonstrated that this syndrome is typically persistent and stable, rather than paroxysmal, and presents primarily with visual disturbances, including geometric pseudohallucinations, false motion in the peripheral fields, halos, flashes of color, trails behind moving objects, and afterimages. The term *flashback* has been supplanted by HPPD. The visual distractions are increased by several factors, including stress, darkness, and marijuana, and are decreased by benzodiazepines.

Unfortunately, although acute, short-lived adverse reactions to hallucinogens are often fairly benign, the chronic, unremitting courses carry a poor prognosis. These long-term consequences appear to be rare, although this has not been thoroughly studied.

Hallucinogens, with the possible exception of MDMA (Cottler, Womack, Compton, & Ben-Abdallah, 2001), are not addictive. MDMA also differs from other hallucinogens in that toxic fatalities due to hyperthermia have occurred with MDMA use.

In a study conducted in the mid-1960s, when LSD was added to suspensions of human white blood cells in vitro, there was more chromosomal breakage than in the cells without LSD. This stimulated a great deal of further investigation and led to a reduction in LSD abuse, but the in vivo animal research and surveys of people who used or were given hallucinogens offered no evidence of genetic damage, birth defects, mutations, or cancer due to hallucinogens.

Use of peyote cactus in small amounts as a sacrament is legal only when used by Native American Church members. Otherwise, use of hallucinogens is prohibited; hallucinogens are categorized under the Controlled Substances Act as Schedule I drugs, which are drugs with no currently accepted medical use and/or high potential for abuse. However, the supposed insightful, epiphanous quality of hallucinogen experiences, and the vivid recall of repressed memories that occurs during use, combined with the relative lack of somatic toxicity, have led to suggested psychotherapeutic uses of hallucinogens, especially in the treatment of mental illness, including Posttraumatic Stress Disorder and substance addiction. Sandoz marketed LSD in 1949 as an adjunct in psychoanalysis. Medical use was halted in the 1960s due to the long-term adverse psychological effects previously outlined and limited evidence of therapeutic benefit. Nonetheless, psychiatric methodology has greatly improved since then, and there is renewed interest in experimentally reexamining hallucinogens (especially those other than LSD, due to LSD's reputation for producing long-lasting psychoses and HPPD) in the therapy of alcoholism and other refractory diseases. For example, although ibogaine itself may not be used therapeutically in the United States due to its neurotoxicity, studies of ibogaine analogs are continuing in animal models in the search for therapeutic agents that are not neurotoxic. Investigators are seeking to determine if it is possible to develop a therapeutic hallucinogen, novel or old, whose benefits outweigh its risks in selected patients.

REFERENCES

Abraham, H. D., Aldridge, A. M., & Gogia, P. (1996). The psychopharmacology of hallucinogens. *Neuropsychopharmacology, 14,* 285–298.

Aghajanian, G. K., & Marek, G. J. (1999). Serotonin and hallucinogens. *Neuropsychopharmacology, 21,* 16S–21S.

Cottler, L. B., Womack, S. B., Compton, W. M., & Ben-Abdallah, A. (2001). Ecstasy abuse and dependence among adolescents and young adults: Applicability and reliability of *DSM-IV* criteria. *Human Psychopharmacology: Clinical and Experimental, 16,* 599–606.

Glennon, R. A. (1996). Classical hallucinogens. In C. R. Schuster & M. J. Kuhar (Eds.), *Handbook of experimental pharmacology: Vol. 118.* Pharmacological aspects of drug dependence (pp. 343–371). Berlin: Springer.

Hofmann, A. (1980). *LSD: My problem child.* New York: McGraw-Hill.

Johnston, L. D., O'Malley, P. M., & Bachman, J. G. (2002). *Monitoring the Future National Survey results on drug use, 1975–2001: Vol. 1. Secondary school students* (NIH Publication No. 02-5106). Bethesda, MD: National Institute on Drug Abuse.

Nichols, C. D., & Sanders-Bush, E. (2002). A single dose of lysergic acid diethylamide influences gene expression patterns within the mammalian brain. *Neuropsychopharmacology, 26,* 634–642.

Sanders-Bush, E. (1994). Neurochemical evidence that hallucinogenic drugs are 5-HT_{1C} receptor agonists: What next? In G. C. Lin & R. A. Glennon (Eds.), *Hallucinogens: An update* (National Institute on Drug Abuse Research Monograph No. 146. NIH Pub. No. 94-3872; pp. 203–213). Washington, DC: U.S. Government Printing Office.

SUGGESTED READING

Hanson, G. R., Venturelli, P. J., & Fleckenstein, A. E. (2002). *Drugs and society* (7th ed.). Sudbury, MA: Jones and Bartlett.

Pellerin, C. (1996). *Trips: How hallucinogens work in your brain.* New York: Seven Stories Press.

Jerry Frankenheim
Geraline Lin
National Institute on Drug Abuse

HALSTEAD-REITAN BATTERY

The Halstead-Reitan Battery consists of a series of individual neuropsychological measures, that in combination permit the skilled examiner to make rather detailed inferences about the integrity of the cerebral hemispheres. Because the brain is the organ of adaptive behavior, brain dysfunction is typically observable in some behavioral aberration. The tests included in the Halstead-Reitan Battery are designed to sample behavior across every possible sphere and assess all major cognitive, sensory, expressive, and motor functions.

Ward Halstead began collecting (and discarding) tests of brain function in the 1930s at his University of Chicago laboratory. His first graduate student, Ralph Reitan, refined the battery, eliminating those tests that failed to discriminate at statistically significant levels. In addition, Reitan began a programmatic series of studies that demonstrated the utility of these tests in identifying patients with brain lesions. Recent studies have demonstrated that the predictive accuracy of the Halstead-Reitan Battery exceeds that of traditional neurological techniques (e.g., angiography and pneumoencephalography), while comparing favorably with newer techniques such as computerized axial tomography.

Many of the subtests included in the Halstead-Reitan Battery are well known and are widely used by nonneuropsychologists. These include the Wechsler Adult Intelligence Scale (WAIS) and the Minnesota Multiphasic Personality Inventory (MMPI). Other tests were developed or adapted specifically for the battery. The Category Test, for example, is regarded as one of the most sensitive measures of cerebral impairment. It consists of a series of 208 stimulus items (slides) that require a manual response from the patient. Positive or negative feedback is given in the form of a bell or buzzer. This novel learning situation is extremely difficult for the brain-impaired patient.

Another excellent general measure of cortical function is the Tactual Performance Test (TPT), which requires that the blindfolded patient place 10 different blocks in their proper place on a modified Seguin-Goddard form board by using first the dominant hand, then the nondominant hand, then both hands together. After the third trial, the patient is asked to draw the board from memory. Other Halstead-Reitan tests include the Speech-Sounds Perception Test, the Rhythm Test, the Finger-Oscillation Test, and Trails A and B. In addition, sensory-perceptual, lateral dominance, and aphasia examinations are included as part of the battery. Cutoff scores suggestive of brain impairment are provided for most tests, and the most sensitive tests are included in the calculation of the Impairment Index, a general measure of cortical dysfunction.

Somewhat different tests are included in two other versions of the Halstead-Reitan Battery that were developed for assessing younger and older children. The children's versions of the battery have not been as well validated as the adult battery.

Recent research on the Halstead-Reitan Battery has focused on head and brain injury, characterizing the types of neuropsychological deficits that occur, and identifying the similarities and differences in mild and more severe head injury. Development of knowledge in this area has added to the value of the Halstead-Reitan Battery, in both clinical evaluation and the area of forensic neuropsychology.

Interest in the Halstead-Reitan Battery continues to grow, spurred by a series of workshops given by Reitan and his colleagues. In addition, graduate students in clinical neuropsychology training programs routinely learn to administer and interpret the Halstead-Reitan Battery. Computer programs have been developed to interpret test results from the battery; these programs typically convert raw test scores into scaled and T scores. Because these programs use exact age and education values in calculating T scores, they may provide data that are more useful for the clinician than raw scores alone. Some researchers and clinicians have begun to supplement the traditional Halstead-Reitan Battery with additional tests such as the Boston Diagnostic Aphasia Examination and the Wisconsin Card Sorting Test.

In sum, it appears that the place of the Halstead-Reitan Battery is secure, both in the history of psychology and in the practice of neuropsychology.

SUGGESTED READING

Heaton, R. K., Grant, I., & Matthews, C. G. (1991). *Comprehensive norms for an expanded Halstead-Reitan Battery: Demographic corrections, research findings, and clinical applications.* Odessa, FL: Psychological Assessment Resources.

Horton, A. M., Jr. (1997). The Halstead-Reitan Neuropsychological Test Battery: Problems and prospects. In A. M. Horton, D. Wedding, & J. Webster (Eds.), *The neuropsychology handbook: Vol. 1. Foundations and assessment* (2nd ed.). New York: Springer Publishing.

Jarvis, P. E., & Barth, J. T. (1994). *Halstead-Reitan Neuropsychological Battery: A guide to interpretation and clinical applications* (pp. 221–254). Odessa, FL: Psychological Assessment Resources.

Reitan, R. M., & Wolfson, D. (1997). Theoretical, methodological, and validational bases of the Halstead-Reitan Neuropsychological Test Battery. In I. Grant & K. M. Adams (Eds.), *Neuropsychological assessment of neuropsychiatric disorders* (2nd ed.). New York: Oxford University Press.

Reitan, R. M., & Wolfson, D. (2001). The Halstead-Reitan Neuropsychological Test Battery: Research findings and clinical applications. In A. S. Kaufman & N. L. Kaufman (Eds.), *Specific learning disabilities and difficulties in children and adolescents* (pp. 308–346). Cambridge, UK: Cambridge University Press.

Danny Wedding

See also: **Luria-Nebraska**

HANDICAP

A handicap is a constellation of physical, mental, psychological, and/or social properties or processes that complicate adaptation, such that optimal development and functioning are not achieved. Other related terms such as *disability* or *impairment* are often used interchangeably; however, there has been a call for greater precision to decrease the stigma associated with various conditions. The World Health Organization (WHO) distinguishes the terms *impairment, disability,* and *handicap,* based on the manifestation of the disorder at the organic, whole-person, and societal level. Thus, *handicap* refers to the effect of a condition on an individual's functioning in a particular setting or situation: A paraplegic woman may be greatly handicapped on the dance floor but not handicapped in an accessible office setting. A handicap is the limitation imposed by social and psychological reactions to the condition. Thus, we maintain that a disability does not necessarily imply a handicap.

Handicaps associated less with a disability than with an individual difference help to clarify this distinction. Consider differences in visual functioning; individuals vary in terms of nearsightedness and farsightedness, and such visual impairment is often corrected with contact lenses or eyeglasses. An individual would be handicapped *only* if self-image were impaired, activity were restricted, visual information was distorted, or if others devalued the person for the impairment or prosthesis. At the same time it is possible that none of these "handicaps" would enter into the individual's adaptation *because vision problems are so common and so well accepted in our culture.* The same disability might be much more handicapping in a developing society where corrective lenses are unavailable.

Two major approaches to conceptualizing handicaps will illustrate the complexity of the transformation of a disability into a handicap. The dominant approach in both professional and lay culture uses disease metaphors for the individual differences represented by the disability. The disability is a negative property setting the individual apart from "normal" people, requiring medically oriented interventions such as diagnosis and treatment. Thus, there is something wrong with the individual, who is seen as needing treatment aimed toward curing, rehabilitating, or at least ameliorating the disability.

This medical orientation predominates in current professional practice and public policy. Its bias is inherent in most major classification systems currently available for categorizing disabilities and handicaps. For instance, the Federal Rehabilitation Act of 1973, Section 504, uses the term *handicap* to refer to a range of conditions including speech, hearing, visual, and orthopedic impairments and cerebral palsy, epilepsy, muscular dystrophy, multiple sclerosis, cancer, diabetes, heart disease, mental retardation, emotional or psychiatric disorders, drug or alcohol addiction, and specific learning disabilities. The particular domain in which the handicap presents can be indicated in a classification schema, as in the concept of educational handicaps—conditions that interfere with a child's academic achievement but have limited impact in other settings such as on the baseball field.

An alternative approach to conceptualizing handicaps considers the handicap a social construction rather than an inherent trait of the disabled individual. This approach maintains that a handicap is a social condition, created by society. A person's bodily or behavioral condition becomes a handicap only to the extent that other people, or the person himself, define it as such. The result of this social definition is to create distinctive environments and behaviors that sequentially remove the person from normal life patterns and, in time, convince all concerned that the person truly is handicapped.

Because most persons sense the social consequences of being different, great effort is exerted to avoid such characterization. Individuals may exert great effort to conceal their differences. These attempts to pass and cover, along with the substantial creations of society to cope with those who are different, provide extensive evidence for the need to examine handicaps as social conditions. This approach suggests directions for prevention and treatment of handicaps—directions that are antithetical to the current approaches of our educational and rehabilitation agencies, which require diagnosis or labeling in order to obtain services necessary to avoid turning a disability into a handicap.

Approaching handicaps as social constructions reveals parallels between handicapped persons and other minority or disadvantaged groups. Discrimination or prejudice against disabled individuals thus becomes a counterpart to racism and sexism, whether in its individual, institutional, explicit, or implicit forms.

The civil rights movement has recently made headway in increasing society's awareness of handicapped people. Legislation and court decisions have moved our society in the direction of more humanitarian and pluralistic approaches. The Rehabilitation Act of 1973, the Education for All Handicapped Children Act (Public Law 94-142), and the Americans with Disabilities Act of 1994 represent this major thrust toward guaranteeing educational, civil, and human rights for handicapped individuals, specifying governmental obligations for ensuring their psychological as well as physical well-being. Under the Americans with Disabilities Act, failing to fully include individuals with disabilities is forbidden, with civil penalties for individuals and institutions that discriminate on this basis.

Concepts and policies such as *deinstitutionalization, mainstreaming, inclusion,* and *normalization* form the basis of these approaches. *Deinstitutionalization* refers to efforts to remove the handicapped from segregated settings, provide for those with special needs in the community, and increase opportunities for optimal and normalized development. *Inclusion* is a newer version of mainstreaming, based on including the disabled from the onset. *Normalization* is a similar concept, applied beyond educational settings, and emphasizes keeping disabled individuals integrated to the greatest possible extent.

Donald L. Wertlieb
Dante S. Spetter

See also: **Mainstreaming**

HAWTHORNE EFFECT

The Hawthorne effect is named for a series of studies conducted from the late 1920s through the 1930s at the Western Electric Company's Hawthorne Works near Chicago. Many textbooks cite these studies as central in the historical development of industrial/organizational psychology. Introductory textbooks and experimental methods texts discuss the Hawthorne effect, although only rarely is reasonable attention given to the overall scope of this research program. Stated in its simplest form, the Hawthorne effect suggests that any workplace change, such as a research study, makes people feel important and thereby improves their performance.

Much of the credit for the Hawthorne studies is often given to F. J. Roethlisberger and W. J. Dickson, who in 1939 published a major book describing the research. As described by them, the Hawthorne studies had five distinct research phases: the illumination experiments, the relay assembly test room experiments, the mass interviewing program, the bank wiring observation room experiments, and the program of personnel counseling.

The illumination experiments had the initial purpose of relating levels of lighting to worker productivity. A number of specific studies were done, but no clear functional relationship could be found between the two variables. Indeed, throughout these illumination studies, the researchers attempted to improve experimental control, apparently believing a well-designed study would answer their question.

The second major phase of the Hawthorne studies was an attempt at studying workers' performance under carefully controlled conditions. For this purpose, five employees were selected and isolated in a separate room, along with a layout operator (i.e., a person who assigns work) and a research observer. In this setting a number of experiments were performed, mostly focusing on differing schedules of rest breaks. Although it is often reported that all experimental conditions in the relay assembly test room led to improved production over the preceding condition, such an interpretation is misleading. Two individuals showed a general tendency to improve production; one showed steady production overall; but two others showed generally decreasing production and so were replaced by more "cooperative" employees. Clearly, the overall trend toward improved production does not necessarily apply to individual workers.

At the completion of the relay assembly test room studies, the researchers began to realize that more was involved than the physical conditions of work. Specifically, it was apparent that the social impact of the research was far greater than the impact of changes in lighting or rest breaks. To clarify this issue, the mass interviewing program was begun. In the following years over 20,000 employees were interviewed.

The fourth phase of the Hawthorne studies grew out of the mass interviewing program. Given the importance of social groups in the workplace, the bank wiring observation room studies were designed as an intensive investigation of such groups. To perform this investigation, 14 men were observed and interviewed for over 6 months, which produced a wealth of data on work groups.

Finally, the fifth phase involved an extensive program of personnel counseling. Counselors were employed who could be approached by employees and confided in as impartial agents. With the opening of such communication channels, supervisors could be assisted in improving their behavior. In general, the researchers reported a number of improvements in intraorganizational communication.

A simplistic view of the Hawthorne effect is unwarranted. Clearly, not everything the experimenters tried led to improved productivity, although the Hawthorne effect is often described in precisely such terms. What is clear, however, is that changes in lighting or rest breaks could not by themselves explain changes in employee performance.

Given the apparent complexity of the Hawthorne effect, a number of people have tried to clarify its nature. Robert L. Kahn has pointed out that the Hawthorne effect cannot be counted on to emerge from all research studies. His analysis suggests that worker participation in important decisions plays a major role in eliciting the effect.

Another approach is taken by H. McIlvaine Parsons, who suggests that principles of operant conditioning and reinforcement can best explain the results of the Hawthorne studies. In this view, day-to-day feedback, combined with an appropriate reward structure, is critical in shaping the behavior of workers.

A third view of the Hawthorne studies suggests that traditional interpretations of these studies rely on the unjustified assumption of capitalist philosophy. These criticisms see the Hawthorne studies from a socialist perspective and suggest that the traditional interpretation is a myth.

It has recently been shown that there are ways to actually increase the likelihood of obtaining the Hawthorne effect. Many action researchers have the goal of bringing about positive changes in such measures as performance, and using goals and feedback and removing obstacles to performance indeed makes positive change more likely.

Regardless of one's personal theoretical orientation, it is clear that the Hawthorne studies constitute an important milestone in industrial/organizational psychology. Certainly, a wealth of data were collected, and although they have long been recognized as imperfect, the studies are still important to consider.

Philip G. Benson
New Mexico State University

See also: **Industrial-Organizational Psychology; Performance Appraisal**

HEAD START

Head Start is a comprehensive intervention program for young children and their families who live in poverty. It is the largest and longest-running federal program established to prepare this population for a successful entry into elementary school. As such, it has served as a national laboratory for the design, study, and refinement of effective intervention techniques.

Head Start was conceived as part of President Lyndon Johnson's War on Poverty—a national campaign to enable the poor to improve their status through self-help and educational opportunities. Whereas most of the war efforts targeted poor adults, Head Start was envisioned as a program to help poor preschoolers begin school on an equal footing with children from wealthier homes. However, with the exception of a few experimental projects, there was little experience or research evidence to suggest how to bolster their school readiness. Johnson's chief strategist in the war, Sargent Shriver, convened a panel of experts in education, physical and mental health, social work, and developmental psychology to design the new program. The group's professional diversity gave Head Start more than a strictly educational focus.

The committee's recommendations were presented to Shriver in February 1965, just a few months before the program was to open its doors. The planning document was based on a "whole child" philosophy that embraced a variety of objectives related to school readiness. Children were to receive inoculations, physical and dental exams, and follow-up treatment if needed. They would eat hot meals and nutritious snacks, and their parents would be taught to provide healthy diets at home. The preschool education component would be developmentally and culturally appropriate, including language and other academic skills as well as experiences to promote social and emotional development. Parents would volunteer in the classrooms, attend classes of their own, and have a role in program administration. Family needs and goals would be assessed and support services provided through the program and links to community agencies. Head Start would develop community partnerships to enhance the availability and delivery of human services. The need for these components was an educated guess at that time but has now proved critical to the success of early intervention.

Head Start opened in the summer of 1965, serving over half a million children and their families. Today the program is housed in the Head Start Bureau in the Administration on Children, Youth and Families. In fiscal year (FY) 2001, over 905,000 children attended Head Start in some 48,500 classrooms nationwide. The majority are 3- and 4-year-olds whose parents have incomes below the federal poverty line. About 13% are children with disabilities. The FY 2002 budget was about $6.5 billion, which allowed the program to serve about half the eligible children (estimates vary). By law, grantees receive 80% of their funding from the federal government and the rest from other, usually community sources.

Each Head Start center must focus on three major activities: child development services (physical and mental health, nutrition, preschool education); family and community partnerships (including parent involvement and social support services); and program design and management (to improve quality and accountability). Although these components must conform to a national set of performance standards, centers are encouraged to adapt their services to local needs and resources. For example, some programs offer home-based services, and an increasing number are extending hours or collaborating with local child care providers to accommodate children whose parents work. Thus it is somewhat misleading to think of Head Start as a single intervention because of the variety in local programming.

Head Start's early administrators never believed that this brief preschool experience would end poverty. They dismissed the then-popular "inoculation model," which held that some quick fix could make up for the past and prevent the future effects of growing up in economically disadvantaged conditions. They encouraged the development of dovetailed programs to serve children and families both before and after the preschool years. A recent example is the Head Start/Public School Early Childhood Transition project, which continued parent involvement and comprehensive services to preschool graduates through third grade. Studies of this and similar programs have shown that extending services into elementary school benefits children's achievement and adaptation. All Head Start programs are now mandated to undertake transition to school activities at least until the young students are settled in their new environment.

Efforts to serve children before the preschool years also began early in Head Start's mission. Mounting evidence that preventive efforts are more effective than remedial ones, and that waiting until a child is 3 or 4 years old is sometimes too late, spurred political support for interventions for very young children. In 1994, congress authorized Early Head Start for families and children from birth to 3 years. Services begin prenatally and include health care, nutrition, parenting education, and family support services. In FY 2001, there were 650 such programs serving over 55,000 infants and toddlers. Initial evaluations have shown many developmental benefits to this approach.

Early evaluations of preschool Head Start focused almost entirely on improvements in children's intelligence. This outcome was highlighted both because the project's goals outlined in the planning document were not very specific and because psychologists in the 1960s were enthralled with the possibility that IQ scores could be raised substantially. The results of such research on Head Start and just about every other early intervention arrived at the same conclusion: IQ scores do increase during preschool (later found to be due to better motivation and familiarity with the testing situation), but these gains fade out after a few years in elementary school. When researchers looked at broader outcomes, they found more lasting benefits. Quality preschool programs raise school achievement, reduce grade repetition and special education placements, and appear to reduce later juvenile delinquency. A major study currently underway is the Family and Child Experiences Survey (FACES), which is following the progress of former Head Start students and their families as well as analyzing qualities of the preschool programs they attended. Results thus far show that Head Start graduates are ready for kindergarten and better able to benefit from later schooling.

Research on Head Start's preschool, demonstrations, and the model programs it inspired has created a large knowledge base on early childhood care and education that did not exist in its founding days. Children who are healthy, have the social and academic skills they need, have parents who are involved in their education, and have families whose basic needs are met are more competent when they arrive at school. To help them attain school readiness, programs must be comprehensive, of high quality, and of long enough duration to make a meaningful difference.

Sally J. Styfco
Yale University

HEADACHE

Headache is one of the most common pain complaints. Over the 10-year period from 1987 to 1996 health care providers saw an increasing number of individuals with pain-related diagnoses, primarily due to an increase in the number of patients with headache.

Description of the Major Types of Headache

Migraine headache is episodic and characterized by a throbbing, pulsating, or pounding type of pain that generally starts on one side of the head, although, as the headache progresses, it often encompasses both sides. It typically starts over an eye or in the temple region and can last anywhere from 2 hours to 3 days. Frequently it is accompanied by nausea and, sometimes, vomiting, as well as sensitivity to noise (termed *phonophobia*) and, especially, light (termed *photophobia*). A migraine can occur on a frequency of two a week to only one or two a year; the average migraineur has one to two headaches a month. Approximately 10% of migraine headache patients have a prodrome—that is, preheadache symptoms that can occur up to 30 minutes before a headache, such as seeing flashing lights or squiggly lines, experiencing a disturbance in speech, or experiencing a tingling, burning, or pricking feeling in the arms or hands (termed *paresthesia*). Those migraine headache sufferers with a prodrome are described as *classic migraineurs;* those without a prodrome are termed *common migraineurs.*

Migraine headache is predominantly a disorder of women during the childbearing years. In prepubertal children, migraine is approximately equally distributed across the sexes. With the onset of menarche, females begin to outnumber males by about 2 or 3 to 1.

Tension headache is generally less episodic and is characterized by a steady, dull ache or pressure that is generally on both sides of the head. It is sometimes described as a tight band or cap around the head, a soreness, or a nagging or vicelike pain. It typically begins in the forehead, temple, back of the head and neck, or shoulder regions, and encompasses the entire head. A tension headache can last from 30 minutes to 7 days. If headaches occurs less than 15 days a month, they are termed *episodic tension-type headache;* if the headaches are experienced 15 or more days a month, they are termed *chronic tension-type headache.* The pain associated with tension headache is considered to be of generally lesser intensity than that of migraine headache. Tension-type headache is believed to be the most prevalent form of headache. It is more common in females than males, with a male to female ratio of approximately 1:1.5. Age of onset is generally in the second decade, and it peaks between the ages of 30 and 39.

Up to half of patients with migraine headache also meet the criteria for tension headache. These individuals have been labeled as *mixed migraine and tension-type headache* or *combined migraine and tension-type headache.* Most clinicians and researchers have typically lumped both pure migraine and mixed migraine and tension headaches together under the label of vascular headache and treated them similarly. Cluster headache, which is a very rare type of headache and tends to be found predominantly in males, is generally diagnosed by its very distinctive temporal pattern: In episodic cluster headache, the patient is headache-free for months to years and then enters a so-called cluster bout. During the cluster bout, the one-sided headaches appear fairly regularly, once or twice per day to every other day. The headaches are described as intense, excruciating pain, as if someone is drilling or boring into the head, that often makes it impossible for the patient to lie still. They last from 15–30 minutes to 2–3 hours. Many patients are so debilitated by this type of headache that it can take hours after the cessation of pain for them to return to a normal level of functioning. The cluster bout lasts several weeks to several months and then disappears. Some poor unfortunates have continuous cluster headaches.

Psychological Treatment Outcome of Headache

A beneficial manner of reporting outcome is the average proportion or fraction of a sample of headache patients who achieve a clinically significant reduction in headache activity, as documented by a daily headache diary. In chronic pain, a patient with 50% or greater reduction in pain activity has traditionally been considered a treatment success.

The three primary psychological approaches to headache are relaxation therapy, biofeedback, and cognitive-behavioral therapy. Because they are felt to have both psychological and physiological effects, the first two approaches are frequently called *psychophysiological interventions.* In practice, they are often combined with each other as well as cognitive-behavioral therapy. Please refer to the appropriate sections of this encyclopedia for more detail concerning these treatments.

Tension Headache

With tension headache, the biofeedback approach used is electromyographic (EMG; muscle tension) feedback from the forehead, neck, and/or shoulders. For relaxation therapy alone, successful treatment outcomes generally range from 40 to 55%; for EMG biofeedback alone, this value ranges from 50 to 60%, and for cognitive therapy, from 60 to 80%. When EMG biofeedback and relaxation are combined, the average number of treatment successes improves from about 50 to about 75%; when relaxation and cognitive therapy are combined, success increases from 40 to 65%.

Migraine Headache

For patients with pure migraine headache, hand surface temperature (or thermal) is the biofeedback modality of choice, and it leads to clinically significant improvement in 40 to 60% of patients. Cognitive therapy by itself achieves about 50% success. A systematic course of relaxation training seems to help when added to thermal biofeedback (increasing success from about 40 to 55%), but cognitive therapy added to the thermal biofeedback and relaxation does not improve outcome on a group basis. Relaxation training alone achieves success in from 30 to 50% of patients, and adding thermal biofeedback boosts that success (from about 30 to 55%).

Combined Migraine-Tension Headache

For patients with both kinds of the primary benign headache disorders (migraine and tension-type), the results with thermal biofeedback alone are a bit lower, averaging 30–45% success; relaxation training alone leads to 20–25% success. The best results come when thermal biofeedback and relaxation training are combined. With this combination treatment, results show 50–55% success rates (adding thermal biofeedback to relaxation raises success from 20 to 55%; adding relaxation therapy to thermal biofeedback increases success from 25% to 55%). Most experts strongly recommend a combination of the two treatments for these headache sufferers.

Cluster Headache

Nonpharmacological interventions have been found to be relatively ineffective for cluster headache, and many practitioners no longer see such patients in their practice.

Special Headache Populations

There is now a sizable body of research attesting to the efficacy of thermal biofeedback with pediatric migraine. In addition, headaches in the elderly can also be effectively treated with biofeedback and relaxation techniques, as can those individuals who consume excessive levels of medication. A number of investigators have demonstrated that a combination treatment including relaxation therapy and biofeedback is efficacious for treating headaches during pregnancy. Because pregnant women are not able to use most pain medications, many experts have suggested that techniques such as the psychophysiological interventions and psychotherapy should be the first-line intervention for headaches during pregnancy.

John G. Arena
Medical College of Georgia
Department of Veterans Affairs

See also: **Coping Strategies; Psychosomatic Disorders**

HETEROSEXUALITY

Sexual Behavior

The idea that sex is strictly for reproduction has deep historical roots in Western culture. Early Christian writers such as Thomas Aquinas promoted the view of sex as sinful, justifiable only in marriage for the purpose of procreation. Greater knowledge, technical advances in contraception, media awareness, and legal decisions have allowed people to separate sexuality from procreation and make personal decisions regarding sexuality. Variations in ethnicity, acculturation, religious orthodoxy, and socioeconomic status account for great diversity in sexuality. Human sexual behaviors cluster primarily around kissing and touching, intercourse (vaginal, anal), oral-genital stimulation, and masturbation. Atypical sexual behaviors, those behaviors that fall outside this range, include noncoercive paraphilias such as fetishism, transvestism, sexual sadism, and sexual masochism, and coercive paraphilias such as exhibitionism, voyeurism, frotteurism, necrophilia, and zoophilia. Because paraphilic behaviors are typically a source of intense sexual pleasure, individuals are generally reluctant to seek treatment and psychotherapy has not proven to be highly effective.

Sexual Response

Sexual Desire

Sexual desire refers to the broad interest in sexual objects or experiences and is generally inferred by self-reported frequency of sexual thoughts, fantasies, dreams, wishes, and interest in initiating and/or engaging in sexual experiences. Definition of this construct is complicated by factors such as attitudes, opportunity/partner availability, mood, and health. Relationship factors, individual preferences for sexual variety and emotional intimacy are closely linked to sexual desire. Androgens appear to also play a role. In males, about 95% of androgens (e.g., testosterone) are produced by the testes; the remainder is produced by the outer adrenal glands. In females, androgens are produced by the ovaries and adrenal glands in quantities much lower than in males (about 20–40 times less; Rako, 1996). In both males and females, decreased testosterone levels due to, for example, orchidectomy (removal of testes) or oophorectomy (removal of ovaries) have been linked to impaired sexual desire.

Sexual Arousal

Closely connected with desire, sexual arousal is defined in both subjective (e.g., feeling sexually excited) and physiological terms (e.g., genital vasocongestion). The primary markers of sexual arousal in both sexes are increased myotonia (muscle tension), heart rate, blood pressure, and vasocongestion (blood engorgement), which leads to penile erection in males, and engorgement of the clitoris, labia, and vagina (with lubrication) in females.

Physiological sexual arousal in males involves signal input from the brain and spinal cord and peripheral nervous systems, and on a complex interplay between neurotransmitters, vasoactive agents, and endocrine factors. Within the penis is a central artery (corpus cavernosum) and veins that exit and drain the erectile bodies. The muscles that line the sinusoidal spaces and the central artery are contracted during the nonerect state. Erection begins with muscle relaxation that is controlled by autonomic nerves and by the release of nitric oxide into the corpus cavernosum. Cyclic guanosine monophosphate (cGMP) mediates the effects of nitric oxide, which causes smooth muscle relaxation, reduces vascular resistance, and allows the erectile bodies to fill with blood. Once the erectile bodies become engorged, the veins are compressed under the penis's tough fibroelastic covering and blood is trapped in the penis. Normally, detumescence (loss of erection) occurs with the release of catecholamines during orgasm and ejaculation.

Physiological sexual arousal in women begins with vasocongestion of the vagina, vulva, clitoris, uterus, and possibly the urethra, and can occur within only a few seconds of sexual stimulation. Vaginal lubrication occurs when the blood vessels of the vaginal wall become engorged with blood, causing fluid to pass between the cells of the vaginal epithelium and emerge on the vaginal wall as sweatlike droplets. These droplets can quickly build up to form a lubricating film that facilitates penetration of the penis. Estrogens, produced predominantly by the ovaries, help maintain the elasticity of the vaginal lining and assist in vaginal lubrication.

Orgasm

In males and females, orgasm is characterized by a peak in sexual pleasure that is accompanied by rhythmic contractions of the genital and reproductive organs, cardiovascular and respiratory changes, and a release of sexual tension. In males, orgasm generally occurs in two stages: emission, which refers to rhythmic muscular contractions that force semen into the ejaculatory ducts, and expulsion, which is the release of semen through the urethra (ejaculation). Unlike males, some females (approximately 15%) are able to experience multiple orgasms, and some women experience orgasm and perhaps ejaculation when the Grafenberg spot, an area along the anterior wall of the vagina, is stimulated. Contrary to Freud's assertion of two distinct types of orgasm in females, clitoral (the "infantile" orgasm) and vaginal (the "mature" orgasm), Masters and Johnson (1966) found no physiological differences in orgasm produced by vaginal versus clitoral stimulation. Other researchers note that intensity of orgasm and emotional satisfaction can differ dependent upon type of stimulation.

Resolution

Following orgasm, physiological responses return to the unaroused state. In males there is a refractory period, a period of time in which it is physiologically impossible to achieve another orgasm. The length of the refractory period is highly variable and depends upon a number of factors including age, novelty of sexual situation, and frequency of sex. The extent to which aging affects the sexual response in both males and females depends largely on psychological, pharmacological, and illness-related factors.

Sexual Dysfunction

Diseases of the neurological, vascular, and endocrine systems (e.g., diabetes, cancer, multiple sclerosis) can impair virtually any stage of the sexual response. Medications used to treat depression, high blood pressure, psychiatric disorders, and cancer, as well as numerous recreational drugs (e.g., barbiturates, narcotics, alcohol abuse, tobacco smoking) can interfere with sexual desire, arousal, and orgasm. Psychological factors contributing to impaired sexual function most commonly include anxiety, relationship concerns, negative attitudes about sex, religious inhibition, and fears of pregnancy.

Low or absent sexual desire (hypoactive sexual desire) is the most common problem of couples going into sex therapy. Approximately 33% of women and 15% of men ages 18–59 report a lack of sexual interest (Laumann, Gagnon, Michael, & Michaels, 1994). Sexual aversion disorder is an extreme, irrational fear or dislike of sexual activity that leads to the avoidance of all or nearly all genital sexual contact with a sexual partner. Arousal difficulties include female sexual arousal disorder—inhibition of the vasocongestive/lubrication response—and male erectile disorder. Women of all ages may experience difficulty with lubrication, although it tends to be a problem more associated with menopause. Erectile problems may be of organic (e.g., circulatory problems, neurological disorders, hormone imbalances) or psychogenic (e.g., performance anxiety) origin. The ability to have erections during REM sleep suggests that the problem is psychological. Approximately 7% of men ages 18–29 years, and 18% of men ages 50–59 years, experience erectile difficulties (Laumann et al., 1999). *Anorgasmia,* which occurs in approximately 24% of women ages 18–59 (Laumann et al., 1999), refers to the inability to attain orgasm. *Premature ejaculation* is defined as ejaculation early on in the sexual scenario and before the person wishes it, and is reported in approximately 29% of men ages 18–59 years (Laumann et al., 1999). *Dysparuenia,* or pain during intercourse, occurs most commonly in females, and generally involves a combination of physical and psychological factors. *Vaginismus* is characterized by involuntary contractions of the muscles in the outer third of the vagina that interfere with penetration of the vagina (e.g., during intercourse, insertion of fingers, tampons, gynecological exam).

REFERENCES

Laumann, E. O., Gagnon, J. H., Michael, R. T., & Michaels, S. (1994). *The social organization of sexuality: Sexual practices in the United States.* Chicago: University of Chicago Press.

Masters, W., & Johnson, V. (1966). *Human sexual response.* Boston: Little, Brown.

Rako, S. (1996). *The hormone of desire.* New York: Harmony Books.

Cindy M. Meston, PhD
University of Texas, Austin

See also: **Sexual Desire**

HIPPOCAMPUS

Ever since Scoville and Milner's 1957 report on the patient H. M., who suffered a profound amnesia following bilateral surgical resection of the medial temporal lobe, it has been clear that the hippocampal region of the brain plays a critical role in memory. There is now considerable knowledge about the anatomical pathways of the hippocampus, about the functional role of the hippocampal region, and about the information encoded by firing patterns of hippocampal neurons.

Anatomy of the Hippocampus

From the perspective of its role in cognition and memory, the hippocampal system is last in a long succession of stages of cortical representation (Van Hoesen, 1982). Neocortical areas that provide information to the hippocampal system include only the highest stages of each neocortical sensory system, plus multimodal and limbic cortical areas and the olfactory cortex. These inputs arrive in three main cortical subdivisions of the parahippocampal region, composed of the perirhinal, parahippocampal, and entorhinal cortices. Superficial layers of parts of the parahippocampal region then project onto the hippocampus itself at each of its main subdivisions.

The main flow of information through the hippocampus involves serial connections from the dentate gyrus to CA3 to CA1, and then to the subiculum (Amaral & Witter, 1989). The intrinsic hippocampal pathway partially preserves the topographical gradients of neocortical input, but there are also considerable divergence and associational connections, particularly at the CA3 step. Outputs of subiculum, and to a lesser extent CA1, are directed back to deep layers of the parahippocampal region, which in turn projects back onto the neocortical and olfactory areas that were the source of cortical inputs. Thus, the hippocampal system is organized for maximal convergence of the final outcomes of cortical processing and is positioned to influence the nature of cortical representations based on an architecture ideal for the formation of associations among them.

Human Amnesia and Animal Models of Hippocampal Function

The early findings on H. M. emphasized the global nature of his impairment, an almost complete failure to learn all sorts of new verbal and nonverbal material (see Corkin, 1984; Eichenbaum & Cohen, 2001). Yet H. M.'s remote autobiographical memories and his capacity for short-term memory were completely intact, leading to the initial view that the hippocampal region plays a specific role in the consolidation of short-term memories into long-term memory. More recent work with H. M. and other amnesic patients has shown conclusively that the impairment in acquiring long-term memories is also circumscribed to a particular type of memory expression. Thus, amnesics can normally acquire new motor, perceptual, and cognitive skills and demonstrate normal sensory adaptations and "priming" of perceptual stimuli; and such implicit learning occurs despite the patients' inability to recall or recognize the learning materials or the events of the learning experience. Based on these distinctions, the kind of memory lost in amnesia has been called *declarative* or *explicit* memory, emphasizing the characteristic capacity for conscious and direct memory expression so devastated following damage to the hippocampal region. Conversely, the collection of capacities preserved in amnesia has been called *procedural* or *implicit* memory, emphasizing the finding that hippocampal-independent memories are characteristically revealed by unconscious and indirect means of expression.

Considerable success has been achieved in developing nonhuman primate and rodent models of human amnesia. Following removal of the same medial temporal structures involved in H. M.'s surgery, monkeys are severely impaired on delayed recognition of objects and show poor retention of rapidly acquired object discriminations. Conversely, they have a preserved ability to acquire slowly learned motor skill and pattern discrimination tasks. In addition, hippocampal damage results in impaired retention of object discriminations learned shortly before the lesion but spares retention of similar discriminations learned long before the damage. These findings parallel the pattern of impaired and spared memory capacities observed in human amnesics.

Further findings from experiments on monkeys and rats that focused on more selective damage within the medial temporal lobe suggest that the surrounding parahippocampal region and the hippocampus may play different roles in memory processing. Selective damage to the hippocampus results in either no deficit or only a mild deficit in recognition memory for specific objects, whereas damage to the parahippocampal region results in a severe impairment. By contrast, damage to either the hippocampus or the parahippocampal region results in impairments in linking memories to support flexible, inferential memory expression. According to one model the parahippocampal region may act as an intermediate-term buffer for convergent perceptual representations, whereas the hippocampus associates these representations into the network of long-term memories (Eichenbaum, 2000).

Information Encoded By Hippocampal Neurons

Complementary evidence on the nature of memory processing accomplished by the hippocampus has been derived from studies of the firing patterns of hippocampal neurons in behaving animals. Consistent with the view that the hippocampus is the ultimate stage of hierarchical processing, the functional correlates of hippocampal cells are "supramodal" in that they appear to encode the abstract stimulus configurations that are independent of any particular sensory input. Most prominent among the functional types of hippocampal principal neurons are cells that fire selectively when a rat is in a particular location in its environment as defined by the spatial relations among multiple and multimodal stimuli (O'Keefe, 1976). In addition, there are many reports of nonspatial behavioral correlates of hippocampal neuronal activity that indicate that hippocampal representation is not limited to the encoding of spatial relations among distal cues (e.g., Wood, Dudchenko, & Eichenbaum, 1999). Even the activity of place cells is influenced by events that are meaningful to the task at hand (e.g., Wood, Dudchenko, Robitsek, & Eichenbaum, 2000). These findings extend the range of hippocampal coding to reflect the global involvement of the hippocampus in memory indicated by the neuropsychological studies and serve to reinforce the conclusion that the hippocampus supports relational representations (Eichenbaum, Dudchenko, Wood, Shapiro, & Tanila, 1999).

A comprehensive and consensual understanding of the role of the hippocampal system in memory remains elusive. Nevertheless, there is an increasing convergence of evidence indicating that the hippocampus represents and relates specific experiences into a network of memories that supports our capacity for declarative memory.

REFERENCES

Amaral, D. G., & Witter, M. P. (1989). The three-dimensional organization of the hippocampal formation: A review of anatomical data. *Neuroscience, 31,* 571–591.

Corkin, S. (1984). Lasting consequences of bilateral medial temporal lobectomy: Clinical course and experimental findings in H. M. *Seminars in Neurology, 4,* 249–259.

Eichenbaum, H. (2000). A cortical-hippocampal system for declarative memory. *Nature Reviews Neuroscience, 1,* 41–50.

Eichenbaum, H., & Cohen, N.J. (2001). *From conditioning to conscious recollection: Memory systems of the brain.* New York: Oxford University Press.

Eichenbaum, H., Dudchencko, P., Wood, E., Shapiro, M., & Tanila, H. (1999). The hippocampus, memory, and place cells: Is it spatial memory or a memory space? *Neuron, 23,* 209–226.

O'Keefe, J. A. (1976). Place units in the hippocampus of the freely moving rat. *Experimental Neurology, 51,* 78–109.

Scoville, W. B., & Milner, B. (1957). Loss of recent memory after bilateral hippocampal lesions. *Journal of Neurology, Neurosurgery, and Psychiatry, 20,* 11–12.

Van Hoesen, G. W. (1982). The parahippocampal gyrus: New observations regarding its cortical connections in the monkey. *Trends in Neurosciences, 5,* 345–350.

Wood, E., Dudchenko, P. A., & Eichenbaum, H. (1999). The global record of memory in hippocampal neuronal activity. *Nature, 397,* 613–616.

Wood, E., Dudchenko, P., Robitsek, J. R., & Eichenbaum, H. (2000). Hippocampal neurons encode information about different types of memory episodes occurring in the same location. *Neuron, 27,* 623–633.

Howard Eichenbaum
Boston University

HISTORY OF CLINICAL PSYCHOLOGY

Clinical psychology is probably the most common specialty within psychology around the world today (Lunt & Portinga, 1996). Its principal aims include the study of psychopathology and its assessment and treatment. This same territory is shared by a number of other professional disciplines, including psychiatry, social work, mental health nursing, and various types of counseling. Compared to professionals in these neighboring fields, present-day clinical psychologists are distinctive in the quality of their training in research, psychometric testing, and behavior therapy.

Within the Western tradition, the earliest influential concepts of psychopathology are those found in the writings attributed to the Greek physician Hippocrates (c. 460–377 B.C.E.), who viewed madness as an illness like any other (Routh, 1998). For example, Hippocrates identified the condition called melancholia as being due to an excess of black bile produced by the pancreas (the very word *melancholia* means "black bile"). Such an imbalance of the internal fluids, or "humors," was treated by administering purgatives, whereas a furious manic state was more likely to be treated by bleeding the patient.

The specialty of psychiatry did not develop until the eighteenth century, and it did so simultaneously in a number of different countries, including England, Italy, France, and the new United States of America. The most famous figure of this era was the physician Philippe Pinel (1745–1826), who was in Paris at the time of the French Revolution. He elaborated the principles of moral treatment of mental patients. The basic idea was that it was not necessary to chain a mental patient to the wall. Instead, one should treat the individual in a kind and considerate way, minimizing coercion. It was during this time that asylums began to be considered as a way of treating the insane and not simply a way of confining them to protect society. In 1838, a French law was passed creating a national system of asylums. Soon afterward, formal organizations of "alienists," or psychiatrists, developed and began to publish scholarly journals. For example, the organization that became the American Psychiatric Association was founded in 1844.

In 1896, a psychological clinic was founded at the University of Pennsylvania by Lightner Witmer (1867–1956), a professor there. This event is generally regarded as the origin of the field of clinical psychology. Witmer, who had obtained his doctorate under Wundt, was especially interested in children with learning problems, including those in reading and spelling as well as general academic retardation. What was especially new was his suggestion that psychologists not only study people but also attempt to help them. He used the techniques being developed by experimental psychologists to study children and worked with teachers, physicians, and others to try to remediate such problems. Witmer trained doctoral students in these activities, and in 1907 founded a journal, *The Psychological Clinic,* in which he outlined his ideas concerning the new field (Witmer, 1907).

In France in 1905, the experimental psychologist Alfred Binet (1857–1911) and a physician, Theodore Simon (1873–1961), developed the first successful intelligence test. This test was quickly translated into English and imported by the United States, where it soon underwent various technical refinements by Lewis M. Terman (1877–1956) and became the Stanford-Binet (Terman, 1916). Administering Binet tests became the most characteristic activity of the first generation of clinical psychologists in the United States. For example, psychologists were incorporated into the clinical team of the first child guidance clinics primarily as intelligence testers. In 1908, psychologist Henry Goddard founded the first psychology internship program at the Vineland School in New Jersey; the program mainly provided extensive experience in such mental testing. The first organization of clinical psychologists, the American Association of Clinical Psychologists, founded in Pittsburgh in 1917, had as one of its purposes the staking out of individual mental testing as the professional domain of clinical psychologists (Routh, 1994).

Before World War II, clinical psychology was a small field. However, even before 1945, the repertoire of clinical psychologists in the area of mental testing expanded greatly, establishing its pattern for the remainder of the century. Herman Rorschach (1884–1922), a Swiss psychiatrist, developed the Rorschach inkblot test. In 1943, psychologist Starke R. Hathaway (1903–1984) and psychiatrist J. C. McKinley published the first edition of the Minnesota Multiphasic Personality Inventory. The *Journal of Consulting Psychology,* now one of the premier journals in clinical psychology, was established in 1937; during its first decade, it was devoted largely to professional issues and to advances in mental testing.

After World War II, clinical psychology was newly supported by government funds and expanded enormously. In the United States, the Veterans Administration and the National Institute of Mental Health requested information about which universities provided adequate training in clinical psychology. The American Psychological Association responded by setting up an official system for accrediting training in clinical psychology. In 1949, the Boulder Conference set the pattern for such programs, which sought to train "scientist-practitioners." In Britain and on the European continent, clinical psychologists began to be incorporated into the national health systems of many countries.

In this era, clinical psychologists have generally expanded their scope of practice beyond mental testing to include various intervention activities. In the postwar United States, the most influential clinical psychologist involved in psychotherapy was no doubt Carl R. Rogers (1902–1987). Other psychologists, such as Hans Eysenck (1916–1997) in Britain, launched the behavior therapy movement.

In conclusion, clinical psychology has emerged from its first century of existence as the largest psychological specialty, with a focus on the study, assessment, and treatment of psychopathology.

REFERENCES

Lunt, I., & Poortinga, Y. H. (1996). Internationalizing psychology. *American Psychologist, 51,* 504–508.

Routh, D. K. (1994). *Clinical psychology since 1917: Science, practice, and organization.* New York: Plenum.

Routh, D. K. (1998). Hippocrates meets Democritus: A history of clinical psychology as psychiatry. In A. S. Bellack & M. Hersen (Eds.), *Comprehensive clinical psychology* (Vol. 1, pp. 1–48). New York: Pergamon.

Terman, L. M. (1916). *The measurement of intelligence.* Boston: Houghton Mifflin.

Witmer, L. (1907). Clinical psychology. *Psychological Clinic, 1,* 1–9.

Donald K. Routh
Florida Gulf Coast University

See also: **Psychotherapy**

HISTORY OF PSYCHOLOGICAL ASSESSMENT

It can be assumed that early humans, well back into prehistory, engaged in informal evaluations of their fellows on such psychological variables as intelligence, aggressiveness, and cooperativeness. In the ancient world, after the dawn of civilization, the two primary methods of systematic assessment were horoscopic astrology and physiognomy. Astrology had the appeal that it was not necessary for the assessor to actually see the subject in order to provide a personality description; its disadvantage was that it was totally invalid, although this was not readily apparent. Physiognomy, based on the subject's physique and style of movement, though also grossly invalid, had at least the advantage that the assessor saw the subject.

Both astrology and physiognomy were immensely popular during the medieval and early Renaissance periods. However, in the latter period, in 1575, in Spain, there appeared a book that proposed the first rational, although still highly tentative, approach to assessment. This was Juan Huarte's *Examen de Ingenios para las Ciencas,* translated into English as *The Tryal of Wits.* Huarte argued that different persons have different talents ("wits") and that these differences are by measurable by experts ("Triers").

In 1691 Christian Thomasius, in what is now Germany, developed a primitive observational system for evaluating individual personalities, and reported quantitative data on several subjects, the first such instance in the history of psychology.

It was in the latter nineteenth century, however, in the person of Francis Galton, in England, that the movement toward scientifically based assessment got genuinely under way. Galton, who was something of a polymath, was passionately interested in measuring and calculating (he was the primary developer of the correlation coefficient) human individual differences. His 1883 book, *Inquiries into Human Faculty and Its Development,* presented a wealth of data on human attributes and capacities.

Although Galton employed the term *test* in something like its present sense, the word became more clearly established in the assessment lexicon by virtue of an important 1890 article, "Mental Tests and Measurements" by James KcKeen Cattell, an American who had spent some time in Galton's laboratory.

The breakthrough to a reasonable degree of accuracy in assessment was in the area of intelligence. In 1904, in Paris, a commission was appointed to devise a method for identifying children to be assigned to special classes. To help in such decisions Alfred Binet and Theodore Simon put together a series of 30 items varying in difficulty (e.g., 1: coordination of head and eyes in following a lighted match; 30: distinguishing between abstract terms) to indicate a child's level of mental development. The Binet-Simon scale proved useful, and later revisions were adopted and improved by others. The most prominent of these was the revision by Lewis M. Terman at Stanford, in 1916. This test—the Stanford-Binet—included the innovation of the intelligence quotient, or IQ (mental age divided by chronological age times 100). The concept of IQ became a part of American culture, as it still is, despite many technical problems that have since appeared.

An early problem with Binet-like tests was that they were not applicable to children with limited verbal skills. In response, psychologists early in the twentieth century developed several performance tests, including the Porteus Maze Test, the Kohs Block Design Test, and the Goodenough Draw-a-Man Test, to assess intelligence. In the same period Arthur S. Otis, an associate of Terman, developed the first of numerous pencil-paper tests roughly measuring intelligence in adults.

The Stanford-Binet had been specifically designed for the individual assessment of children. There was a need, however, for an equally precise measurement for adults. This need was met in 1939, with the publication of David Wechsler's Weschsler-Bellevue Intelligence Scale. Since then numerous additional tests for the assessment of intelligence have been developed. However, the Stanford-Binet and the Wechsler-Bellevue Scales, for both of which recent revisions have appeared, remain the most prominent.

The development of instruments for the assessment of personality and/or psychopathology did not lag far behind. Among the early personality questionnaires were R. S. Woodworth's Personal Data Sheet (used in the first World War to help identify unstable American soldiers); the Bernreuter Personality Inventory; and the Minnesota Multiphasic Personality Inventory (MMPI) by Starke Hathaway and Jovian McKinley in 1943. This latter test proved to be extremely useful and is still a part of the standard assessment armamentarium (it was revised in 1989).

Another early step in personality assessment was the construction of projective techniques (the subject is conceived to unknowingly "project" authentic personality traits into responses). The earliest—and still most popular—of these were the Rorschach and the Thematic Apperception test (TAT). The former instrument, created in 1921 by Herman Rorschach, a Swiss psychiatrist, consists of 10 inkblots in which the subject, reacting imaginatively, "sees" various objects. The interpretive system now most used is that of John E. Exner. The TAT, devised by Christiana Morgan and Henry Murray, consists of various pictures, to some of which the subject reacts by telling stories. Although numerous additional projective tests have since been constructed, the Rorschach and the TAT are still the most prominent.

Psychological assessment frequently includes systematic evaluations of a person's interests. The most important pioneer in this area was Edward K. Strong, a colleague of Terman's at Stanford in the 1920s. Another important area is achievement testing; this was pioneered by Edward Thorndike at Columbia and Terman at Stanford.

Currently, the field of psychological assessment is a thriving, active area. Numerous important new instruments have come to the fore: for example, in personality assessment, the California Personality Inventory, by Harrison Gough, and the Personality Assessment Inventory by Leslie C. Morey. In addition, there have been important new theoretical directions. One of these is behavioral assessment, in which the emphasis is on direct, systematic observation of the subject, rather than on psychological tests. Another new emphasis is on the use of structured interviews, particularly in the assessment of psychopathology. Also, significant advances have been made in neuropsychological assessment. Finally, computer technology is increasingly utilized in assessment, both in test administration and test interpretation.

SUGGESTED READING

DuBois, P. H. (1970). *A history of psychological testing.* Boston: Allyn & Bacon.

Goldberg, L. R. (1971). A historical survey of personality scales and inventories. In P. McReynolds (Ed.), *Advances in psychological assessment* (Vol. 2, pp. 293–336). Palo Alto, CA: Science and Behavior Books.

McReynolds, P. (1986). History of assessment in clinical and educational settings. In R. O. Nelson & S. C. Hayes (Eds.), *Conceptual foundations of behavioral assessment* (pp. 42–80). New York: Guilford Press.

PAUL W. MCREYNOLDS

HOMELESSNESS

Widespread homelessness is an age-old social problem, and a challenge to overcome.

What Is Homelessness?

Homelessness is more than the absence of a permanent address. It is a condition in which a very large and growing portion of people in the United States and most likely the rest of the world find themselves. It means being cut off from relatives, social groups, and community organizations and losing a sense of belonging to society.

Who Are the Homeless?

The homeless come from all walks of life, but the majority are single men. Among them are unemployed as well as the working poor whose average monthly income is $267.00. They are relatively young and disproportionately from minorities (e.g., Blacks, Hispanics) and die at an average age of 50. Among the rapidly growing homeless are single women, adolescents, and families with children. War veterans constitute one of the largest homeless contingents. Over a quarter of those who are homeless have achieved more than a high school education.

Causes

Poverty, unemployment, or other economic conditions may lead to homelessness. Underlying causes of homelessness are extreme poverty and a dearth of affordable housing. Nearly 1 in 5 homeless women and men cite gambling as a cause of their situation.

Large numbers of the homeless have alcohol, drug, or

mental disorders. It is not certain whether these disorders have come about before, during, or after homelessness. Substance Abuse is not considered to be either the cause or the consequence of homelessness, but rather a preexisting condition aggravated by loss of housing.

According to the *single calamity hypothesis,* homelessness grows out of a single crisis. Consequently, it would be difficult to predict which individual characteristics, experiences, and behaviors lead to homelessness. An individual crisis that occurs often to the homeless is a major illness. Thus, the onset of poor health may lead to homelessness and at the same time also be a consequence of it. Another crisis is the loss of a job followed by the lapse into unemployment. Racism, particularly against Blacks, has played a powerful role in bringing about and perpetuating homelessness.

How Many People Are Homeless?

Since the homeless population is transient, the actual number of homeless is uncertain. The number cited is usually based on those times when surveys are made by on-street interviews and counts at shelters, soup kitchens, and other such programs. It is estimated that 750,000 Americans are homeless on any given night and close to 2 million are homeless during the course of a year. There are countless people unaccounted for who manage to live in temporary locations such as subway caves, empty buildings, public areas, and the like.

Consequences

Homelessness often leads to stress, psychiatric disorders, and Substance Abuse: Alcohol abuse is the most prevalent health problem. Nearly two thirds of the homeless suffer from infectious or chronic diseases. Among the homeless are AIDS victims. In addition, the homeless typically lack adequate medical care or access to treatment. Medicaid and other welfare benefits are often unattainable to the homeless.

Children

Children are at greatest risk for the detrimental effects of homelessness, and they suffer the most physical, psychological, and emotional damage. Their physical development may be delayed, and children are susceptible to infectious and communicable diseases.

Among the homeless 3- to 5-year-olds, behavioral problems have been observed. Children older than age 5 frequently act out their anxieties. The foreboding danger for children is the inevitability that they are virtually trapped in poverty with no escape from homelessness. Thus poverty and homelessness may become a self-fulfilling prophecy passed on through the generations.

Bonds between the homeless parents and children weaken because parents are likely to assume a diminished role as disciplinarians and nurturers. Potential for child abuse is rife when the frustrations of homelessness exceed parental self-control.

Far too many homeless children skip school, fail and repeat grades, perform below the average, test poorly in reading and math, and are functionally illiterate.

Adolescents

Homeless adolescents are described as street kids, runaways, throwaways, and system youths who leave social service placements. Frequently, these adolescents come from dysfunctional families in which they are physically and sexually abused.

Health and Substance Abuse problems are common, as are sexual experiences, which make adolescents vulnerable to hepatitis and AIDS.

Lack of supportive and functional families is cited as the key factor associated with homeless adolescents. Large numbers of homeless youths are depressed and at risk for suicide.

Psychological Trauma

The psychological impact of homelessness can be as detrimental to one's self-esteem and well-being as the physical loss of housing. Homeless people may suffer from extraordinary stresses (e.g., psychological trauma resulting from loss of housing, living in a shelter, or victimization). A symptom of psychological trauma is social disaffiliation, breaking the bonds of attachment to significant others and to social institutions. Homelessness leads to distrust of others and isolation.

A second symptom is learned helplessness. Traumatized homeless individuals come to believe that they have no control over their lives and that they must depend on others to fulfill their basic needs. Among the homeless who suffer from traumatic victimization are battered women, some of whom report having been abused in childhood. In addition to social disaffiliation and learned helplessness, traumatized women also may display other dysfunctional symptoms, and many are abusive parents.

Solutions

Homelessness impinges on everyone in some way. When food and shelter are lacking, individuals cannot fulfill their need for self-actualization. Human resources that could be applied to improve the quality of their lives remain untapped.

In our society, because homelessness results from poverty, the first priorities for helping the homeless include building permanent affordable housing, providing income enhancement, and expanding health care.

The magnitude of the problem is so great that many believe only a federal effort to finance and administer such a project could eventually bring about its resolution. Failure to act eventually will be costly to the public and in terms of human suffering. Temporary overcrowded emergency shelters will become a permanent feature of the American landscape, and the homeless will continue to multiply at an uncontrollable and unprecedented rate at home and abroad.

Sheldon S. Brown

See also: **Learned Helplessness**

HOMEOSTASIS

Complex organisms must maintain relatively stable internal environments to survive and move freely through the changing and often adverse conditions that surround them. *Homeostasis* is the name given to this constancy in 1926 by Walter B. Cannon, an American physiologist. Through his work on homeostasis, Cannon created a concept that is a milestone in the history of ideas. It was the culmination of an approach begun some six decades earlier with the work of Claude Bernard, the French physiologist who established the foundations of scientific physiology. Bernard concluded that organisms have evolved toward a greater independence from the changing environment by developing from the blood and bodily fluids an internal environment held stable by its own adjustments. Cannon demonstrated that the activities of homeostasis, often simple if viewed each in isolation, are nevertheless orchestrated by remarkably complex regulatory processes involving the organism across physiological systems and levels of functioning.

In 1925, Cannon described his findings as instances of the maintenance of steady states in open systems. In 1926 he named this steady condition *homeostasis* and offered a set of postulates regarding its nature. In 1929, he discussed the homeostatic regulatory mechanisms identified up to that point. The body, he asserted, was able through homeostatic reactions to maintain stability in the fluid matrix surrounding the body cells, thus controlling body temperature, blood pressure, and other aspects of the internal environment necessary for life. Regulated by the nervous system and endocrine glands, bodily reactions at all levels of complexity were involved in homeostasis, from the speed with which cell metabolism proceeded and produced heat in cold weather, to increases and decreases in the complex processes giving rise to hunger and thirst, with impact on behaviors affecting energy and water intake.

Cannon's concept of homeostasis emerged as a complex statement regarding the existence, nature, and principles of self-regulating systems. He emphasized that complex living beings are open systems made up of changing and unstable components subjected continually to disturbing conditions precisely because they are open to their surroundings in so many ways. While continuously tending toward change, living beings must maintain constancy with regard to the environment in order to preserve circumstances favorable to life. Adjustments within such systems must be continuous and less than perfect. Homeostasis therefore describes a state that is relatively, rather than absolutely, stable.

The concept of the open system challenged all conventional views regarding the appropriate unit of analysis of an entity. If the heart, lungs, kidneys, and blood, for example, are parts of a self-regulating system, then their actions or functions cannot be understood by studying each alone. Full understanding comes only from knowledge of how each acts with reference to the others. The concept of the open system also challenged all conventional views of causality, substituting complex reciprocal determination for any notion of simple serial or linear causality. Homeostasis therefore offered a new perspective both for viewing the behavior of systems of many sorts and for understanding people as members of open systems.

Homeostasis has served as a cornerstone for a number of subsequent developments involving a system perspective of control and causality. Hans Selye's work with stress and disease, and his discovery of the general adaptation syndrome, began with the insight that certain diseases and disorders might arise as the cost of the body's struggle to maintain homeostasis in the face of prolonged disruptive pressure. Selye's view of disease as derangement of homeostasis contributed to a view of health in which the role of medicine is to assist the homeostatic processes to return the organism to the constant state. Norbert Wiener's 1948 cybernetic theory attempted to formulate principles to account for self-regulation across biological and nonliving systems such as computers, a pursuit construed even more broadly in Ludwig von Bertalanffy's general system theory.

Homeostasis research continues to stimulate new perceptions, in recent decades by establishing that learning can play a central role in homeostatic regulation of even physiological systems, such as those involved in the increasing drug tolerance levels found in addictions. In a series of experiments starting in the 1970s, for example, Shepard Siegel showed that increased morphine tolerance in rats involves a learning process. A body of subsequent research supported the conclusion that the increasing levels of drug tolerance associated with repeated drug administrations involve learned homeostatic efforts to restore normal functioning in the presence of drugs that otherwise destabilize normal functioning. With repeated exposure to the drug, the organism learns to produce a pattern of offsetting physiological and/or behavioral responses that counteract the perturbing effects of the drug. In the 1990s, D. S. Ramsay and S. C. Woods demonstrated that, once learned, this pattern of homeostatic responses can even be elicited in anticipation of the drug. Overall, Cannon's system concepts continue to play a central role in organizing our understanding of the nature of our interactions with our inner and outer environments.

Roger E. Enfield
West Central Georgia Regional Hospital, Columbus, Georgia

See also: **Adaptation; Double Bind; General Adaptation Syndrome**

HOMOSEXUALITY

Homosexuality refers to sexual behaviors, desires, attractions, and relationships among people of the same sex, as well as to the culture, identities, and communities associated with them. The term encompasses at least five phenomena that are often, although not always, related. First, it is used to describe any specific instance of sexual behavior with or attraction to a person of one's same sex. Both homosexual and heterosexual behaviors and attractions are common throughout human societies and across species. Second, it refers to ongoing patterns of attraction for sexual or romantic partners of one's own gender, which may or may not be expressed behaviorally.

A third aspect of homosexuality is psychological identity, that is, a sense of self defined in terms of one's enduring attractions to members of the same sex. Individuals who identify as homosexual typically refer to themselves as "gay," with most women preferring the term "lesbian." Some use "queer" as a self-descriptive term, thereby transforming a formerly pejorative label into a positive statement of identity. People follow multiple paths to arrive at an adult homosexual identity. Not everyone with homosexual attractions develops a gay or lesbian identity, and not all people who identify themselves as gay engage in homosexual acts.

A fourth component of homosexuality is involvement in same-sex relationships. Many gay and lesbian people are in a long-term intimate relationship and, like heterosexual pairings, those partnerships are characterized by diverse living arrangements, styles of communication, levels of commitment, patterns of intimacy, and methods of conflict resolution. Heterosexual and homosexual relationships do not differ in overall psychological adjustment or satisfaction. However, antigay stigma often denies same-sex partners the social support that heterosexual spouses typically receive, and even forces many same-sex couples to keep their relationship hidden from others.

Fifth, in the United States and many other societies, homosexuality involves a sense of community membership, similar to that experienced by ethnic, religious, and cultural minority groups. Empirical research indicates that gay men and lesbians in the United States tend to be better adjusted psychologically to the extent that they identify with and feel part of such a community.

The fact that the term homosexuality has multiple meanings highlights the difficulties of defining exactly who is gay. Moreover, many gay people do not disclose their sexual orientation publicly because they fear discrimination and harassment. Consequently, no accurate estimate exists for the proportions of the U.S. population that are homosexual, heterosexual, and bisexual. In North American and European studies during the 1980s and 1990s, roughly 1–10% of men and 1–6% percent of women (depending on the survey and the country) reported having had sexual relations with another person of their own sex since puberty.

Behavioral and Social Science Research on Homosexuality

The American mental health profession regarded homosexuality as an illness for much of the twentieth century. This classification reflected value assumptions and the viewpoints of particular schools of psychoanalysis rather than empirical data obtained scientifically from nonpatient samples. Its accuracy came into question when behavioral scientists began to systematically study the psychological functioning of homosexuals. Beginning with Evelyn Hooker's pioneering research in the 1950s, those studies consistently failed to find an inherent connection between homosexuality and pathology. In 1973, the weight of empirical data, coupled with changing social mores and the emergence of a politically active gay community in the United States, led the American Psychiatric Association to declare that homosexuality would no longer be considered an illness. Since then, the mental health professions have recognized that society's continuing prejudice against homosexuality is often a source of significant stress for gay men and women and sometimes leads to serious psychological distress and maladaptive behaviors. Consequently, many psychologists, psychiatrists, and other professionals are working to remove the stigma historically associated with homosexuality.

When homosexuality was regarded as an illness, its origin or cause was a topic of much speculation. More recently, researchers have recognized that the etiology of heterosexuality is equally puzzling, and scholarly inquiry now addresses the broad question of how sexual orientation develops in any given individual. A satisfactory answer to this question has not yet been found. It is possible that scientists will eventually identify multiple ways in which a person comes to be heterosexual, homosexual, or bisexual, with biological, psychological, and cultural factors all playing a role in this complex process.

Regardless of its origins, a heterosexual or homosexual orientation is experienced by most people in the United States and other Western industrialized societies as a deeply rooted and unchangeable part of themselves. Many adults report never having made a conscious choice about their sexual orientation and always having felt sexual attractions and desires to people of a particular sex. When homosexuality was assumed to be a form of psychopathology, psychiatrists and psychologists often attempted to "cure" it; that is, they tried to change homosexual people into heterosexuals. Even today, some counselors and psychotherapists continue this practice. However, such treatments are widely rejected by mainstream therapists because they are usually ineffective, often harmful to the client, and ethically questionable. Instead, most mental health practitioners working with lesbian and gay clients try to assist them in developing positive feelings about their sexuality, establishing meaningful intimate relationships, and coping with societal stigma.

Scientific studies demonstrate that gay men and lesbians constitute a highly diverse group. Apart from their sexual orientation, they are no more homogeneous than the heterosexual population. Researchers have failed to find significant differences between homosexual and heterosexual people on a wide range of characteristics, including psychological adjustment, the capacity to form and maintain intimate relationships, the ability to be a good parent, the likelihood of victimizing children or adults, and the ability to function effectively in work groups and organizations.

Conclusion

Psychology today regards homosexuality as a different, rather than pathological, form of sexuality. Psychology also recognizes the considerable diversity that exists among gay men and lesbians, and increasingly seeks to address the problems they face as a result of the stigma historically associated with homosexuality in the United States.

Gregory M. Herek
University of California, Davis

HOPE: THE IMPERATIVE HUMAN MOTIVE

The frequency with which we use the word *hope* in our daily interactions reveals the extent to which it is woven into the fabric of our lives. Despite the pervasiveness of hope, however, its meaning may be elusive. Try thinking of a synonym for hope. This probably is more difficult than you had imagined. Given this ubiquitous yet vague nature of hope, we seek to elucidate a concise definition of hope, to provide a brief overview of a theory of hope that is being used in psychology, and to describe the role of this vital motive for adaptive human functioning.

Throughout history, hope has been viewed as a virtue or an emotion—or both. With the emergence of cognitive psychological theories in the 1960s, however, hope began to be seen as an important cognitive construct. In this regard, researchers explored how hope could relieve stress by allowing people to believe that things will get better. Beliefs that outcomes are controllable and that one can influence those outcomes bolster such hope.

Focusing on the antecedents of psychopathology and mental illness, theorists such as Aaron Beck, Lyn Abramson, and Lauren Alloy developed theories of hopelessness—the perception that negative outcomes cannot be avoided. Such hopelessness taps apathy, as well as a general lack of positive expectancies and enthusiasm toward the future.

In contrast to this focus on attempting to avoid negative outcomes, other theorists such as Erik Erikson and Ezra Stotland recognized the significance of hope for adaptive functioning. Erikson viewed hope as resulting from successful negotiation of the first stage of human development—moving from mistrust to trust in the world. Similarly, Stotland defined hope as reflected positive cognitive schemas, or internal belief structures, that predispose our expectations about how our goal-related behaviors will shape the future. Thus, hope involves our perceptions about the probability of goal attainment and the accompanying motivation to reach the goal.

Expanding on these goal-based conceptualizations, C. R. Snyder and his colleagues developed a theory and definition of hope that easily can be measured. In this contemporary theory of hope, the ability to clearly conceptualize goals is accompanied by two additional cognitive processes: the perceived ability to develop specific strategies for attaining the goal (called *pathways*), and the perception that one can muster the requisite motivation to use those chosen pathways (termed *agency*). As such, pathways and agency are both necessary, although neither alone is sufficient for goal attainment. For example, if an individual cannot identify pathways to a goal, no amount of agency will lead to the goal's attainment. Likewise, in the absence of a plan, goal-directed motivation is useless.

Hope as described here is learned over the course of childhood through interactions with a consistently responsive and supportive caregiver who serves as a role model and who acts as a hope-inducing coach. Such interactions teach the child to trust in the consistency of cause-and-effect relationships and to trust that others will be available to lend assistance in attaining personal goals. These high-hope children continue to view others as available and supportive into adulthood. Thus, other people can be viewed as sources of hope agency ("you can do it!") as well as resources for pathways by providing needed information. Over time, high-hope people view the world as consistent and safe and themselves as worthy of support. Hence, they characteristically focus on success and experience positive emotional states.

Although emotions are related to hope, they are not the primary ingredients of hopeful thinking. Goal-directed thoughts are at the core of hope. In hope theory, emotions follow cognitions as the individual pursues valued goals. As the individual initiates the goal pursuit along chosen pathways, which can be conceived of as a collection of incremental subgoals, the experience of success at each stage along the way produces positive emotional experiences. Conversely, lack of success at these subgoal stages leads to negative affect. Thus, emotions feed back and act as affective cues that, when interpreted cognitively, inform people of the correctness of their courses toward goals. Likewise, negative emotions lessen motivation and may lead to a reevaluation of previously chosen pathways.

Over time, hope becomes a traitlike disposition relating to an individual's overall perception that he or she has the ability to attain desired goals. Someone who has experienced minimal success in past goal pursuits may subsequently perceive little chance of successfully pursuing future goals. In this case, the individual quickly gives up when encountering impediments or does not expend the requisite energy to succeed. In contrast, reinforced by positive emotional feedback, higher-hope people develop a large number of goals and identify alternative pathways for reaching those goals in case the original pathways become blocked or fail to yield desired outcomes.

The perceived ability to develop effective strategies for reaching goals, accompanied by positive emotional reinforcement, leads high-hope people to choose challenging goals. Consequently, hope contributes to positive outcomes. In the area of education, for example, research shows that hope is positively related to perceived self-worth, scholastic competence, and social competence, along with higher grades among students from elementary school through the college years. In the area of mental health, hope is a common factor in successful psychotherapy, and it promotes greater psychological well-being, less anxiety, and fewer depressive symptoms.

Because of its adaptive significance, hope provides the basis for developing interventions to improve the quality of life for individuals and for society as a whole. Furthermore, people can be taught to become more hopeful by setting clear goals for their futures, making commitments, and staying the course until they have reached their objectives. Thus, hope is a crucial motive for coping, change, and positive growth.

C. R. Snyder
Hal S. Shorey
Carla Berg
University of Kansas, Lawrence

HUMAN DEVELOPMENT

Life-span developmental psychology proposes that human development occurs from conception to death and that it involves the intricate interweaving of biological, sociocultural, and psychological processes (Baltes, 1987; Baltes, Lindenberger, & Staudinger, 1998). With regard to individual development, this theoretical approach focuses on (1) how single individuals change over time (intra-individual change); (2) differences between individuals during different developmental periods (interindividual variability); and (3) differences in individuals' patterns of change over time (interindividual variability in intra-individual change). Life-span developmentalists assume that human development can be conceptualized consistent with a series of principles and can be studied using research methodologies that capture the complexity of developmental processes.

Human development theorists have debated two issues concerning the continuity and discontinuity in developmental processes. In response to whether there are certain *age periods* (e.g., early childhood) that hold primacy in human development, or whether development occurs at all stages of the life span, the empirical literature supports the conclusion that humans have a capacity for change across the entire life span (Brim & Kagan, 1980) and that "no age period holds supremacy in regulating the nature of development" (Baltes, 1987, p. 613). The second issue, whether development proceeds in a smooth, linear, and *continuous manner* or whether development proceeds through a series of discontinuous stages, is resolved with the recognition that at all stages of the life span, both *continuous* (cumulative) and *discontinuous* (qualitatively different and innovative) processes are at work (Baltes, 1987; Lerner, 1984).

A core principle of human development is its *multidimensionality* and *multidirectionality*. Regardless of the developmental domain, multiple dimensions are required to capture the complexity of behavioral changes over time. The sequencing of changes, the conditions influencing continuity and change, the direction of changes (increasing or decreasing in complexity, frequency, or salience), and the pacing of changes tend to vary across dimensions within any domain. Only through the examination of multidirectional variations in the trajectories of change of multiple dimensions over time can the complexity of human development be elucidated.

The process of human development is not a simple movement toward higher efficiency, such as incremental growth. Rather, throughout life, development always consists of the joint occurrence of *gain* (growth) and *loss* (decline). In contrast to earlier views of human development that focused solely on processes that generated increasing capacity or complexity, life-span models of human development assert that in order to gain capacity in one dimension, loss must occur in another (Baltes, 1987). New adaptive capacities replace or subsume previously functional ones that have been lost. As reserve capacity and the range of plasticity decline in later life, older adults select more carefully the domains of functioning in which they try to maintain high efficacy and, when necessary, rely on compensatory mechanisms to adapt to the demands of the environment within those specialized domains (Baltes & Baltes, 1990).

Plasticity refers to the "processes by which one develops one's capacity to modify one's behavior to adjust to, or fit, the demands of a particular context" (Lerner, 1984, p. 10). This principle presumes the organism's capacity to influence the environment and itself in order to shape the course of its own development. Structural characteristics of the species both create the potential for, and set the constraints on, behavioral plasticity.

Two key propositions of the life-span perspective on human development are *contextual embeddedness* and *dynamic interaction* (Lerner, 1984). Contextual embeddedness refers to the idea that the key phenomena of human life exist at multiple levels (e.g., inner-biological, individual-psychological, social-sociological, cultural-historical, outer-physical/ecological) that influence each other in reciprocal ways. Thus, the task of human developmentalists is to describe and explain how different levels interact and influence each other and to optimize the parameters that affect these interactions and the resulting developmental trajectories (Baltes et al., 1998; Lerner, 1984).

Taken together, the basic principles of life-span development make *multidisciplinary inquiry* a necessity. Developmental changes in human behavior can only be explained by engaging in multiple levels of analysis of both internal and external contexts, leading to the inevitable necessity that development will only be understood when multiple disciplines work together to examine developmental processes.

Although theorists have argued that human development research requires observation over the "period of time during which the developmental phenomena of interest are thought to occur" (Schaie, 1983, p. 1), developmental research has mostly relied on cross-sectional comparisons of different age groups. Although valuable in informing researchers about the possible magnitude and the pattern of age differences in a certain behavior at a given point in time, cross-sectional studies are limited in providing information about developmental changes (Schaie, 1994). Longitudinal studies that track individuals over the course of their development permit (1) the direct identification of intra-individual change; (2) the identification of interindividual variability in intra-individual change; (3) the assessment of the interrelationships among different domains of intra-individual change; (4) the analysis of determinants or correlates of intra-individual change; and (5) the analysis of interindividual variability in the determinants or correlates of intra-individual change (Schaie, 1983). However, longitudinal designs share problems inherent in quasi-experimental designs (Campbell & Stanley, 1967) and confound time-of-measurement and aging effects that render estimates of age effects internally invalid (Schaie, 1983, 1994). *Sequential study designs* address many of these limitations (Schaie, 1994). Life-span developmental psychology has made great progress in the description, explanation, and optimization of human development across the whole life span. The use of longitudinal and sequential research designs has resulted in elaborate multivariate studies of behavioral development, showing that development occurs at all stages of the human life course from conception to death. In general, human development is characterized by processes of continuity and discontinuity, multidirectionality, gains and losses, and modifiability, and has as the ultimate goal the realization of a person's fullest potential.

REFERENCES

Baltes, P. B. (1987). Theoretical propositions of life-span developmental psychology: On the dynamics between growth and decline. *Developmental Psychology, 23,* 611–626.

Baltes, P. B., & Baltes, M. M. (1990). Psychological perspectives on successful aging: The model of selective optimization with compensation. In P. B. Baltes & M. M. Baltes (Eds.), *Successful aging: Perspectives from the behavioral sciences* (pp. 1–34). New York: Cambridge University Press.

Baltes, P. B., Lindenberger, U., & Staudinger, U. M. (1998). Life-span theory in developmental psychology. In W. Damon (Series Ed.) & R. M. Lerner (Vol. Ed.), *Handbook of child psychology: Vol. 1. Theoretical models of human development* (5th ed., pp. 1029–1143). New York: Wiley.

Brim, O. G., Jr., & Kagan, J. (Eds.). (1980). *Constancy and change in human development.* Cambridge, MA: Harvard University Press.

Campbell, D. T., & Stanley, J. C. (1967). *Experimental and quasi-experimental designs for research.* Chicago: Rand McNally.

Lerner, R. M. (1984). *On the nature of human plasticity.* New York: Cambridge University Press.

Schaie, K. W. (1983). What can we learn from the longitudinal study of adult psychological development? In K. W. Schaie (Ed.), *Longitudinal studies of adult psychological development* (pp. 1–19). New York: Guilford Press.

Schaie, K. W. (1994). Developmental designs revisited. In S. H. Cohen & H. W. Reese (Eds.), *Life-span developmental psychology: Methodological contributions* (pp. 45–64). Hillsdale, NJ: Erlbaum.

Sara Honn Qualls
University of Colorado, Colorado Springs

Manfred Diehl
Lise M. Youngblade
University of Florida

HUMAN INTELLIGENCE

The Definition of Intelligence

Intelligence, according to *Webster's New World College Dictionary* (3rd ed.), is "the ability to learn or understand from experience, ability to acquire and retain knowledge; mental ability" (Neufeldt, 1997, p. 702). Such a definition captures many facets of the nature of intelligence, but not necessarily those believed to be key by experts.

Two symposia have sought to ascertain the key features of intelligence according to experts in the field ("Intelligence and its Measurement," 1921; Sternberg & Detterman, 1986). Critical elements of the definition of intelligence, according to experts, are (1) adaptation in order to meet the demands of the environment effectively, (2) elementary processes of perception and attention, (3) higher-level processes of abstract reasoning, mental representation, problem solving, decision making, (4) ability to learn, and (5) effective behavior in response to problem situations. Some experts, however, have been content to define intelligence operationally, simply as the intelligence quotient, or IQ (Boring, 1923). These definitions rely on tests such as those originated by Binet and Simon (1916) to measure judgmental abilities or of Wechsler (1939) to measure verbal and performance abilities.

Laypeople also can be asked to define intelligence, and it turns out that their definitions differ from expert definitions in placing somewhat greater emphasis on social-competence skills. In one study, for example, laypeople defined intelligence in terms of three broad classes of skills: (1) practical problem solving, (2) verbal ability, and (3) social competence (Sternberg, Conway, Ketron, & Bernstein, 1981). Definitions can vary somewhat across occupations (Sternberg, 1985).

Heritability and Modifiability

Whatever human intelligence may be, that aspect of it measured as IQ is both partially heritable—with a heritability coefficient estimated at about .5 (albeit slightly lower in childhood and somewhat higher in adulthood)—and modifiable in at least some degree (Sternberg & Grigorenko, 1997). Indeed, intelligence as measured by IQ tests has been rising steadily through most of the century (Neisser, 1998).

Theories of Intelligence

Another approach to understanding intelligence is through a more elaborated theory. A theory, in contrast to a definition, must provide an explanatory framework and be testable. Theories have been of several different kinds.

Psychometric Theories

The best-known theories are probably psychometric ones. Among these theories, the earliest major one is that of Spearman (1927), who proposed that intelligence comprises a general factor (*g*) of intelligence common to all intellectual tasks, as well as specific factors (*s*), each of which is unique to a given test of intelligence. His proposal was based on his finding of a "positive manifold" among intelligence tests: All tests seemed to be positively intercorrelated, suggesting the existence of a general factor. Spearman's theory still has many proponents today (e.g., Jensen, 1998). Thurstone (1938) disagreed with Spearman, arguing that the general factor was an artifact of the way Spearman analyzed his data. Thurstone suggested that seven primary mental abilities underlie intelligence: verbal comprehension, verbal fluency, number, spatial visualization, inductive reasoning, memory, and perceptual speed. More modern theorists, such as Cattell (1971) and Carroll (1993), have attempted to integrate these two kinds of views, suggesting that intelligence is best understood hierarchically, with a general factor at the top of the hierarchy and narrower factors under it. Cattell proposed two such factors: fluid intelligence, which is involved in reasoning with novel kinds of stimuli, and crystallized intelligence, or stored knowledge base.

Systems Theories

Some theories of intelligence have viewed intelligence as a system. By far the best-known theory of this kind is that of Piaget (1972), according to which intelligence involves an equilibration between two processes: assimilation of new information to fit existing cognitive structures, and accommodation of existing cognitive structures to incorporate information that does not fit into preexisting cognitive structures. Sternberg (1997) has proposed that intelligence comprises three aspects: analytical abilities (used to analyze, evaluate, and critique), creative abilities (used to create, discover, and invent), and practical abilities (used to apply, implement, and use). Gardner (1999) has suggested instead that there are eight multiple intelligences—linguistic, logical-mathematical, spatial, musical, bodily-kinesthetic, naturalist, intrapersonal, and interpersonal—and perhaps existential intelligence as well.

REFERENCES

Binet, A., & Simon, T. (1916). *The development of intelligence in children* (E. S. Kite, Trans.). Baltimore, MD: Williams & Wilkins.

Boring, E. G. (1923, June 6). Intelligence as the tests test it. *New Republic,* 35–37.

Carroll, J. B. (1993). *Human cognitive abilities: A survey of factor-analytic studies.* New York: Cambridge University Press.

Cattell, R. B. (1971). *Abilities: Their structure, growth, and action.* Boston: Houghton-Mifflin.

Gardner, H. (1999). Are there additional intelligences? The case for naturalist spiritual, and existential intelligences. In J. Kane (Ed.), *Education, information, and transformation* (pp. 111–131). Englewood Cliffs, NJ: Prentice Hall.

"Intelligence and its measurement": A symposium. (1921). *Journal of Educational Psychology, 12,* 123–147, 195–216, 271–275.

Jensen, R. B. (1998). *The g factor.* Greenwich, CT: Greenwood.

Neisser, U. (Ed.). (1998). *The rising curve.* Washington, DC: American Psychological Association.

Neufeldt, V. (Ed.). (1997). *Webster's New World College Dictionary* (3rd ed.). New York: Macmillan.

Piaget, J. (1972). *The psychology of intelligence.* Totowa, NJ: Littlefield Adams.

Spearman, C. (1927). *The abilities of man.* London: Macmillan.

Sternberg, R. J. (1985). Implicit theories of intelligence, creativity, and wisdom. *Journal of Personality and Social Psychology, 49,* 607–627.

Sternberg, R. J. (1997). *Successful intelligence.* New York: Plume.

Sternberg, R. J., Conway, B. E., Ketron, J. L., & Bernstein, M. (1981). People's conceptions of intelligence. *Journal of Personality and Social Psychology, 41,* 37–55.

Sternberg, R. J., & Detterman, D. K. (1986). *What is intelligence? Contemporary viewpoints on its nature and definition.* Norwood, NJ: Ablex.

Sternberg, R. J., & Grigorenko, E. L. (Eds.). (1997). *Intelligence, heredity, and environment.* New York: Cambridge University Press.

Thurstone, L. L. (1938). *Primary mental abilities.* Chicago: University of Chicago Press.

Wechsler, D. (1939). *The measurement of adult intelligence.* Baltimore, MD: Williams & Wilkins.

Lloyd G. Humphreys

See also: **Primary Mental Abilities**

HUMAN LOCOMOTION

In the eighteenth century, the investigation of movement was based on the premise that upright stance and gait and also differentiation of hand movements represented a basic requirement for human cultural development. This necessitates that the nervous system must function to automatically balance the body's center of mass over the feet during all motor activities. In other words, every movement must begin and end with a postural adjustment. Nevertheless, basic neuronal mechanisms underlying quadrupedal locomotion remain preserved during human gait.

Analysis of human gait first became possible toward the end of the nineteenth century with the development of photographic recordings of running movements. Later, the technique for recording electrophysiological responses during locomotion was developed and was first demonstrated in cats.

The relative significance of reflexes on central rhythms and programming in locomotion has been addressed. The *central mechanisms* involved in locomotion are reflected in a reciprocal mode of leg muscle activation and a di- or triphasic pattern of antagonistic leg muscle activity following displacement of the feet that is thought to be programmed in its basic structure. This electromyographic (EMG) pattern is assumed be evoked by a multisensory afferent input and generated by spinal interneuronal circuits that are closely connected with spinal locomotor centers. The extent to which the timing of the pattern can be modified by afferent input has not yet been fully explored. A basic requirement of bipedal locomotion is that both legs act in a cooperative manner; each limb affects the strength of muscle activation and the time-space behavior of the other. There exists some evidence that this interlimb coordination is mediated by spinal interneuronal circuits, which are themselves under supraspinal (e.g., cerebral and cerebellar) control.

In regard to the *reflex mechanisms,* short latency stretch reflexes in leg extensor muscles are profoundly modulated during gait mainly by presynaptic inhibition group IA input and less by fusimotor influences. During large translational perturbations a significant contribution of this reflex has not yet been demonstrated. However, they may be involved in the compensation of the small ground irregularities at distinct phases of gait. Compensation for larger displacements during gait is provided by polysynaptic spinal reflexes. This includes an activation of synergistic muscle groups of both legs. These EMG responses are thought to be mediated predominantly by peripheral information from group II (and probably III) afferents, converging with different peripheral and supraspinal inputs onto common interneurons on a spinal level. These reflexes modulate the basic motor pattern of spinal interneuronal circuits underlying the respective motor task.

During recent years, increasing evidence has come up for the crucial importance of load receptor input in the control of bipedal stance and gait in quadrupeds and bipeds. Yet we are still at the beginning of an understanding of its nature and its interaction with other afferent inputs and control mechanisms. Vestibular and visual functions are mainly context dependent and are essential when afferent input from other sources is reduced.

One of the first symptoms of a lesion within the central motor system represents *movement disorder,* which is most characteristic during locomotion in patients with spasticity, cerebellar lesions, or Parkinson's disease. The *clinical* examination reveals typical changes in tendon tap reflexes and muscle tone typical for one of the movement disorders. However, today we know that there exists only a weak relationship between the physical signs obtained during the clinical examination in a passive motor condition and the impaired neuronal mechanisms in operation during an active movement. By the recording and analysis of electrophysiological and biomechanical parameters during a functional movement such as locomotion, the significance of, for example, impaired reflex behavior or pathophysiology of muscle tone and its contribution to the movement disorder can reliably be assessed. Consequently, an adequate treatment should not be restricted to the cosmetic therapy and correction of an isolated clinical parameter but should be based on the pathophysiology and significance of the mechanisms underlying the disorder of functional movement that impairs the patient.

Volker Dietz
University Hospital Balgrist

HUMAN RELATIONS TRAINING

Once heralded by Carl Rogers as "the most important social invention of the twentieth century," human relations training has failed to meet the promise inherent in that statement. Human relations training (HRT), also known as group-dynamics training, encounter groups, sensitivity training, or T-groups (for training), is rarely the focus of either the theory or practice of psychology in the first decade of the twenty-first century. With the possible exception of those committed to a humanistic psychology perspective, HRT has become simply one approach to increasing management and work-group effectiveness.

The process of HRT typically involved a small group of persons, usually 12–15 in number, who would meet together over a specified period of time with the goal of increasing their own self-awareness, their understanding of others, and their knowledge of and skill in small-group dynamics. With the support of a trained facilitator, these process-oriented groups would engage in a variety of discussions, activities, and exercises that would allow participants to both reveal themselves as persons and receive feedback on the reactions of the other members of the group about how these revelations were experienced. As each member of the group provided such feedback, they would learn how congruent their reactions were with those of the others and thus learn more about how effective they were as observers. The key ingredient to promoting changes through HRT was the feedback process in which these various observations and reactions were shared. The facilitator or trainer would explain, model, and monitor the feedback to ensure that all such feedback was behaviorally based, nonjudgmental, and offered in a helpful context. Through this feedback process, participants would learn more about themselves, especially about the impact of their behavior on others. Such training programs typically last from 2 to 5 days.

A useful model for understanding how HRT functions to increase self-awareness is the Johari Window (Luft, 1961), which is presented in Figure 1. In the Johari Window, Quadrant I, the open or public quadrant, represents the behaviors that are known both to the self and to others. Quadrant II, the blind quadrant, represents behaviors known to others but not to the self, while Quadrant III, the hidden or secret quadrant, refers to behaviors known to the self but not to others. The unknown quadrant, Quadrant IV, represents behaviors known to neither the self nor others. Perhaps the most important goal of HRT is to increase the size of the public area (Quadrant I) and to reduce the size of the blind and hidden areas. This increase in the public area is seen as an important way to increase interpersonal competence and effectiveness in human relationships.

One can enlarge one's public area through self-disclosure, thereby reducing the secret area, and through receiving feedback about one's behavior, especially its impact upon others, which reduces the blind area. HRT training is typically designed to elicit a wide range of self-disclosing behaviors that are not typically exhibited by the individual, which permit others to have a broader knowledge of the person. The leader or trainer then encourages the person to request feedback about how those behaviors affect the others in the group. Thus self-disclosure and feedback lead to an increase in the open or public area and, presumably, to increased interpersonal competence. The reduction in the size of both the blind and hidden areas should then reduce the size of the unknown area. All of this is carried out in a laboratory environment that encourages behavioral experimentation and where trust, nondefensiveness, and interpersonal warmth should predominate.

In a similar fashion, the participants in HRT can be helped by the facilitator to observe various group processes as they occur in the course of the program. The various stages of group development can be noted, the various group roles that participants play can be examined, the group's decision-making processes can be reviewed, and so on. Thus HRT is seen as a vehicle for learning both about the self and about group dynamics. The role of the facilitator, also known as the trainer or group leader, in HRT is to

	Known to Self	Not Known to Self
Not Known To Others	I OPEN	II BLIND
Known to Others	HIDDEN III	UNKNOWN IV

Figure 1. The Johari Window (after J. Luft, 1961).

assist the group in setting the structure and norms for the early work of the group and in processing learning, on both individual and group levels.

There are any number of reasons for the loss of interest in HRT on the part of psychologists. The lack of any standardization in HRT, the enormous variations in the training and skills of HRT facilitators, and the reports of serious emotional breakdowns in HRT were all contributors, as was the decline in interest by social psychologists in small-group research (Goodstein & Dovico, 1979). But probably the most important factor was the lack of empirical evidence on the long-term effectiveness of HRT.

The research on the effectiveness of HRT (Campbell & Dunnette, 1968; Dunnette & Campbell, 1968) suggests that although such training does produce positive changes in behavior, there is little evidence that the effects of training transfer to the participants' home environments. One exception to these findings is the report by Hand, Richards, and Slocum (1973), who followed a group of managers for 18 months after they participated in HRT and found that, in contrast to a matched control group, the members of the trained group had more self-awareness and were more sensitive to others, and that their subordinates were also aware of these changes. It is interesting to note that these performance ratings increased only for those trained participants who worked in consultative environments, but not for those in autocratic environments. Yet, overall, the support for the long-term impact of HRT on interpersonal competence is limited, which undoubtedly was an important factor in its demise as an important psychological activity.

Perhaps the most important legacy of HRT, however, is its focus on the importance of feedback in modifying human behavior. This focus may help account for the current interest by psychologists and others in using 360-degree feedback and in managerial coaching based upon that feedback. In 360-degree feedback, an individual is rated by superiors, peers, and subordinates, using a standardized, reliable behavioral rating instrument. These ratings are then compared with the individual's self-rating, and any differences become the basis for coaching to reduce these differences—a process similar in intent to HRT but one based upon a data set with which psychologists are more comfortable.

REFERENCES

Campbell, J. R., & Dunnette, M. D. (1968). The effectiveness of T-group experiences in managerial training and development. *Psychological Bulletin, 70,* 73–104.

Dunnette, M. D., & Campbell, J. P. (1968). Laboratory education: Impact on people and organizations. *Industrial Relations, 8,* 1–45.

Goodstein, L. D., & Dovico, M. (1979). The rise and fall of the small group. *Journal of Applied Behavioral Science, 15,* 320–328.

Hand, H. H., Richards, M. D., & Slocum, J. W. (1973). Organizational climate and the effectiveness of a human relations training program. *Academy of Management Journal, 16*(2), 185–195.

Luft, J. (1961). The Johari window: A graphic model of awareness in interpersonal behavior. *Human Relations Training News, 5*(1), 6–7.

Leonard D. Goodstein

HUNGER

Feelings and Behaviors

The subjective states related to eating are familiar. Hunger, for example, increases during fasts, whether these are voluntary intermeal intervals or externally enforced fasts. Hunger is also elicited by conditioned stimuli, such as Pavlov's legendary bell. The complementary states of satiety are equally familiar. Although the psychology of subjective states of hunger and satiety has been studied for many years, newer methods, including brain imaging, are now making them accessible to neuroscientific analysis.

The functional behavioral unit related to hunger and satiety is the meal. Patterns of spontaneous meal sizes and intermeal intervals are biologically organized, as is evident from the characteristic spontaneous eating patterns displayed by humans and other animals and from the predictable changes in meal patterns in response to various physiological and environmental variables. There are also more elementary biological units of eating behavior than meals. For example, neural networks in the brain stem produce patterns of licks, bites, chews, and swallows of food, and these also vary predictably in many states in ways that modify meal size. These units of eating are attracting increasing attention from neuroscientists who are analyzing how the brain produces eating behavior.

Food Selection and Meal Initiation

Food selection and meal initiation are controlled mainly by conditioned olfactory, visual, temporal, cognitive, and social stimuli. These are usually highly individuated, especially in humans. Two physiological signals are also known to be sufficient for normal meal initiation. First, small, brief, transient declines in blood glucose supply signal hunger. These declines are not hypoglycemia (i.e., decreases in blood glucose that reduce cellular glucose supply), which rarely occurs spontaneously. Second, certain changes in liver metabolism that occur between meals, such as changes in fatty acid oxidation, are sufficient to initiate eating. Gastric contractions are not signals for meal initiation; the referral of "hunger pangs" to the stomach seems an epiphenomenon.

Meal Size

Controls of the maintenance of eating and of the termination of eating determine meal size. Taste, especially sweet taste, is the only known unconditioned stimulus that affects eating once it has begun. Odors are crucial for flavor preferences, but their contribution is conditioned.

Feedback signals from the gastrointestinal tract provide unconditioned controls of meal termination. Most important are stomach volume, which is detected by mechanoreceptors in the gastric muscles, and small intestinal nutrient content, which is detected by chemoreceptors in the intestinal mucosal. Feedback information is encoded in the periphery as neural impulses in the vagus or splanchnic nerves or in the concentration of gut peptide hormones such as cholecystokinin (CCK).

Other feedbacks unrelated to the ongoing meal also control meal size. Most interesting are two hormones whose average blood levels are correlated with body fat content, insulin and leptin. The control of meal size and food intake by body fat can be dramatic or weak, depending, for example, on genetic variation, on the availability, palatability, variety, and energy density of food, and, probably, on conditioning.

Learning

Except the unconditioned effects of taste, all food identification, selection, and preference is learned. Little is known, however, about the complex social and cultural conditioning that so dramatically influences human appetite, producing, for example, the paradoxical preference for capsaicin (chili). Food's rewarding, satiating, metabolic, and toxic effects all support learning. A neutral flavor associated with a satiating food can simultaneously condition preference, so that flavor is preferred, and satiety, so less of foods of that flavor are eaten. Conditioned aversions linking tastes with certain forms of gastrointestinal illness are a dramatic example of a special biological preparedness: A single pairing of taste and illness suffices, the taste-illness interval can be hours, and the learning is very resistant to extinction.

Brain Mechanisms

Neuropharmacological methods, including the measurement of neurochemicals at their site of action in awake, behaving animals, link many specific neurochemical systems in the brain to hunger. Dopamine and endogenous opioids are neurotransmitters crucial for food reward (i.e., for the maintenance of eating during meals, the production of pleasure, and the reinforcement of learning about food). Neuropeptide Y (NPY), norepinephrine (NE), and agouti-related peptide also increase eating, apparently by increasing hunger rather than affecting reward. The most researched neurotransmitter that inhibits eating is serotonin (5-hydroxytryptamine, 5HT), which is important in food reward, CCK's satiating action, and conditioned preferences.

The outlines of the neural networks in the brain underlying eating have begun to take shape. Unconditioned controls of meal size apparently can act in the brain stem to inhibit eating. In the forebrain, the hypothalamus is a crucial node for both conditioned and unconditioned controls of meal initiation and meal size. Reward certainly involves other basal forebrain areas, including the nucleus accumbens and the amygdala. More complex controls involve increasingly wide areas of the forebrain.

Eating Disorders

Both subjective and behavioral aspects of meals are disturbed in eating disorders. The behavioral neuroscience of eating has begun to contribute to understanding these problems. For example, patients with Bulimia Nervosa eat larger than normal meals under laboratory conditions; ingested food is less satiating than normal for these patients, and the decreased satiety is related to decreased CCK secretion.

SUGGESTED READING

Degan, L., Matzinger, D., Drewe, J., & Beglinger, C. (2001). The effect of cholecystokinin in controlling appetite and food intake in humans. *Peptides, 22,* 1265–1269.

Friedman, J. M. (2001). Leptin and the regulation of body weight. *Harvey Lectures, Series 95,* 107–136.

Geary, N. (2001). Estradiol, CCK and satiation. *Peptides, 22,* 1251–1263.

Geary, N., & Smith, G. P. (1999). Appetite. In B. J. Sadock & V. A. Sadock (Eds.), *Comprehensive textbook of psychiatry* (7th ed., Vol. 1, pp. 209–218). Philadelphia: Lippincott Williams & Wilkins.

Grill, H. J., & Kaplan, J. M. (2002). The neuroanatomical axis for the control of energy balance. *Frontiers in Neuroendocrinology, 23,* 2–40.

Langhans, W. (1996). The role of the liver in the metabolic control of feeding. *Neuroscience and Biobehavioral Reviews, 20,* 145–153.

Rosenbaum, M., Leibel, R. L., & Hirsch, J. (1997). Medical progress: Obesity. *New England Journal of Medicine, 337,* 396–407.

Rozin, P. (1986). Food likes and dislikes. *Annual Review of Nutrition, 6,* 433–456.

Sclafani, A. (1997). Learned controls of ingestive behavior. *Appetite, 29,* 153–158.

Smith, G. P. (2000). The controls of eating: A shift from nutritional homeostasis to behavioral neuroscience. *Nutrition, 16,* 814–820.

Spiegelman, B. M., & Flier, J. S. (2001). Obesity and the regulation of energy balance. *Cell, 104,* 531–543.

Woods, S. C., & Stricker, E. M. (1999). Food intake and metabolism. In M. J. Zigmond, L. R. Squire, & J. L. Roberts (Eds.), *Fundamental neuroscience* (pp. 1091–1108). San Diego, CA: Academic Press.

NORI GEARY

See also: Neurotransmitters

HYPERACTIVITY

The term *hyperactivity* refers to both a symptom associated with a variety of medical and behavioral disorders and a common psychopathological syndrome. A range of related terms are often treated interchangeably, including *overactivity, hyperkinesis, minimal brain dysfunction, attention-deficit disorder,* and *Attention-Deficit/Hyperactivity Disorder.* This discussion will address hyperactivity as a descriptor, symptom, and syndrome, emphasizing the disorder currently called Attention-Deficit/Hyperactivity Disorder.

Descriptor

Activity level is an important developmental and temperamental dimension, representing an individual difference among all living beings. Developmental change is expected, as captured in the contrast between a frisky young puppy and a sedentary old dog. Thus, there is a range of behavior considered to be within normal limits. Exceeding these limits in either statistical or clinical terms can be called *overactivity.* Hyperactivity is a continuous form of movement such as squirming, fidgeting, or foot tapping, rather than discrete or episodic movement such as a spasm or a tic.

Overall activity level is one category of temperament: constitutionally based qualities of responsiveness that are evident and relatively stable throughout life. Hyperactivity, as a statistical or clinical extreme, has particular implications for problems in development and adaptation, which can contribute to secondary difficulties for the individual.

Symptom

A common, often primary, symptom, hyperactivity is observed in a variety of medical and behavioral disorders, including bipolar disorder, Schizophrenia, autism, developmental disabilities, metabolic disorders, endocrine disorders, toxic exposure (e.g., lead poisoning), and other neurological conditions (brain tumor, encephalitis, Parkinson's disease, etc.). Hyperactivity is not in itself a cause for concern. Instead, it is a nonspecific symptom whose significance depends on demographic and situational factors and the presence of other physiological characteristics or behavioral symptoms.

Syndrome

Despite the heterogeneity of conditions that include motor excess, there appears to be a set of covarying factors resulting in the identification of a hyperactivity syndrome or disorder. Hyperactivity does not constitute a syndrome in the technical sense of the word, because the particular pattern of symptoms or characteristics does not form a unitary cluster, nor is there adequate evidence of common etiology, both sine qua non of a true syndrome. However, the disorder most closely associated with hyperactivity is Attention-Deficit/Hyperactivity Disorder (ADHD; American Psychiatric Association, 1994). The core symptoms are hyperactivity, distractibility, and impulsivity.

Russell Barkley (1997a, 1997b, 1998) has summarized the research and developed a cohesive theory to explain ADHD and the disability it creates. As a developmental disorder, ADHD is present from birth, and symptoms manifest at a young age (before age 7). Symptoms are persistent rather than episodic and are present across situations. However, hyperactivity may be more obvious in settings where quiet, calm behavior is required and may go virtually unnoticed in unstructured settings where active behavior is allowed or encouraged, which accounts for the difference in a child's presentation in the classroom, on the playground, and at home.

Prevalence estimates range from 3 to 7%, with about 3 times more males than females affected. ADHD was conceptualized as a childhood disorder that one outgrew until longitudinal research showed that although some manifestations of the disorder become less problematic when formal education is completed, the overall pattern persists in at least 30–50% of the affected population. In addition to the primary symptoms, individuals with ADHD are at increased risk for poor academic progress, school difficulties, and poor interpersonal relationships. Increased rates of anxiety and depression, more aggressive and delinquent behavior, and increased rates of Substance Abuse also have been documented. Furthermore, adults with ADHD may have vocational difficulties, increased risk for motor vehicle accidents, and greater marital instability.

Specific etiology of ADHD remains unknown, although professional consensus leans toward biological explanations. Genetic perspectives are supported by the increased incidence of the disorder in relatives of those with ADHD and the overrepresentation of males, although intrafamilial variability does not rule out psychological or behavioral transmission. Organic explanations are supported by observations of similar behavior in individuals with traumatic head injuries, and the prevalence of hyperactivity in some metabolic disorders, suggesting that an acquired illness or injury may contribute to the condition.

Environmental factors associated with ADHD symptoms include toxins such as lead and exposure to radiation and specific medications. Although psychological hypotheses such as particular child-rearing patterns or learning patterns are less well accepted than other theories, these factors affect the course and outcome of the disorder.

Recently, Barkley and others have turned their attention to so-called executive functioning as the core deficit that causes ADHD. Barkley suggests that developmentally, certain types of self-regulation, including regulation of motor behavior and sustained attention, ought to emerge with age. These skills do not adequately develop in people with ADHD. Neuroimaging findings, neuropsychological tests, and laboratory tasks appear to provide converging evidence for this perspective, which identifies behavioral inhibition as the key deficit. However, given the range of factors that may contribute to ADHD, and the high prevalence of the disorder, it is likely that the actual etiology is multifactorial. Furthermore, if the notion of multiple syndromes is borne out, multiple etiologies are likely to be revealed.

Consistent with the variation in etiological hypotheses, assessment and treatment of the disorder is wide-ranging and crosses disciplinary lines with educators, physicians, and mental health providers all claiming ownership of the disorder. Neurodevelopmental, psychological, psychoeducational, and neuropsychological evaluations all are used to identify the disorder. Several valid and reliable parent and teacher rating scales have been developed for identification of ADHD. Many children are identified by their teachers or pediatricians in the absence of a comprehensive assessment, and there are no data comparing the accuracy of each type of diagnosis because there is no definitive test that proves the presence of this disorder. Recent attention has turned toward neuropsychological assessment tools, which may provide greater sensitivity and specificity; however, none of these has sufficient reliability or validity to be the "gold standard" for diagnosis. Consequently, comprehensive multidisciplinary assessment, incorporating parent and teacher reports, cognitive and behavioral assessment, and norm-based rating scales, is particularly desirable in diagnosing ADHD.

Treatment with stimulant medications such as methylphenidate or dextroamphetamine is the most common and most effective, yet controversial, treatment for ADHD. However, it is generally recognized that medication alone is insufficient to address either the primary disorder or its disabling effects. Therefore a variety of cognitive, behavioral, and psychoeducational interventions are necessary adjuncts to medication.

REFERENCES

American Psychiatric Association. (1994). *Diagnostic and statistical manual of mental disorders* (4th ed.). Washington, DC: American Psychiatric Association.

Barkley, R. A. (1997a). *Attention-Deficit/Hyperactivity Disorder and the nature of self-control.* New York: Guilford Press.

Barkley, R. A. (1997b). Behavioral inhibition, sustained attention, and executive functions: Constructing a unifying theory of ADHD. *Psychological Bulletin, 121*(1), 65–94.

Barkley, R. A. (1998). *Attention-Deficit/Hyperactivity Disorder: A handbook for diagnosis and treatment* (2nd ed.). New York: Guilford Press.

Donald L. Wertlieb
Dante S. Spetter

HYPERTENSION

Hypertension, a disease affecting the cardiovascular system and commonly known as high blood pressure, is a major health problem. It is characterized by chronic elevation of diastolic and, typically, systolic blood pressure without demonstrable pathology of either the blood vessels or the heart. Hypertension is a primary cause of adult sickness, disability, and death in the United States, afflicting approximately 50 million persons. Additionally, it is one of the most important risk factors in the promotion of atherosclerotic diseases, kidney failure, congestive heart failure, coronary heart disease, myocardial infarction (heart attack), and cerebrovascular accident (stroke).

Blood pressure occurs on a continuum, with no clear division between normal and elevated pressure. Further, the blood pressure values of concern to a practitioner vary as a function of a patient's history, age, sex, and environment. In general, however, blood pressure is regarded as high when the systolic pressure at rest consistently provides a measurement of 140 mm Hg (millimeters of mercury) or more, and the diastolic pressure is 90 mm Hg or more. Depending upon a variety of factors, a diagnosis of hypertension may or may not be applied when consistent readings above 140/90 (reported as one-forty over ninety) are obtained. Nevertheless, consistent readings above this level do warrant monitoring and perhaps remediation.

If remediation is selected, the treatment strategy depends upon the etiology of the malady. *Primary* or *essential hypertension* refers to an instance in which the cause is unknown, whereas *secondary hypertension* is the result of an identifiable antecedent, such as malfunction of particular endocrine organs, coarctation of the aorta, pregnancy, or oral contraceptive medication. Although secondary hypertension may be ameliorated via surgery or chemotherapy, this category accounts for a relatively small percentage of the cases.

In contrast to the low incidence of secondary hypertension, in about 80% of the patients evidencing hypertension there is no clear cause for the disease. Even though this type of hypertension is of unspecified etiology, it has been recognized for a long time that emotional factors, stress, and a fast-paced lifestyle have an elevating effect on blood pressure. Within this context, much research has been directed toward establishing effective behavioral treatments that may be employed alone or in conjunction with a variety of pharmacological regimens. These behavioral treatments include progressive muscle relaxation, meditation, yoga exercises, autogenic training, biofeedback-assisted relaxation, blood pressure biofeedback, contingency managed aerobics and diet, as well as strategies combining two or more of these programs. In addition, when pharmacological intervention is necessary, a variety of classes of antihypertensions are available. These include B-adrenergic receptor antagonists, calcium channel blockers, diuretics, angiotensin-converting enzyme (ACE) inhibitors, and others. Treatment may involve one agent or a combination of these antihypertensive agents to attain normal blood pressure, or, at least, lower blood pressure to a more acceptable level.

SUGGESTED READING

Berkow, R. (Ed.). (1997). High blood pressure. In *The Merck manual of medical information* (pp. 112–118). Whitehouse Station, NJ: Merck Research Laboratories.

Boone, J. L., & Christiansen, J. F. (1997). Stress and disease. In M. D. Feldman & J. F. Christensen (Eds.), *Behavioral medicine in primary care.* Stamford, CT: Appleton & Lange.

Wesley W. Weinrich

HYPNOSIS

Hypnosis occurs within the context of a special hypnotist-subject relationship, during which suggestions of distortions of cognition, perception, memory, and affect can be responded to by some individuals who are able to control (voluntarily) their levels of consciousness. Hypnosis appears to be characterized by the dissociative subject's ability to temporarily accept as reality suggested distortions of perception, cognition, and affect.

Brief History of Hypnosis

The history of hypnosis begins with Franz Anton Mesmer (1734–1815). His patients gathered around the *baquet*—a tub of water filled with iron filings, with protruding rods held by the patients. The gathered ill became hypnotized, evinced by the ensuing *crisis* or hysterical seizure. A Royal Commission headed by Benjamin Franklin in Paris in 1784 led to the rejection of Mesmer's *animal magnetism.* The alleged therapeutic cures were dismissed as due to mere imagination.

James Braid (1852) introduced the term *hypnosis,* from the Greek *hypnos* (to sleep). Jean-Martin Charcot (1882) considered hypnosis a manifestation of hysteria, in women. Charcot influenced the development of dissociation theorizing by Janet and Prince, and also influenced Freud's observations of the hypnotic abreaction and his development of the concept of unconscious motivation. Freud later gave up hypnosis because, he stated, he could not hypnotize everybody. He did not understand that hypnosis was a characteristic of the individual rather than something done by a hypnotist/therapist. Hippolythe Bernheim (1886) saw hypnosis as "suggestibility"—a view championed by the first major research program in hypnosis, conducted by Clark Hull (1933). Modern counterparts of each of these developments persist.

Characteristics of Hypnosis

A number of standardized scales have been developed that have made it possible to measure hypnosis with high reliability and validity. The scales are based on objective behavioral ratings of responses to subjective suggestions graded in difficulty. Hypnotic responsiveness is unlikely to change over time.

The methodological sophistication of contemporary hypnosis research contributes to general psychological theory, including the evaluation of subjective experience, verbal reports, limits of performance, attention and consciousness, factors involved in the social psychology of the psychological experiment, pain, and clinical practice. Three illustrative areas can be summarized.

Trance Logic

Trance logic is the ability to tolerate logical incongruities. It is not particularly troublesome for the hypnotized person to regress to, for example, 7 years of age. At one level the hypnotized person knows reality exists, but at another level it can be suspended in an effortless absorption in a fantasy world. However, his or her recollection of past experiences may have been contaminated by the contextual aspects of memory. The hypnotized subject's regression may not accurately reproduce childhood experiences. Although the distorted and confabulated material may be important therapeutically, there is a disturbing tendency for hypnosis to be used in forensic applications based on the faulty premise of accurate recall. Hypnotized subjects can lie or confabulate under hypnosis just as easily as in the waking state.

Pain Control

Hypnosis can play an important role in pain control. Hypnotic analgesia involves two distinct processes: (1) Hypnosis can directly reduce pain at a sensory, physiological, or primary level; and (2) expectational or placebolike effects can reduce pain because of the special context in which hypnosis is induced. Thus, there is only a modest correlation between the capacity for hypnosis and the capacity for pain control (and any other therapeutic intervention). This correlation is kept low by the impact of the nonspecific or placebolike factors brought into play in patients who are psychologically ready to give up their symptoms if an intervention is appropriately legitimized.

The profoundly analgesic subject can still report the objective pain stimulus conditions when the hypnotist addresses another part of the hypnotized subject's awareness (Hilgard's "hidden observer"). People operate on multiple cognitive levels (dissociation).

Characteristics of the Hypnotizable Person

The hypnotized subject seems tuned to multiple cognitive pathways and is easily able to distort reality while remaining aware of its existence at other levels of awareness. The hypnotizable person is not gullible, compliant, hysterical, weak-willed, passive, prone to placebo response, or subject to the control of the dominant hypnotist. Instead, he or she has the capacity to become absorbed in ongoing experiences (e.g., becoming lost in fantasy, or identifying with the emotions of a character in a play or movie). He or she reports imaginary playmates as a youngster. The hypnotizable subject may turn up late for experimental appointments—a puzzling finding for those who see hypnosis as role-playing performed to please the hypnotist.

Cognitive flexibility is the hallmark of the hypnotizable person. The hypnotizable person naps and falls asleep quickly at night, and has other characteristics that cluster together to define a dimension involving the "control of consciousness," or a basic individual difference in cognitive flexibility. This flexibility dimension explains why hypnotizability is a significant prognostic index of recovery from psychiatric illness and of the ability to give up symptoms.

Clinical Hypnosis

Professional Training in Clinical Hypnosis

Hypnosis is a technique, not a treatment. Its use must be integrated into the specialized skills of the professional in his or her area of competence. It is the skills of the professional therapist—knowing what to treat, when not to treat, possible side effects and complications—that define safety and efficacy when using the technique.

Training opportunities are available in many universities and medical schools. Two national hypnosis societies offer annual workshops limited to physicians, dentists, psychologists, nurses, and psychiatric social workers: the American Society of Clinical Hypnosis and the Society for Clinical and Experimental Hypnosis. Both societies publish a journal on hypnosis. The International Society of Hypnosis provides a forum for professional colleagues throughout the world.

Clinical Applications

Hypnosis is used to treat many medical, psychological, and behavioral problems. Claims of dramatic clinical results have not usually been well documented. Hypnosis can control pain in cancer and burn patients. It can modify chemotherapy-induced vomiting and nausea and ease discomfort of invasive procedures (e.g., debridement, bone marrow procedures) even with those of moderate hypnotizability. Hypnosis is especially useful in habit control where, for whatever reason, the patient is ready to give up a symptom and needs legitimization and a dramatic intervention to justify change. Hypnosis can establish whether patients have the resources to facilitate mind-body, self-control, and cognitive mastery over their symptoms. Hypnosis helps facilitate relaxation, allow ego strengthening, control anger and other negative emotions, uncover affect with age regression, develop imagery strategies, and facilitate symptom relief.

Summary

A comprehensive psychology of consciousness is probably needed to understand hypnosis. Hypnotic phenomena can provide paradigms for understanding important aspects of the psychopathology of everyday life. Some individuals can experience hypnosis and control different states of consciousness with flexibility.

SUGGESTED READING

Crasilneck, H. B., & Hall, J. A. (1985). *Clinical hypnosis.* New York: Grune & Stratton.

Frankel, F. H. (1976). *Hypnosis: Trance as a coping mechanism.* New York: Plenum.

Fredericks, L. E. (Ed.). (2000). *The use of hypnosis in surgery and anesthesiology.* Springfield, IL: Charles C. Thomas.

Hilgard, E. R. (1977). *Divided consciousness: Multiple controls in human thought and action.* New York: Harcourt, Brace & World.

Frederick J. Evans

HYPNOSIS AS A PSYCHOTHERAPEUTIC TECHNIQUE

Hypnosis is a procedure in which the use of suggestions presented by the therapist or researcher (or self, in the case of self-hypnosis) allows the hypnotized individual to experience changes in sensations, perceptions, thoughts, or behaviors. Hypnosis capitalizes upon an innate cognitive capacity that probably involves imaginative ability, the capacity to concentrate, and an effortless receptivity.

Typically, an induction procedure is used to establish the context in which hypnotic suggestions are presented. Although hypnotic inductions vary, most involve suggestions for relaxation, calmness, and a sense of well-being. On the other hand, active-alert inductions that involve physical activity have also been shown to be effective in establishing responsiveness to suggestion.

The ability to respond to hypnotic suggestions is a stable personality trait that varies little over time or situations. This trait of hypnotic responsiveness is normally distributed with the largest number of individuals able to experience some but not all types of hypnotic suggestions. Hypnotic responsiveness peaks at about 9 to 11 years of age, with a mild decrement taking place in later years. A highly responsive subject will become hypnotized under a host of experimental conditions and therapeutic settings. A low hypnotizable person will not, despite his or her sincere efforts. This trait of hypnotic responsiveness appears to be unrelated to other traits such as trust, interrogative suggestibility, and gullibility. Evidence exists that some highly dissociative individuals are also highly responsive to hypnosis, but for the general population, dissociativity and hypnotic responsiveness are minimally related, if at all.

Even highly hypnotizable subjects remain in control of their behavior when hypnotized and typically continue to be aware of self and surroundings. On the other hand, a major component of the experience of hypnosis is a sense of involuntariness. Kenneth Bowers best described this paradox when he stated, "hypnotic responses can be purposeful without being enacted on purpose." Hypnosis can be thought of as an invitation to experience suggested alterations, which the subject can then either accept or reject. Although amnesia can occur during hypnosis, for the most part this occurs only when explicit suggestions for amnesia are given, and the amnesia is reversible.

Contrary to some popular depictions, hypnosis is not a panacea for recovering forgotten memories. Research indicates that memories recalled under hypnosis may or may not be accurate. Further, difficulty distinguishing true memory from suggested memory arises as a result of increased confidence in memories that can occur under hypnosis. Hypnosis appears to diminish the ability to discriminate between fantasy and reality, and of course it involves enhanced responsiveness to suggestions. Similarly, hypnotic age regression does not enable subjects to return to an earlier point in their life. Observable alterations in behavior or speech following hypnotic age regression are no more childlike than those observed among adults role-playing as children.

Hypnosis is not a form of therapy per se but rather a procedure that can be used within the context of therapy or as an adjunct to medical treatment. Hypnosis is effective for some individuals and for some problems. Thus, hypnosis should be used only by a clinician or researcher who is familiar with the applications and limitations of hypnosis as well as being trained in the area for which hypnosis is being used.

It is well established that hypnosis can be a very effective tool for minimizing both acute and chronic pain for some individuals, and this effect exceeds that of placebo. In 1996, a National Institute of Health Technology Assessment Panel Report found hypnosis to be a viable and effective intervention for alleviating pain with cancer and with other chronic pain conditions. Hypnosis can also be effective for minimizing pain associated with burn treatment, surgical procedures, childbirth, and invasive medical diagnostic procedures. The use of hypnosis can allow the patient to respond in an active manner when faced with pain, can reduce the use of medication, and may facilitate medical compliance. Hypnotic interventions have also been proven to be cost effective and may reduce patient care costs in some instances related to improved outcome, use of less pain medication, and shortened procedure duration. Hypnotic suggestion can be used directly to alleviate the experience of pain, to alter the pain sensation, or to provide distraction from pain. Typically the client will eventually be taught to use self-hypnosis once the effective use of suggestions has been demonstrated.

There is evidence that the addition of hypnotic suggestion to behavioral treatment plans provides some advantage in treating habit disorders. Hypnotic suggestions that alter perceptions can be especially useful in these treatments. For individuals trying to quit smoking, hypnotic suggestions to increase the aversiveness of smoking and minimize withdrawal symptoms can be incorporated into a standard smoking cessation protocol. Similarly, treatment for obesity can incorporate suggestions for aversive reactions to unhealthy foods and an enhanced sense of control over eating behaviors. Augmenting treatment with hypnotic suggestions can also increase confidence in the ability to achieve one's goals and can lead to greater compliance with the selected treatment program. Meta-analytic studies suggest that the effects of treatments for obesity and pain (among other conditions) may be enhanced by the inclusion of hypnosis.

One way in which hypnosis can be used in expressive psychotherapies is to help the patient modulate and work through particularly painful emotional experiences. Suggestions can help to productively direct emotional expression and thereby facilitate affect regulations in the service of cognitive mastery. Further, the use of hypnosis may increase access to painful primary process and symbolic material, as logical, critical thinking tends to be suspended. This allows the therapist and patient to develop creative approaches to solving problems in living, with an emphasis on self-efficacy. Again, because of enhanced receptivity to suggestion, it is important that the therapist be knowledgeable in working with the presenting issues, have a clear clinical formulation, and have the wherewithal to treat the patient with or without hypnosis.

It appears that for some patients, hypnosis can increase receptivity, enhance relatedness, and facilitate symptom resolution. This makes hypnosis a useful tool to be integrated into many forms of treatment for medical and psychological problems.

Brenda J. King
Altru Health System

See also: **Psychotherapy**

HYPOTHESIS TESTING

Research hypotheses are predictions based on reasoning from a theory or past findings about the results of a study. Ideally, hypotheses are specific and concrete so that they indicate specific criteria needed to test them and can be proven or disproven unambiguously. The criteria used to test hypotheses are called *dependent variables.* The process of generating testable hypotheses serves to clarify the questions being asked about a particular research problem. It forces the researcher to specify the concrete data needed to come to a conclusion about the hypothesis as well as how the data will need to be analyzed.

The statistical procedures used to test a hypothesis have, by convention, been set up on the assumption that any differences in the dependent variables are due to chance. The procedures ascertain the probability that any apparent difference is not an actual difference. Consequently, when hypotheses are examined statistically, they must be represented in the null form (i.e., predict no difference). When the statistical analysis indicates that there is a high probability of there being no actual difference among the dependent variables, the null hypothesis is accepted. When the probability of there being no actual difference is low, the null hypothesis is rejected.

When a research hypothesis is supported, it means that the changes in the data cannot be attributed to chance. It also means that causal factors stated in the hypothesis may explain the changes, but it does not prove that they do as long as there are alternative hypotheses. As a result, the process of theory building is not a matter of proving a hypothesis, but rather of eliminating inadequate hypotheses until one continues to survive attempts at disconfirmation.

If a research hypothesis predicts that the dependent variable will change in a particular direction (e.g., become larger or smaller), then the corresponding statistical hypothesis is analyzed by using what is termed a *one-tailed test,* which focuses on only one end of the sampling distribution and analyzes changes in the hypothesized direction. If it is hypothesized that change could occur in either direction, a *two-tailed test* is used.

When deciding whether to reject or accept a statistical hypothesis, two types of error are possible. A *Type I* or *alpha error* occurs when the hypothesis of no difference is rejected, when in fact there was no real change in the dependent variable. Prior to an experiment, a researcher decides how much he or she is willing to risk a Type I error by choosing a level of significance. The level of significance, or alpha, is the probability of a given change in the dependent variable occurring by chance. The typical level of significance used for rejecting the null hypothesis is $p = 0.05$ or 0.01.

A *Type II* or *beta error* occurs when a hypothesis of no change is accepted, when in fact there has been a change. The chances of making this error decrease if alpha (the level of significance) is increased or if the sample size is increased. Reducing the variance within the sample or increasing the magnitude of the experimental effect can also reduce the chances of a Type II error.

Because the probability of one type of error decreases as the probability of the other increases, a researcher must decide which is preferable in a given situation. In instances in which labeling a chance difference as a genuine difference is costly, a conservative approach can be taken by setting the level of significance low. Alternatively, in instances in which it would be costly to overlook any promising leads, a higher level of significance can be set, thus reducing the chances of a Type II error.

The power of a statistical test is the probability of correctly rejecting the hypothesis of no difference. It is equivalent to 1 minus the probability of a Type II error. The power of a statistical test can be increased by using the methods for decreasing the chances of a Type II error mentioned previously.

Statistical significance is not synonymous with practical significance. A decision about practical significance is made independently of statistical procedures and can only be arrived at by individuals who are aware of the specific situation in which the research findings might be applied.

G. K. Lockwood

See also: **Research Methodology; Statistical Inference**

I

IDENTITY FORMATION

There are numerous theoretical approaches illuminating certain areas of identity development (i.e., Kegan's constructive-developmental approach or Blos's object relations approach), but Erik Erikson's (1963, 1968) psychosocial approach to human development appeals to many professionals because of its utility in many areas: clinical, theoretical, and empirical. Erikson's seminal work stressed the importance of history (personal and societal) and social contexts as influencing individuals' lives; consequently, he incorporated these ideas into his concept of identity formation in adolescence.

Erik Erikson developed the construct of ego identity as an adaptive response to Freud's focus on neurotic personalities. He was interested in the development of healthy personalities and created a lifespan stage theory that addressed the development of the healthy ego. Obtaining a healthy ego identity evolves through unconscious and conscious mechanisms interacting dynamically in a process of discovering the self. According to Erikson, there are certain key crises inherent in different periods of a person's life. These crises reflect the person's social maturity and societal expectations. The crises are then categorized into distinct psychosocial stages of development, at which times certain ego strengths emerge as resolutions of these crises.

A person integrates into his or her ego identity the resolution of the crises for each stage of development. Each stage of psychosocial development culminates in a balance of both *syntonic* and *dystonic outcomes.* A syntonic outcome is a positive experience through which the individual strives to attain and consequently maintain the experience in the overall ego structure. Receiving accolades for achievement in school from a significant teacher is an example of a syntonic experience. Conversely, a dystonic outcome is a negative experience whereby the individual strives to avoid and consequently rectify the experience in the overall ego structure. Being the recipient of a disparaging remark from a significant teacher is an example of a dystonic experience. Healthy psychological development occurs when the number of syntonic experiences outweighs dystonic experiences (Waterman, 1993, p. 53).

Adolescence, the fifth stage of psychosocial development, is the crucial period during which identity formation occurs. It reflects the accumulated syntonic and dystonic outcomes of the prior four stages of development. Identity formation is an integration in the self of the prior outcomes related to earlier stages of development. However, as Erikson noted, the formation of identity does not occur in a vacuum. The culture of society is crucial in how the adolescent integrates the prior stages of development. One's culture is shaped by the contexts in adolescents' lives. Hamachek (1985) uses a metaphor of ego growth rings, much like the growth rings of a tree, to facilitate an understanding of how an adolescent integrates the self in relation to contextual conditions when constructing an identity. Erikson's psychosocial stages of development are imbedded in a series of concentric circles such that the width between each ring of development identifies the context, both positive and negative, of growth. Development that is constricted by the environment and made up of mostly dystonic outcomes would show a shorter width in growth for a particular stage, while development that is enriched or expanded by the environment and made up of mostly syntonic outcomes would show a longer width in growth for a particular stage.

Identity development mirrors the outcomes achieved in various domains in a person's life. Erikson delineated the following identity domains where this mirroring or self-reflection occurs. These are (1) vocation; (2) ideologies (religious, political, and economic); (3) philosophy in life; (4) ethical capacity; (5) sexuality; (6) gender, ethnicity, culture, and nationality; and (7) "an all-inclusive human identity" (Erikson, 1968, p. 42). Through growth and integration in these domains, the adolescent's identity becomes integrated, ideally forming a healthy and stable self.

Marcia (1980) applied Erikson's concepts of ego identity into two operational dimensions of exploration and commitment.

> *Exploration* refers to a period of struggle or active questioning in arriving at various aspects of personal identity, such as vocational choice, religious beliefs, or attitudes about the role of a spouse or parenting in one's life. *Commitment* involves making a firm, unwavering decision in such areas and engaging in appropriate implementing activities. (Waterman, 1993, p. 56)

Relative to these two dimensions of exploration and commitment, Marcia delineated four identity statuses that exist for an individual in later adolescence. These four statuses are (1) *identity diffusion,* (2) *identity foreclosure,* (3) *moratorium,* and (4) *identity achievement.* Identity diffused adolescents have not committed to an internally consistent set of values and goals, and exploration is superficial or absent. Identity foreclosed adolescents have committed to a set of values and goals with little or no exploration present. Moratorium adolescents are in the process of committing to a set of values and goals as they are intensely exploring alternatives to their decisions. Identity achieved adolescents have experienced a period of exploration (as in moratorium) and have come to an autonomous resolution of identity by committing to a set of values and goals (Patterson, Sochting, & Marcia, 1993, pp. 10–12; Marcia, 1993, pp. 10–11). These statuses are not static and evolve as one develops. That is why it is not uncommon for some middle-aged adults to change professions or convert to another religion (Kroger, 2000). The culture or context in which one lives provides the framework for instituting a change in the self. Generally these changes lead one through a new phase of moratorium and, finally, achievement. Thus, identity formation involves a dynamic interplay between the intrapsychic self and the contexts in which the person lives.

REFERENCES

Erikson, E. H. (1963). *Childhood and society* (2nd ed.). New York: W. W. Norton.

Erikson, E. H. (1968). *Identity: Youth and crisis.* New York: W. W. Norton.

Hamachek, D. E. (1985). The self's development and ego growth: Conceptual analysis and implications for counselors. *Journal of Counseling and Development, 64,* 136–142.

Kroger, J. (2000). *Identity development: Adolescence through adulthood.* Thousand Oaks, CA: Sage Publications.

Marcia, J. E. (1980). Identity in adolescence. In J. Adelson (Ed.), *Handbook of adolescent psychology* (pp. 149–173). New York: Wiley.

Marcia, J. E. (1993). The ego identity status approach to ego identity. In J. E. Marcia, A. S. Waterman, D. R. Matteson, S. L. Archer, & J. L. Orlofsky (Eds.), *Ego identity: A handbook for psychosocial research* (pp. 3–21). New York: Springer-Verlag.

Patterson, S. J., Sochting, I., & Marcia, J. E. (1993). The inner space and beyond: Women and identity. In G. R. Adams, T. P. Gullotta, & R. Montemayor (Eds.), *Adolescent identity formation: Vol. 4. Advances in adolescent development* (pp. 9–24). Newbury Park, CA: Sage Publications.

Waterman, A. S. (1993). Identity as an aspect of optimal psychological functioning. In G. R. Adams, T. P. Gullotta, & R. Montemayor (Eds.), *Adolescent identity formation: Vol. 4. Advances in adolescent development* (pp. 50–72). Newbury Park, CA: Sage Publications.

Kathleen McKinney
University of Wisconsin, Stevens Point

See also: **Ego Development**

IDIODYNAMICS AND THE IDIOVERSE

There are three universes in the known cosmos: at one extreme, there is a universe of stellar bodies that requires telescopic observation (astronomic), while, at the other extreme, there is the atomic universe of molecules and other particles (microscopic). Between these two realms exists the human idioverse of experiential events.

It is important to recognize that the three universes have in common, at least hypothetically, the dynamic feature of energy expressed in orbital motion or the equivalent. In the case of stellar bodies, the Earth, as a member of the solar system, revolves around the sun and rotates on its axis through the principles of gravitation. By analogy, the members of the remotely observed galaxies presumably behave similarly, but this analogy is hypothetical. At the other extreme, the atoms, which compose molecules, are governed by components or particles with characteristic orbits. The table of the atomic numbers of the chemical elements and other principles of physics and chemistry have analogous properties to those observed for the solar system. Finally, it is here hypothetically postulated that the human idioverse, with its population of events and its characteristic patterns of repetitive markers, will, in future years, be shown to exhibit similar properties. Nervous energy mediated by the brain and the autonomic nervous system are known to express dynamic characteristics which at this point can only be the subject of speculation.

Idiodynamics is the science of the idioverse: the science of behavior from the standpoint of human individuals (Rosenzweig, 1951, 1958, 1986a, 1986b). The idioverse is conceived to be a population of experiential events. Events are the basic units and are defined and observed phenomenologically.

Origin and Development

Idiodynamics had its origin in three areas of empirical investigation: (1) the experimental redefinition of clinically-derived psychoanalytic concepts; (2) the intensive study of individual mental patients, to obtain an anamnesis through interviews, and by administering projective and psychometric techniques; and (3) the reconstruction of the life and work of creative writers, and selected patients, through an approach called *psychoarchaeology.*

The earliest contribution was a formulation by Rosenzweig in his essay, "The Experimental Situation as a Psychological Problem" (1933). It systematically examined the previous methodological literature of experimental psychology in relation to the evidence of the writer's own recent experimental research. The standpoint was that of the reciprocal interactions of the observer and the subject. These interactions were schematically classified, the terms *observer* and *subject* being replaced by *experimenter* (Er) and *experimentee* (Ee). It was shown that in the early German literature just such a reciprocal terminology was employed, that is, *Versuchsleiter* and *Versuchsperson*. The special contribution of the paper was a classification of the various typical, reciprocal interactions encountered in experiments. This advance in experimental psychodynamics and social psychology made only a minor impact until about 20 years later when, in the 1950s, Rosenthal and others began to publish their independent findings on "experimental bias" and related concepts (Rosenthal, 1959, 1966).

This first formulation of the complementarity between experimenter and experimentee (Rosenzweig, 1933) was followed by several other similar ones. In "Schools of Psychology: A Complementary Pattern" (Rosenzweig, 1937), the natural division among the then-prevalent schools was shown to represent a complementary pattern in which a certain type of *problem* achieved resolution by *methods* (and related concepts) appropriate to the problem. In "Some Implicit Common Factors in Diverse Methods of Psychotherapy" (Rosenzweig, 1936), Sherrington's neurological principle of the "final common pathway" (CF/CP) was, without deliberate awareness, applied to the very different field of psychological therapy. Each of these formulations stressed a different kind of complementarity, but all were implicitly guided by the overriding principle.

Another complementary distinction made in idiodynamics was the threefold manner in which behavior may be alternatively *explained: nomothetic, demographic,* and *idiodynamic*. These three explanatory modes, known as "norms," were first designated as universal, group, and individual. They were illustrated by reviewing their roles as modes of association in the history of psychology (Rosenzweig, 1950). The nomothetic modes of association were first described by the early Greek thinkers who distinguished the categories of similarity, contiguity, and so forth. Even in present-day theories of learning, such categories are employed. After Galton's work was published (1879–1880), these categories became the basis for experimental studies of word-association, conducted in Wundt's laboratory of experimental psychology in Leipzig (Trautscholdt, 1883). It was recognized early that certain groups of individuals, including mental patients with a given diagnosis, produced associations peculiar to or characteristic of the group. In this way certain kinds of associations consistently produced by an individual helped to classify him or her as belonging to a given diagnostic group (e.g., the clang associations of the manic patient). Later, in Jung's research on complexes (Jung, 1918), the peculiar significance of certain word associations were seen as pointing to uniquely individual constellations (or complexes) of thought, image, and feeling in a particular person. Jung's insight anticipated the *idiodynamic* orientation.

These three explanatory modes are now designated as *nomothetic, demographic,* and *idiodynamic* to avoid the quantitative emphasis misleadingly implied by the earlier terminology. That confusion is evident in the writing of Gordon Allport (1937), who proposed a new conceptualization of personality that (implicitly) equated each mode with the size of a population. In this way Allport tended to confound the *idiodynamic* with the *idiographic* (Rosenzweig & Fisher, 1997).

Concepts

The idioverse has (1) a core matrix and (2) a *biogenic* medium, on one side, and a *sociogenic* medium, on the other, both of which contribute to the core matrix. These media overlap and converge at the matrix *idiodynamically*. The three types of norms shown in Table 1 are to a considerable extent aligned with the three milieus, shown in Figure 1: the *biogenic,* tending to be used nomothetically; the *sociogenic,* demographically; and the matrix of the idioverse, aligned with *idiodynamic* norms.

There are also three levels of communication by which

Table 1. Three Types of Explanatory and Predictive Norms

Type	Description
Nomothetic (Universal)	Functional principles of general psychology considered valid by and large.
Demographic (Group)	Statistical generalizations derived from particular cultures or classes of individuals.
Idiodynamic (Individual)	Distinctive markers recurring in a given, single population of events (idioverse).

Note: Each type of norm not only involves a different mode of understanding but also implies a cognate basis for predicting and/or controlling behavior.

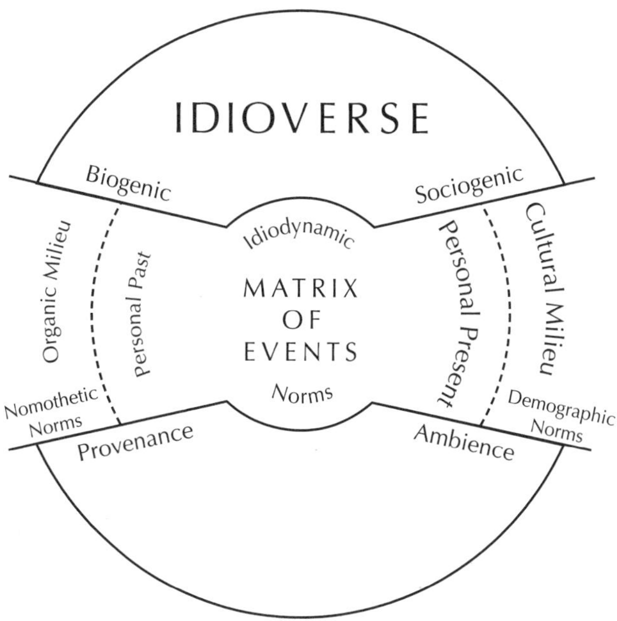

Figure 1. The Idioverse.

the idioverse can be meaningfully understood: the *immediate* or literal level, the *intermediate* or allusive, and the *inframediate* or intimate (Rosenzweig, 1986b). These correspond roughly to the three layers of meaning depicted in the fourteenth century by Dante Alighieri and called by him the *literal,* the *allegoric,* and the *mystical* (Haller, 1973). In the present formulation the first level is similar to Dante's; the second involves not only possible allegory but also other modes of allusion; and the third, instead of being mystical, is recognized as disguised autobiography or other intimate details.

The three levels of communication may be employed to reveal the total meaning inherent in a given idioverse. This technique of discovery is named *psychoarchaeology.* The three levels are studied concurrently, with the assumption that they will not necessarily be represented with equal strength in every production (see Rosenzweig, 1987, for a detailed example of psychoarchaeology).

Psychoarchaeology can be employed with documents such as psychotherapy transcripts, diaries, letters, and the data yielded by projective (psychological) techniques. But the most rewarding results are available in the imaginative productions of creative writers, the elite of whom are almost compulsively involved in veiled self-exposure (Rosenzweig, 1992).

REFERENCES

Adair, J. G. (1973). *The human subject: The social psychology of the psychological experiment.* Boston: Little, Brown.

Allport, G. W. (1937). *Personality: A psychological interpretation.* New York: Holt.

Galton, F. (1879–80). Psychometric experiments. *Brain, 2,* 149–162.

Haller, R. S. (1973). *Literary criticism of Dante Alghieri.* Lincoln: University of Nebraska Press.

Hormuth, S. E. (1986). The sampling of experience in situ. *Journal of Personality, 54,* 262–293.

Jung, C. G. (1918). *Studies in word association.* London: Heinemann.

Larsen, R. J. (1989). A process approach to personality: Utilizing time as a facet of data. In D. Buss & N. Cantor (Eds.), *Personality psychology: Recent trends and emerging directions* (pp. 177–193). New York: Springer.

Rosenthal, R. (1959). The experimental induction of the defense mechanism of projection. *Journal of Projective Techniques, 23,* 357–364.

Rosenthal, R. (1966). *Experimenter effects in behavioral research.* New York: Appleton-Century-Crofts.

Rosenzweig, S. (1933). The experimental situation as a psychological problem. *Psychological Review, 40,* 337–354.

Rosenzweig, S. (1936). Some implicit common factors in diverse methods of psychotherapy. *The American Journal of Orthopsychiatry, 6*(3), 412–415.

Rosenzweig, S. (1937). Schools of psychology: A complementary pattern. *Philosophy of Science, 4*(1), 96–106.

Rosenzweig, S. (1943). The ghost of Henry James: A study in thematic apperception. *Character & Personality, 12,* 79–100. (Reprinted with a postscript in W. Sutton & R. Foster (Eds.), *Modern criticism* (pp. 401–416). New York: Odyssey Press, 1963.)

Rosenzweig, S. (1944). Converging approaches to personality: Murray, Allport, Lewin. *Psychological Review, 51*(4), 248–256.

Rosenzweig, S. (1950). Norms and the individual in the psychologist's perspective. In M. L. Reymert (Ed.), *Feelings and emotions: The Mooseheart symposium* (pp. 327–335). New York: McGraw-Hill.

Rosenzweig, S. (1951). Idiodynamics in personality theory with special reference to projective methods. *Psychological Review, 58*(3), 213–223.

Rosenzweig, S. (1952). The investigation of repression as an instance of experimental idiodynamics. *Psychological Review, 59*(4), 339–345.

Rosenzweig, S. (1958). The place of the individual and of idiodynamics in psychology: A dialogue. *Journal of Individual Psychology, 14,* 3–20.

Rosenzweig, S. (1986a). Background to idiodynamics. *The Clinical Psychologist, 39,* 83–89.

Rosenzweig, S. (1986b). Idiodynamics vis-a-vis psychology. *The American Psychologist, 41,* 241–245.

Rosenzweig, S. (1992). *Freud, Jung and Hall the King-maker: The expedition to America (1909).* St. Louis: Rana House Press; Seattle: Hogrefe & Huber.

Rosenzweig, S., & Fisher, S. (1997). "Idiographic" vis-a-vis "idiodynamic" in the historical perspective of personality theory: Remembering Gordon Allport, 1897–1997. *Journal of the History of the Behavioral Sciences, 33*(4), 405–419.

Trautscholdt, M. (1883). Experimentelle Untersuchungen uber die Association der Vorstellungeu. *Philosophical Studies* (Wundt), *1,* 213–250.

Saul Rosenzweig
Washington University

Amy Hackney
Georgia Southern University

IDIOGRAPHIC–NOMOTHETIC PSYCHOLOGY

Social scientists may choose to formulate either idiographic or nomothetic interpretations of phenomenona. These terms were coined by Wilhelm Windelbrand to describe the work of the natural sciences on the one hand, and, on the other hand, the cultural or human sciences, in which individual cases were studied. An essential conflict defines the two points of view. Scientific generalizations are assumed to be nomothetic or law-like. But for these predictions to be used, they must be applied to particular cases, and individual cases (idiographic analysis) may not conform to general laws.

Idiographic science involves the intensive analysis of

single cases, with the attempt to formulate interpretive statements pertaining only to the case or to the class of phenomena that the case represents. Idiographic interpretations are based on the particularities of a given case. Their claim to validity rests on the power of the descriptions produced by the researcher. These descriptions attempt to capture the perspectives of those studied. It is assumed that different interpretations are likely to be meaningful in different realities. Any interpretation will be shaped by local particulars and interactions between the researcher and those studied.

Nomothetics rests on the claim that scientific laws can be formulated only statistically, through the study and analysis of a large number of randomly selected cases. Nomothetic generalizations are assumed to be time and context free. They do not depend on the specifics of a particular context or case.

The conflict over idiographic and nomothetic models of science and inquiry has plagued the social sciences in general and psychology in particular since the beginning of the twentieth century, although the origins of the debate can be traced to the rise of the human disciplines in the eighteenth and nineteenth centuries.

Fundamental assumptions regarding the nature of inquiry, philosophies of science, and the purposes of the social and psychological sciences are involved in the idiographic–nomothetic debate. Arguments by feminist scholars and scholars of color have sharpened this debate. Such individuals believe that the methods of nomothetic science have often been used as tools of oppression, producing knowledge that is biased in the direction of a male-dominated science. Postpositivist critical theorists and postmodernists also have criticized nomothetic science and its assumption that knowledge is free of bias, personal values, and political ideology. These theorists argue that nomothetic science is often used as a form of political control.

Stated most succinctly, the issue revolves around whether psychology will be a causal science seeking general laws of human behavior or an interpretive, praxis-based discipline seeking greater and deeper understanding of social and psychological processes.

Nomothetic investigators reject idiographic interpretations. They regard them as being unscientific or journalistic. Conversely, ideographic researchers argue that nomothetic studies are of little value because all interpretations are assumed to be contextual and specific to given cases.

Nomothetic Psychology

Nomothetic psychology seeks the discovery of scientific, statistically valid, generalizable laws regarding human behavior. Certain assumptions underlie this point of view. First, causal explanations of social phenomena are sought. A variable-analytic language that rests on the operationalization of variables and concepts is employed, and strict cause–effect models of inference are used. Second, the quantification of mental and behavioral processes is pursued. Third, it is assumed that causal propositions formulated on the basis of the careful study of randomly selected subjects can be generalized to nonobserved populations. Fourth, the nomothetic scientist endeavors to construct (typically) nonnaturalistic experimental laboratory settings in which scientific observations are gathered. Fifth, to the degree that the findings from idiographic methods are used in nomothetic science, they are frequently regarded as useful only for explanatory, descriptive, or illustrative purposes (e.g., pretesting). Sixth, nomothetic theories are deductive and probabilistic and offer functional explanations of phenomena. Idiographic psychology and its methods are regarded as useful only to the extent that they contribute to the construction of scientific theories that meet the foregoing criteria.

Idiographic Psychology

In twentieth century psychology, the work of Gordon Allport is most commonly associated with idiographic psychology, which rests on certain assumptions and methods. In the words of Allport, it is assumed that "psychology will become *more* scientific (i.e., better able to make predictions) when it has learned to evaluate single trends in all their intrinsic complexity, when it has learned how to tell what will happen to *this* child's IQ if we change his environment in a certain way." Allport's assumption requires a deep and sustained interest in the study and analysis of a single case over a long period of time; longitudinal studies are required.

Specifics, not universals, are explored by the idiographic psychologist. Because each individual is assumed to be unique, the psychologist must work with a theory and a set of methods that retain and reveal individual differences. In addition, there is an attempt to permit the individual subject to speak in his or her own language, to secure the meanings that hold for persons in their life world, and to capture those meanings and experiences with methods that are relatively unstructured, open-ended, projective, and interpretive. Personal documents and life histories are used, as are unobtrusive and indirect measures of personality, in combination with other methods and techniques in a triangulated fashion. Naturalistic research conducted in the everyday situations of individuals is favored by the idiographic psychologist.

Etic and Emic Investigations

The contrast between nomothetic and idiographic psychologies may be compared with the *etic* and *emic* controversy in recent anthropological theory. Etic investigations are external, comparative, and cross-cultural. Distance from particular cultures is sought so that general patterns can be discovered. The specific, unique configurations of meaning that pertain within a single culture are set aside in an effort to discover cross-cultural universals. Emic investigations study cultural meanings from the inside, seeking to uncover the cognitive categories and classification systems that members of particular cultures and cultural groupings use. Emic investigations are particularizing; etic investigations are generalizing. Furthermore, emic investigations are framed from the insider's point of view. Emic studies implement the idiographic approach to science, whereas etic studies are committed (usually) to the nomothetic approach.

Thick Versus Thin Descriptions

Thick, as opposed to thin, descriptions go beyond the mere reporting of fact, correlational coefficients, or significance tests to the level of detail, emotion, meaning, nuance, relationship, and interaction. Thick descriptions are emic and idiographic. If combined with the traditional methods of the idiographic psychologist, thick descriptions would permit a deeper probing of the underlying personality and interaction patterns that idiographic psychologists endeavor to discover and understand. Nomothetic psychology primarily rests on thin descriptions, etically discovered.

Progressive–Regressive Method of Sartre

Jean-Paul Sartre proposed a method of inquiry that, in many significant respects, synthesizes the above discussion. The progressive–regressive method of investigation seeks to situate and understand a particular subject or class of subjects within a given historical moment. Progressively, the method looks forward to the conclusion of a set of acts or projects undertaken by the subject (e.g., the production of a novel). Regressively, the method looks backward to the conditions that embed and embody the projects and practices of the subject. By moving forward and backward in time, the subject and his or her projects are situated in time and space. The unique differences in the person's life are revealed while the commonalities and similarities shared with others are likewise revealed. The method also is analytic and synthetic, in that analysis is woven through the main threads of the subject's life in a synthesizing, interpretive fashion.

Feminist Inquiry

Recent developments in feminist scholarship expand the idiographic-emic approaches in new directions. More reflexive epistemologies that place the investigator in the center of the research process are being developed. African American, Hispanic, and Third World feminists are studying how colonial (positivist–nomothetic) discourses misrepresent the lives of women in diverse contexts. Other scholars are challenging the objective biases of the nomothetic approach. This perspective, they assert, assumes that a static world of objects can be studied (not created) by the methods of objective science. They contend that the scientist creates the world that is studied. These researchers note that studies of women have traditionally treated females as static objects to be viewed through the lens of an objective (male-dominated) science. Other feminist scholars are experimenting with new writing forms, including autoethnographies, performance texts, and poetry.

N. K. Denzin

See also: **Idiodynamics and the Idioverse**

THE INSULIN-LIKE GROWTH FACTOR 1 (IGF-I): A KEY MODULATOR OF NEUROGENESIS AND COGNITIVE FUNCTIONS

Activity of insulin-like proteins was discovered in 1957. The precise action of insulin-like growth factor I (IGF-I) remained poorly understood until the production in the 1980s of recombinant human IGF-I. This trophic factor has been well characterized as a factor mediating growth hormone action (Jones & Clemmons, 1995; Isaksson, Ohlsson, Nilsson, Isgaard, & Lindahl, 1991). IGF-I is found in high levels in the blood and is believed to originate mainly from the liver (Pankov, 1999). The detection of the IGF-I gene using molecular techniques showed its presence in several organs, including the brain (Rotwein, Burgess, Milbrandt, & Krause, 1988). Substantial evidence supports the importance of IGF-I and insulin in normal development and maintenance of adequate neuronal functions throughout the entire lifespan. The structure of IGF-I is quite similar to insulin (Isaksson et al., 1991). Interestingly, researchers have suggested that the level of insulin in the brain is quite low and that, in fact, IGF-I could act as insulin in the central nervous system. IGF-I has the capacity to bind to the entire IGF receptor family, including the insulin receptor. High densities of binding sites for IGF-I and insulin are discretely and differentially distributed throughout the brain, with prominent levels localized to the hippocampus. IGF receptors are produced by numerous neuronal and non-neuronal cell types. IGF-I is a well-established stimulant of cell growth, proliferation, and differentiation, and can stimulate glucose transport and prevent cell death (Doré et al., 1997b). These later effects are crucial for survival of postmitotic neurons.

The authors have previously demonstrated that IGF and insulin receptors are tightly regulated and subject to rapid and chronic changes after a multitude of surgical and pharmacological lesions (Doré et al., 1997c; Doré et al., 1996; Kar et al., 1997a). Both the IGF-I and insulin receptors possess similar tyrosine kinase activities, and binding of the ligand to the α-subunit of the receptor induces the autophosphorylation of the β-subunits. One of the key phosphoproteins is the insulin receptor substrate (IRS), which interacts directly with other intracellular signaling substrates, including the phosphatidylinositol 3-kinase/AKT kinase pathway and various other downstream transcription factors (Zheng et al., 2002). Activation of these pathways has been shown to be protective in several chronic and acute neurodegenerative conditions (for example, using models of Huntington and hypoxia (Humbert et al., 2002; Scott et al., 2002)).

IGF-I and Insulin Receptor Levels in Cognition

No significant differences are found in IGF-I or insulin receptor levels in any subfields of the hippocampus of young versus aged rats (Doré, Kar, Rowe, & Quirion, 1997). Furthermore, deficits in cognitive performance do not relate to alterations in the levels of these receptors in aged impaired (AI) compared to aged unimpaired (AU) rats. It thus appears that IGF-I and insulin receptor binding sites are not markedly altered during the normal aging process in rats, and cognitive deficits observed in the Morris water maze are not mirrored by changes in these markers. Accordingly, spatial learning deficits observed in the AI group are not due to alteration in IGFs and/or insulin receptor sites. However, these data do not rule out the potential of altered IGFs or insulin postreceptor signaling efficacy between AU and AI groups (discussed later). These results can also be related to those obtained in the human brain. No significant differences in the levels of IGF-I binding sites were reported in the human cerebral cortex with respect to age, postmortem delays, or medications (Crews, McElhaney, Freund, Ballinger, & Raizada, 1992). In contrast, specific IGF-I binding was increased in the cerebral cortex of Alzheimer's disease (AD) patients, possibly in response to decreased levels of IGF-I (Jafferali, Dumont, Sotty, Robitaille, Quirion, & Kar, 2000).

Regarding insulin receptors, an earlier study reported results similar in 22-month-old (compared to young) Wistar rats, with no significant changes being observed in any brain regions, except for a slight decrement in olfactory bulbs (Tchilian, Zhelezarov, Petkov, & Hadjiivanova, 1990). In contrast, insulin receptor binding was reported to be decreased in aged mouse brain homogenates (Zaia & Piantanelli, 1996). These differences are likely to be species-related. A study on the ontogenesis of the insulin receptor using synaptosomal membranes revealed a general decrease in the human cerebral cortex from development to adulthood (Potau, Escofet, & Martinez, 1991).

Insulin and/or IGF-I Resistance with Aging

In general, aging is associated with insulin resistance. Is it possible that neurons also become resistant (or somewhat diabetic) and that their uptake of glucose is not as efficient to satisfy energy demand? In the periphery, previous studies showed age-related alterations in tyrosine kinase activity (Ruiz et al., 1992). Moreover, despite normal levels of insulin receptors in 20-month-old Wistar rats, it was shown that receptor autophosphorylation was reduced by 25%, in addition to decreased IRS-1 levels. Moreover, insulin-stimulated IRS-1 association with phosphatidyl-inositol 3-kinase (PI3-kinase) was decreased by 70% in the liver and 98% in muscles of 20- versus 2-month-old rats, with no change in PI3-kinase level; the phosphorylation of IRS-2 followed a similar pattern (Carvalho et al., 1996). Interestingly, insulin could not induce sodium/potassium-ATPase activation and plasma membrane hyperpolarization of certain cell types in aged Wistar rats (Frolkis, 1995). It was also demonstrated that peripheral insulin resistance in 24-month-old Wistar rats was accompanied by an impairment in insulin-sensitive, glycosyl-phosphatidylinositol-dependent cellular signaling (Sanchez-Arias et al., 1993). One study divided 24- to 27-month-old Wistar rats into three groups having mild, moderate, and severe reduction in maximal insulin-related kinase activity and found that deficits in the mild and moderate subgroups could be reversed by extensive autophosphorylation (Nadiv, Cohen, & Zick, 1992). It remains to be established whether in aged rats differential alterations in these markers could be correlated with cognitive performance and comparable changes in the IGF-I receptor signaling pathway.

A study was also designed to assess whether cognitive deficits in aging could be partially overcome by increasing the availability of IGF-I in the brain (Markowska, Mooney, & Sonntag, 1998). Male rats of two ages (4 and 32 months) were preoperatively trained in behavioral tasks and subsequently implanted with minipumps to infuse IGF-I or a vehicle into the cerebral ventricles. Animals were retested at 2 and 4 weeks. IGF-I improved working memory in the repeated acquisition and object recognition tasks. An improvement was also observed in the place discrimination task, which assesses reference memory. Moreover, injection of IGF-I antisense oligonucleotides in the inferior olive region elicited a complete inhibition of conditioned eye-blink learning in freely moving rats (Castro-Alamancos & Torres-Aleman, 1994). Furthermore, insulin treatment prevents deficits in water maze learning and long-term potentiation (LTP) in streptozotocin-diabetic rats (Biessels et al., 1998). Taken together, these data indicate a potentially important role for IGF-I (and insulin) in the reversal of age-related behavioral impairments in rodents.

The growth hormone (GH)/IGF-I axis is known to be involved in aging of physiological functions. Recent studies indicate that the GH/IGF-I axis may also be associated with cognitive functioning. For example, Aleman et al. (1999) determined whether age-related decline in circulating IGF-I levels were correlated with cognitive performances. Twenty-five healthy older men with well-preserved functional ability participated in the study. Neuropsychological tests of general knowledge, vocabulary, basic visual perception, reading ability, visuoconstructive ability, perceptual–motor speed, mental tracking, and verbal long-term memory were administered. Performance on the last four tests declined with age, whereas the first four were not as sensitive to aging. Interestingly, the authors found that plasma IGF-I levels were significantly correlated with performances (controlled for education) on the Digit Symbol Substitution test and the Concept Shifting Task, two tests measuring perceptual–motor and mental processing speed. Subjects with higher IGF-I levels performed better on these tests. These data support the hypothesis that circulating IGF-I may play a role in the age-related decline of certain cognitive functions, especially those related to the speed of information processing (Aleman et al., 1999). In another study, Rollero et al. (1998) reported that plasma IGF-I levels were directly correlated with cognitive function as assessed using the Mini Mental State Examination; scores and IGF-I levels were lower in patients with the most advanced cognitive deterioration.

Importance of Controlling Glucose Homeostasis

In aged rats and humans, impaired glucose regulation has been correlated with poor memory performance. Aged (22 to 24 months) and young (3 months) rats were assessed in a battery of behavioral tests that included tasks of learning and place navigation. Following evaluation all animals were analyzed for their local glucose utilization. The decline in performance correlated significantly with the decrement in regional glucose utilization (Gage, Kelly, & Bjorklund, 1984). Moreover, performance in these two tests showed significant correlation with glucose use in brain regions associated with learning processes. These results suggest that learning impairments in aged rats may be related to decreases in glucose utilization.

Interestingly, intraperitoneal glucose injections result in improved learning performance (Long, Davis, Garofalo, Spangler, & Ingram, 1992). For example, effects of a pretraining intraperitoneal glucose injection on learning and memory were tested using the Morris water maze. Glucose injection before a block of trials enhanced spatial memory performance in mice (Li et al., 1998). In aged cognitively impaired Wistar rats, significantly reduced cerebral glucose utilization was observed in various regions associated with learning and memory processes (Wree et al., 1991). Treatment of both neuronal and glial cultured cells with insulin and IGF-I induced a time- and dose-dependent increase in the steady state levels of glucose transporter mRNA (Werner et al., 1989). Severe decreases in brain insulin levels were also observed in aged rabbits, and the expression of the glucose transporters in the Wistar rat brain is altered during aging (Vannucci, 1994). Interestingly, herpes simplex virus vectors bearing a glucose transporter gene were found to protect neurons against a one-hour focal ischemic insult in rats (Lawrence et al., 1996), suggesting a possible treatment strategy to increase glucose transporter availability in the aged brain. Hence, in spite of apparently normal levels of IGF-I and insulin receptor sites in the AU and AI Long Evans rats (discussed earlier), alterations in related signaling pathways and glucose transporters could lead to decreased cognitive abilities. It is thus possible that altered cellular IGF and/or insulin responsiveness is a general feature of aging having functional significance in neurodegenerative diseases by affecting cognitive abilities. Interestingly, experimental desensitization of brain insulin receptors in aged Wistar rats induced abnormalities in glucose utilization, membrane phospholipids, and monoaminergic metabolism, resembling some of the disturbances seen in AD (Hoyer, Muller, & Plaschke, 1994). Links between the onset of AD and diabetes are thus possible, because the latter is a risk factor in AD (Fanelli et al., 1995; Vanhanen et al., 1998).

Using rat hippocampal sections, the authors observed that IGF-I modulates potassium-evoked acetylcholine (ACh) release (Kar et al., 1997b). These data suggest a direct role for IGF-I and its receptors in the regulation of transmitter release in the central nervous system. Evidence indicates that systemic glucose treatment enhances memory while producing a corresponding increase in hippocampal acetylcholine (ACh) release (Ragozzino, Pal, Unick, Stefani, & Gold, 1998). Unilateral intrahippocampal infusions of glucose were examined for enhanced spontaneous cognitive performance and corresponding increases in ACh release. Twelve minutes after a unilateral infusion of glucose, rats were tested in a cross maze for spontaneous alternation behavior with concurrent microdialysis collection. Glucose infusions significantly increased cognitive scores compared to controls, and behavioral testing resulted in increased ACh output in the hippocampus. These results suggest that glucose may enhance cognitive abilities by modulating ACh release. Accumulated evidence (Kar et al., 1997b; Knusel, Michel, Schwaber, & Hefti, 1990) suggests that IGF-I acts as trophic factor as well as a rapid neuromodulator for selected populations of cholinergic neurons, and thus may be of relevance to certain degenerative diseases, particularly AD, in which decreased levels of cholinergic markers are associated with impairments in cognitive functions (Perry, 1986; Quirion, 1993; Selkoe, 1994). In support of a possible role for IGF in AD, it has been shown that IGF-I binding sites are increased in the cortical areas affected by this disease (Crews et al., 1992), and IGF-I can protect/rescue cultured hippocampal neurons from β-amyloid-mediated toxicity (Doré et al., 1997a). Interestingly, glucose levels may also modulate the production and the toxicity of β-amyloid fragments (El Tamer, Raikoff, & Hanin, 1998; Hoyer et al., 1994; Mark, Pang, Geddes, Uchida, & Mattson, 1997), again associating the beneficial effect of IGF-I and brain glucose metabolism.

Crucial Role of IGF-I in Neurogenesis

In most brain regions of highly developed mammals, the majority of neurogenesis is terminated soon after birth. However, new neurons are continually generated throughout life in at least two areas of the adult mammalian brain, the subventricular zone of the lateral ventricle and the subgranular layer of the hippocampal dentate gyrus (Anderson, Aberg, Nilsson, & Eriksson, 2002; Magavi & Macklis, 2002; Reynolds & Weiss, 1992), although the exact phenotype of the most primitive cell in these areas is not yet known. The proliferation, migration, differentiation, and survival of these progenitor cells are regulated by complex interactions between a number of internal and external factors. Enriched environment, psychosocial stress, learning, exercise, age, and a variety of neurotransmitters and growth factors (especially IGF-I) have been shown to modulate the number of new neurons (Magavi & Macklis, 2002).

IGF-I has also been shown to influence not only the developing nervous system, but also adult neurogenesis (Anderson et al., 2002). In vitro and in vivo studies indicate that IGF-I increases proliferation and, in some experimental paradigms, also promotes differentiation toward a neuronal cell lineage (Aberg, Aberg, Hedbacker, Oscarsson, & Eriksson, 2000). However, it is still unclear whether the net increase in new neurons is due to a neuroprotective/survival effect of IGF-I on newborn neurons, rather than an effect on neurogenesis itself (Anderson et al., 2002). Another indication that IGF-I influences neurogenesis under physiological conditions arises from a recent study that has demonstrated that exercise-induced neurogenesis is mediated by uptake of IGF-I into the brain parenchyma. Administering an antibody that blocked passage of systemic IGF-I to the brain during running attenuated hippocampal neurogenesis (Trejo, Carro, & Torres-Aleman, 2001). Hippocampal neurogenesis declines with age, caused at least partially by naturally increased glucocorticoid levels, since adrenalectomized aged rats have levels of neurogenesis very similar to those of young rats (Magavi & Macklis, 2002). Intracerebroventricular administration of IGF-I to old rats increased neurogenesis and reversed cognitive impairments (Lichtenwalner et al., 2001). Stress and depression also inhibit neurogenesis, possibly via the associated reductions in serotonin or increases in circulating glucocorticoids (Magavi & Macklis, 2002). As both of these changes have the potential to downregulate IGF-I production by neural cells, stress may inhibit neurogenesis indirectly via downregulation of IGF-I.

Potential Therapeutic Approaches

It has been reported that intraventricular and subcutaneous supplementation of IGF-I protects immature and adult brains against hypoxic-ischemic injury and ischemia (Hoffmann, Schaebitz, & Schwab, 1999; Loddick et al., 1998; Tagami et al., 1997; Zhu & Auer, 1994). Brain injury is often associated with an increase in IGF levels (Gluckman et al., 1992; Sandberg Nordqvist et al., 1996) and IGF receptors (Bergstedt & Wieloch, 1993). IGF-I has been extensively used clinically (Lewis et al., 1993; Yuen & Mobley, 1995) and has been studied with respect to growth delay, diabetes, and catabolic disorders. Its safety has been well established, although some side effects must be considered, especially in relation to chronic use. One of the counterindications is that IGF-I, due to its characteristic growth-promoting activities, could promote the progression of some tumors (Lewis et al., 1993; Lonning & Lien, 1995). Hence, the design of mimetics, devoid of the side effects of IGF-I, should be developed.

In that regard, a few strategies are worth considering. One approach relates to alterations of IGF-I binding to IGF-binding proteins (IGFBP) in order to increase the level of IGF-I, while the other strategy is based on the design of nonpeptidic mimetics. It is well known that the action of IGF-I is modulated by the IGFBPs (six different forms are well known) (Jones & Clemmons, 1995), which form high-affinity complexes and under most circumstances inactivate IGF-I. It has been suggested that displacement of this large pool of endogenous IGF-I from the binding proteins could elevate free IGF-I levels to elicit neuroprotective effects comparable to those produced by the administration of exogenous IGF-I (Loddick et al., 1998). It was shown that a human IGF-I analog [$Leu^{24,59,60}$ Ala^{31}hIGF-I] with high affinity for IGF-binding proteins, but no biological activity at the IGF-I receptors, increased the levels of free, bioavailable IGF-I in the brain. Intracerebroventricular administration of this analog up to one hour after an ischemic insult to the rat brain had a potent neuroprotective action comparable to that of IGF-I. This ligand also attenuates losses of pyramidal neurons in the hippocampus in a model of toxicity induced by quinolinic acid. Hence, this may represent a novel strategy to increase free IGF-I levels in the brain.

The second strategy is very challenging. It is based on the design of nonpeptidic mimetics. Considering that large polypeptides such as IGF-I do not readily cross the blood–brain barrier, the development of a nonpeptide mimic would be ideal. Recently, a team of researchers has shown the feasibility of this approach by developing L-783,281, a nonpeptidyl mimic acting as an agonist on the insulin receptor (Zhang et al., 1999). A similar strategy could lead to the characterization of an IGF-I mimetic on the basis of similarities between IGF-I and insulin receptors.

In conclusion, knowing the pleotropic actions of IGF-I and insulin on neuronal and nonneuronal cells following injuries, an IGF-I treatment could have therapeutic applications in a number of neurodegenerative disorders, in traumatic brain and spinal cord injuries, and in aging. Several clinical trials have suggested the potential beneficial effect of IGF-I in the nervous system, especially in amyotrophic lateral sclerosis (Lou Gehrig's Disease; Lewis et al., 1993). Development of IGF mimetics is now imperative in order to directly assess the usefulness of IGF-I-like drugs in the treatment of neurodegenerative diseases. A better understanding of the links between IGF-I, brain glucose metabolism, and neurogenesis could also lead to the development of new drugs that would reduce memory loss in disorders such as Alzheimer's disease and other forms of dementia and age-related neurological conditions.

REFERENCES

Aberg, M. A., Aberg, N. D., Hedbacker, H., Oscarsson, J., & Eriksson, P. S. (2000). Peripheral infusion of IGF-I selectively induces neurogenesis in the adult rat hippocampus. *Journal of Neuroscience, 20,* 2896–2903.

Aleman, A., Verhaar, H. J., De Haan, E. H., De Vries, W. R., Samson, M. M., Drent, M. L., et al. (1999). Insulin-like growth factor-I and cognitive function in healthy older men. *Journal of Clinical Endocrinology and Metabolism, 84,* 471–475.

Anderson, M. F., Aberg, M. A., Nilsson, M., & Eriksson, P. S. (2002). Insulin-like growth factor-I and neurogenesis in the adult mammalian brain. *Brain Research. Developmental Brain Research, 134,* 115–122.

Bergstedt, K., & Wieloch, T. (1993). Changes in insulin-like growth factor 1 receptor density after transient cerebral ischemia in the rat. Lack of protection against ischemic brain damage following injection of insulin-like growth factor 1. *Journal of Cerebral Blood Flow and Metabolism, 13,* 895–898.

Biessels, G. J., Kamal, A., Urban, I. J., Spruijt, B. M., Erkelens, D. W., & Gispen, W. H. (1998). Water maze learning and hippocampal synaptic plasticity in streptozotocin-diabetic rats: Effects of insulin treatment. *Brain Research, 800,* 125–135.

Carvalho, C. R., Brenelli, S. L., Silva, A. C., Nunes, A. L., Velloso, L. A., & Saad, M. J. (1996). Effect of aging on insulin receptor, insulin receptor substrate-1, and phosphatidylinositol 3-kinase in liver and muscle of rats. *Endocrinology, 137,* 151–159.

Castro-Alamancos, M. A., & Torres-Aleman, I. (1994). Learning of the conditioned eye-blink response is impaired by an antisense insulin-like growth factor I oligonucleotide. *Proceedings of the National Academy of Sciences, USA, 91,* 10203–10207.

Crews, F. T., McElhaney, R., Freund, G., Ballinger, W. E., Jr., & Raizada, M. K. (1992). Insulin-like growth factor I receptor binding in brains of Alzheimer's and alcoholic patients. *Journal of Neurochemistry 58,* 1205–1210.

Doré, S., Kar, S., & Quirion, R. (1997a). Insulin-like growth factor I protects and rescues hippocampal neurons against beta-amyloid- and human amylin-induced toxicity. *Proceedings of the National Academy of Sciences, USA, 94,* 4772–4777.

Doré, S., Kar, S., & Quirion, R. (1997b). Rediscovering an old friend, IGF-I: potential use in the treatment of neurodegenerative diseases. *Trends in Neuroscience, 20,* 326–331.

Doré, S., Kar, S., Rowe, W., & Quirion, R. (1997). Distribution and levels of [125I]IGF-I, [125I]IGF-II and [125I]insulin receptor binding sites in the hippocampus of aged memory-unimpaired and -impaired rats. *Neuroscience, 80,* 1033–1040.

Doré, S., Krieger, C., Kar, S., & Quirion, R. (1996). Distribution and levels of insulin-like growth factor (IGF-I and IGF-II) and insulin receptor binding sites in the spinal cords of amyotrophic lateral sclerosis (ALS) patients. *Brain Research. Molecular Brain Research, 41,* 128–133.

El Tamer, A., Raikoff, K., & Hanin, I. (1998). Effect of glucose-deprivation on mayloid precursor protein (APP) release from hippocampal slices rat. *Society for Neuroscience Abstracts, 1,* 1006.

Fanelli, C., Pampanelli, S., Calderone, S., Lepore, M., Annibale, B., Compagnucci, P., et al. (1995). Effects of recent, short-term hyperglycemia on responses to hypoglycemia in humans. Relevance to the pathogenesis of hypoglycemia unawareness and hyperglycemia-induced insulin resistance. *Diabetes, 44,* 513–519.

Frolkis, V. V. (1995). The role of "invertors" (intracellular activators) in age-related changes in cell response to hormones. *Experimental Gerontology, 30,* 401–414.

Gage, F. H., Kelly, P. A., & Bjorklund, A. (1984). Regional changes in brain glucose metabolism reflect cognitive impairments in aged rats. *Journal of Neuroscience, 4,* 2856–2865.

Gluckman, P., Klempt, N., Guan, J., Mallard, C., Sirimanne, E., Dragunow, M., Klempt, M., Singh, K., Williams, C., & Nikolics, K. (1992). A role for IGF-1 in the rescue of CNS neurons following hypoxic-ischemic injury. *Biochemical and Biophysical Research Communications, 182,* 593–599.

Hoffmann, T. T., Schaebitz, W. R., & Schwab, S. (1999). Reduction of infarction volume in rats after intraventricular and subcutaneous application of IGF-I. *Journal of Cerebral Blood Flow and Metabolism, 19,* S182.

Hoyer, S., Muller, D., & Plaschke, K. (1994). Desensitization of brain insulin receptor. Effect on glucose/energy and related metabolism. *Journal of Neural Transmission. Supplementum, 44,* 259–268.

Humbert, S., Bryson, E. A., Cordelieres, F. P., Connors, N. C., Datta, S. R., Finkbeiner, S., et al. (2002). The IGF-1/Akt pathway is neuroprotective in Huntington's disease and involves Huntingtin phosphorylation by Akt. *Developmental Cell, 2,* 831–837.

Isaksson, O. G., Ohlsson, C., Nilsson, A., Isgaard, J., & Lindahl, A. (1991). Regulation of cartilage growth by growth hormone and insulin-like growth factor I. *Pediatric Nephrology, 5,* 451–453.

Jafferali, S., Dumont, Y., Sotty, F., Robitaille, Y., Quirion, R., & Kar, S. (2000). Insulin-like growth factor-I and its receptor in the frontal cortex, hippocampus, and cerebellum of normal human and Alzheimer disease brains. *Synapse, 38,* 450–459.

Jones, J. I., & Clemmons, D. R. (1995). Insulin-like growth factors and their binding proteins: Biological actions. *Endocrinology Review, 16,* 3–34.

Kar, S., Seto, D., Doré, S., Chabot, J. G., & Quirion, R. (1997a). Systemic administration of kainic acid induces selective time dependent decrease in [125I]insulin-like growth factor I, [125I]insulin-like growth factor II and [125I]insulin receptor binding sites in adult rat hippocampal formation. *Neuroscience, 80,* 1041–1055.

Kar, S., Seto, D., Doré, S., Hanisch, U., & Quirion, R. (1997b). Insulin-like growth factors-I and -II differentially regulate endogenous acetylcholine release from the rat hippocampal formation. *Proceedings of the National Academy of Sciences, USA, 94,* 14054–14059.

Knusel, B., Michel, P. P., Schwaber, J. S., & Hefti, F. (1990). Selective and nonselective stimulation of central cholinergic and dopaminergic development in vitro by nerve growth factor, basic fibroblast growth factor, epidermal growth factor, insulin and the insulin-like growth factors I and II. *Journal of Neuroscience, 10,* 558–570.

Lawrence, M. S., Sun, G. H., Kunis, D. M., Saydam, T. C., Dash, R., Ho, D. Y., et al. (1996). Overexpression of the glucose transporter gene with a herpes simplex viral vector protects striatal neurons against stroke. *Journal of Cerebral Blood Flow and Metabolism, 16,* 181–185.

Lewis, M. E., Neff, N. T., Contreras, P. C., Stong, D. B., Oppenheim, R. W., Grebow, P. E., et al. (1993). Insulin-like growth factor-I: Potential for treatment of motor neuronal disorders. *Experimental Neurology, 124,* 73–88.

Li, A. J., Oomura, Y., Sasaki, K., Suzuki, K., Tooyama, I., Hanai, K., et al. (1998). A single pre-training glucose injection induces memory facilitation in rodents performing various tasks: Contribution of acidic fibroblast growth factor. *Neuroscience, 85,* 785–794.

Lichtenwalner, R. J., Forbes, M. E., Bennett, S. A., Lynch, C. D., Sonntag, W. E., & Riddle, D. R. (2001). Intracerebroventricular infusion of insulin-like growth factor-I ameliorates the age-related decline in hippocampal neurogenesis. *Neuroscience, 107,* 603–613.

Loddick, S. A., Liu, X. J., Lu, Z. X., Liu, C., Behan, D. P., Chalmers, D. C., et al. (1998). Displacement of insulin-like growth factors from their binding proteins as a potential treatment for stroke. *Proceedings of the National Academy of Sciences, USA, 95,* 1894–1898.

Long, J. M., Davis, B. J., Garofalo, P., Spangler, E. L., & Ingram, D. K. (1992). Complex maze performance in young and aged rats: Response to glucose treatment and relationship to blood insulin and glucose. *Physiology and Behavior, 51,* 411–418.

Lonning, E., & Lien, E. A. (1995). Mechanisms of action of endocrine treatment in breast cancer. *Critical Reviews in Oncology/Hematology, 21,* 158–193.

Magavi, S. S., & Macklis, J. D. (2002). Induction of neuronal type-specific neurogenesis in the cerebral cortex of adult mice: Manipulation of neural precursors in situ. *Brain Research. Developmental Brain Research, 134,* 57–76.

Mark, R. J., Pang, Z., Geddes, J. W., Uchida, K., & Mattson, M. P. (1997). Amyloid beta-peptide impairs glucose transport in hippocampal and cortical neurons: Involvement of membrane lipid peroxidation. *Journal of Neuroscience, 17,* 1046–1054.

Markowska, A. L., Mooney, M., & Sonntag, W. E. (1998). Insulin-like growth factor-1 ameliorates age-related behavioral deficits. *Neuroscience, 87,* 559–569.

Nadiv, O., Cohen, O., & Zick, Y. (1992). Defects of insulin's signal transduction in old rat livers. *Endocrinology, 130,* 1515–1524.

Pankov, Y. A. (1999). Growth hormone and a partial mediator of its biological action, insulin-like growth factor I. *Biochemistry (Mosc), 64,* 1–7.

Perry, E. K. (1986). The cholinergic hypothesis—Ten years on. *British Medical Bulletin, 42,* 63–69.

Potau, N., Escofet, M. A., & Martinez, M. C. (1991). Ontogenesis of insulin receptors in human cerebral cortex. *Journal of Endocrinological Investigation, 14,* 53–58.

Quirion, R. (1993). Cholinergic markers in Alzheimer disease and the autoregulation of acetylcholine release. *Journal of Psychiatry and Neuroscience, 18,* 226–234.

Ragozzino, M. E., Pal, S. N., Unick, K., Stefani, M. R., & Gold, P. E. (1998). Modulation of hippocampal acetylcholine release and spontaneous alternation scores by intrahippocampal glucose injections. *Journal of Neuroscience, 18,* 1595–1601.

Reynolds, B. A., & Weiss, S. (1992). Generation of neurons and astrocytes from isolated cells of the adult mammalian central nervous system. *Science, 255,* 1707–1710.

Rollero, A., Murialdo, G., Fonzi, S., Garrone, S., Gianelli, M. V., Gazzerro, E., et al. (1998). Relationship between cognitive function, growth hormone and insulin-like growth factor I plasma levels in aged subjects. *Neuropsychobiology, 38,* 73–79.

Rotwein, P., Burgess, S. K., Milbrandt, J. D., & Krause, J. E. (1988). Differential expression of insulin-like growth factor genes in rat central nervous system. *Proceedings of the National Academy of Sciences, USA, 85,* 265–269.

Ruiz, P., Pulido, J. A., Martinez, C., Carrascosa, J. M., Satrustegui, J., & Andres, A. (1992). Effect of aging on the kinetic characteristics of the insulin receptor autophosphorylation in rat adipocytes. *Archives of Biochemistry and Biophysics, 296,* 231–238.

Sanchez-Arias, J. A., Sanchez-Gutierrez, J. C., Guadano, A., Alvarez, J. F., Samper, B., Mato, J. M., et al. (1993). Changes in the insulin-sensitive glycosyl-phosphatidyl-inositol signalling system with aging in rat hepatocytes. *European Journal of Biochemistry, 211,* 431–436.

Sandberg Nordqvist, A. C., von Holst, H., Holmin, S., Sara, V. R., Bellander, B. M., & Schalling, M. (1996). Increase of insulin-like growth factor (IGF)-1, IGF binding protein-2 and -4 mRNAs following cerebral contusion. *Brain Research. Molecular Brain Research, 38,* 285–293.

Scott, B. A., Avidan, M. S., & Crowder, C. M. (2002). Regulation of hypoxic death in C. elegans by the insulin/IGF receptor homolog DAF-2. *Science, 296,* 2388–2391.

Selkoe, D. J. (1994). Normal and abnormal biology of the beta-amyloid precursor protein. *Annual Review of Neuroscience, 17,* 489–517.

Tagami, M., Ikeda, K., Nara, Y., Fujino, H., Kubota, A., Numano, F., et al. (1997). Insulin-like growth factor-1 attenuates apoptosis in hippocampal neurons caused by cerebral ischemia and reperfusion in stroke-prone spontaneously hypertensive rats. *Laboratory Investigation, 76,* 613–617.

Tchilian, E. Z., Zhelezarov, I. E., Petkov, V. V., & Hadjiivanova, C. I. (1990). 125I-insulin binding is decreased in olfactory bulbs of aged rats. *Neuropeptides, 17,* 193–196.

Trejo, J. L., Carro, E., & Torres-Aleman, I. (2001). Circulating insulin-like growth factor I mediates exercise-induced increases in the number of new neurons in the adult hippocampus. *Journal of Neuroscience, 21,* 1628–1634.

Vanhanen, M., Koivisto, K., Kuusisto, J., Mykkanen, L., Helkala, E. L., Hanninen, T., et al. (1998). Cognitive function in an elderly population with persistent impaired glucose tolerance. *Diabetes Care, 21,* 398–402.

Vannucci, S. J. (1994). Developmental expression of GLUT1 and GLUT3 glucose transporters in rat brain. *Journal of Neurochemistry, 62,* 240–246.

Werner, H., Raizada, M. K., Mudd, L. M., Foyt, H. L., Simpson, I. A., Roberts, C. T., Jr., et al. (1989). Regulation of rat brain/HepG2 glucose transporter gene expression by insulin and insulin-like growth factor-I in primary cultures of neuronal and glial cells. *Endocrinology, 125,* 314–320.

Wree, A., Kaever, C., Birgel, B., Schleicher, A., Horvath, E., & Zilles, K. (1991). Local cerebral glucose utilization in the brain of old, learning impaired rats. *Histochemistry, 95,* 591–603.

Yuen, E. C., & Mobley, W. C. (1995). Therapeutic applications of neurotrophic factors in disorders of motor neurons and peripheral nerves. *Molecular Medicine Today, 1,* 278–286.

Zaia, A., & Piantanelli, L. (1996). Assay of insulin receptors in mouse brain. *Bollettino della Societa italiana di biologia Sperimentale, 72,* 95–102.

Zhang, B., Salituro, G., Szalkowski, D., Li, Z., Zhang, Y., Royo, I., et al. (1999). Discovery of a small molecule insulin mimetic with antidiabetic activity in mice. *Science, 284,* 974–977.

Zheng, W. H., Kar, S., & Quirion, R. (2002). Insulin-like growth factor-1-induced phosphorylation of transcription factor FKHRL1 is mediated by phosphatidylinositol 3-kinase/akt kinase and role of this pathway in insulin-like growth factor-1-induced survival of cultured hippocampal neurons. *Molecular Pharmacology, 62,* 225–233.

Zhu, C. Z., & Auer, R. N. (1994). Intraventricular administration of insulin and IGF-1 in transient forebrain ischemia. *Journal of Cerebral Blood Flow and Metabolism, 14,* 237–242.

Sylvain Doré
Julia Kofler
Johns Hopkins University

Rémi Quirion
McGill University, Canada

ILLUSIONS

Illusions are misperceptions of the environment. The essential notion of an illusion is that it leads the perceiver to misjudge the stimulus, to have a nonveridical perception. The Müller–Lyer illusion (Figure 1) is a visual illusion, probably the most studied of all visual illusions, in which the perceiver misjudges the length of lines. The lines are equal in length, yet the one on the left is judged to be approximately 25% longer than the other. The illusion has been used to illustrate the unreliability of the senses. Stage lighting, makeup, dress fashions—our visual world is full of the practical application of illusionistic principles.

Illusions are an important part of survival for many species. *Protective coloration* means that an animal takes on coloration similar to that of the environment for protection. Some species have ways to hide in shadows by shading that makes it hard to localize the object and dark streaks that camouflage a conspicuous eye (e.g., the raccoon). Blending in with the background indeed creates a misperception, but not a significant distortion, as when one attributes distance to a physically near object.

Figure 1. The Müller–Lyer illusion. The two horizontal lines are of equal length, but the line on the left appears to be much longer. To make the lines appear subjectively equal, the line on the right must be approximately 25% longer than the one on the left.

We have no systematic ecological classification of all the illusions in nature and in daily life. Illusions occur in all sense modalities. Best studied are the visual illusions. The Müller–Lyer visual illusion already mentioned is also a tactual illusion. In the horizontal–vertical illusion, a horizontal line is bisected by a vertical one of equal length, but the vertical line appears longer. The Poggendorf illusion has an oblique line that intersects two parallel lines. The portion between the parallel lines is blank, and the oblique line appears to exit somewhat below the point where one would infer that it should. The Ponzo illusion has two approaching lines, as in the linear projection of a road in a picture, in which the distant part seems to converge. Two equal lines between the converging lines, one near the front and the other one near the back of the two lines, seem to be of unequal length, the farther line appearing longer.

The ambiguity of empty visual fields and unusual contexts is responsible for many illusions. A fixed dim light in the dark seems to move—an illusion known as the *autokinetic effect,* exhibited by dim stars on a summer night.

The proprioceptive system is responsible for many illusions, one being the drunken walk of the experienced sailor who feels the ship as steady and the dry land as heaving. The aircraft pilot catapulted from a carrier sees objects appear to rise (the oculographic illusion) while the pilot's body feels tilted backward (the oculogravic illusion). The airplane may seem to be climbing too fast, but corrective action—putting the nose of the aircraft down—may result in a crash into the sea. The illusion is particularly compelling at night when visual references are lacking.

Sound localization is ambiguous and is helped by a visual reference. Thus sound is ascribed to the dummy, not to the ventriloquist (the ventriloquist effect). High-pitched sounds, particularly continuous sounds of a single note, are difficult to localize.

The cutaneous "rabbit" is an illusion of localization, of knowing precisely *where* taps are felt on the skin. If one has three contactors four inches apart on the forearm and gives the lower one five separate taps, then the middle one five taps and the last one five taps, the feeling is not of bursts of pulses at three different places, which is what actually happens, but rather of 15 pulses spread out over the forearm, like a "rabbit" running up the arm. This is because localization on the skin is very imprecise. Similarly with hearing: If seven successive sounds are spread over three speakers, a person hears seven sounds in different places—an auditory "rabbit." The visual fovea is very accurate for spatial localization, but successive lights in the periphery of the eye can also give the illusion of coming from more places than are actually in the source. The "rabbit" is multisensory.

Taste illusions are illusions in which the taste of one substance influences the subsequent taste of another. Salt can make water taste sour, and sucrose can make water taste bitter.

Richard D. Walk
George Washington University

***See also:* Perception**

IMPLOSIVE THERAPY

A behavioral procedure devised by T. Stampfl in the 1950s, implosive therapy hypothesizes that neurotic intense anxiety develops as an avoidance mechanism for coping with repressed traumatic experience and that the relative success of avoidance enables anxiety to persist. In implosive therapy, a patient's anxiety is increased to an almost intolerable level by imagining a series of provoking cues, described either by the therapist or by the patient (with the therapist's assistance), until the anxiety dissipates. Proponents believe the technique reinforces anxiety control and extinguishes related public responses by depriving the anxiety of its avoidance function.

SUGGESTED READING

Levis, D. J. (1995). Decoding traumatic memory: Implosive theory of psychopathology. In W. T. O'Donohue & L. Krasner (Eds.), *Theories of behavior therapy: Exploring behavior change.* Washington, DC: American Psychological Association.

Stampfl, T., & Levis, D. (1967). Essentials of implosive therapy: A learning theory–based psychodynamic behavioral therapy. *Journal of Abnormal Psychology, 72,* 496–503.

Forest Hansen

***See also:* Repression**

IMPULSIVITY

Impulsivity is a complex personality dimension that relates to the control of thoughts and behavior. At the extreme it becomes symptomatic of a wide range of impulse control disorders. At less extreme levels it characterizes tendencies to influence behavior in coping with everyday life experiences. Marketing experts are well aware of the role of impulsivity in everyday life decision-making. For example, the displays of magazines and other sundry items at checkout counters in stores are carefully chosen to provide cues for triggering impulsive buying. Impulsive buying can be defined as purchasing a product you had not intended to buy and did not need. If done infrequently, it is not pathological behavior. If done to the extent that it becomes "uncontrollable," it can be pathological. In this respect, impulsivity is similar to blood pressure. Blood pressure, like impulsivity, falls on a continuum from low to high, with the "disorder" of hypertension being defined by the level of the blood pressure and the frequency of elevation. Also, like impulsivity, individuals who have persistently elevated blood pressure may have a different biology and respond differently to treatment than individuals with occasional elevations of blood pressure.

In a general sense, impulsivity is part of a behavioral inhibition system that interacts with behavioral activation or "impulse" systems. The range of impulses in the activation system is broad, as evidenced by the number of behavioral disorders that include impulsivity as a symptom. Examples include disorders of personality (e.g., antisocial and borderline), eating, substance abuse, Attention-Deficit/Hyperactivity Disorder, and impulsive aggression (Intermittent Explosive Disorders).

The characteristics of impulsivity as manifest in these disorders attest to its complexity. Impulsive responses are unplanned and usually unconscious. The cues that trigger the responses can be internal thoughts or external stimuli. The behaviors often result in social sanctions which, even though part of the conscious awareness of the impulsive person before committing the impulsive act, are usually not effective enough in themselves to prevent the acts from occurring. Persons who commit impulsive acts that have negative consequences often experience regret or even remorse after the act because they "knew better." Yet their lack of control of these adverse behaviors will continue until special efforts are made to intervene.

Impulsivity is being widely researched because of its pervasive role in selected psychiatric disorders. One of the problems with researching a complex personality trait like impulsivity is that an interdisciplinary research approach is necessary to understand its complexities. This is not a unique problem for impulsivity research, but research on personality and psychopathology in general suffers from the lack of a model that synthesizes research findings from different disciplines. The lack of an overarching model appears, however, to be changing slowly. Rather than simply noting the importance of cross-disciplinary research, researchers have begun to develop models that recognize the need to study impulsivity and other complex personality traits by synthesizing data from different disciplines within a discipline-neutral framework. This change in theoretical contexts has all of the characteristics of a Kuhnian paradigmatic shift for psychopathology and personality research. Within these emerging models, four categories of constructs and related measurements are recognized: biological, behavioral, social/environment, and cognitive. Obviously, impulsivity will be measured differently within the disciplines represented by each of these four categories. However, the goal is not simply an "adding together" of measurements, but rather the use of theories to synthesize the multimodal measurements. A wide number of measurements within each of the four categories have been used to measure impulsivity.

An example of a *biological* substrate of impulsivity was the identification of an electrical pattern of brain activity recorded while subjects solved cognitive tasks. One of these patterns includes a positive peak of electrical activity that occurs about 300 milliseconds after a relatively rare visual stimulus is presented, also known as a "P300." This peak is significantly smaller in high impulsive subjects and has been related to efficiency of the central nervous system (CNS) in processing information. As measured using this technique, high impulsive subjects process probability-related visual information less efficiently. Another biological characteristic of impulsivity is lower levels of the CNS neurotransmitter serotonin among high impulsive subjects. This has led, in some instances, to the successful intervention in selected impulse control disorders using psychopharmacological agents that increase CNS serotonin levels. Although many of the biological measures appear to be sensitive to levels of impulsivity, it is not clear how specific they are to impulsivity levels per se.

Many forms of *behavioral* measures of impulsivity have been used. One of the more commonly used behavioral measures in both clinical practice and research is the continuous performance task or CPT. In the CPT, subjects have to discriminate among stimuli and indicate their choices by a motor response (e.g., pressing one of two buttons). On these tasks, high impulsive subjects make significantly more errors of commission (responding when they should not have) than low impulsive subjects.

Environmental/social constructs are important in the study of impulsivity because many of the sociocultural cues for impulsive responding, which are acquired at various developmental stages, are learned unconsciously. This implicit learning process can provide the cues for unconscious impulsive acts. These are the cues which, for example, marketing experts capitalize on or which substance abuse patients respond to. Learned cues can become part of a pathological process, as observed, for example, in bulimia. A refrigerator door may become a cue to eat.

Cognitive cues in impulsivity are more difficult to study because cognition is always inferential in nature. Cognition is studied by relating biological and behavioral responses to certain cues or emotional states. However, there are some relatively "pure" cognitive indicators of impulsivity. It has been demonstrated that high impulsive subjects have difficulty, for example, in accurately judging time periods. Subjects with high levels of impulsivity judge time periods as shorter than do subjects with low levels. Thus, when a mother tells a hyperactive child to "wait a minute," his judgment of time will be shorter than that of a nonhyperactive child and his "minute" may be only 10 seconds in duration. These problems in time judgments have been related to "internal clocks" or rate of information processing.

Progress toward better understanding of impulsivity is being made through each of these emerging systems, as exemplified by models like the newly developed "social-cognitive-neurosciences." A discipline-neutral approach that synthesizes the cross-disciplinary substrates of impulsivity will eventually lead to a discipline-neutral definition of impulsivity as an impulsivity index to advance the study of causes and treatments of pathological impulsivity.

Ernest S. Barratt
University of Texas Medical Branch

F. Gerard Moeller
University of Texas Houston Health Science Center

See also: **ADHD; Behavioral Inhibitions**

INDEPENDENT PRACTICE

Whereas psychologists are trained to conduct a wide variety of psychotherapeutic interventions of various styles and approaches, and to assess intellect, aptitude, personality, neuropsychological functioning, and marital adjustment, agency or institutional practice generally restricts the psychologist's practice to those elements required by the institution for which the psychologist works. In the independent practice setting, clinical psychologists tend to work autonomously. They have the opportunity to decide on the best utilization of their own skills and tools.

During the 1950s, there were perhaps 50 psychologists in full-time independent practice in the United States. As of 1995, at least 10,000 psychologists were in full-time independent practice. It is generally agreed that those who enter independent practice in clinical psychology should have the doctorate from an approved training institution, as well as 2 years of postdoctoral supervised experience in clinical psychology. Various states have licensing or certification requirements that represent the journeyman level of competence for independent practice.

Most psychologists committed to independent practice have found that it has considerable advantages. These include

1. The opportunity to offer a broad spectrum of psychological services.
2. The opportunity to develop services that the practitioner knows best, enjoys most, and delivers effectively.
3. The free choice and opportunity to avoid rendering partial, long-delayed, or inappropriate services.
4. Relative freedom from political and bureaucratic constraints and demands.
5. Fair compensation for extra skill, effort, or commitment.

6. The opportunity to become an experienced practicing clinician without loss of status or income.
7. The opportunity to pursue a broadening of skills and training without the constraints of institutional budgets.
8. The option of offering services to anyone without regard to eligibility.
9. The opportunity to make oneself available as a trainer of skill and experience.
10. The option of selecting surroundings, equipment, supporting staff, and the style of service delivery. Excellence and its pursuit is limited only by the practitioner's education, training, ethical constraints, and goodwill.
11. A clearer attribution of success or failure to the practitioner.
12. The opportunity to be the first and last person to see the consumer. Direct access increases the probability of delivery of competent service, more personal involvement, early resolution of misunderstandings, and better evaluation of benefit.
13. The freedom to adjust fees to the consumer's income.
14. Freedom from institutional constraints—real or symbolic.
15. Variety of activity and scheduling flexibility, which are likely to increase the quality of life for practicing professionals.

Surveys indicate that in American communities the range of saturation for full-time independent practitioners of psychology is from 1 per 2500 population to 1 per 135,000. Thus, this particular model for clinical psychologists offering direct consumer service may be the model of the future.

Theodore H. Blau

INDIVIDUAL DIFFERENCES

The communication system developed by humans not only makes them unique in regard to other animals, but also makes individuals unique in regard to one another. Speech and language require adequate physical and neural development and similar sensory experiences for humans to develop the basic skills required in communication. Genetic or physical damage to all or part of the nervous system, inadequate sensory development, or inadequate learning experiences can make individuals different. The age at which experiences occur, as well as emotional factors and opportunities, can contribute to individual uniqueness.

As a result of human uniqueness, psychology has had to turn to more general and less effective group approaches to try to gain information about the individual. Methods of evaluation and statistical techniques had to be developed to make the evaluation results useful. This has taken a great deal of time; as a result, the scientific investigation of individual differences, along with the special factors that exist in each case, is of relatively recent origin. It has become a specialized area within the general field of psychology known as differential psychology.

A major problem in differential psychology is the kind and number of ways an individual can be different. Differences start at conception as a result of the great differences in the chromosomes and genes available in each parent. There are the effects of environment on the selection of chromosomes and genes plus the physical, mental, and emotional state of the mother who carries the child-to-be. Other factors include the nutrition available during the developmental period and after birth, the amount of stimulation available after birth, the types of traumatic experiences that may occur, the others in the individuals' environment, and the kinds of educational experiences available.

The particular genes supplied by the parents are the determiners of the basic physical, mental, and emotional development of the individual. Each set of genes is unique, even in the case of identical twins. Recent studies have found maternal environmental differences that can affect the development of one twin more than they affect the other.

The environment can only modify what is already present. For example, failure to supply something that is needed, such as vitamins or proteins, or the presence of harmful physical or chemical factors can make dramatic changes.

Stimulation is necessary for the normal development of an individual. Sensory deprivation can lead to retardation in motor and mental development.

Traumatic experiences in the form of shocks or insults can create individual differences. A fall in which the head or neck is damaged can affect physical, mental, and emotional development. Emotional experiences of a traumatic nature can have a short-term or long-term effect on intellectual development. A devastating illness can leave physical, mental, and emotional damage in its wake.

Sexual differences are observable after birth. Girls tend to develop faster than boys, and this will affect brain development. Early developers have better verbal than spatial abilities, whereas late developers perform better on spatial than on verbal tasks.

In the area of physical growth a relatively orderly sequence of development exists, primarily based on inheritance. Although the order is relatively the same from child to child, the rate of development can vary tremendously, with some infants reaching the stage of standing or walking months ahead of others. Sex differences play a primary role here: By 5 years of age, girls tend to be 4 months or more ahead of boys. Major differences between the sexes can be seen in the preadolescent growth spurt that occurs toward the end of the childhood period, beginning 2 years before adolescence. The average girl begins her growth spurt shortly after age 10 and achieves adolescence by approximately 12.5 years, with a deceleration of growth by age 14. The average boy begins his growth spurt at about 13 years and achieves adolescence around age 15, with a deceleration of growth after 16.

Learning experiences play such an important part in emotional development that no clear-cut differences in emotional behavior have been found for the two sexes. As a child matures, the emotional characteristics undergo major changes and the type of experiences that generate emotional reactions also changes. Parental attitudes and behavior, the culture, and the environment are all important factors in an individual's emotional development, but so are the individual's own characteristics.

Francis Galton is given credit for the first systematic investigation of individual differences. Convinced that heredity was the major factor in differences among people, he devised a sensory–motor test that discriminated among stimuli. This test has been called the first measure of intellectual potential.

James M. Cattell was interested in the differences between individuals in several areas including academic success. He is said to have used the term "mental test" as early as 1890.

Alfred Binet became interested in individual differences as a result of his work with hypnosis and his observations of the different ways his daughters solved problems. Working with Theodore Simon, he developed the first real intelligence scale in 1905 when he assembled a group of cognitive and sensory tasks in an attempt to identify retarded children in the French school system.

Testing materials and approaches have greatly improved. New techniques for evaluating testing materials and their results have increased the usefulness of these devices. As a result, it is easier today to determine an individual's strengths and weaknesses and then to place that individual in the best existing educational or training program designed to meet his or her needs.

Measurement is the only way that has been found to determine how one person will differ from another in ways that cannot be directly observed. Intellectual functioning is the area most frequently involved in controversy over devices used for measuring individual differences. An individual's intellectual functioning depends on the inherited potential plus an environment that permits the development of that potential. But IQ is not a constant characteristics such as eye color. If IQ scores are accumulated on the same individual over a period of time, there is an increase in the constancy of the scores. This improvement in constancy can be related to the changes that occur as the result of maturation, plus the experiences that improve the individual's ability to deal with information in the nervous system. In addition, learning experiences over a period of time fill in some of the earlier gaps in knowledge until some degree of balance is reached and the scores become more and more alike.

There are many aspects of intelligence not adequately dealt with on an IQ test, which tends to concentrate on abilities most relevant to school learning. An accurate picture of intelligence requires the sampling of performance in a broad range of abilities. The scores obtained reflect experiences that have taken place in and out of educational institutions interwoven with psychological factors pertinent to the particular individual.

No matter what test is used to measure individual differences, there are always additional factors to be considered, such as the individual's physical, mental, and emotional state at the time of the examination; the ability of the individual to understand the directions or to use the materials effectively; the time of day, week, or month; the area used for testing; the temperature; the amount of light available; and the amount of noise in the background. Any one of these things and many more can affect the score of a particular individual on a particular day.

Frederick D. Breslin
Glassboro State College

See also: **Differential Psychology; Life-Span Development**

INDIVIDUALISM

In common usage, *individualism* is defined as leading one's life in one's own way without regard for others. Individualism may be separated from *individuality,* which is the sum of the qualities that set one person apart from others. To *individualize* is to distinguish a person as different from others, whereas to *individuate* is to make a person individual or distinct. Individualism is also distinct from *autonomy,* which is the ability to understand what others expect in any given situation and what one's values are, and to be free to choose how to behave based on either or both. While individuality and autonomy are important aspects of healthy psychological development and health, individualism is not.

Based on the theorizing of Morton Deutsch (1962) and David Johnson and Roger Johnson (1989), individualism may be defined as believing and behaving as if one's efforts and goal attainments are unrelated to or independent of the efforts toward goal attainment of others. Individualism is usually contrasted with cooperativeness and competitiveness. *Cooperativeness* may be defined as believing and behaving as if one's efforts and goal attainments are positively related to the efforts and goal attainments of others, or as if one can achieve one's goals if, and only if, the others with whom one is cooperatively linked obtain their goals. *Competitiveness* may be defined as believing and behaving as if one's efforts and goal attainments are negatively related to the efforts and goal attainments of others, or as if one can achieve one's goals if, and only if, the others with whom one is competitively linked fail to achieve their goals.

There is considerable research comparing the relative effects of individualism, cooperativeness, and competitiveness. These reviews have primarily been conducted by David Johnson and Roger Johnson and their colleagues (Johnson & Johnson, 1989, 1999). Individualism, compared with cooperativeness, tends to be related to: (1) lower beliefs that one is liked, accepted, supported, and assisted by others; (2) less seeking of information from others, and utilizing it for one's own benefit; (3) lower achievement, intrinsic, and continuing motivation, and greater orientation toward extrinsic rewards; (4) less emotional involvement in efforts to achieve one's goals; (5) lower achievement; (6) lower ability to take the cognitive and affective perspective of others; (7) less healthy processes for deriving conclusions about one's self-worth; (8) lower psychological health, as reflected in greater psychological pathology, delinquency, emotional immaturity, social maladjustment, self-alienation, self-rejection, lack of social participation, basic distrust of other people, pessimism, and inability to resolve conflicts between self-perceptions and adverse information about oneself; and (9) less liking for others and more negative interpersonal relationships. There has been very little research comparing individualism and competitiveness.

If the direct evidence is not very favorable toward individualism, the writings in personality and clinical psychology are even less so. The solitary human who avoids relationships and coalitions with others is considered abnormal. Humans are basically interdependent beings, biologically and socially. Effective socialization brings with it an awareness that one cannot achieve one's life goals alone; one needs other people's help and resources. Psychological health requires a realization that one's goals and the goals of others, one's efforts and the efforts of others, and one's success and the success of many different people, are all related and interdependent. Accurately perceiving the interdependence between yourself and others involves an awareness of sharing a common fate (both you and your fellow collaborators will receive the same outcome); a recognition of mutual causation (achieving your goals depends on both your own efforts and those of collaborators); the possession of a long-term time perspective; and an appreciation of the skills, information, competencies, and talents of other people as well as oneself. Individuals high on individualism do not have a high degree of these traits. Individualism often brings with it the following: (1) feelings of alienation, loneliness, isolation, inferiority, worthlessness, depression, and defeat; (2) attitudes reflecting low self-esteem, an emphasis on short-term gratification, and the conviction that no one cares about one or one's capabilities; and (3) relationships characterized by impulsiveness, fragmentation, withdrawal, and insensitivity to one's own and others' needs.

Every person needs to establish a coherent and integrated identity that differentiates him or her as a unique individual, separate and distinct from all others. While the ability to act independently, autonomy, and individuality are all important aspects of developing an identity, individualism is not. Paradoxically, it is from collaborative and supportive relationships that encourage individuality that a mature identity is formed. Self-awareness, self-understanding, differentiating oneself from others, the internalization of values and self-approval, and social sensitivity are all acquired through encouraging and cooperative relationships, not through isolation or leading one's life in one's own way without regard for others.

REFERENCES

Deutsch, M. (1962). Cooperation and trust: Some theoretical notes. In M. Jones (Ed.), *Nebraska symposium on motivation.* Lincoln: University of Nebraska Press.

Johnson, D. W., & Johnson, R. (1989). *Cooperation and competition: Theory and research.* Edina, MN: Interaction Book Company.

Johnson, D. W., & Johnson, R. (1999). *Learning together and alone: Cooperative, competitive, and individualistic learning* (5th ed.). Boston: Allyn & Bacon.

David W. Johnson
Roger T. Johnson
University of Minnesota

See also: **Affiliation Need; Avoidant Personality; Bystander Involvement; Deindividuation; Ethnocentrism; Social Isolation**

INDUSTRIAL–ORGANIZATIONAL PSYCHOLOGY

That branch of psychology concerned with the scientific study of behavior in the workplace and/or the application of psychological knowledge to that setting is known as industrial–organizational psychology. The field stresses both knowledge generation (research) and the application of that knowledge (practice) to better meet the needs of employees and employers.

Industrial–organizational psychology represents the merging of two disciplines of psychology to address behaviors in the workplace. One discipline is individual differences. Psychologists well grounded in the understanding of human abilities brought this knowledge to the workplace and focused upon the match of job demands with individual skills and abilities. The second focus flows from social psychology. This focus, best expressed by Kurt Lewin, is concerned with the attitudes and behaviors of people in social settings encountered in the workplace. At one time industrial psychology referred to the first focus, and organizational psychology to the second. Today the single discipline represents the merger of the two.

Selection and Placement

One of the most important concerns of industrial–organizational psychologists is that of selecting individuals to fill the various work roles in an organization, and placing the employees hired by the organization in jobs so as to create a good match of people to jobs. To accomplish these selection and placement tasks, the following procedures represent major concerns of industrial psychologists.

Job Analysis

A job analysis is the study of the job requirements. It first involves a description of the duties and responsibilities of the person who holds the job. In addition, the job analysis goes beyond the simple description of what must be done to suggest the human characteristics necessary to accomplish the job successfully. It is absolutely necessary that the nature of the job be understood before any attempt is made to select or place persons in the job. In addition to selection, job analyses are also essential for developing compensation systems and guiding career development and training programs. The nature of jobs and their links to many job functions have been greatly facilitated by the recent development of the Occupational Information Network (O*NET), a national database of jobs and job characteristics.

Personnel Assessment

Once the job characteristics have been assessed, it is necessary to assess the characteristics of individuals so as to match persons with jobs. The industrial–organizational psychologist must choose methods for assessing job-relevant individual characteristics that (1) are appropriate for the characteristic being assessed, and (2) possess acceptable psychometric properties of reliability and validity. Since standardized tests of skills and abilities, aptitudes, and/or interests often provide the best means of accomplishing these two objectives, the industrial–organizational psychologist must have a thorough knowledge of the standardized tests available and how to construct and evaluate tests. Situational interviews, assessment centers, biographical data, and a variety of other standardized measures are used to measure individual differences. Finally, it is the professional, ethical, and legal responsibility of the industrial psychologist to develop assessment procedures that are reliable and valid and do not discriminate unfairly against particular groups.

Criterion Development

Once employees are on the job, ways of assessing their effectiveness must be developed. This task encompasses the classical criterion problem that has received considerable attention from industrial psychologists. The development of criteria first involves identifying those job behaviors or outcomes relevant to effective job-role accomplishment, and then developing ways to assess validly and reliably the dimensions identified.

Validation

The final step in the selection and placement process is to evaluate the fit between individual characteristics used for selection and the effectiveness of these individuals on the job. This complex process is referred to as validation or the validity study.

Performance Appraisal

Judgments about the effectiveness of employees' job performance often must be based on subjective evaluations obtained from other individuals. Although these judgments can be made by any of a number of individuals on the job, the task of judging employees' performance is usually accomplished by their immediate supervisors. These evaluations serve a wide variety of functions. Performance evaluations can be used as criteria for validating selection systems. They are also used for determining raises and promotions, to evaluate training effectiveness, and to counsel employees about their performance on the job or their long-term career goals. Subordinates, peers, and supervisors often provide feedback in order to provide employees with information about how their work and interactions are seen from many perspectives. Providing supervisors with appraisals from multiple sources for developmental purposes is currently referred to as 360-degree feedback.

The establishment of appraisal systems requires that rating scales and procedures for using them be developed so that the ratings are as unbiased and accurate as possible. To accomplish this, researchers are faced with complex issues of scale development and policies for conducting such ratings. Major advances have been made in this area. One of the most important involves scaling critical job behaviors and describing them in the job incumbent's own words.

Training

When employees or potential employees do not possess the knowledge, skills, or abilities needed to perform their jobs, they may obtain knowledge and skills through training. Industrial psychologists are involved in all four of the major phases of training. The first phase is a needs analysis, which considers the present and near-future demands of the jobs in the organization and then, in a very real sense, inventories the extent to which the workforce possesses the knowledge and skills that are and will be needed. This analysis considers not only the present employees, but also estimates the losses of personnel through retirement and other forms of turnover during the time period of interest. Once the needs analysis is complete, the industrial psychologist plans training programs to meet these needs. During this second phase, the psychologist applies what is known about human learning and training methods to best facilitate the development of the knowledge and skills needed.

The third phase of the training process is the actual training. Industrial psychologists frequently are involved with conducting training. The ability to deliver training over the Internet, to create relatively high fidelity simulations with computers, and to make use of other recent advances are rapidly changing the nature of training. Finally, the effectiveness of the training should be assessed. It is the responsibility of industrial–organizational psychologists to attempt to build into the conduct of training programs ways to assess their effectiveness.

Work Motivation

The industrial–organizational psychologist deals with motivation at three different levels. First of all, psychologists must have a thorough knowledge of human motivation in general. They need to be aware of current theory and thinking related to motivation, regardless of the setting. At a more work-related level, at least four general motivationally-oriented processes are applied by the industrial psychologist. These are incentive systems, goal setting, participation in decision making, and job design. Incentive systems development involves the association of valued rewards with behaviors that the employer wants to encourage. To use incentives effectively requires a thorough knowledge of what is valued by employees and the likely behavioral effects of making valued outcomes contingent upon performance. In addition, one must be aware of the relative value of the incentives in the marketplace. Goal setting involves the establishment of standards for performance and feedback with respect to those standards. Participation in decision making or autonomy is predicated on the assumption that employees desire to have more say in what goes on at work. Industrial–organizational psychologists often have attempted to build participation into managerial/leadership training, performance appraisal, and other processes in work settings. The success of these procedures has been mixed. To a large extent, it depends on whether one is interested in improving performance or increasing employee satisfaction.

Motivation is affected by having jobs designed so that job incumbents can believe their needs can best be met by behaving in a way that meets the organization's goals. The design of motivationally-focused systems tailors the general motivational strategies to the particular organizational setting, its culture, and its employees. To do this, some combination of the four motivational processes just described is typically used. Increasingly, job design incorporates multiple employees in teams and work groups, where motivation is focused not only on individual task performance but also on the coordination and maintenance of effectively functioning teams.

Job Satisfaction

A great deal of effort has been expended by industrial–organizational psychologists to assess work attitudes. In particular, there is considerable interest in measuring employees' satisfaction with their jobs. Much of the earlier work was motivated by the assumption that the more satisfied people were with their work, the more productive they would be. In the face of repeated failures to show that this was true, later work with job satisfaction has stressed the value of a satisfied work force as an end in itself. Also, information about satisfaction has a great deal of diagnostic potential for the organization. With it, the organization can often identify problem areas and then take action to alleviate these problems.

Job satisfaction measures are most useful when they are a part of a regularly scheduled attitude survey repeated over time in the same organization. Periodic surveys provide feedback from employees on a regular basis, helping to identify trends in changes in attitudes and providing information for supervisors about the feelings of the people who work for them. Such surveys are also frequently used to assess the reactions of customers.

Job Design

Although job design has been mentioned briefly under work motivation, more space needs to be devoted to it, because of its relevance to industrial–organizational psychologists from a broader perspective than motivation. In particular, jobs must be designed to fit the abilities of the individuals who hold the jobs, as well as their motivation. Therefore, industrial–organizational psychologists tend to take one of two general approaches to job design. One is a motivational approach. Recent motivational emphasis has been on changing jobs so that they allow job incumbents more control, autonomy, feedback, and opportunity to be involved in their work. This point of view underlies the area known as job enrichment. With the increasing use of teams in the work setting, job design is also being raised to a level above that of the individual to include coordination, cooperation, helping, and other interpersonal behaviors.

The other orientation toward job design concentrates on individual abilities and attempts to design tasks in jobs to match, as closely as possible, the abilities of the jobholders. This field is known as human factors engineering or ergonomics. This field has been strongly influenced by the information processing capabilities of human beings and machines with respect to the interface between people and computers, and influenced also by the technological advances in robotics. As a result, the field of human factors has become a subset less of industrial psychology than of applied experimental psychology and/or industrial engineering.

Daniel R. Ilgen
Michigan State University

INFERIORITY FEELINGS

Alfred Adler distinguished between inferiority feelings and inferiority complex. Adler assumed a feeling of inferiority on the part of everyone. He pointed out that to be human means to feel inferior. Inferiority feelings were traced to the child's smallness and dependence in a world of adults, and later to the pursuit of perfection.

Feelings of inferiority may serve as a stimulant to healthy, normal striving and development. They become a pathological condition only when the individual is overwhelmed and becomes depressed and incapable of development. Orgler states that Adler found that inferiority complexes can develop from three sources: organ inferiority, spoiling, and neglect. When feelings of inferiority result in avoiding participation in the community, they become a complex.

The word *inferiority* is derived from the Latin *inferus,* meaning "below" or "under." Whenever a person feels inferior, it implies comparison with another person or some standard or norm. Such comparisons are the starting point of much human misery. Next, a host of other negative factors occur, including anger, competitiveness, and a consequent loss of initiative because competition, by focusing one's efforts on a rival, precludes spontaneity. Furthermore, one may act in a superior manner: A superiority complex can compensate for an inferiority complex.

To conquer the feeling of inferiority, two things must be done. First, one must stop comparing oneself to another so as to give full and undivided attention to the problem or task at hand. Second, one must surrender the need to be superior. Renouncing the need for superiority and privilege, one finds one's balance, gains momentum, and ceases to feel inferior.

Inferior self-assessment is always a negative thing, yet sometimes it serves as a stimulus for constructive and useful compensation. Out of weakness and deficiency can grow strength. In such a situation it is not inferiority itself that is advantageous, but the constructive overcoming of weakness and deficiency.

Related to inferiority feelings are feelings of inadequacy. Whereas inferiority implies feeling not as good as someone else, the inadequate person feels unable to cope with tasks. The frame of reference is not another person but the task one cannot handle. Just as, according to Adler, one overcomes inferiority feelings by giving up comparisons and the desire to be superior, so, to overcome inadequacy, one must focus on the task at hand and have the courage to be imperfect.

Donald N. Lombardi
Seton Hall University

INFORMED CONSENT

Informed consent is the ethical and legal obligation psychologists have to obtain consent from persons prior to conducting assessment, treatment, or research. The doctrine of informed consent requires persons to be informed of potential benefits and risks of the contemplated procedures, as well as any possible alternative procedures. Underlying the informed consent doctrine is the principle that allowing individuals to make informed decisions respects each person's autonomy and self-determination.

Three Elements of Consent

Valid consent implies that participation in assessment, treatment, or research is given intelligently, knowingly, and voluntarily. Intelligence, sometimes referred to as competency, is defined as the capacity to comprehend and evaluate specific information that is offered. Psychologists should follow the reasonable patient standard in deciding what information to provide. This standard imparts an affirmative duty on professionals to give as much information as a reasonable patient would desire to make treatment decisions. At a minimum, the following information should be provided to assure informed consent: purpose of the procedure, any potential risks and benefits, alternative procedures available, limits of confidentiality (e.g., mandated reporting of child abuse), general client rights (e.g., the right to withdraw from therapy at any time), qualifications of the professional, and logistical information (e.g., scheduling practices, fee structures, emergency procedures).

Providing required information alone is necessary but not sufficient. In addition, consent must be given knowingly or with appreciation. In order to ensure that a person fully appreciates the information provided, psychologists must regularly question comprehension of the material. One way of assessing comprehension is to ask the person to repeat, in his or her own words, information on the procedure that was presented previously. Finally, the voluntary element of informed consent suggests that such consent may not be coerced or enticed by the professional. For example, psychologists should avoid promising miraculous and timely cures; they should also avoid offering financial incentives for participating in treatment or research studies.

Bases of Informed Consent

Legal Bases

Several legal cases illustrate the importance of obtaining informed consent for treatment (e.g., *Mohr v. Williams,* 1905; *Schloendorff v. the Society of New York Hospital,* 1914; *Canterbury v. Spence,* 1972). Repeatedly, courts have found in favor of patients' being apprised of all relevant information regarding treatment. Failure to do so may constitute battery or assault, and the psychologist may be held legally liable for any damage that results.

In research contexts, federal regulations promulgated by the Department of Health and Human Services legally require psychologists to obtain valid consent prior to initiation of a study. However, in treatment settings, there are no federal or nationwide statutes on informed consent for psychological interventions. Although all states have statutes mandating some type of informed consent procedures for physicians and psychiatrists, not every state specifies that psychologists or other mental health providers must obtain informed consent for psychological treatments. It is incumbent on treating clinicians to be aware of the statutes in the states in which they practice, as laws regarding informed consent for therapy vary across state lines.

Ethical Standards

Ethical codes of conduct clearly dictate that psychologists apply the concept of informed consent in both treatment and research settings. For example, the ethical codes developed by the American Psychological Association (APA) and the American Counseling Association (ACA) both contain sections dealing with informed consent for clinical interventions and research studies. The overarching principles espoused in these ethical codes is that professionals must consider each person's best interests, autonomy, and self-determination.

Research on Informed Consent

Informed consent typically is documented in writing by having the person sign a consent form. There has been little research conducted on the process or effects of utilizing written consent forms. Studies have found that the average length of such forms doubled from 1975 to 1982 and that these forms generally require the reader to have at least a college education in order to comprehend and appreciate the information. Unfortunately, researchers also have found that longer consent forms inhibit the amount of information retained. It appears clear that clients and research participants often agree to engage in procedures that they do not fully understand, which belies the whole idea of informed consent.

Regarding children, only adults are considered able to understand procedural information and to be legally competent to give consent. Therefore, in many states, consent to assess, treat, or study minors must be obtained from a legal guardian or parent. However, some state statutes give minors limited rights to consent to treatment, in particular. Regardless of state law, it is important to involve even young children in the process of obtaining consent, as researchers have found that even young children (i.e., age 7 or above) may be capable of understanding and weighing options.

Several studies have examined the effects of written consent forms on the therapy process. In general, the literature has documented primarily positive results from the use of written informed consent forms. For example, researchers found that the use of more written information increased participants' positive judgments of therapists' experience, likeability, and trustworthiness, particularly with respect to less experienced therapists. In addition, researchers have found that written consent forms do not negatively affect client attendance, nor do they increase the likelihood of premature termination. Despite these promising findings, research has been mixed on the impact of written consent forms on client disclosures in treatment settings. Some studies have found that warning clients of the limits of confidentiality reduces client disclosures, whereas other studies have found that it has no impact. Due to conflicting findings in the literature, further research is needed to clarify the impact of informed consent procedures on client disclosures in treatment settings.

CATHERINE MILLER
Pacific University

See also: **Confidentiality**

INHIBITORY CONDITIONING

At the beginning of the twentieth century, Ivan Pavlov developed the original model of conditioning. In his research, he conditioned dogs to salivate at the sound of a bell by the repeated process of ringing the bell and then presenting food. His research showed that each time the bell and food were paired, the amount of saliva that the dog produced increased. Using the standard terminology, the bell is referred to as the conditioned stimulus (CS), the food is the unconditioned stimulus (US), the salivation in response to the ringing of the bell is called the conditioned response (CR), and each bell–food pairing is called a trial. In this study, Pavlov was interested in the processes that cause the CS to activate or "excite" the behavior of salivation. In this example, the CS is referred to as "excitatory" because it acts to elicit the CR. However, Pavlov was also interested in the processes that are responsible for the "inhibition" of responding. In inhibitory conditioning, the CS acts against the elicitation of a conditioned response.

The standard conditioned inhibition procedure involves two phases. In the first phase, a CS such as a tone is repeatedly paired with the presentation of a food US (T+ trials), until the subject shows a stable salivary response to the tone. As in the previous example, the tone can be considered excitatory because it elicits the CR of salivation. In the second phase of the procedure, two types of learning trials are randomly intermixed throughout the phase. One trial type is the same as that given in the first phase (T+ trials). The second trial type involves the simultaneous presentation of the tone and a second stimulus, such as a light. However, on these compound trials, no food is given (TL– trials). At the beginning of this phase, the dog may salivate on both the T+ trials and the TL– trials. However, as the phase progresses, the dog will eventually stop salivating during the presentation of the compound stimulus, TL, while continuing to salivate during the presentation of the tone alone. Thus, the light may be considered inhibitory because it appears to act against the elicitation of a CR that would have normally been produced by the tone.

Although Pavlov discovered conditioned inhibition in the early 1900s, inhibitory conditioning did not command the serious attention of researchers until over 40 years later when Rescorla (1969) reintroduced the topic by arguing that the candidate inhibitor must pass a both a "summation test" and a "retardation test" in order to be declared a true conditioned inhibitor. For the summation test, a third stimulus is employed. This new stimulus (say, a bell) has already been paired with a US, and is thus known to be excitatory. During the test, the candidate inhibitor (L) is presented in compound with the bell (BL– trials). The light is said to pass the summation test if it is successful in reducing the level of conditioned responding to the bell. In the retardation test, the candidate inhibitor (L) is paired with a US (L+ trials) and the rate at which the light acquires excitatory strength is observed (as measured by the development of conditioned responding). It is said to pass the retardation test if it acquires that strength more slowly than would a neutral or novel stimulus paired with the same US.

Rescorla maintained that a candidate inhibitor must pass both of these tests because a CS could pass either one of these tests alone and still not be a true conditioned inhibitor. For example, if it had only passed the summation test, one could argue that it was merely distracting the animal and drawing the animal's attention away from the excitatory stimulus. If it had only passed the retardation test, then one could argue that the training during the second phase served merely to cause the animal to ignore the stimulus. However, if it passed both tests, neither the "distracting" nor the "ignoring" explanation could work—a stimulus cannot be both distracting and ignored at the same time; it must be a true conditioned inhibitor with the ability to act against the elicitation of a conditioned response.

Rescorla's belief that a conditioned inhibitor must be able to pass these two special tests reflects the concept that excitation and inhibition lie at opposite ends of a single continuum of associative strength. Excitation and inhibition were viewed by Rescorla and others as opposing associative processes that carried opposite signs and counteracted each other (Rescorla & Wagner, 1972). The summation and retardation tests were meant to capitalize on this opposition by pitting the two opposing processes against each other. However, some studies have suggested, and some theories argue, that inhibition is not the symmetric opposite of excitation and that they are not two mutually exclusive associative processes (Matzel, Gladstein, & Miller, 1988; Williams & Overmier, 1988; Zimmer-Hart & Rescorla, 1974). Some researchers have rebelled against the notion of inhibition itself, suggesting that what appear to be the effects of inhibition on conditioned responding are really the effects of varying amounts of excitation in combination with some principle of performance (Gibbon & Balsam, 1981; Miller & Schachtman, 1985). These theories explain the behavioral effect of a putative inhibitory CS in terms of a comparison of the CSs' relative strengths of excitation. For a review of this issue, see Williams, Overmier, and LoLordo (1992).

REFERENCES

Gibbon, J., & Balsam, P. D. (1981). Spreading association in time. In C. M. Locurto, H. S. Terrace, & J. Gibbon (Eds.), *Autoshaping and conditioning theory* (pp. 219–253). San Diego, CA: Academic Press.

Matzel, L. D., Gladstein, L., & Miller, R. R. (1988). Conditioned excitation and conditioned inhibition are not mutually exclusive. *Learning & Motivation, 19*(2), 99–121.

Miller, R. R., & Schachtman, T. R. (1985). Conditioning context as an associative baseline: Implications for response generation and the nature of conditioned inhibition. In R. R. Miller & N. E. Spear (Eds.), *Information processing in animals: Conditioned inhibition* (pp. 51–88). Hillsdale, NJ: Erlbaum.

Rescorla, R. A. (1969). Pavlovian conditioned inhibition. *Psychological Bulletin, 72*(2), 77–94.

Rescorla, R. A., & Wagner, A. R. (1972). A theory of Pavlovian conditioning: Variations in the effectiveness of reinforcement and nonreinforcement. In A. H. Black & W. F. Prokasy (Eds.), *Classical conditioning: II. Theory and research* (pp. 64–99). New York: Appleton-Century-Crofts.

Williams, D. A., & Overmier, J. B. (1988). Some types of conditioned inhibitors carry collateral excitatory associations. *Learning & Motivation, 19*(4), 345–368.

Williams, D. A., Overmier, J. B., & LoLordo, V. M. (1992). A reevaluation of Rescorla's early dictums about Pavlovian conditioned inhibition. *Psychological Bulletin, 111*(2), 275–290.

Zimmer-Hart, C. L., & Rescorla, R. A. (1974). Extinction of Pavlovian conditioned inhibition. *Journal of Comparative & Physiological Psychology, 86*(5), 837–845.

Janice E. McPhee

INNER/OUTER-DIRECTED BEHAVIOR

The problem of internal as compared to external control concerns, first, the circumstances under which one perceives one's own behavior to be determined by forces in the environment or by oneself. Second, it concerns the possibility that even in the same situation, people differ in the processes that govern their own behavior.

Almost any line of research points to the influence of cognitive factors in the selection and control of response. The Würzburg school showed how instructions or task conditions induce in the subject a *set* or particular kind of readiness to respond, which then determines subsequent responses. Following the lead of E. C. Tolman, many psychologists employ the term *expectancy* for this phenomenon. Even more generally, the term *attitude* refers to the regulative function in personality.

A set is essentially defined by experimental conditions and is inferred by effects associated with variations in those conditions. But an attitude requires measurement independent of the situation, such as by a personality test. When differences appear in performance, then, we would link them with intrinsic variations in cognitive structure.

It is usually not sufficient just to assess a personality variable. Its mere presence in the subject does not guarantee that it will influence response. For this reason, an experimenter needs to include conditions that maximize its operation. These conditions include *arousal* or *induction* aimed at the variable in question, and a task that engages the subject's *interest* or commitment enough to involve his or her resources.

Research on internal—as compared to external—control of behavior has employed strategies, on the one hand, of manipulating cognition by extrinsically imposed conditions, and on the other hand, by identifying groups who differ in antecedent assessment of these inferred characteristics. The former approach has to do with sets or expectancies, the latter with attitudes. In neither strategy have the requisite conditions just mentioned always been fully recognized.

Expectancies of Control

Interest in the problem of personal control owes much to research on frustration and its effects—situations in which a person is blocked in attempting to attain a goal. Emotional arousal and aggression may thereby be elicited (although negative effects are typically emphasized, constructive or coping efforts may also be evident). Such reactions vary with the degree of control one has over the threatening conditions. For example, with a threat of electric shock, subjects prefer certainty that the shock will occur to uncertainty or inconsistency, and report less anxiety when they control the shock lever. Other studies bear out the fact that perception of control of aversive stimuli significantly reduces subjective discomfort. Even an illusion of control can influence one's reactions to a situation. The "self-fulfilling prophecy" is another interesting phenomenon in which an expectation about what will happen influences one's behavior. Archibald has reviewed possible interpretations of such effects. An expectation of failure may arouse anxiety so that a person tries to alleviate such feelings, or the aroused state may produce inappropriate effort (trying too hard or paying attention to the wrong cues). Alternatively, an expectation of a favorable outcome may simply increase effort and thereby facilitate performance. A person highly involved in a task may be oriented primarily to preserve self-esteem or some important value. Therefore, the task or goal may be redefined to avoid disconfirmation of the expectation. Thus if one expects to fail, the task may be perceived as too difficult, with an adverse effect on performance. Clearly, no explanation fits all cases.

Reactance

Brehm and others presented a systematic analysis of what occurs when the environment imposes restrictions on a person's freedom to act. Such conditions, Brehm argued, induce arousal, which makes a person act to prevent a further loss of freedom and to reestablish the diminished or threatened freedom. This counterforce he calls "reactance." Experiments have confirmed predictions from this theory.

Origin–Pawn Orientations

De Charms extended Heider's causality proposition. An Origin feels that environmental effects are produced by oneself and thus has a sense of competence and control. A Pawn perceives that events are caused independently of one's actions and thus feels powerless or ineffectual.

Locus of Control

Rotter devised a test for a related attitude. It is conceptualized as general beliefs concerning the relationship between one's own actions and events. *Internal control* is the belief that an event is contingent on one's own characteristics or acts. *External control* is the perception that one's behavior is controlled by forces beyond (or mostly beyond) one's control, such as fate or luck. This distinction has been made by other social scientists as well, such as Fromm and Riesman.

The Internal–External Control Scale gets at one aspect of the expectancy component. The subject is asked to choose between pairs of statements, and the score is the number of "external control" alternatives chosen (thus a low score reflects internal control). For example, in one item there is a choice between making plans confidently and reluctance to do so for fear that bad luck may foil them.

This scale has prompted a great deal of research as well as the development of new measures. Several investigators have employed factor analysis to clarify the components of the scale. In particular one needs to distinguish, as aspects of the external locus, between control by powerful others and control by chance, and between defensive and nondefensive externals. Nondefensive externals assume more personal responsibility for their actions than do defensive externals.

Research shows that internals tend to perceive themselves as capable of controlling events, whereas externals tend to attribute outcomes to luck, chance, or other forces that control them. In general, internals are more confident than externals.

Learned Helplessness

Seligman developed the notion of learned helplessness, which may ensue when one experiences outcomes that occur independently of one's activity (i.e., are uncontrollable). Hiroto and Seligman exposed subjects to an aversive noise or to a concept task. Some of them could "escape" the noise by pressing a button that terminated it. For some subjects the concept problems were unsolvable, whereas for others they were solvable. Control subjects merely listened to the noise or inspected the problems. Next, the subjects either experienced the same conditions again (albeit with instructions that they could do something to escape) or received anagrams to solve the problem. The subjects who received "helplessness training" (inescapable noise or unsolvable problems) displayed learned helplessness in that they were impaired in learning how to escape the noise or solve the anagrams (depending on which sequence they encountered).

Clearly, the attitude of the person ought to influence how a task is treated. Hiroto utilized a test derived from the Rotter scale in an experiment on learned helplessness. One set of instructions emphasized skill; the other emphasized chance. The "no escape" pretreatment produced helplessness effects. But externals were adversely affected regardless of pretreatment or instructions; in fact, internals performed very much like the control subjects. In the helplessness training pretreatment, internals tried more often to escape than did externals. Zuroff has also shown that the effects of helplessness training are to be understood as a function of the subject's expectancies, whether sets or attitudes. In addition, as Koller and Kaplan, and Gregory and colleagues show, it is the lack of explicit cues that adversely affects the performance of externals, in keeping with their greater influence by environmental conditions.

Locus of Control and Reactance

The effects of extrinsically imposed conditions clearly vary as a function of personality characteristics. The interaction between internal–external control and the induction of reactance appears in a study by Cherulnik and Citrin. Subjects rated four attractive posters and were promised a choice of one of them as a reward. However, in a second session, when new ratings were obtained, the poster rated as third highest (identified separately for each subject) was not available. Some students were given *impersonal* instructions (that the shipment of posters inadvertently failed to include that poster); others were given *personal* instructions (that the experimenters had excluded one because evidence indicated that it would not be "meaningful for that student"). A control group merely made the two ratings. When freedom was limited, internals rated the eliminated option much more attractive under *personal* conditions, whereas the externals displayed this effect under *impersonal* conditions. Although restrictions on freedom may have general effects, they are contingent on relevant personality variables.

Perceptions of Causality

Research on attribution processes stemming from conceptualizing by Heider, and on expectancies associated with achievement motivation, converge on the locus of control variable. Theories of achievement motivation and internal–external control share some common features.

Accordingly, Weiner and associates have presented a systematic picture of how internals and externals perceive their performance. Internals tend to attribute their success or failure to their own characteristics—ability and effort—whereas externals attribute their outcomes to factors outside themselves—difficulty or luck. Several studies support this distinction.

Persons high in achievement are especially likely to attribute success to ability and effort, which increases feelings of accomplishment. When failure occurs, the outcome is attributed to lack of effort, which, as an unstable condition, can be increased. These persons prefer tasks of intermediate difficulty in which difficulty can be countered by increased effort to enhance the likelihood of success. They act vigorously because they believe that effort leads to success, and tasks of intermediate difficulty are most likely to benefit from effort.

In contrast, persons low in achievement avoid achievement-related activities because they attribute success to external factors, and effort is not considered to affect the outcome significantly. They give up when failure threatens because they believe that it results from a lack of ability (a stable and uncontrollable factor). These persons prefer easy or difficult tasks, which minimize self-evaluation.

W. E. Vinacke

INSTINCT

The concept of instinct is a very old one, going back to antiquity and the writings of philosophers who were interested in the natural behavior and psychology of animals, including humans. When an act, perception, motive, or goal is said to be instinctive, that means the observer views it as being unlearned and caused by the organism's hereditary make-up. Instincts are often adaptive, in the sense that they aid in the survival of the individual and the species (courting, mating, nestbuilding, and rearing of young in birds, for example). In the early part of the twentieth century, as psychology was struggling to become a recognized science, so many different instincts were attributed to humans that the concept was thought to be unwieldy, and so lost favor in some quarters. Another, more important criticism of the concept of instinct was its antianalytic flavor. If a behavior or perception was labeled instinctive, there was no reason to experimentally analyze its development in the individual because it was thought to come directly from the genes (genes → species-typical behavior). As it became clearer that the genes must influence behavior through the nervous system, the developmental understanding of instinct became genes → nervous system → behavior.

Beginning in the 1920s and 1930s, the popularity of the instinct concept waned in psychology, especially as the behaviorist school of thinking became dominant and much of behavior, perception, and motivation were thought to be learned or acquired rather than innate or instinctive. In the 1920s and 1930s, a small group of zoologists called ethologists became interested in the natural behavior of animals as observed in field settings, and they brought the instinct concept back into the scientific study of animals' perceptions, motives, and actions. They invented a whole new vocabulary for dealing with instinctive behavior: *Releasers* or *sign stimuli* were behavioral or anatomical features of other members of the species that innately triggered *fixed action patterns* (FAPS) that arose from special places in the nervous system that had been put there by genes. The motivational part was seen in the observation that, if the FAPs were not released by encountering the appropriate releaser, they would "go off in a vacuum" (i.e., without being triggered by a sign stimulus). Since the ethologists were zoologists who were trained in the importance of natural selection in the evolution of species, they focused on the reproductive behavior of species, especially birds. They found that each species had their own special set of releasers and innate motor movements (FAPs), and the more closely related the species, the greater the similarity in their releasers and FAPs. In the hands of ethologists, the classical features of instinct were defined as

1. species-typical or species-specific behaviors;
2. not dependent on known forms of learning;
3. adaptive (having survival value);
4. responsive to a narrow range of sensory stimulation (sign stimuli or releasers) provided by other members of the species and not requiring prior exposure to such stimulation;
5. largely or totally unmodifiable by the organism's experience;
6. attributable to hereditary influences operating directly on the nervous system to prepare the animal to behave in an adaptive fashion.

This was an imposing and precise list of defining features of instinct that motivated young, experimentally oriented animal behaviorists (both zoologists and psychologists) to analyze instinctive behavior under laboratory conditions. What was learned is that behavior, perception, and motivation, thought to be instinctive in the strict sense defined above, were more influenced by an animal's prior experience than previously believed to be the case. For example, in the instance of gulls rearing their baby chicks, the chicks come to peck (FAP) at a spot (releaser) on the lower mandible of the parent and the parent regurgitates predigested food that the young eat. In studies by Jack Hailman, it was found that the baby chicks are at first not accurate in their pecking response and only become so during a fairly protracted period of "practice."

In studying the motor patterns involved in courtship displays in various species, George Barlow and others observed significant individual variability in the precision of the motor patterns within every species studied (thus, the *fixed* action pattern became the *modal* action pattern). Moreover, in studying the instinctive perceptual response of newly hatched ducklings to the maternal assembly call of their own species, Gilbert Gottlieb found that in order for the ducklings' response to be species-specific, they had to have heard their own embryonic vocalizations. In the experimental cases in which the embryos were prevented from hearing their own vocalizations, the specificity of the posthatching response to the species maternal call was lost; they were as likely to respond to the maternal call of another species as they were to their own.

In a similar vein, David B. Miller found that the specificity of newly hatched ducklings' freezing response to the maternal alarm call was lost in the absence of their usual embryonic and postnatal experiences. In another remarkable case of a nonobvious prior experience preparing the developing animal to respond adaptively, Joshua Wallman found that preventing newly hatched chicks from seeing their own toes move by covering their feet with white taffeta cloths resulted in the chicks being nonresponsive to mealworms, their favorite food under usual conditions. The list of examples goes on. What do these findings mean? How have they changed our understanding of instinct?

While there can be no doubt that animals exhibit species-typical and species-specific behavior that is adaptive and is often not dependent on known forms of learning such as associative learning or conditioning, that does not mean that the animals' prior experiences, more broadly considered, are irrelevant. The classic concept of instinct was based on the notion that the epigenesis (development) of behavior, perception, and motivation is *predetermined;* that is, that genes give rise to structures that function in a unilinear manner (genetic activity → structure → function). However, as experiments on behavior, the nervous system, and genetic activity have shown, epigenesis is *probabilistic* rather than predetermined, in that the relation among genetic activity, structure, and function is bidirectional rather than unidirectional (genetic activity ⇆ structure ⇆ function ⇆ environment). As a result, the present definition of instinctive behavior includes the prior experiences of the individual, broadly construed. Instinct is an outcome of the probabilistic epigenesis of behavior, perception, and motivation, based on the bidirectional coactions among the environment, function, structure, and genetic activity: Instinct is not a special class of behavior in terms of its determinants.

Gilbert Gottlieb
University of North Carolina, Chapel Hill

INSTRUMENTAL CONDITIONING

Instrumental conditioning represents a form of behavioral change that depends on the temporal relationship (contingency) between a response and an environmental outcome. The response might correspond to pressing a bar, lifting a leg, turning a wheel, or navigating a maze. In the laboratory, the outcome is typically a biologically relevant event, such as food, water, or a frightening shock. Outside the laboratory, behavior can be modified by a variety of events including social praise, access to a sexual partner, or a stimulus that has acquired value (e.g., money). Outcomes capable of modifying an organism's behavior are sometimes called *reinforcers* and the process through which they influence behavior is known as *reinforcement.* Examples of an instrumental contingency include praising a child for waiting quietly or providing a food pellet to a rat whenever it presses a bar. According to Thorndike's law of effect, these contingencies should bring about a lasting change in behavior, leading the child to stand quietly and increasing the frequency with which the rat presses the bar.

It is clear that the timely application of a reinforcer can bring about a dramatic change in behavior. Anyone who has trained a pet using food as a reward, or attempted to influence a roommate's behavior through social reinforcement, has employed a form of instrumental conditioning. It is important to remember, however, that instituting a response-outcome relationship can sometimes affect performance in the absence of instrumental learning. For example, stimuli that regularly predict an aversive event can be associated with the event through a form of Pavlovian (classical) conditioning. This learning can endow the stimuli with the capacity to produce a conditioned response that affects our target behavior. The problem is that this Pavlovian conditioning can lead us to mistakenly conclude that instrumental (response-outcome) learning has occurred, when in fact the behavioral modification actually reflects the acquisition of a stimulus-outcome relation. Similarly, simple exposure to an outcome alone can cause a response to grow stronger (sensitization) or weaker (habituation) in the absence of an instrumental relation. Demonstrating that instrumental learning is at work requires that we eliminate these alternatives.

Outlining some formal criteria can help us determine whether a behavioral change reflects instrumental conditioning. At a minimum, the following conditions must be met: (1) the behavioral modification depends on a form of neural plasticity; (2) the modification depends on the organism's experiential history; (3) the modification outlasts (extends beyond) the environmental contingencies used to induce it; and (4) imposing a temporal relationship between the response and the outcome alters the response.

The first three criteria specify essential conditions for learning. Because performing the response can alter its vigor through a peripheral modification (e.g., muscular exercise or fatigue), it is important to show that the behavioral change is neurally mediated (criterion 1). Changes attributable to neural development or injury do not count as learning (criterion 2). Finally, because instituting an environmental contingency can bring about a temporary mechanical modification in the response, we must show that our training regimen has a lasting effect on behavior (criterion 3).

The fourth criterion specifies the nature of the behavioral change required for instrumental learning: that the behavioral modification depends on the response-outcome relation. Two operations are used to establish this. One involves the inclusion of a yoked control group that receives the reinforcer independent of its behavior. A second technique degrades the essential relation by imposing a temporal gap between the response and the outcome. If the response-outcome relation is essential, both procedures should undermine the response.

Some instrumental behavior is biologically constrained by the organism's evolutionary history (Timberlake & Lucas, 1989). For example, consider the flexion response elicited by an aversive stimulus applied to the base of the foot. Because this response is organized by neurons within the spinal cord, it can be elicited in the absence of feedback from the brain. This reflex can be modified by imposing a response-outcome contingency; if shock is presented only when the limb is extended, the organism quickly learns to maintain its leg in a flexed (up) position. This modification of a reflexive behavior meets the minimum criteria (1–4) for instrumental conditioning. However, learning within the spinal cord appears biologically constrained. Given the same outcome, we cannot arbitrarily train subjects to exhibit either a flexion or an extension.

More sophisticated neural systems can support a greater range of flexibility. Humans can be trained to lift or lower a hand using a variety of reinforcers (i.e., food, money, or shock). Such advanced forms of instrumental conditioning meet two additional criteria: (5) The nature of the behavioral change is not constrained (e.g., either an increase or decrease in the response can be established); (6) The nature of the reinforcer is not constrained (a variety of outcomes can be used to produce the behavioral effect).

The term *instrumental conditioning* has its roots in the reflexive tradition of E. L. Thorndike, J. Konorski, and C. L. Hull. From this perspective, instrumental learning reflects a form of elicited behavior, one that depends on the relationship established between a response and an outcome. An alternative view was suggested by B. F. Skinner, who noted that it is often difficult (or impossible) to specify the eliciting stimulus for advanced forms of instrumental behavior. He referred to this type of behavior as *operant conditioning* and argued that it is emitted, not elicited.

These historical facts continue to influence how the terms are used within the modern learning literature. Skinnerians focus on the experimental analysis of behavior and generally employ the term operant conditioning. The emphasis is on emitted behavior and rate of responding. Those that follow in the tradition of Hull assume that response-outcome relations can affect elicited responses and that associative processes underlie complex instrumental behavior.

Because both instrumental and operant conditioning depend on the response-outcome relation, they are sometimes treated as synonyms. However, in cases where the target response is elicited and/or an attempt is made to explain the behavior in terms of associative mechanisms, the term instrumental conditioning is more appropriate.

REFERENCE

Timberlake, W., & Lucas, G. A. (1989). Behavior systems and learning: From misbehavior to general principles. In S. B. Klein & R. R. Mowrer (Eds.), *Contemporary learning theories: Instrumental conditioning and the impact of biological constraints on learning* (pp. 237–275). Hillsdale, NJ: Erlbaum.

James W. Grau
Texas A & M University

See also: **Operant Conditioning; Reinforcement**

INTEGRITY GROUPS

Integrity groups (IGs) are a community mental health resource for assisting people in coping with problems of living through self-change. These self-help groups were developed by O. Hobart Mowrer. Integrity groups are based on Mowrer's view that many psychosocial disorders are a consequence of individuals breaking commitments and contracts with significant others in their lives. The indicated remedy for helping someone deal with these concerns is to involve the person in a support group of about eight other similarly engaged individuals.

The social learning approach that characterizes these groups consists of a particular constellation of structure, goals, and shared leadership; group intake in which experienced members model appropriate group behavior; behavioral guidelines and ground rules for conducting weekly meetings; a contractual agreement to practice honesty, responsibility, and involvement inside and outside the group; individual commitments for specific behavior change; an expectation that verbal intentions will be translated into actions; and a considerable amount of group support and reinforcement for behavior change. Group members are available to assist one another as needed during the intervals between the weekly 3-hour meetings. The emphasis on self-responsibility and mutual support is expressed in the IG motto: "You alone can do it, but you can't do it alone."

Anthony J. Vattano
University of Illinois, Urbana-Champaign

See also: **Peer Group Therapy**

INTERFERENCE

One of the earliest and most robust findings of experimental psychology is that two event representations in memory can compete with one another. If training on Task A precedes Task B, subsequent testing on Task B may yield impaired (i.e., proactive interference) or facilitated performance relative to control subjects who were not exposed to Task A. Conversely, subsequent testing on Task A may yield impairment (i.e., retroactive interference) or facilitation relative to control subjects who were not exposed to Task B. Such interference is commonly viewed as evidence of competition between the representations of Tasks A and B. Interference (and facilitation) has been observed across a wide variety of subjects (including human and nonhuman species) and tasks. Much of the memory research conducted over the last century has attempted to identify relevant variables (for excellent reviews, old but still relevant, see Postman & Underwood, 1973; Underwood, 1957). The following remarks apply equally to proactive and retroactive interference (and facilitation) except where otherwise noted.

Independent Variables

The most important variables in producing proactive and retroactive interference appear to be (1) the amount of training on each task; (2) the temporal interval between training on the two tasks and between training on each task and testing; and (3) the similarity of the two tasks, the last of which appears central in determining whether interference or facilitation will be observed. Not surprisingly, more extensive training on a task makes it more apt to impact performance on another task and less apt to be impacted by training on another task. The closer in time the two tasks are to one another, the more apt they are to interact, producing interference (or facilitation) on the test task. Given a fixed interval between Task A and Task B training, the retention interval can be manipulated. Unlike the effects of most other independent variables on interference, which are symmetric between the proactive and retroactive cases, lengthening the retention interval decreases retroactive interference and enhances proactive interference, presumably because a significant portion of retroactive interference depends on a recency effect, and recency effects wane with increasing retention intervals (Postman, Stark, & Fraser, 1968). Task similarity appears to be the prime determinant of whether interference or enhancement will be observed.

One of the most systematic attempts to summarize these relationships was by Osgood (1949). Although his principles were elegantly logical, research has found that only some of them are consistently supported. Let us conceptualize a task as consisting of an eliciting stimulus and an acquired response to that stimulus (e.g., in paired-associate learning, Task A eliciting stimulus = chair, response = banana; Task B eliciting stimulus = stool, response = car). Obviously, two tasks with the same eliciting stimuli and same responses are identical, reducing the Task A–Task B sequence to additional training on a single task; consequently, facilitation is anticipated and, of course, observed. Conversely, when the two eliciting stimuli are highly dissimilar and the two responses are also highly dissimilar, little interaction is expected and little is observed. The interesting cases are when the eliciting stimuli are similar and the responses are dissimilar (or incompatible) as in the above example from paired associate learning, and when the eliciting stimuli are dissimilar and the responses are similar. In the former case, interference is ordinarily observed. But in the latter case, the outcome can range from interference to facilitation, and we do not yet have a simple rule for anticipating which outcome will occur other than experience with prior similar situations.

Theoretical Mechanisms

Several different theoretical accounts have been proposed to explain interference. Available evidence suggests that no single account will suffice (which is not to suggest that all proposed mechanisms contribute equally or even at all in each case). Accounts appear to fall into one of three categories (Miller, Greco, Marlin, & Balaz, 1985; Runquist, 1975): (1) competition for a limited capacity processing system at the time of acquisition (often called "processing interference"); (2) competition between tasks for representation in long-term memory over the Task B test retention interval; and (3) competition for retrieval and response generation at the time of testing (often called "trace interference"). Processing interference appears to take place only when the two competing tasks occur close in time. With this type of interference, task similarity is relatively unimportant. (However, more interference can be expected if the two events use the same sensory modality than in different modalities because the limited processing capacity of organisms appears to be largely segregated by sensory modality.) The second mechanism assumes that the two task (or event) representations compete for a place in long-term memory rather than coexisting with one another. This mechanism would be relevant only when the two events are contrafactual (e.g., acquisition and extinction, or conditioning and counterconditioning). Many researchers deny that this second interference mechanism exists, preferring to attribute all evidence cited in support of this mechanism to trace interference. Trace interference has received the greatest amount of attention, and, not surprisingly, theorizing concerning it is most highly developed. The consistent finding concerning this third mechanism is that the greater the similarity between eliciting stimulus of the interfering task (including nominal, contextual, and temporal cues) and the test conditions, relative to the similarity between the eliciting stimulus of the target task and the test conditions, the greater the interference will be (e.g., Bouton, 1993; Tulving & Thomson, 1973).

Generally speaking, temporal variables (i.e., processing interference) appear to have their greatest impact when the intervals separating Tasks A, B, and testing are relatively short (measured in seconds, e.g., Peterson & Peterson, 1959), whereas the impact of task similarity variables (trace interference) seems to be greatest at longer intervals (Runquist, 1975). This suggests that these variables act through fundamentally different mechanisms (Miller et al., 1985). Seemingly, most interference with short intervals separating Tasks A and B reflects competition between A and B for access to a limited capacity short-term memory. In contrast, interference with longer intervals reflects competition for retrieval and for response generation. These relationships have been well known for over 30 years. Contemporary research on interference (e.g., Matute & Pineno, 1998) has given rise to a plethora of hypothesized mechanisms, but they all appear to fall within the three families of accounts described above.

Permanence

Interference effects in principle can be due either to a potentially reversible lapse in performance (an expression failure) or an irreversible absence of information (i.e., failure to acquire information or loss after acquisition). Each of the three types of mechanisms could, in principle, yield reversible or irreversible interference. But the three types of mechanisms are commonly thought to diverge sharply in terms of the interference that they produce being reversible or irreversible. The first and second types of interference are generally viewed as resulting in an irreversible absence from memory of the target task representation. In contrast, the third type of interference is usually viewed as yielding a failure to express information that is still retained in memory. Consistent with this view, interference observed with relatively long intervals between training on the two tasks often can be reversed without additional training on the target task. Spontaneous recovery from retroactive interference is one particularly clear case of this. Priming and variation in retrieval cues at test are other often successful means of obtaining recovery from interference; however, these demonstrations are less compelling evidence of a lapse (rather than an absence) of information, because they potentially tap into different representations of the target task than that which was assessed (and found wanting) originally.

An Applied Example

Interference theory is applicable to many practical situations. For example, one contemporary application of interference theory (and controversy in its explanation) is provided by demonstrations that eyewitness accounts of events are subject to retroactive interference, often originating with leading questions from attorneys. One view is that the representation of the original (target) event is irreversibly altered by the (subsequent) interfering event (in our terminology, mechanism type 2; e.g., Loftus, 1975). In contrast, an alternative view is that the representation of the original event is still present in memory but is less readily retrieved because of the interfering event (trace interference; e.g., McCloskey & Zaragoza, 1985).

REFERENCES

Bouton, M. E. (1993). Context, time, and memory retrieval in the interference paradigms of Pavlovian learning. *Psychological Bulletin, 114,* 80–99.

Loftus, E. F. (1975). Leading questions and the eyewitness report. *Cognitive Psychology, 7,* 560–572.

Matute, H., & Pineno, O. (1998). Stimulus competition in the absence of compound conditioning. *Animal Learning & Behavior, 26,* 3–14.

McCloskey, M., & Zaragoza, M. (1985). Misleading postevent information and memory for events: Arguments and evidence against memory impairment hypotheses. *Journal of Experimental Psychology: General, 114,* 3–18.

Miller, R. R., Greco, C., Marlin, N. A., & Balaz, M. A. (1985). Retroactive interference in rats: Independent effects of time and similarity of the interfering event with respect to acquisition. *Quarterly Journal of Experimental Psychology, 37B,* 81–100.

Osgood, C. E. (1949). The similarity paradox in human learning: A resolution. *Psychological Review, 56,* 132–143.

Peterson, L., & Peterson, M. J. (1959). Short-term retention of individual verbal items. *Journal of Experimental Psychology, 58,* 193–198.

Postman, L., Stark, K., & Fraser, J. (1968). Temporal changes in interference. *Journal of Verbal Learning and Verbal Behavior, 7,* 672–694.

Postman, L., & Underwood, B. J. (1973). Critical issues in interference theory. *Memory & Cognition, 1,* 19–40.

Runquist, W. N. (1975). Interference among memory traces. *Memory & Cognition, 3,* 143–159.

Tulving, E., & Thomson, D. M. (1973). Encoding specificity and retrieval processes in episodic memory. *Psychological Review, 80,* 352–373.

Underwood, B. J. (1957). Interference and forgetting. *Psychological Review, 64,* 49–60.

Ralph R. Miller
State University of New York, Binghamton

INTERNATIONAL PSYCHOLOGY

Psychology has been an international enterprise since its beginning as a modern science over a century ago. When most psychologists use the term "international psychology," they are referring to various forms of organized psychology at the international level, including societies, congresses, journals, and other kinds of scientific and professional exchanges. A review by Adair, Coehlo, and Luna (2002) of international databases in psychology revealed a significant presence of organized psychology in 47 countries and a presence of psychology as a scientific discipline in 22 additional countries. Sometimes the term also designates the social psychology of international relations, or the comparative study of psychological processes across different nations and cultures, as in cross-cultural psychology. These last two meanings of international psychology are dealt with only briefly here.

Social Psychology of International Relations

The systematic use of psychological concepts and methods for the development of theory, research, and policy studies in international relations is a relatively new area of specialization within social psychology. Following World War II, various studies of national stereotypes, attitudes toward war and peace, nationalism, and international affairs made significant contributions to an improved understanding of international relations. Generally interdisciplinary in character, these social–psychological approaches deal with the problems of interaction among nations, often with a goal of reducing tension and promoting international cooperation. Among the kinds of research that deal specifically with the international behavior of individuals are studies of national stereotypes or images, attitudes toward international affairs, national ideology and how it is communicated, and the effects of cross-national contacts upon individual or group behavior. The investigation of intergroup conflict and its resolution has been broadened to include both simulated and naturalistic studies of international negotiation. These and related aspects of psychology applied to international relations are discussed in detail by Herbert Kelman (1965) in his book, *International Behavior: A Social Psychological Analysis.*

International Study of Psychological Processes

Cross-cultural psychology has expanded greatly in the past quarter century. Cross-cultural, comparative approaches are particularly appealing for the study of sociocultural factors in any aspect of human development. The growing realization of parochial limitations in Western psychology, particularly within the United States, has stimulated the development of a new kind of comparative psychology, a comparative psychology of human behavior in markedly different natural settings, rather than a comparative psychology dealing with different animal species. International studies of personality development, cognitive development, and perceptual processes have become commonplace, in spite of the difficult methodological problems encountered in such research.

The most common type of cross-national or cross-cultural study involves only two cultures. Comparisons between two nations are generally very difficult to interpret, because many cultural differences are operating that might provide alternate explanations of the findings, and that cannot be ruled out. The inclusion of subcultural variation and social factors within each nation enhances the likelihood that interpretable results can be obtained. An example of such an international study comparing children studied over a 6-year period in Mexico and the United States is given by Wayne Holtzman, Rogelio Diaz-Guerrero, and Jon Swartz in *Personality Development in Two Cultures.* The intensive study of over 800 children in an overlapping longitudinal design produced clear and uniform differences across the two cultures for many psychological dimensions and test scores, as well as a number of interactions between culture and age, sex, and social class. Six major hypotheses concerning personality differences between Mexicans and Americans were proposed by the authors.

International psychology is only one aspect of cross-cultural psychology, the latter encompassing a much wider range of comparative studies. The search for cultural variation and its consequences for psychological functioning may be limited to a study of cultures within one large multicultural nation, rather than international differences in culture. The first *Handbook of Cross-Cultural Psychology* was published in 1980–1981 in six volumes. Edited by Harry Triandis and William Lambert, the *Handbook* provides a comprehensive review of cross-cultural psychology, the underlying theoretical and systematic approaches, the methodological issues and techniques, and the basic processes that have been studied comparatively, as well as special reviews of developmental psychology, social psychology, and psychopathology as studied from cross-cultural or international perspectives.

Organized Psychology at the International Level

The first International Congress of Psychology was held in 1889, less than 10 years after the founding of the first laboratory of experimental psychology. The rapid exchange of new ideas and methods of research across the different countries of Europe and the Americas produced a truly international psychology with a predominantly Western orientation. Most of the early leading academicians received much of their training in Germany or Great Britain. A long and distinguished series of international congresses served psychology well, but there was clearly a need for an international organization to provide continuity between congresses held only every 3 or 4 years.

At the 13th International Congress of Psychology held in Stockholm in July 1951, the International Union of Psychological Science (IUPsyS) was formally established. The IUPsyS is the only international organization that has as its members national psychological societies rather than individuals. The 11 psychological societies that served as the charter members in 1951 were from Belgium, France, Germany, Great Britain, Italy, Japan, the Netherlands, Norway, Sweden, Switzerland, and the United States. By 2002 the Union had grown to 68 national societies and 12 affiliated international organizations, representing most of the psychologists in every country with an appreciable presence of psychology as both a scientific discipline and an applied profession. *History of the International Union of Psychological Science (IUPsyS)* provides a detailed account of the international nature of organized psychology from its inception in 1889 to 2000 (Rosenzweig, Holtzman, Sabourin, & Belanger, 2000).

Organizing an international congress every 4 years is the most important activity of the Union. The 27th International Congress of Psychology, held in Stockholm, Sweden, attracted nearly 6,000 psychologists and guests who participated in over 680 symposia, workshops, and related scientific sessions. The 28th Congress will be held in Beijing, China on August 8–13, 2004.

The major aims and objectives of the Union are to promote the exchange of ideas and scientific information among psychologists of different countries, to foster international exchange of scholars and students, to collaborate with other international and national organizations in promoting psychology as a science and profession, and to encourage international projects that will further the development of psychology. An example of such projects is the organization of advanced research training seminars for young psychologists held in proximity to the world congresses.

One of the most important projects of the Union in the past was the compilation and publication of the *International Directory of Psychologists.* The fourth edition of the *Directory,* edited by Kurt Pawlik, lists over 32,000 psychologists from 48 different countries, excluding the United States, where the American Psychological Association and the American Psychological Society already publish readily available directories of their members. In the past 15 years the number of psychologists throughout the world has increased so rapidly that a single directory of individuals is no longer possible, even excluding the several hundred thousand psychologists in the United States. Together with Psychology Press, Ltd., the Union electronically publishes specialized international directories of research institutions and resources on compact computer disks, the first of which is *Psychology: IUPsyS Global Resource* (Overmeier & Overmeier, 2002).

In 1975, the three-volume *Trilingual Psychological Dictionary,* edited by Hubert C. J. Duijker and Maria J. van Rijswijk, provided a standard technical vocabulary for translating psychological terms from English, French, or German into either of the other two languages. Since then, the publication of similar bilingual dictionaries for translation between English and another language have greatly expedited standardized translation of psychological works. An example is the *Concise Encyclopedia of Psychology,* edited by Q. C. Jing, which defines in Chinese the many technical terms in psychological science.

Another kind of publication promoting international psychology provides English summaries of articles and books published originally in a different language. The *German Journal of Psychology, French-Language Psychology,* and *Spanish-Language Psychology* have set the standard for the exchange of scientific information across languages. Since nearly 90% of the articles and books in psychology are published originally in English, and since most psychologists can read English, *Psychological Abstracts* and its electronic version, *Psyc-SCAN,* provide readily available, English-language abstracts of articles in the leading psychological journals throughout the world.

Most international organizations in psychology have individuals rather than societies as members. The oldest is the International Association of Applied Psychology, founded in 1920 by Edouard Claparede. As in the case of IUPsyS, the International Association of Applied Psychology sponsors a world congress every 4 years. At the 24th International Congress of Applied Psychology, held in San Francisco in August 1998, applied psychologists from throughout the world participated in symposia, workshops, general sessions, and individual paper presentations devoted to such fields as industrial, clinical, counseling, and school psychology, applied social or experimental psychology, and educational psychology, usually from an international or cross-cultural perspective. Between congresses, the Association sponsors international projects and exchanges such as the International Test Commission. A number of special interest divisions within the Association deal with more narrowly defined international issues in applied psychology.

Smaller international organizations also exist to meet the specialized international interests of psychologists. Illustrative of such organizations are the International Council of Psychologists, the International Association for Cross-Cultural Psychology, the Interamerican Society of Psychology, the European Association of Experimental Social Psychologists, the European Association of Personality Psychology, the European Association of Work and Organizational Psychology, the European Federation of Professional Psychologists, the International Association of French-speaking Psychologists, the International Neuropsychology Society, the International Society of Comparative Psychology, and the International School Psychology Association.

The above associations are comprised almost entirely of psychologists. Some interdisciplinary associations also have large numbers of psychologists as members. Leading examples of such associations are the International Brain Research Organization and the International Society for the Study of Behavioral Development.

The development and status of psychology in different countries and regions of the world vary considerably. As one would expect, the most highly developed scientific psychology exists in North America, Europe, and Japan. Rapid growth in the post-World War II period has also occurred in Australia, Brazil, and Mexico, with several other countries of Latin America and Asia close behind. Surveys of trends in the development and status of psychology throughout the world, as reviewed by Mark Rosenzweig (1992), editor of *International Psychological Science,* suggest that there are well over a half million recognized psychologists throughout the world. The most rapid growth has occurred among practitioners rather than research scientists. The greatest concentration exists in the United States and Canada, followed closely by Western Europe. If one could count all the individuals engaged in some kind of psychological research or practice, the actual number would be far greater. International comparisons are complicated by the fact that some countries may require a doctoral degree for full membership in their national psychological societies and for most professional positions, while other countries may require only a professional certificate after 5 years of university work.

Psychology is a discipline cultivated mainly in the industrialized countries, although the developing countries are rapidly catching up. While the scientific principles of psychology are valid regardless of cultural boundaries and politics, the scientific status of psychology and its social relevance vary greatly throughout the world.

REFERENCES

Adair, J. G., Coehlo, A. E. L., & Luna, J. R. (2002). How international is psychology? *International Journal of Psychology, 37,* 160–170.

Duijker, H. C. J., & van Rijswijk, M. J. (1975). *Trilingual psychological dictionary, Vol. 1: English-French-German. Vol. 2: Francais-Allemand-Anglais. Vol. 3: Deutsch-Englisch-Franzosisch.* Bern, Stuttgart, Vienna: Huber.

Holtzman, W. H., Diaz-Guerrero, R., & Swartz, J. (1975). *Personality development in two cultures.* Austin: University of Texas Press.

Jing, Q. C. (Ed.). (1991). *Concise encyclopedia of psychology* (In Chinese with English headings). Beijing: Chinese Academy of Science (for IUPsyS).

Kelman, H. C. (1965). *International behavior: A social psychological analysis.* New York: Holt.

Overmeier, J. B., & Overmeier, B. (2002). *Psychology: IUPsyS GLOBAL RESOURCE* CD-ROM. *International Journal of Psychology,* Psychology Press Ltd., Taylor & Francis, East Sussex, BN3 2FA, UK.

Pawlik, K. (Ed.). (1985). *International directory of psychologists* (4th ed.). Amsterdam: North Holland.

Rosenzweig, M. R. (Ed.). (1992). *International psychological science.* Washington, DC: American Psychological Association (for IUPsyS).

Rosenzweig, M. R., Holtzman, W. H., Sabourin, M., & Belanger, D. (2000). *History of the International Union of Psychological Science (IUPsyS).* Philadelphia: Psychology Press (Taylor & Francis Group).

Triandis, H. C., & Lambert, W. W. (Eds.). (1980–1981). *Handbook of cross-cultural psychology* (6 Vols.). Boston: Allyn & Bacon.

Wayne H. Holtzman
University of Texas

INTERPERSONAL COMMUNICATION

Attempts at defining interpersonal communication date back to the Golden Age of Greece. Plato and Aristotle discussed communication in terms of rhetoric. However, several millennia later there is still no generally agreed upon scientific definition of communication. According to Webster's *New World Dictionary* (1966), "to communicate" is defined as "to impart, pass along, transmit," and "communication" is defined as "giving and receiving of information, signals or messages by talk, gestures, writing, etc." These definitions are helpful as orientations to this area of study, but lack sufficient detail or specificity for scientific purposes.

The notion of transmission of information has been applied to genetic materials as well as nonorganismic events. An individual might transfer information from one cognitive context to another in a form of intraindividual communication. Furthermore, categories representing intergroup, interorganizational, international, and (in science fiction) intergalactic communication could be developed. Interpersonal communication refers to the transfer of information by a source to a specific target. These communications typically occur in face-to-face interactions, although they may also occur by mail, telephone, television, the Internet, or other electronic means. Lasswell (1948) captured in one sentence much of the subject matter of human communication: "Who says what in what channel to whom with what effect?"

Electrical engineering principles were applied by Shannon and Weaver in 1949 to human communication. Figure 1 shows their model of the communication process. The mind of the communicator may be considered the source of the communication. Presumably, messages originate in the brain and are encoded for transmission to other people. The source must have a means of transmitting information, such as speech, gestures, or writing. The message is encoded and sent as a signal to a receiver, who must decode the message. Thus, the destination of a message is the mind of a target or receiver person.

This information model is helpful in examining some of the more important questions regarding interpersonal communication. It should be noted that the source may unintentionally communicate to others, as when nonverbal cues betray a liar. Of course, the source may not even be aware of a communication. For example, a person may communicate liking for another by maintaining a rather close physical proximity, but may be unaware of doing so.

Intentional communication may be examined in terms of the degree to which the interpretations of the source are accurately received by the target. For some communication theorists it is the sharing of interpretations and not just the exchange of information that lies at the heart of the communication process. Any interference with accurate transfer of information is referred to as *noise* in the system. Noise may be due to ambiguous encoding, problems with channels through which signals are transmitted, or faulty decoding by the target. If, for example, the source transmitted a message in German and the target understood only English, noise would be attributable to the target's inability to decode the communication. If two persons were talking over the telephone but could not hear each other because of static over the lines, noise would be located in the channels being used. One should not construe disagreement between two persons as necessarily caused by noise. A target may be able to take the viewpoint of the source and fully understand the interpretation communicated, but nevertheless disagree with it. Often persons believe they have not been understood, when in reality the target persons disagree with them.

There has often been confusion even among scientists in distinguishing between language and communication. To make the distinction, one must understand the differences between signs, signals, and symbols. Signs are environmental stimuli which the organism has associated with

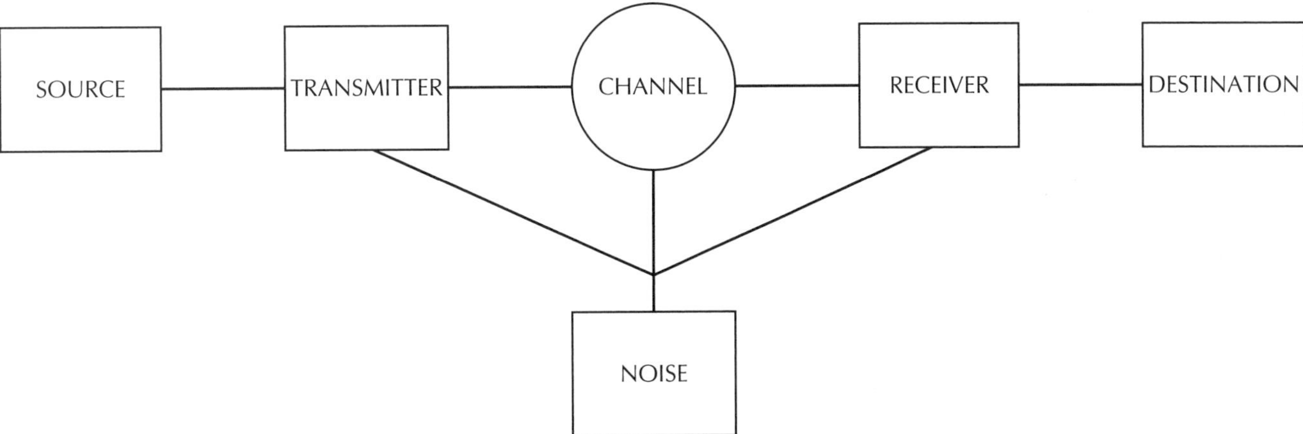

Figure 1. A schematic of a communications system (after Shannon & Weaver, 1949).

other events. For example, a hunter may associate certain prints in the dirt as a sign that a deer has recently passed nearby. Signs are inflexibly and directly related to their associated events.

Signals are signs produced by living organisms. Most animals can use signals in their interaction with other animals. Thus, birds may emit love calls, insects may transmit odors, and monkeys may manifest threat gestures. Research by Gardner and Gardner (1969) has shown that chimpanzees can be taught to use complex signals often taught to deaf and/or mute humans. However, even the most intense training results in fewer than 400 signals learned by these higher primates. Nevertheless, the ability of these animals to communicate is clearly greater than previously thought possible.

A symbol, like a signal, has a referent. However, symbols do not necessarily refer to physical reality and may not have space–time relationships as their referents. Symbols derive their meaning from a community of users and not from a connection with a referent. The use of symbols allows the development of various abstract areas of knowledge such as history, literature, religion, art, and science. Furthermore, it provides the basis for the individual's construction of social reality, including a self. The available evidence (Gardner & Gardner, 1969) indicates that only humans use symbols. Chimpanzees appear to be confined to the existential moment and cannot escape their time–space coordinates. Although they can remember and signal what they did an hour ago, they cannot report what they did yesterday or reveal plans about the future. Thus, it appears that the symbol represents an important discontinuity in phylogenetic development between humans and all other forms of life.

Language is a means of information processing and is used to store, manipulate, create, and transmit information. No analysis of interpersonal communication among humans would be complete without a consideration of the symbolic aspects of language. Two important properties of symbols are that they may refer to classes of things, and they may have multiple meanings. Thus, errors in communication are both frequent and inevitable; that is, noise tends to be an inevitable feature of interpersonal communication.

Situations and relationships with others provide contexts within which persons can share interpretations of communication and hence reduce noise. The individual's definition of the social situation typically involves certain expectations about the behavior of others, the rules that define and regulate interactions, and guides to conduct. These expectations provide a frame of reference within which the person encodes and decodes information. For example, "Did you buy the pot?" means something different when communicated on a street corner between teenagers than when transmitted from a mother to a daughter.

Communication has a number of functions. It allows the coordination of behaviors of individuals in a group. Large corporations and government bureaucracies require a great deal of communication among employees at all levels in order to function at all. Interpersonal communication also allows for instruction, in which one individual helps another to learn skills or develop new frames of reference. Perhaps most important of all, communication functions as a means to influence others. Messages used for purposes of power and influence may be considered actions with as much impact as skeletal behaviors. Thus, communicative actions are sometimes referred to as speech acts.

Speech acts that refer to rewards and punishments take the form of threats or promises which may be contingent or noncontingent in form. A contingent threat specifies that a target must comply with some demand of the source or else suffer some cost to be inflicted by the threatener. A noncontingent threat announces the source's intention to impose some cost on the target without any demand for compliance being made. A contingent promise offers a reward, if the target complies with a request by the source. A noncontingent promise simply announces the source's intention to reward the target. Promises, unlike threats, carry a moral obligation of fulfillment by the source.

There are several speech acts that may be classified as means of information control. Persuasion represents a source's attempt to influence a target's decisions. Among the types of persuasive communication are warnings, mendations, and activation of commitments. Warnings convey expectations of future negative events not controlled by the source, while mendations are predictions of positive events not controlled by the source. Activation of commitments consists of exhortations appealing to the normative values of the target in order to induce some related behavior by the target.

Another classification of speech acts refers to their function as self-presentational. Actors project certain identities to others and engage in various tactics to foster desired identities in the eyes of others. Among the more prominent speech acts devoted to impression management are accounts, entitlements, and enhancements. When a person does something that seems strange, untoward, or abnormal to others, an explanation is usually offered or demanded. The lack of an explanation leaves an unfavorable impression and may lead observers to blame and perhaps punish the actor. Accounts are explanations for untoward behavior and consist of excuses and justifications. Excuses are explanations that deny responsibility for negative effects of behavior. Excuses may deny intention to produce the effects, or may deny that the source had volitional control over the actions in question. Denials of intention refer to lack of foreknowledge, mistake, inadvertence, and accident. Denials of volition may refer to drugs, alcohol, physical disability, or mental illness (insanity). Justifications are explanations of actions that admit responsibility but offer legitimate reasons for them. For example, a person may justify spanking children as a way to teach them not to run out into the street. Justifications may appeal to authority, ideology, norms of justice, self-defense, or self-actualization.

Entitlements are speech acts in which the source attempts to take responsibility for positive events. Enhancements are attempts to embellish the value of the positive consequences. People want credit for positive consequences because they gain approbation and rewards for such actions. The more positive the consequences, the greater the credit; hence, actors are motivated to use enhancement tactics.

Gestures, visual contact, body orientation, and the use of interpersonal space may substitute for verbal communication or may serve as a context within which to interpret verbal communication. In many instances, nonverbal responses act as signals and do not convey symbolic forms of information. For example, eye contact may communicate hostility or love, or indicate that the source is acting deceitfully.

REFERENCES

Gardner, R. A., & Gardner, B. T. (1969). Teaching sign language to a chimpanzee. *Science, 165,* 664–672.

Lasswell, H. D. (1946). Describing the contents of communications. In B. L. Smith, H. D. Lasswell, & R. D. Casey (Eds.), *Propaganda, communication, and public opinion.* Princeton, NJ: Princeton University Press.

Shannon, C., & Weaver, W. (1949). *The mathematical theory of communication.* Urbana: University of Illinois Press.

James T. Tedeschi
State University of New York, Albany

See also: **Communication Skills Training; Interpersonal Perception**

INTERPERSONAL PERCEPTION

The impressions we form of other people serve as important bases for interpersonal interactions. Person perception is a complex topic and clearly different from space perception. The latter is concerned with how perceptions of physical reality are mediated and tends to focus on biochemistry, biophysics, and/or psychophysics; the researcher attempts to relate cognitive factors to physical ones through the pathways provided by the sensory apparatus of the organism. In person perception the observer is concerned with the interior psychological processes of stimulus persons: what are they feeling, what plans do they have for future action, what effects do they intend to produce in the environment, and what causes them to act the way they do? These questions have little to do with sensory mechanisms, but instead are answered by inferences or attributions made by the observer. In a way, person perception is a misnomer which perhaps would be better expressed as "person inferences." Much of the topic is currently referred to as attribution theory, or more generally as social cognition.

In his seminal work, *The Psychology of Interpersonal Relations,* Fritz Heider (1958) noted that there are three differences between the perceptions of objects and persons. First, persons are assumed to experience an interior life and objects are not. Each person experiences thoughts and emotions, and assumes that others do also. Second, objects are not perceived as causes of their own actions, whereas persons are often viewed as first causes. The concept of responsibility is inextricably interwoven with the notion that one acts for one's own interior reasons, rather than in response to the inexorable forces of the environment. Third, persons can deliberately manipulate and exploit the perceiver, while inanimate objects cannot. One purpose of person perception is to allow the observer to predict the probable actions of the stimulus person, so as to anticipate in planning his or her own actions.

The study of person perception is essentially an attempt

to reconstruct the way the average person processes information about other people and the self. The observer is interested in answering the question of why the stimulus person acted as he or she did. Thus, the average person acts as a naive psychologist in seeking explanations for behavior. According to Heider (1958), causes for behavior are attributed to either the environment or the person. Environmental forces may be perceived to be so strong as to move actors around as if they were pawns on a chessboard. On the other hand, the person may be seen as the origin of action, even acting against strong environmental currents. When the action can be attributed to environmental causes, the actor is not held responsible for the positive or negative effects of his or her behavior, but when factors inside the actor are perceived as the origins, the actor is held accountable for the effects.

Much of the work done in the area of attributions is concerned with the rules that observers use in attributing cause to the environment or the person. For example, suppose an automobile swerves toward a sidewalk and runs over and kills a pedestrian. Is the death (an effect) attributable to environmental factors, such as a mechanical failure, or a reaction to another car that sideswiped the automobile and so caused the death? Or is the death attributable to deliberate intention to commit murder, or perhaps to the inebriated condition of the driver? Which of many potential causes actually produced the effect will determine how others react to the driver.

The tendency of observers is to accept the first sufficient cause as the reason for behavior. The impact of any particular cause in producing an effect is discounted, however, if other plausible causes are present. This discounting principle may lead to attributions to both environmental and person causes of behavior. Furthermore, the more effects the observer believes are associated with the actor's behavior, the more plausible causes there can be. Harold H. Kelley (1973), who proposed the discounting principle, also suggested an augmentation principle: the more costs the actor risks in order to act as he or she does, the more likely the observer is to attribute the behavior to person causes. Thus, the more embarrassment, pain, criticism, penalty, or punishment the actor suffers, the more likely an observer will attribute the behavior to something about the person. On the other hand, when the actor does what most other people would do in the same situation, observers would not believe they had learned anything much about this particular actor. The rule of thumb is that the more the actor's behavior deviates from what the observer believes most people would do, the more likely the action is associated with something peculiar about this actor. Of course, different observers may have different expectations about the so-called average or typical person, and hence may apply the augmentation principle somewhat differently.

An observer may observe an actor only once or may have multiple opportunities to witness behavior. Most attributional rules can be categorized as based on either a single observation or on multiple observations. Among the former are the following:

1. *Out-of-role behavior.* People are often rewarded for playing certain roles and meeting the expectations of others. For this reason, people tend to conform to role demands and expectations. When a person violates the norms governing a role, the out-of-role behavior is attributed to the person, who is apparently acting against environmental constraints. Out-of-role behavior can be construed as derivative from the augmentation principle. The person who is out of role has given up customary rewards and is apparently willing to accept negative reactions from others. The action must stem, therefore, from some inner personal factors.
2. *Noncommon effects.* An observer may mentally reconstruct the decision making of the actor in order to understand the choices made. Each choice alternative would presumably bring about desired effects for the decision maker. It may be assumed that the chosen alternative is preferred because it maximizes some value for the actor, at least as compared to the other alternatives. That is, some effect that is noncommon to the decision alternatives is the basis for the decision that is made, and that effect reveals something about the decision maker.
3. *Hedonic relevance.* When the actions of another person have some positive or negative impact on the observer, the latter has a stronger tendency to attribute the behavior to personal causes. That is, the observer is more apt to make environmental attributions when the actor's behavior affects other people than when it affects the observer.
4. *Personalism.* When the observer experiences positive or negative effects from the actor's behavior, consideration will be given to whether those effects were specifically aimed at the observer. When the observer believes the behavior was directed at him or her (personally), the observer more confidently makes a person attribution.

Kelley (1973) has provided a model of the rules used by naive observers in making attributions after multiple observations of an actor. If the observer does not have a ready causal schema within which particular actions are analyzed, causes attributed, and responsibility assigned, he or she will rationally process the data available, much as a scientist would. Suppose, for example, that someone tells you they liked a particular movie. Is this reaction to the movie due to something about the person, or is it because the movie is really good (i.e., an environmental cause)? To answer this question, the observer can assemble all the information he or she has about the movie reviewer. According to Kelley (1973), the following principles will allow the observer to make attributions to the person and/or the environment:

1. *Consistency.* If the reviewer saw the movie more than once and liked it both times, it would seem unlikely that some personal factor such as a temporary mood or state of emotion, which would tend to fluctuate and change over time, could account for the reaction to the movie on both occasions. The movie is part of the physical environment, which is experienced as stable and relatively unchanging, and would seem a more likely cause of the reaction. Thus, consistency of reaction suggests a stable environmental cause, while inconsistent reactions suggest fluctuating personal causes.
2. *Distinctiveness.* If a reviewer likes all movies seen, one would tend to attribute the reaction to personal causes. After all, some movies are excellent, some are good, and then there are the others. A reviewer who does not have distinctive reactions to movies apparently does not react to the differences between them, hence appears to react more on the basis of internal personal factors. Generally speaking, then, the more distinctive the person's response, the more apt an observer is to make an environmental attribution, and the less distinctive the response, the more likely a personal attribution will be made.
3. *Consensus.* If a large number of people react in the same way to a situation, an environmental attribution will be made. However, if a person reacts in a manner different from most other people, a personal attribution is more likely. In the case of the movie reviewer, if a large number of people agree with the reviewer's reaction, it will be attributed to the film and not to anything about the reviewer. However, if the reviewer's reaction is idiosyncratic, the reaction will be attributed to something about the reviewer rather than to the film.

There is a tendency for divergences in attributions between actors and observers. Actors usually cannot do everything they most desire, but must act within the context of obtaining the best outcomes possible under the circumstances. As a result, actors tend to see their own actions as strongly constrained by the environment. On the other hand, as Heider (1958) has noted, the behavior of the actor tends to engulf the perceptual field of the observer. This focus on the actor to the exclusion of the environment is referred to as the fundamental attribution error and leads observers to make stronger personal attributions than do actors. Also, of course, actors have more information about themselves and a wider context of attribution than do observers.

Jones and Davis (1965) have argued that once an observer makes an attribution to personal causes, a corresponding inference will be made from the characterization of the behavior that was observed and the motive that is inferred as underlying that behavior. The observer notes effects that occur in the environment and traces these back to the behavior of an actor. If the behavior is attributed to environmental factors, the information processing ceases. However, if a personal attribution is made, the observer assumes the actor intended the effects observed. Intent implies that the actor has foreknowledge of the effects and the ability to produce them. Intent refers to the effects and not to the behavior in question. If intent is attributed to the actor, a motive for the intention is inferred. The difference between intent and motive is that the former is an "in order to" reason and the latter a "because of" reason. That is, a forward-oriented reason that the behavior was emitted to produce the effects is an intention, whereas a motive is backward looking and gives a reason for wanting to produce those effects.

Correspondent inference assumes a commonality between the nature of a response and the motive attributed for it. For example, domineering people may have a power motive attributed to them. This theory, offered by Jones and Davis (1965), assumes that whenever an observer makes an attribution of cause to the person, a correspondent inference will be made. It must be further assumed that the identification and labeling of responses is unproblematic and is a given, much like the proximal energies of space perception. It can be argued, however, that an action cannot be identified apart from the goals assumed to guide the actor. For example, a man pulling and pushing a pump handle could be described as exercising his back and arm muscles or as pumping water into a trough. Which description is more "accurate" would depend on what the man's goals were believed to be.

Clearly, observers do form overall impressions of other people. Information is gathered from direct observations and from reports by other observers. The first impression of an actor tends to have a stronger impact than later information. This primacy effect may occur because earlier information serves as a context within which later information is interpreted. Some kinds of information are more central in forming overall impressions, and other information is more peripheral or unimportant. For example, describing someone as warm or cold has been shown to have more impact on overall impressions than describing the stimulus person as polite or blunt. Anderson (1965) has proposed mathematical models of how observers process and weigh information provided (in adjectival form) about actors. How likable a person is may be more heavily weighted by some traits than others, and earlier information may be given more weight than later information. The primacy effect may be due to the discounting of later information or may occur by inattention after an early impression is formed. These ideas can be presented in the form of an algebraic weighted averaging model, which has received rather impressive support from empirical studies.

Social psychologists have had a traditional concern about the accuracy with which observers attribute emotional states and personality traits to actors. Observers have been presented idealized paintings, photographs, motion pictures, and live actors portraying various emotions, and have been asked to identify the emotion expressed. If one accepts the labels given to stimuli by scientists as the criterion, then observers are fairly accurate in identifying emotions from viewing only facial expression, hand movements, still photographs, and voice inflections. Furthermore, there is rather good agreement across very different cultures in making these attributions to identical stimuli. The latter finding has provided some support for the Darwinian belief that human expressions have evolved through the phyla. Viewing cues in social context allows observers in all cultures to provide more "accurate" labels of emotional states. But there is a criterion problem with much of this research: There is no satisfactory definition of what exactly an emotion is, hence it is not very clear how one identifies any particular state.

Observers tend to assume that other people will behave consistently over time. To attain a view of the world as orderly and predictable, the observer tries to maintain organized and meaningful impressions of other people. It might even be said that observers will invent some constancy to characterize others, such as underlying stable dispositions, so as to make sense out of the diversity of behavior. Each person tends to develop an implicit theory of personality in which certain kinds of traits and dispositions are viewed as being mutually associated or dissociated. For example, an observer who makes a correspondent inference that another person has a power motive may then construct, through a chain of inferences, a belief that the stimulus person has a series of other traits (strong, exploitative, aggressive, cold, impolite, etc.). While there may be some commonality of implicit personality theories within a given culture, there is considerable variation as well.

Observers will often cluster traits together as descriptive of a particular category of people. This picture in our heads is referred to as a stereotype. A social stereotype exists when a sizable group of people agree on the category-based cluster. A stereotype of Italians, for example, may include that they are musical and passionate. Presumably, if the only information an observer has regarding a given actor is that the individual is Italian, any future interaction between them may be based on the belief that the actor possesses the stereotypical traits. In this sense stereotypes help to organize perceptions and to provide a basis for predicting what strangers are likely to do. While there may be a grain of truth in some stereotypes, at least as they apply to entire groups of people, they tend to present an impoverished and inadequate basis for understanding and interacting with individuals.

An important stereotype recently investigated by social psychologists refers to beautiful women. It is generally believed that beautiful women have more dating opportunities and more socially desirable personalities, and are happier and more intelligent. Beautiful women may also have an advantage in job interviews and performance ratings. However, there is evidence that at higher levels of management, physical attractiveness is an asset for men but a handicap for women.

Most of the literature on interpersonal perception assumes that a stimulus person is inert and merely stands (as for a portrait), while the observer draws inferences from the behavior performed. However, the actor may have much to gain or lose from the impressions given off by behavior, and hence is motivated to affect them in some way. Thus, the actor may engage in one or more of a numerous assortment of possible impression management strategies to negotiate an identity in the eyes of the observer.

Impression management may be defensive in remedying a spoiled identity resulting from negative behaviors, or in warding off negative impressions in advance of behavior. For example, the actor may offer accounts or explanations for a problematic behavior. Such accounts may take the form of excuses, generally helping the observer to make environmental attributions for the behavior, or justifications that argue that the beneficial effects of the behavior outweigh the negative effects. Impression management behaviors may also be assertive in the sense that the actor tries to establish a preplanned identity in the eyes of the observer. For example, when positive effects are produced by behavior, the actor will try to get the observer to make a personal attribution. If a personal attribution is made, the actor will gain responsibility and credit for the positive effects, and is apt to gain approbation or other rewards for so doing.

Rules of decorum and demeanor often require that an observer accept an identity presented by another. To challenge that identity may be taken as an insult and generally would not lead to smooth interactions between the two parties. On the other hand, an observer cannot allow an actor to establish any identity whatsoever, since to do so would give control of the interaction to the actor. Thus, there is a tendency for people to negotiate their identities in front of one another.

The study of interpersonal perception has not yet incorporated the dynamic interaction proposed by impression management theory. The attribution process appears to be static and perhaps relies too much on rational models of information processing. Future focus is likely to examine strategies of impression management and how observers penetrate attempts to control their impressions in forming judgments of actors.

REFERENCES

Anderson, N. G. (1965). Averaging versus adding as a stimulus-combination rule in impression formation. *Journal of Experimental Psychology, 70,* 394–400.

Heider, F. (1958). *The psychology of interpersonal relations.* New York: Wiley.

Jones, E. E., & Davis, K. E. (1965). From acts to dispositions: The attribution process in person perception. In I. Berkowitz (Ed.), *Advances in experimental social psychology* (Vol. 2). New York: Academic Press.

Kelley, H. H. (1973). The process of causal attribution. *American Psychologist, 28,* 107–128.

James T. Tedeschi
State University of New York, Albany

See also: **Social Cognition**

INTERPERSONAL PSYCHOTHERAPY

For at least a century, since Sigmund Freud invented psychoanalysis, psychotherapy has been an important part of psychiatric treatment. Yet until recently, the utility of talking treatments rested on therapists' belief rather than research data. Hundreds of psychotherapies arose, many developed by charismatic therapists, but none had an empirical basis. Only in the last 30 years have psychotherapies been carefully tested to see when they are helpful and when they are not. Interpersonal psychotherapy (IPT) is one of still few psychotherapies to have undergone rigorous testing and been shown to help patients with specific psychiatric diagnoses.

IPT was developed in the early 1970s by the late Gerald L. Klerman, MD; Myrna M. Weissman, PhD; and their colleagues at Harvard and Yale. In planning a medication treatment study for outpatients with Major Depressive Disorder (serious clinical depression), and recognizing that many patients in clinical practice received talking therapy as well as pills, Klerman and Weissman decided to add a psychotherapy to their study. Being researchers, they developed a manual-based treatment that relied on known psychosocial aspects of depression. They knew that serious life events can trigger depressive episodes in individuals who are vulnerable to developing depression, and that, once depressed, many individuals have difficulties in interpersonal functioning that result in further demoralizing life events. In other words, life events affect mood, and mood affects life circumstances, in a potentially vicious cycle. Further, research had shown that social supports provide protection against developing depression, whereas conflicted relationships increase depressive risk.

Based on such findings, and on interpersonal theories by psychiatrists from the 1950s such as Harry Stack Sullivan and the attachment theory of John Bowlby, Klerman and Weissman constructed a psychotherapy manual and trained psychotherapists to use it. What emerged as IPT is a life events-based, diagnostically targeted, straightforward, pragmatic, optimistic, forward-looking rather than past-focused, and empirically rather than theoretically driven treatment. Principles of IPT include

1. A formal time limit, to allow comparison to medications in research trials, and to accelerate treatment results.
2. A supportive, encouraging relationship with the patient.
3. Two definitions of the patient's situation. First, the patient is given the diagnosis of major depression, which is presented as a treatable medical illness rather than a character flaw (which is how the patient often perceives it). Patients are given the "sick role," a temporary status that recognizes they are suffering from an illness and probably cannot function at full capacity. Depressed patients learn to blame the illness when appropriate, rather than guiltily blaming themselves as they are wont to do. The sick role also incorporates the responsibility to work in treatment toward recovery, at which point the patient reassumes a healthy role.
4. The time-limited treatment is then focused on one of four areas: *complicated bereavement* (an aberrant response to the death of a significant other), *role dispute* (a struggle with a significant other), *role transition* (a major life change, such as in job, geography, marital status, or health), or *interpersonal deficits* (a poorly named category that really denotes absence of any of the first three kinds of life events).

In each weekly, 50-minute session, therapist and patient review what has happened between sessions and connections between the patient's recent mood and recent life situations. Sessions focus on the patient's interpersonal skills; for example, depressed patients typically struggle to assert themselves, confront other people, and take social risks. When patients handle interpersonal situations appropriately, therapists reinforce their use of social skills and underscore the link between good social functioning and improved mood. When interpersonal events go badly, therapists help patients to understand what went wrong and to prepare to handle future encounters more adaptively.

Randomized controlled trials of IPT showed that it relieved depression better than control conditions and with roughly equivalent efficacy to antidepressant medications. Moreover, IPT helped patients to build social skills, which medication alone did not. The success of IPT in studies of outpatients with Major Depressive Disorder led to its testing for patients with other mood and nonmood diagnoses, including major depression in medically ill patients, depressed geriatric and adolescent patients, mothers with postpartum depression, Dysthymic Disorder, and as an adjunctive treatment for bipolar disorder; it has also been tested for bulimia, social phobia, Post-Traumatic Stress Disorder, and other conditions. For many of these syndromes, researchers developed new manuals to adapt IPT to the particular psychosocial needs of patients with the target diagnoses. Only in two studies of patients with substance abuse has IPT not been shown to be helpful.

Used mainly as an acute (12 to 16 week) individual treatment, IPT increasingly has been tested in other formats: as couple's therapy, group therapy, telephone therapy, and as a 3-year maintenance treatment for patients with recurrent depression who improved after acute treatment. Indeed, IPT is the only psychotherapy fully tested as a maintenance treatment for patients with recurrent episodes of major depression. Even in a low, once monthly dosage, it protected against relapse better than pill placebo, although not as effectively as high dose maintenance antidepressant medication. In some acute studies and one of the two maintenance studies, the combination of IPT and medication worked better than either treatment alone.

Research on IPT has focused largely on outcome, that is, symptomatic improvement. Its success in this area has led to the inclusion of IPT in American and international treatment guidelines for depression and bulimia. Other research domains also deserve exploration: which of the eclectic ingredients of IPT help which patients; when IPT might be preferable to, or less helpful than, other treatments such as cognitive-behavioral therapy; and how well IPT works in general practice. Some research has begun to reveal biological and psychological outcome predictors as well as neuroimaging brain changes due to IPT. Initially a purely research therapy, IPT is now beginning to expand beyond its research origins into clinical practice, spawning an International Society for Interpersonal Psychotherapy and addressing questions of appropriate standards for certification of IPT proficiency by nonresearch therapists.

John C. Markowitz

See also: **Psychotherapy**

INTERVENING VARIABLE

An intervening variable is an unobservable link between two observed variables. Many of our assumptions about the causes of human behavior postulate an intervening psychological variable that mediates between the stimulus and response. For example, imagine two children on the playground. George bumps Sam, then Sam hits George. The stimulus (being bumped) presumably caused Sam's response (hitting George). However, in order to understand the causal link, we need to postulate an intervening variable. Sam is bumped (the stimulus); Sam thinks, "George hurt me, so it's fair to hurt him back" (the intervening variable); then Sam hits George (the response). The introduction of an intervening variable allows us to understand why people react differently to the same stimulus. For example, William runs away when George bumps him, but David laughs when George bumps him. Perhaps the intervening variable for William is his thought, "George is stronger than I am. If I don't run, he'll hit me again." When George bumps David, David laughs, perhaps because he interprets the bump as another example of George's playfulness or clumsiness.

The intervening variable is not observable. We observe two things: the stimulus (getting bumped by George) and the response (hitting George, running away, or laughing). Psychotherapists work with clients to understand the intervening variables that lead to maladaptive responses. Psychoanalysts may look for intervening variables related to early life experiences. Cognitive therapists may help people replace unacceptable intervening variables (e.g., negative self-talk) with more adaptive ones (e.g., positive self-talk). For example, a client who is afraid of the dark may be taught to redefine darkness as relaxing and nonthreatening. Albert Ellis's rational-emotive psychotherapy is based on the concept that cognitive intervening variables can be changed.

Psychologists explain consistencies in human behavior by postulating intervening variables that are relatively stable characteristics of individuals, such as personality traits or abilities. It might be postulated that Sam is pugnacious, William has low self-esteem, and David has a good sense of humor. This interpretation can be tested by observing the children in a variety of situations.

The interpretation of a response depends on what intervening variable is applied. Imagine that a child just failed an exam. It can be postulated that the intervening variable is competence, the motivation to study hard, or the support of caring parents. Did the student fail because of ability, motivation, or parental assistance? How the intervening variable is interpreted affects the decision about how to help the child improve. Should the child be moved to a lower-level class or be provided with better motivation, or should a therapist or teacher work with the parents? If the wrong intervening variable is selected, the remediation may be ineffective. Psychologists use interviews and tests to assess intervening variables.

Psychological theories postulate intervening variables such as ego strength, locus of control, and cognitive dissonance. These unobservable variables provide theoretical links between stimuli and responses. An effective intervening variable allows psychologists to better understand and predict behavior.

Mary J. Allen
California State University

See also: **Individual Differences; Rational Emotive Behavior Therapy**

INTRINSIC MOTIVATION

Intrinsic motivation is a type of motivation based in people's inherent interest in activities that provide novelty and challenge. Intrinsically motivated behaviors are an expression of an individual's self and do not depend on external reinforcements. Thus, intrinsically motivated behaviors have what is referred to in attribution theory as an internal perceived locus of causality; people experience the causes of these behaviors to be within themselves (deCharms, 1968).

Throughout life, when in their healthiest states, people are active and curious, displaying an eagerness to learn and explore. This natural, intrinsic motivation helps people acquire knowledge about themselves and their world.

Until the 1950s, theories of motivation focused on physiological drives such as hunger, thirst, and sex, proposing that all behaviors are motivated by those drives and their derivatives (Freud, 1962/1923; Hull, 1943). However, as various phenomena emerged that could not be explained by drive theories, White (1959) suggested that a full understanding of motivation required a consideration of psychological needs as a motivational basis for some behaviors. He proposed an intrinsic motivation for interacting effectively with the environment; Deci and Ryan (1985) subsequently stated that the psychological needs for competence and autonomy underlie intrinsic motivation, which flourishes in contexts that allow satisfaction of those needs.

Whereas drive theories implied that humans seek quiescence and minimal stimulation, intrinsic motivation theories suggest that people desire an optimal level of stimulation. The structure of intrinsically motivated behaviors thus involves an ongoing cycle of finding stimulation and working toward quiescence. In other words, people seek and conquer optimal challenges.

Behaviors such as reading a book, solving puzzles, exploring novel spaces, looking at paintings, and playing softball are intrinsically motivating for many people, but not necessarily for all, because intrinsic motivation is a property of the interaction between a person and an activity. For an individual to be intrinsically motivated for an activity, that individual must find the activity interesting.

Intrinsic motivation is typically contrasted with extrinsic motivation. People are extrinsically motivated for an activity when they do it to earn money, avoid censure, or comply with social norms.

Numerous studies have confirmed that, relative to extrinsic motivation, intrinsic motivation leads to better conceptual learning, greater creativity, more cognitive flexibility, and enhanced well-being (see Deci & Ryan, 1985). Consequently, there has been great interest in the conditions that enhance versus diminish intrinsic motivation. Initial studies examined how extrinsic rewards affect intrinsic motivation, and a recent meta-analysis substantiated that tangible extrinsic rewards undermine intrinsic motivation for rewarded activities (Deci, Koestner, & Ryan, 1999).

Additional studies with young children, teenagers, college students, and adults revealed that other external events, such as directives, surveillance, deadlines, threats of punishment, and negative performance feedback also decrease intrinsic motivation. By contrast, events such as offering choice, acknowledging people's feelings, and providing positive performance feedback have been found to enhance intrinsic motivation.

Deci and Ryan (1985) interpreted these results in terms of satisfaction versus thwarting of the basic needs for competence and autonomy. Specifically, people tend to interpret rewards, directives, deadlines, and threats as controllers of their behavior, which thwarts their need for autonomy; in contrast, people tend to experience choice and acknowledgment as support for their autonomy. Similarly, positive feedback tends to satisfy people's basic need for competence, whereas negative feedback tends to thwart that need.

Further studies examined the general interpersonal context or ambience of particular settings such as classrooms or workgroups. For example, investigators found that teachers who were more autonomy supportive (in contrast to being controlling) catalyzed their students' intrinsic motivation and desire for challenge, and that managers who supported their subordinates' autonomy promoted motivation and satisfaction on the job (Deci & Ryan, 2000). In fact, authority figures such as doctors, parents, and coaches have also been found to influence the motivation and behaviors of their patients, children, and athletes, depending on the degree to which they are autonomy supportive versus controlling.

Finally, Deci and Ryan (2000) pointed out that external events such as rewards, feedback, and deadlines can be interpreted differently by different people. That is, many external events such as rewards have both an aspect that *controls* behavior and one that conveys positive competence *information.* If the controlling aspect is more salient, it pressures people toward specific outcomes and undermines their intrinsic motivation. However, if the informational aspect is more salient, it affirms their competence and enhances their intrinsic motivation. Whether the controlling or informational aspect is more salient depends on both the situation and the person.

When the interpersonal context within which rewards or feedback are administered is generally autonomy supportive, the informational aspect of the rewards or feedback tends to be more salient. For example, studies have shown that, although monetary rewards typically diminish intrinsic motivation, they can maintain or enhance it if they are administered in an autonomy-supportive context.

In addition, some people, due to socialization, are inclined to experience events such as rewards and feedback as more informational, whereas others are inclined to experience them as more controlling. Thus, individual differences can lead different people to experience the same external event differently, so the event will have different effects on their intrinsic motivation (Deci & Ryan, 2000).

To summarize, intrinsic motivation flourishes when people are able to satisfy their needs for competence and autonomy while doing interesting tasks. Specific events in the interpersonal environment, such as the offer of rewards, the imposition of deadlines, and the provision of performance feedback can directly affect people's need satisfaction and, thus, their intrinsic motivation. The general interpersonal ambience can also impact people's need satisfaction and intrinsic motivation both directly and by influencing how they experience external events. Finally, people differ in their tendencies to interpret events and environments in ways that support versus thwart need satisfaction and intrinsic motivation.

Because intrinsic motivation is relevant in many walks of life and leads to more positive outcomes than extrinsic motivation, it seems important to support the autonomy and competence of our children, students, clients, employees, and patients.

REFERENCES

deCharms, R. (1968). *Personal causation.* New York: Academic Press.

Deci, E. L., Koestner, R., & Ryan, R. M. (1999). A meta-analytic review of experiments examining the effects of extrinsic rewards on intrinsic motivation. *Psychological Bulletin, 125,* 627–668.

Deci, E. L., & Ryan, R. M. (1985). *Intrinsic motivation and self-determination in human behavior.* New York: Plenum.

Deci, E. L., & Ryan, R. M. (2000). The "what" and "why" of goal pursuits: Human needs and the self-determination of behavior. *Psychological Inquiry, 11,* 227–268.

Freud, S. (1962). *The ego and the id.* New York: Norton. (Original work published 1923)

Hull, C. L. (1943). *Principles of behavior.* New York: Appleton-Century-Crofts.

White, R. W. (1959). Motivation reconsidered. *Psychological Review, 66,* 297–333.

Edward L. Deci
University of Rochester

INTROVERSION–EXTRAVERSION

Carl Jung coined the terms introversion and extraversion to refer to two different psychological types. By introversion, Jung meant a turning inward of the libido (psychic energy), whereas extraversion referred to a directing outward of the libido. Note that either term can be spelled with an "o" or an "a" (that is, either as above or as intraversion and extroversion). Although inconsistent, introversion and extraversion are the spellings used with the Myers–Briggs Type Indicator (MBTI), which is a popular personality assessment instrument based on Jung's type theory.

An introvert's mind, emotions, attention, and so forth are turned inward toward himself or herself. Jung believed that the introvert directs the libido inward because of inferiority feelings, an idea reminiscent of Alfred Adler. Particularly during stressful periods, introverts tend to withdraw into themselves, to avoid others, and to be self-absorbed. With a bent toward self-sufficiency, the introvert's essential stimulation is from within, from his or her inner world of thoughts and reflections. Introverts are frequently reserved and difficult to get to know, tend to bottle up their emotions, and need privacy.

In contrast, extraverts orient primarily to the outer world, focusing their perceptions and judgments on people and things. Extraverts draw energy from other people and external experiences; tend to express their emotions; need relationships more than privacy; and are usually friendly, talkative, and easy to get to know. Extraverts may seem shallow to introverts, whereas introverts may seem withdrawn to extraverts.

On the MBTI, the E-I or extraversion-introversion index is one of four dichotomous scales. The other three are sensing-intuition (S-N), thinking-feeling (T-F), and judgment-perception (J-P).

SUGGESTED READING

Jung, C. G. (1971). Psychological types. In *The collected works of C. G. Jung* (Vol. 6), Bollinger Series XX. Princeton, NJ: Princeton University Press.

Myers, I. B., & Myers, P. B. (1980). *Gifts differing.* Palo Alto, CA: Consulting Psychologists Press.

B. Michael Thorne
Mississippi State University

ISLAM AND PSYCHOLOGY

Introduction

There are two main ways of deciding the truth of an issue. We can believe something is true if we trust the source of the information. For example, Muslims believe that the Quran is divinely constructed. A second path to knowledge is through logical and critical reasoning of experienced phenomena. This is the method of scientific study on which psychology rests. This entry will focus on the primary focus of knowledge, the foundation on which knowledge is based, the methods for acquiring knowledge, the criteria for validating knowledge, and the potential for human change according to each approach.

Psychology examines the physical, cognitive, personality, social, emotional, and moral aspects of human development. Its emphasis is on the material aspects of the human being; the spiritual component, in contrast, is only marginally recognized.

In Islam, Allah created all things, including human beings. Allah created the universe alone and solely sustains and governs it. Human life has a divine and transcendental purpose because humans shall be resurrected in a Divine world (the Hereafter) and be made to account for their lives in this world. In the Islamic view, humans are creatures made of two components: matter and spirit. Humans should strive for the betterment of both in a balanced way. The Quran, which governs human lives, has been divinely formulated so that both components can be cared for in a balanced way. The Islamic Law (Shariah) and hadith (sayings of the prophet Muhammad [Peace Be Upon Him]) form documentation that governs the lives of Muslims everywhere.

Psychology

Source of Knowledge

In psychology as in all other behavioral and social sciences, the source of knowledge is confined to that ascertained by the human intellect and the senses. The primary focus of scientific knowledge is a study of reality, beginning with the material aspects of the universe.

Foundation of Investigation

Faith in reason and the experience of utilizing the scientific method forms the basis for psychological investigation. Psychology recognizes experimentation as the primary tool for verifying knowledge. The essence of logical positivism or empiricism is observation, measurement, and quantification of sense data. In undertaking this observation it is assumed that objective data are neutral and value-free. It is also assumed that the observer has shielded the methodology from the influence of all extraneous variables, confounding variables, personal attitudes, values, and biases by means of rigorous control mechanisms.

The natural and logical consequence of this methodology and its epistemological basis is reductionism. This has led to human behavior being reduced to the level of material bodies that can be studied within the confines of control and observation mechanisms.

Methods of Acquiring Knowledge

Psychological research tests hypothesize relationships and causal explanations. They evaluate the reliability, validity, and underlying factor structure of psychological measures. They also measure the degree of generalizability across samples.

Criteria for Validation

Psychological research is predicated on a particular set of assumptions, which are: (1) Order—scientists believe that events in the world are governed by deducible laws; (2) Determinism—order in events is likely to be causally related; (3) Empiricism—information should be gathered directly through sensory experience; and (4) Parsimony—economy of explanation.

Thus, psychological research is characterized by control of variables, operational definitions of the factors under study, and replicability of results.

Probability for Human Change

Psychological research leads to a range of views on the possibilities of personal development of human capacities. On the one hand, behavioral research suggests that altering stimulus–response relationships can alter behavioral patterns. This type of modification is used in a number of health domains (Sheridan & Radmacher, 1992). On the other hand, humanistic psychology advocates unlimited potential for personal control of individual development. In all cases individual progress is either facilitated or impeded by powerful biological, evolutionary, historical, and social forces.

Islam

Source of Knowledge

In Islam, the study of reality is considered to begin with the metaphysical or spiritual aspects of the universe. Principles of human development, human interaction, and human functioning in all aspects of life are derived initially from the Quran.

Foundation of Investigation

Faith is the belief in the authority of revelation. Belief in revelation as an infallible source of knowledge is an essential article of faith in Islam. This belief influences the search for knowledge and personal meaning in life. Faith in ultimate unknowns also forms part of the fabric of Muslim consciousness.

Methods of Acquiring Knowledge

Prayer is a fundamental pillar of Islam. Believers are enjoined to pray five times each day at set times. Prayer is considered to connect each human being with his/her Creator. This exercise is endorsed by Muslim scholars (Haeri, 1991) as enhancing discernment and understanding. Reading, listening, and understanding the Quran forms the crux of knowledge, since it is on the word of the Quran that all other knowledge is based. Discipline of material self or ego is a requirement for gaining knowledge and wisdom.

Criteria for Validation

The criteria for validation are personal and subjective interpretation of revealed word and associated texts, and consistency with prior interpretations and reflections.

Probability for Human Change

Muslims believe in a single, all-knowing, all-loving Creator who constructed human beings with powers and capacities that can be developed to an infinite extent. The purpose of human life is to fulfill one's potential. Each human being is gifted with certain specific virtues; however, each virtue if carried to its extreme becomes a vice. All life events serve to highlight human virtues. Ultimately, the purpose of life and life events is to bring each human being closer to Allah.

Conclusion

Psychology and Islam illustrate two main methods for obtaining knowledge: through trusting a divine revelation or through objective analysis of experienced phenomena. Both of these methods possess flaws. It is possible to read something from a credible source but misunderstand a particular issue. The possibility of error through personal experience is well documented; for example, optical illusions provide numerous examples of such errors (Gross & McIlveen, 1998). In addition, reason is capable of error, as evidenced by the fact that so many scientists have different explanations for the same set of data. For example, Eysenck (Eysenck Personality Questionnaire) and Cattell (Cattell 16PF) used the same method of factor analysis to arrive at two distinct measures of human personality (Carlson, Buskist, & Martin, 2000).

Finally, teachers of religion have different explanations for the same set of inspired text. For example, two different and unique explanations of personality have been derived from Islamic teachings: the Enneagram (Palmer, 1988) and the Three Levels of Self (Haeri, 1991).

As human life evolves so human understanding also evolves. Psychology and Islam are two world views which have led to two parallel paradigms for understanding human beings and the world in which we live. Each paradigm contributes a unique understanding to this issue. Whilst the language of the two paradigms may be different, their aims and objectives are the same. Although the two methodologies may provide different types of information, both are valid and both are necessary.

REFERENCES

Carlson, R., Buskist, W., & Martin, N. (2000). *Psychology: The science of behaviour.* London: Allyn & Bacon.

Gross, R., & McIlveen, R. (1998). *Psychology: A new introduction.* Oxon: Hodder and Stoughton.

Haeri, Shaykh F. A. (1991). *The journey of the self.* New York: Harper Collins.

Palmer, H. (1988). *The enneagram.* London: Harper & Row.

Sheridan, C. L., & Radmacher, S. A. (1992). *Health psychology: Challenging the biomedical model.* Chichester, UK: Wiley.

Qulsoom Inayat
University of Greenwich, London

ISOMORPHISM

In psychology, the term isomorphism (from the Greek roots *iso* or "same" and *morph* or "form") is identified with Gestalt theory. Gestalt psychologists suggested that objective brain processes underlying and correlated with particular subjective experiences are isomorphic with, that is, have functionally the same structure as, those experiences. This proposal challenged early twentieth century mind/brain theories which viewed the brain as comprised of interconnected, insulated wires and switches rather than as a dynamic system of interdependent electrochemical processes.

One-to-one correspondence between isomorphic phenomena, as in mathematical set theory, is inconsistent with Gestalt theory. For example, two dotted circles, one composed of 30 dots along its circumference and another of 32 dots, are isomorphic in the Gestalt sense of having identical form; the number of dots composing each circle is immaterial as long as there are enough to specify the shape. The form or shape is crucial, not the number of "elements" it happens to have. Two circles, however many "elements" compose them, and irrespective of their color or size, are isomorphic simply because they both display the circular shape. Comparably, two squares are isomorphic even if they are of different sizes, brightnesses, or colors.

The first Gestalt reference to brain processes isomorphic with perceptual processes occurred in a 1912 paper by Max Wertheimer on apparent motion. It suggested brain processes that might correspond to the perception of motion when there is no motion in the physical stimulus. Assume, say, two one-inch vertical lines, x and y, separated horizontally by one inch. If line x is briefly exposed, then disappears, and an instant later line y is exposed, the observer may see not two stationary lines successively exposed, but a single line moving from location x to location y. If the sequence continues, so that right after line y disappears line x is exposed again, then line y reappears almost immediately after line x goes off, and so on, as long as the distance and time relations are appropriate, the perceived result is a single line moving back and forth. If the time between disappearance of one line and appearance of the other is too long, the observer experiences two successively exposed stationary lines in two different places; if the interval is too short (or if there is overlap in the time that both lines are exposed), the observer reports two stationary lines simultaneously exposed in two different places.

What happens in the brain when a single moving line is seen under these conditions? Wertheimer argued that particular parts of the visual cortex are activated when the observer sees the lines, one area of activation corresponding to line x, and another nearby corresponding to line y. Furthermore (and here Gestalt theory deviated from other mind/brain theories), when motion is perceived, there must be some kind of "short circuit" between the brain areas corresponding to line x and line y; this "short circuit" is the brain process isomorphic with the experience of a single moving line.

Wertheimer's hypothesis was elaborated by Kurt Koffka (in his 1935 book) and Wolfgang Köhler (in extensive perceptual experiments). Köhler and his collaborators derived predictions from the theory and validated these predictions experimentally. Köhler and Hans Wallach devoted a monograph (1944) to "figural after-effects," perceived distortions of figures generated by prolonged prior observation of other figures.

Assume, for example, that the perceived distance between two points in the visual field, x and y, is isomorphic with the electrical resistance between their corresponding locations in the visual cortex, X and Y. If the resistance is great, the brain processes X and Y are functionally far apart, and the perceived distance between corresponding points in the visual field, x and y, should be great; if the resistance is small, the perceived distance between their experienced isomorphic counterparts, x and y, should be small.

A change in resistance between two points in the visual cortex should result in a corresponding change in the isomorphic visual experience. Any continuing excitatory process in neural tissue generates a process that inhibits its own continuation. According to isomorphism theory, this inhibition is increased resistance. One way to enhance resistance between two points in the visual cortex, therefore, is excitation with an appropriate visual stimulus. Prolonged stimulation of the brain area corresponding to the space between two points in the visual field by a figure exposed visually in that space should increase resistance in the space, and the same two points in the visual field should therefore appear farther apart than before. Such distortions were indeed found in many of Köhler and Wallach's experiments.

These and further experiments (not only in vision but also in other modalities, such as kinesthesis) made the isomorphism theory widely discussed in the mid-twentieth century. In the 1950s, Karl Lashley and Roger Sperry (and their collaborators) challenged the theory experimentally. They incised the visual cortex of cats and monkeys and inserted insulating material into the cuts, or placed excellent electrical conductors on the surface of or into the animals' visual cortices. These disturbances in the brain's electrochemical characteristics, they argued, should destroy the performance of visual discriminations the animals had learned previously—if isomorphism theory was indeed correct. But these alterations in the brain produced no changes in the animals' ability to make visual discriminations they had learned previously. Köhler argued that field properties of local changes in the electrical characteristics of the brains should reorganize almost instantaneously, and hence no disturbance in visually guided performance would be expected. Neither Lashley nor Sperry rebutted this argument.

The theory was neither corroborated nor refuted by empirical data; neuropsychological researchers studied other issues. Nevertheless, Gestalt theory of physical processes in the brain that are functionally isomorphic with processes in subjective experience remains one significant effort to address the fundamental question of the mind–brain relation.

REFERENCES

Koffka, K. (1935). *Principles of Gestalt psychology.* New York: Harcourt, Brace.

Köhler, W. (1929). *Gestalt psychology.* New York: Liveright.

Köhler, W., & Wallach, H. (1944). Figural after-effects. *Proceedings of the American Philosophical Society, 88,* 269–357.

Lashley, K. S., Chow, K. L., & Semmes, J. (1951). An examination of the electrical field theory of cerebral integration. *Psychological Review, 58,* 123–136.

Sperry, R. W., & Miner, N. (1955). Pattern perception following insertion of mica plates into visual cortex. *Journal of Comparative and Physiological Psychology, 48,* 463–469.

Sperry, R. W., Miner, N., & Myers, R. E. (1955). Visual pattern perception following subpial slicing and tantalum wire implantations in the visual cortex. *Journal of Comparative and Physiological Psychology, 48,* 50–58.

Wertheimer, M. (1912). Experimentelle Studien über das Sehen von Bewegung (Experimental studies of the seeing of motion). *Zeitschrift für Psychologie, 60,* 321–378.

Michael Wertheimer
University of Colorado, Boulder

See also: **Gestalt Psychology**

ITEM ANALYSIS

The major purpose of item analysis is to provide information on the extent to which the individual items making up a test are functioning in a desired manner. This information can then be used to improve the reliability and validity of the test by editing or discarding poor items. An item analysis of an achievement test may also provide diagnostic information on what examinees know and do not know, serving as a basis for instructional planning and curriculum revision.

Item analysis information may be either rational (judgmental) or empirical (statistical). A rational item analysis entails careful inspection of each item to determine whether its content is accurate, congruent with the test specifications, free of cultural or other bias, and not contrary to standard item-writing guidelines. This approach is characteristic of item analyses of criterion-referenced achievement tests, but it can also be applied to norm-referenced tests.

Empirical item analysis involves the calculation of one or more statistical measures of item functioning, including an item difficulty index, an item discrimination (validity) index, and some measure of the functioning of distracters. The difficulty index (p) of an item is computed quite simply as the proportion of people tested who answer the item correctly. The optimum difficulty index varies with the purpose of the test and the type of item.

The procedure for determining an index of the ability of an item to discriminate among examinees attaining different scores on the criterion variable depends on the nature of the criterion and the type of test. The usual internal criteria for an achievement test are the total scores on the test itself, which are rank-ordered and divided into upper (U) and lower (L) groups. In the case of a norm-referenced test, these two groups usually consist of examinees in the top 27% and the bottom 27% of the distribution of total test scores. Then the discrimination index (D) for each item is computed as $D = p_U$ where p_U and p_L are the proportions of examinees in the top and bottom groups, respectively, who answer the item correctly. With an external criterion such as performance ratings or school marks, the item discrimination index is computed as the point-biserial correlation (r_{pb}) between item score (0 or 1) and scores on the criterion continuum. Obviously, the closer either D or r_{pb} is to 1.00, the more valid is the item as a discriminator between high and low scorers on the criterion. Depending on the size of the group of examinees on whom the indexes are computed, D or r_{pb} values as low as 0.20 may prove sufficient for retaining items. It should be noted, however, that selecting items on the basis of D will tend to yield an internally consistent, homogeneous test. In contrast, selecting items on the basis of p_{pb} will usually produce a less homogeneous test, but one with greater validity for predicting an external criterion.

Determination of the discriminative power of items on a criterion-referenced test involves a bit more work than was previously mentioned. W. J. Popham describes two procedures: (1) pretest–posttest differences and (2) uninstructed versus instructed group differences.

Although an item analysis of a multiple-choice test focuses on the difficulty and discrimination indexes of individual items, responses to the incorrect options (distracters) may also be examined. In general, each distracter should be equally attractive to examinees who do not know the answer to an item. Furthermore, the ratio of the number of examinees in the upper group (on the criterion) to the number of examinees in the lower group should be approximately equal for all distracters.

L. R. Aiken

J

JAMES–LANGE THEORY OF EMOTIONS

The James–Lange theory of emotions has been the subject of considerable scientific debate since its publication by James in *Principles of Psychology* (1890). Portions of James's theory had been formulated by the Danish physiologist Lange in 1885. James combined his views with those of Lange, and credited Lange in the name of the theory. It offers a physiological explanation of the constitution, organization, and conditioning of the coarser emotions such as grief, fear, rage, and love in which "everyone recognizes strong organic reverberations," and the subtler emotions, or "those whose organic reverberations are less obvious and strong," such as moral, intellectual, and aesthetic feelings (James, 1890, p. 449).

The general causes of the emotions are assumed to be internal, physiological, nervous processes and not mental or psychological processes. The moods, affections, and emotions that persons experience are "constituted and made up of those bodily changes which we ordinarily call their expression or consequence" (James, 1890, p. 452). A purely disembodied emotion—for example, the emotion of fear without a quickened heartbeat, sharp breathing, or weakened limbs—would be a nonentity for this theory. The emotions are the result of organic changes that occur in the body as a reflex effect of an exciting object or fact confronting the person.

There are three factors in the sequence of an emotional experience: (1) the perception of an exciting fact or object; (2) a bodily expression such as weeping, striking out, or fleeing; and (3) a mental affection or emotion, such as feeling afraid or angry. Many theories of emotion, as well as common sense, place the bodily expressions of weeping, striking out, or fleeing after the emotion of anger or fear. The James–Lange theory alters this sequence, placing bodily expressions between the perception of the exciting fact and the emotion. In everyday terms, this means we cry and then feel sad rather than feeling sad and then crying. "The bodily changes follow directly the perception of the exciting fact . . . our feeling the same as they occur is the emotion" (James, 1890, p. 449; italics in original).

The debate that has surrounded the theory involves the relative importance of central nervous system processes and social environmental factors in the production of emotion (Pribram, 1981). Centralists (including James and Lange) have argued that there are discrete physiological changes for each emotion (Scheff, 1979; Kemper, 1978). Peripheralists argue that there is no discrete physiological change for each emotion (Cannon, 1927; Schachter & Singer, 1962); rather, there is only a bodily state of arousal modified by factors in the social environment. The experimental evidence is inconclusive (Kemper, 1978; Scheft, 1979).

Sartre, in *Sketch for a Theory of the Emotions* (1939), critically evaluated the James–Lange theory from a phenomenological perspective and rejected it on several grounds. First, behavior, physiological or expressive, is not emotion, nor is emotion the awareness of that behavior. Second, the body does not call out its own interpretations, which are given in the field of consciousness of the person. Third, the bodily disturbances present in emotion are disorders of the most ordinary kind and are not the causes of emotion. They ratify emotion's existence for the person and give emotion its believability, but are not its causes. Fourth, to have considered only the biological body independent of the lived body—and the person's consciousness of the body—as the source of emotion was to treat the body as a thing and to locate emotion in disorders of the body. Emotion as a part of the person's lived experiences in the life world has not been given adequate attention by either the centralist or the peripheralist followers of the James–Lange theory.

The James–Lange theory of emotions remains a viable theory today. The factors isolated by the theory are not disputed. Controversy remains over the ordering of the sequence of the factors and on the emphasis to be given to strictly physiological—as opposed to social and psychological—factors and processes (see Barbalet, 1998). However, the historical character of emotional experience suggests that cultural and structural factors strongly influence how emotions are felt and expressed (see Newton, 1998).

REFERENCES

Barbalet, J. A. (1998). *Emotion, social theory, and social structure: A macrosociological approach.* New York: Cambridge University Press.

Newton, T. (1998). The sociogenesis of emotion: A historical sociology? In G. Bendelow & S. J. Williams (Eds.), *Emotions in social life: Critical themes and contemporary issues* (pp. 60–80). London: Routledge.

Perinbanayagam, R. S. (2000). *The presence of self.* Lanham, MD: Roman & Littlefield.

Scheff, T. J. (2001). The emotional/relational world. In J. H. Turner (Ed.), *Handbook of sociological theory* (pp. 255–268). New York: Kluwer.

Norman K. Denzin
University of Illinois

JUST NOTICEABLE DIFFERENCE (JND)

The concept of just noticeable difference (JND), also known as the difference threshold or difference limen (Latin for threshold), derives from early work in the area of classical psychophysics conducted in the mid-nineteenth century. This work was highlighted by the research of Ernst Weber (1795–1878), a German physiologist, whose experimental investigations focused on tactile stimulation and the determination of sensory thresholds. Weber's seminal work in this area was extended and elaborated on by Gustav Fechner (1801–1887), a professor of physics at the University of Leipzig (Germany), who coined the term *psychophysics* to refer to this area of experimental psychology. In 1860, Fechner published the first textbook on psychophysics (*Elemente der Psychophysik*) that highlighted the basic goals of this emerging discipline and the scientific methods that were to be employed to advance knowledge in this area (Watson, 1973).

A primary focus of classical psychophysics was on investigating the relationships between different types of physical stimuli and the sensations they evoked in human (and animal) subjects and in assessing the ultimate sensory capabilities of the organism. Of specific interest was determining thresholds for the detectability of stimuli. Much of the early research in this area focused on the determination of absolute thresholds. While investigators employed various experimental methods, depending on the specific nature of the research, subjects in such studies were typically presented with some stimulus (e.g., auditory, visual, tactile) of very low (and undetectable) intensity. This was then followed by a graded presentation of test stimuli, at increasing levels of stimulus intensity, with the subject's task being to indicate when they were able to detect the stimulus. Presentations of stimuli were continued until stimulus intensity was reached where the stimulus was reported as present. Since subjects in such studies were often found to be quite variable regarding the level of stimulus intensity required for detectability on different trials, experiments most often provided subjects with a number of stimulus presentation trials, with the subjects' absolute threshold being considered as that level of stimulation where the subject reported the stimulus as being present 50% of the time.

While experiments like these were designed to determine absolute thresholds (e.g., the smallest amount of stimulation required for detectability), other studies, specifically relevant to the present topic, focused on the issue of differential sensitivity or difference thresholds. Here the primary question was: To what extent must the intensity of one physical stimulus differ from that of a second physical stimulus for subjects to distinguish one from another? Studies of difference thresholds often employed experimental methods similar to those used in determining absolute thresholds. For example, subjects might be provided with a standard stimulus of a given weight, which could be used for purposes of comparison (the standard stimulus), and then be presented with a graded series of test stimuli which differed from the standard stimulus along the weight dimension. The subject's task would be to indicate whether a test stimulus was the same or heavier (or lighter depending on the nature of the specific study) than the standard stimulus. The primary focus of these studies was on determining the smallest increment in weight necessary for the subject to perceive the test stimulus as different from the standard stimulus (50% of the time). This threshold for the detection of differences in physical stimuli has been referred to by a variety of terms: difference threshold, difference or differential limen, least perceptible difference, or just noticeable difference. The term *just noticeable difference,* often abbreviated JND, is the one most widely accepted in the psychophysics literature. Formally, the JND can be defined as the magnitude of change in a stimulus necessary for it to be perceived as different from another stimulus, as the smallest detectable difference between two stimuli (Levine & Shefner, 1981).

Early work related to just noticeable differences in sensation was subsequently extended by attempts to characterize quantitatively the precise nature of the relationship between increases in the magnitude of physical stimuli and increases in just noticeable differences in detectability. Here, Weber's Law (which was actually popularized by Fechner) states that the amount of increase in stimulation that results in a just noticeable difference is a constant proportion of the standard stimulus. Thus a heavy stimulus must be increased by a larger increment in weight for one to notice a difference between the two objects than a lighter stimulus, where a smaller increment in weight may result in the detection of a difference.

It should be noted that remnants of this early interest in the concepts of absolute and difference thresholds are reflected in the psychological literature even today, although the concept of threshold has to some extent fallen into disrepute (apart from its value in assessing the capacity of sensory systems). This is due, in part, to the influence of contemporary cognitive psychology and current views of the individual as an active processor of information. Specifically, it would seem that notions of thresholds have been largely supplanted by concepts derived from signal detection theory (Green & Swets, 1974), where it is assumed that detectability of stimuli is determined, not only by the sensory capacities of the individual, but also by the nature of the response criteria one adopts in responding to detectability tasks (Levine & Shefner, 1981).

REFERENCES

Fechner, G. T. (1964). *Elemente der psychophysik.* Amsterdam: E. J. Bonnet. (Original work published 1860)

Green, D., & Swets, J. A. (1974). *Signal detection theory and psychophysics.* Huntington, NY: Krieger.

Levine, M. W., & Shefner, J. M. (1981). *Fundamentals of sensation and perception.* Reading, MA: Addison-Wesley.

Watson, C. S. (1973). Psychophysics. In B. B. Wolman (Ed.), *Handbook of general psychology* (pp. 275–305). New York: Prentice Hall.

James H. Johnson
University of Florida

K

KINDLING

Kindling is the development of full-blown seizures in response to repeated subthreshold stimulation of the brain. In the classical sense it involves intracerebral electrical stimulation of various areas of brain, most typically the amygdala, with electric currents that are below those required to produce a local afterdischarge (AD). However, with repeated stimulation, the afterdischarge threshold is decreased (brain excitability is increased) and ADs begin to emerge with increasing duration and complexity, and to spread to other areas of the brain. This process is accompanied by a behavior seizure stage progression through stage I (behavioral arrest), stage II (head nodding and chewing movements), stage III (unilateral forepaw clonus), stage IV (bilateral forepaw clonus with rearing), stage V (rearing and falling), and, following sufficient numbers of stimulation, stage VI (major motor seizures in the absence of exogenous electrophysiological stimulation—a true model of spontaneous epileptogenesis).

Kindling is obviously a model of seizure evolution and progression from triggered to spontaneous seizures. However, from the outset, Goddard and Douglas also described kindling as a model for neuronal learning and memory, as the brain was showing increasing and long-lasting increases in responsivity to repetition of the same stimulus over time. This was apparent using a variety of electrophysiological and behavioral end points, including lowering of the initial AD threshold, increasing AD duration and complexity, increasing spread to other areas of the brain, the concomitant progression of behavioral seizure stages evolution culminating in full-blown triggered seizures, and eventually spontaneous major motor seizures.

Much investigation has revealed a host of biochemical and structural changes associated with both the lasting kindled memory trace and shorter-lived compensatory or endogenous anticonvulsant mechanisms. Both of these processes involve a spatiotemporal evolving set of changes in first and second messenger systems, as well as in growth factors, immediate early genes (IEGs), and late effector genes (LEGs) ultimately associated with changes in neuronal excitability and the balance of neurotrophic and apoptotic processes. Thus, kindling appears to be a useful model for studying the complex cascade of changes in gene expression mediating biochemical and microstructural changes associated with neuronal learning and memory.

However, since seizure end points are not a common manifestation of most psychiatric illnesses, kindling must be considered a nonhomologous model and an analogy for related processes that are likely to occur in other neuroanatomical and biochemical systems that might be more pertinent to behavioral pathology short of a full-blown seizure end point. In this manner, the kindling analogy is used to help further characterize one course of the unipolar and bipolar illness which typically involves the occurrence of early stressors that are initially insufficient to precipitate a full-blown affective episode, but that, with stressor recurrence (parallel to repeated electrical stimulation kindling), may trigger an episode of depression or mania. With sufficient occurrence of these triggered affective episodes, they, too, may begin to occur in the absence of obvious psychosocial precipitants. The data of Kessing and Bolwig and colleagues have validated one of the many predictions based on the kindling model, in that the number of prior hospitalizations for depressive episodes is directly proportional to the vulnerability to a recurrence, as assessed by both incidence and latency to relapse.

Another potential use of the kindling model in conceptualizing some elements of neuropsychiatric disorders is in the realm of loss of therapeutic efficacy of a drug treatment via a tolerance mechanism. Initially, administration of anticonvulsants before each amygdala-kindled seizure is typically associated with a marked reduction or complete suppression of seizure manifestations, depending on the drug. However, with repeated drug administration prior to (but not after) each kindled stimulation, seizures eventually break through most pharmacological interventions based on pharmacodynamic (and not pharmacokinetic) alterations associated with the contingent tolerance.

Loss of efficacy via tolerance has increasingly been recognized as a problem in the treatment of a variety of neuropsychiatric illnesses, including trigeminal neuralgia, Panic Disorder, epilepsy, and the recurrent affective disorders. To the extent that there is parallelism between tolerance mechanisms across these diverse syndromes, manipulations that are found to slow the development of tolerance to the anticonvulsant effects of drugs on amygdala-kindled seizures may provide hints to some of the molecular mechanisms involved and the maneuvers that may be assessed and directly tested in the clinical situation.

The data from the preclinical anticonvulsant tolerance studies of Weiss and associates suggest that tolerance is slowed by: use of higher rather than lower or only marginally effective doses; use of stable rather than escalating doses; use of higher potency drugs, such as valproate instead of carbamazepine or lamotrigine; initiating treatment early in the course of kindled seizure expression rather than late in its course; using combination strategies, such as combining carbamazepine and valproate at doses that for each alone would be associated with more rapid tolerance development.

In terms of approaching treatment when tolerance has already occurred, switching to drugs with different mechanisms of action may be most appropriate because these differently acting drugs are often not associated with cross-tolerance to the initial drug. When tolerance has occurred, returning to a previously effective agent after a period of time off that drug may also be helpful. Tolerance has been associated with the loss of selective endogenous anticonvulsant adaptations and with progression of the primary pathological processes of kindling. Hypothetically, a period of time off a drug would allow the endogenous compensatory adaptations to reemerge; this may be associated with renewed responsivity. Again, each of these potential approaches deserves consideration for its applicability to the clinical realm, and direct tests of the predictive validity of the model are needed. Some preliminary data are already supportive of some of the factors that might show loss of efficacy, such as the fact that lithium carbonate treatment instituted earlier in the course of bipolar illness is much more likely to be effective than when instituted later in the course of illness, after multiple episodes have occurred.

In summary, the development of kindled seizures to a previously subthreshold stimulation most clearly is a model of epileptogenesis, but may also be pertinent for considering molecular mechanisms and pharmacological interventions involved in the progression and treatment of a variety of other neuropsychiatric syndromes. Because the model is not behaviorally homologous for most of these syndromes, one must be particularly cautious about the direct inferences derived. The model would appear to be most useful in the area of conceptualization of mechanisms and interventions underlying syndrome progression and in its heuristic value toward new approaches to treatment and prevention.

SUGGESTED READING

Adamec, R. E. (1990). Does kindling model anything clinically relevant? *Biological Psychiatry, 27,* 249–279.

Clark, M., Post, R. M., Weiss, S. R., Cain, C. J., & Nakajima, T. (1991). Regional expression of c-fos mRNA in rat brain during the evolution of amygdala kindled seizures. *Brain Research and Molecular Brain Research, 11,* 55–64.

Corcoran, M. E., & Moshe, S. L. (Eds.). (1998). *Kindling* (5th ed.). New York: Plenum.

Goddard, G. V., & Douglas, R. M. (1975). Does the engram of kindling model the engram of normal long term memory? *Canadian Journal of Neurological Science, 2,* 385–394.

Goddard, G. V., McIntyre, D. C., & Leech, C. K. (1969). A permanent change in brain function resulting from daily electrical stimulation. *Experiments in Neurology, 25,* 295–330.

Kessing, L. V., Andersen, P. K., Mortensen, P. B., & Bolwig, T. G. (1998). Recurrence in affective disorder: I. Case register study. *British Journal of Psychiatry, 172,* 23–28.

McNamara, J. O. (1988). Pursuit of the mechanisms of kindling. *Trends in Neurological Science, 1,* 33–36.

Post, R. M., & Weiss, S. R. B. (1994). Kindling: Implications for the course and treatment of affective disorders. In K. Modigh, O. H. Robak, & T. Vestergaard (Eds.), *Anticonvulsants in psychiatry* (pp. 113–137). Stroud, UK: Wrightson Biomedical.

Post, R. M., & Weiss, S. R. B. (1996). A speculative model of affective illness cyclicity based on patterns of drug tolerance observed in amygdala-kindled seizures. *Molecular Neurobiology, 13,* 33–60.

Post, R. M., Weiss, S. R. B., Ketter, T. A., Denicoff, K. D., George, M. S., Frye, M. A., Smith, M. A., & Leverich, G. S. (1997). The kindling model: Implications for the etiology and treatment of Mood Disorders. *Current Review of Mood and Anxiety Disorders, 1,* 113–126.

Racine, R. (1978). Kindling: The first decade. *Neurosurgery, 3,* 234–252.

Sato, M., Racine, R. J., & McIntyre, D. C. (1990). Kindling: Basic mechanisms and clinical validity. *Electroencephalography and Clinical Neurophysiology, 76,* 459–472.

Weiss, S. R., & Post, R. M. (1994). Caveats in the use of the kindling model of affective disorders. *Toxicology and Indicators of Health, 10,* 421–447.

Weiss, S. R., & Post, R. M. (1998). Kindling: Separate vs. shared mechanisms in affective disorders and epilepsy. *Neuropsychobiology, 38,* 167–180.

Robert M. Post
National Institute of Mental Health

KINSEY INSTITUTE

The Kinsey Institute for Research in Sex, Gender and Reproduction is a not-for-profit corporation associated with Indiana University, Bloomington. It is the oldest continuously operating institution in the United States, and perhaps the world, focusing on sexuality research; the archiving of art, literature, and scientific materials on sexuality; and public and academic sexuality education.

Alfred C. Kinsey and the Establishment of the Institute for Sex Research

The Institute for Sex Research was established in 1947 by Alfred C. Kinsey, Sc.D. (1894–1956), a professor of zoology and eminent entomologist, and Herman B. Wells, president of Indiana University (Christenson, 1971; Gathorne-Hardy, 1998; Pomeroy, 1972).

The Institute began with Kinsey's 1938 course on marriage, requested by the Association of Women Students (Christenson, 1971). The scant sexuality material then available was primarily clinical or based upon individual opinion and experience. Kinsey began questioning students about their sex lives to provide some empirical data for his course, ultimately developing a 350-question face-to-face interview, encoded to protect subjects' confidentiality. Eventually data were gathered from individuals around the United States. Kinsey conducted 8,000 of the more than 17,000 interviews collected by the Institute from 1938 to 1956 (Gebhard & Johnson, 1979). His application of social science techniques to the documentation of sexual behavior was revolutionary (Reinisch, 1998).

In 1940, Kinsey abandoned entomology to pursue sexuality research. By 1941 support from the National Research Council's Committee for Research in the Problems of Sex (funded by the Rockefeller Foundation) permitted assembly of a full-time research team: biologist Clyde Martin, 1941; psychologist Wardell Pomeroy, 1943; and anthropologist Paul Gebhard, 1946 (Reinisch & Harter, 1994).

Sexual Behavior in the Human Male (Kinsey, Pomeroy, & Martin, 1948), a dry, academic tome based upon 5,300 interviews with American men, was published and became an international bestseller, followed by *Sexual Behavior in the Human Female* (Kinsey, Pomeroy, Martin, & Gebhard, 1953), reporting on 5,940 American women. The two "Kinsey Reports" samples primarily included white, middle class, college educated individuals under 35 years of age. The data on many "taboo" sexual activities challenged contemporary views by revealing that many American men and women had engaged in these activities. These data were still relied upon in the mid-1980s when the emergence of AIDS demanded information on sexual behavior (Institute of Medicine/National Academy of Sciences, 1986).

The volume on female behavior caused a major furor. Congress targeted the Rockefeller Foundation for its funding of the Institute. In 1954 the Rockefeller Foundation withdrew funding of sex research. Proceeds from the "Kinsey Reports" were used for staff salaries. There were also legal expenses when the U.S. Customs Service seized explicit materials intended for the Institute's archives. Kinsey died at 62 of cardiac failure following pneumonia on August 25, 1956. The following year, the seizure battle was won by attorney Harriet Pilpell in the landmark *United States v. 31 Photographs.*

The Low-Profile 1960s and 1970s

Following Kinsey's death, Gebhard was chosen as director. For the next two decades, a low public profile was maintained. The focus was on publication of books from the database, and organizing the expanding collections. *Pregnancy, Birth, and Abortion* (Gebhard, Pomeroy, Martin, & Christenson, 1958), and *Sex Offenders: An Analysis of Types* (Gebhard, Gagnon, Pomeroy, & Christenson, 1965) were published as were books on erotic art and Victorian sexual culture. Reflecting staff interests, from the mid-1960s through the 1970s research related to the sociology of sexuality (Gagnon & Simon, 1973), sexual morality (Klassen, Williams, & Levitt, 1989) and psychosocial aspects of homosexuality (Bell & Weinberg, 1978). NIMH supported some library services and related scholarly materials were compiled.

Expansion of the Kinsey Institute for Research in Sex, Gender, and Reproduction

In 1981 the university mandated that the Institute be overseen by an independent board of trustees. Following Gebhard's retirement, in 1982 they appointed June Machover Reinisch, a developmental biopsychologist, as the third director, and research was expanded to include biomedical and psychobiological issues. In 1983, the Institute was renamed The Kinsey Institute for Research in Sex, Gender, and Reproduction. New research examined the consequences of maternal hormone and drug treatment during pregnancy on the psychosexual development of offspring (Reinisch, Mortensen, & Sanders, 1993). Sexual behavior research was maintained with studies on high-risk sexual behavior related to AIDS and other STDs (Reinisch, Hill, Sanders, & Ziemba-Davis, 1995). A series of research symposia resulted in the Kinsey Institute Series of volumes, including *Masculinity / Femininity* (Reinisch, Rosenblum, & Sanders, 1990), *Adolescence and Puberty* (Bancroft & Reinisch, 1990), *Homosexuality / Heterosexuality* (McWhirter, Sanders, & Reinisch, 1987), and *AIDS and Sex* (Voeller, Reinisch, & Gottlieb, 1990).

Based on the 1982 mandate of the trustees and the university to raise the Institute's public profile, the Institute began providing the public with scientific information on sex, gender, and reproduction (Reinisch, Sanders, Hill, & Ziemba-Davis, 1991). From 1984 to 1993, an internationally syndicated newspaper column, "The Kinsey Report," answered more than 2,900 questions sent by readers from around the world. The Institute produced its third bestseller and first book specifically designed for the general public, *The Kinsey Institute New Report on Sex* (Reinisch, with Beasley, 1990), which was also published in eight other languages.

Central to the Institute's work are its large collections of print items, private papers and diaries, photographs, fine art objects, artifacts, popular ephemera, data archives, films, and videotapes (Reinisch, 1993) encompassing human sexuality from all eras, regions, and cultures. Beginning in the mid-1980s, there was a threefold expansion and renovation of the library and archives facilities, the staff was tripled, patron workspace was expanded, and a new art gallery was installed. In addition, the first curators for the collections were appointed, and full-time technical and information services and inputting the library and archives catalogs on-line was begun.

Recent Years

In 1993, upon Reinisch's retirement, Stephanie A. Sanders, a psychologist and the Institute's associate director, was appointed interim director. The institute's educational, archival, and patron service programs grew, and studies on high-risk sexual behavior (Sanders & Reinisch, 1999) and the effects of prenatal drug exposure on adult behavior (Reinisch, Sanders, Mortensen, & Rubin, 1995) were completed. In 1995, John Bancroft, a British psychiatrist, was appointed as the fourth director. The Institute's research again changed direction, emphasizing sexual functioning and research methodology. The first Kinsey Institute-associated clinics addressing sexual and menstrual cycle–related problems were established. The symposium series was continued with *Researching Sexual Behavior: Methodological Issues* (Bancroft, 1997), *The Role of Theory in Sex Research* (Bancroft, 1999) and *Sexuality in Mid-Life and Beyond.* Renovation and expansion of the facilities continued, computerization of library catalogs was finished, and formal involvement in graduate and professional education was undertaken.

Surviving more than five often turbulent decades during which it was regularly under attack, The Kinsey Institute has remained the premiere academic institution focused on the interdisciplinary study of sex, gender, and reproduction. It continues to develop and maintain extraordinary archives for a wide variety of artistic, cultural, and scientific materials related to human sexuality that remain an unparalleled resource for future generations of scholars, students, and professionals.

REFERENCES

Bancroft, J. (Ed.). (1997). *Researching sexual behavior: Methodological issues.* Bloomington: Indiana University Press.

Bancroft, J. (Ed.). (1999). *The role of theory in sex research.* Bloomington: Indiana University Press.

Bancroft, J., & Reinisch, J. M. (Eds.). (1990). *Adolescence and puberty.* Kinsey Institute Series. New York: Oxford University Press.

Bell, A. P., & Weinberg, M. S. (1978). *Homosexualities: A study of diversity among men and women.* New York: Simon & Schuster.

Christenson, C. V. (1971). *Kinsey: A biography.* Bloomington: Indiana University Press.

Gagnon, J., & Simon, W. (1973). *Sexual conduct: The social sources of human sexuality.* Chicago: Aldine.

Gathorne-Hardy, J. (1998). *Alfred C. Kinsey: Sex the measure of all things—A biography.* London: Chatto & Windus.

Gebhard, P. H., Gagnon, J. H., Pomeroy, W. B., & Christenson, C. V. (1965). *Sex offenders: An analysis of types.* New York: Harper & Row.

Gebhard, P. H., & Johnson, A. B. (1979). *The Kinsey data: Marginal tabulations of the 1938–1963 interviews conducted by the Institute for Sex Research.* Philadelphia: Saunders.

Gebhard, P. H., Pomeroy, W. B., Martin, C. E., & Christenson, C. V. (1958). *Pregnancy, birth and abortion.* New York: Harper Brothers.

Institute of Medicine/National Academy of Sciences. (1986). *Confronting AIDS: Directions for public health, health care, and research.* Washington, DC: National Academy Press.

Kinsey, A. C., Pomeroy, W. D., & Martin, C. E. (1948). *Sexual behavior in the human male.* Philadelphia: Saunders.

Kinsey, A. C., Pomeroy, W. D., Martin, C. E., & Gebhard, P. H. (1953). *Sexual behavior in the human female.* Philadelphia: Saunders.

Klassen, A. D., Williams, C. J., & Levitt, E. E. (1989). *Sex and morality in the U.S.: An empirical inquiry under the auspices of the Kinsey Institute.* Middletown, CT: Wesleyan University Press.

McWhirter, D. P., Sanders, S. A., & Reinisch, J. M. (Eds.). (1987). *Homosexuality / heterosexuality: Concepts of sexual orientation.* Kinsey Institute Series. New York: Oxford University Press.

Pomeroy, W. B. (1972). *Dr. Kinsey and the Institute for Sex Research.* New York: Harper & Row.

Reinisch, J. M. (1993). Preface: George Platt Lynes—A personal perspective. In J. Crump, *George Platt Lynes.* New York: Bullfinch Press, Little Brown.

Reinisch, J. M. (1998). Hoist on another's petard: The misreading of Kinsey's caveats. *Sexualities, 1,* 88–91.

Reinisch, J. M., with Beasley, R. (1990). *The Kinsey Institute new report on sex: What you must know to be sexually literate.* New York: St. Martin's Press.

Reinisch, J. M., & Harter, M. H. (1994). Alfred C. Kinsey. In V. Bullough & B. Bullough (Eds.), *Human sexuality: An encyclopedia.* New York: Garland.

Reinisch, J. M., Hill, C. A., Sanders, S. A., & Ziemba-Davis, M. (1995). High-risk sexual behavior at a Midwest university: A confirmatory survey. *Family Planning Perspectives, 27*(2), 79–82.

Reinisch, J. M., Mortensen, E. L., & Sanders, S. A. (1993). The Prenatal Development Project. *Acta Psychiatrica Scandinavica, Suppl 370,* 54–61.

Reinisch, J. M., Rosenblum, L. A., & Sanders, S. A. (Eds.). (1990). *Masculinity / femininity: Basic perspectives.* Kinsey Institute Series. New York: Oxford University Press.

Reinisch, J. M., Sanders, S. A., Hill, C. A., & Ziemba-Davis, M. (1991). Perceptions about sexual behavior: Findings from a national sex knowledge survey—United States, 1989. *Morbidity and Mortality Weekly Report, 40,* 249–252.

Reinisch, J. M., Sanders, S. A., Mortensen, E. L., & Rubin, D. B. (1995). In utero exposure to phenobarbital and intelligence deficits in adult men. *Journal of the American Medical Association, 274,* 1518–1525.

Sanders, S. A., & Reinisch, J. M. (1999). Would you say you had sex if " "? *Journal of the American Medical Association, 281,* 275–277.

Voeller, B., Reinisch, J. M., & Gottlieb, M. (Eds.). (1990). *AIDS: An integrated biomedical and biobehavioral approach.* Kinsey Institute Series. New York: Oxford University Press.

June M. Reinisch

See also: **Gender Roles; Homosexuality; Sexuality**

L

LANGUAGE ACQUISITION

One of the most amazing human abilities is the mastery by infants of a complex linguistic system within a relatively short amount of time. In the first year of life, and even before, infants are learning important distinctions relevant to speech perception. For example, exposure to speech that occurs before birth enables newborns to recognize their mother's voice (DeCasper & Fifer, 1980), and to use prosodic and acoustic cues to recognize a particular story that was read to them while they were in the womb (DeCasper & Spence, 1986). After birth, infants show the ability to distinguish unfamiliar languages from each other based on rhythmic differences, and an increasing ability to distinguish their native language from other languages (Nazzi, Jusczyk, & Johnson, 2000). In the first half-year of life, infants are able to discriminate both phonetic contrasts that occur and those that do not occur in their native language, but before the first year is up, they generally lose the ability to distinguish contrasts not relevant to their native language (Werker & Tess, 1984). During the latter half of the first year, infants also demonstrate the ability to use different types of information—such as syllable stress, phonotactics (legal combinations of sounds within words), coarticulation, and the likelihood that certain syllables co-occur—to segment the continuous speech stream into words (Johnson & Jusczyk, 2001; Saffran, Aslin, & Newport, 1996).

Language production starts in the first year of life with cooing and babbling, which increases in complexity and mirrors the prosodic patterns of the native language. Children start producing words around their first birthday. Initially, productive vocabulary acquisition is slow. Then, at around 18 months, a burst in vocabulary acquisition occurs. In English, early words tend to be common nouns. With increasing vocabulary size, verbs and adjectives begin to increase in number, followed by growth in grammatical function words such as prepositions and articles (Bates et al., 1994). What words and word classes will be acquired early is probably a function of frequency and saliency in parental input, as well as their phonological or morphological complexity.

When acquiring vocabulary, children must determine the meaning of each new word. When an object is directly labeled, children tend to extend that label to other objects that are similar in shape, rather than to objects that perform the same function but have a different appearance (Graham, Williams, & Huber, 1999). When children are given a new word in the presence of multiple objects, they tend to assign it to a novel object or to an object or part of a known object for which they do not already have a name. There are multiple explanations for this tendency, among them simply that the children's attention is captured by novelty, and thus they associate the new word with what has captured their attention (Smith, Jones, & Landau, 1996).

Grammatically, children start off producing single word utterances. With increasing age, utterances increase in length (generally measured in terms of number of morphemes—i.e., meaningful units, rather than words per se) and sophistication. Early multiword speech tends to leave out unstressed and grammatical elements, although comprehension studies show that children do know what grammatical words are appropriate in a sentence frame (Gerken & McIntosh, 1993), and even children at the one-word stage have mastery of grammatical devices such as word order in comprehension (Hirsh-Pasek & Golinkoff, 1996). Grammatical sophistication increases with age, with predictable patterns of mastery on structures such as negation, questions, passives, and relative clauses.

Theoretical Orientations

Because language learning occurs so quickly, and with such apparent ease, researchers such as Chomsky and Fodor have proposed that language learning is fundamentally different from other cognitive processes and involves an innate, language-specific component. Much of this claim revolves around the mastery of the grammar. Theorists from this camp claim that the linguistic input that a child receives does not contain enough information to allow a child to correctly induce the grammatical structure of the language. Thus, some innate contribution is necessary to overcome this poverty of the stimulus. One particularly influential innate language-specific theory is parameter setting, which proposes that an infant is born with a set of switches, or parameters, that code all possible linguistic variation. These parameters begin with a default setting. Linguistic input then triggers these parameters to be set to the value appropriate for that language. Setting the parameter then grants mastery of particular syntactic structures of that language. This mastery may encompass other structures than that represented in the trigger input. Thus, through the combination of the innate parameters and triggers from the linguistic input, grammatical mastery is achieved.

In contrast to the above viewpoint, other researchers believe that children bring general learning processes to language, and apply these to the input, which contains enough information for the child to figure out the grammar. Indeed, there is ample accumulating evidence that the linguistic input that children receive is not nearly as impoverished as innatists portray. For example, there are differences in phonetic and acoustic properties between content words and grammatical function words that may allow infants to distinguish between them (Morgan, Shi, & Allopenna, 1996). There is also a high, although imperfect, correlation between prosodic and syntactic units in speech, and during the first year of life, infants become sensitive to relevant prosodic cues (see Jusczyk, 1997). These prosodic cues may be exaggerated in the type of speech directed at infants. There is also evidence that children can use a general statistical learning mechanism to rapidly acquire knowledge about the speech stream. For example, with as little as two minutes of exposure to novel connected speech, infants can use co-occurrence regularities to parse the speech stream into words (Saffran, Aslin, & Newport, 1996) and to learn something about the underlying grammatical structure (Gomez & Gerken, 1999). Proponents of the general learning mechanism approach postulate that these and other types of information allow children to bootstrap up from the input to the grammar (see Hirsh-Pasek & Golinkoff, 1996).

REFERENCES

Bates, E., Marchman, V., Thal, D., Fenson, L., Dale, P., Reznick, J. S., Reilly, J., & Hartung, J. (1994). Developmental and stylistic variation in the composition of early vocabulary. *Journal of Child Language, 21,* 85–123.

DeCasper, A. J., & Fifer, W. P. (1980). Of human bonding: Newborns prefer their mother's voices. *Science, 208,* 1174–1176.

DeCasper, A. J., & Spence, M. J. (1986). Prenatal maternal speech influences newborns' perception of speech sounds. *Infant Behavior and Development, 9,* 133–150.

Gerken, L., & McIntosh, B. J. (1993). Interplay of function morphemes and prosody in early language. *Developmental Psychology, 29,* 448–457.

Gomez, R. L., & Gerken, L. (1999). Artificial grammar learning by 1-year-olds leads to specific and abstract knowledge. *Cognition, 70,* 109–135.

Graham, S. A., Williams, L. D., & Huber, J. F. (1999). Preschoolers' and adults' reliance on object shape and object function for lexical extension. *Journal of Experimental Child Psychology, 74,* 128–151.

Hirsh-Pasek, K., & Golinkoff, R. M. (1996). *The origins of grammar.* Cambridge, MA: MIT Press.

Johnson, E. K., & Jusczyk, P. W. (2001). Word segmentation by 8-month-olds: When speech cues count more than statistics. *Journal of Memory and Language, 44,* 548–567.

Jusczyk, P. W. (1997). *The discovery of spoken language.* Cambridge, MA: MIT Press.

Morgan, J. L., Shi, R., & Allopenna, P. (1996). Perceptual bases of rudimentary grammatical categories: Toward a broader conceptualization of bootstrapping. In J. L. Morgan & K. Demuth (Eds.), *Signal to syntax* (pp. 263–283). Mahwah, NJ: Erlbaum.

Nazzi, T., Jusczyk, P. W., & Johnson, E. K. (2000). Language discrimination by English-learning 5-month-olds: Effects of rhythm and familiarity. *Journal of Memory and Language, 43,* 1–19.

Saffran, J. R., Aslin, R. N., & Newport, E. L. (1996). Statistical learning by 8-month-old infants. *Science, 274,* 1926–1928.

Smith, L. B., Jones, S. S., & Landau, B. (1996). Naming in young children: A dumb attentional mechanism? *Cognition, 60,* 143–171.

Werker, J. F., & Tess, R. C. (1984). Cross-language speech perception: Evidence for perceptual reorganization during the first year of life. *Infant Behavior and Development, 7,* 49–63.

Janet L. McDonald
Louisiana State University

LANGUAGE: ITS INTERGROUP PARAMETERS

Language is an integral element of most intergroup relations, as evidenced by the resurrection of Hebrew as a lingua franca in multicultural Israel, the role of French in Quebecois separation, and the revival of Catalan in Spain. But beyond nationalist and ethnic arenas, forms of language (e.g., dialect, nonverbals, and discourse) play key roles in virtually all intergroup situations—as evident in adolescents' distinctive speech styles, patronizing ways of addressing and referring to older adults and the physically challenged, expressions and tone of voice used among gay men, and so forth (see Clément, 1996). In fact, intergroup processes have become core foci in the social psychology of language, as witnessed by their frequent appearance across many different chapters of *The New Handbook of Language and Social Psychology* (Robinson & Giles, 2001).

Much of the research and theory devoted to these issues has its origins in the social identity theory (SIT) of intergroup relations (e.g., Tajfel & Turner, 1979). The latter emerged from European social psychologists' dissatisfaction with reductionist (predominantly North American) approaches that provided explanations of intergroup behavior couched in terms of individual psychology (e.g., frustration-aggression, belief dissimilarity). SIT, in contrast, articulated an explanation in terms of social beliefs about the contextual relations between groups. In particular, it highlighted a social motivation to create or maintain a positive social identity that is realized and constrained by people's beliefs about the place of their in-group in the status hierarchy. These beliefs concern the legitimacy and stability of intergroup status relations as well as beliefs about the feasibility, or lack thereof, of passing into another group.

Different combinations of these beliefs encourage different identity enhancement strategies.

One of the most developed products of this approach has, arguably, been its extension into the realm of language and intercultural communication (e.g., Gudykunst & Ting-Toomey, 1988), one that contributes enormously to our understanding of many language phenomena, including second language learning, code-switching, semilingualism, diglossia, patterns of language attitudes and language shifts, and so forth. An important theoretical force here has been ethnolinguistic identity theory, which has added further criteria (e.g., "group vitality") and brought into sharper focus the specific language strategies that might be used in intergroup settings (see Giles & Coupland, 1991). Group vitality articulates the ways that groups differ with respect to institutional support (e.g., via education and the media), demographic representation (e.g., numbers and concentration of group members), and status variables (e.g., economic control and a historic sense of in-group pride). The more group members perceive their group to possess these facets of vitality, the more likely they are to engage in activities designed to maintain their so-called "psycholinguistic distinctiveness" (via language, dialect, specialized jargon, slang, code words, etc.). Certain caveats notwithstanding, research around the globe has shown that groups possessing high perceived vitality prosper, while those that lack such vitality integrate with dominant groups or die out.

While ethnolinguistic identity theory describes the wider macrosocial processes that frame language use, communication accommodation theory describes the accomplishment of these identity enhancement strategies within microsocial contexts (see Giles & Coupland, 1991). Broadly, language can be used to draw out similarities with an interlocutor (called "convergence"), or it can be used to maintain or enhance social distance (called "divergence"). In an interpersonal context, convergence is assumed to reflect an interlocutor's motive of wanting to be liked; convergence indicates similarity to the recipient which, in turn, can foster social attraction. In intergroup contexts, "upward" convergence by a minority group speaker to the dominant group's language can be found when people are not particularly invested in their group identity; when group boundaries are thought to be surmountable; and when the status distinction is considered to be legitimate and stable. Such convergences would be even more likely if such speakers also construed their group vitality to be relatively low.

At other times, and sometimes even in the same intergroup context, "downward" divergence (i.e., the maintenance or accentuation of a subordinate group's language forms, such as with the Hawaiian language movement) can be found in individuals who are strongly committed to their group; who consider the social boundaries between their group and the dominant group to be impermeable; who construe their group's vitality to be relatively high; and who believe their status inequality vis á vis the outgroup is unstable and illegitimate.

By considering these and other background conditions, we can see how views about bilingualism—as being additive to or detracting from one or another group's identity—can evolve in a society. Indeed, immigrants' supposed "failure" to acquire near-native proficiency in their host community's language can, from an intergroup perspective, be reinterpreted as the immigrants' successful retention of their own group's language in the face of a significant threat to its survival in that milieu. Such a position has profound implications for second language pedagogy and the kinds of social factors deemed necessary to address in teaching people bilingual skills.

As alluded to earlier, this general theoretical backdrop has been confirmed, extended, and applied in a number of intergroup contexts, notably between genders, socioeconomic brackets, different generations, and those of differing physical capacities, as well as in the strategic use of language in sustaining, legitimizing, and subverting social power (see Harwood & Giles, in press). Future work in the study of "intergroup language"—that which is regulated by individuals' awareness of their memberships in various relevant social groups (Hindu, gang member, physician, and so forth)—is likely to move beyond SIT by taking into account theoretical developments in self-categorization theory (Turner, Hogg, Oakes, Reicher, & Wetherell, 1987). This replaces the social motivational mechanism in SIT with a social-cognitive mechanism: group behavior is driven by a search for a maximally meaningful identity that seeks to determine how individuals fit into the world. They achieve this by identifying with groups that simultaneously maximize within-group similarities and between-group differences. Self-categorization theory can lead, potentially, to language-based theories of leadership emergence, stereotyping, social influence, and social attraction. What is more, the same mechanism might be integrated into ethnolinguistic identity and communication accommodation theories, thereby providing a more parsimonious account of language shifts and macrosocial conditions that increases our understanding of who in an particular social group uses which language strategies, addressing also questions of how, when, with what outcomes, and why.

REFERENCES

Clément, R. (Ed.). (1996). The social psychology of intergroup communication. *Special Issue of the Journal of Language and Social Psychology, 15,* 221–392.

Giles, H., & Coupland, N. (1991). *Language: Contexts and consequences.* Pacific Grove, CA: Brooks/Cole.

Gudykunst, W. B., & Ting-Toomey, S., with Chua, E. (1988). *Culture and interpersonal communication.* Newbury Park, CA: Sage.

Harwood, J., & Giles, H. (Eds.). (in press). *Intergroup communication: Multiple perspectives.* New York & Berlin: Peter Lang.

Robinson, W. P., & Giles, H. (Eds.). (2001). *The new handbook of language and social psychology.* Chichester, UK and New York: Wiley.

Tajfel, H., & Turner, J. C. (1979). An integrative theory of intergroup conflict. In W. G. Austin & S. Worchel (Eds.), *The social psychology of intergroup relations* (pp. 33–47). Monterey, CA: Brooks/Cole.

Turner, J. C., Hogg, M. A., Oakes, P. J., Reicher, S. D., & Wetherell, M. S. (1987). *Discovering the social group: Self-categorization theory.* Oxford: Blackwell.

Howard Giles
Scott Reid
University of California, Santa Barbara

See also: **Language; Socialization**

LATE-LIFE FORGETTING

There is considerable public concern that memory loss signals the beginning of Alzheimer's disease or senility. Early diagnosis, combined with intervention and family support, can assist older adults with memory loss to function and to manage life on a daily basis in the least restrictive setting.

The first task for the health professional faced by a patient concerned about memory loss is to ascertain whether the symptoms are indicative of dementia or whether they are the result of normal decline in cognitive abilities associated with the aging process. Even if there is a diagnosis of dementia (defined by the American Psychiatric Association as a loss of intellectual abilities of sufficient severity to interfere with social or occupational functioning), it is important to determine whether the dementia is reversible or not. If the cause is determined promptly, some dementias are reversible, because an almost limitless array of diseases and behavioral disorders can result in a dementing process. Muriel Lezak (1995) points out that memory loss serves as a starting point for differentiating individuals with normal forgetting from those who might warrant a diagnosis of dementia.

Two types of memory impairments are described by Asenath LaRue (1982) to distinguish between normal and nonnormal forgetting. Originally, these were labeled *benign senescent forgetfulness* and *malignant senescent forgetfulness.* Benign forgetfulness was characterized by memory failures limited to relatively unimportant facts but included the ability to recall these at a later time. Most of the forgotten aspects were part of the remote rather than the recent past, and the individual was usually aware of the memory loss and could compensate for it. In some ways, this type of forgetting is not unlike the absentminded professor stereotype. In contrast, malignant forgetfulness of old age included distortion of memories, reduced retention time, and difficulties in remembering recent events and experiences. In addition, disorientation to place, time, and eventually, person also occurred. On the face of it, this seemed to be a straightforward distinction between types of forgetfulness. However, critics have speculated whether benign and malignant senescent forgetfulness are points on a continuum rather than separate conditions.

There have been a number of attempts to define changes in memory associated with normal aging. A National Institute of Mental Health work group was established in 1986 to study and encourage research and communication in this area. This work group published diagnostic criteria for what they termed age-associated memory impairment (AAMI). The criteria for AAMI required the presence of memory complaints based on a gradual onset of memory loss in adults 50 years and older functioning within an acceptable intellectual level (specifically defined by the criteria). To meet the criteria of AAMI, individuals must perform 1 standard deviation (SD) below the average established for younger adults on tests of recent memory. In addition, a number of criteria exclude an individual from meeting the AAMI category. These include the presence of dementia, alcohol dependence, depression, certain neurological disorders, and/or other medical disorders. Current use of psychotropic drugs also would disqualify an individual from meeting the diagnostic criteria. AAMI, it was argued, was designed to describe older adults who have memory problems but who do not suffer from a neurological impairment. It was assumed that AAMI is a normal consequence of aging in a proportion of older individuals.

Richard C. Blackford and Asenath LaRue (1989) took some issue with the measurement aspects of AAMI. They recommended that there should be two categories within AAMI: age-consistent memory impairment and late-life forgetfulness. The criteria for age-consistent memory impairment include performance on 75% of memory tests used that are within +1 SD of the mean established for that participant's age.

The criteria for late-life forgetting requires performance on 50% or more of the tests given that are within 1 to 2 SD below the mean established for that age. The exclusion criteria for each of these subcategories is somewhat similar to those stated previously for age-associated memory impairments. All these categories apply to individuals between the ages of 50 to 79, but exclude individuals 80 and above.

Glenn Smith and others (1991) studied age-associated memory impairment, age-consistent memory impairment, and late-life forgetting by testing 523 cognitively normal older adults living in the community. The researchers did not seek out individuals who complained of memory problems. In fact, they specifically selected participants who did not present memory complaints. After excluding those participants who did not meet criteria (e.g., those who were taking psychotropic medications or had histories of alcohol abuse or who had medical, neurological, or other relevant disorders), they found that 98% of members in one group and 77% of members in another group met criteria for age-associated memory impairments as suggested by the National Institute of Mental Health. The researchers concluded that age-related changes in memory should avoid the implication of disability suggested by the term *impairment*. They believe that a better term would be *age-associated memory decline*. They also recommended that more effort be expended to develop normative data for individuals of advanced age, including the old-old. Finally, the researchers recommended that a specific memory battery be used rather than permitting researchers to select from a range of testing instruments. Glenn Smith and colleagues (1991) also point out that there is wide variability in the diagnosis of early or probable dementia, and the use of the term *impairment* suggests abnormality and disease. They counter that the true meaning of scoring 1 SD below that of younger individuals in decline of memory functions has not been determined. In the meantime, it might be best not to label such declines as pathological. More recent developments include the use of the term *mild cognitive decline* (MCI), which is viewed as a transitional state between normal aging and Alzheimer's disease—recognizing, however, that many individuals with MCI will not develop Alzheimer's disease. Howard Chertkow (2002) suggests that mild cognitive impairment may be the stage in which preventive therapies are most useful, since he estimates that 19 to 50% of individuals with mild cognitive impairments progress to dementia over three years.

REFERENCES

Blackford, R. C., & LaRue, A. (1989). Criteria for diagnosing age associated memory impairment: Proposed improvements from the field. *Developmental Neuropsychology, 5,* 295–306.

Chertkow, H. (2002). Mild cognitive impairment. *Current Opinion in Neurology, 15,* 401–407.

LaRue, A. (1982). Memory loss and aging. *Psychiatric clinics of North America, 5,* 89–103.

Lezak, M. D. (1995). *Neuropsychological assessment* (3rd ed.). New York: Oxford University Press.

Smith, G., Ivnik, R. R., Peterson, R. C., Malec, J. F., Kokmen, E., & Tangalos, E. (1991). Age associated memory impairment diagnoses: Problems of reliability and concerns for terminology. *Psychology and Aging, 6,* 551–558.

Norman Abeles
Michigan State University

LATE-LIFE PSYCHOSIS

The number of elderly persons with psychosis has risen in tandem with the growth of the geriatric population. The predisposing factors include comorbid illnesses, pharmacokinetic alterations, cortical neuron loss, neurochemical changes, social isolation, sensory deficits, cognitive changes, polypharmacy, premorbid personalities, and female gender.

Diagnoses associated with psychosis in the elderly include Delirium, Schizophrenia, Delusional Disorder, Mood Disorder, Dementia, Substance Abuse, medical conditions, neurological conditions, and Substance-Induced Psychotic Disorder.

Cognitive impairment in the elderly, including organic psychosis, has an estimated prevalence rate of 16.8% to 23%. In a study of patients with Alzheimer's disease, 63% developed psychosis. The prevalence rate of delirium in hospitalized elderly is reported to be 11% to 24%.

Structural abnormalities, including white matter hyperintensities and focal brain disease, have been reported in elderly patients with psychotic disorders. Subjects with late onset psychotic disorders have abnormal brain imaging studies, and half had white matter lesions and/or lacunar infarctions.

Delirium

Delirium is an acute state characterized by changes in cognition and consciousness, often accompanied by visual hallucinations and paranoid delusions. Delirium may be superimposed on other neuropsychiatric conditions. Clouded consciousness, poor attention span, and a fluctuating course during the day are features that help in the diagnosis. Early recognition and treatment of the cause are important to reduce the high morbidity and mortality rates associated with this diagnosis. Common causes of delirium include infections; drugs, especially anticholinergics; electrolyte imbalance; arrhythmia; and myocardial infarction. Other causes include transient ischemic attacks, cerebrovascular accidents, structural brain lesions, and withdrawal from prescription medications and substances of potential abuse. Disruption of cerebral metabolism and neurotransmission, particularly of dopamine and GABA pathways, have been implicated in the pathophysiology of delirium. Persistent cognitive deficits may reflect a concurrent dementing illness.

Schizophrenia

Schizophrenia may continue into old age or, rarely, its first episode may occur in patients older than 45. Approximately 15% of all patients with schizophrenia may have onset of symptoms after the age of 45. There are some differences between Late Onset and Early Onset Schizophrenia (LOS and EOS). LOS is more common in women, has fewer negative symptoms, and tends to respond to lower doses of antipsychotic medication than EOS. MRI study of the size of thalami found them to be larger in LOS than EOS.

Symptoms of EOS tend to become less severe with age. Both positive and negative symptoms improve in about 20%

of patients, remain relatively unchanged in 60% of patients, and worsen in only 20% of patients.

Delusional Disorder

As per *DSM-IV,* patients with Delusional Disorder reveal persistent delusions without prominent hallucinations in the absence of Dementia, Schizophrenia, or Mood Disorders. The delusions are nonbizarre and usually circumscribed. Patients are generally resistant to treatment.

Mood Disorder with Psychosis

Mania and depression in the elderly can be associated with psychotic symptoms such as delusions and hallucinations. Elderly patients with psychotic depression are at increased risk for relapse and have more persistent symptoms, suicide attempts, hospitalizations, comorbidity, and financial dependency.

Dementia with Psychosis

Psychotic symptoms can occur in dementia secondary to various etiologies. Alzheimer's disease is the most common cause of dementia, and more than 50% of patients manifest psychotic symptoms during the course of the illness.

Detailed discussion of late life psychotic disorder due to medical or neurological conditions, substance abuse, or prescription drugs is beyond the scope of this brief article and may be found elsewhere.

Treatment of Late-Life Psychosis

A thorough psychiatric and medical assessment is essential before initiation of treatment. Social, behavioral, and environmental interventions should be considered before pharmacotherapy. Antipsychotic drugs, cholinesterase inhibitors, electroconvulsive therapy, mood stabilizers, benzodiazepines, and buspirone are the most commonly used medications.

Pharmacokinetic and pharmacodynamic factors, comorbid medical illnesses, and concurrent medications increase side effects and drug interactions in this population. The geriatric psychopharmacology maxim "start low and go slow" should be followed in the use of these medications. The appropriate starting dose of antipsychotics in the elderly is 25% of the adult dose and daily maintenance dose is 30 to 50%. Antipsychotic medications in the elderly can require 6 weeks or longer for optimum therapeutic effects. Patients with Dementia generally require smaller doses of antipsychotics than patients with Schizophrenia.

Conventional Antipsychotics. The use of conventional antipsychotics is limited because of their increased potential for serious side effects. The advantages include the availability of parenteral preparation for rapid control of agitation and long-acting, injectable preparations for haloperidol and fluphenazine.

Atypical Antipsychotics. The atypical agents are as efficacious in reducing positive symptoms, more efficacious in reducing negative symptoms, and have a much safer side effect profile.

Clozapine has moderate to good efficacy and very low rate of extrapyramidal symptoms (EPS), but has significant other side effects including delirium, somnolence, orthostasis, agranulocytosis, and cardiac effects. Its use requires regular monitoring every 2 weeks for adverse effects on the white blood cell count. Clozapine is the only antipsychotic medication with demonstrated efficacy in the treatment of refractory Schizophrenia.

Risperidone is the most widely studied atypical agent used in treating the elderly. The most frequent side effects reported include sedation, dose dependent EPS, dizziness, and postural hypotension. The advantages include negligible anticholinergic effects, low incidence of EPS and tardive dyskinesia (TD) (at low doses), and efficacy for positive and negative symptoms.

Olanzapine is increasingly being used in the elderly. The side effects include sedation, weight gain, anticholinergic effects, dizziness, and orthostasis. The advantages include low incidence of EPS and good effect on positive and negative symptoms.

Quetiapine is the least studied atypical agent used in treating the elderly. The common adverse effects include somnolence, dizziness, and postural hypotension. Advantages include negligible EPS and minimal anticholinergic effects, with good effectiveness on positive and negative symptoms.

Conclusion

The new atypical antipsychotic agents offer significant advantages over conventional agents in the treatment of psychosis in the elderly. Antipsychotic drugs form part of a comprehensive treatment plan which should include psychosocial, behavioral, and environmental interventions in the management of late-life psychosis.

SUGGESTED READING

American Psychiatric Association. (1994). *Diagnostic and statistical manual of mental disorders* (4th ed.). Washington, DC: Author.

American Psychiatric Association. (1997). Practice guidelines for the treatment of patients with Schizophrenia. *American Journal of Psychiatry, 154*(4 suppl), 1–63.

Belitsky, R., & McGlashan, T. H. (1993). At issue: The manifestations of Schizophrenia in late life: A dearth of data. *Schizophrenia Bulletin, 19,* 683–685.

Brown, F. W. (1993). The neurobiology of late-life psychosis. *Critical Review of Neurobiology, 7,* 275–289.

Corey-Bloom, J., Jernigan, T., Archibald, S., Harris, M. J., & Jeste

D. V. (1995). Quantitative magnetic resonance imaging in late-life Schizophrenia. *American Journal of Psychiatry, 152,* 447–449.

Harris, M. J., & Jeste, D. V. (1988). Late onset Schizophrenia: An overview. *Schizophrenia Bulletin, 14,* 39–55.

Janicak, P. G., Easton, M., & Comaty, J. E. (1989). Efficacy of ECT in psychotic and nonpsychotic depression. *Convulsive Therapy, 5,* 314–320.

Jeste, D. V., Eastham, J. H., Lacro, J. P., Gierz, M., Field, M. G., & Harris, M. J. (1996). Management of late-life psychosis. *Journal of Clinical Psychiatry, 57*(Suppl. 3), 39–45.

Jeste, D. V., Harris, M. J., Krull, A., Kuck, J., McAdams, L. A., & Heaton, R. (1995). Clinical and neuropsychological characteristics of patients with late onset Schizophrenia. *American Journal of Psychiatry, 152,* 722–730.

Jeste, D. V., Lacro, J. P., Gilbert, P. L., Kline, J., & Kline, N. (1993). Treatment of late life Schizophrenia with neuroleptics. *Schizophrenia Bulletin, 19,* 817–830.

Katz, I., Jeste, D. V., Mintzer, J. E., Clyde, C., Napolitano, J., & Brecher, M. (1999). Comparison of risperidone and placebo for psychosis and behavioral disturbances associated with Dementia a randomized double blind trial. *Journal of Clinical Psychiatry, 60,* 107–115.

Kotrla, K. J., Chacko, R. C., Harper, R. G., & Doody, R. (1995). Clinical variables associated with psychosis in Alzheimer's disease. *American Journal of Psychiatry, 152,* 1377–1379.

Lesser, I. M., Jeste, D. V., Boone, K. B., Harris, M. J., Miller, B. L., Heaton, R. K., & Hill-Gutierrez, E. (1992). Late onset psychotic disorder, not otherwise specified: Clinical and neuro imaging findings. *Biological Psychiatry, 31,* 419–423.

Lipowski, Z. (1989). Delirium in the elderly patient. *New England Journal of Medicine, 320,* 578–582.

Madhusoodanan, S., Brecher, M., Brenner, R., Kasckow, J., Kunik, M., & Negron, A. E. (1999). Risperidone in the treatment of elderly patients with Psychotic Disorders. *American Journal of Geriatric Psychiatry, 7,* 132–138.

Madhusoodanan, S., Brenner, R., Araujo, L., & Abaza, A. (1995). Efficacy of risperidone treatment for psychosis associated with Schizophrenia, Schizoaffective Disorder, bipolar disorder or senile Dementia in 11 geriatric patients: A case series. *Journal of Clinical Psychiatry, 56,* 514–518.

Madhusoodanan, S., Brenner, R., & Cohen, C. I. (1999). Role of atypical antipsychotics in the treatment of psychosis and agitation associated with Dementia. *CNS Drugs, 12*(2), 135–150.

Madhusoodanan, S., Brenner, R., Suresh, P., Concepcion, N. M., Florita, C. D., Menon, G., Kaur, A., Nunez, G., & Reddy, H. (2000). Efficacy and tolerability of olanzapine in elderly patients with Psychotic Disorders: A prospective study. *Annals of Clinical Psychiatry, 12*(1), 11–18.

Madhusoodanan, S., Suresh, P., & Brenner, R. (1999). Experience with atypical antipsychotics—Risperidone and olanzapine in the elderly. *Annals of Clinical Psychiatry, (11)*3, 113–118.

Myers, J. K., Weissman, M. M., & Tischler, G. (1984). Six month prevalence of psychiatric disorders in three communities. *Archives of General Psychiatry, 41,* 959–970.

Nelson, J. C., Conwell, Y., Kim, K., & Mazure, C. (1989). Age at onset in late-life delusional depression. *American Journal of Psychiatry, 146,* 785–786.

Pearlson, G., & Rabins, P. (1988). The late-onset psychoses: Possible risk factors. *Psychiatric Clinics of North America, 11,* 15–32.

Sajatovic, M., Madhusoodanan, S., & Buckley, P. (2000). Schizophrenia in the elderly: Guidelines for its recognition and treatment. *CNS Drugs, 13*(2), 103–115.

Sajatovic, M., Perez, D., Brescan, D., & Ramirez, L. F. (1998). Olanzapine therapy in elderly patients with Schizophrenia. *Psychopharmacology Bulletin, 34*(4), 819–823.

Satterlee, W. G., Reams, S. G., Burns, P. R., Hamilton, S., Tran, P. V., & Tollefson, G. D. (1995). A clinical update on olanzapine treatment in schizophrenia and in elderly Alzheimer's disease patients (abstract). *Psychopharmacology Bulletin, 31,* 534.

Street, J., Clark, W. S., & Mitan, S. (1998, December 14–18). *Olanzapine in the treatment of psychosis and behavioral disturbances associated with Alzheimer's disease.* American College of Neuropsychopharmacology 37th Annual meeting, Las Croabas, Puerto Rico, Scientific abstracts: 223.

Targum, S. D., & Abbott, J. L. (1999). Psychoses in the elderly: A spectrum of disorders. *Journal of Clinical Psychiatry, 60*(Suppl. 8), 4–10.

Tariot, P. N. (1996). Treatment strategies for agitation and psychosis in Dementia. *Journal of Clinical Psychiatry, 57*(Suppl. 14), 21–29.

Thorpe, L. (1997). The treatment of psychotic disorders in late life. *Canadian Journal of Psychiatry, 42*(Suppl. 1), 195–275.

S. Madhusoodanan
R. Brenner
M. Spitzer
St John's Episcopal Hospital

C. I. Cohen
State University of New York

LATENT INHIBITION

Latent inhibition (LI) is demonstrated when a previously exposed, unattended stimulus is less effective in a new learning situation than a novel stimulus. The term *latent inhibition* dates back to Lubow and Moore (1959), who intended to design a classical conditioning analog of latent learning. As such, the LI effect was "latent" in that it was not exhibited in the stimulus preexposure phase, but rather in the subsequent test phase. "Inhibition" simply reflected the fact that the effect was manifest as a *retardation* of learning. Since that first demonstration, there have been hundreds of LI-related experiments. LI is extremely robust, appearing in all mammalian species that have been tested and across many different learning paradigms.

The ubiquitous nature of LI suggests some adaptive advantages. Indeed, LI appears to protect the organism from associating irrelevant stimuli with other events. It helps to partition the important from the unimportant, and thus to economize on processing capacity by selectively biasing the organism to more fully process new inputs as opposed to old, inconsequential ones.

Although the term *latent inhibition* is descriptive, the phenomenon has been subject to a number of theoretical interpretations. One class of theories holds that inconsequential stimulus preexposure results in reduced *associability* for that stimulus as compared to a novel stimulus. The loss of associability has been attributed to a variety of mechanisms that reduce attention (see Lubow, 1989 for a review), which then must be reacquired in order for learning to proceed normally.

Alternatively, it has been proposed that LI is a result of *retrieval failure* rather than acquisition failure. Such a hypothesis suggests that following stimulus preexposure, the acquisition of the new association to the old stimulus proceeds normally. However, in the test stage, two competing associations may be retrieved, an earlier stimulus–no consequence association from the preexposure stage and/or the stimulus–unconditioned stimulus association of the acquisition stage. In normal LI, the nonpreexposed group performs better than the preexposed group because there is only the second association to be retrieved, whereas the preexposed group performs poorly because both the first and second associations, which are in competition, are retrieved.

Among those variables that consistently have been shown to modulate the size of the LI effect, and perhaps the most important theoretically is that of context. In virtually all LI studies, the context, unless specifically an experimental variable, remains the same in the stimulus preexposure and test phases. However, if context is changed from the preexposure to the test phase, then LI is severely attenuated. In addition: (1) For context and stimulus preexposure to be effective in producing LI, the two must be preexposed conjointly; (2) Context preexposure after preexposure of the stimulus in that same context (context extinction procedure) has little or no effect on LI; and (3) Preexposure of the context prior to stimulus preexposure in the same context increases the magnitude of LI.

The various stimulus preexposure–context effects have been used to develop a theory of the conditioning of inattention and its modulation to account for both LI in normals and its reduction in schizophrenics. The theory states that normal LI is manifest when the preexposure context reappears in test and sets the occasion for eliciting the stimulus–no consequence association that was acquired during preexposure. As such, the context limits the access of the previously exposed irrelevant stimulus to working memory. In addition, it has been proposed that in schizophrenia, there is a breakdown in the relationship between the preexposed stimulus and the context, such that the context no longer sets the occasion for the expression of the stimulus–no consequence association. Consequently, working memory is inundated with experimentally familiar but phenomenally novel stimuli, each competing for the limited resources required for efficient information processing. This description fits well with the symptoms of schizophrenia, particularly high distractibility, as well as with research findings.

The assumption that the same attentional process that produces LI in normal subjects is dysfunctional in schizophrenics has stimulated considerable research. Evidence to support this contention comes from several sources, including the parallel effects of dopamine activity associated with schizophrenia and with LI. There is much data that indicate that dopamine agonists and antagonists modulate LI in rats and in normal humans. Dopamine agonists, such as amphetamine, abolish LI, while dopamine antagonists, such as haloperidol and other neuroleptics, produce a super-LI effect. In addition, manipulations of putative dopamine pathways in the brain have the expected effects on LI. Thus, hippocampal and septal lesions interfere with the development of LI, as do lesions of the nucleus accumbens (for reviews, see Gray, 1998; Weiner & Feldon, 1997). With human subjects, there is some evidence that nonmedicated schizophrenics show reduced LI compared to medicated schizophrenics and normals, while there are no differences in the amount of LI in the latter two groups. Finally, symptomatically normal subjects who score high on psychotic-prone or schizotypal scales also exhibit reduced LI compared to low psychotic-prone/low schizotypal subjects (for a review, see Lubow & Gewirtz, 1995).

In addition to LI illustrating a fundamental strategy of information processing and providing a useful tool for examining attentional dysfunctions in pathological groups, LI has also been used to explain why certain therapies, such as alcohol aversion treatments, are not as effective as might be expected. On the other hand, LI procedures may be useful in counteracting some of the undesirable side effects that frequently accompany radiation and chemotherapies for cancer, such as food aversion. Finally, LI research has suggested techniques that may be efficacious in the prophylactic treatment of certain fears and phobias (for a review of the practical applications of LI, see Lubow, 1997).

In summary, the basic LI phenomenon represents some output of a selective attention process that results in learning to ignore irrelevant stimuli. It has become an important tool for understanding information processing in general, as well as attentional dysfunctions, and it has implications for a variety of practical problems.

REFERENCES

Gray, J. A. (1998). Integrating schizophrenia. *Schizophrenia Bulletin, 24,* 249–266.

Lubow, R. E. (1989). *Latent inhibition and conditioned attention theory.* New York: Cambridge University Press.

Lubow, R. E. (1997). Latent inhibition and behavior pathology. In W. D. O'Donohue (Ed.), *Learning and behavior therapy* (pp. 107–121). Boston: Allyn & Bacon.

Lubow, R. E., & Gewirtz, J. (1995). Latent inhibition in humans: Data, theory, and implications for schizophrenia. *Psychological Bulletin, 117,* 87–103.

Lubow, R. E., & Moore, A. U. (1959). Latent inhibition: The effect of non-reinforced preexposure to the conditioned stimulus. *Journal of Comparative and Physiological Psychology, 52,* 415–419.

Weiner, I., & Feldon, J. (1997). The switching model of latent inhibition: An update of neural substrates. *Behavioural Brain Research, 88,* 11–26.

Robert E. Lubow
Tel Aviv University, Israel

See also: Schizophrenia

LEARNED HELPLESSNESS

Learned helplessness was discovered when researchers immobilized a dog and exposed it to electric shocks that could be neither avoided nor escaped. Twenty-four hours later, the dog was placed in a situation in which electric shock could be terminated by a simple response. The dog did not make this response; instead, it just sat passively. This behavior was in marked contrast to dogs in a control group that reacted vigorously to the shock and learned to turn it off.

These investigators proposed that the dog had learned to be helpless. When originally exposed to uncontrollable shock, it learned that nothing it did mattered. Shocks came and went independently of behavior. This learning of response-outcome independence was represented as an expectation of future helplessness that was generalized to new situations to produce motivational, cognitive, and emotional deficits. These deficits following uncontrollability have come to be known as the *learned helplessness phenomenon,* and their cognitive explanation as the *learned helplessness model.*

Much of the early interest in learned helplessness stemmed from its clash with traditional stimulus-response theories of learning. Alternative accounts of learned helplessness were proposed by theorists who saw no need to invoke mentalistic constructs, and these alternatives emphasized an incompatible motor response learned when animals were first exposed to uncontrollability. This response was presumably generalized to the second situation, where it interfered with performance at the test task.

Steven Maier and Martin Seligman (1976) conducted a series of studies testing the learned helplessness model and the incompatible motor response alternative. The most compelling argument for the cognitive account comes from the *triadic design,* a three-group experimental paradigm that differentiates uncontrollability from trauma. Animals in one group are exposed to shock that they are able to terminate by making some response. Animals in a second group are yoked to those in the first group, exposed to the identical shocks; the only difference is that animals in the first group control their outcome whereas those in the second do not. Animals in a third group are exposed to no shock at all. All animals are then given the same test task. Animals with control over the initial shocks typically show no helplessness when tested. They act just like animals with no prior exposure to shock. Animals without control become helpless.

Also supporting a cognitive interpretation of helplessness are studies showing that an animal can be "immunized" against the effects of uncontrollability by first exposing it to controllable events. Presumably, the animal learns during immunization that events can be controlled, and this expectation is sustained during exposure to uncontrollable events, precluding helplessness. Other studies show that learned helplessness deficits can be undone by exposing a helpless animal to the contingency between behavior and outcome. The animal is forced to make an appropriate response to the test task, by pushing or pulling it into action. After several such trials, the animal responds on its own. Again, the presumed process at work is cognitive. The animal's expectation of response-outcome independence is challenged during the "therapy" experience, and learning occurs.

Psychologists interested in human problems were quick to see the parallels between learned helplessness as produced in the laboratory and maladaptive passivity as it exists in the real world. Thus began several lines of research looking at learned helplessness in people. First, helplessness in people was produced in the laboratory much as it was in animals, by exposing them to uncontrollable events and seeing the effects on their motivation, cognition, and emotion. Unsolvable problems were usually substituted for uncontrollable electric shocks, but the critical aspects of the phenomenon remained: Following uncontrollability, people show a variety of deficits similar to those observed among animals. Second, researchers proposed various failures of adaptation as analogous to learned helplessness and investigated the similarity between these failures and helplessness. Especially popular was Seligman's (1975) proposal that depression and learned helplessness shared critical features: causes, symptoms, consequences, treatments, and preventions.

It soon became clear that the original helplessness model was an oversimplification when applied to people, failing to account for the range of reactions that people display following uncontrollability. Some people indeed showed pervasive deficits, as the model hypothesized, that were general across time and situation, whereas others did not. Further, failures of adaptation that the learned helplessness model was supposed to explain, such as depression, were sometimes characterized by a striking loss of self-esteem, about which the model was silent.

In an attempt to resolve these discrepancies, Lyn Abramson, Martin Seligman, and John Teasdale (1978) reformulated the helplessness model as it applied to people.

The contrary findings could be explained by proposing that when people encounter an uncontrollable (bad) event, they ask themselves why it happened. Their answer sets the parameters for the helplessness that follows. If their causal attribution is stable ("it's going to last forever"), then induced helplessness is long-lasting. If their causal attribution is global ("it's going to undermine everything"), then subsequent helplessness is manifest across a variety of situations. Finally, if the causal attribution is internal ("it's all my fault"), the individual's self-esteem drops following uncontrollability. These hypotheses comprise the *attributional reformulation* of helplessness theory.

In some cases, the situation itself provides the explanation. In other cases, the person relies on a habitual way of making sense of events that occur, what is called *explanatory style.* Explanatory style is therefore a distal influence on helplessness and the failures of adaptation that involve helplessness. Explanatory style has been studied in its own right, and it has an array of correlates. People who explain bad events with internal, stable, and global causes show passivity; poor problem-solving; depression; anxiety; failure in academic, athletic, and vocational realms; social estrangement; morbidity; and mortality. Explanatory style can be highly stable, sometimes over decades. The self-fulfilling nature of explanatory style—and helplessness per se—explains this stability. At the same time, explanatory style can and does change in response to ongoing life events. Cognitive therapy, for example, can move explanatory style in an optimistic direction.

REFERENCES

Abramson, L. Y., Seligman, M. E. P., & Teasdale, J. D. (1978). Learned helplessness in humans: Critique and reformulation. *Journal of Abnormal Psychology, 87,* 49–74.

Maier, S. F., & Seligman, M. E. P. (1976). Learned helplessness: Theory and evidence. *Journal of Experimental Psychology: General, 105,* 3–46.

Seligman, M. E. P. (1975). *Helplessness: On depression, development, and death.* San Francisco: Freeman.

Christopher Peterson
University of Michigan

See also: **Depression**

LEARNING CURVES

Progress in learning reflects itself in a number of different ways: increases in the rate, probability of occurrence, speed and vigor of responding, decreases in latency (time required to initiate a response), time required to complete a task, and number of errors committed in doing so. These changes in performance are frequently presented in one of a variety of forms called *learning curves,* in which the baseline is most often the number of practice trials but occasionally is time. The vertical axis represents one of the measures just mentioned.

The different measures of learning behave in different ways if the learning involves practice. Amplitude, probability of occurrence, speed of responding, and rate curves show an increase; latencies and other time measures decrease. Probability and percentage of response curves often show a double inflection. Because conditioned responses sometimes do not appear until after several reinforcements, the first portion of the curve may be flat. This portion is followed by a positively accelerated increase, which is soon replaced by a negatively accelerated one as a maximum is approached.

Most learning curves are for groups of subjects, rather than for individuals. For many purposes this creates a problem, especially in experiments where subjects are run to some criterion such as 100% conditioning in a block of trials. Different subjects will take different numbers of trials to reach the criterion, and it becomes difficult to find a baseline against which to plot the response measures to represent the course of acquisition. One solution to this problem is in the use of the *Vincent curve.* The total number of trials required for each subject to reach the criterion is divided into fractional parts such as tenths, and measures are plotted for these portions. This method makes it possible to combine data for subjects whose performances differ widely.

Unfortunately, this and other procedures for combining data may distort the picture of acquisition presented by the learning curve. For one thing, the typical performance of individual subjects in a learning experiment is irregular, showing chance upward and downward excursions. To select the first point at which a subject reaches some arbitrary level as the criterion of learning is very often to stop the learning session at a point that is accidentally high. This fact accounts for at least some of the end spurts obtained in Vincentized data. These appear as rather sudden increases in the final segment of practice. It now seems that they often occur as *criterion artifacts,* because the experiment is terminated after a series of unusually good performances.

Greg A. Kimble

See also: **Operant Conditioning**

LEARNING OUTCOMES, I

The primary means of indicating that learning has occurred is to show that some newly appearing human performances are possible, when required by appropriate circumstances. The inferences that can be made from these changes in performance are to the effect that individuals have acquired some new entities in their long-term memory store—entities not present before the learning occurred. The outcomes of learning, then, are neural states that persist over considerable periods of time, as shown by tests of retention. Because the effects of these states are to make individuals persistently capable of exhibiting particular kinds of performance, it is reasonable to think of them as *learned capabilities*.

Differences in Learned Capabilities

From a broad and practical view, it is of considerable help in defining the boundaries of knowledge in the field of human learning to distinguish some principal types of learning outcomes. The outcomes clearly differ from one another in the performances they make possible. They differ, too, in important respects in the specific conditions optimal for their learning. Presumably, they also differ in the nature of the cognitive structures that represent them in long-term memory.

Varieties of Learning Outcomes

On the basis of the criteria previously described, five kinds of learned capabilities may be distinguished.

1. *Verbal knowledge (declarative knowledge).* This kind of knowledge ranges from single names and labels through isolated "facts" to bodies of organized information. The kind of performance made possible by such knowledge is *stating* (declaring) orally, in writing, or in some other medium.
2. *Intellectual skills (procedural knowledge).* These capabilities enable the individual, by manipulation of symbols, to demonstrate the application of concepts and rules to specific instances. The distinction between "knowing that" (declarative knowledge) and "knowing how" (procedural knowledge) was given prominence by the philosopher Gilbert Ryle.
3. *Cognitive strategies.* These are skills used to direct and influence cognitive processes such as attending, perceiving, encoding, retrieving, and thinking. Cognitive strategies of problem solving were studied in concept identification tasks by Bruner, Goodnow, and Austin. More recently, the effects of cognitive strategies in controlling or modifying other cognitive processes of learning and memory, such as attention, encoding, and retrieval, have been studied extensively. When taught to and deliberately employed by learners, such strategies constitute a major aspect of what is called *metacognition*.
4. *Attitudes.* This fourth kind of learning outcome is generally considered to possess affective as well as cognitive memory components. Attitudes are learned states that influence the choices of personal action the individual makes toward persons, objects, or events.
5. *Motor skills.* Learning outcomes sometimes consist of actions accomplished by smoothly timed muscular movements called motor skills. Most motor skills involve performing procedures, sometimes lengthy ones. The procedure itself may be simple or complex and has been called the *executive subroutine.* This procedure may be learned separately or as an early stage of acquiring the motor skill. Learning the motor skill itself is a matter of acquiring increasing smoothness and precise timing of muscular movement. Often, the executive subroutine has the function of molding part skills into a total skill.

Relation of Learning Outcomes to the School Curriculum

The outcomes of school learning are usually stated as curricula, composed of subject matter content such as reading, writing, mathematics, science, history, and so forth. Each of these subjects usually includes more than one category of learning outcome. Thus, arithmetic is made up largely of intellectual skills, but includes also some essential verbal knowledge about situations in which quantitative concepts are applicable.

Clearly, the five kinds of learning outcomes—verbal knowledge, intellectual skills, cognitive strategies, attitudes, and motor skills—cut across the traditional subject matters of the school curriculum. Each subject area typically seeks to establish more than one kind of capability in students. To achieve optimally effective learning, as well as optimally efficient management of learning, the design of instruction in each subject matter field must take into account the different requirements of each type of learning outcome.

Relation to Other Taxonomies

Perhaps the best-known taxonomy of learning objectives is that proposed by Bloom and his coworkers. Although the categories described in this article have been independently derived from a different theoretical base, they show great similarity to Bloom's topics and are in most respects compatible. The three major strands of the Bloom taxonomy are the *cognitive domain,* the *affective domain,* and the *psychomotor domain.*

Conditions of Learning Favorable for Each Outcome

From learning research and theory, it is possible to specify with reasonable assurance the conditions favorable to the learning that lead to each outcome. These conditions differ somewhat in each case, and the existence of these differences provides a major reason for distinguishing among learning outcomes in designing instruction.

Verbal Knowledge

A number of lines of evidence support the theoretical contention that *prior knowledge* is of great assistance to the learning of new knowledge. The precise nature of the relation between old knowledge and new—in the sense that the former aids the learning and retention of the latter—is presently a matter of active investigation. A second factor of importance for optimal learning is the *organization* of the instructional communication (or other stimulus), which affects the process of encoding. The inclusion of *contextual* cues at the time new knowledge is learned is another condition favoring retention of that knowledge.

Intellectual Skill

The primary condition affecting the learning of intellectual skills is the *accessibility of prerequisite skills.* In contrast to the case of verbal knowledge, these subordinate skills are related to the new skill to be learned as components. The implication is that instruction for optimal learning requires the precise identification of these prerequisite skills, by methods of task analysis. A second condition affecting the retention of intellectual skills is *spaced review* and *practice.* Many basic skills prerequisite to skilled performance in reading, writing, and arithmetic apparently need to be practiced to the level of automaticity.

Cognitive Strategies

Because cognitive strategies are a type of skill, one might expect optimal conditions for learning to be similar to those for intellectual skills. In a sense this is the case: Prerequisite skills must be mastered for cognitive strategies to be learned. However, the prerequisite skills of strategies are often extremely simple, well practiced, and readily accessible. Many strategies of attending, learning, retrieving, and problem solving can be conveyed (or retrieved) by means of a *brief verbal communication.* Some strategies of problem solving, however, do not appear to persist unless practiced in a variety of contexts. Recognition of this fact leads the designers of instruction to suggest that students be given frequent opportunities to solve novel problems.

Attitudes

Although attitudes may be acquired in numerous ways from the experiences of living, it appears that the most dependable deliberate arrangement of conditions for optimal learning involves the technique of *human modeling.* The human model can be an actual human being, a pictured person, or even a printed description. It is most desirable for the model to be perceived by the learners as admirable, credible, and powerful. The procedure leading to attitude learning or modification, according to Bandura, includes two steps: The model (1) communicates or demonstrates the choice of action reflecting the target attitude, and (2) is seen to experience satisfaction and be rewarded for this action choice (vicarious reinforcement). Subsequently, additional strength of attitude can presumably be attained when the learners themselves are reinforced for their choices of personal action.

Motor Skills

The learning of a motor skill often begins, as Fitts and Posner point out, with the acquisition of a cognitive component (actually, an intellectual skill) called the *executive subroutine.* This is the procedural part of the skill. Sometimes separate practice is undertaken of *part skills.* The various components of a complex motor skill come together in *practice of the total skill.* Indeed, it is practice and practice alone that brings attainment of the smoothly timed action that is recognized as a motor skill.

ROBERT M. GAGNÉ

LEARNING OUTCOMES, II

The term *outcome* broadly refers to what an individual has learned as a result of having been engaged in a learning activity of some kind. Within different research perspectives, however, the term takes on a more precise meaning that varies in crucial ways from one perspective to another. These variations, and the assumptions that underlie them, can be examined in relation to *traditional, neo-Piagetian,* and *phenomenographic* research perspectives.

The Traditional Perspective and Its Shortcomings

Within traditional research on learning the outcome of learning is neutral in content and quantitative in character. The experimental procedure commonly followed is to investigate the effect of one or more independent variables on a dependent variable specified in advance. If the resultant findings are in accord with hypotheses derived from a theory, the validity of that theory has been supported.

In all these experiments the dependent variable is in a quantitative form that makes the content of learning invisible; of no interest in itself, it is there simply because there cannot be any learning without a content of some kind. These two aspects of the conventional paradigm of research on learning—the quantitative nature of the dependent variable and the instrumental character of the content of learning—are logically related to a third and superordinate aspect: the aim of arriving at general (and content-neutral) statements about learning, applicable to any kind of subject matter.

Whether this approach is a reasonable basis for psychological research on learning, its relevance to the educational context is questionable. A school is not concerned only with students' acquisition of information and skills: One of its main tasks—indeed, many would argue, *the* main task—is to shape and change pupils' ways of thinking. Thus, schooling should facilitate a transition from commonsense notions of the surrounding world to conceptions more in line with scientific ways of thinking.

The history of science clearly shows that the conceptual frameworks of every scientific discipline have repeatedly gone through radical qualitative shifts, while research on cognitive development points to restructurings of the maturing child's reality that are similar, even if less obvious in their everyday context. To describe outcomes of learning in this particular sense, it is necessary to discover what qualitatively different conceptions of the content of learning are apparent after the teaching/learning process has occurred. To describe the preconditions of learning, it is necessary to find out what qualitatively different preconceived ideas the learners have about the content they will encounter.

In this alternative interpretation, then, *outcomes of learning* are defined as the qualitatively different ways of understanding the content of learning. In what follows, two alternative approaches to this problem will first be examined in turn and then discussed in relation to each other.

A Neo-Piagetian Approach

If learning is conceptualized as was previously described, the distinction commonly made between learning and development becomes somewhat difficult to maintain. Transitions between qualitatively different ways of thinking represent the well-known Piagetian view of cognitive development. It seems easy to understand that the most widespread approach to the description of outcomes of learning has been based on the extension of Piagetian thinking into various subject-matter domains.

It is important to note that these researchers consider their work as studies less of learning than of development. Levels of thinking in different content areas were conceptualized as resulting from the application of general operatory structures to those domains. This was held to be true in both an epistemological and an ontological sense. The former refers to the expectation that the researcher will be able to discern the levels of thinking in a particular content domain by applying the description of the general Piagetian stages to that domain. In contrast, if students exhibit a certain level of thinking in relation to a particular content, they are interpreted as having applied the general operatory structures characteristic for the corresponding stage of development to that particular content.

Research has, however, cast doubt on the validity of this line of reasoning. Flavell and Hundeide, among others, have summarized many investigations challenging the notion of stages and content-free mental structures.

It is nonetheless important to acknowledge what has been achieved. The assumption of stage-related mental structures may not be warranted, in light of the empirical evidence now available of variation in performance on tasks that differ in content and context but are structurally similar. Yet the differences in thinking described are of great interest in themselves, whether the differences are stable across varying contexts and subject matter or not.

Biggs and Collis consider the different levels of thinking identified in these domains as outcomes of learning rather than development-related phenomena. The name they gave to their model of description—SOLO (Structure of the Observed Learning Outcomes)—reflects this. According to these authors, mastering a skill or a knowledge domain can be viewed as a miniature development that can be described in terms of transitions between qualitatively different levels of thinking.

If a group of students who have been dealing with a certain content is observed, it is likely that different students will have advanced to different points. The qualitatively different levels of thinking observed will then appear as qualitative differences (between individuals) in the outcome of learning.

The five general levels of thinking described by Biggs and Collis are as follows:

1. *Prestructural.* A nonexistent, irrelevant, or otherwise inadequate attempt to learn a component is made.
2. *Unistructural.* One relevant component is acquired.
3. *Multistructural.* Several relevant components are acquired, but additively and independently of each other.
4. *Relational.* The components become functionally or conceptually interdependent.
5. *Extended abstract.* The integrated components become part of a more general case, which in fact forms a new mode.

These five levels of thinking correspond to Collis's modification of Piaget's stages: preoperational, early concrete, middle concrete, concrete generalization (originally, early formal), and formal. Biggs and Collis argue that the characteristics that a certain individual's thinking exhibits on various tasks may vary widely, but that the characteristics themselves (in the sense of categories of description) are applicable to the various tasks regardless of content.

A Phenomenographic Approach

The third perspective originates mainly from the work of a Swedish research group. Marton has argued that description of the qualitatively different ways in which people experience, conceptualize, perceive, and understand various aspects of the world around them should be considered as an autonomous scientific specialization, termed *phenomenography*. The arguments for seeing this as an autonomous field of concern are twofold. First, categories of description that characterize people's notions about reality are considered to be of interest in themselves—not the least in educational contexts. Second, such categories cannot be derived from more general properties of the human mind, but must be investigated in their own right.

The relevance of phenomenography to research on learning stems from the conceptualization of learning as a change between qualitatively different ways of understanding a phenomenon or an aspect of reality as contrasted with, for instance, a conceptualization of learning as a memorization of something read or as an acquisition of facts, details, and so on. Because phenomenography is concerned with discerning the different ways in which we understand aspects of the world around us, learning is seen as a transition between phenomenographic categories.

In general, phenomenography offers an alternative way of describing both effects and preconditions of learning and teaching. It aims at making explicit *what* (conception) is changed to *what* (conception). By pinpointing levels of conceptions of fundamental aspects of reality, it identifies a possible dimension of change, and by revealing the everyday ideas about the content of learning and teaching that the students bring with them to the school situation, it increases the likelihood of change.

Similarities and Differences Between the Two Alternative Approaches

As pointed out earlier, within both a neo-Piagetian and a phenomenographic approach, learning is conceptualized as a transition between qualitatively different forms of thought and is thus seen as a miniature development. In a normal school situation it seems quite reasonable to expect that, at the time of a particular observation, different students have advanced to different levels. The outcome of learning will thus be described in terms of qualitative differences. Furthermore, in relation to both ways of describing qualitative differences in the outcome of learning, some correlates have been found in the differing ways in which students set about the learning tasks that account for those differences. Biggs has identified three independent dimensions in study process: utilizing, internalizing, and achieving. The students' ways of studying were found to be highly correlated with learning outcomes.

In spite of these obvious similarities, there is an important difference between the two sets of studies that has to do with the role of content. Biggs and Collis use a general structural model as a point of departure. As the actual content varies in different instances, the realization of categories also will, of course, vary on a concrete level. The structural properties are considered to remain the same, however. Furthermore, they form an explicit hierarchy, as the notion of levels would suggest.

The phenomenographic approach is radically content-oriented because deriving categories of description in relation to various contents of learning is considered to be the main task. The different categories may or may not form a hierarchy in a particular case (of content).

In the SOLO model the description of outcomes of learning takes the form of the application of the general model to new content domains, while in phenomenography each new phenomenon, concept, or principle studied requires the discovery of the qualitatively different ways in which that particular phenomenon, concept, or principle is thought about, experienced, or "lived."

F. I. Marton

LEARNING THEORIES

The field of learning studies how experience produces long-lasting effects in the way that behavior changes with variation in the environment. Learning theory consists of principles that summarize the processes that produce these changes. Learning principles are based upon experimental observations, commonly from the laboratory. Learning theory has two main purposes: (1) to explain existing laboratory findings and aid the discovery of new findings, and (2) to provide plausible accounts of more complex phenomena that occur outside of the laboratory, where well-controlled observations are impossible to obtain. Although learning theory is based on laboratory observations (i.e., experiments), its principles are applicable to general societal concerns such as educational practice and the alleviation of dysfunctional behavior. Laboratory studies of learning usually involve observations of nonhuman animals. The experience of nonhumans can be better controlled, which allows the findings to be attributed to events that take place within the experiment. Although the learning theorist remains open to the possibility that some principles may be unique to humans, biology and neuroscience suggest that basic learning principles are common to most species with which we share an extensive evolutionary history and a common set of physiological processes.

The effect of the *ancestral* environment on behavior is most fundamentally understood through Darwin's principle of natural selection. The central goal of the learning theorist is to develop an account of the effects of the *individual* environment that is as powerful as the principle of natural selection. The search for this principle—a principle of reinforcement—began with the research of Edward L. Thorndike (1932) and Ivan P. Pavlov (1927), and was most explicitly continued in the work of B. F. Skinner (1938) and

Clark L. Hull (1943). Two related experimental procedures are used in the study of reinforcement—classical (or Pavlovian) conditioning and operant (or instrumental) conditioning. Both procedures present the learner with a stimulus that already elicits behavior, generally as a result of natural selection, as with the elicitation of salivation by food. In the classical procedure, the eliciting stimulus is presented after some relatively neutral stimulus, such as a tone or light. In the operant procedure, the eliciting stimulus is presented after some relatively arbitrary behavior, such as pressing a lever. In both procedures, the eliciting stimulus brings about a change in the way the environment affects behavior on future occasions. For example, in the classical procedure the tone comes to evoke salivation, whereas in the operant procedure, the sight of the lever comes to evoke lever pressing (as well as salivation). When these experiences change behavior, the eliciting stimulus is said to act as a *reinforcer.*

What conditions must be present for a stimulus to act as a reinforcer? Experimental work has identified two conditions. The first condition is *contiguity,* and was discovered with both the classical and operant procedures. If the eliciting stimulus is to serve as a reinforcer, it must occur within a very brief time interval (a matter of seconds at most) after the event upon which it is dependent—a stimulus in the classical procedure or a response in the operant procedure (Gormezano & Kehoe, 1981). If the putative reinforcer is delayed, whatever other stimuli or responses may have intervened are affected. The second condition is *discrepancy,* which was not identified until the mid-twentieth century (Kamin, 1969). Laboratory research indicates that not only must a brief interval elapse before the reinforcer occurs; but also the reinforcer must evoke a *change* in ongoing behavior. As examples, in the classical procedure, a stimulus followed by food, and in the operant procedure, lever pressing followed by food do not promote learning if another stimulus already evokes salivation at the moment when food appears. The learning mechanism is engaged only when a would-be reinforcer evokes a change in ongoing behavior. Natural selection has ensured that learning occurs only when the learner is "surprised" to receive the reinforcer.

Although general agreement exists concerning the two conditions needed for learning, learning theories differ among themselves as to how best to state the principle of reinforcement. Two main approaches are considered here—*associationism* and *biobehaviorism.* In the associationist approach, behavioral observations are used to infer the processes that underlie the observed changes in behavior. These inferred processes are called *associations,* following the tradition of British empiricist philosophy. For example, if salivation becomes more likely in the presence of a tone in the classical procedure, a strong tone-food association is inferred. Or, if lever pressing becomes more likely in the operant procedure, a strong lever press-food association is inferred. The nature of the underlying association is often based on tests conducted after original learning. For example, experiments have shown that if lever pressing is followed by food, and then food is separately paired with a noxious stimulus, lever pressing declines in strength. The decline occurs even though lever pressing itself never preceded the noxious stimulus. On the basis of these behavioral observations, the theorist infers that a response-reinforcer association (i.e., a lever press-food association) was formed during the original operant procedure, and that this association was weakened, or devalued, when food was paired with the noxious stimulus in a classical procedure (cf. Colwill & Rescorla, 1986). Historically, most learning theories have been of the inferred-process type, ranging from the earlier theories of Edward Tolman and Clark Hull (see Estes et al., 1954 for a review of earlier theories) to the later theories of William Estes and of Robert Rescorla and Alan Wagner (1972).

In a biobehavioral approach to learning theory, the reinforcement principle is initially stated in terms of behavioral observations only. For example, the discrepancy requirement is defined as a difference between the strength of the response elicited by the reinforcing stimulus (e.g., salivation elicited by food) and the strength of that same response at the moment before the reinforcing stimulus is presented. By contrast, the associationist approach defines the discrepancy requirement as the difference between the maximum associative strength supportable by the reinforcer and the associative strength of prevailing stimuli with that reinforcer. The first definition of discrepancy is stated in behavioral terms; the second in terms of inferred associationist processes. When learning theory is restricted to behavioral terms, it follows the approach of B. F. Skinner, known as *behavior analysis.* When behavior analysis is supplemented by observations at the level of neuroscience, it constitutes a biobehavioral approach. For example, a learned reinforcer—such as a tone that has previously been paired with food—may evoke little behavior. Hence, there is no discrepancy that is readily measurable at the behavioral level. In such cases, a biobehavioral approach points to the observation at the neural level that learned reinforcers can activate the same brain structures as food (Shultz, 1997). Thus, the biobehavioral approach is a synthesis of behavior analysis and neuroscience.

Theories of learning increasingly integrate behavioral and neuroscientific research, which satisfies the need to specify the processes that mediate environment-behavior relations without an appeal to inferred processes. Given the rapid advances in neuroscience, reliance on inferences from behavior is being replaced by direct observations of the neural processes that implement learning. The major remaining task for learning theory is to demonstrate that the principle of reinforcement is sufficiently powerful to provide a compelling account of complex human behavior—memory, language, problem solving, and the like (cf. Donahoe & Palmer, 1994).

REFERENCES

Colwill, R. M., & Rescorla, R. A. (1986). Associative structures in instrumental learning. In G. H. Bower (Ed.), *The psychology of learning and motivation* (Vol. 20, pp. 55–104). New York: Academic Press.

Donahoe, J. W., & Palmer, D. C. (1994). *Learning and complex behavior.* Boston: Allyn & Bacon.

Estes, W. K., Koch, S., MacCorquodale, K., Meehl, P. E., Mueller, C. G., Jr., Schoenfeld, W. N., & Verplanck, W. S. (Eds.). (1954). *Modern learning theory.* New York: Appleton-Century-Crofts.

Gormezano, I., & Kehoe, J. E. (1981). Classical conditioning and the law of contiguity. In P. Harzem & M. D. Zeiler (Eds.), *Predictability, correlation, and contiguity* (pp. 1–45). New York: Wiley.

Hull, C. L. (1943). *Principles of behavior.* New York: Appleton-Century-Crofts.

Kamin, L. J. (1969). Predictability, surprise, attention, and conditioning. In B. A. Campbell & R. M. Church (Eds.), *Punishment and aversive behavior* (pp. 279–296). New York: Appleton-Century-Crofts.

Pavlov, I. P. (1927). *Conditioned reflexes.* New York: Oxford University Press. Reprint. New York: Dover, 1960.

Rescorla, R. A., & Wagner, A. R. (1972). A theory of Pavlovian conditioning. In A. H. Black & W. F. Prokasy (Eds.), *Classical conditioning II* (pp. 64–99). New York: Appleton-Century-Crofts.

Schultz, W. (1997). Adaptive dopaminergic neurons report the appetitive value of environmental stimuli. In J. W. Donahoe & V. P. Dorsel (Eds.), *Neural-network models of cognition* (pp. 317–335). Amsterdam: Elsevier Science Press.

Skinner, B. F. (1938). *The behavior of organisms.* New York: Appleton-Century-Crofts.

Thorndike, E. L. (1932). *The fundamentals of learning.* New York: Columbia University Press.

John W. Donahoe
University of Massachusetts

See also: **Associationism; Natural Selection; Operant Conditioning; Reinforcement**

LEISURE COUNSELING

Leisure counseling emerged as a specialty within the counseling profession only during the 1970s, with its own literature, professional journals, and practitioners. It as yet lacks a substantive theoretical base and solid research support for its concepts, although these are beginning to appear. Leisure counseling has been the province of two professional groups, those concerned with leisure studies (including therapeutic recreation) and those concerned with counseling. There has been a tendency to perceive leisure behavior as a matter of choosing activities, rather than looking at leisure from the point of view of the psychological *meaning* of these activities for the individual.

The recent interest in leisure counseling can in part be traced to increasing affluence in Western Europe and North America, and the decline of the Protestant ethic as a source of individual and societal values. Whereas in previous times of scarcity, work was extolled and leisure denigrated, we are now increasingly turning to leisure as a major source of life satisfaction and meaning. This is especially true for those individuals whose work often lacks meaning and intrinsic interest. Unfortunately, it is precisely those people whose leisure activities are often lacking in variety, challenge, and meaning.

Definitions of Leisure

At least four categories of leisure definitions have appeared in the literature, although they overlap conceptually. *Residual definitions* view leisure as what one does in the time left over after the necessary activities of life have been accomplished. *Activity-related definitions* define leisure by the type of activity in which one engages. Certain activities are considered to be leisure and others defined as work, regardless of the context in which they occur.

Work-related definitions of leisure reflect the value structure of the Protestant work ethic. The first has been called *complementary,* or *spillover,* in which the nature of one's leisure activities is similar to one's work activities. The second type has been called *supplemental* and refers to leisure activities intentionally chosen to be quite different from those typically engaged in while at work. *Compensatory* leisure refers to activities that are designed to reduce or eliminate stresses or tensions that the individual experiences in daily life.

Psychological definitions of leisure tend to stress the meaning of the leisure experience for the individual, rather than the type of activity engaged in or its relation to some other activity. J. Neulinger defines leisure as a state of mind—being at peace with oneself and what one is doing. His concept of leisure revolves around two bipolar constructs: freedom versus constraint and intrinsic versus extrinsic motivation.

Needs and Motives for Leisure

Many personality theorists of diverse orientations note that a basic human task is the development of a sense of competence, mastery, or self-efficacy. It has been found that individuals choose those activities in which they perceive themselves to be competent because participation in such activities elevates one's sense of competence and enhances one's sense of freedom. Furthermore, learning new leisure skills (assuming minimal and increasing competency) enhances one's self-concept, whereas practicing already learned skills only maintains one's existing self-concept.

Other needs and motives for leisure have also been found. People appear to be motivated by a need for optimal arousal and incongruity, or what one might call "novelty value." The level of optimal arousal will, of course, differ from individual to individual, but participation in leisure activities can help satisfy this need for everyone. In addition, leisure is valued to the extent that it provides positive interpersonal involvement.

Emerging Leisure Paradigms

Several comprehensive treatments of the psychological nature of leisure have recently appeared. McDowell has argued that the leisure experience is characteristic of "right-brain thinking," while work consciousness is characteristic of "left-brain thinking." In addition, he has developed the concept of leisure well-being, which he defines as "an esthetic, enjoyable, satisfying, healthful and dynamic leisure-style." McDowell suggests that leisure well-being involves four key components of self-care: coping, awareness–understanding, knowledge, and assertion.

Seppo E. Iso-Ahola considers the four most important determinants of the perception of an experience as leisure to be (in order of importance) (1) perceived freedom to engage in the activity, (2) intrinsic motivation to engage in the activity, (3) whether the activity is related to daily work, and (4) whether the activity is oriented toward final goals or instrumental goals. There is some evidence that, given an already high level of interest in an activity, expected external rewards for engaging in that activity can actually *reduce* the individual's later engagement in it.

The phenomenon of leisure has also been examined from an attributional point of view. Attribution refers to the process by which a person assigns causes to events, behaviors, and outcomes in an attempt to construct causal meaning out of situations. Attributions have been found to have three dimensions: internality–externality (whether the cause resides within or outside the individual); stability–instability (whether the cause is stable over time); and globality–specificity (whether the cause is common to many situations). The positive relationship between perceived freedom and internal causality is quite high; therefore, individuals tend to define leisure as those activities attributed to internal stable causes.

An internal-unstable attribution for the leisure activity would be made when the individual is engaging in new activities in which competence is sporadic. It would be especially useful in this situation to assist the person in attributing success to internal factors, rather than external factors, so that participation in the activity is maintained and is not labeled as "work."

The global–specific dimension refers to attributions of leisure competence (or incompetence) of oneself in relation to perceived competence of others.

Models of Leisure Counseling

Numerous models of leisure counseling have been proposed in the last few years, organized by Tinsley and Tinsley into three categories: (1) leisure guidance, (2) leisure decision making, and (3) leisure counseling. Leisure guidance models stress information-giving techniques that focus on assisting clients in choosing appropriate leisure activities that are interesting to them. In leisure decision-making models, the focus is still on assisting the client in choosing appropriate leisure activities, but there is a greater use of the client–counselor relationship as part of the leisure counseling interaction, as well as a greater awareness and use of the decision-making process. Leisure counseling involves a holistic focus on the total individual and the establishment of a facilitative counseling relationship.

Goals of Leisure Counseling

A primary goal of leisure counseling is to provide for an increase in the clients' perceived competence by engaging in activities at which they can succeed. A second goal is to provide for the clients' increased sense of freedom by engaging in freely chosen, competence-enhancing activities.

Another goal of leisure counseling is to increase an individual's level of optimal arousal and incongruity, an area in which many people are sorely lacking. In principle, this can be accomplished by increasing the variety, challenge, and complexity in one's leisure experience.

Leisure activities can also serve as a trial preparation for subsequent activities: Numerous people have turned hobbies into satisfying occupations. Leisure activities can also satisfy needs that cannot be met through other activities (e.g., work).

E. Thomas Dowd
Kent State University

LEWINSOHN'S MODEL OF DEPRESSION

Lewinsohn's original model of depression (Lewinsohn, Weinstein, & Shaw, 1969) emphasized a "reduced rate of response-contingent reinforcement" as a critical antecedent for depression. Reinforcement was defined by the quality of the patient's interactions with his or her environment. Those person-environment interactions with positive outcomes constitute positive reinforcement. Such interactions strengthen the person's behavior. The term "contingent" refers to the temporal relationship between a behavior and its consequences. The reinforcement must follow the behavior. The model assumed that the behavior of depressed persons does not lead to positive reinforcement to a degree sufficient to maintain their behavior. Hence, depressed persons find it difficult to initiate or maintain their behavior, and become increasingly passive. The low rate of positive reinforcement was also assumed to cause the dysphoric feelings.

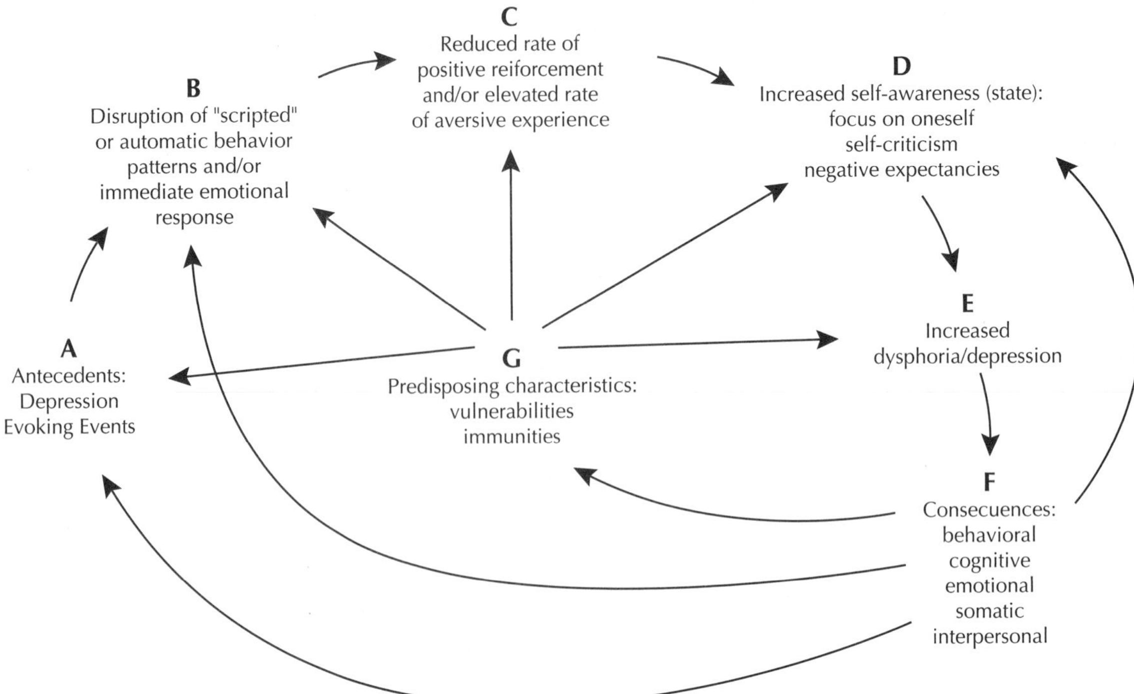

Figure 1. Lewinsohn's model of depression.

A low rate of response-contingent positive reinforcement may occur because (1) events that are contingent on behavior may not be reinforcing; (2) events that are reinforcing may become unavailable; or (3) reinforcers may be available but because of lack of the required skills, the individual is unable to elicit them.

An important supplement to the behavioral position was that the social environment provides reinforcement in the form of sympathy, interest, and concern for depressive behaviors. These reinforcements are typically provided by a small segment of the depressed person's social environment (e.g., the immediate family). Since most people in the depressed person's environment (and eventually even his family) find these behaviors aversive, they will avoid the person as much as possible, thus decreasing the depressed person's rate of receiving positive reinforcement and further accentuating the depression.

A number of different environmental events (e.g., the death of a loved one, separation, rejection, poverty, misfortune) and organismic states and traits (e.g., lack of social skill, physical disease) were presumed to be causally related to a low state of positive reinforcement. Social skill was seen as an area of deficit especially important in the development of depressive behaviors.

On the basis of empirical studies (Grosscup & Lewinsohn, 1980; Lewinsohn & Amenson, 1978; Lewinsohn, Lobitz, & Wilson, 1973; Lewinsohn, Mermelstein, Alexander, & MacPhillamy, 1985; Lewinsohn & Talkington, 1979; Lewinsohn, Youngren, & Grosscup, 1979) the theory was expanded to incorporate a relationship between aversive events and depression. Specifically, it was hypothesized that depressed individuals are more sensitive, experience a greater number of aversive events, and are less skillful in terminating aversive events.

In 1985, Lewinsohn, Hoberman, Teri, and Hautzinger broadened the scope of the previously described theoretical efforts and proposed an "integrative" theory of depression, which is represented in Figure 1.

The earlier model did not assign a causal role to depressotypic cognitions, assuming them to be consequences of the depressed state. The "integrative" theory views the occurrence of depression as a product of environmental as well as dispositional factors. The chain of events leading to the occurrence of depression is postulated to begin with the occurrence of an evoking event or antecedent (A). The occurrence of antecedents is assumed to initiate the depressogenic process to the extent that the antecedents disrupt substantial, important, and relatively automatic behavior patterns of an individual (B). Such disruptions, and the emotional upset they typically engender, are assumed to be related to the occurrence of depression to the extent that they lead to a reduction of positive reinforcement or to an elevated rate of aversive experience (C). In response to these disruptions, the person will attempt to reduce their impact; the person's personal and environmental resources (G) will determine how successful these efforts will be. The inability to reverse the impact of an evolving event is hypothesized to lead to a heightened state of self-awareness (D), that is, a state in which attention is focused internally, which results in individuals becoming more aware of their thoughts, feelings, values, and standards. Increasing self-awareness has been shown to cause individuals to become increasingly self-critical, to produce an increase in the discrepancy between ideal self and perceived self, and to produce dysphoria, which in turn is assumed to lead to some of the cognitive alterations, such as pessimism and attribution of failures to self, that have been emphasized by cognitive theorists. The model assumes that increasing self-awareness (D) and dysphoria (E) lead to many of the cognitive, behavioral, and emotional changes (F) that have been shown to be correlated with depression. These changes (F) are presumed to reduce the individual's ability to cope with the initial and subsequent depression-evoking events. For example, the dysphoria may further reduce the individual's social and other competence. The lack of competence in important spheres of functioning, in turn, may make it more likely that additional depression-evoking events (A) will occur. The proposed model allows for predisposing characteristics of various kinds (G) to either increase (vulnerabilities) or to decrease (immunities) the risks for depressive episode.

As indicated in Figure 1, predisposing characteristics are assumed to affect all elements of the model. A few illustrative examples: an individual with good coping skills would be more likely to be able to reverse the depressogenic cycle by implementing new behaviors to deal with the disruption (B) or by decreasing self-awareness by finding distractions and thereby staying focused on external events. The behavior of significant others in the person's environment may constitute a vulnerability to the extent that they selectively reinforce the depressed individual's symptoms and complaints.

The model allows for "feedback loops" that are seen as important for determining the level of severity and the duration of an episode of depression. Thus, becoming depressed (F) and thinking and behaving in the depressed mode would be expected to interfere with the individual's problem-solving skills (G) and consequently their ability to reverse the disruption (B) and the effects of the disruption (C). Feedback loops set the stage for a vicious cycle, but also for a benign cycle. By reversing any of the components of the model, the depression will be progressively and increasingly ameliorated.

REFERENCES

Ferster, C. B. (1965). Classification of behavior pathology. In L. Krasner & L. P. Ullman (Eds.), *Research in behavior modification* (pp. 6–26). New York: Holt

Grosscup, S. J., & Lewinsohn, P. M. (1980). Unpleasant and pleasant events and mood. *Journal of Clinical Psychology, 36,* 252–259.

Lewinsohn, P. M., & Amenson, C. (1978). Some relations between pleasant and unpleasant mood-related events and depression. *Journal of Abnormal Psychology, 87,* 644–654.

Lewinsohn, P. M., Hoberman, H., Teri, L., & Hautzinger, M. (1985). An integrative theory of depression. In S. Reiss & R. Bootzin (Eds.), *Theoretical issues in behavior therapy* (pp. 331–359). New York: Academic Press

Lewinsohn, P. M., Lobitz, W. C., & Wilson, S. (1973). "Sensitivity" of depressed individuals to aversive stimuli. *Journal of Abnormal Psychology, 81,* 259–263.

Lewinsohn, P. M., Mermelstein, R. M., Alexander, C., & MacPhillamy, D. J. (1985). The unpleasant events schedule: A scale for the measurement of aversive events. *Journal of Clinical Psychology, 41,* 483–498.

Lewinsohn, P. M., & Talkington, J. (1979). Studies on the measurement of unpleasant events and relations with depression. *Applied Psychological Measurement, 3,* 83–101.

Lewinsohn, P. M., Weinstein, M., & Shaw, D. (1969). Depression: A clinical research approach. In R. D. Rubin & C. M. Frank (Eds.), *Advances in behavior therapy* (pp. 231–240). New York: Academic Press.

Lewinsohn, P. M., Youngren, M. A., & Grosscup, S. J. (1979). Reinforcement and depression. In R. A. Depue (Ed.), *The psychobiology of the depressive disorders: Implications for the effects of stress* (pp. 291–316). New York: Academic Press

Skinner, B. F. (1953). *Science and human behavior.* New York: Free Press.

Peter M. Lewinsohn
Oregon Research Institute

See also: **Learning Theories; Reinforcement**

LIBIDO

"Libido is a term used in the theory of the instincts for describing the dynamic manifestation of sexuality." Thus Freud began his 1923 encyclopedia article on the libido theory. He had used the term "libido" as early as 1894. His major theoretical treatise, *Three Essays on the Theory of Sexuality* (1905-1973, p. 255), placed libido at the center of his theories of development and psychopathology. In his *New Introductory Lectures on Psychoanalysis* (1933/1973, p. 95), Freud introduced his review and current synthesis of libido theory, noting that "the theory of instincts is so to say our mythology." Even in his later years libido remained a central construct in psychoanalytic theory, one side of the basic, pervasive, and instinctual dualism: sex and aggression, life and death. The metapsychology of libido's vicissitudes and reorganizations over the course of development through the psychosexual stages—oral, anal, phallic, latency, and genital—formed the core of early psychoanalytic theories of developmental psychology, psychopathology, and clinical practice.

Libido theory is among the most far-reaching and controversial notions in psychoanalysis. Now, as then, libido refers to the sexual biological instinct, drive, or psychic energy. However, whereas libido was not typically discussed in general physicians' offices in Freud's era, modern internists and specialty physicians recognize the importance of healthy sexual functioning as an important indicator of overall health and quality of life. Thus, the term libido may also be used to refer to sexual instincts and sexual desire more generally.

Freud himself had strong allegiance and high hopes for biological causation and explanation, but still broadened his notion of libido to include the sensual as well as the more basic sexual aspects of life. Nonetheless, the relative emphasis upon biological versus social or psychological description still characterizes the ongoing controversy over libido theory. As early as 1916, Jung in his *Psychology of the Unconscious* attacked Freud's theory of libido, arguing that sexuality was only a variant of a more primal, undifferentiated form of psychic energy. In Jung's view, furthermore, sexuality emerged and predominated only in puberty, much later than in Freud's theory, with its focus on infancy and early childhood manifestations of libidinal expression and development. Rapaport replaced the libido concept with a more general, nonspecific drive energy as he cast traditional and id-oriented psychoanalysis into more general ego psychology. The growing concern with the bankruptcy of hydraulic, thermodynamic, and drive discharge models led to the elimination or de-emphasis of libido theory in many recent psychoanalytic reformulations. Klein, one of the most recent and influential systematizers of psychoanalysis, remarked that "in fact, the uncritical acceptance of libido theory with the newer current of ego psychology brings into sharp relief one of the focal dilemmas confronting psychoanalysis" (Klein, 1976, p. 147).

Aside from ongoing controversy over what role, if any, libido plays in psychoanalytic psychology, or with any other theory of behavior or pathology, two abiding domains or concepts derived from libido theory remain useful, especially when their metapsychological nature is appreciated and respected. One domain is the qualitative properties of libido (or any instinctual energy) which serve as structure, process, and organization for the so-called drive. Schafer notes that through variation in degree of anticathexis, cathexis, or hypercathexis of libido, we may posit dreams, symptoms, jokes, rituals, pathology, relationships, therapeutic effects, and so on—the concerns of psychoanalysis. He lists seven qualities of libido (Schafer, 1976, pp. 80–81):

1. Direction (sexual gratification),
2. Urgency or peremptoriness (unremitting pressure for discharge),
3. Mobility (readiness to divert itself into indirect channels when direct channels are blocked),
4. Dischargeability (its being reduced in quantity, hence in impetus, following certain activities),
5. Bindability (its being maintained in a fixed or blocked position by opposing energy),
6. Transformability (loss of its properties of direction, peremptoriness, probability), and
7. Dischargeability (a loss known as desexualization or deinstinctualization), fusibility (its capacity to blend with the energy of aggressive impulses/energy)

The second useful domain of concepts derived from libido theory are those of the developmental progressions of psychosexuality and object relations. In the theory of infantile sexuality, Freud described the maturation and successive reorganization of libido through the oral stage (birth to about 18 months), anal stage (18 to 36 months), phallic stage (three to five years), latency stage (middle childhood), and genital stage (adolescence and adulthood). Libidinal gratification was associated with sensuality or activity focused on each of the so-called erotogenic body zones implied in the stage sequence. Particular qualities of character and pathology were associated with the successes, failures, and compromises at each mutually influential step of the developmental process. A related progression of libido from autoerotism (gratification through one's own body) to narcissism (love of one's "self") and object love (gratification through investment and involvement with other people) complements the psychosexual progression, contributing yet another of the major developmental lines which form the framework for psychoanalytic diagnostic classification.

The scientific status of libido theory and its derived constructs remains to be established by empirical research, an effort abandoned by many in the belief that it is not researchable. Greater understanding will undoubtedly emerge with the coming of improved technology and conceptualization. Until then, libido theory remains an influential—though controversial—girder in the framework that guides a major portion of applied psychology: psychoanalysis.

REFERENCES

Freud, S. (1905/1973). Three essays on the theory of sexuality. In J. Strachey, *The standard edition of the complete psychological works of Sigmund Freud* (Vol. 7). London: Hogarth Press.

Freud, S. (1923/1973). In J. Strachey, *The standard edition of the complete psychological works of Sigmund Freud* (Vol. 18). London: Hogarth Press.

Freud, S. (1933/1973). New introductory lectures on psychoanalysis. In J. Strachey, *The standard edition of the complete psychological works of Sigmund Freud* (Vol. 23). London: Hogarth Press.

Jung, C. (1993). *The basic writings of C. G. Jung.* New York: Modern Library.

Klein, G. S. (1976). *Psychoanalytic theory: An exploration of essentials.* New York: International Universities Press.

Nagera, H. (1990). *Basic psychoanalytic concepts on the libido theory.* London: Karnac Books.

Schafer, R. (1976). *New language of psychoanalysis.* New Haven, CT: Yale University Press.

Donald L. Wertlieb
Tufts University

LIE DETECTION

An instrument that monitors one or more involuntary physiological variables from a person under interrogation is popularly called a lie detector. The most common instrument for this purpose, the *polygraph,* normally monitors breathing movements, relative blood pressure, and electrodermal responses (which are related to the sweating of the palms). It is popularly believed that these or other instruments can identify lying by detecting some response or pattern of responses that is specific to deception, a "Pinocchio response" or pattern of reaction that everyone shows when lying but does not show when answering truthfully. No such specific lie response has ever been objectively demonstrated.

All one can determine from the polygraph chart is that the subject was relatively more disturbed or aroused by one question than by another; one cannot determine why the subject was aroused, whether the question elicited, for example, guilt or fear or anger. Moreover, polygraph responses that are indistinguishable from spontaneous ones can be elicited by biting one's tongue or clenching the toes.

The examiner must therefore try to infer deception from the difference in reaction elicited by different types of questions. Since the 1950s, the standard question format has been the *control question test* or CQT. Relevant questions (e.g., "Did you take the $1000 from the safe?") were intermixed with questions that refer in a general way to prior misdeeds of the subject. In the case of a theft investigation, for example, a control question might be, "Before last year, had you ever taken anything that didn't belong to you?" The objective is to find two or three questions to which (in the opinion of the examiner) the subject's answer is untruthful or, at least, about which the subject is uncertain that his answer is truthful. The theory of the control question test is that an innocent person, able to answer the relevant questions truthfully, will be more disturbed by these control questions and show stronger physiological reactions to them, whereas the guilty person will react most strongly to the relevant questions.

In the *directed lie test,* or DLT, the subject is required to deny such common sins as "Have you ever committed any sort of traffic violation?" The DLT assumes that subjects who answer the relevant questions truthfully will be relatively more disturbed by these directed-lie questions than by questions about the crime of which they are suspected. Most polygraph testing of job applicants or employees in federal security agencies now relies upon the DLT.

A different method of polygraphic interrogation, the *guilty knowledge test* or GKT, attempts to determine whether the suspect recognizes facts or images about the crime that would be known only to someone who had been present at the scene. The GKT consists of a series of multiple-choice questions such as: "The killer wore a ski mask. If you are the killer, you will know the color of the mask. Was it: Brown? Blue? Red? Black? Yellow? Green?" In the GKT, the subject's physiological responses to the incorrect alternatives serve as genuine controls. If he responds differentially to the correct alternatives, then guilty knowledge can be inferred. The GKT is used extensively by police investigators in Israel and in Japan but seldom in the United States.

The lie detector test is very effective in inducing confessions or damaging admissions, at least from unsophisticated suspects. In perhaps 14 states, polygraph evidence is admissible in criminal trials when both sides have so stipulated prior to testing. This normally happens when the prosecution's case is so weak that they offer to drop the charges if the defendant passes the lie detector. The defendant must stipulate, however, that the test results can be used in court against him should he or she fail the test. In its 1993 *Daubert* decision, the Supreme Court ruled that federal judges must at least hold evidentiary hearings whenever lie detector (or other allegedly scientific evidence) is proffered. Such hearings to date have almost invariably led to the exclusion of polygraph test results. In its 1998 *Scheffer* decision, the Supreme Court ruled that the per se exclusion of polygraph evidence does not violate the defendant's Sixth Amendment right to present a defense.

Accuracy of Lie Detection. Polygraph examiners claim very high rates of accuracy, ranging typically from 95% to 99%, but these claims have not been supported by credible research. Because one cannot simulate in the laboratory the emotional concerns of criminal suspects being interrogated in real life, studies of lie detector validity must be done in the field situation. Interrogation of criminal suspects who have failed polygraph tests produces confessions in perhaps 20% of cases, thus verifying the test that produced the confession. Such confessions sometimes clear other suspects in the same case. To determine the accuracy of diagnoses based just on the polygraph recordings, the charts from such verified tests are then scored by a different examiner than the one who administered the test.

But suspects who fail the polygraph and then confess may not generally be representative of guilty suspects. Moreover, because testing of multiple suspects normally ceases after one suspect has been diagnosed as deceptive, suspects verified as innocent by another's confession will usually have been tested prior to the suspect who confessed and their charts scored as truthful. Therefore, field studies based on charts verified by polygraph-induced confessions necessarily overestimate the validity of the polygraph because they exclude charts from guilty suspects who passed the test and also charts from innocent suspects who failed the test. By 1998, four such studies of polygraph accuracy had been published in scientific journals. Where chance accuracy would lead to 50% correct classification, in the four mentioned studies the charts of the innocent suspects were scored as "deceptive" in 39.5% of the cases, indicating that the lie detector tests are strongly biased against the truthful person. The accuracy of the GKT has not yet been adequately studied in real life applications. Laboratory studies agree, however, in showing that the GKT is highly accurate in identifying innocent suspects and, with six or more questions, in identifying guilty suspects as well.

SUGGESTED READING

Gale, A. (Ed.) (1988). *The polygraph test: Lies, truth, and science.* London: Sage

Iacono, W. G., & Lykken, D. T. (1997). The scientific status of research on polygraph techniques: The case against polygraph tests. In D. L. Faigman, D. Kaye, M. J. Saks, & J. Sanders (Eds.), *Modern scientific evidence: The law and science of expert testimony* (pp. 582–618, 627–629, 631–633). St. Paul, MN: West Publishing.

Iacono, W. G., & Lykken, D. T. (1997). The validity of the lie detector: Two surveys of scientific opinion. *Journal of Applied Psychology, 82,* 426–433.

Lykken, D. T. (1998). *A tremor in the blood: Uses and abuses of the lie detector.* New York: Plenum Press.

David Lykken
University of Minnesota

LIFE-SPAN DEVELOPMENT

The point where change occurs throughout the life cycle is critical. Traditional approaches to human development have emphasized change from birth to adolescence, stability in adulthood, and decline in old age. Sears and Feldman have captured the flavor of some of the most important adult changes. The changes in body, personality, and abilities may be great during these later decades. Strong developmental tasks are imposed by marriage and parenthood, by the waxing and waning of physical prowess and of some intellectual capacities, by the children's exit from the nest, by the achievement of an occupational plateau, and by retirement and the prospect of death.

A number of stage-crisis theories have been developed to explain the change adults undergo, the best known being Erikson's theory and, in the popular literature, Gail Sheehy's *Passages.* Many theorists and researchers, however, have not been satisfied with the stage-crisis approaches to adult development. To obtain a more accurate view of adult development, many experts believe that the study of life events adds valuable information. Hultsch and Deutsch point out that our lives are punctuated by transitions defined by various events. Particular emphasis is placed on the stressful nature of these events. Events typically thought of as positive (marriage or being promoted at work), as well as events usually perceived as negative (death of spouse, being fired from work), are potentially stressful. Factors that can mediate such stressful life events include internal resources (physical health, intellectual abilities) and external resources (income, social supports). Adaptation involves the use of coping strategies that result in behavioral change.

Broadly speaking, there are two theoretical approaches to the study of personality development, one focusing on similarities and the other on differences. The stage theories all attempt to describe the universals—not the individual variation—in development. Farrell and Rosenberg suggest a more complex model, one anchored in the idea that individuals are active agents in interpreting, shaping, and altering their own reality.

In a recent discussion of life stress, I. G. Sarason has called attention to the wide array of individual differences in the frequency and preoccupying characteristics of stress-related cognitions. Although the most adaptive response to stress is a task orientation that directs a person's attention to the task at hand rather than to emotional reactions, some individuals are task-oriented while others are not.

Sarason emphasizes that the ability to set aside unproductive worries and preoccupations is crucial to functioning under stress. At least five factors influence how an individual will respond to life stress, according to Sarason:

1. The nature of the task or stress
2. The skills available to perform the task or handle the stress
3. Personality characteristics
4. Social supports available to the person experiencing stress
5. The person's history of stress-arousing experiences and events

But while adults are likely to experience one or more highly stressful events during their lives, an increasing number of individuals are reaching late adulthood in a healthier manner than in the past.

John W. Santrock

See also: **Adult Intellectual Development; Human Development**

LIMBIC SYSTEM

Broca described the "great limbic lobe" of the brain as a large cerebral convolution that lies medially and envelops the brain stem and is common to all mammals (Broca, 1878). The limbic lobe was thought to be important in olfaction due to its dense connections with the olfactory cortex, and was often referred to as the *rhinencephalon* (smell brain). Papez, in 1937, proposed that the rhinencephalon was also important in emotional behavior. In 1952, MacLean coined the term *limbic system* to refer both to a medial part of the

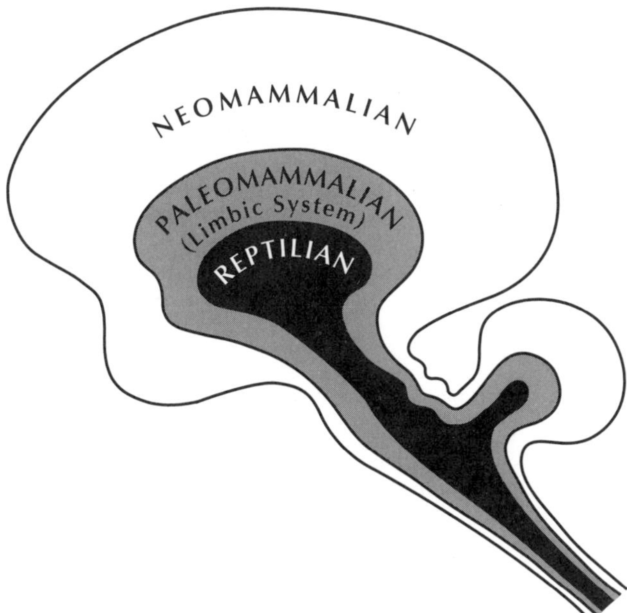

Figure 1. Limbic system of the brain in relation to neomammalian and reptilian structures.

cortex that enveloped the brain stem and to subcortical structures that were tightly associated with this region. He based this grouping not only on its anatomic location but also on evidence that this region was well developed only in mammals, was phylogenetically older than the more peripheral neocortex, and appeared to be important in emotional and social behavior (1990). The limbic, or paleomammalian, system of the brain is shown in Figure 1 in relation to higher cortical (or neomammalian) and deeper brain (or reptilian) structures. MacLean's subdivisions of the limbic system (1990) include the amygdalar, septal, and thalamocingulate divisions shown in Figure 2. Extensive preclinical and clinical observations have suggested that the limbic system is critical in learning, memory, emotions, social behaviors, and autonomic responses. This essay will briefly review the definition and anatomy of the limbic system, describe the three limbic subdivisions, and discuss evidence for and against the limbic system construct.

Definition and Anatomy

Although there is no clear consensus, the following regions are generally considered part of the limbic system: The cortical structures include the cingulate gyrus, subcallosal gyrus, hippocampus, and olfactory cortex. Subcortical regions include the amygdala, septum, pellucidum, epithalamus (habenula), anterior thalamic nuclei, hypothalamus, and parts of the basal ganglia. In addition, several closely linked cortical structures that appear important in emotional behavior are also considered part of this circuit and are often referred to as paralimbic. These regions include the anterior temporal polar cortex, medial-posterior orbitofrontal cortex, and insular cortex (Mesulam & Mufson, 1982).

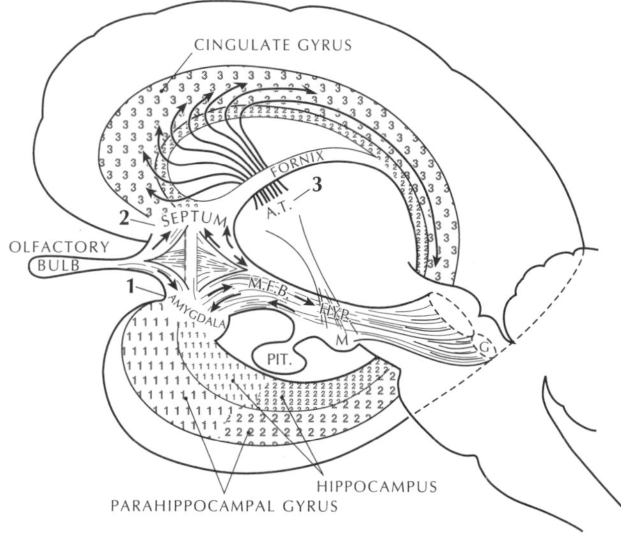

Figure 2. Maclean's subdivisions of the limbic system.

Maclean's Proposed Limbic Subdivisions

Amygdalar Division

MacLean (1990) emphasizes that this region is involved in self-preservation behaviors such as those required in the search for food, including fighting and self-defense. Stimulation of this area in humans may produce fear and anxiety.

Septal Division

The septal region may subserve behaviors related to sexual function and procreation. MacLean (1990) emphasizes that septal stimulation in humans can produce pleasurable sensations and in animals can elicit social grooming as well as genital tumescence.

Thalamocingulate Division

This region represents the phylogenetically newest subdivision of the limbic system. It is present in mammals but not in reptiles. Several typical mammalian social behaviors are associated with this area, including extensive mother–infant bonding, infant crying, and play. Lesions of this region in nonhuman mammals often produce social apathy; even mothers will neglect their young (MacLean, 1990).

In addition to these social functions, the cingulate, particularly its anterior extent, is believed to be important in selective attention and pain (MacLean, 1990).

Evidence for and Against the Limbic System Construct

Extensive research suggests that limbic structures are important in emotional behavior. What is uncertain is the extent to which limbic regions and associated brain structures alone are critical in emotional regulation and whether the limbic system functions as a unified network. Much of the clinical evidence for the unified network concept has come from studies of psychomotor seizures (Jasper, 1964), although recent functional imaging studies in humans also support the notion of a limbic system concept (George et al., 1995). Critics of the limbic system construct (Kotter & Meyer, 1992; LeDoux, 1996) point out that no two authorities can agree on which structures should be included in the limbic system. Also, limbic structures are connected with virtually all areas of the brain, so critics argue that one should then consider the whole brain the limbic system. Moreover, if the limbic system is defined functionally as that part of the brain involved in emotion, evidence suggests that the neocortex may be important in the regulation and recognition of emotions and that limbic regions such as the hippocampus and cingulate are important in functions other than emotion, such as memory, cognition, and selective attention.

Conclusions

Extensive preclinical and clinical observations have suggested that the limbic system structures are critical in emotional behavior. Limbic structures have also been found to be important in social behavior, cognition, and autonomic responses. The limbic system, however, has extensive direct interconnections with all brain regions, and the extent to which the limbic system functions as a network itself remains to be determined. Perhaps the limbic system concept will lose its heuristic appeal as we improve our definitions of emotional states, and the roles of discrete structures and small circuits important in motivation (Kalivas, Churchill, & Romanides, 1999), fear (LeDoux, 1996), and other emotional behaviors. Alternatively, as some imaging studies suggest, we may actually confirm that emotional behaviors do not arise from the activity of single brain regions, but instead emerge from the coordinated action of many connected structures. New techniques in functional imaging and noninvasive regional brain stimulation will allow for direct testing of the limbic system construct in normal function and in psychiatric and medical disorders. Broca's limbic lobe, initially thought to be important by some only in olfaction, is certainly no longer ignored.

REFERENCES

Broca, P. (1878). Anatomie comparee des circonvolutions cerebrales. Le grand lobe limbique et la scissure limbique dans la serie des mammiferes (Comparative anatomy of the cerebral cortex. The limbic lobe and connections in mammalian species). *Review of Anthropology, 1*(2), 456–498.

George, M. S., Ketter, T. A., Parekh, P. I., Horwitz, B., Herscovitch, P., & Post, R. M. (1995). Brain activity during transient sadness and happiness in healthy women. *American Journal of Psychiatry, 152*(3), 341–351.

Jasper, J. J. (1964). Some physiological mechanisms involved in epileptic automatisms. *Epilepsia, 5,* 1–20.

Kalivas, P. W., Churchill, L., & Romanides, A. (1999). Involvement of the pallidal-thalamocortical circuit in adaptive behavior. *Annals of the New York Academy of Science, 29*(877), 64–70.

Kotter, R., & Meyer, N. (1992). The limbic system: A review of its empirical foundation. *Behavioural Brain Research, 52,* 105–127.

LeDoux, J. (1996). *The emotional brain.* New York: Simon & Schuster.

MacLean, P. D. (1952). Some psychiatric implications of physiological studies on frontotemporal portion of limbic system (visceral brain). *Electroencephalographic Clinical Neurophysiology, 4,* 407–418.

MacLean, P. D., (1990). *The triune brain in evolution: Role in paleocerebral functions.* New York: Plenum Press.

Mesulam, M. M., & Mufson, E. J. (1982). Insula of the old world monkey: I. Architectonics in the insula-orbito-temporal component of the paralimbic brain. *Journal of Comparative Neurology, 212,* 1–122.

Papez, J. W. (1937). A proposed mechanism of emotion. *Archives of Neurological Psychiatry, 38,* 722–743.

Mark B. Hamner
Jeffrey P. Lorberbaum
Mark S. George
Medical University of South Carolina

***See also:* Brain**

LITERATURE AND PSYCHOLOGY

The emergence of psychology as a separate discipline in the late nineteenth century brought to the forefront the relation of this new science to the humanities. Two great figures of that time, William James and Sigmund Freud, loomed large in this issue. Both were trained in medicine and psychology, but viewed themselves as psychologists; both were attracted to philosophy; and both were to receive renown as writers. William James's duality was mirrored in his younger brother Henry, whose reputation as a writer is based importantly on his psychological insights and understanding.

It is fitting that Freud should have met William James in 1909 on his only visit to America. As he evolved psychoanalysis, he always understood that humanistic studies were vital to his thinking, and he criticized the lack of such studies in the medical curriculum, especially for the training of someone who was to become a psychoanalyst. The cornerstone of his clinical theory was the Oedipus complex, influenced not only by his clinical observations and his self-analysis, but also by his familiarity with Sophocles' tragedy, which he had translated as a youth. The specific writers who influenced him were many, including Shakespeare, whose works he had read in English as a youth; Goethe, whom he was fond of quoting; and Dostoyevski, whose psychological acumen he so admired. Freud created not just a theory of the human mind, but works of great literary merit. He wrote psychology as literature on a level that has not been equaled since.

Humans are linguistic beasts, and Freud recognized that any comprehensive theory of human behavior must come to grips with this simple fact. Freud used the analysis of language as the foundation on which he erected his theoretical edifice. Freud's analysis of dreaming provided him with his basic concepts concerning the operation of the human mind and its cognitive processes. Concepts with linguistic referents inform his analysis of dreamwork, including censorship, condensation, displacement, secondary revision, and symbolization.

The importance Freud gave to language is reflected in all areas of his thought. He began with an analysis of slips of the tongue and other verbal parapraxes. Similarly, he elaborated how wit and joking are forms of language that reveal the complex workings of the mind. Moreover, Freud evolved a "talking cure," the technique of psychoanalytic therapy in which two people converse as a means of alleviating neurotic suffering.

The concern with transformational processes provides a fundamental meeting ground for psychology and literature. We interpret literature and we interpret dreams, and in this way recognize that hermeneutics, the study of the interpretive process, is central to psychology and literature. Freud was preoccupied with these transformational processes in his theory not only in cognition—as in the distinctions of unconscious versus conscious, primary process versus secondary process, repressed versus return of the repressed, and manifest dream versus latent dream—but also in transformation or vicissitudes of instincts, as in love versus hate.

This transformational or two-language nature of psychoanalysis brings it into congruence with a number of contemporary approaches to language, including the structuralist approach of the French psychoanalyst Jacques Lacan and the deconstructionist approach of Jacques Derrida. However, it is in the transformational-generative theory of language that we find striking similarities to the nature of Freud's thought. The parallel between Freud and Chomsky has been amplified by M. Edelson, who notes that both men posit the presence of deeper structures forming the basis of surface structures, as well as stress the importance of transformational operations by which the language of the deep structure is represented in the language of the surface structure. Echoing Freud's basic distinction between primary process thought and secondary process thought, Fodor assumes a private language that is the precursor of the public language. In consonance with Chomsky's idea of "language and unconscious knowledge," he holds that to learn a language we must have available another private language. Fodor is led to speculate on the "vocabulary" of the code by which the private language is transformed into the public language.

Literature of the late nineteenth and early twentieth centuries, as in the works of Proust and Joyce, exemplifies the concern with levels of language. Joyce's novels can be considered as progressive movements from the public language of the conscious to a predominant emphasis on the private language of the unconscious. It is as if Joyce wished to write in the private language that forms the substrate of all literary works. It is poetry, however, that reveals most directly the transformation process from the private to the public language. The poet's language bridges primary and secondary processes and focuses on the transition from one to the other. Early in this century F. C. Prescott recognized the parallel between such poetic tropes and the process of dreamwork developed by Freud, a parallel subsequently elaborated by the psychoanalyst E. F. Sharpe. Thus, psychoanalysis, literature, and linguistics converge upon transformational operations, and the problem of interpretation of the text, or hermeneutics, becomes a central issue.

Because psychoanalytic interpretations of literature initially emphasized the major developmental themes explicated by Freud, there has been continuing interest in the oral, anal, and phallic aspects of literature, often with predominant emphasis on the Oedipal state of development. With the development of ego psychology within psychoanalysis, psychoanalytic literary criticism took a turn toward emphasizing the more adaptive, synthesizing aspects of literary productivity. The emphasis of ego psychology was to construe literary effort as positive, coping behavior in which the regression was purposive and controlled, otherwise the fantasy emanating from the primary process would become too private and preclude artistic communication with the reader. Erikson's work gave psychoanalytic interpretations of literature a firmer foothold by emphasizing the cohesive, integrative role of the writer's ego identity on the one hand, and his or her place within the context of the social, cultural, and historical forces on the other hand.

Freud turned more to pre-Oedipal issues late in his life, as he distinguished between the psychological development of the male and female child, and recent feminist literary criticism has moved in this direction. Freud maintained that the pre-Oedipal relationship with the mother was of more basic significance for the development of the female child than was the Oedipal period. Such a formulation is central in the feminist approach to problems of female identity formation. The intense interest feminist critics are displaying in this issue of female identity formation in relation to writing is one example of the mutual contribution of literature and psychology in the development of both.

Using a paradigm centering on Oedipal issues, the literary critic Harold Bloom has made bold forays into psychoanalytic concepts in advancing a theory of literature. Bloom emphasizes rhetorical tropes in poetry as manifestations of mechanisms of defense. More generally, Bloom is concerned with the thesis that repression as a defense operates importantly in how writers deal with their literary precursors. Repression operates by causing writers to misread their important precursors, and by otherwise distorting their influence.

Because Bloom's thesis implies that all reading of prior texts is a misreading of these texts, it broaches the important problem of the psychological bases of the reader's response to literature. The foremost theoretician of this issue has been N. N. Holland. It is apparent that every reader of a text responds to the text with some interpretive schema that reflects her or his personality.

Another promising approach is to consider different analyses of the same text by a group of literary critics, in an effort to identify common interpretational structures irrespective of each critic's idiosyncratic interpretation of the text. Such meta-analyses of interpretations of literature bear important similarities to the need in clinical psychology to identify common elements and structures in the interpretive diagnostic and psychotherapeutic efforts of clinicians.

The structuralist view rejects the idea that texts exist to be interpreted, or that they contain truth or meaning. Structuralists seek a systematic "scientific" framework that allows them to reduce texts to basic semiotic categories, such that the experience of the reader is nullified. The text reads itself.

Lacan, influenced by the structural linguistics of Saussure and the structural anthropology of Levi-Strauss, has as a central tenet the idea that the unconscious is structured like a language. Lacan rejects American psychoanalytic ego psychology and its emphasis on the adaptive, synthesizing, and integrative aspects of the ego in literary creativity. In contrast, Lacan stresses the alienated otherness of the ego and self, which he considered central to Freud's concepts of narcissism and identification. The infant first begins to develop its alienated self in what Lacan calls the "mirror stage" of development, such that the mother as a mirror is the basis of the infant's self as the other. Lacan's idea of the mirror stage allows the reintroduction of the concept of *imago* into literary analysis and provides a link between psychoanalytic conceptions and the archetype of Jung.

The deconstructionist program has been strongly influenced by Heidegger, Freud, and Lacan. More severely than Lacan, Derrida wishes to establish the text as both a presence and an absence, such that the text is ultimately effaced. The text of Freud or any writer is erased, deconstructed, or dismantled in order that it can be reconstructed or rewritten so as to show the text what it "does not know." The ultimate effect of Derrida's criticism is to render texts, Freudian or otherwise, open-ended, without closure, never fully fathomed, never fully constructed, or deconstructed. As in Freud's final commentary on psychoanalytic therapy, the text becomes both terminable and interminable.

What might the psychologist learn from literature? Perhaps the most psychologically astute of these poets was William Blake, whose startlingly acute and direct penetrations of the human psyche have yet to be adequately recognized and studied. Not only were his ideas precursors of both Freud and Jung, but the entire corpus of his work, both literary and artistic, also demands an exegesis in its own psychological terms that could yield important conceptualizations of the human personality.

The Romantic turn toward the self is strongly exemplified in Wordsworth, whose poetic texts contain some of the most vivid recapitulations of early childhood experience, including infancy. The complex ideas of Coleridge speak to many contemporary psychological issues, including his concepts concerning imagination and fantasy. The contributions of Keats to psychological understanding have been more generally recognized, including his emphasis on identity as a crucial element in personality formation and his ideas about the creative process, including *negative capability,* his oxymoron for a process reaching into issues central to Freud's theory of dreams.

Psychology, in seeking a systematic understanding of the human personality, needs to be reminded by literature where its conceptions fall short of the depth, complexity, and richness that characterize the human being.

J. Bieri

LOGICAL POSITIVISM

Logical positivism is an approach to philosophy of science that was developed by philosophers in the 1920s and 1930s in Vienna and Berlin (for review see Suppe, 1974). These philosophers pursued a common goal: to rid philosophy of the excesses of metaphysical idealism by clarifying philosophical language. This project called for strict logical and empirical criteria for assigning meaning to terms and truth value to propositions. The logical criteria were those of deductive logic, and the empirical criteria were appropriated from a misreading of Wittgenstein. Members of the Vienna Circle mistook Wittgenstein's quite imprecise claims about "atomic facts" as implying that science contained a language of facts independent from theoretical assumptions. Bloor (1983) has provided a corrective reading of Wittgenstein.

These philosophers wanted to set philosophy straight by making it conform to deductive logic and the meaning criteria of naive empiricist epistemology. In order to correct philosophy and set it on "the sure path of science," the positivist movement concluded that it was necessary to *justify* scientific practice philosophically. The primary concern of philosophy of science was the context of justification, where one could show via a reconstruction of history that scientists' products (i.e. their theories) changed and developed in a pattern consistent with logical reasoning. From this perspective, science is the set of theoretical and empirical propositions devised by physicists, chemists, and biologists to describe and explain the world. Science differs from nonscience by adhering both to logical truth and to empirical truth.

Overall, the logical positivists were not enthusiastic about psychology. Attempts to base the authority of deductive logic on "natural" habits of mind or psychological processes were rejected as psychologism. In order for the truths of logic and mathematics to command the high philosophical status of clear and certain (also transhistorical and universal) truth, it was necessary that these truths be objectively true. By definition, objective truth meant truth independent of subjective experience. Consequently, any attempt to base the truths of logic and mathematics on a study of cognitive contents and/or processes undermined their privileged status and authority.

Epistemologically speaking, the positivist program assumed that the relationship between human perception and the world was uncomplicated, with "basic facts" being "given" in direct observation. Psychologically speaking, the scientist or at least the collective community of scientists was conceived as a perfect information processing device capable of isomorphic inputs and outputs. Moreover, the claim was made that the language of science could be neatly bifurcated into distinct and nonoverlapping sets: (1) basic statements about the world or the language of direct observation (e.g., blue, hard, hot), and (2) theoretical terms (e.g., wavelength, density, kinetic energy) which, when introduced, had to be linked to observation terms via various explicit correspondence rules (i.e., operational definition).

The project of logical reconstruction consisted of demonstrating how new scientific knowledge was achieved through the accumulation of more extensive and accurate observations coupled with rigorous application of deductive logic. Scientific theories were reconstructed as if they were axiomatic systems like the postulates of pure geometry, their only difference being that they also had empirical content. In the later form known as "logical empiricism," the historical picture that emerged was a reconstruction of scientific development in which both rationality, as adherence to deductive logic, and progress, as movement toward ever more comprehensive theories, were inevitable (Feigl, 1970; Hempel, 1965; Nagel, 1961).

The logical positivists and logical empiricists accomplished their reconstruction of science by ignoring many of the particulars of what individual scientists might have done and said. Science as described by the logical positivists and logical empiricists was an abstraction, a set of propositions often taken out of historical context and only loosely tied to people called scientists.

Whether or not scientists actually behaved in the manner described by this reconstruction was deemed irrelevant to the paramount task of establishing that science in the abstract somehow proceeded along logical lines and therefore made valid claims to "Truth." Thus, by focusing on an abstraction called "science," the project of logical reconstruction could be carried forward without entertaining the sort of evidence that might be provided by detailed sociological and psychological studies of scientists' actual practices. As subsequent work in the history of science showed, it is a bitter irony that the philosophical movement that promised to rid philosophy of speculative idealism only reinstated a kind of idealism in the logical reconstruction of science without scientists.

Much of psychology itself was judged by the logical positivists to be defective and in need of the purification they offered (Bergmann, 1940; Carnap, 1932/1959; Feigl, 1945). To complicate matters further, the positivist prescriptions for doing philosophy were widely taken as prescriptions for doing science. This was evident in the often tacit but nevertheless dogmatic adoption of major tenets of positivist philosophy by empirically oriented psychologists (for review see Koch, 1959–1963), who apparently overlooked the antidogmatic stance of most members of the Vienna Circle. Smith's (1986) study of leading behaviorists in the 1930s and 1940s raises doubts about the direct connection between their views and those of the logical positivists, but he also noted that by the 1950s logical empiricism was widely accepted as the standard account of science among psychologists in general. Although some of the logical positivists and logical empiricists advocated types of behaviorism at times, Smith has shown that it is clearly incorrect to call Skinner a logical positivist.

REFERENCES

Bergmann, G. (1940). On some methodological problems of psychology. *Philosophy of Science, 7,* 205–219.

Bloor, D. (1983). *Wittgenstein: A social theory of knowledge.* New York: Columbia University Press.

Carnap, R. (1959). Psychology in physical language. In A. J. Ayer (Ed.), *Logical positivism* (pp. 165–198). New York: Free Press. (Original work published 1932)

Feigl, H. (1945). Operationism and scientific method. *Psychological Review, 52,* 250–259.

Feigl, H. (1970). The "orthodox" view of theories. In M. Radner & S. Winokur (Eds.), *Minnesota studies in philosophy of science IV* (pp. 3–16). Minneapolis: University of Minnesota Press.

Hempel, C. G. (1965). *Aspects of scientific explanation.* New York: Free Press.

Koch, S. (Ed.). (1959–1963). *Psychology: A study of a science* (6 vols.). New York: McGraw-Hill.

Nagel, E. (1961). *The structure of science.* New York: Harcourt, Brace, and World.

Smith, L. D. (1986). *Behaviorism and logical positivism: A reassessment of the alliance.* Stanford: Stanford University Press.

Suppe, F. (1974). The search for philosophic understanding of scientific theories. In F. Suppe (Ed.), *The structure of scientific theories* (pp. 3–232). Urbana: University of Illinois Press.

Arthur C. Houts
University of Memphis

LOGOTHERAPY

The Greek word *logos* denotes meaning, and logotherapy can be defined as a meaning-centered psychotherapy. It was founded by Viktor E. Frankl. The motivational theory underlying Frankl's approach focuses on what he calls "the will to meaning," in counterdistinction to "the will to power" and the "will to pleasure" (the pleasure principle). Today more and more patients complain of a feeling of meaninglessness, and many of the ills and ailments of our time, according to Frankl, can be traced back to this frustration in a "search for meaning." The result of this state of affairs is the neurotic triad: depression, aggression, and addiction. Empirical evidence has been furnished by logotherapists that the feeling of meaninglessness is at the root of the neurotic triad.

No logotherapist can hand out or "prescribe" meanings. It is the objective of logotherapy to *describe* the process of meaning perception by way of a phenomenological analysis, so as to find out how normal people arrive at meaning and consequently at a sense of fulfillment.

From such analysis Frankl has distilled his "logo theory," according to which meaning can be found in doing a deed, creating a work, or experiencing something (art, nature, culture, etc.). Logotherapy also offers a special technique for the treatment of obsessive–compulsive and phobic neuroses. This technique is called *paradoxical intention* and can be defined as having the patient try to do, or wish to have happen, precisely that which he or she fears. The effect is to disarm the anticipatory anxiety that accounts for many of the feedback mechanisms that initiate and perpetuate the neurotic condition. Another logotherapeutic technique, called *dereflection,* is designed to counteract sexual neuroses such as frigidity and impotence.

Viktor E. Frankl

See also: **Psychotherapy**

LONGITUDINAL STUDIES

Longitudinal studies represent a research design wherein individuals or groups are observed or repeatedly assessed over a considerable period of time in order to assess change. The longitudinal study is an important research method in developmental psychology, where time-related phenomena are under investigation. Often the intent is to study behavioral or physiological changes that may occur in subjects as they grow older. Two major approaches have been employed to investigate the time-related trajectory of change: cross-sectional and longitudinal designs. *Cross-sectional* studies measure a given dependent variable (e.g., IQ) in several different age cohorts. In this type of study one might measure IQ in groups that were, for instance, 4, 7, 10, and 12 years old. *Longitudinal* investigations repeatedly assess the dependent variable for the same cohort of subjects over time (e.g., when they are 4, 7, 10, and 12 years of age). Technically, a longitudinal study is any investigation in which repeated measurements are recorded on the same subjects over time. However, the term "longitudinal" is typically not used for studies in which the time span is less than several months or years.

Longitudinal studies have a long history in various specialties of psychology as well as many other fields, ranging from health to sociometric status. The late nineteenth century is generally cited as the time when psychology began to seriously employ longitudinal research. However, the classic study of infants by D. Tiedemann, entitled *Beobachtungen über die Entwicklung der Seelenfähigkeit bei Kindern,* was published in 1787. Early work using longitudinal studies significantly influenced the nature of developmental psychology.

One major strength of longitudinal designs is that researchers are able to follow the same subjects over the period of the study. This permits examination of change in the same individuals as they develop or decline. Consequently, longitudinal investigations permit more direct inferences regarding development than cross-sectional studies. Longitudinal studies with multiple measures such as the examples noted above (i.e., assessments at ages 4, 7, 10, and 12) are also preferred because of strong statistical power in determining the trajectory of a change over time.

Longitudinal designs also present certain methodological difficulties. Since the subjects are measured repeatedly, it is possible that changes may be observed which are partially due to the effects of repeated assessment reliability and the continuing attention or Hawthorne effect over time. Another potential problem is subject attrition: since longitudinal studies often continue for an extended period of time, a certain number of subjects may be lost for a variety of reasons (death, moving, refusal to continue). As with most experimental designs, most problems associated with longitudinal studies can be successfully circumvented by ingenious researchers. Such studies remain an important research strategy in psychology, although they are not frequently undertaken because of the time and expense involved.

SUGGESTED READING

DeShon, R. P., Ployhard, R. E., & Sacco, J. M. (1998). The estimation of reliability in longitudinal models. *International Journal of Behavioral Development, 22,* 493–515.

Gelfand, D. M., Jenson, W. R., & Drew, C. J. (1997). *Understanding child behavior disorders.* Fort Worth, TX: Harcourt Brace.

Maassen, G. H., Goossens, F. A., & Bokhorst, J. (1998). Ratings as validation of sociometric status determined by nominations in longitudinal research. *Social Behavior and Personality, 26,* 259–274.

Maxwell, S. E. (1998). Longitudinal designs in randomized group comparisons: When will intermediate observations increase statistical power? *Psychological Methods, 3,* 275–290.

Clifford J. Drew
University of Utah

LONG-TERM POTENTIATION

Virtually all notions about memory hold dear the central notion that learning relies on the modification of synaptic function. In recent years considerable attention has focused on one particular form of use-dependent synaptic plasticity known as long-term potentiation (LTP). LTP was first discovered by Terje Lomo, who observed that repetitive high frequency electrical stimulations of the pathway from the cortex to the hippocampus resulted in a steeper rise time of the excitatory synaptic potential as well as recruitment of spike activity from a greater number of cells. Moreover, these changes in synaptic and cellular responses to subsequent single shocks lasted several hours, suggesting the possibility of a lasting memory mechanism.

Two key properties of LTP are most notable: First, LTP is *specific* to those synapses activated during stimulation. Other neighboring synapses, even on the same neurons, are not altered. This phenomenon parallels the natural specificity of our memories, and would be a key requirement of any useful cellular memory mechanism. The property of specificity may be key to the storage capacity of brain structures because each cell can participate in the representation of multiple memories composed from distinct subsets of its synaptic inputs.

Second, LTP is *associative* in that potentiation characteristically occurs across multiple inputs that are stimulated simultaneously. The property of associativity is consistent with Hebb's (1949) postulate that increasing synaptic efficacy requires the repeated activation of a presynaptic element AND its participation in the success in firing the postsynaptic cell, as indeed occurs in associative LTP when several inputs are simultaneously active.

Considerable evidence has now accumulated revealing the cellular and molecular mechanisms that mediate the properties of different forms of LTP, as well as the cousin synaptic plasticity mechanism called long-term depression, in both the hippocampus and the neocortex (Bear, 1996; Bliss & Collingridge, 1993; Madison, Malenka, & Nicoll, 1991; Malenka, 1994).

LTP and Memory: Is There a Connection?

As Stevens (1996) once put it, the mechanism of LTP is so attractive that it would be a shame if LTP turned out not to be a memory device. But there should be no doubt about the fact that LTP is not memory; it is a laboratory phenomenon never observed in nature. The best we can hope for is that LTP and memory share some of their physiological and molecular bases. In recent years evidence from two general strategies have emerged to provide supporting connections between LTP and memory.

Behavioral LTP. One strategy is to determine whether learning produces changes in synaptic physiology similar to the increases in synaptic and cellular responses that occur after LTP. Recently, Rogan, Staubli, & LeDoux, (1997) offered the most compelling evidence to date that these aspects of LTP are a consequence of natural learning. In this case the circuit under study was the pathway from the medial geniculate nucleus of the thalamus to the lateral amygdala nucleus that is part of the critical circuit for auditory fear conditioning. These investigators found that repeated pairings of auditory stimuli and foot shocks train rats to fear the tones. Furthermore, this learning experience alters evoked sensory responses to the tones in the same way as LTP in that pathway. Thus, in rats with properly timed tone–shock pairings, tones produce evoked potentials of greater slope and amplitude, just as do electrical stimulus trains applied to this pathway. No enhancement of field potentials was observed with unpaired tone and foot shock presentations, even though this conditioning control leads to as much of a behavioral response (freezing) as paired presentations because even the unpaired control rats learn to freeze to the environmental context where shocks are received. Furthermore, this behavioral LTP is enduring, lasting at least a few days, as long as the behavioral response during extinction trials. Other studies have shown a similar pattern of enhanced strength of connections among neurons in the motor cortex of rats trained on a skilled reaching task (Rioult-Pedotti, Friedman, Hess, & Donoghue, 1998).

Blocking LTP and memory. Perhaps the most compelling and straightforward data on a potential connection between the molecular basis of LTP and memory has come from experiments in which a drug is used to block LTP and, correspondingly, prevent learning. These studies were based on the observations that induction of the most prominent form of hippocampal LTP is dependent on a specific glutamate receptor known as the N-methyl-D-aspartate (NMDA) receptor, and that drugs such as D-2-amino-5-phosphonovalerate (AP5) selectively block the NMDA receptor and prevent hippocampal LTP while sparing normal synaptic transmission. Thus, to the extent that the role of the NMDA receptor is fully selective to plasticity, one might predict these drugs would indeed block new learning without affecting nonlearning performance or retention of learning normally accomplished prior to drug treatment.

Consistent with these predictions, some of the strongest evidence supporting a connection between LTP and memory has come from demonstrations that drug-induced blockade of hippocampal NMDA-receptors prevents hippocampal-dependent spatial learning (Morris, Anderson, Lynch, &

Baudry, 1986). Additional experiments revealed no effect of AP5 on retention of the same spatial learning when training was accomplished prior to drug treatment. This would be fully predicted because NMDA receptors are viewed as required only for the induction of LTP and not for its maintenance. In addition, targeted genetic manipulations have now shown that knocking out NMDA receptors (McHugh, Blum, Tsien, Tonegawa, & Wilson, 1997) or later stages in the cascade of molecular triggers for maintenance of LTP (e.g., Silva, Paylor, Wehner, & Tonegawa, 1992) also results in severe memory impairments. These studies have also shown some restrictions on the role of NMDA-receptor mediated LTP in spatial memory. Recent experiments have indicated that blocking NMDA-dependent LTP does not necessarily prevent the encoding of a new spatial environment (Bannerman, Good, Butcher, Ramsay, & Morris, 1995). However, NMDA-dependent LTP may be necessary to remembering new episodes within a familiar space (Steele & Morris, 1999).

REFERENCES

Bannerman, D. M., Good, M. A., Butcher, S. P., Ramsay, M., & Morris, R. G. M. (1995). Prior experience and N-methyl-D-aspartate receptor blockade dissociate components of spatial learning in the watermaze. *Nature, 378,* 182–186.

Bear, M. F. (1996). A synaptic basis for memory storage in the cerebral cortex. *Proceedings of the National Academy of Science USA, 93,* 13453–13459.

Bliss, T. V. P., & Collingridge G. L. (1993). A synaptic model of memory: Long-term potentiation in the hippocampus. *Nature, 361,* 31–39.

Hebb, D. O. (1949). *The organization of behavior.* New York: Wiley.

Madison, D. V., Malenka, R. C., & Nicoll, R. A. (1991). Mechanisms underlying long-term potentiation of synaptic transmission. *Annual Review of Neuroscience, 14,* 379–397.

Malenka, R. C. (1994). Synaptic plasticity in the hippocampus: LTP and LTD. *Cell, 78,* 535–538.

McHugh, T. J., Blum, K. I., Tsien, J. Z., Tonegawa, S., & Wilson, M. A. (1996). Impaired hippocampal representation of space in CA1-specific NMDAR1 knockout mice. *Cell, 87,* 1339–1349.

Morris, R. G. M., Anderson, E., Lynch, G. S., & Baudry, M. (1986). Selective impairment of learning and blockade of long term potentiation by an N-methyl-D-aspartate receptor anatagonist, AP5. *Nature, 319,* 774–776.

Rioult-Pedotti, M.-S., Friedman, D., Hess, G., & Donoghue, J. P. (1998). Strengthening of horizontal cortical connections following skill learning. *Nature Neuroscience, 1,* 230–234.

Rogan, M. T., Staubli, U. V., & LeDoux, J. E. (1997). Fear conditioning induces associative long-term potentiation in the amygdala. *Nature, 390,* 604–607.

Silva, A. J., Paylor, C. F. R., Wehner, J. W., & Tonegawa, S. (1992). Impaired spatial learning in a-calcium-calmodulin kinase II mutant mice. *Science, 257,* 206–211.

Steele, R. J., & Morris, R. G. M. (1999). Delay dependent impairment in matching-to-place task with chronic and intrahippocampal infusion of the NMDA-antagonist D-AP5. *Hippocampus, 9,* 118–136.

Stevens, C. F. (1996). Strengths and weaknesses in memory. *Nature, 381,* 471–472.

Howard Eichenbaum
Boston University

LOOSE ASSOCIATIONS

The most important source of data for assessing patients with psychiatric disorders is speech behavior during a clinical interview. One critical component of this assessment is the patient's ability to produce coherent conversational discourse.

The sine qua non of disrupted discourse coherence consists of loose associations. A synonymous term currently used is "derailment." Loose associations or derailments are suspected when the listener has significant difficulty following or tracking continuous, conversational speech. The overall intention or focus of the utterance is obscure, and the speaker seems to shift idiosyncratically from one frame of reference to another (Andreasen, 1979a). A typical case of loose associations is illustrated in the following:

Interviewer: Tell me about where you live.

Patient: I live in one place and then another place. They're black and white you know. That's why I love Christmas and stuff because, you know, it's different colors. I used to live in Brooklyn. (Hoffman, Kirstein, Stopek, & Ciccheti, 1982)

Here the patient seems to respond to the interviewer's prompt but then abruptly switches to a Christmas motif that fails to elaborate on the "where I live" theme and does not, in itself, make a point. Of note is that each of the sentences, when considered separately, is quite ordinary and grammatical. Deviance reflects the juxtaposition of phrases and sentences.

A more complex form of loose associations is illustrated by the following (Hoffman, 1986):

Interviewer: Did you ever try to hurt yourself?

Patient: I cut myself once when I was in the kitchen trying to please David. I was scared for life because if David didn't want me then no man would.

Here the patient seems to be talking about two frames of reference, the first pertaining to cutting herself, presumably while preparing food, and the second pertaining to reasons for being suicidal. Shifts between the two frames of reference are expressed without warning to the listener. In other words, the patient did not state, "I never intentionally hurt myself but I was so upset about David that . . ." These shifts of frame ordinarily help the listener to make the transition from one frame of reference to another (Hoffman et al., 1982).

Most typically, loose associations are produced by patients with schizophrenia. However, some patients with aphasia or brain disturbances secondary to drug intoxication or organic encephalopathy may also produce such language disturbances. A related language difficulty is referred to as "flight of ideas," and is typically associated with patients with mania or amphetamine-induced states. Some researchers have not distinguished flight of ideas from loose associations (Andreasen, 1979a), but there is some empirical evidence that the two terms refer to distinct phenomena (Hoffman, Stopek, & Andreasen, 1986). In the case of flight of ideas, conversational speech yields unannounced and disruptive shifts in frame of reference, but is also accompanied by rapid production of speech. Most importantly, the speaker in the former case seems to retain the ability to flesh out particular themes or topics within a particular frame of reference. In contrast, looseness of associations suggests a sustained inability to fully and coherently elaborate on any theme or topic. Although the presence of these language difficulties favors some psychiatric diagnoses over others, they, in themselves, are not diagnostic of a specific disorder. For instance, it has been well established that some apparently normal speakers occasionally produce loose associations (Andreasen, 1979b; Hoffman et al., 1986).

There is some research exploring the cognitive and/or neurobiological basis of loose associations. Some recent studies have suggested that alterations in semantic processing produce loose associations and related language disturbances in patients with schizophrenia (Goldberg et al., 1998; Spitzer, 1997). Another recent study of regional cerebral blood flow using positron emission tomography suggested that these language difficulties arise from an imbalance of regional cerebral activation, with reduced activation in inferior frontal and cingulate brain regions combined with excessive activation in hippocampal regions (McGuire et al., 1998). Additional research on the neurocognitive basis of loose associations is needed.

REFERENCES

Andreasen, N. C. (1979a). Thought, language, and Communication Disorders: I. Clinical assessment, definition of terms, and evaluation of their reliability. *Archives of General Psychiatry, 36,* 1315–1321.

Andreasen, N. C. (1979b). Thought, language, and Communication Disorders: II. Diagnostic significance. *Archives of General Psychiatry, 36,* 1325–1330.

Goldberg, T. E., Aloia, M. S., Gourovitch, M. L., Missar, D., Pickar, D., & Weinberger, D. R. (1998). Cognitive substrates of thought disorder: I. The semantic system. *American Journal of Psychiatry, 155,* 1671–1676.

Hoffman, R. E. (1986). Verbal hallucinations and language production processes in Schizophrenia. *Behavior and Brain Science, 9,* 503–548.

Hoffman, R. E., Kirstein, L., Stopek, S., & Cichetti, D. (1982). Apprehending schizophrenic discourse: A structural analysis of the listener's task. *Brain Language, 15,* 207–233.

Hoffman, R. E., Stopek, S., & Andreasen, N. C. (1986). A comparative study of manic versus schizophrenic speech disorganization. *Archives of General Psychiatry, 43,* 831–838.

McGuire, P. K., Quested, D. J., Spence, S. A., Murray, R. M., Frith, C. D., & Liddle, P. F. (1998). Pathophysiology of 'positive' thought disorder in Schizophrenia. *British Journal of Psychiatry, 173,* 231–235.

Spitzer, M. (1997). A cognitive neuroscience view of schizophrenic thought disorder. *Schizophrenia Bulletin, 23,* 29–50.

Ralph E. Hoffman
Yale University

LOVE

What Is Love?

In romantic relationships, psychologists distinguish between *passionate* love and *companionate* love. Passionate love is defined as an intense longing for union with the other. It is associated with a confusion of feelings: tenderness and sexuality, elation and pain, anxiety and relief, altruism and jealousy (see Hatfield & Rapson, 1993, 1995 for a review of this research). Companionate love, a less intense emotion, is characterized by affection, intimacy, attachment, and a concern for the welfare of the other (see Sternberg, 1998).

Is Passionate Love a Cultural Universal?

Since Darwin's classic treatise on *The Descent of Man and Selection in Relation to Sex,* scientists have debated the universality of romantic love. Once, scientists assumed that passionate love was a Western phenomenon. Today, most assume it to be a cultural universal. In one study, anthropologists selected a sampling of tribal societies from the *Standard Cross-Cultural Sample.* They found that in far-flung societies, young lovers talked about passionate love, recounted tales of love, sang love songs, and talked about the longings and anguish of infatuation. When passionate affections clashed with parents' or elders' wishes, young people often eloped. It appears that romantic love *is* a pan-human characteristic (see Jankowiak, 1995). However, cross-cultural researchers, anthropologists, and historians point out that there is cultural variability in how common such feelings are.

Do Men and Women in Different Cultures Differ in Their Views of Love?

Culture has been found to have a significant impact on how men and women view passionate love. Researchers interviewed young people in America, Italy, and the People's Republic of China about their emotional experiences. They found that in all cultures, men and women identified the same prototypic emotions—joy/happiness, love/attraction, fear, anger/hate, and sadness/depression. Men and women also agreed as to whether emotions were positive experiences (such as joy) or negative ones (such as fear, anger, or sadness). The only exception was in the case of love. Americans and Italians tended to equate love with joy and happiness. Chinese students had a darker view of passion, associating it with sadness, pain, and heartache.

What Do Men and Women Desire In Romantic Partners, Sexual Partners, and Mates?

Throughout the world, young men and women desire many of the same things in a mate. In one cross-cultural study, Buss (1994) asked over 10,000 men and women from 37 countries to indicate what they valued in mates. The cultures represented a tremendous diversity of geographic, cultural, political, ethnic, religious, racial, economic, and linguistic groups. Of utmost importance was love! High on the list of things men and women cared about were character, emotional stability and maturity, a pleasing disposition, education and intelligence, health, sociability, a desire for home and children, refinement, good looks, and ambition.

Scientists have documented that a major determinant of sexual "chemistry" is physical attractiveness. People also tend to fall in love with people who are similar to themselves in attitudes, religious affiliation, values, interests, education, and socioeconomic status.

Do Men and Women Desire the Same Thing in Mates?

Evolutionary psychologists argue that there are major differences in what men and women desire in romantic partners and mates. An animal's "fitness" depends on how successful it is in transmitting its genes to subsequent generations. It is to both men's and women's evolutionary advantage to produce as many progeny as possible. Men and women differ, however, in "ideal" reproductive strategies: men seek quantity, women quality in a mate if they are to maximize reproductive outcomes. This logic led Buss (1994) to propose a "sexual strategies theory" of human mating. Men and women, he argues, are genetically programmed to desire different traits in potential mates. Men prefer women who are physically attractive, healthy, and young, and they desire sexual encounters with a variety of partners. Women seek out men who possess status, power, and money; who are willing to make a commitment; who are kind and considerate; and who like children. Buss and his colleagues have collected considerable evidence in support of these hypotheses.

Many anthropologists, historians, sociologists, and psychologists have sharply criticized the evolutionary approach. They point out that *Homo sapiens* possess an unrivaled ability to adapt—to change themselves and their worlds. Men and women possess different attitudes, these critics continue, not because they are propelled by ancient genetic codes, but because they are responding to different sociocultural realities. For most of human history, men and women who desired passionate liaisons and/or indulged in casual sex were likely to face very different consequences. Is it surprising, then, that even today many women fear risky sexual experiments?

There is evidence from nonhuman primates and from women in societies with few coercive constraints on female sexual behavior, such as the ¡Kung San or modern Scandinavia, that under permissive conditions women are far more active and assertive sexually and far more excited by sexual variety.

Is Passionate Love an Intensely Pleasurable or an Intensely Painful Experience?

For centuries, theorists have bitterly disagreed over what passionate love "really" is. Is it an intensely pleasurable experience or an intensely painful one? Some psychologists argue that passionate love is explained by the same reinforcement principles that explain interpersonal attraction in general. They contend that passionate love is stimulated by intensely positive experiences and dampened by intensely negative ones.

Other theorists take the opposite tack. They argue that passion can be fueled by admiration for a social ideal, a desire to expand one's horizons, a yearning for challenge, mystery, and excitement . . . and sometimes even anger and hostility (see Aron & Aron, 1986). Most social psychologists would probably agree that both pleasure and pain can fuel passion. They would endorse the old adage: "The opposite of love is not hate but indifference."

There are physiological reasons why love might be linked to both pleasure and pain. Physiologically, love, delight, and pain have one thing in common—they are intensely arousing. Joy, passion, and excitement as well as anger, envy, and hate all produce a sympathetic response in the nervous system. This is evidenced by the symptoms associated with all these emotions: a flushed face, sweaty palms, weak knees, butterflies in the stomach, dizziness, a pounding heart, trembling hands, and accelerated breathing. For this reason, theorists point out that either delight or pain (or a combination of the two) should have the potential to fuel a passionate experience.

An abundance of evidence supports the commonsense contention that, under the right conditions, intensely positive experiences such as euphoria, sexual fantasizing, an understanding partner, or general excitement can fuel passion. But there is also some evidence for the more intriguing contention that under the right conditions, anxiety and fear, jealousy, loneliness, anger, or even grief can fuel passion (see Hatfield & Rapson, 1993; Zillmann, 1998).

Strange as it sounds, then, evidence suggests that adrenalin makes the heart grow fonder. Delight is surely the most common stimulant of passionate love, yet anxiety and fear can sometimes play a part.

REFERENCES

Aron, A., & Aron, E. N. (1986). *Love and the expansion of self: Understanding attraction and satisfaction.* New York: Hemisphere.

Buss, D. M. (1994). *The evolution of desire.* New York: Basic Books.

Darwin, C. (1871). *The descent of man and selection in relation to sex.* London: Murray.

Hatfield, E., & Rapson, R. L. (1993). *Love, sex, and intimacy: Their psychology, biology, and history.* New York: HarperCollins.

Hatfield, E., & Rapson, R. L. (1995). *Love and sex: Cross-cultural perspectives.* New York: Allyn & Bacon.

Hatfield, E., & Sprecher, S. (1986). *Mirror, mirror: The importance of looks in everyday life.* Albany, NY: SUNY Press.

Jankowiak, W. (Ed.). (1995). *Romantic passion.* New York: Columbia University Press.

Sternberg, R. J. (1998). *Cupid's arrow: The course of love through time.* Cambridge, UK: Cambridge Press.

Zillmann, D. (1998). *Connections between sexuality and aggression* (2nd ed.). Mahwah, NJ: LEA Press.

Elaine Hatfield
Richard L. Rapson
University of Hawaii

LURIA–NEBRASKA NEUROPSYCHOLOGICAL BATTERY

The Luria–Nebraska Neuropsychological Battery is a neuropsychological assessment battery based on the psychological procedures originated by the Russian neuropsychologist Alexander R. Luria, and subsequently reorganized by Charles J. Golden (Golden, Hammeke, & Purisch, 1978) and his associates into a standardized battery of Luria's tests for the purpose of clinical neurodiagnosis. Luria, like the English neurologist J. Hughlings Jackson and his fellow Russian L. S. Vygotsky, believed that brain–behavior relationships could not be explained satisfactorily by either the localizationist or the equipotentialist theories of brain function. Instead, Luria conceived of behavior as the result of the interactions among all areas of the brain, and favored the use of simple test procedures that reflected relatively uncomplicated patterns of brain interactions, so that functional systems of the brain could be more precisely investigated.

Recognition of Luria in the United States came with the publication of *Higher Cortical Functions in Man* (1962) and *The Working Brain* (1973). Detailed information on Luria's test procedures became available with Anne-Lise Christensen's (1979) *Luria's Neuropsychological Investigation.* Luria's testing methods were not immediately accepted by American clinical neuropsychologists because of the absence of a standardized, quantitative scoring system and of experimental evidence supporting the validity of the test procedures. In addition, Luria's procedures appeared to rely heavily upon clinical judgment rather than objective, verifiable data.

To remedy the psychometric deficits of the Luria techniques, Golden and his colleagues transformed Luria's test items into standardized test procedures with objective scoring systems, and a battery that allowed a clinical evaluation on a quantitative level, like most American tests, as well as a qualitative level, as urged by Luria. The standardized version of Luria's tests assesses major areas of neuropsychological performance, including motor, tactile, and visual skills; auditory abilities; expressive and receptive speech functions; reading, writing, and arithmetic abilities; spatial skills; and memory and intelligence.

Description of the Battery

There are 269 items in the standardized Luria battery, initially referred to as the Luria–South Dakota Neuropsychological Test Battery. Each item is a test of a specific aspect of neuropsychological functioning. Subgroups of items exist which represent performance in the content area implied by the name of the scale, as, for example, the motor functions scale. The names of the scales of the Luria–Nebraska Neuropsychological Battery are as follows:

1. Motor Functions
2. Rhythm (acoustico-motor) Functions
3. Tactile (higher cutaneous and kinesthetic) Functions
4. Visual (spatial) Functions
5. Receptive Speech
6. Expressive Speech
7. Writing Functions
8. Reading Skills
9. Arithmetical Skills
10. Memory
11. Intellectual Processes

Form II of this battery added a twelfth scale, Intermediate Memory, which assesses delayed recall of 10 of the previously administered Memory items.

There are five summary scales, based on some of the items of the clinical scales:

1. Pathognomonic. This scale consists of simple items rarely missed by normals and is highly indicative of brain dysfunction.
2. Right Hemisphere. This scale measures the motor and tactile functioning of the left side of the body.
3. Left Hemisphere. This scale measures the motor and tactile functioning of the right side of the body.
4. Profile Elevation. This scale measures the level of present functioning or degree of behavioral compensation.
5. Impairment. This scale measures the degree of overall impairment.

Since the original publication of this battery, other scales have been developed, including eight localization scales (Frontal, Sensorimotor, Parietal-Occipital, and Temporal scales for each brain hemisphere) and 28 separate factor scales. A 66-item list of qualitative descriptors of test performance is also provided to aid the examiner in evaluating the nature of performance errors.

An impaired performance on any of the scales is determined by comparison with a critical level, which is calculated for each patient with age and education corrections. If a scale exceeds the critical level, the possibility of impairment on that scale is suggested. Two or more scales exceeding the critical level are suggestive of brain damage.

An adaptation for children, The Luria–Nebraska Neuropsychological Battery—Children's Revision, is available for ages 8 to 12. A short form of this battery has been proposed to be used with elderly patients.

The Luria–Nebraska is administered by psychologists as well as by psychology technicians trained in the administration and scoring procedures of the battery. The testing time averages about 2½ hours. The scale scores can be hand-scored, but a computerized service by the test battery's publisher is also available.

Neuropsychological Studies

Several validity studies of the Luria–Nebraska have been completed using normal, brain-damaged, and schizophrenic patients. In 1978, Golden, Hammeke, and Purisch reported the first validity study of the Luria, examining the test items with 50 brain-damaged and 50 control subjects. Of the 269 Luria items, 252 were found to discriminate significantly at the 0.05 level or better, with the remaining 17 items significant at the 0.02 level.

Hammeke, Golden, and Purisch (1978) also studied the 14 scales of the Luria Battery with 50 brain-damaged subjects and 50 controls. The diagnostic accuracy of the scales with the brain-damaged subjects ranged from 64% for the Arithmetic Scale to 86% for the Expressive Speech Scale. The hit rates with the normal subjects ranged from 74% for the Expressive Speech Scale to 96% for the Memory Scale. A discriminant analysis using the 14 scaled scores correctly classified all 50 control patients and 43 of the brain-damaged patients, yielding an overall hit rate of 93%.

Cross-validation of the standardized Luria was reported by Golden, Moses, and colleagues (1981), utilizing 87 patients with localized lesions and 30 control patients. A Luria–Nebraska summary score led to an 74% accuracy rate for determining brain damage. The two hemisphere scales yielded a lateralization hit rate of 78%, whereas the highest localization scale led to a lateralization hit rate of 92% and a localization hit rate of 84%.

The effectiveness of the Luria–Nebraska was compared with the Halstead-Reitan Neuropsychological Battery, recognized as the most widely used standardized battery. Both test batteries were administered to 48 brain-damaged and 60 normal subjects. The results showed a high degree of relationship (all Rs > 0.71, $p < 0.05$) between the 14 Luria–Nebraska scale scores and the major 14 scores of the Halstead-Reitan. Discriminant analysis found both batteries equally effective in identifying the brain-damaged subjects, with hit rates over 85% (Golden, Kane, et al., 1981).

Critique of this battery has noted that it is comprised of test items from Luria's work, but it does not necessarily represent Luria's clinical and qualitative methodology of testing hypotheses concerning a patient's neuropsychological functions or deficits. Support for the battery, on the other hand, has identified the standardization and empirical aspects of this battery as its strongest assets (Anastasi, 1982). Although the validity of this battery with neurologically impaired patients has been confirmed by a number of studies by Golden and his associates, others have been unable to replicate these validation findings. A frequent source of diagnostic errors occur with patients experiencing language impairment, evidently due to the highly verbal nature of many of the test items.

A concise review of this battery is presented in Lezak's (1995) *Neuropsychological Assessment,* including a discussion of concerns about the battery's norms, scale specificity, validation studies, and lateralization capabilities.

REFERENCES

Anastasi, A. (1982). *Psychological testing* (5th ed.). New York: Macmillan.

Christensen, A.-L. (1979). *Luria's neuropsychological investigation* (2nd ed.). Copenhagen, Denmark: Munksgaard.

Golden, C. J., Hammeke, T. A., & Purisch, A. D. (1978). Diagnostic validity of a standardized neuropsychological battery derived from Luria's Neuropsychological Tests. *Journal of Consulting and Clinical Psychology, 45,* 1258–1265.

Golden, C. J., Kane, R., Sweet, J., Moses, J. A., Cardellino, J. P., Templeton, R., Vicente, P., & Graber, B. (1981). Relationship of the Halstead-Reitan Neuropsychological Battery to the Luria–

Nebraska Neuropsychological Battery. *Journal of Consulting and Clinical Psychology, 49,* 410–417.

Golden, C. J., Moses, J. A., Fishburne, F. J., Engum, E., Lewis, G. P., Wisniewski, A. M., Conley, F. K., Berg, R. A. & Graber, B. (1981). Cross-validation of the Luria–Nebraska Neuropsychological Battery for the presence, lateralization, and localization of brain damage. *Journal of Consulting and Clinical Psychology, 49,* 491–507.

Golden, C. J., Purisch, A. D., & Hammeke, T. A. (1985). *Luria–Nebraska Neuropsychological Battery: Forms I and II.* Los Angeles: Western Psychological Services.

Hammeke, T. A., Golden, C. J., & Purisch, A. D. (1978). A standardized, short, and comprehensive neuropsychological test battery based on the Luria neuropsychological evaluation. *International Journal of Neuroscience, 8,* 135–141.

Lezak, M. D. (1995). *Neuropsychological assessment* (3rd ed.). New York: Oxford University.

Luria, A. R. (1962). *Higher cortical functions in man.* New York: Basic Books.

Luria, A. R. (1973). *The working brain.* New York: Basic Books.

Moses, J. A., Jr., & Purisch, A. D. (1997). The evolution of the Luria-Nebraska Neuropsychological Battery. In G. Goldstein & T. M. Incagnoli (Eds.), *Contemporary approaches to neuropsychological assessment* (pp. 131–170). New York: Plenum Press.

William T. Tsushima
Straub Clinic and Hospital

See also: **Halstead-Reitan Battery; Neuropsychology**

M

MAGNETIC RESONANCE IMAGING (MRI)

Magnetic resonance imaging (MRI) is a method that can provide information on both the anatomy and physiological function of the brain. It is a powerful tool for integrating our current understanding of brain function with models of cognition and emotion. *Anatomical MRI* provides a picture of brain structure, whereas *functional MRI* (fMRI) provides information about the physiological function of the brain.

MRI relies on three magnetic fields. A constant magnetic field, known as the static field, aligns all magnetically sensitive particles uniformly, so that perturbations can be detected. In clinical machines, this magnetic field is generally between 0.5 and 1.5 tesla (T) and in "high-field" research machines, it is either 3 or 4 T (as reference, the magnetic field of the earth is 0.0001 T). The perturbation is supplied by a second magnetic field, known as the pulse sequence, which is an oscillating electromagnetic field "tuned" to a set frequency (resonant frequency) of a particular substance, typically hydrogen atoms. The relaxation time, the time it takes for the protons to revert to their original state, is recorded through a radio frequency coil, also known as a receiver coil. Because hydrogen atoms in different substances have different relaxation times, distinct tissues, such as white matter and gray matter, can be differentiated. Information on where in the brain those substances are residing comes from another magnetic field, the gradient field, which varies in intensity over the area being imaged.

Standard anatomical MRI can be used to examine the structural integrity of different brain regions. For example, it can detect reduced cerebral volume with aging or increases in myelination during childhood. Recently developed *diffusion tensor MRI* (DTMRI) provides information about the structural integrity of nerve fibers as well as patterns of anatomical connectivity. This method works by detecting differences in the degree to which water diffuses along each of the three axes of nerve fibers. The axis along which water diffusion is greatest indicates the main directional orientation of white matter tracts, while the degree of diffusion can provide information on the structural integrity of those tracts. Because white matter tracts connect distant brain regions, this method can be utilized to detect disorders that arise from a partial or complete disconnection between brain regions.

Functional MRI (fMRI) detects local changes in other physiological functions, such as cerebral blood flow and blood oxygenation. The most commonly used fMRI method, known as BOLD (Blood Oxygen Level Dependent), takes advantage of the fact that oxygenated blood is more magnetic than deoxygenated blood. Neuronal activity causes a local increase in oxygen-rich blood. Because the local tissue cannot extract all the oxygen supplied, the relative proportion of oxygenated blood to deoxygenated blood increases in that region. This change results in an increased signal from which a measure of brain activation can be derived.

Because we are detecting a change in the signal, fMRI always requires that two conditions be compared: the condition of interest and a baseline condition. The selection of the baseline is critical for interpretation of the results. For example, to determine those regions specifically involved in processing the emotional information contained in faces, brain activation while viewing emotional faces needs to be compared to a baseline of brain activation while viewing nonemotional faces. On the other hand, if the desire is to determine all the brain regions involved in processing emotional faces, then brain activation while viewing emotional faces needs to be compared to a baseline of brain activation while viewing a simple visual stimulus, such as a series of crosses.

The creation and use of fMRI techniques, although burgeoning, are still in the developmental stage. Currently, other fMRI methods such as arterial spin-labeling techniques are being developed and advanced in the hope that they will provide a powerful method of measuring cerebral blood flow. Absolute measures of cerebral blood flow are advantageous because they allow for direct comparisons across individuals, such as younger individuals and older individuals.

fMRI is very useful for a number of reasons. First, it is widely available and can be performed on clinical MRI machines that have been appropriately upgraded to enable these methods. Second, it is a noninvasive technique and does not involve high-energy ionizing radiation. Third, multiple scans can be run on a single individual, allowing clinicians and scientists to examine changes in the brain over time, such as those that occur as a result of practice or treatment regimens. Fourth, it provides superior temporal and spatial resolution relative to other brain imaging methods, such as positron emission tomography (PET). fMRI allows brain activity to be detected in seconds and with an anatomical resolution of 3 to 5 millimeters.

Because MRI can be tuned to specific atoms, it can be utilized to examine the concentration of other biologically-active substances via a method known as *magnetic resonance spectroscopy.* This method is limited in that it provides only very gross information on the location of such substances within the brain (e.g., within the frontal lobe), and cannot be used unless the concentration of the substance is quite high. For example, it remains to be seen whether this method will be able to detect neurotransmitters. One substance examined using this technique is *N*-acetylaspartate (NAA), an amino acid found in high concentration within the nervous system. Reduced NAA is observed when neuronal functioning is less than optimal, such as occurs when pathological processes are acting upon neurons or when the energy metabolism of the brain is compromised. For example, lower levels of NAA in the dorsolateral prefrontal cortex of schizophrenics are associated with poorer cognitive abilities on a test of executive function. The importance of magnetic resonance spectroscopy may increase in the future as high-field MRI systems become more commonplace, and as greater field strength enhances the ability to detect substances at lower concentrations.

Marie T. Banich
University of Colorado

MAINSTREAMING

Mainstreaming dates back to the very beginnings of the field of special education. As the term implies, mainstreaming means educating students with disabilities alongside "typical" students in a general education classroom for at least some portion of a school day. Mainstreaming came into widespread use in the late 1960s as professionals and parents called into question the segregation of students with disabilities in U.S. public schools. Professionals argued that special classes for students, particularly those with mental retardation, could not be justified. The purpose of mainstreaming was to ensure that students with disabilities received individualized planning and support from both general and special education teachers. However, this did not always happen in actual practice. In fact, the term *mainstreaming* fell out of favor when it became associated with placing students with disabilities in general education classes without the necessary support. It was viewed by parents as a means to save money and limit the number of students who could receive specialized services. Such practices gave rise to the term *maindumping.* Although the term *mainstreaming* remains in limited use today as one way to describe educating students with disabilities in general education settings, other descriptors have come into popular use, including *integration, least restrictive environment,* and *inclusive education.*

With the passage of the federal Education of All Handicapped Children Act of 1975 (now the Individuals with Disabilities Education Act [IDEA]), *least restrictive environment* (LRE) became a commonly used term in the United States. LRE describes a process by which students with disabilities are placed in educational settings consistent with their individual educational needs. As defined in IDEA, the intent of LRE is to educate students with disabilities with their typical peers to the maximum extent appropriate. A student is removed from the general education setting only when the nature and severity of the disability are such that education in general education classes with supplementary aids or services cannot be satisfactorily achieved.

Although the concept of LRE suggests a strong preference for students with disabilities to be educated alongside their typical peers, it also states that this should occur only when appropriate. As such, LRE and mainstreaming are not synonymous. A student's LRE may be any one of a "continuum of placements," ranging from the general education classroom to separate educational environments exclusively for students with disabilities. Public schools are required to provide such a continuum for students who cannot be satisfactorily educated in general education classes. Whenever possible, however, students should be educated in or close to the school they would attend if not disabled.

As with mainstreaming, the concept of LRE has been criticized in recent years. The concern is that, despite LRE's strong preference for students to be educated with their typical peers, it also has legitimized and supported the need for more restrictive, segregated settings. Additionally, LRE has created the perception that students with disabilities must go to services, rather than having services come to them. In other words, as students move further from the general education classroom, the resources available to meet their needs increase accordingly.

Whereas LRE is the term most often associated with special education in the United States, *integration* is the term that is most often used to describe programs and services in several other countries. For example, Italy's laws mandate the integration of students with disabilities into general education classes. Australia may be described as moving toward full integration of these students, while to a lesser extent France, England, and Germany all have major initiatives promoting the integration of students with disabilities into general education settings.

In the United States, the term integration is most closely associated with social policy to end separate education for ethnic minority children, specifically students of color. In the landmark *Brown v. Board of Education* in 1954, the U.S. Supreme Court ruled that education must be made available to everyone on an equal basis. Separate education for African-American students was ruled inherently unequal to that of white students. The increasing use of the term *integration* by many professionals and parents to describe the value of educating students with disabilities alongside their typical peers coincided with the U.S. civil rights movement of the 1980s for people with disabilities, a movement that culminated in the passage of the Americans with Disabilities Act (ADA) in 1990. In fact, ADA moved away from the concept of the least restrictive environment as defined in IDEA, mandating that people with disabilities be placed in integrated settings appropriate to their individual needs.

In today's schools, the most widely used term consistent with the original intent of mainstreaming is *inclusive education*. At its most fundamental level, inclusive education promotes the value of students with disabilities attending the same school they would attend were they not disabled. This approach promotes acceptance and belonging, focusing on services and support coming to students within the setting of the general education school and classroom, rather than students with disabilities going to services in a segregated environment. In inclusive classrooms, the intent is for all students to be actively involved, socially accepted, and motivated to learn to the best of their ability.

To achieve this goal, some professionals have argued for specific changes in the educational system. These include providing inclusive services and support in "neighborhood" schools. The proportion of students needing special education should be relatively uniform for all schools within a particular area or district, and should reflect the proportion of people with disabilities in society at large. In such neighborhood schools, students with disabilities could receive the support they need to succeed without being segregated into special classes within the school.

Inclusive education may be defined by the level of participation and support available to the student in the educational setting. Two terms describe these levels: *full inclusion* and *partial inclusion*. Full inclusion is an approach whereby students with disabilities receive all instruction in a general education classroom setting; support services come to the student. With partial inclusion, students with disabilities receive most of their instruction in general education settings but are "pulled out" to another instructional setting when appropriate to their individual needs.

The success of both full and partial inclusion programs depends on the availability of both formal and natural supports in the general education classroom. Formal supports are those provided by, and funded through, the public school system. These include qualified teachers, paraprofessionals, appropriate curriculum materials, and assistive technology aids. Natural supports in an educational setting most often consist of the student's family and classmates. Natural supports emphasize the relationship among children as friends and learning partners.

Michael L. Hardman
University of Utah

MAJOR DEPRESSIVE DISORDER: RECOVERY AND RECURRENCE

Major Depressive Disorder

Major Depressive Disorder (MDD) is characterized by depressed mood or a lack of interest or pleasure in once-enjoyable activities, and associated symptoms (e.g., sleep disturbance, appetite/weight disturbance, difficulty concentrating, worthlessness or exaggerated guilt). To receive a diagnosis of MDD, at least five symptoms must be present most of the day, nearly every day, for at least 2 weeks (American Psychiatric Association [ApA], 1994).

The lifetime and 12-month prevalence of MDD is higher than that of any other major psychiatric disorder (Kessler et al., 1994), and evidence suggests that the prevalence of MDD has been increasing in recent birth cohorts (Lewinsohn, Rohde, Seeley, & Fischer, 1993) while the age at first onset has been decreasing (Klerman & Weissman, 1989). Indeed, approximately 25% of entering college students have previously experienced an episode of MDD (Lewinsohn, Clarke, Seeley, & Rohde, 1994). Although episodes of MDD appear to be self-limiting, the disorder is typically episodic, with high rates of relapse/recurrence.

Remission and Recovery

Over the years, researchers have used various definitions of "remission" and "recovery" from MDD. Guidelines published in recent years (Frank et al., 1991) have increased consistency across studies. There is now some agreement that remission is a period during which full criteria for MDD are no longer met but significant symptoms remain (partial remission), or during which the individual experiences no more than minimal (e.g., two or fewer) symptoms for up to 6 months (full remission). Full recovery is defined as 6 months or longer with no more than two symptoms.

An episode of major depression appears to be self-limiting, in that most cases remit in approximately 6 to 8 months, even if untreated. Recovery rates appear to be similar across children and adult samples. For example, Kessler and Walters (1998) found that, in a community sample of adolescents and young adults, the average length of the longest episode an individual had suffered was 32.5 weeks. Similarly, Kovacs and colleagues (1984a) reported a mean length of 32 weeks for a sample of depressed children. Within 1 year of onset of a major depressive episode, 78% of adults will have recovered (Keller, Lavori, Rice, Coryell, & Hirschfeld, 1986).

Despite the high rate of spontaneous remission of MDD and an average length of six to eight months per episode, a number of individuals suffer significantly longer episodes of depression. While 78% of depressed adults remit within 1 year of onset of MDD, 22% experience a more chronic course. The longer an individual suffers from an episode of MDD, the lower the probability of recovery from that episode. Thus, for individuals who have not recovered within one to two years of onset, the prognosis is relatively poor. The long-term prognosis for individuals who recover more quickly from MDD is also discouraging, in that a large proportion will suffer a relapse or recurrence of the disorder.

Relapse and Recurrence

Relapse is a return of symptoms such that the individual once again meets full criteria for MDD during the period of remission but before recovery. A recurrence, in contrast, is a new episode of MDD with onset occurring after full recovery from the previous episode (Frank et al., 1991). Although these terms have been defined fairly consistently in recent research, much of the earlier research did not differentiate between relapse and recurrence; therefore, these terms will be used interchangeably here.

A recent review of the literature revealed that more than 50% of adults who recover from an episode of MDD again meet criteria for MDD within 3 years of the index episode (Brosse, Craighead, & Craighead, 2002). More specifically, the recurrence rate in adult outpatient samples was found to be 19% to 32% at 1-year follow-up, 36% to 38% after 18 months, 21% to 44% after 2 years, and 43% at 30-months follow-up. In adult samples comprised of both outpatients and inpatients, 24% to 36% experienced a recurrence within 6 months of recovery, increasing to 37% to 40% after 10 to 12 months, 52% by 26 months, 57% by 3 years, 71% by 5 years, and 85% by 15-year follow-up. The highest recurrence rates were reported for inpatient samples. Between 25% and 43% recurred within 6 months of recovery, a rate not achieved in outpatient samples until 18 months after recovery; 51% suffered a recurrence within 9 months, 27% to 55% within 1 year (with only one study reporting a rate lower than 41%), and 54% to 68% within 2 years. Similar rates of relapse and recurrence have been found in children and adolescents with MDD (e.g., Kovacs et al., 1984b).

It appears that each new MDD episode increases the risk of suffering yet another episode (ApA, 1994); additionally, there is some evidence of increasing severity with each new MDD episode, as well as decreased well time between episodes. Preliminary evidence suggests that acute treatment with psychotherapy (e.g., cognitive behavior therapy, interpersonal psychotherapy) provides greater prophylactics against relapse than does pharmacotherapy, and that "maintenance" or "continuation" psychotherapy further protects patients against relapse (e.g., Jarrett et al., 2001). Given the high cost of depression, and the increasing severity of the disorder with each new episode, additional research regarding the prevention of relapse and recurrence of MDD is clearly warranted.

REFERENCES

American Psychiatric Association. (1994). *Diagnostic and statistical manual of mental disorders* (4th ed.). Washington, DC: Author.

Brosse, A. L., Craighead, L. W., & Craighead, W. E. (2002). Relapse and recurrence of Major Depressive Disorder: A decade later. Manuscript submitted for publication.

Frank, E., Prien, R. F., Jarrett, R. B., Keller, M. B., Kupfer, D. J., Lavori, P. W., Rush, A. J., & Weissman, M. M. (1991). Conceptualization and rationale for consensus definitions of terms in Major Depressive Disorder. *Archives of General Psychiatry, 48,* 851–855.

Jarrett, R. B., Kraft, D., Doyle, J., Foster, B. M., Eaves, G., & Silver, P. C. (2001). Preventing recurrent depression using cognitive therapy with and without a continuation phase. *Archives of General Psychiatry, 58,* 381–388.

Keller, M. B., Lavori, P. W., Rice, J., Coryell, W., & Hirschfeld, R. M. A. (1986). The persistent risk of chronicity in recurrent episodes of nonbipolar Major Depressive Disorder: A prospective follow-up. *American Journal of Psychiatry, 143,* 24–28.

Kessler, R. C., McGonagle, K. A., Zhao, S., Nelson, C. B., Hughes, M., Eshleman, S., Wittchen, H., & Kendler, K. S. (1994). Lifetime and 12-month prevalence of *DSM-III-R* psychiatric disorders in the United States. *Archives of General Psychiatry, 51,* 8–19.

Kessler, R. C., & Walters, E. E. (1998). Epidemiology of *DSM-III-R* major depression and minor depression among adolescents and young adults in the national comorbidity survey. *Depression and Anxiety, 7,* 3–14.

Klerman, G. L., & Weissman, M. M. (1989). Increasing rates of depression. *Journal of the American Medical Association, 261,* 2229–2235.

Kovacs, M., Feinberg, T. L., Crouse-Novak, M., Paulauskas, S. L., & Finkelstein, R. (1984a). Depressive disorders in childhood I: A longitudinal prospective study of characteristics and recovery. *Archives of General Psychiatry, 41,* 229–237.

Kovacs, M., Feinberg, T. L., Crouse-Novak, M., Paulauskas, S. L., Pollack, M., & Finkelstein, R. (1984b). Depressive disorders in childhood II: A longitudinal study of the risk for a subsequent major depression. *Archives of General Psychiatry, 41,* 643–649.

Lewinsohn, P. M., Clarke, G. N., Seeley, J. R., & Rohde, P. (1994). Major depression in community adolescents: Age at onset, episode duration, and time to recurrence. *Journal of the American Academy of Child and Adolescent Psychiatry, 33,* 809–818.

Lewinsohn, P. M., Rohde, P., Seeley, J. R., & Fischer, S. A. (1993). Age-cohort changes in the lifetime occurrence of depression and other mental disorders. *Journal of Abnormal Psychology, 102,* 110–120.

Alisha L. Brosse
Erin S. Sheets
University of Colorado at Boulder

MALE SEXUAL DYSFUNCTION

Male Erectile Disorder

Since the advent of pharmacological treatment for male erectile disorder and the ensuing flood of print and television ads, this disorder has become the definitive example of sexual disorders that affect men. Male Erectile Disorder (ED) is defined by an inability to attain or maintain an erection until completion of sexual activity, and is associated with marked distress or interpersonal difficulty (American Psychiatric Association [ApA], 2000). Epidemiological studies have not typically included assessment of sexual disorders, but sex researchers who have studied the prevalence of ED in community samples have found rates ranging from 3% to 9% of men of all ages (Spector & Carey, 1990).

Studies of prevalence in men from ages 40 to 70 have found that approximately 52% of males in this age range experience mild, moderate, or severe erectile difficulties (Feldman, Goldstein, Hatzichristou, Krane, & McKinlay, 1994). Previous estimates of ED complaints in clinical samples have indicated that from 36% to 48% of men who present for treatment in sex clinics have a primary diagnosis of male erectile disorder (Ackerman & Carey, 1995). Current estimates of clinical prevalence are missing, and may be important in describing the change in treatment for erectile dysfunction from sex therapy to pharmacology. Physiologically-based risk factors for ED include older age, alcohol use, nicotine use, and a sedentary lifestyle (Ackerman & Carey, 1995; Tengs & Osgood, 2001). Psychological risk factors include mental disorders and acute emotional states, particularly anxiety and depression (Barlow, 1986; Masters & Johnson, 1970; Wincze & Carey, 1991).

Assessment of ED and its etiological source has long been considered a difficult undertaking for clinicians. Historically, erectile dysfunction was considered a purely psychological disorder that should be treated with traditional behavioral sex therapy techniques (Ackerman & Carey, 1995). More recently, clinical attention has been focused on issues of differential diagnosis and determining the relative importance of psychogenic and organic factors in the etiology and persistence of erection difficulties. Physiological problems such as neurological diseases, hormonal abnormalities, and vascular problems are involved in a considerable percentage of ED cases, with or without corresponding psychological origins (Tanagho, Lue, & McClure, 1988). Many medications have also been implicated in causing erectile difficulty, including the SSRI's (Rosen, Lane, & Menza, 1999).

Psychogenic contributions to ED include the emotional states mentioned earlier as well as dysfunctional cognitions about sexual performance (Cranston-Cuebas & Barlow, 1990; Masters & Johnson, 1970; Weisberg, Brown, Wincze, & Barlow, 2001) and dyadic relationship problems (Leiblum & Rosen, 1988). In addition, a lack of adequate penile stimulation during foreplay, typically a necessary component of erectile attainment in aging males, has been indicated in some mild impairments of functioning (Meggers & LoPiccolo, 2002). Determining the etiological source of ED for each individual requires a medical examination as well as an assessment of psychological factors that play a role in both cause and persistence of problems. As noted by LoPiccolo (1994), the presence of organic impairment does not always negate the need for behavioral treatment. In many cases, men with mild organic impairment are made more vulnerable to erectile failure by psychological, behavioral, and sexual technique factors.

Several medical treatment strategies for ED have been utilized in the past, including penile implants, vacuum devices, and penile injections. The most recent advance in the medical treatment of ED, however, is the medication sildenafil, better known by its trade name, Viagra. Viagra is an effective treatment, showing positive results in 70 to 80 percent of cases treated (Sadovsky et al., 2001). The drug works by reducing venous outflow once blood has been pumped into the cavernous bodies, *not* by increasing arterial inflow. As a result, men who use Viagra still need adequate sexual and emotional stimulation to achieve an erection. Some of the 20 to 30 percent of cases in which Viagra fails are not actually pharmacologic failures, but failures to provide adequate physical or emotional stimulation. Consequently, the use of Viagra is contraindicated in instances where couple systemic issues are the only etiological factors contributing to erectile difficulties. In addition, Viagra is also contraindicated in instances where low desire is the cause of erectile failure, as the drug has not been shown to increase levels of desire.

The predominant themes in the psychological treatment of erectile dysfunction are the reduction of performance anxiety and the increase of sexual stimulation, and this treatment approach is still based largely on the work of Masters and Johnson (1970). One comprehensive study of treatment outcome research for male sexual dysfunctions reported that there is a paucity of well-designed studies to determine the effectiveness of behavioral sex therapy for male erectile disorder (O'Donohue, Swingen, Dopke, & Regev, 1999). However, behavioral sex therapy for ED is included on the list of empirically supported treatments compiled by ApA's Task Force on Promotion and Dissemination of Psychological Procedures (1995).

Premature Ejaculation

While ED is typically a dysfunction of older males, Premature Ejaculation (PE) most frequently occurs in younger men. PE is the persistent or recurrent ejaculation during sexual activity that is associated with minimal stimulation and individual or couple dissatisfaction with duration (ApA, 2000). At the present time, there are no objective criteria for determining the duration of sexual activity that constitutes premature ejaculation. Perhaps it is easier to describe what is not premature ejaculation: Both partners agree that the quality of their sexual activities is not negatively impacted by efforts to postpone ejaculation (LoPiccolo, 1994). Prevalence estimates for PE derived from community samples indicate a rate of disorder between 36 and 38% (Spector & Carey, 1990).

Definitive data on the etiology of premature ejaculation

does not currently exist. Sociobiologists have theorized that it offers an evolutionary advantage and has been built into the human organism (Hong, 1984). However, this theory does not effectively deal with the large variability in duration of intercourse that has been observed both across and within species. Another theory proposed by Kaplan (1974) postulates that men with premature ejaculation are not able to accurately perceive their own level of sexual arousal and thus do not engage in any self-control procedures to avoid rapid ejaculation. One laboratory analogue indicates, however, that men with premature ejaculation were better able to perceive their own levels of sexual arousal when compared to controls (Spiess, Geer, & O'Donohue, 1984).

Rowland, Cooper, and Slob (1996) found that men who experience PE can be differentiated from functional men and men with ED by both a heightened response to vibrotactile penile stimulation and an increase in negative emotion, such as shame and embarrassment, during sexually arousing activities. This evidence supports a psychophysiological model of PE in which a vulnerability of the penile reflex and intensified negative cognitions and affect combine to create problems with ejaculation latency (Strassberg, Kelly, Carroll, & Kircher, 1987). Finally, it has been proposed that premature ejaculation is related to low frequency of sexual activity (Kinsey, Pomeroy, & Martin, 1948). While some research has indicated that sensory thresholds in the penis are lowered by infrequent sexual activity and that premature ejaculation patients do have a low rate of sexual activity (e.g., Spiess et al., 1984), it is possible that premature ejaculation causes low rates of sex, rather than causality being in the opposite direction, as this disorder makes sex an unpleasant failure experience.

The standard treatment for PE involves the pause procedure developed by Semans (1956) and modified into the pause and squeeze technique by Masters and Johnson (1970). Although there has not been a controlled experimental study of the relative effectiveness of the pause procedure versus the pause and squeeze technique, both appear to be effective. Success rates of 90% to 98% "cure" have been reported, and this success has been demonstrated in group and individual treatment as well as in self-help programs (Kilmann & Auerbach, 1979).

More recently, psychopharmacological treatment of PE has been the subject of research. According to Rosen et al. (1999), several uncontrolled studies of SSRI treatment of PE have indicated that pharmacological treatment may be efficacious. Waldinger, Hengeveld, and Zwinderman (1994) found that low doses of clomipramine significantly improved ejaculatory latency and improved sexual satisfaction in men with PE. Similar results have been found for paroxetine, fluoxetine, and setraline (Rosen et al., 1999). While SSRI treatment for PE seems provocative, it is important to remember that serotonergic drugs have well-known deleterious effects on sexual arousal and physicians and clinicians should question whether reducing levels of sexual arousal is a desirable method for lengthening ejaculatory latencies. SSRI treatment of PE is temporary, with latency effects disappearing after treatment is discontinued (Waldinger et al., 1994).

Hypoactive Sexual Desire Disorder (HSDD)

HSDD is a disorder characterized by absent or low desire for sexual activity that is associated with interpersonal difficulty or distress (ApA, 2000). A distinction is made between receptive and proceptive sexual behaviors, with a lack of proceptive behavior most indicative of true low sexual desire (Pridal & LoPiccolo, 2000). HSDD affects both men and women, and it is the most common primary diagnosis in cases of sexual dysfunction. Segraves and Segraves (1991) conducted a large pharmaceutical study for sexual disorders and found that 19% of clients with a primary diagnosis of HSDD were male. Prevalence estimates for community samples indicate a rate of 15% for males (Rosen & Leiblum, 1995).

The three major etiological factors for low sexual desire that have been proposed are hormonal problems, affective-cognitive models, and relationship dynamic theories. Although evidence of hormonal influence on sexual desire in females is inconsistent, research continually shows a relationship between androgens and sexual desire in males (Beck, 1995). Androgens, particularly testosterone, seem to be essential for normal levels of sexual desire in males (Bancroft, 1988). However, testosterone deficiency does not account for all cases of HSDD in males (Schover & LoPiccolo, 1982).

Theories of excessive negative affect may account for some of these non-physiological cases. Kaplan's (1979) theory of intrapsychic anxiety and anger as determinants of low desire has also received empirical support. Studies indicate that increased anger is associated with diminished desire and penile tumescence in men, while anxiety is related to decreased subjective arousal but is not related to tumescence (Beck & Bozman, 1995; Bozman & Beck, 1991).

Relationship dynamic explanations for low drive in men have stressed the adaptive value of low desire for the maintenance of relationship equilibrium (LoPiccolo & Friedman, 1988; Verhulst & Heimen, 1988). Low desire may serve an effective function within the habitual dynamics of the marital relationship. For example, low drive is cited as being a passive-aggressive way for a man to maintain a position of some power and control or emotional distance in a relationship. Finally, it is necessary to mention briefly the adverse effects of many medications on sexual desire, including antihypertensives and psychotropic medications—particularly SSRIs (Rosen et al., 1999).

Low sexual desire has been seen with increasing frequency in clinical practice. In fact, attenuated desire is now the most common complaint among patients seeking therapy (LoPiccolo & Friedman, 1988). However, treatment for low sexual desire can be a complex issue, as people with low sexual desire often have even lower levels of desire for therapeutic intervention. Perhaps because of this, quality treatment outcome measures for low drive are relatively scarce (see O'Donohue et al., 1999). However, some studies have demonstrated good treatment results using a complex, cognitive-behavioral treatment program (LoPiccolo & Friedman, 1988) with a focus on low desire symptomatology (Schover & LoPiccolo, 1982). This focus on specific symptoms is seen as imperative to the success of treatment of low desire, as standard sex therapy often fails to raise desire (Kaplan, 1979).

Male Orgasmic Disorder

Male Orgasmic Disorder, previously referred to as Inhibited Ejaculation, has received very little attention in the therapeutic literature. As initially reported by Masters and Johnson (1970), this remains a relatively rare dysfunction, and etiology remains unclear. Clinical case studies suggest a variety of psychological factors as causes, but there is virtually no empirical support for these theories (Dow, 1981; Schull & Sprenkle, 1980). Male Orgasmic Disorder can, however, result from a number of physiological conditions, such as multiple sclerosis and damage to the hypothalamus. Finally, the inability to reach orgasm may be a side effect of several medications, including anti-hypertensives; sedatives; and anti-anxiety, anti-depressive, and antipsychotic agents (Ban & Freyhan, 1980).

Perhaps due to the ambiguity surrounding the etiology of Male Orgasmic Disorder, relatively little has appeared in the literature regarding treatment. The standard treatment strategies—eliminating performance anxiety and ensuring adequate stimulation—remain the preferred treatment approaches (LoPiccolo, 1994). Additional elements taken from the treatment program for female anorgasmia, including the use of vibrators, certain behavioral maneuvers, and patient role-play of an exaggerated orgasm, also seem to have some success in treating males (LoPiccolo, 1977). For cases caused by organic impairment, some success has been reported with the use of drugs, such as ephedrine sulfate, that work to activate the sympathetic nervous system (Murphy & Lipshultz, 1988). In addition, behavioral modification that leads to increased stimulation of the scrotal, perineal, and anal areas also tends to trigger orgasm. The use of an anal insertion probe is the most effective technique for inducing orgasm and, in fact, is the only effective treatment for severely neurologically impaired patients (Murphy & Lipshultz, 1988).

REFERENCES

Ackerman, M. D., & Carey, M. P. (1995). Psychology's role in the assessment of erectile dysfunction: Historical precedents, current knowledge, and methods. *Journal of Consulting and Clinical Psychology, 63*(6), 862–876.

American Psychiatric Association. (2000). *Diagnostic and statistical manual of mental disorders* (4th ed., rev.). Washington, DC: Author.

Ban, T. A., & Freyhan, F. A. (1980). *Drug treatment of sexual dysfunction.* New York: Karger.

Bancroft, J. (1988). Sexual desire and the brain. *Sexual and Marital Therapy, 12,* 93–107.

Barlow, D. H. (1986). Causes of sexual dysfunction: The role of anxiety and cognitive interference. *Journal of Consulting and Clinical Psychology, 54,* 140–148.

Beck, J. G. (1995). Hypoactive Sexual Desire Disorder: An overview. *Journal of Consulting and Clinical Psychology, 63*(6), 919–927.

Beck, J. G., & Bozman, A. (1995). Gender differences in sexual desire: The effects of anger and anxiety. *Archives of Sexual Behavior, 24*(6), 595–612.

Bozman, A., & Beck, J. G. (1991). Covariation of sexual desire and sexual arousal: The effects of anger and anxiety. *Archives of Sexual Behavior, 20,* 47–60.

Cranston-Cuebas, M. A., & Barlow, D. H., (1990). Cognitive and affective contributions to sexual functioning. In J. Bancroft, C. M. Davis, & D. Weinstein (Eds.), *Annual review of sex research: Vol. 1. An integrative and interdisciplinary review.* Lake Mills, IA: Stoyles Graphic Services.

Dow, S. (1981). Retarded ejaculation. *Journal of Sex and Marital Therapy, 2,* 229–237.

Feldman, H. A., Goldstein, I., Hatzichristou, D. G., Krane, R. J., & McKinlay, J. B. (1994). Impotence and its medical and psychosocial correlates: Results of the Massachusetts Male Aging Study. *Journal of Urology, 151,* 54–61.

Hong, L. K. (1984). Survival of the fastest. *Journal of Sex Research, 20,* 109–122.

Kaplan, H. (1974). *The new sex therapy.* New York: Bruner/Mazel.

Kaplan, H. (1979). *Disorders of sexual desire.* New York: Bruner/Mazel.

Kilmann, P. R., & Auerbach, R. (1979). Treatments of premature ejaculations and psychogenic impotence: A critical view of the literature. *Archives of Sexual Behavior, 8*(1), 81–100.

Kinsey, A. C., Pomeroy, W. B., & Martin, C. E. (1948). *Sexual behavior in the human male.* Philadelphia: Saunders.

Leiblum, S. R., & Rosen, R. C. (Eds.). (1988). *Sexual Desire Disorders.* New York: Guilford Press.

LoPiccolo, J. (1977). Direct treatment of sexual dysfunction in the couple. In J. Money & H. Musaph (Eds.), *Handbook of sexology* (pp. 1227–1244). New York: Elsevier/North Holland.

LoPiccolo, J. (1994). The evolution of sex therapy. *Sexual & Marital Therapy, 9*(1), 5–7.

LoPiccolo, J., & Friedman, J. (1988). Broad-spectrum treatment of low sexual desire: Integration of cognitive, behavioral, and systemic therapy. In S. R. Leiblum & R. C. Rosen (Eds.), *Sexual Desire Disorders.* New York: Guilford Press.

Masters, W. H., & Johnson, V. E. (1970). *Human sexual inadequacy.* Boston: Little, Brown.

Meggers, H., & LoPiccolo, J. (2002). Sex therapy. In M. Hersen & W. Sledge (Eds.), *Encyclopedia of Psychotherapy.* New York: Academic Press.

Murphy, J., & Lipshultz, L. (1988). Infertility in the paraplegic male. In E. Tanagho, T. Lue, & R. McClure (Eds.), *Contemporary management of impotence and infertility.* Baltimore: Williams & Wilkins.

O'Donohue, W., Swingen, D., Dopke, C., & Regev, L. (1999). Psychotherapy for male sexual dysfunction: A review. *Clinical Psychology Review, 19,* 591–630.

Pridal, C. G., & LoPiccolo, J. (2000). Multielement treatment of desire disorders: Integration of cognitive, behavioral, and systemic therapy. In S. R. Leiblum & R. C. Rosen (Eds.), *Principles and practice of sex therapy* (3rd ed.). New York: Guilford Press.

Rosen, R. C., Lane, R. M., & Menza, M. (1999). Effects of SSRIs on sexual functions: A critical review. *Journal of Clinical Psychopharmacology, 19*(1), 67–85.

Rosen, R. C., & Leiblum, S. R. (1995). Hypoactive sexual desire. *Psychiatric Clinics of North America, 18,* 107–121.

Rowland, D. L., Cooper, S. E., & Slob, A. K. (1996). Genital and psychoaffective response to erotic stimulation in sexually functional and dysfunctional men. *Journal of Abnormal Psychology, 105*(2), 194–203.

Sadovsky, R., Miller, T., Moskowitz, M., & Hackett, G. (2001). Three-year update of sildenafil citrate (Viagra®) efficacy and safety. *International Journal of Clinical Practice, 55,* 115–128.

Schover, L., & LoPiccolo, J. (1982). Treatment effectiveness for dysfunctions of sexual desire. *Journal of Sex and Marital Therapy, 8,* 179–197.

Schull, W., & Sprenkle, T. (1980). Retarded ejaculation. *Journal of Sex and Marital Therapy, 6,* 234–246.

Segraves, K., & Segraves, R. T. (1991). Hypoactive Sexual Desire Disorder: Prevalence and comorbidity in 906 subjects. *Journal of Sex and Marital Therapy, 17,* 55–58.

Semans, J. H. (1956). Premature ejaculation: A new approach. *Southern Medical Journal, 49,* 353–357.

Spector, I. P., & Carey, M. P. (1990). Incidence and prevalence of the sexual dysfunctions: A critical review of the empirical literature. *Archives of Sexual Behavior, 19*(4), 389–408.

Speiss, W. F., Geer, J. H., & O'Donohue, W. T. (1984). Premature ejaculation: Investigation of factors in ejaculatory latency. *Journal of Abnormal Psychology, 93,* 242–245.

Strassberg, D. S., Kelly, M. P., Carroll, C., & Kircher, J. C. (1987). The psychophysiological nature of premature ejaculation. *Archives of Sexual Behavior, 16*(4), 327–336.

Tanagho, T., Lue, F., & McClure, R. (Eds.). (1988). *Contemporary management of impotence and infertility.* Baltimore: Williams & Wilkins.

Task Force on Promotion and Dissemination of Psychological Procedures. (1995). Training in and dissemination of empirically-validated psychological treatments: Report and recommendations. *The Clinical Psychologist, 48,* 3–23.

Tengs, T., & Osgood, N. D. (2001). The link between smoking and impotence: Two decades of evidence. *Preventive Medicine: An International Journal Devoted to Practice and Theory, 32*(6), 447–452.

Verhulst, J., & Heimen, J. (1988). A systems perspective on sexual desire. In S. Leiblum & R. Rosen (Eds.), *Sexual desire disorders.* New York: Guilford Press.

Waldinger, M. D., Hengeveld, M. W., & Zwinderman, A. H. (1994). Paroxetine treatment of premature ejaculation: A double-blind, randomized, placebo-control study. *American Journal of Psychiatry, 151*(9), 1377–1379.

Weisberg, R. B., Brown, T. A., Wincze, J. P., & Barlow, D. H. (2001). Causal attributions and male sexual arousal: The impact of attributions for a bogus erectile difficulty on sexual arousal, cognitions, and affect. *Journal of Abnormal Psychology, 110*(2), 324–334.

Wincze, J. P., & Carey, M. P. (1991). *Sexual dysfunction: Guide for assessment and treatment.* New York: Guilford Press.

Heather J. Meggers
Joseph LoPiccolo
University of Missouri

See also: **Antidepressant Medications**

MANAGED MENTAL HEALTH CARE

Managed care is any health care delivery method in which an entity other than the health care provider actively manages both financial and medical aspects of health care. It includes a wide variety of techniques, products, and services that integrate the financing and the delivery of health care. Based on the premise that providers alter practice in response to financial incentives, managed care was created to control the costs, use, and quality of health care by increasing provider accountability to payers, promoting competition, and using practice standards. Managed mental health care (behavioral services) can co-exist with or be delivered within general managed care health systems. Alternatively, they can be separated or "carved out" from general health care plans and contracted to specialized providers who are responsible for utilization control, provider selection, finances, and quality assurance.

Managed care began as prepaid health care, the provision of a set package of services for a pre-established fee. The originators intended to deliver affordable, accessible care to poor and middle-class farmers and laborers who wanted to eliminate unexpected medical bills. Today's critics of managed care say it has failed in this mission. They argue that consolidation of behavioral health care has concentrated control in the hands of a few powerful fiscal organizations. These organizations, say critics, place profit ahead of patient welfare, deny or delay access to necessary treatments and providers, award bonuses for reducing referrals to specialists, and arbitrarily discharge providers who use too many resources. For-profit, industrialized health care has not controlled inflationary medical costs, and over 42 million Americans are without health insurance.

Forms of Managed Health Care

Managed health care evolved swiftly from the 1980s to the present. Forms of managed care and managed mental health care are defined according to: (1) structural characteristics, (2) relationship of provider and patients to systems, and (3) financial arrangements. Methods to reduce costs include reviewing the medical necessity of services, intensive management of high cost cases, regulation of inpatient admissions and length of stay, incentives for selecting less costly forms of care, beneficiary cost sharing, and selective contracting with health care providers. Hybrids blend the characteristics of more than one model as a function of diverse sets of local and regional requirements, state regulations, and specific statutes. The major types of managed health care are as follows:

1. *Utilization review and management* provides evaluation of medical necessity and appropriateness of mental health services prospectively, concurrently, or restrospectively.
2. The *Staff Model Health Maintenance Organization (HMO)* offers services to a defined population for a fixed price (capitation). Providers are salaried employees or contractors who work in specific locations.
3. In the *Independent Practice Association (IPA),* individual providers contract with an HMO to provide care in their own offices. Reimbursement is a prearranged fee-for-service, capitated, or percentage of the subscriber's premium. Providers contribute to risk pools, and hold-backs are incentives to control utilization.
4. *Group model HMOs* contract with groups of providers to devote a specified percentage of practice time to subscribers on a salaried or capitated basis, usually in a central location. Providers share in the group's profit or loss.
5. *Preferred Provider Organization (PPO)* caregivers must offer cost-effective care to a predetermined subscriber group for either discounted rates or a schedule of maximum payments in return for a certain volume of referrals. Consumers can use nonparticipating providers, but receive discounts for using PPO providers. An Exclusive PPO pays only for services from participating providers.
6. *Independent broker models* use a liaison between providers who want to sell and buyers (small business, the self-insured, guilds, etc.) who group together in order to purchase discounted services.
7. The *network model* combines features of the IPA, group and staff models, and contracts with HMOs to provide services. Providers do not provide care exclusively to HMO members and will give care to nonmembers.
8. A *point-of-service* or *open-ended plan* reduces fees or increases benefits to encourage the use of network providers.
9. In an *employee assistance program (EAP),* mental health services are provided to the employee in the workplace or off-site.
10. An *integrated delivery system (IDS)* has a variety of providers, such as a management service, medical foundation, group provider practice, and physician-hospital that work together to provide coordinated, comprehensive care for patient needs, including acute inpatient, outpatient, and prevention services.

REFERENCES

Austad, Carol S. (1996). *Is long-term psychotherapy unethical?* San Francisco: Jossey Bass.

Buck, J., Teich, J., Umlan, B., & Stein, M. (1997). Behavioral health benefits in employer-sponsored health plans. *Health Affairs, 18,* 2, 67–78.

England, M. J. (1999). Capturing mental health cost offsets. *Health Affairs,* March, April, 91–93.

Ginzberg, E., & Ostow, M. (1997). Managed care—A look back and a look ahead. *The New England Journal of Medicine, 336*(14), 1017–1020.

Hastings, D. A., Krasner, W. L., Michael, J. L., & Rosenberg, N. D. (Eds.). (1995). *The insider's guide to managed care.* Washington, DC: The National Lawyers' Association.

Nelson, J. (1987). The history and spirit of the HMO movement. *HMO Practice, 1*(2), 75–86.

Small, R. F., & Barnhill, L. (1998). *Practicing in the new mental health marketplace.* Washington, DC: American Psychological Association.

Starr, P. (1986). *The social transformation of American medicine.* New York: Basic Books.

Wineburgh, M. (1998). Ethics, managed care and outpatient psychotherapy. *Clinical Social Work Journal, 1,* 433–443.

Carol Shaw Austad
Central Connecticut State University

MANAGEMENT DECISION MAKING

A major concern in management has been to understand and improve decision making. Psychologists have proposed various approaches, most based on a "divide-and-conquer" strategy. This strategy involves breaking a large problem into smaller parts. The idea is not new; Benjamin Franklin in a "Letter to Joseph Priestly" (1956) described such a decomposition strategy.

Nobel laureate Herbert Simon outlined the theoretical justification for this approach in his account of "bounded rationality." This concept says that cognitive processing limitations force humans to construct simplified mental models of the world. As Simon observed, a person "behaves rationally with respect to this model . . . (although) such behavior is not even approximately optimal" (1957, p. 198).

There have been two approaches to accounts of management decision making. The first is concerned with development and application of normative decision rules based on formal logic from economics or statistics. The second involves descriptive accounts of how people go about making judgments and decisions.

Normative Analyses

As outlined in John von Neumann and Oskar Morgenstern's seminal 1947 book, *Theory of Games and Economic Behavior*, various techniques exist for making optimal decisions. A distinction is drawn between riskless (or certain) choices and risky (or uncertain) choices.

Multi-Attribute Utility

Multi-attribute utility (MAU) applies to decisions with riskless outcomes. MAU involves estimating utility values for decision alternatives and selecting the alternative with the highest value. The utility for an alternative is obtained from a weighted sum of the part utilities. The MAU approach has been applied to management decisions such as siting new plants and personnel selection.

Decision-Tree Analysis

A decision tree is a graphical model that displays the sequence of choices that make up a risky decision. The approach is based on laying out choice alternatives, uncertain events, and outcome utilities as a series of branches. For each alternative, an expected value (EV) is computed as the average outcome value over all events. The optimal choice is the alternative with the highest EV. Decision trees have been used to guide high-risk decisions such as new product marketing and public policy.

Bayesian Networks

Bayesian networks combine Bayesian probability theory, artificial intelligence, and graphical analysis into a decision-making analytic tool. Starting with a fully connected network, all possible cause-and-effect linkages between nodes are described. Through a process of pruning, the structure is simplified to essential links, resulting in an enormous reduction of complexity. This approach is used to diagnose programming errors and to anticipate military trouble spots.

Descriptive Analyses

Most descriptive analyses were initially concerned with discrepancies between normative rules (e.g., EV) and actual decision behavior. In 1954, Ward Edwards modified EV by introducing subjective probabilities and psychological utilities to produce Subjectively Expected Utility (SEU). This model has become the starting point for descriptions of risky decision behavior and has been used for making lending and family planning decisions.

Social Judgment Theory

Based on the "lens model" concept proposed by Egon Brunswik, Kenneth Hammond developed a comprehensive perspective on judgment and decision making. By adapting multiple regression routines, this approach combines elements of normative and descriptive analyses. Central is the distinction between analytic and intuitive modes of cognition. This approach has been used to describe decisions by highway engineers and medical doctors.

Information Integration Theory (IIT)

Analyses of psychological rules used to combine information from multiple sources reveal that people often average inputs. Norman Anderson has shown that an averaging rule is more descriptive than the adding rule assumed in normative models. Through functional measurement procedures, IIT leads to simultaneous evaluation of processing strategies and psychological values. This approach has been applied to marketing decisions and marital choices.

Heuristics and Biases

Amos Tversky and Daniel Kahneman argued that decisions are made using psychological shortcuts or "heuristics." For instance, "representativeness" means probability estimates are based on the degree of similarity of an event to an underlying source; greater similarity implies more accurate estimates. Heuristics lead to "biases" since relevant information, for example, base rate, is often ignored. This approach has been used to explain suboptimal decisions in management and accounting.

Fast and Frugal Heuristics

Simon developed "bounded rationality" to deal with two interlocking components: limitations of the human mind, and structure of the environment. Gerd Gigerenzer extended these ideas to incorporate "fast and frugal" heuristics that take advantage of environmental constraints. Such heuristics have been found to lead to efficient decisions in medicine and forecasting.

Naturalistic Decision Making (NDM)

Naturalistic decision making was developed by Gary Klein to account for decision making by experts in time-sensitive environments. In fire fighting, for instance, there is no time to make normative choices between options. Instead, experts follow a "recognition-primed decision making" strategy—they seek a single course of action based on experience. The NDM perspective has been applied to decisions by military commanders and medical doctors.

Expert Decision Making

Behind advances in decision research has been the need for psychologists to help professionals make better choices. For instance, considerable effort was extended to understand how clinical psychologists make decisions. Although analyses often reveal that experts are biased decision makers, James Shanteau studied domains in which surprisingly good decisions occur. For example, air traffic controllers and agricultural judges generally make accurate decisions.

Conclusions

Despite the differences between normative and descriptive approaches, there have been many successful applications of behavioral decision theory in management. In large part, the successes reflect Ben Franklin's original insight into problem decomposition: Decision making is almost always improved by breaking a problem into parts, working on the parts separately, and then combining them to make a final decision.

SUGGESTED READING

Arkes, H. R., & Hammond, K. R. (Eds.). (1986). *Judgment and decision making: An interdisciplinary reader.* London: Cambridge University Press.

Franklin, B. (1956). Letter to Joseph Priestly. In *The Benjamin Franklin Sampler.* New York: Fawcett.

Kahneman, D., Slovic, P., & Tversky, A. (1982). *Judgment under uncertainty: Heuristics and biases.* New York: Cambridge University Press.

Shanteau, J., Mellers, B. A., & Schum, D. A. (Eds.). (1999). *Decision science and technology: Reflections on the contributions of Ward Edwards.* Norwell, MA: Kluwer Academic Publishers.

Simon, H. A. (1957). *Models of Man.* New York: Wiley.

Von Neumann, J., & Morgenstern, O. (1947). *Theory of Games and Economic Behavior.* Princeton, NJ: Princeton University Press.

James Shanteau
Kansas State University

MAO INHIBITORS

The MAO inhibitors have important historical, heuristic, and clinical value. Their name is derived from their primary pharmacological action: the inhibition of the activity of the enzyme monoamine oxidase (MAO), which is responsible for the metabolic degradation within neurons of several key monoamine neurotransmitters, including serotonin, norepinephrine, epinephrine, and dopamine.

The MAO inhibitors are among the very first compounds shown to be effective antidepressants. Serendipity played an important role in the discovery of their antidepressant properties. In the 1950s, intensive efforts were launched to develop antibiotic treatments for tuberculosis (TB). An early report of the clinical properties of one of these compounds, iproniazid, described its mood-elevating properties when given to TB patients (Bloch, Doonief, Buchberg, & Spellman, 1954). This fortuitous observation was soon confirmed in controlled trials (Kline, 1984). Several years later, the mechanism of antidepressant activity was found to involve the inhibition of the activity of MAO enzymes (Zeller, 1963). Unfortunately, iproniazid was soon associated with significant liver toxicity, and its use as an antidepressant was discontinued. However, several other compounds with MAO inhibitory activity were then shown to possess antidepressant efficacy.

Shortly after the widespread introduction of the MAO inhibitors into clinical practice, reports emerged regarding severe, at times fatal, hypertensive crises in some patients. Blackwell and colleagues (1967) demonstrated that these reactions were due to the hypertensive effects of tyramine and related compounds in certain foods and beverages. Tyramine can provoke a dramatic elevation in blood pressure, but monoamine oxidase in the gut wall usually breaks it down before it can be absorbed into the body. When the MAO inhibitors block this activity, sudden increases in blood pressure can occur when patients ingest foods that are rich in tyramine. Once this physiological basis for these reactions was recognized, dietary guidelines were developed to allow for the safe use of the MAO inhibitors.

In addition to foods that possess high tyramine content, several medications with sympathomimetic properties are contraindicated for patients receiving MAO inhibitors (see Table 1). These restrictions, and the fear of potentially life-threatening reactions, have substantially diminished the use of these medications, which have now largely been supplanted by the new generation of antidepressants, including the serotonin selective reuptake inhibitors (SSRIs).

The discovery that clinical depression could be successfully treated with the MAO inhibitors had a profound effect on both the practice of clinical psychiatry and on neuroscience research. Coupled with the nearly concurrent discovery of other effective antidepressant (i.e., the tricyclics) and antipsychotic pharmacotherapies, the MAO inhibitors helped to launch the revolution of modern clinical psychopharmacology. Psychiatrists began to incorporate biological therapies into treatment approaches that previously had been dominated by psychodynamic psychotherapy. Also, the relative specificity of action of these medications (i.e., their effectiveness in treating major depression, but not adjustment disorders or normal bereavement) ultimately led to greater emphasis on reliable and valid diagnostic criteria. In the neurosciences, these medications fo-

Table 1. Partial Listing of Food and Medication Restrictions for MAOIs

Foods	Medications
Cheese (except cream cheese)	Tricyclic antidepressants
Overripe fruit (especially banana peels)	Serotonin selective reuptake inhibitors
Fava beans	Meperidine
Sausages and preserved meats	Buspirone
Pickled fish and vegetables	Sympathomimetics (e.g., l-dopa, pseudoephedrine)
Chicken and beef liver	
Red wines, sherry, liquors	
Monosodium glutamate	

Note: This is a partial, representative listing. Patients receiving treatment with an MAO inhibitor should check with their physician for a comprehensive list of prohibited foods and medications.

cused attention on the potential role of the biogenic amine neurotransmitters in the pathophysiology of depression. By blocking the intraneuronal degradation of norepinephrine, serotonin, and dopamine, the MAO inhibitors led to the accumulation of these neurotransmitters and eventually to the release of larger quantities into the synapse, thereby enhancing neurotransmission. These observations of the pharmacological actions of the MAO inhibitors, coupled with their clinical efficacy, formed the basis of several theories postulating that a functional deficit in one or more of these neurotransmitters was responsible for the development of clinical depression. More recently, it has been suggested that the clinical response to the MAO inhibitors may be linked to secondary adaptive changes in various neurotransmitter receptors, and thus their mechanism of action, and the pathophysiology of depression, remain unclear.

There are two types of monoamine oxidase in the human central nervous system and in some peripheral organs. The main substrates for MAO-A activity are the neurotransmitters dopamine, norepinephrine, epinephrine, and serotonin, while dopamine, phenylethylamine, phenylethanolamine, tyramine, and benzylamine are the main substrates for MAO-B. The classic MAO inhibitors (phenelzine, isocarboxazide, and tranylcypromine) irreversibly affect both MAO-A and MAO-B. Newer agents target one of the specific forms of MAO (e.g., selegiline is an MAO-B specific inhibitor) and/or have reversible effects (e.g., moclobemide is a reversible inhibitor of MAO-A).

The primary use of the MAO inhibitors is in the treatment of depression. Several studies have suggested that these medications are especially effective in the treatment of "atypical depression," where the usual physical signs and symptoms of depression are reversed (i.e., hypersomnia rather than insomnia; increased appetite with weight gain rather than decreased appetite with weight loss) (Golden & Nicholas, 2002). There is also substantial research documenting the efficacy of MAO inhibitors in the treatment of panic disorder (Lydiard et al., 1989), although the SSRI's and high potency benzodiazepine derivatives are more widely used. Limited controlled trials have also supported the use of these medications in the treatment of social phobia and posttraumatic stress disorder (Kosten, Frank, Dan, McDougle, & Giller, 1991; Versiani et al., 1992).

Side effects are often more frequent and more severe with MAOIs than with newer antidepressants. The most frequent side effects include orthostatic hypotension, insomnia, dizziness, constipation, blurred vision, and weakness (Krishnan, 1998). Liver damage may occur in rare instances. These side effects, coupled with the concern regarding dietary and medication restrictions and the availability of the new generation of antidepressants, have led to considerable decrease in the use of the MAO inhibitors. However, they are still utilized by many clinicians in the treatment of refractory cases of depression. In the future, the availability of more specific and reversible forms of MAO inhibitors may stimulate their resurgence in clinical practice.

REFERENCES

Blackwell, M., Marley, E., Price, J., & Taylor, D. (1967). Hypertensive interactions between monoamine oxidase inhibitors and food stuffs. *British Journal of Psychiatry, 113,* 349–365.

Bloch, R. G., Doonief, A. S., Buchberg, A. S., & Spellman, S. (1954). The clinical effect of isoniazid and iproniazid in the treatment of pulmonary tuberculosis. *Annals of Internal Medicine, 40,* 881–900.

Golden, R. N., & Nicholas, L. (2002). Atypical depression: Diagnosis, prevalence, and implications for treatment in primary care. *Resident and Staff Physician, 48,* 52–56.

Kline, N. S. (1984). Monoamine oxidase inhibitors: An unfinished picaresque tale. In F. J. Ayd & B. Blackwell (Eds.), *Discoveries in biological psychiatry.* Baltimore: Ayd Medical Communications.

Kosten, T. R., Frank, J. B., Dan, E., McDougle C. J., & Giller E. L. Jr. (1991). Pharmacotherapy for Post-Traumatic Stress Disorder using phenelzine or imipramine. *Journal of Nervous and Mental Disorders, 179,* 366–370.

Krishnan, K. R. R. K. (1998). Monoamine oxidase inhibitors. In A. F. Schatzberg, & C. B. Nemeroff (Eds.), *The American Psychiatric Press textbook of psychopharmacology.* Washington, DC: American Psychiatric Press.

Lydiard, R. B., Laraia, M. T., Howell, E. F., Fossey, M. D., Reynolds, R. D., & Ballenger, J. C. (1989). Phenelzine treatment of Panic Disorder: Lack of effect on pyridoxal phosphate levels. *Journal of Clinical Psychopharmacology, 9,* 428–431.

Versiani, M., Nardi, A. E., Mundim, F. D., Alves, A. B., Liebowitz, M. R., & Amrein, R. (1992). Pharmacotherapy of Social Phobia: A controlled study with meclobemide and phenelzine. *British Journal of Psychiatry, 161,* 353–360.

Zeller, E. A. (1963). Diamine oxidase. In P. D. Boyer, H. Lardy, & K. Myrback (Eds.), *The enzymes* (2nd ed., Vol. 8). London: Academic Press.

Robert N. Golden
University of North Carolina School of Medicine

MARIJUANA

Marijuana smoking remains the most prevalent form of illicit drug use in the United States, Canada, Australia, New Zealand, and some European countries. Cannabis is the generic name for the psychoactive substance(s) derived from the plants *Cannabis sativa* or *indica*. Marijuana (a mixture of flowering tops, leaves, and stems of the dried plant) and hashish (extracted resin from the flowering tops) are the most common forms of cannabis smoked to obtain psychoactive effects. Scientists have identified Δ^9-tetrahydrocannabinol (THC) as the predominant substance in marijuana that produces the subjective "high" associated with smoking the plant.

Marijuana was used in the Western Hemisphere both medically and recreationally as early as the eighteenth century. The Marijuana Tax Act of 1937 prohibited the recreational use of marijuana in the United States. Little scientific investigation was directed toward marijuana until the 1960s and 1970s, when marijuana use increased in Western cultures.

Marijuana use in the United States and other countries continues to provoke controversy. Pro-marijuana supporters argue that cannabis has many positive effects, has only minor adverse consequences, is less harmful than other legalized drugs such as alcohol, and has important medicinal uses. Others point to evidence of the adverse effects of misuse and abuse of marijuana, its addictive potential, its possible link to the use of more harmful drugs such as cocaine and heroin, and the lack of evidence for its efficacy and the availability of alternative medicines for treating specific medical conditions. Conflicting and inconclusive scientific findings have contributed to general misperceptions and confusion regarding marijuana.

Epidemiology

In the United States, conservative estimates from the National Household Survey on Drug Abuse indicate that more than 9.3% of the general population over the age of 12 smoked marijuana during the previous year (over 11 million people), and approximately 20% of these smoked almost daily. Approximately, 13% of those who used marijuana in the previous year met the criteria for marijuana dependence or abuse. Dependence indicates that an individual experiences a cluster of cognitive, behavioral, or physiological symptoms associated with substance use, yet continues to use the substance regularly. Lifetime prevalence rates of marijuana dependence (4 to 5%) in the general population are higher than for any other illicit substance, which is clearly due to the greater overall prevalence of marijuana use. The conditional dependence rate for marijuana, or the risk of developing dependence among those who have ever used marijuana, is substantial, albeit lower than for most other drugs of abuse (9% for marijuana, 15% for alcohol, 17% for cocaine, 23% for heroin, and 32% for tobacco).

Marijuana-Related Problems

The lay and scientific communities have questioned both the addictive potential and the harm that may be associated with marijuana use or abuse. However, recent research indicates that misuse of marijuana can have significant psychosocial and perhaps adverse medical consequences. Acute marijuana use typically produces a mild euphoric state that affects sensory awareness, perception of time, appetite, mood, short-term memory, concentration, attention, motor coordination, blood pressure, and heart rate. These effects are dose dependent and vary greatly across individuals. Such effects are typically not as debilitating as those observed with other substances of abuse (e.g., alcohol, narcotics), but nonetheless can increase the risk of accidents and mistakes when performing physical or mental activities.

The types of problems associated with regular marijuana use have also been well documented. Heavy use has been linked to impairment in memory, concentration, motivation, health, interpersonal relationships, employment, and school performance, as well as lower participation in conventional roles of adulthood, history of psychiatric symptoms and hospitalizations, and participation in deviant activities. These problems appear related to frequency and duration of use. Regarding health issues, chronic use clearly increases the risk of respiratory problems (e.g., bronchitis). Of note, marijuana smoke has more carcinogens than tobacco smoke, yet direct links to lung cancer have not yet been observed. Marijuana impacts many other physical systems (e.g., cardiovascular, reproductive, endocrine, immunological, neurobiological). However, the clinical significance of effects across these systems is generally not considered robust, although much more research is needed to provide definitive information.

Marijuana Dependence

As noted above, the majority of those who try and use marijuana do not become dependent or develop significant problems. But as with other substances of abuse, a significant subset of users does develop a dependence syndrome with consequences that are similar to those associated with other types of drug dependence. For many years, the scientific community debated whether marijuana use could produce dependence. The past 10 to 15 years of basic and clinical research have produced strong evidence that marijuana use can and does produce dependence.

Basic research has identified a neurobiological system specific to the actions of marijuana (cannabinoids). At least two cannabinoid receptors (CB1, CB2) and an endogenous cannabinoid (anandamide) have been identified. The synthesis of cannabinoid antagonists (substances that can block the receptor site and hence the actions of marijuana) has facilitated experiments demonstrating that this brain system works much like neurobiological systems specific to other drugs of abuse (e.g., the endogenous opioid system). Moreover, human and nonhuman studies have demonstrated that a withdrawal syndrome can follow discontinuation of chronic use of marijuana or other cannabinoid-like substances, and that this syndrome has many similarities to other substance withdrawal syndromes. Such withdrawal appears relatively common among heavy marijuana users.

Clinical research indicates that many marijuana users willingly seek treatment for problems related to marijuana abuse. The majority of individuals who seek such treatment meet diagnostic criteria for marijuana dependence. These individuals exhibit substantial psychosocial impairment and psychiatric distress, report multiple adverse consequences and repeated unsuccessful attempts to stop using, and perceive themselves as unable to quit. Marijuana abusers do not typically experience the acute crises or severe consequences that many times drive alcohol-, cocaine-, or heroin-dependent individuals into treatment; however, they show impairment that warrants clinical intervention.

Treatment for Marijuana Abuse or Dependence

Treatment seeking for marijuana abuse is increasing. A more than two-fold increase was observed during the 1990s, such that the number of people seeking treatment for marijuana abuse now approximates the numbers seeking treatment for cocaine and heroin. Clinical trials evaluating treatments for marijuana dependence suggest that this disorder, like other substance dependence disorders, is responsive to intervention, yet the majority of patients have much difficulty achieving and maintaining abstinence. The types of treatment approaches with demonstrated efficacy for other substance dependence disorders (e.g., cognitive-behavioral, coping skills, contingency management, motivational enhancement) also appear effective with marijuana dependence. Interestingly, the response to treatment and relapse rates observed among marijuana-dependent outpatients also appear similar to those observed with other substances of abuse, suggesting that marijuana dependence is not easily treated.

Summary

Much remains unknown about the effects of marijuana on human psychological and physical health. Nonetheless, studies have provided strong evidence that marijuana use can produce multiple adverse effects and that many people experience problems related to marijuana use. The demonstration of causal relationships between marijuana and some of these effects has proven difficult, and the magnitude of risk and functional significance of some effects remains elusive. As with other abused substances, many individuals use marijuana without significant consequence, but others misuse, abuse, or become dependent. Dependence on marijuana develops in much the same way as with other drugs, although in general the associated consequences appear less severe than those associated with alcohol, heroin, or cocaine dependence.

Alan J. Budney
University of Vermont

See also: **Addictions; Dependency**

MARITAL DISCORD

The large volume of research on marital discord and the related constructs of marital conflict and marital dissatisfaction attest to the perceived importance of understanding the problems that sometimes arise in marriage. Of the various terms used in this area of inquiry, "marital satisfaction" is the best defined, referring to an evaluation of the relationship or the partner. Because of their clarity and brevity, measures of marital satisfaction play a prominent role in all areas of marital research. "Marital conflict" is a somewhat broader term than "marital satisfaction" and is used to refer to spousal perceptions, emotions, anticipations, and behavior in relation to some disagreement or area of differing interests. However, marital conflict is not inherently negative and may or may not be associated with marital dissatisfaction. In some cases marital conflict may set the stage for increases in relationship satisfaction, while in others it may be the harbinger of deterioration in the relationship. For this reason, the study of marital conflict is often considered distinct from the study of marital satisfaction, and researchers in this area place considerable importance on direct observation of marital interaction.

"Marital discord" is also a relatively broad term, referring to a state of marital dissatisfaction in conjunction with any of a number of problems that may beset couples and lead to long-standing marital conflict, loss of marital commitment, feelings of estrangement within marriage, or marital dissolution. Because the construct combines a variety of disparate features, measures of marital discord tend to be collections of heterogeneous items. The most comprehensive self-report instrument of marital discord is called the Marital Satisfaction Inventory. This inventory solves the problem of heterogeneous content by assessing each content area using a separate scale. Its primary disadvantage is its overall length of 150 items. Maintaining the distinctions between different terms used in the area has become increasingly important as research in the area of marital discord has developed. Of particular importance is the distinction between marital dissatisfaction and marital conflict, as these two constructs may often diverge in their implications.

On the other hand, measures of marital dissatisfaction and measures of marital discord are often highly correlated and the two terms are sometimes used interchangeably.

Inquiry into the causes, consequences, and correlates of marital discord is driven, in part, by the perceived importance of better understanding the effect of marital discord on numerous processes related to personal and family adjustment. Supporting this perception, much recent research suggests that marital discord and the related constructs of marital dissatisfaction and marital conflict play an important role in individual and family well-being. For example, marital dissatisfaction commonly co-occurs with depression, eating disorders, and some types of alcoholism, as well as physical and psychological abuse of partners. In addition, marital discord and marital dissolution co-vary with problems of delinquency and may presage children's later problems with intimate communication. Similarly, marital discord is associated with poorer health and with specific physical illnesses such as cancer, cardiac disease, and chronic pain. Marital interaction studies suggest possible mechanisms that may account for these links, showing, for example, that hostile behaviors during conflict relate to alterations in immunological, endocrine, and cardiovascular functioning. Better understanding of marital discord therefore offers the potential for more effective treatment of certain types of individual psychopathology and family difficulty and offers hope for better managing their sequelae. In addition, increased understanding of marital discord may also prove useful in developing better health maintenance strategies and in managing chronic health problems.

Inquiry regarding marital discord is also fueled by the perceived importance of developing harmonious marital relationships as an end in itself. Better understanding of marital discord is sought as a way to guide those attempting to develop interventions to relieve marital discord or those developing programs to prevent marital distress and divorce. That is, understanding marital discord is potentially important because enhancing marital satisfaction and alleviating marital discord are desirable goals in their own right.

As these considerations suggest, there is good reason for continuing research on the topic of marital therapy and developing prevention programs designed to prevent a decline in marital satisfaction and the development of marital discord. Because of the need to control for various extraneous effects, randomized clinical trials of various marital therapy programs have been conducted. The results of these trials indicate that substantial benefit may be obtained from several types of marital therapy, including behavioral marital therapy, emotion-focused marital therapy, insight-oriented marital therapy, and cognitive-behavioral marital therapy. Similarly, promising results have been obtained for divorce prevention programs. However, because of the difficulty in conducting randomized clinical trials on preventative intervention and the difficulty in reaching couples at greatest risk for developing marital discord and divorcing, many questions about the utility of preventative programs remain unanswered. Further, despite advances in treatment and prevention efforts, fewer than half of discordant couples receiving marital therapy remain maritally satisfied at long term follow-up. Likewise, the majority of couples in need of prevention services do not seek them out. Accordingly, there is considerable room for progress in the development of marital interventions and divorce prevention programs.

REFERENCES

Fincham, F. D., & Beach, S. R. H. (1999). Marital conflict. *Annual Review of Psychology, 50,* 47–77.

Gottman, J. M. (1999). *The marriage clinic.* New York: Norton.

Hahlweg, K., Markman, H. J., Thurmaier, F., Engl, J., & Eckert, V. (1998). Prevention of marital distress: Results of a German prospective longitudinal study. *Journal of Family Psychology, 12,* 543–556.

Schmaling, K. B. & Sher, T. G. (2000). *The psychology of couples and illness: Theory, research, & practice.* Washington, DC: APA Press.

Steven Beach
University of Georgia

See also: **Marriage Counseling**

MARRIAGE COUNSELING

It has been estimated that within the United States, most people (over 90%) will marry by the end of their lives, and that nearly 50% of recent marriages may end in divorce (Kreider & Fields, 2001). The fact that so many couples have problems in their relationships supports the importance of developing effective approaches to preventing and treating relationship difficulties.

Research has shown that marriage counseling is an effective form of treatment for marital discord. Results from studies comparing treatment groups to no treatment control groups have consistently found that counseling increases relationship satisfaction, which is the most commonly evaluated outcome measure. One way to quantify the impact of treatment is through effect size statistics, which provide information regarding the degree to which counseling is effective. Shadish et al. (1993) reported a mean effect size of .71 across 16 outcome studies that evaluated the effect of marriage counseling on global relationship satisfaction. An effect size of .71 translates into a treatment success rate of approximately 67% for treated couples versus 34% for untreated control couples.

In addition to improving relationship satisfaction, researchers have evaluated marriage counseling as a treatment for mental and physical health problems. Providing couple therapy for mental and physical health problems is based on research findings indicating that when couples have problems in their relationships, there are often co-occurring emotional and behavioral problems (e.g., Whisman, 1999). To date, marriage counseling has been shown to be effective in treating mood disorders, anxiety disorders, alcohol use disorders, and sexual disorders (Baucom, Shoham, Mueser, Daiuto, & Stickle, 1998). Thus, there is evidence that marriage counseling is effective in treating problems traditionally viewed as "individual" problems, as well as treating relationship difficulties.

There are several major theoretical approaches to marriage counseling. One of the most thoroughly researched approaches is behavioral marriage counseling (Jacobson & Margolin, 1979), which focuses on increasing pleasing exchanges (i.e., caring behaviors) between partners, as well as improving communication and problem-solving skills. A related approach focuses not only on modifying behavior, but also on modifying partners' interpretation of that behavior. In this approach, labeled cognitive-behavioral marriage counseling (Epstein & Baucom, 2002), the goal is to teach couples ways of identifying and modifying cognitions that are associated with marital problems. A second treatment approach is emotion-focused marriage counseling, which conceptualizes relationship problems in terms of the disruption of attachment bonds (Greenberg & Johnson, 1988). This approach targets problems of adult attachment insecurity by modifying couples' interaction patterns and the emotional responses that evoke and are evoked by these interactions. A third approach is insight-oriented marriage counseling (Snyder & Wills, 1989), which focuses on helping couples become aware of interaction patterns, relationship cognitions, and developmental issues that are either totally or partially beyond conscious awareness.

In addition to developing different theoretical approaches to working with couples, there has been a recent movement towards developing integrating approaches that cut across treatment modalities. For example, Jacobson and Christensen (1996) have developed an approach to marriage counseling that promotes acceptance between partners, as well as change strategies similar to those emphasized in behavioral marriage counseling. To date, there is little evidence to suggest that these different approaches yield different outcomes in terms of relationship satisfaction. Furthermore, there are few empirically-based guidelines to help match couples with the type of treatment that would be most beneficial to them.

Another important development in marriage counseling has occurred in the area of prevention of relationship problems. Research has shown that cognitive-behavioral approaches to premarital counseling—which typically involve lectures, group or couple discussions, and exercises involving practice of relationship skills—are effective in improving satisfaction and reducing divorce rates. Hahlweg and Markman (1988) reported a mean effect size of .79 across seven outcome studies that evaluated cognitive-behavioral prevention programs, which translates into a treatment success rate of approximately 69% for treated couples versus 32% for untreated control couples.

Although there have been a number of advances in the development and evaluation of marriage counseling, there are several understudied areas needing additional research (Christensen & Heavey, 1999). For example, there is a need for research on the impact of marriage counseling for different types of couples, including nontraditional couples (e.g., same-sex couples, cohabiting couples), older couples, and members of ethnic minority groups. Furthermore, there is a need for research evaluating longer-term outcome following marriage and premarital counseling, and research evaluating the impact of marriage counseling on other types of outcomes (e.g., children, individual functioning).

REFERENCES

Baucom, D. H., Shoham, V., Mueser, K. T., Daiuto, A. D., & Stickle, T. R. (1998). Empirically supported couple and family interventions for marital distress and adult mental health problems. *Journal of Consulting and Clinical Psychology, 66,* 53–88.

Christensen, A., & Heavey, C. L. (1999). Interventions for couples. *Annual Review of Psychology, 50,* 165–190.

Epstein, N. B., & Baucom, D. H. (2002). *Enhanced cognitive-behavioral therapy for couples.* Washington, DC: American Psychological Association.

Greenberg, L. S., & Johnson, S. M. (1988). *Emotionally focused therapy for couples.* New York: Guilford Press.

Hahlweg, K., & Markman, H. J. (1988). Effectiveness of behavioral marital therapy: Empirical status of behavioral techniques in preventing and alleviating marital distress. *Journal of Consulting and Clinical Psychology, 56,* 440–447.

Jacobson, N. S., & Christensen, A. (1996). *Integrative couple therapy: Promoting acceptance and change.* New York: W. W. Norton.

Jacobson, N. S., & Margolin, G. (1979). *Marital therapy: Strategies based on social learning and behavior exchange principles.* New York: Bruner/Mazel.

Kreider, R. M., & Fields, J. M. (2001). *Number, timing, and duration of marriages and divorces: Fall 1996.* Current Population Reports, P70–80. Washington, DC: U.S. Census Bureau.

Shadish, W. R., Montgomery, L. M., Wilson, P., Wilson, M. R., Bright, I., & Okwumabua, T. (1993). Effects of family and marital psychotherapies: A meta-analysis. *Journal of Consulting and Clinical Psychology, 61,* 992–1002.

Snyder, D. K., & Wills, R. M. (1989). Behavioral versus insight-oriented marital therapy: Effects on individual and interpersonal functioning. *Journal of Consulting and Clinical Psychology, 57,* 39–46.

Whisman, M. A. (1999). Marital dissatisfaction and psychiatric disorders: Results from the National Comorbidity Survey. *Journal of Abnormal Psychology, 108,* 701–706.

Mark A. Whisman
University of Colorado

See also: **Behavior Therapy; Marital Discord**

MASOCHISM

Sadomasochism is common among sexual deviations, more prevalent in men than in women. Women who perform sadistic acts for money or to please men are not necessarily sexually excited. Young women who cut their arms with razors do so to obtain relief from psychological distress, not for sexual satisfaction. The literature of this subculture is among the best selling in bookshops and newsagents. It has long exercised a considerable influence upon fashion and the visual images and story content of science fiction. Most animated cartoons and slapstick comedies contain sequences in which extremely painful happenings are presented for enjoyment.

Some sexologists, among them Schrenck-Notzing, preferred the term "algolagnia," emphasizing pleasure in pain, whereas Krafft-Ebing's terms, sadism and masochism include pleasure in humiliation, dominance, and subjection. Sadism takes its name from the writings and exploits of Donatien Alphonse François, Marquis de Sade, found to have been one of the nine prisoners held in the Bastille when it was stormed in 1789. It denotes a condition in which erotic pleasure is derived from inflicting pain or humiliation. The more puzzling condition of masochism, in which erotic pleasure is obtained from being hurt, restrained, or humiliated, is so named after the writings and activities roughly a century later of the Chevalier Leopold von Sacher-Masoch. The coupling of the two names in sadomasochism is important as the two conditions are usually present, albeit with one or the other predominating, in one and the same individual. This individual may also display other deviant interests, for instance in fetishism or transvestism. Freud pointed out that the sexuality of infancy is "polymorphously perverse," and some masochists actually visit "Adult Baby" clubs.

Many of those engaging in sadomasochistic ritual will state that this interaction is all about control and is dictated by the masochist. Their explanations are, however, seldom adequate to the impenetrability of the phenomenon they are addressing. A somewhat simplistic account is given in a medical encyclopedia: a glandular insufficiency, especially of the gonads and adrenals, demanding the stimulation of pain before the subject is able to react to sexual stimuli. Trying to explain masochism without Freud would be like trying to explain gravity without Newton. In 1924, Freud wrote in *The Economic Problem of Masochism:* "The existence of a masochistic trend in the instinctual life of human beings may justly be described as mysterious from the economic point of view. For if mental processes are governed by the pleasure principle in such a way that their first aim is the avoidance of unpleasure and the obtaining of pleasure, masochism is incomprehensible. If pain and unpleasure can be not simply warnings but actually aims, the pleasure principle is paralysed—it is as though the watchman over our mental life were put out of action by a drug. Thus masochism appears to us in the light of a great danger, which is in no way true of its counterpart, sadism. We are tempted to call the pleasure principle the watchman over our life rather than merely over our mental life." Few psychologists would wish to dispute the primacy of this principle. The whole edifice of behaviorism is built upon it. The fact that masochism is sometimes literally a danger to life itself is attested to by the deaths following certain rituals of "bondage" and hypoxyphilia (sexual arousal by oxygen deprivation)—about 50 a year in the United States according to coroners' records of 30 years ago and almost certainly more numerous today.

As Freud pointed out, a child will repeat an unpleasant experience in its play in order to gain control of it. The masochist, who has never grown up, recreates not once, but many times, the situation he fears in order that he shall not, in retrospect, be its hapless victim but, indeed, its instigator. This is not likely to benefit those in his path! It is not difficult to recognize that his "mishaps" are provocations because he will never apologize or express regret as he would if they were truly inadvertent.

Mervin Glasser has, out of his extensive clinical involvement with sadomasochism at the Portman Clinic, London, put his finger on an important and frequently encountered etiological factor: incomplete individuation. He explains it in terms of a "core complex": a pervasive longing for closeness to another person, amounting to a "merging," which invariably awakens the fear of a permanent loss of self as soon as closeness is offered. The flight to a safe distance brings a sense of isolation and, in a vicious circle, the return of longing for union. Aggression, aroused by this threat of obliteration, cannot be directed towards the potentially engulfing person (originally the mother)—it may, however, be focused on the self, and it may be sexualized and the relationship preserved in sadomasochistic mode. Many masochists lack a sense of identity apart from that of their family or their childhood background. Any struggle for autonomy which may have started, perhaps with adolescence, has failed. Some not only have an obvious reluctance to achieve satisfaction in conventional sexual intercourse with a partner, which might be a reluctance due to a sense of guilt, but they even fear such a loss of control as the culmination of a punishment ritual. They would rather masturbate alone afterwards. This confirms Glasser's interpretation that masochists need to regulate their movement toward or away from a partner, ensuring that they do not lose control of the situation in the partner's presence and expose themselves to the danger of being engulfed.

Some masochists describe sexually colored incidents in their childhood involving rubber or plastic articles, and attribute to these incidents their lifelong interest in rubber or shiny plastic as sexual stimuli. Fetishes may bear some resemblance to the "transitional objects" postulated by Donald W. Winnicott. John Bowlby preferred the term *substitute objects,* explaining that inanimate objects, such as teddy bears, have attachment behavior directed toward them because the attachment figure is unavailable. Like the attachment figure, they are sought particularly when a child is tired or sick or upset. One might perhaps add also that when a child is bored, the physical properties of the substitute object itself might become salient. In a final step, they might become sexual stimuli through masturbation. In pursuit of their fetish, some adolescents and adults find themselves confronted with pornographic literature which leads them into the SM scene. What they at first encounter in sex shops as a contiguous interest gradually extends its fascination and becomes central to their deviance. As to the fetishistic paraphernalia on sale in sex shops, a mask or uniform may serve to conceal the ordinary and create a new and powerful identity.

In cases of prolonged illness or severe injury in childhood, the endogenous opioids produced as a biological response to these situations may create an addiction to pain and stress, for they have been reported as many times more addictive than morphine and other exogenous opiates. They were reported definitively by Kosterlitz and Hughes in 1975 in the journal *Nature.* The interest, the controversy and the literature generated by these neuromodulators have, in fact, been immense. The receptors to which they bind have been found in many parts of the human body, but chiefly in pain pathways and limbic regions of the brain. They have been implicated in strenuous physical exercise—an "endorphin rush" has now become part of common parlance. What is firmly established, however, and of prime significance, is that they are, like morphine, both pain-killing and addictive. They are actually produced by pain or stress, and they relieve it by reducing neural excitability. Pleasure, often referred to in the literature as "the reward factor," follows. The practising masochist is a person for whom "normal" sexual release by means of the genitals is at best problematic. Often, the anus and buttocks are more erotogenic than the genitals. If one looks into the childhood of a masochist, one frequently finds an accident or illness involving intense, protracted, physical pain, or repeated beatings, or a situation causing severe, prolonged stress. These events, usually only the beginning of a series, have not only psychological but also physiological consequences, one of these being the release of endogenous opioids. As painful event succeeds event, what happened at first by ill chance is later engineered. He is addictively seeking pain and in some cases he even knows it and explicitly states it.

Thus the etiology of masochism may be predominantly physical through injury, illness, or stress; predominantly psychological through maternal rejection, parental divorce, or death for which the masochist attributes guilt to himself; or a combination of both through corporal punishment, hospitalization, persecution by or envious hatred of siblings, a puritanical home atmosphere where sexual relations are considered sinful or disgusting, or a bullied and miserable school life. Where sadomasochism finds no outlet in sexual activity it is likely to spill over from sexuality into the personality. Particularly in women, martyrdom may be a way of transferring guilt to others. As the neurologist and psychiatrist Kurt Goldstein noted, the healthy personality is characterized by flexible functioning, the damaged personality is rigid; healthy functioning is planned and organized, disturbed functioning is mechanical; the healthy person can delay and anticipate the future, the disturbed personality is bound by the past and the immediate present.

Theodor Reik's depiction of masochism is arguably the most accurate after Freud's. He identifies its quintessential characteristics as a predilection for fantasy, the seeking of suspense, and what he calls the demonstrative feature. (To these one might add rigidity, infantilism, hypocrisy, and passivity.) At the end of *Masochism in Modern Man,* Reik seeks the common denominator in the various manifestations of masochism—sexual deviance and personality disorder alike—and finds it in the formula "victory through defeat." This is indeed the kernel of masochism and there is no doubt that the highly specific victory is total. The man whose aim is to be defeated has achieved a desperate invulnerability. The masochist who operates primarily through deviant sexual practices, the "supersensualist," as Sacher-Masoch styled himself, defiantly obtains gratification in spite of every obstacle, every delay, every embargo. The masochist who, in each situation life presents, systematically ruins his chances of happiness and success, is locked within a vicious circle of guilt, requiring punishment, punishment affording masochistic satisfaction, thus begetting more guilt, requiring more punishment.

Sadomasochism has been described by the psychiatrist Otto Kernberg as a continuum—a spectrum would be another metaphor, with feckless theatrical games at one end and sadistic serial killings at the other. The danger comes when preoccupation with immediate physical pleasure takes over, when other human beings are seen only as insensate means of sexual gratification, and this is indissolubly linked with domination. That at the other end of the spectrum, everyday human relations are shot through with covert sadomasochism is, sadly, as irrefutable as saying that Homo sapiens is a dangerous species.

Of course, masochists have other qualities besides deviance and sometimes, where fantasy is creative as opposed to emprisoning, considerable talents or skills, as in the cases of Gesualdo, Mussorgsky, Bartok, Rousseau, Dostoevsky, Swinburne, C. S. Lewis, T. E. Lawrence, and Yukio Mishima, to mention but a few.

June Rathbone
University College, London

MASTURBATION

Masturbation is the term used to signify any type of autoerotic stimulation. Both males and females indulge in stimulation of the genitals for sexual gratification. The term is also applied to an infant's manipulation of the genitals, a common exploratory behavior in the early years. During adolescence, masturbation becomes one of the main sexual outlets, and remains so for many adults. Michael, Gagnon, Laumann, and Kolata (1994) found that among Americans, 60% of men and 40% of women report that they have masturbated during the past year. Twenty-five percent of men and 10% of women say they masturbate at least once a week. Estimates vary, depending on the studies cited and the specific approaches used in collecting the data.

Of all the areas of sexual behavior, masturbation appears to be subject to the widest variation in reported frequency, owing no doubt to the privacy of this behavior and the shame that has traditionally surrounded it. While in earlier historical periods masturbation was considered a sign of depravity or sinfulness, it is more generally accepted today as a common practice among adolescents and adults, both male and female.

REFERENCES

Michael, R. T., Gagnon, J. H., Laumann, E. O., & Kolata, G. (1994). *Sex in America: A definitive survey.* Boston: Little, Brown.

John Paul McKinney

MEDICAL MODEL OF PSYCHOTHERAPY

The medical model has been applied to several areas, including physical illness, psychiatric illness, and psychotherapy. Although several features distinguish the medical model of psychotherapy from those of physical and psychiatric illness, the models also share similarities. A discussion of applications of the medical model to physical and psychiatric illness will help to define and delineate the medical model of psychotherapy.

The Medical Model of Physical and Psychiatric Illness

The medical model of physical illness rests on the assumption that the etiology of a disease can ultimately be traced to the disruption of internal physiological processes. Further, it is often posited that this disruption is caused by specific pathogens such as viruses, bacteria, toxins, genetic abnormalities, or cellular dysfunction. To relieve symptoms of an illness and return the patient to a state of health, the medical model requires that the practitioner correctly diagnose the disorder, identify the underlying pathology, and provide an intervention that removes, inactivates, or reverses the action of the internal pathogen.

Applied to psychiatric illness, the medical model presupposes that a patient's report of disturbed mood, problematic thoughts, and/or aberrant behavior is caused by the disruption of internal physiological processes such as neurochemical abnormalities or central nervous system damage. Operating from this perspective, a practitioner will attempt to treat the underlying pathology by prescribing or supporting the use of medications, surgical interventions, or electroshock therapy.

The Medical Model of Psychotherapy

The medical model of psychotherapy is based on a set of assumptions similar to those described above. That is, supporters of the medical model of psychotherapy argue that the primary causes of behavior problems may be traced to the dysregulation of internal processes. Unlike the medical model of illness, however, the medical model of psychotherapy replaces biological pathogens with what may be described as *intrapsychic pathogens*—dysfunctional internal psychological processes that give rise to problematic behavior. Many examples of intrapsychic pathogens have been reported in the psychoanalytic and psychodynamic literature, including unconscious conflicts, poor ego development, psychosexual fixations, unconscious defenses, childhood traumas, and impaired object relations (e.g., Fenichel, 1945; Freud, 1933/1964; London, 1986; Luborsky, 1984; Luborsky, Barber, & Crits-Christoph, 1990). Because practitioners endorsing the medical model of psychotherapy view intrapsychic factors as the primary cause of behavior problems, assessment and treatment procedures target presumed internal psychological processes as opposed to external (e.g., situational) processes.

Evaluation of the Medical Model of Psychotherapy

Several criticisms of the medical model of psychotherapy have been put forth by authors who endorse a scientifically-based cognitive-behavioral approach to assessment and therapy (e.g., Barrios, 1988; Hawkins, 1986; Haynes & O'Brien, 2000). First, because internal, unobservable, and hence, unmeasurable intrapsychic processes are cited as the primary cause of behavior, critics argue that the medical model of psychotherapy is more apt to generate nonscientific and untestable explanations of behavior disorders. Second, critics argue that there is very little scientific evidence supporting two critical assumptions underlying the medical model of psychotherapy: (1) that intrapsychic factors are the primary cause of disordered behavior, and (2) that treatments that primarily target intrapsychic factors (e.g., psychodynamic and psychoanalytic approaches) yield better client outcomes relative to interventions that target external factors (e.g., behavioral approaches) or a combination of external and internal factors (e.g., cognitive-behavioral approaches). In fact, several meta-analytic reviews suggest that psychoanalytic and psychodynamic interventions typically produce outcomes that are inferior to behavioral and cognitive-behavioral interventions (e.g., Pinquart & Soerensen, 2001).

A third criticism relates to patient diagnosis and labeling. Specifically, because the medical model locates the cause of disordered behavior within the individual, practitioners who endorse this view may be more apt to believe that their clients have long-standing and less treatable personality-based problems (Brehm & Smith, 1986). In turn, these practitioners may be unrealistically pessimistic about the possibility for client improvement.

Recent changes in mental health care have also adversely affected the acceptance and use of the medical model of psychotherapy. Specifically, because practitioners are now required to demonstrate more clearly that their treatments yield cost-effective outcomes, scientifically supported behavioral and cognitive-behavioral treatments are increasingly used to treat a wide array of psychological disorders (Chambless & Hollon, 1998; Geraty, 1995). Alternatively, because there are limited scientific data supporting the use of interventions that target intrapsychic factors, techniques based on the medical model of psychotherapy are less frequently used in clinical practice (Altshuler, 1990).

To address declining use and the changing health care environment, the medical model approach to psychotherapy is now expanding to include more scientifically supported procedures and to incorporate interdisciplinary techniques (Gabbard, 1994; Weissman, 1994). Although proponents of the model argue that their approach may be less amenable to traditional research techniques than other approaches, increased empirical validation of the medical model approach to psychotherapy is critical for its survival (Strupp, 2001).

Summary

The medical model approach to psychotherapy, like the medical model of illness, rests on the assumption that problematic behavior arises from the disruption of internal pathogenic processes. As a result, assessment and treatment emphasize the measurement and modification of presumed intrapsychic determinants of behavior. Criticisms of the medical model combined with changes in mental health care have reduced the acceptability of this approach and, as a result, it is less frequently used in clinical settings. Adherents of the medical model are calling for changes that will permit inclusion of scientifically-based assessment and treatment procedures. This broadening of the medical model will be needed if it is to survive as an approach to psychotherapy.

REFERENCES

Altshuler, K. Z. (1990). Whatever happened to intensive psychotherapy? *The American Journal of Psychiatry, 147,* 428–430.

Barrios, B. A. (1988). On the changing nature of behavioral assessment. In A. S. Bellack & M. Hersen (Eds.), *Behavioral assessment: A practical handbook* (3rd ed., pp. 3–41).

Brehm S., & Smith T. (1986). Social psychological approaches to behavior therapy and behavior change. In S. L. Garfield & A. E. Bergin (Eds.), *Handbook of psychotherapy and behavior change* (3rd ed., pp. 69–115).

Chambless, D., & Hollon, S. (1998). Defining empirically supported therapies. *Journal of Consulting and Clinical Psychology, 66,* 7–18.

Fenichel, O. (1945). *Psychoanalytic theory of neurosis.* New York: W. W. Norton.

Freud, S. (1964). New introductory lectures in psychoanalysis. In J. Strachey (Ed.), *The standard edition of the complete psychological works of Sigmund Freud* (pp. 7–184). London: Hogarth Press. (Original work published 1933)

Gabbard, G. O. (1994). Mind and brain in psychiatric treatment. *Bulletin of the Menninger Clinic, 58,* 427–446.

Geraty, R. D. (1995). General hospital psychiatry and the new behavioral health care delivery system. *General Hospital Psychiatry, 17,* 245–250.

Hawkins, R. P. (1986). Selection of target behaviors. In R. O. Nelson & S. C. Hayes (Eds.), *Conceptual foundations of behavioral assessment* (pp. 331–385). New York: Guilford Press.

Haynes, S. N., & O'Brien, W. H. (2000). *Behavioral assessment: Principles and practice.* New York: Kleuwer/Plenum.

London, P. (1986). *The modes and morals of psychotherapy* (2nd ed.). New York: Hemisphere.

Luborsky, L. (1984). *Principles of psychoanalytic psychotherapy: A manual for supportive expressive treatment.* New York: Basic Books.

Luborsky, L., Barber, J. P., & Crits-Christoph, P. (1990). Theory-based research for understanding the process of dynamic psychotherapy. *Journal of Consulting and Clinical Psychology, 58,* 281–287.

Pinquart, M., & Soerensen, S. (2001). How effective are psychotherapeutic and other psychosocial interventions with older adults? A meta-analysis. *Journal of Mental Health & Aging, 7,* 207–243.

Strupp, H. H. (2001). Implications of the empirically supported treatment movement for psychoanalysis. *Psychoanalytic Dialogues, 11,* 605–619.

Weissman, S. (1994). American psychiatry in the 21st century: The discipline, its practice, and its workforce. *Bulletin of the Menninger Clinic, 58,* 503–518.

William H. O'Brien
Allison E. Collins
Bowling Green State University

MEMORY DISORDERS

Information learned and events experienced are considered to be more or less permanently stored in memory. To understand memory, an information-processing analogy may be helpful. Information is entered through the senses, operated on, stored, retrieved, and utilized. The operations stage has functions of attaching appropriate cues to information, linking related events, setting priority, and selecting information to avoid confusion.

Obviously, efficient retrieval is the objective of any memory system, but achieving it is not always easy. Retrieval can be hampered by lack of *availability.* When too much information is taken in, memory capacity can be exceeded and information is lost. When too much time elapses between instances of retrieval, old memories fade. Retrieval can also be hampered by lack of *accessibility.* Attaching inappropriate priority to information may lead to failure to recall the highest priority information; poor attention and highly similar cues applied to other information can cause confusion and interference during retrieval. Memory loss due to lack of availability and/or accessibility results in the most frequent, nonpathological form of memory disorder: *forgetting.*

Forgetting due to loss of availability of stored information can occur with too little rehearsal or repetition of the information to be remembered, or when recently acquired information receives priority over previously learned information, making the old information no longer available. A common cause of forgetting is confusion or interference from acoustically or semantically similar information.

Amnesia, or the loss of memory, can be either anterograde or retrograde and is caused by emotional or cortical trauma and by alcohol or barbiturate abuse. Amnesia can be (1) *localized,* so that specific features of the time frame around the trauma fail to be both accessible and available for recall; (2) *selective,* as evidenced in the failure to recall particular events like the death of a loved one, an automobile accident, or war experiences; (3) *generalized,* as evidenced by the inability to recall all one's life events up to and surrounding the time of a traumatic experience; or (4) *continuous,* where there is failure to recall events around the traumatic event and into the present. Generalized and continuous types are much less frequent than localized and selective types.

Memory disorders evidenced during *senility* indicate a clarity in memory for events from the distant past interjected inappropriately into the present. The information recalled is frequently viewed as somewhat trivial by others, but has emotional and situational importance for the person.

Memory disorders are also evidenced by *confabulation* or story telling to fill in for periods of blanking caused by alcohol or substance abuse. Here, substance abuse seems to interfere with the encoding and storage capabilities, so that both availability and accessibility are disrupted for periods that may exceed 48 hours. Similar blanking appears during epileptic episodes and schizophrenic catatonic stupors.

Special cases of memory disorders are evidenced in the intellectually retarded. With them, despite highly rehearsed motor and elemental intellectual exercises, memory is frequently short-term; rarely is it available for the past 24 hours. Other special cases of memory disorders are evidenced by the aphasias. Here, previously learned and frequently used abilities such as reading, speaking, writing, and picture recognition are lost through a neurological disorder that may be precipitated by cortical trauma, stroke, and so on. In such cases, formerly competent readers become *alexic* and lose the ability to read. Others who had had fine motor skills now become *apraxic* and lose the capacity for fine motor movement, and still others who were highly adept socially become *prosopagnostic* and lose the ability to recognize faces.

Dennis F. Fisher

MEMORY, STRESS, AND PROBLEM SOLVING

Can stress likely affect the efficiency of memory and its mechanisms? Generally, it is agreed that the degree of retaining the completeness of an event will determine how effectively its details are encoded, and how easily the memory can be retrieved. This notion was posited as "depth of processing," but recently has been discussed more often in terms of elaboration (Craik & Lockhart, 1972; Craik & Tulving, 1975).

Mandler (1979) suggested that elaboration illustrates the complexity of interstructural links that are developed in the process of encoding, and that these links provide better access at the time of retrieval. These findings about memory and storage retrieval suggest that the restriction of conscious capacity that occurs as a result of stress could have obvious effects on memory functions. Under conditions of stress we tend to remember fewer things that occur and these less well; thus, events will be less elaborately coded under stress. Anecdotal evidence, at least, supports this hypothesis. Unfortunately, there is little experimental evidence on the effects of stress on complex storage and retrieval processes. Available data tend to be rather dated and are limited to supporting the point that stress (frequently defined as failure) impairs memory. The only extensive set of data concerns the effect of stress on short-term memory, and shows that practically any kind of stress, failure experience, or uncontrollable noise will impair short-term memory retrieval. Since short-term memory, as used in the experimental research literature, is to some extent coextensive with span of attention or consciousness, such a finding is not surprising and adds little to our understanding of more complex processes.

Both lay people and mental health professionals recognize the phenomenon that when under stress, the thought processes involved in problem solving demonstrate a kind of narrowing and stereotyping. Because much of problem solving requires the manipulation in consciousness of alternatives, choices, probable and possible outcomes, consequences, and alternative goals, the internal noise of stress and autonomic nervous arousal should and does interfere with problem solving. Thought processes become narrowed in the sense that only the very obvious alternatives are considered and no conscious capacity is available to evaluate other alternatives. The restriction on memory elaboration leads to a similar restriction on elaboration that is present during problem solving under stress. Examples of these consequences appear in the discussions of available data on the problems of central and peripheral processing under stress.

Understanding more precisely the impact of stress on memory and problem solving requires experimental research studies dealing with analyses of problem solving processes under stress. How and when does the introduction of stress (however produced or defined) constrain the available alternatives in the conscious state? Which processes are suppressed or removed from consciousness and in what order? Does the stress-induced inability to solve a problem synergistically further stress reactions because of the failure to solve the problem? How is hypothesis sampling affected by stress conditions? Under what circumstances can the focusing that occurs under stress be beneficial, promoting more efficient problem solving? The research potential is great, yet our preoccupation with the unstressed mind has restricted experimental work on these problems.

REFERENCES

Craik, F., & Lockhart, R. S. (1972). Levels of processing: A framework for memory research. *Journal of Verbal Learning and Verbal Behavior, 11,* 671–684.

Craik, F., & Tulving, E. (1975). Depth of processing and the retention of words in episodic memory. *Journal of Experimental Psychology, 104,* 268–294.

Mandler, G. (1975). Memory storage and retrieval: Some limits on the reach of attention and consciousness. In P. M. A. Rabbit & S. Dornic (Eds.), *Attention and performance* (pp. 499–516). London: Academic Press.

Norman J. Cohen
Bowie State University

MENSTRUATION

Menstruation refers to normal vaginal bleeding that is usually monthly. The endometrium (uterus lining) sheds when a woman is not pregnant. The menstrual cycle refers to the time from the menstrual flow until the day before the next bleeding (commonly called a "period") begins. Normal flow lasts for 3–5 days, and the total amount of fluid is about 20–40 ml (four to eight soaked regular tampons or menstrual pads).

Menstruation is a normal biological phenomenon. However, menstruation is viewed negatively in Western culture. This taboo has lessened during the past decades, and varies with gender and age as well as cultural background.

A young woman in North America has her first menstruation (menarche) at about age 12, although between 10 and 14 years is normal. Menstruation continues cyclically for several decades until the final menstrual period at an average age of 51. A woman is menopausal once she has had a year without menstrual flow. The menopause transition (or perimenopause) occurs during the final years of menstruation and lasts about four years from the start of irregular periods. Perimenopause is a time of change with high or variable estrogen levels, ovulation disturbances, and consequent changes in flow, unpredictability of menstrual cycles, and more intense premenstrual experiences.

The menstrual cycle may also describe the cyclic hormonal changes that are orchestrated by coordination of signals from the brain and pituitary with hormones from the ovary. All estrogen produced during a given cycle is made by the cells of one particular *dominant follicle* (larger nest of cells surrounding one egg). This follicle begins to grow during menstrual flow, increasing in size and in the amount of estrogen it makes to the middle of the cycle. As it enlarges it develops a cyst (small sack) of fluid that may normally grow to 2 to 3 cm in size. Next, the cyst ruptures and the egg is extruded—this is called ovulation. Following ovulation, cells that lined the follicle form a new body, called the corpus luteum, that makes progesterone as well as estrogen. If ovulation does not occur, progesterone levels do not rise and the ovary is left containing a cyst.

Although the typical menstrual cycle is 28 days long and ovulation ideally occurs on day 14, there is wide variation in the length of menstrual cycles and the timing of ovulation. A normal menstrual cycle is between 21 and 36 days long. Luteal phase length (the number of days from ovulation until the next flow starts) is also variable. Normal luteal phase lengths are 10–16 days.

An interested woman can detect three events in the menstrual cycle. One is a sustained rise of about 0.22 degrees Celsius in first morning temperature. This rise follows ovulation by about 24 to 48 hours. Progesterone raises the core temperature through its action in the brain. The temperature rise continues until the end of the menstrual cycle. If a woman is pregnant she will usually not have a period and her temperature will remain elevated.

The second event occurs before ovulation and is the response of glands at the cervix (opening of uterus into the vagina) to the increasing estrogen. Estrogen stimulates production of clear, stretchy mucus that resembles egg white—this creates an ideal environment in which sperm can swim into the uterus. After ovulation (because progesterone suppresses the cervical glands' production), the stretchy mucus disappears. If there is no ovulation, stretchy mucus can be detected throughout the cycle.

Finally, near the middle of the cycle a pituitary hormone called *luteinizing hormone* (LH) can be detected using an over-the-counter urine test kit. This test can tell whether a woman is going to ovulate and is used as an aid to fertility.

When ovulation occurs late in a menstrual cycle, this is called short luteal phase. It is defined as fewer than 12 days between the LH peak and flow or fewer than 10 days between temperature rise and the next menstruation. Short luteal phase cycles are associated with early miscarriages and infertility. In addition, short luteal phases are associated with risks for low bone density (and subsequent osteoporosis). Short luteal phase cycles are common during the first 12 years following menarche and during the menopause transition, but may occur at any time.

Menstrual cycle and ovulation changes are caused by physical or emotional stresses (such as examinations at school, psychological abuse, heavy exercise training, decreased food intake, or being ill). The most subtle of these changes is shortening of the luteal phase length. More intense stress may cause anovulation (lack of ovulation) that may occur in a normal or irregular cycle. Several stressors operating together or young gynecological age (number of years following menarche) may cause oligomenorrhea (cycle lengths longer than 36 days). Absence of menstruation for six months is called amenorrhea.

Emotional stress related to worry about gaining weight (called *cognitive dietary restraint*) in a normal weight woman is associated with short luteal phase cycles and also with higher urinary excretion of the stress hormone cortisol, and with increased risk for osteoporosis.

A woman's physical and emotional experiences fluctuate during her menstrual cycle in concert with hormonal changes. These normal, unremarkable changes are known collectively as *molimina.* Some use this term for all premenstrual changes, but it may be specific for cycles with normal ovulation. Slowly increasing moderate exercise reduces premenstrual symptoms, as does taking supplemental calcium (1200 mg/d).

In the past few decades, the concept of a "premenstrual syndrome" or PMS has arisen. Some women experience a premenstrual exaggeration of the normal ebb and flow of experiences, particularly emotional lability, fluid retention, increased appetite and cravings, and breast tenderness. The *Diagnostic and Statistical Manual of Mental Disorders* (*DSM*) currently includes a diagnosis of Premenstrual Dysphoric Disorder for premenstrual mood changes. There are many publications in the popular and scientific literature on the topic of PMS, but the science behind this designation and the validity of the underlying concepts remain unclear.

Physiological processes that vary across the menstrual cycle include exercise performance, lung function, and glucose metabolism. Additionally, there have been reports of a number of medical conditions that vary across the menstrual cycle. The classical term for these is "catamenial." Some examples include migraine headaches, asthma, and epileptic seizures. In general, the research in this area has been minimal and most studies are not adequately controlled.

Adequate or high levels of estrogen with too little or no progesterone are associated with flow and cycle disturbances and are common after menarche and in perimenopause. Any flow heavier than 16 soaked regular-sized pads or tampons in one period is abnormal and puts a woman at risk of anemia (low blood count). Menstrual cramps (dysmenorrhea) occur before and during flow especially during the teens and often increase in perimenopause. They can be treated with anti-inflammatory medications such as ibuprofen, taken at the first feeling of pelvic heaviness and repeated as soon as cramps start to recur.

Jerilynn C. Prior
Christine L. Hitchcock
University of British Columbia

MENTAL IMAGERY

Around the turn of the century, mental images were frequently mentioned in controversies concerning cognitive experiences. Whether images were crucial to thinking became a significant issue of contention among both theoretical and empirical psychologists in Germany at that time. John B. Watson, the father of behaviorism, regarded mental images as nothing more than mere ghosts of sensations and of no functional significance whatsoever. Subsequently, experimental psychologists ignored the existence of images and worked almost exclusively with linguistic and behavioral associations. More recently, however, mental imagery has become one of the most significant issues in cognitive psychology.

Researchers like Hobart Mowrer, Silvan Tomkins, and others paved the way for the "return of the ostracized." For almost three decades, Allan Paivio has been at the forefront of both research and theory relating memory processes to imagery. His research has led to the conclusion that "imagery variables are among the most potent memory factors ever discovered" (Paivio, 1972, p. 253). Paivio has interpreted his results in terms of a dual coding model which contains the underlying assumption that there are two main modes of coding experience: verbal and imaginal. The dual coding hypothesis has generated a great deal of research (Paivio, 1971, 1990).

Current Imagery Research and Theory

Stephen Kosslyn, Allan Paivio, Alan Richardson, Peter Sheehan, Roger Shepard, Jerome Singer, and many others have demonstrated that imagery plays an important role in learning, memory, language, thinking, problem solving, perception, emotion, motivation, creativity, sexual behavior, and numerous other aspects of human behavior. This research has also revealed the functional characteristics that distinguish imagery from verbal symbolic processes. This differentiation has been further supported by neurophysiological and clinical work. The imagery system, because of its concrete and contextual nature, appears more akin to perception.

While interest and research in imagery have mounted, there certainly has been less than complete agreement concerning the nature and function of images. Over the years, in addition to dual-coding models, several other significant theories have been advanced: U. Neisser's percept analogy; D. Hebb's cell assemblies; T. Moran's propositional model; Kossly, Schwartz, and Pinker's array theory; A. Trehub's neural networks; R. Finke's levels of equivalence; R. Shepard's psychophysical complementarity; Z. Pylyshyn's tacit knowledge account; and G. Hinton's structural descriptions (Sheikh, 1983). These theorists fall into two groups: to use Dennet's terms, the "iconophiles, those attributing a special nature to mental imagery representations and giving the reported special nature of images some important theoretical status, and the iconophobes, those who believe that images are mentally represented in the same way as other forms of thought with no special status accorded to some intrinsic 'spatial' or 'pictorial' nature" (Pinker & Kosslyn, 1983, p. 44). In R. Shepard's words (1978, p. 127), "current controversy concerning mental imagery seems to have focused on two closely related questions: (a) Do the mental images that some of us undeniably experience, play a significant functional role in our thinking or are they mere epiphenomenal accompaniments of underlying processes of very different, less pictorial character? and (b) What exactly are mental images or, more specifically, what sort of physical processes underlie them in the brain, and to what extent are these processes, like pictures, isomorphic to the external objects that they represent?" (Also see Shepard & Gooper, 1982.) The long-standing debate between the iconophiles (favoring depictive representation) and the iconophobes (favoring propositional representations) appears to have been resolved in favor of the former (Behrman & Kosslyn, 1995; Kosslyn, 1994).

Whether images represent a direct encoding of perceptual experiences, an artifact of propositional structuring, or a constructive and reconstructive process has not been of any real concern to the majority of clinicians and experimenters. They assume that everyone experiences mental representations of objects and events, and these representations constitute their subject matter. A definition of imagery such as the one by A. Richardson is implicit in most of these approaches: "Mental imagery refers to all those quasi-sensory or quasi-perceptual experiences of which we are self-consciously aware, and which exist for us in the absence of those stimulus conditions that are known to produce their genuine sensory or perceptual counterparts" (Richardson, 1969, p. 2).

Classification of Images

On the basis of twentieth-century investigations, A. Richardson has identified four classes of mental images which may be compared with respect to clarity, vividness, localization, fixedness or stability, completeness of detail, susceptibility to scanning, and degree of likeness to the sensory percept. The identified classes are: (1) afterimages, (2) eidetic images, (3) thought images (or memory images), and (4) imagination images (Richardson, 1969, 1994).

Afterimages closely resemble percepts, having a strong sensory quality. Usually afterimages result from actual perception of a stimulus object; they are representations of the object's form and, positively or negatively, of its hue.

Eidetic images are another form of percept-like images. Two types of eidetic images are reported: those resembling prolonged afterimages occasioned by percepts, and those originating in memory or the general process of imagination. Both types are characterized by clarity and detail. Existing studies accept the prevalence of eidetics among children, but among adults they are thought to be extremely rare.

Thought images tend to be pallid, fragmented, indefinitely localized, and of brief duration. However, they have the potential for extreme vividness and clarity, and conceivably could be cultivated for these qualities.

Imagination images are significantly influenced by motivational states and generally involve concentrated quasi-hypnotic attention along with inhibition of associations. Imagination images include the following relatively distinct forms: hypnagogic images, perceptual isolation images, hallucinogenic drug images, and sleep deprivation images.

Assessment of Mental Imagery

Self-reports or questionnaires traditionally have been the most frequently utilized method of measuring individual difference in imagery ability. These measures have dealt with three aspects of imagery ability: (1) vividness or clarity of the images, (2) imagery types (whether subjects differ as to the modalities in which the clearest images occur), and (3) imagery control (whether some people can manipulate their images at will better than others).

Another group of methods measures the facets of consciousness that reflect experience more directly. Examples of such measures are the thought-sampling method introduced by Eric Klinger, which aims to assess subjects' "current concerns," and the Experiential Analysis Technique of Sheehan, McConkey, and Cross. The main difference between these types of assessment and self-report inventories is that the former draw upon the ongoing stream of consciousness rather than upon retrospective comments on experience. Thus, they may be more valid for assessing the facets of cognition that distinguish current everyday thought (Sheikh, 1983).

Attempts have also been made to infer imaging ability from behavioral performances. The most compelling performance tests are those developed in conjunction with the assessment of eidetic imagery, for example the Random-Dot Stereogram Test.

Akin to this type of ability test are those that are spatial in nature. These tests often are clearly intended to arouse imagery, but this imagery is generally concerned with the mental manipulation of spatial relationships.

Clinical Uses of Mental Imagery

Although imagery has been an instrument of therapeutic intervention throughout recorded history, recently interest in imagery techniques has greatly expanded and intensified. Several writers have indicated numerous characteristics of the imagery mode that make it an eminently suitable vehicle for clinical work.

Over the years, numerous widely varied, imagery-based therapies have emerged both abroad and in the United States. Evidence is also accumulating that spontaneous and induced visual images are a rich and readily accessible source of diagnostic information (Sheikh, 2003).

REFERENCES

Behrmann, M., & Kosslyn, S. M. (1995). *The neuropsychology of mental imagery.* New York: Pergamon.

Kosslyn, S. M. (1994). *Image and brain: The resolution of the imagery debate.* Cambridge, MA: MIT Press.

Paivio, A. (1971). *Imagery and verbal processes.* New York: Holt, Rinehart and Winston.

Paivio, A. (1972). A theoretical analysis of the role of imagery in learning and memory. In P. W. Sheehan (Ed.), *The function and nature of imagery.* New York: Academic Press.

Paivio, A. (1990). *Mental representations: A dual coding approach.* Oxford, UK: Oxford University Press.

Pinker, S., & Kosslyn, S. M. (1983). In A. A. Sheikh (Ed.), *Imagery: Current theory, research, and application.* New York: Wiley.

Richardson, A. (1969). *Mental imagery.* New York: Springer Publishing.

Richardson, A. (1994). *Individual differences in imagery.* Amityville, NY: Baywood.

Sheikh, A. A. (Ed.). (1983). *Imagery: Current theory, research, and application.* New York: Wiley.

Sheikh, A. A. (Ed.). (2003). *Healing images: The role of imagination in health.* Amityville, NY: Baywood.

Shepard, R. N. (1978). The mental image. *American Psychologist, 33,* 125–137.

Shepard, R. N., & Cooper, L. A. (1982). *Mental images and their transformations.* Cambridge, MA: MIT Press.

Anees A. Sheikh
Marquette University

***See also:* Perception**

META-ANALYSIS

The fundamental problem addressed by meta-analytic procedures is the cumulation of evidence. There has long been a pessimistic feeling in the softer social, behavioral, and biological sciences that progress has been exceedingly slow, at least when compared to the progress of harder sciences, such as physics and chemistry. In particular, it has seemed that the softer (and newer) sciences do not show the orderly progress and development of the harder (and older) sciences. In other words, the more recent work of the harder sciences seems to build directly upon the older work of those sciences, whereas the more recent work of the softer sciences seems often to be starting from scratch.

Cumulating Scientific Evidence

Poor cumulation does not seem to be due primarily to lack of replication, or to the failure to recognize the need for replication. There are many areas of the softer sciences for which we have the results of numerous studies, all addressing essentially the same question. Our summaries of the results of these sets of studies, however, have not been nearly as informative as they might have been, either with respect to summarized levels of statistical significance or with respect to summarized effect magnitudes. Even the best reviews of research by the most sophisticated workers have rarely told us much more about each study in a set of studies than the direction of the relationship between the variables investigated, and whether or not a given significance level was attained. This state of affairs is beginning to change. More and more reviews of the literature are moving from the traditional literary approach to quantitative approaches to research synthesis. The goals of these quantitative approaches of meta-analysis are to help us discover what we have learned from the results of the studies conducted, and to help us discover what we have not yet learned.

Defining Research Results

Before we can consider various issues and procedures in the cumulation of research results, we must become quite explicit about the meaning of the concept "results of a study." It is easiest to begin with what we do not mean. We do not mean the prose conclusion drawn by the investigator and reported in the abstract, the results, or the discussion section of the research report. We also do not mean the results of an omnibus F test with $df > 1$ in the numerator or an omnibus χ^2 test with $df > 1$. (These omnibus tests address vague questions that are rarely, if ever, of scientific interest.)

What we do mean is the answer to the question: What is the relationship between any variable X and any variable Y? The variables X and Y are chosen with only the constraint that their relationship be of interest to us. The answer to this question should normally come in two parts: (1) the estimate of the magnitude of the relationship (the effect size), and (2) an indication of the accuracy, precision, or stability of the estimated effect size (as in a confidence interval placed around the effect size estimate). An alternative to the second part of the answer is one not intrinsically more useful, but one more consistent with the existing practices of researchers; that is, the examination of the significance level of the difference between the obtained effect size and the effect size expected under the null hypothesis (usually an effect size of zero). If the significance level is employed, it should always be reported accurately and never as "significant" or "not significant."

Because a complete reporting of the results of a study requires the report of both the effect size and level of statistical significance, it is useful to make explicit the relationship between these quantities. The general relationship is given by:

$$\text{Test of Significance} = \text{Size of Effect} \times \text{Size of Study}$$

In other words, the larger the study in terms of the number of sampling units, the more significant the results will be. This is true unless the size of the effect is truly zero, in which case a larger study will not produce a result that is any more significant than a smaller study. However, effect magnitudes of zero are not encountered very often.

A Brief Historical Note

We are inclined to think of meta-analysis as a recent development, but it is older than the *t*-test, which dates back to 1908! We can simultaneously describe the early history of meta-analysis and provide a classic illustration of the meta-analytic enterprise. In 1904, Karl Pearson collected correlation coefficients (*r*s); there were six of them with values of .58, .58, .60, .63, .66, and .77. The weighted mean *r* of these six correlation coefficients was .64, the unweighted mean *r* was .63, and the median *r* was .61.

Karl Pearson was collecting correlation coefficients because he wanted to know the degree to which inoculation against smallpox saved lives. His own rough-and-ready summary of his meta-analysis of six studies was that there was a .6 correlation between inoculation and survival—a truly huge effect. An *r* of that magnitude can be thought of as the effects of inoculation changing the proportion of people surviving from 20% to 80%.

When Karl Pearson quantitatively summarized six studies of the effects of smallpox inoculation, a meta-analysis was an unusual thing to do. It is unusual no longer. Indeed, there is an explosion of meta-analytic research syntheses such that a rapidly increasing proportion of all reviews of the literature are in the form of quantitative reviews. The trajectory is such that within just a few years virtually all reviews of the literature in the serious scientific journals of our fields will be quantitative reviews—meta-analyses.

REFERENCES

Cooper, H., & Hedges, L. V. (Eds.). (1994). *Handbook of research synthesis.* New York: Russell Sage.

Pearson, K. (1904, Nov. 5). Report on certain enteric fever inoculation statistics. *British Medical Journal,* 1243–1246.

Rosenthal, R. (1991). *Meta-analytic procedures for social research* (Rev. ed.). Newbury Park, CA: Sage.

Wilkinson, L., & The Task Force on Statistical Inference, APA Board of Scientific Affairs. (1999). Statistical methods in psychology journals. *American Psychologist, 54,* 594–604.

Robert Rosenthal
University of California, Riverside
Harvard University

MILLER ANALOGIES TEST

The Miller Analogies Test consists of 100 verbal analogy items (A is to B as C is to D) drawn from a wide range of academic areas. It is a highly regarded test with reasonably substantial prediction of academic success of potential students in graduate schools in a variety of departments. It measures verbal and reasoning ability and has the technical characteristics of being able to differentiate among high-ability students of varying potential. The test has been shown to predict grades in graduate school in a broad range of areas, and seems to serve this purpose as well as any predictor available, except for those fields involving considerable quantitative material. This test has been the subject of considerable research to support its claims. The Miller Analogies Test was carefully built and access to it is strictly controlled. It has a high level of difficulty, and good aids to help users interpret the scores on the test.

J. William Asher
Purdue University

MIND/BODY PROBLEM

For centuries, scholars have struggled to define the nature of the human being. One of the key questions in this struggle deals with mind, body, and the relationship between them.

There is general agreement that the term "body" refers to the material, physical characteristics of the organism, the activities of which can be studied by the traditional empirical methods of science. There is also general agreement that having a body is at least a part of the nature of being human.

It is the mind (psyche, soul)—the question of whether such an entity exists, and how to define it—that is the crux of the mind/body problem. For some thinkers, the immediate experience of self-awareness constitutes evidence that mind is qualitatively different from the physiological body. At one extreme, the terms *mind* and *mental* have been defined as describing a nonphysical, noncorporeal entity. Such an entity would not necessarily function according to the same laws as would matter. Its existence would thus logically permit acknowledgment of the possibilities of life after death, extrasensory perception, and other nonmaterial phenomena, as well as more traditional mental functions such as learning, memory, and intelligence. The laws of such phenomena need not necessarily relate to those of the body.

Being nonmaterial and nonphysical, the mind cannot be verified or studied by means of input from the physical senses. This feature of mind causes the mind—body problem for those who would study human behavior using empirical methods.

In the interest of solving this dilemma, scholars have developed three main approaches to defining mind in a different manner. The first is one of extreme reductionism. From this viewpoint, mind per se does not exist; it is simply a label for a particular level of biological functioning—specifically, the activity of the brain and nervous system.

The second approach tries to relate the qualitatively dissimilar mind and body by learning about the former from empirical knowledge of the latter. This approach is typically illustrated by inferences concerning the nature of mental activities drawn from observation and correlation of externally observable behavioral characteristics. Such an approach, however, leaves the psychologist with the problem of creating a means for relating the internal activity of the mind to the physically observable behavior of the body.

The third approach is in some ways similar to reductionism, but is not as simplistic. In this perspective, neither mind nor body is viewed as an independent entity. Instead, the human being is viewed as a single composite of mind and body, neither of which has existence without the other. Such viewpoints have come to be called "double aspect."

The defining characteristic of these attempts to solve the mind–body problem is whether the particular definition of the mind aspect best lends itself to study of the mind by the method of rationalism, the method of empiricism, or some combination of the two. Thus, the necessity of interpreting psychological and behavioral data in terms of their correlates with the laws of physics and biology (instead of by independent laws of their own) will depend upon the nature of mind and its relationship, if any, to body.

Without being explicit as to their particular philosophical positions on the mind–body problem, neuropsychologists collectively tend to use methodology by which they correlate either brain activity, loci, or neuronal activity patterns with observable behavior, verbal or otherwise. The phenomenal scope of development of modern technology (including MRI, CT scan, etc.) has broadened the range and complexity of behavior comprising the study of neuropsychology.

At the same time, there has been a resurgence of acceptance of "mind" as an appropriate subject of study in and of itself, as well as in its relationship to the body. A particularly salient review article illustrating the scope of mind/body relationships in current neuroscience can be found in DeAngelis (2002).

REFERENCE

DeAngelis, T. (2002). A bright future for PNI. *Monitor on Psychology, 3*(6), 46–50.

Mary E. Reuder

See also: **Behaviorism; Monism/Dualism; Structuralism**

MINDLESSNESS–MINDFULNESS

Mindlessness may be defined as a state of reduced cognitive activity in which the individual processes cues from the environment in a relatively automatic manner without reference to potentially novel (or simply other) aspects of those cues. Mindfulness, in contrast, is a state in which environmental cues are consciously manipulated, and the individual is engaged in actively constructing his or her environment. This is in marked contrast to the mindless state in which one deals with an already constructed environment.

Mindless information processing may arise either after many repetitions of a particular experience or, in certain instances, after a single exposure. In the former case, as an individual's experience with certain situations accumulates, a cognitive structure of the situation is formed that represents its underlying "semantics." The appearance of similar cues on subsequent occasions will then trigger a mindless sequence of behaviors. Once an activity becomes mindless, the underlying semantics may no longer be available for conscious cognitive manipulation or even for examination. In the latter single-exposure case, reduced cognitive activity does not result from reliance on cognitive structures built up over time, but from reliance on a cognitive structure that one has appropriated from another source.

Mindlessness is pervasive. In fact, for the typical individual, *mindfulness* is expected to occur only (1) when significantly more effort is demanded by the situation than was originally demanded, (2) when the external factors in the situation disrupt initiation or the mindless sequence, (3) when external factors prevent the completion of the behavior, or (4) when negative or positive consequences are experienced that are sufficiently discrepant with the consequences of prior enactments of the same behavior.

Although research has addressed reduced levels of cognitive activity (e.g., automaticity, preattentive processing, and overlearning), a newer theory and a newer term are needed for several reasons. First, mindlessness suggests a more molar unit of analysis than has been examined in the past. Second, mindlessness may come about with and without repeated exposure. Third, mindlessness and mindfulness appear to be qualitatively different, not just quantitatively different (e.g., that which has been processed mindlessly may no longer be available for active conscious cognitive work). Fourth, researchers studying automaticity, for example, have focused on the adaptive function automatic processing serves in freeing conscious attention. Although this is certainly true, all research conducted thus far on mindlessness–mindfulness suggests that it may also be quite maladaptive.

The study of mindlessness has been pursued in several domains: its consequence for competent performance, for the perception of deviance, and for the course of physical disease, as well as its implications for the very study of social psychological processes.

Research has revealed that whether interactions between people were face-to-face or through written communication, and whether they were semantically sound or senseless, they occasioned behavior that appeared mindless as long as the structure of the interaction triggered some overlearned sequence of behavior. With respect to potentially relevant information, people failed to hear what was said and to read what was written.

Because the individual components of the activity progressively drop out with each repetition of an activity, the result is not only that the individual is responding to some abstracted structure but also that the steps of the task become relatively inaccessible. Thus research has found that counter to an analysis that ignored the mindless–mindful distinction, a great deal of practice at a task may render the individual more vulnerable to external factors that bring competence into question. When these factors led subjects to question whether they could do the task, groups that were moderately practiced were able to supply the steps or the activity as evidence of competence and, therefore, did not show performance decrements. Unpracticed and overpracticed groups could not supply the task components and, therefore, showed clear debilitation.

Regarding the perception of deviance, it was reasoned, first, that deviance (novelty) breeds mindfulness. If people are typically mindless vis-à-vis normal individuals, then the people who are deviant in any respect may be perceived as deviant in many respects (and, therefore, labeled, avoided, etc.) not so much because of their deviance but because of the thorough scrutiny prompted by the mindful state. Such a close examination of *any* individual would lead one to notice characteristics that typically go unnoticed and to inappropriately judge these characteristics as extreme or unusual. As predicted, it was found that the perception of the deviant was accurate, but the typical characteristics and gestures that were noticed were evaluated as extreme and unusual. This occurred whether the deviance was positive (e.g., a millionaire) or negative (e.g., an ex-mental patient) but did not occur when the same stimulus person was not given a deviant label.

Additional research investigated mindlessness on initial exposure, that is, mindlessness that results from the formation of premature cognitive commitments to information. A premature cognitive commitment is considered premature because the individual makes a commitment to information and freezes its meaning before considering alternative uses to which the information could be put.

Research found that encouraging decision making in nursing home residents resulted in these residents being happier, healthier, and more alert. A follow-up study also found that they lived longer than comparison groups. Initially, it was thought that the experimental group was a group for whom the researchers had induced a sense of control and responsibility. Because the elderly, especially the institutionalized elderly, are a group for whom routine is the rule, where there is very little to think about, the experimental group might be better seen as a thought-encouraged group, which would suggest that mindfulness may be necessary for survival. Its primary effectiveness in health-related issues, however, may be due to its ability to provoke mindfulness.

Work on mindlessness also has been conducted in an educational setting. Here it was found that when information is initially given in absolute language (e.g., "this is an X"), people form premature cognitive commitments to the information and are oblivious to future creative uses of that information. When instead people are instructed conditionally (e.g., "this could be X"), alternative uses of the information remain available to them. Indeed, later work found that many of the beliefs we hold about learning are mindless. For example, we believe we should learn the basics so well that they become second nature. Now we know that "second nature" is mindless. We believe we should keep the object of our attention still when we want to pay attention to it. If we mindfully varied the target of our attention, instead, we would find paying attention to be easier. We also believe we should delay gratification and so we think learning is difficult. In fact, mindful learning is what we do at play. Drawing novel distinctions, the essence of mindfulness, is the essence of engagement and thus is immediately gratifying.

Research also suggests that our mindfulness is visible and has an effect on other people. Research participants were asked to draw a picture and then copy their drawing three times. One group, however, was given a mindfulness instruction and was asked to make the last copy new in very subtle ways that only they would be aware of. The drawings were then presented to raters in a random order. We found that those drawings mindfully created were preferred. In another investigation, children interacted with an adult whose behavior was either scripted or not. Although the essence of the verbal content was the same, those who interacted with a mindless adult showed a drop in self-esteem.

Research on mindlessness and mindfulness has yielded a wealth of results, spanning a number of diverse issues unified by a common theme: the consequences of reduced cognitive activity. The findings thus far suggest that mindlessness–mindfulness is a central dimension in human functioning, the study of which may perhaps even yield basic laws of human behavior.

Ellen J. Langer

See also: **Automatic Thoughts; Mental Imagery**

MINNESOTA MULTIPHASIC PERSONALITY INVENTORY (MMPI-2)

The most widely researched and used clinical assessment instrument is the Minnesota Multiphasic Personality Inventory (MMPI-2). The MMPI was originally published in the 1940s to assess mental health problems in psychiatric and medical settings, and it rapidly became a standard personality instrument in a wide variety of settings (Hathaway & McKinley, 1940). The popularity of the true-false personality inventory was due in large part to its easy-to-use format and to the fact that the scales have well established validity in assessing clinical symptoms and syndromes (Butcher, 1999). The MMPI underwent a major revision in the 1980s, resulting in two forms of the test—an adult version, the MMPI-2 (Butcher, Dahlstrom, Graham, Tellegen, & Kaemmer, 1989), and an adolescent form, MMPI-A (Butcher et al., 1992). The MMPI-2 is a 567-item inventory comprised of symptoms, beliefs, and attitudes in adults above age 18. The MMPI-A is a 467-item version that is used for assessing young people from ages 14 to 18. This discussion will address only the MMPI-2.

Assessing Protocol Validity

Some people in some settings, when taking psychological tests, are motivated to present themselves in ways that do not disclose accurate information about themselves. For example, in cases where a person is being tested to determine sanity in a pretrial criminal evaluation, the person might be exaggerating symptoms. The initial step in MMPI-2 profile interpretation is the important one of determining whether the client has cooperated with the testing and responded in a frank, open manner. A number of indices are available on the MMPI-2 to aid the clinician in determining whether the client's item responses provide key personality information, or whether they are simply reflecting response sets or deceptive motivational patterns that disguise the true feelings and motivations of the client (Baer, Wetter, Nichols, Greene, & Berry, 1995). Several validity scales have been developed to evaluate the client's approach to the test. Four of these assessment strategies will be described here.

The L Scale

The L scale is a measure of the client's willingness to acknowledge personal faults or problems. Individuals who score high on this scale are presenting an overly favorable picture of themselves. High scorers are claiming virtue not found among people in general. The L scale is particularly valuable in situations like personnel screening or some types of court cases, because people in those settings try to put their best foot forward and present themselves as "better" adjusted than they really are.

The K Scale

The K scale was developed to assess test defensiveness or the tendency to minimize problems. This scale, in addition to serving as an index of defensiveness, serves also as a correction factor to compensate for the tendency of some people to deny problems.

The F Scale

The F scale was developed to assess the tendency of some people to exaggerate their problems or "fake" the test by overresponding to extreme items. The items on this scale are very rare or bizarre symptoms. Individuals who endorse a lot of these items tend to exaggerate symptoms on the MMPI-2, perhaps as a way of trying to convince professionals that they need psychological services. As noted earlier, this motivational pattern is also found among individuals with a need to claim problems in order to influence the court in forensic cases. The F scale can be elevated for several possible reasons. The profile could be invalid because the client became confused or disoriented or responded in a random manner. High F scores are also found among clients who are malingering or producing exaggerated responses in order to falsely claim mental illness (Graham, Watts, & Timbrook, 1991).

TRIN and VRIN Scales

Two inconsistency scales for determining profile validity have been developed in the MMPI-2. These scales are based on the analysis of the individual's response to the items in a consistent or inconsistent manner. The scales are comprised of item pairs that involve responses that are semantically inconsistent; for example, a pair of items that contain contradictory content that cannot logically be answered in the same direction if the subject is responding consistently to the content.

Assessing Clinical Symptom Patterns

The assessment of clinical problems is approached in several ways through the self-reported symptoms and behaviors. We will examine three types of scales that comprise the MMPI-2's problem measures: the traditional clinical scales and profile codes, the MMPI-2 content scales, and the specific problems or supplemental scales. A scale is a group of items from the MMPI-2 item pool that have been shown to measure certain symptom patterns or personality traits. Each item cluster or scale is "normed" on a population of normal individuals. This normative group serves as the reference point to which all profiles are compared.

The MMPI-2 Clinical Scales

The authors of the original MMPI developed the clinical scales to empirically group patients into clinical problem types. For example, they developed scales to assess hypochondriasis (The Hs scale), depression (the D scale), hysteria (the Hy scale), psychopathic deviation (the Pd scale), paranoid thinking (the Pa scale), psychasthenia (the Pt scale), schizophrenia (the Sc scale), and mania (the Ma scale). In addition, two other scales were included on the clinical profile to address problems of sex role identification (the Mf scale) and social introversion and extraversion (the Si scale). In addition to interpretation of single clinical scales, elevations on certain scale patterns or configurations of scores (referred to as profile or code types) are interpreted. These profile types result from clients endorsing two or more of the clinical scales.

Content-Based Scales

The MMPI-2 contains a number of scales that assess the content themes an individual endorses in the item pool. The content scales are homogeneous item clusters that assess unitary themes and represent clear communication about problems to the practitioner. There are 15 content scales measuring different symptom areas and problems; examples include Antisocial Practices (ASP), Bizarre Mentation (BIZ), and Family Problems (FAM).

Special Scales

Several supplemental scales have been developed to assess specific problems, such as the potential to develop problems of addiction (the MacAndrew Addiction Scale or MAC-R, and the Addiction Potential Scale or APS) and whether or not the individual acknowledges having problems with drugs or alcohol. The Marital Distress Scale assesses clients' attitudes toward their marital relationship. These special scales allow the practitioner to assess specific problems that are not addressed in the clinical or content scales.

How the MMPI-2 Is Used

There are many diverse, current applications for the MMPI-2 for evaluating individuals across a wide variety of settings. Contemporary uses include: evaluating clients who are being admitted to an inpatient psychiatric facility; understanding problems and possible treatment resistance of clients entering psychotherapy; providing personality information for therapists to employ in giving the client feedback in psychotherapy; assessing possible personality problems of students applying for a graduate clinical psychology program; measuring behavior problems and symptoms in neuropsychological evaluation of a client with severe head injury; appraising personality factors and psychological adjustment in applicants for an airline pilot position; examining persons who are being tried for murder and are claiming to be not guilty by reason of insanity; and using the test as a research instrument to evaluate the psychological changes in a drug trial. There have been over 25 translations and adaptations of the MMPI-2 for use in other countries. The items and scales have shown remarkable robustness when used in other languages and cultures (Butcher, 1996).

In summary, the MMPI-2 is a self-report personality inventory that provides the test user with scores on a number of scales. These scales assess response attitudes, mental health symptoms and personality traits, and special problems that the client might be experiencing. The MMPI-2 has been widely validated and is used in numerous settings around the world.

REFERENCES

Baer, R. A., Wetter, M. W., Nichols, D., Greene, R., & Berry, D. T. (1995). Sensitivity of MMPI-2 validity scales to underreporting of symptoms. *Psychological Assessment, 7,* 419–423.

Butcher, J. N. (1999). *The MMPI-2: A beginner's guide.* Washington, DC: American Psychological Association.

Butcher, J. N. (1996). *International adaptations of the MMPI-2.* Minneapolis: University of Minnesota Press.

Butcher, J. N., Dahlstrom, W. G., Graham, J. R., Tellegen, A. M., & Kaemmer, B. (1989). *Minnesota Multiphasic Personality Inventory-2 (MMPI-2): Manual for administration and scoring.* Minneapolis: University of Minnesota Press.

Butcher, J. N., Williams, C. L., Graham, J. R., Tellegen A., Ben-Porath, Y. S., Archer, R. P., & Kaemmer, B. (1992). *Manual for administration, scoring, and interpretation of the Minnesota Multiphasic Personality Inventory for Adolescents: MMPI-A.* Minneapolis: University of Minnesota Press.

Graham, J. R., Watts, D., & Timbrook, R. (1991). Detecting fake-good and fake-bad MMPI-2 profiles. *Journal of Personality Assessment, 57,* 264–277.

Hathaway, S. R., & McKinley, J. C. (1940). A multiphasic personality schedule (Minnesota): 1. Construction of the schedule. *Journal of Psychology, 10,* 249–254.

James M. Butcher
University of Minnesota

MOB PSYCHOLOGY

Crowds are defined as "co-acting, shoulder-to-shoulder, anonymous, casual, temporary, and unorganized collectivities" (Brown, 1954, p. 840). According to Floyd Allport (1924), "A crowd is a collection of individuals who are all attending and reacting to some common object, their reactions being of a simple prepotent sort and accompanied by strong emotional responses" (p. 292). Crowds can be subdivided according to whether they are active or passive, the former being a *mob* and the latter an *audience.*

Mobs are further classified according to the dominant behavior of participants: (1) aggressive, (2) escape, (3) acquisitive, or (4) expressive. *Aggressive* mobs, which include riot and lynch mobs, involve a display of aggression toward persons or objects. The dominant behavior of *escape* mobs is one of panic, as during a fire in a theater. Orderly escape is not panic. According to Brown (1954), "Panic is emotional and irrational. The escape behavior of the fear-driven mob must either be maladaptive from the point of view of the individual, or, if personally adaptive, the behavior must ruthlessly sacrifice the interests of others who also seek to escape" (p. 858). *Acquisitive* mobs are similar to escape mobs in that both involve a competition for some object that is in short supply—tickets to the theater in the case of the acquisitive mob, and exits from the theater in the case of the escape mob. *Expressive* mobs represent a wastebasket category that includes all mobs not in the first three categories. Included here is behavior that can best be described by the obsolete word *revelous:* behavior that might be displayed at religious revivals, sporting events, and rock music concerts. LaPiere (1938) believed that such behavior provides a release for the psychological tensions created by social life.

While there is no universal agreement among theorists, certain features tend to be attributed to mobs: (1) like-mindedness or "mental homogeneity," and (2) emotionality. Gustav Le Bon (1903), in his classic work, *The Crowd,* explained the mental homogeneity of mobs in terms of *contagion*—a mechanical, disease-like spreading of affect from one member to another. More recent research (Hatfield, Cacioppo, & Rapson, 1994) suggests that contagion is not mechanical, but rather is dependent on a number of conditions. Milgram and Toch (1969) suggest that the mechanism of *convergence* may also account for the seeming mental homogeneity of mobs: like-minded individuals tend to converge and join mobs. Thus, homogeneity precedes rather than follows from membership in the mob. Brown (1954) questioned the homogeneity of aggressive mobs and suggested that the composition of such mobs could be ordered in terms of mob members' readiness to deviate from conventional norms of society. He identified five types of participants, ranging from the "lawless" whose actions "trigger" the mob, to those "supportive onlookers" who stand on the fringes shouting encouragement.

A central issue in the study of mob behavior is determining why restraints that lead to conventional behavior break down when individuals find themselves in a crowd. Two important mechanisms that account for the violation of conventional behavior in crowds are: (1) the loss of responsibility through anonymity, and (2) the impression of universality. Both mechanisms are enhanced by the size of the crowd. Le Bon (1903) and many others have pointed out that aggressive mob members find it easier to act out their impulses because of the difficulty legal authorities have in singling them out and holding them responsible for their actions. Mob participants will feel safer from legal reprisals in large crowds because the sheer size of the crowd will pose impediments to identification and apprehension by the authorities. Allport (1924), and more recently, Turner and Killian (1957) have contended that an individual is swayed by the mob because of a belief that if everyone else is acting in a certain way, the actions cannot be wrong—the mob simply redefines the norm for "correct" behavior. In their "emergent norm theory," Turner and Killian (1957) take issue with the causal role of emotional contagion, and argue instead that people act the way they do in crowds because the crowd helps to define the situation and the appropriate behavior. In the crowd context, the *less* anonymous one is to coacting peers, the greater the conformity to crowd norms. The greater the number of crowd participants, the stronger the impression of universality. Crowd size has different implications for aggressive as opposed to acquisitive and escape mobs. Whereas in aggressive mobs, a larger number of crowd members enhances belief in anonymity and impressions of universality, in acquisitive and escape mobs, a large number of crowd members increases the competition for scarce resources (e.g., theater tickets, escape exits), thereby amplifying crowd responses.

Mob psychology has attracted little attention from social psychologists in recent years, owing in part to methodological difficulties in studying such phenomena. The last edition of the *Handbook of Social Psychology* to feature a chapter on mob psychology was published in 1969. Similarly, recent social psychology textbooks no longer include a chapter on mob psychology; the last one to do so was written by Roger Brown in 1965.

REFERENCES

Allport, F. H. (1924). *Social psychology.* Boston: Houghton Mifflin.

Brown, R. (1954). Mass phenomena. In G. Lindzey (Ed.), *Handbook of social psychology* (Vol. 2, pp. 833–876). Cambridge, MA: Addison-Wesley.

Brown, R. (1965). *Social psychology.* New York: Free Press.

Hatfield, E., Cacioppo, J. T., & Rapson, R. L. (1994). *Emotional contagion.* New York: Cambridge University Press.

LaPiere, R. T. (1938). *Collective behavior.* New York: McGraw-Hill.

Le Bon, G. (1903). *The crowd.* London: Unwin.

Milgram, S., & Toch, H. (1969). Collective behavior: Crowds and social movements. In G. Lindzey & E. Aronson (Eds.), *The handbook of social psychology* (2nd ed., Vol. 4, pp. 507–610). Reading, MA: Addison-Wesley.

Turner, R. H., & Killian, L. M. (1957). *Collective behavior.* Englewood Cliffs, NJ: Prentice Hall.

Martin S. Greenberg
University of Pittsburgh

MODELING

Psychological theories have traditionally emphasized learning through the rewarding and punishing effects that actions produce. Yet, if knowledge and competencies could be acquired only by direct experience, human development would be severely retarded, not to mention unmercifully tedious and perilous. A given culture could never transmit the complexities of its language, mores, social practices, and essential competencies if they had to be shaped laboriously in each new member solely by response consequences, without the benefit of models to exemplify the cultural patterns. Trial-and-error experience can be a tough teacher; errors can be highly costly and some missteps are deadly. The abbreviation of the acquisition process is, therefore, vital for survival as well as for successful human development. Moreover, the constraints of time, resources, and mobility impose severe limits on the situations and activities that can be directly explored for the acquisition of knowledge and competencies.

Humans have evolved an advanced capacity for learning by observation that enables them to develop their knowledge and competencies from information conveyed by modeling influences. Indeed, virtually all types of behavioral, cognitive, and affective learning resulting from direct experience can be achieved vicariously by observing people's behavior and its consequences for them (Bandura, 1986; Rosenthal & Zimmerman, 1978).

Much human learning occurs either deliberately or inadvertently by observance of the actual behavior of others in one's social environment and the consequences they experience. However, a great deal of information about human values, styles of thinking, behavior patterns, and sociostructural opportunities and constraints is gained from modeled styles of behavior portrayed symbolically through the electronic mass media. The growing importance of symbolic modeling lies in its tremendous scope and multiplicative power. A single model can transmit new ways of thinking and behaving to multitudes of people in widely dispersed locales simultaneously. The accelerated development of electronic technologies has vastly expanded the range of models to which members of society are exposed day in and day out. These electronic systems, feeding off telecommunications satellites, have become the dominant vehicle for disseminating symbolic environments. By drawing on these modeled patterns of thought and action, observers transcend the bounds of their immediate environment.

Not only are social practices being widely diffused within societies, but ideas, values, and styles of conduct are being modeled worldwide. The electronic media are coming to play an increasingly influential role in transcultural and sociopolitical change (Bandura, 1997; Braithwaite, 1994). Because the electronic media occupy a large part of people's lives, the study of acculturation in the present electronic age must be broadened to include electronic acculturation.

Mechanisms of Observational Learning

Observational learning is governed by four component subfunctions. *Attentional processes* determine what people selectively observe in the profusion of modeling influences and what information they extract from ongoing modeled events. Observers' preconceptions, cognitive development, interests, and value preferences influence what they explore and how they perceive what is modeled in the social and symbolic environment.

People cannot be much influenced by modeled events if they do not remember them. A second subfunction concerns *cognitive representational processes.* Retention involves an active process of transforming and restructuring information about modeled events into rules and conceptions for generating new patterns of behavior. In the third subfunction in observational learning—the *behavioral production process*—symbolic conceptions are transformed into appropriate courses of action. Skills are usually perfected through a conception-matching process. Conceptions guide the construction and execution of behavior patterns and the behavior is modified as necessary to achieve close correspondence between conception and action.

The fourth major subfunction concerns *motivational processes.* People do not perform everything they learn. Performance of styles of behavior acquired through modeling are influenced by three types of incentive motivators—direct, vicarious, and self-produced. People are more likely to perform observationally-learned behavior if it results in valued outcomes for them than if it has unrewarding or punishing effects. The observed detriments and benefits experienced by others influence the performance of modeled patterns in much the same way as do directly experienced consequences. People are motivated by the successes of others who are similar to themselves, but discouraged from pursuing courses of behavior that they have seen often result in adverse consequences. Personal standards of conduct provide a further source of incentive motivation. People pursue activities they find self-satisfying and that give them a sense of self-worth but reject those of which they personally disapprove.

Abstract Modeling

Social modeling is not merely a process of behavioral mimicry. Highly functional patterns of behavior, which constitute the proven skills and established customs of a culture, may be adopted in essentially the same form as they are exemplified. There is little leeway for improvisation on how to drive automobiles. However, in many activities, subskills must be improvised to suit different situations. Modeling influences can convey rules for generative and innovative behavior as well. For example, an individual may see others confront moral conflicts involving different matters yet apply the same moral standard to each of them. In abstract modeling, observers extract the rules or standards governing specific judgments differing in content but embodying the same underlying rule. Once people extract the rules, they can use them to judge things and generate new courses of behavior that fit the prototype but go beyond the examples they have seen or heard. Evidence that generative rules of thought and behavior can be created through abstract modeling attests to the broad scope of observational learning (Bandura, 1986; Rosenthal & Zimmerman, 1978).

Modeling can contribute to creativeness in several ways. Originality largely involves synthesizing experiences into new ways of thinking and doing things. When exposed to models of differing styles of thinking and behaving, observers often vary in what they adopt from the different sources and thereby create new blends of personal characteristics that differ from the individual models. Modeling influences that exemplify new perspectives and innovative styles of thinking also foster creativity by weakening conventional mind-sets.

Motivational, Emotional, and Valuational Effects

In addition to cultivating competencies, modeling influences can alter incentive motivation (Bandura, 1986). Seeing others achieve desired outcomes by their efforts can instill motivating outcome expectations in observers that they can secure similar benefits for comparable performances. These motivational effects rest on observers' judgments that they have the efficacy to produce the modeled attainments and that comparable accomplishments will bring them similar beneficial outcomes. By the same token, seeing others punished for engaging in certain activities can instill negative outcome expectations that serve as disincentives.

People are easily aroused by the emotional expressions of others. What gives significance to vicarious emotional influence is that observers can acquire lasting attitudes and emotional and behavioral proclivities toward persons, places, or things that have been associated with modeled emotional experiences. They learn to fear the things that frightened models, to dislike what repulsed them, and to like what gratified them (Bandura, 1992). Fears and intractable phobias are ameliorated by modeling influences that convey information about coping strategies for exercising control over the things that are feared (Bandura, 1997; Williams, 1992). Values can similarly be developed and altered vicariously by repeated exposure to modeled preferences. The actions of models can also serve as social prompts that activate, channel, and support previously learned behavior. Thus, the types of models that prevail within a social milieu partly determine which human qualities, from among many alternatives, are selectively encouraged.

During the course of their daily lives, people have direct contact with only a small sector of the physical and social environment. In their daily routines, they travel the same routes, visit the same familiar places, and see the same group of friends and associates. As a result, their conceptions of social reality are greatly influenced by modeled representations of society in the mass media (Gerbner, 1972). The more their conceptions of the world around them depend on portrayals in the media's symbolic environment, the greater the media's social impact (Ball-Rokeach & De-Fleur, 1976).

Social Diffusion through Symbolic Modeling

Much of the preceding discussion has been concerned with modeling at the individual level. As previously noted, the electronic media are coming to play an increasingly powerful role in transcultural change. In this broader function, symbolic modeling usually serves as the principal conveyer of innovations to widely dispersed areas, especially in early phases of diffusion. Modeling instructs people in new ideas and social practices and designates their functional value.

A number of factors, including perceived self-efficacy to execute the modeled patterns, possession of necessary resources, outcome expectations concerning the costs and benefits of the new styles of behavior in the new milieu, and perceived opportunities and impediments, determine whether people will adopt and put into practice what they have learned observationally (Bandura, 1986, 1997).

People are enmeshed in networks of relationship. They are linked, not only directly, by personal relationships. Because acquaintanceships overlap different network clusters, people become linked to each other indirectly by interconnected ties. These multi-linked social networks provide diffusion paths for the spread of new ideas, lifestyle patterns, and social practices (Granovetter, 1983; Rogers & Kincaid, 1981).

REFERENCES

Bandura, A. (1986). *Social foundations of thought and action: A social cognitive theory.* Englewood Cliffs, NJ: Prentice Hall.

Bandura, A. (1992). Exercise of personal agency through the self-efficacy mechanism. In R. Schwarzer (Ed.), *Self-efficacy: Thought control of action* (pp. 3–38). Washington, DC: Hemisphere.

Bandura, A. (1997). *Self-efficacy: The exercise of control.* New York: Freeman.

Bandura, A., Ross, D., & Ross, S. A. (1963). Imitation of film-mediated aggressive models. *Journal of Abnormal and Social Psychology, 66,* 3–11.

Braithwaite, J. (1994). A sociology of modeling and the politics of empowerment. *British Journal of Sociology, 45,* 445–479.

Gerbner, G. (1972). Communication and social environment. *Scientific American, 227,* 153–160.

Granovetter, M. (1983). The strength of weak ties—A network theory revisited. In R. Collins (Ed.), *Sociological theory 1983* (pp. 201–233). San Francisco: Jossey-Bass.

Rogers, E. M., & Kincaid, D. L. (1981). *Communication networks: Toward a new paradigm for research.* New York: Free Press.

Rosenthal, T. L., & Zimmerman, B. J. (1978). *Social learning and cognition.* New York: Academic Press.

Williams, S. L. (1992). Perceived self-efficacy and phobic disability. In R. Schwarzer (Ed.), *Self-efficacy: Thought control of action* (pp. 149–176). Washington, DC: Hemisphere.

Albert Bandura
Stanford University

MONISM/DUALISM

Monism/dualism refers to a traditional classification of the various types of solutions proposed for the mind–body problem. Such solutions assume that the human being comprises either a single, unified entity (monism) or two qualitatively different, independent entities (dualism). Adherents of each type of solution also tend to differ in epistemology. Monists tend to view empiricism as the primary (even the only) acceptable method of knowledge. Dualists, on the other hand, accept empiricism and rationalism as equally appropriate and valid, each in its own sphere.

Because monists tend to equate knowledge with empiricism, all of their definitions try to equate or reduce mind (or mental functions) to the activity of the brain and nervous system. Thus, in effect, mind and body become one. Mind is defined as being of the materialistic order of things. In the field of psychology, this position gives neuroscience a central focus of importance in the understanding and explanation of behavior. Many neuropsychologists thus view the study of the brain and nervous system as the primary approach to understanding human behavior.

Dualists, in contrast, are faced with the problem of relating the activities of the nonmaterial mind and the material body. Two primary patterns of dualism have prevailed throughout history. The first are the interactionist theories, of which the views of Descartes are considered classic. Modern dualists have not had much success in replacing Descartes's explanation in terms of modern neurological knowledge.

A form of dualism that avoids the difficulty of explaining an interaction is psychophysical parallelism. Mind and body are viewed as acting in concert such that events that affect the one, affect the other; thus, knowledge of one provides information about the other. The isomorphism of mental activity and brain function, as well as the applications of the concepts of topology and field theory by Gestalt psychology, represent a modern version of psychophysical parallelism in present-day thinking.

A key element of dualistic positions as they affect psychology is that when the mind is defined as being a totally separate entity from the materialistic body, conceptualizations of the activity of the mind are not constrained by the laws of materialism. Thus, although mental activity may parallel physiological (or physical) activity, there is no necessity for it to do so. Laws unique to mental activity become acceptable and appropriate. The study of cognitive activity without concern for or consideration of any underlying nervous system activity has led to many attempts to develop such laws of behavior.

Although it is self-evident that the relating of psychological, especially cognitive, behavior to physiological activity implies the taking of a position on the monism-dualism problem, few neuropsychologists (either clinical or research) ever explicitly state a position. However, since the days when Watsonian behaviorism made its great impact, American psychology has been heavily monistic, and the monistic position still prevails in this discipline. Nevertheless, the rise in popularity of existentialism, humanism, and other self-oriented philosophies and their effects on the thinking of psychologists, particularly psychotherapists, have led to revived interest in problems that logically require dualistic positions. Such areas of concern as imageless thought, life after death, and mental telepathy have aroused the interest of serious scientists. Concomitantly, there has arisen new interest in dualism.

Mary E. Reuder

See also: **Behaviorism; Mind/Body Problem; Structuralism**

MORAL DEVELOPMENT

Moral development involves the process by which persons internalize and orient their behavior according to socially sanctioned rules. Three conceptually distinguishable aspects of this developmental process have been highlighted: moral judgment (how one reasons about moral situations), moral behavior (how one acts), and moral emotions (what one feels).

Moral Judgment

Early in the twentieth century, psychologists like James Mark Baldwin and William McDougall began to study the process of moral development. Much contemporary research, however, has been inspired by the cognitive-developmental theory of Jean Piaget (1932). According to Piaget's two-stage account, children progress from a heteronomous morality of constraint to an autonomous morality of cooperation. Although the stages differ on a number of dimensions—including employment of expiatory punishment versus restitution, belief in immanent justice, and unilateral obedience to authority—most research has examined whether moral judgments are based on objective consequences or subjective intentions. In general, research supports an age-related shift from an objective to a more subjective (intentional) conception of moral responsibility.

Kohlberg (1958) extended Piaget's two-stage view by postulating that moral rules and principles are progressively internalized throughout adolescence and into adulthood. The theory comprises three general levels of moral reasoning: preconventional, conventional, and postconventional morality. Each level, in turn, is divided into two specific stages (Kohlberg, 1958).

Preconventional morality is externally oriented. At Stage 1, what is right is defined by avoiding punishment and obeying authority. At Stage 2, hedonistic acts that satisfy personal needs determine what is right. Moral decisions at the *conventional* level are mediated by internalized rules and values. At Stage 3, interpersonal conformity is emphasized; one adheres to rules in order to please and be approved of by significant others. At Stage 4, right is defined in terms of doing one's duty and maintaining the existing social order.

Postconventional reasoners emphasize moral principles with applicability and validity independent of a specific authority or social order. At Stage 5, moral decisions reflect a personal obligation to abide by contractual commitments, including implicit societal contracts. People understand the relativistic nature of rules and laws, but realize the need for contractual agreements to ensure equal justice and protect individual rights. However, rational considerations about social utility may necessitate subsequent changes and revisions of existing laws. At Stage 6, moral decisions are grounded in self-selected rational ethical principles considered to be universally valid.

The central tenet of Kohlberg's formulation—namely, a fixed moral developmental sequence—has been supported by empirical investigations. In particular, research supports the supposition that preconventional morality is a prerequisite for conventional reasoning and both must precede the development of postconventional morality (Colby, Kohlberg, Gibbs, & Lieberman, 1983; Walker, 1989). However, the postconventional stages may not necessarily be found in all samples of adolescents or adults, especially Stage 6, which has been deleted in the revised scoring method (Colby & Kohlberg, 1987).

Critics have underscored the role that social-cultural factors may play in promoting postconventional reasoning, especially experiences within the context of a constitutionally based system of justice. Although Kohlberg's model may not provide *the* universal view of a moral person, it does seem to be relevant to people living in countries with constitutionally based legal systems.

Moral Behavior

The empirical link between moral cognition and action has been elusive: people can exhibit the same behavior for different reasons, and individuals at the same level of moral reasoning may act in different ways. Although some linkages have been reported, relationships between moral reasoning and behavior may not be linear (e.g., Hann, Smith, & Block, 1968). If moral behavior is mediated by moral reasoning, it may be necessary to focus on intraindividual variation over time and situations. For example, knowing that people are conventional moral reasoners may not be sufficient to accurately predict their behavior; the specific normative rules or expectations they hold would also need to be identified. Other relevant factors may include knowing how personally committed people are to translating their reasoning into action and the extent to which they possess the self-regulatory resources to do so.

In the 1920s, a more fundamental issue of moral behavior was addressed by Hartshorne and May. They devised behavioral measures of the extent to which participants would resist the temptation to lie, cheat, and steal in experimental settings. Correlational analyses provided little evidence for a general personality trait of honesty; they advanced the position that moral behavior was situation-specific. Research has continued to support the situation-specificity doctrine of moral behavior (Bersoff, 1999). Of course, not all people yield when confronted by situational temptations and external pressures. Recent research has highlighted the role that individual differences in self-regulatory resources may play in impulse control, temptation resistance, and self-restraint (Baumeister, Heatherton, & Tice, 1994).

Moral Emotion

The psychoanalytic theory of guilt-motivated morality was presented by Sigmund Freud. Briefly, Freud contended that children experience Oedipal/Electra feelings. Fear of paternal retaliation prompts them to introject the same-sexed parent's rules and prohibitions: the superego or conscience is thereby formed. In subsequent situations, children experience self-punishment or guilt when tempted to violate these internalized rules. Research indicates, however, that power-assertive parental practices are associated with an externalized morality: children comply with normative standards because they fear detection and/or punishment (Hoffman, 1994). A more internalized morality results when parental discipline is coupled with explanations about the harmful consequences of children's behavior for others. Such practices may contribute to moral development by enhancing children's tendencies to anticipate the consequences of their actions and to empathically experience another's emotional state (Hoffman, 1994).

The development of postconventional moral reasoning and prudent, inner-directed moral behavior are both associated with principles and explanations that emphasize individual rights and the negative impact that misdeeds have on others. Knowing that people are postconventional moral reasoners, however, may not be sufficient for predicting how they will behave in moral situations. The specific principles they are personally committed to, their motivation to implement them, and whether or not they have sufficient self-regulatory resources may also need to be taken into account.

REFERENCES

Baldwin, J. M. (1897). *Social and ethical interpretations in mental development: A study in social psychology.* New York: Macmillan. (Reprinted, New York: Arno Press, 1973)

Baumeister, R. F., Heatherton, T. F., & Tice, D. M. (1994). *Losing control: How and why people fail at self-regulation.* San Diego: Academic Press.

Bersoff, D. (1999). Why good people sometimes do bad things: Motivated reasoning and unethical behavior. *Personality and Social Psychology Bulletin, 25,* 28–38.

Colby, A., & Kohlberg, L. (1987). *The measurement of moral judgment* (Vols. 1–2). New York: Cambridge University Press.

Colby, A., Kohlberg, L., Gibbs, J., & Lieberman, M. (1983). A longitudinal study of moral judgment. *Monographs of the Society for Research in Child Development, 48*(1–2, Serial No. 200).

Freud, S. (1962/1930). *Civilization and its discontents.* New York: Norton.

Funder, D. C., & Block, J. (1989). The role of ego-control, ego-resiliency, and IQ in delay of gratification in adolescence. *Journal of Personality and Social Psychology, 57,* 1041–1050.

Hann, N., Smith, B., & Block, J. (1968). Moral reasoning of young adults. *Journal of Personality and Social Psychology, 10,* 183–201.

Hartshorne, H., & May, M. A. (1928–1930). *Studies in the nature of character: Vol. I. Studies in deceit; Vol. II. Studies in self-control; Vol. III. Studies in the organization of character.* New York: Macmillan.

Hoffman, M. L. (1994). Discipline and internalization. *Developmental Psychology, 30,* 26–28.

Kohlberg, L. (1958). *The development of modes of moral thinking and choice in the years 10 to 16.* Unpublished doctoral dissertation, University of Chicago.

McDougall, W. (1926/1908). *An introduction to social psychology.* Boston: Luce.

Piaget, J. (1965/1932). *The moral judgment of the child.* New York: Free Press.

Walker, L. J. (1989). A longitudinal study of moral reasoning. *Child Development, 60,* 157–166.

Michael D. Berzonsky
State University of New York, Cortland

See also: **Human Development; Self-Control**

MORPHINE

Morphine is the principal alkaloid of opium, and is used for the control of moderate to severe pain. The word *opium* itself is derived from the Greek name for juice, the drug being obtained from the juice of the poppy, *Papaver somniferum.* Opium contains more than 20 distinct alkaloids. In 1806, Setürner reported the isolation of an opium alkaloid that he named morphine after Morpheus, the Greek god of dreams.

Morphine and other morphinelike drugs (heroin, codeine, or methadone) produce analgesia primarily through their interaction with opioid receptors located in the central nervous system and periphery. The existence of multiple opioid receptors was proposed in 1977 and confirmed by various studies. Soon after the demonstration of these opioid receptors, three classes of endogenous opioid peptides were isolated and identified: the enkephalins, the endorphins, and the dynorphins (Gutstein & Akil, 2001).

Although there are now many compounds with pharmacological properties similar to those produced by morphine, this "old" drug remains the most useful in clinical settings. However, in spite of its efficacy, morphine treatment has some associated problems. Side effects such as nausea, vomiting, constipation, drowsiness, confusion, and the variability in analgesic response between patients are common clinical problems during morphine therapy, with respiratory depression being a less frequent but more serious side effect (Martindale, 2002). Although the development of dependence and/or tolerance is not generally a problem when morphine is used in patients with opioid-sensitive pain, the possibility of tolerance, dependence, and addiction with long-term use may complicate its clinical use and can create barriers to its adequate prescription (Schafer et al., 2001). In fact, the development of tolerance, physical dependence, and addiction with repeated use is a characteristic feature of all the opioid drugs. Tolerance can be defined as a loss of potency of a drug after its repeated administration, so that doses have to be increased to achieve the same effect. Drug addiction of the morphine type is a state arising from repeated administration of morphine or morphinelike drugs (heroin, pethidine, etc.); it is characterized by an overwhelming need to continue taking the drug or one with similar properties. Abrupt withdrawal of morphine or morphinelike drugs from persons physically dependent on them precipitates a withdrawal syndrome (Martindale, 2002). However, when morphine and morphinelike drugs are used correctly in appropriate doses to treat morphine-sensitive pain, tolerance, dependence, and severe side effects are not a clinical problem (McQuay, 1989). What happens when morphine or opioids are given to someone in pain is different from what happens when they are given to someone not in pain (McQuay, 1999). In patients, tolerance may be due to a disease progression or increased nociception, and they may develop a drug-seeking behavior that represents an attempt to get appropriate pain relief (Schug, Merry, & Acland, 1991).

During morphine treatment, common side effects such as nausea, constipation, and drowsiness are usually controlled by appropriate measures. What complicates morphine use in the clinical setting is the variability between patients in their pharmacological responses. Careful evaluation of the morphine dose required to alleviate the pain is needed, given that the effective dose varies not only from patient to patient but also from time to time (because of disease progression and/or tolerance). The correct dose for the patient is that which gives good pain relief during the interval between doses, without producing unacceptable side effects. Another fact that complicates morphine pharmacology is its *pharmacokinetics:* what the body does to the drug. Pharmacokinetics deals with absorption of the drug from the site of administration (oral, rectal, intramuscular), its distribution into the body, its biotransformation, and its elimination from the body. Morphine is a very versatile drug because it can be administered by many different routes (oral, parenteral, spinal). When administered orally, it undergoes extensive biotransformation or metabolism, mainly in the liver. Biotransformation of morphine also occurs when it is administered by other routes, but to a lesser extent. For this reason, oral doses must be much larger than parenteral doses to achieve the equivalent effect. The biotransformation of morphine produces two major and important metabolites, morphine-3-glucuronide (M3G) and morphine-6-glucuronide (M6G). These metabolites are found in the plasma and cerebrospinal fluid after administration of morphine. M6G has pharmacological activity and a more potent antinociceptive effect than morphine. M3G produces stimulatory effects but is devoid of analgesic activity. There are, however, conflicting reports of its effects (antagonism) on morphine and M6G analgesia (Smith, Watt, & Cramond, 1990; Suzuki, Kalso, & Rosenberg, 1993; Faura, Olaso, Garcia Cabanes, & Horga, 1996). It has been suggested that these metabolites may contribute to the global effects of morphine, but the pharmacological activity and real contribution of morphine metabolites remains a mystery despite many years of investigation (Faura, Collins, Moore, & McQuay, 1998).

Given the pharmacological activity of the morphine metabolites and their possible contribution to the global effects of morphine, it is important to specify the factors that can modify the morphine-metabolite relationship. Age of the patient, presence of renal impairment, and route of administration are important factors in the kinetics of morphine and its metabolites. There is evidence that newborn children produce morphine metabolites at a lower rate than children or adults, mainly because of their functional immaturity. Morphine metabolites are eliminated from the body mainly via the kidneys, which is why the presence of renal impairment results in their high plasma concentrations. Intravenous, intramuscular, and rectal administration of morphine result in lower metabolite production than does oral administration (Faura, Collins, Moore, & McQuay, 1998). Although some factors affecting the kinetics of morphine and its metabolites have been determined, the cause of variation in the pharmacological response of morphine remains unknown (Bowsher, 1993).

The available information on morphine confirms that despite the relative lack of knowledge about its pharmacology, this old drug is still the standard against which other analgesic drugs are compared. Its efficacy and safety when properly used make morphine the drug of choice for moderate to severe opioid-sensitive pain.

REFERENCES

Bowsher, D. (1993). Paradoxical pain. *British Medical Journal, 306,* 473–474.

Faura, C. C., Olaso, M. J., Garcia Cabanes, C., & Horga, J. F. (1996). Lack of morphine-6-glucuronide antinociception after morphine treatment. Is morphine-3-glucuronide involved? *Pain, 65,* 25–30.

Faura, C. C., Collins, S. L., Moore, R. A., & McQuay, H. J. (1998). Systematic review of factors affecting the ratios of morphine and its major metabolites. *Pain, 74,* 43–53.

Gutstein, H. B., & Akil, H. (2001). Opioid analgesics. In Goodman & Gilman, *The pharmacological basis of therapeutics* (10th ed, pp. 569–619). New York: McGraw-Hill.

Martindale. (2002). In S. C. Sweetman (Ed.), *The complete drug reference* (33rd ed., pp. 56–59). London: Pharmaceutical Press.

McQuay, H. J. (1989). Opioids in chronic pain. *British Journal of Anaesthesia, 63,* 213–226.

McQuay, H. J. (1999). Opioids in pain management. *The Lancet, 357,* 2229–2232.

Schafer, P. M., Gonzalez Mendez, E., Gjeltema, K., et al. (2001). Opioids for chronic nonmalignant pain. Attitudes and practices in primary care physicians in the UCSF/Stanford Collaborative Research Network. *Journal of Family Practice, 50,* 145–151.

Schug, S. A., Merry, A. F., & Acland, R. H. (1991). Treatment principles for the use of opioids in pain of nonmalignant origin. *Drugs, 42,* 228–239.

Smith, M. T., Watt, J. A., & Cramond, T. (1990). Morphine-3-glucuronide a potent antagonist of morphine analgesia. *Life Sciences, 47,* 579–585.

Suzuki, N., Kalso, E., & Rosenberg, P. H. (1993). Intrathecal morphine-3-glucuronide does not antagonize spinal antinociception by morphine or morphine-6-glucuronide in rats. *European Journal of Pharmacology, 249,* 247–250.

Clara C. Faura Giner
Universidad Miguel Hernandez
Alicante, Spain

MORPHOLOGY

Morphemes are the meaningful elements that comprise the internal or sublexical structure of words. Work on the role of sound structure in language processing is common, but only recently have psychologists begun to examine morphemes as units of sublexical processing. Much of the work on morphemes (morphology) focuses on how language users store and understand words composed of more than one morpheme (complex words) and how they create new ones. Compare the English words *indent, indented,* and *indenture.* There is no way to break down the word *indent* into smaller parts whose meanings together make up the meaning of the whole word, but *indented* and *indenture* each consist of the base morpheme, *indent,* and an affix, either *ed* or *ure.* Most complex words can be described in terms of rules for combining components. In the case at hand, the rules generate a past tense or a nominal from the base morpheme. However, not all complex words can easily be described in these terms. For example, we can tell that the word *forget* consists of the prefix *for* and the base *get,* because *forget* has the same irregular past tense form as *get: got.* Yet there is no rule in modern English forming *forgot* from *get.*

The final component of *fullness* is the suffix *ness.* Its function is to form a noun. It is joined together with the first component, the base adjective *full,* to form a noun with the predictable meaning "condition of being full." The same suffix occurs in many other nouns derived from adjectives (e.g., *fondness, fussiness*) and can also be used to form novel words like *nerdiness* or *emotiveness* whose meanings are understood easily by speakers of English. The fact that nouns like *walkness* or *tableness* are awkward also tells us that there are restrictions on how morphemes combine. Morphemes that appear before or after the base morpheme are called affixes (prefixes and suffixes, respectively). Affixes may vary quite widely in their productivity, the likelihood that they will be used to create new words. Compare the two English suffixes *-ure* and *-ness,* both of which form nouns from adjectives (e.g., *indenture* and *sadness*). The first suffix is completely unproductive in modern English; no new word with this suffix has been added to the language in centuries. The second is highly productive: innovations are common.

Languages differ greatly in the prevalence of complex words and in the way in which morphemes combine to make complex words. Some languages (e.g., Chinese) have very little in the way of combining morphology. Others (e.g., Turkish) are famous for their complex morphology, combining many morphemes within a single word. Rules for combining morphemes also vary across languages. In Serbian or English, for example, morphemes are linked linearly (e.g., *un+forget+ful+ness*). In Hebrew, morphemes can be interleaved with one another (e.g., N-F-L combines with -a-a- to form NaFaL, meaning "he fell," and with -o-e- to form NoFeL, meaning "he falls").

Suffixes such as *ure* and *ness* are examples of derivational affixes, whereas *ed* is an inflectional morpheme. Adding a derivational affix forms a new word and often changes the word class of the base morpheme, as in the *indent, indenture* example above. Derivational formations tend to be semantically somewhat unpredictable, as is also true with this example. Compare, for example the relation of *confess-confession* to *profess-profession.* Inflectional morphology is concerned with the different forms that a word may take, depending on its role in a sentence. English is quite poor inflectionally, but in many other languages (e.g., Serbian or Swahili) each noun, verb, and adjective will have a large number of inflected forms.

Words that are morphologically related tend to have similar orthographic and phonological forms as well as similar meanings. Knowledge about words comprises the mental lexicon. A major research question for psycholinguists is whether morphological knowledge is explicitly represented in the mental lexicon or whether it falls out of the conjoint but nonadditive contributions of similarity from form and meaning. Among theorists who think that morphology is explicitly represented, some describe morphological knowledge in terms of lexical representations that are decomposed into constituent morphemes. Others describe morphological knowledge in terms of a principle of lexical organization among full forms that are related. Another point of discussion is whether all word forms, or only those forms that are irregular with respect to either form or meaning, are stored as wholes in the mental lexicon. When regularity is defined with respect to form, we can ask whether words that undergo a change such as *forget-forgot* are represented differently from words such as *forfeit* whose past tense form (*forfeited*) is regular. When regularity is defined in terms of meaning, we can ask whether the meaning of the base morpheme must be semantically transparent with respect to the complex form in order to be represented in the lexicon in terms of its morphological structure. Similarly, we can ask whether inflected and derived forms are represented in the same manner.

In the psycholinguistic literature, a classical task for exploring morphological knowledge is the lexical decision task. Letter strings are presented visually and skilled readers must decide whether each is a real word. Decision latencies tend to be faster for words composed from frequent than from less frequent components. When words are presented in pairs, a prime and then a target, the temporal interval can vary. Sometimes prime and target are presented in immediate succession at varying intervals. Other times there are intervening items. Decision latencies to the target as a function of the type of prime are measured.

Whether or not reduced similarity in spelling or pronunciation between *forget-forgot* type relatives diminishes the magnitude of facilitation to targets relative to *indent-indented* type pairs appears to depend on the timing relation between them. With respect to meaning, results in Hebrew, Dutch, and Serbian have shown morphological facilitation with semantically opaque as well as transparent morphological relatives. However, there is some evidence that at long (250 milliseconds) but not at very short (50 milliseconds) time intervals, morphological facilitation is greater after semantically transparent morphological relatives than after those that are semantically more opaque. Similarly, facilitation for targets tends to be greater after inflectional than after derivational relatives.

Morphemes and their properties play a critical role in word recognition. Morphology cannot be expressed in terms of similarity of form or meaning alone, although facilitation among morphological relatives is sensitive to similarity of form and meaning. Psychologists study morphology for what it reveals about how the components of words (sublexical structure) contribute to word identification and production.

SUGGESTED READING

Aronoff, M. (1994). *Morphology by itself.* Cambridge, MA: MIT Press.

Aronoff, M., & Fudeman, K. (2003). *Fundamentals of morphology.* Oxford: Blackwell.

Bauer, L. (1983). *English word-formation.* Cambridge, UK: Cambridge University Press.

Bauer, L. (2001). *Morphological productivity.* Cambridge, UK: Cambridge University Press.

Booij, G., & van Marle, J. (annual). *Yearbook of morphology.* Dordrecht: Kluwer.

Feldman, L. B. (Ed.). (1995). *Morphological aspects of language processing.* Hillsdale, NJ: Erlbaum.

Frost, R., & Grainger, J. (Eds.). (2000). *Language and cognitive processes.* London: Taylor and Francis.

Jarema, G., Kehayia, E., & Libben, G. (Eds.). (1999). *Brain and language.* New York: Academic Press.

Matthews, P. H. (1991). *Morphology* (2nd ed.). Cambridge, UK: Cambridge University Press.

Sandra, D., & Taft, M. (Eds.). (1994). *Morphological structure, lexical representation and lexical access.* Hove, UK: Erlbaum.

Spencer, A. (1991). *Morphological theory.* Oxford: Blackwell.

Zwicky, A., and Spencer, A. (Eds.). (1997). *Handbook of morphology.* Oxford: Blackwell.

Laurie B. Feldman
The University at Albany, State University of New York

Mark Aronoff
Stony Brook University, State University of New York

See also: **Phonemes**

MOTION PARALLAX

Various types of information contribute to the visual perception of depth, including binocular disparity—difference between the retinal images due to the separation of the eyes—and pictorial cues such as relative size and interposition. Relative size refers to the difference in visual size according to the distance from the observer of objects of known physical size, while interposition refers to the fact that a relatively close object can partially or totally hide a more distant object. Another source of information derives from the observer's motion. This is *motion parallax*—systematic visual motion of the static environment. The direction of visual motion is opposite to the observer's motion for objects in front of fixation and in the same direction for objects behind fixation; rates of visual motion increase with increasing distance from fixation. Motion parallax also applies to a surface slanted in depth: The visual geometry transforms with the observer's motion, according to the degree of slant. Hence, visual motion is potentially important in the perception of depth. Indeed, this belief has been developed and emphasized in "ecological" treatises (Gibson, 1966).

Evidence that motion parallax is effective comes from simulations: The observer rests his or her head on a movable chin support, while viewing monocularly an array of computer-generated dots. When the observer is stationary, the array appears as a single surface in the plane of the computer screen, as might be expected. However, moving the head generates simulated motion parallax in the array. Even minimal head motion elicits a compelling perception that the display consists of surfaces varying in distance from the observer (Rogers & Graham, 1982).

Does this conclusion apply to *real* stimuli—objects and surfaces truly varying in depth? As indicated above, real stimuli convey pictorial information based, for example, on their believed physical sizes and shapes. An Ames' "distorted-room" stimulus is rich in misleading pictorial information: It is constructed from trapezoidal surfaces slanted in depth to appear as the interior of a cube when viewed from a peephole in the front surface (Ittleson, 1952). Gehringer and Engel (1986) tested an assertion made by Gibson (1966) that the illusion is destroyed if the front surface is removed to permit head motion. In fact, motion had a much weaker effect in reducing the illusion than did binocular viewing, a result corroborated by research in which observers viewed single trapezoidal or triangular surfaces differing in their slant-in-depth (Reinhardt-Rutland, 1996).

How is the conflicting evidence from simulations and real stimuli to be reconciled? A first point is that visual motion is ambiguous: The moving observer may be viewing static objects, the static observer may be viewing moving objects, or the moving observer may be viewing moving objects (Reinhardt-Rutland, 1988). To resolve this ambiguity, effective motion parallax requires *cumulative* processing over time. In contrast, pictorial information is available for *immediate* processing, while binocular disparity relies on *simultaneous* comparison of the retinal images. Studies of real stimuli entail competition between motion and pictorial information; while motion parallax may have a role, rapid judgment is based on pictorial information. This even applies in a motion-rich activity such as driving, where depth judgments of child pedestrians or small automobiles may be wrong because pictorial information based on the sizes of "average" pedestrians and motor vehicles is applied inappropriately (Stewart, Cudworth, & Lishman, 1993).

Depth-from-motion simulations probably rely on the motion of the dots introducing information that is normally conveyed pictorially. An edge conveys the existence of two surfaces; the surface of one side of the edge is at a different distance than the surface of the other side of the edge. Edges are specified pictorially, even by something as simple as a line in a pen-and-ink drawing, but may also be defined by a spatial discontinuity in depth-from-motion simulations. Now an edge does not convey which surface is the closer; other information is required. Rogers and Rogers (1992) suggest that early depth-from-motion simulations had inadvertently included pictorial information in the display that allowed the observer to decide which parts of the array of dots appeared closer and which parts further away. When this pictorial information was eliminated, they found that the depth relationships became ambiguous, confirming that dot motion may be restricted to specifying edges in simulations.

Another form of pictorial information, interposition, is enhanced by motion. For a moving observer, the pattern of interposition changes. At one point in the observer's motion, both objects may be fully visible. At another point, the more distant object may become partially or totally occluded. The changing pattern of occlusion varies systematically with the observer's motion, providing unambiguous information for relative order in depth (Gibson, 1966).

To conclude, motion parallax has a role in depth perception, but it is less important than some have asserted. Its limitation is that it requires time-consuming cumulative processing, while other sources of depth information are available for immediate processing. However, the observer's motion generates information that enhances pictorial information. It is this that may make the observer's motion important in depth perception.

REFERENCES

Gehringer, W. L., & Engel, E. (1986). Effect of ecological viewing conditions on the Ames' distorted room illusion. *Journal of Experimental Psychology: Human Perception and Performance, 12,* 181–185.

Gibson, J. J. (1966). *The senses considered as perceptual systems.* Boston: Houghton-Mifflin.

Ittleson, W. (1952). *The Ames demonstrations in perception.* Princeton, NJ: Princeton University Press.

Reinhardt-Rutland, A. H. (1988). Induced motion in the visual modality: An overview. *Psychological Bulletin, 103,* 57–72.

Reinhardt-Rutland, A. H. (1996). Depth judgments of triangular surfaces during moving monocular viewing. *Perception, 25,* 27–35.

Rogers, B., & Graham, M. (1982). Similarities between motion parallax and stereopsis in human depth perception. *Vision Research, 22,* 261–270.

Rogers, S., & Rogers, B. (1992). Visual and nonvisual information disambiguate surfaces specified by motion parallax. *Perception and Psychophysics, 52,* 446–452.

Stewart, D., Cudworth, C. J., & Lishman, J. R. (1993). Misperception of time-to-collision by drivers in pedestrian accidents. *Perception, 22,* 1227–1244.

Anthony H. Reinhardt-Rutland
University of Ulster at Jordanstown
Newtownabbey, Northern Ireland

MOTIVATED FORGETTING

All of us forget to remember, at least occasionally. Whether it is the name of a relative, an item to purchase at the store, or, more rarely, entire events from our lives, we have all experienced the phenomenon of forgetting. Unlike a digital camcorder, the human memory system does not encode and retrieve data in a mechanical fashion. Only a portion of what is available to our senses is stored in memory (long-term storage), and only a portion of what is stored is available at any given moment to be retrieved. Moreover, even when it is available for retrieval, not everything gets reported.

Sometimes, we forget because our old memories fade with the passage of time or are interfered with as new memories become stored. This is known as retroactive interference. Other times, we find it harder to remember more recent events and easier to remember our older memories because something interfered with the process of storing or retrieving these recent events; this is known as proactive interference. Both are unconscious forms of forgetting; that is, we are unable to recollect information despite energetic efforts to do so.

A less prosaic type of forgetting, however, is labeled "motivated," and it has nothing to do with the passage of time or interference from subsequent experiences. Many of the original ideas regarding "motivated forgetting" stem from Sigmund Freud, who stated that "besides the simple forgetting of proper names, there is another forgetting which is motivated by repression" (Freud, 1938, p. 40). According to Freud, this is particularly the case when dealing with memories of traumatic experiences. Since Freud, many writers and memory researchers frequently mixed these two types memory failure (repression and motivated forgetting) or used them interchangeably.

Some writers and researchers, however, distinguish between repression and motivated forgetting. For some, repression deals with the *unconscious* process of blockading potentially painful memories in order to protect the individual. Motivated forgetting, on the other hand, occurs when the individual *consciously* forgets about painful or embarrassing events (Thompson, Morton, & Fraser, 1997). Therefore, unlike the unconscious forms of forgetting and interference mentioned above, motivated forgetting has at its root a conscious desire to forget or "suppress" events. Unlike repression, where memories are claimed to be unavailable even if the individual tries very hard to recall them, motivated forgetting is associated with the ability to recall unpleasant experiences when we consciously attempt to do so. These memories are only temporarily out of consciousness as a result of a desire to avoid thinking of them.

Some make even finer distinctions within the concept of motivated forgetting. Wegner (1989), for example, proposes two more specific types of forgetting called "directed forgetting" and "thought suppression," both of which are similar to, yet distinct from, motivated forgetting. Although both directed forgetting and thought suppression are defined as "avoiding consciousness of a thought" (Wegner, 1989, p. 9), directed forgetting is used almost exclusively to refer to the forgetting of words. Thought suppression, however, is employed only when dealing with the forgetting of discrete objects, events, or sequences of events, usually because the events are "too unpleasant, embarrassing, or threatening" (Ceci & Bruck, 1995, p. 194).

An example of thought suppression is to ask someone to try not to think of food when they are dieting. Ideally, they will actively engage in experiences that are distracting, such as watching TV or reading a book (Wegner, 1989). In the aftermath of a traumatic or embarrassing event, one might try to distract their thoughts away from this particular event and engage in thoughts about something more pleasant.

One irony about these types of forgetting (motivated, directed, and thought suppression) is that such monitoring techniques may increase the automatic activation of the thought that is supposed to be suppressed (Wegner, Quillian, and Houston, 1996). Therefore, by consciously trying to forget a word or event, one often becomes more likely to remember it, as demonstrated by the "try not to think of a pink elephant" phenomenon.

REFERENCES

Ceci, S. J., & Bruck, M. (1995). *Jeopardy in the courtroom: A scientific analysis of children's testimony.* Washington, DC: American Psychological Association.

Freud, S. (1938). The psychopathology of everyday life. In A. A. Brill (Ed. & Trans.), *The basic writings of Sigmund Freud* (pp. 35–178). New York: The Modern Library.

Thompson, J., Morton, J., & Fraser, L. (1997). Memories for the Marchioness. *Memory, 5,* 615–638.

Wegner, D. M. (1989). *White bears and other unwanted thoughts: Suppression, obsession and psychology of mental control.* New York: Viking Press.

Wegner, D. M., Quillian, F., & Houston, C. E. (1996). Memories out of order: Thought suppression and the disturbance of sequence memory. *Journal of Personality and Social Psychology, 71,* 680–691.

Tomoe Kanaya
Stephen J. Ceci
Cornell University

See also: Unconscious

MOTIVATION

Motivation refers to the energizing states of animals and humans. Motivation leads to the instigation, persistence, energy or arousal, and direction of behavior. Motivation may involve biological survival, as in hunger or thirst, and it involves a wide range of learned processes. *Environmental cues* and *goals* are key in the study of motivation. Motivation may involve approach, such as seeking success on a task, or it may involve avoidance, such as seeking to avoid failure on a task. Many events are motivating, and motivation *disposition* differs from motivation *arousal.* One may become fearful or anxious as a motivational disposition, but this differs from being actually aroused, that is, *motivated,* in a given moment or situation.

Internal states of motivation, such as hunger, are experienced by species other than humans. However, some motivations appear to be uniquely human, such as the striving for excellence in achievement. Motivation plays a major role in psychodynamic theories of personality, like those of Alfred Adler and Sigmund Freud, and the literature in psychopathology addresses problems of disturbance in motivation, such as depression and anxiety. Many internal variables, including emotion, learning, cognition, problem solving, and information processing, are closely related to motivation, especially in the case of humans. Although these internal variables are interrelated, they are independently defined and scientifically investigated (Ferguson, 2000). Motivation has been studied in terms of social and cultural processes as well as from an evolutionary perspective.

Humans have many cognitive representations as goals, such as seeking new friends or striving to get a new job. Motivation, although influenced by external factors, refers to processes internal to the individual. Thus, others can set goals for an individual (Locke & Latham, 1990), as is done when a parent sets a standard for a child's school achievements or an employee's supervisor sets goals for work accomplishment. Often such an external goal is not motivating because the individual internally fails to self-set such a goal.

Intensity of Motivation

Motivation differs not only in kind, such as an individual's being thirsty rather than hungry, but also in intensity. One can be more or less thirsty, more or less hungry. Intensity may be described by a word such as *arousing,* which refers to the energizing aspect of motivation. The energizing effect of heightened motivation can be observed by means of physiological measures as well as by overt responses. Measures of brain waves, skin conductance, heart rate, and muscle tension can identify the intensity dimension of motivation. Under conditions of drowsiness and low excitation, electroencephalographic recordings generally show slow and large brain waves with a regular pattern, while under excited alertness the pattern is one of fast, low, irregular waves. When aroused or excited, individuals also tend to show an increase in muscle potential, as measured by electromyographic recordings, and a decrease in skin resistance. Individual differences lead to variation in physiological responses under arousal.

Animals generally run, turn wheels, and press bars at a faster rate when they have an increased level of motivation. For many species, including humans, heightened motivation tends to increase effort, persistence, responsiveness, and alertness. Some contemporary theorists (e.g., Steriade, 1996) have found cortical desynchronization to be associated with the firing of specific neurons and with signs of behavioral arousal, but a full understanding of arousal processes is not yet available. Physiological, neurochemical, and psychological processes are involved in motivation. Motivation has been shown by health psychologists to affect immunological functioning (Cohen & Herbert, 1996), and in many ways, motivational states have a strong impact on the total health of the individual.

Complex Relationships Between Behavior and Motivation

One cannot infer the existence of a motivation merely by the presence of certain behaviors. For example, aggressive behavior does not presuppose a motivation or drive for aggression. Behavior is due to many factors. This complexity is illustrated by eating disorders such as obesity or bulimia, as well as in everyday life when people who are not food deprived nevertheless crave food when bored or anxious. Likewise, individuals can find food aversive and abstain from eating even when there is a strong tissue need for nourishment (Capaldi, 1996). People may eat when feeling unloved, and individuals may refrain from eating when motivated to seek social approval, obtain a job, or participate in a political hunger strike. Similarly, sexual behavior may occur when individuals seek power, prestige, or social approval rather than sexual gratification related to sexual arousal (McClelland, 1973). Although physiological needs may be powerful sources of motivation, they are neither necessary nor sufficient as the basis for motivation.

External rewards and reward pathways in the brain affect motivation and behavior, especially in addiction. Incentives of all types have been shown to affect motivation. For humans, intrinsic motivation that is internally generated differs from extrinsic motivation that is imposed by external sources (Deci, Kostner, & Ryan, 2001). Adlerian psychologists have found that children trained with encouragement and self-reliance rather than with praise and rewards are more likely to maintain socially constructive behaviors (Dreikurs, Grunwald, & Pepper, 1999; Dreikurs & Soltz, 2001).

Fear and Anxiety

Learning of all kinds, including early life experiences, shapes the way animals and humans respond to stressful and fear-arousing events. Different situations arouse motivation of fear and anxiety for different species and for different individual prior experiences. Stimuli associated with pain come to evoke fear, such that fear occurs when painful stimulation is anticipated. In humans, painful events are often symbolic and not merely physical, such as fear of failure (Atkinson, 1964).

Sigmund Freud postulated that human neurosis has its roots in anxiety. Clinical, field, and laboratory findings have demonstrated that defensive motivations like fear and anxiety are likely to lead to behaviors that interfere with effective task performance and creative problem solving. Task-oriented anxiety can be beneficial when the individual exerts effort toward task mastery, but self-oriented anxiety is likely to engender thoughts that indicate preoccupation with self-worth or personal safety, which interfere with problem solving and limit the amount of attention given to task demands. Fear of failure often leads to behaviors directed toward preventing failure rather than behaviors directed toward attaining success (Covington, 2000; Dweck, 1999).

Anxiety can be measured as both a trait and a state. Usually, but not always, the two show a strong positive correlation. In certain situations persons who have a disposition to be anxious (high trait anxiety) may have low state anxiety, and likewise, under specific circumstances persons of low trait anxiety may be very high in state anxiety. Anxiety can lead to stress-induced illness and lower immune system activity and is associated with lowered productive energy (Thayer, 1989). Memory, attentional control, and retrieval efficiency tend to suffer when an individual is anxious. High trait anxious people are more pessimistic and more prone to take note of threatening information than are persons with low anxiety (Eysenck, 1991).

Anxiety and fear in human beings can relate to actual threats but can also be self-generated. According to Adlerian theory and clinical evidence (Adler, 1927/1959; Dreikurs, 1967), emotions are linked with motivation. For example, a child may develop strong anxiety to get her parents to cater to her whims, or a husband may display marked anxiety as a means of getting his wife to pamper him and provide him service. The complexity of human motivation is well illustrated by anxiety, which can be facilitating as well as debilitating, can alter performance as well as be altered by it, and can serve a variety of interpersonal goals.

Anxiety tends not to lead to effective functioning. Rather, people function effectively when they believe positive outcomes are possible, and when they have self-confidence and confidence in others. When a person feels belonging, bonds with others, and contributes to the welfare of others, the individual functions effectively in many spheres of living. Contemporary writers have written about the need to belong, to feel competent, and to be self-determining, ideas that were formulated by Alfred Adler many decades ago (Adler, 1927/1959).

For humans, self-direction and symbolic processes are fundamental in determining motivation and its effects on behavior. Altruism and prosocial motivation enable humans to establish long-term emotional bonding, to overcome adversity, and to engage in cooperation and creative problem solving. Situational factors as well as intrinsic motivation shape people's cooperative or competitive actions and attitudes. Organismic and species variables are important in studying motivation in a wide range of animals. Additionally, for humans, societal and personal values, cultural and personal experiences, and many situational variables shape motivation and its effect on behavior.

REFERENCES

Adler, A. (1959). *The practice and theory of individual psychology.* Paterson, NJ: Littlefield, Adams. (Originally published 1927)

Atkinson, J. W. (1964). *An introduction to motivation.* New York: Van Nostrand.

Capaldi, E. D. (1996). Introduction. In E. D. Capaldi (Ed.), *Why we eat what we eat: The psychology of eating* (pp. 3–9). Washington, DC: American Psychological Association.

Cohen, S., & Herbert, T. B. (1996). Health Psychology: Psychological factors and physical disease from the perspective of human psychoneuroimmunology. *Annual Review of Psychology, 47,* 113–142.

Covington, M. V. (2000). Goal theory, motivation, and school achievement: An integrative review. *Annual Review of Psychology, 51,* 171–2002.

Deci, E. L., Kostner, R., & Ryan, R. R. (2001). Extrinsic rewards and intrinsic motivation in education: Reconsidered once again. *Review of Educational Research, 71,* 1–27.

Dreikurs, R. (1967). The function of emotions. In R. Dreikurs (Ed.), *Psychodynamics, psychotherapy, and counseling* (pp. 205–217). Chicago: Adler School of Professional Psychology.

Dreikurs, R., Grunwald, B. B., & Pepper, F. C. (1999). *Maintaining sanity in the classroom: Classroom management techniques.* (2nd ed.). Philadelphia: Taylor & Francis.

Dreikurs, R. & Soltz, V. (2001). *Children: The challenge.* New York: Penguin.

Dweck, C. S. (1999). *Self-theories: Their role in motivation, personality, and development.* Philadelphia: Psychology Press.

Eysenck, M. W. (1991). Trait anxiety and cognition. In C. D. Spielberger, I. G. Sarason, Z. Kulcsar, & G. L. Van Heck (Eds.), *Stress and emotion: Anxiety, anger and curiosity* (Vol. 14, pp. 77–84). New York: Hemisphere.

Ferguson, E. D. (2000). *Motivation: A biosocial and cognitive integration of motivation and emotion.* New York: Oxford University Press.

Locke, E. A., & Latham, G. P. (1990). *A theory of goal setting and task performance.* Englewood Cliffs, NJ: Prentice Hall.

McClelland, D. C. (1973). The two faces of power. In D. C. McClelland & R. S. Steele (Eds.), *Human motivation: A book of readings* (pp. 300–316). Morristown, NJ: General Learning Press.

Steriade, M. (1996). Arousal: Revisiting the reticular activating system. *Science, 272*(5259), 225–226.

Thayer, R. E. (1989). *The biopsychology of mood and arousal.* New York: Oxford University Press.

Eva Dreikurs Ferguson
Southern Illinois University, Edwardsville

***See also:* Anxiety**

MULTICULTURAL COUNSELING

Multicultural counseling assumes that each person's identity has been shaped by a great number of cultures and that effective counseling will address these different cultural identities in each client and community of clients. Multiculturalism has emerged as a social, political, economic, educational, and cultural movement during the last two decades. The term *multicultural* implies a wide range of special interest groups, without valuing any one of them as better or worse than others and without denying the distinct, complementary, or even contradictory perspectives that each group brings with it. Multicultural counseling recognizes that each of us belongs to many different cultures at the same time. Within-group differences as well as between-group differences are important in the multicultural perspective (Pedersen, 2000).

Interest in multicultural counseling grew out of the Civil Rights and feminist movements in the 1950s and the community mental health movement of the 1960s, which affirmed that mental health care was the right of all citizens. Popular dissent from the anti-Vietnam War movement and issues of feminism promoted discontent, while protest against inequity was accepted and encouraged by the media. By the 1970s, underuse of mental health services by minorities had become a serious issue. By the 1980s, large numbers of refugees further demonstrated the importance of a multicultural global perspective in counseling. By the 1990s, the rapidly changing demographic balance predicted that one third or more of the nation's school students would be non-White by the turn of the century. The war against terrorism since the year 2001 has further highlighted the lack of understanding among different cultures and countries.

Culture can be defined broadly or narrowly. Much research has contributed to and shaped the multicultural perspective for counseling, which initially was focused on the oppression of minorities by the majority culture. Culture has come to be defined more broadly to include special interest groups defined by ethnographic, demographic, status, and affiliation variables (Sue & Sue, 1999; Ponterotto, Casas, Suzuki, & Alexander, 2001; Pedersen, Draguns, Lonner, & Trimble, 2002).

Multiculturalism is becoming a "fourth force" to supplement the psychodynamic, behavioral, and humanist perspectives, emphasizing that all counseling takes place in a multicultural context (Pedersen, 1998). Behaviors are learned and displayed in a cultural context, so accurate assessment, meaningful understanding, and appropriate counseling intervention must also attend to that cultural context.

Multicultural counseling theory (MCT) (Sue, Ivey, & Pedersen, 1996) helps to clarify multiculturalism as a unified concept. MCT is based on six major propositions about counseling theories as worldviews which form the basis for a multicultural metatheory. These propositions are: (1) each Western or non-Western theory represents a different worldview; (2) the interrelationships that clients and counselors experience in their cultural contexts must be the focus of counseling; (3) a counselor's or client's cultural identity will influence how problems are defined and dictate or define appropriate counseling goals or processes; (4) the ultimate goal of MCT is to expand the repertoire of helping responses available to counselors; (5) conventional roles of counseling are only some of many alternative helping roles available in other cultural contexts; and (6) MCT emphasizes the importance of expanding personal, family, group, and organizational consciousness in a contextual orientation.

There is also resistance to multiculturalism (Mio & Awakuni, 2000; Sue, 1998). Multiculturalism may be perceived as competing with established theories, and is associated with emotional issues of quotas and affirmative action. Multiculturalism is also connected with the postmodern movement. Some critics argue that the same unified counseling criteria should be applied to all cultures. The definition and standards for assessing multiculturalism have been challenged and the ideals of multiculturalism are judged by some to be impractical. Multiculturalism has also been associated with reverse racism and anti-White groups.

The multicultural movement in counseling has promoted research on racial and ethnic identity development. Ponterotto, Casas, Suzuki, and Alexander (2001) describe scales of ethnic identity for American Indians, Blacks, Hispanics, Whites, and other populations that generally include five stages. The first "pre-encounter" stage is the level of least awareness. In the second "encounter" stage, a crisis occurs, followed by a third "immersion-emersion" stage in which cultural identity becomes more explicit. In the fourth "internalization" stage these new insights are internalized. The fifth and final "internalization-commitment" stage represents the highest level of racial/ethnic awareness. These categories of progressive awareness are important for counselors to use in assessing their own competency, as well as for defining constructive growth among clients from different cultural backgrounds.

Members of the APA's Division 17 (Counseling) Education and Training Committee developed a position paper of competencies for multicultural counseling (Sue et al., 1982). These competencies emphasize awareness, knowledge, and skill in a developmental sequence. These competencies have been updated in Sue et al., (1998) and other publications.

The awareness competencies describe the need for counselors to become cognizant of their own cultural heritage while valuing and respecting differences, to be aware of how their own values may affect culturally different clients, to become comfortable with differences in race and belief between clients and counselors, and to know when a minority client should be referred elsewhere.

The knowledge competencies describe the need to have a good understanding of the sociopolitical dynamics between minority and majority cultures, to have specific knowledge and information about the client's particular culture, to have a clear and explicit knowledge of generic and traditional counseling theory and practice, and to be aware of institutional barriers that prevent minorities from using mental health services.

The skill competencies assume that all culturally skilled counselors will be able to generate a wide variety of verbal and nonverbal responses appropriate to the cultural setting and skill level, that counselors will be able to accurately send and receive both verbal and nonverbal messages in each culturally different context, and that counselors will be able to advocate for change within the system or institution appropriately, when changes are necessary, on behalf of their culturally different clients.

These competencies have been adopted by the American Psychological Association as well as the American Counseling Association for professional standards of counseling (Sue et al., 1998).

REFERENCES

Mio, J. S., & Awakuni, G. I. (2000). *Resistance to multiculturalism: Issues and interventions.* Philadelphia: Bruner/Mazel.

Pedersen, P. (1998). *Multiculturalism as a fourth force.* Philadelphia: Bruner/Mazel.

Pedersen, P. (2000). *A handbook for developing multicultural awareness* (3rd ed.). Alexandria, VA: American Counseling Association.

Pedersen, P., Draguns, J., Lonner, W., & Trimble, J. (2002). *Counseling across cultures* (5th ed.). Thousand Oaks, CA: Sage.

Ponterotto, J. G., Casas, J. M., Suzuki, L. A., & Alexander, C. M. (2001). *Handbook of multicultural counseling* (2nd ed.). Thousand Oaks, CA: Sage.

Sue, S. (1998). In search of cultural competencies in psychology and counseling. *American Psychologist, 53,* 440–448.

Sue, D. W., Bernier, J. E., Durran, A., Fineberg, L., Pedersen, P., Smith, C. J., et al. (1982). Cross-cultural counseling competencies. *The Counseling Psychologist, 19*(2), 45–52.

Sue, D. W., Carter, R. T., Casas, J. M., Fouad, N. A., Ivey, A. E., Jensen, M., et al. (1998). *Multicultural counseling competencies: Individual and organizational development.* Thousand Oaks, CA: Sage.

Sue, D. W., Ivey, A. E., & Pedersen, P. B. (1997). *A theory of multicultural counseling and therapy.* Pacific Grove, CA: Brooks/Cole.

Sue, D. W., & Sue, D. (1999). *Counseling the culturally different: Theory and practice* (3rd ed.). New York: Wiley Interscience.

Paul B. Pedersen
Syracuse University
University of Hawaii

See also: **Cross-Cultural Counseling; Postmodernism; Psychotherapy Effectiveness**

MULTIMODAL THERAPY

Multimodal therapy (MMT) provides an integrative assessment and treatment plan that considers the whole person in his or her social network. Multimodal therapy places most of its theoretical underpinnings within a broad-based social and cognitive learning theory, but draws on effective techniques from many disciplines without necessarily subscribing to their particular suppositions (i.e., it espouses technical eclecticism). In MMT one endeavors to use, whenever possible and applicable, empirically supported methods. Thus, its practitioners are at the cutting edge of the field, drawing on scientific and clinical findings from all credible sources.

This technically eclectic outlook is central and pivotal to MMT. It is important to understand that the MMT approach sees *theoretical* eclecticism, or any attempt to integrate different theories in the hopes of producing a more robust technique, as futile and misguided (see Lazarus, 1992, 1997).

Multimodal therapy is predicated on the assumptions that most psychological problems are multifaceted, multidetermined, and multilayered, and that comprehensive therapy calls for a careful assessment of seven parameters or modalities—Behavior, Affect, Sensation, Imagery, Cognition, Interpersonal relationships, and Biological processes. The most common biological intervention is the use of psychotropic Drugs. The first letters from the seven modalities yield the convenient acronym BASIC I.D.—although it must be remembered that the "D" represents not only the drugs commonly used for biological intervention, but the entire panoply of medical and biological factors.

It is assumed that the more a patient learns in therapy, the less likely he or she is to relapse. In other words, therapeutic breadth is emphasized. Over many years, my follow-ups have revealed more durable treatment outcomes when the entire BASIC I.D. is assessed, and when significant problems in each modality are remedied. Multimodal therapy uses several distinct assessment procedures that tend to facilitate treatment outcomes.

Second-order BASIC I.D. assessments may be conducted when therapy falters. For example, an unassertive person who is not responding to the usual social skills and assertiveness training methods may be asked to spell out the specific consequences that an assertive modus vivendi might have on his or her behaviors, affective reactions, sensory responses, imagery, and cognitive processes. The interpersonal repercussions would also be examined, and if relevant, biological factors would be determined (e.g., "If I start expressing my feelings I may become less anxious and require fewer tranquilizers"). Quite often, this procedure brings to light reasons behind such factors as noncompliance and poor progress. A typical case in point concerns a man who was not responding to role-playing and other assertiveness training procedures. During a second-order BASIC I.D. assessment, he revealed a central cognitive schemata to the effect that he was not entitled to be confident, positive, and in better control of his life, because these qualities would show up his profoundly reticent and inadequate father. Consequently, the treatment focus shifted to a thorough examination of his entitlements.

A 35-item *Structural Profile Inventory* (SPI) yields a quantitative BASIC I.D. diagram depicting a person's degree of activity, emotionality, sensory awareness, imagery potential, cognitive propensities, interpersonal leanings, and biological considerations (see Lazarus, 1997). The SPI is particularly useful in couples therapy where differences in the specific ratings reflect potential areas of friction. Discussion of these disparities with clients can result in constructive steps to understand and remedy them.

A method called *tracking* may be employed when clients are puzzled by affective reactions. "I don't know why I feel this way." "I don't know where these feelings are coming from." The client is asked to recount the latest untoward event or incident. He or she is then asked to consider what behaviors, affective responses, images, sensations, and cognitions come to mind.

One client who reported having panic attacks for no apparent reason was able to put together the following string of events. She had initially become aware that her heart was beating faster than usual. This brought to mind an episode in which she had passed out after drinking too much alcohol at a party. This memory or image still occasioned a strong sense of shame. She started thinking that she was going to pass out again, and as she dwelled on her sensations, the cognition only intensified, culminating in her feelings of panic. Thus, she exhibited an S-I-C-S-C-A pattern (Sensation, Imagery, Cognition, Sensation, Cognition, Affect). Thereafter, she was asked to note carefully whether any subsequent anxiety or panic attacks followed what might be called a similar firing order. She subsequently confirmed that her two trigger points were usually sensation and imagery. This alerted the therapist to focus on sensory training techniques (e.g., diaphragmatic breathing and deep muscle relaxation) followed immediately by imagery training (e.g., the use of coping imagery and the selection of mental pictures that evoked profound feelings of calm).

The BASIC I.D. lends itself to other assessment and treatment tactics that keep the clinician on track and enable him or her to address issues that might otherwise have been glossed over. Lazarus (1997) presents these methods in some detail.

Research findings on overall effectiveness of MMT have been conducted by Kwee (1984), a Dutch psychologist, who obtained encouraging results when conducting a controlled-outcome study using MMT with severe obsessive-compulsive patients, and with a group of extremely phobic individuals. Williams (1988), a Scottish psychologist, in a careful controlled-outcome study, compared MMT with other treatments in helping children with learning disabilities. He emerged with clear data pointing to the efficacy of MMT in comparison to the other methods studied.

In essence, it should be understood that MMT is a broad-spectrum orientation, extremely flexible, with which the therapist may match the best and most effective methods with the appropriate treatment style for each individual. It is both brief and comprehensive (Lazarus, 1997).

REFERENCES

Kwee, M. G. T. (1984). *Klinishe multimodale gedragtstherapie.* Lisse, Holland: Swets & Zeitlinger.

Lazarus, A. A. (1992). Multimodal therapy: Technical eclecticism with minimal integration. In J. C. Norcross & M. R. Goldfried (Eds.), *Handbook of psychotherapy integration* (pp. 231–263). New York: Basic Books.

Lazarus, A. A. (1997). *Brief but comprehensive psychotherapy: The multimodal way.* New York: Springer.

Williams, T. (1988). *A multimodal approach to assessment and intervention with children with learning disabilities.* Unpublished doctoral dissertation, Department of Psychology, University of Glasgow.

Arnold A. Lazarus
Center for Multimodal Psychological Services

See also: **Psychotherapy**

MULTIPLE CORRELATION

Multiple correlation is a multivariate analysis method widely used in psychology and other behavioral sciences. It can be considered an extension of bivariate correlation, and indicates the degree of association between one variable and an optimally weighted combination of several other variables. The weights are determined by the principle of least squares so as to minimize the residual, or unrelated, variance.

The multiple correlation ranges in value from zero to one, and is interpreted similarly to a bivariate correlation, if rectilinearity and the other assumptions of the bivariate intercorrelations from which the multiple correlation is computed are reasonable.

In psychology the squared multiple correlation (R^2) frequently is used to estimate the proportion of variance in a dependent variable that is related to a set of independent variables. A related method, multiple regression, is used for predicting a dependent (or criterion) variable from a set of independent (or predictor) variables.

Benjamin Fruchter

See also: **Correlation Methods; Multiple Regression**

MULTIPLE REGRESSION

Multiple regression is a multivariate analysis method that relates a dependent (or criterion) variable (Y) to a set of independent (or predictor) variables (X) by a linear equation.

$$Y' = a + b_1X_1 + b_2X_2 + \ldots + b_kX_k$$

The regression or b weights are usually determined by the principle of least squares, to minimize the sum of the squared deviations of the dependent values from the corresponding predicted values.

In a "stepwise" approach, variables are added (or removed) one at a time from the independent variable set until there is a nonsignificant change. Also, sets of variables may be added (or removed) to evaluate their contribution to the multiple correlation, and an F-test done to determine if their effect is statistically significant. Nonlinear relationships may be evaluated by including higher order terms and/or multiplicative terms on the right-hand side of the equation.

The regression weights are determined most reliably when the independent variables are relatively uncorrelated. The situation in which some of them are highly intercorrelated is "multicollinearity," and tends to yield regression coefficients whose values may fluctuate markedly from sample to sample. Some common uses for multiple regression are

1. To obtain the best linear prediction equation
2. To control for confounding variables
3. To evaluate the contribution of a specific set of variables
4. To account for seemingly complex multivariate interrelationships
5. To perform analysis of variance and covariance by coding the levels of the independent variables

Benjamin Fruchter

See also: **Multiple Correlation**

MULTISYSTEMIC THERAPY

General Description

Multisystemic therapy (MST), developed and refined by Scott Henggeler and his colleagues over the past 25 years, is an intensive family- and community-based treatment for youth presenting with serious clinical problems (e.g., antisocial behavior, substance abuse, emotional disturbance) that focuses on changing the empirically derived determinants of these problems within a broad-based, social ecological framework. MST uses evidence-based interventions designed to attenuate known risk factors and to enhance protective factors at multiple levels of the youth's social ecology. These levels include characteristics of individuals, salient features of encapsulating social environments (e.g., families, schools, peer groups, etc.), and the relations between and among individuals and their relevant social settings (e.g., caregiver-teacher relationships, family-school linkages).

Core Principles

MST therapists are guided by nine core principles that direct them: (1) to assess the fit between identified problems and their broader systemic context; (2) to emphasize the positive and use systemic strengths as levers for change; (3) to promote responsible and decrease irresponsible behavior among family members; (4) to implement present-focused and action-oriented interventions aimed at specific and well-defined problems; (5) to target sequences of behavior within and between multiple systems that maintain the identified problems; (6) to design interventions that fit the developmental needs of the youth; (7) to require daily or weekly effort by family members; (8) to evaluate intervention effectiveness continuously from multiple perspectives with providers assuming responsibility for overcoming barriers to successful outcomes; and (9) to promote generalization of therapeutic change by empowering caregivers to address family members' needs across multiple systemic contexts.

Theoretical Underpinnings

Four theories/perspectives have been especially influential in the formulation of MST (1) *social ecological perspectives* articulating that human development is multiply determined by complex interdependencies of individuals and the nested social environments (families, schools, peer groups, neighborhoods) in which they are immersed; (2) *family systems theories* emphasizing that maladaptive behaviors of youth stem from faulty family communication/problem solving processes and problematic family structures (e.g., cross-generation alliances, inadequate levels of cohesion or adaptability); (3) *social learning / behavioral theories* specifying that externalizing behaviors are learned and maintained because they "pay off" in terms of either positive or negative reinforcement (e.g., achievement of specific resources, escape or avoidance of unwanted outcomes) delivered contingently by caregivers and peers; and (4) *structural-organizational* and *resilience* perspectives emphasizing the importance of protective factors (e.g., strengths of individuals, families, and social systems) in counteracting or buffering negative effects of risk factors, thus potentially yielding relatively adaptive outcomes for high-risk youth and their families.

Empirical Foundations

The aforementioned theories/perspectives have driven a substantial body of empirical research that, in turn, has elucidated the determinants of serious problem behaviors in youth. The malleable determinants have become targets for change in MST intervention programs. Two major types of research have influenced MST interventions and its theory of change: (1) multivariate cross-sectional and passive (nonintervention) longitudinal studies that delineate the correlates/predictors of youth behavioral and emotional problems, and (2) treatment outcome studies that target theory-driven risk/protective factors and yield beneficial results for high-risk youth. For example, both types of research support a social ecological perspective, a central guiding feature of MST. Numerous nonintervention studies indicate that challenging clinical problems of youth are determined by multiple factors at multiple levels of analysis. In addition, treatment outcome studies using ecologically oriented interventions have demonstrated effectiveness in reducing antisocial behavior in adolescents.

Intervention Strategies, Service Delivery, and Treatment Fidelity

Specific MST interventions include strategies from pragmatic family therapies, behavioral parent training, social learning/contingency management approaches, and cognitive-behavioral therapy. Interventions are theory-based, have empirical support, and are delivered strategically and flexibly throughout the treatment process. MST interventions often have the following goals: (1) to reduce unproductive caregiver-youth conflict; (2) to improve caregiver monitoring, limit setting, and family management practices; (3) to enhance family communication and problem-solving mechanisms; (4) to develop adaptive levels of family cohesion and adaptability; (5) to extricate youth from ties with deviant peers and to increase their association with prosocial peers; (6) to increase academic and social competencies; and (7) to increase involvement with prosocial organizations (e.g., religious groups, community recreational facilities).

MST therapists have low caseloads (i.e., four to six families), provide treatment in natural environments (i.e., home, school, and neighborhood settings), schedule sessions at convenient times for families (e.g., evenings and weekends), and maintain availability for interventions 24 hours per day and 7 days per week. Treatment involves approximately 60 hours of direct service extending over 3 to 6 months (and thus is time-limited). These practices likely contribute to the high treatment completion rates evidenced across MST studies.

MST includes comprehensive and continuous quality assurance mechanisms designed to maximize treatment fidelity (e.g., manualization of clinical, supervisory, consultative, and administrative procedures; provision of weekly feedback to therapists from clinical supervisors and MST consultants). Clinical training and supervision focus on therapist adherence to the core MST principles. Adherence scores on a standardized questionnaire completed by caregivers have been associated with positive youth and family outcomes. Empirical support for MST quality assurance mechanisms has been obtained and should facilitate the effective transport of MST nationally and internationally.

Effectiveness Trials

Multiple published outcome studies (including seven randomized clinical trials), and the preliminary results of investigations in progress suggest that MST is an effective treatment for antisocial youth (including substance use problems). MST also shows promise for treating youth experiencing psychiatric emergencies, juvenile sexual offenders, and maltreated children. Evidence regarding the relative cost effectiveness of MST in comparison with traditional services is also encouraging. MST studies have met stringent standards of methodological rigor consistent with high internal validity, and have been conducted in community settings with heterogeneous client populations (using few exclusion criteria), thus bolstering the external validity of results.

Treatment outcome studies consistently have found differences in favor of MST on putative mediators of change (e.g., improved parent-child relationships) as well as ultimate outcomes (e.g., reduced criminal behavior). More recently, mediational analyses conducted on two independent samples of antisocial youth corroborated key features of the theory of change underlying MST. MST improved parenting and global family functioning and reduced youth association with deviant peers; these changes, in turn, were associated with reductions in criminal activity.

W. Glenn Clingempeel
Scott W. Henggeler
Medical University of South Carolina

See also: **Conduct Disorder; Family Therapy**

MYELINATION

The functional unit of the nervous system, the neuron, is equipped with a specialized region for transmitting information called the axon. The speed at which a neuron can convey sensory information to the brain and motor information to the muscles is dependent upon two critical features of its axon: its diameter and the presence of a myelin sheath. By increasing the diameter of an axon, a strategy used in the nervous system of both invertebrates and vertebrates, the conduction velocity of a fiber increases as a result of a lower axolemma resistance to the flow of current.

However, the limits to which the brain can expand in size as a result of this adaptation has prompted a second strategy to evolve that increases the speed of action potential propagation with little axon diameter growth (Hildebrand, Remahl, Persson, & Bjartmer, 1993). This strategy, called myelination, results from a complex interaction between neurons and oligodendrocytes in the central nervous system (CNS) or Schwann cells in the peripheral nervous system (PNS). These two glial cell types are capable of synthesizing a membrane structure, called myelin, which is elaborated into a sheath and wrapped, in a concentric fashion, around an axon (Figure 1).

This sheath of myelin is not continuous along the length of an axon but is laid down as segments of myelin (internodes) that are interrupted, at regular intervals, by areas devoid of myelin. These regions are termed the nodes of Ranvier (Figure 2). Moreover, sodium channels are concentrated at these nodes but virtually absent from regions of axon membrane covered by a myelin sheath. Therefore, when an action potential is triggered, the insulating properties of the myelin sheath and the enrichment of sodium channels at the nodes allows current to be swiftly funneled by passive spread to the next node. This movement of the action potential from node to node is termed *saltatory con-*

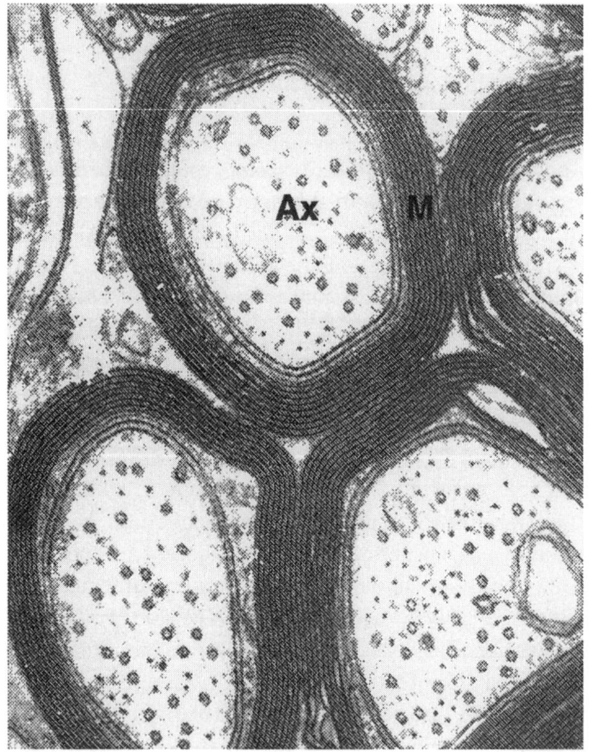

Figure 1. Electron micrograph showing central nervous system axons (Ax) ensheathed with myelin (M) produced by oligodendrocytes.

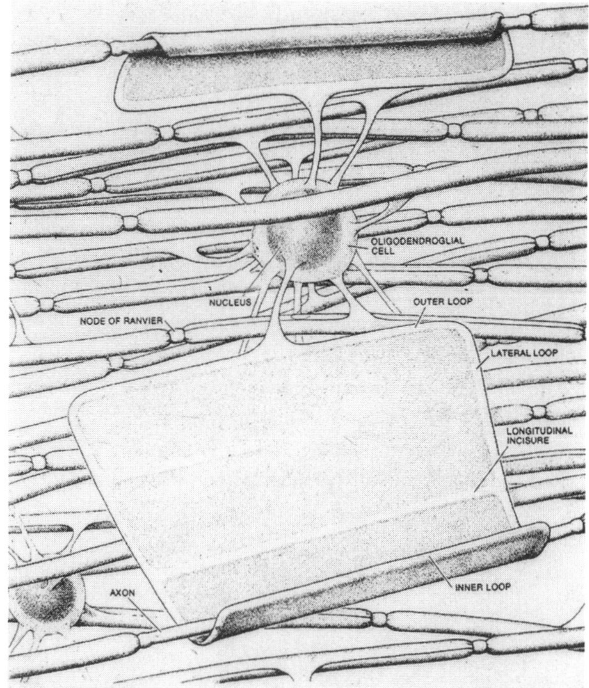

Figure 2. Illustration of an oligodendrocyte ensheathing multiple axons with internodes of myelin.

duction and enables myelinated axons with a diameter of 4μm to convey information at the same speed as unmyelinated axons with a diameter of 500μm. Therefore, axon myelination provides the means by which the nervous system can convey electrical impulses at high speeds in a confined manner. Conversely, any loss of axon myelination, as seen in demyelinating diseases or nervous system trauma, disrupts action potential propagation, resulting in devastating consequences to normal motor and sensory functions (Compston, Scolding, Wren, & Noble, 1991).

Although the interactions that occur between neurons and either Schwann cells or oligodendrocytes produce the same outcome, that is, an axon ensheathed in myelin, myelination in the peripheral and central nervous systems differ in a number of ways (Colello & Pott, 1997). In particular, it has been estimated that a single oligodendrocyte can ensheath 20 to 50 axons with an internode of myelin, whereas, a single Schwann cell will ensheath only one axon with myelin. Consequently, the destruction of one oligodendrocyte will have a larger impact on motor or sensory function than the destruction of one Schwann cell. Moreover, it has been shown that myelin produced from oligodendrocytes and Schwann cells differs to some degree in its biochemical makeup of lipids and proteins (Snipes & Suter, 1995; Campagnoni, 1998). This may explain why some myelin diseases target preferentially either the central or peripheral nervous system. Regardless of differences, myelination in both systems can be regarded as the culmination of events that began with the differentiation of glial cells from mitotically active, migratory precursor cells. Upon becoming postmitotic, these cells proceed to transcribe and translate the genes that make up myelin. The elaboration of myelin into a sheath by the processes of glial cells and the subsequent recognition of target axons are further distinct steps along the pathway leading to myelination. Finally, the initiation of axon ensheathment and the subsequent compaction of the myelin sheath around the axon completes the stages of myelination.

Although the process of myelination enables axons to propagate action potentials quickly and in a compact manner, the complexity of this neuron/glia interaction results in an increased vulnerability of the nervous system to disease. Indeed, there are a large number of identified pathological conditions that primarily target myelin (Hopkins, 1993). These diseases, which can lead to the destruction of the myelin sheath, are categorized as either acquired (i.e., multiple sclerosis) or hereditary diseases (i.e., leukodystrophies). Multiple sclerosis, which is the most common human demyelinating disease, is characterized by the formation of plaques, or areas of demyelinated axons that can develop virtually anywhere in the central nervous system (Figure 3). Although axons can be spared in the plaque regions and remyelinate during periods of disease remission, cumulative axonal loss is thought to provide the pathologic substrate for the progressive disability that most long-term MS patients experience (Bjartmar & Trapp, 2001). These findings suggest that any therapeutic treatment aimed at restoring function in patients with demyelinating disease will need to combine both remyelinating and neuroprotective strategies. Further complicating such therapeutic attempts, however, is the observation that myelin debris, known to be present within demyelinating lesions, includes factors inhibitory for neuronal regeneration after central nervous system injury (Schwab, 2002). Fortunately, the re-

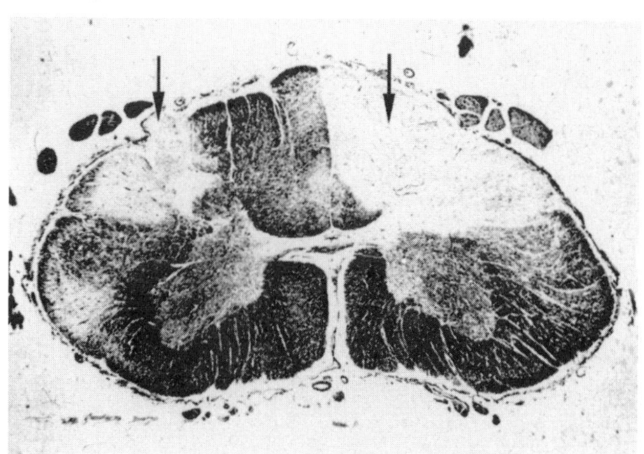

Figure 3. Cross-section of the spinal cord of a patient who had multiple sclerosis showing the loss of myelin (black stain) in fiber tracts of the spinal cord (arrows) responsible for conveying sensory impulses and voluntary movement.

cent identification of receptor molecules with redundant binding activities for such inhibitory factors (Domeniconi et al., 2002; Liu, Fournier, GrandPre, & Strittmatter, 2002) should allow for the development of additional strategies aimed at repairing neurons that have undergone demyelination.

REFERENCES

Bjartmar, C., & Trapp, B. D. (2001). Axonal and neuronal degeneration in multiple sclerosis: Mechanisms and functional consequences. *Current Opinion in Neurology, 14,* 271–278.

Campagnoni, A. T. (1998). Molecular biology of myelin proteins from the central nervous system. *Journal of Neurochemistry, 51,* 1–14.

Colello, R. J., & Pott, U. (1997). Signals that initiate myelination in the developing mammalian nervous system. *Molecular Neurobiology, 15,* 83–100.

Compston, A., Scolding, N., Wren, D., & Noble, M. (1991). The pathogenesis of demyelinating disease: Insights from cell biology. *Trends in Neurosciences, 14,* 175–182.

Domeniconi, M., Cao, Z., Spencer, T., Sivasankaran, R., Wang, K., Nikulina, E., et al. (2002). Myelin-associated glycoprotein interacts with the nogo66 receptor to inhibit neurite outgrowth. *Neuron, 18,* 283–290.

Hildebrand, C., Remahl, S., Persson, H., & Bjartmer, C. (1993). Myelinated nerve fibers in the CNS. *Progress in Neurobiology, 40,* 319–384.

Hopkins, A. (1993). *Clinical neurology: A modern approach.* Oxford: Oxford University Press.

Liu, B. P., Fournier, A., GrandPre, T., & Strittmatter, S. M. (2002). Myelin-associated glycoprotein as a functional ligand for the nogo-66 receptor. *Science, 297,* 1190–1193.

Schwab, M. E. (2002). Repairing the injured spinal cord. *Science, 295,* 1029–1031.

Snipes, G. J., & Suter, U. (1995). Molecular anatomy and genetics of myelin proteins in the peripheral nervous system. *Journal of Anatomy, 186,* 483–94.

Raymond J. Colello
Babette Fuss
Medical College of Virginia

N

NARCOLEPSY

Narcolepsy is a lifelong neurological disorder of rapid eye movement (REM) sleep in which the affected individual has attacks of irresistible daytime sleepiness, cataplexy (sudden muscle weakness in response to emotional triggers like surprise, laughter, fright, or anger), hypnagogic hallucinations (vivid and often terrifying dreams at sleep onset), and sleep paralysis (a momentary inability to move as one is drifting off to sleep). Cataplexy, hypnagogic hallucinations, and sleep paralysis are all manifestations of intrusion of REM sleep onto wakefulness. The entire constellation of symptoms may not be present initially, but appears gradually over a period of 5 to 10 years. Daytime sleepiness and cataplexy are the two most reliable features of narcolepsy. The daytime sleepiness frequently leads to automatic behavior of which the subject is unaware, impairment of memory, concentration, and executive function as well as mood swings. Nighttime sleep is also disturbed, with frequent awakenings, with or without associated periodic limb movements in sleep.

The incidence of narcolepsy in United States is 1.37 per 100,000 persons per year (1.72 for men and 1.05 for women). It is highest in the second decade, followed by a gradual decline thereafter. The prevalence rate is approximately 56 persons per 100,000 persons (Silber, Krahn, Olson, & Pankrantz, 2002). A meta-analysis of 235 subjects derived from three studies found that 34% of all subjects had onset of symptoms prior to age 15, 16% prior to age 10, and 4.5% prior to age 5 (Challamel et al., 1994). Patients frequently report a lag of 5 to 10 years between the onset of clinical symptoms and establishment of the definitive diagnosis, suggesting insufficient awareness of the disorder among health professionals.

Narcolepsy has been described in miniature horses, Brahmin bulls, quarter horses, and about 15 breeds of dogs. Canine narcolepsy has autosomal recessive inheritance, and is related to a deficiency of hypocretin 2 receptors. On the other hand, the murine model of narcolepsy is associated with deficiency of the hypocretin (orexin) ligand. Hypocretin is a peptide that is elaborated in dorsomedial and dorsolateral areas of the hypothalamus. Hypocretin-containing neurons have widespread projections to the forebrain and brain stem. Activation of hypocretin projections leads to up-regulation of arousal mechanisms, increased muscle tone, muscle activity, and metabolic rate.

Human narcolepsy-cataplexy is associated with a marked deficiency hypocretin–1 in the cerebrospinal fluid. In contrast to the autosomal recessive transmission of canine narcolepsy, the pathogenesis of human narcolepsy is more complex, and appears to be related to an interplay between genetic and environmental factors. The histocompatibility antigen DQB1*0602 is present in 90 to 95% of patients with narcolepsy, in contrast to a 25 to 30% prevalence in the general population. Genetic susceptibility per se is, however, insufficient to trigger symptoms, as evidenced by the fact that monozygotic twins may be discordant for the disorder. Environmental stresses like head trauma, systemic infection, or surgery precede the development of clinical symptoms in two thirds of subjects, thus supporting a "two-hit" hypothesis. Rare instances of *secondary narcolepsy* following encephalitis, hypothalamic tumors, central nervous system lymphoma, and vascular malformations also suggest a contribution from acquired factors. It is presumed that low central nervous system levels of hypocretin–1 decrease noradrenergic activity and also lead to disinhibition of the brain stem cholinergic systems, thus triggering both sleepiness and cataplexy.

The diagnosis of narcolepsy is established on the basis of the narcoleptic tetrad (overwhelming sleepiness, cataplexy, hypnagogic hallucinations, sleep paralysis), combined with characteristic findings on the nocturnal polysomnogram and the multiple sleep latency test (MSLT). The nocturnal polysomnogram is a procedure in which the activity of multiple bodily functions, such as the electroencephalogram (EEG), eye movements, chin and leg electromyogram (EMG), airflow, thoracic and abdominal respiratory effort, electrocardiogram, and oxygen saturation, are recorded simultaneously on a strip of moving graph paper or a computer system. The test helps exclude disorders such as obstructive sleep apnea and periodic limb movement disorder which may also impair daytime alertness and mimic narcolepsy. On the morning following the nocturnal polysomnogram, the patient undergoes the MSLT, during which four 20-minute nap opportunities are provided at two hourly intervals in a darkened, quiet room (e.g., at 1000, 1200, 1400, and 1600 hours). The speed with which the subject falls asleep is measured using the EEG, chin EMG, and eye movement recordings. The time between "lights out" and sleep onset is termed the *sleep latency*. The mean sleep latency is calculated by adding the sleep latencies of individual naps and dividing by the total number of naps. The mean sleep latency is markedly shortened to less than 5 minutes in subjects with narcolepsy, as compared to normal values in the 14 to 20 minute range in unaffected controls. Furthermore, unaffected individuals show a transition from wakefulness into REM sleep, while patients with narcolepsy tend to shift from wakefulness directly into REM sleep.

The differential diagnosis of narcolepsy includes insufficient sleep, abnormal sleep hygiene, circadian rhythm disorders like the delayed sleep phase syndrome, the upper airway resistance syndrome, idiopathic hypersomnia, depression, periodic hypersomnia, and abuse of hypnotic/sedative drugs (prescription or over-the-counter).

Narcolepsy requires lifelong treatment. Daytime sleepiness is countered with stimulants like methylphenidate or dextroamphetamine. The side effects include anorexia, nervousness, tics, and insomnia. Modafinil (Provigil), a drug with an unspecified mode of action, is also effective in enhancing alertness and improving psychomotor performance. Gamma hydroxybutyrate also holds promise as an agent for both enhancing alertness and reducing cataplexy. Because cholinergic pathways in the brain stem mediate cataplexy, drugs such as clomimipramine and protryptiline with anticholinergic properties have been used to treat cataplexy. Replacement therapy with hypocretin analogues holds some long-term promise. One to three planned naps per day, each lasting 25 to 30 minutes, are also helpful in enhancing alertness. Supportive psychotherapy and fluoxetine may be needed if the patient develops emotional or behavioral problems.

Because of the increased risk of accidents from sleepiness, patients with narcolepsy should be cautioned against driving and should not work close to sharp, moving machinery. The Narcolepsy Network, Inc. (http://www.narcolepsynetwork.org) is a helpful nonprofit patient support organization.

REFERENCES

Challamel, M. J., Mazzola, M. E., Nevsimalova, S., et al. (1994). Narcolepsy in children. *Sleep, 17S,* 17–20.

Silber, M. H., Krahn, L. E., Olson, E. J., & Pankrantz, S. (2002). Epidemiology of narcolepsy in Olmstead County, Minnesota. *Sleep, 25,* 197–202.

SUGGESTED READING

John, J., Wu, M. F., & Siegel, J. M. (2000). Systemic administration of hypocretin-1 reduces cataplexy and normalizes sleep and waking durations in narcoleptic dogs. *Sleep Research Online, 3,* 23–28.

Kotagal, S., Hartse, K. M., & Walsh, J. K. (1990). Characteristics of narcolepsy in pre-teen aged children. *Pediatrics, 85,* 205–209.

Littner, M., Johnson, S. F., McCall, W. V., Anderson, W. M., Davila, D., Hartse, S. K., Kushida, C. A., Wise, M. S., Hirshkowitz, M., & Woodson, B. T. (2001). Practice parameters for the treatment of narcolepsy: An update for 2000. *Sleep, 24*(4), 451–466.

Thannickal, T. C., Moore, R. Y., Nienhuis, R., Ramanathan, L., Gulyani, S., Aldrich, M., Comford, M., & Siegel, J. M. (2000). Reduced number of hypocretin neurons in human narcolepsy. *Neuron, 27,* 469–474.

SURESH KOTAGAL
Mayo Clinic

See also: **Rapid Eye Movement (REM); Sleep**

NATIONAL INSTITUTE OF MENTAL HEALTH

The National Institute of Mental Health (NIMH), a component of the U.S. National Institutes of Health (NIH), supports and conducts research to reduce the burden of mental and behavioral disorders through a better understanding of mind, brain, and behavior. In the United States, mental disorders collectively account for more than 15 percent of the overall burden of disease, a term that encompasses both premature death and disability associated with illness. The NIMH is the nation's largest single source of support for research on mental disorders, with an appropriated budget of $1.25 billion in fiscal year 2002. Approximately 85% of this budget supports research grants and contracts at universities, hospitals, and other settings throughout the country. The Institute also administers an intramural, or in-house, research program that accounts for about 11% of its budget.

Creation and Early History of NIMH

Although the origins of NIMH can be traced to the federal government's efforts to provide treatment to narcotic addicts in the early twentieth century, more immediate impetus for the Institute's creation was the fact that psychiatric disorders were found to be the largest cause for medical discharges from the military during WWII and accounted for nearly 40% of Selective Service rejections. When these data stimulated congressional interest, Robert Felix, M.D., then director of the U.S. Public Health Service's Division of Mental Hygiene, expanded an earlier proposal to create a federal neuropsychiatric research institute to encompass responsibility for developing the nation's supply of mental health clinical personnel and assisting states to expand community-based mental health treatment facilities. This proposal received a prompt and positive hearing by Congress, which passed the National Mental Health Act (P.L. 79-487) that was signed into law by President Truman on July 3, 1946.

Upon its establishment, NIMH consisted of three extramural funding units focused, respectively, on research grants and fellowships, clinical training, and community services, and the fledgling intramural research program. Research opportunities in the biological, behavioral, and social sciences encouraged steady growth in basic and clinical research; NIMH also invested heavily in training scientists. With respect to developing a national pool of mental health clinicians, stipends to trainees and funding of faculty salaries were the most common means of support, although NIMH strove to accommodate specific needs of various disciplines, funding curriculum development conferences and visiting teacherships in psychology, for example, and funding career teacher and career investigator awards needed to develop mental health research capacity. In the mental health services arena, NIMH worked with states to develop community-based mental health services, stimulating an initiative that grew dramatically after President Kennedy signed a 1963 law authorizing NIMH to fund a national network of community mental health centers (CMHCs) that were anticipated to reduce need for long and costly hospitalization. Key CMHC concepts were early identification and prevention of mental disorders; provision of a comprehensive array of services; and continuity of care.

Over the years, scientific progress and opportunities, public health needs, and political directives have influenced NIMH's research priorities. In 1965, for example, President Johnson pledged to ensure the relevance of federally funded research to social ailments. NIMH responded by creating problem-focused centers to insure that basic and applied research, training, service demonstrations, and related activities would be devoted to critical targets. Centers were created to focus on Schizophrenia and suicide, but also on crime and delinquency, urban mental health, alcohol and drug abuse, minority group mental health, and, under congressional mandate, the prevention and control of rape. In 1970, award of the Nobel Prize to NIMH scientist Julius Axelrod for his studies of neurochemical processes in the brain signaled growing emphasis on research into basic biological and behavioral substrates of mental disorders.

Still, the Institute's involvement in mental health services and its high-profile role in social problems research clearly differentiated it from other NIH components, and in 1967 the NIMH was separated from the NIH. Six years later, the NIMH centers focusing on alcohol and drug abuse were converted to full-fledged institutes, and a new agency, the Alcohol, Drug Abuse, and Mental Health Administration, was created to serve as an umbrella for the three institutes.

By the late 1970s, NIMH's investment in CMHCs had helped transform the mental health care system into a pluralistic system comprising federal, state, local, and private facilities. Deinstitutionalization of long-term residential mental hospitals that had begun with the introduction of effective psychotropic drugs in the 1950s accelerated with the advent of federal reimbursement programs that underwrote services traditionally funded by states. In order to more effectively target services to persons with severe mental illnesses, the NIMH launched in 1977 a pilot Community Support Program (CSP) designed to assist states and communities improve mental health and related support services for adults with chronically disabling mental health problems. The success of the CSP in reducing need for hospitalization came to be widely recognized, and most states invested additional money to complement the start-up investment made by NIMH.

Through the 1970s and 1980s, NIMH refocused mental health clinical training on special areas such as children, the elderly, minorities, and the chronically mentally ill, and on mental health consultation/liaison, given the increasing role of the general medical sector in providing mental health care. By the time NIMH was relieved of clinical training authority in 1992, annual funding for these programs had dwindled to $13 million, from a high point of $98 million in 1969.

In the late 1970s, competition between NIMH research and service priorities was being questioned sharply by many people. NIMH increased its research investment in neuroscience and related brain and behavior research; clinical treatment studies; epidemiology; and an area of emerging interest, mental health services/economics research. Support for this shift and for an intended refocusing of service programs on treatment needs posed by severe mental illness received added impetus in the late 1970s with the emergence of a vocal mental health consumer movement. The National Alliance for the Mentally Ill (NAMI) and, subsequently, the National Depressive and Manic Depressive Association (NDMDA) and the Anxiety Disorders Association of America (ADAA), were key consumers' groups that added an authentic and compelling note of urgency to an advocacy effort that had been borne for many years by the National Mental Health Association.

The shift toward research as the defining mission of the NIMH that occurred during the 1980s was punctuated in 1989 when President George Bush signed into law (P.L. 101-58) a presidential proclamation designating the 1990s the "Decade of the Brain," and again in 1992 when advocacy groups favoring closer ties of mental health science and practice to mainstream medicine supported a reorganization that reunited NIMH's research and research training with the NIH while assigning service responsibilities to a new federal agency. Today, NIMH is exclusively a research institute with four broad scientific priorities: basic research in molecular biology, neuroscience, genetics, and behavior; the translation of new basic knowledge into clinical applications; treatment effectiveness studies that will provide a foundation for evidence-based practice; and research dissemination activities.

Richard K. Nakamura
National Institute of Mental Health

NATIONAL INSTITUTES OF HEALTH

The National Institutes of Health (NIH) is the U.S. federal government's principal agency for the support of medical research. The mission of the NIH is to uncover new knowledge that will lead to improved human health. With a 2001 budget of more than $20 billion, the 27 institutes and centers that comprise the NIH award about 84 percent of the money through a grants program to investigators in universities and other institutions across the United States and to some foreign researchers. A smaller in-house program of research so-called intramural research, is funded on the NIH's campus in Bethesda, Maryland, and ancillary sites.

This present-day configuration emerged after World War II, but the NIH itself traces its roots to 1887, when a one-room bacteriological laboratory was created within the Marine Hospital Service, predecessor agency to the U.S. Public Health Service. Initially, infectious diseases were the primary concern of the laboratory. Beginning in 1902, research expanded into the areas of pharmacology, chemistry, and zoology, and after 1912, research into noncontagious diseases was also included. Basic research, especially in chemistry, became an interest of laboratory scientists in the 1920s and 1930s. In 1937, the first categorical institute, the National Cancer Institute (NCI), was created as a separate entity from the NIH.

During World War II, all NIH research was redirected toward the war effort. In 1944, a Public Health Service reorganization act introduced two features that shaped the subsequent development of the modern NIH. First, the NIH was permitted to award grants in aid of research; second, the NIH was permitted to conduct clinical research. Health-related lobbying groups also convinced Congress to create additional categorical institutes, the first of which was the National Institute of Mental Health (NIMH), authorized in 1946. By 1948, institutes for heart disease and dental research joined existing programs in microbiology and experimental biology and medicine to bring the number of institutes to six.

Other institutes investigated arthritis, eye diseases, neurological diseases, deafness, and diabetes, among other diseases. The National Library of Medicine (NLM) developed bioinformatics, and the Fogarty International Center coordinated international biomedical research activities. In addition to disease-focused components, institutes for research on the broad areas of child health, aging, nursing, and general medical sciences were also added. In recent years, components for human genome research, complementary and alternative medicine, biomedical imaging and bioengineering, and several others have come into the NIH. In 2002, 27 institutes and centers sponsored multiple research initiatives related to their categorical missions. In addition, trans-NIH initiatives seek to coordinate work across institute boundaries. Special disciplinary interest groups, a bioengineering consortium, and a mammalian gene collection reflect other cross-cutting efforts.

In the 1950s, research in psychology and the neurosciences, although technically housed in two separate institutes, shared a common in-house research program. The most highly recognized research growing out of this effort was Julius Axelrod's work on the reuptake phenomenon of neurotransmitters, for which he won a 1970 Nobel prize in "medicine or physiology." Axelrod's work, which built on a biological foundation for mental health research that had begun with the psychopharmacology revolution of the 1950s and 1960s, punctuated the ascendancy of neuroscience research at NIMH as well as at the National Institute on Neurological Diseases and Stroke (NINDS). These two institutes now lead a trans-NIH neurosciences initiative. One of its components is the Human Brain initiative, which supports research on and development of advanced technologies and infrastructure through cooperative efforts among neuroscientists and information scientists. The goal is to produce new digital capabilities in an Internet-based information management system.

In addition to its support of biologically-oriented medical research, the NIH has had a long and growing commitment to behavioral and social scientific research relevant to health. Almost all NIH institutes and centers have played a role, but NIMH has remained the largest single source of support for behavioral research and social science. Following President Lyndon B. Johnson's call in the 1960s to apply research to the alleviation of social and public health problems, NIMH established various topic-focused centers on basic and applied research, training, demonstration grants, and technical assistance related to issues such as crime and delinquency, suicide, inner-city problems, mental health and aging, minority group mental health, and substance abuse and alcoholism. In 1968, NIMH was moved out of NIH to become a part of the newly created Alcohol, Drug Abuse, and Mental Health Administration (ADAMHA). Research components of NIMH, the National Institute on Alcoholism and Alcohol Abuse (NIAAA), and the National Institute on Drug Abuse (NIDA) rejoined the NIH in 1992.

In addition, in the 1970s the National Heart, Lung, and Blood Institute (NHLBI) developed a pioneering extramural program on health and behavior, and the National Institute on Child Health and Human Development (NICHD) as well as the National Institute on Aging (NIA) established broad-ranging programs in support of basic and applied behavioral and social research. In 1979, ADAMHA and NIH jointly commissioned a landmark study by the Institute of Medicine entitled *Health and Behavior: Frontiers of Research in the Biobehavioral Sciences* (Washington, DC: National Academy Press, 1982) that gave direction to NIH's expanding activities in the behavioral and social sciences. Organizationally, NIH recognized the need to coordinate its activities across the institutes and centers, and in 1982 it established the NIH Working Group on Health and Behavior (now called the NIH Behavioral and Social Sciences Research Coordinating Committee). In 1993, Congress established the Office of Behavioral and Social Sciences Research (OBSSR) in the Office of the Director, NIH, in recognition of the key role that behavioral and social factors often play in illness and health. The OBSSR mission is to stimulate behavioral and social sciences research throughout NIH and to integrate these areas of research more fully into other areas of NIH health research, thereby improving the understanding, treatment, and prevention of disease. Currently, about 10 percent of the NIH budget is devoted to behavioral and social sciences research and training across its various programs.

In 1999, Congress made a commitment to double the NIH budget by 2003. The additional monies have been invested in several highly promising lines of research. One achievement from the investment in genomics—the map of the human genome—is perhaps the best known. Other areas include protenomics, the analysis of large sets of proteins with the goal of understanding their function; combinatorial chemistry, which provides a new way to generate large libraries of molecules that can be screened for use as drugs; and new, advanced imaging techniques.

The National Institutes of Health

Office of the Director

Institutes

- National Cancer Institute
- National Eye Institute
- National Heart, Lung, and Blood Institute
- National Human Genome Research Institute
- National Institute on Aging
- National Institute on Alcoholism and Alcohol Abuse
- National Institute of Allergy and Infectious Diseases
- National Institute of Arthritis and Musculoskeletal and Skin Diseases
- National Institute on Biomedical Imaging and Bioengineering
- National Institute of Child Health and Human Development
- National Institute on Deafness and Other Communication Disorders
- National Institute of Dental and Craniofacial Research
- National Institute of Diabetes and Digestive and Kidney Diseases
- National Institute on Drug Abuse
- National Institute of Environmental Health Sciences
- National Institute of General Medical Sciences
- National Institute of Mental Health
- National Institute of Neurological Disorders and Stroke
- National Institute of Nursing Research
- National Library of Medicine

Centers

- Center for Information Technology
- Center for Scientific Review
- John E. Fogarty International Center
- National Center for Complementary and Alternative Medicine
- National Center for Minority Health and Health Disparities
- National Center for Research Resources
- Warren Grant Magnuson Clinical Center

Victoria A. Harden
Raynard S. Kington
National Institutes of Health

NATURAL SELECTION

Definitions of natural selection vary due to the long history of the discussion of this topic. According to Darwin's theory of evolution, natural selection signifies the phenomenon that in the struggle for life only the favorable variants of a potentially much larger progeny survive. Advantageous variations accumulate, and thus descendants finally diverge from the ancestors until—in the long run—new species evolve.

Apart from a few exceptions, most contemporary biologists and other scholars regard natural selection as a real process in nature. However, the evaluation of the extent to which natural selection contributes to the origin of species varies significantly among them. For the neo-Darwinian school of biologists, natural selection is the key process for the origin of all life forms on earth. However, for most other biologists it is of only limited significance and thus largely incapable of explaining the origin of species, and especially higher systematic categories. Between these views all possible intermediates can be found.

Basic problems for the theory of natural selection include: (1) the virtual inaccessibility of past events, and (2) the fact that even at present, putative selection processes are hardly attainable for rigorous scientific investigation.

With regard to the modern synthesis, with its ideas of selection of mutations with "slight or even invisible effects on the phenotype" (Mayr) within a high number of offspring, by the 1950s, French biologists such as Cuenot, Tetry, and Chauvin raised the following objection (according to Litynski, 1961):

> Out of 120,000 fertilized eggs of the green frog only two individuals survive. Are we to conclude that these two frogs out of 120,000 were selected by nature because they were the fittest ones; or rather—as Cuenot said—that natural selection is nothing but blind mortality which selects nothing at all?

If—as in many other cases—only a few out of millions and even billions of individuals are to survive and reproduce, then there is some difficulty in believing that those few should really be the fittest. Strongly different abilities and varying environmental conditions can already turn up during different phases of ontogenesis. Distances between and hiding places of predator and prey, local differences of biotopes and geographical circumstances, and weather conditions and microclimates all belong to the repertoire of infinitely varying parameters. One may therefore agree with King Solomon, who stated in 1000 B.C.: "I returned, and saw under the sun, that the race is not to the swift, nor the battle to the strong . . . but time and chance happeneth to all of them."

Population genetics has attempted to quantitatively assess this problem. Fisher (1930) calculated that new alleles with even 1% selective advantage will routinely be lost in natural populations with more than 90% probability in the next 31 generations. Chance occurrences like genetic drift (random fluctuations of gene frequencies in populations) seem to play a rather underestimated role in nature. Moreover, variation due to modifications can strongly surpass the effects of the mutations mentioned previously.

In spite of the objections listed earlier concerning the limits of natural selection as a general principle in nature, some survival-of-the-fittest apparently takes place. Although largely caused by human activities, the emergence of new alleles and plasmids with strong selective advantage, as in the cases of multiple resistance in bacteria and resistances due to DDT in insect species, have often been cited as evidence of natural selection in action.

The discussion between biologists and other scientists, therefore, deals with the question of the extent to which natural selection takes place in nature, and whether it is actually an omnipotent principle that explains the diversity of all life forms.

To be sufficient, the selective principle considered above depends on adequate numbers of creative mutations to occur, constituting the basis upon which selection will work. However, in large mutagenesis experiments the number of new phenotypes due to mutations regularly proved to be limited and followed a saturation curve (see the *law of recurrent variation,* Lönnig, 2002).

Also, on the morphological/structural level severe difficulties exist for natural selection. A major problem is the origin of irreducibly complex structures. "An irreducible complex system is one that requires several closely matched parts in order to function and where removal of one of the components effectively causes the system to cease functioning" (Behe, 1998, p.179). The often quoted example of the bacterium flagellum with filament, hook, and motor embedded in the membranes and cell wall has not, in fact, been explained by natural selection (for further examples, see Behe, 1996). But even for many simple structural differences, such as the wide variety of different kinds of leaf margins in plants, few selective advantages have been detected so far. Thus, qualitative as well as quantitative limits in generating selectively advantageous mutations point to the limits of the theory of natural selection.

The objection raised by the philosopher Sir Karl Popper that "Darwinism is not a testable scientific theory but a *metaphysical research program,*" that is, natural selection was seen to be "almost tautologous" (1974), has so strongly been contested by neo-Darwinians and others that four years later he retracted some of his arguments and stated that "the theory of natural selection may be so formulated that it is far from tautological" (1978). As evidence, he mentioned the famous textbook example of natural selection termed the "industrial melanism" of the peppered moth (*Biston betularia*).

However, 20 years after Popper's partial retraction, Coyne (1998) and other biologists have stated that the whole case is flawed. They note that: (1) peppered moths normally do not rest on tree trunks, (2) they choose their resting places during the night, and (3) the return of the variegated form occurred independently of the lichens "that supposedly played such an important role" in the evaluation of the phenomenon (for an extensive recent discussion, see Hooper, 2002). Thus, Popper's partial retraction is not substantiated by the only case he mentioned, and his original criticism of metaphysics seems still to be more valid than he later imagined.

In the search for possible alternatives to explain the complexity and divergence of life forms, one of the hypotheses—the concept of Intelligent Design—integrates the difficulties arising from statistical improbabilities as well as the morphological and functional problems that have not been solved by the modern synthesis.

REFERENCES

Behe, M. (1996). *Darwin's black box: The biochemical challenge to evolution.* New York: Free Press.

Behe, M. (1998). Intelligent design theory as a tool for analyzing biochemical systems. In W. A. Dembski (Ed.), *Mere Creation* (pp. 177–194). Downers Grove, IL: InterVarsity Press.

Coyne, J. A. (1998). Not black and white (review of the book of Majerus, M.E.N., 1998, melanism). *Nature, 396,* 35–36.

Hooper, J. (2002). *Of moths and men: Intrigue, tragedy & the peppered moth.* London: Fourth Estate.

Litzynski, Z. (1961). Should we burn Darwin? *Science Digest, 51,* 61–63.

Lönnig, W.-E. (2002). *Mutationen: Das gesetz der rekurrenten variation.* Cologne: Naturwissenschaftlicher Verlag.

Mayr, E. (1998). *Toward a new philosophy of biology.* Oxford, UK: Oxford University Press.

Popper, K. (1978). Natural selection and the emergence of mind. *Dialectia, 32,* 339–355.

Wolf-Ekkehard Lönnig
Heinz-Albert Becker
Max-Planck-Institut für Züchtungsforschung Cologne, FRG

NATURALISTIC OBSERVATION

Naturalistic observation refers to the unobtrusive and nonreactive study of organisms in their native habitat or environment, devoid of researcher manipulation, intrusion, or controls. The naturalness of the study environment, however, is to be interpreted as a continuum rather than as a dichotomy (Dane, 1994). Fossey's (1983) study of the mountain gorillas in their natural habitat in Zaire (1983); Goodall's (1986) study of chimpanzees in the forests of Gombe; and Schaller's study of gorillas in Zaire, pandas in China, and wildlife in the Tibetan steppe (Schaller, 1963, 1993, 1998) are examples of recent naturalistic observation studies conducted by ethologists. In addition to animal ethology, naturalistic observation techniques have been widely used in psychology, anthropology, sociology, and education to study human beings as well. Among the large number of topics that are studied using naturalistic observation techniques are instinctive behavior, imprinting, evolution, play, stimuli, communication and signals, feeding, hunting, learning, memory, adaptation, organizations, courtship and mating, cooperation, competition, migration, environment, depression, mental illness, children at play, and ecology. The studies encompass animals, birds, fish, and human beings.

Though systematic usage of naturalistic observation is of recent origin, it is one of the oldest methodologies in science. The development of naturalistic observation may be roughly divided into three periods: (1) antiquity to 1920, (2) 1920 to 1950, and (3) post 1950s. Its origins can be traced back to prehistoric times, rooted in oral traditions and observable in cave paintings. Many explorers, travelers, and journalists have contributed observational accounts of their own or other societies. During the last century, naturalists including Charles Darwin carried out more systematic fieldwork.

The second period, between 1920 and 1950, has been described as the classical period of ethology (Crist, 1999). This period witnessed basic and comprehensive changes in naturalistic observation research that continue to evolve today. Theoretical perspectives were introduced during the latter part of this period in order to understand and explain animal behavior.

After the 1950s, ecological perspectives and the study of human ethology were introduced (Willems & Raush, 1969). Similarly, sociobiological perspectives, evolutionary psychological approaches, and the area of cognitive ethology were also introduced during this period. Behavior therapists began to use direct observation in collecting specific behavioral data in natural settings (Hutt & Hutt 1970; Johnson & Bolstad, 1973; Mash & Terdal, 1976), and clinicians extended their observations from individuals to organizations. The works of Lorenz, Tinbergen, and von Frisch were awarded the Nobel prize in 1973, and the prize provided a prestigious acknowledgment of the contributions of ethology (Tinbergen, 1985). More recently, ideas from other disciplines such as game theory, optimality theory from economics, and handicap principles from sports have been borrowed to study animal behavior in the context of competing demands for food and safety.

Technology has significantly impacted the naturalistic observation methodology in recent years. The availability of versatile audio equipment, sophisticated digital video equipment, and powerful computers has extended the scope, range, and attractiveness of naturalistic observation and has made possible the dissemination of observations and findings to much larger audiences.

Conducting Naturalistic Observation Studies and Research Issues

Though the naturalistic paradigm has been shared by different disciplines, the research techniques in those fields vary significantly (Arrington, 1943; Brandt, 1972; Denzin & Lincoln, 1994; Dewsbury, 1985; Hammersley, 1992; Liebow, 1967; Lincoln & Guba, 1985; Malinowski, 1953; Pelto & Pelto, 1978; Taylor & Bogdan, 1984; Weick, 1985.) Researchers who study animals have commonly addressed five types of questions. These questions refer to the function, evolution and adaptation, causation, development of behavior, and stages of development. Some of these studies are comparative in nature. Laboratory studies of animals are used to study the physiology and neural control of behavior that is not affected by captivity or the artificiality of the laboratory. Another set of studies covers anthropological, sociological, and educational perspectives focused on understanding and explaining groups, societies, and cultures in different contexts. The complexity of human beings and their social structure has necessitated the use of supplemental tools and techniques such as laboratory studies, interviews, projective techniques, multisite studies, informants, multidimensional rating scales, and content analysis.

At various times, issues have been raised about naturalistic observation's importance, methodological validity and reliability, generalizability, replicability, intrusion by researchers, and interpretation of behavior, especially human behavior. The work of Darwin, for example, has been analyzed and scrutinized for its anthropomorphism (Crist, 1999, pp. 11–51). Questions about sampling raised by Arrington (1943) more than 50 years ago are relevant even today. Nevertheless, naturalistic observers have addressed many of these problems, and it is now generally recognized that social and behavioral sciences cannot always be devoid of researcher selectivity and bias (Asquith, 1991; Haraway, 1989).

Trends

It is clear that naturalistic observation methods have gained legitimacy among academic disciplines. The search for naturalistic conditions or environments even in the context of experimental designs (Gibbons, Wyers, Waters, & Menzel, 1994) is an illustration. Studies of the animal kingdom, fish, and birds have also gained wide popularity among the general public through the media, especially television. Researchers such as Goodall and Fossey are now known outside their own fields. Recent discoveries of the closeness between the animal kingdom and human beings have provided an economic rationale for such studies as well. With the introduction of new topics such as ecology, the debate surrounding controversial topics such as cognitive ethology, and the advent of significant technological breakthroughs, the techniques of naturalistic observation are likely to be even more widely used and accepted in the future.

REFERENCES

Arrington, R. E. (1943). Time sampling in studies of social behavior: A critical review of techniques and results with research suggestions. *Psychological Bulletin, 40*(2), 81–124.

Asquith, P. (1991). Primate research groups in Japan: Orientation and East-West differences. In L. M. Fedigan & P. J. Asquith (Eds.), *The monkeys of arashiyama* (pp. 81–99). Albany: State University of New York Press.

Brandt, R. M. (1972). *Studying behavior in natural settings.* New York: Holt, Rhinehart, and Winston.

Crist, E. (1999). *Images of animals, anthropomorphism and the animal mind.* Philadelphia: Temple University Press.

Dane, F. C. (1994). Survey methods, naturalistic observations and case studies. In A. M. Coleman (Ed.), *Companion encyclopedia of psychology* (pp. 1142–1156). London: Routledge.

Denzin, N. K., & Lincoln, Y. S. (1994). *Handbook of qualitative research.* Thousand Oaks, CA: Sage Publications.

Dewsbury, D. A. (Ed.). (1985). *Studying animal behavior, autobiographies of the founders.* Chicago: University of Chicago Press.

Fossey, D. (1983). *Gorillas in the mist.* Boston: Houghton Miflin.

Gibbons, E. F., Jr., Wyers, E. J., Waters, E., & Menzel, E. W. (Eds.). *Naturalistic environments in captivity for animal behavior research.* Albany: State University of New York Press.

Goodall, J. (1986). *The chimpanzees of Gombe: Patterns of behavior.* Cambridge, MA: Belknap Press.

Hammersley, M. (1992). *What's wrong with ethnography?* New York: Routledge.

Haraway, D. (1989). *Primate visions: Gender, race, and nature in the world of modern science.* New York: Routledge.

Hutt, S. J., & Hutt, C. (1970). *Direct observation and measurement of behavior.* Springfield, IL: Charles C. Thomas.

Johnson, S. M., & Bolstad, O. D. (1973). Methodological issues in naturalistic observations: Some problems and solutions for field research. In L. A. Hamerlynck, L. C. Handy, & E. J. Mash (Eds.), *Behavior change: Methodology, concepts, and practice* (pp. 7–68). Champaign, IL: Research Press.

Liebow, E. (1967). *Tally's corner: A study of Negro street corner men.* Boston: Little Brown.

Lincoln, Y., & Guba, E. (1985). *Naturalistic inquiry.* Beverly Hills, CA: Sage.

Malinowski, B. (1953). *Argonauts of the western pacific: An account of native enterprise and adventure in the archipelagoes of Melanesian New Guinea.* New York: Dutton.

Mash, E. J., & Terdal, L. G. (Eds.). (1976). *Behavior-therapy assessment: Diagnosis, design, and evaluation.* New York: Springer Publishing.

Pelto, P. J., & Pelto, G. H. (1978). *Anthropological research: The structure of inquiry* (2nd ed.). Cambridge: Cambridge University Press.

Schaller, G. B. (1963). *The mountain gorilla: Ecology and behavior.* Chicago: University of Chicago Press.

Schaller, G. B. (1993). *The last panda.* Chicago: University of Chicago Press.

Schaller, G. B. (1998). *The wildlife of the Tibetan steppe.* Chicago: University of Chicago Press.

Taylor, S. J., & Bogdan, R. (1984). *Introduction to qualitative research methods: The search for meanings.* New York: Wiley.

Tinbergen, N. (1985). Watching and wondering. In D. A. Dewsbury (Ed.), *Studying animal behavior, autobiographies of the founders* (p. 455). Chicago: University of Chicago Press.

Weick, K. E. (1985). Systematic observational methods. In E. Aronson & G. Lindzay (Eds.), *Handbook of social psychology* (3rd ed., pp. 567–634). New York: Random House.

Willems, E. P., & Raush, H. L. (Eds.). (1969). *Naturalistic viewpoints in psychological research.* New York: Holt, Rinehart, and Winston.

Subhash R. Sonnad
Western Michigan University

See also: **Anthropology; Ethology**

NATURE–NURTURE CONTROVERSY

The so-called nature–nurture controversy is a family of controversies about the relative roles of heredity (nature) and environment (nurture) in shaping human characteristics. These controversies exist not so much because the scientific questions involved are difficult—although many are—but because the proposed alternative solutions are perceived as having profound implications for cherished beliefs concerning human equality, social justice, and individual responsibility.

Although precursors of the nature–nurture controversy may be found in the writings of the ancient Greeks, its modern form can be traced back fairly directly to the philosopher John Locke (1632–1704) on the one hand, and the naturalist Charles Darwin (1809–1882) on the other.

Locke may be considered the chief ideological father of the nurture side of the controversy. In *An Essay Concerning Human Understanding* (1690), he invoked the metaphor of the mind as a blank sheet of paper on which knowledge is written by the hand of experience. His political view that all men are by nature equal and independent had a strong influence on the theorists of the American and French revolutions. In Locke's own view, human political equality was not inconsistent with an inborn diversity of human tendencies and capabilities. In *Some Thoughts Concerning Education* (1683, §101) he wrote, "Some men by the unalterable frame of their constitutions are stout, others timorous, some confident, others modest, tractable, or obstinate, curious, or careless, quick or slow. There are not more differences in men's faces, and the outward lineaments of their bodies, than there are in the makes and tempers of their minds." Nevertheless, Locke judged the bulk of human variation to be the result of differences in experience (§1): "I think I may say, that of all the men we meet with, nine parts of ten are what they are, good or evil, useful or not, by their education."

Darwin gave the nature side of the controversy its modern form by placing the human mind solidly in the framework of biological evolution. In *The Descent of Man* (1871) and *The Expression of the Emotions in Man and Animals* (1872), Darwin made it clear that human behavior shared common ancestry with the behavior of other animal forms, and that behavioral as well as physical characters were subject to the basic evolutionary mechanism of genetic variation followed by natural selection of the variants most successful in their environments. Darwin's younger cousin, Sir Francis Galton, enthusiastically applied Darwin's ideas to the interpretation of human differences. Galton invented mental testing, and also founded the eugenics movement, which aimed to improve humanity by encouraging the more able to have larger families and the less able to have smaller ones.

Another aspect of the Darwinian continuity of humans with other animals was emphasized by the psychologist William McDougall in the early part of the twentieth century. McDougall developed a social psychology around the doctrine of instincts, the idea that "the human mind has certain innate or inherited tendencies which are the essential springs or motive powers of all thought and action" (McDougall, 1908, p. 20). Examples of such inherited tendencies cited by McDougall were the instincts of gregariousness, self-assertion, curiosity, flight, repulsion, pugnacity, acquisition, construction, parental care, and reproduction.

Both McDougall's instinct doctrine and the Galtonian notion of inherited individual differences in capacities were vigorously rejected in the radical behaviorism of the psychologist John B. Watson, who in 1925 issued a famous challenge: "Give me a dozen healthy infants, well-formed, and my own specified world to bring them up in and I'll guarantee to take any one at random and train him to become any type of specialist I might select . . . regardless of his talents, penchants, tendencies, abilities, vocations, and race of his ancestors" (Watson, 1925, p. 82).

The next few decades of the nature–nurture debate were marked by an increasing emphasis on empirical research, involving identical and fraternal twins, adoptive families, and other informative groups. In a series of 1959 lectures (published in 1962 as *Mankind Evolving*), the geneticist Theodosius Dobzhansky elegantly integrated Darwinian concepts with an appreciation of the role of culture in human evolution and Lockean democratic ideals. By 1960, with the publication of the textbook *Behavior Genetics* by J. L. Fuller, a biologist, and W. R. Thompson, a psychologist, it appeared that the nature–nurture controversy might at last be becoming ordinary science.

The calm was illusory. In 1969 the educational psychologist Arthur R. Jensen published a long article in the *Harvard Educational Review* entitled, "How much can we boost IQ and scholastic achievement?" Jensen took a fairly strong hereditarian position, estimating that about 80% of individual variation in IQ was genetic. To make matters worse, he conjectured that at least part of the persistent disadvantage of U.S. Blacks in IQ test performance was also genetic in origin.

In 1974, the psychologist Leon Kamin in *The Science and Politics of I.Q.* launched an assault on human behavior genetics and its political uses. A more moderate critique was that of the sociologist Christopher Jencks and his colleagues in their book, *Inequality* (1972). Then in 1975, a new front opened up with the publication by the zoologist Edward O. Wilson of *Sociobiology,* which outlined a modern population-genetic basis for the notion that biological instincts might play a central role in human affairs. Not all of the action inspired by these controversies was genteel academic debate—tires were slashed and speakers assaulted. In 1994, a new round of controversy was touched off by R. J. Herrnstein and C. Murray's book *The Bell Curve,* which examined the role of intelligence in American life.

Early in the twenty-first century, with cloning and the sequencing of the human genome in the news, it appears that nature–nurture controversies have not yet run their course. It would not do to conclude, however, that no progress has been made since the days of Locke and Darwin. Modern views of biological evolution, while deriving from Darwin, are more complex, differentiated, and mathematical than his. Modern psychology takes—in its better moments—a vastly more sophisticated view of the organism-environment interplay than the instinct lists of McDougall or the behavioristic battle cries of John B. Watson. Finally, nature–nurture controversialists must accommodate their prejudices to a much larger body of evidence today than in the past. Even though nature–nurture controversies continue, they themselves also evolve.

REFERENCES

Darwin, C. (1871). *The descent of man and selection in relation to sex.* London: Murray.

Darwin, C. (1965/1872). *The expression of the emotions in man and animals.* Chicago: University of Chicago Press.

Dobzhansky, Th. (1962). *Mankind evolving: The evolution of the human species.* New Haven, CT: Yale University Press.

Fuller, J. L., & Thompson, W. R. (1960). *Behavior genetics.* New York: Wiley.

Herrnstein, R. J., & Murray, C. (1994). *The bell curve: Intelligence and class structure in American life.* New York: Free Press.

Jencks, C., Smith, M., Acland, H., Bane, M. J., Cohen, D., Gintis, H., Heyns, B., & Michelson, S. (1972). *Inequality: A reassessment of the effects of family and schooling in America.* New York: Basic Books.

Jensen, A. R. (1969). How much can we boost IQ and scholastic achievement? *Harvard Educational Review, 39,* 1–123.

Kamin, L. J. (1974). *The science and politics of I.Q.* Hillsdale, NJ: Erlbaum.

Locke, J. (1934/1683). *Some thoughts concerning education.* Cambridge, UK: Cambridge University Press.

Locke, J. (1965/1690). *An essay concerning human understanding.* London: Dent.

McDougall, W. (1926/1908). *An introduction to social psychology.* Boston: Luce.

Watson, J. B. (1958/1925). *Behaviorism.* New York: Norton.

Wilson, E. O. (1975). *Sociobiology: The new synthesis.* Cambridge, MA: Harvard University Press.

John C. Loehlin
University of Texas

NEAR-DEATH EXPERIENCES

Near-death experiences are profound psychological events occurring in individuals close to death or facing intense physical or emotional danger. Although the term *near-death experience* and its acronym NDE were not coined until 1975, accounts of similar events can be found in the folklore and writings of most cultures. The phenomenon was first described as a clinical syndrome in 1892, although isolated cases appeared in medical journals throughout the nineteenth century. Once thought to be rare, NDEs have been documented to occur in 10% to 20% of cardiac arrest survivors.

Moody, who coined the term *near-death experience,* used it to refer to an ineffable experience on the threshold of death that may include hearing oneself pronounced dead, feelings of peace, unusual noises, a sense of movement through a dark tunnel, a sense of being out of the physical body, meeting other spiritual beings, meeting a being of light, a life review, a border or point of no return, and a return to the physical body, followed by profound changes in attitudes and values and elimination of one's fear of death. Noyes and Slymen factor-analyzed the features reported by near-death experiencers into (1) mystical elements, such as a feeling of great understanding, vivid images, and revival of memories; (2) depersonalization elements, such as loss of emotion, separation from the body, and feeling strange or unreal; and (3) hyperalertness elements, such as vivid and rapid thoughts and sharper vision and hearing. Ring proposed a model of NDEs unfolding in sequential stages of peace and contentment, detachment from the physical body, entering a darkness, seeing a brilliant light, and entering a supernal realm of existence.

Some investigators have identified different types of NDE. Sabom categorized NDEs as autoscopic, involving an apparent out-of-body experience; transcendental, involving an apparent passage of consciousness into another dimension; or combined, involving features of both types. Greyson classified NDEs as cognitive, dominated by altered thought processes; affective, dominated by changes in emotional state; paranormal, involving purported psychic elements; or transcendental, characterized by apparently mystical or otherworldly features.

Recent studies suggest that how one comes close to death may influence the type of NDE. NDEs dominated by cognitive features, such as temporal distortions, accelerated thoughts, and a life review, are more common in near-death events that are sudden and unexpected than in those that may have been anticipated. NDEs associated with cardiac arrest resemble out-of-body experiences, while those without cardiac arrest are more similar to depersonalization, in which one feels oneself or one's body to be unreal. NDEs occurring to intoxicated persons tend to be bizarre and confused, like hallucinations. Although all elements of the NDE can be reported by individuals who merely perceive themselves to be near death, an encounter with a brilliant light, enhanced cognitive function, and positive emotions are more common among individuals whose closeness to death can be corroborated by medical records.

Retrospective studies of near-death experiencers show them to be psychologically healthy individuals who do not differ from comparison groups in age, gender, race, religion, religiosity, mental illness, intelligence, neuroticism, extroversion, trait and state anxiety, and relevant Rorschach measures. Some studies suggest that the experiencers are good hypnotic subjects, remember their dreams more often, are adept at mental imagery, and tend to acknowledge more childhood trauma and resultant dissociative tendencies than nonexperiencers. It is not known whether these personal traits and recall of prior experiences are the results of an NDE or premorbid characteristics that predispose people to have NDEs when they come close to death.

Several physiological and psychological models have been proposed to explain NDEs, although there has been almost no research testing etiological hypotheses. A plausible psychological explanation suggests that NDEs are products of the imagination, constructed from personal and cultural expectations to protect us from facing the threat of death. However, individuals often report experiences that conflict with their specific religious and personal expectations of death. Although there are some cross-cultural variations in the content of NDEs, these may reflect simply the experiencers' difficulty processing and expressing an experience that is largely ineffable. Specific knowledge individuals had about NDEs previously does not influence the details of their own experiences; people who have never heard or read of NDEs describe the same kinds of experiences as do people who are quite familiar with the phenomenon. Furthermore, children too young to have received substantial cultural and religious conditioning about death report the same kinds of NDEs as do adults; some cases have been reported to have occurred before the child could have acquired any language skills.

Several neurobiological models have been proposed for the near-death experience, invoking the role of endorphins or various neurotransmitters, and linking the NDE to specific sites in the brain. At this point, such models are speculative and none has been tested. A plausible assumption is that NDEs are hallucinations produced either by drugs given to dying patients or by metabolic disturbances or brain malfunctions as a person approaches death. However, many NDEs are recounted by individuals who had no metabolic or organic conditions known to cause hallucinations. Organic brain malfunctions generally produce clouded thinking, irritability, fear, belligerence, and idiosyncratic visions, quite incompatible with the exceptionally clear thinking, peacefulness, calmness, and predictable content that typifies near-death experiences. Visions in patients with delirium are generally of living persons, whereas those in NDEs are almost invariably of deceased persons. Furthermore, patients who are febrile, anoxic, or given drugs when near death report fewer and less elaborate NDEs than do patients who remain drug-free. That finding may suggest that drug- or metabolically-induced delirium, rather than causing NDEs, in fact inhibits them from occurring, or alternatively that delirious patients tend not to recall their experiences upon recovery.

Regardless of their cause, NDEs may permanently and dramatically alter the individual experiencer's attitudes, beliefs, and values. Aftereffects most often reported, corroborated in long-term follow-up studies including interviews with near-death experiencers' significant others, include increased spirituality, compassion and concern for others, appreciation of life, belief in postmortem existence, sense of purpose, and confidence and flexibility in coping with life's vicissitudes, as well as decreased fear of death, interest in materialism, and competitiveness. Although decreased fear of death has been associated with increased suicidal risk, near-death experiencers paradoxically express stronger objections to suicide than do comparison samples, primarily on the basis of increased transcendental beliefs.

REFERENCES

Greyson, B. (1985). A typology of near-death experiences. *American Journal of Psychiatry, 142,* 967–969.

Moody, R. A. (1975). *Life after life.* Covington, GA: Mockingbird Books.

Noyes, R., & Slymen, D. J. (1978–1979). The subjective response to life-threatening danger. *Omega, 9,* 313–321.

Ring, K. (1980). *Life at death: A scientific investigation of the near-death experience.* New York: Coward, McCann and Geoghegan.

Sabom, M. B. (1982). *Recollections of death: A medical investigation.* New York: Harper & Row.

Bruce Greyson
University of Virginia Health System

See also: **Hallucinations; Stress Consequences**

NEOCORTEX

The two cerebral hemispheres comprise the most anterior and visible portion of the mammalian brain. In humans, most of the surface of these hemispheres is covered by highly convoluted neocortex (*cortex,* derived from Greek, means bark or covering). Neocortex is found only in mammals, and is differentiated from more primitive types of cortex by a complex morphology and lamination pattern. This tissue may be considered the "crown jewel" of mammalian evolution, having expanded more than any other brain region during our evolutionary history. The characteristic convolutions of the cortical surface represent a clever geometric solution to the challenge of fitting more of the two-dimensional neocortical sheet into a braincase without unduly increasing the size of the head. In humans, the neocortex occupies about 80% of the brain mass and is essential for rational thought, language, perception, and goal-directed behavior.

The neocortex is approximately 2 mm thick and consists of some 12 billion neurons. About 70% of these are large "pyramidal" shaped cells and the remainder are smaller "stellate" shaped cells. Functionally, cortical neurons may be classified based on whether they excite or inhibit their synaptic targets. Whereas pyramidal neurons are excitatory, different types of stellate neurons may be either excitatory or inhibitory. An imbalance of excitation and inhibition can lead to pathological states such as epileptic seizure activity.

Most of the neocortex is made up of six distinct layers of cell bodies and processes. These layers differ from one another in the size and density of their cell bodies and in the relative proportion of neurons of different types. The functional operations of the neocortex may divided into three general components: (1) reception of neural information from subcortical and cortical brain regions (via synaptic inputs), (2) integration of this information, and (3) organization of output signals that are projected to the many targets of the neocortex.

The cortical layering pattern is related to these basic functions. For example, layer IV of sensory neocortex receives information from lower sensory structures. This information is integrated, and synaptic excitation flows upward and downward to superficial and deeper layers of the cortex. Finally, pyramidal neurons within these various layers further integrate this information and project the results of this processing (in the form of trains of action potentials) to both subcortical and cortical targets. This vertical spread of activation reflects the organization of the cortex into functional columns or modules, which have been found in many cortical regions. Thus, the cortical column represents a basic functional processing unit, consisting of thousands of neurons spanning the six cortical layers. The entire neocortex is thought to contain hundreds of thousands of such functional columns. The power of the mammalian neocortex as an engine of information processing is thought to result, in part, from the simultaneous, parallel operation of thousands of such cortical columns.

Functionally, neocortex can be divided into sensory, motor, and association areas. Each sensory modality has multiple cortical representations that are organized in a hierarchical manner. For example, the primary visual cortex (in the occipital lobe) performs the initial cortical processing of visual information. Higher visual cortical areas are specialized in analyzing color, motion, and other functional aspects of vision. These areas communicate their analyses to the inferotemporal cortex, which is necessary for object recognition. Thus, whereas primary visual cortex is essential for visual sensation, inferotemporal cortex is essential for perception of objects. Other sensory modalities as well as motor-related areas are organized in a similar hierarchical manner. Most of the neocortex (approximately 75%) cannot be divided into sensory or motor areas and is referred to as "association" cortex. There are many such areas, some of which support the highest cognitive abilities such as language, foresight, and abstract reasoning.

Each of the two cerebral hemispheres can be divided into frontal, parietal, occipital, and temporal lobes. These cortical regions are related to certain sensory, motor, or cognitive functions. A brief overview of the main functions and clinical syndromes associated with the cortical lobes is as follows:

The *occipital lobes* are the hindmost cortical lobe and contain regions necessary for vision. The posterior pole of the occipital lobe is known as the primary visual cortex, and lesions here can produce blindness in the contralateral visual field. More specific visual disorders result when brain damage also includes neighboring temporal or/and parietal lobes. For example, lesions to occipitotemporal regions can produce visual agnosias, such as a deficit in recognizing objects, colors, or faces, despite otherwise normal vision.

The *parietal lobes* constitute the dorsal and lateral area of each hemisphere and mediate somatosensory information from the body including touch, pain, temperature, and limb position. The parietal lobes also play an important role in higher visual processing and in attending and integrating sensory information from different modalities. Parietal lobe lesions can often cause a striking deficit called unilateral neglect, in which a patient ignores visual, auditory, and somatosensory information coming from the side of the body contralateral to the brain lesion.

The *temporal lobes* contain cortical areas involved in auditory and higher visual processing and areas crucial for learning, memory, multimodal integration, and emotion. Lesions to the temporal lobes' primary auditory area can cause partial or complete deafness. Lesions to associated areas can cause more selective hearing deficits. For example, temporal lobe lesions in the left hemisphere are often associated with disorders of speech perception, while lesions to the symmetrical areas in the right hemisphere can produce deficits in music perception. Within the temporal lobes are structures that are part of the limbic system, which is phylogenetically older than the neocortex. These structures are crucial for forming long-term memories and for emotional behavior.

The *frontal lobes* occupy almost one half of each cerebral hemisphere in humans. The frontal lobes play a major role in motor activity (control of body movements), participate in language functions, and are important for higher integrative functions, personality traits, emotionality and "executive" control (the translation of thought into action). Damage to the primary motor area can cause paralysis on the contralateral side of the body. Fluent speech production is associated with a region (Broca's area) in the left frontal lobe. A large portion of frontal lobes called the prefrontal cortex is involved in a variety of complex cognitive functions such as problem solving, planning action toward a goal, and using information flexibly.

The two cerebral hemispheres are largely symmetrical in both structure and function. Some important functions, however, are organized primarily within a single hemisphere. The left hemisphere of almost all right-handed and most left-handed people is essential for many language-related functions. Injuries to specific areas of the left hemisphere often result in language related disabilities such as Broca's aphasia (difficulty with speech production), Wernicke's aphasia (difficulty with comprehension), agraphia (inability to write), or alexia (inability to read). In contrast, the right hemisphere is superior for emotional speech intonation (prosody), appreciation of humor, and visuospatial integration such as recognition of objects and faces. A massive fiber bundle, the corpus callosum, is responsible for communication between the two hemispheres and for coordinating their activity. When this pathway is destroyed the two hemispheres may begin to act independently. The careful study of such "split-brain" patients has led to many remarkable insights into neocortical organization.

Katarina Lukatela
Brown University Medical School

Harvey A. Swadlow
University of Connecticut

NEURAL NETWORK MODELS

Models containing networks of neuronlike units are the central feature of "connectionist," "parallel distributed processing," and "spreading activation" theories. Mathematically, neural networks form a system of computation that is cooperative and self-organizing. Behavior that seems to follow a plan, schema, or strategy emerges from the interactions among the units, without the presence of a supervisory system.

Network Units

Each unit in a neural network is described by two rules. First, the *activation rule* combines inputs and generates an output called an activation level. Second, the *learning rule* alters the transmission of activation levels between one unit and the next.

Activation rules explain how neurons perform logical and mathematical operations (McClulloch & Pitts, 1943). Each unit receives activation levels from either sensory receptors or other units. These inputs usually have a value of either 0 or 1. An input value of 1 will activate its connection with the unit. The connection itself has a value between −1 and +1, which is called the *connection weight.* It expresses the efficiency of transmission of the input level across a synapse between units. The total input level to a unit at any one moment is the sum of the active input weights. If the total input level exceeds a threshold value, then the unit will be triggered, and the activation level of its output will rise from 0 to 1.

By manipulating connection weights and threshold values, it is possible to produce common logic functions. For example, an AND function can be constructed if a unit with a threshold of .75 has two inputs, each with a connection weight of .50. If only one input is active, the total input level will be too low to trigger an output. If, however, both inputs are active, the total input level would be 1.0, exceeding the threshold and thereby triggering the output. The same unit can be converted to an OR function either by lowering the threshold value to less than .50 or by raising each input weight to a value greater than .75.

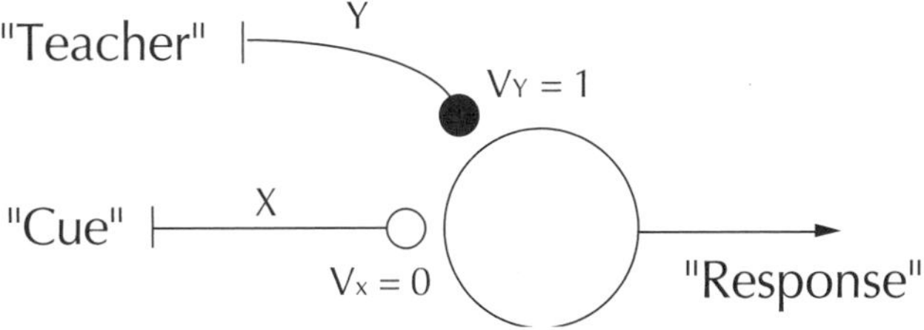

Figure 1. Hebbian adaptive unit, in which X denotes the "cue" input level, V_X denotes an adaptive connection weight, Y denotes the "teacher" input level, V_Y denotes the fixed connection weight, and "response" denotes the output level.

Learning rules for networks are based on the Law of Contiguity (Hebb, 1949, p. 50; James, 1892/1984, p. 226). These rules contend that synaptic transmission increases in efficiency whenever presynaptic activity has been contiguous with postsynaptic activity. Figure 1 shows an example of a unit capable of learning. One input (X), here called the "cue," has no initial connection weight ($V_X = 0$) and thus is unable to trigger the unit. The other input (Y), here called the "teacher," has a fixed, large weight ($V_Y = 1$) that can trigger the unit's "response" output. The cue input provides presynaptic activity, and the teacher input induces postsynaptic activity. In mathematical terms, the change in connection weight (ΔV_X) is a product of the two levels of activity, written as $\Delta V_X = (cXY)$ where c is the learning rate ($0 < c < 1$) (Sutton & Barto, 1981). This formula is usually called the "Hebbian rule."

While the operation of the Hebbian rule depends on the contiguity of activation levels, another widely used rule assumes that learning depends on the difference between the cue's input weight and the teacher's input weight, $\Delta V_X = c(V_Y - V_X)$ (Sutton & Barto, 1981). This rule is known variously as the error-correction rule, the delta rule (Rumelhart, Hinton, & Williams, 1986), the Rescorla-Wagner rule (Rescorla & Wagner, 1972), and the least-mean squares rule (Gluck & Bower, 1988).

Basic Architectures

Layered Networks

Figure 2 shows a layered network. It has a layer of sensory inputs, each of which projects to an intermediate layer of "hidden" units, which send their outputs to a third layer of response units. Layered networks have proved crucial in resolving difficult issues of stimulus representation and

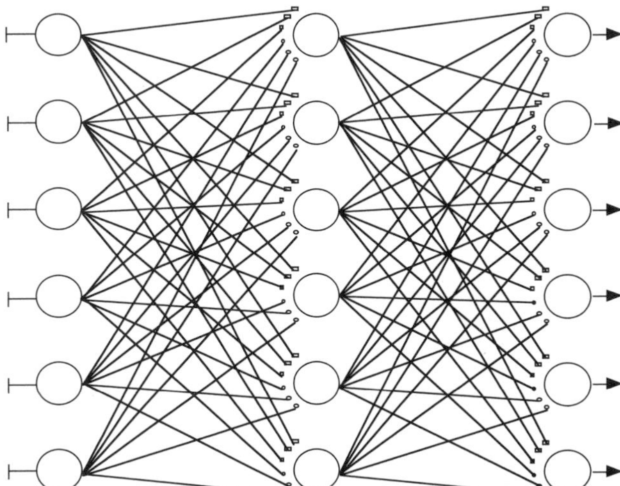

Figure 2. A layered network with three layers. The left-hand layer receives inputs from the environment and projects to the second layer of "hidden" units, which projects to a layer of output units.

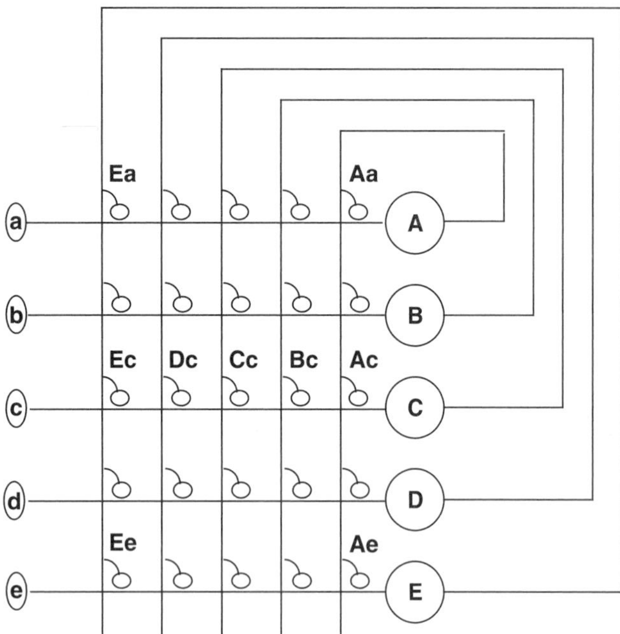

Figure 3. An autoassociative network, in which all output levels can be associated with input levels.

concept formation. Specifically, layered networks provide a basis for learning arbitrary mappings from stimulus input patterns to response output patterns. For example, each distinctive combination of sensory inputs can acquire connections to one of the hidden units. In turn, that hidden unit can acquire a connection with one of the response outputs in the final layer.

Autoassociative Networks

Autoassociative networks feed their outputs back as inputs. Figure 3 shows a small autoassociative network. Each of five units (A, B, C, D, E) receives one external input (a, b, c, d, e). These external inputs have fixed connections that can trigger an output from their respective units. Each unit also receives five recurrent inputs, one from each unit's output including its own. For example, as shown in Figure 3, the C unit has five recurrent connections, designated as Ac, Bc, Cc, Dc, and Ec. These connections are modifiable; whenever an output and an input are both active, a positive connection weight can grow at their intersection, according to a Hebbian rule.

Autoassociative networks can perform three functions that are of interest in psychology:

1. *Pattern completion.* After training, only a portion of the original inputs can retrieve the entire pattern of outputs. If inputs a and e are repeatedly presented together, four interconnections would be established, namely Aa, Ae, Ea, and Ee. Subsequently, the a input alone would trigger both the A and E outputs via the Aa and Ae connections. Likewise, the e input would trigger both outputs via the Ea and Ee connections.

2. *Noise tolerance.* Provided that successive sets of inputs are not entirely random, the pattern of the interconnections will reflect any underlying prototypic set, even if the prototype itself is never presented. Thus, a new set of inputs that is similar to the prototypic set can retrieve the prototypic pattern. This feature of autoassociative networks allows them to be used to explain stimulus generalization, pattern recognition, and categorization.

3. *Superimposed storage.* Autoassociative networks can store a large number of input sets. This feature allows for the retrieval of both prototypic patterns and specific, frequent exemplars (Kohonen, 1984, pp. 160–167; McClelland & Rumelhart, 1985).

REFERENCES

Gluck, M. A., & Bower, G. H. (1988). Evaluating an adaptive network model of human learning. *Journal of Memory and Language, 27,* 166–195.

Hebb, D. O. (1949). *The organization of behavior.* New York: Wiley.

James, W. (1892/1984). *Briefer psychology.* Cambridge, MA: Harvard University Press.

Kohonen, T. (1984). *Self-organization and associative memory.* Berlin: Springer-Verlag.

McClelland, J. L., & Rumelhart, D. E. (1985). Distributed memory and the representation of general and specific information. *Journal of Experimental Psychology: General, 114,* 159–188.

McClulloch, W. S., & Pitts, W. (1943). A logical calculus of the ideas immanent in nervous activity. *Bulletin of Mathematical Biophysics, 5,* 115–133.

Rescorla, R. A., & Wagner, A. R. (1972). A theory of Pavlovian conditioning: Variations in the effectiveness of reinforcement and nonreinforcement. In A. H. Black & W. F. Prokasy (Eds.), *Classical conditioning II* (pp. 64–99). New York: Appleton-Century-Crofts.

Rumelhart, D. E., Hinton, G. E., & Williams, R. J. (1986). Learning internal representations by error propagation. In D. E. Rumelhart (Ed.), *Parallel distributed processing: Explorations in the microstructures of cognition* (Vol. 1, pp. 318–362). Cambridge, MA: MIT Press.

Sutton, R. S., & Barto, A. G. (1981). Toward a modern theory of adaptive networks: Expectation and prediction. *Psychological Review, 88,* 135–171.

E. James Kehoe
University of New South Wales, Sydney, Australia

NEUROCHEMISTRY

Early neurochemists established that the brain is enriched with fatty substances (lipids), many of which are unique to the nervous system. Long, highly unsaturated fatty acids occur as components of brain phospholipids and glycolipids.

The brain also contains cholesterol, but unlike other body organs, has little or no cholesterol ester or triglyceride. The human brain contains about 10% lipids, 10% protein, and 78% water. The remaining 2% consists of DNA, RNA, electrolytes, and other materials. White matter is enriched in nerve axons ensheathed in multilayered, lipid-rich membranes (myelin) produced by oligodendroglia, while gray matter contains mainly neuronal cells and support cells (the astroglia), interposed between the neurons and cerebral blood vessels.

The human brain weighs about 1400 grams, or 2% of body weight. Its pale appearance belies the fact that about 15% of the cardiac output is required to supply it with glucose and oxygen, and to remove metabolic wastes. The brain is efficient in this exchange and thus accounts for about 20% of the resting basal metabolic rate. Chemical energy for the working of the brain is generated in the form of 38 molecules of ATP (adenosine triphosphate) per molecule of glucose metabolized. By means of an intravenously injected glucose analogue (^{14}C-2-deoxyglucose), it was demonstrated that brain metabolism in experimental animals could be regionally activated (e.g., in the occipital cortex during visual stimulation). Stimulated regional cerebral blood flow (rCBF) also occurs. These metabolic correlates of brain activity can be measured noninvasively in human subjects by means of radiolabeled tracers and positron emission tomography (PET). Regional brain activation can also be studied by functional magnetic resonance imaging (fMRI).

While hydrophilic and ionically charged small molecules readily diffuse from blood into most body organs, they are excluded from the brain and spinal cord by the blood-brain-barrier (BBB). Exceptions are glucose, vitamins, essential amino and fatty acids, and other essential nutrients, for each of which special transport systems exist. While the BBB protects the brain, it necessitates molecular legerdemain in designing effective drugs.

The high energy needs of the brain reflect the enormous volume of information it can integrate at great speed: sensory inputs, central processing, storage, and retrieval on the one hand; and neural and neuroendocrine outputs that control the body's vital functions and behavioral expression on the other. All of this is mediated by neurons, via coded electrical messages (conduction) and chemical messages (synaptic transmission).

Neuronal action potentials are conducted down the axon as rapid depolarization waves, typically terminating at the presynaptic region of another neuron. The electrical potential is generated by efflux of neuronal potassium and influx of sodium. Ultimately, the ionically based electrical gradients are restored by neuronal sodium extrusion and potassium influx. The recovery process requires the enzyme Na^+/K^+ATPase, which consumes ATP in the process. While the direction of information flow in neurons is generally unidirectional—from dendrite to cell body to axon—the supply of critical materials within the neuron is centrifugal: from cell body to the farthest reaches of both dendrites and axons. Proteins are formed primarily in the cell body, so cytoskeletal elements (microtubules, neurofilaments, actin, etc.) and organelles, including mitochondria and various vesicular structures, migrate centrifugally to the cell extremities via anterograde axonal transport, under the influence of "molecular motor" proteins, the kinesins. There is also centripetal, or retrograde, flow, mediated by dyneins and thought to transmit information from the synapse to the nucleus, for example to make more neurotransmitters or to initiate repair of damaged nerves.

Arrival of depolarization waves at presynaptic nerve endings initiates the process of neurotransmission with the release of chemical messenger molecules (neurotransmitters) such as acetylcholine, glutamate, gamma-aminobutyrate, glycine, norepinephrine, dopamine, and serotonin. These agents are released into the synaptic cleft in packets, following fusion of synaptic vesicles with the presynaptic membrane. The process of synaptic vesicle exocytosis and reformation by endocytosis involves many specialized proteins. A number of naturally occurring toxic agents, such as black widow spider venom and botulinum toxin, exert their action by disrupting this cycle.

Released neurotransmitters traverse the synaptic cleft and bind to specific membrane-spanning postsynaptic receptor proteins embedded in the plasma membrane, usually of another neuron. Note that the neurotransmitter molecule itself does not enter the postsynaptic cell, and is removed from the synaptic cleft quickly, to constitute an "off" signal. Occupied receptors respond in different ways, most commonly by the opening of ion channels or via an intervening guanine nucleotide binding protein (G-protein) that regulates the formation of an intracellular second messenger molecule, such as cyclic AMP, or of two phospholipid cleavage products, inositol trisphosphate and diacylglycerol. These chemical messages can in turn lead to intracellular calcium release, be amplified by various phosphoprotein/protein kinase cascades, or activate nuclear transcription factors, ultimately leading to a physiological outcome. The entire complex process of synaptic transmission can occur in milliseconds or take minutes. The actions of most neuroactive drugs, including stimulants, sedatives, anxiolytics, and antipsychotic agents, as well as illicit addictive substances, can be traced to their action on one or more steps in synaptic transmission.

Neurochemical studies on memory formation in a number of invertebrate and vertebrate species show that long-term, but not short-term, memory formation requires ongoing protein synthesis. It is generally held that long-term memory formation and other forms of neuroplasticity are mediated by altered synaptic relationships for which synthesis of new protein is required. Such conclusions, initially based on the behavioral effects of antibiotic blocking agents, have been further documented by genetic mutant, transgenic, and "knockout" studies, thus far primarily in fruit flies and mice.

Understanding of neuroscience at the molecular level has improved drug design. For example, administration of

DOPA, a precursor of dopamine that penetrates the BBB, alleviates the symptoms of Parkinson's disease resulting from a brain dopamine deficiency; inhibitors of acetylcholinesterase are effective in treating a brain acetylcholine deficiency in Alzheimer's disease; the blocking of presynaptic serotonin reuptake by fluoxetine (Prozac) relieves depression; a diet low in the amino acid phenylalanine prevents the mental retardation that otherwise occurs in an inborn defect in amino acid metabolism (phenylketonuria [PKU]). Numerous additional genetic defects that produce abnormal behavior have been identified in recent years, and in many instances, the biochemical phenotype, such as a defective protein, has been identified, an important first step in the eventual discovery of effective therapeutic strategies.

SUGGESTED READING

Cooper, J. R., Bloom, F. E., & Roth, R. H. (1996). *The biochemical basis of neuropsychopharmacology* (7th ed.). New York/Oxford: Oxford University Press.

Siegel, G. J., Agranoff, B. W., Albers, R. W., Fisher, S. K., & Uhler, M. D. (Ed.). (1999). *Basic neurochemistry* (6th ed.). Philadelphia/New York: Lippincott-Raven.

Bernard W. Agranoff
University of Michigan

NEUROETHOLOGY

Neuroethology is the study of the neural basis of behavior, or how a certain coordinated pattern of movements (behavior) is planned and produced in response to a key stimulus by the integrated activity of different parts of the nervous system. This field emerged out of traditional ethology, or the study of animal behavior in a natural setting, when ethologists in collaboration with physiologists and anatomists began to investigate the relationship between brain structure/functions and observed behaviors. Main features of neuroethology include multidisciplinarity (with participation of disciplines such as ethology, neuroanatomy, neurophysiology, neuropharmacology, neuroendocrinology, and neuropsychology) and comparative approach (to identify basic principles of organization for the neural correlates of behavior). Aims and features of modern neuroethology have been reviewed in recent years (Spiro & White, 1998; Pfluger & Menzel, 1999).

The Neuroethological Approach

It is known from ethology that species-specific adaptive behaviors are elicited by key stimuli in the animal's environment that release a stereotyped behavioral response (fixed action pattern) when the internal or motivational state of the animal is appropriate. This program is known as an "innate releasing mechanism," although strong influences of learning have been recognized in behavioral responses. Tinbergen (1951) identifies at least seven different levels of neuroethological investigation: (1) the receptors and the sensory processes for identification of key stimuli; (2) the neuronal mechanisms for the localization of key stimuli; (3) the processes for the acquisition, retention, and recall of sensory information; (4) the neural correlates of motivational states; (5) how sensory information is processed to provide an organized motor output (the sensory-motor interface); (6) the neural circuits providing coordinated motor patterns; and (7) the ontogenesis and maturation of the neural elements involved in such processes.

In general, sensory systems are characterized by both anatomical and functional specializations for the detection and localization of the key stimuli (Capranica, 1983). In the brain, sensory systems are organized in the form of topographic maps representing the animal's sensory space. Similarly, motor systems are also topographically organized as maps representing the animal's body plan. Therefore, the sensory-motor interface includes brain mechanisms for communication between sensory and motor maps (Scheich, 1983). The coordinated activity of motor neurons resulting in the behavioral output (fixed action pattern) is likely to be determined genetically (Ewert, 1980). Finally, the whole process is modulated by neural structures influencing the animal's motivational state. For instance, hypothalamic nuclei are known to modulate aggressive (Anderson & Silver, 1998) or reproductive behaviors (Adler, 1983).

Classical studies in neuroethology include those on electrolocation (fish; Heiligenberg, 1991), echolocation (bats; Simmons, 1989), sound localization (owls; Knudsen, 1987), vocal learning (songbirds; Bottjer & Johnson, 1997), navigation and spatial learning (homing pigeons; Casini et al., 1997), and prey-catching behavior (toads; Ewert, 1997).

Genetic Approaches in Neuroethology

The genetic approach may help neuroethological research, especially in organisms such as *drosophila* that constitute classic experimental models for genetic manipulations (Heisenberg, 1997). Identified genetic variants may reveal new properties of neurons and can provide useful tools for interpretation of neuronal circuitries and their roles in complex behavioral systems.

Developmental Neuroethology

The term *developmental neuroethology* has gained a distinctive identity in defining the science that is specifically devoted to the investigation of the ontogeny of neural mechanisms underlying naturally occurring behaviors (Stehouwer, 1992). Issues in developmental neuroethology include, for instance: the roles played by hormones in the ontogeny of neural circuits subserving species-specific behaviors; transient appearance of neural circuits of behavioral relevance that are not retained in mature animals; organization of behavioral sequences during ontogeny; and neural plasticity and learning in behavioral ontogeny.

Computational Neuroethology

Adaptive behavior is classically regarded as the result of the integrated activity of neural circuits. However, adaptive behavior does not depend solely on brain activity, but requires a continuous feedback between the nervous system, the body, and the environment. To understand these interactions, a methodology called *computational neuroethology* has been developed (Chiel and Beer, 1997). It is based on creating joint models of the relevant parts of an animal's nervous system, body, and environment to study the contributions of the components to adaptive behavior and the new phenomena that may emerge from their interactions.

REFERENCES

Adler, N. T. (1983). The neuroethology of reproduction. In J. P. Ewert, R. R. Capranica, & D. J. Ingle (Eds.), *Advances in vertebrate neuroethology* (pp. 1033–1065). New York: Plenum Press.

Anderson, K., & Silver, J. M. (1998). Modulation of anger and aggression. *Seminars in Clinical Neuropsychiatry, 3,* 232–242.

Bottjer, S. W., & Johnson, F. (1997). Circuits, hormones, and learning: Vocal behavior in songbirds. *Journal of Neurobiology, 33,* 602–618.

Capranica, R. R. (1983). Sensory processes of key stimuli. In J. P. Ewert, R. R. Capranica, & D. J. Ingle (Eds.), *Advances in vertebrate neuroethology* (pp. 3–6). New York: Plenum Press.

Casini, G., Fontanesi, G., Bingman, V., Jones, T.-J., Gagliardo, A., Ioalè, P., & Bagnoli, P. (1997). The neuroethology of cognitive maps: Contributions from research on the hippocampal formation and homing pigeon navigation. *Archives Italiennes de Biologie, 135,* 73–92.

Chiel, H. J., & Beer, R. D. (1997). The brain has a body: Adaptive behavior emerges from interactions of nervous system, body and environment. *Trends in Neurosciences, 20,* 553–557.

Ewert, J.-P. (1980). *Neuroethology: An introduction to the neurophysiological fundamentals of behavior.* Berlin: Springer-Verlag.

Ewert, J.-P. (1997). Neural correlates of key stimulus and releasing mechanism: A case study and two concepts. *Trends in Neurosciences, 20,* 332–339.

Heiligenberg, W. (1991). *Neural nets in electric fish.* Cambridge, MA: MIT Press.

Heisenberg, M. (1997). Genetic approaches to neuroethology. *Bioessays, 19,* 1065–1073.

Knudsen, E. I. (1987). Neural derivation of sound source location in the barn owl. An example of a computational map. *Annals of the New York Academy of Sciences, 510,* 33–38.

Pfluger, H. J., & Menzel, R. (1999). Neuroethology, its roots and future. *Journal of Comparative Physiology. A Sensory, Neural, and Behavioral Physiology, 185,* 389–392.

Scheich, H. (1983). Sensorimotor interfacing. In J. P. Ewert, R. R. Capranica, & D. J. Ingle (Eds.), *Advances in vertebrate neuroethology* (pp. 7–14). New York: Plenum Press.

Simmons, J. A. (1989). A view of the world through the bat's ear: The formation of acoustic images in echolocation. *Cognition, 33,* 155–199.

Spiro, J. E., & White, S. A. (1998). Neuroethology: A meeting of brain and behavior. *Neuron, 21,* 981–989.

Stehouwer, D. J. (1992). The emergence of developmental neuroethology. *Journal of Neurobiology, 23,* 1353–1354.

Tinbergen, N. (1951). *The study of instinct.* Oxford, UK: Clarendon Press.

Giovanni Casini
Università della Tuscia, Italy

NEUROIMAGING

Neuroimaging is the use of a variety of different techniques to map the location of different structural and functional regions within the living brain. It can be used clinically, as in identifying the location of a brain tumor, or in research, as in visualizing brain regions involved in complex behaviors or emotional states. The field of neurosciences is undergoing a radical acceleration in knowledge due to the use of these techniques and their potential for expanding our understanding of the brain correlates of thinking, feeling, and acting.

Structural neuroimaging techniques include methods that generate anatomic images of brain structures, while functional neuroimaging generates data that relate to the functioning of the brain, including measures of neuronal activity, cerebral metabolism, chemical composition, or neuroreceptor characteristics. Structural and functional techniques are often used in conjunction with one another as each technique provides different data. Selection of the specific imaging tool depends on whether the information will be used for clinical or research purposes, accessibility of the tool, the cost of the procedure, and the time course available for analyzing the imaging data.

All imaging procedures quantify a parameter for a unit of three-dimensional space within the individual. The measures of three-dimensional space acquired in the imaging techniques are called "voxels." Through quantification the values of the voxels are then arranged in an array to represent their spatial relationship within the living brain. These data are then typically transformed into an image displayed as a plane in two-dimensional space.

Neuroimaging Techniques

Computed Tomography (CT)

Modern brain imaging was revolutionized in the 1970s with the introduction of computerized X-ray tomography. This was one of the first widely practiced and accessible neuroimaging techniques that allowed investigation of the living brain. In CT, multiple X-ray beams of radiation are projected through the object of interest (e.g., brain) and the intensity of the emerging radiation is measured by detectors. Intravenous contrast agents may be used with CT to increase its sensitivity in detecting pathology. CT is particularly good at detecting abnormalities in the bone, calcifications, and acute bleeding. Limitations include exposure to radiation, poor differentiation between soft tissue densities, and circumscribed views of the person being scanned. CT is used primarily in clinical settings.

Magnetic Resonance Imaging (MRI)

In MRI, radio waves immerse a person centered in a magnetic field with the signals absorbed and re-emitted in proportion to the mobile hydrogen ion concentration in the tissue of the person. The absorbed energy is detected by a radio receiver when it is re-emitted. MRI has evolved rapidly and is increasingly used for both clinical and research applications into general cognitive functioning and pathology. The technique is noninvasive (e.g., does not expose one to radiation) and produces images with excellent spatial and temporal resolution. Structural MRI of the brain produces images of brain anatomy, whereas functional MRI (fMRI) produces indirect measures of brain activity through the study of changes in blood flow and blood oxygenation. FMRI uses standard MRI scanners with fast imaging techniques and works on the principle that focal changes in neuronal activity tend to be coupled with changes in brain blood flow and blood volume. FMRI is becoming widely available, but is primarily a research tool. Limitations to MRI include occasional claustrophobia, prohibitive use of metal implants in users, and sensitivity to motion artifacts.

Positron Emission Tomography (PET) and Single Photon Emission Computed Tomography (SPECT or SPET)

In both PET and SPECT a radioactive tracer is injected or inhaled into the blood stream. The tracer is distributed in the brain and emits a photon signal that is detected by the scanner. The techniques measure the regional distribution of radioactive activity, which, depending on the labeled tracer, can measure glucose metabolism, blood flow, or the distribution or density of a receptor. Blood flow and metabolism are typically coupled and are used as a measure of neural activity. A variety of tracers are available in PET, each measuring different parameters (e.g., regional cerebral blood flow, glucose metabolism, or receptor distribution). PET is increasingly used as an advanced technique to identify pathology (e.g., tumors and neuronal degeneration). Water containing oxygen 15 is considered the best and most widely used PET tracer for assessing blood flow in cognitive studies. This tracer is ideally suited for this purpose because its short half-life (2 minutes) allows research subjects to be scanned several times in different cognitive states or doing various tasks. With all techniques involving ionizing radiation, however, there are limits on the total acceptable amount of radiation exposure for the subject.

Future Directions in Neuroimaging

Several other techniques are also being used to reveal how the brain works. Many of these techniques will be used with those described above. Magnetoencephalography (MEG) and electroencephalography (EEG) are tools that can measure neuronal function with submillisecond temporal resolution—which is preferable for studying many cognitive processes. MEG is particularly promising because it can be used to visualize the time course of regions of activation as they become activated during a task. MEG measures signals proportional to electroencephalographic waves emanating from brain electrical activity. Magnetic Resonance Spectroscopy is a rapidly expanding, noninvasive technique that can measure the chemical composition of proton, phosphorus, and carbon-based molecules. The technique generates plots representing the chemical composition of a brain region. Diffusion tensor imaging (DTI) is another rather novel technique that makes use of the ability of MRI to measure the movement and diffusion of water. In certain brain tissues, such as the white matter, this diffusion is along the white matter tracts; thus, the technique can be used to map the presence, direction, and thickness of cerebral white matter fibers. DTI is used in clinical applications to assess the degeneration or remodeling of tissue structures associated with disease. It is used in research applications to study the relationship between structure and function of tissue electrophysiology and biomechanics. Finally, transcranial magnetic stimulation is another tool for the noninvasive manipulation of brain activity that may be combined with traditional imaging tools to help determine whether a particular region is critical for performing a cognitive or motor operation.

Julie Schweitzer
University of Maryland School of Medicine

See also: **Brain; MRI**

NEUROLINGUISTICS

Broadly defined, neurolinguistics is a theory of language and brain. A formal theory of neurolinguistics is developing through interaction in the fields of neurology, psychology, and linguistics. Larnendella urged a simultaneous integration of three distinct perspectives in the formal theory of language and brain: *overt speech and language behavior, covert neuroanatomy and neurophysiology,* and the *functional organization of speech and language systems* as a contingent reality. He emphasized the need to incorporate into neurolinguistic theory implications of nonverbal communication systems of human behavior, of cultural and individual variables developed through environmental modification, and of cognitive information processing and a theory of human cognition.

Neurolinguistics may be described as a study of how information is received through the senses, processed in the neurons and neural pathways of the brain (including the language areas), and expressed in language and behaviors. The most salient sensory modalities for information processing into language are the visual, auditory, and kinesthetic modalities. Optimally, information is received and expressed in all channels with consistency and equal efficiency.

Information processing is concerned with two types of symbols: *theoretical,* related to language, and *qualitative.* Processing the different types of symbols is believed to depend on functions occurring within the left and right hemispheres of the brain. Theoretical symbols such as visual linguistic elements (e.g., the written word), auditory linguistic elements (e.g., the spoken word), visual quantitative elements (e.g., written numbers), and auditory quantitative elements (e.g., spoken numbers) are processed primarily in the left hemisphere of the brain.

Qualitative symbols of a sensory nature, such as sounds, taste, or pictures, are associated with cultural codes or the meanings received from nonverbal expressions, role playing, social distance, or time constraints, and are processed primarily in the right side of the brain. The bilateral symmetry of the brain provides that sights and sounds bringing in information from the external environment will be processed by both hemispheres together.

Neurolinguistic evidence is contributing to the understanding of communication, cognition, culture, and their practical applications. In addition to the study of disordered brain function, experimental techniques have been applied to speech and language processing in individuals who are considered normal. Research has indicated varying responses of individuals who are considered normal in the sensory modalities of vision and audition.

Electrophysiological experiments using auditory and visual stimuli show that auditory responses are significantly greater in the left hemisphere, and visual responses are significantly greater in the right hemisphere.

The right ear outperforms the left ear in hearing and identifying competing digits—a reflection of left-brain dominance for language. A clear left-ear advantage was found for melodies and environmental sounds. The left ear has direct access to the right hemisphere, and the right brain is dominant for music, chords, and nonverbal sounds.

Individuals tend to look up and away when a question has been posed and the answer must be retrieved. The same neurological pathways and structures seem to be used for both external stimulation in a given sensory modality and internal fantasies in that same modality.

Human beings who are considered normal are all endowed with essentially equivalent sensory organs and structures, both anatomically and physiologically. Each individual learns to depend on one sensory system or another as a means of perceiving and understanding the world. The Sensory Modality Checklist assesses an individual's preferred sensory modality for learning and self-expression.

Neuro-Linguistic Programming (NLP) is the study of the structure of subjective experience, or how individuals perceive and understand the world. Neuro-Linguistic Programming is a trademark name for a model of techniques and strategies for interpersonal communication based on some elements of transformational grammar and on the identification of preferred sensory representations for learning and self-expression.

Bandler and Grinder identified the process indicating that the predicates people use are representative of their preferred sensory modalities. An individual who highly values the visual system uses visual process words and predicates (verbs, adjectives, adverbs) such as "clear," "bright," "see," and "perspective."

Bandler and Grinder also describe the nonverbal and physiological cues that people unconsciously use. Eye movements, breathing patterns, body postures, and body types give clues to an individual's preferred sensory modality.

N. A. Haynie

NEUROMUSCULAR DISORDERS

Neuromuscular disorders generally refer to disease processes that affect motor neurons, including axons and the innervation of the motor neurons with muscle fibers. A great many neuromuscular disorders are inherited, although it is common to find no genetic link in some cases. At the onset of symptoms, neuromuscular disease typically manifests itself as an asymmetrical weakness with intact sensation. As the disorder progresses, the symmetry of wasting becomes apparent, with each side of the body manifesting similar rates of muscle atrophy.

Neuromuscular disorders may be most easily characterized in terms of level and degree of motor neuron involvement. Disorders involving the upper motor neuron tracts, such as progressive spastic bulbar paralysis, and demyelinating diseases, such as multiple sclerosis (MS) and amyotrophic lateral sclerosis (ALS), cause bulbar paralysis. Symptoms typically include difficulty speaking and swallowing, and respiratory failure.

MS, a demyelination disorder with axonal degeneration, is the most common disabling neurological condition observed in young adults. Symptom onset typically occurs in the fourth decade of life and is more common in women. It appears to be the result of genetic risk in combination with environmental factors, as the disorder is more common in individuals who have lived in the more Northern and Southern latitudes for at least 15 years and who have family members with MS. There are four types of MS, with the former types being more common than the latter: relapsing-remitting, secondary progressive, primary progressive, and progressive relapsing. Symptoms of MS include ataxia, sensory disturbances, trigeminal neuralgia, tremor, muscle spasticity, ocular impairments, paralysis, generalized fatigue, depression, and impaired concentration and memory. Dementia is also present in some cases.

ALS, also known as Lou Gehrig's disease, often affects both the upper and lower motor neuron tracts. Approximately 5 to 10% of individuals with ALS have an autosomal dominant inheritance pattern linked to chromosome 21. Onset of symptoms is typically in middle adulthood, and is characterized by muscle weakness and atrophy accompanied by subcutaneous muscle twitching in one arm or leg. The symptoms spread across the rest of the body, including the face, pharynx, and tongue, resulting in flaccid quadriplegia, and atrophic and areflexic muscles. Death typically results from respiratory complications and occurs 2 to 4 years after symptom onset. ALS typically has no cognitive component, although some individuals exhibit dementia, so individuals with the disorder are usually aware of their symptoms and can make choices about end-of-life decisions, including the use of respiratory ventilators.

Although it has been eliminated as a wild virus, poliomyelitis is a virus that causes an infection in the anterior horn cells of the spinal cord (motor neurons) and lower brain stem. Polio does not affect cognitive functioning, but results in asymmetric paralysis, muscle fasiculations, and the absence of deep tendon reflexes.

Nonviral neuromuscular diseases occurring with some frequency include myasthenia gravis, myotonic dystrophy, and Duchenne's muscular dystrophy. Myasthenia gravis is a neuromuscular junction disorder caused by an autoimmune response that blocks the nicotinic receptors in the extraocular and facial muscles and is associated with thymus gland abnormalities. The disorder, which typically affects young women and older men, results in fluxuating and asymmetric muscle weakness, but causes no cognitive symptoms. The symptoms of myasthenia gravis include facial and neck muscle weakness, difficulty controlling neck and shoulder muscles, difficulty swallowing, and poor respiratory functioning. In severe cases, this disorder may result in quadriplegia and respiratory distress.

Myotonic dystrophy is a commonly occurring neuromuscular disorder in adults, with symptom onset typically in the third decade of life. Males and females are equally affected as this disorder is carried on chromosome 19. Symptoms appear to have an earlier onset and are more severe when the disorder is inherited from the father. Myotonic dystrophy is also subject to genetic amplification such that the symptoms are more severe and have an earlier onset in successive generations. Early symptoms include facial and distal dystrophy with myotonia, such that following voluntary effort, muscles have prolonged and uncontrolled contractions. Disease progression is slow and variable. Later symptoms can include endocrine system failure, cataracts, cardiac symptoms, personality change, dementia, and limited intelligence.

Duchenne's muscular dystrophy is the most frequently occurring neuromuscular disorder in children. The disorder is sex-linked, with symptoms displayed only in males, but females carry the genetic defect asymptomatically. The symptoms are caused by a failure to produce dystrophin, a muscle-cell membrane protein. First evidence of the disorder is difficulty standing and walking with pseudohypertrophy in the calf muscles during childhood. Gower's sign, wherein boys with Duchenne's appear to "climb their own legs," is highly diagnostic. Progression of the disorder is relatively rapid and by early adolescence, boys with Duchenne's typically require a wheelchair. The disorder is fatal, with death typically resulting from respiratory insufficiency in the late adolescent or young adult years. Duchenne's is sometimes accompanied by mental retardation.

Other, less common motor neuron diseases include Werdnig-Hoffman's disease (hereditary ALS-like symptoms identified in infants), Kugelberg-Welander disease (hereditary ALS-like symptoms identified in children), Oppenheim's disease, progressive neuropathic muscular atrophy, and Dejerine-Scottas' disease. Age at onset, disease progression rate, and years of survival vary.

There are no cures for neuromuscular disorders, although the utility of gene therapies is being investigated in some cases. Treatment of symptoms associated with neuromuscular disorders focuses on avoiding infection and controlling spasticity. Psychological intervention should center around counseling and the maintenance of patient support mechanisms.

Carlin J. Miller
City University of New York, Queen's College

George W. Hynd
Purdue University

See also: **Central Nervous System**

NEURONAL CELL BODY

As a single cell, the neuron is highly specialized in the extent of its regionalization, that is, its structural and functional compartmentalization. Three distinct regions or compartments can be identified in a typical neuron: dendrites, cell body, and axons. The cell body plays two principle roles in the life of a neuron: supporting most of its macromolecular synthesis and serving as the site at which input signals are integrated to determine output signals.

The cell body, also called the neuronal soma, is defined as the compartment of the neuron containing the cell nucleus. In addition to the nucleus, the cell body is the compartment most like a typical animal cell in that it also contains ribosomes, endoplasmic reticulum, the Golgi apparatus, and the other cellular organelles involved in the synthesis, processing, and delivery of macromolecules throughout the cell, for example proteins and membrane components. Axons and dendrites are both narrow extensions of cytoplasm that grow from the cell body during early embryonic development. The synthetic capacity of these other compartments is much reduced compared to the cell body and, in the case of axons, is nearly absent. In addition to lacking synthetic machinery, the extreme length of many neural axons means that its compartment typically has the majority of the cytoplasmic mass of the cell. Thus, the axon grows and is maintained only by being supplied with proteins and membrane components from the relatively smaller mass of its cell body. Disruption in the synthesis, degradation, processing, or subsequent delivery to the axon of macromolecules underlies a variety of neuronal pathologies. In Alzheimer's disease, for example, inappropriate processing of a normal integral membrane protein of brain neurons produces short protein fragments that aggregate to form an insoluble precipitate. This, in turn, leads to neuronal cell death and progressive loss of cognitive function.

In addition to their differences in synthetic function, the three compartments of a neuron differ also in their electrical signaling functions as part of a system of neurons. Dendrites are the input side of neurons, receiving various chemical information from other cells, typically other neurons, and converting it into local electrical signals. The cell body receives this electrical input, both stimulatory and inhibitory, from its entire dendritic arbor and integrates it to produce a net stimulus. This overall stimulus within the cell body then determines the informational electrical output of a neuron, which propagates along the very long and narrow axonal projection. The classic view of this process of integration is that the cell body is the site of essentially passive summing of the various inhibitory and stimulatory inputs to arrive at a net stimulation or inhibition of output, that is, initiation or suppression of action potentials. More recent evidence suggests that the cell body may actively amplify or decrease input signals as part of its integration function determining output.

Structurally, the cell body of neurons is usually a compact, rounded mass of cytoplasm that contrasts with the narrow tapering arbor of dendritic branches, as well as with the exceptionally elongated axonal process. In general, neuronal cell bodies tend to occur in identifiable aggregates within the nervous system at which neuron-to-neuron signaling occurs. In other words, cell bodies and their associated synapses tend to occur in clumps. In the brain, a region with a large number of cell bodies is called a *nucleus.* For example, the lateral geniculate nucleus is the brain region in which visual processing first occurs after the eyes. Outside the brain and spinal cord, aggregates of neuronal cell bodies are called *ganglia.* For example, dorsal root ganglia are found just outside the spinal cord and are aggregates of the cell bodies of sensory neurons from the skin and muscle that relay information about these peripheral tissues to the central nervous system.

Steve R. Heidemann
Michigan State University

NEUROPSYCHOLOGICAL DEVELOPMENT

The growth of the brain and nervous system can be described as if it were a series of changes that occur at particular ages. Although some changes are rapid and dramatic, others are more gradual. Regardless of the rapidity of change, however, these changes generally occur in a fixed sequence.

The first stage of brain development is *cell migration,* during which nerve cells are formed in the inner or ventricular lining of the brain. After formation they migrate from the inner lining through the layers that already exist, to eventually form a new outer layer. This means that structures such as the cortex actually mature from the inner to the outer surfaces.

During the cell migration stage, *axonal growth* manifests itself, as axons begin to sprout from the migrating cells. Axons are the elongated neural process that carries information away from the cell body to be received by other cells down the line. Each axon has a specific target that it must reach if the neuron is to be functional. How each axon locates its target is still an unsolved question.

The *growth of dendrites* is the next major change in the system. This growth does not begin until after the cell reaches its final location after migration. At some stages of dendritic growth there appears to be an overabundance of dendritic branches. Some of these excess or unused branches are eventually lost in a process referred to as "pruning," which is actually a loss of neural material.

The time course of *synapse formation* has been mapped in detail for primates. Synapses begins to form about 2 months before birth and grow rapidly for several months. In humans, synaptic growth is known to continue for at least 2 years after birth. There is some suggestion that experience may affect the survival of synapses. This is based upon the fact that, between about 2 and 16 years of age, there is actually a loss of about 50% of the synapses. One speculation is that only the regularly used synapses survive, with unused synapses disappearing through a process sometimes referred to as "shedding."

While it has been generally believed that neural development is completed after about 2 years of age, in fact growth continues well beyond this point. There is even some suggestion that brain growth occurs at irregular intervals, called "growth spurts" (Banich, 1997). Such spurts occur at around 3 to 18 months and at 2 to 4, 6 to 8, 10 to 12, and 14 to 16 years of age. Except for the first (rather long) spurt, during which brain weight increases by about 30%, each subsequent growth spurt increases brain mass by 5 to 10%. It is tempting to try to correlate these growth spurts with overt changes in development. Thus it may be significant that the first four episodes of rapid brain growth seem to coincide with Piaget's four principal stages of cognitive development.

Other changes in the neural system continue well beyond adolescence. An important factor in the later stages of neuropsychological development is cell loss. For instance, the area of the occipital cortex that receives projections from the fovea of the eye contains about 46 million neurons per gram of tissue in a 20-year-old. In an 80-year-old, however, the neuronal density is reduced by nearly one half, to only 24 million neurons per gram of tissue. This cell loss is believed to account for some of the loss of visual acuity in older individuals (Coren, Ward, & Enns, 1999). Similar losses in other areas of the brain might also be expected to affect normal functioning.

Brain size and mass can also be affected by experience. Exposure to a stimulus rich environment seems to increase brain size, especially in the neocortex. Such enriched stimulus exposure seems to increase the number of dendrites and synapses, especially if the enriched experience occurs early in life. Furthermore, animals with larger brains as a result of more varied experience seem to perform better on a number of behavioral tasks, including those involving memory and learning. In contrast, animals reared from birth with restricted sensory inputs, such as no light to the eyes, possess a reduced number of functioning cells and more abnormal neurons in the appropriate sections of the cortex (e.g., Atkinson, 2000).

Environmental effects in the form of traumas that affect the developing fetus—such as toxic agents, mechanical injury, chemical imbalances, a stressful birth, or a difficult pregnancy—can cause both subtle and dramatic disturbances in neural development. In some cases, changes in function ("soft signs") are used to determine the likelihood that there is some form of damage or disruption in neurological development that cannot specifically be seen in physiological examinations, but must be inferred from behavioral changes.

Generally speaking, neuropsychological development follows a fixed sequence of stages with an initial developmental predisposition, period of environmental vulnerability, period of plasticity, and finally fixed functional properties.

REFERENCES

Atkinson, J. (2000). *The developing visual brain.* New York: Oxford University Press.

Banich, M. T. (1997). *Neuropsychology: The neural bases of mental function.* Boston: Houghton-Mifflin.

Coren, S., Ward, L. M., & Enns, J. T. (1999). *Sensation and perception* (5th ed.). San Diego: Harcourt, Brace, Jovanovich.

Martin, G. M. (1997). *Human neuropsychology.* New York: Prentice Hall.

Stanley Coren
University of British Colombia

NEUROPSYCHOLOGY

Origins of the Term Neuropsychology

Historically, the field of neuropsychology was derived not only from the discipline of psychology, but also from the various related disciplines within the traditional professions of medicine, education, and law (Meier, 1997). The term *neuropsychology* is a combination of the word *neurology,* which is defined as a branch of medicine that deals with the nervous system and its disorders, and *psychology,* which is defined as the study of behavior or the mind (Finger, 1994). One of the first people to combine the words neurology and psychology into neuropsychology was Kurt Goldstein (Frommer & Smith, 1988) in his book *The Organism* (1939). Neuropsychology today is used to describe a field of psychology that principally circumscribes the identification, quantification, and description of changes in behavior that relate to the structural and cognitive integrity of the brain (Golden, Zillmer, & Spiers, 1992).

The Neuropsychologist as a Professional

Most individuals who call themselves neuropsychologists are professionals involved with assessing and treating human patients (i.e., clinical neuropsychology) (Finger, 1994). A majority of neuropsychologists in practice work with either psychiatric or neuropsychological populations in a variety of settings: private practice, university-based medical centers, psychiatric hospitals, general community hospitals, mental health centers, university psychology departments, and prisons (Golden, 1983). Neuropsychologists are involved in specifying the nature of brain-related disorders and applying this information to rehabilitation and education. In order to achieve this, the clinical neuropsychologist is required to establish a comprehensive database of historical and current general medical, surgical, neurological, neuroradiological, pharmacological, developmental, and psychosocial factors underlying the presenting problem (Meier, 1997).

Diagnosis in Neuropsychology

One of the major questions facing neuropsychologists is the differentiation of brain damage from the major psychiatric disorders (Golden, 1983). The reason for the difficulty in differentiation lies in the fact that the range of psychiatric disorders is broad and involves elements of cognitive impairment commonly seen in brain injury. The area of diagnosis for the neuropsychologist includes three subareas. The first subarea involves the identification of the presence of a brain injury in which a differentiation must be made between disorders caused by emotional problems and those caused by injury to the function of the brain. The second subarea involves the specification of the nature of the deficit caused by brain damage, including localizing the injury to specific areas of the brain. The third subarea includes the identification of the underlying process or underlying cognitive disorder (Golden, 1983).

Neuropsychological Assessment

The primary goal of assessment in neuropsychology is to address the relevant neurobehavioral aspects of higher psychological functioning that are considered to be central to understanding the cognitive strengths and deficits of the individual (Meier, 1997). In neurodiagnostic settings, there is an emphasis on the search for dysfunctional aspects of an individual's cognition and behavior that aid in diagnosis of the particular lesion, disease, syndrome, or condition (Golden, Zillmer, & Spiers, 1992). In addition, neuropsychological assessments can also serve as a baseline for a patient's abilities so that a course of recovery or decline in a patient can be evaluated (Golden, Zillmer, & Spiers, 1992).

Neuropsychological assessments are typically organized into standardized or flexible batteries. Standardized batteries are those in which patients take all tests in a given battery. Some examples of standardized neuropsychological batteries include the Halstead-Reitan and the Luria Nebraska test batteries. Both batteries are composed of an established set of tests that assess those neurocognitive functions that are susceptible to disruption from neurologic impairment, including those sustained after head injury (Smith, Barth, Diamond, & Giuliano, 1998). Flexible neuropsychological batteries are those in which the neuropsychologist creates a customized battery of specific tests or modifies a basic battery based on individual patient issues and history (Smith et al., 1998).

Treatment Evaluation

Neuropsychologists may use tests to evaluate the effectiveness of interventions with a client after brain injury. Such interventions may include medical treatment (e.g., surgery for chronic epilepsy), speech therapy, occupational therapy, physical therapy, or whether a particular drug makes a patient better or worse in terms of neuropsychological functioning (Golden, 1983). For instance, a study by Goldberg et al. (1982) found significant improvement in memory after drug treatment (Hanlon, 1994). These studies aid in documenting and evaluating the effects and value of treatment.

Rehabilitation

The primary objective of neuropsychological rehabilitation is to improve the quality of life of individuals who have sustained neurological insult which may involve cognitive, behavioral, emotional, and social factors (Hanlon, 1994). Neuropsychological assessment can serve as a first step in developing a rehabilitation program for a patient because it allows the clinician to fully document the details of the patient's strengths and weaknesses. Documentation integrated with an understanding of brain function allows the clinician to understand the behavioral, cognitive, and emotional effects of an injury (Golden, Zillmer, & Spiers, 1992).

Hanlon (1994) described four primary approaches to cognitive rehabilitation that are currently practiced: (1) the direct retraining approach that involves the use of repetitive drills and exercises; (2) the substitution-transfer model, in which visual imagery is used to facilitate verbal retention, verbal mediation, and elaboration to compensate for visual memory dysfunction; (3) the functional compensation and adaptation model, which involves the use of any and all strategies, techniques, devices, and adaptive equipment that enable the patient to perform tasks that can no longer be performed in a conventional manner; and (4) the behavioral approach, which is based on the principles of learning theory and behavior.

Future Trends in Neuropsychology

The field of neuropsychology continues to expand. Kay and Starbuck (1997) have noted that the relatively low cost of personal computers and the potential of having computers perform labor-intensive scoring and test administration procedures may explain the popularity of computer applications in neuropsychological assessment. However, they also add that computerized testing appears to have had only minimal impact on the field of neuropsychology, probably because of a general resistance to novel methods or to the lack of human-to-human contact.

REFERENCES

Finger, S. (1994). History of neuropsychology. In D. W. Zaidel (Ed.), *Neuropsychology* (pp. 1–28). San Diego: Academic Press.

Frommer, G. P., & Smith, A. (1988). Kurt Goldstein and recovery of function. In S. Finger, T. E. LeVere, C. R. Almli, & D. G. Stein (Eds.), *Brain injury and recovery: Theoretical and controversial issues* (pp. 71–88). New York: Plenum Press.

Goldberg, E., Gerstman, L. J., Mattis, S., Hughes, J. E. O., Bilder, R. M., & Sirio, C. A. (1982). Effects of cholinergic treatment of posttraumatic anterograde amnesia. *Archives of Neurology (Chicago), 39,* 581.

Golden, C. J. (1983). The neuropsychologist in neurological and psychiatric populations. In C. J. Golden & P. J. Vicente (Eds.), *Foundations of clinical neuropsychology* (pp. 163–187). New York: Plenum Press.

Golden, C. J., Zillmer, E., & Spiers, M. (1992). *Neuropsychological assessment and intervention.* Springfield, IL: Charles C. Thomas.

Goldstein, K. (1939). *The organism.* New York: American Book Co.

Hanlon, R. (1994). Neuropsychological rehabilitation. In D. W. Zaidel (Ed), *Neuropsychology* (pp. 317–338). San Diego: Academic Press.

Kay, G. G., & Starbuck, V. N. (1997). Computerized neuropsychological assessment. In M. E. Maruish & J. A. Moses, Jr. (Eds.), *Clinical neuropsychology: Theoretical foundations for practitioners* (pp. 143–161). Mahwah, NJ: Erlbaum.

Meier, M. J. (1997). The establishment of clinical neuropsychology as a psychological speciality. In M. E. Maruish & J. A. Moses, Jr. (Eds.), *Clinical neuropsychology: Theoretical foundations for practitioners* (pp. 1–31). Mahwah, NJ: Erlbaum.

Smith, R. J., Barth, J. T., Diamond, R., & Giuliano, A. J. (1998). Evaluation of head trauma. In G. Goldstein, P. D. Nussbaum, & S. R. Beers (Eds.), *Neuropsychology* (pp. 136–170). New York: Plenum Press.

ANGELICA ESCALONA
CHARLES J. GOLDEN
Nova Southeastern University

NEUROTRANSMITTER RELEASE

Neurons can communicate with each other by direct ion fluxes at "electrical or electrotonic synapses," but more commonly do so by releasing chemical messenger molecules, termed neurotransmitters, from their terminals at "chemical synapses." Depending on the type of neuron or neuroendocrine cell, neurotransmitters are stored either in membrane-bound, electron-lucent synaptic vesicles approximately 50 nm in diameter, or in larger vesicles with dense cores. They are released by appropriate stimuli into the extracellular space, evoking a response in neighboring cells by binding to membrane receptors. They are subsequently eliminated by diffusion, by degradation, or by uptake into presynaptic terminals or neighboring glial cells.

Bernard Katz and his collaborators in the early 1950s were the first to recognize that the end plate potentials recorded electrophysiologically at neuromuscular junctions were the sum of many "miniature" end plate potentials produced simultaneously, each of which represented the release from a single vesicle of a "quantum" comprised of several hundred molecules of the neurotransmitter acetylcholine, ACh. Many other molecules have since been recognized to fulfill the four essential criteria of neurotransmitters, which are: (1) neuronal synthesis, (2) presence in the axon terminal, (3) release from terminals in response to stimulation, and (4) production of a biological effect when applied exogenously to synapses.

Neurotransmitters can be classified according to their chemical structure: *biogenic amines,* principally ACh and monoamines, including the indoleamine, serotonin (5-hydroxytryptamine), and the catecholamines, dopamine, noradrenaline, and adrenaline; *amino acids,* including GABA (γ aminobutyric acid), glutamic acid, and glycine; *peptides,* such as endogenous opioids and substance P; and *neurotransmitters with no chemical similarities,* such as nitric oxide and adenosine.

Neurotransmitters are termed "fast" (e.g., ACh, GABA, etc.) or "slow" (e.g., peptides) and most are rapidly eliminated after release. Peptides, however, represent an exception and can act over long periods far from their release sites. Neurotransmitters are released from neurons in response to the arrival of an action potential or the interaction of specific ligands with membrane receptors, stimuli that trigger opening of voltage-dependent Ca^{2+} channels, allowing Ca^{2+} to enter the nerve terminal. Release kinetics and Ca^{2+} requirements vary considerably between different types of neuron and neuroendocrine cells and also for different types of neurotransmitter. Thus, release from small synaptic vesicles in neurons occurs less than a millisecond after stimulation, while in cultured pheochromocytoma cells the delay can be 200 ms and this increases to up to one second for adrenaline and noradrenaline secretion from large (2 to 500nm diameter) secretory granules in adrenal medullary chromaffin cells. In addition, Ca^{2+} influx at nerve terminals, and thereby neurotransmitter release, can be modulated via presynaptic membrane receptors, such as GABA receptors.

Neurotransmitters are classically considered to be released by a multistep process involving translocation of neurotransmitter storage vesicles to synaptic membranes; vesicle docking at active membrane sites; Ca^{2+}-triggered fusion of vesicle membranes with synaptic membranes and exocytosis of vesicle contents into the extracellular space; and vesicle endocytosis involving clathrin-coated vesicles.

In resting neurons, most synaptic vesicles accumulate in the distal cytoplasm of presynaptic terminals in reserve pools, linked to F-actin by the protein synapsin. Stimulation causes the Ca^{2+} concentration to rise near Ca^{2+} channels, provoking synapsin phosphorylation by specific kinases, which permits vesicles to dissociate from the cytoskeleton and translocate to active synaptic membrane sites. Vesicle docking at these sites is mediated by interactions between highly conserved proteins also implicated in constitutive secretion and intracellular trafficking. These include both soluble cytosolic proteins, such as NSF (**N**-ethylmaleimide **S**oluble **F**actor) and **S**oluble **NSF** **Att**achment **P**roteins (SNAPs), and membrane-bound SNARE (**S**oluble **NSF** **A**ttachment **Re**ceptor) proteins. Synaptobrevin and synaptotagmin have been identified as vesicle membrane SNAREs, and SNAP-25 and syntaxin as synaptic membrane SNAREs. Docking involves formation of NSF/SNAP/SNARE complexes and depends on GTP and small G-proteins. Subsequent Ca^{2+}-dependent ATP hydrolysis enables synaptotagmin and synaptobrevin to dissociate from the complex, permitting vesicles to move even closer to the membrane and fuse with it. This Ca^{2+}-dependent step involves the opening of a fusion pore, in which the vesicle protein synaptophysin may participate, allowing the neurotransmitter inside the vesicle to escape into the extracellular synaptic space. Other vesicular proteins, including cysteine string proteins and syntaxin, may facilitate vesicular association with Ca^{2+} channels, thus helping to prime the transmitter release cascade.

Two alternative mechanisms have been proposed for neurotransmitter release. In the first, the "kiss and run" theory, synaptic vesicles undergo rapid and reversible interactions with the membrane which stop short of complete fusion, but which allow variable amounts of neurotransmitter to diffuse out. This mechanism thus involves the transient formation of a gate with channel properties, which is equivalent to the initial step in vesicle/synaptic membrane fusion in the classical view of neurotransmission. A second contrasting hypothesis abandons the notion of vesicle fusion and suggests that a 200 kDa "gate" protein, termed a "mediatophore," located in the nerve terminal membrane, is alone sufficient for the Ca^{2+}-dependent release step. It estimates that the brief opening of around 10 gate proteins would allow quantal release of neurotransmitter and at the same time generate miniature end plate potentials.

It seems unlikely that neurotransmitters are released by strictly identical mechanisms in all neurons and related cells, because not all proteins thought to be implicated in exocytosis have been detected in all neurons. The markedly different release kinetics for neuroendocrine cells and neurons and for different types of synapses also suggest that regulation differs between cell types. Photoreceptor retinal bipolar cells and hair cells of the inner ear illustrate this dramatically. They possess special "ribbon" synapses, which release neurotransmitters from vesicles according to a graded response depending on the extent of their membrane depolarization. These synapses are specifically adapted to rapid, almost continuous, firing, in contrast to the action potential-triggered periodic bursts of activity from conventional synapses. Thus, in such synapses Ca^{2+} channels differ from those in other neurons by their resistance to inactivation, and translocation of vesicles to active membrane sites is not controlled by synapsin, as in conventional terminals, but occurs by a distinct, more efficient mechanism to satisfy the high firing rate.

Keith Langley
Institut National de la Sainté et de la Recherche Médicale

NEUROTRANSMITTERS

A neurotransmitter is a chemical substance that carries a "message" from the terminal bouton of one nerve cell or neuron across a tiny gap (synapse) to receptor sites on another neuron. Neurotransmitters are, in general, synthesized in the neuron's cell body and stored in tiny sacs called synaptic vesicles.

Nobel Prize winner Otto Loewi is credited with demonstrating synaptic transmission's chemical nature in 1920. Loewi isolated a frog heart with an attached vagus nerve. Stimulating the nerve caused the heart's rate to decrease; when Loewi extracted some of the fluid around the heart and applied it to an unstimulated second heart, the second heart's rate slowed as well. Loewi concluded that stimulating the nerve to the first heart had released a chemical at the synapse between the vagus nerve and the heart, and this chemical had transported the message to the heart to slow down. Because he had stimulated the vagus nerve, Loewi called the mysterious chemical "Vagusstoff." It was later discovered that Vagusstoff was acetylcholine (ACh).

When a neurotransmitter such as ACh diffuses across the synapse, it binds to specific postsynaptic receptors to produce either a local excitatory effect or an inhibitory effect. Whether the postsynaptic neuron passes on the message by producing an action potential depends on the sum of the influences it receives from presynaptic neurons.

A neurotransmitter that remained in the synapse for any length of time would limit the number of messages that could be passed from one neuron to another. Thus, the neurotransmitter is rapidly inactivated almost from the moment of its release. One common method of inactivation is called reuptake, a process through which the neurotransmitter is taken back into the presynaptic neuron from which it was released.

The second major inactivation mechanism is used on ACh and on neuropeptide neurotransmitters and is called enzymatic degradation. In the former case, acetylcholinesterase (AChE) breaks the ACh molecule into two parts, neither of which produces the effect of ACh. Neuropeptides, once released, are degraded by peptidase. Diffusion, the drifting away of neurotransmitter molecules from the synapse, is another inactivation method that occurs with all neurotransmitters.

The brain uses as many as 100 neurotransmitters. For many years, it was believed that each neuron released only one particular neurotransmitter from all its nerve terminals. We now know that many if not most neurons release two or three transmitters, and some may release as many as five or six.

The three major categories of neurotransmitters are biogenic amines, amino acids, and peptides. One biogenic amine—ACh—is found in the brain and spinal cord, and is also the chemical that carries messages from the motor nerves to the skeletal muscles. Other important biogenic amines include dopamine, norepinephrine, epinephrine, and serotonin.

Dopamine is importantly implicated in two major brain disorders: schizophrenia and Parkinson's disease. In Parkinson's disease, cells die in a brain area called the substantia nigra (Latin for "black substance"). In the course of the disease, the "black substance" actually becomes white because of the loss of dopamine-producing cells. Nigral cells normally project dopamine to the neostriatum, which controls motor activities. Without the neurotransmitter, the afflicted individual begins to develop characteristic symptoms such as tremor at rest, rigidity, and bradykinesia. Replacement therapy—supplying drugs to increase the amount of dopamine in the brain (for example, L-dopa)—may work temporarily, but unfortunately, the disease is progressive.

Schizophrenia is also associated with defects in the dopamine system, in this case by increased activity. Major antipsychotic drugs, both typical—such as chlorpromazine (Thorazine)—and atypical—such as resperidone (Risperdal)—block subtypes of dopamine receptors.

Norepinephrine (also called noradrenalin) is the neurotransmitter at the post-ganglionic sympathetic nervous system, and is also found in the brain. Decreased norepinephrine and/or serotonin activity in the brain are thought to contribute to depression. Most drugs used to treat depression increase the release of norepinephrine, serotonin, or both.

Gamma-aminobutyric acid (GABA) is an example of an amino acid neurotransmitter. GABA is the most common inhibitory neurotransmitter in the brain, and the destruction of GABA neurons in a major motor system (the basal ganglia) occurs in Huntington's disease. Symptoms of Huntington's disease include involuntary movements. Antianxiety drugs such as diazepam (Valium) and alprazolam (Xanax) act by stimulating GABA receptors. Other amino acid neurotransmitters include glutamate (the most common excitatory neurotransmitter in the brain), glycine, and aspartate.

The peptide neurotransmitters include the "endorphins," or "endogenous morphine-like substances." Because opiates such as morphine and heroin are so addictive, brain researchers suspected that there were receptors for the opiates in the brain. In 1973, such receptors were found, which led to the further discovery of naturally occurring neurotransmitters with opiate-like properties, which induce analgesia and euphoria. Some functions in which the endogenous opiates have been implicated include the placebo effect, runner's high, and pain relief from acupuncture (but not from hypnotically induced analgesia). Other examples of peptide neurotransmitters include substance P (involved in pain perception), oxytocin (responsible for labor pains), and cholecystokinin (involved in hunger satiety).

In addition to the categories of neurotransmitters discussed, there is a newly discovered group of neurotransmitters that appear to break all the "rules" governing the actions of neurotransmitters. These are soluble gases that are made in all parts of neurons, are released as soon as they are manufactured, and do not affect postsynaptic receptors. The soluble gases identified at this time are nitric oxide and carbon monoxide. Nitric oxide is apparently involved in such disparate functions as penile erection, dilation of blood vessels in areas of the brain that are metabolically active, and learning.

B. Michael Thorne
Mississippi State University

NICOTINE

Nicotine is a pale yellow, highly toxic liquid contained in the leaves of several species of plants. Commercially, nicotine is extracted from dried *Nicotiana tabacum* leaves and used for making insecticides (nicotine sulfate) or tobacco products (Benowitz, 1998). Nicotine is extremely poisonous and can cause respiratory failure, convulsions, nervous system paralysis, and death if consumed in a single dose of 50 mg or more.

Nicotine is typically found in tobacco products such as cigarettes, cigars, snuff, chew, and pipes as well as in insecticides such as Black Leaf (40 percent nicotine sulfate; Benowitz, 1998). Most tobacco products, such as cigarettes, contain 10 milligrams or more of nicotine content (American Cancer Society [ACS], 1997). However, when smoked, a single cigarette delivers approximately 1 to 3 mg of nicotine, as well as 4,000 other chemicals, to the nose, mouth, and primarily to the lungs, where nicotine is quickly assimilated through cell membranes into the pulmonary capillary blood flow (Grunberg, 1999). After inhaling, nicotine is transferred to the brain within approximately 10 seconds from the first puff (National Institute on Drug Abuse [NIDA] 1998).

Because smoking so quickly transports nicotine to the brain, cigarettes provide an efficient and consistent "drug-delivery system" (Hurt & Robertson, 1998; NIDA, 1998). Nicotine affects the mesolimbic system, or the pleasure center of the brain, creating increased levels of dopamine, a neurotransmitter essential to the functioning of the central nervous system and emotion regulation (Brauthar, 1995; Pich, Pagliusi, & Tessari, 1997). An increase of dopamine elicits feelings of euphoria and has been linked to the addictive process. Nicotine also elicits pleasurable feelings such as relaxation, stimulation, and increased attention, reinforcing continued use (Corrigall, Franklin, Coen, & Clarke, 1992; Hurt & Robertson, 1998; Ovid & Pomerleau, 1992).

Because nicotine is so addictive, as well as toxic, tobacco

use is a primary health concern. Cigarette smoking contributes to approximately 400,000 deaths annually in the United States and the majority of these deaths are directly attributable to cancer (ACS, 1999; Peto, Lopez, Boreham, Thur, & Heath, 1992). Nicotine stimulates the division of small cell carcinomas, a cancer cell line, by several hundred percent. As a result, tobacco use is associated with many types of cancers, such as lung, larynx, esophageal, bladder, pancreatic, kidney, and colon cancers (ACS, 1996; Centers for Disease Control [CDC], 1993a). Tobacco use also leads to an increase in heart disease as well as respiratory diseases such as emphysema and chronic bronchitis (CDC, 1993a). Additionally, women who smoke during pregnancy have an increased risk of spontaneous abortion, preterm birth rates, low birth weights, and fetal or infant death (DiFranza & Lew, 1995; Slotkin, 1998).

Effective methods to assist people in quitting smoking can clearly reduce the risk of cancer and health hazards from smoking (CDC, 1993a). Recent advances in the treatment of nicotine dependence offer a variety of options such as behavior modification programs, antidepressants (Zyban), nicotine replacement therapies such as the patch (Nicoderm CQ, Nicotrol, Habitrol, etc.) or nicotine gum (Nicorette), as well as nasal spray (Nicotrol NS) (Henningfield, 1995; Rose, 1996). With the variety of smoking-cessation treatments available, a primary physician can best assist individuals to tailor treatments to effectively meet their needs (Ward, Klesges, & Halpern, 1997).

REFERENCES

American Cancer Society. (1996). *Cancer facts and figures, 1996.* Atlanta, GA: American Cancer Society.

American Cancer Society. (1997). *Cigarette nicotine disclosure report, 1997.* Atlanta, GA: American Cancer Society.

American Cancer Society. (1999). *Surveillance research: Vital statistics of the United States, 1998.* Atlanta, GA: American Cancer Society.

Benowitz, N. L. (1998). *Nicotine safety and toxicity.* New York: Oxford University Press.

Brauthar, N. (1995). Direct effects of nicotine on the brain: Evidence for chemical addiction. *Archives of Environmental Health, 50*(4), 263–267.

Chassin, L., Presson, C. C., Rose, J. S., & Sherman, S. J. (1996). The natural history of cigarette smoking from adolescence to adulthood: Demographic predictors of continuity and change. *Health Psychology, 15,* 478–484.

Centers for Disease Control and Prevention. (1993a). Mortality trends for selected smoking-related diseases and breast cancer-United States, 1950–1990. *Morbidity and Mortality Weekly Report, 42*(44), 857, 863–866.

Centers for Disease Control and Prevention. (1993b). Reasons for tobacco use and symptoms of nicotine withdrawal among adolescent and young adult tobacco users—United States, 1993. *Morbidity and Mortality Weekly Reports, 48*(19), 398–401.

Centers for Disease Control and Prevention. (1995). Symptoms of substance dependence associated with use of cigarettes, alcohol and illicit drugs, 1991–1992. *Morbidity and Mortality Weekly Reports, 44*(44), 830–831.

Corrigall, W. A., Franklin, K. B. J., Coen, K. M., & Clarke, P. B. S. (1992). The mesolimbic dopaminergic system is implicated in the reinforcing effects of nicotine. *Psychopharmacology, 107,* 285–289.

DiFranza, J. R., & Lew, R. A. (1995). Effect of maternal cigarette smoking on pregnancy complications and sudden infant death syndrome. *Journal of Family Practice, 40,* 385–394.

Grunberg, N. (1999). Understanding the facts about nicotine addiction. *The Brown University Digest of Addiction Theory and Application, 18,* 6, S1.

Henningfield, J. (1995). Nicotine medications for smoking cessation. *New England Journal of Medicine, 333,* 1196–1203.

Hurt, R. D., & Robertson, C. R. (1998). Prying open the door to the tobacco industry's secret about nicotine: The Minnesota Tobacco Trial. *Journal of the American Medical Association, 280*(13), 1173–81.

Lichtenstein, E., & Glasgow, R. E. (1992). Smoking cessation: What have we learned over the past decade? *Journal of Consulting and Clinical Psychology, 60,* 518–527.

National Institute on Drug Abuse. (1998). Nicotine addiction. *National Institute on Drug Abuse* (NIH Publication 98-4342). Washington, DC: U.S. Government Printing Office.

Ovid, E. F., & Pomerleau, C. S. (1992). Nicotine in the central nervous system; behavioral effects of cigarette smoking. *American Journal of Medicine, 93,* 1a–7s.

Rose, J. E. (1996). Nicotine addiction and treatment. *Annual Review of Medicine, 47,* 493–507.

Peto, R., Lopez, A. D., Boreham, J., Thun, M., & Heath, C. (1992). Mortality from tobacco in developed countries: Indirect estimation from national vital statistics. *Lancet, 339,* 1268–1278.

Pich, E. M., Pagliusi, S. R., & Tessari, M. (1997). Common neural substrates for the addictive properties of nicotine and cocaine. *Science, 275,* 83–86.

Shiffman, S. (1993). Smoking cessation treatment: Any progress? *Journal of Consulting and Clinical Psychology, 61,* 718–722.

Slotkin, T. A. (1998). The impact of fetal nicotine exposure on nervous system development and its role in sudden infant death syndrome. In N. L. Benowitz (Ed.), *Nicotine safety and toxicity.* New York: Oxford University Press.

Stephenson, J. (1996). Clues found to tobacco addiction. *Journal of the American Medical Association, 275,* 1217–1218.

U.S. Department of Health and Human Services. (1998). *National household survey on drug abuse, 1998.* Atlanta, GA: U.S. Centers for Chronic Disease Prevention and Health Promotion Research.

Ward, K. D., Klesges, R. C., & Halpern, M. T. (1997). Predictors of smoking cessation and state-of-the-art smoking interventions. *Journal of Social Issues, 53*(1), 129–145.

Heather LaChance
Kent Hutchison
University of Colorado at Boulder

See also: **Addiction**

NIGHTMARES

Nightmares are defined as disturbing dreams associated with anxiety or fear that cause an awakening from sleep. Generally, the sufferer quickly becomes alert after awakening and readily recalls the details of the dream. Nightmares are a universal human experience and have engendered much literary attention but only limited empirical research. One aspect of dreams and nightmares that make them difficult to study is the fact that they cannot be directly observed. Dreams can only be recalled following awakening, and the fidelity of recall is not known. For example, it is possible that dream recall is limited to dream events occurring in the period immediately prior to arousal. Further, dream recall is subject to retrieval biases in which the subject will impose order on what can be chaotic mental experience.

Nightmares are associated with rapid eye movement (REM) sleep or light stages of Non-REM sleep. Nightmares typically occur in the last hours of sleep when the sufferer is more easily aroused. Studies that involve awakening subjects at various time points across the sleep period have found that the extent of dream recall increases as a function of time elapsed since sleep onset, irrespective of sleep stage (Rosenlicht, Maloney, & Feinberg, 1994). Thus, nightmares experienced at the end of the sleep period are associated with better recall than those occurring early in the sleep period.

Nightmares are often confused with night terrors, which represent a clinically distinct entity. Night terrors involve an incomplete awakening from deep non-rapid eye movement (NREM) sleep and are associated with disorientation, severe distress, and prominent autonomic arousal. During the night terror, the sufferer, most typically a young child, is difficult to awaken. Following complete awakening, the sufferer usually has absent or vague recall of dream mentation. Night terrors usually occur in the first hours of sleep when non-REM slow wave sleep stages are prominent.

While nightmares are experienced universally, the experience of frequent nightmares is considerably less common. The *Diagnostic and Statistical Manual of Mental Disorders* (American Psychiatric Association [ApA], 1994) include the diagnosis of Nightmare Disorder, which was formerly referred to as Dream Anxiety Disorder. The criteria for this disorder include repeated awakenings from sleep with recall of frightening dreams that lead to significant impairment. Though the precise epidemiology of this disorder has yet to be characterized, the available data suggest that it occurs in 10 to 50 percent of children (ApA, 1994), with a peak incidence between the ages of 3 and 6 (Leung & Robson, 1993) and a decline in frequency with age (Hartmann, 1984). Nightmares occur with less frequency in adults and can be associated with alcohol withdrawal, dopamine stimulating medications, or withdrawal of REM-suppressing medication. Surveys have found that 10 to 29% of college students report having a nightmare once or more per month (Feldman & Hersen, 1967, Belicky & Belicky, 1982). A survey of 1006 adults, ages 18 to 80, in Los Angeles found that 5.3% of respondents reported that "frightening dreams" were a current problem (Bixler, et al. 1979). This survey as well as others (Coren, 1994) have reported a higher prevalence of frightening dreams in women. Unfortunately, little polysomnography data are available in adults with Nightmare Disorder, in part because nightmares are rarely captured in the sleep laboratory. Further, survey data are limited by the fact that subjects are often confused about the difference between night terrors and nightmares (Hartmann, 1984).

There has long been an interest in the relationship between trauma exposure and nightmares (Freud, 1920/1953; Kardiner & Spiegel, 1947; Horowitz, 1976; Brett & Ostroff, 1985; Ross, Ball, Sullivan, & Caroff, 1989). Subjectively, the experience of the nightmare feels as distressing as a traumatic experience during waking life. The nightmare is associated with the full sensory experience of an autonomic fear response. When nightmares occur during rapid eye movement sleep, a sleep stage in which skeletal muscles are atonic, the sufferer may experience a sense of paralysis and an inability to escape. Hartmann, in his studies of frequent nightmare sufferers, found that adult exposure to violent assault increased nightmare frequency, though he was not able to find a history of early childhood trauma (1984). Kales et al. (1980) also found that the onset of nightmares was preceded by "major life events." The National Comorbidity Survey reports a lifetime prevalence of Post-Traumatic Stress Disorder (PTSD) of 10.4% in women and 5.0% in men (Kessler Sonnega, Bronet, Hughes, & Nelson, 1995), which is similar to the gender ratio reported in frequent nightmare sufferers.

At present there are insufficient data to validate the diagnosis of Nightmare Disorder as a separate nosologic entity apart from PTSD. One large study of combat veterans found that frequent nightmares were virtually specific for those diagnosed with PTSD at the time of the survey (Neylan et al., 1998). In this study, combat exposure was highly associated with nightmares, moderately associated with sleep onset insomnia, and only weakly related to sleep maintenance insomnia. These relationships are consistent with the results of the combat veteran twin study (True et al., 1993), which showed that combat exposure was highly correlated with reports of dreams and nightmares and only weakly associated with sleep maintenance insomnia. These observations are also consistent with several other studies that show a low to moderate correlation between nightmares and other domains of sleep disturbance (Coren, 1994; Krakow, Tandberg, Scriggins, & Barey, 1995). Thus, the nightmare appears to be the primary domain of sleep disturbance related to exposure to traumatic stress.

There is no standardized treatment for frequent nightmares. There are a number of small scale open-label trials using sedating antidepressants, cyproheptadine, benzodiazepine, clonidine, guanfacine, and prazosin (Raskind et al., 2002). None of these has been systematically studied in large randomized controlled trials. One novel treatment for repetitive nightmares is dream rehearsal therapy. Nightmare sufferers describe their nightmares in the context of group psychotherapy. They then repetitively rehearse an alternate and nontraumatic outcome to their nightmare narrative. This technique has been found to reduce the frequency and intensity of recurrent nightmares (Krakow et al., 2001).

REFERENCES

American Psychiatric Association. (1994). *Diagnostic and Statistical Manual of Mental Disorders* (4th ed.). Washington, DC: Author.

Belicky, D., & Belicky, K. (1982). Nightmares in a university population. *Sleep Research, 11,* 116.

Bixler, E. O., Kales, A., Soldatos, C. R., Kales, J. D., & Healey, S. (1979). Prevalence of sleep disorders in the Los Angeles metropolitan area. *American Journal of Psychiatry, 136,* 1257–1262.

Brett, E. A., & Ostroff, R. (1985). Imagery and Posttraumatic Stress Disorder: An overview. *American Journal of Psychiatry, 142,* 417–424.

Coren, S. (1994). The prevalence of self-reported sleep disturbances in young adults. *International Journal of Neuroscience, 79,* 67–73.

Feldman, M. J., & Hersen, M. (1967). Attitudes toward death in nightmare subjects. *Journal of Abnormal Psychology, 72,* 421–425.

Freud, S. (1920/1953). Beyond the pleasure principle. In *Complete psychological works* (Vol. 18). London: Hogarth Press.

Hartmann, E. (1984). *The nightmare: The psychology and biology of terrifying dreams.* New York: Basic Books.

Hartmann, E., Russ, D., van der Kolk, B., Falke, R., & Oldfield, M. (1981). A preliminary study of the personality of the nightmare sufferer: Relationship to schizophrenia and creativity? *American Journal of Psychiatry, 138,* 794–797.

Horowitz, M. J. (1976). *Stress response syndromes.* New York: Jason Aronson.

Kales, A., Soldatos, C. R., Caldwell, A. B., Charney, D. S., Kales, J. D., Markel, D., & Cadieux, R. (1980). Nightmares: Clinical characteristics and personality patterns. *American Journal of Psychiatry, 137,* 1197–1201.

Kardiner, A., & Spiegel, H. (1947). *War stress and neurotic illness.* New York: Paul B. Hoeber.

Kessler, R. C., Sonnega, A., Bromet, E., Hughes, M., & Nelson, C. B. (1995). Posttraumatic Stress Disorder in the National Comorbidity Survey. *Archives of General Psychiatry, 52,* 1048–1060.

Krakow, B., Johnston, L., Melendrez, D., Hollifield, M., Warner, T. D., Chavez-Kennedy, D., & Herlan, M. J. (2001). An open-label trial of evidence-based cognitive behavior therapy for nightmares and insomnia in crime victims with PTSD. *American Journal of Psychiatry, 158*(12), 2043–2047.

Krakow, B., Tandberg, D., Scriggins, L., & Barey, M. (1995). A controlled comparison of self-rated sleep complaints in acute and chronic nightmare sufferers. *Journal of Nervous and Mental Disease, 183,* 623–627.

Leung, A. K., & Robson, W. L. (1993). Nightmares. *Journal of the National Medical Association, 85*(3), 233–235.

Neylan, T. C., Marmar, C. R., Metzler, T. J., Weiss, D. S., Zatzick, D. F., Delucchi, K. L., Wu, R. M., & Schoenfeld, F. B. (1998). Sleep disturbances in the Vietnam generation: An analysis of sleep measures from the National Vietnam Veteran Readjustment Study. *American Journal of Psychiatry, 155,* 929–933.

Raskind, M. A., Thompson, C., Petrie, E. C., Dobie, D. J., Rein, R. J., Hoff, D. J., McFall, M. E., & Peskind, E. R. (2002). Prazosin reduces nightmares in combat veterans with posttraumatic stress disorder. *Journal of Clinical Psychiatry, 63*(7), 565–568.

Rosenlicht, N., Maloney, T., & Feinberg, I. (1994). Dream report length is more dependent on arousal level than prior REM duration. *Brain Research Bulletin, 34,* 99–101.

Ross, R. J., Ball, W. A., Sullivan, K. A., & Caroff, S. N. (1989). Sleep disturbance as the hallmark of Posttraumatic Stress Disorder. *American Journal of Psychiatry, 146,* 697–707.

True, W. R., Rice, J., Eisen, S. A., Heath, A. C., Goldberg, J., Lyons, M. J., & Nowak, J. (1993). A twin study of genetic and environmental contributions to liability for posttraumatic stress symptoms. *Archives of General Psychiatry, 50,* 257–264.

Thomas C. Neylan
University of California, San Francisco

NOISE EFFECTS

Noise is defined as unwanted sound. Its intensity is measured in decibels (dB). Zero dB is defined as the weakest noise that a person with normal hearing can just barely detect in quiet surroundings, 55 dB is equivalent to light traffic sounds, and 120 dB is equivalent to jet takeoff from 200 feet away. Most behavioral studies use a modified dB scale, called the *dBA scale,* devised to approximate perceived loudness. This scale assigns higher weights to high-frequency sounds, since they are perceived as louder than low-frequency sounds of equal sound pressure.

Noise pollution is a worrisome problem in the United States. The Environmental Protection Agency (EPA) has estimated that more than 70 million Americans live in neighborhoods noisy enough to be annoying and to interfere with communication and sleep. More than 50% of production workers are exposed to workplace noise loud enough to damage hearing.

Noise is by definition unwanted and therefore frustrating and tension-inducing. As a stressor, it alters the functioning of cardiovascular, endocrine, respiratory, and digestive systems, and is also suspected of having damaging effects on mental health.

The hearing loss effects of noise are well established. The EPA estimates that 1 out of every 10 Americans is exposed to noise levels of sufficient intensity and duration to create permanent hearing losses. Hearing losses do not hurt and are not immediately apparent, but even minor hearing impairments seem to enhance susceptibility to further injury in the middle and late years.

The consequences of noise on performance cannot easily be predicted. They depend on the noise, the performance, the meaning of the sound, and the social context of the person performing. If people have clear warning of the need to react and receive easily visible cues, loud noise shows little or no overall effects on their work. In general, novel or unusual noises are more bothersome than familiar noise. However, familiar noises louder than 95 dBA—especially if unpredictable, uncontrollable, and intermittent—are disruptive. Typically, noise leads to variable performance—moments of inefficiency interspersed with normal and compensatory spurts of efficient performance. The lapses make workers more accident prone.

In academic settings, adverse effects have been documented repeatedly by well-controlled studies that take into account the socioeconomic and racial characteristics of the participants and use comparison groups. Among the effects of noisy homes and schools are impairment of auditory and visual discrimination, reading and visual-motor skills, overall scholastic achievement, and persistence in the face of frustration. One explanation for these effects is that noise disrupts the teaching-learning process, resulting eventually in cumulative deficits. Some investigators believe that the stressful effects of noise are ameliorated when people have accurate expectations about or (at least perceived) control over the noise.

Noise levels influence people's social conduct, as well. A number of experimental studies have found that individuals exposed to noise tend to be less helpful than those not exposed. Sheldon Cohen has suggested that noise causes subjects to focus their attention on salient aspects of the situation so they fail to notice interpersonal cues. Alternatively, decreases in helping might result from feelings of anger or frustration.

L. L. Davidoff

NONASSOCIATIVE LEARNING

From a biological viewpoint, learning is the process of acquiring new knowledge about the environment and the self necessary for survival of the species. Two major classes of learning can be distinguished: nonassociative and associative. In *nonassociative* learning, the subject learns about a stimulus by being repeatedly exposed to it. Three forms of nonassociative learning are distinguished: habituation, dishabituation, and sensitization. Habituation consists in a reduced response upon repeated presentation of the stimulus. For example, when a loud noise is repeatedly presented to a subject, the startle response rapidly habituates. Dishabituation is the recovery of habituation to a given stimulus upon presentation of a new salient stimulus. Sensitization is an increased response to a stimulus upon its repeated presentation. An example of sensitization is the increased response to a mild tactile stimulus after a painful pinch.

Habituation has been well studied in the defensive reflexes of marine mollusk Aplysia. In these studies habituation was found to be due to a decrease in synaptic transmission between sensory neurons and interneurons and motor neurons. With repeated stimulation, the synaptic potential generated by sensory neurons on interneurons and motor cells become progressively smaller because the amount of transmitter released into the synaptic cleft is decreased. After these modifications the reflex response is reduced. This reduction in the synaptic transmission can last for many minutes. Changes in the synaptic connections between several interneurons and motor neurons represent the components of the storage process for the short-term memory for habituation. This memory storage depends on plastic changes in the strength of preexisting connections. Habituation does not depend on specialized memory neurons that store information, but on neurons that are integral components of a normal reflex pathway. Different types of experiences may be stored in different cells that have many functions other than storing information. The duration of the habituation depends on the extent of training: a single training session of 10 stimuli in Aplysia produces a short-term habituation lasting few minutes, but four training sessions produce a long-term change lasting up to 3 weeks.

Habituation takes place also in the central nervous system of mammals. By monitoring in vivo the release of dopamine in different brain areas of rats using the microdialysis technique, it has been found that dopamine in the nucleus accumbens shell is also involved in the habituation phenomenon. Thus in rats, after a feeding of an unusual palatable food, such as Fonzies or chocolate, extracellular dopamine increases in the nucleus accumbens shell, but a second meal of the same food given after either 2 hours, 1 day, or 3 days fails to activate dopaminergic transmission. In addition, the delayed increase after an aversive gustatory stimulus (like quinine solutions) underwent habituation after a single trial. Recovery of responsiveness and of habituation takes place 5 days after the last exposure to the stimulus. In contrast, exposure to Fonzies or chocolate or quinine increases the extracellular dopamine in the prefrontal cortex, and a second exposure after 2 hours is able again to stimulate dopaminergic transmission. Therefore, in the prefrontal cortex, in contrast to the nucleus accumbens, dopamine does not undergo habituation.

Sensitization is a more complex form of nonassociative learning and it is well studied in the gill-withdrawal reflex in Aplysia. A single stimulus can produce a reflex enhancement that lasts minutes (short-term sensitization), and afterwards it can produce an enhancement that lasts days or weeks (long-term sensitization). Short-term sensitization is produced following a single noxious stimulus to the head or tail. Synapses made by the sensory neurons on interneurons and motor neurons become modified. After sensitizing the stimulus, a group of facilitating interneurons that synapse on the sensory neurons, some of which are serotoninergic, become activated. There is an enhanced transmitter release from the sensory neurons because more transmitter than normal is available for release and there is a larger postsynaptic potential in the motor neurons. The consequence is an enhanced activation of interneurons and motor neurons, and thus an enhanced behavioral response (i.e., sensitization).

In long-term sensitization there are similar, but more extended, modifications than in the short-term process. In both short- and long-term sensitization there is an increase in synaptic strength due to the enhanced transmitter release, but long-term facilitation requires the synthesis of new protein and mRNA. Repeated training prolonged activation of protein kinasi A that phosphorylates nuclear regulatory proteins. These proteins affect the regulatory regions of DNA, increasing transcription of RNA and synthesis of specific proteins. One of the newly synthetized proteins restructuring of the axon arbor. With this process sensory neurons can form other connections with the same motor neurons or make new connections with other cells. In both short-term and long-term sensitization, the enhanced responses of the animal to test stimuli depend on enhanced release of the transmitter from sensory neurons to interneurons or to motor neurons at the level of preexisting synapses, but increases in axonal arborization and synaptic contacts are exclusive of long-term sensitization. The enhanced and prolonged activation of interneurons and cells depends on more synaptic connections with sensory neurons.

Studies about gustatory stimuli show that dopamine transmission is activated by unpredicted appetitive or aversive gustatory stimuli in a different manner in the two different compartments of the nucleus accumbens: the medioventral shell and the laterodorsal core. In fact, while dopamine transmission is activated by Fonzies and chocolate feeding, and in a delayed manner by quinine solutions, to a larger extent in the shell than in the core, preexposure to gustatory stimulus inhibits the dopamine response in the shell but potentiates it in the core. The response properties of dopamine transmission in the nucleus accumbens core, while different from those of the nucleus accumbens shell, are similar to those of the prefrontal cortex.

The responsiveness of dopamine transmission to gustatory stimuli in the nucleus accumbens compartments seems to differ in its adaptive properties. While the dopaminergic responsiveness to gustatory stimulus in the nucleus accumbens core is sensitized by preexposure to it, in the shell it is inhibited. Dopamine physically released in the nucleus accumbens shell by gustatory stimulus might enable the association between the stimulus properties and the biological consequences of feeding. By this mechanism, gustatory stimuli are attributed a motivational valence which determines the specific consummatory response to be emitted by the subject upon further encounter of the same food. The potentiation of dopaminergic transmission in the nucleus accumbens core by preexposure to gustatory stimulus is consistent with an activational role of dopamine in the nucleus accumbens, and with the possibility that the release of dopamine in the nucleus accumbens core facilitates the motor expression of motivated behavior.

SUGGESTED READING

Bassareo, V., & Di Chiara, G. (1997). Differential influence of associative and dopamine transmission to food stimuli in rats fed ad libitum. *Journal of Neuroscience, 17*(2), 851–861.

Bassareo, V., & Di Chiara, G. (1999). Differential responsiveness of dopamine transmission to food-stimuli in nucleus accumbens shell/core compartments. *Neuroscience, 3,* 637–641.

Bassareo, V., De Luca, M. A., & Di Chiara, G. (2002). Differential expression of motivational stimulus properties by dopamine in nucleus accumbens shell versur core and prefrontal cortex. *The Journal of Neuroscience, 22*(11), 4709–4719.

Beggs, J. M., Brown, T. H., Byrne, J. H., Crow, T., LeDoux, J. E., LeBar, K., et al. (1999). Learning and memory: Basic mechanisms. In M. J. Zigmond, F. E. Bloom, S. C. Lands, J. L. Roberts, & L. R. Squire (Eds.), *Fundamental neuroscience* (pp. 1411–1454). New York: Academic Press.

Eichenbaum, H. B., Cahill, L. F., Gluck, M. A., Hasselmo, M. E., Keil, F. C., Martin, A. J., et al. Learning and memory: Systems analysis. In M. J. Zigmond, F. E. Bloom, S. C. Lands, J. L. Roberts, & L. R. Squire (Eds.), *Fundamental neuroscience* (pp. 1455–1486). New York: Academic Press.

Kandel, E. R. (1985). Cellular mechanisms of learning and the biological basis of individuality. In E. R. Kandel (Ed.), *Principles of neural science* (pp. 1009–1031). Amsterdam: Elsevier.

Kaplan, H. I., Sadock, B. J., & Grebb, J. A. (1994). Contributions of the psychosocial sciences to human behavior. In *Synopsis of psychiatry* (pp. 157–220). Baltimore: Williams & Wilkins.

Kupfermann, I. (1985). Learning and memory. In E. R. Kandel (Ed.), *Principles of neural science* (pp. 997–1008). Amsterdam: Elsevier.

Moruzzi, G. (1975). Attività innate e attività acquisite. In *Fisiologia della vita di relazione.* UTET ed.

Valentina Bassareo
University of Cagliari
Cagliari, Italy

NONPARAMETRIC STATISTICAL TESTS

Nonparametric statistical methods are based on weaker assumptions than standard parametric procedures such as the t-test, analysis of variance, and inferential procedures associated with the Pearson correlation coefficient. For example, the usual t-test for two independent groups assumes that the scores in the groups are independent and are randomly sampled from normally distributed populations with equal variances. In contrast, nonparametric or distribution-free tests do not make such strong assumptions about the populations.

Although there is agreement that many standard parametric tests are fairly robust with regard to type 1 error when the assumption of normality is violated, the power of these tests may be severely reduced when the populations are not normally distributed. In particular, severe losses of power may occur when the underlying populations are *heavy tailed;* that is, when there are more scores in the extremes of the distributions (outliers) than would be expected for a normal distribution. In certain cases, it may be shown that particular nonparametric tests have considerably more power than the corresponding parametric tests. However, nonparametric tests are not completely free of assumptions, and unless certain conditions are met, do not test the same null hypotheses as the corresponding parametric tests. For example, the Wilcoxon–Mann–Whitney test based on ranks is a commonly used "nonparametric" analog of the independent-groups t-test. The null hypothesis of the t-test is that the population means of the two groups are equal. If one does not wish to make assumptions about the underlying populations, yet wants to make inferences about measures of location such as the mean or median, one must make the assumption (the so-called "shift" assumption) that, whatever their characteristics, the populations are identical except for their locations. Only in this case do the t- and Wilcoxon–Mann–Whitney tests both address the same null hypothesis.

Rationales For Some Classes of Nonparametric Tests and Some Examples

In most nonparametric tests, the original scores or observations are replaced by other variables that contain less information, so that the statistical tests that are used are less influenced by extreme scores. An important class of tests uses the ordinal properties of the data. The original observations are first replaced by the ranks from 1 to N, and subsequent operations are performed only on the ranks. Some of these procedures (but certainly not all) are computationally simple because the means and variances of the first N integers are easily obtained. It has been shown that some of these procedures are equivalent to what would be obtained by first converting the scores to ranks, then performing the standard parametric tests on these ranks.

If equality of population distributions except for location can be assumed, both the Wilcoxon–Mann–Whitney procedure mentioned above and the Kruskal–Wallis procedure, the generalization to more than two conditions, test hypotheses about location with more power than their parametric analogues when the underlying distributions are heavy tailed. If identical distributions cannot be assumed but homogeneity of the variances *of the ranks* can be assumed, Vargha and Delaney (1998) have shown that what is tested is whether there is a general tendency for scores in at least one of the populations to be larger (or smaller) than those in all of the remaining populations, taken together. If this holistic hypothesis is of interest in situations in which homogeneity of variance or ranks cannot be assumed, alternatives to the t-test and ANOVA procedure (such as the Welch test) performed on the ranks are recommended.

Another important class of tests employs information only about whether an observation is above or below some value, such as the median. All values above the median might be assigned a "plus" and those below it a "minus," so that, in effect, they are replaced by a new variable that can take on only two values.

A number of nonparametric analogs exist for repeated-measures ANOVAs and matched-group t-tests. One approach is simply to rank all of the scores, then perform a repeated-measures ANOVA on the ranks. This test is less powerful than the corresponding ANOVA performed on the original scores if the underlying populations have normal distributions. However, when the distributions are heavy tailed, the ANOVA on the ranks can be more powerful. This approach is recommended when samples come from populations that are heavy tailed and symmetric. If the distributions are skewed and the average correlation is not close to zero, the Friedman chi-square test, which involves ranking the scores separately for each subject, will tend to be more powerful.

A very different approach does not depend on the idea of the usual population model of inference, in which inferences are made about parent populations from which the available data have been randomly sampled. Rather, the way in which a sample of scores, however acquired, is distributed across two or more treatment conditions is considered by *permutation tests.* If the scores are distributed in ways that would be unusual had they simply been randomly assigned to conditions, a treatment effect is indicated.

REFERENCE

Vargha, A., & Delaney, H. D. (1998). The Kruskal–Wallis test and stochastic homogeneity. *Journal of Educational and Behavioral Statistics, 23,* 170–192.

SUGGESTED READING

Kepner, J. L., & Robinson, D. H. (1988). Nonparametric methods for detecting treatment effects in repeated-measures designs. *Journal of the American Statistical Association, 83,* 456–461.

Siegel, S., & Castellan, N. J. (1988). *Nonparametric statistics for the behavioral sciences.* New York: McGraw-Hill.

Zimmerman, D. W., & Zumbo, B. D. (1993). The relative power of parametric and nonparametric statistical methods. In G. Keren

& C. Lewis (Eds.), *A handbook for data analysis in the behavioral sciences: Methodological issues* (pp. 481–517). Hillsdale, NJ: Erlbaum.

Arnold D. Well
University of Massachusetts

NONVERBAL COMMUNICATION

Nonverbal communication is the nonlinguistic transmission of information through visual, auditory, tactile, and kinesthetic channels. Like other forms of communication, nonverbal communication involves encoding and decoding processes. Encoding is the act of generating the information and decoding is the act of interpreting the information. Nonverbal encoding processes include facial expressions, gestures, posture, tone of voice, tactile stimulation such as touch, and body movements like moving closer to or farther away from a person or object. Decoding processes involve the use of received sensations combined with previous experience in interpreting and understanding the information. Although nonverbal communication may refer to mass communication such as television, art products, and multimedia productions, in this discussion the emphasis is on interpersonal communication, whether face-to-face or by telephone.

Culture has a significant impact on nonverbal communication. For instance, the ways people use gestures are specific from culture to culture. People in the western world nod their heads to signal agreement, but people in South Asian countries often move their heads from side to side to convey a similar meaning. While westerners interpret the O sign using the finger and thumb as OK, the parking man in Indonesia would use the sign as an order to the driver to put the car's gear shift in a zero position. This misunderstanding will create a problem when the parking man has to push the car for a parking space. Most Asians use gestures like bowing to show their respect to other people. Many Asians are silent when they are disappointed and continue using their usual tone of voice and smiling face even though they are in that emotional state. Most Americans seem more comfortable than Asians in using nonverbal communication to encode their emotional states.

Scientists and practitioners have long been aware of the importance of the relationship between nonverbal communication and emotion. In 1872, Charles Darwin published *The Expression of the Emotions in Man and Animals.* In 1905, Sigmund Freud observed that even though someone does not say anything, parts of the body will move and convey to the observer that something is happening inside. By the 1970s and 1980s, researchers had started to develop refined procedures and technology for measuring the encoding and decoding processes of nonverbal communication. The methods vary from social to physiological and from descriptive to experimental studies. They have generated general laws and measures of individual differences in the transmission of cognitive and affective information.

Paul Ekman has studied extensively facial expression and emotion. He began studying this topic in 1965 by asking a single question: Are facial expression and emotion universal or culture specific? He could not find a simple answer, and that led him to more questions. With Friesen, Ekman originated the Facial Action Coding System (FACS) in 1978. FACS is a reliable rating technique using photographs or a video for encoding and decoding basic emotions such as anger, disgust, fear, happiness, sadness, and surprise. David Matsumoto has also developed an instrument to compare Japanese and American facial expressions.

Another nonverbal cue that helps individuals detect emotions experienced by another person is voice. Using vocal cues, sometimes called paralinguistics or prosody, in 1966 Norman Sundberg developed a Test of Implied Meanings (TIM) using judgments of the "real meanings" of sentences spoken by actors. This test showed differences favoring skilled therapists over others, as well as sex differences favoring females. The most developed and researched paralinguistic test is the Profile of Nonverbal Sensitivity (PONS), developed by Rosenthal, Hall, DiMatteo, and Archer in 1979. The PONS includes visual and auditory stimuli. One of its findings is that facial expression is superior in decoding accuracy as compared to other channels.

Intimacy can be detected from proxemics, or the use of space in gestures, postures, and touching. Patterson reported in 1990 that the more intimate a relationship between individuals, the more nonverbal communication is observed. Proxemics between the two are closer; they do more hugging and touching, although the amount and manner of physical contact is related to culture. In 1990, Hall and Veccia studied touching between the sexes. They found that both men and women touched each other on purpose with the same frequency. The difference was that males tended to put their arms on the females' shoulders, but females put their arms on the males' arms (perhaps related to differences in height).

The expression and perception of mental states is a complex phenomenon that constantly presents challenges in interpersonal communication. How sincere and truthful is a person? How intensely does a companion feel? Is facial expression of emotion universal or culture specific? How do people use gestures, tone of voice, and other nonverbal cues to perceive emotional states in others? Will touch affect others in a positive or negative way? If it is positive, is touch useful for the healing process? Is a measure of nonverbal behavior as an indicator of hospital patients' mental state useful to improve health providers' services? Will increasing contact in a global society require and lead to greater ability to encode and decode mental states in others? How important is nonverbal communication in the negotiation process among politicians and decision makers, and can a better understanding of the mental states of others enhance peace in the global world? These are only a few of many important questions for future research. The advancement of theory and research in nonverbal communication is crucial for improving the understanding of basic processes in human interaction.

Johana E. P. Hadiyono
Gadjah Mada University,
Yogyakarta, Indonesia

NOREPINEPHRINE

Norepinephrine is the main neurotransmitter released from noradrenergic (sympathetic) nerve terminals. The noradrenergic neurons occur in both the central and the peripheral autonomic nervous systems. Central noradrenergic fibers arise in neurons located in the brain stem, mainly in the ventrolateral and the dorsomedial medulla oblongata, the locus ceruleus, and the subceruleus area. In the peripheral autonomic nervous system, noradrenergic neurons are located in the para- and prevertebral sympathetic ganglia from which postganglionic fibers originate and supply various organs and blood vessels.

Chemically, norepinephrine is a catecholamine; "catechol" refers to compounds containing an aromatic benzene ring with two adjacent hydroxyl groups (Kopin, 1985; Pacak, Palkovits, Kopin, & Goldstein, 1995). Catechol itself (1,2 dihydroxybenzene) does not occur as an endogenous compound in animals. Endogenous catechols include the catecholamine precursor, dihydroxyphenylalanine, its amine products (dopamine, norepinephrine, and epinephrine), and their deaminated metabolites.

The first and rate-limiting enzymatic step in norepinephrine biosynthesis is hydroxylation of tyrosine to form dihydroxyphenylalanine (Figure 1). This reaction is catalyzed by tyrosine hydroxylase and requires tetrahydrobiopterin as a cofactor. Free dopamine and norepinephrine in the cytoplasm of dopaminergic and noradrenergic neurons inhibit tyrosine hydroxylase and thereby regulate their own synthesis. Hydroxylation of tyrosine is followed by decarboxylation of dihydroxyphenylalanine by L-aromatic amino acid decarboxylase, and this reaction occurs in the cytoplasm of neuronal and nonneuronal cells to yield dopamine (Kagedal & Goldstein, 1988; Kopin, 1985; Pacak et al., 1995).

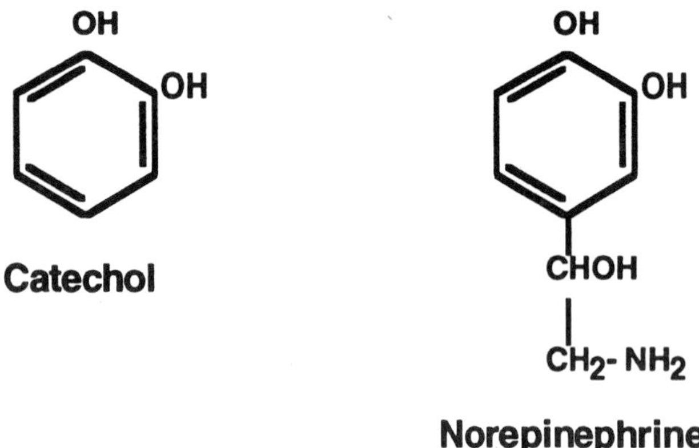

Figure 1. Chemical structure of catechol and norepinephrine.

Dopamine is transported via a nonspecific amine transporter into vesicles found in noradrenergic terminals. In the vesicles hydroxylation of dopamine occurs by dopamine-β-hydroxylase to yield norepinephrine (Kagedal & Goldstein, 1988). In the brain and some peripheral tissues, especially adrenal medulla, norepinephrine is converted to epinephrine by phenylethanolamine-N-methyltransferase.

Upon nerve stimulation, a soluble vesicular content including norepinephrine and other cotransmitters such as chromogranins, neuropeptide Y, dopamine-b-hydroxylase, adenosine triphosphate, and enkephalins are released during noradrenergic nerve terminal depolarization. Sodium and calcium entering nerve terminals during depolarization are thought to evoke exocytosis. In contrast, chloride ions may exert an inhibitory presynaptic effect.

Table 1. Effects of Some Drugs on Noradrenergic Neurotransmission

Drug	Inhibitory effect	Stimulatory effect
Acetylcholine (nicotine receptor)	—	NE release
Acetylcholine	NE release	—
ACTH	—	NE release
Adenosine	NE release	—
Angiotensin II	—	NE release
Clorgyline	Monoamine oxidase-A	—
Cocaine	Uptake–1	—
Desimipramine	Uptake–1	—
Epinephrine (presynaptic β_2-adrenoreceptors)	—	NE release
GABA ($GABA_A$ receptor)	—	NE release
GABA	NE release	—
Glucocorticoids	Uptake–2	—
Lithium	Uptake–1	—
Opioids	NE release	—
Ouabain	Uptake–1	Na^+-mediated efflux
Pargyline	Monoamine oxidase-B	—
Phenoxybenzamine	Uptake–1	—
Prostaglandins E	NE release	—
Reserpine	Vesicular uptake	—
Tricyclic anti-depressants	Uptake–1	—
Tyramine	—	Vesicular release
α-Methyldopa	Dopa decarboxylase	—

Notes: ACTH: adrenocorticotropin; NE: norepinephrine; GABA: gamma-amino butyric acid.

The metabolic disposition of norepinephrine differs in neurons and in nonneuronal cells (Figure 2). Neurons contain monoamine oxidase (a mitochondrial enzyme) but little if any catechol-O-methyl transferase. Axoplasmic norepinephrine is metabolized mainly by deamination in neurons, whereas nonneuronal cells contain catechol-O-methyl transferase as well as monoamine oxidase (Kopin, 1985). The product of norepinephrine deamination, 3,4 dihydroxyphenylglycolaldehyde, is reduced to form 3,4 dihydroxyphenylglycol. Most (60%–80%) of the dihydroxyphenylglycol formed in sympathetic nerve terminals is derived from vesicular norepinephrine. In subjects at rest, plasma dihydroxyphenylglycol levels are determined mainly by vesicular turnover, rather than by reuptake of released norepinephrine. Dihydroxyphenylglycol diffuses freely and rapidly across cell membranes and reaches extraneuronal cells, extracellular fluid, and plasma.

Norepinephrine released from peripheral nerve terminals is removed extensively by reuptake (90%, Uptake-1) and to a lesser degree by extraneuronal uptake (Uptake-2; Kopin, 1985; Pacak et al., 1995). In the brain, the relative roles of these modes of inactivation are poorly understood. Norepinephrine that enters the neurons is largely taken up into vesicles (Table 1). A portion of this norepinephrine (the exact amount of the portion is unknown in brain noradrenergic terminals) is thought to leak out of the vesicles and undergo metabolism in the axoplasm.

Norepinephrine and dihydroxyphenylglycol that enter extraneuronal cells, which, as indicated above, contain catechol-O-methyltransferase as well as monoamine oxidase, are O-methylated to form normetanephrine and further metabolized to methoxyhydroxyphenylglycol. Methoxyhydroxyphenylglycol is also formed from dihydroxyphenylglycol. Plasma normetanephrine accounts for a relatively small proportion (less than 10%) of the total norepinephrine metabolized in the body and is derived mainly from norepinephrine metabolized before entry into plasma and the remainder (45%) from norepinephrine after it enters plasma (Eisenhofer et al., 1995). The extent of nonneuronal metabolism of norepinephrine in the brain is poorly understood. Metoxyhydroxyphenylglycol in plasma is derived mainly either from dihydroxyphenylglycol formed in tissues or from normetanephrine formed in extraneuronal tissues before its entry into plasma. Thus, simultaneous measurements of norepinephrine and its metabolites provide a comprehensive picture of norepinephrine synthesis, turnover, and metabolism in brain and peripheral tissues.

In contrast to sympathetic nerve terminals where norepinephrine is released into the synaptic cleft and acts locally (only a small portion of norepinephrine can reach the

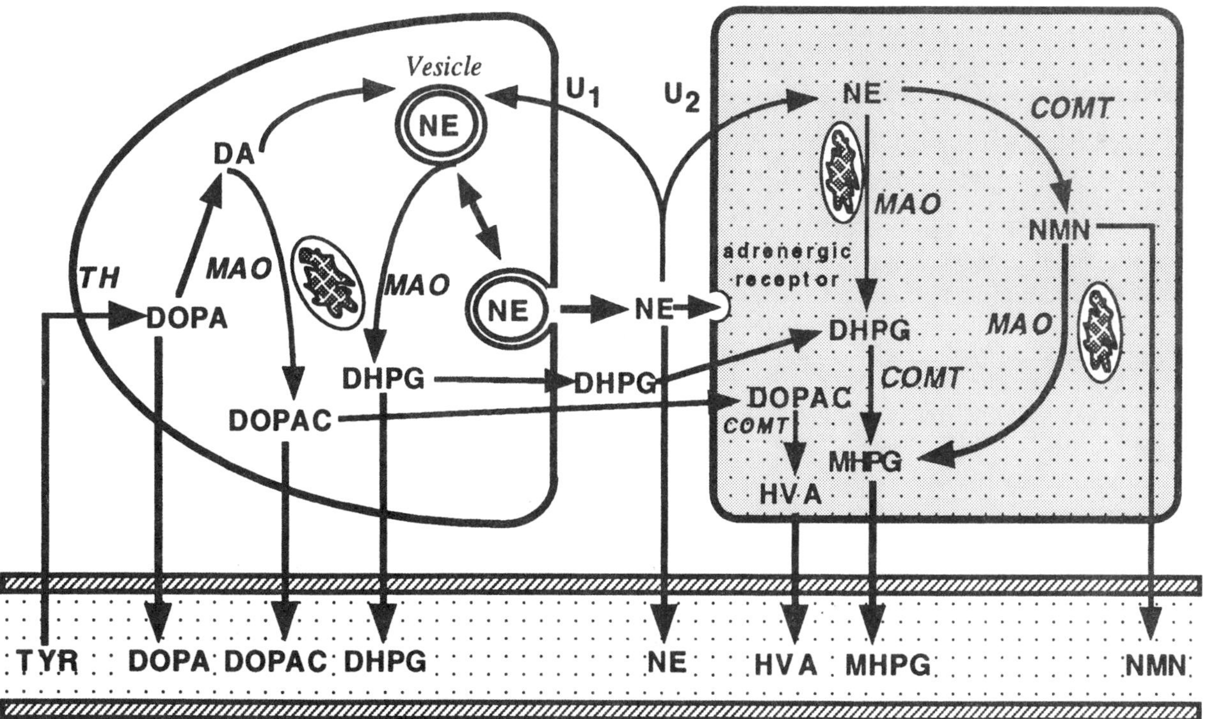

Figure 2. Diagram showing the synthesis, release, uptake, and metabolism of norepinephrine (NE).
Abbreviations: COMT: catechol-*O*-methyltransferase; DA: dopamine; DHPG: dihydroxyphenylglycol; DOPA: dihydroxyphenylalanine; DOPAC: dihydroxyphenylacetic acid; HVA: homovanillic acid; MAO: monoamine hydroxylase; NMN: normetanephrine; TH: tyrosine hybroxylase.

bloodstream) via alpha and beta adrenergic receptors, epinephrine and norepinephrine (approximately 20% of the total body amount) released from the adrenal medulla are secreted directly into the adrenal vein and in a very short time reach all sites in the body except for most brain regions (catecholamines do not cross the blood-brain barrier).

Norepinephrine released from noradrenergic terminals exerts its effect via adrenoceptors (e.g., α_1: blood vessel constriction, uterus, sphincters of gastrointestinal tract and urinary bladder contractions; α_2: feedback inhibition of norepinephrine release; β_1: heart rate increase; β_2: relaxation of blood vessels, bronchi, sphincters of gastrointestinal tract and urinary bladder dilation).

Distinct patterns of sympathoneuronal activation during exposure to different situations have been demonstrated. Orthostasis, hyperthermia, and cold exposure evoke selective norepinephrine release, whereas hypoglycemia evokes large epinephrine responses.

The availability of simultaneous measurements of norepinephrine and its metabolites introduced a novel application of clinical catecholamine neurochemistry: the delineation of neurochemical patterns associated with specific genetic abnormalities (Goldstein et al., 1996). Such abnormalities are seen in phenylketonuria (abnormal phenylalanine and tyrosine hydroxylation), Menkes disease and some forms of orthostatic hypotension (dopamine-β-hydroxylase deficiency or decreased activity), Norrie's disease and aggressive behavior (monoamine oxidase deficiency), and velocardio-facil syndrome and DiGeorge syndrome (decreased catechol-O-methyl transferase activity).

REFERENCES

Eisenhofer, G., Rundquist, B., Aneman, A., Friberg, P., Dakak, N., Kopin, I. J., Jacobs, M.-C., & Lenders, J. W. M. (1995). Regional release and removal of catecholamines and extraneuronal metabolism to metanephrines. *Journal of Clinical Endocrinology and Metabolism, 80,* 3009–3017.

Goldstein, D. S., Lenders, J. W. M., Kaler, S. G., & Eisenhofer, G. (1996). Catecholamine phenotyping: Clues to the diagnosis, treatment, and pathophysiology of neurogenetic disorders. *Journal of Neurochemistry, 67,* 1781–1790.

Kagedal, B., & Goldstein, D. S. (1988). Catecholamines and their metabolites. *Journal of Chromatography, 429,* 177–233.

Kopin, I. J. (1985). Catecholamine metabolism: Basic aspects and clinical significance. *Pharmacology Review, 37,* 333–364.

Pacak, K., Palkovits, M., Kopin, I. J., & Goldstein, D. S. (1995). Stress-induced norepinephrine release in the hypothalamic paraventricular nucleus and pituitary-adrenocortical and sympathoadrenal activity: In vivo microdialysis studies. *Frontiers in Neuroendocrinology, 16,* 89–150.

Karel Pacak
National Institutes of Health

R. McCarty
American Psychological Association

See also: **Neurotransmitters**

NYMPHOMANIA

Broadly speaking, nymphomania refers to the condition of a woman whose sexual desire and/or behavior is referred to by terms like "insatiable," "abnormally intense," "unquenchable," "unrestrained," or "uncontrollable." In practice, the term is poorly defined and often loosely applied. It is usually distinguished from *sexual promiscuity,* but many proposed definitions use the two expressions interchangeably.

A woman who has many sexual encounters, whose lovers are culturally considered to be inappropriate, who is anorgasmic despite frequent sexual contacts, and whose sexual behaviors rarely take place within the context of an intense emotional relationship fits the classical and folkloric stereotype. Furthermore, Levitt points out that the various conceptions of nymphomania neglect the potentially important factor of opportunity as reflected in physical attractiveness, place of residence, type of occupation, and marital status.

Albert Ellis and Edward Sagarin distinguish between *controlled promiscuity* and *endogenous nymphomania.* The former refers to the not-too-unusual, multipartnered existence of a woman who is completely functional, while the latter is "seldom found outside the disturbed wards of mental hospitals." Ellis adds that he has not encountered a single endogenous nymphomaniac in his extensive clinical practice.

E. E. Levitt

See also: **Sexual Deviations**

O

OBSERVATIONAL METHODS

Observations, whether formal or informal, consist of taking note of events or occurrences and making a record of what is observed. Observation is basic to all science, and special methods have been devised to make observations of behavior objective and reliable.

In *controlled observation,* a situation is prearranged or contrived to study the responses of people or animals to certain stimulus conditions. Because controlled observation involves special procedures, *uncontrolled observation,* in which the observer exerts no control over the situation and merely takes note of behavior in situ, is more common.

Much of what is known about the dynamics of personality and mental disorder is the result of observations made by people in clinical settings. The *clinical method* is not completely objective; not only does the therapist–observer affect the patient's behavior, but the patient also affects the reactions of the therapist.

In scientific research it is usually considered advisable for the observers to remain as unobtrusive as possible, not interacting in any way with those being observed. However, if the researcher elects to become a part of the observational situation and be a *participant observer,* the effects of the observer's presence on the behavior of the performers need to be considered in interpreting the research findings.

An important first step in improving the accuracy of observations is to train the observers. Observers must be made aware of the effects of their own biases, conduct, and condition on what is being observed, and of the tendency to confuse fact with interpretation. Furthermore, the influence of the situational context in which observations are made should be taken into account in interpreting the findings.

Obtaining meaningful results from an observational study also demands that the sample of observed behavior be representative, which is usually time-consuming and expensive. To reduce the time, expense, and volume of data obtained from continuous observations of behavior, special data-sampling procedures are employed. In *incident sampling,* only specified behavioral incidents are noted and recorded. A second procedure, *time sampling,* involves making a series of observations, each lasting only a few minutes, over a period of a day or so. Finally, the use of an *observational schedule,* such as a rating scale or checklist filled out during or shortly after the behavioral occurrence, can improve the reliability of observations.

Observations are also made in developmental research, surveys, correlational studies, and even experiments. For example, periodic observations of the development of the same age group of individuals over a period of months or years (*longitudinal investigation*), or of different age groups of people at a specific point in time (*cross-sectional investigation*), are common in developmental research. Content analysis of self-observations recorded in diaries, autobiographies, letters, and other personal documents also provide insight into personality dynamics.

Lewis R. Aiken

See also: **Psychological Assessment**

OBSESSIONS

Obsessions are described in the fourth edition of the *Diagnostic and Statistical Manual of Mental Disorders* (American Psychiatric Association, 1994) as recurrent intrusive thoughts, impulses, or images that produce anxiety or discomfort. Individuals with Obsessive-Compulsive Disorder (OCD) usually try to suppress or neutralize obsessions with other thoughts or actions. Typical themes for obsessions are harming, sexuality, contamination, concerns with disease, religion, superstition, or otherwise neutral thoughts ("What if I cannot stop thinking about my breathing?"). Normally the individuals with OCD know that the obsessions originate in their own mind and are not coming from the outside.

Although pure obsessions (i.e., obsessions without overt compulsions) have traditionally been assumed to be infrequent, treatment centers worldwide have reported between 1.5% and 44% of OCD patients who report no overt compulsions (median = 20%; for a review see Freeston & Ladouceur, 1997). Moreover, epidemiologic studies have found that in the community, the percentage of individuals with OCD suffering from pure obsessions may be as high as 60%.

Several theories have attempted to explain the development of obsessional problems and related compulsions. For example, Mowrer (1960) described a two-stage theory, stating that a fear of specific stimuli is first learned through classical conditioning (stage 1, e.g., the patient feels anxious after thinking a blasphemous thought) and then maintained by operant conditioning (stage 2) as the individual learns to engage in ritualistic behavior to decrease anxiety (e.g., the patient prays compulsively). Thus, rituals are preserved by reinforcing properties of anxiety reduction. Because reinforced behaviors will occur more often in the future, the frequency of rituals increases. Rituals or avoidance behavior maintain the fear response because the sufferer does not stay in contact with the stimulus long enough for the anxiety to extinguish.

More recent theories for the development of obsessional problems have suggested information processing biases and deficits with respect to decision making, failures of inhibition, and memory (for a detailed review see Steketee, Frost, Rheaume, & Wilhelm, 1998). For example, Enright and Beech (1993) showed that OCD patients had difficulty inhibiting the processing of irrelevant, emotionally neutral material. This difficulty may account for the frequency of intrusive thoughts in OCD. The evidence for memory deficits underlying obsessional problems is inconclusive: several studies failed to find deficits but did find a lack of confidence in the sufferers' recall of their own actions (e.g., McNally & Kohlbeck, 1993).

Current cognitive models of OCD characterize intrusive thoughts as normal events that most people experience, indistinguishable from obsessional thoughts with respect to their content. Rachman and DeSilva (1978) found that those intrusive thoughts were reported by almost 90% of a nonclinical sample. Intrusive thoughts develop into obsessions not because of their content but because of the meaning individuals attribute to them. Nonobsessional individuals disregard intrusions and do not evaluate them as important, whereas people with OCD attend to them believing that they are meaningful. The appraisal of the intrusion may depend on underlying beliefs or assumptions acquired in a religious, cultural, or family context. People who appraise the intrusions in a maladaptive way experience negative emotions (e.g., guilt, anxiety) and fear negative consequences. Thus, in seeking ways to reduce discomfort they often engage in neutralizing strategies such as overt compulsions, mental rituals, avoidance behaviors, and attempts to suppress thoughts. However, a series of thought suppression experiments suggested that efforts to suppress specific thoughts resulted in an increase rather than a decrease of those thoughts (Wegner, 1989).

Faulty interpretations of intrusive thoughts have been categorized in several domains (Obsessive Compulsive Cognitions Working Group, 1997) and include overimportance of thoughts, the need to control thoughts, overestimation of threat, intolerance of uncertainty, perfectionism, and excessive responsibility.

Many OCD sufferers attach too much importance to the content and presence of their thoughts, and erroneously believe that other people do not have intrusive thoughts. They may believe that simply because a thought occurs, it is meaningful or indicates that they will act on it. Extreme beliefs about the importance and meaning of thoughts can lead to beliefs about having to exert control over them. For example, if an individual interprets an intrusive thought as indicating "I am evil," it is likely that this interpretation is followed by emotional discomfort and by attempts to remove the intrusion. Like other anxiety disorder sufferers, OCD patients often overestimate both the probability and the severity of negative outcomes; therefore, they may interpret situations as dangerous until proven safe, whereas most people consider a situation safe unless there is an indication of threat. The need for certainty in OCD patients or intolerance of uncertainty is another frequently noted feature of OCD. The tendency of OCD patients to overestimate danger may be related to their difficulties with ambiguous situations and with making decisions. Theories of OCD have linked intolerance of ambiguous situations to perfectionism. For example, OCD patients may feel uncertain about the efficacy of their efforts to minimize harm when a perfect solution cannot be determined. The domain of excessive responsibility has received the most attention in recent studies and refers to the assumption that one has the pivotal power to generate or avert unwanted outcomes (e.g., Salkovskis, 1985). Excessive responsibility can induce guilt which is then reduced by compulsions. Recent studies have tested cognitive treatments that address those cognitive domains (see Steketee et al., 1998).

In summary, several theories have been introduced for the development of obsessional problems. Behavioral, biological, and other theories examining the cognitive aspects of the development of obsessional problems have been proposed. Current cognitive research suggests that obsessional problems are the result of maladaptive interpretations of intrusive thoughts. A better understanding of obsessional problems may result from an integration of these different areas of research.

REFERENCES

American Psychiatric Association. (1994). *Diagnostic and statistical manual of mental disorders* (4th ed.). Washington, DC: Author.

Enright, S. J., & Beech, A. R. (1993). Reduced cognitive inhibition in Obsessive-Compulsive Disorder. *British Journal of Clinical Psychology, 32,* 67–74.

Freeston, M. H., & Ladouceur, R. (1997). *The cognitive behavioral treatment of obsessions: A treatment manual.* Unpublished manuscript.

McNally, R. J., & Kohlbeck, P. A. (1993). Reality monitoring in Obsessive-Compulsive Disorder. *Behaviour Research and Therapy, 31,* 249–253.

Mowrer, O. H. (1960). *Learning theory and behavior.* New York: Wiley.

Obsessive Compulsive Cognitions Working Group. (1997). Cognitive assessment of Obsessive-Compulsive Disorder. *Behaviour Research and Therapy, 35,* 667–681.

Rachman, S., & DeSilva, P. (1978). Abnormal and normal obsessions. *Behaviour Research and Therapy, 16,* 233–248.

Salkovskis, P. M. (1985). Obsessional-compulsive problems: A cognitive-behavioral analysis. *Behaviour Research and Therapy, 23,* 571–584.

Steketee, G., Frost, R. O., Rheaume, J., & Wilhelm, S. (1998). Cognitive theory and treatment of Obsessive-Compulsive Disorder. In M. A. Jenike, L. Baer, & W. E. Minichiello (Eds.), *Obsessive-Compulsive Disorder: Theory and management* (3rd ed., pp. 368–399). Chicago: Mosby.

Wegner, D. M. (1989). *White bears and other unwanted thoughts.* New York: Viking.

Sabine Wilhelm
Massachusetts General Hospital
Harvard Medical School

See also: **Anxiety**

OBSESSIVE-COMPULSIVE DISORDER

Definition

Obsessive-Compulsive Disorder (OCD) is an anxiety disorder that involves two primary symptoms: obsessions and compulsions. *Obsessions* are thoughts, ideas, images, or doubts that are experienced as senseless, unwanted, and distressing. Although the person recognizes the thoughts as irrational, they often evoke anxiety about dreaded consequences. Common themes of obsessions include contamination; terrible mistakes; violent, sexual, or blasphemous thoughts; or thoughts about things not being "just right." *Compulsions* are urges to perform purposeful behavioral or mental rituals that serve to neutralize the anxiety and doubt evoked by obsessional thoughts. Examples include handwashing, checking, asking for reassurance, ordering/arranging, repeating routine activities, counting, and mentally praying or thinking a "good" thought.

Obsessions and compulsions are phenomenologically related. For example, a person with obsessional thoughts concerning contamination from "floor germs" may spend hours washing their hands or other objects thought to be contaminated. Someone with unwanted blasphemous thoughts might repeat prayers until the thought has disappeared. Similarly, a person with fears of causing a house fire may check that appliances are unplugged. Compulsive rituals sometimes take the form of mental acts such as repeating phrases to neutralize "bad" thoughts, attempting to suppress a thought, or mentally reviewing to gain reassurance that a mistake was not made.

Prevalence and Course

The prevalence of OCD is about 2 to 3% in the adult population and 1 to 2% in children. Although it may begin as early as the preschool years, the average age of onset is in the late teens to early twenties. Males tend to develop OCD at a younger age than females. Although the severity of obsessions and compulsions may wax and wane depending on the amount of general life stress, OCD is a persistent condition with a low rate of spontaneous remission. Without effective treatment, a chronic and deteriorating course can be expected.

Etiological Theories

The causes of OCD are largely unknown, yet its development most likely involves a biological vulnerability to anxiety in combination with psychosocial factors. There is no evidence to support psychoanalytic theories of OCD which propose that the interplay of unresolved childhood conflicts contribute to the development of obsessions and compulsions. The current leading theories of OCD include biological, behavioral, and cognitive behavioral explanations.

Biological

Biological models of OCD propose that the underlying pathophysiology of this disorder is abnormal serotonin functioning. In particular, individuals with OCD are thought to have a hypersensitivity in postsynaptic serotonin receptors. Indeed, studies have found evidence for elevated serotonin levels among OCD patients. Moreover, serotonin reuptake inhibitor (SRI) medication is more effective than other forms of pharmacotherapy in the treatment of OCD. It is important to note, however, that whereas some study results support the *serotonin hypothesis* of OCD, others do not support this model. Moreover, a specific mechanism by which serotonin function may be related to OCD symptoms has not been proposed.

Behavioral

Classical behavioral theories posit a two-stage process by which OCD develops and is maintained. In the first stage (fear acquisition), a natural event becomes associated with fear by being immediately paired with an aversive stimulus that evokes anxiety. For example, a knife may acquire the ability to elicit anxiety by being paired with a traumatic experience. In the second stage (maintenance), avoidance and compulsive rituals are negatively reinforced because they result in a reduction in anxiety. For example, if checking that the drawers are locked relieves distress evoked by thoughts of knives, this kind of checking is likely to be repeated whenever thoughts of knives occur. Although there is evidence that obsessional thoughts increase anxiety, and compulsive rituals reduce it, the classical behavioral model of OCD does not adequately explain the development of OCD symptoms.

Cognitive–Behavioral

The inadequacy of classical behavioral theories of OCD led to the development of cognitive–behavioral theories that consider how patients interpret normally occurring intrusive thoughts. This model recognizes that most people have senseless thoughts now and then (e.g., *what if I stabbed someone I care about?*). However, OCD develops if one habitually appraises such thoughts in biased ways that lead to feeling overly responsible and threatened (e.g., *I'm an immoral person for thinking this,* or *my thoughts are equivalent to actions*). The result is preoccupation with the thought (obsessions) and increasingly anxious mood.

The fear and exaggerated sense of responsibility evoked by obsessional thoughts motivates the person with OCD to engage in compulsive rituals to reduce the probability of feared catastrophes. Rituals and avoidance are, however, excessive responses to stimuli and thoughts that are not actually threatening. According to this theory, such responses maintain obsessional anxiety because they (1) result in a short-term reduction in obsessional anxiety, and (2) prevent the person from realizing that their fears were unrealistic in the first place.

Treatment

Two treatments are effective for OCD: SRI pharmacotherapy and cognitive-behavioral therapy (CBT).

Pharmacotherapy

SRIs (clomipramine, fluoxetine, sertraline, paroxetine, fluvoxamine, and citalopram) are the most effective pharmacological treatment for OCD. These medications block the reuptake of serotonin, which is suspected to be related to OCD symptoms. On average, rates of improvement with adequate trials of SRIs (at least 12 weeks) range from 20% to 40%. However, response varies widely from patient to patient and side effects such as nausea, sleep disturbances, or decreased sex drive are common. Importantly, once pharmacotherapy is stopped OCD symptoms return in 85% of patients.

Cognitive–Behavioral Therapy

CBT is based on the behavioral and cognitive-behavioral models of OCD and is the most effective short- and long-term treatment for this disorder. Patients treated with CBT often achieve up to 65% reduction in their OCD symptoms. The two main CBT procedures are (1) exposure with response prevention (EX/RP) and (2) cognitive therapy. Exposure involves prolonged and repeated confrontation with situations that evoke obsessional fears, while response prevention entails refraining from carrying out compulsive rituals. EX/RP is thought to work by demonstrating that obsessional fears are unrealistic and that rituals are unnecessary to prevent feared catastrophes. Cognitive therapy involves using rational discourse to help patients recognize and correct faulty appraisals of intrusive thoughts. It is often used in conjunction with EX/RP.

Jonathan S. Abramowitz
Kristi R. Luenzmann
Mayo Clinic

See also: **Anxiety Disorders: Serotinin**

OCCUPATIONAL INTERESTS

Because of the extensive concern of career development and career counselors with systematic measurement of career interests and adjustment, a general assessment of interests has become of major importance in the field. Among the issues involved have been the adequacy of psychometric approaches to measuring career interests; problems associated with sexism and/or racism in measuring career interests, particularly as these affect the language of the instruments; assumptions underlying the development of the interests; and the norms upon which the scores are based.

Interests are usually operationally defined by the instrument used to measure them, such as the Strong–Campbell Interest Inventory or the Kuder Occupational Interest Survey. Four generic types of interests are usually assumed to exist. *Manifest interests* are represented by the activities in which an individual actually engages; *expressed interests* are those identified by an individual when asked about his or her interests; *inventoried interests* are those measured by various instruments, such as the Strong–Campbell or the Kuder survey; and *tested interests* are inferred on the basis of the knowledge possessed by an individual about various fields of endeavor, on the assumption that the knowledge reflects involvement in pertinent activities.

It is generally agreed that among adolescents occupational interests as measured by inventories predict about as well as do expressed interests, and that adolescents' interests change over time. One reason interests do not predict occupational entry and satisfaction in adolescents well is that such variables as aptitudes, performance, and opportunity intervene significantly to determine occupational entry and achievement.

Most interest inventories are based on the general assumption that individuals who enter and find the same occupation satisfying share numerous characteristics, so the interest inventories strive to measure relevant personal characteristics. Currently, little is known about how interests actually develop, though various theoretical explanations stemming from social learning theory, psychoanalytic theory, and personality theory have been proposed to guide thought and research exploring interest development.

Psychometric Adequacy

Most measures of career interest have followed highly successful examples used by the two leaders in the field—the Strong–Campbell Interest Inventory and the Kuder Occupational Interest Survey. Over the years, these two instruments have increasingly been adapted to incorporate those characteristics of the other instruments that they previously lacked. The Strong–Campbell Interest Inventory in its original version primarily measured individuals' preferences for activities, occupations, and so on, and compared these to the preferences of satisfied employed members of particular occupations. The rationale was entirely empirical and no attempt was made in the development of this instrument to establish any other rationale underlying the score. On the other hand, the original Kuder measures were designed to assess different orientations toward the world that could be translated into interests. Individuals were assumed to possess inclinations toward certain kinds of activities, and these inclinations were assumed to be more related to certain occupations and less related to others. Over the years, many counselors used both instruments together because one provided information about the person and the other provided information about the world of work as it related to the person; as a result, the two instruments complemented each other.

Recognizing that each instrument had its limitations, their developers modified them over the years. The Kuder now includes empirically derived scores as well as the more theoretically derived ones, and the Strong–Campbell also now includes theoretically derived scores based on the Holland type of theory (Holland, 1966) as well as the traditional empirical scales. Potential users may have their own preferences for the psychometric underpinnings of one or the other instrument, but theoretically they measure the same sets of attributes.

These two instruments have dominated the field of interest measurement for more than half a century; other instruments have been developed and can be evaluated through the use of Buros's *Mental Measurements Yearbook,* but none have anywhere near the influence on measuring career interests that these two have had.

Other measures, such as the *Self-Directed Search* (SDS) of J. L. Holland (1979), have also been used widely. The SDS assesses interests differently from the Strong–Campbell or the Kuder Occupational Scales, and theoretical components of the SDS have been incorporated into the Strong–Campbell Interest Inventory. The SDS requires individuals to describe their career-related interests, activities, and competencies in terms of environments to which they might appropriately aspire. The SDS is probably the third most widely used device for measuring occupational interests.

Sexism and Racism in Measurement

All of these instruments have met with difficulties over the years as concerns about racial and sexual biases have heightened among test users. Most obvious in the earlier versions were sex bias leading to assumptions that particular occupations were deemed to be "male" as opposed to "female," which affected the construction of the questions, the norms for the instruments, and the language used to describe interests. Beginning in the 1960s, test users expressed concern that females who showed interest in traditionally male occupations would be inappropriately assessed using traditional instruments, as would males who expressed interest in traditionally female occupations. Since that time, most of the instruments have undergone a number of revisions and their language and normative approaches have been adapted to accommodate these critiques. The Kuder and Strong–Campbell measures now have same-sex and separate-sex normative approaches and sexism has been deleted from the language of the measures. Sexism is not a problem with the SDS, but there is a single set of norms, and, there are some systematic differences in the probability with which females versus males will score on different types that might not be related to eventual occupational membership and satisfaction.

Racism is more subtle and has been addressed less directly because the items are not necessarily racist themselves. However, the normative base, the language patterns, and the experience base is likely to be substantially different for various ethnic and racial groups. These factors may subtly affect the responses of individuals being assessed and their scores, resulting in potentially inappropriate inferences and interpretations of the results.

Samuel H. Osipow
Ohio State University, Columbus

See also: **Psychometrics; Strong Interest Inventory; Test Standardization**

OCCUPATIONAL STRESS

Occupational stress arises from an interaction between people and their jobs and is characterized by changes within people that force them to deviate from their normal functioning. Most theories of occupational stress postulate that stress occurs when environmental stimuli, or workers' appraisals of those stimuli, contribute to changes in workers' well-being or normal behavior.

It is important to note that occupational stress is a related, though distinct, concept from job dissatisfaction. Stress and dissatisfaction can have distinct correlates, and the presence of either stress or dissatisfaction does not necessitate the existence of the other. Therefore, a worker who is not satisfied is not necessarily experiencing occupational stress or the manifestations of that stress.

Personal consequences of occupational stress (i.e., strains) include psychological, physiological, and behavioral responses. Anxiety, depression, boredom, somatic complaints, psychological fatigue, frustration, feelings of futility, emotional exhaustion, and anger represent deleterious psychological outcomes. Physiological outcomes to occupational stress include cardiovascular disease, gastrointestinal disorders, respiratory problems, headaches, bodily injuries, fatigue, and death. Examples of behavioral responses include poor job performance, job-related accidents, absenteeism, disruptive or counterproductive job behaviors such as stealing or spreading rumors, acts of aggression, smoking, turnover, and drug abuse. Organizational consequences of occupational stress include costs associated with absenteeism, tardiness, turnover, poor performance, litigation and settlements, and retirement and health care benefits. Importantly, the data regarding any particular reaction are generally sparse. It is safest to conclude, therefore, that occupational stress can adversely affect an individual's well-being; precisely how these negative outcomes may be manifested remains an open question.

Three general classes of stress-inducing stimuli (i.e., stressors) include organizational characteristics and processes, working conditions and interpersonal relationships, and job demands and role characteristics. Organizational characteristics and processes that lead to an unsupportive organizational climate, inadequate or complicated technological resources, a poor or inequitable pay structure, frequent relocations, poor communications, discriminatory or unfair treatment, ambiguous or conflicting task assignments, shift work, and inadequate feedback can yield occupational stress.

Stressors related to working conditions include crowding, a lack of privacy, noise, excessive temperatures, inadequate or flickering lights, and exposure to hazardous materials. However, the relationship between certain conditions, such as amount of privacy and noise, and resultant strains appears to be more complex, with findings supportive of a curvilinear relationship between the degree of the stressor and well-being. Interpersonal relationships at work characterized by a lack of recognition, acceptance, supportiveness, and trust, as well as those characterized by high levels of competition, mistreatment, harassment, discrimination, and conflict are regarded as stressful.

In terms of job demands, potential stressors include repetitive work, high levels of demand, unpredictability, low levels of control and autonomy, time pressures and deadlines, responsibility for others such as employees or clients, and a discrepancy between skill level and skill utilization. Finally, research on the roles people perform at work suggests that role conflict, role ambiguity, role under- or overload, role-status incongruency, and work-family conflict function as occupational stressors.

It is essential to note that these three classes of occupational stressors are not independent of one another; the existence of one type of stressor influences the likelihood that other types of stressors will be present. For example, characteristics of a particular occupation or organization will impact working conditions and job demands. Therefore, identifying and studying one stressor in isolation, without considering the context in which the stressor occurs, can lead to misleading conclusions.

In addition to the stress associated with work, the absence of work also can be stressful. Although the loss of work is potentially stressful for several reasons, most evidence indicates that the financial repercussions of unemployment are especially devastating to individuals.

Despite researchers' efforts to identify various stressors and strains, several factors contribute to the difficulty in understanding and predicting individuals' reactions to a particular stressor. First, individuals may differ both in their likelihood of encountering certain stressful situations and in their reactions to the same objective stimuli. Therefore, consideration of various characteristics of the individual as well as those in the objective environment is necessary. In particular, the personality trait of neuroticism (or negative affectivity) influences workers' reports of occupational stressors and strains. Although researchers continue to debate the precise mechanisms underlying the role of such individual differences, findings indicate that these traits impact individuals' susceptibility to, perceptions and appraisals of, reactions to, and ability to cope with objective stimuli.

The second difficulty in understanding and predicting occupational stress is appreciating the reciprocal relationship between work and other facets of workers' lives. Examining how work and nonwork-related stressors, strains, and coping mechanisms impact each other is essential in understanding the complexities of occupational stress.

Third, in recent years, researchers have begun to reveal the intricacy of stressor–strain relationships by demonstrating the inadequacy of treating either all stressors or all strains as equivalent or identical to one another. Current research focuses on psychological processes instead of simply the identification of various stressors and strains.

Three general types of organizational interventions exist to reduce occupational stress or mitigate the harmful effects of occupational stress. Efforts to restructure the workplace, redesign the nature of the work, encourage participative management, modify organizational policies and climate, practice team-building, and promote acceptance of diversity are examples of preventive interventions that take place at the organizational level. Preventive strategies that occur at the individual level include helping workers to manage perceptions of stress and perceptions of the work environment; engage in relaxation training; practice effective coping strategies; and participate in healthy physical, spiritual, or emotional outlets. The third and most common type of intervention involves the treatment of employees after they have experienced occupational stress. Examples of these strategies include Employee Assistance Programs, medical treatment, and substance abuse counseling.

Seth A. Kaplan
A. P. Brief
Tulane University

See also: **Employee Assistance Programs**

OLFACTORY CORTEX

One of the most evocative of senses, olfaction produces powerful responses in humans and is used as a primitive but potent form of communication among animals. It is important to sexual attraction and may provide an early alarm signal of potential danger, while disgusting smells may signal the presence of toxins or other contaminants. Brain areas subserving various olfactory abilities, such as olfactory acuity, olfactory identification ability, and olfactory memory, may be differentially affected in various disease states.

Neuroanatomy of Olfaction

The mucous-lined olfactory epithelium of each nasal cavity consists of approximately 50 million receptor cells, which are bipolar neurons having short peripheral dendrites and long central axons. The dendritic processes connect to the mucosal surface, ending in an expanded olfactory knob from which extends a dense mat of cilia that interact with odorants entering the nasal cavity. The olfactory information is conveyed centrally via the axonal processes, which pass through the skull's cribriform plate to the ipsilateral olfactory bulb, situated beneath the orbitofrontal cortical surface. Unlike most sensory systems, there is no direct projection from primary olfactory receptors to neocortex. Neurons then project to *allocortical* (including the hippocampus, pyriform, or primary olfactory cortex) and *paralimbic* (including the orbitofrontal cortex, insula, temporal pole, parahippocampal gyrus, and cingulate) areas.

Olfactory information from each olfactory bulb has five important projections (Kandel, Schwartz, & Jessell, 1991; Pribram and Kruger, 1954). Each bulb communicates with the contralateral olfactory nucleus via the anterior commissure (Powell, Cowan, & Raisman, 1965), allowing rapid cross-hemispheric integration. Further projections pass via the ventral striatum (olfactory tubercle) and medial dorsal nucleus (MDN) of the thalamus to the orbitofrontal cortex (OFC; Potter & Nauta, 1979; Powell et al., 1965). The OFC mediates conscious appreciation and identification of odor (Eichenbaum, Shedlack, & Eckmann, 1983) and is relevant to cognitive aspects of smell (Potter & Butters, 1980), including sensory integration (Harrison & Pearson, 1989). Other axons from the olfactory tract radiate ipsilaterally to the anterior perforated substance and terminate in the amygdaloid complex. Further projections to hypothalamus and midbrain are considered relevant to eating and reproduction (Harrison & Pearson, 1989). Projections from the olfactory bulb also radiate to the pyriform cortex, which subserve olfactory recognition and discrimination, and then pass to the amygdala and the entorhinal cortex. The entorhinal cortex also receives direct projections from the olfactory bulb, where odor information is integrated with other sensory modalities. Polysensory information is then conveyed to the hippocampus. Limbic projections from the olfactory tract are relevant to the affective associations of odors and olfactory memory as well as to odor detection (i.e., olfactory acuity) (Potter & Butters, 1980).

Assessment of Olfaction

The assessment of olfactory function is undertaken using various odorants. *Identification ability* is assessed using scratch-and-sniff "suprathreshold" odors that are microencapsulated and embedded in plastic capsules coated onto labels, as in the standardized University of Pennsylvania Smell Identification Task (UPSIT; Doty, Shaman, & Dann, 1984). *Olfactory acuity* (or *detection*) is assessed using a forced-choice method utilizing graded concentrations of selected odorants that do not produce a trigeminal nerve response (Doty, Gregor, & Settle, 1986). *Odor discrimination* involves assessment of whether odors are the same or different without requiring identification. *Odor recognition* establishes whether an odor has previously been experienced, while *odor memory* requires recall of a previously presented target odorant from a series of odors (Martzke, Kopala, & Good, 1997). Assessment of olfaction in females should consider variations in olfaction with the menstrual cycle, while some steroidal substances may not be detectable by a significant proportion of the population (Albone & Shirley, 1984). Further, the assessment of olfactory function should take into account the decrease in olfactory threshold and identification ability with age (Doty, 1989).

Disorders Affecting the Primary Olfactory Sensory Organs

Temporary or prolonged reduction of olfactory acuity (hyposmia/anosmia) is often caused by diseases affecting the nasal mucosa or epithelium, including allergic, infective, or vasomotor rhinitis. Congestion and swelling of mucous membranes may also result from metabolic and hormonal disorders (Adams & Victor, 1981). As well as acting peripherally on nasal mucosa and epithelium, solvents can interfere with odor identification and odor detection through their action on the central nervous system (Schwartz, Ford, Bolla, Agnew, & Bleeker, 1991). Permanent loss of smell ability may result from exposure to toxins, from influenza and upper respiratory infections, or from traumatic brain injury (TBI). Olfactory deficits due to TBI generally signify orbitofrontal damage, shearing of the olfactory bulbs, or damage to the delicate filaments of the epithelium (Adams & Victor, 1981).

Olfaction in Neurological Disorders

Findings from lesions studies suggest that lesions of the orbital prefrontal regions result in olfactory identification deficits, while olfactory acuity is spared (e.g., Jones-Gotman & Zatorre, 1988). Further, findings of more dramatic olfactory impairment following prefrontal lesions rather than damage to midline structures (e.g., thalamus) are consistent with a hierarchical organization of processing from medio-dorsal thalamic nucleus to entorhinal cortex and then to lateral posterior orbitofrontal cortex (Potter & Butters, 1980).

Studies in temporal lobe epilepsy (TLE) report reductions in olfactory acuity in patients with right temporal lobectomies (Martinez et al., 1993), while olfactory recognition, discrimination, and short-term memory ability are impaired in patients presurgery (Jones-Gotman et al., 1997; Martinez et al., 1993). Discrimination and short-term memory deficits are greater after temporal lobectomy (Martinez et al., 1993). Olfactory identification is relatively preserved in TLE patients presurgery; however, deficits are observed in lobectomized patients with lesions involving the OFC (Jones-Gotman & Zatorre, 1993).

Deficits in olfaction (acuity, memory, and identification) appear early in the course of a number of neurodegenerative disorders, including cortical Dementia of the Alzheimer's Type, and some of the subcortical dementias, namely Parkinson's disease, Huntington's disease, and HIV-related dementia. However, such deficits have not been reported in patients with atypical parkinsonian syndromes, including corticobasal degeneration and progressive supranuclear palsy (see Doty, 2001; Pantelis, Brewer, & Maruff, 2000). These findings are consistent with the nature of involvement of the relevant olfactory circuits in these various disorders, and suggest that smell ability may assist in differential diagnosis. Studies have also found deficits in olfactory memory in chronic alcohol abusers and of identification ability in patients with Korsakoff syndrome (Potter & Butters, 1980). Olfactory identification deficits have also been found in motor neuron disease (MND), multiple sclerosis (MS), and Down syndrome (McKeown et al., 1996).

Olfaction in Psychiatric Disorders

Olfactory deficits are not a prominent feature of depression, consistent with functional imaging studies finding dorsolateral rather than orbitofrontal cortex involvement (see Pantelis et al., 2000). This suggests that olfaction may help to discriminate depressive from dementing disorders (Doty, 2001). Patients with Obsessive-Compulsive Disorder show marked deficits in olfactory identification ability (Barnett et al., 1999), also implicating OFC involvement. Patients with schizophrenia consistently demonstrate deficits of olfactory identification ability and olfactory recognition memory (Moberg et al., 1999), with deficits in identification being found from illness onset, including neuroleptic naive patients (Brewer et al., 2001; Kopala, Clark, & Hurwitz, 1993).

Summary

Olfactory deficits are observed in a number of neurological and psychiatric disorders. Such deficits involve different aspects of olfactory function, which depends on the nature and extent of neurological involvement. There is evidence to suggest that olfactory functions may be dissociable, with the most profound deficits seen in higher order function involving the ability to identify odors, which implicates orbitofrontal cortex involvement. Examination of olfactory disturbances may provide early markers of impending neurological or psychiatric illness and, in some psychiatric disorders including schizophrenia, may be trait markers of the condition.

REFERENCES

Adams, K. M., & Victor, M. (1981). *Principles of neurology.* New York: McGraw-Hill.

Albone, E. S., & Shirley, S. G. (1984). *Mammalian semiochemistry. The investigation of chemical signals between mammals.* New York: Wiley.

Barnett, R., Maruff, P., Purcell, R., Wainwright, K., Kyrios, M., Brewer, W., & Pantelis, C. (1999). Impairment of olfactory identification in Obsessive-Compulsive Disorder. *Psychological Medicine, 29*(5), 1227–1233.

Brewer, W. J., Pantelis, C., Anderson, V., Velakoulis, D., Singh, B., Copolov, D. L., & McGorry, P. D. (2001). Stability of olfactory identification deficits in neuroleptic-naive patients with first-episode psychosis. *American Journal of Psychiatry, 158*(1), 107–115.

Doty, R. L. (1989). Influence of age and age-related diseases on olfactory function. *Annals of the New York Academy of Sciences, 561,* 76–86.

Doty, R. L. (2001). Olfaction. *Annual Review of Psychology, 52,* 423–452.

Doty, R. L., Gregor, T. P., & Settle, R. G. (1986). Influence of intertrial and sniff-bottle volume on phenyl ethyl alcohol odor detection thresholds. *Chemical Senses, 11,* 259–264.

Doty, R. L., Shaman, P., & Dann, W. (1984). Development of the University of Pennsylvania Smell Test: Standardised microencapsulated test of olfactory function. *Physiological Behavior, 32,* 489–502.

Eichenbaum, H., Shedlack, K. J., & Eckmann, K. W. (1983). Thalamocortical mechanisms in odor-guided behavior-1. Effects of lesions of the mediodorsal thalamic nucleus and frontal cortex on olfactory discrimination in the rat. *Brain, Behavior & Evolution, 7,* 255–275.

Harrison, P. J., & Pearson, R. C. A. (1989). Olfaction and psychiatry. *British Journal of Psychiatry, 155,* 822–828.

Jones-Gotman, M., & Zatorre, R. J. (1988). Olfactory identification deficits in patients with focal cerebral excision. *Neuropsychologia, 26,* 387–400.

Jones-Gotman, M., & Zatorre, R. J. (1993). Odor recognition memory in humans: Role of right temporal and orbitofrontal regions. *Brain & Cognition, 22,* 182–198.

Jones-Gotman, M., Zatorre, R. J., Cendes, F., Olivier, A., Andermann, F., McMackin, D., Staunton, H., Siegel, A. M., & Wieser, H.-G. (1997). Contribution of medial versus lateral temporal-lobe structures to human odour identification. *Brain, 120,* 1845–1856.

Kandel, E. R., Schwartz, J. H., & Jessell, T. M. (1991). *Principles of neural science.* London: Elsevier.

Kopala, L. C., Clark, C., & Hurwitz, T. (1993). Olfactory deficits in neuroleptic naive patients with Schizophrenia. *Schizophrenia Research, 8*(3), 245–250.

Martinez, B. A., Cain, W. S., de Wijk, R. A., Spencer, D. D., Novelly, R. A., & Sass, K. J. (1993). Olfactory functioning before and after temporal lobe resection for intractable seizures. *Neuropsychology, 7,* 351–363.

Martzke, J. S., Kopala, L. C., & Good, K. P. (1997). Olfactory dysfunction in neuropsychiatry disorders: Review and methodological considerations. *Biological Psychiatry, 42,* 721–732.

McKeown, D. A., Doty, R. L., Perl, D. P., Frye, R. E., Simms, I., & Mester, A. (1996). Olfactory dysfunction in young adolescents with Down's syndrome. *Journal of Neurology, Neurosurgery and Psychiatry, 61*(4), 412–414.

Moberg, P. J., Agrin, R., Gur, R. E., Gur, R. C., Turetsky, B. I., & Doty, R. L. (1999). Olfactory dysfunction in Schizophrenia: A qualitative and quantitative review. *Neuropsychopharmacology, 21,* 325–340.

Pantelis, C., Brewer, W. J., & Maruff, P. (2000). Olfactory cortex. In W. E. Craighead & C. Nemeroff (Eds.), *The Corsini encyclopedia of psychology and behavioral science* (pp. 1090–1098). New York: Wiley.

Potter, H., & Butters, N. (1980). An assessment of olfactory deficits in patients with damage to the prefrontal cortex. *Neuropsychologia, 18,* 621–628.

Potter, H., & Nauta, W. J. H. (1979). A note on the problem of olfactory associations of the orbitofrontal cortex in the monkey. *Neuroscience, 4,* 361–367.

Powell, T. P. S., Cowan, W. M., & Raisman, G. (1965). The central olfactory connections. *Journal of Anatomy, 99,* 791–813.

Pribram, K. H., & Kruger, L. (1954). Function of the "olfactory brain." *Annals of the New York Academy of Sciences, 58,* 109–138.

Schwartz, B. S., Ford, D. P., Bolla, K. I., Agnew, J., & Bleeker, M. L. (1991). Solvent associated olfactory dysfunction: Not a predictor of deficits in learning and memory. *American Journal of Psychiatry, 148,* 751–756.

Christos Pantelis
Warrick J. Brewer
University of Melbourne, Australia

OPERANT CONDITIONING

Operant conditioning, a term coined by B. F. Skinner in 1937, has several shades of meaning. It is both an experimental procedure and a behavioral process, that is, a characteristic interaction of an organism and its environment observed in species with complex nervous systems. In the latter sense, it is a biological adaptation with a plausible evolutionary interpretation. The study of operant conditioning and related phenomena comprises a substantial research paradigm within psychology in both laboratory and applied settings. This paradigm endorses tightly controlled experiments to discover behavioral principles; the direct extension of those principles to behavior therapy, education, organizational behavior management, and other applications; and the use of the principles as interpretive tools for understanding complex human behavior such as language, memory, and problem solving.

The Operant Conditioning Procedure

In an operant conditioning procedure, a consequence is made contingent upon a behavior; specifically, the experimenter arranges a contingency in which a stimulus is presented if and only if a target behavior has just occurred. For example, an apparatus might be arranged so that, whenever a rat presses a lever, a drop of water drips into a dish from which the rat can drink. If the rat has recently been denied access to water, the strength of the target behavior will change; among other effects, the rate of pressing the lever will increase in that setting and in similar settings. If replications and suitable control conditions demonstrate that this change in strength is in fact due to the contingency, and is not a coincidence, the procedure is an instance of positive reinforcement, and water is called a reinforcing stimulus. If the rat has not been deprived of water, the procedure might have no effect on behavior. Under these conditions, if the rat were forced to drink by squirting water in its mouth, for example, we would expect the rate of lever-pressing to decrease relative to a baseline condition. We then speak of a punishment contingency and of water as a punishing stimulus. Thus both reinforcement and punishment are defined, not by procedures or by the nature of particular stimuli, but by their effects on the probability of behavior under given conditions.

Although Thorndike was the first researcher to study operant conditioning systematically, Skinner was the first to discover that the rate of behavior in freely moving organisms was highly sensitive to a wide variety of independent variables. In experiments using Skinner's methodology, the demonstration of operant principles has been found to be highly reliable in many species. Single-subject designs are preferred, since the behavioral principles of interest are revealed in the detailed interactions of organism and environment and may be obscured by averaging cases. Skinner recognized that appropriate units of analysis in psychology should not be defined in advance by the experimenter, but should be determined empirically, by looking for orderly relationships between the organism and its environment. The units that emerge from such an analysis are three-term contingencies of environment, behavior, and consequence, and no one term can be understood in isolation.

Operant Conditioning as a Behavioral Process

Operant conditioning procedures have revealed that behavior changes in strength or probability when it is followed by biologically important consequences such as access to food, water, sexual activity, or escape from painful stimuli, cold, or excessive heat. Activities that tend to promote survival and reproduction become more frequent, while those that bring harm are reduced or eliminated. Operant conditioning is thus an evolutionary adaptation enabling an organism to adjust to variable environments where nourishment, comfort, potential mates, and danger are not ubiquitous but must be searched for, fought for, or avoided. Food, water, and sexual contact are all examples of unconditioned reinforcers, stimuli that are innately reinforcing under relevant motivating conditions. However, neutral stimuli can acquire a reinforcing function if they are frequently paired with unconditioned reinforcers. Thus we learn to respond to the dinner bell, to hunt for a water fountain, and to approach a member of the opposite sex who smiles at us. In humans, money, fame, and prestige are particularly effective conditioned reinforcers only indirectly related to survival and differential reproduction.

The strengthening of adaptive behavior and the weakening of ineffective behavior is a selection process, analogous in many respects to natural selection. Behavior is variable; even a highly practiced behavior will vary somewhat from one instance to the next. By differentially reinforcing responses with some property, such as relatively forceful lever presses, an experimenter can effect a change in the distribution of responses. More and more forceful lever presses occur to the point that the typical response is wholly unrepresentative of the original distribution of behavior. When organisms are exposed to such programs of gradually changing contingencies—a process called shaping—behavior can evolve and become highly differentiated over the lifetime of the individual, much as the morphology of organisms changes over evolutionary time. The repertoires of the skillful juggler, rock climber, and gymnast have presumably been shaped mainly by programs of intrinsic contingencies, but the repertoires of the seeing-eye dog, the race horse, the mathematician, the engineer, and the historian are likely to have been shaped mainly by programs of contingencies explicitly arranged by trainers or educators.

The Domain of Operant Conditioning

Some response systems, such as respiration, circulation, and digestion, serve a narrow function in the economy of the organism, and it would not be adaptive for them to vary substantially with arbitrary contingencies of reinforcement. In contrast, the orientation of receptors and responses mediated by skeletal muscles, such as the vocal apparatus, limbs, digits, and other effectors, can be recruited for a wide variety of tasks. Operant conditioning can most easily be demonstrated in the latter class of response systems.

It is characteristic of students of operant conditioning to confine their experimental analyses to objective, measurable variables. However, in any experiment some part of the behavior of an organism is always below the threshold of observability. Since this threshold depends upon the tools of the investigator and is not an intrinsic property of behavior, it must be assumed that the principles of operant conditioning apply not only to behavior that can be observed, but also to covert behavior as well. The psychologist's understanding of covert behavior is necessarily interpretive rather than experimental. The principle of reinforcement has proven a powerful tool in such interpretations since the terms of the analysis have been well established in single subjects under analogous conditions in the laboratory. However, the extent to which operant conditioning and other principles of learning provide a sufficient foundation for an interpretation of such phenomena as language, recall, covert problem solving, imagery, and perception remains controversial. Behaviorists argue that these phenomena can all be interpreted with established principles of learning. From this perspective, operant conditioning is the primary principle underlying all adaptive complexity in behavior.

SUGGESTED READING

Catania, A. C. (1998). *Learning.* Upper Saddle River, NJ: Prentice Hall.

Donahoe, J. W., & Palmer, D. C. (1994). *Learning and complex behavior.* Boston: Allyn & Bacon.

Iverson, I. H., & Lattal, K. A. (1991). *Experimental analysis of behavior.* New York: Elsevier.

Skinner, B. F. (1938). *The behavior of organisms: An experimental analysis.* New York: Appleton-Century-Crofts.

Skinner, B. F. (1953). *Science and human behavior.* New York: Macmillan.

Sidman, M. (1960). *Tactics of scientific research.* New York: Basic Books.

Thorndike, E. L. (1898). Animal intelligence: An experimental study of the associative processes in animals. *Psychological Review Monograph Supplements, 2*(4, Whole No. 8).

David C. Palmer
Smith College

See also: **Behaviorism; Learning Theories; Reinforcement Schedules**

OPERATIONAL DEFINITION

Few topics in the area of scientific communication have been as troublesome as that of operational definition. Psychologists have done their share both to clarify and to muddy the waters on this problem, and this article outlines some of the principal facets they need to consider.

Operationism

Operationism was initiated by Harvard University physicist P. W. Bridgman, who had reviewed the history of definitions of fundamental physical concepts like length, space, and time as they were used before Einstein to learn why they required such drastic revisions in Einstein's revolutionary theorizing. Bridgman concluded that the traditional Newtonian definitions had contained substantial amounts of meaning not related to their actual physical measurements (e.g., the assumption of an absolute scale for time); it was this kind of excess meaning that was responsible for Einstein's need to make radical reformulations in these concepts.

Bridgman suggested that to avoid similar roadblocks in the development of physical theory it would be necessary to impose more stringent requirements on the making of definitions. His proposal was that concepts should be defined strictly in terms of the operations used to measure them. As he put it, "The concept is synonymous with the corresponding set of operations."

Bridgman found that nothing was quite as simple and straightforward as it had seemed at first. He subsequently made some strategic retreats from his initially monolithic position, such as acknowledging at least the temporary admissibility of paper-and-pencil operations and accepting the usefulness of abstract concepts.

The idea that the meaning of all concepts should be restricted to the necessary operations underlying them had an immediate appeal for psychologists. Operationism was promulgated early in psychology by S. S. Stevens. Stevens was careful to point out that the operational-definition movement was simply a formalization of the methodology that had always been used by effective scientists, including psychologists.

Unfortunately, the balanced position advanced by Stevens did not quite prove to be the norm. Probably the single most important negative factor was the overselling of the operational ideal, especially as applied to situations in which perfectly operational definitions of psychological concepts were clearly not even approximately feasible. Also, there was the continuing persistence of the more grandly conceived operationism, and the consequent overloading of what should have been merely a fundamental methodological principle with essentially fewer relevant substantive issues of one kind or another. The net result has been that far too little attention has been paid to the central principle.

A good example of the communication difficulties that await the unwary user or reader is afforded by the word *frustration.* Quite apart from the further complications of theoretical nuances, this word is used in at least three distinct ways, which are usually but by no means always kept clearly separated: (a) as a kind of blocking operation that prevents a motivated organism from obtaining a goal or persisting in goal-directed behavior; (b) as the kind of behavior that appears when such a goal-oriented organism is thus blocked; and (c) as some hypothetical inner process that is assumed to be responsible for the overt behavioral responses to the blocking operation.

None of the secondary and tertiary disputes over operationism can eliminate the fact that psychologists all too often simply fail to communicate adequately with each other because they continue to use key terms in a variety of loosely defined and highly ambiguous ways. Some basic considerations need to be emphasized. First, operational definitions are not all-or-none achievements; rather, there is a continuum of operational clarity in definitions, that is, in the degree to which ambiguity and excess meaning have been eliminated. Second, full operational clarity needs to be an objective to be kept clearly in mind throughout all phases of theoretical and empirical research; acceptance of ambiguity must be regarded in many situations as a necessary but, it is hoped, not a permanent condition, and it is important that scientific communicators explicitly recognize this state of affairs rather than simply ignore it and gloss over the problem. Third, substantive issues involving defined concepts must not be allowed to intrude on and confuse the primarily methodological criteria associated with operational definitions. Fourth, it is hoped that recognition of the importance of these considerations serves as a spur to improve definitional clarity and ultimately to help make improvements in theoretical development. Taking this kind of positive approach to the definitional problem should also serve to help free psychologists from the semantic quagmires in which so many of the key concepts are still entangled.

Melvin H. Marx

See also: **Logical Positivism**

OPERATIONALISM

Operationalism is the demand that theoretical terms in science—that is, those that do not refer to something directly observable—be given operational definitions. Operational definition was proposed independently by the physicist Percy Bridgman (who named it) and by the logical positivists, who called it "explicit definition." It was introduced to psychology by S. S. Stevens in 1935, and played an important role in behaviorism. The goal of operationalism was to eliminate from science any concepts that were metaphysical, and to positivists meaningless, ensuring that science would ask only questions that had empirical answers, and would have theories that referred only to meaningful entities.

As empiricists, operationists assume that we can never be in doubt when talking about things we can observe. Thus, the meaning of an observational term such as "red" is unproblematic because it refers to a publicly observable attribute of objects. Uncertainty arises for theoretical terms such as "mass," "drive," "anxiety," and "superego." None of these is publicly observable, even though we have all experienced anxiety or hunger, while two terms, "mass" and "superego," may turn out not to refer to anything at all. Nevertheless, science needs theories and theoretical terms, and operationalists sought to guarantee the cognitive significance of theoretical terms by giving each an operational definition. In an operational definition, we define a theoretical term by linking it to some publicly verifiable operation—a measurement or a manipulation—we can perform on the environment. "Mass" becomes the weighing of an object at sea level, "drive" the withholding of food from an animal for some number of hours, and "anxiety" the score of a subject on the Taylor Manifest Anxiety Test.

The operationalist contends that the operational definition supplies the full meaning of a concept by linking it to unproblematic observation terms; anything more is unscientific surplus meaning. Moreover, operationalists question the scientific legitimacy of any term not operationally definable. Thus, the Freudian concept of the superego might be challenged as hopelessly unscientific, as there is no clear way of defining it in terms of something observable.

Operationalism gained wide assent in psychology, and, despite the death of logical positivism, psychologists continue to use operational definitions for theoretical terms that otherwise might have only mental, nonpublic, and therefore, psychologists fear, nonscientific meanings. Nevertheless, operationalism has been controversial. It has proved difficult, if not impossible, to operationalize all the terms even of physics, leading positivists themselves gradually to abandon operationalism. In psychology, operationalism has been criticized for unduly narrowing psychology's focus, making behaviorism the only acceptable psychology by methodological fiat rather than by superiority of results. That terms be operationalized remains, however, a common requirement of psychological theory.

SUGGESTED READING

Hempel, C. (1965). *Aspects of scientific explanation.* New York: Free Press.

Leahey, T. H. (1980). The myth of operationism. *Journal of Mind and Behavior, 1,* 127–143.

Suppe, F. (1972). Theories, their formulations, and the operational imperative. *Synthese, 25,* 129–164.

Thomas H. Leahey
Virginia Commonwealth University

***See also:* Empiricism; Logical Positivism**

OPIOID RECEPTORS

The effects of opiates, such as heroin or morphine, are consequences of the interactions of these drugs with opioid receptors. Opioid receptors, like receptors for other neurotransmitters, are cell surface proteins that (1) detect the presence of specific neurotransmitter or drug molecules in the extracellular environment, and (2) initiate biochemical changes that alter cellular processes in response to neurotransmitter or drug binding to the receptors. The activation of opioid receptors results in hyperpolarization, reduced neuronal excitability, and the blockade of neurotransmitter release in cells bearing the receptors.

Receptors that specifically bind opiate drugs were demonstrated in 1973, and endogenous peptides that bind these receptors were subsequently purified from brain (Pert & Snyder, 1973; Akil, Watson, Young, Lewis, Khachaturian, & Walker, 1984). There are three major families of endogenous opioid peptides: the endorphins, the enkephalins, and the dynorphins. The terminals of neurons containing endogenous opioid peptides are distributed in the same areas of the nervous system where there are high densities of opioid receptors, and it is believed that the endogenous opioid peptides function as the neurotransmitters or neuromodulators that utilize the opioid receptors. While the specific functions of endogenous opioid peptides are incompletely understood, they have been implicated in a variety of central nervous system functions including nociception, homeostatic function, mood regulation, and reward.

There are three subtypes of opioid receptor, referred to as mu, delta, and kappa receptors. The subtypes are distinguished by distinct binding selectivities, patterns of distribution in brain and spinal cord, and functional properties. Each opioid receptor subtype can be further categorized into subtypes on the basis of binding selectivities, distribution, and function.

Opioid receptors belong to the superfamily of G protein-coupled receptors. G proteins become functionally activated in response to receptor activation and can then initiate functional changes. G proteins can directly influence proteins such as ion channels, and they can also indirectly influence protein functions by interaction with biochemical messenger systems. Opioid receptors couple to both types of G protein.

The most studied messenger system associated with

opioid receptors is the adenylyl cyclase (AC) enzyme that mediates the synthesis of cyclic adenosine monophosphate (cAMP). The cAMP acts as a biochemical messenger that activates cAMP-dependent protein kinase (PKA). PKA is an enzyme that adds phosphorylates to a variety of types of cellular proteins, thus altering their size, charge, and functional capabilities. Opioid receptors can activate an inhibitory G protein (G_i), which inhibits AC activity and cAMP formation and consequently decreases substrate phosphorylation by PKA. Substrates for PKA include neurotransmitter receptors, synaptic proteins, and neurotransmitter synthetic enzymes, all of which can modify neuronal excitability.

Opioid receptors are also coupled to G proteins that can directly regulate ion channel activity and cellular excitability independently of second messenger intervention. Opioid receptors regulate ion channels controlling K^+ and Ca^{++} currents though direct coupling with G proteins. The results of opioid receptor activation are increased K^+ outflow causing hyperpolarization of the membrane potential, and reduced Ca^{++} entry into cells (Duggan & North, 1983). These mechanisms are thought to be important to the opioid blockade of neurotransmitter release, which may be the primary mechanism whereby opiate drugs reduce transmission within pain pathways and produce analgesia.

Opioid receptors of each subtype have been cloned and sequenced in animals and humans (Knapp et al., 1995; Satoh & Minami, 1995). The amino acid sequences indicate that they all contain the seven hydrophobic membrane-spanning domains that are characteristic of the G protein coupled receptor superfamily. The sequences show significant homology, with the greatest homology in the transmembrane regions and in the intracellular regions that connect them.

The three opioid receptor subtypes show distinct patterns of distribution in the nervous system (Mansour, Khachaturian, Lewis, Akil, & Watson, 1988; Tempel & Zukin, 1987). Mu receptors are found in the dorsal horn of the spinal cord, the spinal trigeminal nucleus, periaquaductal gray, and medial thalamus, consistent with a role in morphine-induced analgesia. They are also found in brain stem nuclei that are involved in morphine depression of respiration and stimulation of nausea and vomiting. Mu receptors in the nucleus accumbens, ventral tegmental area of the midbrain are important to morphine effects on mood and reward.

Delta opioid receptors are more restricted in their distribution and are found mainly in forebrain structures (neocortex, caudate-putamen, and amygdala) and the spinal cord and are also thought to participate in analgesia. Kappa receptors are located in the dorsal horn of the spinal cord, and in the hypothalamus where they may regulate neuroendocrine function. Kappa receptors are located in amygdala, dorsal striatum, and in the nucleus accumbens, and in contrast to mu-mediated effects, kappa receptor stimulation can produce dysphoria and psychotomimetic effects.

REFERENCES

Akil, H., Watson, S. J., Young, E., Lewis, M. E., Khachaturian, H., & Walker, J. M. (1984). Endogenous opioids: Biology and function. *Annual Review of Neuroscience, 7,* 223–255.

Duggan, A. W., & North, R. A. (1983). Electrophysiology of opioids. *Pharmacological Review, 35,* 219–282.

Knapp, R. J., Malatynska, E., Collins, N., Fang, L., Wang, J. Y., Hruby, V. J., Roeske, W. R., & Yamamura, H. I. (1995). Molecular biology and pharmacology of cloned opioid receptors. *FASEB Journal, 9,* 516–525.

Mansour, A., Khachaturian, H., Lewis, M. E., Akil, H., & Watson, S. J. (1988). Anatomy of central nervous system opioid receptors. *Trends in Neuroscience, 11*(7), 308–314.

Pert, C. B., & Snyder, S. H. (1973). Properties of opiate receptor binding in rat brain. *Proceedings of the National Academy of Sciences, USA, 70,* 2243–2247.

Satoh, M., & Minami, M. (1995). Molecular pharmacology of the opioid receptors. *Pharmacology and Therapeutics, 68,* 343–364.

Tempel, A., & Zukin, R. S. (1987). Neuroanatomical patterns of the mu, delta, and kappa opioid receptors of rat brain as determined by quantitative in vitro autoradiography. *Proceedings of the National Academy of Sciences, USA, 84,* 4308–4312.

Catharine H. Duman
Yale University

OPPONENT-PROCESS THEORY OF EMOTION

The opponent-process theory of emotion was initially proposed by Solomon in 1970 as a general theory of motivation that focuses on the temporal pattern of changes in the qualitative nature and intensity of emotional/affective states (responses) evoked by sensory events (stimuli). Following an exemplary model developed by Hurvich and Jameson (1957) in their theory of color vision (especially complementary color afterimages), Solomon (1980; see also Solomon & Corbit, 1974) applied the opponent-process system in a parsimoniously elegant form to account for a broad range of psychological phenomena, chief among them addiction and aversion.

A description of the pattern of the affective dynamics underlying the theory begins with the introduction (onset) of either a pleasurable or aversive stimulus which evokes an affective/hedonic reaction (A State) that rises quickly to a peak. The intensity of the hedonic A State (affect/emotion/tone/feeling/mood) then declines to a steady level where it remains as a long as the stimulus quality and intensity are maintained. Immediately following the termination of the stimulus, its affective reaction ends and is replaced by a different affective afterreaction (B State) which is opposite that of the initial hedonic state (i.e., the B State is the opponent of A State). This afterstate (B State) reaches its peak at a slower rate than that of the A State, then decays at a relatively slow rate until the initial neutral affective baseline is eventually reestablished.

An everyday example of the phases of the affective dynamics in the case of a hedonically positive A State (which implies a negative B State) and the events that evoke them might be as follows: News (stimulus) that a long-absent loved one will soon return evokes a positive hedonic state (A State) of joy or happiness (response). If the subject hears subsequent news that plans for the return of the loved one have been canceled, the positive A State will end abruptly and be replaced with a negative hedonic B State of sorrow or unhappiness, which will gradually decay until the neutral hedonic state extant prior to the positive news is reestablished. An example of the affective dynamics in the case of a hedonically negative A State might be one in which news (stimulus) that a loved one is seriously ill evokes a negative hedonic A State of sorrow or unhappiness (response). If subsequent news announces that the diagnosis was in error, the negative A State will end abruptly and be replaced with a positive hedonic B State of joy or happiness which decays gradually until the prior hedonically neutral state returns.

Beyond typical hedonic theories that assume events arouse positive or negative states, the opponent-process theory of emotion proposes that hedonic (affective/emotional) states are automatically opposed by self-regulatory negative feedback loops within the central nervous system, that is, opponent *processes* that reduce the intensity of their respective hedonic *states*. If the A State is positive, its underlying *a* process is opposed by a negative *b* process; and if the A State is negative, its underlying *a* process is opposed by a positive *b* process. Thus, in addition to the "baseline-A-B-baseline" sequence of emotional states illustrated above, the theory posits that each emotional state is accompanied by underlying opponent processes. The intensity and duration of affective states is determined through an analysis of these underlying affective processes. Arousal of the *a* process is accompanied by arousal of its opponent *b* process, a slave process that is slow to rise and slow to decay. The difference between these two processes determines the hedonic quality of emotional experience. (If a > b, then the organism is in the A State; and if b > a, the organism is in the B State.) Because the *a* process ends abruptly with the termination of the stimulus for the A State, and because the *b* process is slow to decay, the termination of the stimulus for the A State will give rise to an opposite or opponent affective state. With frequent arousal of the A State, the *b* process will increase in magnitude and duration, thereby diminishing the intensity of the A State proportionately.

Although the theory does not depend on assumptions of associative learning to account for positive and negative reinforcement effects often applied in theories of addiction, the affective A and B States are subject to Pavlovian/classical conditioning. Thus, the theory accounts for addictive behavior in the absence of any apparent current pleasurable consequences of the addictive substance by pointing to the increase in intensity of the negative B State that accompanies withdrawal from the addictive substance (stimulus for A State) and by pointing to the conditionality of both the A State and the B State. According to the theory, associative processes, though present in cases of acquired motivation, are neither necessary nor sufficient to produce related behaviors. Addictive behaviors are representative of most acquired motives in social contexts. In acquired motivation, affective processes are inevitably involved: namely, contrast, habituation, symptoms of withdrawal, and opposition between states characteristic of the presence or absence of the stimuli.

In the study of addiction, a critical assumption of the theory lies in the effects of frequency of stimulus occurrence (use of addictive substance) and latency between doses on the changes in the intensity and duration of B States (and their underlying b-processes) relative to A states (and their underlying a-processes). According to the theory, the opponent process *b* is strengthened by use and weakened by disuse, whereas the primary affective process *a* is not significantly affected by use. As such, with frequent elicitation, the b-processes will show a shorter latency of response, sharper rise time, greater asymptote, and slower decay time than *a* processes. The effect on hedonic response rate after many stimulations will be a lower peak of the A state (labeled A'), and a more intense, longer-lasting B state (labeled B'). In time the addictive substance (stimulus for A State) offers the addict nothing but relief from the aversive effects of its absence. Because the theory is nonassociative, a major implication of the postulation of opponent-processes is that physiological stress can be caused by pleasurable as well as aversive stimulation. Thus, one should look for disorders of adaptation to types of stresses due to correlated physiological side effects of long duration and often-elicited intense *b* processes.

The theory provides a unique model for understanding a broad range of emotional/motivational phenomena; it is a singular contribution to the behavioral sciences, especially psychology, psychiatry, and psychophysiology. For examples of how the opponent-process theory has been applied in clinical respiratory psychophysiology to account for the anxiolytic effects of single inhalations of large concentrations of carbon dioxide (Wolpe, 1987) and amyl nitrite (Wolpe, 1990), see Ley (1994).

REFERENCES

Hurvich, L. M., & Jameson, D. (1957). An opponent-process of color vision. *Psychological Review, 64,* 384–404.

Ley, R. (1994). An opponent-process interpretation of the anxiolytic effects of single inhalations of large concentrations of carbon dioxide. *Journal of Behavior Therapy and Experimental Psychiatry, 25,* 301–309.

Solomon, R. L. (1980). The opponent-process theory of motivation: The costs of pleasure and the benefits of pain. *American Psychologist, 35,* 691–712.

Solomon, R. L., & Corbit, J. D. (1974). An opponent-process theory of motivation: I. Temporal dynamics of affect. *Psychological Review, 81,* 119–145.

Wolpe, J. (1987). Carbon dioxide inhalation treatments of neurotic anxiety: An overview. *Journal of Nervous and Mental Disorders, 175,* 129–133.

Wolpe, J. (1990). *The practice of behavior therapy* (4th ed.). New York: Pergamon Press.

Ronald Ley
University at Albany, State University of New York

See also: **Addiction; Learning Theories**

OPPOSITIONAL DEFIANT DISORDER

Oppositional Defiant Disorder (ODD) is a recurrent pattern of negativistic, disobedient, and hostile behavior toward authority figures (American Psychiatric Association, 1994). A diagnosis requires that at least four of eight symptoms are present over the course of at least six months. Symptoms include: (1) losing one's temper, (2) arguing with adults, (3) actively defying adults' requests or rules, (4) deliberately annoying others, (5) blaming others for mistakes, (6) being easily annoyed, (7) being angry and resentful, and (8) being spiteful or vindictive (American Psychiatric Association, 1994). Those receiving a diagnosis of ODD exhibit such behaviors at a frequency above what is considered to be developmentally appropriate, and such behaviors lead to significant impairment (e.g., in social or academic functioning). These symptoms need only be present in one setting to receive a diagnosis, and children sometimes exhibit symptoms in the home setting without concurrent problems at school or in the community (American Psychiatric Association, 1994). Estimated rates of ODD in the general population range from 6% to 10% (McMahon & Estes, 1997). Epidemiological research suggests that ODD may be more common in males than females, with gender differences more pronounced at younger ages (Lahey, Miller, Gordon, & Riley, 1999).

ODD involves a broad tendency to respond angrily (Lahey, McBurnett, & Loeber, 2000). Although children with ODD are often verbally aggressive, they do not display the frequent physically aggressive behaviors observed in Conduct Disorder (CD). In fact, these two diagnoses are mutually exclusive and, to be diagnosed with ODD, a child cannot also meet criteria for CD (American Psychiatric Association, 1994). However, Loeber (1990) hypothesized that aggressive behavior, including verbal aggression, in the elementary school years is part of a developmental trajectory that can lead to adolescent delinquency and CD. Indeed, a subset of children with ODD will proceed to develop CD, whereas some children will develop CD without ever meeting diagnostic criteria for ODD (American Psychiatric Association, 1994; Lahey et al., 2000). Longitudinal research indicates that ODD is a strong risk factor for CD in boys, whereas the presence of ODD does not increase the risk for later CD in girls (Rowe, Maughan, Pickles, Costello, & Angold, 2002). Girls with ODD, however, are at greater risk for continued ODD and internalizing disorders (Rowe et al., 2002). In general, children are more at risk for continued behavior problems if they display both overt and covert behaviors across multiple settings (Lochman & Szczepanski, 1999). Likewise, certain environmental risk factors, such as a dysfunctional family setting, socioeconomic disadvantage, or a violence-ridden neighborhood can play a role in moving children along this developmental pathway (McGee & Williams, 1999).

Precursors to ODD may start very early among inflexible infants with irritable temperaments (Loeber, 1990; Sanson & Prior, 1999). Likewise, early behavioral problems, such as impulsivity, overactivity, and mild aggression, may blossom into more serious forms of disruptive behaviors, including ODD (Sanson & Prior, 1999). Children with difficult temperaments and early emerging behavioral problems are at greater risk for failing to develop positive attachments with caregivers and becoming involved in increasingly coercive interchanges with parents and significant adults, such as teachers. Likewise, parents of children with disruptive behavior problems often display high rates of harsh, inconsistent discipline, have unclear rules and expectations, and have low rates of positive involvement, adaptive discipline strategies, and problem solving skills (Lochman & Wells, 1996; Patterson, 1986). Loeber (1990) hypothesized that children begin to generalize their use of coercive behaviors to other social interactions, leading to increasingly oppositional and disruptive behavior with peers and adults and to dysfunctional social–cognitive processes. These dysfunctional processes, in turn, serve to maintain problem behavior sequences. Children with ODD have been shown to use problem solving strategies that rely on aggressive solutions, have difficulties encoding social information accurately, and expect that aggressive solutions will work (Coy, Speltz, DeKlyen, & Jones, 2001; Crick & Dodge, 1994). Such difficulties have been documented as early as preschool and are not accounted for by comorbidity with other disruptive behavior problems, such as Attention-Deficit/Hyperactivity Disorder (Coy et al., 2001). Notably, children with ODD lack insight into their defiant behavior and usually justify their behavior as a reaction to unfair demands (American Psychiatric Association, 1994).

Historically, psychosocial treatment of oppositional, conduct-disordered children has been perceived to be difficult and not very productive. However, in recent years randomized clinical research trials have identified empirically-supported treatments for ODD and CD. Brestan and Eyberg (1998) have identified two parent-training intervention programs with well-established positive effects (Patterson, Reid, & Dishion, 1992; Webster-Stratton, 1994) and ten other programs as probably efficacious for treating disruptive behavior disorders such as ODD. Treatment strategies aimed at parents (e.g., improving parental monitoring and improving consistency in discipline; see Eyberg, Boggs, & Algina, 1995; Peed, Roberts, & Forehand, 1977; Webster-Stratton, 1994; Wiltz & Patterson, 1974), as well as cognitive-behavioral treatments targeting children (e.g., problem solving skills training, anger management, and impulse control; see Feindler, Marriott, & Iwata, 1984; Kazdin, Siegel, & Bass, 1992; Lochman, Burch, Curry, & Lampron, 1984) have led to a reduction in behavioral problems and externalizing symptomatology in children, including those with ODD (Kazdin, 1998; Kazdin & Weisz, 1998; Silverthorn, 2001).

Treatment outcome research indicates that a combination of interventions for both parents and children may be the most efficacious in treating ODD. For example, behavioral parent training programs for parents of children with ODD are most effective when provided in combination with a child-focused problem solving skills training component (Behan & Carr, 2000). Group intervention programs, which are time- and cost-efficient, are usually as clinically effective as individually based programs in treating ODD (Behan & Carr, 2000). Intensive, comprehensive prevention programs have also been developed and evaluated with high risk children starting as early as first grade, and the results indicate that aggressive behavior and other symptoms associated with ODD and CD can be reduced through early intervention (Conduct Problems Prevention Research Group, 1999; Tremblay, LeMarquand, & Vitaro, 1999; Vitaro, Brendgen, Pagani, Tremblay, & McDuff, 1999).

REFERENCES

American Psychiatric Association. (1994). *Diagnostic and statistical manual of mental disorders* (4th ed.). Washington, DC: Author.

Behan, J., & Carr, A. (2000). Oppositional defiant disorder. In A. Carr (Ed.), *What works with children and adolescents?: A critical review of psychological interventions with children, adolescents, and their families* (pp. 102–130). New York: Brunner-Routledge.

Brestan, E. V., & Eyberg, S. M. (1998). Effective psychosocial treatments of Conduct-Disordered children and adolescents: 29 years, 82 studies, and 5,272 kids. *Journal of Clinical Child Psychology, 27,* 180–189.

Conduct Problems Prevention Research Group. (1999). Initial impact of the Fast Track prevention trial for conduct problems: I. The high-risk sample. *Journal of Consulting and Clinical Psychology, 67,* 631–647.

Coy, K., Speltz, M. L., DeKlyen, M., & Jones, K. (2001). Social-cognitive processes in preschool boys with and without Oppositional Defiant Disorder. *Journal of Abnormal Child Psychology, 29,* 107–119.

Crick, N. R., & Dodge, K. A. (1994). A review and reformulation of social information-processing mechanisms in children's social adjustment. *Psychological Bulletin, 115,* 74–101.

Eyberg, S. M., Boggs, S., & Algina, J. (1995). Parent-child interaction therapy: A psychosocial model for the treatment of young children with conduct problem behavior and their families. *Psychopharmacology Bulletin, 31,* 83–91.

Feindler, D. L., Marriott, S. A., & Iwata, M. (1984). Group anger control training for junior high school delinquents. *Cognitive Therapy and Research, 8,* 299–311.

Kazdin, A. E. (1998). Conduct disorder. In R. J. Morris & T. R. Kratochwill (Eds.), *The practice of child therapy* (3rd ed., pp. 199–230). Boston: Allyn & Bacon.

Kazdin, A. E., Siegel, T. C., & Bass, D. (1992). Cognitive problem-solving skills training and parent management training in the treatment of antisocial behavior in children. *Journal of Consulting and Clinical Psychology, 60,* 733–747.

Kazdin, A. E., & Weisz, J. R. (1998). Identifying and developing empirically supported child and adolescent treatments. *Journal of Consulting and Clinical Psychology, 66,* 19–36.

Lahey, B. B., McBurnett, K., & Loeber, R. (2000). Are Attention-Deficit/Hyperactivity Disorder and Oppositional Defiant Disorder developmental precursors to Conduct Disorder? In A. J. Sameroff, M. Lewis, & S. M. Miller (Eds.), *Handbook of developmental psychopathology* (2nd ed., pp. 431–446). New York: Kluwer Academic/Plenum Press.

Lahey, B. B., Miller, T. L., Gordon, R. A., & Riley, A. W. (1999). Developmental epidemiology of the disruptive behavior disorders. In H. C. Quay & A. E. Hogan (Eds.), *Handbook of disruptive behavior disorders* (pp. 23–48). New York: Kluwer Academic/Plenum Press.

Lochman, J. E., Burch, P. R., Curry, J. F., & Lampron, L. B. (1984). Treatment and generalization effects of cognitive-behavioral and goal-setting interventions with aggressive boys. *Journal of Consulting and Clinical Psychology, 52,* 915–916.

Lochman, J. E., & Szczepanski, R. G. (1999). Externalizing conditions. In V. L. Schwean & D. H. Saklofske (Eds.), *Psychosocial correlates of exceptionality* (pp. 219–246). New York: Plenum Press.

Lochman, J. E., & Wells, K. C. (1996). A social-cognitive intervention with aggressive children: Prevention effects and contextual implementation issues. In R. D. Peters & R. J. McMahon (Eds.), *Preventing childhood disorders, substance abuse, and delinquency* (pp. 111–143). Thousand Oaks, CA: Sage.

Loeber, R. (1990). Development and risk factors of juvenile antisocial behavior and delinquency. *Clinical Psychology Review, 10,* 1–42.

McGee, R., & Williams, S. (1999). Environmental risk factors in Oppositional Defiant Disorder and Conduct Disorder. In H. C. Quay & A. E. Hogan (Eds.), *Handbook of disruptive behavior disorders* (pp. 419–440). New York: Kluwer Academic/Plenum Press.

McMahon, R. J., & Estes, A. M. (1997). Conduct problems. In E. J. Mash & L. G. Terdal (Eds.), *Assessment of childhood disorders* (pp. 130–193). New York: Guilford Press.

Patterson, G. R. (1986). Performance models for antisocial boys. *American Psychologist, 41,* 145–166.

Patterson, G. R., Reid, J. B., & Dishion, T. J. (1992). *Antisocial boys.* Eugene, OR: Castalia.

Peed, S., Roberts, M., & Forehand, R. (1977). Evaluation of the effectiveness of a standardized parent training program in altering the interaction of mothers and their noncompliant children. *Behavior Modification, 1,* 323–350.

Rowe, R., Maughan, B., Pickles, A., Costello, E. J., & Angold, A. (2002). The relationship between *DSM-IV* Oppositional Defiant Disorder and Conduct Disorder: Findings from the Great Smoky Mountains study. *Journal of Child Psychology and Psychiatry and Allied Disciplines, 43,* 365–373.

Sanson, A., & Prior, M. (1999). Temperament and behavioral precursors to Oppositional Defiant Disorder and Conduct Disorder. In H. C. Quay & A. E. Hogan (Eds.), *Handbook of disruptive behavior disorders* (pp. 23–48). New York: Kluwer Academic/Plenum Press.

Silverthorn, P. (2001). Oppositional Defiant Disorder. In H. Orvaschel, J. Faust, & M. Hersen (Eds.), *Handbook of conceptualization and treatment of child psychopathology* (pp. 41–56). Amsterdam: Pergamon/Elsevier.

Tremblay, R. E., LeMarquand, D., & Vitaro, F. (1999). The prevention of Oppositional Defiant Disorder and Conduct Disorder. In H. C. Quay & A. E. Hogan (Eds.), *Handbook of disruptive behavior disorders* (pp. 525–555). New York: Kluwer Academic/Plenum Press.

Vitaro, F., Brendgen, M., Pagani, L., Tremblay, R. E., & McDuff, P. (1999). Disruptive behavior, peer association, and Conduct Disorder: Testing the developmental links through early intervention. *Development and Psychopathology, 11,* 287–304.

Webster-Stratton, C. (1994). Advancing videotape parent training: A comparison study. *Journal of Consulting and Clinical Psychology, 62,* 583–593.

Wiltz, N. A., & Patterson, G. R. (1974). An evaluation of parent training procedures designed to alter inappropriate aggressive behavior of boys. *Behavior Therapy, 5,* 215–221.

Tammy D. Barry
Texas A&M University

John E. Lochman
University of Alabama

OPTIC NERVE

The sensory visual system begins with light stimulation of the retinal photoreceptors. The information is transmitted to the retinal ganglion cells and then transits the orbit and the optic canal as the optic nerve. The information then crosses in the optic chiasm, synapses in the lateral geniculate, and projects to the striate cortex. The optic nerve is a tract that is myelinated by oligodendrocytes, and therefore is considered part of the central nervous system. The one million axons not only transmit information about light, contrast, and color but also participate in setting circadian rhythms via projections to the hypothalamus. An intact anterior visual pathway is essential for normal visual function and pupillary reaction.

Anatomy of the Retinal Ganglion Cells

The photoreceptors—the rods and cones—sense light and initiate the neuroelectrical signal, which is processed by the 12 retinal layers. The processed information is then transmitted to individual retinal ganglion cells. Each retinal ganglion cell then sends a myelinated axon to converge at the optic disc (the optic nerve head visible on retinoscopy). Ganglion cells in the macular region provide central vision and send their axons directly from the fovea to the temporal optic disc (the papillomacular bundle). Fibers from the peripheral nasal retina enter the nasal optic disc, while the temporal retinal fibers enter the superior and inferior aspects of the optic disc (superior and inferior arcuate bundles). The ganglion cell axons comprise the nerve fiber layer, which can be viewed with a direct ophthalmoscope. These fibers are best appreciated through a dilated pupil using green illumination. The surface nerve fiber layer derives its vascular supply from the central retinal artery and its branches. Pathologic states of the retina or optic nerve may result in nerve fiber layer loss (ganglion cell axon death) that allows a clearer view of the retinal vessels.

Anatomy of the Optic Nerve Head

The optic nerve head is divided into three regions: retinal (prelaminar), choroidal (laminar), and scleral (retrolaminar). The lamina cribrosa is a grouping of perforations in the choroid and sclera through which the retinal ganglion cells exit. Although there are regional density differences, the connective tissue forms a tight seal that prevents leaking except under very high pressure.

The optic nerve head is composed of ganglion cell axons and a laminar matrix of astrocytes, capillaries, and fibroblasts. The axons account for 90% of the optic nerve head. The size and exit angle of the scleral canal varies from individual to individual. It lies approximately 3 mm nasal to the fovea and is an optically blind region due to the lack of photoreceptors. This blind spot is present on all visual fields, covers at least 5 degrees of visual space and lies 15 degrees temporal to fixation. The central retinal artery is a branch of the ophthalmic artery and pierces the optic nerve sheath inferiorly at 10 to 12 mm behind the globe, then emerges at the center of the disc.

The prelaminar region of the optic nerve head receives blood supply from the four short posterior ciliary vessels. In contrast, the short posterior ciliary, peripapillary choroidal vessels, and pial arterial network (the incomplete circle of Zinn–Haller) perfuse the laminar aspect of the nerve.

Anatomy of the Optic Nerve

The optic nerve has three meningeal layers: the dura, the arachnoid, and the pia. The subarachnoid space is filled with cerebrospinal fluid that is continuous with the central subarachnoid space.

The optic nerve is 50 mm but individual variation is common. In addition to the one millimeter intraocular component (the optic nerve head), the optic nerve has three other portions: intraorbital, intracanalicular, and intracranial. The intraorbital optic nerve segment is the longest and is often serpiginous. The ophthalmic artery, a branch of the internal carotid artery just as it exits the cavernous sinus, perfuses the orbital portion. The intracanalicular portion lies within the optic canal formed by the lesser wing of the sphenoid bone, and receives perfusion from the ophthalmic and internal carotid arteries. The intracranial portion of the optic nerve continues as the optic chiasm and then the optic tracts. The intracranial aspect of the optic nerve has multiple vascular sources, including the internal carotid, anterior cerebral, anterior communicating, and ophthalmic arteries.

The orbital optic nerve is myelinated posterior to the lamina cribrosa and, by definition, extends from the globe to the optic canal. The 20 to 30 mm segment has a redundancy that allows marked proptosis (usually at least 9 mm) prior to tethering of the optic nerve, which may be visualized on neuroimaging. Just prior to entering the optic canal, the optic nerve is enveloped in the annulus of Zinn—a condensation of the tendonous insertions of the recti muscles.

The optic canal runs posterior and medial and has approximate dimensions of 10 mm long by 5 mm wide. The canal is thinnest medially where the optic nerve travels adjacent to the sphenoid sinus and posterior ethmoid cells. In addition to the optic nerve, the canal contains the ophthalmic artery and a sympathetic plexus. The periosteums of the sphenoid bone and the dura of the optic nerve are fused within the canal. The intracanalicular optic nerve is thereby tethered and prone to compression by any space-occupying lesions.

As the optic nerve exits the optic canal it ascends and converges posteromedially to form the optic chiasm. A majority (53%) of ganglion cell axons from the nasal retina cross in the chiasm and join the uncrossed temporal contralateral fibers. These fibers then continue hemi-decussated in the optic tract. The optic chiasm is adjacent to the floor of the third ventricle and inferior to the pituitary gland.

Most ganglion cell axons terminate in one of the six layers of the lateral geniculate, where information is processed and then projected to the visual cortex via the optic radiations. These axons contain visual and pupillomotor information, and some fibers ascend to the hypothalamus and contribute to circadian control of diurnal rhythms.

Common Pathologic States of the Optic Nerve

Optic nerve function can be impaired by changes in its blood supply, or by inflammation, demyelination, or compression. The hallmark of optic nerve dysfunction is the afferent pupillary defect (Marcus Gunn pupil). The involved optic nerve is not transmitting as much light to the visual pathways as does the optic nerve on the normal side, so the involved pupil does not constrict as briskly and redilates more readily. Other findings include impaired color vision, central visual acuity, and a visual field defect. The optic nerve head may be normal, edematous, or pale.

Acute ischemic optic neuropathy occurs in the patient's fifth or sixth decade, and characteristically presents with acute, painless, unilateral loss of vision that is noticed upon awakening. The optic nerve typically has sectoral edema and the most common visual field defect is inferior altitudinal loss. Most patients do not regain normal visual function. Aspirin should be prescribed to prevent contralateral involvement. A sedimentation rate should be obtained to rule out temporal arteritis. If systemic symptoms of malaise, weight loss, or temporal pain are present, a temporal artery biopsy should be performed.

Optic neuritis typically occurs in women in their second or third decade. The visual loss is acute and accompanied by pain that is exacerbated with eye movement. The optic nerve head is often normal, but the visual field is abnormal. An afferent pupillary defect is present unless the contralateral side has been previously damaged. Most patients begin to improve in six weeks and regain near-normal visual function. Recurrent bouts of optic neuritis or magnetic resonance imaging evidence of multifocal periventricular demyelination make the diagnosis of multiple sclerosis likely. Acute visual loss should be treated with a 3-day course of intravenous Methylprednisolone followed by an oral Prednisone taper. Oral corticosteroids alone are contraindicated because they increase the risk of subsequent episodes.

Compressive optic neuropathy may occur from intraorbital tumors, optic nerve tumors, intracranial expansions of the sphenoid wing, or increased intracranial pressure. Enlargement of the extraocular muscles—as seen in thyroid-associated ophthalmopathy—can also compress the optic nerve at the orbital apex. The most common orbital tumor in adults is the cavernous hemangioma. Other, less common masses include schwannomas, neurofibromas, lymphomas, and hemangiopericytomas. Optic nerve meningiomas typically occur in middle-aged women, while optic nerve gliomas present in the first decade without a gender predilection. Sphenoid wing meningiomas are much more common than either of these primary optic nerve tumors. Intervention should be considered when proptosis (globe protrusion due to tumor growth) is dramatic or visual function is significantly impaired. Intraorbital tumors can be surgically excised allowing preservation of vision. Optic nerve tumors, in contrast, can not be removed without resulting in complete visual loss. Sphenoid wing meningiomas are approached intracranially, but complete surgical excision is difficult. External beam radiation is useful for lymphomas, optic nerve meningiomas, and incompletely-excised sphenoid wing meningiomas.

Thyroid-associated ophthalmopathy presents with proptosis, double vision, and periorbital swelling. In less than 10% of cases, the optic nerve becomes compressed by the enlarged extraocular muscles. Intravenous corticosteroids, external beam radiation, and orbital decompression have all been successfully used to relieve the pressure on the optic nerve.

Pseudotumor cerebri (intracranial hypertension) characteristically presents in young, obese women. Transient visual loss, double vision, and headaches precede visual loss. Bilateral optic nerve edema is present in most cases. Neuroimaging should be performed to rule out an intracranial tumor; a lumbar puncture is then performed to confirm elevated intracranial pressure. Diamox (1–2 g/day) is effective in controlling the symptoms and preventing visual loss. A Lumboperitoneal shunt or optic nerve sheath fenestration should be performed if medical management is inadequate.

SUGGESTED READING

Bill, A. (1993). Vascular physiology of the optic nerve. In R. Varma & G. L. Spaeth (Eds.), *The optic nerve in glaucoma* (pp. 37–50). Philadelphia: J.B. Lippincott.

Beck, R. W., & Clearly, P. A. (1993). Optic neuritis treatment trial. *Archives of Ophthalmology, 111,* 773–775.

Hayreh, S. S. (1974). Anatomy and physiology of the optic nerve head. *Transactions of the American Academy of Ophthalmology & Otolaryngology, 78,* 240–254.

Jonas, J. B., & Naumann, G. O. (1993). Optic nerve: Its embryology, histology, and morphology. In R. Varma & G. L. Spaeth (Eds.), *The optic nerve in glaucoma* (pp. 3–26). Philadelphia: J.B. Lippincott.

Kupersmith, M. J., Frohman, L., Sanderson, M., Jacobs, J., Hirschfeld, J., Ku, C., & Warren, F. A. (1997). Aspirin reduces the incidence of second eye NAION: A retrospective study. *Journal of Neuro-ophthalmology, 17*(40), 250–253.

Pollock, S. C., & Miller, N. R. (1986). The retinal nerve fiber layer. *International Ophthalmology Clinic, 26,* 201–221.

Rizzo, J. F., & Lessell, S. (1991). Optic neuritis and ischemic optic neuropathy. *Archives of Ophthalmology, 109,* 1668–1672.

Sadun, A. A. (1998). Anatomy and physiology of the optic nerve. In N. R. Miller & N. J. Newman (Eds.), *Walsh and Hoyt's clinical neuro-ophthalmology* (pp. 57–83). Baltimore: Williams & Wilkins.

Kimberly P. Cockerham
Allegheny Opthalmic and Orbital Associates, Pittsburgh

OPTIMAL FUNCTIONING

The area of optimal functioning was introduced into modern scientific psychology by Marie Jahoda. This area of psychology is a scientific investigation of what the person is capable of becoming, of the best the person can be, and of the way the person can realize any number of personal potentials.

Self-Actualization

Abraham Maslow's (1971) investigation of optimal functioning asserts that there are two basic realms of human need. One, called the D or deficiency realm, is composed of the things we need to be functioning persons. These include the physiological needs such as food and water; the safety needs to be protected from chaos; the love and belongingness needs to be included in a group to protect us from loneliness; and our esteem needs for self-respect and self-esteem. These are needs that must be met for us to be adequate as human beings.

The B needs—our needs for self-actualization and our aesthetic needs—enable us to be self-actualizing human beings. Maslow posited that these B-level needs, or metaneeds, are just as necessary as the D-level needs. If D needs are not met, one becomes ill physiologically and psychologically. If the B-level needs are not met, one develops metapathologies. Following Maslow's lead, Shostrom (1962, 1975) developed two inventories to measure self-actualization. Building directly on Shostrom's work, Jones and Crandall (1986, 1991) developed a short (15-item) index. In contrast, Summerlin and Bundrick (1996) developed a brief index by going back to Maslow's concept of needs hierarchy.

For Maslow, self-actualized persons are aided in their development by intense moments of ecstasy, joy, and insight called peak experiences. There are moments of transcendence that take a person beyond self-actualization to what Maslow called the Z realm, a realm beyond the self that transcends both space and time. Recently, Csikszentmihalyi (1996, 1997) has expanded the notion of peak experience in his concept of "flow."

Beautiful and Noble Persons

Working within the tradition of Maslow's approach, Landsman (1974) developed a system for describing and empirically investigating the optimal functioning person, "the Beautiful and Noble Person." Landsman described his Beautiful and Noble Person as a self that proceeds from: (1) the passionate self, a self-expressive, self-enjoying state; to (2) the environment-loving self, where the person cares deeply for the physical environment and the tasks to be accomplished in the world; and finally to (3) the compassionate self, which enables the person to be loving and caring toward other persons. Working within the Landsman tradition, Privette (2001) has investigated positive and peak experiences in general, as well as in the specific areas of sports and athletic performance (1997) and business (Thornton, Privette, & Bundrick, 1999).

Fully Functioning Person

Rogers (1959, 1980) described his idea of the optimal functioning or, in his terms, "fully functioning" person. In contrast to Maslow, Rogers emphasized the process of being fully functioning as it occurs moment by moment in every person's life, rather than being primarily concerned with describing characteristics of persons. Rogers's emphasis is on process, rather than structural components of the optimally functioning person.

Rogers starts with the assumption that all people have the capacity to actualize or complete their own inner nature. The key is for people to remain in contact with their deepest feelings, which Rogers called organismic experiences. These direct and deeper feelings can be symbolized accurately in the person's awareness or they can be distorted. Optimal functioning is promoted when the person is able to be fully aware of this deeper, direct organismic level. The person must be able to develop the kind of self that is able to be congruent with the person's own deep feelings or experiences.

Psychology of Optimal Persons

Another formulation of optimal functioning centering on the concept of process that emphasizes constant change is Kelly's (1980) formulation of the psychology of an optimal person. The unit of analysis is the personal construct, a bipolar meaning dimension a person might hold, such as seeing people as loving versus rejecting. The personality of the individual is made up of a number of these personal construct dimensions. Kelly's system of optimal functioning requires that each individual use his or her system of personal meaning in order to complete what he termed "full cycles of experiences." By this, he meant that each individual must create his or her own conceptions of the world in such a way that these conceptions are continually tested and reevaluated. The work within this framework has centered on ways to evaluate each of the steps and to promote a progression through these steps as elaborated by Epting and Amerikaner (1980). The concern in construct theory is with the way in which people invent or create themselves rather than with their uncovering or discerning an inner self.

Optimal Personality Traits

Coan (1977) undertook a multivariate study of optimal functioning persons, and later elaborated the theoretical implications of this work. In this empirical approach, Coan employed a battery of tests that included measures pertaining to phenomenal consistency, experience of control, scope of awareness, openness to experience, independence, self-insight, and various other aspects of attitudes, beliefs, and adjustments. The final factor analysis yielded 19 obliquely rotated factors, though no single general factor was found that could represent a global personality trait of self-actualization. Coan suggests, from his analysis as well as from readings of Eastern and Western theories, that five basic attributes characterize the ideal human condition: efficiency, creativity, inner harmony, relatedness, and transcendecy. In a similar fashion, Hanin (1995, 2000) has developed the concept of Zones of Optimal Functioning (ZOF) with regard to athletic performance, suggesting that the ZOF for each individual is unique and dependent on various factors and environmental influences. Recently, Kasser and Ryan (2001) have investigated the relationship between optimal functioning and goal setting with college students.

REFERENCES

Coan, R. W. (1977). *Hero, artist, sage, or saint.* New York: Columbia University Press.

Crandall, R., & Jones, A. (1991). Issues in self-actualization measurement. *Journal of Social Behavior and Personality, 6,* 339–344.

Csikszentmihalyi, M. (1996). *Creativity: Flow and the psychology of discovery and invention.* New York: Harper Collins.

Csikszentmihalyi, M. (1997). *Finding flow: The psychology of engagement with everyday life.* New York: Basic.

Epting, F., & Amerikaner, M. (1980). Optimal functioning: A personal construct approach. In A. W. Landfield & L. M. Leitner (Eds.), *Personal construct psychology: Psychotherapy and personality.* New York: Wiley.

Hanin, Y. L. (1995). Individual zones of optimal functioning (IZOF) model: An idiographic approach to anxiety. In K. Henschen & W. Straub (Eds.), *Sport psychology: An analysis of athlete behavior* (pp. 103–119). Longmeadow, MA: Mouvement.

Hanin, Y. L. (2000). Individual zones of optimal functioning (IZOF) model: Emotion-performance relationship in sport. In Y. Hanin (Ed.), *Emotions in sport* (pp. 93–111). Champaign, IL: Human Kinetics.

Jones, A., & Crandall, R. (1986). Validation of a short index of self-actualization. *Personality and Social Psychology Bulletin, 12,* 63–73.

Kasser, T., & Ryan, R. M. (2001). Be careful what you wish for: Optimal functioning and the relative attainment of intrinsic and extrinsic goals. In P. Schmuck & K. M. Sheldon (Eds.), *Life goals and well-being: Towards a positive psychology of human striving* (pp. 116–131). Kirkland, WA: Hogrefe & Huber.

Kelly, G. A. (1980). A psychology of the optimal man. In A. W. Landfield & L. M. Leitner (Eds.), *Personal construct psychology: Psychotherapy and personality.* New York: Wiley.

Landsman, T. (1974). The humanizer. *American Journal of Orthopsychiatry, 44,* 345–352.

Maslow, A. H. (1971). *The farther reaches of human nature.* New York: Viking.

Privette, G. (1997). Psychological processes of peak, average, and failing performance in sport. *International Journal of Sports Psychology, 28*(4), 323–334.

Privette, G. (2001). Defining moments of self-actualization: Peak performance and peak experience. In K. J. Schneider, J. F. T. Bugental, & J. F. Pierson (Eds.), *The handbook of humanistic psychology: Leading edges in theory, research, and practice.* Thousand Oaks, CA: Sage.

Rogers, C. A. (1959). A theory of interpersonal relationships, as developed in the client-centered framework. In S. Koch (Ed.), *Psychology: A study of science: Vol. III. Formulations of the personal and social context.* New York: McGraw-Hill.

Rogers, C. A. (1980). *A way of being.* Boston: Houghton Mifflin.

Shostrom, E. L. (1962). *Manual for the Personal Orientation Inventory (POI): An inventory for the measurement of self-actualization.* San Diego, CA: Educational and Industrial Testing Service.

Shostrom, E. L. (1975). *Personal Orientation Dimension (POD).* San Diego, CA: Educational and Industrial Testing Service.

Summerlin, J. R., & Bundrick, C. M. (1996). Brief index of self-actualization: A measure of Maslow's model. *Journal of Social Behavior and Personality, 11*(2), 253–271.

Thornton, F., Privette, G., & Bundrick, C. M. (1999). Peak performance of business leaders: An experience parallel to self-actualization theory. *Journal of Business & Psychology, 14*(2), 253–264.

Franz R. Epting
D. Philip
D. I. Suchman
University of Florida

OXYTOCIN

Oxytocin is a peptide hormone and neuromodulator with a range of physiological and psychological effects related to reproduction and social behavior. Oxytocin is produced predominantly in the hypothalamus and oxytocin-containing nerve terminals project to the posterior pituitary for release into general circulation, where it acts as a hormone. Oxytocin plays important roles in regulating both the progression of labor and lactation. Oxytocin is the most potent uterotonic substance known, and pitocin, a synthetic oxytocin, is widely used by physicians to stimulate the progression of labor. Nipple stimulation during nursing stimulates synchronous firing of hypothalamic neurons via a reflex arch, resulting in the pulsatile release of oxytocin from the mother's pituitary gland. This elevation in oxytocin stimulates milk ejection by causing myoepithelial cells in the mammary gland to contract.

Oxytocin-containing nerve terminals also project to sites within the central nervous system, where it acts as a neuromodulator to affect emotionality and behavior. Oxytocin receptors are found in discrete limbic brain areas known to regulate behavior. Most of our understanding of the role of central oxytocin is derived from animal studies, and therefore the findings may or may not be relevant to humans.

Reproductive Behavior

In animal models, central oxytocin facilitates female sexual behavior, or receptivity. Receptivity in rodents is regulated primarily by the sequential actions of ovarian estrogen and progesterone. Estrogen increases oxytocin synthesis and the numbers of oxytocin receptors in regions of the hypothalamus involved in the regulation of sexual behavior. Oxytocin injections into the hypothalamus of estrogen-primed female rats facilitate female sexual behavior, while oxytocin antagonists block this behavior. Oxytocin may also play a role in sexual performance in males. For example, oxytocin levels in the cerebrospinal fluid are elevated after ejaculation in male rats and oxytocin injections decrease the latency to ejaculation. Oxytocin also stimulates the occurrence of spontaneous, noncontact penile erections in male rats. The role of oxytocin in human sexuality is unclear; however, plasma oxytocin levels increase during sexual arousal and peak at orgasm in both men and women.

Social Memory

Animals living in social groups must be able to recognize familiar individuals. Several studies have suggested a role for oxytocin in the formation or expression of social memory. In rodents, social memory is based primarily on olfactory cues and can be quantified by measuring the decrease in olfactory investigation after repeated exposure to the same individual. Low doses of oxytocin enhance the formation of social memory in rats. Mice lacking a functional oxytocin gene fail to recognize individuals even after repeated exposure, but display normal social memory after a single injection of oxytocin. It is not known whether oxytocin plays a significant role in social memory for species in which individual recognition is not based on olfactory cues.

Social Attachment and Affiliation

Strong social attachments are essential for successful reproduction in mammals. Oxytocin is involved in the formation of social attachments between mother and offspring, and in monogamous species, between mates. In many species, virgin females fail to display nurturing behavior toward infants, but females display extensive maternal care for their offspring beginning moments after giving birth. Virgin rats receiving oxytocin injections into the brain display nurturing behavior toward pups, while interfering with oxytocin transmission interferes with the normal onset of maternal care in parturient dams. Once initiated, blocking oxytocin transmission does not interfere with maternal behavior, suggesting that oxytocin is important for the initiation, but not the maintenance, of maternal behavior. In sheep, oxytocin is released in the brain within 15 minutes of delivery of the lamb. Infusion of oxytocin into the brain of an estrogen-primed ewe elicits full maternal responsiveness within 30 seconds. Oxytocin also appears to facilitate the selective bond between the mother and her offspring, probably through an olfactory recognition mechanism. Ewes will allow their own lamb to suckle while rejecting other lambs. Stimulating oxytocin release during exposure to an unfamiliar lamb stimulates the ewe to bond with that lamb even if she has previously bonded with her own lamb. It is unclear whether oxytocin significantly influences the mother–infant bond in humans, although correlational studies suggest that endogenous oxytocin does influence personality traits in postpartum women. Women who give birth by cesarean section have fewer oxytocin pulses during breastfeeding than those who give birth vaginally, and are less likely to describe themselves during the postpartum period as exhibiting a calm personality or high levels of sociality. In mothers delivering by cesarean section, oxytocin levels are correlated with the degree of openness to social interactions and with calmness.

Like the bond between a mother and infant, strong social attachments are formed between mates in monogamous species. Prairie voles are a monogamous species of rodent and have been extensively studied as a model for understanding the neural basis of monogamy. In the prairie vole, oxytocin plays a role in formation of the bond of the female for the male. Infusion of oxytocin into the brain of a female prairie vole even in the absence of mating results in the formation of a pair bond. Oxytocin also enhances nonsexual affiliative behaviors. For example, experiments examining the effects of central oxytocin on social interaction in rodents have shown that oxytocin increases the time spent in physical contact with other individuals. There is speculation that central oxytocin may underlie the reinforcing nature of positive social interactions.

The role of oxytocin in human social relationships remains to be determined. Sex in humans may play a role in strengthening the emotional attachments between partners, and vaginocervical stimulation, nipple stimulation, and orgasm, each components of human sexuality, facilitate oxytocin release.

Anxiety

Oxytocin reduces the physiological reaction to stressful situations. Lactating animals and humans exhibit a clear decreased response to stressors. Lactating rats show an attenuated elevation in stress hormone in response to white noise compared to virgins. Infusion of oxytocin in virgin rats also dampens the elevation of stress hormones in response to stress, suggesting that the increased oxytocin released during lactation may be acting to buffer the individual from environmental stressors. Oxytocin also has anxiolytic effects in behavioral assays of anxiety, such as the elevated plus maze.

Oxytocin is not known to be directly involved in any psychiatric disorders; however, some interesting correlations have been reported. Autism is a disease characterized by, among other symptoms, deficits in social reciprocity in humans. One study has found that autistic children have decreased levels of plasma oxytocin compared to age-matched control children.

SUGGESTED READING

Carter, C. S. (1998). Neuroendocrine perspectives on social attachment and love. *Psychoneuroendocrinology, 23,* 779–818.

Engelmann, M., Wotjak, C. T., Neumann, I., Ludwig, M., & Landgraf, R. (1996). Behavioral consequences of intracerebral vasopressin and oxytocin: Focus on learning and memory. *Neuroscience and Biobehavioral Reviews, 20,* 341–358.

Uvnäs-Moberg, K. (1998). Oxytocin may mediate the benefits of positive social interaction and emotions. *Psychoneuroendocrinology, 23,* 819–835.

Young, L. J. (2001). The neurobiology of social recognition, approach, and avoidance. *Biological Psychiatry, 51,* 18–26.

Larry J. Young
Emory University

P

PAIN: COPING STRATEGIES

From an early age, virtually everyone has experience with brief, relatively mild pain caused by cuts, insect bites, minor burns, bruises, toothaches, stomachaches, and routine medical and dental procedures. In addition to these relatively minor painful experiences, some individuals also will experience acute pain from major trauma, surgery, and invasive medical procedures. Others may even experience persistent pain such as chronic back pain, headaches, or pain secondary to chronic illness such as arthritis. Whenever a person is confronted with a painful situation, there are demands or requirements placed on that individual for certain responses. For example, a child receiving an injection must hold his or her arm still while a needle is inserted into the arm. Individuals spontaneously react in these situations and use various strategies to deal with pain and the demands of the situation.

Cognitive Coping Strategies

Mental strategies or ways to use thoughts or imagination to cope with pain are usually called *cognitive coping strategies.* Distraction involves thinking about other things to divert attention from pain and can be internal, such as imagining a pleasant scene, or external, such as focusing on a specific aspect of the environment. Reinterpreting pain sensations is imagining that the pain is something else, such as numbness or a warm feeling. Calming self-statements refers to statements that one might tell oneself to provide comfort or encouragement (e.g., "I know I can handle this"). Ignoring pain is denying that the pain exists. Wishful thinking, praying, or hoping involves telling oneself that the pain will go away some day by faith, an act of God, or something magical. Fear and anger self-statements are statements one might tell oneself that promote fear or anger, such as "I am afraid I am going to die." Catastrophizing refers to the use of negative self-statements and overly pessimistic thoughts about the future (e.g., "I can't deal with the pain"). Cognitive restructuring refers to a process of recognizing negative thoughts and changing them to more realistic and rational thoughts.

Behavioral Coping Strategies

Overt things that a person might actually do to cope with pain are called *behavioral coping strategies.* Increasing behavioral activity involves actively engaging in activities such as reading or visiting with friends to stay busy and unfocused on pain. Pacing activity involves taking regular, planned rest breaks to avoid overdoing and experiencing increases in pain. Isolation refers to withdrawing from social contact to cope with pain. Resting refers to reclining in bed or on the couch. Relaxation involves attempting to decrease physiological arousal by remaining calm and relaxing muscles. Relaxation also is sometimes referred to as a physiological coping strategy, because it may include direct physical benefits.

Some coping strategies are effective and facilitate good adjustment, whereas other strategies are ineffective and may promote additional pain and suffering. Although intuitively certain strategies appear effective and others seem ineffective, empirical studies are needed to demonstrate the relationship between coping strategies and adjustment. This is especially important because some strategies are effective in one situation but not the next, or for one person but not another.

Chronic Pain

Most individuals probably begin to develop strategies for coping with pain from an early age and from exposure to relatively minor painful experiences. Yet the research in this area has progressed almost backward, with initial studies focusing on coping strategies used by chronic pain populations such as patients with chronic back pain or pain secondary to disease (e.g., arthritis and sickle cell disease).

One of the first instruments designed to assess pain coping strategies systematically was the coping strategies questionnaire (CSQ) developed by Rosensteil and Keefe. The CSQ measures the frequency with which individuals use various cognitive and behavioral coping strategies to deal with pain. Research using the CSQ with chronic pain patients has found that pain coping strategies can be reliably assessed and are predictive of pain, psychosocial adjustment, and functional capacity. Chronic pain patients who are high on catastrophizing and perceived inability to control and decrease pain have higher levels of depression and anxiety and overall physical impairment. Chronic pain patients who take a more active approach to managing pain by using a variety of cognitive and behavioral strategies have been found, in at least some studies, to have better functional adjustment (i.e., remain more active in work and social activities). These results have been replicated across several research laboratories and with several populations of chronic pain patients (chronic back pain, headaches, osteoarthritis, rheumatoid arthritis, and sickle cell disease).

Taken together, the studies with chronic pain populations have generally concluded that although there seem to be some positive effects due to active coping efforts, negative thinking appears to be a more potent adverse influence on adjustment. Also, longitudinal studies have shown that coping strategies measured at one point in time are predictive of adjustment at follow-up. Thus maladaptive copers may continue to be at risk for future adjustment problems.

Stability and Change in Coping Strategies

Because of the significance of coping style in adjustment to chronic pain, researchers have attempted to determine whether the strategies used by individuals to cope with pain tend to be stable or to change over time.

Two approaches have been used to study this issue. The first approach has been to compare coping strategies assessed during a baseline assessment to coping strategies measured at follow-up (e.g., 1 year later) with no systematic intervention occurring between the two assessment periods. Results have shown that without intervention, coping strategies are relatively stable over time, suggesting that some individuals persist in ineffective coping efforts. This stability in coping style appears to be unrelated to changes in disease severity. That is, although disease severity may lessen, this does not automatically translate into improved coping efforts, and even if there is an increase in disease severity over time, this does not necessarily mean that there will be further deterioration in adjustment. Although coping tends to be relatively stable, individuals who do become more and more negative in their thinking may experience even further deterioration in functional capacity and psychosocial adjustment over time.

The second approach to examining changes in pain coping strategies in chronic pain patients has been intervention studies. These studies have attempted to improve pain coping by training individuals in cognitive and behavioral pain coping skills. These studies have shown that with intervention, pain coping skills can be improved, and improvements in pain coping skills translate into improvements of psychosocial and functional adjustment. For example, in one study, Keefe and coworkers trained a group of patients with osteoarthritic knee pain to use relaxation, imagery, distraction, cognitive restructuring, and pacing activity. Compared with a control group, trained subjects had lower levels of pain and psychological disability. Furthermore, individuals in the pain coping skills group who had greatest positive change in their coping strategy use (i.e., increased perceived effectiveness) had the most improvements in physical abilities. Similar findings have been reported across several types of pain problems.

Taken together, these results suggest that without intervention, the strategies an individual uses to cope with chronic pain are relatively stable over time. Change in pain coping skills is possible, however, and cognitive-behavioral approaches appear to provide an effective means to train individuals with various chronic pain problems to use more effective coping strategies.

Acute Pain

Acute pain may result from events ranging from minor experiences to pain secondary to surgery or invasive procedures. As with chronic pain, when an individual is confronted with acute pain, he or she reacts spontaneously and uses various strategies to cope. Because acute pain situations are often also stressful and anxiety provoking, coping strategies used in these situations often include strategies to deal both with pain and with anxiety.

Among the earliest attempts to examine coping strategies used in acute pain situations were studies that described preoperative and postoperative adults as either active or avoidant copers. Active copers were considered persons who approached the painful stimulus (i.e., surgery) by seeking out information, dealing with it rationally, and using cognitive strategies to cope. Avoidant copers (or those high on denial) were those who preferred not knowing information about their surgery or medical procedure, and actually became anxious and experienced more pain when provided with information. Conclusions based on these early studies are limited, however, because studies often attempted to categorize subjects into one of these patterns of coping based on informal interviews of questionable reliability.

More recently, systematic measures for assessing pain coping strategies in acute pain situations have been developed. Butler and coworkers developed the Cognitive Coping Strategy Inventory (CCSI) for use with postoperative pain populations. The inventory consists of subscales that are similar to dimensions found to be important in the measurement of chronic pain coping (i.e., catastrophizing, attention diversion, and imaginative inattention). Items, however, are more relevant to the acute pain experience. Research using the CCSI has found that this questionnaire is reliable and valid, and that coping strategies used by postoperative patients to deal with pain are related to recovery. For example, adults who are high on catastrophizing have higher levels of pain and functional disability after surgery.

Childhood Pain

The investigation of coping strategies in children confronting painful experiences is a relatively new area of research. In contrast to the work with adults in which questionnaires are primarily used to assess pain coping, most studies with children use interviews and observational methods to examine pain coping strategies.

Interview studies have used both open-ended and semi-structured formats to gather information on how children experience pain and what they do in response to it. For example, Ross and Ross interviewed a large sample of school-age children and asked them about the strategies that they used to cope with pain. Some of the children had chronic diseases such as sickle cell disease or hemophilia, but most had no major medical problems and responded in regard to their coping with more minor pain (e.g., cuts and bruises). Responding to open-ended questions, few children reported using self-initiated strategies to cope with pain. Of the small proportion that reported using strategies, distraction, thought stopping, and relaxation were among the more commonly reported strategies.

Observational studies of children coping with pain have focused primarily on children's reactions to painful procedures such as burn therapy or cancer-related treatments (e.g., venipunctures, bone marrow aspirations). In these studies, observers record the frequency of behaviors exhibited by the child such as crying, seeking social support, information seeking, and verbal and motor resistance. Although these behaviors are usually considered a measure of distress, some of the behaviors also can be conceptualized as coping efforts exhibited by the child to manage the pain and stress of the situation.

A few recent studies have found that coping strategies could be reliably assessed using questionnaires in school age children. Using a modified version of the CSQ that was developed for adults, Gil and coworkers found that children who engaged in negative thinking and relied passively on strategies such as resting had more adjustment problems. This pattern of coping was associated with greater reductions in school and social activity, more frequent health care contacts, and more depression and anxiety. Children who took an active approach to managing pain by using a variety of cognitive and behavioral coping strategies were more active and required less frequent health care services.

The KIDCOPE developed by Spirito, Stark, and Williams is a questionnaire that has been designed specifically to assess coping strategies used by children to deal with stressful situations. The child identifies a recent stressful event to provide a context for responding to the coping strategy items. Given that pain is a common problem identified by children with medical problems, the KIDCOPE can be a useful instrument to assess pain coping strategies, especially because it is relatively brief and simple to complete.

Child Age and Sex

Although there appear to be almost no major differences in coping between girls and boys, differences in coping strategy use have been found across different ages. Older children tend to have more coping skills in their repertoire, especially more cognitive coping skills. Some data suggest that older children with chronic pain secondary to disease may rely more on negative thinking and passive coping strategies as they get older. By adolescence, some of their maladaptive coping patterns may become entrenched and resistant to change.

Parents

The relationship of the parent to coping and adjustment in children also has been a recent target of study. A number of studies have evaluated the effects of parent presence versus absence on child coping during painful procedures. Most of these studies have shown that although children exhibit less overt distress when their parents are absent, they may be physiologically and psychologically disturbed by their parents' absence and merely inhibiting their behavioral reaction. Thus, rather than removing the parents, researchers may need to investigate which behaviors of the parent are related to effective versus ineffective coping by children during painful procedures.

Coping strategies used by parents to cope with their own (the parent's) pain also may be related to adjustment in children with pain problems. One study found that parents who took an active approach to managing their own pain had children who remained more active during episodes of sickle cell pain. Furthermore, there appear to be significant relationships between pain coping strategies in parents and in their children, suggesting that children might learn how to cope with pain, in part, by observing their parents' reactions.

Clinical Implications

Coping skills training is now a regular part of most comprehensive approaches to chronic pain management. Multidisciplinary pain programs now often include groups or individual sessions in which patients are trained to use active coping skills and cognitive restructuring techniques to manage pain. Although this type of approach is not routine for the management of most acute pain problems, there is a growing recognition for the need to train coping strategies to those undergoing medical procedures. Perhaps the area that has received the most attention has been in preparing children for surgery or for repeated invasive medical procedures such as burn therapy or cancer-related treatments. Although this is usually not done until after the child has developed a significant problem coping with pain, some clinicians are beginning to recognize the need to help prepare children to cope with painful experiences before they become oversensitized.

Karen M. Gil
Duke University Medical Center

See also: **Self-Control**

PANIC DISORDER

Epidemiology and Course

Panic Disorder (PD) (with and without agoraphobia) is a debilitating condition with a lifetime prevalence of approximately 1.5% (American Psychiatric Association [ApA], 1994). Studies have demonstrated that this prevalence rate is relatively consistent throughout the world. Approximately twice as many women as men suffer from PD. Although PD typically first strikes between late adolescence and the mid-30s, it can also begin in childhood or in later life. Although data on the course of PD are lacking, PD appears to be a chronic condition that waxes and wanes in severity. Consequences of PD include feelings of poor physical and emotional health, impaired social functioning, financial dependency, and increased use of health and hospital emergency services.

Description

As defined in the fourth edition of the *Diagnostic and Statistical Manual of Mental Disorders* (ApA, 1994), the essential feature of PD is the experience of recurrent, unexpected panic attacks. A panic attack is defined as a discrete period of intense fear or discomfort that develops abruptly, reaches a peak within 10 minutes, and is accompanied by at least four of the following 13 symptoms: shortness of breath, dizziness, palpitations, trembling, sweating, choking sensation, nausea/abdominal distress, depersonalization, paresthesias (numbness/tingling), flushes/chills, chest pain, fear of dying, and fear of going crazy or doing something uncontrolled. To warrant the diagnosis of PD an individual must experience at least two unexpected panic attacks followed by at least one month of concern about having another panic attack. The frequency of attacks varies widely and ranges from several attacks each day to only a handful of attacks per year.

The vast majority of PD patients seeking treatment present with agoraphobia. Agoraphobia is the experience of anxiety in situations where escape might be difficult or where help may not be immediately available should a panic attack occur. Common agoraphobic situations include airplanes, buses, trains, elevators, being alone, or being in a crowd. As a result of the anxiety experienced in these situations, individuals often develop phobic avoidance resulting in a constricted lifestyle. The severity of agoraphobia ranges from mild to severe.

Causes Of PD

Following is a brief review of some of the most promising theories about the causes of PD.

Genetics

One line of evidence for a biological etiology of PD comes from studies that demonstrate that panic tends to run in families. These studies have found that approximately one half of all PD patients have at least one relative with PD, that first-degree relatives of PD patients are approximately five times more likely to develop PD than first-degree relatives of normal controls, and that PD and agoraphobia with panic attacks are more than five times as frequent in monozygotic twins than in dizygotic co-twins of patients with PD (Woodman & Crowe, 1995).

Neurotransmitter Theories

Biological theorists attempt to provide an indirect link between PD and specific neurotransmitter systems by assessing the effects of drugs on these neurotransmitter systems. Specifically, they attempt to demonstrate that drugs used to treat panic increase the availability of a specific neurotransmitter or its metabolite, while drugs that induce panic decrease the availability of the same neurotransmitter. An association may also be established by demonstrating that antipanic drugs decrease the availability of a specific neurotransmitter while panic-provoking drugs increase the availability of the same neurotransmitter. Neurotransmitters commonly implicated in the etiology of PD include norepinephrine, serotonin, and gamma-aminobutyric acid (GABA; Papp, Coplan, & Gorman, 1992).

Psychological Theories of PD

Several proposed psychological theories of PD are well supported by empirical data. This suggests that psychological factors are central to the etiology and maintenance of PD.

The cognitive model of PD proposes that panic attacks occur when individuals perceive certain somatic sensations as dangerous and interpret them to mean that they are about to experience sudden, imminent disaster (Clark, 1986). For example, individuals may develop a panic attack if they misinterpret heart palpitations as signaling an impending heart attack. The vicious cycle culminating in a panic attack begins when a stimulus perceived as threatening creates feelings of apprehension. If the somatic sensations that accompany this state of apprehension are catastrophically misinterpreted, the individual experiences a further increase in apprehension, elevated somatic sensations, and so on, until a full-blown panic attack occurs.

Pure behavioral models focus on the fact that panic attacks and agoraphobia are maintained by negative reinforcement. That is, individuals prone to panic attacks and agoraphobia avoid anxiety sensations and situations that may provoke anxiety. This leads to increased sensitization to anxiety symptoms and fuels further avoidance. Support for this model comes from learning theory and animal studies, as well as from treatment studies demonstrating that exposure-based treatments in which patients confront sensations and situations that were previously avoided lead to improvement (Barlow, 2001).

Treatment

Psychotherapy, specifically cognitive-behavioral therapy (CBT), and pharmacotherapy have both been shown to be effective treatments for PD (Wolfe & Maser, 1994). CBT consists of a number of treatment elements including psychoeducation, monitoring of panic, cognitive restructuring, anxiety management skills training, and in vivo exposure. Support for the efficacy of CBT for PD treatment is provided by extensive studies yielding high-quality data.

Four classes of medications have been shown to be effective in the treatment of PD. These medications are *selective serotonin reuptake inhibitors, tricyclic antidepressants, benzodiazepines,* and *monoamine oxidase inhibitors.* Studies demonstrate that medications from all four classes have similar efficacy. The choice of medication for a patient depends on a consideration of possible side effects, medication cost, and other clinical circumstances.

Studies that examine the effectiveness of combining CBT and antipanic medication compared to each modality separately have thus far been inconclusive. However, conventional clinical wisdom suggests that a combination is at least equivalent to either modality alone.

REFERENCES

American Psychiatric Association. (1994). *Diagnostic and statistical manual of mental disorders* (4th ed.). Washington, DC: Author.

Barlow, D. H. (2001). *Anxiety and its disorders* (2nd ed.). New York: Guilford Press.

Clark, D. M. (1986). A cognitive approach to panic. *Behaviour Research and Therapy, 24,* 461–471.

Papp, L. A., Coplan, J., & Gorman, J. M. (1992). Neurobiology of anxiety. In A. Tasman & M. B. Riba (Eds.), *Review of psychiatry* (Vol. 11, pp. 307–322). Washington, DC: American Psychiatric Association Press.

Wolfe, B. E., & Maser, J. D. (Eds.). (1994). *Treatment of Panic Disorder: A consensus development conference.* Washington, DC: American Psychiatric Association Press.

Woodman, C. L., & Crowe, R. R. (1995). The genetics of Panic Disorder. In G. Asnis & H. M. van Praag (Eds.), *Panic Disorder: Clinical, biological, and treatment aspects* (pp. 66–79). New York: Wiley.

William C. Sanderson
Hofstra University

See also: **Antidepressant Medications; Behavior Therapy; Neurotransmitters**

PARADIGMS

Paradigms are rules or regulations that set boundaries and direct actions toward accomplishing a goal successfully (Barker, 1992, p. 32). Kuhn (1970), a scientific historian, focused the attention of the scientific world on paradigms; he believed paradigms fit only the physical scientific world. Paradigms in action amount to a basic set of ideas or concepts that directs an individual's behavior, thereby setting parameters for the individual's standard way of working, or progressing toward a goal. This pattern becomes an individual's way of doing something or solving a problem.

Paradigms are found in every culture. Norms within every culture govern the boundaries of accepted behavior and become the proper way of doing things. When pattern changes occur, thus deviating from the established operating norms of any given situation, Barker (1992, p. 37) referred to this as "a paradigm shift . . . a change to a new game, a new set of rules."

In every generation, changes have been initiated by nonconformists who took risks to make paradigm shifts, because paradigms encourage conformity and the paradigm shifts create confusion. A simple example of a paradigm shift is when a person requests pie instead of the usual cake for a birthday; breaking from the custom of a birthday cake is a paradigm shift.

Within Western culture, many paradigm shifts have occurred. During the early 1900s, the Wright brothers created a paradigm shift with their invention of the airplane. Traditionalists believed that if God wanted humans to fly, we would have wings. Paradigm shifts led to vast changes in communications after the 1940s. Telephone calls, which used to require cranking a box on a party line, were transformed to single-party lines, worldwide calling, car phones, cordless phones, cellular phones, 800 numbers, and so forth. Each improvement marked a paradigm shift. Paradigms themselves range from challengeable to unchallengeable, and may include theories, models, and standards as well as frames of reference, ideologies, rituals, and compulsions (Barker, 1992, p. 35).

Family Institution

Before the 1940s, only a small percentage of women were in the job market, mostly doing office work. The basic paradigm before World War II was that women belonged at home with the children and the men were the breadwinners. At the time, this was an acceptable way of life. By 1950, however, a paradigm shift occurred. More women were entering the professional world. Many women entered the labor market so the family could have "extras," but later the second income became a necessity to survive the economic crunch.

Religion

Many changes have taken place in religious practices, for example, in the Roman Catholic Church since Vatican II. These changes include praying the Mass in the vernacular, the concept of healing of reconciliation, one hour of fasting before receiving communion, fewer statues, face-to-face confession, and increased lay ministries. Such changes met with considerable resistance. Ritzer (1975), in his interpretation of Kuhn's original work, stated that "the paradigm that emerges victorious is the one that is able to win the most converts." As new concepts gain more followers, the resistance to paradigm changes decreases and acceptance emerges.

Cognitive Development

Some presently accepted theories of cognitive growth and development that were originally paradigmatic are those by Erik Erikson, Sigmund Freud, Jean Piaget, and Lev Vygotsky. Another paradigm concerning intelligence is mentioned by Woolfolk (1993, pp. 111–116), and is based on the theories of Alfred Binet, Charles Spearman, L. L. Thurstone, J. P. Guilford, Howard Gardner, Robert Sternberg, and other theorists. Each presents guidelines and boundaries in methodology, standards, models, and procedures, and each specialty is under the whole umbrella of intelligence.

Education

As the needs of a society change, the educational process must change with it, thereby creating a paradigm shift. According to Drucker (1989), traditional education was rather terminal, ending with the attainment of a diploma or degree. However, today, because of continuing rapid changes in technology, education can not terminate at the time of degree completion. Continuing education is required as a result of paradigm shifts. Every employing institution becomes an educational facility as well as a place of employment. Drucker (1989, p. 252) stated "That major changes are ahead for schools and education is certain—the knowledge will demand them and the new learning theories and technologies will trigger them."

Technology

The word *paradigm* is used in all aspects of life because all facets of life have certain boundaries or parameters. Paradigms related to technology are changing rapidly in this highly technological age. Frequently, the changes are so rapid that the paradigm effect does not fully occur because new paradigms are continually being adopted. Our society, as well as the rest of the world, has come a long way from the days of Thomas S. Kuhn's original concept of paradigms.

Naisbitt (1984) stated that our lives and our social institutions are being transformed by the acceptance of the paradigm shift and by the recognition that we must change in order to survive. The paradigm shift alluded to by Naisbitt has taken place much more quickly than anticipated because of the rapid advancements in technology. Peters (1988, p. 518) stated that "integrity has been the hallmark of the superior organization through the ages . . . today's accelerating uncertainty gives the issue new importance."

Paradigm Shifts Over the Past Ten Years

Technology is accelerating very rapidly, thereby creating new paradigms faster than we can understand the present ones. New developments in the field of medicine include laser surgery, lasik surgery (eyes), laparoscopy, appendectomy, cholecystectomy (gallbladder), and many other advances. These are done either on an outpatient basis or a one-day hospitalization. In computer science, the Internet provides such features as the ability to buy and sell instantly, the use of e-mail, and access from anyplace a computer is available. As for telephones, cellular phones are replacing standard phones because you can receive and make calls just about any place. These phones are very compact. Television digital satellite dishes are replacing cable television, and compact discs and digital video discs (DVD) are used with computers and recording apparatus. Music can be heard on the computer via the internet. The invention of the personal digital assistant (PDA) allows individuals to maintain a personal data base. The business world now consists of mergers and acquisitions, a global economy, downsizing, and many more changes. These are just a few broad examples of some new paradigms in the last ten years.

Conclusion

Barker (1992, p. 36) stated, "the interrelationship of all these paradigms is crucial to the success and longevity of any culture or organization." Some paradigms are accepted more rapidly than others. If the need is great for a change, the paradigm shift will emerge quickly.

Paradigm shifts have occurred throughout the centuries, since the beginning of recorded history. As new concepts and ideas emerge, paradigm shifts will continue to occur in order to meet ever-changing human needs.

REFERENCES

Barker, J. A. (1992). *Future edge.* New York: William Morrow.

Drucker, P. F. (1989). *The new realities.* New York: Harper & Row.

Kuhn, T. S. (1970). *The structure of scientific revolution.* Chicago: University of Chicago Press.

Naisbitt, J. (1988). *Megatrends.* New York: W. A. Warner Communication Company.

Peters, T. (1988). *Thriving on chaos.* New York: Alfred A. Knopf.

Ritzer, G. (1975). *Sociology: A multiple paradigm science.* Boston: Allyn & Bacon.

Woolfolk, A. E. (1993). *Educational psychology.* Boston: Allyn & Bacon.

Peter A. Carich

PARADOXICAL INTERVENTION

Paradoxical interventions are psychotherapeutic tactics that seem to contradict the goals they are designed to achieve. For example, a therapist may prescribe that clients have an unwanted symptom deliberately or restrain them from changing. In the classic definition of a therapeutic double-bind or paradox, "an injunction is so structured that it (a) reinforces the behavior the patient expects to be changed, (b) implies that this reinforcement is the vehicle of change, and (c) thereby creates a paradox because the patient is told to change by remaining unchanged" (Watzlawick, Beavin, and Jackson, 1967, p. 241).

References to resolving problems with paradoxical interventions appear as early as the eighteenth century. In this century, Dunlap applied the technique of "negative practice" to problems such as stammering and enuresis. Rosen (1953), through "direct psychoanalysis," encouraged psychiatric patients to engage in aspects of their psychosis in order to prevent relapse, and Frankl (1960) used paradoxical intention to help his patients revise the meaning of their symptoms. The most influential literature on therapeutic paradox, however, derives from Bateson's 1952–1962 project on communication. Bateson, Jackson, Haley, Weakland, and others explored the role of paradoxical "double-bind" communications in resolving as well as creating problems. Influenced by systemic/cybernetic ideas and by the work of master hypnotist Milton Erickson, descendants of the Bateson project such as Haley, Weakland, Watzlawick, Fisch, and Selvini-Palazzoli and colleagues went on in the 1970s to develop family therapy models with paradox as a central feature. Around the same time, Frankl's paradoxical intention technique was adopted by behavior therapists who demonstrated its usefulness with specific symptoms such as insomnia, anxiety, urinary retention, and obsessions.

Although paradoxical interventions have been associated historically with particular theoretical frameworks, the current literature tends to treat them as techniques that can be applied and explained apart from the models in which they were developed. Indeed, paradoxical interventions cut across theoretical boundaries insofar as paradoxical elements can be found in virtually all schools of psychotherapy (Seltzer, 1986). Nevertheless, there are striking differences in how therapists of different theoretical orientations use paradoxical interventions. In comparing cognitive-behavioral and strategic-systemic approaches—the two frameworks most akin to therapeutic paradox—one finds that behavior therapists use "paradoxical intention" to interrupt within-person exacerbation cycles, while strategic-systems therapists use a wider variety of paradoxical interventions and more often focus on between-person (family) interaction. Another difference is that behavior therapists make their rationale explicit, while strategic therapists typically do not. In behavioral applications of paradoxical intention, for example, the therapist teaches the client to adopt a paradoxical attitude, explaining, for example, how the client's intention to force sleep is actually exacerbating the problem, and why a paradoxical intention to stay awake might make sleep come easier. The *intention* here is clearly the client's, not the therapist's, and the client is expected to do (or at least try to do) what he or she is told. In strategic applications, however, the therapist sometimes expects a patient or family to do the opposite of what is proposed, and in this sense the therapist's intention is paradoxical. In contrast to the openly shared, educational rationale of a behavior therapist, strategic therapists attempt to maximize compliance (or defiance) by framing suggestions in a manner consistent (or deliberately inconsistent) with the clients' own idiosyncratic world view (Fisch, Weakland, & Segal, 1982).

Types and Applications

Several schemes for classifying paradoxical interventions have been offered in the literature (Rohrbaugh, Tennen, Press, & White, 1981; Seltzer, 1986). Of the many types, the most commonly used are symptom prescription and restraint from change. Variations of these two techniques—asking clients to engage in the behavior they wish to eliminate or restraining them from changing—have been applied in both individual and family therapy. However, nearly all controlled studies of therapeutic paradox have involved symptom prescriptions with individuals. Based on these studies, Shoham-Salomon and Rosenthal (1987, see below) reported that outcome largely depends on how these interventions are administered.

Most paradoxical interventions involve some combination of prescribing, reframing, and positioning. *Prescribing* means telling people what to do (giving tasks, suggestions, and so on) either directly or indirectly. For example, a therapist might ask a patient to have a panic attack deliberately or prescribe that an overinvolved grandmother take full responsibility for a misbehaving child, expecting that she will back off and let the mother take charge. *Reframing* involves redefining the meaning of events or behavior in a way that makes change more possible. Although reframing resembles interpretation, its goal is to provoke change rather than provide insight—and the accuracy of redefinition is less important than its impact. Thus, Haley described a case in which a wife became more sexually responsive after her frigidity was reframed as a way of protecting the husband from the full force of her sexuality, and Selvini-Palazzoli, Cecchin, Prata, and Boscolo (1978) pioneered the use of "positive connotation," a technique for changing dysfunctional family patterns by ascribing noble intentions to both the identified patient's symptom and the behaviors of family members that support it. *Positioning* is a term for altering the therapist's own role, or potential role, in a problem-maintaining system. Prescribing, reframing, and positioning are interwoven, with each at least implicit in any paradoxical strategy or intervention. Thus, prescribing that someone be deliberately anxious reframes an involuntary symptom as controllable; reframing problem behavior as a protective sacrifice carries an implicit (paradoxical) prescription not to change; and warning against dangers of improvement sometimes helps reverse or neutralize a therapist's role in a problem cycle.

Applications of paradox tend to be most varied and complex in marital and family therapy. In one case, where the focus was on reversing family members' well-intentioned but self-defeating attempt to solve a problem, a therapy team coached the relatives of a depressed stroke victim to encourage him by discouraging him (Fisch et al., 1982). In another case, a therapist asked a depressed husband to pretend to be depressed and asked his wife to try to find out if he was really feeling that way. For extreme marital stuckness, a therapist may recommend paradoxical interventions such as prescribing indecision about whether a couple should separate. The most dramatic examples of paradox with families come from the early work of the Milan team (Selvini-Palazzoli et al., 1978). After complimenting a severely obsessional young woman and her parents for protecting each other from the sadness associated with the death of a family member several years earlier, the team prescribed that the family meet each night to discuss their loss and suggested that the young woman behave symptomatically whenever her parents appeared distraught.

Clinical reports describe successful applications of paradoxical intervention with a wide variety of problems including anxiety, depression, phobia, insomnia, obsessive-compulsive disorder, headaches, asthma, encopresis, enuresis, blushing, tics, psychosomatic symptoms, procrastination, eating disorders, child and adolescent conduct problems, marital and family problems, pain, work and school problems, and psychotic behavior (Seltzer, 1986). Paradoxical strategies appear least applicable in situations of crisis or extreme instability, such as acute decompensation, grief reactions, domestic violence, suicide attempts, or loss of a job, but there have been too few controlled studies to list indications and contraindications with any degree of certainty.

While some authors advocate reserving paradoxical approaches for difficult situations where more straightforward methods have not succeeded or are unlikely to succeed, paradoxical strategies are too diverse for this to make sense as a blanket rule. For example, paradoxical symptom prescription could reasonably be a first line of approach for involuntary symptoms like insomnia that to some extent are maintained by attempts to stave them off.

Change Processes

Explanations of how and why paradoxical interventions work are as diverse as the interventions themselves. Behavioral, cognitive, and motivational processes—alone and in combination—have been proposed to explain change in both individuals and families. At the individual level, a behavioral account of why symptom prescription helps involuntary problems such as insomnia, anxiety, and obsessive thinking is that, by attempting to have the problem, a patient cannot continue in usual ways of trying to prevent it, thus breaking an exacerbation cycle. Cognitive explanations of the same phenomena emphasize that symptom prescription redefines the uncontrollable as controllable, decontextualizes the problem, and in a fundamental way alters the symptom's meaning. A third, rather different change mechanism has been suggested for situations where clients appear to defy or oppose a therapist's directive. Here the client presumably rebels to reduce psychological reactance, a hypothetical motive state aroused by threats to perceived behavioral freedom (Brehm & Brehm, 1981).

Not surprisingly, explanations of how paradoxical interventions promote change at the family-systems level are more diverse and more abstract. Some paradoxical interventions are assumed to interrupt problem-maintaining interaction cycles between people (Fisch et al., 1982), and some, like positive connotation, presumably operate by introducing information into the system or by changing the meaning of the symptom and the family interaction that supports it (Selvini-Palazzoli et al., 1978). Motivational explanations of systems-level change suggest that paradoxical interventions work by activating relational dynamics such as "compression" and "recoil" (Stanton, 1984) or by creating disequilibrium among systemic forces aligned for and against change (Hoffman, 1981).

Some theories of paradoxical intervention attempt to combine or integrate various change processes. For example, Rohrbaugh and colleagues (1981) proposed a compliance-defiance model distinguishing two types of paradoxical interventions. Compliance-based symptom prescription is indicated (a) when an "unfree" (involuntary) symptom like insomnia is maintained by attempts to stave it off, and (b) when the potential for reactance is low (i.e., when clients are unlikely to react against attempts to influence them). Defiance-based interventions, on the other hand, work because people change by rebelling. These are indicated when clients view the target behavior as relatively "free" (voluntary) and when the potential for reactance is high.

Another model of therapeutic paradox originally proposed by Watzlawick et al. (1967) incorporates behavioral and cognitive explanations of change. The therapeutic double-bind—a directive to deliberately engage in involuntary symptomatic behavior—is a mirror image of the pathogenic "be spontaneous" paradox. The only way to obey such a directive is by disobeying it. According to Watzlawick et al. (1967), two possible consequences follow: If the client is not able to produce the symptom on demand, he or she will show less of the problem; if the client does produce the symptom, it will be with a greater sense of mastery and control. In this way clients are "changed if they do and changed if they don't." If the symptomatic behavior itself does not change, at least the client's perception of it changes—and as Raskin and Klein put it, behaviors over which one has control might be sins, but they are not neurotic complaints. Studies by Shoham-Salomon and her colleagues provide empirical support for this "two paths to change" model.

Efficacy

When paradoxical interventions are part of a broader therapeutic strategy, their specific contribution to clinical outcome is difficult to evaluate. Nevertheless, dramatic and seemingly enduring effects on individuals and families have been documented in numerous clinical reports and case studies and in qualitative literature reviews (Seltzer, 1986).

Controlled experimental studies of paradoxical interventions with individual clients have yielded mixed results. Two independent meta-analytic reviews (Hill, 1987; Shoham-Salomon & Rosenthal, 1987) indicate that paradoxical interventions compared favorably to no-treatment control conditions, but comparisons to nonparadoxical treatments have been equivocal. Whereas Hill's (1987) meta-analysis found paradox to be superior, Shoham-Salomon and Rosenthal (1987) found that the overall effect of paradoxical interventions was as large (but no larger than) the average effect size of psychotherapy in general. Research also suggests that some forms of paradoxical intervention may be more effective than others. In Shoham-Salomon and Rosenthal's (1987) meta-analysis, the effect sizes of two positively connoted symptom prescriptions were significantly greater than those of other, nonparadoxical treatments or of symptom prescriptions that did not include a positive frame. Paradoxical interventions were most effective when the therapist either reframed the symptom positively before prescribing it (for example, praising a depressed client's tolerance for solitude or her willingness to sacrifice for the good of others), or explained the paradoxical intention (exacerbation-cycle) rationale in a way that defined the client as not "sick" but "stuck." In a recent study directly testing the importance of positive connotation, Akillas and Efran found that socially anxious men improved more when a prescription to be anxious was presented with a positive frame (rationale) than when it was not. This supports the view that symptom prescriptions work best when they aim to alter the meaning a client attributes to the symptom.

Research on paradoxical interventions is not without limitations. For example, meta-analytic results must be interpreted cautiously because stringent inclusion criteria may compromise the clinical or ecological validity of conclusions. Moreover, as noted above, research in this area has focused almost exclusively on symptom prescription with individuals. There have been too few controlled studies to summarize the efficacy of other forms of therapeutic paradox (restraint from change, for example) or of applications with interactional systems and families.

Ethical Issues

As the popularity of paradoxical therapy increased during the 1980s, concern also grew about ways in which these techniques can be misused. Strategic applications in which therapists do not make their rationale for particular interventions explicit to clients have been criticized as manipulative and potentially harmful to the client–therapist relationship. And in analogue studies, observers of therapy vignettes have rated symptom prescription as less acceptable than straightforward behavioral interventions, even when these vignettes portrayed paradoxical interventions as more effective.

Defenders of strategic therapy, on the other hand, argue that good therapy is inherently manipulative and that therapeutic truth-telling can be not only naive but discourteous. Responsible therapists of all persuasions agree that paradox should not be used for the shock value or power it promises. Encouraging a symptom or restraining people from changing can be disastrous if done sarcastically or from a sense of frustration ("There's the window—go ahead and jump!"). It is also significant that therapists like Haley, Weakland, Palazzoli, and Hoffman, who pioneered the use of paradoxical methods, now give them less emphasis; even therapists well-versed in strategic methods find the term "paradoxical" confusing, inaccurate, and overly loaded with negative connotations. Of particular concern is that the term "paradoxical intervention," cut loose from its theoretical and clinical moorings, is too easily seen as a "quick fix" or a gimmick.

Three guidelines may decrease the potential for misusing paradoxical interventions: First, define behavior positively. When prescribing a symptom or restraining change, avoid attributing unseemly motives to people (like needing to control, resist, or defeat one another); ascribe noble intentions not only to the symptom but to what other people are doing to support it. Second, be especially cautious with challenging or provocative interventions. When restraining clients from change, for example, it is safer to suggest that change may not be advisable than to predict it will not be possible. Finally, have a clear theoretical formulation of how the problem is being maintained and how a paradoxical intervention may help to change that. The most important guideline for paradoxical (or any other) intervention is having a coherent rationale for using it.

REFERENCES

Brehm, S. S., & Brehm, J. W. (1981). *Psychological reactance: A theory of freedom and control.* New York: Academic Press.

Fisch, R., Weakland, J. H., & Segal, L. (1982). *The tactics of change.* San Francisco: Jossey-Bass.

Hill, K. A. (1987). Meta-analysis of paradoxical interventions. *Psychotherapy, 24,* 266–270.

Hoffman, L. (1981). *Foundations of family therapy.* New York: Basic.

Rohrbaugh, M., Tennen, H., Press, S., & White, L. (1981). Compliance, defiance, and therapeutic paradox: Guidelines for strategic use of paradoxical interventions. *American Journal of Orthopsychiatry, 51,* 454–467.

Seltzer, L. F. (1986). *Paradoxical strategies in psychotherapy: A comprehensive overview and guide book.* New York: Wiley.

Selvini-Palazzoli, M., Cecchin, G., Prata, G., & Boscolo, E. L. (1978). *Paradox and counterparadox.* New York: Aronson.

Shoham-Salomon, V., & Rosenthal, R. (1987). Paradoxical interventions. A meta-analysis. *Journal of Consulting and Clinical Psychology, 55,* 22–28.

Stanton, M. D. (1984). Fusion, compression, diversion, and the workings of paradox: A theory of therapeutic/systemic change. *Family Process, 23,* 135–168.

Watzlawick, P., Beavin, J., & Jackson, D. D. (1967). *Pragmatics of human communication.* New York: Norton.

SUGGESTED READING

Frankl, V. E. (1991). Paradoxical intention. In G. E. Weeks (Ed.), *Promoting change through paradoxical therapy* (pp. 99–110). New York: Brunner/Mazel.

Haley, J. (1973). *Uncommon therapy: The psychiatric techniques of Milton H. Erickson, MD.* New York: Norton.

Haley, J. (1987). *Problem-solving therapy* (2nd ed.). San Francisco: Jossey-Bass.

Hunsley, J. (1993). Treatment acceptability of symptom prescription techniques. *Journal of Counseling Psychology, 40,* 139–143.

Madanes, C. (1980). Protection, paradox, and pretending. *Family Process, 19,* 73–85.

Omer, H. (1981). Paradoxical treatments: A unified concept. *Psychotherapy: Theory, research, and practice, 18,* 320–324.

Raskin, D., & Klein, Z. (1976). Losing a symptom through keeping it: A review of paradoxical treatment techniques and rationale. *Archives of General Psychiatry, 33,* 548–555.

Shoham, V., & Rohrbaugh, M. (1997). Interrupting ironic processes. *Psychological Science, 8,* 151–153.

Weeks, G. R. (1991). *Promoting change through paradoxical therapy.* New York: Brunner/Mazel.

Varda Shoham
M. J. Rohrbaugh
University of Arizona

See also: **Cognitive Therapy; Psychotherapy**

PARADOXICAL SLEEP

Paradoxical sleep is a sleep stage characterized physiologically by a lack of muscle tone, rapid eye movements (REMs), and an awake cortical electroencephalographic (EEG) pattern. The "paradox" refers to the disparity between the alert EEG pattern, implying that the person is awake or nearly so, and the indications that the person is actually more deeply asleep than at other times (difficulty in arousing, reduced muscle tone).

The term *paradoxical sleep* was introduced in a 1967 *Scientific American* article on the states of sleep by French researcher Michel Jouvet. Jouvet used the term to describe a period of apparent sleep in cats in which they exhibited high levels of neural activity with completely relaxed neck muscles. In humans, such periods are also characterized by rapid eye movements; sleep researchers use the term *REM sleep* with human subjects but *paradoxical sleep* with animals because many species do not exhibit eye movements.

REM or paradoxical sleep is just one of several stages that a sleeping organism passes through during a sleep bout. One way to categorize the stages is into REM sleep and non-REM (NREM) sleep. Four stages are usually distinguished in NREM sleep, labeled appropriately Stages 1–4, with the stages representing progressively deeper sleep. Stages 3 and 4 are collectively called *slow-wave sleep* (SWS) because the EEG waves are slower than in Stages 1 and 2.

REM sleep is associated with erections in males and vaginal moistening in females, as well as with reports of dreaming. In males at least, the genital changes are not necessarily associated with sex-related dreaming. Dreams also have been reported in SWS, but they are more frequent in REM sleep and generally more elaborate.

Studies of people awakened from REM sleep have answered several questions about dreaming. For example, apparently all normal humans dream, even though many people claim that they do not. When "nondreamers" are awakened during REM sleep, they usually report dreams, although their dreams may be less vivid than those of people who usually remember their dreams upon awakening. Another observation is that dreams last about as long as they seem to.

A number of studies have attempted to determine the function of REM sleep by depriving volunteers of it. In general, subjects awakened during each REM stage and kept awake for several minutes increase their attempts at REM sleep and develop mild, temporary personality changes. Studies of paradoxical sleep deprivation in animals reveal similar increased attempts at REM sleep and some general disturbances, none of which solves the mystery of REM sleep's function.

According to one explanation, sleep is an adaptive mechanism developed to conserve energy at night, when food gathering would be difficult for an animal active in the daytime. However, the evolution of many animals has resulted in regular patterns of locomotor activity, thought to occur approximately every 2 hours, during which food gathering and other activities related to survival might occur. If this 2-hour cycle continued around the clock, the animal would have its sleep periodically interrupted. Thus, in order to get a full night's sleep and continue with the 2-hour activity cycle, the animal enters a period of paradoxical sleep in which only the brain awakens.

Another possibility is that REM or paradoxical sleep is important for strengthening memories. Studies have shown that humans and other mammals increase REM sleep periods following a new learning experience, and without this increase, memory deficits result. However, some have suggested that REM sleep performs just the opposite function: purging useless information from memory. Yet another possibility is that infants spend an inordinate amount of time in REM sleep because such sleep is associated with the development of the brain. About all we can say at this time is that the number of disparate explanations indicates that we really do not know much about the causes and functions of paradoxical sleep.

B. Michael Thorne
Mississippi State University

PARAMETRIC STATISTICAL TESTS

Parametric statistical tests, as opposed to nonparametric or distribution-free tests, are based on various assumptions regarding the characteristics, properties, and form of the distributions of populations from which the data are drawn. A large number of statistical tests are included among the parametric tests, primarily hypothesis-testing procedures derived from the general linear model. These include both univariate and multivariate statistical tests: the *t*-test, univariate and multivariate analysis of variance and covariance (including repeated measures), Pearson product-moment correlation, simple and multiple regression (and variants including logistic regression), Hotelling's T^2, discriminant function analysis, canonical correlation, and multivariate set correlation. When their underlying assumptions are met, parametric statistical tests are generally considered more powerful than their nonparametric alternatives. However, it is more for their versatility than for their statistical power that parametric tests have become the most common tools in behavioral research.

The principal assumptions on which parametric tests are based include independence of the observations, normality of the underlying distributions, homogeneity of variance across groups (for multiple group procedures), continuity of measurement, and equality of intervals of measurement. Additional assumptions may be required for some parametric procedures, such as linearity of regression (Pearson correlation, simple and multiple regression), homogeneity of regression slopes (univariate and multivariate analysis of covariance), and sphericity (univariate and multivariate repeated measures). The principal assumptions for multivariate statistics include independence of the observations, multivariate normal distributions for all dependent variables, and homogeneity of the variance–covariance (dispersion) matrices across groups.

In principle, when assumptions are violated, the significance level (*p* value) associated with a statistical test result may be seriously in error, increasing either Type I or Type II error rates. However, under many circumstances, univariate statistics seem to be quite robust to violations of assumptions. One exception is the violation of the assumption of independence, which is always serious. Robustness may also be compromised under certain conditions, such as when two or more assumptions are violated simultaneously, when sample sizes are very small, when sample sizes are unequal, or when one-tailed significance tests are used. When violation of assumptions is a concern, various remedial techniques can be employed, including data transformations (e.g., square root, arcsine, log) or the use of alternative, specialized analytical procedures (e.g., Welch's *t*-test, generalized estimating equations, nonparametric statistics). The assumptions underlying repeated measures procedures appear to be more restrictive than for univariate tests. Consequently, repeated measures procedures may not be as robust as univariate tests. Although not as much research has been conducted as for univariate procedures, multivariate statistical tests appear to be robust to violation of assumptions under many commonly occurring circumstances.

Joseph S. Rossi
University of Rhode Island

See also: **Confidence Interval; Nonparametric Statistical Tests**

PARASYMPATHETIC NERVOUS SYSTEM

The *parasympathetic nervous system* (PNS) is one of two branches of the autonomic nervous system, which controls the function of organs and glands in the body (called the efferent portion) and senses changes in these organ systems (the afferent portion). The other autonomic branch is called the *sympathetic nervous system* (SNS). The neurons that comprise the efferent PNS arise from either the cranial nerves that exit from the brain stem and spinal cord, or from the sacral (i.e., lower) portion of the spinal cord. Thus, this system is sometimes referred to as the craniosacral branch. Cranial parasympathetic fibers innervate the organs and glands of the head, neck, chest, and upper abdomen, including the upper portions of the gastrointestinal (GI) tract. The sacral parasympathetic fibers innervate the lower GI tract and other organs of the pelvis.

The anatomy of the efferent autonomic nerves to each organ or gland includes preganglionic neurons, which exit the brain or spinal cord, and postganglionic neurons, which directly innervate the target organ. A ganglion is comprised of the cell bodies of the postganglionic neurons and is the region where the pre- and postganglionic neurons communicate with one another. In the PNS, the preganglionic fibers exiting the brain or spinal cord extend across relatively long distances in the body before reaching the ganglion. Typically, PNS ganglia are found very near or even in the wall of the target organ or gland. Thus, the postganglionic neurons are very short, since they extend only from the ganglion to the target organ. The neurotransmitter released by the axon terminals of the preganglionic neurons is acetylcholine. Acetylcholine acts on cholinergic receptors of the nicotinic subtype, which are found on the postganglionic neurons. The neurotransmitter released by the postganglionic neuron onto the target organ or gland is acetylcholine, which activates muscarinic subtype cholinergic receptors. Afferent autonomic fibers from organs to the central nervous system run alongside the same nerves carrying efferent autonomic fibers. The visceral (i.e., organ) afferents comprise a relatively large proportion of the total number of fibers, perhaps 50% or more, in the parasympathetic nerves. Afferent autonomic fibers provide sensory information about the state of an organ, such as stretch of the bladder, and also may relay some pain signals.

The organs and glands controlled by the efferent PNS typically receive input from both branches of the autonomic nervous system, a phenomenon referred to as dual innervation. When organs receive innervation from both autonomic branches, activation in the two branches often, but not always, produces opposite effects on the organ. For example, the heart rate is controlled by both autonomic branches. Increased activity in the parasympathetic branch decreases heart rate, and decreased activity increases heart rate. Conversely, increased activity in the sympathetic branch increases heart rate, whereas decreased activity decreases heart rate. Thus, each of the two branches is capable of bidirectionally influencing the rate at which the heart beats.

When the body is at rest, many of the organs of the body are conserving or actively storing metabolic resources for later use, a process known as anabolism. Often during such states, activity in the parasympathetic system is relatively high compared to periods when the organism is moving, challenged, or distressed. For example, during rest or low levels of bodily activity, digestion of food is a priority for the body. Increased parasympathetic activation enhances digestion by producing increased motility and blood flow, and the secretion of digestive fluids such as acid and enzymes into the gastrointestinal tract. When an organism requires metabolic energy to maintain activity above resting levels, for example in response to a stressor or with physical exertion, activation of the parasympathetic system tends to decrease at the same time that activation of the sympathetic system tends to increase. At very high levels of metabolic need, parasympathetic activation of some organs may cease altogether. Most of the time, the autonomic nervous system operates somewhere between these extremes of low and high energy mobilization. In these cases, PNS effects on the organs and glands will be intermediate and tuned to the specific needs of each organ system.

In addition to the tendency for the two autonomic branches to operate in a reciprocal fashion under extremes of activity or inactivity, the two autonomic branches can operate nonreciprocally and independently. Thus, although a typical pattern of autonomic control consists of the activation of one autonomic branch accompanied by a decrease in activity in the other branch (a reciprocal pattern), this is not the only pattern of response that can occur. The two autonomic branches can have uncoupled effects on an organ with either increased or decreased activity in one autonomic branch in the absence of any change in activity in the other branch. Alternatively, the two branches can exert coactivational effects where there are simultaneous increases or decreases in activity in both autonomic branches. The existence of the nonreciprocal patterns means that one cannot measure function in one autonomic branch and on that basis alone infer the activation level in the other branch.

SUGGESTED READING

Berntson, G. G., Cacioppo, J. T., & Quigley, K. S. (1991). Autonomic determinism: The modes of autonomic control, the doctrine of autonomic space, and the laws of autonomic constraint. *Psychological Review, 98,* 459–487.

Loewy, A. D., & Spyer, K. M. (1990). *Central regulation of autonomic function.* New York: Oxford University Press.

Karen S. Quigley
University of Medicine and Dentistry of New Jersey—New Jersey Medical School and East Orange VA Medical Center

See also: **Central Nervous System; Sympathetic Nervous System**

PARENT MANAGEMENT TRAINING

Parent management training (PMT) employs a therapist as a consultant who works directly with a parent (mediator) to alleviate the problem behavior of a child (target). The basic PMT format consists primarily of instruction by the therapist in parenting techniques, structured modeling, role-plays and practice sessions, and homework assignments for the parent to practice skills with the child. This format is based on the assumption that parenting skills deficits are at least partly responsible for the development and/or maintenance of child problem behaviors, and thus provides parents with a repertoire of skills with which to manage, and eventually improve, the child's behavior as well as improve broader parent-child interactional patterns.

PMT has been utilized as a therapeutic intervention primarily for disruptive or "acting-out" behavior (e.g., aggression, noncompliance, destructiveness) of children. This type of behavior is one of the most frequent causes of referrals for child mental health treatment. Disruptive, aggressive, or delinquent behavior of children and adolescents is a significant problem for society, not only as a direct result of the difficulties caused by such behaviors themselves, but also because such behavioral patterns often persist, or worsen, into adulthood, when their consequences are much greater.

Because the emotional and financial costs associated with disruptive behaviors can be so significant for families and society, clinical researchers have devoted substantial energy to understanding the causes of this behavior and determining ways of treating and preventing it in youth. Countless studies have shown that the family is one of the most consistent areas of a child's life that contributes to both the development and the treatment of disruptive behavior. Positive parenting practices, such as a supportive parent-child relationship, authoritative discipline methods, and close supervision are major protective factors against the development of disruptive behavior. In contrast, negative or coercive parenting practices, such as harsh punishment, psychological control, and negative parent-child interactions contribute to the development of child and adolescent problem behavior. As such, PMT, which targets these areas of parenting, has become the intervention of choice for treating and preventing disruptive behavior problems of children and adolescents. Empirical studies, meta-analyses, reviews, and task force conclusions all provide substantial support for PMT as one of the most effective therapeutic interventions for the disruptive or acting-out behavior of children.

The development of PMT as an empirically validated practice has occurred in three distinct stages: establishment, generalization, and enhancement. The first stage (from 1960 to 1975) involved the establishment of the parent training format and tests of its efficacy as a treatment for child problem behaviors. Early studies, which included a large number of descriptive studies and single-case designs, found support for the short-term efficacy of the parent training model in reducing disruptive child behaviors and improving parenting practices.

The second stage of research was conducted between 1975 and 1985 and focused on the long-term effects and generalization of PMT. Such generalization has been shown to occur in at least four areas: setting (e.g., transfer of behavior changes from the clinic to home or school), temporal (e.g., maintenance of behavior change over time), sibling (e.g., application of new parenting skills with non-targeted children), and behavioral (e.g., concomitant improvements in non-targeted behaviors). The empirical demonstration of the generalization of treatment effects has served to enhance the perceived social validity of parent training (i.e., whether the treatment effects are considered to be clinically or socially important to the client as well as the clients' satisfaction with the treatment).

The third stage of PMT research, which began in 1986 and continues today, examines ways to expand and enhance the PMT curriculum. This line of research has considered a wide range of factors that can impact the implementation and outcome of parent training. For example, the role of developmental variables (e.g., the child's age) has been emphasized in developing and tailoring PMT interventions. As a child increases in age, her or his cognitive abilities and source of primary reinforcement (e.g., parents, peers) change, which leads to changes in intervention strategies. PMT has been found to be more effective with younger than older children, and the families of younger children are less likely to drop out of treatment. With older children, particularly adolescents, PMT interventions may not only be less effective but also more difficult to implement. As another example of the findings from this stage of PMT research, several researchers have considered the contextual factors that can affect PMT, thus broadening the perspectives for treating child disruptive behavior. For example, in addition to the traditional teaching of parenting skills, the PMT paradigm may be modified to include multiple areas of family functioning as targets for intervention (e.g., parental depressive symptoms and/or marital adjustment). More recently, interventions have been designed to involve and coordinate multiple levels of the child's environment, including the home, school, clinic, and community.

PMT programs all share several common or core elements, including: (1) focusing more on parents than on the child; (2) teaching parents to identify, define, and record child behavior; (3) instructing parents in social learning principles (e.g., reinforcement of prosocial behavior, withdrawal of attention for misbehavior through the use of ignoring or time-out); (4) teaching new parenting skills via didactic instruction, modeling, role-playing, and practicing with the child in the clinic and at home; (5) discussing ways to maximize generalization of skills from the clinic to the home; and, when necessary, (6) addressing contextual issues affecting parents (e.g., depressive symptoms), the family (e.g., marital conflict), and the community (e.g., neighborhood violence) which may interfere with the acquisition or maintenance of new parenting skills and the promotion of adaptive child behavior.

Rex Forehand
University of Vermont

Beth A. Kotchick
Loyola College of Maryland

Anne Shaffer
University of Minnesota

PARENTAL APPROACHES

Parents have a legal and moral duty to rear their children. This includes providing for their sustenance and well-being, as well as their social, ethical, and personal development. In order to fulfill this responsibility, parents have to find ways to convey their principles, expectations, and regulations. Thus, the goal of parenting is to raise confident and satisfied children who can function independently and contribute to the welfare of society.

Historically, children were considered property of the father. Fathers had the supreme right to command blind obedience. In addition, religious doctrine mandated that parents make their children god-fearing subjects by requiring them to submit to religious commandments, "to honor thy mother and father." Thus, an authoritarian style of parenting was purported to be the optimal method for transferring the philosophy and practices of the parents to the children.

In the 1900s, psychoanalytic premises stressed attention to children's instinctive needs. Autocratic child rearing practices were seen as contributing to the anxiety of children by precipitously and abruptly addressing their psychosexual developmental needs. Instead, a philosophy of parental permissiveness was seen as the optimal method in order to follow the wisdom of the unconscious. Thus, parents were encouraged to indulge children by practicing a "laissez-faire," nonintrusive approach with their children.

Dreikurs and Grey (1968), students of Alfred Adler, adopted a democratic position of parenting that forged a middle ground of parental authority. They stressed that children should be encouraged to balance freedom with responsibility. The combination of teaching children both freedom and responsibility added new challenges to the task of parenting. Parents no longer had an either/or solution of tyranny or indulgence, but needed to creatively encourage children through natural and logical consequences.

Benefits of Authoritative Parenting

Diana Baumrind's research of more than 30 years supported the benefits of a rational approach to parenting that fostered child development through an artful balance of control and responsiveness. Baumrind (1967, 1971) initially articulated three parental styles of handling authority as *authoritative, authoritarian,* and *permissive.* Later, she added a fourth category called rejecting–neglecting, or parents who were *unengaged.*

In cluster and factor analyses, Baumrind (1989) identified *demandingness* and *responsiveness* as the two major modalities in the parenting process. Demandingness correlates with parental attributes that provide appropriate direction and control. Demanding parents can be *confrontive* even if such a position results in open conflict. Confrontation is contrasted with coercive approaches that demand power without reason. Confrontation of the problem behavior (versus intimidating the child) can result in resolution and negotiation of conflict, which enhances the child's internal decision making, self-esteem, and communication skills. Parents who insist that children embrace individually appropriate levels of responsibility, those who make *high maturity demands,* promote higher levels of prosocial behavior and academic competence. Appropriate parental *monitoring* is preferable to an overly intrusive and constrictive approach, which diminishes an appropriate level of exploration and autonomy. Reinforcement, logical consequences, and rational punishment are methods that can teach children desirable values, attitudes, and behaviors.

Table 1. Parental Styles

Demandingness	Responsiveness: High	Responsiveness: Low
High	Authoritative	Authoritarian
Low	Permissive	Unengaged

The preceding attributes of parental authority, alone, are insufficient to raise healthy, confident, and competent children. Parents who demonstrate *responsiveness* establish a loving environment that is sensitive to and accommodative of the child's needs (Bowlby, 1969). Children who experience *affective warmth* from a parent develop feelings of object permanence and feel securely *attached and bonded* to their environment. These children become attuned to the demands of the parent and are more likely to be cooperative than children with a cold or uninvolved parent. *Reciprocity* is the extent to which parents listen and respond to the needs and feelings of the child. Parents *sensitively attuned* to the child's motivational system can use reciprocity to uncover "win-win" solutions in the intergenerational dialogue. Parents who are responsive model prosocial communications to the child and produce children who authentically desire harmony with their parents.

Authoritative parents, who are high in both responsiveness and demandingness, remain receptive to the needs of the child for attachment and autonomy, but take responsibility for firmly guiding the actions of the child. Authoritarian (autocratic) parents are high in demandingness but low in responsiveness. They set absolute standards for their children and require unquestioned obedience and submission to their authority. Permissive (indulgent) parents are high in indulgence but low in control. These parents put few demands on their children, usually accept their children's impulses, and for the most part, avoid conflict. Unengaged (neglectful-rejecting) parents are low in both authority and nurture. Out of all parental styles, they produce children with the most severe problems because their children are forced to fend for themselves or depend too greatly on their peer group for support.

Cultural Considerations

Baumrind's early research (1967, 1971) began by measuring mostly middle-class, Caucasian children who were being raised by one or both parents. Nonetheless, much of the research holds that authoritative parenting works best across differences of culture, race, gender, socioeconomic factors, and family structure. Therefore, authoritative caregiving can be effective for child rearing regardless of the relationship between caregiver and child. However, Baumrind (1995) cautioned that the blend of demandingness and responsiveness is dependent upon the social and cultural context of the child.

Brofenbrenner (1979/1982) agreed that the optimal balance of freedom and control depends upon the level of stability of the larger society. Due to the massive change of the family's ecology, he suggested that there is a greater need for structure in the modern family. More specifically, Kohn (1977) stated that African American parents often used authoritarian methods to instill obedience and authority in their children to help them adapt to a bicultural reality of minority status in the American culture. Thus, parenting does not occur in isolation of the context.

Similarly, there have been different gender implications of parenting styles. The authoritarian approach emanates from a masculine manner of handling authority, whereas authoritative parenting is much more compatible with female development and feminine use of authority. Gilligan's (1982) research proved that girls respond much more to a consensually-based approach so that they can discover their own voice.

Summary

Research on parental approaches strongly supports an authoritative approach, which blends a flexible balance of demandingness and responsiveness through the child's developmental process. This approach provides the nurture, safety, protection, respect, and responsive limits (Pesso, 1973) that children need to optimize their potential as healthy, confident, and vital members of society. However, parents need to adapt the mixture of demandingness and responsiveness to the idiosyncrasies of the child, culture, and context.

REFERENCES

Baumrind, D. (1967). Child care practices anteceding three patterns of preschool behavior. *Genetic Psychology Monographs, 75,* 43–88.

Baumrind, D. (1971). Current patterns of parental authority. *Developmental Psychology Monographs, 4*(1), 1–103.

Baumrind, D. (1989). Rearing competent children. In W. Damon (Ed.), *Child development today and tomorrow* (pp. 349–378). San Francisco: Jossey-Bass.

Baumrind, D. (1995). *Child maltreatment and optimal caregiving in social contexts.* New York: Garland Publishing.

Bowlby, J. (1969). *Attachment and loss: Vol. 1. Attachment.* New York: Basic Books.

Brofenbrenner, U. (1979/1982). *The ecology of human development.* Cambridge, MA: Harvard University Press.

Dreikurs, R., & Grey, L. (1968). *Logical consequence: A new approach to discipline.* New York: Meredith.

Gilligan, C. (1982). *In a different voice: Psychological theory and women's development.* Cambridge, MA: Harvard University Press.

Kohn, M. L. (1977). *Class and conformity: A study in values* (2nd ed.). Chicago: University of Chicago Press.

Pesso, A. (1973). *Experience in action.* New York: New York University Press.

Russell A. Haber
University of South Carolina

PARTNER ABUSE

Partner abuse, often referred to as intimate partner violence, partner aggression, domestic violence, or spouse abuse, is a very broad term encompassing three diverse categories of abusive behaviors that occur within the context of intimate relationships: physical, sexual, and psychological. Partner physical abuse includes behaviors ranging in severity from those that are unlikely to result in injury (e.g., pushing and grabbing) to those that are life threatening (e.g., choking, kicking, and beating up). Partner sexual abuse refers to any undesired sexual contact that is psychologically or physically coerced. The definition of partner psychological abuse is particularly broad, encompassing behaviors ranging from insulting or swearing at a partner, to threatening a partner, to engaging in jealous behaviors, to isolating a partner from friends and family. In most cases, particularly when the aggression is mild to moderate, partner abuse is bilateral. That is, both partners engage in aggressive or abusive behaviors. However, in our clinical and research experience, in relationships in which women are severely abused and often injured, men are much more likely to be abusers than are women, and women's aggression is often in self-defense (see also Johnson, 1995). Female victims of such severe partner abuse are often referred to as battered women, and their abusive partners are often referred to as batterers.

Given the greater research emphasis on physical abuse as compared with psychological and sexual abuse in intimate relationships, partner physical abuse is the main focus herein.

Prevalence

Partner physical abuse is a relatively common form of violence in our society. The 1975 and 1985 National Family Violence Surveys revealed that each year approximately 12% of married or cohabiting men and women in the United States engage in physical aggression against a partner, and approximately 3 to 5% engage in severe or life-threatening physically assaultive behaviors against a partner (Straus & Gelles, 1990). Partner abuse is not limited to adult heterosexual married and cohabiting relationships, but also occurs in a substantial number of adolescent dating relationships (Halpern, Oslak, Young, Martin, & Kupper, 2001) and same-sex romantic relationships (Renzetti & Miley, 1996). Although the statistics presented above only reflect the prevalence of partner abuse in the United States, partner abuse is currently recognized as an important problem throughout the world (Walker, 1999).

Explanatory Frameworks and Risk Factors

Several explanatory frameworks have been developed to describe the causes of partner abuse. Feminist accounts identify partner abuse as a product of a patriarchal (male-dominated) society. Violence in the home is viewed as one of many expressions of gender-based power inequality in society (Yllö, 1993). Psychological accounts identify partner abuse, particularly severe partner abuse, as a manifestation of the interaction between individual personality traits or personality disorders and other risk factors such as marital dissatisfaction (O'Leary, 1993). Sociological accounts identify position in the social structure as an important causal factor in partner abuse. Substantial research linking variables associated with position in the social structure, such as poverty, age, and race, to partner abuse provides support for this explanatory framework (Gelles, 1993). Numerous other social, psychological, and biological factors, such as anger, depression, witnessing violence as a child, relationship communication problems, and alcohol problems are associated with increased risk for partner abuse perpetration, and may be causally related to such abuse (Schumacher, Feldbau-Kohn, Slep, & Heyman, 2001).

Consequences

As a result of partner abuse, society incurs substantial costs related to physical and mental health care, legal interventions, child welfare, social services, and lost work productivity. At the individual level, partner abuse can have very negative effects, particularly for women. Although women engage in physically aggressive behaviors against a partner at approximately the same rate as men, the findings of the National Violence Against Women Survey indicate that women are significantly more likely to sustain injuries, receive medical care or be hospitalized, receive counseling, and lose time at work as a result of partner abuse victimization than are men (Tjaden & Thoennes, 2000). Violence by a partner is also a surprisingly common cause of death for young women, claiming roughly 2,000 lives annually (Browne & Williams, 1993). Partner abuse has also been associated with negative consequences for individuals who witness the violence as children. The results of a survey of more than 17,000 adult HMO members in California indicated that adults who reported having been raised in environments in which partner abuse occurred were significantly more likely to also report other adverse experiences during childhood, such as child abuse and neglect, than adults who were not raised in such environments. Further, the frequency of witnessing partner abuse as a child was related to self-reported alcoholism, drug use, and feelings of depression in adulthood (Dube, Anda, Felitti, Edwards, & Williamson, 2002).

Intervention and Prevention Strategies

A variety of psychological interventions are currently utilized, particularly psychoeducational and therapy groups for men (and occasionally women) who abuse their partners. Various legal interventions including arrest, prosecution, and restraining orders are also used to manage this problem. For severely abused women, support groups are commonly used along with legal advocates, shelters, social service agencies, and individual therapeutic interventions to help victims leave abusive relationships and rebuild their lives. For women and men in less severely abusive relationships where both the male and female engage in physically aggressive behaviors, couple or marital therapy based interventions designed specifically to reduce psychological and physical aggression can be useful (O'Leary, Heyman, & Neidig, 1999). Dating violence prevention programs in junior high and high school are designed to provide children with education and skills and to foster attitudes that will reduce or prevent partner abuse in their current and future relationships. Partner abuse is clearly a multidetermined problem that is influenced by a variety of psychological and social factors. As a result, this problem requires multifaceted interventions including legal, psychological, social, and medical approaches.

REFERENCES

Browne, A., & Williams, W. R. (1993). Gender, intimacy, and lethal violence: Trends from 1976 through 1987. *Gender and Society, 7,* 78–98.

Dube, S. R., Anda, R. F., Felitti, V. J., Edwards, V. J., & Williamson, D. F. (2002). Exposure to abuse, neglect and household dysfunction among adults who witnessed intimate partner violence as children: Implications for health and social services. *Violence and Victims, 17,* 3–18.

Gelles, R. J. (1993). Through a sociological lens: Social structure and family violence. In R. J. Gelles & D. R. Loseke (Eds.), *Current controversies on family violence* (pp. 31–46), Newbury Park, CA: Sage.

Halpern, C. T., Oslak, S. G., Young, M. L., Martin, S. L., & Kupper, L. L. (2001). Partner violence among adolescents in opposite-sex romantic relationships: Findings from the National Longitudinal Study of Adolescent Health. *American Journal of Public Health, 91,* 1679–1685.

Johnson, M. P. (1995). Patriarchal terrorism and common couple violence: Two forms of violence against women. *Journal of Marriage and the Family, 57,* 283–294.

O'Leary, K. D. (1993). Through a psychological lens: Personality traits, personality disorders, and levels of violence. In R. J. Gelles & D. R. Loseke (Eds.), *Current controversies on family violence* (pp. 7–30), Newbury Park, CA: Sage.

O'Leary, K. D., Heyman, R. E., & Neidig, P. H. (1999). Treatment of wife abuse: A comparison of gender-specific and couples approaches. *Behavior Therapy, 30,* 475–505.

Renzetti, C. M., & Miley, C. H. (1996). *Violence in gay and lesbian domestic partnerships.* New York: Harrington Park Press.

Schumacher, J. A., Feldbau-Kohn, S., Slep, A. M. S., & Heyman, R. E. (2001). Risk factors for male-to-female partner physical abuse. *Aggression and Violent Behavior, 6,* 281–352.

Straus, M. A., & Gelles, R. J. (Eds.). (1990). *Physical violence in American families.* New Brunswick, NJ: Transaction.

Tjaden, P., & Thoennes, N. (2000). Prevalence and consequences of male-to-female and female-to-male intimate partner violence as measured by the National Violence Against Women Survey. *Violence Against Women, 6,* 142–161.

Walker, L. E. (1999). Psychology and domestic violence around the world. *The American Psychologist, 54,* 21–29.

Yllö, K. A. (1993). Through a feminist lens: Gender, power, and violence. In R. J. Gelles & D. R. Loseke (Eds.), *Current controversies on family violence* (pp. 47–62), Newbury Park, CA: Sage.

Julie A. Schumacher
Research Institute on Addictions

K. Daniel O'Leary
State University of New York

PASTORAL COUNSELING

Pastoral counseling is a modern and psychologically sophisticated form of religious caring. Usually offered by a minister, priest, rabbi, chaplain, or other religious worker, pastoral counseling seeks to combine skilled counseling methods with an understanding and application of the moral guidelines and spiritual values of religion.

In contrast to the term *religious counseling,* which is not limited to Christian pastors or to Western systems of belief, the term *pastoral counseling* usually is limited to the help given by religious leaders whose beliefs are based in Judaic/Christian traditions.

The Bible is filled with examples of dedicated men and women who encouraged, guided, supported, confronted, comforted, advised, and in other ways helped people in need. Throughout the Christian era, pastors and other religious workers have engaged in what have come to be known as the four pastoral functions: (a) healing (restoring individuals to wholeness and leading them to advance beyond their previous conditions); (b) sustaining (helping hurting people to endure and to rise above difficult circumstances); (c) guiding (assisting perplexed individuals as they face difficult decisions); and (d) reconciling (reestablishing relationships between people and between individuals and God).

The modern pastoral counseling movement began in the 1920s as a reaction against both traditional theological education, which tended to have little practical and pastoral emphasis, and early psychiatric treatment, which had little place for religious perspectives on healing.

Clinical Pastoral Education (CPE) has developed into a highly organized movement. Much of its work has been in providing standards and guidelines for the training of pastoral counselors; demonstrating to both hospital personnel and theological educators that pastoral involvement is relevant and effective in the treatment of psychological and physical illness; investigating ways in which theology and the psychological sciences can be related; and showing that the personal and spiritual development of seminarians is at least as important as intellectual training for the ministry.

Pastoral counselors of all theological persuasions deal with personal, social, marital, family, and religious problems. Much of the emphasis in pastoral counseling is on coping with present problems, helping those who suffer, and giving spiritual guidance.

Pastoral counseling takes place not only in pastors' offices and church settings but also in hospital rooms, prison cells, parishioners' homes, restaurants, military settings, and funeral homes. Hospital and military chaplains usually identify themselves as pastoral counselors, as do college chaplains and chaplains associated with major league sports teams.

As pastoral counseling has become more popular and its effectiveness more recognized, increasing numbers of pastors are finding themselves swamped with requests for counseling. To meet these needs, several trends have become apparent within the pastoral counseling movement. These include increased communication and cooperation among pastors and professionals in the helping fields; the development of better training programs in seminaries; the stimulation of lay counseling within and through the local congregation; the establishment of pastoral counseling centers; the involvement of pastors in new and established counseling clinics and community centers; the consideration of ways in which problem prevention can be stimulated by and through the church or synagogue; the increased use of sermons and small study groups as ways of stimulating mental and spiritual health; and the development of films, seminars, and training programs that can supplement, replace, and prevent the need for counseling.

Gary R. Collins

***See also:* Counseling; Religion and Mental Health**

PATIENT ADHERENCE

Adherence

Adherence is defined as the extent to which patients follow prescribed regimens (Haynes, Taylor, & Sackett, 1979). Adherence to prescribed treatment regimens supports health promotion (e.g., exercise and diet), treatment of disease, symptom management, and efficient health care delivery. The term *adherence* is used rather than *compliance* because its meaning is more consistent with views of patients as active participants in health care rather than passive recipients of services (e.g., O'Brien, Petrie, & Raeburn, 1992). While this article is limited to medication adherence, the issues are relevant for adherence to other prescribed regimens.

Adherence involves a complex set of behaviors. It requires that patients take a medication at the prescribed time, in the correct amount, using indicated conditions (e.g., with meals). Since adherence failures involve errors of omission, commission, or timing, reported adherence rates need to be defined. Patients are sometimes classified as nonadherent if they are less than 100% adherent, but an 80% level is considered acceptable (O'Brien et al., 1992). Ideal adherence is dependent on the specific medication, treatment goals, and individual factors including age, disease severity, and health-related quality of life.

Measurement

Adherence measures should be unobtrusive, objective, and practical (Rudd, 1979). Biological measures (e.g., blood assays) can be obtrusive, whereas microelectronic monitoring is relatively unobtrusive and objective (Park & Jones, 1997). Although practical, self-reports of adherence and pill counts have been shown to overestimate adherence to medications and therefore are a less desirable method of measuring adherence (Guerrero, Rudd, Bryant-Kosling, & Middleton, 1993; Lee et al., 1996).

Extent and Consequences of Nonadherence

Estimates of nonadherence range from 30 to 60% for a variety of patients, diagnoses, and treatments (e.g., Rogers & Bullman, 1995; Haynes et al., 2002). Nonadherence to medication reduces health outcomes by lowering drug efficacy and producing drug-related illness due to incorrect doses or drug combinations (e.g., Col, Fanale, & Kronholm, 1990). Because adherence is often not monitored (Steele, Jackson, & Gutman, 1990), inadequate assessment of treatment efficacy can occur (Dunbar-Jacob, Burke, & Puczynski, 1995).

Theories of Nonadherence

Social-behavioral theories used to explain nonadherence include the Health Belief Model (Strecher & Rosenstock, 1997), Common Sense Model (Leventhal, Leventhal, Robitaile, & Brownlee, 1999), and Social Learning Theory (Bandura, 1997). Park and colleagues (Park et al., 1999) integrate psychosocial approaches with cognitive theory. They propose that nonadherence is influenced by illness representation, cognitive function, and external aids. Multifactor models recognize that patients must understand how to adhere, accept the prescribed regimen, develop an adherence plan that integrates information for all medications, and then implement the plan (Morrow & Leirer, 1999).

Predictors of Nonadherence

Nonadherence occurs for many reasons: Patients may nonadhere intentionally to avoid side effects (Cooper, Love, & Raffoul, 1982), unintentionally because of barriers (e.g., affordability), or inadvertently because they do not understand or remember how to take the medication.

Illness and Treatment Variables

Nonadherence increases with regimen complexity (e.g., times of day) (Ascione, 1994) and varies with symptoms (O'Brien et al., 1992), medication side effects (Haynes et al., 1979), illness representation (Leventhal & Leventhal, 1999), perceived benefits of treatment, and severity of illness (Strecher & Rosenstock, 1997).

Patient Variables

There is little evidence that nonadherence varies with gender, socioeconomic, or ethnic factors (Dunbar-Jacob et al., 1995). Nonadherence is associated with education, cognitive ability, and age. Less educated patients tend to have lower health literacy (ability to understand basic medical and services information), leading to poor health outcomes and lower utilization of services (Gazmararian et al., 1999). Older adults' nonadherence is a critical problem because they are a growing segment of the population, tend to use more health services, and are vulnerable to the consequences of nonadherence (e.g., Ascione, 1994). Older adults' comprehension of medication information is predicted by education level (Diehl, Willis, & Schaie, 1995) and nonadherence by cognitive decline (Morrell et al., 1997; Park et al., 1992). However, nonadherence may be higher for middle-aged than for young-old adults (ages 65–74; Morrell et al., 1997; Park et al., 1999), perhaps because busy lifestyles increase forgetting.

Provider-Patient Communication

Patient adherence also relates to improved physician communication variables, such as amount of information and partnership building (Hall, Roter, & Katz, 1988).

Reducing Noncompliance

There are few intervention studies with rigorous designs such as randomized control trials (Haynes, McKibbon, & Kanani, 1996; Roter et al., 1998; Haynes et al., 2001). Moreover, interventions targeting adherence alone are not sufficient because the goal is to improve clinical outcomes (e.g., Haynes et al., 2001).

The literature suggests the importance of several interventions, although they tend to be complex and difficult to implement. More convenient care, improved instruction, reminders, self-monitoring, reinforcement, counseling, family therapy, attention, and tailoring the regimen to daily habits are among successful approaches (Haynes et al., 2002). Interventions often involve cognitive or psychosocial approaches.

Cognitive Approaches

Nonadherence is associated with more complex regimens, suggesting that simplifying regimens by reducing or synchronizing times improves adherence (Ley, 1997; Baird et al., 1984). Sensorimotor barriers can be mitigated by simple interventions such as large print on labels and easy-to-open containers (Ascione, 1994). Comprehension and memory problems are addressed by improving instructions, including providing more information and using simple language, clear formats, and organization based on patients' schemas for taking medication (Hartley, 1999; Morrow et al., 1988; Morrow & Leirer, 1999). Pictures in instructions address problems related to limited education and literacy (e.g., Morrow & Leirer, 1999). Nonadherence is reduced by improved packaging (e.g., Wong & Norman, 1987), calendars or other aids that help patients organize (e.g., MacDonald, MacDonald, & Phoenix, 1977), pill organizers if they are correctly loaded (Park & Jones, 1997), and automated telephone messages that support prospective memory and symptom monitoring (e.g., Tanke & Leirer, 1994).

Psychosocial Approaches and Patient Education

Educational programs based on psychosocial approaches focus on intentional nonadherence. There is evidence that they improve adherence by targeting belief-based barriers such as perceived vulnerability to illness and benefits and costs of treatment (Janz & Becker, 1984; Strecher & Rosenstock, 1997). Benefits may occur for reasons in addition to influencing specific beliefs, such as increased patient knowledge (e.g., Brown, 1990) or self-efficacy (e.g., Lorig et al., 1989).

Other Interventions

Several methods attempt to shape adherence behavior, including behavioral contracting (Haynes et al., 1979), feedback (Kruse, Rampmaier, Ullrich, & Weber, 1994), and financial incentives (Giuffrida & Torgerson, 1997). Nonadherence is reduced by increasing social support, which may reflect the influence of significant others on patients' prospective memory, health beliefs, or self-efficacy (Park & Jones, 1997).

Conclusions

Although there are many adherence studies, few have adequately measured adherence, and nonadherence remains a pervasive health care problem (e.g., Haynes et al., 2001). Challenges for future research include the following: There is a need for intervention research based on comprehensive models that address both intentional and unintentional adherence (see Park & Jones, 1997). A complex, patient-based approach is needed, including profiles of nonadherent patients so providers can recommend methods for specific nonadherence conditions. Finally, research should focus on implementing interventions within existing health delivery systems once efficacy has been demonstrated in clinical trials.

REFERENCES

Ascione, F. (1994). Medication compliance in the elderly. *Generations, 18,* 28–33.

Baird, M. G., Bentley-Taylor, M. M., Carruthers, S. G., Dawson, K. G., Laplante, L. E., & Larochelle, P. (1984). A study of the efficacy, tolerance, and compliance of once-daily versus twice-daily metoprolol (Betaloc) in hypertension. *Clinical and Investigative Medicine, 7,* 95.

Bandura, A. (1997). Self-efficacy and health behaviour. In A. Baum, S. Newman, J. Weinman, R. West, & C. McManus (Eds.), *Cambridge handbook of psychology, health, and medicine.* (pp. 160–162). Cambridge, UK: Cambridge University Press.

Brown, S. A. (1990). Studies of educational interventions and outcomes in diabetic adults: A meta-analysis revisited. *Patient Education and Counseling, 16,* 189–215.

Col, N., Fanale, J. E., & Kronholm, P. (1990). The role of medication noncompliance and adverse drug reactions in hospitalizations of the elderly. *Archives of Internal Medicine, 150,* 841–845.

Cooper, J. W., Love, D. W., & Raffoul, P. R. (1982). Intentional prescription nonadherence (noncompliance) by the elderly. *Journal of the American Geriatrics Society, 30,* 329–333.

Diehl, M., Willis, S. L., & Schaie, W. (1995). Everyday problem solving in older adults: Observational assessment and cognitive correlates. *Psychology and Aging, 10,* 478–491.

Dunbar-Jacob, J., Burke, L. E., & Puczynski, S. (1995). Clinical assessment and management of adherence to medical regimens. In P. M. Nicassio & T. W. Smith (Eds.), *Managing chronic illness: A biopsychosocial perspective* (pp. 313–349). Washington, DC: American Psychological Association.

Gazmararian, J. A., Baker, D. W., Williams, M. V., Parker, R. M., Scott, T. L., Green, D. C., Fehrenbach, S. N., Ren, J., & Koplan, J. P. (1999). Health literacy among medicare enrollees in a managed care organization. *Journal of the American Medical Association, 281,* 545–551.

Giuffrida, A., & Torgerson, D. (1997). Should we pay the patient? A review of financial incentives to enhance patient compliance. *British Medical Journal, 3,* 703.

Guerrero, D., Rudd, P., Bryant-Kosling, C., & Middleton, B. (1993). Antihypertensive medication-taking. Investigation of a simple regimen. *Journal of Hypertension, 6,* 586–592.

Hall, J. A., Roter, D. L., & Katz, N. R. (1988). Meta-analysis of correlates of provider behavior in medical encounters. *Medical Care, 26,* 657–675.

Hartley, J. (1999). What does it say? Text design, medical information, and older readers. In D. C. Park, R. W. Morrell, & K. Shifren (Eds.), *Processing of medical information in aging patients* (pp. 233–248). Mahwah, NJ: Erlbaum.

Haynes, R. B., McKibbon, K. A., & Kanani, R. (1996). Systematic review of randomized trials of interventions to assist patients to follow prescriptions for medications *Lancet, 348,* 383.

Haynes, R. B., Montague, P., Oliver, T., McKibbon, K. A., Brouwers, M. C., & Kanani, R. (2001). Interventions for helping patients to follow prescriptions for medications. (Cochrane Review). In *The Cochrane Library, 4,* Oxford: Update Software.

Haynes, R. B., Taylor, D. W., & Sackett, D. L. (1979). *Compliance in health care.* Baltimore: Johns Hopkins University Press.

Janz, N. K., & Becker, M. H. (1984). The health belief model: A decade later. *Health Education Quarterly, 11,* 1–47.

Kruse, W., Rampmaier, J., Ullrich, G., & Weber, E. (1994). Patterns of drug compliance with medications to be taken once and twice daily assessed by continuous electronic monitoring in primary care. *International Journal of Clinical Pharmacology and Therapeutics, 32,* 452–457.

Lee, J. Y., Kusek, J. W., Greene, P. G., Bernhard, S., Norris, K., Smith, D., Wilkening, B., & Wright, J. T. Jr. (1996). Assessing medication adherence by pill count and electronic monitoring in the African American Study of Kidney Disease and Hypertension (AASK) Pilot Study, *American Journal of Hypertension, 9*(8), 719–725.

Leventhal, E. A., Leventhal, H., Robitaile, C., & Brownlee, S. (1999). Psychosocial factors in medication adherence: A model of the modeler. In D. C. Park, R. W. Morrell, & K. Shifren (Eds.), *Processing of medical information in aging patients* (pp. 145–166). Mahwah, NJ: Erlbaum.

Ley, P. (1997). Recall by patients. In A. Baum, S. Newman, J. Weinman, R. West, & C. McManus (Eds.), *Cambridge handbook of psychology, health, and medicine* (pp. 315–317). Cambridge, UK: Cambridge University Press.

Lorig, K., Seleznick, M., Lubeck, D., Ung, E., Chastain, R. L., & Holman, H. R. (1989). The beneficial outcomes of the arthritis self-management course are not adequately explained by behavior change. *Arthritis and Rheumatism, 32,* 91–95.

MacDonald, E. T., MacDonald, J. B., & Phoenix, M. (1977). Improving drug compliance after hospital discharge. *British Medical Journal, 2,* 618–621.

Morrell, R. W., Park, D. C., Kidder, D. P., & Martin, M. (1997). Adherence to antihypertensive medications across the life span. *The Gerontologist, 37,* 609–619.

Morrow, D. G., & Leirer, V. O. (1999). Designing medication instructions for older adults. In D. C. Park, R. W. Morrell, & K. Shifren (Eds.), *Processing of medical information in aging patients* (pp. 249–265), Mahwah, NJ: Erlbaum.

Morrow, D. G., Leirer, V. O., & Sheikh, J. (1988). Adherence and medication instructions: Review and recommendations. *Journal of the American Geriatric Society, 36,* 1147–1160.

O'Brien, M. K., Petrie, K., & Raeburn, J. (1992). Adherence to medication regimens: Updating a complex medical issue. *Medical Care Review, 49,* 435–454.

Park, D. C., Hertzog, C., Leventhal, H. Morrell, R. W., Leventhal, E., Birchmore, D., Martin, M., & Bennett, J. (1999). Medication adherence in rheumatoid arthritis patients: Older is wiser. *Journal of the American Geriatrics Society, 47,* 172–183.

Park, D. C., & Jones, T. R. (1997). Medication adherence and aging. In A. D. Fisk & W. A. Rogers (Eds.), *Handbook of human factors and the older adult* (pp. 257–287). San Diego, CA: Academic Press.

Park, D. C., Morrell, R., Freske, D., & Kincaid, D. (1992). Medication adherence behaviors in older adults: Effects of external cognitive supports. *Psychology and Aging, 7,* 252–256.

Rogers, P. G., & Bullman, W. R. (1995). Prescription medication compliance: A review of the baseline of knowledge. A report of the National Council on Patient Information and Education. *Journal of Pharmacoepidemiology, 2,* 3.

Roter, D. L., Hall, J. A., Merisca, R., Nordstrom, B., Cretin, D., & Svarstad, B. (1998). Effectiveness of interventions to improve patient compliance: A meta-analysis. *Medical Care, 36,* 1138–1161.

Rudd, P. (1979). In search of the gold standard for compliance measurement. *Archives of Internal Medicine, 139,* 627–628.

Steele, D. J., Jackson, T. C., & Gutmann, M. C. (1990). Have you been taking your pills? The adherence monitoring sequence in the medical interview. *Journal of Family Practice, 30,* 294–299.

Strecher, V. J., & Rosenstock, I. M. (1997). The health belief model. In A. Baum, S. Newman, J. Weinman, R. West, & C. McManus (Eds.), *Cambridge handbook of psychology, health, and medicine* (pp. 113–116). Cambridge, UK: Cambridge University Press.

Tanke, E. D., & Leirer, V. O. (1994). Automated telephone reminders in tuberculosis care. *Medical Care, 32,* 380–389.

Wong, B. S. M., & Norman, D. C. (1987). Evaluation of a novel medication aid, the calendar blister-pak, and its effect on drug compliance in a geriatric outpatient clinic. *Journal of the American Geriatrics Society, 35,* 21–26.

Daniel G. Morrow
University of Illinois at Urbana-Champaign

Kathleen C. Insel
University of Arizona

***See also:* Motivation**

PEER COUNSELING

Peer counseling is defined as the performance of limited counselor functions, under counselor supervision, by a person of approximately the same age as the counselee. The majority of peer counseling programs are conducted at the college level, although secondary and elementary schools are also involved. Community mental health agencies and penal systems have developed paraprofessional models using indigenous "natural" leaders and mediators in self-help programs for change.

Peer counselors have been used four ways: (1) as clerical help; (2) as an adjunct to the counseling program, usually in a narrowly defined role such as tutor or information provider; (3) as an aide in a group setting under direct supervision of a counselor; and rarely (4) as an independent agent with the responsibilities of a counselor.

A group counseling model for peer training emphasizes self-awareness, interpersonal and communication skills, and an introduction to counseling skills for higher levels of involvement. The model is theoretically grounded in applied and social learning theory, with attention being given to affective and cognitive development. The training program is based on principles of peer group behavior; the power of peer influence is directed toward positive, effective, and rewarding life skills. Peer counselors are models for their peers; positive behavior is encouraged and developed in the training and exhibited by the peer counselors to influence their contemporaries.

V. Delworth evaluated peer counseling programs to ascertain why they are not more effective in school settings. He concluded that the major failure lies in the fact that these individuals are trained to maintain the status quo of the school. In most of the programs surveyed, peer counselors operate under the direct supervision of the counselor and within the formal hierarchical school structure. This makes it difficult to have an effect on "problem" students whose values are different from those represented by the peer counselors.

The necessary elements for an effective paraprofessional or peer program are that (1) the selection process must identify the natural leaders and helpers, (2) the training must provide access to "system entry" skills, (3) involvement in all aspects of the organization must be encouraged, (4) this involvement must be developmental, and (5) community among the peers must be built.

N. A. Haynie

See also: **Peer Group Therapy; Peer Influences**

PEER GROUP THERAPY

Therapy done in a group by lay people who share common problems is known as peer group therapy. Peer group therapy was lifted to major importance with the beginning of Alcoholics Anonymous (AA).

Peer group therapy uses a high level of self-disclosure, rigorous honesty about personal responsibility for actions done, admission of past wrongs to a member of the group or the group itself, readiness to give up old ways of behaving, the making of amends to people who have been harmed, the turning over of one's will and life to the care of some higher power, and assistance to others as a means of helping the member stay sober.

Other peer groups use much the same format, with some requiring more confrontation. Some groups reported on in the literature are simply peers, but most, other than AA and AA-type groups, also have lay leaders who are minimally trained by someone with a psychology background.

All told, approximately 1,500,000 people are involved in peer group therapy in AA and AA-type groups.

Peer group therapy is also practiced in groups such as Synanon, Daytop, and other communities set up to free people of drug use and to provide continuous living support thereafter. They are structured around an environment of deep love and concern but have a highly confrontative atmosphere with a constant demand for rigorous honesty in every aspect of the ex-addicts' daily lives. Communal living and constant confrontation seem to be required for addicts, whereas alcoholics do not find this necessary.

Many other self-help groups practice peer group therapy: Make Today Count (for cancer sufferers) and Grow groups (started in Australia and now in the United States for people who want to improve their emotional functioning) are two of the larger organizations. In addition, there are groups organized by parents or adults who need help facing a problem with an illness or handicap. Examples are United Cerebral Palsy and the Muscular Dystrophy Association.

A national clearinghouse for all self-help organizations is the Self-Help Center of Evanston, Ill. There are nearly 40 other self-help centers in various stages of operation or development across the country. An estimated 500,000 self-help groups in the United States serve as many as 5 million people.

J. Lair

See also: **Group Counseling; Peer Counseling**

PEER INFLUENCES

High-quality peer relationships are important for all aspects of the development and well-being of children and adolescents. Compared with interaction with adults, interactions with peers tend to be more frequent, more intense, and more varied throughout childhood and adolescence. Traditionally, however, the relationships between children and adults have been viewed as the most important vehicle for ensuring effective socialization and development. Child-child relationships have been assumed to be, at best, relatively unimportant and, at worst, unhealthy influences. Such views were mistaken. Prominent theorists such as Sigmund Freud, George H. Mead, Jean Piaget, Erik Erickson, Lawrence Kohlberg, and many others have argued that high-quality peer relationships are essential for an individual's development and well-being, and hundreds of research studies have validated their views (see Bukowski, Newcomb, & Hartup, 1996; Johnson, 1980; Johnson & Johnson, 1999; Ladd, 1999).

In their interactions with peers, children directly learn attitudes, values, skills, and information unobtainable from adults. Positive peer relationships continue to have a critical impact throughout a person's life.

Prosocial and Antisocial Behavior

Interaction with peers provides support, opportunities, and models for prosocial or antisocial behavior. Peers provide the norms, models, and motivation for engaging in prosocial actions as well as the opportunity for doing so. It is while interacting with peers that a person has the opportunity to help, comfort, and give to others. Without peer interaction, many forms of prosocial values and commitments could not be developed. There is a solid and established link, furthermore, between prosocial behavior and peer acceptance. Rejection by peers tends to promote antisocial actions, such as instrumental and impulsive aggressiveness, disruptiveness, and other negatively perceived behavior.

Impulsiveness

Children frequently lack the time perspective needed to tolerate delays in gratification. However, as they develop and are socialized, the focus on their own immediate impulses and needs is replaced with the abilities to (1) take longer time perspectives, and (2) view their individual desires from the perspectives of others. Peers provide models of, and expectations, directions, and reinforcements for, learning to control one's impulses.

Perspective-Taking Ability

Primarily through interaction with one's peers, egocentrism is lost and increased perspective-taking ability is gained. Perspective taking is a critical competency for cognitive and social development. It has been related to the ability to present and comprehend information, constructively resolve conflicts, willingly disclose personal information, help group problem solving, and display positive attitudes toward others in the same situation. All psychological development may be described as a progressive loss of egocentrism and an increase in ability to take wider and more complex perspectives.

Autonomy

In making decisions concerning what behavior is appropriate, autonomous people tend to consider both their internal values and the expectations of other people, and then to respond in flexible and appropriate ways. Autonomy is the result of the internalization of values derived from previous caring and supportive relationships (internalized values provide guides for appropriate behavior and self-approval) and the acquisition of social skills and social sensitivity (which provide accurate understanding of others' expectations for one's behavior). Peer relationships have a powerful influence on the development of values, social skills, and social sensitivity. Children with a history of isolation from or rejection by peers often are inappropriately other-directed. They may conform to group pressures even when they believe the recommended actions are wrong or inappropriate.

Identity

Throughout infancy, childhood, adolescence, and early adulthood, a person moves through several successive and overlapping identities. Physical, cognitive, and social development and broader experiences and responsibilities all cause changes in self-definition. The final result is a coherent and integrated identity. In peer relationships, children clarify the similarities and differences between themselves and others, experiment with a variety of social roles that help them integrate their own sense of self, clarify their attitudes and values and integrate them into their self-definition, and develop a frame of reference for perceiving themselves.

Aspiration and Productivity

Peers have a strong influence on productivity and aspirations. Supportive relationships with peers are related to using abilities in achievement situations and to academic competence. Peer rejection predicts school absenteeism, grade retention, and adjustment difficulties. The more one's peers value academic excellence and the higher their academic aspirations, the more likely one is to achieve and to seek out opportunities for higher education.

Psychological Health

The ability to maintain interdependent, cooperative relationships is a prime manifestation of psychological health. Poor peer relationships in elementary school predict psychological disturbance and delinquency in high school, and poor peer relationships in high school predict adult pathology. The absence of friendships during childhood and adolescence tends to increase the risk of psychological disorder. Peer rejection predicts loneliness and emotional distress while friendships and peer acceptance are related to socioemotional adjustment. Children adapt better to stressful situations when in the presence of friends or familiar peers. *Peer victimization* exists when children are exposed to abusive processes that promote cognitive-affective states such as insecurity, mistrust, or fearfulness. Peer victimization involves aggressors and their victims, and is linked with a number of adjustment difficulties during childhood, including anxiety, loneliness, depression, and school maladaptation.

Promoting Positive Peer Relationships

To promote positive peer relationships, children should first have continuous opportunities to cooperate with peers and occasionally engage in competitions. Second, children should receive specific training in the social skills needed to build and maintain positive relationships. Third, the norms of caring, support, encouragement, assistance, reciprocity, and so forth should be established. The rights and responsibilities of collaborators and friends should be clear. Finally, a set of civic values needs to be taught and inculcated. Those values include commitment to the well-being of others and to the common good, a sense of responsibility to contribute one's fair share of the work, respect for the efforts of others and for them as people, behaving with integrity, caring for others, showing compassion when others are in need, and appreciating diversity.

REFERENCES

Bukowski, W., Newcomb, A., & Hartup, W. (Eds.). (1996). *The company they keep: Friendship in childhood and adolescence.* New York: Cambridge University Press.

Johnson, D. W. (1980). Importance of peer relationships. *Children in Contemporary Society, 13,* 121–123.

Johnson, D. W. (2000). *Reaching out: Interpersonal effectiveness and self-actualization* (7th ed.). Boston: Allyn & Bacon.

Johnson, D. W., & Johnson, R. (1999). *Learning together and alone: Cooperative, competitive, and individualistic learning* (5th ed.). Boston: Allyn & Bacon.

Ladd, G. (1999). Peer relationships and social competence during early and middle childhood. *Annual Review of Psychology* (Vol. 50, pp. 333–359). Palo Alto, CA: Annual Reviews.

David W. Johnson
Roger T. Johnson
University of Minnesota

See also: **Affective Development; Bonding and Attachment; Development of Human Social Behavior**

PEER TUTORING

Any use of students to coach or tutor one another is usually called "peer tutoring," although when their ages differ, the students are not really members of the same peer group.

Comenius, the sixteenth-century Czech educator, observed what is a routine finding on peer tutoring today, that those doing the tutoring learn more than those who are tutored.

The appeal of peer tutoring for modern educators lies in its effectiveness as a teaching/learning method, rather than in its potential economies. Research studies have been universally supportive of the method.

In a review of research, A. Elliott arrived at the following explanations for the efficacy of peer tutoring:

1. Peer tutoring increases the percentage of time spent on teaching in the classroom period.
2. Peer tutoring provides learners with more feedback as to their performance and provides it promptly.
3. Peer tutoring increases time spent in student talk and decreases time spent in teacher talk.
4. Tutors enjoy an enhanced sense of competence and personal worth.
5. Tutors are enabled to view the teaching/learning situation from the teacher's position and thus are led to make the classroom psychological climate more cooperative and less suppressive and authoritarian.
6. Tutors are able to identify problems of learning and adjustment that have been overlooked by teachers.

Henry C. Lindgren

PERCEPTION

Perception refers to the experience of obtaining sensory information about the world of people, things, and events, and to the underlying process.

The Classical Theory

Successive British empiricist philosophers from Hobbes to Berkeley to Mill viewed all perceptions as learned assemblies of simpler sensory ideas. Scientific study began in 1838 when J. Müller identified the specific part of the nervous system underlying each modality; H. von Helmholtz (Müller's student) subdivided those modalities into elementary sensations, each due to a specific receptor nerve cell reacting to selected stimulation. Thus, the eye's *retina* contains receptors for long, middle, and short wave lengths

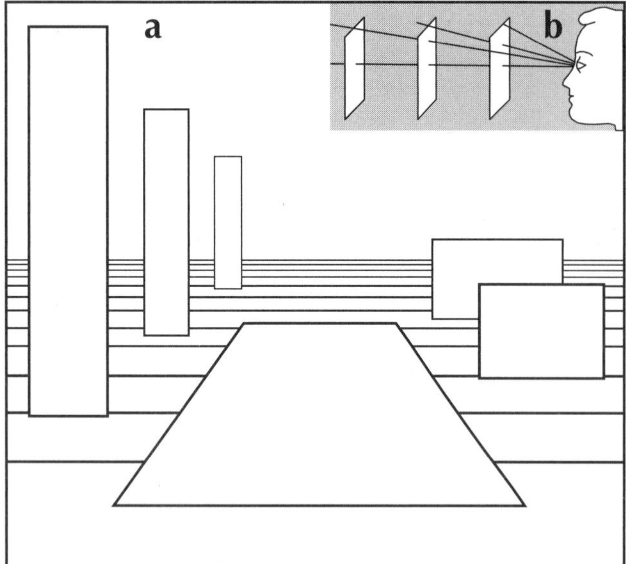

Figure 1. Two dimensional images of a three-dimensional world. (a) Classical pictorial cues to depth and distance. (b) Visual angle as a function of object size and distance.

Source: All figures in this entry are modified from J. Hochberg (in press). Acts of perceptual inquiry: Problems for any stimulus-based simplicity theory. *Acta Psychologica.*

(L, M, S), presumably providing red, green, and blue points of color sensation.

Most perceived properties—shape, distance, movement, and so forth—are not sensations in this theory, but complex learned perceptions, as considered next.

Things in Space: Depth, Constancies, Illusions

Many different three-dimensional objects can provide the same (two-dimensional) retinal image. However, normal environments offer *depth cues.* (Simple examples, studied by fifteenth-century artists, include the perspective illustrated in Figure 1a, and the occluding intersections shown in Figure 4a.) To classical theory, depth perception rests on memories that the depth cues have acquired. These *associations* involve connections formed between simultaneously active nerve cells in the brain. By using depth cues, illumination cues, and learned rules about how such variables relate the object to its retinal image (see Figure 1b), the perceiver unconsciously infers the object's attributes. When we correctly use whatever cues are present, we thereby achieve *size constancy, shape constancy, color constancy,* and so forth. Misperceived attributes, or *illusions,* presumably result from mistaking some pattern for a cue it is not.

In this theory, all perception is learned. Independent sensory receptors analyze stimulation into elementary sensations, and by associating those sensations into perceptual structures, the brain mirrors the environment.

The theory's first problem is that some animal species can respond appropriately to visual depth *without prior visual experience* (E. Thorndyke, chicks; E. J. Gibson and R. Walk, other species); How they do so, however, remains undetermined.

Figure 2. Figure and Ground: When the black pedestal is figure, the white regions are unshaped ground, and when the white faces are figures the black region is unshaped ground.

Organization, Figure/Ground, and the Gestaltist Argument

To *Gestalt* theorists (notably M. Wertheimer, W. Köhler, and K. Koffka) the visual system responds directly to the stimulating energies' overall *configuration* (or Gestalt), not to a point-by-point analysis. In Figure 2, an example of E. Rubin's figure–ground phenomenon, only one region, the pedestal or the pair of faces, is *figure* and has a recognizable shape at any time, while the other is *ground,* extending behind the figure's edge. *Laws of figure–ground organization* therefore determine what objects we see: By the *law of good continuation,* for example, a familiar letter is concealed and revealed in Figures 3a and b, respectively, and the cube in Figure 3d is only a flat pattern in 3c.

Gestalt theory did not replace its opponent. Figure–ground properties and organizational "laws" might just be environmental likelihoods, as E. Brunswik proposed, while no Gestaltist theory explaining such phenomena survives. Research to quantify organizational "laws" does continue, like that by M. Kubovy, as do attempts to replace these laws with the more general principle that one perceives the sim-

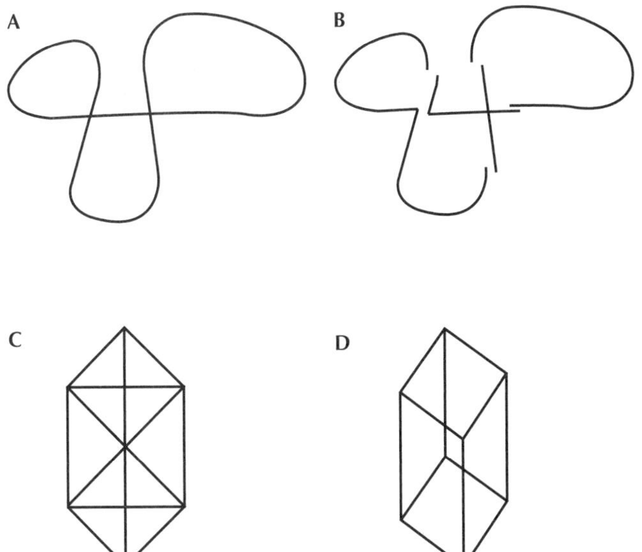

Figure 3. At (a), *good continuation* obscures the familiar shape ("4") that is revealed at (b). The pattern at (c) is *simpler* as a flat pattern than that at (d).

plest organization that fits a particular stimulus pattern—for example, Figure 3c is simpler as a flat pattern than 3d. Such efforts have been undertaken separately by the present author and by F. Attneave, and pursued by E. Leeuwenberg and colleagues. But a general theory of configurations, compatible with modern neurophysiology, has not yet appeared.

Direct Perception Versus Inference

To replace both Helmholtzian and Gestalt approaches, J. J. Gibson proposed that viewers moving through natural environments receive stimulus information that remains constant despite changing conditions (distance, slant, etc.). This allows *direct perception* of objects and layout: No inferences from depth cues are needed. This direct approach generated several sophisticated mathematical analyses of available information, most recently by J. Koenderink and A. van Doorn, and experimental studies of its use (whether "directly" or otherwise), notably by W. Warren.

But the Gibsonian approach, too, has not replaced Helmholtzian inference: Depth cues certainly appear to work, as in pictures and false-perspective illusions, even when they are opposed by motion-generated information signaling a flat surface. Like Gestalt theory, it has yet to connect with what we now know about eye and brain.

Modern Neurophysiology

Helmholtz's assumptions about independent receptor neurons and sensations were wrong. To E. Hering and E. Mach, Helmholtz's contemporaries, neuronal interconnections accounted directly for some perceptual constancies and illusions, assertions mostly accepted today. Hering's argument that the elementary colors are not red, green, and blue sensations, but three opponent pairs originating with interconnected cell pairs, was verified by L. Hurvich and D. Jameson (psychophysically) and by R. DeValois and G. Jacobs (using microelectrodes). Mach's proposal of pattern-sensitive interconnections was verified by D. Hubel and T. Wiesel, using microelectrodes to find cells and brain regions with receptive fields selectively sensitive to shapes and motions. (Some properties and objects we perceive surely reflect the output of specific neural mechanisms.) The retina's topography is preserved upward through several cortical levels, with increasing receptive field size and decreasing resolution from V1 to V4; these levels are all mutually connected in both directions, as P. Lennie maps them, so the highest V4 offers a context-affecting entry level, V1.

Such pattern-sensitive structures and top-down interactions must change our approach to perceptual theory.

Attention and the Moving Eye

Only the small retinal center (the *fovea,* ca 2°) obtains detailed visual information. Within single foveal glances, items that are unfamiliar, unexpected, or of no interest to the viewer may go undetected. To see more, the viewer aims and executes rapid intentional eye movements (*saccades*), getting glimpses of about 1/5sec/glance. Integrating such successive glimpses into a unified perception of an object or scene is not automatic or all-inclusive, as movie editors know well: Figure 4 remains ambiguous when attending point b, even *after* attending a. Detailed information that has been looked at but not *encoded* (stored in working memory, as G. Sperling showed) is usually not followed up. Per-

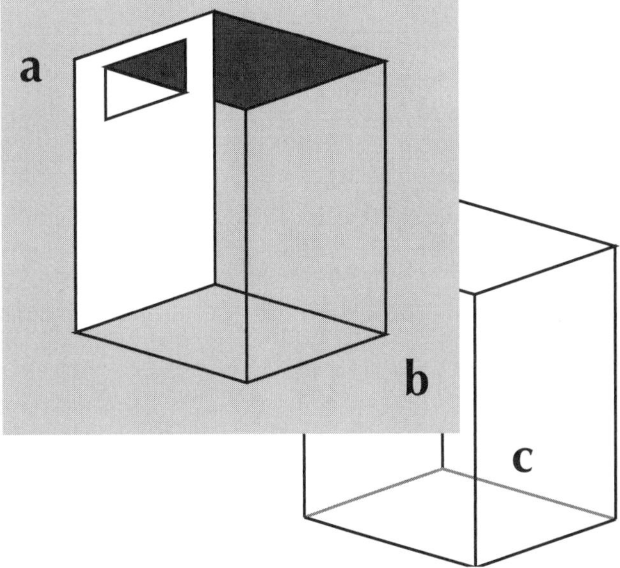

Figure 4. Occlusions at (a) show the white leftmost region to be in front. At lower right (b) the same figure is ambiguous, and can be readily reversed, as in the cube partially shown at (c).

ception is a directed activity, and brain imaging is about to tell us how the different regions participate in attentive perceptual inquiry.

Julian Hochberg
Columbia University

PERCEPTUAL CONTROL THEORY

"Perceptual control theory" is a name adopted by a group of scientists interested in the feedback-system organization of human and animal behavior to distinguish their work from the control theory field of servo engineers. The members are engaged in the development and application of the thesis advanced in W. T. Powers's (1973) book, *Behavior: The Control of Perception.* While a majority of this group are psychologists, it also includes biologists, sociologists, systems engineers, mathematicians, and members of other professions—all finding themselves able to communicate with the common language of Powers's theory, a rather unusual experience in this age of high specialization.

One member of the group, Richard Marken, observed that Powers has not one but two accomplishments to his credit. First, he discovered, or noted, that behavior is the control of perception, contrary to what psychologists have believed ever since Descartes. For Descartes, the environment controlled behavior in the sense that he believed perception of phenomena of the environment stimulates or triggers behavior by entering sensory receptors to set off reflex responses in the organism. Second, Powers developed a theory to explain how behavior does work, showing that feedback-control theory can account for how perceptual variables are maintained against external influences/disturbances by control systems, whether in organisms or robots. The theory he developed finally provided a coherent mechanism for the phenomenon of homeostasis, which had been observed much earlier by biologists but had remained an inexplicable phenomenon.

Although biologists had gradually accepted self-regulatory—homeostatic—mechanisms after Bernard as applying to many bodily functions, the idea that the same principles could account for mental phenomena gained ground more slowly. However, beginning in the 1940s a number of scientists, such as Norbert Wiener, began to suggest that such principles could explain certain aspects of behavior, if not all. Finally, in 1960 the team of W. T. Powers, R. K. Clark, and R. L. McFarland published *A General Feedback Theory of Human Behavior,* which presented the first fully comprehensive view of how all behavior could be accounted for by an integrated assembly of hierarchically-ordered feedback control systems. This work then led to Powers's 1973 book.

The basic scheme is as follows. Behavior occurs via a system comprised of a closed feedback loop in which a variable perceptual signal (PS) is held to a specified value—reference signal (RS)—by the workings of a comparator (C). The comparator subtracts the value of the reference signal from the value of the perceptual signal to obtain an error signal (ES) that is fed into an output mechanism capable of affecting the perceptual signal in such a way as to counteract any disturbance (D) coming from the environment. It does so by driving the perceptual signal back toward (maintains it at) the reference value. The system works to keep minimizing the errorsignal, and in so doing it controls the pertinent, perceived aspect of the environment as a byproduct. Perceptual variables in organisms derive from sensory signals.

Reference signals are previously stored sensory signals. Output mechanisms are ultimately muscles and glands. Powers pointed out a number of examples of feedback circuitry in neuroanatomy in his book and has continued to find additional anatomical evidence in his further work.

Figure 1 shows the feedback loop outlined in its simplest form.

The same scheme is repeated in hierarchical fashion in which the sensory signal is relayed to higher order systems and the output of the order above determines the RS of the order below. This simple schema may be effectively applied to a host of everyday behaviors to explain what is happening. A popular illustration is the action of driving a car. The driver keeps the car in its lane against external disturbances such as wind, curves, bumps, and so forth by monitoring the relationship between the front of the car and the edge of the road, both of which are perceptual variables reducible to a higher order variable: the constancy of that relationship. The latter is thus the presumptive perceptual signal of interest. It is matched in the brain to the reference signal; that is, the desired condition of that relationship, the result being the continual flow of error signals that are minimized by the actions of the driver on the steering wheel.

Powers showed that this analysis could be quantified in

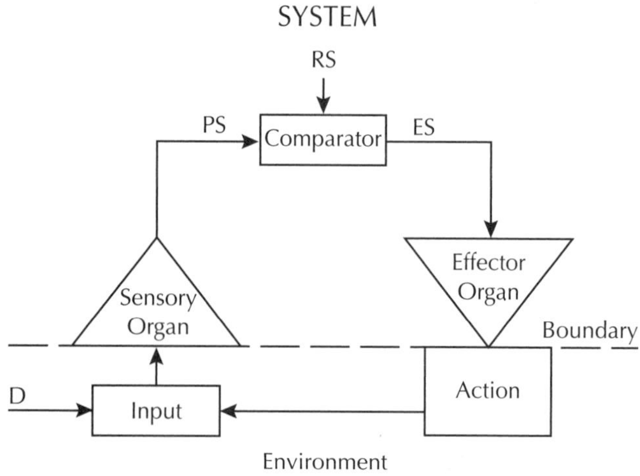

Figure 1. Feedback loop.
Source: Adapted from W. T. Powers, 1973, *Behavior: The Control of Perception.*

simultaneous equations as PS = O + D and ES = PS – RS, where D represents a disturbing condition in the environment, and O, the output of the system, is some function of ES as determined by the properties of the particular system. He applied these equations to many different analyses of behavioral phenomena, adding constants as appropriate to specific systems, and created a number of computer simulations of various types of behavior showing that human actions can be imitated by programs using his functions, the implication being that if a feedback model, and only a feedback model, imitates a human performance, it suggests that the behavior is feedback controlled.

The perceptive reader might have noticed in the above that Powers has also solved the problem of purpose, or intention, that has been a dilemma for stimulus–response psychologists. It is identical with the reference signal. The control system realizes what one intends as the organism's action brings what is being perceived to match the specification that is to be perceived. Powers went on to propose hypothetical answers to many other questions that one might raise about the nature of behavior. He sketched out a hierarchy of control systems to account for the complexity of behavior, in which individual control systems of each level receive their reference signals from the output of systems of the level above.

Another proposal is that of an organizing–reorganizing system powered by an intrinsic system comprised of genetically determined reference settings. He postulated that if any "readings" in the intrinsic system go into an error state (i.e., indicate physical malfunctioning), the reorganizing system would be triggered to inject random signaling into the control-system hierarchy to bring about changes in neural circuitry which, when successful in controlling some new (for that organism) condition, constitutes what we regard as learning. His insight was that only random action could afford the chance to produce a new type of action (in a given organism) because any disturbance to conditions already under control would immediately be nullified by existing systems. A moment's reflection leads one to conceive of how the human being comes to have a learned hierarchy in the first place, starting from only an intrinsic system of genetically given life-supporting systems at birth, acting via the reorganizing system upon a growing mass of uncommitted neurons forming and reforming connections as development proceeds.

Other members of this group have gone on to apply Powers's analysis to a wide variety of experiments and applications based upon the idea that living organisms do not control their environments by controlling their outputs, but instead, by controlling their inputs—their perceptions. Much of this work constitutes a significant advance in the testing of hypotheses by quantitative model building and computer simulation rather than by inferences of causality from correlations, as is commonly practiced in contemporary psychology. This work can be accessed through the information net CSGnet; the Control Systems Group homepage, http://ed.uiuc.edu/csg/csg.html; W. T. Powers's web site, http://home.earthlink.net/~powers_w; and other members' home pages.

Richard J. Robertson

See also: **Behavior Modeling; Control Therapy; Cybernetics; Homeostasis**

PERCEPTUAL DEVELOPMENT

The most active investigations about perceptual development focus on infants' visual and auditory capabilities. Researchers who study these topics have demonstrated impressive creativity and persistence in designing research techniques for assessing early abilities. Two representative methods are the following: (1) the habituation/dishabituation method, in which infants decrease their attention to an object that has been presented many times, and then increase their attention when a new object is presented; and (2) the preference method, in which infants spend consistently longer responding to one object than to a second object.

Visual Development

The retina of a newborn is not fully developed, especially in the central region (fovea) where adult acuity is best. A newborn's visual accuity is about 20/600; that is, newborns can see at 20 feet what an adult with normal acuity (20/20) can see at 600 feet. However, acuity improves with age, until it approximates 20/20 vision at about 3 years of age.

Infants who are younger than 1 month of age do not have functional color vision. However, by 3 months of age, they can discriminate among many different colored stimuli.

With respect to distance perception, 6-month-old babies can use both monocular depth information (e.g., shading, interposition) and binocular depth information (e.g., binocular disparity, with each eye registering a slightly different view of the world). By this age, they also tend to avoid the deep side of a visual cliff, thereby demonstrating that they can apply this visual information about distance.

Young infants also demonstrate constancy. For example, a 3-month-old shows some shape constancy, so that an object seems to stay the same shape, even when viewed from a different angle. A 6-month-old shows good size constancy, so that an object seems to stay the same size, even when viewed from a different distance. In contradiction to Piagetian theory, infants display object permanence by about 4 months of age; an object still exists, even when it is hidden behind another object.

Motion perception also develops in the first months of age. For example, by 5 months, babies can make relatively subtle discriminations in an object's motion. By this age, they also appreciate biological motion, which is the pattern of movement of living things. For example, they can look at a set of moving lights and tell the difference between (1) a pattern of lights representing a moving person and (2) a pattern of random moving lights.

The research on shape perception suggests that infants exhibit several Gestalt laws, such as the law of closure. When adults look at a long rod moving back and forth—but partially concealed by a block—we perceive that the rod is one solid, continuous object, rather than two separate rod fragments. Infants who are 2 months old also display this law of closure, but newborns do not.

With respect to face perception, infants who are 1 *hour* old can move their eyes a longer distance in order to track a facelike stimulus, rather than a stimulus with a scrambled-face design. Infants who are 1 day old will produce more sucking responses to a video of their mother than to a video of a female stranger. These findings have important implications for early face recognition and for the development of emotional attachments.

Auditory Development

Within the topic of auditory development, the majority of the research focuses on speech perception. More than 30 years ago, researchers demonstrated that infants between the ages of 1 and 4 months could distinguish between two similar phonemes, such as /b/ and /p/. We now know that infants can make more than 50 different contrasts between speech sounds. Infants' language environment has an influence on the development of phoneme discrimination. For example, 6-month-old infants reared in an English-speaking environment are highly accurate in distinguishing between two Hindi phonemes, even though English-speaking adults cannot make this particular distinction. However, if the infants continue to be exposed only to English—and not to Hindi—they lose this ability by about one year of age. At this age, they are only sensitive to distinctions that are relevant in their own language environment.

In addition to detecting the differences between speech sounds, infants also appreciate similarities between speech sounds. For example, they reveal an ability that could be called "speech-sound constancy"; that is, they recognize that the phoneme /a/ spoken in a high-pitched woman's voice is the same as the /a/ spoken by a relatively low-pitched man's voice. This ability is important because it allows them to recognize words they have heard before, which had been produced by a different person.

In terms of preferences, 2-day-old newborns can discriminate between their mother's voice and the voice of a stranger. Furthermore, 4-day-old newborns prefer to listen to speech produced in their mother's native language, rather than in another language. For instance, French infants preferred to listen to a stranger speaking French, rather than when the same woman spoke Russian. Newborn infants even prefer to listen to a passage from a children's story that their mothers had read during the last 6 weeks of pregnancy rather than a similar passage from a different children's story. All three studies demonstrate that vocal information is perceived during prenatal development.

By 4 months of age, infants prefer to listen to child-directed language—the exaggerated, high-pitched speech that parents use in speaking to infants—rather than the kind of language directed toward other adults. By 4 months, infants also appreciate that the visual and auditory components of language must be coordinated; the vowel sound from the word "pop" should come from a rounded mouth configuration.

All these auditory skills have important implications for one of the most impressive of cognitive skills: the comprehension and production of spoken language. Developmental psychologists have difficulty explaining how children can rapidly acquire thousands of words between one year of age and the time they start school. The research on infants' auditory abilities demonstrates that they already have a significant head start before they reach their first birthday.

M. W. Matlin

PERCEPTUAL STYLE

A perceptual style means that a person has a characteristic way of perceiving the world. The idea that people perceive the world in different and individual ways is an intriguing one. The uses of color and form by some modern painters in highly individual and somewhat distorted ways have been hypothesized to be based on possible visual defects, so that the artist is truly copying his or her own subjective experience into art. However, this is difficult to prove, as are other hypotheses. Is it truly a perceptual influence or simply a cognitive interpretative one? Somehow, cognitive styles, meaning the way people think, seem a more neutral concept than perceptual styles. Additionally, there is always the problem of reliable and repeatable information.

Young children do seem to perceive the world more globally and as less differentiated than adults do. Not only do they have less developed verbal descriptions, but also their eye and hand movement search patterns are much less differentiated and precise than are those of older children and adults.

Herman Witkin used the concepts of "field independence" and "field dependence" in the 1950s and 1960s to describe individual differences on perceptual tasks. Witkin had three major tasks: an embedded figures task, a rod-and-frame task, and a tilted room task. Field-independent people can ignore the conflicting visual surround to find a hidden figure (embedded figures) or the true vertical (rod-frame, tilted room). The field-dependent subjects are more influenced by the visual surroundings, leading to worse performance on the embedded figures or dependence on the visual framework rather than the true gravitational one in the other tasks. Performance on the three tasks is related. Witkin also related the results to various personality measures. Field independence and field dependence are still heavily researched areas.

The most reliable "perceptual style" is that of immaturity. Children are less able to differentiate the visual field than are adults. In addition to children, brain-injured adults show these same effects.

Richard D. Walk
George Washington University

See also: **Perception**

PERFORMANCE APPRAISAL

Organizations are concerned with performance. Indicators such as profits, sales, number of widgets produced, number of defective widgets, costs of production, downtime, number and severity of accidents, number and length of absences, and so forth are used in evaluating an organization and the units within an organization. Similarly, performance appraisals evaluate performance of individual employees.

Performance appraisals are used in making administrative decisions, for counseling employees, in training and developing employees, for human resources planning, and in the validation of selection procedures. They are utilized in determining pay increases, in making promotional decisions, and in deciding whether an employee is to be discharged.

There is much discontent with performance appraisal systems. Frequent changes in the methods used for making appraisals, and even abandonment of them, are common occurrences.

History

Informal appraisals of performance have been universal throughout history. Formal appraisal systems have been used since at least the third century A.D. Industrial applications can be traced back to Robert Owens, who introduced them in Scotland early in the nineteenth century. The military forces of the United States adopted performance appraisals in 1813, and the federal government did so for its civilian personnel in 1842.

During the twentieth century, the growth of performance appraisal systems has been relatively rapid. Psychologists have played an active role in the development and application of these systems. In recent years, psychologists have become concerned with the applications of such systems and have been involved in efforts to improve their use.

Subsequent to the passage of the Civil Rights Act of 1964, performance appraisal systems have been subjected to legal challenges. In a number of rulings, federal court judges have found that such systems discriminate against minorities and other groups protected by the law.

Methods

For appraising performance, a variety of methods have been developed. From the results of surveys of business and of government organizations, those in use can be classified as essay, rating scales, combined essay and rating scales, and objectives-based. Essays are essentially narrative reports on the performances of individual employees. They describe and evaluate performance. Rating scales are designed to quantify performance, either overall, on separate dimensions, or on a combination of both. Objectives-based appraisals are used in concert with management-by-objectives (MBO) approaches that have been adopted by many organizations in recent years.

Several varieties of rating scales have been developed. The most prevalent are known as "graphic" rating scales and are characterized by requiring the rater to indicate a ratee's performance as to some characteristic—for example, "integrity."

Another, more complex method of rating is referred to as "forced choice." In using this method, a rater is required to select a word or phrase from two or more that best describes the person being rated. The words or phrases composing such combinations are statistically determined, as are the numerical values assigned each word or phrase.

A third rating method, developed during World War II, is known as "critical requirements" or, more commonly, as "critical incidents." The method is based on descriptions of behaviors that reflect either effective or ineffective performance. Once these critical incidents have been collected and edited for a particular occupation, they form the basis for a checklist of behaviors, the critical requirements that can be used in evaluating performance.

Behaviorally anchored rating scales (BARS) are a relatively recent addition to rating scale methods. They emphasize participation by the raters in developing the scales, a procedure called "retranslation," mathematical scaling, careful observations of performance, and logging of observations by the raters.

Behavioral observation scales (BOS) are the most recent addition to rating scale methods. Using critical incidents, behaviors important to effective performance in an occupation are first identified. They are grouped into categories by persons familiar with the work or by a statistical method called "factor analysis." The items describing the behaviors are designed so as to obtain estimates of the frequency with which the behaviors occur. A scoring method provides for total scores by categories of performance and for a total score across categories. Raters using the method are forced to focus on specific behaviors crucial to effective performance in making their observations and recording their observations.

All rating scale methods depend on some person or persons making judgments of performance. Consequently they are essentially subjective. In contrast, objectives-based appraisal methods focus on collecting information that furnishes objective information concerning performance, for example, sales, quantity and quality of goods produced, or frequency of absences.

Research

It is generally recognized that raters tend to make many errors. Among the common errors is the "halo effect," which is a tendency to rate a person the same on all characteristics being rated even though the ratee may perform differently on different aspects of a job. Another common error is referred to as "leniency," a tendency to rate all ratees more favorably than their individual performances would warrant.

It is a common practice in organizations to have supervisors rate their subordinates. Alternative sources, for example, peers, subordinates, outsiders, and the ratee himself or herself, are available.

To develop and validate an appraisal system properly, considerable research is required. The procedures are highly technical and require professional expertise. Unfortunately, many appraisal systems are developed by persons who lack essential knowledge and skills, and thus the validity of such systems is subject to challenge.

After an appraisal system has been implemented, an organization may want to determine the extent to which the system is meeting its objectives. Such an evaluation requires research that may entail extensive collection and analysis of data.

The use of performance appraisals in counseling employees is a relatively recent development. That both judging employee performance and counseling employees on how to improve performance can produce difficulties for a manager seeking to accomplish these objectives became apparent in a series of studies conducted in the General Electric Company. The studies clearly showed that mutual goal setting by a supervisor and a subordinate and avoidance of criticizing the latter's performance are essential if improved performance is to be achieved.

Application

Implementing and maintaining a performance appraisal system requires much effort and involves many of the resources of an organization. Performance appraisal poses many issues, and considerable mutual education may be required if practitioners and researchers are to function as a team.

Appraisal systems tend to depend on ratings of performance, which are inherently subjective. The many attempts to objectify ratings have had little, if any, success. However, objective methods for appraising performance also have many limitations.

The legal issues involving discriminatory aspects of performance appraisal systems are relatively recent. Though future developments with respect to the legal aspects of performance appraisals are difficult to predict, it would appear that organizations and others concerned with such systems, psychologists in particular, must familiarize themselves with viewpoints expressed by the courts and keep abreast of pertinent developments.

Donald L. Grant

See also: **Applied Research**

PERFECTIONISM IN GIFTED ADOLESCENTS

While many gifted students find special programs for their academic achievements challenging, some gifted students are overwhelmed by the simplest of academic demands. These gifted students are often viewed as lazy. While this label may occur as early as junior high school, problems with academics may not appear until high school or even college.

There are multiple reasons for being seen as lazy, including learning disabilities, attention-deficit/hyperactivity disorder, drugs, psychosis, a death, or even a divorce. Many lazy students are early adolescents. They are extremely bright and sensitive and were often the teacher's favorite in elementary school. These gifted early adolescents suffer from a crippling triad of an endless drive for perfectionism coupled with an intense fear of failure, which then triggers an overwhelming shame. In addition, they fear their own unresolved anger and aggressiveness, which become fused with their assertion and prevent them from comfortably asserting themselves in competitive situations.

Self psychology and intersubjectivity, with their emphasis on the early mother–child relationship, help us focus on the child's need to please his or her parents as a major source of gifted individuals' struggle with being judged as lazy. However, only by understanding the entrenched intrapsychic struggle, or the infant morality system (IMS), can one truly help these gifted individuals to overcome their struggle with perfectionism and accompanying issues and, thus, to attain their full potential.

The IMS starts during infancy. The more brilliant the child, the earlier this system of judgment begins and, hence, the more primitive the child's judgments. This system is thus founded on "black and white," "all or nothing," perfectionistic, rigid, cruel, harsh, and unrelenting judgments, which the developing gifted child directs toward him/herself and his/her world. In addition, in trying to develop a sense of order in a chaotic world, these highly sensitive children take responsibility for everything. This entire primitive and judgmental system becomes part of their unconscious life.

Between 3 to 5 years of age, as young children start to integrate into their families, they often give up parts of themselves—some of their thoughts, comments, and actions—in order to fit within the family illusions. While acceptance of the family illusions provides some protection from being abandoned, they, unfortunately, lose a core part of themselves.

Although this IMS is entrenched well before a child's entrance into elementary school, the inherent self-criticalness continually undermines the developing child's self-esteem. Their perfectionism makes it difficult for these brilliant children to hold onto positive comments, whether from teachers, parents, or peers. At the same time, they experience negative comments or interactions as an assault on their budding sense of self.

For most gifted children, everything comes easily during elementary school. However, excessive parental intrusions often prevent fragile gifted students from learning effective problem-solving techniques. In addition, these gifted students may not learn how to deal with boredom, frustration, and delayed gratification—hallmarks of a competent, successful student.

At some point, sometimes as late as college, these gifted students hit a wall. Not knowing how to deal with boredom, frustration, and delayed gratification, they become overwhelmed. Possessing no effective problem-solving skills, other than being "bright" or "cute," these gifted students suddenly find themselves devastated by their first failure. As a consequence, these gifted students, especially early adolescent males, just give up. Suddenly, there are a multitude of excuses for not completing their homework or studying for a test. They become "lazy." With a precipitous drop in their self-esteem, these students frequently become involved with angry, rebellious peers.

Another way to avoid dealing with their rigid perfectionism is to become engaged in self-defeating games. One student made going to college into a joke. He never went to class, never turned in any homework, and never studied for tests. Receiving Cs for his work, he bragged about having done so well with absolutely no work. This young adult's struggle with perfectionism also highlights how these difficulties go beyond academics. During this time, he wanted to buy a very expensive sports car with a six-speed manual transmission. After stalling a friend's car only once during an hour-long practice with a stick shift, and in spite of a lifelong desire to drive a stick shift, he bought his dream car without a stick shift.

An additional area of difficulty for these very mild-mannered, gifted students is their inability to deal with anger. Often, they come from families in which anger is not dealt with comfortably. As a consequence, these students often confuse assertion with aggression. When they try to do well, they feel that they will hurt other students. One teenager who was getting Cs at an all-girls high school said,

> If I start to get As, one of my classmates who used to get an A is going to get a B, then another one of my classmates who used to get a B is going to get a C, another one of my classmates who used to get a C is going to get a D, another one of my classmates who used to get a D is going to get an F, and another one of my classmates who used to get an F is going to fail out of school and it's all my fault and they are going to hate me!

As this student learned to be more comfortable with her assertion and competitiveness, her grades improved drastically.

This entry has attempted to show the reader how, independent of parental influence, perfectionism and fear of failure can be severely debilitating to some gifted teenagers. Intellectually, gifted teenagers often understand their parents' desire for them to achieve, as well as their own struggles with being competitive. However, articulating the primitive nature of their intrapsychic conflicts helps them consciously work on lessening their own internal struggle with perfectionism and their fear of failure. In addition, they must address their fear of being seen as defective, as well as being overwhelmed by the ensuing shame, which they experience as paralyzing.

Poor self-esteem is another important issue for the gifted student. As adolescents often respond better to actions rather than to words, walks, sharing food, and playing boardgames or cards are often helpful in lessening the crippling and overwhelming sense of perfectionism. Once again, it is the crippling need to be perfect, as well as the incredible fear of an imagined catastrophic failure and the resulting overwhelming shame that often drives gifted teenagers to become lazy students.

Douglas Schave
UCLA School of Medicine

PERFORMANCE TESTS

Performance tests require overt, active responses, such as motor or manual behaviors. Such tests frequently measure motor coordination, speed, or perceptual or motor skills. Because of their usual deemphasis on language skills, performance tests have proven useful in the assessment of the physically handicapped, particularly the deaf. A common performance test is a typing test that measures how quickly and accurately one can type. A nonperformance measure of typing might ask multiple-choice questions about typewriter parts, positions of the keys, or selection of font, but would not include actual typing performance.

One of the earliest and most popular performance tests is the Sequin formboard, designed for assessment and sensory-motor training of the mentally retarded. This test requires that 10 differently shaped pieces be placed into correspondingly shaped holes; for example, the round peg must be placed in the round hole. More complex formboards also have been developed. Another classic performance test, the Kohs Block Test, developed in 1923, requires subjects to copy patterns by placing cubes with differently colored sides together. The Porteus Maze Test, originally developed in 1914 as a measure of foresight and planning ability, contains sets of mazes graded in difficulty. These early tests, and others like them, continue to be used on IQ tests such as the Stanford-Binet and Wechsler tests.

The Wechsler intelligence tests produce three IQ scores: verbal, performance, and full scale. The full-scale IQ is a combination of verbal and performance subtests, with the performance subtests requiring subjects to perform tasks such as assembling puzzles, forming blocks into patterns, and arranging pictures in a logical sequence. Analyses of the profile or pattern of the subtests and the verbal and performance IQ scores are frequently carried out to provide descriptions of cognitive strengths and weaknesses and insight into possible localization of brain dysfunction and personality factors. For example, sociopaths and people with left-hemisphere damage are believed to tend to score higher on performance than on verbal items.

Performance tests have been used extensively by the military (for example, flight training simulators to measure pilots' skills) and in business (for example, typing tests). In nonacademic settings, performance tests, when obviously related to job skills, generally are acceptable to those being tested for hiring, placement, retention, or promotion considerations. Academic settings also use performance tests, for example, tests of penmanship and oral reading and writing skills (based upon assessing "work samples").

Although performance tests frequently have greater face validity, nonperformance paper-and-pencil tests remain the most commonly used test format. The paper-and-pencil tests, when administered to people sufficiently experienced in this format, can provide measurements that are valid, less expensive, and more conducive to group testing.

Mary J. Allen
California State University

PERSONAL CONSTRUCT THEORY

Personal Construct Theory (PCT) represents a coherent, comprehensive psychology of personality that has special relevance for psychotherapy. Originally drafted by the American psychologist George Kelly in 1955, PCT has been extended to a variety of domains, including organizational development, education, business and marketing, and cognitive science. However, its predominant focus remains on the study of individuals, families, and social groups, with particular emphasis on how people organize and change their views of self and world in the counseling context.

At the base of Kelly's theory is the image of the *person-as-scientist,* a view that emphasizes the human capacity for meaning making, agency, and ongoing revision of personal systems of knowing across time. Thus, individuals, like incipient scientists, are seen as creatively formulating *constructs,* or hypotheses about the apparent regularities of their lives, in an attempt to make them understandable, and to some extent, predictable. However, predictability is not pursued for its own sake, but is instead sought as a guide to practical action in concrete contexts and relationships. This implies that people engage in continuous extension, refinement, and revision of their systems of meaning as they meet with events that challenge or *invalidate* their assumptions, prompting their personal theories toward greater adequacy.

Kelly formally developed his theory through a series of corollaries, which can be broadly grouped into those concerned with the *process* of construing, the *structure* of personal knowledge, and the *social embeddedness* of our construing efforts. At the level of process, PCT envisions people as actively organizing their perceptions of events on the basis of recurring themes, meanings attributed to the "booming, buzzing confusion" of life in an attempt to render it interpretable. By punctuating the unending flow of experience into coherent units, people are able to discern similarities and differences of events in terms that are both personally significant and shared by relevant others.

At the level of structure, PCT suggests that meaning is a matter of contrast—an individual attributes meaning to an event not only by construing what it *is,* but also by differentiating it from what it *is not.* For example, a given person's unique description of some acquaintances as "laid back" can only be fully understood in the context of its personal contrast—say, "ambitious" as opposed to "uptight." At a broader level, individuals, social groups, and whole cultures orient themselves according to (partially) shared constructs such as "liberal versus conservative," "pro-life versus pro-choice," and "democratic versus totalitarian," which provide a basis for self-definition and social interaction. Especially important in this regard are *core constructs,* frequently unverbalizable meanings that play critical organizing roles for the entirety of our construct systems, ultimately embodying our most basic values and sense of self. Finally, at the level of the social embeddedness of our construing, PCT stresses both the importance of private, idiosyncratic meanings and the way in which these arise and find validation within relational, family, and cultural contexts.

To a greater extent than other "cognitively" oriented theories of personality and psychotherapy, PCT places a strong emphasis on emotional experiences, understood as signals of actual or impending transitions in one's fundamental constructs for anticipating the world. For example, individuals might experience *threat* when faced with the prospect of imminent and comprehensive change in their core structures of identity (e.g., when facing dismissal from a valued career, or abandonment by a partner they counted on to validate a familiar image of themselves). Alternatively, people might experience *anxiety* when confronted with events that seem almost completely alien and uninterpretable within their previous construct system. This attention to the delicate interweaving of meaning and affect has made PCT an attractive framework for contemporary researchers and clinicians concerned with such topics as relational breakdown, trauma, and loss, all of which can fundamentally undercut one's assumptive world, triggering a host of significant emotional and behavioral responses.

As an approach to psychotherapy, PCT stresses the importance of the therapist making a concerted effort to enter the client's world of meaning and understand it "from the inside out," as a precondition to assisting with its revision. In this way the therapist does not assume to be an expert who guides clients toward a more "rational" or "objectively true" way of thinking. Instead, he or she works to help clients recognize the coherence in their own ways of construing experience, as well as their personal agency in making modifications in these constructions when necessary. At times the therapist prompts the client's self-reflection by making use of various interviewing strategies such as the laddering technique to help articulate core constructs, or narrative exercises such as self-characterization methods, as a precursor to experimenting with new ways of construing self and others. Such changes may be further fostered by the creative use of in-session enactment, fixed role therapy (in which clients "try out" new identities in the course of daily life), and other psychodramatic techniques.

A unique feature of PCT is its extensive program of empirical research conducted by hundreds of social scientists around the world. Most of this research has drawn on *repertory grid methods* (see also "Repertory Grid Methods"), a flexible set of tools for assessing systems of personal meanings, which have been used in literally thousands of studies since Kelly first proposed the concept. By providing visual and semantic "maps" of an individual's construct system and its application to important facets of one's life (e.g., relationships with friends, partners, and family members), grids have proven useful in both applied and research settings. Among the many topics investigated using this method are the body images of anorexic clients; the ability of family members to understand one another's outlooks; children's reliance on concrete versus abstract construing of people; and the degree of commonality of work team members in their construing of common projects.

Finally, it is worth emphasizing that PCT, despite its status as the original clinical constructivist theory, remains a living tradition that continues to attract scholars, researchers, and practitioners from a broad range of disciplines. More than many other theories, it has established a sizable following and annual conferences outside of North America, with vigorous programs of training, research, and practice in countries as diverse as Australia, Germany, Spain, and the United Kingdom. As it has grown in influence, it has also begun to articulate with other, more recent "postmodern" traditions of scholarship, including other constructivist, social constructionist, and narrative therapy approaches. While these various perspectives differ in some respects, each draws attention to the way in which personal identity is constructed and transformed in a social context. Likewise, each focuses on the role of language in defining reality, and each suggests a collaborative role for the psychotherapist attempting to assist clients with the problems of living.

SUGGESTED READING

Fransella, F. (1996). *George Kelly.* Thousand Oaks, CA and London: Sage.

Kelly, G. A. (1955). *The psychology of personal constructs.* New York: Norton.

Neimeyer, R. A., & Raskin, J. (Eds.). (2001). *Constructions of disorder: Meaning making frameworks in psychotherapy.* Washington, DC: American Psychological Association.

Neimeyer, R. A., & Neimeyer, G. J. (Eds.). (2002). *Advances in personal construct psychology.* New York: Praeger.

Raskin, J. D., & Bridges, S. K. (Eds.). (2002). *Studies in meaning: Exploring constructivist psychology.* New York: Pace University Press.

Robert A. Neimeyer
University of Memphis

PERSONALITY AND ILLNESS

Personality is an overarching construct used to identify the characteristics (e.g., traits, motives, interests, goals) that influence an individual's unique pattern of thinking, emoting, and behaving. Over the centuries physicians have observed an association between these personal characteristics and predispositions toward illness. Hippocrates, the father of medicine, in 404 B.C.E. concluded, "There is no illness of the body apart from the mind." The ancient English physician Parry of Bath observed, "It's more important to know what sort of person has a disease than what sort of disease a person has." And Sir William Osler, the nineteenth century Canadian physician, often remarked, "The care of tuberculosis depends more on what the patient has in his head than what he has in his chest."

Illness-Prone Personalities

There has been a great deal written about illness-prone personalities. The general assumption is that the beliefs and emotional lives of different personalities predispose them to certain illnesses. The illness-prone personality for which there is the greatest amount of research support is the coronary-prone personality, first identified by Meyer Friedman and Ray Rosenman (1974). The criteria used in identifying this personality include a behavioral syndrome, referred to as the Type A behavior pattern, and certain beliefs regarding one's self-worth. Coronary-prone individuals believe that their worth is derived solely from their accomplishments and that their success results from being able to more, and to do it faster, than the next person. Consequently, they are said to be suffering from "hurry sickness." Because they are driven to produce, they grow impatient with tasks that require delayed responses, and because they frequently engage in multitasking, they are more likely to experience frustration and hostility from encountered barriers to success. Persons possessing these personality characteristics were said to have an increased risk of coronary artery disease. Recent research conducted independently at three universities, however, presents a more complex picture. Accordingly, the increased risk for heart attacks occurs only when Type A characteristics are accompanied by a cynical distrust of others and a tendency to inhibit hostile feelings. Furthermore, this tendency to experience greater amounts of hostility than normal is associated with a significant increase in mortality across all diseases, not just coronary artery disease. In frustrating situations, hostile people dump more epinephrine and norepinephrine into their bloodstreams and wind up with higher blood pressure.

Other illness-prone personalities have been discussed in the literature, though research evidence for the existence of these personalities is much weaker. Considerable attention has been directed, however, to the idea of a carcinogenic personality, often said to be characterized by gross self-devaluation, feelings of helplessness and hopelessness, and the tendency to approach environmental demands in a passive, dependent manner. Examples of other illness-prone personalities cited in the literature include the arthritic personality, the anxious–reactive personality, and the disease-prone personality. An illness-resistant personality, called the "hardy personality," has received attention as well. The chief characteristics of this personality are a sense of control regarding issues in one's life, a tendency to see life demands as challenges rather than stressors, and commitment to one's endeavors because they hold meaning for the person. Recently, optimism also has been viewed as a personality attribute that buffers stress and prevents illness (Seligman, 1990, 1998).

Emotional Expression

Recently, researchers have attempted to determine to what extent personality variables are related to illness. The research question has taken one of two forms: (1) Is there a relationship between specific personality variables and specific illnesses, or (2) Is there a predisposition toward illness in general from the possession of certain personality variables? In a meta-analytic review of 101 studies purporting to investigate the effects of strangulated emotions on vulnerability to illness, Howard Friedman and Stephanie Booth-Keeley (1987) found only weak support for a relationship between specific distressing emotions, such as anxiety, anger, and depression, and specific illnesses, such as asthma, ulcers, arthritis, heart disease, and headaches. However, they found substantial support for a relationship between these distressing emotions and an increased vulnerability to illness in general. Consequently, they considered it appropriate to refer to persons accustomed to strangulating their emotions as having a "disease-prone personality." Hostility and negative affectivity, the tendency to be critical of self and others, in particular have been associated with a variety of illnesses across many studies.

Coping Styles of Differing Personalities

The effects of personality on illness may be mediated by differences in the coping styles adopted by dissimilar personality types. Michael Antoni (1987) found that persons who adopt more passive approaches to distressing events trigger a different set of neurological and endocrine reactions than persons who cope more actively. The helplessness, hyper vigilance, and withdrawal tendencies typical of passive coping are associated with much higher concentrations of cortisol, a stress hormone indicted for its negative effects on immune functioning. It seems that high levels of circulating cortisol sustained over long periods of time kill immune cells and hasten age-related memory loss. Elevated levels of cortisol are frequently found in persons experiencing depression, and chronic depression is associated with higher rates of morbidity and mortality. Thus, passive copers may be conducting chemical warfare against their own bodies.

Locke and Colligan (1986) at Harvard University found the effect of multiple life demands on blood levels of natural killer (NK) immune cells was strongly influenced by the presence or absence of distressing emotions. Medical students who reported high levels of anxiety and/or depression while coping with multiple life demands had diminished NK-cell activity, whereas students facing the same magnitude of life demands but reporting little or no anxiety or depression actually showed higher than normal NK cell activity. Thus, it seems that high demand loads have a watershed effect: Personalities given to experiencing high levels of anxiety and/or depression experience suppression of immune functioning, while personalities devoid of such tendencies appear to have their immune systems further strengthened.

The field of medicine examining the interface of personality features with illness is referred to as psychoneuroimmunology. We now know that there is a direct link between brain structures and immune factors such as the thymus gland, T-lymphocytes, and macrophages. Moreover, we are now discovering that the chemical messengers that operate most extensively in both brain and immune system are dense in neuroanatomical areas that regulate emotion. The traffic seems to go both ways; that is, the brain produces neurochemicals that stimulate receptor sites on immune cells, and the immune system produces biochemicals that stimulate brain cells. Consequently, it seems likely that patterns of thinking typifying different personalities are likely to have differential effects on immune functioning.

In summary, the role of psychological factors conceptualized as features of personalities as causal or aggravating agents of illness is now universally recognized. There is a growing recognition, however, that personality as a construct may be too broad, with too many overlapping meanings, for optimal use in this context. A more rewarding direction for future research should focus attention on the less amorphous constructs often used in defining personalities.

REFERENCES

Antoni, M. H. (1987). Neuroendocrine influences in psychoimmunology and neoplasia: A review. *Psychology and Health, 1,* 3–24.

Friedman, H. S., & Booth-Keeley, S. (1987). The "Disease prone personality": A meta-analytic view of the construct. *American Psychologist, 42*(6), 539–555.

Friedman, M., & Rosenman, R. H. (1974). *Type A behavior and your heart.* New York: Knopf.

Locke, S., & Colligan, D. (1986). *The healer within: The new medicine of mind and body.* New York: The New American Library.

Seligman, M. E. P. (1990, 1998). *Learned optimism: How to change your mind and your life.* New York: Pocket Books

Kenneth B. Matheny
Roy R. Kern
Georgia State University

See also: **Psychoneuroimmunology**

PERSONNEL EVALUATION

Personnel evaluations are formalized practices that provide information about the job performance of employees. Evaluations serve two general purposes: administrative and developmental. Administrative purposes are served to the extent that the evaluations are used to make personnel decisions about such things as salary increases, job assignments, promotions, and selection for training program participation. Developmental uses serve employees by providing feedback about their performance on the job and information that can guide planning for future career roles.

The development of instruments and practices involves at least three major classes of processes and choices: (1) the specification of the performance criteria, (2) the development of performance evaluation measures, and (3) the choice of evaluators.

Performance Criteria

The quality of any personnel evaluation system depends upon the extent to which the major dimensions of performance on the jobs to be evaluated have been identified. These dimensions must be relevant to successful and unsuccessful performance on the job. For example, if one were evaluating the performance of a bank teller, the dimensions of interpersonal interacting with customers, the ability to balance the drawer at the end of the day, and the ability to "interact" with the central computer through individual terminals might represent some of the dimensions of the job on which evaluations should be made. Collectively, the set of dimensions comprises the criteria. Criteria are identified through job analyses.

Criteria can be classified in many different ways. However, psychologists think in terms of two general classes: objective and subjective. Objective criteria are usually part of records kept on employees and, for the most part, are quite straightforward.

Subjective criteria are usually based in some individual's evaluation of the employee's performance. Subjective criteria can be further divided into trait-related and behaviorally related criteria. Examples of trait-related criterion dimensions are friendliness, honesty, aggressiveness, ambition, helpfulness, and work ethic. Behaviorally referenced criteria may include relationships with customers, accuracy of transactions, and skill in working with the equipment interacting with the central computer.

Psychologists almost always favor the use of objective criteria plus subjective criteria that are behaviorally oriented. However, when the overall evaluation is taken into account and it is necessary to compare employees across a wide variety of different types of jobs, the use of behaviorally based evaluations is more difficult. Also, some critical dimensions of work are subjective by nature; for example, cooperation, customer satisfaction, and teamwork.

Performance Measures

Once the criteria have been identified, the next task is to construct ways in which to measure them. Objective criteria, by their very nature, often have standards for their measurement. For subjective measures of performance, evaluation scales must be developed. To do so requires constructing scales that are reliable, valid, unbiased, and as free as possible from contamination.

A wide variety of scaling procedures and practices exist for the construction of such scales. The perfect evaluation scale, or even one that clearly stands out above the rest, has eluded experts. However, the inability to identify one best method for all criteria should not imply that there have been no major advances. Critical behaviors identified by job incumbents and scaled as to their importance for effective job performance work well.

Evaluators

Because of the hierarchical nature of most organizations, with the well-accepted control mechanism whereby supervisors are responsible for the work of their subordinates, most performance evaluations are done by employees' immediate supervisors. It is also common for the next higher level of supervision to endorse the evaluations. In spite of this practice, there is no reason to believe that supervisors are in the best position to provide the evaluation. In fact, work with peer ratings—ratings obtained from others at a level parallel to the employee—shows that peers are excellent sources of evaluations and are often better than supervisors. From the standpoint of the quality of the rating, the best generalization is that quality is a function of the evaluator's ability to observe and judge the dimension in question. Since much work today is carried out by teams, performance evaluations called "360-degree feedback" are frequently completed by superiors, peers, and subordinates. These evaluations are primarily to help employees see how others perceive them rather than for administrative purposes (e.g., raises, promotions, etc.).

Process Concerns

Until the mid-1970s, psychologists working in the area of performance appraisal concentrated almost all of their efforts on the development of performance rating scales and the procedures for using these scales. It was assumed that evaluators had well-formed notions about performance and that all that was necessary was to develop rating scales that would express the raters' judgments accurately. Recently, psychologists have recognized that it is not that simple. Thus, the process of performance appraisal has received much attention. There is now a widespread belief that improvements that can be accomplished through scale construction alone very likely have been reached. It is now time to turn attention to the evaluation process as a whole.

One of the most important aspects of this process was the recognition that the evaluator is faced with a person-perception problem that requires the perception, memory, and recall of events related to employees. From this perspective, it is necessary to understand how people perceive others, how they retrieve from memory information about others, how the performance evaluation procedure for an organization requires them to record their evaluation, and the use(s) to which the ratings will be put.

Finally, in addition to looking at the evaluator, more attention must be paid to the characteristics of the performance setting. Although performance evaluations are of the utmost importance to the psychologists who develop evaluation systems, to the line manager with many other responsibilities, the appraisal process is just another task that must be completed by a certain deadline. Thus, more attention must be paid to the situational conditions in which appraisals take place, to establish conditions that increase the probability of accurate evaluations. Again, the recent trend is to be more cognizant of the situational constraints and to attempt to deal with the personnel evaluation systems and the context as parts of the nature of the performance itself.

Daniel R. Ilgen
Michigan State University

PHENYLALANINE

Phenylalanine

Phenylalanine is an essential hydrophobic aromatic amino acid. The term *essential* in this context means that the amino acid cannot be synthesized endogenously and must be obtained through diet. A common amino acid in proteins, phenylalanine is the immediate precursor of tyrosine, a nonessential amino acid from which catecholamine neurotransmitters are synthesized.

Phenylalanine Metabolism

Phenylalanine not used in protein synthesis is oxidized to tyrosine by the enzyme phenylalanine hydroxylase (Figure 1). This reaction requires a cofactor, tetrahydrobiopterin (BH_4), which is synthesized de novo from guanosine triphosphate. In the reaction, BH_4 is converted to quinonoid dihydrobiopterin, which is reduced back to BH_4 by dihydropteridine reductase. This recycling pathway serves the important function of maintaining the BH_4 cofactor.

Hyperphenylalaninemia

Hyperphenylalaninemias are inborn disorders of phenylalanine metabolism. Normally, about 25% of phenylalanine is used for protein synthesis and the remaining 75% is converted to tyrosine. Hydroxylation of phenylalanine is the principal pathway for phenylalanine runout from body flu-

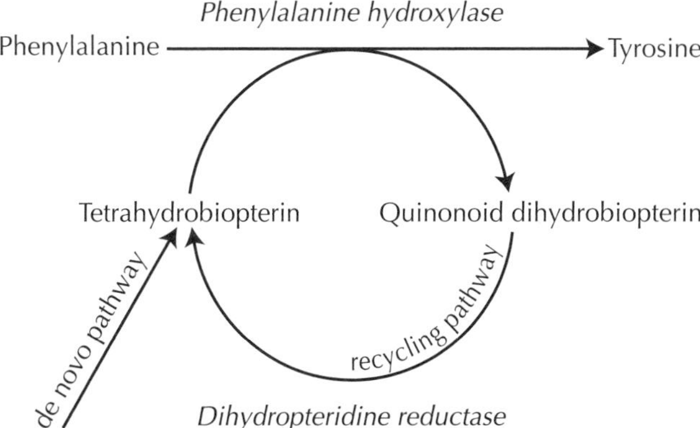

Figure 1. Phenylalanine metabolism. Enzymes are in italicized type. *Source:* Reprinted with permission from Baumeister & Baumeister. (1998). Dietary treatment of hyperphenylalaninemia. *Clinical Neuropharmacology, 21*(1), 18–27.

ids. If this process is impaired, continued input of phenylananine from diet and endogenous sources (i.e., peptide turnover) causes the concentration of phenylalanine in plasma to rise. Impairment of hydroxylation can result from a defect in phenylalanine hydroxylase or, less frequently, in one of the enzymes involved in BH_4 synthesis or recycling. Phenylketonuria (PKU) is a type of hyperphenylalaninemia that is defined on the basis of plasma phenylalanine concentration. When plasma phenylalanine is above an arbitrary threshold (often 16.5 mg/dl) the condition is called PKU. Unfortunately, wide variation exists in the threshold that is employed, leading to differences in clinical practice and incidence estimates. Conditions associated with an elevation of phenylalanine that is below the threshold for PKU are called non-PKU hyperphenylalaninemias.

Clinical Manifestation

Marked elevation of phenylalanine is associated with clinical manifestations most notably involving the central nervous system. Untreated or late-treated PKU usually results in a host of neurologic sequelae including severe mental retardation, seizures, and behavioral (e.g., self-mutilation, aggression, and hyperactivity) and psychiatric (e.g., depression and mania) disorders. A consistent neuropathologic finding is abnormalities in cerebral white matter revealed by magnetic resonance imaging. Persons with non-PKU hyperphenylalaninemia typically have fewer and less severe manifestations.

Recent research has elucidated the relation between genotype and clinical manifestations in the hyperphenylalaninemias. These disorders have an autosomal recessive mode of inheritance. More that 400 distinct mutations of the gene that encodes phenylalanine hydroxylase (located on chromosome 12) have been identified. Severity of the genetic mutation of both alleles correlates with severity of the biochemical and cognitive phenotypes. The presence of a mild mutation on one allele is protective. Intelligence quotient scores tend to be lower when the mutation on both alleles is severe than when one is severe and the other mild. Nevertheless, there is wide variation of IQ within genotype groups due to other influences, such as inherited intellectual disposition and the timing, effectiveness, and duration of treatment.

Aberrant behavior in PKU may be related to neurotransmitter deficiencies. Concentrations of dopamine and serotonin in cerebrospinal fluid have been found to be reduced in persons with hyperphenylalaninemia, and both of these neurotransmitters have been implicated in deviant behaviors that often occur in untreated PKU. The cause of the neurotransmitter deficit is not established, though reduced synthesis is implicated. Two possible bases for reduced synthesis are (1) decreased transport of precursor amino acids to sites of neurotransmitter synthesis due to competition with phenylalanine for transporters; and (2) diminished activity of hydroxylase enzymes. Although in PKU phenylalanine hydroxylase is usually defective, this alone does not appear to reduce catecholamine synthesis, because in the absence of phenylalanine hydroxylase activity tyrosine becomes an essential amino acid and its intake in diet is normally adequate. However, in hyperphenylalaninemias caused by impaired BH_4 synthesis or recycling, activities of tyrosine, tryptophan, and phenylalanine hydroxylase are all diminished because all three enzymes require the BH_4 cofactor. Reduction in tyrosine and tryptophan hydroxylation does interfere with neurotransmitter synthesis.

Treatment

Nervous system damage in PKU is thought to result from phenylalanine toxicity. Recent evidence indicates that the concentration of phenylalanine in the brain is a more important indicator of neurologic risk than the concentration in the blood. Dietary restriction of phenylalanine shortly after birth lowers plasma and brain phenylalanine and prevents major neurologic sequelae. Because early detection and treatment are essential, screening for PKU at birth is now routine in most developed nations. In the past it has been customary to ease dietary restrictions in school-age children on the assumption that the brain is less vulnerable at this time. However, mounting evidence that this practice is associated with behavioral, cognitive, and neurologic deterioration indicates a need to maintain the restricted diet into adolescence or longer. There is evidence that some neurotoxic effects of phenylalanine in persons who were treated early but later removed from diet and in persons not treated early are reversible to some extent by late initiation of a phenylalanine-restricted diet.

Treatment of disorders of BH_4 synthesis or recycling requires additional measures. In these disorders, catecholamine and serotonin neurotransmitters are deficient even when phenylalanine is controlled, because BH_4 is a required cofactor for tyrosine and tryptophan hydroxylase. Treatment with L-dopa and 5-hydroxytryptophan, the immediate precursors of dopamine and serotonin, is necessary to correct deficiencies in these neurotransmitters.

Maternal PKU

Children who do not have hyperphenylalaninemia but who are born to affected women who do not maintain dietary restrictions during pregnancy can suffer various teratogenic effects of phenylalanine, including mental retardation, microcephaly, growth retardation, and heart malformations. This condition is called maternal PKU. Control of blood phenylalanine by maternal dietary restriction from conception to birth is associated with improved fetal outcome. There is a strong inverse relationship between maternal phenylalanine levels above 6 mg/dl during pregnancy and IQ of the child. Fetal vulnerability to phenylalanine is greatest during the first trimester. About 90% of infants born to PKU mothers not maintained on the phenylalanine-restricted diet during pregnancy are severely affected. It has been estimated that without proper maternal control of phenylalanine, the benefits of infant screening and treatment for PKU will be erased in one generation.

Alan A. Baumeister

PHEROMONES

Pheromones are chemical signals that pass between organisms of the same species and have inherent communicatory function. Pheromones likely originated in the earliest life forms and continue to serve as the primary means of communication in many species, including most terrestrial and aquatic invertebrates, fishes, and many mammals. Pheromones are notorious for their potency and specificity, features that are generally attributed to specialized components of the olfactory system. Diverse biochemicals can have pheromonal function; however, with the exception of insects, the pheromones of few animals have been definitively identified. Because pheromones are frequently mixtures of common compounds and can have a variety of functions, the defining characteristic of pheromones lies not in their chemical identity or specific function, but in the ability of conspecifics to recognize them.

Pheromones are most appropriately characterized by their actions, which are generally species-specific, and can include behavioral ("releaser") and/or physiological ("primer") effects. Best known are releaser effects, which are associated with reproduction, aggregation, territory marking/recognition, or alarm. Many terrestrial, aquatic, and aerial species locate and select mates using potent reproductive pheromones. For example, male moths are attracted to the odor of females located hundreds of meters away, male dogs respond to the scent of bitches in heat nearly a kilometer upwind, and male goldfish detect female sex pheromones at concentrations as low as 1 gram in 3 billion liters of water. Aggregation pheromones bring individuals of the same species together and are employed by unicellular slime molds to form fruiting bodies, by migrating lamprey to locate spawning rivers containing the odor of larval lamprey, and by swarming insects. In contrast, terrestrial mammals such as antelopes and badgers use territorial pheromones to maintain spacing. Terrestrial and aquatic organisms commonly use alarm pheromones such as "Schreckstoff," which is released from the skin of injured fish. The potency and specificity of releaser pheromones has led to their application in the management of nuisance species.

Many pheromones with largely physiological (primer) effects are also known. In rodents, juvenile females advance puberty in response to male urinary odor (the Vandenburgh effect) and delay puberty in response to female urinary odor, whereas pregnant females abort preimplantation embryos in response to unfamiliar male odor (the Bruce effect). In goldfish and carp, males exhibit rapid endocrine responses to female steroidal sex pheromones that also affect behavior, demonstrating the multifunctionality of some pheromones.

The chemical nature of pheromones varies enormously and is much better understood in insects than in vertebrates. Pheromones are often compounds that originally served other, related functions. In the goldfish and its relatives, identified sex pheromones are unspecialized hormonal products whose release and detection largely benefits the receivers. However, in other cases, pheromone "donors" have evolved specialized abilities to produce and release pheromonal products, apparently because they derive benefit from doing so. Thus, many insects and ungulates control the release of molecular blends produced in quantity by special glands. Sex pheromones of noctuid moths are precise species-specific mixtures of up to seven fatty acids and related acetates, aldehydes, and alcohols. Among mammals, most pheromones appear to be complex mixtures hidden within the body odor of the donor that benefit both the donor and receiver of the signal, a condition that some mammalian chemical ecologists equate with the use of the term.

Although a range of chemicals can serve as pheromones, the chemical characteristics of pheromones are often related to ecological context. Alarm and sex pheromones of terrestrial insects are often small, volatile compounds that spread and fade quickly. Interestingly, elephants use some of the same volatiles as sex pheromones for close-range communication as moths. Water presents a different challenge, and fish often use relatively small, soluble conjugated steroids as pheromones. In contrast, hyenas mark territories with large molecules that last for months in the hot sun, and rodents mark with long-lived odors that bind with a stable protein, the major urinary protein (MUP).

Where understood, olfactory processing of pheromonal information in invertebrates and vertebrates exhibits striking similarities that include the presence of sexually dimorphic components specialized for pheromonal function. Pheromones are detected by specific sensory hairs located on antennae of invertebrates such as moths and lobsters, while a specific type of receptor neuron, the microvillous cell, appears to mediate responses to pheromones in vertebrates. Invertebrates and vertebrates also exhibit similar organization of the neurons that process pheromonal information. In male moths, axons from receptor neurons project to a specialized subset of glomeruli, the macroglomerular complex (MGC) located in their olfactory lobe. Connections among MGC glomeruli enable males to discriminate pheromone mixtures and adjust flight maneuvers. Pheromone receptor neurons of vertebrates also appear to project to specific glomeruli which in fish are found in medial regions of the olfactory bulb. In terrestrial vertebrates the situation is complex because, with the exception of primates and humans, tetrapods have a dual olfactory system comprised of a main olfactory epithelium and vomeronasal organ (VNO). The latter is located in the roof of the mouth. Although both systems can mediate pheromone responses, the VNO appears to be the primary system for discriminating pheromones because naive rodents that lack a VNO do not respond to some pheromones.

Although responsiveness to pheromones is typically instinctual, some responses can be learned. Honeybees learn to recognize hydrocarbon mixtures on the bodies of nest mates, whom they allow to enter the nest. Young mice imprint on their parent's odor (which appears to be associated with the Major Histocompatability Complex [MHC]) and later avoid it when choosing mates. Similarly, the Bruce effect depends on the ability of female mice to learn male odor during mating.

There are suggestions that human mate choice is influenced by odors associated with the MHC, as people choose partners with different MHC profiles. Pheromones also appear to mediate the menstrual synchrony of women living in close proximity, although the active compounds are unknown. With the advent of molecular techniques, understanding of pheromone identity and function is expected to advance rapidly.

SUGGESTED READING

McClintock, M. K. (2002). Pheromones, odors, and vasnas: The neuroendocrinology of social chemosignals in humans and animals. In D. W. Pfaff, A. P. Arnold, A. M. Etgen, S. E. Farback, & R. T. Rubin, (Eds.), *Hormones, brain, and behavior* (Vol. 1, pp. 797–870). New York: Academic Press.

Sorensen, P. W., Christensen, T. A., & Stacey, N. E. (1998). Discrimination of pheromonal cues in fish: Emerging parallels with insects. *Current Opinion in Neurobiology, 8,* 458–467.

Wyatt, T. D. (2003). *Animal pheromones and behaviour: Communication by smell and taste.* Cambridge, UK: Cambridge University Press.

Peter W. Sorensen
University of Minnesota

Tristram D. Wyatt
University of Oxford, U.K.

PHILOSOPHY OF PSYCHOTHERAPY

Psychotherapy is often considered to be an applied science consisting of a compendium of techniques or approaches validated by empirical research. Alternately, it is viewed as an art form requiring a creative, intuitive, and individualistic approach to clients and their problems. However, psychotherapy can also be regarded as influenced in a fundamental way by broader, philosophical underpinnings that transcend its scientific, human engineering, or artistic dimensions. Examples of some of these domains are: (1) our possessing a priori categories of understanding that are part of therapeutic work, such as certain assumptions about reality, and underlying narrative structures; (2) the inevitability of value-laden issues in therapy; and (3) the presence of societal and cultural influences on the practice of psychotherapy, as well as the effect of psychotherapy on the terms in which people in our society view themselves (Messer & Woolfolk, 1998; Woolfolk, 1998). We will take up each of these three areas in turn.

A Priori Categories of Understanding

Every intellectual endeavor has a starting point that is prior to empirical investigation. Without the conceptual categories that are prior to experience we could not organize the world into objects and events. When we look at the world, we do so through particular lenses or conceptual schemes that influence what we see. Philosophical analysis is a tool for making the properties of these lenses explicit, helping us to understand the concepts that underlie our thinking.

One aspect of the philosophical and cultural *a priori* is referred to by contemporary philosophers as "the Background." It contains the taken-for-granted knowledge and norms that are implicit in our practical and theoretical activities. Consider, as an example of the Background, the contrasting narrative themes underlying different forms of treatment, which often go unrecognized. One typology of narratives describes four such "visions" or viewpoints: romantic, tragic, ironic, and comic (Frye, 1957). From the *romantic viewpoint,* life is an adventure or quest, a drama of the triumph of good over evil, virtue over vice, and light over darkness. It idealizes individuality and authentic self-expression. The romantic vision underpins humanistic approaches to psychotherapy, which stress the value and possibilities of spontaneity, authenticity, and creativity. The *ironic vision,* by contrast, encompasses an attitude of detachment and suspicion, of keeping things in perspective, and of recognizing the fundamental ambiguity and mystery of every issue that life presents. Whereas behavioral and cognitive therapists tend to take client complaints at face value, and humanistic therapists accept most client feelings as authentic expression, psychoanalytic therapists are more likely to look for hidden meanings, paradoxes, and contradictions. This puts them more squarely in the ironic mode.

The *tragic vision* is an acceptance of the limitations in life—not all is possible, not all is redeemable, not all potentialities are realizable. The clock cannot be turned back, death cannot be avoided, human nature cannot be radically perfected. Many aspects of psychoanalysis fall within the tragic vision. People are determined by events of their early childhood, which are subject to repression and beyond their conscious purview. The outcome of psychoanalytic treatment is not unalloyed happiness or all obstacles overcome, but rather the fuller recognition and acceptance of what one's struggles are about, and of the conditions and limitations of life. By contrast, within the *comic vision* the direction of events is from bad to better or even best. Obstacles and struggles are ultimately overcome. Harmony and unity, progress and happiness prevail. Cognitive-behavioral therapy holds out the promise of finding greater happiness through the application of scientific principles of healing, while humanistic approaches emphasize the substantial possibility for gratification. These underlying visions profoundly affect both the process and desired outcomes of these different forms of treatment.

Psychotherapy and Values

Virtually all of the innovators who made significant contributions to psychotherapy, such as Freud, Rogers, Wolpe, Perls, and Beck, considered themselves to be discoverers of morally neutral, scientific knowledge, and viewed psychotherapy as an objective application of that knowledge to the goal of psychological health. By contrast, philosophical analysis helps us to see how values often establish, albeit covertly, the criteria for intervention; influence patterns of therapeutic exploration; and promote standards for client conduct. For example, a middle-aged man comes to a therapist announcing that he is considering leaving his wife for a much younger, recently married woman, and wants help making the decision. A therapist operating within the values of liberal, secular individualism would stress the happiness and contentment of the individual above all else and above all others, encouraging him to explore the issue in these self-directed (some might say "selfish") terms. One who holds to communitarian values might be more inclined to address how the client's decision to leave his wife will cause others to suffer, such as spouses, children, and other family members. Yet another therapist, hewing to religious values such as the sanctity of marriage, might emphasize the psychological and moral consequences of breaking marital vows. Despite claims to the contrary, there is no value-free psychotherapy.

The Intersection of Psychotherapy with Societal and Cultural Worldviews

The institution of psychotherapy is a significant source of, and influence on, contemporary customs, values, and worldviews, and is constantly incorporating them in its purview (Messer & Wachtel, 1997; Woolfolk, 1998). For example, all societies need mechanisms that establish what behavior is to be promoted and what is to be proscribed. Although we most often think of clinicians as healers, they also function as agents of social control. The clinician is granted responsibility for many bizarre, incapable, or destructive individuals whom the rest of society will not or cannot tolerate.

Psychotherapy and its related theory and language are also cultural phenomena that have affected how people think about themselves. For example, lay people refer to Freudian slips, defenses, guilt complexes, conditioned responses, existential angst, identity crises, or discovering their true selves—all terms related to the activity of psychotherapy. Similarly, when they explain their problems in terms of childhood occurrences such as parental neglect or harsh criticism, repressed memories, or learned associations they demonstrate that psychotherapy is far more than a scientific or technical endeavor. Its language constitutes the very belief systems that people employ to make sense out of their lives.

REFERENCES

Frye, N. (1957). *Anatomy of criticism.* Princeton, NJ: Princeton University Press.

Messer, S. B., & Wachtel, P. L. (1997). The contemporary psychotherapeutic landscape: Issues and prospects. In P. L. Wachtel & S. B. Messer (Eds.), *Theories of psychotherapy: Origins and evolution* (pp. 1–38). Washington, DC: American Psychological Association Press.

Messer, S. B., & Woolfolk, P. L. (1998). Philosophical issues in psychotherapy. *Clinical Psychology: Science and Practice, 5,* 251–263.

Woolfolk, R. L. (1998). *The cure of souls: Science, values and psychotherapy.* San Francisco: Jossey-Bass Publishers.

Stanley B. Messer
Robert L. Woolfolk
Rutgers University

See also: **Psychotherapy**

PHINEAS GAGE

On September 13, 1998, a group of brain scientists, including neurologists, neuropsychologists, and neurosurgeons, gathered in the hamlet of Cavendish, Vermont, to commemorate a bizarre anniversary. It was the 150th anniversary of an accident in which a young man named Phineas Gage suffered a brain injury when an iron bar was shot through the front part of his head. The accident itself was remarkable enough—immediately afterward, despite a gruesome wound to the front of his head and brain, Gage was conscious, alert, and talkative, and it seemed rather a miracle that he had even survived. But what followed over the next few decades, and then over the many years since, is what put Cavendish, Vermont, on the scientific map, and the reason why scientists traveled from around the world that late summer day in 1998 to commemorate the anniversary (see Macmillan, 2000).

On September 13, 1848, Phineas Gage was laboring with coworkers to blast a bed for railroad tracks through the rugged, rocky terrain of southern Vermont. While setting an explosive, Gage prematurely triggered an explosion with his tamping iron. The iron was propelled through the front part of his head, entering his left cheek just under the eye, piercing the frontal lobes of his brain, and exiting through the top front part of his head. In light of the comparatively primitive state of medicine in the mid-nineteenth century, Gage's medical recovery was nothing short of astonishing—he survived this massive onslaught with normal intelligence, memory, speech, sensation, and movement. Following this surprising recovery, however, Gage displayed a profound change in personality and social conduct that established him as a landmark case in the history of neuroscience. Before the accident, he had been responsible, socially well-adapted, and well-liked by peers and supervisors. Afterwards, Gage proved to be irresponsible and untrustworthy, irreverent and capricious, with markedly unreliable behavior and little regard for social convention; in short, he was "no longer Gage."

Gage's physician, John Harlow, speculated (very accurately, as it turned out) that there was a causative relationship between the damage to the front part of Gage's brain and the profound change in his personality and social conduct (Bigelow, 1850; Harlow, 1868). Harlow's observations, although never fully appreciated by his contemporaries, hinted at a conclusion that was both radical and prescient: there are structures in the front part of the human brain that are dedicated to the planning and execution of personally and socially adaptive behavior, and to the aspect of reasoning known as rationality. Case reports published over the first several decades of the twentieth century supported Harlow's contention, and modern investigations have documented that the prefrontal region is crucial for moral reasoning, social conduct, planning, and decision-making (Damasio & Anderson, 2003; Tranel, 2002). Moreover, when this region is damaged early in life, the development of social and moral reasoning may be permanently precluded (Anderson, Bechara, Damasio, Tranel, & Damasio, 1999; Anderson, Damasio, Tranel, & Damasio, 2000).

Using tools of modern neuroscience, scientists have performed a detailed reconstruction of the injury to Gage's brain (Damasio, Grabowski, Frank, Galaburda, & Damasio, 1994). From measurements of Gage's skull and the tamping iron (which are part of the Warren Anatomical Medical Museum at Harvard University), scientists were able to reproduce the precise path the tamping iron traversed through Gage's brain. (The skull and iron, which were on display at the 150th anniversary celebration, are remarkably well preserved to this day.) This reconstruction confirmed that the damage included the left and right prefrontal regions, anterior to structures required for motor behavior and speech, in precisely the location that modern studies have highlighted as the key neural underpinning of social conduct and rational decision making.

The importance of the case of Phineas Gage can be more fully appreciated when one considers just how difficult it has been to unravel the cognitive and behavioral functions that are subserved by the prefrontal region of the human brain. The prefrontal sector, situated anterior to the motor/premotor cortices and superior to the sylvian fissure, comprises an enormous expanse of the brain, forming nearly half of the entire cerebral mantle. In humans in particular, this region has expanded disproportionately. Throughout the history of neuropsychology, the psychological capacities associated with the prefrontal region have remained enigmatic and elusive. Beginning with the observations of Phineas Gage, however, the special significance of this region began to be appreciated.

Following on Harlow's prescient writings regarding Gage, other investigators have called attention to the oftentimes bizarre development of abnormal social behavior that can follow prefrontal brain injury (e.g., Eslinger & Damasio, 1985; Stuss & Benson, 1986). The patients have a number of features in common (see Damasio & Anderson, 2003): inability to organize future activity and hold gainful employment, diminished capacity to respond to punishment, a tendency to present an unrealistically favorable view of themselves, and a tendency to display inappropriate emotional reactions. Making this profile especially puzzling is the fact that most of these patients, like Gage, retain normal intelligence, language, memory, and perception. Other scientists have called attention to the striking characteristics of patients with prefrontal lobe brain injury, especially damage to the ventral and lower mesial portions of this region (the "ventromedial prefrontal" sector). Blumer and Benson (1975) noted that the patients displayed a personality profile (which the authors termed "pseudo-psychopathic") featured by puerility, a jocular attitude, sexually disinhibited humor, inappropriate and near-total self-indulgence, and complete lack of concern for others. Stuss and Benson (1986) emphasized that the patients demonstrated a remarkable lack of empathy and general lack of concern about others.

The patients showed callous unconcern, boastfulness, and unrestrained and tactless behavior. Other descriptors included impulsiveness, facetiousness, and diminished anxiety and concern for the future.

It is interesting to note that this personality profile is strikingly similar to that characterized in clinical psychology and psychiatry as psychopathic (or sociopathic) (American Psychiatric Association, 1994). In fact, this condition has been dubbed "acquired sociopathy," to emphasize the fact that prefrontal injured patients often have personality manifestations that are quite reminiscent of those associated with sociopathy (Barrash, Tranel, & Anderson, 2000; Tranel, 1994). The qualifier "acquired" signifies that in the brain-damaged patients, the condition follows the onset of brain injury, and occurs in persons whose personalities and social conduct were previously normal (as in the case of Phineas Gage). Patients with acquired sociopathy have a proclivity to engage in decisions and behaviors that have negative consequences for their well-being. They repeatedly select courses of action that are not in their best interest in the long run, making poor decisions about interpersonal relationships, occupational endeavors, and finances. In short, the patients act as though they have lost the ability to ponder different courses of action and then select the option that promises the best blend of short- and long-term benefit.

As it turned out, the misadventures of Phineas Gage provided crucial early clues about the importance of the prefrontal sector of the brain for social behavior, reasoning and decision-making, and what can generally be called "personality." Phineas Gage's accident was bizarre, to be sure, but its important place in scientific history is firmly secure.

REFERENCES

American Psychiatric Association. (1994). *Diagnostic and statistical manual of mental disorders* (4th ed.). Washington, DC: Author.

Anderson, S. W., Bechara, A., Damasio, H., Tranel, D., & Damasio, A. R. (1999). Impairment of social and moral behavior related to early damage in the human prefrontal cortex. *Nature Neuroscience, 2,* 1032–1037.

Anderson, S. W., Damasio, H., Tranel, D., & Damasio, A. R. (2000). Long-term sequelae of prefrontal cortex damage acquired in early childhood. *Developmental Neuropsychology, 18,* 281–296.

Barrash, J., Tranel, D., & Anderson, S. W. (2000). Acquired personality disturbances associated with bilateral damage to the ventromedial prefrontal region. *Developmental Neuropsychology, 18,* 355–381.

Bigelow, H. J. (1850). Dr. Harlow's case of recovery from the passage of an iron bar through the head. *American Journal of the Medical Sciences, 39,* 13–22.

Blumer, D., & Benson, D. F. (1975). Personality changes with frontal and temporal lobe lesions. In D. F. Benson & D. Blumer (Eds.), *Psychiatric aspects of neurologic disease* (pp. 151–169). New York: Grune & Stratton.

Damasio, A. R., & Anderson, S. W. (2003). The frontal lobes. In K. Heilman & E. Valenstein (Eds.), *Clinical neuropsychology* (4th ed.). New York: Oxford University Press.

Damasio, H., Grabowski, T., Frank, R., Galaburda, A. M., & Damasio, A. R. (1994). The return of Phineas Gage: Clues about the brain from the skull of a famous patient. *Science, 264,* 1102–1105.

Eslinger, P. J., & Damasio, A. R. (1985). Severe disturbance of higher cognition after bilateral frontal lobe ablation: Patient EVR. *Neurology, 35,* 1731–1741.

Harlow, J. M. (1868). Recovery from the passage of an iron bar through the head. *Publications of the Massachusetts Medical Society, 2,* 327–347.

Macmillan, M. (2000). *An odd kind of fame: Stories of Phineas Gage.* Cambridge, MA: MIT Press.

Stuss, D. T., & Benson, D. F. (1986). *The frontal lobes.* New York: Raven Press.

Tranel, D. (1994). "Acquired sociopathy": The development of sociopathic behavior following focal brain damage. In D. C. Fowles, P. Sutker, & S. H. Goodman (Eds.), *Progress in experimental personality and psychopathology research* (Vol. 17, pp. 285–311). New York: Springer.

Tranel, D. (2002). Emotion, decision-making, and the ventromedial prefrontal cortex. In D. T. Stuss & R. T. Knight (Eds.), *Principles of frontal lobe function.* New York: Oxford University Press.

Daniel Tranel
University of Iowa College of Medicine

PHONEMES

Linguistic analyses have traditionally represented the form of speech in terms of *phonemes.* The word *cat,* for instance, can be represented by a sequence of three phonemes: /k/, /æ/, and /t/. Changes in the phonemic construction of a word will result in a different word, or a nonsense word. For example, reordering the phonemes in *cat* can produce other words, such as *act* (/ækt/) or *tack* (/tæk/), whereas replacing the /k/ with a /p/ results in a new word, *pat.* Words like *cat* and *pat* that differ on the identity of a single phoneme are referred to as minimal pairs, and provide a useful source of evidence for defining the phonemic inventory for a language. In an alphabetic language such as English, the phonemic nature of speech is made explicit by the close correspondence between letters and the phonemes they represent. Logographic languages (e.g., Chinese) do not share this correspondence; instead, characters are used to represent whole words.

A further division of speech sounds is possible, into subphonemic units called *phonetic features.* The representation of a phoneme consists of a set of phonetic features, which capture the similarities and differences between groups of phonemes. For example, the difference between the phonemes /t/ and /k/ is largely due to the difference in the place of closure created by the tongue touching the roof of the mouth. The same contrast is found between /d/ and /g/, and between /n/ and /ŋ/ (the final phoneme in "ring"). This contrast can be represented by one or more places of articulation features.

It is important to realize that the abstract notion of a phoneme obscures a great deal of variation in the form of speech. The context in which a phoneme is uttered has a strong effect on the way in which it is articulated, and this results in a wide variation of acoustic forms all being termed the same phoneme. Similarly, the discrete sequences of symbols in a phonemic transcription do not properly represent the temporal structure of the speech waveform, in which information about different phonemes is spread across time or overlapping. A critical issue in the psychological study of speech is whether mental representations of speech reflect the diversity and detail of the speech waveform or the abstractness and simplicity of the phonemic transcription.

Phonemes in Speech Perception

It is clear that some aspects of the organization of speech sounds in perception correspond to phonemic categories. It is possible to create artificial continua using recorded speech or a speech synthesizer in which the extremes correspond to two typical phonemes. Typically adults will show categorical perception of these continua; that is, they will find it difficult to discriminate between two sounds on a continuum that would be classed as the same phoneme, but relatively easy to discriminate between two sounds that cross a phoneme boundary. Infants as young as a month old show similar discontinuities in their perception of these continua. In fact, it seems that early on in development, infants are able to discriminate between speech sounds that are allophonic in their language (i.e., phonetically distinct members of the same phoneme category) but are different phonemes in other languages. This ability is lost in the first year of life, as the infant becomes familiar with the phonemes of his or her native language.

A possible conclusion to be drawn from these studies of infant speech perception is that people are born with an innate universal phonemic inventory, from which the contrasts relevant to the child's native language are consolidated. However, various nonhuman species, such as chinchillas and macaque monkeys, have also shown categorical perception of some phonemic contrasts. So what is innate may in fact be more physical aspects of the auditory system, which provide a basis for discrimination between some sounds but not others. By this view, the phonemic systems of languages have evolved in order to take advantage of these abilities and deficits.

Although categorical perception of phonemes is found from infancy, it is less clear how aware people are of these units. Alphabetic languages lend themselves to a phonemic decomposition of speech by the literate adult. This makes the conscious manipulation and decomposition of speech (such as deciding what the initial phoneme of "spin" might be) a relatively simple task. However, for verbally proficient illiterate adults and speakers of nonalphabetic languages this is not the case. It seems that the existence of the phoneme as a unit at a conscious level relies on more or less explicit teaching through learning to read alphabetic scripts.

The phoneme has been proposed as the initial unit of classification in speech perception at a subconscious level. The assumption is that words are identified by comparison between this representation and stored phonemic representations of words. However, the lack of context-invariant characteristics for many phonemes has weakened this proposal, and other models have been suggested in which speech is mapped onto larger units (e.g., the syllable) or smaller units (e.g., acoustic features) before searching the lexicon for a matching word. The matching process between the speech waveform and the mental lexicon has also proved to be sensitive to a wide range of subtle changes in the form of words, suggesting that very little acoustic detail is discarded during the recognition of spoken words. Currently, there is no consensus on the importance of the phoneme unit in spoken-word recognition.

Phonemes in Speech Production

There is greater agreement among psycholinguists about the role of the phoneme in speech production. Most current models assume that words are selected according to the conceptual requirements of the speaker, and then the phonemes making up that word are selected for articulation, possibly with reference to a store of known syllables. Originally, these models relied on data from speech errors in order to define the units involved in production. Errors are not common in natural speech, but when they do occur many of them involve substitutions, anticipations, or perseverations of phonemes. In the case of Spoonerisms, the substitution results in sequences that correspond to real words (e.g., "you have hissed all the mystery lectures" instead of "you have missed all the history lectures"). These phonemic errors will often preserve the syllabic information related to the phonemes involved, such that syllable-initial phonemes are unlikely to end up at the end of another syllable. Phonemic similarity and whether or not the change would produce a real word are also influential factors in defining the likelihood of a speech error. In the last few years these error data have been augmented by more sophisticated techniques that allow error-free speech production to be studied. These techniques have been particularly useful in mapping out the time course of the various processes in speech production.

Gareth Gaskell
University of York, U.K.

PHONETICS

Phonetics, often defined as the scientific study of speech sounds, encompasses three primary areas of interest: (1) speech sound production, (2) acoustic transmission of speech sounds, and (3) speech sound reception. The field of phonetics is interdisciplinary and draws upon the natural sciences (anatomy, physiology, physics), the social and behavioral sciences (psychology, sociology, anthropology, linguistics), and engineering. In turn, the principles of phonetics are applied in such diverse fields as education (foreign language pedagogy, reading), health care and rehabilitation (speech-language pathology), the humanities (vocal music), and forensics. The phonetic sciences also impact industry; telecommunications, speech recognition software packages, and synthetic speech applications incorporate phonetic principles and are widely available.

A basic goal of phonetics has been to develop reliable and valid conventions for describing speech production. In practice, this is accomplished using two complementary approaches: impressionistic phonetic transcription and instrumental measurement. These procedures are designed to allow one to document speech patterns regardless of the language that is being spoken.

Phonetic Transcription

Several phonetic alphabets have been developed; however, the International Phonetic Alphabet (IPA) is perhaps the best known and most widely used system. The IPA, like the familiar Latin alphabet, uses symbols to represent different speech sounds; however, the IPA differs from traditional orthography in both scope and consistency.

Whereas the Latin alphabet has only 26 letters, the current IPA consists of more than 100 symbols representing the sounds of the world's languages. In addition, IPA symbols have been developed to describe suprasegmental or prosodic aspects of speech (e.g., stress, duration, tone). Diacritic symbols exist for documenting nuances of speech sound production. Thus, the scope of the IPA is much broader than traditional orthography.

The IPA also is more consistent in its representation of speech sounds. In traditional orthography, the relationship between sound and symbol may vary. For example, the letter "c" is pronounced as [s] in some words (e.g., "city") and as [k] in others (e.g., "cap"). A basic principle of the IPA is that each phonetic symbol will represent one (and only one) distinctive sound; accordingly, each sound will be represented consistently by one (and only one) symbol.

The IPA is well suited for the description of individual differences in speaking patterns. It is often used to document dialectal differences, speech performance errors (i.e., slips of the tongue), foreign accent, as well as disordered speech. Extensions to the IPA have been developed to document sounds that are produced only by speakers with disordered speech. Impressionistic phonetic transcription provides valuable information regarding speech production; however, it requires much practice to develop the skill and even experts may disagree on the most appropriate way to render a given production.

Instrumental Measurement

Phoneticians often use specialized laboratory equipment and software to study acoustic and articulatory aspects of speech production. Traditionally, tape-recorded speech signals were examined using an oscilloscope, sound spectrograph, and other instruments to complete acoustic measurements. The spectrograph, for example, allowed the phonetician to examine changes in the frequency and intensity characteristics of conversational speech. Today, advances in processing speed and signal storage have made it commonplace for phoneticians to capture speech signals using microcomputers. The signal may then be retrieved and properties such as frequency, intensity, and duration can be measured. The widespread availability of digital signal processing has stimulated the development of high-quality—yet low-cost—speech analysis software packages.

There also have been many advances in the measurement of articulation. For example, electropalatography (EPG) allows one to examine tongue-to-palate contact during running speech. Another procedure, electromagnetic articulography (EMA), provides a noninvasive means of measuring and graphing movements of the speech organs. Such objective instrumental analyses may be used to quantify speech movements and to refine phonetic transcriptions. In addition, speech instrumentation has been used to provide biofeedback to improve the pronunciation of second language learners and to diagnose and treat speech disorders in children and adults.

The field of phonetics is diverse, and many branches within the field have been described. For example, *experimental phonetics* has been distinguished from *descriptive phonetics*. Experimental phonetics seeks to examine the impact of various conditions upon speech production or perception under controlled conditions, whereas descriptive phonetics seeks to document naturally occurring speech production patterns, often for purposes of classification or to track changes in speech patterns over time (the latter is sometimes referred to as *historical* or *diachronic phonetics*). Likewise, *theoretical phonetics* has been distinguished from *applied phonetics* (also known as *practical phonetics*).

The term *articulatory phonetics* denotes the branch of phonetics devoted to studying the relationship between speech anatomy and sound production. The branch that is concerned with the study of the physics of speech transmission is known as *acoustic phonetics*. A third branch, *auditory phonetics* or *perceptual phonetics*, emphasizes the study of speech sound reception and the factors that influence it. Other specializations have been identified in the field of phonetics, including *linguistic phonetics* (which provides insight into the nature of human language systems), *comparative phonetics* (which discerns similarities and differences among sounds of different languages, often for educational purposes), *clinical phonetics* (which applies phonetics to the study, diagnosis, and treatment of human communication disorders), *neurophonetics* (which emphasizes the relationship between neurology and speech production/perception), and *forensic phonetics* (which applies phonetics to crime investigations such as the use of speech patterns to help identify a perpetrator's identity).

Phoneticians have catalogued the sounds of many of the world's languages. Although universal tendencies have been identified, there is considerable variability in the number and types of sounds that are used by speakers of different languages. Speakers of the Hawaiian language, for example, produce few (approximately 13) distinct sounds, and some languages use even fewer sounds. American English, in contrast, has more than 40 distinct sounds. Speakers of !Xung (an African language) reportedly produce more than 140 distinctive sounds—more than any other known language. The field of phonetics continues to evolve as a scientific discipline to provide insight into the most human of behaviors—speech.

Thomas W. Powell
Louisiana State University Health Sciences Center

PHOTORECEPTORS

Photoreceptors are specialized receptors for translating the absorption of light into electrical signals, which are the language of the nervous system. Photoreceptors have reached the physical limits of light detection and can register the absorption of a single light quantum. On the other hand, our eye can adapt its sensitivity to light levels 10^9-fold higher.

The interior surface of the vertebrate eye is covered by the retina, which is part of the central nervous system. It harbors the photoreceptors as well as neurons that process the information before it is relayed to the brain by the ganglion cells. The retina is inverted, that is, the light falls through all retinal layers before it reaches the photoreceptors (Figure 1). Two types of photoreceptors can be distinguished: the rods (120 million in a human eye) for vision in dim light, and the cones (6 million per eye) for daylight and for color vision. Photoreceptors each have a cell body, an axon that forms synapses with other neurons, and an inner segment that contains the machinery for routine cellular metabolism. Photoelectrical transduction takes place in the outer segment, which contains photopigment molecules, all biochemical components for the signal amplification, as well as the ion channels that are needed to generate the electrical response.

Phototransduction

The ion channels in the outer segment are opened by intracellular messenger molecules, cyclic guanosine-monophosphate (cGMP; Yau & Baylor, 1989; Finn, Grunwald, & Yau, 1996). In the dark, the cGMP concentration in the outer segment is high, channels open, and Na^+ and Ca^{2+} ions enter the cell through these open channels, thereby adjusting the membrane voltage to around –35 mV. At this membrane voltage, the photoreceptor releases transmitter molecules at its synapse. The retinal neurons process this information and relay it to the brain, where it is interpreted as "dark."

Rod outer segments contain a stack of flat, hollow membrane compartments, the discs (Figure 2). The photopigment rhodopsin is found in high concentration within the disc membranes (up to 100 million rhodopsin molecules per rod). Rhodopsin consists of a protein part (the opsin), which is inserted into the disc membrane, and a light absorbing part, the aldehyde form of vitamin A, retinal (Figure 2). Retinal can exist in different forms. The folded 11-cis form of retinal is bound within the rhodopsin. Absorption of a light quantum switches the 11-cis retinal to the elongated all-trans form, which induces a conformational change in the rhodopsin molecule—it becomes "activated." Light-

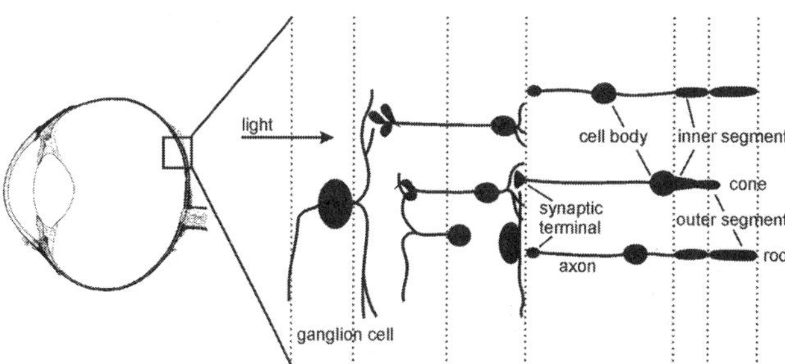

Figure 1. Section through the eye and the retina, showing different retinal cell types.

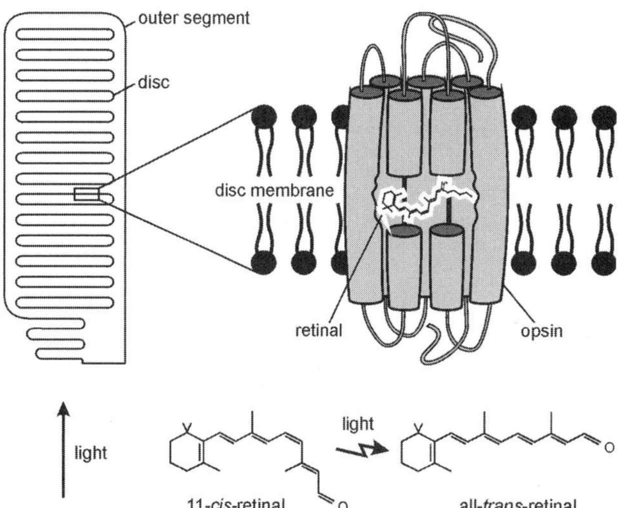

Figure 2. The rod outer segment contains hundreds of discs with millions of rhodopsin molecules.

activated rhodopsin is capable of activating protein molecules called transducin, which in turn activate a third protein class, the phosphodiesterase. The activated phosphodiesterases destroy cGMP molecules, the cGMP concentration falls rapidly, and the ion channels close. As fewer positive ions enter the cell, the membrane voltage becomes more negative and less transmitter is released at the synapse (Yau, 1994). This information is processed further and is interpreted by the brain as "light."

Sensitivity and Adaptation

One light-activated rhodopsin molecule may activate up to 150 transducin molecules, each of which can activate one phosphodiesterase molecule. Each phosphodiesterase can cleave up to 2000 cGMP molecules per second. Due to this high amplification, the absorption of one light quantum leads to the closure of many channels and a measurable change in membrane voltage. With brighter light, more cGMP is destroyed, more channels close and the voltage can reach –70 mV.

Photoreceptor adaptation is only incompletely understood. The internal messenger Ca^{2+} is very important (Kaupp & Koch, 1992). The internal Ca^{2+} concentration is high in the dark, when Ca^{2+} enters through the cGMP-gated channels, but drops rapidly when the channels close upon illumination. Ca^{2+} binding proteins serve as Ca^{2+} sensors and relay the change in Ca^{2+} concentration to their target enzymes in order to adjust their activity. One consequence is the activation of the guanylyl cyclase, which increases cGMP production. Furthermore, the light response becomes truncated. At low Ca^{2+} concentration, light-activated rhodopsin is shut off by the proteins rhodopsin kinase and arrestin, so that fewer tranducin molecules are activated. The gain of the cascade becomes smaller; that is, the cell becomes less sensitive and its operating range increases. Adaptive mechanisms are also postulated in the retinal network; some may follow a circadian rhythm.

Psychophysics

Cones function in a manner similar to that of rods, but are less sensitive. We can distinguish colors because our retina harbors three types of cones whose opsins differ in their sensitivity to light of different wavelengths. Mutations in the cone opsins may result in abnormal color vision. Vision is best in the central retina ("fovea"), where cones are densely packed and the information of each cone is transmitted separately from others to the brain. In the peripheral retina, many photoreceptors converge onto one postsynaptic cell, hence resolution is lower. The fovea contains no rods and is night-blind.

In dark-adapted rods the high signal amplification may need 200 milliseconds to build up the light response, which can last up to a second. But even in light-adapted rods and cones light responses last 15 to 50 ms, thus we cannot resolve more than 60 events per second. Therefore, in our perception, pictures in movies fuse to a continuous motion. In comparison, photoreceptors of many insects would need more than 200 pictures per second for fusion.

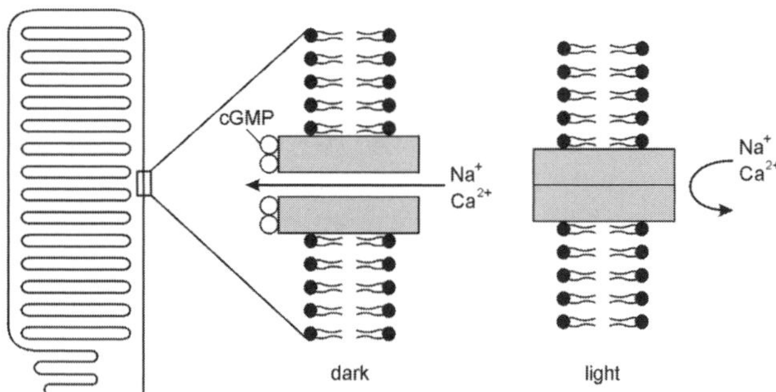

Figure 3. In the dark, ions enter the outer segment through the cGMP-gated channels in the plasmamembrane. Upon illumination, channels close and the influx ceases.

REFERENCES

Finn, J. T., Grunwald, M. E., & Yau, K.-W. (1996). Cyclic nucleotide-gated ion channels: An extended family with diverse functions. *Annual Review of Physiology, 58,* 395–426.

Kaupp, U. B., & Koch, K.-W. (1992): The role of cGMP and Ca^{2+} in vertebrate photoreceptor excitation and adaptation. *Annual Review of Physiology, 54,* 153–175.

Yau, K.-W. (1994). Phototransduction mechanism in retinal rods and cones. *Investigative Ophthalmology and Visual Science, 35,* 9–32.

Yau, K.-W., & Baylor, D. A. (1989). Cyclic GMP-activated conductance of retinal photoreceptor cells. *Annual Review of Neuroscience, 12,* 289–327.

Frank Müller

PHRENOLOGY

Phrenology, now an outmoded theory of personality, originated with the speculations of the physician-anatomist Franz Joseph Gall (1758–1828). Intrigued by a personal inference that individuals with bulging or prominent eyes had good memories, Gall began to look for personality correlates of other features such as broad foreheads, prominent jaws, and so on. Ultimately, he focused his attention primarily on the brain and skull and founded what he called the new science of craniology. Knowledge of the brain and nervous system at that time was vestigial at best. In consequence, much of Gall's early work on his theory included the development of new techniques of dissection, perfection of the construction of brain and skull models, and the amassing of a unique collection of skulls. The superb quality of this supporting anatomical work gave Gall great credibility when he first presented his ideas to the medical community.

Gall's basic belief was that mental functions are located in the brain, and that their exercise and perfection would lead to localized brain development. This, in turn, would lead to appropriate enlargement of the related areas of the surrounding skull. Thus, by a very close scrutiny of the skull and its various prominences, one could obtain a detailed, individualized diagnosis of an individual's personal qualities and characteristics. He was thus the first researcher to postulate what has come to be known as localization of brain function—a precursor of modern neuropsychology in which physiological measures of brain and nervous system activity are correlated with psychological observations.

Around 1800, Spurzheim (1776–1823), a pupil of Gall, joined him on a lecture tour to espouse the new science of phrenology (a term never used by Gall). A dynamic and convincing lecturer, Spurzheim changed the emphasis to stress mostly the detection of the presence of positive faculties and their modifiability by means of strategic training. The approach to "reading bumps" became less akin to medical diagnosis and more to quackery and fortune telling. Correspondingly, phrenology lost its popularity and acceptance by medical groups, but simultaneously became popular with the general public.

SUGGESTED READING

Davies, J. D. (1955). *Phrenology—Fad and Science.* New Haven, CT: Yale University Press.

Spurzheim, J. G. (1827). *Outlines of phrenology: being also a manual of reference for the market busts.* London: Treuttel, Wurtz & Richter.

Winkler, J. K., & Bromberg, W. (1939). *Mind explorers.* New York: World.

Mary E. Reuder

PHYSICAL ATTRACTIVENESS

Physical attractiveness has been defined as "That which represents one's conception of the ideal in appearance; that which gives the greatest degree of pleasure to the senses" (Hatfield & Sprecher, 1986, p. 4).

Artists, philosophers, and scientists have asked if there are any universal standards of beauty. In the fifth century B.C., for example, the Greek philosopher Aristotle proposed that the Golden Mean, a perfect balance, was a universal ideal.

Aristotle appears to have been right. When social scientists asked people to compare individual faces with average faces, they found people greatly preferred the latter. Researchers assembled photographs of men and women's faces. Then, using video and computer techniques, they generated a series of composite faces. Inevitably, students found the composites to be more appealing than any individual face.

Evolutionary psychologists contend that men and women prefer faces that, in a sense, "have it all"—faces that combine the innocence of childhood with the ripe sexuality of the mature. Early ethnologists discovered that men and women often experience a tender rush of feeling when they view infantile "kewpie doll" faces—faces with huge eyes, tiny noses and mouths, and little chins. Later, sociobiologists discovered that men and women are aroused by faces that possess features associated with maturity, especially lush, adult sexuality (for example, thick hair, dewy skin, and full lips) and mature power (for example, high cheekbones or a firm jaw and chin). Recent evidence suggests that people prefer faces that possess *both* assets: large eyes and small noses, full sexual lips, and strong jaws and chins (see Rhodes & Zebrowitz, 2002). Whether these preferences will turn out to be truly universal is not yet known.

Evidence That People are Biased in Favor of the Physically Attractive

Scientists find that most people, most of the time, are biased in favor of the good-looking. The Greek philosopher Sappho contended that "what is beautiful is good." Today, scientists have come to a fuller understanding of just how, where, when, and why physical appearance is important. There seem to be four steps in the stereotyping process:

1. Most people know that it is not fair to discriminate against the unattractive (they would be incensed if others discriminated against *them*).
2. Privately, most people take it for granted that attractive and unattractive people are different. Generally, they assume that what is beautiful is good and what is unattractive is bad.
3. Most people treat good-looking and average people better than they treat the unattractive.
4. As a consequence, a self-fulfilling prophecy occurs. The way people are treated shapes the kinds of people they become. (Hatfield & Sprecher, 1986, p. 36)

There is evidence that people do perceive attractive and unattractive people differently. In one classic experiment, social psychologists showed college students yearbook photographs of men and women who varied markedly in appearance and asked them about their first impressions of the people depicted. Young adults assumed that handsome men and beautiful women must possess nearly all the virtues. The good-looking were assumed to be more sociable, outgoing, poised, interesting, exciting, sexually responsive, kind, nurturing, warm, modest, strong, and sensitive than their homely peers. They were also expected to have happier and more fulfilling lives.

Not only do people think that the attractive are special, but they also treat them that way. Clinicians spend more time with good-looking clients. Teachers reward more attractive students with better grades. Executives are more likely to hire and promote good-looking men and women and to pay them higher salaries. The good-looking are more likely to receive assistance when they are in trouble. Attractive criminals are less likely to get caught, be reported to the authorities, be found guilty, or receive strict sentences than are others.

Society's biases give good-looking men and women a marked advantage in intimate relationships, as well. The attractive have an easier time meeting potential dates and mates, attract more appealing dates and mates, and end up with better dating and marital relationships. If, in spite of all these advantages, things go wrong, they find it easier to start anew.

What effect does such stereotyping have on men and women? It turns out that the good-looking and unattractive are not so different as people assume them to be. Self-esteem and self-concept are positively related to how good-looking people *think* they are, but not to actual appearance. In general, the personalities of the attractive and unattractive differ only slightly, if at all.

Attractive and unattractive people do seem to differ in one critical respect, however. The good-looking appear to be more confident in romantic and social situations and to possess more social skills than their peers. People expect the good-looking to be charming, so they treat them as if they are. As a consequence, the good-looking become more socially skilled.

This self-fulfilling aspect of physical attractiveness was demonstrated in a classic study by M. Snyder, E. Tanke, and E. Berscheid (1977). Men and women at the University of Minnesota were recruited for a study on the acquaintance process. First, men were given a Polaroid snapshot and biographical information about their partners. In fact, the snapshot was a fake; it depicted either a beautiful or a homely woman. Men were then asked their first impressions of this "potential date." Those who believed they had been assigned a beautiful partner expected her to be sociable, poised, humorous, and socially skilled. Those who thought they had been assigned an unattractive partner expected her to be unsociable, awkward, serious, and socially inept. Such prejudice is not surprising; it is known that good-looking people make exceptionally good first impressions.

The next set of findings, however, was startling. Men were asked to get acquainted with their partners via a telephone call. Men's expectations had a dramatic impact on the way they talked to their partners. Men who thought they were talking to a beautiful woman were more sociable, sexually warm, interesting, independent, sexually permissive, bold, outgoing, humorous, and socially skilled than were men who thought their partner was homely. The men assigned to an attractive woman were also more comfortable, enjoyed themselves more, liked their partners more, took the initiative more often, and used their voices more effectively. In brief, men who thought they were talking to a beautiful woman tried harder.

Within the space of a telephone conversation, women (regardless of their true appearance) became what men expected them to be. Women who were talked to as if they were beautiful soon began to sound that way. They became unusually animated, confident, and socially skilled. Those who were treated as if they were unattractive became withdrawn, lacked confidence, and seemed awkward.

The men's prophecies had been fulfilled.

A final observation: The evidence makes it clear that the good-looking have an advantage. However, a careful analysis of existing data makes it clear that the relationship between appearance and advantage is not a straightforward one. The extremely attractive have only a small advantage over their more ordinary peers. What is really important is to be at least average. Alas, it is the unattractive and the disfigured who suffer the greatest social costs of prejudice.

REFERENCES

Hatfield, E., & Sprecher, S. (1986). *Mirror, mirror: The importance of looks in everyday life.* Albany, NY: SUNY Press.

Marquardt, S. R. (2002). See www.beautyanalysis.com.

Rhodes, G., & Zebrowitz, L. A. (2002). (Eds.). *Advances in visual cognition: Facial attractiveness. Evolutionary, cognitive, and social perspectives* (Vol. 1). Westport, CN: Ablex.

Snyder, M., Berscheid, E., & Glick, P. (1985). Focusing on the exterior and the interior: Two investigations of the initiation of personal relationships. *Journal of Personality and Social Psychology, 48,* 1427–1439.

Snyder, M., Tanke, E. D., & Berscheid, E. (1977). Social perception and interpersonal behavior: On the self-fulfilling nature of social stereotypes. *Journal of Personality and Social Psychology, 35,* 656–666.

Elaine Hatfield
Richard L. Rapson
University of Hawaii

See also: **Interpersonal Communication; Self-fulfilling Prophecy**

PHYSIOLOGICAL AND BEHAVIORAL CONCOMITANTS OF AGING

Many behavioral and psychological changes occur as one ages. To illustrate, we have described some of the age-related physiological changes in two sensory systems (vision and hearing), the cardiovascular system, and the musculoskeletal system, and their behavioral and psychological effects. Many of these changes, however, are not inevitable consequences of aging.

Hearing

Various types of age-related hearing losses can occur (i.e., conductive, sensorineural, mixed, and central hearing loss; Heckheimer, 1989). These hearing losses may lead to specific hearing impairments. First, older adults may experience difficulty hearing high-frequency sounds (e.g., children's voices, squeaking brakes). Second, older adults may have trouble hearing information embedded in background noise (e.g., conversations in noisy environments). Consequently, older adults may frequently request that information be repeated, or they may rely on other contextual cues (e.g., lip-reading). Third, older adults may have more difficulty recognizing consonant sounds of shorter durations at lower decibel levels. Therefore, when conversing, older adults may ask speakers to talk louder. Similarly, older adults may increase the volume on radios or television sets. Fourth, older adults may experience more difficulty hearing rapidly presented speech with a low degree of context. Therefore, whenever novel information is spoken rapidly (e.g., messages over public announcement systems), older adult may miss important details. Fifth, older adults may experience difficulty hearing and understanding speech that lacks normal fluctuations in tone and rhythm (e.g., hearing unwavering speech or undifferentiated computer-generated speech).

These age-related declines in hearing may have additional behavioral consequences (e.g., social isolation or depression). Individuals may become irritated with their hearing difficulties and the speech characteristics of others that interfere with auditory perception. Further, older adults may even become paranoid about what others may be saying about them, perceiving others as "mumbling" or speaking softly to purposefully exclude the older listener.

Vision

Several age-related changes occur in the visual system that can have psychological and behavioral consequences. First, older adults require more light to see because of the increased density and opacity of their lenses, and the decreased number of photoreceptors (Whitbourne, 1998). Second, older adults are more likely to experience glare when viewing bright objects, due to the scattering of light within the lens resulting from the increased density. Third, older adults are more likely to experience difficulty with accommodation due to the increased lens density and the loss in flexibility of the eye capsule. Fourth, depth perception decreases with age, caused by the increased density of the lens. Fifth, age-related problems with color discrimination are caused by the increased yellowing of the lens and pigmentation of the vitreous humor. Finally, an age-related decrease in the visual field can be caused by macular degeneration, which is experienced by most individuals in their 70s and 80s.

The behavioral consequences of the foregoing problems can be quite significant. The increased difficulty in seeing objects in reduced light and greater susceptibility to glare can lead individuals to increasingly restrict their evening driving and walking. These changes in vision can also lead to increased accidents and falls resulting from failure to see hazardous objects, and diminished self-esteem resulting from such accidents and restrictions incurred from low vision. Changes in color perception can create difficulties in correctly matching clothing and facial makeup, and sometimes cause others to question the individual's aesthetic sensibilities (Whitbourne, 1998). These changes can also affect one's understanding of color-coded information and diminish one's appreciation of artwork, movies, and scenery. The diminished visual acuity can lead to difficulty reading, watching television, recognizing friends, and learning and remembering the distinctive features of the faces of new acquaintances. Finally, the embarrassment associated with these problems can lead to increased social isolation and decreased social activities.

Cardiovascular and Respiratory System

Age-related changes in the cardiovascular and respiratory systems can have significant behavioral and psychological consequences. However, not all older adults experience the same levels of decline of the cardiovascular and respiratory systems. Exercise, disease, and genetic predisposition are important factors, in addition to the effects of aging, in the determination of cardiorespiratory fitness.

Increased age is often associated with reduced cardiopulmonary fitness. The amount of blood ejected from the heart and the sensitivity of the heart to neural stimulation, which controls the timing and rate of heart contractions, decrease with age.

Aging also results in structural changes of the lungs (e.g., decreased elastic recoil and increased rigidity of chest wall) that limit lung capacity and the efficiency of the gas exchange. The consequences of cardiovascular and respiratory changes may include a decreased ability to cope with physical stress. The older adult may become more easily fatigued and experience shortness of breath more quickly compared to younger adults. Consequently, the older adult may become fearful of activities associated with physical exertion. Likewise, older adults may demonstrate frustration with the limitations associated with cardiovascular and respiratory changes and become more fearful of activities that cause physical exertion, and therefore pursue activities that are more sedentary. All of these limitations can also lead to lowered self-esteem.

Musculoskeletal System

Age-related musculoskeletal changes have important implications for the daily lives of older adults. Muscle mass decreases with age and can lead to increased weakness. Muscle endurance also diminishes with age. Bone mass and porosity decreases, increasing susceptibility to fractures. The joint cartilage also degenerates with age, resulting in increased joint pain and stiffening. Musculoskeletal changes can be reduced (e.g., increased muscle strength and endurance) in both younger and older adults via exercises.

Age-related musculoskeletal changes may result in older adults restricting movements and being less willing to undertake physically demanding tasks. Older adults may become more easily fatigued and more cautious in their movements, particularly on slippery surfaces. Individuals may demonstrate difficulty climbing stairs or rising from a sitting position. Fear of falling may develop because of leg weakness or fear of breaking bones when ambulating. These musculoskeletal changes may restrict participation in enjoyable/leisure activities and diminish self-esteem. The chronic pain sometimes associated with musculoskeletal changes can also lead to depression.

In summary, numerous changes occur in the aging body that can have substantial behavioral and psychological effects. Fortunately, the human body exhibits amazing resilience, accommodation, and adaptation to the aging process.

REFERENCES

Heckheimer, E. (1989). *Health promotion and the elderly in the community.* Philadelphia, PA: W. B. Saunders.

Whitbourne, S. (1998). Physiological aspects of aging: Relation to identity and clinical implications. In B. Edelstein (Ed.), *Clinical geropsychology* (Vol. 7, pp. 1–24). Oxford, UK: Elsevier Science.

Barry A. Edelstein
Jeffrey L. Goodie
Ronald R. Martin
West Virginia University

PHYSIOLOGICAL PSYCHOLOGY (NONREDUCTIONISM)

Any serious consideration of a nonreductionist approach to physiological psychology calls for a prefatory definition in an effort to achieve a thorough comprehension of the pivotal term *reductionism.* The order ranges from physics, the simplest, to sociology, the most complex (Figure 1). The reductionist believes that all the diverse forms of nature are continuous and result from different combinations of the same basic elements. Reductionists conclude that the ultimate nature of the universe is reducible to those fixed and indivisible atomic building blocks. According to reductionists, that is the way to understand all aspects of nature.

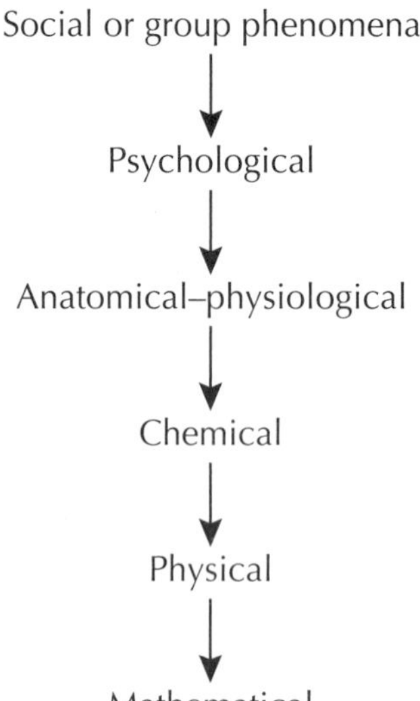

Figure 1. Hierarchy of the sciences arranged according to levels of complexity.

At one time, the reductionist could have safely clung to the belief that at some time in the future, sociological, psychological, biological, and physical events would all be explained in terms of the fixed and eternal building blocks of physics. However, the absolutistic reductionist now is confronted by the embarrassing discovery of contemporary physics that atomic particles themselves have very elusive properties, hardly a dependable base on which to erect a firm theoretical structure.

Reductionism in Biology

For its particular area of investigation, biology segregates living things, both plants and animals. Subdivisions of biology deal with cells (cytology), tissues (histology), anatomy or morphology, physiology, and embryology. Cells, tissues, organs, and organisms have properties beyond those found in molecules. Among them are organization, coordination, control, adaptation, growth or duplication, and repair. Although there are no phenomena in living systems that are not molecular, there also are none that are only molecular.

The cell shows a certain characteristic unity, pattern, order, and integration not found in the molecular constituents of cells. The organism also shows properties that cannot be inferred from its constituent organs. The word *organism* refers to organization, the hallmark of the living thing, plant or animal. It acts as a unit—as a system, not as a collection of independently acting, helter-skelter organs, tissues, cells, or molecules.

Opposed to the notion of reductionism is the concept of

wholeness and levels of integration. According to holism, each cell, tissue, organ, or organism is more than the sum of its parts. A converse statement would say, in effect, that in describing a cell in terms only of its component molecules, some aspects of that cell would be left out. Knowledge of the individual parts would not yield understanding of the whole, except by seeing the role of the parts as an expression of the whole organism.

The concept of integrative levels may help to clarify a nonreductionistic approach to natural events. According to this notion, the order of sciences in Figure 1, from physics up to sociology, reflects levels of integration. Thus, in place of reductionistic continuity, there is discontinuity at each level, beginning at physics. At each higher level, new qualities emerge that were not apparent at lower levels. The implication is that events at each level must be studied at their own level instead of being forced into a lower mold. To reduce phenomena at a higher level to a lower level would be to lose the attributes and structure of the observations that initiated inquiry.

The Role of the Hypothetical Construct

In some sciences, such as physics and biology, some phenomena can be analyzed to the point at which sight and touch give out and the investigator is forced to resort to submicroscopical concepts—an undesirable situation and certainly not one to be emulated. The relationship between what is perceived and what is conceived in explanatory terms sometimes becomes highly attenuated.

How can the troubles that reductionism presents be avoided? A different procedure is tried. This time, a field approach of the interbehavioral type is adopted in investigating psychological occurrences. A first requisite here will be to broaden views to include organism and stimulus object. With this change in orientation, the focus shifts away from the reductionist's concentration on the organism. The center of interest now concerns not what might be imagined to be going on inside the organism, but what transpires between the organism and stimulus object. Their interaction is of paramount, but not exclusive, preoccupation because there are additional observable variables. The interaction requires light to mediate visual interactions and air for auditory interactions. No event occurs in a vacuum, so the setting factors or surrounding conditions in which the event occurs must be noted. All of these aspects of the total event must be seen in system, in their totality. It is hardly possible to overstress the equal emphasis given to the stimulus object, a view that certainly deglamorizes the organism.

Scientists come to accept certain events that fit a dependable regularity or "ideal of natural order" as self-explanatory. There is no need to go behind the scenes or to ask further questions. These occurrences are accepted as the starting point or base for explaining other things. Gravitation offers a convenient example. Note the gravitational interaction between the Earth and the Moon. It would not profit the astronomer to ask, "Why is there gravity?" The fact is that there is gravity, and the problem is to determine how, what, when, and where it operates. A rejection of the rock-bottom concept would be illustrated by an investigator who insisted on tearing apart the Earth and the Moon in an attempt to find the "cause" of gravity. Modern astronomers know better than to join such a foolish enterprise. They accept gravity as a fact that requires no further explanation, and go to work convinced that gravitation just *is*.

The concept of "rock-bottom" can be applied to psychological inquiry. For nonreductionistic physiological psychologists, the organism is rock-bottom. They do not need to dissect it for some imaginary internal "cause" of behavior any more than the astronomer feels compelled to search within the bowels of the Earth or the Moon for the "cause" of gravity. Nonreductionists accept the organism as one of the variables and as a starting point for inquiry, an inquiry that relates the unitary, integrated organism to the stimulus and to other components of the total field. In summary, the difference between reductionistic physiological psychologists and the nonreductionistic variety is what they accept as rock-bottom. For the former, rock-bottom lies somewhere inside the organism's head; for the nonreductionist, the organism itself is rock-bottom.

The Organism as a Locus of Variables

It would appear as if the nonreductionist's acceptance of the organism as rock-bottom implies a complete neglect of the biological aspects of the living copartner of a psychological event. This is not so. On the contrary, the nonreductionist looks on the organism as an important locus of variables than can affect the psychological event. An example using two scenarios in which a boy is reading a book can help make the point in a broad way. In both Event A and Event B, the boy and the book are interacting under definite and specific conditions. Among these are a certain illumination, quiet, 70°F temperature, and so on. However, prior to Event B the boy suffered damage to his brain. The important point is that Event A does not equal Event B. The brain concussion as a significant variable has changed the boy. Thus the boy in Event B is not the same boy as the one who participated in Event A. Therefore, the two events are not comparable. Reading that proceeded smoothly in Event A has been interfered with in Event B by a variable localizable within the biological matrix of the boy.

For the nonreductionist, such an explanation is rock-bottom and it is satisfying, but it only spurs the reductionist to search within the brain somewhere for a "why" kind of explanation for the boy's changed reading behavior. This procedure can only lead us back to "merely conceivable" explanations, which themselves call for verification before they can be used.

The difference between the reductionist and nonreductionist view of the nervous system can be summed up by characterizing the nervous system as a necessary but not a sufficient condition for proper verbal behavior.

Our consideration of the nervous system as a necessary but not sufficient condition of psychological occurrences paves the way for an expanded inquiry into the question of the organism as a locus of variables. Specifically, this calls for an inventory of the anatomical-physiological aspects of the organism that are involved in various psychological events. For example, in speaking, such parts as the oral cavity with lips, teeth, and vocal chords, and the trachea, lungs, and diaphragm participate in interactions. Yet even here there are no absolutes, as people without vocal chords or tongue have been able to produce speech. However, no amount of minute anatomical-physiological description can explain how it is that one person speaks French, another speaks Swedish, and still another speaks Russian. Also, it is granted that a Beethoven born deaf would never have become the superb composer that he was. Yet the fact that he became deaf did not prevent him from composing the bulk of his work after his tragedy. There is a suggestion here of the domination of the flesh by the psychological. Certainly legs and arms are of crucial importance in football or baseball activities; however, some leg amputees can swim. Nevertheless, any departure from an optimal intactness of the organism can act in a negative way. Blindness can prevent visual interactions, but so can absence of illumination. If we think of the former condition as more permanent, how about a sighted person's life imprisonment in a pitch-black dungeon? The two conditions are then equated, and, because either can have devastating consequences, neither condition is exalted above the other, as either can extinguish visual interactions. With the view of the organism as rock-bottom, the nonreductionist holds that a maximal intactness of the organism is desirable.

Conclusions

Because reductionism deals with imputed properties of the nervous system, we must take note of the circular reasoning underlying the hypothetical construct and reject theories that are "merely conceivable." As an alternative, the organism might be regarded as a locus of variables that can either facilitate or interfere with psychological events. As such, they are considered part of the total psychological event. A nonreductionist view avoids problems such as treating the nervous system (1) as causal (i.e., as producing psychological action), and (2) as having dual functions, biological and psychological—problems created by a reductionistic approach.

N. H. Pronko

See also: **Determinism; Mind-Body Problem**

PIAGET'S THEORY

Over the course of 60 years, Jean Piaget (1896–1980), a Swiss biologist and philosopher, formulated a theory of the development of intellectual competence that continues to influence contemporary theories in that field. Piaget maintained that logical thought depended on learning, social cooperation, biological maturation, and *development,* by which he meant a series of fundamental changes such that the later ways of thinking are dependent upon, yet qualitatively distinct from, the earlier ones, always moving in the direction of greater logical consistency. He formulated subsidiary theories of the development of moral judgment and reasoning, perception, images, and memory, always from the perspective of how each was constrained by the various levels of intellectual competence.

Genetic Epistemology

Genetic epistemology is a discipline founded by the American psychologist James Mark Baldwin that draws upon philosophy, psychology, logic, biology, cybernetics, and structuralism and addresses all aspects of such questions as: What is knowing? From whence does it come? What conditions make it possible? Genetic epistemology, as formulated by Piaget, attributed the development of knowledge and intelligence within the individual and within Western scientific cultures to coordinated mechanisms that simultaneously sought to preserve and to modify the underlying structure of the mind and the culture.

Piaget held that the fundamental structures of our minds are not given a priori, but are humanly constructed through evolving systems by which we act on and transform the environment and our own minds. The succeeding levels or stages are always reformulations or reconstructions of our preceding ways of acting on the world and validating knowledge. Subsequent stages are always a more consistent way of acting on the world, and are always more coherent, than the stages that precede them.

The Epistemic Subject

Piaget's theory of intellectual development is about an idealized person, a person who probably does not exist, but who could exist. The person is the *epistemic subject,* the pure knower who has no individual characteristics—no personality, sex, motivation (other than to know), culture, nationality—and the theory is about that person. Although Piaget's theoretical description of a child's competence at logical problem solving does not fully account for what a given child will do in a problem situation, it does characterize what a child can do if no other mitigating factors are present. While the epistemic subject merely understands and knows events, the ordinary person succeeds in any number of tasks, and often without any understanding of this success. In fact, this lag between success on a task and understanding the task is a topic that Piaget addressed in his later work.

The epistemic subject knows those truths that are necessarily true as opposed to those that are merely true. For example, when A = B and B = C, not only is it true empirically that A = C, but it is necessarily true; it must be true, it could not possibly be otherwise, and there is no need to examine A and C in any way to know that A equals C. At its core, Piaget's theory is about the development of truths that have to be as they are and could not conceivably be otherwise.

The Clinical Method

In Piaget's clinical research, each child was seen individually, given some materials or an apparatus to manipulate, and asked questions designed to elicit responses about what he or she did. What the child said or believed about what was done was important, but greater emphasis was placed upon what the child actually did, how the problem was tackled, what errors the child made, and so forth. Invariably, the child was asked to think about a common childhood event, such as flattening a clay ball or playing marbles, in a new way, or to consider a new possibility in an ordinary childlike task, such as lining up sticks in order by their lengths.

The tasks or problems set for the children were usually designed to reveal the structure of the child's reasoning about some epistemological question, such as the nature of causality, necessity, implication, time, or space.

The Stages of Intellectual Development

Piaget claimed only that he had developed a general outline or skeleton of a theory, with gaps to be filled in by others. Even the number of stages of intellectual development varied in his work from time to time, but most accounts set forth four main stages: the *sensorimotor stage* (0–2 years), with six substages; the *preoperational stage* (2–7 years), with two substages; the *concrete operational stage* (7–12 years), with two substages; and the *formal operational stage* (12 years and up). Within each stage and substage, Piaget frequently distinguished three levels: failure, partial success, and success. In the final versions of the theory, development was viewed not as linear progression through the stages, but as an open-ended spiral in which the differentiated forms and content at one level are reworked, restructured, integrated, or synthesized at the higher levels of the spiral.

Sensorimotor Stage

The six substages of this stage show the following developments: The infant exhibits (1) innate reflexes and an inability to think, have purpose, or distinguish him/herself from the surroundings; (2) reflexes extended to repetitive actions; (3) the ability to reproduce fortuitous, pleasant, and interesting events; (4) increased coordination of ways to make the interesting things last; (5) discovery of new ways to produce interesting results; and (6) an ability to represent absent events symbolically. The principal accomplishments are the construction of coordinated movements, which have a grouplike mathematical structure; the construction of representation; and the idea of permanent objects and intentionality.

Preoperational Stage

This stage has often been characterized primarily by what the child cannot do. Thought seems rigidly captured by one aspect of a situation, often the child's own point of view (egocentrism), to the exclusion of other perspectives. Thought, besides being centered on a single salient feature of an event, seems to flow in sequences of simple juxtaposition rather than sequences of logical implication or physical causality. Children's reasons for their responses are often preposterous fabrications, or justifications at any price.

Concrete Operational Stage

The errors the child makes during the preoperational stage are corrected in the subsequent stage, but not uniformly or all at once. The solution to problems is worked out separately in various domains. For example, the notion of invariance (conservation) is acquired separately and sequentially in the following order: number, length and mass, area, weight, time, and volume.

Formal Operational Stage

The young adolescent is able to consider all possibilities and to vary all but one in an analysis of a physical event. The ability to hypothetically vary all but one of the possible dimensions of a situation means that form can be considered and manipulated apart from its content and that reality can be subservient to possibility.

Neo-Piagetian Theory

Subsequent work by "neo-Piagetian" theorists has reinforced and expanded Piaget's constructivist stance. Piaget's followers have argued for ongoing intellectual development beyond adolescence that extends *formal thought* to new areas, but based on structures that are less universal, more domain specific, and associated with areas of schooled expertise. The course of development in this view was taken to be more gradual, less punctuated, more socially and culturally dependent, and more integrated with other mental functions (like emotion and motivation) than in many interpretations of Piaget's initial formulations.

Frank B. Murray
University of Delaware

PICK'S DISEASE

Pick's disease was first described by Arnold Pick in 1892 to describe non-Alzheimer's neuropathological changes in an individual with left anterior temporal atrophy and spared frontal lobes. It is a relatively rare and possibly heritable progressive neurodegenerative disorder appearing 10 to 20% as often as Alzheimer's disease. Duration of the disease from diagnosis to death is 5 to 10 years (Tissot, Constantinidis, & Richard, 1985). The disease typically affects individuals between the ages of 45 and 65 years (Hodges, 1994). In Pick's disease patients, brain imaging and autopsy examinations characteristically display progressive frontotemporal lobar atrophy. Due to clinical overlap with other cortical dementias, neuropathologic confirmation is required to establish a definitive diagnosis of Pick's disease.

Neuropathology of Pick's Disease

Pick's disease results in atrophy of the anterior portion of the frontal lobe and a characteristic atrophy of the anterior portion of the superior temporal gyrus (anterior to the central sulcus) with preservation of the posterior portions of that gyrus. The parietal and occipital lobes are generally spared. The atrophy leaves the gyri with a knife-edge appearance. The lateral ventricles, particularly the frontal horns, are dilated due to the atrophic changes. There is also a characteristic severe loss of the granular neurons that comprise the dentate gyrus of the hippocampal complex. Subcortical structures in which neuronal loss occurs include the basal ganglia, amygdala, nucleus basalis of Meynert, substantia nigra, and locus ceruleus (Hof, Bouras, Perl, & Morrison, 1994; Hansen, 1994). Brain stem and cerebellar areas with connections to the cortex are also typically involved (Braak, Arai, & Braak, 1999; Dickson, 1998). In contrast to severely abnormal computed tomography or magnetic resonance images, electroencephalographic recordings are usually normal.

Neuropathologic features of Pick's disease include severe cerebral cortical neuronal loss, Pick bodies, and ballooned neurons (Pick cells; Giannakopoulos et al., 1996). Pick bodies are intracytoplasmic argyrophilic neuronal inclusions composed of straight filaments, microtubules, and occasional paired helical filaments (similar to those in Alzheimer's disease neurofibrillary tangles; Hof et al., 1994). Although there is some neuronal loss in the nucleus basalis of Meynert, cortical levels of choline acetyltransferase are not reduced in Pick's disease as they are in Alzheimer's disease.

Cognitive Changes in Pick's Disease

Clinical manifestations of Pick's disease reflect the distribution of neuropathological changes. Cognitive deficits typically follow alterations in personality and behavior. Behavior changes may include disinhibition, impulsivity, apathy, and decreased initiative. Patients may begin to exhibit inappropriate social behaviors and neglect personal responsibilities. Emotional changes vary and can include depression, anger, mania, irritability, or lability. Patients commonly lack insight into their behavioral and personality changes. Due to severe atrophy of the frontal lobes, patients with Pick's disease have marked impairments in planning and organizing complex activities, set-shifting, judgment, sequencing, and sustaining attention. Their inability to sustain attention and organize activities can give a misleading impression of memory impairment. However, patients generally have preserved memory function evident by cue-enhanced immediate memory and information retrieval abilities. Patients with Pick's disease may have language disturbances characterized by echolalia and perseveration, reduced production of speech, use of stereotyped phrases, and late mutism. Articulation, syntax, and phonology are generally preserved. General intelligence, orientation, perceptual skills, and visuospatial abilities are often intact. In addition, sensory, motor, and reflex functions remain normal through most of the disease (Mendez, Selwood, Mastri, & Frey, 1993; Hodges, 1994; Mendez et al., 1996).

Comparison of Pick's and Other Neurodegenerative Diseases

As cognitive and behavioral performance progressively deteriorate, it becomes increasingly difficult to differentiate Pick's disease from other cortical dementias such as Alzheimer's disease and necessitates neuropathologic confirmation (Arnold, Hyman, & Van Hoesen, 1994). Pick's disease causes extensive atrophy and gliosis throughout the frontal lobe and anterior temporal lobe, most prominent in cortical layer three. Pick bodies are most evident in the insula and inferior temporal cortex. Loss of hippocampal dentate gyrus granular neurons with relatively preserved pyramidal neurons is characteristic of Pick's disease, while in Alzheimer's disease there is early loss of hippocampal pyramidal neurons with preservation of the dentate gyrus neurons. Nearly three fourths of Pick's disease patients display early personality changes and behaviors such as roaming, hyperorality, and disinhibition, while less than one third of Alzheimer's disease patients have such symptoms. These behaviors correlate with the greater frontal and temporal lobe damage in Pick's disease.

In addition to the clinical overlap of Pick's disease with Alzheimer's disease, the neuropathologic features of Pick's disease overlap with those of frontal lobe dementia, primary progressive aphasia, corticobasal degeneration, and multisystem atrophy. Therefore, attempts have been made to differentiate Pick's disease from progressive supranuclear palsy and corticobasal degeneration (Feany, Mattiace, & Dickson, 1996). All three disorders have abnormalities of cortical and subcortical regions; however, Pick's disease has more cortical involvement, progressive supranuclear palsy has more subcortical damage, and corticobasal degeneration has equal cortical and subcortical pathology. The three disorders all have significant pathology in the substantia nigra, subthalamic nucleus, and locus ceruleus. However, Pick's disease has greater numbers of ballooned neurons than the other diseases; corticobasal degeneration can be distinguished by numerous neuropil threads in gray and white matter and neurofibrillary tangles in the globus pallidus; and progressive supranuclear palsy has numerous tangles in the globus pallidus with few neuropil threads or ballooned neurons. Thus, although there are significant overlaps, neuropathologic changes are relatively distinct for each disorder, suggesting separate pathophysiologic entities. Because of the neuropathologic similarities, these latter disorders have been grouped together under the heading "Pick's complex."

More recently, however, Pick's disease has become subsumed under the rubric of frontotemporal dementia in order to reflect the distribution of the pathologic changes rather than the exact histological subtypes of dementias. Three clinical subtypes of frontotemporal dementia are now recognized by the scientific and medical community: frontotemporal dementia, of which a portion of cases are pathologically confirmed as Pick's disease; semantic dementia; and progressive nonfluent or primary progressive aphasia (Neary et al., 1998).

REFERENCES

Arnold, S. E., Hyman, B. T., & Van Hoesen, G. W. V. (1994). Neuropathologic changes of the temporal pole in Alzheimer's disease and Pick's disease. *Archives of Neurology, 51,* 145–150.

Braak, E., Arai, K., & Braak H. (1999). Cerebellar involvement in Pick's disease: Affliction of mossy fibers, monodendritic brush cells, and dentate projection neurons. *Experimental Neurology, 159,* 153–163.

Dickson, D. W. (1998). Pick's disease: A modern approach. *Brain Pathology, 8,* 339–354.

Feany, M. B., Mattiace, L. A., & Dickson, D. W. (1996). Neuropathologic overlap of progressive supranuclear palsy, Pick's disease and corticobasal degeneration. *Journal of Neuropathology and Experimental Neurology, 55,* 53–67.

Giannakopoulos, P., Hof, P. R., Savioz, A., Guimon, J., Antonarakis, S. E., & Bouras, C. (1996). Early-onset dementia: Clinical, neuropathological and genetic characteristics. *Acta Neuropathologica, 91,* 451–465.

Hansen, L. (1994). Pathology of the other dementia. In R. D. Terry, R. Katzman, & L. Bick (Eds.), *Alzheimer disease* (pp. 167–177). New York: Raven.

Hodges, J. R. (1994). Pick's disease. In A. Burns & R. Levy (Eds.), *Dementia* (pp.739–752). London: Chapman & Hall.

Hodges, J. R. (2000). Pick's disease: its relationship to progressive aphasia, semantic dementia, and frontotemporal dementia. In J. O'Brien, D. Ames, & A. Burns (Eds.), *Dementia* (pp. 747–758). London: Edward Arnold.

Hof, P. R., Bouras, C., Perl, D. P., & Morrison, J. H. (1994). Quantitative neuropathologic analysis of Pick's disease cases: Cortical distribution of Pick bodies and coexistence with Alzheimer's disease. *Acta Neuropathologica, 87,* 115–124.

Mendez, M. F., Selwood, A., Mastri, A. R., & Frey, W. H. (1993). Pick's disease versus Alzheimer's disease: A comparison of clinical characteristics. *Neurology, 43,* 289–292.

Mendez, M. F., Cherrier, M., Perryman, K. M., Pachana, N., Miller, B. L., & Cummings, J. L. (1996). Frontotemporal dementia versus Alzheimer's disease: Differential cognitive features. *Neurology, 47,* 1189–1194.

Neary D., Snowden, J. S., Gustafson, L., Passant, U., Stuff, D., et al. (1998). Frontotemporal lobar degeneration: A consensus on clinical diagnostic criteria. *Neurology, 51,* 1546–1554.

Tissot, R., Constantinidis, J., & Richard, J. (1985). Pick's disease. *Handbook of Clinical Neurology, 2,* 233–246.

Julie A. Testa
University of Oklahoma Health Sciences Center

PITUITARY

The name *pituitary* was applied to the small gland beneath the brain's hypothalamus in the early seventeenth century because of the mistaken notion that the structure made phlegm; hence the name *pituitary,* which literally means "snot gland." Hypophysis is a less colorful name for the pituitary.

For descriptive, embryological, and functional reasons, the pituitary is divided into two lobes: the anterior lobe or adenohypophysis and the posterior lobe or neurohypophysis. The structure is connected to the hypothalamus by the infundibulum or hypophyseal stalk. A schematic drawing of the pituitary is shown in Figure 1.

Anterior Lobe or Adenohypophysis

Because of its role in the control of other endocrine glands, the pituitary is often called the "master gland of the body." This designation is more appropriately applied to the pituitary's anterior lobe than it is to the posterior lobe, as the adenohypophysis manufactures and secretes hormones that regulate the body's most important glands (e.g., the adrenal glands, the thyroid gland, the gonads). In fact, the prefix "adeno-" means *gland.*

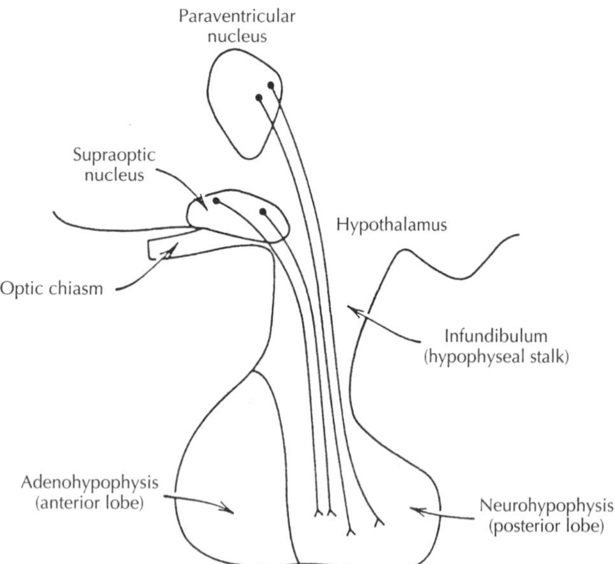

Figure 1. Schematic drawing showing the relationship of the posterior lobe (neurohypophysis) to the hypothalamus. The anterior lobe (adenohypophysis) is functionally connected to the hypothalamus by blood vessels (not shown).

The anterior lobe of the pituitary is derived from skin cells from the roof of the mouth, and the surgical approach to the pituitary is through the roof of the mouth, which will give you a better appreciation of the gland's location in your head. Although it is not in direct neural contact with the brain, the activities of the adenohypophysis are regulated by the hypothalamus, which secretes neurochemicals termed "releasing factors" that travel to the anterior lobe through a system of blood vessels called the hypothalamo-hypophysical portal system.

The releasing factors are peptides and they modulate the secretion of anterior lobe hormones such as somatotropin, thyrotropin, adrenocorticotropin, lactogenic hormone, and the gonadotropins. Each will be discussed briefly.

Somatotropin (STH) is a growth-promoting hormone and, in fact, is usually called *growth hormone*. Its presence at appropriate developmental periods is essential for normal growth. Too much can produce a distorted growth problem called acromegaly; too little results in dwarfism.

Thyrotropin (TSH or thyroid-stimulating hormone) acts on the thyroid gland to promote the synthesis, storage, and release of the thyroid hormones thyroxine (T_4) and triiodothyronine (T_3). Thyroid hormones are involved in the regulation of the body's metabolism.

Adrenocorticotropin (ACTH or adrenocorticotropic hormone) stimulates the production and release of hormones by the adrenal cortex (the adrenal glands are above the kidneys). ACTH triggers the release of glucocorticoids (e.g., cortisol), which are important in carbohydrate metabolism and in the body's resistance to stress. ACTH itself is released in response to physical or emotional stress.

Lactogenic hormone (LTH or prolactin) acts on the mammary glands to promote milk secretion. Prolactin may also be important for the display of parental behaviors in vertebrates.

The *gonadotropins* (luteinizing hormone and follicle stimulating hormone) act on the gonads. Luteinizing hormone (LH) is necessary for ovulation in females. In males, LH acts on cells in the testes to cause them to produce testosterone.

Posterior Lobe or Neurohypophysis

Unlike the anterior lobe, which receives no direct neural innervation, the posterior lobe of the pituitary or neurohypophysis contains the axonic nerve terminals of two hypothalamic nuclei: the supraoptic and the paraventricular. The supraoptic nuclei predominantly synthesize vasopressin, known as antidiuretic hormone (ADH). ADH acts primarily on the kidneys to regulate water balance. Lack of ADH secondary to disease, trauma, or genetic vulnerability causes diabetes insipidus, a serious disorder characterized by excessive drinking and urination.

The paraventricular nuclei predominantly manufacture oxytocin, which is a smooth muscle-contracting hormone. Oxytocin plays an important role in inducing the contractions of the uterine walls during the birth process; that is, oxytocin is responsible for labor pains. In addition, it is required for the release of milk in response to suckling. In males, oxytocin regulates prostate gland function.

B. Michael Thorne
Mississippi State University

PLACEBO

Placebo is derived from the Latin meaning "to placate or please." Shapiro (1960) defines placebo as "any therapy (or that component of any therapy) that is deliberately used for its nonspecific psychologic or physiologic effect, or that is used for its presumed effect on a patient's [symptom or illness] but which, unknown to patient and therapist, is without specific activity for the condition being treated" (p. 109).

The Ubiquitous Placebo

Patients have always been soothed by medicines that do not work psychopharmacologically. The files of the FDA are full of once-new miracle drugs that have mysteriously become ineffective over time.

The placebo response has been positive in studies of adrenal gland secretion, angina pain, blood cell counts, blood pressure, cold vaccine, common cold, cough reflex, fever, gastric secretion/motility, headache, insomnia, measles vaccine, oral contraceptives, pain, pupil dilation/constriction, rheumatoid arthritis, vasomotor function, vitamins, warts, and other ailments. Placebo medication has inhibited gastric acid secretion; soothed bleeding ulcers; and mimicked the effects of amphetamine, ipacac, and LSD, as well as most psychoactive drugs. It has reduced adrenocorticol activity and serum lipoproteins. It has been used in drug withdrawal studies as a substitute for morphine, Talwin injections, and Naloxone. Placebo side effects mimic medication side effects, and placebo effects have been documented in studies of psychotherapy, acupuncture, hypnosis, and behavioral treatments for insomnia and pain. Such surgical and dental procedures as Ligation of mammary arteries for angina pain, and bruxism have been shown to be as ineffective as placebo.

There is a dearth of placebo controlled studies on the plethora of over-the-counter medications, nutritional supplements, and new treatments: Many turn out to be no different from powerful placebos. The mutual expectations and faith in the treatment's efficacy provide the therapeutic ingredient. Theories about the mechanisms underlying placebo effects include discussions of the role of anxiety, conditioning, endorphins, experimenter bias, and suggestion. The role of belief and expectation in mediating the placebo response seems to have the most empirical support.

The placebo response has been viewed as a nuisance variable in methodological studies. It can have powerful negative therapeutic effects, called *nocebo effects*. Patients may show symptoms when they first learn what side effects may be expected, and iatrogenic effects may follow completion of informed consent for medical procedures.

The Placebo Effect in Double-Blind Trials

Placebo response is a control procedure in pharmacological studies. Medication may be given in a double-blind condition so that neither the patient nor the researcher/clinician knows whether a medication or a placebo has been administered. The placebo effect is considered a nuisance variable. Because of the reactive nature of all research, the effects of the interpersonal doctor-patient relationship, and the drug-giving ritual, the expectation is communicated that relief of symptoms is imminent. Under double-blind conditions, the maximized placebo response is subtracted from the active medication effect, leaving the net medication effect.

There are methodological difficulties with the classic double-blind procedure. The researcher rarely collects data from both patient and observer concerning which agent they believe was administered. The investigator's guess about whether a patient has received the drug or the placebo is more correlated with the results than whether the patient received the drug or the placebo. In treatment studies in which the placebo effect is atypically low compared to an active treatment, it is likely that the blind code was inadvertently broken by the many cues influencing a patient's response.

Clinical Significance of Placebo

Beecher (1959) reviewed 15 double-blind studies of morphine treatment of postoperative pain. He reported that 35% of these patients experienced pain reduction comparable to patients given a standard injection of morphine. Beecher's 35% clinical efficacy fails to recognize that even a standard dose of morphine was effective in only about 70% of patients. Evans (1974) used an index of placebo efficiency, comparing the effectiveness of placebo with the effectiveness of morphine, and found placebo was 56% as effective as morphine. Similarly, averaging available double-blind studies since Beecher's review, placebo is about 55% as effective as Aspirin, Darvon compound, Codeine, and Zomax. These consistencies imply that the placebo response is proportional to the assumed efficacy of the treatment itself. Similar ratios are found comparing double-blind studies of antidepressant and sleep medications to placebo.

The placebo effect has powerful positive therapeutic implications. The placebo response is apparently mediated in all treatment contexts by expectancy, anxiety reduction, and cues that emanate from the subtleties of the doctor-patient relationship. Studies have shown that the placebo response is not related to suggestibility, gullibility, conformity, hypnosis, or related traits.

Clinical Applications of Placebo

Under what circumstances should placebos be actively prescribed? Physicians admit they have occasionally used placebos knowingly, but less than their colleagues in other specialties. This unfortunate negative view of the placebo denies the significance of the doctor-patient relationship. Some critics argue that placebos are inherently unethical because deception is involved. From the point of view of the patient, the contract with the physician is to get better; therefore, one might question whether it is unethical to deny treatment that may be effective, inexpensive, and relatively safe.

The placebo has several clinical applications:

1. It involves mechanisms that will lead to improved treatment.
2. Placebo may be a powerful diagnostic tool. For example, anesthesiologists may use placebo nerve blocks for diagnostic purposes. Unfortunately, wrong conclusions may be drawn: Some physicians have incorrectly equated response to a placebo diagnostic test with the belief that the symptom (e.g., pain) is "psychological."
3. A positive placebo response indicates that the patient has the resources to manipulate and control symptoms at some level. A positive placebo response will often predict a positive therapeutic outcome.
4. The nonspecific placebo effects and the specific treatment effects are interactive and cumulative. Place-

bos can sometimes be used as an alternative to medications as a substitute for potentially dangerous drugs, and as an aid in withdrawal from active or addictive medication.

Summary

The placebo effect is a significant part of the total treatment context. The nature of the doctor-patient relationship and the expectations of treatment and cure that are communicated in this context provide the basis for powerful nonspecific therapeutic interventions.

REFERENCES

Beecher, H. K. (1959). *Measurement of Subjective Responses.* New York: Oxford University Press.

Evans, F. J. (1974). The power of the sugar pill. *Psychology Today,* April, 59–74.

Shapiro, A. K. (1960). A contribution to a history of the placebo effect. *Behavioral Science, 5,* 398–450.

FREDERICK J. EVANS

PLANNED SHORT-TERM PSYCHOTHERAPY

Although occasional references to short-term psychotherapy appeared prior to the inauguration of the community mental health movement in the early 1960s, serious examination of brief psychotherapies began at the same time that mental health professionals recognized the importance of serving the mental health needs of the entire community. Time-limited psychotherapy was thought to be a strategy that had the potential for helping greater numbers of clients in the community.

The literature on planned short-term psychotherapy has increased exponentially since then until there are now nearly 200 books and 4,500 published papers on the topic. No school of psychotherapy has been unaffected by this literature. There are now numerous descriptions and outcome studies of planned short-term individual and group approaches to psychodynamically oriented, cognitively and behaviorally oriented, solution-focused, and strategic psychotherapies with both children and adults in both inpatient and outpatient settings.

This growing literature has had a profound impact on the funding and practice of psychotherapy primarily because of its consistent evidence that planned short-term psychotherapies, often as short as a single interview, generally appear to be as effective as time-unlimited psychotherapies, virtually regardless of client characteristics, treatment duration, or therapist orientation. Furthermore, almost identical findings have been reported for short-term inpatient psychiatric care.

Health economists concerned about the alarming increase in the cost of medical care could hardly have been expected to ignore the evidence that, in the case of psychotherapy at least, longer is rarely better. Indeed, were it not for the consistent evidence of the effectiveness of planned short-term psychotherapy, the writings in this field might have ended up simply as a footnote in the ongoing history of psychotherapy. What seems to be happening in the practice of psychotherapy parallels what is happening in general health services. Treatment has become shorter rather than longer, is taking place increasingly in outpatient rather than inpatient settings, and is less, rather than more, invasive.

Planned short-term psychotherapy is not simply less of time-unlimited psychotherapy. Rather, the practice of planned short-term psychotherapy rests on four fundamental principles uniquely associated with it that distinguish it from traditional time-unlimited approaches. Furthermore, evidence suggests that training in these principles and their application improves the clinical effectiveness of therapists.

First, research studies have consistently found that improvement during an episode of psychotherapy is negatively accelerated—very rapid at first, then slowing significantly. Accordingly, therapists who are interested in making the best use of time take advantage of the initial period of rapid improvement by keeping episodes of therapy as short as possible while at the same time encouraging clients to return for additional brief therapeutic episodes when they are needed. Whereas traditionally trained psychotherapists tend to think that when a client returns to treatment it is a sign that the initial treatment episode was a failure (an assertion for which there is little if any empirical evidence), planned short-term psychotherapy is designed to be intermittent—multiple individual brief treatment episodes within an ongoing therapeutic relationship.

Second, brief psychotherapy is especially empowering to the therapist. The evolution from time-unlimited to planned short-term psychotherapy results in a fundamental change in the role of the therapist—from a passive one in which the gradual deconstruction of conflict is observed to a more active one in which the therapist takes a directive stance in helping plan every aspect of the clinical episode. Planned short-term psychotherapy requires an active collaboration between client and therapist in establishing therapeutic goals, conducting the therapeutic episode, and bringing it to an agreed-upon conclusion.

Third, in contrast to traditional time-unlimited psychotherapies that place unique therapeutic importance on the face-to-face clinical contact, planned short-term psychotherapies assume that the time between clinical contacts and after the conclusion of a clinical episode has significant therapeutic potential. Accordingly, the therapeutic episode is designed to use the time between sessions planfully and to start a therapeutic process that can continue after the face-to-face contacts have been brought to an end.

Small changes during the treatment episode may be all that is required to start a process that will lead to significant and long-lasting clinical improvement. An episode of psychotherapy is thought of as a starting place rather than a completion of the change process. In addition, numerous empirical studies have also identified the so-called *sleeper effect,* evidence that the effects of psychotherapy continue, and often increase, long after the therapeutic episode has been concluded. One way that planned short-term psychotherapists build on this sleeper effect is to include a planned follow-up contact into the therapeutic episode. Such posttreatment contacts not only create a unique opportunity to evaluate the consequences of their work, but also appear to extend the life and the effectiveness of therapeutic interventions.

Fourth, time-conscious therapists think of each client contact as a self-contained unit, an opportunity to accomplish a significant, focused piece of clinical work so that additional contacts may not be necessary. A therapeutic episode is thus thought of as a series of single sessions. In contrast to traditional psychotherapists, who tend to underestimate how helpful they can be to people in brief periods of time, therapists who practice planned short-term psychotherapy believe that virtually all clients can be helped and can be helped relatively quickly, regardless of diagnosis or problem severity. The psychological climax of every interview is intended to be a skillful intervention—a well-timed interpretation, a carefully considered activity plan designed to modify undesired behavior, or a proposal whose goal is to change interpersonal interaction.

There are numerous cases, of course, in which psychotherapy needs to be extended in order to achieve satisfactory results. These instances can rarely be predicted in advance, however, and mental health professionals are learning to make time available to treat clients who need longer-term psychotherapy by making sure that all their clients receive only the psychotherapy they need, but no more.

For nearly 40 years the empirical literature has underlined the remarkable efficacy of planned short-term psychotherapy. The theoretical literature is equally impressive in helping put these new clinical practices in a conceptually rich and historically revered context. Mental health professionals, while properly insisting on avoiding undertreatment, are beginning to accept the affirmation of their effectiveness in brief periods of time and are increasingly alert to avoiding overtreatment as well.

SUGGESTED READING

Bloom, B. L. (1997). *Planned short-term psychotherapy: A clinical handbook* (2nd ed.). Boston: Allyn & Bacon.

Bernard L. Bloom
University of Colorado

See also: **Psychotherapy**

PLAY

Play is variously regarded as a "cobweb," an "omnibus term," or even a category not useful for psychology. This is probably so because play manifests itself in so many forms that it is difficult to find a commonality of structure or function in all these activities.

There are two main approaches to an understanding of play, and these are distinguishable in its motivation and goal. In the more commonly held view, play is an exotelic activity and a rehearsal for the acquisition of greater competence. Play is an activity performed generally by children and young people, and exists so that they can rehearse actions that will increase competence and promote maturity. Thus, play is an outcome variable with the reward to be found extrinsic to the activity. Advocates of this view argue that competence is enhanced by appropriate and adequate play opportunities. Some even argue that the very existence of youth is largely for the sake of play.

In the autotelic view, regardless of its form or structure, play is seen to be motivated by an interaction of the conditions of the player with those of the environment (both external and internal). The environment must contain elements conductive to an interchange with elements in the motivational state of the individual. This produces activity characterized by pleasure, interest, and reduction of tension. The elements that produce playful behavior are similar to those that evoke curiosity and produce exploratory behavior.

Piaget, following an exotelic approach, based his taxonomy of play on his theory of cognitive development, arguing that at each stage of development certain types of play become predominant. Thus, in the sensorimotor stage (the first 2 years of life), practice play is common. This consists of repetition of patterns of movement or sound, beginning with sucking and babbling, finally developing into reacting with the environment in ways in which activities are varied systematically and their effects are monitored.

After the second year, the child moves into the preconceptual stage with the ability to master symbolic functions. Games reflect this change by becoming symbolic—games of make-believe. These games are exemplified by the child's use of objects as things different from their apparent intention. Children also begin to place themselves in symbolic relationships with the external world.

During the intuitive stage (ages 4–7), children become interested in games with rules, structured situations, and social interactions with others. Gradually types of rules move from sensorimotor to collective, in that rules initially accepted because they lent structure and reputation later become accepted because of social constraints and group demands. Codification of rules appears about age 11 or 12, when competitive games become the norm.

Berlyne advocated an autotelic approach. His attempts to reduce all definitions of play to a few key concepts produced four recurrent motifs:

1. Playful activities are carried on "for their own sake" or for the sake of "pleasure." They contrast with serious activities, which deal with bodily needs or external threats, or otherwise achieve specifiable, practical ends. He coined the phrase "telic behavior" to describe this distinction in purpose.
2. Many writers stress the "unreality" or "quasi-reality" of play. "Reality" presumably refers to the forms of interaction between the organism and its environment that occupy most of its waking hours.
3. Several authorities have noted the mixture of "tension" and unpleasant excitement in play, and attach importance to it.
4. The final element is the reduction of arousal, relaxation of tension, and relief from conflict that occur in the course of play.

Day developed a taxonomy that includes five types of play and argued that overt characteristics do not always distinguish these types. Instead, they differ mainly in their source and telicity (goal). The five types are as follows:

1. *Exploratory Play.* Exploratory play is motivated by uncertainty concerning objects and events in the environment. It occurs generally as a reaction to novelty or complexity in the environment. The goal of exploratory play is the acquisition of information. The affect during play is pleasure (autotelic play).
2. *Creative Play.* Creative play is a more complex manifestation of exploratory play and requires the ability to symbolize as well as familiarity with the superficial or physical characteristics of the stimulus (toy). There is greater tension during creative play and the goal shifts to the maximization of hedonic pleasure (autotelic play).
3. *Diversive Play.* Diversive play is seen as aimless interaction with the environment in general when boredom has set in. It may take many forms, such as aimless locomotion or alternation among different activities or locations. A common expression of diversive play is the continuous switching of channels on a television set with a remote control (autotelic play).
4. *Mimetic Play.* Mimetic play tends to be repetitious, structured, and symbolic. It is the only form of play that can be considered exotelic because its purpose is the enhancement of competence and mastery. Often the activity is not necessarily considered play, as exemplified by practicing a musical instrument or a sport (exotelic play).
5. *Cathartic Play.* Therapeutic in goal, cathartic play may take any form or shape. Although intrinsic in the sense of reducing arousal, it does not seem to be associated with positive hedonic affect or pleasure (mixed autotelic and exotelic play).

Child therapists often use cathartic play as a treatment modality. They argue that children are generally unable to express their discontent and anxiety verbally, but when allowed to express these in an unstructured milieu rich in fantasy-producing material such as toys, will work through their feelings toward appropriate growth and maturation. Thus, they allow children the opportunity to play and enhance competence while relieving stress. In this case, play is both autotelic and exotelic.

Playfulness

Probably a better approach to the study of play is to avoid the term altogether and to posit that playfulness, together with workfulness, is a condition existing in all acts, whether jobs, games, or schooling. Playfulness is that portion of the activity that is intrinsically rewarding (autotelic) and workfulness is the exotelic portion. Over time and repetition predictability sets in, playfulness ebbs, and activities lose their autotelicity and become workful. Day has taken this approach and devised a questionnaire that measures the proportion of playfulness in different activities, including occupations and games, and measures change in proportions of each over time. High levels of playfulness enhance motivation to participate in these activities, but when autolicity wanes, activities become boring and, unless the extrinsic reward is increased, are often abandoned.

H. I. Day
York University, Toronto, Canada

See also: **Human Development; Play Therapy**

PLAY THERAPY

The term *play therapy* is employed in at least two different ways to describe child psychotherapy. First, the term sometimes refers to particular psychotherapy approaches that centrally emphasize children's play as a means of therapeutic communication and as a modality through which children's problems can be solved (e.g., Bromfield, 1992; Ciottone & Madonna, 1996; Kaduson & Schaefer, 1997; McMahon, 1992; Schaefer, 1993; Singer, 1993). Second, the term *play therapy* is employed more generally to describe individual child psychotherapy. That usage occurs because virtually all therapies rely on children's play at least as a mode of communication (Johnson, Rasbury, & Siegel, 1997), although they differ in whether play is considered central or relatively incidental to the process of change. Such differences of opinion depend upon therapists' theoretical orientations and upon the children's ages and their problems.

Various forms of play are useful in child psychotherapy. Even simple *practice play,* (e.g., bouncing a ball) can help a child relax and become comfortable with the therapist. In addition, *games with rules* (e.g., checkers) can teach children about fair play (e.g., Gardner, 1993). *Symbolic* or *pretend play,* however, is especially important for psychotherapy, because such play expresses children's experiences beyond their limited capacity to verbally explain themselves.

Symbolic play entails engaging in one activity with one object for the purpose of representing a different activity and a different object. Thus, a child might jump about while holding a broomstick, playing "horsie," in order to represent a cowboy riding a horse. Symbolic play can involve toys (e.g., dolls or action figures) or sociodramatic scenes in which children join together to enact stories. Symbolic play represents and communicates children's personal viewpoints about real events as well as their wishes, fears, and other personal reactions to those events (e.g., Bretherton, 1989; Ciottone & Madonna, 1996; Johnson et al., 1997; Schaefer, 1993). For example, children would not play "horsie" unless they were familiar with the possibility of riding horses and had some feelings about this activity. In fact, researchers find that children are especially likely to symbolically enact events and wishes that have aroused their anxiety as well as their desire (Watson, 1994). Symbolic play is "often so revealing of the child's otherwise hidden wishes and percepts (that it) can open the inner world of the child to the therapist" (Coppollilo, 1987, p. 228).

Beyond providing therapists with information about children's internal lives, therapeutic orientations that place a very central value on play propose that engaging in symbolic play is inherently "curative." Symbolic play sometimes provides children with an avenue to actually resolve the anxiety and dilemmas that are expressed symbolically (Bretherton, 1989; Ciottone & Madonna, 1996; Schaefer, 1993; Watson, 1994). For example, play might provide relief by allowing a symbolic expression of experiences that would be too threatening to express directly (Johnson et al., 1997; Watson, 1994). Moreover, while playing, children are "in charge," and they experience the relief of being active and in control, in contrast to the powerlessness they ordinarily experience in threatening situations (Copollilo, 1987; Erikson, 1977; Sarnoff, 1976; Schaefer, 1993). Some authors propose that children construct new ways of coping with their dilemmas when they miniaturize or "model" dilemmas symbolically (e.g., Erikson, 1964, 1977; Watson, 1994).

Client-centered and existential therapists permit considerable uninterrupted play in therapy (Axline, 1947; Ellinwood & Raskin, 1993; Moustakas, 1953). These therapists presume that play is therapeutic insofar as it occurs in the context of an accepting, clarifying, and confidential therapeutic relationship. Such relationships allows children to fully symbolize their subjective experiences and impressions. Although not necessarily accepting this unique emphasis on the curative alliance between children and therapists, all approaches to child therapy do presume that the quality of the relationship is important (Shirk & Saiz, 1992).

In contrast to emphasizing the benefits of unimpeded play, other therapists actively intervene while the child is playing. For example, psychodynamic therapists intervene by providing children with interpretations about the meaning of the wishes, fears, and ways of coping that are represented symbolically (Copollilo, 1987; Singer, 1993). Such interpretations are intended to help children to understand and express their experiences consciously, not only symbolically. Increasingly conscious understanding can provide for increasingly adaptive ways of coping. Moreover, some therapists emphasize the need to explicitly interpret connections between real, traumatizing events and the repetitive play through which some children symbolize such traumas (Silvern, Karyl, & Landis, 1995).

Other therapeutic approaches grant play a somewhat incidental role, rather than a central one. For example, play can be an adjunct to cognitive-behavioral therapy that has a primary goal of teaching new cognitions about the social world and new ways of coping with emotions and social interactions. Kendall and Braswell (1993) suggested that playing out problematic social interactions can reveal children's perspectives and their problematic cognitions that should be corrected. Knell (1993) proposed a cognitive-behavioral approach to play therapy in which therapists structure the child's play, which is integrated into educational techniques such as modeling, role-playing, and reinforcement of adaptive thoughts and behavior.

Whatever the particular approach, play therapy is ordinarily conducted in a therapeutic playroom. To facilitate the therapy process, the playroom is ideally equipped with materials that are suitable for children of different ages and backgrounds. Materials should also be sufficiently varied to encourage enacting diverse themes and personal issues (Johnson et al., 1997). Unstructured materials, including sand, water, and clay, are intended to foster maximum freedom of self-expression. Structured materials such as cars or puppets are often introduced to elicit play about particular themes that deal with feelings, attitudes, and conflicts in family or peer relationships (Johnson et al., 1997). For example, some therapists introduce two doll houses for children who are adjusting to having two homes after adoption or divorce (e.g., Kuhli, 1993). Similarly, toy medical equipment might be introduced to children who are facing a medical procedure (Oremland, 1993).

Instead of focusing on toys, many therapists have adopted Gardner's (1971, 1993b) "mutual storytelling" technique. The therapist begins to tell a story that raises a therapeutic issue; the client finishes the story while the therapist suggests adaptive outcomes.

Although play therapy has traditionally been employed with general emotional and behavioral disorders, in recent years several specialized approaches have been developed for particular life problems. For example, specialized approaches have been developed for children who have been sexually abused (Ciottone & Madonna, 1996; McMahon, 1992), children who have been otherwise traumatized (Silvern et al., 1995; Webb, 1991), children who are undergoing frightening medical procedures (Oremland, 1993), and children with developmental or physical handicaps (Hellendoorn, van der Kooij, & Sutton-Smith, 1994).

Recently, play has been extended beyond its traditional role in individual psychotherapy to other treatment modalities. For example, play techniques have been integrated into family therapy (Gil, 1994). Additionally, school-based programs train socially disadvantaged children to engage in symbolic play with the intention of preventing developmental, psychological, and school problems (Hellendoorn et al., 1994). Play has also been integrated into many parent training approaches (Foote, Eyberg, & Schuhmann, 1998; Strayhorn, 1994). Although the goals of parent training are typically to improve childrearing and discipline, empirical findings have revealed that it is more effective to initially establish playful interactions between children and parents than to immediately focus on discipline skills (Foote et al., 1998).

Since there are many approaches to child psychotherapy, it is important for parents to inquire about therapists' orientations and practices. By itself, the term *play therapy* reveals little about the specific characteristics of a particular therapist's treatment.

REFERENCES

Axline, V. M. (1947). *Play therapy.* Boston: Houghton Mifflin.

Bretherton, I. (1989). Pretense: The form and function of make-believe play. *Developmental Review, 9,* 393–401.

Bromfield, R. (1992). *Playing for real.* New York: Dutton.

Buchsbaum, H., Toth, S. L., Clyman, R. B., Cicchetti, D., & Emde, R. N. (1992). The use of a narrative story stem technique with maltreated children: Implications for theory and practice. *Development and Psychopathology, 4,* 603–625.

Ciottone, R. A., & Madonna, J. M. (1996). *Play therapy with sexually abused children.* Northvale, NJ: Jason Aronson.

Coppolillo, H. P. (1987). *Psychodynamic psychotherapy of children.* Madison, WI: International Universities Press.

Ellinwood, C. G., & Raskin, J. J. (1993). Client-centered/humanistic psychotherapy. In T. R. Kratochwill & R. R. Morris (Eds.), *Handbook of psychotherapy with children and adolescents* (pp. 264–375). Boston: Allyn & Bacon.

Erikson, E. (1964). Toys and reasons. In M. Haworth (Ed.), *Child psychotherapy* (pp. 3–11). New York: Basic Books.

Erikson, E. (1977). *Toys and reasons.* New York: W. W. Norton.

Foote, R., Eyberg, S., & Schuhmann, E. (1998). Parent-child interaction approaches to the treatment of child behavior problems. In T. H. Ollendick & R. J. Prinz (Eds.), *Advances in clinical child psychology* (Vol. 20, pp. 125–143). New York: Plenum Press.

Gardner, R. A. (1971). *Therapeutic communication with children: The mutual storytelling technique.* New York: Science House.

Gardner, R. A. (1993a). Checkers. In C. E. Schaefer & D. M. Cangelosi (Eds.), *Play therapy techniques* (pp. 247–262). Northvale, NJ: Jason Aronson.

Gardner, R. A. (1993b). Mutual storytelling. In C. E. Schaefer & D. M. Cangelosi (Eds.), *Play therapy techniques* (pp. 199–209). Northvale, NJ: Jason Aronson.

Gil, E. (1994). *Play in family therapy.* New York: Guilford Press.

Hellendoorn, J., van der Kooij, R., & Sutton-Smith, B. (Eds.). (1994). *Play and intervention.* Albany: State University of New York Press.

Johnson, J. H., Rasbury, W. C., & Siegel, L. J. (1997). *Approaches to child treatment: Introduction to theory, research, and practice.* Boston: Allyn & Bacon.

Kaduson, H. G., & Schaefer, C. E. (1997). *101 favorite play therapy techniques.* Northvale, NJ: Jason Aronson.

Kendall, P., & Braswell, L. (1993). *Cognitive-behavioral therapy for impulsive children* (2nd ed.). New York: Guilford Press.

Knell, S. M. (1993). *Cognitive-behavioral play therapy.* Northvale, NJ: Jason Aronson.

Kuhli, L. (1993). The use of two houses in play therapy. In C. E. Schaefer & D. M. Cangelosi (Eds.), *Play therapy techniques.* (pp. 63–68). Northvale, NJ: Jason Aronson.

McMahon, L. (1992). *The handbook of play therapy.* London: Tavistock/Routledge.

Moustakas, C. (1953). *Children in play therapy.* New York: Ballantine Books.

Oremland, E. K. (1993). Abreaction. In E. C. Schaefer (Ed.), *Therapeutic powers of play* (pp. 143–165). Northvale, NJ: Jason Aronson.

Sarnoff, C. (1976). *Latency.* New York: Aronson.

Schaefer, C. E. (1993). What is play and why is it therapeutic? In E. C. Schaefer (Ed.), *Therapeutic powers of play* (pp. 1–15). Northvale, NJ: Jason Aronson.

Schaefer, C. E., & Cangelosi, D. M. (Eds.). (1993). *Play therapy techniques.* Northvale, NJ: Jason Aronson.

Shirk, S., & Saiz, C. C. (1992). Clinical, empirical and developmental perspectives on the therapeutic relationship in child psychotherapy. *Development and Psychopathology, 4,* 713–728.

Silvern, L., Karyl, J., & Landis, T., (1995). Individual psychotherapy for traumatized children of abused women. In E. Peled, P. G. Jaffe, & J. L. Edelson (Eds.), *Ending the cycle of violence: Community responses to children of battered women* (pp. 43–76). Thousand Oaks, CA: Sage.

Singer, D. G. (1993). *Playing for their lives.* Toronto: Free Press.

Strayhorn, J. M. (1994). Psychological competence-based therapy for young children and their parents. In C. W. LeCroy (Ed.), *Handbook of child and adolescent treatment.*

Wachtel, E. F. (1994). *Treating troubled children and their families.* New York: Guilford Press.

Watson, M. W. (1994). *Children at play: Clinical and developmental approaches to representation and meaning: The relation between anxiety and pretend play.* New York: Oxford University Press.

Webb, N. B. (1991). *Play therapy with children in crisis.* New York: Guilford Press.

Louise Silvern
Brook McClintic
University of Colorado, Boulder

See also: **Family Therapy**

POLICE PSYCHOLOGY

The origins of American police psychology have been traced back to at least 1916, when Terman attempted to use the then-current Stanford-Binet test, First Edition, to identify "good" prospective police officers in California. His research indicated officers are likely to require a minimum IQ of 80 to adequately perform job duties. Few published contributions to police psychology ensued until the mid-twentieth century, when psychologists began to offer services to various local, state, and federal law enforcement organizations.

Precipitated by the advancements of police psychologists in the 1960s and 1970s, especially those of Reiser (1972) and his associates, a rapidly growing interest developed in providing psychological services to law enforcement agencies. Given the considerable growth during the past dozen years police psychology is likely to be one of the principal directions of future forensic and clinical psychological practice.

What Is It?

Psychological services for law enforcement frequently involve new applications of traditional clinical and industrial-organizational psychological services. Police psychology is a specialty subsection of forensic psychology. Police psychology is the interface between the behavioral sciences and law enforcement.

Police psychological services are generally grouped into two categories: employee services and organizational services. Employee-oriented services generally recognize the employee as the client. Employee assistance services include counseling and assessment requested by the employee. Organizational services recognize the agency as the client and include preemployment psychological evaluations, fitness-for-duty evaluations, and management consultations. Hybrid services (such as crisis counseling) have developed which are both employee-oriented and organizational in nature. Crisis counseling may be requested and organized by the agency, but agency administrators have limited access to the process (Super, 1999). Police psychologists may provide services as agency employees or as contractual consultants, depending on the specific needs and resources of the agency.

Assessment

Approximately one third of police psychologists assist in the selection of recruits for police training and in the selection of trainee graduates for positions in law enforcement. Psychologists conduct fitness-for-duty evaluations of police officers who have been in stressful or physically debilitating interactions while on the job. Psychologists have also participated in the assessment procedures for advanced placements and promotions within the law enforcement community (Blau, 1994).

Psychological assessment techniques, including interviews, objective personality tests, intelligence tests, and in vitro video-based assessment have been used to assist in the selection of law enforcement officers, corrections officers, and special police team members (SWAT, hostage negotiation, undercover agents, child protection specialists, and so forth). The three approaches commonly used in preemployment psychological evaluation include: (1) selection of the best suited applicants; (2) screening out of undesirable applicants; or (3) a combination of the two (Blau, 1994; Super, 1999).

Intervention

Psychologists provide therapeutic services for police officers who are under stress, such as grief counseling for police officers and families. The need for counseling may stem from officers who are injured or killed in the line of duty. Police psychologists provide family counseling, counseling services for the children of police officers, and drug and alcohol counseling. Police psychologists assist in establishing peer counseling teams within the law enforcement agency (Kurke & Scrivner, 1996). Some psychologists offer psychoeducational evaluations for officers' children to address issues that may peripherally affect the officer's ability to discharge sworn duties.

Operations. Psychologists may be requested to provide operational services, including investigative hypnosis, investigative strategies when working with mentally disturbed suspects, hostage negotiation, and offender psychological profiling (Blau, 1994; Reese & Solomon, 1996). Although the above services are frequently viewed by laypersons as being at the core of what police psychologists do, these types of services generally represent a small part of professional activity.

Training. Psychologists provide training in police academies on such topics as offenders, stress recognition and prevention, proper methods of addressing irate citizens' complaints, cultural diversity, interviewing techniques, interpersonal skills, effective communication, impulse control, suicide prevention and intervention, and group behavior. Psychologists provide continuing education for police officers who must earn a specified number of credits every several years to maintain their sworn status. Continuing education topics may range from the psychology of driving to stress inoculation.

Strategic Planning

Generally, law enforcement has been reactive rather than proactive to crime. Modern law enforcement administrators are becoming increasingly more proactive by attempting to address prospective community needs, employing new applications of psychological services, and attempting to address changing community needs. This is at the heart of strategic planning. Psychologists, primarily industrial and organizational psychologists, have been providing strategic planning consultations to police management with increasingly more regularity during the mid and late 1990s. Sensitivity and restraint training are areas that have recently been explored.

Research

One of the most important and most overlooked contributions by police psychologists is research involving the development of local norms, base rates, and predictive effectiveness (Super, 1999). Project funding has become more available as law enforcement administrators become more aware of the potential costs and benefits of research (Blau, 1994).

Why Is This Developing Now?

Police departments are currently being pressed to acquire accreditation. Accreditation is one method of demonstrating an agency's efficiency and modernization. As of 1999, the Commission on Accreditation for Law Enforcement Agencies (CALEA) has accredited 457 local agencies throughout the United States. There are approximately 17,000 local police agencies in the United States. Many of these will seek accreditation to participate in lower-cost risk management insurance plans. Accreditation requires departments to provide various psychological services, including preemployment psychological assessment, fitness-for-duty assessment, and assessment for hostage negotiations and SWAT team applicants. In the near future, accreditation guidelines are likely to require the availability of psychologists, on staff or as consultants, to respond to postcritical incident stress situations.

One of the agency administrator's greatest incentives for seeking psychological services is to decrease the probability of costly litigation against the department. Psychologists are helpful in selecting those people who will do the best possible job as law enforcement officers. Ongoing counseling and training by psychologists help those already working to maintain job skills and emotional stability in a stressful work setting.

What's Next?

Division 18 (Public Service) of the American Psychological Association (APA) has a Police Psychology and Public Safety subsection. Starting in about 1989 with 20 or so members, in 1999 there were approximately 252 members, including three fellows and 22 students in this subsection. Standards for preemployment psychological evaluations and fitness-for-duty evaluations have been developed and are under ongoing revision as new techniques emerge and as new applications of psychology to law enforcement arise. Several graduate institutions have begun to offer courses in police psychology.

REFERENCES

Blau, T. (1994). *Police psychology: Behavioral science services for law enforcement.* New York: Wiley.

Kurke, M., & Scrivner, E. (Eds.). (1996). *Police psychology in the 21st century.* Hillsdale, NJ: Erlbaum.

Reese, J. T., & Solomon, R. M. (Eds.). (1996). *Organizational issues in law enforcement.* Washington, DC: U.S. Department of Justice, Federal Bureau of Investigation.

Reiser, M. (1972). *The police department psychologist.* Springfield, IL: Thomas.

Super, J. T. (1999). Forensic psychology and law enforcement. In A. Hess & I. Weiner (Eds.), *The handbook of forensic psychology* (2nd ed., pp. 409–439). New York: Wiley.

SUGGESTED READING

Reese, J. T., & Scrivner, E. (Eds.). (1994). *The law enforcement family: Issues and answers.* Washington, DC: U.S. Department of Justice, Federal Bureau of Investigation.

Theodore H. Blau
J. T. Supers

POSTMODERNISM

Postmodern themes were discussed within architecture, literary criticism, and sociology in the United States in the 1950s and 1960s. French philosophers addressed postmodernity during the 1970s. Jean-Francois Lyotard has analyzed the status of knowledge in a postmodern age, in particular with respect to legitimation; Michael Foucault has addressed the webs of power and knowledge in historical studies; Jean Baudrillard focused on fascination, seduction, and the media's creating of a hyperreality of simulacra; Jacques Derrida has addressed language and deconstruction; and Jacques Lacan has reinterpreted the psychoanalytic unconscious. In the United States, Jameson has analyzed postmodernism as the logic of late capitalism, and Rorty has developed a neopragmatic approach to postmodernity.

Meanings of Postmodernism

The very term *postmodern* is ambiguous. It may be helpful to discern at least three meanings: postmodernity as referring to a postmodern age; postmodernism as referring to the cultural expression of a postmodern age; and postmodern thought, or discourse, as referring to philosophical reflection on a postmodern age and culture.

Postmodernity refers to an age that has lost the Enlightenment belief in progress and emancipation through more knowledge and scientific research. There is a change from a mechanical, metallurgic production to an information industry, and from production to consumption as the main focus of the economy. It is an age in which the multiple perspectives of the new media tend to dissolve any sharp line between reality and fantasy, undermining belief in an objective reality.

Postmodernism as a cultural expression encompasses art as collage and pastiche, the pop art of Andy Warhol's consumer goods, Las Vegas-style architecture, the media's dissolution of the distinction between reality and image, and the hectic change of perspectives in the rock videos. Also focal are the labyrinthine themes of Borge's stories and the caricatures of the interpretation mania of the modern search for meaning in the novels of Umberto Eco.

Postmodern thought replaces a conception of a reality independent of the observer with notions of language as actually constituting the structures of a perspectival social reality. The modern dichotomy of an objective reality distinct from subjective images is breaking down, and being replaced by a hyperreality of self-referential signs. There is a critique of the modernist search for foundational forms and belief in a linear progress through the acquisition of knowledge.

Psychology in a Postmodern Condition

Human beings were in the center of the Age of Enlightenment. The modern science of psychology was founded on a conception of individual subjects, with internal souls and later internal psychic apparatuses. In a postmodern age, man is decentered, as the individual subject is dissolved into linguistic structures and ensembles of relations. The question arises as to the status of psychology as a science of the individual when the individual has been dethroned from the center of the world. There have been few discussions among psychologists on the consequences of a postmodern culture. Three possible implications of a postmodern approach to psychology are outlined here.

1. The very conception of a psychological science may be so rooted in modernist assumptions that it becomes difficult to understand men and women in a postmodern culture. Other disciplines, such as anthropology, have been more sensitive to the situatedness of human activity in a cultural context.
2. At the other extreme, contemporary psychology could be seen as a postmodern conceptual collage—a pastiche of recycled ideas and methods borrowed from other fields and combined according to the most recent consumer demands of a mass culture. With an extreme adaptability and flexibility, psychology does seem able to move—amoeba-like—into whatever niche opens in the markets for therapy and self-realization, as well as for selection and control of personnel.
3. A third position would involve a psychology that faces the rootedness of human existence in specific historical and cultural situations, and opens new vistas for psychology.

Implications of a postmodern discourse for the science and profession of psychology may be divided into five areas:

Knowledge and Research. A recognition of the heterogeneous and noncommensurable contexts of the everyday world involves a loss of hegemony for formalized experimental and statistical research methods. There is an acceptance of diverse quantitative and qualitative ways of producing knowledge, with a move from knowledge as abstract, objective, and universal to knowledge as ecologically valid, socially useful, and locally situated. Narrative, hermeneutical, and deconstructive approaches are included. Conversation and social practice become the contexts in which the validity of knowledge is negotiated and ascertained.

Professional Knowledge. The professional practice of psychologists is regarded as an important generator of psychological knowledge. While generally discarded by academic psychology, the insights produced by these practices are, however, in line with philosophical analyses of knowledge in a postmodern age, given that they focus on local and narrative knowledge, on the heterogeneous and linguistic knowledge of the everyday world, and on validation through practice. This does not imply a practice devoid of theory, but involves a shift in the focus of theorizing in psychology—from the interior of the individual to the relation of human beings to their world.

Systemic Therapy. The professional field where the implications of a postmodern linguistic shift have been most explicitly taken up is systemic therapy. There is a shift from studying the psyche of the individual self to studying the family as a linguistic system. Pathology is no longer seen as residing in consciousness, nor in the unconscious, but in the structures of language. Indeed the very term "psychotherapist" seems to be inadequate, for the therapist does not attempt to heal some interior "psyche," but works with language and, as a master of conversation, heals with words.

Deconstructing Social Psychology. Ian Parker and John Shotter have attempted a deconstructing of social psychology. They follow Derrida, Foucault, and Lacan in looking at the internal contradictions of these texts; analyzing their social formation; uncovering the power relations at work; and bringing forth the voices not expressed, such as the feminist work on the social construction of gender.

Social Constructionism. Ken Gergen has developed a social constructionism that rejects a substantial conception of the self and replaces the individual with the relationship as the locus of knowledge. He emphasizes the social construction of personal identities, focusing in particular on how communication technologies have led to a multiplicity of knowledge and a recognition of the perspectival nature of reality, and on the self as embedded in a multitude of networks.

Concluding Remarks

A postmodern psychology would involve a move from studying the cognitive mechanisms of an internal psychic apparatus or the inner experiences of a self-realizing self, to examining human activity in a linguistically constituted social world. The focus of interest is moved from the insides of a psychic container to being-in-the-world with other human beings. Concepts such as consciousness, the unconscious, and the psyche recede into the background, while concepts such as knowledge, language, culture, and landscape move into the foreground. A postmodern psychology will involve a move from the archaeology of a psyche to the architecture of the current cultural landscapes.

Steinar Kvale
University of Aarhus, Denmark

See also: Contextualism

POSTTRAUMATIC STRESS DISORDER IN ADULTS

Posttraumatic Stress Disorder (PTSD) is an extreme psychobiological reaction to a psychologically traumatic event characterized by profound disturbances in cognitive, behavioral, and physiological functioning. The diagnosis is applied when an individual has experienced, witnessed, or been confronted with an event involving perceived or threatened loss of life, serious injury, or loss of physical integrity and which evoked intense fear, helplessness, or horror. The types of events that may cause PTSD include sexual or physical assault, military combat, motor vehicle accidents, major disasters, and acts of terrorism.

In the *Diagnostic and Statistical Manual of Mental Disorders,* fourth edition (*DSM-IV*) symptoms of PTSD are organized under three clusters: (1) reexperiencing (e.g., intrusive thoughts, nightmares, flashbacks, and psychophysiological reactivity to reminders of the trauma); (2) avoidance and emotional numbing (e.g., avoiding stimuli associated with the trauma, and inability to experience a full range of emotions); and (3) hyperarousal (e.g., hypervigilance, exaggerated startle response, and sleep disruption). By definition, these symptoms must persist for more than one month and produce clinically significant distress or impairment.

Epidemiological studies have found that the majority of people in the general population will experience a traumatic event meeting the PTSD stressor criterion in the *DSM-IV* during their lifetime, but that only approximately 10% of those will go on to develop PTSD. However, the probability of developing the disorder depends largely on the nature and severity of the traumatic event and higher rates (i.e., closer to 25%) have been observed in select samples of individuals exposed to intense traumas involving interpersonal violence or life threat (e.g., rape survivors and combat veterans).

The relationship between trauma exposure and the development of PTSD is influenced by numerous psychosocial risk factors and individual difference variables. Psychosocial risk factors for PTSD include family history of psychiatric illness, childhood trauma or behavior problems, the presence of psychiatric symptoms prior to the trauma, inadequate social support, and an overreliance on maladaptive coping strategies. Individual difference factors also play a role in the etiology of the disorder. For example, the rate of PTSD in women, after controlling for trauma exposure, is approximately twice as high as the rate for men. In addition, personality traits associated with Introversion and Neuroticism have also been identified as liabilities for PTSD, whereas characteristics such as Hardiness appear to represent resilience factors.

Assessment and Treatment of PTSD

A comprehensive clinical assessment of PTSD should include administration of structured diagnostic interviews, self-report psychometrics, and an evaluation of trauma across the lifespan. Several structured interviews are available and the Clinician-Administered PTSD Scale for the *DSM-IV* and PTSD module of the Structured Clinical Interview for the *DSM-IV* have become standards in the field. Self-report instruments can also assist in diagnosis or provide efficient, low-cost assessment methods for research and screening purposes. Of these, several were constructed specifically for assessing PTSD (e.g., Mississippi Scale for Combat-related PTSD; PTSD Checklist; PTSD Diagnostic Scale). Others were derived from the existing items of major inventories such as the Minnesota Multiphasic Personality Inventory and the Symptom Checklist–90. Finally, instruments such as the Potential Stressful Events Interview and the Traumatic Stress Schedule are used to evaluate trauma across the lifespan.

Treatment for PTSD typically involves the use of psychotherapy, pharmacotherapy, or both. Of the psychotherapies, exposure-based approaches (e.g., systematic desensitization, flooding, prolonged exposure, imaginal and in vivo exposure, and implosive therapy) have received the most attention and empirical support to date. The common feature of each is the practice of gradually exposing the therapy client to trauma-related cues to desensitize and extinguish the accompanying conditioned emotional and physiological reactions. The therapeutic mechanism is generally conceptualized within the framework of classical conditioning; repeated exposure to trauma-related cues (e.g., trauma-related images evoked from memory) in the absence of the feared negative consequences (e.g., the trauma itself) reduces the conditioned fear, anxiety, and avoidance characteristics of PTSD.

A second promising category of empirically validated treatments for PTSD is cognitive restructuring therapy. Based on cognitive therapy principles, this approach is designed to identify and modify dysfunctional trauma-related beliefs and to teach specific cognitive coping skills. The therapy process may also involve tasks that include an element of exposure, such as writing or describing the trauma to uncover trauma-related cognitions.

A third psychotherapy approach is anxiety management, variously referred to as relaxation training, stress inoculation, or biofeedback training. This approach does not focus on the trauma itself, but is instead geared toward teaching an individual the requisite skills for coping with stress, often via the use of relaxation. For this reason, anxiety management is often an adjunctive treatment to trauma-focused treatments.

Pharmacotherapy for PTSD generally targets symptoms of the disorder that it shares in common with the other anxiety disorders and major depression (i.e., hyperarousal, sleep disturbance, and anhedonia) and many medications developed for the treatment of these other disorders have been used to treat PTSD. Although clinical drug trials have shown fairly modest results overall, results suggest that some individuals with PTSD may benefit greatly from pharmacotherapy. The SSRIs (including sertraline, fluoxetine, and paroxetine) are currently the medications of choice for the treatment of PTSD.

Mark W. Miller
Terence M. Keane
VA Boston Healthcare System
National Center for PTSD
Boston University School of Medicine

See also: Trauma

POWER: STRATEGIES AND TACTICS

Introduction

Power refers to the ability to make decisions that have an important impact and that involve others (Greenberg & Baron, 2000; McClelland, 1975; Winter, 1973). Often, power involves controlling the behavior of others, although many times other people voluntarily accept the directives of power holders and do not feel any loss of independence. In everyday language, power refers to "getting one's way" and "having clout." Many people are socialized to distrust power, to feel that only evil and manipulative individuals are interested in acquiring it, and to feel that they themselves should avoid places where powerful people congregate. In reality, and like many complex issues such as economic incentives and government-sponsored housing programs, power is like fire. It can be used for good intentions or it can be used to pursue evil goals. Power, especially the strategies and tactics for its implementation, can be viewed as a tool to be used in efforts toward the goals people set for themselves (Brislin, 1991; Buchanan & Badham, 1999; Somech & Drach-Zahavy, 2002).

Strategies reflect people's careful planning about their future in that they refer to complex sets of behaviors (e.g., resource and network development and developing the image of a winner) that will have many positive implications in their pursuit of power. Tactics, on the other hand, refer to more specific behaviors useful at a certain time and place in the pursuit of specific goals (e.g., sending up trial balloons or creating a lightning rod). Brislin (1991) developed an extensive list of both strategies and tactics useful in the acquisition and use of power. Many depend on respectful and effective working relations with other people.

The Acquisition and Use of Power: Working with Others

Power is an aspect of relationships among people, and most powerful individuals have cordial interactions with a wide variety of others. Although one image of a power holder may be a deranged monarch ordering people to commit drastic deeds, reminiscent of a bad Hollywood movie influenced by Machiavelli, power holders are most often cordial people who communicate well with others (Kotter, 1982). This is especially true in a democracy, where people have various institutional supports such as the legal system, unions, and the media to complain about callous behavior emanating from leaders. Cordial relations with others are necessary because no one person has all the skills or knowledge needed to develop complex projects and to implement them. For example, imagine that two executives want to suggest the development of a new product line. They must convince power holders, necessitating communication skills. They must research the present marketplace, demanding knowledge of survey methods, finance, production, and accounting. They must make predictions about the eventual consumption of the products, demanding knowledge of distribution systems. In addition, legal concerns will be raised at many steps in the planning process. No two people can possess all this knowledge. The two will have to integrate the efforts and talents of others.

These efforts will be made much easier if the two executives know many other people who are part of a circle of acquaintances or network (Nahavandi & Malekzadeh, 1999). These others may be old classmates, members of other departments within the same organizations, people met through community activities, people met at social gatherings, and so forth. People in one's network are not necessarily friends with whom one shares confidences. Rather, people in a network are useful to each other because they exchange favors. If people cease being useful to each other, they drop out of each other's network, although they may enter into another network relationship years later if they become mutually useful again.

The exchanges of favors occur in a manner similar to that described by Cialdini (2000). For instance, one person knows tax law. He or she exchanges a few key pieces of advice with a lawyer who knows what terms found in advertising can be considered part of the public domain. Another person is knowledgeable about the ways that senior executives want proposals presented to them. He or she can exchange this information with another in the expectation that help will be forthcoming on the design of a survey instrument to measure market demands. Similarly, people who are knowledgeable about organizational developments through their active participation in the "grapevine" can exchange information for a variety of favors.

There is a sense of obligation in the exchange of these favors: people are expected to receive and to give. If people do not return favors, they are simply dropped from network membership and find themselves out of various information loops that previously kept them informed about developments in their organizations. Network development and maintenance may seem cold and unfeeling, yet people must be able to exchange favors if they are to develop complex projects and to stay informed about news in large organizations. Many power holders know hundreds of people with whom they can exchange favors, but they cannot become deeply involved in the emotional lives of all them. Becoming comfortable with network development is one of the necessities as people become more sophisticated about the nature of power in decision making.

Becoming More Sophisticated

Some people learn about power as part of their socialization, for instance, when they see their lawyer or politician parents participating in networks, exchanging favors, developing complex plans, and working on their strategies and tactics. Others do not have access to the application of power when they are young and must learn its techniques as adults. One way to become more sophisticated is to participate in voluntary community activities. In addition to developing a network, people can observe the processes of coalition formation, impactful communication of ideas, creation of a winning image, and so forth (Brislin, 1991). A further possibility is to obtain a seat on the community activity's budget committee. No matter what proposal is put forth for the use of money, some people will invariably prefer another use. In observing how successful people use skills, strategies, and tactics to advance their preferred plans, careful observers can learn a great deal about the use of power. They can also learn that the most sophisticated approach is not to view power as an end in itself. Rather, power should be looked on as a tool to be used in compassionate and intelligent leadership.

REFERENCES

Brislin, R. (1991). *The art of getting things done: A practical guide to the use of power.* New York: Praeger.

Buchanan, D., & Badham, R. (1999). *Power, politics, and organizational change: Winning the turf game.* Thousand Oaks, CA: Sage.

Cialdini, R. (2000). *Influence: Science and practice* (4th ed.). Boston: Addison-Wesley.

Greenberg, J., & Baron, J. (2000). *Behavior in organizations* (7th ed.). Upper Saddle River, NJ: Prentice Hall.

Kotter, J. (1982). What effective general managers really do. *Harvard Business Review, 60*(6), 157–167.

McClelland, D. (1975). *Power: The inner experience.* New York: Irvington.

Nahavandi, A., & Malekzadeh, A. (1999). *Organizational behavior: The person-organization fit.* Upper Saddle River, NJ: Prentice Hall.

Somech, A., & Drach-Zahavy, A. (2002). Relative power and influence strategy: The effects of agent/target organizational power on superiors' choice of influence strategies. *Journal of Organizational Behavior, 23,* 167–179.

Winter, D. (1973). *The power motive.* New York: Macmillan.

Richard W. Brislin
University of Hawaii

See also: **Applied Research**

PRECOCIOUS DEVELOPMENT

Precocity refers to an earlier than expected maturation level. The term is often used to refer to untimely ripeness or premature fruiting. A child who is described as precocious has developed earlier and at an accelerated rate when compared to other children of the same age.

Early development can be general or specific in its manifestation. General precocity refers to a child advanced in numerous areas: physical, intellectual, and social. Specific precocity is more often the case and this typically does not present any adverse conditions for the child. However, precocity symptomatic of biological untimeliness is often pathological in that the biological patterns are highly regulated by genetic composition. Any deviations in biological development tend to produce distortions in physical structure. Precocious puberty, by definition, occurs in females before age 8 and in males at age 9 or earlier. Females who display precocious puberty develop pubic hair at an early age. In addition, breast enlargement and contour, increased ovarian and uterine volume, menses at age 9 or younger, and advanced bone age are reported. Males who display precocious puberty show signs of hirsutism or virilization and increased testicular volume (Della Manna, Setian, Damiani, Kuperman, & Dichtchekenian, 2002). Precocious puberty occurs more frequently in the female population at a 10:1 female-to-male ratio. The estimated rate of occurrence in the overall population of children is between 1:5,000 and 1:10,000. (Partsch & Sippell, 2001)

Recent studies have suggested that nutrition and body composition may influence the development of reproductive competence in mammals. Witchel, Arslanian, & Lee (1999) reported no significant relationships between circulating gonadotropin and leptin concentrations. This is important as prior assumptions held that leptin concentrations communicated nutritional status to the neuroendrocrine reproductive axis (Heger, Partsch, Peter, Blum, Kiess, & Sippell, 1999). Gonadotropin-releasing hormone (GnRH) is linked to precocious anatomical development in males and females. GnRH agonist treatment remains controversial, although there is some attempt to standardize treatment protocols (Partsch & Sippell, 2002).

Central nervous system (CNS) abnormalities have also been linked to precocious sexual development. CNS abnormalities include tumors either specific to or with secondary effects on endocrine function. Children with neurodevelopmental disabilities are more at risk for premature sexual development when compared to children without a neurodevelopmental disability (Siddiqi, Van Dyke, Donohue, & McBrier, 1999); this finding has been reported for Williams' syndrome (Cherniske, Sadler, Schwartz, Carpenter, & Pober, 1999). An interesting case study involving monozygotic twin females both with neurofibromatosis type 1 (nf1) found that the sister with optic pathway glioma developed precocious puberty, but the sister without optic pathway glioma did not (Kelly, Sproul, Heurta, & Rogol, 1999). While precocious puberty is often found in neurofibromatosis type 1 patients, it is almost always associated with optic pathway glioma.

Meas et al. (2002) investigated a somewhat paradoxical hypothesis that intrauterine undernutrition may predispose females to serious endocrine consequences that include precocious pubarche and functional ovarian hyperandrogenism. Their study did find that precocious pubarche may be associated with future functional ovarian hyperandrogenism. However, a link between functional ovarian hyperandrogenism and intrauterine undernutrition was not demonstrated.

Another type of specific biological precocity involves premature "old age" in which the young sufferers actually die from symptoms of old age: rapid deterioration of the body and its organs, and so on. Werner syndrome (WS) is a human premature aging disorder characterized by chromosomal instability. WS, a rare autosomal recessive disorder, also produces other age-related diseases.

Precocity of cognitive functions has been reported in the literature for centuries. For example, J. S. Mill is said to have learned Greek by the age of 3! However, there is a dearth of scientific literature to support the anecdotal character of this precocious cognitive development.

While precocious puberty and aging are more clearly biologically traced, it is difficult to discern whether precocious cognitive development is a result of biological factors, environmental influence, or an interactional effect between the two.

REFERENCES

Cherniske, E. M., Sadler, L. S., Schwartz, D., Carpenter, T. O., & Pober, B. R. (1999). Early puberty in Williams syndrome. *Clinical Dysmorphia, 8*(2), 117–121.

Della Manna, T., Setian, N., Damiani, D., Kuperman, H., & Dichtchekenian, V. (2002). Premature thelarche: Identification of clinical and laboratory data for the diagnosis of precocious puberty. *Hospital Clinical Facility Medicine, 57*(2), 49–54.

Heger, S., Partsch, C. J., Peter, M., Blum, W. F., Kiess, W., & Sippell, W. G. (1999). Serum leptin levels in patients with progressive central precocious puberty. *Pediatric Research, 46*(1), 71–75.

Kelly, T. E., Sproul, G. T., Heurta, M. G., & Rogol, A. D. (1999). Discordant puberty in monozygotic twin sisters with neurofibromatosis type 1 (NF1). *Clinical Pediatrics, 37*(5), 301–304.

Lebel, M. (2001). Werner syndrome: Genetic and molecular basis of a premature aging disorder. *Cell Molecular Life Science, 58*(7), 857–867.

Meas, T., Chevenne, D., Thibaud, E., Leger, J., Cabrol, S., Czernichow, P., & Levy-Marchal, C. (2002). Endocrine consequences of premature pubarche in post-pubertal Caucasian girls. *Clinical Endocrinology, 57*(1), 101–106.

Partsch, C. J., & Wippell, W. G. (2001). Pathogenesis and epidemiology of precocious puberty. Effects of exogenous oestrogens. *Human Reproduction Update, 7*(3), 292–302.

Partsch, C. J., & Wippell, W. G. (2002). Treatment of central precocious development. *Clinical Endocrinology and Metabolism, 16*(1), 165–189.

Siddiqi, S. U., Van Dyke, D. C., Donohue, P., & McBrien, D. M. (1999). Premature sexual development in individuals with neurodevelopmental disabilities. *Developmental Medical Child Neurology, 41*(6), 392–395.

Witchel, S. F., Arslanian, S., & Lee, P. A. (1999). Leptin concentrations in precocious puberty or untimely puberty with and without GnRH analogue therapy. *Journal of Pediatric Endocrinology & Metabolism, 12*(6), 839–845.

Robert A. Leark
Craig D. Anderson
Alliant International University
Forensic Psychology Program

PREJUDICE AND DISCRIMINATION

Although often employed interchangeably by lay persons and the media, the terms *prejudice* and *discrimination* possess distinct meanings for most social scientists. The former denotes the possession of *negative attitudes* of a particular kind regarding members of a specific group or category; the latter is the term applied to the *negative actions* that result from prejudicial attitudes and that are directed against the targets or victims of prejudice. Someone who is prejudiced may, in certain situations, practice discrimination.

More specifically, social scientists view prejudice as the possession of negative attitudes targeted at members of some particular group (religious, racial, ethnic, political)—attitudes that give rise to negative or unfavorable evaluations of individuals seen as belonging to that group.

As an attitude, prejudice is seen as having a tripartite nature, comprising cognitive, affective, and behavioral components. A person's beliefs and expectations regarding a particular group constitute the cognitive component of the prejudicial attitude. The term *stereotypes* has come to designate networks or clusters of such beliefs and expectations. The basis of all stereotypes is that all those who belong to a specific category or group—ethnic, religious, racial, political, or any other classification—manifest similar behaviors and possess similar attitudes. The widespread application of stereotypes largely ignores human differences and individual differences.

Individuals who are prejudiced against specific groups will tend to experience intense negative feelings when they come into contact with these groups, either directly or indirectly. The affective component of the prejudicial attitude comes into play here, with profound negative emotional feelings tending to accompany cognitive reactions to objects of prejudice.

The behavioral component of prejudice has engendered the most research interest. Here the concern is the tendency of prejudiced individuals to act in a negative manner towards targets of their prejudice. When such tendencies become manifest in overt behavior, discrimination is said to occur. Numerous constraints upon behavior operate in everyday situations to prevent prejudicial feelings from being transformed into discriminatory behavior. If such obstacles are not present in a given instance, however, the prejudicial thought or tendency may find expression in the behavioral act, which may vary in intensity from the lowest level, mere social avoidance, to acts of extreme violence or even genocide.

The attitudinal nature of prejudice has generated measurement research modeled after much of the attitude literature. The cognitive, affective, and behavioral components of prejudice have all been the subject of research directed at assessing the nature and extent of prejudice in the population at large. The cognitive or belief component of prejudice, the assessment of stereotypes, is generally tapped through a trait-selection procedure. Individuals are given a list of ethnic, religious, racial, and political categories and a list of traits, and are asked to note which traits are associated with which group(s). Information on the affective or feeling component of prejudice is generally derived through the use of attitude scales engineered to measure the level of an individual's positive or negative feelings toward specific groups.

The *social distance scale* is an important tool in research into the behavioral component of prejudice. Subjects are presented with a series of hypothetical relationships between themselves and members of specific groups. The series of items represents increasing levels of closeness or intimacy between respondents and members of various groups (ranging from residing in the same country at the lowest level to intermarriage at the highest level), with the subjects being asked to indicate, for a given group, their willingness to accept individuals from that group into a given level of intimacy.

Florence L. Denmark
Pace University

PRESCRIPTION PRIVILEGES

In March 2002, Governor Gary Johnson of New Mexico signed a law authorizing prescription privileges for properly trained psychologists. "Properly trained" is defined as completing at least 450 hours of coursework, completing a 400 hour/100 patient practicum under physician supervision, and passing a national certification examination. The academic component includes courses in psychopharmacology, neuroanatomy, neurophysiology, clinical pharmacology, pharmacology, pathophysiology, pharmacotherapeutics, pharmacoepidemiology, and physical and lab assessment. Following the passing of the national exam, psychologists licensed to practice in New Mexico become eligible for a two-year license permitting practice under the supervision of a physician. At the end of the two years, following physician approval and a peer review of the prescribing records, the psychologist can apply to practice independently and is expected to maintain a collaborative relationship with the patient's health care practitioner (American Psychological Association Online, 2002).

In addition to New Mexico, psychologists on Guam were able to obtain prescription privileges in 1999. A number of other states have pending legislation on prescription privileges. In 2002 these states included Georgia, Illinois, Hawaii, and Tennessee. A number of state psychological associations have created prescription privileges task forces working for legislative actions on their proposals.

Graduate schools in several states have begun to provide psychopharmacology training, as have some private organizations. According to a recent book (Levant, Sammons, & Paige, 2003), there are currently 11 programs offering postdoctoral training in psychopharmacology, and it is estimated that over 900 psychologists have pursued such training or are in the process of doing so.

Some would argue that prescription privileges are a natural extension of present laws already on the books (e.g., in California) that "establish that psychologists should be knowledgeable about psychopharmacological effects of populations at risk and are encouraged to seek additional education in the area of geriatric pharmacology" (Ch. 1539 of the statutes of 1990). In Hawaii, State House resolution 334-90 recommended a series of roundtable discussions dealing with Hawaii's unserved mental health needs and included "the possibility of allowing appropriately trained psychologists to prescribe psychotropic medications . . . under certain conditions."

Psychologists are not newcomers to the arena of physical interventions. Jansen and Barron (1988), in reviewing this topic, asserted that biofeedback techniques, alarm bells for bed-wetting, galvanic skin responses, and polygraph assessments are examples of physical interventions already used by psychologists. Direct involvement of physical interventions by psychologists have also included behavior management procedures with children. The authors pointed out that even though psychologists have been active in the development of physical interventions, they have been automatically excluded from prescribing medications because they are not physicians.

Meeting Society's Needs: The Public Policy Perspective

Patrick DeLeon has summarized the public policy issue by arguing that the essence of prescriptive authority is to ensure that Americans have access to the highest possible quality of care. In the Foreword of *Prescriptive Authority for Psychologists* (Levant, Sammons, & Paige, 2003), he suggests a model whereby "psychotropic medications are prescribed in the context of an overarching, psychologically based treatment paradigm as opposed to current psychiatric models that have an almost exclusive biological orientation" (p. xiii). He insists that the prescriptive authority agenda involves all of psychology and is an educational agenda that strives to strengthen psychologists' understanding of the workings of the human psyche. On a policy level, he argues that the U.S. health care delivery system is in need of change, and that there is an excessive time lag between the discovery of efficacious treatments and their routine use in patient care. He argues (DeLeon, Fox, & Graham, 1991) that prescriptive authority for psychologists is not only necessary but essential to meet the needs of quality care for the mentally ill and to deal with the problem of excessive medication for the elderly. Until very recently more than half of outpatient mental health visits were conducted by general medical practitioners and nursing home residents were often medicated using drugs to treat mental disorders even though most of these elderly patients were not mentally ill.

At the other end of the age continuum, there is widespread discussion among professionals and the general public as to the justification for medicating children. It has been argued that proper diagnosis is crucial in using medications for children with Attention Deficit Disorder or Attention-Deficit/Hyperactivity Disorder. However, medications may not be necessary with other psychological disorders (DeLeon, Folen, Jennings, Willis, & Wright, 1991). One policy implication raised by these authors is how parents deal with their children. It may be that the parents' inability to cope with children, rather than the child's activity level, is the primary concern. Thus, evaluating the stress level of the parent may lead to a productive course of action without necessarily subjecting children to medication. Clinical child psychologists need to know more about the efficacy of psychoactive drugs for children and about the general area of psychopharmacology.

Opposition to Prescription Privileges

No discussion on prescription privileges would be complete without citing objections to psychologists prescribing drugs. Breggin's *Toxic Psychiatry* (1991) is noteworthy in this regard. Breggin argues that the administration of drugs by psychiatrists is a political and financial issue encouraged by the "psychopharmacological complex" that "pushes biological and genetic theories, as well as drugs, on the society" (p. 408). He argues that psychiatry as a profession must discontinue its financial collaboration with drug companies and must not make inaccurate claims regarding genetic and biological causes of mental illness. Breggin insisted that love, understanding, and psychotherapy are the answers to psychiatric problems. His concerns revolve around the addictive and damaging aspects of drugs, especially if the patient has not been apprised in advance of the effects and consequences of psychotropic medications.

Breggin also takes to task psychologists who advocate prescription privileges. He notes that some psychologists have become envious of the status accorded to psychiatrists and notes that drug companies are sponsoring and funding seminars at meetings of psychologists to discuss the advantages of prescription privileges. Brown (Levant, Sammons, & Paige, 2003) discusses the opposition to prescriptive authority by noting that prescribing medications is foreign to the identity of professional psychology because psychologists have traditionally viewed themselves as dealing primarily with the mind rather than the body. She suggests that studying the impact of biological bases of behavior or the impact of behavior on biological factors is a more recent phenomenon. Also, she points out that most psychologists today perceive the profession of medicine as intimately connected with pharmacology. This association is pervasive, she suggests, even though it is a relatively recent phenomenon; only 100 years ago most medications were available over the counter, as they are in a number of other countries today.

Final Comment

The core argument against prescription privileges is that they should not be granted because they would fundamentally change the nature of psychology. Many psychologists believe that prescription privileges should never be permitted because they violate the fundamental tenets of psychology. Nevertheless, a sizable majority of psychologists do believe that some patients need psychotropic medications at some time in their lives. Moreover, the Task Force on Psychologists' Use of Physical Intervention has defined the practice of psychology as including both physical and psychological interventions (Jansen & Barron, 1988). Fox (1989) pointed out that the use of such physical interventions should occur within the context of improving the quality of services, within the competence of the provider, and in the service of consumer welfare.

Psychology is a relatively young profession and changes are part of any field's development. It certainly does appear that prescription privileges will become part of the practice of psychology in the twenty-first century.

REFERENCES

American Psychological Association Online. (2002, March 6). New Mexico governor signs landmark law on prescription privileges for psychologists. Retrieved September 26, 2002, from http://www.apa.org/practice/nm_rxp.html.

Breggin, P. (1991). *Toxic psychiatry.* New York: St. Martin's Press.

DeLeon, P. H., Folen, R., Jennings, F., Willis, D., & Wright, R. (1991). The case for prescription privileges: A logical evolution of professional practice. *Journal of Clinical Child Psychology, 3,* 254–267.

DeLeon, P. H., Fox, R., & Graham, S. (1991). Prescription privileges: Psychology's next frontier? *American Psychologist, 46,* 384–393.

Fox, R. E. (1989). Some practical and legal objections to prescription privileges for psychologists. *Psychotherapy in Private Practice, 6,* 23–39.

Jansen, M., & Barron, J. (1988). Introduction and overview: Psychologists' use of physical interventions. *Psychotherapy, 25*(4), 487–491.

Levant, R., Sammons, M., & Paige, R. (Eds.). (2003). *Prescriptive authority for psychologists.* Washington, DC: American Psychological Association.

Norman Abeles
Michigan State University

PREVENTION OF MENTAL DISORDERS

The twentieth century witnessed major advances in the diagnosis and treatment of mental disorders. However, concerted work on prevention is just beginning as we enter the twenty-first century. In response to growing awareness of the need for prevention, Congress recently charged the Institute of Medicine (IOM) to convene a Committee on Prevention of Mental Disorders.

In their report (Mrazek & Haggerty, 1994), the IOM Committee proposed that, in order to reduce the indiscriminate use of this concept, the term *prevention* be reserved for interventions administered before the onset of a clinically diagnosable disorder. By contrast, *treatment* consists of interventions designed to ameliorate or cure a mental disorder that has already developed.

Why Prevention?

The alarming prevalence rates of many mental disorders, as well as their devastating consequences for individuals and communities, require that the mental health system move beyond focusing solely on treatment and advance toward the development and implementation of preventive interventions. The Committee identified as promising targets for prevention five disorders with heavy emotional and financial costs: Conduct Disorder, Alcohol Abuse/Dependence, Schizophrenia, Alzheimer's disease, and depressive disorders. Because Major Depressive Disorder arguably poses the most widespread risk on both a national and global level and may be the most likely to be prevented first, it can serve as a model for the prevention of other disorders (Muñoz & Ying, 1993).

In the United States, 17% of adults suffer at least one episode of major depression during their lifetimes (Kessler et al., 1994). The World Health Organization reported that major depression is the number one cause of disability in the world, and—with respect to the burden of disease in the world, taking into account both disability and mortality—major depression was the fourth most important disorder in 1990 and will become the second by 2020 (Murray & Lopez, 1996). Depression has been found to cause dysfunction that is equivalent to or worse than chronic physical illness (Wells et al., 1989), and it also contributes to major causes of death, such as smoking and drinking (Schoenborn & Horm, 1993). With a problem of this magnitude, treatment is not sufficient to reduce prevalence (the total number of affected individuals); prevention of incidence (new cases) must be achieved.

Preventive Interventions for Mental Disorders

The IOM Report identified three levels of preventive interventions. *Universal preventive interventions* target an entire population group (e.g., childhood immunizations). *Selective preventive interventions* target high-risk groups within a community (e.g., home visitation for low-birth-weight children). Risk status is determined on the basis of biological, psychological, or social factors known to be associated with the onset of a disorder, rather than individual risk profiles. *Indicated preventive interventions* target individuals with early signs or symptoms of a disorder who do not yet meet full diagnostic criteria (e.g., parent-child training for children identified as having behavioral problems). In general, the lower the cost and the fewer the possible ill effects of a preventive intervention, the more amenable it is for universal dissemination. Conversely, more costly and potentially risky or burdensome interventions should be reserved for use with individuals who have an indicated risk for the disorder.

The Nature and Scope of Prevention

Some disorders can be fully prevented by individual behavior. For example, alcohol, drug, and nicotine dependence are 100% preventable if an individual chooses not to use those substances. For other disorders, such as depression, individual strategies will reduce risk by some as yet unknown proportion. Similarly, prevention at the community level will reduce the incidence of disorders, rather than eliminating them completely. However, taken together, individual and community-level strategies can significantly lower rates of disorders. For instance, legal and other social interventions such as cigarette tax increases, antitobacco media campaigns, and laws prohibiting smoking indoors modify individual behavior and thus impact rates of smoking initiation and smoking cessation.

It is noteworthy that prevention efforts can be successful even when the causes of a disorder are poorly understood or cannot be modified directly. For instance, phenylketonuria (PKU) is a metabolic disorder resulting from genetic mutation. However, the severe mental retardation produced by PKU can be prevented via strict dietary control. Another example is the classic case of John Snow, who halted the nineteenth-century cholera epidemic in London by removing the handle of a Broad Street water pump even though the specific agent that caused cholera was not yet known. Thus, although scientists do not yet fully comprehend the complex biological and social factors that produce mental disorders such as depression, the development of effective prevention strategies is nonetheless a feasible goal.

Evidence-based prevention services require studies to test their efficacy. For example, to date four randomized controlled trials have been conducted to evaluate whether the onset of major depressive episodes (MDEs) can be prevented. The San Francisco Depression Prevention Research Project evaluated the effects of a cognitive-behavioral prevention course with a sample of 150 primary care, predominantly minority patients and found reductions in depression symptoms but not in MDE incidence rates at 12-month follow-up. A similar pattern of results was obtained in a study of 231 college freshmen using cognitive-behavioral skills training. However, two controlled studies assessing the effects of a cognitive-behavioral coping course on at-risk adolescents reported reductions in the incidence of MDEs at 12-month follow-up. Taken together, results are promising and indicate that it is possible to prevent the onset of major depressive episodes (Muñoz, Le, Clarke, & Jaycox, 2002).

Future Directions

The mental health field will progress in the area of prevention of disorders as the general health care system moves toward parity in the treatment of mental and other disorders. Screening methods to identify cases of mental disorders in primary care settings will eventually be extended to the identification of individuals at risk. As preventive interventions receive empirical support, health care systems will be held accountable for providing those shown to be efficacious. Ultimately, as these interventions become more widespread, we will begin to see measurable drops in the incidence of targeted mental disorders, with a resulting decrease in their prevalence. This will be a major achievement both from the standpoint of lowering health care costs and, more importantly, reducing human suffering.

REFERENCES

Kessler, R. C., McGonagle, K. A., Zhao, S., Nelson, C. B., Hughes, M., Eshleman, S., et al. (1994). Lifetime and 12-month prevalence of *DSM-III-R* psychiatric disorder in the United States: Results from the National Comorbidity Survey. *Archives of General Psychiatry, 51,* 8–19.

Mrazek, P., & Haggerty, R. (1994). *Reducing risks for mental disorders: Frontiers for preventive intervention research.* Washington, DC: National Academy Press.

Muñoz, R. F., Le, H.-N., Clarke, G., & Jaycox, L. (2002). Preventing the onset of major depression. In I. H. Gotlib & C. L. Hammen (Eds.), *Handbook of depression* (pp. 343–359). New York: Guilford Press.

Muñoz, R. F., & Ying, Y. (1993). *The prevention of depression: Research and practice.* Baltimore: Johns Hopkins University Press.

Murray, C. J. L., & Lopez, A. D. (1996). *The global burden of disease: Summary.* Cambridge, MA: Harvard University Press.

Schoenborn, C. A., & Horm, J. (1993). *Negative moods as correlates of smoking and heavier drinking: Implications for health promotion* (Advance data from Vital and Health Statistics No. 236). Hyattsville, MD: National Center for Health Statistics.

Wells, K. B., Stewart, A., Hays, R. D., Burnam, M. A., Rogers, W., Daniels, M., et al. (1989). The functioning and well-being of depressed patients: Results from the Medical Outcomes Study. *Journal of the American Medical Association, 262,* 914–919.

Ricardo F. Muñoz
T. Mendelson
University of California, San Francisco

See also: Depression

PRIMARY MENTAL ABILITIES

One of the earliest accomplishments of the science of psychology was the objective measurement of mental abilities.

In 1904, the British psychologist Charles Spearman argued that intelligence could be characterized as being composed of a general factor (g) common to all meaningful activity and of specific factors (s) that are unique to the different tasks used to measure intelligence. Test instruments that applied the concept of general intelligence were introduced by Binet and Simon in France and by Terman in the United States. American psychologists engaged in educational and occupational selection activities found the concept of general intelligence less useful for predicting success in specific jobs or other life roles. In addition, Thorndike's work on transfer of training had suggested that the notion of generalizability of a single ability dimension was not justified.

Efforts soon began, therefore, to determine whether human abilities could be described along a parsimonious number of distinct substantive dimensions. Initial work along these lines began with the publication of T. L. Kelley's *Crossroads in the Mind of Man* (1928), which advocated the determination of group factors representing distinct skills, such as facility with numbers, facility with verbal materials, spatial relationships, speed, and memory. These efforts were also aided by advances in the methods of factor analysis that allowed the determination of multiple factors, each representing a latent construct represented by sets of independently observed variables.

Most prominently associated with these developments was L. L. Thurstone (1935), who expressed the hope that a careful scrutiny of the relations among a wide array of assessment devices, developed to reflect a given construct as purely as possible, would yield a limited number of dimensions that would reflect "the building blocks of the mind." He administered a battery of 56 simple psychological tests to a large number of children in Chicago schools and applied factor analysis to determine the latent basic ability dimensions represented by these tests. Given the procedures available at the time, he was reasonably successful in showing that fewer than 10 latent constructs were required to explain most individual differences variance in his measures. The factors obtained in this work were consequently labeled the *primary mental abilities*.

Most of the factors identified by Thurstone have been replicated subsequently in work by others. The most important factors, in order of the proportion of individual differences explained, are the following:

Verbal comprehension (V). This factor represents the scope of a person's passive vocabulary, and is most often measured by multiple-choice recognition vocabulary tests.

Spatial Orientation (S). The ability to visualize and mentally rotate abstract figures in two- or three-dimensional space. This ability is thought to be involved in understanding maps and charts and in assembling objects that require manipulation of spatial configurations. This may be a complex factor involving both visualization and the perception of spatial relationships.

Inductive Reasoning (R or I). This is the ability to determine a rule or principle from individual instances, probably involved in most human problem solving. The ability is generally measured using a number or letter series that has several embedded rules; the subject is asked to complete the series correctly.

Number (N). This is the ability to engage rapidly and correctly in a variety of computational operations. The most simple measure of this ability is a test checking sums for addition problems.

Word Fluency (W). This factor represents a person's active vocabulary and is generally measured by free recall of words according to a lexical rule.

Associative Memory (M). Found primarily in verbal tasks involving paired associates or list learning. It is not a general memory factor, evidence for which has not thus far been established.

Perceptual Speed (P). This ability involves the rapid and accurate identification of visual details, similarities, and differences. It is usually measured by letter canceling, simple stimulus, or number comparison tasks.

Other organizational schemes to characterize multiple abilities have been developed by G. H. Thompson (1948) and P. E. Vernon (1960) in England and by J. P. Guilford (1967) in the United States. The latter system actually classified tasks along a three-dimensional higher-order hierarchy in terms of content, product, and operations involved in each task, resulting in a taxonomy of as many as 120 factors, many of which remain to be operationalized.

For the purposes of educational application, L. L. Thurstone and T. G. Thurstone (1949) developed a series of tests at several difficulty levels suitable from kindergarten to high school designed to measure Thurstone's first five factors (V, S, R, N, and W). This battery was updated and revised by T. G. Thurstone in 1962. Measures of the other factors may be found in the kit of factor-referenced tests (1976) developed by the Educational Testing Service.

The primary mental abilities measures have had little use in educational practice in recent years. However, the primary abilities have experienced a revival as a useful measurement instrument for charting the course of abilities in studies of adult development (also see "Adult Intellectual Development"). A special version of the primary abilities tests particularly suitable for work with older adults has also been developed (STAMAT). Factorial invariance of six latent ability dimensions (Inductive Reasoning, Spatial Orientation, Verbal Ability, Numeric Ability, Perceptual Speed, and Verbal Memory) has been demonstrated in longitudinal samples across time and different birth cohorts (as well as across genders) (Schaie, 1996). The validity of the primary mental abilities in adults has also been examined with respect to its relation to measures of practical intelligence and subjective perception of competence, as well as to specific occupational outcomes.

REFERENCES

Binet, A., & Simon, T. (1905). Méthodes novelles pour le diagnostic do niveau intellectuel des anormaux. *L'Aneé Psychologique, 11,* 191.

Ekstrom, R. B., French, J. W., Harman, H., & Derman, D. (1976). *Kit of factor-referenced cognitive tests* (Rev. ed.). Princeton, NJ: Educational.

Guilford, J. P. (1967). *The nature of human intelligence.* New York: McGraw-Hill Testing Service.

Kelley, T. L. (1928). *Crossroads in the mind of man: A study of differentiable mental abilities.* Stanford, CA: Stanford University Press.

Schaie, K. W. (1985). *Manual for the Schaie-Thurstone Adult Mental Abilities Test (STAMAT).* Palo Alto, CA: Consulting Psychologists Press.

Schaie, K. W. (1996). *Intellectual development in childhood: The Seattle Longitudinal Study.* New York: Cambridge University Press.

Spearman, C. (1904). "General Intelligence": Objectively determined and measured. *American Journal of Psychology, 15,* 201–292.

Terman, L. M. (1916). *The measurement of intelligence.* Boston: Houghton Mifflin.

Thomson, G. H. (1948). *The factorial analysis of human abilities* (3rd ed.). Boston: Houghton Mifflin.

Thorndike, E. L., & Woodworth, R. S. (1901). Influence of improvement in one mental function upon the efficiency of other mental functions. *Psychological Review, 8,* 247–262, 384–395, 553–564.

Thurstone, L. L. (1935). *Vectors of mind: Multiple-factor analysis for the isolation of primary traits.* Chicago: University of Chicago Press.

Thurstone, L. L., & Thurstone, T. G. (1949). *Examiner manual for the SRA Primary Mental Abilities Test.* Chicago: Sience Research Associates.

Vernon, P. E. (1960). *The structure of human abilities* (Rev. ed.). London: Methuen.

K. Warner Schaie
Pennsylvania State University

See also: **Testing Methods**

PRIMARY MOTOR CORTEX AND PRIMARY SOMATIC SENSORY CORTEX

The primary motor cortex and the primary somatic sensory cortex represent two principal components of sensory motor integration implemented in the brain. The fundamental function of motor cortex is to control voluntary movements, whereas somatic sensory cortex receives and analyzes tactile, joint, and muscle sensory inputs, sometimes in relation to voluntary movement. From classical perspectives, motor cortex functions as the final cortical output for already processed movement commands, relaying signals from premotor cerebral cortical sites to the spinal cord. Similarly, somatic sensory cortex has often been viewed as a pipe to relay subcortical inputs to higher order cortical sites for further processing. Recent evidence indicates more complex and crucial roles for primary motor cortex and primary somatic sensory cortex in processing motor and somatic sensory information.

Primary Motor Cortex

In the past two decades, new concepts have emerged to explain the function and role of motor cortex in movement control. Instead of resembling an automatic "piano player" superimposed upon spinal cord output, motor cortex appears to have significant functions related to movement planning and learning. The neural substrate for these higher order functions of motor cortex likely relates to the distributed and plastic anatomical and functional organization within motor cortex.

Motor Cortical Organization

Motor cortex has three functional subdivisions, one each for the upper limb, the lower limb, and the head and neck; output from these subdivisions yields the motor commands that elaborate voluntary movement. Previous principles of motor cortex organization indicated a somatotopic pattern resembling a distorted but recognizable body shape—the homunculus—represented upon the surface of the motor cortex. A functional consequence of the homuncular arrangement could be to imply dedication of specific neural elements, such as a cortical column, to controlling one body part, perhaps a finger.

Recent evidence suggests that motor cortex does not have a regular and organized somatotopic pattern. Instead, circuits in motor cortex exhibit a widely distributed, multiple and overlapping representation of the different body parts, though there remains separation between the leg, arm, and head representations. Thus, neural circuits in motor cortex related to finger movements are intermingled and may be shared with circuits for the more proximal movements. The distributed and shared functional organization of motor cortex can provide for flexibility and enormous storage capacity.

Motor Cortex Plasticity and Cognition

Motor function has nearly infinite flexibility, ranging from the capability to learn new simple or complex tasks to recovery from central nervous system damage that might come about through changes in motor cortex internal processing. Flexibility of motor cortex output can be influenced by behavioral or physiological context. For example, changing a posture before moving modifies somatic sensory input that can then yield differing motor cortex output. These effects may be explained by changes in central set by neural facilitation of motor cortex networks, and likely are influenced by local synaptic interactions. Limits seem to exist upon the flexibility of motor cortex representations. In normal individuals, motor cortex sites retain functionality related to the represented movements.

Possibly related to its flexible output, motor cortex has an important role in adapting and learning motor skills. Motor representations in human motor cortex exhibit modification following short-term or long-term experience, such as repeating a finger movement for a few minutes or over weeks. Learning a movement sequence changes the amount of functional activation in motor cortex or the coupling between motor cortex and target structures in the spinal cord. Motor cortex patterns also change when humans learn to associate arbitrary visual signals with already known motor skills.

Neural substrates in motor cortex may provide the basis for motor learning. Plasticity occurs between sites interconnected with internal, or horizontal, connections in motor cortex. Many of these horizontal connections exhibit short- and long-term synaptic plasticity. Blockade of motor cortical synaptic plasticity reduces behavioral manifestations of motor learning or motor cortex output shifts. The coupling of functional studies on motor cortex relationships with motor learning and the new findings on synaptic reorganization of motor cortex suggest the motor cortex does have an important role in skill acquisition.

Motor cortex also plays a role in higher-order motor functions, including cognition. Neurons in motor cortex have functional relationships with movement planning and appear to code for abstract movement features such as direction, movement goal, and target position. The activity of motor cortex can be uncoupled from observable movements or neuronal excitability occurring within motor portions of the spinal cord, such as during mental rehearsal of movements.

Primary Somatic Sensory Cortex

The primary somatic sensory cortex receives detailed sensory information about the skin, muscle, and joints that becomes segregated into anatomically distinguishable subdivisions that separately process sensation related to skin surface deformations or deep joint and muscle sensations. Each subzone has a complete "homuncular" representation of the body surface with little overlap among circuits processing somatic sensory input from nearby body parts. Somatic sensory cortex has a columnar organization, such that neurons aligned vertically process the same type of somatic sensory stimulus impinging on the same point of the body surface, converting raw sensory data into perceptions of stimulus velocity, texture, and form. Somatic sensory cortex relays locally processed information laterally to other body part representations within somatic sensory cortex, and to motor and association areas of the cerebral cortex.

The body representation in somatic sensory cortex exhibits plasticity. Nerve injury or pathological changes deprive cortical zones of crucial inputs; this can yield unresponsive zones, but more commonly causes expansion of neighboring body representations into the denervated cortical territory. Analogous reorganization occurs in relation to experience such as the repetition of sensory-based actions.

In summary, primary motor cortex and primary somatic sensory cortex have complete and complex representations of the body. These two areas represent the major cortical output and input structures for sensory motor integration. Motor and somatic sensory cortex do not function as simple purveyors of already processed motor commands (motor cortex) or of unprocessed somatic sensory inputs. They have key roles as higher-order information processing structures and participate in many aspects of sensory motor integration.

SUGGESTED READINGS

Jones, E. G. (2000). Cortical and subcortical contributions to activity-dependent plasticity in primate somatosensory cortex. *Annual Review of Neuroscience, 23,* 1–37.

Sanes, J. N., & Donoghue, J. P. (2000). Plasticity and primary motor cortex. *Annual Review of Neuroscience, 23,* 393–415.

Jerome N. Sanes
Brown Medical School

PRIMARY PREVENTION OF PSYCHOPATHOLOGY

Primary prevention involves efforts to reduce the future incidence of emotional disorders and mental conditions in populations of persons not yet affected. The efforts are proactive. Primary prevention sometimes is directed at high-risk groups, or at groups approaching high-risk situations or potential life crises. Programs in primary prevention may involve the reduction of organic factors contributing to psychopathology, efforts to reduce avoidable stress, the building of competencies and coping skills, the development of improved self-esteem, and the enhancement of support networks and groups.

The logic of investing in efforts at primary prevention is supported in several ways. For example, the incredible imbalance between the number of people suffering emotional distress and those with mental disorders makes it impossible for individual interventionists to reach those needing help, and this gap is impossible to bridge.

Most of the enormous improvement in the health and increasing longevity of members of our society has come about as a result of the successful application of the methods of primary prevention within the field of public health. Public health prevention methods involve "finding the noxious agent" and taking steps to eliminate or neutralize it, or "strengthening the host."

During the first enthusiasm for the application of public health methods in the field of mental disorder, it seemed just a matter of time until these "mental illnesses" could also be brought under control and eliminated. However, as time has passed, it is gradually becoming apparent that most of the so-called mental illnesses may not have a specific and unique cause.

A high level of stress-causing conditions (e.g., powerlessness, unemployment, sexism, marital disruption, loss of support systems) can cause any of several patterns of emotional disruption (e.g., depression, alcoholism, anxiety, hypertension). In brief, there is a nonspecific relation between causes and consequences.

If our purpose is to reduce the incidence of the different conditions or compulsive lifestyles we refer to as mental disorders, is there any way to think about organizing prevention efforts? The following formula may be helpful:

$$\text{Incidence} = \frac{\text{Organic factors} + \text{Stress}}{\text{Competence} + \text{Self-esteem} + \text{Support networks}}$$

To succeed in preventive efforts is to reduce the incidence of the various forms of emotional disturbance. There are several strategies for accomplishing that purpose. The first is to prevent, minimize, or reduce the number of organic factors. The more an organic factor can be reduced or eliminated, the smaller the resulting incidence will be. Specific examples are as follows:

1. Reduction of the amount of brain damage resulting from lead poisoning or from accidents reduces the resulting mental conditions.
2. Prevention of damaged genes from developing into damaged individuals (after amniocentesis, aborting a fetus with chromosomal abnormalities) prevents the birth of a mentally impaired or brain-damaged infant.
3. Provision of medication to reduce hypertension lowers the incidence of brain injury resulting from strokes.
4. Improvement of the circulation of blood to the brain reduces the rate of later cerebral arteriosclerosis.

A second strategy involves the reduction of stress. Here relationships become more complex. Stress takes many forms. Reducing stress requires changes in the physical and social environment. Environmental stress situations involve a whole complex of interacting variables. Some forms of social stress are a product of deeply ingrained cultural values and ways of life not easily susceptible to change. Stress may result from low self-esteem that becomes a kind of self-fulfilling prophecy. Women and members of ethnic minorities, who learn from earliest childhood that their sex or race is seen as inferior, grow up with lower self-esteem that may be exceedingly difficult to change. Preventive efforts take the form of public education, changes in the mass media, and the reshaping of pervasive value systems. Such efforts encounter the angry resistance of the power forces that get real benefit from the values being criticized.

An area of major research investigation in recent years has been the relationship between stressful life events and the onset of both physical illness and mental disturbance. Studies report correlations between severity of life stresses and the probability of the appearance of specific illnesses in the future. Statistically significant relationships have been found between the stresses of life change and diseases such as tuberculosis, heart attacks, accidents, leukemia, and diabetes. High life stress has been associated repeatedly with subsequent mental and emotional disturbances. Being part of a strong support network reduces the risk of exposure to stress.

The model described by the formula obviously has shortcomings. Often intervention results in changes in all areas. For example, training in a sport may involve regular practice with resulting improvement in physical coordination, bodily health, musculature, circulation, and a sense of physical well-being. At the same time, the subject may experience a reduction of stress as he or she burns up energy in physical activity; meanwhile, improvement in competence in performing the physical requirements of the sport may increase self-confidence and self-esteem. Thus improvement occurs at all levels.

Ultimately, many prevention efforts will require societal change through political action. For this reason, the struggle to redistribute power as a strategy for the prevention of psychopathology has only begun.

George W. Albee
University of South Florida

See also: **Psychotherapy; Self-help Groups**

PRIMARY, SECONDARY, AND TERTIARY GAINS AND SECONDARY LOSSES

Freud defined *primary gain* as a decrease in anxiety from a defensive operation which caused a symptom. *Secondary gain* was defined as interpersonal or social advantage attained by the patient because of the illness. The *Diagnostic and Statistical Manual of Mental Disorders* (*DSM-IV-R*) defined primary gain as the gain achieved from a conversion symptom which in turn keeps a conflict out of awareness. Secondary gain was defined as the gain achieved from the conversion symptom in avoiding a noxious activity or enabling support from the environment. Secondary gain is not a *DSM-III-R* diagnosis. Primary and secondary gains are thought to occur by unconscious mechanisms. The following is a list of possible secondary gains: gratification of dependency needs; gratification of revengeful strivings; fulfillment of need for attachment; desire of patient to prove entitlement for disability; fulfillment of need for oversolicitousness from others; avoidance of hazardous work conditions; fulfillment of need for sympathy and concern; permission to withdraw from unsatisfactory life role; need for sick role; financial rewards; acquisition of drugs; manipulation of spouse; maintenance of family status; maintenance of family love; domination of family; freedom from given socioemotional role; and contraception.

Tertiary gains are attained from a patient's illness by someone other than the patient. It is not known whether these occur at a conscious or unconscious level. The following is a list of possible tertiary gains: Collusion on the part of the significant other to focus on patient's somatic complaints; diversion of attention from existential issues (cancer/death); enjoyment of change in role for significant other; financial gain; sympathy from social network; decreased family tension; and resolution of marital difficulties.

It is not clear whether secondary gains are the same as reinforcers. It appears that operationally some are the same; the gain may be the reinforcer. Secondary gains, however, are a more unconscious motivation for the observed behaviors.

Abnormal illness-affirming states include the following *DSM-IV-R* diagnoses: somatoform disorders (Conversion Disorder, Hypochondriasis, Somatization Disorder, Pain Disorder); factitious disorders (including Munchausen Syndrome); and malingering. In all these diagnoses, secondary gain is thought to be responsible for the production of some or all of the patient's signs and symptoms.

Secondary losses may also result from a patient's disability. The following is a list of possible secondary losses: economic loss, loss of opportunity to relate to others through work, loss of family life, loss of recreational activities, loss of comfortable and clearly defined role, loss of respect and attention from those in helping roles, loss of community approval, social stigma of being chronically disabled, guilt over disability, negative sanctions from family, and loss of social support. Patients act in spite of these losses even though the secondary losses far outweigh the secondary gains. This problem with the economy of secondary gains and losses is a direct challenge to the integrity of the secondary gain concept.

Secondary gain is often incorrectly equated with malingering. The term has also been equated with financial rewards associated with disability, which in turn is equated with malingering. Suspicion of malingering usually interferes with treatment and development of empathy. Moreover, secondary gain issues are often used as an excuse for treatment failure. Treating professionals often ignore the concept of secondary loss and focus only on secondary gain. If all patients in a medical facility were examined for alleged secondary gains, most would be found to have one or more secondary gains; however, the identification of an apparent secondary gain does not necessarily mean that this gain has had an etiological or reinforcing effect on the illness.

David A. Fishbain
University of Miami

PRIMARY SOMATOSENSORY CORTEX

The somatosensory cortex was defined in earlier human studies as the cortical region the stimulation of which provoked subjective somatosensory experiences. It was defined in various other mammals as the cortical region where somatosensory-evoked potentials were recorded after stimulation of the periphery. The cortical areas involved in the somatosensory processing are distributed widely in the parietal lobe, the postcentral gyrus, posterior parietal regions, and lateral regions. They form a connected network with serial (hierarchical) and parallel cortico-cortical connections. Among them, the primary somatosensory cortex (or the first somatosensory cortex [SI]) is defined as the area where the shortest-latency, evoked potentials are recorded after stimulation of the periphery. It receives direct and strongest projections from the thalamic ventrobasal complex—specific relay nuclei mainly for the dorsal column-lemniscal system that conveys innocuous somatosensory signals from the periphery.

Anatomy

The SI of primates is composed of four different cytoarchitectonic areas of Brodmann: areas 3a, 3b, 1, and 2 in the postcentral gyrus. The thalamic ventrobasal complex projects mainly to areas 3a and 3b. Sensory signals from deep tissues—muscles or joints—project mainly to area 3a, while those from the superficial tissues—skin or intra-oral mucous membrane—project mainly to area 3b. Areas 1 and 2 receive fewer projections from the thalamic ventrobasal complex and instead receive cortico-cortical projections from areas 3a and 3b and some additional projections from the thalamic association nuclei. All four cytoarchitectonic subdivisions of SI have connections to the second somatosensory cortex (SII) in the lateral regions (see Jones, 1986; Burton & Sinclair, 1996).

Somatotopic Representation of the Body Surface

It is generally accepted that the sensory cortex is characterized by topological and orderly representation of the receptor sheet. In the primary somatosensory cortex of the primate, the oral cavity, face, hand, arm, trunk, leg, and foot are represented somatotopically along the lateral-medial axis of the postcentral gyrus. Penfield and Boldrey (1937) invented a homunculus to describe such an arrangement. The somatotopic representation of the body over the cortical surface was demonstrated in various other mammals by recording evoked potentials. The cortical tissue devoted to each body-part representation is not even. That part of the body which is exaggerated differs among animals. In primates, the cortical region devoted to the representation of the oral cavity, face, hand, or foot is much larger compared to that for the trunk or proximal limbs (see Burton & Sinclair, 1996).

Hierarchical Processing in the Finger Region

Modern microelectrode techniques to record single neuronal activity in awake animals enabled scientists to analyze detailed organization of the enlarged cortical finger representation in the monkey (Burton & Sinclair, 1996). In the finger region of area 3b in the monkey, functionally unique parts of fingers (i.e., tips, ventral glabrous surfaces, and dorsal surfaces) are represented separately, forming different subdivisions of area 3b. In areas 1 and 2, progressive interphalangeal or interdigital integration takes place along the rostro-caudal axis of the postcentral gyrus; thus, receptive fields of neurons in areas 1 and 2 become larger, covering more than one phalange of a finger, or more than one finger. The interdigital integration is more remarkable in the ulnar fingers than in the radial ones. There are unique types of neurons in areas 1 and 2 with selectivity to specific features of stimulus, such as the direction of a moving stimulus; the presence of an edge or rough surface; those that are activated better or solely by the monkey's active hand movements, including reaching; or those facilitated or inhibited by attention. Diversity in the receptive field of cortical neurons was pointed out also in conjunction with a cortical column (a perpendicular array of neurons). There are a number of additional observations in favor of serial hierarchical processing.

The integration proceeds to combine information from the bilateral sides in the higher stages of hierarchical processing: A substantial number of neurons with bilateral or ipsilateral receptive fields are found in the caudalmost part (areas 2 and 5) of the postcentral finger region (Iwamura, Iriki, & Tanaka, 1994). Bilateral integration is seen also in other body parts. The bilateral receptive fields are large and the most complex types found in this gyrus. The distribution of the bilateral receptive field neurons roughly corresponds to that of callosal connections in this gyrus.

Plastic Changes in the Representation of Fingers

After extensive training to use three fingers together, there emerged in area 3b of owl monkey neurons with multidigit receptive fields, which were never seen in untrained animals (Wang, Merzenich, Sameshima, & Jenkins, 1995). Blind persons who use three fingers together to read Braille frequently misperceive which of the fingers actually touches the text. In these subjects an expansion and dislocation of SI hand representation was found by magnetic source imaging technique (Sterr et al., 1998). The representation area of fingers measured by magnetic source imaging increased in the left hand in string players, possibly as the result of extensive training (Elbert, Pantev, Weinbruch, Rockstroh, & Taub, 1995).

Attributes of Tactile Perception Represented in Cortical Activity

Cortical activities representing spatio-temporal patterns of tactile skin stimulation such as flutter-vibration, motion, direction, length, velocity of tactile stimulus, surface texture, spatial form, and so on, have been studied (see Burton & Sinclair, 1996). DiCarlo, Johnson, and Hsiao (1998) found that 94% of area 3b neurons in the finger region contained a single central excitation, as well as regions of inhibition located on one or more sides of the excitatory center. It was thus indicated that area 3b neurons act as local spatio-temporal filters and may contribute to form and texture perception.

Cortical Representation of Pain

Single-cell recordings in the monkey established that nociceptive pathways project to areas 3b and 1 of the primary somatosensory cortex. Pain has a sensory component in addition to its strong emotional component, and is processed by multiple distributed cortical loci. The SI cortex is involved in the sensory-discriminative aspect of pain, especially stimulus localization, while intensity may be coded by multiple cortical areas (see Treede, Kenshalo, Gracely, & Jones, 1999).

REFERENCES

Burton, H., & Sinclair, R. (1996). Somatosensory cortex and tactile perceptions. In L. Kruger (Ed.), *Touch and pain* (pp. 105–177). London: Academic.

DiCarlo, J. J., Johnson, K. O., & Hsiao, S. S. (1998). Structure of receptive fields in area 3b of primary somatosensory cortex in the alert monkey. *Journal of Neuroscience, 18,* 2626–2645.

Elbert, T., Pantev, C., Wienbruch, C., Rockstroh, B., & Taub, E. (1995). Increased cortical representation of the fingers of the left hand in string players. *Science, 270,* 305–307.

Iwamura, Y., Iriki, A., & Tanaka, M. (1994). Bilateral hand representation in the postcentral somatosensory cortex. *Nature, 369,* 554–556.

Jones, E. G. (1986). Connectivity of the primate sensory-motor cortex. In E. G. Jones & A. Peters (Eds.), *Cerebral cortex, sensory-motor areas and aspects of cortical connectivity* (Vol. 5). New York: Plenum Press.

Penfield, W., & Boldrey, E. (1937). Somatic motor and sensory representation in the cerebral cortex of man as studied by electrical stimulation. *Brain, 60,* 389–443.

Sterr, A., Muller, M. M., Elbert, T., Rockstroh, B., Pantev, C., & Taub, E. (1998). Changed perceptions in Braille readers. *Nature, 391,* 134–135.

Treede, R.-D., Kenshalo, D. R., Gracely, R. H., & Jones, A. K. P. (1999). The cortical representation of pain. *Pain, 79,* 105–111.

Wang, X., Merzenich, M. M., Sameshima, K., & Jenkins, W. M. (1995). Remodelling of hand representation in adult cortex determined by timing of tactile stimulation. *Nature, 378,* 71–75.

Yoshiaki Iwamura
Kawasaki University of Medical Welfare, Japan

PRIMING

Priming is a long-term memory phenomenon that increases the efficiency of processing repeated stimuli. Most long-term memory tasks comprise three phases: (1) a study phase in which stimuli are encoded, (2) a retention interval in which an unrelated task is performed, and (3) a test phase in which memories of the encoded stimuli are retrieved. Retrieval can be measured either as a conscious recollection of the study-phase stimuli, or as a nonconscious change in processing speed, processing accuracy, or response bias accrued to the recently studied material. Retrieval tasks that require conscious and deliberate reconstruction of the study-phase experience are referred to as explicit (Schacter & Graf, 1986), direct (Richardson-Klavehn & Bjork, 1988), or declarative (Cohen & Squire, 1980). Retrieval tasks that require no reference to the study-phase experience are referred to as implicit, indirect, or procedural.

Priming memory is revealed on implicit tasks. In the test phase of a priming memory experiment, the subject is asked to perform a task that is ostensibly unrelated to the study-phase task, but in actuality, requires repeated processing of studied stimuli and new processing of unstudied stimuli. In some tasks, processing of the identical study-phase stimuli is required (identity or direct priming). In other tasks, processing of stimuli that are related to the study-phase stimuli is required (indirect priming). Priming memory is calculated as the difference in performance between repeated versus new stimuli, which reflects memory acquired in the study phase and retrieved in the test phase.

Priming is not limited to previously known items or well-known associations between items (e.g., *bird-stork*). Priming has been demonstrated using novel items such as nonsense pseudowords (e.g., *blurk*) (e.g., Bowers, 1994), or nonrepresentational line patterns and designs (e.g., Schacter, Cooper, & Delaney, 1990). Further, priming for new associations has been shown by presenting unrelated pairs of words together in a study phase (e.g., *table-pride, window-potato, mountain-pride*), and then comparing test-phase priming for identical pairs (*table-pride*) versus recombined pairs (*window-stamp*). People show greater priming for the identical than the recombined pairs, thereby demonstrating priming for a novel association between two words created by their random pairing at study (e.g., Graf & Schacter, 1985).

Priming is not a unitary memory phenomenon. Any given task invokes multiple cognitive mechanisms that drive multiple kinds of priming. For example, a functional dissociation between tasks that invoke primarily *perceptual* or *conceptual* processes in priming has been demonstrated in studies with young subjects (Blaxton, 1989). Perceptual priming tasks draw upon processes concerned with the visual, auditory, or tactual form of a target stimulus. These tasks yield priming that is maximal when stimuli are analyzed for perceptual features at study and at test, and diminished by study-test changes in perceptual features (e.g., auditory-to-visual modality and word-to-picture notation). Conceptual priming tasks draw upon processes concerned with the content or meaning of a target stimulus. These tasks yield priming that is maximal when stimuli are analyzed for conceptual features at study and test, and insensitive to study-test changes in perceptual features.

Neuropsychological and neuroimaging studies have begun to reveal the neural mechanisms supporting priming memory. Amnesic patients with focal bilateral damage to mesial-temporal and/or diencephalic structures have normal levels of priming memory for the very materials they cannot recall or recognize (Cermak, Blackford, O'Connor, & Bleich, 1988; Gabrieli et al., 1994; Graf, Squire, & Mandler, 1984; Warrington & Weiskrantz, 1968, 1970). Priming memory is also intact in patients with progressive damage to subcortical nuclei due to Parkinson's disease (without dementia; Bondi & Kaszniak, 1991) and Huntington's disease (Heindel, Salmon, Shults, Walicke, & Butters, 1989). Thus, the neural substrate supporting priming memory does not appear to include limbic, diencephalic, or subcortical circuits.

Studies of patients with Alzheimer's disease (AD) have suggested what neural substrates may underlie priming memory (Fleischman & Gabrieli, 1999). AD is characterized by degeneration of mesial-temporal structures, which, as in focal amnesia, results in profoundly impaired recall and recognition. Unlike focal amnesia, AD is additionally characterized by progressive and selective damage to association neocortices, which causes deficits in multiple cognitive domains as well as reduction or failure of some kinds of priming memory. These findings suggest that association neocortex may be the critical neural substrate underlying priming memory.

Some kinds of priming memory remain robust in AD, and the pattern of preservation and loss in priming parallels the regional distribution of neuropathological change that occurs in the disease. Posterior cortical regions are relatively preserved early in the course of AD (e.g., Damasio, Van Hoesen, & Hyman, 1990), and so is perceptual priming (e.g., Fleischman et al., 1995; Park et al., 1998; Postle, Corkin, & Growdon, 1996), whereas anterior cortical regions are damaged in AD (e.g., Damasio, Van Hoesen, & Hyman, 1990), and conceptual priming is impaired (e.g., Monti et al., 1996; Salmon, Shimamura, Butters, & Smith, 1988). These AD findings converge with findings from neuroimaging activation studies (Blaxton et al., 1996; Buckner et al., 1995; Schacter, Alpert, Savage, Rauch, & Albert, 1996; Squire et al., 1992) and focal lesion studies (Fleischman et al., 1995; Gabrieli, Fleischman, Keane, Reminger, & Morrell, 1995; Keane, Gabrieli, Mapstone, Johnson, & Corkin, 1995) that have demonstrated a posterior cortical locus for visual perceptual priming and have implicated regions of left frontal cortex (Gabrieli, Desmond, Demb, & Wagner, 1996) and left frontal and temporal cortex (Blaxton et al., 1996) in conceptual priming.

Priming as a long-term memory phenomenon independent of conscious forms of long-term memory is a relatively recent discovery. Initial studies date back 25 to 30 years, but the most intensive research in the area has been done only in the past 10 years.

REFERENCES

Blaxton, T. A. (1989). Investigating dissociations among memory measures: Support for a transfer-appropriate processing framework. *Journal of Experimental Psychology: Learning, Memory, and Cognition, 15,* 657–668.

Blaxton, T. A., Bookheimer, S. Y., Zeffiro, T. A., Figlozzi, C. M., Gaillard, W. D., & Theodore, W. H. (1996). Functional mapping of human memory using PET: Comparisons of conceptual and perceptual tasks. *Canadian Journal of Experimental Psychology, 50,* 42–54.

Bondi, M. W., & Kaszniak, A. W. (1991). Implicit and explicit memory in Alzheimer's disease and Parkinson's disease. *Journal of Clinical and Experimental Neuropsychology, 13,* 339–358.

Bowers, J. S. (1994). Does implicit memory extend to legal and illegal nonwords? *Journal of Experimental Psychology: Learning, Memory, and Cognition, 16,* 404–416.

Buckner, R. L., Petersen, S. E., Ojemann, J. G., Miezen, F. M., Squire, L. R., & Raichle, M. E. (1995). Functional anatomical studies of explicit and implicit memory retrieval tasks. *The Journal of Neuroscience, 15,* 12–29.

Cermak, L. S., Blackford, S. P., O'Connor, M., & Bleich, R. B. (1988). The implicit memory ability of a patient with amnesia due to encephalitis. *Brain and Language, 7,* 145–156.

Cohen, N. J., & Squire, L. R. (1980). Preserved learning and retention of pattern-analyzing skill in amnesia: Dissociation of knowing how and knowing that. *Science, 21,* 207–210.

Damasio, A. R., Van Hoesen, G. W., & Hyman, B. T. (1990). Reflections on the selectivity of neuropathological changes in Alzheimer's disease. In M. F. Schwartz (Ed.), *Modular deficits in Alzheimer-type dementia* (pp. 83–99). Cambridge, MA: MIT Press.

Fleischman, D. A., & Gabrieli, J. D. E. (1999). Long-term memory in Alzheimer's disease. *Current Opinion in Neurobiology, 9*(2), 240–244.

Fleischman, D. A., Gabrieli, J. D. E., Reminger, S. L., Rinaldi, J. A., Morrell, F., & Wilson, R. S. (1995). Conceptual priming in perceptual identification for patients with Alzheimer's disease and a patient with right occipital lobectomy. *Neuropsychology, 9,* 187–197.

Gabrieli, J. D. E., Desmond, J. E., Demb, J. B., & Wagner, A. D. (1996). Functional magnetic resonance imaging of semantic memory processes in the frontal lobes. *Psychological Science, 7,* 278–283.

Gabrieli, J. D. E., Fleischman, D. A., Keane, M. M., Reminger, S., & Morrell, F. (1995). Double dissociation between memory systems underlying explicit and implicit memory in the human brain. *Psychological Science, 6,* 76–82.

Gabrieli, J. D. E., Keane, M. M., Stanger, B. Z., Kjelgaard, K. S., Corkin, S., & Growdon, J. H. (1994). Dissociations among structural-perceptual, lexical-semantic, and event-fact memory systems in Alzheimer, amnesic and normal subjects. *Cortex, 30,* 75–103.

Graf, P., & Schacter, D. L. (1985). Implicit and explicit memory for new associations in normal and amnesic patients. *Journal of Experimental Psychology: Learning, Memory and Cognition, 11,* 501–518.

Graf, P., Squire, L. R., & Mandler, G. (1984). The information that amnesic patients do not forget. *Journal of Experimental Psychology: Learning, Memory, and Cognition, 10,* 164–178.

Heindel, W. C., Salmon, D. P., Shults, C. W., Walicke, P. A., & Butters, N. (1989). Neuropsychological evidence for multiple implicit memory systems: A comparison of Alzheimer's, Huntington's and Parkinson's disease patients. *The Journal of Neuroscience, 9,* 582–587.

Keane, M. M., Gabrieli, J. D. E., Mapstone, H. C., Johnson, K. A., & Corkin, S. (1995). Double dissociation of memory capacities after bilateral occipital-lobe or medial temporal-lobe lesions. *Brain, 118,* 1129–1148.

Monti, L. A., Gabrieli, J. D. E., Reminger, S. L., Rinaldi, J. A., Wilson, R. S., & Fleischman, D. A. (1996). Differential effects of aging and Alzheimer's disease on conceptual implicit and explicit memory. *Neuropsychology, 10,* 101–112.

Park, S. M., Gabrieli, J. D. E., Reminger, S. L., Monti, L. A., Fleischman, D. A., Wilson, R. S., et al. (1998). Preserved priming across study-test picture transformations in patients with Alzheimer's disease. *Neuropsychology, 12,* 340–352.

Postle, B. R., Corkin, S., & Growdon, J. H. (1996). Intact implicit memory for novel patterns in Alzheimer's disease. *Learning and Memory, 3,* 305–312.

Richardson-Klavehn, A., & Bjork, R. A. (1988). Measures of memory. *Annual Review of Psychology, 39,* 475–543.

Roediger, H. L., & McDermott, K. B. (1993). Implicit memory in normal human subjects. In H. Spinnler & F. Boller (Eds.),

Handbook of neuropsychology (Vol. 8, pp. 63–131). Amsterdam: Elsevier.

Salmon, D. P., Shimamura, A. P., Butters, N., & Smith, S. (1988). Lexical and semantic priming deficits in patients with Alzheimer's disease. *Journal of Clinical and Experimental Neuropsychology, 10,* 477–494.

Schacter, D. L., Alpert, N. M., Savage, C. R., Rauch, S. L., & Albert, M. S. (1996). Conscious recollection and the human hippocampal formation: Evidence from positron emission tomography. *Proceedings of the National Academy of Sciences of the United States of America, 93,* 321–325.

Schacter, D. L., Cooper, L. A., & Delaney, S. M. (1990). Implicit memory for unfamiliar objects depends on access to structural descriptions. *Journal of Experimental Psychology: General, 119,* 5–24.

Schacter, D. L., & Graf, P. (1986). Preserved learning in amnesic patients: Perspectives from research on direct priming. *Journal of Clinical and Experimental Neuropsychology, 8,* 727–743.

Squire, L. R., Ojemann, J. G., Miezen, F. N., Petersen, S. E., Videen, T. O., & Raichle, M. E. (1992). Activation of the hippocampus in normal humans: A functional anatomical study of memory. *Proceedings of the National Academy of Sciences of the United States of America, 89,* 1837–1841.

Warrington, E. K., & Weiskrantz, L. (1968). New method of testing long-term retention with special reference to amnesic patients. *Nature, 217,* 972–974.

Warrington, E. K., & Weiskrantz, L. (1970). The amnesic syndrome: Consolidation or retrieval? *Nature, 228,* 628–630.

Debra A. Fleischman
Rush University Medical Center

See also: Declarative Memory

PROBABILITY

Probability theory is important to psychology because it is the foundation upon which statistics is based, and statistics are the tools for conducting empirical research. The basic notions of chance and probability have a very long history. Gambling, the throwing of dice, and randomization procedures such as the drawing of lots are very ancient, if not prehistoric. While these concepts were vague by modern standards, it is surprising that even the simplest sort of probability calculus was not invented until relatively recent times. Why this did not take place much earlier is a matter of some mystery and controversy.

Systematic work leading to a formal appreciation of probability did not begin until around 1650, when the idea of relative frequencies and the likelihood of particular events based on gathered data began to take hold. The primary motivation for the study of probability at this time (besides gaming) was the establishment of actuarial tables based on local death records, initially compiled to keep track of the progress of the plague afflicting London late in the sixteenth century. In a sense, the origin of modern statistics and probability theory can be seen as a result of the plague, an idea that undoubtedly resonates with the feelings of many students beginning the study of statistics and probability!

Graunt (1620–1674) was the first to organize mortality records so as to make probabilistic inferences based on actual proportions and relative frequencies of events. For example, he argued in reasonably modern terms that one need not fear dying insane ("a Lunatick in Bedlam") because the odds against it were quite high (about 1500 to 1). About the same time, the analysis of "games of chance" provided the basis for further development of probability theory in the work of Pascal (1623–1662), Fermat (1601–1665), Huygens (1629–1695), and Bernoulli (1654–1705). This work saw the first development of a true mathematical foundation or theory of probability.

Early in the eighteenth century work on the binomial distribution was begun by Bernoulli and continued later by de Moivre (1667–1754). Bernoulli also developed the theorem that eventually became known as the "Law of Large Numbers," probably one of the most important events in the development of probability theory as it relates to statistical testing. The work of Laplace (1749–1827), a French astronomer and mathematician, was also significant. His two main treatises on the theory of probability and the "laws of chance," published in 1812 and 1814, provided the foundation upon which probability theory is based. This work led eventually to the development of the method of least squares, the law of errors, and the normal distribution by Laplace, Gauss (1777–1855), and others early in the nineteenth century.

One of the first practical applications of this work was in astronomy. The general problem was the necessity of fitting observations to theoretical distributions so as to be able to reject discrepant observations, not unlike many modern applications in the behavioral sciences. When astronomers became concerned with errors of measurement early in the nineteenth century they eagerly seized upon the work of Gauss. The oldest of the "exact" sciences, it is perhaps ironic that astronomy was the first to systematically apply the principles of probability. Particularly interested in the work of Gauss was the Prussian astronomer Bessel (1784–1846), who in 1818 devised the concept of the "probable error," a precursor of the standard error and comparable, in modern terms, to a 50% confidence interval. Thus many of the ingredients necessary for the development of statistical tests and statistical inference—probabilistic inference, distribution theory, methods of least squares, and the probable error—were all present before 1850.

Extension of the use of the probable error from astronomy to the biological and social sciences was first proposed by the Belgian astronomer and mathematician Quetelet (1796–1874). Before Quetelet, it is fair to say that the word *statistics* retained its original meaning, referring primarily to descriptive data about the state, or "political arithmetic." Quetelet was the first to envision the utility of combining statistics with probability theory to develop a social science based on the Law of Large Numbers. The most famous example of Quetelet's work was his description of the frequency distribution of the heights of 100,000 French army conscripts. He noted that the distribution closely followed the normal curve, and he computed its probable error. Using this information, Quetelet calculated the number of conscripts expected in each height category and compared these to the observed numbers. He found the number of conscripts in the lowest category, just below the minimum height requirement, considerably exceeded the expected number, while the frequency in the category just above the cutoff was deficient by the same amount. He ascribed the discrepancy to fraud, asserting that such an occurrence could not have arisen through measurement error.

Quetelet's work greatly influenced the subsequent work of Galton (1822–1911), and through Galton, had great impact on the founders of modern statistics early in the twentieth century, including Karl Pearson (1857–1936) and Fisher (1890–1962). The influence of Quetelet's work was substantial because it was the first to present the principles of probability in terms accessible to nonmathematicians and to suggest specific applications for probability theory beyond the evaluation of measurement error in the physical sciences. Quetelet expounded the view that social phenomena were subject to quantitative laws just as physical phenomena obeyed the laws of Newton and Kepler. He believed that the fusion of statistics and probability could reveal the underlying laws of nature governing human behavior, leading ultimately to his concept of *l'homme moyen,* the average man. Such a view nicely fit the mechanistic philosophy that resulted from the scientific revolution of the seventeenth century, the legacy of Newton and Descartes. Ironically, this philosophy was soon demolished in the physical sciences by the quantum revolution, but it became the dominant force in the developing science of human behavior and remains so today.

Joseph S. Rossi
University of Rhode Island

***See also:* Parametric Statistical Tests**

PROPAGANDA

Propaganda is the advancement of a position or view in a manner that attempts to persuade rather than to present a balanced overview. Propaganda often carries the connotation of a government activity, although persuasive communications are, of course, regularly used in the private or voluntary sector.

In marketing products or services, public relations and advertising activities represent a form of propaganda, since they are not necessarily interested in communicating the whole truth, but in selective communication of information for the purpose of encouraging sales.

In the United States, one popular use of the concept of propaganda is to describe persuasive communications with which we are not in sympathy. If someone else does it, it might be described as propaganda, with negative connotations. If we do it, the communication will be designated in some other way. Thus, the official vehicle for American overseas propaganda in World War I was called the Committee on Public Information.

Propaganda, seeking to effect attitude change, can be contrasted with education, which seeks to communicate knowledge. The study of propaganda can be regarded as a branch of several larger fields, such as mass communication, mass persuasion, attitude change, and psychological warfare.

Propaganda use increases in wartime, as one indirect method of fighting the war. In a war situation, "white" propaganda identifies its source, "gray" propaganda gives no source, and "black" propaganda attributes the material to a source other than the one that actually produced it. The first systemic study of wartime propaganda was conducted after World War I by H. D. Lasswell. He studied each side's success in achieving four objectives: demoralizing the enemy, mobilizing hatred against the enemy, maintaining the friendship of neutrals, and possibly obtaining their cooperation. The British were probably most successful in associating themselves with humanitarian war aims. Lasswell demonstrated that it is more productive to analyze propaganda in terms of content categories than in terms of presumed effects because of difficulty in measuring effects.

In military propaganda, which seeks to subvert the morale of an enemy, the target is the potential waverer, who is still fighting but has lost any enthusiasm. To expect such persons to surrender on the basis of propaganda is unrealistic, but they might be encouraged to permit themselves to be captured, under appropriate circumstances.

Between World Wars I and II in the totalitarian countries, propaganda was used quite openly and nonevaluatively as a descriptor, so that Josef Goebbels in Hitler's Germany was proudly identified as the head of the country's Propaganda Bureau. America has generally described its agencies that do comparable work as engaging in "information" or "communication" activities. In the United States, propaganda has carried negative loading especially since the 1930s, when it was identified with the efforts of Germany and Italy to obtain favorable views of their new political organizations. Indeed, for many years after World War II, the content of American propaganda communication overseas was not available in this country, for fear that it could be used for domestic political purposes.

The Institute for Propaganda Analysis was established before World War II in New York City by a number of academic scholars for the purpose of educating the general public in the techniques employed by the fascist countries in their proselytizing activities. Systemic content analysis was used by the Institute in its efforts to inform the American public about the menace of fascist propaganda. In addition, the Institute defined 11 propaganda techniques: selecting the issue, stacking the cards, simplification, name calling, glittering generalities, transfer, testimonials, plain folks, bandwagon, hot potato, and stalling. The scholars of the Institute believed that by identifying the mechanisms of foreign propaganda, its ability to influence Americans would be undercut.

During World War II, systematic content analyses were conducted of the writings and other communications of native fascist groups and of German Nazi output. A comparison of these two kinds of content, admitted as evidence in court, contributed to the conviction of some native fascist groups in federal trials for the crime of sedition. Other publications and radio stations were cleared of the charge, using similar content analysis techniques as evidence.

The intensive American studies of propaganda approaches during World War II, the results of which were used to indoctrinate our military personnel with film series like "Why We Fight," led to major subsequent research programs in psychology departments at Yale and other universities. These programs conducted basic research on the formation and modification of attitudes and the role of personality characteristics, such as influenceability.

It is possible that influenceability or persuasibility by propaganda and other persuasive communications is a general trait, but research on the subject has had only moderate success in identifying its correlates. Propaganda is most likely to be effective with people who are already in favor of the views it is promoting. If they are not in favor, they may not expose themselves to it. If they are not in favor, but are exposed to it, they may not comprehend the message because they fail to identify with it or because they change its frame of reference.

One avenue in the study of propaganda involves the analysis of fear appeals in persuasion. Dependent variables studied include such issues as drivers' intention to use seat belts and parents' willingness to obtain appropriate inoculations against disease for their children. Although the results are not consistent, there is an overall tendency in producing attitude change from propaganda for a positive relationship between the intensity of fear arousal and the amount of attitude change that subsequently occurs.

In the study of political propaganda, it may be useful to measure the amount and kinds of emotionalization, often by counting the incidence of emotionalized words or concepts. Another approach involves measuring the different kinds of sources for assertions and claims, in terms of the prestige and social status of the persons to whom a viewpoint is attributed.

The rapid expansion of the Internet at the end of the twentieth century led to considerable fear that it would become a significant vehicle for the efficient spreading of various kinds of undesirable or antisocial propaganda, especially among young people. This seems unlikely for at least three reasons: (1) The Internet's system of routers minimizes communicators' secrecy and facilitates tracking message sources; (2) It is relatively easy to put up a new web site to contradict another site's messages; and (3) Internet clutter interferes with messages being received and absorbed.

In addition, many young people who grew up with the Internet were familiar with the revelations generated by Watergate, the Vietnam War, the Cold War, and the savings and loan and corporate accounting scandals around the turn of the century. These revelations help to reinforce cynicism about the integrity and motivations of some of the major institutions that disseminate propaganda. Even without the Internet, however, propaganda will continue to be important as long as there is competition between nations, political parties, and marketers, and in other adversarial situations in which communication is a tool.

Charles Winick
R. L. Norman
City University of New York

PROSOCIAL BEHAVIOR

Prosocial behavior has traditionally been defined as responses that have no obvious benefits for the responder, but are beneficial to the recipient (i.e., actions that benefit another person without any expected reward for the self). A significant number of studies have found evidence of concern for others beginning in infancy and developing throughout childhood and adolescence. Girls have generally been thought to be (or capable of being) more prosocial than boys; however, the majority of research has not found appreciable gender differences in prosocial behavior. Both internal and external mechanisms have been proposed as determinants of prosocial behavior.

The family and caretaker milieu have been suggested to be critical contributors as models and sources of specific standards of prosocial behavior. Parents and caretakers of children who exhibit prosocial behavior are typically prosocial in their own actions and seek to promote such actions. For example, they point out models of prosocial behavior and direct children toward stories, television programs, movies, and videos that illustrate cooperation, sharing, and empathy and encourage generosity, helpfulness, and sympathy. These significant adults also employ inductive disciplinary methods as opposed to power-assertive practices. Interactions with siblings and peers also provide opportunities for trying out caring behavior and learning to see others' points of view, as well as offering models and reinforcers of prosocial behavior.

From middle childhood through adolescence, cognitive development relative to perspective taking—the capacity to imagine what others may be thinking and feeling—increases the potential to act prosocially. While perspective taking can vary greatly among children and adolescents of the same age, cognitive maturity as well as interactions with adults and peers who explain their viewpoints and emotional experiences encourage noticing another's perspective. Interactions that provide practice in perspective taking have been shown to increase empathy and promote prosocial responding.

Motives for prosocial behavior change with the development of more mature moral reasoning. Young children tend to exhibit egocentric motives, such as the desire to earn praise and avoid disapproval. They weigh the benefits and costs to themselves and consider how they would like others to behave towards them. As moral reasoning develops, children become less self-centered and adopt societal standards of "being good" which eventually become internalized in the form of higher-level principles and values.

As individuals mature, they understand more, are better able to grasp the consequences of their behavior, and learn to accept and act upon general principles of morality. Cultures vary in the extent to which they foster prosocial behavior. Traditional collectivist cultures tend to inculcate prosocial values more than cultures that emphasize competition and individual achievement. External emphases have focused on situational determinants of prosocial behavior. Two major theoretical approaches for understanding prosocial behavior have stressed the importance of the situation or setting: a reinforcement explanation of why persons sometimes help others, and a cognitive analysis of the manner in which perceptions and judgments can influence behavior. From the point of view of some learning theorists, prosocial responses occur because they have been rewarded in the past. In addition to direct experiences, individuals are also influenced by their expectations about future rewards or punishments.

Among factors found to affect prosocial behavior are external determinants such as the presence of bystanders. The presence of more than one bystander in an emergency situation tends to inhibit the responses of each person present. This bystander inhibition appears to be a function of individuals' uncertainty about the situation. People respond less when circumstances are ambiguous, when they are unfamiliar with the surroundings, and when they are unsure of the behavioral norms of a particular setting.

Internal factors found to affect prosocial behavior include such variables as the mood a person is experiencing. Helping behavior increases when individuals are in a positive mood. Prosocial behaviors enhance and prolong an already positive mood; positive moods promote thinking about the rewarding nature of prosocial behavior. While prosocial behavior can offer a means to escape a negative mood, negative moods tend to encourage greater self-focus and thus decreased attention to others. Prosocial behavior also varies as a function of the relative balance of perceived costs and perceived rewards.

SUGGESTED READING

Eisenberg, N., & Fabes, R. A. (1998). Prosocial development. In N. Eisenberg (Ed.), *Handbook of child psychology: Vol. 3. Social, emotional, and personality development* (5th ed., pp. 701–778). New York: Wiley.

Eisenberg, N., Zhou, Q., & Koller, S. (2001). Brazilian adolescents' prosocial moral judgment and behavior: Relations to sympathy, perspective-taking, gender-role orientation, and demographic characteristics. *Child Development, 72,* 518–534.

Singer, J. L., & Singer, D. G. (1998). "Barney and Friends" as entertainment and education: Evaluating the quality and effectiveness of a television series for preschool children. In J. K. Asamen & G. L. Berry (Eds.), *Research paradigms, television, and social behavior* (pp. 305–367). Thousand Oaks, CA: Sage.

Charles H. Huber

See also: **Bystander Involvement; Modeling; Moral Development**

PSEUDODEMENTIA

The American Psychiatric Association's *Diagnostic and Statistical Manual of Mental Disorders,* fourth edition (*DSM-IV*) describes dementia as an organic mental syndrome characterized by global impairment in memory severe enough to interfere with the ability to work or severe enough to interfere with the ability to carry out social activities. Memory loss in dementia can be associated with faulty judgment, a tendency to avoid new tasks, and problems with impulse control. Friends and family may also note personality changes. The *DSM-IV* generally assumes that dementia has an underlying organic cause.

For dementia to be diagnosed, there must be evidence of impairment in short-term as well as long-term memory. In addition, one of the following must be present: (1) impairment in abstract thinking as noted, for example, by impaired performance in such tasks as defining words and concepts and finding similarities and differences in related words; (2) impaired judgment; (3) other impairments of higher cortical functioning, which can include problems in carrying out language or motor functions; or (4) changes in personality.

If no findings point to an organic basis for dementia, the manual advises that an organic cause can still be assumed if no other factors can be found as causative agents. *Pseudodementia* refers to nonorganic factors that can account for symptoms of dementia. Initially, this condition was named depressive pseudodementia under the assumption that depression will cause cognitive symptoms, including memory impairments. Andrew A. Swihart and Francis J. Pirozzolo (1988) pointed out that pseudodementia as a diagnostic category is not clearly defined, explaining that characteristic features of pseudodementia include reversibility of memory and other intellectual impairments once the nonorganic disorder has been accurately diagnosed and treated. In contrast, dementia is not reversible and is usually progressive even though there may be long, plateaulike periods.

Most often, pseudodementia occurs in individuals over the age of 50, although it can occur at any age. Asenath LaRue, Connie Dessonville, and Lissy F. Jarvik (1985) noted that 30% of individuals diagnosed with pseudodementia may be incorrectly classified. Some individuals tend to improve without treatment, whereas others respond to treatment for depression. Although it is often difficult to apply clinical criteria to differentiate between demented and depressed individuals, there have been a number of attempts to do so. Memory loss for recent events is about the same as for distant events (demented patients often have greater memory loss for recent events). Pseudodemented patients' emotional reactions (coping, affective state, concern about disability, and general complaints) tend to be emphasized in contrast to demented patients, and previous psychological problems are more frequently reported, though the ability to concentrate may be relatively intact. Overall, performance on neuropsychological assessment tasks may be more variable, with a greater likelihood of "don't know" answers as opposed to "near misses." Most authorities agree that pseudodementia is especially difficult to diagnose. Furthermore, this diagnosis has not been demonstrated to be conclusive and is often based more on an overall pattern of diagnostic signs and the overall clinical history of the patient other than on specifically pertinent symptom constellations.

The previously cited authors (LaRue, Dessonville, & Jarvik, 1985) suggested that pseudodementia represents a consciousness-raising diagnosis that encourages health service providers to be cautious in making a diagnosis of dementia, because this often results in termination of active treatment attempts. Andrew Swihart and Francis J. Pirozzolo (1988) pointed out that just because dementia is eventually irreversible, efforts at treating demented patients should not cease.

Steven Zarit and Judy Zarit (1998) discuss pseudodementia under the rubric of the association of dementia and depression. They, along with other authorities, suggest that it is not accurate to assume that pseudodementia is reversible, though it is always important to evaluate potential reversible elements. Sergio Starkstein and Robert Robinson (1993) emphasize the impact of depression on cognitive functioning and go on to speculate that perhaps there is a different mechanism operating for patients with left-side brain lesions as opposed to right-side lesions. They found that patients with right hemisphere lesions with depression do not show the same cognitive impairments as do patients with left hemisphere lesions.

There is a lack of consensus for the diagnosis of pseudodementia. Carl Salzman and Janice Gutfreund (1986) argue that pseudodementia is neither pseudo nor dementia. They insist that it is a genuine impairment of memory secondary to depression without impairment of other mental processes. They believe it is helpful to differentiate patients both on the basis of mood and cognitive functions as well as on the basis of age. They use a four-category descriptive system, starting with the young-old (under the age of 80) who are mildly to moderately depressed. Then come the young-old who are severely depressed, followed by the old (older than 80 yrs.) who are mildly to moderately depressed: this is followed by the old who are severely depressed. These authors contend that the assessment of memory loss as a function of depression is relatively easy for the first group and increasingly difficult for the other three groups. In their opinion, the over-80 and severely depressed group may not be amenable to accurate assessment.

Muriel Lezak (1995) notes that the assumption underlying the diagnosis of pseudodementia is that the patient is neurologically sound. However, she points out that individuals with and without organic diseases have been given this diagnosis and that the pseudodementia diagnosis is often given when depressive symptoms are strongly noted and the diagnosis of primary dementia is not warranted.

The importance of distinguishing between depression and dementia in the elderly is vital. Very often, physicians will prescribe antidepressant medications if they suspect that a patient may be depressed. Although this may be helpful for younger patients, it may be less helpful for older patients, because antidepressant medications may be toxic for the elderly and, almost paradoxically, the chemical nature of some antidepressant drugs may actually produce memory impairment. Every effort should be made to differentiate dementia from pseudodementia, recognizing that neither dementia nor pseudodementia is a clearly defined category and that the assessment of pseudodementia is fraught with great difficulties, especially for those over 80 who are severely depressed.

REFERENCES

LaRue, A., Dessonville, C., & Jarvik, L. F. (1985). Aging and mental disorders. In J. Birren & K. W. Schaie (Eds.), *Handbook of the psychology of aging*. New York: Van Nostrand Reinhold.

Lezak, M. D. (1995). *Neuropsychological assessment* (3rd ed.). New York: Oxford University Press.

Salzman, C., & Gutfreund, J. (1986). Clinical techniques and research strategies for studying depression and memory. In L. Poon (Ed.), *Handbook for clinical memory assessment of older adults*. Washington, DC: American Psychological Association.

Starkstein, S. E., & Robinson, R. G. (1993). *Depression in neurologic disease*. Baltimore: Johns Hopkins University Press.

Swihart, A., & Pirozzolo, F. (1988). The neuropsychology of aging and dementia: Clinical issues. In H. A. Whitaker (Ed.), *Neuropsychology studies of nonfocal brain damage: Dementia trauma* (pp. 1–60). New York: Springer-Verlag.

Zarit, S. H., & Zarit, J. M. (1998). *Mental disorders in older adults: Fundamentals of assessment and treatment.* New York: Guilford Press.

Norman Abeles
Michigan State University

See also: **Depression; Late-life Forgetting**

PSI CHI

Psi Chi, the National Honor Society in Psychology, provides academic recognition to outstanding students interested in psychology. In its 73 years of existence it has also become an important source of opportunities for the intellectual, ethical, and social responsibility development of psychology students as it seeks to promote the highest ideals of the science and profession of psychology. Psi Chi is the oldest student organization in psychology still in existence and has the largest membership of any psychology-related organization in the world. Since its inception, Psi Chi has inducted over 420,000 members. It was the first organizational affiliate of the American Psychological Association (APA).

At both the local and national levels, Psi Chi seeks to enhance excellence in psychology. Membership is open to undergraduate and graduate students for whom psychology is a primary interest and who meet or exceed the minimum qualifications for membership (e.g., hours in psychology, grade point average, class rank). Individual membership is for life. Psi Chi is an affiliate of both the APA and the American Psychological Society and is also a member of the Association of College Honor Societies. It undertakes cooperative and mutually beneficial programming with Psi Beta, the National Honor Society for Community and Junior colleges.

Organization

The association has local chapters at over 1,000 U.S. higher education institutions, varying in size from small liberal arts colleges to large state universities. A council of elected members functions as a governing body, making decisions, setting policy, and facilitating the ongoing operation of the organization with the approval of the local chapters. National Council members consist of the president, past president, and president-elect; six vice-presidents representing geographical regions (Eastern, Midwestern, Rocky Mountain, Southeastern, Southwestern, and Western); and the executive officer. Day-to-day operations of administration, publication, promotion, record keeping, and so forth occur at the National Headquarters in Chattanooga, Tennessee, under the guidance of the executive officer.

Local chapters are organized and run by students with the help of faculty advisors. Officers are elected from the membership. Within the guidelines of the national organization, officers and members are responsible for recruiting and inducting new members, as well as planning and executing educational and social meetings and programs.

History

The idea for a national organization for students in psychology arose in a conversation between Frederick Lewis and Edwin Newman at the University of Kansas in 1927. A committee to study its feasibility was formed at a psychology meeting in May 1928, and additional work was undertaken at the APA convention in 1928. A constitution was written and approved at the first national meeting of the organization. This was held in conjunction with the Ninth International Congress of Psychology at Yale University, September 4, 1929. The organization began under another name but became officially known as Psi Chi in 1930. There were 22 charter chapters of the organization. In 1930 a newsletter was initiated, and the first *Psi Chi Handbook* appeared in 1932.

Issues confronted early on by Psi Chi included appropriate activities for the organization, who should be admitted to membership—with one exception the early chapters were all from larger colleges and universities—and the question of honorary members. During World War II national meetings were not held, but the postwar years saw considerable growth in the number of chapters and members. In addition to change associated with growth, the 1950s saw the first Psi Chi student research award (1950), the formal affiliation of Psi Chi with APA (1958), and the initiation of Psi Chi–sponsored speakers at the annual APA meeting (1959). This program has featured many distinguished scholars including, for example, E. G. Boring, Otto Klineberg, Jerome Bruner, Rollo May, Neal Miller, Carl Rogers, and B. F. Skinner. More recently, changes in the organization have involved the addition of several awards and grants, changes in the structure of the National Council, and the designation and affirmation of Psi Chi as an honor society rather than a professional society. Over the years Psi Chi has enjoyed and benefited from strong leadership from the National Council, the National Office, and local chapters. Undoubtedly the most notable leadership contributions were those of Ruth H. Cousins, who from 1958 to 1991—during most of which she served as executive director—provided tireless and inspired leadership that shaped the identity and efficiency of the modern Psi Chi organization.

Functioning

Local chapters engage in a wide variety of activities addressing the academic, social, and service needs of the membership. Invited speakers; student recognition of excellence in teaching; sessions on applying to graduate school; research fairs; student-faculty social gatherings; volunteering at mental health, childcare, medical, and charitable facilities; group research projects; university and collegiate service activities; field trips; and tutoring services are just a few examples of the many varied activities undertaken by local chapters. Individually, these activities afford opportunities for incidental and direct learning, professional exploration, recognition of accomplishments, good-natured fellowship, and the exercise of leadership. Collectively, these activities augment and enrich the curricular experiences of students in psychology.

The national organization sponsors student paper and poster sessions at regional and national meetings and provides certificate recognition of outstanding student scholarship, as well as supporting student research more generally. For example, it now provides monetary support for undergraduate research conferences. It provides research awards for undergraduate and graduate students, research grants for students and faculty, and recognition awards for outstanding chapters and faculty advisors. Currently, Psi Chi provides $180,000 annually through its grants and awards programs. Psi Chi publishes *Eye on Psi Chi,* a quarterly magazine featuring articles of interest to psychology students and faculty. Issues such as preparing for graduate school, career planning, and increasing the vitality of Psi Chi chapters, as well as information regarding meetings and Psi Chi awards and grant programs are routinely presented. Finally, the organization publishes the *Psi Chi Journal of Undergraduate Research,* which presents original empirical research primarily designed, conducted, and written by undergraduate members.

Warren H. Jones
University of Tennessee

PSYCHOANALYTIC STAGES

Psychoanalytic stages, or psychosexual stages, are stages of psychosexual development postulated by Sigmund Freud to account for personality development. Based on the assumption that early childhood experiences significantly influence adult personality, social experiences at each stage presumably leave some permanent residue in the form of attitudes, traits, and values acquired at that stage. Further, it is assumed that a certain amount of sexual energy (libido) is present at birth and thereafter progresses through these psychosexual stages. More specifically, Freud theorized that the central theme running through personality development is the progression of the sex instinct through four universal stages—oral, anal, phallic, and genital. A period of *latency* intervenes between the latter two psychosexual stages but, strictly speaking, it is not a stage. Freud assigned crucial significance to the first three stages, termed *pregenital* stages, in the formation of adult character structure.

The Oral Stage

During the oral stage of psychosexual development, which lasts approximately throughout the first year of life, the primary erogenous zone is the mouth. Through activities associated with the mouth—sucking, swallowing, biting—infants experience their first continuous source of pleasure, and thus the mouth region becomes a focal point of rudimentary psychosexual satisfaction. Fixation in the oral-aggressive phase (enter teeth), earmarked by biting and chewing activities, may result in a bitingly sarcastic, argumentative, and hostile adult personality. From the psychoanalytic perspective, then, there is little wonder why people experience serious difficulties in giving up such verbal behaviors—ultimately their psychological roots can be traced back to the first year of life.

The Anal Stage

During the second and third years of life, the primary erogenous zone is the anus. Children at this stage are thought to derive considerable pleasure from temporary retention of feces (i.e., permitting minor pressure to be exerted against the lower intestine and anal sphincter) or expulsion of feces (i.e., immediate tension reduction). With the onset of parentally controlled toilet training, however, the child's pleasures in this regard encounter the stiff opposition of social restraints, and various fixations may thus occur. Reflecting the assumption of the importance of early childhood experience in personality formation, Freudians believe that their approach to toilet training forges the way for the development of adult productivity and creativity.

The Phallic Stage

The genitals become the primary erogenous zone during the phallic stage of psychosexual development, which extends from the fourth through the fifth years of life. During this stage, children can be observed examining their sex organs, masturbating, and showing interest in matters pertaining to birth and sex. But perhaps more important, this period of life serves as the stage on which the most critical psychological drama of childhood is played out—the Oedipus complex. Freud theorized that every child unconsciously wishes to possess the opposite-sexed parent and simultaneously dispose of the same-sexed parent.

Freud believed that the boy experiences intense conflict over his incestuous desires toward the mother and fears retaliation from the father for such desires. Specifically, the small boy fears that the father will discover his sexual desires and retaliate by cutting off the boy's penis.

The little girl during the phallic stage is depicted as discovering that, unlike her father, she lacks a penis. Immediately following this anatomical discovery, the girl wishes she had one—a desire which, in psychoanalytic theory, is called *penis envy.* Penis envy in girls is roughly equivalent psychologically to castration anxiety in boys, and together, penis envy and castration anxiety are known as the castration complex in Freudian theory.

Failure to resolve the Oedipus conflict and unresolved Oedipal feelings lie at the root of many psychological disorders, when viewed from the perspective of psychoanalytic theory.

The Genital Stage

As the Oedipus complex becomes resolved, the child is presumed to move into a period of latency (lasting approximately from age 6 to 12) in which the sex instinct remains relatively dormant and psychic energy is redirected into nonsexual activities, such as school and athletics. With the onset of puberty, however, genital sexuality is reawakened and the genital stage of psychosexual development, extending from puberty until death, begins. During the genital stage, narcissistic strivings become fused with, and largely transformed into, the seeking of heterosexual relationships involving mutual gratification. Thus the adult genital personality type, the successful end product of psychosexual development in psychoanalytic theory, is characterized by a capacity for mature heterosexual love, responsible concerns beyond the self, and productive living in society.

SUGGESTED READING

Freud, S. (1920). *A general introduction to psychoanalysis* (J. Riviere, Trans.). New York: Washington Square Press.

Daniel J. Ziegler
Villanova University

PSYCHOENDOCRINOLOGY

Hormones are substances, such as steroids and peptides, synthesized and released from endocrine glands, cell clusters, or specialized cells and spread over the brain, lungs, or gastrointestinal tract. Several of these hormones exist both in the brain and peripheral organs, where they act as an endocrine or paracrine messenger, or even as a neurotransmitter. Most endocrine activities vary with sex and age, and many show pronounced variations over the course of the month or even the day.

Psychological events profoundly modulate the release of hormones either directly, via the brain, or indirectly, via the autonomic nervous system. These hormones, in turn, influence psychological events either directly or indirectly. Psychoendocrinology is interested in investigating the interface between the endocrine systems and mood, cognition, and behavior. Most of this research is presently done in animal experiments. However, the ability to assess steroids in saliva has considerably facilitated research with human subjects. Furthermore, new and highly sensitive immunoassays, advances in neuroendocrine techniques, and the development of specific pharmacological tools have rapidly increased our knowledge in psychoendocrinology.

The hypothalamic-pituitary-adrenal axis (HPAA) has been of particular interest as the major pathway through which the brain responds to psychological stress. Corticotropin-releasing factor (CRF) from cells of the paraventricular hypothalamus acts as a releasing hormone for adrenocorticotropin (ACTH) in the pituitary, and ACTH releases corticosteroids from the adrenal cortex. Corticosteroids (cortisol, corticosterone) are essential for the body and allow psychological and physical adaptation to stressors. In addition, they exert a negative feedback on the release of CRF and ACTH. Disturbances of the HPAA are associated with both mental and physical illness. CRF can easily be activated by stress and promotes depression, anxiety, and other forms of behavioral pathology. By activating the autonomic nervous system, CRF further links psychological stress to gastrointestinal and cardiovascular disorders. Although homeostasis of the HPAA is maintained by negative feedback, permanently enhanced and lowered glucocorticoid levels have been observed under prolonged stress. While hypercortisolemia is associated with depression, cognitive dysfunction, inflammatory diseases, and the metabolic syndrome, hypocortisolemia has been found in patients with fibromyalgia, chronic pelvic pain, irritable bowel disease, chronic fatigue syndrome, and Posttraumatic Stress Disorder. The molecular mechanisms by which CRF and glucocorticoids facilitate these disorders are presently under investigation. New techniques allow researchers to assess receptor function and receptor polymorphisms, and to identify regions in the human body where hormones exert their behavioral effects.

The hypothalamic-pituitary-gonadal axis (HPGA) and the hypothalamic-pituitary-thyroid axis (HPTA) are other important endocrine pathways linking psychological events to organic function. Both systems are comparably controlled by negative feedback. Sexual cues can stimulate the HPGA, while stress inhibits the HPGA via CRF, thus promoting stress-induced infertility. Sex steroids such as testosterone, progesterone, and estradiol profoundly affect brain function, behavior, cognition, and mood. Such effects can become clinically relevant, as in the premenstrual syndrome or postpartum depression. Hyperthyroidism, which is usually caused by organic diseases, leads to psychological alterations such as irritability, hyperactivity, and heat intolerance. Hypothyroidism, on the other hand, provokes lethargy, depression, fatigue, and cold intolerance. Other hormones from the anterior pituitary, such as prolactin and growth hormone (GH), are also released by stress. However, there is not yet a clear picture of the role of these hormones in stress-related disorders.

Vasopressin and oxytocin are peptide hormones, mainly released by the posterior pituitary. Vasopressin has vasoconstrive and antidiuretic properties, and has been considered relevant for stress effects on blood pressure and enuresis nocturna. Recent evidence suggests that it is beneficial for psychoendocrinology not to separate the role of a given substance from its function as an endocrine messenger or a neurotransmitter. Oxytocin promotes labor in pregnant women when the baby's head distends the uterus wall, and the release of milk is initiated by the suckling newborn. Oxytocin is closely associated with social attachment and bonding, and a social partner again initiates both psychological events. Therefore, it seems that another significant individual within a reproductive context activates this substance, both as a neurotransmitter and as a hormone. While oxytocin receptor functions are facilitated by estrogens, testosterone modulates vasopressin receptors. For example, it has been shown that the flank-marking behavior of hamsters is regulated by vasopressin, but strongly dependent upon testosterone.

Recent evidence has shown that endocrine systems are strongly influenced by pre- and postnatal events. Stress or infections of the mother, raising glucocorticoid levels, or reduced maternal care after birth seem to result in a lifelong programming of specific hormone receptors. There is already strong evidence that these determinants account for later vulnerability for hypertension, diabetes II, and visceral obesity. Even later in life, chronic and traumatic stress can induce permanent endocrine changes and enhance vulnerability for specific diseases.

The endocrine system closely and bidirectionally interacts with both the autonomic nervous system and the immune system. Thus, psychoendocrinology has to consider the full interplay of biological events, which affect cognitive, affective, and behavioral events and disturbances. The rapid acquisition of data and information has already been successfully transferred into clinical applications: several endocrine challenge tests have already been developed to aid in the diagnosis of mental and stress-related disorders. Additionally, new therapeutic treatments can be developed: After the discovery of the important role of CRF and CRF-receptors in depression, for example, a new group of antidepressants is presently being developed that block the respective CRF-receptors. Furthermore, new tools—such as the intranasal application of neuroactive hormones like melanocortin, insulin, vasopressin, oxytocin, or leptin—provide new routes for psychoactive drugs.

New hormones are continously being discovered, and it is clear that these discoveries will continue to stimulate psychoneuroendocrinology research. The peptides PYY 3-36 or ghrelin, for example, are gut-derived hormones, both of which regulate food intake via effects on the central nervous system. Obviously, both hormones will contribute considerably to our understanding of food intake and eating disorders, thus illustrating the complexity and potential benefits of research in psychoendocrinology.

Dirk H. Hellhammer
Christine Philippsen
University of Trier, Germany

PSYCHOLOGICAL ASSESSMENT

Psychological assessment is considered one of the most important functions in applied psychology. In psychological assessment the practitioner uses observation, interviews, and psychological tests to gain information about the client's personality characteristics, symptoms, and problems in order to arrive at practical decisions about their behavior. In an assessment study the practitioner identifies the main sources of a client's problems and attempts to predict the likely course of events under various conditions.

Mental health patients may present with behavioral, emotional, or physical discomforts that are often difficult for a clinical practitioner to understand initially. Usually, in mental health settings a clinical psychologist attempts to understand the nature and extent of the patient's problem through a process of inquiry that is similar to the way a detective might approach a case: by collecting evidence and using inductive and deductive logic to focus on the most likely factors. Assessment of mental disorders is usually more difficult, more uncertain, and more protracted than it is for evaluation of many physical diseases. Yet early assessment of mental health problems is extremely important in clinical practice—no rational, specific treatment plan can be instituted without at least some general notion of what problems need to be addressed.

In order for psychological assessment to proceed effectively, the person being evaluated must feel a sense of rapport with the clinician. The assessor needs to structure the testing situation so that the person feels comfortable. Clients need to feel that the testing will help the practitioner gain a clear understanding of their problems, to understand how the tests will be used, and to understand how the psychologist will incorporate test results in the clinical evaluation.

What does a clinician need to know in a psychological

assessment? First, of course, the problems must be identified. Are they of a situational nature; that is, have they been precipitated by some environmental stressor, or are the problems more pervasive and long-term? Or is it perhaps some combination of the two? Is there any evidence of recent deterioration in cognitive functioning? How long has the person had the symptoms and how is he or she dealing with the problem? What, if any, prior help has been sought? Are there indications of self-defeating behavior or low self-esteem, or is the individual using available personal and environmental resources? Following are several important areas to be considered in a psychological assessment.

Personal History

It is important to have a basic understanding of the individual's history and development, family history (whether the person has relatives with a history of mental illness), intellectual functioning, personality characteristics, and environmental pressures and resources. For example, how does the person characteristically respond to other people? Are there excesses in behavior present, such as eating or drinking too much? Are there notable deficits, for example in social skills? Does the person show any inappropriate behavior?

Personality Factors

Assessment needs to include a description of any relevant long-term personality characteristics. Has the person behaved in deviant or bizarre ways in particular situations; for example, in circumstances requiring submission to legitimate authority? Do there seem to be personality traits or behavior patterns that predispose the individual to behave in maladaptive ways across a broad range of situations? Does the person tend to become dependent on others to the point of losing his or her identity? Is the person able to accept help from others? Is the person capable of accepting appropriate responsibility for others' welfare? Such questions are necessarily at the heart of many assessment efforts.

Social Situations

It is also important to evaluate the social contexts in which the individual functions. What environmental demands does the person face? What emotional support or special stressors exist in the person's life?

The diverse information about the individual's personality traits, behavior patterns, and environmental demands must be integrated into a consistent and meaningful picture often referred to as a *dynamic formulation* because it describes the current situation and provides hypotheses about what is driving the person to behave in maladaptive ways. The clinician should try to arrive at a plausible explanation; for example, a reason why a normally passive and mild-mannered man suddenly flew into a rage and became physically abusive toward his wife. The formulation will allow the clinician to develop hypotheses that might explain the client's future behavior. What is the likelihood that the person would get worse if the problems are left untreated? Which behaviors should be the initial focus of change, and what treatment methods are likely to be most efficient in producing this change? What changes might reasonably be expected if the person were provided a particular type of therapy?

Clients who are being assessed in a clinical situation are usually highly motivated to be evaluated and usually like to know the results of the testing. They usually are eager to give some definition to their discomfort. In many situations it is important to incorporate information from a medical evaluation into the psychological assessment in order to rule out physiological abnormalities that may be causing or contributing to the problem.

Clinical assessment attempts to provide a comprehensive picture of an individual's psychological functioning and the stressors and resources in his or her life situation. In the early stages of the process, the assessment psychologist attempts to obtain as much information about the client as possible—including present feelings, attitudes, memories, demographic facts, and important formative life events—and trying to fit the diverse pieces together into a meaningful pattern. Starting with a global technique, such as a clinical interview, clinicians may later select more specific assessment tasks or tests. The following procedures are some of the methods that may be used to obtain the necessary data.

The Assessment Interview

The assessment interview is usually the initial and often the central information source in the assessment process. This is usually a face-to-face interaction in which information about various aspects of a patient's situation, behavior, past history characteristics, and personality is acquired. The initial interview may be relatively open in format, with an interviewer deciding about his or her next question based on the client's answers to other ones, or it may be more structured so that a planned set of questions is followed. In structured interviewing the clinician may choose from a number of possible interview formats whose reliability has been established in research. The structured interviewing approach is likely to be more reliable but may be less spontaneous than the free-response interview.

Clinical interviews can be subject to error because they rely upon human judgment to choose the questions and process the information. The assessment interview can be made more reliable by the use of rating scales that serve to focus inquiry and quantify the interview data. For example, the person may be rated on a three-, five-, or seven-point scale with respect to suicide potential, violence potential, or other personality characteristics, depending upon the goals of the assessment.

The Clinical Observation

One of the most useful assessment techniques that a clinician has for gaining patient-relevant information is direct observation. Observation can enable the clinician to learn more about the person's psychological functioning; for example, personal hygiene, emotional responses, and such pertinent characteristics as depression, anxiety, aggression, hallucinations, or delusions. Clinical observation is probably more effective if conducted in the natural environment (such as a classroom or home); however, it is more likely to take place upon admission to or in the clinic or hospital ward.

Clinical observation can provide more valuable information in the clinical situation if it is objectively structured; for example, the use of structured rating scales helps maintain objectivity. The most useful rating scales are those that enable a rater to indicate not only the presence or absence of a particular behavior but also its prominence. Standard rating scales can provide a quantifiable format for rating clinical symptoms. For example, the Hamilton Anxiety Rating Scale (Hamilton, 1959) specifically addresses behavior related to the experience of intense anxiety and has become almost the standard for assessing anxiety states. Observations made in clinical settings by trained observers can provide behavioral data useful in ongoing clinical management of patients, for example, to focus on specific patient behaviors to be changed.

Psychological Tests

Psychological tests are standardized sets of procedures or tasks for obtaining samples of behavior. A client's responses to the standardized stimuli are compared with those of other people having comparable demographic characteristics, usually through established test norms or test score distributions. Psychological tests are useful diagnostic tools for clinical psychologists in much the same way that blood tests or X-ray films are useful to physicians in diagnosing physical problems. In all these procedures, problems may be revealed in people that would otherwise not be observed. The data from tests allow a clinician to draw inferences about how much the person's psychological qualities differ from those of a reference norm group, typically a sample of "normal" persons. Psychological tests have been developed to measure many psychological attributes in which people vary. Tests have been devised to measure such characteristics as coping patterns, motive patterns, personality factors, role behaviors, values, levels of depression or anxiety, and intellectual functioning.

Two types of psychological tests are typically incorporated in psychological assessments in clinical practice—intelligence tests and personality tests.

Intelligence Tests

In many cases it is important to have an evaluation of the person's level of intellectual functioning. The clinician can assess intellectual ability with a wide range of intelligence tests. For example, if the patient is a child, the Wechsler Intelligence Scale for Children-Revised (WISC-III) or the current edition of the Stanford-Binet Intelligence Scale might be used for measuring the child's intellectual ability. For measuring adult intelligence, the Wechsler Adult Intelligence Scale-Revised (WAIS-III) is the most frequently used measure.

Individually administered intelligence tests—such as the WISC-R, WAIS-III, and the Stanford-Binet—are labor-intensive and typically require 2 to 3 hours to administer, score, and interpret. The information obtained about the cognitive functioning of patients, however, can provide useful hypotheses about the person's intellectual resources and ability to deal with problems.

Personality Tests

The clinician would likely employ several tests designed to measure personal characteristics. Personality tests are of two general types—projective and objective tests.

Projective Techniques

Projective techniques are unstructured tasks; for example, the clinician might use ambiguous stimuli, such as incomplete sentences which the person is asked to complete. The individual's responses to these ambiguous materials are thought to reveal a great deal about their personal problems, conflicts, motives, coping techniques, and personality traits. One important assumption underlying the use of projective techniques is that the individual (in trying to make sense out of vague, unstructured stimuli) tends to "project" their own problems, motives, and wishes into the situation, because they have little else on which to rely in formulating their responses to these materials. Projective tests are considered to be valuable in providing clues to an individual's past learning and personality. The three most frequently used projective tests are the Sentence Completion Test, the Thematic Apperception Test (TAT), and the Rorschach. Due to space considerations this article will examine only the Rorschach and the TAT.

The Rorschach test was developed by the Swiss psychiatrist Rorschach in 1911. Using 10 inkblot pictures, the person is instructed to look at each card and tell "what it looks like or reminds you of." After the initial responses to all the cards are recorded, the examiner then goes back through the responses to determine "what about the inkblot made it look the way it did." Once the responses are obtained, the clinician must then interpret them—this normally involves scoring the protocol according to a standard method in order to determine what the responses mean. The most widely used and reliable scoring system is the Exner Comprehensive System (Exner, 1993). The indexes resulting from the scoring summary are then employed to explore the literature to determine the meaning of the responses. Experience with the instrument is extremely important in arriving at useful hypotheses about clients.

The Thematic Apperception Test (TAT) was introduced in 1935 by Morgan and Murray as a means of studying personality traits. The TAT uses a series of pictures about which a subject is instructed to create stories. The content of the pictures is highly ambiguous as to actions and motives, so that people tend to project or attribute their own conflicts and worries into their stories. Interpretation of the stories is impressionistic. The interpreter reads the constructions and determines what potential motives and behavioral tendencies the respondent might have that led them to "see" the pictures in the ways they did. The content of the TAT stories is thought to reflect the person's underlying traits, motives, and preoccupations.

Projective tests, like the Rorschach and TAT, can be valuable in many clinical assessment situations, particularly in cases where the task involves obtaining a comprehensive picture of a person's personality makeup. The great strengths of projective techniques are their unstructured nature and their focus on the unique aspects of personality. However, this is also a weakness, because their interpretations are subjective, unreliable, and difficult to validate. In addition, projective tests typically require a great deal of time to administer and advanced skill to interpret. The clinician must also employ more objective tasks in order to put the client's symptoms and behavior in an appropriate perspective.

Objective Personality Scales—The MMPI-2 Objective tests are *structured* in that they use questions or items that are carefully phrased. In giving alternative responses as choices, they provide a more controlled format than projective instruments and thus are more amenable to quantifiable response analysis, which in turn enhances the reliability of test outcomes. The most widely used of the major structured inventories for personality assessment is the Minnesota Multiphasic Personality Inventory (MMPI), now known as the MMPI-2 after a revision in 1989 (Butcher, Dahlstrom, Graham, Tellegen, & Kaemmer, 1989). It is described here because it is the most widely studied test in this class of instruments, and because in many ways it is the most successful of the class.

The MMPI was introduced for general use in 1943 by Hathaway and McKinley. Today, it is the most widely used personality test for both clinical assessment and psychopathologic research in the United States and is the assessment instrument most frequently taught in graduate clinical psychology programs. Moreover, translated versions of the MMPI-2 are widely used internationally (Butcher, 1996). The MMPI-2 consists of 567 items covering topics ranging from physical symptoms to psychological problems to social attitudes. Normally, subjects are encouraged to answer all of the items either *true* or *false*.

The MMPI-2 is interpreted using scoring scales that have been devised to measure clinical problems. The MMPI clinical scales were originally developed by an empirical item-selection method. The pool of items for the inventory was administered to a large group of normal individuals and several quite homogeneous groups of clinical patients who had been carefully diagnosed. Answers to the items were then analyzed to see which ones differentiated the various groups. On the basis of these findings, the clinical scales were constructed, each consisting of the items that were answered by one of the patient groups in the direction opposite to the predominant response of the normal group. This method of item selection, known as empirical keying, produced scales that were valid in predicting symptoms and behavior. If a person's pattern of true/false responses closely approximate that of a particular group, such as depressed patients, it is a reasonable inference that he or she shares other psychiatrically significant characteristics with the group—and may in fact be functioning "psychologically" like others in that group.

Each of these clinical scales measures tendencies to respond in psychologically deviant ways. Raw scores of a client are compared with the scores of the normal population, many of whom did (and do) answer a few items in the critical direction, and the results are plotted on the standard MMPI-2 profile form. By drawing a line connecting the scores for the different scales, a clinician can construct a profile that shows how far from normal a patient's performance is on each of the scales. The Schizophrenia scale, for example, is made up of the items that schizophrenic patients consistently answered in a way that differentiated them from normal individuals. People who score high (relative to norms) on this scale, though not necessarily schizophrenic, often show characteristics typical of the schizophrenic population. For instance, high scorers on this scale may be socially withdrawn, have peculiar thought processes, may have diminished contact with reality, and in severe cases may have delusions and hallucinations.

One extremely useful feature of the MMPI-2 is that it contains a number of scales to evaluate test-taking attitudes. It includes a number of validity scales to detect whether a patient has answered the questions in a straightforward, honest manner. For example, there is one scale that detects lying or claiming extreme virtue and several scales to detect faking or malingering. Extreme endorsement of the items on any of these measures may invalidate the test.

The MMPI-2 is used in several ways to evaluate a patient's personality characteristics and clinical problems. The traditional use of the MMPI-2 is as a diagnostic standard. The individual's profile pattern is compared with profiles of known patient groups. If the client's profile matches that of a particular group, information about patients in this group can suggest a broad descriptive diagnosis for the patient under study. A second approach to MMPI interpretation is referred to as content interpretation. This approach is used to supplement the empirical interpretation by focusing on the content themes in a person's response to the inventory. For example, if an individual endorses an unusually large number of items about depression, a clinician might well conclude that the subject is preoccupied with low mood.

Applications of Clinical Assessment

Assessment in Mental Health Settings

Most clinical assessment is undertaken in medical, psychiatric, or prison settings to evaluate the mental health status of people with problems. The practitioner would administer, score, and interpret the battery of tests, usually at the beginning of the clinical contact, and develop an integrated report. The report would likely focus on such tasks as developing mental health treatment plans (Beutler & Berran, 1995).

Psychological Assessment in Forensic or Legal Cases

One of the fastest-growing applications of psychological tests involves their use in evaluating clients in court cases. Psychological tests have been found to provide valuable information for forensic evaluations—particularly if they contain a means of assessing the person's test-taking attitudes (such as the MMPI-2, which contains several measures that provide an appraisal of the person's cooperativeness or frankness in responding to the test items). Many litigants or defendants in criminal cases attempt to present themselves in a particular way (for example, to appear disturbed in the case of an insanity plea or impeccably virtuous when trying to present a false or exaggerated physical injury). These motivations to "fake good" or "fake bad" tend to result in noncredible test patterns.

Because of their scientific acceptability, well-known psychological tests, such as the WAIS-III and MMPI-2, are widely accepted by courts as appropriate assessment instruments. In order for a test to be allowed into testimony, it must be shown to meet an accepted scientific standard. The primary means of assuring that tests are appropriate for court testimony is that they are standardized and are not experimental procedures (Ogloff, 1995). Psychological assessments in court cases can provide information about the mental state of felons on trial, assess the psychological adjustment of litigants in civil court cases, and aid in the determination of child custody in divorce cases.

Psychological Tests in Personnel Screening

The use of personality tests in employment screening has a long tradition; the first formal use of a standardized personality scale in the United States was implemented to screen out World War I draftees who were psychologically unfit for military service (Woodworth, 1920). Today, personality tests are widely used for personnel screening in occupations that require great public trust. Some occupations, such as police officers, airline flight crews, fire fighters, nuclear power plant workers, and certain military specialties require greater emotional stability than most other jobs. Maladaptive personality traits or behavior problems in such employees can result in public safety concerns. For example, someone who behaves in an irresponsible manner in a nuclear power plant control room could significantly endanger the operation of the facility and the safety of the surrounding community. The potential for problems can be so great in some high-stress occupations (e.g., air traffic controllers) that measures need to be taken in the hiring process to evaluate applicants for emotional adjustment.

Personnel screening for emotional stability and potentially irresponsible behavior requires a somewhat different set of assumptions than clinical assessment. One assumption is that personality or emotional problems, such as poor reality contact, impulsivity, or pathological indecisiveness, would adversely affect the way in which a person would function in a critical job. Psychological tests should not be the sole means of determining whether a person is hired. Psychological tests are more appropriately used in the context of an employment interview, a background check, and a careful evaluation of previous work records.

Summary

Psychological assessment is one of the most important and complex activities undertaken by clinical psychologists. The goals of psychological assessment include describing the individual's symptoms, identifying possible causes, evaluating the severity of the problem, and exploring the individual's personal resources, which might be valuable in the decisions to be made.

A broad range of psychological assessment methods is used for gathering relevant psychological information for clinical decisions about people. The most flexible assessment methods are the clinical interview and behavioral observation. These methods can provide a wealth of clinical information. Psychological tests are used to measure personality characteristics by employing standardized stimuli for collecting behavior samples that can be compared with those of other individuals through test norms. Two different personality testing methods have been employed: projective tests, such as the Rorschach, in which unstructured stimuli are presented to a subject who then "projects" meaning or structure onto the stimulus, thereby revealing "hidden" motives, feelings, and so on; and objective tests, or personality inventories, in which a subject is required to read and respond to itemized statements or questions. Objective personality tests usually provide a cost-effective way of collecting personality information. The MMPI-2 provides a number of clinically relevant scales for describing abnormal behavior. Psychological tests are widely used for making clinical decisions in mental health settings, forensic applications, and personnel screening for positions that require emotionally stable employees.

REFERENCES

Beutler, L. E., & Berran, M. R. (1995). (Eds.). *Integrative assessment of adult personality.* New York: Guilford Press.

Butcher, J. N. (1996). *International adaptations of the MMPI-2.* Minneapolis: University of Minnesota Press.

Butcher, J. N., Dahlstrom, W. G., Graham, J. R., Tellegen, A., & Kaemmer, B. (1989). *Minnesota Multiphasic Personality Inventory-2 (MMPI-2): Manual for administration and scoring.* Minneapolis: University of Minnesota Press.

Exner, J. (1993). *The Rorschach: A comprehensive system* (Vol. 1). New York: Wiley.

Hamilton, M. (1959). The assessment of anxiety states by rating. *British Journal of Medical Psychology, 32,* 50–55.

Morgan, C. D., & Murray, H. A. (1935). A method for investigating fantasies. *Archives of Neurology and Psychiatry, 34,* 289–306.

Ogloff, J. (1995). The legal basis of forensic application of the MMPI-2. In Y. S. Ben-Porath, J. R. Graham, G. C. N. Hall, R. D. Hirschman, & M. S. Zaragoza (Eds.), *Forensic applications of the MMPI-2.* Thousand Oaks, CA: Sage.

Woodworth, R. S. (1920). *The Personal Data Sheet.* Chicago: Stoelting.

James N. Butcher
University of Minnesota

See also: **Bender Gestalt; Questionnaires**

PSYCHOLOGICAL HEALTH

All psychotherapeutic systems have a view of human nature, a concept of disease etiology, and a vision of psychological health. The intention of therapy is to work toward the vision of psychological health as defined by each particular orientation. The vision of psychological health as defined by each approach is predicated upon and consistent with its view of human nature. These views can be understood as paradigms, or "world hypotheses" that professionals operate from in pursuing their work. While such paradigms are necessary to make sense out of our lives and work, they can also be limiting. For example, psychology has traditionally been pathology based, viewing psychological health as the mere absence of symptoms, as evidenced by the *Diagnostic and Statistical Manual of Mental Disorders.*

Reflecting a dissatisfaction with pathology-based clinical and mental health classifications, some researchers are developing and empirically investigating models of positive health, including non-Western models. These investigations suggest that elimination of pathology may give us the concept of the "average" or "normal" rather than a concept of true positive or "optimal" psychological health.

Five Views of Human Nature and Psychological Health

This section presents five views of human nature and their respective views of psychological health—the goal of therapy (Table 1).

Biomedical Approach

View of Human Nature. The biomedical paradigm, which guides modern medicine and psychiatry, views human nature as determined in large part by our biological/physiological processes. An example is the biomedical approach to depression. Assessment leads to a precise diagnosis for which an organic cause is identified (e.g., lack of serotonin), then a treatment specific to the pathology is prescribed (e.g., SSRI—serotonin specific reuptake inhibitor).

Goal of Therapy. The goal of therapy is to alleviate undesired symptoms via medication, restore biochemical homeostatis, and thereby achieve "psychological health."

Psychodynamic Approach

View of Human Nature. Psychodynamic psychology views behavior as a product of competing instincts, needs, and impulses. Although there are many schools, all subscribe to the same basic premise, namely that man is, in Freud's terms, "lived by unknown and controlled forces" which originate in the amoral id. Since these mental forces are unconscious, a person is not fully aware of how they are manifested, and the result of this conflict is neurosis, or "mental illness."

Goal of Therapy. From a psychodynamic view of human nature, psychological health is achieved by uncovering the repressed facts of the self—"to make the unconscious conscious"—and bringing these repressed desires, fears, and depressions into consciousness: "Where id was, ego shall be."

Behavioral/Cognitive Approach

View of Human Nature. The cognitive-behavioral approach views human nature as a *tabula rasa,* a blank slate. The individual is motivated by environmental stimuli and social interactions (or cognitive representations of the two). Therefore, psychological maladjustment is likely to result

Table 1. Comparison and Contrast of Five Schools of Psychotherapy

Subject	Biomedical	Psychodynamic	Cognitive-Behavioral	Humanistic-Existential	Transpersonal
View of human nature	Primarily biological/ physiological processes.	Ruled by unconscious, amoral id.	Blank slate. Determined by environmental stimuli, or cognitive representations of stimuli.	Innately self-actualizing (H). Existence precedes essence (E).	Interconnected. Capable of going beyond ego identity.
Goal of Psychotherapy	Normalize chemical imbalances.	To make the unconscious conscious, "where id was, ego shall be."	Competently respond to environment. Reinterpret illogical cognitions.	Foster self-actualization (H). "Choices" create authentic self (E).	Go beyond identification with limited ego. See interconnection with others and world.

from maladaptive learning, reinforcement patterns, and/or cognitive distortions.

Goal of Therapy. A cognitive-behavioral approach teaches clients to identify and reinterpret the illogical notions that underline their distressing symptoms. Psychological health is achieved when maladaptive patterns (cognitive and behavioral) are recognized and changed, consequently alleviating undesired symptoms.

Humanistic/Existential Approach

View of Human Nature. The humanistic/existential approach views the individual as neither controlled by a "genetic" amoral id nor by external stimuli. The humanistic approach instead views the individual as constantly changing or "becoming," with an innate self-actualizing nature. The existential approach argues there is no innate self-actualizing nature—existence precedes essence—and therefore a person must "create his/her authentic self." The unhealthy person, from a humanistic/existential perspective, is one who restricts the task of openly discovering and making sense of his or her existence, turns away from the responsibility of creating choices, and fails to relate to others and the world authentically in the present moment.

Goal of Therapy. The goal of humanistic/existential therapy is to foster self-actualization, allowing the client to assume full responsibility for developing his/her identity. Ultimately, this entails authentically encountering the human environment, facing the inevitability of isolation and mortality, and realizing that if I cannot choose my fate, I can nevertheless choose my attitude toward it.

Transpersonal Approach

View of Human Nature. The transpersonal approach views human nature as having an interconnected "essence" and an innate motivation toward values that transcend the self.

Goal of Therapy. Within the transpersonal tradition, the goal of therapy is to extend the identity or sense of self beyond the "narrow self" so that individuals realize their interconnection with others and the world. The qualities of the healthy person include realizing the limits of ego identity, developing compassion, opening oneself up to peak experiences, being aware of unitive consciousness, and embracing ultimate values.

Toward a More Systemic Approach to Psychological Health

Each of the above traditions has a view of human nature and an understanding of psychological health based on its own paradigmatic view. A more complete view of psychological health may need to integrate the unique perspective offered by each tradition in order to maximize health on the physical, mental, social, and spiritual levels.

Such a multilevel systemic view of psychological health is complementary, rather than exclusive, addressing issues and pathologies at various developmental levels. For example, a comprehensive treatment plan for depression, depending upon the client, may include addressing biochemical imbalances (biomedical), learning coping strategies to handle environmental stressors and behavioral repertoire deficits (behavioral), interpreting cognitive distortions (cognitive), overcoming lack of trust in oneself (humanistic), examining unconscious psychodynamic and intrapsychic conflicts (psychodynamic), and exploring meaning and ultimate spiritual questions (existential/transpersonal).

Thus, a more comprehensive view of psychological health may best be achieved by honoring the strengths of each tradition, from the biomedical through the transpersonal. It would include the traditional measures such as positive affect, life satisfaction, positive sense of control, self-determination, and self-acceptance. It would also extend the criteria to include sensitivity to the body and its needs (e.g., physical well-being), increased depths of relationship (interpersonal well-being), purpose in life, personal growth, self-actuality, and realizing the limits of ego identity (e.g., existential, spiritual well-being). Clearly, more research is needed to help evolve a systemic, multilevel, and integrative definition of psychological health.

Such knowledge has the potential to considerably augment both clinical practice and even society as a whole.

Deane H. Shapiro, Jr.
University of California, Irvine

Craig Santerre
University of Arizona

Shauna Shapiro
University of Santa Clara

Johan A. Astin
California Pacific Medical Center

See also: **Cognitive Therapy; Control Therapy**

PSYCHOLOGICAL SCIENCE

Psychological science is concerned with the application of scientific method and principles to the study of a set of questions that traditionally have been categorized as psychological in nature. It also refers to the body of theories and facts about the questions and issues that have emerged from this process. Psychological science is different from mere philosophical speculation about psychological questions. It also is different from the so-called self-help literature that deals in an intuitive way with problems of living. Psychological science requires empirical observation and experimental verification of its speculations, which are often cast as, and considered to be, scientific theories. Defined in this way, psychological science is the discipline of all but a few university departments of psychology.

Because of the development in the past quarter century of the multidisciplinary program called cognitive science, we must make further distinctions. Cognitive science, called the "mind's new science" by Howard Gardner (1985), represents a coalition of approaches that includes aspects of the disciplines of psychology, linguistics, philosophy, neuroscience, computer science, and anthropology. We are, however, faced with a problem: how to differentiate cognitive science from psychological science per se. Pending further developments, for the time being we can conceptualize psychological science as a science dealing with traditionally psychological questions. Psychological science has its own methodology and a philosophy that resists the reduction of psychological questions to brain processes, arguing that such questions must be understood in their own context, on their own terms. Some would argue that psychological processes are based upon emergent properties and functions of the intact functioning organism that require their own set of assumptions and logic. Whether ultimately true or not, such a stance defines a set of issues that can mark off psychological science as a domain separate and distinct from cognitive science.

Psychological questions, at least historically, deal with mental processes and conscious experience or awareness of one's existence and the world in which one exists, a concept that is closely related to mind. Going back to antiquity, humans have speculated about the nature of mind, of the relationship of mind to the world in which they live, of the relationship of mind to the body of which it is a part, of the nature of knowledge and how it is acquired, and of the relationship between mind and human action. Such philosophical speculation constituted a major focus of such notable thinkers as Plato and Aristotle and of a range of philosophers following the Renaissance, including Descartes, Hobbes, Locke, Berkeley, and Kant. Of these, Kant is remembered for his insistence that there could be no science of psychology. This opinion was based on his belief that mental events were not measurable; thus, there could be no mathematical analysis or description of them. Furthermore, according to Kant, mental events were brief and subject to distortion by the observation process itself, and mental events could not be produced by experimental means; they had their own existence and obeyed their own laws and whims. There simply could not be a science dealing with such an unmanageable and even nonphysical subject matter.

The development of psychological science required the emergence of a sophisticated view of science and then a demonstration of the relevance of the scientific method to psychological questions. These requirements seem to have been satisfied around the middle of the nineteenth century, at which time many of Kant's objections appear to have been surmounted by methodological advances leading to pertinent discoveries in physiology. If a date can be provided for the birth of psychological science, perhaps it would be 1874, the year that Wilhelm Wundt's *The Principles of Physiological Psychology* was published. The Preface to this work begins with this remarkable statement: "This book which I here present to the public is an attempt to work out a new domain of science" (p. v).

Both in response to the shortcomings of Wundt's introspective procedure and as a result of early successes in animal psychology, another methodological approach, the behaviorist movement, emerged in the first half of the twentieth century. In part, behaviorism has been seen as an outgrowth of what has been called functionalistic psychology, which is concerned with explaining the function of mind and how mind could be implicated in the coping behavior of humans as well as other animals. But it soon seemed apparent that human and animal behavior could be studied in their own right. The behaviorist approach, as formulated by John B. Watson in 1913, was "a purely objective experimental branch of natural science. . . . Introspection forms no essential part of its methods" (p. 158). Mind and conscious experience were ruled out as topics of scientific investigation because they were not directly observable. Behaviorism, at least in the United States, became a dominant force in psychology and formed the basis for a substantial portion of research publications from 1920 through 1960.

Modern-day cognitive psychology emerged in the 1970s, approximately 100 years after the birth of psychological science, and today is almost synonymous with experimental psychology. Cognitive psychology's subject matter returns to questions of mind, but not in the form conceptualized by Wundt. Rather than examining the nature of conscious experience from the perspective of the observer of that experience, cognitive psychology focuses on theoretical mental processes as they are manifested in observable measures such as accuracy and response time. In this approach, specific characteristics of mental processes are hypothesized and the observable consequences of assumptions about the characteristics are derived. Experiments are then conducted to determine whether or not the hypothesized consequences occur, with a positive result bolstering confidence in the power of the theoretical assumptions. This form of experimentation has as its empirical base observable responses made by the experimental subject, responses that depend on the activities of the hypothesized processes under investigation. From this perspective, cognitive psychology can be viewed as a return to an earlier view about the subject matter of psychological investigation, but with the adoption of the sophisticated and objective methodology of behaviorism. In this view, psychology's focus is not on the structure of conscious experience, but on the task of identifying and explicating the processes that are involved in attention, memory, pattern recognition, linguistic behavior (speaking, listening, and reading), thinking, problem solving, and associated problems.

The history of psychological science from its beginnings in the laboratory of Wundt to the present day reveals a great broadening of its concern. Wundt's experimental procedures were generally limited to the question of identifying the elements of the structure of mind conceptualized as conscious experience. The behavioristic movement substituted a concern with the functioning of animal and human organisms interacting with an environmental context. Present-day cognitive psychology has returned to questions of mental activity, but with a different goal than that of Wundt. Along the way, psychology has adopted a number of methodologies and procedures that extended its scope, and it grew by encompassing a number of areas related to its main goal. Psychology adopted the analytic methodology of statistics and in many areas was able to harness mathematical models to augment its growing methodological armament. The methods and goals of psychological science were applied to a wide variety of psychological questions and in a variety of settings. Today, the introductory textbook in psychology displays a broad array of applications of the methodology of psychological science, ranging from basic subfields of psychology such as perception, learning, cognition, and personality to such topics as drug abuse, mental illness, and gender differences—all areas in which our knowledge has been extended through psychological science.

REFERENCES

Gardner, H. (1985). *The mind's new science: A history of the cognitive revolution.* New York: Basic Books.

Watson, J. B. (1913). Psychology as the behaviorist sees it. *Psychological Review, 20,* 158–177.

Wundt, W. (1904). *Principles of physiological psychology* (5th ed.) (E. Tichener, Ed.). New York: MacMillan. (Original work published 1874)

Alan Boneau

See also: **Behaviorism**

PSYCHOLOGY AND PHILOSOPHY

Concerns that are now typically part of contemporary psychology—What is the nature of the mind? What causes human happiness? How do humans come to believe or know?—were until the end of the last century part of the concerns of philosophers. In the latter part of the nineteenth century, investigators such as Wilhelm Wundt took an experimental approach to these questions and contemporary psychology was born. Although empirical and experimental methods allow psychologists to address questions commonly outside the scope of philosophy (e.g., What is the incidence of depression?), philosophical concerns continue to influence these empirical pursuits. One clear example of such influence is the general agreement among psychologists that research takes place within a context of philosophical assumptions: What is science? What counts as evidence? What inferences are legitimate to make given the data?

Naturalized Epistemology

Arguably, the central philosophical problem within psychology is the problem of knowledge. Psychologists want to gain and use knowledge, and seek to construct epistemologically sound methods for doing so. Thus, the question "What method(s) can be used to gain knowledge about a particular subject matter?" is of central concern in contemporary psychology. It is central for three reasons: (1) Scientific psychology has made slow progress, and it is difficult not to blame this at least partially on the limitations of its research methods; (2) The phenomena studied by psychologists may be sufficiently different from the phenomena studied by other natural scientists that the wholesale adoption of the methods of natural science for use in psychology may be inappropriate; and (3) Psychology empirically investigates learning, that is, the acquisition of knowledge, and therefore may inform our conceptions of epistemology. Such approaches to epistemology are referred to as *naturalized* epistemology because they take empirical findings regarding learning into account. Naturalistic approaches to epistemology are endorsed not only by psychologists, but also by prominent philosophers such as W. V. O. Quine and Karl Popper.

The Good Life

Psychologists are increasingly drawn into the domain of ethics, a domain previously relegated to clergy and philosophers. Ethics has to do with the good life, asking questions such as "What is the good?" "How ought I act?" and "Is happiness the ultimate goal in life?" Psychological research, in particular work done by clinical and social psychologists, is viewed by some as providing insight into these important questions. Psychological well-being, for example, is a collection of positive attributes that might be comparable to what philosophers refer to as virtues. Psychologists and philosophers alike agree that variables like good health, positive outlook, quality friends and social network, and a developed sense of self are all implicated in humans' ability to flourish. As with epistemology, there are those who believe that empirical evidence can provide answers to ethical questions. Although most thinkers agree that empirical findings can help people to more effectively realize their goals, it is a matter of great controversy as to whether or not such findings can help to define what is good or virtuous.

Philosophy of Mind

Otherwise known as the mind-body problem, the problematic nature of this field of inquiry is typically traced to Descartes's (in)famous articulation of *substance dualism* (though both Plato and Aristotle weighed in on the issue). Two broadly construed solutions have been proposed to the mind-body problem: *dualism* and *monism.* Though the mind-body problem has changed significantly since Descartes's time, being construed now as the problem of consciousness, the various "solutions" to this problem suggested by thinkers throughout history still address the same fundamental issue.

Substance dualism is the thesis that there is an essential difference between minds (mental phenomena) and bodies (physical phenomena); that is, mind is an essentially thinking substance and body is an essentially extended substance. Given this bifurcation of reality into two separate and unconnected domains, subsequent thinkers have developed theories aimed at ameliorating the difficulties associated with our common sense intuition that the mind and body do, in fact, interact. *Psychophysical interactionism* stipulates that bodily (brain) states cause corresponding mental states which, in turn, are capable of causally instantiating subsequent bodily states. *Epiphenomenalism* is the thesis that bodily (brain) states cause corresponding mental states, but that these mental states are causally inefficacious with respect to bringing about subsequent bodily states. As such, epiphenomenalism is a one-way interaction: body to mind, but not the other way around. *Psychophysical parallelism* avoids the problem of interaction altogether by claiming that mental and physical states run parallel to one another, like two clocks each showing the same time, but do not interact.

Monism is the thesis that all of the objects of reality are of one kind. As such, monism is the explicit denial of the dualistic claim that mind and body are essentially different. Given our predilection toward discussing the topic in terms of the "mental" and the "physical," monistic theories are devoted to describing how one of these terms is reducible, or identical, to the other. *Idealism* is a kind of monism that states "all things are essentially mental or, at least, depend upon the mind for their existence." *Materialism* is a kind of monism that states "all things are physical," that is, the mind is just the brain. *Phenomenalism* is a less popular variety of monism that stipulates that all empirical statements (including, but not limited to, statements about mental and physical states) are reducible to actual or possible phenomenal appearances. In general, any monistic theory that reduces both mind and body to another, more fundamental reality or substance is labeled a *dual aspect theory.*

Free Will and Determinism

As psychological explanations of human behavior become more precise, belief in free will becomes more difficult to entertain. One who maintains that "humans are free agents" claims (at least implicitly) that (1) our psychological understanding of the causes of human behavior underdetermines the actual range and complexity of observed behavior; and (2) no future scientific advances will eventuate in a theory that adequately accounts for the full range of human behavior. Those who adopt a deterministic position need not necessarily claim that current psychological theory does, in fact, account for the entire range of human behavior. Rather, the determinist need only stipulate that such an all-embracing scientific account of human behavior is possible.

William O'Donohue
University of Nevada, Reno

PSYCHOLOGY AND THE LAW

The field of psychology and law began to develop within the last century and is currently in its greatest period of growth and expansion. The interaction between the disciplines of psychology and law has greatly increased over the past few decades in three overlapping areas: forensic psychology, legal psychology, and psychological jurisprudence. In forensic psychology, psychologists act as experts, practitioners, researchers, and/or consultants with respect to legally relevant clinical areas (such as competency to stand trial, insanity, or civil commitment to psychiatric hospitals). Legal psychology uses applied and empirical research methods to study a range of issues of importance to the legal system (e.g., eyewitness accuracy, police selection, procedural justice, jury decision making, and legal assumptions about human behavior relevant to the rights of defendants, victims, children, and mental patients). Finally, psychological jurisprudence is that area of the field in which efforts to develop a philosophy of law and justice based on psychological values is the main focus.

Evidence of recent growth in psychology and law can be seen in the publication of numerous books and the creation of book series in psychology and law; the creation of journals and periodicals specifically targeted towards psychology and legal issues; the establishment of the American Psychology-Law Society, the American Academy of Forensic Psychology, and the American Board of Forensic Psychology; and the development and expansion of educational and internship experiences. Many graduate programs have developed degree programs in which a specialization or concentration in psychology and law can be obtained, and a number of universities have established joint degree programs in psychology and law in which both a PhD and a law degree are obtained (Bersoff et al., 1999). This article provides a broad overview of the major areas in which psychologists in the field of psychology and law are engaged. Psychologists are often asked to testify in court both about psychological evaluations of individuals and about research findings that may be applicable to a specific criminal or civil court case (see Brodsky, 1999; Ceci & Hembrooke, 1998, for discussion of the role of expert witnesses).

Psychology and law can be conceptualized as encompassing both sides of the justice system (civil and criminal) as well as two broad aspects of psychology (clinical and experimental). Professionals who practice mainly within the civil-clinical area of the field focus on clinical activities within the civil justice system, including conducting evaluations for civil commitment or evaluations of risk for violence among psychiatric patients, or providing psychological treatment for these issues. In addition, researchers working within this area of the field might focus their efforts on developing and evaluating treatment programs or developing and validating assessment instruments to evaluate these civil issues. Professionals who work mainly within the civil-experimental area of the field focus on researching topics at the intersection of psychology and the civil justice system. Examples of such issues include civil commitment criteria, policies, and practices; the right to refuse treatment; and mental health law and policy implications.

Professionals who practice mainly within the criminal-clinical area of the field focus on clinical issues relevant to the criminal justice system and the defendants within this system. Such clinical issues might include evaluations of competency to stand trial, mental state at the time of the offense (insanity), mitigation at sentencing, or risk for future offending, as well as the treatment of offenders (for an overview, see Melton, Petrila, Poythress, & Slobogin, 1997). Researchers within this area of the field might focus on developing and validating instruments for the various types of evaluations or on developing and evaluating treatment programs for various types of offenders or issues (e.g., Heilbrun & Griffin, 1999). Professionals who work mainly in the criminal-experimental area of the field focus on conducting research and advancing knowledge with respect to various aspects of the criminal justice system, such as eyewitness testimony and accuracy, jury deliberations and decision making, police selection, criminal investigation techniques, or punishment and sentencing.

One area that has attracted increased attention in both research and practice is the assessment of violence potential. Research has provided substantial insights into the risk and protective factors that are associated with violent behavior, and this research has changed how we approach risk assessment. Indeed, psychologists have shifted from trying to predict dangerousness to the assessment of risk, which involves thinking about and assessing those factors that will increase or decrease the probability that an individual will become violent in the future. Instead of attempting to make a prediction about a particular individual (and whether he or she is dangerous), the focus changed to an examination of those situational and dispositional factors that would increase or decrease the probability that a particular individual would become violent. Several risk assessment instruments have been developed to guide evaluators through a consideration of particularly important and empirically-derived variables for both adults and juveniles (e.g., Corrado, Roesch, Hart, & Gierowski, 2002; Kropp, Hart, Webster, & Eaves, 1995; Webster, Douglas, Eaves, & Hart, 1997).

The above categorization is, obviously, very broad and simplistic. Many professionals within the field of psychology and law perform multiple activities, which include but are not limited to teaching, research, supervision, expert testimony, consultation, evaluation, and treatment, and which often span more than one of the categories described above.

The discipline of psychology has begun to make an impact upon the discipline of law and continued research and practice is crucial to furthering our understanding of how psychology and the law interact with respect to particular issues. Experts within the field of psychology and law need to continue to conduct research and provide testimony and evidence to help formulate policy recommendations and suggested improvements to the legal systems (both criminal and civil).

The field of psychology and law will, no doubt, continue

to grow and expand in the years to come. It will be important for well-trained professionals to continue to teach, consult, testify, evaluate, treat, supervise, and conduct research in all the various aspects of psychology and law in order to continue to expand and refine this field.

REFERENCES

Bersoff, D. N., Goodman-Delahunty, J., Grisso, J. T., Hans, V. P., Poythress, N. G., & Roesch, R. G. (1997). Training in law and psychology: Models from the Villanova conference. *American Psychologist, 52,* 1301–1310.

Brodsky, S. L. (1999). *The expert expert witness: More maxims and guidelines for testifying in court.* Washington, DC: American Psychological Association.

Ceci, S. J., & Hembrooke, H. (Eds.). (1998). *Expert witness in child abuse cases: What can and should be said in court.* Washington, DC: American Psychological Association.

Corrado, R. R., Roesch, R., Hart, S. D., & Gierowski, J. K. (2002). *Multi-problem violent youth: A foundation for comparative research on needs, interventions, and outcomes.* NATO Science Series. Amsterdam: IOS Press.

Heilbrun, K., & Griffin, P. (1999). Forensic treatment: A review of programs and research. In R. Roesch, S. D. Hart, & J. R. P. Ogloff (Eds.), *Psychology and law: The state of the discipline* (pp. 241–274). New York: Kluwer Academic/Plenum Press.

Kropp, P. R., Hart, S. D., Webster, C. D., & Eaves, D. (1995). *Manual for the spousal assault risk assessment guide* (2nd ed.). Vancouver: The British Columbia Institute Against Family Violence.

Melton, G. B., Petrila, J., Poythress, N. G., & Slobogin, C. (1997). *Psychological evaluations for the courts: A handbook for mental health professionals and lawyers* (2nd ed.). New York: Guilford Press.

Webster, C. D., Douglas, K. S., Eaves, D., & Hart, S. D. (1997). *HCR-20: Assessing risk for violence* (version 2). Burnaby, BC: Mental Health, Law, and Policy Institute, Simon Fraser University.

Ronald Roesch
Simon Fraser University

Patricia A. Zapf
John Jay College

See also: **Competency to Stand Trial; Expert Testimony; Forensic Psychology; Right to Refuse Treatment; Right to Treatment**

PSYCHOLOGY IN CHINA

Early History

Chinese psychological thought may be traced as far back as 500 B.C. in diverse philosophical, political, and other writings. A distinctive feature of ancient Chinese philosophy was its emphasis on education in cultivating human personality. The great Chinese philosopher Confucius (551–479 B.C.), who had profound influence on the development of China's cultural history, was one of the first scholars to discuss the essence of human nature and how it can be modified through education. Later, Xun Zi (313–328 B.C.) developed a systematic theory of knowledge stressing that the mind is capable of knowing the external world and that human nature can be modified by external influences. These examples indicate the richness of psychological thought embodied in ancient Chinese philosophy. Problems such as the mind-body relationship, the acquisition of knowledge, and the nature-nurture controversy were discussed together with other general philosophical and epistemological issues.

Modern Chinese scientific psychology came into existence after China had more contact with the West. During the first decades of the twentieth century the first group of Chinese students went to Europe and the United States to study psychology, returned to China, and established psychology as an independent scientific discipline. Notably, the famous Chinese educator Cai Yuanpei studied in Wundt's laboratory in Leipzig in 1908, returning to China in 1912. In 1917 Cai became president of Peking University, and with his support the university established the first psychology laboratory in China. During this period psychology was taught in some pedagogical institutions, and many teaching materials were translations from Japanese textbooks. In 1921 the Chinese Psychological Society was founded, and the first psychology journal appeared in 1922. With the introduction of the Western educational system into China, psychology expanded rapidly.

In 1937, the Japanese invasion of China resulted in the occupation of a large part of China, causing serious setbacks in the progress of psychology. The occupation lasted until the end of World War II.

Psychology After the Founding of the People's Republic of China

The People's Republic of China was founded in 1949. Chinese psychologists started a movement for reform and independence from Western influences. The new psychology took Marxist philosophy as its guiding principle; psychology in the then-Soviet Union was looked upon as the model. During this period, social psychology and psychological testing were abolished on the grounds that the former ignored the class nature of society, and the latter favored the selection of children of the elite class into schools. Following the educational system in the Soviet Union, there were no independent departments of psychology in Chinese universities. Psychology was a secondary discipline in the departments of philosophy or education.

After 1949, psychology was frequently attacked by leftist political ideologists as an imported Western bourgeois ideology, the mouthpiece of capitalistic individualism. Critics argued that many psychological experiments conducted in the laboratory failed to reflect real-life situations. These attacks on psychology set the stage for the liquidation of psychology between 1966 and 1976, the period of the well-known Cultural Revolution. This time psychology was uprooted completely as a scientific discipline. Scientific research and teaching institutions in psychology were dissolved, and psychologists were dispatched to the countryside to work on the farms. The Cultural Revolution ended in 1976.

Recent Developments

From 1978 on, the Chinese government launched a policy of reform and opening up to the outside world. The change has pushed Chinese psychology into a new era of development. There are now more than 30 departments of psychology in Chinese universities, and the Chinese Psychological Society now has about 5,000 members. Chinese psychology has since moved into the international community. The Chinese Psychological Society joined the International Union of Psychological Science (IUPsyS) in 1980. Many exchanges were established between Chinese universities and universities in other countries.

As experimental psychology has become less affected by ideology, cognitive theory has penetrated into many fields of psychology. Basic research in cognitive processes has increased, and studies of perception, memory, and learning have attracted consistent interest. The Chinese language, as an ideographic language with a unique writing and structural system, has attracted much attention in attempts to understand its acquisition and learning processes. Studies have included the ideographic and sound characteristics of Chinese characters, their reading and comprehension, and the hemispheric laterality of information processing of Chinese language. Exciting findings have been reported in this field.

Neuropsychology is also a field of interest; studies have included the neural mechanism of memory, memory changes in aging, the effects of drugs on behavior, and psychoimmunology. Recently, studies have been made using Positron Emission Tomography and Functional Magnetic Resonance Imaging on basic cognitive functioning.

The areas of developmental and educational psychology have always been lively fields of research in China. There are 300 million children in China, and any new knowledge in this field would have implications for the cultivation of an entire generation. About half of the 5,000 Chinese psychologists now work in teacher training universities or pedagogical institutes. The Ministry of Education in China is advocating a Quality-Oriented Education program to give children a comprehensive education—morally, intellectually, physically, and aesthetically. Such an education is achieved by improving teaching methods, revising curriculum arrangement, stressing moral education, and requiring students to participate in social activities.

Psychologists also work in other practical fields in which psychology can make effective contributions to society. Health psychology and psychological counseling are becoming popular in China. A large number of counseling centers have been established in schools and social institutions. Personnel selection and human resource evaluation centers have been set up to aid in the selection of government employees and workers in industrial and commercial enterprises. Other newly developed applied fields are industrial psychology and managerial psychology. The economic reform of China calls for the introduction of new methods of management in industrial enterprises. Incentives and motivational studies have been carried out to promote efficiency. Managerial assessment methods are being introduced from Western countries and adapted for domestic use.

Psychology in China, after having undergone full-fledged development for only 30 years after the Cultural Revolution, has developed into a mature scientific discipline able to serve society in both its basic and its applied fields.

REFERENCES

Jing, Q. C. (1994). Development of psychology in China. *International Journal of Psychology, 29,* 667–675.

Jing, Q. C., & Fu, X. L. (2001). Modern Chinese psychology: Its indigenous roots and international influences. *International Journal of Psychology, 36,* 408–418.

Qicheng C. Jing
Institute of Psychology, Chinese Academy of Sciences

PSYCHOLOGY IN GERMANY

In the first third of the twentieth century, Germany was among the leading nations in scientific psychology, and German was an important language for psychological publications. Today, the impact of German psychology on the scientific community is rather small (Keul, Gigerenzer & Stroebe, 1993; Montada, Becker, Schoepflin, & Baltes, 1995). First, we will discuss reasons for the decline of German psychology. Second, we will outline the status of today's German psychology.

Decline of Psychology in Germany

The obvious reason for the decline of German psychology was the Nazi regime (1933–1945). Most eminent psychologists, mainly Jews, were harassed, fired, and either emigrated, committed suicide, or were killed. In all, 130 psychologists from German universities emigrated, including

29 full professors (Geuter, 1986), and after the war, only a few (14 according to Geuter, 1986; e.g., Bondy and Düker) returned. Simultaneously, 79 psychology professors employed at the German universities during the Nazi regime remained in their positions after 1945 (Geuter, 1986), in spite of the fact that most of them received their positions for political reasons and not because of scientific excellence.

A first restructuring of the German university system and psychology was triggered by the student revolts of 1968. German universities became open to a larger number of students, and the number of employed scientists in psychology increased about tenfold. However, only a few well-trained and internationally competitive psychologists worked in Germany, Austria, or Switzerland. As a consequence, the scientific output and the international reputation of German psychology did not substantially improve.

German Psychology Today

In Germany today about 50 university departments or institutes of psychology exist, with somewhat more than 400 professors (full professors and "habilitierte" associate professors) holding research and teaching positions. In addition, there are about 30 departments or institutes of medical psychology, with about 90 professors. The curriculum is tightly regulated by nationwide study and examination guidelines, and therefore universities do not greatly differ in teaching and examination topics. Distribution of students to universities is regulated by a national agency on the basis of pre-university grades. Since there are far more applicants to study psychology than available openings, this nationwide selection process gives universities and professors no opportunity to select students, and does not allow students to choose departments with proven excellence. As a consequence, competition between universities for students and state money until now has been weak. Only recently, rankings (although of questionable validity) for universities and study subjects were published, and only recently did states begin to distribute modest amounts of research money on the basis of proven scientific scholarship.

Most recent reviews conclude that the research resources for psychology in Germany are comparable to or even better than those in the United States, Britain, Canada, Australia, France, the Netherlands, or Israel. However, the scientific output, the international reputation, and the reception of German psychology were found to be mediocre. For example:

- Physics and chemistry in Germany contribute about 3 to 4% of the publication in international journals, while the corresponding number for psychology is below 0.5%.
- 42% of the German professors in psychology did not publish within a five-year period (1986–1990) any article which was listed in the SSCI (Keul et al., 1993).
- A considerable number of German psychologists never or rarely publish in English (Basler & Schieferbein, 1995; Keul et al., 1993; Montada et al., 1995). However, it is now recognized that publications in German have a 5 to 10 times lower citation rate than publications in English.
- An evaluation of *Psychological Review* and *Psychological Bulletin* articles between 1975 and 1992 revealed that German contributions are rare, comparable with the Netherlands, Israel, and Sweden, although these countries all have substantially smaller populations, fewer full professorships, and fewer research resources (Keul et al., 1993). In addition, most publications of German psychologists in APA journals come from a few institutes (Montada et al., 1995).

These problems are mainly acknowledged now, and several proposals have suggested ways of improving scientific output, as well as international reception and citation of German psychology (e.g., Gigerenzer et al., 1999).

The slow but continuous increase in the proportion of publications in international journals by German psychologists, mainly driven by a subgroup of productive psychologists, indicates progress (Becker, 1994). German psychophysiologists and social psychologists in particular have received international acknowledgement in their fields (Keul et al., 1993).

An asset of the German science system that greatly helped to overcome the decline of psychology in Germany after the war and to improve the reputation of German psychology is the German Research Foundation (DFG, Deutsche Forschungsgemeinschaft). Based on the lessons learned during the Nazi regime, the peer review process and the rules for grant applications do not allow any political or economic influences or pressures. Grant award decisions are based only on peer review and scientific reputation. The grant money awarded to psychology has continuously increased within the last few years, a sign that the quality and international reputation of psychology in Germany is improving.

REFERENCES

Basler, H.-D., & Schieferbein, J. (1995). Zur wissenschaftlichen Produktivität in der Medizinischen Psychologie. *Psychologische Rundschau, 46,* 36–41.

Becker, J. H. (1994). Publizieren produktive deutschsprachige Psychologen zunehmend in englischer Sprache? *Psychologische Rundschau, 45,* 234–240.

Birbaumer, N. (in press). Psychologie 1933 bis heute. *Zeitschrift für Psychologie* (Sonderband: Deutschsprachige Psychologie im 20. Jahrhundert edited by F. Klix).

Birbaumer, N., & Flor, H. (in press). Deutsche Psychophysiologie 2000. *Zeitschrift für Psychologie* (Sonderband: Psychologie 2000 edited by F. Klix).

Bourne, L. E. J., & Russo, N. F. (1998). *Psychology.* New York: Norton.

Geuter, U. (1986). *Daten zur Geschichte der deutschen Psychologie.* Göttingen: Hogrefe.

Gigerenzer, G., Rösler, F., Spada, H., Amelang, M., Bierhoff, H. W., & Ferstl, R. (1999). Internationalisierung der psychologischen Forschung in Deutschland, Österreich und der Schweiz: Sieben Empfehlungen. *Psychologische Rundschau, 50,* 101–113.

Keul, A. G., Gigerenzer, G., & Stroebe, W. (1993). Wie international ist die Psychologie in Deutschland, Österreich und der Schweiz? Eine SCCI-Analyse. *Psychologische Rundschau, 44,* 259–269.

Montada, L., Becker, J. H., Schoepflin, U., & Baltes, P. B. (1995). Die internationale Rezeption der deutschsprachigen Psychologie. *Psychologische Rundschau, 46,* 186–199.

Strobl, M. (1998). Universities seek to atone for Nazi past. *Nature, 391,* 112–113.

Paul Pauli
University of Wuerzburg, Germany

Niels Birbaumer
University of Tuebingen, Germany

PSYCHOLOGY IN ICELAND

Psychologists in Iceland have been trained in various countries. An undergraduate course in psychology was started at the University of Iceland in 1971, but postgraduate training in psychology had to take place abroad until 1999, when a postgraduate MA course in psychology began at the University of Iceland. Initially most Icelandic psychologists completed their training in Denmark, but later they sought their training in other countries (e.g., Norway, Sweden, Germany, France, England, Scotland, United States, Canada, Australia).

The Icelandic Psychological Association (IPA) was established in 1954, and the current membership is 177. Within the association there are three divisions: clinical, educational, and rehabilitation psychology. The office of the IPA is housed at the Academics Union Bandalag Hàskòlamanna (BHM).

The profession of psychology in Iceland is regulated by law #40/1976, which protects the title and to some extent the function of psychologists. The accrediting committee of the Icelandic Psychological Society is consulted by the Ministry of Health, which is the awarding authority of accreditation for psychologists in Iceland. Only those who have the right to call themselves psychologists can apply for positions advertised for psychologists. Psychologists are permitted to practice psychotherapy.

Four specialties are recognized within psychology in Iceland and regulated by bylaw #158/1990: clinical psychology, rehabilitation psychology, educational psychology, and organizational/occupational psychology. Only those who have been accredited by the Ministry of Health to practice as psychologists can embark upon postgraduate training in one of these specialties; this training lasts 4½ years. During this time the trainee has to work under the supervision of a specialist within specified areas for a stipulated number of months. The trainee receives 120 hours of personal supervision from at least two specialists and 40 hours of group supervision (1 hour per week/40 hours per year). The trainee has to complete 300 hours of didactic training. Finally, the trainee has to conduct a research project and publish in a refereed journal before becoming recognized as a specialist in one of the areas above.

Most of the psychologists in Iceland are employed by health, social, and school services. There are about 10 psychologists working full time and about 30 part time in private practice. The services rendered by psychologists and specialists in psychology in private practice are not reimbursed by the national health services, private insurance, or the social services. Patients are either self-referred or referred by a physician or the social services. Many practicing psychologists consult with corporations and industry.

Eirikur Ö. Arnarson
University of Iceland, Reykjavik

PSYCHOLOGY IN SPAIN

Despite the fact that the history of Spanish psychology shows a marked lack of continuity, it is possible to pinpoint a number of outstanding figures whose work achieved international dimensions.

Juan Luis Vives (1492–1540), born in Valencia in the year in which Columbus first stepped foot on American soil, attempted to focus his contemporaries' attention on the direct observation of human behavior rather than on such indefinable concepts as the soul or the mind. Vives constantly stressed the need for making the most of direct experience as the most reliable source of knowledge.

Juan Huarte de San Juan (1529–1588) in his book, *Examen De Ingenios Para las Ciencias,* presented an ingenious theory about the relationship between psychology and physiology, explaining how good vocational guidance can be built upon this relationship. Apart from its interest as a pioneer attempt in the field of applied psychology, the book is also worth mentioning for its determinist stand, its incipient evolutionism, and the importance it places on the influence of environmental factors.

Santiago Ramón y Cajal (1852–1934), is credited with theories and discoveries on nerve cells and synapse that paved the way for a considerable amount of research work in psychophysiology. Emilio Mira y López (1896–1964) was probably the first Spanish-speaking psychologist to show an interest in behaviorism, and one of the first to study the work of Sigmund Freud. His published writings include works on psychoanalysis, legal psychology, psychiatry, evolutive psychology, vocational guidance, and experimental psychology.

Ramón Turró (1854–1926), undertook the forceful defense of the experimental method, personifying the spirit of Claude Bernard in the mentalist scene that prevailed in Spain at the turn of the century. A great admirer of Ivan P. Pavlov, Turró pursued some interesting experiments with newly born animals to determine how they learn their first specific responses as a basis for all later knowledge. Turró's standpoint on many subjects was truly original.

International psychological trends found their way into Spain, and were welcome there, but with different degrees of success.

One of the key figures in introducing scientific psychology into Spain was Luis Simarro (1851–1921). A member of the Institución Libre de Enseñanza, a movement that attempted the political and social renewal of Spain through the renewal of its educational system.

The phenomenology and Gestalt movements found their way into Spain a little later, thanks to people such as José Ortega y Gasset (1883–1955), who tried to open the country to the trends in psychology and philosophy that appeared in Europe after Wundt. About the same time, the "Geneva School" also started to show its influence in the country, an influence still noticeable today.

In 1917, following ideas advanced in Germany by Hugo Münsterberg in 1911, an Instituto de Orientación Profesional (Institute for Vocational Guidance) was established in Barcelona. This was one of the first centers of applied psychology in the world. Mira y López was elected to head the Institute.

José Germain had studied with Claparède in Geneva, with Wolfgang Köhler in Berlin, and with Pierre Janet in Paris. After the Civil War, he helped to bridge the gap between the postwar generations and the scientific psychology that was trying to become established in Spain in the early 1930s. In 1948, the Consejo Superior de Investigaciones Científicas (Higher Council of Scientific Research) founded the Department of Experimental Psychology with Germain as principal. Among those who worked for the Department were Pinillos, Siguán and Yela. Some years later, they were to be the first professors of psychology in Spanish universities in charge of establishing the systematic study of psychology.

In 1953, the Escuela de Psicología y Psicotecnia de la Universidad de Madrid (Madrid University's School of Psychology and Psychotechnics) was inaugurated. The first attempt to establish university studies of a purely psychological nature, this school was open only to postgraduate students. In 1964, a similar center was set up in Barcelona. Eventually, in 1968, the universities of Madrid and Barcelona began to offer five-year courses in psychology for undergraduates. Their example was soon followed by the remaining Spanish universities.

The last 20 years have been marked by a considerable expansion in Spanish psychology. By the end of the twentieth century there will be more than 30,000 licenced psychologists in the country. The fields of research and application have expanded from health psychology and sports psychology to forensic psychology and traffic psychology. Interdisciplinary areas, such as psycho-oncology and psychoneuroimmunology, are also developing and, in a growing number of hospitals, psychologists are included in palliative care teams. Spanish psychologists are now working on topics such as adherence to new AIDS antiretroviric drugs, anorexia and bulimia, addictive behaviors, counseling, burnout, and so on.

R. Bayés

PSYCHOLOGY OF MEN

The study of sex and gender differences in psychology has a long and distinguished history. However, a field of psychology explicitly and intentionally devoted to the study of the psychology of men is a relatively recent development. Beginning as a response to the feminist critique of traditional gender roles that gained prominence in the late 1960s, the psychology of men has blossomed into a prominent specialization within developmental, clinical, and counseling psychology. The American Psychological Association has established a division, The Society for the Psychological Study of Men and Masculinity, devoted to the psychology of men. In addition, a number of national organizations, such as the National Organization of Men Against Sexism, have sections and interest groups devoted to issues pertaining to the psychology of men.

The psychology of men traces its roots to the feminist analysis of traditional gender roles. Social scientists and psychologists interested in the psychology of men followed the lead of feminist researchers and studied the restrictive and detrimental effects of male gender role socialization. Some of these effects included difficulties in intimate emotional relationships, inhibitions on male-male friendships, restriction of emotional expression, excessive devotion to work and competition, drug and alcohol problems, and interpersonal violence.

In institutions of higher education, psychologists studied restrictive gender role socialization as it related to both men and women. As these researchers disseminated their findings through conferences and publications, a subarea of gender psychology devoted to the psychology of men began to develop. Psychologists working in this area began to build scientific support for feminist-inspired critiques of traditional gender roles as applied to boys and men. The development and use of psychological assessment instruments to measure the negative impact of this restrictive masculine gender role socialization further enhanced the scientific credibility of the emerging field of the psychology of men.

Scholars studying the psychology of men have documented the existence of psychological stress associated with adherence to traditional masculine gender roles. Historically, traditional masculine gender roles have been defined as an overvaluing of competition and toughness, a devaluing of emotional expression, and an aversion to behaviors and activities associated with femininity. Research demonstrated that attempts by men to adhere to these aspects of the masculine gender role were associated with restricted emotional expression, value conflicts between occupational or vocational achievement and devotion to family, inhibitions on affection between men, and excessive preoccupation with power, competition, and control. Men who experienced conflict in these aspects of their lives also experienced increased levels of stress, anxiety, depression, physical problems, and a host of other detrimental psychological symptoms.

As academic psychologists researched aspects of strain associated with adherence to the traditional masculine gender role, practicing psychologists began to develop networks of men and women who were devoted to challenging the social problems that resulted from such adherence. At least three distinct men's movements emerged from these efforts. First, a movement called the mythopoetic men's movement, spearheaded by the poet Robert Bly, was marked by the publication of his popular book *Iron John* in 1990. This movement was devoted to supporting men as they examined the personal meaning of masculinity in their lives. This movement utilized a number of different venues to achieve its goals, including workshop formats, weekend retreats, individual psychotherapy, and at times men's counseling groups specifically dedicated to this endeavor. A second men's movement, called the men's rights movement, emerged from networks of men working together to fight what were perceived to be inequities in the judicial system. Problems that some men associated with divorce or child custody proceedings were an impetus for the advancement of the men's rights movement. Finally, the profeminist men's movement was organized to address issues of social justice that were largely based on feminist critiques of American culture. Aspects of these critiques include the discrepancy in pay between women and men, violence directed toward women by men, and other aspects of oppression perceived to be a result of traditional masculine ideology and socialization.

Today, researchers in the psychology of men have extended their inquiry into specific problem areas for men, such as male depression, violence, suicide, and men's health problems. In addition, a number of psychologists are examining why boys tend to perform poorly in school settings, and why boys are more frequently diagnosed with behavior and learning problems in these settings. Research has demonstrated that over the span of a typical educational experience, boys tend to perform much more poorly than girls on a number of achievement and outcome measures.

In addition, a number of clinical and counseling psychologists have been developing specific assessment and intervention methods geared toward helping male clients in educational, hospital, and clinic settings. Some of these methods include the use of all-male psychotherapy groups and masculine-specific counseling and therapy methods designed to reduce the stigma many men feel when they seek help for personal problems. An important benefit of such efforts may be that more men will seek help for the stresses associated with efforts to conform to the traditional masculine gender role.

Sam V. Cochran
University of Iowa

PSYCHOMETRICS

The field of psychometrics generally considers quantitative psychological data. Such data normally emerges from test responses, although it may come from other measures. Psychometric theory (e.g., Nunnally, 1978; Lord, 1980) provides mathematical models for considering responses to test items, tests, and sets of tests. Applied psychometrics implements these models and applies their analytic procedures to test data (e.g., Thorndike, 1982). Four concerns of psychometrics include norming and equating, reliability, validity, and item analysis. There are both theoretical formulations for each of these four categories and actual procedures to be performed in estimating the usefulness of a test in a specific instance.

Norming and Equating

Norming and equating procedures are used in developing test score reporting systems. Norming is part of test standardization and involves administering the examination to a representative sample of individuals, determining various levels of test performance, and translating raw test scores to a common metric. There are two scoring models: linear and nonlinear transformations. Linear transformations change the mean and standard deviation of the raw test scores, but maintain all other aspects of the raw score distribution; the relative positions of examinees are unchanged. The purpose of linear transformations is to provide test results on scales with which test users are familiar, and hence to increase the amount of information and meaning carried in a score.

Three nonlinear transformations are common: normalization transformations, percentile equivalents, and developmental norms. Normalization transformations fit the test score distribution to a normal curve while maintaining the original rank-ordering of the examinees. Percentile equivalents express each score as the proportion of examinees falling at or below that score. Developmental norms are converted scores that express test performance relative to normal development, typically either years of age or schooling. Age equivalents such as mental age describe test performance in terms of behavior typical for children of various ages. Age and grade equivalent scores are often used, but have extreme psychometric and interpretative problems (Anastasi & Urbina, 1997; Thorndike, 1982).

When there are numerous forms of the test, tests are normally equated. While all forms should measure the attribute with equal precision, raw scores from different forms customarily have varying percentile equivalents. Equating brings forms to a common scale (see Kolen & Brennan, 1995). Angoff (1971) and Thorndike (1982) also describe equating methods.

The past 30 years have led to a family of models of test scores called item response models (IRT). These models permit scaling of tests and test items using methods presumably independent of the population from which the test data emerge, and are explained by Hambleton, Swaminathan, and Rogers (1991); Lord (1980); and Thorndike (1982).

Reliability

Both reliability and validity refer to the generalizability of test scores—assessing the reasonableness of inferences about test scores (Cronbach, Gleser, Nanda, & Rajaratnam, 1972). Reliability concerns inferences made about consistency of measurement. Consistency is defined by tradition as a family of relationships: temporal stability, comparability of tests proposed to be equivalent, homogeneity within a single test, and comparability of judgment-based assessments made by raters. A procedure called the "test-retest" method is used to establish the reliability of a test by administering the test and then waiting a short period (e.g., 2 weeks) before administering the same test again to the same group. In the alternate-forms method, multiple parallel measures are developed and both are administered to a sample of examinees. Both of the above methods use the correlation coefficient between the two sets of measurements as the reliability coefficient, an index that ranges from 0.00 to 1.00 and denotes the percentage of test variance that is reliable. Using raters essentially as parallel forms is called inter-rater reliability and is often used when expert judgments are needed.

Each of the above procedures flows from what has been called the classical or parallel testing model of reliability (Campbell, 1976; Nunnally, 1978). In this model, each test score is perceived as the sum of two independent components: true score and error. True scores may be thought of either as perfect measurement of the attribute in question, were such assessment possible, or as the average of an infinite number of testings. Error is defined as randomly occurring deviations from the true score. Under these conditions, it follows that when two sets of purportedly parallel measurements are correlated with one another, the resultant correlation coefficient is equal to the proportion of the individual differences resulting from the test that are due to true score differences—statistically, the ratio of true score variance to the variance of obtained scores.

An alternate model to the parallel testing model is the domain sampling model. This model requires that a test constructor define the universe of behaviors of interest. Reliability is defined as the ability of the given test to predict an individual's score on all tests in that universe. Among the reliability estimation procedures that emanate from this model are various internal consistency formulations that estimate the correlation between the test and the universe from the average correlations between items on the test.

A third model, the generalizability model (Cronbach et al., 1972; Stanley, 1971) goes a step beyond the domain sampling model; it assumes that one may generalize over dissimilar conditions as well as similar conditions. Thus, in the domain sampling model, a researcher may estimate the reliability between two PhD-level psychologists, whereas in the generalizability model, one could estimate the extent to which one may generalize from a PhD-level psychologist to another professional. One can generalize from one set of scores or observations to others collected at another time or under somewhat different conditions, for instance. Generalizability bridges the gap between reliability and validity.

Validity

Validity refers to the quality with which a measurement procedure permits the desired inferences. Because psychologists make a number of different kinds of inferences using tests and measurements, there have traditionally been several kinds of validity: predictive validity, content validity, and construct validity. Predictive validity has been used to assess the ability of measurement devices to infer success on the job or in advanced education. Typically, the predictive measure is correlated with some quantified assessment of job or school success, called a criterion. Thus, tests used for admission to graduate or profession schools are frequently correlated with grades at that school. The resultant correlation coefficient is called the validity coefficient. Furthermore, because a single instrument is often not able to predict a criterion as well as would be desired, multiple predictors are used, often with the statistical procedure of multiple regression. This procedure weights the various predictive tests to achieve maximal prediction of the criterion. A methodology has also been developed to insure that predictions from tests do not favor one group or discriminate against another. In general, findings of such "differential validity" have been quite rare.

When the purpose of a test is to assess mastery of skills within some behavioral domain, content validity is often involved. The content validity of a test is typically judged by determining how well the domain has been covered. Those who are expert in the test domain generally make such judgments. Careful and detailed description of the domain prior to test construction and implementation of procedures to insure adequate sampling from all aspects of the domain are critical for content validity.

In recent years, it has become accepted that construct validity subsumes predictive and content validity (Geisinger, 1992; Messick, 1989). The critical question asked with regard to construct validity is how well a given test measures the trait(s) it is supposed to be measuring. The construct validity of a test is rarely determined by a single study; rather, it is the gradual accumulation of evidence that provides conclusions regarding construct validity. Procedures implemented to insure content validity and predictive validity research may be used as part of the evidence needed for the construct validation of an instrument. Anastasi & Urbina (1997) provide a good introduction to construct validity and Messick (1989) offers a rather complete summarization.

One key part of validity, as acknowledged by many test theorists (e.g., Messick, 1989), relates to test fairness. If a test is valid, then it should not lead to scores that differ inappropriately among groups as divided by various racial, ethnic, or gender lines, among others. Considerable effort has been put forth over the past 25 years to help psychologists and others develop and use psychological measures fairly (Sandoval, Frisby, Geisinger, Scheunemann, & Grenier, 1998).

Item Analysis

Item analysis procedures are generally employed in test construction and refinement with the purpose of selecting items to maximize a test's utility. Descriptions of the techniques overviewed here may be found in Henrysson (1971) or Thorndike (1982). Most item analysis procedures either (1) look at the number of examinees answering the item correctly and incorrectly, (2) correlate individual items with other variables, or (3) check items for bias.

Conclusion

This article has of necessity omitted numerical concepts, but psychometrics is a quantitative discipline, as perusing the references will demonstrate. The aim of the four quantitative concepts presented in this entry is to improve the quality of data in psychology. The use of norms make test scores communicate information more effectively; equating tests makes scores from varying forms of the same examination comparable. In general, the value of any psychological measuring device is defined by its validity, and the reliability of a measurement procedure limits the validity of the device (i.e., when individual differences on a test are due to random fluctuation, any correlations with that instrument would generally be considered to be randomly based as well). Thus, psychometrics is a discipline that employs numbers, but it is also a discipline that evaluates itself quantitatively.

REFERENCES

Angoff, W. H. (1971). Scales, norms, and equivalent scores. In R. L. Thorndike (Ed.), *Educational measurement* (2nd ed., pp. 508–600) Washington, DC: American Council on Education.

Anastasi, A., & Urbina, S. (1997). *Psychological testing* (7th ed.). Upper Saddle River, NJ: Prentice Hall.

Campbell, J. P. (1976). Psychometric theory. In M. D. Dunnette (Ed.), *Handbook of industrial and organizational psychology* (pp. 185–222). Chicago: Rand McNally.

Cronbach, L. J., Gleser, C. C., Nanda, N., & Rajaratnam, N. (1972). *The dependability of behavioral measurements.* New York: Wiley.

Geisinger, K. F. (1992). The metamorphosis in test validation. *Educational Psychologist, 27,* 197–222.

Hambleton, R. K., Swaminathan, H., & Rogers, H. J. (1991). *Fundamentals of item response theory.* Newbury Park, CA: Sage.

Henrysson, S. (1971). Gathering, analyzing, and using data on test items. In R. L. Thorndike (Ed.), *Educational measurement.* (2nd ed., pp. 130–159). Washington, DC: American Council on Education.

Kolen, M. J., & Brennan, R. L. (1995). *Test equating: Methods and practices.* New York: Springer.

Lord, F. M. (1980). *Applications of item response theory to practical testing problems.* Hillsdale, NJ: Erlbaum.

Messick, S. (1989). Validity. In R. L. Linn (Ed.), *Educational measurement* (3rd ed., pp. 13–104). New York: American Council on Education/Macmillan.

Nunnally, J. C. (1978). *Psychometric theory* (2nd ed.). New York: McGraw-Hill.

Sandoval, J., Frisby, C. L., Geisinger, K. F., Scheunemann, J. D., & Grenier, J. R. (Eds.). (1998). *Test interpretation and diversity.* Washington, DC: American Psychological Association.

Stanley, J. C. (1971). Reliability. In R. L. Thorndike, (Ed.), *Educational measurement* (2nd ed., pp. 356–442) Washington, DC: American Council on Education.

Thorndike, R. L. (1982). *Applied psychometrics.* Boston: Houghton Mifflin.

Kurt F. Geisinger
University of St. Thomas

See also: **Reliability; Validity**

PSYCHONEUROENDOCRINOLOGY

Psychoneuroendocrinology is the study of endocrine functions ultimately controlled by the brain. In turn, many brain processes underlying mood and cognition are influenced by the hormonal products of the various endocrine organs. The main endocrine functions of the body organize development and growth, reproduction, homeostatis (temperature, fluids, minerals, and energy balance), and immunity. Although endocrine dysfunctions are often produced by direct organic disorders, many endocrine disorders have been traced to abnormal brain processes. Thus, the discipline of psychoneuroendocrinology focuses on an exploration of the relationships between mind, brain, and endocrine systems. The following account briefly describes the major constituents of the neuroendocrine systems, and focuses on how the brain, moods, and cognition regulate, and are regulated by, hormones.

General Principles

Most vital endocrine functions in humans are directly influenced by a relatively small brain region—the hypothalamus (roughly 0.003% of the entire brain mass). The neurosecretory cells that regulate the garden pea-sized pituitary (*master*) gland at the base of the brain are located in the middle third of the hypothalamus. The important neuroendocrine cell groups in this region consist of the paraventricular and arcuate nuclei. Different groups of cells in these nuclei are responsible for the direct release of some hormones in the bloodstream. These hypothalamic influences are mediated by direct axonal projections through the *infundibular stalk* to the *posterior lobe* of the pituitary. They control functions such as water balance through the release of antidiuretic hormone (vasopressin), and control uterine contraction and milk-production/ejection in pregnant and lactating women, respectively, through the release of the hormone oxytocin.

However, the majority of tropic hormones are synthesized and released by the *anterior lobe* of the pituitary, through the secretion of special hypothalamic peptides termed *releasing factors.* Upon their secretion, these releasing hormones enter capillaries at the level of the *median eminence* that coalesce to form *portal vessels* that run through the infundibular stalk and terminate in vascular sinuses in the anterior lobe of the pituitary. The range of functions associated with anterior pituitary hormones includes maturation and growth, immunity, stress responsivity reproduction, energy, and metabolism, broadly defined. Thus, although the pituitary gland is responsible for the release of many hormones acting on body tissues and end-organs, it is admirably enslaved by the hypothalamus, and by *negative feedback* effects of the released hormones. Negative feedback inhibition is an important regulatory mechanism whereby hormone release acts at several levels, including the pituitary, hypothalamus, and even brain areas that project to the hypothalamus, to reduce its own further release and thus help reduce deviations from optimal set points that are detrimental to organisms. The hypothalamus and the brain circuits associated with its activity play a critical role in endocrine functions, and, in turn, endocrine status has a significant impact on brain processes subserving affect and cognition.

Hormones, Mood, and Cognition

Most hormones play a significant role in affect and cognition. An example is cortisol, which is secreted by the adrenal cortex under the influence of the anterior pituitary peptide adrenocorticotropin hormone (ACTH). Cortisol hypersecretion, such as in Cushing's disease, produces psychological changes ranging from hyperphagia, insomnia, and euphoria to anxiety, panic, and mania. On the other hand, a significant number of individuals diagnosed with major depression present signs of adrenal hypertrophy and increased circulating levels of cortisol. The mechanisms hypothesized to mediate increased cortisol levels in clinically depressed patients have implicated increased activity at the level of the hypothalamus, and dysregulation of brain serotonergic and noradrenergic systems. A *reduction* of circulating cortisol levels, observed in patients with Addison's disease (adrenal atrophy and insufficiency), is itself correlated with irritability, apprehension, mild anxiety, and inability to concentrate. Thus, low or high circulating cortisol levels produce psychiatric symptoms.

The mechanisms whereby low cortisol levels affect mood and other cognitive functions are poorly understood. Normalization of cortisol levels usually improves the psychological profiles of these patients, and a variety of antidepressant treatments also lead to cortisol normalization in depressed patients. Learning is also influenced by circulating cortisol levels and evidence of poor memory with either too much or too little cortisol has been documented.

Similar observations are reported with thyroid hormones (T_3 and T_4), which are crucial for normal brain development and function. Hypothyroidism during fetal life (a condition known as *cretinism*) produces short stature, sexual immaturity, and severe mental defects in afflicted individuals. In adulthood, hypothyroidism is often associated with depression, bipolar disorder, low energy, appetite and sleep changes, poor concentration, memory impairments, and apathy. The similarity of these symptoms with clinical depression routinely prompts clinicians to test thyroid functions to distinguish between the two conditions. The reverse interaction between affective illnesses, particularly major depression, and thyroid hypofunction has also been documented recently. As with cortisol, hyperthyroidism (as in Grave's disease) presents with several psychiatric symptoms including insomnia, irritability, agitation, major depression, Attention-Deficit/Hyperactivity Disorder, paranoia, and most often, Generalized Anxiety Disorder. Exactly how thyroid hormone dysregulation produces affective disorders, particularly major depression and rapid-cycling bipolar disorder, is mostly unknown. Lower thyroid hormone levels have been suggested to reduce β-adrenergic receptor activity and central serotonin activity, states often associated with a variety of affective disorders.

Growth hormone (GH—also known as somatotropin) dysregulation similarly has a variety of interactions with affect and cognition. Perhaps the most famous phenomenon associated with GH hyposecretion in children is psychosocial dwarfism, a state of short stature sustained by parental abuse. GH deficiency in adults is associated with higher incidence of affective disorders, lack of energy, and impaired self-control. GH hypersecretion can also result in affective disorders, increased appetite, and loss of drive and libido, without observable changes in intelligence or memory functions. Treatments that normalize GH levels ameliorate the psychologic symptoms produced by GH dysregulation. A similar picture emerges with sex hormones, which are believed to be responsible for disturbances in memory retrieval, anger, moodiness, and anxiety associated with premenstrual syndrome (PMS) in 30% of cycling women, and perhaps some cases of major depression associated with childbirth and menopause. Elimination of ovarian cycling in PMS, or estrogen replacement at menopause, can be effective treatments for these conditions. On the other hand, several affective illnesses, as well as physical and psychological stress, are well known to interfere with sexual functions in general and with their associated hormones and cycles.

There are thus clear psychological outcomes associated with endocrine imbalances, most of which are ameliorated with hormonal normalization. Likewise, psychiatric conditions encompassing several mood disorders have a significant impact on most endocrine functions. These observations suggest a close connection between the brain substrates underlying affect and the control of endocrine systems, a connection that essentially remains to be uncovered.

SUGGESTED READING

Akil, H., Campeau, S., Cullinan, W. E., Lechan, R. M., Toni, R., Watson, S. J., & Moore, R. Y. (1999). Neuroendocrine systems I: Overview—Thyroid and adrenal axes. In M. J. Zigmond, F. E. Bloom, S. C. Landis, J. L. Roberts, & L. R. Squire (Eds)., *Fundamental neuroscience* (pp. 1127–1150). San Diego, CA: Academic Press.

Campeau, S. (2002). Psychoneuroendocrinology. In V. S. Ramachandran (Ed.), *Encyclopedia of the human brain* (vol. 4, pp. 83–101). San Diego, CA: Academic Press.

Frohman, L., Cameron, J., & Wise, P. (1999). Neuroendocrine system II: Growth, reproduction, and lactation. In M. J. Zigmond, F. E. Bloom, S. C. Landis, J. L. Roberts, & L. R. Squire (Eds.), *Fundamental neuroscience* (pp. 1151–1187). San Diego, CA: Academic Press.

McEwen, B. S. (1994). Endocrine effects on the brain and their relationship to behavior. In G. J. Siegel, B. W. Agranoff, R. W. Albers, & P. B. Molinoff (Eds.), *Basic neurochemistry* (pp. 1003–1023). New York: Raven Press.

Nemeroff, C. B. (1992). *Neuroendocrinology.* Boca Raton, FL: CRC Press.

Nemeroff, C. B. (1999). *The psychiatric clinics of North America—Psychoneuroendocrinology* (Vol. 21, no. 2). Philadelphia: W. B. Saunders.

Schulkin, J. (1999). *The neuroendocrine regulation of behavior.* Cambridge, UK: Cambridge University Press.

Serge Campeau
University of Colorado at Boulder

See also: **Anxiety; Depression; Pituitary**

PSYCHONEUROIMMUNOLOGY

Psychoneuroimmunology (PNI) is the study of behavioral-neural-endocrine-immune system interactions. It emerged from the realization that the immune system does not operate autonomously, as had been assumed by those who conceptualized it as a closed system, driven by challenges from foreign substances (*antigens*), and regulated by soluble products produced and released by immune cells (e.g., lymphokines, cytokines, monokines). Although antigens do initiate immune responses, and cytokines (such as interleukin-1) do regulate immune processes, data now demonstrate that there are *bidirectional communication pathways* between the immune system and central nervous system (CNS), with each providing important regulatory control over the other (Maier, Watkins, & Fleshner, 1994). The general function of the immune system is to identify and eliminate antigens that enter the body, such as pathogenic microorganisms (bacteria, viruses), fungi, parasites, tumors, and toxic chemicals. It also acts as a regulatory, repair, and surveillance infrastructure, preventing its components from turning against each other and assisting in tissue repair after injury.

The most important cells in the immune system are the thymus (or T) cells, and the leukocytes or white blood cells, of which there are three major categories: granulocyte cells, monocytes (called macrophages when they mature), and lymphocytes—bone marrow (or B) cells, responsible for the production and secretion of antibodies. There are three general types of T cells: Cytotoxic T cells are capable of destroying target cells; natural killer (NK) cells destroy virally infected cells and certain tumors; and helper T cells enhance the immune response. The latter cells are the primary targets of the human immunodeficiency virus (HIV).

Immune function can require global alterations involving the entire organism as well as local processes, and only the CNS can orchestrate such widespread outcomes in a coordinated fashion. Thus, the CNS must be able to exert control over some aspects of the immune response. Conversely, in order to accomplish this function, the CNS must receive information about events in the body, such as infectious agents that have penetrated the skin, and the status of the immune processes. Hence, the immune system exerts control over neural function, and the CNS exerts control over the immune system. These neural-immune interactions permit psychological events to enter the matrix; if neural processes regulate immune processes, then potentially they can impact behavior, emotion, and cognition. PNI studies these complex interactions.

One branch of the immune system can be referred to as the *antibody-mediated subsystem,* which operates through the bloodstream by means of antibodies produced by B cells. When activated by an antigen, B cells produce any of five known types of antibodies; for example, type IgE tends to increase during stress and is responsible for allergic reactions (e.g., wheezing and sneezing as reactions to pollen or house dust). The action of B cells in the antibody-mediated subsystem is influenced by T cells and macrophages, which belong to the immune system's other branch, *the cell-mediated subsystem.* They produce "messenger" substances (e.g., cytokines, lymphokines, monokines) that impact other immune cells. A tumor cell can be attacked by macrophages after being covered with antibodies, or can be killed directly by NK cells. Helper T cells facilitate the function of the killer T cells and the B cells; as a result, innate immune mechanisms operate as a first line of defense against invading pathogens. In addition, the immune system is influenced by neuroendrocrine outflow from the pituitary gland. Two pathways link the brain and the immune system: the autonomic nervous system (ANS) and neuroendrocrine outflow by way of the pituitary. Both routes provide biologically active molecules capable of interacting with cells of the immune system. The potential interactions between neuroendocrine and immune processes is shown by observations that immune cells activated by immunogenic stimuli are capable of producing neuropeptides (Ader, Cohen, & Feltin, 1995).

A laboratory example of CNS involvement in the modulation of immunity is the classical Pavlovian conditioning of antibody- and cell-mediated immune responses. When a distinctly flavored drinking solution (the conditioned stimulus) is paired with injection of an immunosuppressive drug (the unconditioned stimulus), the subsequent antibody response is attentuated in conditioned animals reexposed to the conditioned stimulus (Ader & Cohen, 1991). In Pavlovian terms, an antigen can be thought of as an unconditioned stimulus that elicits an immune response. These data may assist the understanding of how immune activity can decrease as a result of exposure to stimuli that are not ordinarily immnosuppressive. For example, women who had undergone a number of chemotherapy treatments for ovarian cancer displayed immunosuppression after simply returning to the hospital for additional treatment.

When a transplant reaction occurs, it is a result of the cell-mediated immune response. Cell-mediated immunity is also responsible for delayed types of allergy or hypersensitivity. A person sensitive to tuberculin as a result of exposure to tuberculosis will develop an area of reddening and hardness of the skin shortly after the injection within the skin. PNI studies also implicate psychosocial factors in the predisposition to, and the initiation and progression of, diseases involving somatization (Wickramasekera, 1998). The chain of psychophysiological events has not been firmly established, but changes in several components of both antibody- and cell-mediated immunity have been associated with naturally occurring and experimentally induced behavioral and emotional states. For example, the degree of students' loneliness can moderate their immune reactions (Kiecolt-Glaser, 1999).

PNI has triggered a paradigm shift in the understanding of immunoregulatory functions. This new paradigm may provide an understanding of the means by which psychosocial factors and emotional states influence the development and progression of infectious autoimmune and neoplastic diseases. However, most studies have examined only one measure of immunity at one point in time with a circumscribed sample. It will take a considerable amount of research to distill general principles from these specific findings.

REFERENCES

Ader, R., & Cohen, N. (1991). The influence of conditioning on immune responses. In R. Ader, D. L. Felton, & M. Cohen (Eds.), *Psychoneuroimmunology* (2nd ed., pp. 611–646). San Diego, CA: Academic Press.

Ader, R., Cohen, N., & Felton, D. (1995). Psychoneuroimmunology: Interactions between the nervous system and the immune system. *The Lancet, 345,* 99–103.

Kiecolt-Glaser, J. K. (1999). Stress, personal relationships, and immune functioning: Health implications. *Brain, Behavior, and Immunity, 13,* 61–72.

Maier, S. F., Watkins, L. R., & Fleshner, M. (1994). Psychoneuroimmunology: The interface between behavior, brain, and immunity. *American Psychologist, 49,* 1004–1017.

Wickramasekera, I. (1998, Spring). Out of mind is not out of body: Somatization, the high risk model, and psychophysiological psychotherapy. *Biofeedback,* pp. 8–11, 32.

Stanley Krippner
Saybrook Graduate School

PSYCHOPATHIC PERSONALITY

The Antisocial Personalities

The psychiatric problem surrounding the psychopathic personality is to understand why an intelligent and rational person might persist in antisocial behaviors in the face of risks and actual punishments that would inhibit most similar impulses in a normal individual. Defined generally, antisocial personality can be regarded as a family of disorders, comprising at least two genera, which are themselves divisible into "species." One genus might be labeled *sociopaths* and would include those persons of broadly normal temperament who pass through the stages of conduct disorder and delinquency into adult antisocial personality because of parental malfeasance. Although our species evolved a capacity for socialization—for acquiring a self-monitoring conscience, feelings of empathy, altruistic motivations, and a sense of communal responsibility—it appears that, like our capacity for language, this latent talent must be elicited, shaped, and reinforced during childhood. This socialization of children once was the responsibility of the extended family. Judging from the low crime rates that are characteristic of traditional societies still living in extended family groups, most children were successfully socialized in our ancient "environment of evolutionary adaptation." Most modern societies, however, entrust this function only to the child's parents and his peers, and the incidence of sociopathy has risen accordingly. Especially at risk are children reared by single mothers; about 70% of adjudicated delinquents in the United States were reared without the participation of their biological fathers.

A second genus consists of persons whom we might label *psychopaths* and would include species of organic dysfunction or abnormality. Some pathologically impulsive individuals seem to have a specific defect of inhibitory control. Some hyperactive children mature into impulsive psychopaths. Other persons have tyrannical sexual hungers or explosive, uncontrollable tempers or an apparent short-circuiting of aggressive and sexual instincts. These affective disturbances appear to be constitutional in origin and would obviously predispose affected individuals toward antisocial behavior.

The Primary Psychopath

A thoughtful and influential essay on the clinical characteristics of the psychopathic personality, *The Mask of Sanity,* was published in 1941 by psychiatrist Hervey Cleckley. Cleckley's psychopath, "while not deeply vicious, carries disaster lightly in each hand." He may be intelligent and often displays great charm, enhanced undoubtedly by his lack of nervousness or other neurotic manifestations. Yet he is fundamentally unreliable, has a remarkable disregard for truth, and seems incapable of real love or emotional attachment. His antisocial behavior often appears to be inadequately motivated. He takes needless risks, giving the appearance of poor judgment, and shows an indifference to punishment by failing to learn from unpleasant experience. He lacks genuine remorse or shame, often rationalizing his behavior or placing the blame on others. He has a "specific loss of insight," that is, an inability to appreciate how others feel about him or to anticipate how they will react to his outrageous conduct. Notably, in perhaps three cases out of four, "he" is likely to be male.

Cleckley was persuaded that this syndrome results from some deep and probably constitutional defect involving an inability to experience the normal affective accompaniments of experience. Alternatively, it has been suggested that this type of psychopath is distinguished by nothing more exotic than a low "fear IQ." All mammals can experience fear and can learn to associate anxiety with impulses that have been punished or with other stimuli that signal danger. Some people develop conditioned fear responses much more readily than other people do and have high "fear IQs." A child at the low end of this same continuum will be difficult to socialize by the usual techniques of discipline that depend so heavily upon the use of fear and punishment. He may frustrate and antagonize his parents so as to be deprived of the important experience of that prototypic love. It is possible that the average child learns to identify with others as part of a self-protective effort to predict their behavior. Being relatively unconcerned with what others might do or think, the relatively fearless child may invest less effort in this aspect of social learning. One who does not readily identify with others may not readily empathize with others, nor introject their values as required for the normal development of conscience and the capacity for guilt. Fear, and its allies shame, guilt, and embarrassment, seem to be largely responsible for preventing most of us from occasionally committing some of the same misdemeanors that constitute the antisocialism of the psychopath. And the absence of fear, the happy-go-lucky insouciance that emerges when shyness, self-consciousness, guilt, and apprehension are dispelled, is a cardinal attribute of "charm." An important and paradoxical corollary of the "fear IQ" hypothesis is that the child at risk for psychopathy should not be considered sick or defective. His is the stock from which heroes are made. With the right sort of parenting—cultivating a sense of pride and self-respect to substitute for the weak inhibitions of fear and guilt—these children may grow up to be explorers and adventurers, test pilots and astronauts of the kind Tom Wolfe admired in his book *The Right Stuff.*

D. T. Lykken showed in 1957 that the primary psychopath is slow to condition fear to warning signals, tends to ignore painful electric shock in a situation where normals learn to avoid the shock, and seems generally to be less influenced than the average person by reactions of fear or embarrassment. These findings have been replicated and extended by other investigators, most notably by Robert Hare in a series of studies spanning 30 years. Hare has shown, for example, that the primary psychopath displays abnormally little electrodermal arousal in anticipation of a painful shock or a loud blast of noise. Using a startle/stimulus paradigm, C. J. Patrick has shown that frightening or aversive scenes, which enhance startle responses in normal subjects, affect primary psychopaths as do attractive or interesting scenes, by reducing startle.

A genetically determined "low fear IQ," interacting with environmental influences (the style and consistency of parenting, etc.), could promote a tendency toward psychopathy. On the other hand, the vast majority of biological relatives of primary psychopaths are not psychopaths themselves.

David T. Lykken
University of Minnesota

PSYCHOPHYSICS

Psychophysics is the quantitative study of the relation between stimulus and sensation or sensory response. As such, it is concerned with the following questions: (1) How much stimulation is required to produce a sensation or sensory response? (2) How much must a stimulus be changed for the change to be detected? (3) In what way or ways must a stimulus be changed to be perceptually equivalent to another? and (4) How does the sensation or sensory response change with changes in stimulus magnitudes? Answers to these questions, among others, are provided by psychophysical methods. These consist of the three classical methods (limits, adjustment, and constant stimuli) advanced, but not originated, by Gustav T. Fechner (1801–1887) for use in determining thresholds, numerous suprathreshold psychophysical scaling methods used for deriving measures of sensation magnitude, and signal detection theory methods used in providing measures of basic sensory sensitivity, minimally contaminated by motivational and attitudinal biases. Although employed primarily with human subjects, several of the psychophysical methods have been adapted for studying nonhuman sensitivity.

Classical Psychophysics

"By psychophysics," wrote Gustav T. Fechner in his *Elements of Psychophysics* (1966/1860), "I mean a theory which, although ancient as a problem, is new here insofar as its formulation and treatment are concerned; in short, it is an exact theory of the relation of body and mind." Specifically, Fechner attempted to devise a precise and quantitative way of measuring the mind by providing a measure of sensation magnitude.

The idea that strong stimuli generate strong sensations and weak stimuli generate weak sensations was not new. The task was to determine how strong the corresponding sensation was for a given stimulus. Quantitative attempts to do this date back, at least, to the time of the Greek astronomer Hipparchus (160–120 B.C.), who invented the stellar magnitude scale categorizing visible stars into six categories from faintest (sixth magnitude) to brightest (first magnitude). This scale was subsequently found to be approximated by a logarithmic function and consequently was redefined as a logarithmic scale by the British astronomer N. R. Pogson (1829–1891). The concept of a faintest visible star suggests there may be even fainter and invisible stars. Correspondingly, other stimulus dimensions could be divided into perceptible and imperceptible parts. The concept of such a division was incorporated into psychology by Johann Friedrich Herbart (1776–1841) as the threshold (or doorway) into consciousness. The idea of a threshold was influential in Fechner's analysis.

But once into consciousness, how intense is the resulting sensation? This is the basic question of psychophysics. Fechner proposed one answer: $R = k \log (I/I_o)$. The sensation magnitude (R) in Fechner's law varies directly with the logarithm of the stimulus intensity-to-threshold (I/I_o) ratio. An alternative formulation was proposed by the physicist J. A. F. Plateau (1801–1883), who arrived at a power function to describe the sensation of brightness. This formulation has been advanced for other senses as well as vision by S. S. Stevens (1906–1973) in a large number of experiments and theoretical articles (summarized in his *Psychophysics: Introduction to its Perceptual, Neural, and Social Prospects* (1975). The general equation for Stevens' power function is $R = CI^n$, where the sensation magnitude (R) varies directly with the stimulus magnitude (I) raised to a power (n). The value of n depends upon which sense is being stimulated but is considered to be relatively constant over time and across (normal) observers. The constant (C) in the equation is determined by the measurement units used.

These two theoretical formulations—Fechner's law and Stevens' law—describe differently the way sensation magnitude changes with stimulus intensity. Although both state that R increases monotonically with stimulus intensity, different predictions are made about the amount of the increase. Much experimental work has been done using numerous psychophysical methods in an attempt to determine which fits the data better. For example, by using the method of magnitude estimation (which has the observer assign numbers proportional to the stimulus magnitudes), results consistent with Fechner's law would appear as a line when graphed in semilogarithmic coordinates, while those consistent with Stevens' law would be a line in log–log coordinates. Findings have largely supported Stevens' law over Fechner's law, particularly for power functions for which the exponent is 1.0 or larger (e.g., length, duration, electric shock), and for which the predicted results clearly diverge. In those cases for which the exponent is small (e.g., brightness of an extended source or loudness of a sound), data variability may mask the smaller difference in predictions made by the two laws.

Signal Detection Theory

Motivation, expectation, and attitude are biases possessed by the observer in psychophysical threshold determinations. On trials in which no stimulus is presented ("catch trials"), "yes" responses occur (indicating perception of a nonexistent stimulus). This circumstance in signal detection theory (SDT) is called a false alarm. Correct detection of the stimulus (responding with "yes" when the stimulus is present) is termed a hit. Changes in motivation, expectation, or attitude can increase the hit rate, but at the expense of elevating the false alarm rate. Classical psychophysics attempted to keep the false alarm rate low so that false alarms could safely be ignored in threshold determinations. Signal detection theory gives equal consideration to both hit and false alarm rates in determining an alternative index of sensitivity, which is designated d'. The details for computing d' depend upon the SDT procedure used, and alternative sensitivity indices are used (e.g., percent correct).

The motivational, expectancy, and attitudinal biases are collectively treated as the observer's criterion, which is estimated from the false alarm rate. The criterion can be manipulated by changing the proportion of signal trials (and so informing the observer), by instructing the observer to be more lenient or strict, or by changing the payoffs for different decisions. When data are plotted with hit rate along the ordinate and false alarm rate along the abscissa, different levels for the observer's criterion yield different data points along what is called a receiver operating characteristic (ROC) curve. Different ROC curves are generated by different signal levels, but all points on the same ROC curve represent the same level of detectability. Thus sensory and nonsensory factors can be separately identified.

Applications

Psychophysical theory and methods have found application not only in the analysis of basic sensitivity to stimuli but also in screening for sensory deficits (where an individual's threshold is compared with known normal values), in the design of equipment and signaling devices in engineering psychology, in the study of memory using signal detection techniques, and in the comparative evaluation of clinical diagnostic tests.

SUGGESTED READING

Baird, J. C. (1997). *Sensation and judgment: Complementarity theory of psychophysics.* Mahwah, NJ: Erlbaum.

Falmagne, J.-C. (1985). *Elements of psychophysical theory.* New York: Oxford University Press.

Fechner, G. T. (1966). *Elements of psychophysics* (D. H. Howes & E. G. Boring, Eds.; H. E. Adler, Trans.). New York: Holt, Rinehart and Winston. (Original work published 1860)

Green, D. M., & Swets, J. A. (1966). *Signal detection theory and psychophysics.* New York: Wiley.

Macmillan, N. A. (2002). Signal detection theory. In H. Pashler (Ed. in Chief) & J. Wixted (Vol. Ed.), *Stevens' handbook of experimental psychology: Vol. 4. Methodology in experimental psychology* (pp. 43–90). New York: Wiley.

Macmillan, N. A., & Creelman, C. D. (1991). *Detection theory: A user's guide.* New York: Cambridge University Press.

Marks, L. E. (1974). *Sensory processes: The new psychophysics.* New York: Academic Press.

Marks, L. E., & Gescheider, G. A. (2002). Psychophysical scaling. In H. Pashler (Ed. in Chief) & J. Wixted (Vol. Ed.), *Stevens' handbook of experimental psychology: Vol. 4. Methodology in experimental psychology* (pp. 91–138). New York: Wiley.

Stebbins, W. C. (Ed.) (1970). *Animal psychophysics: The design and conduct of sensory experiments.* New York: Appleton-Century-Crofts.

Stevens, S. S. (1975). *Psychophysics: Introduction to its perceptual, neural, and social prospects.* New York: Wiley

Swets, J. A. (1996). *Signal detection theory and ROC analysis in psychology and diagnostics: Collected papers.* Mahwah, NJ: Erlbaum.

George H. Robinson
University of North Alabama

PSYCHOPHYSICS AND COMPUTATIONAL MODELING OF MOTION PERCEPTION

We live, we walk or drive, we turn our head or shift our gaze in a world full of living or humanly created objects that move themselves. In consequence, the image on our retina is never still, and visual motion processing is a distributed and continuous activity of nervous systems, of which we only become aware when we have to solve specific problems, such as catching a ball or assessing the approach of a vehicle. So it is not surprising that motion perception has a long tradition as a research topic (Wade, 1998), starting from classical observations of the waterfall illusion: After prolonged exposure to visual motion, for instance when watching a stream of water, static objects are perceived as moving in the opposite direction—also referred to as motion after-effect. A typical aspect of traditional psychophysics is the attempt to trick the visual system by creating motion sensations from still images, which led to practical applications like "movies." The study of motion-perception-like phenomena in animal systems, from insects to primates, has provided valuable clues to the neural basis of motion processing, and suggested computational models that are increasingly relevant for machine vision. Thus, motion vision can be regarded as an exemplar for the understanding of perception in terms of its underlying brain mechanisms.

Basic Processing Steps

Experiments carried out by Exner in the late nineteenth century mark a fundamental step towards the functional understanding of motion perception. Electric sparks elicited the sensation of apparent motion when presented in rapid succession as alternating between two locations

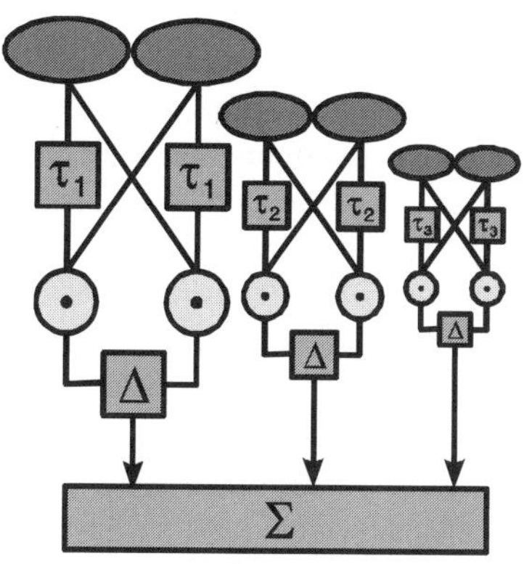

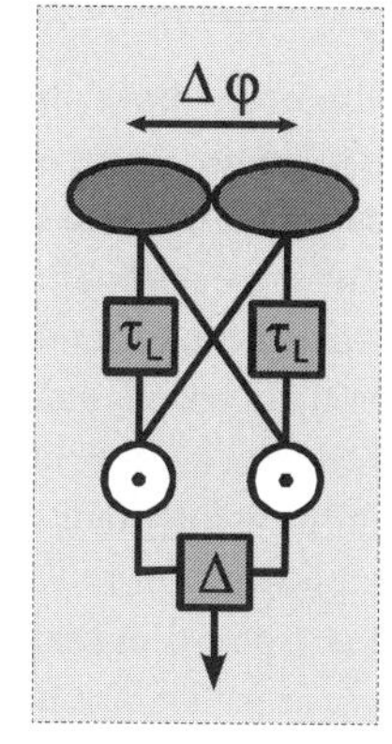

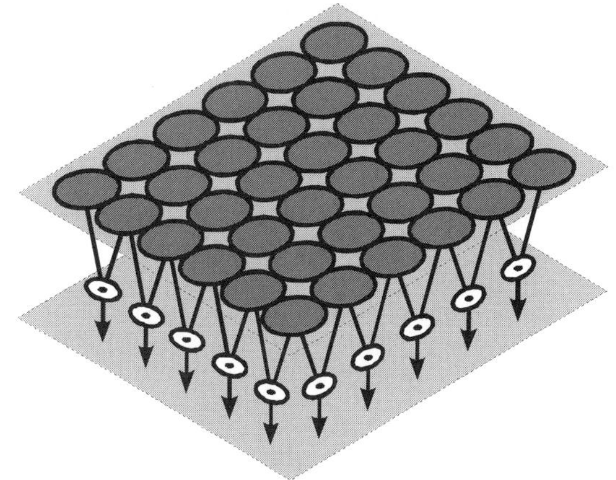

Figure 1. Models of motion perception: elementary motion detector (EMD, middle), two-dimensional arrays (right), spatiotemporal pooling (left).

that could not be resolved with synchronous presentation. This experiment not only demonstrates motion as an independent perceptual entity, but also suggests the basic components of a mechanism to detect visual motion by defining the crucial components of a minimum motion stimulus. For half a century, real and apparent motion stimuli were studied mainly in the framework of a Gestalt psychology seeking to define the crucial attributes that constitute a particular motion percept, before low-level mechanisms returned to the center of attention in the second half of the twentieth century. An elementary motion detector model (EMD), which was originally derived from the analysis of insect vision, turned out to be rather successful in describing the function of a variety of visual systems. The EMD (Figure 1, center) consists of four fundamental operations: (1) two input elements, separated by the sampling base $\Delta\varphi$, pick up luminance signals from neighboring locations in the visual scene; (2) temporal filters delay the input signals with a time constant τ; (3) the original signal from one location interacts with the filtered signal from the other location (multiplication); and (4) the outputs of two mirror-symmetric subunits are subtracted (opponency, indicated by Δ). Whereas the magnitude of the final EMD output does depend on the speed, contrast, and spatial properties of the stimulus, the direction of motion is clearly reflected by the sign of the output (Borst & Egelhaaf, 1989). Thus motion is detected with a small number of simple operations, all of which can be easily realized with neural processing elements.

Local Motion Detection

A number of perceptual features can be expected from this EMD model that represent a class of "correlation" or "motion energy" models. The specific spatial and temporal tuning of the EMD, related to $\Delta\varphi$ and τ, is often used as the fingerprint of this mechanism, eliciting a maximum response for moving gratings at a constant rate of light change (a "temporal frequency optimum"). This and other predictions from the EMD model are consistent with behavioral and physiological evidence from a wide range of animal species. In particular, motion detection and direction discrimination, as well as motion after-effects, depend on temporal frequency, suggesting that EMD design principles are implemented in human vision. Another, even more obvious prediction derived from the EMD model is the existence of displacement limits for motion detection—that is, pattern displacement will no longer be detected once it moves beyond the sampling base of the EMD. This is exactly what was found in a number of experiments where stimuli were generated from randomly distributed dots, which do not allow the identification of objects without motion being detected in the first place. Based on the displacement limits for such Random Dot Kinematograms, a "short-range" process that relies on spatiotemporal correlation, is distinguished from a "long-range" process that identifies and tracks features or objects during a motion sequence (Braddick, 1980).

Motion Integration

The basic motion detection mechanism, and the EMD model, is just the starting point for a cascade of processing steps in which such local filters are combined in various ways.

- Spatial or temporal pooling helps to reduce noise that is inherent to neural processing and is ambient in natural scenes.
- Two-dimensional arrays of motion detectors (Figure 1, right) are required to analyze distributions of motion signals, such as the characteristic "flowfields" generated by movements of the observer (Gibson, 1979) or the boundaries between regions which are characterized by different velocities (to detect camouflaged objects).
- For speed estimation it is necessary to integrate the outputs from EMD units that are tuned to different

spatiotemporal frequencies (by variation of $\Delta\varphi$ and τ, see Figure 1, left). This operation is important for a number of motor control tasks, and can also lead to the reduction of noise (Zanker & Braddick, 1999).

- Motion detectors may operate on a variety of inputs, such as luminance, color, texture, or motion itself. Additional nonlinear processing steps give rise to "first-" and "second-order" motion detection, finally leading to a parallel and hierarchical processing system which is able to extract a wide variety of motion cues (Cavanagh & Mather, 1989).

The complexity indicated by this brief overview of possible interactions between local motion detectors reflects the scope and the significance of motion vision tasks confronting the visual system with an immense flow of visual information, which need to be solved effortlessly when navigating safely through everyday life.

REFERENCES

Borst, A., & Egelhaaf, M. (1989). Principles of visual motion detection. *Trends in Neuroscience, 12,* 297–306.

Braddick, O. J. (1980). Low-level and high-level processes in apparent motion. *Philosophical Translations Society London Behavior, 290,* 137–151.

Cavanagh, P., & Mather, G. (1989). Motion: The long and short of it. *Spat. Vision, 4,* 103–129.

Gibson, J. J. (1979). *The ecological approach to visual perception.* Hillsdale, NJ: Erlbaum.

Wade, N. J. (1998). *A natural history of vision.* Cambridge, MA: MIT Press.

Zanker, J. M., & Braddick, O. J. (1999). How does noise influence the estimation of speed? *Vision Research, 39,* 2411–2420.

JOHANNES M. ZANKER
University of London

See also: **Gestalt Psychology; Perception**

PSYCHOPHYSIOLOGY

Psychophysiology is the study of mental or emotional processes as revealed through involuntary physiological reactions that can be monitored in an intact subject. In psychophysiological research the independent variables will usually be psychological, while the dependent variables will be physiological changes that can be recorded peripherally either as electrical signals (e.g., brain waves, muscle potentials, the electrocardiogram) or as pressure, volume, or temperature changes (e.g., breathing movements, blood pressure, skin temperature).

Psychophysiological Measurement

The immediate object of psychophysiological measurement is to generate an electrical signal that faithfully mimics the manner in which the physiological phenomenon being measured varies over time. Once the phenomenon has been represented as an electrical signal, it can easily be amplified or filtered, visualized as a tracing on a computer screen, and stored for later playback and analysis. Some psychophysiological phenomena, such as the electroencephalogram (EEG), the electromyogram (EMG), and the electrocardiogram (ECG), are already electrical signals generated in the body and their measurement requires only a pair of electrodes, appropriately placed to pick up the biological voltage and connected to the input of an amplifier that will boost this voltage until it is strong enough to be recorded in some way. Electrodes used in psychophysiology are junctions where the flow of electric current changes from electronic, in the wires of the external circuitry, to ionic, in the skin and other tissues. Such an interface is subject to electrochemical processes that can produce polarization. A polarized electrode acts like a high-pass filter that discriminates against slow or low-frequency changes. Relatively nonpolarizing electrodes are available, typically made of silver coated with silver chloride. An electrode paste or electrolyte is applied between the skin surface and the electrode; the properties of this conductive paste are also important for successful recording.

Phenomena such as pressure or temperature changes can be converted into electrical signals by means of an appropriate transducer. For example, a thermister is a device whose electrical resistance varies reliably with temperature; by passing a weak electric current through a thermister probe and amplifying the voltage developed across it, one can produce a signal that accurately represents changes in temperature. A strain gauge, similarly, changes in resistance as it is flexed and can therefore act as the "sense organ" of a pressure transducer or of a device for measuring, for example, breathing movements.

Some psychophysiological phenomena that do not produce signal voltages directly may involve changes in the electrical properties of tissue that can be measured by passing an external sensing current through the tissue; the electrical conductance of the palmar skin is one example. The standard technique for measuring the skin conductance response (SCR) involves applying a constant voltage of 0.5 volt between two nonpolarizing electrodes attached to the palmar skin surface and measuring the small direct-current flow (less than 10 microamperes per square centimeter) through the tissues.

Noise

The modern world is literally full of electrical "noise," electromagnetic emanations from television transmitters, electric motors, passing autos, fluorescent lights, and so forth, which the human body picks up as an antenna does. Bioelectric signals originating in the body, similarly, become noise when they are not the signal one wants to measure but appear nonetheless in one's recordings. Noise of biological origin, as when eye movements affect the EEG or when the ECG shows up unwanted in the electrodermal channel, requires special solutions. Sometimes reorientation of the electrodes will suffice. If the noise consists mainly of frequencies outside the bandwidth of the desired signal, a bandpass filter may provide the solution. A third approach is to measure the noise directly in a separate channel and then subtract it from the signal channel by electronic inversion and summation.

Analyzing the Data

The variance of a sample of scores on some psychophysiological variable can be partitioned thus:

$$\sigma_\omega^2 = \sigma_\psi^2 + \sigma_\phi^2 + \sigma_\varepsilon^2 \qquad (1)$$

where σ_ψ^2 is the variance due to individual differences in the underlying psychological variable of interest, σ_ϕ^2 is the orthogonal component of variance due to physiological differences, and σ_ε^2 represents measurement error. If skin conductance level (SCL), represented by ω, is being measured, for example, ψ might be central nervous system (CNS) arousal or "energy mobilization," ϕ would reflect individual differences in the density and activity of volar sweat glands, and ε would increase with variations in cleaning the skin surface, in positioning of the electrodes, in the area of skin contacting the electrolyte, and so on.

Underlying most psychophysiological measurement is the implicit assumption that ω is a monotonically increasing function—and, it is hoped, a simple linear function—of the underlying variable of interest, ψ, as in:

$$\omega = a + b\psi + \varepsilon. \qquad (2)$$

Using SCL again as the example, the parameter a would represent this subject's minimum SCL when sudomotor activity is zero, while b would be determined by the reactivity of the entire electrodermal system, that is, the increase in conductivity produced by a unit increase in ψ. (Very similar assumptions are implicit in most psychological measurement.) The problem is that the parameters a and b also vary, often within the same individual from time to time, and certainly from one individual to another. This is the variation represented by σ_ϕ^2, in equation 1. The job of the psychophysiologist is, first, to ensure that the physiological variable chosen (ω) *is* linearly related to ψ, at least approximately, and then to try to minimize both measurement error σ_ε^2, and also σ_ϕ^2, the variance due to physiological variability, within subjects or between subjects, which also must be regarded as error variance in this context.

SUGGESTED READING

Andreassi, J. L. (2000). *Psychophysiology* (4th ed.). Mahwah, NJ: Erlbaum.

Backs, R. W., & Boucsein, W. (Eds.) (2000). *Engineering psychophysiology: Issues and applications.* Mahwah, NJ: Erlbaum.

Cacioppo, J. T., Tassinary, L. G., & Berntson, G. B. (Eds.). (2000). *Handbook of psychophysiology* (2nd ed.). Cambridge, UK: Cambridge University Press.

Stern, R. M., Ray, W. J., & Quigley, K. S. (2001). *Psychophysiological recording today* (2nd ed.). Oxford, UK: Oxford University Press.

David T. Lykken
University of Minnesota

PSYCHOSEXUAL STAGES

In Sigmund Freud's (1938) personality theory, development is described in terms of stages defined by the specific expression of sexual, or libidinal, urges. Those areas of the body—the erogenous zones—that give rise to libidinal pleasure at specific ages are identified as the focus of each developmental stage. Thus the pleasure derived from sucking liquids and mouthing foods is the focus of the first developmental period, the *oral stage.* The satisfaction surrounding the retaining and expelling of feces defines the second, *anal stage.* The *phallic stage* refers to the period in which the young child begins to explore and derive pleasure from the genitals. These three stages, called the pregenital stages, span, respectively, the first year of life, the second two years, and the years from three to five, roughly.

The pregenital stages are followed by a period of supposed psychosexual quiescence, the *latency period,* which lasts until the onset of puberty. Puberty, however, brings with it a resurgence of the pregenital urges, which now focus specifically on the pleasures deriving from the genital organs; thus the name of this final developmental period, the *genital stage.*

Libidinal urges in Freudian theory are not equatable with genital sexuality. For example, three of the psychosexual stages are "pregenital." The term *libido* is meant to define a broad concept of mental sexual energy occurring even in infancy. Nor do the stages refer only to male sexuality, despite the masculine language. For example, the phallic stage refers to the last pregenital stage of both sexes.

Oral Stage

The oral stage of development is characterized by a need for nurturance and by pleasure derived primarily from activities of the mouth and lips, such as sucking, mouthing, and swallowing of food, as well as, later, the biting and chewing of food. These early gratifications are said to be the precursors of the development of later character traits. Thus, the two main sources of oral pleasure, oral incorporation and biting (seen as aggressive), may be the prototypes for later habits and personality traits. Oral incorporation as a predominant trait may lead to the acquisition of material things and acquisitiveness in personal relationships. An oral aggressive style may include such behavior traits as "biting" sarcasm, "chewing out" an opponent, and spewing out an invective. Dependency and need for approval are seen as main components of the oral character. Some evidence for this relationship has been found by Joseph Masling et al. (1968), who found that conforming college students gave a significantly greater number of "oral-dependent" responses on the Rorschach test, when compared with less conforming subjects.

Anal Stage

The anal stage extends approximately from one year of age to two, when bowel and bladder control is a primary task, and the pleasure and pain derived from expelling and retaining feces are the main libidinal outlet. The toddler in the anal period is growing in independence and self-assertion. Freud saw the events surrounding the task of toilet training as crucial for later character formation. A child who is harshly trained and severely punished for accidents before acquiring control may express rage by defecating at will at inappropriate times or by being selfish and stingy (anal retentive). Conversely, the child who is rewarded and praised for control efforts becomes the generous (anal expulsive) and often creative individual. Overindulgence can lead to messiness and vagueness (Maddi, 1972, p. 273).

Phallic Stage

Between 2 and 3 years of age, the child begins more active body exploration. The locus of erotic pleasure shifts from the anus to the genitals as the young child discovers the pleasurable effects of masturbation. One of the main tenets of Freudian theory, the Oedipus complex, has its origins in this stage. Named for the mythical Greek king of Thebes who killed his father and married his mother, the Oedipus complex refers to the child's incestuous desire for the opposite-sexed parent. In the boy, the simultaneous pleasure from autoerotic activity coupled with a desire for the mother and a rivalry with his father generates anger in his father, which the boy perceives as a threat. Since the erotic pleasure emanates from the genitals, the boy assumes that the father may destroy them. Freud called this perceived threat *castration anxiety.*

The resolution of the Oedipus complex in the girl is not as clear in Freudian theory. Since castration to the girl appears to be a *fait accompli,* she blames her mother, whom she sees as sharing her plight, and envies the male for his organ and favored position and power. Freud's term for this condition was *penis envy.* The girl gradually gives up her attachment to her father and begins to identify with her mother.

Genital Stage

After a period of psychosexual quiescence, termed latency, puberty brings with it a resurgence of the phallic strivings and more realistic capabilities for their expression. Once again, masturbation becomes a source of erotic satisfaction, and appears so nearly universal and urgent that Freud called this adolescent impulse *onanism of necessity.* Armed with full adult genitalia and sexual drives, the growing adolescent shifts his or her affection from parents to peers, first of the same sex (a brief homosexual phase, just after puberty), and then of the opposite sex. In the fully integrated adult, the psychosexual urges most often find expression in activity with an opposite-sexed partner of roughly the same age. More important, these urges no longer are purely narcissistic, as they were in the pregenital stages. The psychosexual urges now extend and generalize to altruism, friendship, sharing, and loving of a more adult nature.

REFERENCES

Asch, S. E. (1956). Studies of independence and conformity: I. A minority of one against a unanimous majority. *Psychological Monographs, 70*(9, Entire No. 416), 1–70.

Freud, S. (1969/1938/1935/1920). *A general introduction to psychoanalysis.* New York: Pocket Books.

Maddi, S. R. (1976/1972/1968). *Personality theories: A comparative analysis* (3rd ed.) Homewood, IL: Dorsey Press.

Masling, J., Weiss, L., & Rothschild, B. (1968). Relationships of oral imagery to yielding behavior and birth order. *Journal of Consulting and Clinical Psychology, 32,* 89–91.

John Paul McKinney

PSYCHOSOMATIC DISORDERS

The term *psychosomatic disorder* generally refers to a type of physical condition in which the etiology or course is related to significant psychological factors. A psychosomatic disorder involves a demonstrable organic pathology, such as a duodenal ulcer, or a known pathophysiological process, such as a migraine headache. These conditions usually include such disorders as rheumatoid arthritis, asthma, and essential hypertension, and are not limited to a single physiological system.

Psychosomatic disorders, also known as psychophysiologic disorders, were not specifically listed in the fourth edition of the *Diagnostic and Statistical Manual of Mental Disorders,* fourth edition (*DSM-IV*), but are referred to as "psychological factors affecting medical condition," and in the ninth edition of the *International Classification of Diseases* (*ICD-9*) as "psychic factors associated with diseases classified elsewhere."

Historical Background

Psychosomatic concepts have roots in ancient philosophical thoughts about mind-body relationships. Emperor Huang Ti (c. 2697–2597 B.C.) recorded in his *Classic of Internal Medicine* keen observations on the etiology, diagnosis, treatment, and prognosis of psychosomatic illnesses. Herbal doctors of the Babylonian-Assyrian civilization (c. 2500–500 B.C.) considered sin to be the source of sickness and exorcism to be the cure, with mind and body interaction being central to their concept of disease.

Socrates (496–399 B.C.) and Hippocrates (466–375 B.C.) also offered early acknowledgment of the role of mental factors in health and disease. Heinroth in 1818 first employed the word "psychosomatic," a term later popularized by German psychiatrist Jacobi. Scientific medicine achieved major progress toward the end of the nineteenth century, with an emphasis on physical disease, as a result of the discoveries in morbid anatomy, microbiology, and biochemistry. The gap between the biological and the psychological aspects of illness remained until a rapprochement began to develop in the early twentieth century, largely because of the work of Freud, Pavlov, and Cannon. Freud's elaboration of the unconscious, Pavlov's studies of the conditioned reflex, and Cannon's notion of fight and flight reactions offered important psychological concepts that stimulated the growth of the psychosomatic approach in health care.

A psychosomatic movement began in Germany and Austria in the 1920s, and many Europeans, such as Alexander, migrated to the United States, bringing along the European interest in psychosomatic disorders. In 1939, the birth of the journal *Psychosomatic Medicine,* under the editorship of Dunbar, reflected the growing interest in this field in the United States. Important volumes began to appear in the 1940s and 1950s, including Weiss and English's *Psychosomatic Medicine,* Alexander's *Psychosomatic Medicine,* and Grinker's *Psychosomatic Research.*

Early psychosomatic methodology consisted mainly of clinical observations. By the late 1950s, an increasing number of psychologists were engaged in laboratory and clinical psychosomatic experiments. There was a declining interest in researching psychoanalytic concepts in psychosomatic problems, accompanied by a growing trend toward experimental research studying human biological response to hypnotic techniques, conditioning, and sensory input and deprivation. Psychosomatic research with animals provided a large body of scientific information, with relevant implications for human physiology and clinical practice.

Theoretical Concepts

Although Freud never mentioned "psychosomatic disorder" in his writings, he stressed the role of psychic determinism in somatic conversion hysteria. Freud's followers provided further refinement of psychoanalytic concepts vis-à-vis psychosomatic phenomena, including Dunbar's description of personality profiles (e.g., the ulcer personality, the coronary personality, and the arthritic personality), as well as Alexander's analysis of psychodynamic patterns underlying asthma, ulcers, arthritis, hypertension, and other disorders.

Important psychosomatic concepts also emerged in nonpsychoanalytic schools. Corticovisceral theory prevailed in Eastern Europe, dominated by Pavlovian neurophysiology and conditioning research. In the United States, psychological stress theory, such as Cannon's concept of bodily homeostasis, Wolff's research on the adaptive biological responses, and Selye's work on pituitary adrenal responses formed the foundation for psychosomatic research and clinical approaches. Social or ecological concepts have also been elaborated, as in the early Midtown Manhattan Project or the more recent life-change studies by Rahe and Holmes.

Type of Disease

In 1950, Alexander listed seven classic psychosomatic diseases: essential hypertension, peptic ulcer, rheumatoid arthritis, hyperthyroidism, bronchial asthma, colitis, and neurodermatitis. More recently, the extensive classification system of the ninth *International Classification of Diseases* provided a comprehensive list of psychosomatic disorders, including the following:

1. Psychosomatic disorders involving tissue damage, such as asthma, dermatitis, eczema, gastric ulcer, mucous colitis, ulcerative colitis, urticaria, and psychosocial dwarfism.
2. Psychosomatic disorders not involving tissue damage, such as psychogenic torticollis, air hunger, psychogenic hiccup, hyperventilation, psychogenic cough, yawning, cardiac neurosis, cardiovascular neurosis, neurocirculatory asthenia, psychogenic cardiovascular disorder, psychogenic pruritus, aerophagy, psychogenic cyclical vomiting, psychogenic dysmenorrhea, and teeth grinding. A psychosomatic syndrome can also be categorized according to the major organ systems affected.

In the following, psychological factors may be a cause or an aggravating stress that affects the course of the disorder.

1. Gastrointestinal disorders: gastric and duodenal ulcers, ulcerative colitis, anorexia nervosa, bulimia, obesity, irritable colon, spastic colitis.

2. Respiratory disorders: asthma, hyperventilation, tuberculosis.
3. Skin disorders: neurodermatitis or eczema, pruritus, urticaria, psoriasis, skin allergies, herpes.
4. Musculoskeletal disorders: rheumatoid arthritis, temporomandibular jaw syndrome, muscle contraction headache.
5. Metabolic and endocrine disorders: thyrotoxicosis, myxedema, diabetes mellitus, Addison's disease, Cushing's syndrome, parathyroid disease, hypoglycemia.
6. Gynecological and obstetrical disorders: menstrual disorders (premenstrual tension, menorrhagia, pseudocyesis), conception and pregnancy (sterility, spontaneous abortion).
7. Cardiovascular disorders: coronary artery disease, essential hypertension, congestive heart failure, vasodepressive syncope, migraine headaches, angina pectoris, arrhythmia, cardiospasm, tachycardia.
8. Hematological disorders: hemophilia.
9. Others: immune diseases, chronic pain syndrome, allergic reactions.

Treatment

The early roots of psychosomatic medicine consisted of psychoanalytically oriented therapies, such as those of Alexander and his associates. In more recent decades, nonanalytic psychotherapies have become more prominent. With the increasing sophistication in pharmacotherapies, psychiatrists find the use of psychotropic medications helpful, including various tranquilizers and antidepressants. Group psychotherapy is especially suitable for certain psychosomatic patients, such as those with bronchial asthma, who find relief in meeting others with similar concerns and learn to identify and verbalize significant feelings related to this condition.

In cases where psychosomatic reactions may be the result of learned patterns of behavior—for example, certain sexual dysfunctions—behavior therapy is an effective therapeutic method. Behavioral approaches have been demonstrated to be effective components of interventions for hypertension, arthritis, pain, obesity, and bulimia nervosa.

Recent decades have seen a rapid growth in psychologists' employment of behavior modification techniques, exercise, and relaxation therapies, such as Jacobson's progressive relaxation, Luthe's autogenic training, and biofeedback to treat headaches and other stress-related disorders. In addition, principles and methods of transcendental meditation, yoga, controlled breathing, and Morita therapy have also been used with psychosomatic disorders.

SUGGESTED READING

Kaplan, H. I., & Saddock, B. J. (1995). *Comprehensive textbook of clinical psychiatry* (6th ed.). Baltimore: Williams & Wilkins.

Stoudemire, A. (Ed.). (1995). *Psychological factors affecting medical conditions.* Washington, DC: American Psychiatric Press.

William T. Tsushima
Straub Clinic and Hospital

See also: **Behavior Therapy; Psychotherapy**

PSYCHOSTIMULANT TREATMENT FOR CHILDREN

The putative efficacy of psychostimulants as a first-line treatment for children with Attention-Deficit/Hyperactivity Disorder (ADHD) is well documented and deserved. Few treatments provide benefit to such a large percentage of individuals affected with a particular disorder and improve functioning in multiple domains. Positive effects are ascertained in an estimated 50% to 96% of children with ADHD, depending on the stringency with which positive response is defined and the particular outcome variable targeted. For example, positive treatment response is estimated to occur in 70% of children undergoing psychostimulant therapy, whereas an overall 96% improvement rate in behavior problems is demonstrated when response is defined as improvement on any one of several alternative psychostimulants. Conversely, others have shown response rates to vary between 53% and 94% for academic efficiency and teacher-rated classroom behavior, respectively, when positive response is evaluated using psychometric indices such as statistically derived normative comparison scores (Rapport, Denney, DuPaul, & Gardner, 1994).

The breadth of domains shown to improve with psychostimulant treatment is equally impressive. These include direct observations of children's attention, behavior, and academic performance (Rapport et al., 1994), parent/teacher ratings of social deportment, performance on a wide range of clinic-based neurocognitive tests, tasks, and paradigms (for a review, see Rapport & Kelly, 1991), peer relationships and interpersonal behavior, and even participation in some extracurricular activities. Titrating MPH (i.e., determining the correct dosage), however, has become increasingly more complex in recent years. Issues related to determining appropriate dosage and which behaviors or variables to target for intervention are discussed below.

Titrating Psychostimulants

Methylphenidate (MPH) is currently the most widely prescribed psychostimulant for treating children with ADHD, albeit several alternative formulations such as Concerta, Metadate, and Adderall are now available and their effects on behavior last substantially longer than those obtained from a standard tablet of MPH. Adderall is the best studied of the alternatives. It appears to be therapeutically equivalent to standard MPH in affecting behavior; however, limited information is available concerning its effects on cognitive function in children.

Several misconceptions concerning both the initial titration of and dosage effects associated with psychostimulants prevail. Popular among these is the notion that a child's gross body weight should be used to establish initial dosage parameters, using a milligram of medicine per kilogram of body weight (mg/kg) ratio—the implicit assumption being that heavier children require more medicine than do lighter-weight children. Two studies have addressed this issue in recent years, with both reporting a lack of relationship (not even a trend) between children's body weight and clinical response to methylphenidate (MPH).

A more complicated issue concerns the dose-response nature of psychostimulants. For example, there is widespread belief that different behavioral domains are optimized at widely discrepant dosage levels in children. Many clinicians believe that lower dosages optimize cognitive performance whereas higher dosages are needed to optimize behavior and manageability in the classroom. Neither comprehensive literature reviews (see Rapport & Kelly, 1991) nor direct observations of children receiving psychostimulant treatment while working in classroom or laboratory environments have supported this contention. Instead, both classroom behavior and cognitive performance (including academic performance) have been found to be affected at similar dosage levels, usually within the middle to higher dosage range when using MPH (Rapport et al., 1994). It should be stressed, however, that these results are based on average responses of large groups of children. The optimal dosage for a particular child must be carefully determined in the context of a controlled medication trial.

Selecting Appropriate Target Behaviors

Most children are prescribed psychostimulants by their primary physician and seen routinely in an office setting for purposes of monitoring treatment effectiveness (including the possibility of emergent symptoms or side effects). Physicians, in turn, rely primarily on parent and teacher reports to (1) establish whether a child has shown a favorable response to the medication, and (2) determine the most effective dosage. What would appear to be a relatively straightforward endeavor is in fact complicated by a number of factors. Neither children nor their parents are particularly astute at delineating positive treatment effects. Because of the relatively short behavioral life of MPH (approximately 4 to 5 hours from time of ingestion) and dissimilarities between the home and classroom setting (particularly the fewer cognitive demands associated with the former), parents are not ideally situated to judge treatment effectiveness. Moreover, the findings of a recent study reveal that neither initial presenting characteristics of the child (e.g., level of pretreatment hyperactivity, age) nor changes in particular behavioral domains (e.g., attention, reduced impulsivity) portend improvement in other important areas such as academic functioning (Denney & Rapport, 1999). Conversely, improved academic functioning nearly always coincides with improved behavior. The essence of this finding is that children's academic performance in the classroom should serve as the primary target for titrating psychostimulants in children. Assessment of this domain can be accomplished by using the Academic Performance Rating Scale (APRS; DuPaul, Rapport, & Perriello, 1991) or a similar instrument that provides a valid index of children's classroom academic performance.

Conclusions

The use of psychostimulants as a therapeutic regimen to treat children with ADHD remains a controversial topic. A majority of children derive clear and sustained benefit from this therapeutic modality, although most experienced clinicians and researchers concur that neither this nor any treatment regimen used alone adequately addresses the multifaceted difficulties associated with ADHD. When used, a controlled medication trial incorporating a wide range of dosages is recommended owing to the unique response children exhibit to psychostimulants. Outcome assessment should, at the very least, include multiple, standardized, treatment-sensitive measures across settings (home and school) throughout the duration of the clinical trial as well as at scheduled intervals thereafter to assess continuity and maintenance of treatment effects. Finally, clinical indices of improvement should ideally include measures from both the behavioral and cognitive (academic) domains, owing to the latter variable's established relationship with long-term academic achievement and adult outcome.

REFERENCES

Denney, C. B., & Rapport, M. D. (1999). Predicting methylphenidate response in children with Attention Deficit Hyperactivity Disorder: Theoretical, empirical and conceptual models. *Journal of the American Academy of Child and Adolescent Psychiatry, 38,* 393–401.

DuPaul, G. J., Rapport, M. D., & Perriello, L. M. (1991). Teacher ratings of academic skills: The development of the Academic Performance Rating Scale. *School Psychology Review, 20,* 284–300.

Rapport, M. D., Denney, C., DuPaul, G. J., & Gardner, M. (1994). Attention Deficit Disorder and methylphenidate: Normalization rates, clinical effectiveness, and response prediction in 76 children. *Journal of the American Academy of Child and Adolescent Psychiatry, 33,* 882–893.

Rapport, M. D., & Kelly, K. L. (1991). Psychostimulant effects on learning and cognitive function: Findings and implications for children with Attention Deficit Hyperactivity Disorder. *Clinical Psychology Review, 11,* 61–92.

Mark D. Rapport
Matt Alderson
University of Central Florida

See also: **Attention-Deficit/Hyperactivity Disorder (ADHD)**

PSYCHOSURGERY

Psychosurgery, by definition, implies the destruction of brain tissue for the relief of severe, persistent, and debilitating psychiatric symptomatology. Its use can be traced back with early archeological evidence of trepanation in 2000 B.C. (Valenstein, 1980). However, the first widespread application of psychosurgical procedures to psychiatric patients began in the late 1930s, reached its peak in the 1960s, and began to decline in the 1970s (Weingarten & Cummings, 2001).

In the first half of this century, the technique most frequently used for creating lesions was frontal lobotomy, wherein fibers in the frontal lobes were cut bilaterally. Initially this was accomplished by placing a cutting instrument through a cannula into burr holes drilled through the skull, or by placing it through the bony orbits above the eyes, and then rotating the instrument. More precise placement of lesions became possible during the 1950s as a result of the invention of a stereotaxic instrument that held the head in a fixed position. A knife or electrode could then be lowered into the brain at a point predetermined by a set of three-dimensional coordinates as defined by a brain map or atlas. In this manner, well-localized lesions could be made. This treatment was initially used largely for the treatment of Schizophrenia. The use of knife cuts was gradually replaced by the use of electric currents or radiofrequency waves delivered through electrodes. Some neurosurgeons have also used cryoprobes, radioisotopes, proton beams, ultrasound, and thermocoagulation for this purpose (Weingarten & Cummings, 2001).

Emotional changes occur in a variety of neurological disorders including epilepsy, stroke, and trauma. Clinically, it has been noted that lesions in distinctly different areas of the brain will disrupt emotional processing at different levels or stages. Therefore, a common feature shared by theories of emotional dysfunction is that multiple brain systems are involved (Borod, 2000; Davidson, Pizzagalli, Nitschke, & Putnam, 2002; LeDoux 2000). Some theories accent the role of the right hemisphere in emotion, and other theories emphasize frontal-cortical-subcortical system connections. Still others have advanced modular models that combine concepts from lateral dominance with ideas about the brain's other axes (dorsal-ventral and anterior-posterior). Here, the right hemisphere's putative role in emotion is modified by a valence hypothesis: The right hemisphere controls negative emotions, while the left controls positive emotions. In more recent years, psychosurgery has been used in the treatment of refractory obsessive-compulsive disorder and in refractory depression.

In the main, psychosurgery has targeted bilateral brain systems. The most effective early targets for relief of psychiatric symptoms appear to involve the medial and ventral areas of the frontal lobes. Other regions of the brain with well-defined connections to specific frontal areas have been selected as targets for psychosurgery. These connecting regions include the cingulum, the amygdala, several areas in the thalamus and hypothalamus, and anterior portions of the internal capsule (to interrupt frontothalamic projections). The term *tractotomy* refers to the interruption of fiber tracts connecting frontal areas with lower brain centers, and it has been used in the treatment of severe depression, anxiety, and Obsessive-Compulsive Disorder. Amygdalotomy has been effective in some patients with aggressive behaviors associated with temporal lobe epilepsy (Jasper, Riggio, & Goldman-Rakic, 1995). Pallidotomy in patients with severe Parkinson's disease restores, in some cases, relatively normal motor function (see Lang & Lozano, 1998). It remains to be seen, however, how long the beneficial effects last.

Since psychosurgery for psychiatric patients has often been performed on apparently normal brain tissue, its practice has generated considerable controversy. The National Commission for the Protection of Human Subjects of Biomedical and Behavioral Research supported several intensive investigations on the use and efficacy of psychosurgery. As indicated in a resultant report by the U.S. Department of Health, Education and Welfare and the follow-up reports published in Valenstein's book (Valenstein, 1980), the Commission considered many pros and cons, including risks and benefits. Opponents of the use of psychosurgery have compared it to the abuses of human subjects in biomedical experiments carried out in Germany during World War II. Those in favor of psychosurgery have argued that its prohibition would rob patients of their right to effective medical treatment by limiting the scope of procedures available.

On the basis of the diverse and extensive information reviewed by the Commission, recommendations were made to the U.S. Department of Health and Human Services (DHHS) regarding the use of psychosurgery. One recommendation encouraged DHHS to support evaluative studies of the safety and efficacy of the procedures, and two other recommendations detailed conditions for, and approval of, their limited use with institutionalized individuals. Obviously psychosurgery is a topic that involves many ethical, scientific, and legal concerns, and there is no easy resolution of the controversy associated with its use.

REFERENCES

Borod, J. C. (Ed.). (2000). *The neuropsychology of emotion.* New York: Oxford University Press.

Davidson, R. J., Pizzagalli, D., Nitschke, J. B., & Putnam, K. (2002). Depression: Perspectives from affective neuroscience. *Annual Review of Psychology, 53,* 545–574.

Jasper, J. H., Riggio, S., & Goldman-Rakic, P. (Eds.). (1995). *Epilepsy and the functional anatomy of the frontal lobe.* New York: Raven Press.

Lang, A. E., & Lozano, A. M. (1998). Medical progress: Parkinson's disease. *New England Journal of Medicine, 339*(16), 1130–1143.

LeDoux, J. E. (2000). Emotion circuits in the brain. *Annual Review of Neuroscience, 23,* 155–184.

Valenstein, E. S. (Ed.). (1980). *The psychosurgery debate: Scientific, legal and ethical perspectives.* San Francisco: Freeman.

Weingarten, S. M., & Cummings, J. L. (2001). Psychosurgery of frontal-subcortical circuits. In D. G. Lichter & J. L. Cummings (Eds.), *Frontal-subcortical circuits in psychiatric and neurological disorders* (pp. 421–435). New York: Guilford Press.

Marlene Oscar-Berman
Boston University School of Medicine, and Department of Veterans Affairs Healthcare System, Boston Campus

PSYCHOTHERAPY

Definition and Utilization

What is psychotherapy? Although originally defined as one-on-one sessions between a patient and therapist with the intent of changing the inner workings of the patient's psychological life, over the last several decades psychotherapy has broadened in its formats, participants, procedures, and focus (there are now over 250 different forms of psychotherapy) so that any definition of psychotherapy must be far-ranging enough to encompass the full spectrum of different "psychotherapies." What relaxation therapy, family therapy, cognitive therapy, group therapy, insight-oriented therapy, play therapy (with children), exposure therapy—to name a few—have in common is a set of psychological or behavioral procedures, delivered by one or more therapists, designed to change the thoughts, feelings, somatic symptoms, or behaviors of one or more participants who are seeking help.

Although the practice of psychotherapy is not regulated, it is generally delivered by psychologists, psychiatrists, social workers, family therapists, psychiatric nurses, pastoral counselors, or addiction counselors. Surveys have found that 2.2% to 4.4% (depending on the city) of the United States population makes at least one visit to a mental health specialist in a 6-month period (Hough, Landsverk, Karno, & Burnam, 1987). People who seek psychotherapy do so for a variety of reasons, including treatment for an ongoing psychiatric disorder such as Agoraphobia or depression, difficulty coping with recent stressful life events, or desire for more success or satisfaction with life.

History

Psychotherapy in its modern form can be traced to Sigmund Freud in the late nineteenth century. Psychoanalysis was developed as a long-term treatment designed to bring to the patient's awareness repressed unconscious conflicts. Despite the large number of brands of psychotherapy today, only a few general schools have continued to be influential. The psychodynamic, or analytic, school continued to develop over the twentieth century. Under the influence of Sandor Ferenczi, Otto Rank, Franz Alexander, and Thomas French, the analytic school shifted towards shorter-term treatments that included increased therapist activity. Modern psychodynamic therapy evolved in the 1970s under the influence of Malan, Mann, Sifneos, and Davanloo, who encouraged a focal treatment that explored patients' maladaptive interpersonal styles within the context of time limits. In the 1980s, Luborsky and Strupp and Binder published manuals for implementing short-term dynamic psychotherapy. These treatments focus mainly on the interpretation of maladaptive relationship patterns as they influence the patient's current relationships and functioning, provided in the context of a supportive therapeutic relationship.

Closely related to dynamic treatments, the interpersonal school was first described by Harry Stack Sullivan. Sullivan focused on interpersonal relationships as they influenced the development of the patient's personality. In 1984, Klerman, Weissman, Rounsaville, and Chevron published a manual for interpersonal psychotherapy. This treatment emphasizes the patient's current interpersonal relationships. Unlike dynamic treatments, developmental factors and maladaptive relationship patterns as they are expressed in the therapeutic relationship are not given direct attention.

Carl Rogers developed the client-centered school of psychotherapy. This approach focuses on the psychological climate created by the therapist. An environment characterized by genuine acceptance, sensitive understanding, and empathic understanding is believed to foster within the patient the ability to reorganize his or her personality. Unlike dynamic therapy, the climate of the therapeutic relationship alone is believed to foster the patient's gains.

The behavioral school of psychotherapy has also remained influential. Behavior therapy has its base in learning theory. The model postulates that symptoms are a result of learned behaviors that are subject to direct manipulation by contingency management and classical conditioning. Techniques focus on modifying behavior through positive and negative reinforcement and desensitization.

The cognitive school of psychotherapy was founded by Albert Ellis in the 1950s. In Rational Emotive Therapy, problems are seen as a result of faulty expectations and irrational thoughts. The goal of this treatment is to teach patients to modify their thinking patterns. In 1979, Aaron Beck published a manual of cognitive therapy for depression. This treatment focuses on identifying, testing the validity of, and correcting the dysfunctional beliefs that underlie the patient's cognitions.

These types of psychotherapy are applied in both an individual and group format. In individual therapy, the therapist works one-on-one with the patient, while group formats may include couples, families, or groups of strangers brought together to work on a specific topic. The family systems approach to psychotherapy focuses on each family member as coequal in importance. The therapist helps the members identify problems in the family system and reorganize themselves as an effective family unit.

A recent trend to emphasize the common factors across the various schools of psychotherapy has paved the way for the movement toward integration of different approaches. Many practitioners find it useful to borrow techniques from multiple schools to maximize patient benefit. Cognitive and behavioral techniques are often used in combination and are seen as important complements to each other in the therapeutic process.

Another recent trend has been toward brief, rather than long-term, treatment. This trend has been influenced in part by research conducted on brief therapy, and in part because of the need to contain health care costs (i.e., most insurance companies will only pay for a limited number of sessions of psychotherapy).

Research on Psychotherapy

Although many are skeptical of psychotherapy as a treatment, it has been investigated in research studies more than any other medical procedure, with well over 1,000 studies of psychotherapy performed to date. Extensive reviews of the research literature have concluded that, broadly speaking, psychotherapy works. Research is now directed toward the more specific question of finding out which type of psychotherapy procedure works best with identified types of patient problems or disorders, and developing new techniques for enhancing treatment benefits. Other research examines psychotherapy as it is delivered in the community—its effectiveness, cost, and dose-response relationships. Still yet another form of psychotherapy research (process studies) looks at what actually happens during psychotherapy sessions and attempts to unravel the relationship between the actions of the therapist in sessions and changes in the patient(s).

Research on specific treatment procedures for different problems and disorders has led to recommendations about which psychotherapy procedures have sufficient empirical support. These recommendations are based largely upon the results of studies in which patients are randomly assigned to psychotherapy versus a control group (e.g., a waiting list or a psychological or pill placebo). Specific psychotherapies have received strong empirical support as treatments for Obsessive-Compulsive Disorder, Major Depressive Disorder, Panic Disorder, Agoraphobia, and Generalized Anxiety Disorder (Chambless et al., 1996). For these disorders, the relative effectiveness of psychotherapy compared to psychotropic medication, or the combination of medication and psychotherapy, is of high public health significance and is a topic of much ongoing research.

Studies of psychotherapy as it is practiced in the community have yielded important data on the number of treatment sessions that are necessary to help patients achieve a recovery from their symptoms. About a year of treatment (58 sessions) is needed to produce symptomatic recovery for 75% of patients (Kopta, Howard, Lowry, & Beutler, 1994). While brief psychotherapy may be of help to many, these data suggest that longer-term psychotherapy may still be needed for other patients to reach full recovery. Other community-based studies of psychotherapy examine the extent to which treatments developed and tested under ideal conditions in academic settings can be exported to the types of therapists and patients who participate in psychotherapy in community settings.

REFERENCES

Chambless, D., Sanderson, W. C., Shoham, V., Johnson, S. B., Pope, K. S., Crits-Christoph, P., Baker, M., Johnson, B., Woody, S. R., Sue, S., Beutler, L., Williams, D. A., & McCurry, S. (1996). An update on empirically validated therapies. *The Clinical Psychologist, 49,* 5–18.

Hough, R. L., Landsverk, J. A., Karno, M., & Burnam, M. A. (1987). Utilization of health and mental health services by Los Angeles Mexican Americans and non-Hispanic whites. *Archives of General Psychiatry, 44,* 702–709.

Kopta, S. M., Howard, K. I., Lowry, J. L., & Beutler, L. E. (1994). Patterns of symptomatic recovery in psychotherapy. *Journal of Consulting and Clinical Psychology, 62,* 1009–1016.

Paul Crits-Cristoph
Mary Beth Connolly Gibbons
University of Pennsylvania

See also: **Cognitive Therapy; Existential Psychotherapy**

PSYCHOTHERAPY EFFECTIVENESS

Psychotherapy effectiveness means that psychotherapy can accomplish its intended or expected result. To be effective, psychotherapy must reliably produce a desirable outcome in the treatment of emotional, behavioral, and/or cognitive dysfunctions.

More research on the effectiveness of psychotherapy is being conducted currently than ever in the history of psychotherapy. A number of factors have spurred interest in psychotherapy research, including the maturation of the field of psychotherapy, increasing acceptance of mental health treatment (resulting in a greater demand for services), and changes in the economics of health care that have caused payers to demand more accountability about the effectiveness of providers' treatments. A great demand exists to evaluate the effectiveness of psychotherapies based upon objective information derived from controlled studies as opposed to the opinions of professionals.

Background of Psychotherapy Effectiveness

In the past, many researchers have questioned the effectiveness of psychotherapy. In 1952, Hans Eysenck investigated whether psychotherapy was an effective treatment by studying the outcome data for 8,053 clients reported in 24 research articles. His key dependent measures were discharge data from New York Hospital and improvement from patients seeking insurance settlements. Eysenck's results showed that two thirds of all neurotics who entered psychotherapy improved within 2 years, but two thirds of neurotics who did not enter therapy also improved (Eysenck, 1952). In a review of additional studies, Eysenck reached the general conclusion that patients who received psychotherapy fared no better than control subjects. Eysenck's claim that no conclusive evidence showed that psychotherapy with neurotics was more effective than no psychotherapy stirred controversy and stimulated interest in answering the fundamental research question, Is psychotherapy beneficial and effective?

Numerous investigators reanalyzed the original research upon which Eysenck based his conclusions and found greater rates of improvement in the therapy samples and a lower rate of spontaneous remissions in the control subjects. New interpretations of Eysenck's data led authors to conclude that the results of psychotherapy are positive, with a minority of patients showing no improvement or deterioration. As the controversy evolved, the scientific community of psychotherapy researchers more closely scrutinized the methodology used to evaluate the effectiveness of therapy and recognized that while rigorous scientific assessment of psychotherapy was necessary, it was also complex. In order to draw valid conclusions about the effectiveness of psychotherapy, multiple factors needed to be controlled. Researchers were challenged to try to find a universal, standardized definition or operational definition of psychotherapy; to use methodological strategies for measuring outcomes that are reliable and valid; and to resolve ethical issues about withholding treatment. The following variables needed to be controlled: The nature of the sample; amount and quality of therapy; nature and onset of duration of pathology; preciseness of the definition of disorders; comparability of cases across studies; duration and rigorousness of follow-up; patient, therapist, and process variables; and independent outcome assessments.

As methodological sophistication increased, researchers developed meta-analysis, a quantitative procedure that allowed them to examine the statistical significance of the size of effects across multiple psychotherapy studies and to draw conclusions about aggregate results. Smith and Glass (1977) conducted the first meta-analytic study of significance, in which they reviewed 475 studies, computed an effect size statistic, and concluded that those who received psychotherapy were better off than 80% of those who received no treatment. Other meta-analytic studies were conducted and based upon numerous reviews of the literature using both traditional and meta-analytic approaches, researchers concluded that psychotherapy is helpful and has clinically significant effects. Not everyone benefits from psychotherapy and some even suffer from iatrogenic or negative effects, but planned, systematic efforts of trained therapists to relieve psychological distress were more effective than placebo control groups, waiting lists, or no treatment control groups, and patients who showed initial changes in therapy generally maintained the changes.

Once it was established that there were general positive effects of psychotherapy, the next question posed was "Which psychotherapeutic technique is most effective?" Overall, there is no clear evidence to show that one therapy is superior over another over the long term. Some studies show that some specific techniques (behavioral, cognitive, eclectic) are helpful in the treatment of specific circumscribed behaviors such as stuttering, phobias, compulsions, childhood aggression, or sexual problems. Thus, the most current thematic research question is "What are the specific effects of specific interventions by specific therapists on specific symptoms or patient types?"

While the available research measuring the effectiveness of psychotherapy varies in quality, with earlier research being less scientifically rigorous than more recent research, the methodology has improved continuously so more recent studies meet more stringent criteria. As more and more studies are conducted to test the effectiveness of psychotherapy, hopefully more rigorous scientific parameters are applied. The gold standard or ideal efficacy study methodology is one that contrasts one type of therapy with a comparison group under well-controlled conditions and thus empirically validates the therapy. In such an ideal study, patients are randomly assigned to treatment and control conditions, controls are rigorous, treatments are manualized, patients are seen for fixed periods, target outcomes are well operationalized, and raters and diagnosticians are blind to patient assignment (Seligman, 1995). The trend toward the empirical validation of modern psychotherapy is growing, with increasing numbers of studies showing that the effectiveness of psychotherapy is a good measure of psychotherapy's worth.

REFERENCES

Eysenck, H. J. (1952). The effects of psychotherapy: An evaluation. *Journal of Consulting Psychology, 16,* 319–324.

Seligman, M. (1995). The effectiveness of psychotherapy: The *Consumer Reports* study. *American Psychologist, 50*(12), 965–974.

Smith, M., & Glass, G. (1977). Meta-analysis of psychotherapy outcome studies. *American Psychologist, 32*(9), 752–760.

Carol Shaw Austad
Central Connecticut State University

See also: Meta-Analysis; Psychotherapy

PSYCHOTHERAPY RESEARCH

Psychotherapy research is concerned primarily with the evaluation of the impact and process of psychological interventions across various forms of treatment (e.g., individual, couple, group) for clinical disorders (e.g., depression), problems of living (e.g., marital discord), and medical conditions (e.g., chronic pain). It is also concerned with characteristics of the client and therapist as they relate to the process and outcome of treatment.

Psychotherapy Outcome

With regard to outcome, more than 50 years of research has shown that psychotherapy works: It is more effective than the absence of treatment, placebo, and pseudotherapies (Lambert & Bergin, 1994). Based on the findings of controlled clinical trials (e.g., Chambless & Hollon, 1998), researchers have been able to identify a large number of empirically supported treatments (ESTs) for specific clinical problems experienced by adults, adolescents, and children (see Kendall & Chambless, 1998). However, with the exception of a number of specific problems and related treatments (e.g., cognitive-behavioral therapy for Panic Disorder), comparative outcome research suggests that the impact of different forms of psychotherapy tends to be equivalent (Lambert & Bergin, 1994).

Although psychotherapy works, there are clear limitations to its impact. For example, even though the EST movement demonstrates that a large number of individuals can benefit from psychotherapy when applied in controlled clinical trials, it is not clear how these findings might generalize to clinical practice in natural settings. In addition, a number of clients terminate treatment prematurely, do not respond to therapy, and/or even deteriorate (Garfield, 1994). As a strategy to increase the beneficial impact of treatment, therapists have attempted to integrate or selectively prescribe techniques associated with different therapeutic orientations (Castonguay & Goldfried, 1994). However, with just a few notable exceptions (see Glass, Victor, & Arnkoff, 1993), these integrative efforts have yet to receive considerable empirical attention.

Psychotherapy Process

Whereas outcome research focuses on whether or not psychotherapy works, process research investigates how it works (or fails to work). Researchers (see Beutler, Machado, & Allstetter Neufeldt, 1994; Garfield, 1994; Orlinsky, Grawe, & Parks, 1994) have studied process variables related to the *therapist* (e.g., adherence to treatment manuals), *client* (e.g., emotional experience), *client–therapist relationship* (e.g., working alliance), and *structure of treatment* (e.g., duration of therapy). Examination of such variables, among many others, is in line with the two main goals of process research: (1) describing what happens in treatment, and (2) identifying factors that foster or impede client improvement.

With respect to the descriptive function of process research, several studies have shown that therapists can adhere to treatment protocols and that different forms of treatment can be discriminated based on the therapist's use of prescribed techniques (e.g., DeRubeis, Hollon, Evans, & Bemis, 1982; Hill, O'Grady, & Elkin, 1992). However, studies have also demonstrated that there are important differences between what therapists do and what they say they do. For example, just as psychodynamic therapists have been shown to apply supportive interventions presumably more native to behavior therapy (e.g., prescription of daily activities; Wallerstein & Dewitt, 1997), behavior therapists have also been shown to demonstrate higher levels of empathy than psychodynamic therapists (Sloane, Staples, Cristol, Yorkston, & Whipple, 1975).

With regard to its function of identifying helpful and hindering aspects of treatment, process research has uncovered a number of variables that have been linked positively with outcome (Orlinsky et al., 1994). Among them, the quality of the therapeutic alliance has shown to be the most robust predictor of improvement (Constantino, Castonguay, & Schut, 2002). According to Lambert (1992), common factors (such as the alliance) and placebo effects account for approximately 45% of the variance in therapy outcome.

Process research has also provided support for the therapeutic importance of variables assumed to be unique to particular approaches. For example, the use of homework has been linked to improvement in cognitive therapy (CT;

e.g., Burns & Nolen-Hoeksema, 1991). On the other hand, researchers have found other techniques prescribed by the CT manual to be either unrelated to or negatively associated with improvement (e.g., Castonguay, Goldfried, Wiser, Raue, & Hayes, 1996). Similar mixed findings with regard to prescribed interventions have also been found in other forms of treatment (e.g., psychodynamic, see Schut & Castonguay, 2001).

Client and Therapist Characteristics

Psychotherapy researchers have also been interested in examining characteristics of clients and therapists. A large number of demographic variables have been investigated (e.g., age, ethnicity), but none of them appear to account for a significant part of the outcome variance (Beutler et al., 1994; Garfield, 1994). However, a number of other client and therapist characteristics have been shown to relate to psychotherapy process and outcome. For example, in different forms of psychotherapy for depression, clients' pretreatment level of perfectionism has been negatively related to the therapeutic alliance and outcome (e.g., Blatt, Quinlan, Pilkonis, & Shea, 1995). Also negatively related to outcome is the therapist's level of emotional disturbance and distress (Beutler et al., 1994). Moreover, Henry, Schacht, and Strupp (1990) have found that the therapist's hostility toward self is predictive of negative process in the client–therapist relationship.

Studies have also examined whether the matching of client, therapist, and/or treatment variables could improve the impact of therapy. With few exceptions, however, this research has lead to a paucity of reliable findings. Among these exceptions is the work of Beutler et al. (1991), who demonstrated that clients with an externalized coping style improved more in a symptom-oriented treatment (i.e., CT) than clients with an internalized style of coping who responded most to an insight-oriented treatment (i.e., supportive/self-directive therapy [S/SD]). Beutler et al. (1991) have also found that whereas clients high in reactance level (those who resist being controlled by others) fare better in a nondirective type of treatment (i.e., S/SD) than in directive forms of therapies (i.e., focused-expressive therapy and CT), clients low in reactance respond more to CT than S/SD.

Conclusion

Research has offered considerable information with regard to the impact and process of psychotherapy. Moreover, this information is being further refined with the emergence of more sophisticated methods to assess treatment processes (e.g., task analysis; Rice & Greenberg, 1984). Presently, however, it seems fair to say that psychotherapy research has had a limited impact on clinical practice. For example, although the current ESTs represent for many researchers the embodiment of the scientific-practitioner model, they are perceived by many clinicians as irrelevant academic efforts, if not major threats to valid clinical practice (see Castonguay, Schut, Constantino, & Halperin, 1999). Fortunately, efforts to bridge the gap between researchers and clinicians have begun to emerge (Newman & Castonguay, 1999), which holds the promise of improving the effectiveness of psychotherapy and better understanding its process of change.

REFERENCES

Beutler, L. E., Engle, D., Mohr, D., Daldrup, R. J., Bergan, J., Meredith, K., et al. (1991). Predictors of differential response to cognitive, experiential, and self-directed psychotherapeutic procedures. *Journal of Consulting and Clinical Psychology, 59,* 333–340.

Beutler, L. E., Machado, P. P. P., & Allstetter Neufeldt, S. (1994). Therapist variables. In A. E. Bergin & S. L. Garfield (Eds.), *Handbook of psychotherapy and behavior change* (4th ed., pp. 229–269). New York: Wiley.

Blatt, S. J., Quinlan, D. M., Pilkonis, P. A., & Shea, M. T. (1995). Impact of perfectionism and need for approval on the brief treatment of depression: The National Institute of Mental Health Treatment of Depression Collaborative Research Program revisited. *Journal of Consulting and Clinical Psychology, 63,* 125–132.

Burns, D. D., & Nolen-Hoeksema, S. (1991). Coping styles, homework compliance, and the effectiveness of cognitive-behavioral therapy. *Journal of Consulting and Clinical Psychology, 59,* 305–311.

Castonguay, L. G., & Goldfried, M. R. (1994). Psychotherapy integration: An idea whose time has come. *Applied and Preventative Psychology, 3,* 159–172.

Castonguay, L. G., Goldfried, M. R., Wiser, S., Raue, P. J., & Hayes, A. H. (1996). Predicting outcome in cognitive therapy for depression: A comparison of unique and common factors. *Journal of Consulting and Clinical Psychology, 64,* 497–504.

Castonguay, L. G., Schut, A. J., Constantino, M. J., & Halperin, G. S. (1999). Assessing the role of treatment manuals: Have they become necessary but non-sufficient ingredients of change? *Clinical Psychology: Science and Practice, 6,* 449–455.

Chambless, D. L., & Hollon, S. D. (1998). Defining empirically supported therapies. *Journal of Consulting and Clinical Psychology, 66,* 7–18.

Constantino, M. J., Castonguay, L. G., & Schut, A. J. (2002). The working alliance: A flagship for the "scientist-practitioner" model in psychotherapy. In G. S. Tryon (Ed.), *Counseling based on process research: Applying what we know* (pp. 81–131). Boston: Allyn & Bacon.

DeRubeis, R. J., Hollon, S. D., Evans, M. D., & Bemis, K. M. (1982). Can psychotherapies for depression be discriminated? A systematic investigation of cognitive therapy and interpersonal therapy. *Journal of Consulting and Clinical Psychology, 50,* 744–756.

Garfield, S. L. (1994). Research on client variables in psychotherapy. In A. E. Bergin & S. L. Garfield (Eds.), *Handbook of psychotherapy and behavior change* (4th ed., pp. 190–228). New York: Wiley.

Glass, C. R., Victor, B. J., & Arnkoff, D. B. (1993). Empirical research on integrative and eclectic psychotherapies. In G. Stricker & J. R. Gold (Eds.), *Comprehensive handbook of psychotherapy integration* (pp. 9–25). New York: Plenum Press.

Henry, W. P., Schacht, T. E., & Strupp, H. H. (1990). Patient and therapist introject, interpersonal process, and differential psychotherapy outcome. *Journal of Consulting and Clinical Psychology, 58,* 768–774.

Hill, C. E., O'Grady, K. E., & Elkin, I. (1992). Applying the collaborative study psychotherapy rating scale to rate therapist adherence in cognitive-behavior therapy, interpersonal therapy, and clinical management. *Journal of Consulting and Clinical Psychology, 60,* 73–79.

Kendall, P. C., & Chambless, D. L. (1998). Special section: Empirically supported psychological therapies. *Journal of Clinical and Consulting Psychology, 66,* 3–163.

Lambert, M. J. (1992). Psychotherapy outcome research: Implications for integrative and eclectic therapists. In J. C. Norcross & M. R. Goldfried (Eds.), *Handbook of psychotherapy integration* (pp. 94–129). New York: Basic Books.

Lambert, M. J., & Bergin, A. E. (1994). The effectiveness of psychotherapy. In A. E. Bergin & S. L. Garfield (Eds.), *Handbook of psychotherapy and behavior change* (4th ed., pp. 143–189). New York: Wiley.

Newman, M. G., & Castonguay, L. G. (1999). Reflecting on current challenges and future directions in psychotherapy: What can be learned from dialogues between clinicians, researchers, and policy makers? *Journal of Clinical Psychology / In Session, 55,* 1407–1413.

Orlinsky, D. E., Grawe, K., & Parks, B. K. (1994). Process and outcome in psychotherapy—Noch einmal. In A. E. Bergin & S. L. Garfield (Eds.), *Handbook of psychotherapy and behavior change* (4th ed., pp. 270–376). New York: Wiley.

Rice, L. N., & Greenberg, L. S. (1984). *Patterns of change: Intensive analysis of psychotherapy process.* New York: Guilford Press.

Schut, A. J., & Castonguay, L. G. (2001). Reviving Freud's vision of a psychoanalytic science: Implications for clinical training and education, *Psychotherapy, 38,* 40–49.

Sloane, R. B., Staples, F. R., Cristol, A. H., Yorkston, N. J., & Whipple, K. (1975). *Psychotherapy versus behavior therapy.* Cambridge, MA: Harvard University Press.

Stiles, W. B. (1988). Psychotherapy process-outcome correlations may be misleading. *Psychotherapy, 25,* 27–35.

Wallerstein, R. S., & DeWitt, K. N. (1997). Intervention modes in psychoanalysis and in psychoanalytic psychotherapies: A revised classification. *Journal of Psychotherapy Integration, 7,* 129–150.

Louis G. Castonguay
Pennsylvania State University

Michael J. Constantino
Stanford University Medical Center

Alexander J. Schut
McLean Hospital–Harvard Medical School

See also: **Cognitive Therapy; Psychotherapy**

PSYCHOTHERAPY TRAINING

Psychotherapy training has two aspects. One concerns the models of training in graduate programs, while the second aspect focuses on the way in which psychotherapy is learned.

Training Models

Since the end of World War II, a number of conferences (often known by the location where they were held, such as the Boulder, Vail, Swampscott, or Norman conferences) and articles emanating from these conferences have defined models of clinical, counseling, and community psychology training programs. These models usually invoke an image of training that weaves together didactic and applied competencies. The didactic components include mastering research and statistical analysis as well as basic processes such as learning, cognition, psychopathology, and psychophysiology. The applied components include interviewing, assessment, and psychotherapy. David Shakow (1969) developed a model curriculum in which the student begins clinical training concurrently with his or her didactic studies. The student's initial exposure to clinical work might take the form of sitting in with experienced interviewers, assessors, and psychotherapists. In subsequent years the student usually takes on more responsibility in assessment and psychotherapy, still under the supervision of more senior clinicians, while simultaneously progressing through the didactic studies. Shakow's hope was that the student would then structure a thesis (for the master's degree) or a dissertation (for the PhD) that was methodologically sound and clinically important. Such clinically relevant research takes time to come to fruition.

Regrettably, implementation of the Shakow model has become weakened by several forces. First, academic psychologists find greater likelihood of rewards (promotion, tenure, and grants) from conducting research that might be more methodologically driven and fewer rewards for supervising clinical activities (Hess & Hess, 1983). Thus the student's clinical activities are not as valued in the advisor's eyes to the same degree as pure research endeavors. Similarly, clinicians in the field who might have been receptive to research in past decades are now pressed to spend more of their time generating third-party payments. Clinical research detracts from their fee-bearing activities. These two forces account for some of the division of the academic from the clinical that was of one cloth in the Shakow model.

Manuals that detail psychotherapeutic treatment of defined problems are suppose to increase the effectiveness of psychotherapy in this era of managed care and attention to the "bottom line." For well-defined and common problems during research trials, both experienced and relatively inexperienced professionals can use manuals effectively. However, manualized treatment is far from universally accepted. Critics argue that this approach stifles the therapist's exploration of the patient's life, which may cause therapists to miss important underlying problems that may accompany the presenting complaint. Indeed, Lehman, Gorsuch, and Mintz (1985) found that most presenting complaints mask the real problem for which the patient is seeking treatment.

Psychotherapy effectiveness studies continue to show that there are salutary effects to therapeutic interventions. (Seligman, 1995; Smith & Glass, 1977). These effects seem to be related to the therapist's style and personality ("nonspecific" therapy factors) more than to a particular theoretical bent or persuasion of the therapist. Again influence by managed care, recent research efforts focus on therapeutic efficacy; that is, getting the highest dose-effect benefit possible to cut spiraling costs of patient care, irrespective of the client's needs.

The advent of the PsyD, or doctorate of psychology, degree-granting programs has been another influence on psychotherapy training. PsyD programs emphasize hands-on training rather than the research and basic processes approach of the PhD programs. Before a student can earn the doctorate in either program, the student must complete an internship. The internship exposes the student to a more varied types of clients (adult and child, inpatient and outpatient) with a variety of problems (psychosis, anxiety disorders, personality disorders, and medical conditions with psychological sequelae). Some professionals feel that competence in psychotherapy develops only after a minimum of five years of postdoctoral clinical work, during which the student-psychotherapist can see changes in a number of patients' lives over time and learn how his or her skills affect people.

Psychotherapy Supervision

Psychotherapy supervision is the modality by which students learn psychotherapy. Hess (1980) summarized the models of supervision that include the supervisor in the roles of lecturer, teacher, peer, monitor, learned elder, and therapist. A number of theories postulate stages through which the student psychotherapist is presumed to pass. These include the demystification of psychotherapy, the acquisition of technical skills, and the beginning of mastery of complex skills and judgments, such as timing of interventions and tailoring techniques to the particular patient. Similarly, supervisors are presumed to pass through stages en route to becoming accomplished supervisors. Swain (1981) found that supervisors perceive supervisee performance along five dimensions: (1) clinical sense, as exemplified by listening skills, maintaining poise, and allowing the client to make decisions; (2) preparation for supervision and psychotherapy, such as organizing materials before sessions; (3) theoretical and cognitive knowledge, such as the ability to relate clinical material to theoretical concepts; (4) self-awareness and appropriate disclosure, such as access to feelings about patients that can be discussed in supervision; and (5) boundary management, as shown by being on time for appointments, knowing clinical rules, and attending to record keeping. Aldrich (1982) found that students regard supervisors along eight stable dimensions: defensiveness, professionalism, experience as a clinician, theoretical base, experience as a teacher, appropriate interest in the supervisee's life, likeableness, and ability to motivate.

In recent years, more attention has been devoted to models of supervision, to an interpersonal theory of supervision, and to qualitative research (Watkins, 1997). The small number of supervisees in any particular setting and the competing demand for service fee generation hinder efforts to conduct nomothetic and quantitative research. Research concerning models of supervision, effectiveness of intervention and learning strategies, and assessment of changes as a function of supervision in both the neophyte psychotherapist and his or her clients needs to be conducted. Nonetheless, the qualitative research that is emerging shows how supervisors benefit psychotherapists-in-training (Ladany & Muse-Burke, 2001).

REFERENCES

Aldrich, L. G. (1982). *Construction of a scale for the rating of supervisors of psychotherapy.* Unpublished master's thesis. Auburn, AL: Auburn University.

Hess, A. K. (1980). Training models and the nature of psychotherapy supervision. In A. K. Hess (Ed.), *Psychotherapy supervision: Theory, research and practice* (pp. 15–25). New York: Wiley.

Hess, A. K., & Hess, K. D. (1983). Psychotherapy supervision: A survey of internship training practices. *Professional Psychology, 14,* 504–513.

Ladany, N., & Muse-Burke, J. L. (2001). Understanding and conducting supervision research. In L. J. Bradley & N. Ladany (Eds.), *Counselor supervision: Principles, process, and practice* (3rd ed., pp. 304–329). Philadelphia: Brunner-Routledge.

Lehman, R. S., Gorsuch, R. L., & Mintz, J. (1985). Moving targets: Patients' changing complaints during psychotherapy. *Journal of Consulting and Clinical Psychology, 53,* 49–54.

Seligman, M. (1995). The effectiveness of psychotherapy: The *Consumer Reports* study. *American Psychologist, 50,* 965–974.

Shakow, D. (1969). *Clinical psychology as science and profession: A forty-year odyssey.* Chicago: Aldine.

Smith, M. L., & Glass, G. V. (1977). Meta-analysis of psychotherapy outcome studies. *American Psychologist, 32,* 752–760.

Swain, D. (1981). *Behaviorally anchored rating scales for recipients of psychotherapy supervision: Instrument construction.* Unpublished master's thesis. Auburn, AL: Auburn University.

Watkins, C. E., Jr. (Ed.). (1997). *The handbook of psychotherapy supervision.* New York: Wiley.

Allen K. Hess
Auburn University, Montgomery, AL

See also: **Psychotherapy**

Table 1. Summary of Four Factors in the Mediation of Teacher Expectancy Effects

Factor	Brief Summary of the Evidence
Central Factors	
Climate (affect)	Teachers appear to create a warmer socioemotional climate for their "special" students. This warmth appears to be at least partially communicated by nonverbal cues. (Estimated effect size $r = .29$).
Input (effort)	Teachers appear to teach more material and more difficult material to their "special" students. (Estimated effect size $r = .27$).
Additional Factors	
Output	Teachers appear to give their "special" students greater opportunities for responding. These opportunities are offered both verbally and nonverbally (e.g., giving a student more time in which to answer a teacher's question). (Estimated effect size $r = .17$).
Feedback	Teachers appear to give their "special" students more differentiated feedback, both verbal and nonverbal, as to how these students have been performing. (Estimated effect size $r = .10$).

Note: Even the smallest effect size *r* listed above reflects a difference in performance levels of 55% versus 45%; the larger effect size *r*s listed above reflect a difference in performance levels of 64% versus 36%.

PYGMALION EFFECT

The term *Pygmalion effect* refers broadly to the effects of interpersonal expectations, that is, the finding that what one person expects of another can come to serve as a self-fulfilling prophecy. These effects of interpersonal self-fulfilling prophecies have come to be called *Pygmalion effects* in general, but especially so when the interpersonal expectancy effects occur in an educational context.

Early Laboratory Experiments

The earliest studies of Pygmalion effects were conducted with human participants. Experimenters obtained ratings of photographs of stimulus persons from their research participants, but half of the experimenters were led to expect high photo ratings and half were led to expect low photo ratings. In the first several such studies, experimenters expecting higher photo ratings obtained substantially higher photo ratings than did experimenters expecting lower photo ratings.

To investigate the generality of these interpersonal expectancy effects in the laboratory, two studies were conducted employing animal subjects. Half of the experimenters were told that their rats had been specially bred for maze (or Skinner box) brightness and half were told that their rats had been specially bred for maze (or Skinner box) dullness. In both experiments, when experimenters had been led to expect better learning from their rat subjects, they obtained better learning from their rat subjects (Rosenthal, 1966, 1976).

Pygmalion Effects in the Classroom

Researchers hypothesized that if rats became brighter when expected to by their experimenters, then perhaps children could become brighter when expected to by their teachers. Accordingly, all of the children in one study were administered a nonverbal test of intelligence, which was disguised as a test that would predict intellectual "blooming." The test was labeled "The Harvard Test of Inflected Acquisition." There were 18 classrooms in the school, three at each of the six grade levels. Within each grade level the three classrooms were composed of children with above average ability, average ability, and below average ability, respectively. Within each of the 18 classrooms, approximately 20% of the children were chosen at random to form the experimental group. Each teacher was given the names of the children from his or her class who were in the experimental condition. The teachers were told that these children's scores on the "Test of Inflected Acquisition" indicated that they would show surprising gains in intellectual competence during the next 8 months of school. The only difference between the experimental group and the control group children, then, was in the mind of the teacher.

At the end of the school year, 8 months later, all the children in the school were retested with the same nonverbal test of intelligence. The children from whom the teachers has been led to expect greater intellectual gain showed a significantly greater gain than did the children in the control group (Rosenthal & Jacobson, 1968, 1992).

Domains Investigated

A dozen years after the Pygmalion effect classroom study was completed, the research literature on interpersonal expectancy effects had broadened to include 345 experiments that could be subsumed under one of eight domains of research: human learning and ability, animal learning, reaction time, psychophysical judgments, laboratory interviews, person perception, inkblot tests, and everyday situations (Rosenthal, 1991). After another dozen years, the overall mean effect size of the 479 studies was found to be an *r* of .30. An *r* of that magnitude can be thought of as the effects of interpersonal expectations changing the proportion of people performing above average from 35% to 65%.

The Four-Factor Theory

A considerable amount of research has been summarized, employing meta-analysis, that suggests how teachers may treat differently those children for whom they have more favorable expectations. Table 1 summarizes these differences as four factors, two that are primary and two that are somewhat smaller in their magnitude of effect (Harris & Rosenthal, 1985).

Current Research

The most recent work, and that currently in progress, continues to examine the effects of interpersonal expectancies in an ever widening circle of contexts. Pygmalion effects in management, courtrooms, nursing homes, and a variety of classrooms are under investigation. It has been shown that organizational effectiveness can be increased by raising leaders' expectations, that juries' verdicts of guilty can be increased by assigning them judges (to instruct them) who believe the defendant to be guilty, that the depression levels of nursing home residents can be reduced by raising the expectation levels of caretakers, and that teacher expectations can serve as self-fulfilling prophecies in other countries and for more than simply intellectual tasks. In all these cases the mediating variables are receiving special attention, with rapidly growing evidence that much of the mediation is occurring by means of unintended nonverbal behavior (Ambady & Rosenthal, 1992; Babad, 1992; Eden, 1990).

REFERENCES

Ambady, N., & Rosenthal, R. (1992). Thin slices of expressive behavior as predictors of interpersonal consequences: A meta-analysis. *Psychological Bulletin, 111,* 256–274.

Babad, E. (1992). Teacher expectancies and nonverbal behavior. In R. S. Feldman (Ed.), *Applications of nonverbal behavioral theories and research* (pp. 167–190). Hillsdale, NJ: Erlbaum.

Eden, D. (1990). *Pygmalion in management: Productivity as a self-fulfilling prophecy.* Lexington, MA: D. C. Heath.

Harris, M. J., & Rosenthal, R. (1985). Mediation of interpersonal expectancy effects: 31 meta-analyses. *Psychological Bulletin, 97,* 363–386.

Rosenthal, R. (1966). *Experimenter effects in behavioral research.* New York: Appleton-Century-Crofts; enlarged edition, Irvington, NY, 1976.

Rosenthal, R. (1991). *Meta-analytic procedures for social research* (Rev. ed.). Newbury Park, CA: Sage Publications.

Rosenthal, R., & Jacobson, L. (1968). *Pygmalion in the classroom.* New York: Holt, Rinehart and Winston; expanded edition, Irvington, NY, 1992.

Robert Rosenthal
University of California, Riverside
Harvard University

See also: **Self-fulfilling Prophecy**

Q-SORT TECHNIQUE

The Q-sort technique is a general method for eliciting a detailed, subjective description of a stimulus. This description is quantitative and based on explicit, internal reference points. The letter *Q* was used by the inventor of the technique, Stephenson (1935, 1936), to indicate the affinity of the data provided by the technique for use in Q-type analyses (based on correlations between persons, in contrast to R-type analyses based on correlations between variables). The Q-sort technique is used for two quite distinct purposes: First, as originally devised by Stephenson, the technique is a broadly applicable scaling method that can articulate the personal subjective understanding and experience of the respondent in great detail. Alternatively, when respondents describe the same stimulus, intersubjective agreement across descriptions provides a basis for drawing inferences about the stimulus. In the former approach, the focus is on the perceiver; in the latter approach, the focus is on the perceived. The perceiver-focused approach is utilized most often in studies of social and political attitudes that are conducted in political science (see Brown, 1980, for a detailed account of this approach, and McKeown and Thomas, 1988, for a more concise survey). The second approach, predominant in psychology, follows Block's (1961) adaptation of the method for personality assessment. In this application, the stimulus is a target person who is typically described by multiple judges who are acquainted with the target.

Q-Sort Procedure

The Q-sort method requires a set of items that might be used to describe any member of a class of stimuli. The respondent, or judge, sorts the items (typically words or phrases printed on separate cards) into ordered categories ranging from extremely characteristic of the target stimulus to extremely uncharacteristic of the target stimulus. The number of items that may be placed in each category is fixed, and each category has a preassigned numerical label that becomes the score of the items placed in that category. A rank ordering of items can be viewed as an example of the Q-sort method, in which the number of items and the number of categories are equal in number. More typical is the California Adult Q-Set (Block, 1961), which contains 100 items to be sorted into 9 categories to form a quasi-normal distribution (the number of items to be placed in categories 1 to 9, respectively, are 5, 8, 12, 16, 18, 16, 12, 8, and 5).

The fixed distribution of the Q-sort forces the judge to identify which items are most and least descriptive of the target person relative to the other items in the Q-set. Thus, if the Q-item is "friendly toward strangers," the judge compares the degree to which this item is an apt description of the target, compared to the other items. This is in marked contrast to the typical procedure in which judges would be asked whether the target, when compared with others, is friendly toward strangers. Ratings obtained using the explicit internal frame of reference created by the use of a fixed distribution were labeled *ipsative* by Cattell (1944) to distinguish them from the more usual normative ratings.

The ipsative character of the Q-sort is the source of both strengths and limitations of the method (Ozer, 1993). Among the benefits are that it encourages the judge to apply considerable thought and effort to the numerous judgments, and removes judge differences in the distribution of ratings, thereby controlling for certain types of judge error and bias. Nonindependence among the item placements is the source of specific problems with Q-sort method. Mean item differences across groups or in the same group over time are difficult to interpret (Ozer & Gjerde, 1989). Ipsativity also presents difficulties for statistical procedures that assume independence among items (Clemans, 1966).

Types of Q-Sets

In Stephenson's (1953) description of Q-methodology, Q-items were construed as members of a population that are sampled for use in particular studies. Block (1961) identified both practical and scientific reasons for the use of a standard set of items to compose a particular Q-set. Numerous Q-sets have been developed for various purposes, but in general there are two broad types of item domains. Some Q-sets define a broad domain of item content and have relatively little redundancy among items. For example, Block's (1961) California Adult Q-Set provides near-comprehensive coverage of personality. Other Q-sets focus on a much narrower range of content and assess just a few, or even one, primary construct. The Attachment Q-Set (Waters & Dean, 1985), which includes content clusters for particular attachment styles, is a well-known example of this second approach.

Evaluation and Use of Q-Sort Data

When judges' descriptions of target stimuli are used to make inferences about the target, it is important to establish that there is substantial agreement among judges. Either the average item reliability or the average reliability of each target description is typically computed for this purpose (see Block, 1961; Ozer, 1993). The composite judge evaluations may be analyzed like any other rating data, but they also invite application of other sorts of analyses based on either the correlation between persons or the correlation between the description of the same person over multiple occasions. Such methods have been employed with some frequency in personality psychology, where correlations between the Q-sorts of different persons have been used to develop taxonomies of personality (e.g., Block, 1971); correlations between different Q-sort descriptions of the same person at different ages have been used to assess personality consistency and change (e.g., Ozer and Gjerde, 1989).

REFERENCES

Block, J. (1961). *The Q-sort method in personality assessment and psychiatric research.* Springfield, IL: Charles C. Thomas.

Block, J. (1971). *Lives through time.* Berkeley, CA: Bancroft Books.

Brown, S. R. (1980). *Political subjectivity: Applications of Q methodology in political science.* New Haven, CN: Yale University Press.

Cattell, R. B. (1944). Psychological measurement: normative, ipsative, interactive. *Psychological Review, 51,* 292–303.

Clemans, W. V. (1966). An analytical and empirical examination of some properties of ipsative measures [Monograph]. *Psychometric Monographs, 14,* 1–56.

McKeown, B., & Thomas, D. (1988). *Q Methodology.* Newbury Park, CA: Sage Publications.

Ozer, D. J. (1993). The Q-sort method and the study of personality development. In D. C. Funder, R. D. Parke, C. Tomlinson-Keasey, & K. Widaman (Eds.), *Studying lives through time: Personality and development* (pp. 147–168). Washington, DC: American Psychological Association.

Ozer, D. J., & Gjerde, P. F. (1989). Patterns of personality consistency and change from childhood through adolescence. *Journal of Personality, 57,* 483–507.

Stephenson, W. (1935). Correlating persons instead of tests. *Character and Personality, 6,* 17–24.

Stephenson, W. (1936). The foundations of psychometry: Four factor systems. *Psychometrika, 1,* 195–209.

Stephenson, W. (1953). *The study of behavior: Q-Technique and its methodology.* Chicago: University of Chicago Press.

Waters, E., & Deane, K. E. (1985). Defining and assessing individual differences in attachment relationships: Q-methodology and the organization of behavior in infancy and early childhood. In I. Bretherton & E. Waters (Eds.), Growing points of attachment theory and research (pp. 41–65). *Monographs of the Society for Research in Child Development, 50*(1–2, Serial No. 209).

Daniel J. Ozer
University of California, Riverside

See also: **Attachment Styles; Reliability**

QUALITY OF LIFE

Quality of life has become a popular concept that is used by politicians, marketing executives, media and sports personalities, and members of the public. There is an extensive scientific literature on the subject by health practitioners and social scientists. Scholars in ancient China and Greece were interested in quality of life, and renewed interest in it occurred in times of enlightenment in the centuries that followed. In recent history, quality of life emerged as a political entity in the United States in the 1950s and in Europe in the 1960s. Several U.S. presidents, such as Eisenhower, Johnson, and Nixon, popularized the term in presidential commissions and in their speeches. The focus on quality of life in the last half century has increased because there has been a general recognition that the health of countries must be judged in something more than gross economic terms and that the health of individuals is something beyond the absence of illness.

The economic focus led to the development of social indicators directed at objectively measuring the quality of life of populations. In 1970 the Organization for Economic Cooperation and Development (OECD) encouraged member countries to develop and report measures of social well-being for their constituents. This resulted in a number of countries reporting such social indicators as the number of schools per person, the number of hospital beds per person, and the number of health care professionals per person. It soon became apparent that, while social indicators provided information about cultural entities (towns, states, and countries), they provided little or no information about the quality of life of individuals within these entities. This prompted researchers in a number of countries, including the United States, Canada, Europe, and Australia, to assess the subjective or perceived quality of life of population samples within their countries. Perhaps the earliest such study was by Bradburn in 1969. He surveyed two samples (N = 2,787 and N = 2,163) from several metropolitan areas in the United States. The measure he employed was the effect balance score, which was based on ratings of positive and negative effect. It was assumed to be indicative of quality of life. Campbell, Converse, and Rogers carried out a second important study in the United States in 1976. They sampled 2,160 individuals selected to be representative of the national population. Participants were asked to rate their satisfaction in a number of life domains and to rate their satisfaction with their life as a whole. Subsequent to these early cross-sectional studies, the methods of assessing quality of life in the population at large have become more complex.

In 1947 the World Health Organization promulgated a definition of health that suggested that health was not just the absence of illness, but was also a state of physical, psychological, and social well-being. This definition provoked health professionals to start to view the impact of their interventions in a context broader than just symptom recovery. Thus, in the last three decades, there has been a proliferation of what have come to be known as Health Related Quality of Life (HRQOL) measures. Global and specific HRQOL measures have been developed in most branches of health care, including cardiology, cancer, epilepsy, urology, psychiatry, and general medicine, to name just a few. One of the most ambitious projects is that of the World Health Organization Quality of Life Group (1998), who are developing a global health measure of quality of life that can be employed with people from differing cultures worldwide.

Despite the popular and scientific interest in quality of life, there is little agreement on what is meant by the term *quality of life*. As Evans (1997) noted, quality of life has been used interchangeably with well-being, psychological well-being, subjective well-being, happiness, life satisfaction, positive and negative affect, and the good life. There is in fact a high degree of similarity among many of these measures, and statistical analyses with samples of the general population indicate that measures of life satisfaction, positive and negative affect, and quality of life are highly related to each other and form a single factor (Evans, 1997). Most researchers in the field believe that quality of life is a multidimensional concept, and there is fair agreement as to the majority of subdomains within the construct. There is some disagreement concerning the method by which measures in each of the subdomains should be aggregated to form an overall measure of quality of life.

The quality-of-life area has an abundance of measures and a paucity of theoretical models. Two prominent models are the bottom-up and top-down models of quality of life. Proponents of the top-down model argue that our general quality of life influences quality of life in the specific domains of our life, hence the focus of research should be on these global measures. Those who advocate the bottom-up model propose that the quality of our life in each life domain affects our overall quality of life, thus the specific domains should be the focus of research. Another current line of research is the identification of factors that influence an individual's quality of life. There is increasing evidence that personality dimensions, such as self-esteem, locus of control, extraversion, neuroticism, and hardiness, to name but a few, influence an individual's quality of life. This network of relationships could form the basis for a more elegant theory in the field. Recent attempts to measure quality of life across the many cultures around the world also have potential to provide some of the parameters that would define a quality-of-life theory. Emphasis in the future will be on the development of quality-of-life theoretical models, which will inform current measurement issues.

REFERENCES

Evans, D. R. (1997). Health promotion, wellness programs, quality of life and the marketing of psychology. *Canadian Psychology, 38,* 1–12.

The World Health Organization Quality of Life Group. (1998). The World Health Organization Quality of Life Assessment (WHOQOL): Development and general psychometric properties. *Social Science and Medicine, 46,* 1569–1585.

David R. Evans
University of Western Ontario

QUESTIONNAIRES

Questionnaires are inventories used to gather various kinds of information. Questionnaires are typically self-administered, self-report devices and are similar to interviews (face to face or over the telephone). Among the advantages of questionnaires are their relatively low cost as a means of gathering data, a general freedom from bias on the part of an interviewer, the large number of individuals who may be asked to respond, the sense of anonymity that respondents may feel, the temporal flexibility afforded the respondent, the possibility of directly linking research questions and survey results, the relative economy of data collection, and the ease of data coding and analysis for interpretation of the results (Kidder, 1981). One disadvantage of questionnaires relates to return rates; frequently, only a small fraction of those provided with a questionnaire complete it. Also, respondents may not be honest or may permit subtle biases to influence their responses. Furthermore, many Americans are still unable to read and write well enough in English to complete a questionnaire.

Questionnaires are used in both basic and applied research and in either experimental or correlational research. For example, many psychologists who investigate personality use survey questionnaires, and surveys may also be used as dependent variables in experiments. In applied research, questionnaires are often used in program evaluations, job analyses, needs assessments, and market research. These include personality variables, attitudes, values, beliefs, interests, and descriptions of past and present behavior. Furthermore, because most questionnaire research is correlational, causal attributions are generally inappropriate. However, it is the experimental design, rather than the nature of the variable per se, that dictates the ability to make causal statements.

Types of Questionnaires

Most questionnaires are composed of numerous questions and statements. Statements are frequently used to determine the extent to which respondents agree or disagree with a given thought, concept, or perspective. This agree-disagree format is often referred to as Likert scales, after the industrial psychologist Rensis Likert who pioneered their use and analysis. Survey questions may be of two general types: free response or response selection. Free-response questions are often open ended; response-selection questions are close-ended or fixed-alternative questions. Chief advantages of response-selection questions are ease of response and of data entry for data analysis. Answers to free-response questions, on the other hand, must first be categorized, scored, and coded. Because this process often demands a trained professional, the process is inevitably time consuming as well as expensive. Furthermore, respondents may find detailing their answers in writing to be laborious and may choose not to respond or to give short, inadequate responses.

There are a number of steps involved in developing a questionnaire properly. An example listing of these steps follows: specifying the objectives of the study, designing the questionnaire itself, drafting it, editing it, developing instructions for it, pretesting it, revising it, developing a sampling plan for administering it, executing the survey-data collection, data analysis, and reporting the results. Only a few of these steps are mentioned below.

The goals of the study be detailed; such work may lead to the elimination of unnecessary items and result in a higher response rate. The objectives then form an outline of the questionnaire. Once topics for questions are provided, decisions regarding the best item formats may be made (e.g., free-response or response-selection questions). Bouchard (1976) reported that questionnaire construction is still primarily an art form, and Bouchard provided various general rules based on both research and experience that may improve questionnaire construction.

Both introductions and instructions are advisable. Good introductions increase the rate of returned questionnaires. Some researchers send postcards to potential respondents in advance of the survey advising them of the survey. Cover letters that explain the purpose and importance of the questionnaire are strongly recommended. Instructions should be clear and as simple as possible. If the survey is to be returned in the mail, a stamped, addressed envelope should be included.

Pretesting the questionnaire is essential. Interviews with or written comments from respondents may highlight potential difficulties that may be avoided. Occasionally, when many respondents specify "other" responses to certain response-selection questions, new options can be added.

Statistical analyses used for other psychological measures (interitem correlations or reliability and validity studies) are frequently appropriate for questionnaires.

Two recurring problems in questionnaire research are response biases and nonrespondents. In many studies, respondents either avoid threatening questions or try to make themselves seem better; this latter response style is known as social desirability. Bradburn, Sudman, & associates (1980) make a number of recommendations to reduce this effect. Explanatory introductions to threatening questions help, as do promises of confidentiality. Permitting respondents to write sensitive answers rather than simply checking an answer is also beneficial. Another potentially useful strategy is asking respondents to describe friends or "people like themselves" rather than themselves.

Increasingly, questionnaires are being used in cross-cultural research. In such cases, the translation of a questionnaire from one language to another is required. Cautions need be involved in such instances, especially because language and culture must both be addressed (Geisinger, 1994).

Achieving an adequate and unbiased sample is perhaps the biggest concern in questionnaire research. The non-response problem is twofold. First, many individuals do not respond to surveys. Furthermore, nonrespondents frequently differ from respondents. Strategies to increase return rates help include appeals and offers of small rewards, for example. Another approach is to interview a random sample of nonrespondents.

Because of their relative ease, low cost, and low-intrusion value, questionnaires are certain to continue to be frequently used as data-collection devices in psychology. Solutions to problems such as those mentioned are likely to be sought. Even if good solutions are found, it is unlikely that experimental methodology will relinquish its preeminent status in psychology since causal relationships are more easily discerned with it. Nonetheless, questionnaire use is increasing, and this growth will likely continue.

REFERENCES

Bouchard, T. J., Jr. (1976). Field research methods: Interviewing, questionnaires, participant observation, systematic observation, unobtrusive measures. In M. D. Dunnette (Ed.), *Handbook of industrial and organizational psychology* (pp. 363–413). Chicago: Rand McNally.

Bradburn, N. M., Sudman, S. O., & associates. (1980). *Improving interview method and questionnaire design.* San Francisco: Jossey-Bass.

Geisinger, K. F. (1994). Cross-cultural normative assessment: Translation and adaptation issues influencing normative interpretation of assessment instruments. *Psychological Assessment, 6,* 304–312.

Kidder, L. H. (1981). *Research methods in social relations* (4th ed.). New York: Holt, Rinehart, and Winston.

Kurt F. Geisinger
University of St. Thomas, Houston

See also: **Psychometrics; Self-Report and Self-Ratings**

R

RACISM

The term *racism* is a relatively recent one that dates back only to 1936. Although many definitions of racism have been proposed, an all-inclusive definition has yet to be agreed upon, particularly as researchers have identified a variety of racisms (Richards, 1997). Moreover, different levels of analysis have been adopted to study racism, including individual, interpersonal, intergroup, and institutional approaches (Augoustinos & Reynolds, 2001).

Central to many definitions of racism is the belief in a biological hierarchy between racial and ethnic groups, as well as associated social practices that maintain and reproduce different status positions of groups based on such beliefs. The belief that differences between social groups are biologically driven implies that such variability is fundamental and fixed. These essentialist beliefs lead to the categorization of people into groups based on assumptions that surface characteristics (e.g., skin color) reflect deeper essential features, and these in turn are believed to be inherent and unchangeable and to reflect the real nature of the groups they represent. It has been argued, however, that contemporary racism—commonly referred to as the *new racism*—is less about beliefs in a biological hierarchy between groups and increasingly about beliefs in the cultural superiority of a dominant group's values, norms, and practices. Another variant of contemporary racism rejects the notion of a cultural hierarchy altogether and instead emphasizes the need and desirability of the separate development of groups, claiming that it is not in human nature for us to coexist peacefully with culturally different others.

There has been a tendency within psychology to use the terms *prejudice* and *racism* interchangeably. Jones (1997), however, makes the case that racism is distinct from prejudice. Prejudice has commonly been defined as negative attitudes and behavior toward a social group and its members. Prejudice is typically regarded as an individual phenomenon, whereas racism is a broader construct that links such individual beliefs and behavior to broader social and institutional norms and practices that systematically disadvantage particular groups. The second important difference between prejudice and racism relates to the role of power. At an individual level, a person can display prejudice, but this in itself does not necessarily constitute racism. Central to racism is the ability of dominant groups systematically to exercise power over outgroups. It is important that the power one group has over another transforms prejudice into racism and links individual prejudice with broader social practices (Jones, 1997).

Practiced at a structural and cultural level, racism maintains and reproduces the power differentials between groups in the social system (Jones, 1997). Racism practiced at this broad societal level has been referred to as institutional and cultural racism. Institutional racism refers to the institutional policies and practices that are put in place to protect and legitimize the advantages and power one group has over another. Institutional racism can be overt or covert, intentional or unintentional, but the consequences are that racist outcomes are achieved and reproduced. Cultural racism occurs when the dominant group defines the norms, values, and standards in a particular culture. These mainstream ideals permeate all aspects of the social system and are often fundamentally antagonistic with those embraced by particular minority groups (e.g., African Americans in the United States). In order to participate in society, minority groups often have to surrender their own cultural heritages and adopt those of the dominant group (e.g., the White majority).

Old and New Forms of Racism

By the early 1970s researchers had discerned a notable change in racial attitudes in the United States and other Western countries. Survey studies were indicating that blunt, hostile, segregationist, and White supremacist beliefs were less openly acceptable to members of the White majority. A distinction began to be made between old-fashioned racism, which is blunt, hostile, segregationist, and supremacist, and modern or symbolic racism, which in contrast is subtle and covert and, paradoxically, endorses egalitarianism. Modern racism rejects racial segregation and notions of biological supremacy and is instead based on feelings that certain social groups transgress important social values such as the work-ethic, individualism, self-reliance and self-discipline: values that are embodied in the Protestant ethic. Symbolic or modern racism justifies and legitimates social inequities based on moral feelings that certain groups violate such traditional values.

Other accounts of the new racism include ambivalent racism and aversive racism (Dovidio & Gaertner, 1986).

Both provide similar models of the new racism, positing that contemporary racial attitudes have become complex, contradictory, and multidimensional. In the ambivalent racism model, pro-Black and anti-Black sentiments are seen to coexist within the person and to reflect different value structures held by the individual. Pro-Black attitudes reflect humanitarian and egalitarian values that emphasize equality and social justice, whereas anti-Black attitudes reflect individualism, the Protestant ethic, hard work, individual achievement, and self-reliance. Similarly, the aversive racism model emphasizes the coexistence of a contradictory complex of attitudes: on the one hand, liberal-egalitarian principles of justice and equality, and on the other, a residue set of negative feelings and beliefs about particular groups that are learned early in life and that are difficult to eradicate completely. In both of these accounts, individuals strive to maintain a nonprejudiced image, both to themselves and to others, and struggle unconsciously to resolve the internal psychological ambivalence that is produced by maintaining a contradictory set of attitudes and beliefs. By justifying and legitimizing social inequalities between groups on the basis of factors other than race, members of dominant groups can avoid attributions of racism and thus maintain and protect a nonprejudiced self-image. Contemporary racism is therefore seen as more insidious and difficult to identify because of its subtle and covert nature. This has led to the development of new scales and unobtrusive methodologies to identify and measure this more subtle racism.

These accounts of the new racism tend to locate racism primarily within the psychological and cognitive domain of the individual. One recent approach that emphasizes the ambivalent and contradictory nature of contemporary racism, but explicitly avoids making claims about the psychology of individual perceivers, is discursive psychology (Wetherell & Potter, 1992). Discursive psychology views racism as interactive and communicative and as located within the language practices and discourses of a society. It is through everyday language practices, both in formal and informal talk, that relations of power, dominance, and exploitation become reproduced and legitimated. The analytic site for discursive psychology is the way in which discursive resources and rhetorical arguments are put together to construct different social and racial identities and to provide accounts that legitimate these differences and identities as real and natural. Discursive psychology locates these language practices, or ways of talking, at a societal level, as products of a racist society rather than as individual psychological or cognitive products. The analytic site therefore is not the prejudiced or racist individual, but the discursive and linguistic resources that are available within an inequitable society. This approach has been able to identify how linguistic resources are combined in flexible and contradictory ways to reproduce and justify racist outcomes in modern liberal democracies.

REFERENCES

Augoustinos, M., & Reynolds, K. (2001). (Eds.). *Understanding prejudice, racism, and social conflict.* London: Sage.

Dovidio, J. F., & Gaertner, S. L. (1986). (Eds.). *Prejudice, discrimination, and racism.* Orlando, FL: Academic Press.

Jones, J. M. (1997). *Prejudice and racism* (2nd ed.). New York: McGraw-Hill.

Richards, G. (1997). *"Race," racism and psychology: Towards a reflexive history.* London: Routledge.

Wetherell, M., & Potter, J. (1992). *Mapping the language of racism: Discourse and the legitimation of exploitation.* London: Harvester Wheatsheaf.

Martha Augoustinos
University of Adelaide

See also: **Attitudes; Discrimination; Prejudice and Discrimination**

RAPE

Definition

Definitions of rape are varied. However, most jurisdictions currently define rape as nonconsensual completed or attempted vaginal or anal penetration by the penis, hands, fingers, or other objects, or of the mouth by the penis, through the use of force or threats or when the victim is unable to consent (e.g., due to age or illness). Historically, rape was defined as a crime perpetrated by a man against a woman other than his wife. Today, rape of a spouse is a crime in all states and male victims are recognized, but rape of women by men is 10 times more common than rape of men. Therefore, rape is considered a form of gender-based violence. In 8 of 10 cases, rape is perpetrated by someone the victim knows. Most victims are young, between the ages of 12 and 24.

Prevalence

Rape is a major social and public health problem of national-crisis proportions. According to the Bureau of Justice Statistics, rape is one of the most underreported crimes, which makes it very difficult to count. Underreporting is due in large part to the high level of social stigma and shame associated with rape. Women who say they were raped often are not believed and frequently are blamed in some way for the rape. Some segments of society still believe in rape myths (e.g., women deserve to be raped if they dress provocatively), and these beliefs are stronger when the victim of rape is the wife of the perpetrator.

Incidence and prevalence are two ways to measure the frequency of rape. *Incidence* focuses on the number of acts in a given period, often the last year. Some have argued that the use of incidence rates alone to measure rape may disguise rape as an infrequent crime because respondents may feel uncomfortable reporting rape that occurred recently. *Prevalence* rates may be more useful because they focus on the number of people victimized over a longer period of time, commonly the lifetime, without regard to when or how many times. Questions about lifetime prevalence may produce more accurate estimates because they make respondents more comfortable and may be easier for respondents to answer. In addition, studies that use several behaviorally specific questions such as, "Has anyone ever physically forced you to have sexual intercourse without your consent?" (instead of asking, "Were you raped?") have led to more disclosure. The 1995–1996 National Violence Against Women Survey in the United States found a lifetime prevalence of 18% for women and 3% for men. Studies of wife rape have found lifetime prevalence for women between 10% and 14%. The National College Women Sexual Victimization Study estimated that between 1 in 4 and 1 in 5 college women are raped during their college years.

Vulnerability and Risk

Researchers have examined factors that increase vulnerability to victimization and risk factors for perpetrating sexual assault. Vulnerability research seeks to uncover factors that may increase the likelihood for victimization. Although the focus is on victims, identifying vulnerability factors is distinct from victim blaming. Victim blaming mistakenly assigns responsibility for victimization to victims (e.g., if a woman was drunk when she was raped, it is her fault). One of the most often replicated indicators of risk for adult rape victimization is a previous history of child sexual abuse; however, the risk accounted for by this predictor is not large. Drug use, but not alcohol consumption, was found to be causally related to rape in the largest U.S. longitudinal study to date. Aside from gender and age, personal characteristics of victims are not very good predictors of victimization. Some researchers have concluded that risks for adult victimization are best understood as aftereffects of childhood victimization. For example, women who were sexually abused as children may be more likely to use drugs habitually, which in turn increases the likelihood for future victimization. For some women, rape and sexual assault are repeated at different life stages, and evidence suggests that childhood abuse followed by revictimization in adolescence is the most provocative pattern for future sexual assaults. In sum, the key factors associated with rape victimization are ones over which victims have no control: being young, female, and having a previous history of sexual abuse.

Risk for perpetration is more important to understand than vulnerability to victimization, as victims will exist as long as perpetrators keep offending. Many single-factor theories exist to explain rape perpetration, but rape appears to be complex. A combination of societal, relational, and individual factors including biological and psychological characteristics may be necessary to explain perpetration. The confluence model attempts to do that, proposing that male sexual aggression results from an impersonal-promiscuous orientation to sex, hostile attitudes toward and mistrust of women, and sexual arousal from the domination of women, all of which are shaped by adverse childhood experiences. Many researchers have recognized the important role of societal factors such as patriarchy (the political, economic, and social domination of women by men) in understanding rape perpetration. Research has pointed to factors such as media images (e.g., pornography), sexist attitudes toward women, and male peer support for violence, which, combined with individual factors and previous histories of violence, serve to encourage and legitimate rape perpetration.

Consequences

The physical and psychological impacts of rape victimization are numerous. Immediate physical consequences can include vaginal trauma, broken bones, bruises, sexually transmitted diseases, and pregnancy. Longer term physical health effects also have been found in rape victims, such as chronic pelvic, head, and back pain; gastrointestinal disorders; and high-risk sexual behavior. Immediate psychological consequences may include fear of revictimization, shock, denial, and withdrawal. Ongoing psychological manifestations of rape can include chronic depression, Post-Traumatic Stress Disorder (PTSD), lowered self-esteem, anxiety, sexual problems, suicide ideation and attempts, and alcohol or drug dependency, and these may last for several years. Repeat victims are more likely to suffer from more severe and long-term consequences.

Conclusion

Rape is a ubiquitous problem with serious and long-term consequences. There are always limitations in measuring rape, and neither official crime data nor surveys can by themselves get at the full extent of the problem. Specific and explicit questions are critical in facilitating disclosure of rape, and consistency in questions across surveys is important to compare findings. In order to decrease rape and help victims, it is important to identify and understand risk factors and consequences of rape. More research is needed to measure rape victimization and perpetration across less studied populations such as people of color, gays and lesbians, the homeless, the elderly, and the mentally ill. Understanding the full spectrum of societal-, relational-, and individual-level influences on perpetration is imperative to inform prevention. Preventive efforts focused specifically on perpetrators are important to eradicate this problem.

Kathleen C. Basile
Centers for Disease Control and Prevention

Mary P. Koss
University of Arizona

RAPID EYE MOVEMENT (REM) SLEEP

The two major phases of sleep are rapid eye movement (REM) sleep and nonrapid eye movement (NREM) sleep (Gillin et al., 2000). REM sleep is often called dreaming (or D) sleep because dreams are reported by about 70–80% of persons awakened during this period. It also has been referred to as paradoxical sleep because the brain paradoxically seems to be in an activated state that is similar to, but not identical to, the waking state. For example, brain metabolism is normal or slightly increased during this period. REM sleep is characterized by an activated electroencephalogram (EEG) pattern (low-voltage, fast-frequency brain waves), muscular paralysis (with the exception of diaphragmatic and ocular muscles), periodic bursts of rapid eye movements, and instability of the autonomic nervous system (e.g., variable blood pressure, heart rate, and respiration). In men, penile erections occur during REM sleep, which can be evaluated in sleep studies to distinguish organic and psychological causes of impotence. Finally, nightmares occur almost exclusively during REM sleep. By contrast, NREM sleep encompasses the other four stages of sleep, including the deepest state of sleep, where the EEG pattern is less activated (high-voltage, slow-frequency brain waves), autonomic function is slower and steadier, brain metabolism is decreased, and there is no muscular paralysis or rapid eye movements. Moreover, less than 30% of persons report dreaming during NREM sleep. For this reason, night terrors (which differ from nightmares) occur during NREM sleep.

The time from falling sleep to the first onset of REM sleep is referred to as REM latency, which is normally about 70–100 minutes and progressively shortens in normal elderly persons to about 55–70 minutes. The amount of REM sleep also tends to decline with age. Approximately 50% of the sleep in babies is spent in REM sleep, which decreases to about 25% by age 4, remains relatively constant throughout adult life, and then begins to decline again after age 60. The number of rapid eye movements during a REM period is referred to as REM density. REM and NREM sleep oscillate throughout the night with a cycle length of approximately 90–100 minutes. The relative proportion of time spent in REM sleep increases during the course of the night while NREM time decreases. Sleep deprivation is normally followed by several nights of increased REM sleep with shortened REM latency, referred to as REM rebound.

Sleep and dreaming have long been an area of clinical and scientific interest in psychology, psychiatry, and neuroscience (Nofzinger et al., 1999). For example, the similarity between hallucinations and the often bizarre and strange content of most dreams naturally stimulated interest in studying REM sleep in patients with schizophrenia and other psychiatric disorders. Although such studies did not support the hypothesis that hallucinations represent waking dreams, further research in depression often found that REM latency is shortened to less than 60 minutes, REM density and the amount of REM sleep are increased, and the distribution of REM sleep is shifted to the earlier part of the night, compared to normal subjects. These findings had been considered a potential biological marker for depression, but shortened REM latency also has been found in some patients with other psychiatric disorders. Patients with schizophrenia and psychotic depression can have extremely short REM latencies, sometimes occurring immediately at the onset of sleep (sleep-onset REM) (Howland 1997). Increased REM sleep and shortened REM latency also occur in patients during the acute period of abrupt withdrawal from alcohol, benzodiazepines, and other sedative-hypnotic drugs. There is some evidence that shortened REM latency might be a genetic marker for depression within families. Many effective treatments for depression (including antidepressant drugs and electroconvulsive therapy) are associated with a decrease (or even suppression) of REM sleep and a lengthening of REM latency. Curiously, total sleep deprivation and even more selective sleep deprivation (i.e., waking patients during the onset of REM sleep throughout the night) has an antidepressant effect in many depressed patients, but this phenomenon is transient, and depression usually returns again after a complete night of sleep.

Abnormalities in REM sleep have been described in two neurologic disorders. In narcolepsy, sleep-onset REM periods are very common. These patients abruptly fall asleep, and they often report hypnogogic hallucinations, which are vivid dream-like states that are likely related to the rapid occurrence of sleep-onset REM periods. Patients with narcolepsy also develop cataplexy, which is the sudden brief loss of muscle tone during waking periods. This may be related to the muscular paralysis normally associated with REM sleep. These findings suggest that narcolepsy is characterized by dysregulated control of REM-NREM sleep. In REM behavior disorder, the normal paralysis of REM sleep is lost. These patients show complex vocal and motor behaviors during REM sleep and often appear to enact the dream content. This is similar to what is seen in animals with selective brain-stem lesions described previously.

Despite many decades of research, the precise function of sleep is not certain (Reiser, 2001). Sleep studies in various animal species suggest that NREM sleep evolved earlier than did REM sleep. These findings and other studies have suggested that NREM sleep might have a primary role in the conservation and restoration of energy, whereas REM sleep might be especially important to the development and maintenance of cognitive functioning.

REFERENCES

Gillin, J. C., Seifritz, E., Zoltoski, R. K., & Salin-Pascual, R. J. (2000). Basic science of sleep. In B. J. Sadock & H. I. Kaplan (Eds.), *Comprehensive textbook of psychiatry* (7th ed., pp. 199–209). Baltimore: Williams & Wilkins.

Howland, R. H. (1997). Sleep-onset rapid eye movement periods in neuropsychiatric disorders: Implications for the pathophysiology of psychosis. *Journal of Nervous and Mental Disease, 185,* 730–738.

Nofzinger, E. A., Keshavan, M., Buysse, D. J., Moore, R. Y., Kupfer, D. J., & Reynolds, C. F. (1999). The neurobiology of sleep in relation to mental illness. In D. S. Charney, E. J. Nestler, & B. S. Bunney (Eds.), *Neurobiology of mental illness* (pp. 915–929). New York: Oxford University Press.

Reiser, M. F. (2001). The dream in contemporary psychiatry. *American Journal of Psychiatry, 158,* 145–153.

Robert H. Howland
University of Pittsburgh School of Medicine

RATER ERRORS

Rater errors refer to mistakes made by raters when they use a rating scale to indicate the performance of an individual. The task competence of the rater, as well as the rater's sex, social position, race, religion, and age, have all been found to have effects on the rating given. While many of these errors are idiosyncratic, the following types of rating errors are common across many situations.

The *leniency* error occurs when average ratings tend to be higher than the midpoint of a scale because of pressure on the rater to rate subordinates high, a perception that subordinate rating reflects that of the rater, and the prescreening of students or subordinates before evaluation time. The effect of this error is to reduce variability between individuals. The harshness error is the same situation in reverse.

The *central tendency* error occurs when the rater checks the midpoint of the scale continuously. This can come about because of a hesitancy to "play God" or because extreme ratings (unsatisfactory or poor) require additional support and may have drastic effects on the rater's relationship with the subordinates.

The *halo effect* occurs when one trait affects the way all others are measured. Halo effect implies a positive generalization to other traits; *devil effect* implies a negative one.

The *sequential* error occurs when the particular order of traits has a special effect on the following ones, such as the halo effect.

The *logical* error occurs when a rater correlates specific traits in a manner believed to be consistent with the performance on others. The logical error is more complicated than the halo error.

The *recency* error occurs when an incident close in time to the rating has a greater effect on the rater than it would have had it happened much earlier. This is especially a problem when the incident is an emotional one such as a grievance, accident, or fight.

Rater errors pose special problems for the issues of reliability and validity. Furthermore, ratings that differ in time may accurately reflect a change in behavior even though this difference would demonstrate an artificial lack of reliability. High interrater reliability is a useful tool if both raters are knowledgeable about the individual being rated.

The problem caused by rater error for rating validity is the most serious problem of all because ratings are frequently used when a more objective measure cannot be developed. To the extent that rater errors exist and are not statistically adjusted out, the validity of the ratings is seriously contaminated.

Many strategies have been developed to reduce the impact of rater errors. These include training for raters, statistical adjustment for systematic differences between raters (e.g., leniency), and development of alternative evaluation strategies such as behaviorally anchored rating scales, ranking methods, forced choice, and the force distribution techniques.

L. Berger

RATING SCALES

In contrast to the items on a checklist, which require only a yes-no decision by the respondent, on rating scale items the respondent (rater) must make an evaluative judgment on some multicategory continuum. Introduced by Francis Galton in the nineteenth century, rating scales have been widely employed in business, industry, educational institutions, and other organizational contexts to evaluate various behavioral and personality characteristics. Such ratings are usually made by another person (e.g., a supervisor or peer), but individuals can also rate themselves.

Types of Rating Scales

On a numerical rating scale, the rater assigns to the person being rated (ratee) one of several numbers corresponding to particular descriptions of the characteristic being rated. A simple example of a numerical scale for rating a person on friendliness is to assign an integer from 0 to 4, depending on how friendly the person is perceived as being. Also illustrative of a numerical rating scale is the semantic differential technique, used extensively in studies of the connotative meanings of various concepts. Another widely used rating method is a graphic rating scale, in which the rater checks the point on the line corresponding to the appropriate description of the ratee.

On a standard rating scale, the rater supplies, or is supplied with, a set of standards against which ratees are to be compared. An example is the man-to-man rating scale, used for many years by the U.S. Army to rate officers on promotability. A man-to-man scale is constructed for rating individuals on a given trait, such as leadership ability, by having the rater think of five people who fall at different points along a hypothetical continuum of leadership ability. Then the rater compares each person to be rated with these five individuals and indicates which of them the ratee is most like in leadership ability.

On a forced-choice rating scale, raters are presented with two or more descriptions and are asked to indicate the one that best characterizes the ratee. If there are three or more descriptions, raters also may be told to indicate which description is least characteristic of the ratee.

Errors in Rating

An advantage of the forced-choice rating method is that it does a better job than other types of scales in controlling for certain errors in rating. Two errors are giving ratings that are higher than justified (leniency error) or lower than justified (severity error). Other errors are checking the average or middle category too often (central tendency error) and rating an individual highly on a certain characteristic or behavior simply because he or she rates highly in other areas (halo effect). Raters may also make the contrast error of rating a person higher than justified merely because a preceding ratee was very low or rating a person lower than justified because a preceding ratee was very high.

L. R. Aiken

RATIONAL EMOTIVE BEHAVIOR THERAPY

Rational emotive behavior therapy (REBT, formerly rational emotive therapy) is a theory of personality and a system of psychological treatment developed in the 1950s by Albert Ellis. It emphasizes the role of unrealistic expectations and irrational beliefs in human misery. The therapy's *A-B-C theory* of personality holds that emotions follow largely from cognitions and not from events. For example, should a family quarrel be followed by extreme anxiety, REBT asserts that emotional consequence C was not caused by activating event A but rather by some irrational belief or beliefs B about the nature or meaning of the quarrel, such as "I am an awful person" or "Without their approval, I cannot go on."

Ellis traces the origins of his insight about human upset back nearly 200 years to the writing of the later Stoic, Epictetus. In about C.E. second century, his disciple. Marcus Aurelius, emperor of Rome, wrote in his *Meditations,* "It is not this *thing* which disturbs you, but your own judgment about it. . . . Take away the opinion and there is taken away the complaint." REBT seeks to overcome disturbances caused by false beliefs and also to ameliorate the human predisposition toward crooked thinking that permits false beliefs to flourish. REBT theory considers emotional disturbance in the light of human nature in both its biological and social aspects.

Biological Origins of Personality

The lowest organisms may show complex, instinctive behavior in the apparent absence of learning. Such behaviors tend to be found in all members of a species and are performed in fixed stereotypical ways. For the most part, humans lack these fixed, universal behaviors, instead possessing a highly evolved capacity to acquire behaviors through learning and to retain them through habit. What is preprogrammed in humans is the clear predisposition to learn and form habits. Such predispositions make some sorts of things easier to learn than others. Children easily learn the desire to be loved rather than hated and readily prefer satisfaction of a want to its frustration. REBT stresses, however, that the predisposition to think is often the predisposition to think crookedly. The capacity to learn includes the capacity to learn nonsense. Among human predispositions with unfortunate consequences are tendencies to acquire desires for obviously hurtful things, to shed even grotesquely inappropriate habits only with great difficulty, and to think in terms of absolutes that distort even relatively accurate beliefs into disturbingly inaccurate ones.

Social Origins of Personality

Ellis found that many faulty cognitions appear throughout Western culture, such as beliefs that to have value one must be loved or approved of by virtually everyone and that it is a catastrophe when things go other than the way one wishes. Exaggerated, absolutistic beliefs establish impossible expectations. Thus, while people tend by nature to be happiest when their interpersonal relationships are best, most emotional disturbances result from caring too much about the opinions of others and from holding catastrophic expectations about the consequences of breached relationships.

Personality and Disturbance

REBT holds that because we are human, it is easy to learn to disturb ourselves and very hard to stop. Accordingly, REBT devotes considerable attention to the mechanisms by which disturbance is perpetuated. If thoughts are the cause of emotional upsets, then thinking is the means by which disturbance is perpetuated: People disturb themselves and perpetuate their own misery through habitual internal verbalizations of irrational beliefs. Regardless of the origins of an irrational belief, it is maintained only by use. Eliminate the irrational thought and the upset dissipates. Eliminate the irrational thinking and the problem will not recur. People tend to be happier and more effective when they reduce their natural human tendency toward irrational self-reindoctrination and begin to think and behave more rationally.

REBT Approaches to Treatment

Although REBT therapists employ a wide variety of specific techniques in therapy, the intent is to minimize or eradicate irrational beliefs and to foster a more rational lifestyle. The therapist seeks to reeducate the client and to break down old patterns and establish new ones, using logic, reason, confrontation, exhortation teaching, prescription, role-playing, behavioral assignments and more. The central technique is disputation, a logicoempirical analysis through which irrational beliefs are identified and challenged.

Ellis has said that effective psychotherapy blends full tolerance of the client as an individual with a ruthless, hardheaded campaign against his self-defeating ideas, traits, and performances. The initial goal of therapy is to help the client achieve three insights. The first is that while self-defeating behaviors and emotional malfunctions have origins in the past and provocations in the present, their current and proximal cause lies with one's irrational beliefs, not with one's parents, history, or circumstances. The second insight is that these irrational, magical beliefs remain in force only because of the continued mixed-up thinking and foolish behaviors that reinforce them. People remain disturbed for only so long as they continue to reindoctrinate themselves. The third insight is that insights do not correct crooked thinking. Only hard work and practice can do this.

Fundamental to REBT is a broad campaign to push clients to work against their major irrational premises on several fronts. Humans can think rationally about their irrational thinking. REBT relies primarily on cognitive methods to show clients the flawed nature of their expectations, demands, and beliefs and to teach them to think more rationally. Emotive procedures, however, may also be used. Role-playing, for example, may elicit actual occurrences of irrational beliefs, upsets and behavioral tendencies, which can then be logically analyzed and corrected. Emotive methods are also employed to evoke feelings and reactions leading directly to changes in attitudes or values. As an active, directive, educative approach, REBT from the beginning used behavioral methods, both in the office and through homework assignments. Perfectionistic clients may be instructed to fail deliberately at some real task to observe the noncatastrophic nature of the consequences. Shy persons may be required to take progressively larger risks in social settings to learn that failure is neither inevitable nor intolerable.

Once clients begin to behave in ways that challenge their major behavioral beliefs, they are encouraged to continue to do so because actions may in fact speak louder than words in maintaining positive change. Ellis observed that people are rarely able to keep disbelieving their profoundly self-defeating beliefs unless they persistently act against them.

Depending on clinical needs, REBT often incorporates cognitive, emotive, and behavioral elements within a single case or single complex intervention. Regardless of the methods used, it remains constant: to help clients to foster what Ellis described as their natural human tendencies to gain more individuality, freedom of choice, and enjoyment and to help them discipline themselves against their natural human tendencies to be conforming, suggestible, and unenjoying.

Roger E. Enfield
West Central Georgia Regional Hospital
Columbus, GA

See also: **Cognitive Therapy; Psychotherapy**

READING DISABILITIES (ASSESSMENT)

Dyslexia is a common learning disability that affects the ease with which children learn to read and spell. Poor phoneme awareness is believed to make the major contribution to this difficulty learning to read and spell. Phoneme awareness refers to the ability to detect, manipulate, and order the individual sounds (phonemes) within words. Difficulty with this process makes learning the alphabetic code more difficult, leading to the reading and spelling difficulties that are the hallmark of dyslexia.

A good evaluation for dyslexia has several major components and taps several sources of information. These components include a careful history, quantitative test results, and a qualitative analysis of errors.

It is most efficient to obtain a developmental history questionnaire from parents prior to a meeting to review the child's history. Because there is a substantial genetic contribution to developmental dyslexia, a careful family history should be taken, which inquires about difficulties with reading, spelling, learning foreign languages, or other language difficulties in the child's parents and other close blood relatives. Early developmental histories of children with dyslexia are typically normal, although there may be some slight speech delay or articulation difficulties. The child with dyslexia typically shows some difficulty with learning letter names and sounds in kindergarten, although there is considerable variability in this regard. In mildly affected or quite bright children who are educationally advantaged, there may be little concern about progress in kindergarten. Other children show striking difficulties with learning the alphabet in spite of much extra help. Difficulty with learning to read and spell is typically noted in the early grades. Parents should be carefully queried about the child's spontaneous spelling because many children with dyslexia are able to learn words for a spelling test only to forget them very quickly and thus are occasionally not described as poor spellers early on. Difficulty with learning the multiplication tables is a very common problem and is related to difficulties with rote verbal memory that are typically seen in children with dyslexia. For older children, there are often concerns about poor spelling and slow, effortful reading, which often leads to poorer performance on timed tests. Finally, learning a foreign language is typically difficult.

Following the gathering of history, testing is conducted with the child. A typical assessment battery might take approximately 3 to 4 hours or even more, depending on whether there are other related questions. A description of specific tests in a sample battery follows, but other tests that assess the same functions and skills could be substituted. The important issue is that the various functions and skills described be evaluated.

The first major area that should be assessed is general intellectual ability, for which the Wechsler Intelligence Scale for Children–III (WISC-III) is one recommended instrument. Dyslexia cannot be diagnosed based on WISC-III scores, but there are some score patterns and some qualitative observations that can be helpful. Specifically, scores are often somewhat weaker on the Arithmetic and Digit Span subtests, which both require verbal working memory among other capacities. On the Performance scale, the Coding subtest, which requires learning a new symbolic code and good visuomotor skill, is often somewhat weak. Qualitatively, word-finding difficulties are often evident on the Picture Completion subtest as the child may correctly locate the missing element in the picture but be unable to provide the name quickly. Likewise, on the Information subtest, it is not uncommon for the child to make errors on relatively easier items where specific names of people or months are required, even though more difficult items that are more conceptual are subsequently passed.

After general intellectual ability, another major function to be assessed is phonological processing. The Comprehensive Test of Phonological Processing (CTOPP) is one useful test battery for this purpose. The Woodcock-Johnson III also has a useful Sound Awareness subtest. The Lindamood Test of Auditory Conceptualization is another useful test in this category. All of these tests tap the child's ability to isolate and manipulate phonemes within words. Weakness in this area is a core underlying deficit in dyslexia. The CTOPP additionally has a Rapid Naming Cluster, which taps lexical retrieval by having the child rapidly name letters and numbers.

Another area that needs careful assessment is the child's skill levels in reading and written language and preferably also in math. The Woodcock-Johnson III Psychoeducational Battery has subtests covering the necessary areas, but other batteries are also certainly appropriate. It is important to test the child's single-word reading, nonsense-word reading (Word Attack), spelling, and calculation skill.

In addition to testing single-word and nonsense-word reading, it is also important to test contextual reading in a way that takes time into account. It is not unusual for a child with dyslexia to obtain a score close to grade level on an untimed test of reading; their genuine deficit may not become readily apparent until the rate and accuracy of their reading are taken into account. The Gray Oral Reading Test–4 is a good instrument for assessing reading in this way because it provides scores for reading rate, accuracy, and comprehension. Another test that taps reading rate is the Test of Word Reading Efficiency, in which the child reads lists of sight words and nonsense words in a specified time, and the score is based on the number of words which the child is able to read. In addition to the quantitative scores on these reading tests, a qualitative analysis of errors should be made, which can be helpful in guiding remedial efforts. In assessing spelling, it is important that a dictation-type test (rather than multiple choice) be used so that a qualitative analysis of the types of spelling errors can also be made. Children with dyslexia are particularly prone to dysphonetic errors (errors that indicate poor tracking of the sound sequence in the word). This kind of qualitative analysis is also useful in guiding remedial efforts.

The evaluation should conclude with a feedback conference with parents at which results are carefully explained and recommendations made. Because the most important goal of an assessment for dyslexia is to provide guidance about appropriate interventions, the information from the evaluation should be summarized in a written report. Interventions can be thought of in terms of two broad categories: remediation and compensation. Remediation refers to direct teaching to improve the child's weak skills, and there are numerous effective programs for this purpose. These share a focus on the child's poor phoneme awareness and mastery of the alphabetic code in highly structured and programmatic ways. A good remedial program also includes considerable practice in contextual reading, using techniques such as guided oral repetitive reading to address the difficulties children with dyslexia have with achieving silent reading. Compensation refers to various procedures that teachers and others can use in order to facilitate the child's learning and guard self-esteem while remedial efforts are being undertaken. Like remediation, these must be geared to the individual needs of the child and include, for example, more time on tests, some relaxation of spelling requirements on in-class work, caution in asking younger poor readers to read aloud in class, and various methods of assisting with the difficulty with math fact memorization that can interfere with the child's math progress.

Finally, it should be emphasized that the knowledgeable assessment of dyslexia is particularly important because so much can be done to help the child with dyslexia when this condition is correctly identified and remediated.

MARGARET W. RIDDLE
University of Denver

RECIPROCAL INHIBITION

Central nervous systems (CNSs) together with peripheral reflex loops form the basis of all animal movements. It has long been recognized that the CNS is primarily responsible for generating the motor-neuron firing patterns that underlie repetitive movements—that is, those that have a rhythmic expression (Delcomyn, 1980). An important aim in neurobiology is to identify the neuronal circuits underlying these rhythmic behaviors and to understand how the rhythmic motor patterns arise from neuronal connections and neuronal properties (Friesen & Stent, 1978).

The term *reciprocal inhibition* refers to a model or concept that was formulated at the beginning of the previous century by Brown (1911) to explain the neuronal origins of rhythmic walking movements. This first explanation for how a circuit of neurons can cause alternating limb movements was formulated long before specific neuronal circuits were identified. At that time, experiments by several researchers, including Brown, demonstrated that the stepping movements of animal limbs could be elicited even in deafferented mammalian preparations. That is, cats that had sensory axons severed to remove all possibility of sensory feedback from the periphery to the CNS could still perform at least the rudiments of stepping movements. These experiments led to the concept that a CNS oscillator exists within the vertebrate spinal cord to generate the neuronal impulse patterns that lead to repetitive animal movements. Brown's model for this central spinal oscillator envisioned two sets of neurons coupled by reciprocal (i.e., mutually) inhibitory synapses (Figure 1, panel A) for each limb or even for each joint. Because of the synaptic inhibitory connections, only one of the two inhibitory neurons (or perhaps pools of inhibitory neurons) can be active at any one time. Moreover, the activity of the two neurons alternates (Figure 1, panel B). With appropriate connections to motor neurons, output of these inhibitory neurons can control the activity of first flexor and then extensor motor neurons. Thus, the alternating neuronal patterns generated by the central circuit can drive the appropriate impulse patterns needed to command rhythmic flexion and extension, and hence to forward and backward movements of individual limbs (Brown, 1911).

A. CNS Circuit

B. Circuit Output

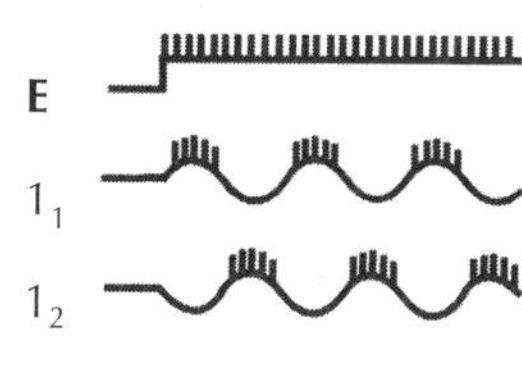

C. Dynamics

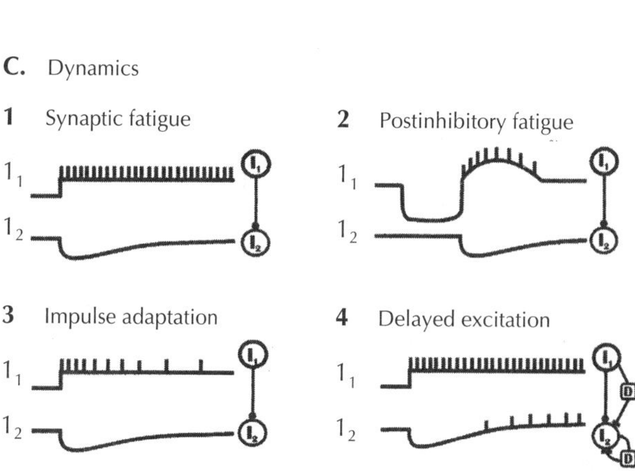

Figure 1. Model of reciprocal inhibition. A. *Circuit diagram.* Three neurons, one excitatory (E) and two inhibitory (I_1 and I_2) are interconnected by excitatory (—|) and inhibitory (—o) synapses. The output of this circuit (B.) consists of antiphasic membrane potential oscillations and impulse bursts generated by the two inhibitory neurons when the excitatory cell is active. C. *Dynamic properties important for reciprocal inhibition.* Insets to the right illustrate synaptic interactions. Upper traces in each part show the activity of presynaptic neurons; lower traces illustrate the effects on postsynaptic cells. C1. *Synaptic fatigue.* Excitatory drive to I_1 generates an initially large, then declining, hyperpolarization in I_2. C2. *Postinhibitory rebound.* When neuron I_1 is hyperpolarized briefly, the termination of the inhibition is followed by an excitatory response whereby the membrane potential overshoots rest to generate a burst of impulses. This PIR causes transient inhibition in neuron I_2. C3. *Impulse adaptation.* Excitatory drive to neuron I_1 elicits a train of impulses whose frequency declines with time. The effect on neuron I_2 is hyperpolarization, whose amplitude gradually decreases. C4. *Delayed excitation.* D designates delayed onset of excitation, which might either be synaptic or cellular.

Simple reciprocal inhibition alone cannot generate oscillations. Rather, additional dynamic (time-varying) properties are needed to ensure that mutually inhibitory neurons do not act as a simple, bistable switch (Friesen & Stent, 1978). Brown (1911) proposed two such dynamic properties: synaptic fatigue, a synaptic property; and postinhibitory rebound (PIR), a cellular property. If the strength of synaptic interactions is labile in a reciprocally inhibitory circuit, continuous excitation of either neuron will only transiently inhibit the other one (Figure 1, panel C1). If both neurons of the reciprocally inhibitory pair receive continuous excitatory input, the result will be antiphasic oscillations, as demonstrated by the following consideration. If neuron 1 is activated first, it will inhibit neuron 2 until the synapse fatigues. Once the synapse has weakened, neuron 2 will be relieved of inhibition and will be activated by the excitatory input, shutting off neuron 1. While neuron 2 is active, the synaptic terminal of the inhibited neuron recovers from fatigue and can once again inhibit neuron 2 when the synapse from neuron 2 to neuron 1 has weakened sufficiently for neuron 1 to become reactivated.

In neurons expressing the dynamic property PIR, the membrane potential overshoots the resting level at the termination of an inhibitory, hyperpolarizing input (Figure 1, panel C2). Also termed *paradoxical excitation,* this property provides transient excitatory drive when inhibition ceases. Membrane properties that can generate PIR include inactivation of a sodium conductance, such as is associated with the nerve impulse, and activation of an excitatory, inward current by membrane hyperpolarization (Calabrese & Arbas, 1989). As Brown (1911) realized, postinhibitory rebound in a circuit consisting of two reciprocally inhibitory neurons can suffice to generate stable, antiphasic oscillations (Perkel & Mulloney, 1974).

Two additional dynamic properties that can contribute to rhythmicity in neuronal circuits have been proposed. One cellular property is impulse adaptation, in which a continuously excited neuron emits a train of impulses with decreasing frequency (Figure 1, panel C3). The effect of adaptation, like that of synaptic fatigue, is to limit the duration of inhibition, again ensuring that a pair of mutually inhibitory neurons alternates activity, rather than forming a bistable switch. A final dynamic effect is delayed excitation, which can arise either because of complex circuit properties in which the inhibitory interaction between cells is superceded in time by synaptic excitation or because of hyperpolarization-induced excitatory currents. Rather than reducing the amplitude of the inhibitory interaction, these two cellular and circuit properties act as sources of delayed excitatory drive to overcome synaptic inhibition (Figure 1, panel C4).

Brown's (1911) neuronal model for rhythm generation is known either as reciprocal inhibition or as the half-center model. Although reciprocal inhibition served as the only important conceptual model for generating rhythmic movements for many years, it was first authenticated experimentally by the finding that reciprocal inhibition is one component of the rhythm-generating mechanism in the pyloric system of the lobster stomatogastric ganglion (Miller & Selverston, 1985). Since then, the model has been applied with success to a variety of neuronal circuits that generate animal behavior (Friesen, 1994). Examples include swimming movements in lamprey, tadpoles, the marine mollusks *Clione* and *Tritonia,* and the leech. The rhythmic contraction of leech heart tubes provides an especially well-described preparation in which reciprocal inhibition generates the oscillations (Calabrese & Arbas, 1989).

REFERENCES

Brown, T. G. (1911). The intrinsic factors in the act of progression in the mammal. *Proceedings of the Royal Society of London, 84,* 308–319.

Calabrese, R. L., & Arbas, E. A. (1989). Central and peripheral oscillators generating heartbeat in the leech Hirudo medicinalis. In J. W. Jacklet (Ed.), *Cellular and neuronal oscillators* (pp. 237–267). New York: Marcel Dekker.

Delcomyn, F. (1980). Neural basis of rhythmic behavior in animals. *Science, 210,* 492–498.

Friesen, W. O. (1994). Reciprocal inhibition: A mechanism underlying oscillatory animal movements. *Neuroscience and Biobehavior Review, 18,* 547–553.

Friesen, W. O., & Stent, G. S. (1978). Neural circuits for generating rhythmic movements. *Annual Review of Biophysics & Bioengineering, 7,* 37–61.

Miller, J. P., & Selverston, A. I. (1985). Neuronal mechanisms for the production of the lobster pyloric motor pattern. In A. I. Selverston (Ed.), *Model neural networks and behavior* (pp. 37–48). New York: Plenum.

Perkel, D. H., & Mulloney, B. (1974). Motor pattern production in reciprocally inhibitory neurons exhibiting postinhibitory rebound. *Science, 185,* 181–183.

W. Otto Friesen
University of Virginia

REFLECTIVE LISTENING

Reflective listening is a way to communicate empathy, an important element of psychotherapeutic interaction. Carl Rogers wrote that

> being empathic has several facets. It means entering the private perceptual world of the other and becoming thoroughly at home in it. It involves being sensitive, moment to moment, to the changing felt meanings which flow in this other person, to the fear or rage or tenderness or confusion or whatever, that he/she is experiencing. It means temporarily living in his/her life, moving about in it delicately without making judgments, sensing meanings of which he/she is scarcely aware, but not trying to uncover feelings, since this would be too threatening. It includes communicating your sensings of his/her world as you look with fresh and unfrightened eyes at elements of which the individual is fearful. It means frequently checking as to the accuracy of your sensings, and being guided by the responses you receive. You are a confident companion. By pointing to the possible meanings in the flow of his/her experiencing you help the person to focus on this useful type of referent, to experience the meanings more fully, and to move forward in the experiencing.
>
> To be with another in this way means that for the time being you lay aside the views and values you hold for yourself in order to enter another's world without prejudice. In some sense it means that you lay aside your self and this can only be done by a person who is secure enough [to] not get lost in what may turn

out to be the strange or bizarre world of the other, and [to] comfortably return to his own world when he wishes. (Rogers, 1975)

The importance of empathic listening has been written about in many approaches to psychotherapy including client-centered, self psychology, psychoanalysis, Gestalt, existential, focusing-oriented, pretherapy, child therapy, marital and couple therapy, disaster-recovery therapy, and clinical supervision. Some emphasize the importance of nonverbal components of empathy. Empathy shares aspects of mental discipline with meditation. Empathic ability is not strongly associated with academic or diagnostic proficiency.

Reflective listening involves holding a distinct set of attitudes toward the person being listened to. There is an acceptance of the content of the person's awareness. The listener trusts the resources of the speaker to evaluate, analyze, and decide and therefore does not give advice and suggestions about what to do or how to perceive. When listening, one is nondiagnostic and nonevaluative.

Communicating one's empathy is often best accomplished by using much the same language as the person in order to avoid possible connotations of different language that would not be correct for the speaker. This does not mean limiting oneself to literally what was said. The listener senses for and reflects meanings not yet clear, some not yet mentioned in words, that have been expressed nonverbally. Frequently communicating one's empathy, as often as a couple of times per minute to stay in close contact, gives the speaker ample opportunities to correct misunderstandings or to revise what he or she says to articulate experiencing as it evolves.

Listening has useful effects: In the process of being accurately and caringly understood, feelings and ideas change in problem-solving, insight-producing, tension-releasing, responsibility-building, and conflict-reducing ways. In addition, the person gets the message that his or her experience makes sense and that he or she is worthy of being taken seriously.

Paradoxically, this powerful way to foster change involves the listener's studiously not pushing for change. The listener accepts what the speaker says on the speaker's terms, without dispute.

Eugene Gendlin (1981, 1996) clarified the *object* to which the listener listens. The *bodily felt sense* is more inclusive than what one is clearly aware of consciously, including everything felt at the moment, even if only vaguely and subliminally. It often has opposing impulses in it. It is not a static object but changes from moment to moment as events proceed. It is this fluid object that the listener reflects.

Through research, Gendlin, Rogers, and others came to believe that certain attitudes, when directed toward the bodily felt sense, resulted in more positive personality change than did other attitudes. These attitudes include patience, gentleness, warmth, interest, respect, curiosity, and an expectation that something new can be discovered. This is in contrast to attitudes of criticism, control, evaluation, or neglect.

Listening creates an interactional opportunity for the speaker to experience and have supported his or her own capacities for solving problems, for identifying the part he or she contributes to interpersonal difficulties, for building self-esteem, and for sorting out complicated personal concerns and motives. The common helper attitudes of evaluation, diagnosis, analysis, and advice seem to have the opposite effect: that of stopping this kind of process in favor of an attitude of dependence on (or resistance to) the guidance of external authority.

Reflecting is a limited metaphor for empathic listening. It does not adequately convey the change produced by good listening, nor the way in which it is an intimate relationship event. The speaker experiences the calming, enlightening embrace of an affectionately indifferent, accepting attitude democratically encompassing all presently experienced emotions, thoughts, sensations, and images. This embrace, provided by the listener, enables the speaker to move toward unconditional acceptance and understanding of his or her subtle and complex experiencing. Ann Cornell (1994) refers to this intrapersonal attitude as the "radical acceptance of everything." It has a remarkable power to release one's energy to move forward in constructive ways.

Reflective listening is valued beyond psychotherapy. Thomas Gordon recommends it to parents as a means of maintaining open and trusting relationships with their children and to health care professionals for improving relations with patients. Teachers who are rated more empathic have been shown to achieve greater student involvement in educational settings. Empathic listening has also been found helpful for school administrations in dealing with parents. It plays a role in improving intimacy in spousal relationships. Clinical and vocational supervision situations also benefit from this skill. Many conflict management and mediation approaches use reflective listening as a core technique. Writings about building community emphasize the value of empathic listening techniques. Some philosophical writings also cite this form of communication as a beneficial dialectical method.

Kenneth Clark (1980) believed that empathy utilizes the most recently evolved part of the brain and that it counterbalances egocentric power drives. Thus, reflective listening may have great social significance toward collective solutions to resource allocation and peaceful human relations.

REFERENCES

Clark, K. (1980). Empathy: a neglected topic in psychological research. *American Psychologist, 35,* 187–190.

Cornell, A. W. (1994). The Radical Acceptance of Everything. Available at http://focusingresources.com/articles/radical acceptance.html

Gendlin, E. T. (1981). *Focusing* (2nd ed., Rev. ed.). New York: Bantam.

Gendlin, E. T. (1996). *Focusing-oriented psychotherapy: A manual of the Experiential Method.* New York: Guilford Press.

Rogers, C. R. (1975). Empathic: An unappreciated way of being. *Counseling Psychologist, 5,* 2–10.

James R. Iberg
Adjunct Faculty Argosy University, Illinois School of Professional Psychology / Chicago Campus

See also: **Experiential Psychotherapy**

REFLEXES

A reflex is the central nervous system's least complex, shortest-latency motor response to sensory input. The expression of a reflex is an involuntary, stereotyped contraction of muscles determined by the locus and nature of the eliciting stimulus. Reflexes may be elicited by stimulation of any sensory modality. There are many reflexes; an exhaustive listing is not provided here. Rather, the principles that apply to all reflexes are described using a few examples.

The simplest reflex is the myotatic, or muscle stretch, reflex. This reflex can be elicited from any skeletal muscle, but the best known example is the patellar, or knee-jerk, reflex. The anatomical basis of the myotactic reflex is the monosynaptic (one synapse) connection between the sensory fibers that detect stretch on a muscle and the alpha (tr) motor neurons that supply nerve fibers to that same muscle. The sensory fibers have their cell bodies in the dorsal root ganglia. One end of the sensory fiber terminates in the sensory end-organ for muscle stretch, known as the muscle spindle. The other end of the nerve fiber enters the spinal cord through the dorsal root and dorsal horn and terminates in the ventral horn of the spinal cord on an a motor neuron.

Muscle spindles are embedded in the mass of each striated muscle. They are arranged in parallel with the extrafusal muscle fibers that contract when the motor nerves supplying them are stimulated. The central portion of the spindle is nonmuscular and receives the sensory nerve ending. When the central portion of the spindle is stretched, the sensory nerve increases its rate of production of action potentials. The axons that provide the input for the stretch reflex are the largest of the sensory nerve fibers and are called type Ia. Conduction is very rapid in these nerves. This fact, and the fact that they each make a monosynaptic contact with a motor neuron supplying the extrafusal muscle fibers, ensures that the reflex contraction of the whole muscle in response to stretch is very rapid. When the muscle contracts, the muscle spindle shortens; the stimulus for sensory discharge is reduced, and the rate of action potential production in the sensory fibers decreases or stops.

In addition to a nonmuscular sensory middle, the muscle spindle has muscular tissue attached to each of its ends. These muscular endings of the muscle spindle are called intrafusal muscles and do not contribute to the contractile strength of the muscle. They are innervated by their own type of motor neuron called the gamma (γ) motor neuron. Motor areas in the brain, particularly in the reticular formation, send axons that influence the γ motor neurons and through this connection can modulate the stretch reflex by changing the tension on the nonmuscular central portion of the spindle.

The stretch reflex demonstrates the basic principles of all reflexes. A sensory, or afferent, limb is necessary. Severing the dorsal roots eliminates the stretch reflex. The eliciting stimulus is specific. The reflex is produced by stretch on the muscle, not by touch, pain, or some other stimulus. A motor, or efferent, limb is necessary. Severing the ventral roots eliminates the reflex. The efferent response is specific. Only the muscles that are stretched will reflexively contract. The reflex is graded. The greater the stretch, the greater the contraction.

More complex reflex arcs also exist. The anatomy of these reflexes includes the interposition of one or more interneurons between the afferent and efferent limbs of the reflex. These reflexes, therefore, have more than one synapse and are called polysynaptic. The Golgi tendon organ reflex provides an example of the simplest polysynaptic reflex. The sensory end-organ is found in the tendon; its cell body is in a dorsal root ganglion. Increased tension on the tendon, usually produced by contraction of the muscle to which it is attached, is the eliciting stimulus that increases activity in the tendon organ afferent fiber. The tendon organ afferent fiber synapses on an interneuron in the spinal cord. This interneuron inhibits as a motor neuron, thus decreasing activity in its efferent axon. Because this axon returns to the muscle to which the stretched tendon is attached, the muscle relaxes and the tension on the tendon is reduced.

The muscle stretch reflex and the Golgi tendon organ reflex work in concert to provide the basis for rapid regulation of the degree of contraction of the muscle. For example, these reflexes are useful for quick adjustments to change the position of the foot as a person hikes across uneven ground.

Other polysynaptic reflexes are involved in movement of whole limbs and the coordination of different limbs. These reflexes incorporate more interneurons. The divergent (from one neuron to several neurons) and convergent (from several neurons to one neuron) connections of the interneurons form the basis of these complex reflexes. An example is provided by a person who steps barefooted on a sharp object and reflexively withdraws the injured foot. The sensory input is pain. The pain afferents enter the dorsal horn of the spinal cord and continue to its ventral division, where they synapse on interneurons. Some of these interneurons excite motor neurons that cause the flexor muscles of the affected leg to contract to lift the foot, while other interneurons serve to inhibit the motor neurons that supply the extensor muscles of the same leg. This permits the leg to withdraw quickly and smoothly from the noxious stimulus.

Other neurons receiving pain input send axons across the midline of the spinal cord and excite the motor neurons for extensors of the opposite leg and inhibit those that innervate that leg's flexors. This causes the leg to stiffen and provide support. Furthermore, interneurons relay information up and down the spinal cord to produce intersegmental reflexes that coordinate muscle contraction of the trunk and upper limbs. The entire reflex is known as the flexion–crossed extension reflex.

The spinal cord reflexes form the basis for maintenance and adjustment of posture. Brain motor systems influence spinal cord reflexes via input to interneurons and the γ motor neurons to produce normal movement and modulate reflexes. Changes in spinal cord reflexes may indicate pathology in the brain motor systems. For example, damage to the motor cortex or to axons originating in this part of the brain produces increased reflex response to muscle stretch.

Several optic reflexes exist. An example is the direct light reflex, which is the constriction of the pupil to light. It requires an intact retina, optic nerve, midbrain, and third cranial nerve, but not the lateral geniculate nucleus or visual cortex. If light is restricted to one eye only, a crossing pathway at the pretectal level of the mid-brain produces constriction of the pupil opposite to the one into which the light is introduced; this is called the consensual light reflex. Several reflex changes (accommodation reflex) also occur when the eyes are directed toward a near object. These include convergence of the eyes as the medial recti contract, thickening of the lens, and pupillary constriction. Many components of the visual system are involved in this reflex, including the retina, optic nerve, occipital cortex, superior colliculus, lateral geniculate nucleus, and nuclei of the oculomotor nerve.

Reflexes can also be elicited from stimulation of sensory input from the viscera. The baroreceptor reflex is an example of such an autonomic reflex. An increase in blood pressure stretches receptors in large vessels near the heart. This increases afferent input to nucleus tractus solitarius of the medulla. Neurons in the nucleus tractus solitarius relay activity to the motor nucleus of the vagal nerve, as well as to the spinal cord autonomic neurons, and heart rate and blood pressure decrease.

REFERENCES

Goldberg, M. E., Eggers, H. M., & Gouras, P. (1991). The ocular motor system. In E. R. Kandel, J. H. Schwartz, & T. M. Jessell (Eds.), *Principles of neural science* (3rd ed., pp. 660–667). New York: Elsevier.

Gordon, J., & Ghez, C. (1991). Muscle receptors and spinal reflexes: The stretch reflex. In E. R. Kandel, J. H. Schwartz, & T. M. Jessell (Eds.), *Principles of neural science* (3rd ed., pp. 564–580). New York: Elsevier.

May, P. J., & Corbett, J. J. (1997). Visual motor system. In D. E. Haines (Ed.), *Fundamental neuroscience* (pp. 399–416). New York: Churchill Livingstone.

Mihailoff, G. A., & Haines, D. E. (1997). Motor system 1: Peripheral sensory, brainstem, and spinal influence on ventral horn cells. In D. E. Haines (Ed.), *Fundamental neuroscience* (pp. 335–346). New York: Churchill Livingstone.

Naftel, J. P., & Hardy, S. F. P. (1997). Visceral motor pathways. In D. E. Haines (Ed.), *Fundamental neuroscience* (pp. 418–429). New York: Churchill Livingstone.

Pearson, K. G. (1993). Common principles of motor control in vertebrates and invertebrates. *Annual Review of Neuroscience, 16,* 265–297.

Michael L. Woodruff
East Tennessee State University

REHABILITATION PSYCHOLOGY

Rehabilitation psychology is a specialty area of practice within the broad field of psychology. Rehabilitation psychology is the application of psychological knowledge and understanding on behalf of individuals with disabilities and society through such activities as research, clinical practice, teaching, public education, development of social policy, and advocacy. Professionals who provide rehabilitation psychology services are called rehabilitation psychologists. Rehabilitation psychologists participate in a broad range of activities including clinical care, program development, service provision, research, education, administration, and public policy.

Rehabilitation psychologists work in diverse settings including acute care hospitals and medical centers, inpatient and outpatient physical rehabilitation units/centers, nursing homes and assisted living centers, community agencies specializing in services for a particular type of disability (e.g., cerebral palsy, multiple sclerosis, deafness), and other types of settings such as pain and sports injury centers and cardiac rehabilitation facilities. They may work for private facilities or for such government facilities as Veterans Administration hospitals and centers. Rehabilitation psychologists serve individuals throughout the life span, from early childhood through late adulthood. Many rehabilitation psychologists are full-time university or college faculty and focus primarily on teaching and research. Others may work in or consult industry, provide expert legal testimony, or conduct assessments and evaluations for insurance agencies. Rehabilitation psychologists advocate for improvement of life conditions for people with disabilities; as such they are involved in the development and promotion of legislation such as the Americans with Disabilities Act.

Rehabilitation psychologists who provide clinical and counseling services assist individuals in coping with, and adjusting to, chronic, traumatic, or congenital injuries or illnesses that may result in a wide variety of physical, sensory, neurocognitive, emotional, and developmental disabilities. These may include (but are not limited to): spinal cord injury; brain injury; stroke; amputations; neuromuscular disorders; medical conditions with the potential to limit functioning and participation in life activities such as cancer, AIDS, multiple sclerosis, or limb weakness; chronic pain; congenital or chronic developmental disorder such as mental retardation; severe psychiatric disability; substance abuse; burns and disfigurement; deafness and hearing loss; blindness and vision loss; and other physical, mental, and emotional impairments compounded by cultural, educational, or other disadvantages.

Rehabilitation psychologists provide services with the goal of increasing function and reducing disability, activity limitations, and restrictions on societal participation. The person served is seen as an active partner in the treatment process, and, thus, the services provided take into account the person's preferences, needs, and resources. Consistent with the World Health Organization's recently adopted International Classification of Functioning, Disability, and Health (ICF), the rehabilitation psychologist works with the individual with a disability to address personal factors impacting on the ICF domains of activities and participation. This includes assessing and addressing neurocognitive status, mood and emotions, desired level of independence and interdependence, mobility and freedom of movement, self-esteem and self-determination, and subjective view of capabilities and quality of life as well as satisfaction with achievements in specific areas such as work, social relationships, and being able to go where one wishes beyond the mere physical capability to do so. Rehabilitation psychologists take the influences of culture, ethnicity, gender, residence and geographic location, relative visibility, and assumption of disability on attitudes and available services into account when planning services and interventions. Rehabilitation psychologists explore with individuals environmental barriers to their participation and activity performance and the means to address these barriers including accommodations and adaptations in existing structures or materials, the use of assistive technology, and the use of personal assistance services. For individuals with severe disabilities or chronic illnesses, a blend of these products and services is often most beneficial.

The rehabilitation psychologist provides services to families and primary caregivers as well as other significant people in the individual's social-community circle (e.g., teachers, employers, clergy, friends). The goal of rehabilitation psychology is to assist the individual (and those significant others who are involved in treatment planning and ongoing provision of support) in achieving optimal physical, psychological, and interpersonal functioning by addressing the obstacles preventing the highest level of personal and social functioning. Rehabilitation psychologists view persons served holistically, and they seek to broaden opportunities for maximum individual functioning as well as functioning and participation in social relationships, social activities, education, employment, and the community.

Some rehabilitation psychologists work within a broad variety of health care settings and with a broad range of persons with varying disabilities, whereas others specialize in a particular area of clinical practice. Regardless of setting or area of specialization, the rehabilitation psychologist is consistently involved in interdisciplinary teamwork and provides services within the network of biological, psychological, social, environmental, and political environments to assist the persons served in achieving desired rehabilitation goals. Thus, in addition to working directly with the persons served and their families, rehabilitation psychologists often serve an important role in providing consultations regarding disability and health issues to attorneys, courts, government agencies, educational institutions, corporate facilities, and insurance companies.

Rehabilitation psychologists have completed doctoral degrees in psychology and have had extensive predoctoral and postdoctoral training in health care settings. Further, rehabilitation psychologists providing clinical services are usually required to be licensed in order to provide services in their state of practice and to receive reimbursement for services from health insurance payers. The American Board of Professional Psychology (ABPP) recognizes rehabilitation psychology as a specialty area of practice within psychology. The ABPP's definition of rehabilitation psychology was a significant and primary source in the development of the present description.

Although rehabilitation psychologists belong to many professional organizations relevant to their area of practice and specialization, the major organization representing rehabilitation psychology is the American Psychological Association, Division of Rehabilitation Psychology (http://www.apa.org/divisions/div22/). This division publishes a scholarly journal and newsletter and sponsors sessions relevant to rehabilitation psychology research and practice at the annual APA conference as well as other education venues for psychologists and other health professionals.

The American Psychological Association can be contacted for a list of rehabilitation psychologists in the United States as well as those members who live outside the United States. Finally, there are excellent textbooks available on the general topic of rehabilitation psychology as well as books on areas of specialization within this field.

Marcia J. Scherer
Institute for Matching Person and Technology

Kelly L. Blair
West Tennessee Rehabilitation Center

Martha E. Banks
ABackans Diversified Computer Processing

Bernard Brucker
University of Miami School of Medicine

John Corrigan
Ohio State University

Stephen Wegener
Johns Hopkins University

REINFORCEMENT

Thorndike's statement of the law of effect reads as follows:

> The law of effect is that: Of several responses made to the same situation, those which are accompanied or closely followed by satisfaction to the animal will, other things being equal, be more firmly connected to the situation, so that, when it recurs, they will be more likely to recur; those which are accompanied or closely followed by discomfort [annoyance] to the animal will, other things being equal, have their connections to that situation weakened, so that, when it recurs, they will be less likely to occur. The greater the satisfaction or discomfort, the greater the strengthening or weakening of this bond.

With the development of reinforcement theory, chiefly at the hands of Clark L. Hull, the key terms in the law of effect, *satisfaction* and *discomfort,* became positive and negative reinforcement. Positive and negative reinforcement are theoretical concepts just as Thorndike's satisfaction and discomfort were. These effects are created by the manipulation of more objective conditions, positive reinforcers (rewards and satisfiers in Thorndike's terms) and negative reinforcers (punishers and annoyers in Thorndike's terms). Whether the effect is positive or negative, reinforcement depends on whether the positive or negative reinforcer is delivered or withheld. Positive reinforcement may be produced either by the presentation of a reward or by withholding a punishment when a particular response occurs; negative reinforcement may be produced either by the presentation of a punisher or by withholding a reward when a particular response occurs. These four arrangements define a basic classification of types of operant conditioning: (1) *reward training*—food is delivered when the rat presses the lever in the Skinner box; (2) *active avoidance training*—the rat avoids electric shock by crossing to the opposite side of a shuttle box; (3) *passive avoidance training*—the rat receives electric shock if it steps down from a platform onto a grid; (4) *omission training*—the rat receives food only if it fails to press the bar in the Skinner box.

Greg A. Kimble

See also: **Operant Conditioning**

REINFORCEMENT SCHEDULES

In operant conditioning theory, a behavior is maintained by its consequences, that is, by the reinforcing or punishing events that follow the behavior. The relationship between a behavior and its consequences is called a contingency. Reinforcement generally operates on an intermittent schedule of some sort. Skinner pointed out that reinforcement may be scheduled in many ways and demonstrated that subtle differences in scheduling can generate dramatic differences in behavior.

Four basic schedules of reinforcement have been studied in detail. Two are ratio schedules, in which the presentation of a reinforcer is contingent on the number of responses emitted by the organism. In a fixed ratio (FR) schedule, every *n*th response is reinforced. In a variable schedule (VR), responses are reinforced on a certain average ratio, but the number of responses required for reinforcement varies unpredictably from reinforcement to reinforcement. The other two basic schedules are interval schedules, which are defined by the length of time that must elapse between reinforcements. The first response to occur after this time has elapsed is reinforced. In fixed interval (FI) schedules, this interval remains constant from reinforcement to reinforcement; in variable interval (VI) schedules, the intervals between reinforcements vary randomly about some mean interval.

In addition to these four basic schedules, there are a number of other schedules, such as differential reinforcement of low rates of response (DLR), differential reinforcement of other behaviors (DRO), and various complex and concurrent schedules, which are combinations of the four basic schedules.

Each schedule has a particular effect on behavior. Ratio schedules generally produce high rates of response, and interval schedules produce lower rates of response. Variable schedules, particularly variable interval schedules, produce a remarkably stable pattern of behavior. Behaviors maintained under variable schedules are also highly resistant to extinction. This fact helps to explain why it is so difficult to extinguish undesirable behaviors, since most behaviors are maintained under variable schedules.

Robert A. Shaw
Brown University

See also: **Operant Conditioning; Reinforcement**

RELATIONSHIP THERAPY

Relationship therapy refers to several forms of psychotherapy that invoke the relationship between the therapist and client as the effective change mechanism. In contrast, insight and behavior change are the mechanisms of change for psychoanalysis and behavior modification, respectively. Additionally, the term *relationship therapy* has come to refer to treating relationships as the focus of therapy.

The Relationship as the Mechanism of Change

Two central theorists of relationship therapy are Martin Buber (1974) and Harry Stack Sullivan (1953), although

Carl Rogers (1951) and Eric Berne (1964) played important roles in the development of the theory and practice of relationship therapy.

Buber saw the essence of human living as the encounter in a direct experience between one person and another (I-Thou), rather than as the act of one person's seeing another (and being seen) as an object or through the barriers and filters of social roles (I-It). The humanizing influence of one person's I-Thou experiencing on the other allows the other to feel fully human. Buber saw people not as static diagnostic entities such as neurotics or schizophrenics to be treated (which would be I-It relationships) but as humans in need of a direct I-Thou relationship with another human. Thus the therapist, who is the expert in human relationships, provides a chance for the person to encounter another in dialogue or the I-Thou experience. This experience is the curative element and, in its more general form, is both the prophylactic and antidote to the oppression of a mechanistic and increasingly bureaucratic society that makes people into *its* rather than *thous.* Buber's influence catapulted with the 1922 publication of *I and Thou* (1958), reached a peak in the 1950s and 1960s, and remains a force in pastoral and humanistic counseling today.

For Sullivan, personality develops as a function of the relationship. For example, an infant born to a teenage mother who consequently could not go to college would be viewed by that mother differently than would a baby who was born to a long-childless couple who desired a baby. The parents' reactions constitute appraisal that is reflected back to the developing person either overtly, by verbal and other behavior, or covertly, by facial and emotional expression and by vocal tone. The developing self contributes to personality or, to use Sullivan's term, the *envelope of energy transformation.* Abnormal behavior is the stereotyped response, or *parataxic distortion,* to others for whom the response is not fitting. The psychotherapist begins the four stages for treatment with the inception or initial sizing-up of the patient and of one another and processes to the reconnaissance, which is the more formal history taking of the patient. The therapist is ever mindful of the emotional tone from moment to moment in each session and for each topic. The problematic areas are scrutinized during the detained inquiry, and progress is summarized in the termination phase. Anxieties or insecurities are revealed during the examination of the patient's life, although various warps or strains in the relationship are seen in slips of the tongue, stuttering, misused words, and gestures inconsistent with verbal statements or with the mood of the moment. The therapist might sense these moods of the moment via Sullivan's reciprocal emotions or through the strains or pulls produced by the patient during the session. This sensing of the other may result in the therapist's responding in a way that the patient can use to examine his or her experience. The therapeutic and unusual response may allow the patient to unhook, or behave in a new way because their old behaviors did not bring about the usual and desired response from the therapist. The therapist provides a noncondemning environment for such experimenting. Sullivan's influence is strong but not generally acknowledged currently.

Rogers saw humans as motivated to grow when provided with the right conditions. These conditions could be supplied within the counseling or therapeutic context when the right relationship was presented. The basic ingredients include the theorist's unconditional positive regard, empathic understanding, and congruence of feelings that were communicated to the patient in the therapeutic relationship. Berne saw games or enactments of the scripts we learn early in life within relationships in which people assume one-up and one-down roles. Thus one person might play parent or caretaker to another person's child or help-seeking role.

Contemporary Developments

Relationship as the Therapeutic Modality

Recently, the traditional metaphors from the several dominant theoretical perspectives have grown brittle with age. The theoretical approaches have gravitated toward realizing the role of the relationship as the force accounting for effectiveness in psychotherapy. Psychoanalytic approaches have developed the idea of intersubjectivity as a way of including the role of the relationship between the psychoanalyst and the analysand as the change mechanism in therapy. Intersubjectivity denotes the interpersonal transactions in psychotherapy and the way by which corrective emotional experiences transpire. The corrective emotional experience might occur when the therapist responds in a different and asocial fashion to a set of patient behaviors that previously elicited a particular and stereotyped response. Thus, a sexually seductive or coy behavior by a patient that does not elicit a sexual advance from the therapist provides the patient with the opportunity to experience him- or herself differently. The patient might now have to examine why he or she might be stuck in the role of using him- or herself as a sexual object in order to interact with others.

Behavioral approaches recognize relationship factors by increasingly employing such notions as nonspecific therapist factors and the role of context in behavior change. This contrasts with the more traditional use of behavioral reinforcement as the central and sole source of change in effective behavioral therapy. The role of the therapist's personality in structuring the relationship and the use of the theorist-in-relationship are more realistic approaches to how behavior change works. The shift in behavioral theory and practice accords well with the therapy effectiveness research. Such research has found that the curative aspects of psychotherapy center on the nature of the relationship and the working through of patient problems.

Treating the Relationship

Traditional Sullivanian thinking has developed into systems theory. Variants of systems theory focus on treating the relationship. The family therapy theories developed by Bowen (1978), Haley (1963), Madanes (1981), Minuchin (1974), and Satir (1967, 1972) are prime examples of relationship therapies. Another group of therapists who focused on relationships concern themselves with conducting marital therapy. John Mordechai Gottman (1995) has been foremost in his research and treatment program for defining marital troubles and their treatment. Relationship treatments tend to be time limited; active in interventions; problem focused; present oriented; interpersonal; and oriented to coping, identifying assets, and improving relationships.

REFERENCES

Berne, E. (1964). *Games people play.* New York: Grove.

Bowen, M. (1978). *Family therapy in clinical practice.* New York: Jason Aronson.

Buber, M. (1934). *I and thou.* New York: Scribner's.

Gottman, J. M. (1995). *Why marriages succeed or fail.* New York: Simon & Schuster.

Haley, J. (1963). *Strategies of psychotherapy.* New York: Grune & Stratton.

Klerman, G. L., & Weissman, M. M. (Eds.). (1993). *New applications of interpersonal psychotherapy.* Washington, DC: American Psychiatric Press.

Madanes, C. (1981). *Strategic family therapy.* San Francisco: Jossey-Bass.

Minuchin, S. (1974). *Families and family therapy.* Cambridge MA: Harvard University Press.

Rogers, C. R. (1951). *Client-centered therapy.* Boston: Houghton-Mifflin.

Satir, V. (1967). *Conjoint family therapy: A guide to theory and technique.* Palo Alto, CA: Science and Behavior Press.

Satir, V. (1972). *Peoplemaking.* Palo Alto, CA: Science and Behavior Press.

Sullivan, H. S. (1953). *The interpersonal theory of psychiatry.* New York: Norton.

Allen K. Hess
Auburn University, Montgomery, AL

See also: **Interpersonal Psychotherapy**

RELIABILITY

The reliability of a test refers to its consistency or stability. A test with good reliability means that the test taker will obtain the same test score over repeated testing as long as no other extraneous factors have affected the score. In the real world, of course, a test taker will rarely obtain the exact same score over repeated testing. The reason for this is that repeated assessments of any phenomenon will always be affected by chance errors. Thus, the goal of testing is to minimize chance errors and maximize the reliability of the measurement with the recognition that a perfectly reliable measure is unattainable. Although a highly reliable test will not yield identical scores for a participant from Time 1 to Time 2, the scores will tend to be similar. For example, on a 7-point Likert scale, a participant whose score is high on an item at Time 1 will tend to score high on that same item at Time 2. The reliability of a test must be established before its validity can be determined (the validity of a test is the extent to which a test accurately measures the construct that it purports to measure). Yet reliability alone does not indicate that the measurement accurately assesses the concept in question. Thus, a measure of IQ may be highly reliable, yielding consistent scores over long periods of time, but it may not be an accurate measure of the concept of intelligence. Reliability is only the first step in establishing the scientific acceptance of a measure, but it is a required step. The two most common forms of reliability are test-retest reliability and scale reliability.

Test-retest reliability is a measure of a test's consistency over a period of time. Test-retest reliability assumes that the construct being measured is relatively stable over time, such as personality temperaments or intelligence. A good test manual should specify the sample, reliability coefficient, and the length of the test-retest interval. Manuals for most popular objective tests report intervals of about one week to one month. If the trait is likely to change over time (e.g., state anxiety), test makers generally choose a shorter interval (e.g., one week). Test-retest reliabilities are reported and interpreted as correlation coefficients. Test-retest reliabilities are considered to be excellent if they are .90 or better and good if they are about .80 or better. If a trait is thought to be relatively stable but the test-retest reliability coefficient for a test of that trait is around .50, it may mean that the measure is unreliable. There may be too few questions on the test, or the questions may be poorly worded (e.g., double negatives are difficult for nearly everyone). It is also possible that some extraneous variable or variables intervened on the trait during the test-retest interval. One final problem for the interpretation of test-retest reliabilities is that they may be spuriously high because of practice effects or memory effects. A respondent may do better on the second testing because the trait being assessed improves with practice. In addition, some people may respond similarly to a test because they remember many of the answers that they gave on the test earlier. One possible solution to this problem is the use of alternate forms. Some popular tests come with an alternate form, but most do not. If a test user is interested in a trait's change over time and is worried about practice or memory effects, alternate forms of the test may be given.

Scale reliability (commonly called internal consistency) is a measure of how well the items on a test relate to each other. The most common statistic for scale reliability is

Cronbach's coefficient alpha, which is the virtual standard of scale reliability in objective testing. One intuitive way of interpreting Cronbach's alpha is to view it as an average of all of the correlations of each item with every other item on a test. The alpha coefficient is interpreted much like a correlation coefficient and ranges from 0.00 to 1.00. Values above approximately .80 are considered good and generally reflective of reliable (internally consistent) scales.

The alpha coefficient is dependent, however, on three other variables. First, all things being equal, shorter scales or tests (less than about eight items) will yield lower alpha coefficients than will longer scales or tests. This also means that scales or tests with seven or less items may possess reliability that is not reflected in the alpha coefficient. Scales or tests of 30 or more items will often yield alpha coefficients around .90, and even a random selection of more than about 30 items on a test will meet the minimum standard of internal consistency (e.g., .80). Second, the alpha coefficient is dependent on a high first factor concentration (i.e., the scale or test is measuring a single concept or trait). For example, if there is a scale measuring psychoticism and the items were derived to measure equally two major components of psychoticism (aberrant thinking and social withdrawal), the coefficient alpha will be lower than a different measure of psychoticism that assesses only one underlying concept (like aberrant thinking). Third, the alpha coefficient will be dependent on the number of participants who take the test. A higher number of participants (generally above 200) will yield higher alpha coefficients, whereas a lower number of participants (less than 100) will yield lower alpha coefficients. In summary, the scientific community views values of Cronbach's alpha above .80 as acceptable and reliable. It is also important to note that shorter scales or tests (with fewer than approximately eight items) may still be reliable and yet yield alpha coefficients below .80. Scales or tests with a large number of items (around 30 or more) may sometimes yield spuriously high alpha coefficients. Thus, it is important when evaluating the scale reliability of a test to take into account the number of items, the underlying construct or factor structure, and the number of participants. Once evidence of reliability is firmly established for a test, then validity studies can be initiated.

Frederick L. Coolidge
Daniel L. Segal
University of Colorado at Colorado Springs

See also: **Psychometrics; Validity**

RELIGION AND HEALTH

Religion and medicine have long been fused in response to illness and death. A common idea across ancient cultures was that sickness was a result of violation of ethical or religious standards. In short, sickness was the result of sin (Kinsley, 1996). Today, the connections between religion and health, both physical and mental, have withstood the scrutiny of scientific inquiry. While methodological difficulties exist, the quality of research into the topic is improving, moving from anecdotal compilations to correlational reports and controlled studies. Work continues on a variety of fronts to better understand the mechanisms linking religion-spirituality and health variables.

Religion and Well-being

Exploratory studies designed to determine the paradigms for wellness across a person's life span consistently name religion as a characteristic necessary for optimal health (Frankel & Hewitt, 1994; Wilcock et al., 1999). Meisenhelder and Chandler (2001) report that high frequency of prayer is associated with greater vitality and general health. Similarly, Ayele, Mulligan, Gheorghiu, and Reyes-Ortiz (1999) report that intrinsic religious activity (e.g., prayer, Bible reading) was significantly positively correlated with life satisfaction. Positive associations between religion and general well-being are evident along the continuum of human aging. Holt and Jenkins (1992) emphasized the importance of religion to older persons and stressed the need for gerontologists to exhibit greater awareness of religion as a health enhancer. Other studies conclude that traditional Judeo-Christian beliefs and behaviors may be related to wellness in later life (Burbank, 1992; Foley, 2000; Fry, 2000; Levin & Chatters, 1998). In an exhaustive examination of 630 data-based studies, Koenig (2001) demonstrated that most mainline religions meeting criteria for traditions and accountability tend to promote positive experiences across the life span.

Religion and Mental Health

Frequency of church attendance has been reported to be negatively related to depression, with frequent churchgoers being about half as likely to be depressed as nonchurchgoers (Koenig, Hays, George, & Blazer, 1997). Woods, Antoni, Ironson, and Kling (1999a, 1999b) report that greater use of religion as a coping mechanism resulted in fewer symptoms of depression and anxiety in two distinct samples of HIV-infected individuals. Another study (Mickley, Carson, & Soeken 1995) theorized that religion can have either a positive (e.g., encouraging social cohesiveness, helping establish meaning in life) or a negative (fostering excessive guilt or shame, using religion as an escape from dealing with life problems) impact on mental health. The same study reported that people who demonstrate high levels of intrinsic religiousness tend to have less depression, less anxiety, and less dysfunctional attention seeking. They also display high levels of ego strength, empathy, and integrated social behavior. Studies suggest that religious-spiritual resources can buffer psychological distress associated with trauma (Rosik, 2000), bereavement (Golsworthy & Coyle, 2001), and sexual assault (Chang et al., 2001).

Not all studies, however, speak to the positive association between religion and mental health. Higher religiosity scores have been demonstrated to be associated with obsessions (Lewis, 2001), schizotypy (Joseph & Diduca, 2001), and dissociation (Dorahy & Lewis, 2002).

Religion and Physical Health

Pargament, Koenig, Tarakeshwar, and Hahn (2001), in a study of nearly 600 medically ill Americans over the age of 55, found that subjects reporting high religious struggle scores were at significantly greater risk of all-cause mortality than those subjects reporting little religious struggle. Likewise, another study reports that subjects describing themselves as "secular" had a significantly higher risk of myocardial infarction (MI) compared with subjects describing themselves as "religious," and this risk was independent of other, more traditional MI risk variables (Friedlander, Kark, & Stein, 1986). Steffen et al. (2002) reported an association between religious coping and lower ambulatory blood pressure in African Americans. Another study reports that absence of strength and comfort from religion following elective open-heart surgery predicted greater mortality (Oxman, Freeman, & Manheimer, 1995). In an intriguing study, Leibovici (2001) conducted a double-blind, randomized control trial examining the effects of remote prayer on 3,393 adults with bloodstream infection and reported that those subjects who were prayed for displayed significantly shorter hospital stays, shorter duration of fever, and lower death rates than those not prayed for. However, Sloan and Bagiella (2002) and Thoresen and Harris (2002) urge caution in interpreting these studies and speak to the need for rigorous examination of reported associations between religion and health.

Mechanisms

The Immune System

While studies examining the impact of religion on the immune system are few, they are methodologically sound and offer intriguing results. One study reports an inverse relationship between frequent attendance at religious services and interleukin-6, an inflammatory cytokine and putative immune system regulator (Koenig et al., 1997a). Another study (Woods et al., 1999a) reports that subjects displaying high levels of religious behavior (e.g., attending religious services, praying) had significantly higher levels of T-helper inducer cell (CD4+) counts and higher CD4+ percentages. Schaal et al. (1998) reported that religious expression was positively correlated with natural killer (NK) cell number, T-helper cell counts, and total lymphocytes in women with metastatic breast cancer.

Increased Social Support

Religion is often practiced in the fellowship of others. Frequent religious involvement may be associated with better health due to an expansion of the social support network. A long tradition of research in social epidemiology has demonstrated the salutary nature of social support (House, Landis, & Umberson, 1988) as well as social support's ability to exert a strong and positive influence over a person's ability to deal with and recover from serious illness (Cohen & Willis, 1985; Taylor, Falke, Shoptaw, & Lichtman, 1986).

Less Fear of Death

Most major religions speak to a continued and happy existence after life on earth is over. As such, another mechanism in the link between religion and health may be the lessened fear of death that religious people tend to display. Modell and Guerra (1980) reported that fear of death led to significant postsurgical complications in 75% of the patients they studied. In a case review of older men undergoing treatment for advanced throat cancer, Pressman, Larson, Lyons, and Humes (1992) found evidence suggesting that a lack of death anxiety explained as a belief in God played a more important role in mediating surgical anxiety than did other coping abilities.

Less Health-Risking Behaviors

Still another factor in the mechanism linking religion and health may be that religious behavior leads to less participation in those behaviors known to be in direct opposition to good health. Jarvis and Northcott (1987) reviewed the practices of members of nine major religions and found significant differences from nonpracticing controls in two main areas: Most religions (1) prescribe behavior that prevents illness or death or that assists in treatment of sickness and (2) proscribe behavior that is harmful to life or that would hinder treatment. Woods and Ironson (1999), in their examination of the role of religiosity-spirituality in medically ill patients, reported that those patients identifying themselves as religious were more apt to cite their religious beliefs as the reason they did not smoke, did not drink, and chose healthy diets than did those patients not identifying themselves as religious. Several studies report positive correlations between reported religiosity and abstinence from alcohol and controlled substances, as well as responsible sexual activity (Avants et al., 2001; Fierros & Brown, 2002; Hammermeister et al., 2001; Holder et al., 2000; Washington & Moxley, 2001).

Methodological Considerations

While the examination of religion and spirituality's role as factors in physical and mental health has yielded consistently positive results, methodological concerns exist—primarily in defining the construct itself to ensure validity and generalizability of any findings. Some studies define religion as the number of times one attends religious services; others use subject self-identification; and still others use belief in God as their definition of religion. Recent headway has been made in the development of instruments designed to make the distinction between religion and spirituality (Ironson & Woods, 1998). Carefully defining the constructs would not only facilitate assessment, it would also address the often confusing nature of what is being measured when one measures religion.

Another concern relates to inadequate control for potentially moderating or mediating variables in most of the studies published to date. It is possible that what appears at first glance to be an association between religion and health may actually be mediated by social support, healthy diet, or any of a myriad of potentially confounding variables.

REFERENCES

Avants, S., Warburton, L., & Margolin, A. (2001). Spiritual and religious support in recovery from addiction among HIV-positive injection drug users. *Journal of Psychoactive Drugs, 33*(1), 39–45.

Ayele, H., Mulligan, T., Gheorghiu, S., & Reyes-Ortiz, C. (1999). Religious activity improves life satisfaction for some physicians and older patients. *Journal of the American Geriatrics Society, 47*(4), 453–455.

Burbank, P. (1992). An exploratory study: Assessing the meaning in life among older adult clients. *Journal of Gerontological Nursing, 18*(9), 1123–1134.

Chang, B., Skinner, K., & Boehmer, U. (2001). Religion and mental health among women veterans with sexual assault experience. *International Journal of Psychiatry in Medicine, 31*(1), 77–95.

Cohen, S., & Willis, T. (1985). Stress, social support, and the buffering hypothesis. *Psychological Bulletin, 98,* 310–357.

Dorahy, M., & Lewis, C. (2001). The relationship between dissociation and religiosity: An empirical evaluation of Schumaker's theory. *Journal for the Scientific Study of Religion, 40*(2), 315–322.

Fierros, R., & Brown, J. (2002). High risk behaviors in a sample of Mexican-American college students. *Psychological Reports, 90*(1), 117–130.

Foley, L. (2000). Exploring the experience of spirituality in older women finding meaning in life. *Journal of Religious Gerentology, 12*(1), 5–15.

Frankel, G, & Hewitt, W. (1994). Religion and well-being among Canadian university students; the role of faith groups on campus. *Journal for the Scientific Study of Religion, 33*(1), 62–73.

Friedlander, Y., Kark, J., & Stein, Y. (1986). Religious orthodoxy and myocardial infarction in Jerusalem: A case control study. *International Journal of Cardiology, 10*(1), 62–73.

Fry, P. (2000). Religious involvement, spirituality and personal meaning for life: Existential predictors of psychological well-being in community-residing and institutional care elders. *Aging and Mental Health, 4*(4), 375–387.

Golsworthy, R., & Coyle, A. (2001). Practitioner's accounts of religious and spiritual dimension in bereavement therapy. *Counseling Psychology Quarterly, 14*(3), 183–202.

Hammermeister, J., Flint, M., Havens, J., & Peterson, M. (2001). Psychological and health-related characteristics of religious well-being. *Psychological Reports, 89*(3), 589–594.

Holder, D., Durant, R., et al. (2000). The association between adolescent spirituality and voluntary sexual activity. *Journal of Adolescent Health, 26*(4), 295–302.

Holt, M., & Jenkins, M. (1992). Research and implications for practice: Religion, well being/morale, and coping behavior in later life. *Journal of Applied Gerontology, 11*(1), 101–110.

House, J., Landis, N., & Umberson, D. (1988). Social relationships and health. *Science, 241,* 540–545.

Ironson, G., & Woods, T. (1998). *IWORSHIP: An unpublished assessment instrument of religious and spiritual dimensions.* Coral Gables, FL: University of Miami.

Jarvis, G., & Northcott, H. (1987). Religion and differences in morbidity and mortality. *Social Science and Medicine, 25,* 813–824.

Joseph, S, & Diduca, D. (2001). Schizotypy and religiosity in 13–18 year old school pupils. *Mental Health, Religion, and Culture, 4*(1), 63–69.

Kinsley, D. (1996). *Health, healing and religion: A cross-cultural perspective.* Upper Saddle River, NJ: Prentice Hall.

Koenig, H. (2001). Religion and medicine: II. Religion, mental health, and related behaviors. *International Journal of Psychiatry in Medicine, 31*(10), 97–109.

Koenig, H., Cohen, H., George, L., Hays, J., Larson, D., & Blazer, D. (1997a). Attendance at religious services, interleukin-6, and other biological parameters of immune function in older adults. *International Journal of Psychiatry Medicine, 27,* 233–250.

Koenig, H., Hays, J., George, L., & Blazer, D. (1997b). Modeling the cross-sectional relationships between religion, physical health, social support, and depressive symptoms. *American Journal of Geriatric Psychiatry, 5,* 131–144.

Leibovici, L. (2001). Effects of remote intercessory prayer on outcomes in patients with bloodstream infection. *British Medical Journal, 323*(7327), 1450–1451.

Levin, J., & Chatters, L. (1998). Religion, health, and psychological well-being in older adults: Findings from three national surveys. *Journal of Aging and Health, 10*(4), 504–531.

Lewis, C. (2001). Cultural stereotype of the effects of religion on mental health. *British Journal of Medical Psychology, 74*(3), 359–367.

Meisenhelder, J., & Chandler, E. (2001). Frequency of prayer and functional health in Presbyterian pastors. *Journal for the Scientific Study of Religion, 40*(2), 315–322.

Mickley, R., Carson, V., & Soeken, K. (1995). Religion and adult mental health: State of the science in nursing. *Issues in Mental Health in Nursing, 16*(4), 345–360.

Modell, J., & Guerra, F. (1980). Psychological problems in the surgical patient. In F. Guerra & J. A. Aldrete (Eds.), *Emotional and psychological responses to anesthesia and surgery.* New York: Grune & Stratton.

Oxman, T., Freeman, D., & Manheimer, E. (1995). Lack of social participation or religious strength and comfort as risk factors for death after cardiac surgery in the elderly. *Journal of Psychosomatic Medicine, 57*(1), 5–15.

Pargament, K., Koenig, H., Tarakeshwar, N., & Hahn, J. (2001). Religious struggles as a predictor of mortality among medically ill elderly patients: A 2-year longitudinal study. *Archives of Internal Medicine, 161*(15), 1881–1885.

Park, H., Bauer, S., & Oescher, J. (2001). Religiousness as a predictor of alcohol use in high school students. *Journal of Drug Education, 31*(3), 289–303.

Pressman, P., Larson, D., Lyons, J., & Humes, D. (1992). *Religious belief, coping strategies, and psychological distress in seven elderly males with head and neck cancer.* Unpublished manuscript.

Rosik, C. (2000). Utilizing religious resources in the treatment of dissociative trauma symptoms. *Journal of Trauma and Dissociation, 1*(1), 69–89.

Schaal, M., Sephton, S., Thorenson, C., et al. (1998, August). *Religious expression and immune competence in women with advanced cancer.* Paper presented at American Psychological Association, San Francisco.

Sloan, R. P., & Bagiella, E. (2002). Claims about religious involvement and health outcomes. *Annals of Behavioral Medicine: Special Issue: Spirituality, Religiousness and Health: From Research to Clinical Practice, 124*(1), 14–21.

Steffen, P., Hinderliter, A., Blumentahl, J., & Sherwood, A. (2001). Religious coping, ethnicity, and ambulatory blood pressure. *Psychosomatic Medicine, 63*(4), 523–530.

Taylor, S., Falke, R., Shoptaw, S., & Lichtman, R. 91986). Social support, support groups, and the cancer patient. *Journal of Consulting and Clinical Psychology, 54,* 608–615.

Thorensen, C. E., & Harris, A. H. S. (2002). Spirituality and Health: What's the evidence and what's needed. *Annals of Behavioral Medicine: Special Issue: Spirituality, Religiousness and Health: From Research to Clinical Practice, 24*(1), 3–13.

Washington, O., & Moxley, D. (2001). The use of prayer in group work with African-American women recovering from chemical dependency. *Families in Society, 82*(1), 49–59.

Wilcock, A., van der Arend, H., Darling, K., Scholz, J., Siddall, R., Snigg, C., & Stephens, J. (1999). An exploratory study of people's perceptions and experiences of wellbeing. *British Journal of Occupation Therapy, 61*(2), 75–82.

Woods, T., Antoni, M., Ironson, G., & Kling, D. (1999a). Religiosity is associated with affective and immune status in symptomatic HIV-infected gay men. *Journal of Psychosomatic Research, 46*(2), 165–176.

Woods, T., Antoni, M., Ironson, G., & Kling, D. (1999b). Religiosity is associated with affective status in symptomatic HIV-infected African-American women. *Journal of Health Psychology, 4*(3), 317–326.

Woods, T., & Ironson, G. (1999). Religion and spirituality in the face of illness: How cancer, cardiac, and HIV patients describe their spirituality/religiosity. *Journal of Health Psychology, 4*(3), 393–412.

Teresa E. Woods.
Elizabeth Mullen
University of Wisconsin–Madison

See also: **Psychomatic Disorders; Somatopsychics**

RELIGION AND MENTAL HEALTH

Religion is an organized system of beliefs, practices, and rituals designed to facilitate closeness to the sacred or transcendent—whether that be God, a higher power, ultimate truth, or ultimate reality—and to foster an understanding of one's relationship and responsibility to others in living together in a community. Religion includes not only attendance at religious services and involvement in religious community activities involving scripture study or prayer but also private personal religious practices such as prayer, meditation, study of scriptures, reading inspirational literature, and private worship. Religion also includes personal religiousness, degree of religious commitment, and religious motivation (the extent to which religious beliefs are the object of the person's ultimate concern in life).

Mental health includes both positive and negative emotional and cognitive functioning. Positive mental health has to do with constructs such as well-being, life satisfaction, joy, peace, hope, optimism, and meaning and purpose, as well as the ability to engage in satisfying social relationships and productive work. Negative mental health involves dissatisfaction, unhappiness, boredom, meaninglessness, and pessimism, as well as the presence of mental conditions that seriously interfere with social and occupational functioning, such as depressive disorder, anxiety disorder, mania as part of bipolar disorder, schizophrenia and other psychotic disorders, personality disorders, substance abuse, and cognitive disorders.

Until about a decade ago, mental health professionals commonly thought that religion was associated with neurosis and negative health outcomes. Sigmund Freud described religion as the obsessional neurosis of humanity (Freud, 1927). Psychologist Albert Ellis said that "the less religious they are, the more emotionally healthy they will tend to be" (Ellis,1980). Psychiatrist Wendell Watters said, "Christian doctrine and teachings are incompatible with many of the components of sound mental health, notably self-esteem, self-actualization and mastery, good communication skills, related individuation and the establishment of supportive human networks, and the development of healthy sexuality and reproductive responsibility" (Watters, 1992). These statements, however, were typically based on personal experiences and clinical experiences with psychiatric patients, not on unbiased systematic assessment of adults in the general population who for the most part are mentally intact.

In the past 10 years increased attention has been paid to the relationship between religion and mental health, especially in nonpyschiatric populations. What has been found is quite different from what was just suggested by some leaders in the field of mental health. The *Handbook of Religion and Health* (Koenig, McCullough, & Larson, 2001) reviews 724 quantitative studies on the relationship between religion and a wide range of mental health outcomes as described in the definition of mental health just provided. Nearly 480 of those studies (66%) found a statistically significant relationship between religious involvement and better mental health, greater social support, or less substance abuse. For example, both in the United States, where religion is prevalent, and in Europe, where religious involvement is low, studies find that those who are less religious experience more depression and recover more slowly from depression. A number of clinical trials in patients with depression and anxiety disorders have found that religious interventions achieve faster improvement or remission of symptoms than does secular psychotherapy or no treatment. These studies have involved Christian, Muslim, and Buddhist interventions.

Not only may religious beliefs and practices help to protect against mental disorder and speed recovery, but there is evidence that religious involvement is even more strongly associated with positive emotions. Of a total of 100 studies identified in the preceding review, 79 found statistically significant positive correlations between religiousness and variables such as well-being, hope, and optimism. Of 20 studies examining the relationship between religious involvement and social support, 19 found that the religious person had not only more social support but also a higher quality of support that was more likely to endure over time, especially in situations where the person was physically ill or otherwise unable to reciprocate. Similarly, 15 of 16 studies found that religious people appear to have more purpose and meaning in life than do those who are less religious, especially when experiencing physical illness and disability. Even Sigmund Freud admitted that "only religion can answer the question of the purpose of life. One can hardly be wrong in concluding that the idea of life having a purpose stands and falls with the religious system" (Freud, 1930).

Why is religion generally associated with better mental health? There are quite rational reasons why this might be so. First, as noted earlier, religion provides a positive, optimistic worldview that gives life meaning and purpose and provides hope. Again, this is especially true during times of physical illness, dependency, bereavement, and other situations characterized by powerlessness and loss of control that destroy meaning and foster hopelessness. Second, religion provides rules and regulations to help guide decisions concerning one's self and one's relationships with others. These guidelines often encourage such behaviors as forgiveness, thankfulness, generosity, altruism, and other prosocial activities. They also discourage unhealthy coping behaviors such as alcohol or drug use, sexual indiscretions, and gambling that can destroy both personal and family well-being. As a result, religion may actually help to reduce the amount of stress that a person ultimately experiences. This relationship, however, is complicated by the fact that many people also turn to religion in response to stress.

Third, religion helps to create and maintain social connections that are important for combating isolation and loneliness. Religious motivations for providing support to others (i.e., "Love thy neighbor as thy self"), which are present in all major religious traditions, motivate people to continue to provide support even when they do not feel like doing so. Religion provides intrinsic rewards for altruistic activities that do not depend on reciprocal efforts by the receiver (i.e., God will reward). As people respond to religious teachings to reach out and care for others, they find themselves experiencing greater fulfillment, meaning, and joy. Both the receiving and giving of social support are particularly important at times when people tend to withdraw into themselves, as during physical illness or as they grow older, when there is a tendency to become preoccupied with aches and pains and losses, which often leads to anxiety and depression.

This does not mean that religion is always associated with better mental health or greater personal or social well-being. Religious beliefs can be associated with excessive guilt, anxious ruminations over religious teachings, and prejudice against others and may restrict and limit life rather than make it fuller and more satisfying. In general, however, it appears that the positive influences of religion on mental health outweigh the negative.

REFERENCES

Ellis, A. (1980). Psychotherapy and atheistic values: A response to A. E. Bergin's "Psychotherapy and religious values." *Journal of Consulting and Clinical Psychology, 48,* 635–639.

Freud, S. (1927/1962). Future of an illusion. *Standard edition* (p. 43). London: Hogarth Press.

Freud, S. (1930/1962). Civilization and its discontents. *Standard edition* (p. 25). London: Hogarth Press.

Koenig, H. G., McCullough, M., & Larson, D. B. (2001). *Handbook of religion and health: A century of research reviewed.* New York: Oxford University Press.

Watters, W. (1992). *Deadly doctrine: Health, illness, and Christian God-talk* (p. 140). Buffalo, NY: Prometheus Books.

Harold G. Koenig
Duke University Medical Center

REPERTORY GRID METHODS

Developed within personal construct theory, repertory grid methods represent a widely used set of techniques for studying personal and interpersonal systems of meaning. Because of their flexibility, repertory grids (or *repgrids*) have been used in approximately 3,000 studies of a broad variety of topics, ranging from children's understandings of physical science principles and consumer preferences to formal structures of self-reflection within cognitive science and the mutual validation of belief systems between friends. However, their most consistent area of application has probably been in the clinical domain, where grids have been used to assess the properties of meaning systems of different groups of persons (e.g., those diagnosed as thought disordered or agoraphobic), and how these change over the course of treatment.

The role construct repertory test (or *reptest*) was initially designed by George Kelly, the author of personal construct psychology (PCP), as a means of assessing the content of an individual's repertory of role constructs—the unique system of interconnected meanings that define his or her perceived relationships to others. In its simplest form, the reptest requires the respondent to compare and contrast successive sets of three significant people (e.g., my mother, my father, and myself) and to formulate some important way in which two of the figures are alike and different from the third. For example, if prompted with the previous triad, a person might respond, "Well, my mother and I are very trusting of people, whereas my dad is always suspicious of their motives."

This basic dimension, being trusting of people rather than suspicious of their motives, would then be considered one of the significant themes or constructs that the person uses to organize, interpret, and approach the social world, as well as to define his or her role in it. By presenting the respondent with a large number of triads of varying elements (e.g., a previous romantic partner, best friend, a disliked person, one's ideal self), the reptest elicits a broad sampling of the personal constructs that constitute the person's outlook on life and perceived alternatives. These constructs can then be interpreted impressionistically, used as the basis for further interviewing of the respondent, or categorized using any of a number of reliable systems of content analysis, conducted either manually or using available computer programs.

Although the results of the reptest are often revealing, most contemporary users prefer to extend the method beyond the simple elicitation of constructs by prompting the respondent subsequently to rate or rank each of the elements (e.g., people) on the resulting construct dimensions. For example, using the triadic comparison method just described, a respondent might generate a set of 15 constructs (e.g., trusting vs. suspicious; moved by feelings vs. rational; has ambition vs. no goals; young vs. old), which might be arrayed in 15 rows on a sheet of paper. She might then be asked to assign a number to each of 10 elements (e.g., my mother, father, self, partner) arranged in columns going across the sheet, representing where each figure would fall on, say, a 7-point scale anchored by the poles of each construct. For instance, "mother" might be seen as 1 on trusting versus suspicious, representing very trusting, whereas "father" might be placed at 5 on this same scale, representing moderately suspicious. The intersection of the 15 construct rows with the 10 element columns forms the grid, and the matrix of 150 specific ratings it contains is amenable to a wide range of analyses. In practice, repertory grids can be virtually any size, from six constructs and elements to literally hundreds of each for a given respondent. However, most research indicates that the amount of new information about the person's meaning system in a domain (e.g., perceptions of acquaintances) begins to peak once approximately 15 to 20 constructs and a similar number of elements have been sampled. Although the repgrid was originally devised as an interview-based or paper-and-pencil measure, most contemporary users rely on any of a number of computer programs for their elicitation and analysis, such as the popular *WebGrid II* program available via the Internet.

Although the specific element ratings on important constructs are often informative in themselves (e.g., seeing that a respondent views her father as suspicious and having no goals, but also as rational), it is typically more helpful to conduct a comprehensive analysis of the grid to discern larger patterns. This might involve correlating and factor analyzing the matrix of ratings to see at a glance which constructs "go together" for the respondent (e.g., everyone who is trusting may also be seen as moved by feelings), or to learn what people are most and least alike in the respondent's view. These linkages among constructs often suggest why people remain stuck in symptomatic patterns, as when a client resists reconstruing himself as happy instead of depressed because the former is associated with being superficial as opposed to deep. Similarly, patterns of identification among elements in a grid can be clinically informative, and some of these (e.g., degree of correlation between actual self and ideal self) may provide useful indexes of progress in psychotherapy.

An interesting feature of grid technique is that it combines aspects of both idiographic assessment, which strives to reveal unique dimensions of a given respondent's outlook, and nomothetic research, which seeks general patterns across people. Thus, the format of the repgrid essentially guides the respondent in constructing his or her own questionnaire (by eliciting the individual's own constructs and relevant elements or figures to rate) while permitting comparisons across different people or groups. For example, depressed individuals, relative to others, tend to show not only distinctive themes in the content of their constructs (e.g., more self-references and more morally evaluative themes) but also distinctive overall structure (e.g., tighter intercorrelations among constructs and more polarized or extreme perceptions). This blend of projective and objective testing has made grid technique useful to both clinicians and scientists seeking to understand how different persons and groups organize their view of themselves and the world.

Describing a few of the problems to which repgrids have been applied gives some idea about the range and flexibility of the method. Grids have been used to study the long-term adjustment of survivors of incest, who carry with them a sense of distance from other people decades after the sexual abuse. They have also been used to measure processes of identification with other clients and therapists within group therapy settings and to predict who is most likely to benefit from this form of treatment. Grids have been applied to the study of the development and breakdown of romantic relationships and friendships, by looking at the degree of convergence between partners in the way they construe experiences at increasingly intimate levels. Other investigators have relied on grids to understand the distinctive differences in the knowledge structures of experts and novices in a given domain and to refine the discriminations made by assembly line workers in detecting product flaws. As the use of these methods continues to grow with the dissemination of ever more powerful computerized systems for their elicitation and analysis, it seems likely that repertory grids will become an increasingly popular tool for both helping professionals and social scientists.

REFERENCES

Bell, R. C. (1990). Analytic issues in the use of repertory grid technique. In G. J. Neimeyer & R. A. Neimeyer (Eds.), *Advances in personal construct psychology* (Vol. 1, pp. 25–48). Greenwich, CT: JAI.

Bringmann, M. (1992). Computer-based methods for the analysis and interpretation of personal construct systems. In G. J. Neimeyer & R. A. Neimeyer (Eds.), *Advances in personal construct psychology* (Vol. 2, pp. 57–90). Greenwich, CT: JAI.

Neimeyer, G. J. (1993). *Constructivist assessment.* Thousand Oaks: CA: Sage.

Neimeyer, R. A., & Neimeyer, G. J. (Eds.). (2002). *Advances in personal construct psychology.* New York: Praeger.

Robert A. Neimeyer
University of Memphis

See also: **Constructivism; Personal Construct Psychology**

REPRESSION

One of the cornerstones of psychoanalytic theory and therapy is the psychological defense mechanism that protects a person from unwanted or unbearable feelings, impulses, or memories. Throughout his life Sigmund Freud, the founder of psychoanalysis, claimed that the purpose of psychoanalytic therapy was to lift the repression that excluded unacceptable mental contents from awareness and to "make the unconscious conscious." In 1893 he and his collaborator Josef Breuer argued that repression operated on memories of traumatic events and that allowing these memories back into consciousness, together with the emotion that originally accompanied them, could bring about a permanent cure for hysteria. In 1896 Freud adapted this idea and claimed a unique role for the repression of memories of early sexual traumas. By the beginning of the new century he had already abandoned this stance in favour of the position which was to become part of mainstream psychoanalysis, namely that repression operated primarily on infantile drives and wishes rather than on memories of actual events.

What did Freud mean by *repression*? He used the term in two main ways and often failed to distinguish between them. One usage referred to a process whereby unwanted material is turned away before it reaches awareness at all (Freud called this *primary repression*). Rather than quietly remaining in the unconscious, however, this material is likely to reenter awareness in disguised ways, such as in slips of the tongue. In his second usage of the term, Freud proposed that a person becomes aware of unwanted mental contents (such as derivatives of this original repressed material) and then deliberately attempts to exclude them from consciousness (Freud called this *repression proper* or *after-expulsion*).

Although there is little empirical evidence to support the notion of primary repression, many contemporary memory researchers would have little problem with Freud's other use of the term. Originally, psychologists saw forgetting as being simply a passive process involving the gradual decay of the memory trace over time or the trace being made less accessible because of interference by later learning of similar material. Today it is widely believed that efficient mental functioning depends on flexible excitatory and inhibitory mechanisms that select relevant material and exclude unwanted material from entering consciousness. In a number of different types of experiments, researchers have found that people who are instructed to forget certain items because they are irrelevant, or who repeatedly practice ignoring them and retrieving something else, do find it harder to remember these items later. A plausible explanation is that these effects are due to an inhibitory mechanism preventing the retrieval of the to-be-forgotten items, a concept that is not dissimilar from after-expulsion.

Intriguingly, there appears to be a substantial group of people (*repressors*) who have difficulty in recalling negative information, although they are no different from others when it comes to positive information. They also tend to deny feeling anxious even when there is physiological evidence that they are highly aroused. Repressors consistently take longer to recall negative incidents from their own past, although they are no slower to recall positive incidents. They are also more successful at forgetting negative material when instructed to do so in an experimental task. With these characteristics, most memory theorists would expect their lives to have been happier than average, but in fact the opposite seems to be the case. These paradoxical findings are consistent with the idea of defense mechanisms posited by psychoanalytic theory.

Do these experimental findings generalize, so that people may first forget and later remember not just words but also significant traumatic incidents that they have experienced? A growing number of prospective and retrospective studies have found that a substantial proportion of clients in therapy for the effects of child sexual abuse (somewhere between 20% and 60%) report having periods in their lives (often lasting for several years) when they could not remember that the abuse had taken place. People have reported forgetting nonsexual as well as sexual traumas, and many of the incidents have received some corroboration. Consistent with Breuer and Freud's original observations, the recovery of many of these memories was accompanied by intense emotion. These recent findings strongly suggest that it is indeed possible to forget and later remember traumatic incidents but do not say anything about whether repression is the mechanism involved or rule out the likelihood that some seemingly recovered memories may not be accurate. Some researchers have speculated that deliberate forgetting, motivated by fear of the consequences of disclosure or of the disruption of close attachments, could help to explain how children abused by someone they know well could come to forget their ill-treatment. Repeated ignoring of the abuse and rehearsal of positive interactions with the perpetrator could have the effect of preventing recall of abusive interactions and reduce the long-term accessibility of these memories.

Freud's emphasis on the importance of defenses against unwanted mental contents and his analysis of some symptoms in these terms have clearly been borne out. Repression, in the sense of a deliberate attempt to exclude unwanted thoughts, feelings, or memories, no longer seems an outlandish notion but has parallels in our modern view of memory and forgetting. The systematic mental avoidance and forgetting of disturbing material appears to be both possible and reasonably common among people who have been traumatized, although the mechanisms are not yet understood. Other aspects of the theory of repression have not been supported, however. The notions of repression as a fully unconscious defense, or as one that is directed at infantile wishes and feelings, have not received empirical support. If anything, it is the earlier 1893 formulation of Breuer and Freud that has benefited most from recent empirical studies. Another primary tenet, that the lifting of repression is the essential element in recovery, has also not been supported. Freud had already discovered by the mid-1890s that its therapeutic value was very limited, but this did not stop him from continuing to place it at the core of the psychoanalytic method.

Chris R. Brewin
University College of London

See also: Memory; Trauma

RESEARCH METHODOLOGY

A general axiom of science is that there is no knowledge without comparison. Measurement in psychology generally is rather imprecise. There are also a relatively large number of variables, and these variables vary over time. Thus the creativity of the researchers enters.

To be able to infer a causal relationship is called the *internal validity* of the research design. Finally, these research relationships and cause-and-effect statements must be shown to generalize, which is called the *external validity.*

Experimental versus Passive Observational Research Designs

There are two broad types of research design: experimental research designs and passive observational designs. In the first type, variables are systematically imposed on or withheld from the subjects. In the passive observational design the researcher merely observes participants under many natural conditions and records the participants' scores and describes their condition and surroundings.

True Experiments

Within experimental designs, there are two major subtypes: true experiments and quasi-experiments. In true experiments, the participants involved in the research are randomly allocated to experimental groups and control groups.

Quasi-experiments

In quasi-experiments no random allocation of participants to groups has been made. Quasi-experiment groups are formed naturally or via the intervention of others. Further, pretreatment measures also must be available. A major difference in the quasi-experiment is that often the groups are unequal initially. However, many times in quasi-experiments groups do differ initially. After experimental treatment, they may be either more different or less different on the criteria than they were initially. Either way suggests that the treatment may cause the effect.

A major type of quasi-experiment is the interrupted time series design. It occurs when participants are observed periodically over time and a treatment is applied or a condition arises at some point or at several specified points in that time span.

Passive Observational Research Design

The second major classification of research designs is the passive observational type—those that are not experimental and often involve intrinsic variables that cannot be applied and withheld, such as socioeconomic level, grade point average, and intelligence level. The passive observational studies can be categorized into four major types of research designs: prediction and classification, sampling and survey, quantitative descriptive, and qualitative descriptive. These last two categories especially encompass a very large number of variations and methods.

Prediction and Classification

These involve K variables, $K - 1$ of which are used to predict the future (or even current) status, and the Kth variable is a predicted interval variable. In classification analyses, the Kth variable defines classification categories such as college major or religious affiliation. It is known from Sawyer's 1966 study that all types of data available should be used. The results of regression procedures for prediction have never been surpassed.

Sampling and Survey Studies

The purpose of this design is to describe a large population. It is done by selecting a representative group, called the sample, from the population and making the descriptive observations.

Quantitative Descriptive Design

This design also includes a large number of variations. Typically, the observations are made at or near one interval of time on a single group. All observations are quantified via the use of ratings, scales, test scores, and the like.

Qualitative Descriptive Design

Qualitative research is used to discover new variables and new relationships among old and new variables. Some of the methods and areas included in this broad natural observational category are case study, ecological, psychoanalytical, social, clinical, and personality. This type of research is of major use where only one or a small number of participants are involved.

Threats to Internal Validity

Findings in any research can occur by chance alone as the result of naturally occurring variability over time and by random fluctuations in measurement systems. This is called instability, and it is controlled by statistical analysis.

It is known that all observed scores on variables (except average scores) are biased, too high and too low. High scores are biased upward, and low scores are biased downward. When used to measure rather atypical subjects, the bias can be marked. Future observations are expected to change and to be nearer to the average. This threat to internal validity is called regression toward the mean. "Threats to internal validity" is the phrase in research design that interpreters of data use to describe the set of questions they have about possible inaccuracies in interpretation of cause-and-effect relationships among research variables.

Maturation is another threat because participants grow and develop on their own with the passage of time irrespective of what a researcher does to them. Mortality is the systematic reduction of groups of participants because of dropouts, absences, people moving away, and so on. Selection is the systematic choosing or self-selection of people for a treatment or condition who may be different for some groups before the treatment. History is the threat that involves changes in conditions surrounding the research. Instrumentation is a threat that involves changes in the observers' standards over time. Testing involves the distinct effect of gains in participants' scores simply as the result of having previously taken a test.

There are also four affective threats to internal validity: imitation, compensatory rivalry, compensatory equalization, and demoralization. These result from emotional changes in subjects and administrators to adjust for the fact that they were not "favored" by receiving an experimental treatment.

External Validity and Meta-analysis

Finally, external validity is the sum of the characteristics of research that allow the cause-and-effect statements made (as the result of good internal validity) to be generalized to participants, treatments, and criteria not used in the research but similar to them.

Meta-analysis

The external validity of research findings is markedly enhanced when a number of studies of the same general treatment variable can be combined. This procedure is called meta-analysis. In meta-analysis, the major conditions of the research on the criterion variables and the strength of treatment effect are determined. The relationship of most interest is the set of research condition variables and the criterion variable. As the result of this analysis, numerous research condition variables may be shown to have no influence on a set of criteria, and therefore researchers can generalize the results from a number of studies without regard to these extraneous conditions.

SUGGESTING READING

Hedges, L. V., & Olkin, I. (1985). *Statistical methods for meta-analysis.* Orlando, FL: Academic Press.

Sawyer, J. (1966). Measurement and prediction, clinical and statistical. *Psychological Bulletin, 66*(3), 178–200.

Shadish, W. R., Cook, T. D., & Campbell, D. T. (2002). *Experimental and quasi-experimental designs for generalized causal inference.* Boston: Houghton Mifflin.

Vockell, E., & Asher, J. W. (1995). *Educational research* (2nd ed.). Englewood Cliffs, NJ: Macmillan-Prentice Hall.

J. William Asher
Purdue University

See also: **Meta-Analysis**

RESIDENTIAL ALTERNATIVES

Throughout the course of one's life, the need for residential care may arise. This need may be generated by a variety of reasons, such as a need for physical rehabilitation, or because of mental or physical illness, loss of shelter, or old age.

The current trend in residential alternatives is toward person-centered planning, in which individuals choose where and with whom they live (Braddock, Hemp, Bacfedler, & Fujina, 1995). This trend typically employs natural environments as the venue for such services. Natural environments might be the person's own home with supports or another house or apartment where supports are shared.

Sometimes, however, a natural environment is not indicated for an individual, and there are many other specialized residential alternatives for people who require more care. Residential alternatives most often are thought to be institutions, emergency shelters, orphanages, and nursing homes. These, however, are but a few of the alternatives available for people in need of care. The following are some of the other residential alternatives.

A *boarding home* is one in which unrelated individuals reside without supervision. Most boarding homes are privately operated and serve as a less expensive alternative to apartment or home living. The term *hospice* is often used interchangeably with boarding home.

Convalescent hospitals afford long-term residential care for those who require extensive rehabilitation or nursing care or who are terminally ill. Convalescent hospitals can be privately or publicly operated.

Foster homes are provided by families who open their houses to children who require shelter. Most children who receive foster care require such service because of the loss of parents or guardians. Foster care may be provided for developmentally disabled children who require specialized training outside of their natural homes. Foster parents are usually trained in effective parenting practices and are usually paid for their services by state or county social service agencies. Foster parents are not adoptive parents, as adoption results in a legal name change for the child, as well as legal guardianship of the child by the adoptive parent.

Group homes are provided by public and private agencies for children and adults who require supervised residential care. Unlike foster care programs, group homes generally have up to eight unrelated people residing with supervisory personnel. These supervisory personnel are identified as teaching parents by Fixsen, Wolf, and Phillips (1973) and as house parents/house couples by Holmes (1998).

The very name *halfway house* connotes a transition home. Generally, halfway houses are operated by public or private agencies for the express purpose of facilitating a person's movement from a highly supervised residential setting to independence in the community. Halfway houses also have been called *transitional homes*.

An *intermediate care facility* offers residential services to people with developmental disabilities. Unlike group homes, many intermediate care facilities are located on institutional grounds and follow a medical model, according to Stripling and Ames (1977). Intermediate care facilities are sponsored by the federal government but are administered by the states.

A *nursing home* is a privately or publicly operated long-term care setting for the terminally ill, handicapped, or aged. Unlike convalescent hospitals, nursing homes do not have ready access to all the necessary life-support services that some long-term convalescent patients require.

An *orphanage* is a residential care center designed to offer shelter to homeless children. Unlike foster care settings, most orphanages are operated by religious organizations, but a few are sponsored by public and nonsectarian private agencies.

A *psychiatric hospital* is a residential hospital designed primarily for persons requiring psychiatric care. Unlike institutions for individuals with developmental disabilities, psychiatric hospitals specialize in offering services to the mentally ill. Most psychiatric hospitals are publicly operated.

A *residential school* is one in which the educational training programs are located on the same premises or under the same auspices as the residential program. Residential schools are available to children with or without special needs in the form of preparatory schools. Residential schools can be either privately or publicly operated.

Respite care is a short-term residential service provided to individuals who require temporary shelter, primarily in cases of emergency, family crisis, family vacation, or trial separation. Respite care services can be found as a subunit in many private or public residential settings or in centers designed solely for such services.

A *retirement home* is a residential alternative designed specifically for senior citizens. Retirement homes can follow many different models, including boarding homes, residential cottages, and apartments. Most retirement homes are privately operated.

A *sanitorium* is a residential alternative designed for the treatment of chronic disease and disorders, such as tuberculosis and various forms of mental illness. Sanitoriums generally follow a medical hospital model for service delivery. Most sanitoriums are publicly operated.

A *state school* is an institutional school for children with special needs. Not unlike many residential schools, state schools have residences and educational-training opportunities located on the same site. To a large extent, a cottage residence model is followed at state schools. State schools are publicly operated.

Supervised apartments are living alternatives for adults with special needs who are capable of independent living (Holmes, 1990). Supervised apartments can be found either in clusters or randomly located in an apartment complex. People residing in supervised apartments are regularly monitored by human services personnel to make certain that their personal and social needs are being met. Supervised apartments can be either privately or publicly sponsored.

REFERENCES

Braddock, D., Hemp, R., Bacfedler, L., & Fujina, G. (1995). *The state of the state in developmental disabilities.* Washington, DC: Association on American Mental Retardation.

Fixsen, D. L., Wolf, M. M., & Phillips, E. L. (1973). Achievement Place: A teaching family model of community-based group homes for youth in trouble. In Hammerlynch et al. (Eds.), *Behavior modification.* Champaign, IL: Research Press.

Holmes, D. L. (1990). Community based services for children and adults with autism. *Journal of Autism and Developmental Disorders, 20,* 339–351.

Holmes, D. L. (1998). *Autism through the life span: The Eden model.* Bethesda, MD: Woodbine House.

Stripling, T., & Ames, S. (1977). Intermediate care facilities for the mentally retarded. *Federal Programs Information and Assistance Project, 54,* 61180/6-02.

David L. Holmes
The Eden Institute

See also: **Halfway Houses**

RETICULAR ACTIVATING SYSTEM

The ascending reticular activating system (ARAS) is the collection of anatomical and neurochemical systems proposed to underlie cortical electroencephalographic signs of arousal and the correlated behavioral activities of alerting and attention. The concept of the ARAS was first formulated by Moruzzi and Magoun in 1949. Based on the effects of either stimulation or destruction of parts of the reticular formation of the brain stem, these authors concluded that "a background of maintained activity within this ascending brain stem activating system may account for wakefulness, while reduction of its activity either naturally, by barbiturates, or by experimental injury and disease, may respectively precipitate normal sleep, contribute to anesthesia, or produce pathological somnolence." While the accuracy of this prescient formulation has occasionally been challenged during the past 50 years, its general validity is still recognized, and its underlying neural substrates have been described.

The anatomical basis of the ARAS is the reticular formation (RF). The RF extends from the caudal medulla to the rostral midbrain. Its neurons form the core of the brain stem, in which are embedded the specific nuclear groups that supply the cranial nerves with axons. The ascending and descending long sensory and motor pathways of the brain stem pass through and around the reticular formation. Its neurons tend to have long axons with many branches. For example, a single RF neuron may have an axon that branches to reach the dorsal column nuclei, the spinal cord, and the hypothalamus. Because of such extensive branching, the neurons of the RF are capable of exerting profound effects on the general level of activity of the brain and spinal cord.

Projections from the RF to the diencephalon are involved in behavioral and electroencephalographic arousal and correspond to the ARAS. There are at least three aspects of arousal: (1) altering of consciousness to become more alert, often with increased concentration on selected stimuli; (2) appearance of orienting reactions if arousal is produced by introduction of a novel stimulus; and (3) desynchronization of the electroencephalogram (EEG).

The RF influences arousal through two anatomically distinct routes. One pathway extends from the RF through the hypothalamus, ventral thalamus, and basal forebrain to influence the cortex; this pathway is most probably involved in producing generalized arousal that makes the differences between sleep and waking. The second pathway extends from the RF to the reticular and intralaminar nuclei of the dorsal thalamus and probably participates in alerting reactions and alpha blocking.

In addition to having different pathways by which it influences different aspects of arousal, the RF can be divided into nuclear groupings according to anatomical and neurochemical criteria. The most convenient anatomical categorization is made along the medial-lateral dimension. The raphe nuclei are found in the midline of the RF. A large-celled region is found in the central core of the RF, and a small-celled division is located in its lateral portion. These large, medial-lateral divisions may be subdivided along the rostral-caudal length of the RF. The nucleus gigantocellularis is the large-celled nucleus of the medulla. It gives rise to reticulospinal axons that influence movement. In the pons, the nuclei pontis caudalis and oralis take the place of the nucleus gigantocellularis and also give rise to reticulospinal axons. However, these nuclei, especially the rostral-lying pontis-oralis, have many ascending projections and are involved in regulation of cortical arousal.

Some reticular nuclei may also be defined according to neurotransmitter content. Nuclei that contain norepinephrine have been identified in the medullary and pontine RF. The most extensively studied of these is the locus coeruleus. The ascending projections of this nucleus are involved in increasing wakefulness and in selective attention and may be involved in alternating between non-REM (slow-wave) and REM sleep. Dopamine-containing neurons are found in several nuclei of the midbrain tegmental area. The best known of these nuclei is the substantia nigra. Loss of the dopaminergic neurons from the substantia nigra leads to Parkinsonism. There is some evidence that other dopaminergic nuclei participate in maintenance of waking, possibly by influencing the hypothalamus. Some nuclei within the rostral reticular formation utilize acetylcholine as a transmitter; their output forms the part of the ARAS that includes the ventral thalamus and basal forebrain. They may also influence other reticular formation regions to regulate REM sleep. Serotonin, the neurotransmitter produced by the raphe nuclei, has also been implicated in modulation of arousal. Lesions of the raphe or inhibition of serotonin synthesis produces insomnia. The insomnia induced by reduction in serotonin decreases with time after the insult, suggesting an alternative pathway for decreasing arousal. However, the marked initial effects of destruction of the raphe or permanent inhibition of serotonin synthesis, contrasted with the fact that enhancement of serotonin levels leads to decreased electrocortical arousal and slow-wave sleep, suggest an important role for this transmitter in the regulation of arousal.

REFERENCES

Moruzzi, G., & Magoun, H. W. (1949). Brain stem reticular formation and activation of the EEG. *Electroencephalography and Clinical Neurophysiology, 1,* 455–473.

SUGGESTED READING

Role, L. W., & Kelly, J. P. (1991). The brain stem: Cranial nerve nuclei and the monoaminergic systems. In E. R. Kandel, J. H. Schwartz, & T. M. Jessell (Eds.), *Principles of neural science* (3rd ed., pp. 683–699). New York: Elsevier.

Steriade, M. (1996). Arousal: Reordering the reticular activating system. *Science, 272,* 225–226.

Michael L. Woodruff
East Tennessee State University

RETT SYNDROME

Rett syndrome is a pervasive neurodevelopmental disorder that affects almost solely females. It is marked by a period of apparently normal development for 6–18 months followed by rapid and severe physical and mental deterioration (Brown & Hoadley, 1999). Many of the handicapping features of Rett syndrome stem from apraxia or dyspraxia (inability to perform voluntary motor movements), which interferes with virtually every body movement. The apraxia and absence of verbal skills make assessment of intelligence difficult, but most affected girls ultimately test in the severely retarded range. The syndrome appears to be an X-linked dominant disorder largely owing to a mutation of the methyl-CpG-binding protein 2 gene (MeCP2; Van den Veyver & Zoghbi, 2000).

Although estimates vary, Rett syndrome occurs in about 1 in every 15,000 female births worldwide and affects all racial and ethnic groups. Occurrence appears to be random. Recurrence rates within the same family are less than .4%, indicating that most cases arise through spontaneous mutation (International Rett Syndrome Association [IRSA], 2002). A few males have had symptoms similar to those of Rett syndrome (developmental regression, loss of the ability to walk and make purposeful hand and finger movements, progressive scoliosis, and seizures), but none has had classic Rett. The possibility that males with the syndrome may have a more severe form of the disorder is supported by a report of severe neonatal encephalopathy and infant death of the brother of a girl with Rett syndrome. The infant boy and his sister had the same MECP2 gene mutation (Geerdink et al., 2002). Rett syndrome is apparently lethal prenatally to most affected males.

Rett syndrome has necessary, supportive, and exclusionary criteria. Necessary characteristics include

1. Apparently normal pre-, peri-, and early postnatal development
2. Deceleration of head growth beginning from 3 months to 3 years of age
3. Loss of acquired skills (voluntary hand skills, verbal and nonverbal communication skills) beginning from 3 months to 3 years of age
4. Appearance of obvious mental retardation in early childhood
5. Appearance of intense and persistent hand stereotypies, including hand wringing, squeezing, washing, patting, and rubbing and mouthing and tongue pulling
6. Gait abnormalities in ambulatory cases

Supportive criteria include breathing dysfunctions, bloating and marked air swallowing, electroencephalogram abnormalities, seizures, spasticity, muscle wasting, peripheral vasomotor disturbances, scoliosis, hypotrophic small and cold feet, and growth retardation. Exclusionary criteria include signs of storage disease, retinopathy or optic atrophy, microcephaly at birth, existence of metabolic or other hereditary degenerative disorder, neurological disorder from severe infection or head trauma, intrauterine growth retardation, and peri- or postnatal brain damage. The syndrome may also appear in atypical variants that may be diagnosed in females showing at least three primary and five supportive criteria for classic Rett syndrome. Less restrictive criteria may also be used when evaluating males with symptoms suggestive of Rett.

Classic Rett syndrome generally develops through a four-stage sequence of behavioral and physical changes first described by Hagberg and Witt-Engerström (1986). However, not all affected children show all the features of each stage, and the age of onset, duration of transition from stage to another, and duration of each stage are highly variable. The stages can be summarized as follows:

1. Early-onset stagnation (begins around 6–18 months; duration of months). Developmental stagnation, de-

celeration of head growth, hyptonia; diminished eye contact, communication, hand-use ability; diminished interest in play and the environment; development of random movements

2. Rapid developmental regression (begins around 12–36 months; duration of weeks to months). Appearance of hand stereotypies, including hand wringing, washing, and mouthing; onset of sleep disturbances, breathing irregularities, and seizure-like spells; deterioration of cognitive functioning, hand use, and expressive language; appearance of behavior that may resemble, and be diagnosed as, autism
3. Pseudostationary (begins around preschool age; duration until about 10 years of age). Decrease in autistic-like features; gait and stance become fixed; increased severity of mental retardation, breathing irregularities, bruxism, body rigidity, and seizures; development of scoliosis
4. Late motor deterioration (begins around 10 years of age; duration lifelong). Loss of or decrease in expressive or receptive language and any remaining motor functions, including chewing, swallowing, and walking; increase in rigidity, scoliosis, and muscle wasting.

No cure or effective treatment for Rett syndrome is available, although some symptoms can be managed. Treatment is specific to the individual and the severity of the symptoms at any particular time. A multidisciplinary approach is necessary, typically beginning with treatment by a neurologist and developmental pediatrician. Lifelong physical, occupational, and speech therapy are often necessary, as are academic, social, vocational, and supportive services. Each symptom needs a specific treatment for alleviation, such as medication for seizures and agitation, and braces, surgery, and physical therapy for scoliosis (IRSA, 2002; *WE MOVE*, 2002). Behavior modification has had limited effectiveness in treating the syndrome (e.g., Brown & Hoadley, 1999).

A child diagnosed with Rett syndrome will live well into her 40s, but quality of life is severely compromised at best. Some functioning may show brief spontaneous recovery, but prognosis is poor, and the progressive course of the disorder is currently irreversible. Affected girls will require lifelong close care and supervision, placing a heavy burden on their caretakers. Families may benefit from early and maintained counseling (Brown & Hoadley, 1999).

The recent discovery of the genetic basis and advances in biotechnology have led to several promising avenues of research. These include discovering the mechanisms by which the mutated MeCP2 gene manifests itself; determining how to silence the effects of the mutation; and developing treatment, such as stem cell transplants, that may halt or reverse the course of the disorder (National Institute of Health, 2001).

REFERENCES

Brown, R. T., & Hoadley, S. L. (1999). Rett syndrome. In S. Goldstein & C. R. Reynolds (Eds.), *Handbook of neurodevelopmental and genetic disorders in children* (pp. 459–477). New York: Guilford Press.

Geerdink, N., Rotteveel, J. J., Lammens, M., Sistermans, E. A., Heikens, G. T., Gabreels, F. J., et al. (2002). MECP2 mutation in a boy with severe neonatal encephalopathy: Clinical, neuropathological, and molecular findings. *Neuropediatrics, 33*, 33–36.

Hagberg, B., & Witt-Engerström, I. (1986). Rett syndrome: A suggested staging system for describing impairment profile with increasing age toward adolescence. *American Journal of Medical Genetics, 24*(Suppl. 1), 47–59.

International Rett Syndrome Association (IRSA). (2002). Retrieved from http://www.rettsyndrome.org

Van den Veyver, I. B., & Zoghbi, H. Y. (2000). Methyl-CpG-binding protein 2 mutations in Rett syndrome. *Current Opinion in Genetics and Development, 10*, 275–279.

WE MOVE. (2002). *Rett syndrome*. Retrieved from http://www.wemove.org/rett.html

Sarah L. Hoadley
Robert T. Brown
University of North Carolina at Wilmington

REWARDS AND INTRINSIC INTEREST

It is usually assumed that giving rewards for performing a task increases future motivation for and engagement in that activity. A large body of research supports this assumption (Baldwin & Baldwin, 1998; Sarafino, 1996). In the early 1970s, however, studies began to find that under certain conditions the opposite effect seemed to occur: External rewards for performing an intrinsically interesting activity *undermined* subsequent interest in and performance of that task.

Demonstrating and Explaining an Undermining Effect of Rewards

The procedure that has generally been used to demonstrate this undermining effect is illustrated by the research of Lepper, Greene, and Nisbett (1973). Preschool children who pretested as being interested in the target activity of drawing with magic markers were assigned to reward and control conditions. Some children were shown a Good Player Award that they would get for drawing pictures, but the control subjects were not. After drawing the pictures, the children who expected the reward received it, and the controls did not. Later, all the children were secretly observed while the drawing materials and other activities were freely available, with no prizes offered to anyone. The children who previously expected and received rewards for drawing spent less time playing with the drawing materials than did those who had not received a reward. This undermining effect was soon demonstrated with older children and college students using a variety of tasks and material rewards (deCharms & Muir, 1978; Lepper & Greene, 1976).

The explanation given by Lepper and his colleagues (1973; Lepper & Greene, 1976) for the undermining effect of rewards is called the *overjustification hypothesis.* If an external reward is offered and provided for engaging in an initially enjoyable task, individuals perceive the target activity as overjustified because a reward is not necessary. They infer that engaging in the activity was "basically motivated by the external contingencies of the situation, rather than by any intrinsic interest in the activity itself" (Lepper et al., 1973, p. 130). Another theory proposes that rewards can reduce feelings of self-determination (Deci & Ryan, 1985).

Current Status of the Undermining Effect

On the face of it, the idea that rewards reduce people's interest in activities that they enjoy seems to contradict common sense and observation. After all, many people get paid for work that they enjoy and continue to work hard even though they receive paychecks. Research since the 1970s has produced mixed findings, and many studies have reported no decrease in interest after people got rewards for performing enjoyable activities (Cameron & Pierce, 1994; Dickinson, 1989; Flora, 1990). The undermining effects of rewards seem to occur only under limited conditions (Eisenberger & Cameron, 1996; but see also Lepper, Keavney, & Drake, 1996; Ryan & Deci, 1996). Rewards sometimes undermine motivation under three conditions:

1. *High initial interest.* Rewards can undermine very high interest but enhance motivation when there is less initial interest (Calder & Staw, 1975; Sarafino & DiMattia, 1978).
2. *Tangible and salient rewards.* Tangible rewards, such as candy or money, sometimes undermine interest in a task, especially if the reward is salient, such as when a child focuses attention on it (Sarafino, 1984). However, praise as a reward usually enhances motivation for the task (Dollinger & Thelen, 1978; Eisenberger & Cameron, 1996).
3. *The norm is for no reward.* If a person believes that people are not normally given a reward for the activity, being given a reward can undermine interest. If the person believes it is normal and appropriate to receive a reward for the activity, however, the reward increases motivation (Staw, Calder, Hess, & Sandelands, 1980).

Finally, when reduced interest does occur, these decrements are usually minor, transient if the person continues to perform the task following the reward, and unlikely at all if performance meets or exceeds stated standards or receives repeated rewards (Dickinson, 1989; Eisenberger & Cameron, 1996). Thus it appears that rewards can undermine people's interest in enjoyable activities under limited conditions, but the likelihood, strength, and durability of these effects are slight.

REFERENCES

Baldwin, J. D., & Baldwin, J. I. (1998). *Behavior principles in everyday life* (3rd ed.). Upper Saddle River, NJ: Prentice Hall.

Calder, B. J., & Staw, B. M. (1975). Self-perception of intrinsic and extrinsic motivation. *Journal of Personality and Social Psychology, 31,* 599–605.

Cameron, J., & Pierce, W. D. (1994). Reinforcement, reward, and intrinsic motivation: A meta-analysis. *Review of Educational Research, 64,* 363–423.

deCharms, R., & Muir, M. S. (1978). Motivation: Social approaches. *Annual Review of Psychology, 29,* 91–113.

Deci, E. L., & Ryan, R. M. (1985). *Intrinsic motivation and self-determination in human behavior.* New York: Plenum Press.

Dickinson, A. M. (1989). The detrimental effects of extrinsic reinforcement on "intrinsic motivation." *Behavior Analyst, 12,* 1–15.

Dollinger, S. J., & Thelen, M. H. (1978). Overjustification and children's intrinsic motivation: Comparative effects of four rewards. *Journal of Personality and Social Psychology, 36,* 1259–1269.

Eisenberger, R., & Cameron, J. (1996). Detrimental effects of reward: Reality or myth? *American Psychologist, 51,* 1153–1166.

Flora, S. R. (1990). Undermining intrinsic interest from the standpoint of a behaviorist. *Psychological Record, 40,* 323–346.

Lepper, M. R., & Greene, D. (1976). On understanding "overjustification": A reply to Reiss and Sushinsky. *Journal of Personality and Social Psychology, 33,* 25–35.

Lepper, M. R., Greene, D., & Nisbett, R. E. (1973). Undermining children's intrinsic interest with extrinsic reward: A test of the "overjustification hypothesis." *Journal of Personality and Social Psychology, 28,* 129–137.

Lepper, M. R., Keavney, M., & Drake, M. (1996). Intrinsic motivation and extrinsic rewards: A commentary on Cameron and Pierces's meta-analysis. *Review of Educational Research, 66,* 5–32.

Ryan, R. M., & Deci, E. L. (1996). When paradigms clash: Comments on Cameron and Pierce's claim that rewards do not undermine intrinsic motivation. *Review of Educational Research, 66,* 33–38.

Sarafino, E. P. (1984). Intrinsic motivation and delay of gratification in preschoolers: The variables of reward salience and length of expected delay. *British Journal of Developmental Psychology, 1,* 149–156.

Sarafino, E. P. (1996). *Principles of behavior change: Understanding behavior modification techniques.* New York: Wiley.

Sarafino, E. P., & DiMattia, P. A. (1978). Does grading undermine intrinsic interest in a college course? *Journal of Educational Psychology, 70,* 916–921.

Staw, B. M., Calder, B. J., Hess, R. K., & Sandelands, L. E. (1980). Intrinsic motivation and norms about payment. *Journal of Personality, 48,* 1–14.

Edward P. Sarafino
The College of New Jersey

See also: **Intrinsic Motivation; Motivation; Reinforcement**

RHYTHM

The concept of rhythm has many meanings. The broadest definition that covers all meanings of the word seems to be that of Plato: "Rhythm is order in movement." One might instead propose: "Rhythm is order in succession."

Patterns of temporal order can be found in areas greatly diverse. Here we consider temporal order in three of these—cosmology, biology, and perception. There are similarities between the first two areas, but neither relates to the third.

Cosmic rhythms are known on the basis of experiences independent in time, such as the rhythm of the seasons; the rhythm of the moon, which affects tides; and especially the rhythm of day and night, which has considerable repercussion on our daily lives.

Biological rhythms are numerous in the vegetable and animal kingdoms. If one considers the organism of the human being alone, almost all the body functions are rhythmical.

These rhythms comply with the different systems whose periodicity is endogenous, but they can play the role of synchronizer as one relates to another. Clearly, as the foundation, there is the nightly rhythm. However, humans can transcend the nightly rhythm for a time, such as by living in artificial conditions, in the far North, or even in space. This circadian rhythm differs for its natural duration in being somewhat longer than 24 hours.

The waking-sleeping rhythm, which is more flexible, also would appear to comply with an oscillating system. One finds it in persons in free-running situations, without the influences of the nightly rhythm. It is used to regulate the lives of astronauts in space where the successions of light and darkness are much more rapid.

Yet, although the waking-sleeping rhythm is profoundly altered by social conditions (night work) or geographic considerations (transmeridian flights), one can ascertain that these new rhythms in the long run can serve as synchronizers for the body temperature rhythm, which then adjusts itself to the rhythm of the activity.

These adaptations are important; not only do feelings of well-being or weariness depend on the temperature rhythm, but also degrees of alertness and often levels of performance are affected.

These rhythms then are defined as endogenous; their period of time scarcely varies, but their phases can be displaced through synchronization with a rhythm of the same time period (e.g., the influence of activity rhythm on temperature).

Next we find rhythms acquired through habit (conditioning). Thus it is with the rhythms of hunger, linked to our eating habits with repercussions on our degree of alertness. Weekly rhythms also exist, related in particular to weekend resting, which, come Monday morning, causes slight difficulties with readaptation to the routine of work, whether in the classroom or in the factory.

Perceptual Rhythms

When one speaks of rhythm, one thinks immediately of music and poetry—that is of the recurrence at equal intervals of one or several elements organized in unified structures. This simple description means that, in these cases, there is a perception of the order in the succession.

The perception of rhythm leads us to ask two fundamental questions: (1) What are the temporal limits in which succession is perceived? and (2) What is the nature of structures that lend themselves to repetition?

Temporal Limits of Perceived Rhythm

As the basis for the perception of rhythm, there is the capacity for apprehending successive elements in a unity analogous to our capacity for apprehending a portion of space in a visual angle.

This capacity for apprehending is often called *psychic present* because it corresponds to a perception in which there are simultaneously successive elements. Such is our ability to perceive a simple phrase, such as a telephone number. The psychological present has limits that relate both to the duration and the nature of the elements. Thus one can perceive the succession of two identical sounds that go from the threshold of 0.1 second to a duration of 1.8 seconds. Beyond this duration, the sounds become elements perceived as independent of each other.

But how many elements can one perceive in this present?

Here one must distinguish discrete elements from those that form a structure. Although we are able to apprehend about five letters of the alphabet presented out of order, we can perceive 12 syllables forming a verse. In a perceived structure, be it repeated or not, we perceive subgroups called chunks. The more a perceptual unity is subdivided, the longer the psychic present can be, under the condition that no internal interval exceeds 1.8 seconds. The regular repetition of equal situations thus no longer gives the perception of merely a unity (as that of a phrase) but of a rhythm, as is the case in music, poetry, and dance.

This leads us to consider the rapidity of succession, or tempo. Tempo is referred to as the rapidity with which the elements of a structure succeed themselves and the structures within themselves.

For the rhythmic unity to be clearly perceived, it is necessary that the duration between elements be sufficiently rapid. In significantly slowing the poetic diction or musical execution, one suppresses the perception of the rhythm.

Rhythmic Structures

Consider the simplest example, in which a single sound is repeated at intervals of 0.4 second. These sounds are perceived as linked to each other. When listened to with care, they are perceived as grouped in twos (more rarely in threes). If one analyzes this perception, one begins to see that these groups appear distinct from each other in one or two aspects—either a lengthening of the duration between the groups (pause) or the accentuation of one of two elements.

Artistic Rhythms

Clearly, artistic rhythms are, in the order of temporality, perceived rhythms. It is important to see whether there is a connection between what is done spontaneously by creative artists and the laws of rhythm derived through experimental procedures.

Temporal Limits

Rhythms produced in poetry and music have periods of duration that register perfectly in the indicated perceptual limits. The average length of the rhythmic measures is 3.2 seconds. For lines of poetry, according to J. E. Wallin, the average duration is 2.7 seconds.

For a number of elements of substructures in music, the composer rarely exceeds six beats, and the listener generally hears units of two or three beats. In poetry, the number of syllables rarely exceeds 12, and each line is scanned in two, three, or four parts by accents or pauses.

The structure of rhythmical units perfectly illustrates the preceding analyses. For want of documents, we know through Aristoxene de Tarente (fourth century B.C.) that rhythm is a succession of durations and that these durations are not arbitrary. There is a minimum of indivisible duration and multiples of this duration by two or three, so that rhythm is analyzed as a more or less complex series of shorts and longs, that is, of series of durations. This is also true of dance, music, and chant—arts that were not dissociated. Such was the case in Greek and Latin poetry. Today, depending on the language and customs, poetry is more of the syllabic type, with regular sequences of accents, and in classical poetry, rhyme provides a supplementary indication.

In the classical music of our time, the composer disposes of a set of durations that are exceedingly numerous because the possible durations are binary divisions of a very long note, the semibreve. This is divided into minims, crotchets, quavers, and so on, without counting further gradations. A composer, in a piece that is homogeneous from the point of view of tempo, makes principal use of two notes that stand in a ratio of two or three (quaver and crotchet, or double quaver-quaver, sometimes double quaver-semiquaver), and this in a proportion of 70% to 80%. Evidently there are short notes, long notes, and silences. We believe that these accidents are the creations of the artist, who seeks to escape the determinisms that demand the preferential use of only two periods of duration, the shortest of which is the most frequent.

How might one explain this spontaneous prevalence, perpetuated by usage, of only two durations in rhythmical structures? One might recall a general law that one often finds working in the domain of perceptions: the understanding of a simplification through a double process of assimilation of the elements only slightly different from each other, and of a distinction that tends to overestimate the differences not reduced by assimilation. But in the case of durations used in rhythms, one must remember the notion of transmitted information. In the scale of absolute perceived durations, it has been established that one cannot distinguish a number of durations greater than two or, at most, three.

Here we see a constraint on temporal perception that has imposed itself on artists of all times. It also imposed itself on those who created an alphabet on the basis of intermittent lengths, such as the Morse code based on a system of dots and dashes.

Rhythms of Movements

To study the laws of rhythm, we have made use of perceptions as well as aspects of motor production. One must first note that perceived rhythms, especially in the arts, are rhythms produced by human motor or verbal activities. There is, in effect, a harmony between the rhythms produced and the rhythms perceived. This harmony manifests itself, in particular, in the fact that heard rhythms elicit a very real motor induction whose movements also are periodic. The phenomenon is observable from the earliest age. A child at the age of 1 year can rock gently upon hearing a rhythmical musical piece, and even adults tend to restrain spontaneous movements upon hearing music.

This spontaneity is also revealed by our difficulty in stressing a beat that, for example, lies between two normal accents, or what is called syncopation. Normally it takes considerable practice to execute two different rhythms with separate hands to create a polyrhythm.

To return to the spontaneous synchronization of music, one clearly sees that the movement accompanies the principal accent point, but if the structure is long and complex, synchronal movements are created with secondary accent points. It all works as though the induced accompanying movements are to remain interlocked, which means that the interval that separates them must be distinctly less than 1.8 seconds.

Motor induction and synchronization give other than

perceptual qualities to the rhythms. The audiomuscular harmony brings about emotional reactions characteristic of the perception of rhythm. Besides, spontaneous synchronization allows for the socialization of rhythmical activities, such as in dance, orchestral music, and choral singing. This socialization of activities is always a source of stimulation.

Spatial Rhythms

One speaks less of spatial rhythm than one does of auditory rhythm. In describing a monument, for example, one speaks more readily of form or proportion. Quite naturally there are successions, but they register in a three-dimensional context, which gives rise to further problems.

When considering only linear successions, it is observed that they often are like rhythmic structures with regular repetitions of identical elements, as a tree-planted avenue, or by a repetition of binary, or even tertiary, structures with regular spacings between the groupings. One may even find in rows of windows, for example, more complex structures with elements that are varied but of a repetitive nature.

P. Fraisse

RIBOSOME

The prokaryotic ribosome represented by the *E. coli* ribosome has a molecular mass of 2.5 million daltons and a volume of 3 million cubic Ås (Yonath & Franceschi, 1998) and is designated a 70S particle. The 70S ribosome has three tRNA binding sites: the acceptor (A), the peptidyl (P), and the exit (E) site. It is made up of dissociable subunits, a 30S subunit (0.8 million) and a 50S subunit (1.7 million). The 30S subunit is a complex of one large RNA strand (16S RNA, 1,542 bases long) and 21 proteins (denoted S1 to S21). The 50S subunit is a complex of two RNA strands (23S rRNA, 2,904 bases long; 5S RNA, 120 bases long) and at least 33 proteins (denoted L1 to L34; there is no L8). X-ray crystallography and nuclear magnetic resonance (NMR) have been applied to determine the high resolution structure of a number of ribosomal proteins and limited regions of RNA and of protein RNA complexes. Thanks to the progress in the crystallography of ribosomes, reasonably accurate structural models for the subunits and for one or two complexes of 70S ribosomes are available (Ban et al., 1998; Moore, 1998; Yonath, private communication, 1998). The relative spatial arrangements of each ribosomal component are now understood (resolution approximately 7–10 Å). In addition, cryoelectron microscopy elucidated the structure of the 70S ribosome and complexed ligands such as tRNA, mRNA, EF-G, and EF-Tu at 7- to 10-Å resolution. Other approaches helping us to understand the structure of ribosomes include neutron scattering, immuno-electron microscopy, fluorescence energy transfer, cross-linking and chemical footprinting. On the basis of the information obtained by these studies, computer-based, three-dimensional models of ribosomes have been built.

The most extensive studies on eukaryotic ribosomes were conducted on rat ribosomes (Wool, Chan, & Gluck, 1996). Although these eukaryotic ribosomes are in principle similar to their prokaryotic counterparts, important differences do exist. Mammalian ribosomes (80S particles) are composed of 40S and 60S subunits. The 40S subunit has 18S RNA and 33 proteins, while the 60S subunit has three RNAs—5S, 5.8S, and 26S—and 47 proteins. Mammalian ribosomal proteins have an average molecular weight of 18,500 and contain 165 amino acids. They are very basic, with an average isoelectric point of 11.05. A common feature of mammalian ribosomal proteins is the repetition of short amino acid sequences, generally of three to eight. The number of genes encoding the ribosomal protein is 12, but there is no evidence that more than one gene is functional. Ribosomal proteins from all eukaryotic species are closely related and appear to be derived from a common ancestral gene.

Function of Ribosomes

The function of ribosomes is to synthesize protein from aminoacyl tRNA according to the information in the messenger RNA (mRNA) with the help of soluble protein factors. Protein synthesis can be divided into four steps: translation initiation, peptide chain elongation, translation, termination (release of the completed chain), and disassembly of the posttermination complex for the recycling of the translational machinery.

Translation Initiation

During the protein synthesis initiation process, the small ribosomal subunit binds to the mRNA and positions the initiation codon of the mRNA into the ribosomal decoding center at the P- (peptidyl-) site. The second codon on the mRNA is at the ribosomal A- (acceptor-) site. The charged initiator tRNA is bound at the ribosomal P-site. The resulting ribosome:mRNA:initiator-tRNA complex is called the initiation complex. Bacteria and organelles (mitochondria and chloroplasts) of eukaryotes form the initiation complex in much the same way. The analogous process in the cytoplasm of the eukaryotes differs from that of prokaryotes in several respects, and the prokaryotic and eukaryotic translation initiations are described separately.

Prokaryotic Translation Initiation. Three soluble factors, IF1, IF2, and IF3, are involved in this process. The first event of the initiation process is the dissociation of the released free 70S ribosome into its large and small subunits via one of the two known functions of IF3 (Gualerzi & Pon, 1990). IF3 also prevents subunit reassociation and helps the 30S subunit to bind to the initiation site of mRNA. The initiator fMet-tRNA^{fMet} and mRNA, with appropriate initiation signals, bind the 30S subunit. This process takes place in random order (Wu, Iyengar, & RajBhandary, 1996). The initiation site of mRNA usually has the ribosome binding sequence (Shine-Dalgarno [SD] sequence), a few nucleotides (optimally 3–9) upstream of the initiation codon (AUG > GUG > UUG > AUU). Base pairing between this SD sequence and a few nucleotides at the 3′ end of the 16S rRNA is important for the selection of the translational start site of mRNA by the 30S subunit (Hui & De Boer, 1987; Jacob, Santer, & Dahlberg, 1987).

In some cases translation may occur from mRNAs lacking an SD sequence; alternative mechanisms therefore exist (Sprengart & Porter, 1997)—for example, bridging the mRNA to the ribosome by the S1 ribosomal protein, which recognizes U-rich stretches in the 5′ untranslated region. Base pairing with 16S rRNA nucleotides 1082 to 1093 and 1343 to 1355 with the 5′ untranslated sequence of mRNAs plays a role in this case. Other mechanisms include base pairing with 16S rRNA nucleotides 1469 to 1483, with mRNA sequences downstream from the initiation codon.

In all cases, the interaction between the 16S rRNA and the mRNA is such that the initiation codon is positioned at the decoding center of the ribosome in the 1400/1500 nucleotide region of the 3′ end of the 16S rRNA. Association of the 30S subunit and mRNA, and the concomitant translation initiation, may occur at several different initiation points along the bacterial polycistronic mRNA.

IF2, the largest of the three initiation factors, promotes the binding and correct positioning of fMet-tRNA^{fMet} to the P-site of the ribosome and prevents the participation of elongator aminoacyl-tRNA in the initiation process. This is achieved by specific recognition of the blocked (formylated) amino group of initiator fMet-tRNA^{fMet} by IF2 (Hartz, McPheeters, & Gold, 1989; Wu & RajBhandary, 1997). IF2 functions as a carrier of fMet-tRNA^{fMet} to the 30S ribosomal P-site in much the same way as EF-Tu functions as a carrier of aminoacyl-tRNAs to the A-site of 70S ribosomes (see the section Peptide Chain Elongation). The sites of fMet-tRNA^{fMet} contacting IF2 have been studied by footprinting experiments and were found primarily within the T loop and the minor groove of the T stem. The footprints of IF2 on fMet-tRNA^{fMet} in the binary fMet-tRNA^{fMet}·IF2 complex and in the 30S·IF2·fMet-tRNA^{fMet}·AUG complex are similar. This suggests that the interactions between IF2 and either the isolated fMet-tRNA^{fMet} or the P-site-bound fMet-tRNA^{fMet} are essentially the same (Wakao et al., 1989). In addition, IF2 interacts with the 3′ end of the initiator tRNA and protects the ester linkage in fMet-tRNA^{fMet} from deacylation (Petersen, Roll, Grunberg-Manago, & Clark, 1979). No effect of IF2 on the reactivity pattern of the 16S rRNA in the protection assays was seen, suggesting that this factor interacts primarily through protein-protein interactions with the ribosome in the initiation complex (Moazed, Samaha, Gualerzi, & Noller, 1995).

IF3, bound to the 30S subunit, recognizes the anticodon stem of the initiator tRNA and helps to prevent the binding of elongator tRNAs to the 30S initiation complex (Hartz et al., 1989). Furthermore, IF3-dependent protection of 16S rRNA from chemical modification is found in the vicinity of a region that is also protected by P-site–bound tRNA. This indicates that the IF3 may also interact with the anticodon domain of fMet-tRNA^{fMet} or influence the properties of the 30S P-site during initiation (Moazed et al., 1995). The placement of IF3 by cryoelectron microscopy on the 30S subunit allows an understanding in structural terms of the biochemical functions of this initiation factor (McCutcheon et al., 1999).

IF1 is the smallest of the three initiation factors. It stimulates the activity of IF2 and IF3 on formation of the 30S initiation complex. The affinity of IF2 to the ribosome is increased in the presence of IF1 (Gualerzi & Pon, 1990). Footprinting revealed that the binding of IF1 to the 30S ribosomal subunit protects the same nucleotides in 16S rRNA from modification as the EF-Tu–dependent binding of aminoacyl-tRNA to the ribosomal A-site (Moazed et al., 1995). This suggests that during initiation, IF1 binds to the ribosomal A-site at the same position as the anticodon domain of the aminoacyl-tRNA during elongation. Thus, the function of IF1 may be to prevent the premature binding of elongator aminoacyl-tRNA to the A-site during the initiation process, and a complex of IF1 and IF2 interact with the ribosomal A-site, mimicking the structure of the elongation factor G (Brock, Szkaradkiewicz, & Sprinzl, 1998). As these initiation factors and EF-G fulfill a similar function in placing a tRNA to the ribosomal P-site, structural similarities between them may indicate similar molecular mechanisms of action.

The 30S initiation complex forms the 70S initiation complex by association with the 50S ribosomal subunit. Concomitant with this process, IF1 and IF3 are ejected. The process is stimulated by IF2, whose GTPase activity is activated, and IF2 is released upon hydrolysis of GTP. At this stage, the fMet-tRNA^{fMet} is located in the ribosomal P-site, ready to form the first peptide bond. The mechanism of initiation in bacteria has been extensively reviewed (Gualerzi & Pon, 1990; Hartz et al., 1989; RajBhandary & Chow, 1995).

Initiation in the Cytoplasm of Eukaryotic Cells. One peculiar feature of eukaryotic mRNAs is that the 5′ end of most of them has a structure called a cap. This is a structure involving methylated guanine triphospho nucleotide, ^{7}mGpppN, where N denotes any base. Many factors are involved in the eukaryotic initiation process and are designated as eIFs. A cap-dependent mechanism accounts for the translation of the vast majority of cellular mRNAs. An alternative cap-independent initiation mechanism is responsible for translation of a small number of mRNAs (Gray & Wickens, 1998). The process of initiation is similar in germ line cells and during embryogenesis as well (Jackson & Wickens, 1997).

In both the cap-dependent and the cap-independent pathways, the initiation proceeds via formation of a 43S preinitiation complex consisting of the 40S ribosomal subunit, a ternary complex of eIF2·GTP·Met-tRNA$_i^{Met}$ (the initiator tRNA in eukaryotes is not formylated in contrast to its prokaryotic counterpart), and eIF3. Ribosomes at physiological Mg^{2+} concentration (>1 mM) predominantly exist as 80S monosomes. The equilibrium between 80S monosomes and dissociated subunits is shifted toward dissociation by eIF3, eIF1A (alternative name eIF-4C), and eIF3A (alternative name eIF6). EIF3 and eIF1A bind to the 40S subunits, while eIF3A binds to the 60S subunit, making 40S subunits available for initiation (Hershey, 1991; Merrick, 1992; Pain, 1996). EIF1A is a single subunit factor with basic N-terminus and acidic C-terminus.

eIF-3 consists of at least 8 polypeptides in mammalian cells and *S. cerevisiae* and 10 polypeptides in wheat germ cells. This initiation factor remains bound to the 40S subunit and is necessary for the stable binding of the eIF2·GTP·Met-tRNA$_i^{Met}$ ternary complex (Gray & Wickens, 1998; Merrick, 1992; Merrick & Hershey, 1996) to the small subunit. eIF3A (one of the proteins of eIF3 complex), which remains bound to the 60S subunit, is a single subunit protein (Merrick, 1992).

eIF2 consists of three subunits: γ, β, and α. The γ-subunit possesses the GTP-binding elements. In the absence of GTP, eIF2 is not able to bind to initiator tRNA. Based on cross-linking studies, both the γ- and the β-subunits bind to Met-tRNA$_i^{Met}$ (Gaspar et al., 1994). The main known function of the α-subunit is to link translation to regulatory circuits via the presence of a conserved phosphorylation site (Ser51 in mammalian cells) present in its sequence. When the α-subunit is phosphorylated, eIF2 loses its ability to replace its spent GDP with GTP. In addition, the phosphorylated α-subunit segregates the nucleotide exchange factor eIF2B from the rest of eIF2 by tightly binding to it. This makes eIF2B less available for replacing the GDP with GTP on the eIF2·GDP binary complex. As a consequence, availability of the eIF2·GDP·Met-tRNA$_i^{Met}$ ternary complex for the initiation decreases, fewer 43S preinitiation complexes are formed, and translation decreases (Gray & Wickens, 1998; Pain, 1996).

In the cap-dependent pathway, this 43S preinitiation complex is then recruited at the 5′ end of the mRNA, involving the ^{7}mGpppN cap structure on the 5′ end with the association of eIF4 group initiation factors, including 4F and B. The complex is frequently called the 48S preinitiation complex.

The eIF4F consists of three subunits with distinctive functions: eIF4E, eIF4A, and eIF4G. eIF4E is a cap-binding protein; eIF4A has an ATP-dependent RNA helicase activity; and eIF4G has affinity in its N-terminal third to eIF4E (Lamphear, Kirchweger, Skern, & Rhoads, 1995; Mader, Lee, Pause, & Sonenberg, 1995), while its C-terminal two-thirds has affinity to both eIF3 and eIF4A (Lamphear et al., 1995). Therefore, eIF4G bridges the cap structure of the mRNA (via eIF4E), the 40S subunit of the ribosome (via eIF3), and eIF4A (Hentze, 1997; Jackson & Wickens, 1997). Both eIF4E and eIF4G have been shown to participate in regulatory circuits affecting translation in the initiation step (Gray & Wickens, 1998; Hentze, 1997; Jackson & Wickens, 1997).

It has been shown in *S. cerevisiae* that the poly(A) tail-stimulated translation is mediated by a protein, Pab1p, which binds to a stretch of 10 A nucleotides at the 3′-ends of mRNAs. Pab1p acts synergistically with the cap structure but also can work in its absence and exerts its stimulatory effect via binding to the eIF4G.

There is also growing evidence that some signal transduction/phosphorylation systems positively regulate translation via the involvement of eIF4E. Thus, the eIF4E binding protein 1 (4E-BP1) strongly binds eIF4E and sequesters it from entering the eIF4F initiation complex. Phosphorylation of 4E-BP1, elicited, for instance, by insulin, makes eIF4E available for eIF4G binding and hence increases 48S preinitiation complex formation.

Another eIF4 group factor (but not part of eIF4F), eIF4B joins the 48S preinitiation complex and stimulates the unwinding of the secondary structures in the 5′ untranslated region of the mRNA via eIF4A (Lawson et al., 1989; Rozen et al., 1990). EIF4B also interacts with eIF3; this ability may aid in binding the 43S preinitiation complex to the mRNA (Merrick, 1992).

The 40S ribosomal subunit, with the associated initiation factors, has to relocate from the cap through the 5′-untranslated region (5′-UTR) of the mRNA to the site of initiation, which is generally 100 to 150 nucleotides downstream along the mRNA. This process is termed scanning (Kozak, 1978) or shunting (Gray & Wickens, 1998). In the scanning model, the preinitiation complex migrates along the mRNA in a continuous manner from the 5′-UTR to the initiation site. In the shunting model, scanning toward the initiation site is discontinuous; the preinitiation complex hops over secondary mRNA structures, which in themselves are inhibitory for the scanning. The scanning is an ATP-dependent process and is dependent on eIF1 and eIF1A (Pestova et al., 1998).

The scanning preinitiation complex selects the site of initiation generally at the location of the first initiation codon, overwhelmingly AUG but occasionally GUG or CUG (Kozak, 1989, 1994). Sometimes it is not the first initiation codon, mainly when the ORF is preceded by short ORFs (sORFs), and the ORF is not translated when translation of sORF is prevented (Hinnebush, 1996). RNA:RNA interactions may play a role in positioning the initiation codon in the decoding center of the 40S ribosomal subunit, although it is not so apparent as in prokaryotes (Sprengart & Porter, 1997). There is a consensus sequence of approximately 10 nucleotides for the initiation site (Kozak, 1994). The most important positions are a purine, at −3 position, and a G, at +4 position, where A of the initiator AUG codon is position +1. The fidelity of interaction between the codon and the complementary anticodon loop of the initiator tRNA is controlled by both eIF3 (Naranda, MacMillan, Donahue, & Hershey, 1996) and eIF2 (Pain, 1996).

In the alternative cap-independent initiation pathway, a *cis*-acting mRNA element (the internal ribosome entry segment [IRES]) promotes direct access of the 43S preinitiation complex to the initiation codon and can even allow several cycles of translation of a covalently closed circular mRNA (Chen & Sarnow, 1995). Although IRES is similar in strictly operational terms to the Shine and Dalgarno sequence of prokaryotic mRNAs (Pestova, Shatsky, et al., 1998), IRES is much larger. Internal entry was first discovered with picornavirus RNA, and evidence for its existence has widened since then (Bernstein, Shefler, & Elroy-Stein, 1995; Gan & Rhoads, 1996; Jackson & Kaminski, 1995). Internal initiation of viral mRNA allows some viruses whose mRNAs do not have a cap structure to shut down the translation of most of the cellular mRNAs during viral infection via cleavage of eIF4G. This gives the advantage to the virus, which will then use all cellular protein synthesis machinery for its own replication. The cleavage separates eIF4G into an amino-terminal one-third portion that binds the cap-binding initiation factor eIF4E, and a carboxy-terminal two-thirds fragment that binds eIF3 and the helicase eIF4A.

After the initiation site is selected by the 40S subunits, the 60S ribosomal subunit associates with the complex forming of the 80S ribosome. This step requires eIF5 and the energy of hydrolysis of the GTP bound to eIF2 in the preinitiation complex. The hydrolysis is catalyzed by eIF5, which has GTPase motifs in its sequence (Chakravarti & Maitra, 1993; Das, Chevesich & Maitra, 1993). Upon association of the large subunit, initiation factors are released, and the 80S ribosome is ready to enter the elongation cycle.

Peptide Chain Elongation

For catalyzing peptide chain elongation, the ribosome has three tRNA binding sites: the acceptor (A) site, the peptidyl (P) site, and the exit (E) site (Agrawal & Frank, 1999; Frank, 1997; Moore, 1997, 1998; Nyborg & Liljas, 1998). The ribosomal A-, P-, and E-sites are situated in the cavity between the large and small subunit interface, with the E-site positioned toward the L1 arm side of the large subunit, the A-site positioned toward the L7/L12 arm on the opposite side of the large subunit, and the P-site in between the other two sites. The A- and P-sites span the large and the small subunit, whereas the E-site is localized to the large subunit only.

Peptide chain elongation takes place in the absence of soluble factors, though very slowly (Wilson & Noller, 1998). Under physiological conditions, the prokaryotic ribosome requires elongation factors EF-Tu, EF-Ts, and EF-G. These factors are single-subunit proteins, except for EF-Ts, which forms a dimer (Czworkowski & Moore, 1996; Green & Noller, 1997). In eukaryotes, three factors function for peptide chain elongation: EF-1α (a monomeric protein) corresponds to EF-Tu; eEF-1$\beta\gamma$ (composed of two subunits) corresponds to EF-Ts; and eEF-2 (a monomeric protein) corresponds to the prokaryotic EF-G (Hershey, 1991; Merrick, 1992). An additional factor, eEF-3, which stimulates the translation 5- to 30-fold, has been identified only in yeast and fungi (Merrick, 1992). This factor is necessary for the removal of the deacylated tRNA from the E-site, which has a stronger affinity for tRNA in eukaryotes (especially in fungi) than in prokaryotes (Spahn & Nierhaus, 1998).

The repetitive elongation cycle proceeds in three consecutive steps: aminoacyl-tRNA binding to the ribosomal A-site, peptide bond formation, and translocation of the ribosome one codon towards the 3′-end on the mRNA with concomitant translocation of the deacylated tRNA from the P-site to the E-site, and the peptidyl-tRNA from the A-site to the P-site together with the mRNA movement.

In the first step of chain elongation, the elongator aminoacyl-tRNA is brought to the ribosomal A-site as a ternary complex: aminoacyl-tRNA·EF-Tu (EF-1α in the cytoplasm of eukaryotic cells)·GTP (Pape, Wintermeyer, & Rodnina, 1998; Rodnina, Fricke, Kuhn, & Wintermeyer, 1995; Rodnina, Pape, Fricke, Kuhn, & Wintermeyer, 1996; Rodnina, Pape, Fricke, & Wintermeyer, 1995). The initial rapid and reversible phase is a codon-independent complex formation between the ribosome and the ternary complex. With the cognate aminoacyl tRNA, the subsequent event, inducing the GTPase conformation of EF-Tu and the ribosome-induced GTP hydrolysis, proceeds at a rate four orders of magnitude higher than in the case of binding a noncognate ternary complex. The affinity of the cognate aminoacyl tRNA to the A-site is greatly influenced by whether the E-site is occupied with deacylated tRNA according to the allosteric model (described below), because the configuration of ribosomes is greatly influenced by tRNA on the E-site (Spahn & Nierhaus, 1998).

During the binding process, the anticodon end of the aminoacyl tRNA binds to the A-site of the 30S subunit. The opposite end of the complex contacts the L7/L12 region of the 50S subunit, and the amino acid on the acceptor end of the tRNA is held by the elongation factor so that it is not yet accessible for the peptidyl transferase center on the 50S subunit (Krab & Parmeggiani, 1998; Nyborg & Liljas, 1998; Stark et al., 1997). When the GTP of the ternary complex is hydrolyzed by the GTPase activity of the elongation factor, EF-Tu undergoes a second conformational change, which leads to the release of the aminoacyl-tRNA from the ternary complex. Subsequently, in a rotational movement, the acceptor end of the aminoacyl-tRNA becomes positioned into the large subunit part of the A-site and becomes accessible for the peptidyl transferase center on the 50S subunit (accommodation step; Nyborg & Liljas, 1998; Stark et al., 1997). In the eukaryotic system, the binding of aminoacyl tRNA proceeds in a similar way with EF-1α (corresponding to EF-Tu). Because both the prokaryotic EF-Tu and the eukaryotic EF-1α bind GDP with high affinity, an additional elongation factor, EF-Ts in prokaryotes and EF-1βγ in eukaryotes, helps to regenerate the GTP form of these factors.

The next step is the peptide bond formation. The peptidyl transferase activity is an inherent property of the ribosomes. Peptide bond formation is catalyzed by the large ribosomal subunit (Green & Noller, 1997; Maden, Traut, & Monro, 1968; Nierhaus, Stuhrmann, & Svergun, 1998). The peptidyl-transferase is located at the interface side of the subunit below the central protuberance of the 50S subunit. In vitro ribosome reconstitution experiments and the finding that the peptidyl transferase activity of *Thermus aquaticus* ribosomes is very resistant to protein extraction procedures point to the ribosomal proteins L2, L3, and the 23S rRNA as prime candidates for exerting the activity.

The next step is translocation; but before a discussion of translocation, the two models of the ribosomal tRNA binding site must be introduced. They are the hybrid site (Moazed & Noller, 1989) and the allosteric α-ε–site models (Burkhardt, Junemann, Spahn, & Nierhaus, 1998; Czworkowski & Moore, 1996; Dabrowski, Spahn, Schafer, Patzke, & Nierhaus, 1998; Green & Noller, 1997; Hershey, 1991; Merrick, 1992; Nierhaus, 1990; Nierhaus et al., 1998; Spahn & Nierhaus, 1998; Wilson & Noller, 1998).

In the hybrid site model, the main feature is that one portion of tRNA (3′ end) bound to the large subunit moves independently of the other portion (anticodon part) during peptide chain elongation. Loading of the aminoacyl-tRNA occurs in two well defined steps: In the first step, the aminoacyl-tRNA occupies only the small subunit portion of the A-site; the second step leads to the full occupation of the A-site. Before peptidyl transfer, the peptidyl-tRNA is in the P-site and the aminoacyl tRNA is in the A-site. After the peptidyl transfer (peptide bond synthesis), the peptidyl-tRNA is bound to the A-site of the 30S subunit at the anticodon portion while the acceptor portion of the peptidyl-tRNA with peptide group is bound to the P-site of the large subunit. At the same time, the anticodon portion of the deacylated tRNA (formed as a result of the peptide bond formation) remains at the P-site of the 30S subunit, while the CCA end (the acceptor end) of the tRNA moves to the E-site of the large subunit. Translocation moves the anticodon portion of the deacylated tRNA, together with the mRNA, to the E-site so that the deacylated tRNA fully occupies the E-site. On the other hand, the anticodon portion of the newly elongated peptidyl-tRNA moves, together with the mRNA, to the P-site of the 30S subunit. Thus, the peptidyl-tRNA is now fully situated in the P-site.

The allosteric α-ε model stems from the finding that the ribosomal binding domains of the A-site and of the P-site–bound tRNAs in the pretranslocation state ribosome do not change significantly when these tRNAs are translocated to the P- and E-sites respectively. This suggests that the microenvironment for the tRNAs remains very similar in both states, although there are considerable conformational changes in the ribosome itself. Therefore, the ribosome behaves as if it had a movable block preserving the contact sites for the tRNAs during translocation. The α part of the ribosome preferentially binds an acylated tRNA (aminoacyl or peptidyl tRNA) and covers the A- or P-site. The ε part of the ribosome preferentially binds a decylated tRNA and covers the P- or E-site. At the pretranslocation step, the α part is found only at the A-site; after translocation, the ε part is located exclusively at the E-site. In the posttranslocational state, two high-affinity sites (P and E) exist. It is known that aminoacyl tRNA can bind to the posttranslocational state ribosomes (Triana-Alonso, Chakraburtty, & Nierhaus, 1995) at the A-site. Therefore, the α-ε model postulates the third nonmovable decoding site, ∂. The affinity of the ∂-site is increased when the E-site is emptied due to the allosteric effect of the E-site on the affinity and fidelity of the A-site. The ∂-site is separated from the α-ε domain in the post-state but overlaps with the α domain at the prestate.

Translocation is the movement of the mRNA, tRNA, and ribosome complex by one codon length toward the 3′ end for about 12Å (Wadzack et al., 1997). Two tRNAs are relocated from the A- and P-sites to the P- and E-sites, respectively. The role of EF-G·GTP (eEF-2·GTP in eukaryotes) in this process is mainly to reduce the activation energy barrier between the pre- and the posttranslocational states, which is about 90 kJ/mol under physiological conditions (Schilling-Bartetzko & Nierhaus, 1992). In support of this concept is the fact that in the absence of the elongation factors, translocation is still possible at a reduced speed (Bergemann & Nierhaus, 1983; Schilling-Bartetzko et al., 1992). During the translocation step, the GTP of the elongation factor is hydrolyzed. The EF-G·GDP (eEF-2·GDP in eukaryotes) complex loses its affinity for the ribosome and is released. A striking similarity in the overall shape of the EF-G·GDP (Czworkowski, Wang, Steitz, & Moore, 1994) and the aminoacyl-tRNA·EF-Tu·GTP (Nissen et al., 1995) complexes were found recently. This leads to the speculation that the two macromolecules may share common ribosomal structures for their binding and some kind of common mechanism in their function (Wilson & Noller, 1998).

The elongation cycle is the most energy-requiring process in protein biosynthesis. It essentially takes two high-energy phosphates brought about by elongation factor·GTP complexes and two high-energy phosphates used to generate each aminoacyl-tRNA (ATP + AA + tRNA $\rightarrow$ AMP + PP_i + AA-tRNA). Thus, the formation of each peptide bond costs four high-energy phosphates for the cell.

Translation Termination

When the prokaryotic ribosomes engaged in the peptide chain elongation come to the end of the open reading frame, the termination codon, UAA, UAG, or UGA, is placed in the A-site (acceptor site) of the ribosomes. The release of completed chain takes place at this point with the help of certain factors. With most of the prokaryotes, except for *M. genitalium,* the smallest free-living organism, three soluble factors RFs (release factors) 1, 2, and 3 are involved. RF1 functions with UAA and UAG, while RF2 functions with UAA and UGA (Scolnick, Tompkins, Caskey, & Nirenberg, 1968). Regions in helix 34 and 44 of the 16S RNA (Brown & Tate, 1994; Goringer, Hijazi, Murgola, & Dahlberg, 1991) have been implicated in the recognition of the stop codon. RF1 and RF2 are composed of two domains, one responsible for recognition of the stop codon and the other responsible for hydrolysis of the ester linkage between 3′ OH of tRNA and COOH of amino acid (Brown & Tate, 1994; Moffat & Tate, 1994). The function of RF3 is to promote the recycling of RF1 (Freistroffer et al., 1997; Grentzmann, 1998). As for the relationship between RF2 and RF3, RF3 either stimulates recycling of RF2 (Freistroffer et al., 1997) or simply promotes the binding of RF2 to the termination complex (Grentzmann et al., 1998). The differential effect of RF3 on RF1 and RF2 is supported by the in vivo experiment in which RF3 was shown to act preferentially on RF2 (Grentzmann et al., 1995). During the action of RF3 in vitro, GTP is required (Grentzmann et al., 1998); this is understandable because RF3 has the GTPase motif (Grentzmann et al., 1994) and ribosome-dependent GTPase activity (Grentzmann et al., 1998).

The process of the completed peptide chain release in eukaryotes is similar but somewhat different. Only two factors, eRF1 and eRF3, are involved. eRF1 functions for recognition of all three termination codons (Frolova et al., 1994), and eRF3 functions as GTPase only in the presence of eRF1 and ribosomes (Frolova et al., 1996). ERF3 is essential for cell survival (Ter-Avanesyan et al., 1993). The human eRF3 is 138 amino acids long (Jean-Jean, LeGoff, & Philippe, et al., 1996) and therefore much shorter than prokaryotic RF3. In yeast eRF3 was first recognized as SUP35 (Kushnirov et al., 1988; Stansfield & Tuite, 1994), the omnipotent suppressor if damaged by mutation. In a similar manner, the yeast eRF1 was first recognized as SUP45 (Stansfield et al., 1995), which was later identified as RF1 by sequence homology with mammalian RF1 (Frolova et al., 1994).

eRF3 of yeast (Sup35 protein) is capable of propagating a specific conformation that gives rise to the [psi+] nonsense suppressor determinant (Wickner, 1994). This is due to the fact that eRF3 of yeast with [psi+] phenotype has prion-like characteristics. Sup35 protein (yeast eRF3) molecules interact with each other through their N-terminal domain in [psi+] but not in [psi–] cells (Patino, Liu, Glover, & Lindquist, 1996; Paushkin, Kushnirov, Smirnov, & Ter-Avanesyan, 1996). Thus, cells containing this form of eRF3 (Sup35p) show a depletion in the levels of soluble functional eRF3 that is sequestered in high–molecular weight, prion-like fibers. Though isogenic [psi+] and [psi–] strains show no difference in growth rates under normal laboratory conditions, [psi+] strains exhibit enhanced tolerance to heat and chemical stress, compared to [psi–] strains. Thus, the prion-like determinant [psi+] is able to regulate translation termination efficiency in response to environmental stress.

Ribosome Recycling

The termination step described in the preceding section leaves behind the ribosomal posttermination complex; the next step is disassembly of that complex. In *E. coli,* this process is catalyzed by two factors: elongation factor G (EF-G; Hirashima & Kaji, 1972, 1973) or RF3 (Grentzmann et al., 1998) and ribosome recycling factor (RRF, originally called ribosome releasing factor; Janosi, Shimizu, & Kaji, 1994). In addition to disassembly of the posttermination complex, RRF appears to help maintain translational fidelity during chain elongation (Janosi, Ricker, & Kaji, 1996). Discovered in 1970 (Hirashima & Kaji, 1970), RRF is present in every organism (Janosi, Hara, Zhang, & Kaji, 1996; Janosi, Ricker, & Kaji, 1996) and is essential (Janosi et al., 1994) for maintenance of life in all bacteria except archaebacteria (*Archaea:* Bult et al., 1996). *M. genitalium,* being the smallest free-living organism, with only 500 genes, manages without RF2 and RF3 (Fraser et al., 1995), but it retains RRF, suggesting the importance of RRF.

When RRF was omitted in the in vitro translation system, ribosomes remaining on the mRNA reinitiated unscheduled translation from the triplet next to the termination codon (Ryoji, Berland, & Kaji, 1981). Upon inactivation of RRF in vivo, a ribosome may frame-shift into all possible frames and may slide downstream as many as 10 to 45 nucleotides before it randomly starts translation of the mRNA (Janosi et al., 1998).

Eukaryotic RRF is an organelle protein (e.g., in chloroplasts or mitochondria) that is involved in protein synthesis within the organelles in much the same way bacterial RRF functions (Rolland et al., 1999). This conclusion is further supported by the fact that translation in chloroplasts is similar to that in prokaryotes (Danon, 1997; Harris, Boynton, & Gillham, 1994) and the fact that yeast (Kanai et al., 1998) and human (Zhang & Spremulli, 1998) RRF may be a mitochondrial protein. It should be noted that none of the Archeons contains RRF. Archeons, in between eukaroytes and prokaryotes in their phylogenetic development, have a protein synthesis system similar to that of eukaryotic cytoplasm. This suggests that the eukaryotic homologues of RRF are involved in the organelle protein synthesis but not in the cytoplasmic protein synthesis. This raises a question as to the factors responsible for the disassembly of the post-termination complex involved in the cytoplasmic protein synthesis in eukaryotes. This is an important question, which should be answered in near future. Four review articles on RRF have been published (Janosi, Hara, Zhang, & Kaji, 1996; Janosi, Ricker, & Kaji, 1996; Kaji & Hirokawa, 1999; Kaji, Teyssier, & Hirokawa, 1998).

REFERENCES

Agrawal, R. K., & Frank, J. (1999). Structural studies of the translational apparatus. *Current Opinion in Structural Biology, 9,* 215–221.

Ban, N., Freeborn, B., Nissen, P., Penczek, P., Grassucci, R. A.,

Sweet, R., Frank, J., Moore, P. B., & Steitz, T. A. (1998). A 9 Å resolution X-ray crystallographic map of the large ribosomal subunit. *Cell, 93,* 1105–1115.

Bergemann, K., & Nierhaus, K. H. (1983). Spontaneous, elongation factor G independent translocation of *Escherichia coli* ribosomes. *Journal of Biological Chemistry, 258,* 15105–15113.

Bernstein, J., Shefler, I., & Elroy-Stein, O. (1995). The translational repression mediated by the platelet-derived growth factor 2/c-sis mRNA leader is relieved during megakaryocytic differentiation. *Journal of Biological Chemistry, 270,* 10559–10565.

Brock, S., Szkaradkiewicz, K., & Sprinzl, M. (1998). Initiation factors of protein biosynthesis in bacteria and their structural relationship to elongation and termination factors. *Molecular Microbiology, 29,* 409–417.

Brown, C. M., & Tate, W. P. (1994). Direct recognition of mRNA stop signals by *Escherichia coli* polypeptide chain release factor two. *Journal of Biological Chemistry, 269,* 33164–33170.

Bult, C. J., White, O., Olsen, G. J., Zhou, L., Fleischmann, R. D., Sutton, G. G., et al. (1996). Complete genome sequence of the methanogenic archaeon, *Methanococcus jannaschii. Science, 273,* 1058–1073.

Burkhardt, N., Junemann, R., Spahn, C. M. T., & Nierhaus, K. H. (1998). Ribosomal tRNA binding sites: Three-site models of translation. *Critical Reviews in Biochemistry and Molecular Biology, 33,* 95–149.

Chakravarti, D., & Maitra, U. (1993). Eukaryotic translation initiation factor 5 from *Saccharomyces cerevisiae:* Cloning, characterization, and expression of the gene encoding the 45,346-Da protein. *Journal of Biological Chemistry, 268,* 10524–10533.

Chen, C.-Y., & Sarnow, P. (1995). Initiation of protein synthesis by the eukaryotic translational apparatus on circular RNAs. *Science, 268,* 415–417.

Czworkowski, J., & Moore, P. B. (1996). The elongation phase of protein synthesis. *Progress in Nucleic Acids Research and Molecular Biology, 54,* 293–332.

Czworkowski, J., Wang, J., Steitz, T. A., & Moore, P. B. (1994). The crystal structure of elongation factor G complexed with GDP, at 2.7 Å resolution. *EMBO Journal, 13,* 3661–3668.

Dabrowski, M., Spahn, C. M. T., Schafer, M. A., Patzke, S., & Nierhaus, K. H. (1998). Protection patterns of tRNAs do not change during ribosomal translocation. *Journal of Biological Chemistry, 273,* 32793–32800.

Danon, A. (1997). Translational regulation in the chloroplast. *Plant Physiology, 115,* 1293–1298.

Das, K., Chevesich, J., & Maitra, U. (1993). Molecular cloning and expression of cDNA for mammalian translation initiation factor 5. *Proceedings of the National Academy of Sciences, USA, 90,* 3058–3062.

Frank, J. (1997). The ribosome at higher resolution: The donut takes shape. *Current Opinion in Structural Biology, 7,* 266–272.

Fraser, C. M., Gocayne, J. D., White, O., Adams, M. D., Clayton, R. A., Fleischmann, R. D., et al. (1995). The minimal gene complement of *Mycoplasma genitalium. Science, 270,* 397–403.

Freistroffer, D. V., Pavlov, M. Y., MacDougall, J., Buckingham, R. H., & Ehrenberg, M. (1997). Release factor RF3 in *E. coli* accelerates the dissociation of release factors RF1 and RF2 from the ribosome in a GTP-dependent manner. *EMBO Journal, 16,* 4126–4133.

Frolova, L., LeGoff, X., Rasmussen, H. H., Cheperegin, S., Drugeon, G., Kress, M., et al. (1994). A highly conserved eukaryotic protein family possessing properties of polypeptide chain release factor. *Nature, 372,* 701–703.

Frolova, L., LeGoff, X., Zhouravleva, G., Davydova, E., Philippe, M., & Kisselev, L. (1996). Eukaryotic polypeptide chain release factor eRF3 is an eRF1- and ribosome-dependent guanosine triphosphatase. *RNA, 2,* 334–341.

Gan, W., & Rhoads, R. E. (1996). Internal initiation of translation directed by the 5′-untranslated region of the mRNA for eIF4G, a factor involved in the picornavirus-induced switch from cap-dependent to internal initiation. *Journal of Biological Chemistry, 271,* 623–626.

Gaspar, N. J., Kinzy, T. G., Scherer, B. J., Humbelin, M., Hershey, J. W., & Merrick, W. C. (1994). Translation initiation factor eIF-2: Cloning and expression of the human cDNA encoding the gamma-subunit. *Journal of Biological Chemistry, 269,* 3415–3422.

Goringer, H. U., Hijazi, K. A., Murgola, E. J., & Dahlberg, A. E. (1991). Mutations in 16S rRNA that affect UGA (stop codon)-directed translation termination. *Proceedings of the National Academy of Sciences, USA, 88,* 6603–6607.

Gray, N. K., & Wickens, M. (1998). Control of translation initiation in animals. *Annual Review of Cellular Development and Biology, 14,* 399–458.

Green, R., & Noller, H. F. (1997). Ribosomes and translation. *Annual Review of Biochemistry, 66,* 679–716.

Grentzmann, G., Brechemier-Baey, D., Heurgué, V., Mora, L., & Buckingham, R. H. (1994). Localization and characterization of the gene encoding release factor RF3 in *Escherichia coli. Proceedings of the National Academy of Sciences, USA, 91,* 5848–5852.

Grentzmann, G., Brechemier-Baey, D., Heurgué-Hamard, V., & Buckingham, R. H. (1995). Function of polypeptide chain release factor RF-3 in *Escherichia coli:* RF-3 action in termination is predominantly at UGA-containing stop signals. *Journal of Biological Chemistry, 270,* 10595–10600.

Grentzmann, G., Kelly, P. J., Laalami, S., Shuda, M., Firpo, M. A., Cenatiempo, Y., & Kaji, A. (1998). Release factor RF-3 GTPase activity acts in disassembly of the ribosome termination complex. *RNA, 4,* 973–983.

Gualerzi, C. O., & Pon, C. L. (1990). Initiation of mRNA translation in prokaryotes. *Biochemistry, 29,* 5881–5889.

Harris, E. H., Boynton, J. E., & Gillham, N. W. (1994). Chloroplast ribosomes and protein synthesis. *Microbiology Review, 58,* 700–754.

Hartz, D., McPheeters, D. S., & Gold, L. (1989). Selection of the initiator t-RNA by *Escherichia coli* initiation-factors. *Genes and Development, 3,* 1899–1912.

Hentze, M. W. (1997). eIF4G: A multipurpose ribosome adapter? *Science, 275,* 500–501.

Hershey, J. W. B. (1991). Translational control in mammalian cells. *Annual Review of Biochemistry, 60,* 717–755.

Hinnebush, A. G. (1996). Translational control of GCN4: Gene specific regulation by phosphorylation of eIF2. In J. W. B. Hershey, M. B. Mathews, & N. Sonenberg (Eds.), *Translational control* (pp. 199–244). Cold Spring Harbor, NY: Cold Spring Harbor Laboratory Press.

Hirashima, A., & Kaji, A. (1970). Factor dependent breakdown of polysomes. *Biochemistry and Biophysics Research Communications, 41,* 877–883.

Hirashima, A., & Kaji, A. (1972). Purification and properties of ribosome-releasing factor. *Biochemistry, 11,* 4037–4044.

Hirashima, A., & Kaji, A. (1973). Role of elongation factor G and a protein factor on the release of ribosomes from messenger ribonucleic acid. *Journal of Biological Chemistry, 248,* 7580–7587.

Hui, A., & De Boer, H. A. (1987). Specialized ribosome system: Preferential translation of a single mRNA species by a subpopulation of mutated ribosomes in *Escherichia coli. Proceedings of the National Academy of Sciences, USA, 84,* 4762–4766.

Jackson, R. J., & Kaminski, A. (1995). Internal initiation of translation in eukaryotes: The picornavirus paradigm and beyond. *RNA, 1,* 985–1000.

Jackson, R. J., & Wickens, M. (1997). Translational controls impinging on the 5′-untranslated region and initiation factor proteins. *Current Opinion in Genetic Development, 7,* 233–241.

Jacob, W. F., Santer, M., & Dahlberg, A. E. (1987). A single base change in the Shine-Dalgarno region of 16S rRNA of *Escherichia coli* affects translation of many proteins. *Proceedings of the National Academy of Sciences, USA, 84,* 4757–4761.

Janosi, L., Hara, H., Zhang, S., & Kaji, A. (1996). Ribosome recycling by ribosome recycling factor (RRF): An important but overlooked step of protein biosynthesis. *Advances in Biophysics, 32,* 121–201.

Janosi, L., Mottagui-Tabar, S., Isaksson, L. A., Sekine, Y., Ohtsubo, E., Zhang, S., et al. (1998). Evidence for *in vivo* ribosome recycling, the fourth step in protein biosynthesis. *EMBO Journal, 17,* 1141–1151.

Janosi, L., Ricker, R., & Kaji, A. (1996). Dual functions of ribosome recycling factor in protein biosynthesis: Disassembling the termination complex and preventing translational errors. *Biochimie, 78,* 959–969.

Janosi, L., Shimizu, I., & Kaji, A. (1994). Ribosome recycling factor (ribosome releasing factor) is essential for bacterial growth. *Proceedings of the National Academy of Sciences, USA, 91,* 4249–4253.

Jean-Jean, O., LeGoff, X., & Philippe, M. (1996). Is there a human [psi]? *Comptes Rendus de l'Academie des Sciences, 319,* 487–492.

Kaji, A., & Hirokawa, G. (1999). *The ribosome: Structure, function antibiotics and cellular interactions: Disassembly of post termination complex by RRF (ribosome recycling factor), a possible new target for antimicrobial agents.* Washington, DC: American Society of Microbiology.

Kaji, A., Teyssier, E., & Hirokawa, G. (1998). Disassembly of the post-termination complex and reduction of translational error by ribosome recycling factor (RRF): A possible new target for antibacterial agents. *Biochemical and Biophysical Research Communications, 250,* 1–4.

Kanai, T., Takeshita, S., Atomi, H., Umemura, K., Ueda, M., & Tanaka, A. (1998). A regulatory factor, Fel1p, involved in depression of the isocitrate lyase gene in *Saccharomyces cerevisiae:* A possible mitochondrial protein necessary for protein synthesis in mitochondria. *European Journal of Biochemistry, 256,* 212–220.

Kozak, M. (1978). How do eukaryotic ribosomes select initiation regions in messenger RNA? *Cell, 15,* 1109–1123.

Kozak, M. (1989). Context effects and inefficient initiation at non-AUG codons in eucaryotic cell-free translation systems. *Molecular and Cellular Biology, 9,* 5073–5080.

Kozak, M. (1994). Determinants of translational fidelity and efficiency in vertebrate mRNAs. *Biochimie, 76,* 815–821.

Krab, I. M., & Parmeggiani, A. (1998). EF-Tu, a GTPase odyssey. *Biochimica et Biophysica Acta, 1443,* 1–22.

Kushnirov, V. V., Ter-Avanesyan, M. D., Telckov, M. V., Surguchov, A. P., Smirnov, V. N., & Inge-Vechtomov, S. G. (1988). Nucleotide sequence of the *SUP2 (SUP35)* gene of *Saccharomyces cerevisiae. Gene, 66,* 45–54.

Lamphear, B. J., Kirchweger, R., Skern, T., & Rhoads, R. E. (1995). Mapping of functional domains in eukaryotic protein synthesis initiation factor 4G (eIF4G) with picornaviral proteases: Implications for cap-dependent and cap-independent translational initiation. *Journal of Biological Chemistry, 270,* 21975–21983.

Lawson, T. G., Lee, K. A., Maimone, M. M., Abramson, R. D., Dever, T. E., Merrick, W. C., & Thach, R. E. (1989). Dissociation of double-stranded polynucleotide helical structures by eukaryotic initiation factors, as revealed by a novel assay. *Biochemistry, 28,* 4729–4734.

Maden, B. E. H., Traut, R. R., & Monro, R. E. (1968). Ribosome-catalysed peptidyl transfer: The plophenylalanine system. *Journal of Molecular Biology, 35,* 333–345.

Mader, S., Lee, H., Pause, A., & Sonenberg, N. (1995). The translation initiation factor eIF-4E binds to a common motif shared by the translation factor eIF-4 gamma and the translational repressors 4E-binding proteins. *Molecular and Cellular Biology, 15,* 4990–4997.

McCutcheon, J. P., Agrawal, R. K., Philips, S. M., Grassucci, R. A., Gerchman, S. E., Clemons, W. M., Jr., et al. (1999). Location of translational initiation factor IF3 on the small ribosomal subunit. *Proceedings of the National Academy of Sciences, USA, 96,* 4301–4306.

Merrick, W. (1992). Mechanism and regulation of eukaryotic protein synthesis. *Microbiology Review, 56,* 291–315.

Merrick, W. C., & Hershey, J. W. B. (1996). The pathway and mechanism of eukaryotic protein synthesis. In J. W. B. Hershey, M. B. Mathews, & N. Sonenberg (Eds.), *Translational control* (pp. 31–69). Cold Spring Harbor, NY: Cold Spring Harbor Laboratory Press.

Moazed, D., & Noller, H. F. (1989). Intermediate states in the movement of transfer RNA in the ribosome. *Nature, 342,* 142–148.

Moazed, D., Samaha, R. R., Gualerzi, C., & Noller, H. F. (1995). Specific protection of 16S rRNA by translational initiation factors. *Journal of Molecular Biology, 248,* 207–210.

Moffat, J. G., & Tate, W. P. (1994). A single proteolytic cleavage in release factor 2 stabilizes ribosome binding and abolishes peptidyl-tRNA hydrolysis activity. *Journal of Biological Chemistry, 269,* 18899–18903.

Moore, P. B. (1997). Ribosomes: Protein synthesis in slow motion. *Current Biology, 7,* R179–R181.

Moore, P. B. (1998). The three-dimensional structure of the ribosome and its components. *Annual Review of Biophysics and Biomolecular Structure, 27,* 35–58.

Naranda, T., MacMillan, S. E., Donahue, T. F., & Hershey, J. W. (1996). SUI1/p16 is required for the activity of eukaryotic translation initiation Factor 3 in *Saccharomyces cerevisiae. Molecular and Cellular Biology, 16,* 2307–2313.

Nierhaus, K. H. (1990). The allosteric three-site model for the ribosomal elongation cycle: Features and future. *Biochemistry, 29,* 4997–5008.

Nierhaus, K. H., Stuhrmann, H. B., & Svergun, D. (1998). The ribosomal elongation cycle and movement of tRNAs across the ribosome. *Progress in Nucleic Acids Research and Molecular Biology, 59,* 177–204.

Nissen, P., Kjeldgaard, M., Thirup, S., Polekhina, G., Reshetnikova, L., Clark, B. F. C., & Nyborg, J. (1995). Crystal structure of the ternary complex of Phe-tRNA^{Phe}, EF-Tu and a GTP analog. *Science, 270,* 1464–1472.

Nyborg, J., & Liljas, A. (1998). Protein biosynthesis: Structural studies of the elongation cycle. *FEBS Letters, 430,* 95–99.

Pain, V. M. (1996). Initiation of protein synthesis in eukaryotic cells. *European Journal of Biochemistry, 236,* 747–771.

Pape, T., Wintermeyer, W., & Rodnina, M. V. (1998). Complete kinetic mechanism of elongation factor Tu-dependent binding of aminoacyl-tRNA to the A-site of the *E. coli* ribosome. *EMBO Journal, 17,* 7490–7497.

Patino, M. M., Liu, J. J., Glover, J. R., & Lindquist, S. (1996). Support for the prion hypothesis for inheritance of a phenotypic trait in yeast. *Science, 273,* 622–626.

Paushkin, S. V., Kushnirov, V. V., Smirnov, V. N., & Ter-Avanesyan, M. D. (1996). Propagation of the yeast prion-like [psi(+)] determinant is mediated by oligomerization of the *SUP35*-encoded polypeptide chain release factor. *EMBO Journal, 15,* 3127–3134.

Pestova, T. V., Borukhov, S. I., & Hellen, C. U. (1998). Eukaryotic ribosomes require initiation factors 1 and 1A to locate initiation codons. *Nature, 394,* 854–859.

Pestova, T. V., Shatsky, I. N., Fletcher, S. P., Jackson, R. J., & Hellen, C. U. (1998). A prokaryotic-like mode of cytoplasmic eukaryotic ribosome binding to the initiation codon during internal translation initiation of hepatitis C and classical swine fever virus RNAs. *Genes and Development, 12,* 67–83.

Petersen, H. U., Roll, T., Grunberg-Manago, M., & Clark, B. F. (1979). Specific interaction of initiation factor IF2 of *E. coli* with formylmethionyl-tRNA f Met. *Biochemical and Biophysical Research Communications, 91,* 1068–1074.

RajBhandary, U. L., & Chow, C. M. (1995). Initiator tRNAs and initiation of protein synthesis. In D. Soll & U. RajBhandary (Eds.), *tRNA: Structure, biosynthesis and function* (pp. 511–527). Washington, DC: American Society of Microbiology.

Rodnina, M. V., Fricke, R., Kuhn, L., & Wintermeyer, W. (1995). Codon-dependent conformational change of elongation factor TU preceding GTP hydrolysis on the ribosome. *EMBO Journal, 14,* 2613–2619.

Rodnina, M. V., Pape, T., Fricke, R., Kuhn, L., & Wintermeyer, W. (1996). Initial binding of the elongation factor Tu·GTP·aminoacyl-tRNA complex preceding codon recognition on the ribosome. *Journal of Biological Chemistry, 271,* 646–652.

Rodnina, M. V., Pape, T., Fricke, R., & Wintermeyer, W. (1995). Elongation factor Tu, a GTPase triggered by codon recognition on the ribosome: Mechanism and GTP consumption. *Biochemistry & Cell Biology, 73,* 1221–1227.

Rolland, N., Janosi, L., Block, M. A., Shuda, A., Teyssier, E., Miege, C., Cheniclet, C., Carde, J.-P., Kaji, A., & Joyard, J. (1999). Plant ribosome recycling factor homologue is a chloroplastic protein and is bactericidal in *Escherichia coli* carrying temperature-sensitive ribosome recycling factor. *Proceedings of the National Academy of Sciences, USA, 96,* 5464–5469.

Rozen, F., Edery, I., Meerovitch, K., Dever, T. E., Merrick, W. C., & Sonenberg, N. (1990). Bidirectional RNA helicase activity of eukaryotic translation initiation factors 4A and 4F. *Molecular and Cellular Biology, 10,* 1134–1144.

Ryoji, M., Berland, R., & Kaji, A. (1981). Reinitiation of translation from the triplet next to the amber termination codon in the absence of ribosome-releasing factor. *Proceedings of the National Academy of Sciences, USA, 78,* 5973–5977.

Schilling-Bartetzko, S., Bartetzko, A., & Nierhaus, K. H. (1992). Kinetic and thermodynamic parameters for tRNA binding to the ribosome and for the translocation reaction. *Journal of Biological Chemistry, 267,* 4703–4712.

Scolnick, E., Tompkins, R., Caskey, T., & Nirenberg, M. (1968). Release factors differing in specificity for terminator codons. *Proceedings of the National Academy of Sciences, USA, 61,* 768–774.

Spahn, C. M. T., & Nierhaus, K. H. (1998). Models of the elongation cycle: An evaluation. *Biological Chemistry, 379,* 753–772.

Sprengart, M. L., & Porter, A. G. (1997). Functional importance of RNA interactions in selection of translation initiation codons. *Molecular Microbiology, 24,* 19–28.

Stansfield, I., & Tuite, M. F. (1994). Polypeptide chain termination in *Saccharomyces cerevisiae. Current Genetics, 25,* 385–395.

Stansfield, I., Jones, K. M., Kushnirov, V. V., Dagkesamanskaya, A. R., Poznyakovski, A. I., Paushkin, S. V., et al. (1995). The products of the *SUP45* (eRF1) and *SUP35* genes interact to mediate translation termination in *Saccharomyces cerevisiae. EMBO Journal, 14,* 4365–4373.

Stark, H., Rodnina, M. V., Rinke-Appel, J., Brimacombe, R., Wintermeyer, W., & van Heel, M. (1997). Visualization of elongation factor Tu on the *Escherichia coli* ribosome. *Nature, 389,* 403–406.

Ter-Avanesyan, M. D., Kushnirov, V. V., Dagkesamanskaya, A. R., Didichenko, S. A., Chernoff, Y. O., Inge-Vechtomov, S. G., et al. (1993). Deletion analysis of the *SUP35* gene of the yeast *Saccharomyces cerevisiae* reveals two nonoverlapping functional regions in the encoded protein. *Molecular Microbiology, 7,* 683–692.

Triana-Alonso, F. J., Chakraburtty, K., & Nierhaus, K. H. (1995). The elongation factor 3 unique in higher fungi and essential for protein biosynthesis is an E-site factor. *Journal of Biological Chemistry, 270,* 20473–20478.

Wadzack, J., Burkhardt, N., Junemann, R., Diedrich, G., Nierhaus, K. H., Frank, J., et al. (1997). Direct localization of the tRNAs within the elongating ribosome by means of neutron scattering (proton-spin contrast-variation). *Journal of Molecular Biology, 266,* 343–356.

Wakao, H., Romby, P., Westhof, E., Laalami, S., Grunberg-Manago, M., Ebel, J. P., et al. (1989). The solution structure of the *Escherichia coli* initiator tRNA and its interactions with initiation factor 2 and the ribosomal 30S subunit. *Journal of Biological Chemistry, 264,* 20363–20371.

Wickner, R. B. (1994). [URE3] as an altered Ure2 protein: Evidence for a prion analog in *Saccharomyces cerevisiae. Science, 264,* 566–569.

Wilson, K. S., & Noller, H. F. (1998). Molecular movement inside the translational engine. *Cell, 92,* 337–349.

Wool, I. G., Chan, Y.-L., & Gluck, A. (1996). Mammalian ribosomes: The structure and the evolution of the proteins. In J. W. B. Hershey, M. B. Mathews, & N. Sonenberg (Eds.), *Translational control* (pp. 685–711). Cold Spring Harbor: Cold Spring Harbor Laboratory Press.

Wu, X. Q., Iyengar, P., & RajBhandary, U. L. (1996). Ribosome-initiator tRNA complex as an intermediate in translation intiation in *Escherichia coli* revealed by use of mutant initiator tRNAs and specialized ribosomes. *EMBO Journal, 15,* 4734–4739.

Wu, X. Q., & RajBhandary, U. L. (1997). Effect of the amino acid attached to *Escherichia coli* initiator tRNA on its affinity for the initiation factor IF2 and on the IF2 dependence of its binding to the ribosome. *Journal of Biological Chemistry, 272,* 1891–1895.

Yonath, A., & Franceschi, F. (1998). Functional universality and evolutionary diversity: Insights from the structure of the ribosome. *Structure, 6,* 679–684.

Zhang, Y., & Spremulli, L. L. (1998). Identification and cloning of human mitochondrial translational release factor 1 and the ribosome recycling factor. *Biochimica Et Biophysica Acta, 1443,* 245–250.

Akira Kaji
University of Pennsylvania

L. Janosi
Exponential Biotherapies, Inc.

RIGHT TO REFUSE TREATMENT

Past failures and current successes in the area of treatment have led to a paradoxical state of affairs: We involuntarily commit individuals for treatment, yet these very individuals frequently assert a right to refuse treatment.

Past failures regarding the hospitalized and involuntary patient have been well documented. Hospitalization per se, the therapeutic milieu of the hospital, and traditional talk therapy have not led to recovery, cure, and discharge rates. The patient rights movement, the right to treatment, and the right to treatment in the least restrictive setting have been endorsed by several courts and legislatures.

The legal roots of such a right to refuse derives from both common law, where, under tort law, informed consent is needed before medical or psychological treatments are initiated, and from constitutional law. Constitutionally, the first, fourth, eighth, and fourteenth amendments have been offered to establish such grounds.

The implications and questions, as well as dilemmas, for the continued treatment of involuntary patients are many, and the reactions of therapists are being heard. For one, is informed consent possible? Can an involuntarily hospitalized patient, who may have been institutionalized for many years, give competent, knowing, and voluntary consent? Might not the therapist be a double agent—also concerned with ward management or invested in a research project, as well as in the welfare of the patient? Are therapists not in a double bind—faced with suits for not treating and suits for treating? Will patients now be entrapped by both their psychoses and their rights? Will this lead to a challenge to psychology to develop nonmedical treatments that are both effective and consent worthy? At this stage, the questions and issues have surfaced far faster than the solutions.

Norman J. Finkel
Georgetown University

See also: **Psychology and the Law; Right to Treatment**

RIGHT TO TREATMENT

In 1960 Morton Birnbaum, a physician and lawyer, proposed "The Right to Treatment." Although the Constitution does not speak directly about such a right or mention hospitalization, involuntary commitment, or treatment, Birnbaum reasoned that the eighth and fourteenth amendments, those dealing with cruel and unusual punishment and deprivation of liberty without due process and equal protection, could be construed to imply such a right. The issue is this: When states commit individuals to psychiatric hospitals on *parens patriae* grounds (i.e., because they are mentally ill and in need of treatment) or because they are incompetent to stand trial, is there not also the promise and obligation to provide treatment?

The first test case was *Rouse v. Cameron,* in which Judge Bazelon argued that such a right does exist. More recent cases bring to light the many complicated questions, issues, and implications facing the courts, communities, patients, mental health practitioners, legal advocates, and other branches of government.

The 1970s brought the revolution and litigation of patients' rights to the foreground; along with it have come a fresh examination of involuntary commitment procedures and hospital practices and the knowledge that our treatments have not fulfilled our promises.

Norman J. Finkel
Georgetown University

See also: **Psychology and the Law; Right to Refuse Treatment**

RIGIDITY

Although the term *rigidity* has no precise definition, one offered by Chown (1959) comes closest to a working definition. Chown stated that rigidity describes behaviors that include the inability to change habits, sets, attitudes, and discriminations. Moreover, it can be said that rigidity is especially apparent when a person's behavior fails to change even though the demands of new situations require different behaviors.

Many terms in psychology refer to rigidity, including perseveration, conservatism, dogmatism, anality, intolerance of ambiguity, and compulsiveness. Terms such as flexibility, lability, tolerance of ambiguity, and, to some degree, creativity have served as labels for tendencies contrasted with rigidity. As Chown stated, these terms have been used rather loosely. Therefore, it is highly unlikely that rigidity is a single psychological construct or personality factor. However, it is valuable to examine some specific subtypes of rigidity in order to seek some common relationships among them.

Rigidity as Perseveration

In the *Abilities of Man,* Spearman (1927/1970) presented a law of inertia that stated that cognitive processes are slow both to start and to finish and then questioned whether there would be individual differences in inertia. Along these lines, Cattell (1935) isolated two factors of trait rigidity: *inertia,* in which the person is unable to switch between two well-established skills, and *dispositional rigidity,* which refers to the inability to apply an old skill to a new but different situation.

In his studies of neurological patients, Goldstein (1934/1959) noted that it was common to see patients who were unable to shift from one task to another. In addition, when faced with difficult tasks involving abstract thought, some patients would blurt out immediate but incorrect answers. In the 1940s, Goldstein and Scheerer (1941) developed a test battery that contained a variety of sorting and classification tasks. They found that individuals who had brain damage could often sort a group of objects according to one classification scheme (e.g., color) but would be unable to shift to another scheme (e.g., shape).

Goldstein believed that under ordinary circumstances, the healthy person functions as a whole system with well-integrated and articulated subsystems. However, with brain damage, the integrity of the system is destroyed, and the person is unable to handle the complexity required by abstract problems. Goldstein stated that the rigid, concrete behavior shown by patients with brain damage was not a simple deficit, but rather was an attempt to reduce complexity and to make a potentially overwhelming situation more manageable. Thus, Goldstein was able to link perseveration, brain injury, and concreteness into one pattern.

Laboratory studies conducted by Luchins (1942) and Maltzman and Morrisett (1953) indicated that when subjects were repeatedly presented with problem-solving tasks that at first had a fixed solution formula, they often rigidly continued to use the same solution formula for subsequent problems, even though these new tasks could be solved in a variety of ways. Although these authors attributed rigidity to task variables, other researchers were inspired to find individual differences in problem-solving perseveration by using these tasks and attempting to find correlations with measures of other ability and personality traits.

Intolerance of Ambiguity

A number of researchers and theoreticians, including T. W. Adorno, Else Frenkel-Brunswik, Milton Rokeach, Erich Fromm, David Shapiro, Stephen Breskin, Louis Primavera, and Bernard Gorman have noted a fairly consistent constellation of traits that includes strict obedience to authority figures, intolerance of opposing opinions, prejudice, a tendency to construct an oversimplified view of the world, a tendency to employ sharply polarized or black-white cognitive constructs, and a cynical view of human nature. Numerous studies have indicated that this constellation is not limited to rigid social and political beliefs alone but extends to many laboratory tasks as well.

The development of such authoritarian and dogmatic personality patterns has been attributed to socialization practices that include blind, unquestioning obedience to parents and other authority figures and discipline practices that emphasize power and coercion, rather than reasoning, induction, and explanations of personal moral choices. Therefore, the rigid person has been constantly exposed to situations that state that there are absolute rules to be followed and that deviations from such rules will be met with severe punishment.

Discussions of rigid, authoritarian, and dogmatic belief systems have been extended to psychopathology. Clinically, highly dogmatic and rigid behaviors can be observed in obsessive-compulsive and paranoid patients. Such patients' thoughts and actions are replete with examples of logical contradictions, rigid and overselective constructions of situations, and complaints of being driven to perform certain actions.

In *Neurotic Styles* (1965) and in *Autonomy and Rigid Character* (1981), Shapiro explored a paradox in these disorders; namely, that although patients claim to be rigidly following and driven by principles seen as alien to their selves, people consciously plan and execute behaviors instrumental in supporting these beliefs. Shapiro reconciled this paradox by noting that the mandated shoulds and oughts are the beliefs of important authority figures. Although the rigid person does not desire to carry out these demands, he or she feels powerless to disobey them. For example, an obsessive patient may know that it is useless to worry but also believes that a display of conscientiousness to others is the proper thing to do. Thus, the person is placed in a conflict between beliefs about his or her own lack of personal efficiency and the presumed power of others over the self.

An Integration of Approaches

How can observations that rigid people display perseveration, concreteness, intolerance of ambiguity, and avowals of authority-centered beliefs be subsumed under a single term? Perhaps an explanation may be found by using Jean Piaget's theory of cognitive development.

Throughout his many writings, Piaget had shown how new cognitive schemes develop through the clash of two opposite adaptive tendencies: assimilation (the tendency to fit new knowledge into existing schemes) and accommodation (the tendency to modify behavior according to the demands of the situation). Either tendency alone could be properly considered to be rigidity. However, through situations in which assimilation is checked by accommodation, and vice versa, new and more flexible equilibrated schemes are formed (Piaget, 1968).

Piaget had shown how early thought is characterized by overassimilation and overaccommodation and cogently demonstrated that young children and adults with mental retardation employ one-dimensional, rigid, "centered" cognitive strategies in comparison with the multidimensional, flexible, "decentered" strategies employed by older children and normal adults. According to Piaget, affective and moral development is inseparable from cognitive development. Therefore, the rigid behaviors found in intellectual tasks have their parallels in the lack of autonomy, the perseveration, and the rigid constructions of personal and interpersonal values found in social behaviors.

It may be that rigidity, in both the intellectual and affective domains, is a manifestation of unbalanced schemes in which either accommodation or assimilation predominates. As many factors, including cognitive immaturity, neurological damage, and authority-oriented child-rearing practices, may hinder the development of adequately equilibrated schemes, rigidity may stem from many different roots.

REFERENCES

Adorno, T. W., Frenkel-Brunswik, E., Levinson, D. J., & Sanford, R. N. (1950). *The authoritarian personality.* New York: Harpers.

Breskin, S. (1968). Measurement of rigidity, a non-verbal test. *Perceptual and Motor Skills, 27,* 1203–1206.

Cattell, R. B. (1935). On the measurement of perseveration. *British Journal of Educational Psychology, 5,* 76–92.

Chown, S. M. (1959). Rigidity: A flexible construct. *Psychological Bulletin, 56,* 195–233.

Fromm, E. (1965). *Escape from freedom.* New York: Avon Books. (Original work published 1941)

Goldstein, K. (1959). *The organism: A holistic approach to biology derived from psychological data in man.* New York: American Book. (Original work published 1934)

Goldstein, K., & Scheerer, M. (1941). Abstract and concrete behavior: An experimental study with special tests. *Psychological Monographs, 53*(2, Whole No. 239).

Gorman, B. S., & Breskin, S. (1969). Non-verbal rigidity, creativity, and problem solving. *Perceptual and Motor Skills, 29,* 715–718.

Luchins, A. S. (1942). Mechanization in problem solving: The effect of *Einstellung. Psychological Monographs, 54*(Whole No. 248).

Maltzman, I., & Morrisett, L., Jr. (1953). Different strengths of set in the solution of anagrams. *Journal of Experimental Psychology, 45,* 351–354.

Piaget, J. (1968). *Six psychological studies.* New York: Vintage.

Piaget, J. (1981). *Intelligence and affectivity: Their relationship during child development.* Palo Alto, CA: Annual Reviews. (Original work published 1953)

Primavera, L. H., & Higgins, M. (1973). Nonverbal rigidity and its relationship to dogmatism and Machiavellianism. *Perceptual and Motor Skills, 36,* 356–358.

Rokeach, M. (1960). *The open and closed mind.* New York: Basic Books.

Shapiro, D. (1965). *Neurotic styles.* New York: Basic Books.

Shapiro, D. (1981). *Autonomy and rigid character.* New York: Basic Books.

Shapiro, D. (1994). Paranoia from a characterological standpoint. In J. M. Oldham & S. Bone (Eds.), *Paranoia: New psychoanalytic perspectives* (pp. 49–57). Madison, CT: International Universities Press.

Spearman, C. E. (1970). *The abilities of man: Their nature and measurement.* New York: AMS Press. (Original work published 1927)

Bernard S. Gorman
Nassau Community College and Hofstra University

See also: **Learned Helplessness; Obsessive-Compulsive Disorders**

RITUAL BEHAVIOR

Ritual is a conventionalized joint activity that is given to ceremony, involves two or more persons, is endowed with special emotion and often sacred meaning, is focused around a clearly defined set of social objects, and when performed, confers upon its participants a special sense of the sacred and the out-of-the-ordinary (Denzin, 1974, p. 272). When a ritual is performed, ritual participants through their actions convey their respect to themselves to "some object of ultimate value . . . or to its stand-in" (Goffman, 1971, p. 62). A ritual consists of interrelated activities and acts, termed *rites,* and is performed within sacred or special interactional situations, termed *ritual settings.* Ritual performances legitimitize the selves of the ritual performers and solidify their standing within a social relationship's or a social order's hierarchy of morality. Ritual may grow out of any sector of group life, including sexual, economic, political, religious, legal, and interpersonal arenas of discourse and interaction (Douglas, 1975, pp. 60–61). Rituals permit few variations and are subject to the pressures of interactional normalization. They have the features of drama and involve the reenactment of cultural and world views held to be salient and central by human groups (Geertz, 1973; Harrison, 1912). Modifying Bateson (1972) slightly, one may say that *ritual* is the name of a frame for action, and within the frame of ritual, individuals act ritualistically.

Durkheim (1912) divided ritual into two categories: positive and negative, or sacred and profane. Positive rituals bring interactants together in ways that support their social relationship and permit offerings of various kinds, including the giving of gifts and greetings (Goffman, 1971). Negative or avoidance rituals, commonly termed taboos, protect the individuals and their properties from the intrusions of others.

Religious rituals, in contrast to interpersonal rituals, are the rules of conduct that prescribe how a person should comport him- or herself "in the presence of . . . sacred objects" (Durkheim, 1912, p. 41). Interpersonal rituals are "brief rituals one individual performs for and to another, attesting to civility and good will on the performer's part and to the recipient's possession of a small patrimony of sacredness" (Goffman, 1971, p. 63). According to many observers, including Goffman, interpersonal rituals have replaced sacred rituals in contemporary Western societies. A confusion over interpersonal, religious, and cultural rituals characterizes many of the developing nations of the world today (Geertz, 1973).

Rituals may be performed, as Malinowski (1913), Radcliffe-Brown (1922), Frazer (1890), Smith (1889), Durkheim (1912), Levi-Strauss (1962), van Gennep (1909), and Warner (1962) have argued, for purely magical, mystical, or religious reasons; so as to mark or gain some control over the uncontrollable, often occurrences in the natural world; transgressions of the group's moral code; or the existential certainties of birth, death, and the life cycle transitions from status position to status position within the group's social structure (e.g., child to adult, male to husband and father, female to wife and mother, etc.). Rituals are also enacted for the emotional effects the performance bestows on individuals. Participation may be voluntary or obligatory, large or small in numbers of participants, and negative or positive in tone, and often it will be connected to sacred (religious) and secular (political and interpersonal) calendars (Warner, 1962).

Ritual performances require the organization and focusing of ritual acts around stand-in objects whose presence is required for the ritual to be accomplished. These objects include, at a minimum, actors (performers and audiences), settings or stages for the ritual performance, a class of previously selected objects to be acted on during the occasion of ritual display, and a script, or prearranged interactional text, that will be followed, spoken, and enacted. Stand-in objects may include wedding rings, hymns, music, food, drink, and talk. The meanings of the ritual derive from the actions that persons direct toward these stand-in objects and toward themselves.

Serial ritual display characterizes ritual performances. In no sense can a ritual be accomplished all at once; it must proceed through phases, which are scheduled, interconnected, and made up of sequences of small ritual acts or rites. Ritual meals (Douglas, 1975) display this feature of serial ritual display. The social organization of ritual activities, in terms of serial ritual display, reveals the underlying power and control hierarchies in a group's social structure (Leach, 1968).

Social Relationships and Ritual

Social anthropologists, sociologists, and social psychologists "claim that their special field is the study of social relationships" (Leach, 1968, p. 524). While social relationships cannot be studied directly, the interactions that occur between individuals can be, and to the extent that these interactions are ritualized and conventionalized, ritual becomes a principal means for studying social relationships. Goffman's (1971) analysis of supportive and remedial interchanges, rituals of ratification, access, and departure in interpersonal rituals suggests that rituals serve to separate and join persons simultaneously. Greetings, for instance, maintain distance between persons, while joining them, if only momentarily, in a shared interactional exchange.

Perhaps more important than this joining and separating feature of rituals in social relationships is the fact that they have meaning only within the context of social relationships. That is, in social relationships, persons find and confirm their identities, and in these relationships, they join their actions to the ongoing fabric of the social life of their group. Rituals become one of several avenues (others include routines and problematic acts) for bridging the gap between persons and the social order, and provide a salient bond for connecting persons to one another.

At a deeper relational level, it can be argued that persons are connected to their societies through ritual ties. Thus ceremonies such as the coronation of the queen in England are seen by Shils and Young (1953) as instances of national communion in which ordinary, everyday individuals are drawn together into the moral fabric of their society. The queen and her coronation ritually embody all that being English entails and means. Participation in the ritual by members of the audience symbolically accomplishes a joining of the person with the society. It is a paradox that the rituals that stand nearest to the core of a society (coronations, inaugurations, etc.) are most typically at the society's most distant, peripheral interpersonal edges. Thus, core interpersonal rituals of the person and the group often stand in contradistinction to the core, sacred values and rituals of society at large (Shils, 1976).

Ritual as Interaction

Ritual must be understood as interaction, and not in static, strictly structural terms. While rituals do, in the abstract, stand outside and above persons, their lived meaning resides in the world of face-to-face interaction wherein they are acted on, defined, produced, and interpreted. When a number of persons join hands around a table and begin reciting the Lord's Prayer in unison, they are interactionally, collectively, and conjointly engaging in a shared ritual activity. With eyes closed, left hand clasping the extended right hand of the person to the left, right hand clasping the left hand of the person to the right, they, individually and interactionally, join and offer their presence to the collective presence of the group. Their voices are embodiments of their physical presence and participation in the ritual. Each individual is a part of the ritual, just as the ritual becomes a part of each person. The interactional accomplishment of a ritual requires individual and collective participation; but most important, it requires interaction. Ritual, then, is symbolic interaction, and should be studied as such (see Blumer, 1969).

Alternative Views of Ritual

The foregoing suggests that the meaning of ritual lies in interaction, not in rituals per se or in abstract structures. There are, however, alternative ways of formulating ritual. Rituals may be studied semiotically and structurally, in terms of the binary oppositions that constitute the inner or primary text of the ritual (Barthes, 1967; Levi-Strauss, 1962, 1963). Thus, paired oppositions within rituals and myths (male-female, life-death, near-far, old-young, etc.) may be examined and fitted together within a structural totality.

Rituals may be studied dramaturgically and their symbolic and cultural contents may be given special attention. Rituals may be studied in terms of the power they are intended to produce, just as they may be conceptualized as beliefs in illusion or in myth, magic, or religion. However, when ritual action transforms people's relationships to themselves, to others, and to their environment, more than the belief in an illusion is involved. Rituals and the actions they entail are real and consequential in their interactional implications, especially when the meanings of the ritual carry over into other sectors of the group's and the individuals' lives.

Conclusions

The import of ritual in everyday life may be summarized in terms of the following three assertions:

1. That which a group takes to be problematic will be subjected to pressures to make those problematic objects, acts, and events predictable and routine. This is necessary if orderly actions are to be taken toward them.
2. Groups and relationships display constant negotiated struggles over what is problematic, routine, and predictable.
3. At the heart of organized group life lies a complex network of rituals—interpersonal, positive, negative, sacred, and secular—that are communicated to newcomers to the group and that, when taught and successfully performed, lead to systematic ways of making everyday group life predictable, ordinary, and taken for granted.

An understanding of the everyday, taken-for-granted features of group life requires the systematic study of ritual. The understanding of how persons are connected to others and to the society at large demands similar study. Rituals stand at the intersection of the individual and society and require detailed examination by the disciplines of social anthropology, sociology, social psychology, psychology, religion, and philosophy. Indeed, Rosaldo (1993) suggests that ritual is best viewed as a busy intersection, as a place where a number of distinct and important cultural processes intersect. The notion of ritual as a busy intersection anticipates the more contemporary view of culture as a complex, ongoing process. In this view culture is not a self-contained whole made up of coherent, stable, unchanging patterns and rituals (Rosaldo, 1993).

REFERENCES

Bateson, G. (1972). *Steps to an ecology of mind.* New York: Ballantine.

Durkheim, E. (1912). *The elementary forms of religious life.* London: Allen & Unwin.

Goffman, E. (1971). *Relations in public.* New York: Basic Books.

SUGGESTED READING

McLaren, P. (1998). *Schooling as ritual performance* (3rd ed.). New York: Routledge.

Schechner, R. (1995). *The future of ritual.* New York: Routledge.

Norman K. Denzin
University of Illinois

ROSENZWEIG PICTURE-FRUSTRATION (P-F) STUDY

The Rosenzweig Picture-Frustration (P-F) study is a semi-projective technique of personality diagnosis that has been successfully used for the past half-century both as a clinical device and as an investigative procedure. It was developed as a method for exploring concepts of frustration theory and examining some dimensions of projective methodology (Rosenzweig, 1945). Based on earlier experiments on psychodynamic concepts, including frustration, repression, and directions and types of aggression, an Adult Form appeared in 1948. A Children's Form for ages 4 to 13 was published four years later, and in 1964 a form for Adolescents was added.

The P-F consists of a series of 24 cartoon-like pictures, each depicting two persons involved in mildly frustrating situations of common occurrence. Facial features and other expressions of emotion are deliberately omitted from the pictures. The figure at the left is always shown saying words that help to describe the frustration of the other individual. In the blank caption box above the frustrated figure on the right, the subject is asked to write the first reply that enters his or her mind.

It is assumed as a basis for P-F scoring that the examinee unconsciously or consciously identifies with the frustrated individual in each picture and projects his or her own bias into the responses given. To define this bias, scores are assigned to each response under two main dimensions: direction of aggression and type of aggression. Direction of aggression includes extraggression (EA), in which aggression is turned onto the environment; intraggression (IA), in which it is turned by the subject onto him- or herself; and imaggression (MA), in which aggression is evaded in an attempt to gloss over the frustration. It is as if extraggressiveness turns aggression *out,* intraggressiveness turns it *in,* and imaggressiveness turns it *off.* Type of aggression includes obstacle-dominance (OD), in which the barrier occasioning the frustration stands out in the response; ego (etho) defense (ED), in which the ego of the subject predominates to defend itself, and need-persistence (NP), in which the solution of the frustrating problem is emphasized by pursuing the goal despite the obstacle. From the combination of these six categories, there result for each item nine possible scoring factors.

It is essential to observe that aggression in the P-F and in the construct on which it is based in not necessarily negative in implication. In the context of the P-F, aggression is generically defined as assertiveness, which may be either affirmative or negative in character. Need-persistence represents a constructive (sometimes creative) form of aggression, whereas ego (ethos) defense is frequently destructive (of others or of oneself) in import. This point is particularly noteworthy because in many technical theories of aggression this distinction is overlooked and aggression is thought to be practically synonymous with hostility or destructiveness. Common parlance, when not contaminated by psychoanalytic or other psychological conceptualizations comes close to the broader usage of the term *aggression,* which the P-F Study employs.

Although the scoring of the P-F is always phenotypic (according to the explicit wording used in the response), interpretation is genotypic, involving three kinds of norms: universal (nomothetic), group (demographic), and individual (idiodynamic). Statistical data used in interpretation refer to group norms, that is, the extent to which the individual performs vis-à-vis the group to which he or she belongs (based on age, sex, etc.). Individual (idiodynamic) norms, which derive from the unique wording of the responses and in interrelation of the scored factors in the protocol, complement the group norms. Universal (nomothetic) norms are represented by the constructs on which the instrument is based, and these underlie both group and individual norms. A Group Conformity Rating (GCR) measures the subject's tendency to agree with the modal responses of a normal population sample.

Interscorer reliability has been found to be 85% for the adult form. The results of a retest reliability, with some variations, have been demonstrated to be high. The various scoring categories selectively showed significant reliability as determined by the split-half method, but by the retest method the major scoring dimensions of the P-F have been demonstrated to agree with significant reliability.

The P-F has been studied for both construct (criterion-related) and pragmatic validity with significantly positive results. In addition to the clinical purposes for which the P-F study was originally intended, it has been used as a screening or selection device in business, industry, and schools and for research on cultural differences. In particular, the GCR has proved to be of value. The categories of "etho-defense" and "need-persistence" also have been shown to have differentiating potential, and some positive results have been obtained for obstacle-dominance. The results of P-F in hospital and clinic settings have proved useful, but an exclusive reliance on the P-F as a symptom-differentiating tool in such contexts is not recommended. Used in conjunction with other tests or as part of a configuration index, the technique has significant potential.

The published evidence for P-F reliability and validity are summarized in the *Basic Manual* (Rosenzweig, 1978b) and discussed in detail in the book *Aggressive Behavior and the Rosenzweig Picture-Frustration Study* (Rosenzweig, 1978a).

It is important to observe that the P-F Study is one of the few projective methods that directly apply a systematic theory of behavior, in this case, of aggression. Moreover, by employing in its scoring the three types of norms (nomothetic, demographic, and idiodynamic), the instrument is compatible with the general theory of personality known as idiodynamics.

The P-F has been translated and adapted, with standardization, in nearly all the countries of the Americas, Europe, and Asia and thus has become a natural tool for cross-cultural investigation. It is particularly noteworthy that the Japanese have intensively pursued the relationship between the constructs of frustration theory and the standpoint of idiodynamics, and a Japanese book on this topic is in preparation.

REFERENCES

Rosenzweig, S. (1945). The picture-association method and its application in a study of reactions to frustration. *Journal of Personality, 14,* 3–23.

Rosenzweig, S. (1978a). *Aggressive behavior and the Rosenzweig Picture-Frustration Study.* New York: Praeger.

Rosenzweig, S. (1978b). *Basic Manual for the Rosenzweig Picture-Frustration (P-F) Study.* St. Louis: Rana House. (Distributed by Psychological Assessment Resources, Odessa, FL.)

SUGGESTED READING

Clarke, H. J., Fleming, E. E., & Rosenzweig, S. (1947). The reliability of the scoring of the Rosenzweig Picture-Frustration Study. *Journal of Clinical Psychology, 3,* 364–370.

Pareek, U. N. (1958). Reliability of the Indian adaptation of the Rosenzweig P-F Study (Children's Form). *Journal of Psychological Researches, 2,* 18–23.

Pichot, P., & Danjon, S. (1955). La fidelite du Test de Frustration de Rosenzweig. *Revue de Psychologie Appliquee, 5,* 1–11.

Rauchfleisch, U. (1978). *Handbook zum Rosenzweig Picture-Frustration Test (PFT)* (Vols. 1–2). Bern, Switzerland: Hans Huber.

Rosenzweig, S. (1944). An outline of frustration theory. In J. M. Hunt (Ed.), *Personality and the behavior disorders* (Vol. 1, pp. 379–388). New York: Ronald Press.

Rosenzweig, S. (1950). Frustration tolerance and the picture-frustration study. *Psychological Service Center Journal, 2,* 109–115.

Rosenzweig, S. (1951). Idiodynamics in personality theory with special reference to projective methods. *Psychological Review, 58,* 213–223.

Rosenzweig, S. (1960). The Rosenzweig Picture-Frustration Study, Children's Form. In J. Zubin & A. Freedman (Eds.), *Projective techniques with children* (pp. 149–176). New York: Grune & Stratton.

Rosenzweig, S. (1970). Sex differences in reaction to frustration among adolescents. In J. Zubin & A. Freedman (Eds.), *Psychopathology of adolescence* (pp. 90–107) New York: Grune & Stratton.

Rosenzweig, S. (1977). Outline of a denotative definition of aggression. *Aggressive Behavior, 3,* 379–383.

Rosenzweig, S. (1978). An investigation of the reliability of the Rosenzweig Picture-Frustration (P-F) Study, Children's Form. *Journal of Personality Assessment, 42,* 483–488.

Rosenzweig, S., & Adelman, S. (1977). Construct validity of the Rosenzweig Picture-Frustration (P-F) Study. *Journal of Personality Assessment, 41,* 578–588.

Rosenzweig, S., Ludwig, D. J., & Adelman, S. (1975). Retest reliability of the Rosenzweig Picture-Frustration Study and similar semiprojective techniques. *Journal of Personality Assessment, 39,* 3–12.

Rosenzweig, S., & Rosenzweig, L. (1952). Aggression in problem children and normals as evaluated by the Rosenzweig P-F Study. *Journal of Abnormal and Social Psychology, 47,* 683–687.

Rosenzweig, S., & Sarason, S. (1942). An experimental study of the triadic hypothesis: Reaction to frustration, ego-defense, and hypnotizability: I. Correlational approach. *Character and Personality, 11,* 1–19.

Saul Rosenzweig
Washington University

RUSSIAN NEUROPSYCHOLOGY AFTER LURIA

Now, when the psychologists all over the world have commemorated the centennial anniversary of the birth of A. R. Luria (1902–1977), we can realize his continuous enormous influence to different branches of Russian neuropsychology.

The Problem of Interhemispheric Specialization and Interaction

Research has revealed interhemispheric specialization for different forms of memory (Korsakova & Mikadze, 1982; Simernitskaya, 1978) as well as greater vulnerability of the right hemisphere to cerebral pathology and lower compensating capabilities (Vasserman & Lassan, 1989). The right hemisphere was proved slower in information processing than the left one (Krotkova, Karaseva, Moskovichyute, 1982) and less able to regulate and accelerate mental activity (Homskaya, Efimova, Budyka, & Enikolopova, 1997). It was also shown that each hemisphere is specific for different types of reasoning such as empirical or logical reasoning as well as for intensity and stability of human emotions, and there are unilaterally and bilaterally realized functions, or a competence of each hemisphere (Homskaya & Batova, 1998; Meerson & Dobrovolskaya, 1998). Each mental activity is realized through the interaction of both hemispheres, each making a specific contribution. New evidence proves that interhemispheric differences can be revealed both on cortical and subcortical levels. Cognitive defects specific for the left hemisphere are more evident in cortical lesions, whereas subdominant syndromes appear predominantly after subcortical lesions of the right hemisphere (Moskovichyute, 1998).

Subcortical Brain Pathology

A good model for studying cognitive disturbances due to subcortical damages is Parkinson's disease (PD; Glozman, 1999b; Korsakova & Moskovichyute, 1985). The pattern of cognitive disturbances in persons with PD is a specific combination of natural brain alterations appearing with age and specific impairments caused by the disease. This pattern is not the sum of both components but a qualitatively new complex of symptoms. Quantitative and qualitative integration of Lurian procedures was proved necessary to reveal these data (Glozman, 1999a).

Dementia should not be considered as an obligatory component of PD, and it is not limited to the symptoms of so-called subcortical dementia. It includes some cortical cognitive disorders, the pattern of which is different from that of Alzheimer's disease (AD).

Neuropsychology of Older Persons

Luria's (1973) conception of three functional units of the brain may help to differentiate normal and abnormal aging (Glozman, 1999b; Korsakova, 1998). In the normal elderly, the functioning of the first unit—that of activation—is predominantly disturbed, and this is manifested in general slowness, aspontaneity in all activities, increased inhibition of memorized information by interfering stimuli, and restriction of the volume of mental activities when different programs must be simultaneously retained and realized. The normal aging represents a stage of individual development, necessitating a change in strategies, voluntary selection and use of new forms of mediating mental activity. In pathological atrophic states, such as AD or senile dementia, not only these symptoms are aggravated, but defects in functioning of the two other cerebral units are also demonstrated. Progression of cognitive disturbances leading to the appearance of vascular dementia is predominantly due to regulatory and operational deficits connected to cortical brain regions. A corticalization of the cognitive and executive disturbances thus occurs. The evolution of AD is realized by the consecutive frontalization and subcorticalization of impairments, that is, by superimposed neurodynamic and regulatory impairments upon operational ones.

Developmental Neuropsychology

The further growth of developmental neuropsychology in Russia follows two main lines: study of individual features during the development of cognitive functions (Akhutina, 1998, 2001; Mikadze & Korsakova, 1994) and analysis of interhemispheric interaction in abnormal development (Semenovich, 2002).

Neuropsychological diagnosis of causes responsible for learning problems revealed heterogeneity in the maturation of brain structures and connections in the development of functional systems and significance of a correspondence between the child's abilities and exigencies of the learning programs. The emphasis of the assessments is a modification from diagnostic evaluation to prognostic and corrective suggestions. The neuropsychological assessment should emphasize the subject's strengths, which are important in his or her correction (rehabilitation) program and predict his or her ultimate integration into society. This principle was first realized in aphasiology as the so-called socio-psychological aspect of rehabilitation (Tsvetkova, 1985; Tsvetkova et al., 1979) and then in studies of interrelations between communication disorders and personality in different nosological groups (Glozman, 2002) and in developmental neuropsychology.

Neuropsychology of Individual Differences

Neuropsychology of individual differences is an application of neuropsychological concepts and methods to the assessment of healthy subjects that tries to explain normal functioning by using principles of cerebral organization, particularly characteristics of interhemispheric asymmetry (motor, acoustic, and visual) and interhemispheric interaction (Homskaya & Batova, 1998; Homskaya et al., 1997). The authors identified 27 possible profiles of lateral brain organization and their correlation to aspects of cognitive, motor, and emotional activity of the normal subjects, as well as their adaptive abilities.

To summarize, three main trends can be seen in the development of neuropsychology in the former Soviet Union:

1. Extensive further expansion of research and practice, that is, embracing numerous new domains and nosological patient groups
2. Combination of qualitative and quantitative approaches
3. A social and personality-based orientation

REFERENCES

Akhutina, T. V. (1998). Neuropsychology of individual differences in children as a basis for the application of neuropsychological methods at school. In E. D. Homskaya & T. V. Akhutina (Eds.), *First international Luria memorial conference proceedings.* Moscow: Russian Psychological Association Press.

Akhutina, T. V. (2001). Neuropsychological approach to the diagnosis and correction of writing disabilities. In *Modern approaches to the diagnosis and correction of speech troubles.* Saint Petersburg, Russia: Saint Petersburg University Press.

Glozman, J. M. (1999a). *The quantitative evaluation of neuropsychological assessment data.* Moscow: Center of Curative Pedagogics Press.

Glozman, J. M. (1999b). Russian neuropsychology after Luria. *Neuropsychology Review, 9*(1), 33–44.

Glozman, J. M. (2002). *Communication and the health of the personality.* Moscow: Academia.

Homskaya, E. D., & Batova N. Y. (1998). *Brain and emotions.* Moscow: Russian Pedagogical Agency Press.

Homskaya E. D., Efimova, I. V., Budyka, E. V., & Enikolopova, E. V. (1997). *Neuropsychology of individual differences.* Moscow: Russian Pedagogical Agency Press.

Korsakova, N. K. (1998). Neuropsychogerontology: Development of A. R. Luria's school of ideas. In E. D. Homskaya & T. V. Akhutina (Eds.), *First international Luria memorial conference proceedings.* Moscow: Russian Psychological Association Press.

Korsakova, N. K., & Mikadze, Y. V. (1982). Neuropsychological studies of memory: Results and perspectives. In E. D. Homskaya, L. S. Tsvetkova, & B. V. Zeigarnik (Eds.), *A. R. Luria and modern psychology.* Moscow: Moscow University Press.

Korsakova, N. K., & Moskovichyute L. I. (1985). *Subcortical structures and mental processes.* Moscow: Moscow University Press.

Krotkova, O. A., Karaseva, T. A., & Moskovichyute, L. I. (1982). Lateral differences in the time course of higher mental functions in endonasal glutamic acid electrophoresis. *Voprocy Neurohirurgii, 3,* 48–52.

Luria, A. R. (1973). *The working brain: An introduction to neuropsychology.* London: Penguin Books.

Meerson, Y. A., & Dobrovolskaya, N. V. (1998). Disorders in perception of absolute and relative objects localization in spatial depth (depth agnosia) after focal damage of the right or left cerebral hemisphere. In E. D. Homskaya & T. V. Akhutina (Eds.), *First international Luria memorial conference proceedings.* Moscow: Russian Psychological Association Press.

Mikadze, Y. V., & Korsakova, N. K. (1994). *Neuropsychological diagnosis and correction of primary school children.* Moscow: Inteltex.

Moskovichyute, L. I. (1998). Cerebral hemisphere asymmetry on the cortical and subcortical levels. In E. D. Homskaya & T. V. Akhutina (Eds.), *First international Luria memorial conference proceedings.* Moscow: Russian Psychological Association Press.

Semenovich, A. V. (2002). *Neuropsychological diagnostics and correction of children.* Moscow: Academia.

Simernitskaya, E. G. (1978). *Hemispheric dominance.* Moscow: Moscow University Press.

Tsvetkova, L. S. (1985). *Neuropsychological rehabilitation of patients.* Moscow: Moscow University Press.

Tsvetkova, L. S., Glozman, J. M., Kalita, N. G., Maximenko, M. Y., & Tsyganok, A. A. (1979). *Socio-psychological aspect of aphasics rehabilitation.* Moscow: Moscow University Press.

Vasserman, L. I., & Lassan, L. P. (1989). Effect of lateralization of subcortical stereotaxic destruction on post surgery dynamics of mental functions in subjects with epilepsy. In *Clinical aspects of the problem of brain functional asymmetry.* Minsk, Belarus.

Janna Glozman
Moscow State University

S

SADISM

The origin of the term *sadism* is associated with the Marquis de Sade, a French writer (1740–1815). He wrote novels in which he describes scenes of torture and killing in a sexual context (Hucker, 1997). In the *DSM-IV* (American Psychiatric Association [ApA], 1994), sadism is defined as a paraphilia and is included in the section on sexual and gender identity disorders. A diagnosis of sadism requires the following criteria: "over a period of at least 6 months, recurrent, intense sexually arousing fantasies, sexual urges, or behaviors involving acts (real, not simulated) in which the psychological or physical suffering (including humiliation) of the victim is sexually exciting to the person" and "the fantasies, sexual urges, or behaviors cause clinically significant distress or impairment in social, occupational or other important areas of functioning" (ApA, 1994, p. 530). According to Dietz, Hazelwood, and Warren (1990), the essence of sadism is not the suffering of the victim but the complete power over the victim; in fact, "there is no greater power over another person than that of inflicting pain on her" (p. 165).

Sexual sadism may be expressed in fantasies only, in sexual behaviors with a consenting partner (e.g., bondage, mild torture) or in sexual aggressions (e.g., rape, sexual murder). The incidence of sadistic fantasies such as humiliating a woman (14.9%) or beating up a woman (10.7%) is not infrequent among men in the general population (Crépault & Couture, 1980). In addition, 5% of males and 2% of females obtained sexual gratification from inflicting pain in mutually consenting sexual activities (Hunt, 1974). Finally, a significant proportion of sexual aggressors and sexual murderers of women acted out sadistic behaviors during their offences (Groth & Birnbaum, 1979; Knight & Prentky, 1990; Ressler, Burgess, & Douglas, 1988).

The childhood and adolescence of sexually sadistic criminals are characterized by a blend of violence, sex, and social isolation. A number of sexually sadistic criminals have an ambivalent relationship (love/hate) with their mothers. In addition, a number of sexually sadistic criminals reported that they were physically victimized by an authoritarian father. Following these inadequate interactions with their parents, they developed an inadequate attachment style characterized by a withdrawn attitude and social isolation (Brittain, 1970). During adolescence, they developed a low self-esteem due to failures in social and sexual interactions. Then, deviant sexual fantasies and paraphilic behaviors (e.g., exhibitionism, voyeurism, fetishism) became their main source of emotional stimulation and gratification (MacCulloch, Snowden, Wood, & Mills, 1983). Deviant sexual fantasies become sadistic in order to maintain a high level of sexual arousal.

Adult sexually sadistic criminals are introverted, shy, and socially inept and isolated. They rarely show violence, but they have an interest in guns and detective magazines (Brittain, 1970). In addition, they often establish a reputation as a solid citizen (Dietz et al., 1990). Finally, they have a rich fantasy life and are engaged in a diversity of paraphilic behaviors (Gratzer & Bradford, 1995).

Regarding their personality, sexually sadistic criminals are usually described as psychopathic and narcissistic (Dietz et al., 1990). Such a diagnosis is congruent with their lack of empathy during their crimes and with their view of themselves as supercriminals. However, their usual way of relating to others is instead characterized by avoidant (e.g., low self-esteem) and schizoid (e.g., withdrawn) personality disorder traits (Proulx, 2001).

The criminal offences of sexual sadists are well planned and organized (Ressler et al., 1988). They choose an unknown victim who is taken to a place selected in advance. Often, the victim is kept in captivity for more than 24 hours (Dietz et al., 1990). During the crime, the victim is tortured and humiliated (Grubin, 1994). Frequently, foreign objects are inserted into the victim's vagina or anus (Warren, Hazelwood, & Dietz, 1996). Finally, the victim is usually killed by strangulation (Brittain, 1970).

After the crime, sexual sadists behave normally until their next offense (Podolsky, 1965). They report no guilt or remorse. They usually feel a great relief of tension after the crime. Finally, they may consider that they are superior to the police because they avoid detection. In fact, as suggested by Brittain (1970), a sexual sadist "may feel himself to be inferior, except as regard to his offence" (p. 199).

REFERENCES

American Psychiatric Association. (1994). *Diagnostic and statistical manual of mental disorders* (4th ed.). Washington, DC: Author.

Brittain, R. (1970). The sadistic murderer. *Medicine, Science, and the Law, 10,* 198–207.

Crépault, E., & Couture, M. (1980). Men's erotic fantasies. *Archives of Sexual Behavior, 9,* 565–581.

Dietz, P. E., Hazelwood, R. R., & Warren, J. (1990). The sexually sadistic criminal and his offenses. *Bulletin of the American Academy of Psychiatry and the Law, 18,* 163–178.

Gratzer, T., & Bradford, J. M. W. (1995). Offender and offence characteristics of sexual sadists: A comparative study. *Journal of Forensic Sciences, 40,* 450–455.

Groth, N. A., & Birnbaum, H. J. (1979). *Men who rape.* New York: Plenum Press.

Grubin, D. (1994). Sexual murder. *British Journal of Psychiatry, 165,* 624–629.

Hucker, S. J. (1997). Sexual sadism: Psychopathology and theory. In D. R. Laws & W. O'Donohue (Eds.), *Sexual deviance: Theory, assessment, and treatment* (pp. 194–209). New York: Guilford Press.

Hunt, M. (1974). *Sexual behavior in the 1970s.* New York: Playboy Press.

Knight, R. A., & Prentky, R. A. (1990). Classifying sexual offenders: The development and corroboration of taxonomic models. In W. L. Marshall, D. R. Laws, & H. P. E. Barbaree (Eds.), *Handbook of sexual assault: Issues, theories, and treatment of the offender* (pp. 23–52). New York: Plenum.

MacCulloch, M. J., Snowden, P. R., Wood, P. J. W., & Mills, H. E. (1983). Sadistic fantasy, sadistic behaviour and offending. *British Journal of Psychiatry, 143,* 20–29.

Podolsky, E. (1965). The lust murderer. *Medico-Legal Journal, 33,* 174–178.

Proulx, J. (2001, November 7–10). *Sexual preferences and personality disorders of MTC-R3 rapists subtypes.* Paper presented at the 20th Annual Research Conference of the ATSA, San Antonio, TX.

Ressler, R. K., Burgess, A. W., & Douglas, J. E. (1988). *Sexual homicide: Patterns and motives.* New York: Lexington Books.

Warren, J. I., Hazelwood, R. R., & Dietz, P. E. (1996). The sexually sadistic serial killer. *Journal of Forensic Sciences, 41,* 970–974.

Jean Proulx
Éric Beauregard
University of Montreal

SADISTIC RITUAL ABUSE

Sadistic ritual abuse (SRA; Goodwin, 1992), also known as satanic ritual abuse or ritual abuse has been defined as a "method of control of people of all ages consisting of physical, sexual, and psychological mistreatment through the use of rituals" (Rhoades, 1999, p. 844).

Levels and Symbols of Satanism

Satanism has been defined in four levels (Simandl, 1997): (1) the experimental-dabbler, typically a teenager; (2) nontraditional, self-styled satanists, individuals or small groups obsessed with satanic themes; (3) organized traditional satanists, organized religious groups that are protected by religious freedom under American law, such as the Church of Satan; and (4) occultic networking or transgenerational cults, SRA groups perpetuated through family generations and the focus of this article (Ryder, 1992).

Commonly reported satanic symbols (Pulling, 1989) include the pentagram, inverted pentagram, hexagram (Star of David), cross of Nero (peace symbol or broken cross), swastika, anarchy symbol, thaumaturgic triangle, udjat (all-seeing eye), scarab, lightning bolts, the number 666, ankh, inverted cross, black mass indicator, an emblem of Baphomet, the symbol of the Church of Satan, and the cross of confusion.

The SRA Controversy

The Satan Seller (Warnke, 1972) and *Michelle Remembers* (Smith & Pazder, 1980) introduced SRA to public awareness. The FBI first received reports of possible SRA activity in 1983 (Lanning, 1991). The initial explosion of interest in and controversy surrounding SRA in Christian (Passantino & Passantino, 1992), professional (Mulhern, 1992; Putnam, 1991), and law enforcement circles (Hicks, 1991; Lanning, 1989) was soon supplanted by the controversy over "recovered memory" and the "backlash" (Myers, 1992) against reported survivors of sexual abuse and their therapists. In 1998, the potential legal suits against mental health professionals were estimated to be in the thousands (Brown, Scheflin, & Hammond, 1998).

More books than journal articles have been written on SRA, including reported survivors (Ryder, 1992), a parent accused of sexual abuse (Pendergrast, 1995), journalists (Nathan & Snedeker, 1995), researchers (Loftus & Ketcham, 1994), therapists (Fraser, 1997; Ross, 1995; Sakheim & Devine, 1992; Yapko, 1994), fictionalized accounts of SRA (James, 1994; Larson, 1991), and children's books on SRA (Sanford, 1990).

The basic controversy is over whether such cults exist, and if they do exist, how they are organized and how they conspire to abuse people (Sakheim & Devine, 1992). Alternative explanations for SRA allegations include pathological distortion; traumatic memory; normal childhood fears and fantasy; and misperception, confusion, and trickery by perpetrators (Lanning, 1992); overzealous interveners (Ganaway, 1992); contaminating effects from the media, society, parents, and professionals (Ganaway, 1989; Jones, 1991); a social delusion (Mulhern, 1994); a moral panic (Victor, 1998); SRA training seminars (Mulhern, 1992); and "misdiagnosis, and the misapplication of hypnosis, dreamwork, or regressive therapies" (Coons, 1994).

Research with the Word Association Test (WAT; Leavitt & Labott, 1998; also Leavitt, 1998) and Rorschach (Leavitt & Labott, 2000) suggested that an experience base was shared by individuals reporting SRA that was not found in individuals who did not report satanic abuse (even if they did report sexual abuse). The increased production of satanic word associations was not found to be associated with high hospital or media exposure.

The SRA controversy broadened with the recovered memory debate and the formation of the False Memory Syndrome Foundation (Goldstein, 1992). A number of states amended their statutes of limitations to grant delayed discovery, wherein adult survivors of childhood sexual abuse could sue their reported abusers (Crnich & Crnich, 1992). Five states (Louisiana, Missouri, Texas, Idaho, and Illinois) have passed laws addressing the ritual abuse of children (Simandl, 1997). Ritual abuse prosecutions (Tate, 1994) and research by therapists (Jonker & Jonker-Bakker, 1991; van der Hart, Boon, Jansen, 1997) in Europe have shown that SRA is not just a North American phenomenon.

Ritual Abuse of Children

Snow and Sorensen (1990) conducted a study of ritualistic child abuse in five separate neighborhood settings. They discovered that in four out of five neighborhoods, three distinct components of the sexual abuse appeared: incest, juvenile perpetration, and the adult ritual sex ring.

Finkelhor and Williams (1988) conducted a 3-year study of sexual abuse in day care centers in America and noted that 13% of the cases involved ritualistic abuse. Kelly (1989) found that the ritualistically abused children experienced significantly more types of sexual abuse, severe physical abuse, and threats of being watched by Satan.

Child Therapeutic Issues

Gould (1992) noted that the three factors of drugs, hypnosis, and intolerable abuse leading to dissociation, combined with the ritualistic abuse of children, before the age of 6 often create "amnesic barriers," making spontaneous disclosure of abuse unlikely.

Gould (1992) developed a twelve-category checklist for signs and symptoms of ritualistic abuse in children. Therapy involved play therapy with the gradual disclosure of the abuse to the therapist and nonabusive parents (Gould, 1992). The therapist was to be active in the treatment in structuring the therapeutic activities and providing motivation to the child to address issues that otherwise the child may avoid, including possible multiplicity and mind-control programs (Gould & Cozolino, 1992). Treatment is typically done in three stages (Herman, 1992), such as engagement, the trauma work, and resolution (Waters & Silberg, 1996), addressing the five domains (Silberg, 1996) of cognitive, affective, physical, interpersonal, and spiritual.

Ritual Abuse of Adolescents

Tennant-Clark, Fritz, and Beauvais (1989) noted a psychosocial profile of high occult participants in adolescents: chemical substance abuse, low self-esteem, negative feelings about school, poor self-concept, low desire to be considered a good person, negative feelings about religion, high tolerance for deviance, negative feelings about the future, low social sanctions against drug use, and feeling blamed (p. 768). Simandl (1997) saw these teens as having an undue fascination with death, torture, and suicide; alienation from family and religion; drastic change in grades; and a "compulsive interest in occult material, fantasy role games, and films and videos (all with themes of death, torture, and suicide)" (pp. 216–217).

Adult Survivors of Childhood Ritual Abuse

Young, Sachs, Braun, and Watkins (1991) reported a study of 37 adult patients with dissociative disorder who reported ritual abuse as children. All reported abusive rituals during satanic worship. The types of abuses reported were, in order of decreasing percents, sexual, witnessing and receiving physical pain or torture, witnessing animal mutilation or killings, death threats, forced drug usage, witnessing and forced participation in human adult and infant sacrifice, forced cannibalism, marriage to Satan, buried alive in coffins or graves, forced impregnation, and sacrifice of one's own child.

Adult Therapeutic Considerations

Clinical presentations are often dissociative (Leavitt, 1994) and posttraumatic stress disorder symptoms, in addition to "cult-related phenomena, bizarre self-abuse, and unremitting eating, sleep, and anxiety disorders" (Young & Young, 1997, p. 69). Treatment would thus involve principles and techniques that have been found to be effective with posttraumatic stress disorder and dissociative disorders (Kluft, 1985; Putnam, 1989, 1997; Silberg, 1996; van der Kolk, 1987; van der Kolk, McFarlane, & Weisaeth, 1996; Whitfield, 1995).

Treatment typically involves the three stages of safety-stability, trauma work, and integration (Herman, 1992; Rhoades, 1995a), while taking precautions to help prevent false memory allegations (Rhoades, 1995a, 1995b, 1995c). Treatment methods include abreaction; hypnosis; expressive therapies such as journaling, art, and sand tray; medication; hospitalization, including voluntary restraints (Young, 1992; van der Kolk, 1987; van der Kolk, McFarlane, & Weisaeth, 1996) and 12-step groups as an adjunct to therapy (Shaffer & Cozolino, 1992).

REFERENCES

Brown, D., Scheflin, A. W., & Hammond, D. C. (1998). *Memory, trauma treatment, and the law.* New York: W. W. Norton.

Coons, P. M. (1994). Reports of satanic ritual abuse: Further implications about pseudomemories. *Perceptual and Motor Skills, 78,* 1376–1378.

Crnich, J. E., & Crnich, K. A. (1992). *Shifting the burden of truth: Suing child sexual abusers—A legal guide for survivors and their supporters* (pp. 207–248). Lake Oswego, OR: Recollex.

Finkelhor, D., & Williams, L. M. (with Burns, N.). (1988). *Nursery crimes: Sexual abuse in day care.* Newbury Park, CA: Sage.

Fraser, G. A. (Ed.). (1997). *The dilemma of ritual abuse: Cautions and guides for therapists.* Washington, DC: American Psychiatric Press.

Ganaway, G. (1989). Historical truth versus narrative truth: Clarifying the role of exogenous trauma in the etiology of multiple personality and its variants. *Dissociation, 21*(4), 205–220.

Ganaway, G. (1992). Some additional questions: A response to Shaffer and Cozolino, to Gould and Cozolino and to Friesen. *Journal of Psychology and Theology, 20*(3), 201–203.

Goldstein, E. (with Farmer, K.). (1992). *Confabulations: Creating false memories—Destroying families.* Boca Raton, FL: SIRS Books.

Goodwin, J. (1992, November). *Pre-conference workshop: Sadistic ritual abuse issues in the 1990's.* Comments made at the Ninth International Conference on Multiple Personality Dissociative States, Chicago.

Gould, C. (1992). Diagnosis and treatment of ritually abused children. In D. K. Sakheim & S. E. Devine (Eds.), *Out of darkness.* New York: Lexington Books.

Gould, C., & Cozolino, L. (1992). Ritual abuse, multiplicity, and mind-control. *Journal of Psychology and Theology, 20*(3), 194–196.

Herman, J. L. (1992). *Trauma and recovery.* New York: Basic Books.

Hicks, R. (1991). *In pursuit of Satan: The police and the occult.* New York: Prometheus Books.

James, S. (1994). *Dabblings: A journey of horror and hope.* Gresham, OR: Vision House.

Jones, D. (1991). Ritualism and child sexual abuse. *Child Abuse and Neglect, 15,* 163–170.

Jonker, F., & Jonker-Bakker, I. (1991). Experiences with ritualistic child sexual abuse: A case study from the Netherlands. *Child Abuse and Neglect, 15,* 191–196.

Kelly, S. (1989). Stress responses of children to sexual abuse and ritualistic abuse in day care centers. *Journal of Interpersonal Violence, 4*(4), 502–513.

Kluft, R. P. (Ed.). (1985). *Childhood antecedents of multiple personality.* Washington, DC: American Psychiatric Press.

Lanning, K. (1989, October). Satanic, occult, ritualistic crime: A law enforcement perspective. *Police Chief,* 62–83.

Lanning, K. (1991). Ritual abuse: A law enforcement view or perspective. *Child Abuse and Neglect, 15,* 171–173.

Lanning, K. (1992). A law-enforcement perspective on allegations of ritual abuse. In D. K. Sakheim & S. E. Devine (Eds.), *Out of darkness* (pp. 109–146). New York: Lexington Books.

Larson, B. (1991). *Dead air.* Nashville, TN: Thomas Nelson.

Leavitt, F. (1994). Clinical correlates of alleged satanic abuse and less controversial molestation. *Child Abuse and Neglect, 18*(4), 387–392.

Leavitt, F. (1998). Measuring the impact of media exposure and hospital treatment on patients alleging satanic ritual abuse. *Treating Abuse Today, 8*(4), 7–13.

Leavitt, F., & Labott, S. M. (1998). Revision of the Word Association Test for assessing associations of patients reporting satanic ritual abuse in childhood. *Journal of Clinical Psychology, 54*(7), 933–943.

Leavitt, F., & Labott, S. M. (2000). The role of media and hospital exposure on Rorschach response patterns by patients reporting satanic ritual abuse. *American Journal of Forensic Psychology, 18*(2), 35–55.

Loftus, E., & Ketcham, K. (1994). *The myth of repressed memory.* New York: St. Martin's Press.

Mulhern, S. (1992). Ritual abuse: Defining a syndrome versus defending a belief. *Journal of Psychology and Theology, 20*(3), 230–232.

Mulhern, S. (1994). Satanism, ritual abuse, and multiple personality disorder: A sociohistorical perspective. *International Journal of Clinical and Experimental Hypnosis, 42*(4), 265–288.

Myers, J. E. B. (Ed.). (1992). *The backlash: Child protection under fire.* Thousand Oaks, CA: Sage.

Nathan, D., & Snedeker, M. (1995). *Satan's silence: Ritual abuse and the making of a modern American witch hunt.* New York: Basic Books.

Passantino, B., & Passantino, G. (1992). The hard facts about satanic ritual abuse. *Christian Research Journal, 14*(3), 20–27.

Pendergrast, M. (1995). *Victims of memory: Incest accusations and shattered lives.* Hinesburg, VT: Upper Access.

Pulling, P. (1989). *The devil's web.* Lafayette, LA: Huntington House.

Putnam, F. W. (1989). *Diagnosis and treatment of multiple personality disorder.* New York: Guilford Press.

Putnam, F. W. (1991). The satanic ritual abuse controversy. *Child Abuse and Neglect, 15,* 175–179.

Putnam, F. W. (1997). *Dissociation in children and adolescents: A developmental perspective.* New York: Guilford Press.

Rhoades, G. F. (1995a). *Dissociative identity disorder (DID / MPD)* (two audio cassettes). Pearl City, HI: L. L. Maxwell.

Rhoades, G. F. (1995b). *Sadistic ritual abuse* (two audio cassettes). Pearl City, HI: L. L. Maxwell.

Rhoades, G. F. (1995c). *Traumatic memory* (three cassette tapes). Pearl City, HI: L. L. Maxwell.

Rhoades, G. F. (1999). Ritual abuse. In R. J. Corsini (Ed.), *The dictionary of psychology* (p. 844). Philadelphia: Brunner/Mazel.

Ross, C. A. (1995). *Satanic ritual abuse: Principles of treatment.* Toronto, Ontario: University of Toronto Press.

Ryder, D. (1992). *Breaking the circle of satanic ritual abuse.* Minneapolis, MN: CompCare.

Sakheim, D. K., & Devine, S. E. (1992). Introduction: The phenomenon of satanic ritual abuse. In D. K. Sakheim & S. E. Devine (Eds.), *Out of darkness* (pp. xi–xix). New York: Lexington Books.

Sanford, D. (1990). *Don't make me go back mommy: A child's book about satanic ritual abuse.* Portland, OR: Multnomah Press.

Shaffer, R., & Cozolino, L. (1992). Adults who report childhood ritualistic abuse. *Journal of Psychology and Theology, 20*(3), 188–193.

Silberg, J. (Ed.). (1996). The five-domain crises model: Therapeutic tasks and techniques for dissociative children. In J. Silberg (Ed.), *The dissociative child: Diagnosis, treatment, and management* (pp. 113–134). Lutherville, MD: Sidran Press.

Simandl, R. J. (1997). Teen involvement in the occult. In G. A. Fraser (Ed.), *The dilemma of ritual abuse: Cautions and guides for therapists.* Washington, DC: American Psychiatric Press.

Smith, M., & Pazder, L. (1980). *Michelle remembers.* New York: Congdon and Lattes.

Snow, B., & Sorensen, T. (1990). Ritualistic child abuse in a neighborhood setting. *Journal of Interpersonal Violence, 5*(4), 474–487.

Tate, T. (1994). Press, politics and paedophilia: A practitioner's guide to the media. In V. Sinason (Ed.), *Treating survivors of satanist abuse* (pp 182–194). London: Routledge.

Tennant-Clark, C., Fritz, J., & Beauvais, F. (1989). Occult participation: Its impact on adolescent development. *Adolescence, 24*(96), 757–772.

van der Hart, O., Boon, S., & Jansen, O. H. (1997). Ritual abuse in European countries: A clinician's perspective. In G. A. Fraser (Ed.), *The dilemma of ritual abuse: Cautions and guides for therapists* (pp. 137–163). Washington, DC: American Psychiatric Press.

van der Kolk, B. A. (Ed.). (1987). *Psychological trauma.* Washington, DC: American Psychiatric Press.

van der Kolk, B. A., McFarlane, A. C., & Weisaeth, L. (Eds.). (1996). *Traumatic stress: The effects of overwhelming experience on mind, body, and society.* New York: Guilford Press.

Victor, J. (1998). Moral panics and the social construction of deviant behavior: A theory and application to the case of ritual child abuse. *Sociological Perspectives, 41*(3), 541–565.

Warnke, M. (1972). *The Satan seller.* Plainfield, NJ: Logos International.

Wassil-Grimm, C. (1995). *Diagnosis for disaster: The devastating truth about false memory syndrome and its impact on accusers and families.* Woodstock, NY: Overlook Press.

Waters, F., & Silberg, J. (1996). Therapeutic phases in the treatment of dissociative children. In J. Silberg (Ed.), *The dissociative child: Diagnosis, treatment, and management* (pp. 135–166). Lutherville, MD: Sidran Press.

Whitfield, C. L. (1995). *Memory and abuse: Remembering and healing the effects of trauma.* Deerfield Beach, FL: Health Communications.

Yapko, M. D. (1994). *Suggestions of abuse: True and false memories of childhood sexual trauma.* New York: Simon & Schuster.

Young, W. C. (1992). Recognition and treatment of survivors reporting ritual abuse. In D. K. Sakheim & S. E. Devine (Eds.), *Out of darkness* (pp. 249–278). New York: Lexington Books.

Young, W. C., Sachs, R., Braun, B., & Watkins, R. (1991). Patients reporting ritual abuse in childhood: A clinical syndrome. *International Journal of Child Abuse and Neglect, 15,* 181–189.

Young, W. C., & Young, L. J. (1997). Recognition and special treatment issues in patients reporting childhood sadistic ritual abuse. In G. A. Fraser (Ed.), *The dilemma of ritual abuse: Cautions and guides for therapists* (pp. 65–104). Washington, DC: American Psychiatric Press.

George F. Rhoades, Jr.
Ola Hou Clinic

SADNESS

Until recently, the study of emotion was primarily left to novelists and poets, who have provided some of the most poignant analyses of emotions such as sadness, whether from the Bible—"They that sow in tears shall reap in joy" (Psalms)—or from Shakespeare:

> Give sorrow words. The grief that does not speak
> Whispers the o're fraught heart, and bids it break. (*Macbeth*)

Psychology had ignored the challenges laid down in Charles Darwin's famous study of emotion, *The Expression of the Emotions in Man and Animals* (published in 1872) and in earlier philosophical analyses by Descartes, Plato, and Aristotle. However, the past few decades have seen an exponential increase in interest in the study of emotion.

Sadness, like other emotions, is easy to experience or recall yet hard to describe or define. The main reason is that emotions are complex, multilevel states that include a number of important elements; namely, important external or internal events that typically lead to sadness, an interpretation and appraisal of the significance of those events, a physiological state characteristic of the emotion, a state of readiness to act in a way appropriate to the emotion, the possible conscious awareness of the emotion state, and overt behavior. In addition, these states are experienced in important social and cultural contexts, which may have complex rules about expression, suppression, or transformation of the emotions. Some of these points are elaborated in the following.

The most characteristic focus in sadness tends to be on events that include loss or failure, either real or imagined, in the past, the present, or the future. There is an appraisal of loss or failure, in which the lost object or goal varies in degree of importance and type; it could be a person, a place, an ambition that has not been attained, an object of personal value (e.g., a special pen, an important gift), or a loss of an ideal or moral value. The focus of sadness is therefore on the appraisal of loss of one or more goals across one or more domains. The loss need not be permanent but could be a temporary separation from a loved one or a loved place or even sadness experienced at the return to a loved one or a loved place following a period of separation. Moreover, the focus of the loss may be on a significant other rather than oneself, for example, one's child's failing an exam or being ill or injured. Indeed, the loss may be communal rather than personal, as in the loss of a head of state, a favorite film star, or failure by one's national team in the World Cup. Although sadness is typically classified as a negative emotion, there are many types of sadnesses that are experienced positively, such as sadness following a film or novel or the bitter-sweet combination of sadness and happiness experienced in nostalgia.

One of the dominant approaches within psychology to the study of emotions such as sadness is that of the basic emotions approach. This approach follows in the traditions of Descartes and Darwin and emphasizes the possibility that there is a limited set of innate emotions that occurs universally across all cultures and from which other more complex emotions are derived. One of the major exponents of the basic emotions approach has been Paul Ekman, who has shown that facial expressions of emotions such as sadness are recognized and experienced across a wide range of cultures. Although there is no clear agreement as yet about the exact number of basic emotions, the emotions of sadness, anger, anxiety, disgust, and happiness would be on most emotion theorists' lists of basic emotions. However, the approach is not without its critics, both from within psychology and from other areas such as anthropology, where the issue of cultural relativity versus universality has been keenly debated for a wide range of psychological and social functions. All involved in the debates agree that the *expression* of emotions, especially in adults, varies considerably across individuals and cultures both currently and historically. In fact, sadness provides some of the best examples of this variation; thus, in different times and places it has been seen as anything varying from a weak, "feminine," negative emotion leading to a loss of status for males to that of a highly desirable aesthetic state connected with high creativity (e.g., in Elizabethan England) or a state leading to compassion for others (e.g., in Catherine Lutz's study of the Ifaluk Islanders).

The modern approaches to emotion are also characterized by an emphasis on the function of emotion and reject the long-dominant Platonic view that emotions are the antithesis of reason and that they are simply disruptive of normal functioning. In the case of sadness, the functions seem to range from a period of reflective self-examination in which current goals and relationships are reexamined and reevaluated (emphasized more in individualistic Western cultures) to the seeking of help from others or offering of help to others (emphasized in the more collectivist Eastern cultures). In the infant, cries of distress early on develop into sadness by about 3 months of age with a characteristic facial expression, crying, and tears. Tears (i.e., other than as a reflex for lubrication of the eye) as part of the expression of emotion are uniquely human and illustrate the importance of the social signaling function of the face. They do not, however, occur only in sadness but can appear also with, for example, joy or laughter; as with sadness, they are an expression of the intensity of the emotion experienced.

Finally, the basic emotions approach emphasizes that a range of more complex emotions is derived from sadness because of an increase in the intensity of the emotion, because of the different circumstances in which the emotion can be experienced, or because of the combination or blending of sadness with other basic emotions. The more extreme variants of sadness seen in grief, bereavement, and mourning or in disorders derived from sadness such as depression have been widely studied in psychology, whereas the milder, everyday variants have received little attention. The experience of extreme grief consequent on the loss of an attachment figure can be seen as the major loss of mutual goals, roles, and plans that the loss of attachment figures entails. Because of the evolutionary base to attachment, the universal experience of grief across cultures must in part have an innate basis and is likely therefore to involve the operation of an automatic or unconscious route to emotion. It has been suggested that the focus on the extreme and the abnormal may perhaps represent something of our own cultural problems with sadness and its expression, especially in these extreme circumstances.

Michael J. Power
University of Edenburgh

SAVANT SYNDROME

In their *Psychiatric Dictionary,* Hinsie and Campbell (1974) noted that in early times "idiot referred to any person who lived as a recluse in a private world" (p. 377). The French term *savant* means a person of knowledge (Hill, 1978). Rimland (1978), who coined the term *autistic savant,* described an idiot savant or autistic savant as an individual who can perform various mental feats at a level far beyond the capacity of any normal person, but whose general intellectual level is very 'low.'

Those believing that subnormal intelligence is due to mental retardation have traditionally referred to such an individual as an idiot savant. Those who believe, as Rimland does, that subnormal intellectual functioning results from autism, refer to the individual as an autistic savant. Treffert (1998, 2002), who has performed an extensive investigation, prefers the term *savant syndrome.*

Savant syndrome is very rare, with estimates of fewer than 0.5% of the developmentally disabled population presenting its symptoms. In addition, there appear to be more males with the disorder than females (6:1) (Fox, 2002).

Whether the person is labeled an idiot savant or autistic savant or as having the more inclusive savant syndrome, the presenting behavior is the same: general subnormal intelligence combined with superior intellectual abilities in one or more of the areas of music, memory, art, pseudoverbal, mathematics, geography, motor coordination, calendar, and extrasensory perception (Sacks, 1995).

REFERENCES

Hill, A. L. (1978). Savants: Mentally retarded individuals with special skills. In N. Ellis (Ed.), *International review of research in mental retardation* (Vol. 9, pp. 99–126). New York: Academic.

Hinsie, L., & Campbell, R. (1974). *Psychiatric dictionary.* London: Oxford University Press.

Rimland, B. (1978). *Infantile autism: The syndrome and its impli-*

cations for a neural theory of behavior. Englewood Cliffs, NJ: Prentice Hall.

Sacks, O. (1998). *An anthropologist on mars.* New York: Knopf.

Treffert, D. A. (1998). The idiot savant: A review of the syndrome. *American Journal of Psychiatry, 145,* 563–572.

Treffert, D. A., & Wallace, G. L. (2002). Islands of genius. *Scientific American,* 76–85.

David L. Holmes
The Eden Institute

SCHIZOPHRENIA, ADOLESCENT AND CHILDHOOD

Similar to adults, both adolescents and prepubertal children may suffer from Schizophrenia. Historically, both youths with either Schizophrenia or Autistic Disorder were diagnosed under the rubric of childhood psychosis. This phenomenon was likely a reflection of the fact that young people with either Schizophrenia or Autistic Disorder can have profound impairments in interpersonal functioning and substantial disturbances of thinking and behavior. Within the past three decades, it has subsequently become clear that juvenile-onset Schizophrenia and Autistic Disorder are in fact separate conditions with distinct presentations. When juveniles do suffer from Schizophrenia, they suffer from the same symptoms as adults with this condition. These may include hallucinations (most often auditory), delusions, grossly inappropriate affect, avolition, poverty of thought or speech, disorganized behavior, and disorganized speech.

However, as young people may have imaginary friends, experience eidetic imagery, and be generally less organized in their speech and behaviors than adults, accurately determining whether a child or teenager truly is suffering from a psychotic illness can be a difficult task. Further complicating accurately accepting or rejecting a diagnosis of schizophrenia in a young person is that the differential diagnosis of Schizophrenia in youths is quite extensive.

Besides developmentally expectable phenomena that are not pathological, numerous psychiatric syndromes can present with symptoms of psychosis. The most common of these include depression, bipolar disorder, Anxiety Disorders, substance-related conditions, Personality Disorders, behavioral disorders, and pervasive Developmental disorders. In addition, developmental speech and language disorders as well as the corrective self-talk that may be seen in some youths with developmental disabilities can lead an examiner to believe that a young person is experiencing hallucinations. Of note, there appears to be a group of young people who have perceptual disturbances and substantial difficulties with affect regulation, interpersonal functioning, and behavioral control that are referred to as being multidimensionally impaired. Whether these youths suffer from a condition that should be considered within the Schizophrenia spectrum of illnesses remains to be seen and is a topic of ongoing research.

It should be remembered that there are medications that are commonly prescribed to children and teenagers as well as some general medical conditions (predominantly neurological or endocrinological) that may also lead to symptoms of psychosis in young people. In fact, it appears that most children who subjectively describe hallucinations are not suffering from a psychotic illness. It is not surprising that many youths who initially receive the diagnosis of Schizophrenia are subsequently found not to be suffering from a psychotic illness.

Although the average age at onset of illness for patients with Schizophrenia is the third decade of life, approximately one third of all patients with Schizophrenia develop this illness during the teenage years. However, childhood onset of Schizophrenia is considered quite rare; very few patients develop this illness prior to age 10. As Schizophrenia occurs in approximately 1% of adults, adolescent Schizophrenia is a relatively common phenomenon. Despite this fact, a relatively modest amount of research has focused on adolescent Schizophrenia.

The longitudinal course of juvenile-onset Schizophrenia has many similarities to the natural history of this illness in adults. For example, most young people with Schizophrenia have developmental difficulties that antecede the development of the symptoms of psychosis that define this syndrome. In this age group, the onset of illness is usually not acute, but insidious. In fact, it is not uncommon for young people with Schizophrenia to have psychotic symptoms for months or years prior to being correctly diagnosed. Unfortunately, numerous studies have consistently reported that adolescent onset of Schizophrenia puts patients at high risk for a poor outcome.

Neurobiological studies have reported that young patients with Schizophrenia have findings that are distinct from typically developing youths. These include structural differences in cerebral morphology and eye tracking.

Although it is generally recommended that a multimodal approach be employed for young people with Schizophrenia, the cornerstone of treatment for adolescents and children with this illness is antipsychotic medication. Unfortunately, there have been only a few methodologically rigorous studies in this patient population. Pharmacotherapy for juvenile-onset Schizophrenia is complicated by the observation that young patients appear to be at higher risk than adults for developing antipsychotic-related extrapyramidal side effects. It also appears that earlier age at onset is associated with a greater propensity for lack of response to the typical antipsychotic agents. For these reasons, most clinicians now prescribe atypical antipsychotics to treat young people with Schizophrenia in hopes of improving the rates of symptomatic response and reducing the rates of extrapyramidal side effects seen with the typical antipsychotics.

Open label studies have reported that risperidone, olanzapine, and quetiapine may be effective treatments for adolescents with Schizophrenia. Clozapine appears to be a rational treatment for those youths who do not respond to other forms of pharmacotherapy. However, young patients appear to be at higher risk than adults for clozapine-related neurological side effects such as seizures.

Besides pharmacotherapy, it is recommended that psychosocial interventions be employed in this condition. As young patients with Schizophrenia may have impairments in working memory and attention, many of these youths may benefit from special education services that consider these issues. It is generally recommended that psychosocial treatments not only involve the affected youth but also include the patient's family. Patients and their families may benefit from supportive and psychoeducational therapies. Youths may also derive benefit from social skills training. Families and patients often find utilizing case management and becoming part of community-based support groups to be quite helpful.

Although symptom amelioration is vital, the ultimate goal of treatment for children and teenagers with Schizophrenia is to provide these vulnerable youths the best opportunity to achieve developmentally appropriate academic goals while enjoying rich and fulfilling relationships with their peers and loved ones.

Robert L. Findling
Nora K. McNamara
University Hospitals of Cleveland

SCHOOL ADJUSTMENT

School adjustment is a multidomain construct comprising social, behavioral, and academic competencies. School interest and motivation, academic achievement, peer relationships, and classroom conduct are among the many variables involved in school adjustment. A child's school adjustment depends on the match between his or her competencies and the demands of the school environment and may fluctuate across schools, years, and classrooms or across different domains within the same year.

The school environment and the children's experiences inside and outside of school impact school adjustment. Concurrent physical and cognitive development, as well as stressful life events, peer relationship problems, and family relationships, impinge on children's school adjustment, as does the changing school environment. Within and across schools, considerable variability exists in terms of educational resources, academic and behavioral expectations, teacher and parent involvement, extracurricular activities, classroom management strategies, class size, and other aspects of the school environment. School transitions (e.g., the transition to middle school) may be particularly challenging for children due to increased social, behavioral, and academic demands. Although most children adapt to school transitions comfortably, rates of adjustment problems are elevated during school transitions.

Commonly examined markers of school adjustment include achievement and grade information, competence and problem behaviors, frequency of school absence, comfort and involvement with the school environment, anxiety or avoidance behaviors, and negative attitudes about school. Chronic poor school adjustment can lead to low achievement, school dropout, delinquency, and psychosocial maladjustment. Because adjustment in the early primary grades is related to later school adjustment, it is important to prevent poor school adjustment early in children's school careers. Interventions designed to reduce poor school adjustment target the mismatch between children's competencies and the demands of the educational environment by addressing children's competencies, parental involvement, and school environmental demands.

SUGGESTED READING

Perry, K. E., & Weinstein, R. S. (1998). *The social context of early schooling and children's school adjustment. Educational Psychology, 33*(4), 177–194.

Stephen A. Erath
Kelly S. Flanagan
Pennsylvania State University

SCHOOL DROPOUT

The term *dropout* denotes one who officially enrolls in a program but does not complete it. As it pertains to education and schooling, a dropout is one who neither completes requirements for graduation nor receives a high school diploma. High school graduation is interpreted as receiving a high school diploma on completion of the required course credits and enrollment duration, but not an equivalence certificate. High school completion is interpreted as having fulfilled all of the requirements for high school graduation including receipt of a high school diploma, or having received an alternative form of certification, the most commonly known of which is the general equivalency diploma (GED).

Many school districts and states use the cohort method to predict future graduation numbers and define dropouts. A cohort is a group of people enrolling or participating in a specific project or program with an anticipated or expected completion date. For high school graduation, an entering 9th grade cohort or group has a four-year expected completion date. This completion is usually recognized formally by an official graduation and presentation of a high school diploma. Thus, using the cohort method to define dropouts requires different assumptions or information about students who do not graduate from secondary school within four years from the time that they enroll.

If a school computes dropout rates using the cohort method, based on students who did not graduate on time and are no longer enrolled, it may make the assumption that students who do not graduate with their cohort have left the school and are not enrolled anywhere else. The aforementioned method neglects the fact that some students could have transferred to another school, still are on schedule to graduate after four years, and should not be counted as dropouts. Other students may have been retained in their grade and are enrolled in school, so their dropout status is not determined after four years. Even if a school determines that a cohort student lacking four-year graduation status has not been retained in grade, transferred to another school, or home schooled, the student still may not be a dropout. In this case, nondropouts include students who may have graduated early by skipping a grade or who passed the GED, which technically makes them high school completers, and not dropouts.

The term *dropout,* thus, is best defined as students who entered secondary school with a particular cohort, withdrew from both formal and informal schooling, and did not complete secondary school or receive an equivalent credential. Such a conceptualization focuses more on the fact that the students withdrew from the educational system and less on the amount of time it took them to complete secondary school or the type of credential received. This definition takes into consideration factors such as grade retention, school transfer, early graduation, and alternative certification.

Additional types of definitions of dropouts include event rates and status rates. Event rate definitions of dropouts include the number of students who drop out of high school during a given academic year. Status rate definitions include the number of persons within an age range (e.g., 16–24) who have neither graduated from nor completed high school. Some reasons why students become high school dropouts include low achievement levels, the need to work, teenage pregnancy, incarceration, illness, and death.

Olotokunbo Fashola
Johns Hopkins University

SCHOOL LEARNING

School learning is both formal and informal. Formal learning is associated primarily with instructional processes and content applied by teaching staff. Less directly, it also stems from school-wide socialization processes, such as exposure to institutional standards and their enforcement. Informal learning at school, sometimes called the hidden curriculum, is associated with experiences of success and failure and with modeling and social persuasion.

Determinants of School Learning

A reciprocal determinist view of behavior emphasizes transactions between person and environment (Bandura, 1978; Lewin, 1951; Walsh, Craik, & Price, 1992). From this perspective, school learning is the product of the interplay among student and school variables. Each student brings to school adaptive, assimilated schemata consisting of capacities and attitudes accumulated over time, as well as current states of being and behaving. These variables transact with each other and with variables encountered at school and in coping with school requirements outside school (Adelman & Taylor, 1994).

Variables related to formal school learning encompass not only instructional processes and content but also the physical and social contexts in which instruction and related practice are the primary focus. Informal learning is the product of the many variables impinging on a student during times when instruction is not the agenda and occurs in settings such as the playing field, eating areas, and hallways, as well as in classrooms.

Types of School Learning

The impact of transacting variables can lead to four types of learning (Adelman & Taylor, 1993):

1. *Desired learning:* changes and expansion of capacities and attitudes in keeping with the school's goals
2. *Deviant learning:* changes and expansion of capacities and attitudes not in keeping with the school's goals
3. *Disrupted learning:* interference with learning functions, including possible confusion that distorts attitudes and decreases capacities
4. *Delayed and arrested learning:* little change or possibly a decay in capacities and attitudes

These outcomes are accompanied by concomitant shifts in current states of being and behaving.

Person-Environment Match

Bodies of relevant research range from basic research on learning and social learning to applied research on teaching and schooling. Theoretical underpinnings are rooted in the paradigm of person-environment match or fit (D. E. Hunt & Sullivan, 1974; J. M. Hunt, 1961; Piaget, 1952; Vygotsky, Vygotsky, & John-Steiner, 1980). With respect to formal school learning, the paradigm broadly proposes that the better the match, the more likely it is that instruction will lead to desired outcomes. Conversely, the poorer the match, the less likely it is that desired outcomes will be achieved. Concern about quality of the match arises at the outset of instruction and remains throughout.

The problem of creating a good match in teaching is viewed broadly as that of establishing an appropriate challenge to the adaptive, assimilated schemata of a student. In theory, some degree of appropriate match is always feasible.

The concept of the match can be operationalized using observer or actor viewpoints or both. For example, the psychological perspective of the teacher may be the sole referent in deciding which student characteristics are considered, which instructional processes and content are used, and whether an appropriate match is established. In contrast, some teachers decide how to proceed and judge quality of fit based on student perspectives.

Matching Motivation and Developed Capability

Efforts to optimize the person-environment match focus on *both* motivation and development. Cognitive-affective theories underscore the necessity of addressing individual differences in motivation as a primary concern in creating an optimal match for learning. The focus is on four broad considerations.

First, motivation is considered a key antecedent condition—a prerequisite to school learning. Poor motivational readiness may be a cause of inadequate and problem functioning, a factor that maintains such problems, or both. Thus, strategies are called for that can result in a high level of motivational readiness (including reduction of avoidance motivation and reactance) so that a student is mobilized to participate and learn.

Second, motivation is a key ongoing process concern; processes must elicit, enhance, and maintain motivation so that the student stays mobilized. For instance, a student may value a specific outcome but may not be motivated to pursue certain processes for obtaining it or may be motivated at the beginning of an activity but not maintain that motivation.

Third, it is necessary to avoid or at least minimize conditions likely to produce avoidance and reactance. Of particular concern are activities that students perceive as unchallenging and uninteresting, overdemanding, or overwhelming and procedures that seriously limit a student's range of options or that are experienced as overcontrolling and coercive.

Finally, development of intrinsic motivation is an outcome concern (Deci & Ryan, 1985). This requires strategies to enhance stable, positive, intrinsic attitudes that mobilize a student's ongoing pursuit of desirable ends outside the school context and after graduation.

Matching a student's level of developed capability is another primary consideration in facilitating school learning. Variations in functional capacity stem from differences related to given areas of development. To facilitate an appropriate match, functional differences are accommodated through modifying processes and content to account for development lag and development that meets or surpasses expectations.

In general practice, overall patterns are considered in designing instruction to fit groups of students, with the observed patterns reflecting both accumulated capacities and attitudes. Such patterns may be described in terms of student differences, diversity, assets, deficits, and disabilities observed in a given classroom and school. Researchers and practitioners interested in patterns of functional differences find it useful for observation and measurement purposes to stress four performance dimensions: (1) rate (the pace of performance), (2) style (preferences with regard to ways of proceeding), (3) amount (the quantity of produced outcomes), and (4) quality (care, mastery, and aesthetic features demonstrated in performance; Gagne, 1985).

Environmental Factors

Facilitating school learning by focusing on the environmental side of the person-environment match has two facets: (1) directly enhancing facilitative factors and (2) minimizing extrinsic factors that are barriers to learning. Research of relevance to these matters comes from ecological and environmental psychology, systems theory and organizational research, and the study of social and community interventions. Examples of key variables include setting and context characteristics associated with school learning; characteristics of persons in the setting; and task, process, and outcome characteristics. With specific respect to barriers to learning, the focus is on factors that are insufficient to stimulate learning, exceed the student's capacity for accommodative modification, or are so intrusive or hostile that they disrupt learning.

Because teachers can affect only a relatively small segment of the physical environment and social context in which school learning occurs, increasing attention is being given to analyses of school-wide factors and combinations of school, home, and community variables.

REFERENCES

Adelman, H. S., & Taylor, L. (1993). *Learning problems and learning disabilities: Moving forward.* Pacific Grove, CA: Brooks/Cole.

Adelman, H. S., & Taylor, L. (1994). *On understanding intervention in psychology and education.* Westport, CT: Prager.

Bandura, A. (1978). The self system in reciprocal determinism. *American Psychologist, 33,* 344–358.

Deci, E. L., & Ryan, R. M. (1985). *Intrinsic motivation and self-determination in human behavior.* New York: Plenum Press.

Gagne, R. M. (1985). *The conditions of learning and theory of instruction* (4th ed.). Fort Worth, TX: Holt, Rinehart & Winston.

Hunt, D. E., & Sullivan, E. V. (1974). *Between psychology and education.* Chicago: Dryden Press.

Hunt, J. M. (1961). *Intelligence and experience.* New York: Ronald Press.

Lewin, K. (1951). *Field theory and social sciences.* New York: Harper & Row.

Piaget, J. (1952). *The origins of intelligence in children.* New York: International Universities Press.

Vygotsky, L. S., Vygotsky, S., & John-Steiner, V. (Eds.). (1980). *Minds in society: The development of higher psychological processes.* Cambridge, MA: Harvard University Press.

Walsh, W. B., Craik, K. C., & Price, R. H. (Eds.). (1992). *Person-environment psychology: Models and perspectives.* Hillsdale, NJ: Erlbaum.

Howard Adelman
University of California, Los Angeles

SCHOOL REFUSAL BEHAVIOR

School refusal behavior refers to a child's refusal to attend school and to difficulties remaining in classes for an entire day. The behavior is apparent in school-age youth who miss entire school days, skip classes, or arrive to school late (excluding legitimate absences). However, the behavior also refers to youth who show severe behavior problems in the morning to try to stay home from school as well as youth who attend school with great dread. School refusal behavior affects up to 28% of youth at some time in their lives and can lead to several negative consequences. In the short term, for example, school refusal behavior may lead to family conflict, legal trouble, declining grades, social alienation, and distress. In the long term, extensive school refusal behavior may lead to delinquency, school dropout, and occupational, economic, and social problems in adulthood.

Many cases of school refusal behavior involve diverse symptoms. For example, these youth often have general and social anxiety, fear, depression, somatic complaints (e.g., headaches and stomachaches), and withdrawal. In addition, however, these youth also show many disruptive behaviors such as noncompliance, defiance, aggression, tantrums, clinging, refusal to move, and running away from school or home. In many cases of school refusal behavior, a mixture of these symptoms is present. In general, school refusal behavior is not largely related to gender, income level, or race, although dropout rates tend to be highest for Hispanics and African Americans.

Historically, school refusal behavior has been defined in different ways, and many terms have been used to describe the population. School phobia, for example, often refers to youth who are fearful of something at school, although few children in this population report specific fears. School refusal generally refers to youth who are anxious about school. This may include youth with separation anxiety or those who become worried at the prospect of being apart from parents or significant others. Truancy often refers to youth who refuse school without parental knowledge and who show other delinquent acts. The phrase *school refusal behavior* was designed as an umbrella term to include all of these children.

Treatment for youth with school refusal behavior usually begins with a systematic assessment by a school or mental health professional. In most cases, assessment includes the child, parents, school officials, and relevant others. Assessment may consist of interviews, questionnaires, observations of the family and child, standardized tests, daily ratings of distress, and reviews of school records, among other methods. A thorough medical examination should also be conducted to identify any genuine physical ailments (e.g., ulcers, migraines). Clinicians often focus on the various forms (e.g., anxiety, depression, noncompliance) as well as on the functions of school refusal behavior, or reasons why the behavior continues over time. Identified reasons for school refusal behavior include desires to escape from painful items at school, to obtain attention from parents, and to pursue tangible rewards outside of school (e.g., sleeping late, riding one's bicycle, being with friends). Many children refuse school for a combination of these reasons as well.

Common examples of school-related items that children sometimes avoid include buses, fire alarms, gymnasiums, playgrounds, hallways, animals, and transitions from one place to another (e.g., classroom to cafeteria). Common examples of school-related people that children sometimes avoid include peers (e.g., bullies), teachers, and principals. Common examples of school-related situations that children sometimes avoid include tests, recitals, athletic performances, and writing or speaking before others. Many children, however, refuse school not because of something painful there but because they wish to pursue something more appealing outside of school (e.g., time with parents or friends).

Treatment for school refusal behavior usually depends on its forms and functions. For children who refuse school because of anxiety while attending, treatment often focuses on the child to help him or her master anxiety and gradually return to school. This is done by educating the child about his or her anxiety, helping the child relax muscles and control breathing, changing irrational thoughts that might prevent attendance, and gradually reintegrating the child back into school. The latter is usually done by having the child identify classes or time periods during the day that he or she likes most (e.g., lunch and science class). The child initially attends these times only and reports different thoughts and other anxiety-based symptoms that occur. Over time, the child gradually increases classroom attendance, working to control anxiety, until full-time attendance is achieved.

For children who refuse school for attention, parent training is often used. In this approach, parents are encouraged to design set routines in the morning, daytime (if the child is home from school), and evening. A child's compliance to these routines is rewarded, and noncompliance is punished. The child is also required gradually to reattend school and face appropriate consequences for successes and failures. Parents are sometimes instructed forcibly to bring a child to school under certain circumstances (e.g., no anxiety present, cooperation with school officials, two adults present).

For children who refuse school for tangible rewards outside of school, family therapy is often used. In this approach, family members (e.g., parents and teenager) are encouraged to design contracts that increase rewards for school attendance and decrease rewards for absenteeism. The latter sometimes involves increasing supervision of the child and escorting him or her from class to class. Related procedures include communication skills training to reduce conflict and increase negotiation among family members and peer refusal skills training so that youth can appropriately refuse offers to miss school.

School refusal behavior is a serious problem that must be addressed quickly and must involve the cooperation of the child, parents, educators, and relevant others (e.g., therapist, dating partners, medical professionals). In addition, ongoing monitoring of the child is necessary to prevent relapse and address any new problems that may occur during the academic year. Early introduction to new school settings and starting the typical weekday routine one to two weeks before the start of school is often recommended as well.

Christopher A. Kearney
University of Nevada, Las Vegas

See also: **Anxiety; Family Therapy**

SCHOOLS OF PROFESSIONAL PSYCHOLOGY

Most psychologists are educated in academic departments of psychology. Even those entering such professional fields as clinical or counseling psychology usually pursue their graduate studies in departmental programs comparable in size and administrative structure to programs in experimental, developmental, or social psychology. Increasing numbers of psychologists preparing for careers in practice, however, are educated in schools of professional psychology administratively comparable to schools of law, medicine, engineering, or business. The earliest schools of professional psychology were free-standing institutions, unaffiliated with universities. Currently, many of the schools are situated in universities, although many others continue to operate independently.

Schools of professional psychology are distinguished by several characteristics. First, their explicit mission is to prepare students for careers in practice. Second, their organizational structure is that of a school or college rather than of a departmental program. This status carries several consequences. The chief administrator is usually a dean. The academic unit is accorded a high degree of autonomy in defining its curriculum, selecting faculty, admitting students, and other matters of policy and procedure. Administrative resources and controls are relatively direct, usually through officers of the central administration in university-based schools and through boards of directors in free-standing schools. Enrollments are typically much larger than in departmental programs.

A third characteristic of professional schools is that the curriculum is specifically designed to prepare people for professional work. Supervised experience in psychological practice is therefore emphasized throughout graduate study as well as in an internship. A dissertation is required in the programs of nearly all professional schools, but the inquiry is conceived as a form of practice, not as an end in itself. Fourth, the faculties include large numbers of practitioners, and all faculty members are ordinarily expected to maintain some involvement in professional activity. Finally, the degree awarded on completion of graduate study is in nearly all cases the doctor of psychology (PsyD) degree rather than the doctor of philosophy (PhD).

The forerunner of contemporary schools of professional psychology was the program in clinical psychology at Adelphi University. When the Adelphi program was approved by the American Psychological Association Committee on Accreditation in 1957, it became the first accredited program whose primary objective was to educate clinicians for practice, instead of to educate them as scientists or scientist-practitioners. Prior to that time, all of the clinical and counseling programs in the United States and Canada had followed the Boulder model of education that was defined in a conference on the training of clinical psychologists in Boulder, Colorado, in 1949. The conference held that clinical psychologists were to be trained in academic psychology departments, prepared to conduct research as well as to practice psychology, and awarded the PhD degree on completion of graduate studies. The early Adelphi program preserved the administrative structure that was common to other departmental programs, changed the curriculum mainly by introducing more supervised clinical experience than usual, and retained the PhD as the terminal degree. It differed fundamentally from all other programs at the time, however, by affirming the legitimacy of direct education for psychological practice, with or without the promise of contributory research.

The first institution administratively organized as a school for practitioners of psychology was the Graduate School of Psychology in the Fuller Theological Seminary.

Psychologists were initially brought into the seminary faculty to train clergy in pastoral counseling, but in time they expanded their activities to form a comprehensive doctoral program combining clinical psychology with theological studies. The Fuller school was established in 1965.

Large-scale development of schools of professional psychology did not begin, however, until the California School of Professional Psychology was founded in 1969. Overwhelmed by demands for psychological services in an increasingly populous state and frustrated by repeated refusals of academic psychologists to increase the size and implicitly change the emphases of their tiny, research-oriented clinical programs, a group of practitioners resolved to create their own professional school that would be independent of any university. Faculty were to be practicing professionals, teaching on a part-time basis. The curriculum duplicated the Adelphi pattern and, as at Adelphi, the PhD degree was to be awarded to graduates. Capital funds were obtained from several private benefactors. For the first year, the founding group offered their time as administrators and faculty free of charge as an operational endowment. The plan was approved in 1969, and in 1970 the California School of Professional Psychology admitted students to its first two campuses, in San Francisco and Los Angeles. Additional campuses were opened in San Diego and Fresno over the next two years.

In 1973 another conference on professional training in psychology was held in Vail, Colorado. The conference concluded that psychology had matured sufficiently to justify creation of explicit professional programs, in addition to those for scientists and scientist-professionals. Professional schools were recognized as appropriate settings for training, and the PsyD degree was endorsed as the credential of choice on completion of graduate requirements in practitioner programs. Over the following years, schools of professional psychology were established in many locations throughout the United States. Some were in universities, and some were in free-standing institutions. Some awarded the PhD; others awarded the PsyD degree. The Graduate School of Applied and Professional Psychology, established at Rutgers University in 1974, was the first university-based professional school to offer the PsyD. At Rutgers, as in the Illinois PsyD program that preceded it, a scientist-practitioner program leading to the PhD was maintained for students interested primarily in research. This pattern—a relatively large school of professional psychology designed expressly to train practitioners and awarding the PsyD degree alongside a smaller PhD program to prepare students for research careers—has since been adopted by several other universities and independent professional schools. Toward the end of the 20th century, more than 35 professional schools were in operation, approximately half in universities and half as free-standing institutions. During this period, nearly one-third of students receiving doctorates in clinical psychology were graduated from professional schools.

As the schools have evolved, they have changed in several ways. Early faculties in free-standing schools were employed almost entirely on a part-time basis. Proportions of full-time faculty in the independent schools have increased over the years, and professional schools in universities employed large proportions of full-time faculty from the beginning. Psychological centers, analogous to the teaching hospitals of medical schools, are now an integral part of nearly all professional schools and provide the controlled settings in which faculty and students offer public services, students are trained, and research is conducted. Dissertation requirements, which were eliminated completely in some of the early schools, are now an essential part of nearly every program, though the emphasis on direct education for practice and the view of systematic investigation as a form of professional service has been retained. The PsyD degree has replaced the PhD degree in almost all of the professional schools in operation at this time.

In 1976 the National Council of Professional Schools was established to provide a forum for exchange of information among professional schools, to develop standards for the education and training of professional psychologists, and to improve in every way possible the educational process so that graduates would serve public needs most effectively. Later, the name of the organization was changed to the National Council of Schools and Programs of Professional Psychology to acknowledge the inclusion of some 20 programs that share the fundamental aims, curricula, and degree-granting practices of professional schools but differ in their smaller enrollments and departmental administrative structures. Through a series of conferences and reports, the council has conducted self-studies, defined curricula, and established means for quality assurance among its member organizations. Along with the Council of Graduate Departments of Psychology and the Councils of University Directors of Clinical, Counseling, and School Psychology, the National Council of Schools and Programs of Professional Psychology is an influential participant in shaping educational policy in American psychology.

SUGGESTED READING

Peterson, R. L., Peterson, D. R., Abrams, J. C., & Stricker, G. (1997). The National Council of Schools and Programs of Professional Psychology educational model. *Professional Psychology: Research and Practice, 28,* 373–386.

Stricker, G., & Cummings, N. A. (1992). The professional school movement. In D. K. Freedheim (Ed.), *History of psychotherapy: A century of change.* Washington, DC: APA Books.

Donald R. Peterson
Rutgers University

See also: **American Psychological Association**

SCIENTIFIC METHOD

The scientific method is a set of procedures designed to establish general laws through developing and evaluating theories that attempt to describe, explain, and predict phenomena. Hypotheses are made from such theories; the hypotheses are evaluated using objective, controlled, empirical investigations; and conclusions are open to public scrutiny, analysis, and replication.

Conclusions about reality can be made in at least four different ways: on faith ("I believe that God created heaven and earth"), on common sense or intuition ("I feel that women have a maternal drive"), on logic ("I think, therefore I am"), or on the analysis of empirical data (the scientific method).

The scientific approach is analytical. Complex events are analyzed into relevant variables; relationships among these variables are investigated; and theories consistent with the empirical results are created and critically evaluated. For example, if disease is more common among the poor, the scientist may postulate a set of variables that are the cause of this phenomenon, such as differences in diet, education, medical availability, environmental factors, and genetic susceptibility. Then empirical data are collected to analyze the effect of such variables on disease so that a general theory can be constructed and tested by other scientists.

The scientific method involves a critical approach to data analysis and interpretation. Issues of observer bias (the researcher who only sees or emphasizes the results that are consistent with a theory), subject bias (the subject who cooperates with the researcher by conforming to the experimenter's expectations), and confounding or extraneous variables (alternative variables that could explain the observed phenomena) receive serious attention as scientists interpret the results of their studies.

The scientific method involves a broad array of alternative procedures ranging from carefully observing the variables as they naturally occur to collecting data under controlled situations with subjects randomly assigned to conditions. Scientific research design can be grouped into three major categories. Studies can be designed to describe events, to describe correlational relationships among events, or to establish cause-and-effect relationships between events. Descriptive and correlational studies can be used to provide information for theory construction and hypothesis testing. Causal research allows the researcher to establish the direct effect of one variable on another, rather than simply to establish that two variables may correlate.

An important maxim to remember is that correlation does not imply causation. Two variables may correlate with each other, although neither causes the other. For example, literacy rates and levels of air pollution may correlate across countries. Literacy does not cause air pollution, and air pollution does not cause literacy; both variables may be caused by the demands of an industrialized society. To establish a cause-and-effect relationship, the researcher must demonstrate that by manipulating or controlling the causal variable, a change in the affected variable systematically occurs. This is a scientific experiment. Sometimes, however, this is impossible. For example, to see if being orphaned causes personality disorders, the researcher would have to select a random sample of children and make them into orphans. Because this clearly is unethical, psychologists sometimes must rely on correlational evidence and cannot provide scientific evidence for some cause-and-effect theories.

Scientists construct theories out of a collection of building blocks, and research studies and their results provide these blocks. Theories fall if the cumulative evidence does not support their construction, and theories built on a solid foundation of supporting evidence survive. A single study, by itself, rarely is considered a sufficient basis on which to accept or discard a theory. Replication (producing duplicate studies) and cross-validation (conducting studies by defining variables in different ways or using different types of samples) are necessary for the scientific community to accept the validity of a scientific theory. They also provide evidence for refining theories, to delimit more carefully conditions under which a theory holds true.

Probably one of the easiest research methodologies is the archival method, which involves seeking information from public and private records, such as newspapers or diaries. For example, research on sexism in the media could be based on content analyses of randomly selected newspapers, magazines, and radio and television programs.

Another type of scientific method involves an in-depth case study of a particular individual. Clinical psychologists may examine a patient to learn how the patient's symptoms relate to various factors in the environment or to treatment strategies. The systematic observation method can be extended from the case study of an individual to the study of entire groups. For example, naturalistic observations might be made of children as they play in a school yard or of wild animals as they roam their natural habitats. These observations can lead to theories (e.g., how dominance hierarchies are established in animals) or can be used to test hypotheses based on theories (e.g., a theory may lead to the hypothesis that children have fewer arguments when they have recently eaten).

Naturalistic observation data collected in real-life settings generally are less artificial than data collected under carefully controlled laboratory settings, so generalizing results with the former may be more valid. However, the data are only of a descriptive or correlational nature, so cause-and-effect conclusions cannot be made.

An alternative research strategy is the use of surveys, questionnaires, and structured interviews. Subjects knowingly participate as research participants and provide the data in response to specific questions. The questions can be presented in writing (e.g., an attitude survey or personality test) or orally (e.g., an individual IQ test or public opinion poll). The quality of the data depends on the cooperation and honesty of the subjects, as well as on the quality of the questions asked. Survey techniques allow for the collection of large amounts of data under fairly standardized conditions.

Observational methods provide data for descriptive or correlational studies. Only an experiment in which the researcher manipulates the causal variable (the independent variable) and observes the effect on the affected variable (the dependent variable) can lead to conclusions about causality. It is crucial that all other variables that may affect the dependent variable (extraneous or nuisance variables) be controlled for so that results can be unambiguously interpreted.

Mary J. Allen
California State University
Office of the Chancellor

SCL-90-R

The SCL-90-R is a 90-item self-report symptom inventory developed by Leonard R. Derogatis in the mid-1970s to measure psychological symptoms and psychological distress. It is designed to be appropriate for use with individuals from the community, as well as individuals with either medical or psychiatric conditions. The SCL-90-R assesses psychological distress in terms of nine principal symptom dimensions and three summary scores termed global scores. The principal symptom dimensions are labeled Somatization (SOM), Obsessive-Compulsive (OBS), Interpersonal Sensitivity (INT), Depression (DEP), Anxiety (ANX), Hostility (HOS), Phobic Anxiety (PHOB), Paranoid Ideation (PAR), and Psychoticism (PSY). The global measures are referred to as the Global Severity Index (GSI), the Positive Symptom Distress Index (PSDI), and the Positive Symptom Total (PST).

The SCL-90-R and its companion scales represent the current expression of a long measurement tradition. This progression proceeded most directly from a self-report instrument termed the Hopkins Symptom Checklist (HSCL) developed by Derogatis and his colleagues several years earlier than the SCL-90-R. The HSCL shares common characteristics and item content with a number of prior self-report instruments, most notably the Cornell Medical Index developed several decades before. A number of SCL-90-R items can be traced all the way back to the original self-report symptom inventory, Woodworth's Personal Data Sheet, developed to screen American Expeditionary Force soldiers for psychiatric disorder in World War I.

The SCL-90-R is one component of an integrated series of psychological distress instruments. There are two additional brief self-report scales in the series: the Brief Symptom Inventory (BSI), which is a 53-item version measuring the same nine primary symptom dimensions and three global scales, and the BSI-18, published in 2000 as a short screening version of the scale. The BSI-18 is focused on only the Somatization, Depression, and Anxiety dimensions and includes a Total summary score. Comparable dimension scores on the three instruments correlate very highly with each other. The three instruments require 12–15 minutes, 9–12 minutes, and 3–4 minutes respectively to complete.

In addition, the SCL-90 Analogue Scale and the Derogatis Psychiatric Rating Scale, two matched companion clinician rating scales, are also components in the series. The two rating scales, which differ primarily in level of complexity, enable the measurement of psychological distress status via skilled clinician judgments, measured on the same principal symptom dimensions as the respondent's self-report.

To enable more accurate and meaningful interpretation of SCL-90-R, BSI, and BSI-18 score profiles, all three instruments have gender-keyed norms. Norms were developed in such a manner that standardized scores for the various tests have actuarial properties, which means that they translate into accurate percentiles, much like college SAT or GRE scores. Norms based on community adults, community adolescents, psychiatric outpatients, and psychiatric inpatients are available for the SCL-90-R and the BSI. Adult community norms and comprehensive norms for cancer patients have been developed so far for the BSI-18.

Numerous studies testing the consistency of the tests' dimension scores across various important respondent characteristics such as gender and age have demonstrated high consistency. In addition, numerous studies evaluating the predictive and construct validity and reliability of the tests' dimension and summary scores have been conducted over the years in multiple samples and populations. These investigations have repeatedly demonstrated the instruments to be valid and consistent as measures of psychological symptoms and emotional distress. The scales have also repeatedly shown high and selective convergence with other tests that measure the same constructs and have been appropriately uncorrelated with other tests that measure distinct and unrelated constructs.

Currently, the SCL-90-R and its progeny have been utilized in close to 2,000 published clinical studies in an extraordinarily broad spectrum of applications. The instruments have been employed in diagnostic and treatment applications concerning mental health status in an extensive range of medical conditions including cardiovascular, oncologic, endocrine, neurologic, and surgical, as well as with psychiatric disorders. They have consistently demonstrated their sensitivity to pharmacotherapeutic, psychotherapeutic, and other treatment interventions and have repeatedly proven their capacity to register systematic, clinically meaningful changes in psychological distress levels.

The SCL-90-R has been translated into 28 languages including Spanish, French, German, Italian, Russian, Portuguese, Dutch, Swiss, Japanese, Chinese, Korean, Vietnamese, Hebrew, and Arabic. The complete line of tests is published and distributed by National Computer Systems (NCS) of Minnetonka, Minnesota.

Leonard R. Derogatis
University of Maryland

SELECTIVE ATTENTION

Within the field of cognitive psychology, selective attention refers to the differential processing of simultaneous sources of information. Perhaps the best-known real-life example of selective attention is one in which a person is capable of listening to a single voice in a room full of people talking at the same time, while apparently being oblivious to all other conversations. This instance of auditory selective attention was described by Cherry (1953) when he noted that while a person may have appeared to be selectively attending to only his or her own conversation while ignoring all other voices, that person sometimes noticed important stimuli, such as his or her own name. Cherry referred to this so-called *cocktail-party phenomenon* when he framed many of the principle questions about selective attention.

One of the main questions about selective attention concerns what factors make it easy or difficult. Much of the research on this question in auditory selective attention makes use of a dichotic listening task, in which two different auditory messages are presented simultaneously, one to each ear, via headphones. Participants are instructed to attend selectively to one of the messages and repeat, or shadow, this relevant message as quickly and accurately as possible. In general, participants have little difficulty shadowing the relevant message; that is, they can quickly and accurately repeat the relevant message in the attended ear while repeating very little, if any, of the irrelevant message in the unattended ear. Findings from modified dichotic listening task studies seem to indicate that selectivity occurs on the basis of the spatial location of the messages, as well as on the basis of frequency differences between the relevant and irrelevant messages. For example, if each of the two messages is played simultaneously at equal intensity in both ears (eliminating differences in spatial location as determined by variances in interaural intensity) using the same voice (eliminating differences in frequency), selectivity of just one message becomes considerably more difficult (Cherry, 1953). Selectivity improves, however, if the voices of the two messages differ in pitch; for example, the ease of shadowing increases when the irrelevant message is delivered by a different gender (Treisman, 1964). Shadowing is also improved when spatial localization is produced by introducing even moderate differences in interaural intensity between the two messages (Treisman, 1964).

The factors affecting the ease of selective attention has been an issue also with respect to the visual modality. That is, what factors make it easier or more difficult for a person to attend selectively to a particular visual stimulus while excluding others? Visual selective attention is often studied using a visual filtering task in which participants are asked to attend selectively to one visual stimulus embedded within an array of visual distracter items. Other tasks involve superimposing two different videotaped events onto a single video. Participants are instructed to selectively attend to one visual scene and press a button whenever an unusual event occurs in the relevant scene. Results seem to suggest that the ease with which participants can selectively attend to the relevant visual stimulus depends on the degree to which the relevant and irrelevant stimuli differ in terms of simple physical attributes, such as location, color, size, and brightness (Pashler, 1998).

Since Cherry first drew attention to the topic of selective attention in the early 1950s, two structural models of selective attention have been proposed. So-called early selection models of Broadbent (1958) and Treisman (1964) viewed selective attention in the context of an information-processing model in which incoming stimuli are successively transformed from basic sensory attributes into more complex semantic representations. Selective attention was seen as a type of filter or bottleneck that restricted the flow of information through the system. According to Broadbent and Treisman, this bottleneck occurred early in the information-processing system, such that only low-level perceptual characteristics could be perceived prior to attentional selection. Thus, early-selection theories suggest that higher level semantic characteristics cannot be perceived early in processing. In contrast, late-selection theories hold that the bottleneck occurs later in the information-processing system, such that higher level, abstract processing of meaning can occur before attentional selection takes place (Deutsch & Deutsch, 1963). Even though several decades have passed since the articulation of this issue, the question of whether selection occurs early or late has remained largely unresolved.

This question of whether selective attention takes place early in stimulus processing, before semantic analysis of any stimulus, or whether it takes place later in processing, after semantic analysis of all stimuli, has preoccupied researchers for many years. Research on this question also makes use of the dichotic listening task. Results from these types of studies show that participants can remember almost nothing about the content of the irrelevant message but are able to note if the gender of the speaker is switched or if the irrelevant message is replaced with a tone (Cherry,

1953). These results seem to indicate that selection takes place before the stimulus has been analyzed on the basis of its meaning. However, other studies have shown that participants are able to notice the insertion of their name into the irrelevant message (Moray, 1959) and that they sometimes shift their shadowing from the relevant message to the irrelevant message when, midway through a shadowing task, messages are switched between ears (Treisman, 1960).

In visual modality studies, evidence for semantic processing of unattended stimuli is also somewhat mixed. Experiments reported by Underwood (1981) involved presentation of central (relevant) and right (irrelevant) parafoveal word stimuli in order to determine whether semantic attributes of the irrelevant word would influence processing of the relevant word. Following presentation of the word stimuli, participants were asked to respond by naming the category to which the relevant word belonged. It was found that the latency of the category-naming response was influenced by the semantic relationship between the relevant and irrelevant words. However, in several other studies of a similar nature, no semantic biasing or priming effects were observed (Inhoff & Rayner, 1980; Paap & Newsome, 1981).

REFERENCES

Broadbent, D. E. (1958). *Perception and communication.* New York: Pergamon.

Cherry, C. (1953). Some experiments on the recognition of speech with one and two ears. *Journal of the Acoustical Society of America, 25,* 975–979.

Deutsch, J. A., & Deutsch, D. (1963). Attention: Some theoretical considerations. *Psychological Review, 70,* 80–90.

Inhoff, A. W., & Rayner, K. (1980). Parafoveal word perception: A case against semantic preprocessing. *Perception and Psychophysics, 27,* 457–464.

Moray, N. (1959). Attention in dichotic listening: Affective cues and the influence of instructions. *Quarterly Journal of Experimental Psychology, 11,* 56–60.

Paap, K. R., & Newsome, S. L. (1981). Parafoveal information is not sufficient to produce semantic or visual priming. *Perception and Psychophysics, 29,* 457–466.

Pashler, H. E. (1998). *The psychology of attention.* Cambridge, MA: MIT Press.

Treisman, A. M. (1960). Contextual cues in selective listening. *Quarterly Journal of Experimental Psychology, 12,* 242–248.

Treisman, A. M. (1964). The effect of irrelevant material on the efficiency of selective listening. *American Journal of Psychology, 77,* 533–546.

Underwood, G. (1981). Lexical recognition of embedded unattended words: Some implications for reading processes. *Acta Psychologica, 47,* 267–283.

Janice E. McPhee
Florida Gulf Coast University

SELF-CONTROL

Psychology has had a long and stormy relationship with concepts relating to human agency. Willpower, will, and self-control have all been part of the battle. Late nineteenth century psychology textbooks still discussed will and self-control in terms of the individual as an initiator of action. American psychology after G. Stanley Hall, and German psychology after Ach and Lewin, moved away from those notions toward concepts of drive and motive and voluntary and involuntary physiological responses. This trend represented an effort in psychology to disavow its parent, philosophy, and avoid potential mentalistic and teleological concepts of human action.

But the concept of self-control will not go away. It is an essential component of philosophy related to classic terms such as choice, free will, determinism, and self. Self-control is relevant in law and society in the sense of personal responsibility for one's actions, competence to stand trial, and punishment and consequences for behavior. It plays a role in religious and spiritual traditions where concepts of self-restraint, internal self-regulation, and management of external behavior (e.g., right speech, right action) are integral.

Views of Self-Control in Different Psychological Traditions

Each psychological tradition has been forced to grapple with and define self-control. For the classical Freudian, it was "where id was, ego shall be"; for the ego psychologist, it was for the autonomous ego to learn to regulate and exercise greater independent control and mastery over instincts.

Early radical behaviorists argued that the concept of self-control was unnecessary because all behavior could be determined by environmental causes. More recent views place a prime importance on the capacity of the individual to develop greater cognitive and behavioral self-control and self-regulation. Self-control has been defined by various behavioral theorists as the response of an organism made to control the probability of another response, engaging in a low probability behavior in the absence of immediate external constraints, delay of gratification, and self-efficacy.

Humanistic psychologists have stressed the importance of the individual moving away from other direction toward self-direction and autonomy. Existentialists argue that personal control is realized through exercising our freedom to make choices. Transpersonal psychology holds two seemingly paradoxical views regarding control: (1) Individual efforts are important to gain active control of our self, mind, and passions, and (2) surrendering active control is also essential, and this, too requires a type of self-control—the control to let go, forgive, and accept.

Toward Multideterministic Models of Self-control

The majority of current thinking in psychology has moved beyond simplistic unideterministic, absolute models of personal control that argue that there is only one major variable involved in human agency. Examples of unideterministic models include radical behaviorists (like strict cultural determinists) who posited that there was no such thing as personal self-control. Radical existentialists maintained that the individual was totally responsible for personal self-control. Biological determinists theorized that biology at the cellular, biochemical level determines thought and behavior (control upward).

Current, larger models involve reciprocal (and omni-) determinism suggesting that control involves a mutual interaction among many variables. For example, the environment influences the individual, but the individual can exert personal control on the environment (self-controlling the environment). Further, just as biology can influence consciousness, consciousness can influence biology (self [as consciousness] controlling the mind and behavior).

These larger models have also refined thinking about the *self* in *self-control.* Self-control can be seen as potentially occurring on multiple levels. When a person controls him- or herself, what is occurring descriptively is that the self as agent is having an effect on the self as object. From this descriptive viewpoint (not implying self-duality), the self as agent or object can be referred to linguistically as the whole person (totality); one's mind, brain, cognitions, and feelings; one's body; or one's behavior. For example, I (self as agent: totality) am learning to control my anger (self as object: feelings). My mind (self as agent) is helping me learn to relax my body (self as object: body). By practicing meditation (self as agent: cognitive focusing), I am learning to be more forgiving and accepting (self as object: emotions).

Thus, self-control as a multidimensional construct implies a process movement away from reflexive action to conscious choice awareness and personal responsibility. The belief system on which the construct is based is that individuals are not absolutely determined, can gain more autonomy and free choice, and have the ability to effect change in their lives on some level.

Self-Control Strategies and Goals of Self-Control

A self-control strategy refers to a family of techniques that an individual practices in a regular, systematic manner to influence cognitive and behavioral activity in a desired direction. Self-control techniques include behavioral self-control, hypnosis, biofeedback, meditation, and guided imagery, among others. These techniques utilize certain components, which can be analyzed and compared based on the following variables: nature of cognitive statements and instructions, type of images used, where and how attention is focused, what is self-observed, the nature of breath regulation, environmental strategies (e.g., stimulus cues), and behavioral practices.

During the past three decades psychologists and health care professionals have developed and refined a number of effective control strategies to help individuals change self-cognitions, reinterpret and transform emotions, change perceptions, and modify their behaviors. These strategies involve one of three goals: to help the individual change the environment, to change their behavior, and to change their consciousness (e.g., cognitive control to impose meaning on or interpret events).

Critical in the development of self-control and the use of self-control strategies is the concept of choice, or decisional control: that is, What is the goal for which the person wishes to develop and exercise self-control? Several schools of thought are now beginning to integrate the traditional change model of self-control with an acceptance model of self-control. For example, a person who dislikes his or her body image may make a choice to learn self-control strategies involving an assertive change mode of control such as exercising more and developing healthier eating habits. Or such individuals may choose to learn self-control strategies involving meditation and cognitive instructions of self-acceptance to honor their bodies as they are. Depending on the person and the circumstances, either self-control goal may be healthy and bring about a sense of control and well-being.

Further, the two goals do not need to be an either-or, mutually exclusive situation: An individual can learn to accept and honor his or her body as it is while at the same time developing an exercise program and healthier eating habits. Although there is no comparable concept in Western psychology (or even in English), the Chinese language suggests this possibility of harmonizing change and acceptance modes of self-control through *dongjing:* the proper and balanced combination of the two different modes of control.

By noticing how frequently thoughts, feelings, and actions intersect with issues of self-control, we can begin to realize that this construct, though multifaceted and difficult to grasp, is a critical aspect of our daily lives: personally, interpersonally, and societally.

Deane H. Shapiro, Jr.
Johanna Shapiro
University of California, Irvine

John A. Astin
California Pacific Medical Center

Shauna Shapiro
University of Santa Clara

SELF-DETERMINATION

The science of psychology was built on the assumption that behavior is lawful. This led behaviorists to propose that behavior is controlled by associative bonds that develop through reinforcement processes (Hull, 1943; Skinner, 1953). From that perspective, behavior is beyond people's control; in other words, it is not self-determined.

Beginning in the 1950s, cognitive concepts such as expectancies, goals, and decisions replaced associative bonds as the process underlying behavioral regulation (Lewin, 1951; Tolman, 1959). People were said to behave in order to attain goals, outcomes, or reinforcements. Thus, their behavior is not controlled by past reinforcements but depends on decisions to pursue future outcomes. As Nobel laureate Roger Sperry (1977) stated, people do have some capacity to choose their own behaviors based on their thoughts and feelings.

This change in focus from past reinforcements to expectations about future outcomes was a dramatic shift, and social learning theorists such as Bandura (1989) argued that self-motivation involves people pursuing outcomes that they feel able to attain. Implicit in that view is the assumption that there is only one type of motivation, that motivation varies only in amount. The amount of people's motivation depends on their expectations that behavior will lead to reinforcements and on their feeling competent to do the behavior.

Other theorists have identified serious problems with that perspective (Deci & Ryan, 1991). Even casual reflection reveals that there are different kinds of motivation. In other words, motivation varies not only in amount but also in orientation or type. Sometimes people behave with a full sense of willingness, with a sense of freedom and excitement, finding the task quite enjoyable. Other times they behave while feeling coerced, with the sense that they have to do the behavior even though they do not want to. In both cases they are motivated, and they might even have equal amounts of motivation; however, the type or orientation of motivation is clearly very different, and the consequences of the two types of motivation will be different.

As an example, think of employees who are highly motivated to produce a product because they are paid a certain amount for each unit produced. They would probably feel pressured to produce, and they might even feel a sense of alienation from the job itself. After all, the job is just an instrument for obtaining money. In contrast, think of employees who are motivated because they have the desire to perform well and because they find the job interesting and important. They too might have a very high level of motivation, but unlike the others they would be working with a sense of commitment and enjoyment. The job itself is important to them.

These two examples convey the distinction between *intrinsic motivation,* which refers to doing something because it is inherently interesting or enjoyable, and *extrinsic motivation,* which refers to doing something because it leads to a separate outcome. Intrinsically motivated behaviors do not require reinforcements and thus do not operate by the same expectancy principles as extrinsic motivation. In fact, intrinsic motivation is the prototype of self-determination, whereas extrinsic motivation that involves feeling coerced by reward contingencies does not constitute self-determination. In short, in spite of the social-learning perspective, only some motivated behaviors are self-determined, volitional, and agentic.

Self-determination involves experiencing a sense of choice about what one is doing, and research has now shown that while intrinsic motivation is the model of self-determination, extrinsically motivated behavior can also become self-determined. This occurs through the processes of internalization and integration of behavioral regulations (Ryan & Deci, 2000). Internalization involves taking in a regulation, and integration involves fully transforming it into one's own. Thus, there are different forms of extrinsic motivation: one in which the regulation is external to the person; one in which the regulation has been internalized but not integrated; and one in which the regulation has been fully integrated. Although the latter two both represent internal motivation, only integration involves a full sense of volition and personal commitment.

Together, intrinsic motivation and fully integrated extrinsic motivation are the bases for self-determination, and more than three decades of research have shown that the quality of experience and performance varies as a function of the degree to which a behavior is self-determined. Those behaviors that are more self-determined are associated with a stronger sense of personal commitment, greater persistence, more positive feelings and self-perceptions, better quality performance, and better mental health (Deci & Ryan, 1985). Thus, given the relation of self-determination to both personal experience and performance outcomes, the critical question concerns how to promote self-determination.

Studies have shown that one factor affecting how self-determined people will be in doing behaviors is whether the behaviors are valued by others to whom they feel connected. This suggests that the starting point for facilitating self-determination in others is providing them with a sense of personal relatedness. Further, people must feel competent at the target behaviors in order to be self-determined in carrying them out. For example, people will be more likely to internalize and integrate a goal if they have the relevant skills and understanding to succeed at it. Thus, supporting competence by offering optimal challenges and providing effectance-relevant feedback will also facilitate self-determination. Finally, for people to become self-determined with respect to a behavior, they must grasp its meaning to them, have their own perspective acknowledged, and feel a sense of choice about doing the behaviors. In other words, facilitating self-determination in others also requires providing them with supports for autonomy (Deci, Eghrari, Patrick, & Leone, 1994; Deci & Ryan, 1991).

In sum, self-determination, which is based in intrinsic motivation and integrated extrinsic motivation, has been associated with a variety of positive performance and affective outcomes in the areas of education, parenting, work, health care, and sport and has been found to depend on interpersonal supports for relatedness, competence, and autonomy (Ryan & Deci, 2000).

REFERENCES

Bandura, A. (1989). Human agency in social cognitive theory. *American Psychologist, 44,* 1175–1184.

Deci, E. L., Eghrari, H., Patrick, B. C., & Leone, D. R. (1994). Facilitating internalization: The self-determination theory perspective. *Journal of Personality, 62,* 119–142.

Deci, E. L., & Ryan, R. M. (1985). *Intrinsic motivation and self-determination in human behavior.* New York: Plenum.

Deci, E. L., & Ryan, R. M. (1991). A motivational approach to self: Integration in personality. In R. Dienstbier (Ed.), *Nebraska symposium on motivation: Vol. 38. Perspectives on motivation* (pp. 237–288). Lincoln: University of Nebraska Press.

Hull, C. L. (1943). *Principles of behavior.* New York: Appleton-Century-Crofts.

Lewin, K. (1951). Intention, will, and need. In D. Rapaport (Ed.), *Organization and pathology of thought* (pp. 95–153). New York: Columbia University Press.

Ryan, R. M., & Deci, E. L. (2000). Self-determination theory and the facilitation of intrinsic motivation, social development, and well-being. *American Psychologist, 55,* 68–78.

Skinner, B. F. (1953). *Science and human behavior.* New York: Macmillan.

Sperry, R. W. (1977). Bridging science and values: A unifying view of mind and brain. *American Psychologist, 32,* 237–245.

Tolman, E. C. (1959). Principles of purposive behavior. In S. Koch (Ed.), *Psychology: A study of a science* (Vol. 2, pp. 92–157). New York: McGraw-Hill.

Edward L. Deci
University of Rochester

See also: **Motivation; Self-Control; Intrinsic Motivation**

SELF-EFFICACY

People contribute to their own functioning and well-being through mechanisms of personal agency. Among the mechanisms of personal agency, none is more central or pervasive than people's beliefs in their capability to exercise control over their own functioning and over environmental events (Bandura, 1997). Efficacy beliefs are the foundation of human agency. Unless people believe that they can produce desired results by their actions, they have little incentive to act or to persevere in the face of difficulties. That self-efficacy beliefs play an influential role in human adaptation and change is amply documented by meta-analyses that combine the findings of numerous studies in different spheres of functioning (Holden, 1991; Holden, Moncher, Schinke, & Barker, 1990; Multon, Brown, & Lent, 1991; Stajkovic & Luthans, 1998).

Sources of Self-Efficacy

People's beliefs about their efficacy are constructed from four principal sources of information. The most effective way of instilling a strong sense of efficacy is through mastery experiences. Successes build a robust belief in one's personal efficacy. Failures undermine it, especially if frequent failures occur in early phases in the development of competencies. Development of resilient self-efficacy requires experiences in overcoming obstacles through perseverant effort. The second method is by social modeling. Models serve as sources of competencies and motivation. Seeing people similar to oneself succeed by perseverant effort raises observers' beliefs in their own capabilities. Social persuasion is the third mode of influence. Realistic boosts in efficacy can lead people to exert greater effort, which increases their chances of success. People also rely partly on their physiological and mood states in judging their capabilities. The fourth way of altering self-efficacy beliefs is to enhance physical states, reduce stress and depression, and correct misinterpretations of somatic states.

Efficacy-Activated Processes

Self-efficacy beliefs regulate human functioning through four major processes. They include cognitive, motivational, emotional, and selection processes.

Cognitive Processes

The effects of self-efficacy beliefs on cognitive processes take various forms. Much human behavior, being purposive, is regulated by forethought embodying cognized goals. Personal goal-setting is influenced by self-appraisal of capabilities. The stronger the perceived self-efficacy, the higher the goal challenges people set themselves, and the firmer their commitment to meeting them.

Most courses of behavior are initially shaped in thought. People's beliefs about their efficacy influence the types of anticipatory scenarios they construct and rehearse. Those who have a high sense of efficacy visualize success scenarios that provide positive guides for performance. Those who judge themselves as inefficacious are more inclined to visualize failure scenarios, which undermine performance by dwelling on personal deficiencies and on how things will go wrong. A major function of thought is to enable people to predict the occurrence of events and to create the means for exercising control over those that affect their daily lives. It requires a high sense of efficacy to stick with the laborious cognitive activity needed to extract predictive and operational knowledge from information that contains many ambiguities, redundancies, and uncertainties. The stronger the perceived self-efficacy, the more effective people are in their analytic thinking and in constructing successful courses of action.

Motivational Processes

Beliefs of personal efficacy play a central role in the self-regulation of motivation. Most human motivation is cognitively generated. In cognitive motivation, people motivate themselves and guide their actions anticipatorily through the exercise of forethought. They form beliefs about what they can do; they anticipate likely outcomes of prospective actions; and they set goals for themselves and plan courses of action designed to realize valued futures. Different theories—attribution theory, expectancy-value theory, and goal theory—have been built around these various forms of cognitive motivators.

Perceived self-efficacy operates as a central factor in each of these forms of cognitive motivation (Bandura, 1986, 1991). Efficacy beliefs bias the extent to which people attribute their successes and failures to personal capabilities or to external factors. People act on their beliefs about what they can do, as well as their beliefs about the likely outcomes of various actions. The effects of outcome expectancies on performance motivation are, therefore, partly governed by self-beliefs of efficacy. There are many activities which, if done well, guarantee valued outcomes, but they are not pursued by people who doubt they can do what it takes to succeed. Perceived self-efficacy also contributes in several ways to motivation through goal systems (Bandura, 1991; Locke & Latham, 1990). It is partly on the basis of efficacy beliefs that people choose what challenges to undertake, how much effort to expend in the endeavor, and how long to persevere in the face of obstacles and failures.

Human attainments and positive well-being require an optimistic sense of personal efficacy (Bandura, 1986, 1997) because ordinary social realities are strewn with difficulties. In a world full of impediments, failures, adversities, setbacks, frustrations, and inequities, people must have a robust sense of personal efficacy to sustain the perseverant effort needed to succeed.

Affective Processes

People's beliefs in their coping capabilities also play a pivotal role in the self-regulation of affective states (Bandura, 1997). There are four principal ways in which self-efficacy beliefs affect the nature and intensity of emotional experiences. Such beliefs create attentional biases and influence how potentially aversive life events are construed and cognitively represented; they affect the exercise of control over perturbing thought patterns, and they sponsor courses of action that transform distressing and threatening environments into more benign ones (Williams, 1992). These alternative paths of affective influence are amply documented in the self-regulation of anxiety arousal and depressive mood.

People who believe they can exercise control over potential threats do not conjure up apprehensive cognitions and, hence, are not distressed by them. But those who believe they cannot manage potential threats experience high levels of anxiety arousal. They dwell on their coping deficiencies, view many aspects of their environment as fraught with danger, magnify the severity of possible threats, and worry about perils that rarely, if ever, happen. Through such inefficacious thought they distress themselves and constrain and impair their levels of functioning. It is not the sheer frequency of perturbing cognitions, but the perceived inefficacy to turn them off, that is the major source of distress.

In addition, people with a high sense of efficacy to manage unpleasant emotional states by palliative means can get themselves to relax, direct their attention to favorable things, calm themselves, and seek support from friends, family, and others. For those who believe they can get relief in these ways, anxiety and sadness are easier to tolerate.

A low sense of efficacy to gain and maintain what one values contributes highly to depression in at least three ways. One route is through unfulfilled aspiration. People who impose on themselves standards of self-worth which they judge unattainable drive themselves to bouts of depression. A second efficacy route to depression is through a low sense of social efficacy to develop social relationships that bring satisfaction to one's life and cushion the adverse effects of chronic stressors. A low sense of social efficacy contributes to depression both directly and by curtailing development of socially supportive relationships. The third route to depression is through thought-control efficacy. People live in a psychic environment largely of their own making. Much human depression is cognitively generated by dejecting, ruminative thought. A low sense of efficacy to exercise control over ruminative thought contributes to the occurrence, duration, and recurrence of depressive episodes.

Selection Processes

The final way in which self-beliefs of efficacy contribute to human adaptation and change concerns selection processes (Bandura, 1995). Beliefs of personal efficacy shape the courses of lives by influencing selection of activities and environments. People tend to avoid activities and situations they believe exceed their coping capabilities, but they readily undertake challenging activities and pick social environments they judge themselves capable of handling. Any factor that influences choice behavior can profoundly affect the direction of personal development. This is because the social influences operating in selected environments continue to promote certain competencies, values, and interests long after the decisional determinant has rendered its inaugurating effect. Career choice and development is but one example of the power of self-efficacy beliefs to affect the course of life paths through choice-related processes (Lent, Brown, & Hackett, 1994).

People with a low sense of efficacy in a given domain of functioning shy away from difficult tasks, which they tend to perceive as personal threats; have low aspirations and weak commitment to the goals they choose; turn inward on their self-doubts instead of thinking about how to perform successfully; dwell on obstacles, the consequences of failure, and their personal deficiencies when faced with difficulties; attribute failures to deficient capability; slacken their efforts or give up quickly in the face of difficulties; are slow to recover their sense of efficacy after failures or setbacks; and are prone to stress and depression. People who have a strong sense of efficacy, by contrast, approach difficult tasks as challenges to be mastered rather than as threats to be avoided; set challenging goals and sustain strong commitment to their goals; concentrate on how to perform successfully rather than on disruptive personal concerns in the face of problems; attribute failures to insufficient effort or deficient knowledge and skills that are remediable; redouble their effort in the face of obstacles; quickly recover their sense of efficacy after failures or setbacks; and display low vulnerability to stress and depression.

REFERENCES

Bandura, A. (1986). *Social foundations of thought and action: A social cognitive theory.* Englewood Cliffs, NJ: Prentice Hall.

Bandura, A. (1991). Self-regulation of motivation through anticipatory and self-regulatory mechanisms. In R. A. Dienstbier (Ed.), *Perspectives on motivation: Nebraska symposium on motivation* (Vol. 38, pp. 69–164). Lincoln: University of Nebraska Press.

Bandura, A. (Ed.). (1995). *Self-efficacy in changing societies.* New York: Cambridge University Press.

Bandura, A. (1997). *Self-efficacy: The exercise of control.* New York: Freeman.

Holden, G. (1991). The relationship of self-efficacy appraisals to subsequent health related outcomes: A meta-analysis. *Social Work in Health Care, 16,* 53–93.

Holden, G., Moncher, M. S., Schinke, S. P., & Barker, K. M. (1990). Self-efficacy of children and adolescents. A meta-analysis. *Psychological Reports, 66,* 1044–1046.

Lent, R. W., Brown, S. D., & Hackett, G. (1994). Toward a unifying social cognitive theory of career and academic interest, choice, and performance. *Journal of Vocational Behavior, 45,* 79–122.

Locke, E. A., & Latham, G. P. (1990). *A theory of goal setting and task performance.* Englewood Cliffs, NJ: Prentice Hall.

Multon, K. D., Brown, S. D., & Lent, R. W. (1991). Relation of self-efficacy beliefs to academic outcomes: A meta-analytic investigation. *Journal of Counseling Psychology, 38,* 30–38.

Schwarzer, R. (Ed.). (1992). *Self-efficacy: Thought control of action.* Washington, DC: Hemisphere.

Stajkovic, A. D., & Luthans, F. (1998). Self-efficacy and work-related performance: A meta-analysis. *Psychological Bulletin, 124,* 240–261.

Williams, S. L. (1992). Perceived self-efficacy and phobic disability. In R. Schwarzer (Ed.), *Self-efficacy: Thought control of action* (pp. 149–176). Washington, DC: Hemisphere.

Albert Bandura
Stanford University

See also: **Behavioral Inhibition; Motivation**

SELF-FULFILLING PROPHECY

Historically, prophecies have been generally associated with individual prophets as in the Old Testament or individual deities as in the case of the Greeks. Prophets and prophecies in the traditional meaning are not in vogue now, but it is now being recognized that social beliefs and expectations often affect social reality. The phenomenon of social beliefs affecting social facts or creating a social reality is referred to as self-fulfilling prophecy. A popular example of such a phenomenon from the 1930s would be a run on a bank and a resulting foreclosure of that bank because of rumors of financial risks associated with that bank, despite its financial solvency.

The term self-fulfilling prophecy is associated with two sociologists, W. I. Thomas and Robert K. Merton. Merton popularized the concept of self-fulfilling prophecy, which was based on the idea posited by Thomas, now often referred to as the Thomas theorem. The basic premise of the Thomas theorem is that "if men define these situations as real, they are real in their consequences" (Janowitz, 1966, p. 301). The idea, however, was not new, and many famous names in the past, including Shakespeare, Pirandello, and Freud, had made use of it. Moll, a hypnotist, distinctly stated that prophecy causes its own fulfillment in the case of his subjects. The concept addresses the general relationship between social beliefs and expectations and their outcomes. According to Merton, the self-fulfilling prophecy is, in the beginning, a false definition of the situation evoking a new behavior, which makes the originally false conception come true (Merton, 1968, p. 477). A self-fulfilling prophecy can take place at an individual, group, or organizational level and could be international in scope. An individual may have self-imposed expectations or expectations from external sources. The concept of self-fulfilling prophecy can also be used to illustrate prejudices toward minority groups around the world.

Application and Testing

The concept has been refined, modified, extended, tested, and incorporated in many disciplines such as sociology, psychology, education, child development, military, business, industry, and health practices. A number of other terms are being used as synonyms, variations, and antonyms for self-fulfilling prophecy. In addition to the term self-defeating prophecies, suggested by Merton, variations of the theme called self-destroying prophecies, self-frustrating predictions, and self-confirming predictions have appeared in the literature (Sztompka, 1986, p. 234). Similarly, in educational research, the term Pygmalion effect is used instead; Galatea effect is used to indicate rising expectations of the employees, and Golem effect is used to denote negative consequences in industrial research.

Labeling theory in sociology asserts that when deviant behavior earns an individual a label as a deviant, the reaction of others toward him because of that labeling may push the individual to accept the identity of a deviant and thus further commit other deviant acts. Some psychologists who have studied this process for the last 50 years are of the opinion that beliefs and expectations can create individual or social realities (Fleming & Manning, 1994). Allport (1950), for example, suggested that suspicion of hostile intentions between two countries could trigger a conflict between them. In experimental situations, the self-fulfilling prophecy is called expectancy effect and demand characteristics. These characteristics were also experimentally demonstrated by Rosenthal (1966). Psychologists have extended their research in self-fulfilling prophecy to nonverbal behavior and less formal types of interaction and effects of labeling inside and outside organizations such as mental institutions. Psychologists in general have tried to provide the dynamics of the process, sequence, and combination of motives, the attitudes and goals involved in self-fulfilling prophecy, and the constraints and conditions under which it works. In the medical literature, the self-fulfilling prophecy or placebo effect to relieve pain or affect healing has been very widely documented since the 1940s, from the treatment of warts to the healing of damaged tissues. The prevalence of voodoo is another example of the power of placebo effect.

Educational research studies have indicated that the teacher's positive or negative expectations often come to be shared by the students, frequently in the direction of the prior anticipations of the teachers, and this phenomenon is called the Pygmalion effect after the Greek mythological character (Jones, 1977; Rosenthal, 1966; Tauber, 1997). Although there is criticism of this concept in the field of education that it is self-fulfillment of the self-fulfilling prophecy (Wineburg, 1987), teacher expectation bias effects have been acknowledged by many educational researchers. Similarly, parental expectations of children are often shared by the children themselves. In the military, business, and industrial research, the concept of self-fulfilling prophecy has been used to increase productivity, sales, and performance. Workshops are conducted in order to outperform the competition by communicating to the employees that they are capable of meeting the increased expectations (Eden, 1990).

What happens when prophecy fails? A book by the same title gives an interesting account of the rationalizations involved in a direct prophecy about the end of the world, which did not materialize (Festinger, Riecken, & Schachter, 1956). Philosophers and psychologists use the concept of confirmatory bias to account for the acceptance of a statement that was only partially confirmed and partially proved to be false. Of course, many prophecies are neither self-fulfilling nor inevitable. All prophecies are subject to change, failure, or defeat. Merton has pointed out that the initial definition of the situation needs to be abandoned before the prophecy can be broken. The dire predictions about Y2K were self-defeating because a massive number of projects were established to attack the problem.

The research literature attests to the scope of the applications as well as to the limitations of the phenomenon of self-fulfilling prophecy. For example, labeling is not very effective in the case of major offences such as murder. In the case of Y2K, for example, some people decided not to travel on the eve of the year 2000, but some others ignored it. Such prophecies will continue to provide interesting case studies, as they illustrate the possibilities and problems involved in understanding the process, power, and limitations of the phenomenon of self-fulfilling prophecy.

REFERENCES

Allport, G. W. (1950). The role of expectancy. In H. Cantrill (Ed.), *Tensions that cause wars.* Urbana: University of Illinois Press.

Becker, H. S. (1963). *Outsiders: Studies in the sociology of deviance.* New York: Free Press of Glencoe.

Eden, D. (1990). *Pygmalion in management: Productivity as a self-fulfilling prophecy.* Lexington, MA: Lexington Books.

Festinger, L., Riecken, H. W., & Schachter, S. (1956). *When prophecy fails.* Minneapolis: University of Minnesota Press.

Fleming, J. H., & Manning, D. J. (1994). Self-fulfilling prophecies. In V. S. Ramachandran (Ed.), *Encyclopedia of human behavior* (Vol. 4, pp. 89–97). San Diego: Academic Press.

Janowitz, M. (Ed.). (1966). *W. I. Thomas on social organization and social personality selected papers.* Chicago: University of Chicago Press.

Jones, R. A. (1977). *Self-fulfilling prophecies: Social, psychological and physiological effects of expectancies.* Hillsdale, NJ: Erlbaum.

Lemert, E. M. (1951). *Social pathology.* New York: McGraw Hill.

Merton, R. K. (1968). *Social theory and social structure* (Enlarged ed.). New York: Free Press.

Rosenthal, R. (1966). *Experimenter effects in behavioral research.* New York: Appleton-Century-Crofts.

Rosenthal, R., & Jacobson, L. (1968). *Pygmalion in the classroom: Teacher expectation and pupils' intellectual development.* New York: Holt, Rinehart and Winston.

Sztompka, P. (1986). *Robert K. Merton: An intellectual profile.* New York: St. Martins Press.

Tauber, R. T. (1997). *Self-fulfilling prophecy: A practical guide to its use in education.* Westport, CT: Praeger.

Wagar, W. W. (1963). *The city of man, prophecies of a modern civilization in twentieth century thought.* Boston: Houghton Mifflin.

Wineburg, S. S. (1987). The self-fulfillment of the self-fulfilling prophecy. *Educational Researcher, 16*(9), 28–37.

Wineburg, S. S., & Shulman, L. S. (1990). The self-fulfilling prophecy: Its genesis and development in American education. In J. Clark, C. Modgil, & S. Modgil (Eds.), *Robert K. Merton, consensus and controversy* (pp. 261–281). London: Falmer Press.

Subhash R. Sonnad
Western Michigan University

See also: **Pygmalion Effect**

SELF-HELP GROUPS

The primary goal of self-help groups (sometimes called mutual aid or mutual help groups) is to achieve psychological or behavioral gains for their members, who typically address a single problem or condition and who are committed to two principles: that people who are coping or have coped with a personal problem are better helpers than professionals who do not have firsthand experience and that such people help themselves by helping each other.

Origins and Present Status

Various strains of ancestry have been cited: a tradition of mutual support by family, community, church, and ethnic group members; trade unions and cooperatives; Christian group-confessional religious practices; and the American (U.S.) value of self-reliance. Whatever the antecedents, contemporary self-help groups have evolved at least partly to meet therapeutic needs that often are not, or are not adequately, dealt with by existing social institutions.

Alcoholics Anonymous (AA) is the oldest, largest, and best known ongoing self-help group. Founded in 1935 by Bill W. and Dr. Bob, it is organized by and for alcoholics (with offshoots Al-Anon and Al-Ateen for relatives and friends). Although described in the 1937 publication *Alcoholics Anonymous,* AA was little known to the general public until a 1944 *Saturday Evening Post* article. It now has well over a million members in 100 countries. Its 12-step program has been adopted by many other groups (e.g., Gamblers Anonymous, Overeaters Anonymous, Narcotics Anonymous, Debtors Anonymous). Other early self-help organizations are Recovery, Inc., founded in 1937 by psychiatrist Abraham Low for former patients of mental health institutions, and Synanon, founded in the 1950s by Charles Dederich for drug addicts (and, later, ex-convicts).

Self-help groups grew in number in the late 1950s and early 1960s. One directory listed 265 in 1963. Another listed 650 local chapters from 120 different self-help organizations in 1982 in the Chicago area alone. In 1993 Alfred H. Katz estimated 750,000 self-help groups in the USA with 10 to 15 million members. Some see this growth as a major movement in psychotherapy, a fourth force following the third force of humanistic psychotherapy.

In 1976 both the *Journal of Applied Behavior Science* and *Social Policy* had special issues on self-help. U.S. Surgeon General C. Everett Koop organized a national workshop on self-help and public health in 1987. There are national and state self-help clearinghouses of information and similar centers in Canada, Australia, Israel, Japan, and a dozen European countries.

Types of Groups

Levy's (1976) classification of self-help groups is instructive:

- *Type I.* This aims primarily at behavioral control or change, especially for addicts and compulsives. Examples are AA, Gamblers Anonymous, TOPS (Take Off Pounds Sensibly), and Parents Anonymous (coping with child-abuse tendencies).
- *Type II.* Members of this type share a stressful status or condition, sometimes a particular physical health problem (e.g., Mended Hearts for those who have had heart surgery; Make Today Count for cancer patients, families, and friends; Reach to Recovery for women who have had mastectomies; in 1995 Riessman and Carroll claimed a self-help group for every major illness listed by the World Health Organization); others have members coping with mental illness (e.g., Schizophrenics Anonymous); still others focus on such crises as rape, murder of one's child, and suicide; and another subcategory deals with life transitions (Geriatric Rap, Widow-to-Widow, Parents Without Partners) or transitions toward normality (for former mental patients, ex-convicts, Vietnam War veterans).
- *Type III.* These groups include people felt to be discriminated against because of sex, race, class, or sexual orientation.
- *Type IV.* Individuals in this type work toward general self-actualization and enhanced effectiveness. Levy (1976) includes Mowrer's (1972) Integrity Groups under this classification, which covers many consciousness-raising groups.

Therapeutic Factors in Self-help Groups

1. *Shared experiences or situations,* helping people feel immediately understood and thus not psychologically alone. Commonality tends also to reduce defensiveness and encourage self-revelation with its cathartic utility and reduction of shame.

2. *Helping others.* The helper therapy principle of self-help groups, first enunciated by Frank Riessman in 1965, posits that the more group members help others, the more they are helped themselves. Helpers feel greater competence, make learning gains, receive social approval, practice and thereby self-reinforce desirable role behavior, and achieve more objectivity concerning their particular problem.
3. *Ongoing support network.* Members receive supportive praise at their meetings. Typically, support extends virtually around the clock with members on call.
4. *Information sharing.* Much benefit comes from receiving information, whether technical or part of folk wisdom, including everything from explaining medical jargon to child-rearing advice. Some groups keep abreast of current research and treatment modalities.
5. *Finding models.* Membership provides opportunities to observe how others cope effectively.
6. *Gaining feedback.* In the openness and honesty that typify self-help groups, members' behaviors tend to be accurately observed and commented on. Such directness, in a supportive atmosphere, helps people find their way.
7. *Learning special methods.* With some self-help groups such as AA and other 12-step programs, successful coping is closely linked to following special procedures. Members learn and perpetuate them, and many find the structure valuable.

Self-help Versus Professional Psychotherapy

The relationship between self-help groups and professional and institutional helpers has varied from antagonism to close cooperation. Professional group psychotherapy typically differs from self-help in significant ways: Professionals have formal training and credentialing; their help is paid for and time-limited; they do not expect reciprocal emotional support; and they operate from an explicit theoretical base that claims empirical support. For some self-help groups, independence from the authority, methods, and funding of professionals is a matter of principle (and sometimes of antiprofessional rhetoric).

But even self-help advocates acknowledge ways in which professionals have started, advised, and legitimized some groups. Among professional therapists who have founded self-help groups are Low (Recovery, Inc.), Mowrer (Integrity Groups), and Phyllis Silverman (Widow-to-Widow). Perhaps a third of self-help groups began with assistance of professional helpers. Interaction among professionals and laypersons often occurs in groups related to physical health. Organizations such as AA gain endorsements by psychiatrists and clinical psychologists. The National Institute of Mental Health has sponsored studies of self-help groups and of their interactions with professional workers and institutions. Cooperation between self-help groups and professional psychologists and psychotherapists seems to be increasing.

Evidence of the effectiveness of self-help groups is largely anecdotal. Research is difficult by their very nature (i.e., anonymity, transient membership, lack of record keeping). Aside from such issues, challenges to some groups might be raised about questionable founding premises and pressures toward conformity. But Riessman and Carroll (1995) put the movement in a larger psycho-socio-political context: "A major reason for the current resonance of the self-help approach relates to the significant world problems to which a self-help model is potentially responsive, including widespread feelings of powerlessness and alienation . . . and of isolation; widespread addictions; . . . the tremendous expansion of chronic illnesses," and a host of other social, political, and even professional problems and limitations.

REFERENCES

Alcoholics Anonymous. (1976). *Alcoholics Anonymous.* New York: A. A. World Services (Original work published 1937)

Katz, A. H. (1993). *Self-help in America: A social movement perspective.* New York: Twayne.

Levy, L. H. (1976). Self-help groups: Types and psychological processes. *Journal of Applied Behavioral Science, 12,* 310–322.

Mowrer, O. H. (1972). Integrity groups: Basic principles and procedures. *Counseling Psychologist, 3,* 7–33.

Riessman, F. (1965). The "helper" therapy principle. *Social Work, 10,* 27–32.

Riessman, F., & Carroll, D. (1995). *Redefining self-help: Policy and practice.* San Francisco: Jossey-Bass.

TKTK Journal of Applied Behavioral Science, 12(3). (1976). Self-help groups [Special issue].

TKTK *Social Policy, 7*(2). (1976).

Forest W. Hansen

See also: **Twelve-Step Programs**

SELF: LOOKING-GLASS CONCEPT

The looking-glass concept of self is commonly attributed to Charles Horton Cooley (1902), who, in elaborating on William James' (1890) discussion of the social self, suggested that a reflected self arises when individuals appropriate a self-feeling on the basis of how they think they appear in the eyes of other individuals. Cooley stated, "A social self of this sort might be called the reflected or looking-glass self: *Each to each a looking-glass / Reflects the other that doth pass*" (1902, p. 184).

While Cooley is credited with the looking-glass metaphor, its appearance in literature can actually be traced to the works of Adam Smith, who, in *The Theory of Moral Sentiments,* stated, "We examine our persons limb by limb, and by placing ourselves before a looking-glass, or by some expedient, endeavor as much as possible to view ourselves at the distance and with the eyes of other people" (1892, p. 162). Society, he suggested, provides the mirror in which individuals can see themselves as spectators of their own behavior: "This is the only looking-glass by which we can, in some measure, with the eyes of other people, scrutinize the propriety of our own conduct" (1892, p. 164).

The metaphor of the looking glass carries a double meaning in Smith's and Cooley's formulations. In everyday life, individuals see their faces, figures, and dress in the glass and "are interested in them because they are ours, and pleased or otherwise with them according as they do or do not answer to what we should like them to be" (Cooley, 1902, p. 184). In interactions with others, it is necessary for one to imagine how he or she appears in the eyes of the other. The other becomes the mirror and forms his or her interpretation of the individual given that individual's gestures, facial expressions, and statements. Anselm Strauss has captured this relationship with the other in the title of his essay on identity, "Mirrors and Masks" (1958).

The self-idea that incorporates self-feeling, according to Smith and Cooley, has two principal components—the imagination of the other's judgment of that appearance and some sort of "self-feeling, such as pride or mortification" (Cooley, 1902, p. 184). The self-feeling is appropriate on the basis of the imagined judgment of the other. This imputed sentiment, taken from the other and directed inward, to the self, moves the individual. The evaluation of the other, in whose mind the person sees the self, determines this self-feeling. Cooley states, "We are ashamed to seem evasive in the presence of a straightforward man, cowardly in the presence of a brave one, gross in the eyes of a refined one, and so on" (1902, p. 184).

The basic structure of self-feeling is threefold, involving (1) a feeling for one's self, (2) a feeling of this feeling, and (3) a revealing of the self through this feeling (Heidegger, 1982). The other directly enters into this process, imaginatively, for it is the other's presence that provides the grounds against which self-feeling is judged and felt. The feeling person feels the self in emotion. Self-feeling is central to an understanding of the empirical social self (James, 1890).

Cooley elaborated the looking-glass self-concept in a brief comment in "On a Remark of Dr. Holmes" that "six persons take part in every conversation between John and Thomas" (1927, p. 200). There is a real John, John's ideal John (never the real John), and Thomas's ideal John, and there are three parallel Thomases. The matter then becomes more complicated; in everyday life, 12 persons participate in every interaction, six on each side. For example, Alice, who has a new hat, meets Angela, who has a new dress. In this situation, there is the real Alice, Alice's idea of herself in her new hat, her idea of Angela's judgment of her new hat, and her idea of what Angela thinks she thinks of herself in her new hat. Also, there is Angela's actual idea of what Alice thinks of herself, and six analogous phases of Angela and her dress (Cooley, 1927).

Self-feelings move through these imputed and imagined reactions of each interactant to the other's real and imagined judgments of their social selves. Every interaction is peopled by many selves, with always more persons present in a situation than there are real bodies (Maines, 1978; Stone, 1981; Strauss, 1958). The strength of Cooley's formulation lies in its emphasis on the multiplicity of definitions, feelings, and meanings that arise in any situation in which two persons come together for interaction. Multiple awareness contexts of interaction characterize such situations (Glaser & Strauss, 1967).

The looking-glass self-concept is basic to the symbolic interactionist theory of interaction and remains central to current social psychological theorizing on the social self and on emotion. The centrality of the self and of self-processes in the study of emotional feeling and emotional expression is pivotal in current neuropsychological formulations of emotion (Pribram, 1981). Cooley's concepts of self-feeling and the looking-glass self warrant reexamination in light of this fact.

Cooley's arguments are quite compatible with more contemporary theories of the self that stress its gendered, semiotic, and performative character (see Butler, 1997; Dunn, 1998; Wiley, 1994).

REFERENCES

Butler, J. (1997). *Excitable speech: A politics of the performative.* London: Routledge.

Dunn, R. G. (1998). *Identity crises: A social critique of postmodernity.* Minneapolis: University of Minnesota Press.

Perinbanayagam, R. S. (2000). *The presence of self.* Lanham, MD: Roman & Littlefield.

Scheff, T. J. (2001). The emotional relational world. In J. H. Turner (Ed.), *Handbook of sociological theory* (pp. 255–268). New York: Kluwer.

Wiley, N. (1994). *The semiotic self.* Cambridge, UK: Polity Press.

Norman K. Denzin
University of Illinois

***See also:* Deindividuation; Interpersonal Perception**

SELF-MONITORING

Self-monitoring refers to an assessment procedure in which individuals are asked to notice and document target behaviors as they occur in natural settings. Self-monitoring is one of the most direct forms of behavioral assessment (Cone, 1978), and it is often employed when the use of trained observers is not feasible. Self-monitoring is also the most direct form of assessment available when target responses are private by nature (e.g., thoughts and feelings) or by convention (e.g., sexual behavior). In self-monitoring, recordings are made as the target behavior occurs. For this reason, self-monitored data are less vulnerable to errors or distortion that can occur when reporting information from memory. In addition to recording the occurrence of a target behavior, the self-monitor may be asked to record features of the context as well as potential consequences of the target behavior. This information is useful in designing behavioral strategies for intervention.

There are several procedures for self-monitoring. If a target behavior is fairly low in frequency, each occurrence can be recorded in an ongoing frequency count. Frequency counts may be burdensome for the self-recorder if a target behavior occurs very often. Frequently occurring behaviors might be self-recorded within predetermined time intervals (e.g., two mornings out of a week) or estimated at intervals (e.g., recording every two hours). While some information may be lost, these latter methods may produce greater compliance than would frequency counts.

When it is important to consider the amount of time spent engaged in a target behavior, the self-monitor can record the duration for each occurrence. This information is probably more precise for responses that have a more salient onset and ending, such as studying. Other activities, such as worrying, may begin with less notice. Self-recorders may be asked to estimate the starting time when they find themselves engaged in this type of target activity.

Particularly in the early stages of clinical assessment, it may be difficult to identify specific behaviors to target for change. For example, an individual might want to target anger but may not be able to specify particular responses that are disruptive or problematic. Even when target behaviors are readily identified, it is often desirable to collect as much information as possible concerning the circumstances and potential consequences associated with these behaviors. In these cases, diary formats may be preferred. Diary formats allow the self-recorder to supply more elaborate and narrative descriptions of their behavior and the environment in which it occurs. As problem areas are revealed, assessment can focus on more specific target behaviors using more structured self-monitoring forms.

Aside from its value as an assessment tool, self-monitoring appears to have beneficial treatment effects. This is because the frequency of self-monitored behaviors changes when individuals begin to self-monitor. This phenomenon is termed *reactivity* (Nelson, 1977). Reactivity poses problems for assessment in that the procedure for measurement changes the frequency of the behavior being assessed. However, these reactive behavior changes tend to benefit the client because self-monitored behaviors tend to change in desirable ways. Unwanted behaviors become less frequent when self-monitored, whereas desirable behaviors become more frequent with self-monitoring. Reactive effects are typically small and short-lived. However, they are immediate and may encourage continued investment in behavior change.

Several factors can detract from the accuracy and utility of self-monitored data. As noted earlier, the procedure involves two separate responses. The self-recorder must first notice the occurrence of the behavior and then make the necessary recording. Both responses must occur for consistent and accurate information to be collected, and problems may arise that interfere with one or both. For example, self-monitors may have difficulty noticing behaviors that are not clearly specified and defined. Alternatively, clearly defined target behaviors may be difficult to notice. For example, a person might be asked to self-record instances when they have the thought "I'm a failure." Although the thought may be clear, it may be so fleeting or ego-syntonic that the person does not notice each instance. Other factors can influence whether a noticed behavior is actually recorded. Failure to record might occur when forms are difficult to access or when target behaviors are socially unacceptable. Alternatively, highly desirable behaviors might be overrecorded. When compliance is problematic, self-recorders might complete forms all at once just before returning them to the assessor rather than collecting the data in an ongoing fashion.

Many of the aforementioned difficulties can be alleviated by implementing procedures that have been shown to enhance the accuracy of self-monitored data. These include (1) clearly defining target behaviors, (2) requiring that recordings be made immediately after the target behavior occurs, (3) providing training to self-monitors, (4) emphasizing the importance of accurate data collection and providing reinforcement for accurate data collection, (5) minimizing the number of target behaviors being monitored at one time, and (6) regularly checking the accuracy of self-monitored data and informing self-monitors that their accuracy will be checked (see Korotitsch & Nelson-Gray, 1999, for a review).

The accuracy of self-recordings can sometimes be checked through comparison with data collected by observers. For example, a spouse or roommate might occasionally collect observations to compare with self-recordings of an insomniac. For some target behaviors, other measurements can corroborate self-monitored data. For instance, regularly collected measurements of weight might be compared to self-monitored food intake in a weight reduction program.

In conclusion, self-monitoring is a widely used assessment device because of its convenience, the accuracy of collected data under conditions specified earlier, and the initial therapeutic benefits due to reactivity.

REFERENCES

Cone, J. D. (1978). The Behavioral Assessment Grid (BAG): A conceptual framework and a taxonomy. *Behavior Therapy, 9,* 882–888.

Korotitsch, W. J., & Nelson-Gray, R. O. (1999). An overview of self-monitoring research in assessment and treatment. *Psychological Assessment, 11*(4), 415–425.

Nelson, R. O. (1977). Methodological issues in assessment via self-monitoring. In J. D. Cone & R. P. Hawkins (Eds.), *Behavioral assessment: New directions in clinical psychology.* New York: Brunner/Mazel.

William J. Korotitsch
Rosemery O. Nelson-Gray
University of North Carolina, Greensboro

See also: **Self-Control; Self-Report and Self-Ratings**

SELF-REPORT AND SELF-RATINGS

Self-report assessment methods are those in which individuals are asked to summarize their behavior and report this information retrospectively. Self-report measures include interviews, questionnaires, self-ratings, and cognitive assessment methods such as think-aloud procedures. Self-report is the most indirect method for assessing overt behavior. However, it is the most direct method available for assessing behaviors that cannot be readily observed, such as thoughts and feelings.

Interviews, questionnaires, and rating scales are the most widely used self-report methods. Interviews vary in the degree to which they are structured (confined to particular areas of inquiry) and standardized (with uniform procedures for administration and scoring). Unstructured interviews follow no predetermined order and vary in content depending on the responses and concerns that are raised. This open-ended approach is often a useful starting point in clinical assessment. In contrast, structured interviews contain specific questions that are administered in a set sequence. These interviews are generally designed for nonprofessionals to administer and are frequently used to establish a psychiatric diagnosis for research purposes. More commonly used by clinicians is the semistructured interview. These interviews also follow a format; however, they allow the interviewer to pursue additional information when necessary and demand more clinical judgment.

Questionnaires are easily administered and are highly efficient in terms of cost and time. Questionnaires can generally be divided into broad and specific types (Korotitsch & Nelson-Gray, 1999). Broad questionnaires assess general functioning in multiple life areas, multiple diagnostic categories, or multiple psychological constructs such as traits. Specific or brief questionnaires focus on particular behaviors or areas of functioning. For example, one brief questionnaire might assess recent symptoms of depression, whereas another might assess the thoughts and beliefs that are often associated with depression. Broad questionnaires provide more comprehensive information, but they require more time and resources to administer, score, and interpret. Broad questionnaires also tend to be less sensitive to small or specific changes in behavior over time. For these reasons, broad questionnaires are usually administered infrequently, such as before and after treatment. Specific questionnaires are more often used to assess ongoing behavior change throughout treatment.

Many questionnaires have available norms. They can be administered to very large groups of people, and a particular score can be compared to the population average to determine whether it falls outside of the normal range. Norms may also be used to determine whether treatment results in scores that fall closer to the average range. This information can be collected frequently and used to assess ongoing progress in treatment.

Self-ratings require respondents to generate numerical ratings of the response being assessed. For example, rather than reporting specific symptoms of anxiety, it can be rated on a scale of 1 to 7. Rating scales can be constructed for virtually any phenomenon an assessor is interested in measuring and are useful when no appropriate specific questionnaires are available. Bloom, Fischer, and Orme (1995) offer guidelines for constructing individualized self-rating scales.

Cognitive assessments require individuals to verbalize their thoughts in a particular situation. For instance, a phobic might be asked to verbalize his thoughts while approaching an airplane. Persons might be asked to verbalize thoughts continually (think-aloud), to report their most recent thought when given a cue (thought sampling), or to recall thoughts immediately after the situation (thought listing). These methods yield a wealth of information, but the data can be difficult to quantify and compare across individuals.

Self-report methods have several disadvantages. The accuracy of self-reported data can be difficult to determine. Information may be omitted, added, or distorted because of natural errors and imperfections in memory. Self-reports might also be based on personal beliefs or theories concerning the causes and stability of one's own behavior (Ross, 1989). Self-reported information can also be minimized or withheld when undesirable behaviors are being assessed. Similarly, more desirable responses may be exaggerated.

Self-report can also be influenced by response biases such as answering true to questions regardless of their content. Many broad questionnaires include scales that assess response bias and the tendency to provide inconsistent or inaccurate information. However, most brief scales cannot assess these biases. A final concern is that self-report measures must be designed with careful attention to the level of sophistication and the clarity of questions. Inaccurate information can often be traced to misleading, complex, or ambiguous questions.

Self-report measures are widely used in psychology because they are economical, quantifiable, and easy to administer. More important, many self-report measures have published norms to aid in interpretations of a given score. They can also be used to assess subjective or private experiences that cannot be observed directly. There has been rapid proliferation of specific questionnaires over the past 20 years (Froyd, Lambert, & Froyd, 1996). An excellent resource to aid clinicians in choosing appropriate questionnaires is provided by Fischer and Corcoran (1994). A more in-depth discussion of self-report methods is provided by Korotitsch and Nelson-Gray (1999).

REFERENCES

Bloom, M., Fischer, J., & Orme, J. (1995). *Evaluating practice: Guidelines for the accountable professional.* Englewood Cliffs, NJ: Prentice Hall.

Fischer, J., & Corcoran, K. (1994). *Measures for clinical practice: A sourcebook* (2 vols., 2nd ed.). New York: Macmillan.

Froyd, J. E., Lambert, M. J., & Froyd, J. D. (1996). A review of practices of psychotherapy outcome measurement. *Journal of Mental Health, 5,* 11–15.

Korotitsch, W. J., & Nelson-Gray, R. O. (1999). Self-report and physiological measures. In S. C. Hayes, D. H. Barlow, & R. O. Nelson-Gray (Eds.), *The scientist-practitioner: Research and accountability in the age of managed care* (2nd ed., pp. 320–352). New York: Allyn & Bacon.

Ross, M. (1989). Relation of implicit theories to the construction of personal histories. *Psychological Review, 96,* 341–357.

William J. Korotitsch
Rosemery O. Nelson-Gray
University of North Carolina, Greensboro

See also: **Reliability; Self-Monitoring**

SEPARATION DISTRESS/ANXIETY

Distress resulting from separation from an attachment figure has been accepted as an attribute of normal infant development since the early part of this century (Bowlby, 1973; Freud, 1909/1955). Bowlby interpreted the distress that infants displayed to maternal separation as reflecting their anxiety at being left alone. Indeed, he saw fear of being left alone as the root cause of generalized human anxiety (Bowlby, 1973). In normal development, distress due to separation appears between the ages of 7 and 12 months and peaks around 15 to 18 months of age. This inverted U-shaped curve to the onset, peak, and diminution of distress to separation has been found across various cultures among which the pattern of rearing has varied considerably. For example, Fox (1977) found this pattern among infants raised on an Israeli kibbutz (where infants slept separately from their mothers and were cared for by a primary caregiver other than the mother). Barr, Konner, Bakeman, and Adamson (1991) reported a similar developmental function for infants raised among the !Kung bushmen in the Kalahari Desert, as did Kagan and Klein (1973) for infants raised in rural Guatemala. The common developmental change in separation distress across cultures most probably reflects universal changes in the infant's abilities to understand and represent its mother's disappearance from view. Thus, this behavior should not be considered as maladaptive but rather as a normative part of early development.

There are reports of individual differences in the tendency to display distress to separation. Davidson and Fox (1989), for example, reported a pattern of greater right frontal electroencephalogram (EEG) activation associated with a temperamental disposition to cry in response to maternal separation. Similar findings by Fox, Bell, and Jones (1992) suggest modest stability of frontal asymmetry over time.

Although normative changes in distress to separation find it diminishing around 18 to 24 months of age, instances of continued distress response to separation from mothers have been described in the child clinical literature. These instances were described under the heading of separation anxiety. Freud (1895/1959) first conceived of the concept of anxiety neurosis in 1895 and suggested that anxiety was a symptomatic consequence of a repressed libido. Only later, in 1926, did he begin to take note of separation anxiety. The psychoanalytic perspective viewed separation anxiety as a tendency for adults to experience apprehension after the loss of a significant other (Freud, 1926). Freud's later studies led him to conclude that anxiety was an emotion that resulted from the experience of traumatic events. Since that time, separation anxiety has been studied in a variety of contexts, including the attachment literature. It was not until the 1980s that separation anxiety was considered a discrete clinical diagnostic category. The *Diagnostic and Statistical Manual of Mental Disorders,* third edition (*DSM-III*) designated separation anxiety disorder (SAD) as one of the three anxiety disorders of childhood and adolescence (American Psychiatric Association, 1980). Current diagnostic criteria of SAD include excessive anxiety with respect to separation from an attachment figure (most commonly the mother or primary caregiver) or separation from familiar surroundings such as home.

Children experiencing SAD may exhibit both behavioral and physiological symptoms such as extreme distress, terror, hyperventilation, or heart palpitations when anticipating separation. Children with SAD seek to avoid separation from attachment figures and, not surprisingly, are most commonly referred to clinicians as a result of a hesitancy or unwillingness to attend school. Similarly, both sleep disturbances and refusals to sleep are also characteristic of SAD.

Studies that examine comorbidity of psychiatric disorders indicate that children and adolescents with SAD are commonly diagnosed with other disorders as well. One half of children with SAD are diagnosed with other anxiety disorders, and one third are diagnosed with depression. It has been suggested that children with SAD may have become overly dependent on the attachment figure, often after a stressful life event such as illness or the loss of a loved one (Erickson, 1998). SAD occurs in approximately 2% to 4% of children and adolescents, and those with this disorder may be at increased risk for psychopathology in adulthood. Current treatment approaches to SAD include behavioral interventions, psychotherapy, and family interventions as well as psychopharmacological treatments.

The literature on childhood anxiety has recently emphasized the important influence of temperament factors (Kagan, Resnick, Clarke, Snidman, & Garcia-Coll, 1984) in this area. It has been found that the incidence of childhood anxiety disorders is greater in children who exhibit the temperamental characteristic of behavioral inhibition (Biederman et al., 1990). This characteristic, described as the tendency to withdraw from novel or social situations, may be related to separation anxiety.

Separation distress is a normative response across different caregiving and cultural contexts for infants to display distress on separation from the caregiver. This behavioral response appears during the second half of the first year of life and is no longer present by the beginning of the third year of life. The behavioral pattern is distinct and apparently unrelated to the phenomenon known as separation anxiety. Little is known currently about the etiology of separation anxiety in young children. Current research suggests that there may be a temperamental basis to withdraw from discrepancy or novelty. Such a bias may in some instances lead to the behavioral pattern known as separation anxiety in children.

REFERENCES

American Psychiatric Association. (1980). *Diagnostic and statistical manual of mental disorders* (3rd ed.). Washington, DC: Author.

Barr, R. G., Konner, M., Bakeman, R., & Adamson, L. (1991). Crying in !Kung San infants: Test of the cultural specificity hypothesis. *Developmental Medicine and Child Neurology, 33,* 601–610.

Biederman, J., Rosenbaum, J. F., Hirshfield, D. R., Faraone, S. V., Bolduc, E. A., Gersten, M., Meminger, S. R., Kagan, J., Snidman, N., & Resnick, J. S. (1990). Psychiatric correlates of behavioral inhibition in young children of parents with and without psychiatric disorders. *Archives of General Psychiatry, 47,* 21–26.

Bowlby, J. (1973). *Separation, anxiety and anger: Vol. 2. Attachment and loss.* New York: Basic Books.

Davidson, R. J., & Fox, N. A. (1989). Frontal brain asymmetry predicts infants' response to maternal separation. *Journal of Abnormal Psychology, 98,* 127–131.

Erickson, M. T. (1998). *Behavior disorders of children and adolescents: Assessment, etiology, and intervention.* New Jersey: Prentice Hall.

Fox, N. A. (1977). Attachment of kibbutz infants to mother and metapelet. *Child Development, 48,* 1228–1239.

Fox, N. A., Bell, M. A., & Jones, N. A. (1992). Individual differences in response to stress and cerebral asymmetry. *Developmental Neuropsychology, 8,* 161–184.

Fox, N. A., Kimmerly, N. L., & Schaeffer, W. D. (1991). Attachment to mother/attachment to father: A meta-analysis. *Child Development, 62,* 210–225.

Freud, S. (1959). Inhibitions, symptoms and anxiety. In J. Strachey (Ed.), *The standard edition of the complete psychological works of Sigmund Freud* (Vol. 20, pp. 77–175). London: Hogarth Press.

Freud, S. (1955). Analysis of a phobia in a five-year-old boy. In J. Strachey (Ed.), *The standard edition of the complete psychological works of Sigmund Freud* (Vol. 10, pp. 1–149). London: Hogarth Press. (Original work published 1909)

Freud, S. (1959). On the grounds for detaching a particular syndrome from neurasthenia under the description "anxiety neurosis." In J. Strachey (Ed.), *The standard edition of the complete psychological works of Sigmund Freud* (Vol. 3, pp. 87–116). London: Hogarth Press. (Original work published 1895)

Kagan, J., & Klein, R. E. (1973). Cross-cultural perspectives on early development. *American Psychologist, 28,* 947–961.

Kagan, J., Resnick, J. S., Clarke, C., Snidman, N., & Garcia-Coll, C. (1984). Behavioral inhibition to the unfamiliar. *Child Development, 55,* 2212–2225.

Kirsten M. VanMeenen
Nathan Fox
University of Maryland

See also: **Behavioral Inhibition**

SEROTONERGIC NEURONS

The serotonergic neurons are one of the diffusely organized projection systems in the central nervous system (CNS). Considerable research carried out over the past 40 years has clearly established the serotonergic system as a major neurotransmitter system subserving a number of important physiological and psychological functions. Although Page and his collaborators succeeded in the isolation and identification of serotonin (5-HT) more than five decades ago (1948) (Page 1976), the distribution of these neurons and their cell bodies in the CNS have been identified only after the availability of fluorescent histochemistry and immunocytochemical methods (1964). The distribution of serotonergic neurons and their cell bodies in the CNS was originally identified using fluorescent histochemistry

(Dahlstrom & Fuxe, 1964; Ungerstedt, 1971), and subsequently by more sensitive immunocytochemical methods. Serotonin is synthesized from the aromatic amino acid L-tryptophan into the serotonin neuron.

Distribution and Physiological Function of the Serotonergic Neuron

In the CNS, serotonergic neurons are limited to a group of brain-stem reticular formation nuclei, the raphe nuclei. Dahlstrom and Fuxe (1964) originally described nine serotonergic cell groups, which they named B1 through B9. Most of these groups are associated with the raphe nuclei and the reticular region of the lower brain stem from which they project rostro-caudally, and thus to virtually all areas of the CNS receive serotonergic inputs. The serotonergic neurons in the midbrain and pontine dorsal and median raphe project to higher brain centers: cerebral cortex, cerebellum, hippocampus, thalamus, hypothalamus, and basal ganglia. In contrast, serotonergic cell bodies in the ventral medulla, caudal pons, and pontomesencephalic reticular formation provide long descending projections to the spinal cord. The origins of the serotonergic projections to the dorsal horn are the neurons of the raphe magnus and adjacent reticular formation and are involved mainly in pain sensation. The serotonergic neurons that terminate in the ventral horn arise primarily from the raphe obscurus and raphe pallidus nuclei and facilitate motor activity. The preganglionic sympathetic neurons of the intermediolateral column in the thoracic cord also receive serotonergic input, mostly from the ventrolateral medulla, and are involved in blood pressure regulation and perhaps other autonomic functions. The pathways from the midbrain raphe to the prefrontal cortex may mediate depressive and cognitive effects of serotonin. The pathway from the midbrain raphe to basal ganglia likely underlies the role of serotonin in the pathophysiology of obsessive-compulsive disorder (OCD). This pathway also is thought to be related to the regulatory action of serotonin on locomotion. The regulatory functions of serotonin on emotions, anxiety, and memory are thought to be related by the pathway from the raphe to the limbic cortex. The pathway from midbrain raphe to hypothalamus might mediate the effects of serotonin on appetitive behaviors. Sexual function mediated by serotonin might be related to the descending pathways from the raphe to the spinal cord. Moreover, the serotonergic system has been implicated in the regulation of circadian rhythms through its actions on the suprachiasmatic nucleus (SCN). Recent data suggest that along with excitatory amino acids, serotonin may be important in the neutral pathway that mediates the transmission of photic information to the circadian system. Recently, it has been demonstrated that the serotonergic system also has a link to neuroadaptive changes that occur in substance dependence. For example, extracellular serotonin levels decreased dramatically during cocaine withdrawal.

The action of serotonergic neurons, as a whole, is complex, and it is difficult to understand how specific changes in serotonin neurotransmission affect specific behaviors or neurological functions. This issue becomes even more challenging by the molecular cloning of more than 14 serotonin receptor subtypes, each with its own expression pattern, coupling mechanism, and pharmacological profile. Moreover, serotonergic nerve terminals may contain other neurotransmitters, such as acetylcholine (ACh), noradrenaline (NE), substance-P (SP), enkephalins, thyrotropin-releasing hormone (TRH), calcitonin gene-related peptide (CGRP), and postraglandins. The physiological response to serotonergic innervation reflects the nature of the postsynaptic receptors. The 5-HT_{1B}, and 5-HT_{1D} receptors are autoreceptors, and they regulate further release of 5-HT through inhibition of adenyl cyclase. These receptors are both somatodendritic and terminal autoreceptors. The somatodendritic autoreceptors suppress cell firing and are believed to play a role in collateral inhibition among serotonergic neurons. These autoreceptors also lead to reduction in serotonin synthesis and release in the areas to which the cells project by inhibiting neuronal activity. In contrast, terminal autoreceptors are not believed to influence cell firing but instead inhibit serotonin release, and possibly also synthesis from the nerve terminals. Most serotonergic synapses are inhibitory, though some are excitatory.

The involvement of the serotonergic system in motor function in vertebrates was indicated initially by its dense axon terminal innervation of motoneurons in both the brain stem and spinal cord. Secondary motor structures, such as the basal ganglia, substantia nigra, and habenula, also receive significant serotonergic input as noted. Administration of serotonergic agonists produces a motor syndrome in rats: head shakes, hyperreactivity, tremor, hindlimb abduction, lateral head weaving, and reciprocal forepaw treading. Extracellular recordings in conjunction with microiontophoresis of serotonin onto motoneurons in the rat facial motor nucleus or in the spinal cord ventral horn showed that when serotonin interacts with excitatory influences on motoneurons, it produces a strong facilitation of neuronal activity (via 5-HT_2 receptors). Administration of serotonergic agonists directly into the trigeminal nerve in cats produced an increase in the amplitude of the electromyography (EMG) of both the masseter muscle and an externally elicited jaw-closure reflex.

Serotonergic System and Relevance to Disease and Therapy

Studies of the serotonergic system over the last few decades have brought clinical evidence suggesting that altered serotonin function is involved in the pathophysiology of depression, anxiety, and OCD. The strongest support for these comes from studies demonstrating that a variety of serotonergic drugs, especially those that block the reuptake of synaptically released serotonin into the presynaptic terminal, are frequently effective in treating depression, anxiety, and OCD. Moreover, recent studies suggest that combined 5-HT_{2A}- and 5-HT_{2C}-receptor antagonists such as clozapine alleviate some of the symptoms (especially negative symptoms) of schizophrenia and that aberrant function of the serotonergic system may indeed be a major component of the disease. Moreover, alterations in serotonin uptake have been demonstrated in postmortem tissue studies in the limbic systems of schizophrenic patients. In addition, there is some evidence to suggest that there may be serotonergic dysfunction in at least some patients with anorexia nervosa. Animal studies using the motoneuron disease model (Wobbler mouse) suggested that sprouted serotonergic fibers in the cervical spinal cord could have excitotoxic effects on motoneurons and thus be causal to the loss of motoneurons (Bose & Vacca-Galloway, 1999).

REFERENCES

Bose, P., & Vacca-Galloway, L. L. (1999). Increase in fiber density for immunoreactive serotonin, substance P, enkephalin and thyrotropin-releasing hormone occurs during the early presymptomatic period of motoneuron disease in Wobbler mouse spinal cord ventral horn. *Neuroscience Letters, 260*(3), 196–200.

Dahlstrom, A., & Fuxe, K. (1964). Evidence for the existence of monoamine-containing neurons in the central nervous system. *Acta Physiologica Scandinavia, 232*(Suppl.), 1–55.

Page, I. H. (1968). *Serotonin.* Chicago: Year Book Medical Publishers.

Page, I. H. (1976). The discovery of serotonin. *Perspective in Biology and Medicine, 20,* 1–8.

Ungerstedt, U. (1971). Steriotaxic mapping of the monoamine pathways in the rat brain. *Acta Physiologica Scandinavia, 367* (Suppl.), 1–48.

Prodip Bose
Jolly Bose
University of Florida McKnight Brain Institute

SEROTONIN (5-HYDROXYTRYPTAMINE, 5-HT)

Serotonin (5-hydroxytryptamine, 5-HT) is an indoleamine neurotransmitter and hormone that has many actions in the central nervous system (CNS) and periphery. Serotonin was initially described as a hormone in the serum from clotted blood that caused vasoconstriction, hence the term serum-tonic factor, or serotonin. Serotonin was purified from blood and identified as 5-hydroxytryptamine in 1949. In 1953 serotonin was first detected in the central nervous system. The first serotonin receptors termed "D" and "M" types were characterized in guinea pig intestinal smooth muscle in 1957 (Gaddum & Picarelli, 1957). Serotonin achieved the status of neurotransmitter in 1963 when it was localized in neurons of the raphe nuclei. The first serotonin receptors in the CNS, the serotonin-1 and serotonin-2 receptors, were described in 1979, which triggered an explosion of investigation and discovery in the serotonergic system that continues unabated to the present (Peroutka & Snyder, 1979). The gene that encodes the 5-HT_{1A} receptor was the first serotonin receptor gene cloned and sequenced in 1986, which rapidly led to the identification of many new and unexpected serotonin receptors (Kobilka et al., 1987). By 1998 there were at least 15 distinct serotonin receptor types identified and grouped into seven broad families.

Serotonin is an evolutionarily old neurotransmitter. All metazoan species with organized nervous systems appear to use serotonin as a neurotransmitter. Serotonergic neurons, receptors, and serotonin-mediated behaviors have been described in the nematode *C. elegans,* fruit fly *D. melanogaster,* crayfish, mouse, rat, cat, pig, chimpanzee, and humans, among others. Serotonin has been shown to participate in many different behaviors, including feeding and satiety behaviors, mating and copulatory behaviors, nociception, circadian rhythmicity, arousal, sleep and REM sleep production, perception, temperature regulation, aggression, and seizure vulnerability.

In primates, serotonin exists in the CNS and the periphery. In humans approximately 90% of total body serotonin is in the gastrointestinal (GI) tract; 8% is in platelets; and the CNS has the remaining 1–2%. All of the serotonin in the body is synthesized de novo, as dietary serotonin is rapidly degraded in the GI tract. The biosynthetic pathway for the production of serotonin is identical in the GI tract and CNS. The amino acid tryptophan is the precursor from which serotonin is produced (Figure 1). Tryptophan is converted to 5-hydroxytryptophan (5-HTP) by tryptophan hydroxylase. This is the rate-limiting step and is dependent on the concentration of tryptophan. The 5-HTP is rapidly converted to 5-hydroxytryptamine (serotonin) by aromatic amino acid decarboxylase. The serotonin in serum is synthesized and secreted by cells in the GI tract and subsequently concentrated in the platelets. Despite its high intracellular concentrations, serotonin is not synthesized in platelets. The amount of serotonin synthesized in the CNS is controlled by the serum concentration of tryptophan (Maes et al., 1990). The serum concentration of tryptophan determines the amount that crosses the blood-brain barrier, which in turn controls the amount of serotonin synthesized in the brain (Carpenter et al., 1998).

In the brain, serotonin is synthesized in neurons of the raphe nuclei. The serotonergic cells of the raphe nuclei have axons that project widely throughout the CNS. The rostral raphe nuclei supply ascending serotonergic axons that innervate cortical and limbic structures, and the caudal raphe nuclei have descending axons that innervate the

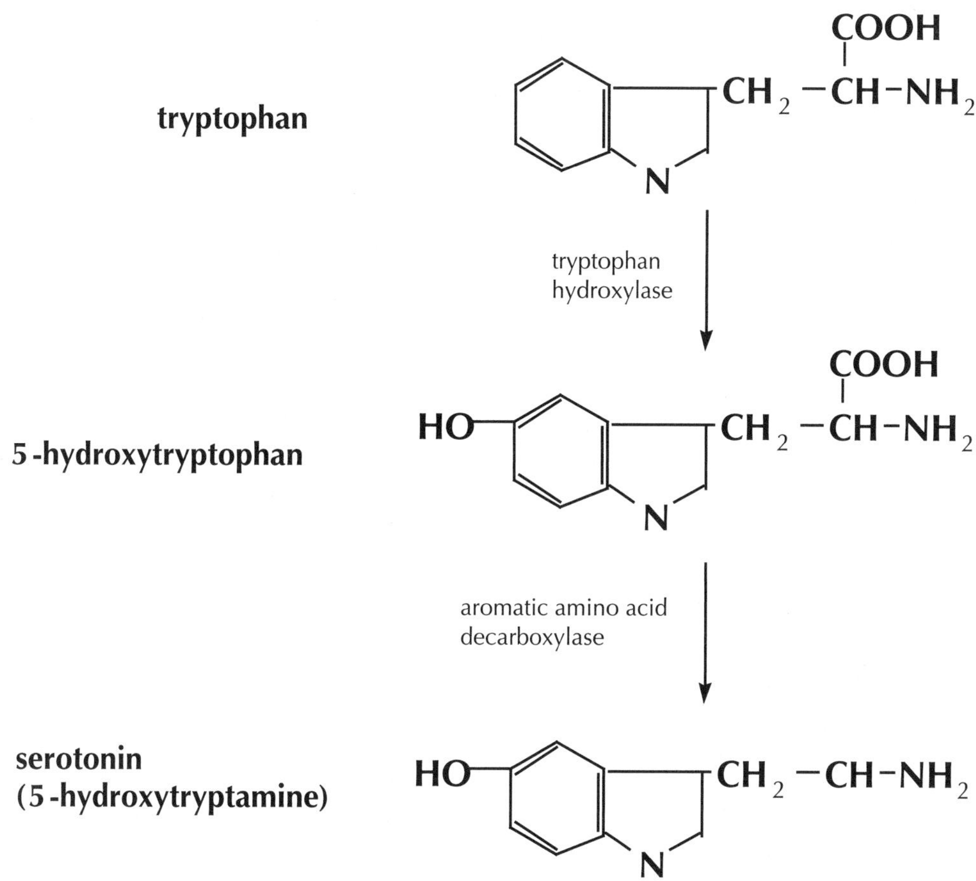

Figure 1. Biosynthetic pathway for serotonin.

spinal column. The serotonergic axons also project back onto the serotonergic cell bodies in the raphe and in this way regulate their own firing rate. The anatomical structure of the serotonergic system—with all of the transmitter being synthesized in a relatively small number of cells that in turn project widely throughout the brain—is the reason that serotonin is able to modulate so many different neurobehavioral and cognitive processes.

Depolarization of the membrane of the axon terminal causes serotonin to be released into the synapse. The serotonin diffuses across the synapse and binds to postsynaptic serotonin receptors. Transmission is terminated by the actions of the serotonin transporter (SERT) that pumps the serotonin back into the presynaptic neuron. In the CNS, the SERT is exclusively on the axon terminals of serotonergic neurons. The SERT on platelets is identical to the SERT on serotonergic neurons in the CNS (Lesch, Wolozin, Murphy, & Riederer, 1993). The SERT is the site of action of many different types of antidepressants including the specific serotonin reuptake inhibitors (SSRIs). The SERT is also the site of action of drugs of abuse including cocaine and MDMA (Ecstasy).

At least 15 different serotonin receptors have been identified and grouped into families according to molecular and pharmacological homology. The 5-HT_3 type is a ligand-gated ion channel receptor similar to the nicotinic cholinergic receptor, whereas the other serotonin receptors are 7-transmembrane, G-protein coupled receptors. Several of the serotonin receptors have been implicated in the pathophysiology of major mental illnesses. The 5-HT_{2A} receptor has been implicated in the biology of depression and schizophrenia. This receptor is the site of action of some antidepressants (trazodone, nefazodone) and of atypical antipsychotics (clozapine, olanzapine, etc.), and it is one of the sites of action of LSD and other hallucinogenic drugs. The advent of molecular biology has revealed that there are many more serotonin receptors than initially posited and that this system is much more complex than previously anticipated. The actual biological function of most of the new serotonin receptors remains obscure. Certain of the serotonin receptors, the 5-HT_{1A} and 5-HT_{1B} subtypes, also function as the perikaryal and terminal autoreceptors, respectively, further modulating the firing rate of 5HT neurons.

The serotonergic system has been hypothesized to participate in the pathophysiology of major depression, schizophrenia, anxiety disorders, impulse control disorders, suicide, and substance use disorders. A large and concerted research effort has been devoted to studying the role of the serotonergic system in these conditions (Maes & Meltzer, 1995; Meltzer & Lowy, 1987). The evidence that connects the serotonergic system to these different syndromes comes both from the measurement of serotonergic function and from the actions of various pharmacological agents.

Clearly, the serotonin system is highly complex. Serotonin participates in the regulation of many different neurobehavioral and cognitive processes. Dysfunction of the serotonergic system appears to play a role in the pathophysiology of major mental illnesses. Drugs that modify serotonergic function can be both psychotherapeutic (antidepressants, antipsychotics, anxiolytics) or agents of abuse (MDMA, cocaine, LSD, etc.). Knowledge of the structure and function of the serotonergic system is in its infancy but is currently in a period of exponential expansion, and new discoveries reported with astonishing regularity.

REFERENCES

Carpenter, L. L., Anderson, G. M., Pelton, G. H., Gudin, J. A., Kirwin, P. D., Price, L. H., Heninger, G. R., & McDougle, C. J. (1998). Tryptophan depletion during continuous CSF sampling in healthy human subjects. *Neuropsychopharmacology, 19*(1), 26–35.

Gaddum, J. H., & Picarelli, Z. P. (1957). Two kinds of tryptamine receptor. *British Journal of Pharmacology and Chemotherapy, 12,* 323–328.

Kobilka, B. K., Frielle, T., Collins, S., Yang-Feng, T., Kobilka, T. S., Franke, U., Lefkowitz, R. J., & Caron, M. G., (1987). An intronless gene encoding a potential member of the family of receptors coupled to guanine nucleotide regulatory proteins. *Nature, 329,* 75–79.

Lesch, K. P., Wolozin, B. L., Murphy, D. L., & Riederer, P. (1993). Primary structure of the human platelet serotonin uptake site: Identity with the brain serotonin transporter. *Journal of Neurochemistry, 60,* 2319–2322.

Maes, M., Jacobs, M.-P. Suy, E., Minner, B., Leclercq, C., Christiaens, F., & Raus, J. (1990). Suppresant effects of dexamethasone on the availability of plasma L-tryptophan and tyrosine in healthy controls and depressed patients. *Acta Psychiatrica Scandinavica, 81,* 19–23.

Maes, M., & Meltzer, H. Y. (1995). The serotonin hypothesis of major depression. In Floyd E. Bloom & H. Y. Meltzer (Ed.), *Psychopharmacology: The fourth generation of progress* (pp. 933–944). New York: Raven Press.

Meltzer, H. Y., & Lowy, M. T. (1987). The serotonin hypothesis of depression. In H. Y. Meltzer (Ed.), *Psychopharmacology: The third generation of progress* (pp. 513–526). New York: Raven Press.

Peroutka, S. J., & S. H. Snyder (1979). Multiple serotonin receptors: Differential binding of [^{3}H]-serotonin, [^{3}H]-lysergic acid diethylamide and [^{3}H]-spiroperidol. *Molecular Pharmacology, 16,* 687–699.

Steven J. Garlow
Emory University School of Medicine

SEVERITY OF PSYCHOSOCIAL STRESSORS SCALE

The Severity of Psychosocial Stressors Scale was developed for Axis IV of the third edition and revised third edition of the *Diagnostic and Statistical Manual of Mental Disorders.* The scale assessed precipitating stressors in mental disorders in the year prior to evaluation and formed part of the multiaxial system of modern diagnosis designed to improve the view of patients' background, symptoms, and functioning. The Severity Scale was founded on research on stressors that took place in the 1960s and 1970s, particularly the Holmes-Rahe Scale, which rated stressful life events along a hierarchy of severity.

The Severity Scale was divided into six categories of stress that ranged from no stress to catastrophic stress. Ratings were made by clinicians based on their assessment of the stress experienced by an average person. Some examples of stressors include school graduation (mild stress), job loss (moderate), unemployment (severe), severe chronic illness (extreme), and death of a child (catastrophic).

Research has distinguished the impact of time-limited events from that of more deleterious chronic stressors. For example, years of unemployment will likely be more stressful than a recent job loss. Consequently, the Severity Scale in the *DMS III-R* was rated for either acute events lasting less than six months (e.g., death in the family) or enduring conditions lasting more than six months (e.g., chronic illness). In addition, separate scales were provided for assessing stressors in adults (e.g., marital problems) and in adolescents or children (e.g., rejection by parents).

The Severity Scale was intended to help clinicians plan treatment, understand etiology better, and predict course and outcome. For treatment, information on specific stressors helps clinicians plan interventions to cope with the stress.

In terms of etiology, research on most mental disorders suggests that many factors may be involved as influences or causes. These factors may include social (external) events in combination with biologic or genetic (internal) dispositions. According to current diathesis-stress or vulnerability models of pathology, an inherent or biological vulnerability (diathesis) in an individual may be triggered by a stressful life event. Similar models have been used to elucidate the causes and outcomes of medical illnesses such as diabetes or coronary heart disease.

In terms of prognosis, theorists have suggested that acute symptoms precipitated by specific stressors that are external to the disorder may have a better prognosis than symptoms whose onset is gradual and less related to stress. For example, outcome research has distinguished good-prognosis, reactive schizophrenia (with acute onset and precipitating stress) from poor-prognosis, process schizophrenia (with gradual onset and no precipitating stress). Similar dichotomies and prognoses have been noted for mood disorders and alcoholism.

However, a review of the research (Skodol, 1991) reported several difficulties with the Severity Scale and with assessing stress in general. The scale did not seem to be widely used by clinicians. The reliability and validity of the scale were also questioned. Reliability ratings were generally low, in part due to the difficulties of rating stress. Validity was also moderate to poor for various disorders. Precipitating stress was a poor predictor of the course of illness in the psychotic disorders such as schizophrenia; the most positive predictive results occurred in depression—but not on a uniform basis. Nonetheless, significant results were generally in the hypothesized direction, with severe stressors associated with better outcomes. In addition, the prevalence of stressors varied by diagnosis. They were more likely to be found in disorders such as major depression and anxiety disorders than in schizophrenia (Skodol, 1991).

Explanations for problems with the scale included the following:

1. Clients' stressors reports were retrospective and subject to memory distortions.
2. The rating was often subjective and reflected what clinicians thought was stressful. Some clinicians focused on stressors ignored by other clinicians.
3. The background for assessment was average functioning rather than the distinct impact of the event on the individual. Critics suggest that the same stressor may have different effects on different clients.
4. The impact of multiple stressors, which often occurs, was difficult to assess. For example, a recently widowed person may also experience financial problems and social isolation.
5. The impact of continuous daily "hassles" (rather than single, major events) could not be accurately assessed. For example, the concept of *expressed emotion,* in which hostile, critical comments within families have been found significantly to impact relapse in several disorders, is difficult to assess by the Severity Scale.

Another major criticism was that only risk factors or negative stress, but not protective factors such as social supports and personal resources, were assessed. Increasingly, research has suggested that positive events, personal strengths, and social attachments may be of more import than deficits, symptoms, or negative events in predicting outcome. Positive protective factors such as social networks often mitigate the impact of stressful events.

Most important, some theorists suggest that the illness process itself may decide the protective or risk factors experienced by the individual. In other words, stressful events may be the result of the illness rather than the cause. For example, prospective, longitudinal research findings have shown that depressed individuals are more vulnerable to experiencing negative events than are non-depressed individuals (Cui & Vaillant, 1997). Individuals with severe mental disorders are more likely (because of their illness) to be unemployed or divorced or to experience other negative life events as a consequence of the illness, and these events may in turn exacerbate the illness. Conversely, some mentally healthy individuals actually seek some types of stressors (e.g., job changes) as opportunities for creativity. To a great extent, internal and external risk and protective factors are involved in complex, developmental interactions across the life span, and it is quite difficult to unravel the causes and consequences of a mental disorder.

Because of these myriad problems, the Severity Scale was dropped and replaced with a new Axis IV in the *DSM-IV:* Psychosocial and Environmental Problems. The new Axis IV is a simple notation of problems in nine possible areas such as economic problems. There are no restrictions on the number or types of events that clinicians can note, and severity ratings are not made. The new Axis IV scale in the *DSM-IV* is simpler than the Severity of Psychosocial Stressors Scale. It is hoped that the new scale will be more widely used and informative to clinicians planning treatment.

REFERENCES

Cui, X., & Vaillant, G. E. (1997). Does depression generate negative life events? *Journal of Nervous and Mental Disease, 185*(3), 145–150.

Skodol, A. E. (1991). Axis IV: A reliable and valid measure of psychosocial stressors? *Comprehensive Psychiatry, 32*(6), 503–515.

Jerry F. Westermeyer
Adler School of Professional Psychology

SEX BIAS IN MEASUREMENT

Bias in measurement is an issue when groups respond differently to items in an achievement, ability, or aptitude test, or in other types of measures, such as interest inventories. Sex bias in measurement is an issue when men and women respond differently to such items. The issue has particularly important implications for women's educational and occupational choices, as it has for members of minority groups.

Although the terms *bias* and *unfairness* have often been used interchangeably, the consensus among those who have studied bias seems to be to use the term bias to refer to intrinsic features of a test—its content, the construct or constructs it purports to measure, and the context within which the content is placed. *Unfairness,* however, refers to ethical questions about how the test results are used. Shepard further defines bias as occurring when two individuals with equal ability but from different groups do not have the same probability of success on a test item.

Sex bias and sex fairness in measurement have been investigated mainly with reference to interest, achievement, and aptitude tests, and to a lesser extent with reference to personality measures. Many of the differences between men and women in test performance have been attributed to differences in the socialization process—different expectations regarding early childhood behavior, interests, and achievement; exposure to different sets of experiences, including courses each was encouraged to take in school; and the stereotyping of occupations as men's work and women's work, with the latter encompassing mainly low-level, dead-end occupations in which most women workers are found.

In Interest Measurement

Until relatively recently, interest inventories—especially those with occupational scales—focused mainly on preferences for male-oriented activities. Only recently have there been attempts to build sex-balanced interest scales, with the number of items in a scale favored by one sex balanced by the number of items favored by the other sex. The National Institute of Education study of sex bias in interest measurement included guidelines for sex-fair inventories such as the reporting of scores on all scales, regardless of sex of the criterion group, to both women and men; and more sex-fair interpretation of inventory results.

In Achievement and Aptitude Testing

After the ninth grade, item context as well as content and gender balance in testing are important variables in sex differences in performance, especially in mathematics and science. Carol Dwyer related findings that in tests of verbal ability, all other things being equal, males obtained higher scores when the material was set in the context of business, science, practical affairs, mechanical principles, or mathematics. Females scored higher when the material was drawn from the arts, the humanities, or an understanding of human relations. There was no conclusive evidence as to whether these differences were the result of familiarity with the context, motivational considerations associated with the context, or some combination of the two. Tittle also described a study in which, while basic mathematical processes remained the same, when item context was manipulated experimentally to describe materials or settings more familiar to males or to females, sex differences in performance resulted. In aptitude testing, sex bias and fairness issues are perhaps best illustrated by Lee Cronbach's comments on the Armed Services Vocational Aptitude Battery. Cronbach pointed out that, among other weaknesses, the battery was poorly designed for use with women. Lack of trade and technical information (for instance, the ability to identify a carburetor) would be scored as low trade and technical aptitude, or ability to learn.

The Magnitude of Male-Female Differences

An important factor in dealing with questions of sex bias and sex fairness in measurement is the actual size of measured differences in ability. Janet Hyde describes a meta-analysis she applied to studies on verbal, quantitative, visual-spatial, and visual-analytic spatial differences between males and females. Although the differences had been described as "well established," Hyde found that they were, in fact, not large. Gender difference accounted for only 1% of the variance in verbal and quantitative ability, 4% of the variance in visual-spatial ability, and approximately 2.5% of the variance of visual-analytic spatial ability. These quantities, she concluded, were too small to account for the differences in the occupational distributions of men and women in occupations such as engineering.

A Question of Social Justice

Messick pinpointed two critical questions: (1) Is the test good as a measure of the characteristics it is interpreted to assess? (2) Should the test be used for the proposed purpose in the proposed way? The first question is concerned with the psychometric properties of the test, especially construct validity. The second is an ethical question, and to answer it the proposed use of a test must be justified in terms of social values. These questions apply not just to matters of selection or personality assessment, but to all psychological and educational measurement, including construct-based ability tests and content-sampled achievement tests.

Esther E. Diamond

SEX DIFFERENCES IN MATHEMATICS

Sex differences in mathematical aptitude favoring males have been reported for several years. Not until junior high school, however, do such sex differences become obvious. Girls then tend to excel on computational tasks, whereas boys excel on tasks requiring mathematical reasoning ability. Although the sex difference in overall mathematical reasoning ability is large, the sex difference in certain kinds of mathematics achievement is even larger. As compared with males, females complete fewer high school and college mathematics courses from a given competency level, have a lower rate of entry into quantitative fields in college for a given number of mathematics courses completed in high school, and have a lower rate of persistence in quantitative fields.

Several hypotheses have been proposed to account for these differences. The masculine-identification hypothesis states that it is necessary for one to identify psychologically with a male to have interest and ability in mathematics.

The social-reinforcement hypothesis states that sex-related differences in mathematics achievement are due, at least in part, to differential social conditioning and expectations for boys and girls.

Fennema and Sherman proposed that the sex difference in mathematical reasoning ability is simply a function of the fact that boys take more mathematics courses than do girls. Differential course taking is the result of socialization forces. Benbow and Stanley presented data that contradict this theory. They believe that some combination of endogenous and exogenous variables probably causes more boys than girls to reason well mathematically. What interactions of factors such as environment, female versus male hormones, physiologically induced differences in activity levels, and different brain-hemisphere lateralization might be responsible cannot as yet be ascertained.

Camilla P. Benbow
Vanderbilt University

See also: **Learning Outcomes, I and II; School Learning**

SEX DIFFERENCES: DEVELOPMENTAL

The best established sex differences are in the areas of life experiences and biology. They generally are considered to cause smaller and less well-established sex differences in the psychological areas of cognitive and social-emotional characteristics.

Cognitive areas showing sex differences include verbal and mathematics achievement and visual-spatial performance; the social-emotional area showing the most consistent sex difference is that of aggression. The developmental periods during which these sex differences occur vary somewhat by area.

Girls tend to excel at verbal tasks during infancy and young childhood. The existence of sex differences in verbal achievement during the elementary school years is not as clear, although many more boys than girls have trouble learning to read. Starting in early adolescence, females tend to achieve higher average scores than males on many kinds of verbal tasks, including lower level skills such as spelling and punctuation through high-level skills such as comprehension of difficult reading material and verbal analogies. The average female advantage continues through middle age and perhaps through old age, although there is very little relevant research on the elderly. Prior to adolescence, the sexes are quite similar in mathematics achievement. Starting some time during adolescence, males on average tend to score higher than females on mathematics tests.

There are at least two major components to visual-spatial performance: analytic (including, e.g., disembedding figures from backgrounds and constructing block designs) and nonanalytic (including mental rotations and reproducing spatial relations). Prior to adolescence, the sexes are similar in performance on both components. Starting in early adolescence, males tend to have higher average scores than females in both areas. The male advantage may continue into old age, although again there is little research in this area. The sexes, however, do *not* differ in spatial performance in nonvisual modalities such as touch or hearing.

Male children, on average, are more aggressive than female children from about age 2 through adolescence and college age. This pattern is found cross-culturally. The results for adults are not as clear. A review by Ann Frodi did not find that men always display more physical aggression; she did find, however, that men reported themselves as being more aggressive and hostile than women are.

Life Experience Differences

Starting at birth, girls and boys are treated differently in many socialization areas. Adults expect boys and girls, and women and men, to differ in the physical, personality, and cognitive characteristics contained in the sex-role stereotypes, although they profess to hold similar behavioral goals for their own children regardless of sex.

Education is differentiated by sex, with increasing differentiation occurring as educational level increases. Students are exposed to sex differentiation in the various occupations found in schools. Men fill most administrative and custodial jobs and tend to teach mathematics, social studies, and science in secondary schools. Women fill most of the clerical and secretarial jobs and teach most elementary school grades and language arts in secondary schools. Although about equal percentages of females and males graduate from high school, more males are encouraged to continue, so the percentage of females continually drops as the level of the educational degree increases.

While in school, more boys than girls are encouraged and actually take the advanced mathematics and sciences courses, prerequisites to many majors in college, and more girls than boys take language courses. Correspondingly, in higher education, more females major in humanities and education, whereas more males major in scientific fields. In vocational training, women are concentrated in the domestic, health, and office staff programs, and men are enrolled in technical, agricultural, and trade-industry programs; these differences by sex lead to lower paying jobs for most women.

There also are sex differences related to family life and to work. All cultures have some division of labor by sex, usually based on mobility. Cross-culturally, men often are responsible for tasks that require travel; women usually are responsible for work that allows them to remain near home and take major child care responsibility. Both sexes perform tasks requiring strength.

There are sex differences in physical and mental health.

Males have shorter average life spans, and a higher proportion of males die prenatally and throughout life. However, women visit physicians and therapists more often. The largest sex difference for mental health problems is for depression.

Sex differences in health, both physical and mental, are mediated by marriage. Married men have lower average rates of death and illness than unmarried men. The healthiest women, however, are those who never marry.

As greater opportunities become available, some of the sex differences in life experiences are narrowing, primarily because increasingly more women are choosing to participate in activities, education, training, and jobs that have been considered culturally male appropriate. However, the gap in sex-differentiated pay scales has not narrowed; it appears to be widening.

Biological Sex Differences

Several biological areas exhibit sex differences. These include genes, hormones, brain organization, and physical characteristics. Prenatal sexual development depends on a sequence involving chromosomes, hormones, and the environment. The sequence begins with the combination of an X or Y chromosome from the father paired with an X chromosome from the mother. Testicular hormones must be present prenatally to result in a biological male, regardless of the chromosomes present; without these hormones, a biological female develops. Genetic differences related to the sex chromosomes are one possible biological influence on sex-role development and on psychological sex differences.

Differences in brain structure and function also have been theoretically implicated in psychological sex differences and sex roles. Generally, the right hemisphere of the brain is related to performance on spatial tasks and to processing several items of information concurrently while the left hemisphere is linked to performance on verbal tasks and to individual processing of information items. There may be small sex differences in brain organization, but even if they do exist, they cannot explain psychological sex differences.

Sex hormones also have been proposed as one possible biological influence. Currently, however, hormonal sex differences do not explain psychological sex differences.

There may be monthly hormonal variations associated with some sex differences in perceptual and social-emotional characteristics. Some women experience changes in activity levels, sensory thresholds, and moods related to their menstrual cycles. However, there is no evidence, despite a great deal of research, that women's menstrual cycles are related to their cognitive performances.

There are several physical sex differences; for example, on average, men are taller, heavier, and stronger than women. Girls, on average, have higher physical maturation rates than boys, and the same may be true for the maturational rate of the central nervous system. Girls reach puberty between 1½ and 2 years earlier, on average, than boys. The rate of physical maturation does seem to be related to visual-spatial skills; for both sexes, later maturers have better visual-spatial skills than do early maturers. There is no relationship between maturation rate and verbal skills.

Conclusions

Many psychologists studying the relationships among biological, life, and psychological sex differences conclude that biological sex differences do not explain psychological sex differences. Biological factors may set the potential for psychological characteristics, but the environment often overcomes the biological differences and controls the sex differences that do and do not appear in psychological characteristics.

Candace G. Schau

See also: **School Learning; Sex Differences**

SEX THERAPY, FEMALE

Sex therapy starts with the correct diagnosis of the sexual dysfunction presented by the patient. Making a correct diagnosis is not an easy task due to the vague diagnoses provided by the *Diagnostic and Statistical Manual of Mental Disorders* (*DSM-IV-TR*; American Psychiatric Association [ApA], 2000), the high comorbidity of sexual dysfunctions, and the lack of age-related norms for the female sexual response. The common agreement is to look at medical etiology of the sexual complaints and then to follow with the investigation of personal and relational aspects. After this initial phase, the most liberal therapists discuss potential goals and patient expectations, which are not limited to sexual intercourse but could include skills such as communication and assertiveness or feelings of enjoyment and comfort during sexual behaviors. The techniques used in sex therapy vary according to treatment goals, dysfunction, and patient characteristics. Because sex therapy employs a symptom-oriented approach, much of the rationale is borrowed from the cognitive-behavioral school. In order to select the most appropriate form of sex therapy and therapy goals, the therapist must consider patient characteristics such as age, sexual orientation, ethnic background, and cultural expectations.

Sexual Desire Disorders

Hypoactive Sexual Desire Disorder

Women with Hypoactive Sexual Desire Disorder (HSDD) complain of a low interest in general sexual activities.

There are currently no empirically validated treatments for HSDD. Sex therapy techniques generally consist of 15 to 45 sessions of cognitive therapy aimed at restructuring thoughts or beliefs that may adversely impact sexual desire (e.g., "women should not initiate sexual activities," "sex is dirty") and to address negative underlying relationship issues. Behavioral approaches are utilized to teach patients to express intimacy and affection in both nonsexual (e.g., holding hands, hugging) and sexual ways, to incorporate new techniques into their sexual repertoire that may enhance their sexual pleasure, and to increase sexual communication. Testosterone is effective in restoring sexual desire in women with abnormally low testosterone levels (e.g., secondary to removal of the adrenal glands, bilateral removal of the ovaries, menopause).

Sexual Aversion Disorder

Defined as the avoidance of sexual genital contact with a partner, Sexual Aversion Disorder (SAD) has a high comorbidity with history of sexual abuse, vaginismus, and dyspareunia. Treatment for this condition often combines couples therapy and cognitive therapy and focuses on solving conflict areas within the couple, such as emotional differences and issues of control. Anxiety reduction techniques such as systematic desensitization are used when the aversion is accompanied by strong feelings of anxiety. Systematic desensitization consists of identifying a hierarchy of sexual activities that provoke anxiety and then pairing relaxation techniques with imagining the sexual activity. The goal is for the patient to feel relaxed while imagining each sexual activity and eventually while actually engaging in each sexual activity. Some therapists feel that, during treatment of sexual abuse survivors, trauma-related issues need to be resolved before SAD is addressed.

Arousal Disorders

Female Sexual Arousal Disorder

Female Sexual Arousal Disorder (FSAD) is operationalized as the difficulty in reaching and maintaining vaginal lubrication or genital swelling until the completion of the sexual activity (ApA, 2000). Recently, theorists have argued that diagnosis of FSAD should consider not only the physiological dimension of sexual arousal (i.e., lubrication) but the psychological experience as well. Women of all ages may experience difficulty lubricating, although it tends to be more of a problem in later life, typically after menopause. Female Sexual Arousal Disorder is generally assessed and treated in conjunction with Female Orgasmic Disorder or HSDD. To date, there are no validated treatments that focus exclusively on treating female arousal problems, although a number of pharmacological agents for enhancing vaginal engorgement and lubrication are currently under investigation. Techniques are often employed to help the patient become aware of her anxiety or her sexual turn-off thoughts, emotions, or behaviors. To help facilitate arousal, the patient is sometimes trained in the development of sexual fantasies, communication skills, sexual assertiveness, sensate focus, and the use of erotica or vibrators. Lubricants such as K-Y Jelly or Astroglide are often recommended to help compensate for decreased lubrication. Recently, the Federal Drug Administration approved a handheld battery-operated device called EROS-CTD for the treatment of FSAD. This suction device is placed over the clitoral tissue and draws blood into the genital tissue.

Orgasm Disorders

Female Orgasmic Disorder

Female Orgasmic Disorder (FOD) is defined in the *DSM-IV-TR* as the delay or absence of orgasm following a normal sexual excitement phase. The cognitive-behavioral treatment approach has received the greatest amount of empirical support for treating FOD. Reported success rates range between 88% and 90%. This therapy technique aims at reducing anxiety-producing thoughts associated with sexual activities and increasing positive behavioral experiences. The treatment is moderately short, averaging 10 to 20 sessions. The major treatment components include sensate focus, directed masturbation, and systematic desensitization. Sensate focus involves exchanging physical caresses, moving from nonsexual to increasingly sexual touching of one another's body over an assigned period of time. Directed masturbation involves a series of at-home exercises that begin with visual and tactile total body exploration and move toward increased genital stimulation with the eventual optional use of a vibrator. Directed masturbation is the technique with the best success rates, whereas systematic desensitization is particularly useful when anxiety plays a primary role in the dysfunction. Couples therapy, which focuses on enhancing intimacy and increasing communication, has also been used for the treatment of FOD, but the success rates of this approach have not been well established.

Sexual Pain Disorders

Dyspareunia

Dyspareunia refers to genital pain associated with intercourse (ApA, 2000). Vulvar vestibulitis is the most common type of premenopausal dyspareunia, whereas vulvar or vaginal atrophy is mostly reported by postmenopausal women. Women with these types of dyspareunia complain of pain in the vulvar area or anterior portion of the vagina upon penetration. The assessment of the type of dyspareunia should include information on the location, quality, intensity, time course, and meaning of the pain. The few studies that have examined treatment efficacy showed a moderate success rate of cognitive-behavioral techniques and biofeedback. The cognitive-behavioral approach includes education and information about dyspareunia, training in progressive muscle relaxation and abdominal breathing, Kegel exercises to train the patient to identify vaginal tenseness and relaxation, use of vaginal dilators, distraction techniques to direct the patient's focus away from pain cues, communication training, and cognitive restructuring of negative thoughts. During biofeedback, the patient is instructed to contract and relax her vaginal muscles while a surface electromyographic sensor inserted in her vagina provides her with feedback on muscular tenseness.

Vaginismus

Vaginismus is the involuntary contraction of the outer third of the vagina, which impedes penetration of fingers, tampons, or penis. Sex therapy for vaginismus often consists of a form of systematic desensitization that involves instructing the woman to insert graded vaginal dilators into her vagina. The woman's control over the insertion of the dilators is an important aspect of the therapy. The role of the partner in the exercise is passive if the partner is at all present. The emotional and psychological aspects of vaginismus are approached through patient education and control. Exercises that reduce anxiety and substitute anxiety-provoking thoughts with positive sexual thoughts are sometimes used in conjunction with the behavioral techniques.

REFERENCES

American Psychiatric Association. (2000). *Diagnostic and statistical manual of mental disorders* (4th ed., Text rev.). Washington, DC: Author.

Cindy M. Meston
Alessandra Rellini

See also: **Sexual Desire; Sexual Arousal; Orgasm; Sexual Pain**

SEXUAL DESIRE

Sexual desire is commonly defined as a wish, need, or drive to seek out and/or respond to sexual activities, or the pleasurable anticipation of such activities in the future. It is an appetitive state distinct from genital arousal and sexual activity. The mechanisms underlying sexual desire are not well known, although it is frequently believed to have both biological and psychological components.

A number of biological factors are likely to play a role in sexual desire, including testosterone, serotonin, and dopamine. In humans, testosterone is the most widely studied of these to date. It has been shown that testosterone administered to hypogonadal men can restore sexual desire to normal levels. However, testosterone given to nonhypogonadal men does not consistently increase desire, and the majority of studies assessing testosterone treatment for women with low desire have not been successful. Dopamine and serotonin play a role in the sexual motivation of animals, but little research in this area has yet been conducted in humans.

The psychological components of sexual desire are believed to stem from both intrapsychic and interpersonal factors. Social influences also play a role in the expression and experience of sexual desire. The effect of the interactions between these elements on the development and manifestation of sexual desire is not clearly understood.

There are currently two disorders associated with sexual desire: hypoactive sexual desire disorder (HSDD) and sexual aversion disorder (SAD). HSDD is defined as persistent or recurrent deficiencies in sexual fantasies and desire for sexual activity, taking into account factors that affect sexual functioning, such as age and the context of a person's life. To meet the diagnostic criteria for HSDD, such a deficiency must cause marked distress or interpersonal difficulty. SAD, in contrast, is characterized by persistent or recurrent extreme aversion to, and avoidance of, almost all genital sexual contact with a partner. As with HSDD, the aversion or avoidance must cause marked distress or interpersonal difficulty. Interestingly, no diagnoses are associated with excessive, or hyperactive, sexual desire.

Current estimates suggest an annual prevalence of disorders of desire of approximately 23% in the US (Laumann, Paik, & Rosen, 1999), although some studies indicate that this figure may be significantly higher. The occurrence of desire disorders is believed to be on the rise, and dysfunctions of sexual desire are present in over 50% of couples seeking sex therapy, making them the most common problem at sex therapy clinics (Schover & LoPiccolo, 1982). In the early phase of research in this area, researchers estimated that women experienced desire disorders at twice the rate of men, but there is increasing evidence that these rates are equalizing across genders (Kaplan, 1995; Schover & LoPiccolo, 1982); some studies have found the rates in men approaching those in women.

Although very little research has been done on disorders of desire in general, the vast majority of research has focused on HSDD rather than SAD. HSDD, however, is the subject of much disagreement among researchers, including issues of prevalence, diagnostic criteria, etiology, and treatment methods. Indeed, some argue that the diagnosis itself merely pathologizes normal human variation in desire levels (i.e., low desire becomes a problem only when one's partner has a higher level of desire). Such areas of disagreement are exacerbated by the difficulty in accurately measuring levels of sexual desire. In the absence of a consensus regarding what constitutes the most salient aspects of sexual desire (e.g., frequency of sexual behavior, frequency of sexual fantasy, intensity of sexual urges, etc.), researchers frequently are in disagreement even as to how to measure sexual desire.

Despite these difficulties, research to date indicates that HSDD responds less favorably to treatment than dysfunctions of orgasm or arousal and requires more treatment sessions to achieve positive results. Treatment of HSDD is complicated by the high prevalence (41%) of other comorbid sexual dysfunctions in patients with HSDD (Segraves & Segraves, 1991). Indeed, in many recurring cases of orgasm or arousal dysfunction, relapse may be due to an underlying desire disorder that was not successfully treated.

Major factors related to the development of HSDD are marital conflict, current or past depression, religious orthodoxy, and use of oral contraceptives. A number of commonly used medications (e.g., antidepressants, anticonvulsants, and antihypertensive agents) are also associated with a decrease in sexual desire (for a more complete listing of medications associated with decreased desire, see Finger, Lund, & Slagle, 1997).

A number of psychological treatments for low sexual desire have been proposed and evaluated to date. Such treatments include modified versions of standard sex therapy, marital therapy, cognitive-behavioral therapy, and orgasm consistency training. All of these treatments have shown some degree of success, although the characteristics likely to predict who will respond to which treatment have not been fully explored, and overall response in most of these studies is lower than for many other disorders. In addition, a number of medications have been evaluated in the treatment of low sexual desire, but most have either failed to show efficacy or require further examination to confirm preliminary findings. Future research is expected to expand the range of pharmacological and psychological options available for the treatment of disorders of desire.

REFERENCES

Finger, W. W., Lund, M., & Slagle, M. A. (1997). Medications that may contribute to sexual disorders: A guide to assessment and treatment in family practice. *Journal of Family Practice, 44,* 33–43.

Kaplan, H. S. (1995). *The sexual desire disorders: Dysfunctional regulation of sexual motivation.* New York: Brunner/Mazel.

Laumann, E. O., Paik, A., & Rosen, R. C. (1999). Sexual dysfunction in the United States: Prevalence and predictors. *JAMA: The Journal of the American Medical Association, 281,* 537–544.

Piletz, J. E., Segraves, K. B., Feng, Y. Z., MacGuire, E., Dunger, B., & Halaris, A. (1998). Plasma MHPG response to yohimbine treatment in women with hypoactive sexual desire. *Journal of Sex & Marital Therapy, 24,* 43–54.

Schover, L. R., & LoPiccolo, J. (1982). Treatment effectiveness for dysfunctions of sexual desire. *Journal of Sex & Marital Therapy, 8,* 179–197.

Segraves, K. B., & Segraves, R. T. (1991). Hypoactive sexual desire disorder: Prevalence and comorbidity in 906 subjects. *Journal of Sex & Marital Therapy, 17,* 55–58.

Tracie D. Giargiari
University of Colorado at Boulder

***See also:* Sexuality**

SEXUAL DEVELOPMENT

According to Sigmund Freud's psychoanalytic theory of personality, sexuality begins in infancy (Freud, 1938). The development of sexuality is a major part of the development of personality. According to Freud, the individual passes through several psychosexual stages: oral, anal, phallic, and genital, each named for the erogenous zone that gives rise to the main libidinal cathexis of that period.

Behaviorally, puberty marks the onset of human genital sexuality. Puberty begins between approximately 10 and 14 years of age for females and between 12 and 16 years of age for males. Hypothalamic stimulation of the pituitary gland causes secretion of pituitary hormones, including those directed to the gonads (gonadotropic) and to the adrenal glands (adrenocorticotropic). These glands, in turn, secrete the hormones responsible for the physical changes at puberty: a rapid increase in growth, the development of secondary sex characteristics, and the development of the reproductive capacity. James Tanner outlined the chronological sequence of the appearance of secondary sex characteristics (often referred to as Tanner stages). In addition, the individual experiences an increase in sexual awareness and a heightening of sexual drives. Sexual activity, including kissing, petting, and even intercourse, is a frequent component of the adolescent experience.

Although intercourse is most often considered in the context of marriage, the incidence of premarital coitus has increased over the years. David Kallen (1980) reviewed the North American studies reported between 1900 and 1980 and noticed several major changes over those years:

1. *Percentage of adolescents reporting coitus.* The data clearly indicate an increase in the number of high school and college students reporting having had intercourse.
2. *Proportions of males versus females reporting coitus.* In the past, the percentage of males reporting having had coitus was higher than the percentage of females. Kallen found that this had changed. Owing to the increased percentage of females reporting coitus, the proportion for males and females was almost identical by 1980.
3. *Age at first coitus.* Coitus is being reported at an earlier age. Estimates vary from 10% to 25% of 15-year-olds reporting intercourse, with the greater percentage being males. By age 17, approximately one third report having experienced coitus, with almost no difference between the sexes.
4. *Number of partners.* There has been a growing tendency among adolescents to limit their sexual experience to one partner within a given time period.
5. *Type of relationship.* Not only are adolescents less promiscuous in terms of the number of their partners, but there is also a greater tendency to experience sex-

uality in a relationship of love and affection. This has traditionally been true for females. It now appears to be the norm for most males as well.

REFERENCES

Freud, S. (1969/1938/1935/1920). *A general introduction to psychoanalysis.* New York: Pocket Books.

Kallen, D. J. (1980). Les adolescents decident de leur sexuality. In *Collection bioethique, Les cahiers du Centre de Bioethique, Institut de Recherches Cliniques de Montreal, 3, Medicine et adolescents.* Quebec: Le Presses de L'universite Laval.

John Paul McKinney
Michigan State University

SEXUAL DEVIATIONS

Sexual deviations, or *paraphilias,* are psychosexual disorders characterized by sexual arousal in response to objects or situations that are not part of normative sexual arousal-activity patterns and that in varying degrees may interfere with the capacity for reciprocal affectionate sexual activity. This term simply emphasizes that the deviation (para) is in that to which the individual is attracted (philia). It encompasses a number and variety of sexual behaviors that, at this time, are sufficiently discrepant from society's norms and standards concerning sexually acceptable behavior as to be judged deviant.

In the *Diagnostic and Statistical Manual of Mental Disorders* (*DSM*) from the American Psychiatric Association paraphilias are classified as of several types: (1) preference for use of a nonhuman object for sexual arousal; (2) repetitive sexual activity with persons involving real or simulated suffering or humiliation; and (3) repetitive sexual activity with nonconsenting partners.

Traces of paraphilias are commonly found in the realm of normal sexuality. It is only when such activities become the focal point of sexual gratification, and thereby displace direct sexual behavior with a consenting adult partner, that paraphilias may be said to exist.

The causes of paraphilias are seen as psychogenic rather than biogenic and hence depend very much on the paradigm one adopts within psychopathology. For example, within the psychoanalytic paradigm, these disorders are viewed as a consequence of aberrations occurring during psychosexual development in early childhood; in the behavioristic paradigm, they are seen as unadaptive sexual behavior resulting from learning and conditioning experiences; in the humanistic paradigm, they presumably represent particular outgrowths of each individual's unique, albeit distorted, subjective world of experience.

Types of Paraphilias

What follows is a brief description of each recognized paraphilia, following the *DSM* categorization and description system.

Fetishism

Fetishism is essentially characterized by the use of nonliving objects or, less frequently, parts of the human body as the preferred or exclusive method of producing sexual excitement. These objects or body parts (called *fetishes*) are essential for sexual satisfaction in the fetishist and constitute the focal point of sexual arousal. Fetishists are almost always males. The objects involved in fetishism can be quite varied and commonly include women's underpants, shoes, stockings, and gloves; parts of the body that typically become fetishes include breasts, hair, ears, hands, and feet.

Transvestism

In the psychosexual disorder of transvestism, there is recurrent and persistent cross-dressing by a heterosexual male for the purposes of his own sexual arousal. The gamut of transvestism extends from secretive and solitary wearing of female clothes, through sexually relating to one's spouse while so attired, to appearing in public cross-dressed and accompanied by extensive involvement in a like-minded subgroup.

Zoophilia

Zoophilia is marked by the use of animals as the repeatedly preferred or exclusive method of achieving sexual excitement. The animal may serve as the object of sexual intercourse or may be trained to excite the paraphiliac sexually by means of licking or rubbing. In this disorder, the animal is preferred regardless of other available sexual outlets.

Pedophilia

Pedophilia (from the Greek, meaning "love of children") is essentially characterized by a preference for repetitive sexual activity with children. Such activity may vary in intensity and includes stroking the child's hair, holding the child close while covertly masturbating, manipulating the child's genitals, encouraging the child to manipulate one's own, and, less frequently, attempting intromission. A youngster of any age up to puberty may be the object of pedophiliac attention, and force is seldom employed.

Exhibitionism

Exhibitionism is characterized by repetitive acts of exposing one's genitals to an unsuspecting stranger for the purpose of producing one's own sexual excitement. Normally no further contact is sought.

Voyeurism

Voyeurism is fundamentally characterized by the repetitive seeking out of situations in which the individual looks ("peeps") at unsuspecting women who are either naked, undressing, or engaging in sexual activity. Voyeurs, almost always males, derive intense sexual excitement from their peeping behavior. They usually either masturbate to orgasm during the voyeuristic activity or immediately afterward in response to the scene witnessed. Further sexual contact with the observed woman (usually a stranger) is rarely sought, and most voyeurs, like exhibitionists, are not physically dangerous.

Sexual Sadism

The widely used term *sadism* derives from the infamous Marquis de Sade, who, for erotic purposes, perpetrated such cruelty on his victims that he eventually was committed as insane. Sexual sadism refers to a disorder essentially characterized by the infliction of physical or psychological suffering on another person as a method of stimulating one's own sexual excitement and orgasm. Moreover, persistent sexually stimulating fantasies of this nature are also experienced by the individual. In some instances, the sadistic activities function as stimulants in building up to sexual relations, while in others the sadistic practices alone are sufficient for complete sexual gratification. Although the partners of sadists may be consenting or nonconsenting, the majority of sadistic behavior seems to occur in a relationship with a willing partner.

Sexual Masochism

The essential feature of sexual masochism is sexual excitement produced in an individual by his or her own suffering. That is, in this disorder the preferred or exclusive means of achieving sexual gratification is being humiliated, bound, beaten, whipped, or otherwise made to suffer. Such situations may be sufficient in themselves for full sexual gratification, or they may be a necessary prelude to direct sexual behavior, such as intercourse. Like sadism, then, masochism essentially involves suffering; unlike sadism, the suffering here is inflicted on oneself rather than on others.

Atypical Paraphilia

In the *DSM* atypical paraphilia is a residual category for individuals with paraphilias that cannot be classified in any of the other categories. These disorders include coprophilia (feces), frotteurism (rubbing), klismaphilia (enema), mysophilia (filth), necrophilia (corpse), telephone scatologia (lewdness), and urophilia (urine).

D. J. Ziegler
Villanova University

See also: **Sexual Development**

SEXUAL HARASSMENT

The United States government decided that employees have a right to feel free from discrimination while at work, and the statute that speaks to this right is Title VII of the Civil Rights Act of 1984. This law prohibits discrimination on the basis of "race, color, religion, sex, and national origin." Sexual harassment is considered to be a form of discrimination.

Definition of Sexual Harassment

Several components make up the definition of sexual harassment. First, to be considered *sexual* harassment, the conduct involved must be sexual in some way. However, this can include innuendos, jokes, pictures, leering, gestures, or other types of sexual behaviors that do not involve actual physical contact. A second component of the definition involves the recipient's perception of the sexual conduct as unwelcome. Many people meet their future mates at work, so coworkers may date, flirt, or behave in a sexual manner with one another. However, this behavior is not considered sexual harassment if both people deem it to be consensual. The sexual conduct must be unwelcome in order to constitute harassment.

The third component of the definition is that the conduct is committed or permitted by a person who is in a position of authority. Although the perpetrator of sexual harassment can be a supervisor or a coworker, the responsibility for preventing sexual harassment in the workplace is placed on the employer or supervisor. In fact, if a visitor to a business behaves in a sexually inappropriate manner, the employer can be held accountable if he or she had some knowledge of the risk and did not take adequate steps to create a safe work environment.

The reasonable-person rule comprises the fourth component to the definition of sexual harassment. The U.S. Equal Employment Opportunity Commission (EEOC) was created to develop the guidelines for interpreting Title VII and investigate violations. However, the EEOC guidelines are strongly influenced by judgments made by the federal courts, including the U.S. Supreme Court. For many years after Title VII was passed, the courts used the reasonable-person standard to evaluate whether certain sexual conduct was unreasonable. This standard changed for several years, between 1988 and 1991, when federal judges indicated that what is reasonable to a male may not be reasonable to a female employee. Accordingly, the EEOC recommended that questionable conduct should be judged from the viewpoint of the female employee. This standard was changed again in the early 1990s when the EEOC returned to using the reasonable-person standard. Many courts have followed suit, but final decisions are made on a case-by-case basis.

The final component to the definition of sexual harassment involves how the unwelcome sexual conduct impacts the employee's job. A person's job can be affected by sexual harassment in three ways: The employee's ability to fulfill job requirements can be hampered by the unwelcome sexual conduct; his or her opportunities for career advancement can be impeded; or the sexual harassment may create what is called a hostile work environment.

Types of Sexual Harassment

Most sexual harassment cases can be categorized as either *quid pro quo* or *hostile work environment.* Quid pro quo cases are those in which the harasser either directly or indirectly conveys that the person's job is at stake, that career advancement will be jeopardized, or that the employee will suffer some type of penalty for refusing to respond to the sexual conduct. In contrast, hostile work environment occurs when the unwelcome sexual conduct produces a work atmosphere that the victim perceives to be antagonistic, intimidating, or hostile. In either type of sexual harassment, the perpetrator never has to state that the victim will suffer negative consequences for noncompliance. These outcomes are either implied or perceived. The results of a large, national telephone survey of women demonstrated that only one in six harassers ever explicitly states that the victim will experience employment ramifications for noncompliance.

A woman or a man can perpetrate sexual harassment, and the victim can be either gender. In cases where the perpetrator and victim are of the same gender, the victim no longer needs to prove that the harasser is homosexual. In other words, heterosexuals can still commit sexual harassment against someone of the same gender. In these instances, the sexual conduct may be used to make the harasser feel powerful, and he or she may not even feel sexually aroused by the situation.

As a result of a U.S. Supreme Court ruling, victims of sexual harassment no longer have to prove that they have been damaged in some way—physically, economically, or psychologically—by the sexual harassment. However, there is evidence that female victims of sexual harassment are more likely to meet criteria for major depression and posttraumatic stress disorder during their lifetime than are women who have never experienced sexual harassment.

Responses to Sexual Harassment

There are several responses that a victim of sexual harassment can exhibit. Many victims initially try to ignore the unwelcome sexual conduct, particularly if it is not physical (e.g., leering, gestures, jokes). About three quarters of sexual harassment victims will ask the perpetrator to stop the harassing behavior; unfortunately, however, a majority of harassers continue. Furthermore, there is some evidence that about one in four harassers may take action against the victim as a result of being asked to cease their behavior.

Because people perceive words and behaviors differently, pointing out the offensive behavior and requesting that it stop are recommended in situations where the victim does not have safety concerns. Documenting the unwelcome sexual conduct is also recommended and should include detailed descriptions of the conduct, exact times and dates when it occurred, and who may have witnessed it. If a company has a sexual harassment policy, the employee can follow the rules outlined in that policy. Telling a supervisor about the sexual harassment enables the employer to take necessary action to remedy the situation and once again create a safe work environment. Because the employer is held accountable for sexual harassment, arming the employer with detailed information empowers both the victim and the authorities.

If a victim of sexual harassment chooses to file a claim with the EEOC, he or she must file within 180 days of the last incident of sexual harassment, and the company must have at least 15 employees. The EEOC can provide a right to sue letter to be used in civil litigation. An employee who is being sexually harassed can also file a claim under the state fair employment practice (FEP) statutes. However, victims' identities are not protected in FEP claims like they are with EEOC claims. FEP laws also vary from state to state, whereas the EEOC falls under the federal umbrella.

Summary

Sexual harassment involves unwelcome sexual conduct that is committed or permitted by a person in a position of authority that can lead to perceived or real negative work consequences or creates a hostile work environment. The harasser may be a supervisor or coworker, male or female, and of the opposite or same sex as the victim. Asking the perpetrator of sexual harassment to stop usually does not lead to the cessation of the harassment, and employees are encouraged to follow their company's sexual harassment policy and notify a person in a position of authority who can help restore a safe work environment. Victims of sexual harassment are at risk for major depression and posttraumatic stress disorder, although proving that a victim suffered psychological consequences is no longer required as evidence that sexual harassment occurred. Victims of sexual harassment can contact the EEOC for information and guidance and to file complaints within 180 days of the last incident of harassment.

Bonnie S. Dansky
Rochelle F. Hanson
Medical University of South Carolina

SEXUAL INTERCOURSE, HUMAN

Human sexual intercourse, or coitus, is one of the most common sexual outlets among adults. Although it is usually considered in the context of marriage, premarital and extramarital intercourse are also widely practiced. Adolescents appear to be engaging in sexual intercourse more frequently than in the past. Although cultures differ widely in their acceptance of premarital intercourse, U.S. customs have been traditionally more restrictive than most.

Sexual intercourse generally refers to penile penetration of the vagina, the most common sexual expression between opposite-sexed partners practiced in the United States. In a large national survey study of over 3,000 participants, Laumann, Gagnon, Michael, and Michaels (1994) found that 95% of men and 97% of women reported that they had experienced vaginal intercourse. Other sexual techniques with opposite-sex partners include anal intercourse and oral sex (both cunnilingus, i.e., male mouth on female genitalia, and fellatio, i.e., female mouth on male genitalia). These sexual expressions are far less common, however, than vaginal intercourse both in terms of life incidence and most recent experience.

In practice, North American sexual customs have changed from a double standard in which sexual intercourse was permissible for males but not for females to a standard of permissiveness with affection. Many adolescents and adults, however, still adhere to a standard of abstinence until marriage as an ideal. Despite that, the age at first intercourse has steadily declined over the past 40 years, according to Laumann et al. (1994).

Cultures also differ in the preferred manner of experiencing intercourse. Whereas American partners prefer a face-to-face, man-above position, this practice is by no means a universal preference. In *Human Sexuality,* McCary (1967) noted that whereas 70% of American males had never copulated in any other manner, this technique was relatively rare in other cultures. As do many authors of texts and manuals on human sexuality, McCary describes alternative patterns with their respective physiological and psychological advantages.

REFERENCES

Laumann, E. O., Gagnon, J. H., Michael, R. T., & Michaels, S. (1994). *The social organization of sexuality: Sexual practices in the United States.* Chicago: University of Chicago Press.

McCary, J. L. (1967). *Human sexuality.* New York: Van Nostrand.

John Paul McKinney

SEXUAL ORIENTATION, ROOTS OF

No one is certain why a majority of individuals are heterosexual and a minority are homosexual or why some of us accept the sex in which we are born and others do not. Most clues, however, point to genetic and endocrine forces interacting with social experiences. These biological factors set a bias with which the individual meets society to effect sexual orientation and sexual identity. Not everyone, however, sees biology as playing so strong a role.

The strongest evidence that sexual orientation has a biological basis comes from studies of human families and twins. Classical studies in this area were done in the 1950s with identical and fraternal male twin pairs in which at least one of the twins in each pair, at the onset of the study, admitted to homosexual behavior. Among these twins, it was found that if one of the identical twins was homosexual, so, too, was his brother. Among the nonidentical brothers, on the other hand, the twins were essentially similar to the general male population.

A slew of studies soon followed that reported identical twins not concordant for homosexuality, and theories that held to a genetic component to homosexuality lost support. Alfred Kinsey as well as Masters and Johnson also argued that homosexuality was of social rather than biological origin.

Subsequent research since the 1980s, however, supports a biological component to sexual orientation. In one set of studies, almost 200 families were examined in which at least one member was openly known to be homosexual. A set of heterosexual index individuals were controls. The investigators then inquired of the sexual orientation of all siblings. Their basic finding was that if a family contained one son who was homosexual, 20% to 25% of his brothers would also be homosexual. If an index brother was heterosexual, the chance of other brothers being homosexual was only 4% to 6%. Another study reported findings of behavioral concordance among six pairs of monozygotic twins reared apart in which at least one member of each pair was homosexually active. More recent research strongly supported these original findings. One such study of 110 pairs of twins found that half of identical twin brothers of self-identified homosexual men were also homosexual, compared with 22% of fraternal twins and 11% of unrelated adoptive brothers. Separate and additional research in the United States and Australia similarly found a high concordance for homosexuality among identical twins. These data indicate that genetic makeup has a significant influence on male sexual orientation. Among females, studies also show a link between genetics and orientation but not as strong as that for the males.

New avenues of research are being followed. One line of investigation finds a birth order effect relative to male homosexuality. Younger brothers are more likely to be androphilic than older brothers. Some type of immune response within the mother during pregnancy, with later male children, has been hypothesized. Another type of research has reported results that are conflicting. Investigators have consistently found that fingerprint patterns significantly differ between males and females. These characteristics are being probed to see if they correlate with sexual orientation. Some studies find the effect, while others do not. Because these patterns are formed before birth, social forces cannot be involved.

Research has also found that certain brain structures differ between heterosexuals and homosexuals. Dutch researchers found that a region of the brain called the suprachiasmatic nucleus is much larger in androphilic than in gynecophilic males. American investigators have found a region of the hypothalamus (INS 3) that is smaller in androphilic males and women than in gynecophilic males. The brains of lesbians have yet to be examined. Others also have found that different areas of the brain differ between men and women. Such structural differences may yet be found to differ among heterosexual and homosexual individuals.

Many studies document instances in which biological bases for heterosexuality and maleness override the social conditioning of rearing males as girls. In probably the best known case, the John/Joan story, a male infant whose penis had been accidentally burned off was raised as a girl (pseudonym Joan). Despite efforts by family and therapists to have Joan adjust to this situation, she rebelled. As soon as this child was able, he switched to living as a male (pseudonym John) and sought surgery to remove his breasts—induced by physician-administered estrogen—and fashion a penis. John developed as a gynecophilic male with strong manly mannerisms and attitudes. He now lives as a married male with adopted children.

Research from other cultures also is instructive. Among a group of individuals in the Dominican Republic, it was found, due to a genetic quirk, that some males were born with female-appearing genitalia. Their parents raised them as girls. However, this same genetic condition resulted in a penis and scrotum developing by puberty. Despite having been raised as girls from birth, 17 of 18 of these teenagers then switched, on their own, to life as the heterosexual males they felt themselves to be. Males born in Gaza and raised as girls (with a similar but different genetic condition) were found to desire similarly to live as males. Other investigators in other parts of the world found somewhat the same. For these latter cases, some argue that the parents knew in advance they would be switching their children's gender so that these subjects do not constitute a true test of the nature-nurture issue. This can be true for some of the latter cases studied, but it does not hold for the early cases before their association with modern medicine. Nature seems to have a strong influence.

These findings are not to say that culture and society are not influential in shaping an individual's sexual orientation. However, these social and cultural forces seem to be superimposed on certain biological givens. In so doing, they modify the frequency and character of the demonstrated behaviors but not the impulse for the behavior.

Milton Diamond
University of Hawaii

SEXUAL SUBCULTURES

The term *homosexual* refers to private behavior, the term *gay* to public behavior and association with a subculture. Although the majority of homosexually oriented individuals are probably closed about their activities, others are open about their sexual preferences and often are identified by various mannerisms and activities. These observable traits may be effeminate ones by males or masculine ones by females. These may be natural expressions of the self or part of highly formalized codes that signal group identity. Many of the social cues used to signal erotic interest are the same for homosexuals and heterosexuals (e.g., eye contact, use of double entendres). Yet for male and female homosexuals moving in a primarily heterosexual (*straight*) and often hostile world, certain clues are useful: subtle uses of voice tone, stance, mannerisms, and code words, and frequenting known contact places such as bars, galleries, coffee and bath houses, or park areas.

The visibility and social acceptance of homosexual activity has varied with time and place. There is probably more visibility and acceptance of homosexuality and other sexual preferences in the West today than ever before. There is no evidence, however, that same-sex behavior or other activities are any more or less prevalent than in the past. Transsexuality became more visible as surgical techniques become increasingly available; transsexual people could turn wish to reality. Intersexuality has only in the last decade or so opened up as a publicly recognized phenomenon even though it is as ancient as life itself.

Ambiphilic behavior also came to be more openly discussed in the 1990s than in the past. There is again no evidence that it is any more prevalent than at any other prior era. Bisexuals appear more often to congregate with homosexuals than heterosexuals but see themselves, and might well be considered, in a category of their own. As lesbians have done before them, they call for recognition as separate from homosexuals in general, with particular group needs and interests.

Women who prefer same-sex erotic and love-activities, exclusively or occasionally, used to be called *romantic friends* in Victorian times. Even more so than males, they were a secret minority in the West whose visibility became public only after World War II. Into the 1970s they were lumped with males as female homosexuals or female gays. Later, for political reasons they preferred to be called lesbians because it gave them identity as a group. They often prefer that the term *gay* refer only to males. Although many common needs exist among male and female homosexuals, lesbians have some special needs. In particular, they feel most strongly about not being stereotyped. As with individuals of any other grouping, they can be feminine or macho, conservative or liberal, devout or atheist, uninterested in orgasm or orgasm-driven, promiscuous or monogamous, in the closet or out of it, and attractive or plain. Their motivations or reasons for identifying with the lesbian community are often broader than those for male homosexuals. Some women will engage in same-sex activity for (feminist) political reasons, whereas comparable activity is nonexistent among males. For political and strategic reasons, however, groups of lesbians, gays, bisexuals, and transgendered individuals often come together. They identify the group with a label such as "Hawaii LGBT."

It should be simultaneously mentioned that there are many individuals who have sex with members of their own sex but do not consider themselves homosexual, lesbian, or gay or associate with the gay scene. For this reason, as well as others, those involved with AIDS research, for example, use the designation "males who have sex with men" (MSM) instead of referring to homosexual behaviors.

In any culture, clothes are symbols of maleness or femaleness and mark affiliation or separateness. Clothes serve in obvious ways to keep the genders distinct and readily identifiable. There is demonstrably a great deal of psychic and social investment in clothing, and many people are disturbed that others do not keep inviolate the clothes, and thus group identity, that society expects and prefers. For children younger than six, or somewhat older, it is often clothing (or hair style or occupation of adults) rather than genitals that determines their understanding of gender and serves as their means of identifying man from woman. In this regard, it is significant to mention cross-dressing subcultures, of which there are many. Most often, cross-dressing activities are done in private. The motivations for cross-dressing are many. This might be for comfort when the individuals claim to feel relaxation in dressing in clothes of the other gender. Some claim that cross-dressing allows them to express their full personality, incorporating aspects of both genders. For such persons, homosexual activity or fantasies are not necessarily part of the exercise. In other cases, however, there is a definite heterosexual or homosexual erotic component to the activity. The cross-dressed individual might be thus aroused and follow the activity with masturbation, intercourse, or another activity ranging from autoasphyxia to sadomasochistic play. Certainly, cross-dressing behavior might be associated with a desire totally to shift gender. This would be the typical story for transsexuals.

In most democratic societies, from the United States and Great Britain and Japan to European and Latin American countries, social groups exist to accommodate all the subcultures mentioned and many others as well. It is probably true to say that almost every paraphilia or sex-associated interest or fetish has a social group associated with it. These might be quite open in the culture or very much hidden. Aside from those mentioned already, there are social groups for sadomasochistic activities, mate or partner exchanges (wife swapping), social nudism, and so on. Any good Web search will uncover several social groups to meet the desires of most anyone.

MILTON DIAMOND
University of Hawaii

See also: **Gender Roles; Homosexuality**

SEXUALITY: ORIENTATION, IDENTITY, AND GENDER

Sexual orientation refers to the erotic-love-affectional partners a person prefers. In lay usage one often speaks of a person as a homosexual or heterosexual, and indeed people often refer to themselves the same way. Such usage, however, often links together those whose regular sexual partners are of the same sex with those whose same-sex encounters are rare. The terms heterosexual, homosexual, and bisexual are better used as adjectives, not nouns, and are better applied to behaviors, not people. The term *homosexual* is best reserved for those whose sexual activities are exclusively or almost exclusively with members of the same sex, the term *heterosexual* for those whose erotic companions are always or almost always with the opposite sex, and the term *bisexual* for those with more or less regular sexual activities with members of either sex.

Lately Diamond encourages the terms *androphilic, gynecophilic,* and *ambiphilic* to describe the sexual-erotic partners one prefers (andro = male; gyneco = female, ambi = both; philic = to love). Such terms obviate the need to define specifically the sex of the subject and focus on the desired partner. This usage is particularly advantageous when discussing transsexual or intersexed individuals. These latter terms also do not carry the social weight of the former ones.

To sexologists and others that study sex, *sexual identity* refers to the way one views the self as a male or female. One's inner conviction of sexual identity may or may not mirror the outward physical appearance, the gender role society imposes, or the role one develops and prefers. These distinctions are crucial particularly in regard to transsexualism and the intersexed. In the real world, the *transsexual,* like others, is identified in terms of overt sexual anatomy. Transsexuals are reared as society views them. Nevertheless, the self-image of transsexuals is of the opposite sex. Their physical realities are in conflict with their mind's image. *Gender identity* is the recognition of how one is viewed within society. The female-to-male (FtM) transsexual has the sexual identity of a male but recognizes that society treats her as a woman. She strives to reconcile the two identities with masculinizing surgery and lifestyle. For a male-to-female (MtF) transsexual the situation is reversed. For transsexuals it is more satisfactory to change the body than the mind.

An *intersexed* individual is one born with physical characteristics that are both male and female. For example, an individual can be XX in chromosomal configuration but have a male-like phallus; another individual might have XY chromosomes and have a vagina. Intersexed individuals might identify as female, male, or intersexed.

Sexual identity is an aspect of life tangentially related to sexual orientation. Any individual, even if transsexual or intersexed, may be androphilic, gynecophilic, or ambiphilic. In everyday terms, anybody may identify as homosexual or see their identity as heterosexual. Similarly, people might identify themselves as transsexuals or intersexed. This use of the terms is affiliative: It is as if one might identify as an American or a Unitarian.

One's *gender, gender pattern,* or *gender role* is different, though related, to the concept of orientation and identity. Gender and gender role refer to society's idea of how boys and girls or men and women are expected to behave and be treated. A sex role is the acting out of one's biological predisposition or the manifestation of society's imposition. The terms *boys* and *girls* and *men* and *women* are social terms; the terms *male* and *female* are biological terms. A male may be raised as a boy but grow to live as a woman and vice versa. For most people, their identity, orientation, and gender are in concert. The typical male sees himself as such, has masculine behavior patterns (a combination of biologically and socially determined behaviors), is treated as a male by society, and prefers to have sexual interactions with females. The typical female sees herself as such. She has feminine behavior patterns (also a combination of biologically and socially determined behaviors), is treated as a female by society, and prefers to have sexual interactions with males. Variations occur when an individual prefers erotic relations with one of the same sex or when a male sees himself as a female (male transsexual), a female sees herself as a male (female transsexual), or an intersexed individual elects to follow aspects of androgynous life.

It is thus obvious that one's sexual profile as a male or female or man or woman is not necessarily simple. At least five components are needed to describe adequately a person in sex and gender. A mnemonic for recalling these is PRIMO: gender Patterns (roles), Orientation, and Identity have been discussed. *Mechanisms* are inherent physiological factors that structure significant features of erotic life. Well-known and sexually obvious mechanisms are male penile erection and female lubrication as functions of erotic arousal. *Reproduction,* both in its basic physiology and all its social and cultural features, is another main component of sexuality.

A typical gynecophilic male sees himself as a male, lives as a man, enjoys his penis, and prefers erotic relations with a woman. An androphilic male also sees himself as a male, lives as a man, and also enjoys his penis but prefers to have erotic relations with another man. In contrast, the male transsexual sees himself as a female, prefers to live as a woman, wants to have his penis removed and replaced with a vulva and vagina, and wants to have breasts. As often as not, he will be androphilic and view this as a heterosexual encounter because he sees himself as a female. No typical male homosexual would want to have his penis removed and replaced with a vagina: This, however, is the frequent desire of the male transsexual. For a female transsexual the converse is true. Although she may not always opt to have a penis and scrotum constructed to replace her vagina and labia, she usually wants her breasts removed and her periods to cease because they are constant and visible reminders of what she feels she is not. Intersexed individuals are of such great variety that no consistent description would hold for all.

REFERENCE

Diamond, M. (2002). Sex and gender are different: Sexual identity and gender identity are different. *Clinical Child Psychology and Psychiatry,* 7(3), 320–334.

Milton Diamond
University of Hawaii

See also: **Sexuality**

SHAM RAGE

There has been much research in the area of sham rage, which has been characterized as an affective and pathological aggressive state. Attempts to understand better the anatomical substrate associated with sham rage, using primarily stimulation and ablation procedures throughout the entire limbic system, have unfortunately produced somewhat confusing results. Research on sham rage has often yielded contradictory data, perhaps because of the diffuse interconnections between the limbic system and other brain areas, which themselves may be partly responsible for the complex emotional and motoric behavior associated with the disorder. Moreover, the use of different species in the investigation of sham rage has produced varied results, further muddling our understanding of this behavioral and emotional phenomenon. The present description outlines the most consistent neurological findings of sham rage in both animals and humans. The major connections from the limbic system, and the amygdala in particular, to other brain regions are then elucidated. In conclusion, a general model of hostility and sham rage is presented.

One of the primary findings in the study of animal rage is that temporal lobe ablation produces placidity, whereas temporal region arousal generally yields hostility. Experiments conducted in the 1930s produced data supporting this notion, finding that bilateral fronto-temporal ablation tamed previously aggressive rhesus monkeys. Further development for this concept occurred in the late 1950s and early 1960s, when researchers found that the ablation of the amygdaloid bodies (within the temporal lobe) promoted pacification in the Norway rat. Around the same time, researchers demonstrated that temporal lobe stimulation produced a rage-like response in conjunction with the intensification of negative affective behaviors. It has been generally accepted that the amygdaloid bodies play a particularly important role in the production of hostile behavior.

Animal research also indicates that septal arousal, as opposed to arousal of the amygdaloid body, may play an integral role in producing emotional calming and placidity. Some of the earliest research demonstrated that septal lesions caused sham rage, whereas septal stimulation yielded an apparently pleasant state. Septum stimulation was apparently rewarding, as animals continuously pressed a lever to stimulate their own septal regions.

Researchers generally support the notion that humans experience similar emotional and behavioral sequalae as animals from septal and amygdaloid dysfunction. For example, using noninvasive procedures, amygdaloid lesions in humans have been found to produce a placid response. Moreover, partial complex seizures within the temporal lobes have been documented occasionally to cause nonpurposeful violence and, though hotly contested, perhaps purposefully directed rage. Irrespective of a temporal lobe seizure's sequelae, stereotactic amygdaloidectomy has been found to decrease rage behavior in highly aggressive patients who have a seizure disorder. Moreover, as in animals, human septal dysfunction (from tumor) has been associated with irritability and rage.

Given the extensive interconnections of the amygdala with other brain structures that promote the fight-or-flight response, it is easy to understand the amygdala's role in sham rage. Specifically, amygdaloid activation promotes arousal (and behavioral output) of the lateral hypothalamus (producing tachycardia, galvanic skin response increase, pupil dilation, and blood pressure elevation), parabrachial nucleus (panting, respiratory distress), ventral tegmental area, locus coeruleus, dorsal lateral tegmental nucleus (behavioral electroencephalographic arousal, increased vigilence), and periventricular nucleus (corticosteroid release for the stress response). Thus, amygdaloid hyperactivation may not produce sham rage itself. Rather, it initiates a chain of neuroanatomical events that produce their own cognitive, emotional, and behavioral features. When summated, these features equate to sham rage. Similarly, amygdaloid body lesion produces the reverse pattern of behavior (placidity).

Both data and theory have supported the notion that the hypothalamus is integral to rage production. The septum and amygdala are both extensively interconnected with the hypothalamus, thus providing neuroanatomical support for a hypothalamic role in rage. Indeed, lesion studies with cats and case studies with humans support the role of the hypothalamus in rage production. It is thus proposed that the hypothalamus acts to balance the septum and amygdaloid regions to promote normal levels of hostility and that prefrontal and temporal regions also interact (via the inhibitory uncinate tract) to yield stable aggression levels. Given these theories, it would then be expected that lesion of the septum or hypothalamus or stimulation of the amygdaloid bodies may produce sham rage.

Heath A. Demaree
Jennifer L. Robinson
Case Western Reserve University

SHAMANISM

Shamanism may be humankind's most enduring healing tradition, having survived for tens of thousands of years on all continents except Antarctica. Because of their psychological techniques, shamans are sometimes described as the world's first psychologists and psychotherapists. Shamans are often confused with other healing practitioners such as priests, mediums, and witch doctors, and do in fact often fill these roles. However, they can be distinguished and defined as practitioners whose activities include a method of gaining information by voluntarily entering alternate states of consciousness, in which they experience themselves, or their spirits, traveling to other realms at will, and there obtaining information and power with which to benefit others.

There has been considerable confusion over the psychological status of shamans, who have been dismissed as tricksters, pathologized as psychologically disturbed, or elevated to sainthood. Until recently the conventional academic view was that shamans and shamanism were the products of primitive or pathological minds, and diagnoses such as hysterical epileptic, psychotic, and schizophrenic were applied liberally. However, this appears to reflect a number of unfortunate biases, including ethnocentrism, the well-known tendency to dismiss or diagnose unfamiliar experiences, the confusion of clinic and culture, the pathologizing tendency of psychoanalysis, and lack of researchers' personal familiarity with shamanic experiences and alternate states. Several studies describe shamans as being exceptionally healthy, effective, and powerful and many of their experiences and states as being carefully cultivated, culturally valued, and phenomenologically distinct.

The opposite view, that shamans are virtual saints whose experiences and states of consciousness are equivalent to those of advanced yogis and meditators, has recently become widespread in the popular culture. However, although many shamans are compassionate, some are wiley tricksters, and phenomenological analyses show that shamanic experiences are quite distinct from yogic and meditative ones.

Shamanic techniques include both physical and psychological approaches. One of their central and defining techniques is the shamanic journey. Here they enter an alternate state of consciousness, experience leaving their body and roaming as free spirits throughout the universe, and acquire knowledge and power (especially from other spirits) to bring back to their tribespeople. To obtain the requisite state of consciousness, shamans employ preparatory ritual and ascetic practices and then use combinations of ritual, rhythm (usually involving drums, rattles, singing, and dancing), and occasionally psychedelics. Psychedelics, such as ayahuasca in South America, are used in a sacred context for spiritual, diagnostic, or therapeutic purposes. As such, they are culturally valued and have apparently not been subject to misuse or abuse.

Shamans are ontological realists, meaning that they take the realms they visit and the spirits they meet to be objective, independent realities. Contemporary psychological perspectives might view them as mind-created images akin to guided imagery, guided visualizations, or Jung's active imagination. Whatever one's philosophical interpretation, it seems that shamans can intuitively access valuable diagnostic, therapeutic, and life wisdom from their experiences.

Other techniques include physicalisms of diet, massage, manipulation, and herbal treatments (which are currently being researched by ethnobotanists). Psychological diagnostic techniques include an early projection test using a rock and assessment of muscle tension as an index of conflict.

Psychotherapeutic approaches include specific techniques such as confession, catharsis, music, ritual, and trance induction. Nonspecific approaches include expectation, attention, suggestion, and group support. The entire therapeutic process occurs within what Jerome Frank calls a shared healing myth, meaning that both shaman and patient share beliefs concerning the nature, cause, and appropriate means for curing illness. The net effect of all these factors probably includes a strong placebo effect.

From the shaman's perspective, the therapeutic factors are spiritual or psychic as much as, or more than, psychological or physical. Although research and meta-analysis evidence for some psi phenomena appear to be becoming more solid, studies of psi in shamans have been inconclusive, and most researchers decide the matter according to their personal belief systems. Whatever one's belief, however, it is clear that shamanism represents an extraordinarily widespread and enduring tradition of psychological and medical practices that have been used across centuries and cultures.

REFERENCE

Frank, J. (1973). *Persuasion and healing* (2nd ed.). Baltimore: Johns Hopkins University Press.

Roger Walsh
University of California College of Medicine

See also: **Mind/Body Problem; Placebo**

SHARING OF BELIEFS IN GROUPS

Many of an individual's beliefs are shared by few individuals, by members of a small group, by members of a society, or even by the majority of human beings. Shared beliefs are usually acquired from external sources and are disseminated through interpersonal communication networks or via societal mechanisms of communication.

Of special importance for group life are those shared beliefs that play a determinative role in the development of social identity, solidarity, interdependence, unity, and coordination of group activity—all are necessary conditions for the functioning of social systems. These beliefs are formed on the basis of common experiences of group members and exposure to the same channels of communication. Furthermore, groups not only form these shared beliefs but also make special effort to disseminate them among group members and maintain them.

From the perspective of a century, it can be noted that although the interest in shared beliefs is as long as the history of modern psychology, it has never been a major focus of study, except at the beginning of the emerging discipline. Distinguished early psychologists were interested in questions of how groups think, how they form common mental products, or of what nature the shared thoughts are. Durkheim (1898) labeled collectively shared cognitive products *collective representations,* which consist of the totality of beliefs and sentiments common to average members of the same society. LeBon (1895/1968) focused on the *collective mind* of a crowd, which guides contagious and common behaviors. McDougall (1920), who is considered to be one of the first professed social psychologists, introduced the controversial concept of *group mind,* referring to the continuity of shared thoughts, sentiments, and tradition despite the turnover of group members. Within the realm of early psychology should be noted also the work of Lev Vygotsky, the renowned Russian social developmental psychologist. Vygotsky argued that thinking and reasoning are always products of social activity molded by society. This social activity allows the transmission of common symbolic tools that are internalized through the mediation of language and used in joint action (Vygotsky, 1962).

After the first wave of psychologists who were preoccupied with collective mental products, the interest in this topic somewhat faded away until it reappeared in the work of the three founding fathers of modern social psychology: Muzafer Sherif, Kurt Lewin, and Solomon Asch. All three were interested in group behavior and recognized that group membership affects individuals' perception of their world. Sherif (1936) demonstrated in a series of experiments how individuals in a group form a joint norm (i.e., shared belief) and how it becomes part of their repertoire that affects their perception and judgment. Lewin (1948) focused on the study of psychological forces that influence the group at any given moment and assumed that any prediction of group behavior must take into account group goals, group standards, group values, and the way a group sees its own situation and that of other groups. Asch (1946), in turn, spoke about group members' *mutually shared field,* which enables them to understand the viewpoints of others and form shared actions, feelings, or ideas.

The work of Moscovici (1988) on social representation is the most extensive elaboration of shared beliefs in the recent work of social psychology. On the basis of Durkheim's conception of collective representation, he focused on the plurality and diversity of representations within a group or society and their continuous evolution through communication.

Recently, a new interest in shared beliefs has emerged from several different directions. This new line of research does not necessarily use the term shared beliefs, but in social cognitive tradition presents the term *shared cognition* (e.g., Hardin & Higgins, 1996; Resnick, Levine, & Teasley, 1991). The work by Bar-Tal (1990, 2000) and by Fraser and Gaskell (1990) analyzes shared beliefs in groups and societies that play important functions in the formation and maintenance of social identities and in guiding social behaviors. Bar-Tal (1990) introduced the concept of group beliefs, which denotes convictions that group members are aware of sharing and consider them as defining their groupness. In this conception, group beliefs play important roles in such group processes as schism, mergence, subgrouping, and disintegration. Another direction of investigating shared beliefs emerged in the study of small groups, with the assumption that they play a determinative role in group formation and functioning (e.g., Hinsz, Tindale, & Vollrath, 1997; Klimoski & Mohammed, 1994; Nye & Brower, 1996; Tindale, Meisenhelder, Dykema-Engblade, & Hogg, 2001). According to this line of study, group members can act interdependently only when they form an understanding of goals, norms, and procedures. The development for such understanding is a condition for the successful and efficient performance of small groups.

In all groups and societies, however, shared beliefs have significant social, political, and cultural functions. First of all, shared beliefs have an important influence on group behavior. Coordinated behaviors of group members always have an epistemic basis. In the majority of cases, group members, in addition to common understanding, need rationale and justification for their social behaviors in order to take part in coordinated activities. In this role, shared beliefs in a group are often used as a rationale for social behaviors because group members share them and consider them often as truthful.

The acquired shared beliefs play a further role in the formation of new shared knowledge because there is continuous reciprocal interaction between the shared beliefs and new experiences of the society. On the one hand, the new experiences serve as a source for the formation for new shared beliefs of a group, and on the other hand, the already-accumulated shared beliefs serve as a prism through which the new experiences are understood and new beliefs are formed. Shared beliefs in a group allow a firm construction of group reality in spite of the fact that their contents often concern ambiguous social events, abstract concepts, and information that in most cases is not observed firsthand or experienced. The study of shared beliefs in groups thus opens new avenues for understanding the world of groups as well as of individuals.

REFERENCES

Asch, S. E. (1946). Forming impressions of personality. *Journal of Abnormal and Social Psychology, 41,* 258–290.

Bar-Tal, D. (1990). *Group beliefs: A conception for analyzing group structure, processes, and behavior.* New York: Springer-Verlag.

Bar-Tal, D. (2000). *Societal beliefs of ethos: A social psychological analysis of a society.* Thousand Oaks, CA: Sage.

Durkheim, E. (1898). Representations indiviuelles et representations collectives. *Rev. de Metaphysique, 6,* 274–302.

Fraser, C., & Gaskell, G. (Eds.). (1990). *The social psychology of widespread beliefs.* Oxford, UK: Clarendon Press.

Hardin, C. D., & Higgins, E. T. (1996). Shared reality: How social verification makes the subjective objective. In R. M. Sorrentino & E. T. Higgins (Eds.), *Handbook of motivation and cognition* (Vol. 3, pp. 28–84). New York: Wiley.

Hinsz, V. B., Tindale, R. S., & Vollrath, D. A. (1997). The emerging conceptualization of groups as information processors. *Psychological Bulletin, 121,* 43–64.

Klimoski, R., & Mohammed, S. (1994). Team mental model: Construct or metaphor. *Journal of Management, 20,* 403–437.

Le Bon, G. (1968). *The crowd: A study of the popular mind* (2nd ed.). Dunwoody, GA: Norman S. Berg. (Original work published 1895)

Lewin, K. (1948). *Resolving social conflicts.* New York: Harper & Row.

McDougall, W. (1920). *The group mind.* New York: G. P. Putnam's Sons.

Moscovici, S. (1988). Notes towards a description of social representations. *European Journal of Social Psychology, 18,* 211–250.

Nye, J. L., & Brower, A. M. (Eds.). (1996). *What's social about social cognition? Research on socially shared cognition in small groups.* Thousand Oaks, CA: Sage.

Resnick, L. B., Levine, J. M., & Teasley, S. D. (Eds.). (1991). *Perspectives on socially shared cognition.* Washington, DC: American Psychological Association.

Sherif, M. (1936). *The psychology of social norms.* New York: Harper.

Tindale, R. S., Meisenhelder, H. M., Dykema-Engblade, A. A., & Hogg, M. A. (2001). Shared cognition in small groups. In M. A. Hogg & R. S. Tindale (Eds.), *Blackwell handbook of social psychology: Group processes* (pp. 1–30). Oxford, UK: Blackwell.

Vygotsky, L. S. (1962). *Thought and language.* Cambridge, MA: MIT Press.

Daniel Bar-Tal
Tel Aviv University

SHYNESS

Definition and Categories

Shyness is a universal human emotion, sometimes viewed as a blend of fear and interest. As a personality trait, shyness is defined as excessive self-consciousness characterized by negative self-evaluation, discomfort, and/or inhibition in social situations that interferes with pursuing interpersonal or professional goals. Shyness can occur at any or all of the following levels: cognitive (e.g., excessive negative self-evaluation), affective (e.g., heightened feelings of anxiety or embarrassment), physiological (e.g., racing heart), and behavioral (e.g., failure to respond appropriately). Shyness may be triggered by a variety of situational cues. Among the most typical situations are interactions with authorities, strangers, members of the opposite sex, and unstructured social settings. Although similar in expression, introverts, like extraverts, do not fear social situations but simply prefer solitary activities. Shy individuals prefer to be with others but are restrained by evaluation concern.

Prevalence and Diagnosis

The percentage of adults in the United States reporting that they are shy has escalated from 40% (± 3%) since the 1970s up to 50% in the 1990s and 60% in recent samples. Another 40% indicated they were shy previously but no longer; 15% were situationally shy; and only 5% believed that they were never shy. Most clinical referrals for shyness meet criteria for generalized social phobia (i.e., extreme discomfort and avoidance), and many meet criteria for avoidant personality disorder (i.e., longstanding rejection sensitivity and a belief in one's social inadequacy). Other comorbid diagnoses are dysthymia, generalized anxiety disorder, specific phobias, dependent personality disorder, schizoid personality disorder, and, in a small percentage, obsessive-compulsive and paranoid personality.

Consequences

Shy individuals take less advantage of social situations, date less, are less expressive, and experience more loneliness than do nonshy people. Shy men have been found to marry and have children later, have less stable marriages, delay establishing careers, and exhibit lower levels of career achievement than their nonshy peers. A perceived inability to socialize, along with a pessimistic outlook for social interactions, may become an excuse for anticipated failure and a self-handicapping strategy (e.g., "I can't do it because I am shy"). Finally, severe shyness continuing into later life can result in social isolation, loneliness, and even chronic illness and a shorter life span.

Genetics and the Interactionist Interpretation of Shyness

Research suggesting a genetic contribution to behavioral inhibition proposes that 15% to 20% of newborns exhibit an inhibited temperament characterized by high reactivity (e.g., excessive crying and vigorous movement of head and limbs) to novel stimulation. Such infants tend to exhibit more timid behavior (e.g., playing near the primary caretaker) and have relatives who report more childhood shyness. An interactionist interpretation of trait shyness suggests that these tendencies may interact with environmental variables such as being teased or bullied, dominating older siblings, family conflict, and overprotective parenting, leading to excessive concern about social evaluation and painful self-consciousness. Finally, the development of shyness in adolescence is usually due to experiences of rejection and self-blame for perceived failure in social domains.

Neurological Bases

The neurological foundation of shyness is centered in the amygdala and hippocampus. The amygdala appears to be implicated in the association of specific stimuli with fear. The more general pervasive conditioning of background factors related to the conditioning stimuli is known as contextual conditioning. This diffuse contextual conditioning occurs more slowly and lasts longer than traditional classical conditioning. It is experienced as general apprehension in situations that become associated with fear cues, such as classrooms and parties. Contextual conditioning involves the hippocampus, crucial in learning and memory, as well as the amygdala. The bed nucleus of the striate terminalis (BNST) is also involved and extends to the hypothalamus and the brain stem. The hypothalamus triggers the sympathetic nervous system and associated physiological symptoms, among them, trembling, increased heart rate, muscle tension, and blushing.

Culture

Cross-cultural research confirms the universality of shyness. A large proportion of participants in all cultures reported experiencing shyness—from a low of 31% in Israel to a high of 57% in Japan and 55% in Taiwan. In Mexico, Germany, India, and Canada, shyness was closer to the 40% reported in the United States. Explanations of cultural differences in shyness have focused on the distinction between collectivist cultures, which promote interdependence, thus fostering concerns about giving offense, and individualistic cultures, which promote independence, fostering self-presentational concerns. How cultures assign credit for successful actions and blame for failures also contributes to the experience of shyness if credit is externalized and blame internalized.

Treatment

Treatment includes an initial assessment (e.g., structured clinical interview, shyness inventory, fear of negative evaluation scale, depression inventory) and exposure to a hierarchy of feared situations, usually simulated in treatment sessions and in vivo, cognitive retraining, and social skills training. A treatment program that includes these elements is the 26-week Social Fitness Training (SFT) at the Shyness Clinic near Stanford University. Features of SFT, which contribute to its ecological validity, are in-group simulated exposures of feared situations, using group members and outside confederates, between-session in vivo exposures (e.g., making conversation) called behavioral homework, and the skills tool kit (like tennis drills or calisthenics) for adaptive social behavior. The kit includes emotion regulation, developing trust and intimacy, assertiveness, negotiation, empathy, and converting maladaptive thoughts, including attributions and negative relational schemas, to more adaptive cognitive patterns. As exemplified by SFT, treatment programs must consider the cognitive, behavioral, physiological, and emotional components that constitute each individual's experience of shyness.

SUGGESTED READINGS

Carducci, B. J. (1999). *Shyness: A bold new approach.* New York: HarperCollins.

Henderson, L. M., & Zimbardo, P. G. (2002). Shyness as a clinical condition: The Stanford model. In R. Crozier & L. Alden (Eds.), *The international handbook of social anxiety* (pp. 431–447). New York: Wiley.

Zimbardo, P. G. (1998). *Shyness: What it is, what to do about it.* Reading, MA: Perseus.

Lynne M. Henderson
The Shyness Institute

Philip G. Zimbardo
Stanford University

Bernardo J. Carducci
Indiana University Southeast

SICKLE CELL DISEASE

Clinical Features

Sickle cell disease (SCD) refers to a group of genetic disorders that affect approximately 1 of every 400 African American newborns. The disease results from the inheritance of two abnormal alleles responsible for hemoglobin formation, at least one of these alleles being the sickle cell allele (HbS). In SCD, vascular occlusion occurs when sickled red blood cells block small blood vessels. This can cause both acute and chronic complications, including acute chest syndrome, aseptic necrosis of hips or shoulders, retinopathy, leg ulcers, cerebral vascular accidents, and chronic anemia.

Repeated episodes of severe pain, often referred to as painful crises, are the most common and disabling complication of SCD. Painful episodes are usually recurrent and unpredictable. Pain may be located in almost any area of the body, commonly the extremities, joints, low back, and abdomen. The frequency and severity of pain are highly variable, from long periods of almost no pain to painful episodes several times per month. Medical management attempts to minimize intravascular sickling and then reduce pain. This is often done with aggressive narcotic medications given orally for mild pain or intravenously for severe pain. Frequently, hospitalizations and emergency room visits are necessary.

Until recently, most parents of children with SCD did not know their newborn had the illness until their child began experiencing medical problems. Often, the problems that occur in infants and young children with SCD are severe and can be life threatening. Without proper medical treatment, death may occur, and indeed one of the periods in life in which individuals are at greatest risk for death from this disease is in the first 5 years of life. Recently, newborn screening has become more routine, and now newborns are often identified early. Although it is still common for some individuals to die suddenly and unexpectedly before age 40, many individuals live long and productive lives.

Lifestyle Consequences

Individuals with SCD still encounter significant stressors related to their disease. In children, these include retarded growth, delayed puberty, and frequent clinic visits and hospitalizations. These stressors can affect peer relationships, self-concept, and school attendance. Given their cognitive development, young children may have difficulty understanding pain and the meaning of repeated hospitalizations. They may experience feelings of helplessness and fear of the unknown and may have difficulty expressing feelings to their parents and medical professionals. Behavioral problems, especially internalizing behavioral problems, or the more silent forms of psychological distress (e.g., anxiety and depression) may occur.

As children enter adolescence and young adulthood, their disease may interfere with social relationships, academic performance, and occupational and family planning. Fears related to their illness may interfere with individualization, maturation, and separation.

Adults face decisions regarding selecting a partner and having children, issues that are often complicated by the fact that SCD is hereditary. Many adults may have problems meeting job and family responsibilities. Disability and unemployment are common, and thus so are financial problems. As adults age, they may encounter more complications related to their illness and more frequent episodes of pain. As adults approach the average life span of someone with SCD, anxiety, depression, or even preoccupation with death may occur.

The emotional reactions that can occur in individuals with SCD are often complicated by inadequate recognition and treatment of pain by health care professionals. Many physicians and nurses have not had sufficient hands-on experience treating SCD pain, and thus they may be uncomfortable with aggressive medication management. Sometimes frequent hospitalization and emergency room visits are misinterpreted as drug-seeking behavior or faking pain. Although drug-related problems may occur in individuals with SCD, excessive concern over drug addiction by health care providers can lead to undermedication and inadequate pain management. Some individuals who have frequent frustrating encounters with inexperienced health care professionals become discouraged and alienated from the health care system.

Coping with Pain and Stress Related to Illness

Individuals with SCD cope well, are often able to work, remain active in social and recreational activities, and are well adjusted psychologically. Many others, however, cope poorly, lead more limited lives, and become depressed and overly reliant on health care services for their pain management. Although some of the variability in adjustment is a result of disease severity, psychological factors, including coping strategies and social support, are significantly related to psychosocial and functional adjustment across the life span.

In adults, several factors have been related to good adjustment to SCD. Adults who have lower levels of daily stress, higher efficacy expectations, and high levels of family support have better psychological adjustment. Adults who take an active approach to coping with pain by using multiple cognitive and behavioral strategies such as diverting attention and calming self-statements are more active in household, work, and social activities. Other psychosocial factors have been associated with poorer adjustment to SCD. Adults from conflicted families and adults who use palliative coping methods for dealing with stress have poorer psychological adjustment. Overall poor psychosocial and functional adjustment also occurs in individuals who deal with pain by catastrophizing, engaging in fear and anger self-statements, and using passive strategies such as resting while neglecting to use other strategies when an episode of pain occurs. This pattern of pain coping has been associated with more severe pain; greater reductions in household, social, and occupational activities during painful episodes; and more frequent hospitalizations and emergency room visits.

In children and adolescents, there are similar relationships among these dimensions of coping, family support, and adjustment. It is interesting that factors in the parents such as maternal adjustment and the pain-coping strategies that parents use are also related to the child's adjustment. Furthermore, coping strategies in parents and their children are related, possibly because children learn to cope with their own pain by observing their parent's reactions to pain.

There is a growing recognition for the need to treat individuals with this disease from a multidisciplinary perspective. There are now comprehensive SCD centers that emphasize the importance of integrating psychosocial and educational programs with clinical and basic science research. The goals of these centers often include providing multiple types of psychological treatments such as biofeedback and individual and family therapy along with traditional medical management approaches to enhance pain management and overall coping in patients and their families.

Karen M. Gil
Duke University

See also: **Pain: Coping Strategies**

SIMULTANEOUS CONDITIONING

Dual-task methodology involves assessing performance when individuals perform two tasks simultaneously, and in cognitive neuroscience the dual-task approach is a means to test hypotheses about shared brain substrates of behavioral processes. Simultaneous conditioning uses the dual-task design and is part of a long tradition of psychological research (see Pashler, 1994, for a review). A general model for use in localization of behavioral functions is called the *functional cerebral space model* (Kinsbourne & Hicks, 1978). In this model, performance of an ongoing behavior is predicted to activate regions in the brain that are the substrates for that behavior. In a dual-task paradigm in which two behaviors are performed simultaneously, a second region of activation associated with the second task also occurs. The closer in the brain the regions activated by the two tasks are to each other, the greater the chance that there will be interference between them due to overflow of activation from one to the other.

Using the functional cerebral space approach, experiments are designed to compare simultaneous task performance under two conditions: (1) conditions in which the tasks are hypothesized to involve a common neural system and (2) conditions in which the tasks are hypothesized to involve separable neural systems. Interference should be obtained when the tasks share a common neural substrate, but there should not be interference when the tasks use separate neural systems. Eye-blink classical conditioning is a form of associative learning for which the essential brain circuitry has been almost entirely identified (Thompson, 1986). Simultaneous conditioning or the application of the dual-task approach using eye-blink classical conditioning and other behaviors is a way to test hypotheses about shared brain substrates with classical conditioning.

In the delay eye-blink classical conditioning procedure, the conditioned stimulus (CS), a tone, is presented first and followed after a delay (in most studies with humans the delay is about half a second) by a corneal air puff unconditioned stimulus (US), and the CS and US end together. Early in the conditioning process, when the first paired CS-US presentations are made, participants respond by producing a reflexive eye-blink unconditioned response (UR) to the US. After an average of 40 paired presentations of the CS and US, young adult participants produce conditioned responses (CRs) by blinking before the onset of the US. The well-learned response or CR is an eye blink to the tone occurring just before the onset of the air puff US. Although the response is timed precisely, the participant typically has little awareness of blinking to the tone CS. This absence of awareness that learning is occurring coupled with the fact that medial temporal-lobe circuits are not essential for acquisition qualifies delay eye-blink conditioning as a nondeclarative form of learning.

The neural circuitry for this form of learning has been documented in nonhuman mammals using a variety of techniques (see Steinmetz, 1996; Thompson & Krupa, 1994, for reviews) and extended to humans in studies of neurological patients (Woodruff-Pak, 1997) and in brain imaging studies in normal human adults (e.g., Logan & Grafton, 1995). The neural pathways for eye-blink classical conditioning involve sensory pathways for the CS and US that converge in the cerebellum on the same side (ipsilateral) as the eye that receives the air puff. The association between the tone CS and airpuff US occurs at two loci within the cerebellum: the interpositus nucleus in nonhuman mammals (globose nucleus in humans) and cerebellar cortex. Using this clear delineation of the eye-blink classical conditioning circuitry, we can undertake behavioral dual-task studies to examine whether tasks interfere with one another and draw implications about the locus of activation of these tasks.

Papka, Ivry, and Woodruff-Pak (1995) conducted a dual-task study to test the hypothesis that timed-interval tapping and eye-blink classical conditioning are both dependent upon cerebellar cortical substrates. Eye-blink conditioning was assessed with a 400-ms delay paradigm, and concurrent with conditioning, separate groups of subjects were tested on a timed-interval tapping task, an explicit memory recognition task, a choice reaction-time task, or, for a baseline control, video watching. The hypothesis was that simultaneous conditioning and timed-interval tapping performance would produce interference, whereas simultaneous conditioning and memory recognition, choice reaction time, or video watching would not produce interference. This hypothesis was supported, and Papka et al. reported selective interference between eye-blink conditioning and timed-interval tapping but not during any of the other simultaneous conditioning situations.

A task developed to test motor learning is rotary pursuit, in which the participant holds a stylus on a rotating circular disk. With practice, the time that the participant is able to keep the stylus on target increases, and errors of going off the target decrease. Simultaneous conditioning with rotary pursuit produced little or no interference, suggesting separate neural substrates for the two tasks (Green & Woodruff-Pak, 1997). Word-stem completion priming is a form of learning in which previous experience with a word makes it more likely to be cued by a word stem. Additional work in our laboratory indicated that simultaneous conditioning with word-stem completion priming produced no interference with either task, supporting the contention that these two forms of learning have separate neural substrates (Green, Small, Downey-Lamb, & Woodruff-Pak, in press).

A stronger test of the separability of these two nondeclarative forms of learning and memory was carried out in my laboratory by testing young and older adults on simultaneous conditioning and word-stem completion. The fact that older adults tend to perform more poorly as the complexity of the task is increased is interpreted as an indicator of limited processing resources. The perspective of a diminution of processing capacity in older adulthood is longstanding (e.g., Birren, 1964; Welford, 1958), and contemporary research addressing issues such as aging and working memory continue to reinforce this position. From the perspective that older adults have a diminished processing capacity, it follows that older adults might be impaired in simultaneous conditioning and word-stem completion priming even though younger adults are not impaired in this dual-task situation. Comparing groups of younger and older adults on simultaneous conditioning and priming and comparing their performance to conditioning and priming as single tasks, Downey-Lamb (1999) found no evidence of interference in the simultaneous condition for the young or older adults. Thus, simultaneous conditioning studies demonstrate tasks that do not share the same neural substrate as well as tasks that share cerebellar substrates.

REFERENCES

Birren, J. E. (1964). *The psychology of aging.* Englewood Cliffs, NJ: Prentice Hall.

Downey-Lamb, M. M. (1999). *Dual task performance in younger and older adults: Evidence for brain structures engaged during nondeclarative tasks.* Unpublished doctoral dissertation, Temple University.

Green, J. T., Small, E. M., Downey-Lamb, M. M., & Woodruff-Pak, D. S. (in press). Dual task performance of eyeblink classical conditioning and visual repetition priming: Separate brain memory systems. *Neuropsychology.*

Green, J. T., & Woodruff-Pak, D. S. (1997). Concurrent eyeblink classical conditioning and rotary pursuit performance: Implications for independent nondeclarative systems. *Neuropsychology, 11,* 474–487.

Kinsbourne, M., & Hicks, R. E. (1978). Functional cerebral space: A model for overflow, transfer and interference effects in human performance: A tutorial review. In J. Requin (Ed.), *Attention and performance* (Vol. 7, pp. 345–362). Hillsdale, NJ: Erlbaum.

Logan, C. G., & Grafton, S. T. (1995). Functional anatomy of human eyeblink conditioning determined with regional cerebral glucose metabolism and positron-emission tomography. *Proceedings of the National Academy of Sciences, USA, 92,* 7500–7504.

Papka, M., Ivry, R. B., & Woodruff-Pak, D. S. (1995). Selective disruption of eyeblink classical conditioning by concurrent tapping. *Neuroreport, 6,* 1493–1497.

Pashler, H. (1994). Dual-task interference in simple tasks: Data and theory. *Psychological Bulletin, 116,* 220–244.

Steinmetz, J. E. (1996). The brain substrates of classical eyeblink conditioning in rabbits. In J. R. Bloedel, T. J. Ebner, & S. P. Wise (Eds.), *The acquisition of motor behavior in vertebrates* (pp. 89–114). Cambridge, MA: MIT Press.

Thompson, R. F. (1986). The neurobiology of learning and memory. *Science, 233,* 941–947.

Thompson, R. F., & Krupa, D. J. (1994). Organization of memory traces in the mammalian brain. *Annual Review of Neuroscience, 17,* 519–549.

Welford, A. T. (1958). *Ageing and human skill.* London: Oxford University Press.

Woodruff-Pak, D. S. (1997). Classical conditioning. In R. J. Bradley, R. A. Harris, & P. Jenner (Series Eds.) & J. D. Schmahmann (Vol. Ed.), *International review of neurobiology: Vol. 41. The cerebellum and cognition* (pp. 341–366). San Diego: Academic Press.

Diana S. Woodruff-Pak
Temple University

SINGLE PARENTHOOD

Single parenthood results when a parent divorces (57%), a child's parents are not married (33%), or a parent becomes widowed (6%; Rawlings & Saluter, 1995). The number of single-parent families in the United States increased from 9% of the general population in 1960 to 28% in 1990 and is expected to increase in relation to two-parent families into the twenty-first century (Rawlings & Saluter, 1995).

Finer (1974) set forth a comprehensive international report on single-parent families. The report noted that single-parent families were faced with problems such as social isolation and loneliness, financial hardships, and pressures on children to be responsible for domestic duties that are beyond their capabilities.

Research on single parenthood has tended to focus on the impact on children and the impact on parents.

Impact on Children

Although some children from single-parent families do quite well psychologically, overall there is an increased risk for psychological and behavioral problems. A review of the literature by Hilton, Desrochers, and Devall (2001) shows that single-parent children, as compared to intact families, tend to have lower levels of psychological well-being (Amato & Keith, 1991); internalizing problems such as anxiety, depression, withdrawal, and inhibition (Holden, 1997); externalizing problems such as noncompliance, acting out, and aggression (Holden, 1997); school performance deficits (Acock & Demo, 1994); and health problems (Dawson, 1991). Hetherington, Cox, and Cox (1978) also found that many of these problems surface during the first year following divorce (e.g., children tend to be more aggressive, oppositional, distractible, and demanding).

Crossman and Adams (1980) described two social-psychological theories that can be used to understand the potential negative effects of divorce on children. Crises theory suggests that divorce is an undesirable and stressful event that can have adverse consequences for a family member. According to crisis theory, children who are the most sensitive to the stressors associated with divorce tend to experience the most problems.

Zajonc (1976) provides a second theoretical perspective that suggests that divorce can undermine the amount of time that the parent and child spend interacting, thereby creating negative consequences. According to Zajonc's theory, single parents tend to have less time to spend with their children because of additional role demands. The children's social and cognitive development thus tends to suffer because they do not have enough time to interact with their parents.

Impact on Parent

The most common initial reaction to single parenthood is depression. Often the parent feels victimized, alone, and angry. He or she tends to worry about unpredictable income and poor housing and to feel inadequate (Miller, 1980). Other emotional reactions experienced by single parents include guilt or a sense of failure about a marriage breakdown, grief, fear, anxiety, confusion, and, in some cases, relief (Burgess & Nystul, 1977). The advent of single parenthood may also result in increased strain on the single parent's time, energy, emotions, and ability to work (Burgess & Nystul, 1977).

There has been a limited amount of research on the factors associated with successful single-parent families. Barry (1979) identified tasks for the adjustment period and tasks for the new family period that promote a positive single-parenthood experience.

Tasks for the Adjustment Period

1. Family members must recognize that changes have occurred within the family and that they will affect each member.
2. It must be realized that it will take time for each family member to experience the full impact of these changes.
3. Each family member needs to be allowed to mourn the loss of the parent who has left the family.
4. The limits and opportunities of the new situation must be assessed realistically.
5. The parent should try to understand, and to be accepting and supportive of, the children's attempts to react and adjust to the situation.
6. Parents should seek professional help for themselves and their children if progress on these tasks is not occurring.

Tasks for the New Family Period

1. The role of the parent who has left the family must be clarified in a manner that maximizes meaningful ongoing involvement by the noncustodial parent.
2. Problem-solving and decision-making skills should be applied to the full range of familial concerns such as sibling relationships and financial planning.
3. Communication and leadership skills should be used to readjust family roles for parents and children.
4. Realistic goals (short- and long-term) should be established for each family member and addressed in an ongoing, meaningful manner.
5. Social networks should be established that support the personal goals that are set.
6. Positive parenting principles should be practiced.

Recent Research Trends

To a large degree, research on single parenthood has focused on single mothers and been generalized to all parents (Hilton et al., 2001). More recently, researchers have analyzed the single-parenthood experience in terms of single mothers, single fathers, and intact families. Hilton and Devall (1998) noted that divorce tends to have a positive effect on the parenting of fathers (when they become single parents) and a negative effect on mothers (when they become single parents). Single fathers were also rated to be as effective (in terms of positive parenting) as single and married mothers and rated more positive (in terms of parenting) than married fathers (Hilton et al., 2001; Hilton & Devall, 1998). Collectively, the research relating to single fathers appears to have significant implications for custody decisions.

Financial strain has been identified as an important factor in undermining a woman's ability to adjust to the role in single parenthood. In this regard, Hilton et al. (2001) noted that single mothers have 47% the annual income of intact families, whereas single fathers have 86% of the annual income of intact families.

Coley (1998) evaluated the effects of father figures on children's socialization experiences. She found that divorced fathers had a more positive effect on children's achievement than did never-married father figures. Culture and gender were also important in terms of promoting socialization. African American children (vs. Anglos) and females (vs. males) benefited more from a father figure.

REFERENCES

Acock, A., & Demo, D. H. (1994). *Family diversity and well-being.* Thousand Oaks, CA: Sage.

Amato, P. R., & Keith, B. (1991). Parental divorce and well-being of children: A meta-analysis. *Psychological Bulletin, 110,* 26–46.

Barry, A. A. (1979). A research project on successful single-parent families. *American Journal of Family Therapy, 7,* 65–73.

Burgess, P., & Nystul, M. S. (1977). The single parent family: A review of the literature. *Australian Child and Family Welfare, 8,* 19–26.

Coley, R. L. (1998). Children socialization experiences and functioning in single-mother households: The importance of fathers and other men. *Child Development, 69*(1), 219–230.

Crossman, S. M., & Adams, G. R. (1980). Divorce, single parenting, and child development. *Journal of Psychology, 106,* 205–217.

Dawson. (1991). Family structure and children's health. *Vital Statistics Series, 10* (data from the National Health Interview Survey, No. 1978). Hyattsville, MD: Department of Health and Human Services.

Finer, M. (1974). *Report of the committee on one parent families.* London: Her Majesty's Stationery Office.

Hetherington, D. M., Cox, M., & Cox, R. (1978). *Family interaction and the social, emotional, and cognitive development of children following divorce.* Presented at the Symposium on the Family: Setting Priorities, Institute for Pediatric Service of Johnson and Johnson, Washington, DC.

Hilton, J. M., Desrochers, S., & Devall, E. L. (2001). Comparison of role demands, relationships, and child functioning in single-mother, single-father, and intact families. *Journal of Divorce and Remarriage, 35*(1–2), 29–56.

Hilton, J. M., & Devall, E. L. (1998). Comparison of parenting and children's behavior in single-mother, single-father, and intact families. *Journal of Divorce and Remarriage, 29*(3–4), 23–54.

Holden, G. W. (1997). *Parents and the dynamics of child rearing.* Boulder, CO: Westview Press.

Miller, J. R. (1980). Problems of single parent families. *Journal of New York State Nurses Association, 11,* 5–8.

Rawlings, S. W., & Saluter, A. (1995). *Household and family characteristics: March 1994* (U.S. Bureau of the Census, Current Population Reports, P-20, No. 477). Washington, DC: Government Printing Office.

Zajonc, R. B. (1976). Family configuration and intelligence: Variations in scholastic aptitude scores parallel trends in family size and the spacing of children. *Science, 192,* 227–236.

MICHAEL S. NYSTUL
New Mexico State University

SINGLE-PARTICIPANT RESEARCH DESIGNS

Single-participant research designs involve the intensive study of one organism continuously or repeatedly across time. The organism may be a person or a single molar unit such as an industrial organization or a political unit. As with conventional group designs based on reasonably large samples of participants, single-participant designs are employed to determine whether different variables are related or whether a treatment or intervention causes some effect on relevant response measures. There are situations in which it is more meaningful, more convenient, more ethical, and less expensive to study one or very few participants intensively than to study many participants. A basic difference between group and single-participant designs is that one or very few observations are generally obtained from each participant in group designs, whereas many observations are obtained from one (or very few) participant across time in the case of single-participant designs. The design categories of (1) correlational, (2) quasi-experimental, and (3) experimental that frequently are used to classify different types of group designs also can be used to classify various single-participant designs.

Correlational Designs

Single-participant correlational designs involve a collection of scores obtained across time (a time series) on some dependent variable of interest and, in addition, either (1) a series of scores on some other variable collected at the same time points (the concomitant series) or (2) a log of events that occur during the time series. An analysis is then carried out to determine whether changes on the dependent-variable time series are associated with changes in the concomitant series or the occurrence of events that have been recorded.

Quasi-Experimental Design

The quasi-experimental AB design consists of two phases: the baseline or A phase and the intervention or B phase. Data are collected during the A phase to describe the behavior before the treatment is introduced. After the baseline data are collected, the experimenter introduces an intervention, and data continue to be collected during the B phase. A major weakness of the AB design is that it is often difficult to know if some condition other than the intervention has changed between the A and B phases. Stronger designs are required to cope with this problem.

Experimental Designs

Three single-participant experimental designs are described here; others exist but are slight variants of these basic designs. Each of these designs provides greater certainty that a planned intervention is responsible for a change observed in time-series data than is provided by the AB quasi-experiment.

Reversal Designs

The direct extensions of the AB design are the ABA (baseline-intervention-baseline) and ABAB (baseline-intervention-baseline-intervention) designs. The ABAB design is often referred to as a reversal design in the behavior modification literature because the intervention condition is said to be reversed (more appropriately, withdrawn) after it is first applied. The advantage of these designs is that there is repeated demonstration of the effect of changing conditions that are manipulated by the experimenter. There are many situations, however, in which it is illogical to expect the behavior to revert to a preintervention level or impractical (or unethical) to reintroduce early conditions. Other single-participant designs can solve these problems.

Multiple Baseline Designs

Most of the difficulties associated with reversal designs can be solved with some version of the multiple baseline design. In a sense, this design is a collection of AB designs. Data are collected on two or more baseline series, and an intervention is applied to each one. Because the intervention is introduced in a staggered manner to the various baselines, it is implausible that some event unrelated to the intervention is the cause of the apparent effect on each series.

Single-Participant Randomized Experiments

Unlike the previously described designs, the single-participant randomized experiment does not employ a different condition throughout each of a small number of phases. Instead, the order of administration of two (or more) different conditions is randomized. A disadvantage of this approach is that the logic of the design dictates the use of treatments having very rapid effects that will not carry over long enough to contaminate the other treatments.

Comparison of Single-Participant and Group Designs

Single-participant and group designs differ in terms of several important characteristics, including data collection problems, the question answered, and data analysis. Many variables (both independent and dependent) are not easily (or at reasonable cost) employed repeatedly. This aspect of single-participant designs is perhaps the most limiting.

At a general level, both single-participant and group experimental designs provide an answer to the question of whether there is a treatment effect. They differ in terms of how the effect is defined and studied. The ABAB design, for example, provides important information on the form of change across time (both within and between phases) for a single participant, whereas the between-groups design provides an estimate of the intervention magnitude (generally at one time point) for a specified population of participants. The usefulness of the information obtained from each design depends on the type of external validity of greatest relevance.

Visual analysis (rather than statistical inference) is the norm for single-participant designs; however, a trend is developing among some researchers to employ formal statistical methods regardless of design.

SUGGESTED READINGS

Barlow, D. H., & Hersen, M. (1984). *Single case experimental designs: Strategies for studying behavior change.* New York: Pergamon Press.

Guyatt, G. H., Heyting, A., Jaeschke, R., Keller, J., Adachi, J. D., & Roberts, R. S. (1990). N of 1 randomized trials for investigating new drugs. *Controlled Clinical Trials, 11,* 88–100.

Hayes, S. C. (1992). Single-case experimental design and empirical clinical practice. In A. E. Kazdin (Ed.), *Methodological issues and strategies in clinical research* (pp. 491–521). Washington, DC: American Psychological Association.

Johnston, J. M., & Pennypacker, H. S. (1993). *Strategies and tactics of behavioral research* (2nd ed.). Hillsdale, NJ: Erlbaum.

Johnston, J. M., & Pennypacker, H. S. (1993). *Readings for strategies and tactics of behavioral research* (2nd ed.). Hillsdale, NJ: Erlbaum.

Kazdin, A. E. (1982). *Single-case research designs.* New York: Oxford University Press.

Bradley E. Huitema
Western Michigan University

SIXTEEN PERSONALITY FACTOR QUESTIONNAIRE

The Sixteen Personality Factor Questionnaire (16PF) is one of the most widely used, theory-based instruments for assessing normal-range personality characteristics in adults. The test has been translated into nearly 50 languages and is used to evaluate a set of 16 reasonably independent characteristics that predict a wide range of socially significant criteria. Adaptations of the original questionnaire have been developed for assessing personality in younger populations, effectively extending the age range of the test to 6 years old.

Raymond B. Cattell and a series of coauthors developed the test over a period of many decades following extensive research intended to clarify the basic organization of human personality. Cattell was interested primarily in identifying a relatively small set of *source traits* that could be used to explain variations in the much larger set of surface characteristics observable in behavior and recorded in language. Cattell began his search with the English lexicon because he was convinced that "all aspects of human personality which are or have been of importance, interest, or utility have already become recorded in the substance of language" (Cattell, 1943, p. 478). Whether it is true that language exhaustively delimits personality, it is certainly true that language extensively describes personality. About the time Cattell began his studies, Allport and Odbert (1936) had identified about 18,000 words in the unabridged English dictionary that described aspects of human behavior. When Cattell eliminated terms that were essentially evaluative (e.g., adorable, evil) or metaphorical (e.g., alive, prolific) or that described temporary states (e.g., rejoicing, frantic), 4,504 terms remained. Cattell began with that list and conducted a series of analyses to eliminate overlap among them. His analyses encompassed a variety of perspectives (e.g., peer ratings, self-reports), populations (e.g., undergraduates, military personnel, working adults), and methodologies (e.g., cluster analysis, factor analysis). By beginning his search with the entire universe of trait names and conducting the reduction systematically, Cattell reasoned that the set finally remaining must be judged to be source traits. In the same way that water, for example, could be conceptualized as a weighted combination of elementary molecules (two parts hydrogen, one part oxygen), Cattell believed that human characteristics such as adaptability or competitiveness could be conceptualized as weighted combinations of this small set of source traits.

The first publication of the 16PF did not occur until 1949, more than a decade after Cattell began his studies. Since then the test has undergone five major and several minor revisions. The most recent, in 1993, was the last Cattell completed before his death in 1998.

The current test contains 185 items, requires 35–50 minutes to complete, and has a 5th-grade reading level. The test can be scored by hand, but computerized scoring and an extensive array of interpretive reports are also available. Many of the items in the test are statements (e.g., "I get embarrassed if I suddenly become the center of attention in a social group") to which the examinee responds by choosing from three options (true, uncertain, false). Others present a set of contrasted choices (e.g., "If I could, I would rather exercise by (a) fencing or dancing, (b) uncertain, (c) wrestling or baseball"). The test provides scores for 16 primary scales and five global factors. The global factors result from factor analyses of the 16 primary scales and are conceptualized as major organizing influences behind the primary scales. The average test-retest scale reliability coefficient for the primary scales is .83 after a few weeks and .72 over a period of two months. Corresponding values for the global scales are slightly higher. Internal consistency reliabilities of the primary scales average .75.

The primary scales of the test, which are designated by alphanumeric symbols, are as follows: A—Warmth, B—Reasoning, C—Emotional Stability, E—Dominance, F—Liveliness, G—Rule-Consciousness, H—Social Boldness, I—Sensitivity, L—Vigilance, M—Abstractedness, N—Privateness, O—Apprehension, Q_1—Openness to Change, Q_2—Self-Reliance, Q_3—Perfectionism, and Q_4—Tension. The five global factors (Extroversion, Anxiety, Tough-Mindedness, Independence, and Self-control) assess features similar to those described as the Big Five in personality research. The 16PF can also be scored for approximately 100 scales that derive from years of empirical research on 16PF applications in clinical, counseling, and organizational psychology. The 16PF provides three response style indicators: Impression Management, Infrequency, and Acquiescence. These scales help identify unusual response patterns that may affect the validity of the profile.

The extensive body of research findings that have accumulated over time enhances interpretation of the 16PF. A great deal is known, for example, about how test scores relate to career preference, job performance, academic achievement, creativity, interpersonal relationships, and marital satisfaction. Clinical research with the test suggests that it can be useful in understanding the dynamics of adjustment and personality disorders, addiction, and spousal abuse.

The 16PF is used primarily to provide an objective determination of what a person is like and, therefore, to tell what the person is likely to do in various situations. For example, will the person function effectively in jobs that require a strong technical orientation? Can she be counted on to finish things she starts? Will he be an effective leader? Are these the kinds of people who are likely to handle high-stress situations well?

The 16PF's content overlaps with that of other omnibus instruments designed to assess normal-range personality, such as the California Psychological Inventory, the NEO Personality Inventory, and the Personality Research Form. However, the multivariate model that underlies the 16PF is distinct from those on which these other instruments are built, and the 16PF is embedded within a broader theoretical framework that Cattell developed to address individual differences in learning and human development (Cattell, 1979, 1980).

Since 1949, the 16PF has developed into a widely used instrument for assessing adult personality. A long history of empirical research and an origin within a well-established theory provide a rich source of interpretation for test users.

REFERENCES

Allport, G. W., & Odbert, H. S. (1936). Trait-names, a psycholexical study. *Psychological Monographs, 47.*

Cattell, R. B. (1943). The description of personality: Basic traits resolved into clusters. *Journal of Abnormal and Social Psychology, 38,* 476–506.

Cattell, R. B. (1979). *Personality and learning theory: Vol. 1. The structure of personality in its environment.* New York: Springer.

Cattell, R. B. (1980). *Personality and learning theory: Vol. 2. A systems theory of maturation and structured learning.* New York: Springer.

Samuel E. Krug
MetriTech, Inc.

See also: **Self-Report and Self-Ratings**

SLEEP CYCLE

In mammals including humans and in birds, sleep has a cyclic structure. Sleep electroencephalogram (EEG) recordings reveal the alternating occurrence of periods of non–rapid eye movement (nonREM) and rapid eye movement (REM) sleep. One sleep cycle consists of one nonREM and one REM period. Normal adult humans have 3 to 6 sleep cycles per night (see Figure 1).

The major portion of slow wave sleep (SWS) is found during the first nonREM period. In all sleep cycles the duration of the nonREM period is longer than that of the REM period. However, the nonREM-REM ratio changes across the sleep cycles with an increasing duration of REM periods throughout the night. Similarly REM density (the amount of REMs during REM periods) increases. The mean duration of sleep cycles in human adults is widely constant and ranges intraindividually from about 85 to 115 min. The average duration of the first sleep cycle is about 70 to 100 min; the average length of the second and the following cycles is approximately 90 to 120 min.

The duration of the sleep cycle in a certain species is correlated to the ratio of the body volume and body surface. Therefore, in mice it is about 7 min, and in elephants 180 min.

Sleep is affected by age, illness, and drug use. The cyclic structure of sleep exists already in the newborn, though

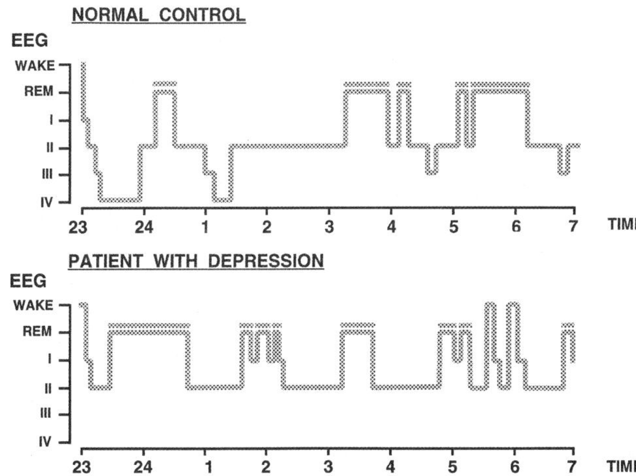

Figure 1. Hypnograms of a young normal control patient and an elderly patient with depression (REM, rapid eye-movement sleep; I–IV, stages of nonREM sleep).

with a shorter period (about 50–60 min) than in adults. Newborns and infants spend most of the time asleep. They sleep polyphasically and have the highest amount of REM sleep (about 50% of sleep). The amount of REM sleep decreases during childhood and adolescence, and then remains widely stable for several decades. During senescence it may decrease. SWS, however, shows a sharp decrease during adolescence followed by a further decline. In women menopause is a major turning point in the decrease of SWS, whereas in men a continuous decrease occurs.

During depression, changes in sleep are similar to those found in aging. These include a disturbed sleep continuity, decrease of SWS and disinhibition of REM sleep (shortened REM latency [the interval between sleep onset and first REM period], prolonged first REM period, and enhanced REM density; see Figure 1). Differences between patients with depression and age-matched controls may be restricted to the first sleep cycle with a shorter REM latency and a decreased amount of SWS in the patients (Lauer et al., 1992). Due to synergism of depression and aging, elderly depressed patients show the most distinct sleep-EEG changes. Sleep onset REM periods (SOREMPs, e.g., a REM latency shorter than 10 min) may occur during depression. In healthy subjects, SOREMPs occur rarely. Patients with narcolepsy also frequently show SOREMPs. In young patients with depression, a shift of the major portion of SWS from the first to the second sleep cycle is a robust finding. Severe disruption of the sleep-wake cycle is a symptom of Alzheimer dementia and is one of the major problems of managing these patients.

Most antidepressants suppress REM sleep. REM suppression is linked to the prolongation of the REM latency. Various substances differ in their ability to suppress REM sleep. Furthermore, this effect depends on the dosage. Potent suppressors like clomipramine may abolish REM sleep totally. Cessation of antidepressants is followed by a REM rebound. However, some antidepressants are effective but do not diminish REM sleep. Trimipramine and mirtazapine even enhance REM sleep in depressed patients (Sonntag et al., 1996).

There are interactions between the sleep cycle and various other ultradian rhythms. In males, spontaneous erections (nocturnal penile tumescence, or NPT) occur in a rather strict association with REM periods. Renin is the key enzyme of the renin-angiotensin-aldosterone system regulating water and salt metabolism. Plasma renin activity (PRA) shows oscillations of about 90 min strongly linked to the nonREM-REM sleep cycles. PRA increases in nonREM sleep and decreases in REM sleep. Increases of SWA and PRA are connected (Brandenberger et al., 1994).

The sleep cycle underlies a complex regulation. REM-on and REM-off neurons of the brain stem are thought to trigger the alternations of nonREM and REM episodes. Cholinergic neurons at the junction of the pons and the midbrain begin to discharge before the onset of REM. EEG activation is promoted via cholinergic projections to the thalamus, and projections to the reticular formation enhance excitability and discharge activity in these effector regions for REM phenomena. In turn, these mesopontine cholinergic neurons are modulated by the REM-suppressing norepinephrinergic locus coeruleus and serotonergic dorsal raphe projections (McCarley, Greene, Rainnie, & Portas, 1995). Furthermore, various neuropeptides participate in sleep regulation. A reciprocal interaction of growth hormone-releasing hormone (GHRH) and corticotropin-releasing hormone (CRH) influences the amount of SWS and nocturnal hormone secretion. GHRH promotes SWS and GH and inhibits cortisol, whereas CRH prompts the opposite effects. Changes of the GHRH-CRH ratio probably contribute to changes of sleep during aging (decline of GHRH activity) and depression (CRH overactivity; Steiger & Holsboer, 1997). Administration of vasoactive intestinal polypeptide, which is found in marked concentrations in the suprachiasmatic nucleus, decelerated the nonREM-REM cycle in young men and advanced the occurrence of the cortisol rise.

REFERENCES

Brandenberger, G., Follenius, M., Goichot, B., Saini, J., Spiegel, K., Ehrhart, J., & Simon, C. (1994). Twenty-four-hour profiles of plasma renin activity in relation to the sleep-wake cycle. *Journal of Hypertension, 12,* 277–283.

Lauer, C. J., Krieg, J. C., Garcia-Borreguero, D., Özdaglar, A., & Holsboer, F. (1992). Panic disorder and major depression: A comparative electroencephalogramic sleep study. *Psychiatry Research, 44,* 41–54.

McCarley, R. W., Greene, R. W., Rainnie, D., & Portas, C. M. (1995). Brainstem neuromodulation and REM sleep. *Neurosciences, 7,* 341–354.

Sonntag, A., Rothe, B., Guldner, J., Yassouridis, A., Holsboer, F., & Steiger, A. (1996). Trimipramine and imipramine exert different effects on the sleep EEG and on nocturnal hormone secretion during treatment of major depression. *Depression, 4,* 1–13.

Steiger, A., & Holsboer, F. (1997). Neuropeptides and human sleep. *Sleep, 20,* 1038–1052.

Axel Steiger
Max Planck Institute of Psychiatry

SLEEP DISORDERS

The field of sleep medicine has grown to comprise a broad spectrum of syndromes, disorders, and diseases. The predominance of psychology and psychiatry in the field has given way to increasing neurology and pulmonary medicine involvement, and most centers prefer a multidisciplinary approach. Comprehensive sleep disorders centers, accredited by the American Academy of Sleep Medicine (AASM), provide clinical assessment, polysomnography, and treatment for patients. The AASM has developed a diagnostic and classification manual for sleep disorders, as well as evidence-based standards of practice.

Sleep-related breathing disorders are the most common diagnoses made in sleep centers. Based on a random sample of 602 employed people between 30 and 60 years of age, Young et al. (1993) estimated that 4% of men and 2% of women meet diagnostic criteria for sleep apnea syndrome. Obesity, large neck circumference, and hypertension are associated with sleep apnea. Most patients are loud snorers and are sleepy during the day, although these complaints often come from family members rather than the patients themselves.

The polysomnogram provides objective evidence of sleep apnea. Airflow, chest and abdominal movement, and oxygen saturation are monitored continuously during the night. Sleep stages are identified by recording the electroencephalogram, eye movements, and chin muscle tone. Initially, breathing was assessed by counting the number of episodes of complete cessation of airflow lasting more than 10 seconds. More recently, decreases of airflow and arousals related to diminished breathing have been recognized as being clinically significant as well. Treatment decisions are based on an apnea-hypopnea index that combines all sleep-related breathing events, as well as oxygen saturation, cardiac arrhythmia, and daytime symptoms.

The cause of sleep apnea appears to be susceptibility of the upper airway to collapse during inspiration when muscle tone decreases with sleep onset. The most common treatment for sleep-related breathing disorders is continuous positive airway pressure (CPAP) delivered by a mask over the nose. Patients are titrated during polysomnography for the minimum pressure that resolves apnea, eliminates snoring, and improves the sleep pattern. Regular use of CPAP usually improves daytime sleepiness and blood pressure control. Treatment alternatives have been developed for patients unable to tolerate CPAP, including upper airway surgery and oral appliances.

Restless legs syndrome and periodic limb movement disorder are associated with prolonged latency to sleep onset and daytime sleepiness. Patients complain of crawling sensations or involuntary jerking of the legs, particularly during the evening or when sitting for prolonged periods. During polysomnograms, sensors detect muscle contractions or overt movements of the legs recurring at regular intervals of about 30 seconds. The movements may cause brief bursts of waking electroencephalographic activity or increased heart rate. The clinical significance of these movements is debated, but with adequate treatment many patients report resolution of the restlessness, improved concentration during the day, and decreased daytime sleepiness.

Insomnia may arise from a variety of causes, and a variety of treatments is available. Sleep-onset insomnia arises from anxiety disorders or jet lag and is often perpetuated by psychophysiological conditioning. The anxiety component may respond to cognitive behavioral therapy or relaxation techniques. A stimulus-deconditioning protocol specific to patients with insomnia has been developed and demonstrated to be effective.

Sleep maintenance insomnia and early morning awakening are hallmarks of depression. Patients with depression who undergo polysomnography also have a shortened latency to rapid eye movement (REM) sleep. This biological marker of depression may appear before a clinical depression is present and may persist despite adequate treatment. Tricyclic antidepressants usually have a beneficial effect on sleep continuity and mood. REM sleep latency may also be normalized. Serotonin reuptake inhibitors also suppress REM sleep but may increase the number of awakenings during the night.

Narcolepsy typically presents at about age 18 with excessive daytime sleepiness. Classically, patients have irresistible sleep attacks as well as accessory symptoms including cataplexy (a sudden loss of muscle tone with strong emotion or surprise), sleep paralysis (an inability to move for several minutes on awakening or at sleep onset), hypnagogic hallucinations (visual, tactile, or auditory sensations, often occurring in association with sleep paralysis) and automatic behaviors. There is a strong association with an HLA antigen and probably a genetic susceptibility to narcolepsy. Recent studies have linked narcolepsy with low levels of hypocretin (orexin) in the central nervous system.

Establishing a diagnosis of narcolepsy requires a polysomnogram followed by a Multiple Sleep Latency Test (MSLT). The MSLT provides an objective measure of sleepiness, as defined by the tendency to fall asleep during the day. The presence of REM sleep during two or more of the 20-minute naps on the MSLT is considered consistent with a diagnosis of narcolepsy. Narcolepsy often responds to treatment with stimulants. Methylphenidate and pemoline have been used for many years; modafanil is a recent alternative. Due to the potential for tolerance and elevation of blood pressure, amphetamines are usually reserved for patients who fail other therapies. Cataplexy reaches a level requiring treatment in some patients. Antidepressants, either tricyclics or serotonin reuptake inhibitors, are effective in controlling cataplexy.

Patients with parasomnias are infrequently seen at sleep disorders centers but are of theoretical interest as they may represent dissociation of aspects of sleep stages. Intrusions of waking behaviors in non-REM sleep include sleepwalking, night terrors, episodic nocturnal wandering, and nocturnal eating disorders. Although extremely common and usually benign in adolescents, parasomnias in adults may be accompanied by violence and therefore require treatment. REM behavior disorder is a failure of the normal muscle paralysis that prevents movement during REM sleep, thus representing an intrusion of wakefulness during REM sleep. Patients with this disorder act out their dreams, occasionally causing significant injuries.

With increasing diagnostic accuracy and improved treatment efficacy, public awareness of sleep disorders has increased markedly. Research efforts are underway to determine whether treatment of sleep-related breathing disorders decreases the risk of heart attack and stroke. Sleep apnea and other disorders causing daytime sleepiness contribute to automobile accidents, employee absenteeism, and mood disorders, among other significant consequences. Sleep disorders centers provide a focus for diagnosis and treatment as well as a resource for research and teaching.

SUGGESTED READINGS

American Sleep Disorders Association. (1997). *ICSD: International classification of sleep disorders: Diagnostic and coding manual* (Rev. ed.). Rochester, MN: Author.

Chokroverty, S. (Ed.). (1999). *Sleep disorders medicine: Basic science, technical considerations, and clinical aspects* (2nd ed.). Boston: Butterworth, Heinemann.

Hauri, P. J. (Ed.). (1991). *Case studies in insomnia.* New York: Plenum.

Kryger, M. H., Roth, T., & Dement, W. C. (Eds.). (2000). *Principles and practice of sleep medicine* (3rd ed.). Philadelphia: W. B. Saunders.

Young, T., Palta, M., Dempsey, J., Skatrud, J., Weber, S., & Badr, S. (1993). The occurrence of sleep-disordered breathing among middle-aged adults. *New England Journal of Medicine, 328,* 1230–1235.

Richard Rosenberg
Evanston Hospital

SLEEPER EFFECT

A sleeper effect in persuasion is a delayed increase in the impact of a persuasive message. In other words, a sleeper effect occurs when a communication shows no immediate persuasive effects, but, after a period of time, the recipient of the communication becomes more favorable toward the position advocated by the message. As a pattern of data, the sleeper effect is the opposite of the typical finding that induced opinion change dissipates over time.

The term *sleeper effect* was first used by Hovland, Lumsdaine, and Sheffield (1949) to describe opinion change produced by the U.S. Army's *Why We Fight* films used during World War II. Specifically, Hovland et al. found that the film *The Battle of Britain* increased U.S. Army recruits' confidence in their British allies when the effect of this film was assessed nine weeks after it was shown (compared to an earlier assessment).

Hovland et al. (1949) interpreted their findings in terms of a dissociation discounting cue hypothesis. According to this hypothesis, a sleeper effect occurs when a persuasive message is presented with a discounting cue (such as a low credible source or a counterargument). Just after receiving the message, the recipient recalls both message and discounting cue, resulting in little or no opinion change. After a delay, as the association between message and discounting cue weakens, the recipient may "remember what was said without thinking about who said it" (Hovland, Janis, & Kelley, 1953, p. 259). In other words, a sleeper effect occurs because of a spontaneous dissociation of a message and a discounting cue over time.

Hovland and Weiss (1951) provided a test of the dissociation hypothesis by giving participants persuasive messages attributed to either a trustworthy or an untrustworthy source. The results showed an increase in the percentage of people agreeing with the message given by the untrustworthy source four weeks after the presentation compared to immediately after the message was received.

The Hovland and Weiss (1951) study gave the sleeper effect scientific status as a replicable phenomenon and the dissociation discounting cue hypothesis credibility as the explanation for this phenomenon. The sleeper effect was discussed in almost every social psychology textbook of the time, appeared in related literatures (e.g., marketing, communications, public opinion, and sociology), and even obtained some popular notoriety as a lay idiom.

However, in 1974 Gillig and Greenwald were unable to produce a sleeper effect. In their studies, over 600 participants received messages attributed to a low credible source. Unlike the Hovland and Weiss (1951) study, the results revealed no indication of a sleeper effect.

The Gillig and Greenwald (1974) research raises an important question: Is the sleeper effect a reliable phenomenon? Studies by Gruder et al. (1978) and by Pratkanis, Greenwald, Leippe, and Baumgardner (1988) answered "yes" to this question and have specified empirical conditions needed for producing a sleeper effect. In both the Gruder et al. and Pratkanis et al. studies, reliable sleeper effects were obtained when (1) message recipients were induced to pay attention to message content by noting the important arguments in the message, (2) the discounting cue came after the message, and (3) message recipients rated the credibility of the message source immediately after receiving the message and cue. For example, in one experiment, participants underlined the important arguments as they read a persuasive message. After reading the message, subjects received a discounting cue stating that the message was false and then rated the trustworthiness of the message source. This set of procedures resulted in a sleeper effect.

The procedures developed by Gruder et al. (1978) and by Pratkanis et al. (1988) are sufficiently different from earlier studies to warrant a new interpretation of the sleeper effect. As a replacement for the dissociation hypothesis, Pratkanis et al. proposed a differential decay interpretation. According to this hypothesis, a sleeper effect occurs when (1) the impact of the message decays more slowly than the impact of the discounting cue and (2) the information from the message and from the discounting cue is not immediately integrated to form an attitude (and thus the discounting cue is already dissociated from message content).

Although much of the research on the sleeper effect has focused on the discounting cue manipulation, researchers have developed other procedures for producing sleeper effects, including (1) delayed reaction to a fear-arousing message, (2) delayed insight into the implications of a message, (3) leveling and sharpening of a persuasive message over time, (4) dissipation of the effects of forewarning of persuasive intent, (5) group discussion of a message after a delay, (6) the dissipation of reactance induced by a message, (7) delayed internalization of the values of a message, (8) wearing-off of initial annoyance with a negative or tedious message, (9) delayed acceptance of an ego-attacking message, and (10) delayed impact of minority influence. Although these other procedures for obtaining a sleeper effect have been less well researched, they may indeed be more common in everyday life than sleeper effects based on the differential decay hypothesis.

REFERENCES

Gillig, P. M., & Greenwald, A. G. (1974). Is it time to lay the sleeper effect to rest? *Journal of Personality and Social Psychology, 29,* 132–139.

Gruder, C. L., Cook, T. D., Hennigan, K. M., Flay, B. R., Alessis, C., & Halamaj, J. (1978). Empirical tests of the absolute sleeper effect predicted from the discounting cue hypothesis. *Journal of Personality and Social Psychology, 36,* 1061–1074.

Hovland, C. I., Janis, I. L., & Kelley, H. H. (1953). *Communication and persuasion.* New Haven, CT: Yale University Press.

Hovland, C. I., Lumsdaine, A. A., & Sheffield, F. D. (1949). *Experiments on mass communications.* Princeton, NJ: Princeton University Press.

Hovland, C. I., & Weiss, W. (1951). The influence of source credibility on communication effectiveness. *Public Opinion Quarterly, 15,* 635–650.

Pratkanis, A. R., Greenwald, A. G., Leippe, M. R., & Baumgardner, M. H. (1988). In search of reliable persuasion effects: III. The sleeper effect is dead. Long live the sleeper effect. *Journal of Personality and Social Psychology, 54,* 203–218.

Anthony R. Pratkanis
University of California, Santa Cruz

SMALL SAMPLE STATISTICS

The notion of small sample or small-n statistics was first developed by Gosset, a statistician working at the Guinness Brewery in the United Kingdom. One of his duties was to analyze samples of freshly brewed stout. Due to the inherent variability in the nature of the brewing process and the length of time required to test samples, Gosset experimented with the idea of substantially reducing the number of samplings taken from the very large number of available barrels. He found that the sampling distribution for small samples differed markedly from the normal distribution. Further, the distribution changed depending on the size of the sample, giving rise to a whole family of distributions. The results of his experiments with small samples led to the development of the t distribution, which Gosset published in 1908 using the pseudonym Student. In addition to being the first to recognize explicitly and deal with the problem of small samples, Gosset was also the first to combine experimental design with statistical testing and probably also the first to suggest anything like the .05 level as a reasonable criterion for rejecting the null hypothesis. Although not immediately recognized as such, Gosset's work with small samples was a critical breakthrough in the history of statistics, leading to the development of a number of other procedures, including the analysis of variance.

The t distribution, like the normal (z) distribution, applies to the testing of the null hypothesis that two samples have been randomly selected from the same population and that the calculated statistics (mean and standard deviation) are unbiased estimates of the population parameters. However, unlike the z, the t distribution for small samples does not require prior knowledge or precise estimates of the population mean and standard deviation. Whereas both the z and t distributions are symmetrical, the t distribution becomes increasingly platykurtic as sample size decreases. Platykurtic curves are less asymptotic (i.e., heavier in the tails) compared to the normal curve. This difference leads to marked discrepancies between corresponding t and z scores, especially for small sample sizes. For example, a t of 2.57 with 5 degrees of freedom (df) is associated with a probability (p) value of .05 (two-tailed), whereas for the normal distribution a z score of only 1.96 is required for $p = .05$. A t value of 2.57 with df = 5 indicates statistical significance at the 5% level. For the normal curve, a z of 2.57 would indicate statistical significance at the 1% level.

Extension of Gosset's work on the t distribution to more than two groups was accomplished by the British statistician Fisher, perhaps the most influential statistician of the twentieth century. Fisher proposed the first theoretical formulations of the analysis of variance and the *F* distribution in a series of classic works starting around 1925. As with the *t* distribution, the *F* distribution is represented by a family of distributions. However, whereas the *t* distribution is characterized by a single df, the *F* distribution is characterized by two separate degrees of freedom, one representing between-groups variability and one within-groups variability (error).

What Constitutes a Small Sample?

Although there is no definitive answer to this question, it is conventional to set the cutoff between a small and a large sample at about 30. Though arbitrary, this judgment stems from comparing the *t* and *z* distributions and noting that discrepancies between *t* and *z* decrease as df increases and that *t* approaches *z* quite closely long before it reaches its limit at df = infinity, when $t = z$. Convergence between *t* and *z* becomes rather rapid at and beyond df = 30. For example, for df = 30, the comparative values for *t* and *z* are, respectively, 2.042 and 1.960 for $p = .05$, 2.750 and 2.576 for $p = .01$, and 3.646 and 3.291 for $p = .001$.

Other Small Sample Statistics

The *t* test and the analysis of variance *F* test procedures were explicitly designed for use with small samples, although they are valid for large samples as well. There are, however, many other statistical methods applicable to small samples, including primarily the nonparametric, or distribution-free, methods. These techniques were designed mainly for use with data that do not fit the definition of either ratio or interval levels of measurement but rather are either ordinal or nominal measures. For nonparametric statistics, no assumptions are made regarding parameters, especially relating to variance estimates. For this reason, nonparametric methods are sometimes used for ratio and interval scale measures when sample sizes are small and there is a likelihood that some of the underlying parametric assumptions are being violated. Among the procedures that have been used in such situations are Fisher's exact test, Kendall's tau, the Kruskal-Wallis *H* test, the Mann-Whitney *U* test, the median test, the sign test, Spearman's rho, and Wilcoxon's *t* test. However, it should be noted that parametric procedures have been shown to be robust to violations of many of their underlying assumptions and that use of nonparametric procedures in such cases may lead to decreased statistical power.

A relatively new approach to small-sample statistical analysis is time-series analysis (TSA). This procedure is appropriate for repeated and equally spaced observations on single units or even single subjects, making it the ultimate in small-sample statistical procedures. Because TSA involves repeated observations, serial dependency (autocorrelation) in the data is an important issue. Identification of an appropriate underlying statistical model is necessary to evaluate and remove serial dependency from the data. This is typically accomplished using one of several alternative autoregressive integrated moving average (ARIMA) models. The most widely used procedures in the social and behavioral sciences involve interrupted TSA. These techniques have wide utility in applied research because of their ability to estimate intervention (interruption) effects and to identify patterns in the data such as trend effects, cyclical (seasonal) variation, and patterns of serial dependency.

Joseph S. Rossi
P. F. Merenda
University of Rhode Island

See also: **Nonparametric Statistical Tests; Parametric Statistical Tests; Probability**

SMOKING BEHAVIOR

Epidemiology

Recent estimates indicate that approximately 60 million Americans (about 29% of the population) and one third of the world's adult population smoke cigarettes. According to the Centers for Disease Control, over 440,000 deaths per year in the United States are attributable to smoking. Worldwide, an estimated 4 million deaths can be attributed to smoking and use of other tobacco products. During the past few decades, overall rates of smoking prevalence have decreased in Western countries. However, in the 1990s, rates increased for certain groups, including women and high school students. Although prevalence rates for men are four times higher (47%) than those for women (12%), rates for men are currently decreasing while rates for women are increasing. Prevalence rates for Native Americans and Caucasians are higher than for African Americans, Latinos, and Asian Americans. Prevalence rates of cigarette smoking and other tobacco use continue to rise for both adolescents and adults in developing countries. The leading consumer of cigarettes worldwide is China, where current estimates indicate that approximately 300 million people (or 67% of the population) smoke cigarettes.

Health Effects

Cigarette smoke contains over 4,000 substances, including at least 50 carcinogens. Levels of tar and nicotine in cigarettes have decreased in the past few decades; however, levels of certain carcinogens have increased. Cigarette smoking is the major cause of chronic bronchitis and emphysema. Approximately one fifth of heart disease-related deaths are attributable to cigarette smoking. Lung cancer caused by smoking is currently the leading cause of cancer deaths in the United States. Smoking also contributes to the development of at least 10 other types of cancer, including cancers of the oral cavity, larynx, esophagus, pancreas, stomach, bladder, and cervix.

Individual Differences in Initiation and Progression to Dependence

Recent literature indicates that certain cultural, genetic, and other factors may provide important information about causes of smoking initiation and progression to nicotine addiction.

Cultural Factors

Prevalence rates for cigarette smoking also have shown important ethnic and gender differences. For example, smoking initiation is more common among White high school students than among non-White students. This discrepancy is especially pronounced in adolescent females. Over two times as many White females smoke compared to African American females. Ethnic and gender differences in risk factors for initiation may include differential effects of peer and family influence and different perceptions of the negative consequences of smoking. Different cultural expectations from smoking may also contribute to these differences; for example, White female adolescents may be at increased risk due to expectancies that smoking helps control weight and mood.

Personality Factors

Researchers have not been able to identify an addictive personality or a group of personality factors that are common to all cigarette smokers. However, certain personality traits are consistently associated with smoking behavior, including higher stress, lower arousal, higher impulsivity and sensation seeking, and neuroticism.

Genetic Factors

Results from family, adoption, and twin studies indicate that smoking initiation results largely from genetic influences (about 50–60%) and shared environmental influences (about 20%, higher for adolescent onset). Factors contributing to progression to nicotine dependence are primarily genetic (about 70%). Current research on candidate genes for nicotine dependence has focused on genes that may influence the rewarding effects of nicotine, craving for nicotine, and sensitivity to nicotine.

Treatment

Treatment for nicotine dependence includes self-help, psychological, and pharmacological interventions. Unaided attempts to quit have shown less than a 10% success rate in leading to long-term abstinence. Advice from a physician has been found to lead to cessation rates of up to 10%. Behavioral therapy alone has demonstrated quit rates of 20%. The most promising results have been shown by combined use of medication and behavioral therapy.

Psychological interventions for quitting smoking include psychoeducation (information about smoking and health, quit strategies, and group discussion), behavioral skill training (monitoring situations, practicing cigarette-refusal skills, and relaxation techniques), and cognitive exercises such as reframing thoughts about smoking and smoking situations.

The most common pharmacological treatment used for nicotine addiction is nicotine replacement therapy (NRT). NRT involves administration of nicotine in various forms, including a skin patch, a nasal spray, an oral inhaler, and a chewing gum. These medicinal forms of nicotine prevent symptoms of nicotine withdrawal without inducing the reinforcing effects of smoking. Long-term (6–12 months) abstinence rates for treatment with NRT alone are about 20–25%. Higher abstinence rates may occur when several NRT methods are used together (e.g., patch and gum). Combined with behavioral therapy, long-term abstinence rates may be up to 35–40%.

Another pharmacologic treatment for nicotine dependence is bupropion hydrochloride or Zyban, the first non-nicotine agent approved for cessation of smoking. Cessation rates using bupropion range from 10% to 25%, depending on the dose. The proposed mechanism of bupropion involves reduction of craving and a decrease in the physiological symptoms of nicotine withdrawal.

Finally, researchers are currently examining the possibility of a nicotine vaccine. In animal models, antibodies specific to nicotine have been shown to alter the distribution, and thus the pharmacological effects, of the substance. The proposed vaccine may act by either reducing the uptake of nicotine by the brain or inhibiting the reinforcing effects of nicotine. This vaccine, if effective, is expected to be most beneficial to adolescents who smoke but have not yet become dependent. Other groups that may benefit from such a vaccine are adolescents who have not yet begun smoking, current smokers who are trying to quit smoking, and former smokers interested in avoiding relapse.

Annie R. Peters
Kent E. Hutchison
University of Colorado at Boulder

SOCIAL CLIMATE RESEARCH

Social climate (psychological climate, social context) is typically defined as the perceptions of a social environment that tend to be shared by a group of people. Climate is rooted in perception ("how I see the way things are done or how people treat each other around here"). Culture refers more to the beliefs, values, and norms that comprise the interdependent experiences and practices of larger collectives ("what we—as a group—should do and why and how we do it"; Denison, 1996; Schneider, 1990). Like meteorological or atmospheric climate, social climate is relatively distinctive across groups (as the Tropics differ from the Himalayas); is dynamic or changeable within groups (like the seasons); and can influence behavior (like an individual's choice of clothing). Social climate research has grown considerably since White and Lippitt's (1960) early experiments comparing democratic, autocratic, and laissez-faire leadership in small groups of children. The concept and measurement of social climate have since been applied across widely diverse disciplines both within and outside the field of psychology.

Such diversity, and its parallel with atmospheric climate, can be demonstrated through a random sampling of recent research. Regarding distinctiveness, separate studies suggest that climates differ between support and therapy groups (Toro, Rappaport, & Seidman, 1987), between hospital units (Johnson, Rosenheck, & Fontana, 1997), and between multiuser Internet groups and face-to-face groups (Sempsey, 1998). Changes in the prevailing social climate have been seen as important in attitude assessment, such as in changing attitudes towards women (Twenge, 1997), and important to clinicians who modify services to fit social trends (Lyth, 1990). Studies of climate change have ranged in subjects from animal behavior (e.g., lizard aggression; Klukowski & Nelson, 1998) to organizations (e.g., small colleges; Oakley, 1997). A positive work climate has also been shown to relate to behavior or productivity (Brown & Leigh, 1996).

Researchers have developed questionnaires assessing social climate in diverse settings and content areas. These include family settings (see Knight & Simpson, 1999), adolescent peer groups (Simpson & McBride, 1992), organizational wellness (Bennett & Lehman, 1997), university teaching environments (Mateo & Fernandez, 1995), organizational learning (cf. transfer of training climate; Bennett & Lehman, 1999a), among the institutionalized elderly (Fernandez-Ballesteros, Montorio, & Fernandez de Troconiz, 1998), work-group use of alcohol (Bennett & Lehman, 1998), and hospital wards (Moos & Lemke, 1996). Perhaps the most studied aspect of climate is social cohesiveness (group pride and interdependence; Mullen & Copper, 1994).

Dimensions of Social Climate Research

Given this diversity, it helps to identify the important dimensions of social climate research. Moreover, recent emphasis on self-report measures is often not based on strong theory or methodology. Theory, measurement, and the new direction of research in social climate can benefit from some taxonomy. Six different dimensions are used here (Figure 1). These are (1) level of analysis issues (whether method/theory is sensitive to multilevel effects); (2) temporality (sensitivity to change and developmental processes); (3) type of setting (whether climate applies to one or many settings); (4) the dimension or domain studied; (5) consideration of social health; and (6) homogeneity (e.g., agreement, diversity, or multicultural processes).

Levels of Analysis

As described by Dansereau and Alutto (1990) and by Klein, Dansereau, and Hall (1994), the measurement of climate may be based on individual perceptions often referred to as psychological climate (Level 1). These perceptions may be aggregated by summing or averaging scores, such as across members of a work group or classroom (Level 2). Multiple groups can be combined into collectives such as work departments or schools (Level 3). These may be aggregated into microsocietal entities such as organizations or school districts (Level 4), which may then be combined into higher level or macrosocietal entities—for example, the state of an industry, profession, or educational system (Level 5). Researchers have focused on Level 1 measurement, but recent efforts have used multilevel statistical techniques (e.g., hierarchical linear modeling; Bryk & Raudenbush, 1992). Examples include group-level cohesiveness, which predicts courteous behaviors (Kidwell, Mossholder, & Bennett, 1997), and neighborhood cohesiveness/social integration, which predicts taking safety precautions against crime (Rountree & Land, 1996). Levels of analysis are critical for assessing such things as cross-level congruence and codetermination, as well as bottom-up versus top-down processes (see Kozlowski & Salas, 1997).

Temporality

Group facilitators and coaches use models of group development that anticipate and guide shifts in social climate (e.g., forming, storming, norming, and performing; Tuckman, 1965). Organizational psychologists are increasingly being called on to improve the climate of a business or workplace (e.g., Schneider, 1990). Despite strong interest in application of ideas of climate change, little has been written about the temporal qualities of climate. For example, how do the boundaries and shape of social climate change over time? Which dimensions are changeable and at what rate? Answers to such questions may come from related studies of time in work groups (McGrath, 1990) and dynamic systems in social psychology (Vallacher & Nowak, 1994).

Setting

As just seen in the review, researchers examine social climate within diverse settings. Thus, measures are often developed for specific rather than universal application. Pre-

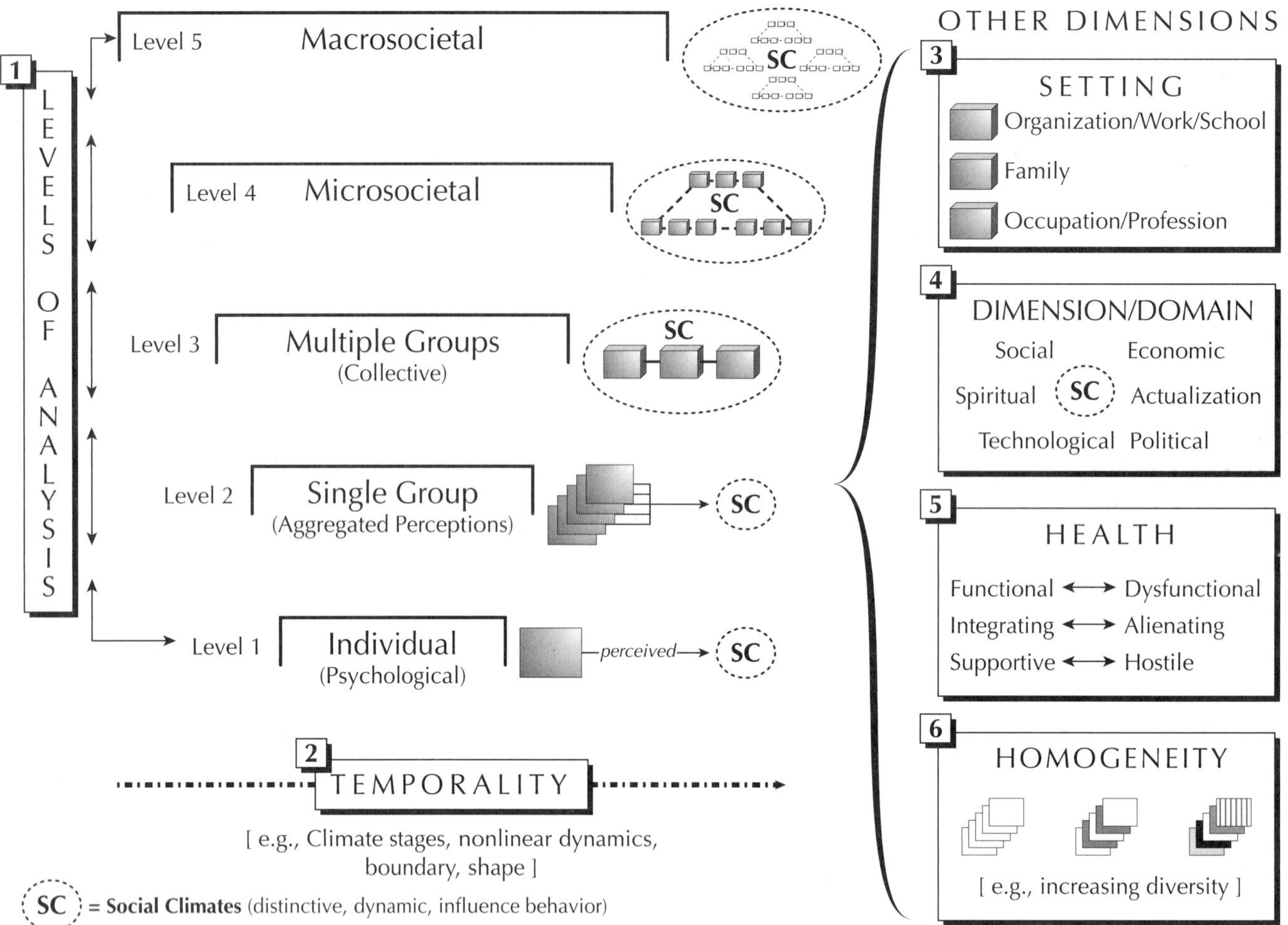

Figure 1. Six dimensions of research into social climates.

dominantly, these have been in organizations (e.g., service, safety, and team climate), schools (e.g., social order, study climate), family settings (e.g., affective involvement, conflict), and some specific occupations or professions (e.g., academic and healthcare).

Dimensions and Domains

Most studies of social climate view it as multidimensional, with anywhere from 3 to 10 different factors. Factor analysis is often used to support multidimensionality. Kopelman, Brief, and Guzzo (1990) view all work climates as having five core dimensions: goal emphasis, means emphasis, reward orientation, task support, and socioemotional support. Denison (1996) also derives five dimensions found across both culture and climate research: structure, support, risk, identity, and standards. It should be noted that social climate overlaps with group-level perceptions in a variety of domain and event areas. Domains include spiritual (church, prayer group), sociotechnical (Internet, shared equipment), economic (distress due to job scarcity), actualization/leisure (self-help groups, shared hobbies), and political (common leaders, partisan loyalty). Researchers have also examined the climate of events or occasions within domains (e.g., holiday seasons, trade shows, business meetings, competitive events, conventions).

Social Health and Safety

Social support or health is a dimension found or implied in nearly all climate measures, and many climate researchers explore the degree to which a group is healthy or unhealthy. For example, studies examine the degree to which the social climate supports substance use (e.g., smoking in adolescents [Byrne & Reinhart, 1998]; drinking at work [Bennett & Lehman, 1999b]). Studies of social integration (vs. alienation), social health, and workplace safety (Cox, 1998) also examine social climate.

Homogeneity and Heterogeneity

Recent research suggests that climate may not always be perceived in the same way by the people who comprise the social group. From a methodological standpoint, researchers have yet to determine how much within-group variability is due to error variance, to actual disagreement, or to some other critical factor such as cultural or gender diversity. Here, the study of social climate borrows from studies of perception within groups (Gigone & Hastie, 1997), measurement of agreement (James, Demaree, & Wolf, 1984), and the field of relational demography (Harrison, Price, & Bell, 1998).

REFERENCES

Bennett, J. B., & Lehman, W. E. K. (1997). Employee views of organizational wellness and the EAP: Influence on substance use, drinking climates, and policy attitudes. *Employee Assistance Quarterly, 13*(1), 55–71.

Bennett, J. B., & Lehman, W. E. K. (1998). Workplace drinking climate, stress, and problem indicators: Assessing the influence of teamwork (group cohesion). *Journal of Studies on Alcohol, 59*(5), 608–618.

Bennett, J. B., & Lehman, W. E. K. (1999a). Change, transfer climate, and customer orientation: A contextual model and analysis of change-drive training. *Group and Organizational Management, 24*(2), 188–216.

Bennett, J. B., & Lehman, W. E. K. (1999b). Employee exposure to coworker substance use and negative consequences: The moderating effects of work group membership. *Journal of Health and Social Behavior, 40,* 307–322.

Brown, S. P., & Leigh, T. W. (1996). A new look at psychological climate and its relationship to job involvement, effort and performance. *Journal of Applied Psychology, 81*(4), 358–368.

Bryk, A. S., & Raudenbush, S. W. (1992). *Hierarchical linear models: Applications and data analysis methods.* Newbury Park, CA: Sage.

Byrne, D. G., & Reinhart, M. I. (1998). Psychological determinants of adolescent smoking behaviour: A prospective study. *Australian Journal of Psychology, 50*(1), 29–34.

Cox, T. R. (Ed.). (1998). The study of safety climate and safety culture [Special section]. *Work and Stress, 12*(3).

Dansereau, F., & Alutto, J. A. (1990). Level-of-analysis issues in climate and culture research. In B. Schneider (Ed.), *Organizational climate and culture* (pp. 193–236). San Francisco: Jossey-Bass.

Denison, D. R. (1996). What is the difference between organizational culture and organizational climate? A native's point of view on a decade of paradigm wars. *Academy of Management Review, 21*(3), 619–654.

Fernandez-Ballesteros, R., Montorio, I., & Fernandez de Troconiz, M. (1998). Personal and environmental relationships among the elderly living in residential settings. *Archives of Gerontology and Geriatrics, 26*(2), 185–198.

Gigone, D., & Hastie, R. (1997). Proper analysis of the accuracy of group judgments. *Psychological Bulletin, 121*(1), 149–167.

Harrison, D. A., Price, K. H., & Bell, M. P. (1998). Beyond relational demography: Time and the effects of surface- and deep-level diversity on work group cohesion. *Academy of Management Journal, 41*(1), 96–107.

James, L. R., Demaree, R. G., & Wolf, G. (1984). Estimating within-group interrater reliability with and without response bias. *Journal of Applied Psychology, 69,* 85–98.

Johnson, D. R., Rosenheck, R., & Fontana, A. (1997). Assessing the structure, content, and perceived social climate of residential posttraumatic stress disorder treatment programs. *Journal of Traumatic Stress, 10*(3), 361–376.

Kidwell, R. E., Jr., Mossholder, K. W., & Bennett, N. (1997). Cohesiveness and organizational citizenship behavior: A multilevel analysis using work groups and individuals. *Journal of Management, 23*(6), 775–793.

Klein, K. J., Dansereau, F., & Hall, R. J. (1994). Levels issues in theory development, data collection, and analysis. *Academy of Management Review, 19*(2), 195–229.

Klukowski, M., & Nelson, C. E. (1998). The challenge hypothesis and seasonal changes in aggression and steroids in male northern fence lizards (*Sceloporus undulatus hyacinthinus*). *Hormones and Behavior, 33*(3), 197–204.

Knight, D. K., & Simpson, D. D. (1999). Family assessment. In P. J. Ott, R. E. Tarter, & R. T. Ammerman (Eds.), *Sourcebook on substance abuse: Etiology, epidemiology, assessment, and treatment* (pp. 236–247). Boston: Allyn & Bacon.

Kopelman, R. E., Brief, A. P., & Guzzo, R. A. (1990). The role of climate and culture in productivity. In B. Schneider (Ed.), *Organizational climate and culture* (pp. 282–318). San Francisco: Jossey-Bass.

Kozlowski, S. W., & Salas, E. (1997). An organizational systems approach for the implementation and transfer of training. In K. Ford (Ed.), *Improving training effectiveness in work organizations* (pp. 247–290). Hillsdale, NJ: Erlbaum.

Lyth, I. M. (1990). A psychoanalytical perspective on social institutions. In E. Trist, H. Murray, & B. Trist (Eds.), *The social engagement of social science: A Tavistock anthology: Vol. 1. The socio-psychological perspective* (pp. 463–475). Philadelphia: University of Pennsylvania Press.

Mateo, M. A., & Fernandez, J. (1995). Evaluation of the setting in which university faculty carry out their teaching and research functions: The ASEQ. *Educational and Psychological Measurement, 55,* 329–334.

McGrath, J. E. (1990). Time matters in groups. In J. Galegher, R. E. Kraut, & C. Egido (Eds.), *Intellectual teamwork: Social and technological foundations of cooperative work* (pp. 23–61). Hillsdale, NJ: Erlbaum.

Moos, R. H., & Lemke, S. (1996). *Evaluating residential facilities: The multiphasic environmental assessment procedure.* Thousand Oaks, CA: Sage.

Mullen, B., & Copper, C. (1994). The relation between group cohesiveness and performance: An integration. *Psychological Bulletin, 115*(2), 210–227.

Oakley, K. L. (1997). Different destinies: Organizational transformation at two Midwestern Catholic women's colleges, 1965–1990. *Dissertation Abstracts International, 57*(11-A), 4615.

Rountree, P. W., & Land, K. C. (1996). Burglary victimization, perceptions of crime risk, and routine activities: A multilevel analysis across Seattle neighborhoods and census tracts. *Journal of Research in Crime and Delinquency, 33*(2), 147–180.

Schneider, B. (Ed.). (1990). *Organizational climate and culture.* San Francisco: Jossey-Bass.

Sempsey, J. J. (1998). A comparative analysis of the social climates found among face to face and Internet-based groups within multi-user dimensions. *Dissertation Abstracts International, 59*(3-B), 1414.

Simpson, D. D., & McBride, A. A. (1992). Family, friends, and self (FFS) assessment scales for Mexican American youth. *Hispanic Journal of Behavioral Sciences, 14*(3), 327–340.

Toro, P. A., Rappaport, J., & Seidman, E. (1987). Social climate comparison of mutual help and psychotherapy groups. *Journal of Consulting and Clinical Psychology, 55*(3), 430–431.

Tuckman, B. W. (1965). Developmental sequences in small groups. *Psychological Bulletin, 63,* 384–399.

Twenge, J. M. (1997). Attitudes toward women, 1970–1995: A meta-analysis. *Psychology of Women Quarterly, 21*(1), 35–51.

Vallacher, R. R., & Nowak, A. (Eds.). (1994). *Dynamical systems in social psychology.* San Diego: Academic Press.

White, R. K., & Lippitt, R. (1960). *Autocracy and democracy: An experimental inquiry.* New York: Harper.

J. B. Bennett
Texas Christian University

SOCIAL COGNITION

The field of social cognition is concerned with the cognitive activity that mediates and accompanies social behavior. It provides an analysis of how stimulus information is initially encoded, organized (and transformed) in memory, and drawn on as the person moves through the social world.

Social cognition, which is neither a single theory nor a narrow empirical domain, refers instead to a particular conceptual level of analysis used in the joint explanation of human thought and social behavior. The level of analysis is molecular rather than molar. Theorists working within this orientation use mental constructs at the level of individual thoughts, categories, and concepts. These constructs are abstract enough to encompass a wide range of content domains (e.g., thoughts about people, traits, situations, animals, and works of art). Most researchers in this field, though mentalistic, do not restrict themselves to the study of conscious thought. The mental constructs are usually defined so as to leave open the question of consciousness.

Workers in the fields of cognitive psychology, psycholinguistics, and artificial intelligence became preoccupied with higher order cognitive processes and grew interested in explaining complex types of human information processing, such as the comprehension and retention of stories, action sequences, and other thematically coherent stimulus ensembles.

The concept of a schema provided the initial meeting ground for the social and cognitive research groups. The elements of our cognitive world do not exist in some random, unrelated array. Rather, they are interassociated into higher order structures.

The schema concept was quite congenial to social psychologists because they already had been using a number of schema-like concepts. These included such terms as stereotype, norm, value, attitude, and implicit personality theory. Some workers in social cognition have developed taxonomies of schemas to aid in establishing conceptual similarities across different topics. Some of the categories proposed are person, role, event, trait, pictorial (or visual), and social group. Taxonomies have also been developed from the cognitive-process point of view that classify schemas in terms of their conceptual properties.

Information-Processing Perspective

The social cognition approach views the human mind as an information-processing system. Information is received from the stimulus world, processed through the cognitive system, and drawn on when engaging in social behavior.

One stage of information-processing deals with the problems of encoding and organization. A second information-processing topic area deals with the problem of cognitive retrieval. What determines the flow of thought, and how do we access prior information and inferences when engaging in social behavior?

There is also the problem of implicit retrieval that occurs in the case of more or less spontaneous social responses. A search for previously acquired information can be bypassed when a behaviorally relevant schema is available.

A third category of issues has to do with information integration. People often face situations for which they have no adequate schemas. Especially when people anticipate encountering such situations often in the future, it is in their interest to develop a new schema to deal with the kinds of variations found in this setting.

A fourth topic area is response selection. How do people survey their response alternatives, tacitly select one, and behaviorally implement it? Communication context and knowledge of the audience's point of view can affect how and when cognitive responses are transmitted.

Unresolved Issues

Social cognition researchers have generally avoided the issue of how cognitive systems are energized. An allied concern is the role of cognitive systems in regulating motivational energies.

Social environments are exceedingly complex. The amount and diversity of information contained in a social interaction are enormous. How does the person arrive at a particular organizational mode? Does the mode fluctuate from one point in the conversation to another, and is it possible to encode (and store) the information in two or more ways simultaneously? This kind of question becomes salient when adopting the level of analysis characteristic of the social cognition perspective.

T. Ostrom

SOCIAL CONSTRUCTIONISM

Social constructionism is an account of knowledge-generating practices, scientific and otherwise. At this level, constructionist theory offers an orientation toward knowledge making in the psychological sciences, a standpoint at considerable variance with the empiricist tradition. At the same time, social constructionism contains the ingredients of a theory of human functioning; at this level, it offers an alternative to traditional views of individual and psychological processes. Constructionist premises also have been extended to a variety of practical domains, opening new departures in such fields as therapy, organizational management, and education.

Assumptions and Antecedents

Social constructionism is not wedded to a fixed set of principles. Rather, it is more properly considered as a continuously unfolding conversation in which various positions may be occupied, elaborated, or vacated as the dialogue proceeds. Several themes are typically located in writings that identify themselves as constructionist. It is typically assumed that accounts of the world—scientific and otherwise—are not dictated or determined in any principled way by what there is. Rather, the terms in which the world is understood are generally held to be social artifacts, products of historically situated interchanges among people. Thus, the extent to which a given form of understanding prevails within a culture is not fundamentally dependent on the empirical validity of the perspective in question but rather on the vicissitudes of social process (e.g., communication, negotiation, communal conflict, rhetoric). This line of reasoning does not detract from the significance of various forms of cultural understanding. People's constructions of the world and self are essential to the broader practices of a culture, justifying, sustaining, and transforming various forms of conduct.

Simultaneous to the developments in social thought and literary theory, political events of the 1960s stimulated large numbers of scholars to reconsider the traditional scientific claims of value neutrality. With increasing degrees of sophistication and indignation, scholars influenced by critical school formulations demonstrated ways in which ordinary and unchallenged assumptions within the sciences lent themselves to unfair distributions of economic resources and political power. These concerns expanded exponentially as the feminist movement began to flourish, and inquiry mounted into the injurious implications of taken-for-granted assumptions embedded within theories, methods, and policies of the sciences. Scholars also became increasingly vocal over the ways in which social science assumptions carried racist values, championed selfish or narcissistic ways of life, or served as a means of subverting non-Western ways of life. For many such scholars, the works of Michel Foucault, which demonstrated the relationship between regimes of language and power relations, also proved pivotal. All of these endeavors demonstrated the extent to which accounts of the world are inseparable from broader social practices.

The Social Construction of Knowledge

The social constructionist view favored by this composite of developments has begun to furnish a replacement for traditional empiricist accounts of psychological science. In the process of this replacement, one may discriminate between two phases: deconstructionist and reconstructionist. In the former phase, pivotal assumptions of scientific rationality, along with bodies of empirically justified knowledge claims, are placed in question. Essentially, this work represents an elaboration and extension of the early antifoundationalist arguments, now informed by the additional developments within the literary and critical domains.

Within the reconstructive phase, the chief focus is on ways in which scientific inquiry, informed by constructionist views, can more effectively serve the society of which it is a part. Although such issues are at the forefront of contemporary discussion, more a matter of debate than decision, several broad themes are apparent. When applied to the domain of psychological study, they suggest the following.

1. *Practical empiricism.* Constructionists are critical of traditional claims that scientific knowledge, in the form of propositional networks, can yield logically derived predictions in a variety of practical settings. However, this is not to negate the possibility of practical prediction itself. Thus, for the constructionist the enormous array of empirical technologies is largely misused, serving primarily those who seek to sustain substantively empty theories within a community of scientific peers. In contrast, observational techniques, measuring devices, and statistical technologies can be used effectively to assess current conditions (e.g., cultural well-being, contours of conflict, homelessness), to evaluate the efficacy of various programs (e.g., community shelters, job training, conservation), and to draw trend lines for deliberating the future (e.g., planning for day care needs, drug-counseling facilities, employment-retraining centers). Of course, the terms of such study would always be culturally constructed, but there is nothing about constructionism that demands the abandonment of intelligibilities (or ways of life) by virtue of recognizing their communally constituted character.
2. *Conceptual innovation.* Although constructionism favors a shift of empirical efforts from the decontextualized setting of the laboratory to sites of practical activity, it also thrusts theoretical activity into a new and more significant role. For the constructionist, the

traditional view that theories should provide accurate accounts of the world is placed in question. Rather, it is argued, language gains its meaning and significance from its function within relationships. Language is a major means by which relationships are carried out. Thus the theoretical language of psychology should be evaluated not in terms of verisimilitude but in terms of its contribution to cultural life. From this standpoint, the practical value of theoretical formulations does not await the drawing of derivative predictions; rather, as psychological discourse gains intelligibility within the culture (through education, the media, the mental health professions, and the like), it becomes a usable resource within the sphere of daily relationships. Thus, scholarly work in psychology—in the form of innovative theorizing—may have enormous potential for the society. For as new theoretical lenses are made available, new options may open in problem domains of long standing. New ways of understanding conflict, of seeing the educational process, of appreciating group differences, and so on, may become available as a cultural resource. This is not to abandon empirical work at the level of scholarly inquiry. However, research procedures at this level primarily serve purposes of vivification; they give theoretical ideas—both descriptions and explanations—a sense of palpability. They enable others to see the world in particular terms.

3. *Valuative reflection.* In the empiricist tradition, the primary criteria for critical assessment of scientific work were methodological. The chief question to be asked of a given formulation was whether it was a valid account of the phenomenon. For the constructionist, however, the crucial question to be asked of a theoretical formulation is how it can or will function within the broader society. What institutions and actions the theory sustains, what is challenged by the formulation, and what new options are opened are all questions of paramount concern. To address such questions fully requires deliberation of a moral and political character. Does a given formulation sustain desirable or undesirable forms of cultural life? Does it undermine cherished institutions? Does it promote human welfare? Such questions necessarily move scientific deliberation from the realm of *is* to *ought*. From the constructionist standpoint, such deliberation should become a normal part of scientific training, and contributions to the dialogue should play a featured role in the books and journals of the field.

Social Constructionist Inquiry in Psychology

Social constructionist views not only provide metatheory for the science of psychology but also are reasserted at the level of psychological theory itself. That is, in providing an account of the knowledge-making activities of scientists, they also offer a way of understanding patterns of human action more generally. Three active areas of inquiry are illustrative.

Major efforts are devoted to exploring the discursive construction of reality. Here investigators attempt to demonstrate the processes by which persons construct the world and self through language. Typically employing techniques of discourse analysis, many investigators explore patterns of existing construction (e.g., cultural assumptions about the developing child); the media construction of homosexuality; the public construction of acquired immunodeficiency syndrome (AIDS); or the available discourses for describing intelligence, the environment, or cultural conflict. Much of this research is used for purposes of generating social change. By elucidating common assumptions, investigators hope that people may be emancipated from the taken-for-granted. In contrast, other investigators attempt to demonstrate the limits of our constructive frameworks. For example, Smedslund attempts to axiomatize cultural understandings of the mind, arguing that it is impossible for cultural participants—including scientific psychologists—to formulate an intelligible proposition that violates these assumptions. Still other scholars are concerned with the ways in which the cultural discourses and conversational positions are used to construct personal identity in ongoing relationships.

A second line of constructionist inquiry is into psychological processes themselves. However, rather than viewing such processes as universal and transhistorical, constructionists are more centrally concerned with individual functioning as it is socially constituted, both in history and culture. How is it that people come to account for their mental life in the ways they do and to perform in such a way that these constructions are made real to both self and others? Historical analysis thus attempts to reveal the ways in which psychological processes were constituted in previous eras and to assess the cultural conditions either favoring a given constitution of the mental world or rendering it dysfunctional.

Kenneth J. Gergen

See also: **Control Therapy; History of Clinical Psychology; Logical Positivism; Postmodernism; Systems and Theories**

SOCIAL DESIRABILITY

Social desirability is the tendency for individuals to present themselves in a generally favorable fashion. Within the fields of psychological testing in general and personality assessment in particular, the concept of social desirability has fueled heated debates for decades. Arguments have focused on the definition of social desirability, its pervasiveness, problems it presents for the interpretation of psychological tests, and methods for its control.

Social desirability has variously been defined as the tendency to give culturally sanctioned and approved responses (Crowne & Marlowe, 1960), to provide socially desirable responses to statements in self-description, or to describe oneself in terms judged as desirable and to present oneself favorably. Noted here is an emphasis on a style of responding irrespective of the specific personality content dimension to be measured by a psychological test. Consequently, a potential problem for a self-report personality test is whether an elevated score represents a high standing on the test's content dimension or a greater tendency to present oneself favorably. For example, does a high score on a particular self-report scale of ambitiousness reflect a test taker's true level of ambitiousness or the respondent's tendency to answer test items in terms of social desirability? The existence of such ambiguous interpretations has generated substantial debate and research.

Research indicates that there are two facets to social desirability (Paulhus, 2002). The first aspect concerns the self and a belief in one's own ability. Phrases used to label this facet include sense of own general capability and egoistic bias. The second component focuses on an orientation toward others, and its labels have included interpersonal sensitivity and moralistic bias. It should be noted that individual scales designed to assess social desirability may measure either or both of these facets.

Some assessment experts believe that self-report tests that have been developed without explicit attempts to minimize the influence of social desirability could be saturated with this stylistic influence. Consequently, any interpretations from such tests are ambiguous and suspect. In contrast to this perspective is the belief that social desirability is itself a personality variable that may be a legitimate component of individual differences. For example, it might be argued that a strong belief in one's own abilities (i.e., social desirability) is a legitimate aspect of the concept of ambitiousness. This, however, then presents a problem: If social desirability is a feature of many different constructs of personality (e.g., ambitiousness, friendliness, neatness, etc.) and social undesirability (i.e., negative social desirability) is a facet of various components of psychopathology (e.g., depression, hostility, alienation), then these constructs are not truly and legitimately independent and should not be theorized, measured, or reported as such.

Various methods have been proposed for coping with social desirability in self-report tests. First, a forced-choice response format could be used for a test. Response options for any test item would then be matched for social desirability. Second, test items could be selected for a scale based on those items being more strongly representative of the psychological concept of interest than social desirability. This would involve a test construction strategy that used some form of item selection from an initial larger pool of test stimuli in which items had been somehow measured for appropriate content and inappropriate response bias (e.g., social desirability). Third, test instructions could be tailored to reduce the likelihood that test takers will be influenced by social desirability. For example, a statement to test takers indicating that the test contains an index for monitoring inaccurate responses could serve to reduce socially desirable responding. Fourth, social desirability could be statistically removed from the score generated on the test. This would require the use of a social desirability scale, the score on which would then be used to adjust the initially obtained score for the psychological concept of interest.

Even though the rancorous debates of the 1960s concerning social desirability have mellowed into more polite disagreements, heated arguments do flare up intermittently. Test developers and users are well advised to be aware of the issues. To construct tests of personality or psychopathology without due consideration of noncentral influences on test responding (e.g., social desirability) is to flirt with theoretical and operational disaster.

REFERENCES

Crowne, D. P., & Marlowe, D. (1960). A new scale of social desirability independent of psychopathology. *Journal of Consulting Psychology, 24,* 349–354.

Paulhus, D. L. (2002). Socially desirable responding: The evolution of a construct. In H. I. Braun & D. N. Jackson (Eds.), *The role of constructs in psychological and educational measurement* (pp. 37–48). Mahwah, NJ: Erlbaum.

Ronald R. Holden
Queen's University

SOCIAL FACILITATION

The question of social facilitation research is how the presence of another person affects performance. If you play a musical instrument alone or in front of an audience, is your performance typically better or worse? If you type with no one around, compared to someone else merely working in the background or observing you, how do these conditions affect both the speed and accuracy of your typing?

Allport (1924) first used the term *social facilitation* for "an increase in response merely from the sight or sound of others making the same movement" (p. 262), although it now refers to either an increase or a decrease in response and from a person who might not be making the same movement. Vaughan and Guerin (1997) argued that an earlier experiment by Triplett (1898), commonly said to be the first in social facilitation, was not related.

The factors affecting performance in the presence of another person were comprehensively delineated by Allport (1924) and Dashiell (1935) and include competition (rivalry), modeling, encouragement or social reinforcement, arousal, monitorability, imitation, group membership, distraction, and evaluation (Guerin, 1993). There is evidence for each of these, and they have separate research literatures.

Social facilitation research has probably held together as a distinct topic only because of the work of Robert Zajonc. Zajonc (1965) first hypothesized that new or poorly learned actions would be made worse by the presence of another person, whereas well-learned actions would be facilitated. For example, an accomplished flute player would perform better with other people present, whereas a poor or beginner flute player would do worse. This formed a simple 2×2 experimental design with participants performing alone or with someone else present and performing either a well-learned or a new behavior. At least 15 theories for this were proposed between 1965 and 1993, and at least 100 tests have been based on this simple design (Guerin, 1993).

The second hypothesis of Zajonc (1965) was that apart from the factors mentioned earlier, there might still be effects from just the mere presence of another person, a term first used by Burnham (1910, p. 766). This negative definition led researchers to attempt to control for all other factors while measuring performance changes. However, it was difficult to control for so many other factors, and only 91 out of 313 studies had suitable controls (Guerin, 1993). The most common fault was to have an experimenter present in the Alone condition.

It has been argued that this whole research endeavor was unsuccessful not only because all the factors could not easily be controlled, but also because a single measure was typically used as evidence for both social facilitation and the alternative theory (Guerin, 1993). Theories were needed of what mere presence was rather than what it was not so that independent measurements could be made of performance and the theoretical mechanism.

Of the reliable effects that have been found using the simple designs and single measures, there are two main ones. First, when someone else is present, people tend to behave in accordance with socially expected standards of performance. This leads to conformity with what they think the experimenter wants them to do, which is usually to try harder at their performance and to do well, but only when they believe that they can be monitored (when there can be consequences) by the experimenter. The second main effect found is an increase in alertness or attention. That is, people are more attentive to what is going on, more rule-governed or verbally governed in their behavior, when someone is present than when they are alone. This impacts on their performance in different ways: If the task is difficult or new, they will do worse if they are paying attention elsewhere (Sanders, 1984); if the task is easy, they might be more relaxed if they have time to watch what people are doing (Guerin, 1993).

There is also a large social facilitation research literature with nonhuman animals. The findings seem to reflect what the species normally does alone or in groups (Guerin, 1993). Normally solitary animals (cats) will become fearful if put in the presence of another animal and will therefore reduce feeding but increase other aggressive or defensive behaviors. Animals that normally live in groups (rats) will tend to interact socially and eat less but play more when put together. Chicks put together in groups become less fearful but do not interact and therefore eat more than when alone.

The problem, then, is similar to that suggested for human studies. If only a single measure is used, such as the facilitation or inhibition of feeding, then there are contradictory findings: Rats eat less in groups but chicks eat more. If the whole context or social ecology is measured, the contradictions disappear: Rats use their time together to groom and play and therefore stop eating, whereas the chicks reduce their fear activities when in groups and spend the extra time eating. The problems of social facilitation research with humans also come down to this: that too much reliance has been made of simple designs and sparse measures. It is not enough to know that people type less when someone else is present with them; we need to measure what they are doing instead. It has also been argued that all behavior is social for humans, even when alone (Guerin, 2001).

REFERENCES

Allport, F. (1924). *Social psychology.* New York: Houghton Mifflin.

Burnham, W. H. (1910). The group as a stimulus to mental activity. *Science, 31,* 761–766.

Dashiell, J. F. (1935). Experimental studies of the influence of social situations on the behavior of individual adults. In C. Murchison (Ed.), *A handbook of social psychology* (pp. 1097–1158). Worcester, MA: Clark University Press.

Guerin, B. (1993). *Social facilitation.* Cambridge, UK: Cambridge University Press.

Guerin, B. (2001). Individuals as social relationships: 18 ways that acting alone can be thought of as social behavior. *Review of General Psychology, 5,* 406–428.

Sanders, G. S. (1984). Self-presentation and drive in social facilitation. *Journal of Experimental Social Psychology, 20,* 312–322.

Triplett, N. (1898). The dynamogenic factors in pacemaking and competition. *American Journal of Psychology, 9,* 507–533.

Vaughan, G. M., & Guerin, B. (1997). A neglected innovator in sports psychology: Norman Triplett and the early history of competitive performance. *International Journal of the History of Sport, 14,* 82–99.

Zajonc, R. B. (1965). Social facilitation. *Science, 149,* 269–274.

Bernard Guerin
University of Waikato

SOCIAL INFLUENCE

Social influence may be defined as the capacity to affect the outcomes of oneself, others, and the environment. The use of social influence may be direct (within interpersonal interaction) or indirect (through group norms and values). All human interaction involves influence. There are three different perspectives on social influence: the trait factor, dynamic interdependence, and the bases of power.

Trait-Factor Perspective

The trait-factor approach to social influence may be traced to Aristotle, whose rhetoric dealt at some length with the characteristics of an effective influencer and gave detailed advice on the techniques of persuasion (Johnson & Johnson, 2003). From the trait-factor point of view, social influence is a function of the characteristics of: (1) the person exerting the influence, (2) the person receiving the influence, and (3) the influence attempt itself. This view is based on two assumptions. First, a person's traits—not circumstances, fortune, or opportunities—explain the person's behavior (certain people are born influencers and others are not). Second, people are rational in the way they process information and are motivated to attend to a message, learn its contents, and incorporate it into their attitudes. The major post–World War II application of the trait-factor approach to social influence was the Yale Attitude Change Program headed by Carl Hovland (Hovland, Lumsdaine, & Sheffield, 1949). Most of the research in this program focused on the effects of a single attempt to influence an audience with a message delivered through the mass media. When a politician gives a speech to an audience, for example, the contact between the communicator and the receiver of the communication is brief and is not repeated. Moreover, the communication is one-way; there is no interaction between the two parties. Because single instances of one-way communication are essentially static, a trait-oriented theory is quite helpful in analyzing them.

Much of the post–World War II research on social influence stemmed from Hovland's wartime studies of propaganda and was organized around the theme question, Who says what to whom and with what effect? Investigators have usually broken this question down into variables relating to the source (the characteristics of the communicator), the message (the characteristics of the communication), and the receiver (the characteristics of the person receiving the message). Social influence occurs when a credible and attractive communicator delivers an effectively organized message to a vulnerable or influenceable audience.

The two most researched aspects of communicators are credibility and attractiveness. The credibility of communicators depends on their perceived ability to know valid information and on their perceived motivation to communicate this knowledge without bias. More specifically, credibility depends on objective indicators of relevant expertise, perceived reliability as an information source, lack of self-interest in the issue, warmth and friendliness, confident and forceful delivery of the message, and considerable social support from others. The attractiveness of communicators depends on their facilitation of the receiver's goal accomplishment, physical appearance, perceived similarity, perceived competence, warmth, and familiarity.

Messages that inspire fear with specific instructions for action, messages that acknowledge opposing viewpoints, and the size of the discrepancy between the content of the message and the receiver's position all promote social influence. Influence attempts are aimed at a receiver. The receiver's self-esteem, present attitudes, forewarning of the intention to influence, practice in defending a position, and intelligence all affect the success of an influence attempt. Furthermore, actively role-playing a previously unacceptable position increases its acceptability to the receiver.

The trait-factor approach to social influence is weak both logically and empirically in situations in which two or more individuals are constantly interacting.

Dynamic-Interdependence Perspective

Dynamic means in a constant state of change; *interdependence* means that each member's actions affect the outcomes of other members. The dynamic-interdependence view of social influence posits that influence exists in relationships, not in individuals; that is, a person cannot be an influencer if there is no influencee (Johnson & Johnson, 2003). For influence to be constructive, it must occur in a cooperative (not competitive) context. In a cooperative context, influence is used to maximize joint benefits and promote the achievement of mutual goals. In a competitive context, influence is used to gain advantage and promote one's own success at the expense of others. Influence attempts in a competitive context result in resistance. *Resistance* is the psychological force aroused in an individual that keeps him or her from accepting influence.

When individuals work together to achieve mutual goals, social influence is inevitable. They must influence and be influenced by each other, each modifying and adjusting his or her behavior to respond to what the other person is doing. The speed of conversation, the attitudes expressed, and the phrasing of messages are all influenced by the others with whom one is interacting. The use of influence is essential to all aspects of relationships. Goals cannot be established, communication cannot take place, leadership cannot exist, decisions cannot be made, and conflicts cannot be resolved unless there is mutual influence. The degree of influence is dynamic in that it constantly changes as the individuals make progress in obtaining their goals, as their costs (in energy, emotion, time, etc.) of working collaboratively vary, and as other relationships become available in which the goals might be better achieved. If the individuals make progress toward achieving the goals, the costs of working together are low, and no other relationships are as rewarding, then the ability of the individuals involved to influence each other increases.

Bases-of-Influence Perspective

According to social exchange theory, influence is based on the control of valued resources. The more an individual wants a specific resource, the more power the people who control the resource have over him or her. Different types of influence can be specified based on what types of resources are under a person's control (Raven, 1992). There are six possible bases for a person's social influence: one's ability to reward, one's ability to coerce, one's legal position, one's capacity as a referent with whom others wish to identify, one's expertise, and one's information. Each of these sources (reward, coercion, legitimacy, referent capacity, expertise, information) enables one to influence others.

REFERENCES

Hovland, C., Lumsdaine, A., & Sheffield, F. (1949). *Experiment on mass communication.* Princeton, NJ: Princeton University Press.

Johnson, D. W., & Johnson, F. (2003). *Joining together: Group theory and group skills* (8th ed.) Boston: Allyn & Bacon.

Moscovici, S. (1985). Innovation and minority influence. In S. Moscovici, G. Mugny, & E. Van Avermaet (Eds.), *Perspectives on minority influence* (pp. 9–51). Cambridge, UK: Cambridge University Press.

Raven, B. (1992). A power/interaction model of interpersonal influence: French and Raven thirty years later. *Journal of Social Behavior and Personality, 7,* 217–244.

David W. Johnson
Roger T. Johnson
University of Minnesota

SOCIAL ISOLATION

Social interaction is integral to mental health across development. Lack of social interaction, or social isolation, not only is a painful experience but also can negatively impact child development. For infants and young children, lack of interaction with a primary caretaker can lead to marked delays in cognitive, socioemotional, linguistic, and motoric development. Furthermore, dysfunctional parent-child interaction patterns can contribute to child social incompetence and social isolation. For school-age children and adolescents, peer interaction becomes an increasingly important socializing agent that provides them with opportunities for social, emotional, and cognitive development. Through interpersonal interaction, children develop the skills of collaboration, perspective taking, empathy, and social competence, which help to promote prosocial behavior and decrease inappropriate, immature, or annoying behavior. The development of these social skills also contributes to children's healthy academic and emotional adjustment, decreasing the likelihood of negative social experiences, such as peer neglect or rejection and isolation.

Social isolation can lead to feelings of loneliness, low self-esteem and alienation, negative self-concept and powerlessness, increased shyness and anger, decreased creativity, depression, social and academic difficulties, and in some cases delinquent behavior and violence. Recent studies suggest that social anxiety may be a precursor to social isolation and that the loneliness that accompanies social isolation uniquely contributes to more severe emotional problems. Additionally, distinctions have been drawn between children who are deliberately isolated by their peers because of cognitive immaturity and inappropriate behavior and children who are passively or anxiously withdrawn. Different characteristics and outcomes may be related to these two dimensions of social isolation, which would also have implications for treatment. Although early developmental research suggested that many withdrawn children outgrow their isolate behaviors, there is evidence that for some children, social isolation is an enduring experience. For these children, the negative effects of social isolation may persist beyond childhood, leading to maladjustment in adolescence and adulthood, including poor educational attainment, occupational status, and psychological well-being.

Socially isolated children seldom initiate contact with others or respond to the invitations of others. These children tend to be ignored and neglected by their peers due to their lack of a conspicuous presence. Recent research regarding the effects of technological advances, such as the Internet, on adjustment suggests that these advances offer new outlets for socialization for isolated youth, although they may not decrease emotional difficulties and loneliness and may lead to weaker social ties. Identification and treatment of social isolation often occurs within academic settings where teachers become aware of withdrawn children's social difficulties. Socially isolated children can be identified through observation or sociometric measures. Additionally, children's self-perceptions of social support and social networks can provide information about experiences of social isolation.

As a treatment for social isolation, social skills training targets deficiencies in social skills performance, such as the ability to interpret interpersonal situations correctly and seek entry into a peer group competently. Such training helps socially withdrawn children learn skills for developing and maintaining gratifying relationships with others. Added components to social skills training interventions may include pairing socially isolated children with socially competent peers, rewarding children for positive social behavior, and addressing any emotional experiences of socially isolated children that may be inhibiting social interaction. Within these intervention approaches, socially isolated children have an opportunity to learn positive social skills, initiate social interactions and friendships, and learn ways to cope with negative affect.

SUGGESTED READING

Rubin, K. H., & Asendorpf, J. B. (Eds.). (1993). *Social withdrawal, inhibition, and shyness in childhood.* Hillsdale, NJ: Erlbaum.

KELLY S. FLANAGAN
STEPHAN A. ERATH
Pennsylvania State University

See also: Shyness

SOCIAL NEUROSCIENCE

Neuroscientists and cognitive scientists have collaborated for more than a decade with the common goal of understanding how the mind works. The focus of this work has been relatively restricted, however, as more complex aspects of the mind and behavior that involve conspecifics and their products (e.g., norms, culture) have fallen outside of the purview of cognitive neuroscience. Social neuroscience emerged in the early 1990s to address these kinds of questions at the information-processing, neural, and computational levels of analysis (Cacioppo & Berntson, 1992).

The notion of a social neuroscience is not as oxymoronic as it might first seem. Evolutionary forces operating over thousands of years have sculpted the human genome to be sensitive to and succoring of relationships with others. Affiliation and nurturant social relationships, for instance, are essential for physical and psychological well-being across the lifespan (Cacioppo, Berntson, Sheridan, & McClintock, 2000). Disruptions of social connections, whether through ridicule, separation, divorce, or bereavement, are among the most stressful events that people endure (Gardner, Gabriel, & Diekman, 2000), and social isolation is as large a risk factor for broad-based morbidity and mortality as are high blood pressure, obesity, and sedentary lifestyles even after statistically controlling for known biological risk factors, social status, and baseline measures of health (House, Landis, & Umberson, 1988). The case of Phineas Gage in the late 1800s vividly established the importance of the frontal cortex for orchestrating normal social discourse (MacMillan, 1999), and various other cortical and subcortical nuclei involved in social cognition have now been identified (Adolphs, 1999).

Social neuroscience has emerged as a pullulating scientific perspective for several additional reasons. Theoretical insights into the mechanisms underlying social processes, as well as ways of testing otherwise conflicting theoretical accounts of social behavior, have come from theory and research in the neurosciences (Berntson, Boysen, & Cacioppo, 1993; Clark & Squire, 1998). Reciprocally, the study of social processes, including work on social factors as moderators of various specific mechanisms, has challenged existing theories in the neurosciences, resulting in refinements, extensions, or complete revolutions in theory and research in the neurosciences (Glaser & Kiecolt-Glaser, 1994). In addition, just as genetic constitution affects a wide array of social behaviors, the social environment has also been shown to shape genetic expression, neural structures, and biochemical processes (Liu et al., 1997).

In an early review, Cacioppo and Berntson (1992) coined the term *social neuroscience* and outlined several organizing principles for multilevel integrative research. The first, the principle of multiple determinism, specifies that a target event at one (e.g., a molar) level of organization can have multiple antecedents within or across levels of organization. For example, both research on individual differences in the susceptibility of the endogenous opioid receptor system and on the role of social context have contributed to our understanding of drug abuse.

The second, the principle of nonadditive determinism, specifies that properties of the whole are not always readily predictable from the properties of the parts. In an illustrative study, the effects of amphetamine on behavior of nonhuman primates were indeterminate until each primate's position in the social hierarchy was considered (Haber & Barchas, 1983). The inclusion of this social factor revealed an orderly relationship, such that amphetamines increased the dominant behavior in primates high in the social hierarchy and increased submissive behavior in those low in the social hierarchy.

The third, the principle of reciprocal determinism, specifies that there can be mutual influences between microscopic (e.g., biological) and macroscopic (e.g., social) factors in determining behavior. For example, not only has the level of testosterone in nonhuman male primates been shown to promote sexual behavior, but the availability of receptive females influences the level of testosterone in nonhuman primates (Berntstein, Gordon, & Rose, 1983). The implication of this and the preceding principles is that multilevel analyses spanning neural and social perspectives contribute to scientific investigations of complex human behavior and foster more comprehensive accounts of cognition, emotion, behavior, and health.

REFERENCES

Adolphs, R. (1999). Social cognition and the human brain. *Trends in Cognitive Sciences, 3,* 469–479.

Berntson, G. G., Boysen, S. T., & Cacioppo, J. T. (1993). Neurobehavioral organization and the cardinal principle of evaluative bivalence. *Annals of the New York Academy of Sciences, 702,* 75–102.

Berntstein, I. S., Gordon, T. P., & Rose, R. M. (1983). The interaction of hormones, behavior, and social context in nonhuman primates. In B. B. Svare (Ed.), *Hormones and aggressive behavior* (pp. 535–561). New York: Plenum Press.

Cacioppo, J. T., & Berntson, G. G. (1992). Social psychological contributions to the decade of the brain: The doctrine of multilevel analysis. *American Psychologist, 47,* 1019–1028.

Cacioppo, J. T., Berntson, G. G., Sheridan, J. F., & McClintock, M. K. (2000). Multilevel integrative analyses of human behavior: Social neuroscience and the complementing nature of social and biological approaches. *Psychological Bulletin, 126,* 829–843.

Clark, R. E., & Squire, L. R. (1998). Classical conditioning and brain systems: The role of awareness. *Science, 280,* 77–81.

Gardner, W. L., Gabriel, S., & Diekman, A. B. (2000). Interpersonal processes. In J. T. Cacioppo, L. G. Tassinary, & G. G. Berntson (Eds.), *Handbook of psychophysiology.* New York: Cambridge University Press.

Glaser, R., & Kiecolt-Glaser, J. K. (1994). *Handbook of human stress and immunity.* San Diego: Academic Press.

Haber, S. N., & Barchas, P. R. (1983). The regulatory effect of social rank on behavior after amphetamine administration. In P. R. Barchas (Ed.), *Social hierarchies: Essays toward a sociophysiological perspective* (pp. 119–132). Westport, CT: Greenwood Press.

House, J. S., Landis, K. R., & Umberson, D. (1988). Social relationships and health. *Science, 241,* 540–545.

Liu, D., Diorio, J., Tannenbaum, B., Caldji, C., Francis, D., Freedman, A., Sharma, S., Pearson, D., Plotsky, P. M., & Meaney, M. J. (1997). Maternal care, hippocampal glucocorticoid receptors, and hypothalamic-pituitary-adrenal responses to stress. *Science, 277,* 1659–1662.

MacMillan, M. (1999). *An odd kind of fame: Stories of Phineas Gage.* Cambridge, MA: MIT Press.

John T. Cacioppo
Catherine J. Norris
University of Chicago

SOCIAL PSYCHOPHYSIOLOGY

Social psychophysiology is characterized by the use of noninvasive procedures to study the relationships between actual or perceived physiological events and the verbal or behavioral effects of human association. The field represents the intersection of social psychology and psychophysiology. Social psychology, the older of the two spawning disciplines, is directed toward understanding the reportable and behavioral effects of human association, whereas psychophysiology employs noninvasive procedures to study the interrelationships between physiological events and a person's reportable or overt behavior. Social psychology, generally partitioned into conceptual areas of research (e.g., attitudes, aggression, altruism), is replete with abstract theories based largely on verbal data. Psychophysiology, in contrast, is generally partitioned into anatomical areas of research (e.g., cardiovascular gastrointestinal) and is laden with sophisticated physiological measures, instrumentation, and observations with uncertain psychological significance. Social psychophysiology has emerged from these disparately focused disciplines for the purposes of understanding the psychological significance of physiological events and explaining complex behaviors in biological terms.

The perspective on human behavior epitomized by social psychophysiology is quite old. It dates back to at least the third century B.C. Articles bearing the imprint of a social psychophysiological perspective began appearing in the psychological literature in the 1920s with reports about the changes in the breathing of poker players when they were bluffing and about the galvanic skin responses (GSRs) of students finding themselves possessing attitudes shared by few peers. The first summary of empirical research in social psychophysiology was published by Kaplan and Bloom in 1960. The review dealt with the physiological concomitants of social status, social sanction, definition of the situation, and empathy. An optimism was expressed that the field of social psychophysiology had come of age. At about the same time, John Lacey published a critical and cogent review in which he argued that there was little consistency in the literature on which to build bridges between psychophysiological data and psychological constructs.

Nevertheless, investigations of the reciprocal influence of social and physiological systems began to broaden in scope and increase in number. In 1962 Schacter and Singer published their influential two-factor theory of emotions: that the sensations derived from a large and unexpected increase in physiological arousal could be experienced as widely different emotions, depending on the circumstances covarying with these sensations. Leiderman and Shapiro represented a different vein of research: Evidence was presented for the dramatic impact that social factors such as conformity pressures have on physiological responding.

The attractiveness of psychophysiological procedures was tempered, however, by three formidable barriers: (1) the paucity of conceptual links between the psychophysiological data and social psychological constructs; (2) the technical sophistication and expensive instrumentation required to collect, analyze, and interpret psychophysiological data in social psychological paradigms; and (3) the inevitable pitting of social psychological and psychophysiological procedures against one another in studies of construct validation. Three distinct strategies developed for dealing with those barriers. One strategy was simply to dismiss physiological factors as irrelevant, at least at present, to the study of social cognition and behavior, and to dismiss social factors as too molar to contribute to an understanding of psychophysiological relationships. A second strategy was to view the physiological factor important in the study of social processes as being a diffuse, perceptible change in physiological arousal. This view provided the rationale for conducting research with little or no psychophysiological recording equipment and expertise, as it followed from this reasoning that any single physiological response, or even sensitive measures of interoceptive sensations, reflected a person's physiological arousal at any given moment (cf. Cacioppo & Tassinary, 1990).

The third approach more often involved collaborative efforts by psychophysiologists and social psychologists. The strategy followed was to narrow the breadth of the social issue under investigation while increasing the depth (levels) of the analysis. For instance, rather than viewing physiological arousal as the sine qua non of organismic influences on social cognition and behavior, specific patterns of physiological responses were conceived as reflecting or influencing specific social processes. Experiments exemplifying this approach are characterized by the simultaneous measurement of multiple physiological, verbal, and behavioral responses in a single session and by interpretations that entertain highly specific, reciprocal, and (at least initially) biologically adaptive influences between social and physiological systems. Studies of the incipient and transient patterning of facial muscles during social interaction, impression formation, or social influence are illustrative.

During the past two decades, the increasing utility for investigators to be informed about various levels of human behavior ranging from the physiological to the sociocultural resulted in a convergence among the three research strategies outlined as the barriers to social psychophysiological research were overcome. The nonelectrophysiological procedures developed by earlier investigators to study the effects of arousal on social processes, for example, posed interesting questions regarding the actual physiological basis for the obtained data. Technical advances increased the accessibility of psychophysiological methods, and psychophysiologists began to grapple with the acute and chronic effects of interpersonal factors and the social context on physiology. This, in turn, led to contributions to the fields of social and health psychology. Additionally, developments in noninvasive brain imaging and cognitive neuroscience have further contributed to the bridging of the abyss between psychophysiological data and psychological constructs. Clearly, the barriers once separating biological and social approaches are no longer major obstacles to integrative, multilevel analyses of human behavior.

SUGGESTED READINGS

Blascovich, J. (2001). Social psychophysiological methods. In H. Reis & C. Judd (Eds.), *Advanced methodological sourcebook for social psychology* (pp. 117–137). London: Cambridge University Press.

Cacioppo, J. T., & Petty, R. E. (1983). *Social psychophysiology: A sourcebook.* New York: Guilford Press.

Cacioppo, J. T., & Tassinary, L. G. (1990). Inferring psychological significance from physiological signals. *American Psychologist, 45,* 16–28.

Gardner, W. L., Gabriel, S., & Diekman, A. B. (2000). Interpersonal processes. In J. T. Cacioppo, L. G. Tassinary, & G. G. Berntson (Eds.), *Handbook of psychophysiology* (pp. 643–664). New York: Cambridge University Press.

Kaplan, H. B., & Bloom, S. W. (1960). The use of sociological and social-psychological concepts in physiological research: A review of selected experimental studies. *Journal of Nervous and Mental Disease, 131,* 128–134.

Schachter, S., & Singer, J. E. (1962). Cognitive, social and physiological determinants of emotional state. *Psychological Review, 69,* 379–399.

John T. Cacioppo
Edith Rickett
University of Chicago

Tyler S. Lorig
Washington and Lee University

SOCIAL SUPPORT

The term *social support* refers to supportive relationships that arise between oneself and friends, family members, and other persons (Friis & Sellers, 1999). The concept embodies material and emotional resources that accrue through one's relationships with others (Friis & Taff, 1986). Social support results in the feeling that one is cared for, loved, esteemed, and valued or is part of a network of mutual interpersonal commitments (Cobb, 1976). In addition, social contact, received emotional support, and anticipated support are interrelated. Increased social contact is associated with increased emotional support and perceptions of support availability. Persons who have high levels of social support are thought to confront stressful or adverse conditions more successfully than do those who lack social support. Conversely, those who have inadequate levels of social support may be at risk of experiencing deleterious consequences for their own mental and physical health.

Mechanisms of Social Support

The protective effects of social support against stressful occurrences are thought to arise from several mechanisms, one being the encouragement (e.g., kind words from a close confidant) that one may receive when faced with adverse circumstances. The other is the availability of material aid and resources for dealing with challenges or adversity. For example, when one is confronted with the need to move to a new house, the availability of many friends to help with the move is indeed reassuring. Thus, social support enhances the individual's ability to cope with changes and crises, which are inevitable in life (Cobb, 1976).

Social Support Versus Social Network Ties

A distinction exists between supportive relationships and the total number of social ties that the individual has. Social support denotes perceived emotional support that one receives from, or the value that one attributes to, social relationships. In contrast, the term *social network ties* is a more quantitative concept that embraces the number, structure, or pattern of ties that one has with other people or organizations. The mere existence of social ties is neither a necessary nor a sufficient condition for social support, nor is the absolute number of ties strongly correlated with social support. In fact, some types of social ties may be intrusive, stressful, or, at best, perfunctory. Close friendships and relationships with partners, spouses, or family members that are perceived as valuable or helpful engender social support. Social relationships, including those with family members and significant others, may be at best a mixed blessing: Many of the stresses that we experience evolve from our interactions with others. These stresses may arise from interactions with our very own family members, who may experience different intensities and outcomes of stress. Research has demonstrated the differential effects of spousal ties on men and women, the former being more likely to receive positive, protective effects from the marital relationship.

The Buffering Model of Social Support

The term *buffering* (sometimes called *moderating*) suggests that the impacts of noxious stimuli or stresses are attenuated by the availability of social support; absence of support, according to the buffering hypothesis, is linked to experiencing of the full consequences of stressful situations (Cobb, 1976; Kaplan, Cassel, & Gore, 1977; LaRocco, House, & French, 1980). The stress-buffering effect is more likely to occur when the social network is perceived as ready to provide assistance. The buffering model has also been extended to social network ties by specifying that they may lessen the adverse psychological consequences of stress (Friis & Nanjundappa, 1989). The buffering role of social support is attractive to practitioners, who view social relationships as more amenable to change than are the conditions in which adversity arises. Theorists posit that social support buffers some stressors more effectively than others, depending on the nature of the stressor. For example, a person who experiences a socially acceptable stress (such as personal illness) may be more likely to seek assistance from social support resources than would one who is confronted with a less socially acceptable stress, such as substance abuse (Mitchell, Billings, & Moos, 1982).

Sources of Social Support

Variations in the effects of support are believed to be related to the source of support; these effects may be conditioned by marital status, age, and gender. For example, support from spouses or friends may be more important than support from other network ties. Marital status, found to be salient in the social support process, causes married older adults to have more contact with family members than with friends and to receive more emotional support than unmarried older adults receive. An apparent paradox arises when comparing gender differences in social support. Some data suggest that women, in comparison to men, give and receive more support yet tend to have higher rates of psychological distress (Fuhrer, Stansfield, Chemali, & Shipley, 1999).

Social Support and Health-Related Outcomes

Investigators have examined the association among stress, social support, and mental and physical health outcomes, the latter including complications of pregnancy, all-cause mortality, chronic disease, and immune status. For example, isolated elderly persons who live in the community may be at higher risk of mortality than those who maintain social engagement. As a second example, immune status as a function of social support was studied among the spouses (assumed to be experiencing severe, chronic life stresses) of cancer patients; in comparison to those with low levels of support, spouses with higher levels of social support had better indexes of immune function.

Social Support and Mental Disorders

Much research has addressed the role of stressors and social support in the etiology of mental disorders. Noting that individuals vary considerably in their vulnerabilities to stressors, some authorities believe that social support may help to explain why some individuals who face high levels of stress do not develop psychiatric disorders (Lin & Dean, 1984). Absence of social support may be linked to psychiatric symptoms, especially depressive symptoms. Studies of patients who were suffering from depression reported that they had significantly less social support than did control patients. Not only do some researchers believe that the presence of social support plays a crucial role in the positive functioning of psychiatric patients, but lack of social support has also been associated with rehospitalization for depression.

REFERENCES

Cobb, S. (1976). Social support as a moderator of life stress. *Psychosomatic Medicine, 38,* 300–314.

Friis, R. H., & Nanjundappa, G. (1989). Life events, social network ties, and depression among diabetic patients. In J. Humphreys (Ed.), *Human stress: Current selected research* (Vol. 3, pp. 147–162). New York: AMS.

Friis, R. H., & Sellers, T. A. (1999). *Epidemiology for public health practice* (2nd ed.). Gaithersburg, MD: Aspen.

Friis, R. H., & Taff, G. A. (1986). Social support and social networks, and coronary heart disease and rehabilitation. *Journal of Cardiopulmonary Rehabilitation, 6,* 132–147.

Fuhrer, R., Stansfeld, S. A., Chemali, J., & Shipley, M. J. (1999). Gender, social relations and mental health: Prospective findings from an occupational cohort. *Social Science and Medicine, 48,* 77–87.

Kaplan, B. H., Cassel, J. C., & Gore, S. (1977). Social support and health. *Medical Care, 15,* 47–58.

LaRocco, J. M., House, J. S., & French, J. R. P. (1980). Social support, occupational stress, and health. *Journal of Health and Social Behavior, 21,* 202–218.

Lin, N., & Dean, A. (1984). Social support and depression: A panel study. *Social Psychiatry, 19,* 83–91.

Mitchell, R. E., Billings, A. G., & Moos, R. H. (1982). Social support and well-being: Implications for prevention programs. *Journal of Primary Prevention, 3,* 77–98.

Robert H. Friis
California State University, Long Beach

See also: Socialization

SOCIALIZATION

Agents and Theories of Socialization

Socialization is the process of becoming a social being. During this process, individuals acquire ways of learning, thinking, acting, and feeling that enable them to familiarize themselves with the culture and participate in the social process. The main agents of socialization typically include family, peers, schools, media, and religion. Although the socialization process is most evident during childhood and adolescence, it covers the entire course of the life span. Erikson's eight stages illustrate the enduring process of socialization. The term *resocialization* emphasizes socialization as a process that never ends. A clear example of resocialization is what happens when someone joins a branch of the armed services. The uniforms, the regulations, and the regimen require the new recruit to learn new behaviors and attitudes appropriate to the new role.

There are at least two commonly used approaches to the study of socialization. The first approach emphasizes the individual and the development of the individual in the context of the culture and society. Studies from the field of psychology focus on topics such as stages involved in cognitive development, life course stages, and personality development. The second approach is a social perspective that emphasizes the development of the social self and the process of social and cultural transmission between generations. This is the major focus of socialization research among sociologists and cultural anthropologists.

With regard to cognitive development, the work of Piaget is especially important. Piaget identified four stages of cognitive development: sensorimotor, preoperational, concrete operational, and formal operational. Important at each stage is one's functioning in relation to the environment. This is accomplished in two ways: assimilation that involves modifying the environment in order to fit with an existing cognitive scheme and accommodation that entails modifying oneself in response to environmental demands.

An expected outcome of child and adolescent socialization is moral development. Freud's psychoanalytic theory emphasizes the affective component of morality. Children are viewed as motivated to act in accordance with their ethical principles in order to experience positive affects such as pride and to avoid negative moral emotions such as guilt and shame. Cognitive-developmental theory emphasizes the cognitive aspects of moral reasoning: the way the individual conceptualizes right and wrong and makes decisions about how to behave. For Piaget, the moral judgment of young children is characterized by an emphasis on abiding by the rules. The moral judgment of the older child, however, is characterized by the individual's viewing rules as arbitrary agreements that can be challenged. According to Piaget, moving from an authoritarian moral code to one based more on autonomy requires both cognitive maturation and social experience. For Kohlberg, moral judgment is the most important factor in moral behavior. Other factors that are necessary for moral judgment to become moral action include the situation and its pressures, motives and emotions, and a general sense of will or purpose. Kohlberg contended that a moral choice involves choosing between two or more universal values as they conflict (e.g., concerns of affection and truth).

The approaches to development of the social self are represented by Cooley and Mead. Cooley's concept of the looking-glass self suggests the importance of others in the development of one's self. The individual imagines how his behavior appears to others and, based on his perceptions of others' judgments, the self develops. According to Mead, the idea of the self emerges as one acquires language and interacts with others. The self is a gift to the individual from society.

Recent Issues

A number of issues widely discussed in the literature in recent years include peer groups, feminist perspectives, inadequate socialization, gender role socialization, and multigroup diversity. The significance of peer groups in the socialization process has been widely studied since the 1950s but has recently begun to gain more attention. Peer groups are increasingly important as the family system has been subjected to significant changes that include single-parent child rearing, stepparent socialization, multiple-parent siblings, and fragmentation of family roles and responsibilities.

Harlow's studies reported that peer groups could contribute to the socialization process of baby rhesus monkeys without a mother. Even in the concentration camps of Germany during World War II, groups of adolescents helped each other, and many children are believed to have survived as a result of such peer bonding. Similarly, countries as diverse as Brazil, Kenya, and Egypt have adolescents living with other adolescents in groups in order to survive. The significance of siblings and peer groups in the caring and socialization of children in Cameroon and India, for example, has also drawn attention to the contribution of peer groups in the socialization process among comparative researchers.

The contribution of feminist perspectives has resulted in a shift in the emphasis directed to socialization, especially since the contributions of Chodorow and Gilligan. Chodorow utilized a psychoanalytic perspective to build on Freud's work and suggested that the sense of mothering in women was not biological, but rather a result of an ongoing relationship between mother and child. Gilligan's perspective on morality is marked by its recognition that men and women do not have identical patterns of moral development. She is critical of the major approaches of Piaget, Erikson, and Kohlberg because their findings may apply only to men and thus disadvantage women. Her research shows that concerns about both justice and care are represented in moral dilemmas, but males are more likely to have an abstract justice focus, and women are more likely to have a care focus due to the differential socialization process undergone by men and women.

Inadequate socialization is an explanation sometimes given for deviant behavior. Deviant subcultures provide a means for individuals to establish identity, even if it is a negative identity. Recent tragic events like school shootings in various areas throughout the United States are often explained, at least in part, by alluding to a failure in socialization. The media, with their emphasis on violent acts, are also targeted. It is important, however, not to mistake correlation for causation. Many other variables are involved in attempting to understand these recent violent events.

During the early stages of socialization, the child develops an awareness of himself or herself as male or female. Sex-appropriate behavior is emphasized whenever it is transgressed. In peer groups, nontraditional behavior is apt to be punished. This is especially the case for boys. Children will be rewarded, then, when they act in a way that is consistent and appropriate for their sex. More recently, sexual orientations other than heterosexuality are being more openly pursued, including bisexuality and homosexuality.

Although social class and ethnic distinctions in socialization have not been neglected in the past, multicultural perspectives in socialization are gaining attention. Multicultural perspectives include issues of class, race, language, and other ethnic viewpoints. The goals of socialization and the process of socialization vary significantly by social class, race, and ethnicity. For example, the exercise of discipline, values, attitudes, and belief systems may vary from group to group within the same culture.

In addition, topics within areas of socialization, such as child development, adolescence, and family socialization studies, have become specialties in their own right, and thus many more topics such as processes of learning, deviance, and emotions are being addressed in the context of socialization.

SUGGESTED READINGS

Chodorow, N. (1978). *The reproduction of mothering: Psychoanalysis and the sociology of gender.* Berkeley: University of California Press.

Cooley, C. H. (1964). *Human nature and the social order.* New York: Schocken Books. (Original work published 1902)

Erikson, E. H. (1980). *Identity and the life cycle.* New York: Norton.

Gilligan, C. (1982). *In a different voice: Psychological theory and women's development.* Cambridge, MA: Harvard University Press.

Ginsburg, H., & Opper, S. (1969). *Piaget's theory of intellectual development.* Englewood Cliffs, NJ: Prentice Hall.

Harlow, H. F., & Harlow, M. K. (1962). Social deprivation in monkeys. *Scientific American, 207*(5), 136–146.

Kohlberg, L. (1981). *The psychology of moral development: The nature and validity of moral stages.* New York: Harper & Row.

Mead, G. H. (1934). *Mind, self, and society.* Chicago: University of Chicago Press.

Piaget, J. (1932). *The moral judgement of the child.* London: Routledge & Kegan.

Piaget, J., & Inhelder, B. (1969). *The psychology of the child* (H. Weaver, Trans.). New York: Basic Books.

Janelle L. Wilson
University of Minnesota Duluth

Subhash R. Sonnad
Western Michigan University

See also: **Eriksonian Development Stages; Piaget's Theory; Human Development; Multicultural**

SOCIETY FOR RESEARCH IN CHILD DEVELOPMENT

The Society for Research in Child Development (SRCD) was established in 1933 as a professional organization to promote research on child development. The goal of the SRCD is to advocate for research in all relevant disciplines, including research that crosses disciplinary lines and research that is basic as well as applied. Currently, there are over 5,500 members who come primarily from psychology and human development disciplines but also from fields such as anthropology, history, sociology, biology, and neuroscience and professions such as pediatrics, child psychiatry, nursing, education, public health, and law.

Membership in the SRCD is open to individuals actively engaged in research or in teaching child or human development or those involved in the application of knowledge through advocacy, policy, or practice. Student memberships are available to postdoctoral, graduate, and undergraduate students as well. The organization and its members seek to promote the exchange of information across relevant disciplines as well as the application of research findings.

The SRCD was the outcome of the Committee on Child Development established by the National Research Council, the research arm of the National Academy of Sciences, in 1922. The goal was to find ways to promote research on children and families, which was generally lacking in American society at the time. The well-known experimental psychologist Robert S. Woodworth served as chair. During its years, the committee effectively fostered interest in the field by awarding fellowships, initiating conferences, and promoting publications. *Child Development Abstracts and Bibliography* (*CDAB*) actually began in 1927 as the first journal devoted entirely to child development issues. In 1933, at the recommendation of the committee, the SRCD was formed. Initially, there were approximately 400 members.

During the 70 years since its founding, the SRCD has become the major professional organization promoting research and application of research for children and families. Currently, its executive offices in Ann Arbor employ nine staff members, and its Office for Policy and Communications, located in Washington, DC, has two staff members. There are several standing committees in addition to the Society's Governing Council and Publications Committees. These include the Committee on Ethnic and Racial Issues, the Ethical Conduct Committee, the International Affairs Committee, the History of Child Development Committee, and the Policy and Communication Committee.

Publications

Publication of *Child Development* and the *Monographs of the Society for Research in Child Development,* as well as the *Social Policy Reports* and the Society's Newsletter, *SRCD Developments,* is a major part of the SRCD's endeavors. *CDAB* ceased publication in 2002 because there now are numerous online bibliographic sources and search systems that essentially cover the former journal's content. However, *Child Development* and *Monographs* continue to be among the most cited and most highly circulated of the many journals in the field. The *Social Policy Reports,* first published in 1984, provide summaries and commentaries of key issues and policies relevant to children and families. Analyses of current and pending legislation are often included as well. These are published three to four times a year and are available online.

Biennial Meetings

The SRCD holds its research meetings biennially, in the spring of odd-numbered years. Attendance typically exceeds 5,000 registrants, and the program, which runs for three and a half days, contains almost 3,000 presentations, including invited addresses, symposia, discussion hours, and poster presentations. The content is truly interdisciplinary and deals with many aspects of policy and application as well as theory-driven research.

Policy and Communications

The Office of Policy and Communications, in Washington, DC, deals with many issues, including acting as liaison with federal funding agencies and congressional committees, as well as various outlets for communications. One of its primary activities is the administration and supervision of the Science Fellows Program. Supported externally, there are two types of fellows, congressional and federal office. Each year, five to eight fellows serve the SRCD and learn about the operation of offices to which they are assigned while playing important staff roles as well. More than 100 fellows have gone on to important positions in local, state, and federal government as well as in the nonprofit sector.

International Presence

An important aspect of the SRCD that has grown rapidly in recent years is its involvement in international activities. This is reflected in the fact that it now has over 800 members from countries outside the United States, representing over 50 countries. Reports of research by scholars from other countries and studies conducted in other countries are appearing with increasing frequency both in the SRCD's journals and at its biennial meetings. Additionally, the SRCD's commitment to the use of research in public and social policy has expanded to consideration of the translation of research to policy in other parts of the world. It is becoming increasingly apparent that all societies and nations are concerned with the health and well-being of their children and families.

In its 70 years, the SRCD has established itself as a major influence in promoting quality research, obtaining resources to facilitate research further, communicating the knowledge gained, and promoting the application of findings to policy and practice.

John W. Hagen
University of Michigan

Kevin Karg

SODIUM-POTASSIUM PUMP

Three families of membrane proteins hydrolyze ATP to obtain the energy needed for the transport of ions against their electrochemical gradients: V-type ATPases (e.g., transporters of hydrogen ions into lysosomal vacuoles and synaptic vesicles), F-type ATPases (e.g., the ATP synthase of the mitochondrial inner membrane), and P-type ATPases (which share a common asp~P reactive site and include the calcium ATPase of the cell membranes and the sarcoplasmic reticulum, the H-K ATPase of the stomach and elsewhere, and the sodium-potassium ATPase found on almost every animal cell membrane). The sodium-potassium ATPase (Na-K ATPase) pumps sodium out of the cell in exchange for potassium. This process consumes a quarter of the basal metabolic rate and has profound consequences on the cell volume, ionic composition, and membrane potential, as well as on fluid transport across epithelial surfaces (DeWeer, 1985).

Functional Properties of the Sodium-Potassium Pump

The sodium-potassium pump is perfectly reversible—capable of consuming ATP to pump sodium out, and potassium into, the cell, as well as generating ATP by the reverse exchange of potassium for sodium. The function of the pump molecule is determined solely by the concentration of extracellular potassium and intracellular sodium, ADP and ATP; under physiological conditions, the cycle always consumes ATP to remove sodium from the cell.

Maintenance of Cell Volume

The Na-K ATPase is a powerful tool for countering the tendency of extracellular water to enter the cell, driven by the oncotic pressure of cell proteins. One immediate consequence of pump activity is that potassium becomes concentrated within the cell. Because cells are relatively permeable to potassium, chemical forces will tend to favor the loss of this extra potassium from the cell (cells are relatively impermeable to sodium at rest, so there will be little movement of that ion). Efflux of potassium, an osmotically active cation, will obligate the movement of chloride, a permeable anion, out of the cell to preserve electroneutrality. Because osmotic forces move water and potassium (or chloride) at a ratio of approximately 500:1, the Na-K ATPase is a particularly efficient water pump (Dwyer, 1998).

Establishment of a Membrane Potential

As the Na-K ATPase continues to operate, potassium will accumulate, and cell chloride will deplete, each establishing concentration gradients across the cell membrane. Consequently, diffusion potentials develop that are electrically negative for both ions. When steady state is reached, the electrical forces on the cell's permeable ions just counter their chemical gradients, and the resting cell membrane potential is established (Hille, 1992).

Transport of Fluid across Epithelial Surfaces

The existence of a sodium gradient allows the cell to use other transport proteins to move a wide variety of solutes, nutrients, and waste products into and out of the cell in a process termed *secondary transport.* Both electrical forces (the negative resting membrane potential) and chemical forces (the sodium concentration gradient) provide energy to couple the uphill transport of one or more molecules to the energetically favorable movement of sodium. Thus it is possible to absorb large quantities of fluid from the intestinal lumen by the cotransport of sodium and sugars or amino acids into epithelial cells lining the small intestine. Although most epithelia locate the Na-K ATPase on the basolateral aspect, neuroepithelia such as the choroid plexus and pigmented epithelia of the retina place the Na-K ATPase on the apical surface in order to better regulate potassium and bicarbonate concentrations in the brain (Rizzolo, 1999).

Electrogenic Property of the Na-K ATPase

Three sodium ions move out of the cell for every two potassium transported into the cell, generating a small electrical current. When the ratio of membrane surface area to cell volume is high, such as in nerve processes, the pump current is sufficient to hyperpolarize the membrane by up to 11 millivolts, potentially altering the electrical excitability of the nerve (DeWeer, 1985).

Metabolic Control of Pump Activity

The pump rate depends on intracellular sodium and extracellular potassium, with half-maximal stimulation at 10 to 20 mM sodium and 1.5 to 2.5 mM potassium. Minute-to-minute control of pump activity is modulated by a variety of protein kinases and phosphatases, with the identity of the Na-K ATPase subunit and the kinase or phosphatase determining whether the final result is stimulatory or inhibitory. Dopamine, for instance, inhibits the pump by an indirect cAMP-mediated inhibition of protein phosphatase 1. In the long term, pump activity is controlled by changing the number or type of the Na-K ATPase subunit present in the cell membrane (Blanco & Mercer, 1998).

Structure of the Sodium-Potassium Pump

The Na-K ATPase is a heterotrimeric protein integral to the cell membrane. The 112 kDa α-subunit contains the site where ATP is hydrolyzed, as well as the ouabain/digitalis inhibitory binding site, the sodium, and much of the potassium-binding site. The 40 to 60 kDa β-subunit shepherds the α-subunit to the cell surface, participates in the binding of potassium, and contains a very large, highly glycosylated extracellular domain that can act as an adhesion molecule, for instance, on glial cells. The 8 to 14 kDa γ-subunit is a hydrophobic polypeptide of uncertain function.

Various isoforms of both the α- and β-subunits are found in human cells, with the α_1- and β_1-subunits being the most common dimers. Identifiable nerve cells contain characteristic combinations of α_1-, α_2-, and/or α_3-subunits: for instance, in the eye, amacrine cells express α_2-subunits, bipolar cells express α_3, horizontal cells express α_1 and α_3, and ganglia cells express all three α isoforms. Glial cells can express α_2 or α_3 isoforms. The functional consequence of the highly specific tissue distribution of a multiplicity of subunit combinations may lie in differences in kinetic or thermodynamic parameters of the specific heterotrimers or in a differential sensitivity to metabolic control (Blanco & Mercer, 1998).

REFERENCES

Blanco, G., & Mercer, R. (1998). Isozymes of the Na-K ATPase: Heterogeneity in structure, diversity in function. *American Journal of Physiology, 275,* F633–F650.

Dwyer, T. M. (1998). *Osmotically active particles and the cell.* 10/12/2003. Retrieved from http://physiology.umc.edu

Gullans, S. R. (2000). Metabolic basis of solute transport. In D. W. Seldin & G. Giebisch (Eds.), *The kidney: Physiology and pathophysiology* (pp. 215–245). New York: Raven.

Hille, B. (2001). *Ionic channels of excitable membranes* (3rd ed.). Sunderland, MA: Sinauer.

Rizzolo, L. J. (1999). Polarization of the Na-K ATPase in epithelia derived from the neuroepithelium. *International Review of Cytology, 185,* 195–235.

Terry M. Dwyer
UMMC

SOMATOPSYCHICS

Definition

The term *somatopsychics* is derived from the Greek terms *soma,* meaning body, and *psyche,* which has become an English term as well. Somatopsychics refers to psychological effects engendered by somatic conditions. Such psychological states range from normal, to mild mood alterations (like irritability due to low blood sugar), to major psychiatric conditions.

Somatopsychics needs to be contrasted with psychosomatics. Psychosomatic mechanisms operate when psychological conditions produce physical symptoms, such as dry mouth and nervous sweating as a result of stress. The distinction between psychosomatic and somatopsychic is clear in most cases and in theory, but in reality, when phenomena of both kinds become intertwined and feed on each other, causes and effects are difficult to disentangle. When somatic and psychological causes successively bring about effects that begin to serve as the cause for the next level of effects, an etiological spiral evolves, making it difficult to identify the degrees to which psychosomatic or somatopsychic factors contributed to the final outcome. For example, stress leads to tachycardia (psychosomatic effect), which in turn causes uneasiness and anxiety (somatopsychic outcome), resulting in a headache (psychosomatic effect), which may trigger irritability (somatopsychic effect).

Neither the concept nor the term is new, but not all researchers are using the term *somatopsychics* correctly, which has created some confusion. Many have used the popular term *psychosomatic* in lieu of somatopsychic when referring to a body-mind connection, regardless of the direction in which the cause and effect arrow points.

Linguistics attests to the recognition of somatopsychic connections. For example, the thymus gland, considered to be the seat of emotions, was named after the Greek word for mood, *thymos,* while hysteria, formerly believed to be related to the uterus, was labeled after the Greek term for uterus, *hyster.*

History

Somatopsychic connections were understood by Hippocrates, Aristotle, and Galen. In the 1700s Lammetrie's "L'homme machine" functioned on a somatopsychic basis. Cabanis perceived the mind as a function of the brain. Gall's phrenology led to Lombroso's somatically based theory about the criminal mind. Fechner's theory of psychophysical parallelism asserted that every physical event has a psychological correlate and vice versa. Lotze, Ribot, and Galton prominently emphasized the somatic basis of psychological processes. Among prominent promoters of somatic hypotheses of mental illness, in the second half of the 19th and at the beginning of the 20th century, were Broca (localization of brain functions), Taine (nerve reflexes), Müller, Weber, Wundt, Jakobi, Griesinger, Westphal, Meynert, Kraepelin, Bleuler, and Wernicke, who used the specific term *somatopsychic.* Meynert, for example, not only argued for an etiology of mental illness rooted in brain pathology but also supported it with specific observations concerning destruction of fibers, blood flow to the brain, and so on. Kretschmer connected body build and personality and proposed a corresponding affinity toward a specific mental illness. Sheldon's body based theories about temperament followed. Around 1900 Pavlov established scientific proof for four personality types based on distinguishable patterns of nervous system reactivity.

In 1913/1973 Karl Jaspers presented several etiologies of mental illness, among them the somatopsychic etiology, which is divided into three parts: (1) brain pathology (trauma, tumors, infection, vascular system–related pathology, genetic deficits, deterioration due to aging, etc.), (2) physical illness producing symptomatic psychoses (infectious diseases, endocrine disorders, uremia, etc.), and (3) effects of toxic substances (morphine, cocaine, carbon monoxide, alcohol, etc.).

With the rapid expansion of biomedical research in the twentieth century, evidence for a somatic basis of many psychological disturbances mounted and in the 1970s lent credence to orthomolecular psychiatry. The theories of Pauling, Kety, Rimland, Pfeiffer, Osmond, and others identified specific mental disorders as somatopsychic effects of biological etiology. They countered adverse genetic, biochemical, nutritional, and environmental conditions with megavitamin and/or mineral therapy to treat and prevent mental illness.

Richard C. W. Hall's landmark 1980 book brought the

concept of somatopsychics into focus. With his colleagues he documented and cataloged psychological presentations of physical illness as well as psychological side effects of pharmacological agents. Additional somatopsychic outcomes were reported to be related to genetic factors, to normal physical changes such as hormonally induced biorhythms or life phase changes, as well as to toxic substances, including gases, and to ambient environmental conditions.

Research into the somatic etiology of mental disorders is growing rapidly, forecasting a more accurate understanding of mental illness and leading to a new, largely somatopsychically based systematization and to new codification of mental illness.

Somatopsychics of Everyday Life

Everyday life is full of experiences illustrating etiology and effects of somatopsychic mechanisms. Parents are familiar with the mood changes that occur in children when they are hot, tired, or hungry. But people of all ages get irritable because of low blood sugar, heat, and fatigue. Effects of sensory overload, such as noise or heat, and many forms of sensory extremes, including sensory deprivation, are reflected in psychological sequelae. Total sensory deprivation as used in some prisons can lead to psychotic states and hallucinations. On the other hand, enjoyable sensations trigger psychological effects as well. Scents can evoke pleasant feelings that may include seductive messages. Music can be stimulating or calming, depending on tone, volume, and rhythm.

Diminished alertness and reactivity are well documented in fatigued drivers of motor vehicles. Fatigue is a generally recognized factor in diminished capacity to function mentally, particularly in learning. In fact, one of the earliest psychological tests was developed by Ebbinghaus (1897) to study fatigue in school children. Limitations of reasoning ability are easily accepted as an effect of a not-yet matured brain in young children but cause concern when they are the result of a deteriorating brain in an aging person.

Hormones are known to cause emotional changes in adolescence and in pregnancy and menopause and are related to mood swings in premenstrual syndrome. Postpartum depression is attributed to the birth-related sudden disruption of the hormone levels accompanying pregnancy.

Somatopsychic effects of common-use substances are well recognized: the stimulating effects of caffeine and nicotine, as well as the initially relaxing but later depressing and judgment-impairing effects of alcohol. Many toxic substances have more than a somatic impact. Lawsuits alleging lead poisoning cite outcomes of learning disabilities, lethargy, and so forth. Carbon monoxide exposure (car exhaust, cooking gas) can lead to memory deficits, apathy, and depression. Brain trauma due to insults from various causes like forceps birth, domestic abuse, accidents, or brain surgery may result in mental deficiencies, adverse emotional reactions, and personality changes. In rare cases trauma has caused a state of euphoria.

Sports-related somatopsychic phenomena include the runner's high, attributed to endorphins, and the SCUBA divers' rapture of the deep, a state of nitrogen narcosis that expresses itself in a euphoric, drunk-like state accompanied by cognitive impairment and poor judgment. High altitude exposure affects mountain climbers and skiers along with inactive sightseers. Apart from physical distress it may cause irritability, impaired judgment, and in extreme cases panic attacks, delirium, and hallucinations.

Light availability affects mood. Diminished presence of daylight in the northern and southern regions, as in Alaska and Scandinavia, causes depression in many people. *Wetterfühligkeit,* more readily acknowledged in Europe, refers to weather sensitivity. It implies that a person's vascular system is affected by weather conditions, particularly changes in barometric pressure affecting the emotional state. The Föhn, the oppressive, warm alpine winds, are blamed for migraine headaches as well as for bringing on depression and even suicide in susceptible individuals.

Disruption of circadian rhythm, especially when resulting in sleep deprivation, reduces optimal physical and mental performance and also appears to play a major role in depression. Leading causes are jet lag and shift work, particularly when shift cycles alternate as soon as the body has begun to adjust.

Medical Illness Producing Psychological/Psychiatric Symptoms

The American Psychiatric Association's *Diagnostic and Statistical Manual of Mental Disorders,* fourth edition recognizes the existence of somatopsychic conditions as long as a general medical condition or a specific substance caused the mental disorder, but it does not explicitly label the mechanism involved as somatopsychic. Such recognized medical conditions likely to generate psychological or psychiatric effects include brain tumors, head trauma, neoplasms, neurological, endocrine, and cardiovascular conditions, specific infections, autoimmune disorders, hepatic and renal disease, and fluid or electrolyte imbalance. Several researchers have pointed out that side effects of medical illness or substance impact may lead to a misdiagnosis of mental illness, which most likely preempts the needed treatment of the underlying condition. Missed early interventions due to missed diagnoses can endanger the patients' life, as in brain tumors. Misleading symptoms depending on tumor site can include personality, affective and cognitive changes, altered perceptions, anxiety and depression, tactile or visual hallucinations, and depression.

Selected Examples of Somatopsychic Effects

Substance-Related Somatopsychics

Somatopsychic effects may be related to a substance of abuse or to withdrawal from it. They also occur when a person incurs a deficit or accumulates a toxic amount of a needed substance, such as a vitamin or mineral. Psychotic, mood, and anxiety disorders, for instance, may be associated with intoxication with and/or withdrawal from many substances. Phencyclidine (PCP), for example, causes a sense of emotional numbing, detachment and isolation, and change in body and spatial images. If it triggers a psychotic episode, the symptoms may be indistinguishable from those of schizophrenia.

Common-use substances like alcohol, caffeine, and nicotine have their somatopsychic effects: Caffeine increases energy and alertness and acts as a mood elevator, but anxiety, fatigue, and depression are bound to follow at abstinence. Somatopsychic effects of alcohol consumption vary, ranging from elevated mood, impaired judgment, anger, rage, and violence to fatigue, or may lead to dysphoria and depression. Memory deficits are common after heavy drinking. Excessive, long-term use can lead to amnestic disorder, dementia, and delirium. Nicotine use increases arousal, vigilance, and concentration and reduces stress and irritability. Severe irritability follows withdrawal.

Malnutrition alters emotional reactivity and cognitive efficacy (starvation, poverty, dieting). Somatopsychic effects due to nutritional deficiencies, though present in the general population, have been noted prominently in the elderly due to both insufficient intake and diminished absorption capacity. Incorrect diagnoses of organic brain syndrome, paranoia, or depression have been made in patients suffering from nutritional deficits. Vitamin and mineral deficiencies can lead to irritability, confusion, mental deterioration, dementia, delusions, disorientation, apathy, hallucinations, depression, anxiety, and so on. Accumulation of toxic amounts of vitamins and minerals can generate similar outcomes. Toxic levels of copper may even mimic psychosis indistinguishable from bipolar disorder or schizophrenia.

Somatopsychics of Mental Disorders and Other Psychological Conditions

Some mental conditions are exclusively of somatic etiology. Most types of mental retardation and autism fit this category. Not as clear-cut are the etiologies of schizophrenia, mood, and anxiety disorders. These disorders, depending on type and severity, are believed to arise from psychogenic and/or somatogenic conditions. Stress can interact with genetic predisposition. In addition, psychological factors can precipitate a psychosomatic outcome. Depending on the resulting somatic condition, it may become the somatic basis for a mental disorder. A selection of recognized etiologies follows. The samples provided are not intended to be all-inclusive.

1. *Mental retardation.* Most cases of mental retardation are somatically based.
   a. Mental retardation related to the *prenatal* period includes chromosomal disorders, inborn errors of metabolism, disorders of the urea cycle, developmental disorders of brain formation such as hydro- and microcephalus, maternal malnutrition, and substance abuse or illness (measles, diabetes).
   b. *Perinatal* phase. A healthy fetus can develop into a child with mental retardation due to unfavorable birth-related events, such as maternal sepsis, and birth delays, umbilical cord accidents, head trauma, and so on. Other etiologies are neonatal disorders, such as infections or intracranial hemorrhage.
   c. Severe malnutrition in the *postnatal* phase is a leading cause of mental retardation. Other damaging factors are head injuries, lead and mercury poisoning, aspirin-related Reye syndrome, childhood onset of metabolic disorders, infections, postimmunization disorders, parasitic infestations such as malaria, seizure disorders, and so on.
2. *Autism.* This has been related to bilateral brain damage in early life, genetic roots, neurochemical and immunological factors, deficient oxygen delivery to the brain, in utero insults, and so forth.
3. *Schizophrenia.* While the evidence for somatic etiologies of SCH is increasing, no singular somatic cause of schizophrenia has been identified. The following are some of the more widely recognized somatopsychic etiologies of SCH. They center on (1) genetic factors; (2) environmental factors, including maternal malnutrition and effects of infectious agents or antibodies operating prenatally; (3) lipid dysfunction; (4) abnormal brain lateralization and/or abnormal hemispheric communications, brain damage occurring as a result of abnormal prenatal brain development, head injury, hypoxia, and so forth; (5) neurodevelopmental errors and neurological malfunction; (6) extreme prematurity at birth; and (7) biochemical deficiencies or imbalances. The broad variety of etiologies producing schizophrenic symptoms calls for a new, somatopsychically based understanding of the disorder.
4. *Depression.* While there is psychogenic depression in response to negative life events, depression also has undisputed somatopsychic etiologies. They include genetics, biorhythms (circadian rhythms, sleep length, and quality), and environmental (sunlight deprivation) and biochemical factors, like activity of monoaminergic neurons, norepinephrine, serotonin- and thyrotropin-releasing hormones (TRH), dopamine deficiency, reuptake of norepinephrine, serotonin and dopamine, and others. In women, hormone-related depression has been associated with premenstrual syndrome, pregnancy, the postpartum period, and menopause.
5. *Mania.* In addition to genetics, mania has been related to various somatic etiologies, such as excess epinephrine and serotonin production, cerebral trauma, left hemisphere injury, sleep disruption, and CD4 count in HIV-infected patients.

6. *Anxiety.*
   a. Research has found that a single dominant gene causes a predisposition to panic disorder. A panic experience can be triggered when the autonomic nervous system is activated by agents like caffeine, yohimbine, lactic acid, increased CO inhalation, and so on. One hypothesis theorizes that patients with panic disorder may chronically be in a higher state of arousal.
   b. Obsessive compulsive disorder is classified as an anxiety disorder, and its somatopsychic etiology is increasingly recognized. Among such etiologies are genetics, abnormal brain structures, and a dysfunction of the serotonergic system.

Outlook

The rapidly expanding body of scientific findings has broadened knowledge about the role of somatic factors in the etiology of psychological and psychiatric presentations. Unless a condition is strictly psychogenic, symptoms are less significant in defining a disorder than their somatic origin is. Identical symptoms of psychopathology can result from vastly different somatic etiology. Somatopsychic research calls for a reassessment of the historically evolved understanding of so-called mental illness, which needs to be redefined in biological-medical terms, accepting etiology as the defining category, no matter how serious the side effects of mental and emotional disturbance are. Many of the old categories, based on symptoms, cannot adequately accommodate disorders that are now understood etiologically and diagnosed with the help of innovative scientific methods and defined by new and different standards. Expected new terminology portraying mental illness largely as a side effect of somatic conditions can remove stigmatization of mental patients and will encourage them to seek timely treatment. More accurate diagnoses invite more precisely targeted interventions, which will improve the efficacy of treatment.

REFERENCES

Bleuler, E. (1995). *Lehrbuch der Psychiatrie* (5th ed.). Berlin: Spinger. (Original work published 1911)

Broca, P. (1876). *Sur la topographie cranio-cerebral.* Paris: Leroux.

Cabanis, P. J. G. (1802). *Rapport du physique et du morale de l'homme.*

Ebbinghaus, H. (1897). *Grundzüge der Psychologie.* Leipzig: Veit.

Fechner, G. T. (1860). *Elemente der Psychophysik.* Leipzig: Breitkopf & Härtel.

Fechner, G. T. (1882). *Revision der Hauptpunkte der Psychophysik.* Leipzig: Breitkopf & Härtel.

Gall, J. F. (1925). *Sur les fonctions du cerveau et sur celles des chacune des ces parties.* Paris: Bailliere.

Galton, F. (1907). *Antechamber of consciousness.* London: Dent.

Griesinger, W. (1845). *Pathologie und Therapie der physischen Krankheiten.* Stuttgart: Adolph Krabbe.

Hall, R. C. W. (1980). *Psychiatric presentations of medical illness: Somatopsychic disorders.* New York: Spectrum.

Hall, R. C. W., Gardner, E. R., Strickney, S. K., LeCann, A. F., & Popkin, M. K. (1980). Physical illness manifesting as psychiatric disease. *Archives of General Psychiatry, 37,* 989–995.

Hall, R. C. W., & Beresford, T. P. (1984). *Handbook of psychiatric diagnostics* (Vols. I & II). New York: Spectrum.

Hall, R. C. W., Beresford, T. P., & Blow, F. C. (1987). Depression and medical illness: An overview. In Oliver G. Cameron (Ed.), *Presentations of depression: Depressive symptoms in medical and other psychiatric disorders.* New York: Wiley.

Hawkins, D., & Pauling, L. (1973). *Orthomolecular psychiatry—treatment of schizophrenia.* San Francisco: Freeman.

Hoffer, A. (1962). *Niacin therapy in psychiatry.* Springfield, IL: Thomas.

Jakobi, M. (1830). *Beobachtungen über die Pathologie und Therapie der mit Irresein verbundenen Krankheiten.* Elberfeld: Schoenian'sche Buchhandlung.

Jaspers, K. (1913/1973). *Allgemeine Psychopathologie* (9th ed.). Berlin: Springer.

Kety, S. (1972). Toward hypotheses for a biochemical component in the vulnerability of schizophrenia. *Seminars in Psychiatry, 4,* 233–258.

Kety, S. (1976). Genetic aspects of schizophrenia. *Psychiatric Annals, 6,* 11–32.

Kraepelin, E. (1893) *Psychiatrie* (4th ed.). Leipzig: Meiner.

Kretschmer, E. (1967). *Körperbau und Charakter* (25th ed.). Berlin: Springer.

Lammetrie, J. (1748). L'homme machine. In *Ouevres philosophiques.* Hildesheim: Olms.

Lipps, G. F. (1899). *Grundriss der Psychophysik.*

Lombroso, C. (1896). *L'uomo delinquente* (5th ed.). Turin: Fratelli Bocca.

Lotze, R. H. (1852). *Mezidinische Psychologie oder Physiologie der Seele.* Leipzig: Weimann.

Meynert, R. (1889). *Klinische vorlesungen über Psychiatrie auf wissenschaftlichen Grundlagen.* Vienna: W. Braumüller.

Müller, G. E. (1879). *Zur Grundlegung der Psychophysik.* Göttingen: Vandenhoeck & Ruprecht.

Müller, G. E. (1882). *Revision der Hauptpunkte der Psychophysik.* Göttingen: Vandenhoeck & Ruprecht.

Osmond, H. (1973). Come home psychiatry! The megavitamin treatment and the medical model. *Psychiatric Opinion, 10,* 14–23

Pauling, L. (1968). Orthomolecular psychiatry. *Science, 160,* 265–171.

Pauling, L. (1974). On the orthomolecular environment of the mind: Orthomolecular theory. *American Journal of Psychiatry, 131,* 1251–1257.

Pfeiffer, C. C. (1976). Psychiatric hospital versus brain biocenter. *Journal of Orthomolecular Psychiatry, 5,* 28–34.

Pavlov, I. P. (1966). *Essential works of Pavlov.* New York: Bantam.

Ribot, T. (1885). *Les maladies de la memoire.* Paris: Bailliere.

Ribot, T. (1888). *Les maladies de la personalite.* Paris: Alcan.

Rimland, B. (1974). Infantile autism. Status of research. *Canadian Psychiatric Association Journal, 19,* 130–133.

Sheldon, W. H. (1942). *The varieties of temperament.* New York: Harper.

Taine, H. (1870). *De l'intelligence.* Paris: Hachette.

Wernicke, C. (1874). *Der aphasische Symptomkomplex: eine psychologische Studie auf anatomischer Basis.* Breslau: Cohn & Weigert.

Wundt, W. (1874). *Grundzüge der physiologischen Psychologie.* Leipzig: Engelmann.

ERIKA WICK
St. John's University, New York

SOMATOSENSORY FUNCTION

Somatosensory function is the ability to interpret bodily sensation. Sensation takes a number of forms, including touch, pressure, vibration, temperature, itch, tickle, and pain. The somatosensory system allows individuals to interpret sensory messages received from the body and consists of sensory receptors located in the skin, tissues, and joints; the nerve cell tracts in the body and spinal cord; and brain centers that process incoming sensory information (Figure 1).

Sensory information is first detected in at least six specialized sense organs in the skin, categorized by rapid or slow response characteristics. Rapid responses occur in hair-follicle receptors, which detect hair movement in hair-covered skin. Hairless skin contains receptors called Meissner's corpuscles that respond rapidly to sudden displacements of skin and low-frequency vibration of up to 80 cycles/s. Another rapid sense receptor, found in hairy and hairless skin, is the Pacinian corpuscle. Pacinian corpuscles respond to sudden skin displacements and to high-frequency vibration, sensing signals at 30 to 800 cycles/s. These rapid sense receptors detect movement across skin, as well as vibration and fast but subtle changes in pressure. Sense receptors with slower responses include Merkel's disks, responsive predominantly to skin indentation; Ruffini endings, which respond to skin stretch, and free nerve endings, which detect touch, pressure, pain, and thermal sensations. These slower receptors occur in both hairy and hairless skin. Free nerve endings are present also in arterial walls and joint surfaces. Various types of nerve endings in joints, tendons, and muscles provide input for kinesthesis, the knowledge of the position and movement of one's body parts. Visceral sensation comes largely from nerve endings in the muscles surrounding the viscera. The viscera themselves are fairly insensitive to touch, temperature, and pain.

The sensory receptors send their information to the spinal cord through peripheral afferent nerves in the arms, legs, body, and head. A total of 31 pairs of nerves (one member of each coming from either side of the body) enter the spinal cord from the body, and four so-called cranial nerves supply sensory information from the head, including structures such as the tongue and pharynx. As the nerves enter the spinal cord, they make connections, or synapses, within the cord tissue. The sensory information then travels to the brain via two major pathways.

The two pathways that convey sensory information from spinal cord to brain serve largely different functions. The dorsal column–lemniscal system transmits mainly touch and pressure information and consists of large and fast nerve fibers that transmit signals at rates of 30 to 110 m/s. The fast information flow enables sensations of movement

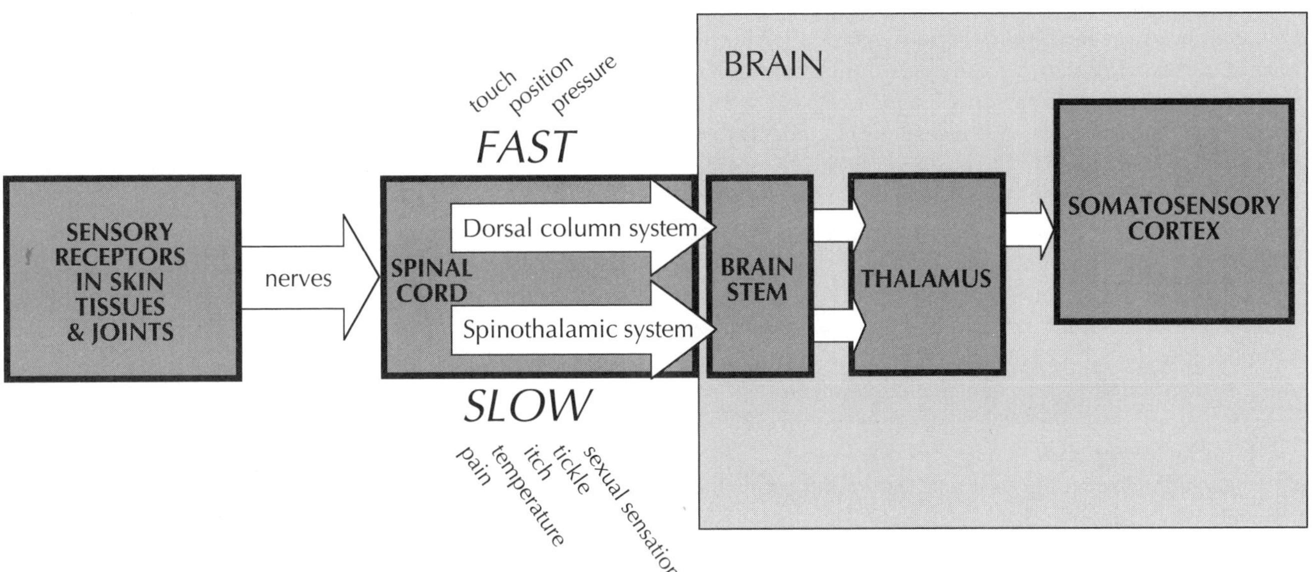

Figure 1. The somatosensory system and its components.

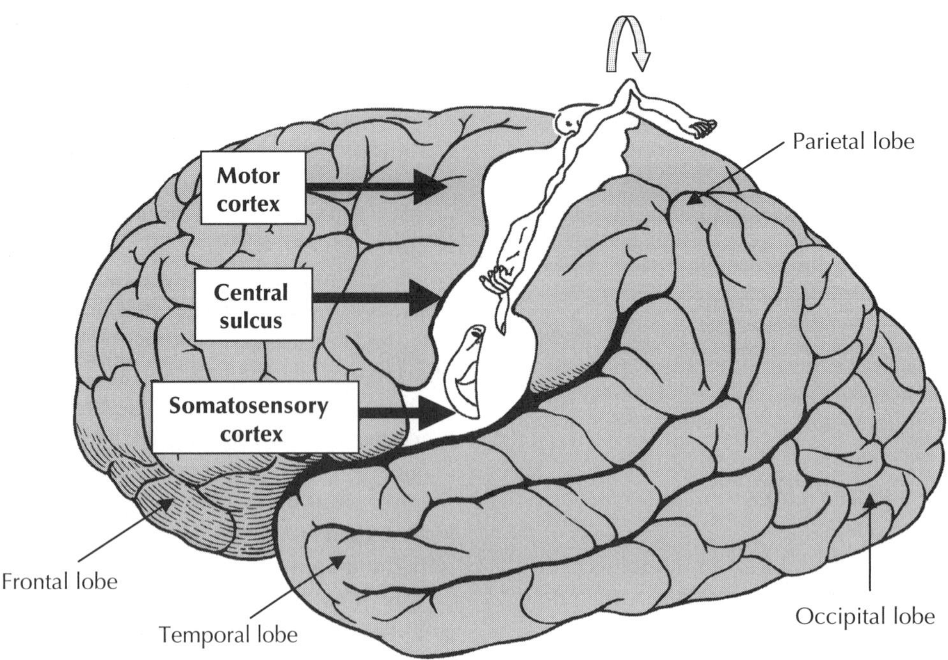

Figure 2. Human somatosensory cortex (white shading) is separated from motor cortex by the central sulcus. The spatial organization of bodily sensation shown as an homunculus, which continues along the inner surface of the brain's hemisphere (folding arrow).

across skin to be detected, as well as rapidly repetitive signals to be ultimately sensed as vibration. In addition, this pathway transmits information with high spatial resolution. Touch sensations are localized with a high degree of accuracy, and fine discriminations in intensity can be made. These processes are due to a key characteristic of this system: rapid adaptation, in which a response to a persistent stimulus dies away quickly.

The second system is the spinothalamic system. This slower, low-resolution pathway transmits mainly information relating to pain, temperature, tickle, itch, and sexual sensations. Typical signal transmission rates range from 8 to 40 m/s and are generally slow because information is sent down smaller nerves than in the dorsal column system. The ability to transmit rapid repetitive signals is poor; spatial resolution is fairly crude; and the spinothalamic system does not adapt quickly. This is important because a persistent sensation of hot, cold, or pain will stimulate the individual to remove the affected body part from a noxious and potentially damaging stimulus.

When fibers from the dorsal column and spinothalamic system enter the spinal cord, their connections are quite different. The dorsal column system fibers take two directions: the so-called lateral and medial branches. Fibers from the lateral branch make synapses in the spinal cord, which ultimately produce spinal cord reflexes and a pathway connecting the spinal cord and the brain's cerebellar hemispheres, structures that play a key role in motor control. Fibers from the medial branch travel to the brain stem to a structure called the medulla. Here the fibers decussate, or cross, from one side of the body to the other. From the medulla, tactile information flows through the medial lemniscus to the thalamus of the brain.

By contrast, in the spinothalamic system some fibers synapse and then decussate locally in the spinal cord. The spinothalamic system sends its information forward via two major routes. First, crossed fibers travel to two regions of the thalamus: one set goes to the same thalamic region as the dorsal column fibers, whereas the other travels to another part of the thalamus. Second, crossed and uncrossed fibers are sent to the reticular nuclei in the brain stem and the thalamus. These latter connections are important for the chronic pain perception. The increased arousal that these signals produce explains why it is difficult to sleep when one is in pain.

The thalamus is the brain's relay station for sensory input, including vision and hearing. From the thalamus, the tactile information travels to a brain region called somatosensory cortex (Figure 1). Somatosensory cortex is the primary brain region dealing with sensation. It lies in the parietal lobe (Figure 2), namely on a surface and fold of brain known as the postcentral gyrus and the central sulcus, respectively. The central sulcus separates the sensory cortex from the motor cortex.

Each side of the body's surface is mapped to somatosensory cortex of the contralateral, or opposite, side of the brain. Sensation in the pharynx, tongue, and teeth is located below that of the face and hands, which in turn are located in regions below those for the trunk and legs (Figure 2). Sensation in the feet and genitalia are located in the cortex that lies between the two hemispheres of the brain. (The arrangement of motor cortex follows a similar topo-

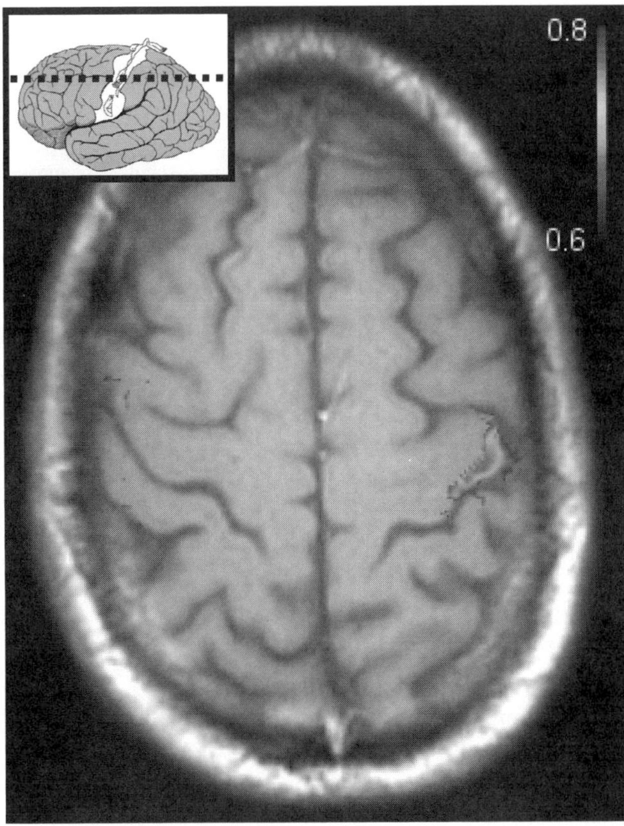

Figure 3. Brain activation study of hand somatosensory cortex elicited by brushing the fingers and palm using functional magnetic resonance imaging at 3 Tesla (graded bar displays correlation coefficient range for $p < 0.01$ level). The horizontal broken line on the brain (inset) indicates display plane for the activation image.

graphical organization. Hence, injuries to these brain regions can be localized from observed impairments in sensory and motor functions of various parts of the body.) The spatial map of somatosensory cortex is not a precise representation of the body. The hands, face, and lips take up a disproportionately large part of the map. These body parts typically are the most sensitive and supply the most information about a contacting stimulus relative to other body areas such as the back. The distorted somatosensory map of the body's surface is often known as the sensory homunculus (Figure 2). Noninvasive activation studies of somatosensory cortex in response to tactile stimulation of a particular body part, such as the hand (Figure 3), are now possible and are beginning to be used routinely in presurgical planning for tumor and epilepsy surgery.

The secondary somatosensory cortex, located slightly below and behind the primary somatosensory cortex in each hemisphere, also deals with sensory information. It receives its input from two thalamic regions predominantly via the spinothalamic system, in addition to receiving input from the primary somatosensory cortex.

The analysis of tactile information in the brain does not stop at somatosensory cortices. We can recognize objects when our eyes are closed by running our fingers over them or by moving them around in our hands. This is possible because the somatosensory (and also motor) cortices send information to other brain regions that perform these sophisticated functions.

Aina Puce
West Virginia University School of Medicine

SPATIAL MEMORY

Spatial memory is ubiquitous. Almost every action takes place in space and requires some form of spatial memory. In addition, spatial memory can be studied easily in animals, which often have outstanding spatial capabilities. Consider, for instance, the memory capabilities of food-storing birds. During autumn, many birds store seeds that they retrieve later on (often several months after the storing episode), when the environment does not provide the necessary amount of fresh food. Thus an individual bird will store hundreds of food items in numerous caches scattered throughout its home range. Retrieving these food caches will depend at least partly on the bird's memory for their locations. For example, laboratory experiments demonstrate that Clark's nutcrackers show excellent retention of many spatial locations over time periods greater than 9 months. Other observations suggest that scrub jays remember more than just spatial locations. They also remember what type of food has been cached and whether it is perishable.

Such capabilities are not unique to birds but are found in many rodents as well. For example, laboratory rats perform very well on the radial maze, a memory task in which they have to gather food at the end of the arms of a radial maze. As arms depleted of food are not rebaited, rats learn to avoid locations that have already been visited. They form a memory of depleted arms based on a representation of the food locations relative to the configuration of visual cues within the testing environment (Roitblat, 1987). Rats are also very proficient at the water maze navigation task, in which they must find a safe platform in a pool filled with water. As the start position is changed from trial to trial and the platform is not visible, the animal cannot apply rigid solutions to the problem. Instead, it must rely on the visual cues located outside the swimming pool so as to infer the platform location. Rats quickly learn to swim directly toward the platform, even when novel start points are used. Thus, they learn the platform location relative to the environment and are able to plan direct paths, whatever their current location. Other studies suggest that the rat's spatial memory encompasses the general structure of space. Such cognitive maps allow rats to use efficient novel paths when the circumstances require it; for example, they can make detours when previously available paths are blocked (Poucet, 1993).

Among the brain areas that support spatial memory, the hippocampus, a structure that lies below the cortex in mammals, has received much attention in recent years. Damage to the hippocampus induces dramatic and permanent deficits in spatial tasks. Rats with such lesions are impaired in the water maze navigation task and have an impaired spatial memory in the radial maze. Their spatial patterns of exploration are also strongly altered, and they fail to detect spatial changes in a familiar environment (see Poucet & Benhamou, 1997, for a review). However, critical evidence is provided by the existence of cells that carry a spatial signal. Such cells can be classified as place cells and head direction cells. Place cells are found in the hippocampus proper. A place cell fires rapidly when the rat is in a restricted portion of the environment independently of the animal's heading and is usually silent elsewhere (O'Keefe, 1976). Each place cell has its own specific firing location. Head direction cells are found primarily in the postsubiculum, an area closely related to the hippocampus. The firing pattern of head direction cells depends only on the heading of the animal and is independent of its location (Taube, 1998). Each head direction cell has its own specific preferred firing direction. Both head direction cells and place cells share many properties, including being under the control of visual and idiothetic (motor-related) inputs. Thus, the two types of cells have access to the same information and form a tightly connected functional neural network that provides the animal with information about both its location and its heading. Their cooperative function is hypothesized to allow the rat to navigate efficiently in its current environment.

Cells that carry somewhat similar spatial signals have been found in the hippocampus of nonhuman primates, suggesting a comparable function in higher species (Ono, Nakamura, Nishijo, & Eifuku, 1993). In addition, recent evidence based on functional neuroimaging of brain activity during navigation in familiar yet complex virtual-reality environments suggests that the human hippocampus also plays a special role in spatial navigation. Activation of the right hippocampus is strongly associated with spatial knowledge and navigation (Maguire et al., 1998). This finding bears a direct relation to animal studies and supports the hypothesis that the role of the hippocampus in spatial memory should be extended to other mammal species, including humans. Further work will be necessary, however, to understand how the hippocampus interacts with other structures (e.g., the parietal cortex) thought to be important for the representation of spatial information.

REFERENCES

Maguire, E. A., Burgess, N., Donnett, J. G., Frackowiak, R. S. J., Frith, C. D., & O'Keefe, J. (1998). Knowing where and getting there: A human navigation network. *Science, 280,* 921–924.

O'Keefe, J. (1976). Place units in the hippocampus of the freely moving rat. *Experimental Neurology, 51,* 78–109.

Ono, T., Nakamura, K., Nishijo, H., & Eifuku, S. (1993). Monkey hippocampal neurons related to spatial and nonspatial functions. *Journal of Neurophysiology, 70,* 1516–1529.

Poucet, B. (1993). Spatial cognitive maps in animals: New hypotheses on their structure and neural mechanisms. *Psychological Review, 100,* 163–182.

Poucet, B., & Benhamou, S. (1997). The neuropsychology of spatial cognition in the rat. *Critical Reviews in Neurobiology, 11,* 101–120.

Roitblat, H. L. (1987). *Introduction to comparative cognition.* New York: Freeman.

Taube, J. S. (1998). Head direction cells and the neurophysiological basis for a sense of direction. *Progress in Neurobiology, 55,* 225–256.

Bruno Poucet
Centre National de la Recherche Scientifique

SPECIFIC HUNGERS

A specific hunger is an increased preference (or craving) for a specific food or flavor at a particular time, such as during conditions of vitamin deficiency. It is distinguished from a consistent preference for a particular food or flavor, such as the fact that some people like jalapeños and others do not. It is also distinguished from pica, which is a preference for eating something apparently useless or harmful, such as clay.

Specific hungers were first documented by Curt Richter (1943, 1947), who found that rats would adaptively modify their intake of carbohydrates, fats, proteins, sodium, calcium, the B vitamins, vitamin E, and others at various times. For example, adrenalectomized rats increase their intake of sodium chloride (NaCl) to compensate for the excessive salt they lose when they urinate. Parathyroidectomized rats increase their calcium intake, again in response to increased need. Pregnant and nursing rats increase their intake of proteins and calcium. Later researchers demonstrated that rats also increase their preference for high-protein diets after a period of protein deficiency (DiBattista & Holder, 1998).

The specific hunger for sodium chloride apparently depends on an innately programmed mechanism that can be triggered by sodium need. A rat that becomes deficient in NaCl immediately shows an enhanced preference for foods and liquids containing NaCl or containing the similar-tasting, but toxic, LiCl (Nachman, 1962; Richter, 1956). This preference depends on changes in the taste of the salt solution (Scott, 1992) and is greatly weakened after damage to the chorda tympani, the nerve responsible for taste from the anterior tongue (Frankmann, Sollars, & Bernstein, 1996). That is, salty substances taste better when the body needs them. Anecdotal evidence suggests that humans have similar mechanisms for sodium hunger (Wilkins &

Richter, 1940). Thus, the salt craving reported by athletes after extensive sweating or by women during heavy menstrual bleeding has a biological basis.

In contrast, other specific hungers develop by trial-and-error learning, largely by process of elimination (Rozin, 1967; Rozin & Kalat, 1971). For example, if a calcium- or thiamine-deficient rat is offered several foods, one of which contains the needed nutrient, it shows no immediate preference, but gradually learns an aversion to the deficient foods and thus an apparent preference for the food containing the nutrient. That is, what appears to be a preference or craving for one food is often an avoidance of the other choices. Similarly, rats on a diet deficient in certain amino acids learn an aversion to that diet and therefore prefer a new and potentially better diet (Wang, Cummings, & Gietzen, 1996). However, a rat on a deficient diet prefers an old, "safe" diet to both the deficient diet and any new, untested one.

Many specific hungers or cravings remain unexplained, however. For example, many people report a marked craving for chocolate at certain times. The chocolate craving is particularly common among women around the time of menstruation. One hypothesis has been that chocolate acts as a kind of tranquilizer or in some other way counteracts the discomfort of menstruation—and presumably discomfort at other times as well. However, providing either tranquilizers or hormonal treatments does not weaken the chocolate cravings of menstruating women (Michener, Rozin, Freeman, & Gale, 1999). It is possible that people learn a preference for chocolate because of some benefit and then maintain the habit even when it is not needed. However, the data currently available do not explain chocolate cravings.

A new kind of specific hunger has been observed that cannot be described as a taste craving. Some chimpanzees and possibly other primates occasionally chew and suck the bitter pith of the plant *Vernonina* or swallow whole leaves with rough edges without chewing them (Huffman, 2001; Lozano, 1998). From their facial expressions, they do not appear to enjoy the taste, and people who have tried the pith or leaves describe them as bitter and foul-tasting. The pith and leaf eating are common only during the rainy season, which is also the time of the greatest spread of the intestinal parasite *Oesophagostomumi,* a nematode. Chimpanzees that engage in pith and leaf eating usually appear to be in poor health, with diarrhea, lethargy, and weight loss. In at least a few documented cases, chimpanzees that ate pith or leaves showed improved health afterward, and there was a decrease in their number of intestinal parasites. Thus it would appear that chimpanzees have discovered the value of these plants as medications, as have, in fact, the indigenous humans of the same regions (Huffman, 2001). Some biologists, however, remain skeptical. First, none of the researchers has adequately documented that the leaves and bitter pith that chimpanzees sometimes eat have better parasite-killing properties than other available plants. Second and more important, it is difficult to imagine how chimpanzees could have learned the medicinal value of plants. Chimpanzees generally keep to a consistent diet and seldom try eating various plants at random. What is the chance that an ill chimpanzee would try eating a bitter-tasting wood, consume enough to do some good, and associate the recovery with the bad-tasting substance? Researchers vary in how plausible they consider this scenario, but we need not assume that each individual learns the behavior independently. If chimpanzees have indeed learned to self-medicate to combat parasites, they presumably rely heavily on social learning—that is, imitation of others that have already developed this behavior. Social learning of food preferences and aversions is well documented in several species, including rats (Galef, 1996), and it seems likely that chimpanzees would be highly adept at this kind of learning. Still, more field research and laboratory research will be needed to explore the possibility that chimpanzees have learned the medical value of certain plants.

REFERENCES

DiBattista, D., & Holder, M. D. (1998). Enhanced preference for a protein-containing diet in response to dietary protein restriction. *Appetite, 30,* 237-254.

Frankmann, S. P., Sollars, S. I., & Bernstein, I. L. (1996). Sodium appetite in the sham-drinking rat after chorda tympani nerve transection. *American Journal of Physiology, 40,* R339–R345.

Galef, B. G., Jr. (1996). Food selection: Problems in understanding how we choose foods to eat. *Neuroscience and Biobehavioral Reviews, 20,* 67–73.

Huffman, M. A. (2001). Self-medicative behavior in the African great apes: An evolutionary perspective into the origins of human traditional medicine. *BioScience, 51,* 651–661.

Lozano, G. A. (1998). Parasitic stress and self-medication in wild animals. *Advances in the Study of Behavior, 27,* 291–317.

Michener, W., Rozin, P., Freeman, E., & Gale, L. (1999). The role of low progesterone and tension as triggers of perimenstrual chocolate and sweets cravings: Some negative experimental evidence. *Physiology and Behavior, 67,* 417–420.

Nachman, M. (1962). Taste preferences for sodium salts by adrenalectomized rats. *Journal of Comparative and Physiological Psychology, 64,* 237–242.

Richter, C. P. (1943). The self-selection of diets. In *Essays in biology in honor of Herbert M. Evans* (pp. 501–505). Berkeley: University of California Press.

Richter, C. P. (1947). Biology of drives. *Journal of Comparative and Physiological Psychology, 40,* 129–134.

Richter, C. P. (1956). Salt appetite of mammals: Its dependence on instinct and metabolism. In P. P. Grasse (Ed.), *L'instinct dans le comportement des animaux et de l'homme* (pp. 577–632). Paris: Masson.

Rozin, P. (1967). Specific aversions as a component of specific hungers. *Journal of Comparative and Physiological Psychology, 64,* 237–242.

Rozin, P., & Kalat, J. W. (1971). Specific hungers and poison avoidance as adaptive specializations of learning. *Psychological Review, 78,* 459–486.

Scott, T. R. (1992). Taste: The neural basis of body wisdom. In A. P. Simopoulos (Ed.), *Nutritional triggers for health and in disease* (pp. 1–39). Basel: Karger.

Wang, Y., Cummings, S. L., & Gietzen, D. W. (1996). Temporal-spatial pattern of c-Fos expression in the rat brain in response to indispensable amino acid deficiency: 2. The learned taste aversion. *Molecular Brain Research, 40,* 35–41.

Wilkins, L., & Richter, C. P. (1940). A great craving for salt by a child with cortico-adrenal insufficiency. *Journal of the American Medical Association, 114,* 866–868.

James W. Kalat
North Carolina State University

SPEECH AND HEARING MEASURES

Clinical, industrial, forensic, and research purposes are among those served by speech and hearing measurement. The nature of the tests and procedures used depends on the purposes of the testing.

Speech-Language Measures

Speech Communication Systems

For purposes such as development of telephone fidelity, speech may be measured by experimental psychologists or engineers in terms of sound wave properties such as frequency, amplitude, and sound waveform. The amount of power given off by a speaker and the distribution of that power over time may also be measured. Researchers have devised graphical methods, which use mathematical Fourier analysis of the waveform, for analyzing speech into its component frequencies. Researchers also use electrical methods such as the sound spectrograph, which notes the changes in intensity-frequency pattern as a function of time. Visual patterns (spectrograms) may be obtained and compared for various words or phrases. The efficacy of speech communication systems may be measured by use of laboratory articulation testing methods. Forensic investigators and others may apply these patterns for voiceprints, which are unique to each individual. Speech and hearing scientists also use such methods in research.

Physiological Function

Physiological aspects of speech and voice production have been studied by such methods as electrophysiological and cinefluorographic methods. Studies of respiration may be tied to voice production, which requires a flow of air between the vocal bands. Computerized study of the variables of phonation (voice production) yields information that may be of both research and clinical use for determining deviant or disordered voice parameters. With ongoing development of technology, magnetic resonance imaging (MRI), functional magnetic resonance imaging (fMRI), positron emission tomography (PET scans), single photon emission computerized tomography (SPECT imaging), and computerized axial tomography (CAT, or CT, scans) may be used for studies of brain function of various aspects of both normally functioning and disordered speech and hearing activities. Such methods now permit observation of brain activity during specific tasks, rather than only conjecture and inference from aspects of overt behavior that previously could not be more centrally observed. In this way, researchers have been investigating ongoing aspects of listening, speaking, reading, writing, musical listening, singing, dyslexia, sign language usage, and other kindred language, speech, and hearing phenomena.

Language

Assessment of language disorders may include tests of various aspects of language function, such as grammar, syntax, pragmatics, sequencing, memory, word retrieval, and other subareas. These are viewed in relation to age, language environment, and other relevant information about the individual being tested. Numerous test instruments have been normed for various populations. These instruments can yield information about developmental level and potential development of disordered language when used by appropriately trained professionals for research or clinical purposes.

Both observational and experimental techniques for the measurement of various aspects of verbal context of speech and other areas of speech and language have been developed. Interdisciplinary approaches to child language have included consideration of sociological, psychological, physiological, linguistic, and other such variables.

Clinical Assessment of Speech-Language Function

Evaluation of speech-language function for clinical purposes entails assessment of one or more of a number of subareas of speech and language. These subareas may include auditory perception for speech and language function; articulation, or phonology (the production of speech sounds); voice, or phonation and resonance; language perception, processing, and production; and fluency (which includes stuttering). There are also instruments to evaluate pragmatics, or the appropriate use of speech and language in interactional context. Language and speech recall, memory, and sequencing functions, as well as phonological awareness of speech sounds (needed for reading and writing), may also be assessed.

Personnel qualified to administer clinical evaluations include certified speech-language pathologists and certified audiologists who have been awarded the Certificate of Clinical Competence (CCC) in speech-language or in audiology by the American Speech-Language-Hearing Association

(ASHA) based in Rockville, Maryland. State licensure may be alternate evidence of qualification. Audiologists have been developing additional certification criteria. When determining etiology and planning treatment of voice and hearing problems, referral for medical evaluation should always be considered in the assessment plan.

Although numerous standardized tests continue to be developed, because of the variability of multicultural and regional norms, speech-language evaluation frequently also includes informal assessment by qualified professionals to rule out misidentification of regional or bilingual patterns as being clinically diagnostic of disorders that are not there. Clinical assessment of bilingual speakers is a growing area of need that also requires the services of certified or licensed bilingual professionals.

Hearing Measurement

Measurement of hearing for research purposes has included study ranging from localization of sound in space to electrical responses from the central auditory system, in order to yield information that may be of both experimental and clinical interest.

Clinically, pure-tone audiometers generate vibrations that may be adjusted to vary the intensity (loudness) of tones ranging from low to high frequency (pitches). By indicating when each tone is heard, an individual may be assessed for the threshold of hearing throughout the audible range of frequencies. An audiogram is used to graph the results of the test. Hearing loss, in decibels, is recorded for frequencies tested. The type of hearing loss may then be determined by evaluating the data obtained from audiometric and other clinical tests. Middle-ear function may be assessed by audiologists and auditory researchers via indirect measurement of acoustic impedence that yields information about the mechanical properties of the middle-ear transmission system, which may be altered by the acoustic reflex of the muscles of the middle ear.

Technological Influences on Applications

Technological development has led to more direct translation of audiogram data into hearing aid design and adjustment to meet individual needs of hard-of-hearing people. Digital, reprogrammable hearing aids have also been developed. Cochlear implants may be used for infants and older individuals in specific cases of extreme deafness. At this time, such implants do not restore hearing but may transmit impulses from certain audible frequencies that, with therapeutic training, may provide assistance in identifying common sounds such as ringing telephones and doorbells. Cochlear implants may also be helpful in teaching oral speech recognition and production to profoundly deaf individuals. Ongoing technological advances have been yielding even further improvement in the benefit of such implants for some individuals.

Barbara B. Mates, Ph.D.
City College of New York, CUNY, and New School University, New York

SPORT-PERFORMANCE INTERVENTIONS

Conventional wisdom suggests that if athletes want to improve in sport, they should simply practice more. Often, however, what is lacking is not athletes' physical training, but rather their mental skills. Sport-performance interventions focusing on the ability to reach optimal performance states (i.e., the zone), management of arousal and anxiety, self-talk, imagery, goal setting, and modeling have been found to contribute positively to sport performance. Research indicates that performance-enhancement treatment packages that combine two or more of these psychological techniques are particularly effective.

Optimal Performance States

Some sport performances transcend the ordinary. In these instances, athletes may describe themselves as being "in the zone" or as having had a "peak performance." Athletes may also describe this experience as a "flow state," where they are totally involved in the present performance moment. Many sport psychology interventions are designed to help athletes enhance their psychological skills with the ultimate goal of helping athletes reach the peak performance state more often.

Arousal and Anxiety

People who experience anxiety in most situations are considered to have trait anxiety. This anxiety differs from the state anxiety that athletes may experience in sport-performance situations. State anxiety has cognitive (e.g., worry, emotional distress) and somatic (e.g., rapid heart rate, sweaty hands) components. Although a level of physiological arousal is necessary for sport performance, research indicates that excessive anxiety is associated with poor sport performances.

A number of theoretical models have been proposed to explain the relationship between arousal and performance (e.g., inverted-U theory, drive theory, individual zone of optimal functioning, and catastrophe theory). These theories all state that a minimum level of arousal is necessary for sport performance and that the amount of arousal that is needed for optimal performance differs across individuals and sport tasks. All of these theories except drive theory also posit that both underarousal and overarousal are associated with decrements in sport performance.

Athletes may use several strategies to manage their anxiety and arousal. Cognitive reappraisal approaches work on the assumption that excessive arousal is caused by problematic thought patterns. Changing particular cognitions or the situations that cause these cognitions can help moderate arousal levels, thus enhancing performance. Physiological anxiety-reduction interventions work by affecting physical parameters. For example, techniques such as diaphragmatic breathing and progressive relaxation have been shown to reduce physiological arousal. Hypnosis has also been used to help athletes regulate arousal and enhance performance.

Self-Talk

Self-talk, an overt or covert dialogue with oneself, has been used to help athletes focus attention, correct errors, maintain self-confidence, and moderate activation levels. Research has shown that use of positive or instructional self-talk is associated with enhanced performance. Although negative self-talk may serve a motivating function on occasion, its use has more widely been associated with poor sport performances. The mechanisms by which self-talk affects performance have not been determined.

Imagery

Imagery is the process by which stored sensory experiences are internally recalled and performed in the absence of external stimuli. Imagery can be used to build confidence, practice specific skills, control emotional reactions, improve concentration, practice strategy, and cope with pain and injury. When using imagery, athletes are typically advised to use all their senses, including the kinesthetic (movement) sense, to imagine positive sport outcomes. Many practitioners combine imagery with relaxation, but research has indicated no added benefit for using relaxation in combination with imagery.

Researchers have compared the performance effects of imagery alone to physical practice and to a combination of imagery and physical practice. Results indicate that the combination of imagery and physical practice is generally more effective in enhancing performance than is either physical practice or imagery alone. It should be noted, however, that the utility of imagery in enhancing performance for any particular athlete may depend on the personality, skills, and task involved. As with physical sport skills, the effectiveness of imagery for sport performance enhancement is improved by practice.

Goal Setting

A goal is something that an individual is trying to accomplish, an objective or an aim. A body of research literature in sport and industrial settings has demonstrated that difficult, specific, and challenging goals lead to better performance than do easy goals, vague ("do your best") goals, or no goals. Additional goal-setting strategies have been suggested to enhance performance, including setting long- and short-term goals, setting goals for practice and competitions, writing down goals, setting individual and team goals, developing goal-achievement strategies, providing support for goals, and evaluating goals.

A number of variables that interfere with the effective implementation of goal setting have been identified. Common goal setting problems include (1) failing to set specific, measurable goals; (2) setting too many goals at the beginning; and (3) failing to monitor and readjust goals.

Modeling

Modeling, or observational learning, has been used by athletes to modify sport-related thoughts, emotions, and behaviors. Research indicates that observing models who are learning skills at or near the skill level of the athlete and hearing the feedback that those models receive is more effective in enhancing performance than is watching models who can perform a skill flawlessly. Overall, athletes who are motivated and attend to the model, remember what was presented, and attempt to reproduce what they have observed benefit most from modeling interventions.

Sport Psychology Consultants

Sport-performance intervention services are provided to athletes primarily by sport psychologists. Because sport psychology is an interdisciplinary field, sport psychology practitioners may be trained in psychology, the sport sciences, or both. The Association for the Advancement of Applied Sport Psychology (AAASP) certifies professionals with specialized training and applied experience in sport psychology. Members who are certified consultants are listed on the organization's web site at http://www.aaasponline.org. The United States Olympic Committee also maintains a registry of sport psychology consultants.

Summary

A number of techniques (e.g., management of arousal and anxiety, self-talk, imagery, goal setting, and modeling) have been used to enhance sport performance. Use of these sport-performance interventions may help athletes reach optimal performance states more easily and often. Using sport psychology intervention strategies in combination and practicing them regularly may be particularly useful in enhancing sport performance.

Judy L. Van Raalte
Britton W. Brewer
Springfield College

See also: **Anxiety; Modeling; Sport Psychology**

SPORT PSYCHOLOGY

The discipline of sport psychology is dedicated to the investigation of the relationship between psychological factors and exercise and sport. Sport scientists and sport psychologists use physical activity settings to examine issues of competition, performance enhancement, skill acquisition, children's development through sport, team interaction, and the maintenance of physical and mental health.

In 1897 Triplett (1897) conducted what is considered to be the first sport psychology experiment. He found that cyclists competing against other individuals performed better than those performing against the clock or against a standard goal. Coleman Griffith is often credited with founding the first sport psychology laboratory in 1925 at the University of Illinois. He was known for his rigorous investigations of psychomotor skill development, learning theory applied to sport, and the role of personality in performance. In the 1930s he joined the Chicago Cubs organization and became the first psychologist in professional sports.

Development in the field proceeded slowly until the 1960s, when Olgive and Tutko (1966) attempted to integrate psychological assessment and personality theory into sport psychology by developing a test that they hoped would help predict athletic performance. During this same period, Richardson (1967) and other researchers began exploring imagery or mental practice interventions for performance enhancement. However, it was not until 1972 that Richard Suinn (1972) brought sport psychology into contact with contemporary clinical psychology when he applied cognitive-behavioral interventions to athletes in an attempt to improve performance. He reported that training elite skiers in relaxation and imagery skills, combined with a behavioral rehearsal technique, improved performance. Based on Suinn's (1972) work, mental practice interventions for performance enhancement became more intricate and began to resemble the growing body of clinical interventions.

In addition to imagery and mental rehearsal, modern sport psychology encompasses a broad range of interventions directed at improving performance. A major focus of these efforts has been on athletes' ability to manage arousal and anxiety. Many interventions include an anxiety management component intended to allow athletes to modify their level of arousal to match the demands of competition. These interventions mirror the clinical anxiety reduction, stress management, and problem-solving motivational work prevalent with clients experiencing anxiety or depression.

Sport psychologists are also interested in goal setting and its effects on performance. This work has been influenced by industrial-organizational psychology, in which the use of goal setting has become a reliable technique for behavior change. Goal setting is thought to enhance motivation for involvement and promote more positive self-evaluation of training and competitive performance. These changes may facilitate task performance and thus lead to performance change.

Kirschenbaum (Kirschenbaum & Bale, 1980) proposed that athletic skill development can be viewed as a self-regulatory process and that performance is a test of the athlete's skill in self-directed cognition and action. Self-monitoring and self-instruction interventions are used to teach athletes successfully to execute a physical skill, monitor their performance, evaluate their performance against some standard or goal, and alter the execution of physical skills. Such processes are intended to enable athletes to transfer their performance-improvement skills to other tasks and settings.

Although these intervention strategies for performance enhancement should be relevant to athletes of all ages and skill levels, most controlled evaluations of these interventions occur with nonelite and recreational athletes. A quantitative review of such studies found that these interventions are more effective than control conditions (Whelan, Meyers, & Donovan, 1995).

Although performance enhancement is the most visible component of sport psychology, the field is much broader. Another major area of research is sport and exercise behavior across the life span. Sport psychologists are interested in physical skill acquisition and development and focus on such areas as modeling of skills, attention in skill acquisition and performance, and decision making. Other topics include children's psychological development through sport, children's motivation for participation in sport, why children discontinue participation in sport, stress and burnout, and effective coaching practices in youth sport.

Much of sport and exercise takes place in a group or team context. Thus, sport psychologists are also interested in group dynamics. Attention is given to issues such as what makes a group successful, the development and characteristics of leaders of successful groups, and the development and deterioration of group cohesion.

It is accepted that regular participation in sport and exercise enhances an individual's physical health. Sport psychologists also attempt to understand how participating in physical activity affects an individual's psychological well-being. Research has indicated that aerobic exercise is associated with reductions in levels of anxiety and depression. Exercise has also shown positive effects on other aspects of emotional life, including increasing feelings of control as well as improving self-confidence and cognitive functioning. The psychological and physiological benefits associated with exercise throughout the life span support the increasing importance of exercise as one ages.

Exposure at the 1984 Los Angeles Olympic Games brought a dramatic increase in attention to the field of sport psychology, as well as a corresponding increase in the growth of the field. Several journals dedicated to disseminating information in the area of sport and exercise psychology were introduced. These journals include the *Journal of Applied Sport Psychology,* the *Journal of Sport and Exercise Psychology,* and the *Sport Psychologist.* Several professional organizations are dedicated to the advancement of sport and exercise psychology, including the Association for the Advancement of Applied Sport Psychology, Division 47 of the American Psychological Association, and the North American Society for the Psychology of Sport and Physical Activity. Members of these organizations include psychologists and sport scientists who study psychological influences on sport and physical activity. In addition to the dissemination of new and relevant research, these organizations are also committed to establishing and upholding professional standards for the competent and ethical practice of sport psychology.

Although it has been over a century since the initial empirical investigation of psychological influences on sport behavior, the science and profession of sport psychology are broad and vibrant. Performance enhancement may be the most visible domain of sport psychology, but the field includes the study of children and the elderly, teams and leaders, and emotional as well as physical health. With sport and exercise continuing to play a meaningful role in our culture, the study of these behaviors will continue to have a place in the science and practice of psychology.

REFERENCES

Kirschenbaum, D. S., & Bale, R. M. (1980). Cognitive-behavioral skills in golf: Brain power golf. In R. M. Suinn (Ed.), *Psychology in sports: Methods and application* (pp. 334–343). Minneapolis: Burgess.

Ogilve, B. C., & Tutko, T. A. (1966). *Problem athletes and how to handle them.* London: Pelham.

Richardson, A. (1967). Mental Practice: A review and discussion: Part I. *The Research Quarterly, 38,* 95–107.

Suinn, R. M. (1972). Behavioral rehearsal training for ski racers. *Behavior Therapy, 3,* 519–520.

Triplett, N. (1897). The dynamic factors in peacemaking and competition. *American Journal of Psychology, 9,* 507–533.

Whelan, J. P, Meyers, A. W., & Donovan, C. (1995). Competitive recreational athletes: A multisystemic model. In S. M. Murphy (Ed.), *Sport psychology interventions* (pp. 71–110). Champaign, IL: Human Kinetics.

Ryan K. May
Marietta College

Andrew W. Meyers
University of Memphis

STATISTICAL INFERENCE

The process of drawing conclusions about a population on the basis of samples (in effect, subsets) drawn randomly from the population is statistical inference. It is widely used in psychology because whole populations can rarely be measured. The logic of statistical inference is the same regardless of the particular problem and techniques employed. On the basis of a sample, the researcher wishes to make statements about what is probably true of the population.

Measures taken on samples are called *statistics;* comparable measures of the population are called *population parameters.* A statistic is calculated on a specific and finite set of data. It will not necessarily equal the population parameter unless the sample is infinitely large, thus including the whole population. Instead, any sample is likely to yield statistics that differ from the true population parameters. The problem becomes one of deciding how accurately each statistic reflects the corresponding population parameters. The application of statistical inference, therefore, requires knowledge of probability theory.

The actual process of statistical inference often begins with setting up the *null hypothesis* (H_0): The researcher assumes that a sample statistic (commonly a mean) was drawn from a population with known parameters. If comparisons between samples are required, the researcher assumes that each group (and its corresponding statistics) was sampled from the same population.

The null hypothesis is retained or rejected on the basis of how likely the observed outcome is. Standardized *test statistics* (such as z, t, F, and chi-square), whose values have known probabilities, are used to evaluate sample statistics in relation to variability. If the difference between groups is largely relative to the amount of variability in the data, the researcher rejects the null hypothesis and concludes that the observed difference was unlikely to have occurred by chance alone: The result is statistically significant. In psychology, researchers customarily reject the null hypothesis if the observed outcome (in effect, the computed test statistic) is so extreme that it could have occurred by chance with a probability of less than 5% ($p < 0.05$).

Because statistical inferences are based on probability estimates, two incorrect decisions are possible: Type 1 errors, in which the null hypothesis is rejected although true, and Type 2 errors, in which the null hypothesis is retained although invalid. The former results in incorrect confirmation of the research hypothesis and the latter in the failure to identify a statistically significant result.

A. Myers

STATISTICAL POWER

Hypothesis testing involves contrasting two rival hypotheses. The null hypothesis specifies that nothing special is happening. The alternative hypothesis specifies that something is happening. For example, the null hypothesis might state that two groups have the same mean or that the correlation between two variables is zero. The alternative hypothesis can be directional or nondirectional. A directional hypothesis states the direction of the phenomenon; for example, Group 1 has a higher mean than Group 2, or the correlation is larger than zero. A nondirectional hypothesis does not specify the direction of the effect but states that the effect does exist; for example, the two groups have different means, or the correlation is not zero. Statisticians begin by assuming that the null hypothesis is true and reject the null hypothesis only if the observed results are quite unlikely under this assumption. Based on some assumptions concerning the study, for example, a random sample, and a normally distributed dependent variable, the researcher can calculate the probability of rejecting the null hypothesis when it is true (alpha) and the probability of rejecting the null hypothesis when the alternative hypothesis is true (the statistical power of the test). Because the researcher wants to reach the correct conclusion, good studies are designed to have low alpha and high power. A correct null hypothesis is unlikely to be rejected if alpha is low, and a correct alternative hypothesis is likely to be concluded if power is high.

Researchers generally use an alpha level that is no larger than .05. They reject the null hypothesis only if the sample results are in the extreme 5% of the range of possible outcomes if the null hypothesis were true. When the null hypothesis is rejected, the researcher concludes that the results are statistically significant and generally specifies the significance probability, that is, the alpha associated with the outcome. For example, the researcher may conclude that the correlation is significant, $p < .01$, meaning that the null hypothesis of zero correlation could be rejected using an alpha less than .01. A more extreme result has a smaller significance probability, such as $p < .005$ or $p < .0001$.

Because the traditional approach is designed to keep alpha low, researchers must be careful to ensure that the power of their tests is reasonably high. Power estimates can be made before data are collected, and research studies with insufficient power can be redesigned to improve power. There are four principal strategies to increase power: increase alpha, specify directional hypotheses, increase the sample size, and increase the effect size.

Increasing alpha increases power. Researchers are more likely to reject the null hypothesis when alpha is higher, so they become more likely to conclude that a correct alternative hypothesis is true. A second way to increase power is to specify directional hypotheses. This allows the researcher to concentrate the alpha risk at only those outcomes that are consistent with the directional hypothesis. For example, a test on a correlation coefficient using a nondirectional hypothesis and an alpha of .05 might reject the null hypothesis for observed correlations below –.60 or above +.60. Outcomes between –.60 and +.60 are expected to occur 95% of the time when the null hypothesis is true, whereas outcomes outside of this range are expected only 5% of the time in this situation. If the researcher could specify a directional hypothesis, such as a positive correlation, the decision might be to reject the null hypothesis for all correlations above +.55. If the observed correlation were .58, the researcher could not reject the null hypothesis for the nondirectional hypothesis but could reject the null hypothesis for the directional hypothesis, giving the test more power. (Unfortunately, if the directional hypothesis postulates the wrong direction, the researcher will not find significant results and will be in error.) A third way to increase power is to increase the sample size. Statistics based on larger samples are more stable, allowing more precise estimation of population characteristics. This increased precision makes it more likely that correct alternative hypotheses are detected. The last way to increase power is to increase the effect size. The effect size is the strength of the relationship being studied. For example, to demonstrate that different types of birds have different sized eggs, one could compare ostriches to hummingbirds, with an enormous effect size, rather than compare chickens with ducks, with a smaller effect size. Studies examining large effect sizes are more likely to reject the null hypothesis, giving them more power.

Researchers want studies with low alpha and high power so that they are likely to reach accurate conclusions. They generally control alpha by not allowing it to exceed .05, and they have strategies to increase power. A well-designed study may have a larger alpha, a directional hypothesis, a large sample size, or a large effect size. Researchers consider all these options when they design studies so that they are likely to reach accurate conclusions about the variables being studied.

Mary J. Allen
California State University
Office of the Chancellor

See also: **Hypothesis Testing**

STATISTICAL SIGNIFICANCE

Researchers often employ statistical tests to evaluate the results of their studies. The term *statistical significance* is used in relation to the use of these tests. If a researcher's results or data reflect statistical significance, an interpretation that the outcomes are not likely due to chance is thought appropriate.

Statistical tests basically evaluate the results of an investigation in light of chance occurrences. These tests permit the researcher to assess the probability that such results might have been due to chance. For example, one might be comparing the recall performance of two groups and find that there were mean correct responses of 25 and

42 for Groups A and B respectively. It is important for the researcher to determine how frequently such differences might be expected by chance alone.

The term *statistically significant* is applied to results where the probability of chance is equal to or below an agreed-upon level. Most psychologists accept a 5% (or lower) probability of chance as being statistically significant. This is typically reported as $p < .05$, which means that if the study were replicated 100 times, these same results would attain fewer than five times due to chance. Another frequently used level of significance is the 1% level, which is generally reported as $p < .01$. In this case one would expect to observe the results by chance only one time out of 100. These significance levels are based on convention and are widely accepted, but they are not derived from mathematical justification. There are some differences among various disciplines regarding what is considered statistically significant.

Statistical significance may be determined for both tests of difference and tests of relationship. For difference questions, one can establish how often such differences would be obtained due to chance. For relationship questions, one can assess how often a given relationship level (correlation coefficient) would be observed due to chance. Statistical significance and the resulting decision regarding the likelihood of an effect due to chance are influenced considerably by the research design employed.

SUGGESTED READINGS

Aron, A., & Aron, E. N. (1999). *Statistics for psychology* (2nd ed.). Upper Saddle River, NJ: Prentice Hall.

Cortina, J. M., & Dunlap, W. P. (1997). On the logic and purpose of significance testing. *Psychological Methods, 2,* 161–172.

Kurtz, N. R. (1999). *Statistical analysis for the social sciences.* Boston: Allyn & Bacon.

McClelland, G. H. (1997). Optimal design in psychological research. *Psychological Methods, 2,* 3–19.

Thompson, B., & Snyder, P. A. (1998). Statistical significance and reliability analyses in recent *Journal of Counseling and Development* research articles. *Journal of Counseling and Development, 76,* 436–441.

Clifford J. Drew
University of Utah

See also: **Probability**

STEPCHILDREN

Studies of stepfathers suggest that the entrance of a stepfather into a previously father-absent home has a positive effect on boys' cognitive and personality development; the effects on girls' cognitive and personality development are virtually uncharted. In one observational study of family interaction in stepfather, divorced-mother custody, and intact families, boys in stepfather families showed more competent social behavior than did boys in intact families. By contrast, girls in stepfather families were observed to be more anxious than girls in intact families. Boys showed more warmth toward their stepfather than did girls. Boys in stepfather families also tended to show more mature behavior than did boys from divorced homes.

In a recent comparison of children in father-custody, stepmother, and intact families, observations indicated some consistent sex differences: Boys were observed to be less competent during social interaction with both their stepmother and their biological father than were girls. Combined with the data collected by Santrock and colleagues on stepfather families, an intriguing scenario of sex of child, sex of custodial parent, and type of stepparent family unfolds. During the early years of the stepfamily, children are confronted with many changes, adjustments, and possible new attachments. The disequilibrium created by the father's remarriage seems to produce a positive effect for his daughter but a negative effect for his son. His children have already undergone at least one major traumatic change in their lives, that is, the severing of their parents' marriage. Several years after the divorce, boys whose fathers have obtained custody seem to have adjusted well, and the same is true for girls whose mothers have custody. The entrance of a stepmother may produce conflict for a boy, and the entrance of a stepfather may do the same for girls.

John W. Santrock

STEPPARENTS

The number of remarriages in which children are involved has been growing steadily. Approximately 10% to 15% of all households in the United States are comprised of stepfamilies. A review of the stepparent literature presents mixed findings. Some researchers have found no differences between stepparent and intact families, whereas others have found significant differences suggesting that stepparent families have more difficulties and problems.

Although an extensive amount of information about divorced families has been obtained in recent years, the efforts to understand the psychological climate of stepparent families have not been as extensive. One recent investigation represents the first attempt to observe actual social interaction in stepparent families. The most consistent findings suggested that the stepfather and biological mother showed more competent parenting when the child was a male than was the case for comparable intact families. Further analyses indicated that, in the sample studied, marital conflict was greater in the intact-family boy's home than in the stepfather boy's home. These data clearly suggest that parenting techniques in stepparent families are not necessarily inferior to those in intact families.

There are virtually no data that compare stepfather or stepmother families with divorced-mother or father-custody families. Mothers with custody seem to have a particularly difficult time with sons, and some evidence suggests that fathers with custody may be more competent in rearing sons than daughters.

John W. Santrock

STIMULUS GENERALIZATION

Stimulus generalization refers to a tendency to respond to a stimulus similar in character to, and yet discriminably different from, a stimulus to which the animal was originally trained. Pavlov (1927) and his associates first demonstrated this phenomenon in laboratory experiments with dogs. After experiencing a succession of paired stimuli, such as a tone with food, the dog eventually comes to salivate reliably to the tone. If a test phase is instituted following this training so that the dog experiences tones varying in similarity to the original tone but without the food, its responding to the new stimuli declines as the test stimuli became more dissimilar to the training stimulus. This outcome is referred to as stimulus generalization, and this gradient of responding reflects the extent to which the training stimulus controls responding. A flat gradient implies that the original stimulus exercises little control over the response; in other words, there is complete generalization. In contrast, a steep gradient suggests little or no generalization; responding is confined largely to the training stimulus. Although the demonstration of generalization gradients appears straightforward, their measurement, the variables that affect them, and their role in the learning process are complex.

Stimulus similarity is usually measured with reference to some physical dimension of the stimulus such as wavelength, size, or intensity, although psychophysical units are used occasionally. The number of responses made to each test stimulus results in an *absolute* generalization gradient. Absolute gradients can be transformed into *relative* gradients by expressing responses to a test stimulus as a proportion of the total number of responses made to all stimuli during the test phase or to responses made previously to the training stimulus. Relative gradients correct for conditions in which wide variation in responding exists among subjects. Which type of gradient to use depends on whether the scale corrects for floor or ceiling effects, remains unchanged when a manipulated variable has no effect on the gradient, or makes the results consistent with other experiments. A common practice is to report both types of gradients.

Schedules of reinforcement, degrees of learning to the training stimulus, and the animal's motivational state influence the extent to which responses generalize to other stimuli. In early studies, reinforcement followed the training stimulus on every occasion. A disadvantage with this procedure was that limited responding occurred to test stimuli because each test trial was also an extinction trial. To offset extinction effects, researchers began reinforcing training stimuli intermittently; however, it was soon apparent that reinforcement schedules directly affected the generalization gradients. Schedules influence the extent to which incidental contextual cues present during the training and test phases affect responding. For example, when the average time interval between reinforcements is lengthened, responding to test stimuli increases, which results in flatter gradients (Haber & Kalish, 1963; Hearst, Koresko, & Poppen, 1964). Presumably, response-produced stimuli that occur during the interval between reinforcements provide additional information as to when the reinforcement will occur, and this stimulation is still present during the generalization test phase (Thomas & Switalski, 1966).

As a general rule, the more experience with the training stimulus prior to generalization testing, the less generalization is observed. In effect, more training results in a steeper gradient (Hearst & Koresko, 1968; Razran, 1971). An exception occurs when external stimulation is uniform and proprioceptive cues control responding. Under this condition the gradient is flat regardless of the training received on the original stimulus (Margoluis, 1955; Walker & Branch, 1998).

Interest in motivational effects on stimulus control stems from Hull's (1943) hypothesis that motivation and habit combine multiplicatively to determine performance. This counterintuitive notion predicts that performance improves with higher levels of motivation, implying higher and steeper absolute gradients with increasing motivation. Although the results of several studies support the hypothesis (e.g., Newman & Grice, 1965), others report contrary findings (e.g., Broen, Stroms, & Goldberg, 1963). Resolution of this issue came from the recognition that motivation's effect on stimulus generalization depends on the discriminability between training and test stimuli. If the discrimination between training and test stimuli is easy, high levels of motivation produce steep slopes. However, when the stimuli are difficult to discriminate, higher levels of motivation result in flatter gradients (Kalish & Haber, 1965).

Gradients may be either excitatory or inhibitory. Excitatory gradients are generated by a decline in responding as test stimuli become more dissimilar to the training stimulus. In contrast, stimuli predicting the absence of reinforcement control the tendency not to respond, and this control can be measured by an increase in responding as the similarity between the original inhibitory stimulus and the test stimuli decreases (Honig, Boneau, Burstein, & Pennypacker, 1963; Jenkins & Harrison, 1962; Karpicke & Hearst, 1975).

Learning theories assign an important theoretical role to stimulus generalization. It not only facilitates survival—behavior resulting in finding food, securing a mate, or escaping a predator may generalize to new but similar situations—but it is also viewed as a process that underlies more complex learning phenomena (Hull, 1943; Spence, 1936).

Conditioning-extinction theory is a major representative of this approach (Hull, 1943, 1952; Spence, 1956). The theory assumes that excitation (a tendency to respond) develops to a stimulus paired with reinforcement and that the excitation generalizes to other similar stimuli. Similarity, inhibition (a tendency not to respond) accrues to the stimulus predicting the absence of reinforcement, and the tendency not to respond also generalizes to similar stimuli. If the original excitatory and inhibitory stimuli are situated along the same physical continuum, there may be an overlap of excitatory and inhibitory gradients. This overlap in the gradients allows for the arousal of contradictory impulses of responding or not responding among the stimuli. Eventually, the animal chooses one stimulus over another because the net excitation (excitation minus inhibition) of the selected stimulus exceeds the net excitation of the unselected stimulus. Conditioning-extinction theory was extended with some success to complex discrimination phenomena such as the peak shift effect, transfer of discrimination, and transposition (Hanson, 1959; Logan, 1971; Spence, 1942).

Even so, the original cast of the theory can account neither for the selective nature of associations nor for the development and utilization of cognitive strategies. In its original form it assumed that any detectable stimulus serving as a signal for reinforcement or nonreinforcement would acquire excitatory or inhibitory properties. But this is not the case: The organization of the neural apparatus determines whether associations between conjoint events will be formed (Garcia & Koelling, 1966), which determines whether stimuli activate tendencies to respond or not. Moreover, the formation of associations depends on the animal's previous learning history. Stimuli that provide no new information about impending events or that are less reliable or valid predictors of reinforcement form either no or weakened associations with significant and consequential events that they precede, as is the case in blocking (Kamin, 1968) and learned overshadowing (Rickert, Lorden, Dawson, Smyly, & Callahan, 1979; Wagner, Logan, Haberlandt, & Price, 1968). The decrement in responding to either redundant or less valid stimuli in the blocking and learned overshadowing paradigms is much greater than the theory predicts. Although efforts to accommodate these phenomena have met with some success (e.g., Rescorla & Wagner, 1972), this version has difficulty predicting the magnitude of generalization decrements in related phenomena (e.g., external inhibition).

More recently, Pearce (1987) suggested that the inability of previous theories to accommodate some of these findings rests on their assuming that the context in which the stimulus is presented has no effect on the stimulus's capacity to elicit responding. Pearce's model argues that context is crucial in determining the extent of generalization. The model posits a limited-capacity memory buffer that stores the current overall pattern of stimulation. If this pattern is followed by a reinforcing event, the representation is stored as a stimulus-reinforcement association in long-term memory. On a later occasion, any change in context results in a stimulus pattern that produces a different content in the buffer, resulting in the formation of a slightly different association. The strength of responding is determined by the correspondence or similarity between the original and the later association.

Pearce's account of stimulus generalization accommodates a wide range of phenomena. When events only moderately correlated with an outcome are paired with either an event that perfectly predicts the occurrence of an outcome or one that predicts its absence, humans judge such events as less valid than they actually are, a finding consistent with Pearce's model (Baker, Vallee-Tourangeau, & Murphy, 2000). Nakajima (1998) trained pigeons to arrays of compound stimuli. In the test phase, during which the positive and negative features of these stimuli were rearranged in different ways, responses to the new compounds were consistent with deductions from the model. Other results that are also consistent with the model have shown that a cue's validity in signaling impending events is jointly determined by the cue and its context (Murphy, Baker, & Fougnet, 2001).

Although the scope of associative theory can apparently be widened to accommodate processes of associative selection, understanding the relation between cognitive processes and associative mechanisms appears necessary to provide a complete account of discrimination and generalization. For example, applying rules to solve discrimination problems may result in behavior that cannot be accommodated in current theories. Learning set reversals was an early example. Bessemer and Stollnitz (1971) found that monkeys abandon response tendencies associated with reinforcement and choose objects previously paired with nonreinforcement based on information from the immediately preceding trial. These data suggest that the use of generalization as an explanatory device requires specifying the conditions under which it and these more complex processes interact.

REFERENCES

Baker, A. G., Vallee-Tourangeau, F., & Murphy, R. A. (2000). Asymptotic judgment of cause in a relative validity paradigm. *Memory and Cognition, 28,* 466–479.

Bessemer, D., & Stollnitz, F. (1971). Retention of discriminations and an analysis of learning sets. In A. M. Schrier & F. Stollnitz (Eds.), *Behavior of nonhuman primates* (Vol. 4, pp. 1–58). New York: Academic Press.

Broen, W. E., Jr., Stroms, L. H., & Goldberg, D. H. (1963). Decreased discrimination as a function of increased drive. *Journal of Abnormal and Social Psychology, 67,* 345–352.

Garcia, J., & Koelling, R. A. (1966). The relation of cue to consequence in avoidance learning. *Psychonomic Science, 4,* 123–124.

Haber, A., & Kalish, H. I. (1963). Prediction of discrimination from generalization after variations in schedules of reinforcement. *Science, 142,* 412–413.

Hanson, H. M. (1959). Effects of discrimination training on stimulus generalization. *Journal of Experimental Psychology, 58,* 321–333.

Hearst, E., & Koresko, M. B. (1968). Stimulus generalization and the amount of prior training on variable-interval reinforcement. *Journal of Comparative and Physiological Psychology, 66,* 133–138.

Hearst, E., Koresko, M. B., & Poppen, R. (1964). Stimulus generalization and the response-reinforcement contingency. *Journal of the Experimental Analysis of Behavior, 7,* 369–380.

Honig, W. K., Boneau, C. A., Burstein, K. R., & Pennypacker, H. S. (1963). Positive and negative generalization gradients obtained under equivalent training conditions. *Journal of Comparative and Physiological Psychology, 56,* 111–116.

Hull, C. L. (1943). *Principles of behavior.* New York: Appleton-Century-Crofts.

Hull, C. L. (1952). *A behavior system.* New Haven, CT: Yale University Press.

Jenkins, H. M., & Harrison, R. H. (1962). Effect of discrimination training on auditory generalization. *Journal of Experimental Psychology, 59,* 246–253.

Kalish, H. I., & Haber, A. (1965). The prediction of discrimination from generalization following variations in deprivation level. *Journal of Comparative and Physiological Psychology, 60,* 125–128.

Kamin, L. J. (1968). Predictability, surprise, attention, and conditioning. In B. Campbell & R. Church (Eds.), *Punishment and aversive behavior* (pp. 279–296). New York: Appleton-Century-Crofts.

Karpicke, J., & Hearst, E. (1975). Inhibitory control and errorless discrimination learning. *Journal of the Experimental Analysis of Behavior, 23,* 159–166.

Logan, F. A. (1971). Essentials of a theory of discrimination learning. In H. H. Kendler & J. T. Spence (Eds.), *Essays in neobehaviorism: A memorial volume to Kenneth W. Spence* (pp. 265–282). New York: Appleton-Century-Crofts.

Margolius, G. (1955). Stimulus generalization of an instrumental response as a function of the number of reinforced trials. *Journal of Experimental Psychology, 49,* 105–111.

Murphy, R. A., Baker, A. G., & Fougnet, N. (2001). Relative validity of contextual and discrete cues. *Journal of Experimental Psychology: Animal behavior processes, 27,* 137–152.

Nakajima, S. (1998). Further investigation of responding elicited by BC and C after A+, AB–, ABC+ training. *Quarterly Journal of Experimental Psychology Section B: Comparative and physiological psychology, 51,* 289–300.

Newman, J. R., & Grice, G. R. (1965). Stimulus generalization as a function of drive level, and the relation between two levels of response strength. *Journal of Experimental Psychology, 69,* 357–365.

Pavlov, I. P. (1927). *Conditioned reflexes* (G. V. Anrep, Trans.). London: Oxford University Press.

Pearce, J. M. (1987). A model for stimulus generalization in Pavlovian conditioning. *Psychological Review, 94,* 61–73.

Razran, G. (1971). *Mind in evolution.* Boston: Houghton Mifflin.

Rescorla, R. A., & Wagner, A. G. (1972). A theory of Pavlovian conditioning: Variations in the effectiveness of reinforcement and nonreinforcement. In A. Black & W. F. Prokasy (Eds.), *Classical conditioning II* (pp. 64–99). New York: Appleton-Century-Crofts.

Rickert, E. J., Lorden, J. F., Dawson, R., Jr., Smyly, E., & Callahan, M. F. (1979). Stimulus processing and stimulus selection in rats with hippocampal lesions. *Behavioral and Neural Biology, 27,* 454–465.

Spence, K. W. (1936). The nature of discrimination learning in animals. *Psychological Review, 44,* 430–444.

Spence, K. W. (1942). The basis of solution by chimpanzees of the intermediate size problem. *Journal of Experimental Psychology, 31,* 257–271.

Spence, K. W. (1956). *Behavior theory and conditioning.* New Haven, CT: Yale University Press.

Thomas, D. R., & Switalski, R. W. (1966). Comparison of stimulus generalization following variable-ratio and variable-interval training. *Journal of Experimental Psychology, 71,* 236–240.

Wagner, A. R., Logan, F. A., Haberlandt, K., & Price, T. (1968). Stimulus selection in animal discrimination learning. *Journal of Experimental Psychology, 76,* 171–180.

Walker, D. J., & Branch, M. N. (1998). Effects of variable-interval value and amount of training on stimulus generalization. *Journal of the Experimental Analysis of Behavior, 70,* 139–163.

Edward J. Rickert
Georgia Institute of Technology

See also: **Contextualism**

STRESS CONSEQUENCES

Stressors encountered by humans may comprise major insults ranging from the loss of loved ones, unexpected calamities (hurricane, tornado, flood, war, accident), and financial distress, or they may involve a series of day-to-day annoying experiences. Both the severe and less intrusive stressors may influence physiological and behavioral processes, and both have been implicated in the provocation or exacerbation of a large number of illnesses, including the classical psychosomatic disorders and depressive illness, cardiovascular disease, as well as those that involve immune dysfunction.

The *stress response* has been considered as the homeostatic or adaptive biological and/or behavioral response (allostasis) to a stimulus that is appraised as being aversive. In general, stressors elicit behavioral responses to attenuate the challenge, and concurrently peripheral and central nervous system neurochemical alterations occur that may be of adaptive significance. Among other things, they may be essential in order that animals be prepared to respond appropriately to impending as well as ongoing stressors. Moreover, these biological changes may be necessary for the organism to react with appropriate emotional and behavioral responses, initiate and maintain effective defensive strategies, initiate processes that will protect the organism from pathogenic stimuli, limit overreaction of other neurochemical systems that might themselves lead to pathology, and minimize the physical and psychological impact of the aversive stimuli.

One of the fundamental, and most frequently examined, physiological responses elicited by stressors is the activation of the hypothalamic-pituitary-adrenal (HPA) axis. This system is readily stimulated not only by psychological or physical stressors but also by systemic stressors (e.g., immune activation), although they may do so by activation of a different neural circuit. Ordinarily, when a stressor is encountered, the paraventricular nucleus of the hypothalamus is activated, giving rise to the release of corticotropin-releasing hormone (CRH) from terminals located at the median eminence. This hormone stimulates the anterior pituitary, promoting the release of ACTH into circulation, which in turn stimulates the release of cortisol (or corticosterone) from the adrenal cortex. Cortisol is thought to play an integral role in facilitating adequate responses to stressful events and may serve to prevent overshoot of immune reactions.

It would be most adaptive for certain neurochemical responses to be mounted rapidly, regardless of the psychological attributes of the stressors (e.g., controllable vs. uncontrollable; predictable vs. unpredictable). Those systems that are necessary for immediate responses to contend with stressors (e.g., activation of the sympathetic nervous system), and even fundamental immune responses that act against pathogenic stimuli, should react comparably to both controllable and uncontrollable stressors. In contrast, those central systems that are uniquely involved in the appraisal of stressors would be influenced by the psychological attributes of the stressor. It is well known, for instance, that uncontrollable stressors provoke behavioral disturbances (reminiscent of depressive states) that are not as readily induced by controllable stressors. Some investigators have interpreted these differences as reflecting learned helplessness provoked as animals learn that they have no control over their environment. Others, however, have attributed the behavioral disturbances to the neurochemical alterations that may be unique to uncontrollable aversive events. Generally, stressors promote increased utilization and synthesis of neurotransmitters within particular regions of the brain. These include norepinephrine (NE), dopamine (DA), serotonin (5-HT), acetylcholine (ACh), GABA, and various peptides. Under conditions where behavioral control over the stressor is unavailable, greater strain is placed on neuronal systems, and consequently they may become overly taxed. The excessive utilization of neurotransmitters (or the decline of the transmitter secondary to excessive utilization) in certain brain regions may result in a net decline of the transmitter, thus leading to greater vulnerability to pathological states.

In addition to the immediate effects, stressful events may proactively influence the response to later stressor experiences. It seems that stressors may result in the sensitization of processes that promote central neurochemical functioning so that reexposure to the same stressor (and even to alternate stressors) at a later time may result in the neurochemical changes occurring more readily. Thus, such sensitization processes may contribute to the induction of stressor-related illnesses even at lengthy intervals following a trauma and may be responsible for the high rates of relapse associated with illnesses such as depression. It is important to note that in addition to simple sensitization effects, cross-sensitization has been observed so that stressors increase the response to drugs such as amphetamine and cocaine. Likewise, it has been shown that the administration of cytokines, signaling molecules of the immune system, may result in a sensitization effect so that the response is vastly increased on their reexposure. Thus, in considering the impact of stressors, one should consider not only the immediate repercussions but also the increased vulnerability that develops to later stressor experiences. It is also important to note that the sensitization grows with the passage of time and hence may be a contributing factor to illnesses that likewise appear to be linked to temporal processes (e.g., posttraumatic stress disorder).

The proactive effects of stressors are particularly notable among animals that had encountered distress early in life. For instance, studies in animals have shown that when pups are separated from the mother for several hours a day during early postnatal development, the adult response to stressors is particularly pronounced. In contrast, those animals that received early life stimulation (particularly those that received frequent licking and grooming) tended, as adults, to be more resilient to the impact of stressors.

Intuitively, one would imagine that the behavioral and neurochemical impact of acute stressors would be exacerbated with repeated stressor experiences. In fact, however, following chronic stressor regimens, some of the behavioral disturbances ordinarily provoked in rats and mice may be attenuated. This sort of adaptation is not limited to the behavioral effects of stressors but has been reported also with respect to physiological processes, including neurochemical and immunological functioning. For instance, the NE reductions ordinarily observed after acute stressors may be absent following protracted or repeated insults owing to a compensatory increase in the synthesis of the transmitter. As the stressor experience continues, however, the wear and tear on the system may become excessive (allostatic load) and may lead to increased vulnerability to pathological outcomes. It is thought that under such conditions vulnerability is increased with respect to mood, neurodegenerative, and immunologically related disorders.

Hymie Anisman
Carleton University

STRESS RESPONSE

There are three current stress model paradigms—environmental, psychological, and biological. Regardless of its etiology, stress exerts a powerful influence on the physiology of every bodily system via its impact on both the cognitive and physiological processes of the central nervous system (CNS). In a normal and beneficial stress response, the challenge is resolved or adapted to, and functioning returns to an appropriate base level. When these responses do not maintain homeostasis and resistance fails due to inadequate, inappropriate, or excessive activation of the compensatory systems, there is high risk of physical and psychological damage.

Due to its variety of specialized extero- and interoceptive sensory transducers and its unique integration capacity, the CNS plays a major role in the defense against and adaptive response to stress. Stress responses begin with cerebral alterations that lead to behavioral changes—in content, emotions, and speech—and alterations in central and peripheral neurotransmitters that effect changes in the physiology of other organ systems. The manifold defense mechanisms directed against stressors to which an organism is subjected form a single and highly integrated regulatory system. This system includes (1) the complex subcortical CNS networks linking the integrative centers of the hypothalamus, brain stem, and limbic system; (2) their major nervous outputs through the peripheral nervous system controlling behavioral and neurovegetative adaptive responses through sympathetic and parasympathetic components; (3) the neurohormonal outputs originating in the endocrine neurons of the hypothalamus; and (4) the immune system.

The normal stress response involves synergistic activation of the sympathetic-adrenal medullary (SAM) and hypothalamic-pituitary-adrenocortical (HPA) systems through their primary CNS effects of corticotropin-releasing hormone and factor (CRH and CRF, respectively). Central CRF systems supply the critical signal for activation of behavioral, emotional, autonomic, and endocrine responses to stressors. They activate cortical limbic, hypothalamic, and pituitary mechanisms that promote adaptive changes in the face of an acute threat. Aggression, the focus of attention on the threat, arousal, vigilance, and the shutdown of sexual and feeding behaviors result. As the adrenal medulla secretes catecholamines and the adrenal cortex secretes glucocorticoids, blood flow is increased to the CNS, and fuel is made available for immediate skeletal muscle activity, in part through gluconeogenesis. Glucocorticoids also cause immunosuppression, theoretically inhibiting the inflammatory response to any injury endured during the threat and postponing it until the organism has escaped to safety. Although this latter effect of glucocorticoids is useful during immediate threat, it may provoke or sustain illness through immunosuppression in the setting of persistent, chronic stress. Glucocorticoids also appear to be critical in the shutdown of the stress response. They suppress the effect of CRH and very likely inhibit catecholamine activity in the locus ceruleus in the SAM system.

Of those two systems, the HPA system exerts significant homeostatic control over the stress response. There is clear evidence of HPA activity in the context of overwhelming, chronic threats and distress, including major depression, where hypercortisolism and other findings support HPA activation (Leonard & Song, 1996). The effects of chronic stress differ from the sequelae of acute, limited stress. A state of persistent, uncontained stress is pathological, and loss of neurobiological control over the stress response could be a factor in the development of cancer, various psychiatric disorders (e.g., depression, posttraumatic stress disorder [PTSD], and alcohol addiction; Ehlert, Gaab, & Heinrichs, 2001), and other medical conditions (hypertension, asthma, and gastrointestinal and reproductive dysfunction; Brier, 1989).

Repeated stress and resultant hypercortisolism have consequences for brain function, especially the hippocampus because of its high concentration of glucocorticoid receptors. The hippocampus is essential for learning through its effect on episodic and declarative memory and is especially important for the memory of context of the time and place where events with a strong emotional basis occurred. Thus, hippocampal impairment decreases the reliability and accuracy of such memories. This may contribute to the degree to which events may be perceived as stressful when, had context memory functions been normal, the circumstances of those events might have been perceived as nonthreatening. The mechanism for stress-induced hippocampal dysfunction and memory impairment is twofold. First, acute stress elevates adrenal steroids and suppresses neuronal mechanisms that subserve short-term memory involving the hippocampus and temporal lobe. These effects are reversible and relatively short-lived. Second, repeated stress causes atrophy of dendrites of pyramidal neurons in the CA3 region of the hippocampus, doing so through a mechanism involving glucocorticoids and excitatory amino acid and other (e.g., serotonin) neurotransmitters released during and in the aftermath of stress. Although this atrophy is reversible as long as stress is short-lived, prolonged stress lasting many months or years may, among other things, be capable of killing hippocampal neurons (Sapolsky, 1996). Stress-related disorders such as recurrent depressive illness, PTSD, and Cushing's syndrome are associated with atrophy of the human hippocampus measured by magnetic resonance imaging (Bremner, 1999).

The hippocampus is also a regulator of the stress response and exerts a largely inhibitory effect to promote shutoff of the HPA axis stress response. Recent evidence suggests that the hippocampal influence on the hypothalamic CRF neurons is via the bed nucleus of the stria terminalis and involves the regulation of an inhibitory output to these neurons (Herman & Cullinan, 1997).

Other areas in the limbic system (e.g., cingulate gyrus and amygdala) and frontal brain regions also have higher concentrations of glucocorticoid receptors. Although less is known about the impact of glucocorticoids in these regions, the same general picture as in the hippocampus may hold, particularly early in life when these regions are developing rapidly and forming interconnections (Hatalski, Guirguis, & Baram, 1998; Schneider, 1992).

A third stress response component is composed of endogenous opioid (EO) release. Hypercortisolism in the HPA system is accompanied by activation of the EO system. Stress-induced analgesia involving EO peptides has been demonstrated in animals and humans, both in association with nociceptive stimuli and in response to nonpain, cognitive stress. Since the original demonstration of the EO receptor by Pert and Snyder in 1973, various opioid peptides such as β-endorphin and enkephalins have been identified. These EOs are produced in sites including the pituitary and adrenal glands, linking the EO system to the HPA and SAM components of the stress response. Theoretically, release of EOs modulates emotional response to stressors through calming effects by reducing pain and perhaps by altering immune function.

There is now clear evidence of reciprocal interactions between the immune system (IS) and the CNS (Webster, Tonelli, & Sternberg, 2002). Most hormones secreted during the stress response have immunologic effects. Anatomical and functional connections have been demonstrated between the IS and the CNS; and cytokines, neuropeptides, and neuromediators have been shown to modulate cells of the two systems via receptors on neurons and lymphocytes. It has become apparent that the IS and CNS are tightly interconnected and interdependent and that they interact during development and in the induction of CNS pathology (Herbert & Cohen, 1993). It has also been extensively documented that individuals experiencing acute, subacute, and chronic psychological stress are immunodepressed and that stress is linked with higher morbidity.

Interindividual variation in stress responsiveness depends on three principal factors. The first is how the individual perceives and interprets the situation. If the stimulus is seen as a threat, then behaviors and physiological responses ensue that can have further consequences; otherwise, responses either are not precipitated or differ from stress responses and are also more benign. The second aspect of individual differences concerns the condition of the body itself. For example, metabolic imbalances leading to obesity and diabetes can increase an individual's vulnerability to stress and may have a genetic component (Brindley & Rolland, 1989). The ability of individuals to cope with the same stressor may be vastly different. Differences in coping skills depend on a combination of many factors, including genetics, training, religion, environment, education, coping skills, gender, age, self-esteem, past experiences, nationality, family stability, social relationships, and perceived social supports.

The final major factor is the nature of the stressor itself. Stressors can be characterized in a variety of ways: by etiology (e.g., physical, emotional-cognitive, or both); by duration (acute, chronic, or both); by complexity (due to a single event or multiple factors); by temporal nature (from the past, present, or future); or by intensity (mild, moderate, or severe). The pattern in which stressors are presented also impacts responses. Baum, Cohen, and Hall (1993) categorized stress duration through the use of a $2 \times 2 \times 2$ matrix that crossed duration of the event, duration of the perceived threat, and duration of stress response. This matrix suggests a more sensitive approach to understanding the role of stress duration (e.g., the difference between a persistent stressful event that is no longer appraised as stressful or responded to with a stress response, and a stressful event that has terminated but continues to be appraised as a stressful event and is responded to with a stress response, e.g., a traumatic experience).

The idea that cumulative levels of stress may have deleterious effects on health and longevity has long intrigued investigators dating from the early work on homeostasis and continuing with the work of Cannon (1939), Selye (1956), and others on the pathologic consequences of excessive physiologic activation. However, much of the early work focused on the effects of stress on specific, individual biologic parameters and associated health consequences. Recently, McEwen and Stellar (1993) broadened Sterling and Eyer's (1988) concept of allostatic load to mean a cumulative, multisystem view of the long-term effects of the physiologic response to stress. McEwen (1998) described four types of allostatic load situations, each with a differing potential for short- and long-term effects: (1) frequent stress exposure with appropriate adaptation; (2) lack of adaptation to the same repeated stressor; (3) prolonged response due to delayed or absent shutdown after the stressor is terminated; and (4) inadequate responses to the stressor that trigger compensatory increases in others.

Stress is universal: It is found in every person, every culture, and every generation. It is a broad-based phenomenon that exists as a continuum. Individuals showing various stress response patterns are likely to be distributed differently across gradients of socioeconomic status but not confined exclusively to one part of the gradient. Thus, it is important to distinguish between characteristics of groups and the vulnerability of individuals. Further work is necessary to understand the various forms of stress responses and their relationship to health and disease in individuals.

REFERENCES

Baum, A., Cohen, L., & Hall, M. (1993). Control and intrusive memories as possible determinants of chronic stress. *Psychosomatic Medicine, 55*(3), 274–286.

Bremner, J. D. (1999). Does stress damage the brain? *Biological Psychiatry, 45*(7), 797–805.

Brier, A. (1989). Experimental approaches to human stress research: Assessment of neurobiological mechanisms of stress in volunteers and psychiatric patients. *Biological Psychiatry, 26*(5), 438–462.

Brindley, D. N., & Rolland, Y. (1989). Possible connections between stress, diabetes, obesity, hypertension and altered lipoprotein metabolism that may result in atherosclerosis. *Clinical Science, 77*(5), 453–461.

Cannon, W. (1939). *The wisdom of the body.* New York: Norton.

Ehlert, U., Gaab, J., & Heinrichs, M. (2001). Psychoneuroendocrinological contributions to the etiology of depression, posttraumatic stress disorder, and stress-related bodily disorders: The role of the hypothalamus-pituitary-adrenal axis. *Biological Psychology, 57*(1–3), 141–152.

Hatalski, C. G., Guirguis, C., & Baram, T. Z. (1998). Corticotropin releasing factor mRNA expression in the hypothalamic paraventricular nucleus and the central nucleus of the amygdala is modulated by repeated acute stress in the immature rat. *Journal of Neuroendocrinology, 10,* 663–669.

Herbert, T. B., & Cohen, S. (1993). Stress and immunity in humans: A meta-analytic review. *Psychosomatic Medicine, 55*(4), 364–379.

Herman, J. P., & Cullinan, W. E. (1997). Neurocircuitry of stress: Central control of the hypothalamo-pituitary-adrenocortical axis. *Trends in Neurosciences, 20*(2), 78–84.

Leonard, B. E., & Song, C. (1996). Stress and the immune system in the etiology of anxiety and depression. *Pharmacology, Biochemistry, and Behavior, 54*(1), 299–303.

McEwen, B. S. (1998). Protective and damaging effects of stress mediators. *New England Journal of Medicine, 338*(3), 171–179.

McEwen, B. S., & Stellar, E. (1993). Stress and the individual: Mechanisms leading to disease. *Archives of Internal Medicine, 153*(18), 2093–2101.

Pert, C. B., & Snyder, S. H. (1973). Opiate receptor: Demonstration in nervous tissue. *Science, 179*(77), 1011–1014.

Sapolsky, R. M. (1996). Why stress is bad for your brain. *Science, 273*(5276), 749–750.

Schneider, M. L. (1992). Prenatal stress exposure alters postnatal behavioral expression under conditions of novelty challenge in rhesus monkey infants. *Developmental Psychobiology, 25*(7), 529–540.

Selye, H. (1956). *The stress of life.* New York: McGraw-Hill.

Sterling, P., & Eyer, J. (1988). Allostasis: A new paradigm to explain arousal pathology. In S. Fisher & J. Reason (Eds.), *Handbook of life stress, cognition and health* (pp. 629–649). New York: Wiley.

Webster, J. I., Tonelli, L., & Sternberg, E. M. (2002). Neuroendocrine regulation of immunity. *Annual Review of Immunology, 20,* 125–163.

Kathrine L. Peters
University of Alberta

STRIATE CORTEX

The striate cortex (area 17 or V1) is the primary visual cortex involved in conscious visual perception. It is located on both banks of the calcarine fissure in the occipital lobe. Each hemisphere has a precise, retinotopic representation of the contralateral visual field. The vertical meridian is represented at the V1/V2 (secondary visual cortex) border; the horizontal meridian bisects it midway; and the contralateral lower and upper visual fields are found in the cuneus and lingual gyrus, respectively. The map is skewed, favoring central visual field representation, and magnification changes from ~4 mm of cortex/degree at 1° centrally to ~0.5 mm/degree at 25° from the center of gaze.

The striate cortex is ~1.5 to 2 mm thick and has six cellular layers (I to VI). Layer IV (granular layer) is expanded into IVA, IVB, and IVC (IVCα and IVCβ). IVA and IVCβ receive input from the parvocellular layers of the lateral geniculate nucleus (LGN), whereas IVCα receives magnocellular LGN input. Layer IVB is the stripe of Gennari and contains cortico-cortical fibers. The koniocellular (small-celled) LGN layers project to layers II and III puffs. Signals from layer IV are relayed to supragranular and infragranular layers. Supragranular neurons project to other cortical areas, whereas infragranular neurons project primarily to the superior colliculus and the LGN.

While the receptive fields (RFs) of retinal ganglion cells and LGN neurons are circular with concentric center-surround antagonism, only the first-stage cortical neurons in layer IVC and layers II and III puffs have similar RFs. Most striate cortical neurons have elongated RFs and respond best to lines, bars, slits, borders, and edges with a specific orientation. They also prefer moving or flickering light stimuli than stationary lines, and layer IVB cells are also direction selective. Hubel and Wiesel (1968) described simple and complex units in the striate cortex of cats and monkeys. Simple cells receive input from three or more LGN neurons and have discrete ON and OFF RFs that respond to stimuli of specific orientation and position. Complex cells receive input from a number of simple cells with the same orientation preference. Their RFs do not have discrete ON and OFF regions, and they respond to stimuli of specific orientation and width, but not necessarily of specific length and position. These and other properties uncovered by many investigators characterize cortical neurons according to their preference for color, direction, orientation, high or low spatial frequencies, eye dominance, and contrast sensitivity.

The striate cortex is organized into vertical columns extending from layer I to VI, in which cells share similar functions. Ocular dominance columns (ODCs) segregate cells dominated by one or the other eye. Although most cells are binocular, those in layer IV are strictly monocular. Orientation columns partition cells by orientation preference (e.g., vertical, horizontal, and oblique at various angles). ODCs are ~0.5 mm wide in humans, and orientation columns are only ~50 μm in diameter. These two sets of columns interdigitate with one another and with other functional columns, such as those for color and spatial frequencies.

The primate striate cortex has an extremely regular array of cytochrome oxidase-rich zones in layers II and III. Cytochrome oxidase is a mitochondrial energy-generating enzyme, and these regions are metabolic hot spots, named puffs, supragranular blobs, dots, patches, or spots. Puffs

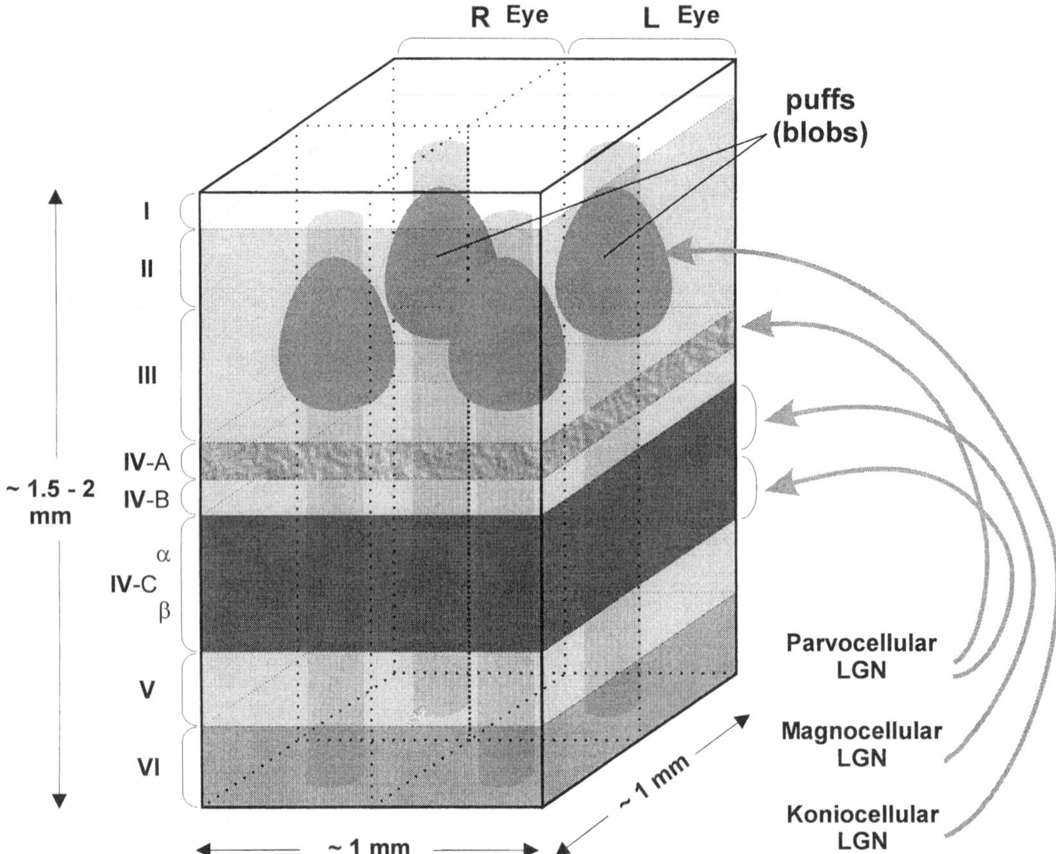

Figure 1. A schematic diagram of the striate cortex showing cytochrome oxidase-rich (darker) and -poor regions. Layers IVC, IVA, II/III puffs (blobs) and, to a lesser extent, VI receive geniculocortical projections and are moderately to intensely labeled. Each puff is centered on an ocular dominance column (right-eye R or left-eye L), the very center of which also exhibits slightly higher levels of cytochrome oxidase (rod-like shading from layers II to VI). Orientation columns (not shown) are intermingled within each ocular dominance column. A module contains the minimal and necessary sets of orientation columns, ocular dominance columns, and puffs/blobs to analyze a small locus in the visual field.

are laid down before birth in the macaque but after birth in the human. They receive direct geniculate input from the konio layers and are centered on ODCs. Cells within puffs have RF properties that are distinctly different from those in the interpuffs.

Puffs	Interpuffs
Cytochrome oxidase-rich	Cytochrome oxidase-poor
Monocular	Binocular
High spontaneous activity	Low spontaneous activity
Receptive field mostly circular; color-opponent center-surround	Receptive field rectangular; ON- or OFF-center with antagonistic flanks
Orientation-nonspecific	Orientation-specific
Respond to low spatial frequency gratings	Respond to high spatial frequency gratings
Greater color selectivity	Lesser color selectivity
Input: IVCβ and koniocellular LGN layers	Input: IVCβ
Output: mainly thin stripes of V2	Output: mainly interstripes of V2

A 1 to 2 mm^2 piece of visual cortex would contain sufficient neural machinery to process visual signals from a particular point in the visual space, such as size, shape, color, luminance, movement, and depth. It would include the minimal and necessary sets of ODCs, orientation columns, and puffs (blobs) centered on ODCs. This is known as a cortical module.

The major neurotransmitter of cortical projection neurons is glutamate, the universal excitatory transmitter. GABA is the key transmitter of inhibitory interneurons. Other neurochemicals, such as calbindin, calmodulin, neuropeptide Y, parvalbumin, somatostatin, substance P, and nitric oxide probably serve modulatory roles.

Information from the geniculocortical pathway is channeled to over 30 extrastriate cortical areas in the occipital, parietal, and temporal lobes. These multiple streams process different attributes of the visual stimuli: color, contrast, form, and movement. The "what" (or ventral) stream for object recognition is channeled to the inferotemporal cortex. It is subdivided into two parvocellular (P) streams: one for color, form, and movement, the other for color and contrast. The "where" (or dorsal) stream is the magnocellular (M) stream for spatial localization and is concerned with contrast, movement, and stereopsis. It goes to the parietal cortex. The koniocellular stream mediates another pathway via the cortical puffs. However, much cross talk exists among visual cortical centers.

If the signal from one eye is disrupted by infection, patching, strabismus, astigmatism, lesion, or other abnormalities during the critical period of postnatal development, cortical neurons that receive input from the nonaffected eye will become dominant and command more synaptic space at the expense of cells representing the deprived eye. Behaviorally, the individual may suffer from amblyopia, poor depth perception, poor pattern perception, or frank blindness in that eye. It is interesting that binocular deprivation is less detrimental than monocular deprivation because of the importance of binocular competition.

Recent work has demonstrated that mature neurons remain capable of responding to altered functional demands (reviewed in Wong-Riley, 1994). When impulse activity of one eye is blocked in adult monkeys, deprived cortical neurons down-regulate their cytochrome oxidase and other neurochemicals (GABA, glutamate, NMDA receptors, nitric oxide synthase, and others). Synaptic reorganization can also occur in the mature visual cortex, and changes are reversible when there is no denervation.

In recent years, functional magnetic resonance imaging (fMRI) has uncovered in the living human visual cortex many analogous subdivisions previously mapped in the macaque brain.

REFERENCES

Hubel, D. H., & Wiesel, T. N. (1968). Receptive field and functional architecture of monkey striate cortex. *Journal of Physiology, 195,* 215–243.

Wong-Riley, M. T. T. (1994). Primate visual cortex: Dynamic metabolic organization and plasticity revealed by cytochrome oxidase. In A. Peters & K. Rockland (Eds.), *Cerebral cortex: Vol. 10. Primary visual cortex in primates* (pp. 141–200). New York: Plenum.

SUGGESTED READINGS

DeYoe, E. A., Carman, G., Bandettini, P., Glickman, S., Wieser, J., Cox, R., Miller, D., & Neitz, J. (1996). Mapping striate and extrastriate visual areas in human cerebral cortex. *Proceedings of the National Academy of Sciences, USA, 93*(6), 2382–2386.

Hendry, S. H. C., & Calkins, D. J. (1998). Neuronal chemistry and functional organization in the primate visual system. *Trends in Neuroscience, 21,* 344–349.

Horton, J. C., & Hedley-Whyte, E. T. (1984). Mapping of cytochrome oxidase patches and ocular dominance columns in human visual cortex. *Philosophical Transactions of the Royal Society of London, B, 304,* 255–272.

Kaas, J. H. (1995). Human visual cortex: Progress and puzzles. *Current Biology, 5,* 1126–1128.

Livingstone, M. S., & Hubel, D. H. (1984). Anatomy and physiology of a color system in the primate visual cortex. *Journal of Neuroscience, 4,* 309–356.

Tootell, R. B. H., Silverman, M. S., Hamilton, S. L., Switkes, E., & De Valois, R. L. (1988). Functional anatomy of macaque striate cortex: V. Spatial frequency. *Journal of Neuroscience, 8,* 1610–1624.

Ungerleider, L. G., & Haxby, J. V. (1994). "What" and "where" in the human brain. *Current Opinion in Neurobiology, 4,* 157–165.

Margaret T. T. Wong-Riley
Medical College of Wisconsin

STRONG INTEREST INVENTORY

The Strong Interest Inventory (SII) was published in 1995, the latest in a series of revisions of a test originally developed by E. K. Strong, Jr., in the 1920s. It contains 317 questions that require the test taker to respond "like," "indifferent," or "dislike" to a variety of occupations, activities, school subjects, and types of people; to indicate preferences between paired options (such as dealing with things vs. dealing with people); and to mark "yes," "no," or "?" to a series of self-descriptive statements.

The SII was developed on the basis of over 60 years of experience with earlier versions of the test and continues the tradition of a counseling instrument that over the years has been used in thousands of research studies and has been given to millions of people. The test must be computer scored, and scores reflect 6 General Occupational Themes, 25 Basic Interests, 211 Occupations (102 occupations separately normed for men and women, plus 7 occupations with single-sex norms), and 4 Personal Styles. Although all people take the same test, separate male and female norms are applied because sex difference in interest patterns frequently occur.

The purpose of the SII is to provide information to the person and professional counselor or personnel officer to aid in academic and career decision making. Scores reflect the person's interests, rather than abilities. The occupational scales compare the person's responses on items known to discriminate between people in the career and men or women in general. For example, the male score for accountant is based on items that have been empirically demonstrated to differentiate between male accountants and men in general. People who choose careers consistent with their interests have been shown to stay with their career choices longer than people who enter careers inconsistent with their interests.

The SII is widely accepted by academic and career counselors as one of the best and most useful tests available for this purpose. It should be used and interpreted in conjunction with trained counselors.

Mary J. Allen
California State University
Office of the Chancellor

See also: **Career Counseling**

STROOP EFFECT

The Phenomenon

Since psychology's earliest days, we have known that the time to name objects or their properties is considerably longer than the time to read the corresponding words. Cattell (1886) demonstrated this in his dissertation: Saying "horse" to a picture of a horse or "blue" to a color patch took more time than did reading the word *horse* or *blue.* Cattell attributed this difference to the automaticity of word reading, developed through extensive practice.

Fifty years later, John Ridley Stroop combined these two dimensions into a single task (1935/1992; for a biographical sketch, see MacLeod, 1991b). In his dissertation, Stroop printed words in incongruent colors (e.g., the word *red* in blue ink). Asked to read the word and ignore the color, people had little difficulty relative to a control condition where all words appeared in normal black ink. However, asked to name the ink color and ignore the word, people were extraordinarily slow and error-prone relative to a control condition of color patches without words.

This difficulty in ignoring incongruent color words while color naming has come to be called the Stroop effect, or Stroop interference. Following Cattell's lead, the effect is seen as resulting from word reading being so automated that it cannot be prevented even when it disrupts performance. As the gold-standard measure of attention, this effect is one of the largest and most stable phenomena in cognitive psychology, having served as a fundamental tool in hundreds of investigations (for a review, see MacLeod, 1991a). As evidence of its impact, many other analogous interference situations have emerged over the years; Figure 1 illustrates a few of these.

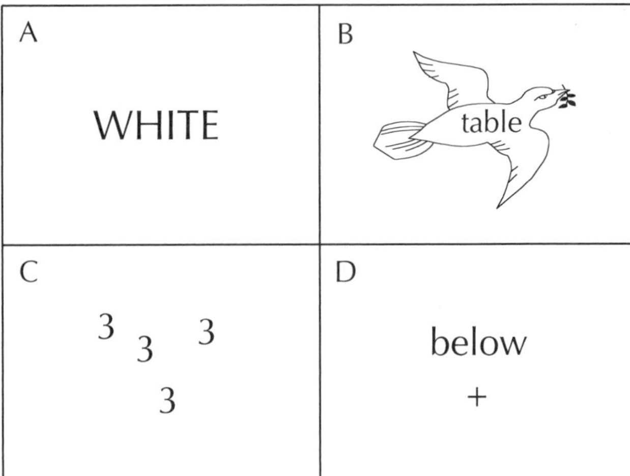

Figure 1. Variations of the Stroop effect. Panel A is the classic task, in which one must name the print color of the word, ignoring the word itself (i.e., say "black"). Panel B is the most frequently studied variant, in which one must name the picture, ignoring the word printed on it (i.e., say "bird"). In Panel C, the task is to count the number of characters, ignoring their identity (i.e., say "four"); in Panel D, the task is to indicate where the word appears with respect to the fixation cross (i.e., say "above"). All panels represent the case that produces interference relative to a control condition.

The Explanations

For many years, the prevalent explanation of Stroop interference was the relative speed of processing account (see Dyer, 1973), in which performance is seen as a kind of horse race in which the wrong horse (the word) beats the right one (the color). This view derives from Cattell's data. More recently, theorists have argued that interference results from people having to execute a controlled process (color naming) in the face of an automatic process (word reading). This explanation derives more from Cattell's theory, and automaticity is viewed as a continuum that develops with practice (MacLeod & Dunbar, 1988).

Most recently, theories have come to emphasize the strength of the connection between particular stimuli and appropriate responses. This is most evident in the new connectionist (neural network) models, notably that of Cohen, Dunbar, and McClelland (1990). Here, a layer of stimulus units (the words and colors) is modulated by task demand units (which set the task as either color naming or word reading). Learning occurs via changing the strength of connections to a layer of intermediate (hidden) units, with the results passed forward to a final output layer containing the responses. Such models do quite well at capturing many crucial findings.

Intriguing Aspects of the Stroop Effect

We now know a great deal about the Stroop effect and the factors that influence it. Clearly, differential practice on the two dimensions is crucial. However, this does not mean that differential speed of processing the two dimensions is the mechanism, as shown by studies that have presented the color information well before the word, thereby giving color a head start, yet have found no reverse interference of color on word reading (Glaser & Glaser, 1982). Indeed, the idea of automaticity has not gone unchallenged either, given that undermining the likelihood of reading the word, such as by coloring only a single letter (Besner, Stolz, & Boutilier, 1997), reduces the effect.

The Stroop task is now widely used as a benchmark measure of attention and automaticity and often appears on standardized tests and in experiments outside cognitive psychology. It's important to note that the effects on the color naming of words are not restricted to color words, but can occur for noncolor words if they are primed by prior presentation (e.g., Warren, 1972). This has led to numerous priming studies, most notably the recent work on the emotional Stroop effect (for a review, see Williams, Mathews, & MacLeod, 1996). Here, time to name the print colors of noncolor words is greater for words related to an individual's anxiety (e.g., *web* for a person with a spider phobia; *exam* for a test-anxious person) than for neutral words (e.g., *chair*), presumably due to chronic priming. The emotional Stroop effect is now used as a diagnostic tool for the existence of and the successful treatment of anxiety disorders.

In addition, new brain imaging techniques that permit localization of cognitive activity, such as positron-emission tomography (PET) and functional magnetic resonance imaging (fMRI), have also been applied to the Stroop effect, with converging results. Like many other attentional tasks, the Stroop effect shows activity in the anterior cingulated cortex, one of the brain centers associated with cognition, and particularly with attention (e.g., Carter, Mintun, & Cohen, 1995; see MacLeod & MacDonald, 2000, for a review).

Overall, then, this seemingly simple demonstration task that has been with us for over 65 years continues to be very fruitful in our exploration of how attention, a fundamental aspect of human cognition, works. We can expect it to be put to continuing creative use in the exploration of cognition and cognitive neuroscience.

REFERENCES

Besner, D., Stolz, J. A., & Boutilier, C. (1997). The Stroop effect and the myth of automaticity. *Psychonomic Bulletin and Review, 4,* 221–225.

Carter, C. S., Mintun, M., & Cohen, J. D. (1995). Interference and facilitation effects during selective attention: An $H_2{}^{15}O$ PET study of Stroop task performance. *Neuroimage, 2,* 264–272.

Cattell, J. M. (1886). The time it takes to see and name objects. *Mind, 11,* 63–65.

Cohen, J. D., Dunbar, K., & McClelland, J. L. (1990). On the control of automatic processes: A parallel distributed processing account of the Stroop effect. *Psychological Review, 97,* 332–361.

Dyer, F. N. (1973). The Stroop phenomenon and its use in the study of perceptual, cognitive, and response processes. *Memory and Cognition, 1,* 106–120.

Glaser, M. O., & Glaser, W. R. (1982). Time course analysis of the Stroop phenomenon. *Journal of Experimental Psychology: Human Perception and Performance, 8,* 875–894.

MacLeod, C. M. (1991a). Half a century of research on the Stroop effect: An integrative review. *Psychological Bulletin, 109,* 163–203.

MacLeod, C. M. (1991b). John Ridley Stroop: Creator of a landmark cognitive task. *Canadian Psychology, 32,* 521–524.

MacLeod, C. M., & Dunbar, K. (1988). Training and Stroop-like interference: Evidence for a continuum of automaticity. *Journal of Experimental Psychology: Learning, Memory, and Cognition, 14,* 126–135.

MacLeod, C. M., & MacDonald, P. A. (2000). Inter-dimensional interference in the Stroop effect: Uncovering the cognitive and neural anatomy of attention. *Trends in Cognitive Sciences, 4,* 383–391.

Stroop, J. R. (1992). Studies of interference in serial verbal reactions. *Journal of Experimental Psychology: General, 121,* 15–23. (Original work published 1992)

Warren, R. E. (1972). Stimulus encoding and memory. *Journal of Experimental Psychology, 94,* 90–100.

Williams, J. M. G., Mathews, A., & MacLeod, C. (1996). The emotional Stroop task and psychopathology. *Psychological Bulletin, 120,* 3–24.

Colin M. MacLeod
University of Toronto

See also: **Brain Imaging; Interference; Priming**

STRUCTURAL PLASTICITY AND MEMORY

Several structural changes in the basic-wiring diagram of the brain have been related to memory storage. These include alterations in the number and pattern of synaptic connections (Moser, 1999), translocation of polyribosomal aggregates to the synaptic spines (Weiler, Hawrylak, & Greenough, 1995), and complex changes in the shape and size of synaptic contact zone (Rusakov et al., 1997). The search for neuronal proteins whose expression correlates with synaptic remodeling has led to the discovery of the growth-associated protein GAP-43, also termed B-50, F1, pp46, and neuromodulin. GAP-43 is a presynaptic membrane phosphoprotein that plays a key role in guiding the growth of axons and modulating the formation of new connections. Neuroplasticity events such as axonal regeneration following nerve injury (Benowitz, Rodriguez, & Neve, 1990) and changes in synaptic efficacy elicited by long-term potentiation (LTP; Meberg, Gall, & Routtenberg, 1993), which is thought to underlie certain forms of learning and memory, determine an increase in GAP-43 expression. Basal values of GAP-43 protein, determined by quantitative immunohistochemistry in selected rat brain regions (Figure 1), are age-dependent. The highest levels of GAP-43 can be found in the adult rat and considerably lower levels in aged rats (Figures 2 and 3). The decrease of GAP-43 content in 31-month-old rats (aged) as compared to that in 18-month-old rats (adult) was statistically significant in hippocampal dentate gyrus (–54%), cingulate cortex (–42%), and olfactory bulb (–38%; see Figure 2). These latter regions of the rat brain exhibit a high degree of plasticity in adulthood but are severely impaired during aging, whereas the other regions investigated (viz., CA1 and cerebellar cortex) maintain a constant, though scarce, capacity of sustaining synaptic remodeling throughout life. The age-dependent decrease of the neuron density innervating the regions that showed this marked loss in GAP-43 immunoreactivity is of particular interest in the analysis of these findings. Hilar hippocampal neurons and cortical neurons providing the bulk of innervation to the inner molecular layer of dentate gyrus and to the cingolate cortex, respectively, show a 20% to 30% decrease in aged (as compared to adult) rats (Coleman & Flood, 1987). The primary neurons of the olfactory epithelium sending afferents to the nerve fiber layer in the olfactory bulb show a striking

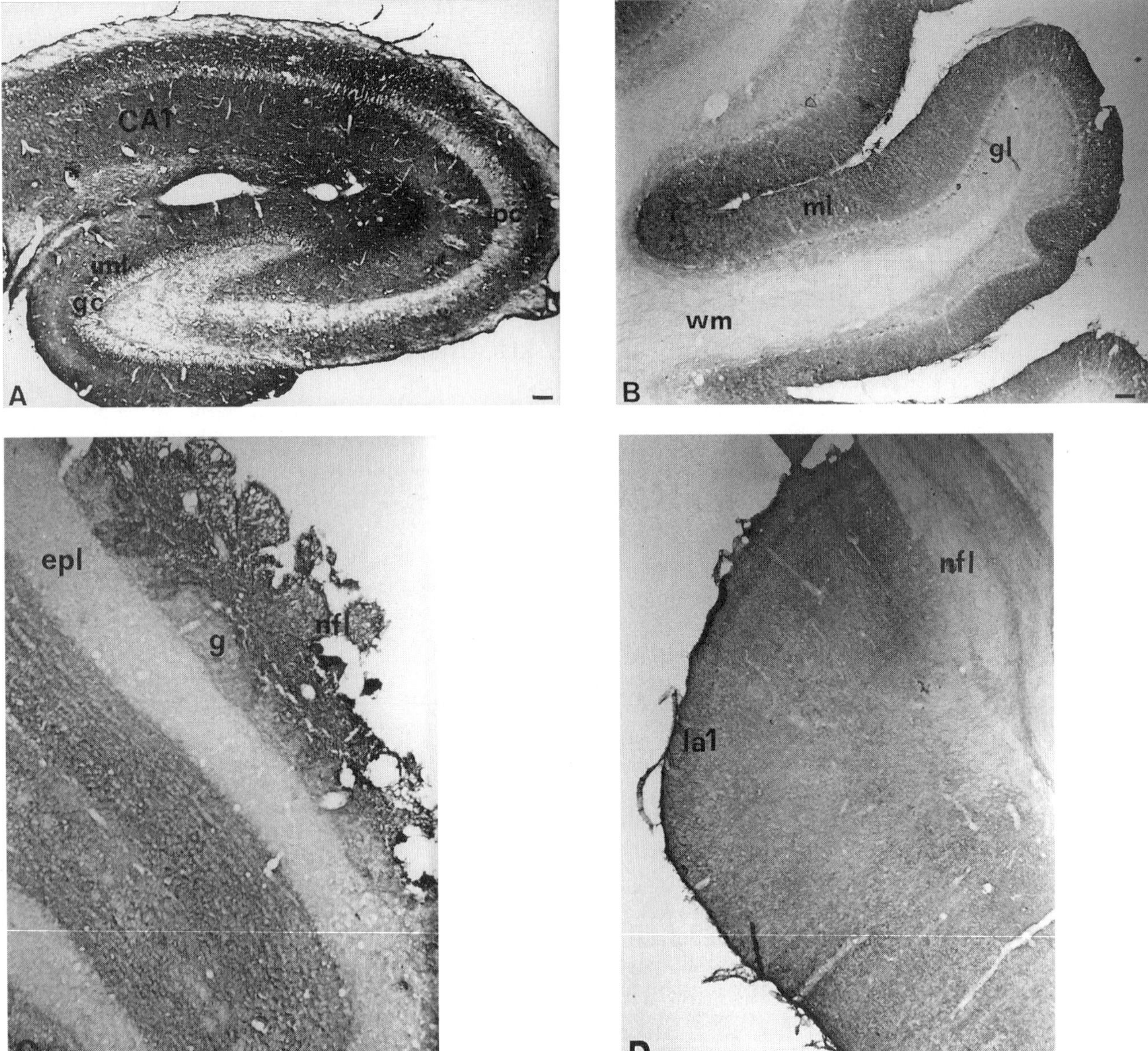

Figure 1. GAP-43 distribution in different brain regions. A: coronal section of ventral hippocampus; neuronal cell soma within the piramidal (pc) and granular layers (gc) are unlabeled while a moderately dense staining is present in the CA1 stratum radiatum (CA1) and in the inner third of the dentate gyrus molecular layer (iml). B: cerebellar cortex; labeling is intense in the molecular layer (ml), lighter in the granule layer (gl) and in the white matter. C: portion of the olfactory bulb; the staining is virtually absent in the external plexiform layer (epl), moderate in the glomeruli (g), and intense in the nerve fiber layer (nfl). D: cingulated cortex. Dense immunolabeling is present in Layer 1 (la1). The underlying neuropil layers are lightly stained. Bars: A, B, and D = 100 μm; C = 300 μm.

decrease in the aged rat, reaching a 48% reduction compared to that in the adult (Hinds & McNelly, 1981). The issues discussed previously indicate that at least two regions showing high levels of GAP-43 in the adult rat brain—namely, the inner molecular layer of the dentate gyrus and Layer 1 of the cingulated cortex—significantly decrease their ability to sustain synaptic turnover during aging. It has been demonstrated that the hippocampus is involved in memory acquisition and consolidation (Shephard, 1988b), whereas the cingulated cortex is reported to be a center for the expression of emotional behavior (Shephard, 1988a). Both these functions are markedly altered in elderly subjects (Timiras, 1994).

REFERENCES

Benowitz, L. I., Rodriguez, W. R., & Neve, R. L. (1990). The pattern of GAP-43 immunostaining changes in the rat hippocampal formation during reactive synaptogenesis. *Molecular Brain Research, 8,* 17–23.

Coleman, P. D., & Flood, D. G. (1987). Neuron numbers and dendritic extent in normal aging and Alzheimer's disease. *Neurobiology of Aging, 8,* 521–545.

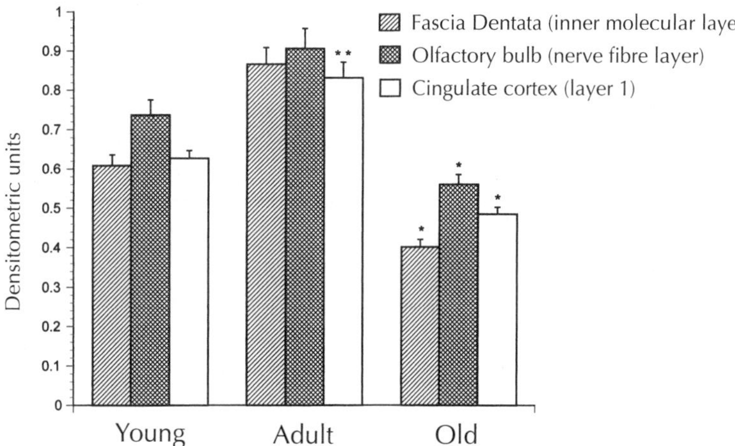

Figure 2. GAP-43 densitometry (mean ± SEM) in the inner molecular layer of dentate gyrus, in the nerve fiber layer of olfactory bulb, and in the layer 1 of cingulate cortex for the 3 age groups. $^{*}p < 0.01$ vs. adult rats. $^{**}p < 0.01$ vs. young rats, two-way ANOVA, multiple contrasts.

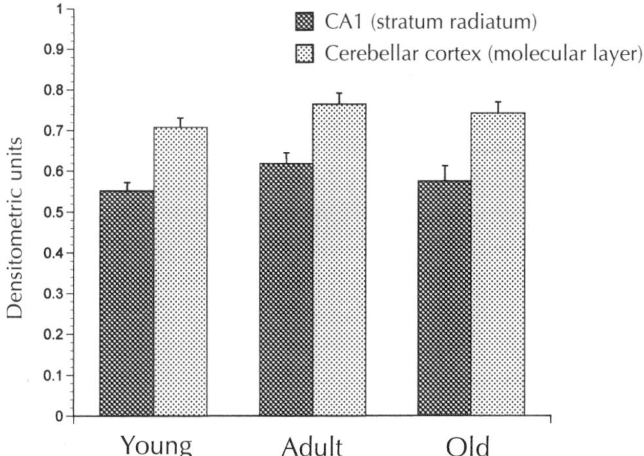

Figure 3. GAP-43 densitometry (mean ± SEM) in the CA1 stratum radiatum and in the molecular layer of cerebellar cortex. No comparisons between the age groups were statistically significant.

Hinds, J. W., & McNelly, N. (1981). Aging in the rat olfactory system: Correlation of changes in the olfactory epithelium and olfactory bulb. *Journal of Comparative Neurology, 203,* 441–453.

Landfield, P. W., Braun, L. D., Pitler, T. A., Lindsey, J. D., & Lynch, G. (1981). Hippocampal aging in rats: A morphometric study of multiple variables in semithin sections. *Neurobiology of Aging, 2,* 265–275.

Meberg, P. J., Gall, C. M., & Routtenberg, A. (1993). Induction of F1/GAP-43 gene: Expression in hippocampal granule cells after seizures. *Molecular Brain Research, 17,* 295–299.

Moser, M. B. (1999). Making more synapses: A way to store information? *Cellular and Molecular Life Science, 55,* 593–600.

Rusakov, D. A., Davies, H. A., Harrison, E., Diana, G., Richter-Levin, G., Bliss, T. V., & Stewart, M. G. (1997). Ultrastructural synaptic correlates of spatial learning in rat hippocampus. *Neuroscience, 80,* 69–77.

Shephard, G. M. (Ed.). (1988a). *Neurobiology* (2nd ed., pp. 579–580). New York: Oxford University Press.

Shephard, G. M. (Ed.). (1988b). *Neurobiology* (2nd ed., pp. 605–610). New York: Oxford University Press.

Timiras, P. S. (1994). Aging of the nervous system: Functional changes. In P. S. Timiras (Ed.), *Physiological basis of aging and geriatrics* (2nd ed., pp. 103–114). Boca Raton, FL: CRC Press.

Weiler, I. J., Hawrylak, N., & Greenough, W. T. (1985). Morphogenesis in memory formation: Synaptic and cellular mechanisms. *Behavioral Brain Research, 66,* 1–6.

Tiziana Casoli
Neurobiology of Aging Laboratory

STRUCTURALISM

As a school or system of psychology, structuralism had its antecedents in British philosophy of the eighteenth and nineteenth centuries. John Locke had established the empirical tradition by stating that all knowledge came from experience, and the mind at birth was a tabula rasa (blank tablet). Locke opposed the continental philosophers, such as René Descartes, who claimed that some ideas were inborn.

Structuralism began formally with the teachings and writings of Wilhelm Maximillian Wundt (1832–1920) in the late nineteenth century. Historians of psychology generally agree that Wundt founded the first psychological laboratory in 1879 in Leipzig. Many important experiments were performed in Wundt's laboratory: reaction time, color mixing, afterimages, psychophysics, and word associations. Wundt's interpretation of the nature of psychology became the first psychological system or framework within which one could organize the facts and theories of psychology.

At the turn of the century, many young pioneers in psychology came to study with Wundt at the University of Leipzig—among them Hall, Cattell, and Titchener. Edward Bradford Titchener (1862–1927) took Wundt's psychology to the United States, where he named the system *structuralism.* He modified and enlarged Wundt's basic tenets and headed the experimental laboratory at Cornell University.

Both Wundt and Titchener defined psychology as the study of consciousness or conscious experience. This kind of knowledge was dependent on the experiencing individual as opposed to experience independent of the individual, which was the subject matter of physics and chemistry. This definition focused psychology on human experience. Throughout the first three decades of the twentieth century, structuralism was a dominant school in American psychology. By the early 1930s, however, the system was beginning to decline in popularity.

For Titchener, there were three classes of elements of experience: sensations, feelings, and images. The elements of sensation came from the various senses: vision, hearing, taste, smell, touch, the muscular sense, and various organic senses. For Wundt, feelings—the inner experience—had three dimensions: pleasantness-unpleasantness, excitement-calm, and strain-relaxation. Titchener proposed only the pleasantness-unpleasantness dimension, stating that Wundt's other dimensions could be reduced to actual sensations. The images that constituted the third class of elements were like weak sensations. Titchener concluded that there were a total of 43,415 different sensory experiences.

Titchener also believed that these elements had dimensions of attributes. There was *intensity,* which referred to how strong or weak the sensations were. *Quality* referred to the kind of experience, as in a particular pitch or tone. *Duration* referred to how long the experience lasted. *Clarity* involved the place an experience had in consciousness. Those experiences at the focus of consciousness would be very clear, whereas those at the fringe would be vague. Finally, Titchener described the attribute of *extensity* or volume, which he believed applied only to visual experience.

Attention referred to the arrangement of conscious elements. It could be voluntary, as when one intentionally directs one's attention to a particular object. Habitual attention was developed with repetition, as when a mother attends regularly to the signals from her child. Finally, involuntary attention could be exemplified by a sudden flash of lightning or a clap of thunder.

In experience, the elements were combined. The means by which this combination could occur was *association.* This was the so-called glue that held the elements together. Titchener and Wundt borrowed the laws of association from the tradition of the British empiricists and associationists.

Both Wundt and Titchener had distinguished the two worlds of experience: the mental (consciousness) and the physical. The relationship between these two worlds could be explained through psychophysical parallelism. For instance, the experience of a particular color had its parallel in the length of light wave, or an experience of a certain pitch had its parallel in the frequency of the sound wave.

One aspect of experience that Wundt failed to explain was the meaning of a particular idea or set of experiences. Therefore, Titchener constructed his context theory of meaning. Here meaning was divided into core and context.

The methodology of structuralism was introspection and experimentation. Introspection was of special importance in analyzing experiences. Titchener maintained that science was dependent on observation and that introspection was one of the methods. In his *Outline of Psychology,* Titchener laid down certain rules for the introspectionist to follow: (1) One must be unbiased; (2) one must have complete control and not allow one's attention to wander; (3) one's body and mind must be fresh and not fatigued or exhausted; and (4) one must feel well, be of good temper, and be interested in the experience being introspected. Titchener warned against the stimulus error, which constituted a reading into the experience of associations from one's past that would contaminate the raw experience.

Structuralism no longer exists as a systematic position. It was very much limited to what psychologists could study in their minds; it had no applications. In 1933 Edwin Boring, a student of Titchener at Cornell, wrote *The Physical Dimensions of Consciousness,* in which he tried to correlate the attributes of consciousness with characteristics of impulses going along the sensory nerves to the brain. Intensity supposedly correlated with the rapidity of the impulse and quality with a patterning of the impulses, but this was purely hypothetical.

What is left of structuralism is to be found in various aspects of sensory psychology, but in a way, structuralism fulfilled its purpose. It set psychology out as a discipline separate from philosophy with a methodology of investigation at least in part experimental. Introspection, as a method, was subjective and qualitative. As psychology was being directed toward a broader scope, to include behavior of both animals and humans, along with applications to the world outside the laboratory, structuralism was eclipsed.

REFERENCES

Boring, E. (1933). *The physical dimensions of consciousness.* New York: The Century Company.

Titchener, E. B. *An outline of psychology.* New York: Macmillan.

Robert W. Lundin
The University of the South

See also: **Monism/Dualism**

STRUCTURED AND SEMISTRUCTURED CLINICAL INTERVIEWS

The past few decades have witnessed a shift among clinical psychologists and psychiatrists toward the increased use of a more formal clinical interview process. It has become commonplace to categorize clinical interviews, based on the degree of structure imposed by the interviewer, into one of three subtypes: structured, semistructured, and unstructured. The unstructured interview is characterized by the clinician's refraining from the use of prescripted queries or a predetermined order of content coverage (Shea, 1990; Wiens, 1990). In direct contrast, a structured interview comprises predetermined questions presented in a predefined order, with tightly operationalized criteria used for interpretation (Beutler, 1995). Semistructured interviews are something of a hybrid case. Like structured interviews, they consist of predetermined questions presented in a predefined order; however, following the predetermined questions, the interviewer is free to follow up as necessary to obtain sufficient information.

Semistructured interviewing, like structured interviewing, is concerned with obtaining sufficient information for reliable and valid rating with respect to some particular content domain (e.g., diagnostic category, symptom severity, level of function, etc.). It differs only in that it allows clinicians more latitude to formulate queries in making a rating. Accordingly, the present chapter subsumes both semistructured and structured interviews under the rubric of the structured interview.

The Shift from Unstructured to Structured Interviews

The increasing use of structured interviews may be traced to the confluence of several historical developments. In the 1960s and 1970s there was growing recognition that the traditional method of diagnosis (i.e., the unstandardized, unstructured interview) was highly unreliable (see Hersen & Bellack, 1988). Structured interviews thereby became an invaluable means of assessing each disorder within the *Diagnostic and Statistical Manual of Mental Disorder* third edition (*DSM-III;* American Psychiatric Association, 1980) in a systematic fashion (Shea, 1990). Another development has been the recent increase in the influence of managed care organizations (MCOs). MCOs, by virtue of concerns for cost containment, have provided an impetus for the widespread use of structured interviews, inasmuch as such interviews allow more valid and accurate diagnosis with minimal prerequisite clinician training (Wiens, 1990).

The Structured Interview: Advantages and Disadvantages

There are several advantages in comparison with unstructured interviewing. Due to their explicit use of operationalized criteria, structured interviews facilitate higher levels of interrater reliability than do unstructured interviews (Segal, 1997; Segal & Falk, 1998). Standardization in administration decreases the amount of both criterion and information variance (Segal, 1997; Segal & Falk, 1998). Structured interviews also attenuate the need for clinical judgment and permit the clinician to rely on operationalized criteria and interpretation based on normative values. In addition, two different interviewers utilizing the same interview are less likely to elicit discrepant information due to differences in interviewing techniques. Due principally to its superior reliability and validity, structured interviewing is now the accepted gold standard of *DSM*-based diagnostic assessment. Descriptions of the most commonly employed structured interviews are listed in Table 1.

Another advantage is that administration and interpretation of the interviews requires less training than for unstructured interviews. Nonetheless, they do require a considerable amount of specialized training, not only because the initial training in interview administration is extensive, but also because retraining is necessary to prevent interviewer drift.

Structured interviews are also capable of providing information tailored to the researcher's or clinician's needs. For example, the relevant sections of a structured interview may be employed to elicit information to address a specific referral question or diagnostic issue. Alternatively, for a more thorough intake assessment, an omnibus diagnostic interview may be employed to screen a patient across the entire spectrum of disorders.

There are a few notable limitations with structured interviews. They constrain an interviewer's freedom in exploring relevant issues to suit the needs of the client (Beutler, 1995). For example, clients may not reveal information unless they are comfortable with the interviewer; thus, questions that are not tailored to the needs of the patient or that proceed in a forced manner may actually result in the patient's revealing less information or being untruthful (Scheiber, 1994; Sullivan, 1954). Finally, clinicians who employ structured interviews lack flexibility in exploring their clinical intuitions when interviewing (Beutler, 1995).

Structured Interviewing: Clinical Considerations

Despite the limited amount of free time available during a structured interview, the clinician is faced with the need to establish rapport quickly with the client in order to obtain accurate and complete information (Beutler, 1995; Scheiber, 1994). Beutler (1995) recommended that the clinician "ensure that the desired expectation and mind set are developed by the patient" (p. 99) by interviewing in a quiet, protected area to provide a relaxing therapeutic milieu of safety and collaboration. In addition, the clinician can, with the skillful use of nonverbal communication (e.g., body posture, etc.), convey a sense of empathy and positive regard throughout the process. Finally, the interviewer will do well to provide the client beforehand with information (e.g., interview format, etc.) that gives the individual some sense of control during the interview process (Beutler, 1995). With such considerations in mind when administering an SI, the clinician can often ascertain important clinical information while simultaneously establishing a positive clinical alliance for subsequent assessment or intervention procedures.

Table 1. Commonly Employed Structured Diagnostic Interviews

Name	Description	Psychometric Properties	Strengths	Limitations
Structured Clinical Interview for *DSM-IV* (SCID; First et al., 1995)	Semistructured; patient and nopatient versions; specified modules; assesses Axis I disorders	kappa = .72–.84 (Williams et al., 1992)	Length based on need; computer scoring	Limited Likert scale; moderate training
Schedule for Affective Disorders and Schizophrenia (Endicott & Spitzer, 1978)	Semistructured; based on Research Diagnostic Criteria for Axis I disorders; specified modules	ICC = .84–1.00 (Endicott & Spitzer, 1978); kappa = .63–1.00 (Spitzer et al., 1979)	Assesses past and present psychopathology	Limited Likert scale; no reliable computer scoring; reliance on clinical judgment; extensive training
Diagnostic Interview Schedule (Robins et al., 1981)	Structured; investigation of mental illness in general population; assesses Axis I disorders	kappa = .60–.80 (Robins et al., 1981)	Designed for nonprofessionals; 1-hour administration; computer scoring	Closed-ended questions; dichotomous scoring with no clarification; assesses only symptoms
International Personality Disorder Examination (Loranger et al., 1994)	Semistructured; specified modules; assesses Axis II disorders based on *DSM* and ICD-10 criteria	kappa = .51–.87; stability = .52 (Loranger et al., 1994)	Uses 5-year inclusion rule; requests examples for scoring	Limited Likert scale; requires extensive training and clinical judgment; 2–3 hour administration
Structured Clinical Interview for *DSM-IV* (SCID-II; First et al., 1994)	Semistructured; screening questionnaire available; specified modules; assesses Axis II disorders	kappa = .48–.98 (Maffei et al., 1997)	Screening component; open-ended follow-up questions	Limited Likert scale; questions grouped together by disorder; extensive training and clinical judgment required

Note: Information on instrument strengths and limitations is abstracted from Segal and Falk (1998).

REFERENCES

American Psychiatric Association. (1980). *Diagnostic and statistical manual of mental disorders* (3rd ed.). Washington, DC: Author.

Beutler, L. E. (1995). The clinical interview. In L. E. Beutler & M. R. Berren (Eds.), *Integrative assessment of adult personality.* New York: Guilford Press.

Endicott, J., & Spitzer, R. L. (1978). A diagnostic interview: The Schedule for Affective Disorders and Schizophrenia. *Archives of General Psychiatry, 35,* 837–844.

First, M. B., Spitzer, R. L., Gibbon, M., & Williams, J. B. W. (1995). *Structured Clinical Interview for Axis I DSM-IV Disorders–Patient Edition (SCID-I/P, Version 2.0).* New York: Biometrics Research Department, New York State Psychiatric Institute.

First, M. B., Spitzer, R. L., Gibbon, M., Williams, J. B. W., & Benjamin, L. (1994). *Structured Clinical Interview for DSM-IV Axis II Personality Disorders (SCID-II, Version 2.0).* New York: Biometrics Research Department, New York State Psychiatric Institute.

Helzer, J. E., Robins, L. N., Taibleson, M., Woodruff, R. A., Reich, T., & Wish, E. D. (1977). Reliability in psychiatric diagnosis. *Archives of General Psychiatry, 34,* 129–133.

Hersen, M., & Bellack, A. S. (1988). DSM-III and behavioral assessment. In A. S. Bellack & M. Hersen (Eds.), *Behavioral assessment: A practical handbook* (pp. 67–84). New York: Pergamon.

Loranger, A. W., Sartorius, N., Andreoli, A., Berger, P., Buchheim, P., Channabasavanna, S. M., Coid, B., Dahl, A., Diekstra, R. F. W., Ferguson, B., Jacobsberg, L. B., Mombour, W., Pull, C., Ono, Y., & Reiger, D. A. (1994). The International Personality Disorder Examination. *Archives of General Psychiatry, 51,* 215–224.

Maffei, C., Fossati, A., Agostoni, I., Barraco, A., Bagnato, M., Donati, D., Namia, C., Novella, L., & Petrachi, M. (1997). Interrater reliability and internal consistency of the Structured Clinical Interview for DSM-IV Axis II Personality Disorders (SCID-II), version 2.0. *Journal of Personality Disorders, 11,* 279–284.

Robins, L. N., Helzer, J. E., Croughan, J., & Ratcliff, K. S. (1981). National Institute of Mental Health Diagnostic Interview Schedule. *Archives of General Psychiatry, 38,* 381–389.

Scheiber, S. C. (1994). The psychiatric interview, psychiatric history, and mental status examination. In R. E. Hales & S. C. Yudofsky (Eds.), *The American Psychiatric Press textbook of psychiatry* (2nd ed.). Washington, DC: American Psychiatric Press.

Segal, D. L. (1997). Structured interviewing and DSM classification. In S. M. Turner & M. Hersen (Eds.), *Adult psychopathology and diagnosis.* New York: Wiley.

Segal, D. L., & Falk, S. B. (1998). Structured interviews and rating scales. In A. S. Bellack & M. Hersen (Eds.), *Behavioral assessment: A practical handbook* (4th ed., pp. xxx). Needham Heights, MA: Allyn & Bacon.

Shea, S. C. (1990). Contemporary psychiatric interviewing: Integration of DSM-III-R, psychodynamic concerns, and mental status. In G. Goldstein & M. Hersen (Eds.), *Handbook of psychological assessment* (2nd ed.). New York: Pergamon Press.

Spitzer, R. L., Williams, J. B. W., & Nee, J. (1979). DSM-III field trials: Initial interrater diagnostic reliability. *American Journal of Psychiatry, 136,* 815–817.

Sullivan, H. S. (1954). *The psychiatric interview.* New York: Norton.

Wiens, A. N. (1990). Structured clinical interviews for adults. In G. Goldstein & M. Hersen (Eds.), *Handbook of psychological assessment* (2nd ed.). New York: Pergamon Press.

Williams, J. B. W., Gibbon, M., First, M. B., Spitzer, R. L., Davies, M., Borus, J., Howes, M. J., Kane, J., Pope, H. G., Rounsaville, B., & Wittchen, H. (1992). The Structured Clinical Interview for DSM-III-R (SCID): Multisite test-retest reliability. *Archives of General Psychiatry, 49,* 630–636.

Phan Y. Hong
Stephen S. Ilardi
University of Kansas

STRUCTURED CLINICAL INTERVIEW FOR DIAGNOSIS

Since the 1970s, the perception of the low reliability of psychiatric diagnosis and the need for homogeneous research groups have stimulated the improvement of classification systems of psychiatric disorders. The establishment of specific diagnostic criteria for each mental disorder, with inclusion and exclusion criteria, as well as criteria for evaluation of severity and duration of symptoms, significantly enhanced the reliability of psychiatric diagnosis.

Nevertheless, the refinement of operational diagnostic criteria fails to control other sources of low reliability, such as the interviewer's behavior and expectations and variations in the information obtained from the patient. To overcome these difficulties, structured and semistructured interview instruments have been developed, based on different classification systems. The development of these instruments is intermingled with the development of the classification systems on which they are based. The instruments began to play an important role not only in research but also in clinical practice and in the training of mental health professionals.

One of the first structured interviews was the Present State Examination (PSE), which aimed at describing psychopathological phenomena in a reliable and objective way (Wing, 1983). The PSE consists of 140 items, 107 referring to symptoms described by the patient and 33 referring to behavior observed by the interviewer. It includes a glossary with comprehensive and precise definitions of each item, the evaluation of which depends on knowledge of psychopathology, clinical judgment, and training with the instrument. The PSE results in a psychological profile that allows clinical diagnoses through the Catego computer program. These diagnoses are based on a conceptual framework strongly influenced by classical psychopathology and are not comparable to any other diagnostic classification system.

The structured clinical interviews are made of closed-ended questions and can also be conducted by lay interviewers after specific training. Rating depends exclusively on the answer given by the person interviewed, and the interview is usually brief. Examples of this kind of interview are the National Institute of Mental Health's Diagnostic Interview Schedule (DIS) and the Composite International Diagnostic Interview (CIDI). The DIS (Robins, Helzer, Croughan, & Ratcliff, 1981) was developed as part of a large epidemiological study performed in the United States (NIMH-ECA), and it is based on three classification systems. Answers to the questions are codified, and the final diagnosis is established from an analysis made by a specific computer program. The CIDI (Robins et al., 1988) was elaborated for epidemiological studies as well, and its questions are modified items from the DIS and PSE.

Interview instruments such as the Schedule for Affective Disorders and Schizophrenia (SADS) and the Structured Clinical Interview for the *DSM-IV* (SCID) can be classified as semistructured interviews because their open-ended questions allow some flexibility. These features of semistructured interviews require familiarization with the diagnostic criteria of the system on which the interview is based and training in the instrument. Because rating is based on clinical judgment and not only on the answer given by the interviewee, only mental health professionals should apply these instruments.

The SADS (Endicott & Spitzer, 1978) aims at the identification of the 25 diagnostic categories. Reliability coefficients obtained with SADS were significant for the majority of the disorders studied and were better than those for most of the reports available at the time of their publication.

Although SADS has been well accepted, it had some limitations because it does not include all mental disorders and it gives little attention to psychosocial assessment. Due to these shortcomings, the SCID was published in the 1980s; it has the same outline of SADS but is based on criteria and diagnostic categories proposed by the American Psychiatric Association (*DSM-III-R* and *DSM-IV;* APA, 1994).

The SCID (Spitzer, Williams, Gibbon, & First, 1992) can be applied to patients as well as to individuals not identified as patients. The interviewer is encouraged to use all sources of information available. Questions are grouped according to diagnosis or criterion, and the scores and diagnostic criteria are integrated into the structure of the interview so that several hypotheses are successively tested. When an essential diagnostic criterion of a particular disorder is not fulfilled, remaining questions on the disorder may be ignored.

The SCID begins with an overview session, which follows the general process of a nonstructured clinical interview. From this overview, the interview is organized in modules that generally refer to the diagnostic classes of the *DSM-IV.* This organization allows the evaluation of a few modules only. Studies of SCID reliability have generally yielded satisfactory results.

The good reliability indexes obtained with these instruments have enabled studies with more precise information about the clinical picture, evolution, prognosis, and comorbidity of several mental disorders. Nevertheless, the use of structured and semistructured clinical interviews relies on familiarization with the instrument. For this purpose, adequate training with the instruments is fundamental and should follow the instructions provided by the instruments themselves.

REFERENCES

American Psychiatric Association. (1994). *Diagnostic and Statistical manual of mental disorders, IV.* Washington, DC: Author.

Endicott, J., & Spitzer, R. L. (1978). A diagnostic interview: The schedule for affective disorders and schizophrenia. *Archives of General Psychiatry, 35,* 837–844.

Robins, L. N., Helzer, J. W., Croughan, J., & Ratcliff, K. S. (1981). National Institute of Mental Health diagnostic interview schedule: Its history, characteristics, and validity. *Archives of General Psychiatry, 38,* 381–389.

Robins, L. N., Wing, J., Wittchen, H. U., Helzer, J. E., Babor, T. F., Burke, J., Farmer, A., Jablenski, A., Pickens, R., Regier, D. A., Sartorius, N., & Towle, L. H. (1988). The composite international diagnostic interview: An epidemiologic instrument suitable for use conjunction with different diagnostic systems and different cultures. *Archives of General Psychiatry, 45,* 1069–1077.

Spitzer, R. L., Williams, J. R., Gibbon, M., & First, M. B. (1992). The structured clinical interview for DSM-III-R: I. History, rationale, and description. *Archives of General Psychiatry, 49,* 624–629.

Wing, J. K. (1983). Use and misuse of the PSE. *British Journal of Psychiatry, 143,* 111–117.

Christina M. Del-Ben
University of São Paulo

***See also:* Diagnosis; Reliability**

STUDY METHODS

Outside the classroom, the primary means by which students learn have long been the preparation of homework assignments, other guided-study activities monitored by a teacher, and independent study on special projects. The requisite studying typically involves reading and remembering written materials, drilling on exercises so as to master specific skills, and preparing and presenting materials for evaluation by a teacher. In addition to textbooks, students often use library resources to acquire specialized information from printed reference materials or from audiovisual sources. Most studying involves working alone, although students often join together to clarify and plan assigned study activities, to obtain feedback or help on assignments, to review completed homework material, or to review for an upcoming examination. Studying traditionally has required a wide variety of activities. The advent of new educational technology based on televised and computer-assisted instruction likely will bring about changes in these traditional study approaches.

Observers have noted wide variations in the study methods typically employed by students. The time and place for studying, the physical conditions of the study environment, and the employment of specific study mechanics were some of the many factors observed. In spite of the lack of consistency seen, a large number of how-to-study books, guides, and tests have been published to assist students in improving study skills. Many schools and colleges offer study skills instruction.

Robinson, originator of the SQ3R method for reading textbooks, presented the approach following several years of research on the reading problems encountered by failing, average, and superior students. This study method, or some variation of it, has been included in most how-to-study books published subsequently. Five steps comprise the SQ3R method:

1. *Survey* the chapter.
2. *Question* by turning headings into questions to be answered while reading.
3. *Read* actively by underlining key phrases and marking main points.
4. *Recite* the main points to yourself in your own words to check your learning.
5. *Review* periodically to refresh your memory and ensure retention.

Pauk developed the five-step Cornell system for taking notes as the product of extensive trial and experiment based on learning theory. The steps are as follows:

1. During the lecture, *record* as many meaningful facts and ideas as possible in the main column of the notes.
2. After the lecture, *reduce* these ideas and facts into key words and phrases listed in the recall column.
3. Cover the main column and *recite* the main facts and ideas to yourself using the cues provided by the recall column.
4. *Reflect* on the material and write your own ideas and opinions in a separately organized summation.

5. Periodically *review* the notes quickly to ensure that the material is remembered.

Brown and Holtzman employed direct observation, interviews, and questionnaires to develop the Survey of Study Habits and Attitudes (SSHA). Specific suggestions for implementing efficient study skills and effective academic attitudes were derived directly from the SSHA.

Many how-to-study guides and study skills inventories have been published, but there appears to be considerable disagreement as to what constitutes good study habits. Some researchers have turned to the investigation of motivational factors. Following an intensive review of existing how-to-study literature, Brown concluded that attitudinal and motivational characteristics were of potentially greater importance than the purely mechanical procedures of studying. More important was what motivated the student to acquire or not acquire, and to use or not use, methods for effective studying.

The following topics are included in most study skills courses: using time efficiently, developing concentration skills, organizing the study area, reading and marking textbooks, skimming articles, summarizing concepts, organizing and outlining material, improving remembering, building vocabulary, taking lecture notes, taking reading notes, setting meaningful goals, conducting library research, writing in-class themes, writing topic reports, studying mathematical material, studying scientific material, preparing laboratory reports, making oral reports, reviewing for examinations, desensitizing test anxiety, taking objective tests, writing essay examinations, and taking problem tests.

Beginning in the early 1960s, the rapid expansion in educational opportunities for the economically disadvantaged resulted in the admission of large numbers of nontraditional students who were relatively ill-prepared for the academic demands of higher education. Without effective assistance in acquiring needed learning skills, these students found that the open door to educational opportunity quickly became a revolving door to academic oblivion. Concern about their low level of academic preparedness led to the creation of special learning centers with programs designed to help these students acquire the learning skills necessary for academic success.

Since its introduction, the concept of a college-wide learning assistance center to provide broad-based services for all students appears to have been widely accepted. Fiscally, however, the movement is struggling for full administrative recognition and acceptance. In the future, the development and implementation of new educational technologies, including computer-based instructional systems, should further expand the role and scope of learning assistance activities in both secondary and higher education.

W. F. Brown

See also: **School Learning**

SUBLIMINAL INFLUENCE

Subliminal influence is defined as the use of persuasion tactics delivered below the threshold of awareness. Although the term *subliminal perception* is well defined in the psychological literature, the term *subliminal influence* is used to refer to a grab bag of techniques ranging from flashing words quickly onto a movie screen, to backward phrases in rock music, to cleverly hidden images in advertisements (see Pratkanis, 1992).

Scientific research has consistently failed to support claims for the effectiveness of subliminal persuasion. In general, researchers have found that people can minimally process subliminal messages (e.g., extracting meaning from a single word presented outside of awareness) but cannot process complex subliminal messages (Greenwald, 1992; Pratkanis & Greenwald, 1988). Regardless of the level of processing, subliminal messages have not been shown to influence behavior.

Opinion polls show that most Americans believe that subliminal messages can influence behavior (Synodinos, 1988). Much of this belief in subliminal persuasion has been stimulated by sensational claims that have appeared in the mass media.

For example, in the late 1950s, James Vicary, an advertising expert, circulated a story claiming that he had secretly flashed the words "Eat Popcorn" and "Drink Coke" onto a movie screen. Vicary claimed an increase in Coke sales of 18% and a rise in popcorn sales of almost 58%. In the 1970s Wilson Bryan Key (1973) proclaimed that subliminal implants were routinely placed in print advertisements. Also in the 1970s, parents and ministers began to evidence concern that rock music contained backward messages often of a Satanic nature. In the 1990s manufacturers of subliminal self-help tapes claimed that their tapes could change personality and behavior. In 1990 the rock band Judas Priest was placed on trial for allegedly putting the subliminal implant "Do it" in one of their songs, causing the suicide deaths of two teenage boys.

Given public belief, it is useful to ask, How effective are subliminal messages in changing and motivating behavior? The conclusion from over 100 years of research is that subliminal messages are incapable of influencing behavior. In a comprehensive review of the literature, Moore (1982) concluded, "There is no empirical documentation for stronger subliminal effects, such as inducing particular behaviors or changing motivation. Moreover, such a notion is contradicted by a substantial amount of research and is incompatible with experimentally based conceptions of information processing, learning, and motivation." Other reviewers have reached the same conclusion, noting that proclaimed subliminal effects often fail to replicate and that studies claiming to find subliminal influence are methodological flawed and unsound (see Eich & Hyman, 1991; Pratkanis & Greenwald, 1988).

Consider Vicary's claim for increased sales of popcorn

and Coke because of subliminal messages. In 1958 the Canadian Broadcast Corporation conducted a replication of this study by flashing the message "Phone Now" during a popular television show ("Phone Now," 1958). Telephone usage did not go up during the period. Later, Vicary admitted, "Worse than the timing, though, was the fact that we hadn't done any research, except what was needed for filing for a patent" (Danzig, 1962).

Key's work has been criticized on methodological grounds. For example, Key (1973) reported a study in which 62% of students who saw a Gilbey Gin ad that supposedly contained the word sex embedded in ice cubes reported feeling aroused and sensuous. However, Key did not include a control group (students who saw a similar ad without the implant), and thus we cannot know if these feelings were aroused because of the alleged implant, in spite of it, or for some other reason.

Vokey and Read (1985) conducted an extensive program of research showing that backward messages are ineffective in altering behavior. They found that subjects could not distinguish between backward nursery rhymes, Christian, satanic, pornographic, or advertising messages.

Several studies have investigated the efficacy of subliminal self-help audiotapes. For example, Pratkanis, Eskenazi, and Greenwald (1994) had participants listen to subliminal self-help tapes designed to improve either self-esteem or memory. Some participants received mislabeled tapes—a memory-improving tape labeled as a self-esteem tape and vice versa. After five weeks of listening, the results showed no improvement in self-esteem or memory abilities. To date there have been nine independent investigations of subliminal self-help tapes—all failing to find an effect consistent with manufacturers' claims (see Pratkanis, 1992).

In the trial of Judas Priest, Judge Jerry Carr Whitehead ruled in favor of the band. His ruling stands as a summary judgment of the power of subliminal persuasion: "The scientific research presented does not establish that subliminal stimuli, even if perceived, may precipitate conduct of this magnitude (i.e., suicide deaths)."

REFERENCES

Danzig, F. (1962, September 17). Subliminal advertising: Today it's just historic flashback for researcher Vicary. *Advertising Age.*

Eich, E., & Hyman, R. (1991). Subliminal self-help. In D. Druckman & R. A. Bjork (Eds.), *In the mind's eye: Enhancing human performance* (pp. 107–119). Washington, DC: National Academy Press.

Greenwald, A. G. (1992). New look 3: Unconscious cognition reclaimed. *American Psychologist, 47,* 766–779.

Key, W. B. (1973). *Subliminal seduction.* Englewood Cliffs, NJ: Signet.

Moore, T. E. (1982). Subliminal advertising: What you see is what you get. *Journal of Marketing, 46,* 38–47.

"Phone now," said CBC subliminally—but nobody did. (1958, February 10). *Advertising Age,* p. 8.

Pratkanis, A. R. (1992). The cargo-cult science of subliminal persuasion. *Skeptical Inquirer, 16,* 260–272.

Pratkanis, A. R., Eskenazi, J., & Greenwald, A. G. (1994). What you expect is what you believe (but not necessarily what you get): A test of the effectiveness of subliminal self-help audiotapes. *Basic and Applied Social Psychology, 15,* 251–276.

Pratkanis, A. R., & Greenwald, A. G. (1988). Recent perspectives on unconscious processing: Still no marketing applications. *Psychology and Marketing, 5,* 339–355.

Synodinos, N. E. (1988). Subliminal stimulation: What does the public think about it? *Current Issues and Research in Advertising, 11,* 157–187.

Vokey, J. R., & Read, J. D. (1985). Subliminal messages: Between the devil and the media. *American Psychologist, 40,* 12311239.

Anthony R. Pratkanis
University of California, Santa Cruz

SUBLIMINAL PERCEPTION

Beginning with the end of the 1950s, a great deal of public concern was expressed when it was claimed that a method existed for presenting advertising messages that could influence behavior at an unconscious level. A typical example might be at a movie theatre, where the message "Buy popcorn" could be given during the film, and even though viewers were not consciously aware of its presence, they might still be motivated to purchase popcorn. The procedures involved quickly flashing messages on the screen at a size, speed, or brightness that was too insignificant to produce conscious awareness. Such stimuli are called *subliminal,* from the Latin for below (*sub*) the threshold for consciousness (*limen*). Subliminal perception comes about when such stimuli, even though apparently unnoticed, appear to exert an effect on later behavior.

There is still controversy as to whether subliminal stimuli have the ability to persuade in advertising settings. Many researchers note that stimuli that are intended to be subliminal may occasionally make it into our consciousness. It has often been suggested that it is only on those occasions when the stimulus actually is detected (even if these are statistically rare) that the message can have any effect. Thus, to persuade people to any great extent, the message cannot be truly subliminal but has to reach consciousness, at least occasionally (e.g., Smith & Rogers, 1994).

The problem with the study of subliminal perception was that it caught the attention of the popular media, and many of the claims made for subliminal persuasion were extravagant and bizarre. For instance, there were claims that people were being manipulated through subliminal sexual symbolism, which was hidden in television and even magazine advertisements. Strange stories were published in which it was suggested that teenagers were being deliberately exposed to subliminal stimuli in musical recordings, which were placed there by revolutionaries and terrorists who wanted to stir aggressive responses in them. Some religious groups claimed that subliminal messages in films, television, and musical recordings were being used by devil worshippers to undermine the morals of the public and to gain them new converts. Such suggestions could never be convincingly substantiated, however these apparent associations with fringe groups and marginalized social activities, plus a lot of bad science, brought the whole topic into disrepute for many years.

Over the years three lines of research have rehabilitated the study of subliminal perception. These are based on what is called the mere exposure effect (Zajonc, 2002). This is a phenomenon that demonstrates that simple repeated exposure to a stimulus, even if it is not consciously noticed or attended to, can produce positive feelings for that stimulus when it is later encountered. This effect has proven to be a robust, reliable phenomenon, showing that people tend to prefer stimuli that they have seen before, no matter what they are—whether drawings, photographs, nonsense words, or even social behaviors of people. One important aspect of these findings is that the effect seems to be quite primitive. People do not need to be consciously aware that they have seen the stimulus, nor do they have to be able to remember ever encountering it before. In fact, a number of studies have suggested that the emotional effect associated with mere exposure is even greater if the stimuli are subliminal (e.g., Bornstein & D'Agonstino, 1992).

Clinical psychologists have cited another aspect of how emotional factors play a role in subliminal perception. This is in the case of perceptual defense. Typical examples occur in experiments in which observers are briefly shown nonsense syllables or figures and are asked to identify them. If some of the stimuli presented had been previously associated with painful electric shock, they might now be expected to be somewhat anxiety producing. In general, it is found that such negative emotional stimuli are recognized less readily than are neutral stimuli—as if the observers are defending themselves from the painful memories evoked by seeing such stimuli. Still, it is possible to show that perception has taken place subliminally. This is done through the use of physiological measures of anxiety, such as the galvanic skin response, which registers the person's negative emotional state for the stimuli, even though the observer cannot consciously identify them. This process, in which there is an emotional response but no conscious awareness of the stimulus, is sometimes also called *subception.*

The most recent, and probably the most active, lines of research involving subliminal perception have involved cognitive psychologists. They have returned to this process due to their interest in an effect called *priming,* in which the occurrence of one stimulus may make it easier to perceive a later stimulus that is related to it in some way. For example, a priming study involving word recognition might first briefly present the prime word, which is followed by a complex *masking stimulus* that prevents the prime word from being consciously seen, followed by a target word. Thus we might briefly present the word "nurse" and follow it with a semantically related word (one that has an associated meaning) such as "doctor" or an unrelated word such as "carrot." Typically, priming is shown when the person responds more quickly to the related word than to the neutral word. It is believed that the prime word has somehow activated cognitive processes associated with the first stimulus, making the stimuli that come later easier to process (see Neely, 1991). The label *priming* comes from the fact that older water pumps often needed to be primed by first having some water poured into the pump chamber before they could efficiently draw additional fluid up from the well.

One of the interesting aspects of priming is that the priming stimulus does not have to be conscious, but can be totally unconscious or subliminal (e.g., Klinger & Greenwald, 1995). During the course of such research, it has become clear that subliminal perception may actually trigger associations that are necessary for us to read quickly and process written information efficiently. Thus we register data from the words that are still ahead of us on the printed page subliminally. Our unconscious perception of this material makes it easier for us to recognize those words and ideas when we encounter them later, as our eyes move down the text, because these associations have already been subliminally primed (Sereno & Rayner, 1992). This suggests that subliminal perception is not a rare psychological oddity but may be a common and integral component in the way that we process information from our environment.

REFERENCES

Bornstein, R. F., & D'Agonstino. (1992). Stimulus recognition and the mere exposure effect. *Journal of Personality and Social Psychology, 63,* 545–552.

Klinger, M. R., & Greenwald, A. G. (1995). Unconscious priming of association judgments. *Journal of Experimental Psychology: Learning, Memory, and Cognition, 21,* 569–581.

Neely, J. H. (1991). Semantic priming effects in visual word recognition: A selective review of current findings and theories. In D. Besner & G. Humphreys (Eds.), *Basic processes in reading: Visual word recognition* (pp. 264–336). Hillsdale, NJ: Erlbaum.

Sereno, S. C., & Rayner, K. (1992). Fast priming during eye fixations in reading. *Journal of Experimental Psychology: Human Perception and Performance, 18,* 173–184.

Smith, K. H., & Rogers, M. (1994). Effectiveness of subliminal messages in television commercials: Two experiments. *Journal of Applied Psychology, 79,* 866–874.

Zajonc, R. B. (2002). Mere exposure: A gateway to the subliminal. *Current Directions in Psychological Science, 10,* 224–228.

Stanley Coren
University of British Columbia

SUCCESSIVE APPROXIMATION (SHAPING)

The terms *successive approximation* and *shaping* are shorthand for the phrase "successive reinforcement of closer and closer approximations to the target behavior" (Skinner, 1953). This procedure is distinct from other operant reinforcement methods (e.g., chaining) in that it relies on both reinforcement and extinction applied to a changing set of criteria responses (Galbicka, 1994). The target, or terminal, response is either infrequent or novel to the organism (i.e., has never been performed), limiting the utility of direct reinforcement of the response. Shaping, as the name implies, involves slow transformations of the organism's behavior over time, much like the process of shaping clay into a fine piece of pottery. Initially, a gross or distal response is sufficient for the delivery of reinforcement. In time, a more similar response is required. This process continues until only the terminal response elicits reinforcement.

Shaping is a powerful tool for expanding the repertoire of organisms, including humans. Shaping may be intentional or unintentional, depending on whether the behavior was produced from planned or accidental reinforcement (i.e., contrived vs. natural consequences).

Examples

1. *Planned shaping.* Molly would like to teach her 1-year-old daughter Sally to call her mommy. Sally currently does not say mommy, but she does say "ma" occasionally. Molly begins to pay extra attention (e.g., says "Great job, Sally" and smiles) when Sally says "ma." Soon Sally says "ma" often. Molly decides it is now time for Sally to say something more similar to mommy, so she no longer praises her for simply saying "ma." Instead, Molly reinforces Sally for saying "ma" twice in a row, which sounds like "moma." This process continues until moma is shaped into mommy.
2. *Accidental shaping.* Timmy is a 3-year-old boy without a history of tantrums. Timmy is bored with shopping at the store, and he begins to whine. His father Don tries to console him by picking him up, talking to him, and giving him something with which to play. The next time Timmy is bored while shopping, he begins to whine. Don appears to have accidentally reinforced Timmy's whining in similar situations. However, whining is no longer sufficient to get Don's attention (i.e., extinction). Timmy changes his whining to wailing, which does catch Don's attention (i.e., extinction burst). Now Don tries to console him as he did before. This process continues, and each time Timmy's behavior escalates in order to gain his father's attention. Ultimately, Timmy tantrums to gain the attention of his father. Hence, Don inadvertently shaped this tantrumming response in Timmy.

Considerations

Although shaping may be accidental, programmed shaping may be of more use to clinicians, parents, and teachers. To shape behavior successfully, Martin and Pear (1999) indicated four factors to be considered.

1. *Specifying the final desired behavior.* The final desired behavior, or terminal behavior, should be well specified. This includes topography (shape or form), intensity, frequency, context, and antecedent conditions. By defining the target behavior with this level of clarity, caretakers and providers will be more likely to apply the shaping procedure consistently.
2. *Choosing the starting behavior.* The starting behavior must occur at a rate likely to receive reinforcement during the training session. This necessity will help select the starting behavior from among the class of possible starting behaviors, even if other behaviors more closely resemble or approximate the target behavior. For example, Molly might have mistakenly chosen to start with Sally saying "mommy," a word not yet within her repertoire.
3. *Choosing the shaping steps.* Prior to shaping, one should consider the likely permutations between the starting behavior and the terminal behavior. Because complex behavior is comprised of multiple chains or patterns of response, the possible permutations may be limitless. Nonetheless, decisions regarding which approximations are sufficient to qualify as progress toward the target behavior must be made. The exact rules for this process are not well specified in the literature. Typically, the new criterion should result in reinforcer delivery at least 50% but not more than 80% of the time. A rate less than 50% is likely to result in an effect similar to extinction of variable ratio schedules, whereby the behavior slowly varies and then tapers off. This is sometimes also referred to as ratio strain. A rate higher than 80% is likely to create inflexibility when the next criterion for success is initiated.
4. *Moving along at the correct pace.* Shaping protocols are typically flexible; if the organism fails to display the new approximation response, simpler steps may be created to facilitate learning. Likewise, when progress is more rapid than expected, criteria for reinforcement may be raised (i.e., more advanced steps may be attempted).

Additional Considerations

In addition to the four typical considerations, it is also important to consider selecting reinforcers, tracking progress, and choosing target behaviors.

- *Selecting reinforcers.* Often overlooked in discussions of shaping, reinforcer selection may be the most important consideration in shaping. Rewards are not the same as reinforcers; reinforcers by definition increase the probability of occurrence of the preceding behavior. Have the person help choose the reinforcer, if possible. Then monitor the shaping process to see if the response frequency is increasing. If it is not, you are not using a reinforcer.

- *Tracking progress.* Progress is not a given in behavioral psychology. Data need be collected to evaluate progress. Data are needed to determine reinforcer effectiveness, pacing of steps, and strength of new responses. A graph of the data employing a changing-criterion design will help consolidate most aspects of the shaping program into a single, simple form.
- *Choosing target behaviors.* Shaping is a highly effective tool for teaching new behavior. Shaping may be used to change behavior even when the organism, or person, is unaware that it is being shaped. Careful consideration should be taken when deciding to use shaping, and target behaviors must be appropriate and beneficial for the organism. Take the time to consider the ethics of your decision, and involve the participant in this process if applicable.

REFERENCES

Galbicka, G. (1994). Shaping in the 21st century: Moving percentile schedules into applied settings. *Journal of Applied Behavior Analysis, 27*(4), 739–760.

Martin, G., & Pear, J. (1999). *Behavior modification: What it is and how to do it* (6th ed.). Englewood Cliffs, NJ: Prentice Hall.

Skinner, B. F. (1953). *Science and human behavior.* New York: MacMillan.

David B. Hatfield
Devereux Cleo Wallace

See also: **Operant Conditioning**

SUICIDAL BEHAVIOR AMONG YOUTH

Epidemiology

Adolescent suicide completions and attempts are public health problems (U.S. Department of Health and Human Services, 2001). Although suicide is uncommon in childhood, it is the fourth leading cause of death in 10- to 14-year-olds and the third leading cause of death for adolescents ages 15–19 (www.cdc.gov). The suicide rate for young people has tripled since 1950, and among adolescents the rate has stabilized at 11 suicides per 100,000 (Goldsmith, Pellmar, Kleinman, & Bunney, 2002). Firearms, hanging, and suffocation are the most common means for suicide completions in youth (www.cdc.gov). Within a 12-month period, approximately 20% of adolescents in the United States seriously consider attempting suicide; 16% develop a suicide plan; 8% attempt suicide; and 3% attempt suicide in a manner requiring emergency medical attention (Centers for Disease Control and Prevention [CDC], 1998b, 2000).

Suicidal ideation and attempts are more common among adolescent females than males (CDC, 1998b). However, completions are more common in boys than girls (5:1; National Center for Health Statistics, 2000). Although historically, suicide rates have been lower among African American than Caucasian youth, the gap has narrowed recently (CDC, 1998a). The highest youth suicide rate is among Native American males (Wallace, Calhoun, Poweel, O'Neil, & James, 1996). Latino youth do not appear to be overrepresented among completed suicides.

Risk Factors

Genetic and Biological

A family history of suicidal behavior increases the risk of attempted and completed suicide (Glowinski et al., 2001; Gould & Kramer, 2001). The role of genetic factors is further supported by twin and adoption studies (Roy, 1992). Early studies on the link between serotonin abnormalities and suicidal behavior in youth suggest an association similar to that reported among adults (Gould & Kramer, 2001).

Psychopathology

A major psychological risk factor for youth suicide and suicide attempts is a history of a prior suicide attempt (Gould & Kramer, 2001). Psychiatric disorders found to be risk factors for the continuum of suicidal behavior include mood, anxiety, disruptive behavior, substance use, and personality disorders (Borowsky, Ireland, & Resnick, 2001; Esposito & Clum, 2002; Zimmerman & Asnis, 1995). A history of prior mental health care is often noted in youth who attempt suicide (Stewart, Manion, Davidson, & Cloutier, 2001).

Cognitive Factors

Cognitive factors associated with suicidal behavior among youth include low self-esteem, hopelessness, negative automatic thoughts, maladaptive attributional styles, and external locus of control (Nock & Kazdin, 2002; Wagner, Rouleau, & Joiner, 2000; Yang & Clum, 2000).

Stressful Life Events

Early negative life events are associated with later suicidality in youth (Yang & Clum, 2000). Adolescent suicide attempters report higher rates of stressful life events 12 months prior to the attempt (Davidson & Linnoila, 1991). Specific life stresses include fights with parents, breakups with a romantic partner, loss of a parent due to death or divorce, and legal or disciplinary problems (Gould & Kramer, 2001).

Family

Parental psychopathology is associated with suicidal ideation, attempts, and completions in youth (Gould & Kramer, 2001). Changes in the composition of the family, such as death, parental separation, divorce, or other losses, also put adolescents at increased risk for suicidal behavior (Gould & Kramer, 2001; Wagner, 1997). The experience of physical or sexual abuse is a risk factor that has been replicated across several studies (Wagner, 1997). Other family risk factors include poor family or parent-child communication, parent-child discord, family aggression, and low family cohesiveness (Gould & Kramer, 2001; Wagner, 1997).

Peer Relationships

Suicidal youth tend to evince impaired social skills, poor interpersonal relationships, and deficient problem-solving skills, making them vulnerable to engaging in suicidal behavior in response to negative stressors (Yang & Clum, 1994). Perceived peer rejection and the lack of close friendship support serve as risk factors for suicidal ideation and attempts (Prinstein, Boergers, Spirito, Little, & Grapentine, 2000). Lifetime prevalence rates of physical and sexual dating violence are associated with suicidality (Sileverman, Raj, Mucci, & Hathaway, 2001). Further, a burgeoning literature reveals that same-sex romantic attachments and relationships increase an adolescent's risk for suicidal behavior (Borowsky et al., 2001). Gay adolescents are two to three times more likely to attempt or commit suicide than are their heterosexual peers (Radkowsky & Siegel, 1997).

Imitation and Contagion

Direct or indirect exposure to suicide is associated with suicidal behavior among youth (Spirito, Brown, Overholser, & Fitz, 1989). Person-to-person contact with another individual who has attempted suicide is linked with suicidal behavior (Borowsky et al., 2001). Indirect exposure to suicide, through media coverage of suicide attempts or fictional accounts of suicide, also is linked with suicidal behavior among adolescents (Gould, 2001). Furthermore, the intensity of media coverage of suicides of well-known celebrities is positively related to suicidal behavior.

Socioenvironmental Factors

Difficulties in school and school absence pose suicide risks for youth (Gould & Kramer, 2001). To date, limited data are available on the effects of socioeconomic status on suicidal behavior in youth.

Protective Factors

Data from the National Longitudinal Study of Adolescent Health revealed that perceived parent and family connectedness were protective against suicide attempts for adolescent males and females across racial-ethnic groups (Borowsky et al., 2001). Emotional well-being was found to be a protective factor for females, and high grade point average was a protective factor for males (Borowsky et al., 2001). The endorsement of more reasons for living protects youth from attempting to kill themselves (Gutierrez, Osman, Kopper, & Barrios, 2000).

Assessment

Berman and Jobes (1991) stressed the importance of a multifocused assessment of suicidality and outlined six dimensions: imminent risk, lethality and intent, predisposing conditions and precipitating factors, psychopathology, cooperation with the interviewer, and coping skills and resources. Using these data, the clinician may screen for levels of risk of suicidal behavior. More recently, the American Academy of Child and Adolescent Psychiatry (AACAP, 2001) presented practice parameters for the assessment of suicide ideators and attempters that underscore the importance of evaluating the suicidal behavior, assessing underlying conditions and risk factors, and determining the risk for death or repetition. The practice guidelines note that such assessment may include the use of specialized suicide scales and instruments that tap related constructs and risk factors.

Crisis Management and Intervention

Management of a suicidal youth is focused on keeping the individual physically safe and alive until the crisis has passed. Optimally, there is a service delivery system that includes emergency room interventions, inpatient services, and short- and long-term outpatient services available for youth who attempt to kill themselves (AACAP, 2001; Rotheram-Borus, Piancentini, et al., 1996; Rotheram-Borus, Walker, & Ferns, 1996; Spirito, Boergers, Donaldson, Bishop, & Lewander, 2002).

Cognitive-behavioral, interpersonal, dialectical-behavior, psychodynamic, family systems, and integrationist approaches may be applied to suicidal youth (AACAP, 2001). Cognitive-behavioral treatment is structured and focuses on building interpersonal, coping, and problem-solving skills. Empirical data suggest that cognitive-behavioral strategies that increase coping skills are useful in decreasing suicidal ideation and suicide attempts (Rotheram-Borus, Piancentini, Miller, Graae, & Castro-Blanco, 1994; Rudd & Joiner, 1998). Dialectical-behavior therapy with suicidal adolescents with a diagnosis of borderline personality disorder appears to be associated with reduced rates of psychiatric hospitalization (Miller, Rathus, Linehan, Wetzler, & Leigh, 1997). A time-limited, home-based family intervention has been found to be helpful for those suicidal youth who also are depressed (Harrington et al., 1998). Further, developmental group psychotherapy, which combines problem-solving, cognitive-behavioral, dialectical-behavior, and psychodynamic group psychotherapy approaches, was found to be more effective than routine care in reducing suicidal behavior and behavioral disorders and enhancing school attendance (Wood, Trainor, Rothwell, Moore, & Harrington, 2001). To date, no clinical trials have ascertained the efficacy of psychopharmacological interventions (AACAP, 2001). Nonetheless, medications may be essential in stabilizing and treating the psychological conditions often observed in suicidal children and adolescents.

Prevention

There has been a proliferation of suicide prevention strategies over the past 10 to 15 years, and there was a recent call to action for the systematic development, evaluation, and implementation of such prevention efforts (U.S. Department of Health and Human Services, 2001). The School Health Policies and Programs Study found that 26% of states required suicide prevention at the elementary school level; 42% required prevention programs at the middle or junior high level; and 46% mandated programs during the senior high school years (www.cdc.gov).

Suicide prevention strategies aim to identify suicidal youth and refer them to intervention programs that target the reduction of risk factors. Several case-finding strategies have been used to increase the recognition and referral of suicidal youth (AACAP 2001; Gould & Kramer, 2001). Case-finding strategies can be accomplished via the provision of school-based suicide awareness curricula, large-scale screening efforts, gatekeeper training, crisis centers and hotlines, media counseling to minimize imitative suicide, and training health care professional to improve the recognition and treatment of mood disorders. Suicide awareness programs aim to facilitate self-disclosure and increase awareness of suicidal behavior among peers so that youth can secure help for their suicidal peers (Hazell & King, 1996). Large-scale screening efforts, which may be conducted in schools, forensic settings, treatment programs, and primary care providers' offices, incorporate self-report and individual interviews in a multistage assessment of risk factors associated with suicide attempts and completions (Shaffer & Craft, 1999). Once these at-risk youth are identified, they may benefit from such youth suicide prevention efforts as Counselors Care (C-CARE) and Coping and Support Training (CAST; Randell, Eggert, & Pike, 2001). The purpose of gatekeeper training is to develop the competence of natural community helpers (e.g., teachers, clergy, and coaches) to identify youth at risk for suicidal behavior and their level of risk and to make appropriate referrals once they identify the young people in need (Kalafat & Elias, 1995). Even though there is limited data on the efficacy of telephone crisis services for youth, hotlines may prove useful if their use were increased and optimized (Gould & Kramer, 2001). Guidelines have been promulgated to support sensible and responsible media coverage of youth suicide by both the Centers for Disease Control and Prevention and the American Foundation for the Prevention of Suicide (AACAP, 2001). Finally, there is some evidence that training for primary care providers on the evaluation of mood disorders and suicidality may be associated with reduced rates of suicidal behavior and more appropriate interventions (Rihmer, Rutz, & Pihlgran, 1995). One final risk-factor reduction strategy that deserves mention relates to the restriction of lethal means, such as the recent efforts at restricting access to firearms, safer prescribing regarding antidepressant medications, and emission controls (Gould & Kramer, 2001).

Postsuicide Intervention

There has been an increase in the number of available school- and community-based postvention programs, programs that target family members, friends, fellow students, and community members following a suicide. Unfortunately, little empirical investigation has been conducted to determine the effectiveness of these programs (Gould & Kramer, 2001). Of course, long-term support and services also need to be easily accessible for families and friends grieved by the loss of a loved one (AACAP, 2001).

REFERENCES

American Academy of Child and Adolescent Psychiatry. (2001). Practice parameter for the assessment and treatment of children and adolescents with suicidal behavior. *Journal of the American Academy of Child and Adolescent Psychiatry, 40*(Suppl. 7), 24S–51S.

Berman, A. L., & Jobes, D. A. (1991). *Adolescent suicide assessment and intervention.* Washington, DC: American Psychological Association.

Borowsky, I. W., Ireland, M., & Resnick, M. D. (2001). Adolescent suicide attempts: Risks and protectors. *Pediatrics, 107,* 485–493.

Centers for Disease Control and Prevention. (1998a). Suicide among Black youths: United States, 1980–1995. *Morbidity and Mortality Weekly Report, 47,* 193–196.

Centers for Disease Control and Prevention. (1998b). Youth-risk behavior surveillance: United States, 1997. *Morbidity and Mortality Weekly Report, 47*(SS-3).

Centers for Disease Control and Prevention. (2000). 1999 Youth Risk Behavior Surveillance: Sadness and suicide ideation and attempts. *Morbidity and Mortality Weekly Report, 49*(SS-05), 1–96.

Davidson, L. E., & Linnoila, M. (Eds.). (1991). *Risk factors for youth suicide.* New York: Hemisphere.

Esposito, C. L., & Clum, G. A. (2002). Psychiatric symptoms and their relationship to suicidal ideation in a high-risk adolescent community sample. *Journal of the American Academy of Child and Adolescent Psychiatry, 41,* 44–51.

Glowinski, A. L., Bucholz, K. K., Nelson, E. C., Fu, Q., Madden, P. A., Reich, W., & Heath, A. C. (2001). Suicide attempts in an adolescent female twin sample. *Journal of the American Academy of Child and Adolescent Psychiatry, 40,* 1300–1307.

Goldsmith, S. K., Pellmar, T. C., Kleinman, A. M., & Bunney, W. E. (Eds.). (2002). *Reducing suicide: A national imperative.* Washington, DC: National Academy Press.

Gould, M. (2001). Suicide and the media. In H. Hendin & J. J. Mann (Eds.), *The clinical science of suicide prevention. Annals of the New York Academy of Sciences.* New York: New York Academy of Sciences.

Gould, M., & Kramer, R. A. (2001). Youth suicide prevention. *Suicide and Life Threatening Behavior, 31*(Suppl.), 6–31.

Gutierrez, P. M., Osman, A., Kopper, B. A., & Barrios, F. X. (2000). Why young people do not kill themselves: The Reasons for Living Inventory for Adolescents. *Journal of Clinical Child Psychology, 29,* 177–187.

Harrington, R., Kerfoot, M., Dyer, E., McNiven, F., Gill, J., Harrington, V., Woodham, A., & Byford, S. (1998). Randomized trial of a home-based family intervention for children who have deliberately poisoned themselves. *Journal of the American Academy of Child and Adolescent Psychiatry, 37,* 512–518.

Hazell, P., & King, R. A. (1996). Arguments for and against teaching suicide prevention in schools. *Australian and New Zealand Journal of Psychiatry, 27,* 653–665.

Kalafat, J., & Elias, M. (1995). Suicide prevention in an educational context: Broad and narrow foci. *Suicide and Life Threatening Behavior, 25,* 123–133.

Miller, A. L., Rathus, J. H., Linehan, M. M., Wetzler, S., & Leigh, E. (1997). Dialectical behavior therapy adapted for suicidal adolescents. *Journal for the Practice of Psychiatry and Behavioral Health, 3,* 78–86.

National Center for Health Statistics. (2000). *Suicide rates per 100,000 living population (all ages) 1998 [GMWK 291].* Washington, DC: U.S. Department of Health and Human Services.

Nock, M. K., & Kazdin, A. E. (2002). Examination of affective, cognitive, and behavioral factors and suicide-related outcomes in children and young adolescents. *Journal of Clinical Child and Adolescent Psychology, 31,* 48–58.

Prinstein, M. J., Boergers, J., Spirito, A., Little, T. D., & Grapentine, W. L. (2000). Peer functioning, family dysfunction, and psychological symptoms in a risk factor model for adolescent inpatients' suicidal ideation severity. *Journal of Clinical Child Psychology, 29,* 392–405.

Radkowsky, M., & Siegel, L. J. (1997). The gay adolescent: Stressors, adaptations, and psychosocial interventions. *Clinical Psychology Review, 17,* 191–216.

Randell, B. P., Eggert, L. L., & Pike, K. C. (2001). Immediate post intervention effects of two brief youth suicide prevention interventions. *Suicide and Life Threatening Behavior, 31,* 41–61.

Rihmer, Z., Rutz, W., & Pihlgran, H. (1995). Depression and suicide on Gotland: An intensive study of all suicides before and after a depression-training programme for general practitioners. *Journal of Affective Disorders, 35,* 147–152.

Rotheram-Borus, M. J., Piancentini, J., Miller, S., Graae, F., & Castro-Blanco, D. (1994). Brief cognitive behavioral treatment for adolescent suicide attempters and their families. *Journal of the American Academy of Child and Adolescent Psychiatry, 33,* 508–517.

Rotheram-Borus, M. J., Piancentini, J., Van Rossem, R., Graae, F., Cantwell, C., Castro-Blanco, D., & Feldman, J. (1996). Enhancing treatment adherence with a specialized emergency room program for adolescent suicide attempters. *Journal of the American Academy of Child and Adolescent Psychiatry, 35,* 654–663.

Rotheram-Borus, M. J., Walker, J. U., & Ferns, W. (1996). Suicidal behavior among middle-class adolescents who seek crisis services. *Journal of Clinical Psychology, 52,* 137–143.

Roy, A. (1992). Genetics, biology, and the family. In R. W. Maris, A. L. Berman, J. T. Maltsberger, & R. I. Yufit (Eds.), *Assessment and prediction of suicide* (pp. 574–588). New York: Guilford Press.

Rudd, M. D., & Joiner, T. (1998). The assessment, management, and treatment of suicidality: Toward clinically informed and balanced standards of care. *Clinical Psychology: Science and Practice, 5,* 135–150.

Shaffer, D. A., & Craft, L. (1999). Methods of adolescent suicide prevention. *Journal of Clinical Psychiatry, 60,* 70–74.

Sileverman, J. G., Raj, A., Mucci, L. A., & Hathaway, J. E. (2001). Dating violence against adolescent girls and associated substance use, unhealthy weight control, sexual risk behavior, pregnancy, and suicidality. *Journal of the American Medical Association, 286,* 572–579.

Spirito, A., Boergers, J., Donaldson, D., Bishop, D., & Lewander, W. (2002). An intervention trial to improve adherence to community treatment by adolescents after a suicide attempt. *Journal of the American Academy of Child and Adolescent Psychiatry, 41,* 435–442.

Spirito, A., Brown, L. S., Overholser, J. C., & Fitz, G. (1989). Attempted suicide in adolescence: A review and critique of the literature. *Clinical Psychology Review, 9,* 335–363.

Stewart, S. E., Manion, I. G., Davidson, S., & Cloutier, P. (2001). Suicidal children and adolescents with first emergency room presentations: Predictors of six-month outcome. *Journal of the American Academy of Child and Adolescent Psychiatry, 40,* 580–587.

U.S. Department of Health and Human Services. (2001). *National strategy for suicide prevention: Goals and objectives for action.* Rockville, MD: U.S. Department of Health and Human Services.

Wagner, B. M. (1997). Family risk factors for child and adolescent suicidal behavior. *Psychological Bulletin, 121,* 246–298.

Wagner, K. D., Rouleau, M., & Joiner, T. (2000). Cognitive factors related to suicidal ideation and resolution in psychiatrically hospitalized children and adolescents. *American Journal of Psychiatry, 157,* 2017–2021.

Wallace, L. J. D., Calhoun, A. D., Poweel, K. E., O'Neil, J., & James, S. P. (1996). *Homicide and suicide among Native Americans, 1979–1992.* Atlanta, GA: Centers for Disease Control and Prevention, National Center for Injury Prevention and Control.

Wood, A., Trainor, G., Rothwell, J., Moore, A., & Harrington, R. (2001). Randomized trial of group therapy for repeated deliberate self-harm in adolescents. *Journal of the American Academy of Child and Adolescent Psychiatry, 40,* 1246–1253.

Yang, B., & Clum, G. A. (1994). Life stress, social support, and problem-solving skills predictive of depressive symptoms, hopelessness, and suicidal behavior in an Asian student population: A test of a model. *Suicide and Life Threatening Behavior, 24,* 127–139.

Yang, B., & Clum, G. A. (2000). Childhood stress leads to later suicidality via its effect on cognitive functioning. *Suicide and Life Threatening Behavior, 30,* 183–198.

Zimmerman, J. K., & Asnis, G. M. (1995). *Treatment approaches with suicidal adolescents.* New York: Wiley.

Nadine J. Kaslow
Emory Family Medicine Clinic

Emily B. Jackson
Kafi S. Bethea
Emory University School of Medicine

SULLIVAN'S INTERPERSONAL THEORY

Interpersonal theory is a theory of interpersonal relations developed by Harry Stack Sullivan largely in the 1930s and 1940s.

Key Concepts

Sullivan emphasized the social aspects of human nature. He defined psychiatry, personality, and key assessment and treatment concepts in interpersonal terms. Performances, or interactions in the interpersonal field, are the means by which disturbances are formed, revealed, and treated. Sullivan also emphasized the crucial role of anxiety in personality formation and disturbance.

The Social Nature of Human Nature

In *Conceptions of Modern Psychiatry,* Sullivan (1953) defined personality as "the relatively enduring pattern of recurrent interpersonal situations which characterize a human life." Even hermits maintain an interpersonal life, through imagery, memory, and fantasy. Dynamisms, which are characteristic patterns of internal or overt social behavior, are the smallest meaningful unit of study of an individual. Dynamisms may involve thinking, feeling, or acting in relation to other people, who need not be present or even real.

That behavior often reflects relationships with persons not actually present was a cornerstone of Sullivan's approach. He perceived the distorting effects of such relationships in the troubled behavior of his patients. The inner aspect of this distortion he called personifications—images one holds of self or others, with their attendant feelings and impulses and ideas. Stereotypes are widely shared personifications, positive or negative. Personifications built up in one relationship may be triggered in another, with consequent distortions of thinking, feeling, and acting, as when a person perceives and relates to an employer as though to an overly critical and demanding parent.

Anxiety

Anxiety can be the most crucial formative influence in the interpersonal field, and its origins are the origins also of personality and of self. Their common roots lie in the helpless nature of infants, who survive only if nurtured. The distressed infant cries. A caregiver responds. The cry becomes a communication within a relationship and the first tool of need reduction. Over time, such interactions acquire two consequences: satisfaction arising from need reduction, and security arising from the preservation of a necessary relationship.

Threats to biological survival bring fear. Threats to security bring anxiety, which may be devastatingly powerful for a being lacking the maturity and experience to manage or dampen it. Given sufficient experience of anxiety, its subsequent avoidance may become the central goal for the infant or young child. Patterns in the interpersonal field have both inner and outer aspects, and the objectively helpless infant may begin to preserve security subjectively through the dynamism of sleep.

The growing dynamism of self (Sullivan's word for the complex of processes that come increasingly to monitor, evaluate, and regulate activities in the interpersonal field) seeks above all else to preserve security. Behaviors bringing approval from significant others are strengthened; behaviors bringing disapproval are inhibited and may be eliminated.

The processes of awareness and behavior control are increasingly bent on preserving security through conforming to the expectations of others. When disapproval attaches to behaviors or events that cannot be managed by the child, however, the child must control the experience rather than the event. When confronted by a threat to security, such as parental disapproval of anger, the child may disown the angry feelings through selectively not paying attention to them and by not giving them labels. Thus, while the anger does not cease to exist, the child ceases being aware of it. Sullivan called this process dissociation. Security is preserved by removing awareness from an undesired aspect of personality, which paradoxically places that aspect beyond the corrective effects of experience and may permit it to continue unmodified into adulthood.

Even more common in the preservation of security are parataxic distortions by which significant aspects of self or others are misperceived, mislabeled, and misunderstood in ways that lessen their anxiety-producing properties. The young child is in prolonged transition from the disconnected jumble of sensory experiences and perceptual impressions characterizing infancy toward a mature mode of rational, logical experience that even adults often fail to maintain. This transitional mode, called the parataxic by Sullivan, is characterized by a primitive associational sense of causality and by developing language use. Still in the process of learning firm and consistent concepts, labels, and meanings, the child's idiosyncratic and personalistic use of language in speech and thought facilitates parataxic distortions. Thus the self, central to each person's understanding of his or her own nature, may become isolated from that nature and therefore from all interpersonal relations. Mental health is restored through increasing awareness of one's interpersonal relations.

Performances

Children dominated by the preservation of security grow up to have very distorted understandings of their performances in the interpersonal field. The deceptions they practice on themselves are often facilitated by persuading others to perceive them as they wish to be seen or, at the least, by preventing others from seeing them as they fear they might really be. All children go through this. It is the way in which cultures preserve their characteristics. Proscribed patterns are inhibited; desired patterns flourish. When children receive the broad, persistent, and intense disapproval of significant others, however, they become more than conforming: They become emotionally disturbed. They misperceive not only their own performances but also those of others because of personifications built through disturbing interactions with significant others. They readily perceive the characteristics of these personifications and relate more to them than to the people actually present. Such troubled and isolated adults approach interpersonal situations warily and communicate in guarded, defensive, and sometimes bizarre ways as a result of the myriad distortions they superimpose on the actual situation.

Sullivan developed numerous strategies for detecting distortions in interpersonal relations and the often subtle manifestations of anxiety that accompany them and for relating to disturbed people in such a way that they could begin to experience the truths behind the evasions, thus expanding the self. Central to his methods was the conviction that all the therapist can objectively know is performance in interpersonal situations. All else is inference. Even the patient's effort to describe internal experience becomes a performance in the interpersonal field, and its content is therefore suspect. Sullivan perceived the therapist as a participant in the performances of the patient and considered that the data of assessment and treatment arise in this process of participant observation. The psychiatric interview is a special kind of interpersonal relation that demands great skill on the part of the therapist. Sullivan's greatest contributions may lie in his sensitivity to the isolation and anxiety of the disturbed persons he treated, in his broad perspective on the processes giving rise to their human misery, and in the richness of his therapeutic strategies on their behalf.

REFERENCE

Sullivan, H. S. (1953/1940). *Conceptions of modern psychiatry* (p. 111). New York: Norton.

Roger E. Enfield
West Central Georgia Regional Hospital

See also: **Psychotherapy; Social Influence**

SURVEYS

Opinion, attitude, and interest surveys are unlike traditional tests in that they are self-report measures in which the persons responding indicate what they feel or think; there are no right or wrong answers. The person responding to the survey is generally asked to rate each item on some type of rating scale—from *most* to *least,* or *strongly agree* to *strongly disagree,* or simply on a scale of anywhere from 3 to 10 points.

The Gallup Poll and the Harris Poll are two of the better-known opinion surveys. Much market research is also of the opinion survey variety.

Attitude surveys are generally used to measure such things as how people feel about social or personal objects or issues. Examples are the Job Attitude Scale and the Attitudes Toward Women Scale.

Interest surveys measure preferences for certain activities; these usually are work-related activities, but some surveys also measure preferences for play or leisure activities, or for activities related to school subjects. Interest surveys are generally used for career and educational exploration and planning. There are two principal types—those with internally built, homogeneous scales; and those with externally, or empirically, built criterion scales. Surveys of the former type are based on clusters of internally related items, with each cluster representing a basic interest dimension, such as outdoor, artistic, mathematical, or literary interest. Examples are the Kuder Preference Record, Vocational; the American College Testing Program Interest Inventory; and the Self-Directed Search. Scores are based on a comparison between the individual's responses and those of a representative sample of people in various grade or age ranges. Criterion, or empirically developed, scales, however, are based on the item responses of people in the criterion group or occupation represented by the scale. Scores represent the degree of similarity with the responses of people in the criterion groups. The validity of an interest survey is generally measured by how well it predicts the occupation or activity a person will enter, or how well satisfied the person will be with that occupation or activity. Empirically developed interest surveys generally are expected to meet an additional requirement: They must be able clearly to discriminate, or distinguish, members of one occupation from members of other occupations. Examples of empirically developed interest surveys are the Kuder Occupational Interest Survey and the Strong-Campbell Interest Inventory.

Esther E. Diamond

SYMPATHETIC NERVOUS SYSTEM

The sympathetic nervous system (SNS) is one of two branches of the autonomic nervous system, which controls the function of organs and glands in the body (called the efferent portion) and senses changes in these organ systems (the afferent portion); the other autonomic branch is the parasympathetic nervous system (PNS). The neurons that comprise the efferent SNS arise from the thoracic and lumbar portions of the spinal cord (i.e., the middle of the cord). Thus, this system is sometimes referred to as the thoracolumbar branch. Sympathetic fibers originating from the thoracic cord innervate organs of the head, neck, chest and upper abdomen. Sympathetic fibers originating from the lumbar cord innervate the lower gastrointestinal (GI) tract and other organs of the pelvis.

The anatomy of the efferent autonomic nerves to each organ or gland includes preganglionic neurons, which exit the spinal cord, and postganglionic neurons, which directly innervate the target organ. A ganglion is comprised of the cell bodies of the postganglionic neurons and is the region where the pre- and postganglionic neurons communicate with one another. In the SNS, the preganglionic fibers that exit the spinal cord are typically short, and many of them synapse within a chain of ganglia found just outside the bony vertebral column housing the spinal cord. Other sympathetic preganglionic fibers pass to additional ganglia that do not form part of the sympathetic chain but that are still some distance from the target organ or gland. Typically, then, the postganglionic fibers of the SNS are relatively long since they extend from a ganglion distant from the target organ. The neurotransmitter released by the axon terminals of the preganglionic neurons is acetylcholine. Acetylcholine acts on cholinergic receptors of the nicotinic subtype, which are found on the postganglionic neurons. The neurotransmitter released by the postganglionic neurons onto the target organ or gland is typically norepinephrine, with one exception, the sweat glands, where the sympathetic nerves release mostly acetylcholine with only a small, possible contribution by neurons containing norepinephrine. Afferent autonomic fibers from organs to the central nervous system run alongside the same nerves carrying efferent autonomic fibers. The visceral (i.e., organ) afferents comprise a relatively small proportion of the total number of fibers, less than 20% in some sympathetic nerves. Afferent autonomic fibers provide sensory information about the state of an organ, such as stretch of the bladder, and also relay pain signals. It has been hypothesized that the sympathetic afferents relay mostly pain information and play only a minimal role in visceral sensations needed for bodily regulation (e.g., signals from the GI tract indicating that food is present and needs to be digested).

The organs and glands controlled by the efferent SNS typically receive input from both branches of the autonomic nervous system, a phenomenon referred to as dual innervation. When organs receive innervation from both autonomic branches, the activity in the two branches often produces opposite effects on the organ. For example, the heart rate is controlled by both autonomic branches. Increased activity in the sympathetic branch increases heart rate, whereas decreased activity decreases heart rate. Conversely, increased activity in the parasympathetic branch decreases heart rate, and decreased activity increases heart rate. Thus, each of the two branches is capable of bidirectionally influencing the rate at which the heart beats. A notable exception to the general rule of dual innervation is the sweat glands, which are innervated only by the SNS.

When the body is physically active or engaged in taxing mental activities, the organs of the body tend to mobilize and use resources in a process called catabolism. Often during such states, activity in the SNS is relatively high compared to periods when the organism is resting quietly. For example, during mental distress or engagement, or when there are high levels of bodily activity, the body has an immediate need for more energy. For example, increased sympathetic activation enhances blood flow to muscles needed to perform work by increasing heart rate and shunting blood from areas of low immediate need such as the GI tract to areas of high need like the exercising muscles. Once the immediate metabolic need has been met, activation of the sympathetic system tends to decline at the same time that activation of the parasympathetic system tends to increase. Most of the time, the autonomic nervous system operates somewhere between these extremes of low and high energy mobilization. In these cases, SNS effects on the organs and glands will be intermediate and tuned to the specific needs of each organ system. Thus, even in a person at rest, ongoing sympathetic activity helps to maintain a resting level of tone (i.e., constriction) on the arteries supplying skeletal muscle.

In addition to the tendency for the two autonomic branches to operate in a reciprocal fashion under extremes of activity or inactivity, the two autonomic branches can operate independently. Thus, although a typical pattern of autonomic control consists of the activation of one autonomic branch accompanied by a decrease in activity in the other branch (a reciprocal pattern), this is not the only pattern of response that can occur. The two autonomic branches can have uncoupled effects on a target organ with either increased or decreased activity in one autonomic branch in the absence of any change in activity in the other branch. Alternatively, the two branches can exert coactivational effects where there are simultaneous increases or decreases in activity in both autonomic branches. The existence of nonreciprocal patterns means that one cannot measure function in one autonomic branch and on that basis alone infer the activation level in the other branch.

SUGGESTED READING

Berntson, G. G., Cacioppo, J. T., & Quigley, K. S. (1991). Autonomic determinism: The modes of autonomic control, the doctrine of autonomic space, and the laws of autonomic constraint. *Psychological Review, 98,* 459–487.

Loewy, A. D., & Spyer, K. M. (1990). *Central regulation of autonomic function.* New York: Oxford University Press.

Karen S. Quigley
University of Medicine and Dentistry of New Jersey—New Jersey Medical School and East Orange VA Medical Center

See also: **Central Nervous System; Parasympathetic Nervous System**

SYNAPTIC COMPETITION

Synapses converging onto a neuron or muscle fiber compete with each other for control of the electrical excitation of the target cell. In a process driven by the relative activity patterns of the individual synapses and the postsynaptic cell, the efficacy of some synapses is strengthened whereas other synapses are weakened or eliminated altogether. Synaptic competition allows for an experience-dependent editing of neuronal circuits both during development and in the mature nervous system.

Synaptic Competition During Development: Activity-Dependent Refinement of Neuronal Connections

During development, mechanisms of synaptic competition and synapse elimination refine initially established projection patterns. This process allows for input-specific modification of an innate, genetically programmed neuronal circuitry.

At the developing neuromuscular junction, synaptic competition ensures that twitch muscle fibers are innervated by a single motoneuron only. All muscle fibers initially receive inputs from multiple motoneurons that are comparable in synaptic strength. In a competitive process between inputs that is marked by gradual decrease of synaptic strength and loss of muscle fiber surface area covered by synapses of losing inputs, inputs of all but one motoneuron eventually retract. This process appears to depend on the unequal or asynchronous neuronal activity of the convergent inputs, suggesting that the myocyte somehow compares the relative activity of motoneuron inputs and acts to weaken undesired while strengthening desired synapses.

The interplay between the genetically programmed initial establishment and later activity-dependent refinement of connections has been extensively studied in the development of topological and functional organization of sensory afferents to the neocortex, such as the projections from the lateral geniculate nucleus of the thalamus to the primary visual cortex. In the mature nervous system, these afferents to Layer 4 of the cortex are segregated into eye-specific columns, so-called ocular dominance columns. Thorsten Wiesel and David Hubel (1963) observed that, following deprivation of vision in one eye during a critical developmental period, ocular dominance columns from the nondeprived eye expanded at the expense of columns from the deprived eye and visual cortical neurons received inputs mostly from the nondeprived eye. Recent evidence suggests that the formation of ocular dominance columns occurs before the onset of vision and is itself not a consequence of synaptic competition (Crowley & Katz, 2002). Nevertheless, these experiments demonstrate the critical influence of activity-dependent synaptic competition on the modification of ocular dominance in the primary visual cortex and illustrate the functional refinement of thalamocortical connections during development.

Synaptic Competition in the Adult: Plasticity of Cortical Maps and Memory

Even in adults, cortical representations of sensory input are by no means fixed entities but are continuously modified by experience. Michael Merzenich and coworkers have documented the role of activity-dependent competition in the plasticity of topographic maps in the somatosensory cortex (Jenkins et al., 1990; see also Buonomano & Murzenich, 1998). Deafferentation of an area results in an expansion of neighboring receptive regions into that area, increasing the cortical representation of the body surface neighboring that whose cortical input has been ablated. Similarly, increased sensory stimulation of a region leads to an expansion of its representation in the somatosensory cortical map. Analogous sensory experience–evoked changes have been observed in the primary visual and auditory cortical areas.

The hypothesis that synaptic competition and the resulting activity-dependent changes in synaptic strength also underlie learning and memory has captivated many neuroscientists for the past five decades. The psychologist Donald Hebb postulated in 1949 that associative memory has its cellular basis in a persistent strengthening of synapses of a presynaptic neuron onto a postsynaptic neuron, if the former repetitively takes part in firing the latter. Tim Bliss and Terje Lømo (1973) provided an experimental correlate to this postulate when they discovered a long-term potentiation (LTP; on the order of hours to days) of hippocampal dentate gyrus granule cell responses to perforant path stimulation after tetanic stimulation of that projection. LTP, and its counterpart, long-term depression (LTD), have since been observed at synapses in many brain regions. Abundant, albeit circumstantial evidence suggests that synaptic competition and plasticity are the fundamental cellular mechanisms of learning and memory. For instance, memory formation relies on many of the same molecular requirements as synaptic plasticity. Furthermore, experimental manipulation of synaptic plasticity in awake animals also modulates the ability to acquire memories (see Martin et al., 2000 for a review).

Cellular Mechanisms Underlying Synaptic Competition

The cellular and molecular mechanisms of synaptic competition are likely to depend on the molecular composition of the synapses involved. The mechanism of synaptic competition at a major class of glutamatergic synapses in the central nervous system has received much attention. Reminiscent of Hebb's postulate, LTP at these synapses is produced when presynaptic firing repeatedly precedes postsynaptic firing by a short time span (10–15 ms). Conversely, LTD is produced when postsynaptic firing repeatedly occurs shortly before presynaptic firing. This spike timing–dependent plasticity (STDP) allows for a bidirectional modulation of synaptic strength in the competition between cartels of coordinately active synapses. It has several mechanistic features: (1) Action potentials, initiated in the axon-initial segment, back-propagate into the dendritic tree. (2) Detection of the temporal order of pre- and postsynaptic activation relies on the activation of calcium conductances, such as the ligand- and voltage-gated NMDA-type glutamate receptor. (3) The local calcium concentration, thought to be a nonlinear function of time and membrane depolarization, activates varying sets of signaling cascades. (4) These signals may lead to a relocalization of AMPA-type glutamate receptors or a modulation of their conductance that causes an immediate change in synaptic strength. (5) The long-lasting maintenance of these changes may require alterations of gene expression and/or structural changes including the establishment of new and the elimination of old synaptic contacts (Sjostrom and Nelson, 2000).

REFERENCES

Bliss, T. V. & Lomo, T. (1973). Long-lasting potentiation of synaptic transmission in the dentate area of the anaesthetized rabbit following stimulation of the perforant path. *Journal of Physiology, 232,* 331–356.

Buonomano, D. V., & Merzenich, M. M. (1998). Cortical plasticity: From synapses to maps. *Annual Review of Neuroscience, 21,* 149–186.

Crowley, J. C., & Katz, L. C. (2002). Ocular dominance development revisited. *Current Opinion in Neurobiology, 12,* 104–109.

Hebb, D. O. (1949). *The organization of behavior: A neuropsychological theory.* New York: Wiley.

Jenkins, W. M., Merzenich, M. M., Ochs, M. T., Allard, T., & Guic-Robles, E. (1990). Functional reorganization of primary somatosensory cortex in adult own monkeys after behaviorally controlled tactile stimulation. *Journal of Neurophysiology, 63,* 82–104.

Martin, S. J., Grimwood, P. D., & Morris, R. G. (2000). Synaptic plasticity and memory: An evaluation of the hypothesis. *Annual Review of Neuroscience, 23,* 649–711.

Sjostrom, P. J., & Nelson, S. B. (2002). Spike timing, calcium signals and synaptic plasticity. *Current Opinion in Neurobiology, 12,* 305–314.

Wiesel, T. N. & Hubel, D. H. (1963). Single-cell responses in striate cortex of kittens deprived of vision in one eye. *Journal of Neurophysiology, 26,* 1003–1017.

Stefan Krueger
Reiko M. Fitzsimonds
Yale School of Medicine

SYSTEMS AND THEORIES

In American psychology, systems and theories historically have been closely associated. For this reason it is important that students of psychology know at least the essence of the major systems that have influenced and, to a lesser degree, continue to influence psychological thought.

Systems

A system of psychology may be defined as "an organization and interpretation of . . . data and theories . . . with special assumptions (postulates), definitions, and methodological biases."

The systems that have been most influential in American psychology are generally agreed to be structuralism, functionalism, behaviorism, Gestalt psychology, and psychoanalysis. The first two are now mainly of historical significance, although the role of a continuing kind of diffuse functionalism is noted in the following.

Structuralism

Structuralism was primarily the product of Wilhelm Wundt, who is credited with establishing the first formal psychological laboratory. Its American form was almost single-handedly shaped by Titchener. Wundt and Titchener conceived of psychology as a kind of mental chemistry. Their objective was to analyze conscious experience into its components using a highly refined form of introspection.

Functionalism

Functionalism developed essentially as a protest against the inadequacies of structuralism. Its theme was that all sorts of behavior, along with the conscious experience analyzed by the structuralists, should be grist for the psychologist's mill.

Although clearly anticipated by William James, functionalism as a formal system was founded by John Dewey and James Angell. The system espoused such diverse conceptual and practical efforts as Darwinian evolutionary theory and the mental testing movement. The common element that bound these diverse interests together was their function—their role in determining both behavior and conscious experience, the two subject matters of psychology.

Behaviorism

The most colorful and influential figure in the development of systematic psychology during the early twentieth century in the United States was John B. Watson, the outspoken founder of the behavioristic system. He developed the position that all that psychology has to study is behavior. During the latter half of the twentieth century, B. F. Skinner replaced Watson as the focus of attention, both positive and negative. Like Watson, Skinner initially worked with animal subjects. His systematic behaviorism was implemented in *operant conditioning,* which stressed emitted behavior rather than the elicited behavior involved in Pavlovian, or classical, conditioning. Also like Watson, Skinner was concerned with practical applications; the best known of these is *behavior modification,* a clinical technique that ignores internal states of the organism and focuses on changes in behavior.

Gestalt Psychology

Gestalt psychology was founded by Max Wertheimer and his two junior colleagues, Wolfgang Kohler and Kurt Koffka. The basic theme was that naive and unsophisticated perceptual experiences should be taken as givens—that is, accepted as they are—rather than reduced to any presumed elements. Phrased differently, the basic and now familiar proposition was that the whole is more than the sum of its parts.

Psychoanalysis

Sigmund Freud's enormously provocative psychoanalytic system left enduring marks on psychology as well as on many other disciplines. Although psychologists differ widely in their evaluation of psychoanalysis, there can be little doubt that Freud's contributions have greatly enriched our understanding of human behavior. The impact of psychoanalysis, with its stress on early development and largely, if not wholly, unconscious sexuality as determinants of neurosis and psychosis, has been greatest on clinical psychology.

Theories

A theory may be defined as an attempt to explain some set of empirical events, particularly when assumptions are made as to how to bridge gaps in available knowledge about underlying factors. Theories vary widely in their organization and scope, from the simplest of hunches, through hypotheses of various sorts that deal with specific empirical predictions, to large-scale systems of deductively related laws. The role of the more informal theorizing is in special need of emphasis because of the much greater attention typically paid to the formal types of theory.

The term *model* has come to serve as a kind of synonym for theory. In its original usage, model referred to an explanatory effort that was based on some better supported explanatory framework in another discipline, such as the use of a mathematical formulation as a basis for deriving experimental tests in psychology.

Deductive theory is characterized by the derivation of propositions, to be tested empirically, on the basis of logically related prior premises.

Inductive theory operates in exactly an opposite manner. It allows disparate bits and pieces of data to accumulate and to be gradually articulated into theoretical propositions without any explicit guidance (in its ideal form at least).

Functional theory attempts to remedy the major faults of deductive and inductive theories. It proceeds cautiously with respect to the empirical basis from which it is generated, but at the same time it is explicitly guided.

M. H. Marx

See also: **Behaviorism; Gestalt Psychology; History of Psychology; Structuralism**

T

TARDIVE DYSKINESIA

Tardive dyskinesia (TD) is the most troublesome and feared extrapyramidal side effect (EPS) of long-term conventional antipsychotic drug therapy. Tardive dyskinesia has been defined as an extrapyramidal hyperkinetic movement disorder characterized by involuntary, repetitive, and irregular abnormal movements, present for a minimum of 4 weeks and occurring after a minimum of 3 months of cumulative classical antipsychotic drug (i.e., neuroleptic [NL]) exposure (Kane et al., 1992).

The presence of TD has been related to poor treatment compliance and, due to its associated stigma, to an important deterioration in quality of life. Even though TD is often not severe and may even improve in a significant proportion of cases (Gardos et al., 1994), the severe, disabling, progressive, and irreversible cases (even though a minority) constitute a permanent threat in long-term antipsychotic or NL treatment because it is still not possible to predict either who is going to develop TD or of what type or severity (Larach, Zamboni, Mancini, & Gallardo, 1997).

Epidemiology of Tardive Dyskinesia

The prevalence of TD has been reported to range from 3% to 62%, with a mean prevalence of around 20% and a cumulative incidence of 5% for each year of NL exposure. For patients over 50 years of age, cumulative incidence rises to 50% or more after 3 years of NL exposure. The natural history of TD, as suggested on long-term follow-up studies, tends to have a fluctuating course and an overall trend toward amelioration with time, although some researchers have found chronic persistent dyskinesia in more than half of the patients in long-term follow-up studies (Kane, 1995).

Risk Factors

The best-identified risk factor is age, with patients under the age of 40 years having about a 10% risk of developing TD; this risk increases five- to sevenfold in elderly patients. Gender differences show that the ratio of women to men developing TD is 1.7:1 and that women tend to have more severe TD and more spontaneous dyskinesias. Vulnerability to drug-induced acute and chronic EPS, secondary to disruption of the nigro-striatal system, is of particular concern in children, who are at special risk because of their immature brains. The presence of schizophrenic negative or deficit symptoms, affective disorders, structural brain abnormalities, diabetes mellitus, and smoking have also been identified as risk factors for TD. Whether the use of either depot neuroleptics or concomitant long-term therapy with such drugs as anticholinergics and lithium presents a special risk still remains controversial. The prolonged use of those NL drugs that are not marketed as NL in the treatment of nonpsychotic conditions—drugs that include many antiemetics, various NL-type dyspeptic agents, and some NLs with marked antidepressant effects (e.g., amoxepine)—frequently constitutes the risk of extended NL exposure without the physician's being aware of that risk (Casey, 1995b).

Clinical Features of Tardive Dyskinesia

Clinical features include involuntary, repetitive, and irregular movements affecting different body regions: facial muscles (usually in older adults) involving the lips, jaw, and tongue (bucco-linguo-masticatory dyskinesia), frequently accompanied by involuntary grimacing and spasmodic eye-blinking; and axial musculature and extremities (usually in children and younger patients) involving any type or combination of choreic, athetotic, myoclonic, and dystonic movements. Tardive dyskinesia usually includes other tardive EPS features such as tardive dystonias and tardive akathisia, considered to be tardive because they also appear after prolonged NL exposure. Dystonic features convey a more severe and disabling picture. As with all extrapyramidal syndromes, movements disappear during sleep and worsen with stress.

The severity and complexity of the movements in TD impair motor functions and psychosocial interaction and produce subjective discomfort symptoms. Motor feature impairment can involve difficulties with speech or swallowing; inability to wear dentures; ulcerations of the mouth mucosae; impairment for daily routines such as walking, sitting, and standing; and significant progressive weight loss that may become a life-threatening condition. These impairments produce different levels of psychological distress that range from no awareness of discomfort to different levels of embarrassment, desperation, and hopelessness, and even to suicidal ideation and behavior (Casey, 1995a).

Early detection of TD may be possible by observing mild and poorly defined movements such as grimacing or facial tics (especially of the eyes and lips); chewing or other bucal movements; mild and fine vermicular movements of the tongue; and rocking and limb restlessness in the absence of the subjective discomfort of akathisia.

Differential Diagnosis

The psychotic motor features of schizophrenia, such as stereotypies, mannerisms, and bizarre postures, should first be ruled out. Other hyperkinetic idiopathic syndromes, such as some rarely spontaneous dyskinesias observed in psychotic patients never exposed to NLs, or others such as senile dyskinesias and Meige's and Tourette's syndromes, should be considered. Secondary dyskinesias caused by systemic diseases such as lupus erythematosus, Sydenham's chorea, Henoch-Schonlein's purpura, chorea gravidium, hyperthyroidism, and hypoparathyroidism, and by hereditary diseases such as Huntington's and Wilson's diseases, should be sorted out. Brain lesions caused by cerebrovascular accidents, tumors, and brain chemical poisoning must also be regarded, as should postencephalitic dyskinesias. Other drug treatments that may produce reversible and irreversible dyskinesias, such as amphetamines, tricyclic antidepressants, antihistamines, phenytoin, oral contraceptives, and L-dopa (in the treatment of Parkinson's disease) should be considered as causes (Casey, 1995b).

Pathophysiology

The pathophysiology of TD remains unknown because there have been no consistent, demonstrable abnormalities found in neurochemical and postmortem receptor studies. The DA nigro-striatal pathways would be functionally abnormal through mechanisms related to the increase in the number of DA receptors secondary to prolonged DA receptor blockade, changes in sensitivity, and poorly understood pre- and postsynaptic DA receptor interactions. High liability for acute EPS seems to be related to increased TD risk. The difficulty with NLs or the so-called typical or classical antipsychotics is that their effective antipsychotic dose range produces more than 70% of D2 receptor blockade in the basal ganglia, an amount very close to the dose needed for the appearance of EPS (around 80% D2 receptor blockade; Farde et al., 1992). The prevailing question in this case is whether the DA role is primary or modulatory. The combination of low D2 and high serotonin (5HT2) receptor blockade activity seems to reduce the risk for EPS symptoms by an (as yet) unclarified mechanism. It appears that serotonin receptor blockade probably modulates DA activity by increasing DA in the substantia nigra as well as in the prefrontal area (Meltzer, 1993). The new generation of antipsychotic drugs—the so-called atypical or novel antipsychotics—has been developed based on these blockade strategies to widen the margin between the dose required for the antipsychotic effect and the dose that causes EPS occurrence.

On the other hand, other, even less confirmed neurochemical theories and substrates have been considered: noradrenergic, cholinergic, and GABAergic; neuropeptide dysfunction (cholecystokinin, substance P, neurotensin, somatostatin); disturbances in mineral metabolism (iron); glucose-insulin-NL interaction; neurotoxicity in the basal ganglia due to high oxidative metabolism caused by increased catecholamine turnover; and so on. Such theories have led the way to miscellaneous pharmacological strategies in the treatment of TD; among them, the more widely used benzodiazepines have helped some patients. Treatment with vitamin E (alpha-tocopherol) at high doses has also been tried, with variable clinical results (Casey, 1995c).

Treatment

The treatment of TD remains highly empirical. At present, there is no definite, effective, standard, safe TD treatment, and it is not possible at this time to predict the treatment response to a specific agent. Thus, prevention continues to be the best strategy regarding TD (Gardos & Cole, 1995). The use of first-line atypical antipsychotics (e.g., risperidone, olanzapine, and quetiapine) for the long-term maintenance treatment of schizophrenia and for some forms of severe affective disorders represents in varying degrees the most relevant factor in TD prevention because of the low incidence of EPS associated with these drugs. Clozapine, the best representative agent of the atypical antipsychotics and for which there are virtually no reports of dystonia or definite TD causation, has been reported to be especially effective in ameliorating or resolving roughly 60% of moderate to severe TD with dystonic disabling features (Larach et al., 1997; Lieberman et al., 1991). Its wide and first-line use is limited by the potential of blood dyscrasia and by the necessity of regular blood tests. Treatment of TD with atypical antipsychotics should be maintained long enough to avoid rebound and to ensure full therapeutic effect. Ideally, periodic video recording during standard examinations is advisable for long-term follow-up and outcome assessment (Larach et al., 1997). The definite effectiveness of atypical antipsychotics in the treatment of overt TD cases still awaits further testing.

REFERENCES

Casey, D. E. (1995a). Motor and mental aspects of extrapyramidal syndromes. *International Clinical Psychopharmacology, 10*(Suppl. 3), 105–114.

Casey, D. E. (1995b). Neuroleptic-induced acute extrapyramidal syndromes and tardive dyskinesia. *Psychiatric Clinics of North America, 16*(3), 589–610.

Casey, D. E. (1995c). Tardive dyskinesia: Pathophysiology. In F. E. Bloom & D. J. Kupfer (Eds.), *Psychopharmacology: The fourth generation of progress* (pp. 1497–1502). New York: Raven Press.

Farde, L., Norström, A.-L., Wiesel, F.-A., Paulli, S., Halldin, C., & Sedvall, G. (1992). Positron emission tomographic analysis of central D1 and D2 dopamine receptor occupancy in patients treated with classical neuroleptics and clozapine: Relation to extrapyramidal side effects. *Archives of General Psychiatry, 49,* 538–544.

Gardos, G., Casey, D., Cole, J. O., Perenyi, A., Kocsis, E., Arato, M., Samson, J. A., & Conley, C. (1994). Ten-year outcome of tardive dyskinesia. *American Journal of Psychiatry, 151,* 836–841.

Gardos, G., & Cole, J. O. (1995). The treatment of tardive dyskinesias. In F. E. Bloom & D. J. Kupfer (Eds.), *Psychopharmacology: The fourth generation of progress* (pp. 1503–1511). New York: Raven Press.

Kane, J. M. (1995). Tardive dyskinesia: Epidemiological and clinical presentation. In F. E. Bloom & D. J. Kupfer (Eds.), *Psychopharmacology: The fourth generation of progress.* New York: Raven Press.

Kane, J. M., Jeste, D. V., Barnes, J. R. E., et al. (1992). *Tardive dyskinesia: A task force report of the American Psychiatric Association.* Washington, DC: American Psychiatric Association.

Larach, V., Zamboni, R., Mancini, H., & Gallardo, T. (1997). New strategies for old problems: Tardive dyskinesia (TD) review and report on severe TD cases treated with clozapine with 12, 8 and 5 years of video follow-up. *Schizophrenia Research, 28,* 231–246.

Lieberman, J. A., Saltz, B. L., Johns, C. A., Pollack, S., Borenstein, M., & Kane, J. (1991). The effects of clozapine on tardive dyskinesia. *British Journal of Psychiatry, 158,* 503–510.

Meltzer, H. Y. (1993). Serotonin receptors and antipsychotic drug action. *Psychopharmacology Series, 10,* 70–81.

VERONICA W. LARACH
Universidad de Chile

TASK DESIGN

The simplification and standardization of the tasks comprising a job have long been advocated as means of enhancing productivity in organizations (Taylor, 1903). Indeed, these strategies have been shown to lead to simplified production scheduling, lowered training costs, and reduced expenditures for labor through the employment of lower-skilled, more interchangeable, and cheaper workers (cf. Aldag & Brief, 1979). However, simplified and standardized tasks are perceived by job incumbents as monotonous, leading them to feel bored and dissatisfied with their work; in turn, this boredom and dissatisfaction presumably cost employers in terms of increased absenteeism and turnover and reduced production output (Hulin & Blood, 1968).

To counteract these costs, job enlargement (Kilbridge, 1960) and job enrichment (Herzberg, 1968) have been advocated as alternative task-design strategies. Conceptually, however, the two strategies are quite similar and can be thought of as entailing the design of jobs to include a wider variety of tasks and to increase the job incumbent's freedom of pace, responsibility for checking quality, and discretion over method. For the most part, the research addressing the two strategies has taken the form of testimonial evidence; thus, one is unable to assert few, if any, generalizations regarding their efficacy (Aldag & Brief, 1979).

Building on the works of Turner and Lawrence (1965) and Hackman and Lawler (1971), Hackman and Oldham (1975) advanced a model to guide more rigorous research aimed at enhancing both theory and practice. They asserted that through various psychological states, five core dimensions influence job incumbents' affective and behavioral reactions to their jobs. These core dimensions are (1) skill variety—the degree to which a job requires a variety of different activities; (2) task identity—the degree to which the job requires the completion of a whole and identifiable piece of work; (3) task significance—the degree to which the job has a substantial impact on the lives or work of other people; (4) autonomy—the degree to which the job provides substantial freedom, independence, and discretion to the incumbent in scheduling work and in determining the procedures to be used in carrying it out; and (5) feedback—the degree to which carrying out the work activities required by the job results in the incumbent's obtaining direct and clear information about the effectiveness of his or her performance. Critical reviews of the research generated by the Hackman and Oldham model indicate that the core job dimensions are likely to lead to higher levels of job satisfaction on the part of job incumbents but do not appear to influence their behaviors significantly (Aldag, Barr, & Brief, 1981; Roberts & Glick, 1981).

More recently, knowledge enlargement, which involves adding requirements to the job for understanding procedures or rules relating to the organization's products, has been advanced as an alternative to task enlargement. It has been shown to yield more satisfaction as well as less overload and fewer errors (Campion & McClelland, 1993). Additionally, in response to manufacturing-process innovations such as just-in-time inventory control and total quality management, it has been advocated that one consider how worker flexibility and employee learning and development might be encouraged by job design (Parker, Wall, & Jackson, 1997). Thus, greater attention should be focused on the context in which jobs are embedded.

Salancik and Pfeffer's (1978) social information processing model explicitly considers the importance of social context in the subjective construction of job attitudes. For example, the model posits that in the process of forming job perceptions, job incumbents rely on what their coworkers say. However, evidence in support of the model has not been promising. Critical reviews have suggested that greater attention be paid to factors such as the employee's past experiences and susceptibility to influence by others (Zalesny & Ford, 1990).

The question of how to design tasks to enhance employee motivation, and thus productivity, remains open. Clearly, personal experiences and intuition lead one to believe that the contents of jobs do vary in terms of their motivational potentials. Until that potential is verified empirically and its costs and benefits are compared with those strategies advanced by Taylor's principles of scientific management, a scientific psychology of task design will be more of an aspiration than a reality.

REFERENCES

Aldag, R. J., Barr, S. H., & Brief, A. P. (1981). Measurement of perceived task characteristics. *Psychological Bulletin, 90,* 415–431.

Aldag, R. J., & Brief, A. P. (1979). *Task design and employee motivation.* Glenview, IL: Scott, Foresman.

Campion, M. A., & McClelland, C. L. (1993). Follow-up and extension of the interdisciplinary costs and benefits of enlarged jobs. *Journal of Applied Psychology, 78,* 339–351.

Hackman, J. R., & Lawler, E. E. (1971). Employee reactions to job characteristics. *Journal of Applied Psychology, 55,* 259–286.

Hackman, J. R., & Oldham, G. R. (1975). Development of the Job Diagnostic Survey. *Journal of Applied Psychology, 60,* 159–170.

Herzberg, F. (1968). One more time: How do you motivate employees? *Harvard Business Review, 46,* 53–62.

Hulin, C. L., & Blood, M. R. (1968). Job enlargement, individual differences, and worker responses. *Psychological Bulletin, 69,* 41–55.

Kilbridge, M. D. (1960). Reduced costs through job enrichment: A case. *Journal of Business, 33,* 357–362.

Parker, S. K., Wall, T. D., & Jackson, P. R. (1997). "That's not my job": Developing flexible employee work orientations. *Academy of Management Journal, 40,* 899–929.

Roberts, K. H., & Glick, W. (1981). The job characteristics approach to task design: A critical review. *Journal of Applied Psychology, 66,* 193–217.

Salancik, G. R., & Pfeffer, J. (1978). A social information processing approach to job attitudes and task design. *Administrative Science Quarterly, 23,* 224–253.

Taylor, F. W. (1903). *Shop management.* New York: Harper.

Turner, A. N., & Lawrence, P. R. (1965). *Industrial jobs and the worker: An investigation of response to task attributes.* Boston: Harvard Graduate School of Business Administration.

Zalesny, M. D., & Ford, J. K. (1990). Extending the social information processing perspective: New links to attitudes, behaviors, and perceptions. *Organizational Behavior and Human Decision Processes, 47,* 205–246.

R. M. Butz
Arthur P. Brief
Tulane University

TASTE AVERSION LEARNING

The acquired aversion to a particular food resulting from experience with that food is known as taste aversion learning (TAL), or conditioned taste aversion. The terms *avoidance* and *flavor* may also be used to refer to this effect, yielding synonyms such as flavor aversion learning, conditioned taste avoidance, and so on. Although the process was first elucidated in studies of radiation sickness, TAL is now recognized as an intrinsic behavior that allows vertebrates to learn about toxic foods.

TAL contributes to an animal's ability to limit intake of poisonous food items. It can be thought of as a hardwired system linking the nose and mouth with the gastrointestinal tract and the brain. The brain integrates signals regarding the flavor and physiological effects produced by ingestion of toxic foods. These integrated signals become a memory that helps animals determine which foods are safe to eat and which are not. Without TAL, animals would likely repeatedly eat the same toxic foods.

Learned taste aversions arise from a sequence of events that begin with the ingestion of a food item. Though not required, aversions occur more readily when unfamiliar (novel) foods are ingested. The flavor of the food serves as a cue called the conditioned stimulus (CS). The flavor cue allows the specific food item to be identified when encountered on future occasions. The next, and most important, event in the process is subsequent occurrence of gastrointestinal distress (i.e. nausea or emesis). The pharmacological source of the illness is known as the unconditioned stimulus (UCS) and may be present in the food or delivered separately. For example, both CS (the flavor of the plant) and UCS (the toxin) are ingested when a toxic plant is eaten. Conversely, a cancer patient may eat a particular food (CS) and suffer nausea from radiation treatments (UCS).

Conditioned aversions are formed experimentally by delivering the UCS shortly after the food is consumed. Lithium chloride is commonly used for this purpose. The nausea produced by lithium chloride is rapidly associated with the food. Although aversions can be formed from a single exposure to the UCS, repeated exposures to the UCS may be required to generate persistent aversions. For example, a single UCS exposure can produce an aversion to a novel food item, but multiple exposures are often needed to form aversions to familiar foods. If familiar and novel foods are followed with a single UCS exposure, an aversion will be formed to the novel food.

The mode of action of the UCS is critical to forming aversions. Stimuli that negatively impact the emetic system (like lithium chloride) are required to produce aversions to associated flavor cues. Stimuli that do not produce nausea are less likely to initiate flavor aversions. Learning occurs whether the delay between CS and UCS exposure is a few seconds or many hours.

TAL is an affective (i.e., subconscious) process that does not require cognitive learning. However, cognitive learning may generate aversions to other sensory attributes of the food such as color or texture. This is why poisonous insects often exhibit aposematic warning colors for protection. These visual cues allow the insects to advertise their toxicity without having to be eaten first. Avoidance of a specific cue may continue even when the UCS is not present. Aversion to a cue in the absence of a consequence produces an effect known as *Batesian mimicry.* Some nonpoisonous insects are called mimics because they have evolved visual cues that mimic the colorations of poisonous insects. The species that possess both CS and UCS are known as models. Mimics are avoided as if they are models because they possess the cue associated with illness.

Because ingestion of a mimic does not produce negative consequences for the consumer, aversion to the cue will be greatly diminished if the mimic is repeatedly eaten. Extinction (complete loss of the aversion) will occur as subjects learn that ingestion of the cue does not produce illness. Extinction occurs rapidly when subjects are forced to ingest items that contain the CS but not the UCS. However, ingestion of the model after extinction may produce spontaneous recovery of the aversion, which may occur months after extinction. Conversely, latent inhibition describes the lack of an aversive response when subjects are exposed to the model following extinction. Latent inhibition is an example of the conflict that occurs when foods thought to be safe suddenly cause illness.

Transfer of avoidance from one food item to another containing a similar cue is known as *generalization.* Generalized cues that closely resemble the CS are most likely to be avoided. In addition to flavors, other sensory cues are subject to generalization. This phenomenon causes animals to assume that all similar foods must also cause illness. However, extinction of generalized aversions will occur if the UCS is not present in the new food that contains the cue.

Even with this learning process in place, animals often ingest toxic plants or prey anyway. Learning processes fail for a variety of reasons. For instance, not all toxins produce the gastrointestinal distress required for learning. Delays between CS ingestion and illness also diminish food aversions. Although delays of many hours do not interfere with learning, delays between ingestion and symptomatic consequences can be several years with some toxins. Learning processes may also fail when the environment changes. Herbivores in unfamiliar environments will ingest familiar toxic plants and avoid unfamiliar nutritious ones, even though illness results from ingestion of poisonous plants.

TAL is a hardwired memory that is formed affectively yet lends itself to further development through cognitive processes. There are several principal aspects of TAL. Namely, it is robust, is highly specific, is acquired rapidly, occurs with a single exposure, and is tolerant of time delay between presentation of CS and onset of UCS effects. These features make it an important mechanism in foraging behavior because animals with this memory need not relearn that certain food items are toxic every time they are encountered.

Bruce A. Kimball
Dale L. Nolte
USDA National Wildlife Research Center

TASTE PERCEPTION

Sense of Taste

Taste is one of five senses that may be involved in sensory evaluation, each sense being associated with a different type of receptor. The sense of taste is important because of its role in food recognition, selection, and acceptance. The final criteria by which food is judged and wins acceptance relate to sensory properties: How does it look? How does it taste? How does it smell? Individuals use their senses to determine whether a product is edible and whether it pleases them. The first is a judgment, the second a reaction; and the more favorable the reaction, the more likely the product is to be acceptable (Woods, 1998).

Taste Receptors

Taste or gustatory sensations occur with stimulations of chemoreceptors in taste buds on the tongue, soft palate, and throat, the majority being on the tongue. The taste buds are small, oval-shaped protruberances containing two types of cells.

The surface of the tongue is rough because of the presence of papillae, which vary in size and shape. The largest are the circular circumvallate papillae, which contain taste buds, and these papillae form an inverted V shape at the back of the tongue. Fungiform papillae, which are mushroom shaped and also contain taste buds, are located on the tip and at the sides of the tongue (Arvidson, 1979). Moderate numbers of taste buds are present in foliate papillae, which occur in the palate and at the back of the throat. Evidence of anatomical influences on the different sensitivities between individuals has been provided by Miller and Bartoshuk (1991) and Bartoshuk, Duffy, and Miller (1994), who correlated counts of papillae and taste buds with taste sensitivity.

Stimulation of Receptors

Saliva is an important component of taste function. It acts as a solvent and enables contact between the taste stimulus and the plasma membranes of the gustatory hairs, where a generator potential initiates a nerve impulse. Moistening of the mucus membrane in the mouth by saliva is increased when food is in the mouth.

Chewing stimulates secretion of saliva via receptors in the brain stem known as the superior and inferior salivating nuclei (Tortora & Anagnostakos, 1984). The stimuli of thought, sight, and smell may lead to anticipation of taste sensation before the food is placed in the mouth, resulting in saliva secretion. These stimuli are based on learned behavior, memory, and psychological response and form the basis for the expression, "It makes my mouth water."

Primary Tastes

It is generally accepted in sensory science that there are four primary tastes that stimulate taste buds at specific areas of the tongue. Each primary taste is designated as such by the responses of taste buds to different chemical stimulants. Studies on single taste buds have demonstrated that most taste buds can be stimulated by more than one primary taste stimulus (Collings, 1974). As a general rule, however, the specificity theory works well for demonstrating the taste sensation of each of the four primary tastes: sweet, salty, sour, and bitter. Sweet is the sensation recognised predominantly at the tip of the tongue, salty and sour sensations at the sides, and bitter at the back. The standards used to demonstrate the primary tastes are based on solutions of sucrose (sweet), sodium chloride (salty), citric acid (sour), and quinine sulphate or caffeine (bitter).

Some substances normally associated with one particular taste sensation may demonstrate other taste sensations over a range of concentrations. Saccharin, which has considerable use as an intense sweetener, can taste bitter as well as sweet. Work by Helgren, Lynch, and Kirchmeyer (1955) demonstrated that some individuals recognize a bitter taste in saccharin at certain concentrations. This bitterness was originally thought to be due to different preparation procedures but was shown in the study to be inherent in the particular structure of the saccharin molecule to which some individuals demonstrated sensitivity.

Another example of differences in taste sensitivity between individuals is the phenomenon of bitter taste blindness. This was originally studied using phenylthiourea (phenylthiocarbamide). Fox (1932) and Blakeslee (1932) discovered that 20% of the population were unable to detect any bitterness in solutions of the compound. More recent studies into taste blindness have been carried out using the compound 6-n-propothiouracil, which correlates with the phenylthiourea response but is less toxic (Lawless, 1980).

When examining responses to primary tastes, it has been shown that some individuals confuse bitter with sour. This occurs not because of a lack of ability to differentiate but because the two primary tastes are frequently present together in many products, such as lemons and grapefruit. This confusion can easily be rectified by demonstration using standard solutions.

Threshold Levels

Absolute or detection threshold is the lowest perceivable energy level of a physical stimulus, or the lowest perceivable concentration in the case of a chemical stimulus (Lawless & Heymann, 1998). Recognition thresholds are the minimum levels of concentration at which the characteristic taste of stimulant is evident. As a general rule, the concentration of the recognition threshold is slightly higher than that of the detection threshold.

Absolute thresholds vary between individuals and even with a single individual. Sensitivity is affected by emotional and environmental factors as well as by the substance under investigation. Difference thresholds relate to the amount by which a stimulus must change before it becomes a just noticeable difference (JND). Early work on this by Weber and Fischer forms the basis for much of today's sensory methodology (Amerine, Pangborn, & Roessler, 1965).

Measurement of threshold levels has been used extensively in studies of the psychophysics of taste. This concerns the functional relationship between stimulus and response. That is, the physical stimuli are measured and related to psychological sensation (Coon, 1986).

Adaptation of Taste

Continuous stimulation of the sense of taste, as with the other senses, results in adaptation. This occurs very quickly after contact with the taste stimulant but is slower after 2 to 3 seconds. Complete adaptation to taste can occur in 1 to 5 minutes and involves a psychological adaptation in the central nervous system (Tortora & Anagnostakos, 1984). When food is being tasted, adaptation involves the senses of both taste and smell.

Taste and Flavor

Flavor is the total sensation realized when a food or beverage is placed in the mouth. The senses of smell and taste involve chemoreceptors, and it is the combination of these with other receptors such as the mechanoreceptors of touch and electromagnetic receptors of sight that leads to the overall perception of flavor. When food or drink is consumed, the primary tastes are recognized on the tongue along with textural and other associated sensations in the mouth and on the palate. Identity is conferred as a result of the movement of volatile components of the food from the back of the mouth into the olfactory area, where the smell mechanism operates. Often when a loss of the sense of taste is indicated, it is really a loss of the sense of smell (Murphy & Cain, 1980). This situation arises with people suffering from the common cold or from an allergy and who complain that they cannot taste. In fact, their taste sensations may not be impaired; the olfactory mechanisms are affected because volatile components from foods are prevented from entering the olfactory system by mucus.

Taste Aversion

Taste acceptance varies considerably between individuals and also with single individuals. Cabanac and Duclaux (1970) demonstrated that hunger influences the degree of acceptability and pleasantness of the sweet taste. Acceptance and preference in relation to food quality depends on a combination of physiological and psychological response. Taste aversion is a type of classical conditioning that occurs when illness follows consumption of a particular food; a negative association is developed with that food, which is subsequently avoided (Logue, 1986). Taste aversion can also occur as a result of drug treatment, especially in cancer patients (Bernstein, 1978; Bernstein & Webster, 1980).

Umami

The four taste qualities sweet, sour, salty, and bitter are adequate for most investigations involving sensory evaluation. Umami is the description for the mouthfilling sensation of monosodium glutamate (MSG), 5^1 inosine monophosphate (IMP), and 5^1 guanine monophosphate (GMP; Kawamura & Kare, 1987). Often described as flavor enhancers, these substances are the subject of ongoing discussions on whether umami can be considered as a separate taste category.

REFERENCES

Amerine, M. A., Pangborn, R. M., & Roessler, E. B. (1965). *Principles of sensory evaluation of food.* New York: Academic Press.

Arvidson, K. (1979). Location and variation in number of taste buds in human fungiform papillae. *Scandinavian Journal of Dental Research, 87,* 435–442.

Bartoshuk, L. M., Duffy, V. B., & Miller, L. J. (1994). PTC/PROP tasting: Anatomy, psychophysics and sex effects. *Physiology and Behaviour, 56,* 1165–1171.

Bernstein, I. L. (1978). Learned taste aversions in children receiving chemotherapy. *Science, 200,* 1302–1303.

Bernstein, I. L., & Webster, M. M. (1980). Learned taste aversion in humans. *Physiology and Behaviour, 25,* 363–366.

Blakeslee, A. F. (1932). Genetics of sensory thresholds: Taste for phenylthiocarbamide. *Proceedings of the National Academy of Sciences, USA, 18,* 120–130.

Cabanac, M., & Duclaux, P. (1970). Obesity: Absence of satiety aversion to sucrose. *Science,* 496–497.

Collings, V. B. (1974). Human taste response as a function of locus on the tongue and soft palate. *Perception and Psychophysics, 16,* 169–174.

Coon, D. (1986). *Introduction to psychology* (4th ed.). St. Paul, MN: West.

Fox, A. L. (1932). The relationship between chemical constitution and taste. *Proceedings of the National Academy of Sciences, USA, 18,* 115–120.

Helgren, F. J., Lynch, M. J., & Kirchmeyer, F. J. (1955). A taste panel study of the saccharin off taste. *Journal of the American Pharmaceutical Association, 14,* 353–355, 442–446.

Kawamura, Y., & Kare, M. R. (1987). *Umami: A basic taste.* New York: Dekker.

Lawless, H. T. (1980). A comparison of different methods for assessing sensitivity to the taste of phenylthiocarbamide (PTC). *Chemical Senses, 5,* 247–256.

Lawless, H. T., & Heymann, H. (1998). *Sensory evaluation of food: Principles and practices.* New York: Chapman & Hall.

Logue, A. W. (1986). *The psychology of eating and drinking.* New York: Freeman.

Murphy, C., & Cain, W. S. (1980). Taste and olfaction: Independence vs. interaction. *Physiology and Behavior, 24,* 601.

Tortora, G. J., & Anagnostakos, H. P. (1984). *Principles of anatomy and physiology* (4th ed.). New York: Harper and Ross.

Woods, M. P. (1998). Taste and flavour perception. *Proceedings of the Nutrition Society, 57,* 603–607.

Margaret P. Woods
Queen Margaret University College

TELEOLOGICAL PSYCHOLOGY

The word *teleology* devolves from the Greek *telos,* which means an end in the sense of an intended goal or target for the sake of which behavior is carried out. Something that is done intentionally can be said to begin in choice, or to serve a purpose. The adjective *teleological* (or *telic*) in the phrase teleological psychology thus tells us that here is a psychology in which organisms—especially human organisms—behave as they do after they have put down or framed some kind of predicating assumption. Meaning is vital here. As any dictionary will reveal, "to mean" is literally "to intend." This style of explanation places a good deal of responsibility on the behaving individual. In contrast, a nonteleological psychology would deny that people have actual control over their intentions and purposes, for they are under a continuous shaping by their heredity and environment. This style of explanation is termed a mechanical psychology. For centuries, there has been a dispute between the teleologists and the mechanists in disciplines such as religion, philosophy, and science. To date, psychology has been predominantly in favor of mechanistic accounts—at least in academic centers. Nevertheless, the ancient debate over the nature of behavior continues.

To understand more fully the disagreement between the two types of psychology we must first grasp what it means to say that anything existing has been *caused* in some fashion. Aristotle advanced the ruling theory of causation, in which he named four kinds of causes as being responsible for a thing's existence or an event's occurrence. First is the material cause, or substance (e.g., wood, mud, flesh, bone matter) that "makes things up." Next is the efficient cause, which provides the thrust to move things along or assemble them in some way (energy, gravity, electricity, etc.). A third responsibility is the formal cause or pattern in events as well as the various shapes that things assume in becoming recognizable (a tornado, mathematical equation, plan, etc.). Fourth, we have the final cause, by which is meant the reason, purpose, or intention for the sake of which things exist or come about (goals, retributions, plans, etc.).

There are at least three kinds of teleological theories found in the history of philosophy: human, natural, and deity. We see a human teleology in Socrates' (470–400 BC) discussion of businessmen risking dangerous sea voyages for the sake of a possible profit (an end that motivates things). There is also a natural teleology, as when Aristotle (384–322 BC) suggests that leaves on the branches of trees exist for the sake of providing shade for the fruit that grows on them, concluding thereby that nature is always involved in some form of purpose. We also have various forms of deity teleology, which claim that the natural order unfolds for the sake of a divine plan reflecting the deity's intention. This latter use of final causation was to bring telic description into decline in science.

Most philosophers in the empirical tradition retained their belief in a deity, but they fashioned a rigorous method of practicing science that did not rely on such a deity teleology to make its descriptive case or to establish its validity. The aim of all so-called proper natural scientists was to reduce observed identities and actions to underlying mechanical processes. In effect, *reductionism* means to reformulate formal and final cause explanation into material and efficient cause explanation.

Teleological explanation drew precedents from continental philosophy. The tie binding all these views is an appreciation of the role that human conceptualization (mind) plays in the understanding and creation of experience (reality). Reductionism is rejected in favor of a form of human teleology in which the person is viewed as framing the reason, creative purpose, or willful intention for the sake of which behavior is carried out.

It could be argued that psychology as a unique scientific discipline began with G. T. Fechner's desire to prove that human beings are in fact teleological organisms. His distinctive psychophysical methods (average error, constant stimuli, limits) and famous (Weber-Fechner) law were the combined fruits of Fechner's efforts to show that consciousness (telic mind) was the inner patterned unity of a corporeal system (nontelic matter). However, he brought a deity as well as a human teleology into his telic explanations, which turned away colleagues and students alike.

Hermann von Helmholtz more than anyone else influenced the early course of psychological explanation, sending it in the direction of reductionism. He argued that the constancy principle (conservation-of-energy principle) applied with equal validity to the explanation of human behavior as to the explanation of inanimate, physical events. Psychologists must reduce behavioral explanation to basic forces, according to Helmholtz. Concepts of mass energy, force, and thence motion were familiar to Newtonian physics, which construed them in terms of *only* material and efficient causation. Such scientific explanations turned nature into a complex mechanism in which no deity's plan or human's intention played a role whatsoever. In a fascinating historical parallel, the youthful Sigmund Freud was to be influenced by Brucke to frame the libido theory of psychoanalysis, which reduced thoughts to underlying forces in the constancy-principle sense.

Advocates of an openly teleological explanation of behavior have been prevalent in psychology. Both Alfred Adler and Carl G. Jung endorsed teleological explanations of the human being. In the more academic circles, William James' fiat of will and William McDougall's purposive psychology were early efforts to add to the Helmholtzian reductionism a formal-final causal explanation that ever eluded it. Notable efforts to provide a telic side to behavioral description can be seen in Gordon Allport's functional autonomy and in Gardner Murphy's concept of canalization. A classic confrontation occurred when Carl R. Rogers (teleologist) debated B. F. Skinner (mechanist) over whether people had freedom and control in their personal behavior. No final decision was reached, of course.

A view being advanced by a growing number of psychologists today is that there may be room for teleological explanations in their field. Difficulties with the mechanistic conception of reinforcement in conditioning adult humans have led these psychologists to question the assumption that behavior is manipulated without a person's conscious awareness of what is taking place and a resultant intention to carry out the implications of such knowledge. Relying on formal and final causation to account clearly for such behavior may be introduced in the not too distant future.

Joseph F. Rychlak
Loyola University of Chicago

TERRITORIALITY I

Territoriality refers to behavior associated with the acquisition, maintenance, and defense of a territory. In animals, territories are geographical areas that surround the home. These areas are protected from other members of the same species, and normally conspecifics are not even allowed entry. In humans, the concept of territoriality is similar, but it often takes different forms.

In animals, territoriality is usually thought of as instinctive and adaptive behavior. Because each group is separated from the others, the density of a population can be maintained at a level that facilitates food gathering, reproduction, and the control of aggression. These spaces can change in size.

Territoriality in humans takes more flexible forms. It is unclear whether this behavior in humans has instinctual or learned origins, but it is certain that people's use of territories is different from that of animals. First, there are several different kinds of human territories. People typically have one or two *primary territories,* such as the home or office, which are places in which a great deal of time is spent and that are owned and personalized on a more or less permanent basis. People also have *secondary territories,* defined as places where they spend less time and in which ownership is transient. People control secondary territories only when they are in them. Public territories are places that people use but that are not owned by an individual or a small group. Parks, beaches, and other such areas are public because they are owned by an extremely large group.

Humans are also more flexible than animals in their defense of territory. Social and cultural mechanisms that fulfill many of the survival needs provided by territoriality among animals make defense of territory less often necessary among people.

The ways in which animals and humans denote territorial control also differ. Many animals rely on scent to notify others that they own a space, such as by urinating along its boundaries to provide clear cues. Humans typically use visual markers. Studies have indicated that people paint and decorate territories to denote ownership.

Aggressive defense of territory does occur among humans, although less often than among animals. This defense often takes milder forms than fighting. In the case of defense of well-established territories, physical aggression is less likely to occur.

Andrew S. Baum
University of Pittsburgh Cancer Institute

TERRITORIALITY II

There is disagreement concerning the best way to define territoriality. Classically, a territory is any defended area.

Animals of many species occupy specific portions of their habitats from which they exclude other members of the species. A male stickleback fish in breeding condition will defend an area around a nest against intruding males. This is the essence of territoriality. What is remarkable is that an animal that might lose a contest in a neutral area or in the territory of another individual typically will win while in its own territory.

Perhaps the most important fact concerning territories is the diverse nature of different patterns grouped together under this one term. Wilson lists five types. Type A territories are large, defended areas within which animals can mate, court, and gather most of their food. Various species of fishes, lizards, and birds occupy such all-purpose territories. Type B territories also are relatively large and are used for breeding, but the residents go elsewhere to feed. Nightjays and reed warblers occupy such territories. Type C territories are small defended areas around a nest, as found in many colonial birds. There is room for little more than breeding. Type D territories are pairing or mating territories; animals go to these territories to mate but, in contrast to the first three types, raise their young elsewhere. Birds such as the sage grouse and ungulates such as the Uganda kob form such leks. Type E territories are the roosting positions or shelters used by many species of bats, starlings, and domestic pigeons.

Thus territories vary along several dimensions. They may or may not be used for feeding, mating, or rearing of the young, depending on the species. The number of residents varies from a single male, a mated male–female pair, or a whole group of animals that defend the territory. Most territories relate to a fixed location. An interesting borderline case can be found with bitterlings, a small species of fish that lays eggs in the mantle cavities of certain species of mussels and that defends the area around the mussels, even if they move. It is important when trying to generalize from territory in animals to similar phenomena in humans that one remember the diversity of animal territoriality.

Territorial defense need not always entail overt fighting; song or odors can serve to mark an area as occupied. In a typical experiment on the function of bird song, some males are removed from their territories and replaced with loudspeakers that do or do not continue to emit the songs. Intrusion by conspecifics is delayed when songs are played. In other experiments, devocalized males have difficulty in keeping out intruders. It seems as though males must sing to keep their space.

The concept of territory often has been applied to humans in a variety of contexts. Members of a nation may defend a border, members of a gang may defend their turf, and suburban homeowners may defend their property. Indeed, Sebba and Churchman looked within the homesite to view the dwelling unit as composed of segments of space appropriate for use by different individuals or clusters of individuals. In another experiment, androstenol was shown to be a human odor that functioned to space males. By treating half of the stalls in a public restroom with the chemical, the experimenters found males to avoid marked territories. Models of economic defensibility in relation to resources have been applied to human populations by anthropologists.

Donald A. Dewsbury

TERTIARY PREVENTION

The concept of tertiary prevention arises from the public health preventive services model (Commission on Chronic Illness, 1957; Last, 1992). In this model, preventive services are categorized into primary, secondary, or tertiary interventions. The goal of primary prevention is to decrease the prevalence of disease via reduction in its rate of occurrence.

Primary prevention is therefore directed at eliminating etiologic factors, thereby reducing the incidence of the disease or eradicating it entirely (Greenfield & Shore, 1995). A classic example of primary prevention is the use of immunization against measles and rubella to eliminate neonatal neurological impairment caused by these diseases. Secondary prevention works to reduce prevalence (a function of both duration and rate of occurrence of the illness) by decreasing the illness's duration through early intervention and effective treatment. Tertiary prevention refers to interventions that aim to reduce the severity, discomfort, or disability associated with a disorder through rehabilitation or through the reduction of the acute and chronic complications of the disorder (Fletcher, Fletcher, & Wagner, 1988; Mrazek & Haggerty, 1994).

Certain interventions may be considered to be either secondary or tertiary prevention. For example, the use of psychotropic medications and psychotherapies may serve at different times as secondary or tertiary preventive measures. Early intervention and use of these as effective treatments can decrease the duration of the illness and may represent secondary prevention. However, in individuals with a chronic relapsing illness, the use of psychotherapy and psychotropic medications to prevent relapse to a symptomatic stage of the illness would constitute tertiary prevention. For example, maintenance antidepressant medication to prevent relapse to a symptomatic stage of mood disorder can be viewed as tertiary prevention. Another example would be the use of group psychotherapy to prevent relapse in currently abstinent individuals with substance use disorders. Other interventions that diminish social impairment or disability among those with chronic conditions also represent tertiary prevention—for example, vocational rehabilitation or social skills training for those with chronic psychotic disorders. Overall, most tertiary preventive interventions for psychiatric disorders fall into the category of maintenance treatments for chronic conditions. Such maintenance interventions include (1) interventions that are aimed at increasing compliance with long-term treatment and whose goal is to reduce relapse and recurrence and (2) aftercare treatments, such as rehabilitation, whose goal is to improve social and occupational function (Mrazek & Haggerty, 1994).

Examples of Tertiary Prevention

Most examples of tertiary prevention within mental health are found in the maintenance, treatment, and rehabilitation of individuals with chronic mental disorders. Schizophrenia is a chronic psychotic disorder with onset usually in late adolescence and an overall prevalence in the United States of approximately 1%. The combination of relatively high prevalence and early onset imposes a large burden of personal suffering and need for treatment and rehabilitative services due to the morbidity and chronic disability the disorder engenders. Tertiary preventive interventions are, therefore, quite important in this population in the form of rehabilitation and prevention of relapse (Preventing schizophrenic relapse, 1995). Medication nonadherence may be responsible for 40% of all exacerbations of schizophrenia that result in hospitalization. In addition, the illness generally interferes with a number of areas of functioning.

A number of tertiary preventive interventions have been designed to improve functioning, increase medication adherence, and reduce relapse, and thereby decrease overall disability due to the illness. Comprehensive psychosocial treatments such as those involving Assertive Continuous Care (Stein, 1990) and behavioral rehabilitation (Anthony & Liberman, 1986; Liberman, Falloon, & Wallace, 1984) can improve patients' medication adherence and help with a number of psychosocial aspects of life, including vocational and recreational activities. For example, behavioral rehabilitation uses a multidisciplinary team to provide services that can help increase adherence to medication and provide support and direction in other areas of the patients' lives, including work, family, and social interactions (Kopelowicz & Liberman, 1995).

Depressive disorders are among the most common psychiatric disorders. For example, the prevalence of major depressive disorder at any one time is estimated to be 2% to 4% in the community, 5% to 10% among primary care outpatients, and 10% to 14% among medical inpatients (Katon & Schulberg, 1992). Depressive illness is generally chronic and relapsing and can have significant social and economic consequences for the affected individual (Montgomery, Green, Baldwin, & Montgomery, 1989). Tertiary prevention of depressive disorders, therefore, usually focuses on decreasing the likelihood of relapse and recurrence. At least 50% of recurrent episodes of depression are preventable by adequate prophylaxis with antidepressant medication (Montgomery et al., 1989). For major depression, antidepressant treatment for a minimum period of 6 to 9 months following the resolution of symptoms is indicated to decrease the risk of recurrence. In addition, a common tertiary preventive intervention for bipolar disorder is maintenance medication with a mood stabilizer with or without an antidepressant to minimize the risk of another manic or depressive episode (Goodwin & Jamison, 1990).

Tertiary prevention of substance use disorders involves relapse prevention and rehabilitation. Considerable evidence suggests that patient involvement in ongoing treatment is helpful in maintaining abstinence, limiting the total duration of relapses, and improving overall long-term outcome (Greenfield & Shore, 1995; Higgins et al., 1994; McLellan, Luborsky, Woody, O'Brien, & Druley, 1983; O'Malley, Jaffe, & Chang, 1992). Programs that help individuals maintain abstinence from substances or limit the duration of relapse are effective tertiary preventions; they include aftercare participation such as training in relapse prevention or coping skills, behavioral treatment, involvement in Alcoholics Anonymous, and methadone maintenance (Galanter & Kleber, 1999).

REFERENCES

Anthony, W. A., & Liberman, R. P. (1986). The practice of psychiatric rehabilitation. *Schizophrenia Bulletin, 12,* 542–559.

Commission on Chronic Illness. (1957). *Chronic illness in the United States* (Vol. 1). Cambridge, MA: Harvard University Press.

Fletcher, R. H., Fletcher, S. W., & Wagner, E. H. (1988). *Clinical epidemiology: The essentials* (2nd ed.). Baltimore: Williams & Wilkins.

Galanter, M., & Kleber, H. D. (Eds.). (1999). *Textbook of substance abuse treatment* (2nd ed.). Washington, DC: American Psychiatric Press.

Goodwin, F. K., & Jamison, K. R. (1990). *Manic-depressive illness.* New York: Oxford University Press.

Greenfield, S. F., & Shore, M. F. (1995). Prevention of psychiatric disorders. *Harvard Review of Psychiatry, 3,* 115–129.

Higgins, S. T., Budney, A. J., Bickel, W. K., Foerg, F. E., Donham, R., & Badger, G. J. (1994). Incentives improve outcome in outpatient behavioral treatment of cocaine dependence. *Archives of General Psychiatry, 51,* 568–576.

Katon, W., & Schulberg, H. (1992). Epidemiology of depression in primary care. *General Hospital Psychiatry, 14,* 237–247.

Kopelowicz, A., & Liberman, R. P. (1995). Biobehavioral treatment and rehabilitation of schizophrenia. *Harvard Review of Psychiatry, 3,* 55–64.

Last, J. M. (1992). Scope and methods of prevention. In J. M. Last & R. B. Wallace (Eds.), *Public health and preventive medicine* (pp. 3–10). Norwalk, CT: Appleton & Lange.

Liberman, R. P., Falloon, I. R. H., & Wallace, C. J. (1984). Drug-psychosocial interactions in the treatment of schizophrenia. In M. Mirabi (Ed.), *The chronically mentally ill: Research and services.* New York: SP Medical and Scientific.

McLellan, A. T., Luborsky, L., Woody, G. E., O'Brien, C. P., & Druley, K. A. (1983). Predicting response to alcohol and drug abuse treatments: Role of psychiatric severity. *Archives of General Psychiatry, 40,* 620–625.

Montgomery, S. A., Green, M., Baldwin, D., & Montgomery, D. (1989). Prophylactic treatment of depression: A public health issue. *Neuropsychobiology, 22,* 214–219.

Mrazek, P. J., & Haggerty, R. J. (Eds.). (1994). *Reducing risks for mental disorders: Frontiers for preventive intervention research.* Washington, DC: National Academy Press.

O'Malley, S. S., Jaffe, A. J., & Chang, G. (1992). Naltrexone and coping skills therapy for alcohol dependence: A controlled study. *Archives of General Psychiatry, 49,* 881–887.

Preventing schizophrenic relapse [Medical news and perspectives]. (1995). *Journal of the American Medical Association, 273,* 6–8.

Stein, L. I. (1990). Comments by Leonard Stein. *Hospital and Community Psychiatry, 41,* 649–651.

Shelly F. Greenfield
McLean Hospital

See also: **Drug Rehabilitation**

TEST STANDARDIZATION

Test standardization is the establishment of uniform procedures for test administration and scoring. If psychological measurement is defined as the use of rules to assign numbers to relative quantities of psychological constructs associated with persons, then test standardization is the determination and explication of those rules. Without standardization, measurement is only an informal process that varies from examiner to examiner. Historical impetus for the concern with control on the part of examiners arose from nineteenth-century experimental psychologists from Leipzig, where work demonstrated that minor variations in giving instructions and making observations resulted in differences (Anastasi & Urbina, 1997). The first standardized tests appeared in the early part of the twentieth century, when E. L. Thorndike and others extended the principles learned in a laboratory to psychological measurement. DuBois (1970) elaborated the history of standardized testing.

The *Standards for Educational and Psychological Testing* (American Educational Research Association et al., 1999) provides an outline of procedures that test publishers and users should follow to ensure proper implementation of standardization procedures. Control of test administration procedures is largely accomplished by instructions specified in test manuals. For example, test authors must develop test manuals that clearly describe (1) test administration directions under which norming, reliability, and validity data were gathered and (2) scoring directions to minimize scoring errors. Regarding directions for test administrators, such matters as time limits, procedures for marking answer sheets and scoring tests, and instructions for guessing must be provided in the test manual. Those conditions under which changes to test administration procedures may be made and how questions from test takers should be answered should be specified. Clemens (1971) provided detailed consideration of test administration (mostly for tests administered in group settings). Regarding procedures for scoring test responses, the *Standards for Educational and Psychological Testing* (1999) specify that detailed instructions for scoring both subjective and objective tests should be furnished in the test manual, and, in the case of subjectively graded tests, the extent of agreement between scorers should be enumerated, differentiating the extent of interscorer reliability by levels of scorer training, if possible. Manuals should detail qualifications needed to administer and score the test in question. Test users are expected to follow carefully the standardized procedures as described in the manual when administering a test and, given these procedures, to enable all test takers to perform their best. One should keep favorable conditions for testing consistent with standardization procedures. Test users are charged with checking all details of test scoring meticulously for accuracy.

Another aspect of test standardization is the development of test norms. To establish norms, a test constructor administers the test under standardized conditions to a large, representative sample. Representative means that the sample resembles the persons for whom the test is intended. The data from this experimental testing allow the test constructor to identify the normative or typical behavior (e.g., the 50th percentile) and other percentiles. These values, in conjunction with reliability and validity information, permit professional test users to interpret test scores properly.

Three potential advantages of standardized psychological tests are evident. First, standardized tests are frequently of higher quality than locally constructed tests. Because these tests may be employed by a large number of client-users, much more expense and professional time can be spent at all stages of the test construction (e.g., preparing test outlines, editing items, item analysis, test revision, etc.). Second, using standardized examinations may free psychologists and other professionals from spending time on test construction and other evaluative activities and permit them to employ time on other more important matters—therapy, instruction, and score interpretation. Last, the use of standardized measures facilitates communication among professionals. Scores on tests administered under proper conditions communicate information about individuals, groups, and scientific findings effectively to others. One important disadvantage of standardized measures is that due to their availability, standardized tests may be used inappropriately. For example, a standardized selection test for industry might be used in a situation in which it has neither been intended nor validated. Similarly, a local school program with unique goals could not be effectively evaluated with a nationally standardized test with its broad-based orientation.

The term *standardized tests* is sometimes applied to those tests that are simply extensively (e.g., nationally) normed. However, norms are usually useful only if they relate to test scores achieved under uniform conditions. In fact, before norming a test can begin, detailed conditions of standardization must be finalized and described for examiners. Tests administered under conditions differing from those for which the test is intended will yield scores that are difficult to interpret.

One special case of test score interpretation where tests often must be administered under nonstandardized conditions is for individuals with disabilities. The Americans with Disabilities Act (1990) requires that tests be administered with appropriate accommodations. That such groups of test takers are small makes validation and interpretation more difficult (Geisinger, 1994; Sandoval, Frisby, Geisinger, Schennemann, & Grenier, 1998), but early validation efforts with nationally standardized college admissions measures seem promising (Willingham et al., 1988).

REFERENCES

American Educational Research Association, American Psychological Association, & National Council on Measurement in Education. (1999). *Standards for educational and psychological testing.* Washington, DC: American Educational Research Association.

Anastasi, A., & Urbina, S. (1997). *Psychological testing* (7th ed.). Upper Saddle River, NJ: Prentice Hall.

Clemens, W. C. (1971). Test administration. In R. L. Thorndike (Ed.), *Educational measurement* (2nd ed., pp. 188–201). Washington, DC: American Council on Education.

DuBois, P. H. (1970). *A history of psychological testing.* Boston: Allyn & Bacon.

Geisinger, K. F. (1994). Psychometric issues in testing students with disabilities. *Applied Measurement in Education, 7,* 121–140.

Sandoval, J., Frisby, C. L., Geisinger, K. F., Scheunemann, J. D., & Grenier, J. R. (Eds.). (1998). *Test interpretation and diversity.* Washington, DC: American Psychological Association.

Willingham, W. W., Ragosta, M., Bennett, R. E., Braun, H., Rock, D. A., & Powers, D. E. (1988). *Testing handicapped people.* Boston: Allyn & Bacon.

Kurt F. Geisinger

See also: **Psychometrics**

TESTING METHODS

The development of tests in psychology is undoubtedly one of the greatest contributions of psychology as a discipline. Psychology has evolved as a useful discipline in a large variety of institutions in our society (e.g., clinical and counseling settings, industry, medicine, and the schools) primarily because of its model of diagnosis and treatment (Anastasi, 1979), in which treatments are applied largely on the basis of assessments made about the current functioning of an individual, group, or organization. Assessments of many different kinds can be made, and it is probably safe to report that if one can imagine every possible human characteristic, behavior, thought pattern, or tendency, some psychologist has attempted to measure it. The many kinds of psychological measurement can be typified along a variety of facets, some of which are best identified as dichotomies and others as continuous.

One of the primary issues in differentiating psychological measures relates to the content of the domain that is being measured. Specifically, most psychological constructs that are measured can be identified as either cognitive or noncognitive measures. Cognitive measures include those that assess normal abilities (e.g., intelligence), special abilities (e.g., artistic or quantitative aptitude), and achievement (which tends to be information and concepts learned in instructional programs). Noncognitive measures generally assess personality, interests, attitudes, beliefs, and so on. One operational difference between the two domains is that questions on cognitive measures tend to be answered correctly or incorrectly or in some cases to vary in their degree of correctness. Noncognitive measures, on the other hand, measure the strength of one's tendencies, sometimes in a bipolar manner. Thus, scales may have two endpoints, such as masculinity-femininity or introversion-extraversion. Responses to questions or ratings that place a respondent along a continuum concerning one of these dimensions are not correct or incorrect; they simply represent differences. This fundamental distinction among cognitive and noncognitive measures in psychology is quite important.

Within cognitive measures, one of the most important and common distinctions is that of ability and achievement. The distinction between abilities and achievement is one of degree, although these characteristics are often mistaken to be qualitatively different, a difference where some occasionally falsely perceive abilities as genetically determined and achievement as rather environmentally influenced. Anastasi and Urbina (1997) defined achievement tests as "designed to measure the effects of a specific program of instruction or training" (p. 475). Achievement tests measure the effects of relatively uniform experiences, especially of instructional events. Ability tests assess behavior that is manifested based on the cumulative influence of the many experiences of all aspects of life. Both ability and achievement reflect learning from one's environment; however, ability tests measure the effects of learning under relatively uncontrolled and often seemingly random life conditions, whereas achievement tests measure the effects of learning that occurred under more known and controlled conditions (Anastasi & Urbina, 1997).

Another major distinction among methods of psychological measurement concerns the nature of the responses by the test taker—specifically, whether the test taker responds with a constructed response or selects a response from among a number of possibilities. These distinctions can relate to the measurement of almost any psychological characteristic, whether cognitive or noncognitive, and they are most often written. On typical classroom tests developed by teachers, for example, a fill-in-the-blanks-type question is a constructed response question, and a multiple-choice question is a selected response question. Selected response questions are generally much easier to score quickly and are hence known as objective-type questions. Essay tests and other types of educational products (e.g., realistic samples of schoolwork performed by students or work samples provided by employees) are much more difficult to score and generally involve expert judgment (Coffman, 1971; Wiggins, 1973). Within the area of personality, measurement can also differ along this dimension. Objective-type measures use true-false or similar types of questions and typically match responses to representative patterns provided by previously identified groups of people. Projective techniques are a common kind of personality measure in which the examined individual provides an interpretation of relatively unstructured stimuli, such as ink blots or ambiguous pictures. The examiner provides a structure to the response in scoring it. These scoring methods, whether for essay questions or projective techniques, must be carefully and explicitly developed in advance to ensure both reliable and valid responses and interpretations of such responses (Wiggins, 1973). Professional test developers attempt to align the types of tests and test components or items (such as multiple-choice, fill-in, essay, short written answer, oral responses) to the nature of the characteristics or knowledge being assessed (Adkins, 1974; Hakel, 1998; Millman & Greene, 1991). Oral responses are common in individually administered tests.

Tests may be administered a number of different ways. Many tests (e.g., many intelligence tests and projective personality measures) are given by a professional examiner to individuals one at a time. Group tests are administered to a number of test takers at one time and often tend to be objectively scorable. Increasingly, many measures are administered via computer. Individual and computer-based tests can adapt to the responses of the test taker. For example, in many computer-adaptive tests (CATs), answering questions correctly sends one to more difficult questions, whereas incorrect responses lead to easier questions in the attempt to assess the test taker most accurately using appropriate questions. A testing professional who administers a test individually can ask probes or appropriate questions and can make certain prescribed test adaptations in accordance with the procedures for test administration as described in the test manual.

Tests can be purchased or built locally by professionals. The former tests are typically called standardized (see "Test Standardization") and are typically sold by test publishers, and the scores or results can be interpreted in terms of norms (statistical distributions of the population of individuals who have taken the test). Norms are typically useful only if they relate to test scores achieved under uniform conditions. Most locally constructed tests do not have such norms or interpretative information, but they may be specifically adapted to the local use in question.

All psychological measures are evaluated using similar criteria, such as test validity. These criteria are explained briefly in "Psychometrics" entry and in a more elaborate fashion in Anastasi and Urbina (1997) or the *Standards for Educational and Psychological Testing* (American Educational Research Association et al., 1999).

REFERENCES

Adkins, D. C. (1974). *Test construction: Development and interpretation of achievement tests* (2nd ed.). Columbus, OH: Merrill.

American Educational Research Association, American Psychological Association, & National Council on Measurement in Education. (1999). *Standards for educational and psychological testing*. Washington, DC: American Educational Research Association.

Anastasi, A. (1979). *Fields of applied psychology* (2nd ed.). New York: McGraw-Hill.

Anastasi, A., & Urbina, S. (1997). *Psychological testing* (7th ed.). Upper Saddle River, NJ: Prentice Hall.

Coffman, W. E. (1971). Essay examinations. In R. L. Thorndike (Ed.), *Educational measurement* (2nd ed., pp. 271–302). Washington, DC: American Council on Education.

Hakel, M. D. (Ed.). (1998). *Beyond multiple choice: Evaluating alternatives to traditional testing for selection*. Mahwah, NJ: Erlbaum.

Millman, J., & Greene, J. (1989). The specification and development of tests of achievement and ability. In R. L. Linn (Ed.), *Educational measurement* (3rd ed., pp. 335–366). New York: American Council on Education.

Wiggins, J. S. (1973). *Personality and prediction: Principles of personality assessment*. Reading, MA: Addison-Wesley.

Kurt F. Geisinger
University of St. Thomas

See also: Psychometrics

THEORETICAL CONSTRUCTS

It is relatively easy to name directly observable behaviors like eating and running. What accounts for these behaviors is a much more difficult task. When the relevant antecedent conditions are known, such as the presentation of a noxious stimulus (for running) or the presentation of food after it has been withheld (for eating), researchers can begin to understand such behaviors. But there is more to the problem than simply identifying antecedent conditions. Attributing overt behaviors to presumed covert intraorganismic functions, such as fear and hunger, requires the naming of those functions. Such naming is essentially the problem of theoretical constructs.

Hypothetical Constructs and Intervening Variables

Theoretical constructs within psychology are thus hypothesized internal processes presumed to underlie specified overt behaviors. An influential distinction between two types of such constructs was made by MacCorquodale and Meehl. Hypothetical constructs are defined as complex internal processes with meanings that are not entirely confined to the relationship between the stimulating conditions and the ensuing behaviors (i.e., they contain surplus meaning). The basic problem with the hypothetical constructs as thus defined is that the presence of such additional, unspecified meaning allows an indeterminate amount of ambiguity to cloud the fundamental definition of the construct and so reduce its theoretical usefulness.

Intervening variables are more restricted concepts. Their meanings are strictly circumscribed by the specified stimulus-response relationships (i.e., the antecedent environmental conditions and the consequent behaviors). The intervening variable is whatever occurs within the organism (presumably within the brain) that accounts for the observed stimulus-response relationship.

Such narrow definitions are not easy for psychologists to live with. Intervening variables as thus defined have been criticized as being sterile. This criticism is rebutted by pointing out that it is not the intervening variable itself that should be so accused but the theoretical use to which it is put. That rebuttal notwithstanding, intervening variables were never popular in psychological theory construction and seem to have become less popular in recent years. Nevertheless, at least some approximation to a fully operational definition, such as is provided by the intervening-variable type of construct, holds promise for more effective theorizing in psychology. Some examples may help to support this opinion.

Examples of Intervening Variables

Here, two uses of intervening variables are considered that illustrate their potential value, especially as tools in the development of theory. Mowrer and Viek kept all laboratory rats in their experiment hungry. They allowed rats in the experimental group to turn off noxious electric shock by jumping off the floor. The shock was given 10 seconds after the rats started to eat food offered on a stick pushed up through the floor bars. Matched controls in contiguous cages had a shock of exactly the same intensity and duration, but these rats were unable to turn it off. The rats in the experimental group ate more of the food and started to eat faster than the control rats. This difference could not be attributed to any physical difference in the shock. Mowrer and Viek explained the behavioral difference by attributing a sense of helplessness to the control rats. The subsequent development of the learned helplessness problem, in which first animal and later human subjects were used, illustrates the way in which more extensive experimental and theoretical work can have both broader and deeper ramifications than an initial experimental demonstration of an intervening variable.

In a second early experiment, modeled on the Mowrer and Viek experimental design, Marx and Van Spanckeren used seizure-sensitive laboratory rats (subjects that had been found to be susceptible to seizures—then called audiogenic—when stimulated by high-frequency, high-intensity sound in a physically restricted environment such as a cage). Vertical poles were placed in the centers of two contiguous cages. An experimental and a control rat, matched for susceptibility to seizure on the basis of prior tests, were then placed in the contiguous cages and the noxious sound stimulation presented. The experimental rat was able to turn off the sound by tilting the pole; the control rat could not do so. Because the sound stimulation came from a centrally located speaker, placed between the cages, any behavioral differences could not be attributed to strictly physical factors but could be attributed to the difference in treatment (i.e., to the more active role of the experimental rat in the management of the noxious stimulus). The results were that the control animals showed both quicker and more frequent seizures. Marx and Van Spanckeren attributed this difference to a presumed sense of control in the experimental rats, thus offering a positive internal function as an intervening variable to account for their greater resistance to seizure.

Contributions of Tolman and Hull

The use of intervening variables in psychological theory was first suggested by E. C. Tolman. Tolman later stated that he had come to favor the more comprehensive, less restricted hypothetical construct. Looking back on his earlier theoretical work, he commented,

> My intervening variables are generally speaking mere temporarily believed-in, inductive, more or less qualitative generalizations which categorize and sum up for me various empirically found relationships. . . . And they are not primarily neurophysiological . . . but are derived rather from intuition, common experience, a little sophomoric neurology, and my own phenomenology.

Clark Hull, in developing a grandly conceived hypothetico-deductive behavior theory, attempted to use intervening variables (e.g., habit strength, reaction potential, and inhibition) in a much more systematic and formalized manner. He used them as both theoretical tools—stimulants to and directors of empirical research—and theoretical concepts embedded in the propositions of his formal theory. There was much criticism of these intervening variables, which were regarded as too specific for the theory (e.g., specifying the weight in grams of the food rewards in some of the research with rats).

An Operational Continuum

It is helpful to think of the hypothetical concept and the intervening variable as belonging on opposite ends of an operational continuum rather than as discrete, absolutely different types of constructs. Progressive improvement in the operational clarity of theoretical constructs can then be regarded as a more reasonable objective in psychological theory construction than any quick-fix of constructs with ambiguous or unspecified meanings.

The intervening variable seems to be more appropriate when used as a tool in theory construction than when used as an element in a fully formalized theory. Scientists are well aware that the phenomena they investigate are complex and not readily reducible to such interpretations. If the more straightforward and simplified concepts, such as intervening variables as here defined, are to be of maximum value, they must be gradually introduced and carefully refined in preliminary types of theory construction or theorizing. Attempting premature placement in highly formalized theory, as Hull did, is to invite rejection.

M. H. Marx

See also: **Operant Conditioning; Operational Definition**

THEORIES OF FAMILY DEVELOPMENT

General Description and Early Formulations

Family development theory focuses on changes over time in family structure, roles of family members, developmental tasks, stressors and crises, and adaptive and maladaptive coping mechanisms. Historically, theorists conceptualized the family development as consisting of predictable stages and normative transitions through which most families evolve across the life cycle. E. M. Duvall's early work in the late 1950s, for example, defined the family life cycle as consisting of eight developmental stages: (1) married couple without children; (2) childbearing families (oldest child from birth to 30 months); (3) families with preschool children (oldest child from 2.5 to 6 years); (4) families with school-age children (oldest from 6 to 13 years); (5) families with adolescents (oldest from 13 to 20 years); (6) families that are launching children from the home (from first child to last child to leave home); (7) middle years including empty-nest syndrome to retirement; (8) and aging families extending from retirement to the death of both spouses. Duvall's model focused on the intact nuclear family (two biological parents living with their children)—the most common family structure at the time—and was based on the assumption that most families evolve through this predictable sequence of stages in accordance with a similar timetable.

Reformulations of Stage Theories

Coinciding with the dramatic rise in marital transitions (e.g., divorce, remarriage, and redivorce) in subsequent decades, R. Hill and other family theorists formulated more complex stage theories (i.e., greater variability in the number, types, and timing of stages with concomitant alterations in developmental tasks) taking into account the prevalence and diversity of single-parent families and stepfamilies. Considering a divorce rate of nearly 50% extending over three decades and the fact that most divorced people remarry (many of whom have children from prior marriages), the burgeoning diversity of family structures required a reformulation of Duvall's original theory of the family life cycle. Stage theories persisted but were now defined in terms of marital stability or instability, whether one or both remarried partners had children from prior marriages (i.e., simple vs. complex stepfamilies), custody arrangements (e.g., stepfather vs. stepmother families), the presence or absence of children from the remarriage (i.e., his, hers, and ours), and the ages and life-cycle stages of individual family members. In addition, family development theorists, buttressed by a plethora of empirical research comparing these permutations and combinations of family structures, became aware that the developmental tasks and concomitant functional and dysfunctional coping mechanisms varied widely across these diverse and changing family forms. Adaptive mechanisms for coping with life-cycle changes often differed from what worked in traditional nuclear families. For example, biological parents disciplining and showing affection to children may be adaptive, but the same parenting practices in newly formed stepfamilies often backfired and was maladaptive.

Challenges to Stage Theories of Family Development

The increasing diversity of family structures beyond those formed as a result of marital transitions (e.g., couples who live together but never marry, never-married parents, families of different cultures and racial groups, biracial couples, gay and lesbian couples, etc.) has led family development scholars in recent years to question the universality assumptions (i.e., families evolve through similar life transitions) of prior theories as well as the capacity of stage theories to capture the inordinate variations in life cycles of all families. Moreover, transitions that still occur in most families (e.g., birth of a first child) may occur simultaneously or in close temporal proximity to other changes and stressors (e.g., divorce, death of parent), which, within the context of different cultural groups and family structures, make the prediction of the types and timing of life changes exceedingly difficult. Additional problems with stage theories include their overly parsimonious focus on single generations in defining stages (e.g., aging families are comprised of members at other generational levels; the launching stage focuses on parents and deemphasizes adolescents and young adults who are leaving home) and their inadequate attention to family processes and the interdependencies of individual growth trajectories and those of families as a collective unit.

Beyond Stage Theories: The Search for Unifying Frameworks

Family development theorists have begun to identify unifying frameworks that transcend stages, address both the commonalities and diversities of family life, adopt a multigenerational perspective, and consider the intersections of individual and family change processes. For example, T. Laszloffy recently articulated a systemic family development (SFD) model, which integrates family crisis theory and family systems theory in conceptualizing families' and individuals' responses to stressful life events and transitions. According to SFD, common processes that all families experience are external and internal stressors that challenge family members to change their roles and interactional patterns in order to cope effectively. In accordance with H. McCubbin's family crisis theory, families cope adaptively (i.e., make the necessary changes) or maladaptively (i.e., get stuck and experience a crisis) depending on an interaction of family members' individual and collective coping resources as well as their interpretations of the stressful events. A pileup of stressors (i.e., multiple stressors occurring within a short period of time) presents a greater challenge to a family's capacity to adapt. Families differ, however, in the number, types, and timing of stressors and life transitions; in their coping resources and interpretations of stressful events; and in whether specific stressors or combinations of stressors lead to crises or successful reorganizations in structure and process. The SFD model also directs attention to a multigenerational model in which different generations within the same family may experience developmental stressors simultaneously (e.g., the first generation begins school, the second generation moves across the country, and the third generation experiences death of marital partner); and, consistent with family systems theory, the effects of stressors on individuals across generations are presumed to be interdependent (e.g., how the second generation copes affects how the first and third generations cope) and varied in their effects on individual family members and the family as a whole.

Consistent with D. Cicchetti's structural-organizational perspective on individual development, a new generation of family development theorists is considering whether families' successful mastery of prior developmental challenges enhances competencies and expectations for success and hence predicts adaptive resolutions of subsequent stressors and life transitions. For example, whether future challenges to family functioning are viewed collectively and/or individually as unmanageable crises or as opportunities for growth may depend on competencies acquired and on success/failure experiences during prior life transitions and stressors. In addition, family development theorists now assume that there may be multiple pathways to adaptive and maladaptive outcomes for families experiencing similar stressors and life transitions.

REFERENCES

Cicchetti, D. (1984). The emergence of developmental psychopathology. *Child Development, 55,* 1–7.

Duvall, E. M. (1957). *Family development* (1st ed.). Philadelphia: J. B. Lippincott .

Laszloffy, T. A. (2002). Rethinking family development theory: Teaching with the systemic family development (SFD) model. *Family Relations, 51,* 206–214.

McCubbin, H., & Figley, C. (1983). *Stress and the family: Coping with normative transitions.* New York: Bruner/Mazel.

W. Glenn Clingempeel
Fayetteville State University

Scott W. Henggeler
Medical University South Carolina

See also: **Family Therapy**

THOUGHT DISTURBANCES

Thought, conscious and unconscious, serves the purposes of generating and monitoring communications, regulating activity, creating, proposing, and problem solving on both verbal and nonverbal levels. Thought disturbances can be observed in a continuum ranging in severity from the normally occurring breaks in attention to the pathological.

Some of the less serious thought disturbances are evidenced by hyperkinetic children whose attention is short-lived and whose tasks are interrupted by a seeming need to perform motor movement. Writers and composers also experience thought disturbances, such as blank periods during which, while all other normal functioning is intact, the ability to keep on with the writing or composing task seems impaired.

Frequently, psychoneuroses such as phobic reactions and anxiety reactions can be attributed to irrational ideas. Many of these irrational ideas are accompanied by poor self-statements. Other psychoneurotic thought disturbances are evidenced in obsessive thoughts where frequently occurring judgmental thinking interferes with normal functioning. Disputation of these thoughts can lead to clear logical thinking.

Psychosomatic symptoms are thought disorders that reflect the individual's inability to cope with anxiety and stress, which are transformed into physiological symptoms that can interfere with normal daily functioning as with many other psychoneurotic thought disorders.

Psychotic thought disturbances are usually accompanied by symptoms of *delusion,* where false beliefs of persecution or megalomania predominate, and *hallucinations,* where the organism generates its own stimulation in any or all of the sensory modalities. Although these thought disturbances are serious in their own right, they are generally attached to other types of pathological behavior, such as Delirium, Dementia, and Schizophrenia.

Delirium is a disturbance of varying severity of consciousness. The subject may be in any state from fully awake to coma, and there is evidence of disorders in cognitive function, thinking, and perception. Delirium is a result of cerebral dysfunction without any destruction of tissue and seems to originate from metabolic, chemical, or toxic disturbances. Delirium is generally transitional and disappears with the removal of the metabolic, chemical, or toxic elements.

Dementia syndrome, however, is a thought disorder related to cortical tissue damage evidenced by diminished intellectual capacity during clear consciousness. Personality, amnesiac, and disorientation changes occur as well. Here the fully alert patient does not grasp the present. Memory deficits and poor concentration are in evidence. Language deteriorates to the point of being childlike, and normal routine thoughts seem labored. Most disturbing is that many patients are aware of their cognitive difficulty and exhibit other secondary emotional disturbances.

Schizophrenia is an example of a psychogenic thought disorder. The schizophrenic's thought disorder seems to demonstrate a conscious sacrifice of physical and emotional life for some alternative "cocooned" existence for the perceived welfare of others. The thought disorder seems to direct an escape for survival as shown by a continual downward adjustment of functioning in an irrational struggle to stay alive. Withdrawal from social contact and emotional involvement occurs, as does regression toward a lower level of intellectual function. This exclusionary nihilistic thought disturbance exhibits itself in paranoid, catatonic, hebephrenic, and simple types.

Dennis F. Fisher

THURSTONE SCALING

Thurstone scaling, also known as the method of equal-appearing intervals, is a technique devised by Louis L. Thurstone for constructing quantitative attitude measurement instruments. The first step in Thurstone scaling is to gather a large number of statements representing a wide range of opinions about the attitude object (e.g., capital punishment). Statements ranging from extremely negative through neutral to extremely positive are drawn from persons holding varying viewpoints or from the popular literature. These statements are then independently sorted by judges into 11 piles of equal-appearing intervals ranging from least favorable toward the object (1) through neutral (6) to most favorable (11). The median and semi-interquartile range (Q) of the judges' scores for each statement are then calculated, and statements with large Q values are discarded as ambiguous. The remaining statements are item-analyzed for internal consistency, and inconsistent statements are discarded as irrelevant.

What remains from this process is a pool of consistent,

unambiguous statements with scale values (median judges' scores) ranging from 1 to 11. The attitude scale itself is then constructed by including two or more statements from each of the 11 intervals on a questionnaire. Respondents check all of the statements with which they agree; the median scale values of the statements endorsed by respondents are their attitude scores. If the item pool is large enough, several parallel scales can be constructed, and the reliability of the attitude score can be determined.

Thurstone's technique is time-consuming and has been largely supplanted in popularity by newer techniques for developing measures of attitude. However, Thurstone scaling is a major step in the development of behaviorally anchored rating scales, mixed-standard rating scales, and weighted checklists for measuring work performance.

William I. Sauser, Jr.
Auburn University

See also: **Rating Scales**

TIME-SERIES ANALYSIS

The statistical analysis of data that have been collected on a single unit (e.g., a person, family, or organization) at equally spaced time intervals (or in a continuous form) is a time-series analysis. Time-series methods are employed to describe the relationship between variables (e.g., biochemical measures in person A and the behavior of person A), to forecast (predict) future behavior, to describe the statistical nature of a process, and to estimate intervention effects.

A major difference between time-series and conventional methods is the nature of the designs to which they are applied. Time-series designs generally involve the collection of a large number of observations across time on a single participant or unit, whereas conventional designs generally involve only one or a few observations on a reasonably large number of participants. This difference in design characteristics often leads to a need for analytic methods that are not necessary in the analysis of most conventional designs. Time-series analyses, unlike most conventional analyses, are characterized by (1) formal evaluations of the assumption of independent errors, (2) analytic strategies to accommodate lack of independence if it exists, and (3) models that contain terms to describe how behavior changes across time.

Time-Series Domains

Approaches to time-series modeling generally fall into one of two major categories: time domain models and frequency domain models. Although there is a mathematical correspondence between the two, they represent different ways of conceptualizing the nature of time series, and they are designed to focus on different descriptive features of the data.

Time Domain Models

Time domain models contain parameters that are used to relate the behavior of process Y to other variables and to the history of process Y. For example, certain time domain models known as autoregressive moving-average (ARMA) models relate the current value Y_t of the time-series to earlier values of the series and to values of present and past random errors. A more general modeling approach that allows for the modeling of data that contain random trends is known as ARIMA (autoregressive integrated moving average). ARIMA models have become popular in the behavioral sciences; software for estimating the parameters of these models is widely available. However, the recommendation that sample size be reasonably large (a minimum of 50–100 is typical) before attempting such modeling has recently led to the development of alternative procedures for small samples. Some of these alternatives are closely related to conventional regression models.

The key issues in the selection of an adequate time-series analysis are the questions to be answered, the nature of the process that generates trend (if any), and whether the errors are independent. Some version of ARIMA or a simpler alternative model is usually chosen. Certain versions of time-series regression models are appropriate in some situations in which it was previously thought that ARIMA models were required. Because independence of the errors is assumed by conventional regression models, however, it is necessary to identify and model dependency among the errors if it exists.

If the dependency is not modeled, inferential tests on the parameters of the model, confidence intervals, and predictions based on ordinary regression methods will be distorted. Under some conditions the distortion can be severe. Hence, a preliminary step in the application of regression models to time-series data is to determine whether the errors of the model are approximately independent. A test of the hypothesis of independent errors is often carried out for this purpose.

If the errors are not independent, the model should be modified by either identifying and including in the model additional variables responsible for the dependency or accommodating the dependency by including terms in the model that describe it. The former should be attempted before the latter. When the latter approach is taken, several different types of coefficient are available to describe various types of dependency among the errors.

A typical time-series regression model contains parameters to describe systematic trends and other deterministic changes such as intervention effects across time as well as parameters to describe patterns among the errors of the model. A practical problem associated with models of this type is that the time series should contain a minimum of about 50 observations if typical time-series regression methods (based on generalized least-squares) are used to carry out the analysis. Recently developed computer-intensive methods, however, provide adequate estimation with fewer observations.

Frequency Domain Models

Whereas a time domain model represents an attempt to explain current behavior of the series using time and other variables (including previous errors) as predictors, frequency domain models focus on breaking down the total series variation into basic frequency components. Frequency is related to the number of cycles of the response measure that occur during a defined period of time. Frequency domain methods (called harmonic analysis, periodogram analysis, and spectral analysis) provide a decomposition of the time-series variance into proportions that are explained by different cycles (if any).

SUGGESTED READING

Box, G. E. P., Jenkins, G. M., & Reinsel, S. G. (1994). *Time-series analysis, forecasting and control.* San Francisco: Holden-Day.

Glass, G. V., Willson, V. L., & Gottman, J. M. (1975). *Design and analysis of time-series experiments.* Boulder: University of Colorado Press.

Huitema, B. E., & McKean, J. W. (2000). Design specification issues in time-series intervention models. *Educational and Psychological Measurement, 60,* 38–58.

McCleary, R., & Welsh, W. N. (1992). Philosophical and statistical foundations of time-series experiments. In T. R. Kratochwill & J. R. Levin (Eds.), *Single-case research design and analysis: New directions for psychology and education* (pp. 41–91). Hillsdale, NJ: Erlbaum.

McKnight, S. D., McKean, J. W., & Huitema, B. E. (2000). A double bootstrap method to analyze linear models with autoregressive error terms. *Psychological Methods, 5,* 87–101.

Warner, R. M. (1998). *Spectral analysis of time-series data.* New York: Guilford Press.

Bradley E. Huitema
Western Michigan University

TOILET TRAINING

The practice of toilet training children is the cause of a great deal of anxiety and frustration for parents and has resulted in debates among professionals. In *The Problem of Anxiety,* Freud (1936) suggested that inappropriate toilet training can result in lifetime trauma for the child. Others submit that the process of toilet training reinforces the self-centered nature of the young child. Wenar (1971) stated that "toilet training enhances the sense of power in the toddler whose thinking is naturally inclined to be omnipotent" (p. 76).

Whether one harbors anxiety over the prospects of toilet training one's child or views the process as a natural phenomenon that will, in time, run its course, the question remains: "What approach should parents take in toilet training their children?" Two psychologists who have examined toilet training philosophies and practices and have developed a strategy sensitive to the range of ideas are Azrin and Foxx. In their book *Toilet Training in Less Than a Day,* Azrin and Foxx (1974) developed a toilet training program that is responsive to the psychoanalytic emphasis on the possible effect of harsh toilet training on later personality, the medical knowledge about toilet training, the importance of Pavlivian learning, operant learning, imitation and social influence.

How and When

Azrin and Foxx (1974) suggest that there are four preliminary considerations to regard before commencing toilet training: age, bladder control, physical readiness, and instructional readiness. They submit that at age 20 months the child is usually capable of being toilet trained. They further submit that a child is ready for toilet training when the child demonstrates bladder control by strength of the urine stream as well as the quantity of urine eliminated. Readiness is also indicated when the child presents good finger and hand coordination (enough to pick up objects) and also is capable of walking independently. Finally, Azrin and Foxx suggest that toilet training readiness is indicated when the child can follow simple directions or imitate actions.

Once it is determined that a child is ready for toilet training, specific procedures can be followed that task-analyze the child's bowel and bladder elimination and the steps necessary for successful toilet training (Holmes, 2003).

Special Problems

Numerous articles have been written on subjects pertaining to toilet training problems. Ellis (1963) addressed the special needs of disabled individuals. Mowrer & Mowrer (1938) addressed nighttime wetting, and Wagner and Paul (1970) discussed bowel accidents. Whether one adheres to a psychoanalytic, behavioristic, or other viewpoint, there is consensus among theoreticians and practitioners that toilet training is a most important developmental milestone. Well-informed parents with a clearly defined approach will be most helpful to the child navigating the course of toilet training.

REFERENCES

Azrin, N., & Foxx, R. (1974). *Toilet training in less than a day.* New York: Simon & Schuster.

Ellis, N. R. (1963). Toilet training and the severely defective patient: An S-R reinforcement analysis. *American Journal of Mental Deficiency, 68,* 48–103.

Freud, S. (1936). *The problem of anxiety.* New York: Norton.

Holmes, D. L. (2003). *The Eden curriculum: Vol. 1. Core curriculum* (2nd ed.). Princeton, NJ: Eden Press.

Mowrer, O. H., & Mowrer, W. M. (1938). Enuresis: A method for the study and treatment. *American Journal of Orthopsychiatry, 8,* 426–459.

Wagner, B. R., & Paul, G. L. (1970). Redirection of incontinence in chronic mental patients: A pilot project. *Journal of Behavior Therapy and Experimental Psychiatry, 1,* 29–38.

Wemar, C. (1971). *Personality development from infancy to adulthood.* Boston: Houghton Mifflin.

David L. Holmes
The Eden Institute

***See also:* Operant Conditioning**

TOUCH THERAPY RESEARCH

Touch therapy or massage therapy is defined as manipulation of body tissues by the hands for wellness and the reduction of stress and pain. Its therapeutic effects derive from its impact on the muscular, nervous, and circulatory systems. Massage therapy sessions usually combine several techniques, including Swedish massage (stroking and kneading), shiatsu (pressure points), and neuromuscular massage (deep pressure). Oils are typically used, and aromatic essences are often added for further effect. The sessions also feature soft background music, usually classical or new age music.

The practice of massage has been in the world since before recorded time. The equivalent to the word *massage* can be found in many classic texts including the Bible and the Ayur-Veda. Hippocrates, as early as 400 B.C. talked about the necessity of physicians being experienced in the art of rubbing. Ancient records from China and somewhat later from Japan refer to massage therapy, and it was also widely used by other early cultures including Arabs, Egyptians, Indians, Greeks, and Romans. During the Renaissance, massage spread throughout Europe, and Swedish massage was developed early in the nineteenth century.

Based on existing research, clients who receive massage therapy are expected to show improved mood state and affect and decreased anxiety and stress hormone levels (salivary cortisol). These changes have been highly significant based on observations of the client, self-reports by the client, and saliva assays for cortisol. In addition, whenever the electroencephalogram is recorded, changes occur in the direction of heightened alertness. Longer term changes also measured in research have typically been evaluated after four weeks of treatment. These changes invariably include a decrease in depression (measured by self-report and elevated serotonin and dopamine levels), lower stress (as measured by urinary cortisol, norepinephrine, and epinephrine levels), improved sleep patterns (as measured by an activity watch), and enhanced immune function (an increase in natural killer cells). Changes have also been noted on clinical measures that are specific to different conditions or considered by clinicians to be gold standards for those conditions. For example, increases have been noted in pulmonary functions including peak air flow for children with asthma, and decreased blood glucose levels have been reported for children with diabetes following a month of bedtime massages from parents. Another example is a significant increase in weight gain in premature infants given three massages per day over a 10-day period. These changes are unique to these conditions and would not be expected to occur generally across medical conditions.

Although the primary indications have been for wellness and a reduction of stress and pain, there are many other ways in which massage therapy is clinically useful, including the following: (1) pain reduction during painful procedures such as childbirth labor, and massage therapy prior to debridement for burn patients; (2) pain reduction in chronic pain conditions such as juvenile rheumatoid arthritis, fibromyalgia, premenstrual syndrome, lower back pain, migraine headaches, and carpal tunnel syndrome; (3) alleviation of depression and anxiety, such as in bulimia, anorexia, and chronic fatigue; (4) stress reduction including job stress and separation stress; and (5) immune disorders including HIV and breast cancer following an associated increase in natural killer cells, which are the front line of the immune system and ward off viral cells and cancer cells, as well as for the autoimmune conditions already mentioned, including diabetes and asthma. Although some therapists have warned of contraindications for massage, there is virtually no research supporting concerns such as infectious or contagious skin conditions, high fever, scar tissue, varicose veins, and tumors.

Many massage therapists are located in private clinics in the community, spas, workout clubs, hair salons, hotels, airports, and even sometimes at car washes. Unfortunately, although massage therapy used to be routinely practiced in hospitals (as recently as the 1950s), it is rarely seen in hospitals today. The costs are relatively low ($1 per minute is the going rate), and the therapy has been shown to be cost-effective. For example, $4.7 billion per year could be saved in medical costs if all premature infants were massaged. That figure derives from 470,000 infants who are born prematurely each year being massaged and discharged 6 days early at a hospital cost savings of $10,000 per infant. Similarly, using senior citizen volunteers as therapists for infants has been cost-effective and has resulted in lower stress hormones and fewer trips to the doctors' office following one month of the therapists' massaging the infants. Similar cost-effective figures are likely to emerge for other conditions because they too benefit from the lower stress hormones (cortisol), enhanced immune function, more infrequent illness, and greater wellness resulting from massage therapy.

SUGGESTED READING

Field, T. (1998). Massage therapy effects. *American Psychologist, 53,* 1270–1281.

Field, T. (1999). *Touch therapy research.* London: Harcourt Brace.

Field, T. (2001). *Touch.* Cambridge, MA: MIT Press.

Tiffany M. Field
University of Miami

See also: Growth Hormones

TOWER OF HANOI PROBLEM

The Tower of Hanoi is a classical puzzle applied in the psychology of problem solving and cognitive skill learning. In the standard version, it consists of three vertical wooden pegs and a variable number of wooden disks, usually three to six, with different diameters. The disks have a hole in the middle and are stacked on the left peg in the order of diameter, the largest at the bottom. The task is to transfer the disks to the right peg with a minimum of moves. Disks may be moved only from one peg to another. Any peg may serve as a temporary target for any disk. Only one disk may be moved at a time, and larger disks must not be placed above smaller ones. Performance is measured by the number of moves, the time required to complete the task, or both. In addition, different types of errors can be classified and assessed. The minimum number of moves is $2^n - 1$, where n is the number of disks (e.g., 31 for the five-disk version). Approximate mean performances on the first attempt are 22 moves and two minutes for the four-disk and 64 moves and 10 minutes for the five-disk version. In aged subjects, mean baseline performance declines.

The problem can be broken down to n similar subgoals (i.e., moving the next-largest disk to the right peg). Before one of these key moves is possible, the corresponding disk is isolated (alternately) on the left or middle peg, and all smaller ones are stacked on the remaining peg. Thus goal and subgoals, as well as lower-order subgoals, are self-similar and require an equivalent strategy. At any stage, it is crucial to decide, by counting disks, where to make the first move; otherwise, the process of unloading can lead to a blockade of the current target peg. Naive subjects tend to apply less efficient, ad-hoc strategies or the trial-and-error approach.

The Tower of Hanoi problem requires visuospatial abilities (i.e., visual imagery and visuospatial working memory) for the mental manipulation of disk configurations. It also requires spatial long-term memory for the retention of move sequences. In normal subjects, a measure of spatial ability has, among several cognitive variables, been found to correlate highest with the time required to solve the four-disk problem. In amnesiac patients, performance was highly correlated with residual declarative memory capacity (Schmidtke, Handschu, & Vollmer, 1996). It is furthermore assumed that performance depends on frontal lobe or executive function. Patients with lesions to the frontal lobe of the brain were reported to require more time and moves to solve the Tower of Hanoi, as well as related problems derived from it. The deficit of these patients has been assigned to deficits of planning and to an inability to resolve goal-subgoal conflicts (Goel & Grafman, 1995; Morris, Miotto, Feigenbaum, Bullock, & Polkey, 1997). The Tower of Hanoi problem is sensitive but not specific to prefrontal dysfunction. In other patient groups, subnormal performances have been attributed to impairments of spatial memory or strategy formation. Since the problem involves several cognitive capacities, its value as a neuropsychological test is limited.

Repeated execution of the problem leads to improvement of performance. In the four-disk version, many normal subjects achieve a ceiling level of performance within few attempts. Higher numbers of disks require considerably more trials. The rules and basic procedure (i.e., moving small stacks of disks from one peg to another) are quickly proceduralized. Perfect performance requires explicit (declarative) knowledge of the strategies mentioned earlier. Before this level is achieved, relapses (i.e., markedly worse single performances) occur even at advanced stages of learning. Procedural learning of the Tower of Hanoi problem thus involves both declarative and nondeclarative components, whose exact contribution is difficult to determine. The problem has also been employed as a paradigm for the study of skill learning (procedural learning) in cognitively impaired subjects, specifically in patients with amnesia and basal ganglia disease. Amnesiac patients, who may not remember having encountered the problem before, usually make considerable progress over trials. However, their learning is slowed in comparison to normal subjects. This is likely due to their deficient declarative memory for strategies, as well as to deficits of planning and other cognitive capacities that typically go along with amnesia. Word fluency, applied as a measure of prefrontal function, has been found to correlate with measures of learning of the Tower of Hanoi problem (Schmidtke et al., 1996). Negative effects of age on the rate of learning have inconsistently been shown.

Variants of the Tower of Hanoi problem have been developed to study planning and problem solving in normal subjects, psychiatric patients, and patients with organic brain damage. As an alternative to moving the whole stack of disks to another peg, the defined goal can be a rearrangement of disks from one given configuration to another. Isomorphs of the problem (e.g., the Monster Problems) involve an analogous problem space and set of rules but different outer appearance (Kotovsky, Hayes, & Simon, 1985). The Tower of London (Shallice, 1982) has been applied in a number of versions. It is thought to depend more on planning and less on visuospatial abilities. Originally, it involves three beads of different colors and three pegs of different lengths that can carry one, two, and all three beads, respectively. From variable starting positions, the beads have to be rearranged to patterns shown on cards on which the number of moves needed is also indicated. Difficulty varies from one to five moves. Computerized versions use colored balls and touch-sensitive screens. In normal subjects, functional imaging studies of the task showed, among other areas, activation of the dorsolateral prefrontal bilaterally, the lateral parietal cortex bilaterally, and the left anterior cingulate gyrus (Baker et al., 1996).

REFERENCES

Baker, S. C., Rogers, R. D., Owen, A. M., Frith, C. D., Dolan, R. J., Frackowiak, R. S. J., & Robbins, T. W. (1996). Neural systems engaged by planning: A PET study of the Tower of London task. *Neuropsychologia, 34,* 515–526.

Goel, V., & Grafman, J. (1995). Are the frontal lobes implicated in "planning" functions? Interpreting data from the Tower of Hanoi. *Neuropsychologia, 33,* 623–642.

Kotovsky, K., Hayes, J. R., & Simon, H. A. (1985). Why are some problems hard? Evidence from the Tower of Hanoi. *Cognitive Psychology, 17,* 248–294.

Morris, R. G., Miotto, E. C., Feigenbaum, J. D., Bullock, P., & Polkey, C. E. (1997). The effect of goal-subgoal conflict on planning ability after frontal- and temporal-lobe lesions in humans. *Neuropsychologia, 35,* 1147–1157.

Schmidtke, K., Handschu, R., & Vollmer, H. (1996). Cognitive procedural learning in amnesia. *Brain and Cognition, 32,* 44–467.

Shallice, T. (1982). Specific impairments of planning. *Philosophical Transactions of the Royal Society of London, B, 298,* 198–209.

Klaus Schmidtke
Center for Geriatric Medicine and Gerontology Freiburg

TOXICITY AND NEUROPROTECTIVE EFFECTS OF CARBON MONOXIDE: CONSEQUENCES TO SUICIDE AND SURVIVAL

Introduction

Previous work has focused mainly on the toxic physiologic effects of inhaled carbon monoxide (CO) gas arising from exogenous sources. CO toxicity is often associated with suicide attempts, and inhaling motor vehicle exhaust fumes is a leading cause of poisoning deaths in America. Recently, it has been demonstrated that CO can be produced endogenously through the actions of heme oxygenase (HO), an enzyme that generates CO by degrading heme. The search for a specific enzyme that can generate CO was stimulated by the finding that nitric oxide (NO), another endogenously produced biologically active gas, can be enzymatically obtained through nitric oxide synthase. Low concentrations of endogenously generated CO appear to have a neuroprotective function, whereas higher levels achieved by inhaling exogenous CO produce severe neurotoxicity.

Endogenous Formation of Carbon Monoxide by Heme Oxygenase

Heme oxygenase degrades heme, which by opening the porphyrin ring generates CO. Heme in the cell is a key component of many essential enzymes (e.g., myoglobin, catalase, glutathione peroxidase, cytochrome, soluble guanylate cyclase, superoxide dismutase, nitric oxide synthase, etc.), and regulation of the free cellular levels is tightly controlled. Heme oxygenase activity can be modulated either by changing the expression levels or via posttranscriptional modifications. CO is a gas that can travel freely throughout intracellular and extracellular compartments. The literature regarding the physiologic role of CO is complex, and many controversies have yet to be resolved (Alkadhi, Al-Hijailan, Malik, & Hogan, 2001; Linden, Narasimhan, & Gurfel, 1993; Maines, 1996; Meffert, Haley, Schuman, Schulman, & Madison, 1994; Poss, Thomas, Ebralidze, O'Dell, & Tonegawa, 1995; Verma, Hirsch, Glatt, Ronnett, & Snyder, 1993).

Two isoforms of HO have been distinguished and well studied (Doré et al., 2002; Ewing & Maines, 1997; Shibahara, Muller, Taguchi, & Yoshida, 1985). HO1 was the first to be isolated (Shibahara et al., 1985). It is an inducible enzyme that is concentrated in tissues such as the spleen and liver. On the other hand, HO2 is constitutive and has been suggested to be the neuronal isoform (Rotenberg & Maines, 1990). HO2 is most concentrated in the brain, accounting for the vast majority of HO activity in the brain (Doré et al., 1999, & Doré et al., 2002). HO1 is inducible in glia cells by hyperthermia (Ewing, Haber, & Maines, 1992), in Alzheimer's disease (Schipper, Cisse, & Stopa, 1995), in global ischemia (Takeda et al., 1996), in transient ischemia (Doré et al., 1999), in subarachnoid hemorrhage (Kuroki, Kanamaru, Suzuki, Waga, & Semba, 1998), and by experimentally injected lysed blood into striatum and cortex (Matz, Weinstein, & Sharp, 1997). Very few studies have been able to detect significant changes in the HO2 protein levels after different stimuli, and modulation of its activity could be a key element to understanding its function in the brain (Doré et al., 2002). One study demonstrated that mice with a genetic deletion of HO2 had infarct volumes twice those of normal control mice after 1 h of middle cerebral artery occlusion and 23 h reperfusion (Doré et al., 1999). Taken together, these results suggest that increasing intraneuronal HO activity provides neuroprotection. Modulation of HO2 activity may be crucial in neuron survival. HO2 might function either as a detoxifying agent of heme (a pro-oxidant), which is released from heme-containing proteins or from extravasation of blood/hemoglobin, or by generating CO, which could have physiologic neuroprotective capabilities.

Effects of Carbon Monoxide on Brain Functions

The affinity of CO for several proteins is generally lower than the affinity of nitric oxide for the same proteins; however, the longer half-life of CO could be a key factor in modifying several key enzymes containing a heme moiety. At a cellular level, physiologic levels of CO generated from degradation of intracellular heme are likely to have biologic actions on several heme-containing proteins. For example, CO may act as a vasodilator by binding to soluble guanylate cyclase and modulating its activity, as discussed later (Maines, 1996; Verma et al., 1993). CO can also act by opening calcium-activated potassium channels (KCa^{2+} channels; Wang & Wu, 1997).

CO has also been reported to have specific anti-inflammatory and antiapoptotic effects (Brouard et al., 2002; Otterbein et al., 2003). The mechanism of protection against apoptotic-like cell death by which CO would act has been suggested to be mediated through the activation of a transduction pathway involving the p38 kinase (Otterbein et al., 2000). This cascade has been previously demonstrated in endothelial cells. When these cells are exposed to inflammatory stimuli, they become activated through the expression of inflammatory proteins. Through the generation of protective genes (heme oxygenase would be among them), these cells are protected against the effects of triggering the apoptotic cascade (Otterbein et al., 2003). Through this process, CO would be generated and would act as a cytoprotective molecule that would limit the deleterious effects of the triggered inflammatory process (Otterbein et al., 2000, 2003).

By competing with sites that generally bind NO, CO may lead to an increase in free levels of NO. By itself, NO is a potent activator of guanylate cyclase and can participate in vasodilation. On the other hand, NO is very reactive and could stimulate the production of related free radicals, which can cause cellular damage often observed as nitrotyrosylation of proteins. Damage due to the generation of free radicals can be either to the cell or the blood vessels, depending on where NO is being dissociated from heme. Thus, even at relatively low concentrations, CO can produce oxidative stress and subsequent cell death. Using animal models, oxidative damage in rats has been observed with CO levels at 1,000 ppm for 40 minutes or as little as 50 ppm for 1 hour. These exposures are sufficient to cause an increase in nitrotyrosine and nitrosylated proteins (Ischiropoulos et al., 1996; Thom, Fisher, Xu, Garner, & Ischiropoulos, 1999). It was suggested that since CO does not modify the activity of the enzyme nitric oxide synthase, a total decrease in NO bound to heme proteins of the platelets would be the possible origin of the free NO. Interestingly, it's been reported that in rats, as little as 50 ppm of CO ventilation for 1 hour was sufficient to allow detection of nitrosylation (Thom et al., 1999). Even low levels of CO of sufficient duration are enough to trigger a cascade generating toxic free radicals (Thom et al., 2000).

Specific brain regions (especially central white matter) are differentially sensitive to damage by CO (Kindwall, 1996). According to the dose and duration of CO exposure, apoptotic and necrotic neuronal death similar to hypoxia-induced ischemia becomes particularly evident in the globus pallidus, hippocampus, cerebral cortex, and cerebellar Purkinje neurons (Piantadosi, Zhang, Levin, Folz, & Schmechel, 1997). The specific vulnerability of these brain regions to CO toxicity could be due to damage to the endothelial walls or directly by transendothelial CO diffusion. Further investigations are necessary to clarify the cellular effect of physiologic levels of CO and its toxic levels at supra-physiological concentrations.

In contrast, NO and CO have been known to play a significant role in establishing memory, especially in regard to long-term potentiation (LTP). They are in a unique family of gas neurotransmitters; these gases cannot be stored in synaptic vesicles and are thus believed to be generated on demand. As mentioned earlier, heme oxygenase is a specific enzyme that generates CO. HO2 is present in high concentrations mainly in the testes and in the brain. In the nervous system, it accounts for the majority of HO action and is discretely localized in neurons and also interestingly colocalized tightly with the guanylate cyclase enzyme (Verma et al., 1993). By generating CO, HO is likely to modulate levels of cyclic GMP (cGMP) by affecting enzyme activity. The use of general HO inhibitors has implicated a role for HO/CO in establishing LTP (Linden et al., 1993), although the specific role of CO in this pathway remains to be firmly established. Interestingly, the authors have demonstrated a trend toward a decrease in HO2 expression levels in ages rats compared to young rats. (Law et al., 2000) When the aged rats are split into two groups based on the presence or absence of cognitive impairment, the impaired rats have higher HO2 levels, suggesting a possible compensatory mechanism. This could possibly help restore cognitive function by increasing the HO2 expression (Law et al., 2000).

Inhalation of Exogenous Carbon Monoxide

CO is known to be toxic, and the inhalation of high concentrations can cause death. CO is an odorless, colorless, and tasteless product of incomplete fuel combustion. Accidental CO poisoning at home occurs more frequently during the winter and is generally due to defective or improper household appliances that use combustible fuel, such as gas, oil, coal, kerosene, or wood, as well as to poor ventilation. Accidental CO poisoning can also occur in other locations as reported in indoor ice-skating rinks, with outdoor tractors, or on motorboats (*JAMA*, 1996; Silvers & Hampson, 1995). CO detectors installed in homes have significantly reduced the incidence of CO poisoning.

Some CO toxicity is accounted for by the fact that CO saturates hemoglobin and impairs its ability to transport oxygen. The affinity of CO to Hb is approximately 200 times higher than that to oxygen. During CO inhalation, the amount of CO bound to heme groups on the hemoglobin increases, generating carboxy-hemoglobin, which consequently decreases the amount of oxygen being carried to tissue and brain. Hypoxia is then likely to affect normal cellular function. The brain has a very high metabolic rate of O_2 consumption, and impaired blood flow causes a rapid loss of consciousness. The brain has a complex array of mechanisms that limit damage following even the smallest changes in tissue oxygenation. During hypoxic states, arteriolar dilation occurs, improving O_2 transport. In the case of CO hypoxia, changes in cerebral blood flow are strictly correlated to the amount of COHb. In addition, by binding on heme-containing proteins, such as the cytochrome system, CO is likely to impair electron transport and also affects leukocytes, platelets, and endothelium, which can also generate a cascade of events leading to oxidative stress damage (Hardy & Thom, 1994).

Death from the inhalation of CO is a commonly used method for people attempting suicide. In newer model vehicles that have catalytic converters, less CO is released from the exhaust system. The catalytic converter was introduced in the 1970s and had a CO emission rate as low as 6g/minute. By 1989 the average new car emitted CO at about 0.22g/min. With the recent introduction of three-way catalytic converters, the reduction in CO emissions is close to 99%. The lower CO exposure during suicide attempts has led to a modified clinical symptom presentation (Vossberg & Skolnick, 1999). Patients are more likely to remain alive after hours of exposure, compared to death within 30 minutes in a closed environment with a vehicle without a catalytic converter.

Recovering patients are likely to have been exposed to a lower concentration of CO but for a longer period. Nonspecific symptoms of CO exposure include headache, nausea, fatigue, mental confusion, clumsiness, impaired judgment, stupor, and coma. Neurologic consequences of CO exposure include traditional cerebrovascular malfunctions, peripheral neuropathies, acute psychosis, cortical blindness, and memory problems (Choi, 1983). Neuroimaging studies indicate that the perivascular zone is a primary target for CO toxicity. Secondary hemorrhagic necrosis may generate focal pathology (Silverman, Brenner, & Murtagh, 1993). Most of the neurologic damage has been reported to occur within the first 6 hours of acute CO exposure, although delayed neurologic complications (e.g., disorientation, bradykinesia, gait disturbances, aphasia, aprasia, incontinence, and cogwheel rigidity) are evident up to 40 days postexposure; (Hardy & Thom, 1994). Close monitoring and follow-up of these patients is essential for optimal recovery.

Summary

In conclusion, at high concentrations, CO can produce serious brain damage. However, at physiologic concentrations, CO is emerging as a unique molecule with beneficial effects. More studies are necessary to understand the complex function of this simple diatomic gas. Once considered to be similar to an inert gas, it now appears that CO has multiple biologic actions. Additional study of this molecule should aim at further exploring the positive effects of CO while gaining a better understanding of treatment following sublethal accidental or intentional exposure.

REFERENCES

Alkadhi, K. A., Al-Hijailan, R. S., Malik, K., & Hogan, Y. H. (2001). Retrograde carbon monoxide is required for induction of long-term potentiation in rat superior cervical ganglion. *The Journal of Neuroscience, 21,* 3515–3520.

Brouard, S., Berberat, P. O., Tobiasch, E., Seldon, M. P., Bach, F. H., & Soares, M. P. (2002). Heme oxygenase-1-derived carbon monoxide requires the activation of transcription factor NF-kappa B to protect endothelial cells from tumor necrosis factor-alpha-mediated apoptosis. *The Journal of Biological Chemistry, 277,* 17950–17961.

Choi, I. S. (1983). Delayed neurologic sequelae in carbon monoxide intoxication. *Archives of Neurology, 40,* 433–435.

Doré, S. (2002) Decreased activity of the antioxidant heme oxygenase enzyme: Implications in ischemia and in Alzheimer's disease. *Free Radical Biology & Medicine, 32,* 1276–1282.

Doré, S., Sampei, K., Goto, S., Alkayed, N. J., Guastella, D., Blackshaw, S., Gallagher, M., Traystman, R. J., Hurn, P. D., Koehler, R. C., & Snyder, S. H. (1999). Heme oxygenase-2 is neuroprotective in cerebral ischemia. *Molecular Medicine, 5,* 656–663.

Ewing, J. F., Haber, S. N., & Maines, M. D. (1992). Normal and heat-induced patterns of expression of heme oxygenase-1 (HSP32) in rat brain: hyperthermia causes rapid induction of mRNA and protein. *Journal of Neurochemistry, 58,* 1140–1149.

Ewing, J. F., & Maines, M. D. (1997). Histochemical localization of heme oxygenase-2 protein and mRNA expression in rat brain. *Brain Research. Brain Research Protocols, 1,* 165–174.

Hardy, K. R. & Thom, S. R. (1994). Pathophysiology and treatment of carbon monoxide poisoning. *Journal of Toxicology. Clinical Toxicology, 32,* 613–629.

Ischiropoulos, H., Beers, M. F., Ohnishi, S. T., Fisher, D., Garner, S. E., & Thom, S. R. (1996). Nitric oxide production and perivascular nitration in brain after carbon monoxide poisoning in the rat. *The Journal of Clinical Investigation, 97,* 2260–2267.

JAMA (1996). Carbon monoxide poisoning at an indoor ice arena and bingo hall— Seattle, 1996. From the Centers for Disease Control and Prevention. *JAMA, 275,* 1468–1469.

Kindwall, E. P. (1996). Delayed sequelae in carbon monoxide poisoning and the possible mechanisms. In D. G. Penney (Ed.), *Carbon Monoxide* (pp. 239–252). Boca Raton, FL: CRC Press.

Kuroki, M., Kanamaru, K., Suzuki, H., Waga, S., & Semba, R. (1998). Effect of vasospasm on heme oxygenases in a rat model of subarachnoid hemorrhage. *Stroke, 29,* 683–688.

Law, A., Doré, S., Blackshaw, S., Gauthier, S., & Quirion, R. (2000).

Alteration of expression levels of neuronal nitric oxide synthase and haem oxygenase-2 messenger RNA in the hippocampi and cortices of young adult and aged cognitively unimpaired and impaired Long-Evans rats. *Neuroscience, 100,* 769–775.

Linden, D. J., Narasimhan, K., & Gurfel, D. (1993). Protoporphyrins modulate voltage-gated Ca current in AtT-20 pituitary cells. *Journal of Neurophysiology, 70,* 2673–2677.

Maines, M. (1996). Carbon monoxide and nitric oxide homology: Differential modulation of heme oxygenases in brain and detection of protein and activity. *Methods of in Enzymology, 268,* 473–488.

Matz, P. G., Weinstein, P. R., & Sharp, F. R. (1997). Heme oxygenase-1 and heat shock protein 70 induction in glia and neurons throughout rat brain after experimental intracerebral hemorrhage. *Neurosurgery, 40,* 152–160.

Meffert, M. K., Haley, J. E., Schuman, E. M., Schulman, H., & Madison, D. V. (1994). Inhibition of hippocampal heme oxygenase, nitric oxide synthase, and long-term potentiation by metalloporphyrins. *Neuron, 13,* 1225–1233.

Otterbein, L. E., Soares, M. P., Yamashita, K., & Bach, F. H. (2003) Heme oxygenase-1: Unleashing the protective properties of heme. *Trends in Immunology, 24,* 449–455.

Otterbein, L. E., Bach, F. H., Alam, J., Soares, M., Tao Lu, H., Wysk, M., Davis, R. J., Flavell, R. A., & Choi, A. M. (2000). Carbon monoxide has anti-inflammatory effects involving the mitogen-activated protein kinase pathway. *Nature Medicine, 6,* 422–428.

Piantadosi, C. A., Zhang, J., Levin, E. D., Folz, R. J., & Schmechel, D. E. (1997). Apoptosis and delayed neuronal damage after carbon monoxide poisoning in the rat. *Experimenal Neurology, 147,* 103–114.

Poss, K. D., Thomas, M. J., Ebralidze, A. K., O'Dell, T. J., & Tonegawa, S. (1995). Hippocampal long-term potentiation is normal in heme oxygenase-2 mutant mice. *Neuron, 15,* 867–873.

Rotenberg, M. O., & Maines, M. D. (1990). Isolation, characterization, and expression in Escherichia coli of a cDNA encoding rat heme oxygenase-2. *The Journal of Biological Chemistry, 265,* 7501–7506.

Schipper, H. M., Cisse, S., & Stopa, E. G. (1995). Expression of heme oxygenase-1 in the senescent and Alzheimer-diseased brain. *Annals of Neurology, 37,* 758–768.

Shibahara, S., Muller, R., Taguchi, H. & Yoshida, T. (1985). Cloning and expression of cDNA for rat heme oxygenase. *Proceedings of the National Academy of Science of the United States of America, 82,* 7865–7869.

Silverman, C. S., Brenner, J., & Murtagh, F. R. (1993). Hemorrhagic necrosis and vascular injury in carbon monoxide poisoning: MR demonstration. *American Journal of Neuroradiology, 14,* 168–170.

Silvers, S. M., & Hampson, N. B. (1995). Carbon monoxide poisoning among recreational boaters. *JAMA, 274,* 1614–1616.

Takeda, A., Kimpara, T., Onodera, H., Itoyama, Y., Shibahara, S., & Kogure, K. (1996). Regional difference in induction of heme oxygenase-1 protein following rat transient forebrain ischemia. *Neuroscience Letters, 205,* 169–172.

Thom, S. R., Fisher, D., Xu, Y. A., Garner, S., & Ischiropoulos, H. (1999). Role of nitric oxide-derived oxidants in vascular injury from carbon monoxide in the rat. *American Journal of Physiology, 276,* H984–H992.

Thom, S. R., Fisher, D., Xu, Y. A., Notarfrancesco, K., & Ischiropoulos, H. (2000). Adaptive responses and apoptosis in endothelial cells exposed to carbon monoxide. *Proceedings of the National Academy of Science of the United States of America, 97,* 1305–1310.

Verma, A., Hirsch, D. J., Glatt, C. E., Ronnett, G. V., & Snyder, S. H. (1993). Carbon monoxide: a putative neural messenger. *Science, 259,* 381–384.

Vossberg, B., & Skolnick, J. (1999). The role of catalytic converters in automobile carbon monoxide poisoning: a case report. *Chest, 115,* 580–581.

Wang, R., & Wu, L. (1997). The chemical modification of KCa channels by carbon monoxide in vascular smooth muscle cells. *The Journal of Biological Chemistry, 272,* 8222–8226.

Ronald L. Cowan
Harvard University

Sylvain Doré
Johns Hopkins University

TRAIT PSYCHOLOGY

Trait psychology is an approach to the theory and measurement of personality relying heavily on the concept of *trait* as a fundamental unit. Traits are defined in various ways. At the simplest level, they are seen as relatively enduring descriptive characteristics of a person. At a somewhat broader level, traits are defined as predispositions to behavior that are both enduring (i.e., having temporal consistency) and wide ranging (i.e., having cross-situational consistency). Gordon Allport asserted that traits also had a physiological basis. Allport also differentiated between common traits, found at some strength in all persons in a given culture, and unique traits, peculiar to an individual. The strongest, most pervasive dispositions within a person, he called cardinal traits.

A term frequently associated with trait is *type.* A trait is a single continuous dimension of personality, but a type is a more complex pattern of characteristics that serves as a model for categorizing people. Early in this century, Carl Jung identified sets of opposite personality types with extraverted versus introverted attitudes, and intuiting versus sensing and thinking versus feeling functions, now measured by the Myers-Briggs Type Indicator. Hans Eysenck and most other trait theorists see personality as organized hierarchically with major predispositions encompassing a set of related traits; for instance, the extraverted type includes traits such as sociability, impulsiveness, and activity.

Another term often contrasted with trait is *state,* which refers to a temporary condition, such as a mood, whereas trait refers to a long-range predisposition. In testing for state anxiety, for instance, C. D. Spielberger asks whether the person feels upset now; in testing for the corresponding trait, he asks if the person is generally, often, or constantly upset.

In many personality theories, traits occupy an important position as the basic units inferred from behavior. Several theorists use a trait-and-factor model; that is, they build systems empirically by factor analyzing a variety of items to produce basic scales or a variety of tests to produce higher level factors. The major personality theorists of this kind are Raymond Cattell, Eysenck, and J. P. Guilford. Each has developed tests for constructs they see as basic traits.

Two issues regarding traits are particularly prominent. The first is the question of the number and kind of traits. Instead of Cattell's 16 factors for questionnaire data, Eysenck identified three: extraversion, emotionality (neuroticism), and psychotism. Other widely used dimensional systems emphasizing interpersonal relations have identified two major axes—friendliness-hostility and dominance-submission—with many degrees of variation between them arranged in a circle. These two axes parallel the features frequently mentioned in organizational psychology—the socioemotional versus the task-oriented aspects of roles.

The other significant issue is the question of the cross-situational consistency of traits. The early work of Hartshorne and May temporarily shattered the belief in consistency of such traits as honesty by demonstrating that children who cheat on an examination do not necessarily lie or cheat in other circumstances. Yet intuitively we feel that people are consistent. By 1972 Eysenck had concluded that the trait position had been upheld and accepted. However, about that time, the much greater attention to the environment and the rise of behavioral psychology led to further attacks on traits, especially by W. Mischel. However, Mischel and others subsequently have recognized that there is considerable consistency among some characteristics. Mischel and P. K. Peake noted that temporal and situational consistency should be separated. The former is high and the latter low in reliability. Using a cognitive prototypical approach, they proposed a resolution of the dilemma, saying that the perception and organization of personality consistencies depend on identifying the key features (the prototypes, or best examples of a characteristic) in personality rather than on behavioral-level consistency in situations.

Norman D. Sundberg
University of Oregon

TRANSCENDENTAL MEDITATION

Various types of meditation have been practiced for over 2,500 years. Many Eastern cultures have included forms of meditation as an important part of their religious and spiritual enrichment (e.g., Zen, yoga). More recently, the West has taken an interest in the practice of transcendental meditation (TM) as taught by Maharishi Mahesh Yogi. It is promoted as a means to help increase energy, reduce stress, and have a positive effect on mental and physical health. The actual practice of TM involves sitting upright, with the eyes closed, and silently repeating a mantra whenever thoughts occur. The meditation is said to be effortless, enjoyable, and relaxing. The individual is instructed to meditate for 20 minutes in the morning before breakfast and 20 minutes in the evening.

Research on Transcendental Meditation

Numerous research studies have investigated the efforts of TM on physiological and psychological processes. These studies are summarized in the following.

Physiological Effects

In 1970 Wallace reported that a number of physiological states occurred during the practice of TM (e.g., significant decrease in respiration rate, heart rate, oxygen consumption, and skin conductance). West (1979) noted that Wallace's findings were supported by several other researchers (i.e., a decrease in heart rate: Dhanaraj & Singh, 1976; a decrease in respiration rate and oxygen consumption: Treichell, Clinch, & Cran, 1973; and a decrease in skin conductance: Walrath & Hamilton, 1975).

West (1980) also noted that TM has a significant effect on electroencephalogram (EEG) readings:

1. During the beginning of meditation, alpha amplitude increases, and alpha frequency may slow by 1–3 Hz.
2. During the middle of the meditation, trains of theta rhythms occur, often intermixed with alpha.
3. During deep meditation, bursts of high-frequency beta of 20–40 Hz can occur.
4. At the end of meditation, alpha may continue even while the eyes are open.

It is thought that EEG readings may be useful in monitoring the individual's response to meditation. Those with atypical EEG readings may need to obtain additional TM instruction or may not be able to use it effectively.

Research has attempted to compare TM to napping, eyes-closed rest, and contemplation meditation in terms of physiological and cognitive ability. Wallace (1999) noted that regular practitioners of TM (as compared to those who close their eyes and rest) had significantly more changes in the autonomic and central nervous system associated with EEG alpha coherence patterns.

Orme-Johnson (2001) compared TM, napping, and contemplation meditation to a no-treatment control group in terms of seven cognitive tasks associated with the following instruments (Test for Creative Thinking-Drawing Production, Constructive Thinking Inventory, Group Embedded Figures Test, State and Trait Anxiety, Inspection Time, and Culture Fair Intelligence Test). Results showed TM practitioners to be superior on seven out of seven compared to the control. Contemplation meditation was superior in two of seven areas of cognitive functioning (Inspection Time and Embedded Figures). Napping did not improve cognitive functioning on any of the seven cognitive variables as compared to the control group. In addition, the TM group was superior to the contemplation group on five variables.

Education

The Science of Creative Intelligence (SCI) is an educational program based on the philosophical foundations of TM (Thuermer, 2002). It is a consciousness-based educational approach that suggests that intellectual functioning can be enhanced by daily meditation (e.g., stress reduction and creative problem solving).

Personality

Transcendental meditation appears to have a positive effect on personality functioning and well-being. For example, Nystul and Garde (1977) found that individuals practicing TM for a mean of 3 years had significantly more positive self-concepts on the Tennessee Self-Concept Scale in terms of total positive, identity, self-satisfaction, personal self, and moral ethical self. TM has also been associated with increases in self-control, happiness, and self-actualization and decreases in psychopathology, such as psychosis, anxiety, and depression (Seeman, Nidick, & Banta, 1972; Hjelle, 1974; Nystul & Garde, 1977, 1979).

Therapy

West (1979) noted that studies have shown TM practitioners to stop or to decrease dramatically the usage of nonprescribed drugs (e.g., Shafi, Lavely, & Jaffe, 1975). Transcendental meditation has also been used as an adjunct to psychotherapy. For example, Vahia, Doongaji, Kapoor, Ardhapurkar, and Ravindra (1973) found that yoga and meditation significantly reduced the anxiety of psychoneurotics. Meditation procedures similar to TM have also been used in the treatment of obesity (Berwick & Oziel, 1973) and claustrophobia (Boudreau, 1972).

The Dropout Phenomenon

Over 50% of the individuals who begin TM stop practicing after 1 year of training (Zuroff & Schwarz, 1980). There are several explanations for this high dropout rate. Otis (1974) noted that a significantly high percentage of neurotic individuals are attracted to TM. They appear to have high expectations and are looking for a quick solution to complicated psychological problems. When TM does not provide them with the answers, they tend to stop practicing it. Nystul and Garde (1979) also found that individuals who stopped practicing TM had significantly more of the characteristics of psychosis than did those who practiced TM regularly.

There may also be some dangers associated with TM that could account for the high dropout rate. For example, TM has been known to cause severe depression, attempted suicide, and schizophrenic breaks (Lazarus, 1976). The negative effects of TM most often result with individuals who overmeditate for 3 hours or more at a time (Carrington, 1977). People who do not overmeditate also may find the practice of TM too stressful. As one meditates, many suppressed and repressed thoughts and feelings may be brought into awareness. One may become overwhelmed by these thoughts, thus resulting in a pathological reaction.

Violence Prevention

A somewhat controversial area of research investigated the potential of TM on reducing violence in society. Hagelin et al. (1999) conducted an innovative study that involved 4,000 individuals practicing TM in Washington, DC, from June 7 to July 30, 1993. It was concluded that the influx of individuals practicing TM reduced collective levels of homicide, rape, assaults, and robberies by 15.6%, though definitive conclusions could not be reached. Results also suggested that a permanent group of 4,000 individuals practicing TM could potentially promote a long-term reduction in serious crime.

REFERENCES

Berwick, P., & Oziel, L. L. (1973). The use of meditation as a behavior technique. *Behavior Therapy, 4,* 743–745.

Boudreau, L. (1972). TM and yoga as reciprocal inhibitors. *Journal of Behavior Therapy and Experimental Psychiatry, 3,* 97–98.

Carrington, P. (1977). *Freedom in meditation.* New York: Anchor/Doubleday.

Dhanaraj, V., & Singh, M. (1976). Effect of yoga relaxation and transcendental meditation on metabolic rate. In D. Orme-Johnson, L. Donash, & J. Farrow (Eds.), *Specific research on the transcendental meditation program, collected papers.* Livingston Manor, NY: MIU Press.

Hagelin, J. S., Rainforth, M. V., Orme-Johnson, D. W., Cavanaugh, K. L., Alexander, C. N., Shatkin, S. F., Davies, J. L., Hughes, A. O., & Ross, E. (1999). Effects of group practice of the transcendental meditation program on preventing violent crime in Washington, DC: Results of the national demonstration project, June–July 1993. *Social Indicators Research, 47*(2), 153–201.

Hjelle, L. (1974). Transcendental meditation and psychological health. *Perceptual and Motor Skills, 39,* 623–628.

Lazarus, A. A. (1976). Psychiatric problems precipitated by transcendental meditation. *Psychological Reports, 39,* 601–602.

Nystul, M. S., & Garde, M. (1977). A comparison of the self-concepts of regular transcendental meditators and nonmeditators. *Psychological Reports, 41,* 303–306.

Nystul, M. S., & Garde, M. (1979). The self-concepts of regular transcendental meditators, dropout meditators, and nonmeditators. *Journal of Psychology, 103,* 15–18.

Orme-Johnson, D. W. (2001). Three randomized experiments on the longitudinal effects of the transcendental meditation technique on cognition. *Intelligence, 29*(5), 419–440.

Otis, L. S. (1974). If well integrated but anxious try TM. *Psychology Today, 7,* 45–46.

Seeman, W., Nidick, S., & Banta, T. (1972). Influence of transcendental meditation on a measure of self-actualization. *Journal of Counseling Psychology, 19,* 184–197.

Shafi, M., Lavely, R., & Jaffe, R. (1975). Meditation and the prevention of alcohol abuse. *American Journal of Psychiatry, 132,* 942–945.

Thuermer, K. (2002). Transcendental education: Meditations on the Maharishi road to academia and nonviolence. *Independent Schools, 61*(2), 34–41.

Treichell, M., Clinch, N., & Cran, M. (1973). The metabolic effects of transcendental meditation. *Physiologist, 16,* 472.

Vahia, N., Doongaji, D., Kapoor, S., Ardhapurkar, I., & Ravindra, N. S. (1973). Further experience with the therapy based upon concepts of pantanjali in the treatment of psychiatric disorders. *Indian Journal of Psychiatry, 15,* 32–37.

Wallace, R. F. (1999). Autonomic and EEG patterns during eye-closed rest and transcendental meditation TM practice: The basis for a neural model of TM practice. *Consciousness and Cognition, 8*(3), 302–318.

Wallace, R. K. (1970). Physiological effects of transcendental meditation. *Science, 167,* 1751–1754.

Walrath, L., & Hamilton, D. (1975). Autonomic correlates of meditation and hypnosis. *American Journal of Clinical Hypnosis, 17,* 190–197.

West, M. (1979). Meditation (review article). *British Journal of Psychiatry, 135,* 457–467.

West, M. (1980). Meditation and the EEG. *Psychological Medicine, 10,* 369–375.

Zuroff, D. C., & Schwarz, J. C. (1980). Transcendental meditation versus muscle relaxation: A two year follow-up of a controlled experiment. *American Journal of Psychiatry, 137,* 1229–1231.

Michael S. Nystul
New Mexico State University

TRANSSEXUALISM

Terminology

The term *transsexual* has existed in the professional literature since the early 1920s (Hirschfeld, 1923). In the currently widely used psychiatric classification system of the *Diagnostic and Statistic Manual of Mental Disorders,* fourth edition (*DSM-IV;* American Psychiatric Association, 1994), the term *transsexualism* was replaced by gender identity disorder (GID). This term is used for individuals who show a strong and persistent cross-gender identification and a persistent discomfort with their anatomical sex as manifested by a preoccupation with getting rid of one's sex characteristics or the belief that one was born the wrong sex.

Development

Individuals may develop a gender identity disorder at the age of 2 or 3 years, but not all children with GID turn out to be adult transsexuals. It is estimated that about 10–20% will appear to be transsexual after puberty (Cohen-Kettenis, 2001; Zucker & Bradley, 1995).

Both environmental factors and biological factors have been put forward to explain atypical gender development. Children with and without GID indeed appear to differ in terms of parental psychopathology. They also differ in child-related factors such as temperament and appearance. Although retrospective studies in adult transsexuals have shown differences in recalled child-rearing patterns between transsexuals and normative groups (e.g., warmth, rejection), these parental behaviors might have been a consequence of the child's gender problem rather than a determinant (for reviews see Cohen-Kettenis & Pfäfflin, 2003; Zucker & Bradley, 1995). The specific mechanisms leading to GID clearly remain to be elucidated.

Potential biological determinants of transsexualism have been found in studies among subjects with an abnormal pre- and perinatal endocrine history. They seem to be at higher than normal risk for GID (Zucker, 1999). Furthermore, a sexually dimorphic brain nucleus (the BSTc) of transsexuals appeared to be completely in the size range of the opposite sex (for reviews see Cohen-Kettenis & Pfäfflin, 2003; Zucker & Bradley, 1995).

Prevalence

Prevalence estimates of transsexualism among the population aged 15 years and above are based mainly on the number of transsexuals treated at major centers or on responses of registered psychiatrists to surveys concerning their number of transsexual patients within a particular region. The numbers vary widely across studies. The estimated prevalence now varies between 1:10,000–40,000 men and 1:30,000–100,000 women (Bakker, van Kesteren, Gooren, & Bezemer, 1993; Weitze & Osburg, 1998).

Treatment

As psychotherapy is inadequate for a crystallized cross-gender identity, sex reassignment is considered to be the best treatment option. The recommended procedure in the Standards of Care of the International Harry Benjamin

Gender Dysphoria Association (an international professional organization in the field of transsexualism; Meyer et al., 2001) is to come to the final, surgical, decision in phases. First, a diagnosis is made on formal psychiatric classification criteria. Then, one's capability to live in the desired role and the strength of the wish for sex reassignment is tested during the real-life experience. The social role change during the real-life experience is usually supported by hormonal therapy. Surgery changes the genitals and other sex characteristics only after a successful real-life experience.

As a result of hormonal therapy in male-to-female transsexuals (MFs), bodily hair growth diminishes drastically, as do penile erections, sexual appetite, and upper body strength. In addition, female sex characteristics develop, such as breasts and a more female-appearing body shape due to a change of body fat around the waist, hips, shoulders, and jaw. Sometimes, facial hair removal techniques are necessary, and speech therapy is necessary for a successful demasculinization. In female-to-male transsexuals (FMs), androgens are used for the induction of male body features, such as a low voice, facial and body hair growth, and a more masculine body shape.

In MFs a vagina is constructed and, in cases of unsatisfactory responsiveness of breast tissue to estrogens, a breast enlargement is performed. In FMs breast reduction takes place in all cases. Because phalloplasty is still in an experimental phase, some FMs prefer to have a neoscrotum, testical prosthesis, and meatidoioplasty, in which the enlarged clitoris (due to hormone therapy) is transformed into a microphallus (Hage & Mulder, 1995).

Results of Sex Reassignment

Pfäfflin and Junge (1998) extensively reviewed 79 studies between 1961 and 1991 that evaluated the effects of reassignment. Since 1991, several more follow-up studies have appeared (for a review, see Cohen-Kettenis & Pfäfflin, 2003). Satisfactory results are reported in 87% of the MFs and 97% of the FMs. FMs usually fare better than their MF counterparts. Negative results, such as severe postoperative regrets to the point of returning to the original gender role, are estimated to be around 1%. From the follow-up studies one may infer that the currently employed, often extensive, diagnostic methods are sufficiently strict.

REFERENCES

American Psychiatric Association. (1994). *Diagnostic and statistical manual of mental disorders* (4th ed.). Washington, DC: Author.

Bakker, A., van Kesteren, P., Gooren, L. J. G., & Bezemer, P. D. (1993). The prevalence of transsexualism in the Netherlands. *Acta Psychiatrica Scandinavica, 87,* 237–238.

Cohen-Kettenis, P. T. (2001). Gender identity disorder in DSM? *Journal of the American Academy of Child and Adolescent Psychiatry, 40,* 391.

Cohen-Kettenis, P. T., & Pfäfflin, F. (2003). *Making choices: Transgenderism and intersexuality in childhood and adolescence.* Thousand Oaks, CA: Sage.

Hage, J. J., & Mulder, J. W. (Eds.). (1995). *Plastische chirurgie van het genitale gebied (Plastic surgery of the genital area).* Leeuwarden, Netherlands: NVPRC.

Hirschfeld, M. (1923). Die intersexuelle Konstitution. *Jahrbuch der sexuellen Zwischenstufen, 23,* 3–27.

Meyer, W. (Chairperson), Bockting, W. O., Cohen-Kettenis, P. T., Coleman, E., DiCeglie, D., Devor, H., Gooren, L. J. G., Hage, J. J., Kirk, S., Kuiper, A. J., Laub, D., Lawrence, A., Menard, Y., Patton, J., Schaefer, L., Webb, A., & Wheeler, C. C. (2001). Standards of Care for Gender Identity Disorders of the Harry Benjamin International Gender Dysphoria Association, Sixth Version. *International Journal of Transgenderism, 5.* Retrieved from http://www.symposion.com/ijt/soc_2001/index/htm.

Pfäfflin, F., & Junge, A. (1998). Sex reassignment: Thirty years of international follow-up studies: A comprehensive review, 1961–1991. *International Journal of Transgenderism.* Retrieved from http://www.symposion.com/ijt/books/index.htm.

Weitze, C., & Osburg, S. (1998). Empirical data on epidemiology and application of the German transsexuals' act during its first ten years. *International Journal of Transgenderism, 2.* Retrieved from http://www.symposion/com/ijt/ijtc0303.htm.

Zucker, K. J. (1999). Intersexuality and gender identity differentiation. *Annual Review of Sex Research, 10,* 1–69.

Zucker, K. J., & Bradley, S. J. (1995). *Gender identity disorder and psychosexual problems in children and adolescents.* New York: Guilford Press.

P. T. Cohen-Kettenis
University Medical Center Utrecht

TRANSVESTISM

In the psychosexual disorder of *transvestism,* there is recurrent and persistent cross-dressing by a heterosexual male for the purposes of his own sexual arousal. That is, the man achieves sexual satisfaction simply by putting on women's clothing, although masturbation (and heterosexual intercourse) is often engaged in once the individual is attired in female garb. Although anxiety, depression, guilt, and shame are often associated with the desire to cross-dress, the transvestite continues to do so because of the considerable satisfaction derived from the practice.

While transvestism is a comparatively rare disorder, some research has been conducted on it. To illustrate, it has been found that the typical transvestite is probably married (about two thirds are), and if married, has children (about two thirds do). Moreover, the overwhelming majority of transvestites assert that they are exclusively heterosexual, and the most common transvestic behavior consists of cross-dressing at home in secret. Concerning their psychological makeup, transvestites as a group are no more neurotic or psychotic than matched control groups, although they do tend to be more controlled in impulse expression, more inhibited in interpersonal relationships, more dependent, and less involved with other people. More than three fourths of transvestites consider themselves to be a different personality when cross-dressed, perhaps experiencing in female clothing a significant facet of their psychological makeup that cannot otherwise be expressed.

Finally, transvestism needs to be distinguished from transsexualism, fetishism, and homosexuality because each of these is sometimes confused with this disorder. In *transsexualism* there is a chronic sense of discomfort and inappropriateness about one's anatomic sex, a persistent wish to be rid of one's own genitals, a desire to live as a member of the opposite sex, and never any sexual arousal associated with cross-dressing; the great majority of transvestites consider themselves male, and erotic arousal is centered on dressing in women's clothing. Although articles of female clothing are involved in both *fetishism* and transvestism, fetishists do not dress in them, whereas transvestites do. Finally, while some male *homosexuals* may occasionally cross-dress to attract another male or to masquerade in theatrical fashion as a woman, the act itself is not sexually stimulating for them. For transvestites, the cross-dressing itself is the focal point of sexual stimulation, and no attempt is made to invite the sexual attention of other males.

Daniel J. Ziegler
Villanova University

TRAUMA

Definition

Trauma can be conceptualized as both an event and a reaction. A traumatic event is one in which an individual experiences actual or threatened serious injury or death (American Psychiatric Association [ApA], 2000). Examples of traumatic events include military combat, sexual assaults (e.g., rape or child sexual abuse), interpersonal physical assaults (e.g., a mugging), natural or manmade disasters, terrorist attacks, and motor vehicle accidents (ApA, 2000; Kessler, Sonnega, Bromet, Hughes, & Nelson, 1995).

In addition to being an event, trauma can also be conceptualized as a reaction. An individual's response to a traumatic event often involves intense emotions, such as fear, helplessness, or horror (ApA, 2000). The individual's emotional response and subjective appraisal of the situation are an integral part of the definition of trauma. Thus, witnessing an event in which another individual is seriously injured or killed or learning about the violent death or injury of a close friend or family member may also be considered traumatic (APA, 2000).

Difference Between Stress and Trauma

It is important to differentiate between stress and trauma. Stress is a reaction to events in the environment (Resick, 2001). These environmental events (stressors) can be negative, such as a hassle at work, or positive, such as getting married. Individuals experience stress also in response to more serious problems, such as divorce or financial strain. Although these experiences are difficult, they result in stress reactions, not trauma reactions (Resick, 2001).

Psychological Sequelae to Trauma

Posttraumatic Stress Disorder

In order to be diagnosed with posttraumatic stress disorder (PTSD), an individual must experience a traumatic event in which he or she feels threatened with death or serious injury and experiences intense emotions, such as fear, helplessness, or horror. Exposure to such a traumatic event results in three clusters of pathological symptoms: reexperiencing, avoidance, and arousal (ApA, 2000). The trauma may be reexperienced through intrusive memories, nightmares, flashbacks, or psychological or physiological distress at reminders of the trauma. The avoidance cluster of symptoms includes avoidance of any stimuli reminiscent of the trauma (from places and people to subjective thoughts and feelings), as well as a general numbing of responsiveness (e.g., feeling detached from others or having a restricted range of affect). Finally, individuals with PTSD suffer from arousal symptoms such as insomnia, irritability, difficulty concentrating, hypervigilance, and an exaggerated startle response. To meet diagnostic criteria, these symptoms must endure for at least one month and must cause problems in life functioning.

Acute Stress Disorder

Whereas PTSD can first be diagnosed 1 month after exposure to a traumatic event, acute stress disorder (ASD) can be diagnosed as soon as 2 days after exposure (ApA, 2000). Similar to PTSD, ASD results from exposure to a traumatic event in which the individual feels threatened by death or serious injury and experiences intense emotions, such as fear, helplessness, or horror. In addition, the individual must experience some dissociative symptoms either during or after the event. Dissociative symptoms include feeling emotionally numb or detached from the situation, feeling in a daze, and having the sense that the experience is somehow unreal or that the experience is not happening (ApA, 2000). Similar to the PTSD diagnosis, ASD also involves reexperiencing, avoidance, and arousal symptoms. The symptoms must cause the individual distress or cause impairment in functioning.

Adjustment Disorder

Adjustment disorder can be diagnosed within 3 months of exposure to a traumatic event for individuals reporting more distress than would normally be expected from the stressor. This distress is manifest through emotional or behavioral changes that cause significant impairment (APA, 2000).

Other Symptoms

Other disorders can cooccur with PTSD, ASD, or adjustment disorder. One of the most commonly cooccurring disorders is depression. In a national survey of more than 5,000 individuals, nearly half of individuals meeting criteria for PTSD also met criteria for depression (Kessler et al., 1995). PTSD has also been associated with higher rates of substance use, especially among war veterans (Kulka et al., 1990). In addition, PTSD has been associated with other anxiety disorders, such as panic disorder, social phobia, and generalized anxiety disorder (Kessler et al., 1995).

In addition to other diagnoses, there are a number of responses that are often associated with PTSD. For example, individuals with PTSD often experience dissociative symptoms during or after the traumatic event (Griffin, Resick, & Mechanic, 1997; van der Kolk & Fisler, 1995). Deficits in memory specific to the trauma, as well as deficits in short-term memory in general, have also been noted (Bremner et al., 1993; Briere & Conte, 1993). Not only psychological reactions, but also sustained physiological reactions have been well documented (Friedman, 2001; Yehuda, Giller, Levengood, Southwick, & Siever, 1995).

Risk Factors

It is important to note that not all individuals who experience a traumatic event develop a psychological disorder. For example, in a prospective study of rape victims, 94% of the participants endorsed enough symptoms to be diagnosed with PTSD one week after the rape (Rothbaum, Foa, Riggs, Murdock, & Walsh, 1992). However, when assessed 3 months after the rape, only 47% met PTSD criteria (Rothbaum et al., 1992). These statistics suggest that most rape victims experience intense PTSD symptoms immediately following the rape. Over half of the victims naturally recover from these symptoms over time. The others, however, remain symptomatic.

Researchers have begun to identify risk factors for developing a psychological disorder after exposure to trauma. Gender seems to be one such factor; research suggests that more women than men develop PTSD (Brewin, Andrews, & Valentine, 2000; Kessler et al., 1995). Individuals lacking social support are also at greater risk for developing a psychological disorder (Brewin et al., 2000). In addition, those who dissociate during a trauma are more likely to have lingering psychopathology (O'Toole, Marshall, Schureck & Dobson, 1999). There are also some characteristics of the trauma itself that increase the likelihood of developing PTSD. For example, it seems that interpersonal traumas, such as war or sexual assault, more often result in PTSD than do natural traumas, such as an earthquake or fire (Kessler et al., 1995).

REFERENCES

American Psychiatric Association. (2000). *Diagnostic and statistical manual of mental disorders* (4th ed., Text Rev.). Washington, DC: Author.

Bremner, J. D., Scott, T. M., Delaney, R. C., Southwick, S. M., Mason, J. W., Johnson, D. R., Innis, R. B., McCarthy, G., & Charney, D. S. (1993). Deficits in short-term memory in posttraumatic stress disorder. *American Journal of Psychiatry, 150,* 1015–1019.

Brewin, C. R., Andrews, B., & Valentine, J. D. (2000). Meta-analysis of risk factors for posttraumatic stress disorder in trauma-exposed adults. *Journal of Consulting and Clinical Psychology, 68,* 748–766.

Briere, J., & Conte, J. (1993). Self-reported amnesia for abuse in adults molested as children. *Journal of Traumatic Stress, 6,* 21–31.

Friedman, M. J. (2001). *Posttraumatic stress disorder.* Kansas City, MO: Compact Clinicals.

Griffin, M. G., Resick, P. A., & Mechanic, M. B. (1997). Objective assessment of peritraumatic dissociation: Psychophysiological indicators. *American Journal of Psychiatry, 154,* 1081–1088.

Kessler, R. C., Sonnega, A., Bromet, E., Hughes, M., & Nelson, C. B. (1995). Posttraumatic stress disorder in the National Comorbidity Survey. *Archives of General Psychiatry, 52,* 1048–1060.

Kulka, R. A., Schlenger, W. E., Fairbanks, J. A., Hough, R. L., Jordan, B. K., Marmar, C. R., & Weiss, D. S. (1990). *Trauma and the Vietnam War generation: Report of findings from the National Vietnam Veterans Readjustment Study.* New York: Brunner/Mazel.

O'Toole, B. I., Marshall, R. P., Schureck, R. J., & Dobson, M. (1999). Combat, dissociation, and posttraumatic stress disorder in Australian Vietnam Veterans. *Journal of Traumatic Stress, 12,* 625–640.

Resick, P. A. (2001). *Stress and trauma.* Philadelphia, PA: Psychology Press.

Rothbaum, B. O., Foa, E. B., Riggs, D. S., Murdock, T., & Walsh, W. (1992). A prospective examination of post-traumatic stress disorder in rape victims. *Journal of Traumatic Stress, 5,* 455–475.

van der Kolk, B. A., & Fisler, R. (1995). Dissociation and the fragmentary nature of traumatic memories: Overview and exploratory study. *Journal of Traumatic Stress, 8,* 505–525.

Yehuda, R., Giller, E. L., Levengood, R. A., Southwick, S. M., & Siever, L. J. (1995). Hypothalamic-pituitary-adrenal functioning in posttraumatic stress disorder: Expanding the concept of the stress response spectrum. In M. J. Friedman, D. S. Charney, & A. Y. Deutch (Eds.), *Neurobiological and clinical consequences of stress: From normal adaptation to post-traumatic stress disorder* (pp. 351–365). Philadelphia, PA: Lippincott-Raven Press.

Julie M. Mastnak, M.A.
Patricia A. Resick, Ph.D.
Center for Trauma Recovery
University of Missouri-St. Louis

See also: **Posttraumatic Stress Disorder**

TRICHOTILLOMANIA

Trichotillomania is a disorder that involves the repeated pulling of one's hair, resulting in noticeable hair loss. Individuals with trichotillomania experience internal sensations of anxiety or tension that immediately precede pulling (and/or an attempt to resist pulling) and subside only after pulling. Cosmetic complaints resulting from hair loss are a primary concern for persons with trichotillomania, but complications in social, occupational, psychological, and medical functioning are also common. Although hair pulling is rarely performed in public, hair loss often results in negative social interactions and the avoidance of many social and occupational settings. In addition to these social and occupational disturbances, a variety of physical and psychological sequelae can accompany trichotillomania. Gastrointestinal problems resulting from trichobezoars (hairballs) associated with trichophagia (eating of hair), dermatological problems, and comorbid psychological problems such as obsessive-compulsive disorder (OCD), mood disorders, and anxiety disorders can cooccur. Although hair pulling resembles a compulsion, trichotillomania appears to be more of a problem with impulse control and is therefore classified as an impulse control disorder.

Demographics

The prevalence of trichotillomania is unclear, but it has been estimated that 0.5% to 2% of college students meet or have previously met diagnostic criteria for trichotillomania. A considerably higher percentage of individuals engage in hair pulling at subdiagnostic levels. Little epidemiological data exist for children or older adults. Adults with trichotillomania are more likely to be female than male, but this gender difference appears to be less exaggerated in children.

Course and Patterns

Trichotillomania can begin at any age but typically starts in adolescence and is often preceded by a significant life event or problem. Hair pulling occurs most frequently from the scalp, eyebrows, and eyelashes, but can involve any body region with hair (e.g., pubic region, arms, legs). Hair pulling typically involves the pulling of only one hair at a time. Prior to the actual removal of a hair, individuals with trichotillomania often engage in a variety of prepulling behaviors including touching, stroking, and manipulating hairs and/or wrapping the hair around a finger. Although hairs are most commonly pulled with the fingers, some individuals pull hairs with cosmetic utensils such as a tweezers. After the hair is removed, individuals engage in a variety of postpulling behaviors including discarding, manipulating, sucking, chewing, or biting the hair. In addition, some individuals engage in trichophagia.

There are two types of hair pulling: automatic and focused. Automatic hairpulling occurs outside of the individual's awareness. Because individuals are unaware of their pulling, they frequently catch themselves pulling, often after removing a considerable number of hairs. Automatic pulling most commonly occurs when an individual is engaged in an activity that requires a high degree of concentration. Focused pulling, in contrast, involves pulling in which the individual is fully aware of the act. Individuals who engage in this type of hair pulling often seek specific situations or settings in which to pull (e.g., the bathroom). Individuals who engage in focused pulling often report an overwhelming urge or need to pull and report that pulling satisfies this urge by making it less intense or making it go away. In addition, individuals who engage in focused pulling report that attempts to suppress pulling makes the urge more intense. Typically, persons with trichotillomania engage in both automatic and focused pulling.

Etiology

Although the cause of trichotillomania is unknown, some experts contend that trichotillomania has genetic or neurobiological underpinnings. Two neurotransmitter systems, serotonin and dopamine, are thought to play a role in trichotillomania. In addition, it has been hypothesized that individuals who pull hair have an increased tolerance for pain, possibly due to abnormalities in the opiate system (a neurochemical involved in the regulation of pain sensation).

From a behavioral perspective, hair pulling appears to remove or reduce the anxiety or tension that precedes it, thus making individuals more likely to pull in the future (i.e., negative reinforcement). It is also hypothesized that, for some individuals with trichotillomania, hair pulling is positively reinforced by stimulation to the site of pulling or to the fingers (positive reinforcement).

Assessment and Treatment

Hair pulling associated with trichotillomania is typically evaluated and monitored through indirect measures such as interviews and questionnaires. Two commonly used questionnaires are the Massachusetts General Hospital Hairpulling Scale and the National Institute of Mental Health Trichotillomania Scales. When direct measures are used, they usually include event recording (recording each time a hair is pulled), hair collection, and photographs of affected areas (collected across several days to monitor and rate the regrowth of hair).

The most common treatments for trichotillomania are pharmacotherapy and behavior therapy. Because hair pulling often resembles the compulsive behavior found in OCD, some of the first drugs used to treat trichotillomania were those used for treating compulsions. Serotonin reuptake inhibiters (SSRIs), a form of antidepressants affecting levels of serotonin, were among the first used and continue to be one of the most commonly prescribed medications.

Common SSRIs for trichotillomania include clomipramine and fluoxetine. Additionally, some individuals respond well to a combination of SSRIs and neuroleptics, which affect levels of dopamine. The most common neuroleptics used in combination with SSRIs are pimozide and risperidone. Several other pharmacological treatments have been used with varying degrees of success (e.g., tricyclic antidepressants, monoamine oxidase inhibitors, opiate antagonists).

The most effective behavioral treatment for trichotillomania is habit reversal, a multielement treatment shown to be effective for treating a variety of repetitive behaviors. The components of habit reversal include awareness, competing response, and social support training. With the help of a trained therapist, an individual first becomes more aware of pulling by learning to recognize high-risk situations (who, what, where), thoughts, and feelings (e.g., urges) that indicate that he or she is about to pull. After awareness is obtained, the individual learns to engage in a response that is incompatible with hair pulling (e.g., fist clenching) before the pulling occurs. Social support is used to prompt the individual to use this competing response and to provide encouragement throughout the treatment process.

Douglas W. Woods
Michael B. Himle
University of Wisconsin-Milwaukee

See also: **Antidepressant Medications**

TRICYCLIC ANTIDEPRESSANTS

The tricyclic antidepressants were first introduced in the early 1960s and soon became widely used for the treatment of depression. The introduction of the tricyclics, along with the development of the phenothiazine antipsychotics for the treatment of Schizophrenia and the use of lithium for treatment of bipolar illness, ushered in the modern era of psychopharmacology. The robust effectiveness of the tricyclics is somewhat offset by their problematic side effects, and although in recent years they have been largely supplanted by the selective serotonin reuptake inhibitors (SSRIs) as first line treatment, the tricyclics still remain a widely used treatment for depression and other psychiatric and neurologic syndromes.

Clinical Pharmacology

The tricyclic antidepressants are so named because all of the compounds share a three-ring substructure and differ primarily in the side chain attached to the middle ring (see Figure 1). The most frequently prescribed are imipramine, amitriptyline, desipramine, and nortriptyline. (Note that

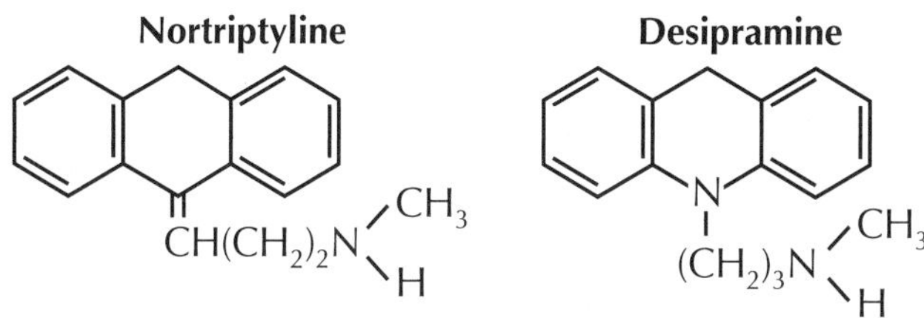

Figure 1. Tricyclic antidepressants compounds.

desipramine and nortriptyline are simply the demethylated metabolites of imipramine and amitriptyline, respectively.)

The tricyclics are lipid soluble and are given orally; they are well absorbed from the gastrointestinal tract. There is considerable first-pass effect in the liver, where the drugs are metabolized by transformation of the tricyclic nucleus and alterations of the side chain. The critical step in metabolism is hydroxylation at the 2 position of the ring, thereby creating a water-soluble metabolite that is then secreted from the body.

A critical advance in maximizing the effectiveness of tricyclics has been the documentation of a strong correlation between plasma level of antidepressant and clinical outcome (Glassman et al., 1985). In patients treated with desipramine and imipramine, there is a threshold effect such that maximum response is achieved at plasma levels over 150 ng per ml and 200 ngs per ml, respectively. Patients treated with nortriptyline have a curvilinear response, or therapeutic window, in which maximum response is achieved when the plasma level is in the range between 50 and 150 ng per ml (see Figure 2).

Mechanism of Action

The major effect of the tricyclic antidepressants is to block the reuptake of monoamine neurotransmitters. The secondary amine tricyclics, desipramine and nortriptyline, block the reuptake of norepinephrine more specifically, whereas the tertiary amine tricyclics, imipramine and amytriptyline, to some degree block the reuptake of both norepinephrine and serotonin. Competitive blockade of the serotonin and norepinephrine uptake pumps is believed to potentiate monoaminergic neurotransmission. However,

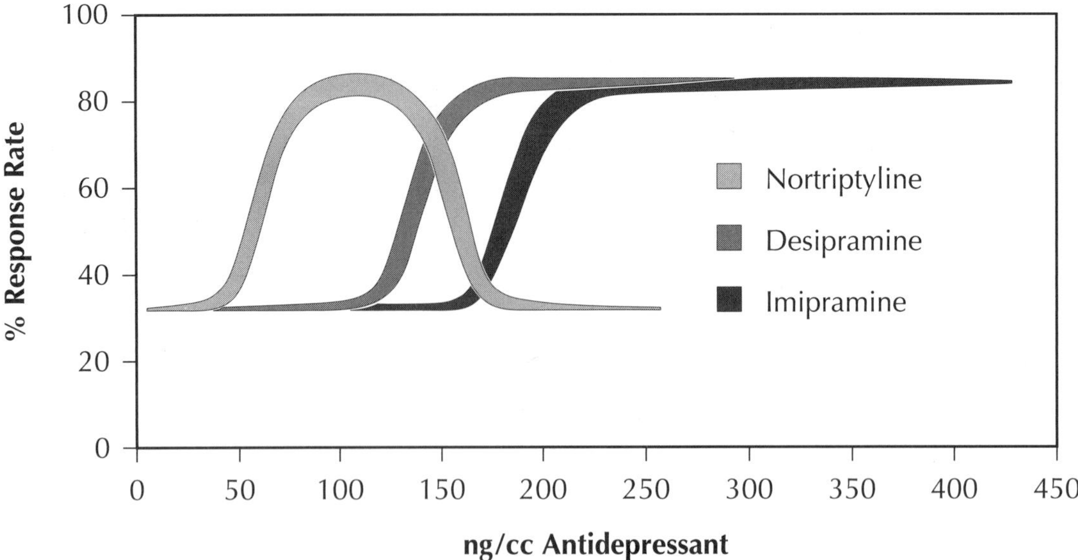

Figure 2. The relationship between blood levels and outcome: Comparison of three antidepressants.

even though blockade of amine uptake occurs within 12 hours, the antidepressant effects of the tricyclics do not occur for several weeks. Recent studies have focused on second messenger systems as critical mediators between receptor activity and gene transcription; this process may explain both antidepressant activity and delay of onset of action (Nestler, Terwilliger, & Duman, 1989).

Side Effects

Despite their robust effectiveness, the clinical use of tricyclic antidepressants has been limited by their side effects. The problems range from minimal seriousness with high nuisance value that can markedly reduce patient compliance, to problems of potential lethality in certain patient populations. The most frequent side effects of tricyclics are due to their peripheral anticholinergic (antimuscarinic) effects, which account for dry mouth, constipation, tachycardia, and blurred vision (Richelson, 1989). In older patients, the anticholinergic effect can result in urinary retention and acute confusional states. The tricyclics also block histamine receptors, which may be related to the significant weight gain that is associated with long-term treatment in some patients.

Another frequent and significant side effect of the tricyclic antidepressants is orthostatic hypotension (Richelson, 1989). This effect results in part from peripheral alpha-adrenergic receptor blockade and occurs in approximately 10% of patients treated with tricyclics. Orthostatic hypotension can result in serious injury and fatalities.

The cardiovascular effects of the tricyclics account for most of the morbidity and mortality associated with these medications (Roose & Glassman, 1989). The tricyclics are Type 1A antiarrhythmic drugs and have a quinidine-like action on the heart that results in an antiarrhythmic effect and slowing of cardiac conduction. Consequently, tricyclics can be dangerous in patients with preexisting conduction system disease such as bundle branch block and can increase mortality in patients with ischemic heart disease. When taken in overdose, tricyclics are frequently lethal due to heart block and ventricular tachycardia. The extensive cardiovascular effects of the tricyclic antidepressants serve as a reminder that the therapeutic label of a medication (an antidepressant) does not necessarily describe all of the systems that are significantly affected. The clinician must be equally aware of the effects of a medication other than the intended mechanism of action.

Clinical Indications

The tricyclic antidepressants are effective in the treatment of unipolar major depressive disorder (Richelson, 1989). They are also effective in the treatment of a bipolar depressive episode. However, because their use can cause a switch into mania, it is standard practice for a depressed bipolar patient to be treated with both a mood stabilizer and an antidepressant. Studies have also established the effectiveness of the tricyclics in the treatment of dysthymia, a form of chronic mild depression that often presents early in life (Kocsis, 1997).

Despite being labeled antidepressants, the tricyclics also produce significant benefit in the treatment of certain anxiety disorders, notably panic attacks and generalized anxiety (Roy-Byrne & Lydiard, 1989). Tricyclics have been shown to decrease significantly the rate of binges in patients with bulimia, although they have been ineffective in the treatment of anorexia nervosa (Walsh et al., 1997). Tricyclics are also used for the treatment of other conditions that are not considered primarily psychiatric but that often are accompanied by affective or anxiety symptoms. Notable among these conditions are irritable bowel syndrome, migraine headaches, and chronic pain.

Although the tricyclic antidepressants have been largely supplanted by the SSRIs as the first-line treatment for depressive or anxiety disorders, they remain widely used compounds. Up to 40% of depressed patients do not achieve remission when treated with an SSRI alone, and it is common clinical practice to combine an SSRI with a tricyclic as a second treatment strategy. Furthermore, some types of depressive disorders may preferentially respond to the tricyclics compared to the SSRIs (e.g., the melancholic subtype of depression). In addition, age may affect response to antidepressant medication, and in the geriatric patient, tricyclics may be more effective than SSRIs (Roose & Suthers, 1998). A recent study showed that nortriptyline in combination with monthly interpersonal psychotherapy is an effective treatment to prevent recurrence of depression in the geriatric population (Reynolds et al., 1999). Unfortunately, the nuisance and potentially dangerous side effects of tricyclics are greatest in the older population. All of the tricyclics are available as generic compounds and so are significantly less expensive than most other antidepressants. In summary, the tricyclics remain in widespread clinic use, but their problematic side-effect profile means that they are rarely used as a first-line treatment for depression.

REFERENCES

Glassman, A. H., Schildkraut, J. J., Orsulak, P. J., et al. (1985). APA Task Force: Tricyclic antidepressants—Blood level measurements and clinical outcome: An APA Task Force Report. *American Journal of Psychiatry, 142,* 155–162.

Kocsis, J. H. (1997). Chronic depression: The efficacy of pharmacotherapy. In A. H. S. Akiskal & G. B. Cassano (Eds.), *Dysthymia and the spectrum of chronic depressions* (pp. 66–74). New York: Guilford Press.

Nestler, E. J., Terwilliger, R. Z., & Duman, R. S. (1989). Chronic antidepressant administration alters the subcellular distribution of cyclic AMP-dependent protein kinase in rat frontal cortex. *Journal of Neurochemistry, 52,* 1644–1647.

Reynolds, C. F., Frank, E., Perel, J. M., Imber, S. D., Cornes, C., Miller, M. D., Mazumdar, S., Houck, P. R., Dew, M. A., Stack, J. A., Pollock, B. G., & Kupfer, D. J. (1999). Nortriptyline and interpersonal psychotherapy as maintenance therapies for recurrent major depression: A randomized controlled trial in patients older than 59 years. *Journal of the American Medical Association, 281*(1), 39–45.

Richelson, E. (1989). Antidepressants: Pharmacology and clinical use. In T. B. Karasu (Ed.), *Treatments of psychiatric disorders* (p. 1773). Washington, DC: American Psychiatric Press.

Roose, S. P., & Glassman, A. H. (1989). Cardiovascular effects of tricyclic antidepressants in depressed patients with and without heart disease. *Journal Clinical Psychiatry, 50*(Suppl.), 1–18.

Roose, S. P., & Suthers, K. M. (1998). Antidepressant response in late-life depression. *Journal of Clinical Psychiatry, 59*(Suppl. 10), 4–8.

Roy-Byrne, P. P., & Lydiard, R. B. (1989). New developments in the psychopharmacologic treatment of anxiety. In P. P. Roy-Byrne (Ed.), *Anxiety: New findings for the clinician* (pp. 151–178). Washington, DC: American Psychiatric Association.

Walsh, B. T., Wilson, G. T., Loeb, K. L., Devlin, M. J., Pike, K. M., Roose, S. P., Fleiss, J. L., & Waternaux, C. (1997). Medication and psychotherapy in the treatment of bulimia nervosa. *American Journal of Psychiatry, 154,* 523–531.

Steven P. Roose
Columbia University

Vanessa Pesce
Late-Life Depression Clinic

TRUST

Trust is "the expectancy of positive (or nonnegative) outcomes that one can receive based on the expected action of another party in an interaction characterized by uncertainty" (Bhattacharya, Devinney, & Pillutla, 1998, p. 462). Trust is both a dispositional (personality) variable and a temporary state.

Trust as a Dispositional Variable

Those who are trusting tend to give others the benefit of the doubt unless they have clear evidence that someone is untrustworthy. In social dilemma situations, they expect others to cooperate (Komorita & Parks, 1994), and they avoid using deception (Rotter, 1980). Trust is negatively related to Machiavellianism and authoritarianism (Deutsch, 1960; Gurtman, 1992).

Those who distrust sometimes make sinister attribution errors, explaining another's negative actions in terms of hostile interpersonal motives (Kramer, 1994). Distrust and trust are usually considered opposite poles on one continuum even though they may be qualitatively different (Lewicki, McAllister, & Bies, 1998).

Trust as a Temporary State

Research investigating trust as a temporary state often explores one of three themes:

1. *Trust and cooperative motivational orientation.* In this theme, trust is a cognitive and emotional state related to cooperative motivational orientation (MO). Thus, in some situations (e.g., prisoner's dilemma experiments) cooperative behavior reflects trust (Kee, 1969; McAllister, 1995).

2. *Trust and predictability.* This theme suggests that a person who behaves consistently is trustworthy (e.g., Butler, 1991). Predictability allows others to anticipate whether a person will keep his or her word—called knowledge-based trust (Shapiro, Sheppard, & Cheraskin, 1992). Even if a person is not cooperative, if he or she is consistent, then others can devise strategies for dealing with that person. Finally, a pattern of repeated, cooperative behavior can establish trust (Kramer, 1999; Lindskold, 1978).
3. *Trust and a problem-solving perspective.* This theme relates trust to a problem-solving orientation in bargaining. Kimmel, Pruitt, Magenau, Konar-Goldband, and Carnevale (1980) observed that trust increases information sharing and problem-solving efforts, yet it has little effect on negotiated payoffs (also see Kee, 1969). This paradox may occur because trust improves the quality of the parties' relationship rather than increases their ability to resolve specific issues. Indeed, friends are often less likely than strangers to discover integrative bargaining solutions because maintaining the trusting relationship is more important than are short-term payoffs (Halpern, 1994).

   Shapiro et al. (1992) suggested that trust is maximized when the cooperative MO perspective and the problem-solving perspective merge into what they call identification-based trust. Here, each side internalizes the other's interests, developing shared interests.

Antecedents of Trust

Numerous social factors such as benevolence can create trust (Kramer, 1999; Mayer, Davis, & Schoorman, 1995). Mental shortcuts called cognitive heuristics also facilitate trust or distrust—sometimes erroneously. For example, people selectively notice, recall, and evaluate certain information (e.g., vivid evidence of betrayal) when deciding whether to trust another (Ross & LaCroix, 1996).

Consequences of Trust

There are numerous consequences of trust, including a willingness to be vulnerable to another (Pruitt, 1981). Trust may also enhance relationships, causing greater empathy and mutual concern (Lewicki, Saunders, & Minton, 1999).

However, trust can prove unwise (Wicks, Berman, & Jones, 1999). The trusting party is unlikely to recognize evidence of betrayal. Trust may also lead to using fewer objective standards and verification mechanisms to ensure compliance (Ross & LaCroix, 1996). Thus, trust may sometimes cause someone to be blind to another person's untrustworthy behavior.

In conclusion, psychologists see trust as both a dispositional trait and a temporary state. Within the latter perspective, research themes have emerged investigating trust and cooperative MO, predictability, and problem solving. Trust is a social, affective, and cognitive phenomenon with numerous antecedents; if correctly placed, trust may yield lasting benefits to the involved parties.

REFERENCES

Bhattacharya, R., Devinney, T., & Pillutla, M. (1998). A formal model of trust based on outcomes. *Academy of Management Review, 23,* 459–472.

Butler, J. K., Jr. (1991). Toward understanding and measuring conditions of trust: Evolution of a Conditions of Trust inventory. *Journal of Management, 17,* 643–663.

Deutsch, M. (1960). Trust, trustworthiness, and the F-scale. *Journal of Abnormal and Social Psychology, 61,* 138–140.

Gurtman, M. (1992). Trust, distrust, and interpersonal problems: A circumplex analysis. *Journal of Personality and Social Psychology, 62,* 989–1002.

Halpern, J. J. (1994). The effect of friendship on personal business transactions. *Journal of Conflict Resolution, 38,* 647–664.

Kee, H. (1969). The development, and the effects upon bargaining, of trust and suspicion. *Dissertation Abstracts International, 70,* 4017A–4018A.

Kimmel, M. J., Pruitt, D. G., Magenau, J., Konar-Goldband, E., & Carnevale, P. (1980). Effects of trust, aspiration and gender on negotiation tactics. *Journal of Personality and Social Psychology, 38,* 9–23.

Komorita, S. S., & Parks, C. D. (1994). *Social dilemmas.* Madison, WI: Brown & Benchmark.

Kramer, R. M. (1994). The sinister attribution error: Paranoid cognition and collective distrust in organizations. *Motivation and Emotion, 18,* 199–230.

Kramer, R. M. (1999). Trust and distrust in organizations: Emerging perspectives, enduring questions. *Annual Review of Psychology, 50,* 569–598.

Lewicki, R. J., McAllister, D., & Bies, R. J. (1998). Trust and distrust: New relationships and realities. *Academy of Management Review, 23,* 438–458.

Lewicki, R. J., Saunders, D., & Minton, J. W. (1999). *Negotiation* (3rd ed.). Burr Ridge, IL: Irwin/McGraw-Hill.

Lindskold, S. (1978). Trust development, the GRIT proposal, and the effects of conciliatory acts on conflict and cooperation. *Psychological Bulletin, 85,* 772–793.

Mayer, R. C., Davis, J., & Schoorman, F. D. (1995). An integrative model of organizational trust. *Academy of Management Review, 20,* 709–734.

McAllister, D. (1995). Affect- and cognition-based trust as foundations for interpersonal cooperation in organizations. *Academy of Management Journal, 38,* 24–59.

Pruitt, D. G. (1981). *Negotiation behavior.* Orlando, FL: Academic Press.

Ross, W. H., Jr., & LaCroix, J. (1996). Multiple meanings of trust in negotiation theory and research: A literature review and an integrative model. *International Journal of Conflict Management, 7,* 314–360.

Rotter, J. B. (1980). Interpersonal trust, trustworthiness, and gullibility. *American Psychologist, 35,* 1–7.

Shapiro, D. L., Sheppard, B. H., & Cheraskin, L. (1992). Business on a handshake. *Negotiation Journal, 8,* 365–378.

Wicks, A. C., Berman, S., & Jones, T. (1999). The structure of optimal trust: Moral and strategic implications. *Academy of Management Review, 24,* 99–116.

William H. Ross
University of Wisconsin at La Crosse

TWELVE-STEP PROGRAMS

In 1935 Bill Wilson, a stockbroker, and Bob Smith, a physician, met for the first time in Akron, Ohio. Both men were struggling with the disease of alcoholism. Bob did not want another person preaching to him about staying sober, but he agreed to see Bill for a few minutes. The two men talked about their common problem and shared their experiences. Bill explained that he was not there to keep Bob sober; he was there to keep himself sober. He had a spiritual awakening during his last detoxification, but it was not enough to keep him sober. He had just lost a business deal, and he was thinking about drinking to ease the pain. Medical science had no answer for the chronic alcoholic at the time. The men talked for hours, and they struck a bond. They found that if they talked about their common problems, they could overcome the compulsion to drink. From this first meeting, Alcoholics Anonymous (AA) was born. AA is a fellowship of men and women who share their strength and hope with each other that they may solve their common problem with alcoholism. The Big Book of Alcoholics Anonymous, first published in 1939, listed the twelve steps that are suggested as a program of recovery. Many other groups have used the twelve steps to develop similar programs of recovery, including Narcotics Anonymous, Cocaine Anonymous, Overeaters Anonymous, Emotions Anonymous, Gamblers Anonymous, and Sexaholics Anonymous.

Twelve-step programs revolve around regular attendance at group meetings, sponsorship with another more experienced member, and a spiritual journey to a higher power. Alcohol and drug treatment facilities using the twelve steps as the foundation of treatment began with Hazelden in 1949 and have spread around the world.

The Twelve Steps

1. We admitted we were powerless over alcohol—that our lives had become unmanageable.
2. We came to believe that a Power greater than ourselves could restore us to sanity.
3. We made a decision to turn our will and our lives over to the care of God *as we understood Him.*
4. We made a searching and fearless moral inventory of ourselves.
5. We admitted to God, ourselves and another human being the exact nature of our wrongs.
6. We were entirely ready to have God remove all these defects of character.
7. We humbly asked Him to remove our shortcomings.
8. We made a list of all persons we had harmed, and became willing to make amends to them all.
9. We made direct amends to such people wherever possible, except when to do so would injure them or others.
10. We continued to take personal inventory and when we were wrong, promptly admitted it.
11. We sought through prayer and meditation to improve our conscious contact with God as we understood Him, praying only for the knowledge of His will for us and the power to carry that out.
12. Having had a spiritual awakening as the result of these steps, we tried to carry this message to alcoholics and to practice these principles in all our affairs. (Alcoholics Anonymous, 1976)

Either a counselor or a sponsor walks recovering persons through the twelve steps. First, recovering persons need to admit how powerless their life is over the addictive substance or behavior. This is accomplished by sharing recurrent psychological, social, or physical problems caused by or exacerbated by the addiction. Recovering individuals need to see that whatever they tried to do to bring their illness under control failed. They might have been able to stay clean for a short period of time, but they always returned to the addiction. Then they are encouraged to come to believe that a Power greater than themselves can restore them to sanity. At first that might be the recovery group, but soon they come to think about God. In Step 3 the individuals make a decision to turn their life and will over to the care of God as they understand Him. This is a spiritual program, not a religious one, so the addicts are allowed great leeway in choosing the higher power of their own understanding. Then addicts are encouraged to clean house by taking a personal inventory. This is a thorough autobiography including their life story and all assets and liabilities. In Step 5 recovering persons verbalize to themselves, god, and another human being the exact nature of their wrongs. This eases the guilt of the past and prepares for a new life in recovery. In Step 6 addicts become ready to give all defects of character over to the care of God. Then in Step 7 they ask God to remove all of these shortcomings. Step 8 involves making a list of everyone harmed by the addiction, and Step 9 encourages the addict to make direct amends whenever possible without hurting anyone. In Step 10 addicts take a daily personal inventory encouraging themselves when they succeed and correcting old behavior when necessary. Step 11 is where they seek conscious contact with god through prayer and meditation and ask God for specific direction. In Step 12 addicts continue to monitor themselves and carry the recovery message to persons still suffering.

REFERENCE

Alcoholics Anonymous (3rd ed.). (1976). New York: Alcoholics Anonymous General Service Office.

Robert R. Perkinson
Keystone Treatment Center

See also: **Self-Help Groups**

TWO-PROCESS LEARNING THEORY

The central premise of two-process learning theory is that the laws of classical and instrumental conditioning are not functionally equivalent. During the first half of the twentieth century, the general trend was to treat classical and instrumental conditioning as obeying the same laws (Guthrie, 1935; Hull, 1929, 1943). Nevertheless, even during its formative period, learning theory had expressed an alternative view. As early as 1928, Miler and Konorski had distinguished between two forms of conditioned response: Type I was Pavlov's secretory conditioned response (CR), formed by establishing a positive correlation between the conditioned stimulus (CS) and the unconditioned stimulus (US); Type II differed from the classical CR in that its occurrence was dependent on its consequences. Despite the early work of Konorski and others (Hilgard, 1937; Schlosberg, 1937; Skinner, 1938) regarding the adequacy of uniprocess theories of learning, it was not until drive reduction theory encountered theoretical problems accounting for avoidance learning that two-process theory emerged to challenge the prevailing view. In drive reduction theory, the motive for the avoidance response derived from the occurrence of an aversive US and the reinforcement of the response from US termination. However, because the avoidance response prevents the US from occurring, the theory cannot account for the learning or maintenance of avoidance behavior (Kimble, 1961).

To resolve this problem, Mowrer (1947, 1950) proposed that avoidance learning was the result of two processes. Fear-instigated avoidance behavior and the reduction of fear following the avoidance response maintained the behavior. Classical conditioning established the fear reaction to the CS by pairing the CS with an aversive US. This view contrasted sharply with Hull's (1929) account. Hull had argued that the cessation of an aversive US was reinforcing. By demonstrating that there was no difference in the conditioning of fear when the onset of the aversive US coincided with the CS or when the CS was coincident with both the onset and the offset of the aversive event, Mowrer showed that fear was formed through classical conditioning. In this case, classical conditioning established the association between the CS and the fear CR. Once aroused, fear motivated instrumental behavior. Reducing the fear reinforced the response that was successful in removing the CS. Cast in this form, two-process theory assigned considerable importance to classical conditioning; the processes established by this form of learning functioned as motivators or reinforcers mediating instrumental behavior.

Ironically, Hull (1929, 1931) provided the hypothetical mechanism that served as the basis for extending two-process theory to appetitive behavior. For Hull, components of the consummatory response became anticipatory following repeated presentations of the US. These fractional anticipatory goal reactions (r_g) were associated with stimuli that antedate (and hence signal) the appetitive US. The r_g mechanism also produced sensory aftereffects, which were symbolized as s_g. Although Hull used $r_g - s_g$ as an associative mechanism to explain disrupted behavior following a change in the quality of a reward, later theorists employed it as a device that mediated incentive motivation: $r_g - s_g$ somehow selectively energized responses that had previously been successful in enabling the animal to encounter a goal object (Logan, 1960; Seward, 1952; Spence, 1956).

Because fear and $r_g - s_g$ were treated as implicit peripheral CRs, considerable research was devoted to determining their role in mediating instrumental behavior. Classically conditioned responses such as heart rate and salivation were used to index these implicit events and the temporal relationship between them and instrumental responses. After an exhaustive review of the literature, Rescorla and Solomon (1967) concluded that the strategy of indexing these inferred events by overt CRs and mapping their relationship to instrumental activity failed because there was no temporal consistency between the observable Pavlovian CRs and the sequence of instrumental responses. In the course of an experiment, the CR might precede, occur coincident with, or follow the instrumental response (Sheffield, 1965).

Rescorla and Solomon (1967) argued that a more promising approach was to view the events established by classical conditioning as central states and to determine their role indirectly using a transfer-of-control paradigm. The transfer-of-control procedure involves multiple stages of training. Classical or instrumental conditioning is given during the first stage of learning; then, depending on which of the two conditioning procedures was first administered, subjects receive the other conditioning procedure. In the third or test phase, while the animal is engaged in instrumental activity, the Pavlovian CS is administered. Facilitation or disruption of the instrumental response following the presentation of the CS is taken as evidence that the CS has evoked a central state (Mellgren & Ost, 1969; Shapiro & Miller, 1965).

Trapold and Overmier (1972) questioned the notion that classical and instrumental training establishes distinct Pavlovian and instrumental processes. They suggested instead the adoption of a more neutral terminology, namely, response-independent and response-dependent learning. One implication of this usage is a greater reciprocity between the two forms of learning: Response-independent learning is not necessarily a result of classical conditioning, even though the process established by this type of learning may affect instrumental behavior. Moreover, the representation formed during response-dependent learning may interact with stimulus-stimulus associations (Alloy & Ehrman, 1981).

The initial formulation of two-process theory held that the laws governing the formation of associations were different although what was learned (viz., stimulus-response associations) were the same. By contrast, the current view argues that classical and instrumental conditioning obeys the same laws. They differ, however, in the sort of associations established by the two training procedures. Classical conditioning promotes the formation of stimulus-stimulus (S-S) associations, whereas instrumental conditioning results in the establishment of response-stimulus (R-S) associations (e.g., Dickinson, 1980; Mackintosh, 1974). One problem with this analysis is that some forms of classical conditioning (e.g., second-order conditioning) seemingly form S-R associations (Rescorla, 1974). Logan (1988) proposed a possible resolution of this dilemma. He argues that the second-order stimulus (CS_2) establishes two mediating links to the CR. One involves an association between CS_2 and representations of consequent events such as the first-order CS (CS_1) or the US; a second mediating link is response-produced stimulation generated from the CR. The salience of these associative connections determines which one controls the CR. Presumably, the sensory properties of the US are more salient than the stimulation produced by the UR in first-order conditioning; but with second-order conditioning, CR-produced feedback is more salient than sensory qualities of CS_1.

A second problem concerns the nature of response selection in instrumental conditioning. Whereas S-S associations can explain the initiation of behavior by assuming that the CS evokes a representation of the US, which in turn elicits the CR, R-S learning must rely on the formation of two separate representations: one between the context and the US, and the other between the US and the response. The excitation necessary for response evocation must flow from the US to the response. This conceptualization does not enjoy a substantial empirical base (Mackintosh, 1983).

Dickinson's (1989) expectancy theory of conditioning provides a possible resolution to this conundrum. The theory retains a mechanistic associationistic explanation for classical conditioning but advances an intentional, cognitive account for nonautomatic forms of instrumental behavior. The mechanistic account suffices for response elicitation in classical conditioning and assigns a role for Pavlovian processes in mediating some types of instrumental learning that evidence automaticity, but voluntary behavior involves the activation of expectancies. Thus, when an animal experiences a contingency between its behavior and some outcome, an expectancy embodying the content of the contingency is formed. The association formed by the contingency is mapped into a declarative structure that represents the actual state of affairs. The content of the representation is of the form "this action leads to that reinforcer." If the content of this belief is accompanied by a relevant motivational state that serves to enhance the desirability of the reinforcer, then the activated expectancy results in the issuance of a command to execute the response. Thus, knowledge and desire form the basis of voluntary behavior through some sort of computational process. The nature of the psychological mechanism (if, indeed, there is one) that captures the intentionality of instrumental conditioning remains, as Dickinson himself pointed out, open.

REFERENCES

Alloy, L. B., & Ehrman, R. N. (1981). Instrumental to Pavlovian transfer: Learning about response-reinforcer contingencies affects subsequent learning about stimulus-reinforcer contingencies. *Learning and Motivation, 12,* 109–132.

Dickinson, A. (1980). *Contemporary animal learning theory.* Cambridge, UK: Cambridge University Press.

Dickinson, A. (1989). Expectancy theory in animal conditioning. In S. Klein & R. R. Mowrer (Eds.), *Contemporary learning theories: Pavlovian conditioning and the status of traditional learning theory* (pp. 279–308). Hillsdale, NJ: Erlbaum.

Guthrie, E. R. (1935). *The psychology of learning.* New York: Harper & Row.

Hilgard, E. R. (1937). The relationship between the conditioned response and conventional learning experiments. *Psychological Bulletin, 34,* 61–102.

Hull, C. L. (1929). A functional interpretation of the conditioned reflex. *Psychological Review, 36,* 498–511.

Hull, C. L. (1943). *Principles of behavior.* New York: Appleton-Century-Crofts.

Kimble, G. A. (1961). *Hilgard and Marquis' conditioning and learning.* New York: Appleton-Century-Crofts.

Logan, F. A. (1960). *Incentive.* New Haven, CT: Yale University Press.

Logan, F. A. (1988). Hybrid theory: What is learned in classical conditioning? *Psychological Reports, 63,* 915–919.

Mackintosh, N. J. (1974). *The psychology of animal learning.* New York: Academic Press.

Macintosh, N. J. (1983). *Conditioning and associative learning.* New York: Oxford University Press.

Mellgren, R. L., & Ost, W. P. (1969). Transfer of Pavlovian differential conditioning to an operant discrimination. *Journal of Comparative and Physiological Psychology, 67,* 323–336.

Miller, S., & Konorski, J. (1928). Sur une forme particuliere des reflexes conditionnels. *Social Biology, 99,* 1155–1157.

Mowrer, O. H. (1947). On the dual nature of learning: A reinterpretation of "conditioning" and "problem-solving." *Harvard Educational Review, 17,* 102–148.

Mowrer, O. H. (1950). *Learning theory and personality dynamics.* New York: Ronald.

Rescorla, R. A. (1974). US-inflation after conditioning. *Journal of Comparative and Physiological Psychology, 86,* 101–106.

Rescorla, R. A., & Solomon, R. L. (1967). Two-process learning theory: Relationships between Pavlovian conditioning and instrumental learning. *Psychological Review, 74,* 151–184.

Schosberg, H. (1937). The relationship between success and the laws of conditioning. *Psychological Review, 44,* 379–394.

Seward, J. P. (1952). Introduction to a theory of motivation in learning. *Psychological Review, 59,* 405–413.

Shapiro, M. M., & Miller, T. M. (1965). On the relationship between conditioned and discriminative stimuli and between instrumental and consummatory response. In W. F. Prokasy (Ed.), *Classical conditioning: A symposium.* New York: Appleton-Century-Crofts.

Sheffield, F. D. (1965). Relation between classical conditioning and instrumental learning. In W. F. Prokasy (Ed.), *Classical conditioning: A symposium.* New York: Appleton-Century-Crofts.

Skinner, B F. (1938). *The behavior of organisms: An experimental analysis.* New York: Appleton-Century-Crofts.

Spence, K. W. (1956). *Behavior theory and conditioning.* New Haven, CT: Yale University Press.

Trapold, M. A., & Overmier, J. B. (1972). The second learning process in instrumental conditioning. In A. A. Black & W. F. Prokasy (Eds.), *Classical conditioning: II. Current research and theory.* New York: Appleton-Century-Crofts.

Edward J. Rickert
Georgia Institute of Technology

See also: **Operant Conditioning**

U

UNCONSCIOUS

The unconscious is a hypothetical construct used to describe behaviors, phenomena, material, processes, and so on that are out of immediate awareness (English & English, 1958/1974). Prior to Freud, this concept was used to explain a variety of behavior, such as dissociation, mesmerism, and trancework. Freud initiated the formal term *unconscious* (Rychlack, 1981). Later, Erickson and Rossi refined it via Ericksonian hypnotherapy and state-dependent memory learning and behavior systems or the mind-body approaches (Erickson, Rossi, & Rossi, 1976; Rossi, 1993).

Definitions of the unconscious vary depending on one's theoretical perspective. English and English (1958/1974) found 39 distinct meanings.

Historical Views

Psychoanalysis

Sigmund Freud was the first modern-day theorist to explore personality in depth. He divided awareness into three levels: (1) conscious awareness, (2) preconscious awareness, and (3) unconscious awareness. Conscious awareness includes any materials, experiences, learnings, perceptions, feelings, or thoughts in immediate awareness. The preconscious—an intermediate level—consists of any materials that enter conscious awareness. The unconscious comprises all repressed thoughts, feelings, behaviors, memories, experiences, learnings, defense mechanisms, sexual impulses, instincts, id impulses, wishes, dreams, psychological conflicts, and so on and remains outside awareness (Hall & Lindsey, 1978; Norby & Hall, 1974).

Hypnotic, Ericksonian Views

Erickson worked with various processes of the unconscious (Erickson et al., 1976; Havens, 1985). His view of the unconscious, developed through trancework, consisted of a reservoir of past memories, or a storehouse of learning patterned from experiences (Beahrs, 1971; McGarty, 1985; Yapko, 1986). The unconscious is considered to be a positive constructive process. The work of Erickson connected the trance state to unconscious functioning (Yapko, 1984).

Trance provides access to the unconscious process. Specific trance (or subconscious) behaviors include age regression (remembering past memories without prior conscious recollections); age progression (experiencing futuristic scenarios before the actual events occur); hidden observer phenomena (imagining watching oneself doing something); dissociation; catalepsy (muscular suspension or immobility and rigidity in the limbs, based on concentration/suggestion); ideodynamic or psychomotor behaviors (involuntary behavioral movements—finger movements, hand movements, etc.—outside ordinary conscious awareness); autohypnosis; anesthesia (by suggestions and concentration); amnesia; automatic writing; imagery; time distortion; eye closure; and relaxation (Carich, 1990a; Erickson et al. 1976). Lankton and Lankton (1983) furthered the Ericksonian view of the unconscious by emphasizing a right-hemispheric physiological base along with behaviors and processes such as spatial modes, pantomine (nonverbal movement), involuntary movements, imagery, sensory modalities, intuition, artistic-creative tendencies, literalism, psychophysiological functioning, music, symbolic representations/meanings, rhythmic patterning, and spontaneity.

Rossi (1993) took a psychophysiological view of the unconscious along with the previously stated Ericksonian views. He postulated that the key to the unconscious processes and the issue of causality is the state-dependent memory learning and behavior (SDML&B) system. Rossi (1987) explained state-dependent memory as "what is learned and remembered is dependent upon one's psychophysiological state at the time of the experience" (p. 372).

The SDML&B system is considered to stem from the limbic-hypothalamic system, which regulates much of human behavior and brain activity through information substances or messenger molecules. These regulatory processes are the substance of the unconscious. Rossi (1993) further contended that behaviors and/or learning consist of encoding perceptions into state-dependent memories at the limbic-hypothalamic level. More specifically, learning, memories, and perceptions are transduced into information via molecular processes within the brain, whereas sensory input is transduced through cellular interaction. This, then, is primarily the basis of the unconscious processes. Rossi (1993) also related this with psychophysiological rhythms (circadian and ultradian cycles). Ultradian cycles are the natural rest cycles that facilitate rest states (Rossi

& Nimmons, 1991) and provide a window into the unconscious. The conceptual meaning of the unconscious is controversial. Research into the unconscious and the related concepts of hypnosis and dissociation is continuing. Kihlstrom (1987) cited research suggesting that humans cognitively process information that is not in immediate awareness. Epstein (1994, p. 710) explained that "the cognitive unconscious is a fundamentally adaptive system that automatically, effortlessly, and intuitively organizes experience and directs behavior. . . . Most information processing occurs automatically and effortlessly outside of awareness."

Consciousness is best viewed on a continuum, ranging in degrees, or levels, from the storage of information and the processing of that information in immediate awareness to a lack of awareness (unconsciousness).

Applications

Among the applications of the unconscious are changing behaviors and resolving problems. To accomplish these goals, the unconscious must be accessed and used. People are generally self-programmed through a series of choices based on a variety of experiences. Many problems are self-programmed at unconscious levels (unconscious choices or choices made at unconscious levels) and need to be reprogrammed at unconscious levels. Some methods of accessing and using the unconscious are internal visualization or imagery, fantasy and daydreams, dreams, self-talk, music, art, body rhythms (basic rest activity cycles), relaxation, and hypnotic techniques.

Imagery is the internal visualization of some image or scenario with a theme (Aroaz, 1982, 1985). By using imagery, fantasy, and daydreams, one gains the experience that something actually happened. When using imagery, one should use sensory modes (auditory [hearing], kinesthetic [movement], taste, and smell; Aroaz, 1982, 1985). To prepare for upcoming events, one should develop a detailed image or scenario of the event and reactively rehearse the scenario, imagining successfully completing the task.

Aroaz (1982, 1985) suggested that self-talk is a type of hypnotic suggestion that self-programs one's mind at an unconscious or subconscious level. By monitoring one's self-statements and changing them, one can reprogram one's unconscious belief systems.

Other ways to access unconscious processes and change dysfunctional behavior are through hypnosis and relaxation techniques that can directly access unconscious processes. For more information on hypnotic techniques, see Hammond (1990) and Carich (1990a, 1990b).

Rossi (1987, 1993) emphasized the importance of the body's naturalistic rhythms (ultradian rest cycles). The unconscious can be accessed by taking advantage of rest cycles (Rossi & Nimmons, 1991).

Both music and art can serve as pathways to the unconscious if one has learned to be receptive. Literally, most music and artwork involve unconscious elements (Lankton & Lankton, 1983).

REFERENCES

Aroaz, D. L. (1982). *Hypnosis and sex therapy.* New York: Brunner/Mazel.

Aroaz, D. L. (1985). *The new hypnosis.* New York: Brunner/Mazel.

Beahrs, J. O. (1971). The hypnotic psychotherapy of Milton H. Erickson. *American Journal of Clinical Hypnosis, 14*(2), 73–90.

Carich, M. S. (1990a). The basics of hypnosis and trancework. *Individual Psychology, 46*(4), 401–410.

Carich, M. S. (1990b). Hypnotic techniques and Adlerian constructs. *Individual Psychology, 46*(2), 1660–1677.

English, H. B., & English, A. C. (1974). *A comprehensive dictionary of psychological and psychoanalytical terms.* New York: McKay. (Original work published 1958)

Epstein, S. (1994). Integration of the cognitive and the psychodynamic unconscious. *American Psychologist, 99*(8), 704–724.

Erickson, M. H., Rossi, E. L., & Rossi, S. I. (1976). *Hypnotic realities: The induction of clinical hypnosis and forms of indirect suggestion.* New York: Irvington.

Hall, C. S., & Lindsey, G. (1978). *Theories of personality.* New York: Wiley.

Hammond, D. L. (Ed.). (1990). *Handbook of hypnotic suggestions and metaphors.* New York: Norton.

Havens, R. (1985). *The wisdom of Milton H. Erickson.* New York: Irvington.

Kihlstrom, J. (1987). The cognitive unconscious. *Science, 237,* 1445–1452.

Lankton, S., & Lankton, C. H. (1983). *The answer within: A clinical framework of Ericksonian hypnotherapy.* New York: Brunner/Mazel.

McGarty, R. (1985). Relevance of Ericksonian psychotherapy to the treatment of chemical dependency. *Journal of Substance Abuse Treatment, 2,* 147–151.

Norby, V., & Hall, C. (1974). *A guide to psychologists and their concepts.* San Francisco: Freeman.

Rossi, E. L. (1987). From mind to molecule: More than a metaphor. In J. K. Zeig & S. Gilligan (Eds.), *Brief therapy: Myths, methods, and metaphors* (pp. 445–472). New York: Brunner/Mazel.

Rossi, E. L. (1993). *The psychobiology of mind-body healing: New concepts in therapeutic hypnosis.* New York: Norton.

Rossi, E. L., & Nimmons, D. (1991). *The 20 minute break: New concepts in therapeutic hypnosis.* Los Angeles: Tarcher.

Rychlack, J. F. (1981). *Introduction to personality and psychotherapy* (2nd ed.). Boston: Houghton Mifflin.

Yapko, M. D. (1984). *Trancework: An introduction to clinical hypnosis.* New York: Irvington.

Yapko, M. D. (1986). What is Ericksonia hypnosis? In B. Zilbergeld, M. G. Edelstein, & D. L. Aroza (Eds.), *Hypnosis: Questions and answers* (pp. 223–231). New York: Norton.

Mark S. Carich

See also: **Hypnosis**

UNIVERSAL HEALTH CARE

Universal health care, also known as national health insurance (NHI), is defined as health care for all residents of the United States funded by the federal government under its single-payer system. There are many examples of universal health care throughout the world (e.g., the United Kingdom, Sweden, Canada), and, in fact, the United States remains the only industrialized nation without government-sponsored single-payer health care.

NHI would constitute a wide-scale, comprehensive redistribution of health care services. Because there would be no aspect of the health care sector that would not be significantly affected, its potential implementation galvanizes every stakeholder to adopt a strong pro or con position. The American Medical Association (AMA) opposes it because it would further erode its already weakened—and once virtually monopoly—status. The private health insurance industry that in the decade of the 1990s burgeoned into various versions of managed care opposes it because it wants no increase in a federal health bureaucracy that would impede its growth. The welfare sector favors it because it would bring health care to every resident and would guarantee the continuation of a welfare system that recently has been subjected to severe cutbacks.

Widespread interest in universal health care began in the 1930s. During this era of the Great Depression, not only was there high unemployment, but also there was no private health insurance. The AMA successfully campaigned against government-sponsored health care, calling it socialized medicine, and instead favored the expansion of county medical clinics to meet the needs of the unemployed. During this same period the Blue Cross/Blue Shield plans were created as the first of a long series of private-sector solutions to the need for extended health care coverage.

During World War II a far-reaching private-sector alternative to government sponsored health care inadvertently emerged. The nation had to relocate millions of Americans to work in the defense industry. Wages were frozen by law, so increased compensation could not be used to lure potential workers from the rural areas. The government permitted health coverage in lieu of money, and because millions of Americans could not afford to pay the doctor, the incentive was successful. The labor unions liked the security it accorded their members, and they made employer-sponsored health care a permanent issue at the collective bargaining table. Thus, with almost all employed persons having health care paid by their employers, the private sector had achieved nearly universal health coverage, at least for those with jobs.

This phenomenon prompted the proponents of government-sponsored universal health care to change their strategy. Because most of the labor force seemed satisfied with employer-sponsored health insurance, they directed their attention to the millions of unemployed, disabled, and elderly Americans. Seemingly overnight, Titles 18 and 19 were added to the Social Security Act, and thus in the mid-1960s Medicare and Medicaid were born. These programs expanded through the years, and by 2000 it could be said that the federal government covered the health care of 50% of Americans. There was no universal government plan, but the combination of all federal health programs (Medicare, Medicaid, Veterans Administration, CHAMPUS, Federal Employees Benefits Program, Indian Affairs, etc.) made the United States government by the year 2000 the largest single payer of health care in the world.

Shortly after the enactment of Medicare and Medicaid, strong interest in universal health care again emerged, championed by Senator Edward (Ted) Kennedy, who had become the chair of the U.S. Senate Subcommittee on Health. Referring in the early 1970s to what he called the "patchwork quilt" of inefficient, duplicative health care in America, he initiated hearings toward the objective of a government-sponsored universal system. NHI seemed imminent when the pendulum abruptly swung the other way. Senator Russell Long, also a Democrat and chair of the overarching Senate Finance Committee, replaced Senator Kennedy with Senator Herman Talmage. The Congress went in the opposite direction and enacted in 1974 the bipartisan HMO Enabling Act. This funded new health maintenance organizations and laid the groundwork for the managed health care era of the 1980s and 1990s, a far-reaching alternative that saw a near-universal system through the industrialization of the private sector.

The Jackson Hole Group, composed of a number of prominent health economists, saw managed competition as the solution to the spiraling costs of health care. They envisaged a system in which an employer provided each employee with a list of approved plans, as many as 20, with various degrees of coverage and copayments, and with some plans requiring the employee to supplement the employer's basic payment. The employee was empowered with knowledge of quality and extensiveness and had an annual choice from among competing plans. The managed care plans that emerged in the 1980s were only partial implementations of this concept, lacking full disclosure and employee choice, but they filled an economic gap. By 2000 there were 175 million Americans who were covered under some form of managed health care. This burgeoning growth was fueled in part by the enactment of Diagnosis Related Groups (DRGs) in 1983, a system in which hospitals are paid for the number of days allotted for each of over 300 diagnostic categories. Because failure to meet the allotments meant that a hospital would lose money, companies designed toward efficiency of care suddenly appeared and prospered.

A serious effort to expand into government-sponsored universal health care was mounted by the Clinton administration. Hillary Rodham Clinton chaired an ill-fated task force in 1993 and 1994 that attempted to meld the concept of managed competition with a federal single-payer plan. It was hampered because it operated in secrecy, and no one was certain what the objectives were. A number of lawsuits under the so-called sunshine laws elicited the fact that most of the task force members were government employees. Most of the prominent health economists who had been invited to join the task force defected, and with its support base eroded, this most recent plan was short-lived.

Currently, the future of universal health care under a government single-payer system is uncertain. There is renewed interest because of increasing problems, but a belief persists among elected officials that tackling health care reform is political suicide. Among the latest problems are the steadily increasing numbers of uninsured (reportedly near 40 million) and the failings of managed care that have brought the health system to the verge of chaos. Judging from the past 60 years, it might be predicted that whatever private or public sector solutions are sought, the federal government's role in providing health care, either directly or indirectly, will increase. Medicare will continue to expand, at first perhaps into prescription drug coverage, as will other government programs. Most health economists oppose government-sponsored health care because the very nature in which it is proposed would ensure that it would go the way of Medicare, Medicaid, and other federal health programs that from their inception were designed to be inefficient. Most ideas on the horizon have their incentives in the wrong direction, encouraging higher costs, waste, and even fraud. Still other health economists have a much different perspective and see the health system to be on the verge of collapse. In their view, a federal single-payer plan is ultimately inevitable. The subject of universal health care continues to evoke strong pro and con positions and little certainty.

Nicholas A. Cummings
University of Nevada, Reno

See also: **Psychotherapy**

UNSTRUCTURED CLINICAL INTERVIEW

The clinical interview has long been regarded as a foundational element of psychiatric and clinical psychological practice (Sullivan, 1954; Wiens, 1976). The interview format, of course, affords the clinician the direct opportunity to solicit from the patient salient, firsthand information regarding his or her presenting problems and the exigencies thereof. This assessment information typically proves germane to the ongoing process of case conceptualization (e.g., diagnosis) and the formulation of appropriate intervention strategies (Scheiber, 1994). In addition, under many circumstances the clinical interview involves the interviewer in the process, not just in assessment, but also in implementing de facto interventions (i.e., acting as an agent of salubrious clinical change during the interview itself).

Despite the existence of literally thousands of assessment instruments—personality inventories, symptom checklists, historical reviews, and so forth—in actual clinical practice the interview is still the most frequently employed assessment procedure (Beutler, 1995). Unlike many other assessment methods, the interview requires no additional expense on the part of therapist or patient; further, it may be tailored to meet the unique needs of each individual patient, may be modified to accommodate implicit or explicit temporal constraints, and may subserve the important function of assisting in the development of rapport and understanding between clinician and patient.

There are three distinctive subtypes of clinical interviewing, most commonly referred to as structured, semistructured, and unstructured. In a structured clinical interview, the interviewer proceeds in verbatim fashion through a predetermined list of questions, each of which may be answered by the patient with short, factual responses (Pope, 1979). Because the structured interview has considerable potential to be experienced by both clinician and patient as contrived and inflexible, such an approach is rarely employed in routine clinical practice, and even in research settings it is less frequently employed than is a related, but more flexible format—the semistructured interview. In the semistructured format, the clinician employs a scripted set of initial queries (still asked verbatim) but is permitted to compose ad hoc follow-up questions tailored to the task of obtaining all necessary clinically relevant information. The Structured Clinical Interview for *DSM-IV* (SCID; First, Spitzer, Gibbon, & Williams, 1995), Longitudinal Interval Follow-up Evaluation (LIFE; Keller et al., 1987), and Anxiety Disorders Interview Schedule–IV (ADIS-IV; DiNardo, Brown, & Barlow, 1994) all serve as examples of commonly employed semistructured interviews.

In rather stark contrast, the unstructured interview does not rely on an a priori set of specified questions; instead, the interview content develops as an emergent result of the clinician-patient interaction. Although the clinician may enter the interview with a set of content domains about which he or she might wish to gather information (e.g., the patient's presenting problems, current level of adaptive function, available social support, prominent psychosocial stressors, coping style, characteristic ego defense mechanisms, etc.), the clinician in an unstructured format quite deliberately refrains from *directing* the interviewee through a predetermined list of queries regarding such content. Rather, the clinician affords the client ample license to initiate and specify much of the interview content and the pace of content coverage. The clinician's role in such an interview format may be defined principally as *skillful interaction,* as opposed to the structured interviewer's role of *skillful direction.* It is to be noted, however, that unstructured interviewing, in comparison with more structured interview formats, has received relatively little in the way of research support vis-à-vis the validity and reliability of the clinical inferences derived therefrom (Segal, Hersen, & Van Hasselt, 1994). Nevertheless, the unstructured interview remains the most commonly employed form of interviewing in the clinical setting (Beutler, 1995).

The unstructured interview format, of course, is closely tied historically to psychoanalytic practice. Within a psychoanalytic conceptual framework, the clinician's creation of an unstructured context is considered to be the essential prerequisite for the patient's subsequent communication of unconscious material (e.g., in the form of so-called transference reactions, free associations, and so forth). It is noteworthy, however, that use of the unstructured interview is not limited to psychoanalytic practice. In fact, unstructured interviewing may be employed by clinicians across the theoretical spectrum, although certainly the focus of the interview will vary somewhat according to the clinician's theoretical orientation. For example, a psychodynamic clinician might show keen interest in the discussion of material regarding the patient's childhood history and familial dynamics (Pope, 1979), whereas a behavior therapist would be more likely to provide subtle reinforcement (e.g., by attending more carefully) for the patient's reporting of specific and detailed information concerning present difficulties and the environmental antecedents and sequelae of such functional problems (Sarwer & Sayers, 1998). The behavior therapist would also likely play a more active role in the interview (e.g., asking more questions) than would her psychodynamic counterpart, while still operating within the broad bounds of the unstructured format by virtue of the deliberate avoidance of predetermined queries.

In the view of many practicing clinicians, the unstructured interview is the format of choice for the efficient gathering of useful clinical information, chiefly due to the extraordinary flexibility associated with the unstructured format. As Johnson (1981) stated, "although haphazard questioning should be avoided, the interview must be loosely enough structured so that the interviewer can pursue avenues of inquiry that present themselves during the course of the interview" (p. 86). Similarly, in order for an interview to be optimally effective, it must be organized around the patient, rather than around a specific psychiatric interview format (MacKinnon & Michels, 1971). Likewise, clinicians from the Rogerian tradition hold that the unstructured format, by virtue of its implicit insistence that the clinician attend to the issues and topics raised by the patient (rather than vice versa), may more easily facilitate the establishment of a positive therapeutic alliance (e.g., Rogers, 1951). However, as we will see, despite the possible intuitive appeal of the aforementioned claims, they have received very little in the way of empirical corroboration.

Format Variables

Unstructured interviewing is a difficult skill to acquire. It is not surprising, therefore, that clinical training programs (e.g., master's and doctoral programs of clinical psychology, counseling psychology, social work, and—less so—psychiatric residency programs) typically devote considerable attention to the development of such skills among their students. Interviewing is typically taught with an overt emphasis on the cultivation of listening skills (as opposed to questioning skills, per se), perhaps because it is not uncommon for the novice clinician to conduct interviews in an ineffectual manner that might charitably be described as a barrage of questions. The acquisition of solid unstructured interviewing skills typically requires considerable practice, in addition to a capacity on the part of the interviewer for critical self-reflection (in order to learn from one's inevitable interviewing missteps) and a recognition of the fact that the interview is based, ultimately, on a human relationship (Johnson, 1981). In an attempt to facilitate the training of interviewing skills, various clinical theorists have subdivided the interview into discrete phases, steps, or objectives.

Harry Stack Sullivan, a seminal figure in both the theory and practice of American psychiatry, was one of the first clinicians to give extensive attention to the interview process. In his still-influential book, *The Clinical Interview* (1954), he described four principal stages characteristic of the unstructured interview (along with the caveat that such stages be recognized as "hypothetical, fictional, abstract, and artificial"). These four stages Sullivan termed the *inception,* the *reconnaissance,* the *detailed inquiry,* and the *termination.* The inception includes the clinician's welcoming of the patient and the establishment of what is to be expected from the interview. The reconnaissance stage consists of questioning regarding the patient's history, social situation, and therapeutic needs. During the inquiry stage, the clinician begins to test various clinically relevant hypotheses, especially those germane to the patient's presenting set of problems. The fourth stage, termination, refers to the delicate process of ending the interview in mutually satisfactory fashion.

A somewhat related, contemporary description of the unstructured interview process is to be found in Shea's (1988) proposed five-phase structural model. This model suggests a broad interview outline that may prove especially helpful for the beginning interviewer and that appears applicable to most forms of unstructured interviewing, regardless of the theoretical context within which the interview occurs. Phase one, the introduction, refers to the initial contact between patient and therapist. During this phase, the therapist may attempt to put the patient at east with conversational small talk and to educate the patient about the interview process itself. Phase two, the opening, entails the clinician's encouraging the patient to provide a first-person account of presenting problems, elicited by a statement such as "Tell me what brought you to therapy." Phase three is the body of the interview. During this phase, the interviewer works to gather relevant information based on material presented during the opening. Such information will subsequently be used by the clinician in the process of case conceptualization and treatment planning. During the closing phase, the interviewer begins the simultaneous process of summarizing material covered during the interview and communicating the clinician's own conceptualization of the manner in which the patient's problems may be optimally addressed—a process that often helps foster a sense of hopefulness in the patient (Frank & Frank, 1991). The final phase, termination, describes the formal cessation of the interview and the exiting of the patient. Shea's model nicely illustrates the point that although the interview format may remain unstructured (inasmuch as the questions and wording thereof are not planned prior to the session), the interviewer typically retains a general idea of the sequence and flow of the interview.

Relationship Variables

Regardless of its degree of structure, the interview process provides the clinician with an implicit opportunity to cultivate a therapeutic alliance with the patient. Moreover, the flexibility of the unstructured situation permits the therapist considerable latitude to respond empathically to the stated concerns of the patient while also providing the patient with an opportunity to observe the clinician's distinctive interpersonal style in action. What, though, are the actual strategies to be employed by the interviewer in promoting a positive working alliance? On the basis of considerable clinical observation and research evidence, Carl Rogers (1961) suggested a set of general principles that may guide the clinician in such an endeavor, among them (1) maintaining a nonjudgmental attitude toward the patient and toward the material that he or she relates during the interview, (2) viewing the patient with unconditional positive regard, (3) reflecting accurate empathy, and (4) conveying a sense of authenticity and genuineness. In a similar vein, Othmer and Othmer (1994) identified a set of guiding principles that may be employed by the clinician to help facilitate clinician-patient rapport, notably, putting the patient at ease with the interview situation (e.g., by greeting the patient in a warm yet professional manner), determining the source of the patient's suffering and showing appropriate empathy, assessing the patient's own (subjective) understanding of his or her problems, communicating a sense of being on their side, and acting as a credible clinical expert.

Research

Despite the ubiquity of the unstructured interview in clinical practice, it is noteworthy that there is a paucity of research concerning its clinical utility. Nevertheless, a handful of published investigations have some bearing on this issue. Following is a brief summary of the relevant literature.

As noted previously, the unstructured interview is employed primarily as a method of clinical assessment—that is, as a means of gathering information pertinent to case conceptualization (e.g., diagnosis) and treatment planning. But how valid and reliable is the information obtained in the unstructured interview format? With respect to the assignment of *DSM*-based diagnoses, the scant available evidence suggests that unstructured interviews may be inferior to structured and semistructured diagnostic interviews with respect to both the reliability and validity of interview-based diagnoses (Segal et al., 1994; Vitiello, Malone, Buschle, & Delaney, 1990; Widiger, Sanderson, & Warner, 1986; Young, O'Brien, Gutterman, & Cohen, 1987). In fact, it appears that structured interviewing exhibits psychometric properties superior to unstructured interviewing even regarding the assessment of the patient's psychiatric social history (Ferriter, 1993) and treatment expectations (Ruggeri, Dall'Agnola, Agostini, & Bisoffi, 1994). Additional support for the hypothesis of the generally poor psychometric properties of unstructured interviews comes from a recent meta-analysis of the use of structured versus unstructured interview formats in employment selection decisions (McDaniel, Whetzel, Schmidt, & Maurer, 1994). Finally, there is some evidence that the unstructured interviewer's own beliefs and preconceptions may exert a biasing effect on the interview process itself, affecting what the patient is willing to discuss in the ongoing reciprocal process of selecting seemingly pertinent information (Gordon, 1969).

In light of the continued widespread utilization of unstructured interviewing as a principal source of information on which clinical diagnoses are assigned, it is rather puzzling that clinical researchers have given so little attention to clarifying the extent to which such a practice may be regarded as reliable and valid. Certainly, on the basis of the scant available evidence, there is some reason to question the psychometric soundness of such a practice, but it is equally clear that more systematic evaluation is necessary before any unequivocal conclusions may be drawn. Similarly, we are aware of no published investigations of the claim that unstructured interviews are superior to structured interviews in the facilitation of the therapeutic alliance. This would appear, therefore, to be another important domain for future clinical investigation.

REFERENCES

Beutler, L. E. (1995). The clinical interview. In L. E. Beutler & M. R. Berren (Eds.), *Integrative assessment of adult personality* (pp. 94–120). New York: Guilford Press.

DiNardo, P., Brown, T., & Barlow, D. (1994). *Anxiety Disorders Interview Schedule for DSM-IV.* Albany, NY: Greywind.

Ferriter, M. (1993). Computer aided interviewing and the psychiatric social history. *Social Work and Social Sciences Review, 4,* 255–263.

First, M. B., Spitzer, R. L., Gibbon, M., & Williams, J. W. B. (1995). *Structured Clinical Interview for Axis I DSM-IV Disorders–Patient Edition (SCID-I/P, Version 2.0).* New York: Biometrics Research Department, New York State Psychiatric Institute.

Frank, J. D., & Frank, J. B. (1991). *Persuasion and healing: A comparative study of psychotherapy.* Baltimore: Johns Hopkins University Press.

Gordon, R. L. (1969). *Interviewing: Strategies, techniques, and tactics.* Homewood, IL: Dorsey.

Johnson, W. R. (1981). Basic interviewing skills. In C. E. Walker (Ed.), *Clinical practice of psychology: A guide for mental health professionals.* Elmsford, NY: Pergamon Press.

Keller, M. B., Lavori, P. W., Friedman, B., Nielsen, E., Endicott, J., & McDonald-Scott, P. A. (1987). The Longitudinal Interval Follow-up Evaluation: A comprehensive method for assessing outcome in prospective longitudinal studies. *Archives of General Psychiatry, 44,* 540–548.

MacKinnon, R. A., & Michels, R. (1971). *The psychiatric interview in clinical practice.* Philadelphia: W. B. Saunders.

McDaniel, M. A., Whetzel, D. L., Schmidt, F. L., & Maurer, S. D. (1994). The validity of employment interviews: A comprehensive review and meta-analysis. *Journal of Applied Psychology, 79,* 599–616.

Othmer, E., & Othmer, S. C. (1994). *The clinical interview using DSM-IV: Vol. 1. Fundamentals.* Washington, DC: American Psychiatric Press.

Pope, B. (1979). *The mental health interview: Research and application.* Elmsford, NY: Pergamon Press.

Rogers, C. (1951). *Client-centered therapy.* Boston: Houghton-Mifflin.

Rogers, C. (1961). *On becoming a person.* Boston: Houghton-Mifflin.

Ruggeri, M., Dall'Agnola, R., Agostini, C., & Bisoffi, G. (1994). Acceptability, sensitivity and content validity of the VECS and VSSS in measuring expectations and satisfaction in psychiatric patients and their relatives. *Social Psychiatry and Psychiatric Epidemiology, 29,* 265–276.

Sarwer, D. B., & Sayers, S. L. (1998). Behavioral interviewing. In A. S. Bellack & M. Hersen (Eds.), *Behavioral assessment: A practical handbook* (4th ed.). Boston: Allyn & Bacon.

Scheiber, S. C. (1994). The psychiatric interview, psychiatric history, and mental status examination. In R. E. Hales & S. C. Yudofsky (Eds.), *The American Psychiatric Press textbook of psychiatry* (2nd ed.). Washington, DC: American Psychiatric Press.

Segal, D. L., Hersen, M., & Van Hasselt, V. B. (1994). Reliability of the Structured Clinical Interview for DSM-III-R: An evaluative review. *Comprehensive Psychiatry, 35,* 316–327.

Shea, S. C. (1988). *Psychiatric interviewing: The art of understanding.* Philadelphia: W. B. Saunders.

Sullivan, H. S. (1954). *The psychiatric interview.* New York: W. W. Norton.

Vitiello, B., Malone, R., Buschle, P. R., & Delaney, M. A. (1990). Reliability of *DSM-III* diagnoses of hospitalized children. *Hospital and Community Psychiatry, 41,* 63–67.

Widiger, T. A., Sanderson, C., & Warner, L. (1986). The MMPI, prototypal typology, and borderline personality disorder. *Journal of Personality Assessment, 50,* 540–553.

Wiens, A. N. (1976). The assessment interview. In I. B. Weiner (Ed.), *Clinical method in psychology.* New York: Wiley.

Young, J. G., O'Brien, J. D., Gutterman, E. M., & Cohen, P. (1987). Research on the clinical interview. *Journal of the American Academy of Child and Adolescent Psychiatry, 26,* 613–620.

Stephen S. Ilardi
Ann D. Branstetter
University of Kansas

V

VALIDITY

Validity refers to the extent to which a test accurately assesses the construct it purports to measure. Essentially, validity has to do with the meaningfulness and usefulness of the specific inferences made from test scores. For a measure of psychoticism, the question of its validity would be whether it actually measures psychotic traits or psychotic behavior. There is an old adage that states a test can be reliable (i.e., stable and consistent) but not valid, but a test cannot be valid without first being reliable. The question of a test's validity is both an empirical issue and a theoretical one. The validity of any psychological test cannot be absolutely established but only relatively established because there is no gold standard of validity in measurement. There are also many different types of validity, including face, content, criterion, and construct validity.

Face validity is perhaps the simplest type of validity. Face validity can refer to a single item or to all of the items on a test, and it indicates how well the item reveals the purpose or meaning of the test item or the test itself. For example, the test item "Recently I have thought of killing myself" has obvious face validity as an item measuring suicidal ideation. The downside of items on tests with clear face validity is that they may be easily manipulated by respondents, either to deny or hide problems or to malinger or exaggerate problems. Some psychometricians appreciate tests that lack face validity but still possess general validity. Tests or items that still measure what they purport to measure but lack face validity are harder for respondents to manipulate.

The *content validity* of a test refers to the adequacy of sampling of content across the construct or trait being measured. Given the published literature on a particular trait, are all aspects of that concept represented by items on the test? Consider an example of conduct disorder in childhood. If a literature search reveals two major aspects of a conduct disorder, namely delinquency and aggression, then the items on the tests should measure these two aspects in relatively equal proportion. Some test makers also rely on experts in that field. The test makers will devise a means of summarizing what the experts claim to be the nature of a particular construct and then create test items to reflect what the experts' consensus was about that construct. Items measuring a trait should appear in equal proportion to what the literature search reveals or what the experts claim about that particular construct.

Criterion validity (also called predictive or concurrent validity) refers to the comparison of scores on a test with some other external measure of performance. The other measure should be theoretically related to the first measure, and their relationship can be assessed by a simple correlation coefficient. Some psychometricians further divide criterion validity into predictive or concurrent validity. With predictive validity, the new test is given to a group of participants who are followed over time to see how well the original assessment predicts some important variable at a later point in time. In concurrent validity (which is far more common), a proposed test is given to a group of participants who complete other theoretically related measures concurrently (at the same point in time). How can a test maker demonstrate concurrent validity if he or she is the first to create such a test? Unfortunately, this is not done as easily. The test maker must use other forms of validity (other than concurrent) if there are no other known measures of that construct. This problem is particularly thorny for diagnostic measures in psychology. Because there are no definitive biological markers and no blood tests used for the diagnosis of any mental disorder, this lack of a so-called gold standard for diagnostic accuracy makes it difficult to assess the criterion-related validity of any psychological test.

Construct validity refers to the extent to which a test captures a specific theoretical construct or trait, and it overlaps with some of the other aspects of validity. This requires a test to be anchored in a conceptual framework or theory that delineates clearly the meaning of the construct, its uniqueness, and its relationship to other variables measuring similar domains. Psychometricians typically assess construct validity by giving other measures of a trait along with the new proposed measure of a trait and then testing prior hypothesized relationships among the measures. In the example of the new Jones Conduct Disorder scale, Jones might also give measures of attention-deficit/hyperactivity disorder (ADHD), altruism, and executive functions deficits (organization and planning problems). Jones might hypothesize that if the new measure of conduct disorder possesses construct validity, then it should correlate positively with ADHD (because the literature suggests a strong comorbidity among the two disorders), correlate negatively with altruism (which might be a clinical intuition without evidence from the literature), and correlate positively with executive function deficits (also consistent with the literature). Note that the hypothesized relationships include a mixture of what the construct should show a meaningful positive relationship to and show a meaningful negative relationship to. The new measure should also show weak relationships to other constructs that are theoretically unrelated to it (e.g., eye color or depression). The type of relationships found, if they are consistent with expected results, help to establish the construct validity of the new test.

There is no single method for determining the construct validity of a test. Usually, many different methods and approaches are combined to present an overall picture of the construct validity of a test. Besides the correlational approach described earlier, another frequently used method is factor analysis. A factor analysis helps a test maker clarify the underlying nature of a new test, and it can help the test maker in modifying the new test to make it better (e.g., more comprehensive, more consistent with the literature, etc.).

Another method of establishing a test's construct validity is discriminant validity. For example, a group of repeat male juvenile offenders should score higher on the new conduct disorder scale than would a group of choirboys. School bullies should score higher than their victims on the conduct disorder scale. All of these methods and designs should be used to establish the construct validity of a test. A test manual should report all of the evidence for a test's construct validity, and the more evidence there is, the better.

Frederick L. Coolidge
Daniel L. Segal
University of Colorado at Colorado Springs

See also: **Psychometrics; Reliability; Validity**

VIDEO: MAJOR APPLICATIONS IN BEHAVIORAL SCIENCE

Video is used in psychology and neuroscience to gather and disperse information and to help people change (behavior, feelings, attitudes) and as experimental stimuli. These uses are summarized here (cf. Dowrick, 1991).

Analyzing and Documenting

The most extensive use of video in behavioral science is to capture and analyze the actions and interactions of humans and other species. Video has been widely used in the analysis of motor activity, nonverbal communication, and social interaction and for medical diagnosis and surveillance. Recently, digital video equipment has replaced high-speed cine film in the analysis of complex movements in dance and athletics. Comparative psychologists have used video to study animal behavior from the courtship of the praying mantis to language development in gorillas.

Video analysis of facial expression is a highly developed methodology that has been extended to social interactions. With enough resources, video allows any level of analysis once a coding system has been operationalized. It is also possible to take video (moving) X rays for medical clarification in such situations as the inability to swallow.

Video can be used in surveillance, such as in sleep laboratories (with infrared lighting) or from cameras mounted in the motor vehicles of drug-influenced drivers. Sometimes video is used for more general documentation, such as tracking clients' progress through treatment.

Educational Videos

Videos, including CDs and DVDs, are often designed for the purposes of instructing and informing. Research into this medium has been unsystematic, although some training packages have been thoroughly evaluated. Most information influencing production (style, length, pace, etc.) comes from the entertainment and public relations industries. A rapidly expanding strategy involves interactive multimedia, in which computer software uses the student's responses to alter exposure to learning materials and tasks. Promising applications can be listed under three broad headings.

The first is classroom education—in schools (e.g., multimedia for learning to read), in universities (e.g., illustrations of attribution theory), and on the job (e.g., supported employment). Applications in this area increasingly include digital technology. The second area is clinical treatment preparation. Patients and family members are shown previews of medical procedures. The third area is lifestyle education, including childhood development and consequences of drug use. Some use, with much promise, exists for special populations (e.g., deaf, physical disabilities).

Peer Modeling

To support people in learning skills, video is widely used to provide demonstrations of effective behavior by a like-person in a like-situation. The range of professional training applications go from divorce mediation to flying an airplane. Other productive areas are social skills, daily living, and sport. The potential for appropriately designed modeling videos for diverse populations is promising but underdeveloped.

Strategies for video-based modeling have not extended much beyond those for live models (similar, multiple, coping). However, there is clear advantage in the potential for repetitive review (with unvarying information), close-ups, slow motion, and so on to the benefit of the learning situation and lower costs.

Self-Modeling

Self-modeling is a procedure in which people see themselves showing only adaptive behavior (Dowrick, 1999). Although video is the best known medium for this procedure, audiotapes, photographs, stories in print, role play, and individuals' imaginations are also used. Researched interventions exist for a wide variety of applications: disruptive behavior, selective mutism, anxiety, Olympic sports, social skills, safety, and others.

The most effective form of self-modeling uses *feedforward,* a term coined to refer to images of desired skills not yet achieved, often created by scripting and editing. For example, a child cannot read independently, but he can point at the words and repeat a phrase at a time; these elements can be videotaped separately and edited to look like realistic independent reading.

A related strategy is *positive self-review,* which refers to watching selectively compiled best examples of skills infrequently or inconsistently achieved. For example, a volleyball player might view videos of her best service, overhead slam, and so on after a full day of many attempts.

Self-modeling videos are typically 2–3 minutes long and reviewed about once a day, for a total of six or more viewings, for maximum effect. They can be reviewed again after 2 or 3 months if a maintenance booster is desired.

Self-Confrontation and Feedback

The practice of video feedback is frequently used, although its theoretical basis remains in dispute. Seeing oneself in personally demanding situations can improve self-assessment. Video feedback is thus applied in many ways: competitive sports, professional skills, interpersonal communication, and so on. It appears to be most effective when the behavior to achieve improvement is clearly indicated and some additional support (e.g., coaching) is provided.

Another value of viewing oneself on video may come from motivational or emotional impact. The effect of seeing a poor performance on video, without being able to undo it, can range from despair and anxiety to increased engagement and determination to succeed. Thus the procedure is risky.

Scene Setting

The use of video to promote discussions, memories, emotions, or judgments is common but understudied in practice. The use of interpersonal process recall (reviewing videotapes to reexamine thoughts and feelings associated with specific actions) has been widely used to teach interviewing and counseling.

The term *triggers* was coined to refer to videos that provoke discussions in group learning experiences. These are typically very short, unresolved vignettes on contentious topics (e.g., child abuse, cultural attitudes). Vignettes are seldom reported in therapy, except some promising uses in social skills training, exposure therapy, and sex therapy. A related use of video is the developmental impact for people (e.g., teens with emotional disturbance, criminal offenders) who take part in scripting and producing their own videos, sometimes airing them on public access television.

Experimental Stimuli

Many research studies mention the use of video vignettes, but the methodological principles are minimally defined. Video content may provide the independent variable (e.g., scowling in one vignette, smiling in another), or video may be contrasted with another medium (e.g., seeing oneself in videos vs. a mirror). It is common to use a single vignette, creating different conditions by labeling (e.g., "she has attention deficit" vs. "she is disruptive") or using different categories of subjects (e.g., experts vs. novices).

Video can even be a dependent variable, as when subjects adjust a distorted image to meet some criterion (e.g., perception of body size).

Conclusion

The potential for using video in behavioral science is ready for another expansion. Improving technology and easier editing, with or without computers, present new opportunities.

REFERENCES

Dowrick, P. W. (1991). *Practical guide to using video in the behavioral sciences.* New York: Wiley.

Dowrick, P. W. (1999). A review of self modeling and related interventions. *Applied and Preventive Psychology, 8,* 23–39.

Peter W. Dowrick
University of Hawaii at Manoa

See also: **Modeling**

VINELAND SOCIAL MATURITY SCALE

Originally developed by Edgar A. Doll, the Vineland Social Maturity Scale represented an early attempt to measure social competence. Doll, in his *Measurement of Social Competence,* defined social competence as "a functional composite of human traits which subserves social usefulness as reflected in self-sufficiency and in service to others" (1953, p. 3). This component of human behavior has also been termed *adaptive behavior,* has been incorporated as a major component in the definition of mental retardation, and has been the focus of considerable measurement effort over the past few decades.

The Vineland evaluates social competence from a developmental perspective and was normed on males and females from birth to 30 years of age. Assessment using the Vineland typically involves interviewing a person who is familiar with the individual being evaluated (e.g., parent, sibling). The interview is intended to determine the behaviors customarily performed by the target person. In some circumstances observations or direct interviews with the person being assessed are used.

Multiple revisions of the Vineland have been undertaken. Now entitled the Vineland Adaptive Behavior Scales (VABS), it consists of multiple scales including the Classroom Edition, the Interview Edition-Survey Form, and the Interview Edition-Expanded Form. The VABS covers birth through early adulthood and older individuals with disabilities. Third parties still represent major sources of information with the Classroom Edition being completed by teachers and the Interview Edition-Expanded Form being administered to parents. Several assessment domains are addressed, including communication skills, daily living skills, socialization, motor skills, and maladaptive behavior. The VABS samples a variety of behavioral elements, making it useful for a variety of clinical applications. The VABS has also established itself as a useful measurement tool for a broad range of research on developmental status and intellectual conditions ranging from Alzheimer's disease to the effects of social circumstances such as poverty. Although questions have been raised about its norm group, the sample was reasonably large and was drawn nationally. Considerable training is needed to administer the assessment, and care must be taken in scoring and interpretation.

SUGGESTED READING

Aiken, L. R. (1997). *Psychological testing and assessment* (9th ed.). Boston: Allyn & Bacon.

Coll, C. G., Buckner, J. C., Brooks, M. G., Weinreb, L. F., & Bassuk, E. L. (1998). The developmental status and adaptive behavior of homeless and low-income housed infants and toddlers. *American Journal of Public Health, 88,* 1371–1373.

Crayton, L., Oliver, C., Holland, A., Bradbury, J., & Hall, S. (1998). The neuropsychological assessment of age related cognitive deficits in adults with Down's syndrome. *Journal of Applied Research in Intellectual Disabilities, 11,* 255–272.

Doll, E. A. (1953). *Measurement of social competence.* Circle Pines, MN: American Guidance Service.

Gregory, R. J. (1996). *Psychological testing: History, principles, and applications* (2nd ed.). Boston: Allyn & Bacon.

Clifford J. Drew
University of Utah

VIRTUAL REALITY EXPOSURE THERAPY

Virtual reality (VR) offers a new human-computer interaction paradigm in which users are no longer simply external observers of images on a computer screen but are active participants within a computer-generated three-dimensional virtual world. Virtual environments differ from traditional displays in that computer graphics and various display and input technologies are integrated to give the user a sense of presence or immersion in the virtual environment.

The most common approach to the creation of a virtual environment is to outfit the user with a head-mounted display (HMD). HMDs consist of separate display screens for each eye, along with some type of display optics and a head-tracking device. This technology integrates real-time computer graphics, body tracking devices, visual displays, and other sensory input devices to immerse a participant in a computer-generated virtual environment that changes in a natural way with head and body motion. For some environments, users may also hold a second position sensor or joystick in their hands, allowing them to manipulate or move around the virtual environment, for example, to use a virtual hand to push an elevator button and ascend.

Exposure therapy is the treatment of choice for many of the anxiety disorders, especially when avoidance is a prominent symptom. Virtual reality exposure therapy (VRE) has been introduced as a new medium of exposure therapy; it is intended to be a component of a comprehensive treatment package and is recommended at the point in therapy at which exposure therapy would be introduced. It has the advantages of allowing time-consuming exposure therapy without leaving the therapist's office and offers more control over exposure stimuli and less exposure of the patient to possible harm or embarrassment. In VRE the therapist makes appropriate comments and encourages continued exposure until anxiety habituates. The patient is allowed to progress at his or her own pace. The therapist simultaneously views on a video monitor all of the virtual environments with which the patient is interacting and therefore is able to comment appropriately. The therapist is present in the room at all times, although she or he is not visible to the patient wearing the HMD, which covers the eyes. For loud virtual environments such as the Virtual Vietnam, the therapist communicates with the patient via a microphone heard over the earphones. VRE has been applied to several anxiety disorders at this point in time.

VRE was incorporated in the treatment of acrophobia (fear of heights) in the first published controlled study to apply VR to the treatment of a psychological disorder (Rothbaum et al., 1995). Subjects were repeatedly exposed to virtual footbridges of varying heights and stability, outdoor balconies of varying heights, and a glass elevator that ascended 50 floors. VRE was effective in significantly reducing the fear of and improving attitudes toward heights, whereas no change was noted in the waiting-list control group. More important, 7 of the 10 who completed VRE treatment exposed themselves to height situations in real life during treatment, although they had not been instructed to do so.

VRE was compared to standard exposure (SE) therapy and to a waiting list (WL) control in the treatment of the fear of flying (Rothbaum, Hodges, Smith, Lee, & Price, 2000). Treatment consisted of eight individual therapy sessions conducted over six weeks, with four sessions of anxiety management training followed by either exposure to a virtual airplane (VRE) or exposure to an actual airplane at the airport (SE). For participants in the VRE group, exposure in the virtual airplane included sitting in the virtual airplane, taxi, takeoff, landing, and flying in both calm and turbulent weather. The results indicated that each active treatment was superior to WL and that there were no differences between VRE and SE. Participants receiving VRE or SE showed substantial improvement on all measures. By the 6-month follow-up, 90% of treated participants had flown since completing treatment. It is important that participants maintained their treatment gains one year following treatment completion (Rothbaum, Hodges, Anderson, Price, & Smith, in press).

VRE has also been adapted for Vietnam combat veterans with posttraumatic stress disorder (PTSD). There are two Virtual Vietnam environments: a virtual clearing and a virtual Huey helicopter. The virtual clearing, often referred to as a landing zone, includes several trees and a bunker surrounded by jungle. The virtual Huey helicopter flies over Vietnam terrain, which includes rice paddies, jungle, and a river. Audio effects include the sound of the rotors (blades), gunfire, bombs, engine sounds, radio chatter, and male voices yelling "Move out! Move out!" Visual effects include the interior of the helicopter in which the backs of the pilot's and copilot's heads are visible, as well as the instrument control panel, and the view out of the side door, including aerial shots of other helicopters flying past, clouds, and the terrain below. The therapist assists the patient in imaginal exposure to his most traumatic memories while immersed in Vietnam stimuli. Preliminary evidence suggests this Virtual Vietnam may hold promise (Rothbaum, Hodges, Ready, Graap, & Alarcon, 2001).

Applications are in place or are currently being developed for the fears of driving, thunderstorms, and public speaking, as well as for several agoraphobic situations such as shopping malls.

REFERENCES

Rothbaum, B. O., Hodges, L. F., Anderson, P. L., Price, L., & Smith, S. (in press). Twelve-month follow-up of virtual reality exposure therapy for the fear of flying. *Journal of Consulting and Clinical Psychology.*

Rothbaum, B. O., Hodges, L. F., Kooper, R., Opdyke, D., Williford, J., & North, M. M. (1995). Effectiveness of virtual reality graded exposure in the treatment of acrophobia. *American Journal of Psychiatry, 152,* 626–628.

Rothbaum, B. O., Hodges, L. F., Ready, D., Graap, K., & Alarcon, R. (2001). Virtual reality exposure therapy for Vietnam veterans with posttraumatic stress disorder. *Journal of Clinical Psychiatry, 62,* 617–622.

Rothbaum, B. O., Hodges, L. F., Smith, S., Lee, J. H., & Price, L. (2000). A controlled study of virtual reality exposure therapy for the fear of flying. *Journal of Consulting and Clinical Psychology, 68,* 1020–1026.

Barbara O. Rothbaum
Emory University School of Medicine

See also: **Behavior Therapy**

VISUAL ILLUSIONS

Illusions have fascinated students of vision for over 2,000 years, but what constitutes an illusion has changed over that period. Almost the whole of visual science is now concerned with illusions—if these are defined as systematic departures of perceptual from physical measurements of a stimulus. But what is the physical description of a stick that is partially immersed in water? It is straight if the stick itself is measured, but not if a photograph is taken of it partially immersed. For this reason (among others), a distinction is made between the distal and proximal stimuli (the physical stimulus and its projection onto the retina). If the light striking the retina (the proximal stimulus) has been transformed in some way, it would be remiss not to incorporate that knowledge in the analysis of its perception. Therefore, psychologists would say that an illusion occurs when there is a mismatch between the proximal stimulus and perception. Theories of illusions abound, and none is widely accepted; a more modest (neuroscience) approach involves relating particular effects to known processes in the visual system.

Illusions are better understood when intermediate measures of stimulus processing are correlated with perception. For example, the radiating spokes seen in Figure 1A can be related to the optics of the eye: Dynamic changes in the axis of transient astigmatism could lead to these effects. The light and dark dots that are visible at the intersections of the lines in Figure 1B have been interpreted in terms of the activity of concentric receptive fields at early stages in visual processing. It is possible to classify illusions according to the levels in the visual system to which the distortions are assigned.

Many cells in the visual cortex respond to lines or edges in specific orientations, and in monkey cortex they have orientation bandwidths of around ±20 deg of the preferred orientation. Illusions of orientation provide possible matching neural correlates. The horizontal parallel lines in Figure 1C do not appear so when intersected by inclined lines. The perception of orientation must be based on the activity of many orientation selective cells and with interactions between them. The Zöllner illusion could point to a bias in the peak of the distribution by the surrounding contours, mod-

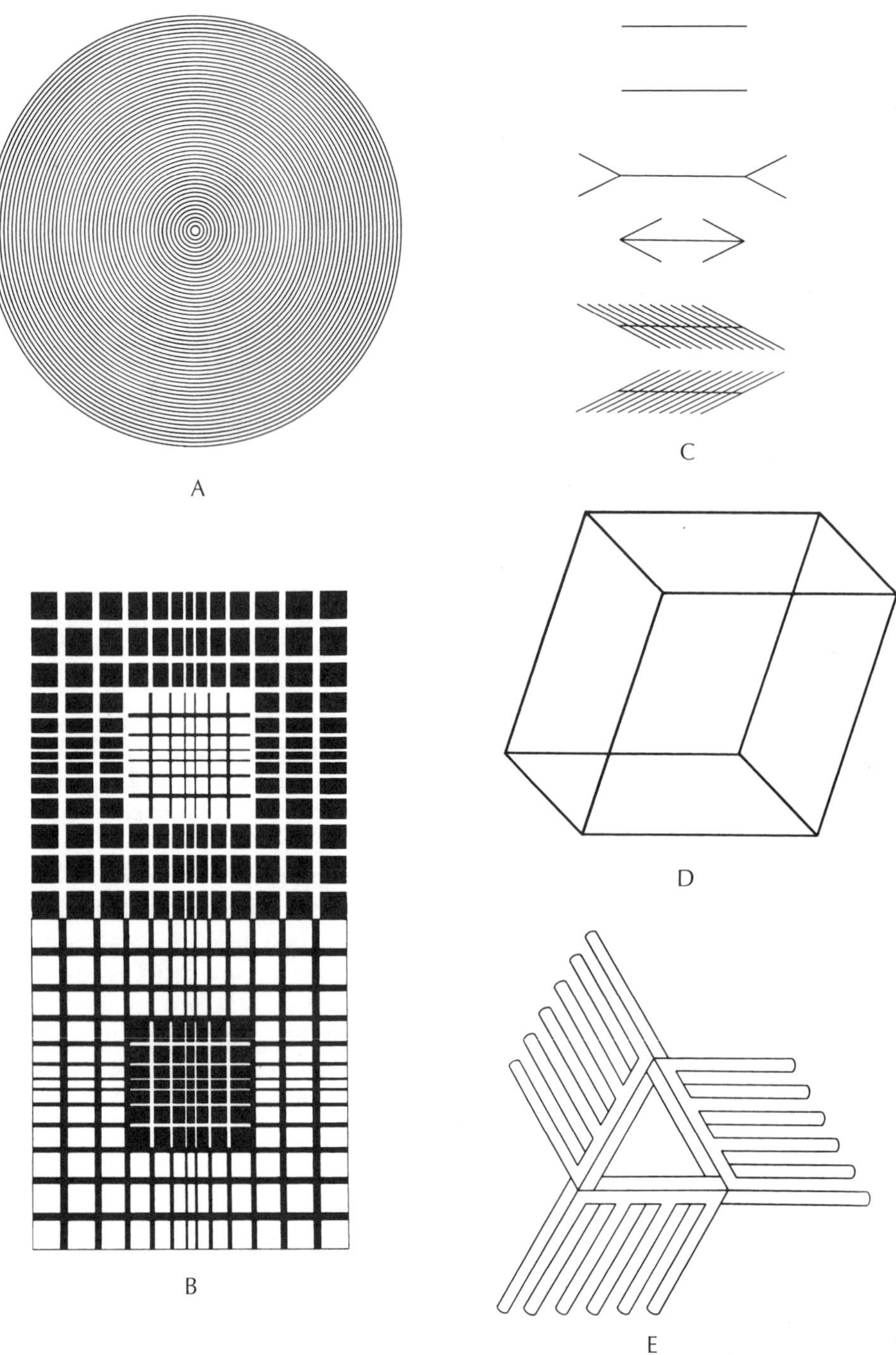

Figure 1. (A) Purkinje's illusion. (B) Hermann-Herring grids. (C) The paired horizontal lines are the same length and parallel in each of the three cases, but their apparent lengths can be modified by attaching fins to the ends (Müller-Lyer illusion), and the apparent orientation can be changed by the directions of the intersecting lines (Zöllner illusion). The gaps between the cross-hatched lines produce illusory contours. (D) Necker rhomboid. (E) Double impossible figure.

ification of the receptive field properties of particular cells by their immediate context, or neural inhibition from the cells with similar receptive field orientations. In addition to the simultaneous biasing of perceived orientation, there are tilt aftereffects: Observation of inclined lines for some seconds results in subsequently viewed vertical lines appearing tilted in the opposite direction. Such simple manifestations are only correlations, and the link between correlation and causation is notoriously tenuous. Increasingly, studies measure both perception and neurophysiology in the same animals so that this link can be strengthened.

Visual illusions are mostly associated with certain figures produced in the late nineteenth century (Figure 1C). The Müller-Lyer figure provides a compelling illusion of perceived length, and it has been studied experimentally perhaps more than any other, but its basis remains elusive. Visual illusions are generally classified as distortions of orientation or size, and for a long time the former have been taken to provide the better links with neuroscience, but the situation is now changing. Functional distinctions between dorsal and ventral streams of visual cortical processing have been attributed to defining an object's location and identity, respectively. A current reinterpretation is in terms of perception and action: The dorsal stream is said to be concerned with motor control and the ventral with perceptual representation. The difference between the way size illusions look to us and the way we respond to them is taken to support the latter distinction. While our perception is distorted by these patterns, our motor control is not. If sticks were positioned in place of the horizontal lines in the Müller-Lyer figure, observers would adjust their fingers to the appropriate physical length rather than their perceived inequality.

Visual neuroscience is generally concerned with neural and behavioral responses to contours or colors. For the distal stimulus, contours are usually defined as luminance discontinuities, and these can be enhanced by lateral inhibition at early stages of visual processing. However, some stimuli involve seeing discontinuities of brightness where no luminance differences exist. They can be induced by line terminations as in the case of the gaps in the Zöllner figure. Such illusory contours behave much like physical ones—they interact with one another and can produce aftereffects.

Pictures provide allusions to objects, and tricks can be played with the transition from three to two dimensions. Pictures incorporate ambiguities and impossibilities that are rarely or never present in objects. One such ambiguity is the depth that is represented in simple line drawings (Figure 1D): The front face appears to be pointing either down and to the right or up and left. The picture is interpreted as representing a three-dimensional structure, but there is insufficient detail (for occluding contours, perspective convergence, or texture) to define which parts would be near and which far. However, both depth interpretations are not entertained simultaneously: The perception flips from one possibility to the other, so that the apparent depth undergoes reversals. Other pictures are far more paradoxical and have been called impossible. A rectangular rod can be depicted by three lines and a quadrilateral, whereas a cylinder can be described by only two lines and an ellipse (Figure 1E). They are called impossible figures because the solid objects to which they allude could not be constructed.

Pictorial allusions, like ambiguities and impossibilities, are fascinating to figure out, but it is not readily apparent whether there are corresponding links to neuroscience. Indeed, searching for them might point us in the wrong direction because such ambiguities rarely occur with objects. Pictures are complex symbolic stimuli that have a relatively recent history in evolutionary terms. Understanding pictures generally and distortions within them will probably require a more cognitive interpretation.

Nick J. Wade
University of Wade

VISUAL IMPAIRMENT: PSYCHOLOGICAL IMPLICATIONS

Among the most important functions that normally rely on visual capacity are orientation in space as well as the recognition and coordination of behavioral options to be executed in the environment. In humans, cultural techniques such as reading also depend heavily on visual capacity. Vision can also be regarded as a typical environment-related capability; that is, vision is essential for the transaction between the person and his or her environment, especially the physical environment. In contrast, hearing is more concerned with communication (i.e., the social environment).

Clarification of Terms

Terms that are most often, and sometimes interchangeably, used in the literature as well as in the practical field are visual impairment, blindness, legal blindness, and low vision. The term *legal blindness* denotes individuals eligible for government and agency benefits and services. Legal blindness is defined as a visual acuity of 20/200 or less in the better eye with the best correction (normal visual acuity is defined as 20/20, that is, a person with a visual acuity of 20/200 must be at 20 feet to see what a person with normal sight sees at 200 feet distance) or a visual field of no more than 20 degrees (the normal visual field is 175 to 180 degrees). Visual impairment not meeting these criteria can nevertheless interfere with independent functioning and the activities of daily living as well as psychological outcomes, which has been underscored by terms such as *low vision.* Frequently, a visual acuity of 20/70 or less is used as a criterion for low vision; also, difficulty or disability in reading normal newspaper print using the best possible correction has been applied in survey and epidemiology research as a functional definition of low vision.

Prevalence

Although vision loss can occur through the whole life span, it should be noted that about 70% of those affected by visual impairment are beyond the age of 60 years and that about 90% of these have experienced their loss only late in their lives. The positive age correlation persists into very old age:

Whereas around 15% of those 65 and older suffer from visual impairment, the percentage roughly doubles in those aged 85 years and over. Aging minorities and elderly African Americans reveal higher prevalence data due to higher percentages in some other chronic conditions that are associated with visual impairment (e.g., diabetes). In sum, visual impairment is predominantly a challenge for older adults who experience this chronic condition late in life and frequently with an irreversible and progressive course.

Psychological Approaches and Findings

Visual impairment can be seen from a diversity of psychological approaches: Theories of psychological development (psychomotor, cognitive, social) predominantly find application on early life visual impairment. By and large, no severe deviations from normal psychological development should be expected in visually impaired children, and potential deficits present at a certain period in early childhood should always be framed within a broader perspective. For example, compensation techniques such as the development of a haptic frame of reference as well as better use of the hearing system normally are very effective tools for managing a good life into adulthood.

In adulthood, the loss of control probably becomes a major phenomenal feature of vision loss. Theories of stress and coping are especially helpful to consider these consequences of age-related visual impairment. In stress and coping theories, the onset of visual impairment is seen as a permanent stressor that warrants the use of adaptive strategies in order to minimize negative psychological consequences. According to a body of empirical evidence, there can be no doubt that age-related visual impairment is associated with negative consequences in the behavioral and emotional domain. With respect to the former, lower functioning in the activities of daily living and especially the more difficult instrumental activities of daily living (e.g., cooking, shopping, or banking) were found. Regarding the emotional domain, a heightened rate of depression and lower subjective well-being are among the most frequently replicated findings. With respect to the most successful coping strategies in order to deal with these negative consequences, currently the best research answer is that this process is highly individual. Problem-focused coping is not always most effective, and escape strategies may be helpful in some cases as well. Additional variables to explain interindividual differences are comorbidity and subjective evaluations of the vision loss, whereas the objective visual impairment reveals weaker association, particularly regarding negative affective consequences.

Theories of person-environment transactions are important for visually impaired persons of all ages due to the general impact that a vision loss has on the person-environment relation. Nevertheless, person-environment transaction may be particularly worth considering in the later years because it is generally assumed that older adults are more strongly affected by the physical environment in terms of barriers and other hindrances. Person-environment transactions operate, however, on the more subjective level as well. For example, blind elders differed from healthy or mobility-impaired persons in their patterns of place attachment, emphasizing especially the cognitive bonding to their home environment more strongly ("I know my home like the back of my hand"). Also in line with this observation, visually impaired older adults are very creative in person- and environment-related compensation efforts to counteract their visual loss and should thus not be seen as mere pawns of environmental conditions.

Intervention

There are very effective rehabilitation strategies with respect to visual impairment in all periods of the life span. Most critical is training in orientation and mobility as well as training in the performance of day-to-day tasks. Both of these skills are very important in maintaining the highest possible level of independent functioning and autonomy; self-help groups also contribute significantly to the maintenance of rehabilitative success and to coping with the daily challenges caused by the vision loss. However, there is reason to assume that comprehensive ophthalmological rehabilitation, which includes the best visual correction aids as well as the systematic improvement of everyday competence, is broadly applied in the earlier years but still not the rule in the later years of life. Among the reasons for this are the negative image of old age, information deficits in both patients and their doctors, and the simple fact that often no rehabilitation site is readily accessible (e.g., for elders living in rural areas). Probably, this situation is still more unsatisfactory with respect to African American older adults and the elderly from minority population groups. In any case it is important to acknowledge that rehabilitation can be very effective with older adults as well, with the clear consequence of a significant and persisting increase in independence and general quality of life.

Hans-Werner Wahl
Frank Oswald
German Centre for Research on Ageing

VOCABULARY TESTS

The 1994 *Tests in Print IV* listed 40 English vocabulary tests (some being out of print). But these lists are only the tip of the iceberg. Along with vocabulary subsections of numerous intelligence and achievement tests are various verbal tests with high correlations with vocabulary, which require knowledge of words and which measure much the same function: verbal analogies, same-opposite, synonyms, verbal classification, and the like.

Vocabulary tests have many attractions. If it can be assumed that all respondents have grown up in the same general environment and have had similar opportunities to acquire words, vocabulary scores tend to reflect aptitude. However, much instruction is directed toward acquiring concepts in a special area, so that growth in vocabulary is an important aspect of growth in knowledge. Vocabulary is a basic component of reading and writing skills, and it is a prerequisite for many forms of intellectual endeavor.

The high intercorrelations of vocabulary items result in high reliabilities, both by internal consistency and by alternate forms. Empirical validities in situations requiring intellectual abilities also tend to be high because many intellectual activities are almost synonymous with the manipulation of verbal concepts.

P. H. DuBois

VOCATIONAL REHABILITATION

The first Vocational Rehabilitation Act (Public Law 236) in the United States was passed by the Congress on June 2, 1920. This act placed a heavy emphasis on vocation and defined rehabilitation as "the rendering of a person disabled fit to engage in a remunerative occupation."

In theory, then, vocational rehabilitation would be directed to individuals disabled in some way and would be the endeavor of choice for those of incapacity. It would be distinguished from similar undertakings designed with initial training as a goal—such endeavors as career development, vocational guidance, and job training. In practice, however, many disabled persons select from available resources to meet their personal goals, often without regard to such formal definitions or the professionals' intentions.

Personal practices serve to obscure statistical trends and leave definitions imprecise. They occur not without reason, however. They reflect practical considerations. An individual might choose one program over another because it is closer geographically. The stigma associated with vocational rehabilitation, and the disability giving rise to its need, may represent another reason. S. Olshansky suggested that the disabled person often suffers from not one but a variety of types of stigma—relating to physical appearance, stereotypical ideas associated with receiving public assistance, and even attitudes regarding race, color, or religion. As medicine and science continue to produce results that increasingly prolong life, vocational rehabilitation may be called on more and more to contribute to the quality of that life.

Stanley Berent
University of Michigan

W

WALDORF EDUCATION

Also known as Steiner education, Waldorf education is based on the philosophy of Rudolf Steiner (1861–1925), an Austrian scientist and scholar who was asked to create a school for the children of the workers at the Waldorf-Astoria cigarette factory in Stuttgart, Germany. The first school was organized in 1919, and the movement has since become international with more than 800 schools worldwide.

Teaching is based on Steiner's conception of humans as spiritual beings with repeated earthly lives. Thus, a child is neither a blank slate to be filled with knowledge nor an animal to be civilized, but is viewed by the teacher as bringing undisclosed potentials in various stages of development. The task of education is to allow these various potentials to develop to their full capacities.

Steiner's view of child development holds that the time at which a subject is introduced, as well as the manner in which it is presented, is of utmost importance. The curriculum integrates the arts, sciences, and humanities, and teaching is done from an artistic point of view, taking into account that individuals learn at different rates and in different ways. The stress of Waldorf education is on the development of the whole human being—socially, artistically, physically, and intellectually.

Waldorf schools may begin with a nursery class and go through high school, depending on the particular school. Following the preschool and kindergarten years, a class teacher begins with a group of first graders and, ideally, continues with the group through eighth grade, supported by various specialist teachers. In high school, each class has a sponsor, and all subjects are taught by specialists. There is no principal or head, but all pedagogical decisions are made by members of a college of teachers who share responsibility for the curriculum and program. Teacher training begins with at least two years of postgraduate work at Waldorf institutes. Professional development continues at weekly faculty meetings and yearly regional conferences.

Bonnie Ozaki-James
Honolulu Waldorf School

WEBER'S LAW

On the basis of experiments with stimuli of pressure, lifted weights, and visual distance (line lengths), along with reported observations of others, Ernst Heinrich Weber (1795–1878), professor of anatomy at the University of Leipzig, concluded that rather than perceiving simply the difference between stimuli being compared, humans perceive the ratio of the difference to the magnitude of the stimuli. A similar finding had already been made by the French physicist and mathematician Pierre Bouguer (1698–1758) for visual brightness. Gustav T. Fechner (1801–1887), formerly a student of Weber's and later also a professor at the University of Leipzig, translated this conclusion into the familiar mathematical form used today. Thus, Weber's law is usually given as either $\Delta I/I = k$ or $\Delta I = kI$ where ΔI is the change required for a just noticeable difference (JND) in stimulation, I is the stimulus magnitude, and k is a constant for the particular sense. The value of k is termed the Weber ratio. This second formulation shows more clearly the proportional change in stimulation required for a JND. If, for example, the stimulus magnitude is doubled, the amount of change required for a JND is also doubled.

Over the years since Weber's formulation, it has been observed that k is not strictly constant over the entire stimulus range but increases for low and high intensities. It is, however, valid for a large range of intermediate intensities for the various senses.

Representative values of the Weber ratio for intermediate ranges include the following: brightness, 0.02–0.05; visual wavelength, 0.002–0.006; loudness (intensity measure), 0.1–0.2; auditory frequency, 0.0019–0.035; taste (salt), 0.15–0.25; smell (various substances), 0.2–0.4; cutaneous pressure, 0.14–0.16; deep pressure, 0.013–0.030; visual area, 0.06; line length, 0.04.

SUGGESTED READING

Baird, J. C., & Noma, E. (1978). *Fundamentals of scaling and psychophysics.* New York: Wiley.

Boring, E. G. (1942). *Sensation and perception in the history of experimental psychology.* New York: Appleton-Century-Crofts.

Laming, D. (1986). *Sensory analysis.* London: Academic Press.

Weber, E. H. (1978). *The sense of touch* (H. E. Ross & D. J. Murray,

Trans.). London: Academic Press. (Original work published 1834 [*De Tactu*] and 1846 [*Der Tastsinn*])

George H. Robinson
University of North Alabama

WEIGHT CONTROL

Obesity has become a global epidemic. Twenty-seven percent of American adults are obese, and an additional 34% are overweight. The prevalence of overweight children has doubled in the last 20 years. Paradoxically, this has occurred while there have been major scientific, medical, and commercial efforts to develop effective means of weight control. One limitation is that these methods have been based on a medical model that emphasizes causes and remedies for individuals. More recently, obesity is considered a public health crisis that demands innovative public policy interventions. This chapter highlights advances in treating obesity, the important issue of stigma, and suggestions for public policy research.

Obesity is a difficult condition to treat. The most optimistic estimates are that 25% of people lose weight and keep it off, leading some experts to emphasize prevention. Yet even if prevention becomes a major priority, the vast numbers of people already overweight deserve compassion and effective care. A number of treatments have been examined.

Commercial and Self-Help Programs

Diet books, community-based self-help groups, and commercial weight loss programs are the most prevalent but least tested approaches to weight control. Consumers and professionals are left to guess about their safety and effectiveness. The Federal Trade Commission has called for commercial weight loss programs to disclose information about the results of treatment, so in the future consumers may be able to make educated decisions about choosing one of these approaches.

Group Behavioral Treatment

Many universities and hospitals offer professionally led group behavioral treatment for obesity, consisting typically of 16 to 20 weekly meetings. Key components are food records, monitoring of physical activity, behavioral strategies to prevent overeating, and cognitive strategies to promote effective coping with stressors and eating triggers. Calorie prescriptions are given, and increasing both programmed and lifestyle physical activity is strongly emphasized. The meetings provide social support and encouragement.

The results of these treatments are well documented; a 20-week program typically results in a 9% weight loss (i.e., 8.5–9.0 kg). Without further treatment, clients typically regain one third of this weight in a year and continue regaining weight over time. A priority in these programs is helping clients recognize the benefits of 5–15% weight losses and facilitating maintenance of weight loss over time.

Very-Low-Calorie Diets and Portion Controlled Diets

A more intensive approach is the liquid very-low-calorie diet (VLCD), which provides 400 to 800 kcal per day. Clients lose twice as much weight initially compared to traditional behavioral treatment, but they regain weight more quickly. At 1-year follow-up, the two approaches have comparable results.

One challenge in weight control is measuring and calculating the calories of foods, so some studies have assessed the effect of providing clients with prepackaged meals. Clients adhere better to low-calorie diets when food is provided than when using a self-selected menu.

Medication

Two medications are currently approved by the FDA for weight loss and maintenance, sibutramine (Meridia) and orlistat (Xenical). Average weight loss with medication alone is around 7–8% at one year, which is comparable to behavioral group treatment. Combining sibutramine with behavioral treatment improves outcome to the range of 10–15%.

Maintenance of Weight Loss

Maintaining weight loss is difficult. Historically, maintenance has been evaluated by providing an intervention, measuring weight loss, and then telling patients to continue making changes on their own and measuring weight loss again at follow-up. If people regain weight, some believe the treatment failed. An alternate view is that treatment *did* work, which is proven by the fact that clients gained weight when it ended. The challenge is finding treatment approaches that are innovative and flexible enough to encourage adherence over the long term.

Obesity is a chronic disorder like diabetes, not a curable condition like an ear infection. A chronic care model, however, conflicts with the desire of many overweight individuals to lose weight quickly and then forget about vigilance. Most successful maintainers continue thinking carefully about food and exercise for the rest of their lives.

Physical Activity

Professionals debate diet approaches, but there is clear consensus that physical activity is central to weight control and leads to benefits apart from weight loss. There is clear documentation that physical activity level is the best predictor of long-term weight control. Other findings suggest that exercising at home leads to better adherence than does going out to a center and that exercising in several small bouts (i.e., 10 minutes) is just as effective as exercising in one longer bout (i.e., 40 minutes). Lifestyle activity (e.g., taking stairs instead of the elevator, parking at the far end of the lot, walking rather than driving to destinations) is as effective as programmed exercise in increasing cardiovascular fitness.

Recent research raises the possibility that people can be fit at any size and that being fit and fat is better than being unfit and normal weight. This is a helpful concept, as it provides incentive for all individuals to increase their level of physical fitness, regardless of its impact on weight and body size. Increasing activity may be easier than losing weight; hence, some in the field believe that activity should be emphasized over weight loss.

Surgery

Surgery may be the best treatment option for people with considerable weight to lose. The two most common procedures are gastric bypass and vertical banded gastroplasty. These procedures result in weight losses in the 25–30% range, which is associated with significant improvements in medical conditions. These procedures seem to be gaining popularity, and further research is needed on how best to evaluate candidates and identify predictors of successful outcomes. Laparoscopic procedures are technically complicated but can greatly reduce surgical complications and speed recovery.

Different treatments work for different people, so it is unlikely that one best treatment will ever emerge. A more fruitful avenue for research may be to search for the best fit between individuals and programs.

Stigma of Obesity

Obesity is a highly stigmatized condition, and obese individuals experience bias and discrimination in many domains of life, including education, employment, and access to medical care. Some argue that the stigma of obesity serves as an incentive for people to try to lose weight. This is faulty logic—if social pressure to be thin worked, we would not have an obesity epidemic. A climate of blame and criticism not only makes weight loss more difficult but also can lead to emotional distress and further eating disturbance. Research is needed on how to ameliorate the stigma of obesity and provide effective coping methods to those who experience it.

Public Policy Approaches

While individual treatments may work for specific people, we believe that reversing the obesity epidemic requires public policy changes that will influence the population's diet and physical activity. The following ideas have been proposed: (1) Regulate food advertising aimed at children; (2) prohibit fast foods and soft drinks from schools; (3) subsidize the sale of healthy foods; (4) tax unhealthy foods; and (5) provide resources for physical activity. The impact of these policy changes on the health of a community is worthy of further study.

Conclusion

Obesity, along with the poor diet and inactivity that cause it, are major contributors to disease. Obesity is now associated with more chronic illness and greater health care costs than is smoking. The nation must be bold in its response to the epidemic, or the problem will grow worse. Prevention must be a priority, but safe and effective treatments must be available to both adults and children who struggle with their weight.

Marlene B. Schwartz
Kelly D. Brownell
Yale University

WERNICKE-LICHTHEIM MODEL OF LANGUAGE PROCESSING

The functional-anatomical model of language processing formulated by Wernicke and Lichtheim in the late 19th century has provided a useful introduction to aphasia for generations of clinicians. Thirteen years before Wernicke's famous monograph, Broca had revolutionized the study of aphasia by linking speech production deficits to frontal lobe damage (Broca, 1861). Wernicke brought these observations together with new data from aphasic patients with temporal lobe lesions, providing the first neuroanatomical account of both language comprehension and production (Wernicke, 1874). Lichtheim's expanded version of this model was influential because of the diagrammatic clarity with which it was able to predict aphasia syndromes from isolated lesions in functional centers or pathways linking the centers (Lichtheim, 1885; Table 1 and Figure 1).

Wernicke Aphasia

Wernicke's area, marked A in the diagram, is the center containing auditory word forms (*Wortklangbilder*). These word forms (the phonological lexicon in more recent terminology) contain information about the sounds of words, essential for decoding speech sound input and for guiding the production of words. Damage to A thus causes impaired speech comprehension as well as incorrect selection or sequencing of phonemes during speaking (phonemic para-

Table 1. Aphasia Syndromes

	Lesion Site				
	A	M	A-to-M	A-to-B	B-to-M
Syndrome	Wernicke	Broca	Conduction	TC Sensory	TC Motor
Spontaneous speech	paraphasic	nonfluent	paraphasic	paraphasic	nonfluent
Spontaneous writing	paragraphic	nonfluent	paragraphic	paragraphic	nonfluent
Naming	impaired	impaired	paraphasic	anomic	anomic
Repetition	paraphasic	nonfluent	paraphasic	nl	nl
Reading aloud	paraphasic	nonfluent	paraphasic	impaired	nl
Auditory comprehension	impaired	nl	nl	impaired	nl
Written comprehension	impaired	nl	nl	impaired	nl

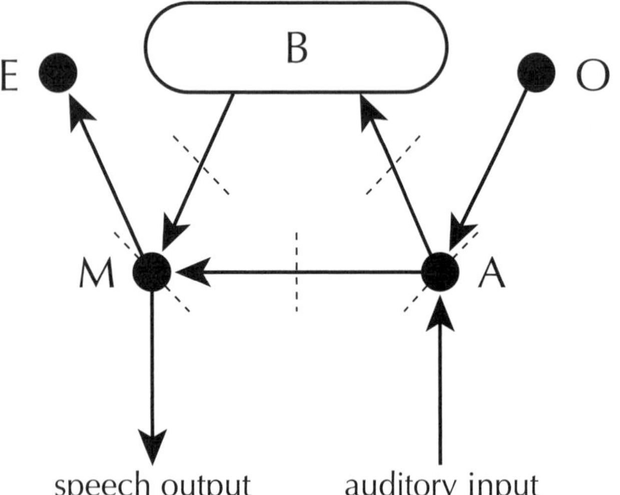

Figure 1. Wernicke-Lichtheim model of language processing.

phasia). Repetition, which requires both speech sound decoding and production, is also impaired, typically with severe paraphasia. In the classical version of the model, the sound images of words being read must be activated by input from the visual center (center O in the diagram) before reading comprehension can occur, and the sound images of words one intends to write are used to guide the motor images used for writing (stored in center E in the diagram). Thus, damage to A also causes alexia and paragraphia. The deficits resulting from a lesion in A are collectively called Wernicke aphasia.

Wernicke localized A to the left superior temporal gyrus (STG). Later authors held widely varying views on the location of Wernicke's area, including some for whom the area encompassed middle temporal, angular, and supramarginal gyri as well as STG (Bogen & Bogen, 1976). A strongly localizationist view, originated by Liepmann, Kleist, and others and popularized in recent times by Geschwind and his students, places A in the posterior STG, particularly in the planum temporale or posterior dorsal STG (Geschwind, 1971). Lesions restricted to the left planum temporale appear to cause only the paraphasic speech component without comprehension disturbance or alexia (Benson et al., 1973; Kleist, 1962). Patients with Wernicke aphasia, including the patients reported by Wernicke himself, have had large lesions extending well beyond the STG (Damasio, 1989; Henschen, 1920–1922; Wernicke, 1874). Comparative studies in nonhuman primates and functional imaging data from humans strongly implicate the posterior STG in auditory functions (Binder, Frost, Hammeke, Rao, & Cox, 1996; Galaburda & Sanides, 1980); this region is thus no longer considered a center for multimodal language processing but probably participates in the sensory analysis of complex sounds, including speech.

Broca Aphasia

A second main component of the model is Broca's center for motor word images (*Wortbewegungsbilder*, marked M in the diagram), which contains motor programs used for movement of the vocal apparatus during speech. Damage to M causes impaired speech production without affecting comprehension. The speaking deficit may be extreme, with complete or nearly complete mutism, or speech may be effortful and nonfluent, with a marked decrease in the length of phrases and the rate of word production. Because M is a final common output node for all speech behaviors, repetition, naming, and reading aloud are all similarly affected. Lichtheim believed that writing movements also depend on input from M; thus, inability to write is often considered a feature of the syndrome. The deficits resulting from a lesion in M are collectively called Broca aphasia. Broca and other early aphasiologists localized M to the pars opercularis of the left inferior frontal gyrus (Brodmann's area 44), but later authors have variously included pars triangularis (area 45) and ventral premotor cortex (area 6) in the definition of Broca's area. Lesions restricted to the left pars opercularis do not cause the full syndrome, but rather a transient deficit of articulation without writing or naming disturbance (Alexander, Benson, & Stuss, 1989; Mohr et al., 1978). Patients with Broca aphasia, including the patient reported by Broca himself, typically have large lesions extending into insula, sensorimotor cortex, parietal operculum, and middle frontal gyrus (Mohr, 1976).

Conduction Aphasia

Damage to connections between A and M also cause impairment of speech production, a syndrome known as conduction aphasia. Comprehension remains intact because A is spared, and speech remains fluent and well-articulated because M is spared. Although Wernicke predicted that such a lesion would cause difficulty producing whole words (anomia), patients with conduction aphasia show instead a disturbance characterized by phonemic paraphasia (Kohn, 1992). Emphasis is often placed on repetition deficits in conduction aphasia, but the same errors typically occur in all speech output tasks. The concept of conduction aphasia as a disconnection syndrome led to the popular view that the critical lesion is in white matter (external capsule and/or arcuate fasciculus) connecting superior temporal to inferior frontal cortex. Evidence for such a localization is scant, however, and typical patients with the syndrome have cortical lesions affecting the posterior STG, posterior insula, or parietal operculum (Benson et al., 1973; Damasio & Damasio, 1980; Kleist, 1962).

Transcortical Aphasia

A third main component of the model is the concept field (*Begriffsfeld*), described as a widely distributed, bihemispheric system containing information about the polysensory properties of objects (center B in the diagram). Comprehension is achieved when the auditory word form makes contact with this polysensory information, while speech production requires that the polysensory concepts activate corresponding motor word images. Because of its widely distributed nature, the concept field could not be damaged by a focal lesion. Focal lesions, however, could sever connections between the concept field and more focal language centers, causing the so-called transcortical syndromes. Repetition is normal in such cases because the A-to-M circuit is intact. Lesions between A and B prevent activation of concepts by auditory word images, causing impaired auditory and written word comprehension with intact repetition. This syndrome is known as transcortical sensory aphasia and is usually caused by damage to the posterior ventrolateral left temporal lobe (posterior middle or inferior temporal gyri) or angular gyrus (Alexander, Hiltbrunner, & Fischer, 1989). Lesions between M and B prevent activation of motor speech centers by concepts, causing nonfluent speech with intact repetition. This syndrome is known as transcortical motor aphasia and is caused by damage to the left middle frontal or superior frontal lobe (Alexander, Benson et al., 1989; Rapcsak & Rubens, 1994). Brain regions in which lesions cause transcortical aphasia have recently been implicated in operations involving verbally encoded semantic knowledge (Binder et al., 1997; Damasio, Grabowski, Tranel, Hichwa, & Damasio, 1996; Démonet et al., 1992; Vandenbergh, Price, Wise, Josephs, & Frackowiak, 1996). The deficits observed in transcortical aphasia may thus be due to direct damage to, rather than disconnection of, these knowledge retrieval systems.

Current Status of the Model

Many advances have been made since the 19th century in our understanding of language processing, and it is not clear that the Wernicke-Lichtheim model in its simple form can accommodate this information. For example, the model has almost nothing to say about syntactic processes or about how spoken or written nonsense words ("brillig," "slithy," "toves") are perceived and pronounced. Empirical observations not accounted for include a variety of context effects in letter and phoneme perception, spared language abilities in auditory or visual modalities, comprehension disturbances in patients with frontal lesions, word frequency effects and short-term memory phenomena in conduction aphasia, spelling regularity and lexicality effects in reading and writing, category-specific naming and comprehension disturbances, and so on. Underlying these difficulties is the fact that the model itself contains little in the way of explicit detail regarding how various transformations—sound to word, print to word, word to concept, concept to word, word to motor sequence—are actually accomplished.

The model has not been entirely abandoned, however, for two reasons. First, the enormous amount of data from modern aphasiology, functional imaging, and cognitive linguistic research has yet to be integrated in a widely-accepted, comprehensive alternative. Second, the range of models employed in the clinical setting may be limited to those that can be readily communicated to students in a diagrammatic or tabular format (Table 1). The Wernicke-Lichtheim model, particularly in its current simplified form, thus continues to serve a useful role as initial common ground for the interested student of aphasiology.

REFERENCES

Alexander, M. P., Benson, D. F., & Stuss, D. T. (1989). Frontal lobes and language. *Brain and Language, 37,* 656–691.

Alexander, M. P., Hiltbrunner, B., & Fischer, R. S. (1989). Distributed anatomy of transcortical sensory aphasia. *Archives of Neurology, 46,* 885–892.

Benson, D. F., Sheremata, W. A., Bouchard, R., Segarra, J. M., Price, D., & Geschwind, N. (1973). Conduction aphasia: A clinicopathological study. *Archives of Neurology, 28,* 339–346.

Binder, J. R., Frost, J. A., Hammeke, T. A., Cox, R. W., Rao, S. M., & Prieto, T. (1997). Human brain language areas identified by functional MRI. *Journal of Neuroscience, 17,* 353–362.

Binder, J. R., Frost, J. A., Hammeke, T. A., Rao, S. M., & Cox, R. W. (1996). Function of the left planum temporale in auditory and linguistic processing. *Brain, 119,* 1239–1247.

Bogen, J. E., & Bogen, G. M. (1976). Wernicke's region—where is it? *Annals of the New York Academy of Sciences, 290,* 834–843.

Broca, P. (1861). Remarques sur le siège de la faculté du langage articulé: Suivies d'une observation d'aphemie. *Bulletin de la Société Anatomique de Paris, 6,* 330–357.

Damasio, H. (1989). Neuroimaging contributions to the understanding of aphasia. In F. Boller & J. Grafman (Eds.), *Handbook of neuropsychology* (pp. 3–46). Amsterdam: Elsevier.

Damasio, H., & Damasio, A. R. (1980). The anatomical basis of conduction aphasia. *Brain, 103,* 337–350.

Damasio, H., Grabowski, T. J., Tranel, D., Hichwa, R. D., & Damasio, A. R. (1996). A neural basis for lexical retrieval. *Nature, 380,* 499–505.

Démonet, J.-F., Chollet, F., Ramsay, S., Cardebat, D., Nespoulous, J.-L., Wise, R., Rascol, A., & Frackowiak, R. (1992). The anatomy of phonological and semantic processing in normal subjects. *Brain, 115,* 1753–1768.

Galaburda, A., & Sanides, F. (1980). Cytoarchitectonic organization of the human auditory cortex. *Journal of Comparative Neurology, 190,* 597–610.

Geschwind, N. (1971). Aphasia. *New England Journal of Medicine, 284,* 654–656.

Henschen, S. E. (1920–1922). *Klinische und anatomische Beitrage zur Pathologie des Gehirns.* Stockholm: Nordiska Bokhandeln.

Kleist, K. (1962). *Sensory aphasia and amusia.* London: Pergamon.

Kohn, S. E. (Ed.). (1992). *Conduction aphasia.* Hillsdale, NJ: Erlbaum.

Lichtheim, L. (1885). On aphasia. *Brain, 7,* 433–484.

Mohr, J. P. (1976). Broca's area and Broca's aphasia. In H. Whitaker & H. Whitaker (Eds.), *Studies in neurolinguistics* (pp. 201–236). New York: Academic Press.

Mohr, J. P., Pessin, M. S., Finkelstein, S., Funkenstein, H. H., Duncan, G. W., & Davis, K. R. (1978). Broca aphasia: Pathologic and clinical. *Neurology, 28,* 311–324.

Rapcsak, S. Z., & Rubens, A. B. (1994). Localization of lesions in transcortical aphasia. In A. Kertesz (Ed.), *Localization and neuroimaging in neuropsychology* (pp. 297–329). San Diego: Academic Press.

Vandenberghe, R., Price, C., Wise, R., Josephs, O., & Frackowiak, R. S. J. (1996). Functional anatomy of a common semantic system for words and pictures. *Nature, 383,* 254–256.

Wernicke, C. (1874). *Der aphasische Symptomenkomplex.* Breslau, Poland: Cohn & Weigert.

Jeff R. Binder
Medical College of Wisconsin

WISDOM

Some Historical Background to the Study of Wisdom

Since the beginnings of human culture, wisdom has been viewed as the ideal endpoint of human development (Baltes & Staudinger, 2000). Historically, wisdom was conceptualized in terms of a state of idealized being, as a process of perfect knowing and judgment (as in King Solomon's judgments), or as an oral or written product such as wisdom-related proverbs. It is important to recognize that the identification of wisdom with individuals (e.g., wise persons), the predominant approach in psychology, is but one of the ways by which wisdom is instantiated. Wisdom is considered an ideal that is difficult to be fully represented in the isolated individual.

Two main lines of argument have been in the center of the historical evolution of the concept of wisdom: the distinction between philosophical and practical wisdom, and the question of whether wisdom is divine or human. Archeological-cultural work dealing with the origins of wisdom-related texts in China, India, Egypt, Old Mesopotamia, and the like has revealed a cultural and historical invariance with regard to wisdom-related proverbs and tales. This relative invariance suggests that the body of knowledge and skills related to wisdom have been culturally selected because of their adaptive value for humankind.

Psychological Approaches to the Definition of Wisdom

A first approach to the definition of wisdom from a psychological perspective is its treatment in dictionaries. The *Oxford Dictionary,* for instance, includes in its definition of wisdom, "Good judgment and advice in difficult and uncertain matters of life."

In a next step, psychologists further specified the content and formal properties of wisdom-related phenomena. G. Stanley Hall and other writers emphasized that wisdom involves the search for the moderate course between extremes, a dynamic between knowledge and doubt, a sufficient detachment from the problem at hand, and a well-balanced coordination of emotion, motivation, and thought. In line with dictionary definitions, such writings refer to wisdom as knowledge about the human condition at its frontier, knowledge about the most difficult questions of the meaning and conduct of life, and knowledge about the uncertainties of life—about what cannot be known and how to deal with that limited knowledge (for an overview, see Sternberg, 1990).

Implicit (Subjective) Theories about Wisdom

Most empirical research on wisdom in psychology so far has focused on further elaboration of the definition of wisdom. Moving beyond the dictionary definitions of wisdom, research explored the nature of everyday conceptions or implicit (subjective) theories of wisdom.

From this research on implicit theories of wisdom (for a review, see Sternberg, 1990), it is evident that people in Western samples hold fairly clear-cut images of the nature of wisdom. Four findings are especially noteworthy. First, in the minds of people, wisdom seems to be closely related to wise persons and their acts as carriers of wisdom. Second, wise people are expected to combine features of mind and character and balance multiple interests and choices.

Third, wisdom carries a very strong interpersonal and social aspect with regard to both its application (advice) and the consensual recognition of its occurrence. Fourth, wisdom exhibits overlap with other related concepts such as intelligence, but it also carries unique variance.

Explicit Theories and Assessment of Wisdom

A more recent line of empirical psychological inquiry on wisdom addresses the question of how to measure behavioral expressions of wisdom. Within this tradition, three lines of work can be identified: (1) assessment of wisdom as a personality characteristic, (2) assessment of wisdom in the Piagetian tradition of postformal thought, and (3) assessment of wisdom as an individual's problem-solving performance with regard to difficult life problems.

Within personality theories, such as Erik Erikson's, wisdom is usually conceptualized as an advanced if not the final stage of personality development. A wise person is characterized, for instance, as integrating rather than ignoring or repressing self-related information, by having coordinated opposites, and by having transcended personal agendas and turned to collective or universal issues.

Central to neo-Piagetian theories of adult thought is the transcendence of the universal truth criterion that characterizes formal logic. This transcendence is common to conceptions such as dialectical, complementary, and relativistic thinking. Such tolerance of multiple truths, that is of ambiguity, has also been mentioned as a crucial feature of wisdom.

There is also work that attempts to assess wisdom-related performance in tasks dealing with the interpretation, conduct, and management of life. This approach defines wisdom as "an expert knowledge system in the fundamental pragmatics of life permitting exceptional insight, judgment, and advice involving complex and uncertain matters of the human condition" (Baltes, Smith, & Staudinger, 1992).

The body of knowledge and skills associated with wisdom as an expertise in the fundamental pragmatics of life entails insights into the quintessential aspects of the human condition, including its biological finitude and cultural conditioning. More specifically, wisdom-related knowledge and skills can be characterized by a family of five criteria: (1) rich factual knowledge about life, (2) rich procedural knowledge about life, (3) life span contextualism, (4) value relativism, and (5) awareness and management of uncertainty (see Baltes et al., 1992, for an extensive definition).

To elicit and measure wisdom-related knowledge and skills, in this approach participants are presented with difficult life dilemmas such as the following: "Imagine that a good friend of yours calls you up and tells you that he/she can't go on anymore and has decided to commit suicide. What would you be thinking about; how would you deal with this situation?" The five wisdom-related criteria are used to evaluate these protocols.

Part of the Berlin paradigm also is a general framework outlining the conditions for the development of wisdom. The empirical work based on this ontogenetic model and the measurement paradigm produced outcomes consistent with expectations. It seems that wisdom-related knowledge and judgment emerge between the age of 14 and 25 years; afterward, growing older is not enough to become wiser (Staudinger, 1999). However, when age was combined with wisdom-related experiential contexts, such as professional specializations specifically involving training and experience in matters of life, higher levels of performance were observed. In line with the historical wisdom literature, which portrays wisdom as the ideal combination of mind and virtue, it was found that wisdom-related performance was best predicted by measures located at the interface of cognition and personality, such as a judicious cognitive style, creativity, and moral reasoning.

Is There Wisdom-Related Potential?

Given the fact that wisdom-related performance had been successfully operationalized, the question arose whether it was possible to increase wisdom-related knowledge and judgment. It should also be noted that, not surprisingly, the overall level of wisdom identified was below or around the theoretical mean of the scale, thus leaving a lot of room for improvement.

One study took into account that higher performance levels may be found if two minds can interact before responding to the wisdom dilemma. And indeed, when two individuals usually interacting about life problems in everyday life had a chance to do so before they individually responded to wisdom tasks, the performance level was increased by one standard deviation (Staudinger & Baltes, 1996). The second study focused on one of the five wisdom-related criteria, value relativism. Participants were trained to think about life problems located at different regions of the world. At posttest, participants trained in the knowledge-activating strategy outperformed the control group by more than half a standard deviation (Baltes & Staudinger, 2000).

Conclusion and Future Directions

The concept of wisdom represents a fruitful topic for psychological research. The study of wisdom emphasizes the search for continued optimization and the further evolution of the human condition, and in a prototypical fashion, it allows for the study of collaboration among cognitive, emotional, and motivational processes. We expect that future research on wisdom will be expanded in at least three ways: (1) the further identification of social and personality factors and life processes relevant for the ontogeny of wisdom, (2) the exploration of wisdom as a meta-heuristic aimed at orchestrating mind and virtue toward human excellence, and (3) the contribution of wisdom research to building a psychological art of life.

REFERENCES

Baltes, P. B., Smith, J., & Staudinger, U. M. (1992). Wisdom and successful aging. In T. Sonderegger (Ed.), *Nebraska symposium on motivation: Vol. 39* (pp. 123–167). Lincoln: University of Nebraska Press.

Baltes, P. B., & Staudinger, U. M. (2000). Wisdom: A metaheuristic to orchestrate mind and virtue towards excellence. *American Psychologist, 55,* 122–136.

Staudinger, U. M. (1999). Older and wiser? Integrating results on the relationship between age and wisdom-related performance. *International Journal of Behavioral Development, 23,* 641–664.

Staudinger, U. M., & Baltes, P. B. (1996). Interactive minds: A facilitative setting for wisdom-related performance? *Journal of Personality and Social Psychology, 71,* 746–762.

Sternberg, R. J. (Ed.). (1990). *Wisdom: Its nature, origins, and development.* New York: Cambridge University Press.

Ursula M. Staudinger
Dresden University

WORK AND PLAY

The technological character of advanced modern civilizations has tended to segregate work and play. A further extension of these segregations is to differentiate the motivations for work and play. This suggests that work is characterized by activities engaged in for the purpose of staying alive and that play refers to activities engaged in for their own sake. E. S. Bordin has proposed that work and play can be seen as involving various combinations of effort, compulsion, and spontaneity.

Effort and compulsion are intimately related. The greater the effort and the longer it endures, the stronger the pressure toward cessation and rest becomes. What sustains effort against the accumulating counterpressure is inner interest and involvement or externalized threats of punishment or annihilation, which, in turn, can be internalized and experienced as an inner compulsion, for example, to stay alive. Spontaneity refers to that element of interest, self-investment, and self-expression that transforms an effortful performance that might have been experienced as alienated toil into a creative, joyful self-expression. This transformed activity epitomizes play.

Work and Play in Childhood

The bulk of the observation of play has been directed toward the immature. In young animals and children, observers stress the excess energy expended and the usefulness of play as a means toward mastery. Therapists working with children utilize this concept of play. Similarly, children are seen as using play to try out and prepare for anticipated adult roles.

The history of education has been marked by concern with preserving spontaneity concerned with maintaining appropriate levels of directed effort. Observers of children's play have noted that the fluid, spontaneous play of the young child soon gives way to formalizations of rules, which introduces restraining boundaries to spontaneity. The physical and intellectual development of the child is accompanied by more sophisticated play with its demands for mastery. Thus, growth and maturation are accompanied by ever-increasing participation by compulsion and effort. Play has become more than a simple joyful expression of energy in which effort is background.

Work and Play in Vocation

Virtually all persons face the necessity of securing the material means of staying alive or for additional comforts. In work-intensive societies, there was more room for men and women to mix the process of working for a livelihood with flexibility for self-expression. Our modern machine-dominated technological society challenges the preservation of these elements in work.

Is there any way to protect against work as alienated toil? Marxist philosophers such as Herbert Marcuse argue that under socialism in which the worker feels in control of the larger process of production, the greater economies in productivity afforded by the utilization of the machine can be converted into greater free time, making possible the assimilation of work into play. He argues that the experience of alienated labor is dictated by the excess repression exerted by capitalism to maintain that economic system.

Psychologists and industrial sociologists point out that many highly skilled jobs and professions require and permit long-term commitments and the flexible expressions of self that mix the compulsion, effort, and spontaneity marking the fusion of work and play. Research on personality development and the psychological characteristics and requirements associated with various occupations and occupational families has provided the base for helping individuals seeking vocational commitments to channel their choices toward optimal reconciliations of the wishes for material returns with their desires for satisfaction in work.

There remains the question of whether this can apply to all jobs. The Marxist answer accepts the antihumanistic element in the machine-human interface and only seeks to limit its duration. R. Blauner found that the worker's relation to the technological organization of the work process and the social organization of the factory determines whether he or she experiences a sense of control rather than domination, a sense of meaningful purpose rather than isolation, and a sense of spontaneous involvement rather than detachment and discontent. These views have spawned many efforts through job enlargement, job rotation, or drastic redesign to achieve for workers desirable levels of intrinsic satisfaction in their work life.

Work and Play in Leisure and Retirement

Surveys of workers' use of nonwork time finds them engaged in second jobs, educational activities, household chores, and child care. Some of this reflects the same economic pressures that make work a necessity. But these data also suggest that a major motivation in leisure time activity is not the removal of effort, but relaxation of the pressure of compulsion.

E. S. Bordin

WORKING MEMORY

Everyday cognitive tasks, such as language comprehension, reasoning, and decision making, often require one to keep relevant information in mind while processing other information. For example, mental arithmetic requires keeping track of the intermediate results from relevant computations and integrating them to reach the correct answer. A system or a set of processes that supports such maintenance of task-relevant information during the performance of a cognitive task is called *working memory.* As reflected by the fact that it has been considered the mind's work space, working memory is a central construct in cognitive psychology and cognitive neuroscience.

The notion of working memory evolved from an earlier conception of short-term memory. Like working memory, short-term memory is a system for enabling temporary maintenance of information, but its maintenance functions are primarily for the sake of memorization (e.g., remembering an unfamiliar phone number until it is dialed) and are far removed from other cognitive processes that support active thinking. In contrast, the central idea behind working memory is that its maintenance functions are in the service of complex cognition and fundamentally support performance of complex cognitive tasks. In other words, the memory part of working memory is not passive and static, but active and working, as its name indicates.

A Multicomponent View of Working Memory

There are a number of well-developed models and theories of working memory (for an overview, see Miyake & Shah, 1999), but the best known model is the multicomponent model developed by Alan Baddeley (1986). According to this model, working memory is a system that consists of three major subsystems. Two of the subsystems, called the phonological (or articulatory) loop and the visuospatial sketchpad, are specialized slave systems whose primary functions are the temporary maintenance and processing of speech-based phonological information and of visual and spatial information, respectively. Each subsystem is assumed to consist of two separable components, a passive phonological store and an active rehearsal process for the phonological loop (Baddeley, 1986) and a visual component (visual cache) and a spatial component (inner scribe) for the visuospatial sketchpad (Logie, 1995). The remaining subsystem is called the central executive and is a general-purpose control structure that regulates the operations of the two slave systems and modulates the flow of information within working memory.

The tripartite structure of Baddeley's (1986) model has been supported by various sources of evidence, particularly with respect to the separability of the two slave systems. For example, secondary tasks that tap the phonological loop's functions, such as repeating a familiar phrase over and over (called articulatory suppression), impair the maintenance of phonological information but not visuospatial information (Baddeley, 1986), whereas secondary tasks that tap the visuospatial sketchpad's functions, such as viewing dynamic visual noise (called the irrelevant picture paradigm), impair the maintenance of some types of visual information but not verbal information (Quinn & McConnell, 1996). In addition, individuals with brain damage have demonstrated selective impairments in the phonological loop or the visuospatial sketchpad (Gathercole, 1994). More recently, neuroimaging studies have produced evidence suggesting that different neural circuits may mediate the maintenance of phonological and visuospatial information (Smith & Jonides, 1999).

Within the framework of this multicomponent model, the main focus of current research is to specify the organization and functions of the central executive, the least understood subsystem of working memory. Although it has been criticized as a homunculus or a theoretical ragbag, interest in understanding this crucial component has been rising (Miyake & Shah, 1999). In particular, researchers have started to specify the subcomponents or subfunctions of the central executive (Baddeley, 1996), as well as the role of the prefrontal cortex in the executive control of behavior (Smith & Jonides, 1999).

More recently, Baddeley (2000) proposed a possible fourth subcomponent of working memory, called the episodic buffer. This buffer is thought to be responsible for integrating or binding multiple sources of information derived from different memory systems (e.g., binding items in the phonological loop with relevant pieces of information in long-term knowledge) and temporarily maintaining the resulting multimodal representations within working memory. Although this new concept helps resolve some difficulties that the original tripartite version of the model had faced, it remains to be seen whether the episodic buffer will become as widely accepted as the other subsystems.

Measurement of Working Memory and Its Role in Complex Cognition

The capacity of short-term memory has traditionally been assessed with a simple span task that requires participants to repeat back a list of digits or words in correct sequence. In contrast to such storage-oriented measures, currently used measures of working memory capacity require participants to perform a dual task, namely the simultaneous processing of some information and remembering of to-be-recalled items. The best-known measure of this kind is the reading span test (Daneman & Carpenter, 1980), in which participants read sentences aloud while remembering the final word of each sentence for later recall. Performance on this task has been shown to correlate well with complex cognitive tasks, such as reading comprehension. According to a meta-analysis (Daneman & Merikle, 1996), the average correlation between the reading span score and global comprehension measures like the Nelson-Denny Reading Test was .41 and was significantly higher than that between traditional short-term memory measures and comprehension measures (.28 for word span and .14 for digit span). Following this success, a number of variants have been developed, including the operation span, counting span, and spatial span tests (Engle, Tuholski, Laughlin, & Conway, 1999; Shah & Miyake, 1996).

These complex span tasks have served as useful research tools to examine the role of working memory in various complex cognitive tasks. Tasks examined in some depth include language comprehension, language learning, spatial thinking, retrieval from memory, and problem solving and reasoning (see Miyake & Shah, 1999, for some illustrative examples of this line of research). Although the extent to which the capacities measured by the complex span tasks is domain-specific or domain-general is under debate, the proposal that working memory capacity may be a key component of general fluid intelligence (Engle et al., 1999) further underscores the importance of working memory in complex cognition.

REFERENCES

Baddeley, A. D. (1986). *Working memory.* New York: Oxford University Press.

Baddeley, A. D. (1996). Exploring the central executive. *Quarterly Journal of Experimental Psychology, 49A,* 5–28.

Baddeley, A. D. (2000). The episodic buffer: A new component of working memory? *Trends in Cognitive Sciences, 4,* 417–423.

Daneman, M., & Carpenter, P. A. (1980). Individual differences in working memory and reading. *Journal of Verbal Learning and Verbal Behavior, 19,* 450–466.

Daneman, M., & Merikle, P. M. (1996). Working memory and language comprehension: A meta-analysis. *Psychonomic Bulletin and Review, 3,* 422–433.

Engle, R. W., Tuholski, S. W., Laughlin, J. E., & Conway, A. R. A. (1999). Working memory, short-term memory, and general fluid intelligence: A latent variable approach. *Journal of Experimental Psychology: General, 128,* 309–331.

Gathercole, S. E. (1994). Neuropsychology and working memory: A review. *Neuropsychology, 8,* 494–505.

Logie, R. H. (1995). *Visuo-spatial working memory.* Hove, UK: Erlbaum.

Miyake, A., & Shah, P. (Eds.). (1999). *Models of working memory: Mechanisms of active maintenance and executive control.* New York: Cambridge University Press.

Quinn, J. G., & McConnell, J. (1996). Irrelevant pictures in visual working memory. *Quarterly Journal of Experimental Psychology, 49A,* 200–215.

Shah, P., & Miyake, A. (1996). The separability of working memory resources for spatial thinking and language processing: An individual differences approach. *Journal of Experimental Psychology: General, 125,* 4–27.

Smith, E. E., & Jonides, J. (1999). Storage and executive processes in the frontal lobes. *Science, 283,* 165–166.

SUGGESTED READING

Andrade, J. (Ed.). (2001). *Working memory in perspective.* Hove, UK: Psychology Press.

Logie, R. H., & Gilhooly, K. J. (Eds.). (1998). *Working memory and thinking.* Hove, UK: Psychology Press.

Miyake, A. (2001). Individual differences in working memory: Introduction to the special section. *Journal of Experimental Psychology: General, 130,* 163–168.

Miyake, A., & Shah, P. (Eds.). (1999). *Models of working memory: Mechanisms of active maintenance and executive control.* New York: Cambridge University Press.

Smith, E. E., & Jonides, J. (1997). Working memory: A view from neuroimaging. *Cognitive Psychology, 33,* 5–42.

Akira Miyake
University of Colorado at Boulder

Z

ZEIGARNIK EFFECT

Work by Bluma Zeigarnik (1927) established the fact that subjects ranging widely in age tended to remember interrupted tasks better (and with greater frequency) than they did tasks they had completed.

What amounted to common-sense observation constituted the impetus for a series of germinal experiments by Zeigarnik. In a typical study, subjects were asked to perform a series of different tasks, ranging from 15 to 22 in number. Some tasks were of a manipulatory nature (such as stringing beads); others clearly involved the application of mental ability (such as puzzles). For half of the activities, subjects were allowed to continue until they were finished. In the case of a puzzle, for example, work might proceed until a solution was found. In the remainder of the activities (one half of the total), the experimenter asked subjects to stop working on a given task and to move on to something else. Following the activity or task session, the tasks were removed from the subjects' view, and each was asked to recall and to jot down some of the activities in which they had been involved. Most subjects were able to recall a number of tasks immediately but required some deliberation time to recall others. Results of the study confirmed Zeigarnik's initial hypothesis. The number of unfinished or incompleted tasks (designated *I*) that were recalled was significantly higher than was the number of completed tasks (designated *C*). By and large, subjects taking part in Zeigarnik's research were twice as likely to recall incompleted tasks as completed ones.

In the series of Zeigarnik studies, the recall ratio for tasks interrupted at the middle or toward the end (tasks nearing completion) was higher than for tasks interrupted at or near the beginning of work on them. This finding attested to the increasing involvement of a subject in moving a given task along to completion. The *I/C* ratio was seen to increase as the subject moved nearer and nearer to the goal of a satisfactory task solution.

During the course of her research, Zeigarnik discovered that persons who could be easily classified as being ambitious (high achiever) had a higher *I/C* ratio than did persons of average ambition. Ambitious (high achiever) subjects forgot completed tasks at a faster rate than did those of average ambitiousness. If task interpretation were to be interpreted by subjects as signifying that they had failed, generating an ego-threatening situation, the *I/C* ratio would be further increased, with subjects tending to recall incompleted tasks with greater frequency than before.

Studies have found that the Zeigarnik effect is sensitive to a number of factors that may be difficult, if not impossible, to control within the context of a laboratory study: (1) The Zeigarnik effect is less likely to appear if the subject is, to some extent, ego-involved in the task; (2) the effect is more likely to appear if the interruption of the task does not seem to be part of the experimental game plan; and (3) the effect is most likely to appear if the subject has set a genuine level of aspiration in the interrupted task, that is, has not come to the conclusion that the thing is impossible or beyond his or her capacity.

REFERENCE

Zeigarnik, Bluma. (1927). Ueber das Behalten von erledigten un enerledigten Handlungen. *Psychol. Forsch., 9,* 1–85.

Florence L. Denmark
Pace University

ZEITGEBERS

Physiological functions such as temperature, blood pressure, blood nutrients and hormones, and sleep-wake cycles fluctuate in a rhythmic pattern the period of which is 24 hours. Such fluctuations are called circadian rhythms, meaning "about a day." The cycle length or period of circadian rhythms under constant, aperiodic conditions, such as constant light or constant darkness, typically deviates from a 24-hour period. Under these conditions circadian rhythms are said to be free running because they no longer are entrained or synchronized by exogenous factors to a constant period in relation to the environment. When the young adult circadian system runs free, its periodicity is typically closer to 25 hours than 24 hours. This is due to certain critical exogenous factors that can synchronize circadian rhythms into stable period and phase relationships with the external day-night cycle. These exogenous factors are termed *zeitgebers* (time keepers) and include both physical and social factors (Aschoff, Hoffman, Pohl, & Wever, 1975).

How Zeitgebers Entrain Circadian Rhythms

In many animals, light is the primary zeitgeber that entrains circadian cycles (Aschoff, 1981; Pittendrigh, 1981). The brain pathway by which light entrains circadian rhythms has been clearly elucidated in animal studies (Moore & Eichler, 1972). This neuronal circuit involves ocular mechanisms (Reme, Wirz-Justice, & Terman, 1991) and a projection from the retina directly to a nucleus in the base of the brain called the suprachiasmatic nucleus (SCN; Moore & Lenn 1972). The suprachiasmatic nucleus has been called the body's biological clock (Rusak, 1989; Rusak & Haddad, 1993; Rusak & Zucker, 1979).

Photic and Nonphotic Zeitgebers

It appears that nonphotic factors such as social factors or social rhythms may also be important in the setting of circadian rhythms in human subjects (Aschoff, Fatranska, & Giedke, 1971; Mrosovsky, 1996; Wever, 1975, 1979, 1988). As well as acting as a direct zeitgeber, social rhythms can indirectly determine when a person is exposed to physical zeitgebers such as daylight and darkness. Moreover, social rhythms also determine when a person goes to bed or gets up and thus set the timing of their sleep-wake cycles. Social entrainment begins soon after birth so that an offspring's eating and sleeping schedules become synchronized with those of siblings and parents.

Social rhythms are maintained by a variety of factors such as occupation, marital status, presence or absence of children, and recreational activities. Thus, interruption of these factors has the potential for disruption of normal circadian timing. The mechanism by which social rhythms participate in entrainment of biological rhythms is unknown. Some authors have suggested, based on animal studies, that social interactions or behavioral activity might cause a nonspecific increase in arousal, which could then feedback on the pacemaker in the SCN (Mrosovsky, Reebs, Honrado, & Salmon, 1989; Turek & Losee-Olsen, 1986; Van Reeth & Turek, 1989). Recently, Moore and Card (1990) proposed that social Zeitgebers may entrain the SCN through a specific neuropeptide Y pathway that involves the intergeniculate leaflet. It has also been suggested that nonphotically entrainable oscillators may exist outside the SCN (Mikkelsen, Vrand, & Mrosovsky, 1998; Mistlberger, 1992).

Consequences of Disruptions of Zeitgebers

A loss or disruption of a zeitgeber can have important consequences on physiological and psychological functioning. Transmeridian flight has been demonstrated to be a potent source of rhythm disruption (jet lag). When a person takes a transmeridian flight, he or she will be exposed to new physical and social time cues (zeitgebers). Shift work represents another case of rhythm disturbance. It is perhaps not surprising that in addition to the jet lag-like symptoms of sleep disruption, malaise, and gastrointestinal disorders (Rutenfranz, Colquhoun, Knauth, & Ghauta, 1977), shift work has been found to be associated with increases in divorce (Knutsson, Akerstedt, Jonsson, & Orth-Gome, 1986; Tepas & Monk, 1987), increased risk of heart disease (Knutsson et al., 1986), difficulty concentrating and irritability (Rutenfranz et al., 1977), and heavier use of caffeine and alcohol (Gordon, Cleary, Parlan, & Czeisler, 1986; Monk, 1988; Regestein & Monk, 1991).

Zeitgebers and Depression

Photic Zeitgebers

Several recent theories have focused on changes in zeitgebers as an etiology of depression. The effect of physical zeitgebers on the development of depressive symptoms has been stressed by researchers who have studied seasonal affective disorder (SAD; Lewy, Sack, & Singer, 1984; Rosenthal et al., 1984). The classic presentation of SAD is the occurrence of depressive symptoms that begin late in autumn and resolve in spring. One treatment used for SAD is bright light exposure in early morning and/or late afternoon in order to approximate the daylight levels of a summer day (see Lewy et al., 1980; Kripke, 1982). Some patients with SAD do obtain relief from depressive symptoms using bright light exposure.

Nonphotic Zeitgebers

Although many studies suggest that light may play a role in the etiology and treatment of seasonal depressive disorders, studies in nonseasonal depression have not demonstrated any consistent therapeutic effect of bright light. Some theories have stressed the role of social zeitgebers in the onset and course of affective illness. In one model, certain life events and difficulties (Brown & Harris, 1986; Brown, Harris, & Peter, 1973), particularly those that involve separation or loss such as death, divorce, loss of job, moving, and so on are viewed as a loss of social zeitgebers. A loss of social zeitgebers, in turn, is postulated to produce changes in social rhythms, or the rhythmicity of the activities of daily life. Disruption in social rhythms are then thought to lead to changes in biological rhythms. Ultimately, it is postulated that chronic disruption of social and biological rhythms can lead to the onset, in vulnerable individuals, of depression. Whether a person actually becomes ill following the loss of a social zeitgeber is thought to depend on certain vulnerability factors such as genetic-familial loading, social supports, past history of affective episodes, and personality variables (Ehlers, Frank, & Kupfer, 1988; Ehlers, Kupfer, Frank, & Monk, 1994; Frank et al., 1994; Healy & Waterhouse, 1995).

REFERENCES

Aschoff, J. (1981). *Handbook of behavioral neurobiology: Vol. 4. Biological rhythms*. New York: Plenum Press.

Aschoff, J., Fatranska, M., & Giedke, H. (1971). Human circadian rhythms in continuous darkness: Entrainment by social cues. *Science, 171,* 213–215.

Aschoff, J., Hoffman, K., Pohl, H., & Wever, R. A. (1975). Re-entrainment of circadian rhythms after phase-shifts of the Zeitgeber. *Chronobiologia, 2,* 23–78.

Brown, G. W., & Harris, T. (1986). Stressor, vulnerability and depression: A question of replication (Editorial). *Psychological Medicine, 16,* 739–744.

Brown, G. W., Harris, T. O., & Peto, J. (1973). Life events and psychiatric disorders: Part II. Nature of causal link. *Psychological Medicine, 3,* 159–176.

Ehlers, C. L., Frank, E., & Kupfer, D. J. (1988). Social Zeitgebers and biological rhythms: A unified approach to understanding the etiology of depression. *Archives of General Psychiatry, 45,* 948–952.

Ehlers, C. L., Kupfer, D. J., Frank, E., & Monk, T. H. (1994). Biological rhythms and depression: The role of Zeitgebers and zeitstorers. *Depression, 1,* 285–293.

Frank, E., Kupfer, D. J., Ehlers, C. L., Monk, T. H., Cornes, C., Carter, S., & Frankel, D. (1994). Interpersonal and social rhythm therapy for bipolar disorder: Integrating interpersonal and behavioral approaches. *Behavior Therapist, 17,* 143–149.

Gordon, N. P., Cleary, P. D., Parlan, C. E., & Czeisler, C. A. (1986). The prevalence and health impact of shiftwork. *American Journal of Public Health, 76,* 1225–1228.

Healy, D., & Waterhouse, J. M. (1995). The circadian system and the therapeutics of the affective disorders. *Pharmacology & Theraputics, 65,* 241–263.

Knutsson, A., Akerstedt, T., Jonsson, B. G., & Orth-Gomer, K. (1986). Increased risk of schemic heart disease in shift workers. *Lancet, 2,* 89–92.

Kripke, D. F. (1982). Phase-advance theories for affective illness. In T. A. Wehr & F. K. Goodwin (Eds.), *Circadian rhythms in psychiatry* (pp. 41–69). Pacific Grove, CA: Boxwood Press.

Lewy, A. J., Sack, R. A., & Singer, C. L. (1984). Assessment and treatment of chronobiologic disorders using plasma melatonin levels and bright light exposure: The clockgate model and the phase response curve. *Psychopharmacology Bulletin, 20,* 561–565.

Lewy, A. J., Wehr, T. A., Goodwin, F. K., Newsome, D. A., & Markey, S. P. (1980). Light suppresses melatonin secretion in humans. *Science, 210,* 1267–1269.

Mikkelsen, N., Vrand, N., & Mrosovsky, N. (1998). Expression of Fos in the circadian system following nonphotic stimulation. *Brain Research Bulletin, 47,* 367–376.

Mistlberger, R. E. (1992). Nonphotic entrainment of circadian activity rhythms in suprachiasmatic nuclei-abated hamsters. *Behavioral Neuroscience, 106,* 192–202.

Monk, T. H. (1988). Coping with the stress of shift work. *Work and Stress, 2,* 169–172.

Moore, R. Y., & Card, J. P. (1990). Neuropeptide Y in the circadian timing system. *Ann NY Acad Sci, 611,* 247–257.

Moore, R. Y., & Eichler, V. B. (1972). Loss of circadian adrenal corticosterone rhythm following suprachiasmatic lesions in rats. *Brain Research, 42,* 201–206.

Moore, R. Y., & Lenn, N. J. (1972). A retinohypothalamic projection in the rat. *The Journal of Comparative Neurology, 146,* 1–14.

Mrosovsky, N. (1996). Locomotor activity and non-photic influences on circadian clocks. *Biological Reviews of the Cambridge Philosophical Society, 71,* 343–372.

Mrosovsky, N., Reebs, S. G., Honrado, G. I., & Salmon, P. A. (1989). Behavioural entrainment of circadian rhythms. *Experientia, 45,* 696–702.

Pittendrigh, C. S. (1981). Circadian systems: Entrainment. In J. Aschoff (Ed.), *Handbook of behavioral neurobiology: Vol. 4. Biological rhythms* (pp. 95–124). New York: Plenum Press.

Regestein, Q. R., & Monk, T. H. (1991). Is the poor sleep of shift workers a disorder? *American Journal of Psychiatry, 148,* 1487–1493.

Reme, C. E., Wirz-Justice, A., & Terman, M. (1991). The visual input stage of the mammalian circadian pacemaking system: I. Is there a clock in the mammalian eye? *Journal of Biological Rhythms, 6,* 5–29.

Rosenthal, N. E., Sack, D. A., Gillin, J. C., Lewy, A. J., Davenport, Y., Mueller, P. S., Newsome, D. A., & Wehr, T. A. (1984). Seasonal affective disorder a description of the syndrome and preliminary findings with light therapy. *Archives of General Psychiatry, 41,* 72–80.

Rusak, B. (1989). The mammalian circadian system: Models and physiology. *Journal of Biological Rhythms, 4,* 121–34.

Rusak, B., & Haddad, G. (1993). Neural mechanisms of the mammalian circadian system. *Journal of Biological Rhythms, 8* (Suppl.), S1–S108.

Rusak, B., & Zucker, I. (1979). Neural regulation of the circadian rhythms. *Physical Review A, 59,* 449–526.

Rutenfranz, J., Colquhoun, W. P., Knauth, P., & Ghata, J. N. (1977). Biomedical and psychosocial aspects of shift work: A review. *Scandinavian Journal of Work, Environment, & Health, 3,* 165–182.

Tepas, D. I., & Monk, T. H. (1987). Work schedules. In G. Salvendy (Ed.), *Handbook of human factors* (pp. 819–843). New York: Wiley.

Turek, F. W., & Losee-Olson, S. (1986). A benzodiazepine used in the treatment of insomnia phase shifts the mammalian circadian clock. *Nature, 321,* 167–168.

Van Reeth, O., & Turek, F. W. (1989). Stimulated activity mediates phase shifts in the hamster circadian clock induced by dark pulses or benzodiazepines. *Nature, 339,* 49–51.

Wever, R. A. (1975). The circadian multi-oscillator system of man. *International Journal of Chronobiology, 3,* 19–55.

Wever, R. A. (1979). *The circadian system of man: Results of experiments under temporal isolation.* New York: Springer-Verlag.

Wever, R. A. (1988). Order and disorder in human circadian rhythmicity: Possible relations to mental disorders. In D. J. Kupfer, T. H. Monk, & D. J. Barchas (Eds.), *Biological rhythms and mental disorders* (pp. 253–346). New York: Guilford Press.

CINDY L. EHLERS
Scripps Research Institute

Z-PROCESS

The Z-process is a psychotherapeutic and attachment system, incorporating ethological and attachment principles, developed to overcome resistance to human bonding and growth. The autistic child shows self-destructive aggression and does not direct aggression toward other people. The Z-process treatment of autistic children led to the conclusion that such psychopathology results from a failure to develop two bonding behavior networks essential for the growth of viable attachment: (1) body contact, necessary for intimacy and basic trust; and (2) eye-face contact, necessary for the direction, integration, and focus of complex emotional and cognitive social behavior. A disturbance in these bonds is called the *Medusa complex,* which is corrected by holding the child in "protest" while maintaining eye-face contact. Niko Tinbergen and his collaborators have reported significant success in using the holding approach with autistic children.

R. W. Zaslow

See also: **Bonding and Attachment**

Z-SCORE

The z-score, also known as the standard score, is the result of a transformation of raw data, and this conversion can be summed up as follows: Something minus its mean divided by its standard deviation. The "something" in this statement is usually one of two things: a raw data point within a set of observations or the observed mean of a sample of data. When such a transformation is applied to all observations within a data set, the first step of subtracting the mean from each individual observation has the effect of re-centering the distribution at a mean of zero. Because dividing all observations within a data set by a constant results in the standard deviation of the distribution being similarly reduced by that factor, the second step in the transformation results in a standard deviation of one for the distribution of z-scores. Thus, when a distribution of scores is converted to z-scores, the resulting distribution is centered at a mean of zero with a standard deviation of one. In addition, a distribution of z-scores retains the shape of its parent distribution. It follows from this attribute that when the parent distribution is normally distributed, so too will be the corresponding z-score distribution. When the size of the sample gets very large, this normal distribution of z-scores is given a special name, the standard normal distribution (see Figure 1), which is discussed in more detail later.

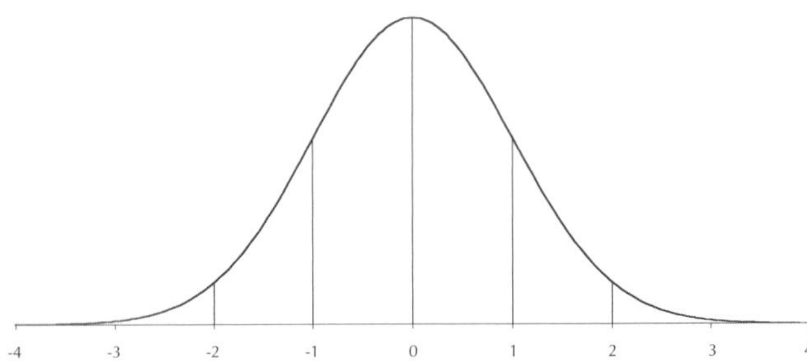

Figure 1. *Z*-scores.

The *Z*-Score as a Descriptive Statistic

A z-score for something indicates its location in relation to the mean of the distribution from which it was drawn. Specifically, a z-score is interpreted as how many standard deviations a score is above (positive z-score) or below (negative z-score) its mean. Returning to our general definition of a z-score as "something minus its mean divided by its standard deviation," we arrive at the following formula for converting an observation from a sample to a z-score:

$$z = (x - \bar{x})/s$$

in which $\bar{x}$ is the sample mean from which x is drawn and s is the standard deviation. To illustrate with an example, suppose that in a sample of adult males, the average weight is 185 lb, and the standard deviation is 15 lb. The z-score for an observation of 170 lb would be (170 – 185)/15 = –1.0. Therefore, we know that a man weighing 170 lb in this sample is 1.0 standard deviation below the mean. A z-score thus conveys the following information about its corresponding raw score: (1) how many standard deviations away from the mean of the distribution the score is, indicated by the absolute value of the score, and (2) whether the score falls above or below the mean of the sample, indicated by the sign of the score (see Figure 1). All z-scores, whether resulting from the transformation of raw data points or means of samples, are interpreted in this way.

The use of z-scores instead of raw sample data or even other measures of relative standing is preferable for several reasons. First, because the unit of measurement for z-scores is standard deviations in relation to the mean of a group of data, observations from different samples or populations can be compared directly with a common metric. Second, although other indexes of relative standing exist (e.g., percentile rank), not all preserve a 1:1 relationship with the parent distribution as the z-score does. For instance, a move from the 80th to 89th percentile (a difference of 9 percentile units) might represent a change of 10 units in the distribution of raw data, whereas a move from the 90th to 99th percentile (still a difference of 9 percentile units) might represent a change of 15 units in the raw data. On the other hand, a particular difference between z-scores, regardless of which two z-scores are examined to produce that difference, will always represent the same discrepancy between the corresponding raw scores in the parent distribution.

The Z-Score as an Inferential Statistic

When used as an inferential statistic, the z-score is not calculated from a particular data point within a sample, but rather from a sample mean. When a study sample is selected, it is basically drawn from a distribution of samples; thus, individual cases are not being sampled, but rather a particular mean. When the observed mean of a sample is converted to a z-score, we are thus calculating how deviant this study mean is from the mean of its hypothetical distribution, which is composed of all possible means that could be observed with samples of the same size. The definition of a z-score, "something minus its mean divided by its standard deviation," when the "something" is a sample mean, is given by the formula

$$z = \bar{x} - \mu/(\sigma/\sqrt{n})$$

Here, $\bar{x}$ is the sample mean being transformed. Again, because $\bar{x}$ is a sample mean, it was drawn from a distribution of sample means of a particular variable. According to the central limit theorem, as sample sizes get larger, this sampling distribution of means will approximate a normal distribution with a mean of μ and a standard deviation of $\sigma/\sqrt{n}$. Here, μ is the population mean for variable x, σ is the population standard deviation, and n is the size of the samples composing the sampling distribution for variable x.

The fact that the sampling distribution of means for a variable will always be normal with samples of sufficient size is not trivial and is in fact central to the utility of the z-score as an inferential statistic. Recall that a distribution of z-scores will retain the shape of its parent distribution. Because the sampling distribution of means is normal, so too will be the corresponding z-score distribution, the standard normal distribution. A z-score table has been derived for this distribution, detailing the proportion of cases that are more extreme (i.e., are further from the mean) than any given z-score (see Table 1). Basically, the standard normal distribution can be thought of as a pie, with an area of 1.0; when we cut this pie at a particular z-score value, we can determine what area of the pie lies on either side of the cut. Areas under the curve associated with particular z-scores are found in the z table and are shown pictorially in Figure 2. The key is that these areas reflect probabilities associated with the corresponding z-scores. Thus, if we look at Figure 2, we see that the proportion of the curve lying beyond a z-score of +1.0 is approximately .16. Because the standard normal distribution is normal, and thus symmetrical, a z-score of −1.0 also cuts off a proportion of .16 in the lower tail. Another way to say this is that the probability of selecting a z-score of 1.0 or greater from the standard normal distribution is .16, or that approximately 16% of observations in a normally distributed population will be greater than an observation producing a z-score of 1.0. Notice that the information in Figure 2 corresponds to proportions that can be found in the z table: Looking under the z-score column, we see that the area beyond a z-score of 1.0 is .1587. If we were not dealing with a normal distribution, we could not compare our calculated z-scores to this table of proportions to determine how extreme (i.e., improbable) a given z-score is, greatly limiting our inferential abilities. How this table is used for inferential purposes is discussed next.

Table 1. Selected Values of z From the z Table.

z	Area beyond z
0.0	.5000
0.33	.3707
0.5	.3085
1.0	.1587
1.5	.0668
2.0	.0228
2.5	.0062
3.0	.0014

Note: Proportions of total are under the normal curve.

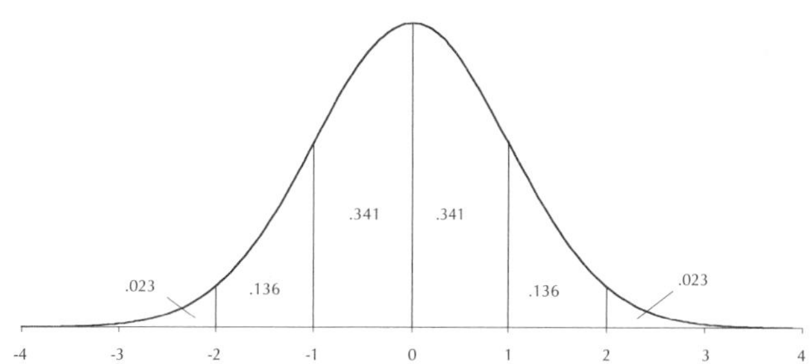

Figure 2. Z-scores and corresponding areas under the normal curve.

Because it is only hypothesized that a study sample is drawn from a particular population of given μ and σ, we can test our assumption by computing a z-score for the observed sample mean in order to determine if it is significantly different from the population mean (recall that this is also the mean of the sampling distribution of means for that variable). If the sample mean differs greatly from the population mean (i.e., produces a large z-score), then it might be concluded that the study sample was drawn from another sampling distribution with a more similar mean. But how do we determine if our sample mean is significantly different from the population mean? How improbable would a z-score and its corresponding sample mean have to be within a particular sampling distribution of means to decide that it is probably not drawn from that population? After all, just because an event is improbable does not mean that it is impossible. In psychology, the convention is to conclude that a *z*-score is significant (i.e., significantly different from the population mean to which it is being compared) if the probability of observing such a *z*-score is .05 or less. To return to our pie analogy, this means that the observed *z*-score cuts off a total of 1/20 of the pie in either one or both tails, depending on the hypothesis (i.e., a proportion of .05). In such a case, the null hypothesis that states that the sample mean equals the population mean for a given variable is rejected. The implication is that the study sample appears to have been drawn from a population distinct from that to which it was compared, a population with a mean more similar to its own. Fortunately, this test of significance is quite simple, as we can use the *z*-score table to determine the probability of obtaining any *z*-score.

Let's return to our weight example to illustrate. Assume that we want to test whether our group of adult men discussed earlier—say there are 25 of them—has been drawn from a population in which the mean is known to be 200 lb and the standard deviation is 25 lb. Because we calculated that the mean of our sample is 185 lb, the corresponding *z*-score is $(185 - 200)/(25/\sqrt{25}) = -.33$. Going to the *z* table, we see that the probability of obtaining a *z*-score of –.33 is .3707, well above .05. Thus, we conclude that observing a mean of 185 lb in a sample of 25 adult men is not so improbable given a population of the parameters mentioned. Thus, we would not determine that our sample mean is statistically different from the given population mean, and thus probably does not represent a different sampling distribution.

Joshua W. Madsen
University of Colorado at Boulder

BIOGRAPHIES

ABELES, NORMAN (b. 1928) Abeles is best known for his research on the interaction between mood and memory in older adults. He established the Clinical Neuropsychological Laboratory at Michigan State University. He has been president of the American Psychological Association and is very involved in its government.

ADLER, ALFRED (1870–1937) Adler founded the school of Individual Psychology. He saw the individual in its unity and goal orientation operating as if according to a self-created life plan, later called *lifestyle.* Drives, feelings, emotions, memory, the unconscious, and all processes are subordinated to the lifestyle.

AINSWORTH, MARY D. S. (1913–1999) Ainsworth devoted a lifetime to researching infant-mother relationships and introduced a 20-minute controlled laboratory technique called the *strange situation.* She extended her research into attachment beyond infancy by examining other affectional bonds throughout the life cycle.

AKIL, HUDA Akil's research primarily focuses on the brain biology of stress and depression and on the biology of endorphins and other molecules related to substance abuse. Her research takes a broad-based approach, examining the system at a cellular, molecular, and integrative level.

ALBEE, GEORGE (b. 1921) Albee's research focused on the prevention of psychopathology. He established the Vermont Conference on the Primary Prevention of Psychopathology and played a constructive role in defining the importance of prevention of disorders.

ALLPORT, FLOYD HENRY (1890–1978) Allport is considered to be the father of social psychology. In his theories and research he set a direction in social psychology that was followed by psychologists in that area for several decades.

ALLPORT, GORDON WILLARD (1897–1967) Allport regarded personality as the natural subject matter of psychology. His approach was eclectic, drawing on a wide variety of sources.

ALMEIDA, EDUARDO (b. 1937) Almeida conducted a program for the development of competence in school children from Mexico City. He also developed an instrument for studying public opinion.

AMES, LOUISE B. (1908–1996) Ames's books have been standard references on the developmental processes for both psychologists and parents.

ANASTASI, ANNE (1908–2001) Anastasi is most closely associated with the development of differential psychology. Her research centered chiefly on factor analysis, problems of test construction, and the interpretation of test scores.

ANGELL, FRANK (1857–1939) Angell established a laboratory at Stanford University. His research centered on psychophysics, especially auditory sensation.

ANGELL, JAMES ROLLAND (1867–1949) Angell stated that functional psychology was the study of mental operations, that psychology should be considered a study of the functional utilities of consciousness, and that psychology is concerned with the relationship between the body and the environment.

ANGYAL, ANDRAS (1902–1960) Angyal asserted that there are two basic patterns of motivation: striving toward mastery and striving toward love.

ANSBACHER, HEINZ L. (b. 1904) Ansbacher is the prime interpreter of Alfred Adler. His most important contribution is his clarification of Adler's concepts of lifestyle and social interest.

ANZIEU, DIDIER (b. 1923) Anzieu's main psychological concepts are *group delusion, skin ego, paradoxical transference,* and *creative psychological work.*

ARISTOTLE (384–322 B.C.) A student in Plato's Academy in Athens, Aristotle created a new science of logic, the art and method of correct thinking. He used his concepts—form, matter, substance, cause, potentiality, actuality, and substratum—as tools for problem solving. In Aristotelian thought, knowledge is expanded to include two classifications: theoretical science and practical science.

ASCH, SOLOMON (1907–1996) Asch is best known for performing a series of experiments to determine the effects of social pressures on single individuals.

ASTON-JONES, GARY Aston-Jones's major research interest is the role of brainstem neuromodulatory systems in attention, affect, and motivation. These interests have led him to focus on monoamine neurons that project to the forebrain, especially with regard to their role in mental functions and dysfunctions.

ATKINSON, RICHARD C. Atkinson's research has dealt with problems of memory and cognition. He is best known for the Atkinson-Shiffrin model, a theory of memory that has helped in clarifying the relationship between brain structures and psychological phenomena.

AUSTAD, CAROL DONNA SHAW (b. 1946) Austad conducted research on the practice of psychotherapy in the managed-care setting.

AVENERIUS, RICHARD (1843–1896) Avenerius hypothesized that there was a system "C" on which consciousness depended. The significance of this concept lies in its influence on Titchener.

AXELROD, JULIUS (1912–1983) Axelrod discovered much of what we know about norepinephrine, serotonin, and dopamine, including their metabolic fates. He discovered the uptake sites for monoamines that represent the basis for the mechanism of action of the serotonin reuptake inhibitors as antidepressants.

AZUMA, HIROSHI (b. 1926) Azuma's work centers on the cognitive development of children, concept learning, and methods of instruction.

BACON, SIR FRANCIS (1561–1636) Bacon stated that in science there are two kinds of experiments: those that shed light and those that bring fruit. He was the first to call a halt to medieval speculation and superstition.

BADDELEY, ALAN (b. 1934) Baddeley demonstrated that long-term memory tends to rely heavily on meaning, as opposed to short-term memory, which relies more heavily on sound or speech coding.

BAIN, ALEXANDER (1818–1903) Bain stressed two basic laws of association: similarity and contiguity. He believed that sensations and feelings come together in close succession and in such a way that, when one of them is brought to mind, the other will most likely occur.

BAIRD, JOHN WALLACE (1873–1919) Baird was regarded as Titchener's most representative follower. He made systematic experimental introspection of the higher mental processes the central research topic of Clark University.

BAKARE, CHRISTOPHER G. M. (b. 1935) Bakare devised a statistical technique for identifying the "kernel of truth" in interethnic stereotypes to understand the conflicts that plague Africa's development.

BALDWIN, JAMES MARK (1861–1934) Known as a founding father of developmental psychology, Baldwin developed a thoroughgoing Darwinian genetic psychology. He stressed intentional action as the instrument of selection in mental development.

BALTES, PAUL B. (b. 1939) Baltes, a pioneer of life-span developmental psychology, emphasizes that individuals continue to maintain a capacity for change across the entire life span.

BANDURA, ALBERT (b. 1925) Bandura assigns a central role to cognitive, vicarious, self-regulative, and self-reflective processes in human coping and adaptation.

BARBER, THEODORE X. (b. 1927) Barber, a distinguished hypnosis researcher and theoretician, delineated three paradigms of responsive hypnotic subjects: positively set, fantasy-prone, and amnesia-prone hypnotic virtuoso.

BARKER, ROGER G. (1903–1990) Barker helped establish the Midwest Psychological Field Station, a pioneering center for research in environmental psychology that investigates relationships between environment and behavior.

BARLOW, DAVID H. (b. 1942) Barlow's work is in the areas of anxiety disorders, sexual problems, and clinical research methodology. His research continues to focus on developing new treatments for childhood anxiety disorders and exploring early psychological and social factors that create vulnerabilities for the development of anxiety disorders.

BARTLETT, FREDERIC C. (1886–1979) Bartlett is best remembered for his outstanding achievement in directing research regarding memory. His work is best represented by his classic book, *Remembering.*

BASOV, MIKHAIL YAKOVIEVICH (1892–1931) Basov was a Soviet psychologist who opposed a mechanistic point of view. He believed that heredity and environment both contributed to human growth and development, their roles changing from one phase of development to another.

BATESON, GREGORY (1904–1980) Bateson conducted anthropological research with the Baining and the Sulka of the Gazelle Peninsula and with the Iatmul of New Guinea. Later in life he explored the causes of maladjustments and mental disorders.

BATESON, WILLIAM (1861–1926) Bateson is best known for his contributions to the establishment of the Mendelian concept of heredity. Bateson named the new science "genetics" and extended his efforts to a study of chromosomes and genes.

BAYÉS, RAMÓN (b. 1930) Bayés is one of the founders of diverse entities in Spain, such as the introduction of behavior modification. He wrote the first Spanish book on behavioral pharmacology.

BAYLEY, NANCY (1899–1994) Among Bayley's seminal studies are longitudinal research on the life span; techniques for measuring behavioral, motor, and physical development; and assessment of interactions between behavioral and biological development.

BEACH, FRANK A. (1911–1988) Known for his work in human and animal sexual behavior, Beach published his findings in *Patterns of Sexual Behavior.* In this book, sex is reviewed from cultural and evolutionary perspectives.

BECK, AARON T. (b. 1921) Beck developed his cognitive theory and therapy of psychopathology in the 1960s and 1970s. The various inventories he developed to test his new theory are among the most widely used psychological instruments.

BEEBE-CENTER, JOHN G. (1897–1958) Beebe-Center was an investigator of hedonic aspects. As a result of his studies of taste thresholds and the scaling of taste values, he developed a psychological scale of taste named the *gust scale.*

BEERS, CLIFFORD W. (1876–1943) Beers developed manic-depressive disorder and for 3 years was a patient in several hospitals. Following his recovery, he organized the first Society for Mental Hygiene in 1908. He authored the classic book *The Snakepit.*

BÉKÉSY, GEORG VON (1899–1972) Békésy is best known for his work in audition. He devised many new tools, such as the Békésy audiometer for measuring loss of hearing.

BÉKHTEREV, VLADIMIR M. (1857–1927) Békhterev is best known for his work on associated reflexes (usually referred to by Ivan Pavlov's term *conditioned reflexes*).

BELL, SIR CHARLES (1774–1842) Bell is known for his discovery that the sensory fibers of a mixed nerve enter the spinal cord at the dorsal root, whereas the motor fibers of the same nerve leave the cord by a ventral root.

BENEDICT, RUTH F. (1887–1948) Most of Benedict's research dealt with the origins of Native American cultures. She saw in each culture an assemblage of elements from many other cultures.

BENTON, ARTHUR L. (b. 1909) Benton's teaching and research career covered a variety of aspects of clinical neuropsychology, including hemispheric cerebral dominance, brain injury in childhood, aphasia, perceptual disabilities, and the development of neuropsychological assessment procedures.

BERNE, ERIC L. (1910–1970) Berne was the founder of transactional analysis, a system of group therapy that takes its name from analyzing interactions between individuals in terms of three ego states in each of us: the child, the parent, and the adult.

BETTELHEIM, BRUNO (1903–1990) Bettelheim was concerned with autistic and psychotic children. His theories tended to be psychoanalytic in opposition to the more biological approaches to childhood psychoses. He is well known for the case of "Joey, the Mechanical Boy."

BIEDERMAN, JOSEPH (b. 1947) Biederman has been concerned with the genetics and development of ADHD. He has made significant contributions to the understanding of the relationship of ADHD to comorbid disorders, especially bipolar disorders.

BIJOU, SIDNEY W. (b. 1908) Bijou was the director of the Child Research Laboratory and the Institute of Research in Exceptional Children at Champaign-Urbana Illinois, and the founding editor of the *Journal of Experimental Child Psychology.* With Donald Baer, he coauthored three influential books regarding human development from a behavioral perspective.

BINET, ALFRED (1857–1911) Binet acquired much of his data on intelligence by studying his daughters. He developed a test that became the first scale for the measurement of intelligence. This test was modified by Terman at Stanford University and became the Stanford-Binet Intelligence Test.

BINGHAM, WALTER V. (1880–1952) During World War I, Bingham served as executive secretary of the committee on classification of personnel in the U.S. Army. He was one of a small group that developed intelligence testing for the Army.

BLAKE, ROBERT R. (b. 1918) Blake has provided insight into group and intergroup dynamics, concentrating particularly on the organizational impact of group norms and the resolution of intergroup conflict.

BLAU, THEODORE H. (1928–2003) Blau has performed research on the nature and effects of mixed cerebral dominance. He proposed a neuropsychological/social influence theory of Schizophrenia as well as producing work on community interventions.

BLEULER, EUGEN (1857–1939) Bleuler introduced concepts such as neologism, word salad, and negative speech into the descriptive vocabulary of Schizophrenia, as well as the notions of autism and ambivalence.

BLOOM, BERNARD (b. 1923) Bloom established the nationally recognized doctoral program in community/clinical psychology at the University of Colorado at Boulder. His major work was on very short-term therapy.

BOAS, FRANZ (1858–1942) Boas wanted to make anthropology a rigorous and exact science. In many of his investigations he noted parallel developments in widely separated areas.

BODER, DAVID PABLO (1886–1961) After the Russian Revolution, Boder traveled to Mexico, where he was placed in charge of psychological research in penal institutions. Later, he established a psychological museum in the United States.

BOLLES, ROBERT C. (b. 1928) Bolles's research ranged over different areas of animal motivation and later focused on avoidance behavior. He developed the concept of species-specific defense reactions.

BONNET, CHARLES (1720–1793) Bonnet and Condillac used the analogy of a human as a statue. Condillac had avoided physiology, but Bonnet wrote of nervous fluids and agitation of the nerve fibers. He may have anticipated the doctrine of the "specific energies of nerves."

BORGATTA, EDGAR F. (b. 1924) Borgatta's early research focused on role-playing techniques and sociometric analysis. Later, his research addressed the formal properties of small groups and the structure of interaction processes, as well as scaling and statistical analysis.

BORING, EDWARD G. (1886–1968) Boring's *History of Experimental Psychology* is a widely accepted classic. It brought together the creative scientist and the *Zeitgeist,* or spirit of the times, and explained how their interaction affected the direction of psychology.

BORKOVEC, THOMAS D. (b. 1944) Borkovec has focused on theories of anxiety development and the treatment of Generalized Anxiety Disorders.

BOUCHARD, JR., THOMAS J. (b. 1937) Bouchard's career has primarily focused on human individual differences. His major contribution has been estimating the various types of environmental and genetic influences on human psychological and medical/physical characteristics.

BOWDITCH, HENRY PICKERING (1840–1911) Bowditch was the first to demonstrate the all-or-nothing law of nerve transmission in heart muscle fibers. The principle that nerves cannot be fatigued is known as Bowditch's law.

BOWER, GORDON HOWARD (b. 1932) Bower's early research involved operant conditioning with lower animals. His interests then turned to problems in human learning, including mathematical models of learning. Bower played a major role in the development of cognitive psychology.

BOWLBY, JOHN (1907–1990) Bowlby is known for his work on the ill effects of maternal deprivation on personality development and for formulating attachment theory as a way of conceptualizing a child's tie to his or her mother.

BRADLEY, FRANCIS HERBERT (1846–1924) Bradley emphasized the importance of individuals to find themselves first as a whole and then bring themselves into line with the world of completely harmonized experience with an infinite coherent unity.

BRAID, JAMES (ca. 1795–1860) Braid generally is credited as the discoverer of hypnosis, although the phenomenon had been known and practiced earlier by Mesmer, Elliotson, and Esdale. His significance is that he removed the phenomenon from the realm of mystical explanation.

BRAY, W. CHARLES II (1904–1982) Bray's research was mostly on hearing, especially on electrical potentials in the cochlea and auditory nerve action in response to sounds. His work initiated the field of auditory electrophysiology.

BRENMAN-GIBSON, MARGARET (b. 1918) Best known for her work on altered states of consciousness and their uses in psychoanalytic psychotherapy, Brenman-Gibson has extended this interest to the creative state in writers.

BRENTANO, FRANZ (1838–1917) Brentano, in opposition to Wilhelm Wundt's views, proclaimed that the primary method of psychology was observation—not experimentation. He differentiated the act of seeing color from the sensory content of color.

BRETT, GEORGE S. (1879–1944) Brett is primarily known for his monumental three-volume work, *A History of Psychology.* He traced psychology from its earliest beginnings in ancient Greece to the twentieth century.

BREUER, JOSEPH (1842–1905) Prior to his first encounters with Freud, Breuer had been treating a young woman known as Anna O. Along with hypnosis, he had been using the talking-out method in treating her symptoms. He discovered that, if placed under hypnosis and encouraged to talk out her feelings and recall her past experiences, she felt better after being removed from the hypnotic state. Breuer worked in collaboration with Freud in Vienna.

BREZNITZ, SHLOMO (b. 1936) Breznitz discovered and documented the phenomenon of *incubation of threat,* whereby fear of danger grows with anticipation.

BRIDGMAN, PERCY W. (1882–1961) Seeking to clarify the nature of physical concepts, Bridgman introduced the notion of operational definition: A concept is to be defined in terms of the operations by which it is observed.

BROADBENT, DONALD E. (1926–1993) Primarily an occupational or "human factors" psychologist, Broadbent was probably best known for an early advocacy of information-processing models for memory in human beings.

BROCA, PAUL (1824–1880) Although later research indicated that speech is too complicated a mechanism to be confined to one specific area of the brain, Broca is best known today for this. This area of the brain became known as "Broca's area."

BRUCH, HILDE (1904–1984) Bruch's research focused on childhood obesity, anorexia nervosa, and the relationship of eating disorders to Schizophrenia development.

BUNNY, W. E. After a long stretch at NIMH, Bunny became chair of Psychiatry at the University of California, Irvine, and has made pioneering breakthroughs in research spanning from the biology of Schizophrenia to mood disorders.

BURT, CYRIL L. (1883–1971) Burt was a leading British psychologist, especially in the areas of child development and statistics. He is a pioneer in the development of child guidance clinics in England and developed techniques of factor analysis. The integrity of his research methods and data has been severely criticized.

BUTTERS, NELSON (1937–1995) Butters's major contribution was to theories and assessment of neuropsychology.

CALKINS, MARY (1863–1930) Calkins invented the method of paired associates for the study of memory.

CAMPBELL, DONALD T. (1916–1996) Campbell was best known for his methodological writings, of which "Convergent and Discriminant Validation by the Multitrait-Multimethod Matrix" (Campbell and Fiske), and *Experimental and Quasi-Experimental Designs for Research* (Campbell and Stanley) are the best known. Later in life, his writings focused on philosophy of science issues.

CANNON, WALTER B. (1871–1945) Cannon's research on emotion and its effect on digestive processes was especially important for the field of psychology. Further exploration in this area led him to discoveries of other adaptive changes in the physiology of the body under emotion and stress. A critique of William James's theory of emotion led to Cannon's substitute theory, now known as the Canon-Bard Theory of Emotion.

CATANIA, CHARLES (b. 1936) As a behavioral pharmacologist, Catania has written on topics in the experimental analysis of behavior, including learning, reinforcement schedules, and verbal behavior.

CATTELL, JAMES McKEEN (1860–1944) The theme of Cattell's research was individual differences. His work contributed to the practical and applied psychology that was functional and uniquely American.

CATTELL, RAYMOND B. (1905–1998) Cattell derived his distinction in psychology from multivariate factor analysis and from numerous tests measuring various aspects of personality and intelligence that he developed.

CHA, JAE-HO (b. 1934) Cha was responsible for identifying a class of social perceptual phenomena, including dissonance effect and perceptual constancies, that he named the *discounting effect.*

CHAPANIS, ALPHONSE (1917–2002) Sometimes called the father of human factors, or ergonomics, Chapanis acquired his taste for applied work while wrestling with the difficult problems encountered by the men who had to fly and fight in the military aircraft of World War II.

CHARCOT, JEAN-MARTIN (1825–1893) Charcot is best known for his studies on hypnosis and hysteria. He believed that hypnosis was a condition peculiar to hysterical patients and a useful method for investigating hysterical predispositions.

CHARNEY, DENNIS (b. 1951) Charney has worked primarily in biological bases and treatments of mood and anxiety disorders.

CHAVEZ, EZEQUIEL A. (1868–1946) Chavez was considered by James Mark Baldwin to be the pioneer of Mexican psychology. He promoted educational reform that permitted him to teach the first psychology course in Mexico.

CHELPANOV, GEORGII IVANOVICH (1862–1936) For Chelpanov, the brain was the seat of the soul, through which psychology could be expressed. The soul was distinct from matter, but through proper experimental techniques it could be studied and understood.

CHEN, LI (b. 1902) Chen's work, mostly in the area of industrial psychology, has made significant contributions to the development of modern Chinese psychology. His study on the differentiation and integration of the *g* factor was recognized as a landmark in understanding intellectual development.

CHILD, IRVIN L. (1915–2000) During the 20th century, Child was one of the prominent figures in child development. He was also concerned with major societal factors, such as poverty, that had an impact on development.

CHOI, DENNIS Choi has contributed importantly to current understanding of mechanisms responsible for neuronal cell death after acute central nervous system insults, including NMDA receptor-mediated excitotoxicity, excessive calcium or zinc influx, and programmed cell death.

CHOMSKY, A. NOAM (b. 1928) Chomsky views the understanding of language as genetically determined and developing comparably to other bodily organs. He argues that learning a language is both species-specific and species-uniform: Only humans have the capacity for language acquisition, and all languages share a common underlying logical structure.

CLARK, KENNETH B. (1914–2000) Clark's research on the effect of segregation on the personality development of children was influential in the U.S. Supreme Court's historic 1964 *Brown v. Board of Education of Topeka, Kansas* decision. Along with his wife, Dr. Mamie Phipps Clark, Clark worked tirelessly to increase the participation of low-income groups in decisions on education, housing, employment and training, and economic development.

COIE, JOHN D. (b. 1940) The primary focus of Coie's research has been the development and prevention of serious antisocial behavior. He theorized that person-based effects on the social environment mediate the overall development of psychopathology and violence.

CORNELIUS, HANS (1863–1910) Cornelius maintained that the form quality was an attribute of experience and must be perceived as a whole (not broken down into individual experiences), as Wundt had suggested.

CORSINI, RAYMOND J. (b. 1914) The original editor of the *Corsini Encyclopedia of Psychology and Behavioral Science,* Corsini is best known for his unique style of dealing with problems in counseling and psychotherapy.

COUÉ, EMILE (1857–1926) Coué, a chemist, studied hypnotism under Bernheim and Liébeault. He claimed that, by means of autosuggestion, ideas that caused illness might be suggested away. His statement, "Every day in every way I am becoming better and better," has become proverbial.

COYLE, JOSEPH T. (b. 1943) Coyle discovered the loss of cholinergic cells in Alzheimer's disease and invented the radioenzymatic assay for catecholamines that revolutionized the field. Most recently he has been working on the role of glutamate in the biology of Schizophrenia.

CRAIGHEAD, W. EDWARD (b. 1942) Craighead has worked on the relationship of cognitive dysfunction and depression. Most recently his work is on prevention of first episode and recurrence of depression among adolescents.

CRONBACH, LEE J. (1916–2001) Cronbach's research was concerned with new approaches to the validation of psychological tests. In education psychology, he has stressed the relationship between classroom practices and basic psychological principles, particularly those of generalization and the transfer of training.

DAHLSTROM, W. GRANT (b. 1922) Dahlstrom focused on the assessment of personality. He played a major role in the evaluation and development of the MMPI-II.

DARLEY, JOHN GORDON (1910–1990) Darley's publications were in the areas of vocational interest measurement, student performance in higher education, student counseling, individual differences, social psychology, and psychometric theory.

DARWIN, CHARLES (1809–1882) Darwin's work influenced psychology in many ways. It changed the goal of psychology to the study of the organism's adaptation to its environment and placed increasing emphasis on individual differences among members of the same species.

DAVIS, MICHAEL (b. 1942) Davis pioneered research on the neurobiology of emotion with an emphasis on the amygdala.

DAVISON, GERALD C. Davison's research focuses on the relationships between cognition and a variety of behavioral and emotional problems via his articulated thoughts in simulated situations. His book *Clinical Behavior Therapy* (coauthored with M. Goldfried) is regarded as one of the definitive texts on the ways theory and research in cognitive behavior therapy are translated into clinical application.

DENMARK, FLORENCE L. (b. 1936) A pioneer in the field of the psychology of women, Denmark's most significant research has emphasized women's leadership and leadership styles, the interaction of status and gender, women in cross-cultural perspective, and the contributions of women to psychology.

DESCARTES, RENÉ (1596–1650) Descartes is renowned as the father of modern philosophy. He emphasized the individual thinker: the question of what a particular person may know, rather than what people may know. A rationalist, he defined knowledge as judgments or statements that can be said to be certain or indubitable, and he denied that sense experience can lead to knowledge in this way.

DEUTSCH, MORTON (b. 1920) Under the influence of K. Lewin's dictum, Deutsch believed that there was nothing so practical as a good theory. His classic study on the effects of cooperation and competition was the taking-off point for much of his subsequent work, which helped to stimulate the development of a movement toward cooperative learning in schools.

DEWEY, JOHN (1859–1952) Dewey's paper "The Reflex Arc Concept in Psychology" is usually credited with establishing functionalism as a defined school of psychology, rather than just an orientation or attitude.

DINGLEDINE, RAYMOND (b. 1948) Dingledine's most significant research accomplishments are the discoveries that glycine is a coagonist of NMDA receptors; that the transition between interictal and ictalstates in the high potassium model of seizures involves shrinkage of extracellular space; that one amino acid residue controls calcium permeation in glutamate receptor channels; that the channel-lining domain of glutamate receptor subunits is a reentrant loop rather than a transmembrane domain; and that the potency of certain ifenprodil analogues as NMDA receptor antagonists is enhanced at ischemic pH.

DOLLARD, JOHN (1900–1980) Dollard's studies achieved a remarkable synthesis of psychoanalysis, experimental psychology of learning and motivation, sociological analysis of social structure, and anthropological awareness of cultural variation.

DONDERS, FRANS C. (1818–1889) Donders is most prominently known for his studies on reaction time.

There were appreciable individual differences among observers. The particular reaction time, as it differed from one astronomer to another, became known as the *personal equation.*

DOWNEY, JUNE ETTA (1875–1932) Downey was the first psychologist to study individual differences in temperament. She developed the Will Temperament Test.

DREIKURS, RUDOLF (1897–1972) Dreikurs, an Adlerian, pioneered group psychotherapy and developed the "double interview" in therapy. He was deeply concerned with social equality, which he viewed as the basis for mental health.

DUBOIS, PAUL-CHARLES (1848–1918) Dubois may be considered the first psychotherapist in the modern tradition in that he believed in "moral persuasion" in dealing with the mentally ill—that is, in simply talking with patients in an attempt to reason with them.

DUNBAR, HELEN FLANDERS (1902–1959) Dunbar demonstrated that psychosomatic disorders were emotional in origin and related the specific type of disorder to personality characteristics.

DUNCKER, KARL (1903–1940) Duncker's publications cover a broad range of subjects, including problem solving, perception, motivation, systematic psychology, and philosophical issues.

DUNNETTE, MARVIN D. (b. 1926) Dunnette developed procedures for selecting and appraising research scientists, sales personnel, and clerical employees.

EBBINGHAUS, HERMANN (1850–1909) Ebbinghaus was the first psychologist to investigate learning and memory experimentally. He invented the nonsense syllable procedure, which revolutionized the study of association and learning.

ECCLES, JOHN C. (b. 1903) Eccles, an interactionist and personalist, views the mind and brain as separate and distinct entities. He offered a "liaison between brain and mind hypothesis" to explain the interactive process.

EHRENFELS, CHRISTIAN VON (1859–1932) Ehrenfels was a forerunner of the Gestalt movement. Asch credits Ehrenfels and Wertheimer as the major influences on his use of Gestalt in social psychology.

EISDORFER, CARL (b. 1930) Eisdorfer has specialized in research on aging. He was founding editor of the *Annual Review of Gerontology and Geriatrics.*

ELKIND, DAVID (b. 1931) Elkind is perhaps best known for his attempt to extend, integrate, and apply Piagetian theories to educational and social problems of children and youths.

ELLIOTSON, JOHN (1791–1868) Elliotson practiced mesmerism at the University College Hospital in London with positive results and gave it professional acceptance. He treated patients suffering from a variety of nervous disorders and also employed hypnosis as an anesthetic.

ELLIS, ALBERT (b. 1913) After practicing psychoanalysis, Ellis rebelled against its dogma and inefficiency, experimented with several other methods, and started his own system, now known as Rational-Emotive Behavior Therapy (REBT).

ELLIS, HAVELOCK (1859–1939) Ellis concluded that homosexual behavior was congenital. Masturbation, he stated, was a legitimate source of mental relaxation. Ellis also objected to Freud's application of adult sexual terms to infants.

ENDLER, NORMAN S. (b. 1931) Endler's interaction model of anxiety postulates that trait and state anxiety are multidimensional and that interactions evoking state anxiety occur between persons and situations only when person factors and situational stress are congruent.

ENTWISTLE, NOEL J. (b. 1936) Entwistle implemented two 5-year programs of research on student learning in higher education. One involved psychometric tests to predict degree performance; another focused more on learning processes.

ERIKSON, ERIK H. (1902–1992) Erikson is known for his work in developmental psychology. He coined the term *identity crisis* and described the human life cycle as comprising eight stages.

ERON, LEONARD D. (b. 1920) Eron's longitudinal research with medical students had some influence on the reorganization of medical curricula at the time. His remarkable longitudinal study on the learning of aggression in children (whose 40-year follow-up he recently conducted) demonstrated that aggressive behavior is stable over time and across generations and that its development is affected by observational learning.

ESCALONA, SIBYLLE K. (b. 1915) Escalona's primary interest was normal development in infancy and early childhood. She was among the first to undertake extensive systematic studies of normal infant behavior in naturalistic settings.

ESDAILE, JAMES (1808–1859) Esdaile, a British surgeon, began practicing hypnosis in India after having read of Elliotson's work. He used hypnosis to induce anesthesia. In operations to remove scrotal tumors, Esdaile reported reducing mortality rates from 50 to 5 percent.

ESQUIROL, JEAN ÉTIENNE (1772–1840) A successor to Philippe Pinel, Esquirol was one of the first, if not the first, to apply statistical methods to clinical studies of the mentally ill.

ESTES, WILLIAM K. (b. 1919) Estes brought statistical theory to bear upon Guthrie's learning theory. He developed a statistical theory of learning predicated on the principle of contiguity.

EVANS, DWIGHT L. (b. 1944) Evans has had a long-standing clinical and research interest in depression. His research has focused on the neurobiology of stress and depression, and he conducted clinical drug trials specializing in depression and related mood disorders.

EVANS, RICHARD I. (b. 1922) Evans is best known as a pioneer in oral history, instruction via film and television, and human problem-oriented research (prejudice, juvenile delinquency, health) in social psychology.

EWALD, JULIUS RICHARD (1855–1921) Ewald was interested in the central nervous system and had a special interest in the physiology of receptor end organs. He developed the pressure-pattern theory of hearing, which challenged the resonance theory of Helmholtz.

EYSENCK, HANS J. (1916–1997) Eysenck researched the areas of personality theory and measurement, intelligence, social attitudes and politics, behavioral genetics, and behavior therapy. He was one of the pioneers in the development of behavior therapy in England.

FABRE, JEAN HENRI (1823–1915) Fabre described many aspects of insect behavior, including the relationship between the sex of the egg and the dimensions of the cell in the solitary bee. He opposed Darwin's theory of evolution.

FAIRBURN, CHRISTOPHER G. (b. 1944) One of the world's leading authorities on the treatment of Bulimia Nervosa. His model of the disorder underlies most cognitive-behavioral interventions for it.

FECHNER, GUSTAV THEODOR (1801–1887) Fechner is best remembered for his development of psychophysics. For the first time scientists could measure the mind; by the mid-19th century, the scientific methods were being applied to mental phenomena.

FERENCZI, SANDOR (1873–1933) Ferenczi was interested in the relationship between biology and psychoanalysis and extended the work of Freud.

FERRIER, SIR DAVID (1843–1928) Ferrier was noted for his contributions regarding the localization of brain functions. He was the first to locate the visual center in the occipital lobes, and his work led to important advances in brain surgery.

FERSTER, CHARLES B. (1922–1981) Ferster was dedicated to an operant behavioral approach to psychology. His writings and research ranged from basic behavioral research to its applications in education and clinical psychology.

FESTINGER, LEON (1919–1989) Festinger further developed cognitive dissonance theory, which states that people whose behavior is in discord with their thoughts will restructure their thoughts and behavior to mutual agreement.

FICHTE, JOHANN GOTTLIEB (1762–1814) Fichte was one of the successors to Kantian philosophy and psychology. He stressed the freedom of the human will in contrast to the determinism found in the physical sciences.

FISCHER, HARDI (b. 1922) Fischer is an experimental psychologist who was especially concerned with the relationships among visual perception, epistemology, and developmental psychology.

FISHER, RONALD A. (1890–1962) Fisher gave psychology the analysis of variance, analytic techniques for small samples, the concept of null hypothesis, and the notion of significant/insignificant as a continuum rather than a dichotomy.

FLAMENT, CLAUDE (b. 1930) Flament's publications covered various topics: social influence, in-group behavior, structural balance cognitive theory, qualitative data analysis, and ordered set theory.

FLAMMER, AUGUST (b. 1938) Flammer's research centered on question asking, selective memory, influence of titles, encoding, free discourse, perspective shifts, and individual differences.

FLAVELL, JOHN H. (b. 1928) Flavell's research style was to think of important cognitive competencies that others had not studied and then to investigate their development from childhood.

FLOURENS, PIERRE (1794–1867) Flourens confirmed the Bell-Magendie law—the separation of the nervous system into sensory and motor divisions.

FLOURNOY, THÉODORE (1854–1920) Flournoy was the initiator of scientific psychology in Switzerland, where he founded the first psychological laboratory. His research included studies on reaction time, imaging, sensation, and hypnosis.

FLÜGEL, JOHN CARL (1884–1955) Flügel's best-known work is *A Hundred Years of Psychology,* which reflects broad historical scholarship in psychology.

FOA, EDNA B. (b. 1942) Foa has devoted her academic career to studying the psychopathology and treatment of anxiety disorders, primarily Obsessive-Compulsive Disorder and Posttraumatic Stress Disorder. She is one of the world's experts in the treatment of these disorders.

FOPPA, KLAUS (b. 1930) Foppa has worked mainly in the field of verbal communication, especially on the development of children's communicative skills, for which he developed several methods of analysis.

FOREL, AUGUSTE-HENRI (1848–1931) Forel was the first to achieve biological preparations of human brain specimens and was also the first to describe parabiosis (the joining together of two animals for experimental research).

FOWLER, RAYMOND D. (b. 1930) Fowler is recognized for his innovative work in computer interpretation of the MMPI. His system has been translated into most major European languages and is considered a prototype for other computer-based testing systems. He served effectively for many years as the executive director of the American Psychological Association.

FRAISSE, PAUL (b. 1911) Fraisse is best known for his contributions to time and rhythm psychology. He also has contributed considerably to the development of psychology as a science in France.

FRANK, ELLEN (b. 1944) Frank's work has focused on treatment and maintenance of obtained treatment effects for mood disorders. She has been a leader in the evaluation and modification of interpersonal psychotherapy.

FRANK, JEROME D. (b. 1909) Frank's major research has led to the formulation of the demoralization hypothesis, the concept that the main healing power of psychotherapy lies in features that combat demoralization. His most important work *Persuasion and Healing*.

FRANKL, VIKTOR E. (b. 1905) Frankl's logotherapy is predicated on "man's search for meaning," based to some degree on his experiences as an inmate of Nazi concentration camps, which he effectively survived.

FRANKLIN, BENJAMIN (1706–1790) Franklin showed that the afterimage will be positive on the dark field of the closed eye and negative when the eyes are open and fixed on a white piece of paper. He was better known for his intellectual contributions to early political development within the United States.

FRANZ, SHEPERD I. (1874–1933) Franz surgically removed parts of animals' brains to study the effects of their removal on behavior. Removing the frontal lobes of the animals' brains resulted in the loss of recently acquired habits.

FRENKEL-BRUNSWIK, ELSE (1908–1958) Frenkel-Brunswik is best known for her major part in *The Authoritarian Personality* and for her empirical delineation of the concept of intolerance of ambiguity.

FREUD, ANNA (1895–1982) The daughter of Sigmund Freud, she was a specialist in children's psychoanalysis who championed the needs of children, applying her father's theories.

FREUD, SIGMUND (1856–1939) Freud developed a personality theory explaining human motivation and expanded his theory to include more than just treatment for the disturbed. He consistently ranks among the most influential writers in history.

FRIJDA, NICO H. (b. 1927) Frijda developed a general theory of emotion, integrating the study of emotion into the information-processing framework, while still supporting phenomenological and clinical viewpoints.

FRISCH, KARL VON (1886–1982) Von Frisch is best known for his study of communication in honeybees. He isolated the visual, olfactory, and gustatory cues involved in the communication, and demonstrated that honeybees navigate by using the sun for orientation.

FROEBEL, FRIEDRICH (1782–1852) Froebel believed that the goal of education was to develop or unfold the innate potential of the individual. The child was assumed to be inherently good; thus, all human evil arises from wrong educational methods.

FROMM, ERICH (1900–1980) Fromm acknowledged humankind's biological past, but he stressed humankind's social nature. The general theme of productive love permeates much of Fromm's writings.

FROMM, ERIKA (1910–2003) Fromm is best known for developing an ego psychological theory of hypnosis. She frequently referred to herself as a "rebel against orthodoxy," referring to Freud's psychoanalytic theory.

GAGNÉ, ROBERT M. (b. 1916) Gagné performed a series of studies on the acquisition of knowledge and distinguished motor and sensory nerves. He also identified learning hierarchies and mathematics learning.

GALEN (ca. 130–200) Galen codified the then extant knowledge of medicine, anatomy, and medically pathological personalities into general personality theory (the humoral theory). He developed a more systematic classification system than had previously been utilized.

GALL, FRANZ JOSEF (1757–1828) Gall is credited with being a pioneer in brain mapping or brain localization. Phrenology's basic premise, however, was invalidated when it was discovered that the skull and the brain's topography are not in accord.

GALTON, FRANCIS (1822–1911) Galton made seminal contributions in a variety of fields: classification of fingerprints, genetics, statistics, anthropometry, and psychometry. He was the first scientist to formulate clearly the nature-nurture question.

GALVANI, LUIGI (1737–1798) Galvani investigated electrical phenomena in animal organisms. His work stimulated many further developments in the understanding of electrical phenomena in living organisms.

GARCIA, GUILLERMO DAVILA (1902–1968) Garcia's fundamental research and teaching interest was in psychopathology. He founded the first Latin American group of cross-cultural studies.

GARCIA, JOHN (1917–1986) Garcia is known for his studies on selective and adaptive learning mechanisms and the modification of predatory behavior with conditioned taste aversions.

GATZ, MARGARET (b. 1944) Gatz has made major contributions to the area of behavioral medicine. She is especially well known for her work among older adults.

GEMELLI, AGOSTINO (1878–1959) Gemelli was attracted to sociology, philosophy, and religion. He initiated and stimulated new areas of research, and he gave Italian psychology a stronger sense of identity and respectability.

GERMAIN, JOSÉ (1897–1986) Germain established scientific psychology in Spain in the early 1930s. He promoted the study, adoption, and application of psychological tests.

GESELL, ARNOLD L. (1880–1961) Gesell greatly influenced child-rearing practices in the 1940s and 1950s. He took a strictly constitutional or physiological approach in which cultural or learning factors played little part.

GIBB, CECIL A. (b. 1913) Gibb's major contributions have been to university administration and educational leadership. His publications have been in the areas of personality, leadership, and executive behavior.

GIBSON, ELEANOR J. (1910–2002) Gibson's research has embraced learning in humans and animals, studies of controlled rearing in animals, development of reading skills, and especially perceptual development in infants and young children.

GIBSON, JAMES J. (1904–1979) Gibson is primarily known for his research and theories of perception. He became a leader of a new movement by considering perception to be direct, without any inferential steps, intervening variables, or associations.

GILBRETH, FRANK B. (1868–1924) Gilbreth analyzed bricklaying to determine the best way of doing it. In his book *Motion Study,* he extended the micromotion study to other areas of construction work.

GILBRETH, LILLIAN E. (1878–1972) Gilbreth applied motion study to household management. She also offered seminars on general micromotion principles.

GLASSER, WILLIAM (b. 1925) Glasser formulated reality therapy, which states that persons are born with basic needs, the primary being the need to belong and to be loved and the need to gain self-worth and recognition.

GODDARD, HENRY H. (1866–1957) An early student of the causes of mental retardation, Goddard argued for hereditary intelligence and was an advocate of eugenics.

GOETHE, JOHANN WOLFGANG VON (1749–1832) Goethe influenced psychology in two different areas: color vision and the theories of Sigmund Freud. He mistrusted experimentation but had great faith in intuitive observation.

GOLDSTEIN, KURT (1878–1965) Goldstein developed a set of tests to measure the loss of abstract attitude in patients with organic brain disease. He observed that brain-injured patients tended to persevere when pushed to perform tasks they could no longer do.

GOODENOUGH, FLORENCE L. (1886–1959) Goodenough was most widely known for the Draw-a-Man Test, which asks the child to draw a figure. This test is scored not for artistic ability but for the presence of details.

GOODWIN, FRED (b. 1936) A major leader in the discovery of patterns of etiology and treatments for Bipolar Disorder.

GORMAN, JACK M. (b. 1951) Gorman's research interests include the neuroanatomy and neurotransmitter function in Panic Disorder, the neuroendocrinology of depression, and the neuroimmunology of Schizophrenia.

GOSSETT, WILLIAM S. (1876–1937) An English statistician and pioneer in the development of modern statistical methods, Gossett derived the statistic t (Student's t), widely used in tests of differences among means of small samples.

GOUIN DÉCARIE, THÉRÈSE (b. 1923) Gouin Décarie designed the first operational scale to assess cognitive development in infancy.

GRACE, ANTHONY A. (b. 1955) Grace's research has focused on the physiology and anatomy of the dopaminergic system and its postsynaptic targets in the basal ganglia, thalamus, and cortex, with an emphasis on the system's role in Schizophrenia. His first major contribution to the field of Schizophrenia research was the discovery of antipsychotic drug-induced depolarization block in dopamine cells.

GRAHAM, FRANCES (b. 1918) Graham related physiological changes in autonomic and brain activity to perceptual-cognitive function, especially during early development.

GREENOUGH, WILLIAM T. Greenough is regarded as the major figure in the research that concluded that the formation of new synaptic connections between nerve cells was a fundamental aspect of memory storage in the brain.

GREGORY, RICHARD L. (b. 1923) Gregory undertook studies on size constancy during motion. He developed the notion that perceptions are predictive hypotheses, somewhat like scientific hypotheses.

GRONER, RUDOLF (b. 1942) Groner's main work is a "generalized hypothesis theory" of cognitive activity. In its most general form, a series of model variants are constructed by specifying assumptions in a systematic and exhaustive way.

GUILFORD, JOY PAUL (1897–1987) Guilford made numerous factor analytic investigations of personality traits, including intellectual abilities, culminating in his structure-of-intellect model.

GUILLAUME, PAUL (1878–1962) Guillaume concentrated mostly on child psychology and on the study of anthropoids. He wrote on the epistemology of scientific psychology, which helped strengthen the foundations of this discipline.

GUION, ROBERT M. Guion has been a leader in the development of industrial psychology and organizational behavior. He has served as a mentor for numerous leaders in organizational and industrial psychology.

GULLIKSEN, HAROLD O. (1903–1996) Gulliksen studied mathematical psychology. As an examiner in social sciences, he was part of a group that developed objective tests for college-level courses.

GUTHRIE, EDWIN R. (1886–1959) Guthrie was a learning theorist. He stated that learning is simply a matter of a stimulus-response association by contiguity.

GUTTMAN, LOUIS H. (1916–1987) Guttman's positions relate to his major interest in psychometrics, nonparametric analysis, and social psychology.

HAGA, JUN (b. 1931) Haga incorporates the study of language into the theory and practice of teaching. He holds that meaning is conveyed by logical and emotive functions of language.

HALL, CALVIN S. (1909–1985) Hall's contributions to the study of dreams are the application of quantitative content analysis to large samples of dreams and a cognitive theory of dreams and dream symbolism. He wrote extensively about personality theory and theorists.

HALL, G. STANLEY (1844–1924) Hall founded and promoted organized psychology as a science and profession, especially with APA. He also was involved in many aspects of child development and education. He brought Freud to the United States to speak to leaders in the field of psychology.

HALL, MARSHALL (1790–1837) Hall distinguished voluntary activities from conscious ones, which are dependent on the higher centers of the brain.

HAMILTON, SIR WILLIAM (1788–1836) In revolt against the British associationists, Hamilton held that the first principle of psychology was the unity and activity of the human mind.

HARLOW, HARRY F. (1905–1981) Harlow is best known for his studies on infant monkeys raised with surrogate mothers. He found that extended social deprivation led to severe disruption of later social behavior.

HARTLEY, DAVID (1705–1765) Hartley is considered the founder of British associationism. He was one of the earliest physiological psychologists to attempt to relate association of ideas with brain vibrations.

HATFIELD, ELAINE C. (b. 1937) Hatfield's main contribution is theorizing and researching areas once thought to be impossible to investigate: passionate and compassionate love, intense emotion, and interpersonal equality.

HEALY, WILLIAM (1869–1963) Healy developed performance tests to supplement the Stanford-Binet Intelligence Scale, of which the Healy Picture Completion Test is perhaps the most widely known and used. He pioneered in the establishment of guidance clinics for problem children; these clinics were frequently located at university settings.

HEBB, D. O. (1904–1985) Hebb's experiments confirmed the importance of early experience in the growth of mind and intelligence and, at maturity, the continued need of exposure to a normal sensory environment for mental health.

HECHT, SELIG (1892–1947) Hecht showed that the smallest amount of light that can be detected under the most ideal viewing conditions is very close to the physiological limit.

HECKHAUSEN, HEINZ (1926–1988) Heckhausen constructed TAT measures for the independent assessment of "hope of success" and "fear of failure." These measures became the base of the rapidly growing German achievement motivation research.

HEGEL, GEORGE FRIEDRICH (1770–1831) Hegel saw reason, not experience, as the first principle. Modern notions of self-consciousness, self-actualization, consciousness raising, and self-concern are direct outgrowths of neo-Hegelian idealism.

HEIDBREDER, EDNA (1890–1985) Heidbreder's varied interests included schools, systems, and theories of psychology; the psychology of cognition; and testing and measurement.

HEIDEGGER, MARTIN (1889–1976) Heidegger is considered to be the bridge between existential philosophy and existential psychology. He believed that humans must accept that death is inevitable and nothingness will follow.

HEIDER, FRITZ (1896–1988) Heider worked in Kurt Koffka's research laboratory on problems related to deafness. His concepts are found in his book *The Psychology of Interpersonal Relations*.

HELMHOLTZ, HERMANN VON (1821–1894) Helmholtz formulated the mathematical foundation for the law of conservation of energy. He influenced the experimental approach to psychological problems, especially in perception and sensation.

HERBART, JOHANN FRIEDRICH (1776–1841) Herbart believed that the mind could be a compound of smaller units. He brought to psychology the notion that the mind could be quantified and influenced Wundt and Freud with his book.

HERING, EWALD (1834–1918) Hering fostered the doctrine of nativism, the view that one can judge space and depth in an inherent way. The Gestalt psychologists later took up this idea.

HERRMANN, THEO (b. 1929) Herrmann is best known for his work in cognitive psychology, psychology of language, and philosophy of psychological science.

HILGARD, ERNEST R. (1904–2001) Hilgard's research interests were primarily in the psychology of learning and motivation, and after World War II he focused his attention on social psychology and hypnosis research.

HINDE, ROBERT A. (b. 1923) Hinde's work on bird behavior entailed comparative studies of courtship behavior, analysis of motivational conflicts, and the study of habituation.

HIPPOCRATES (460–377 B.C.) Hippocrates took Thales' four elements (earth, air, fire, water) and related them to their four corresponding bodily humors (black bile, blood, yellow bile, phlegm).

HIRSCH, JULES Hirsch has worked on clinical research related to the physiology of appetite and eating disorders.

HOBBES, THOMAS (1588–1679) Hobbes is considered the father of British empiricism and associationism. Influenced by Galileo's concept of motion, he concluded that psychological (mental) activities were motions in the nervous system.

HÖFFDING, HARALD (1843–1931) Höffding believed that mental functions could best be understood through simplicity and identity, analysis, and synthesis. He viewed the central fact of psychology as being the will.

HOLLINGWORTH, HARRY L. (1880–1956) Hollingworth employed reintegration as a general principle and saw it as the basis of an improved association psychology.

HOLLINGSWORTH, LETA S. (1886–1939) Hollingsworth's interests centered upon children. Her work emphasized the fact that children with serious problems and children with high intelligence may suffer from emotional difficulties that worsen in adolescence.

HOLT, EDWIN B. (1873–1946) An early behaviorist, Holt believed strongly that psychology should study "the specific response relationship."

HOLT, ROBERT R. (b. 1917) Holt strove to integrate the best of the two approaches of clinical and statistical prediction.

HORAS, PLÁCIDO A. (b. 1916) Horas endeavored to establish integrative bonds between discordant trends in contemporary psychology. He believed that psychology should emanate from a biophysical conception of human behavior, emphasizing its cognitive aspects.

HORNEY, KAREN D. (1885–1952) Horney abandoned the standard Freudian orthodoxy because of the issue of female sexuality. She stated that Freud's stress on the sexual instinct was completely out of proportion. She developed her own theory of neuroticism, which has had a major impact on verbal psychotherapy.

HORST, A. PAUL (b. 1903) Horst's goal was to solve complex human problems using rigorous mathematical and quantitative techniques rather than rhetoric and semantics.

HOSHINO, AKIRA (b. 1927) Hoshino is best known for his study of culture shock, a review and critical theory of sojourners' assimilation and adjustment to a new culture and reentry into their own culture after a long stay abroad.

HOVLAND, CARL L. (1912–1961) Hovland is credited with numerous contributions, primarily to social psychology, among them the sleeper effect, communicator credibility, the preferred value of stating a conclusion, and valuable effects due to the order of presenting propaganda.

HULL, CLARK L. (1884–1952) Hull's most important contribution to psychology lies in his theory of learning, considered one of the most important theories of the twentieth century.

HUME, DAVID (1711–1776) In the *Treatise of Human Knowledge* Hume wrote: "Mind is nothing but a bundle or collection of different perceptions unified by certain relations and suppos'd tho' falsely to be endowed with a perfect simplicity and identity."

HUNT, J. McVICKER (1906–1991) Best known for his two-volume publication *Personality and Behavior Disorders,* Hunt referred to himself as an interactionist and not an environmentalist. He was one of the last general psychologists.

HUNT, THELMA (1903–1992) Hunt's research was in the personnel psychology field, where she developed tests to meet problems stemming from the Civil Rights Act and government regulatory and court measures relating to tests.

HUNTER, WALTER S. (1889–1953) Hunter believed that an objective, behavioristic approach to psychology should not continue to be used with a subject matter imposed on it by philosophy.

HUSSERL, EDMUND (1859–1938) Husserl was the founder and most prominent exponent of *phenomenology,* which affirmed that philosophical inquiry begins with the phenomena of consciousness, and only phenomena of consciousness can reveal to us what things essentially are.

HYMAN, STEVEN E. (b. 1952) Hyman, past director of the National Institute of Mental Health, directed an active research program in molecular neurobiology, focusing on how neurotransmitters, especially dopamine and glutamate, alter the expression of genes in the striatum and thereby produce long-term changes in neural function that can influence behavior.

IKEDA, HIROSHI (b. 1932) Ikeda believes that the most essential thing in psychological study is scientific data collection and measurement, and because Japanese psychology needed more systematic disciplines, he devotes himself to promoting the scientific ideas of research.

IRITANI, TOSHIO (b. 1932) Iritani launched a new field of psycholinguistics. In his *New Social Psychology,* he proposed a broad, integrative unification of social psychological phenomena in the areas of politics, economy, population, geography, and history.

ITARD, JEAN-MARC-GASPARD (1775–1838) Itard was a pioneer in the study of mental deficiency, having attempted to train Victor, the so-called wild boy of Aveyron. Although his efforts with Victor met with little success, he developed methods that proved useful in training individuals with limited intellectual abilities.

IWAO, SUMIKO FURAYA (b. 1935) Regarding the relationship between the knowledge about and attitude toward foreign people, Iwao's findings suggest a linear positive relationship between knowledge and attitude, whereas if the amount of knowledge is large the relationship is negative.

JAENSCH, ERICH R. (1883–1940) Jaensch is best known for his work on eidetic imagery. He proposed two biotypes: The B-type was a vivid memory image under voluntary control; the T-type, which was not under voluntary control, he believed to be related to under activity of the parathyroid.

JAHODA, MARIE (1907–2001) Two connecting threads were inherent in Jahoda's professional life: preventing social psychology from splitting into psychological and sociological branches and engaging in problem-centered rather than method-centered work.

JALOTA, SHYAM SWAROOP (b. 1904) Jalota is best known for his pioneering work for standardized tests of general mental ability in Hindi. He formulated a hypothesis that "each human experience carries within it the active or latent seeds of contrary impulses."

JANET, PIERRE (1859–1947) Janet developed a system of psychology and psychopathology that he called "*psychologie de la conduite*" (psychology of conduct or behavior). A decrease in psychic energy was a central belief in Janet's explanation of mental disorders.

JANIS, IRVING LESTER (1918–1990) According to the Janis-Feisrabend hypothesis, an argument is most effective when the positive side is advanced before the negative. Also, he demonstrated experimentally that hostile individuals are less susceptible to persuasion.

JAMES, WILLIAM (1842–1910) James is considered America's greatest psychologist because of his brilliant clarity of scientific writing and his view of the human mind as functional and employing adaptive mental processes, in opposition to Wundt's analysis of consciousness into elements.

JAMISON, KAY REDFIELD (b. 1946) Jamison is best known for her historical research demonstrating that many famous poets, writers, and musicians suffered from Bipolar (manic-depressive) Disorder. In *An Unquiet Mind* she describes her own experience with Bipolar Disorder.

JASPERS, KARL (1883–1969) Jaspers distinguished three modes of being: being-there, being-oneself, and being-in-itself. Being-there referred to the objective, real world. Being-oneself meant one's personal existence. Being-in-itself involved an ability to transcend the known world and to know other worlds.

JASTROW, JOSEPH (1863–1944) Jastrow wrote about the occult, psychic research, mental telepathy, spiritualism, and hypnosis. He was, at least in part, a believer in psychic phenomena. He attacked Freudian theory, likening it to a house built of playing cards.

JENNINGS, HERBERT S. (1868–1947) Jennings's work was particularly important to psychology in two areas: He disproved the local action theory of tropisms, and he also demonstrated that mutations were likely to involve very small changes in organisms.

JENSEN, ARTHUR R. (b. 1923) Jensen hypothesized that both individual and racial differences in abilities are in part a product of the evolutionary process and have a genetic basis. His ideas came to be termed *jensenism,* often pejoratively.

JING, QUICHENG (b. 1926) Jing's books *Colorimetry* and *Human Vision* were the first books on visual science in China. He also has published studies of the psychological development of Chinese children.

JOHN, ERWIN R. (b. 1924) John is known for his material theory of memory. He hypothesized a statistical configuration theory of learning based on Lashley's conclusions. John also argued for mass action rather than learning centers in the brain.

JOHNSON, VIRGINIA (b. 1925) Johnson is credited, along with her colleague Masters, for helping to bring sex therapy to the forefront of psychology.

JONES, MARY COVER (1896–1987) Jones is most prominent as the first researcher to remove a fear in a child—the case of Peter. She worked with the preeminent behaviorist J. B. Watson, who had left psychology for personal reasons and followed a career in business.

JUDD, CHARLES H. (1873–1946) Judd studied the process of reading by photographing eye movements. He described how number consciousness was a function of reasoning and other high mental processes.

JUDD, LEWIS L. (b. 1930) Judd is an expert in biological psychiatry and clinical psychopharmacology, and his extensive research contributions include investigations into the effects of psychopharmacological agents on both brain mechanisms and symptom patters of depression, Bipolar Disorder, and Schizophrenia.

JUNG, CARL (1875–1961) Jung's personality system included three levels of the psyche: (a) the ego, (b) the personal unconscious, and (c) the deeper collective unconscious. He suggested that therapy include a great deal of dream interpretation. More recently, his theory has served as the basis for personality subtyping.

KAGAN, JEROME (b. 1929) Kagan has researched various aspects of the development of children, including variation in the cognitive styles called reflectivity and impulsivity, and the maturation of memory, self-awareness, and moral sense over the first 2 years of life.

KALIN, NED (b. 1951) Kalin has provided remarkable data in a series of experiments related to the biology of emotion using nonhuman primates.

KAMIYA, JOE (b. 1925) Kamiya's research involves the psychophysiology of consciousness and heightened awareness, altered states of consciousness, and transpersonal consciousness.

KANDEL, ERIC R. (b. 1929) Kandel is Nobel Laureate for his work on the nature of synaptic transmission in Aplysia, an invertebrate, and how such processes modulate transmission in higher organisms.

KANT, IMMANUEL (1724–1804) Kant rejected the view of the mind as mental substance. For him, mental processes could not be measured because they had only the dimension of time, not space. Psychology could never be an experimental science.

KANTOR, JACOB R. (1888–1984) Kantor proposed a systematic psychology called interbehaviorism. It shares with the behavioristic tradition a denial of mind or mental activity in favor of an objective approach.

KATONA, GEORGE (1901–1981) Katona's major contributions are his studies of consumer expectations and behavior found in such works as *Aspirations and Affluence, A New Economic Era,* and *Essays on Behavioral Economics.*

KATZ, DAVID (1884–1953) The same color, Katz discovered, can appear to the viewer in different modes, such as surface or film color, or as bulky, shiny, transparent, or luminous. His findings demonstrated the influence of the total visual field on color perception.

KAZDIN, ALAN E. (b. 1945) A majority of Kazdin's work has focused on treatment of aggressive and antisocial children referred for inpatient or outpatient treatment. His contributions to the field of psychology reflect the melding of intervention research with his interests in evaluation methodology.

KELLER, FRED S. (1899–1996) Keller was a psychologist who applied principles of operant conditioning to real-life human behavior. Much of his work centered on educational techniques to improve classroom learning and memory of learned materials.

KELLER, MARTIN (b. 1946) Keller is a leader in long-term studies of the course and treatment of mood and anxiety disorders.

KELLEY, HAROLD H. (b. 1921) Kelley's major contributions, all in social psychology, have been to the theory of small groups, including attribution theory dealing with the perception of causes of behavior, and to the study of close relationships.

KELLOGG, WINTHROP N. (1898–1972) When their son Donald was 10 months old, Kellogg and his wife Luella obtained a 7-month-old chimpanzee, who was then raised as a sibling. Despite equal treatment, the son surpassed the ape after 9 months.

KELLY, GEORGE A. (1905–1967) Kelly's theory of *personal constructs* is a broad, inclusive personality theory based on the notion that each individual attempts to anticipate and control his or her environment.

KELLY, LOWELL E. (1905–1986) Kelly instituted a longitudinal study of 300 engaged couples that lasted from 1939 to 1980. One of his conclusions was that marital compatibility is due to only a small function of sex and social attributes.

KIERKEGAARD, SOREN A. (1813–1855) Kierkegaard anticipated depth psychology, depersonalization, and the crisis of the will. He understood the peculiar modern malaise of "spiritlessness." He is best known as a Scandinavian philosopher.

KIESOW, FEDERICO (1858–1940) Among the many areas researched by Kiesow are taste, sensitivity, thermic and tactile points, geometric illusions, the Weber-Fechner Law, eidetic imagery, psychophysics, and the specific function of the sense organs.

KILTS, CLINTON D. (b. 1951) Kilts's major accomplishments include the further contribution of novel methods and approaches in neurochemistry and drug monitoring, including a careful and comprehensive description of the pharmacology, regulation, anatomy, and stress reactivity of dopamine-containing neurons innervating the rodent amygdaloid complex.

KINSEY, ALFRED C. (1894–1956) The Kinsey reports provided the first quantified, thorough description of many diverse human self-reports of sexual experience. The data also put to rest many misconceptions about sexuality. Recently Kinsey's work and the institute he founded have come under heavy criticism.

KINTSCH, WALTER (b. 1932) Kintsch, director of the Institute of Cognitive Sciences at the University of Colorado, played a major role in the transition from learning theory to cognitive psychology.

KLAGES, LUDWIG (1872–1956) Klages believed that the body and soul interacted and that the point of this interaction was the human personality. An individual personality was a system of dynamic relationships.

KLERMAN, GERALD (1928–1992) Klerman was among the most influential American psychiatrists. In addition to playing a major role in government mental health policies, he codeveloped interpersonal psychotherapy with his wife, Myrna Weissman.

KLINEBERG, OTTO (1899–1992) Klineberg described differences in various psychological characteristics such as intelligence, emotions, and personality in various races including the Chinese, Native Americans, and African Americans. His general conclusion was that these differences are by and large culturally determined.

KLOPFER, BRUNO (1900–1971) Klopfer's major work was *The Rorschach Technique.* It became the single most authoritative source on the Rorschach test.

KLÜVER, HEINRICH (1897–1979) Klüver developed the method of equivalent and nonequivalent stimuli for studying behavior and determined the role of the brain, particularly the striate cortex, in vision.

KOCH, SIGMUND (1917–1996) Koch argued that psychology is not a coherent science but rather a collectivity of discrete and often incommensurable psychological studies, many of which require methods more like those of the humanities than the natural sciences.

KOFFKA, KURT (1886–1941) Koffka was a founder of the Gestalt psychology movement; of the three founders (Koffka, Kohler, and Wertheimer), he was particularly noted for his extensive publications.

KOHLBERG, LAWRENCE (1927–1987) Kohlberg is best known for his research on moral development in children. Following the lines of Piaget, Kohlberg stated that children followed moral development in three stages.

KÖHLER, WOLFGANG (1887–1967) Köhler, along with Wertheimer and Koffka, was a founder of the Gestalt psychology movement, of which he was particularly noted as the public spokesman.

KONORSKI, JERZY (1903–1973) Konorski pursued his life's pervading goal, to learn "how the brain works," formulated when he was about 20 years of age. His most important book was *Integrative Activity of the Brain.*

KOOB, GEORGE F. Koob is known as an authority on the neurobiology of emotional behavior, addiction, and stress. His investigations have provided significant information about the CNS action of drugs and the neuropharmacological basis of psychopathology.

KORNADT, HANS-JOACHIM (b. 1927) Kornadt has specialized in cross-cultural research, particularly concerning the development of aggression.

KRAEPELIN, EMIL (1855–1926) Through careful observation of many patients and statistical tabulation of symptoms, Kraepelin concluded that there were two major mental disorders: dementia praecox and the manic-depressive psychosis. His work on classification eventually served as a model for the *Diagnostic and Statistical Manual* of the American Psychiatric Association.

KRAFFT-EBING, RICHARD VON (1840–1902) *Psychopathia Sexualis* is Krafft-Ebing's best-known work. He took a purely constitutional approach. All sexual variations were based on genetic defects, but masturbation could hasten or even produce disorders.

KRASNER, LEONARD (b. 1924) Influenced particularly by the experimental orientation of Fred Keller, Krasner's research efforts focused on the development of a behavioral approach in clinical psychology. Along with Leonard Ullmann, he published the first text in abnormal psychology to offer a systematic behavioral model.

KRETSCHMER, ERNST (1888–1964) Kretschmer is best known for his typology within the framework of constitutional psychology: Body structure/physiology determines personality.

KRISHNAN, K. RANGA RAMA (b. 1956) Krishnan's work has focused primarily on neurobiological dysfunctions associated with mood disorders and Alzheimer's disease. A major effort of his collaboration has been to investigate the structural changes that occur among depressed elderly humans.

KÜLPE, OSWALD (1862–1915) Külpe began to believe that the analysis of consciousness involved more than what Wundt had suggested. He concluded that thinking could occur in the absence of mental images or sensations and termed this *imageless thought.*

KUPFER, DAVID J. (b. 1941) Kupfer has made major contributions to the understanding of mood disorders. His work on sleep dysregulation as it relates to depression is particularly noteworthy.

LADD, GEORGE TRUMBULL (1842–1920) Ladd believed that consciousness should operate to solve problems, although he granted that there is a biological side to the nervous system. From his view, the function of the mind is to adapt, and in adapting it must look to the future.

LADD-FRANKLIN, CHRISTINE (1847–1930) Ladd-Franklin is best known for her theory of color vision. Her theory is based on that of F. C. Donders, but with a developmental or genetic focus.

LAMARCK, JEAN-BAPTISTE DE MONET DE (1744–1829) Lamarck developed the theory of evolution. One of his views accounted for the inheritance of acquired characteristics, which Lamarck thought was necessary to explain cumulative changes.

LA METTRIE, JULIEN OFFROY DE (1709–1751) La Mettrie saw humans as machines, which gives him a place in the history of behaviorism. In his later years he developed the doctrine of hedonism, asserting that pleasure is the goal of life and that all motivation is selfish.

LANG, PETER (b. 1930) Lang's early work concerned models of anxiety and behavior therapy. Over his career he expanded his model of human behavior and examined the relationship of cognitive and psychophysiological functioning.

LANGE, CARL GEORG (1834–1900) Unlike W. James, Lange distinguished emotion from passion. He believed that emotions included joy, sorrow, fear, and anger, while passions referred to love, hate, and admiration.

LASHLEY, KARL (1890–1958) Lashley formulated two principles of brain functioning: mass action and equipotentiality.

LAZARUS, ARNOLD A. (b. 1932) Lazarus is the developer of multimodal therapy based on the simultaneous consideration of Behavior, Affect, Sensation, Imagery, Cognition, Interpersonal relations, and Drugs (BASIC-ID) for both diagnosis and treatment of psychological disorders.

LAZARUS, RICHARD S. (1922–2003) Lazarus mounted efforts to generate a comprehensive theoretical framework for psychological stress and undertook programmatic research based on these formulations.

LE BON, GUSTAVE (1841–1931) Le Bon developed a doctrine of the hierarchy of races. The criteria he set up involved the degree of reasoning ability, power of attention, and mastery of instinctual needs.

LEE, CHANG-HO (b. 1936) Lee has been developing an Oriental model of counseling and psychotherapy. The emphasis in his model includes educative dialogue, integrational approach, tolerance training, asset reinforcement, and enhancing social interest.

LEIBNITZ, GOTTFRIED WILHELM (1646–1716) Leibnitz believed that mind and body followed their own laws in perfect agreement. Leibnitz's parallelism was one solution to the mind-body problem that has concerned philosophers and psychologists for centuries.

LEONTIEV, ALEKSEI (b. 1903) Leontiev believed in the cultural-historical theory, which attempted to use Marxist doctrine as a basis for human development. Besides accounting for human psychological processes, the theory held that when persons interact, psychological processes develop.

LERNER, ARTHUR (b. 1915) Lerner regards all literary genres as vital sources for understanding behavior; he holds that one's cognitive and unconscious understanding is shaped by the language, symbols, metaphors, and similes that influence one's growth and development.

LERNER, RICHARD M. (b. 1946) Lerner is currently a leading developmental psychologist. He was one of the first psychologists to write about plasticity of the developing brain.

LEVY, STEVEN Levy is one of the leaders of psychoanalysis. He was recently appointed editor of the *Journal of the American Psychoanalytic Association.*

LEWIN, KURT (1890–1947) Lewin developed a topological vectoral psychology. Topology investigates the properties of space; vectors consider forces or dynamics.

LIÉBAULT, AMBROISE-AUGUSTE (1823–1904) Liébault's use of hypnosis marked the beginning of psychotherapy. Along with H. Bernheim, he founded the Nancy School and treated patients with hypnosis. He argued that hypnosis was a matter of suggestion.

LIEBERMAN, JEFFREY (b. 1948) Lieberman is a pioneer researcher in the area of first episode of Schizophrenia and its treatment.

LINDZEY, GARDNER (b. 1920) Lindzey is best known for his contributions to the fields of personality, social psychology, and behavior genetics. His book *Theories of Personality* (coauthored with C. S. Hall) was the first of its kind, leading the way for many others and for courses designed after this landmark publication.

LINEHAN, MARSHA M. (b. 1943) Linehan's primary research is in the application of cognitive and behavioral models to suicide behaviors, drug abuse, and Borderline Personality Disorder. She is best known for developing Dialectical Behavior Therapy.

LOCKE, JOHN (1632–1704) Locke was the first of the British empiricists and bridged the gap between the rational continental philosophers such as Descartes, Leibnitz, and Spinoza. He helped to promote a new attitude toward knowledge that was fostered in the upcoming empirical tradition.

LOEB, JACQUES (1859–1924) Loeb's theory of the tropism as applied to animal behavior represented a return to the mechanistic view set forth earlier by René Descartes, which stated that animals acted like machines.

LORENZ, KONRAD (1903–1989) Lorenz never conducted a formal experiment, and his descriptive observations were often anecdotal. He infuriated his more conventional colleagues by saying, "If I have one good example, I don't give a fig for statistics."

LOTZE, HERMANN (1817–1881) Lotze is known for his doctrine of local signs, typical of nineteenth-century thought, in which philosophical concepts, rather than empirical data, dominated the interpreted physiology of sense organs.

LUNDIN, ROBERT W. (b. 1920) Lundin's book *An Objective Psychology of Music* was a protest against the mentalistic approaches to the psychology of music presented by Carl Seashore and Max Schoen. He attempted to establish musical behavior on firm empirical grounds.

LURIA, ALEXANDER R. (b. 1902) Luria developed theories of language disorders and of the functions of the frontal lobe. He believed that cell groups must be organized in systems of zones working in concert, each performing its role in the complex system.

MACCOBY, ELEANOR E. (b. 1917) Maccoby is best known for her work on gender differences and the role of parent-child relationships on socialization.

MACCORQUODALE, KENNETH (1919–1986) MacCorquodale's career was intertwined with that of P. Meehl in their combined work in the philosophy of science and learning theory, most notably that of E. C. Tolman. MacCorquodale and Meehl are well known for their joint article "On a Distinction between Hypothetical Constructs and Intervening Variables."

MACH, ERNST (1838–1916) Mach has been identified as a positivist and believed that sensations were the data of all science. In his view, all science is observational, and the primary data of observation are sensations.

MAGENDIE, FRANÇOIS (1783–1855) Magendie contended that the seat of sensations was in the spinal cord and that the cerebrum perceived the sensations from the cord. This being the case, the cerebrum could reproduce the sensations, thus accounting for memory.

MAHER, BRENDAN A. (b. 1924) Maher's early work was focused on the model of motivational conflict as the origin of neurotic behavior. Later, he investigated the nature of language disturbances found in the schizophrenias. In 1970, Maher wrote a seminal paper demonstrating that the prevailing belief that delusions arise from a basic defect in reasoning was not consistent with the empirical evidence.

MAIER, STEVE (b. 1941) Maier, an experimental psychologist, has been a leader in development of neuroscience. He earlier studied learned helplessness, but more recently he has investigated stress and neural pathways.

MAIMONIDES, MOSES (1135–1204) Maimonides rejected the notion of a personal immortality. For him, the capacity for individual thinking disappeared with the destruction of the body, yet an individual might increase in understanding and knowledge and so attain a kind of immortality.

MAKARENKO, ANTON SEMYONOVICH (1899–1939) Makarenko's *The Road to Life* has been cited by most Soviet psychologists. His work developed a theory that became the basis of Soviet personality research and educational practices.

MALEBRANCHE, NICOLAS de (1638–1715) De Malebranche rejected Descartes's interactionism in favor of the doctrine of occasionalism. According to this view, one event does not cause another but is simply an occasion for God, the cause of all things, to cause the second event to occur.

MARLATT, ALAN (b. 1941) A leading authority on behavioral interventions and relapse prevention of alcoholism.

MARX, KARL HEINRICH (1818–1883) The starting point of Marx's socialism is the doctrine of class struggle. This provided the key to two of his most widely known doctrines: a materialist conception of history and the theory of surplus value.

MARX, MELVIN H. (b. 1919) Marx's research interests generally focused on various problems in the fields of learning and cognition. He contributed to our understanding of how human subjects are able to judge the frequencies with which events have occurred. His later work called attention to the pervasiveness and significance in everyday life of the inference process.

MASLOW, ABRAHAM H. (1908–1970) Maslow considered his basic approach to psychology to fall within the broad range of humanistic psychology, which he characterized as the "third force" in American psychology, the other two being behaviorism and psychoanalysis.

MASTERS, WILLIAM (1916–2001) With his colleague, Johnson, Masters conducted seminal work on sexual functioning and dysfunctions. Their work has clarified various myths regarding sexuality, and it has served as a basis for much of sex therapy.

MATARAZZO, JOSEPH D. (b. 1925) The foci of Matarazzo's research include intellectual and neuropsychological functioning, nonverbal indices of empathy and related psychological processes, and the role of lifestyle risk factors in health and illness.

MAY, ROLLO (b. 1909) May is known for his vanguard leadership in humanistic psychology, articulating existential tenets of the *encounter, choice, authenticity, responsibility, transcendence,* and other existential hypotheses.

MAYBERG, HELEN Mayberg is best known for her work in the field of functional brain imagery in mood disorders.

McCLELLAND, DAVID C. (1917–1998) McClelland developed a method of measuring human needs through content analysis of imaginative thought.

McDOUGALL, WILLIAM (1871–1938) McDougall described an instinct as having three aspects: (1) a predisposition to notice certain stimuli, (2) a predisposition to make movements toward a goal, and (3) an emotional core.

McEWEN, BRUCE S. (b. 1938) McEwen studies environmentally regulated, variable gene expression in the brain mediated by circulating steroid hormones and endogenous neurotransmitters in relation to brain sexual differentiation and the actions of sex, stress, and thyroid hormones on the adult brain.

McGAUGH, JAMES L. (b. 1931) McGaugh's research has revealed that memory consolidation is influenced by drugs affecting several neuromodulatory and neurotransmitter systems. Other findings indicate that adrenal stress hormones modulate consolidation, and that these effects are mediated by noradrenergic activation of the amygdala.

McGUIRE, WILLIAM J. (b. 1925) McGuire developed a probability model of thought systems and has also worked on theories regarding the self-concept, attitude change, and personality correlates of persuasion. He also contributed to the psychology of science by developing a "perspectivist" approach describing how researchers do and should develop psychological knowledge.

McKEACHIE, WILBERT J. (b. 1921) Much of McKeachie's research has been concerned with attribute treatment interactions, particularly with respect to those teaching variables interacting with student motivation, such as test anxiety.

MEAD, GEORGE H. (1863–1931) For Mead, the self was an object of awareness rather than a system of processes. At birth there is no self because a person cannot enter one's own experiences directly.

MEAD, MARGARET (1901–1978) Mead pioneered in research methods that helped to turn cultural anthropology into major science. Throughout her career she promoted the importance of environmental influences, women's rights, and racial harmony.

MEEHL, PAUL E. (1920–2003) Meehl's monograph, *Clinical versus Statistical Prediction,* aroused wide interest (and dissent) and is considered a classic work in psychology. He is considered one of the intellectual giants of 20th-century psychology.

MELZACK, RONALD Along with Patrick Wall, Melzack developed the innovative gate control theory of pain. He also helped reveal the neural areas and pharmacological mechanisms involved in pain. Melzack developed the McGill Pain Questionnaire to obtain measures of the multiple dimensions of subjective pain experience, and he later developed the neuromatrix model of brain function, which plays a major role in explaining phantom limb pain.

MERLEAU-PONTY, MAURICE (1907–1961) Merleau-Ponty's primary concern was an understanding of the relationship between consciousness and nature. For him, *nature* referred to external events in their causal relationships. Consciousness, however, was not subject to causality.

MESMER, FRANZ ANTON (1734–1815) Mesmer is commonly recognized as the founding father of modern hypnosis. He attempted to build on the rock of Newtonian ideas to find some basis for understanding human illness and cures.

MEYER, ADOLF (1866–1950) Meyer is best known for his theory of psychobiology, which emphasized the importance of a biographical study for understanding all aspects of an individual's personality.

MILGRAM, STANLEY (1933–1984) Milgram's best-known studies were on the dynamics of obedience to authority. As a result, he found an unexpectedly high rate of obedience. His obedience work has become one of the best-known pieces of research in the social sciences.

MILL, JOHN STUART (1806–1873) Mill believed that a combination of mental events resulted in something totally new that was not present in the original experiences, a notion that became identified as *mental chemistry.*

MILLER, GEORGE A. (b. 1920) Miller was the first to demonstrate trial-and-error learning motivated by electrical stimulation of the brain.

MILLER, NEAL E. (1909–2002) Miller pioneered the application of learning theory to behavioral therapy and the use of chemical and electrical stimulation to analyze the brain's mechanisms of behavior, homeostasis, and reinforcement. His work with animals profoundly aroused the interest and focus of the scientific community in the field of biofeedback.

MILNER, BRENDA (b. 1918) Milner's work has involved the intellectual effects of temporal lobe damage in humans. She has also explored memory disorders and the effect of brain lesions or injury on cerebral organizations.

MISCHEL, WALTER (b. 1930) The model of personality developed by Mischel incorporates social, cognitive, and emotional processes and variables into the conceptualization of personality. His model takes systematic account of the role of the situation in interaction with the characteristics of the person, into the expressions of behavioral consistency.

MISIAK, HENRYK (1911–1992) Misiak's experimental research focused on the perception of intermittent light, particularly on various parameters and applications of critical flicker frequency (CFF).

MONTESSORI, MARIA (1870–1952) Montessori used her scientific background to create universal principles and special methods and materials for a new pedagogy.

MORENO, JACOB L. (1892–1974) Moreno developed the technique of psychodrama, a method of psychotherapy that depends on dramatic role playing.

MORGAN, CONWAY LLOYD (1852–1936) Morgan is best known for the Lloyd Morgan's Canon, an application of the Law of Parsimony to an explanation of animal behavior.

MORITA, SHOMA (1874–1938) Morita developed a new form of psychotherapy, generally known as Morita Therapy, that combined psychotherapy and Zen Buddhism. To gain insight, the patient must be in harmony with the universe.

MOWRER, O. HOBART (1907–1982) Mowrer's best-known and probably most enduring practical contribution is a means of treating nocturnal enuresis known as the bell-and-pad method. His more substantive contribution was his two-factor theory of learning, language, and interpersonal psychology.

MÜLLER, JOHANNES (1801–1858) Müller is best known for his doctrine of the "specific energies of nerves," which states that, regardless of how it is stimulated, each sensory nerve will lead to only one kind of sensation.

MÜNSTERBERG, HUGO (1863–1916) Münsterberg exposed the fraudulence of popular mystics and occult figures, and he generally applied psychology to everyday life.

MURPHY, GARDNER (1895–1979) Murphy's biosocial approach to psychology was recognized as one of the most vital and influential movements in the field.

MURRAY, HENRY A. (1893–1988) Murray developed his taxonomy of needs to characterize people's directions in their lives and activities. Thus, he developed a systematic and dynamic approach to personality.

MUSSEN, PAUL HENRY (1922–2000) Mussen is best known for his research and writings in developmental psychology. His research involved the study of developmental processes in preschool children, generosity in children of nursery school age, and the impact of television cartoons on children's aggressive behavior.

MYASISHCHEV, VLADIMIR N. (1893–1973) Myasishchev suggested that conditioned reflexes might not be an adequate explanation of human motor behavior.

NAKANISHI, SHIGETADA (b. 1942) Nakanishi and colleagues developed a novel cloning strategy to isolate receptors and ion channels by combining electrophysiology and the Xenopus oocyte expression system, and they applied this strategy to the molecular cloning of glutamate receptors. Nakanishi and colleagues also elucidated the molecular nature of neuropeptide and vasoactive peptide receptors.

NATHAN, PETER E. (b. 1935) Nathan has extensively researched basic psychosocial variables associated with alcoholism. He has investigated such diverse issues as alcohol abuse and dependence, syndromal diagnosis, and psychotherapy outcomes.

NEISSER, ULRIC (b. 1928) Neisser is best known for three books: *Cognitive Psychology,* which helped to establish that field; *Cognition and Reality,* which attempted to reorient it; and *Memory Observed: Remembering in Natural Contexts,* which introduced the ecological approach to the study of memory.

NEMEROFF, CHARLES B. (b. 1949) Nemeroff's research has concentrated on the biological bases of the major neuropsychiatric disorders, including affective disorders, Alzheimer's disease, Schizophrenia, and anxiety disorders.

NESTLER, ERIC J. (b. 1954) The goal of Nestler's research is to better understand how the brain adapts to repeated perturbations under both normal and pathological conditions. His laboratory has discovered several adaptations that occur in the brain in response to chronic drug exposure and has provided evidence that these adaptations are responsible for certain behavioral features of addiction.

NETTER, PETRA (b. 1937) Netter initiated research activities in the field of sensory suggestibility in relation to pain tolerance and placebo response.

NEWCOMB, THEODORE M. (1903–1984) Newcomb was among the first psychologists to identify himself with social psychology. He showed that an individual's characteristics and group memberships interacted to influence attitude changes after leaving college.

NIETZSCHE, FRIEDRICH WILHELM (1844–1900) Nietzsche was convinced that psychology should consider the will to power as the primary human motive.

NOIZET, GEORGES (b. 1925) Noizet's main work deals with strategies in the comprehension of utterances and with evaluative judgments.

NÚÑEZ, RAFAEL (b. 1921) Núñez is best known for his research on Mexican personality characteristics. He searched for methods of understanding the psychological problems of the lower economic classes in Latin America.

NUTTIN, JOSEPH R. (1909–1988) Nuttin was one of the first psychologists to formulate an integrated cognitive theory of human selective learning. He is also known for his theory of human motivation in terms of behavioral relations required for optimal functioning.

O'BRIEN, CHARLES (b. 1937) O'Brien is best known for his studies on the causes and treatment of substance disorders.

OKONJI, MICHAEL OGBOLU (1936–1975) Okonji conducted research focused on child rearing, especially the relationship between the field-independence perspective of Herman Witkin and the intellectual perspective of Jean Piaget.

OLDS, JAMES (1922–1976) Olds and Milner were able, by chance, to produce pleasurable effects by electrically stimulating the brain. This led them to assume that a "reward mechanism" exists in the brain and serves as a motivational apparatus.

O'LEARY, K. DANIEL (b. 1940) O'Leary has investigated behavioral procedures for reducing aggressive and hyperactive behavior in children, the ways in which marital discord affects children, and risk factors and treatments for men and women in physically aggressive relationships. He also helped develop a marital therapy treatment for individuals experiencing marital discord and depression.

OSGOOD, CHARLES EGERTON (1916–1991) Osgood's experimental research has centered around the role of meaning within the context of learning theory. He developed the Semantic Differential Method while searching for a tool to quantify meaning.

OTIS, ARTHUR SINTON (1886–1964) Otis developed the Otis Group Intelligence Scale, which incorporated, for the first time, completely objective scoring and multiple-choice items, the keys to group testing and administration by minimally trained personnel.

OVERMEIER, JAMES BRUCE (b. 1938) Overmeier's research spans specialties of learning, memory, stress, psychosomatic disorders, and their biological substrates. This research has been carried out with a variety of species of laboratory animals and with human client volunteers with Down syndrome, Korsakoff's syndrome, or Alzheimer's disease.

PARAMESWARAN, E. G. (b. 1935) Parameswaran, known for his approach to the study of personality, is a pioneering researcher in the area of developmental psychology in India.

PATTERSON, GERALD R. Patterson and his colleagues have made numerous contributions to understanding of child and adolescent aggression. He has developed and evaluated behavioral interventions to prevent and treat aggression.

PAUL, GORDON (b. 1935) Paul's work helped to form the foundation for the evidence-based practice movement in psychology. His clinical research demonstrated the utility of psychosocial principles for understanding and cost-effective nonpharmacological treatment of problems ranging from anxiety disorders to Schizophrenia.

PAVLOV, IVAN PETROVICH (1849–1936) Pavlov's methodology and his greatest scientific achievement was conditioning, a technique that significantly influenced the development of psychology.

PEARSON, KARL (1857–1936) Pearson contributed to the development of the biological, behavioral, and social sciences. His application of mathematical and statistical methods ranks among the great achievements of science. He developed widely used correlation statistics.

PECJAK, VID (b. 1929) Pecjak studied concepts and conceptual interrelations and symbols and their cultural dependence. He found that some symbols are universal, whereas others are unique to individual cultures.

PEDERSEN, PAUL B. (b. 1936) Pedersen conducted research in Indonesia, Malaysia, and Taiwan that emphasized interdisciplinary area studies, with special attention to core values as they are influenced by cultural perspectives.

PEIRCE, CHARLES SANDERS (1839–1914) Peirce held that the domain of knowledge could be so characterized that general assertions could be proven true of all knowledge and that all knowledge depended on logic that made such a characterization possible.

PENFIELD, WILBER GRAVES (1891–1976) Among Penfield's contributions were the development of neurosurgical treatment of certain forms of epilepsy and the discovery that electric stimulation of certain parts of the cortex can evoke vivid memories of past life experiences.

PERL, EDWARD ROY (b. 1926) Perl's first studies in neuroscience utilized electroencephalography and responses of the cerebral cortex to sensory input. Subsequently, his work focused on reflex and somatosensory mechanisms of the mammalian spinal cord. He is widely recognized for pioneer efforts in the documentation of the existence and function of nociceptors.

PERLOFF, ROBERT (b. 1921) Perloff has contributed to psychology through his research on consumer behavior and evaluation studies relating to mental health and educational programs.

PERLS, FREDERICK (FRITZ) (1893–1970) Perls's major contribution to psychology was the development of a new method of psychotherapy, which he named Gestalt therapy, an outgrowth and a rejection of psychoanalysis.

PETERSEN, ANNE C. (b. 1944) Petersen's research interests have included adolescent biopsychosocial development and mental health. She was a leader in demonstrating scientifically the importance of considering the influence of biological change on psychological and social changes in adolescence. She has also investigated the increased risk for depression among adolescent girls.

PETERSON, DONALD R. (b. 1923) Peterson's research has involved topics such as the diagnosis of subclinical schizophrenia, children's behavior disorders, juvenile delinquency, parent-child relationships, and the interaction process in marital relationships. In addition, his trait-based research contributed to the "big five" conceptions of personality structure that were later commonly accepted.

PFAFFMAN, CARL (1913–1994) Pfaffman conducted research on taste and other chemical senses and attempted to find basic relationships between the physiological and psychological aspects of organisms.

PFLÜGER, EDUARD FRIEDRICH WILHELM (1829–1910) Pflüger's research involved studies of the nervous system. He became involved in the controversy over whether reflexes are conscious or unconscious.

PIAGET, JEAN (1896–1980) Piaget studied the relationships formed between the individual knower and the world he or she endeavors to know. His two most important concepts of genetic epistemology are *functional invariants* and *structures.*

PIERON, HENRI (1881–1964) Pieron's work focused on psychophysiology. During an early part of his career, he studied the mechanisms of sleep in animals, but the psychophysiology of sensations constituted the center of his scientific work.

PILLSBURY, WALTER BOWERS (1872–1960) Pillsbury is probably best known as an historian of psychology. His *History of Psychology* details the growth of psychology from philosophy.

PINEL, PHILIPPE (1745–1856) Pinel made a plea for more humane treatment of the insane, who, at that time, were regarded by many as wicked and possessed by demons. He offered an alternative explanation that related disturbed behavior to brain malfunctions.

PINILLOS, JOSÉ (b. 1919) Pinillos is best known for his work on social attitudes and political stereotypes and for his analysis of the F-scale.

PIZZAMIGLIO, LUIGI (b. 1937) Pizzamiglio contributed to the introduction of psycholinguistic models to explain aphasia and hemispheric dominance for cognitive abilities.

PLATO (427–347 B.C.) Plato's influence on Western thought has been inestimable, extending to metaphysics, epistemology, ethics, politics, mathematics, and several branches of natural science.

PLOTINUS (204–270 A.D.) Plotinus described the soul as a unitary entity, completely separate from the body, that is indestructible and immortal. He believed the soul's relation to the body was one of collateral existence, not mixing with the body but dwelling beside it, thus having an existence of its own.

PONZO, MARIO (1882–1960) Ponzo's research was in general and experimental psychology, including the histology and psychophysiology of taste, and tactile and thermic stimulus localization in different regions of the skin.

PORTEUS, STANLEY DAVID (1883–1972) Porteus began his best-known work in psychology, his Maze Test, as a supplement to Henry H. Goddard's 1909 translation of Alfred Binet's intelligence tests that would avoid the culture factor.

PRIBRAM, KARL H. (b. 1919) Pribram has investigated mind-brain problems with a focus on their philosophical implications, drawing on laboratory data to support his premises.

PRINCE, MORTON (1854–1929) Prince described the biography of a multiple personality who had three distinct personalities that alternated with each other, characterized as the saint, the devil, and the woman. Two of the personalities had no knowledge of the others.

PURKINJE, JAN EVANGELISTA (1787–1869) An extensive researcher of sensory elements in the phenomenological tradition, Purkinje described how colors emerged from darkness at dawn.

QUAY, HERBERT C. (b. 1927) Quay's major research contributions include his taxonomic work in both juvenile and adult offenders, his early work in the education of children with behavior disorders, and his later work in the experimental psychopathology of childhood and the adolescent disorders.

QUETELET, LAMBERT ADOLPHE JACQUES (1796–1874) Quetelet extended the notion of the normal distribution as being the true state of affairs rather than simply measurement error.

RACHMAN, STANLEY J. (b. 1934) Rachman, working with Eysenck, was responsible for much of the early work on behavior therapy in England. He was the founding editor of *Behavior Research and Therapy.*

RAIMY, VICTOR (1913–1987) Raimy proposed that changes in the self-concept would be used to chart the course of psychotherapy as well as general changes in personality. In his theory, the self-concept is seen as a guide or map that persons consult when faced with choices.

RAINA, MAHARAI K. (b. 1943) Raina has been involved in research on the National Talent Search Scheme in India. He has concentrated on longitudinal studies of the talented and the role of creativity in the talent search.

RAMON Y CAJAL, SANTIAGO (1832–1934) Ramon y Cajal is called the father of present-day physiological psychology. His techniques for tracing neurons histologically remain a basic approach to physiological psychology.

RANK, OTTO (1884–1939) Rank sought to develop an alternative scientific approach built on the person as both a voluntary interpreter of meaning and an initiator of action. His earlier conception of the birth trauma was largely replaced by more complex ideas. He also rejected the aim, shared by Freud and most of academic psychology, of mechanistic explanation of human behavior or experience with a cause-effect paradigm.

RAO, K. RAMAKRISHNA (b. 1932) Rao's contributions to psychology, both theoretical and experimental, focus mainly on aspects such as psi, which receive little attention in conventional psychology.

RATH, RADHANATH (b. 1920) After his early specialization in psychophysics, Rath turned to social psychology. While involved in the reorientation of primary school education and textbooks he performed intensive research in the area of early education.

RAVIV, AMIRAM (b. 1939) Raviv's research areas include prosocial behavior, pupils' attributions of success and failure, social climate in various settings, and issues related to the role of school psychologists.

RAZRAN, GREGORY (1901–1973) Razran conducted extensive research in the area of classical conditioning by relating the various types of learning to levels of evolutionary development.

REICH, WILHELM (1897–1957) Reich parted from psychoanalysis as his pursuits led him into realms the analysts could not or would not follow. For him, emotions came to mean the manifestation of a tangible, demonstrable biological energy (*orgone*).

REID, THOMAS (1710–1796) Reid proposed that not only did people possess minds, but also any individual mind knew more than it possessed. He also proposed faculty psychology.

REIK, THEODOR (1888–1969) Although a believer in many psychoanalytical concepts, Reik disagreed with Freud over certain matters of love and sex. He believed that true romantic love has little to do with sex—that it is felt most strongly when the loved one is absent.

RESCORLA, ROBERT A. (b. 1940) Rescorla's early work led to the development of the "truly random control" procedure, together with the contingency view of conditioning. He also helped form an influential theory of elementary learning processes, the Rescorla-Wagner model, which continues to be one of the touchstones for thinking about Pavlovian conditioning.

RESNICK, ROBERT J. (b. 1940) Resnick's clinical and research interests were attention-deficit disorders. He filed the landmark "Virginia Blues" litigation establishing the autonomous practice of psychology.

REUCHLIN, MAURICE (b. 1920) Reuchlin has asserted that, in research, the content of the data and the context of the research, as well as statistical findings, must be considered.

REYKOWSKI, JANUSZ (b. 1929) Reykowski is best known for developing a theory of intrinsic motivation applied to prosocial behavior.

RHINE, JOSEPH BANKS (1895–1980) Rhine, considered the father of experimental parapsychology, spent over 50 years in active research that brought psychic research from the closed séance rooms of mediums into open laboratories of scientists.

RIBES-IÑESTA, EMILIO (b. 1944) Partly responsible for the introduction of experimental psychology into Mexico, Ribes-Iñesta contributed to the development of the first professional and graduate research programs on behavior modification and behavior analysis.

RIBOT, THEODULE (1839–1916) Together with Alfred Binet and Pierre Janet, Ribot was a founder of modern French psychology. He stressed motivational forces in personality development, which resulted in what we today would call a dynamic psychology.

RICHTER, CURT PAUL (1894–1988) Richter's research included such areas as spontaneous behavior in rats, energy biological clocks, galvanic skin response, and rhythms, as well as nutrition and self-selection of diets in rats.

RIVERS, WILLIAM HALSE (1864–1922) Rivers became interested in neurology and medical psychology during World War I. With Elliot Smith and T. H. Pear, he was the first to recognize "shell shock" as a distinct clinical entity.

ROGERS, CARL RANSOM (1902–1987) Rogers developed a psychotherapeutic system, which during the 1950–1960 era was second in popularity only to that of Freud, in which the therapist acts as a facilitator. In everyday terms his form of therapy is called *nondirective*.

ROKEACH, MILTON (1918–1988) What people believe, why they believe, and what difference it makes are the recurring themes that preoccupied Rokeach during his research career. His work on human values is already considered a classic book.

ROMANES, GEORGE JOHN (1848–1894) Romanes, a student of behavior, chose to use the anecdotal method that he culled from both the scientific and popular literature. He criticized the tendency to attribute human characteristics, such as insight, to animals.

RORSCHACH, HERMANN (1884–1922) Rorschach extended the inkblot technique to measure the entire personality.

ROSENZWEIG, SAUL (b. 1907) Rosenzweig is best known for his studies and theories of frustration and aggression. He has also studied tolerance for frustration and has noted that the spoiled child is ill equipped to handle frustration.

ROT, NIKOLA (b. 1910) Three areas are central in Rot's empirical research: psychological characteristics of judgments, attitudes, and problems connected to self-management.

ROTTER, JULIAN B. (b. 1916) Rotter's major contribution has been the development of social learning theory (SLT), in which he tried to integrate the two great traditions in psychology: the stimulus-response (or reinforcement) theories and cognitive (or field) theories.

ROYCE, JOSEPH R. (1921–1989) Royce's major experimental research focused on determining the gene correlates of factors of emotion.

ROYCE, JOSIAH (1855–1916) Royce taught that truth could be proven, that an absolute mind exists, and that human beings can grasp truth.

RUBIN, EDGAR (1886–1951) Rubin is best known for his dissertation on the figure/ground distinction. Under some circumstances, figure and ground can reverse.

RUBINSTEIN, SERGEI LEONIDOVICH (1889–1960) Rubinstein formulated these principles of Soviet psychology: Mind is a function of matter, and the human psyche is a function of historical evolution, the unity of consciousness, and the unity of theory and practice.

RUSH, JOHN A. (b. 1942) Rush has conducted clinical investigations that span both biological and psychosocial issues in mood disorders in adults, children, and adolescents. His research efforts contributed to the development of effective pharmacological and cognitive-behavioral therapies for depressed patients and those with bipolar disorders.

RUSSELL, ROGER W. (1914–1998) Russell was one of the first to search for neurochemical mechanisms underlying normal and abnormal behavior.

RUTHERFORD, WILLIAM (1839–1899) Rutherford is known in psychology chiefly for his 1886 "Telephone Theory" of hearing.

RUTTER, MICHAEL (b. 1933) Perhaps the leading child psychiatrist in the world, Rutter wrote about and conducted research on numerous child disorders.

SAKEL, MANFRED (1900–1957) Sakel is primarily known for his discovery of the insulin coma treatment for Schizophrenia.

SAPOLSKY, ROBERT (b. 1957) Sapolsky has examined the cellular and molecular mechanisms underlying glucocorticoid-induced hippocampal neurotoxicity and its relevance to hippocampal damage during aging. Another line of Sapolsky's research involves examining relationships among social rank, personality, and patterns of stress-related disease in wild baboons.

SALTER, ANDREW (1914–1996) Salter's *Conditioned Reflex Therapy* was a major contribution to the founding of behavior therapy; he was also a cofounder of the Association for the Advancement of Behavior Therapy. His *Case against Psychoanalysis* offended many in the psychiatric establishment.

SANFORD, EDMUND CLARK (1869–1924) As an innovator of psychological apparatus, Sanford developed the vernier pendulum chronoscope, which once was a standard instrument for studying reaction time.

SAPIR, EDWARD (1884–1939) Sapir's study of language in Native American tribes was an early contribution to linguistic anthropology.

SCARR, SANDRA WOOD (b. 1936) Scarr explored genetic variability in human behaviors through twin, adoption, and intervention studies.

SCHACHTER, STANLEY (1922–1997) Schachter developed a cognitive theory of emotion in which he established that people cannot discriminate one emotion from another unless they have some cognitive indication of to what their feelings relate.

SCHAIE, K. WARNER (b. 1928) Schaie's principal contributions are long-term longitudinal research on adult intellectual development and study in the area of developmental research methodology.

SCHATZBERG, ALAN (b. 1944) Schatzberg has provided an enhanced understanding of the biology of psychotic depression.

SCHOPENHAUER, ARTHUR (1788–1860) Schopenhauer stressed the redemption of the soul from its sensual bonds. According to him, human beings have an obligation to sensual things, but the final goal is to rise above the senses into the bosom of a peaceful Nirvana.

SCHUMANN, FRIEDRICH (1863–1940) Schumann studied many visual forms and illusions without finding any necessity to appeal to the concept of form-quality. Instead, this could be accounted for by the laws of attention as well as eye movements.

SCOTT, WALTER DILL (1869–1955) Scott transferred his psychological insights into the world of work and introduced the business uses of psychology into advertising, selling, and consumer behavior. Thus, he created a new field-industrial psychology.

SCRIPTURE, EDWARD WHEELER (1864–1945) Scripture coined the term *armchair psychology* to describe those psychologies that state theories and speculations without experimental verification.

SEARS, ROBERT R. (1908–1989) Sears's initial interests in physiological psychology shifted to personality and motivation. He performed numerous verification studies on psychoanalytic concepts.

SEASHORE, CARL EMIL (1866–1949) For many years, Seashore devoted his experimental efforts to the study of music psychology. His thesis was that musical talent consisted of many different capacities.

SECHENOV, IVAN MIKHAILOVICH (1829–1905) The founder of Russian physiology, Sechenov was a mentor to Ivan Pavlov and instrumental in bringing psychology and science together.

SEGUIN, EDOUARD (1812–1880) Seguin originated sense and muscle training techniques whereby children with mental retardation were given intensive exercise in sensory discriminations and in the development of muscle control.

SELIGMAN, MARTIN E. P. (b. 1942) Seligman reformulated the learned helplessness model, claiming that attributions governed the expression of helplessness. More recently, he has developed and implemented applications of "Positive Psychology."

SELYE, HANS (1907–1982) Selye formulated a code of behavior based on the laws that govern the body's stress resistance in dealing with personal, interpersonal, and group problems.

SERPELL, ROBERT (b. 1944) Serpell's research centered on the application of attention theory to various aspects of child development, notably perceptual errors on Western intelligence tests and second-language learning in Zambia.

SHAFFER, DAVID A British psychiatrist, Shaffer has studied suicide as it relates to mood disorders and externalizing behaviors among adolescents.

SHAKOW, DAVID (1901–1982) Shakow is best known for his role in the development and descriptions of models for training in clinical psychology. The "Shakow Report" set the training model as a Ph.D. according to the "Boulder Model of Combined Training in Science and Practice."

SHERIF, CAROLYN (1922–1982) Sherif collaborated with her husband Muzafer Sherif in a series of important studies regarding changing racial attitudes. She went on to make major contributions to social rejection theory and the roles of women in psychology. She was among the "four mothers" of psychology.

SHERIF, MUZAFER (1906–1988) Sherif initiated a series of naturalistic experiments on group formation, intergroup conflict, and cooperation.

SHELDON, WILLIAM HERBERT (1899–1977) Sheldon developed an empirical basis for the structural theory of personality first suggested by Hippocrates and Galen. Sheldon refined what were essentially Kretschmer's three basic body types.

SHERRINGTON, CHARLES SCOTT (1857–1952) Sherrington published studies on color vision and flicker and wrote on the tactual and muscular senses. He introduced the terms *interoceptor, exteroceptor,* and *proprioceptor.* Wolpe based much of his work on relaxation training on Sherrington's ideas, even though they were later called into question.

SHNEIDMAN, EDWIN S. (b. 1918) Shneidman is a suicidologist and thanatologist who has researched death and suicide.

SIGUAN, MIGUEL (b. 1918) Siguan has been a pioneer in the field of infant language, attempting to explain the origins of verbal language as arising from nonverbal communication.

SIMON, HERBERT A. (1916–2001) Simon has pioneered in creating information-processing psychology and has been active in the fields of mathematical economics and organization theory.

SINGER, GEORGE (b. 1922) Singer's major contributions to psychological research are in perception: eating, drinking, and drug intake behaviors, and the application of biochemical methods to the assessment of stress programs.

SINGH, SHEO DAN (1932–1979) Singh established India's first Primate Research Laboratory. His major areas of interest were the impact of urban conditions on the development of social, emotional, and cognitive behavior and the brain chemistry of rhesus monkeys.

SKINNER, BURRHUS FREDERICK (B. F.) (1904–1990) Skinner took a completely objective approach to psychology. He contended that learning occurs as a result of some kind of reinforcement, either positive or negative.

SMITH, M. BREWSTER (b. 1919) Smith studied anti-Semitism, race prejudice, and moral judgment in the student activists of the 1960s. He sought to link the complementarities of scientific and humanistic psychology by focusing on selfhood or personality.

SNYDER, SOLOMON H. (b. 1938) Snyder and colleagues were the first to identify opiate receptors in the brain, a discovery that opened the door to an increased understanding of the actions of addictive drugs. In addition, to challenge the notion that brain cells could not reproduce, Snyder and colleagues concocted a growth medium in which a colony of neurons functioned normally and also multiplied.

SOBELL, LINDA (b. 1947) Sobell's work has focused on problems with alcohol consumption. Her early work with Mark Sobell triggered a major controversy on "controlled drinking."

SOLOMON, RICHARD LESTER (1919–1992) Solomon's research involved numerous areas of experimental psychology. Of particular importance were his various studies of traumatic avoidance learning in dogs. In these studies, he explored many parameters of the problem, some of which later became known as "learned helplessness."

SPEARMAN, CHARLES EDWARD (1863–1945) Spearman discovered that individual differences on all tests of mental abilities are positively intercorrelated in representative samples of the general population.

SPENCE, JANET TAYLOR (b. 1923) Spence developed the Manifest Anxiety Scale as a vehicle for testing her and Kenneth Spence's theory about the interactions between task characteristics and drive or arousal level in determining task performance. In the later years of her career, she focused on masculinity and femininity and how they related to performance.

SPENCE, KENNETH W. (1907–1967) In the philosophy of science and the tenets of logical empiricism, Spence sought the bases on which psychology could proceed as an objective, empirical science.

SPENCER, HERBERT (1820–1903) Spencer considered associationism the most binding psychological principle. Along with his contemporary, Alexander Bain, he brought the entire movement of British associationism to an end.

SPERRY, ROGER WOLCOTT (1913–1994) Sperry's finding, the split-brain phenomenon, created considerable discussion among neuropsychologists and led to the dual personality theory.

SPIELBERGER, CHARLES (b. 1927) Spielberger's research interests have focused on personality and learning, stress, anxiety, and curiosity, and the experience, expression, and control of anger. With adaptations in 52 languages and dialects, his State-Trait Anxiety Inventory is the standard international self-report measure of anxiety.

SPINOZA, BENEDICT BARUCH (1632–1677) Spinoza's philosophy was rationalistic and deductive. Human beings, as a manifestation of God, reflect the psychophysical parallelism that prevails throughout the universe. People have two aspects, mind and body, which are basically one.

SPRANGER, EDUARD (1882–1963) Spranger identified six types of people in terms of their life goals and values that operated apart from any biological drives or needs.

SPURZHEIM, JOHANN GASPER (1776–1832) Spurzheim, a phrenologist, identified 37 faculties of the mind, each related to a specific cortical location. His grouping of the faculties into mental, motive, and vital types anticipated Sheldon's somatotypes.

SQUIRE, LARRY R. (b. 1941) Squire's studies of human memory provided some of the first evidence for the biological reality of multiple memory systems. In addition, the work of Squire and colleagues led to the establishment of an animal model of human amnesia in the monkey and eventually to the identification of the anatomical components of the medial temporal lobe memory system.

STEINER, RUDOLF (1861–1925) Steiner founded the first Waldorf School, now the largest nonsectarian private school system in the world. He taught that the development of humankind's intellectual and spiritual faculties could lead to a "spiritual science."

STEKEL, WILHELM (1868–1940) Stekel stressed the teaching role of the analyst and saw the therapeutic relationship as an active partnership. He believed that the goals of the patient are important and that the patient should be led to distinguish between genuine and false goals.

STEVENS, CHARLES F. (b. 1934) Stevens's research centers on mechanisms responsible for synaptic transmission. He has investigated various mechanisms used by the central nervous system for the short- and long-term regulation of synaptic strength, and he has used a combination of methods to elucidate the molecular basis of neurotransmitter release at synapses.

STEVENS, STANLEY SMITH (1906–1973) Stevens found that physical continua generally conform to a psychophysical power law rather than Gustav Fechner's logarithmic law.

STOUT, GEORGE FREDERICK (1860–1944) Stout rejected mental chemistry and criticized associationists for confusing the "presented whole" with the "sum of its presented components." Thus, Stout anticipated the Gestalt cry that "the whole is greater than the sum of its parts."

STRATTON, GEORGE MALCOLM (1865–1957) Stratton wore special lenses that reversed the field of vision, up for down and right for left, during his waking hours for 8 consecutive days. After 3 days he was able to make relatively automatic and skilled movements and adjust to seeing an inverted world.

STRICKLAND, BONNIE (b. 1936) Strickland's research of students involved in the civil rights movement demonstrated that internal locus of control beliefs are related to direct social action. She has also investigated the mental health status of lesbians and gay men, the effects of discrimination on children's development, and various factors leading to the greater incidence of depression among women.

STRONG, EDWARD KELLOGG, JR. (1884–1963) Strong spent most of his career measuring vocational interests. His later publications dealt with the variation of interests over time, including a large group studied 18 years after completing college.

STRUPP, HANS H. (b. 1921) Strupp viewed the nature of the psychotherapist's influence and the patient's susceptibility to that influence as one of the core problems in psychotherapy research. He conducted several studies on verbal psychotherapy.

STUMPF, CARL (1848–1946) Stumpf's *Tonpsychologie* was the first work on the psychology of music. One of the most important aspects of this work was his theory of consonance and dissonance in music.

STUNKARD, ALBERT J. (b. 1922) Stunkard conducted extensive research on eating patterns and hunger with animals. He subsequently has completed numerous investigations of the effectiveness of various behaviorally based weight loss programs.

SULLIVAN, ARTHUR M. (b. 1932) Sullivan investigated teaching and learning at the remedial level as well as at the first- and second-year university level. The teaching and remedial programs that he devised resulted in dramatic increases in academic success.

SULLIVAN, HARRY STACK (1892–1949) Not only is personality couched in interpersonal relations, Sullivan believed, but also the patient-therapist interpersonal relationship is critical for successful therapy. His model served as the basis of Klerman and Weissman's *Interpersonal Psychotherapy.*

SUNDBERG, NORMAN D. (b. 1922) Sundberg emphasizes both the "horizontal" and the "vertical": "horizontal" in the sense of knowledge across cultures, communities, and applied activities, and "vertical" in the sense of an appreciation of time, of the history and future of the life span.

SUPER, DONALD E. (1910–1994) Super is most often associated with career development theory and its applications. After contributing first to the applications of differential psychology to vocational guidance and personnel selection and classification, he shifted his attention to developmental approaches to vocational choice and development.

SZASZ, THOMAS S. (b. 1920) Szasz is best known for his proposition that mental illness is a myth and for his uncompromising opposition to psychiatric coercions and excuses.

SZEWCZUK, WLODZIMIERZ L. (b. 1913) Szewczuk found three necessary conditions for any memorization: an active attitude, association with earlier experience, and association with emotional reactions.

TAYLOR, FREDERICK WINSLOW (1856–1915) Taylor founded the area of industrial efficiency. He prescribed the time study with standardized tools and procedures organized by a planning department. Equipment was redesigned to be consonant with human abilities.

TEPLOV, BORIS MIKHAILOVICH (1886–1965) Teplov related individual differences to the nervous system, stressing the importance of involuntary reflexes in a manner first studied by Ivan Pavlov.

TERMAN, LEWIS MADISON (1877–1956) Terman's major research contribution to American psychology was his work in intelligence testing and his evaluation of gifted persons.

THOMAS AQUINAS (1225–1274) In his *Summa Theologica,* Thomas Aquinas stated that some things can be known by faith only, others by reason only, and still others by both revelation and rational proof. As humans seek truth, they are also seeking the final good.

THOMPSON, RICHARD F. (b. 1930) In collaboration with W. Alden Spencer, Thompson developed criteria for habituation and evidence that the basic process is a form of synaptic depression that occurs presynaptically.

THOMSON, GODFREY H. (1881–1955) Thomson regarded the mind as comprising a very large number of "bonds," similar to Thorndike's "connections." Any mental act would draw on a sample of bonds, while other acts would draw on some of the same and some that were different.

THORNDIKE, EDWARD LEE (1874–1949) Thorndike taught that psychologists should study behavior, not mental elements or conscious experience. He did fundamental work in understanding learning and also preceded Pavlov's *law of reinforcement* with his *law of effect.*

THURSTONE, LOUIS LEON (1887–1955) Thurstone is best known for his contributions to factor analysis. His multiple factor theory has endured; however, with the advent of electronic computers, his centroid method of factor extraction has been replaced by more exact methods.

TILLICH, PAUL (1886–1965) Tillich believed that religious questions arise from human situations and therefore are practical and not primarily theoretical. He was strongly influenced by existentialism.

TINBERGEN, NIKOLAAS (1907–1988) Many of Tinbergen's works have become classics in both psychology and biology, including his work on courting behavior in sticklebacks, orienting behavior in wasps, and the behavior of grayling butterflies.

TITCHENER, EDWARD BRADFORD (1867–1927) Titchener brought structuralism to the United States from Wundt's laboratory in Leipzig. He was a dominant figure in the early years of American psychology.

TOLMAN, EDWARD CHASE (1886–1959) Tolman is primarily known for his theory of learning. Many psychologists consider this a cognitive field theory, although in his many experiments, primarily with the white rat, he always stressed behavior. He is usually credited with introducing the concept of the intervening variable into psychology.

TRIANDIS, HARRY C. (b. 1926) Triandis focused his work on social factors in cross-cultural research.

TULVING, ENDEL (b. 1927) Tulving has collaborated with Kanneman for much of his career, and they have made major contributions to cognitive psychology and decision theory.

TYLER, LEONA E. (1906–1993) Tyler's work focused on assessment and test construction theory.

ULLMAN, LEONARD P. (b. 1930) Studies of verbal operant conditioning led Ullman and colleagues to a direct, rather than indirect, formulation of the development, maintenance, and change of behavior. The thread in Ullman's work is that being precedes essence—that the focus of study should be overt behavior, which is observable, rather than personality, which is inferred after the fact.

UNDERWOOD, BENTON J. (1915–1994) Underwood's research efforts were devoted to the field of human learning. He explored many facets of verbal learning processes, including problems in retroactive and proactive inhibition, distributed practice, and the role of meaningfulness in associative learning, as well as a variety of variables that contribute to the degree of remembering and forgetting following verbal learning.

UZNADZE, DMITRII NIKOLAYEVICH (1886–1950) Uznadze is best known for his theory of "set" as an objective approach to the unconscious.

VAIHINGER, HANS (1852–1933) Vaihinger is known for his philosophy of "as-if": Something can work as if true even though it is false and recognized as false.

VERNON, PHILIP E. (1905–1987) Vernon conducted a series of comparative studies of abilities in different parts of the world, from Tanzania to the Arctic.

VERPLANCK, WILLIAM S. (b. 1916) Verplanck showed that successive psychological judgments are not independent of one another, as theory dictated.

VITELES, MORRIS (1898–1996) Viteles structured the field of industrial psychology as it is today. His emphasis on the need for a solid experimental basis for industrial applications helped to counter conversion of industrial psychology into industrial psychotechnology.

VYGOTSKY, LEV SEMYONOVICH (1896–1934) Vygotsky opposed the reflexology of Bekhterev, arguing that a study of mind was necessary because it distinguished humans from lower animals. However, he rejected introspection as a method.

WALKER, C. EUGENE (b. 1939) Walker's research has involved psychological testing and measurement, behavioral approaches to psychotherapy, and the effects of pornography on behavior. His interests also include hyperactive behavior in children, child abuse, and juvenile and adolescent sex offenders.

WALLON, HENRI (1879–1962) Wallon saw emotion as a physiological fact with humoral and physiological aspects, mediating between sensations and the social world.

WANG, ZHONG-MING (b. 1949) Wang has been active in the areas of reward systems design, group attributional training, high-tech innovations, judgment and decision making, and decision support systems.

WARD, JAMES (1843–1924) Even though Ward was considered by many to be a philosopher more than a psychologist, he was instrumental in establishing the first psychological laboratory at Cambridge.

WARREN, HOWARD CROSBY (1867–1934) Warren is best known as a writer and editor. He was a contributor to James Baldwin's *Dictionary of Philosophy and Psychology* and published the *Dictionary of Psychology,* which was a standard work for many years.

WASHBURN, MARGARET FLOY (1871–1939) Washburn's research included work on individual differences, color vision in animals, and aesthetic preferences by students for colors and speech sounds.

WATSON, JOHN B. (1878–1958) The founder of American behaviorism, Watson established its two tenets: psychology as an objective science and psychology as the science of behavior.

WATT, HENRY JACKSON (1879–1925) Watt's main contribution involved the study of experience as it occurred in word associations.

WEBB, WILSE BERNARD (b. 1920) Webb's research emphasized the role of individual differences and biological rhythms as determinants of sleep deprivation and performance, and also the effects of aging.

WEBER, ERNST HEINRICH (1795–1878) Weber's main research concern was in the field of sensory physiology. He found that the point of just noticeable difference bears a constant relationship to the standard. This relationship is expressed in a formula by Gustav Fechner, who identified it as Weber's law.

WECHSLER, DAVID (1896–1981) Wechsler applied his creative efforts to the development and standardization of intelligence scales that bear his name and to the substitution for Binet's Mental Age of a Deviation Quotient.

WEINBERGER, DANIEL One of the foremost investigators in the biology of Schizophrenia. More recently he has made breakthroughs on the genetic basis of emotional reactivity.

WEISS, JAY (b. 1941) One of the foremost investigators in rodent models of depression. Recently he has been working on why certain cancer patients develop depression.

WEISSMAN, MYRNA (b. 1940) Weissman's research is concerned with the epidemiology of psychiatric disorders in the community and the treatment and genetics of affective and anxiety disorders. She was a co-developer with her husband, Gerald Klerman, of interpersonal psychotherapy. She received her Ph.D. from Yale in 1974.

WERNER, HEINZ (1890–1964) Werner held that development proceeds from the undifferentiated and unarticulated to the differentiated and articulated.

WERTHEIMER, MAX (1880–1943) Wertheimer was one of the founders of Gestalt psychology. He suggested that the whole is quite *different* from the sum of clinical psychology.

WERTHEIMER, MICHAEL (b. 1927) Wertheimer's research career began with the study of sensory and perceptual processes but soon broadened to include cognition, individual differences, psycholinguistics, person perception, and eventually the history of psychology. He was the son of Max Wertheimer.

WHIPPLE, GUY MONTROSE (1876–1941) Whipple warned the American Psychological Association (APA) against charlatans and otherwise unqualified practitioners who were making inroads into clinical psychology. As a result, the APA set forth procedures for qualifying psychologists.

WHITE, ROBERT W. (1904–2001) White made a timely contribution to theory when he published *Motivation Reconsidered: The Concept of Competence,* which was soon followed by other papers on competence.

WHITE, WILLIAM ALANSON (1870–1937) White abolished the various forms of physical restraint that had been used at St. Elizabeth's hospital, replacing them with concerned humane treatment.

WICKENS, DELOS D. (1909–1988) Wickens's research activities were almost equally divided between work with human and animal subjects, a distribution expressing a bias toward addressing a basic psychology process by the most promising means.

WILCOX, RICHARD E. (b. 1947) Wilcox's work has focused on the behavioral and brain-chemistry changes induced in brain dopamine systems by dosing with dopamine agonist antiparkinson drugs, psychostimulants, and endurance-training regimens. These studies have shown that chronic stimulation of brain dopamine receptors produces adaptations in dopamine synthesis, metabolism, and release.

WILLIAMS, JOANNA P. (b. 1935) Williams has performed research on beginning reading instruction, with a focus on phonemic skills and on reading comprehension (main idea and theme identification and critical reading).

WILSON, EDWARD OSBORNE (b. 1929) Wilson's sociobiology claims that the human body with its social behavior serves to perpetuate the genes. He believes that people exist for the sake of their genes. "The organism is only DNA's way of making more DNA."

WILSON, G. TERENCE (b. 1944) Wilson's recent research has focused on eating disorders, particularly Bulimia Nervosa. He has written extensively on theories of behavior therapy. He is a former President of the Association for the Advancement of Behavior Therapy.

WITKIN, HERMAN A. (1916–1979) Witkin contributed greatly to the conceptualization of the relation between cognitive styles and personality. He believed people generally move from field dependence to field independence as they mature.

WITMER, LIGHTNER (1861–1956) Witmer established the first psychological clinic at the University of Pennsylvania. He also founded *The Psychological Clinic.* In the first issue he called for the establishment of a new helping profession, to be termed clinical psychology.

WOLFF, CHRISTIAN VON (1679–1754) Wolff stressed an active mind rather than one made up of the mere elements of experience as Locke had suggested. The mind consisted of faculties or functions such as knowledge, remembrance, feeling, and willingness.

WOLMAN, BENJAMIN B. (1908–2000) Wolman developed the interactional approach to psychotherapy, which is based on the idea that every person experiences emotional difficulties throughout life.

WOLPE, JOSEPH (1915–1997) The central point of Wolpe's research was experimental studies on the production and cure of neuroses in animals. Neuroses were produced by learning and were reversible by learning. Techniques for treating human neuroses were derived from these findings. Wolpe was one of the early founders of behavior therapy.

WOODWORTH, ROBERT SESSIONS (1869–1962) For Woodworth, the subject matter of psychology was both behavior and consciousness. He believed that behaviorists such as John Watson, who had rejected consciousness or the mind, had left out a legitimate aspect of psychology.

WUNDT, WILHELM (1832–1920) Wundt's systematic efforts established psychology as a new and recognized science in Germany during the 19th century. Using this method of introspection, students and researchers investigated the subject matter of immediate experience.

YERKES, ROBERT MEARNS (1876–1956) Yerkes invented an experimental maze to study animal learning and the evolution of intelligence through the animal species. From his experiments he formed the Yerkes-Dodson law.

YOUNG, PAUL THOMAS (1892–1978) Young is known for his studies in sound localization using a pseudophone in which the auditory inputs are reversed. He found that auditory localization is significant, particularly when the sounding object cannot be seen.

YOUNG, THOMAS (1773–1829) As a result of his interest in vision, Young became prominent in psychology. He described and measured visual astigmatism. By measuring the focal length of the eye, he demonstrated that the accommodation was attributable to the changing shape of the lens.

ZAJONC, ROBERT B. (b. 1923) Zajonc's interest has been drawn to the relationship between family structure and intellectual development. Later in his career he studied the relationship between cognition (thoughts) and emotions (feelings).

ZAPOROZHETS, ALEXANDER (1905–1981) Zaporozhets is best known for his concept of *perceptual action* and his theory of voluntary actions. He elaborated a concept of perceptual action that bound together the problems of sensorimotor skills and cognitive development.

ZEIGARNIK, BLÛMA (b. 1900) Zeigarnik is best known for her formal test of Lewin's theory that attainment of a goal or successful locomotion toward a positive valence relieves tension.

ZIGLER, EDWARD (b. 1930) Zigler's work cuts across the fields of mental retardation, mental health and psychopathology, intervention programs for economically disadvantaged children, preschool education, and out-of-home care for children of working parents. His work in mental retardation is frequently noted in efforts toward more enlightened treatment of individuals with disabilities.

ZIMBARDO, PHILIP G. (b. 1933) Zimbardo simulated prison conditions at Stanford and discovered that student "inmates" became deindividualized and lost time perspective. He has conducted numerous experiments in applied social psychology.

ZUBIN, JOSEPH (1900–1990) Zubin was instrumental in developing techniques of observation and behavior models in psychopathology from physiological, behavioral, genetic, and psychosocial perspectives.

AUTHOR INDEX

SUBJECT INDEX